THE ROUGH GUIDE TO

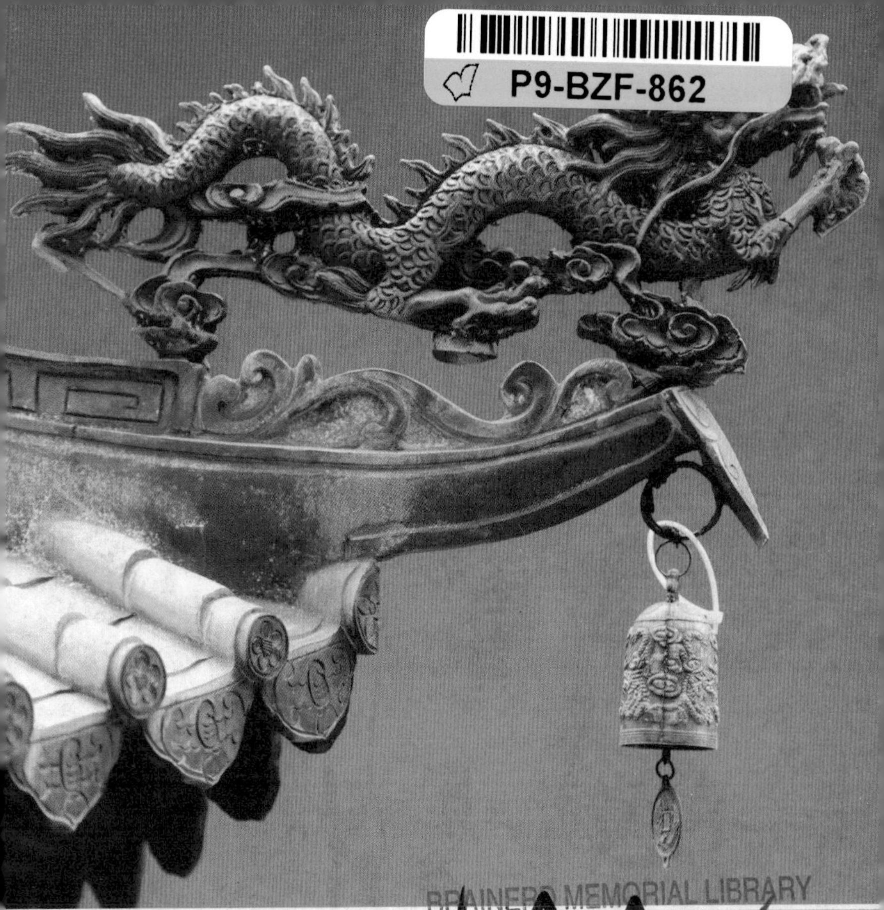

Southeast Asia

ON A BUDGET

This fourth edition updated by

Edward Aves, Emma Boyle, Kiki Deere, Simon Foster, Paul Gray, Anthon Jackson, Anna Kaminski, Shafik Meghji, John Oates, Gavin Thomas and Steve Vickers

roughguides.com

Contents

OPPOSITE ANGKOR THOM, CAMBODIA **PREVIOUS PAGE** THIAN HOCK KENG TEMPLE, SINGAPORE

Introduction to Southeast Asia

With its tempting mix of volcanoes, rainforest, rice fields, beaches and coral reefs, Southeast Asia is one of the most stimulating and accessible regions for independent travel in the world. You can spend the day exploring thousand-year-old Hindu ruins and the night at a rave on the beach; attend a Buddhist alms-giving ceremony at dawn and go whitewater rafting in the afternoon; chill out in a bamboo beach hut one week and hike through the jungle looking for orang-utans the next.

In short, there is enough here to keep anyone hooked for months, and the average cost of living is so low that many Western travellers find they can afford to take their time. The region comprises Brunei, Cambodia, Indonesia, Laos, Malaysia, Myanmar, the Philippines, Singapore, Thailand and Vietnam, and, as useful gateways to the region, we have also included Southeast Asian neighbours **Hong Kong and Macau**. Though the region has long been on the travellers' trail, it doesn't take too much to get off the beaten track – whether it's to discover that perfect beach or to delve into the lush surrounds of the rainforest.

The **beaches** here are some of the finest in the world, and you'll find the cream of the crop in Thailand, the Philippines and Malaysia, all of which boast postcard-pretty, white-sand bays, complete with azure waters and wooden beach shacks dotted along their palm-fringed shores. The clear tropical waters also offer supreme diving opportunities for novices and seasoned divers alike.

Southeast Asia's myriad **temple complexes** are another of the region's best-known attractions. The Hindu Khmers left a string of magnificent monuments, the most impressive of which can be seen at Angkor in Cambodia, while the Buddhists' most impressive legacies include the colossal ninth-century stupa of Borobudur in Indonesia and the temple-strewn plain of Bagan in Myanmar.

Almost every visitor to the region makes an effort to climb one of the spectacular **mountains**, whether getting up before dawn to watch the sun rise from Indonesia's Mount Bromo or embarking on the two-day trek to scale Mount Kinabalu in Malaysia.

ABOVE MONKS, CAMBODIA **OPPOSITE** CHINESE NEW YEAR CELEBRATIONS, ILOILO, PHILIPPINES

Tribal culture is a highlight of many visits to less explored areas, and among the most approachable communities are the tribal groups around Sa Pa in Vietnam, the Torjan of Sulawesi in Indonesia, known for their intriguing architecture and ghoulish burial rituals, and the ethnic minority villages surrounding Hsipaw in Myanmar.

Where to go

Many travellers begin their trip in **Thailand**, which remains the most popular destination in Southeast Asia, with some of the world's best beaches and islands, traditional hill towns and plenty of cultural stimulation. Neighbouring **Laos**, with its burgeoning tourist industry, is still perhaps the best country to explore if you're looking to escape the crowds, and for many people a slow boat down the Mekong here is still the quintessential Southeast Asian experience. To the west, **Myanmar** (Burma) has seen a huge increase in visitor numbers since the removal of a fifteen-year tourism boycott, with travellers flocking to explore the country's remarkable temples, landscapes and culture.

Heading east brings you to **Vietnam**, with its impressive old Chinese towns, two vibrant, rapidly changing and very different cities and some stunning scenery, from the northern mountains to southern beaches. From here it's easy to cross into neighbouring **Cambodia**, where the fabulous temple ruins at Angkor remain a major draw.

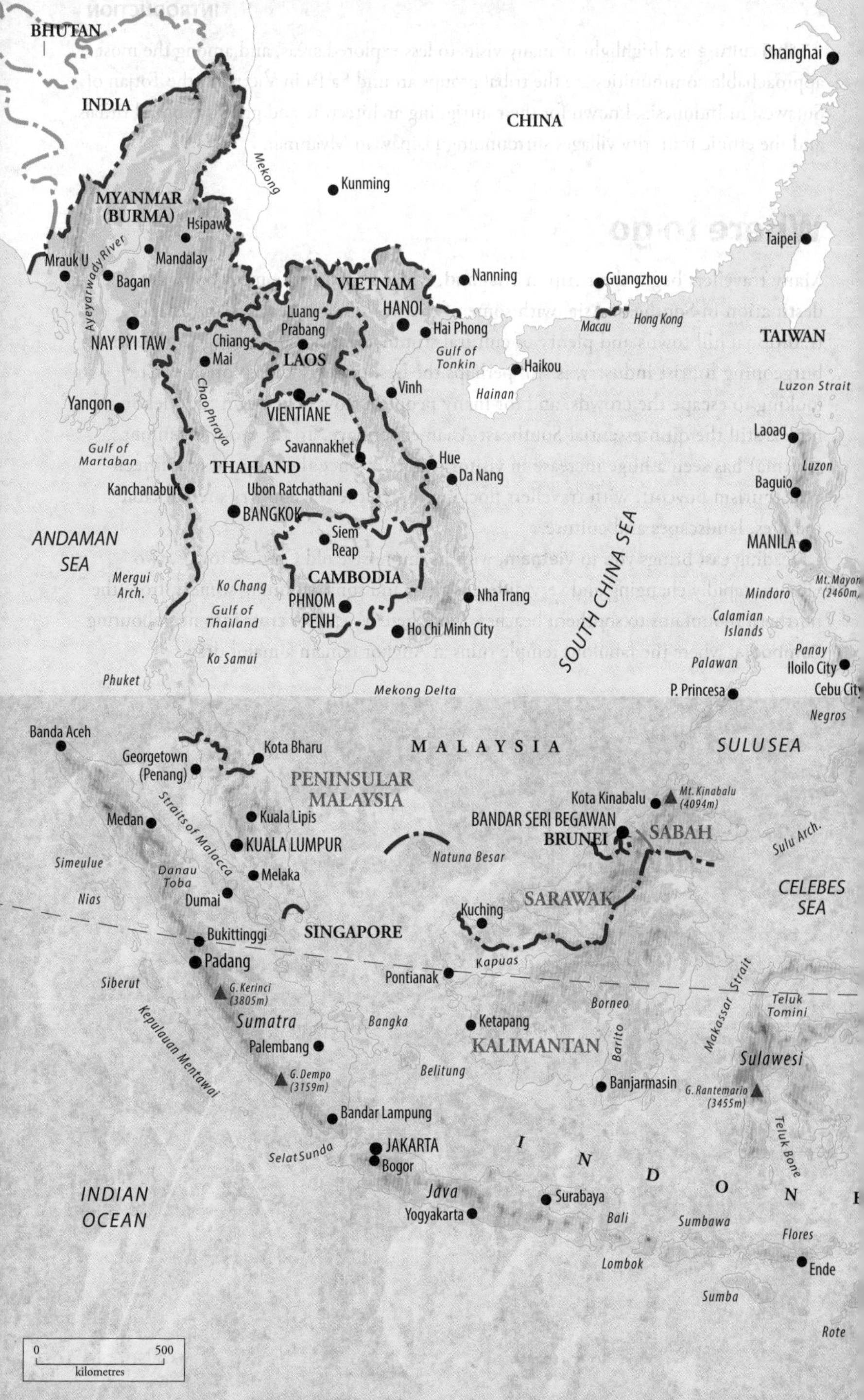

BHUTAN
INDIA
CHINA
Shanghai
Kunming
Mekong
MYANMAR
(BURMA)
Hsipaw
Mandalay
Mrauk U
Bagan
Ayeyarwady River
NAY PYI TAW
Taipei
Nanning
Guangzhou
VIETNAM
HANOI
Hai Phong
Macau
Hong Kong
TAIWAN
Luang
Prabang
LAOS
Chiang
Mai
Gulf of
Tonkin
Haikou
Hainan
Luzon Strait
Vinh
VIENTIANE
Yangon
Chao Phraya
Gulf of
Martaban
Savannakhet
THAILAND
Hue
Da Nang
Laoag
Luzon
Baguio
Kanchanaburi
Ubon Ratchathani
BANGKOK
Siem
Reap
SOUTH CHINA SEA
MANILA
ANDAMAN
SEA
Mergui
Arch.
Ko Chang
CAMBODIA
PHNOM
PENH
Nha Trang
Mindoro
Mt. Mayon
(2460m)
Gulf of
Thailand
Ho Chi Minh City
Calamian
Islands
Ko Samui
Panay
Iloilo City
Palawan
Phuket
Mekong Delta
P. Princesa
Cebu City
Negros
Banda Aceh
Kota Bharu
MALAYSIA
SULU SEA
Georgetown
(Penang)
PENINSULAR
MALAYSIA
Kota Kinabalu
Mt. Kinabalu
(4094m)
Medan
Straits of Malacca
Kuala Lipis
BANDAR SERI BEGAWAN
BRUNEI
SABAH
KUALA LUMPUR
Natuna Besar
Sulu Arch.
Simeulue
Danau
Toba
Melaka
Nias
Dumai
SARAWAK
CELEBES
SEA
Kuching
Bukittinggi
SINGAPORE
Padang
Kapuas
Pontianak
Siberut
G. Kerinci
(3805m)
Makassar Strait
Teluk
Tomini
Kepulauan Mentawai
Borneo
Sumatra
Bangka
Ketapang
Palembang
KALIMANTAN
Barito
Sulawesi
G. Dempo
(3159m)
Belitung
Banjarmasin
G. Rantemario
(3455m)
Bandar Lampung
Teluk Bone
JAKARTA
Selat Sunda
Bogor
INDONE
INDIAN
OCEAN
Java
Surabaya
Yogyakarta
Bali
Sumbawa
Flores
Lombok
Ende
Sumba
Rote
0
500
kilometres

JAPAN

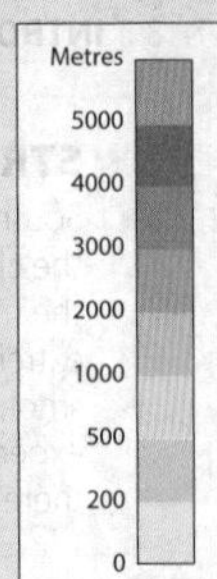

PHILIPPINE SEA

PACIFIC OCEAN

THE PHILIPPINES

Guam

Samar

Leyte

Yap

Cagayan de Oro

Mindanao

Palau

Davao

MOLUCCA SEA

Manado

Equator

MALUKU

Biak

Kep. Sula

JAYAPURA

Seram

Buru

WEST PAPUA

New Guinea

BANDA SEA

Kep. Kai

Kep. Aru

PAPUA NEW GUINEA

New Britain

S I A

Wetar

Babar

Kep. Tanimbar

TIMOR-LESTE

Timor

ARAFURA SEA

Darwin

AUSTRALIA

STREET FOOD

Southeast Asia boasts some of the world's tastiest cuisines, and the really good news is that the cheapest is often the best, with markets and roadside hawkers unbeatable places to try the many local specialities. Night markets, in particular, are great for tasting different dishes at extremely low prices – sizzling woks full of frying noodles, swirling clouds of spice-infused smoke and rows of glistening fried insects all make for an unforgettable gastronomic experience. With each country, each region and even each town having its own specialities, there's so much variety that your tastebuds will never get bored.

South of Thailand, **Malaysia** deserves a leisurely exploration, boasting beautiful beaches, good diving, and some rewarding jungle hikes. East Malaysia, which shares the large island of Borneo with Indonesia's Kalimantan province and the little kingdom of **Brunei**, offers adventurous (if costly) travel by river through the jungle and nights in tribal longhouses. **Singapore**, along with Bangkok and Hong Kong, is a major gateway to the region; though relatively pricey, it has a fascinating mix of old and new, and after you've been on the road for a while you may find its more Westernized feel quite appealing.

From Singapore or Malaysia it's a boat ride or short flight to **Indonesia**. It could take you a lifetime to explore this vast and varied archipelago, with fantastic volcanic landscapes, an unparalleled diversity of tribal cultures, decent beaches and diving, and lots of arts and crafts.

Northeast of Indonesia, a flight away from mainland Southeast Asia, and consequently less visited, **the Philippines** has some of the best beaches and most dramatic diving in the whole region, along with some wonderful Spanish architecture, incredible rice terraces, and unique wildlife, making it well worth the detour from the main tourist trail.

When to go

Southeast Asia sits entirely within the tropics and so is broadly characterized by a hot and humid climate that varies little throughout the year, except during the two annual monsoons. Bear in mind, however, that each country has myriad microclimates; for more detail, consult the introduction to each chapter.

The **southwest monsoon** arrives in west-coast regions at around the end of May and brings daily rainfall to most of Southeast Asia by mid-July (excepting certain east-coast areas, explained on p.10). From then on you can expect overcast skies and regular downpours until October or November. This is not the best time to travel in Southeast Asia, as west-coast seas are often too rough for swimming, some islands become inaccessible, and poorly maintained roads may get washed out. However, rain showers often last just a couple of hours a day and many airlines and guesthouses offer decent discounts at this time.

The **northeast monsoon** brings drier, slightly cooler weather to most of Southeast Asia (east-coast areas excepted) between November and February, making this period the best

OPPOSITE FROM TOP PADDY FIELD NEAR SIEM REAP, CAMBODIA; YOUNG ORANG-UTANS, BORNEO

LOCAL TRANSPORT

Tuk-tuk, bemo, jeepney, songthaew, moto, *remorque*, cyclo – the names are endless, as are the types of vehicle, which can be anything from modern minivans to three-wheel buggies. You'll soon become familiar with the different ones as you travel around, particularly in the more remote parts of the region. Noisy, bumpy and often jam-packed with people, these vehicles are a world away from the slick, air-conditioned transport systems you'll find in Asia's big cities. In some places the larger vehicles run as buses on fixed routes – bemos and jeepneys in Indonesia and the Philippines respectively, for example – but more often they are share-taxis or taxis. Negotiate the fare before you get in, make sure you know whether you're chartering the whole vehicle or just a seat in one, and, as you would anywhere in the world, take sensible precautions when travelling alone and at night.

overall time to travel in the region. The main exceptions to the above pattern are the east-facing coasts of Vietnam, Thailand and Peninsular Malaysia, which get rain when the rest of tropical Asia is having its driest period, but stay dry during the southwest monsoon. If you're planning a long trip to Southeast Asia, this means you can often escape the worst weather by hopping across to the other coast. Indonesia and Singapore are hit by both monsoons, attracting the west-coast rains from May through to October, and the east-coast rains from November to February.

ABOVE CAGDANAO ISLAND, PHILIPPINES **OPPOSITE FROM TOP** BEACH NEAR EL NIDO, PHILIPPINES; KO TAO, THAILAND; KUTA, LOMBOK, INDONESIA

Southeast Asia's best beaches

Offshore islands, Sihanoukville (Cambodia) The coastal waters off Sihanoukville (p.102) are peppered with tropical islands lapped by clear, balmy seas, many graced with white-sand beaches. Offering stretches of sand that are infinitely more peaceful than those on the mainland, they're great places to hole up in for a few days and drink in the idyllic surroundings.

Kuta, Lombok (Indonesia) The main development on Lombok's south coast, the quiet fishing town of Kuta (p.298) is an excellent base to kick back by the sea. The town's own sweeping strand accommodates both sun-worshippers and surfers, while the surrounding beaches are some of the island's most stunning: rent a bike and head west to Are Goleng and Mawun or east to Seger and Tanjung Aan.

Pulau Perhentian (Malaysia) Malaysia's most beautiful beaches are found on the twin islands of Pulau Perhentian – Perhentian Kecil and Perhentian Besar (p.457) – where crystal-clear waters lap against secluded, white-sand strands. Offshore wreck dives and snorkel sites offer opportunities for beginners and pros alike.

El Nido (Philippines) Though El Nido's main beach (p.663) is a little scruffy, the surroundings are truly inspirational – this iridescent bay is the jumping-off point for the enchantingly beautiful Bacuit archipelago, 45 jungle-smothered outcrops of limestone riddled with karst cliffs, sinkholes and idyllic lagoons.

Ko Tao (Thailand) Ko Tao (Turtle Island), so named because its outline resembles a turtle nose-diving towards Ko Pha Ngan, is home to a clutch of beautiful beaches (p.794). The rugged shell of the turtle is crenellated with secluded coves, while Hat Sai Ree, the turtle's underbelly, is a long curve of classic beach backed by palm trees.

Phu Quoc (Vietnam) Vietnam's largest offshore island, Phu Quoc (p.911) rises from its slender southern tip like a genie released from a bottle. Virtually unknown by outsiders a decade ago, it has now cast a spell on enough visitors to challenge Nha Trang as Vietnam's top beach destination.

Architectural wonders

1 BOROBUDUR, INDONESIA
Page 198

The biggest Buddhist stupa in the world, covered in delicately sculpted reliefs.

2 ESPLANADE – THEATRES ON THE BAY, SINGAPORE
Page 675

The strikingly modern "durians" house one of the city-state's most exciting entertainment complexes.

3 BAGAN, MYANMAR
Page 552

Few vistas match the sight of Bagan's two thousand temples, stupas and monasteries.

4 LUANG PRABANG, LAOS
Page 368

Luang Prabang's colonial houses and red-roofed Buddhist temples have won it a place on the UNESCO World Heritage list.

5 ROYAL CITY OF HUE, VIETNAM
Page 869

A majestic citadel and grand imperial mausoleums dotted along the Perfume River.

6 ANGKOR WAT, CAMBODIA
Page 92

This immense Hindu temple complex is nothing short of magnificent.

7 CITY SKYLINE, HONG KONG
See box, page 139

One of the most impressive urban vistas in the world.

1

2

3

4

5

6

7

Eat like a local

1 NASI GORENG, INDONESIA
Page 169

You'll find many variants of this classic snack: fried rice with shredded meat and vegetables.

2 DIM SUM, HONG KONG
See box, page 125

Dim sum – a selection of little dumplings and dishes – is the classic Cantonese way to start the day.

3 AMOK DT'RAY, CAMBODIA
Page 70

In this mild Cambodian curry, fish is mixed with coconut milk and seasonings before being wrapped in banana leaves and baked.

4 MOHINGAR, MYANMAR
Page 524

Breakfast on catfish soup with vermicelli, onions, lemongrass, garlic, chilli and lime.

5 CHILLI CRAB, SINGAPORE
Page 671

Try the quintessential Singaporean dish, stir-fried crab in a sweet, sour and spicy tomato chilli, at one of the city's numerous hawker centres.

6 PHO, VIETNAM
Page 830

You'll find steaming bowls of pho, pronounced "fur", across Vietnam.

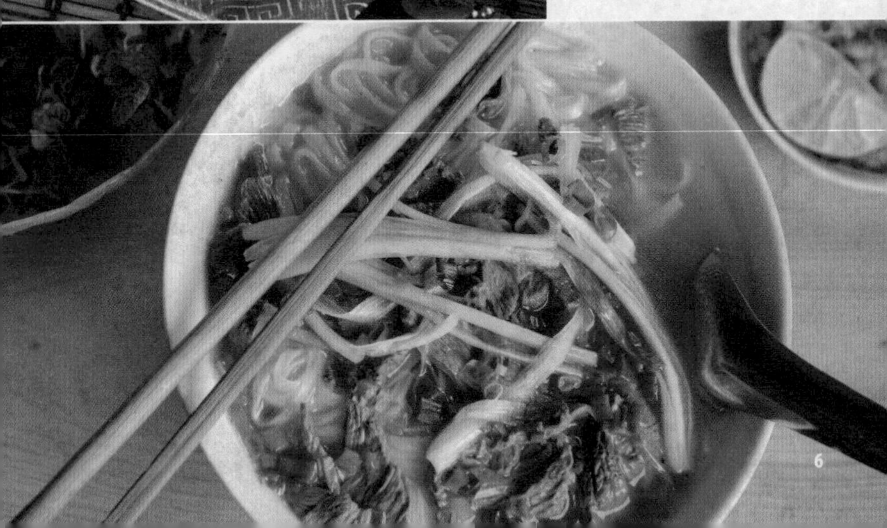

1
2
3
4

5

The great outdoors

1 G-LAND, INDONESIA
Page 211
Indonesia's world-class surf is best tackled from April to October.

2 THE NORTHWESTERN CIRCUIT, VIETNAM
Page 856
Take a mountain-bike tour of Vietnam's mountainous far north.

3 LUANG NAMTHA, LAOS
Page 383
Strike out into the wild highlands on a tour from Luang Namtha, visiting hill-tribe villages en route.

4 THE VISAYAS, THE PHILIPPINES
Page 631
Meet loggerhead turtles or whalesharks on a marine exploration of the Visayas.

5 MOUNT KINABALU, MALAYSIA
Page 502
Southeast Asia's highest peak is a challenging but straightforward two-day hike.

6 BUKIT LAWANG, INDONESIA
Page 223
Observe orang-utan antics at Bukit Lawang in Sumatra.

7 KRABI, THAILAND
Page 808
Discover your own lonely bays and mysterious lagoons on a sea-kayak tour of Krabi.

6

7

Get away from it all

1 GILI MENO, INDONESIA

Page 292

Take a ride on an outrigger on Indonesia's "honeymoon island", Gili Meno.

2 TREKKING AROUND SA PA, VIETNAM

Page 857

See a different side to Vietnam on a hike to ethnic-minority villages around Sa Pa.

3 WAT PHOU, CHAMPASAK, LAOS

Page 396

Explore the spellbinding pre-Angkorian ruins of Wat Phou.

4 BANAUE RICE TERRACES, THE PHILIPPINES

Page 621

The stairways to heaven; for the best view, trek through them to Batad.

5 KHAO SOK NATIONAL PARK, THAILAND

Page 801

Kayak through the humid jungle, then spend the night in a lakeside rafthouse.

6 HSIPAW, MYANMAR

Page 581

Explore the trekking routes from this once sleepy backwater in Shan State.

2

3
4
5
6

Itineraries

You can't expect to fit everything Southeast Asia has to offer into one trip and we don't suggest you try. On the following pages is a selection of itineraries that guide you through the different countries, picking out a few of the best places and major attractions along the way. For those taking a big trip through the region you could join a few together – across from northern Thailand into Laos and down the mighty Mekong, for example. There is, of course, much to discover off the beaten track, so if you have the time it's worth exploring the smaller towns and villages further afield, finding your own deserted island, perfect hill town or just a place you love to rest up and chill out.

VIETNAM

Few countries have changed so much over such a short time as Vietnam. Today, the country is a veritable phoenix arisen from the ashes. Many visitors find a vast number of places to visit that intrigue and excite them in Hanoi, Ho Chi Minh City and the other major centres; but despite the cities' allure, it's the country's striking landscape that most impresses.

❶ **Hanoi** Vietnam's historical, political and cultural capital, an animated maze of old merchant streets and grand French-colonial architecture. **See p.837**

❷ **Ha Long Bay** Sail around this UNESCO World Heritage Site, where two thousand limestone karsts jut out of the shimmering turquoise waters. **See p.851**

❸ **Sa Pa** Bustling market town nestled in the northern mountains that's a popular base for tours to ethnic minority villages, and as the starting point for a scenic train ride back to Hanoi through the dramatic landscape of Vietnam's northwestern circuit. **See p.857**

❹ **Hue** Tranquil yet engaging city famous for its nineteenth-century imperial architecture, and as a base for tours to the DMZ. **See p.869**

❺ **Hoi An** Charmingly seductive sixteenth-century merchant town, offering excellent shopping opportunities and an attractive beach. **See p.877**

ABOVE FLOATING MARKET, VIETNAM; RICE PADDIES, BALI

❻ Nha Trang The country's pre-eminent party town, with a popular municipal beach, boat trips to nearby islands, diving, snorkelling and nearby Cham architecture. **See p.883**

❼ Mui Ne Watersports hub with a vast stretch of golden, palm-shaded beach, laidback backpacker hangouts and sand dunes. **See p.887**

❽ Da Lat Vietnam's premier hill station and the gateway to the Central Highlands. **See p.893**

❾ Phu Quoc Vietnam's largest island, a restful place fringed with sandy beaches and an offshore archipelago perfect for diving and snorkelling. **See p.911**

❿ Mekong Delta Interconnecting canals and rivers cut through lush rice paddies; hop on a boat to visit one of the region's vibrant floating markets. **See p.906**

⓫ Ho Chi Minh City Vietnam's bustling second city; an effervescent collusion of French colonial style and brash, cosmopolitan youth. **See p.896**

MYANMAR (BURMA)

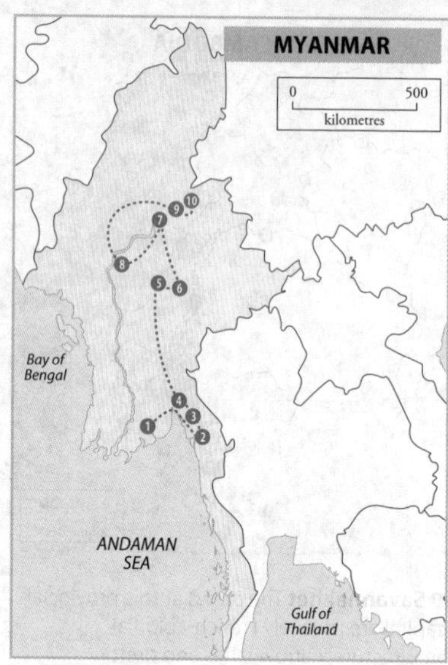

This is a fascinating time to discover Myanmar, previously cut off from the Western world for decades. Beyond the country's rice paddies, temples and beautiful mountain scenery, you'll find people eager to introduce foreigners to their country and culture. It's an enchanting destination.

❶ Yangon Start your trip exploring the colonial-era buildings, street markets and glorious Shwedagon Paya in the former capital, Yangon. **See p.531**

❷ Mawlamyine Once the capital of British Lower Burma, this is now Myanmar's third-largest city. **See p.548**

❸ Hpa-an Take the boat from Mawlamyine to Hpa-an where you can watch the sun rise over the serene Kan Thar Yar Lake. **See p.549**

❹ Kyaiktiyo The precariously balanced Golden Rock at Kyaiktiyo is one of the holiest Buddhist sites in the country. **See p.547**

❺ Kalaw Use Kalaw as a base for one- or two-day treks to visit ethnic-minority villages. **See p.562**

❻ Inle Lake Sample traditional life (or try your luck "leg rowing") on this stunning stretch of water. **See p.565**

❼ Mandalay Watch the sun set over the commercial hub of northern Myanmar from Mandalay Hill. **See p.569**

❽ Bagan Take a hot-air balloon ride at dawn over these awe-inspiring temples. **See p.552**

❾ Pyin Oo Lwin Botanical gardens beckon at this former hill station. **See p.579**

❿ Hsipaw Ride the train across Goteik viaduct to reach Hsipaw, an increasingly popular trekking base. **See p.581**

LAOS AND CAMBODIA

Once little visited, Laos and Cambodia are now firmly established on the Southeast Asian tourist trail. From forest-clad hills and impenetrable jungle to white-sand beaches and relaxed offshore islands Cambodia packs a lot into a small area. Landlocked Laos remains one of Southeast Asia's most beguiling destinations; its people are undoubtedly one of the highlights of any visit.

❶ Houayxai to Luang Prabang The unmissable two-day trip down the Mekong River ends in beguiling Luang Prabang, the city of golden spires. **See box, p.386**

❷ Vang Vieng A natural playground with stunning scenery; the perfect place for cycling, caving, and floating down the river on an inner tube. **See p.364**

❸ Vientiane A charming capital boasting a number of interesting temples, good restaurants and the chance to indulge in a relaxing herbal sauna. **See p.356**

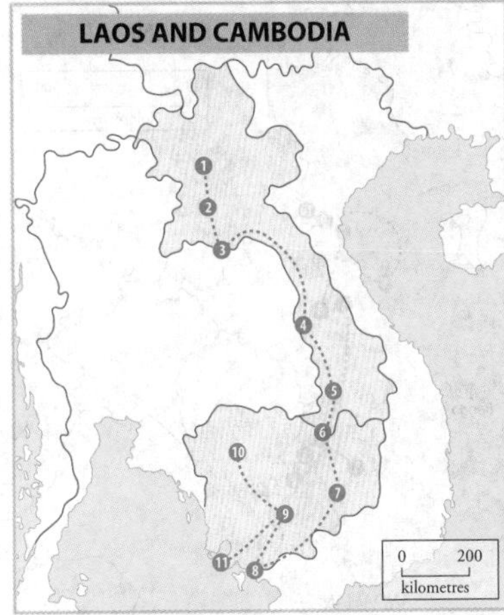

❹ Savannakhet The draws at this provincial capital are its lovely French-colonial architecture, narrow lanes and pretty shophouses. See p.388

❺ Champasak This sleepy little town makes the perfect base to explore the atmospheric Khmer ruins of Wat Phou. See p.395

❻ Si Phan Don Spend your days chilling out in a hammock on one of the four thousand islands scattered across the Mekong, before picking up a minibus to Stung Treng in Cambodia. See p.397

❼ Kratie The unassuming town of Kratie is home to a colony of rare freshwater Irrawaddy dolphins. See p.113

❽ Kampot A lazy riverside town surrounded by fields and in the shadow of the abandoned French hill station on Bokor Mountain. See p.108

❾ Phnom Penh A pleasant sprawl of shophouses and boulevards, lustrous palaces and engrossing museums. See p.76

❿ Angkor An easy bus ride takes you to Siem Reap and the world-famous temples of Angkor. From here it's a straightforward journey to Bangkok, or back to Phnom Penh to continue. See p.87

⓫ Sihanoukville Cambodia's only proper beach resort provides travel-worn tourists with a chance to relax, party and sun-worship on its sandy beaches, before heading on to Vietnam. The offshore islands, now easily accessible, are Southeast Asia's next big thing. See p.102

BANGKOK AND NORTHERN THAILAND

The clash of tradition and modernity in Thailand is most intense in Bangkok, the first stop on almost any itinerary. Within its historic core you'll find resplendent temples, canalside markets, a forest of skyscrapers and some achingly hip bars and clubs. The forested mountains of the north, meanwhile, are set apart from the rest of the country by their art, architecture, exuberant festivals and Burmese-influenced cuisine.

❶ Bangkok Immerse yourself in Thailand's frenetic capital, with its grand palaces, noisy tuk-tuks and thriving, crowded markets. See p.710

❷ Kanchanaburi A mix of charming rafthouses, waterfalls and lush hills, this place is a popular and chilled-out backpackers' haunt. See p.727

❸ Ayutthaya Rent a bicycle and explore the remarkable, extensive ruins of this ancient capital. See p.732

❹ Sukhothai The elegant temple remains in Old Sukhothai attest to its former glory. See p.739

❺ Umphang If you fancy breaking free of the tourist route, head for this lovely, isolated place surrounded by majestic mountains that are perfect for trekking. See p.743

❻ Chiang Mai The complete backpacker package: vibrant markets, hill treks to ethnic minority villages, glorious temples and delectable cuisine. See p.744

❼ Pai Amble through Pai's arty night market and finish the evening in one of the town's excellent live-music bars. See p.758

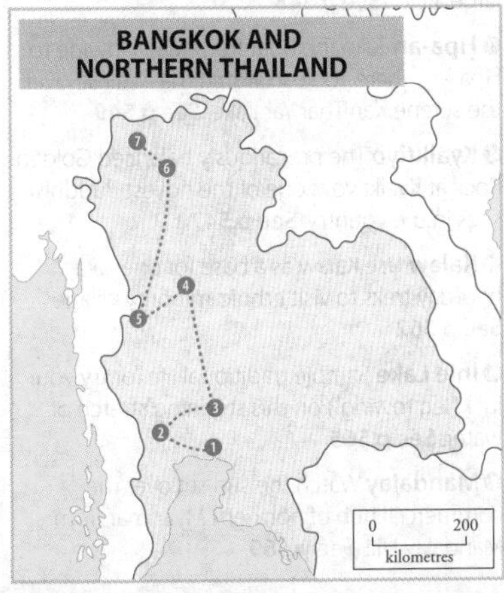

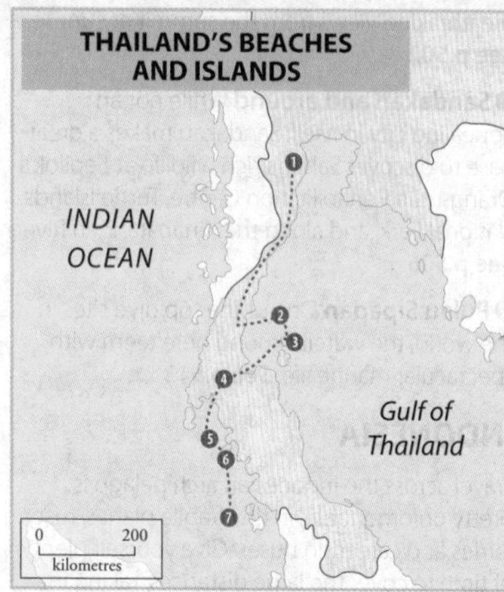

THAILAND'S BEACHES AND ISLANDS

Sand and sea are what many Thai holidays are about, and with over 3000km of tropical coastline, there are plenty of white-sand beaches to choose from. You can dive, swim and sunbathe year-round, for when the monsoon rains are battering one coast you merely have to cross to the other to escape them.

❶ **Phetchaburi** Retains an old-world charm with its historic shophouses, fascinating wats and Rama IV's fabulous hilltop palace. **See p.782**

❷ **Ko Tao** Rough, mountainous, jungle interiors, secluded east-coast beaches, a tastefully developed west-coast beach life and numerous dive schools to choose from. **See p.794**

❸ **Ko Pha Ngan** Famous for its pre-, post-, in-between and actual full-moon parties, Ko Pha Ngan also offers a few, as yet, untainted paradise beaches. **See p.790**

❹ **Khao Sok National Park** Tropical jungle, dotted with dramatic limestone crags, this is one of the most bio-diverse places on the planet. **See p.801**

❺ **Ko Phi Phi** An ugly tourist village that's host to undeniably fun all-night parties is offset by beautiful (yet crowded) Long Beach, great snorkelling and diving, and the magnificent Maya Bay. **See p.811**

❻ **Ko Lanta** Manages to combine a relaxed island getaway experience with spectacular sunsets and good nightlife. **See p.813**

❼ **Ko Lipe** While rapidly becoming overdeveloped, you will still find pockets of paradise here, and the stunning Ko Tarutao National Marine Park is yours to explore. **See p.818**

SINGAPORE AND MALAYSIA

From the fast-paced capital and charming colonial towns to the laidback Perhentian Islands and remote national parks, Malaysia is a varied country that warrants several weeks of exploration. Singapore is a useful gateway to the region, but don't be surprised if this futuristic, captivating city waylays you for longer than you expected.

❶ **Singapore** An easy introduction to Southeast Asia, with an array of tourist-friendly pleasures: shopping, markets, zoos, temples and delicious food. **See p.667**

❷ **Melaka** This old colonial town with a fascinating mix of cultures makes an ideal first stop in Malaysia from either Singapore or Indonesia. **See p.465**

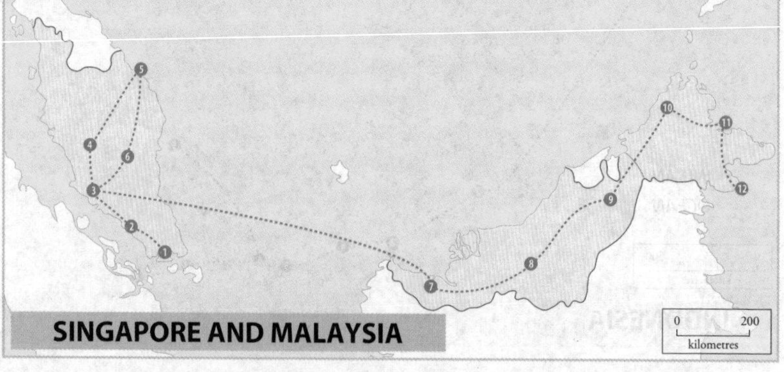

3 **Kuala Lumpur** Visit the thriving capital, packed with modern architecture, monuments, galleries and markets. **See p.421**

4 **Cameron Highlands** The cooling heights of the Cameron Highlands entice the crowds at weekends who come to enjoy the spectacular, lush scenery. **See p.433**

5 **Perhentian Islands** A pair of stunning small islands, with white-sand beaches and buckets of charm, this is the perfect place to kick back and relax. **See p.457**

6 **Taman Negara National Park** Explore the spectacular and ancient rainforests of Malaysia's interior. Taking the Jungle Railway from Kota Bharu in the northeast is a meandering, scenic way to reach it. **See p.450**

7 **Kuching** Sarawak's capital is an attractive, relaxed city that makes a good base for visits to Iban longhouses. **See p.476**

8 **The Batang Rajang** A journey along this 560km river takes you past isolated forts and logging wharfs, and through little-visited towns and longhouses into the true heart of Sarawak. **See p.485**

9 **Gunung Mulu National Park** Sarawak's premier national park bursts with flora and fauna, and is home to the impressive limestone spikes of the Pinnacles. **See p.490**

10 **Kinabalu National Park** An exhausting, exhilarating trek up Mount Kinabalu, the highest peak in Southeast Asia, is rewarded with breathtaking views from the summit at sunrise. **See p.502**

11 **Sandakan and around** While not an appealing city in itself, Sandakan makes a great base to discover Sabah's rich wildlife at Sepilok's Orang-utan Rehabilitation Centre, Turtle Islands National Park, and along the Kinabatangan River. **See p.506**

12 **Pulau Sipadan** One of the top dive sites in the world, the waters around here teem with spectacular marine life. **See p.513**

INDONESIA

Travel across the Indonesian archipelago is pretty unforgettable, in tiny fragile planes, rusty ferries and careering buses. Give yourself plenty of time to cover the large distances, taking in the country's soaring volcanoes, awe-inspiring dive sites, memorable wildlife and laidback island retreats.

1 **Bukit Lawang and Danau Toba** There's plenty to discover among the beautiful scenery of northern Sumatra: Bukit Lawang is home to the famous orang-utan centre, while further south lies the vast lake Danau Toba, with pleasant island resorts and fascinating traditional villages. **See p.223 & p.228**

2 **Jakarta** Whether you're travelling from Sumatra or Singapore, you may end up in the frenetic capital, where it's worth taking time to explore the interesting museums and enjoy the vibrant nightlife. **See p.177**

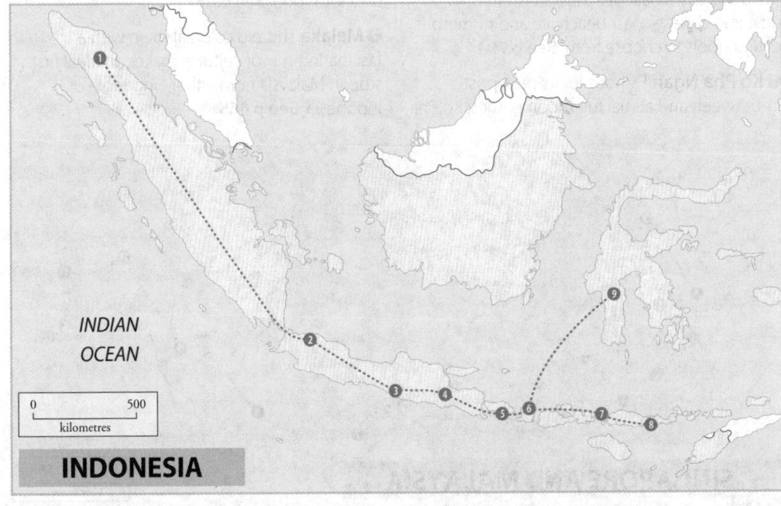

❸ Yogyakarta The cultural heart of Java, with a fascinating walled royal city, Yogya is a centre for Javanese arts and also the best place to base yourself for visiting the magnificent temples of Borobudur and Prambanan. **See p.190**

❹ Gunung Bromo A vast volcanic crater, with the still-smoking Gunung Bromo rising up from its base; the pre-dawn hike up the crater rim is well worth the effort for the dramatic sunrise views over a spectacular landscape. **See p.208**

❺ Bali The laidback Hindu island is still the most popular destination in the archipelago, with great nightlife, perfect surf, beautiful scenery and the chilled-out cultural centre of Ubud. **See p.241**

❻ Lombok Just a short hop from Bali, head to the awesome Gunung Rinjani for a few days' trekking, or to the Gili Islands, just off the northwest coast, for some fabulous diving. **See p.282**

❼ Komodo and Rinca Enjoy close encounters with the fearsome Komodo dragon. Overnight trips can be organized from Labuanbajo on Flores, or from Lombok. **See p.304**

❽ Flores A fertile, mountainous island, Flores has one of the most alluring landscapes in the country. The three craters of Kelimutu each contain a lake of vibrantly different colours. **See p.305**

❾ Tanah Toraja You'll probably have to backtrack to Bali before travelling up to Sulawesi, where the major attraction is the highlands of Tanah Toraja, home to a fascinating culture and flamboyant festivals. **See p.330**

THE PHILIPPINES

Graced by dazzling beaches, year-round sun and numerous opportunities for diving, island-hopping and surfing, the Philippines has long attracted a steady stream of foreign visitors. Yet there's far more to these islands than sand and snorkelling. Beyond the coastline are places to visit of a different nature; mystical tribal villages, ancient rice terraces, jungle-smothered peaks and crumbling Spanish churches.

❶ Manila The Philippine capital can appear sprawling and seedy, but it has a compelling energy all of its own. It's also the most convenient gateway to some of the country's more inaccessible areas. **See p.597**

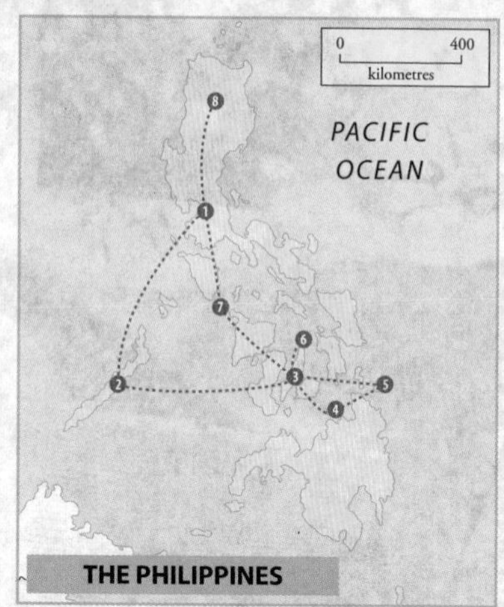

❷ Palawan A prehistoric landscape of underground rivers, giant lizards, shockingly beautiful limestone islands and some of the best wreck-diving in the world. **See p.660**

❸ Cebu city The Philippines' second city is nearly as frenetic as Manila, and an inevitable stop as you island-hop around the Visayas. **See p.634**

❹ Camiguin Easily reached from Cebu City, this small volcanic island offers some of the country's most appealing adventure activities and a laidback, bohemian arts scene. **See p.657**

❺ Siargao This small teardrop-shaped island located off the northeastern coast of Cagayan de Oro draws crowds of enthusiastic surfers eager to ride Cloud 9, one of the world's most acclaimed reef breaks. **See p.658**

❻ Malapascua and Bantayan For a slice of island living complete with limited electricity and captivating sunsets, these islands off the tip of Cebu are the Visayas at their best. **See p.641 & p.639**

❼ Boracay One of the world's most beautiful beaches, with nightlife to rival Manila, Boracay is still an unmissable stop on any trip to the Philippines. **See p.651**

❽ The Cordilleras For a Philippine experience a world away from the sun-drenched beaches of the south, head north to the cool mountain villages of the Igorot tribes, nestled among jaw-dropping rice-terrace scenery. **See p.615**

NONG KHAI, THAILAND

Basics

Getting there

The quickest and easiest way to get to Southeast Asia is by air. One of the cheapest options is to buy a flight to one of the region's gateway cities, such as Singapore or Bangkok, and make onward travel arrangements from there. If you're keen to combine your trip with a visit to India or China, you could consider a stopover or open-jaw ticket, which flies you into one country and out of another, allowing you to explore overland in between. If you're planning a multi-stop trip, then a Round-the-World or Circle Asia/Pacific ticket offers good value; the least expensive and most popular routes include one or more "surface sectors" where you have to make your way between point A and point B by road, rail or sea or by a locally bought flight. As an alternative to air travel, you could consider taking one of the world's classic overland trips, the Trans-Siberian Railway, through Russia and Mongolia to China, and continue from there to Indochina.

The biggest factor affecting the price of a ticket is the time of year you wish to travel. **High season** for many Asian destinations is over Christmas (when much of the region is experiencing its driest period), during the UK summer holidays, and over Chinese New Year. As such, you should book well in advance during these periods. Some airlines and travel agents charge more than others, so it's always good to shop around. Discount-flight agents often offer the best deals. You can also get good deals if you are a **student** or are **under 26** with discount agents such as STA and the Canadian company Travel CUTS.

Flying into Southeast Asia on a one-way ticket is fairly inexpensive and gives you plenty of options for onward travel, but it could cause **problems at immigration** (for example in Indonesia; see p.164). Stricter officials might ask to see proof of your onward or return transport, while others will be more satisfied if you can give details of a convincing onward route, with dates. Showing proof of sufficient funds to keep you going (even if this just means flashing a couple of credit cards) will also placate immigration officials. It's pretty rare for you to be asked for this information, but there's no harm in being prepared.

In some countries, you may have to apply for a **visa** in advance if arriving on a one-way ticket, rather than being granted one automatically at immigration, so always check with the relevant embassy before you leave. If you are continuing overland, you should research visa requirements at the border crossings before leaving home. Details on **overland transport** from neighbouring Southeast Asian countries are given in the introduction to each chapter.

Flights from the UK and Ireland

It's usually more expensive to fly **from the UK and Ireland** nonstop than to change planes in Europe, the Middle East or Asia en route. Some European airlines offer competitive fares to Asia from **regional airports** such as Glasgow, Manchester, Dublin and Belfast, although prices may often be higher than flights from London; Manchester is the only regional airport from where you can fly direct to destinations like Singapore and Hong Kong.

One of the cheapest and most useful **gateways** to Southeast Asia is **Bangkok**. London–Bangkok flights start at about £550 return, rising during peak times (July, Aug, Dec), and take a minimum of twelve hours. Another competitively priced and popular gateway city is **Singapore**. London–Singapore flights start at around £600 return, again rising during peak times (mid-July to Sept), and take at least twelve hours; flights to Kuala Lumpur are similarly priced.

If you want to go to China as well as Southeast Asia, consider buying a flight to **Hong Kong**. Direct London–Hong Kong flights start at about £550 return, and take at least eleven hours. Hong Kong gives you easy and inexpensive local transport

A BETTER KIND OF TRAVEL

At Rough Guides we are passionately committed to travel. We believe it helps us understand the world we live in and the people we share it with – and of course tourism is vital to many developing economies. But the scale of modern tourism has also damaged some places irreparably, and climate change is accelerated by most forms of transport, especially flying. All Rough Guides' flights are carbon-offset, and every year we donate money to a variety of environmental charities.

options into Guangdong province, from where you could continue west into Vietnam, and on into Laos.

If you're planning to fly from London to Vientiane, Phnom Penh, Manila or Yangon, you will have to change planes in Bangkok or Singapore, as there are currently no direct flights to these destinations, although you can now fly direct from London to Hanoi and Ho Chi Minh City in Vietnam on Vietnam Airlines. Vietnamese visas are still easier to obtain in Bangkok than in London, however, so it may be worth building in a stopover just for that.

A one-year open RTW ticket from London taking in Hong Kong, Singapore (with surface travel to Bangkok), Sydney, Auckland, the Cook Islands and Los Angeles costs from £1200, although basic options are around £600. The cheapest time to begin your RTW trip is usually post-Easter to mid-June.

Flights from the US and Canada

There's no way around it: **flights from North America** to Southeast Asia are long. With the exception of nonstop services to Singapore, Bangkok and Hong Kong from the US West Coast, all flights, including so-called "direct flights", will require a stop somewhere along the way. But this means you can take advantage of the **stopovers** offered by many airlines.

Numerous airlines run daily flights to **Bangkok** from major East and West Coast cities, usually making one stop, though it is possible to fly direct from Los Angeles. Flying time from both the West Coast via northern Asia and from New York via Europe is around eighteen hours. Departing from the West Coast, expect to pay from US$880 return, a bit more from the East Coast. From Canada, the flight takes around seventeen hours (from Vancouver via Hong Kong) or around twenty (from Toronto via Europe). Prices start from around Can$960 from either Vancouver or Toronto. **Singapore** is served from New York, Los Angeles (nonstop) and San Francisco; flying eastbound is more direct but still involves at least 22 hours' travelling time. Prices start around US$970 from New York; or US$830 from Los Angeles and San Francisco. From Toronto or Montreal, prices start at Can$1150 and, from Vancouver, Can$1050.

Fly via **Hong Kong** if you wish to visit mainland Asia. The cheapest low-season fare from the US West Coast is around US$870 for the round trip and typically includes a connection in Taiwan or Korea. A direct flight costs more and takes at least fourteen hours. From the East Coast, direct flights to Hong Kong take at least fifteen hours and the cheapest fares from New York start from around US$910. The best options for flights **from Canada** to Hong Kong include nonstop flights from Vancouver (13hr) and Toronto (15hr). Fares from Canada's west coast start at around CAN$760.

An RTW itinerary might be New York–Dubai–Singapore–Hong Kong–New York for around US$2160.

Flights from Australia and New Zealand

The cheapest way to get to Southeast Asia **from Australia and New Zealand** is to buy a one-way flight to one of the region's gateways such as Denpasar (Bali), Jakarta, Singapore, Kuala Lumpur, Bangkok or Hong Kong, and carry on from there by air, sea or overland.

Airfares from east coast **Australian gateways** are all pretty similar, although nonstop flights are sometimes cheaper from Darwin and Perth. **From New Zealand**, you can expect to pay about NZ$200–400 more from Christchurch and Wellington than from Auckland. Return fares to Indonesia, Malaysia, the Philippines and Brunei can be as little as Aus$400/NZ$800, while to Thailand, Indochina and Hong Kong you can expect to pay from Aus$450/NZ$1050.

A RTW ticket from Sydney to Singapore, taking in Bangkok, London, Berlin, New York and Los Angeles, starts at around Aus$2549; one from Auckland to Singapore, taking in Los Angeles, Las Vegas, London, Munich and Bangkok, costs from NZ$2899.

Agents and operators

Agents

Flight Centre UK ⓣ 0844 800 8660, Australia ⓣ 133 133, Canada ⓣ 1877 967 5302, New Zealand ⓣ 0800 243 544, South Africa ⓣ 0860 400 727, US ⓣ 1 877 992 4732, ⓦ flightcentre.com. Discounted flights, tours, packages and hotel bookings.

North South Travel UK ⓣ 01245 608291, ⓦ northsouthtravel.co.uk. Friendly, competitive travel agency, offering discounted fares worldwide. Profits are used to support projects in the developing world, especially the promotion of sustainable tourism.

STA Travel Australia ⓣ 134 782, New Zealand ⓣ 0800 474 400, South Africa ⓣ 0861 781 781; UK ⓣ 0871 230 0040, US ⓣ 1 800 781 4040, ⓦ statravel.com. Worldwide specialists in independent travel; also student IDs, travel insurance, car rental, rail passes, and more. Good discounts for students and under-26s.

Student Flights Australia ⓣ 1800 046 462, ⓦ studentflights.com.au. Flights and round-the-world tickets, plus adventure travel, hotel bookings, rail passes and TEFL placements, for students and budget travellers.

Trailfinders UK ⓣ 020 7368 1200, Ireland ⓣ 01 677 7888, Australia ⓣ 1300 780 212; ⓦ **trailfinders.com.** One of the best-informed and most efficient agents for independent travellers.

Tour operators

An organized tour is worth considering if you're after a more energetic holiday, have ambitious sightseeing plans and limited time, are uneasy with the language and customs, or just don't like travelling alone. The specialists listed below can also help you get to more remote areas and organize activities that may be difficult to arrange yourself, such as extended, multi-country tours, rafting, diving, cycling and trekking. Some also arrange volunteering opportunities. Unless stated otherwise, the prices refer to the land tour only, so you'll need to factor in extra for flights.

FROM THE UK AND IRELAND

Destinations Dublin ⓣ 01 435 0092, ⓦ **destinations.ie.** Specialists in Far Eastern and exotic destinations.

Earthwatch Institute UK ⓣ 01865 318838, ⓦ **earthwatch.org.** A wide range of opportunities to assist archeologists, biologists and community workers in homestays. Prices start at around £1400 for seven days.

Exodus UK ⓣ 020 8675 5550, ⓦ **exodus.co.uk.** Overland trips aimed at 18–45-year-olds, including the 16-day "Cycle Indochina and Angkor" (from £2149 including flights from London).

Explore UK ⓣ 0845 013 1537, ⓦ **explore.co.uk.** Heaps of options throughout Southeast Asia, including tours that explore the Angkor ruins in Cambodia and the jungles of Borneo.

Imaginative Traveller UK ⓣ 0845 287 2949, ⓦ **imaginative-traveller.com.** Broad selection of tours to less-travelled parts of Asia, including walking, cycling, camping, cooking and snorkelling. Their "A Tale of Two Islands (Bali and East Java)" tour costs £757 for 15 days.

Intrepid Travel UK ⓣ 0800 781 1660, ⓦ **intrepidtravel.com.** A wide range of holidays, including adventure and overland, plus a "basix" range for more budget-conscious travellers.

Symbiosis UK ⓣ 01845 123 2844, ⓦ **symbiosis-travel.com.** Environmentally aware outfit that offers specialist-interest holidays in Southeast Asia, cycling trips, and trekking through jungles and longhouse communities of Sarawak and Sabah.

FROM THE US AND CANADA

Adventure Center US ⓣ 1 800 228 8747, Canada ⓣ 1866 338 8735, ⓦ **adventure-center.com.** Offering numerous affordable Southeast Asian tours, including "Best of Indochina", a massive forty-day trip taking in both well-known and off-the-beaten-track destinations from US$2920.

Adventures Abroad US & Canada ⓣ 1 800 665 3998, ⓦ **adventures-abroad.com.** Specializing in small-group tours, including a twenty-day tour of Vietnam and Cambodia for around US$3500.

Geographic Expeditions US ⓣ 1 800 777 8183, ⓦ **geoex.com.** Specialists in "responsible tourism" with a range of customized tours and/or set packages, their trips are perhaps a bit more demanding of the traveller than the average specialist.

Mountain Travel-Sobek US ⓣ 1 888 831 7526, ⓦ **mtsobek.com.** Both group and private custom-made tours to Laos, Vietnam, Thailand, Malaysia, Indonesia and Cambodia.

Pacific Holidays US ⓣ 1800 355 8025, ⓦ **pacificholidaysinc.com.** Fairly inexpensive tour group. Trips include a fourteen-day "Best of Southeast Asia" sightseeing tour of Bangkok, Bali, Singapore and Hong Kong from US$3290.

FROM AUSTRALIA AND NEW ZEALAND

The Adventure Travel Company New Zealand ⓣ 03 364 3400 or ⓣ 04 494 7180, ⓦ **adventuretravel.co.nz.** NZ's one-stop shop for adventure travel and agents for Intrepid, Peregrine, Guerba Expeditions and a host of others.

Adventure World Australia ⓣ 1300 295 049, ⓦ **adventureworld.com.au**, New Zealand ⓣ 0800 238 368, ⓦ **adventureworld.co.nz.** Agents for a vast array of international adventure travel companies.

Allways Dive Expeditions Australia ⓣ 1800 33 82 39, ⓦ **allwaysdive.com.au.** All-inclusive dive packages with a choice of accommodation for every budget to prime locations throughout Southeast Asia.

Asia Travel Experts Australia ⓣ 1800 22 22 44, ⓦ **asiatravelexperts.com.** This experienced company offers economical packages to Vietnam, Thailand and Indonesia.

Earthwatch ⓣ 03 9682 6828, ⓦ **earthwatch.org/australia.** Volunteer work on projects in Borneo, Cambodia and Thailand.

Gecko's Grassroots Adventures ⓣ 03 8601 4444, ⓦ **geckosadventures.com.** Numerous tours of Thailand and most of Southeast Asia, from Aus$1100 for two weeks in Vietnam.

Intrepid Adventure Travel Australia ⓣ 1300 018 871, ⓦ **intrepidtravel.com.** Small-group tours to China and Southeast Asia with an emphasis on cross-cultural contact and low-impact tourism.

OWH (Overseas Working Holidays) Australia ⓣ 1300 651 639, ⓦ **owh.com.au**; New Zealand ⓣ 0800 314 448, ⓦ **owh.co.nz.** Volunteer in Cambodia, Vietnam and Thailand with this established outfit, and take your pick from teaching, conservation and childcare.

Stray Travel Australia ⓣ 1300 733 048; New Zealand ⓣ 09 526 2140, ⓦ **straytravel.asia.** This backpakcer-oriented company runs a network of hop-on, hop-off bus services covering Cambodia, Laos, Thailand and Vietnam.

The Surf Travel Co Australia ⓣ 02 9222 8870; ⓦ **surftravel.com.au.** A well-established surf travel company that can arrange accommodation and yacht charters in Indonesia, as well as give the lowdown on the best surf beaches in the region.

Travel Indochina Australia ⓣ 1300 138 755, ⓦ **travelindochina.com.au.** Offers low-impact hand-crafted tour packages, using mid- to top-range hotels.

World Expeditions Australia ⓣ 1300 720 000, New Zealand ⓣ 0800 350 354; ⓦ **worldexpeditions.com.** Committed to responsible travel and sustainable tourism, World Expeditions are specialists in small-group treks and adventure holidays.

AVERAGE DAILY TEMPERATURES AND RAINFALL

This climate chart lists average maximum daily temperatures and average monthly rainfall for the capital cities of Southeast Asia. Bear in mind, however, that each country has myriad microclimates, determined by altitude and proximity to the east or west coast among other factors; for more detail, see the "when to go" box in the introduction of each chapter.

	Jan	Feb	Mar	Apr	May	June	July	Aug	Sept	Oct	Nov	Dec
BANGKOK, THAILAND												
max (°C)	32	33	34	35	34	33	32	32	32	31	31	31
max (°F)	89.5	91.5	93	95	93	91.5	89.5	89.5	89.5	88	88	86
Rainfall (mm)	8	20	36	58	198	160	160	175	305	206	66	5
HANOI, VIETNAM												
max (°C)	20	21	23	28	32	33	33	32	31	29	26	22
max (°F)	68	69.5	73.5	82.5	89.5	91.5	91.5	89.5	88	84	78.5	71.5
Rainfall (mm)	18	28	38	81	196	239	323	343	254	99	43	20
HONG KONG & MACAU												
max (°C)	18	17	19	24	28	29	31	31	29	27	23	20
max (°F)	64.5	62.5	66	75	82.5	84	88	88	84	80.5	73.5	68
Rainfall (mm)	33	46	74	137	292	394	381	367	257	114	43	31
JAKARTA, INDONESIA												
max (°C)	29	29	30	31	31	31	31	31	31	31	30	29
max (°F)	84	84	86	88	88	88	88	88	88	88	86	84
Rainfall (mm)	300	300	211	147	114	97	64	43	66	112	142	203
KUALA LUMPUR, MALAYSIA												
max (°C)	32	33	33	33	33	33	32	32	32	32	32	32
max (°F)	89.5	91.5	91.5	91.5	91.5	91.5	89.5	89.5	89.5	89.5	89.5	89.5
Rainfall (mm)	159	154	223	276	182	119	120	133	173	258	263	223
MANILA, THE PHILIPPINES												
max (°C)	30	30	31	33	34	34	33	31	31	31	31	31
max (°F)	86	86	88	91.5	93	93	91.5	88	88	88	88	88
Rainfall (mm)	23	23	13	18	33	130	254	432	422	356	193	145
NAY PYI TAW, MYANMAR (BURMA)												
max (°C)	30	32	36	39	37	34	34	33	33	33	30	28
max (°F)	86	90	97	102	99	93	93	91	91	91	86	82
Rainfall (mm)	5	2	9	33	154	160	198	229	186	131	37	7
PHNOM PENH, CAMBODIA												
max (°C)	31	32	34	35	34	33	32	32	31	30	30	30
max (°F)	88	89.5	93	95	93	91.5	89.5	89.5	88	86	86	86
Rainfall (mm)	7	10	40	77	134	155	171	160	224	257	127	45
SINGAPORE												
max (°C)	30	31	31	31	32	31	31	31	31	31	31	31
max (°F)	86	88	88	88	89.5	88	88	88	88	88	88	88
Rainfall (mm)	252	173	193	188	173	173	170	196	178	208	254	257
VIENTIANE, LAOS												
max (°C)	28	30	33	34	32	32	31	31	31	31	29	28
max (°F)	82.5	86	91.5	93	89.5	89.5	88	88	88	88	84	82.5
Rainfall (mm)	5	15	38	99	267	302	267	292	302	109	15	3

Getting around

Local transport across Southeast Asia is uniformly good value compared to public transport in the West, and is often one of the highlights of a trip, not least because of the chance to fraternize with local travellers. Overland transport between neighbouring Southeast Asian countries is also fairly straightforward so long as you have the right paperwork and are patient; full details on cross-border transport options are given throughout the Guide. Travelling between countries by bus, train or boat is obviously more time-consuming than flying, but it's also cheaper and can be more satisfying.

Local transport

Not surprisingly, the ultra-modern enclaves of Singapore and Hong Kong boast the fastest, sleekest and most efficient transport systems in the region. Elsewhere, **long-distance buses** are the chief mode of travel in Southeast Asia, which, though often frequent, can be fairly nerve-wracking. Standards vary across the region, and often between different companies that cover the same route. At the bottom end seats are usually cramped and the whole experience is often uncomfortable, so wherever possible, try to book a pricier but more comfortable a/c bus for overnight journeys – or take the train. Shorter bus journeys can be very enjoyable, however, and are often the only way to get between places. Buses come in various shapes and sizes; full details of all these idiosyncrasies are given in each chapter.

Trains are generally the most comfortable way to travel any distance. Thailand and Peninsular Malaysia both have decent train networks and rolling stock, while Indonesia's is a notch below them, but still a better option than buses on Java. Vietnam's train system is also good for some journeys, and again it's often worth paying extra for more comfort on longer routes.

Taxis come in many forms, including the infamous **tuk-tuk** (three-wheeled buggies with deafening two-stroke engines), rickshaws powered by a man on a bicycle, or simply a bloke on a motorbike (usually wearing a numbered vest); only conventional taxis in the major cities have meters, so all prices must be bargained for and fixed before you set off. In many riverine towns and regions, it's also common to travel by taxi boat.

Regular **ferries** connect all major tourist islands with the mainland, and often depart several times a day, though some islands become inaccessible during the monsoon. In some areas, **flying** may be the only practical way to get around. Tickets are usually reasonably priced, especially if the route is covered by one of the region's growing number of low-cost airlines (see below).

In most countries, **timetables** for any transport other than trains and planes are vague or non-existent; the vehicle simply leaves when there are enough passengers to make the journey profitable for the driver. The best strategy is to turn up early in the morning when most local people begin their journeys. For an idea of frequency and duration of transport services between the main towns, check the "Arrival and departure" details in each chapter. **Security** is an important consideration on public transport (see p.43).

Throughout Southeast Asia it's possible to rent your own transport, though in Vietnam you can't rent self-drive cars. **Cars** are available in all major tourist centres, and range from flimsy Jimnys to a/c 4WDs; you will need your international driver's licence. If you can't face the traffic yourself, you can often hire a **car with driver** for a small extra fee. One of the best ways to explore the countryside is to rent a **motorbike**. They vary from small 100cc Yamahas to more robust trail bikes and can be rented from guesthouses, shops or tour agencies. Check the small print on your insurance policy and if you're renting a bigger bike (125cc and above), make sure your licence covers it. **Bicycles** are also a good way to travel, and are readily available to rent. Don't forget to check that the bicycle's in working order before you set off.

Low-cost regional airlines

The airlines listed below are some of the best-known options for getting from country to country.

AirAsia Kuala Lumpur **T** 600 85 9999, **W** airasia.com. AirAsia flies extensively to many places throughout the region and even to India, Japan and Australia. Frequent daily flights leave from their Kuala Lumpur hub to popular destinations such as Bali, Bangkok, Brunei, Ho Chi Minh City, Hong Kong, Jakarta, Kota Kinabalu, Manila, Phnom Penh, Phuket, Vientiane and Yangon; while a number of flights also leave from Bangkok to places including Bali, Chiang Mai, Hanoi, Hong Kong, Jakarta, Krabi and Singapore.

Bangkok Airways Bangkok **T** 02 270 6699, **W** bangkokair.com. Regular flights from Bangkok to Chiang Mai, Luang Prabang, Phnom Penh, Phuket, Siam Reap and Singapore.

MAJOR BORDER CROSSINGS, OVERLAND AND SEA ROUTES

The following is an overview of those land and sea crossings that are both legal and straightforward ways for tourists to travel between the countries of Southeast Asia. The information is fleshed out in the accounts of relevant border towns within this book. Long-distance tourist buses often run between major destinations, making cross-border travel simpler and quicker, but there are also numerous options by local transport.

TO BRUNEI

From Malaysia Boats to Brunei depart daily from Lawas and Limbang in northern Sarawak, and from Pulau Labuan in Sabah, itself connected by boat to Kota Kinabalu. From Miri in Sarawak, many buses travel daily to Kuala Belait, in Brunei, with some continuing direct to the capital, Bandar Seri Begawan.

TO CAMBODIA

From Vietnam Four border crossings: at Moc Bai to Bavet (buses run from HCMC to Phnom Penh); two crossings just north of Chau Doc on the Bassac River (by bus and boat); and from near Ha Tien over the border (Prek Chang) to Kep (by *xe om* only).

From Thailand Six border crossings: the key routes are from Aranyaprathet to Poipet (with connections to Siem Reap and Phnom Penh); the coastal crossing at Hat Lek, near Trat, then to Cham Yeam; and two more recently opened crossings from northeast Thailand – the Chong Chom–O'Smach border pass near Kap Choeng in Thailand's Surin province and the little-used Sa Ngam–Choam crossing.

From Laos One border crossing, at Veun Kham–Dom Kralor, on the route between Stung Treng and Si Phan Don.

TO HONG KONG AND MACAU

From China By train from Beijing to Hong Kong (via Guangzhou in Canton). Boats from China dock at China Ferry Terminal in Hong Kong and the Terminal Maritimo in Macau.

TO INDONESIA

From Malaysia and Singapore Several routes by boat from Malaysia and Singapore to ports in Sumatra including: Penang to Medan; Melaka to Dumai or Pekanbaru; Johor Bahru and Singapore to Pulau Batam and Pulau Bintan, in Indonesia's Riau archipelago (and on to Sumatra); and from Port Klang, near Kuala Lumpur, to Dumai. By bus from Kuching (Sarawak) to Pontianak (Kalimantan). By ferry from Tawau (Sabah) to Pulau Nunukan and Pulau Tarakan in northeastern Kalimantan.

TO LAOS

From Thailand Five main border crossings (by various combinations of road, rail and river transport): Chiang Khong to Houayxai; Nong Khai to Vientiane; Nakhon Phanom to Thakhek; Mukdahan to Savannakhet; and Chong Mek to Pakse.

From Vietnam Six border crossings: the Lao Bao Pass, 240km from Savannakhet (buses from Hue and Da Nang to Savannakhet); at Cau Treo, 105km from Vinh (buses from Da Nang to Savannakhet and Vientiane); the Bo Y crossing 80km from Kon Tum (buses to Attapu); Tay Trang crossing, near Dien Bien Phu, to Muang Khoua (buses from Dien Bien Phu to Muang Khoua); Nam Can to Nong Het, east of Phonsavan in Laos (buses from Vinh to Phonsavan); and the more remote, seldom-used Na Meo, east of Sam Neua.

From China By bus from Jinghong in China's southwestern Yunnan province to Oudomxai and Luang Namtha, via the border crossing at Boten.

From Cambodia One crossing, at Dom-Kralor-Veun Kham.

Cebu Pacific Air Philippines ⓣ 2702 2888, ⓦ cebupacificair.com. Flights to 35 domestic locations within the Philippines plus regular services to all main Asian cities including Brunei, Hong Kong, Kuala Lumpur, Singapore and Bangkok.

Dragonair Hong Kong ⓣ 3193 3888, ⓦ dragonair.com. A subsidiary of Cathay Pacific, Dragonair fly to destinations across the Asia Pacific region including Hanoi, Kota Kinabalu, Phnom Penh, Manila and Phuket.

TO MALAYSIA AND SINGAPORE

From Thailand Though there are buses and trains from Bangkok via Hat Yai into Malaysia, these routes are currently advised against because of political unrest in southern Thailand; check the latest situation before travelling (see box, p.819). The western routes are safer, particularly from Satun, from where you can take local transport to Kuala Perlis and Pulau Langkawi or Alor Setar; also by ferry from Ko Lipe to Pulau Langkawi.

From Indonesia Several routes by boat from Sumatra including: Medan to Penang; Dumai to Melaka; Tanjung Balai to Port Klang; from Pulau Batam and Pulau Bintan in the Riau archipelago to Johor Bahru and Singapore. From Kalimantan, you can take a bus from Pontianak to Kuching (12hr) in Sarawak. Or you can cross into Sabah on a ferry from either Pulau Tarakan (3hr) or Pulau Nunukan (1hr) to Tawau – a day's bus ride southeast of Kota Kinabalu.

From Brunei Direct boats from Bandar Seri Begawan to Limbang and Lawas (Sarawak), and Pulau Labuan (just off Sabah). Also, direct buses from Bandar Seri Begawan to Miri in Sarawak (via Seria and Kuala Belait) and Kota Kinabalu in Sabah (8hr).

TO MYANMAR (BURMA)

Check the status of border crossings before you travel.

From Thailand There are five border crossings: Ranong–Kawthaung, Three Pagodas Pass (Sangkhlaburi–Payathonzu; day-trips only), Ban Phu Nam Ron–Htee Khee, Mae Sot–Myawaddy and Mae Sai–Tachileik.

From China Organized tour groups can cross between Ruili (Yunnan province) and Muse.

TO THAILAND

From Malaysia and Singapore Travel to some areas of southern Thailand (such as Hat Yai) is not recommended (see box, p.819); check the latest situation before travelling. The safest routes are by minibus from Kangar to Satun and by boat from Kuala Perlis and Pulau Langkawi to Satun, and from Langkawi to Ko Lipe.

From Laos There are five main border crossings: Houayxai to Chiang Khong; Vientiane across the first Friendship Bridge to Nong Khai; Thakhek to Nakhon Phanom; Savannakhet to Mukdahan; and Pakse to Chong Mek.

From Cambodia Six border crossings: Poipet to Aranyaprathet; by bus from Sihanoukville via Koh Kong and Hat Lek to Trat in east Thailand; across the two border crossings from Pailin (easiest at Phsa Prom and one further north at Daung Lem) to Chanthaburi province in northeast Thailand; via the Chong Chom–O'Smach border pass to Surin; and the little-used Sa Ngam–Choam crossing.

From Vietnam By bus from Vietnam, via the Lao Bao Pass, Savannakhet in Laos and then across the Second Friendship Bridge to Thailand.

TO VIETNAM

From Laos Six border crossings: the Lao Bao Pass and the Cau Treo pass, near Vinh (buses via both from Vientiane and Savannakhet to Da Nang or Hue); the Bo Y crossing (from Attapeu to Kon Tum in Vietnam's Central Highlands); Tay Trang (from Muang Ngoi to Dien Bien Phu); Nong Het Nam Can (from Phonsavan to Vinh); and the remote, seldom-used Na Meo crossing (east of Sam Neua).

From Cambodia Four crossings: Moc Bai (buses from Phnom Penh, and from Moc Bai on to Ho Chi Minh City); two crossings just north of Chau Doc in the Mekong Delta (boat or bus); and the Xa Xia/Ha Tien border crossing near Kep and Kampot in Cambodia to Ha Tien in Vietnam.

From China Three crossings: Lao Cai (from Kunming in China by bus, or by direct train from Beijing to Hanoi); Mong Cai (by bus from Guangzhou); and the Huu Nghi border crossing (by bus or train from Pingxiang or Nanning).

Garuda Jakarta ⓣ 021 2351 9999, ⓦ garuda-indonesia.com. Indonesia's national airline. Frequent flights from Denpasar and its hub at Jakarta to Kuala Lumpur and Singapore, plus numerous domestic and regional destinations.

Jet Star Asia Singapore ⓣ 800 6161 977, ⓦ jetstar.com. Daily flights from Singapore to Bangkok, Bali, Ho Chi Minh City, Hong Kong, Jakarta, Kuala Lumpur, Macau, Manila and Phnom Penh, and less frequent flights to Siem Reap.

Lao Airlines Vientiane ⓣ 021 212 057, ⓦ **laoairlines.com.** Frequent flights from Vientiane and Luang Prabang to Bangkok, Chiang Mai, Hanoi and Siem Reap, as well as flights to Phnom Penh and Singapore, and within Laos.

MASwings Sabah and Sarawak ⓣ 1300 883 000, ⓦ **maswings.com.my.** The best-value fares to the biggest variety of destinations within Malaysian Borneo.

Nokair Bangkok ⓣ 02 627 2000, ⓦ **nokair.com.** Frequent daily flights from Bangkok to Chiang Mai, Koh Phi Phi and Phuket.

Silk Air Singapore ⓣ 6223 8888, ⓦ **silkair.com.** Daily flights from Singapore to Kota Kinabalu, Kuala Lumpur, Kuching, Phnom Penh, Phuket, Siem Reap and Yangon, and less frequent flights to Chiang Mai, Lombok and Balikpapan.

Thai Airways Bangkok ⓣ 02 545 3690, ⓦ **thaiairways.com.** Frequent daily flights from Bangkok to Hanoi, Ho Chi Minh City, Hong Kong, Kuala Lumpur, Macau, Manila, Phnom Penh, Phuket, Singapore and Vientiane.

Tiger Airways Singapore ⓣ 65 680 84437, ⓦ **tigerairways.com.** Daily flights from Singapore to Bangkok, Ho Chi Minh City, Kuala Lumpur, Macau, Penang and Phuket, and less frequent flights to Hanoi, Jakarta and Kuching.

Vietnam Airlines Hanoi ⓣ 04 3832 0320, ⓦ **vietnamairlines.com.** Regular daily flights from Hanoi and Ho Chi Minh City to Siem Reap and Vientiane, plus daily flights to Bangkok, Hong Kong, Kuala Lumpur, Luang Prabang, Phnom Penh and Singapore.

Accommodation

You'll rarely have a problem finding inexpensive accommodation in Southeast Asia, particularly if you stick to the main tourist areas. The mainstays of the travellers' scene are guesthouses (also known as bungalows, homestays or backpackers'), which can be anything from a bamboo hut to a three-storey concrete block.

Guesthouses and hotels

A standard **guesthouse** room will be a simple place with one or two beds, hard mattresses, thin walls and a fan – some, but not all, have a window (usually screened against mosquitoes), and the cheapest ones share a bathroom. Always ask to see several rooms before opting for one, as standards can vary widely within the same establishment.

> **ACCOMMODATION PRICES**
>
> All accommodation prices in this guide represent the cost of the cheapest double room available in high season.

For a **basic double room** with shared bathroom in a guesthouse that's in a capital city or tourist centre, rates start at about US$3 in Cambodia, Indonesia and Laos, US$6 in Thailand, US$8 in Malaysia and Vietnam, US$10 in Myanmar, US$15 in the Philippines, and a rather high US$25 in Brunei, Hong Kong and Singapore.

In smaller towns and beach resorts, rates can be significantly lower, and prices everywhere are usually negotiable during low season. **Single rooms** tend to cost about two-thirds the price of a double, but many guesthouses also offer dorm beds, which can cost as little as US$3 a night. More specific accommodation costs are given in the Basics section of each chapter. Many places now provide useful **facilities**, such as restaurants, travellers' notice boards, internet, safes for valuables, left-luggage, laundry and tour-operator desks. At most guesthouses, **check-out time** is noon; during high season it's worth arriving as early as possible to ensure you get a room, unless you've got one booked already. Although many hostels and guesthouses still don't accept telephone bookings (language is also a barrier), an increasing number now allow you to book your accommodation online.

If you venture to towns that are completely off the tourist circuit, you'll find that the cheapest accommodation is usually the bland and sometimes seedy **cheap urban hotels** located near bus and train stations. These places are designed for local businesspeople rather than tourists and may double as brothels; they tend to be rather soulless, but are usually inexpensive and clean enough.

For around US$15–40 almost anywhere in Southeast Asia except Singapore and Hong Kong, you can get yourself a comfortable room in a smart guesthouse or small **mid-range hotel**. These are often very good value, offering pleasantly furnished rooms, with private hot-water bathroom, and quite possibly a/c, a fridge and a TV as well. Some of these also have a swimming pool.

Hostels

Hostels are common in major destinations throughout the region, and many are more stylish and secure than their guesthouse counterparts.

Village accommodation

In the more remote and rural parts of Southeast Asia, you may get the chance to stay in **village accommodation**, be it the headman's house, a family home, or a traditional longhouse. Accommodation in these places usually consists of a mattress on the floor in

THE JOY OF BED BUGS

A bugbear of travellers all over the world is that an inexpensive place to lay your head sometimes equals a cosy night with small, scurrying strangers. **Bed bugs** are pesky little biters that lie uninvited in your bed, sealed into the creases and seams of the mattress. Tell-tale signs are small spots of dry blood on the mattress or sheet, or you may even see the small, pinhead-sized bugs themselves in the sides of the mattress. The joy of bed bugs is their ability to be transported from place to place. They'll worm their way into sleeping bags, sheets and even clothing, ensuring that wherever you lay your hat is their home too.

a communal room, perhaps with a blanket and mosquito net, but it's often advisable to take your own net and blanket or sleeping bag. As a sign of appreciation, your hosts will welcome gifts, and a donation may be in order, too. But in reality, the chance of encountering this kind of arrangement is quite rare. Some countries such as Laos forbid tourists from sleeping in homes that aren't approved by the government as tourist accommodation.

Camping

As accommodation is so inexpensive in Southeast Asia and there are few campsites, there's no point taking a tent. The only times when you may need to **camp** are in the national parks or when trekking, and you may be able to rent gear locally. Bungalow owners usually take a dim view of beach campers. Beaches, especially in tourist areas, are often unsafe at night, particularly for women by themselves.

Bathrooms

In most places in Southeast Asia, you can expect bathrooms with Western-style facilities such as sit-down toilets and either hot or cold-water showers. In rural areas, on some beaches, and in some of the most basic accommodation, however, you'll be using a **traditional Asian bathroom**, often referred to as a **mandi**, where you wash using the scoop-and-slosh method. This entails dipping a plastic scoop or bucket into a huge vat or basin of water and then sloshing the water over yourself. The basin functions as a water supply only and not a bath; all washing is done outside it and the basin should not be contaminated by soap or shampoo. **Toilets** in these places will be Asian-style squat affairs, flushed manually with water scooped from the pail that stands alongside; **toilet paper** tends to clog these things up, so if you want to avoid an embarrassing situation, learn to wash yourself like the locals do.

Food and drink

One of the highlights of a trip to Southeast Asia is its fabulous cuisine: from fresh Thai green curries to Lao larp (a "salad" of minced meat mixed with garlic, chillies, shallots, toasted rice, galangal and fish sauce), the variation of mouthwatering dishes is endless.

Each country has its own national dishes, but they also demonstrate influences from abroad – Vietnamese cuisine, for example, has many Chinese elements – and in large Southeast Asian cities it's always possible to find establishments specializing in Western and Indian food. Fresh fruit is always available (see box, p.36). Eating customs differ from country to country; see the separate chapters for further information on these. You can't buy alcohol in Brunei, but in other countries the most popular tipple is beer, rather than wine.

Water

Most **water** that comes out of taps in Southeast Asia has had very little treatment, and can contain a whole range of bacteria and viruses – always stick to bottled, boiled or sterilized water. Except in the furthest-flung corners of Southeast Asia, **bottled water** is on sale everywhere. Be wary of salads and vegetables that have been washed in tap water, and note that **ice** is not always made from sterilized water.

The only time you're likely to be out of reach of bottled water is when trekking into remote areas, in which case you must boil or sterilize your water.

General precautions

Most health problems experienced by travellers are a direct result of food they've eaten. Avoid eating uncooked vegetables and fruits that cannot be peeled, and be warned that you risk ingesting worms and other parasites from dishes containing raw meat or fish. Cooked food that has been sitting out for an undetermined period of time should also be treated with suspicion. Avoid sharing glasses

TROPICAL FRUITS OF SOUTHEAST ASIA

You'll find fruit offered everywhere – neatly sliced in glass boxes on hawker carts, blended into delicious shakes at night-market stalls, and served as dessert in restaurants. Here are some of the region's less familiar fruits:

Custard apple (soursop) Knobbly, grey-green skin hiding creamy, almond-coloured blancmange-like flesh and many seeds.

Durian The most prized, and expensive, fruit, with a greeny-yellow, spiky exterior. Inside, it divides into segments of thick, yellow-white flesh that give off a disgustingly strong stink that's been compared to a mixture of mature cheese and caramel.

Guava Green, textured skin and sweet, crisp flesh that can be pink or white and is studded with tiny edible seeds.

Jackfruit Large, pear-shaped fruit with a thick, bobbly, greeny-yellow shell protecting sweet, yellow flesh. Green, unripe jackfruit is sometimes cooked as a vegetable in curries.

Mangosteen The size of a small apple, with smooth, purple skin and a fleshy inside that divides into succulent, white segments that are sweet though slightly acidic.

Papaya (paw-paw) Similar in size and shape to a large melon, with smooth, green skin and yellowy-orange flesh.

Pomelo Looks rather like a grapefruit, though it is slightly drier and sweeter and has less flavour. Often used in salads.

Rambutan The bright-red soft, spiny exterior has a white, opaque fruit of delicate flavour, similar to a lychee.

Salak (snakefruit) Teardrop-shaped, the *salak* has a brown, scaly skin like a snake's, and a bitter taste.

Sapodilla (sapota) Small, brown, rough-skinned ovals that look a bit like kiwi fruit and conceal a grainy, yellowish pulp that tastes almost honey-sweet.

Starfruit (carambola) A waxy, pale-green fruit with a fluted, almost star-like shape. It resembles a watery, crunchy apple. The yellower the fruit, the sweeter its flesh.

and utensils. The amount of money you pay for a meal is no guarantee of its safety; in fact, food in top hotels has often been hanging around longer than food cooked at busy roadside stalls. Use your common sense – eat in places that look clean, avoid reheated food and be wary of shellfish.

Health

The vast majority of travellers to Southeast Asia suffer nothing more than an upset stomach, so long as they observe basic precautions about food and water hygiene (see p.35), and research pre-trip vaccination and malaria prophylactic requirements.

The standard of **local healthcare** varies across the region, with Laos and Myanmar having the least advanced systems (it is best to get across the border and go to a Thai hospital) and Singapore boasting world-class medical care. If you have a minor ailment, it's usually best to head for a pharmacy – most have a decent idea of how to treat common ailments and can provide many medicines without prescription. Otherwise, ask for the nearest doctor or hospital. Details of major hospitals are given throughout each chapter and there's an overview of local healthcare under "Medical care and emergencies" in the "Basics" section of each country covered. If you have a serious accident or illness, you may need to be evacuated home or to Singapore, so it's vital to arrange **health insurance** before you leave home.

When planning your trip, **visit a doctor** at least two months before you leave, to allow time to complete any recommended courses of vaccinations or anti-malarial tablets. For up-to-the-minute **information**, call the travellers' health phone lines or visit a travel clinic. In the UK, pick up the Department of Health's free publication, *Health Advice for Travellers*, available at the post office. The content of the booklet, which contains immunization advice, is also available at Ⓦdh.gov.uk. There are also several helpful websites (see p.39).

General precautions

Bacteria thrive in the tropics, and the best way to combat them is to keep up standards of personal hygiene. Frequent **bathing** is essential and hands should be washed before eating, especially in countries where cutlery is not traditionally used. Cuts or scratches can become infected very easily and should be thoroughly cleaned, disinfected and bandaged to keep dirt out.

Ask locally before **swimming** in freshwater lakes and rivers, including the Mekong River, as tiny

worms carrying diseases such as bilharzia infect some tracts of fresh water in Southeast Asia. The worm enters through the skin and may cause a high fever after some weeks, but the recognizable symptoms of stomach pain and blood in the urine only appear after the disease is established, which may take months or even years. At this point, some damage to internal organs may have occurred.

Many countries in Southeast Asia have significant **AIDS** problems. Condoms are available at pharmacies throughout the region, though the quality is not always reliable: it's best to bring a supply with you, take special care with expiry dates and bear in mind that condoms don't last as long when kept in the heat. Blood transfusions, intravenous drug use, acupuncture, dentistry, tattooing and body piercing are also high-risk.

Inoculations

No compulsory vaccinations are required for entry into any part of Southeast Asia, but health professionals strongly recommend that travellers to the region get **inoculations** against the following common and debilitating diseases: typhoid, hepatitis A, tetanus and polio. In addition, you may be advised to have some of the following vaccinations, for example, if travelling during the rainy season or if planning to stay in remote rural areas: rabies, hepatitis B, Japanese encephalitis, diphtheria, meningitis and TB. If you're only going to Hong Kong and Macau, you may not have to get any inoculations. If you've been in an area infected with yellow fever during the fourteen days before your arrival in Southeast Asia, you will need to bring your yellow fever certificate with you to prove you've been vaccinated against the disease.

Malaria

All of Southeast Asia lies within a **malarial zone**, although in many urban and developed tourist areas there is little risk (see box, p.38). Most health professionals advise travellers on a multi-country trip through Southeast Asia to take full precautions against malaria, which is a very dangerous and potentially fatal disease. Information regarding malaria is constantly being updated, so it's absolutely essential to get medical advice before you travel.

Malaria is caused by a parasite in the saliva of the anopheles mosquito that is passed into the human when bitten by the mosquito. There are many strains of the disease, and some are resistant to particular prophylactic drugs. The following are the most common anti-malarial tablets: chloroquine (Avloclor or Nivaquine) and proguanil (Paludrine), mefloquine (Lariam), doxycycline (Vibramycin) and Malarone (atovaquone-proguanil). The first three can be bought from pharmacies, but may have to be ordered in if you are going for a long trip, while the final three require a prescription from your doctor. All the malaria prevention medicines must be started before you travel, so make sure that you visit the doctor or pharmacy in good time. Chloroquine, proguanil and mefloquine should be started a week in advance, while Malarone and doxycycline can be taken one to two days prior to travelling. It's absolutely essential to finish your course of anti-malarial drugs, as there is some time delay between being bitten and the parasites emerging into the blood: taking all your medicine will cover the incubation time, eliminating the risk of infection.

None of the drugs is one hundred percent effective, and it is equally important for the **prevention of malaria** to stop the mosquitoes biting you. Mosquitoes are mainly active from dusk until dawn, and during this time you should wear trousers, long-sleeved shirts and socks, and smother yourself and your clothes in mosquito repellent containing the chemical compound DEET: shops all over Southeast Asia stock it. DEET is strong stuff, and if you have sensitive skin a natural alternative is citronella (sold as Mosi-guard in the UK), which is made from a blend of eucalyptus oils. At night, you should either sleep under a mosquito net sprayed with DEET or in a room with screens across the windows. Accommodation in tourist spots nearly always provides screens or a net (check both for holes), but if you're planning to go way off the beaten track, you can either take a net with you or buy one locally from department stores in capital cities. Mosquito coils – widely available in Southeast Asia – also help keep the insects at bay.

The **symptoms** of malaria are fever, headache and shivering, similar to a severe dose of flu and often coming in cycles, but a lot of people have additional symptoms. You will need a blood test to confirm the illness, and the doctor will prescribe the most effective treatment locally. If you develop

TELL YOUR DOCTOR WHERE YOU'VE BEEN

Some of the **illnesses** you can pick up in Southeast Asia may not show themselves immediately. If you become ill within a year of returning home, tell your doctor where you have been.

MALARIAL OR NOT?

Areas infected with malaria are constantly changing, so find out what the current situation is from your doctor before travelling.

Brunei Extremely low malarial risk.
Cambodia Malarial in all forested and hilly rural areas, in Siem Reap and along the Thai and Laos borders. Phnom Penh, Sihanoukville and Battambang have a very low malarial risk.
Hong Kong and Macau Extremely low malarial risk outside of northern rural areas.
Indonesia Very malarial, though low risk on the tourist resorts of Bali and Java.
Laos Very malarial though risk is minimal in Vientiane.
Malaysia Malarial, especially in Sabah and Sarawak, but low risk on the Peninsula.
Myanmar High risk of malaria across the country, apart from Mandalay and Yangon.
Philippines Malarial except on the majority of the Visayas Islands (except Romblon Island).
Singapore Extremely low malarial risk.
Thailand Generally low malaria risk, but very high risk along the borders with Cambodia, Laos and Myanmar, as well as northern Kanchanaburi province, and parts of Trat province (but low risk on Ko Chang).
Vietnam Malarial, but low risk in Hanoi, Ho Chi Minh City, the coastal plains between them and the northern Red River Delta.

flu-like symptoms any time up to a year after returning home, you should inform a doctor that you have been to a country where malaria is present and ask for a blood test.

Dengue fever

A nasty disease that's becoming more and more widespread is **dengue fever**, a virus carried by mosquitoes which bite day and night. There's no vaccine or tablet available to prevent the illness, which causes fever, headache and joint and muscle pains, as well as possible internal bleeding and circulatory-system failure. There is no specific drug to cure it, and the only treatment is lots of rest, liquids and Panadol (or any other acetaminophen painkiller, *not* aspirin, which can increase chances of haemorrhaging), though more serious cases may require hospitalization. It is vital to get an early medical diagnosis and get treatment.

Heat problems

Travellers unused to tropical climates regularly suffer from **sunburn** and **dehydration**. The important thing is to make sure that you drink enough water, wear suntan lotion and limit your exposure to the sun. As you sweat in the heat you lose salt, so you may want to add some extra to your food. A more serious result of the heat is **heatstroke**, indicated by high temperature, dry red skin and a fast, erratic pulse. As an emergency measure, try to cool the patient off by covering them in sheets or sarongs soaked in cold water and turn the fan on them; they may need to go to hospital, though. **Heat rashes**, **prickly heat** and **fungal infections** are also common: wear loose cotton clothing, dry yourself carefully after bathing and use medicated talcum powder.

Stomach problems

If you travel in Asia for an extended period of time, you are likely to come down with some kind of stomach bug. For most, this is just a case of **diarrhoea**, caught through bad hygiene, or unfamiliar or affected food, and is generally over in a couple of days. **Dehydration** is one of the main concerns if you have diarrhoea, so rehydration salts dissolved in clean water provide the best treatment. **Gastroenteritis** is a more extreme version, but can still be cured with the same blend of rest and rehydration. You should be able to find a local brand of **rehydration salts** in pharmacies in most Southeast Asian towns, but you can also make up your own by mixing three teaspoons of sugar and one of salt to a litre of water. You will need to drink as much as three litres a day to stave off dehydration. Eat non-spicy, non-greasy **foods**, such as young coconut, dry toast, rice, bananas and noodles, and steer clear of alcohol, coffee, milk and most fruits. Since diarrhoea purges the body of the bugs, taking blocking **medicines** such as Imodium is not recommended unless you have to travel.

The next step up from gastroenteritis is **dysentery**, diagnosable from blood and mucus in the (often blackened) stool. Dysentery is either amoebic or bacillary, with the latter characterized by high fever and vomiting. Serious attacks will require antibiotics, and hospitalization.

Giardia can be identified by foul-smelling wind and burps, abdominal distension, evil-smelling stools that float, and diarrhoea without blood or pus. Don't be over-eager with your diagnosis though, and treat it as normal diarrhoea for at least 24 hours before resorting to flagyl antibiotics.

Viruses

The frequency with which travellers suffer from these infectious diseases makes a very strong case for inoculation (see p.37). **Hepatitis A** is a water-borne viral infection spread through water and food. It causes jaundice, loss of appetite, and nausea and can leave you feeling wiped out for months. Seek immediate medical help if you think you may have contracted it. Havrix is a vaccination against hepatitis A, which can last for over 20 years provided you have had a booster 6–12 months after your first jab. You can also vaccinate against **hepatitis B**, which is transmitted by bodily fluids during unprotected sex or by intravenous drug use.

Cholera and **typhoid** are generally spread when communities rely on sparse water supplies. The initial symptoms of cholera are a sudden onset of watery, but painless, diarrhoea. Later, nausea, vomiting and muscle cramps set in. Cholera can be fatal if adequate fluid intake is not maintained. Copious amounts of liquids, including oral rehydration solution, should be consumed and medical treatment should be sought immediately. Like cholera, typhoid is also spread in small, localized epidemics. Symptoms can vary widely, but generally include headaches, fever and constipation, followed by diarrhoea. Vaccination against typhoid is recommended for all travellers to Southeast Asia.

Bites and stings

The most common irritations for travellers come from tiny pests and the danger of infection is to or via the bitten area, so keep bites clean. **Fleas**, **lice** and **bed bugs** (see box, p.35) adore grimy sheets, so examine your bedding carefully, air and beat the offending articles and then coat yourself liberally in insect repellent. Scabies, which cause severe itching by burrowing under the skin and laying eggs, might affect travellers who stay in hill-tribe villages.

Ticks are nasty pea-shaped bloodsuckers that attach themselves to you if you walk through long grass. A dab of petrol, alcohol, Tiger Balm or insect repellent, or a lit cigarette, should make them let loose and drop off; whatever you do, don't pull them off, as their heads can remain under the skin, and cause infection. Bloodsucking **leeches** can be a problem in the jungle and in fresh water. Get rid of them by rubbing them with salt, though anti-tick treatments also work. Apply **DEET** or **Dettol** to the tops of your boots and around the lace-holes. Specially woven leech socks are also available to buy in specialist travel shops back home and often locally in leech-infested areas; recommended for the squeamish.

Southeast Asia has many species of both land and sea **snakes**, so wear boots and socks when hiking. If **bitten**, the number one rule is not to panic. Stay still in order to slow the venom's entry into the bloodstream. Wash and disinfect the wound, apply a pressure bandage as tightly as you would for a sprain, splint the affected limb, keep it below the level of the heart and get to hospital as soon as possible. **Scorpion** stings are very painful but usually not fatal; swelling usually disappears after a few hours.

If stung by a **jellyfish**, the priority treatment is to remove the fragments of tentacles from the skin – without causing further discharge of venom – which is most easily done by applying vinegar to deactivate the stinging capsules. The best way to minimize the risk of stepping on the toxic spines of sea urchins, sting rays and stone fish is to wear thick-soled shoes, though these cannot provide total protection; sea-urchin spikes should be removed after softening the skin with a special ointment (like Tiger Balm), though some people recommend applying urine to help dissolve the spines. For sting-ray and stone-fish stings, alleviate the pain by immersing the wound in very hot water – just under 50°C – while waiting for help.

Rabies is transmitted to humans by the bite of infected animals; **tetanus** is an additional danger from such bites. All animals should be treated with caution, particularly monkeys, cats and dogs. Be extremely cautious with wild animals that seem inexplicably tame, as this can be a symptom. If you do get bitten, scrub the wound with a strong antiseptic and then alcohol and get to a hospital as soon as possible. Do not attempt to close the wound. The incubation period for the disease can be as much as a year or as little as a few days; once the disease has taken hold, it will be fatal.

Medical resources for travellers

AUSTRALIA AND NEW ZEALAND

Travellers' Medical and Vaccination Centre ⓣ 1300 658 844, ⓦ **traveldoctor.com.au.** Lists travel clinics in Australia, New Zealand and South Africa.

UK AND IRELAND

Fit for Travel Ⓦ **fitfortravel.nhs.uk.** Up-to-date travel health information from the NHS.

Hospital for Tropical Diseases Travel Clinic Ⓣ **0845 155 5000** or Ⓣ **020 3456 7890,** Ⓦ **thehtd.org/Travelclinic.aspx.**

MASTA (Medical Advisory Service for Travellers Abroad) Ⓦ **masta-travel-health.com** or Ⓣ **020 7731 8080** for the nearest clinic.

Tropical Medical Bureau Ireland Ⓣ **1850 487 674,** Ⓦ **tmb.ie.**

US AND CANADA

Canadian Society for International Health Ⓣ **613 241-5785,** Ⓦ **csih.org.** Extensive list of travel health centres.

CDC (Centers for Disease Control and Prevention) Ⓣ **1 800 232 4636,** Ⓦ **cdc.gov/travel.** Official US government travel health site.

International Society for Travel Medicine Ⓣ **1 404 373 8282,** Ⓦ **istm.org.** Has a full list of travel health clinics.

Culture and etiquette

Although the peoples of Southeast Asia come from a huge variety of ethnic backgrounds and practise a spread of religions, they share many social practices and taboos, many unfamiliar to Westerners. You will get a much friendlier reception if you do your best to be sensitive to local mores, particularly regarding dress. Country-specific social and religious customs are dealt with in the relevant chapters.

Dress

Appearance is very important in Southeast Asian society, and dressing neatly is akin to showing respect. Clothing – or the lack of it – is generally what bothers Southeast Asians most about tourist behaviour. You need to **dress modestly** whenever you are outside a tourist resort, and in particular when entering homes and religious buildings, and when dealing with people in authority, especially when applying for visa extensions. For women, that means below-knee-length skirts or trousers, a bra and sleeved tops; for men, long trousers. "Immodest" clothing includes thong bikinis, shorts, vests, and anything that leaves you with bare shoulders. Most Southeast Asian people find **topless** and nude bathing extremely unpalatable. If you wash your own clothes, hang out your **underwear** discreetly.

Visiting temples, mosques and shrines

Besides dressing conservatively, always take your **shoes** off when entering temples, pagodas and mosques. **Monks** are forbidden from having close contact with women, which means that as a female, you mustn't sit or stand next to a monk, even on a bus, nor brush against his robes, or hand objects directly to him. When giving something to a monk, the object should be placed on a nearby table or passed via a layman. All **Buddha images** are sacred, and should never be clambered over. When sitting on the floor of a monastery building that has a Buddha image, never point your feet in the direction of the image.

When visiting a **mosque**, women must cover their shoulders and possibly their heads as well (bring a scarf or shawl).

Many religions prohibit **women** from engaging in certain activities – or even entering a place of worship – during menstruation. If attending a **religious festival**, find out beforehand whether a dress code applies.

Social practices and taboos

In Buddhist, Islamic and Hindu cultures, various parts of the body are accorded a particular status. The **head** is considered the most sacred part of the body and the **feet** the most unclean. This means that it's very rude to touch another person's head – even to affectionately ruffle a child's hair – or to point your feet either at a human being or at a sacred image. Be careful not to step over any part of people who are sitting or lying on the floor (or the deck of a boat), as this is also considered rude. If you do accidentally kick or brush someone with your feet, apologize immediately and smile as you do so.

Public displays of sexual affection like kissing or cuddling are frowned upon across the region, though friends (rather than lovers) of the same sex often hold hands or hug in public.

Most Asians dislike **confrontational behaviour**, such as arguing or shouting, and will rarely outwardly display irritation of any kind.

Religion

Religion pervades every aspect of life in most Southeast Asian communities, dictating social practices to a much greater extent than in the West. All of the

world's major faiths are represented in the region, but characteristic across much of Southeast Asia is the syncretic nature of belief, so that many Buddhists, Hindus and Muslims incorporate animist rituals into their daily devotions as well as occasional elements of other major faiths.

Buddhism

Buddhists follow the teachings of Gautama Buddha who, in his five-hundredth incarnation, was born in present-day Nepal as **Prince Gautama Siddhartha**, to a wealthy family during the sixth century BC. At an early age, Siddhartha renounced his life of luxury to seek the ultimate deliverance from worldly suffering and strive to reach **Nirvana**, an indefinable, blissful state. After several years he attained enlightenment and then devoted the rest of his life to teaching the Middle Way that leads to Nirvana.

His **philosophy** was built on the Hindu theory of perpetual reincarnation in the pursuit of perfection, introducing the notion that desire is the root cause of all suffering and can be extinguished only by following the eightfold path or Middle Way. This **Middle Way** is a highly moral mode of life that encourages compassion and moderation and eschews self-indulgence and antisocial behaviour. But the key is an acknowledgement that the physical world is impermanent and ever-changing, and that all things – including the self – are therefore not worth craving. Only by pursuing a condition of complete detachment can human beings transcend earthly suffering.

In practice, rather than set their sights on Nirvana most Buddhists aim only to be **reborn** higher up the incarnation scale. Each reincarnation marks a move up a kind of ladder, with animals at the bottom, women figuring lower down than men, and monks coming at the top. The rank of the reincarnation is directly related to the good and bad actions performed in the previous life, which accumulate to determine one's **karma** or destiny – hence the obsession with "**making merit**". Merit-making can be done in all sorts of ways, including giving alms to a monk or, for a man, becoming a monk for a short period.

Schools of Buddhism

After the Buddha passed into Nirvana in 543 BC, his doctrine spread relatively quickly across India. His teachings, the Tripitaka, were written down in the Pali language and became known as the **Theravada School of Buddhism** or "The Doctrine of the Elders". Theravada is an ascetic form of Buddhism, based on the principle that each individual is wholly responsible for his or her own accumulation of merit or sin and subsequent enlightenment; it is prevalent in **Thailand**, **Laos** and **Cambodia** as well as in Sri Lanka and Myanmar.

The other main school of Buddhism practised in Southeast Asia is **Mahayana Buddhism**, which is current in **Vietnam**, and in **ethnic Chinese communities** throughout the region, as well as in China itself, and in Japan and Korea. The ideological rift between the Theravada and Mahayana Buddhists is comparable in scale to the one that divides Catholicism and Protestantism. Mahayana Buddhism attempts to make Buddhism more accessible to the average devotee, easing the struggle towards enlightenment with a pantheon of Buddhist saints or bodhisattva who have postponed their own entry into Nirvana in order to work for the salvation of all humanity.

Chinese religions

The **Chinese communities** of Singapore, Hong Kong, Macau, Malaysia, Vietnam and Thailand generally adhere to a system of belief that fuses Mahayana Buddhist, Taoist and Confucianist tenets, alongside the all-important ancestor worship.

Ancestor worship

One of the oldest cults practised among both city dwellers and hill-tribes people who migrated into Southeast Asia from China is that of **ancestor worship**, based on the fundamental principles of filial piety and of obligation to the past, present and future generations. Practices vary, but all believe that the spirits of deceased ancestors have the ability to affect the lives of their living descendants, rewarding those who remember them with offerings, but causing upset if neglected. At funerals and subsequent anniversaries, paper money and other **votive offerings** are burnt, and special food is regularly placed on the ancestral altar.

Confucianism

The teachings of **Confucius** provide a guiding set of moral principles based on piety, loyalty, humanitarianism and familial devotion, which permeate every aspect of Chinese life. Confucius is the Latinized name of K'ung-Fu-Tzu, who was born into a minor aristocratic family in China in 551 BC and worked for many years as a court official. At the age of 50, he set off around the country to spread his ideas on social and political reform. His central tenet was the importance

of **correct behaviour**, namely selflessness, respectfulness and non-violence, and loyal service, reinforced by ceremonial rites and frequent offerings to heaven and to the ancestors.

After the death of Confucius in 478 BC, the doctrine was developed by his disciples, and by the first century AD, Confucianism had absorbed elements of Taoism and evolved into a **state ideology** whereby kings ruled under the Mandate of Heaven. Social stability was maintained through a fixed hierarchy of relationships encapsulated in the notion of filial piety. Thus children must obey their parents without question, wives their husbands, students their teacher, and subjects their ruler.

Taoism

Taoism is based on the **Tao-te-ching**, the "Book of the Way", traditionally attributed to **Lao Tzu** ("Old Master"), who is thought to have lived in China in the sixth century BC. A philosophical movement, it advocates that people follow a central path or truth, known as Tao or "The Way", and cultivate an understanding of the nature of things. The Tao emphasizes effortless action, intuition and spontaneity; it cannot be taught, nor can it be expressed in words, but can be embraced by virtuous behaviour. Central to the Tao is the duality inherent in nature, a tension of complementary opposites defined as **yin** and **yang**, the female and male principles. Harmony is the balance between the two, and experiencing that harmony is the Tao.

In its pure form Taoism has no gods, but in the first century AD it corrupted into an organized religion venerating a deified Lao Tzu, and developed highly complex rituals. The vast, eclectic pantheon of Taoist **gods** is presided over by the Jade Emperor, who is assisted by the southern star, the north star, and the God of the Hearth. Then there is a collection of immortals, genies and guardian deities, including legendary and historic warriors, statesmen and scholars. Confucius is also honoured as a Taoist saint.

Islam

Islam is the youngest of all the major religions, and in Southeast Asia is practised mainly in **Indonesia**, **Malaysia**, **Singapore** and **Brunei**. It was founded by **Mohammed** (570–630 AD), a merchant from Mecca in Arabia, who began, at the age of forty, to receive messages from Allah (God). On these revelations Mohammed began to build a new religion: Islam or "Submission", as the faith required people to submit to God's will. Islam quickly gained in popularity in Southeast Asia, not least because its revolutionary concepts of equality in subordination to Allah freed people from the feudal Hindu caste system that had previously dominated parts of the region.

The Islamic religion is founded on the **Five Pillars**, the essential tenets revealed by Allah to Mohammed and collected in the **Koran**, the holy book that Mohammed dictated before he died. The first is that all Muslims should profess their faith in Allah with the phrase "There is no God but Allah and Mohammed is his prophet". The act of praying is the second pillar. Five daily prayers can be done anywhere, though Muslims should always face Mecca when praying, cover the head, and ritually wash feet and hands. The third pillar demands that the faithful should always give a percentage of their income to charity, while the fourth states that all Muslims must observe the fasting month of **Ramadan**. This is the ninth month of the Muslim lunar calendar, when the majority of Muslims fast from the break of dawn to dusk, and also abstain from drinking and smoking. The reason for the fast is to intensify awareness of the plight of the poor. The fifth pillar demands that every Muslim should make a pilgrimage to Mecca at least once in their lifetime.

Hinduism

Hinduism was introduced to Southeast Asia by Indian traders more than a thousand years ago, and spread across the region by the Khmers of Cambodia who left a string of magnificent castle-temples throughout northeast Thailand, Laos, and most strikingly at Angkor in Cambodia. The most active contemporary Hindu communities live in **Singapore** and **Malaysia**, and the Indonesian island of **Bali** is also a very vibrant, if idiosyncratic, Hindu enclave.

Central to Hinduism is the belief that life is a series of reincarnations that eventually leads to spiritual release. The aim of every Hindu is to attain **enlightenment** (*moksa*), which brings with it the union of the individual and the divine, and liberation from the painful cycle of death and rebirth. *Moksa* is only attainable by pure souls, and can take hundreds of lifetimes to achieve. Hindus believe that everybody is reincarnated according to their **karma**, this being a kind of account book that registers all the good and bad deeds performed in the past lives of a soul. Karma is closely bound up with caste and the notion that an individual should accept rather than challenge their destiny.

A whole variety of **deities** are worshipped, the most ubiquitous being Brahma, Vishnu and Shiva.

Brahma is the Creator, represented by the colour red and often depicted riding on a bull. As the Preserver, **Vishnu** is associated with life-giving waters; he rides the garuda (half-man, half-bird) and is honoured by the colour black. Vishnu also has several avatars, including Buddha – a neat way of incorporating Buddhist elements into the Hindu faith – and Rama, hero of the Ramayana story. **Shiva**, the Destroyer or, more accurately, the Dissolver, is associated with death and rebirth, and with the colour white. He is sometimes represented as a phallic pillar or lingam. He is the father of the elephant-headed deity **Ganesh**, generally worshipped as the remover of obstacles.

Animism

Animism is the belief that all living things – including plants and trees – and some non-living natural features, such as rocks and waterfalls, have **spirits**. It is practised right across Southeast Asia, by everyone from the Dayaks of Sarawak and the hill tribes of Laos to the city dwellers of Bangkok and Singapore, though rituals and beliefs vary significantly. As with Hinduism, the animistic faiths teach that it is necessary to live in harmony with the spirits; disturb this harmonious balance, by upsetting a spirit for example, and you risk bringing misfortune upon yourself, your household or your village. For this reason, animists consult, or at least consider, the spirits before almost everything they do, and you'll often see small **offerings** of flowers or food left by a tree or river to appease the spirits that live within.

Travel essentials

Costs

Your **daily budget** in Southeast Asia depends both on where you're travelling and on how comfortable you want to be. You can survive on £13/$20 a day in most parts of Cambodia, Laos, Indonesia, Malaysia, Thailand and Vietnam, around £14/$22 a day in the Philippines, £15/$25 a day in Myanmar, £25/$35 in Hong Kong, and on £18/$40 in Singapore, but for this money you'll be sleeping in very basic accommodation, eating at simple food stalls, and travelling on local non-a/c buses.

In some countries, prices for tourist accommodation and foreigners' restaurants are quoted in **US dollars**, though the local equivalent is always acceptable.

Travellers soon get so used to the low cost of living in Southeast Asia that they start **bargaining** at every available opportunity, much as local people do. Most buyers start their counterbid at about 25 percent of the vendor's opening price, and the bartering continues from there. But never forget that the few pennies you're making such a fuss over will go a lot further in a local person's hands than in your own.

Price tiering exists in parts of Southeast Asia, with foreigners paying more than locals for public transport, hotels and entry fees to museums and historical sites. Remember that prices vary within individual countries, especially when you enter more remote areas. Very few **student discounts** are offered on entry prices.

Tipping isn't a Southeast Asian custom, although some smarter restaurants expect a gratuity, and most expensive hotels/guesthouses add service taxes.

Crime and personal safety

Travelling in Southeast Asia is generally safe and unthreatening, though, as in any unfamiliar environment, you should keep your wits about you. The most common hazard is opportunistic theft, which can easily be avoided with a few sensible precautions. Occasionally, political trouble flares in the region, so before you travel you may want to check the official government advice on international trouble spots (see box, p.44). Most experienced travellers find this official advice less helpful than that offered by other travellers – online travellers' forums are useful (see p.48). In some countries, there are specific year-round dangers such as kidnapping (southern Philippines), and unexploded ordnance (Laos, Cambodia, Vietnam); details of these and how to avoid them are described in the introduction to the relevant country.

General precautions

As a tourist, you are an obvious target for opportunistic **thieves** (who may include your fellow travellers), so don't flash expensive cameras or watches around. Carry travellers' cheques, cash and important documents (airline tickets, credit cards and passport) under your clothing in a **money belt**. It's a good idea to keep $100 cash, photocopies of the relevant pages of your passport, insurance details and travellers' cheque receipts separate from the rest of your valuables.

Ensure that **luggage** is lockable and keep important documents on your person rather than in outer pockets. A **padlock** and chain, or a cable

lock, is useful for doors and windows at inexpensive guesthouses and beach bungalows, and for securing your pack on **buses**, where you're often separated from your belongings. If your pack is on the top of the bus or boat, make sure it is attached securely, and keep an eye on it whenever the bus or boat pulls into a station, jetty or port. Be especially aware of pickpockets on buses, who usually operate in pairs: one will distract you while another does the job. On **trains**, either cable-lock your pack or put it under the bottom bench-seat, out of public view. Be wary of accepting food and drink from strangers on long overnight bus or train journeys: there is a rare possibility that it's drugged in order to knock you out while your bags are stolen.

Some guesthouses and hotels have **safe-deposit boxes** or lockers, which solve the problem of what to do with your valuables while you go swimming. The safest lockers are those that require your own padlock, as valuables sometimes get lifted by hotel staff. Padlock your luggage when leaving it in hotel or guesthouse rooms.

Violent crime against tourists is not common in Southeast Asia, but it does occur. Obvious precautions include securing locks at night, and not travelling alone at night in an unlicensed taxi, tuk-tuk or rickshaw. Think carefully about motorbiking alone in sparsely inhabited and politically sensitive border regions. If you're going hiking on your own for a day, inform hotel staff of your route so that they can look for you if you don't return when planned.

Con artists and scams

Con artists are usually fairly easy to spot. Always treat **touts** with suspicion – if they offer to take you to a great guesthouse/jewellery shop/untouristed village, you can be sure there'll be a huge commission in it for them, and you may end up being taken somewhere against your will. A variation involves taxi drivers assuring you that a major sight is closed for the day, so encouraging you to go with them on their own special tour.

Some, but by no means all, **travel agencies** in the backpackers' centres of Southeast Asia are fly-by-night operations. Although it's not necessarily incriminating if a travel agent's office seems to be the proverbial hole in the wall, it may be a good idea to reject those that look too temporary in favour of something permanent and thriving. In Vietnam in particular, travel agents and guesthouses will copy the name of a successful and reputable company, so always double-check the address to ascertain that it is actually the place that's recommended.

Reporting a crime

If you are a victim of theft or violent crime, you'll need a **police report** for insurance purposes. Try to take someone along with you to the police station to translate, though police will generally do their best to find an English-speaker. Allow plenty of time for any involvement with the police, whose offices often wallow in bureaucracy; you may also be charged "administration fees" for enlisting their help, the cost of which is open to sensitive negotiations. You may also want to contact your **embassy** – see the "Directory" section of the nearest capital city for contact numbers. In the case of a medical emergency, you will also need to alert your **insurance company**.

Drugs

Drugs penalties are tough throughout the region – in many countries there's even the possibility of being sentenced to death – and you won't get any sympathy from consular officials. Beware of drug scams: either being shopped by a dealer or having substances slipped into your luggage. If you are arrested, or end up on the wrong side of the law for whatever reason, you should ring the consular officer at your embassy immediately.

OFFICIAL ADVICE ON INTERNATIONAL TROUBLE SPOTS

The following sites provide useful advice on travelling in countries that are considered unstable or unsafe for foreigners.

Australian Department of Foreign Affairs Ⓦ dfat.gov.au. Advice and reports on unstable countries and regions.

British Foreign and Commonwealth Office Ⓦ fco.gov.uk. Constantly updated advice for travellers on circumstances affecting safety in more than 130 countries.

Canadian Foreign Affairs Department Ⓦ international.gc.ca. Country-by-country travel advisories.

US State Department Travel Advisories Ⓦ travel.state.gov/travel. Website providing "consular information sheets" detailing the dangers of travelling in most countries of the world.

Electricity

In most parts of the region, electricity is supplied at an almost equal balance of 220 and 230V, though socket type varies from country to country, so you should bring a travel plug with several adaptors. Specific details are given in the introduction to each chapter. Power cuts are common, so bring a torch.

Gay and lesbian travellers

Homosexuality is broadly tolerated in Southeast Asia, if not exactly accepted. Thailand and the Philippines have the most public and developed **gay scenes** in the region, and gay travellers are generally made to feel welcome in both places. Indonesia, Cambodia, Laos and Vietnam all have less visible gay communities, but they do exist and homosexuality is not illegal in any of them. The situation is less rosy in more conservative Malaysia, and travellers there should be especially discreet – despite this, there are gay bars and meeting places in Kuala Lumpur and Penang. In Singapore, though there is a gay scene, sodomy is illegal, and the government gives mixed messages on its attitude to homosexuality. Homosexuality is illegal in Myanmar and discrimination widespread.

The tourist-oriented gay sex industry is a tiny but highly visible part of Southeast Asia's gay scene, and is most obvious in Thailand where gay venues are often nothing more than brothels.

For detailed **information** on the gay scene in Southeast Asia, check out the **websites** Ⓦ utopia-asia.com, which is an excellent resource for gay travellers to all regions of Asia and has travellers' reports on gay scenes across the region, and Ⓦ fridae.asia, which lists gay city guides within Asia.

Contacts for gay and lesbian travellers

IN THE UK

Gay Travel Ⓦ **gaytravel.co.uk** Online gay and lesbian travel agent with listings.

IN THE US AND CANADA

Damron Company Ⓣ 1 800 462 6654 or Ⓣ 415 255 0404, Ⓦ **damron.com.** Publisher of Damron Accommodations, which lists hundreds of accommodations for gays and lesbians worldwide.

International Gay & Lesbian Travel Association Ⓣ 1 954 630 1637, Ⓦ **iglta.org.** Keeps a list of gay- and lesbian-friendly travel agents, worldwide, and accommodation.

IN AUSTRALIA AND NEW ZEALAND

Gay Travel Ⓣ 1800 429 8728, Ⓦ **gaytravel.com.** Trip-planning and bookings.

Rainbow Travel Australia Ⓣ **02 9191 2979, New Zealand** Ⓣ **0800 123 669,** Ⓦ **rainbowtourism.com.** Works with regional gay and lesbian travel agencies to offer tours as well as accommodation throughout Southeast Asia, such as homestays in Hanoi.

Insurance

Wherever you're travelling to in Southeast Asia, you must have adequate travel insurance. Before buying a policy, check that you're not already covered: student health coverage often extends during holidays and for one term beyond the date of last enrolment, and your home insurance policy may cover your possessions against loss or theft even when overseas.

Most policies exclude so-called dangerous sports unless an extra premium is paid: in Southeast Asia, this can mean scuba diving, whitewater rafting and bungee jumping, though probably not trekking. Read the small print and benefits tables of prospective policies carefully.

You should definitely take **medical coverage** that includes both hospital treatment and medical evacuation; be sure to ask for the 24-hour medical emergency number. Keep all medical bills and, if possible, contact the insurance company before making any major outlay. Very few insurers will arrange on-the-spot payments in the event of a major expense – you will usually be reimbursed only after going home, so a credit/debit card could be useful to tide you over.

When securing **baggage cover**, make sure that the per-article limit will cover your most valuable possession. If you have anything stolen, get a copy of the police report, otherwise you won't be able to

claim. Always make a note of the policy details and leave them with someone at home in case you lose the original.

Internet

Internet access is widespread in Southeast Asia. Wi-fi is often offered for free, and can be found in establishments ranging from coffee houses and backpacker lodges to some of the smallest airports and big city malls.

Laundry

There are few coin-operated laundries in Southeast Asia, but most guesthouses and hotels will wash your clothes for a reasonable price.

Left luggage

Most guesthouses and hotels will store luggage for you, though sometimes only if you make a reservation for your anticipated return; major train stations and airports also have left-luggage facilities.

Mail

Travellers can receive mail in any country in Southeast Asia via **poste restante**. The system is universally fairly efficient, but tends only to be available at the main post office in cities and popular tourist destinations. Most post offices hold letters for a maximum of one month, though some hold them for up to three, and others seem to hold them forever. Mail should be addressed: Name (family name underlined or capitalized), Poste Restante, GPO, Town or City, Country. It will be filed by family name, though it's always wise to check under your first initial as well. To collect mail, you'll need to show your passport and may have to pay a small fee.

Money

The easiest way to carry your money is in the form of plastic; ATMs are fairly widespread, except in the smallest towns and most rural areas. Banks charge a handling fee of about 1.5 percent per transaction when you use your debit card at overseas ATMs.

Some hotels and a growing number of restaurants, shops and travel agents accept American Express, Visa, MasterCard and Diners Club credit cards. However, surcharging of up to five percent is rife, and theft and forgery are major industries – always demand the carbon copies and destroy them immediately. It's sensible not to rely on plastic alone; you may want to consider **travellers' cheques** in US dollars, UK pounds sterling, euros or the local currency. Hold on to the **receipt** (or proof of purchase), as some exchange places require seeing it before cashing your cheques. Most **international airports** have exchange counters, which is useful, as you can't always buy Southeast Asian currencies before leaving home. Tourist centres also have convenient **exchange counters** where rates can compare favourably with those offered by the banks, but always establish any **commission** first – the places that display promising rates may charge a hefty fee, and be careful of some common scams, including miscalculating amounts (especially when there are lots of zeros involved), using a rigged calculator, folding over notes to make the amount look twice as great and removing a pile of notes after the money's been counted.

Wiring money

Wiring money through a specialist agent is fast but expensive. The money wired should be available for collection, usually in local currency, from the company's local agent within twenty minutes of being sent via Western Union or MoneyGram; both charge on a sliding scale, so sending larger amounts of cash is better value.

American Express MoneyGram UK and Ireland Ⓣ 0800 8971 8971, US & Canada Ⓣ 1 800 666 3947, Australia & New Zealand should visit their local agent; Ⓦ moneygram.com.

Western Union UK Ⓣ 0800 731 1815, Ireland Ⓣ 1800 395 395, US & Canada Ⓣ 1 800 325 6000, Australia Ⓣ 1800 173 833, New Zealand Ⓣ 0800 085 253; Ⓦ westernunion.com.

Phones

You can **phone** home from any city or large town in Southeast Asia. One of the most convenient ways of doing so is over the internet, with a provider such as Skype (Ⓦ skype.com), enabling you to make internet calls at the price of a local call, and free computer to computer calls. An expensive alternative is to take a **telephone charge card** from your phone company back home, to charge calls to your account.

In most places national telecommunications offices or post offices tend to charge less than private telephone offices and guesthouses for international calls. In phone centres where there's no facility for reverse-charge calls, you can almost always get a "**call-back**". Ask the operator for a minimum (one-minute) call abroad and get the phone number of the place you're calling from; you can then be called back directly at the phone centre.

IDD CODES

To phone abroad from the following countries, you must first dial the international access code, then the IDD country code, then the area code (usually without the first zero), then the phone number:

INTERNATIONAL ACCESS CODES WHEN DIALLING FROM:

Australia T **0011**
Brunei T **00**
Cambodia T **00**
Canada T **011**
Hong Kong T **001**
Indonesia T **001, 008**
Ireland T **00**
Laos T **14**
Macau T **00**
Malaysia T **00**
Myanmar T **00**
New Zealand T **00**
Northern Ireland T **048**
The Philippines T **00**
Singapore T **001, 002**
South Africa T **00**
Thailand T **001**
UK T **00**
US T **011**
Vietnam T **00**

IDD COUNTRY CODES

Australia T **61**
Brunei T **673**
Cambodia T **855**
Canada T **1**
Hong Kong T **852**
Indonesia T **62**
Ireland T **353**
Laos T **856**
Macau T **853**
Malaysia T **60**
Myanmar T **95**
New Zealand T **64**
The Philippines T **63**
Singapore T **65**
South Africa T **27**
Thailand T **66**
UK T **44**
US T **1**
Vietnam T **84**

Mobile phones

If you want to use your **mobile** in Southeast Asia, check with your provider whether it will work abroad, and what the call charges are. Generally speaking, UK, Australian and New Zealand mobiles should work fine in Southeast Asia. However, with US mobile phones only tri-band models are likely to function outside the US.

You are likely to be charged extra for incoming calls when abroad, as the people calling you will be paying the usual rate. For further information about using your phone abroad, check out W telecomsadvice.org.uk/features/using_your_mobile_phone_abroad_roaming.htm. If you're in a country for a while it's worth buying a local pre-pay SIM card, but you'll need to get your phone "unlocked" before you leave home.

Tourist information

Although some Southeast Asian countries have no dedicated tourist information offices abroad, there's plenty of information available online.

Tourist offices abroad

Local tourist information services are described in the introduction to each chapter.

Brunei W bruneitourism.travel. Contact your nearest Bruneian embassy or consulate (see p.48).

Cambodia W tourismcambodia.org. UK & Ireland T 020 8451 7850.

Hong Kong and Macau W discoverhongkong.com; Australia and New Zealand T 02 9283 3083; Canada T 416 366-2389; UK and Ireland T 020 7432 7700; US: New York T 212 421 3382, Los Angeles T 323 938 4582, W macautourism.gov.mo; Australia T 02 9264 1488; New Zealand T 09 308 5206; UK and Ireland T 020 8334 8325; US T 310 545 3464; US: California T 310 545 3464, New York T 646 227 0690.

Indonesia W indonesia.travel. Contact the relevant consulate or embassy (see p.49).

Laos A few, basic tourist offices abroad. Attempting to contact and extract information from Lao embassies often results in frustration. The most useful source of information is W visit-mekong.com/laos/.

Malaysia W tourism.gov.my; Australia: Sydney T 02 9299 4441, Perth T 08 9481 0400; Canada T 604 689-8899; New Zealand contact the embassy (see p.49); South Africa T 011 268 0292; UK and Ireland T 020 7930 7932; US: Los Angeles T 213 689 9702, New York T 212 754 1113.

Myanmar W myanmar-tourism.com. Contact your nearest Burmese embassy or consulate (see p.49).

The Philippines W wowphilippines.com.ph; Australia and New Zealand T 02 9279 3380; Canada: contact nearest office in the US (see below); UK and Ireland T 020 7835 1100; US: Los Angeles T 213 487 4525, New York T 212 575 7915, San Francisco T 415 956-4060.

Singapore Ⓦ yoursingapore.com; Australia Ⓣ 02 9290 2888; Canada: contact nearest office in the US (see below); New Zealand Ⓣ 0800 608 506; UK and Ireland Ⓣ 020 7484 2710; US: Los Angeles Ⓣ 323 677-0808, New York Ⓣ 212 302 4861.

Thailand Ⓦ tourismthailand.org; Australia and New Zealand Ⓣ 02 9247 7549; Canada: contact nearest office in the US (see below); UK and Ireland Ⓣ 020 925 2511; US: Los Angeles Ⓣ 323 461 9814, New York Ⓣ 212 432 0433.

Vietnam Ⓦ vietnamtourism.com. Contact the relevant embassy (see opposite).

Useful websites

For country-specific websites see the relevant country introduction.

AsianDiver Ⓦ **uw3some.com.** Online version of the divers' magazine, with good coverage of Southeast Asia's diving sites, including recommendations and first-hand diving stories.

Internet Travel Information Service Ⓦ **itisnet.com.** Specifically aimed at budget travellers, this site is a useful resource on many Southeast Asian countries, regularly updated by travellers and researchers. Info on airfares, border crossings, visa requirements and hotels.

Open Directory Project Ⓦ **dmoz.org/Recreation/Travel.** Scores of backpacker-oriented links, including many Asia-specific ones, plus travelogues and message boards.

Tales of Asia Ⓦ **talesofasia.com.** Reliable practical advice on border crossings, overland travel and assorted off-road adventures across Cambodia, Vietnam, Thailand, Indonesia, Malaysia and Singapore.

Tourism Concern Ⓦ **tourismconcern.org.uk.** Website of the British organization that campaigns for responsible tourism. Plenty of useful links to politically and environmentally aware organizations across the world, and a particularly good section on the politics of tourism in Myanmar.

TravelFish Ⓦ **travelfish.org.** A frequently updated online resource on eight of the most popular Southeast Asian countries, dedicated to backpackers. There's a useful message board, plus you can read travellers' reviews and get advice on specific trip planning.

Travellers' forums

Rough Guides Ⓦ **roughguides.com.** Award-winning site for independent travellers, with online travel guides, features and a community section.

Virtual Tourist Ⓦ **virtualtourist.com.** Interactive site that allows travellers to post reviews and photos of destinations, accommodation, restaurants, and travel-related advice.

Time zones

The region is covered by four time zones. Cambodia, west Indonesia (Java, Sumatra, Kalimantan Barat and Kalimantan Tengah), Laos, Thailand and Vietnam are **7 hours ahead of GMT**, 12 hours ahead of New York, 15 hours ahead of LA, 3 hours behind Sydney and 5 hours behind Auckland. Brunei, Hong Kong and Macau, central Indonesia (Bali, Lombok, Nusa Tenggara, Sulawesi and south and east Kalilmantan), Malaysia, the Philippines and Singapore are all **8 hours ahead of GMT**, 13 hours ahead of New York, 16 hours ahead of LA, 2 hours behind Sydney and 4 hours behind Auckland. Eastern Indonesia (Irian Jaya and Maluku) is **9 hours ahead of GMT**, 14 hours ahead of New York, 17 hours ahead of LA, 1 hour behind Sydney and 3 hours behind Auckland. Myanmar is 6-and-a-half hours ahead of GMT. No countries in the region use daylight saving time.

Visas

Country-specific advice about visas, entry requirements, border formalities and visa extensions is given in the introduction at the beginning of each chapter. As a broad guide, the only countries in Southeast Asia for which citizens of the EU, the US, Canada, Australia and New Zealand need to buy a visa in advance are: Vietnam (a pre-arranged "visa-on-arrival" can be sourced from a Vietnamese travel agency, but it's better to get one from a Vietnamese embassy/consulate; from US$25); Indonesia (purchase a visa for US$25 on arrival at the airport or from a local consulate if travelling overland); and Myanmar (purchase in advance at an embassy or consulate; $20–30).

However, different rules usually apply if you're staying more than thirty days or arriving overland; in **Indonesia** you can only get a thirty-day visa on arrival at certain designated air and seaports (see p.164). However, as all visa requirements, prices and processing times are subject to change, it's always worth double-checking with embassies. Most countries require your passport to be valid for at least six months from your date of entry. Some also demand proof of onward travel or sufficient funds to buy a ticket. For the most up-to-date information, see the Basics section of each country.

Embassies and consulates abroad

It's usually straightforward to get visas for your next port of call while you're on the road in Southeast Asia. Details of neighbouring Southeast Asian embassies are given in the "Directory" section of each capital city within each country chapter.

Brunei Ⓦ gov.bn. Australia: 10 Beale Crescent, Deakin, ACT 2600, Canberra Ⓣ 02 6285 4500; Canada: 395 Laurier Ave E, Ottawa, ON K1N 6R4 Ⓣ 613 234-5656; New Zealand: Contact the embassy in Canberra; UK and Ireland: 19–20 Belgrave Square, London SW1X 8PG Ⓣ 020 7581 0521; US: 3520 International Ct NW, Washington DC 20008 Ⓣ 202 237 1838.

Cambodia Australia: 5 Canterbury Crescent, Deakin, ACT 2600 ⓣ 02 6273 1259; Canada: 903-168 Chadwick Court, V7M 3L4, North Vancouver ⓣ 604 980 1718; New Zealand: Contact the embassy in Australia; UK and Ireland: 64 Rondesbury Park, Brent, London NW6 7AT ⓣ 020 8451 7850; US: 4530 16th St NW, Washington DC 20011 ⓣ 202 726 7742, 866 UNO Plaza, Suite 420, New York 10017 ⓣ 212 223 0676, 422 Ord St, Suite G, Los Angeles, CA 90012 ⓣ 213 625 7777.

Hong Kong and Macau Contact your nearest Chinese embassy. ⓦ fmprc.gov.cn/eng/wjb/zwjg/2490/. Australia: 15 Coronation Drive, Yarralumla, Canberra ACT 2600, ⓣ 02 6273 4780, 39 Dunblane Street, Camperdown, NSW 2050 ⓣ 02 8595 8002; Canada: 515 St Patrick St, Ottawa, ON K1N 5H3 ⓣ 613 789 3434; Ireland: 40 Ailesbury Rd, Baillsbridge, Dublin 4 ⓣ 01 269 1707; New Zealand: Unit 2, 6 Glenmore St, Kelburne, Wellington 6011 ⓣ 04 472 1382; South Africa: 972 Pretorius Street, Arcadia 0083, Pretoria ⓣ 12 431 6500; UK: 49–51 Portland Place, London W1B 1JL ⓣ 020 7299 4049; US: 3505 International Place NW, Washington DC 20008 ⓣ 202 495 2266.

Indonesia ⓦ indonesianembassy.org.uk. Australia: 8 Darwin Ave, Yarralumla, Canberra, ACT 2600 ⓣ 02 6250 8600; 20 Harry Chan Ave, Darwin, NT 0801 ⓣ 089 43 0200; 72 Queens Rd, Melbourne, VIC 3004 ⓣ 03 9525 2755; 134 Adelaide Terrace, East Perth, WA 6004 ⓣ 08 9221 5858; 236–238 Maroubra Rd, Maroubra, Sydney NSW 203 ⓣ 02 9344 9933; Canada: 55 Parkdale Ave, Ottawa, ON K1Y 1E5 ⓣ 613 724 9929; New Zealand: 70 Glen Rd, Kelburn, Wellington, 6012 ⓣ 04 475 8697; South Africa: 949 Schoeman St, Arcadia, Pretoria ⓣ 12 342 3350; UK and Ireland: 38 Grosvenor Square, London W1K 2HW ⓣ 020 7499 7661; US: 2020 Massachusetts Ave NW, Washington DC 20036 ⓣ 202 775 5200.

Laos It's much easier to apply for a visa in Bangkok than in the West. ⓦ laoembassy.com. Australia: 1 Dalmain Crescent, O'Malley, Canberra, ACT 2606 ⓣ 02 6286 4595; Canada: Contact embassy in Washington (see below); France: 74 av Raymond Poincaré, 75116, Paris ⓣ 01 45 53 02 98; New Zealand: Contact embassy in Canberra; UK and Ireland: Contact embassy in France or Thailand; US: 2222 S St NW, Washington DC 20008 ⓣ 202 332 6416, 317 East, 51st Street, New York 10022 ⓣ 212 832 0095.

Malaysia ⓦ kln.gov.my. Australia: 7 Perth Ave, Yarralumla, Canberra, ACT 2600 ⓣ 02 6120 0300, with offices in Perth ⓣ 08 9225 7055 and Melbourne ⓣ 03 9573 5400; Canada: 60 Boteler St, Ottawa, ON ⓣ 613 241-5182; Ireland: Level 3A–5A, Shelbourne House, Shelbourne Road, Ballsbridge, Dublin 4 ⓣ 01 667 7280; New Zealand: 10 Washington Ave, Brooklyn, Wellington ⓣ 04 385 2439; South Africa: 1007 Schoeman St, Hatfield, Pretoria 0083 ⓣ 12 342 5990; UK: 45–46 Belgrave Square, London SW1X 8QT ⓣ 020 7235 8033; US: 3516 International Court NW, Washington DC 20008 ⓣ 202 572 9700.

Myanmar ⓦ mofa.gov.mm. Australia: 22 Arkana Street, Yarralumla, Canberra, ACT 2600 ⓣ 02 6273 3811, ⓔ mecanberra@bigpond.com. Canada: 336 Island Park Drive, Ottawa, K1Y 0A7 ⓣ 613 232 9990, ⓦ meottawa.org. Ireland: Contact the embassy in the UK. New Zealand: Contact the embassy in Australia. UK: 19A Charles Street, London W1J 5DX ⓣ 020 7148 0740, ⓦ myanmarembassylondon.com. US: 2300 Street NW, Washington DC 2008 ⓣ 202 332 3344, ⓦ mewashingtondc.com.

The Philippines ⓦ dfa.gov.ph/. Australia: 1 Moonah Place, Yarralumla, Canberra, ACT 2600 ⓣ 02 6273 2535; Canada: 130 Albert St, Suite 900, Ottawa ⓣ 613 233 1121; Ireland: Hainault House (4th Floor), 69–72 St. Stephen's Green, Dublin 2 ⓣ 01 407 4040; New Zealand: 50 Hobson St, Thorndon, Wellington ⓣ 04 4729 848; South Africa: 54 Nicolson St, Mucklenuek, 0181 Pretoria ⓣ 12 346 0451; UK: 6–8 Suffolk St, London SW1Y 4HG ⓣ 020 7451 1780; US: 1600 Massachusetts Ave NW, Washington DC 20036 ⓣ 202 4679300.

Singapore ⓦ mfa.gov.sg. Australia: 17 Forster Crescent, Yarralumla, Canberra, ACT 2600 ⓣ 02 6271 2000; Canada: 1700, 1095 West Pender St, Vancouver ⓣ 604 622-5281; New Zealand: Level 7, Revera House, 48–54 Mulgrave St, Wellington 6011 ⓣ 04 470 0850; South Africa: 980–982 Schoeman St, Arcadia, Pretoria 0083 ⓣ 012 430 6035; UK and Ireland: 9 Wilton Crescent, London SW1X 8SP ⓣ 020 7235 8315; US: 3501 International Place NW, Washington DC 20008 ⓣ 202 537 3100.

Thailand ⓦ thaiembassy.org. Australia: 111 Empire Circuit, Yarralumla, Canberra, ACT 2600 ⓣ 02 6206 0100, consulate in Sydney; Canada: 180 Island Park Drive, Ottawa, ON K1Y 0A2 ⓣ 613 722 4444; New Zealand: 110 Molesworth St, Thorndon, Wellington ⓣ 04 4768 616; South Africa: 248 Hill St, Arcadia, Pretoria ⓣ 12 342 4600; UK and Ireland: 29–30 Queen's Gate, London SW7 5JB ⓣ 020 7589 2944; US: 1024 Wisconsin Ave NW, Washington DC ⓣ 202 944 3600.

Vietnam ⓦ vnembassy.net. Australia: 6 Timbarra Crescent, O'Malley, Canberra, ACT 2606 ⓣ 02 6286 6059; Canada: 470 Wilbrod St, Ottawa, ON K1N 6M8 ⓣ 613 236 0772; New Zealand: Level 21, Grand Plimmer Tower, 2–6 Gilmer Terrace, Wellington 6011 ⓣ 04 473 5912; South Africa: 87 Brooks St, Brooklyn, Pretoria ⓣ 12 362 8119; UK and Ireland: 12–14 Victoria Rd, London W8 5RD ⓣ 020 7937 1912; US: 1233 20th St NW, Suite 400, Washington DC 20036 ⓣ 202 861 0737.

Travellers with disabilities

Aside from Hong Kong and Singapore, which have wheelchair-accessible public transport, most Southeast Asian countries make few provisions for people with disabilities. Pavements are usually high, uneven, and lack dropped kerbs, and public transport is not wheelchair-friendly. On the positive side, however, most disabled travellers report that help is never in short supply, and wheelchair-users with collapsible chairs may be able to take cycle rickshaws and tuk-tuks, balancing their chair in front of them. Also, services in much of Southeast Asia are very inexpensive for Western travellers, so you should be able to afford to hire a car or minibus with driver for a few days, stay at better-equipped hotels, and take some internal flights. You might also consider hiring a local tour guide to

accompany you on sightseeing trips – a native speaker can facilitate access to temples and museums, or perhaps book a package holiday – see below for useful contacts. Carry a doctor's letter with you about any drug prescriptions you have for when you're passing through airport customs, as this will ensure that you don't get hauled up for narcotics transgressions.

Contacts for travellers with disabilities

IN AUSTRALIA AND NEW ZEALAND

Disabled Persons Assembly ⓣ 04 801 9100, ⓦ dpa.org.nz. Resource centre with lists of travel agencies and tour operators for people with disabilities.

National Disability Services ⓣ 02 6283 3200, ⓦ nds.org.au. Represents more than 700 not-for-profit organizations online and also has offices nationwide.

IN THE UK AND IRELAND

Access Travel ⓣ 01942 888 844, ⓦ access-travel.co.uk. Flights, transfers, car hire and accommodation.

Irish Wheelchair Association ⓣ 01 818 6400, ⓦ iwa.ie. Useful information provided about travelling abroad with a wheelchair.

Tourism for All ⓣ 0303 303 0146, ⓦ tourismforall.org.uk. Provides advice for overseas travel and free lists of accessible accommodation abroad.

IN THE US AND CANADA

Access-Able ⓦ access-able.com. Online resource for travellers with disabilities.

Society for Accessible Travel and Hospitality (SATH) ⓣ 212 447 7284, ⓦ sath.org. Organization that actively represents travellers with disabilities.

World on Wheelz ⓣ 1800 578 8958, ⓦ worldonwheelz.com. Specializes in accessible travel for wheelchair-users, slow walkers and seniors with special needs.

Women travellers

Southeast Asia is generally a safe region for women to travel around alone. That said, it pays to take the normal precautions, especially late at night when there are few people around on the streets; after dark, take licensed taxis rather than cycle rickshaws and tuk-tuks.

Be aware that a common Asian perception of Western female travellers is of sexual availability and promiscuity. This is particularly the case in the traditional Muslim areas of Indonesia and Malaysia, as well as southern Thailand and the southern Philippines, where lone foreign women can get treated contemptuously however decently attired. Most Southeast Asian women **dress modestly** and it usually helps to do the same, avoiding skimpy shorts and vests, which are considered offensive (see p.40). Some Asian women travelling with white men have reported cases of serious harassment – something attributed to the tendency of Southeast Asian men (particularly in Vietnam) to automatically label all such women as prostitutes. Be wary of invitations to drink with a man or group of men if there are no other women present. To many Southeast Asian men, simply accepting such an invitation will be perceived as tacit agreement to have sex, and some will see it as their "right" to rape a woman who has "led them on" by accepting such an invitation and then refused to follow through. Women should also take care around Buddhist monks. It should go without saying that monks who touch women (something strictly against the Buddhist precepts) or who suggest showing you around some isolated site – such as a cave – should be politely but firmly rebuffed. The key is to stay aware without being paranoid.

OMAR ALI SAIFUDDIEN MOSQUE

Brunei

HIGHLIGHTS

❶ **Ambuyat** Get your chopsticks around Brunei's slithery national dish. **See p.54**

❷ **Omar Ali Saifuddien Mosque** Admire Brunei's most photogenic mosque reflected in its own private lagoon. **See p.56**

❸ **Kampong Ayer** Visit the largest stilt village in the world. **See p.57**

❹ **Royal Regalia Museum** See the presents given to one of the world's richest men. **See p.58**

❺ **Ulu Temburong National Park** Go wildlife-spotting and climb above the jungle canopy. **See p.61**

HIGHLIGHTS ARE MARKED ON THE MAP ON P.53

ROUGH COSTS

Daily budget Basic US$50, occasional treat US$70
Drink Watermelon juice US$4.50
Food *Ambuyat* for two US$12
Hostel/budget hotel US$12/US$55
Travel Bus: BSB–Kota Kinabalu (172km; 8–9hr) US$30

FACT FILE

Population 412,238
Language Bahasa Malaysia, though English is also widely spoken
Religion Muslim, with Buddhist and Christian minorities
Currency Brunei dollars (B$)
Capital Bandar Seri Begawan
International phone code ☎ + 673
Time zone GMT + 8hr

1

Introduction

Surrounded by Sarawak on Borneo's northern coast, the tiny but thriving sultanate of Brunei combines rampant consumerism and notable wealth with Islamic conservatism. Most famous as the home of one of the world's richest men, for those with a bit of time and some cash to spend, the state offers a few hidden surprises. With its decorative architecture and streets flooded with brand-new cars, the capital, Bandar Seri Begawan, can often feel a world away from its Malaysian neighbours. Further afield, the remote Ulu Temburong National Park offers untouched virgin rainforest teeming with flora and fauna.

Budget travel is difficult here; accommodation is more expensive than in Sarawak and Sabah, and if you wish to travel outside of the capital, your only options are renting a car (though petrol is cheap) or joining a tour. Many of Brunei's pulling points can be found on a much grander scale, for a fraction of the cost, in the neighbouring Malaysian states. But for those looking for a sense of serenity off the beaten track, Brunei is a good stopover.

Resident Bruneians experience a quality of life that is unlike anywhere else in Southeast Asia: education and healthcare are free; houses, cars and even pilgrimages to Mecca are subsidized; and taxation on personal income is unheard of. You won't see any scooters here, and all the cars look as if they've just rolled out of a showroom. The explanation for this is simple: oil, first discovered in 1929 at the site of the town of Seria. Brunei's wealth is all down to the natural resources pumping through its veins, so it will be interesting to see how the county fares when the "black gold" runs out in twenty years' time.

WHEN TO GO

The **climate** is hot and humid, with average temperatures in the high twenties to early thirties all year round. Lying 440km north of the equator, Brunei has a tropical weather system so, even if you visit outside the wet season (usually Nov–March), there's every chance you'll get caught in some rain. If you wish to meet the **sultan** himself, the best time to come is at the end of Ramadan (see p.56) when the palace throws open its doors for three days.

CHRONOLOGY

c. Seventh century Chinese records suggest that a forerunner to the Brunei state – referred to as "Po ni" – has trading relations with China, exporting birds' nests, hornbill ivory and timber.

1370 Sultan Mohammed becomes the first sultan.

Mid-1400 Sultan Awang Alak der Tabar marries a princess from Melaka and converts to Islam. By the end of the century Brunei is independent and trade with Malacca flourishes.

Fifteenth century After the fall of Malacca in 1511, many wealthy Muslim merchants decamp to Brunei, accelerating its conversion to Islam, and bolstering its position as a trading centre.

1526 The Portuguese establish a trading post in Brunei.

1578 Spain's forces take the capital of Brunei, only to be chased out days later by a cholera epidemic.

1588 & 1645 Brunei raided by the Spanish again.

1660s Feuding between the princes results in civil war. Brunei languishes in obscurity for more than 150 years.

1839 Fortune-seeker James Brooke arrives near Kuching, helps the sultan to quell a rebellion, and demands the governorship of Sarawak in return. Brooke and his successors take Brunei's former territories to create the present-day territory of Sarawak.

January 1846 British gunboats quell a court coup; in return Pulau Labuan is ceded to the British Crown.

1888 The British declare Brunei a protected state, with responsibility for its foreign affairs.

1890 The cession of the Limbang region, literally splitting Brunei in two.

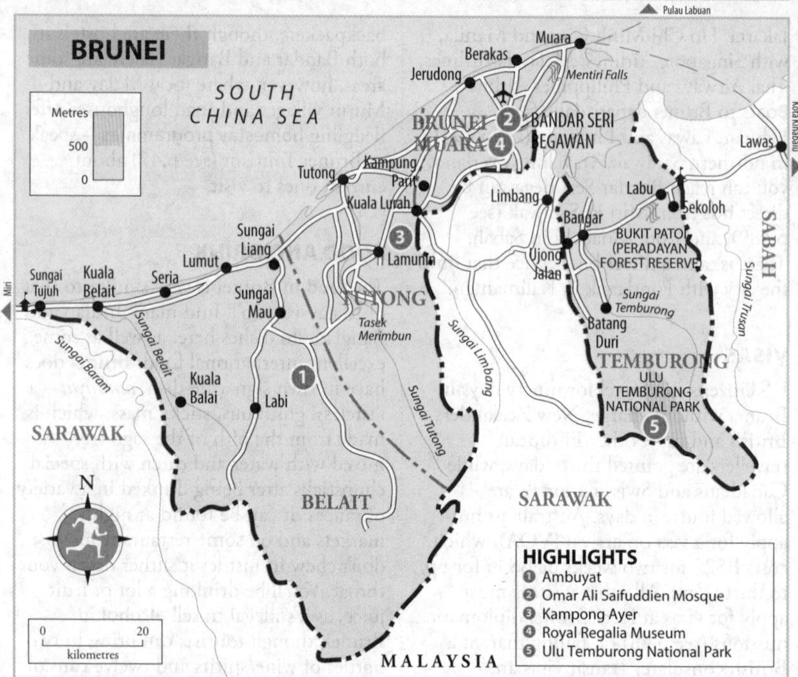

1906 The British set up a Residency in Brunei.

1929 The discovery of the Seria oilfield; extraction begins.

1941–45 The Japanese occupation; after their defeat Brunei becomes a British Protectorate again.

1959 The British withdraw – but still control defence and foreign affairs – and a new constitution enshrining Islam as the state religion is established.

1962 Left-wing Brunei People's Party win the election but after the sultan refuses to let them form a government, the ensuing violence is crushed with the assistance of the British Army. The sultan starts ruling by decree under emergency powers that largely remain in place today.

1963 Brunei is the only Malay state that chooses to remain a British dependency rather than join the Malaysian Federation.

October 5, 1967 Following the voluntary abdication of his father, the current sultan, Sultan Hassanal Bolkiah (see box, p.58), takes the throne.

1970s As oil prices escalate, Bruneians – especially the sultan – grow rich.

January 1, 1984 Brunei gains full independence from Britain and is declared a "democratic monarchy".

1991 A conservative, religious ideology is introduced, which presents the sultan as defender of the faith; the sale of alcohol is banned.

1998 The sultan's playboy brother (and finance minister) Jefri is sued for embezzling nearly B$3bn of state funds: the court reduces his living expenses to a meagre US$300,000 a month.

2004 The sultan revives Brunei's 20-seat legislative council after two decades.

2007 Brunei, Indonesia and Malaysia sign a "Rainforest Declaration" designed to protect the natural habitats of Borneo's rare species.

2009 Brunei celebrates 25 years of independence.

2011 Brunei stages its biggest energy exhibition ever, with exhibitors at the Energy Expo including energy-efficient technology, biofuels and oil and gas.

2013 The Sultan announces the implementation of Sharia law from 2014 onwards, with adulterers to be stoned and public flogging for Muslim consumers of alcohol.

ARRIVAL

Brunei can be reached by air, land or sea. Some long-haul **flights** (principally between the UK and Australia) have stopovers at Brunei International Airport, while Royal Brunei Airlines, Malaysia Airlines and AirAsia run connecting flights from surrounding Sabah and Sarawak; there are also regular flights to other regional hubs, including Singapore, Kuala Lumpur, Bangkok, Hong Kong,

Jakarta, Ho Chi Minh City and Manila, with Singapore Airlines, Malaysia Airlines, Thai Airways and Philippines Airlines. **Boats** to Brunei depart daily from Labuan, Lawas and Limbang (see p.493) in northern Sarawak. Travelling overland, you can reach Bandar Seri Begawan by direct **bus** from Miri in Sarawak (see p.489), and Kota Kinabalu in Sabah. There is even a direct bus service that links the city with Pontianak in Kalimantan.

VISAS

US citizens can travel for ninety days in Brunei without charge, New Zealanders, British and most other European travellers are granted thirty days, while Canadians and Swiss nationals are allowed fourteen days. Australians must apply for a visa on arrival (VOA), which costs B$25 for two weeks or B$35 for up to thirty days. All other visitors must apply for visas at local Brunei diplomatic missions (see p.48) or, failing that, at a British consulate. Transit visas are available for 72-hour stays.

GETTING AROUND

Downtown Bandar Seri Begawan is small and easy to explore on foot; the rest of the city is covered by a network of inexpensive buses (B$1 per ride). For a cheap "tour", hop on bus #1 – the circle line. While there are regular services to towns in the districts of Tutong, Kuala Belait and Seria from Bandar, buses are non-existent south of the main coastal roads, and **taxis** are expensive. A short hop to the water village of Kampong Ayer, straight across the Sungai Brunei river, should set you back around B$0.50; diagonal crossings are more expensive. Apart from that, the only time you're likely to use a **boat** is to get to the Temburong district, which is cut off from the rest of Brunei by the Limbang corridor of Sarawak.

ACCOMMODATION

Accommodation in Brunei is much more expensive than in Sabah and Sarawak, and the country is not well set up for backpackers, though there are hostels in both Bandar and Bangar. There are some areas, however, where local Malay and Murut villages and Iban longhouses offer fledgling **homestay programmes** – speak to Brunei Tourism (see p.47) about current ones to visit.

FOOD AND DRINK

The **food** in Brunei is very similar to that of Malaysia; you'll find many Indian and Bangladeshi dishes here, as well as some excellent international food. Brunei does have its own signature dish, *ambuyat* – a tasteless, glutinous, sticky mass, which is made from the pith of the sago tree mixed with water and eaten with special chopsticks after being dunked in a variety of sauces. It can be found at night markets and on some restaurant menus; don't chew it; just let it slither down your throat. You'll be drinking a lot of fruit juice, as it's illegal to sell **alcohol** in Brunei, though tourists can bring in two bottles of wine/spirits and twelve cans of beer, which must be declared.

Cafés are generally open from 7am to 9pm and **restaurants** from 11am to 10pm, usually waiting until the last customer leaves. There are a number of **night markets** around the capital with hawker stalls that are open from late afternoon until the early hours.

CULTURE AND ETIQUETTE

The Ministry of Religious Affairs actively fosters and promotes **Islam**, which as a state religion has a great influence on the country's culture, customs and traditions. Brunei is more conservatively Islamic than neighbouring Malaysia and it's important to dress modestly. Women should cover their shoulders and legs – ensure skirts and shorts are below knee-length. For men, T-shirts with sleeves and long shorts or trousers are considered respectable.

SPORTS AND ACTIVITIES

Some seventy percent of Brunei's land area is covered by primary rainforests,

1

much of it protected. The best area for **trekking** is the Temburong district, an area of pristine jungle largely undiscovered by tourists. The principal national park, Ulu Temburong, can be visited independently, though most people choose the easy option of visiting as part of a tour from Bandar (see p.60).

COMMUNICATIONS

Brunei has an efficient postal system; it takes around a week for postcards to reach Europe and the USA. There are a number of **internet cafés** around Bandar, most with headsets for Skype, charging around B$3 per hour. There are also numerous free wi-fi hotspots scattered about town. Otherwise, **International** (IDD) **calls** can be made from call centres using the 095 access code for B$0.30–0.50 per minute. Local prepaid SIM cards with either DST or B-Mobile cost B$30 and **local calls** cost B$0.05–0.30. To phone abroad from Brunei, dial ⓣ00 + IDD country code + area code minus first 0 + subscriber number.

CRIME AND SAFETY

Brunei in general has very little crime and travellers rarely experience any trouble. Note that the possession of **drugs** – whether hard or soft – carries a hefty prison sentence, trafficking is punishable by death by hanging and Sharia law could be applied to tourists for petty crime.

MEDICAL CARE AND EMERGENCIES

Medical services in Brunei are modern and excellent, and staff speak good English. Tourists must pay for medical services upfront, and the cost depends upon the level of treatment required.

EMERGENCY NUMBERS

Ambulance ⓣ**991**
Fire brigade ⓣ**995**
Police ⓣ**993**

BRUNEI ONLINE

ⓦ**brudirect.com** Daily local and international news.
ⓦ**bruneitourism.travel** Brunei Tourism's website has a wealth of information – from seven-star hotels to local markets – though it is a little out of date.
ⓦ**thanislim.com** Brunei's premier food blogger reviews the country's best eats.

The main **hospital** is RIPAS Hospital in Bandar (see p.61), which has modern facilities and Western-trained staff.

Oral **contraceptives** and condoms are available at pharmacies; tampons, however, are not.

INFORMATION AND MAPS

In addition to Brunei Tourism's offices (see p.47), look out also for the glossy quarterly *Borneo Insider's Guide* (ⓦborneoinsidersguide.com) magazine.

Nelles East Malaysia **map** has the best coverage of Brunei, while the free *Official Map of Brunei Darussalam* is sometimes found in the tourist offices.

MONEY AND BANKS

Brunei's **currency** is the Brunei dollar, which is divided into 100 cents; you'll see it written as B$, or simply as $. The Brunei dollar is tied to the Singapore dollar, the two currencies used interchangeably in both countries with the exception of the S$2. Notes come in B$1, B$5, B$10, B$50, B$100, B$500, B$1000 and B$10,000 denominations; coins are in denominations of 1, 5, 10, 20 and 50 cents (c). At the time of writing, the **exchange rate** was B$2.01 to the British pound, B$1.68 to the euro, and B$1.25 to the US dollar.

There's no shortage of **ATMs** in BSB; many accept all types of credit and debit card. Money-changing outfits offer better exchange rates than banks.

Major **credit cards** are accepted in most hotels and large shops. Banks will **advance cash** against MasterCard, Visa, American Express or other Maestro, Plus or Cirrus cards.

OPENING HOURS AND HOLIDAYS

Government offices in Brunei open Monday to Thursday and Saturday 7.45am to 12.15pm and 1.30pm to 4.30pm; **shopping centres** open daily 10am to 9pm. **Banking hours** are Monday to Friday 9am to 4pm and Saturday 9am to 11.00am. **Post offices** are open Monday to Thursday and Saturday 8am to 4.30pm, and 8am to 11am and 2pm to 4pm on Fridays.

Most of Brunei's **public holidays** are based on the Islamic calendar and change annually according to the lunar calendar, so check with the tourist office. During **Ramadan**, Muslims spend the ninth month of the Islamic calendar fasting in the daytime; during this time it is culturally sensitive for tourists not to eat or smoke blatantly in public during daylight hours.

PUBLIC HOLIDAYS

Jan 1 New Year's Day
3 Jan 2015; 12 Dec 2016 Maulidur Rasul (Prophet Mohammad's birthday)
19 Feb 2015; 8 Feb 2016 Chinese New Year
Feb 23 Brunei National Day
16 May 2015; 5 May 2016 Israk Mikraj (Ascension of the Prophet)
May 31 Royal Brunei Armed Forces' Day
18 June 2015; 6 June 2016 First day of Ramadan
4 July 2015; 22 June 2016 Nuzulul Qu'ran (Revelation of the Koran day)
July 15 Sultan's Birthday
17 July 2015; 5 July 2016 Hari Raya Aidil Fitri (End of Ramadan)
4 Oct 2014; 23 Sept 2015; 13 Sept 2016 Hari Raya Aidil Adha (Festival of Sacrifice)
25 Oct 2014; 14 Oct 2015; 2 Oct 2016 Hijrah (Islamic New Year)
Dec 25 Christmas Day

FESTIVALS

Brunei National Day The sultan and 35,000 other Bruneians watch parades and fireworks at the Sultan Hassanal Bolkiah National Stadium, just outside Bandar.
Brunei Royal Armed Forces' Day Bandar's square hosts parades and displays.
Sultan's Birthday A fortnight of parades, lantern processions, traditional sports competitions and fireworks.
Hari Raya Aidil Fitri The sultan declares his home, the Istana Nurul Iman, open to the public for three days. All visitors meet the man himself and receive gifts.

Bandar Seri Begawan

The capital of Brunei is **BANDAR SERI BEGAWAN**, also known as BSB or simply Bandar. There is a striking contrast here between the modern buildings and wide, quiet streets of downtown and the lively, colourful, traditional stilt houses across the river in Kampong Ayer, the world's largest water village and home to nearly a quarter of the sultanate's population. The city's main sights can easily be covered in a couple of days. However, central BSB's peace at night and sense of space provide a welcome contrast to the chaos of most Southeast Asian cities.

As recently as the middle of the nineteenth century, BSB was little more than a sleepy water village, but with the discovery of oil came its evolution into the modern, hugely congested waterfront city of today.

WHAT TO SEE AND DO

Downtown Bandar is hemmed in by water. To the east is Sungai Kianggeh; to the south, the wide Sungai Brunei; and to the west, Sungai Kedayan, which runs up to the Edinburgh Bridge. The **Omar Ali Saifuddien Mosque** is Bandar's most obvious point of reference. Central BSB is a fairly small place and easily navigable on foot.

The Omar Ali Saifuddien Mosque

At the very heart of the city is the white, golden-domed **Omar Ali Saifuddien Mosque** (non-Muslim visitors: Sat–Wed 8.30am–noon, 1.30–3pm & 4.30–5.30pm, Fri 4.30–5.30pm). Built in classical Islamic style, it was commissioned by and named after the father of the present sultan, and completed in 1958. The floors and walls of the sumptuous interior are made of fine Italian marble; the UK is responsible for the stained-glass windows and chandeliers, while Saudi Arabia has provided the finest carpets. Topping the cream-coloured building is a golden dome, adorned inside with a mosaic

comprising more than three million pieces of Venetian glass. Its 44m-high minaret is the tallest building in central BSB; no other building is allowed to top that.

The mosque is surrounded by an artificial lagoon; the stone boat sitting in the water is a replica of a sixteenth-century *mahligai* (royal barge).

Kampong Ayer

Kampong Ayer's stilt villages have occupied this stretch of the Sungai Brunei for hundreds of years. This "Venice of the East" – the largest water village in the world – is home to an estimated thirty thousand people, their dwellings connected by a maze of wooden promenades. These villages have their own clinics, mosques, schools, a fire brigade and a police station; the homes have piped water, electricity and TV. The waters, however, are distinctly unsanitary, and the houses susceptible to fire.

There is far more life in the villages than in central Bandar, and the meandering pathways make it an intriguing place to explore on foot; enter via the bridge just behind the Yayasan Complex, or pay one of the boatmen to ferry you across the choppy grey waters on a speedboat (from B$1).

Visit the **Kampong Ayer Cultural and Tourism Gallery** (Sat–Thurs 9am–5pm; Fri 9–11.30am & 2.30–5pm; free) across the river for an insight into the history of Kampong Ayer and displays on its cottage industries, such as weaving, woodwork and pottery. Climb the observation tower for panoramic views of the stilt village and speedboats whizzing across the chocolate-coloured water.

Boat tours

Boatmen hanging around the waterfront will do their best to convince you to take a **boat tour**, which is the best way to see the water village, as well as the Istana (see p.59) and the mangroves beyond, where there's an excellent chance of seeing proboscis monkeys, monitor lizards and even crocodiles. You'll need to negotiate the length and price of your tour; standard

1

tours are around B$35–40 and take an hour or so. To get the most out of it, it's best to pay a bit more and go with Danny (see p.60), as he's good at spotting wildlife and will also be able to tell you the history of the city – something that's beyond the reach of many boatmen with their limited English.

Royal Regalia Museum

The centrally located **Royal Regalia Museum** (Sun–Thurs 9am–5pm, Fri 9–11.30am & 2.30–5pm, Sat 9.45am–5pm; free) is dedicated almost entirely to the Sultan of Brunei and is the most entertaining museum in Bandar. A series of captioned photos of the sultan traces his path from jug-eared child to absolute monarch via a stint at the Sandhurst Military Academy, painting a rather flattering portrait of his life. Standout exhibits include the sultan's enormous, gold-winged Royal Chariot in the main hall; and a golden throne, crown, keris (ceremonial dagger) and gold hand, used to support the sultan's chin during the coronation, behind glass on the first floor. Other first-floor galleries are filled with **exotic objects** given to the sultan as gifts by foreign heads of state; spot the bronze falcon from Ukraine, Nazca lines pins from Peru and framed calligraphy resembling a boat.

The Brunei Museum

The **Brunei Museum** (Sat–Thurs 9am–5pm, Fri 9–11.30am & 2.30–5pm; free), about 5km east of Sungai Kianggeh on Jln Kota Batu (bus #39), has several galleries varying in quality. The undoubted highlight is the **Islamic Art Gallery** – a collection of artefacts from the sultan's personal collection – where, among the riches on display, are beautifully illuminated antique copies of the Koran from around the world, tiny Korans whose script can be read only with a magnifying glass, ninth-century Arabic calligraphy from Iran, astronomy equipment from the eighth century and quirkier items such as a wooden boot with an inlaid mother-of-pearl compass. Also interesting is the **Malay Culture Gallery**, whose dioramas allow glimpses of social traditions, such as the sweetening of a newborn baby's mouth with honey or dates, and the disposal of its placenta in a *bayung*, a palm-leaf basket which is either hung on a tree or floated downriver.

The wing devoted to the oil industry gives no clue as to Brunei's exit strategy when the oil runs out.

The Jame 'Asr Hassanil Bolkiah Mosque

It's an ongoing debate whether the **Jame 'Asr Hassanil Bolkiah (State) Mosque** (also known as the Kiarong Mosque; Mon–Wed & Sat 8am–noon, 2–3pm & 5–6pm; Fri 5–6pm; Sun 10.30am–noon, 2–3pm & 5–6pm; closed Thurs), set in harmonious gardens near the commercial suburb of Gadong, has a distinct edge over the Omar Ali Saifuddien Mosque, at least in sheer size. With its sea-blue roof, 29 golden domes representing Brunei's 29 sultans, and slender minarets, this is

THE SULTAN OF BRUNEI

Brunei's twenty-ninth sultan, **Hassanal Bolkiah**, is reported to be one of the world's richest monarchs, worth a cool US$22 billion. His list of assets includes: the 1788-room Istana Nurul Iman (see opposite); family homes in London, LA, New York and Paris; two Boeings; five aircraft hangars to house his five thousand cars; and climate-controlled stables for his two hundred polo ponies. His yearly expenditure lists US$2.52m on badminton lessons, US$2.5m on masseuses and acupuncturists and nearly US$100,000 on guards for his exotic-bird cages.

This information all became public after he accused his younger brother, Prince Jefri, of siphoning off US$16bn during his thirteen years as finance minister. A court battle ensued and after fifteen years it ruled in the sultan's favour. Jefri was dealt a crushing blow and ordered to hand over two hotels, three houses, diamonds, cherished paintings and cash. But when your older brother is the Prime Minister, Defence Minister, Supreme Commander of the Armed Forces, Supreme Head of Islam and Chief of Police, as well as sultan, who was he to argue?

Brunei's largest mosque, constructed to commemorate the silver jubilee of the sultan's reign in 1992.

Buses #01, #20 and #22 skirt the grounds of the mosque, 3km from the centre en route to the shopping area of Gadong.

The Istana Nurul Iman

The official residence of the sultan is sited along the banks of the Sungai Brunei, 4km west of the capital. Bigger than either Buckingham Palace or the Vatican, the Istana is a monument to self-indulgence, with 1788 rooms, including a staggering 257 bathrooms and a royal banquet hall that can seat four thousand. Designed by Filipino architect Leanrdo Locsin, it is a blend of traditional and modern, with Islamic motifs, such as arches and domes, and sloping roofs fashioned on traditional longhouse designs, combined with all the mod cons you'd expect of a homeowner whose fortune is estimated at US$22 billion. Still, from the outside it looks remarkably like an airport terminal. The palace is open to the general public for three days after Ramadan, when you get to shake hands with the sultan himself and get a goodie bag.

Empire Hotel & Country Club

Ever wondered what a US$1.1 billion folly looks like? If so, it's worth taking a bus to this beyond-extravagant **hotel**, built on the orders of less-than-prudent Prince Jefri as lodging for the guests of the royal family. The hotel is now a luxurious resort with touches such as the US$500,000 gold-and-Baccarat crystal lamps in the lobby and the Emperor Suite (home to Michael Jackson during his reclusive period), which goes for only B$17,000 a night. You don't have to stay here in order to bask in the opulence; a flying visit and an inexpensive cup of tea in the lounge suffices. Since bus #57 runs only three times daily, plan a leisurely visit or arrange a taxi back (B$35).

ARRIVAL AND DEPARTURE

By plane Brunei International Airport (Lapangan Terbang Antarabangsa; ☎02 331747, ⓦcivil-aviation.gov.bn) is 8km north of the city. There are free public phones beyond passport control, a tourist information booth and ATMs. Taxis to the centre cost around B$30 (around B$40 after 9pm). Alternatively, bear right as you exit arrivals into the free parking zone where you can catch a bus (#23, #24 or #34; every 15min; 6.30am–6pm; B$1) into town. Brunei airport departure tax is B$5 for flights to east Malaysia and B$12 to all other destinations.

Destinations Bangkok, Thailand (daily; 4hr); Hong Kong (daily; 3hr 30min); Kota Kinabalu, Sabah (daily; 40min); Kuala Lumpur, Malaysia (daily; 2hr 20min); Kuching, Sarawak (3 weekly; 1hr 10min); Manila, Philippines (several daily; 2hr); Singapore (daily; 2hr).

By boat "Flying coffin" boats (thus named because of their shape and possibly because of the occasionally hair-raising ride) run between the Jalan Residency jetty 2km east of the centre of Bandar and Bangar.

Destinations Bangar (roughly hourly between 6am–4.30pm; 45min).

By bus Long-distance buses from Sabah and Sarawak arrive at and depart from the large car park opposite the Royal Regalia Museum (see opposite). Buses from Kalimantan arrive at the bus terminal inside the multi-storey car park on Jalan Cator. Jesselton Express (☎02 714 5734, ⓦsipitangexpprress.com) runs to Kota Kinabalu, Sabah via Limbang, Bangar and Lawas (see box below), while PHLS Express (☎02 771668, ⓦphls38.com.bn) serves Miri, Sarawak via Seria and Kuala Berait. For a marginally pricier but more convenient option for Miri, it's possible to arrange door-to-door pick-up via Mrs Lee of *Dillenia Guesthouse* (see p.490). S. J. S. Executive Bus (☎02 713 0686, ⓦsjsbus.wordpress.com) runs to Pontianak, Kalimantan.

Destinations Kota Kinabalu, Sabah (daily at 8am; 9hr); Miri, Sarawak via Kuala Belait (5 daily; 4hr); Pontianak (daily at 9am; 26hr).

INTO MALAYSIA: KOTA KINABALU

You can now take a direct air-conditioned bus from Bandar to **Kota Kinabalu** in Sabah. There are eight immigration stops along the way – the first as you leave Brunei, the second on entering Sarawak at Kuala Lurah and the third departing Sarawak, which is followed by number four, re-entering Brunei at Ujong Jalan. The remaining four stops are, in order, on departing Brunei again, re-entering Sarawak at Labu, departing Sarawak, and then on entering Sabah at Pantai. Along the way, the bus stops for a 45-minute lunch break and the nine-hour journey is a good way of appreciating Borneo's scenery.

1

GETTING AROUND

By bus Local buses leave from the bus station on Jln Cator, right in the centre of town (6.30am–6pm; from B$1). There are six lines – Northern, Circle, Southern, Central, Western and Eastern – and routes are clearly displayed in the bus station, with an explanatory map. Frequency varies and some buses (#57 and #58) run rather erratically.

By taxi There are set fares to get to most locations in Bandar, with a fifty percent surcharge after 10pm; from the city centre to the Brunei Museum costs about B$10; B$15 to Gadong; B$30 to the airport; B$35 to the Serasa Wharf in Muara and B$35–40 to the *Empire Hotel*. Taxis wait outside the bus station on Jln Cator or you can call one on ⊤ 02 222214.

By water taxi The jetty below the intersection of Jln Roberts and Jln McArthur is the best place to catch a motorized canoe across the river to Kampong Ayer (B$1).

INFORMATION AND TOURS

Tourist information You can pick up tourist info and decent maps from the information counter at the airport (daily 8am–noon & 1.30–5pm), the Kampong Ayer Cultural & Tourism Gallery (see p.57) and the Old Customs House on the waterfront (Sat–Thurs 9am–5pm, Fri 9–11am & 2.30–5pm).

Tour operators Danny (⊤ 073 880 1180) is a freelance tour guide who usually hangs around the Jln Cator bus station wearing a beret and waistcoat with a Confederate-flag design; he is a treasure trove of local information who can arrange onward travel and excellent boat tours (see p.57). Sunshine Borneo Tours (⊤ 02 446509, Ⓦ exploreborneo.com), an offshoot of the Kuching-based Borneo Adventure (see box, p.482), run tours to Ulu Temburong National Park – both day-trips and overnight stays. Borneo Guide (⊤ 02 426923 or ⊤ 08 766798, Ⓦ borneoguide.com) specializes in eco-programmes around Brunei and beyond; day-trips to Ulu Temburong National Park include meals, the canopy walk, a short jungle hike and a visit to a longhouse; overnight visits also available.

ACCOMMODATION

There's not a lot of choice when it comes to central accommodation, budget or otherwise, but unless you have your own wheels, it's not particularly convenient to be based anywhere else.

Jubilee Hotel Jln Kampung Kianggeh ⊤ 02 228070, Ⓦ jubileehotelbrunei.com. This central high-rise lacks the *Terrace*'s swimming pool, but its clean yet uninspiring rooms are comparable. The "superior" rooms come with kitchenettes, and the rate includes breakfast, airport pick-up and transfers to one BSB attraction of your choice. The downstairs restaurant serves good local dishes. Double **B$95**

KH Soon Resthouse 140 Jln Pemancha ⊤ 02 222052, Ⓦ khsoon-resthouse.tripod.com. Situated right by the bus station, this is a sprawling guesthouse with spartan rooms and largely indifferent staff. The a/c rooms are large and most are en suite, but they could be cleaner and it's worrying to see electricity sockets next to the showers. Dorm **B$18**, double **B$35**, en-suite double **B$40**

Pusat Belia Jln Sungei Kianggeh ⊤ 02 222900, Ⓦ bruneiyouth.org.bn. By far the cheapest and best option for backpackers, this youth centre has sparklingly-clean single-sex four- and ten-bed dorms with a few facilities. There's a huge pool downstairs for guests to use (B$1.50) and an internet café (closed on Sun) next door. The rarely-staffed reception is open between 7.45am and 4.30pm, with staff supposedly on call until 10pm. Ask at the internet café to contact them for you – they're usually not far away. Dorm **B$15**

★ **Terrace Hotel** Jln Tasek Lama ⊤ 02 243554, Ⓦ terracebrunei.com. Though the compact rooms at this central hotel are a little musty, they come with double beds, cable TV, in-room kettles and free use of the swimming pool. There's wi-fi in the lobby; the gym is an extra B$5/hr and the restaurant serves tasty Chinese and Malay dishes. Double **B$65**

EATING AND DRINKING

Bandar has a decent eating scene that ranges from excellent night-markets and street stalls serving local specialities to a wealth of international cuisine.

Aminah Arif Unit 2–3, Block B, Rahman Bldg, Spg 88, Kiulap Ⓦ aminaarif.com.bn; bus #20 to the Kg Kiulap stop. Don't want to leave without sampling Brunei's signature dish? This is one of the best places to try it. Bring a friend and go for the "*ambuyat* special" (B$16 for two). If sago gloop just isn't for you, there are plenty of noodle, rice and soupy dishes to choose from. Daily noon–10pm.

CA Mohamed Unit 202, Yayasan Complex, Jln McArthur. On the top floor above the food court (above the *KFC*), this local favourite is famous for its Indian Muslim dishes, such as *murtabak*, a good number of veggie options and its delicious, inexpensive lunch specials which include soup, a main with rice and a drink (B$7). Daily noon–8pm.

Coffee Bean & Tea Leaf 67 Jalan Sultan. A favourite with travellers, expats and lunching office workers, Borneo's answer to *Starbucks* offers an extensive menu of teas, coffees and ice-blended drinks, great cakes (B$3.90), hearty breakfasts, large sandwiches (smoked salmon, Cajun chicken) and inexpensive pasta dishes (B$10) – all in an a/c, wi-fi-enabled environment. Daily 9am–10pm.

Kaisen Sushi Jln McArthur, next door to *Port View Café*. The austere decor at this classy Japanese restaurant belies the variety and colourfulness of its dishes – from imaginative sushi roll sets (from B$8) to tempura, rice dishes and *yakitori*, accompanied by fresh fruit juices or Japanese tea. Daily noon–10pm.

Lim Ah Siaw Pork Market Jln Teraja. Eating pork in Brunei is an illicit pleasure, since it's forbidden to raise pigs in this country. This cheerful, casual eatery attached to a market serves all things porky, from pork belly to BBQ ribs. If that's not your thing, there's *asam* prawn, mango fish rice and other treats to choose from. Mains from B$6. Daily 7am–10pm.

★ **Pasar Malam Gadong** Jln Pasar Gadong. Not far from The Mall in Gadong, this neatly organized night-market is a feast for the senses and the best place to try Malay-style noodle and rice dishes, as well as Brunei's national dish – *ambuyat*. There are not many places to sit down, though, as most folks get takeaway. Dishes from B$3.50. Daily 4–10pm.

Taman Selera Jln Tasek Lama & Jln Stoney. Located in a park opposite the *Terrace* hotel, this night-market is home to more than twenty stalls serving a mix of Malay and international food. *Roti john* (omelette sandwich with or without meat) is a popular snack among locals and the satay and the seafood dishes are excellent. Daily 5–10pm.

Tamu Kianggeh Jln Sungai Kianggeh. The food stalls at this colourful produce market across a bridge serve good, cheap *soto ayam* (spicy chicken noodle soup), satay, *nasi campur* (mixed rice), *kelupis* (glutinous rice steamed in a leaf) and other Malay staples. Mains from B$2. It's at its busiest and best on weekends. From 5pm.

DIRECTORY

Bookshops Paul & Elizabeth Book Services, 2nd Floor, Yayasan Complex, Jln Pretty.

Embassies and consulates Australia, Level 6, DAR Takaful IBB Utama, Jln Pemancha (☎ 02 229435); Canada, 5th Floor, Jalan McArthur Building, 1 Jln McArthur (☎ 02 220043); Indonesia, Lot 4498, Simpang 528, Kg Sungei Hanching Baru, Jln Muara (☎ 02 330180); New Zealand, c/o Deloitte & Touche, 5th floor, Wisma Hajjah Fatimah, 22–23 Jln Sultan (☎ 02 222422); UK, Level 2, Block D, Yayasan Complex, Sultan Hassanal Bolkiah, Jln Pretty (☎ 02 222231); US, impang 336-52-16-9, Jln Kebangsaan (☎ 02 220384).

Exchange There are many cash-only moneychangers on Jln McArthur with identical rates, and a variety of banks with ATMs on Jln Sultan, including HSBC.

Hospitals The RIPAS Hospital (☎ 02 242424), across Edinburgh Bridge on Jln Putera Al-Muhtadee Billah, has the best equipment, 24hr emergency services and English-speaking staff.

Internet La Ling Cyber Café, 2nd floor, Yayasan Complex (daily 9am–9pm; B$3/hr).

Laundry Superkleen, opposite *Brunei Hotel*, Jln Pemancha (Sat–Thurs 9am–6pm).

Pharmacies Yin Chee Dispensary, Jln Bunga Kuning; Khong Lin Dispensary, G3A, Wisma Jaya, Jln Pemancha.

Post office The GPO (Mon–Thurs & Sat 7.45am–12.15pm & 1.30–4.30pm; Fri 8–11am & 2–4pm) is at the intersection of Jln Elizabeth Dua and Jln Sultan.

Shopping malls Yayasan Complex (Jln Pretty; 10am–10pm); Centrepoint and The Mall complexes (same hours) in Gadong.

Temburong District

The sparsely populated and seldom visited **Temburong** district is Brunei's great expanse of untouched jungle, and the country's greatest natural attraction. Temburong's nondescript main town, **Bangar**, is the gateway to the pristine forest that lies within – protected in **Ulu Temburong National Park**, easily visited as a day-trip or overnight with one of Bandar's tour companies (see opposite).

ULU TEMBURONG NATIONAL PARK

Undoubtedly one of Brunei's highlights, the lowland rainforest of **Ulu Temburong National Park** is home to rich flora and fauna with Borneo's famous proboscis monkey a guaranteed sight on any trip. The park consists of 500 square kilometres of pristine rainforest, with only a tiny fraction of it open to visitors, who come here for short jungle hikes, swimming in a waterfall and a canopy walk.

Day-trips to the park typically start with a hair-raising "flying coffin" journey from Bandar to Bangar. Boats scream through narrow mangrove estuaries that are home to crocodiles and proboscis monkeys, swooping around corners at a 45-degree angle. From the Bangar jetty, it's a twenty-minute drive south to the jetty at the small kampung of **Batang Duri**. From here you make your way upstream to **Ulu Temburong Park Headquarters** along Sungai Temburong; this stretch is very shallow in dry season, and when the water level is low you may have to get out and help pull the boat over rocks. Otherwise, it's an exhilarating thirty-minute trip, with the boatman deftly propelling the *temuai* (Iban longboat) around the submerged logs and rocks and riding the rapids.

Canopy Walk

After you register at the Park Headquarters, it's another short trip upriver to where a long, steep set of stairs, followed by often muddy steps with rope handrails, leads up to the base of the **Canopy Walk**. The park's main attraction consists of an aluminium walkway suspended between towers – the highest rising 60m above the jungle floor. The view from the top is breathtaking: you can see Brunei Bay to the north and Gunung Mulu Park in Sarawak to the south.

If your guide speaks good English, it's a bonus since they can explain the workings of the canopy ecosystem, which supports insects, birds, snakes and more. The walkway and towers are a bit wobbly in the wind, but perfectly sturdy; sunscreen and a hat are important, as you're exposed to the elements up there.

If you're on a day-trip, as opposed to staying overnight, you're at a bit of a disadvantage, since you'll be on the canopy walk at the hottest time of day, when animals and birds are hiding; the best time to go up is early in the morning or late in the afternoon.

Waterfall

After the canopy walk, the longboat whisks you off back past the park headquarters and along a series of bouncy river rapids to a little side stream, which you wade through for a few minutes before reaching an idyllic little waterfall. The pool beneath the waterfall is deep enough to splash around in, and if you stay still, you will feel a tickling sensation as the small fish living in that pool nibble on the dead skin of your feet, giving you a natural pedicure.

The waterfall trip is followed by lunch and a return trip to Bandar in a "flying coffin", possibly stopping at a modern longhouse along the way. If you stay overnight, you can take part in jungle hikes and river-related activities.

ACCOMMODATION

Sumbiling Eco Village Ⓣ 02 426923, Ⓦ borneoguide.com/ecovillage. A few minutes downstream from Batang Duri, this rustic eco-camp is run by Borneo Guide (see p.60) in conjunction with the local Iban community. The rooms are basic but have fans and mosquito nets. The Iban food on offer is delicious. Apart from visiting the Ulu Temburong Park nearby, you can also go inner-tubing on the river and trekking in the jungle. Two days & one night B$245 per person, including meals.

Ulu Ulu Resort Ⓣ 02 441791, Ⓦ uluuluresort.com. This riverside lodge, built of sturdy hardwood, is the only place to stay in the park itself, with a mix of doubles and chalets, as well as its own cinema. Price includes transport from Bandar and full board; activities cost extra. Two days & one night B$290.

ANGKOR WAT

Cambodia

HIGHLIGHTS

❶ **Silver Pagoda** This temple is adorned with more than five thousand silver tiles. **See p.77**

❷ **Choeung Ek** Infamous killing fields featuring a memorial temple containing thousands of human skulls. **See p.85**

❸ **Angkor Wat** Unforgettable temple, crowned with soaring towers. **See p.92**

❹ **Angkor Thom** Walled city crammed with ancient monuments. **See p.93**

❺ **Tonle Sap lake** Miniature inland sea dotted with dozens of floating villages. **See p.98**

❻ **Island hopping** Cambodia's southern islands are a picture of pure shores, turquoise seas and tranquillity. **See p.102**

HIGHLIGHTS ARE MARKED ON THE MAP ON P.64

ROUGH COSTS

Daily budget Basic US$15–20, occasional US$30
Drink Angkor beer US$1.50
Food Khmer mains US$3–4
Hostel/budget hotel US$3–5/US$7–8
Travel Phnom Penh–Siem Reap: bus/shared taxi 6–8hr, US$6–8

FACT FILE

Population 15.2 million
Language Khmer
Religions Theravada Buddhism (96 percent), Islam, Christianity, Animism
Currency Riel (r), US dollar
Capital Phnom Penh
International phone code ☎ +855
Time zone GMT +7hr

Introduction

Having left its troubled past largely behind, Cambodia is fast becoming one of Southeast Asia's hottest destinations. Lured by ancient temples, relatively unspoilt beaches and a wide range of natural attractions from dense forests to majestic rivers, tourists have been flocking to the country in increasing numbers over the past decade. Infrastructure is improving fast, too, with new roads bringing once remote destinations within increasingly easy reach – although getting around is still a time-consuming affair. The temples of Angkor are now very much on the tourist mainstream, attracting some two million visitors a year, but much of the rest of the country remains relatively untouched and little visited, guaranteeing a warm welcome from the country's irrepressibly friendly and cheerful inhabitants. Go now, before the coach parties arrive.

The Kingdom of Cambodia occupies a modest wedge of land, almost completely hemmed in by Vietnam, Laos and Thailand. Most visitors head straight for the stunning **Angkor ruins**, a collection of more than one hundred temples dating back to the ninth century. Once the seat of power of the Khmer Empire, Angkor

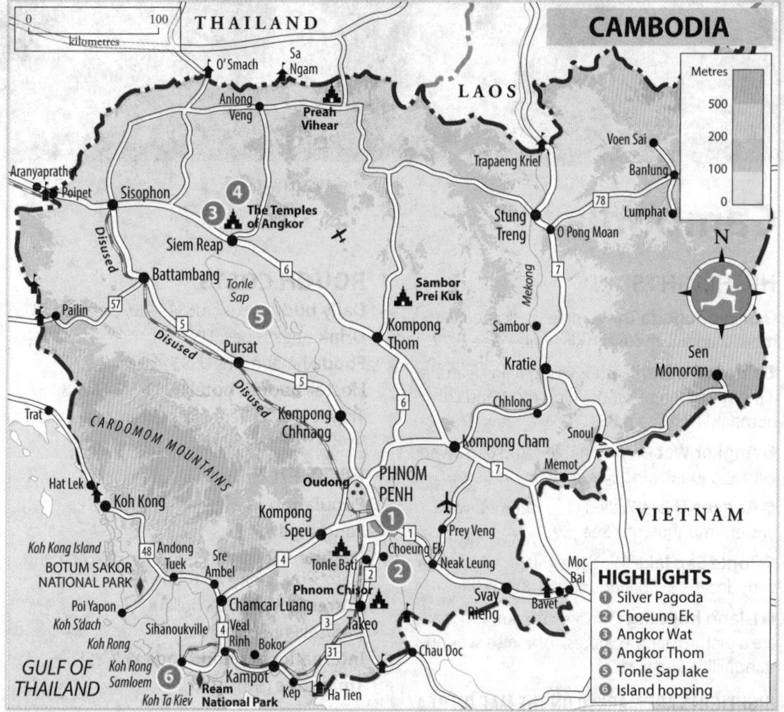

is royal extravagance on a grand scale, its imposing features enhanced by a dramatic setting amid lush jungle and verdant fields.

The capital, **Phnom Penh**, is also an alluring attraction in its own right. Wide, sweeping boulevards and elegant, if neglected, French colonial-style facades lend the city a romantic appeal. However, there's also stark evidence that you're visiting one of the world's poorest countries. Halfway between Angkor and Phnom Penh, it's worth stopping off for a day at **Kompong Thom** to make a side trip to the pre-Angkor ruins of **Sambor Prei Kuk** where there is scarcely another tourist in sight.

Miles of **unspoilt beaches** and remote islands offer sandy seclusion along the southern coastline. Although **Sihanoukville** is the main port of call, it's easy enough to commandeer transport to nearby hidden coves and offshore islands. **Ratanakiri** province in the northeastern corner of the country, with its hill tribes and volcanic scenery, is also becoming increasingly popular with visitors, while neighbouring **Mondulkiri** is less well known, but equally impressive, offering dramatic woodlands, villages and mountains. **Battambang** in the central plains, Cambodia's second city, is a sleepy provincial capital, and the gateway to a region rich in Khmer Rouge history.

WHEN TO GO

Cambodia's **monsoon climate** creates two distinct seasons. The southwesterly monsoon from May to October brings heavy rain, humidity and strong winds – especially in the latter two months – while the northeasterly monsoon from November to April produces dry, hot weather, with average temperatures rising from 25°C in November to around 32°C in April. The best months to visit are December and January, as it's dry and relatively cool, though Angkor is at its most stunning during the lush rainy season.

CHRONOLOGY

First century AD The area to the west of the Mekong Delta, along the trading route from India to China, begins to become an important commercial settlement, known by the Chinese as Funan.

Sixth century Now known as Chenla, the region is occupied by small, disparate fiefdoms operating independently. The temples of Sambor Prei Kuk date from this time.

Early ninth century Rival Chenla kingdoms are united by Jayavarman II, and the Khmer Empire's greatest period, known as the Angkorian period, begins. Jayavarman II establishes the religious cult of the *devaraja* (god-king). The empire lasts for 39 successive kings.

c.1181–1219 The reign of Jayavarman VII, the last major Angkor king. After reclaiming Angkor from the Champa Empire he embarks on a massive programme of construction, culminating in the creation of Angkor Thom.

Fourteenth century The Thai army mounts raids on Cambodian territory, virtually destroying Angkor Thom.

Mid-fifteenth century The capital of Angkor is abandoned in favour of more secure locations to the south; the Khmer Empire is in irreversible decline.

1594 The Khmer capital falls to the Thais; vast swathes of land are lost in tribute payments to both Siam and Vietnam.

1863 King Norodom, wanting to reduce Thai control and secure his own position, exchanges mineral and timber rights with the French in return for military protection.

1904 King Norodom dies; the following three kings are chosen by the French.

1941 Eighteen-year-old Prince Norodom Sihanouk succeeds King Monivong; World War II interrupts French control and Japan invades.

1945 Following the Japanese surrender, King Sihanouk campaigns for independence; France, preoccupied by Vietnam, grants it.

May 1954 Independence is formally recognized by the Geneva Conference. Sihanouk abdicates, installing his father Norodom Suramarit as king, to fight in the elections.

1955 Sihanouk's party, The People's Socialist Community, wins every seat in the newly formed parliament. Political opposition is ruthlessly repressed, and communist elements, the "Khmer Rouge", flee to the countryside.

1960 Sihanouk's father dies and Sihanouk appoints himself Chief of State, in a further gesture of despotic power.

1960s Despite publicly declaring neutrality over the Vietnam conflict, Sihanouk allows the North Vietnamese to use Cambodian soil for supplying the Viet Cong.

1969–73 The US covertly bombs Cambodia's eastern provinces where they believe Viet Cong guerrillas are hiding. Thousands of Cambodian civilians are killed or maimed.

1970 General Lon Nol and Prince Sisowath Matak depose Sihanouk. The Viet Cong are ordered to leave, but instead push deeper into Cambodia, pursued by US and South Vietnamese troops. As the country turns into a battlefield, the Khmer Rouge regroup and begin taking control of large areas.

2

April 17, 1975 Khmer Rouge forces march into Phnom Penh to the cheers of the Cambodian people – but subsequently institute a brutal regime to eradicate all perceived opposition, killing between one and two million people.
1978 Invading Vietnamese forces reach Phnom Penh and a Vietnamese-backed government led by Hun Sen is established; the Khmer Rouge flee to the jungle near the Thai border. A rival Chinese-backed government-in-exile is created, dominated by the Khmer Rouge, and headed by Sihanouk; the international community recognizes this in opposition to Vietnam.
1987 Negotiations between the Hun Sen's government and the coalition led by Sihanouk begin, and the Vietnamese agree to start withdrawing troops.
1991 The Paris Peace Accords are signed. Sweeping powers are granted to the UN Transitional Authority in Cambodia (UNTAC) to supervise control of the country and implement free elections, although little disarmament is achieved.
1993 Despite assassinations and intimidation tactics, there is a nearly ninety-percent turnout at the elections; a fragile coalition between the royalist FUNCINPEC party and Hun Sen's Cambodian People's Party (CPP) is agreed.
1994 The Khmer Rouge are outlawed, and though they still control the north and northwest, an amnesty begins to attract some defections.
1996 Notorious senior Khmer Rouge commander Ta Mok arrests Pol Pot and sentences him to life imprisonment; more defections follow.
April 1998 As Cambodian troops encroach on the last Khmer Rouge strongholds, Pol Pot dies, possibly of a heart attack, or possibly executed by his own cadres.
July 1998 Hun Sen's CPP wins another election; an alliance is negotiated, with Hun Sen as sole prime minister.
2004 King Sihanouk abdicates and invites one of his sons, Norodom Sihamoni, to replace him as king.
2008 Hun Sen wins another election with a sixty-percent majority. UN-backed war crime trials of former Khmer Rouge leaders begin. The first to stand trial is Duch, head of S21 prison in Phnom Penh (see p.80) – he is eventually sentenced to life in prison.
2008–11 Repeated clashes between Cambodian and Thai troops around the disputed border temple of Preah Vihear.
June 2012 The trials of top-ranking Khmer Rouge leaders Nuon Chea, Khieu Samphan, Ieng Sary and his wife Ieng Thirith commence amid allegations that the court is bowing to government pressure to act favourably towards powerful and wealthy Khmers who were previously mid-level Khmer Rouge commanders. Ieng Sary subsequently dies in early 2013, while his wife is declared mentally unfit to stand trial.
Oct 2012 Norodom Sihanouk, Cambodia's "King-Father", dies of a heart attack aged 89.
July 2013 In fresh elections, Hun Sen's CCP wins a narrow victory over Sam Rainsy's Cambodian National Rescue Party, amid allegations of electoral fraud. Widespread protests erupt sporadically during later 2013 and into 2014.
Oct 2013 The trials of the two remaining Khmer Rouge leaders finally conclude – with a verdict expected in 2014.
Jan 2014 Four unarmed textile workers shot dead by police during anti-government protests in Phnom Penh.

THE KHMER ROUGE

Born of radical communism and wartime opportunism, the **Khmer Rouge** defined the darkest period in Cambodia's history, leaving a legacy that will last for generations. The ragtag band of communist guerrillas, led by French-educated Saloth Sar (subsequently known as **Pol Pot**), first began to garner popular support during the American bombings of eastern Cambodia. After King Sihanouk was deposed (see p.65), the Khmer Rouge took advantage of the chaos to seize territory, eventually marching into Phnom Penh to the cheers of Cambodians longing for peace. But the party, known simply as **Angkar**, immediately began to act on their deranged designs to create a socialist utopia by transforming the country into an agrarian collective. The entire population of Phnom Penh and other provincial capitals was forcibly removed to the countryside to begin new lives as peasants working on the land. They were the lucky ones. Pol Pot ordered the mass extermination of intellectuals, teachers, writers, educated people, and their families. Even wearing glasses was an indication of intelligence, a "crime" punishable by death. The brutal regime lasted four years before invading Vietnamese forces captured Phnom Penh in 1978; by this time, between one and three million Cambodians had perished in the genocide.

Driven into the jungle, the Khmer Rouge installed themselves near the Thai border and continued to wage guerrilla warfare against the occupation government, supported by an international community fearful of communist expansionism. It wasn't until Ieng Sary, one of Pol Pot's trusted inner circle, defected in 1996, causing a split in the Khmer Rouge ranks, that the tide began to turn. Pol Pot himself was found dead two years later, having been convicted by his own troops of murder. To this day no one knows for sure how he died.

ARRIVAL

There are **flights** to Phnom Penh from Paris, Kuala Lumpur, Singapore, Seoul, Bangkok, Vientiane, Ho Chi Minh City, and several cities in China including frequent connections with Hong Kong. Siem Reap's international airport is also reached from most of these cities. Travelling **overland** into Cambodia is possible from neighbouring Thailand, Vietnam and Laos.

OVERLAND FROM LAOS

It's possible to cross from Laos at the **Trapaeng Kriel–Nong Nok Khiene/Dong Kalwa** crossing between Stung Treng and Si Phan Don.

OVERLAND FROM THAILAND

There are six entry points from Thailand: the border crossing at **Aranyaprathet**, near Poipet; two crossings at **Pailin**; the coastal border at **Hat Lek** to Cham Yeam, west of Koh Kong (see box, p.778); the reopened crossings in northeast Thailand, at the **Chong Chom–O'Smach** border pass, near Kap Choeng in Thailand's Surin province (see box, p.769); and the little-used **Sa Ngam–Choam** border in Si Saket province.

OVERLAND FROM VIETNAM

From Vietnam, seven crossings are open to foreigners. The busiest (on the main highway between Ho Chi Minh City and Phnom Penh) is at **Moc Bai–Bavet** (see box, p.905). There are three border posts in southern Cambodia including two near the Vietnamese town of **Chau Doc** (see box, p.910) and one at **Ha Tien** (see box, p.916), east of Kep on the coast. There are three further, although little-used, crossings open in Eastern Cambodia including the **O Yadaw–Le Tanh** border post between Banlung and Pkeiku.

VISAS

All foreign nationals except those from certain Southeast Asian countries need a **visa** to enter Cambodia. **Tourist visas**, valid for thirty days, cost US$20 and are issued on arrival at the airports in Phnom Penh and Siem Reap; two passport photos are required. You may be able to pay an extra $1–5 to have the one from your passport copied, depending on the mood of the official. However, there have been reports of people being denied visas for not having a photo. Cambodian visa officials are notoriously unfriendly as well as corrupt. It's also possible to obtain a visa on arrival at all overland border crossings, although Cambodian border officials have been known to inflate the price. To avoid the risk, you may prefer to take care of your tourist visa online in advance (ⓦevisa.mfaic.gov.kh), though these e-visas are not valid at some of the more obscure overland crossing points – check the website for details. **E-visas** cost $20 for the visa plus an additional $5 and take three days to process; you'll need to provide a digital photograph.

Extending a tourist visa is officially done at the Department of Immigration, Pochentong Road, opposite the airport in Phnom Penh (Mon–Fri 8–10.30am & 2.30–4.30pm). You'll need one passport photo and next-day service costs $60. Given the location of the offices, it's easier to take advantage of the extension services offered by travel agents and guesthouses; they can do the running around for you and charge just a couple of dollars' commission. A tourist visa can only be extended once, for one month. If you wish to stay longer you'll need a business visa. You are charged 50,000 riel ($12.50) per day for overstaying your visa.

> **AIRPORT DEPARTURE TAX**
>
> There is a US$6 departure tax on domestic flights; there is no longer a departure tax on international flights.

GETTING AROUND

Transport in Cambodia is all part of the adventure. Massive improvements to the national highway network in the past few years have made getting around the country much easier than it once was, with many formerly dirt roads now surfaced and new highways built. Even so, getting from A to B remains a time-consuming process: roads are still

narrow and bumpy, while regular wet-season inundations play havoc with transport (and often wash away large sections of tarmac in their wake). Regular **boats** run between Phnom Penh, Siem Reap and Battambang, although these are even slower than travel by road, while the last passenger **train** departed in 2009. Fortunately, Cambodia isn't a big country, and most journeys between major centres take no more than a couple of hours – even the trip between Phnom Penh and Siem Reap can now be done in as little as five hours.

The rapidly expanding **bus** system provides connections between all major towns and is likely to be your standard means of transport. **Minibuses** and **share taxis** can be useful if you want to get somewhere not served by bus. They also cover all the same routes as the buses do, and often slightly faster, although any slight savings of time are usually far outweighed by the sardine-like conditions on board. In short, buses are generally preferable unless you're in a serious rush – in which case you probably shouldn't be in Cambodia at all.

BUSES

Buses are the cheapest (and usually the most convenient and comfortable) way to get around, connecting all major cities and towns. Some smaller places aren't yet on the bus network, and others – Banlung, Sen Monorom and Pailin, for example – have only one or two services a day.

All buses are privately run, operated by a growing number of companies. Phnom Penh Sorya are the biggest; others include Rith Mony, GST, Paramount Angkor and Capitol Tours, while other companies like Giant Ibis and Mekong Express operate luxury express buses on the most popular routes.

Buses generally arrive and depart from their respective company offices. Unfortunately, this means there are no bus stations or suchlike in which to get centralized information about the timetables and fares of all the various services available. Some guesthouses or tour operators can provide this information; otherwise you'll have to visit all the individual bus company offices in order to get this information. Fares are generally much of a muchness on all but the most-travelled routes, although you might find one company's timings more convenient than another's.

MINIBUSES

Minibuses provide the main alternative to buses, at a similar price. These generally serve the same routes as buses, and also go to smaller destinations not served by bus. They also tend to be slightly faster. On the downside, most usually get absolutely packed and can be horribly uncomfortable, especially for taller travellers (there's little legroom at the best of times, unlike the buses, which are relatively luxurious in comparison). There are also a few "luxury minibus" services on the main inter-city and international routes (Mekong Express's "limousine bus" services, for example), although these get mixed reviews, and you can never be entirely certain of what you're getting until it's possibly too late.

SHARE TAXIS

Share taxis are generally slightly more expensive but also slightly quicker than buses and minibuses; they also serve local destinations off the bus and minibus network. On the downside, like minibuses they get absurdly packed. Three or even four people on the front passenger seat is the norm – although you can pay roughly double the standard fare to have it to yourself, or indeed pay to hire the entire taxi. The driving can often be slightly hair-raising too. Shared taxis usually leave from the local transport stop. There are no fixed schedules, although most run in the morning, leaving when (very) full.

LOCAL TRANSPORT

Motorcycle taxis, commonly called **motos**, are the most convenient way of getting around town and are inexpensive – short journeys cost around $1. English-speaking drivers can usually be found outside hotels, guesthouses and other tourist spots. Non-English-speaking

drivers will often nod enthusiastically in a show of understanding, only to proceed to the nearest guesthouse or tourist site. You can hire a moto for the day to visit sights in and around towns all over the country. For trips within a 20km radius, a daily rate of around $15 is the norm.

Three-wheeled **cyclos** (cycle rickshaws) are a more relaxing way to trundle around Phnom Penh, but are only practical for shorter trips. Cyclo fares are subject to negotiation, usually costing a little more than motos ($1–2), and a little more still in the midday heat or pouring rain. Faster and more comfortable are **tuk-tuks**, motorbike-drawn rickshaws that ply the roads of most major cities. These can comfortably carry up to four people – although the under-powered engines tend to struggle with more than a couple of people on board. Fares are usually around $1–3 for short trips around town. With motos, cyclos and tuk-tuks, agree a fare in advance.

Taxis aren't really used for short hops around town. There are only a few metered taxi services in Phnom Penh. Otherwise, cars are rented by the day, or by the journey.

VEHICLE RENTAL

Renting a **motorbike** is the most practical self-drive option for Cambodia's backcountry roads. At the rental shops in Phnom Penh, you can pick up a fairly good 250cc trials bike ($25/day), which should be able to handle most terrain, while elsewhere basic bikes can go for as little as $5/day. **Cars** tend to come with a driver. They're almost exclusively white Toyota Camrys, and cost around $50–70 per day depending on mileage.

If you do intend to **self-drive** any vehicle in Cambodia, bear in mind that road conditions are unpredictable. Really, it's only practical if you've had experience of driving in Southeast Asia already.

Officially, vehicles drive on the right, but **traffic regulations** in Cambodia are flexible and you may encounter people driving on the left. Traffic on the roads from Phnom Penh to Sihanoukville and Kompong Cham is heavy and hectic, but much lighter elsewhere.

Bicycles are available to rent cheaply (usually about $1–3 a day), and except in Phnom Penh, where traffic is intimidating, cycling is a pleasant way to explore.

TRAINS

There have been no passenger **train** services in Cambodia since 2009. Plans to restore and reopen Cambodia's dilapidated railway network with Australian assistance have hit major (possibly terminal) delays, and it seems unlikely any progress will be made for the next two or three years at least.

BOATS

Regular **ferries** run between Phnom Penh and Siem Reap, and Siem Reap and Battambang. Conditions are fairly cramped so don't expect the luxury that the foreigner prices imply. Many tourists opt to sit on the roof for the views and sunbathing.

PLANES

Cambodia Angkor Air runs **domestic flights** between Siem Reap and Phnom Penh, and Phnom Penh and Sihanoukville. Flights are around $70 return, although by the time you've got to and from the airports it's not an awful lot quicker than going by bus.

ACCOMMODATION

There are basic hotels in every provincial town, usually in fairly featureless modern concrete blocks. In general, expect to have an en-suite shower (sometimes, but not always, with hot water). The cheapest **hotel** rooms go for a bargain $7 or so. Almost all hotel rooms have double beds as standard – if you ask for a double room, you'll get one with two double beds in it.

Tourist-oriented **budget guesthouses** are springing up in towns across the country, though you'll find most of them in Phnom Penh, Siem Reap and Sihanoukville. In some places it's possible to get a bed for as little as $3 if you don't mind basic facilities or the lack of a window. Throughout the country, you'll pay around $5–7 more per night for air

2

ADDRESSES

Many roads in Cambodia have no names, and those that do are often known by a number rather than a name, so for example, 50 Street 125 means building number 50 on Street 125. Throughout the chapter, where street names are nonexistent, we have located places by describing their location or giving a nearby landmark.

conditioning, which is in fact a bargain considering the high price of electricity. Prices given in the text relate to the cost of the cheapest double room, but most establishments will offer more luxurious rooms as well. **Camping** is theoretically illegal in Cambodia, but is a possibility in some places – for example, on the beaches and islands of the south coast. In the dry season, all you need is a mosquito net and hammock for a comfortable night's sleep.

Electricity is usually supplied at 220 volts, through plugs of the two-flat-pin variety. Power cuts and surges are much less common than they once were, but not unknown.

FOOD AND DRINK

Cambodian food is heavily influenced by China, with **stir-fries** featuring on most menus. Some dishes are similar to Thai cuisine, although usually considerably milder, with herbs being used for flavouring rather than spices and chilli served on the side rather than being blended into the dish. Even **curry dishes**, such as the delicious coconut milk and fish **amok**, tend to be served very mild. **Rice** is the staple food, while **noodles** are eaten more for breakfast – when they're served as a soup – and as a snack. Hygiene standards may not match what you're used to, but produce is always fresh. At street stalls though, given the lack of refrigeration, it's as well to make sure that the food is piping hot. If you have a choice, pick somewhere that's busy.

WHERE TO EAT

The cheapest Khmer cuisine is to be found at **street stalls** and **markets**, which is where you'll find dishes more like the ones the locals eat at home. There are usually one or two dishes on offer at each stall – perhaps pigs'-organ soup, fried noodles or a tasty filled baguette. If you're ordering soup, you can pick and choose the ingredients to taste. These stalls are dirt cheap – you can certainly get a meal for around $1 – though the portions tend to be on the small side. Some baguette and noodle stalls are open throughout the day, but many more crop up around sunset.

Khmer restaurants are the next step up, recognizable by their beer signs outside. In the evenings, the better ones fill up early on, and most places close soon after 9pm. Buying a selection of dishes to share is the norm: dishes typically cost $1.50–3. Some places have an English-language menu although most don't, in which case you'll just have to practise your Khmer or point at what other diners are eating.

Tourist restaurants are plentiful in Phnom Penh, Siem Reap and Sihanoukville, though standards vary enormously. Menus generally feature Khmer dishes alongside a range of Western offerings (not always resembling what you might expect to be served back home). These places generally cost a little bit more than local restaurants, with mains at around $3–5 (or $7–15 in more upmarket restaurants). Western-oriented restaurants tend to stay open later than their Khmer counterparts, usually closing around 11pm, or even later if they double as bars.

KHMER FOOD

A standard **meal** in Cambodia consists of rice, plus two or three other dishes, either a fish or meat dish, and a steaming bowl of soup. Flavours are dominated by fish sauce, herbs – especially lemon grass (particularly in soup) – coconut milk, galangal and tamarind.

Cambodia's national dish, **amok**, features in various forms on virtually every menu in the country – a mild yellow curry with a rich coconut-milk sauce traditionally baked in banana leaves. The classic version of amok is served with fish (**amok dt'ray**), although chicken amok is now equally common.

Fish turns up in many other dishes, particularly around the Tonle Sap, where freshwater fish are particularly abundant. Popular dishes include **dt'ray chorm hoy** (steamed fish), **dt'ray aing** (grilled fish) and **sumlar mjew groueng dt'ray** (Cambodian fish soup with herbs).

For snacks, try **noam enseum j'rook** (sticky rice, soy beans and pork served in a bamboo tube) or **noam enseum jake** (sticky rice and banana). Baguettes (**noam pang**) are always a handy snack food, especially when travelling. Vendors have a selection of fillings, normally pork pâté, sardines, pickled vegetables and salad.

There are some surprisingly tasty **desserts** to be found at street stalls, markets and some restaurants, many of them made from rice and coconut milk. They're very cheap, so you could try a selection. Succulent **fruits** are widely available at the markets. Rambutan, papaya, pineapple, mangosteen and dragonfruit are delicious, and bananas incredibly cheap. Durians grow in abundance in Kampot, and are, according to Cambodians, the world's finest; they're in season from late March.

DRINKS

If you want to reduce the chance of stomach problems, don't drink **tap water** and don't take **ice** out on the streets, although it's generally safe in tourist bars and restaurants. Bottled, sealed water is available everywhere. Other thirst-quenchers are the standard international **soft drinks** brands, available in bottles or cans, and a few local variants. Freshly squeezed sugar-cane juice is another healthy roadside favourite, although the tastiest Khmer beverage has to be **dteuk krolok**, a sweet, milky fruit shake, to which locals add an egg for extra nutrition.

Cambodian **coffee** is quite unlike anything you'll have tasted back home. Beans are traditionally roasted with butter and sugar, plus various other ingredients which might include anything from rum to pork fat, giving the beverage a strange, sometimes faintly chocolately aroma – something of an acquired taste. It's often served (and generally tastes better) as black ice coffee. If you order it white, it comes with a slug of condensed milk already in the glass. Chinese-style **tea** is commonly drunk with meals, and is served free in most restaurants. You'll only find Western tea in tourist restaurants.

The most popular local brew is **Angkor beer**, a fairly good lager, owing in part to the use of Australian technology at the Sihanoukville brewery, although there are numerous other brands available, including the confusingly soundalike (and very similar-tasting) Anchor Beer.

CULTURE AND ETIQUETTE

Cambodians are extremely conservative, and regardless of their means do their very best to keep clean; you'll gain more respect if you're well turned out and modest in your dress. Men should wear tops and women avoid skimpy tops and tight shorts. Particularly offensive to Cambodians is any display of public affection between men and women: even seeing foreigners holding hands is a source of acute embarrassment. Cambodia shares many of the same attitudes to **dress** and **social taboos** as other Southeast Asian cultures (see p.40).

Tipping is common only in Western restaurants – a dollar or two is generally adequate, and much appreciated.

SPORTS AND OUTDOOR ACTIVITIES

Cambodia's lack of tourist infrastructure, combined with the continuing danger of landmines, has made trekking and mountain biking difficult (if not downright dangerous) in the past. However, an increasing number of opportunities are appearing for travellers hankering to get outdoors.

For **trekking**, the place to be is the northeast, particularly Banlung and Sen Monorom, where local guides can lead groups or individuals on treks into the surrounding jungle and Virachey National Park (p.117) lasting anything from a day to a week. Another good place

2

to hike is in the forested hills around Koh Kong, gateway to the pristine Cardamom Mountains (see p.107).

For **diving**, there are a number of PADI dive shops in Sihanoukville, all of which offer certification courses, fun dives and "discover diving" outings for beginners (see p.106).

Cycling and **kayaking** are slowly taking off in the northeast around the Mekong. Kratie and Stung Treng are the best places to organize trips. **Mountain biking** is a bit more difficult to organize, although for those with some cash to spare, several companies in Phnom Penh organize bike trips down to the coast and into the surrounding villages. Pepy (T 023 222804, W pepyride.org) leads tours in support of local education programmes, though you should contact them in advance.

COMMUNICATIONS

To send anything by **mail** it's best to use the main post office in Phnom Penh, as all mail from the provinces is consolidated here anyway. International post is often delivered in around a week, but can take up to a month, depending on the destination. **Poste restante** is available at the post offices in Phnom Penh, Siem Reap and Sihanoukville post offices.

To **phone abroad** from Cambodia, dial T 001 + IDD country code + area code minus first 0 + subscriber number. You can make international calls from most post offices, although these are usually expensive, as are calls made from hotel and guesthouse phones. Phone shops (with can be found around most Cambodian markets) offer cheaper calls, often using a mobile rather than a landline; even cheaper are calls via Skype, available at many internet cafés. It's also easy to pick up a local SIM card to access cheap international phone-call rates.

There are **internet cafés** in all major towns; prices vary considerably, but are usually $0.50–1 per hour. **Wi-fi** is also widely available even in fairly out-of-the-way places; most of the hotels and restaurants listed in the guide section offer it for free.

CAMBODIA ONLINE

W **bayonpearnik.com** Travel information, listings and local gossip with a humorous twist, produced and written by expats.
W **canbypublications.com** Online version of the free tourist guides available in Phnom Penh, Sihanoukville and Siem Reap, full of up-to-date information about food, lodging and transport.
W **talesofasia.com** Reliable practical advice on border crossings, overland travel and assorted off-road adventures; mainly Cambodia, though it covers several other countries as well.

CRIME AND SAFETY

The **security situation** in Cambodia has improved significantly over the last few years and all areas covered in this book are safe to travel in, but be very aware of the fact that Cambodia is one of the most heavily mined countries in the world, and also has significant quantities of unexploded ordnance (UXO) lying around.

Mines and ordnance apart, there is still a culture of guns in Cambodia, and there have been incidents of armed robbery against locals and tourists alike. **Gun crime** is a regular occurrence in Phnom Penh (although considerably less common elsewhere in the country), usually reaching a peak at festival times, most notably Khmer New Year. Don't be paranoid, but, equally, be aware that a small but significant number of visitors continue to be mugged at gunpoint (and occasionally shot), even in busy and touristed areas. Given this, it's a very good idea to keep all valuables well out of sight. If you are unfortunate enough to find yourself being robbed, on no account resist – the consequences if you do so could possibly be fatal. It's also worth making sure that all bags are hidden between your legs if travelling by moto – snatch-and-grab robberies have also been reported, with victims occasionally being pulled off the back of motos by the straps of their bags during attempted grabs.

EMERGENCY NUMBERS
Police ☎ **117**
Fire ☎ **118**
Ambulance ☎ **119**

There are plenty of civilian and military **police** hanging around, whose main function appears to be imposing arbitrary fines or tolls for motoring "offences". Of the two, the **civilian police**, who wear blue or khaki uniforms, are more helpful. Military police wear black-and-white armbands. If find yourself in need of actual police assistance, your best bet is the **tourist police** offices in major cities; they generally speak some English.

LANDMINES

The war has ended, but the killing continues. Years of guerrilla conflict have left Cambodia the most densely mined country in the world. The statistics are horrendous: up to six million **landmines** in the country; more than forty thousand amputees; and hundreds of further mine victims every year. The worst affected areas are the province of Battambang and the border regions adjacent to Thailand in the northwest, namely Banteay Meanchey, Pailin and Preah Vihear provinces.

Although the risk is very real for those who work in the fields, the threat to tourists is minimal. The main **tourist areas** are clear of mines, and even in the heavily mined areas, towns and roads are safe. The main danger occurs when striking off into fields or forests, so the simple solution is to stick to known safe paths. If you must cross a dubious area, try to use a local guide, or at least ask the locals "**mee-un meen dtay**?" ("Are there mines here?"). Look out for the red mine-warning signs, and on no account touch anything suspicious.

MEDICAL CARE AND EMERGENCIES

Clinics and hospitals in Phnom Penh are equipped to deal with most ailments (see p.84). Sihanoukville and Siem Reap have limited facilities, but generally medical facilities outside Phnom Penh are poor. For serious **medical emergencies**, it's best to try to get your insurance company to transfer you to Bangkok. We've provided general emergency telephone numbers (see box above), although in a crisis it's best first of all to enlist the help of your hotel, and secondly to immediately contact your travel insurance company back home for additional back-up and support.

Street-corner **pharmacies** throughout Cambodia are well stocked with basic supplies, and money rather than a prescription gives easy access to anything available, though beware of out-of-date medication. Standard shop hours (see p.76) apply at most of these places, but some stay open in the evening. More reputable operations with English- and French-speaking pharmacists can be found in Phnom Penh and Siem Reap, where a wider variety of specialized drugs is available.

INFORMATION AND MAPS

Cambodia has a network of basic **tourist offices**, although they're desperately starved of resources and generally don't have much information (even if they're open, which often they're not), so it's better to ask at local guesthouses.

Most **maps** of Cambodia are horribly inaccurate and/or out of date. Far and away the best is Reise Know-How's Kambodscha map (that's "Cambodia" in German), beautifully drawn on un-rippable waterproof paper, and as detailed and up-to-date as you could hope, given Cambodia's ever-developing road network.

MONEY AND BANKS

Cambodia's official unit of currency is the **riel**, abbreviated to "r". **Notes** come in denominations of 100, 200, 500, 1000, 2000, 5000, 10,000, 20,000, 50,000 and 100,000. US dollars are used throughout the country as a second currency, interchangeable with riel at an almost universally recognized rate of $1 = 4000r. Prices are quoted in a mix of dollars and riel (or sometimes both). In

2

2

KHMER

Khmer is the national language of Cambodia. Unusually for the region, it is not a tonal language, which theoretically makes it easier to master. However, the difficulty lies with pronunciation, as there are both vowels and consonant clusters that are pronounced unlike any sounds in English. What follows here is a phonetic approximation widely used for teaching Khmer. (People and places throughout this chapter follow the commonly used romanized spellings rather than the phonetic system used below.)

PRONUNCIATION

Most consonants follow English pronunciation, except the following:

bp a sharp "p" sound, between the English "b" and "p"
dt a sharp "t" sound, between the English "d" and "t"
hs soft "h"
n'y/ñ as in "canyon"
a as in "ago"
aa as in "bar"
ai as in "Thai"
ao as in "Lao"
ay as in "pay"
ee as in "see"
eu as in the expression of disgust "uugh"
i as in "fin"
o as in "long"
oa as in "moan"
oo as in "shoot"
ou similar to "cow"
OO as in "look"
u as in "fun"

GREETINGS AND BASIC PHRASES

Hello	*soo-a s'day*
How are you?	*sok sa-bai jee-a dtay?*
Fine, thanks	*sok sa-bai jee-a dtay*
Goodbye	*lee-a hou-ee*
Excuse me	*soam dtoah*
Please	*soam*
Thank you	*or-gOOn*
Can you speak English?	*nee'ak jeh ni-yee-ay reu dtay?*
I don't understand	*k'nyom s'dup meun baan dtay*
Yes (male)	*baht*
Yes (female)	*jahs*
No	*dtay*
Where is the?	*... noo-ee- naa?*
Ticket	*som-bot*
Airport	*jom nort yoo-un hoh/aa- gaah-sa-yee-un-taan*
Boat (no engine)	*dtook*
Boat (with engine)	*karnowt*
Bus/coach	*laan tom/ laan krong*
Taxi	*dtak-see*
Car	*laan toit*
Bicycle	*gong*
Bank	*tor-nee-a-gee-a*
Post office	*bprai-sa-nee*
Passport	*li-keut ch'lorng dain*
Hotel	*son-ta-gee-a*
Motorbike taxi	*moto/motodub*
Restaurant	*poa-cha-nee-ya-taan*
Please stop here	*soam chOOp tee neeh*
Left/right	*ch'wayng/s'dam*
Do you have any rooms?	*nee'ak mee-un bon-dtOOp dtay?*
How much is it?	*t'lai bpon maan?*
Cheap/expensive	*taok/t'lai*
Single room	*bon-dtOOp*
A/c	*graiy moo-ay maa-seen dtro-chey-at*
Electric fan	*dong-harl*
Mosquito net	*mOOng*
Toilet paper	*gra-daah*
Telephone	*dtoo-ra-sup*

practice, it's absolutely fine to pay in either dollars or riel (calculated according to the $1 = 4000r exchange rate), or even in a combination of the two (equally, you'll often be given change in a mix of currencies). It's a bit of a headspin to start with, but worth getting to grips with as soon as you can in order to avoid rip-offs or misunderstandings. Note too that the Cambodian economy runs, unusually, entirely on paper. There are no riel **coins** in circulation, and US coins aren't recognized either. In addition, note that **Thai baht**, abbreviated to "B", are also widely used in the border areas.

The easiest way of accessing funds in Cambodia is via the country's good

EMERGENCIES

Help!	*choo-ee!*
Are there any mines here?	*mee-un meen dtay?*
Accident	*kroo-ah t'nak*
Please call a doctor	*soam hao kroo bphet moak*
Hospital	*moo-un dtee bphet*
Police station	*bpohs bpoli*

NUMBERS

1	*moi*
2	*bpee*
3	*bai*
4	*bpoo-oun*
5	*bprahm*
6	*bprahm-moi*
7	*bprahm bpee/ bprahm bpeul*
8	*bprahm-bai*
9	*bprahm-bpoo-oun*
10	*dop*
11, 12, 13, etc	*dop moi/moi don dop, dop bpee/ bpee don dop, dop bai/bai don-dop*
20	*m'pay*
30, 40, 50, etc	*saam seup, sai seup, haa seup*
100	*moi roy*
101	*moi roy moi*
200, 300, 400, etc	*bpee roy, bai roy, bpoo-oun roy*
1000	*moi bpoa-un*
10,000	*moi meun*

FOOD AND DRINKS GLOSSARY

lerk gai-o	Cheers!
dtai bon-lai soam	Only vegetables, please
k'nyom niam sait dtey, sait dt'ray	I don't eat meat or fish
k'nyom chong …	I'd like …

Rice and noodles

Geautiev	noodle soup
mee chaa	fried noodles
bai	cooked rice
bai chaa	fried rice

Fish, meat and vegetables

bong-kong	shrimp/prawn
bon-lai	vegetables
bpayng boh	tomato
bpoat	corn
dom-loang barang	potato
dtee-a	fish
dt'ray	duck
dtray-meuk	squid
g'daam	crab
moa-un	chicken
sait	meat
sait goa	beef
sait j'rook	pork

Basics

bpong	egg
bpong moa-un chien	fried eggs
dtao-oo	tofu
m'tayh	chilli
nOOm-bpung	bread
om-beul	salt
plai cher	fruit
s'gor	sugar

Drinks

bee-yair	beer
dteuk dtai	tea
dteuk groatch-grobaight	orange juice
dteuk doing	coconut milk
dteuk k'nai choo	palm wine
dteuk sot moi dorb	bottle of water
dteuk om bpow	sugar-cane juice
dteuk sot	drinking water
ka-fei dteuk doh goa	coffee with milk
gaa-fay khmao	coffee (black)
ot dak dteuk kork	no ice

network of **ATMs** (money is dispensed in dollars). You'll find Canadia and Acleda ATMs in every town of any consequence (Canadia ATMs accept foreign Visa and MasterCards, Acleda ATMs accept Visa cards only), plus various other ATMs in larger places. Note, however, that many charge a commission fee of up to $5 – Canadia ATMs are all commission-free, and should be your first port of call. **Credit-card advances** are available in Phnom Penh, Siem Reap, Sihanoukville and Battambang, but don't rely on them as a source of cash, as systems are unreliable. **Travellers' cheques** can be changed at most banks for a small commission, normally two percent.

2

OPENING HOURS AND HOLIDAYS

Opening hours vary, and even posted "official" times tend to be flexible. In theory, **office hours** are Monday to Saturday 7.30am to 5.30pm, with a siesta of at least two hours from around 11.30am. **Banking hours** are generally Monday to Friday 8.30am to 3.30pm, and many banks are also open on Saturday morning. **Post offices** (7am–5pm, or later), markets, **shops** (7am–8pm, or later), travel agents and many tourist offices open every day.

PUBLIC HOLIDAYS

January 1 International New Year's Day
January 7 Victory Day, celebrating the liberation of Phnom Penh in 1979 from the Khmer Rouge
February (variable) Meak Mochea, celebrating Buddhist teachings and precepts
March 8 International Women's Day
April 13/14 (variable) Bonn Chaul Chhnam (Khmer New Year)
April/May (variable) Visaka Bochea, celebrating the birth, enlightenment and passing into nirvana of the Buddha
May 1 Labour Day
May (variable) Bonn Chroat Preah Nongkoal, the "Royal Ploughing Ceremony"
May 13–15 (variable) King Sihamoni's Birthday
June 1 International Children's Day
June 18 Her Majesty the Queen Mother's Birthday
September 24 Constitution Day
Late Sept/early Oct (variable) Bonn P'chum Ben, "Ancestors' Day"
October 15 King Father's Commemoration Day, celebrating the memory of Norodom Sihanouk.
October 23 Anniversary of the Paris Peace Accords
October 30–November 1 (variable) King Sihanouk's Birthday
November 9 Independence Day
Early November Bonn Om Tuk, "Water Festival"
December 10 UN Human Rights Day

FESTIVALS

Festivals tend to be fixed by the lunar calendar, so dates vary from year to year.

Bonn Chaul Chhnam (April 13 or 14) Khmer New Year is the most significant festival of the year, a time when families get together, homes are spring-cleaned and people flock to the temples with elaborate offerings.

Bonn P'chum Ben (late Sept) "Ancestors' Day" is one of the most important events in the festive calendar. Families make offerings to their ancestors in the 15 days leading up to it, and celebrations take place in temples on the day itself.

Bonn Om Tuk (early Nov) The "Water Festival" is celebrated every year when the current of the Tonle Sap, which swells so much during the rainy season that it actually pushes water upstream, reverses and flows back into the Mekong River. The centre of festivities is Phnom Penh's riverbank, where everyone gathers to watch boat racing, an illuminated boat parade and fireworks.

Phnom Penh and around

Cambodia's capital, **PHNOM PENH**, sprawls west from the confluence of the Mekong and Tonle Sap rivers. As you approach from the airport, the city is a confusing mess, its main boulevards choked with motos and other traffic and lined with generic low-rise, concrete blocks. Despite initial impressions, however, the heart of Phnom Penh has a strong appeal. The French influence is evident in the colonial shophouses lining the boulevards, with the occasional majestic monument or public building animating the cityscape. The Phnom Penhois are open and friendly, and the city itself is small enough to get to know quickly. Phnom Penh may not have much in the way of tourist attractions – the majority of sights can be covered in a day or two – but many visitors end up lingering, if only to soak up the unique indolent atmosphere of the city.

WHAT TO SEE AND DO

Phnom Penh **city centre** can be loosely defined as the area between Monivong Boulevard and the Tonle Sap River, stretching as far north as Chroy Chung Va Bridge, and as far south as Sihanouk Boulevard. Its tourist hub is the scenic Sisowath Quay, from where most of the sights and monuments are easily accessible.

Sisowath Quay and around

The heart of Phnom Penh life is a small, fairly nondescript square of land at the

junction of **Sisowath Quay** and Street 184, in front of the Royal Palace. It's here that Cambodians used to congregate to listen to declarations and speeches from the monarch, and where Khmer families still gather in the evenings and at weekends. Picnics, games, kite-flying and perhaps a cup of **dteuk k'nai choo** are the order of the day. Running to the north and south, pedestrianized Sisowath Quay is lined with tall palms on one side, and bars, cafés and restaurants on the other. In the middle of the day the area is quiet, but as evening draws in, it is transformed into a popular and lively social centre with aerobics classes taking centre stage. For a short cruise up the Tonle Sap, particularly popular around sunset, boats can be rented along the shore for about $10 per person per hour.

The Royal Palace

Behind the park, set back from the riverbank on Sothearos Boulevard, stand the **Royal Palace** and adjacent **Silver Pagoda** (daily 8–11am & 2–5pm; $6.25), the city's finest examples of twentieth-century Khmer-influenced architecture. Both are one-storey structures – until the Europeans arrived, standing above another's head (the most sacred part of the body) was strictly prohibited.

The **palace** itself is strictly off-limits, but it's possible to visit several buildings within the compound, even when the king is around – a blue flag flies when he is in residence.

At the entrance, visitors are directed to the palace compound first, an oasis of order and calm. Head straight for the main building in the centre of the compound, the exquisite **Throne Hall**, guarded on either side by statues of naga. Inside, the ceiling is adorned with colourful murals recounting the Hindu legend of Ramayana.

As you leave the Throne Hall via the main stairs, on your left you'll see the **Elephant Pavilion** where the king waited on coronation day and mounted his elephant for the ceremonial procession. A similar building on the right, the **Royal Treasury**, houses the crown jewels, royal regalia and other valuable items. In front and to the left, bordering Sothearos Boulevard, is the **Moonlight Pavilion**, where the king used to address his subjects.

Across the complex, back towards the Silver Pagoda stands the quaint, grey **Pavilion of Napoleon III** (closed at the time of writing). Originally erected at the residence of Empress Eugénie in Egypt, it was packed up and transported to Cambodia as a gift to King Norodom, great-grandfather to the current king, who constructed the first palace here.

The internal wall of the **Silver Pagoda courtyard** is decorated with a fabulous, richly coloured and detailed mural of the Ramayana myth, painted in 1903–04 by forty Khmer artists. The Silver Pagoda takes its name from the floor of the temple, completely covered with silver tiles – 5329 to be exact – and is also known as Wat Preah Keo Morakot ("Temple of the Emerald Buddha"), after the famous **Emerald Buddha** image, made from baccarat crystal, that is kept here.

Returning to the stupa-filled courtyard, seek out the artificial Mount Mondop to see one of the Buddha's extremely large footprints.

The National Museum

Just north of the Royal Palace on Norodom Boulevard, the grand, red-painted structure that houses the **National Museum** (daily 8am–5pm; $5) is a combination of French design and Cambodian craftsmanship. Its four galleries, set around a tranquil courtyard, shelter an impressive array of ancient relics, art and sculpture covering Cambodian history from the sixth century to the present day. Some of the sculpted heads from the bridge at Angkor Thom are exhibited, as is the original statue of Yama God of the Underworld from Angkor's Terrace of the Leper King. The catalogue of exhibits continues to grow as treasures hidden from the Khmer Rouge are rediscovered.

An interesting exhibit from more recent history is the king's boat cabin, a portable wooden room used by the king for travelling on the Tonle Sap.

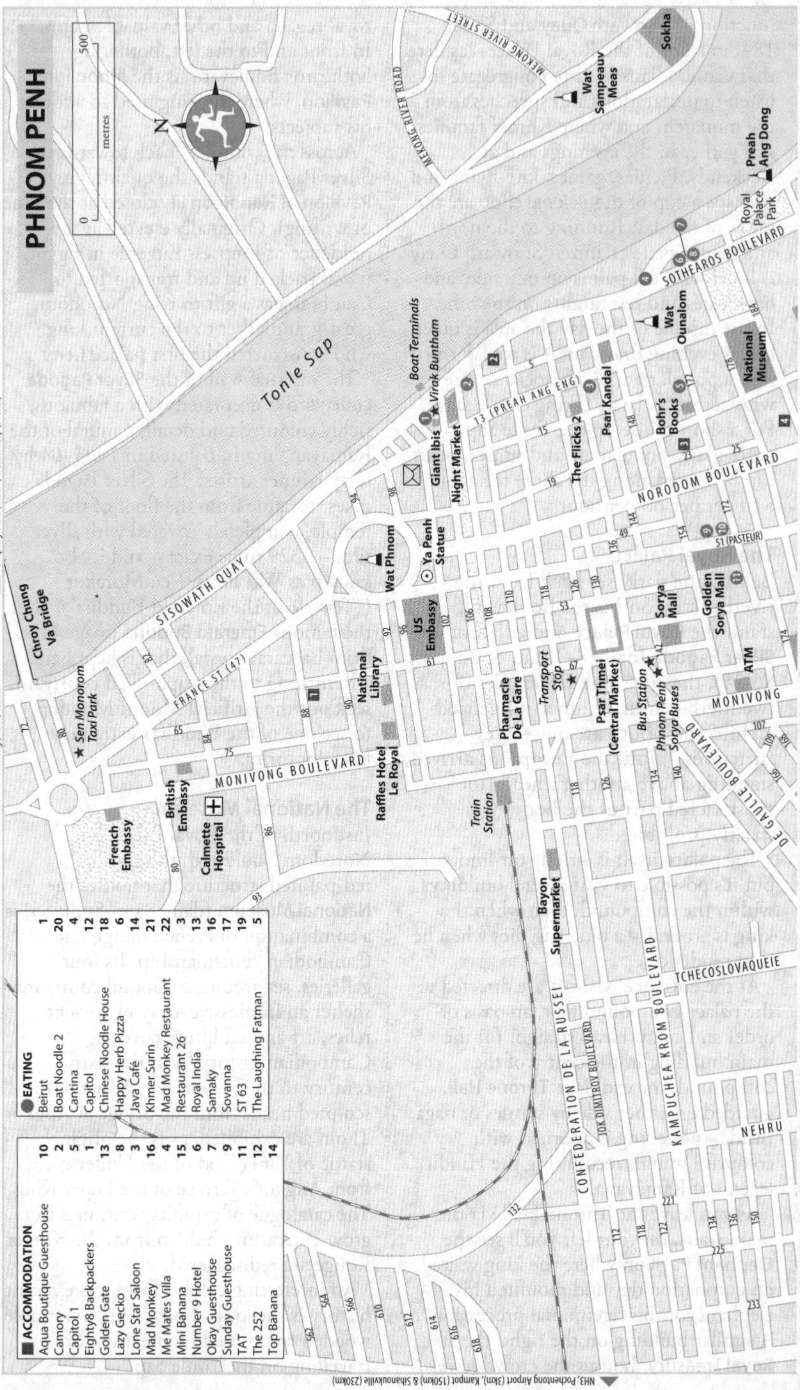

PHNOM PENH

■ ACCOMMODATION	
Aqua Boutique Guesthouse	**10**
Camory	**2**
Capitol 1	**5**
Eighty8 Backpackers	**1**
Golden Gate	**13**
Lazy Gecko	**8**
Lone Star Saloon	**3**
Mad Monkey	**16**
Me Mates Villa	**4**
Mini Banana	**15**
Number 9 Hotel	**6**
Okay Guesthouse	**7**
Sunday Guesthouse	**9**
TAT	**11**
The 252	**12**
Top Banana	**14**

● EATING	
Beirut	**1**
Boat Noodle 2	**20**
Cantina	**4**
Capitol	**12**
Chinese Noodle House	**18**
Happy Herb Pizza	**6**
Java Café	**14**
Khmer Surin	**21**
Mad Monkey Restaurant	**22**
Restaurant 26	**3**
Royal India	**13**
Samaky	**16**
Sovanna	**17**
ST 63	**19**
The Laughing Fatman	**5**

0 500 metres

N

Oudong (40km)
Kompung Cham (145km) & Siem Reap (310km)
NH3, Pochentong Airport (3km), Kampot (150km) & Sihanoukville (230km)

Tonle Sap
Chroy Chung Va Bridge
Sen Monorom Taxi Park
French Embassy
British Embassy
Calmette Hospital
Sisowath Quay
France St (47)
Monivong Boulevard
National Library
Raffles Hotel Le Royal
Wat Phnom
US Embassy
Ya Penh Statue
Boat Terminals
Giant Ibis
Virak Buntham
Night Market
Mekong River Road
Mekong River Street
Train Station
Pharmacie De La Gare
Transport Stop
Bayon Supermarket
Confederation de la Russei
Jok Dimitrov Boulevard
Kampuchea Krom Boulevard
Tchecoslovaqueie
Nehru
Psar Thmei (Central Market)
Bus Station
Phnom Penh Sorya Buses
Sorya Mall
Golden Sorya Mall
ATM
De Gaulle Boulevard
Monivong
51 (Pasteur)
Norodom Boulevard
13 (Preah Ang Eng)
The Flicks 2
Psar Kandal
Bohr's Books
Wat Ounalom
Wat Sampeauv Meas
Sokha
Sothearos Boulevard
National Museum
Royal Palace Park
Preah Ang Dong

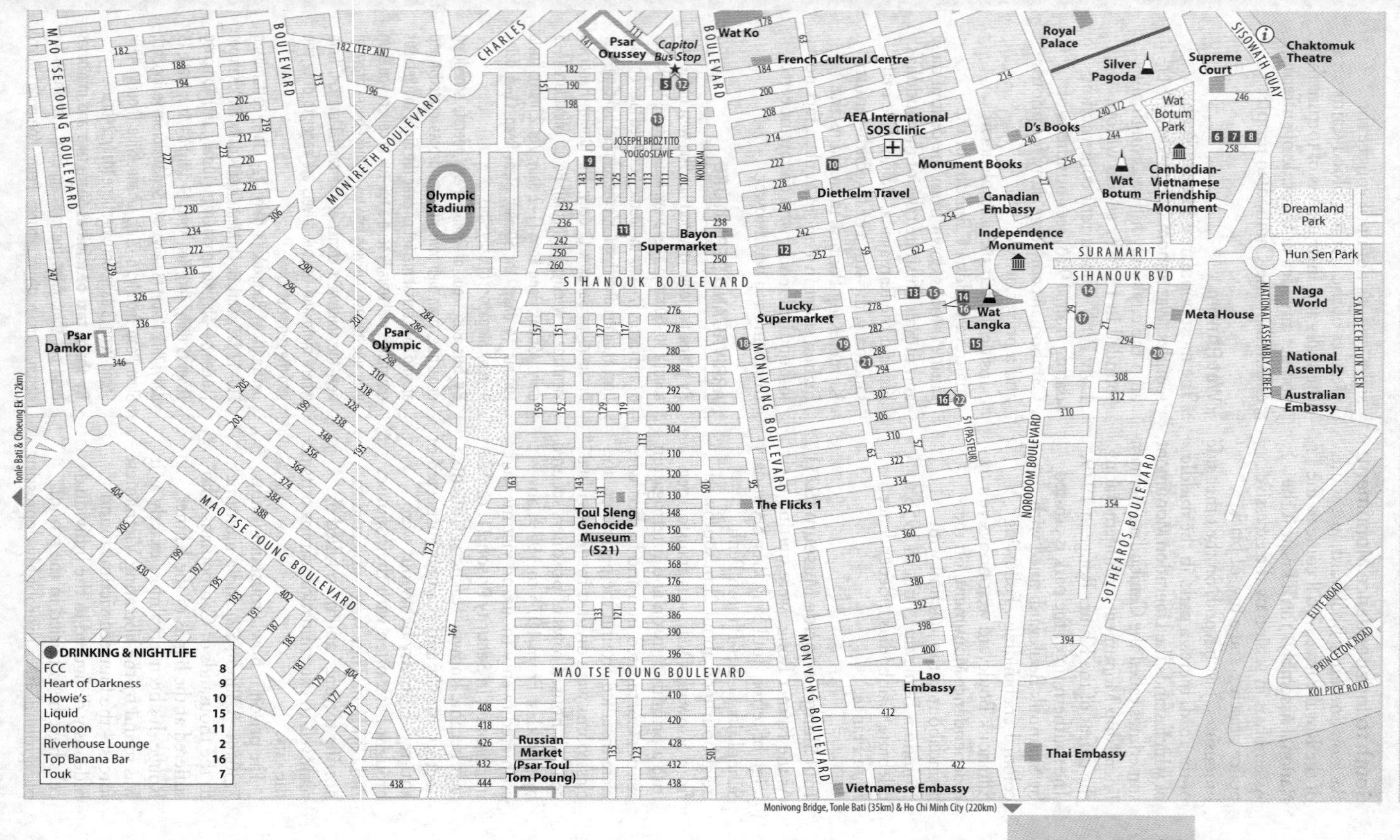
Wat Ko
Psar Orussey
Capitol Bus Stop
Charles
Boulevard
182 (Tep An)
Mao Tse Toung Boulevard
French Cultural Centre
Royal Palace
Silver Pagoda
Supreme Court
Sisowath Quay
Chaktomuk Theatre
Wat Botum Park
AEA International SOS Clinic
D's Books
Joseph Broz Tito Yougoslavie
Noukan
Monireth Boulevard
Olympic Stadium
Monument Books
Wat Botum
Cambodian-Vietnamese Friendship Monument
Dreamland Park
Diethelm Travel
Canadian Embassy
Bayon Supermarket
Independence Monument
Suramarit
Hun Sen Park
Sihanouk Boulevard
Sihanouk Bvd
Naga World
Lucky Supermarket
Wat Langka
Meta House
Psar Damkor
Psar Olympic
National Assembly
National Assembly Street
Samdech Hun Sen
Australian Embassy
Monivong Boulevard
51 (Pasteur)
Norodom Boulevard
Toul Sleng Genocide Museum (S21)
The Flicks 1
Sothearos Boulevard
Tonle Bati & Choeung Ek (12km)
Elite Road
Princeton Road
Koi Pich Road
Lao Embassy
Thai Embassy
Russian Market (Psar Toul Tom Poung)
Vietnamese Embassy
Monivong Bridge, Tonle Bati (35km) & Ho Chi Minh City (220km)
DRINKING & NIGHTLIFE
FCC 8
Heart of Darkness 9
Howie's 10
Liquid 15
Pontoon 11
Riverhouse Lounge 2
Top Banana Bar 16
Touk 7

South to Independence Monument

Back on Sothearos Boulevard, just south of the Royal Palace, you'll come to the **National Assembly**. You'll know if the Assembly is in session by the excessive police presence and a row of black limousines. Just beyond, on the other side of the road, there's a park, in the middle of which stands the **Liberation Monument**, sometimes called the Cambodia–Vietnam Friendship Monument, commemorating the defeat of the Khmer Rouge in 1979. The southern tip of the park is crossed by Sihanouk Boulevard, lined with colonial-era buildings. Following Sihanouk Boulevard west brings you to **Independence Monument**, on the roundabout at the junction with Norodom Boulevard, built in 1958 to celebrate Cambodia's independence from France.

Toul Sleng Genocide Museum (S21)

As the Khmer Rouge were starting their reign of terror, Toul Svay Prey Secondary School, in a quiet Phnom Penh neighbourhood about 2km southwest from Sisowath Quay, was transformed into a primitive prison and interrogation centre. Corrugated iron and barbed wire were installed around the perimeter, and classrooms were divided into individual cells, or housed rows of prisoners secured by shackles. From 1975 to 1979, an estimated twenty thousand victims were imprisoned in **Security Prison 21**, or S21 as it became known. Teachers, students, doctors, monks and peasants suspected of anti-revolutionary behaviour were brought here, often with their spouses and children. They were subjected to horrific tortures, and then killed or removed to extermination camps outside the city.

The prison is now a **museum** (daily 7.30am–5.30pm; $2) and a monument to the thousands of Cambodians who suffered at the hands of the Khmer Rouge. It's been left almost exactly as it was found by the liberating Vietnamese forces – the fourteen victims found hideously disfigured in the individual cells have been buried in the school playground. It's a thoroughly depressing sight, and it's not until you see the pictures of the victims, blood stains on the walls and instruments of torture that you get any idea of the scale of suffering endured by the Cambodian people.

Wat Phnom

The most popular of Phnom Penh's temples, **Wat Phnom** (dawn–dusk; $1), atop the city's only hill, was originally founded in 1373 by a local widow, Lady Penh. The current construction, dating from 1926, sees hundreds of Cambodians converge daily for photos and a prayer or two.

Inside the temple, a resplendent Maitreya Buddha ("Buddha of the Future") looks down from the central dais, and murals illustrate tales of the Buddha's life and the Ramayana. Behind the main sanctuary, the stupa of fifteenth-century Khmer King Ponhea Yat remains the highest point in Phnom Penh, a fact not lost on the French, who commandeered the shrine as a watchtower.

ARRIVAL AND DEPARTURE

By plane Pochentong Airport lies 9km west of the city, about a 30–60min journey away. Taxis charge $9, tuk-tuks $7 and motos $2–4 for the journey. Licensed taxis operate from a counter directly outside the terminal building.

Destinations Bangkok (7 daily; 1hr 10min); Hanoi via Vientiane (5 weekly; 3hr 10min); Ho Chi Minh City (4–5 daily; 45min); Hong Kong (1–2 daily; 2hr 25min); Kuala Lumpur (4 daily; 1hr 50min); Siem Reap (1–4 daily; 45min); Singapore (4 daily; 2hr).

By bus Buses out of Phnom Penh operate scheduled departures from their own offices or depots located in and around the central market or near the night market. Bus companies will usually send a tuk-tuk to collect you from your guesthouse. Arriving into town, most buses draw up near the southwest corner of the central market, from where moto and tuk-tuk drivers are eager to drive you into the centre of town.

Destinations Bangkok (3 daily; 12–13hr); Battambang (10–12 daily; 6hr); Ho Chi Minh City (14 daily; 6hr); Kampot (10 daily; 4–5hr); Kompong Cham (10 daily; 2hr); Kompong Thom (5 daily; 4hr); Koh Kong (3 daily; 6–7hr); Kratie (3 daily; 7hr); Poipet (8 daily; 8hr); Sen Monorom (daily; 8hr); Siem Reap (hourly; 6–7hr); Sihanoukville (hourly; 4hr); Stung Treng (3 daily; 8hr); Vientiane (daily; 24hr).

By share taxi or minibus Share taxis and minibuses head out throughout the morning from Psar Thmei for destinations north of Phnom Penh: Kompong Thom,

Stung Treng, Siem Reap, Kompong Cham, Kratie, Battambang, and through to Sisophon and Poipet. If you're going a long way, get there by 6 or 7am, as drivers like to complete the trip in daylight. For destinations closer to town you'll easily be able to get a share taxi until early afternoon, after which departures become less frequent as fewer people will be travelling. For the southern destinations of Sihanoukville and Kampot, shared transport leaves from Psar Damkor, southwest of the city centre; fares to the coast are in the region of $6/person. Taxis are the only option for Bavet, on the Vietnam border; they leave in the mornings from the Psar Olympic, south of the Olympic Stadium. Note that if you're going to HCMC, it's much easier to take a direct bus. For Sen Monorom, shared transport departs daily at 6am from Street 70, near Wat Phnom.

Destinations All daily: Bavet (for Vietnam; 3hr); Kampot (4hr); Koh Kong (6hr); Kratie (4hr 30min); Sen Monorom (6hr); Sihanoukville (3–4hr); Sisophon (6hr); Stung Treng (6hr 30min).

By boat Express boats dock at the terminals just east of the post office on Sisowath Quay. The journey to Siem Reap takes around 5hr, subject to variations in the river's flow, and is a much pricier alternative to the bus (tickets cost $25 for foreigners). Boats leave at 7am. To Chau Doc, for Vietnam, there are around 3 departures a day (from $25; 4hr 30min). Boats have allocated seating; you can buy your ticket at the dock the day before or on the morning of departure.

INFORMATION

Tourist information The airport has a tourist information desk (variable hours), with a list of accommodation and travel agents. Most guesthouses and hotels have reliable information. The free quarterly *Phnom Penh Visitors' Guide* (Ⓦ canbypublications.com) has a wealth of information on activities and sights around the city, plus a useful map; you'll find it in restaurants, guesthouses and bars, as well as online.

Tour agencies There is a wealth of tour agencies around Phnom Penh, but most are geared towards large groups. For independent budget travellers the best bet is often to arrange a tour through a guesthouse such as *Mad Monkey*, *Okay* or *Top Banana*, which all offer tour services.

GETTING AROUND

By bus Phnom Penh has no public bus service.

By moto Motorcycle taxis, or motos, are the most convenient way of getting around the city and are inexpensive. Expect to pay $1 for a short hop, or up to $3 for a longer journey. Prices go up after dark and in the rain. You can also hire a moto driver for a day – explain to the driver exactly where you want to go and negotiate a price beforehand. A good English-speaker will charge around $12–15/day for his services as driver and guide.

By taxis Taxis are not hailed on the street – you can either book them over the phone or pick one up at Monivong Boulevard near the Psar Thmei, where they tend to gather. Negotiate the fare in advance. Taxis are also available for hire for the day: expect to pay $30–70 depending on distance travelled. Baileys Taxi Service (Ⓣ 012 890000) offers a 24hr taxi service with experienced, reliable English-speaking drivers.

By tuk-tuk Tuk-tuks are everywhere in Phnom Penh, and for groups of two or more they are usually the cheapest (though not the quickest) way to get around. Negotiate the fare in advance, and expect to pay around $2–4 per trip within the city centre.

By bike The many bike rental outlets near *Capitol Guesthouse* charge around $3/day. Lucky! Lucky! (413 Monivong Blvd; Ⓣ 023 212788) charges $7/day for a 110cc moped, $12/day for a 250cc off-road bike, with discounts on rentals of a week or longer. Helmets are provided but no insurance. It's worth paying the 1000r to park in the many moto compounds around the city – thieves are rather partial to unattended Hondas.

ACCOMMODATION

The backpacker vibe is to be found either on St 258, St 172 or, increasingly, around the BKK1 neighbourhood.

STREET 258

Lazy Gecko Café & Guesthouse 1D St 258 Ⓣ 012 619924, Ⓔ lazygeckocafe@gmail.com. A popular backpacker café with a handful of clean and simple rooms – some with flatscreen TV – and a buzzing café below. Double **$7**

Number 9 Hotel 7C St 258 Ⓣ 023 984999, Ⓦ number9hotel.com. Phnom Penh's first "boutique" backpackers, with a sleek and modern bar-restaurant, a/c rooms and a sun-trap rooftop jacuzzi. Double **$15**

Okay Guesthouse 3BE St 258 Ⓣ 012 300804, Ⓦ okay-guesthouse.com. A friendly, family-run hostel and bustling backpacker restaurant. Rooms are basic but clean. It's also a good spot for booking local tours to the Killing Fields or the S21 prison museum. Double **$6**

CENTRAL PHNOM PENH

Aqua Boutique Guesthouse 126 St 63 (on the corner of 278 and 57) Ⓣ 023 217536, Ⓦ aqua-boutique-guesthouse.com. Opulent wood-panelled rooms decked out with carved timber beds, dressing tables, TVs, DVD players, tea/coffee facilities and safes; the suites come with lounges or balconies. Staff are warm and helpful, and breakfast is included. Double **$38**

★ **Camory** 167 Sisowath Quay Ⓣ 012 664567, Ⓦ camoryhostelandrestaurant.com. This laidback hostel has just a few a/c dorms, the largest with a fab balcony overlooking the river. Beds have individual reading lights, and rates

2

2

include breakfast, served in the excellent ground-floor restaurant. Dorm $12

Capitol 1 14 St 182 ⓣ 023 548409, ⓦ capitolkh.com. The *Capitol* empire is a backpacking institution in Phnom Penh. Backpackers arrive here by the busload for the cheap accommodation, food and tours. Indeed, it offers the most comprehensive selection of inexpensive tours in Phnom Penh, and can help arrange onward transport. If minibusing all the central sights in one day is your bag, sign up here. Rooms are a bit cell-like, but are cheap and plentiful. Double $5

Eighty8 Backpackers St 88 ⓣ 023 5002440. In a slightly out-the-way location, but still within walking distance of Wat Phnom and the riverside. Rooms and dorms are sparse but clean and functional. The big draw here is the outdoor pool. Dorm $7, double $20

Lone Star Saloon 30 St 23 ⓣ 012 577860, ⓦ lonestar cambodia.com. Friendly, Texas-owned guesthouse with four cavernous rooms (the largest sleeps four) above a popular bar-restaurant serving supersized portions of southern cuisine. All rooms have safes, TVs and DVD players. Double $25

Me Mates Villa 21AB St 184 ⓣ 023 5003250, ⓦ memates place.com. Its location a few minutes' walk from the Royal Palace and National Museum is hard to beat, and the a/c dorms (some, including the female-only, don't have windows), although small, have wide bunks, and are cleaned daily. There are big lockers and hot-water showers, a nice communal courtyard and a decent restaurant. Dorm $6

Sunday Guesthouse 97 St 141 ⓣ 012 848858, ⓦ sunday guesthouse.hostel.com. Friendly guesthouse with helpful staff and a family atmosphere. There are nightly (7pm) video screenings of *The Killing Fields* in the restaurant, where internet is also available, and clean fan or a/c rooms. Double $8

TAT 52 St 125 ⓣ 012 921211, ⓦ tattooguesthouse.com. The decently sized, bright rooms in this cheerful guest-house mostly come with en-suite facilities. The lounge has internet, communal TV and video, and the rooftop restaurant serves cheap Cambodian and Western food. Double $8

★TREAT YOURSELF

The 252 19 St 252 ⓣ 023 6331252, ⓦ the-252.com. Chicly designed boutique hotel with swimming pool, restaurant, bar and super-friendly staff. Rooms are contemporary, stylishly moulded from polished cement, and feature beautiful soft furnishings, all mod cons and lovely bathrooms. For more space, opt for one with a private balcony. $50

BKK1

Golden Gate 9 St 278 ⓣ 023 427618, ⓦ goldengatehotels .com. A variety of adequate rooms available in two buildings, but the impressive lobby outclasses the rooms themselves. Similar accommodation is available next door at the smaller *Golden Bridge* and *Golden Sun* hotels. Double $20

★Mad Monkey 26 St 302 ⓣ 097/987091, ⓦ phnom penhhostels.com. Run by three cheery English lads, and situated in the swish BKK1 district, this European-standard flashpacker hostel is gaining a big rep for its spacious chill-out area, a/c dorms with extra-large bunk beds, smart private rooms, lively pub and super-slick restaurant. Dorm $7, double $14

Mini Banana 135 St 51 ⓣ 023 726854, ⓦ mini .topbanana.biz. The quieter and much more chilled sister to party HQ, *Top Banana*, this is the place to stay if you want all the same friendly vibes but at a slightly lower decibel. Rooms – with fan or a/c – are clean, cosy and comfortable. Dorm $4, double $9

★Top Banana 9E St 278 ⓣ 012 885572, ⓦ topbanana .biz. Phnom Penh's premier party haunt, *Top Banana* is the stuff of backpacking legend in this part of the world, largely thanks to its raucous bar and the smiley, fun-loving owner, Sovy. Newly upgraded rooms mean you can grab a decent rest between the inevitable partying. Dorm $6, double $10

EATING

Street stalls, where budget travellers can fill up on noodle dishes or filled baguettes, spring up in different places at various times of day: markets are a good place for a daytime selection, as is the riverside in the early evening. The more fashionable street-corner restaurants are concentrated just south of the junction of Sihanouk and Monivong boulevards. Phnom Penh is also filled with innumerable reasonably priced restaurants aimed at expats and tourists, with more opening up all the time; expect to pay from $4–7 for a simple main course.

KHMER AND OTHER RESTAURANTS

Beirut 117 Sisowath Quay, nr the night market ⓣ 023 720111. Close to a handful of bus offices, and near the river, this popular Lebanese joint is the go-to place for *meshwiri* kebabs, meaty *shawarmas* ($3) and mezze platters (from $4). Daily 11am–11pm.

Boat Noodle 2 57 Sothearos Blvd ⓣ 012 774287. Smart Khmer and Thai restaurant, serving a good red curry with pork (16000 riel) as well as innumerable varieties of fried rice and stir-fries. Daily 11am–11pm.

Chinese Noodle House 553 Monivong Blvd. Freshly pulled noodles, sunk into soups or fried, are standouts at this no-frills food joint, and the pork and chive dumplings ($1.50) are divine. Daily 7am–9pm.

Khmer Surin 9 St 57 ⓣ 012 887320. Stunning Khmer-Thai restaurant with walkways leading over little ponds, fountains, and romantic tables tucked away in corners. The food lives up to the decor; try the seafood *amok* ($6). Daily 10am–10pm.

Restaurant 26 Cnr sts 13 & 136. Busy Khmer corner café serving filling *bai sach chrouk* (pork and rice) (5,000 riel) breakfasts; it opens way before dawn and is one of few places you can fuel up before catching an early morning bus. Daily 4am–6.30pm.

Royal India 21 St 111, just south of *Capitol Guesthouse* ⓣ 023 6922205. The most consistently good north Indian food in town, all at economical prices, is served with a smile at this simple restaurant. The halal menu is comprehensive and includes chicken and mutton curries ($3), freshly made veggie samosas and tasty sweet lassis. Daily 10am–10pm.

★**Sovanna** 2C St 21. A Phnom Penh favourite serving excellent Khmer food to locals and in-the-know expats. Everything on the menu is worth a try, be it stir-fried dishes like beef *lok-lak* (12,000 riel) or grilled river fish (10,500 riel). Daily 4–11pm.

ST 63 179E, St 62 (near St 294) ⓣ 015 647062. Its interiors might be minimal, but *ST 63*'s food (Asian/Khmer, with a few European dishes) is generously portioned, and very cheap. Most mains, such as stir-fried ginger pork, cost $3 and vegetarians are well catered for (pumpkin curry, $2). Service is friendly, if a little slow. Beer 75 cents, cocktails and wine $2.50. Daily 7am–10pm.

WESTERN RESTAURANTS

Cantina 347 Sisowath Quay ⓣ 023 222 502. Operated by long-time Phnom Penh icon Hurley Scroggins, this iconic place on the riverfront is as renowned for its Mexican food as it is for its tequila. Burritos from $4. Sun–Fri 3–11pm.

Capitol 14 St 182. Expect cheap and cheerful travellers' dishes at this busy street-corner café. BLTs and fried rice dishes from $2.50. Daily 7am–9pm.

Happy Herb Pizza 345 Sisowath Quay ⓣ 097 9943225. Cheap pizza and pasta. A large "special" pizza ($12) is perfect for two. Daily 10am–10pm.

Java Café 56 Sihanouk Blvd ⓣ 023 987420. Fill up on soups, salads and home-made muffins ($2) in a/c cool or unwind on a balcony overlooking the Independence Monument, where you can also browse rotating art exhibitions. Daily 7am–10pm.

The Laughing Fatman 43 St 172 ⓣ 012 765591. A standout along St 172 for its friendly service and great-value, big-portioned meals, which include Khmer staples for $2–3 and Western dishes such as burgers (from $3), grilled fish and pizza. The $2 passion mojitos are superb. Daily 7am–11pm.

★**Mad Monkey Restaurant** St 302 ⓣ 023 987091. So much more than just backpacker fare is served in this buzzing hostel bar-restaurant. Come for the great tapas and comfort food like cottage pie ($6.50). Daily 7am–10pm.

Samaky 9E St 51 & 278 ⓣ 023 226958. At this friendly restaurant opposite Wat Langka a Dutch chef serves up a good mix of Western salads and Asian fusion dishes such as roast duck and noodles ($6).

DRINKING AND NIGHTLIFE

For most Khmers, nightlife centres around an early evening meal out, followed by a tuneful burst of karaoke: the southern end of Monivong Blvd has a particular concentration of the larger, glitzy joints. However, Western nightlife tastes are more than catered for, and you'll always find a crowd in established favourites such as the *Top Banana*, *Heart of Darkness* and *Pontoon*, many going strong well into the wee hours. Outlets at the *Golden Sorya Mall*, on St 51, serve cheap food and drinks 24hr a day.

BARS

★**Foreign Correspondents' Club (FCC)** 363 Sisowath Quay ⓣ 023 724014. Less foreign correspondents' club than a Southeast Asian version of Bogart's bar in the film *Casablanca*. The balmy air, whirring ceiling fans and spacious armchairs invite one to spend a hot afternoon getting slowly, purposefully smashed (happy hour 5–7pm). Beer from $2. Daily 7am–midnight.

Howie's 32 St 51. Located near the *Heart of Darkness*, *Howie's* is the place to go after the former invariably disappoints. It's worth arriving early to stake out a table on the pavement outside and down an Anchor Draught ($2). Nightly from 6pm.

Liquid 3B St 278 ⓣ 023 720157. A trendy bar with a pool table and an extensive drinks list (mojito $3.50), as well as Western food (mains $5.50). A great place to drink away another warm evening. Mon–Fri 9am–midnight, Sat–Sun 2pm–midnight.

★**Top Banana Bar** *Top Banana*, 9E St 278. If you want to have a drink, get rowdy and meet fellow backpackers, then this rooftop guesthouse bar is just the spot. Live music, beer pong and dancing on the furniture are standard behaviour until the wee hours. Sound like a regular and order the house speciality cocktail, wingman (dark rum and lemonade), for $2.75. Daily 8am–3am.

Touk 1st Floor, cnr Sisowath Quay and St 178. Serves cheaper drinks than its neighbour, the *FCC*, yet the river views from its wraparound balcony are every bit as good; their daily 2-for-1 happy hour (4.30–7.30pm) is a steal, given the locale. Daily 8am–midnight.

CLUBS

Heart of Darkness 26 St 51. Overrated, but it's been here for ages and is one of those places everybody has to visit once. Buy a T-shirt, but wait until you get home to wear it. Daily 9pm–5am.

Pontoon 10 St 172. Phnom Penh's largest club is a perennial favourite among the expat crowd, with regular visiting DJs (Goldie played in recent times), a beautiful amber bar, an intriguing range of cocktails and comfy couches to lose yourself in. They also host a popular drag show, Shameless, every Thurs night. Sun–Thurs 9pm–4am, Fri–Sat 9pm–5am.

ENTERTAINMENT

Cinemas The Flicks 1 & 2, sts 95 & 136 respectively (*theflicks-cambodia.com*), are volunteer-staffed community movie houses screening Western, arthouse and Cambodian films ($3.50/person) in intimate sofa-filled a/c rooms. Otherwise, Meta House, 37 Sothearos Blvd (meta-house.com), offers free afternoon Cambodian documentary screenings (4pm) and more mainstream nightly films (7pm; $2), as well as live music, visual poetry and art exhibitions.

Traditional arts Unfortunately, cultural events in Phnom Penh are few and far between. The ancient tradition of Cambodian classical dance, which originated in the twelfth century, was all but wiped out in the 1970s, and performances at the Chaktomuk Theatre (023 725119) on Sisowath Quay are still infrequent – check the listings in the Friday edition of the *Cambodia Daily*. The theatre also occasionally hosts Khmer plays and musical shows. Alternatively, on Fri & Sat at 7.30pm, Sovanna Phum, 166 St 99, host hour-long shadow puppetry, classical and folk dance performances a little way south of town ($10).

SHOPPING

Bookshops Monument Books (111 Norodom Blvd; 023 223622) stocks a wide range of English books. Secondhand books are sold at D's Books (79 St 240; 017 770014), which has over five thousand titles in (among others) English, French and German.

Markets A trip to one of the capital's numerous markets is essential, if only to buy the red-checked *krama* (traditional chequered scarf), popular with Khmers and visitors alike. The markets are liveliest in the morning; many vendors have a snooze at midday for a couple of hours and things wind down by 5pm. Vendors at the Art Deco Psar Thmei (just ask moto drivers for "psar"), at the eastern end of Kampuchea Krom Blvd, are wise to the apparently limitless funds of all *barangs* (Westerners), and will price their wares accordingly. It's a pretty tight squeeze just trying to get past all the stalls. Electronic goods, T-shirts, shoes and wigs are all in abundance here. A stroll around the Russian Market (Psar Toul Tom Poung), in the southern end of town at the junction of 163 and 440 streets, is a colourful and often more rewarding experience. It's a good balance of tourist-oriented curios and stalls for locals, with jewellery, gems, food, souvenirs, furniture and motorbike parts all grouped in their own sections. Don't expect an easy bargain – you'll have to work hard to pay the locals' price.

Supermarkets Bayon Supermarket, 33–34 St 114 (8am–9pm); Lucky Supermarket, 160 Sihanouk Blvd (8am–9pm); Pencil Supermarket, 15 St 214 (7am–9pm).

DIRECTORY

Banks and exchange There are a few ATMs at the airport and many more downtown. Travellers' cheques can be cashed at virtually any bank around town for a commission of two percent. The best rates for changing foreign currency into riel can be found with the money-changers in and around Psar Thmei.

Dentists International SOS Dental Clinic, 161 St 51 (023 216911), has English-speaking staff.

Embassies and consulates Australia, 16B National Assembly St (023 213470); Canada, 11 St 254 (023 213 470); Laos, 15–17 Mao Tse Toung Blvd (023 983632); Thailand, 196 Norodom Blvd (023 726306); UK, 27–29 St 75 (023 427124); US 1 St 96 (023 728000); Vietnam, 436 Monivong Blvd (023 726274).

Hospitals and clinics For any travel-related illness, tests or vaccinations, head to the International SOS Clinic at 161 St 51 (023 816911) or the Tropical & Travellers' Medical Clinic, 88 St 108 (023 306802).

Immigration department For visa extensions, it's easier to go to one of the travel agents in town or to your guesthouse – they'll charge between $5 and $10 commission. The Department of Immigration (Mon–Fri 8–10.30am & 2.30–4.30pm; 017 812763) is well out of town on Russian Blvd opposite the airport, although you'll need to go there for other immigration queries.

Internet There are outlets all over town, with access around $2/hr (usually open 8am–8pm).

Pharmacies Trained English-speaking pharmacists are available at Pharmacie de la Gare, corner of Monivong and Pochentong boulevards (Mon–Sat 7am–7pm, Sun 7am–5pm), which stocks a good selection of Western pharmaceuticals. Alternatively, look for the branches of U-Care around town.

Post office The main post office is east of Wat Phnom, on St 13 between sts 98 and 102 (Mon–Sat 8am–6pm).

Tourist police 012 942484 or 097 7780002 (English, French and Italian spoken); Office in Ministry of Interior, 275 Preah Norodom.

AROUND PHNOM PENH

Escaping into Phnom Penh's surrounding **countryside** for some peace and fresh air is very easy – it doesn't take long to get out past the shantytown suburbs, and the majority of roads that extend from the capital are in fairly good condition.

INTO VIETNAM

The popular 245km trip from Phnom Penh to HCMC has become easier and cheaper over the last few years, and it's now possible to take **public transport** all the way. Several companies operate full-sized buses or express a/c minibuses all the way to HCMC for $10–15 (until 1.30pm). The alternative is to get yourself a place in a share taxi ($5) to **Bavet**, and then find a minibus to HCMC (US$4) after crossing the border (a 500m or so walk); there are plenty of touts at Bavet to help you out. However you get to the border, allow time to clear **immigration** and note that the border closes at 8pm. The city-to-city trip takes about six to seven hours, including immigration formalities. Be aware that Vietnam visas are not available at the border; you can pick one up at the Vietnamese Embassy at the southern end of Monivong Boulevard in Phnom Penh (Mon–Fri 8–11am & 2.30–4.30pm) for around $60, depending on your nationality and how quickly you need it, but guesthouses can usually organize this for a few dollars more.

The route through **Chau Doc** is more complicated than crossing at Bavet; you'll have to get to Neak Leung and then take a boat down the Mekong to the border, where you can pick up a moto for the short ride to the immigration point on the Bassac River. Alternatively, take an express boat to Chau Doc from Sisowath Quay (from $25). In either case, you'll need to have a valid visa.

For details of the border crossing at Prek Chak (Ha Tien), see the Vietnam chapter (see box, p.916).

Choeung Ek (The Killing Fields)

A visit to **CHOEUNG EK** (daily 7am–5.30pm; $3; audioguide $3), 12km southwest of Phnom Penh and signposted from Monireth Boulevard, is a sobering experience. It was here in 1980 that the bodies of 8985 people, victims of Pol Pot and his Khmer Rouge comrades, were exhumed from 86 mass graves. A further 43 graves have been left untouched. Many of those buried here had suffered prolonged torture at S21 prison (see p.80), before being led to their deaths. Men, women and children were beaten to death, shot, beheaded, or tied up and buried alive.

The site is dominated by a tall, white, hollow stupa that commemorates all those who died from 1975 to 1979, displaying thousands of unearthed skulls on glass shelves. A pile of the victims' ragged clothing lies scattered underneath. A pavilion has a small display of the excavation of the burial pits, and a handwritten sign nearby (in Khmer and English) outlines the Khmer Rouge atrocities, a period described as "a desert of great destruction which overturned Kampuchean society and drove it back to the stone age". Although Choeung Ek is by far the most notorious of the killing fields, scores of similar plots can be found all over Cambodia, many with no more than a pile of skulls and bones as a memorial. To get to Choeung Ek, a return moto will cost you $8–10 return (30min).

Central Cambodia

Central Cambodia is a forgotten territory, stretching from north of Phnom Penh through sparsely populated countryside right up to the Thai border. The region is hardly a popular tourist destination, although a steadily improving road network is now making some of its impressive but formerly remote temples much more easily accessible. These are rewarding destinations if you're itching to get off the tourist trail, and compared to Angkor Wat they're practically deserted. Centrepiece of the region is **Kompong Thom**, the only town of any size hereabouts. Thankfully, it's no major expedition if you want to see **Sambor Prei Kuk**, where there are three groups of well-preserved brick-built temples.

KOMPONG THOM

Located roughly midway between Phnom Penh and Siem Reap on National Route 6, **KOMPONG THOM** is the gateway to the pre-Angkor temple ruins of **Sambor Prei Kuk**, 30km northeast. The town itself is little more than a busy transport stop, but it's a friendly place, and with a passable selection of inexpensive accommodation and food. The main features are a

double-bridge over the Sen River – where the old one has been left alongside the new one, built with Australian assistance (hence the kangaroos at each end) – and gaudy Wat Kompong Thom, the local **temple**, with its massive leopard and rhino statues standing guard outside.

2

ARRIVAL AND DEPARTURE

By bus Buses generally stop opposite the market on the main road, not far from the taxi transport stop. Most transport is just passing through, so make sure your driver knows you want to get off here. You won't have to walk more than 500m from here to reach a hotel or guesthouse, but there are plenty of moto and tuk-tuk drivers around if you need one.

Destinations Phnom Penh (8 daily; 4hr; $6); Siem Reap (8 daily; 2hr; $5).

By share taxi or minibus These leave between around 6am and 2pm. The transport stop is in the square one block east of the main road opposite the *Arunras Hotel*. Share taxis cost around $6/seat from Phnom Penh and Siem Reap.

Destinations Kompong Cham (3hr); Phnom Penh (4hr); Siem Reap (2hr).

ACCOMMODATION

Arunras Hotel and Guesthouse National Route 6 ⓣ 012 961294. Housed in adjoining buildings, with the hotel rooms slightly more luxurious and modern; the building has Kompong Thom's only elevator, a fact about which the proprietors are immensely proud. Both offer clean, good-value rooms ($6 extra for a/c), with guesthouse doubles from $8 and hotel rooms starting a dollar cheaper. Double $7

Stung Sen Royal Garden National Route 6 ⓣ 062 961228. On the main road overlooking the river, with welcoming, English-speaking staff. The comfy rooms all have TV, a/c and hot water. Double $20

EATING

Inexpensive food stalls at the market, on the main road just south of the bridge, are open from early morning to mid-afternoon, and the night market sets up outside the east entrance to the market from late afternoon.

Arunras Hotel National Route 6 ⓣ 062 961294. Lively hotel restaurant, busy with both locals and tourists. The menu features a big range of excellent Chinese and Khmer dishes (mains $3–4.50), plus superb coffee – but no Western options. Daily 7am–10pm.

Run Amok! Dekchaumeas, near the Riverside ⓣ 017 916219, ⓦ facebook.com/runamok.kh. Run by a Kiwi–Khmer couple, with excellent hamburgers (meat and veggie) and pizzas, plus mouthwatering Khmer dishes and good ice cream – try the palm sugar and peanut flavour. Mains around $3–6. Daily 5–10pm.

DIRECTORY

Banks and exchange There are ATMs at the Canadia Bank (Visa and MasterCard) and the Acleda Bank, 500m south of the market (Visa only).

Internet There are a couple of (nameless) internet places down the road running west from the *Arunras Hotel* (2500 riel/hr), and another on the main road one block south of the river.

Post office Next to the *Arunras Hotel* on the main road (daily 11am–10.30pm).

SAMBOR PREI KUK

The site of the major seventh-century Chenla capital known as Ishanapura, **Sambor Prei Kuk** once boasted hundreds of temples, although most have crumbled or been smothered by the encroaching forest. Three fine sets of towers remain, however – well worth the excursion and modest entrance fee ($3).

The site is divided into three groups: north, central and south. If you've come with a driver, he may know of temples that have recently been uncovered, as new sites are being cleared all the time.

The north group (closest to the car park), known as **Prasat Sambor Prei Kuk**, is distinguished by the reliefs of the central sanctuary tower. These depict **flying palaces**, said to be the homes of the gods who guard the temples. In spite of their age, you can make out figures and the floors of the palace. Also look out for the cute reliefs of winged horses and tiny human faces.

The central group is relatively more recent than the other two, dating from the ninth century, although only the main sanctuary tower, **Prasat Tor**, remains – particularly photogenic, with sprouting vegetation and reproduction lions flanking the entrance steps. Intricate foliage carvings are still visible on the south lintel.

The south group, **Prasat Neak Pean**, was the most important temple at Ishanapura. Inside the brick-walled enclosure stand several unusual octagonal towers decorated with further flying palaces and (on the west side of the inner wall) some elaborate but eroded bas-reliefs in a line of roundels.

ARRIVAL AND DEPARTURE

By moto or tuk-tuk Motos and tuk-tuks cost around $8/$15 return. The site is about 15km east of National Route 64; about an hour to reach from Kompong Thom.

Angkor

The world-renowned temples of **Angkor**, in northwest Cambodia, stand as an impressive monument to the greatest ancient civilization in Southeast Asia. Spiritually, politically and geographically, Angkor was at the heart of the great Khmer Empire. During the Angkorian period, the ruling god-kings (*devarajas*) built imposing temples as a way of asserting their divinity, leaving a legacy of more than one hundred temples built between the ninth and fifteenth centuries.

The nearest town to the temples is **Siem Reap**, which has established itself as the base from which to make your way round Angkor, a tradition begun by an American, Frank Vincent Jr, who borrowed three elephants from the governor of Siem Reap in 1872 to explore the ruins. These days, there are plenty of motos, tuk-tuks and taxis on hand for the journey.

SIEM REAP

SIEM REAP is far and away Cambodia's most touristy town, and the hordes of foreign visitors can come as a bit of a culture shock if you've spent long in other parts of the country – although you'll enjoy the incredible range of tourist-friendly facilities and brilliant collection of restaurants and bars. Despite the vast number of tourists, it's retained a surprising amount of its original small-town charm.

Psar Chas

The old colonial heart of Siem Reap around the riverfront and lively **Psar Chas** market remains the most interesting part of town, still sporting many of its original French-era shophouses – now transformed into buzzing cafés, bars and shops. Just north is the main tourist area, centred on the raucous **Pub St**, as it's now known, for obvious reasons.

Artisans d'Angkor

A short walk west of Psar Chas, **Artisans d'Angkor** (daily 7.30am–6.30pm; free; ⓣ063 963330, ⓦartisansdangkor.com) offers a fascinating snapshot of Cambodian arts and crafts collected under one roof, with artesans producing gorgeous (but very pricey) wood and stone carvings, lacquer-work, gilding and silver-working. The centre also produces its own silk at the Angkor Silk Farm (daily 8am–5pm; free), 16km west of Siem Reap. Free buses run from Artisans d'Angkor to the farm (daily 9.30am & 1.30pm).

Angkor National Museum

A visit to Siem Reap's **Angkor National Museum** (Angkor Wat Rd, 1.5km north of the centre; daily 8.30am–6.30pm; $12, students $6; ⓦangkornational museum.com) is an essential adjunct to a visit to the temples themselves – the only downside is the extortionate entrance fee. Choice pieces of ancient Khmer sculpture are beautifully exhibited in vast galleries, while multimedia presentations provide plenty of background on Cambodian history, heritage and religion.

ARRIVAL AND DEPARTURE

By plane Besides flights to Phnom Penh, there are an increasing number of international connections. Transport between the town and airport costs around $6–7; some

INTO THAILAND AT POIPET

From Siem Reap it's a three-hour bus or taxi ride to the busy border crossing at **Poipet** (around 6–7 buses/minibuses daily; $6–7). Thai visas are issued on the spot. Once in Thailand, you can take a tuk-tuk to Aranyaprathet from where you can head on to Bangkok by bus (every 30min, last one 6pm; 4hr) or train (2 daily leaving at 6.40am & 1.55pm, arriving Bangkok 12.05pm and 11.30pm; latest times can be checked at ⓦthairailways .com). For information about entering Cambodia at Aranyaprathet, see the Thailand chapter (see box, p.774).

2

hotels and guesthouses pick you up or take you there for free.

Destinations Bangkok (1hr 10min); Hanoi (2hr); HCMC (1hr 20min); Kuala Lumpur (3hr); Phnom Penh (40min); Sihanoukville (1hr 10min); Singapore (3hr 20min); Vientiane (3hr).

By bus Buses arrive/leave from the Chong Kov Sou bus station 3km east of town, although some also pick up/drop off at one of the various bus company offices along the south end of Sivatha Boulevard near Psar Chas, or at the junction of National Route 6 and Pokambor Ave, just north of the centre.

Destinations Bangkok (6 daily; 9–12hr); Battambang (4 daily; 4hr); Kompong Cham (2 daily; 4hr); Kompong Thom (20 daily; 2hr); Phnom Penh (20 daily; 6–8hr); Poipet (10 daily; 3hr); Sihanoukville (3 daily; 10hr).

By share taxi or pick-up Share taxis arrive and depart from the market, Psar Leu, to the east of the city, a hectic transport hub from where you can easily catch a tuk-tuk or moto into town, or walk (20min).

By boat Boats cruise into the port, around 12km south of Siem Reap (the exact distance varies with the level of the lake), passing the touristy floating village of Kompong

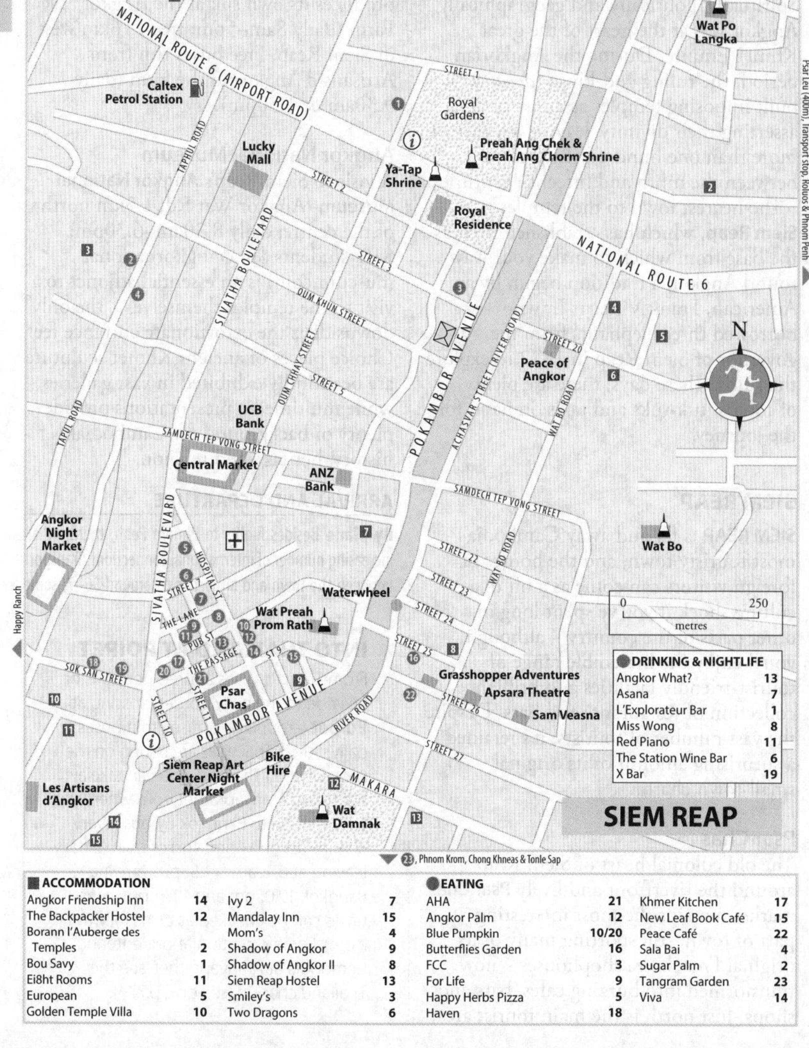

Khneas en route. Guesthouse reps will be keen to offer a free ride into town, so it's a good idea to decide beforehand where you want to stay; otherwise, there are plenty of motos ($3) and tuk-tuks ($5). Boats leave from the port at 7am for Phnom Penh ($35) and at 8am for Battambang ($25). When the water level is really low (Feb–May) the express boats for Phnom Penh moor some way out, and you'll be taken out to them on a smaller craft. You'll need to book your ticket at least a day ahead – two days ahead March–Nov – when often just one boat runs on each route. If you buy your ticket from a guesthouse or hotel, a minibus will collect you, although this may mean setting out as early as 5.30am; otherwise, you'll have to make your own way to the port.

Destinations Battambang (daily; 6hr wet season, up to 8hr in the dry); Phnom Penh (daily; 5–6hr).

GETTING AROUND

The town is small enough to walk across from top to bottom in not much more than 20min or so. There are also plentiful motos and tuk-tuks (both $1/2 for shorter/longer trips around the centre), plus bicycles for rental (from $2/day) at numerous places.

INFORMATION AND TOURS

Tourist information There are three tourist offices in town, one in the southwest corner of the Royal Gardens, one on Sivatha Boulevard near Psar Chas, and one on the way to the temples. It's possible to hire government-licensed temple guides here ($25/day), and also arrange a car and driver (from $30/day). The useful *Siem Reap Angkor Visitors Guide*, published three times a year and available from some hotels, guesthouses and the tourist offices, contains detailed listings of places to stay, eat and drink; it's also available online at Ⓦ canbypublications.com.

ACCOMMODATION

Most budget accommodation is largely concentrated in two areas: in and around Psar Chas, and in the various streets running east of the river (particularly around St 20). There's an excellent selection, and standards are high, although equally prices are generally a bit higher than elsewhere in Cambodia, with many places offering a/c rooms only.

AROUND PSAR CHAS

Angkor Friendship Inn Psakrom St Ⓣ 063 965197, Ⓦ angkorfriendshipinn.com. Friendly family-run guesthouse, popular with long-stay visitors, offering excellent-value a/c rooms, all en-suite with hot water. There's also a nice courtyard seating area plus small pool. B&B. Double **$16**

Ei8ht Rooms Off Sivatha Blvd Ⓣ 063 969788, Ⓦ ei8htrooms.com. Attractive guesthouse spread over two buildings with twelve nicely furnished rooms, all with a/c and hot water, decorated in bold colours. Double **$16**

★ **Golden Temple Villa** Off Sivatha Blvd Ⓣ 012 943459, Ⓦ goldentemplevilla.com. Hugely popular guesthouse in lush gardens with a range of bright, colourfully decorated rooms with a/c, hot water, DVD player and fridge. Complimentary tea, coffee and bananas are available all day, and a free 1hr massage is included. Good value – and booking advised. Double **$15**

Ivy 2 Just off Pokambor Av Ⓣ 012 380516, Ⓦ ivy-guesthouse.com. In a rustic old ivy-clad wooden house, this is a Siem Reap guesthouse like they all used to be – basic, but with bags of character. Downstairs is a laidback café with bar and pool table, upstairs is a nice little veranda, while accommodation is in a mix of simple fan rooms (with cold water) and slightly posher a/c rooms (with hot water; from $10). Double **$6**

★ **Mandalay Inn** Psakrom St Ⓣ 063 761662, Ⓦ mandalayinn.com. Long-running Siem Reap stalwart, and still the best cheapie in the city centre with a range of comfortable fan and a/c rooms (from $16), all with hot water and fridge. The super-helpful staff can arrange all kinds of tours, and there's also a rooftop gym, internet access and a good little restaurant. Double **$10**

Shadow of Angkor Pokambor Av Ⓣ 063 964774, Ⓦ shadowofangkor.com. Old-style Siem Reap guesthouse, set upstairs in a lovely old colonial shophouse by the river, with an attractive restaurant below. Rooms (all with a/c and hot water) are a bit bare and basic for the price, but for location and atmosphere it can't be beaten. Double **$15**

Smiley's Taphul Rd Ⓣ 012 686060, Ⓦ smileyguesthouse.com. From humble beginnings this guesthouse has grown enormously, but remains one of Siem Reap's better budget options. Rooms (optional a/c from $4; some with hot water) are clean and bright, and there's a peaceful little downstairs café. Double **$8**

EAST OF THE RIVER

The Backpacker Hostel 7 Makara Ⓣ 012 313239, Ⓦ angkorbackpacker.com. One of Siem Reap's cheapest sleeps, with beds on top of the five-storey building under a rooftop awning, like a semi-outdoor dorm. It's pretty basic (and at the top of many steps), although the beds themselves are comfortable, and come with nets. Dorm **$3**, double **$10**

★ **Bou Savy** Off Airport Rd Ⓣ 063 964967, Ⓦ bousavyguesthouse.com. Excellent guesthouse – despite the inconvenient location – particularly popular with volunteers and long-staying guests thanks to its home-from-home atmosphere. There's a mix of rooms (all en-suite with hot water and fridge; a/c doubles from $18) and the sociable little plant-strewn courtyard café is a nice place to hang. Advance bookings recommended. B&B. Double **$12**

2

★TREAT YOURSELF

Borann l'Auberge des Temples North of NR6 ☎ 063 964740, Ⓦ borann.com. Intimate little lodge with just twenty rooms in five bungalows spread around extensive gardens stuffed with trees and shrubs. Rooms are beautifully designed with traditional Khmer styling (but no TVs – which adds to the general sense of peace), and there's a big pool and decent restaurant. $59

European Off St 20 ☎ 012 582237, Ⓦ european-guesthouse.com. Quiet and friendly and with large, spotless a/c rooms (all en-suite with hot water) set around an attractive, shady garden. Double $18

Mom's Wat Bo St ☎ 012 630170, Ⓦ momguesthouse.com. Long-running place, more of a hotel now than a guesthouse, but still owned by the same original family. Rooms (all en-suite with hot water, a/c, safe and fridge) are spacious, spotless and attractively furnished, and there's also a nice little pool. B&B. Double $22

Shadow of Angkor II Wat Bo St ☎ 063 760363, Ⓦ shadowofangkor.com. Competitively priced (albeit fairly characterless) modern hotel with pool, restaurant and spacious a/c rooms, some kitted out with traditional Khmer wood furniture. Double $20

Siem Reap Hostel 7 Makara, ☎ 063 964660, Ⓦ thesiemreaphostel.com. Siem Reap's best hostel – a lot more comfortable and stylish than your average backpacker dive. Beds are in a mix of attractive dorms and well-equipped a/c rooms, and there's also a small spa and pool, library, pool table, yoga classes, movie screenings and more. Dorm $5, double $28

★Two Dragons St 20 ☎ 063 965107, Ⓦ twodragons-asia.com. One of the best of the many family guesthouses in this part of town, popular with local expats and long-stay visitors. The spacious and attractively furnished rooms all come with a/c, hot water and cable TV, and there's a small restaurant out front serving up a good range of Thai, Khmer and Western food. Double $15

EATING

Siem Reap has a huge selection of restaurants catering to tourist tastes; for something more authentic and affordable, head for the markets and the cheap fruit stalls on the eastern side of the river near National Route 6.

AHA The Passage ☎ 063 965501, Ⓦ shintamani.com. One of the hippest little restaurants in town, with urban-chic decor and excellent Khmer and contemporary Asian food given an international twist (mains $7–10). Come for dinner or just a drink and a plate of international tapas. Daily 11.30am–9.30pm.

Angkor Palm Hospital St ☎ 063 761436, Ⓦ angkorpalm.com. Smart-looking but budget-friendly restaurant offering an above-average selection of authentic Khmer cooking – although you'll have to get the waiters to explain what's in some of the more recondite dishes. Mains cost just $3.50–5, although rice is an extra $2. Daily 9am–10.30pm.

Blue Pumpkin Hospital St. The original branch of this hugely popular café-cum-bakery (now with outlets all round town). Construct your own snack or picnic from a wide selection of freshly baked breads, sandwiches, cakes, shakes and ice creams. A second branch is located nearby on Sivatha Blvd. Daily 6am–11pm.

Butterflies Garden St 25 ☎ 063 761 211, Ⓦ butterfliesofangkor.com. Tranquil garden café with colourful butterflies (bought from local children and released every few days) flitting between the tables. The menu features the usual Khmer ($4–5) and Western ($5–8) mains. Daily 8am–11pm.

FCC Pokambor Av ☎ 063 760280, Ⓦ fcccambodia.com. Siem Reap's branch of the Foreign Correspondents' Club provides a memorable setting for top-notch Western and Asian food (mains around $8) or a drink at the attractive terrace bar. Daily 7am–midnight (bar open from 5pm).

For Life The Lane ☎ 012 545426, Ⓦ forliferestaurant.com. A local expat favourite, slightly away from the tourist hordes, serving excellent, authentic Khmer food at very competitive prices, with almost everything for $4 (including rice) or under. Daily 11am–11pm.

Happy Herbs Pizza Hospital St ☎ 092 459525. One-stop backpackers' café with a menu as long as your arm and featuring just about every kind of dish you could think of, including good breakfasts, myriad Khmer dishes ($3.50) and some of the best pizzas in town ($6.50). Daily 7.30am–9pm.

Haven Sok San St ☎ 078 342404, Ⓦ havencambodia.com. Peaceful Swiss-run restaurant tucked away on a quiet(ish) side street and helping to train disadvantaged local kids. Food features well-prepared and presented Khmer and Asian classics ($5–6) plus a small but well-chosen selection of Western dishes ($6–7). Booking is usually essential, although you might get lucky at lunch during the low season. Mon, Tues & Thurs–Sat 11.30am–2.30pm (last orders), Wed 11.30am–2.30pm (last orders) & 5.30–9.30 (last orders).

Khmer Kitchen The Passage ☎ 063 966353, Ⓦ khmerkitchens.com. Inexpensive, family-run restaurant that provides great authentic Khmer home cooking with the occasional modern twist, plus a few Thai dishes. All mains $4 (including rice). Daily 10.30am–11pm.

New Leaf Book Café Off Pokambor Ave ☎ 063 766016, Ⓦ newleafbookcafe.org. Good-looking and sociable little café with lots of secondhand books for sale lined up

around the walls. Good coffee and drinks list, including local sombai (rice wine infused with fruits and spices), plus the usual café fare and a few Khmer and Western mains ($4–7). Try the delicious iced coffee and the simple but very satisfying Khmer chicken rice. Daily 7am–9.30pm.

Peace Café St 26 ⓣ 092 177127, ⓦ peacecafeangkor.org. Rustic little garden vegetarian café serving up a good range of Western snacks, salads and light meals (around $4) plus cheaper Asian mains and various breakfasts. Daily 7am–9pm.

Sala Bai Taphul St ⓣ 063 963329. Hospitality school which opens to customers for training purposes; the inexpensive, daily-changing menu features a mix of Western and Khmer dishes according to what students are learning to cook at any particular moment (lunch set menus $9/11). Reservations advised, and sometimes closed July–Sept. Mon–Fri 7–9am & noon–2pm.

★**Sugar Palm** Taphul St ⓣ 012 818143. ⓦ thesugarpalm.com. Attractively rustic pavilion restaurant under a huge wooden house – perfect for a romantic candlelit dinner. The menu focuses on authentic Khmer fare with a short but inventive selection of dishes (mains $6–7) – frogs' legs with basil, for example, or squid with black Kampot pepper, plus flavoursome pomelo and green mango salads. Mon–Sat 11.30am–3pm & 5.30–10pm.

★**Tangram Garden** South of the centre ⓣ 097 726111, ⓦ tangramgarden.com. This relaxed garden restaurant is just a short walk south of town but feels surprisingly peaceful and rural, especially after dark. The small but perfectly formed menu (mains $7–8) features a mix of good-value Western charcoal-grilled dishes (pork ribs, genuine New Zealand steaks and so on) alongside reinvented traditional Khmer dishes. Daily except Tues 11.30am–2.30pm & 5.30–10pm (mid-April to mid-Oct open for dinner only).

Viva Hospital St ⓣ 092 209154, ⓦ ivivasiemreap.com. Wildly popular Mexican restaurant serving up tasty cover versions of all the usual Tex-Mex classics (around $5). The restaurant's signature margharitas are cheap and go down fast – as do many of the punters come closing time. Daily 6am–midnight.

NIGHTLIFE

Siem Reap is a bustling place, with bars targeted at foreigners opening up all over town, especially on the notorious "Pub Street": you can easily while away a week or so visiting a different venue each evening.

Angkor What? Pub St ⓣ 012 731152. "Promoting irresponsible drinking since 1998", *Angkor What?* is the dark heart of the raucous Pub Street scene – a grungy, graffiti-covered Black Hole of Siem Reap into which crazed punters insert themselves nightly in search of cheap beer, loud music and members of the opposite sex. Daily 4pm–3am.

DANCE AND MUSIC

Siem Reap is a good place to take in a cultural **Khmer** performance of classical dance, often known as "Apsara dancing", packaged with dinner by several of the hotels and bars around town; try *Temple Bar*, *La Noria* or *Angkor Village*.

★**Asana** Between St 7 and The Lane ⓣ 092 987801, ⓦ asana-cambodia.com. Occupying the last surviving wooden house in central Siem Reap, with piles of rice and flour sacks doubling as seats upstairs, and a swinging hammock-bed to lounge in below. Above-average prices, but well worth it, particularly for the moreish *sombai* and Asian-style cocktails. Daily 11am– midnight or later.

L'Explorateur Bar *Victoria Angkor* hotel. Siem Reap's most enjoyable colonial-style bar, and the perfect place for cocktails or an after-dinner coffee or *digestif*, either in the period-style a/c interior or on the sultry terrace. Not as pricey as you might expect (beers and coffee $3, cocktails $7), especially during the daily happy hour (5–7pm). Daily 7am–11.30pm.

★**Miss Wong** The Lane ⓣ 092 428332, ⓦ misswong.net. Alluring little retro-Shanghai-style bar. The excellent cocktails (around $5) come with a pronounced Asian twist – Singapore slings, lemongrass collins, apricot and kaffir lime martini and so on – and there's good food too. Daily 6pm–1am.

Red Piano Pub St ⓣ 063 964750. One of Pub Street's more civilized drinking spots, especially if you can bag one of the coveted street-side wicker armchairs. Daily 7am–midnight.

The Station Wine Bar St 7 ⓣ 097 850 4043, ⓦ thestationwinebarsiemreap.com. Chic, very gay-friendly modern wine bar offering an unrivalled selection of wines, plus numerous other tipples. Also hosts regular cabaret, drag and talent shows. Daily 4pm–late.

X Bar Sivatha Blvd. Grungy rooftop bar that pounds out hard rock and heavy metal until late, with live bands on Wed and Fri at around 9pm and a DJ most other nights, plus a big-screen TV showing live sports. Daily 2pm–3/4am.

DIRECTORY

Banks and exchange There are plenty of banks and ATMs throughout Siem Reap – the Canadia Bank at the junction of Sivatha Blvd and Hospital Rd is particularly convenient, and commission-free.

Hospital and clinics The Royal Angkor International Hospital, National Route 6 (2km from the airport; ⓣ 063 761888, ⓦ royalangkorhospital.com), has some of the better medical services including call-out service, 24-hour emergency care, ambulance, translation and evacuation

★TREAT YOURSELF

Siem Reap is a great place to try an inexpensive spa treatment featuring Khmer or other types of massage. One of the best is *Body Tune* (T 063 764141, W bodytune.co.th), just east of Psar Chas, where you can rejuvenate with Thai and Swedish massage, aromatherapy and body scrubs (from $12/hr).

2

to Bangkok. The government-run Siem Reap Provincial Hospital, 500m north of Psar Chas (T 063 963111), is basic and to be used only as a last resort.

Internet In addition to widely available wi-fi there are numerous internet cafés around town – try the huge (but nameless) place near Psar Chas between X Bar and the Haven restaurant (open 24hr; 3000 riel/hr).

Post office Pokambor St (daily 7.30am–5.30pm).

Supermarkets For basic provisions, there are numerous mini-markets dotted around the centre including a useful cluster along Sivatha Boulevard opposite the western end of Pub St. There's a well-stocked supermarket in the Angkor Trade Centre on Pokambor Av just north of Psar Chas.

Tourist police Junction of Sivatha St and National Route 6 T 063 760215.

THE TEMPLES OF ANGKOR

In 802, Jayavarman II declared himself universal god-king, becoming the first of a succession of 39 monarchs to reign over what was then the most powerful kingdom in Southeast Asia. So the **Angkor era** was born, a period marked by gargantuan building projects, the design and construction of inspirational **temples** and palaces, the creation of complex irrigation systems and the development of magnificent walled cities. However, as resources were channelled into ever more ambitious construction projects, Angkor became a target for attacks from neighbouring **Siam**. Successive invasions culminated in the sacking of Angkor in the fifteenth century and the city was abandoned to the jungle. Although Khmers knew of the lost city, it wasn't until the West's "discovery" of Angkor by a French missionary in the nineteenth century that international interest was aroused.

WHAT TO SEE AND DO

More than one hundred Angkorian monuments lie spread over some 3000 square kilometres of countryside around Siem Reap. The best-known monuments are the vast temple of **Angkor Wat** and the walled city of **Angkor Thom**, while jungle-ravaged **Ta Phrom** and exquisitely decorated **Banteay Srei** are also popular sites. The **Roluos** ruins are significant as the site of the empire's first capital city and as a point of comparison with the later architectural styles of **Banteay Kdei** and **Ta Keo**. Many of the artefacts on display at the temples of Angkor are not originals – **thefts** of the valuable treasures have been a problem since the 1970s and the majority are now copies.

Angkor Wat

Built in the twelfth century as a temple (and subsequently mausoleum) for Suryavarman II, **Angkor Wat** represents the height of Khmer art, combining architectural harmony, grand proportions and detailed artistry. Approaching along the sandstone causeway across a broad moat and through the western gate, you're teased with glimpses of the central towers, but it's not until you're through the gate that the full magnificence of the temple comes into view. The causeway, extending 300m across the flat, open compound, directs the eye to the proud temple and its most memorable feature, the distinctive conical-shaped towers, designed to look like lotus buds.

Continuing east along the causeway, you'll pass between the wat's library buildings and two ponds, and mount a flight of steps to the **Terrace of Honour**. The terrace is the gateway to the extraordinary **Gallery of Bas Reliefs**, a covered gallery which extends around the perimeter of the first level. The carvings cover almost the entire wall – 700m long, 2m high – depicting religious narratives, battle scenes and Hindu epics. The best-known carving, **the Churning of the Ocean of Milk**, in the East Gallery, depicts the myth of creation: gods (*devas*) and evil spirits (*asuras*) churn the ocean for a thousand years to produce the elixir of immortality, creating order out of chaos.

VISITING THE TEMPLES

The temples are officially open daily from 5am till 6pm, although Banteay Srei closes at 5pm.

TRANSPORT

There are a number of transport options to get to and around Angkor Wat from Siem Reap: your choice will depend on your time frame, your budget and which temples you intend to visit. Hiring a tuk-tuk is the best way to get around (tours of the Grand Circuit temples, lasting most of a day, can be had for just $12). For one person, a moto (Grand Circuit around $10) can serve a similar purpose, but will be less comfortable. If you have time to spare, renting a bicycle (around $3/day from numerous outlets in Siem Reap) is perhaps the most enjoyable way to explore the temples. Distances are manageable, and the terrain is almost completely flat, although be aware that exploring the temples, with their endless steps, can be pretty tiring, so don't try to cover too many in a day.

ENTRY PASSES

Entry passes are required to enter the Angkor area, and must also be shown at all the temples. At the main entrance, on the Siem Reap–Angkor Wat road, three categories of pass are available: one day ($20), three days ($40, to be used within one week) or seven days ($60, to be used within one month). You need to go here to purchase your ticket even if you want to visit the Roluos temples, which are, frustratingly, in the opposite direction. Most people find it adequate to buy the three-day pass, which gives enough time to see all the temples in the central area and to visit the outlying temples at Roluos and Banteay Srei. If you're short on time, you can cover Angkor Wat, the Bayon, Ta Phrom and Banteay Srei in one full day.

The detail and sharpness of the images make this one of the greatest stone sculptures ever created.

Returning to the Terrace of Honour and walking towards the central chamber, you'll pass through the cruciform galleries linking the first and second levels. On the right-hand side is the **Gallery of One Thousand Buddhas**, though only a handful of figures now remain. The walls of the courtyard on the next level are carved with numerous detailed *apsaras*, celestial nymphs. There is a total of 1850 of these figures in Angkor Wat, each individually carved with unique features. A neck-wrenchingly steep staircase leads up to the topmost third level (you'll probably have to queue to get up), from where various Buddha images look down from the central sanctuary on the temple below.

Angkor Thom

Angkor Thom, 2km north of Angkor Wat, was the last and greatest capital of the Angkor era, built during the late twelfth and early thirteenth centuries. The immense city is enclosed within a square of defensive walls, 8m high and 3km long on each side, themselves surrounded in turn by a 100m-wide moat – although of the original wooden houses which once filled the space inside the walls no trace remains. Certainly more spectacular and extravagant than any Western city at the time, Angkor Thom was an architectural masterpiece, home to perhaps a million inhabitants. Now only the city's great religious monuments, built in imperishable stone, remain as a testament to the city's former grandeur.

There are five gateways set in the walls around Angkor Thom, four covering each of the cardinal points and the fifth, the Gate of Victory, set in the east wall leading directly to the Royal Palace compound. Each gateway is approached via a **stone causeway** crossing the wide moat. On each causeway, 54 god images on the left and 54 demons on the right depict the myth of the Churning of the Ocean of Milk, as featured in the East Gallery of Angkor Wat. Each of the five sandstone **gopuras** is crowned with four large heads, facing the points of the compass, flanked by an image of the Hindu god Indra riding a three-headed elephant.

If you're approaching from Angkor Wat, you will probably enter Angkor Thom through the South Gate. Directly north, at

2

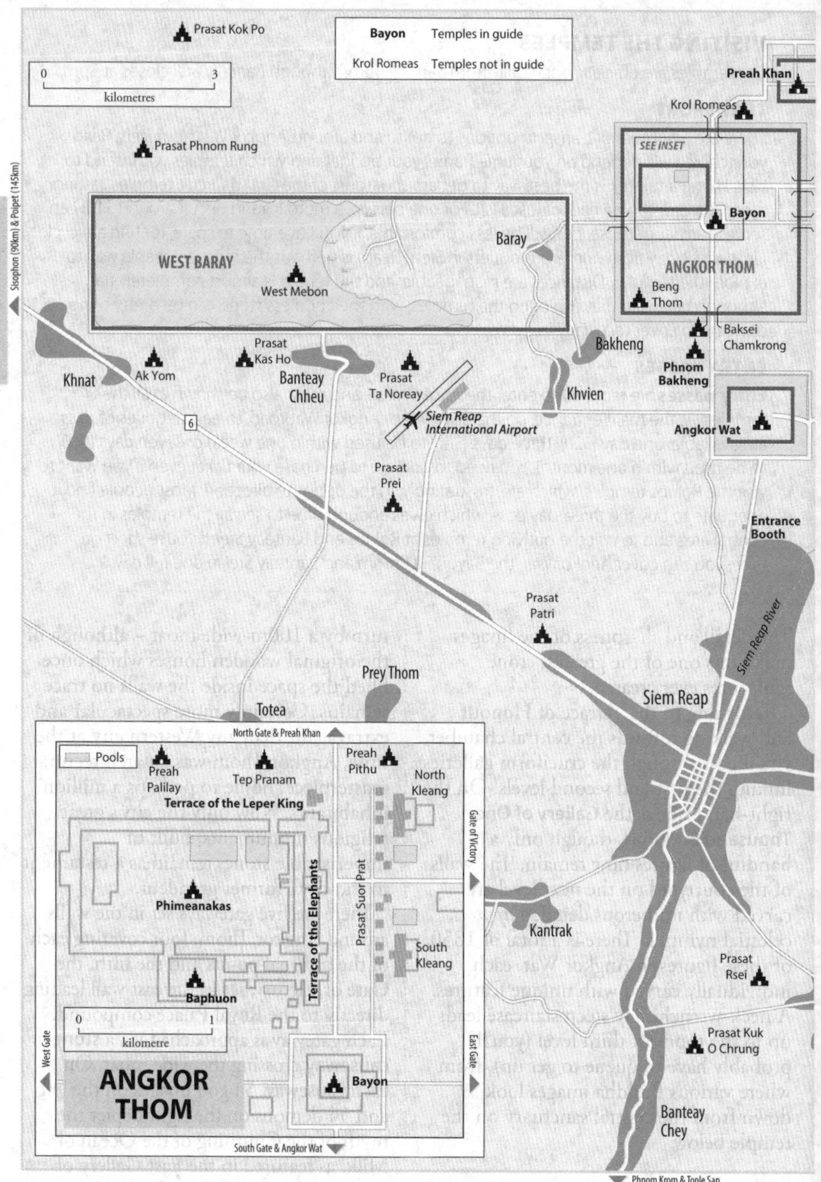

the centre of the walled city, is the **Bayon**. Despite its poor workmanship and haphazard sculpting, this is one of Angkor's most endearing temples, its unusual personality defined by large carved faces adorning the sides of its 54 towers. Although small, it's actually a confusing temple to navigate, largely owing to its complex history. Bayon was built on top of an earlier monument, follows an experimental layout and was added to at various times. Although originally a Buddhist temple, it has a Hindu history too, and themes of both religions can be

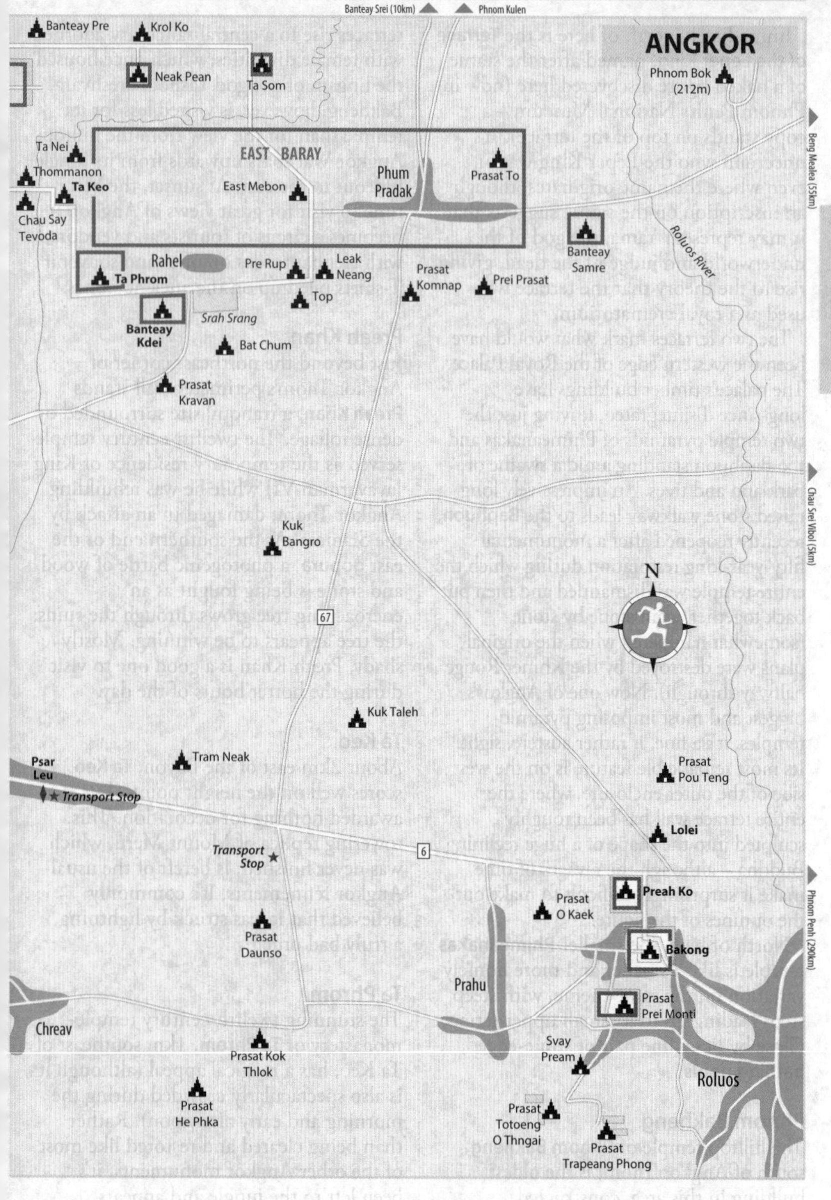

found in the excellent bas-reliefs carved on the walls of the galleries.

Past here is the **Terrace of the Elephants**, extending 300m to the north. Three-headed elephants guard the stairway at the southern end; before ascending, be sure to view the terrace from the road, where a sculpted frieze of hunting and fighting elephants adorns the base of the terrace. The terrace originally supported wooden pavilions and reception halls and would have been used by the king as a ceremonial viewing platform and a place from which to address his citizens.

2

Immediately north of here is the **Terrace of the Leper King**, named after the statue of a naked figure discovered here (now in Phnom Penh's National Museum – a copy stands on top of the terrace). It's uncertain who the Leper King was or even where the name originates, though an inscription on the statue suggests that it may represent Yama, the god of the underworld and judge of the dead, giving rise to the theory that the terrace was used as a royal crematorium.

The two terraces mark what would have been the western edge of the Royal Palace. The palace's timber buildings have long-since disintegrated, leaving just the two temple pyramids of Phimeanakas and the Baphuon standing amid a swathe of parkland and trees. An impressively long raised stone walkway leads to the **Baphuon**, recently reopened after a monumental fifty-year-long restoration during which the entire temple was dismantled and then put back together again stone by stone (somewhat hampered when the original plans were destroyed by the Khmer Rouge halfway through). Now one of Angkor's biggest and most imposing pyramid-temples, it's a fine, if rather austere, sight. Its most remarkable feature is on the west side of the outer enclosure, where the entire terrace wall has been roughly sculpted into the shape of a huge reclining Buddha – although the ravages of time make it surprisingly difficult to make out the outlines of the figure.

North of here, the smaller **Phimeanakas** temple is like a smaller and more homely variation on the same theme, with steep steps leading up to its small upper terrace. Close by lies a fine pair of stone-edge **bathing pools**.

Phnom Bakheng

The hilltop temple of **Phnom Bakheng**, south of Angkor Thom, is the oldest building in this area, constructed following Yasorvarman's move westwards from Roluos. The state temple was built from the rock of the hill on which it stands. It originally boasted 108 magnificent towers set on a spectacular pyramid, although only part of the central tower now remains. The five diminishing terraces rise to a central sanctuary adorned with female divinities, which once housed the lingam of the god Yashodhareshvara. Bakheng, however, is visited less for its temple than for the view from the hilltop; Angkor Wat soars upwards from its jungle hideout to the east. At sunset, the best time to visit for great views of Angkor, it becomes a circus of tourists and vendors, with elephant rides on offer and souvenir T-shirts piled up on the ancient stones.

Preah Khan

Just beyond the northeast corner of Angkor Thom's perimeter wall stands **Preah Khan**, a tranquil site surrounded by dense foliage. The twelfth-century temple served as the temporary residence of King Jayavarman VII while he was rebuilding Angkor Thom, damaged in an attack by the Siamese. At the southern end of the east **gopura**, a photogenic battle of wood and stone is being fought as an encroaching tree grows through the ruins: the tree appears to be winning. Mostly shady, Preah Khan is a good one to visit during the hotter hours of the day.

Ta Keo

About 2km east of the Bayon, **Ta Keo** scores well on the height points, but is awarded nothing for decoration. This towering replica of Mount Meru, which was never finished, is bereft of the usual Angkor refinements. It's commonly believed that it was struck by lightning, a truly bad omen.

Ta Phrom

The stunning twelfth-century temple-monastery of **Ta Phrom**, 1km southeast of Ta Keo, has a magical appeal (although it is also spectacularly crowded during the morning and early afternoon). Rather than being cleared and restored like most of the other Angkor monuments, it's been left to the jungle and appears roughly as it did to the Europeans who rediscovered these ruins in the nineteenth century. Roots and trunks intermingle with the stones and seem almost part of the structure, and the temple's cramped corridors reveal half-hidden reliefs, while valuable carvings litter the floor.

Jayavarman VII originally built Ta Phrom as a Buddhist monastery, although Hindu purists have since defaced the Buddhist imagery. The temple was once surrounded by an enclosed city. An inscription found at the site testifies to its importance: more than twelve thousand people lived at the monastery, maintained by almost eighty thousand people in the surrounding villages.

Banteay Kdei

Southeast of Ta Phrom and one of the quieter sites in this area, **Banteay Kdei** is a huge twelfth-century Buddhist temple, constructed under Jayavarman VII. It's in a pretty poor state of repair, but the crumbling stones create an interesting architecture of their own. Highlights are the carvings of female divinities and other figures in the niches of the second enclosure, and a frieze of Buddhas in the interior court. Opposite the east entrance to Banteay Kdei is the **Srah Srang** or "Royal Bath", a large lake which was probably used for ritual ablutions.

Roluos group

Due east of Siem Reap close to the small town of **Roluos** are three of Angkor's oldest temples: **Bakong**, **Preah Ko** and **Lolei**. The relics date from the late ninth century, the dawn of the Angkorian era, and a time when the emphasis was on detail rather than size.

South of National Route 6, the first temple you come to is **Preah Ko**, built by Indravarman I as a funerary temple for his ancestors. It's in poor condition, but is charming; the highlights are the six brick towers of the central sanctuary, which sit on a low platform at the centre of the inner enclosure.

Cambodia's earliest temple-mountain, **Bakong** is made up of five tiers of solid sandstone surrounded by brick towers. Entering from the east across the balustraded causeway you'll come into the inner enclosure through a ruined **gopura**; originally eight brick towers surrounded the central sanctuary, but only five remain standing. In the heart of the enclosure is a five-tiered pyramid. Twelve small sanctuaries are arranged symmetrically around the fourth tier, and above you on the summit is the well-preserved central sanctuary – if you're wondering why it's in such good condition, it's because it was rebuilt in 1941.

Return to the main road for the sanctuary of **Lolei**, built by Yashovarman I on an artificial island. Its four collapsing brick-and-sandstone towers are only worth visiting for the Sanskrit inscriptions in the door jambs that detail the work rosters of the temple "slaves"; a few carvings remain but are badly eroded.

Banteay Srei

Further afield, the pretty tenth-century temple of **Banteay Srei** is unique among its Angkorian peers. Its miniature proportions, unusual pinkish sandstone and intricate ornamentation create a surreal effect, enhanced by its astonishingly well-preserved state. The journey to the site, about 30km northeast of Angkor Wat, takes about an hour. Tour groups start arriving en masse from 8.30am, and because of its small size, it gets crowded quickly – arriving earlier than this, or later in the afternoon (after 3/4pm), helps avoid the crowds.

From the entry tower, across the moat, the tops of the three intricate central towers and two libraries are visible over the low enclosure wall, their rose-pink sandstone a surreal sight against the green backdrop of the jungle. Inside, the enclosure is a riot of intricate decoration and architecture, with wall-niches housing guardian divinities enclosed in carved foliage and panels extravagantly decorated with scenes from Hindu mythology.

Western Cambodia

The flat plains fanning out from Phnom Penh and stretching all the way to the border with Thailand are the nation's agricultural heartland – Battambang province is popularly known as the "rice-bowl" of Cambodia on account of its fertile rice-paddies and other tropical

2

produce. Centrepiece of the region (and Cambodia's second city) is **Battambang**, an agreeable town, home to some of the country's finest surviving French-colonial architecture, and an enjoyably relaxed place to hang out for a few days.

Southeast from here stretches the vast **Tonle Sap** lake, home to dozens of picturesque floating villages, which swells to more than 8000 square kilometres during the rainy season before contracting spectacularly once again during the dry.

2

The entire region is sandwiched between the **Cardamom Mountains** in the southwestern corner of the country and the **Dangrek Range** in the north. A perfect hideout, these frontier hills were home to the Khmer Rouge guerrillas for nearly twenty years from 1979. The towns within the former occupied territories, such as the remote frontier outpost of **Pailin**, are not attractive places, as you might expect after twenty years of war and isolation, but the countryside is stunning in places and has a Wild West appeal. Many of the residents in these areas are still loyal to the memory of the Khmer Rouge, whose legacy also lives on in the myriad mines which still dot the countryside hereabouts – on no account wander from clearly marked roads or paths.

BATTAMBANG

BATTAMBANG is Cambodia's second-biggest city, though you wouldn't think so from its laidback atmosphere, and it's a world apart from Phnom Penh's urban bustle. It's keen to move up in the world, however – and the French-colonial-era shophouses now sport an increasing array of fancy restaurants and bars. That said, the unhurried central market, Psar Nat, is still the busiest Battambang gets.

WHAT TO SEE AND DO

There are two pleasant **temples** within walking distance of the town centre – **Wat Piphithearam** and **Wat Dhum Rey Sor**. Further afield are **Phnom Sampeu** and **Wat Banan** which make lovely day-trips out of the city – a tuk-tuk/moto will take you to both for about $18/12, and the combined entrance ticket costs $2.

Also worth a visit is the quirky "**Bamboo Railway**", running along a stretch of disused track just outside Battambang. A dozen or so "trains" run up and down the line on demand, each consisting of a small bamboo platform set on top of a metal undercarriage and powered by motorbike engines – a fun way to get a glimpse of Battambang's lush hinterlands. The line starts 7km from Battambang (return by moto/tuktuk $4/6) with twenty- to thirty-minute trips up and down the line costing $5 per person.

Wat Sampeu

Some 15km southwest of Battambang, a large temple complex squats atop the lopsided hill of **Phnom Sampeu** (said to resemble a sinking boat when seen in profile with nearby **Phnom G'daong**). It's a colourful sight, although nowadays better known for its tragic associations with the Khmer Rouge, who used it as a prison, many of whose inmates were killed on the mountaintop.

A breathless twenty-minute hike up steep steps takes you to the top of the hill, dotted with a sprawling cluster of assorted modern shrines and stupas. Directly below the summit of the hill and the main vihara, steps lead down to the sombre, bat-infested **Laang Lacaun** ("Theatre Cave"), gloomy even at midday beneath its vast slab of overhanging rock. Thousands of people were killed here, thrown to their deaths by Khmer Rouge cadres through an opening in the rocks above. A few of the victims' smashed skulls and bones have been collected in an ornate metal cage as a lasting memorial to Khmer Rouge atrocities.

Wat Banan

Reached from Phnom Sampeu via a ferociously bumpy back-country road, the modest temple of **Wat Banan** looks almost like a dilapidated miniature of Angkor Wat, with its five conical towers rising out of the trees at the summit of a 70m-high hill. It's a steep clamber up to the top but worth it to see the detailed lintels, beheaded *apsaras*, and views out over endless paddies, with Phnom Sampeu clearly visible to the north.

2

ARRIVAL AND DEPARTURE

By bus Buses arrive and depart from their various bus company offices near the transport stop in the northwest of town, just off National Route 5. Bus tickets can be bought through many hotels and guesthouses, which can also arrange to have you picked up and taken to your bus.

Destinations Phnom Penh (9 daily; 6hr); Poipet (4 daily; 3hr); Siem Reap (4hr).

By share taxi and minibus These leave from the transport stop unless you're going to Pailin, in which case you should join a share taxi in the south of town, near the start of Route 10 at Psar Leu ($6). They leave from early morning until midday – it's a dusty journey.

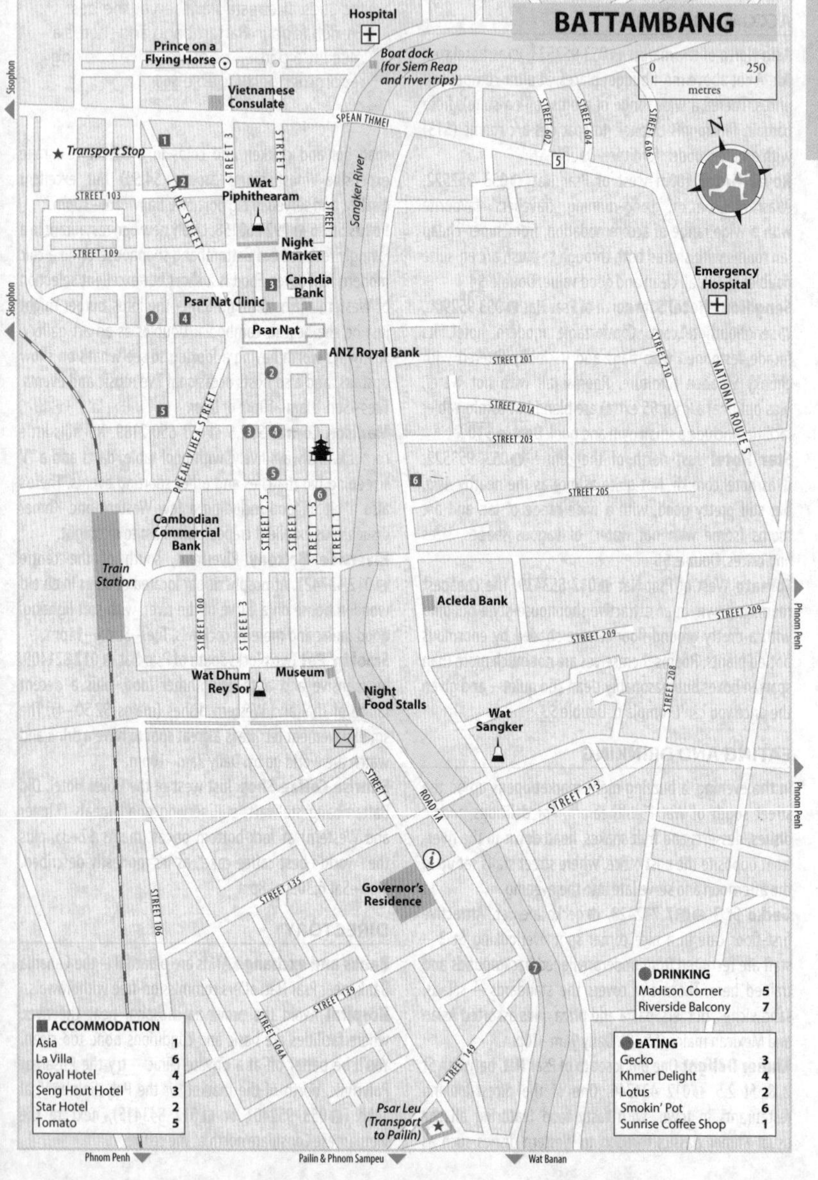

Destinations Pailin (1hr 30min); Phnom Penh (6hr); Poipet (2hr 30min); Siem Reap (3hr 30min).

By boat The boat dock is on the river, a few hundred metres north from the centre of town; hotel reps and English-speaking moto drivers meet the boats, so you'll have no trouble getting to your accommodation speedily. Boats depart daily at 7am for Siem Reap (6hr in the wet season, up to 8hr in dry) and cost $25.

2

ACCOMMODATION

Asia North of the market ⓣ 053 953523, ⓦ asrhotel.com.kh. A cut above most budget places, at ultra-competitive prices. There's a wide range of rooms (all en-suite), from bargain fan rooms through to spacious a/c rooms ($13) with ornate wooden furniture. Double **$6**

Royal Hotel 100m west of Psar Nat ⓣ 053 952522, ⓦ asrhotel.com.kh. Long-running travellers' favourite with a wide range of accommodation, from super-cheap fan rooms with shared bath through to plush a/c en-suite doubles ($12), all clean and good value. Double **$4**

Seng Hout Hotel 50m north of Psar Nat ⓣ 053 952900, ⓦ senghouthotel.com. Comfortable modern hotel, its facade festooned with flags and its lobby littered with chunky wooden furniture. Rooms (all with hot water, plus optional a/c for $5 extra) are bland but comfortable; facilities include a small gym and pool. Double **$10**

Star Hotel Just north of the centre ⓣ 053 953522, ⓦ asrhotel.com.kh. Not quite as nice as the nearby *Asia*, but still pretty good, with a wide range of fan and a/c rooms (some with hot water) of various shapes, sizes and prices. Double **$8**

Tomato West of Psar Nat ⓣ 012 853439. The cheapest rooms in town, in an attractive shophouse-style building with a pretty ground-floor terrace shaded by enormous potted plants. Rooms themselves are not much more than spartan boxes but reasonably clean and quiet – and given the price you can't complain. Double **$3**

EATING AND DRINKING

In the evening, a buzzing night-market opens up on the street south of Wat Piphithearam. For delicious noodle dishes, desserts and fruit shakes, head down to the river-front opposite the post office, where street stalls set up in the afternoon and serve late into the evening.

Gecko St 3 ⓣ 017 712428, ⓦ geckocafe.net. Attractive first-floor café in a nice corner spot overlooking St 3 – staff are recruited from underprivileged backgrounds and trained here. The menu covers the standards – salads, sandwiches, burgers, pasta and pizza, plus assorted Asian and Mexican mains ($5–8). Daily 9am–10pm.

Khmer Delight One block south of Psar Nat, between St 2 & St 2.5 ⓣ 012 434746. One of the nicest-looking restaurants in town, with tasty food featuring all the usual Khmer classics through to Western dishes such as spag bol and chicken and chips in a basket – a mite expensive (most mains around $4.50) but excellent quality, and served in big portions. Daily 7am–10pm.

★TREAT YOURSELF

La Villa East of the river ⓣ 053 730151, ⓦ lavilla-battambang.com. Seven-room boutique retreat in a renovated 1930s merchant's house. Rooms (all a/c) have plenty of colonial ambience (albeit not much furniture) and come with DVD player, and tea- and coffee-making facilities. The restaurant serves the best French food in Battambang and there's a nice little garden pool. Advance booking recommended. Double **$65**

Lotus St 2.5 ⓣ 092 260158. Lively new bar-restaurant in a lovingly restored old Battambang shophouse given a chic modern makeover. Food is a short but excellent selection of Western mains (around $5) – the lotus burger might just be the best in Cambodia. Doubles as an art gallery, so always worth having a looking to see what's on show upstairs, and also hosts occasional live music and events. Tues–Sun 10am–10pm or later.

Madison Corner St 2.5 ⓣ 053 650 2189. No-frills little corner bar, always lively, with pool table, darts and a TV screening big matches and other sporting events. There's also a bit of food including a few Western and Khmer dishes, plus excellent crêpes. Daily 7am to midnight.

Riverside Balcony Riverfront, south of the centre ⓣ 012 437421. Atmospheric bar located upstairs in an old wooden house on a curve of the river, with soft lighting, good music and moreish cocktails. Tues–Sun 4–11pm.

Smokin' Pot Two blocks south of Psar Nat ⓣ 012 821400. Inexpensive and authentic Khmer food, plus a decent range of Thai and Western dishes (mains $2.50–4). The small pavement terrace is a great spot to have a drink and watch the world go by. Daily 7am–10pm.

Sunrise Coffee Shop Just west of the Royal Hotel. Old Battambang stalwart, still serving good meals (Khmer and Western) at rock-bottom prices (mains $2–3), plus the "world's best coffee cake", as it's modestly described. Mon–Sat 6.30am–8pm.

DIRECTORY

Banks and exchange ATMs are plentiful – the Canadia Bank, near Psar Nat, offers commission-free withdrawals.

Hospital Avoid the provincial hospital near the river, where facilities are basic and conditions none too clean. You'll be better off at a private clinic – try the Phsarnat Polyclinic, north of the market, or the Polyclinique Visal Sokh (ⓣ 053 952401 or ⓣ 012 843415), next to the Vietnamese Consulate north of the centre.

Internet Try the well-equipped World Tel on St 2, or World Net, diagonally opposite between sts 2 and 1.5 (both daily 7am–8pm and charging 2000 riel/hr). Most hotels and restaurants have free wi-fi.

Post office On the riverside (daily 8am–4pm). You can also make phone calls from here.

PAILIN

Some 80km southwest of Battambang, **PAILIN** is a dusty little frontier town. The only link to the rest of the country is the recently surfaced National Route 57 from Battambang, and once you arrive there's really no reason to be here unless you're crossing the border into Thailand. The town has a wild and edgy atmosphere, and remains one of the most heavily mined regions in the country: high up and surrounded by jungle, it was long a Khmer Rouge stronghold, supplied with food and weapons from the nearby Thai border.

WHAT TO SEE AND DO

Pailin was once famous for its **gem mining**, though the land is now pretty much mined out. All you're likely to see today are a few dealers in the **market**, ready to hand over cash for rough, uncut stones pulled from the ground.

INTO THAILAND AT PAILIN

The easier of the two borders in the Pailin area to cross is the one at **Psar Pruhm** (7am–8pm), 20km from town (30min; shared taxi around $5, moto $2.50). At the border, a small market and three rather incongruous casinos entertain an almost exclusively Thai clientele – the Thai side of the border is known as Ban Pakkard. If you're crossing the border here, take a share taxi to Chanthaburi for B200 (see p.777), from where there are buses to Bangkok and Trat (for Ko Chang). Thai visas are issued on the spot. Entering Cambodia from here, you should expect the same immigration scams you'll get at any of the country's other border crossings, though you'll probably have the advantage of not being caught in a crush of tourists. The other border access point to Thailand, the Daung Lem border crossing at **Ban Laem**, further north, is extremely difficult to reach without your own vehicle.

The hill of **Phnom Yat** houses a small pagoda, its outer wall decorated with startling images of people being tortured in hell – tongues are pulled out with pliers, women drowned, people stabbed with forks and heads chopped off.

ARRIVAL AND DEPARTURE

By bus There's currently just one bus daily to/from Pailin (run by Paramount Angkor), which continues to/from the border crossing at Psar Pruhm. The transport stop is at the central market.

Destinations Battambang (1hr 30min).

By share taxi Share taxis arrive at and depart from the market in the centre of town. Most only go to Battambang (1hr 30min), from where you'll probably have to change to get transport elsewhere.

ACCOMMODATION

Bamboo Guesthouse 4km out of town on the road towards the border ⓣ 012 405818. A pleasant refuge from central Pailin with a range of wooden bungalows in an attractive garden, all with hot water and a/c. The restaurant is one of the best around, serving Khmer and Thai food, plus a few Western options. Double $13

Pailin Ruby West of the traffic circle on the main road through town ⓣ 055 636 3603. The best and least unruly (Pailin attracts a lot of truckers) place to stay in town. Rooms are clean and pleasant enough, with en-suite bathrooms, TV and chunky wood furniture; hot water and a/c cost an extra $5. Double $7

EATING

Eating in Pailin is no gastronomic delight, but the guesthouses do decent food and there are plenty of stalls in the market and cheap restaurants nearby.

Leang Sren Restaurant In the north of town, just by the temple. Wholesome, spicy soups and decent Khmer food from $2. Daily 8am–9pm.

The southwest

To the southwest of Phnom Penh the Cardamom and Elephant mountains rise up imposingly from the plains, as if shielding Cambodia's only stretch of coast from the world. Indeed, only a few places along the coast are accessible by road. The most popular destination is the beach resort of **Sihanoukville**, whose sandy shores are the launching point for trips to **Ream National Park** and remote and

sparsely populated islands in the Gulf of Thailand. Further east along the coast are the city of **Kampot** and the quaint coastal village of **Kep**. On Cambodia's western border, **Koh Kong** serves as a transit point for visitors arriving from or leaving for Thailand, and is also an ecotourism gateway offering treks into the lush jungle of the Cardamoms.

The accessible areas of the southwest are well served by public **transport**. National Routes 3 and 4 are in a fairly good state of repair, while regular fast ferries and boats service the islands.

SIHANOUKVILLE

The closest that Cambodia gets to a full-blown beach resort, **SIHANOUKVILLE** is somewhat ramshackle, a place where building-site detritus is more common than swaying palm trees. Nevertheless it should be visited, if only as a launching pad to the stunning islands of Koh Rong, Koh Ta Kiev and Koh Rong Samloem. Sihanoukville has a few decent sandy beaches (but nothing spectacular by Southeast Asian standards), fresh seafood, and affordable facilities to go around. It works as a decent place to refuel and unwind, especially if you've been travelling hard on the provincial Cambodian roads. Moreover, lazy days on the beach can be complemented by an evening of partying at one of the town's vibrant nightspots. If you're visiting during high season or a holiday weekend, though, be prepared to battle the crowds.

WHAT TO SEE AND DO

The **town** itself is inland, with its centre around the market; sprawling over a large peninsula, it's ringed by beaches and has many mid-range hotels. The backpacker area is along **Serendipity Beach Road** leading down to the southern corner of the peninsula. Here, you'll find plenty of guesthouses, cheap Western-oriented restaurants and a smattering of late-night bars.

Angkor Brewery

The **Angkor Brewery** is located just north of the town centre. Free tours (Wed 3–5pm), with an open bar, can be arranged through the guesthouses that sell Angkor Beer.

Beaches

Victory Beach is a wide, sandy beach sparsely sprinkled with bars and restaurants. The Victory Hill area has a seedy reputation, being a favourite of middle-aged gentleman looking for "hired company"; however, its quieter hassle-free shoreline seems little affected and is a popular place for families. Beyond Victory Hill is **Hawaii Beach**, a favourite with Khmer families. Next along is **Independence Beach**, named after a seven-storey 1960s monolith, the **Independence Hotel**, a luxury resort which sits at its western end. The bay curves gently, with a line of drinks stalls and shaded huts. As it sweeps round, rocks and small, secluded bays allow some privacy. As you continue east, you reach the less-visited **Sokha Beach**, the almost exclusive preserve of a huge luxury resort. Closest to town are **Serendipity** and **Ochheuteal** beaches (essentially the same beach with the former being the main hub of activity), where you'll find the busiest backpacker vibe. The area has a broad range of accommodation, bars and restaurants, as well as the usual sunbeds, umbrellas and tubes ($1). It's definitely worth making the trip 3km southeast of the town to **Otres Beach**, the most impressive of Sihanoukville's seaside offerings, where you can enjoy not only long stretches of golden sand but also a bohemian bar and restaurant scene.

Offshore islands

As the crowds swell and developments get out of hand in Sihanoukville, many are opting to use the town as a launching point to get to the unspoilt islands off the coast, where rustic bungalow developments are mushrooming. *Crusoe Island* (see p.105) on **Koh Ta Kiev** is a brilliant option, while **Koh Rong** is the largest and most developed, with a buzzing backpacker strip on its south-eastern corner (Koh Touch), clustered near the main pier. Neighbouring **Koh Rong Samloem** has a growing number of

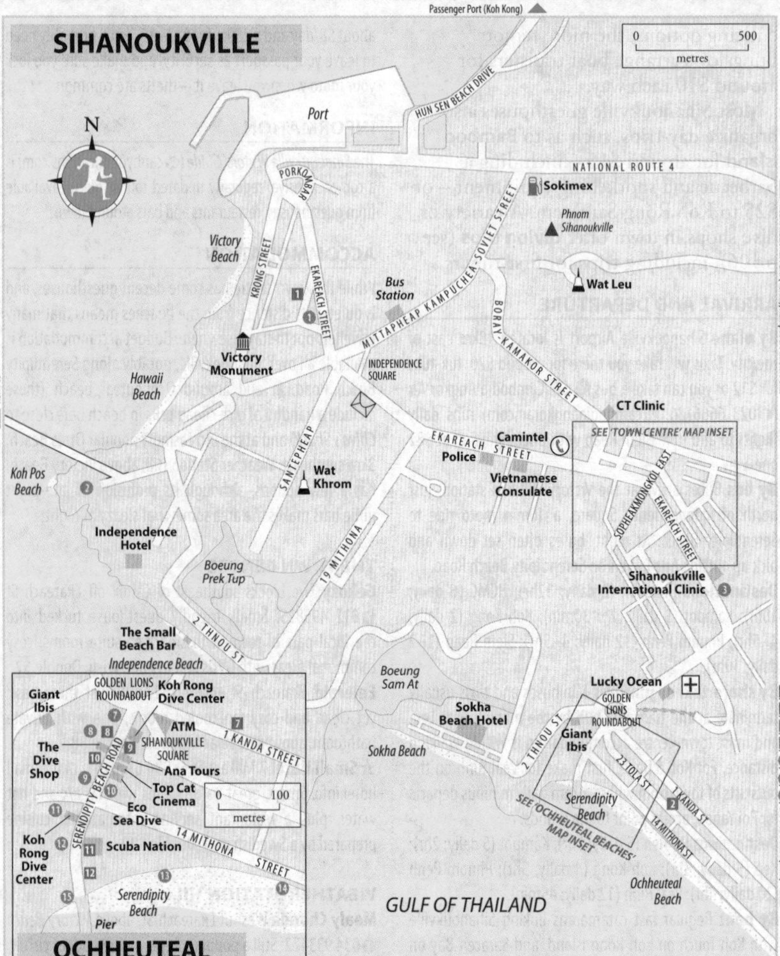

SIHANOUKVILLE
Passenger Port (Koh Kong)
0 500 metres
Port
HUN SEN BEACH DRIVE
NATIONAL ROUTE 4
PORKOMBAR
Sokimex
Phnom Sihanoukville
Ream National Park (18km), Kampot & Phnom Penh
Victory Beach
KRONG STREET
EKAREACH STREET
Bus Station
MITTAPHEAP KAMPUCHEA-SOVIET STREET
Wat Leu
BORAY-KAMAKOR STREET
Victory Monument
INDEPENDENCE SQUARE
Koh Pos
Hawaii Beach
CT Clinic
SEE 'TOWN CENTRE' MAP INSET
Caminteil
Police
EKAREACH STREET
SANTEPHEAP
Wat Khrom
Vietnamese Consulate
SOPHEAKMONGKOL EAST
EKAREACH STREET
Koh Pos Beach
Independence Hotel
Boeung Prek Tup
19 MITHONA
Sihanoukville International Clinic
The Small Beach Bar
2 THNOU ST
Independence Beach
Boeung Sam At
Lucky Ocean
GOLDEN LIONS ROUNDABOUT
Sokha Beach Hotel
Giant Ibis
2 THNOU ST
Sokha Beach
23 TOLA ST
1 KANDA ST
14 MITHONA ST
Serendipity Beach
SEE 'OCHHEUTEAL BEACHES' MAP INSET
& Otres Beach (3km)
Ochheuteal Beach
GULF OF THAILAND
GOLDEN LIONS ROUNDABOUT
Giant Ibis
Koh Rong Dive Center
ATM
The Dive Shop
SIHANOUKVILLE SQUARE
1 KANDA STREET
Ana Tours
SERENDIPITY BEACH ROAD
Top Cat Cinema
0 100 metres
Eco Sea Dive
14 MITHONA STREET
Koh Rong Dive Center
Scuba Nation
Serendipity Beach
Pier
OCHHEUTEAL BEACH

TOWN CENTRE
Psar Pinchecom
KAMAKOR
SOPHEAKMONGKOL NORTH
OMUI STREET
BORAY
STREET 109
SOPHEAKMONGKOL WEST
Transport Stop
STREET 108
STREET 109
SOPHEAKMONGKOL EAST
@ ABC Computer
STREET 108
Old Transport Stop
Psar Leu
Phnom Penh Sorya Transport
EKAREACH STREET
ATM
ATM
Eco Sea Dive
Caltex
Mottah
Virak Buntham
Capitol Bus Station
7 MAKARA
EKAREACH STREET
Samudera
0 200 metres
Orange Supermarket
Canadia Bank

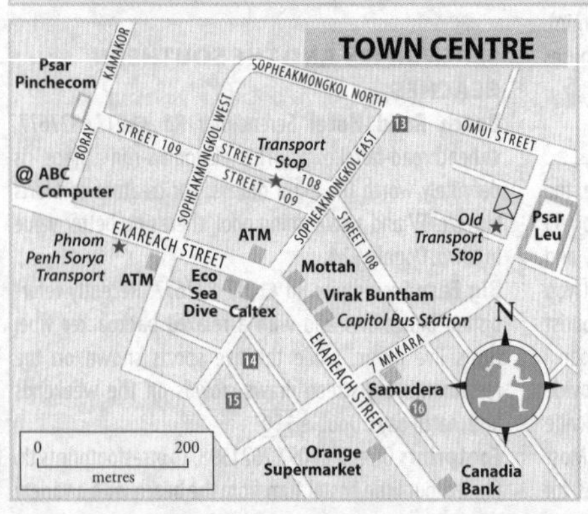

EATING

Corner Bar	1
Delicious	11
Done Right	5
Happa	9
Holy Cow	3
Mick and Craig's	7
Starfish Café	16
Sunshine Café	6
Treasure Island Seafood	2

DRINKING & NIGHTLIFE

Blame Canada	4
Dolphin Shack	13
Jay Jay's	15
Maybe Later	12
Monkey Republic	8
Sessions	14
Utopia	10

ACCOMMODATION

Aqua	7
Beach Road Hotel	9
Big Easy	10
Emerald	13
Footprints	4
Gekozy	15
Hacienda	5
Mealy Chenda	1
MoHaChai	11
Monkey Republic	8
Mushroom Point	3
New Sea View Villa	12
Orchidee	2
Sea Garden	6
Small Hotel	14

enticing options; the more remote bungalows arrange boat transfers for around $10 each way.

Most Sihanoukville guesthouses also organize day-trips, such as to **Bamboo Island** for around $15 – including a barbecue and snorkelling equipment – or $25 to Koh Rong Samloem. A variety of dive shops in town offer **diving trips** (see p.106), including trips for first-timers.

ARRIVAL AND DEPARTURE

By plane Sihanoukville Airport is located 18km east of the city. Taxis will take you there for around $20, tuk-tuks for $12 or you can take a bus for $6. Cambodia Angkor Air (T 023 6666786, W cambodiaangkorair.com) runs daily flights to and from Siem Reap with prices starting at $82 one-way.

By bus Buses arrive at the Victory Hill bus station, just north of Independence Square, a 10min moto ride to Serendipity Beach. At night, buses often set down and pick up outside Ana Travels on Serendipity Beach Road.

Destinations Bangkok (2 daily; 12hr); HCMC (6 daily; 10hr); Kampot (8 daily; 2hr 30min); Koh Kong (2 daily; 4–5hr); Phnom Penh (12 daily; 4–5hr); Siem Reap (1–2 daily; 10hr).

By share taxi or minibus Minibuses and taxis usually terminate at the transport hub by the market, Psar Leu, and most town-centre accommodation is within walking distance. For Koh S'Dach, first make for Veal Rinh on the outskirts of town from where a 7am daily minibus departs for Poi Yapon, access point to the islands.

Destinations Ha Tien (5 daily; 5hr); Kampot (5 daily; 2hr); Kep (5 daily; 3hr); Koh Kong (4 daily; 5hr); Phnom Penh (20 daily; 4hr); Veal Rinh (12 daily; 45min).

By boat Regular fast catamarans linking Sihanoukville with Koh Touch on Koh Rong island, and Saracen Bay on neighbouring Koh Rong Samloem, are offered by Koh Rong Dive Center (booking office on Serendipity Beach Rd; W kohrong-divecenter.com; $25/$35 return; 45/60min). Other island transfers are arranged either by guesthouses or dive companies.

GETTING AROUND

By moto and tuk-tuk Motos and tuk-tuks are the principal form of local transport. For motos, reckon on $3 from town to the beaches or Weather Station Hill, and about twice that for tuk-tuks. It's worth noting that you pay a premium if you hail a moto or tuk-tuk outside tourist hubs like *Monkey Republic* along Serendipity Beach Road.

Motorbike rental If lazing on the beach doesn't provide enough excitement, and you want to explore Sihanoukville and the area, the best option is to rent a motorcycle. Most guesthouses provide this service: a 125cc bike goes for about $8/day and a 250cc for $12–15. You'll probably need to leave your passport as security, and make sure you lock your moto when you leave it – thefts are common.

INFORMATION

The *Sihanoukville Visitors' Guide* (W canbypublications.com) is a comprehensive, regularly updated tourist guide, available from guesthouses, restaurants and bars around town.

ACCOMMODATION

While the town centre has some decent guesthouses, and is quieter, its distance from the beaches means that many travellers opt to stay elsewhere. Budget accommodation is available all over Sihanoukville, notably along Serendipity Beach Road, in and around Ochheuteal beach (these include a handful of dirt-cheap cells in beach bars close to *Chiva's Shack*) and at the increasingly popular Otres Beach, 3km southeast. Weather Station Hill, above Victory Beach, has a few options, although its profusion of late-night girlie bars makes the area somewhat sleazy at night.

THE TOWN CENTRE

Gekozy Two blocks southeast of Caltex off Ekareach St T 012 495825. Small, friendly guesthouse tucked into the local part of town with smart en-suite rooms, cosy communal areas with DVDs aplenty and wi-fi. Double **$7**

Emerald Ekareach St T 097 7527490. Just three basic yet clean and cosy fan-cooled rooms, one with private bathroom, above a popular Irish pub. Double **$8**

★**Small Hotel** 7 Makara St T 034 6306161, W thesmallhotel.info. Smart, great-value rooms with TV, a/c and hot water, plus a restaurant serving international cuisine prepared by a Swedish chef. Double **$20**

WEATHER STATION HILL

Mealy Chenda West of Ekareach St, above *Victory Beach* T 034 933472. Still a popular player on the budget circuit, thanks to its low prices, sociable atmosphere and decent restaurant. Double **$8**

SERENDIPITY AND THE SOUTHERN BEACHES

Beach Road Hotel Serendipity Rd T 017 827677, W beachroad-hotel.com. This Estonian-run place is definitely worth the extra dollars. For creature comforts like a/c, TV and a swimming pool, there's no better value in town. Double **$24**

Big Easy Serendipity Rd T 017 827677. Recently refurbished bungalows and with a relaxed backpacker vibe. Hosts live music, while the live sports shown on the restaurant's big screen draws crowds on the weekends and match days. Double **$10**

Footprints Otres 2 T 097 2621598, W otresfootprints.tk. Chilled-out little hostel 10m from the beach with a variety

of dorms and timber-panelled doubles and triples, plus a cosy communal TV area and safe bike parking. Dorm $6, room $15

Aqua 7 Polawai St, next to Cambodian Resort T 034 934582. W aquasihanoukville.com. Fair-value guesthouse, 10min walk to the beach, with, for the moment at least, views from its pool terrace over a rare patch of green. Rooms are clean and all have a/c and minibars (those upstairs are better). Double $30

Hacienda Otres Village, next to the market, 750m inland from Otres 2 beach T 070 814643, E haciendaotres @outlook.com. Sociable hostel with a free 10-bed dorm ($3 for the first night, free thereafter), over-water bar-restaurant, garden-encircled bungalows and free bicycles for getting to the beach. Double $9

MoHaChai Serendipity Rd T 034 933586, W mohachai .com. Take a superior a/c room with TV and hot water, a rustic bungalow with private veranda or opt for a budget room; all are en suite. There's a cheery bar out front, plus games area and in-house dive centre, Scuba Nation (see p.106). Double $6

Monkey Republic Serendipity Beach Rd T 012 490290, W monkeyrepublic.info. This hostel was completely rebuilt in 2013 following a fire and is now home to sparkling double and quad en-suite rooms and a welcoming pub-style bar-restaurant. Stay here to be right in the thick of the action. They don't take bookings so arrive at checkout time (noon) to bag a room. Double $8

Mushroom Point Otres Beach T 078 509097, W mushroompoint.com. With its mushroom-shaped bungalows, circular beds and hippy decor this might be one of the most unique beach sleeps in Asia, and it's just metres from one of the prettiest stretches of sand in Sihanoukville. Dorm $7, double $25

New Sea View Villa Serendipity Beach Rd T 017 918966, W sihanoukville-hotel.com. A range of big, clean twin and triple rooms, some with a/c and tubs, offering good value if you're in a group though they tend to fill up fast. There's also a very pleasant little restaurant out front. Double $15

Orchidée One block back from Ochheuteal Beach on Tola St T 034 933639, W orchidee-guesthouse.com. Fully equipped, spacious rooms (TV, a/c and hot water), with a pleasant breakfast terrace, a shady garden setting and a pool. Double $20

Sea Garden Otres 1 T 096 2538131, W sea-garden.se. Chilled-out bungalows at the far end of the beach, which are basic but clean (shared facilities). There's a good bar-restaurant, nice lounge and helpful owners. Booked rooms are released after 3pm. Double $14

OFFSHORE ISLANDS

Crusoe Island Koh Ta Kiev T 097 2539082, W crusoe island.asia. Opt to stay in tents, pitch your hammock over the sand or kip down in one of four bungalows. The island is 55min away by boat; $10 return. Tent $6, hammock $2, bungalow $15

Island Boys Koh Rong E kohrongislandboys@gmail .com. Tiny rooms and dorms with paperthin walls and shared bathrooms above Koh Touch's liveliest bar. Dorm $6, Double $12

Lonely Beach Koh Rong T 081 343457, W lonely-beach .com. A relaxed guesthouse set on Koh Rong's quieter and more idyllic northern shores. Dorm $10, bungalow $30

The Fishing Hook Koh Rong Samloem T 081 332718. A cute over-water homestay with just four dorm beds, friendly owners and great food, located in the heart of rustic M'Pai Bay Village. Dorm $5

Sun Island Eco Village Koh Rong Samloem T 077 765069, W sun-island-eco-village.com. Sea-facing tents and no-frills rooms with private or shared bathrooms, 24hr solar power and good food. Double $20

EATING AND DRINKING

Sihanoukville has a good selection of Western-oriented restaurants and bars. In town, most places are either clustered along Ekareach St at the junction with Sopheakmongkol East, home of the night market, or along the southern end of Serendipity Beach Rd. Most of the Western places stay open beyond midnight, and a couple only shut when the last person leaves. The best Khmer food – and also the best value in town – is found in the clutter of food stalls to the eastern side of Golden Lion roundabout.

RESTAURANTS AND CAFÉS

Corner Bar Weather Station Hill T 012 479395. Popular bar-restaurant serving sandwiches, great pizzas and other Western dishes from $3. Delivery service, too. Screens sports events. Daily noon–late.

Delicious North Plaza, off Serendipity Beach Rd T 012 574603. Tiny family-run café famed for *roti canai* ($1.50), cheap local and Western dishes, including decent pizza (from $3) and big breakfasts. A bottle of wine costs just $6. Daily 6.30am–midnight.

Done Right Otres 1 T 097 9361441. While not on the beach, the dining terrace of this hippy Swedish-owned hostel overlooks a pretty garden, and the European food on offer is fab; try the yummy Swedish meatballs ($6) or their "bad ass" salza burger ($5.50). Daily 9am–11pm.

★ **Happa** Serendipity Beach Rd T 034 934380. A stylish Japanese teppanyaki restaurant where food is grilled in front of you. The best spot for seafood in town. Tapas-style dishes $4–6. Daily 5–10pm.

Holy Cow Ekareach St T 012 478510. Set in an old wooden house, just back from the main drag, this is a laidback spot for dining on an inexpensive Khmer and Western menu (jacket potato, $3). Daily 7am–9.30pm.

Mick and Craig's Serendipity Beach Rd ⓣ034 934845. Delicious Western grub for the discerning budget traveller, including sandwiches, quiches, grills, BBQs and curries from $5. Packed out most nights. Daily 7am–11pm.

Starfish Café Off 7 Makara, behind Samudera Supermarket. Delicious Western bread, cakes ($2), scones and other goodies served in a garden, or for takeaway. Arts and crafts by Rajana Fairtrade are sold here, and there's also massage upstairs – all profits go to *Starfish*'s grassroots charity, which supports medical care, housing projects and community workshops in Cambodia. Daily 7am–5pm.

2

Sunshine Café Otres 1 ⓣ012 828432. Simple beach restaurant serving up legendary fish sandwiches and Khmer specialities including *ban chow*, Cambodian pancakes with seafood and Khmer spices ($3), best washed down with a fruit shake. Daily 9am–11pm.

Treasure Island Seafood Between Hawaii and Independence beaches ⓣ012 830505 A gem of a restaurant serving Chinese food, with the emphasis on succulent seafood and fish, set on its own small, sunset-facing beach. Moderately priced, with seafood dishes, such as grilled squid, from $6. Daily 9am–9pm.

BARS AND CLUBS

All bars and clubs are open daily and some stay open 24hr. Ochheuteal Beach is party central.

Blame Canada Otres 1. You'll find plenty of atmosphere at this buzzing pirate-themed beach bar, dotted with plenty of cushioned satellite chairs, a pool table and sunset-worthy upper deck for sipping cocktails (from $3.50). Daily 7am–midnight.

Dolphin Shack Ochheuteal Beach. Loud and proud beach bar with nightly parties, fireshows and even the occasional mud-wrestling competition. Vodka buckets cost $4, beer 50c. Also runs booze cruises and hosts full-moon parties. Open 24hr.

Jay Jay's Serendipity Beach. The spot for late-night revelry. With bronzed backpackers covering themselves in body-paint and dancing on the bar till dawn, this is Sihanoukville's very own slice of Haad Rin Beach. Whisky and Red Bull buckets $5. Daily 5pm–late.

★**Maybe Later** Serendipity Beach Rd ⓣ097 8695264. This lively joint stocks an eye-popping range of rum and tequila, and also serves very good Mexican food into the early hours. Daily 5pm–2am.

★**Monkey Republic** Between Golden Lion Roundabout and Serendipity Beach. Most nights start with people meeting for a few early drinks at *Monkey*, popular among both tourists and expats alike for its wide drinks selection including Guinness, cider and even Jagermeister, and good, hearty food. Happy-hour beer 75¢. Daily 8am–midnight.

Sessions Serendipity Beach. Fun beach bar with deck chairs, dancing platform and oceanfront location. Worth a visit on the nights when they throw impromptu parties. Draught beer 75c during the 4–7pm and all day Monday happy hour. Daily 11am–late

Utopia Between Golden Lion Roundabout and Serendipity Beach. Popular late-night club with dance music, $2.50 cocktails, a swimming pool and a huge 25-person hot tub. Could be a great place if it weren't for the hordes of prostitutes that linger looking for drunken prey. Beer $1. Daily 10am–late.

DIRECTORY

Banks and exchange ATMs are readily available on Serendipity Beach Rd and near Caltex downtown. Canadia Bank, Ekareach St, east of 7 Makara St, for cash on MasterCard and MoneyGram; First Union Commercial Bank, on the corner of Ekareach and Sopheakmongkol streets. You can change dollars for riel at the Acleda Bank, also on Ekareach St.

Cinema Just next to *Beach Road*, the tiny Top Cat cinema on Serendipity Beach Road is open from 11am till late and has private screening rooms where you can pick your own movies, and a big screen playing relatively new releases ($4.50).

Diving To arrange a trip, contact: EcoSea Dive (ⓣ034 934631, ⓦecoseadive.com); Scuba Nation, whose headquarters are at *Mohachai* guesthouse (ⓣ023 604680, ⓦdivecambodia.com); or The Dive Shop (ⓣ034 933664, ⓦdiveshopcambodia.com), next to Monkey Republic on Serendipity Beach Rd. All also offer National Geographic courses. Prices start at $320 for the PADI Open Water, or $65 for one fun dive.

Hospitals and clinics Sihanoukville International Clinic (ⓣ012 738803), on Ekareach St, has a 24hr emergency service. CT Clinic on Borei-Kamakor Rd (ⓣ034 936666) offers a complete service, has English-speaking doctors and accepts credit cards.

Internet ABC Computer on Ekareach St west of the town centre ($1/hr) has a few terminals.

Police On Ekareach St between Independence Square and the town centre (ⓣ093 666261 or ⓣ093 666260).

Post office The main post office is one block behind Krong St, near Independence Monument. You can get stamps and post items at the smaller branch office opposite the market (daily 8am–4pm).

Supermarkets Samudera Supermarket, 7 Makara St, 50m from Ekareach St (daily 6am–10pm), or Lucky Ocean, 200m north of the Golden Lions roundabout, on Ekareach St (daily 7.30am–10pm).

REAM NATIONAL PARK

Ream National Park, also known as Preah Sihanouk National Park, located 18km east of Sihanoukville, is one of the most accessible national parks in Cambodia, and a great place to explore the country's unique, unspoilt natural environment. Its 210 square kilometres include evergreen and mangrove forests, sandy beaches,

coral reefs, offshore islands and a rich diversity of flora and fauna.

The rangers at the park headquarters (daily 7.30–11am & 2–5pm; ⓣ012 875096) are extremely helpful, and can arrange **boat trips** (about $50 for the boat, or $10 per person for large groups) along the Prek Toek Sap estuary to the fishing village of Thmor Tom and on to the idyllic Koh Sam Pouch Beach. The river is bordered by mangroves, and you're likely to see kingfishers, sea eagles and maybe monkeys along the way. Alternatively, go for a guided walk ($8 per person, about 2hr) along forested nature trails.

ARRIVAL AND DEPARTURE

To get to the park headquarters from Sihanoukville head along National Route 4 to Ream village, turning right down the track next to the airport.

By moto or tuk-tuk A moto/tuk-tuk will cost $10/$15 from Sihanoukville.

On a tour Joining a group from a guesthouse costs about $20 per person depending on number in the group.

KOH S'DACH

The small island of **KOH S'DACH** (King's Island) is the fishing capital of Cambodian waters, just off Koh Kong province in the Gulf of Thailand. If you've time for a detour and with time on your hands, the area is worth exploring.

The real reason for stopping here is to get out in a boat to explore the coast – just off the north shore of Koh S'dach you'll find brilliantly coloured coral within paddling distance. A cluster of **islands** nearby – Koh Samai, Koh Samot, Koh Chan and Koh Totang – are all within a boat's row and boast good reefs for snorkelling. A fishing boat to the islands is open to negotiation: $30 a day seems to be the going rate. Alternatively, you can hop in one of the small, fibreglass boats that go across to the mainland (around $1) where there are also some fine, deserted beaches. Thai **Baht** is also accepted on the island.

ARRIVAL AND DEPARTURE

By bus To get to Koh S'Dach, take the 7am minibus from Veal Rinh, 45min from Sihanoukville, to Poi Yapon jetty, or alternatively jump aboard a Koh Kong-bound bus and alight at Andoung Tuek, where you can easily find a moto or minibus the rest of the way.

ACCOMMODATION AND EATING

You can buy snacks and local food at the market, and a well-stocked, if pricey, local store sells beer, snacks and sundries.

Mean Chey ⓣ011 983806. The island's guesthouse, *Mean Chey* is on the western side of the island. It has its own pier so when you arrive at Poi Yapon make it clear to the boat driver where you're going. Accommodation is in basic blue concrete en-suite bungalows. Double **$10**

Yvonne's Next door to *Mean Chey*. A simple restaurant serving good fish, pasta and pizzas. Daily 9am–9pm.

KOH KONG

Boat schedules and border opening times used to conspire to make an overnight stop in **KOH KONG** a necessity. Since the border post extended its hours to 8pm, you no longer have to stay, though a few days exploring the surrounding area is well rewarded. Several **islands** lie near to the town, the largest of which is **Koh Kong Island** itself (not to be confused with the mainland town of Koh Kong), which boasts seven beautiful beaches on the seaward side (although sandflies can be a problem). You can charter a six-person boat for $80 (or $25 per person on day-trips with local operators) for the two-hour trip. Don't consider this between June and October due to rough seas.

Situated on the eastern bank of the Kah Bpow River, Koh Kong was historically an insular outpost, its prosperity based on fishing, logging and smuggling. These days, however, it's the border that brings

ECO ADVENTURES IN KOH KONG

Koh Kong is an emerging ecotourism destination; day-trips to waterfalls and Koh Kong Island, and treks into the lush jungle of the Cardamoms are offered by the reliable Ritthy at Koh Kong Eco Adventure Tours (ⓦkohkongeco adventure.com). For riverine kayaking trips, try Neptune (ⓦneptuneadventure-cambodia.com), whose base is a chilled-out guesthouse on the banks of the serene Tatai River, 18km east of town, itself a lovely place to stay ($25).

2

in the trade. A new bridge, nearly 2km long, crosses the river, and a left turn shortly after the bridge takes you eventually to **Koh Yor Beach**, a pretty strip of sand dotted with low-key restaurants. Despite the fact that much of the rich sandalwood forest has been transported to Thailand, the area around the town is beautiful and remains largely unspoilt.

2

ARRIVAL AND INFORMATION

By bus Buses usually drop off east of town near the Acleda Bank, a $1–2 moto ride into town.

Destinations Phnom Penh (5 daily; 6hr); Sihanoukville (3 daily; 4hr).

By share taxi or minibus If you're coming by road from Sihanoukville, get out at the market or the port, from where you can easily walk to guesthouse accommodation.

Information Koh Kong town is not a large place, and you can get around on foot, but motos are not expensive at just 2000 riel a trip. There's an Acleda Bank on the north side of the market, or you can change baht and dollars on Street 2 at Ratha Exchange (7am–5pm).

ACCOMMODATION

Accommodation options have improved remarkably in recent years, although expect the inevitable irritation of moto drivers taking commission, so know where you're going or book ahead.

Kaing Kaing Guesthouse on the riverfront, near the old boat dock ⓣ 035 6747111. There isn't much English spoken, but the rooms (fan and a/c) are clean and bright; many have river-view balconies and some sleep up to four. Great location. Double $10

Blue Moon Chicken Farm Rd ⓣ 016 946079, ⓔ bluemoonkohkong@yahoo.com. Small guesthouse 300m from the riverfront with clean, if dark, en-suite fan and a/c rooms with TVs. Also runs popular jungle treks. Double $6

Rasmey Buntham Guesthouse Southeast of the market ⓣ 016 797989. Good-sized rooms set around a central lobby, with pool to the rear. Staff can help with travel arrangements, and operate an internet café next door (5000 riel/hr). Double $6

INTO THAILAND: KOH KONG

From **Koh Kong**, it's a 12km tuk-tuk/moto ride ($8/$3) to the border crossing at Cham Yeam (daily 7am–8pm). Fifteen-day Thai visas for most passports are arranged on the spot. From Hat Lek, on the Thai side of the border, minibuses leave for Trat (see p.777), 91km northwest, roughly every 45 minutes between 7am and 5pm (1hr–1hr 30min; 120 baht); Trat has regular connections on to Ko Chang.

EATING AND DRINKING

Baan Peakmai *Asian Hotel*, riverside ⓣ 035 936667. A smart a/c restaurant serving some of the best food in town (Thai mostly, but some Khmer dishes too) including a delicious green chicken curry ($5) and many vegetarian dishes. Daily 6.30–9.30am, 11am–2pm & 5–10pm.

★ **Blue Bar** Thmorda Garden Resort, 169 Neuk Kok Village, 3km from town, on the western side of the river. Relaxed over water bar with a surprisingly chic design; sip cold beers ($1) from hammocks or cushion-plumped day beds overlooking the river. The food is also good and there are free kayaks for exploring the river. Daily noon–10pm.

Bob's Ice Cream & Bar Southeast of the roundabout ⓣ 016 326455. Expats flock here for the Western food and great coffee, although the ice cream's nothing special. Daily 8am–11pm.

KAMPOT

KAMPOT, with its riverside location, backdrop of misty Bokor Mountains and terraces of French shophouses, is one of the most attractive of Cambodia's provincial towns. It's also the staging post for side trips to Kep, and a pleasant place to spend an afternoon browsing the market, strolling along the Teuk Chhou River, heading into the mountains to explore caves and visiting pepper plantations. The river marks the western boundary of the town, with the new market to the north and the roundabout in the centre.

Bokor, the French-colonial ghost town, is perched high in the mountains above Kampot. Parts of the town look like they were shut up just yesterday, and the eerie atmosphere is electrifying. A US$100 million development is however changing the face of the mountain; a plush hotel and casino have already been completed with plans mooted for villas, golf courses, water parks and even a cable car up a portion of the mountain. A newly completed 32km road now makes access easy. All guesthouses organize tours ($15).

ARRIVAL AND DEPARTURE

By bus A handful of buses run frequently to and from Phnom Penh ($5–8; 3–6hr), some taking a circuitous route via Kep ($3; 45min), which can take up to 6hr. There are ticket desks adjacent to the transport stop.

By moto or tuk-tuk A moto to Kep costs around $8, a tuk-tuk $12, a taxi $20; the journey takes 45min.

By share taxi or minibus Leaving from either the market or the transport stop in the southeast of town, off the road to Kep, shared taxis to Phnom Penh (12 daily; 4–5hr; $5) and Sihanoukville (10 daily; 2hr 30min; $4) leave regularly throughout the day.

ACCOMMODATION

IN TOWN

Blissful Guesthouse On a quiet side street about 1km south of the traffic circle ⓣ 012 513024, ⓦ blissfulguesthouse.com. Popular Western-run place with inexpensive rooms; all beds have mosquito nets. There's also a comfy chill-out room upstairs and a travellers' restaurant downstairs. Dorm $2, double $4

Long Villa In the north of town, west of the market ⓣ 012 731400. Cosy en-suite rooms in a wooden villa with a pleasant patio restaurant out front and all travellers' services including help with transport, guided transport and motorbike rental. Double $6

Magic Sponge Off Salt Workers Roundabout ⓣ 017 946428, ⓦ magicspongecambodia.com. Colourful rooms, a brill six-bed penthouse dorm, a crazy golf course, Indian food and a happening bar make this a great option for those looking for something a little quirky. Dorm $3, double $9

Orchid Guesthouse Off Salt Workers Roundabout, opposite *Blissful* ⓣ 092 226996. Rooms and small bungalows (fan or a/c) in a pleasant, orchid-filled garden. Helpful staff also run a variety of tours of the area, and can arrange moto rental. Double $7

Paris Guesthouse Cnr Old Market St, near Captain Chim's ⓣ 033 6902340. A quiet, family-run Khmer guesthouse in a top town-centre location offering clean fan and a/c en-suite rooms with TVs. Great value. Double $10

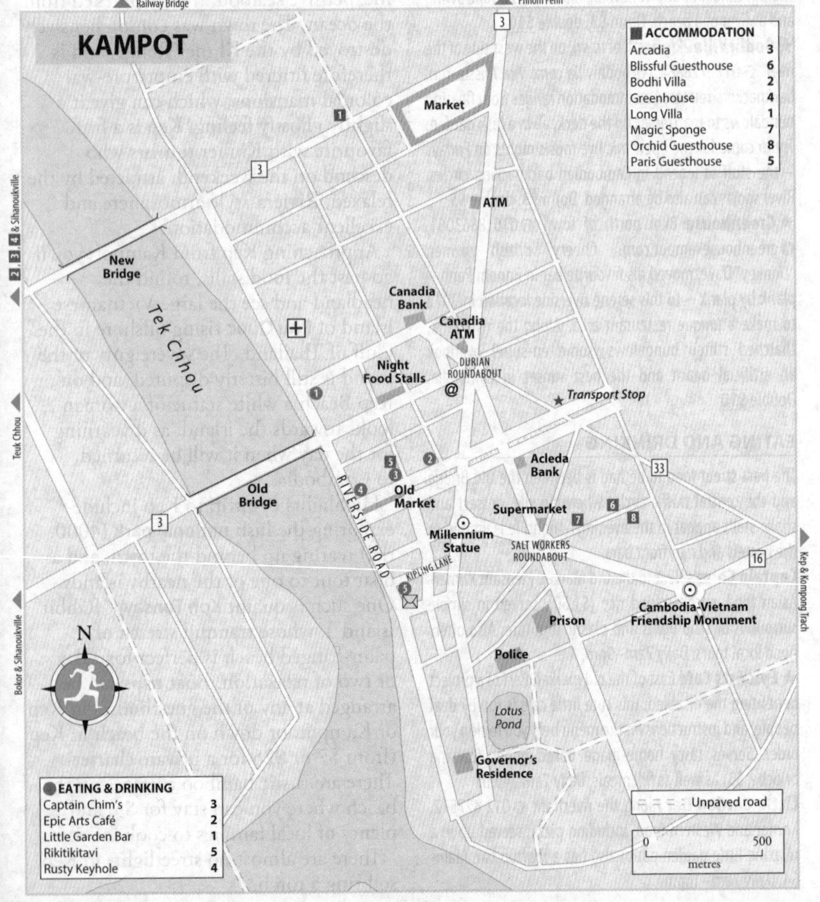

2

★TREAT YOURSELF

Veranda Natural Resort T 036 6388588, W veranda-resort.com. Located on the hill behind the town, this stylish complex of bungalows connected by elevated wood-and-stone walkways offers a range of sophisticated rooms. The sea-facing bar, restaurant and gorgeous pool ($7) are worth visiting even if you're not staying here. $70

OUT OF TOWN

Arcadia 7km north of town T 012 560164, W arcadia backpackers.com. Well worth the hike, this isolated hostel – formerly known as *Utopia* – with dorms, rooms and stilted huts, is a chilled backpackers' joint with friendly owners and regular weekend parties. Activities include tubing, canoeing and volleyball, and there's a rope swing and a sliver of a beach. Dorm $3, double $10

★**Bodhi Villa** 2km north of town, on the west side of the river T 012 728884, W bodhivilla.com. An Aussie-run, backpackers' retreat. Accommodation ranges from floating bungalows to mattresses on the deck, all in a lush garden. Try to come for the open-mic live music nights on Fridays – the stuff of legend in Cambodian backpacking circles. River sports can also be arranged. Dorm $3, double $5

★**Greenhouse** 8km north of town T 016 8863061, W greenhousekampot.com. Cheery British owner, "Donkey" Dave, moved his favourite bar in Phnom Penh – plank by plank – to this serene riverside location in 2012 to make a unique restaurant area. Along the riverbank, thatched stilted bungalows (some en-suite) overlook an artificial beach and the best sunset in Cambodia. Double $10

EATING AND DRINKING

The best street food to be had is between the Old Bridge and the central traffic circle, where noodle, dessert and shake stalls appear in the evenings. Nightlife is limited to the hostels and riverfront bars.

Captain Chim's Next to the Old Market. Pleasant Khmer-Asian food, such as fried rice ($1.50), served in simple surrounds of strip lights and plastic furniture. Also offers good local tours. Daily 7am–9pm.

★**Epic Arts Café** East of the old market. Part of a project benefiting the disabled, this cute little café is run by deaf people, and instructions on the menu help you to sign your order. Serves tasty home-made baked goods (banana brioche, $3) as well as full meals. Daily 7am–4pm.

Little Garden Bar Along the riverfront T 012 427572. Khmer and Western food, including pizza, served up in a relaxing little garden patio; also has a rooftop bar. Mains $4. Daily 7am–10pm.

Rikitikitavi Along the riverfront T 017 306557. Splash out on Khmer or Western mains such as fish and chips ($5.75), sit on the polished wood patio and admire the gorgeous views. Also does take-away sandwiches and a great apple pie ($3). Daily 7am–10pm.

Rusty Keyhole Along the riverfront T 012 679607. One of the busiest places in town, with cheap and tasty salads and sandwiches ($2–4), plus Premier League football on TV. Daily 11.30am–10pm.

KEP

Some 25km southeast of Kampot, **KEP** itself may not have much of a beach, but its breezy seaside character and palm-shaded walks are seductive nonetheless. The town is renowned throughout Cambodia for its delicious, inexpensive seafood, freshly plucked from the ocean. The town was comprehensively destroyed by the Khmer Rouge, and is therefore littered with empty pre-war colonial mansions, which can give it a slightly ghostly feeling. Kep is a firm favourite with Khmer tourists who descend on the weekend, attracted by the relaxed, Riviera-style atmosphere and excellent accommodation.

Approaching Kep from Kampot, you'll go past the food stalls, round the headland and see the large Vietnamese island of **Phu Quoc** rising offshore in the Gulf of Thailand. The sovereignty of the island is still bitterly disputed, and on Kep Beach a white statue of a woman looks towards the island, as if yearning for the day when it will be returned to Cambodia.

Highlights of a trip to Kep include exploring the lush **national park** (4000 riel) rearing up behind the town, and a boat tour to one of the nearby islands. One such is quaint **Koh Tonsay** ("Rabbit Island"), whose tranquil stretch of palm-fringed beach is perfect for a day or two of relaxation. Boat trips can be arranged at any of the guesthouses in Kep or Kampot, or down on the beach in Kep (from $7 or $25 for a private charter). There are rustic bamboo cottages on the beach where you can stay for $5, and plenty of local families to cook for you.

There are almost no streetlights in Kep, so bring a torch.

ARRIVAL AND DEPARTURE

By bus A few big buses still travel via Kep from Phnom Penh to Kampot ($3), but the journey is long and circuitous. Destinations Kampot (5 daily; 45min); Phnom Penh (5 daily; 3hr).

By share taxi or minibus You'll be dropped off and picked up at Kep beach, about 1km south of the town centre where motos can take you to your guesthouse.

By moto or tuk-tuk A moto/tuk-tuk to Kampot costs $10/$15 (45min).

ACCOMMODATION

Bacoma Street 33A, 200m south of the Vishnu statue ⓣ 088 4112424, ⓦ bacoma.weebly.com. The squeaky-clean stone-walled thatched bungalows here are superb value, and set in tranquil gardens. There's also a movie hut, top food and helpful owners. Double $10

Kepmandou 200m east of Rabbit Island Pier ⓣ 097 3359982. Handy for Rabbit Island, this friendly sea-facing hostel has quirky little rooms, with or without windows, a big first-floor communal area, pool table, cinema room and simple kitchen. Double $4

Kukuluku 2km north of market roundabout on the main road ⓣ 036 6300150. Cheap fan and a/c rooms and a light, airy dorm on a small sliver of beach, with café-bar (serving yummy crêpes) and small garden with petite pool. Dorm $5, room $15

★ **Treetop Bungalows** Pepper St, off the main road just west of town ⓣ 012 51519, ⓦ keptreetop.com. The mini-village of lofty stilted bungalows feels like a childhood fantasy. It's on the hillside, with terrific sea views and surrounded by lush gardens. Double $28

EATING

Kep is heaven for the seafood connoisseur. The crab market on the western seafront is the place for crustaceans; further on, the stalls around the centre cook up grilled fish, chicken and other delights, but only during the day.

INTO VIETNAM: HA TIEN

You can hire a moto to the border crossing near Kep at Prek Chang (**Ha Tien**; daily 7am–6pm) for around $10 for the half-hour-long trip. Bear in mind that you need to be in possession of a Vietnam visa as they are not available on the spot. On the Vietnam side, you can hire a moto ($3) to either Ha Tien or Ba Hon, from where you can catch a boat to the island of Phu Quoc or a bus to Ho Chi Minh City. Tour companies and guesthouses in Kampot can arrange share taxis and minivans to do the whole journey.

Kep Lodge Pepper St, near Treetop Bungalows ⓣ 092 435330. Set in lush gardens, *Kep Lodge* has an extensive Khmer and Western menu including Swiss specialities such as röstis ($6.50) and indulgent cheese fondue ($9). Cheaper sandwiches and burgers are also available (from $3.50). You can use the pool for $5, and it's a good place for sunset cocktails. Daily 7am–10pm.

★ **Kimly** Next to the crab market. Known by locals as the pick of the crab-shacks, this is just the spot to try the local favourite, Kampot pepper crab ($7.50), and the menu is in English. Daily 9am–10pm.

Toucan Centre of the Crab Market ⓣ 097 8531057. Open late, this is the closest Kep gets to a party bar with cheap beers, tapas, pool table and over-water deck for sunset cocktails ($3.50). Daily 9am–3am.

2

Eastern Cambodia

Running south from Laos, the mighty **Mekong** forms a natural boundary between eastern Cambodia and the rest of the country. Many travellers pass through en route to or from Laos, although the attractive riverside towns of **Kompong Cham**, **Kratie** and **Stung Treng** are increasingly attracting visitors in their own right.

Stretching away to one side of the Mekong, Cambodia's remote **eastern uplands** remain stuck in their own isolated world, still largely untouched by the march of development (although the region's forests have suffered terribly from uncontrolled logging). If you like nature and wildlife, this is the place to be, and despite rampant deforestation significant patches of dense, unspoilt rainforest survive, still alive in places with rare wildlife and rushing waterfalls – although to reach them takes a certain amount of time, effort and money.

Tucked away in the far northeast, hilly **Ratanakiri** province is bordered by Vietnam to the east and Laos to the north. The upland forests here are home to around twelve distinct groups of **chunchiet** (indigenous hill tribes) who still make up a significant proportion of the population, despite the arrival of growing numbers of Khmer. The

chunchiet now forego traditional dress for modern clothing but remain among the most deprived people in Cambodia, with poor education and healthcare, and practically no way of making a living other than their traditional slash-and-burn farming.

2

South of here the province of **Mondulkiri**, in the far east of the country, bordering Vietnam, is even less developed and discovered but boasts a similar range of wild attractions including a high proportion of chunchiet, waterfalls and beautiful landscapes – its forested highlands occasionally interrupted by grassy fields and gentle hills that would look more at home in rural England. The climate is not dissimilar either: the temperature is a mere 18°C on average in the dry season, and nights can be surprisingly chilly.

During the **American War**, the eastern provinces were heavily bombed by the US to flush out the Viet Cong from the Ho Chi Minh Trail. These attempts proved largely unsuccessful, and thousands of Cambodian civilians were killed, wounded or left homeless. It was during this period that the Khmer Rouge began gathering strength and momentum in the area. Pol Pot used the remote northeastern provinces to hide from Sihanouk's troops, while receiving support from his communist brothers in the Viet Minh.

KOMPONG CHAM AND AROUND

The east's largest city and capital of the province of the same name, **KOMPONG CHAM** was one of Cambodia's largest and most cosmopolitan cities during the colonial era but is now something of a sleepy backwater – even more so since the opening of the huge Japanese-funded bridge across the Mekong rendered local ferry services obsolete. All routes into the east pass through here, and although there's no need to stop, it's a nice place to do so.

It's well worth taking a stroll along the banks of the massive Mekong, about 1.5km wide here, to look at the delightful but crumbling colonial buildings. **Wat Pra Tohm Nah Day Doh**, on the riverbank about 1km south of the bridge, also merits a visit. Fronted by a huge standing Buddha, its grounds are scattered with intriguing statues of people and animals, while a forest of miniature stupas stabs up into the sky.

Wat Nokor

The most interesting sight around town is **Wat Nokor**, about 2km north of the centre just off National Route 7. Much of the original eleventh-century temple survives, with a garishly coloured modern vihara now inserted rudely into the heart of the ancient ruins. It's an art historian's nightmare but has a certain gruesome fascination even so, with luminous modern murals and columns framed by ancient laterite walls, still showing traces of the black paint applied during the days of Khmer Rouge occupation.

Phnom Bpros and Phnom Srei

About 12km further out of town past Wat Nokor rise the twin temple hills of **Phnom Bpros** and **Phnom Srei**, "Man and Woman Mountains". According to legend, in ancient times women had to ask men to marry them. Fed up with this, the women challenged the men to see who could build the best temple by daybreak – the winners would win the right to be proposed to. When the women realized they were lagging behind, they built a huge fire, which the men took to be the rising sun. The men headed for bed while the women carried on building, producing a magnificent temple and winning the right to receive proposals.

ARRIVAL AND DEPARTURE

By bus Buses arrive and depart from their various offices in the centre of town, all within a 10min walk of the riverfront and guesthouses.

Destinations Banlung (1 daily; 9hr, $9); Kratie (5 daily; 3hr 30min); Phnom Penh (13 daily; 3hr); Siem Reap (3 daily; 5hr); Stung Treng (1 daily; 7hr).

By share taxi or minibus Taxis and minibuses are found at the market and are especially quick if heading north to Kratie and beyond.

Destinations Kratie (2hr 30min); Phnom Penh (2hr 30min); Stung Treng (6hr).

ACCOMMODATION AND EATING

There's an excellent string of tourist-oriented places to eat and drink along the riverfront. Around the market, you'll find some decent food stalls and noodle shops.

Lazy Mekong Daze Riverfront. Simple little backpacker café with a pool table serving a decent range of Asian and Western food (most mains $3.50–5) – a good place for breakfast or a sundowner, watching the sun dipping down into the Mekong. Daily 7.30am–10pm.

Mekong Crossing Riverfront ☎017 801788. Always lively, this bar-restaurant is the town's best place for a drink, either in the cosy interior or lounging on a wicker chair on the terrace outside. There's also a decent menu of Asian and Khmer staples (mains $2.50–3.50) plus pricier Western dishes. Daily 6am–10pm.

Mekong Hotel On the riverfront a short way north of the bridge ☎042 941536. The best-value accommodation in town. The large rooms (a/c $18) are beginning to show signs of age, but they're spotless, and with good views if you get one on the riverfront side. Double $8

Mekong Sunrise Riverfront ☎088 805 7407. Popular new backpacker place in a prime riverfront location. Rooms (private bathroom $3 extra, a/c $5 extra) are simple but decent value, and it's also a good place to sort out transport and tours. Tends to fill up quickly, so arrive early or reserve in advance. Double $5

Mittapheap North of the market ☎042 941565. One of the best deals in town, this friendly little hotel provides neat and clean tiled rooms with TV and fridge (a/c $6 extra). Excellent value, if you don't mind being a few minutes' walk from the river. Double $6

Smile Riverfront ☎017 997709. The top restaurant in town, run as a training centre for orphans and vulnerable children and serving up excellent Khmer food, bursting with flavour, plus a decent range of Western dishes, salads, sandwiches and snacks. Mains around $4. Daily 6am–10pm.

KRATIE AND AROUND

Life ticks by slowly in **KRATIE** (pronounced "Kracheh"). This tiny, indolent town on the Mekong is an unexpected delight, with a wonderful hotchpotch of colonial terraces and traditional old Khmer buildings – sturdy wooden structures, with dark-red roof tiles and often a decorative flourish of colour. There's not much to do in the town itself, which stretches lazily along the west bank of the river, but it makes a good base for exploring the surrounding countryside.

About 11km north of Kratie along the river is peaceful **Phnom Sambok**, a lushly forested twin-peaked hill. The dense trees hide a meditation commune and a small temple on the higher summit.

Around 10km further north along the same road, **Kampie** provides the best riverside vantage point from which to view a pod of rare freshwater **Irrawaddy dolphins**, of which it's thought that no more than a hundred remain in the Mekong. A small group of these snub-nosed dolphins lives in this area of rapids, with virtually guaranteed sightings if you take the official boat trip ($9) – although you may also be able to spot them, most distantly, from the river bank.

The easiest way to visit these places is to hire a moto ($6 return) or tuk-tuk ($12), although there is also an enjoyable cycle ride along the beautiful riverside road. If you can spare a full day, you could also include a visit to **Sambor**, some 35km north of Kratie, the site of an ancient pre-Angkorian capital (moto $12, tuk-tuk $20).

ARRIVAL AND DEPARTURE

By bus Buses stop at their various company offices along the riverside, just west of the market. Several companies run morning buses to Phnom Penh and Kompong Cham ($5), and there's a once-daily bus to Banlung ($11). Tickets can be bought from various guesthouses and restaurants around town. Note that the road between Kratie and Stung Treng is currently in a very bad state of repair.

Destinations Banlung (1 daily; 6hr); Kompong Cham (daily; 3hr 30min); Phnom Penh (5 daily; 7hr); Stung Treng (1 daily; 3hr 30min).

By share taxi or minibus Taxis will usually drop you off en route; otherwise, the transport stop is one block north of the market. Share taxis and minibuses leave from the transport stop and are the quickest way to travel between Kratie and Kompong Cham ($6), and are also quicker to Phnom Penh ($8). Heading south, some share taxis also save time by taking the rougher but much more direct route along the river via Chhlong; buses take a much more roundabout route inland via Snoul.

Destinations Banlung (5hr); Kompong Cham (2hr 30min–3hr); Phnom Penh (6hr); Sen Monorom (4hr); Stung Treng (3hr).

ACCOMMODATION

★ **Balcony** Riverfront, north of the centre ☎016 604036, Ⓦbalconyguesthouse.net. Popular guesthouse with balcony restaurant and bar overlooking the river. The spacious fan rooms come with shared or (for an extra $2) private bathroom – there are just seven rooms though, so best to book in advance. Double $6

2

Oudom Sambath Hotel Riverfront, north of the centre ☎012 965944. Large and long-established hotel, a bit worn around the edges but still pretty good value. More expensive rooms come with a/c, balconies and Mekong views. Double $7

U Hong Guesthouse (Also signed "You Hong"); North side of the market ☎012 957003. The cheapest beds in town – although rooms (fan only) are fairly basic, and those at the front can be a bit noisy. Nice restaurant and good tour and travel services. Double $5

2

U Hong II Guesthouse Riverfront ☎085 885168. Neat, clean fan rooms at competitive rates – nicer (and quieter), albeit slightly more expensive, than the original *U Hong*. There's an excellent restaurant downstairs and it's also a good place to sort out transport and tours. Double $7

EATING AND DRINKING

Snack and drink stalls set up every evening by the riverside.

Red Sun Falling Riverfront ☎011 465606. This cosy café is a great place to either start or end your day, with the best selection of Western breakfasts (carb-up with the "Super Full Monty", $6), good, cheap Asian mains ($2–2.50) plus comforting Western favourites including chicken and chips, salads and shakes. Daily 7am–9pm.

Tokae Riverfront ☎097 297 2118. Attractive little restaurant, romantically candlelit after dark, serving good breakfasts and an above-average range of Asian dishes at below-average prices (most mains $2–2.50), including a better than usual vegetarian selection. Daily 6.30am–10pm.

STUNG TRENG

For most people, **STUNG TRENG** is just a staging post on the way to Laos, but the surrounding countryside is beautiful and can be explored by boat, moto or bicycle. Hotel and guesthouse owners can arrange visits to a silk weaving centre, fruit orchards, lakes and waterfalls, and boat trips to remote villages.

One of the most popular outings is a Mekong trip to the **Laos border** (the border crossing itself is at Trapaeng Kriel), offering the possibility of some dolphin-spotting and a glimpse at the waterfalls that make the river impassable here.

ARRIVAL AND DEPARTURE

By bus All road transport arrives and leaves from the transport stop on the riverfront. Bus tickets can be bought through the Riverside Guesthouse and Ponika's Palace.

Destinations Kompong Cham (1 daily; 7hr); Kratie (3 daily; 4hr); Phnom Penh (3 daily; 10hr).

By share taxi or minibus Share taxis and pick-ups leave from the transport stop at around 7.30am and then intermittently through the day, depending on demand.

Destinations Banlung (2hr); Kompong Cham (6hr); Kratie (3hr 30min); Laos border (1hr; see box below); Phnom Penh (8hr).

ACCOMMODATION AND EATING

The market in Stung Treng is exceptional, serving delicious Khmer food of the type people cook at home; throughout the day and into the evening, you can fill up easily for around $1.

Ponika's Palace Just northeast of the market ☎012 916441. There's nothing particularly palatial about this simple little family-run, tourist-oriented café, offering economical Khmer food (mains $3–4) and more expensive Western dishes. Decent Western breakfasts too, plus baguettes, burgers, pancakes and the like. Daily 6am–10pm.

Riverside Guesthouse By the transport stop ☎012 439454. The epicentre of Stung Treng's very modest travellers' scene. The best of the bright, clean rooms (a/c $6 extra) are at the front, though they're not for light sleepers as they overlook the transport stop. Owner Mr T is a great source of information about local tours and onward travel. The passable café downstairs has a big, traveller-friendly menu featuring lots of Asian mains ($3–3.50) and Western

INTO LAOS: TRAPAENG KRIEL–DONG KALAW

Cambodia's only border crossing into Laos is at Trapaeng Kriel, 57km north of Stung Treng. The road to the border is in good condition, with the journey taking just over 1hr. The border itself is open daily 7am–5pm; Laos visas (roughly $30–40 depending on nationality) are issued on the spot if you don't have one already. Several companies run through-buses from Cambodia to destinations in Laos including Don Det (around $15) and Pakse ($17), while some minibuses also cover the same routes. Tickets for buses and minibuses can be bought at guesthouses in Stung Treng, Banlung and elsewhere.

Entering Cambodia, visas are issued on arrival (roughly $30–40, depending on your nationality). If you're not arriving on a through-bus, there's onward transport in shared taxis and minibuses from the border to Stung Treng, and possibly further south to Kratie, Kompong Cham and even Phnom Penh depending on how early and how lucky you get.

staples – baguettes, pancakes, spaghetti and so on (daily 6.30am–10.30pm). Double $6

Tonle Guesthouse 500m west of town on the riverfront ⓣ 092 674990. In an attractive modern villa set in a shady garden, this guesthouse serves as a vocational tourism training centre for disadvantaged local youngsters. The four simply furnished but comfortable rooms (fan only) open onto an airy communal lounge. Bathrooms are shared and meals are available but need to be pre-booked. Double $8

BANLUNG AND AROUND

The sprawling town of **Banlung**, almost 600km northeast of Phnom Penh, only became the provincial capital in 1979, replacing the Khmer Rouge capital of Voen Sai (which had in turn replaced Lumphat, which had been devastated by American bombs). The town is a good base for trips and treks into the surrounding area to visit chunchiet villages and the forests of the nearby Virachey National Park.

WHAT TO SEE AND DO

2

Banlung may be the provincial capital, but not a lot happens here. At its heart is the **market**, especially lively in the early morning when local chunchiet come in to sell fresh produce and forest foods, setting out their produce on the pavement in front of the market building.

Yeak Laom Lake

Banlung's best-known sight is the dramatic **Yeak Laom Lake**, 4km east of town ($5 return by moto), created by a

volcanic eruption many thousands of years ago. It's a 3km walk around the beautiful lakeside path, through stands of bamboo and dense green forest, the tranquillity interrupted only by the occasional bird call. A swim in the clean, turquoise waters is a good way to cleanse yourself of the penetrating dust from Banlung's red dirt roads.

2

Phnom Svay

On the western edge of Banlung, the easy ten-minute climb up **Phnom Svay**, behind the pretty **Wat Eisay Patamak**, is well worth it for the glorious views of the O Traw Mountains. All of this is lost on the 5m-long Reclining Buddha, which lies at the summit, his eyes closed.

The waterfalls

East of Banlung the countryside is dotted with a trio of impressive waterfalls: Ka Chhang and Katieng (roughly 4km from Banlung), and Chha Ong (8km from Banlung). At **Chha Ong**, water sprays from a rock overhang into a small jungle clearing. There's nowhere to swim, but brave visitors shower under the smaller column of water. **Ka Chhang** and **Katieng** are pretty but rather less impressive, although elephants are available for short rides (around $10/hr).

ARRIVAL AND DEPARTURE

All road transport arrives at the transport stop near the market; National Route 78 from the junction at O Pong Moan just south of Stung Treng has been upgraded and is now in superb condition (although the road between Kratie and O Pong Moan is in contrastingly poor nick). Hotel and guesthouses are the best places for sorting out onward transport. Share taxis and pick-ups ($3) make the trip between Banlung and Voen Sai (1hr) from the transport stop when full.

By bus There are very few buses to or from Banlung – most transport is by minibus or shared taxi.

Destinations Kompong Cham (1 daily; 6hr); Kratie (1 daily; 4hr); Phnom Penh (1 daily; 9–10hr).

By share taxi and minibus Transport goes to Stung Treng ($7) and then on to Kratie (another $6).

Destinations Kratie (4hr); Stung Treng (2hr).

By motorbike Some intrepid travellers are biking around this corner of the country. It's the only way of getting to Sen Monorom from Banlung (9hr) – dry season only. You can rent a bike or hire a driver; enquire at *Treetop Eco Lodge* or local tour operators.

ACCOMMODATION

Backpacker Pad Between the town centre and Boeung Kansaing ⓣ092 785 259, ⓔbanlungbackpackerpad@yahoo.com. On a dusty back road between town and lake, this is Banlung's last resort for die-hard budget travellers, with super-cheap accommodation in poky little windowless box rooms (en suite for an extra $1) or an even cheaper dorm. Plus points include the free wi-fi and pool table, and it's also a good place to arrange trips, bus tickets and bike rental. Dorm $2, double $4

★**Tree Top Eco Lodge** ⓣ012 490333, ⓦtreetop-ecolodge.com. Banlung's most original place to stay, with accommodation in bungalows scattered across a thickly wooded hillside and connected by a picturesque network of raised walkways. The bungalows themselves (all en suite, fan only) are fairly basic, although the stone-pebbled bathrooms are a nice touch. More expensive ones have hot water, and some also have nice balconies with hammocks to loll in. There's also a restaurant and free wi-fi, and staff can arrange tours and onward travel. Double $7

Tribal West of the centre ⓣ075 650 8555, ⓦtribalhotel.ekhmerbuys.com. Long-running Banlung institution, although now somewhat past its best. The wood-panelled rooms are spacious but a bit gloomy (and could be cleaner), although perfectly OK for the price (a/c $12). The attractive attached restaurant is a major plus, and staff can also sort out transport and tours. Double $7

Yaklom Hill Lodge 6km east of town, beyond the Hill Tribe Monument ⓣ011 790510, ⓦyaklom.blogspot.co.uk. For real isolation this eco-resort is hard to beat, with fifteen stilted wooden bungalows dotted amid jungly grounds. Rooms (fan only) are simply but nicely furnished, although there are communal showers only, and the electricity goes off nightly at 9pm. B&B $15

★TREAT YOURSELF

Terres Rouges Lodge Boeung Kansaing ⓣ012 770650, ⓦratanakiri-lodge.com. Luxurious guesthouse in lush gardens near the lake. The lodge's wooden buildings look a bit like a miniature Khmer village given a chic modern makeover, with standard rooms in the main building, plus more luxurious accommodation in private bungalows arranged around a beautiful garden. Rooms (all a/c) are individually decorated with traditional fabrics and artefacts. There's also a good restaurant and a decent-sized pool, plus a small spa. Double $52

EATING

A'Dam East of the centre ⓣ 012 411115. This little pavilion restaurant is generally quiet (sometimes bordering on comatose), but the food more than compensates, with a good selection of fresh and flavoursome Chinese dishes, plus a few Thai and Khmer options (mains $2.50–3). Daily 8am–10pm.

Café Alee East of the centre. The newest kid on the Banlung block, with a telephone directory-sized menu stuffed with all the usual Western and Khmer favourites (mains $2.50–4) – from cookies and fruit bread through to pancakes and popcorn, plus an interesting selection of local coffees. Doubles as the office of DutchCo (see below) in the evenings. Daily 7am until late.

Gecko House East of the centre ⓣ 012 422228. In a kind of jungle lodge-style thatched construction, *Gecko* is usually the liveliest place, and can get a bit of a party atmosphere if there are enough trekkers in town. The big menu features Thai, Khmer Western and Chinese options (mains $4–5.50), although the slightly above-average prices aren't always reflected in the quality. Daily 8am–11pm.

DIRECTORY

Banks and exchange There are ATMs at the Canadia Bank (Visa and MasterCard) and Acleda Bank (Visa only) in the centre of town.

Internet Try Srey Mon Internet Café, near the *Tribal Hotel*, or the well-equipped GreenNet close by on the side road just before *A'Dam* restaurant. Both charge $1/hr and are open from around 9am to 9pm.

VOEN SAI AND VIRACHEY NATIONAL PARK

The road north of Banlung winds its way past numerous chunchiet villages until, after around 38km, it reaches the village of **VOEN SAI**, located on the San River, the headquarters of Virachey National Park and one of the most accessible villages in the region.

Covering more than 800,000 acres, **Virachey National Park** is a haven for a variety of endangered species, including deer, rare hornbills, and kouprey, the almost-extinct jungle cow; tigers are also said to lurk here, although most sightings appear to have occurred after a few too many bottles of Angkor beer. The only way of getting into the park is on one of the various **treks** (1–7 nights) organized through the park headquarters in Banlung, northeast of the market (daily 8–11am & 2–5pm in theory, assuming there's someone around to sit behind the desk; ⓣ 075 974013, ⓔ virachey@camintel.com). Prices start from around $90 per person per night for the short treks in a group of two, falling to as little as $40 per night in larger groups on longer treks. All treks feature a visit to a chunchiet village, a night or two in a hammock and a ride downriver on a bamboo raft. Excellent (and relatively affordable) treks and other trips in and around the park are also run by **DutchCo**, (c/o *Café Alee* ⓣ 017 571682, ⓦ EcotourismCambodia.info).

2

Voen Sai itself is home to an unusual mix of **ethnic minorities**, predominantly Lao and Chinese, but also Kreung. A small boat (2000 riel) connects Voen Sai with villages on the opposite bank – to the right, there is a small Lao settlement, and to the left a Chinese community. It's best to visit these places with a local guide, as you'll need someone to act as an interpreter and smooth the way. The easiest way to get to **Voen Sai** is to rent a moto from Banlung (around $12).

SEN MONOROM AND AROUND

The smallest of all Cambodia's provincial capitals, **SEN MONOROM** (420km from Phnom Penh), is slowly coming onto the tourist radar, and has a surprisingly good selection of places to stay and eat. It's a friendly little place, too, with a small-town atmosphere, and makes a good base from which to explore the surrounding countryside and chunchiet villages.

WHAT TO SEE AND DO

Locals will direct you to the **Monorom Falls** (Sihanouk Falls), a peaceful nook on the edge of the jungle where a 10m-high cascade of water drops into a swirling plunge pool. You can either walk the few kilometres here or hire a moto along the easy road. The path ends at the top of the waterfall, where brave (and possibly stupid) souls hurl themselves into the deep water during the rainy season. The more distant but spectacular **Bou Sraa Falls**, about 40km northeast from Sen Monorom, can be reached by moto by

way of a stunningly beautiful forest trail. The falls themselves are a dramatic two-tiered affair, with more than 30m of water gushing into a jungle-clad gorge.

There are hundreds of chunchiet villages around Sen Monorom, but some are not keen on foreign visitors, so it's best to take a local as a guide and interpreter. One of the largest and easiest villages to access is **Phulung** (about 8km north of Sen Monorom), inhabited by Bunong, the majority chunchiet group in Mondulkiri. The curious huts have woven wooden walls and thatched roofs almost to the floor. Three or more families often live in one hut, but you'll be lucky to see more than a handful of people during daytime, as they're out working in the fields.

2

Phulung is also the starting point for half- or full-day **elephant treks** ($15/30), which you can arrange through guesthouses in Sen Monorom. More memorable (and humane) interactions can be had at the pioneering **Elephant Valley Project** (10km northwest of Sen Monorom; day-visit $70, or $40 including a half day's volunteer work; longer visits also available; ⓣ099 696041, ⓦelephantvalleyproject.org), offering the chance to walk with elephants and observe them in their natural habitat – but not to ride them.

ARRIVAL AND DEPARTURE

Sen Monorom lies on a side road which branches off the main highway at Snoul. You might be encouraged to buy a ticket to Snoul and pick up onward transport from there, although this is very hit and miss, and you might end up hanging around for hours, or even possibly overnight.

By bus There are a couple of buses daily between Sen Monorom and Phnom Penh ($12) via Kompong Cham, run by Phnom Penh Sorya and Rith Mony.

Destinations Kompong Cham (4hr 30min); Phnom Penh (8hr).

By share taxi or pick-up These run either direct from Phnom Penh (7hr; $15) or Kompong Cham (4hr). You will get *very* dusty in a pick-up, unless you sit in the cab.

INFORMATION

To see most sights, you'll need to engage the help of a guide. You can book reliable guides at your guesthouse or at the tourist office behind the post office (the white building just off the airstrip). They don't come cheap, though, starting at around $25/day. Another good place to get local information is at *Green House*, next to the market (ⓣ017 905659, ⓦgreenhouse-tour.blogspot.co.uk). Staff here can organize guides, and can also arrange rental of 250cc trail bikes for $15/day. Expect to pay $25 for a moto for the return trip to Bou Sraa.

ACCOMMODATION

★**Nature Lodge** 2km north of town ⓣ012 230272, ⓦnaturelodgecambodia.com. Idyllic little eco-lodge, tucked away in a valley north of town, with accommodation in wooden cabins (fan and hot water) dotted amid the trees, plus a rustic little restaurant, bar and library. Double $10

Phanyro 500m from town (coming from Phnom Penh turn right opposite the *Pich Kiri* guesthouse) ⓣ017 770867. Attractive guesthouse with accommodation in a cluster of neat bungalows (with fan and hot water) lined up on a hill just outside town. Popular with visiting NGOs, so it's worth booking ahead. Double $7

Pich Kiri On the uphill stretch on the way into town just east of the market ⓣ012 932102. Sen Monorom's longest-running guesthouse; the cheapest rooms are slightly musty with fan and cold water only; plusher rooms in the classy new block ($15) come with a/c and hot water. There's also a great restaurant and leafy garden. Double $6

EATING

Banana's 500m down the hill east of the market ⓣ092 412680. This Dutch-owned place is the classiest of Sen Monorom's modest selection of restaurants, set in a mini-jungle by the river and serving up good Western food ranging from schnitzels to coq au vin. The food isn't cheap (mains around $7), but servings are generous and the quality's high. Daily 9am–10pm.

Khmer Kitchen Off the main road in the centre of town, within sight of the bus stop along from *Green House*. The Khmer barbecue, where you can choose from fish, chicken or beef with salad and rice, costs $5. Daily 8am–9pm.

Mondulkiri Pizza Behind the hospital ⓣ0975 222219. Recently opened restaurant in a cute little bamboo building with a lively atmosphere and the best pizza (around $5) you could reasonably expect in the wilds of Mondulkiri. Daily 10am–9pm.

Sovannkiri Just south of the centre on the main road (NH76) to Kompong Cham ⓣ097 474 4528. Australian-Khmer-run place with a great selection of local and Western dishes including good burgers and steaks, plus cheap beer. Mains $2–6. Daily 8am–10pm.

DIRECTORY

Banks and exchange There's an ATM at the Acleda Bank (Visa only) opposite *Green House*.

SUNSET FROM VICTORIA PEAK

Hong Kong & Macau

HIGHLIGHTS

❶ **Victoria Peak** Take the Peak Tram and admire Hong Kong's skyline from above. **See p.135**

❷ **Star Ferry** The cheapest tour of Victoria Harbour is on one of Hong Kong's iconic ferries. **See p.137**

❸ **Outlying Islands** Visit the world's largest seated Buddha and go hiking. **See p.141**

❹ **Dining scene** Gorge yourself on any cuisine imaginable in Kowloon and Central. **See p.147**

❺ **Macau Tower** Go bungee jumping from Macau's highest vantage point. **See p.154**

❻ **Macanese Food** Try the Portuguese classics with a Chinese twist. **See p.157**

HIGHLIGHTS ARE MARKED ON THE MAP ON P.121 & P.150

ROUGH COSTS

Daily budget Basic US$35, occasional treat US$60

Food Noodle soup, fried rice US$5–7

Drink Tsingtao US$5.50–7

Hostel/budget hotel US$20/65

Travel Bus: Central–Stanley US$1.10–1.40; MTR: Tsim Sha Tsui–Central US$1.10

FACT FILE

Population 7.072 million in Hong Kong; 591,900 in Macau

Language Cantonese and English in Hong Kong; Cantonese and some Portuguese in Macau

Currency Hong Kong dollar (HK$); pataca (MOP$) in Macau

International phone code ☎852 in Hong Kong (☎01 from Macau); ☎853 in Macau

Time zone GMT + 8hr

Introduction

An extraordinary, vibrant and crowded territory of more than seven million people, Hong Kong is undoubtedly one of the world's great cities. The view of Hong Kong Island's skyscrapers from across the harbour is one of the most stunning urban panoramas on earth, and this insomniac metropolis buzzes with a contagious energy day and night. Varied and dynamic, Hong Kong is many places to many people: traditional temples with smouldering incense and fortune-tellers; rugged rural escapism with waterfalls and pristine beaches; and a vibrant eating and drinking scene, from streetside noodle shacks to Michelin-starred haute cuisine. Its compact size and enviably efficient transport system make it perfect for a brief stopoff, but there's more than enough to keep you hooked for weeks. Tiny Macau offers similar contrasts, with a unique fusion of Portuguese and Chinese architecture and traditions firmly resisting the ever-increasing number of glitzy casinos.

Since their **handover** to China, in 1997 for Hong Kong and 1999 for Macau, the people of both cities have found themselves in a unique position: subject to the ultimate rule of Beijing, they live in a semi-democratic capitalist enclave – a "Special Administrative Region (SAR) of China". Hong Kong's per capita **GNP** doubled in the first decade of Chinese rule yet the inequality of incomes is staggering: the conspicuous consumption of the few hundred super-rich (all Cantonese), for which Hong Kong is famous, tends to mask the fact that most people work long hours and live in crowded, tiny apartments. There is a lot of wealth, but Hong Kong is also vastly more expensive than its Southeast Asian neighbours.

Sixty kilometres west from Hong Kong across the Pearl River Delta, the tiny former Portuguese trading enclave of **Macau** may seem a geographic and economic midget compared to its high-rise cousin but it's catching up quickly. Macau is booming like never before – thanks largely to a recent, rapid and vast expansion of gambling in the territory. Development has already changed the character of this formerly sleepy colonial backwater beyond recognition (and construction of a land link to Hong Kong – a series of bridges and tunnels – due to be completed in 2016, is well under way), but old Macau is still very much in evidence and the historic centre boasts UNESCO World Heritage status. With a colonial past pre-dating that of Hong Kong by nearly three hundred years, Macau's historic buildings – from old fortresses to Baroque churches to faded mansion houses – are plentiful, and almost every

WHEN TO GO

Hong Kong and Macau's **climate** is subtropical. The best time to visit is between October and April, when the weather is cooler, humidity levels drop and the flowers are in bloom. Between December and February, it can get quite cool but the skies are generally clear. The temperature and humidity start to pick up in mid-April, and between late June and early September readings of 30°C and 95 percent humidity or more are the norm. During typhoon season, from May to September, ferry and airline timetables can be disrupted by bad weather. If a category T8 typhoon is on its way, offices and shops will close and public transport will shut down. Fortunately, typhoons usually don't last too long.

tiny backstreet holds a surprise. South of the main city, on **Taipa** and **Coloane**, are beaches, parks and quiet villages where you can sample a unique cuisine blending Asian, European and African influences.

CHRONOLOGY

HONG KONG

4000–2500 BC The earliest inhabitants of the Hong Kong area are Neolithic hunter-gatherers and fishermen.

214 BC Region is conquered by Chinese emperor Qin Shi Huang and incorporated into imperial China for the first time.

1000–1400 AD The Five Clans – Tang, Hau, Pang, Liu and Man – build their walled villages in what is now the New Territories.

1557 Dutch and French traders come to the region, following the Portuguese traders in Macau.

1683 British East India Company establishes a base in China's Guangzhou province, and trades for silk, porcelain and tea.

1773 British shiploads of opium arrive from India and demand for the drug explodes in China.

1839 The first Opium War starts. Commissioner of Guangzhou, Lin Zexu, forces the British to surrender their opium, before ceremonially burning it.

1840 A naval expeditionary force is dispatched from London; it blockades ports and seizes assets up and down the Chinese coast for a year.

1841 British naval landing party plants the Union Jack at Possession Point on Hong Kong Island.

1842 The Treaty of Nanking cedes to Britain "in perpetuity" a small offshore island called Hong Kong, opens five ports to foreign trade, abolishes the monopoly system of trade and exempts British nationals from Chinese law.

1856–1860 Second Opium War: after more blockades and a march on Beijing, China cedes Britain the Kowloon peninsula and Stonecutters Island.

1898 As the Qing dynasty declines, Britain secures a 99-year lease on one thousand square kilometres of land north of Kowloon, known as the New Territories.

1907 The drug trade is voluntarily dropped as Hong Kong merchants switch from trade to manufacturing.

1941–45 Japanese forces occupy Hong Kong along with the rest of eastern China.

1949 As mainland China falls to the communists, many merchants, particularly from Shanghai, move to Hong Kong.

1966–67 With the Cultural Revolution in full flow on the mainland, pro-Red Guard riots break out in Hong Kong. However, there is little support from Mao's regime and they fizzle out.

1984 The Sino-British Joint Declaration is signed. Britain agrees to relinquish the territory as long as Hong Kong maintains a capitalist system for at least fifty years.

1988 The Basic Law is published as the constitutional framework for the one country, two systems policy.

1989 The Tiananmen Square massacre occurs in Beijing. In the biggest demonstration in Hong Kong in modern times, a million people take to the streets in protest.

1992 Chris Patten becomes the last Governor and introduces a series of reforms, including increasing the voting franchise for the 1995 Legislative Council elections (Legco) from 200,000 to 2.7 million people.

1997 Britain hands Hong Kong over to China. Beijing disbands Legco, and Tung Chee Hwa, a shipping billionaire, becomes the first Chief Executive of the Hong Kong Special Administrative Region (SAR) of the People's Republic of China. Within days, the Asian Financial Crisis begins and Hong Kong's economy goes into recession.

2003 The SARS outbreak causes widespread panic and disruption, and leads to just under three hundred deaths.

July 1, 2003 500,000 protestors take to the streets against a proposed anti-subversion bill, Article 23, that will restrict civil liberties; in September the bill is withdrawn.

March 2005 Chief Executive Tung Chee Hwa resigns; Donald Tsang succeeds him.

2007 Hong Kong's first contested election for Chief Executive is won by Tsang.

August 2008 Beijing hosts the Summer Olympics; the equestrian events are held in Hong Kong.

2008 Beijing rules out direct democratic elections until at least 2017.

December 2009 Hong Kong hosts the East Asian Games.

2010 Formal talks held between Chinese officials and the Opposition Democratic Party – habitually hostile to Beijing – are the first since the 1997 handover.

September 2012 More than one hundred thousand protestors turn out for the anti-national education protests.

MACAU

500 AD Macau is part of the Maritime Silk Road between Guangzhou and Southeast Asia.

1513 The Portuguese arrive in China's Pearl River Delta.

1557 The Portuguese persuade local Chinese officials to rent them a strategically placed peninsula at the mouth of the delta, known as Macao, which means "the goddess of the sea". As the only foreigners permitted to trade with China, the Portuguese become sole agents for merchants across a whole swathe of east Asia and grow immensely wealthy.

1641 The Portuguese lose Melaka in Malaysia to the Dutch; Macau's trading links are cut and its fortunes wane.

1842 Once the British have claimed Hong Kong to the east, Macau's status as a backwater is definitively settled.

1847 Licensed gambling is introduced as a desperate means of securing some kind of income.

1848–1870s Macau is the centre of the "coolie" slave trade, with slave ships departing for South America with slaves kidnapped in southern China.

1851 & 1864 Portugal occupies Taipa and Coloane.

1966 Violent riots erupt, but China does not want the Portuguese to leave due to potential economic shock to Hong Kong.

1974 Fascist dictatorship ends in Portugal, and all Portuguese colonies are relinquished, but China turns down the Portuguese offer to leave Macau.

1984 After agreement with Britain over Hong Kong, China agrees to negotiate the return of Macau as well.

1987 The Sino-Portuguese Joint Declaration is signed, making Macau a "Special Administrative Region" (SAR) of China, effectively a semi-democratic capitalist enclave subject to Beijing.

1999 China assumes formal sovereignty of Macau; it is the last European colony in Asia to be handed back.

2002 Hong Kong tycoon Stanley Ho's monopoly on casinos ends and Macau's gambling industry booms as mainlanders are given greater freedom to travel.

2004 The opening of Las Vegas Sands Casino ushers in a new style of super casino, and a new era of increased foreign investment.

December 2009 Macau celebrates its tenth anniversary of reunification with China.

2013 Macau holds a legislative election, with the pan-democracy AMN party receiving the most votes.

ARRIVAL

Hong Kong can be reached by land, sea or air. It is a major regional hub for flights from the US, Europe and Asia. **Trains** from Guangzhou, Beijing and Shanghai in China arrive at Hung Hom station on the Kowloon peninsula. You can take a bus from here to eastern Hong Kong Island, or else to the Star Ferry terminus, where you can catch a ferry over to Central on Hong Kong Island.

Boats from mainland China and Macau arrive at the China Ferry Terminal on Canton Road, in downtown Kowloon. Ferries from Macau also arrive at the Hong Kong–Macau Ferry Terminal in Sheung Wan, just west of Central on Hong Kong Island. From here you can catch a bus, underground train or tram to other parts of Hong Kong.

Hong Kong international **airport** (hkairport.com) is situated on Lantau Island. It is linked to Hong Kong Island and Kowloon by the high-speed Airport Express train and buses. There are direct bus services from the airport to Shenzhen and Guangzhou in mainland China, as well as cities in the Pearl River

delta, the latter also served by fast Skypier ferry connections.

You can also fly directly to Macau (see p.156).

VISAS

Most nationalities need only a valid passport to enter **Hong Kong**, although the length of stay varies. British citizens get 180 days, whereas citizens of the EU, Canada, Australia, New Zealand and the US can stay for up to 90 days, and South Africans are allowed 30 days. Check the latest visa requirements at ⓦimmd.gov.hk. The easiest way to **extend your stay** is to go to Macau and come back.

To enter **Macau**, citizens of the EU, Australia, New Zealand, South Africa, Canada, and the US need only a valid passport and can stay for a period between 30 and 90 days. The simplest way to **extend your stay** is to go to Hong Kong and re-enter Macau at a later date.

GETTING AROUND

Hong Kong's public transport system is efficient, extensive and inexpensive, although crowded during rush hour. The MTR (Mass Transit Railway) system – overground, underground and light rail – and the main bus routes are easy to use. Few taxi drivers are fluent in English, however, so get someone to write down your destination in Chinese characters.

For details of public transport in Macau, see later in the chapter (p.157).

ACCOMMODATION

Hong Kong has plenty of budget accommodation, most of which is located in Kowloon. The lion's share of the budget market is taken up by **guesthouses** – flats converted to hold as many tiny private rooms (singles, doubles, triples and quads) as possible. These typically come with equally tiny bathrooms where you can shower while sitting on the loo, a/c, TVs, kettles and telephones. Tall Westerners may discover that the majority of beds will be too short for them. Solo travellers won't have trouble finding rooms, but may find that the price of a single is mostly more than half the price of a double. Doubles cost around HK$450–700, while singles range from HK$200–420. The majority of these guesthouses are located in high-rises, the names of which tend to end with "…Mansions" and thus unrealistically raise your expectations.

An alternative is to stay in **youth hostels**, most of which are also located in high-rises, though you do get a few in more peaceful, out-of-the-way locations. These typically come with common area, lockers, and a plethora of information on the city. Dorm prices can be as low as HK$140. Free wi-fi is found in all accommodation reviewed.

Accommodation in **Macau** is generally more expensive, as there is a dearth of cheap lodgings, and tends to consist of guesthouses rather than hostels. As most cater for mainland tourists, many won't speak English, making it difficult to book some of them in advance. Prices often shoot up at weekends. To get the best rates for many guesthouses, book your room through an external website and, if possible, in advance.

3

FOOD AND DRINK

One of the great culinary capitals of the world, Hong Kong offers not only superb, native Cantonese cooking but the full gamut of regional Chinese cuisines and perhaps the widest range of international restaurants of any city outside Europe or North America. This is due in part to the cosmopolitan nature of the population, but also, perhaps more importantly, to the incredible seriousness attached to dining by the local Chinese. Hong Kong residents eat out regularly, and foodie culture thrives.

In Macau, Macanese food is a tempting blend of Portuguese and Asian, and Portuguese and Chinese restaurants also abound. In both Hong Kong and Macau, the **water** is fit for drinking.

HONG KONG

As well as the joys of *dim sum* – a Hong Kong speciality meaning "little eats", and other Cantonese dishes – the city offers

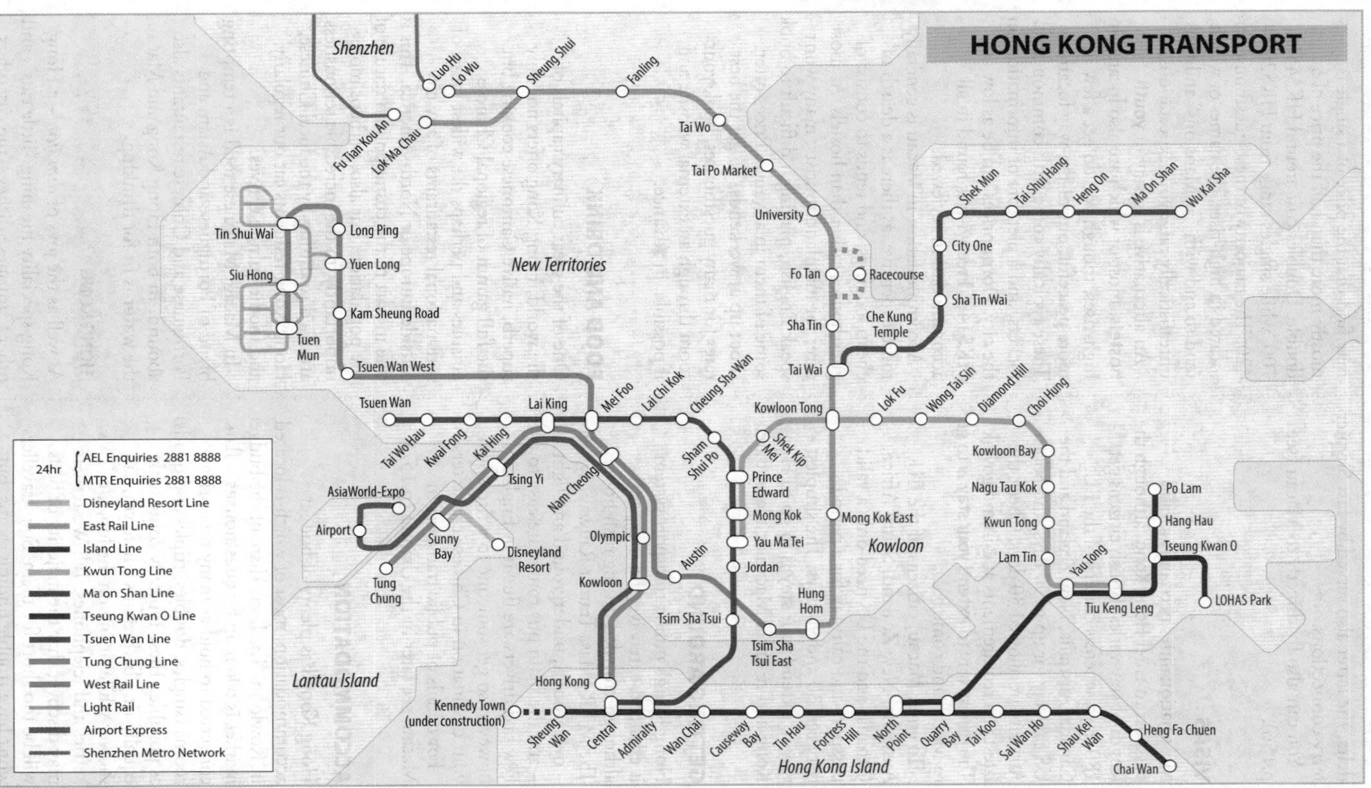
HONG KONG TRANSPORT
Shenzhen
Luo Hu
Lo Wu
Sheung Shui
Fanling
Fu Tian Kou An
Lok Ma Chau
Tai Wo
Tai Po Market
University
Fo Tan
Racecourse
Sha Tin
Tai Wai
Shek Mun
Tai Shui Hang
Heng On
Ma On Shan
Wu Kai Sha
City One
Sha Tin Wai
Che Kung Temple
Tin Shui Wai
Long Ping
Yuen Long
Siu Hong
Kam Sheung Road
Tuen Mun
Tsuen Wan West
New Territories
Tsuen Wan
Tai Wo Hau
Kwai Fong
Kwai Hing
Lai King
Mei Foo
Lai Chi Kok
Cheung Sha Wan
Sham Shui Po
Shek Kip Mei
Kowloon Tong
Lok Fu
Wong Tai Sin
Diamond Hill
Choi Hung
Kowloon Bay
Nagu Tau Kok
Kwun Tong
Lam Tin
Yau Tong
Tiu Keng Leng
Po Lam
Hang Hau
Tseung Kwan O
LOHAS Park
Tsing Yi
Nam Cheong
AsiaWorld-Expo
Airport
Sunny Bay
Disneyland Resort
Tung Chung
Olympic
Kowloon
Austin
Prince Edward
Mong Kok
Yau Ma Tei
Jordan
Mong Kok East
Kowloon
Hung Hom
Tsim Sha Tsui
Tsim Sha Tsui East
Lantau Island
Hong Kong
Kennedy Town (under construction)
Sheung Wan
Central
Admiralty
Wan Chai
Causeway Bay
Tin Hau
Fortress Hill
North Point
Quarry Bay
Tai Koo
Sai Wan Ho
Shau Kei Wan
Heng Fa Chuen
Chai Wan
Hong Kong Island
24hr AEL Enquiries 2881 8888
MTR Enquiries 2881 8888
Disneyland Resort Line
East Rail Line
Island Line
Kwun Tong Line
Ma on Shan Line
Tseung Kwan O Line
Tsuen Wan Line
Tung Chung Line
West Rail Line
Light Rail
Airport Express
Shenzhen Metro Network

everything from fiery Sichuan cookery to veggie-friendly Yunnan cuisine. You'll also find excellent Indian and Malaysian curry houses, sushi bars, Vietnamese, Italian, French and Korean restaurants, British pub-style food and varied cheap **street stalls** (*dai pai dongs*). All budgets are catered for; many restaurants also offer limited lunchtime menus which are half the price of eating out at dinnertime. English or picture **menus** are widely available. Most restaurants will add a ten percent **service charge** to your bill.

The kind of **snacks** you'll find at the *dai pai dongs* and many indoor food halls and canteens (called *cha chan tengs*) include seafood, noodle soups, *congee* (savoury rice porridge) and buns stuffed with *char siu* pork, and shouldn't cost more than HK$50 for a large meal. **Milk tea** (black tea with evaporated or condensed milk strained through a large "tea sock") is a signature Hong Kong beverage and most street stalls sell this steaming brew from dawn.

The most common Chinese food in Hong Kong is **Cantonese**, from China's southern Guangdong province. Dishes consist of extremely fresh food, quickly cooked and only lightly seasoned. Popular ingredients are fruit and vegetables, fish and shellfish, though the cuisine is also known for more unusual ingredients such as fish maw and chicken's feet.

Beijing cuisine is heavier than Cantonese, based around a solid diet of wheat and millet buns, noodles, pancakes and dumplings, accompanied by dark soy sauce and bean paste, white onions and cabbage. Mongol and Muslim influences include hotpots and grilled roast meats.

Shanghai cuisine is characterized by delicate forms and light, fresh, sweet flavours, sometimes to the point of becoming precious – tiny meatballs steamed in a rice coating are known as "pearls".

Szechuan food is the antithesis of Shanghai cuisine. Szechuan peppercorns, chillies, garlic, ginger and spring onions are used heavily, and cooking processes include techniques such as dry frying and smoking.

DIM SUM

A veritable institution, *dim sum* is a breakfast or midday meal consisting of small savoury buns, dumplings, pancakes and other small dishes, all washed down with copious amounts of jasmine tea. Traditionally these delicious eats are wheeled through the restaurant on trolleys, with punters choosing whichever takes their fancy. There are only a couple trolley *dim sum* places left in Hong Kong, one of which is *Lin Heung Tea House* (see p.147). Most dishes cost HK$13–50 and dumplings and buns usually come in portions of three or four.

Yunnan cuisine utilizes some unusual ingredients, such as the blossoms and shoots of numerous plants, plenty of vegetables and herbs; expect the likes of pineapple rice, tofu with jasmine blossoms and chicken steamed in a pot with tonics and herbs.

In most Chinese restaurants, the usual **drink** with your meal is **jasmine tea**, often brought to your table as a matter of course. **Beer** is also popular. All restaurants and bars are non-smoking.

Drinking in bars can be expensive, so it's best to make good use of happy hours to avoid drifting into insolvency. Choose your poison – from a vast selection of bottled lagers (including Chinese Tsingtao), imported brews, wine and cocktails. Bars stay open until 2 or 3am.

MACAU

The Portuguese elements of **Macanese food** include fresh bread, cheap imported wine and good coffee, as well as an array of dishes ranging from *caldo verde* (vegetable soup) to *bacalhau* (dried salted cod). One of Macau's most interesting Portuguese colonial dishes is **African chicken**, a concoction of Goan and east African influences, comprising chicken grilled with peppers and spices. Macau is also justly acknowledged for the exceptional quality of its sweet, flaky custard tarts or *natas*. Straightforward **Cantonese restaurants**, often serving *dim sum* for breakfast and lunch, are also plentiful.

Most restaurants in Macau don't open as late as they do in Hong Kong – although bars do. If you want to eat later than 10pm, you'll probably end up either in a hotel (many of which have 24hr coffee bars that also serve snacks) or in the NAPE (Novos Aterros do Porto Exterior) bar-restaurant area.

Drinking here is not quite as expensive as in Hong Kong, but not far off. Most drinking takes place in the casinos, and bars can often feel very empty even at weekends, although some stay open till dawn.

3

CULTURE AND ETIQUETTE

Generally speaking, Hong Kong and Macau people are not as concerned as other Asian cultures about covering the skin – girls often wear skirts as short as those in the West. However, **bathing topless** on any of Hong Kong's beaches is illegal. To avoid faux pas, point with your palm rather than your index finger, avoid wearing white in a social setting as it's the colour of mourning, and don't feel obliged to leave a tip (though some restaurants add 10 percent gratuity to the bill). If you're invited to someone's house, bring a gift (not a clock or anything in a set of four – a very unlucky number) and present it with both hands. If you're given a gift, refuse it first before accepting, as accepting straight away makes you look greedy. If out to dinner with Hong Kongers, don't take the last bit of food on a serving plate, which is considered impolite.

SPORTS AND ACTIVITIES

Hong Kong residents in particular are keen sporting spectators. **Horse racing**, inseparable from gambling and therefore illegal in mainland China, is a popular pastime, and both Sha Tin and Happy Valley racecourses have weekly meets during the season (see p.133). The other huge sporting draw is the **Rugby Sevens**, which takes place over three days at the end of March. As the name implies, teams have seven players instead of fifteen, and this international tournament has become a major fixture in Hong Kong's calendar.

Hong Kong also offers some amazing opportunities for **outdoor activities**, from hiking and scuba diving to windsurfing on the tiny island of Cheung Chau. For those seeking more extreme activities, the Macau Tower offers the highest commercial **bungee** platform in the world (see p.154).

COMMUNICATIONS

From Hong Kong, **airmail** takes three days to a week to reach Europe or North America; from Macau between five days and a week.

Local calls from private phones in **Hong Kong** are free, public **phones** are cheap (HK$1 for 5 minutes) and **phonecards** (from HK$10–100) are widely available (try 7-Eleven). You can make **international calls** from International Direct Dialling (IDD) phones. Hong Kong SIM cards can be bought for less than HK$50 and local calls from mobiles are inexpensive.

In Macau, local calls are free from **private phones**, MOP$1 from payphones. Instructions tend to be in both Portuguese and English.

Internet access, particularly free wi-fi, is available in most hostels and guesthouses. Purchase a PCCW account online to access more than 7000 wi-fi hotspots in Hong Kong. In Macau, you can access free wi-fi in touristy areas using the user name and password "wifigo"; you have to reconnect after 45-minute sessions.

CRIME AND SAFETY

You're very unlikely to encounter any trouble in Hong Kong or Macau. To avoid **pickpockets**, keep money and wallets in hard-to-reach places and be careful when getting on and off packed public transport. Men should avoid strip bars where the Neanderthals at the door will make sure you fork out for hugely expensive drinks for the "girls".

EMERGENCY NUMBERS

In both Hong Kong and Macau, dial ☎ **999** for fire, police and ambulance.

HONG KONG AND MACAU ONLINE

discoverhongkong.com The Hong Kong Tourist Board's fantastic website is packed with information, and their interactive itinerary planner can transform your visit. Download free mobile apps such as Discover Hong Kong and Hong Kong city walks.

hkoutdoors.com For an insight into Hong Kong's hidden side, as well as practical information on mountain biking, sea kayaking, birdwatching and hiking.

macautourism.gov.mo Not quite as good as the Hong Kong website but still handy for its travel information, lists of guesthouses and suggested tours.

Carrying some form of **identification** is a legal requirement: for a traveller this means your passport. Most police officers speak some English, and will quickly radio help for you if they can't understand and you have a major problem. **Drug possession** carries stiff penalties in both Hong Kong and Macau.

MEDICAL CARE AND EMERGENCIES

Pharmacies (daily 9am–6pm or 24hr in hospitals) are marked with a red-and-white cross and sell many medications over the counter without a prescription. Contraceptives and antibiotics are also available over the counter. Hong Kong pharmacies have a registered pharmacist on-site who usually speaks English.

Medical care in Hong Kong (see p.150) is generally of an excellent standard, but does not come cheap. If you need a doctor, you'll have to pay for any treatment or medicines prescribed, so make sure you have adequate travel insurance. Note that both doctors and **dentists** are known as "doctor" in Hong Kong. Both of Macau's hospitals (see p.158) offer 24hr emergency services.

MONEY AND BANKS

ATMs throughout both Hong Kong and Macau accept international cards.

Hong Kong's unit of **currency** is the Hong Kong dollar (HK$); it is divided into one hundred cents. Bills come in denominations of $10, $20, $50, $100, $500 and $1000, and there are 10 cent, 20 cent, 50 cent, $1, $2, $5 and $10 coins. At the time of writing, the exchange rate was around HK$12 to the **pound sterling**, HK10.3 to the euro, and it's pegged at HK$7.75 to the US dollar. There are no restrictions on taking any currency in and out of Hong Kong.

The unit of **currency** in Macau is the pataca (abbreviated to MOP$ in this book; often seen as M$, MOP or ptca), which consists of one hundred avos. At the time of writing, the **exchange rate** was £1 to MOP$12.50, US$1 to MOP$ 8 and €1 to MOP$10.5. Bills come in MOP$10, 20, 50, 100, 500 and 1000 denominations, and there are 10-, 20- and 50-avo coins, as well as MOP$1, 2, 5 and 10 coins. The pataca is pegged to the Hong Kong dollar at the rate of MOP$103.2 to HK$100, and the two currencies are interchangeable in Macau, though you get slightly less for your Hong Kong dollars. Try to get rid of your patacas before heading to Hong Kong.

All the **major credit cards** are accepted in the larger hotels, but most guesthouses and restaurants still expect payment in cash.

OPENING HOURS

In both Hong Kong and Macau, **offices** are generally open Monday to Friday 9am–5.30pm, with lunch hour between 1–2pm; **shops** are open daily 10am–8pm or later in busy tourist areas like Causeway Bay and Tsim Sha Tsui. **Banks** are open Monday to Friday 9am–4.30pm and Saturday 9am–12.30pm; **post offices** are open Monday to Friday 9.30am–5pm and Saturday 9.30am–1pm, and **restaurants** tend to be open 11am–3pm & 6–11pm or else 11am–11pm. **Government offices** close on public holidays and some religious festivals.

PUBLIC HOLIDAYS

Hong Kong's public holidays are changing as China jettisons the old colonial holidays in favour of its own

3

CANTONESE

Cantonese is the official language of Hong Kong, with Mandarin a fast-growing second. English is widely spoken among the well educated and many in the tourist trade (although not many taxi drivers), otherwise, people speak only basic English. The vast majority of people in Macau speak Cantonese and some also speak Portuguese and English. Cantonese is a tonal language, which means that the tone a speaker gives to a word will determine its meaning. As a simple two-letter word can have up to nine different meanings depending on the pitch of the voice, the Romanized word is really only an approximation of the Chinese sound.

PRONUNCIATION

oy as in b**oy**
ai as in f**i**ne
i as in s**ee**
er as in **ur**n
o as in p**o**t
ow as in n**ow**
oe as in **oh**
or as in l**aw**

WORDS AND PHRASES

Good morning	*Joe sun*
Hello/how are you?	*Lay hoe ma?*
Thank you/excuse me	*M goy*
Goodnight	*Joe tow*
Goodbye	*Joy geen*
I'm sorry	*Doy m joot*
Can you speak English?	*Lay sik m sik gong ying man?*
Yes	*Yow*
No	*Mo*
I don't understand	*Ngor m ming bat*
What is your name?	*Lay gew mut yeh meng?*
My name is …	*Ngor gew …*
I am from England/ America	*Ngor haiying may gwok yan*
Where are these places? (while pointing to the place name or map)	*Ching mun, leedi day fong hai been do ah?*
Train	*For chair*
Bus	*Ba-see*
Ferry	*Do lun schoon*
Taxi	*Dik-see*
Airport	*Fay gay cherng*
Hotel	*Jow deem*
Hostel	*Loy gwun*
Restaurant	*Charn Teng*
Toilets	*Chee saw*
Police	*Ging chat*

NUMBERS

The number two changes when asking for two of something – **lerng wei** (a table for two) – or stating something other than counting – **lerng mun** (two dollars).

1	*yat*
2	*yee*
3	*saam*
4	*say*
5	*mm*
6	*lok*
7	*chat*
8	*bat*
9	*gow*
10	*sap*
11, 12, 13, etc	*sap yat, sap yee, sap aam*

celebrations. For now, the following public holidays are observed. Sundays are also classed as public holidays.

Macau observes all of the holidays listed below with the exception of the HKSAR Establishment Day.

HONG KONG AND MACAU

January 1 New Year
February 19, 2015; February 8, 2016 Chinese New Year
April 3–5, 2015; March 25–27, 2016 Easter (holidays on Good Friday, Easter Saturday and Easter Monday)
April 4 Ching Ming
May 1 Labour Day
May 25, 2015; May 14, 2015 Buddha's birthday
June 20, 2015; June 9, 2016 Tuen Ng (Dragon Boat) Festival
July 1 Hong Kong SAR Establishment Day
September 27, 2015; September 15, 2016 Mid-Autumn Festival
October 1 China National Day
October 2, 2014; October 21, 2015; October 10, 2016 Chung Yeung
December 25 Christmas Day
December 26 Boxing Day

20, 21, 22, 23, etc	*yee sap, yee sap yat, yee sap yee, yee sap saam*
30, 40, 50, etc	*saam sap, say sap, mm sap*
100	*yat bat*
1000	*yat cheen*

FOOD AND DRINKS GLOSSARY

Ordering food

Mai daan	Bill/check
Fai tzee	Chopsticks
La sow ho choy	House speciality
Gay dor cheen?	How much is that?
Ngor hi fut gow toe/ ngor tzee sik soe	I'm a Buddhist/ vegetarian
Ngor serng yew …	I would like …
Choy daan/toe choy/ Ying man choy daan	Main/set menu/ English menu

Drinks

Beh tsow	Beer
Ga fay	Coffee
Char	Tea
Kong tuen soy	Mineral water
Poe toe tsow	Wine

Staple foods

Ah choy	Bean sprouts
Ow yok	Beef
Dou chi jiang	Black bean sauce
Gai	Chicken
Lar jew	Chilli
Hi	Crab
Daan chow faan	Egg fried rice
Yue	Fish
Lok yip soe choy	Green leafy vegetables
For war	Hotpot
Yok choon	Kebab
Meen tew	Noodles
Tong meen	Noodle soup
Jew yok	Pork
Ha	Prawns
Bak faan	Rice (boiled)
Chow fann	Rice (fried)
Jook	Rice porridge congee
How aap	Roast duck
Dow foo	Tofu
Wun dung tong	Wonton soup

Vegetables and eggs

Dun herng goo	Braised mountain fungus
Dow foo soe choy	Fried beancurd with vegetables
Herng la ke tzee tew	Spicy braised aubergine
Soe choy tong	Vegetable soup

Dim Sum (Yum Cha)

Char sew bao	Barbecue pork bun
Hai yok ha gow/gow	Crab and coriander dumpling
Daan tat	Custard tart
Faan sue woo gow	Fried taro and mince dumpling
Gow tzee	Joazi steamed pork dumplings
Leen yong bau	Lotus paste bun
Yuet beng	Moon cake – sweet bean paste in flaky pastry
Ha peen	Prawn crackers
Ha gow	Prawn dumpling
Tzee ma ha dor zi	Prawn paste on fried toast
Wo teet	Shanghai fried vegetable dumpling
Chun goon	Spring roll

ADDITIONAL MACAU PUBLIC HOLIDAYS

November 2 All Souls' Day
December 8 Feast of Immaculate Conception
December 20 Macau SAR Establishment Day

FESTIVALS

With roots going back hundreds (even thousands) of years, many of Hong Kong's festivals are highly symbolic and are often a mixture of secular and religious displays and devotions. On these occasions, there are dances and Chinese opera performances at temples, with plenty of noise and offerings – food and paper goods that are burned as gifts to the dead. The normal Chinese holidays are celebrated in Macau, plus some Catholic festivals introduced from Portugal, such as the procession of Our Lady of Fatima from São Domingos Church annually on May 13 (although this is no longer a public holiday).

As the Chinese use the lunar calendar, many festivals fall on different days, even different months, from year to year; for

exact details, contact the Hong Kong or Macau tourist offices (discoverhongkong.com and macautourism.gov.mo).

FESTIVAL CALENDAR

Chinese New Year (Feb 19, 2015; Feb 8, 2016). The most important festival celebrated in Hong Kong and Macau; the entire population participates and there are spectacular firework displays over the harbour.

Tin Hau Festival (May 11, 2015; April 29, 2016). Particular to Hong Kong in honour of the Goddess of Fishermen, large seaborne festivities take place at Joss House Bay on Sai Kung peninsula.

Tuen Ng (Dragon Boat) Festival (June 20, 2015; June 9, 2016). In Hong Kong, with races along the coast in long, narrow boats.

Yu Lan (Hungry Ghost) Festival (Aug 27, 2015; Aug 16, 2016) Hong Kong's Chiu Chow community appease evil spirits by burning fake money, cooking up sacrifices and performing live Chinese operas and dramas in public parks all around the Territory.

Mid-Autumn Festival (Sept 27, 2015; Sept 15, 2016). Chinese festival, almost as popular as Chinese New Year. Celebrations are more public in Hong Kong and Macau.

Wine and Dine Festival (Oct/Nov). A four-day epicurean festival to kick off November's annual wine and dine month, featuring restaurant promotions, street carnivals and wine-tasting events.

Hong Kong

The territory of **HONG KONG**, whose name means "fragrant harbour", comprises an irregularly shaped peninsula abutting the Pearl River Delta to the west, and a number of offshore islands, which cover more than a thousand square kilometres in total. The southern part of the peninsula, **Kowloon**, and the island immediately south of it, **Hong Kong Island**, are the principal urban areas of Hong Kong. They were ceded to Britain "in perpetuity", but were returned to China at midnight on June 30, 1997. Since then, it has been renamed the **Hong Kong Special Administrative Region (SAR)** of the People's Republic of China.

The island of Hong Kong offers traces of the old colony – from English place names to ancient trams trundling along the shore – among superb modern architecture and futuristic cityscapes, as well as plentiful opportunities for **hiking** and bathing on the **beaches** of its southern shore. Kowloon, in particular its southernmost tip, **Tsim Sha Tsui**, is the budget accommodation centre of Hong Kong, and boasts fantastic shopping, from lofty international designers to traditional markets. The **offshore islands**, including **Lamma** and **Lantau**, are locally famous for their fresh fish restaurants, scenery and tranquillity, while the **New Territories**, north of Kowloon, is where you find remnants of ancient walled villages, splendid temples and some great hiking and biking terrain.

HONG KONG ISLAND

As the oldest colonized part of Hong Kong, its administrative and business centre and site of some of the most expensive real estate in the world, **Hong Kong Island** is, in every sense, the heart of the whole territory. Despite its size, just 15km from east to west and 11km from north to south, the island encompasses the best the territory has to offer in one heady hit: lavish temples to consumer excess, the vivid sights and smells of a Chinese wet market and (away from the north shore's steel and concrete mountains) surprising expanses of sandy beach and forested nature reserves.

WHAT TO SEE AND DO

The territory's major financial and commercial quarter, Central, lies on the northern shore of Hong Kong Island overlooking Victoria Harbour. East of Central are **Wan Chai** and lively **Causeway Bay**, while in the opposite direction is the **Western District**, rather older and more traditional in character. Towering over the city, **The Peak** is a highlight of any trip to the city, offering magnificent views and great walking opportunities.

On its south side, Hong Kong Island straggles into the sea in a series of dangling peninsulas and inlets. The atmosphere is quieter here than on the north shore. You'll find not only separate seafront suburbs such as **Aberdeen**, its busy bay full of boats and sampans, and **Stanley**, with its waterfront bazaar, but

also beaches, such as **Repulse Bay** and **Deep Water Bay**, the **Ocean Park** amusement park, and, further east, the remote and pretty village of **Shek O**. Buses are plentiful to all destinations on the southern shore, and Aberdeen is linked to Central by a tunnel under The Peak. Nowhere is more than an hour from Central.

Central

Central extends out from the Star Ferry Pier a few hundred metres in all directions. Right next to the Star Ferry Pier is the engrossing **Hong Kong Maritime Museum** (Mon–Fri 9.30am–5.30pm, Sat & Sun 10am–7pm; HK$30; ⓦhkmaritime museum.org), its three floors subtly lit to resemble a ship's interior and its partly interactive exhibitions ranging from an overview of China's maritime history to the creation of Victoria Harbour, with a wealth of period objects, paintings, nautical instruments, boat models and photography.

Easily recognizable from the tramlines that run up and down here, **Des Voeux Road** used to mark Hong Kong's seafront before the days of reclamation. East along Des Voeux Road, you'll find Statue Square on your left towards the shore, and, immediately south, the magnificently high-tech, "inside-out" **HSBC Building**, designed by Sir Norman Foster in 1958 – at the time of construction one of the most expensive office blocks ever built (US$1 billlion). A few hundred metres east is the 300m-high blue glass geometric shard of the **Bank of China** tower, designed by Chinese-American architect I.M. Pei, with splendid panoramic views of the city from the public viewing gallery on the 43rd floor (Mon–Fri 8am–6pm; free).

South of Queen's Road the land begins to run uphill. The **Mid-Levels Escalator Link** is a giant series of escalators that runs 800m straight up the hill (downwards only 6–10am; upwards 10.20am–midnight) servicing the expensive **Mid-Levels** residential area, favoured by expats, as well as the thriving restaurant district of **SoHo**, with the steep pedestrian stretch of **Graham Street market** lined with stalls overflowing with fresh produce. Nearby **Lan Kwai Fong** is equally good for eating and drinking, with long queues of Hong Kongers in business attire snaking their way to the flavour-of-the-moment restaurants at lunchtimes and after work.

A short but steep walk away are the **Hong Kong Zoological and Botanical Gardens** (daily 6am–10pm; zoo and aviaries to 7pm; free), one of the world's leading centres for captive breeding of endangered mammals and home to more than 160 species of birds in well-kept aviaries. From the eastern exit, a ten-minute walk along Garden Road brings you to the vast **Hong Kong Park** (daily 6am–11pm; free); The highlight here is the wonderful **Edward Youde Aviary** (daily 9am–5pm; free), with ninety species of birds in a rainforest setting; look out also for a couple of art museums and another showcasing tea ware.

Wan Chai

In the 1950s and 1960s, **Wan Chai** – the area stretching east of Central – was known throughout east Asia as a thriving red-light district, catering in particular for US soldiers on leave from Korea and Vietnam. Lockhart Road is still home to plenty of **bars**, while Jaffe Road to the north is lined with **restaurants**. Local hipsters hang out at "Hipsterville" – the area comprising St Francis, Moon and Star streets. There are also several ethnic enclaves here: Fujian Town at North Point, and Lil' Jakarta. When it comes to shopping, Wan Chai is one of the best places in town to stock up on electronics.

Just north of Gloucester Road is the **Hong Kong Arts Centre** (2 Harbour Road; ⓦhkac.org.hk; daily 10am–6pm; free; ⓜAdmiralty, exit E2), featuring a cinema and art galleries that host interesting exhibitions, such as the recent one on designer toilets, and other cultural events. Pick up a free copy of the monthly listings magazine *ArtsLink* here.

South of Queens Rd East, along Stone Nullah Lane, is the largest Taoist temple on Hong Kong island – **Pak Tai Temple** (daily 8am–5pm), honouring its namesake, a deity of the sea whose 3m-tall copper likeness graces the main hall.

3

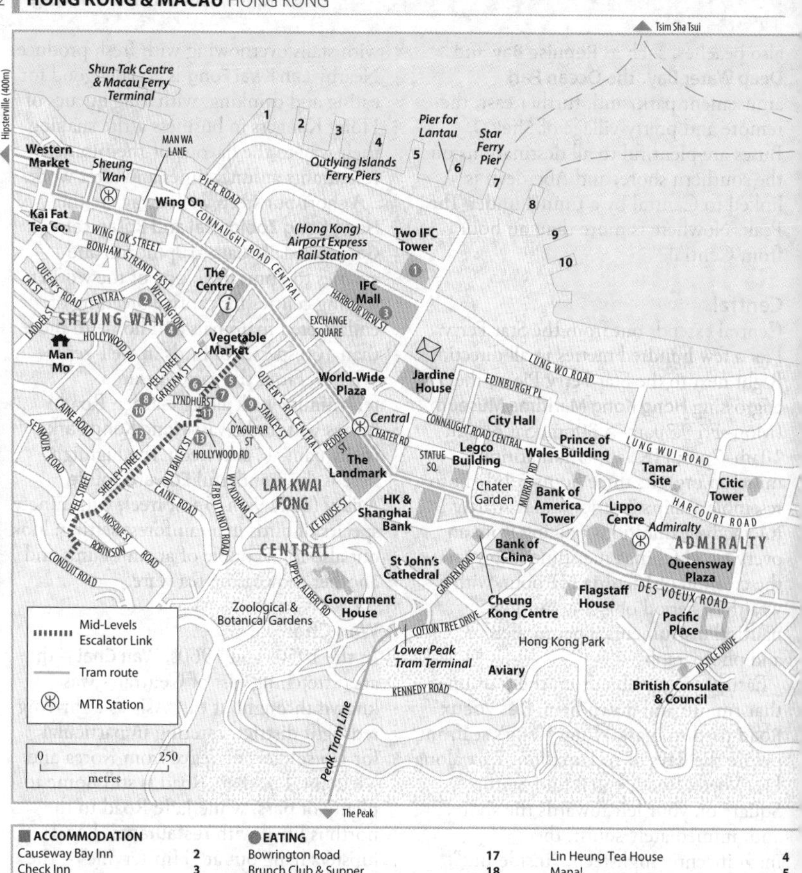

ACCOMMODATION	
Causeway Bay Inn	2
Check Inn	3
Life on a Boat – Moksha	4
YesInn @ Causeway Bay	1
Y-Loft	5

EATING	
Bowrington Road	17
Brunch Club & Supper	18
Chilli Fagara	10
Crystal Jade La Mian Xiao Long Bao	19
Dumpling Yuan	6
Hainan Shaoye	14
Lin Heung Tea House	4
Mana!	5
Nagahama No 1 Ramen	2
Nam Kee Spring Roll Noodle	9
Lil' Siam	12
Nha Trang	7

Causeway Bay

East of Wan Chai, **Causeway Bay** is a lively district packed with shops and restaurants. It's centred between the eastern end of Lockhart Road and the western edge of Victoria Park – Hong Kong's largest piece of public greenery. Trams run here along Yee Wo Street, a continuation of Hennessy Road from Wan Chai.

The main activity in Causeway Bay is shopping – for fashion, electronics and homewares. Near the eponymous MTR station you'll find **Jardine's Crescent**, a narrow alleyway packed with market stalls selling cheap clothes, jewellery and knick-knacks. On the shore, in front of the *Excelsior Hotel* on Gloucester Road, stands the **Noonday Gun** – immortalized in Noël Coward's song *Mad Dogs and Englishmen* – which is fired every day at noon. The eastern part of Causeway Bay, where it meets Wan Chai, is dominated by the vast **Victoria Park** (daily 24hr). On weekdays it's a good place to watch nimble local residents practising tai chi, on Sundays Indonesian maids come picnicking here, during the mid-autumn festival the park fills with people carrying lanterns, and just before the Chinese New Year the place becomes an immense flower market.

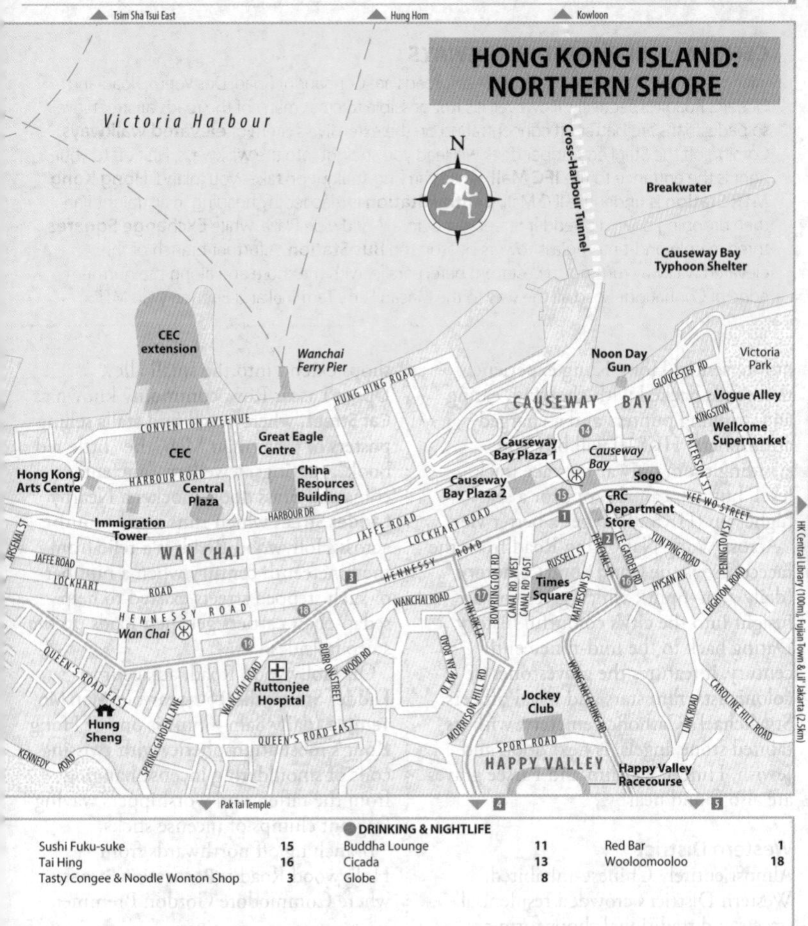

Out in the bay is the Causeway Bay **typhoon shelter** that used to protect fleets of junks and sampans, but these days it protects yachts from the onslaught of the waves and the wind.

Inland from Hennessy Road, on the corner of Matheson and Russell streets, is Causeway Bay's most famous shopping plaza, the half-moon-shaped **Times Square**, fronted by a huge video screen. Just to the west of Times Square lies one of the city's best wet markets – **Bowrington Road Market** – where you can watch the sellers expertly dismembering poultry, fish and meat in the mornings and then grab a bite to eat at the food stalls that stay open until the evening.

Happy Valley

The low-lying area extending inland from the shore south of Wan Chai and Causeway Bay is known as Happy Valley, and means only one thing for the people of Hong Kong: horse racing or, more precisely, gambling. The **Happy Valley Racecourse** (Sept–June Wed 7–10.30pm; HK$10; ⓦhappyvalleyracecourse.com), reachable by tram, dates back to 1846. Immense fortunes have been won and lost here over the past 150 years and Wednesday night at the races is a

CENTRAL'S ELEVATED WALKWAYS

Inland from the shore, the main west–east roads are Connaught Road, Des Voeux Road and Queen's Road respectively. However, it's not possible to cross many of the roads at street level, so pedestrians are better off concentrating on the extensive system of **elevated walkways**. Coming off the Star Ferry upper deck will lead you straight into the walkways. First off to your right is the entrance to the **IFC Mall**, while carrying straight on takes you inland. **Hong Kong MTR Station** is under the IFC Mall; **Central Station** is reached by heading in a straight line then dropping down to Pedder Street just before Worldwide Plaza, while **Exchange Square**'s three marble-and-tinted-glass towers sit atop the **Bus Station**. A further branch of the elevated walkway runs northwest from here, parallel with the shore and along the northern edge of Connaught Road all the way to the Macau Ferry Terminal and Sheung Wan MTR.

quintessential Hong Kong experience, the stands packed with cheering, eating and drinking punters and a charged atmosphere. HK$10 will buy you standing room only at the race track level, but you can also opt for a seat higher up (HK$20) to get a better view.

Across Wong Nai Ching Road from the racecourse is the **Hong Kong Cemetery** (daily 7am–6pm), which gives you an insight into the city's colourful history. Dating back to the mid-nineteenth century, it features the gravestones of colonialists, film stars and naval officers. St Michael's Catholic cemetery, with its tainted stone angels, is next door, and Jewish, Hindu, Muslim and Parsee graves are also found nearby.

Western District

Almost entirely Chinese-inhabited, Western District's crowded residential streets and traditional shops form a striking contrast to Central. **Sheung Wan** spreads south up the hill from the seafront at the modern Shun Tak Centre, a fifteen-minute walk along the elevated walkway from Exchange Square in Central, though you'll get more flavour of the district by hopping on a "ding ding" along Des Voeux Road. Head south to the area around **Bonham Strand East** for an intriguing range of specialist shops selling traditional Chinese medicine, all manner of dried creatures from the sea and personalized stone seals (along Man Wa Lane).

Running from partway up the Mid-Levels escalator to the Western District is **Hollywood Road**, lined with antique and curio shops. The antique shops extend into the small alley, Upper Lascar Row, commonly known as **Cat Street**, where you'll find stalls selling posters of Chairman Mao, the "little red book", carvings, jewellery, "ancient" coins and brass door knockers. Nearby **Ladder Street** which runs north–south across Hollywood Road, is a relic from the nineteenth century when a number of such stepped streets existed to help sedan-chair carriers get their loads up the steep hillsides.

On Hollywood Road, adjacent to Ladder Street, the 150-year-old **Man Mo Temple** (daily 8am–6pm) is one of Hong Kong's most atmospheric, with twisting coils of smouldering incense hanging from the rafters and worshippers waving fragrant clumps of incense sticks.

Branching off northwards from Hollywood Road is **Possession Street**, where Commodore Gordon Bremmer,

THE LAST JUNK IN HONG KONG

Most travellers hold romantic images of Victoria Harbour filled with traditional Chinese wooden junks rigged with scarlet sails – the old workhorses of the waves – but these have long been decommissioned. Today just a single one remains: the lovingly restored **Duk Ling** (2508 1234, dukling.com.hk), typical of junks built 150 years ago, which now offers trips around the harbour. You can choose to sail from either Kowloon's public pier or Tsim Sha Tsui (Thurs 2 & 4pm, Sat 10am & noon), or Central Pier 9 on Hong Kong Island (Thurs 3 & 5pm, Sat 11am & 1pm; HK$100); book your spot in advance.

and the British marines under his command, planted the Union Jack in 1841 to take possession of Hong Kong Island for the British crown; there are no plaques to commemorate this.

The Peak

The uppermost levels of the 552m hill that towers over Central and Victoria Harbour have always been known as Victoria Peak (or simply "The Peak"), and, in colonial days, the area was populated by upper-class expats. Today The Peak offers some extraordinary panoramic views over the city and harbour below, as well as pleasant, leisurely walks. See ⓦthepeak.com.hk for more information.

The Peak Tram drops you at the terminal in the **Peak Tower**. This building and the **Peak Galleria** across the road are full of souvenir shops and pricey bars and restaurants, some with spectacular views. The Peak Tower charges HK$30 to access its **Sky Terrace 428** viewing gallery (Mon–Fri 10am–11pm; Sat & Sun 8am–11pm), or you can buy a ticket that combines the tram and the terrace (HK$53 one-way, HK$65 return). The **view** from the top of the Peak Galleria is almost as good, the only difference being that it's free of charge. For more great vistas, follow Mount Austin Road to Victoria Peak Garden, formerly the site of the Governor's residence, burnt down to the ground by the Japanese in World War II. Another great alternative is to circumambulate The Peak along the 3.5km loop formed by the Harlech Road, due west of the Peak Terminal, and Lugard Road on the northern slope, which sweeps around The Peak before curving back to the terminal.

An excellent way to descend The Peak is to **walk**, the simplest route being to follow the sign pointing to Hatton Road, from opposite the picnic area on Harlech Road. A very clear path leads all the way through trees, eventually emerging after about 45 minutes in Mid-Levels, near the junction between Kotewall Road and Conduit Road. Catch bus #13 or minibus #3 from Kotewall Road to Central, or you can walk east for about 1km along Conduit Road until you reach the top end of the Mid-Levels Escalator (see p.131), and follow that down into Central. The tourist office supplies useful maps (see p.145).

Aberdeen

Situated on the quieter south side of Hong Kong Island, **Aberdeen** is where Hong Kongers come for a seafood lunch. A tiny minority of Aberdeen's residents still live on **sampans** (small motorized boats) in the narrow harbour that lies between the main island and the offshore island of Ap Lei Chau – a tradition that certainly preceded the arrival of the British in Hong Kong, and a way of life that is now facing extinction. A time-honoured and enjoyable tourist activity in Aberdeen is to take a **sampan tour** around the harbour (around HK$68 for 30min). The trip offers great photo opportunities of the old houseboats jammed together, complete with dogs, drying laundry and outdoor kitchens. You'll also pass boat yards and floating restaurants, especially spectacular when lit up at night. The most famous is *Jumbo Kingdom*, created by Stanley Ho in the style of a giant floating imperial palace; Dragon Court is overpriced but the 3rd floor *dim sum* is great. To reach Aberdeen,

RIDING THE PEAK TRAM

Half the fun of The Peak is the ascent on the **Peak Tram**, a cable-hauled funicular that's been climbing 396 vertical metres to the terminus since 1888 in just eight minutes – a remarkable piece of engineering. To find the Lower Peak Tram Terminal in Central, catch bus #15C (HK$4.20) from the Central Bus Terminus near the Star Ferry (10am–11.40pm), or walk up Garden Road – it's a little way up the hill from St John's Cathedral. The Peak Tram itself (daily 7am–midnight; HK$28 one-way, HK$40 return; ⓦthepeak.com.hk) runs every ten to fifteen minutes. If you want to see the sunset from up high, start queuing no later than 4pm; Sundays and public holidays are the busiest times and best avoided.

OCEAN PARK

Ocean Park (daily 10am–7.30pm; HK$320; oceanpark.com.hk), Hong Kong's gigantic **theme and adventure park**, combines the rollercoasters of Thrill Mountain with a host of animal attractions. Waterfront's Grand Aquarium – the world's largest aquarium dome – features an impressive collection of marine life, including sharks and jellyfish, while you can catch dolphin and killer whale shows at Marine World, on the Summit headland, reachable from the main Waterfront entrance by cable car and funicular. The stars of Amazing Asian Animals are four giant pandas and rare red pandas, then there are aviaries, a rainforest and Polar World to explore. The park also plays an active role in wildlife conservation. It's situated just east of Aberdeen; take bus #629 from Admiralty MTR station, #70 & #75 from Central, #72 & #92 from Causeway Bay or #973 from Tsim Sha Tsui. Get off just after you exit the Aberdeen tunnel.

catch **bus** #7 or #70 from Central, #72 from Causeway Bay or #73 or #973 from Stanley. There are also regular **boat** connections between Aberdeen and nearby Lamma Island (see p.141).

Repulse Bay and beyond

The wide, sandy beach of **Repulse Bay**, an upmarket suburb on the southern coast of Hong Kong Island, is very popular with locals. The bay's unusual name may stem from the British fleet's repulsion of pirates there in 1841. Near the southeast end of the beach is a **Kwun Yam Shrine** (dedicated to the goddess of the sea; daily 8am–8pm), surrounded by a wide variety of deity and animal statues. In front of the shrine is **Longevity Bridge**, the crossing of which is said to add three days to your life. Several kilometres northwest of Repulse Bay is **Deep Water Bay**, a more secluded inlet with a beach and a wakeboarding centre, and without Repulse Bay's crowds. You can reach Repulse Bay on **buses** #6, #6X or #260 from Central, #63 or minibus #40 from Causeway Bay, or #973 from Tsim Sha Tsui East.

Stanley

Straddling the neck of Hong Kong's southernmost peninsula is **Stanley**, a moderately sized residential village, with a sweeping European-styled promenade, and large numbers of pubs, bars and restaurants. A little way to the north of the bus stop is **Stanley Main Beach**, popular with windsurfers. Walk downhill from the bus stop and you'll soon find kitschy **Stanley Market** (open during daylight hours) and, beyond, a seafront promenade. Strolling west along the seafront, you'll come to another **Tin Hau Temple** (daily 8am–8pm), completely rebuilt since 1767. Inside, there's a large, blackened tiger skin, the remains of an animal shot near here in 1942.

Next to the temple stands the colonnaded **Murray House**, an officers' barracks dating back to 1844 that's been reconstructed here, brick by brick, after being moved from its spot in Central where the Bank of China Tower stands today.

If you follow Wong Ma Kok Rd south from the bus station, you'll come across the **Stanley Military Cemetery** (daily 8am–5pm; bus #6A); its graves from the 1840s and 1940s allow you to appreciate the toll that diseases and the Japanese invasion took on Hong Kong respectively. Buses #73 and #973 run between Aberdeen and Stanley. All the buses that go to Repulse Bay also go to Stanley.

Shek O

In the far east of the island, **Shek O** is Hong Kong's most remote and exclusive settlement – house numbers on Shek O Road refer not to location but to when the owner became a member of the golf club and therefore allowed to build here. A strong surf pounds the wide, white **beach**, and during the week it's more or less deserted.

Big Wave Bay, a fifteen-minute walk from Shek O, past the Shek O Golf & Country Club, offers windsurfing, and on the headland above the bay is one of Hong Kong's **prehistoric rock carvings**.

To get to Shek O, catch bus #9 (30min; HK$7.20) from the bus terminal outside the **Shau Kei Wan** MTR station (exit A3) on the northeastern shore of Hong Kong Island. It's a picturesque journey over hills during which you'll spot first the sparkling waters of the Tai Tam Reservoir, then Stanley (to the southwest) and finally Shek O itself, appearing below.

Alternatively, jump off at Cape Collinson near To Tei Wan Village, and walk to Shek O along the **Dragon's Back** ridge, one of Hong Kong's most famous hikes (2–3hr), which boasts spectacular views and is part of the 50km Hong Kong Trail (see box, p.142); you can also paraglide and abseil from here. To reach the trail, head into Shek O Country Park and follow signs to Shek O Peak. The tourist office brochure (Ⓦdiscoverhongkong.com), *The Inside Guide to Hikes and Walks in Hong Kong*, has full details.

KOWLOON

A 4km strip of the mainland grabbed by the British in 1860 to add to their offshore island, **Kowloon** was part of the territory ceded to Britain "in perpetuity" and was accordingly developed with gusto and confidence. With the help of land reclamation and the diminishing significance of the border between Kowloon and the New Territories at Boundary Street, Kowloon has, over the years, just about managed to accommodate the vast numbers of people who have squeezed into it. Today, areas such as Mong Kok, jammed with soaring tenements, are among the most densely populated urban areas in the world (in places shoehorning 100,000 people into each square kilometre).

Kowloon is more down-to-earth and ethnically diverse than the financial playground of Hong Kong Island's northern shore. The view from the Tsim Sha Tsui East Promenade towards the wall of skyscrapers across the harbour is one of the most unforgettable city panoramas, especially at night.

WHAT TO SEE AND DO

Tsim Sha Tsui is the tourist heart of Hong Kong, complete with ethnic enclaves, and **Nathan Road** – lined with shops and budget hotels – is its main artery, leading down to the harbour. Hong Kong's major museums (Ⓦmuseums.gov.hk) are also found here; if you're keen to visit them all, buy a HK$30 pass from one of seven participating museums (including all those listed here) for unlimited weekly access or take advantage of free museum entry on Wednesdays.

The part of Kowloon north of Tsim Sha Tsui – encompassing **Yau Ma Tei** and **Mong Kok** – is rewarding to walk around, with authentic Chinese neighbourhoods and interesting markets.

Tsim Sha Tsui

The **Star Ferry Pier**, for ferries to Hong Kong Island (see box below), is right on the southwestern tip of the **Tsim Sha Tsui** peninsula. The **Hong Kong Cultural Centre**, about 100m east of the Star Ferry Pier, contains concert halls, theatres and galleries, including, in an adjacent wing, the superb **Museum of Art** (daily except Thurs 10am–6pm, Sat 10am–8pm;

THE STAR FERRY

Dating back to 1888, the Star Ferry, with its legendary fleet of vessels such as the *Twinkling Star* that ply Victoria Harbour, is a beloved part of the city's history. It was a Star Ferry that brought governor Sir Mark Aitchinson Young to Tsim Sha Tsui in 1941, to surrender to the Japanese, and it was at the Tsim Sha Tsui pier that rioters gathered in 1966 to protest a five-cent hike in ticket prices. The Star Ferry was founded by Dorabjee Nowrojee, a Parsi from Bombay who bought a steamboat for his family's use, at a time when the locals were crossing the harbour in sampans. Riding one of the boats today is a quintessential Hong Kong experience, not to mention the cheapest way to get a tour of one of the world's most spectacular harbours (HK$2.50) as you make the ten-minute journey between Kowloon and Central; photos are best taken from the bottom deck.

3

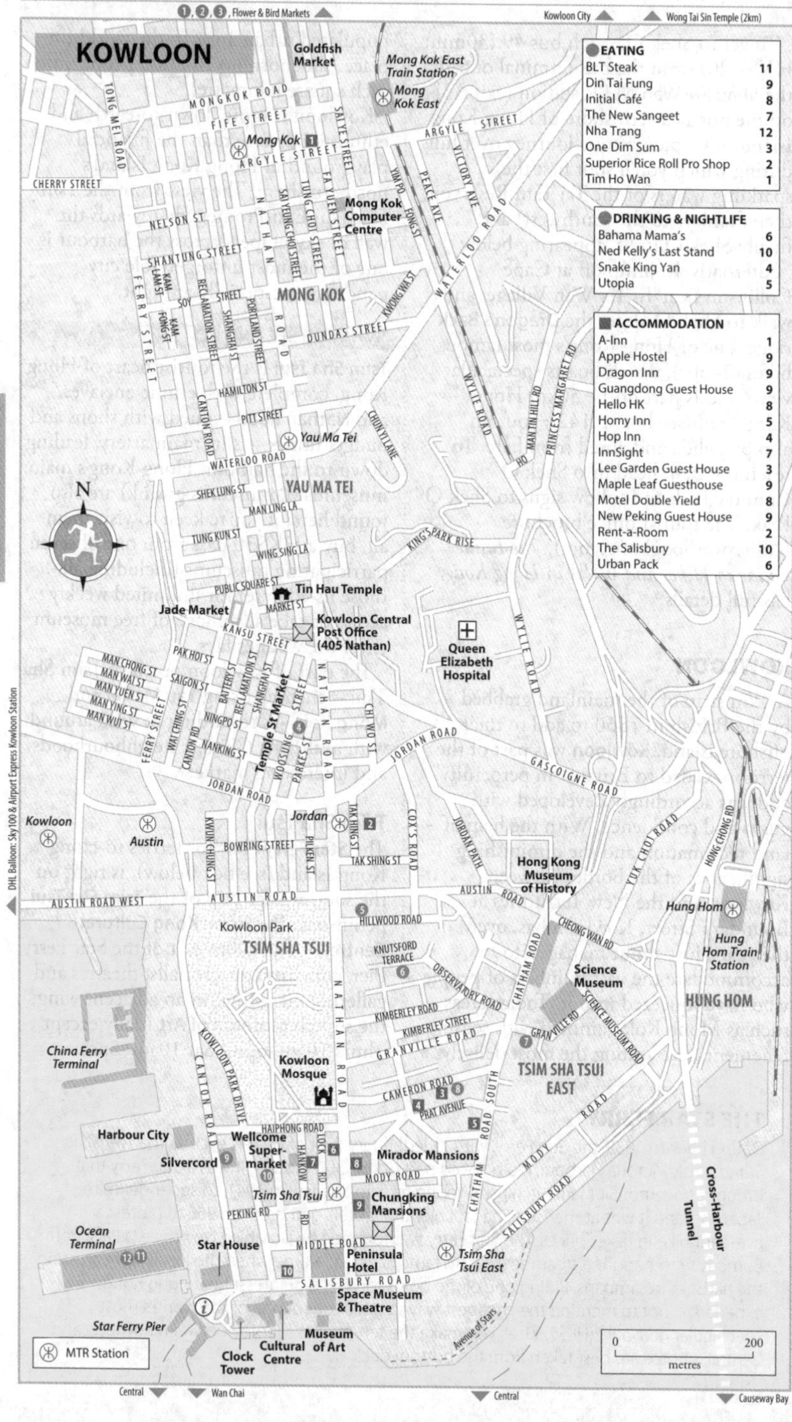
KOWLOON
1, 2, 3, Flower & Bird Markets
Kowloon City
Wong Tai Sin Temple (2km)
EATING
BLT Steak 11
Din Tai Fung 9
Initial Café 8
The New Sangeet 7
Nha Trang 12
One Dim Sum 3
Superior Rice Roll Pro Shop 2
Tim Ho Wan 1
DRINKING & NIGHTLIFE
Bahama Mama's 6
Ned Kelly's Last Stand 10
Snake King Yan 4
Utopia 5
ACCOMMODATION
A-Inn 1
Apple Hostel 9
Dragon Inn 9
Guangdong Guest House 9
Hello HK 8
Homy Inn 5
Hop Inn 4
InnSight 7
Lee Garden Guest House 3
Maple Leaf Guesthouse 9
Motel Double Yield 8
New Peking Guest House 9
Rent-a-Room 2
The Salisbury 10
Urban Pack 6
Goldfish Market
Mong Kok East Train Station
Mong Kok East
Mong Kok
Mong Kok Computer Centre
MONG KOK
Yau Ma Tei
YAU MA TEI
Tin Hau Temple
Jade Market
Kowloon Central Post Office (405 Nathan)
Queen Elizabeth Hospital
Temple St Market
Jordan
Kowloon
Austin
Hong Kong Museum of History
Hung Hom
Hung Hom Train Station
HUNG HOM
Kowloon Park
TSIM SHA TSUI
Science Museum
TSIM SHA TSUI EAST
China Ferry Terminal
Kowloon Mosque
Harbour City
Silvercord
Wellcome Super-market
Mirador Mansions
Tsim Sha Tsui
Chungking Mansions
Ocean Terminal
Star House
Peninsula Hotel
Tsim Sha Tsui East
Space Museum & Theatre
Star Ferry Pier
Clock Tower
Cultural Centre
Museum of Art
Avenue of Stars
Cross-Harbour Tunnel
MTR Station
0 200 metres
DHL Balloon: Sky100 & Airport Express Kowloon Station
Central
Wan Chai
Central
Causeway Bay
TONG MEI ROAD
MONGKOK ROAD
FIFE STREET
ARGYLE STREET
SAI YE STREET
CHERRY STREET
NELSON ST
SHANTUNG STREET
FERRY STREET
KAM LAM ST
SOY STREET
KAM FONG ST
RECLAMATION STREET
SHANGHAI ST
PORTLAND STREET
NATHAN ROAD
SAI YEUNG CHOI STREET
TUNG CHOI STREET
FA YUEN STREET
YIM PO FONG ST
PEACE AVE
VICTORIA AVE
WATERLOO ROAD
KWONG WA ST
DUNDAS STREET
HAMILTON ST
PITT STREET
CANTON ROAD
CHUN YI LANE
WYLIE ROAD
MAN TIN HILL RD
PRINCESS MARGARET RD
HO
SHEK LUNG ST
MAN LING LA
TUNG KUN ST
WING SING LA
KING'S PARK RISE
PUBLIC SQUARE ST
MARKET ST
KANSU STREET
PAK HOI ST
MAN CHONG ST
MAN WAI ST
MAN YUEN ST
MAN YING ST
MAN WUI ST
SAIGON ST
BATTERY ST
WAI CHING ST
NINGPO ST
NANKING ST
WOOSUNG ST
PARKES ST
CHI WO ST
JORDAN ROAD
GASCOIGNE ROAD
KWUN CHUNG ST
BOWRING STREET
PILKEN ST
TAK HING ST
TAK SHING ST
COX'S ROAD
JORDAN PATH
YUK CHOI ROAD
HONG CHONG RD
AUSTIN ROAD WEST
AUSTIN ROAD
HILLWOOD ROAD
KNUTSFORD TERRACE
CHEONG WAN RD
CHATHAM ROAD
OBSERVATORY ROAD
KIMBERLEY ROAD
KIMBERLEY STREET
GRANVILLE ROAD
GRANVILLE RD
SCIENCE MUSEUM ROAD
KOWLOON PARK DRIVE
CAMERON ROAD
PRAT AVENUE
CHATHAM ROAD SOUTH
MODY ROAD
HAIPHONG ROAD
HANKOW RD
LOCK RD
PEKING RD
MIDDLE ROAD
SALISBURY ROAD

3

HK$10, Wed free; Ⓦmuseums.gov.hk). The Fine Arts section is unlike anything you'll see in the West: scroll paintings depicting landscapes and other aspects of nature alongside exquisite calligraphy displays. Also worth a look are the ceramics through the ages in the Chinese Antiques Gallery and the section of contemporary Hong Kong art.

Further east, at 10 Salisbury Road, the domed **Hong Kong Space Museum** (Mon & Wed–Fri 1–9pm, Sat & Sun 10am–9pm; HK$10, Wed free; Ⓦmuseums.gov.hk) houses somewhat dated exhibitions, such as "moon-walking" displays devoted to space exploration and a shop selling dehydrated astronaut ice cream. The attached **Space Theatre** presents IMAX-style shows, such as "Dynamic Earth", for an additional fee (HK$24–32).

Salisbury Road runs parallel to the waterfront and is dominated by large hotels, such as the iconic Peninsula Hong Kong that dates back to 1928. Running north from Salisbury Road, neon-lit **Nathan Road** boasts Hong Kong's most concentrated collection of electronics shops, tailors, jewellery stores and fashion boutiques. The nearby **Kowloon Park** (Nathan Rd & Austin Rd; daily 6am–midnight) is a sprawling green space dotted with enormous banyan trees; on Sunday afternoons you can catch Kung Fu Corner displays here.

Over on Chatham Road South, east of Nathan Road, is one superbly presented museum that no visitor should miss: the **Hong Kong Museum of History** (daily except Tues 10am–6pm, Sun 10am–7pm; HK$10, Wed free; Ⓦhk.history.museum). The "Hong Kong Story" walks you through the territory's history, from prehistoric times, through the colonial period and the Opium Wars to the growth of Hong Kong's urban culture and return to China in 1997. You'll see national costume, a replica junk, re-created dwellings of the Tanka boat people, a retro grocery store, video footage from World War II that features interviews with prisoners of war, displays on annual Chinese festivals and much, much more.

THE SYMPHONY OF LIGHTS

At 8pm every night Hong Kong's spectacular skyline becomes the scene of the world's largest light show, when more than forty buildings are illuminated during a fourteen-minute extravaganza of lights, music and lasers that symbolizes and celebrates Hong Kong's energy, spirit and diversity. The best views are from the promenade to the east of the Star Ferry.

Opposite is the **Hong Kong Science Museum** (Mon–Wed & Fri 1–9pm, Sat & Sun 10am–9pm; HK$25, Wed free; Ⓦhk.science.museum), with three floors of entertaining hands-on exhibits that demonstrate the laws of physics and the workings of light, sound and the technology used in computers, among others. It's particularly popular with children.

3

Yau Ma Tei

Yau Ma Tei, beginning north of Jordan Road, is full of high-rise tenements and busy streets. **Temple Street**, running north off Jordan Road, a couple of blocks west of Nathan Road, becomes a packed **night market** after around 7pm every day, selling fake brand clothing, Hello Kitty umbrellas, watches and souvenirs. Street stalls serving noodle dishes, grilled seafood and more line the sides of the pedestrianized street, and at the northern end you'll find fortune-tellers and, occasionally, impromptu performances of Chinese opera. Just to the north is the local **Tin Hau Temple** (daily 8am–8pm), off Nathan Road, tucked away between Public Square Street and Market Street. This tiny, ancient temple, dedicated to the goddess of the sea, sits in a small concrete park, usually teeming with old men gambling on card games under the banyan trees. A couple of minutes' walk west of the Tin Hau Temple, just under the Gascoigne Road flyover, is the **Jade Market** (Mon–Sat 10am–5pm), which has several hundred stalls offering jade items; be sure to barter hard and don't go for expensive pieces unless you can tell your jade from your nephrite.

3

Mong Kok and traditional markets

North of Yau Ma Tei is **Mong Kok**. At the corner of Nelson Street and Fa Yuen Street, you can pick up incredibly cheap hardware and bargain software at the **Mong Kok Computer Centre** – though that's only worthwhile if you really know your electronics, as the sellers speak very limited English. A few hundred metres north of here in the direction of Prince Edward MTR are two traditional markets: **Flower Market** (daily 7am–7pm), in Flower Market Road, and the **Yuen Po Street Bird Garden** (daily 7am–8pm), at the eastern end of the same street, where it meets the MTR flyover. The flower market is at its best in the run-up to Chinese New Year, when many people come to buy chrysanthemums and orange trees to decorate their apartments for good luck. Many local men bring their own songbirds to the Bird Garden for an airing; as well as the hundreds of birds on sale here, along with their intricately designed bamboo cages, there are live crickets – whose fate is bird-feed, and you may see the birds being fed live caterpillars held by chopsticks.

Outer Kowloon

Head a few hundred metres north of Mong Kok and you reach **Boundary Street**, which marks the symbolic border between Kowloon and the New Territories.

The main attractions in this area are well to the northeast of Boundary Street. The **Sik Sik Wong Tai Sin Temple** (daily 7am–5.30pm; suggested donation HK$2; Ⓜ Wong Tai Sin, exit B2) consists of sprawling grounds filled with colourful, incense-scented temple buildings, and throngs of worshippers practising Taoism, Buddhism and Confucianism – more than any other temple in Hong Kong (especially during Chinese New Year). Big, bright and colourful, it offers a glimpse into the practices of modern Chinese religions: solemn devotees kneel and pray, wave lighted incense sticks, present food and drink to images of deities, or have their fortune read with *chim* (bamboo sticks), which are shaken out of boxes onto the ground and interpreted by on-site fortune-tellers.

One stop further east, Diamond Hill MTR takes you to the tranquil **Chi Lin Nunnery** (daily 9am–4.30pm) and **Nan Lian Garden** (daily 7am–7pm; free). The nunnery is a Tang Dynasty reproduction and is built of wood, without the use of a single nail, in striking contrast to the tower blocks looming all around it. The serene Nan Lian Garden has a circular walk (around 1hr) that takes in a carp pond, golden pagoda and a small bonsai tree collection. There's an excellent vegetarian restaurant here, specializing in mushroom and vegetable dishes (lunch from HK$100).

The New Territories

They make up 86 percent of Hong Kong's territory, yet the vast **New Territories** are little-explored by visitors, most of whom stick to Hong Kong Island and Kowloon. There is so much to see here, from temples, monasteries and the remains of the original walled villages to pristine beaches, marshlands for birdwatching and hiking around the Prover Cove Reservoir (see box, p.142).

Take the MTR northwest along the West Rail Line to Tuen Mun, then switch to Light Rail lines 610 or 615 and alight at Tsing Shan Tsuen to hike up to the **Tsing Shan Monastery** (daily 8am–8pm), Hong Kong's oldest temple, founded 1500 years ago, rebuilt in 1926 and accessible by a 30-minute steep walk uphill. Parts of the iconic Bruce Lee film, *Enter the Dragon*, were shot here, and there's a slightly creepy charm to the more decayed shrines.

GETTING HIGH IN HONG KONG

For some of Hong Kong's best panoramas, head for the **Sky 100** observation deck (1 Austin Road West, daily 10am–9pm; HK$168; Ⓦ sky100.com.hk; Ⓜ Kowloon Station) at the International Commerce Centre – Hong Kong's highest skyscraper. It sits on the building's 100th floor (nearly 400m up) and the 360-degree views, supplemented by maps and interactive exhibits, are particularly striking at night.

Tin Shui Wan MTR station is the starting point for the 1km-long **heritage trail** that takes you past Hong Kong's only surviving ancient pagoda and through three partially walled villages. At the other end of the trail, near Ping Shan Light Rail station, stop by the **Ping Shan Tang Clan Gallery** (follow the signs and walk uphill; daily 9am–6pm), a museum dedicated to the Tang clan – the first to settle in Hong Kong five hundred years ago. You'll also find the impressive **Tang Ancestral Hall** and the **Yu Kiu Ancestral Hall** here – the largest of their kind in the city.

You can also take the MTR East Rail Line to Tai Po to visit the lively **Tai Po Market** and the bustling Farmers' Market (Sundays only), or take bus #64K to Ng Ting Chai for a hike through the bamboo groves to **Man Tak Monastery** (30min) and the **Ng Tung Chai Waterfall**, a twenty-minute walk further uphill.

THE OUTLYING ISLANDS

Hong Kong's **outlying islands** offer a striking contrast to the nonstop buzz of the city in the form of peaceful seascapes, old fishing villages, hilly hikes and relative rural calm, almost entirely free of motor vehicles.

Lamma Island

Lying just to the southwest of Aberdeen, **Lamma** is the closest island to Hong Kong Island, with a spine of greenery-clad hills, a few sandy beaches, and lots of seafood restaurants, particularly at Yung Shue Wan village. There are two possible **ferry** crossing points, from Central to either Yung Shue Wan via Pak Kok Tsuen, or Sok Kwu Wan, and from Aberdeen to Yung Shue Wan via Mo Tat Wan. The best way to appreciate much of the island is to take a boat to Pak Kok Tsuen or Mo Tat Wan, then hike from one to the other (3 hours or so) to catch the boat back. Bring plenty of drinking water; the well-signposted, paved hiking trails that run up and down the hills are relatively steep and there's little shade.

Mo Tat Wan Beach is wide and peaceful and located on the eastern spur of the island. A twenty-minute walk along the coast takes you to **Sok Kwu Wan**, its row of seafood restaurants built out over the water and fish farms in the harbour. The trail continues to the main village of **Yung Shue Wan** (1hr 15min), passing the **kamikaze caves** where the Japanese stored boats filled with explosives during World War II and the wide crescent of **Hung Shing Yeh Beach**, good for swimming and

3

FERRIES TO THE ISLANDS

Three separate companies operate ferries to the outlying islands: New World First Ferry (walkhongkong.com), Hong Kong & Kowloon Ferry Co (walkhongkong.com) and Discovery Bay Transportation Services (hkri.com). The following is a selection of the most useful island **ferry services**. Schedules differ slightly on weekends (services usually start later in the morning), when prices also rise.

TO CHEUNG CHAU

From Outlying Islands Ferry Piers (Pier 5): 24hr service (at least hourly; 1hr; HK$12.60 slow, HK$24.60 fast). There are also nine sailings daily between Mui Wo on Lantau and Cheung Chau.

TO YUNG SHUE WAN, LAMMA ISLAND

From Outlying Islands Ferry Piers (Pier 4): first boat out 6.30am, last boat back 11.30pm (roughly every 20–30min; 30min; HK$16.10).

From Aberdeen (via Pak Kok Tsuen): first boat out 6am, last boat back 9.10pm (10 daily; 40min; HK$17.50).

TO SOK KWU WAN, LAMMA ISLAND

From Outlying Islands Ferry Piers (Pier 4): first boat out 7.20am, last boat back 10.40pm (11 daily; 45min; HK$19.80).

From Aberdeen (via Mo Tat Wan): first boat out 8am, last boat back 9pm (8 daily; 45min; HK$17.50).

TO MUI WO (SILVERMINE BAY), LANTAU ISLAND

From Outlying Islands Ferry Piers (Pier 6): first boat out 6.10am, last boat back 11.30pm (every 30–40min; 30–60min; HK$14.50 slow, HK$28.40 fast).

sunbathing. This stretch is particularly popular with local hikers, but you don't have to go far to find yourself in blissful solitude: walk along the trail to Pak Kok Tsuen and you'll pass through a lovely bamboo grove, or take a detour to deserted Tung O beach along a trail that branches off before you reach the kamikaze caves.

Cheung Chau Island

Cheung Chau is just south of Lantau and an hour from Hong Kong by ferry. Despite its minuscule size of 2.5 square kilometres, Cheung Chau is the most heavily populated of all the outer islands, and the narrow strip between its two headlands is jam-packed with tiny shops, markets and seafront restaurants.

As well as delicious alfresco meals, the island offers some good **walks** and several temples, the most important being the colourful two-hundred-year-old **Pak Tai Temple** (daily 7am–5pm), a few hundred metres northwest of the ferry pier. For a few days in late April or early May the temple is the site of one of Hong Kong's liveliest and most unusual events, the **Tai Chiu (Bun) Festival**, which sees participants scale a 20m bamboo tower covered with buns.

The main beach on the island, the scenic but crowded **Tung Wan Beach**, is due west of the ferry pier. Windsurf boards (from HK$100/hr) and kayaks (from HK$65/hr) are available for rent during the summer months at the nearby **Windsurfing Centre** (ⓦccwindc.com.hk). To walk round the southern half of the island, follow signs from here for the **Mini Great Wall**, which is actually a ridge leading past some interesting rock formations. As a general rule, paths branching off to the right take you back towards the village, while left forks keep you going round the coast. Past the cemetery, follow signs down to **Pak Tso Wan** for a peaceful, secluded beach. It's also worth detouring to the Cheung Po Tsai cave on the island's westernmost tip; pirates used it to stash their booty in the eighteenth century. A similar signposted circular walk covers the northern half of the island. Each loop takes about three hours.

Lantau Island

With wild countryside, monasteries, old fishing villages and secluded beaches, **Lantau Island** – twice the size of Hong Kong Island – offers the best quick escape from the city. Former governor Crawford Murray MacLehose declared all areas of Lantau more than 200m above sea level a country park; so Lantau remains relatively peaceful.

HONG KONG OUTDOORS

Hong Kong is not just a heaving metropolis, and there are ample opportunities for hiking and biking. The islands of **Lamma** and **Cheung Chau** provide easy, paved walks around headlands, while **Lantau**, especially in the southwest corner, offers spectacular mountains, sea views and camping. Hong Kong Island is bisected by the 50km-long **Hong Kong Trail**: passing through five country parks, it's best done in segments. Further afield, the area around **Plover Cove Reservoir** in the New Territories, reachable by taking East Rail Line MTR to Tai Po Market stop and then by bus #75K, is prime hiking and biking country, with rugged trails of varying lengths and difficulty ratings. **Sai Kung Peninsula**, affectionately known as the "back garden", also has tremendous outdoor appeal, boasting watersports, snorkelling, trekking and the Territory's second tallest mountain – Ma On Shan – which peaks at a challenging 702m.

The free Hong Kong Tourist Board brochure **The Inside Guide to Hikes and Walks in Hong Kong** provides basic maps and information on walks around Hong Kong, and the helpful Discover Hong Kong website (ⓦdiscoverhongkong.com) provides detailed info on hikes, including e-books. You can also consider investing in Pete Spurrier's thorough *Serious Hiker's Guide to Hong Kong* (available in most bookshops). Decent trainers are enough for most walks.

If you don't fancy heading off into the wilderness alone, try **Walk Hong Kong** (ⓦwalkhongkong.com); they offer excellent, highly informative guided walks in English or German, while **Kayak and Hike** (ⓦkayak-and-hike.com) explore Sai Kung by kayak and on foot.

The island's biggest attraction is found high up on the Ngong Ping Plateau, in the western part of the island. The **Po Lin Monastery** (daily 9am–6pm; free) is the largest temple in the whole territory of Hong Kong, though it's more of a tourist draw than a spiritual retreat these days. Hundreds of visitors ascend the 268 steps to pay their respects to the 23m-high bronze **Tian Tan Buddha** (daily 10am–6pm), the largest seated bronze outdoor representation of Lord Gautama in the world, weighing in at 202 tonnes. The monastery makes for a particularly lively spectacle around Buddha's birthday. If you're hungry, the *Po Lin Vegetarian Restaurant* (11.30am–4.30pm) serves filling multi-course meals (HK$60).

The most spectacular way of reaching the "Big Buddha" is to take the **Ngong Ping 360 cable car** (Mon–Fri 10am–6pm, Sat & Sun 9am–6.30pm; HK$105 one-way, HK$150 return; Ⓦnp360.com.hk). The ride takes about half an hour, and presents sweeping views over northern Lantau. The pricier Crystal cabins (HK$160 one-way, HK$235 return) have clear glass floors – not for those with vertigo. The Po Lin Monastery (Ngong Ping in bus schedules) can also be reached by bus #2 from Mui Wo, bus #23 from Tung Chung (the village by the power cable-car terminus) and bus #21 from Tai O.

Right on the far northwestern shore of Lantau, the little fishing village of **Tai O** specializes in processing salt fish (hence the smell), and you'll find dried seafood heaped on tables in the little market area. Constructed over salt flats and a tiny offshore island, this community of stilt houses and quiet narrow lanes has become a weekend outing spot for Hong Kongers. The picturesque walk to **Lung Ngam Monastery** across the Sun Kei bridge takes you past houses built out of old boats and on to hillside views and mangroves. You can reach Tai O by bus #1 from Mui Wo, #21 from the Po Lin Monastery or #11 from Tung Chung.

If you take the ferry to Lantau from Pier 6 at the Outlying Islands ferry terminal on Central or from Cheung Chau island, you arrive at the sleepy town of **Mui Wo**, which has a decent enough beach at Silvermine Bay just to the northwest of town. Buses #1, #2 and #4 run from Mui Wo past several more beaches along the south coast, the **Cheung Sha Beach** being the most appealing.

3

ARRIVAL AND DEPARTURE

BY PLANE

Hong Kong International Airport (Ⓣ2181 8888, Ⓦhongkongairport.com) is 34km west of Central on the north coast of Lantau Island and is served by more than 100 airlines from more than 160 destinations worldwide, including numerous cities in mainland China.

Destinations Bangkok (17 daily; 2hr 30min); Beijing (18 daily; 3hr 30min); Chengdu (4 daily; 2hr 30min); Guangzhou (2 daily; 50min); Ho Chi Minh City (7 daily; 2hr 45min); Jakarta (8 daily; 4hr 30min); Kuala Lumpur (14 daily; 2hr); Kuching (2 daily; 4hr 30min); Manila (12 daily; 2hr); Nanjing (4 daily; 2hr); Phnom Penh (daily; 2hr 30min); Phuket (14 daily; 2hr 30min); Seoul (12 daily; 3hr 30min); Shanghai (18 daily; 2hr 10min); Singapore (20 daily; 4hr); Sydney (daily; 9hr); Tokyo (17 daily; 4hr 30min); Xian (daily; 2hr 45min).

Airport Express The quickest (and priciest) way to get to and from the airport is via the high-speed Airport Express line of the MTR (daily 6am–1am; Ⓦmtr.com.hk), which links Hong Kong in Central (HK$100; 24min), Kowloon (HK$90; 20min) and Tsing Yi (HK$60; 12min) MTR stations and runs every 10–12min. If taking the Airport Express, it's worth getting the Airport Express Travel Pass (see box, p.144).

Airbuses Frequent Airbuses (daily 6am–midnight) are cheaper than the Airport Express; buy tickets on-board or from airport customer service counters. The #A11 goes to Causeway Bay on Hong Kong Island via Sheung Wan, Central, Admiralty and Wan Chai (HK$40; 70min), the #A12 goes direct to Central (HK$45; 50min) and the #A21 goes to Hung Hom MTR Station via Tsim Sha Tsui, Jordan, Yau Ma Tei and Mong Kok (HK$35; 75min). All buses have equivalent (though less regular) night services and none gives change; this is available from the transport centre at the airport, as are Octopus cards (see box, p.144).

Taxis Taxis into the city are metered and reliable, but it's a good idea to have the name of your lodgings written down in Chinese characters to show the driver. It costs HK$230–240 to get to Tsim Sha Tsui (20–30min) and about HK$290–300 for Hong Kong Island (30–50min). There's a HK$5 surcharge for every piece of luggage in the boot.

BY FERRY

You can travel to a number of Chinese cities directly from Hong Kong. Tickets can be bought in advance from a branch of CTS (Ⓦctshk.com), online or from the booths in the terminals themselves.

China Ferry Terminal Located just a 10min walk west from Nathan Rd in Kowloon. Destinations include Macau (every 30min; 7am–10.30pm; HK$151 weekdays, HK$166 weekends) and several stops in the Pearl River Delta (also served by the Hong Kong–Macau Ferry Terminal), including Shekou (6 daily; 50min; HK$110) and Zhuhai (7 daily; 1hr 10min; HK$190), though not central Guangzhou or Shenzhen.

Hong Kong–Macau Ferry Terminal Turbojets and catamarans to Macau leave from the Hong Kong–Macau Ferry Terminal in Sheung Wan on Hong Kong Island (every 15min from 7am–midnight, hourly from midnight–7am; HK$151 Mon–Fri, HK$163 Sat & Sun) and take an hour. There's also a Cotai Jet service running from Shun Tak directly to Taipa, for the Cotai Strip casinos (every 30min; 7am–midnight; HK$151 Mon–Fri, HK$163 Sat & Sun; 1hr).

3

Hong Kong International Airport Skypier ferry services operate from the airport to several Chinese destinations (as well as Macau): Zhuhai, Zhongshan, Dongguan, Shekou, Fuyong, Nansha and Shenzhen (see hongkongairport.com for timetables and tariffs). Using this service, it's possible to transfer direct to China without passing through Hong Kong immigration (although you'll need the correct Chinese visa for all destinations bar Macau). Buy your ticket from the desks in the transfer area on Arrivals level 5, near the immigration counters.

BY TRAIN

The simplest way to reach mainland China is by direct train from Hung Hom or simply by crossing the border at Lo Wu/Lok Ma Chau. Tickets are obtainable in advance from CTS offices or on the same day from the Hung Hom MTR Station. For more information, check it3.mtr.com.hk.

Hung Hom MTR Station Located to the east of Tsim Sha Tsui. You can transfer to the MTR East Rail line for one stop to East Tsim Sha Tsui Station, a short walk from Nathan Rd. Destinations Beijing (on alternate days; 3.15pm; 24hr; from HK$574); Guangzhou East (hourly; 7.25am–7.24pm; 1hr 45min; from HK$190; Shanghai (on alternate days; 3.15pm; 19hr; from HK$508).

Lo Wu/Lok Ma Chau MTR Stations The furthest MTR stations along the East Rail Line are easy gateways to Shenzhen. The border crossing at Lok Ma Chau is open 24 hours, while the Lo Wu crossing operates between 6.30am and midnight.

BY BUS

There are regular daily bus services to Guangzhou and Shenzhen operated by China Travel Service (CTS; ctshk.com); these take about one hour longer than the direct train and drop you off at Hung Hom, Sheung Wan, Wan Chai and Causeway Bay (frequent from 5.15am–10.15pm; 2–3hr; HK$100).

GETTING AROUND

By MTR The MTR (Mass Transit Railway; mtr.com.hk) is Hong Kong's underground and overground train system, which operates from roughly 6am–1am and consists of nine coloured lines and a Light Rail network that covers the northwest Northern Territories. You can buy single-journey tickets (HK$4–25) from machines in the stations, or use the slightly better value and more convenient Octopus Card (see box below).

By tram The narrow, double-decker trams (hktramways.com) are a great way to travel along the north shore of Hong Kong Island. They are quite slow, but give you a great view of the neighbourhoods you are passing through. Trams run between 6am and midnight and the longest run is from Kennedy Town in the west to Shau Kei Wan in the east (change at Western Market). Destinations are displayed at the front, and all trams, bar those to Happy Valley, run east–west. Board at the back, and pay the driver (HK$2.30; no change given) when you get off.

By bus The single- and double-decker a/c buses take you pretty much anywhere in the territory. Pay the exact amount as you board. The main bus terminal in Central is at Exchange Square, a few minutes' walk west of the Star Ferry Pier, though some buses also start from the ferry pier's concourse. In Tsim Sha Tsui, the main bus terminal is

THE OCTOPUS CARD

The rechargeable **Octopus Card** (octopus.com.hk) "smart card" can be used for travel on the MTR, Light Rail, the Airport Express, trams, ferries, buses and green minibuses. You can buy an Octopus Card from the airport terminal and from any MTR station; it costs HK$150, with a refundable deposit of HK$50 and HK$100 worth of credit. You can add value to it via machines in MTR stations. Octopus fares are around five percent cheaper than regular fares on the MTR, and since buses, trams and minibuses don't give change, using an Octopus Card prevents you from overpaying. The card is also available as an **Airport Express Travel Pass** (HK$220/300, including one/two trips on the Airport Express and three consecutive days of unlimited travel on the MTR), an **MTR Tourist Day Pass** (HK$55 for 24 hours of unlimited travel on the MTR) and a **Tourist Cross-boundary Travel Pass** (HK$85/120 for one/two days of consecutive travel plus two single journeys to/from Lo Wu/Lok Ma Chau stations). When you leave Hong Kong, just hand the card back at the airport or an MTR terminal to get your HK$50 deposit.

right in front of the Star Ferry Pier. Bus fares vary from around HK$2 to HK$52.

By taxi Taxis in Hong Kong are not expensive, starting at HK$20 (HK$15 in Lantau), with a HK$5 per piece of luggage. Note that there is a toll to be paid (around HK$10) on any trips through a tunnel and drivers are allowed to double this, on the grounds that they have to get back again. Many taxi drivers do not speak English, so have your destination written down in Chinese.

By ferry One of the most enjoyable (and cheapest: HK$2–3) modes of transport is the Star Ferry between Kowloon and Hong Kong Island (see box, p.137). Ferries run every 6–12 minutes between Tsim Sha Tsui and Central (daily 6.30am–11.30pm; 9min), and between Tsim Sha Tsui and Wan Chai (daily 7.20am–11pm; 8min). Regular ferries also run to the outlying islands (see box, p.141).

INFORMATION

Tourist information The super-efficient Hong Kong Tourism Board (HKTB; Ⓦ discoverhongkong.com) has several handy offices: one in the arrivals area of the airport (daily 7am–11pm), at the Star Ferry Concourse in Tsim Sha Tsui (daily 8am–8pm) and in the Peak Piazza on Hong Kong Island (daily 9am–9pm). There's also a HKTB multilingual telephone service (daily 9am–6pm, Ⓣ 2508 1234).

Listings publications Countless leaflets on what to do, including *Where* magazine and *City Life*, can be picked up at HKTB outlets. The free *HK Magazine* (Ⓦ hk-magazine.com), published every Friday, contains excellent up-to-date information on restaurants, bars, happy hours, clubs, concerts and exhibitions. *Time Out* magazine has an HK edition, available throughout the Territory (Ⓦ timeout.com.hk).

Tours There are some excellent themed tours run by individual companies but bookable through HKTB. Otherwise, Walk In Hong Kong (Ⓦ walkin.hk) organize outstanding specialized walking tours for small groups, taking you off the beaten path to the city's cemeteries, venerable old shops selling traditional Chinese medicine, North Point and other characterful neighbourhoods; tours typically last two hours and cost around HK$160. Splendid Tours & Travel (Ⓦ splendid.hk) offer six-hour cruises along the Sai Kung coastline, and a "come horseracing" tour that takes you for a night out at the races (Sept–June). Eco Travel (Ⓦ ecotravel.hk) run an excellent tour to the New Territories Geopark that takes in interesting rock formations, a walled Hakka village, feng shui trees and more.

ACCOMMODATION

HONG KONG ISLAND

The budget rooms on Hong Kong Island are mostly in Causeway Bay, some near Sogo and others towards Leighton Rd. They tend to be more expensive than Kowloon, but comparatively quieter.

Causeway Bay Inn Flat A, 1st floor, Percival House, 77–83 Percival St Ⓦ causewaybayinn.com; Ⓜ Causeway Bay; map pp.132–133. Just three comfortable, modern en-suite rooms – two with twin beds and one a double – decorated in pastel shades, with TVs, a/c and mini fridges. You get an entrance code for your room as there doesn't tend to be anyone manning the reception. Perfect for a quiet stay. Double **HK$390**

Check Inn 273 Hennessy Rd Ⓣ 2155 0175, Ⓦ checkinnhk.com; Ⓜ Wan Chai; map pp.132–133. Friendly, colourful hostel that's perfect for night owls who like pub crawls and socializing. Lockers are on the small side, luggage space is at a premium and getting up on the top bunks requires a certain degree of acrobatic skill, but the staff are very helpful. Dorm **HK$220**

Life on a Boat – Moksha Shum Wan Rd, Wong Chuk Hang, Aberdeen Ⓦ airbnb.co.uk/rooms/65117; buses #36S, #29A; map pp.132–133. One of the more unusual accommodation options in town, *Moksha* is a wooden junk converted into a cute houseboat, currently moored in Aberdeen harbour. The compact cabins are wonderfully cosy, the hosts are welcoming and helpful, breakfast is included and you get to catch a sampan to shore every day. Two-night minimum stay. **HK$750**

★ **YesInn @ Causeway Bay** 2nd floor, Nan Yip Building, 472 Hennessy Rd Ⓣ 2213 4567, Ⓦ yesinn.com; Ⓜ Causeway Bay; map pp.132–133. Bright and colourful, with a chillout area and rooftop garden that encourage mingling, a good mix of single-sex and mixed dorms and private rooms, and beds big enough for Westerners, *YesInn* wins points for comfort and efficiency. Nice extras include iPads that you can borrow and 24hr tea and coffee. Dorm **HK$159**, double **HK$398**

Y-Loft 238 Chai Wan Rd Ⓣ 3721 8989, Ⓦ youthsquare.hk; Ⓜ Chai Wan; map pp.132–133. Don't be put off by the rather remote location at the end of the MTR: the area is blissfully untouristy and you're well positioned to explore Shek O and the south side of Hong Kong Island. The doubles and triples are immense by Hong Kong standards and all come with giant flat-screen TVs and wheelchair access. Double **HK$770**

KOWLOON

Most of the accommodation listed below is within a 15min walk of the Star Ferry Pier – conveniently central, though very touristy.

A-Inn Rooms 809 & 1304, 8th floor, Sincere House, 83 Argyle St Ⓣ 9533 6817, Ⓦ ainnhongkong.hostel.com; Ⓜ Mong Kok; map p.138. More like a budget hotel than a hostel, *A-Inn* has compact doubles, triples and quads with plasma-screen TVs. There's no common room, so it's good for a quiet stay rather than for meeting fellow travellers. Very convenient location right next to the MTR station. Double **HK$400**

3

3

Hello HK A-7, 6th floor, Mirador Mansions, 54–56 Nathan Rd ☎ 3995 4171, ⓦ helloinn.blogbus.com; Ⓜ Tsim Sha Tsui; map p.138. Run by the ever-smiling Ivan, this is a contender for best Hong Kong hostel – though with only six rooms, you must book ahead. Rooms are clean, bright and have bathrooms (with shower cubicles) and LCD TVs, though only two have windows. DVD players are available on request and there's a Chinese visa outlet next door. Double HK$540

Homy Inn Union Mansion, 33–35 Chatham Rd ☎ 8100 0189, ⓦ homyinn.com.hk; Ⓜ Tsim Sha Tsui; map p.138. In spite of the misspelled name, this place is, in fact, very homey and the staff get top marks for going out of their way to ensure your Hong Kong stay is a good one. There are clean, functional singles, doubles and family rooms, all with crisp white linens. Double HK$540

★ **Hop Inn** 9th floor, James S. Lee Mansion, 33–35 Carnarvon Rd ☎ 6753 5757, ⓦ hopinn.hk; Ⓜ Tsim Sha Tsui; map p.138. Colourful little en-suite rooms, each one individually decorated by a local artist, clear glass bathrooms and extra-helpful staff. No common room but a friendly, sociable vibe prevails. Double HK$380

InnSight 9 Lock Rd ☎ 2369 1151, ⓦ innsight.hk; Ⓜ Tsim Sha Tsui; map p.138. Just four individually decorated en-suite rooms with a/c and TVs – two doubles, a twin and a single – in a great location and with very helpful owners. Double HK$580

Lee Garden Guest House Block A, 8th floor, Fook Kiu Mansion, 36 Cameron Rd ☎ 2367 2284, ⓦ starguesthouse.com.hk; Ⓜ Tsim Sha Tsui; map p.138. Friendly owner Charlie Chan and his son Raymond offer a comfortable range of clean, small singles, doubles and triples (all with windows), that feel more like a hotel than a guesthouse. Cheaper rooms share facilities. The Chans also own the similar *Star Guest House* (6th floor, 21 Cameron Rd; ☎ 2723 8951). *Lee Garden* double HK$450, *Star Guest House* double HK$450

Motel Double Yield A-9, 8th floor, Mirador Mansions, 54–56 Nathan Rd ☎ 6144 7072; Ⓜ Tsim Sha Tsui; map p.138. Pristine, newly renovated, modern guesthouse, consisting of just five rooms. Rooms come with kettles and small TVs. Double HK$600

Rent-a-Room Flat A, 2nd floor, Knight Garden, 7–8 Tak Hing St ☎ 2366 3011, ⓦ rentaroomhk.com; Ⓜ Jordan; map p.138. This clean hotel offers two floors of decent-sized rooms – singles, doubles, triples and quads – as well as a whole range of facilities including money-changing and laundry. Rooms are a bit featureless but come with phones, a/c, fridges and kitchenettes. Discounts available for longer stays and security is top-notch. Double HK$700

The Salisbury 41 Salisbury Rd ☎ 2268 7888, ⓦ ymcahk.org.hk; Ⓜ Tsim Sha Tsui; map p.138. The Salisbury is all about location. Yes, the lodgings are a bit basic, if newly renovated, but the harbour-view rooms offer the same vista as the venerable *Peninsula Hotel* next door for a fraction of the price. Other perks include a tour desk, helpful staff and self-service laundry. Double HK$1100

Urban Pack Unit 1410, Hai Phong Mansion, 99–101 Nathan Rd ☎ 2732 2271, ⓦ urban-pack.com; Ⓜ Tsim Sha Tsui; map p.138. Funky "designer hostel" decorated in bright colours, where the staff make you feel like family. The dorms might be a little cramped, but the place is super-clean and you may find yourself extending your stay because of the welcoming vibe. Dorm HK$180

CHUNGKING MANSIONS

Chungking Mansions is an apartment block at 36–44 Nathan Rd with the highest concentration of budget guesthouses in Kowloon. It's an ethnic enclave of immigrants from India and Africa and has an unforgettable atmosphere: on the ground floor alone, you can visit an internet café, eat a great curry, get a haircut, buy a mobile phone, change money and buy new clothes. Above the second floor, the building is divided into five blocks, lettered A to E, each served by two lifts, and usually attended by long queues. The building may feel a bit like a firetrap, but fire safety is at acceptable levels these days, and there's CCTV. Guesthouses vary widely – from dingy flophouses to spotless little places – and there are usually young men loitering at the entrance, dishing out business cards and trying to entice you to stay at their particular guesthouse. Below are several recommended places; if you arrive without a reservation, never agree to stay without inspecting the rooms first, and even if you do have a reservation, the less scrupulous touts may try to tell you that your guesthouse is dirty/has closed down, so take it with a pinch of salt.

Apple Hostel B-3, 10th floor, Block B ☎ 2369 9802, ⓦ applehostel.hostel.com; Ⓜ Tsim Sha Tsui; map p.138. Friendly place with tiny singles and doubles and minuscule bathrooms where you can shower while sitting on the loo. That said, everything is spotless, towels are changed daily and every room comes with a phone and kettle. Wi-fi is semi-reliable. Double HK$400

Dragon Inn B-2, Flat B, 3rd floor, Block B ☎ 2368 2007, ⓦ dragoninn.info; Ⓜ Tsim Sha Tsui; map p.138. Well-organized, friendly and secure hostel-cum-travel agent with singles, doubles and triples. The newer rooms verge on the luxurious and there's even a "honeymoon room", though you have to wonder who'd spend their honeymoon at Chungking Mansions. Double HK$360

Guangdong Guest House B-2, 5th floor, Block B, ⓦ guangdonghostel.com; Ⓜ Tsim Sha Tsui; map p.138. Friendly, helpful Simon oversees various configurations of compact rooms: singles, doubles, triples and quads. All are clean and come with a/c and phones, but as elsewhere in Chungking Mansions, the rooms tend to be curry-scented during the day. Double HK$600, quad HK$1100

Maple Leaf Guesthouse E-4, 12th floor, Block E ⓣ 9325 6152, ⓦ mapleleafguesthouse.hostel.com; Ⓜ Tsim Sha Tsui; map p.138. Welcoming, secure guesthouse with compact, well-lit rooms and equally compact bathrooms. Double **HK$440**

★ New Peking Guest House A-1, 12th floor, Block A ⓣ 2723 8320, ⓦ chungking-mansions.hk/A12-2.htm; Ⓜ Tsim Sha Tsui; map p.138. Spotless guesthouse with toothbrushes, fridge and electrical converters provided by the friendly management. Take your pick from singles, doubles, triples and quads. Double **HK$700**

EATING AND DRINKING

CENTRAL

Most cheap eating in Central can be found along Wellington St and along either side of the Mid-Levels Escalator. Further east, you'll find plenty of choice on Jaffe Rd and in the streets near Times Square. If you want to eat during peak lunch and dinnertime hours, be prepared to queue.

★ Chilli Fagara 51A Graham St Ⓜ Central or Sheung Wan; map pp.132–133. The crimson decor at this thimble-sized Sichuan restaurant gives you some idea of what to expect: beautiful, heat-laden dishes, such as tender chunks of fish in a sweet chilli sauce and red hot chilli prawns that'll bring a tear to your eye – a challenge even to the brave. Set lunch HK$88. Daily 11.30am–2.30pm & 5–11.30pm.

Dumpling Yuan 69 Wellington St Ⓜ Central; map pp.132–133. This efficient Pekinese restaurant lists a good mix of meaty and veggie choices among its dumpling offerings. Tuck into pork and leek, mixed jellyfish or lamb with chives (HK$37). Another branch at 259 Queen's Rd East (Ⓜ Wan Chai). Daily 10am–11pm.

Lil' Siam 38 Elgin St, Central Ⓜ Central; map pp.132–133. Thai restaurant that rises above the competition with its authentic dishes such as *som tum* (spicy papaya salad), red curry with roast duck, banana blossom salad and sticky rice with mango. Lunch set menu a bargain at HK$88. Daily noon–11pm.

Lin Heung Tea House 160–164 Wellington St Ⓜ Sheung Wan; map pp.132–133. One of the last surviving *dim sum* places in Hong Kong where the tiny bites are brought round on trolleys, *Lin Heung* is barely controlled bedlam spread over several floors. Just point at the steamed dumplings, buns, pork ribs, rice with chicken and fish maw and other dishes as the trolleys pass by. Best enjoyed with a group of friends. Dishes from HK$15. Daily 6am–11pm.

Mana! 92 Wellington St Ⓜ Sheung Wan; map pp.132–133. The self-described "fast slow food" at this organic vegetarian and vegan café consists of flatbreads topped with grilled tofu and roast vegetables, mezze platters of hummus and olives, hearty soup of the day and portobello mushroom and haloumi burgers. Mains from HK$70. Daily 10am–10pm.

Nagahama No 1 Ramen 14 Kau U Fong Ⓜ Sheung Wan; map pp.132–133. One of many super-popular ramen noodle joints, *Nagahama* uses a pork bone soup base that gives its chunky, slurpable noodles their distinctive flavour. Large portions, tiny place, so put on your queuing shoes. Mains from HK$80. Daily 11.30am–10pm.

Nha Trang 88–90 Wellington St Ⓜ Sheung Wan; map pp.132–133. Packed out at lunchtimes and evenings with expats and locals alike, this Vietnamese joint offers the likes of *bun bo xao* – cold vermicelli salad with lemongrass beef – pho, pork belly simmered in coconut milk and fresh spring rolls bursting with herbs. Mains from HK$55. There's another branch on the ground floor of the Ocean Terminal, Harbour City, Canton Rd (Ⓜ Thim Sha Tsui). Daily noon–4.30pm & 6.30–10.30pm.

Tasty Congee & Noodle Wonton Shop Shops 3016–3018, IFC Mall, 1 Harbour View St Ⓜ Hong Kong, exit E1; map pp.132–133. Shoppers at the luxury IFC Mall pile into this simple restaurant to feast on the signature prawn wontons, noodle soup, prawn congee and flat rice noodles stir-fried with beef; less standard offerings include boiled jellyfish strips and stewed pork feet. Mains from HK$35. Daily 11.30am–10.45pm.

WAN CHAI AND CAUSEWAY BAY

Bowrington Road Ⓜ Causeway Bay; map pp.132–133. This tiny alley boasts two culinary treats. The "Cooked Food Centre" (daily 6am–2am) has a dozen open kitchens serving great authentic food at rock-bottom prices (Hainan chicken with rice and soup; HK$40), but you'll need to point for your dinner as little English is spoken. In the evening, locals perch on plastic stools to enjoy deliciously fresh and varied seafood dishes from the hole-in-the-wall restaurants. Prices are reasonable – razor clams in black bean sauce HK$75.

Brunch Club & Supper 1st floor, 13 Leighton Rd Ⓜ Causeway Bay; map pp.132–133. Cosy and relaxed, this is a great place for the morning after the night before, with brunch sets ranging from muesli and yogurt to eggs with chorizo, smoked salmon and goat's cheese. It's worth getting out of bed for the chocolate truffle tart alone (HK$28). Happy hour 6–9pm daily. Also at 70 Peel St (Ⓜ Central). Sun–Thurs 9am–11pm, Fri & Sat 9am till late.

Crystal Jade La Mian Xiao Long Bao Shop 310, 3rd floor, Tai Yau Plaza Ⓜ Wan Chai; map pp.132–133. Retro Shanghainese diner specializing in steamed dumplings and noodle dishes. The more unusual dishes include smoked duck with tea leaves. Mains from HK$70. Daily 11am–10.30pm.

Hainan Shaoye Shop P311, 3rd floor, World Trade Centre, 280 Gloucester Rd Ⓜ Causeway Bay; map pp.132–133. Bright, busy restaurant specializing in Singaporean and Malaysian dishes. Try the *bak kut teh* (pork ribs simmered in herb broth) or the noodle dishes such as *mee goreng*. Lunch set from HK$70. Daily 11.30am–2.30pm & 6–10.30pm.

3

Nam Kee Spring Roll Noodle Co 1st floor, San Kei Tower, 56–58 Yee Wo St Ⓜ Causeway Bay; map pp.132–133. Choose from eight meat options for a perfect bowl of steaming hot noodles in aromatic broth – delicious pork belly noodles cost HK$29. Also at 66–72 Stanley St (Ⓜ Central). Mon–Sat 7.30am–11pm & Sun 11am–11pm.

Sushi Fuku-suke 11th floor, Macau Yat Yuen Centre, 525 Hennessy Rd Ⓜ Causeway Bay; map pp.132–133. Decor at this authentic Japanese restaurant consists of simple, clean lines, and the sushi and sashimi sets are top-notch, courtesy of the chef from Tokyo. Lunch sets from HK$165. Daily noon–3pm & 6–11pm.

★**Tai Hing** Shop J, ground floor, Po Ming Building, 54 Lee Garden Rd; Ⓜ Causeway Bay; map pp.132–133. Busy *siu-mei* (roast) specialist with roast duck, goose and pork glistening in the window. The friendly staff don't speak much English but they're helpful, and succulent dishes, including hunks of roast pork, crispy crackling, rice and *kankun* (HK$55) are served up in no time at all. Daily 7am–11.30pm.

3

KOWLOON

You can take your pick from a multitude of stalls and cafés on Temple St and the surrounding area. Prat Avenue has a wide variety of Asian choices, while Knutsford Terrace is good for international food – albeit slightly pricey. Chungking Mansions (see p.146) is the place for inexpensive curries – just follow your nose.

BLT Steak Shop G62, ground floor, Ocean Terminal, Harbour City Ⓜ Tsim Sha Tsui; map p.138. *Bistro Laurent Tourondel* is all about beef – porterhouse, New York strip, ribeye, you name it. Lighter options available for the less carnivorous and lunch sets start from HK$120. Daily noon–10.30pm.

Din Tai Fung Shop 130, 3rd floor, Silvercord, Canton Rd Ⓜ Tsim Sha Tsui; map p.138. Large, bright Shanghainese restaurant specializing mostly in dumplings. The speciality is the *shao long bao*, but it's hard to go wrong with noodle soup or pork and truffle dumplings. Dishes from HK$35. Also at Shop 3–9, GF, 68 Yee Woo St (Ⓜ Causeway Bay). Daily 11.30am–10pm.

Initial Café 48 Cameron Rd Ⓜ Tsim Sha Tsui; map p.138. Appealing coffee house whose distressed decor and mismatched chairs scream shabby chic. All-day breakfasts and waffles are particularly good; the salads, pastas and noodle dishes won't wow your tastebuds but are inexpensive and filling. Mains from HK$60. Daily 8.30am–6pm.

The New Sangeet 7Shop UG06, Toyo Mall, Inter-Continental Plaza, 94 Granville Rd Ⓜ Tsim Sha Tsui; map p.138. Specializing in northern Indian food, this contemporary restaurant has a particularly good-value lunchtime (HK$88) and dinnertime set menu (HK$130). Tandoori dishes stand out from the à la carte. Daily 11am–11.30pm.

★**One Dim Sum** Kenwood Mansion, 15 Playing Field Rd Ⓜ Prince Edward, exit A; map p.138. One of two Michelin-starred cheapies in Hong Kong, this compact *dim sum* joint is perpetually packed with punters who come for the *chiu chow* dumplings, the rice rolls with prawns and barbecued pork, chicken rice and congee. Look for the line of stools by the door; queues move quickly. Dishes HK$13–20. Daily 11am–1am.

Superior Rice Roll Pro Shop 373 Portland St Ⓜ Prince Edward; map p.138. Small joint popular with locals that specializes in eight types of rice rolls: barbecued pork, dried shrimp, vegetable and a few other select flavours. Ask for an English menu. Rice rolls from HK$14. Daily 9am–9pm.

Tim Ho Wan 8 Kwong Wa St Ⓜ Mong Kok; map p.138. Hong Kong's cheapest Michelin-starred restaurant. The *dim sum*'s the star at this tiny establishment; everything is freshly made in house, and the *char siew bao* (BBQ pork buns; HK$14) and the *chiu chow* dumplings are renowned. Queues can be lengthy around mealtimes, so go late morning or early afternoon when there are fewer people. Daily 10am–9.15pm.

NIGHTLIFE

Drinking in Hong Kong is expensive and a beer will normally set you back at least HK$50; however, most bars operate happy hours where drinks may be discounted by as much as fifty percent. Many bars have Ladies' Nights, usually on Wednesday or Thursday, where women can easily stay out all night without spending anything. The most concentrated collection of bars is in Central, spreading from the long-standing, popular Lan Kwai Fong to the network of streets leading into and including the upmarket SoHo area. Rubbing shoulders with the "hostess bars" in Jaffe and Lockhart roads in Wan Chai are a dozen or more regular clubs and bars. Tsim Sha Tsui's nightlife scene is somewhat sparse compared to Hong Kong Island, but there are a few bars, lounges and clubs found near the harbour and Jordan. Check out Ⓦ hiphongkong.com to find out what's hot at the moment.

HONG KONG ISLAND

Buddha Lounge L/G Amber Lodge, 23 Hollywood Rd, Central Ⓜ Central; map pp.132–133. Small and cosy bar decorated with Buddha images that kicks off late, with a superb sound system and DJ sets until the very early hours. Nightly drinks specials, Tuesday ladies' night and a happy hour from 4–10pm. Mon–Sat 1pm–late.

Cicada 4 Shelly St, SoHo Ⓜ Central; map pp.132–133. Delicious Asian tapas such as minted lamb dumplings (HK$75) perfectly complement lychee bellinis and other happy hour cocktails (HK$35) from 3–8pm at this wine bar-cum-restaurant. The closely packed tables overlooking the escalators get booked up quickly with out-of-office crowds. Daily noon–2am.

Globe 45–53 Graham St, SoHo Ⓜ Central; map pp.132–133. Immense bar known for serving T8, the first cask-conditioned ale to be brewed in Hong Kong, with a supporting cast of imported beers and solid comfort food. Happy hour 10am–8pm. Mon–Sat 10am–2am.
Likuid 58–62 D'Aguilar St Ⓜ Central, exit D2; map pp.132–133. All sensuous curves and super high-tech lighting, this is a hot clubbing spot that attracts a trendy crowd. Dress nicely. Happy hour 6–10pm. Daily 5pm–late.
Red Bar 4th floor, IFC Mall, 8 Finance St, Central Ⓜ Hong Kong; map pp.132–133. Fabulous rooftop bar facing out over the harbour and the Kowloon skyline, with a huge cocktail menu (from HK$85) and nightly DJ sets. Happy hour 6–9pm. Daily 11.30am till late.
★ **Wooloomooloo** 31st floor, 256 Hennessy Rd Ⓜ Wan Chai; map pp.132–133. Situated above the acclaimed steakhouse of the same name, this rooftop bar has fantastic 270-degree views over Victoria Harbour and Happy Valley, comfy rattan sofas and friendly staff. Cocktails from HK$65. Daily 11.45am–2.30pm & 6pm till late.

KOWLOON

Bahama Mama's 4–5 Knutsford Terrace Ⓜ Tsim Sha Tsui, exit B1; map p.138. A beach-bar theme, completed with surfboards and an outdoor terrace that prompts party-crowd antics. DJs on Fridays and Saturdays and a young, exuberant crowd. Happy hour 5–9pm. Open 4pm till late.
Ned Kelly's Last Stand 11a Ashley Rd Ⓜ Tsim Sha Tsui, exit L5; map p.138. Decked out with Oz-related parapher-nalia and named after a gun-slinging Australian convict, this lively pub is a favourite with expats and tourists. Happy hour 11.30am–9pm. Daily 11.30am–late.
Snake King Yan 80a Woo Sung St, Yau Ma Tei Ⓜ Jordan, exit A; map p.138. The speciality at this shop, straight out of a Chinese B-movie, is rice wine mixed with snake bile, believed to increase male virility. Try it if you dare. Daily 10am–9pm.
Utopia 26th floor, Hon Kwok Jordan Centre, 7 Hillwood Rd Ⓜ Jordan; map p.138. Views to rival Hong Kong Island's fancier bars, draught beers on tap, a good selection of wines from around the world and a wide selection of cocktails, accompanied by some highly munchable finger food. Happy hour 4.30–9pm. Daily noon–late.

SHOPPING

In Tsim Sha Tsui, Causeway Bay and Wan Chai, daily shop opening hours are generally 11am–11pm; in Central, it's 10am–7pm.
Arts and crafts G.O.D. (Leighton Centre, Sharp St East, Ⓜ Causeway Bay) stands for "goods of desire" and specializes in retro gifts with a twist. Homeless (28 Gough St, Central; Ⓜ Sheung Wan) stocks all sorts of quirky gifts – both practical and for decoration – and gadgets for the home. Hollywood Rd, Central, and the adjoining "Cat St" (see p.134) are a good bet for mah jong sets and Mao memorabilia.
Bookshops Book Attic (Cockloft, 2 Elgin St, Soho) is a cosy secondhand bookshop where you can sip a quiet cuppa while browsing through the wide selection. Page One (Shop 922, 9th floor, Times Square, 1 Matheson St; Ⓜ Causeway Bay) has a large selection of travel guides, maps and English-language fiction.
Clothes Local casual-wear chain stores, including Giordano, Wanko and Bossini, have branches all over the city. Local designers to look out for include Nude is Rude (7 Lan Kwai Fong; Ⓜ Central, exit D2), with casual wear by Marisa Zeman; Ranee K (25 Aberdeen St; Ⓜ Central) offers bold prints and textures, combined with styles both from the east and the west, and Daydream Nation (2nd floor, Hong Kong Arts Centre, 2 Harbour Rd; Ⓜ Wan Chai), with creative clothing and accessories aimed at a youthful audience, designed by a brother and sister team.
Electronics Wan Chai Computer Centre (1st floor, Southorn Centre, 130–138 Hennessy Rd; Ⓜ Wan Chai) is a veritable cornucopia of everything digital and electronic. Mong Kok Computer Centre (8 Nelson St; Ⓜ Mong Kok) is another one-stop shop for anything electronic, but there's a language barrier and you need to know exactly what you're looking for.
Jewellery and accessories 9th Muse (Unit 1204, One Lyndhurst Tower, 1 Lyndhurst Terrace; Ⓜ Central) stocks hand-crafted handbags and jewellery that have been tempting the local fashionistas for years, and it's not too expensive. If you're looking for jade, try the special Jade Market in Yau Ma Tei (see p.139).
Tea At Ming Cha (12th floor, Flat D, Wah Ha Factory Building, 8 Shipyard Lane; Ⓜ Taikoo) friendly and knowledgeable staff will help you find gift tea packs amid their large selection. Lam Kie Yuen Tea Co (105–107 Bonham Strand East; Ⓜ Sheung Wan, exit A2) is a venerable institution, selling tea since 1955. The choice is immense and includes fermented varieties for connois-seurs; you can try before you buy.

DIRECTORY

Banks and exchanges Banks and ATMs are found throughout Hong Kong, and travellers' cheques can be exchanged at branches of the Bank of China. Banks offer good exchange rates.
Embassies and consulates Australia, 23rd & 24th floors, Harbour Centre, 25 Harbour Rd, Wan Chai ☎ 2827 8881; Canada, 11th–14th Floor, One Exchange Square, 8 Connaught Place, Central ☎ 3719 4700; China, 7th Floor, China Resources Building, Lower Block, 26 Harbour Rd, Wan Chai ☎ 3413 2300; New Zealand, Rm 6501, Central Plaza, 18 Harbour Rd, Wan Chai ☎ 2511 7218; South Africa, Rms 2612–1222, Regus Business Centre, 12th floor, China Resources Building, 26 Harbour Rd, Wan Chai

3

CHINESE VISAS

To enter China, you'll need a pre-arranged **visa**. The official consular website states that all visas are required to be processed in your home country, though travel agencies and hotels, even the cheapest hostels, in Hong Kong offer this service. However, it's best to check before you travel. A **single-entry visa** costs from HK$200 with a four-day wait, HK$400 if you want it within three days (express) or HK$500 for the rush two-day service. You can also get more expensive **multiple-entry visas**. Some passport-holders, including British and US, may have to pay significantly more (HK$360 and HK$1100 respectively for the standard four-day service). The Ministry of Foreign Affairs is on the 3th floor, China Resources Building, 26 Harbour Rd, Wan Chai (Mon–Fri 9am–noon & 2–5pm; 3413 2300, fmcoprc.gov.hk).

2577 3279; UK, 1 Supreme Court Rd, Admiralty 2901 3000; US, 26 Garden Rd, Central 2523 9011.

Hospitals Emergency care is excellent. Private hospitals include Hong Kong Central Hospital, 1 Lower Albert Rd, Central 2522 3141, and Hong Kong Baptist Hospital, 222 Waterloo Rd, Kowloon Tong, 2339 8888. Ambulances (dial 999) take you to a public hospital; foreign visitors have to pay a hefty fee for the use of emergency services, so make sure you have travel insurance.

Internet Free wi-fi is available at the vast majority of lodgings, as well as public libraries, parks, and numerous cafés and bars. You can also get a free 60min PCCW wi-fi pass at HKTB visitor centres.

Laundry Various in Kowloon, including on the ground floor of Golden Crown Court, Nathan Rd (one block north of *Mirador Mansions*; red entrance). Sunshine Laundry on Sharp St West, just under the flyover from Times Square in Causeway Bay, is friendly, efficient and open 24hr.

Left luggage In the departure lounge at the airport (daily 5.30am–1.30am), at major MTR stations and in the China Ferry Terminal in Tsim Sha Tsui. Most lodgings will store your luggage for a few days, though some may charge for this.

Police Call 999 in an emergency.

Post office The General Post Office is at 2 Connaught Place, Central (Mon–Sat 8am–6pm, Sun 9am–5pm), just west of the Star Ferry Pier. The Kowloon main post office is at 10 Middle Rd, Tsim Sha Tsui (Mon–Sat 9am–6pm, Sun 9am–2pm).

Telephone services Local phone codes are free. For international calls, use Skype or buy phonecards, such as PCCW's Hello card, from PCCW branches and 7-Eleven stores and use a public payphone.

Macau

Macau is a city with a split personality: its UNESCO World Heritage Portuguese fortresses and crumbling churches jostle for space with ultramodern casinos in the only city in China where gambling is legal. This melange of Portuguese and Chinese food, winding historic lanes, Taoist temples and modern skyscrapers gives it a character very distinct from nearby Hong Kong.

Macau comprises three distinct parts: the **peninsula**, linked by bridge to the island of **Taipa**, and beyond that the former island of **Coloane**, now joined to Taipa by an ever-widening strip of land reclamation home to the majority of the casinos.

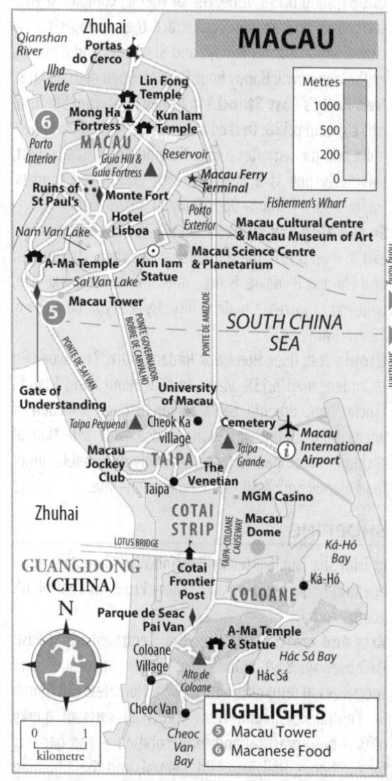

The peninsula of Macau, the location of the original old city and most of the historic sights (as well as the city amenities), is entirely developed right up to the border with China in the north. Taipa and Coloane used to be just dots of land supporting a few small fishing villages, and although Coloane is still relatively tranquil, the opening of the new airport, a third bridge from the mainland and a huge reclamation and casino-building programme mean that much of Taipa, barring its historical centre, has become a rather soulless city suburb.

Although many travellers base themselves in Hong Kong and cover Macau just on a day-trip, a short visit means running yourself ragged; it's well worth staying overnight and allowing yourself at least a couple of days to explore at leisure.

MACAU PENINSULA

The peninsula is compact and it's possible to get around most of it on foot; handy buses ply several main routes, making exploration easier. The town of Macau was born in the south of the peninsula, around the bay-front road known as the **Praia Grande**, and grew out from there. The most important road today, **Avenida de Almeida Ribeiro**, cuts across from southeast (where it's known as Avenida do Infante d'Henrique) to west, taking in the *Hotel Lisboa*, one of Macau's most famous landmarks. The road exits on its western end at the **Porto Interior** (Inner Harbour), near the old docking port, from which foreigners can still depart for the mainland city of Shenzhen in Guangdong. The western part of Almeida Ribeiro is also the budget-hotel area, and some of the streets immediately inland from here are worth poking around. **Rua da Felicidade**, hung with red lanterns, is where part of *Indiana Jones and the Temple of Doom* was shot and is now full of discreet guesthouses, restaurants, aromatic *pastelarias* (pastry shops) and colourful stalls.

The northern part of the peninsula up to the border with China is largely residential, though there are a couple of interesting temples.

Largo do Senado

The attractive **Largo do Senado** (Senate Square) marks the downtown area and bears the unmistakeable influence of southern Europe. At the northern end of the square stands the imposing sixteenth-century Baroque church, **São Domingos** (daily 10am–6pm; free), while to the south, across the main road, stands the **Leal Senado** (Tues–Sun 9am–9pm; free), generally considered the finest Portuguese building in the city. Step into the interior courtyard here to see blue-and-white Portuguese tiles around the walls; up the staircase from the courtyard, you reach first a formal garden and then the richly decorated **senate chamber** itself. In the late sixteenth century, all of the colony's citizens would cram into this hall to debate issues of importance. The senate's title, *leal* (loyal), was earned during the period when Spain occupied the Portuguese throne and Macau became the final stronghold of those loyal to the true king. Today, the senate chamber is still used by the municipal government of Macau. Adjacent to the chamber is the wood-carved **Senate Library** (Mon–Sat 1–7pm), whose collection includes many fifteenth- and sixteenth-century books, which visitors are free to browse.

The area around Rua Central heading south from Almeida Ribeiro is dotted with interesting buildings, especially those in the Largo de Santo Augustino and the Largo de Lilau, one of the earliest Portuguese residential areas.

São Paulo

A few hundred metres north of Largo do Senado stands Macau's most famous landmark, the **church of São Paulo**, once hailed as the greatest Christian monument in east Asia. Constructed at the beginning of the seventeenth century, it dominated the city for two hundred years until its untimely destruction by fire in 1835. Luckily, however, the facade did not collapse – richly carved and laden with statuary, the cracked stone still presents an imposing sight from the bottom of the steps leading up from the Rua de São Paulo. Behind the facade are

the **Na Tcha Temple** (daily 8am–5pm), dedicated to the child god of war in 1888 to fight the plague in the city, and a small section of the old city walls, built nearly five hundred years ago.

Fortaleza do Monte and Museum of Macau

Immediately east of São Paulo looms another early seventeenth-century monument, the impressive **Fortaleza do Monte** (daily 7am–7pm; free), which presents a startling contrast to the bristling modernity of Macau. Built between 1617 and 1626, this imposing fortress covers an area of 10,000 square metres. It was only once used in a military capacity: to repel the Dutch in 1622, when it succeeded in blowing up the Dutch magazine with a lucky shot from a cannonball. It also houses the excellent, partially interactive **Museum of Macau** (Tues–Sun 10am–6pm; MOP$15; Ⓦ macaumuseum.gov.mo), which provides a wonderful introduction to the territory, with the two cultures – Chinese and Portuguese – presented side by side, from early oracle bone script and China's unique inventions (gunpowder, paper, printing and compass-making) to Portugal's maritime achievements. You can press buttons to hear the cries of different street hawkers, learn about firework-making and check out the latest architecture in the contemporary Macau gallery.

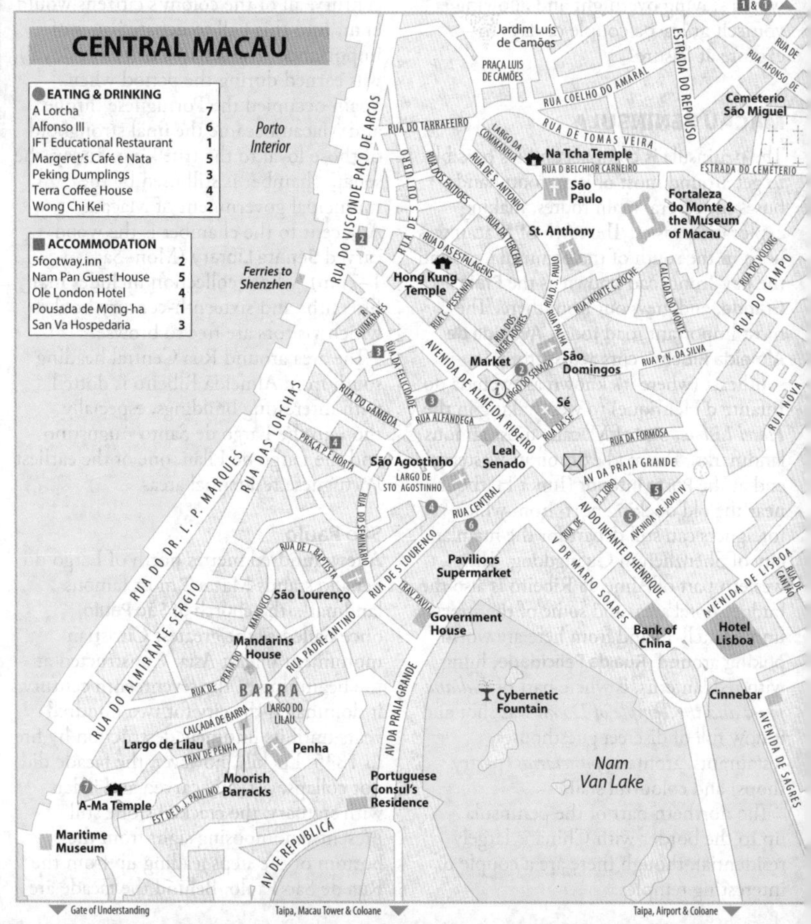

Around Praça Luís de Camões

One of the nicest parts of Macau lies a few hundred metres northwest of São Paulo around **Praça Luís de Camões.** North, facing the square, is the **Jardim Luís de Camões** (daily 6am–10pm; free), a shady park full of tai chi enthusiasts built in honour of the great sixteenth-century Portuguese poet, Luís de Camões, who is thought to have been banished here for part of his life. Immediately east of the square lies the **Cemeterio Sao Miguel** (daily 8.30am–5.30pm; free), where all the non-Catholic traders, visitors, sailors and adventurers who happened to die in Macau in the early part of the nineteenth century are seeing out eternity.

Colina da Guia and around

Colina da Guia is Macau's highest hill, and its summit is crowned by the seventeenth-century **Guia Fortress** (daily 9am–5.30pm), the dominant feature of which is a charming whitewashed **lighthouse**, added in the nineteenth century and the oldest anywhere on the Chinese coast. It's still in operation, competing with the casinos to light up the sky at night, and in the small gallery next to it there are the different typhoon warning symbols on display (same hours). You can take a **cable car** (Tues–Sun 8am–6pm; MOP$3) up the hill from the Flora Garden or climb the steps underneath it. At the top there are some superb views over the whole peninsula,

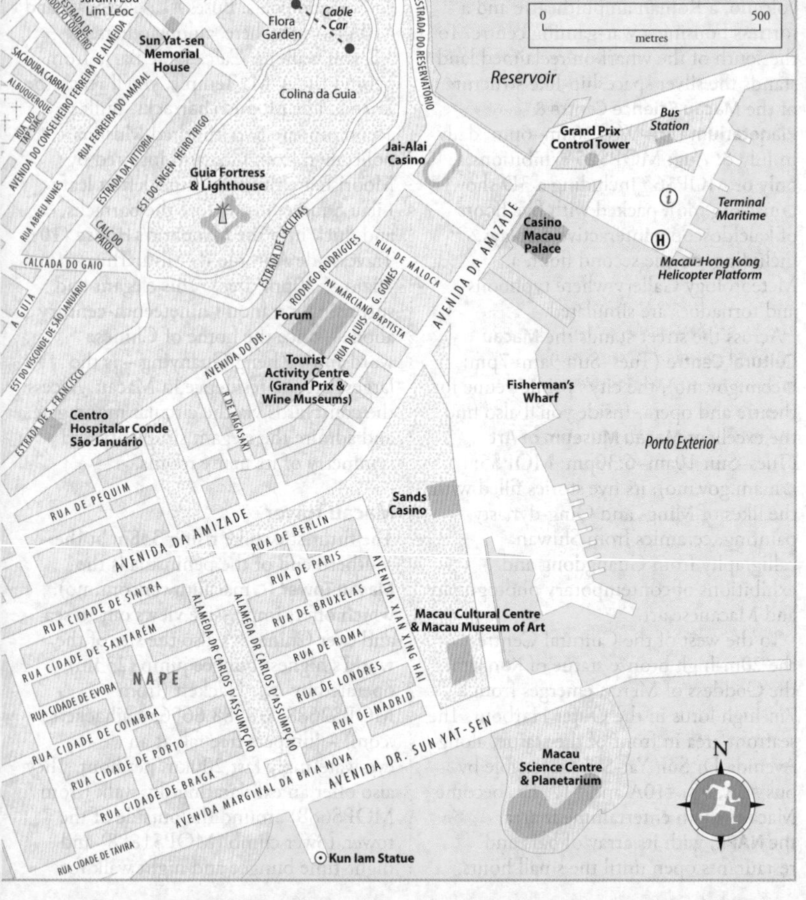

including, on a clear day, a glimpse of Lantau Island far to the east. Buses #2, #9, #17, #19 and #22 stop near the cable car.

Several blocks away, along Avenida do Coronel Mesquita, look for the round stone table inside the grounds of the four-hundred-year-old **Kun Iam Temple** (daily 10am–6pm; buses #12, #17, #18, #23); it is here that the first treaty of trade and friendship was signed between the US and China in 1844. The Goddess of Mercy herself stands in the incense-scented main hall.

Outer Harbour

3

Built on reclaimed land south of the Terminal Maritimo, **Fisherman's Wharf** is a rather bewildering array of amusements, shops and restaurants that includes a fake volcano, a Roman amphitheatre and a fortress housing a war-gaming centre. To the south of the wharf on reclaimed land stands the silver spaceship-like structure of the **Macau Science Centre & Planetarium** (Fri–Wed 10am–6pm; daily in July & Aug; MOP$25 exhibitions only or MOP$65 including a 3D show; Ⓦmsc.org.mo), packed with five floors of kaleidoscopic interactive displays, including, on the second floor, a Meteorology Gallery where typhoons and tornadoes are simulated.

Across the street stands the **Macau Cultural Centre** (Tues–Sun 9am–7pm; Ⓦccm.gov.mo), the city's prime venue for theatre and opera. Inside you'll also find the excellent **Macau Museum of Art** (Tues–Sun 10am–6.30pm; MOP$5; Ⓦmam.gov.mo), its five stories filled with the likes of Ming- and Qing-dynasty painting, ceramics from Shiwan, calligraphy from Guangdong and exhibitions of contemporary photography and Macanese art.

To the west of the Cultural Centre, the 20m-high bronze statue of **Kun Iam**, the Goddess of Mercy, emerges from a 7m-high lotus in the Outer Harbour. The seafront area in front of the statue, along Avenida Dr Sun Yat-Sen (accessible by bus #3A, #8, #10A and #12, has become Macau's main entertainment area, **the NAPE**, with its array of bars and restaurants open until the small hours.

The Barra District

The southwestern side of the Macau peninsula is known as the **Barra district**. Situated underneath Barra Hill overlooking the Inner Harbour, the celebrated **A-Ma Temple** (daily 7am–6pm; free) may be six hundred years old in some sections. Dedicated to the goddess A-Ma, whose identity blurs from Queen of Heaven into Goddess of the Sea (who is also known as Tin Hau), the temple is an attractive jumble of altars among the rocks, greenery and coils of incense.

Immediately across the road from the A-Ma Temple, on the seafront, stands the **Maritime Museum** (daily except Tues 10am–5.30pm; MOP$10), a well-presented collection covering old explorers, seafaring techniques, equipment, models and dragon boats. Buses #1, #2, #5, #7 and #10A swing by here, among others.

If you walk up Calçada de Barra from behind the A-Ma Temple, you'll reach the fortress-like **Moorish barracks**, built to accommodate two hundred Muslim policemen from Goa and inspired by Moorish architecture. Turn left at leafy Lilau Square, just before the barracks, and duck into the **Mandarin's House** (10 Travessa de Antonio da Silva; Thurs–Tues 10am–5.30pm; free). This elegant and surprisingly tranquil nineteenth-century abode – once the home of Chinese wordsmith Zheng Guanying – is the largest private residence in Macau. Access the courtyards via the circular moon gate and admire the elegant simplicity and symmetry of its many rooms.

Macau Tower

The futuristic spike rising 338m at the southern end of the peninsula is the **Macau Tower** (Ⓦmacautower.com.mo), which offers impressive views out to sea and over China. It's also the site of the world's highest bungee jump (233m), operated by A.J. Hackett (from MOP$2688; Ⓣ8988 8656, Ⓦajhackett.com) – jumpers free fall at an eye-wateringly fast 200km per hour. They also offer an exhilarating sky walk (from MOP$688) around the outside of the tower, tower climb (MOP$1888) and night-time bungee and night walk for

nocturnal daredevils. For the less adventurous, there are two observation decks (Mon–Fri 10am–9pm, Sat & Sun 9am–9pm; MOP$80). The road north from here up to the Praia Grande takes about fifteen minutes on foot, or take bus #9A, #18, #23, #26 or #32.

TAIPA

Until the eighteenth century, **Taipa** was two islands separated by a channel, the silting up of which subsequently caused the two to merge into one. The same fate has now befallen Taipa and Coloane, except that this time land reclamation is the culprit – the two islands have been fused to make space for large-scale development. Most of the plots of land have been bought up by mega casinos, so Taipa will continue to change beyond recognition over the next few years.

Taipa Village

Taipa Village on the southern shore, with its old colonial promenade, is a pleasant place to wander. There isn't much more than a few streets to the modern village, where the buses stop, though you'll find some great restaurants around the central north–south alley, **Rua do Cunha**, and, to the west – on the right as you face the shore – a couple of ancient temples in the vicinity of a quiet old square, which has benches perfectly sited for people-watching. Along Rua Correia da Silva, the **Museum of Taipa & Coloane History** (Tues–Sun 10am–6pm; MOP$5) features excavated relics from the two villages, as well as scale building models.

The village is reachable by buses #22, #25, #26A, #28A and #33. Buses #25 and #33 also stop at the **Pou Tai Temple** (daily 9am–6pm), Macau's largest temple complex north of the village, its main feature an enormous statue of Lord Gautama.

Avenida da Praia

The island's real interest lies a few minutes' walk to the east of Taipa Village, in the former waterfront area. Here, as though frozen in time, is a superb old colonial promenade, the **Avenida da Praia**, complete with its original pale-green houses, public benches and street lamps. The beautifully restored mansions overlook what was the sea – but is now the back of the *Venetian Hotel*. The five mansions are open to the public; of particular interest are the **House of the Islands** (Tues–Sun 10am–6pm; MOP$5) or its old photos of Taipa and Coloane, and the **Taipa House Museum** (Tues–Sun 10am–6pm; MOP$5), which gives you some idea of what domestic life was like at the beginning of the twentieth century.

The Cotai Strip and Macau's casinos

An area of reclaimed land billed as "Asia's Las Vegas", the **Cotai Strip**, lined with immense casinos, sits between the villages of Taipa and Coloane, has its own ferry service and, in practice, its own border crossing. The biggest and brashest of the casinos is the Venetian (Ⓦvenetianmacao.com), its interior decorated with three million sheets of gold leaf and featuring a **gondola ride** on the canal past rows of plasticky Venetian buildings. Games include blackjack, roulette, baccarat and sands stud poker. Newer additions to the strip include the City of Dreams (Ⓦcityofdreamsmacau.com), a place to let loose and join in the bimonthly Red Dragon – the biggest poker tournament in Asia. One Macau gambling institution that's not on the Cotai Strip is the Grand Lisboa (Ⓦgrandlisboa.com). Macau's tallest building, it resembles a psychedelically-lit pineapple by night and features more than 730 slot machines and 430 gaming tables spread over four floors.

COLOANE

Coloane peninsula is considerably bigger than Taipa, yet the village is smaller, leaving you with plenty of forested hills to explore and beaches to relax on.

A-Ma Temple complex and around

The first attraction is the **Parque de Seac Pai Van** (Tues–Sun 8am–6pm; free), a large park with a **Giant Panda Pavilion** (Tues–Sun 10am–1pm & 2–5pm; MOP$10; Ⓣ2833 7676, Ⓦmacaupanda.org.mo). The Pavilion's cute panda pair

was gifted to Macau by the Chinese government in December 2009 in honour of its tenth anniversary of reunification. On top of the nearby hill is a 20m-tall white marble **statue** of the goddess A-Ma who gave Macau its name. Just below lies the impressive **Tian Hou Temple** (daily 8am–7.30pm) with its multi-tiered roofs and crowds of worshippers lighting incense under strings of red lanterns. The temple is part of the A-Ma Cultural Village, which includes a good vegetarian restaurant, museum and retreat. Any bus heading to/from Coloane Village will drop you here (#15, #21A, #25, #26, #26A or #50).

From behind the small eating area opposite the temple you can join up with the **Coloane trail**, part of a network of well-signposted, straightforward walks around the peninsula. Follow the signs and a half-hour walk will take you down to **Hac Sa Reservoir**; the path then continues across the road and down to the eponymous black-sand beach – the most popular in Macau.

Coloane Village

The buses all stop at the roundabout in pretty **Coloane Village** on the western shore, overlooking mainland China just across the water. In the shore-side mud you'll see old men fishing with nets, and it's a pleasant spot for a coffee and a scrumptious Portuguese egg tart from *Lord Stow's Bakery* (see p.158). Wandering along the seafront you'll also find the unexpected yellow-and-white **St Francis Xavier Chapel** (daily 10am–8pm), which is fronted by a plaza flanked by appealing alfresco European-style restaurants. A few hundred metres beyond this is the **Tam Kong Temple** (daily 8.30am–6pm) housing a metre-long whale bone, carved into the shape of a dragon boat, to the right of the main altar.

Beaches

Coloane's beaches are pleasant and not usually crowded. Tree-lined, black-sand **Hac Sa Beach** on the eastern shore is the most popular and reachable by buses #21A, #25 and #26A from Almeida Ribeiro; you could stop off at **Cheoc Van Beach** to the south on your way. It's also possible to walk most of the way round the headland between the two. Both beaches have good facilities including showers, toilets and street barbecue stalls as well as some decent, though pricey, restaurants nearby.

ARRIVAL AND DEPARTURE

By plane Macau International Airport is a mini-hub mostly used by budget airlines operating limited routes around Southeast Asia. It's perched on Taipa Island (Ⓦ macau-airport.com) and connected by airport bus #AP1 (MOP$4.20) to the ferry terminal and the Chinese border.

Destinations Beijing (3 daily; 3hr); Shanghai (8 daily; 2hr); Xiamen (2 daily; 1hr); Taiwan (10–11 daily; 1hr 30min); Bangkok (8–9 daily; 2hr); Chiang Mai (daily; 4hr); Manila (2–3 daily; 2hr); Kuala Lumpur (4–5 daily, 3hr 45min); Seoul (2–3 daily; 4hr 30min); Osaka (4 weekly; 4hr); Singapore (1–2 daily; 4hr); and Tokyo (4 weekly, 4hr 40min), as well as an increasing number of other Chinese and Asian cities.

By ferry Every day, large numbers of vessels make the one-hour journey between the Macau Ferry Terminal ("Terminal Maritimo") in the Outer Harbour and Hong Kong – both Central and Kowloon. The terminal is connected to the budget-hotel area on Almeida Ribeiro by #3A, #10 and #10A buses. Allow 40min before departure for queues with luggage and passport control. Daytime tickets are valid on all boats earlier than the stated time. The main boat service is the 24hr Turbojet (Ⓦ turbojet.com.hk) route (every 15min, 7am–midnight, then roughly every 30–60min) from the Hong Kong–Macau Ferry Terminal and the China Ferry Terminal in Hong Kong. Tickets cost from HK$151 one-way; prices rise at weekends, public holidays and on night boats (5.45pm–6.30am) when you should book ahead. Cotai Jet (Ⓦ cotaijet.com.hk) also run high-speed catamarans from the Hong Kong–Macau Ferry Terminal both to the Macau Ferry Terminal and the Taipa Temporary Ferry Terminal near the Cotai Strip (every 30min, 7am–1am; HK$151), from where there are complementary buses to all the major casinos. Carry-on luggage allowance is 10kg in economy class but large bags can be checked in.

By bus You can walk across the Chinese border (daily 7am–midnight) at the border gate in the far north of the peninsula, into Zhuhai Special Economic Zone; buses #3, #5 and #9 connect the border gate with Avenida de Almeida Ribeiro and Rua da Praia Grande. Once in mainland China, you can easily pick up a bus to Guangzhou or Dongguan; there also are direct buses to the two cities from Macau Airport. Alternatively, cross via the Lotus Bridge at the Cotai Frontier Post (9am–8pm) on the block of reclaimed land joining Taipa and Coloane; take buses #15, #21A, #25 or #26A.

GETTING AROUND

By bus Buses operate from 6am until just after midnight. The flat bus fare on the peninsula is MOP$3.20; MOP$4.20 to Taipa; MOP$5 to Coloane Village and MOP$6.20 to Hac Sa Beach; only exact fares are accepted, so hoard your small change or get the rechargeable Macau Pass, available from numerous supermarkets and convenience stores (MOP$130, including the refundable MOP$30 deposit). The Macau Tourist Map, available from Macau Government Tourist Office outlets, shows all the bus routes. Buses #3 and #3A run between the ferry and the city centre; both also run to the border crossing, as does bus #5. Buses #21A, #25 and #26A are the most convenient routes to Taipa and Coloane, while the airport is served by buses #AP1, #26, #MT1 and #MT2.

By taxi Flag fall for the first 1.6km is MOP$13, with MOP$2.30 for each 230m thereafter. Surcharges include: MOP$5 if you're coming from the airport, MOP$2 if you're crossing to Taipa, and MOP$3 for each item of luggage in the boot. Taxi drivers speak little English.

INFORMATION

Tourist information The Macau Government Tourist Office (MGTO; Ⓣ28315566, Ⓦmacautourism.gov.mo) has offices in several locations, the most useful being the Macau Ferry Terminal (daily 9am–10pm; Ⓣ2872 6416), at Macau International Airport (daily 10am–7pm; Ⓣ2886 1418) and in Hong Kong at the Macau Ferry Terminal, Room 336–337, Shun Tak Centre, 20 Connaught Rd (daily 9am–8pm; Ⓣ2857 2287). All dish out free maps and plenty of pamphlets on sights and attractions, and the website is useful for upcoming cultural events listings.

ACCOMMODATION

Guesthouses and cheap hotels are clustered at the western end of Almeida Ribeiro, spreading out from the Porto Interior. Prices usually go up by at least MOP$50 at weekends and all hotels charge fifteen percent tax, so make sure that's included in the price. Booking online tends to be cheaper than walk-ins, and many places get booked up at the weekends.

MACAU PENINSULA

5footway.inn 8 Rua da Constantino Brito Ⓣ2857 3247, Ⓦ5footwayinn.com; bus #3. This boutique guesthouse is a Singapore export, and a welcome one at that. Expect spotless rooms with crisp linens, wooden floors, a/c, touches of modern art and lightning-fast wi-fi. Doubles, triples and quads available; great value if travelling with friends. Double MOP$720

Nam Pan Guest House 2nd floor, 8 Avenida de D Joao IV Ⓣ2848 2842; buses #3, #5 and #10. The central location is a winner here, and the eight wi-fi enabled rooms are clean and decent. The downsides are that you'll have to lug your luggage up to the 3rd floor via a narrow staircase, and the staff are disinterested at best. Double MOP$580

Ole London Hotel Rua Praça de Ponte E Horta 4–6 Ⓣ2893 7761, Ⓦolelondonhotel.com; buses #2, #7, #10A. A 5min trot from Largo do Senado, this ambitious hotel offers bright, compact rooms, with wi-fi and room service in a convenient location near the Inner Harbour. Double MOP$480

★**Pousada de Mong-ha** Colina de Mong-Ha Ⓣ2851 5222, Ⓦift.edu.mo/pousada; buses #5, #12, #22, #25. The pousada's awkward hilltop location can be forgiven on account of its helpful English-speaking staff, individually decorated en-suite rooms (all non-smoking) with Oriental art and fixtures, and delicious buffet breakfasts. There's a peaceful rooftop garden, two good restaurants, and it's within Mong-Ha Park, site of an old Portuguese fort. Double MOP$700

San Va Hospedaria 56–67 Rua da Felicidade Ⓦsanvahotel.com; buses #3, #3A, #10, #10A. *San Va*'s basic rooms, in a traditional wooden house with shared facilities, have a fantastic location and wi-fi. Walls don't quite meet the ceiling, so you may feel as if you're in bed with your neighbours and some rooms are windowless. The staff speak no English, but are friendly and have a list of useful questions on the desk for you to point at. Double MOP$190

EATING

Most restaurants in Macau serve Chinese and Portuguese food. If you want something different head to the NAPE, although it will be pricier than anywhere else on Macau.

MACAU PENINSULA

Alfonso III 11a Rua Central. Small, dimly lit restaurant that's a favourite with the local Portuguese community. Mains, such as the gut-bustingly large portion of fried Macanese rice, will keep you going for days and service can only be described as brusque. Mains from MOP$100. Daily noon–10pm.

IFT Educational Restaurant Colina de Mong-Ha; buses #5, #12, #22, #25. The trainee chefs at this establishment really deliver when it comes to good Macanese and Portuguese food. Feast on the likes of stewed pork with tamarind, codfish rice and white bean and chorizo salad. Lunch buffet MOP$80. Mon–Fri 12.30–10.30pm.

Margeret's Café e Nata Rua Comandante Mata e Oliveira. A Macau institution, with street-side benches where you can tuck into inexpensive, chunky sandwiches, pizzas, home-baked quiches and muffins. Macau's creamy egg tarts (*natas:* MOP$8) don't get any better. Mon–Sat 6.30am–8pm, Sun 9am–7pm.

Peking Dumplings 5 Travessa do Atero Novo; buses #3, #3A, #10. This tiny, informal eatery serves different kinds of dumplings to a loyal local crowd. Choose from steamed

★TREAT YOURSELF

Less than two percent of the population speaks Portuguese, but Macanese food is still heavily influenced by its colonial past, blending Asian, European and African influences. Here are two of the most famous places worth splashing out on:

A Lorcha 289 Rua do Almirante Sergio ☎ 2831 3193; buses #1, #5, #10. A local institution, "The Sailboat" serves an extensive menu of expertly cooked Macanese dishes (mains from MOP$100), such as oxtail stew. Standouts include the heart-stopping *serradura*, a spectacular cream-and-biscuit dessert. Book ahead on weekends. Daily except Tues 12.30–3pm & 6.30–11pm.

Fernando's 9 Praia de Hac Sa, Coloane. An institution among local expats with the casual, cheerful atmosphere of a Mediterranean bistro and great Portuguese dishes such as prawn in clam sauce, pork ribs and grilled chicken (mains from MOP$80). They don't take reservations, and even if you get there early (essential at weekends) you may still have to wait for a table. Situated just 50m from the Hac Sa Beach bus stop; there's no sign so follow your nose. Daily noon–late.

3

meaty dumplings, dumplings in soup, fried dumplings and more. Mains from MOP$30. Daily 11am–11pm.

Terra Coffee House Largo do Santo Agostinho 1; buses #3, #6, #19, #33. Fantastic little coffee house where the baristas really know their beans. Have your brew hot or iced. Daily 11am–8pm.

Wong Chi Kei 51 Rua Cinco de Outubro; buses #8A, #18A, #19, #26. At the original location of this smart noodle shop you can munch on shrimp roe noodles, crab congee, wonton noodle soup and more. The beer is also cheap and there's a history of noodles on the place mat to educate you while you wait. Mains start from MOP$32. There's another branch at 17 Largo do Senado. Daily 8.30am–11pm.

TAIPA AND COLOANE

Galo Rua do Cunha 45, Taipa; buses #11, #15, #22, #30, #33. A good place to sample tasty Portuguese food right in the middle of Taipa Village; go for the fish in tomato sauce, African chicken or the clams in garlic, and skip the oily steak. They have another, more expensive, branch called *Dom Galo* in the NAPE. Mains from MOP$60. Mon–Fri 11.30am–3pm & 6–10.30pm, Sat & Sun 11.30am–10.30pm.

Lord Stow's Bakery Coloane Town Square; buses #21A, #25, #26A. A leading contender for Macau's best egg custard tart (MOP$8). Either luxuriate in the a/c at *Lord Stow's Café* just around the corner, or head down to the waterfront with your tarts, still warm from the oven. Thurs–Tues 7am–10pm, Wed 7am–7pm.

Nga Tim Cafe 1 Rua Caetano, Coloane; buses #21A, #25, #26A. A busy family restaurant with gingham tablecloths opposite St Francis' Chapel, serving delicious Chinese-Portuguese food. Service is slow but the owner is quite a character. Macau-style aromatic duck HK$68. Daily noon–1am.

Pou Tai Restaurant Inside the Pou Tai temple; buses #25, #33. Generous helpings of strictly vegetarian dishes in an atmospheric temple setting. Mains from MOP$40. Mon–Sat 11am–8pm, Sun 9am–9pm.

NIGHTLIFE

Although drinking isn't a major pastime in Macau and can be expensive, a cluster of new bars and night-time cafés lies in the stretch of reclaimed land just southwest of the ferry terminal and in front of the new Kun Iam statue (follow signs to NAPE).

Casablanca Café 1369–1373 Rua Cidade de Tavira; buses include #3, #3A, #5X, #8, #9, #10, #10A. This place has a 1930s Hollywood theme. A covered colonnade and wicker chairs protect it from the weather, and the terrace is a good spot for people-watching. Inside, catch up on the football or play pool. Things don't get going until around midnight. Beer MOP$50. Daily noon–late.

Cinnebar Wynn Macau, Rua Cidade de Sintra, NAPE; buses #8, #10A, #23. Amiable bar serving decent cocktails and malt whiskies; choose from the refined indoor setting or the relaxed outdoor area in the garden. Daily noon–late.

Moonwalker 1361 Rua Cidade de Tavira; buses #8, #10A, #23. This is one of the larger bars on the waterfront, with action spread over two floors and live music every night except Tues from 10pm; open until 6am at the weekends. Daily 1pm–late; daily happy hour 4–8pm daily. Beer MOP$30.

DIRECTORY

Banks and exchange Most ATMs dotted around Macau accept international cards.

Hospitals and pharmacies There is a 24hr emergency department at the public Centro Hospitalar Conde São Januário, Estrada do Visconde São Januário (☎ 2831 3731; English spoken) and several pharmacies in Largo do Senado.

Laundry Hotels and to a lesser extent hostels offer a laundry service. Alternatively, use the one that is handily located right next to the San Va Hospedaria on Rua da Felicidade.

Police The main police station is on Rua Central and operates 24hr. In an emergency, call ☎ 999. There's also an SOS Tourist Hotline on ☎ 112.

Post office Macau's General Post Office is on the east side of Largo do Leal Senado (Mon–Fri 9am–6pm, Sat 9am–1pm).

BOROBUDUR

Indonesia

❶ **Borobudur** The biggest Buddhist stupa in the world. **See p.198**

❷ **Orang-utans** See these enchanting creatures at Bukit Lawang. **See p.223**

❸ **Ubud** Bali's cultural capital with art galleries, dance performances and festivals. **See p.258**

❹ **Gunung Rinjani** Climb one of Indonesia's highest mountains. **See p.296**

❺ **East Kalimantan** Explore Borneo's remote rivers and jungles. **See p.323**

❻ **Tanah Toraja, Sulawesi** Gorgeous scenery, traditional architecture and vibrant festivals. **See p.330**

HIGHLIGHTS ARE MARKED ON THE MAP ON PP.160–161

ROUGH COSTS

Daily budget Basic US$25–30/occasional treat US$35–55

Drink Bintang beer US$2.25

Food *Nasi campur* US$2.50

Hostel/budget hotel US$13

Travel Shuttle bus: Kuta–Ubud (1hr 30min) US$4; Flight: Jakarta–Denpasar (1hr 40min–2hr) US$55

FACT FILE

Population 250 million

Language Bahasa Indonesia

Currency Indonesian rupiah (Rp)

Capital Jakarta

International phone code Ⓣ + 62

Time zone GMT + 7–9hr. Bali is one hour ahead of Java

Introduction

The Indonesian archipelago spreads over 5200km between the Asian mainland and Australia, all of it within the tropics, and comprises 17,000 islands to explore. Its ethnic, cultural and linguistic diversity is correspondingly great – more than 500 languages and dialects are spoken by its 250 million people, whose fascinating customs and lifestyles are a major attraction.

Indonesia is ripe with highlights across the archipelago, beginning in **Medan** on Sumatra's northeast coast. From here, the classic itinerary runs to the thick jungles and **orang-utan sanctuary** at Bukit Lawang and down towards the lakeside resorts on Pulau Samosir in Southeast Asia's largest lake, **Danau Toba**. Further south, the area around the laidback town of **Bukittinggi** appeals because of its flamboyant Minangkabau architecture, the beautiful scenery around Danau Maninjau and the rafflesia reserves in the hills. Many travellers then hurtle through to **Java**, probably spending no more than a night in the traffic-clogged capital **Jakarta** in their rush to the ancient cultural capital of **Yogyakarta** – the best

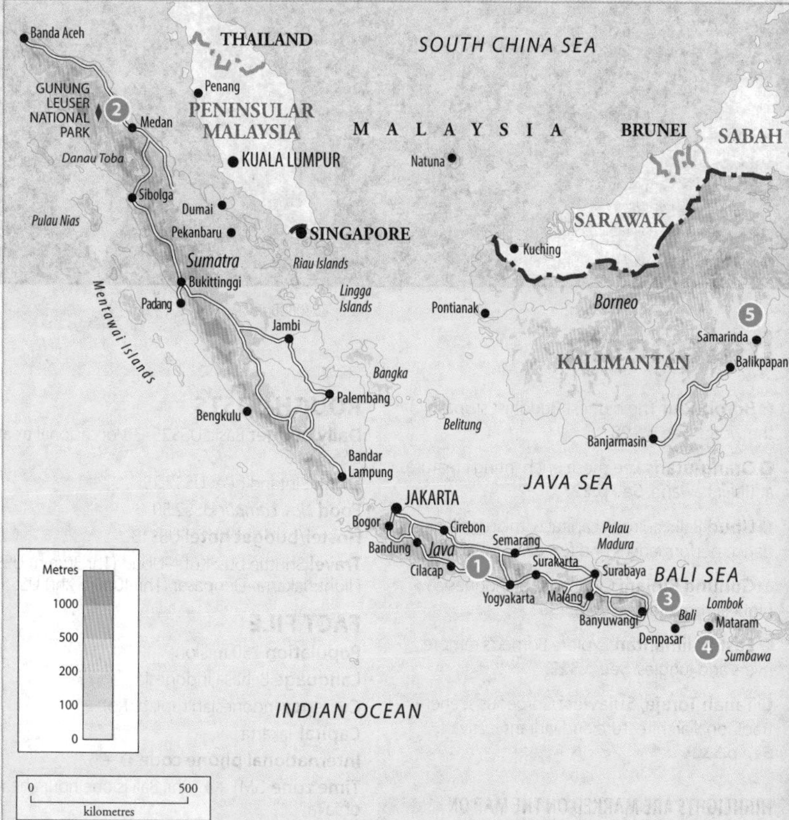

base for exploring the huge **Borobudur** (Buddhist) and **Prambanan** (Hindu) temples. Java's biggest natural attractions are its volcanoes, most famously Gunung Merapi on the outskirts of Yogya and East Java's **Gunung Bromo**, where travellers brave a sunrise climb to the summit.

Just across the water from Java sits **Bali**, the long-time jewel in the crown of Indonesian tourism, a tiny island of elegant temples, verdant landscape and fine surf. The biggest resorts are in the party conurbation of **Kuta-Legian-Seminyak**, with the more subdued beaches at **Lovina** and **Candi Dasa** appealing to travellers not hellbent on nightlife. Most visitors also spend time in Bali's cultural centre **Ubud**, whose lifeblood continues to be painting,

WHEN TO GO

The whole Indonesian archipelago is tropical, with **temperatures** at sea level always between 21°C and 33°C, although cooler in the mountains. In theory, the year divides into a wet and dry season, though it's often hard to tell the difference. Very roughly, in much of the country, November to April are the wet months (Jan and Feb the wettest) and May through to October is dry. However, in northern Sumatra, this pattern is effectively reversed. The **peak tourist season** is between mid-June and mid-September and again over the Christmas and New Year season. This is particularly relevant in the major resorts, where prices rocket and rooms can be fully booked for days, and sometimes weeks, on end.

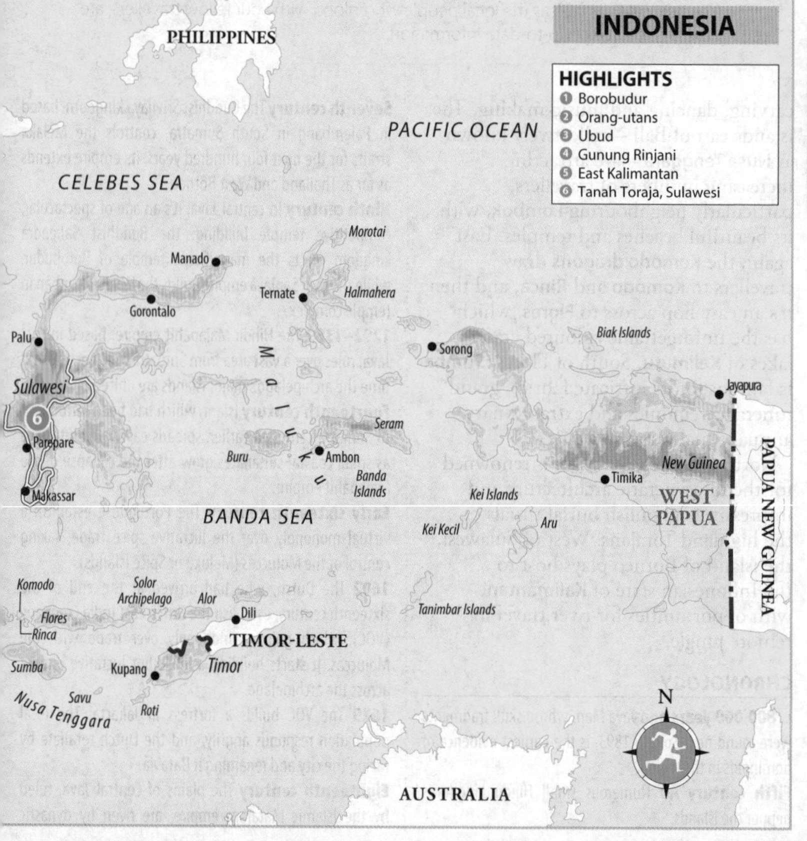

4

SAFETY IN INDONESIA

The militant Islamic Jemaah Islamiyah terrorist group has been responsible for numerous bombs in Indonesia, most notably the **Bali bomb** of 2002, which killed more than two hundred people and left the country's entire tourist industry in tatters. Subsequently there were bombings at the *Marriott* hotel in Jakarta in August 2003, the Australian embassy in Jakarta in September 2004, Bali again in October 2005 and Jakarta's *JW Marriott* and *Ritz-Carlton* hotels in July 2009. Terrorism remains a threat, though there is no need to be more alarmed here than you would be anywhere else frequented by tourists in Southeast Asia.

Caution is advised in the trouble spots around the **Maluku Islands** and **central Sulawesi** where the situation remains unsettled. Much of the trouble dates back to 1999, and the horrifying chaos of the elections of the newly independent state of East Timor. Riots in many parts of the archipelago pitched Muslims against their Christian neighbours, while locals in other provinces, inspired by the success of East Timor in winning its independence, began to fight for the secession of their own province. The **Maluku Islands** in particular were devastated by an internecine war that left thousands dead. A measure of calm has returned to the islands, and travellers are now trickling back.

The security situation can also be unpredictable in other trouble spots such as **Aceh** in northern Sumatra, and the Poso region of **central Sulawesi** (see box, p.327). We also do not cover remote and little-visited **West Papua** (formerly known as Irian Jaya), whose ongoing separatist struggle has in the past resulted in violence against foreigners, or East Timor's neighbour, **West Timor**. If you insist on visiting Indonesia's more unsettled areas, make sure you are fully aware of the latest situation, and heed any warnings given out by your foreign office (see box, p.44), as well as the local people who, along with your fellow travellers, are usually the best source of up-to-date information.

carving, dancing and music-making. The islands east of Bali – collectively known as **Nusa Tenggara** – are attracting increasing numbers of travellers, particularly neighbouring **Lombok**, with its beautiful beaches and temples. East again, the **Komodo dragons** draw travellers to **Komodo** and **Rinca**, and then it's an easy hop across to **Flores**, which has the unforgettable coloured crater lakes of **Kelimutu**. South of Flores, **Sumba** is famous for its intricate fabrics, grand funeral ceremonies and extraordinary annual ritual war, the *pasola*.

North of Flores, **Sulawesi** is renowned for the idiosyncratic architecture and impressively ghoulish burial rituals of the highland Torajans. West of Sulawesi, the island of Borneo plays host to the Indonesian state of **Kalimantan**, with opportunities for river travel in remote jungle.

CHRONOLOGY

c. 800,000 years ago Java Man, whose skull fragments were found near Solo in 1893, is the earliest evidence of hominoids in the region.

Fifth century AD Numerous small Hindu kingdoms pepper the islands.

Seventh century The Buddhist Srivijaya kingdom, based in Palembang in South Sumatra, controls the Melaka straits for the next four hundred years. Its empire extends as far as Thailand and West Borneo.

Ninth century In central Java, it's an age of spectacular, competitive temple building: the Buddhist Saliendra kingdom erects the magnificent temple of Borobudur, while the rival Sanjaya empire builds the Hindu Prambanan temple complex.

1292–1389 The Hindu Majapahit empire, based in East Java, rules over a vast area from Sumatra to Timor, the first time the archipelago's major islands are united.

Fourteenth century Islam, which had been introduced to Sumatra centuries earlier, spreads eastwards into Java as small coastal sultanates grow after the collapse of the Majapahit empire.

Early sixteenth century The Portuguese establish a virtual monopoly over the lucrative spice trade, taking control of the Moluccas (Maluku or Spice Islands).

1602 The Dutch, who had arrived at the end of the sixteenth century, establish the Dutch East India Company (VOC), which gains a monopoly over trade with the Moluccas. It starts building a loose but lucrative empire across the archipelago.

1619 The VOC builds a fortress in Jakarta. The local population responds angrily, and the Dutch retaliate by razing the city and renaming it Batavia.

Eighteenth century The plains of Central Java, ruled by the Islamic Mataram empire, are riven by dynastic

disputes, known as the Three Wars of Succession. The last one (1746–57) divides the empire into three sultanates, two at Solo and one at Yogyakarta. The Dutch then subjugate the entire territory.

1799 The VOC folds and the Dutch government (under a French Protectorate) takes possession of its territories.

1811 The British, under Sir Thomas Stamford Raffles, attack and pick off the islands one by one, landing at Batavia in 1811.

1816 With the end of the Napoleonic Wars, the territories return to the Dutch, who are soon embroiled in bloody disputes with opponents of their rule.

1830 The Dutch devise the Cultural System whereby Javanese farmers must grow cash crops for sale in Europe at a huge profit. Java becomes one giant plantation, to the detriment of indigenous farmers.

1870 onwards The Dutch gradually implement more progressive policies, but this coincides with some devastating natural disasters. Later, irrigation, healthcare and education programmes are started.

1894–1920 The Dutch expand into previously independent territories: Lombok in 1894, Bali in 1906 and Aceh in 1908. By 1910 the Dutch have conquered nearly all of Indonesia; West Papua is the last to fall, in 1920.

1927 Achmed Sukarno founds the pro-independence Partai Nasional Indonesia (PNI). The Dutch outlaw the party and imprison Sukarno in 1931, later exiling him.

1942–45 Indonesia is occupied by the Japanese.

August 17, 1945 Sukarno reads a Declaration of Independence, but it is not recognized by the Allies, who return the territory to the Dutch.

1946–49 War with the Dutch, who withdraw in December 1949. The new Republic of Indonesia is established with Sukarno as president.

1949–65 Sukarno presides over a system he calls guided democracy – in reality authoritarian rule. He forges ties with the Soviet Union, and is sympathetic to the communist party, against the Indonesian army.

September 30, 1965 A group of communists (with whom Sukarno is thought to be in cahoots) abduct and execute a number of leading generals, claiming they are preventing an army-led coup. General Suharto eventually seizes control from them.

1965–67 Suharto launches a purge against the communists, during which it's thought at least 500,000 people die. He restores relations with the West and aid pours into Indonesia. In 1967 Suharto is named acting president.

1970s Indonesia benefits from rising oil prices – its biggest export.

December 1975 Indonesia invades East Timor, which had been granted independence by Portugal the previous year.

1997 Southeast Asia's currency crisis. The value of the rupiah plummets. There are widespread demonstrations, and riots take place in major cities.

May 21, 1998 Suharto steps down after 32 years and his vice-president, B.J. Habibie, takes over. In early November there's more rioting, with demands that Suharto be tried on charges of mismanagement and corruption.

1999 Though the Indonesian Democratic Party of Struggle, led by Megawati Sukarnoputri, Sukarno's daughter, win the elections, Indonesia's parliament chooses Gus Dur as president, with Megawati vice-president.

1999 East Timor gains independence. Other far-flung Indonesian provinces begin to become more vocal – and violent – in their struggle for sovereignty.

2002–05 There is a series of bombings – first in a nightclub and Irish bar in Kuta, Bali, in 2002, and next at the *Marriott* in Jakarta in August 2003, the Australian Embassy in September 2004, and Bali again in October 2005.

December 26, 2004 A devastating tsunami hits the country, leaving more than 160,000 Indonesians dead or missing.

August 15, 2005 A peace deal is signed between the Indonesian government and separatist Free Aceh Movement (GAM), ending three decades of fighting.

January 2008 Suharto dies. His legacy is mixed: he oversaw the country's economic growth, but was accused of – and evaded prosecution for – massive corruption, and many human rights abuses, including the deaths of hundreds of thousands.

July 17, 2009 The bombings of the *Ritz-Carlton* and *JW Marriott* hotels in Jakarta kill nine people and injure more than fifty.

September 2009 An earthquake with a magnitude of 7.6 rocks the city of Padang in West Sumatra; more than 1300 people are killed and more than one million people are left homeless.

October 25, 2010 The eruption of Mount Merapi in Java kills 353 people and causes the evacuation of 350,000 while covering Borobudur in volcanic ash.

June 2012 Bombmaker Umer Patek is sentenced by a Jakarta court to 20 years in prison for his role in the 2002 Bali terrorist attacks.

June 2013 Government fuel price hikes spark violent protests.

ARRIVAL AND DEPARTURE

Jakarta's Sukarno-Hatta Airport and Bali's Ngurah Rai Airport are the main international air gateways into Indonesia, with direct flights from several Australian cities and destinations throughout Asia. The archipelago also boasts international airports at Medan, Makassar, Manado, Surabaya and Yogyakarta – with connections mainly with other Southeast Asian airports.

Indonesia has good ferry connections with Malaysia and Singapore and there are occasional cargo boats from the Philippines.

FROM MALAYSIA AND SINGAPORE

A variety of ferries and speedboats depart from Penang (see p.437), on the west coast of Peninsular Malaysia, to **Medan**, and from Malacca (see p.465) in southern Malaysia to **Dumai** or **Pekanbaru**. You can also take ferries from Johor Bahru (see box, p.472), in far southern Malaysia, and Singapore to Sumatra via the islands of **Batam** and **Bintan**; and from Port Klang (see p.426), near Kuala Lumpur, to **Tanjung Balai** and Dumai in Sumatra.

There are two entry points between **East Malaysia and Kalimantan**. You can catch a bus between the capital of Malaysian **Sarawak** at Kuching (see p.479) to West Kalimantan's capital, Pontianak; alternatively, you can cross from the East Malaysian state of **Sabah** by catching a two- or three-hour ferry (see p.514) to **Pulau Nunukan** or **Tarakan** from Tawau, two days' bus ride southeast of Kota Kinabalu.

VISAS

Citizens of the UK, Ireland, most of Europe, Australia, New Zealand, Canada and the US can get thirty-day visas (US$25) on arrival from any of Indonesia's **official immigration gateways**, though it's worth checking beforehand as Indonesian visa regulations are notoriously prone to change. Official gateways include major international airports – such as Jakarta, Denpasar (Bali), Yogyakarta, Solo, Surabaya and Medan – and several seaports, including Padang Bai in Bali, Tanjung Priok for Jakarta, Pulau Batam and Pulau Bintam (between Singapore and Sumatra), and Medan on Sumatra. If you're arriving in Indonesia through a more remote air- or seaport, check whether you need to obtain a visa from an Indonesian consulate in advance. For a full list of official gateways see Ⓦindonesianembassy.org.uk.

You can get a **sixty-day visa**, but only by applying in advance from an Indonesian consulate; the cost is US$55 and the process takes three to five days, though this varies from one consulate to the next. A visa is most easily obtained in Singapore, Penang or Kuala Lumpur. Note that you must show your ticket out of the country when applying for a visa, whether you're applying at the embassy or the port. A visa-on-arrival can be extended once for up to thirty days for a fee of Rp250,000 (sixty-day visas can currently be extended several times); this process also usually takes a few days. When applying for an extension of your visa, bring photocopies of the photo page in your passport, your Indonesian visa, and your flight ticket out of Indonesia.

Those entering the country via a **non-designated gateway** must get a visa from an Indonesian consulate (see p.49) before travelling. Further details on the latest situation can be found at Ⓦindonesianembassy.org.uk.

GETTING AROUND

Delays are common to all forms of transport in Indonesia – including major flights – caused by weather, mechanical failure, or simply not enough passengers turning up, so you'll save yourself a good deal of stress if you keep your schedule as flexible as possible.

BUSES, MINIBUSES AND TRAINS

Buses are inexpensive, easy to book, and leave roughly on time. But they're also slow, cramped and often plain terrifying: accidents can be devastating. Where there's a choice of operators on any particular route, ask local people which bus company they recommend. **Tickets** are sold a day or more in advance from the point of departure or bus company offices – which are not necessarily near the relevant **bus station** (*terminal*). Where services are infrequent it's a good idea to buy tickets as early as possible. Tell the driver your exact destination, as it may be possible to get delivered right to the door of your hotel. The average **long-distance bus** has padded seats but little leg- or

> **AIRPORT DEPARTURE TAX**
>
> The **airport departure tax** varies from airport to airport, but can be up to Rp150,000 for international flights, and Rp10,000–40,000 for domestic flights.

headroom; it's worth forking out for a luxury bus, if available, which costs roughly twice as much but will have reclining seats. You'll get regular meal stops at roadhouses along the way. On shorter routes, you'll use minibuses, widely known by their Balinese tag, **bemo**. Other names for local transport include *taksi* (*bemo* in Kalimantan), *pete-petes* (in Sulawesi), and *travel* (share taxis in Flores as well as northern Sumatra, often consisting of shiny SUVs). Once on their way, they're faster than buses and cheaper; fares are handed over on board, and rarely advertised. You may also have to pay for any space your luggage occupies. It's almost impossible to give the **frequency** with which *bemos* and public buses run; if no frequency is given in the text, they are frequent, roughly hourly. Journey times given are the minimum you can reasonably expect.

In resort areas such as Bali, a more pleasant option is **tourist shuttle buses** – though far more expensive than local services, these will take you between points as quickly as possible. The longest-established firm on Bali and Lombok is **Perama** (@peramatour.com), who have offices in most major tourist destinations and produce a useful leaflet outlining their routes.

In Java, **trains**, run by PT Kereta API, are often preferred over buses for being more comfortable and reliable. Additionally, train stations are generally far more centrally situated than the typically far-flung bus terminals. You're also less likely to get ripped off at the train ticket window (*loket*).

BOATS AND FERRIES

While air travel is becoming more popular it is still possible to travel between islands by boat. Public ferries run regularly on the shorter crossings between neighbouring islands, such as between Sumatra and Java, Java and Bali, and Bali and Lombok, for example. In more visited areas you'll find tourist boat services, and combined long-distance bus and boat options. However, with the advent of cheap domestic flights, ferry services are becoming less frequent and poorer value as they compete with the airlines.

Pelni (@pelni.com) currently operates around 25 **passenger liners**, most of which run on weekly or monthly circuits and link Java with ports on all the main island groups between Sumatra and Papua (map pp.166–167). The best place for up-to-date information on routes is the **local Pelni office** (listed under "Moving on" for each town in this guide), which should have complete timetables of all the ferries serving their ports. Comprehensive timetables for Pelni's coverage across the whole country can be picked up from their head office in Jakarta. The vessels are well maintained, and as safe and punctual as any transport in Indonesia can be. **Tickets** are available from Pelni offices two or three days before departure, but it's best to pay an agent to reserve these for you as early as possible. You can only buy tickets for services that depart locally.

Accommodation on board is usually divided into two or four classes. All are good value and include meals; cabins also have large lockers to store your luggage. First class consists of a private cabin with a double bed, washroom, TV and a/c – generally US$60–100 a day depending on the route, with prices and facilities working downwards from there. If all classes are full, then the only option is to sleep in the corridors, stairwells or on deck (buy a rattan mat, and get to the port early to stake out your spot on the floor). Lock luggage and chain it to something immovable. Fourth-class food is edible at best, so stock up in advance.

There are also three **ASDP fast ferries**, two of which connect Surabaya on Java with Bali and Nusa Tenggara, and one of which sails north from Surabaya to Kalimantan. While not cheap, the service is good, and ferries take less than a third of the time of Pelni vessels.

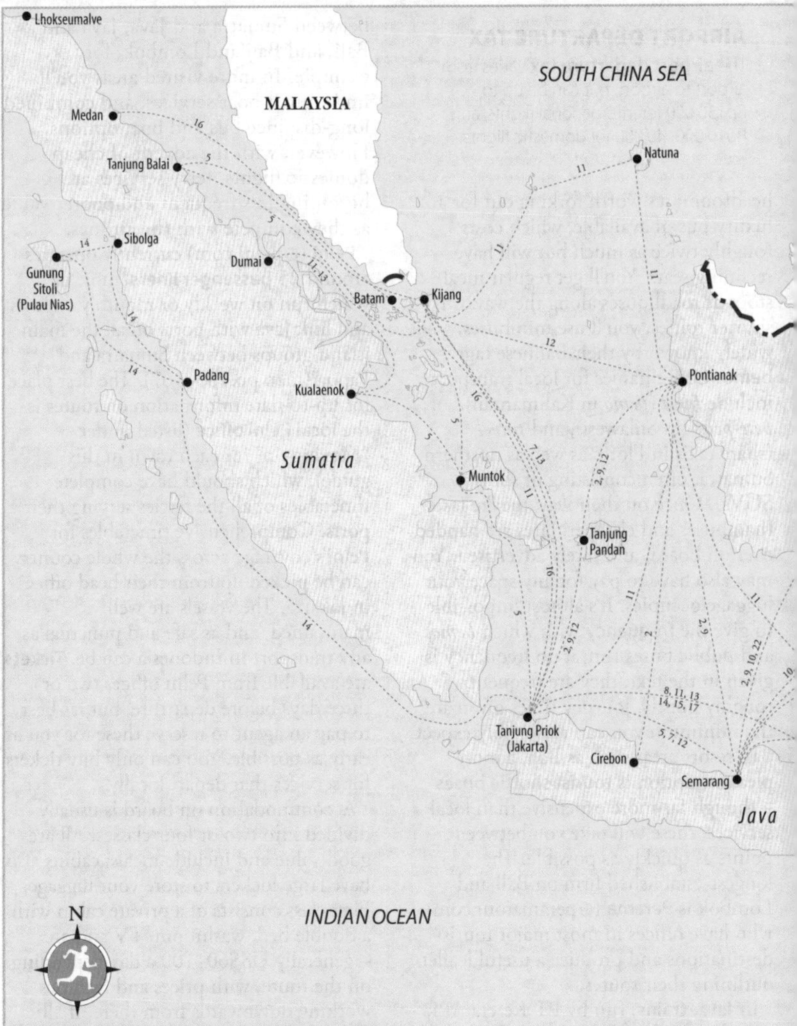

USEFUL PELNI ROUTES

	NAME OF FERRY	MAIN PORTS OF CALL	FREQUENCY
1	KM Kelimutu	Wanci, Bau Bau, Bima, Makassar	monthly
2	KM Lawit	Semarang, Pontianak	monthly
3	KM Tidar	Surabaya, Parepare, Makassar	fortnightly
4	KM Tatamailau	Timika, Tual, Agats, Sorong, Kaimana	irregular
5	KM Sirimau	Semarang, Larantuka, Makassar, Batulicin	fortnightly
6	KM Awu	Surabaya, Sabu, Kumai, Kupang, Ende, Bima	monthly
7	KM Ciremai	Surabaya, Bau Bau, Makassar, Dobo, Ambon	fortnightly
8	KM Dobonsolo	Surabaya, Tanjung Priok, Makassar, Sorong, Bitung	fortnightly
9	KM Leuser	Pontianak, Semarang, Tanjung Pandan, Suarabaya, Kumai	weekly
10	KM Binaiya	Batulicin, Parepare, Semarang, Surabaya	weekly
11	KM Bukit Raya	Tanjung Priok, Pontianak, Letung, Kijang	fortnightly

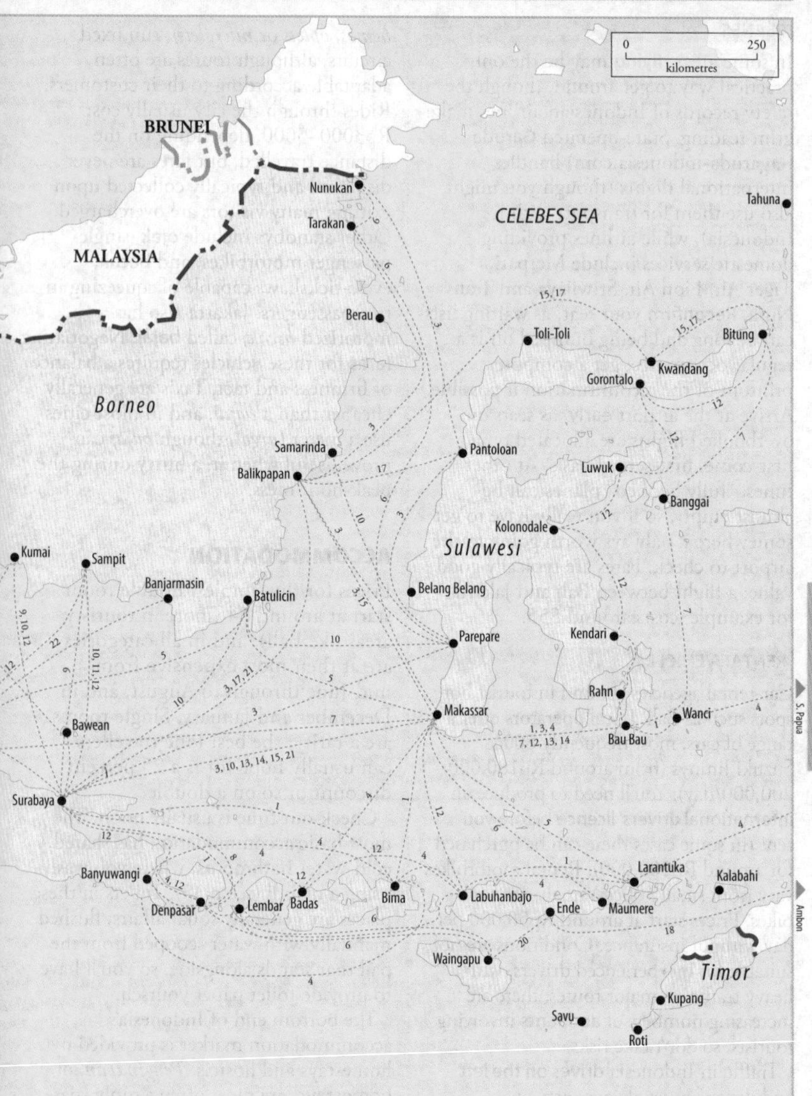

	NAME OF FERRY	MAIN PORTS OF CALL	FREQUENCY
12	KM Tilongkabila	Bau Bau, Raha, Bitung, Makassar	irregular
13	KM Bukit Siguntang	Tarakan, Parepare, Bau Bau, Tanjung Priok	monthly
14	KM Lambelu	Makassar, Surabaya, Tanjung Priok, Ambon	irregular
15	KM Sinabung	Bitung, Semarang, Makassar, Banggai	fortnightly
16	KM Kelud	Belawan, Tanjung Priok, Tanjung Balai Karimun	weekly
17	KM Doro Londa	Bitung, Sorong, Balikpapan, Surabaya	fortnightly
18	KM Pangrango	Geser, Bula, Ambon, Leti, Namrole	fortnightly
19	KM Sangiang	Ternate, Sanana, Ambon, Bitung	fortnightly
20	KM Wilis	Ende, Waingapu, Makassar, Kupang	fortnightly
21	KM Umsini	Nunukan, Balikpapan, Surabaya, Makassar	every two/four days
22	KM Egon	Semarang, Kumai, Banjarmasin,	every two days

4

PLANES

In some areas, **flying** may be the only practical way to get around, though the safety records of Indonesian airlines make grim reading. State-operated **Garuda** (ⓦgaruda-indonesia.com) handles international flights (though you might also use them for transport within Indonesia), while airlines providing domestic services include Merpati, Tiger Air, Lion Air, Sriwijaya and Trans Nusa. **Reconfirm** your seat, as waiting lists can be long and being bumped off is a regular occurrence; get a computer printout of the reconfirmation if possible. Arrive at the airport **early**, as seats on overbooked flights are allocated on a first-come, first-served basis. At other times, "fully booked" planes can be almost empty, so if you really have to get somewhere it's always worth going to the airport to check. Fares are typically good value: a flight between Bali and Jakarta, for example, costs around $55.

RENTAL VEHICLES

Car-rental agencies abound in tourist hot spots such as Bali. Local operators offer a range of cars, most frequently 800cc Suzuki Jimnys (from around Rp180,000–200,000/day). You'll need to produce an **international drivers' licence** before you rent (in some cases these can be purchased for around Rp200,000). Rental motorbikes vary from small 100cc Yamahas to trail bikes. Prices start at around Rp50,000 per day without insurance. Conditions are not suitable for inexperienced drivers, with heavy traffic on major routes; there are increasing numbers of **accidents** involving tourists, so don't take risks.

Traffic in Indonesia **drives on the left** and drivers must always carry an international driving licence and the vehicle registration documents. Passengers in the front of a vehicle must wear a seatbelt by law, and all motorcyclists must wear a helmet. The **police** carry out regular spot checks, and you'll be **fined** for any infringements.

URBAN TRANSPORT

In cities, colour-coded or numbered minibuses known as **angkots** (also called *bemos*, *oplets* or *microlets*), run fixed circuits, although routes are often adaptable according to their customers. Rides through the city usually cost Rp3000–5000, depending on the distance travelled, but fares are never displayed and typically collected upon exiting; many visitors are overcharged. Other standbys include **ojek**, single-passenger motorbikes, and **becak**, cycle-rickshaws capable of squeezing in two passengers. Jakarta also has motorized *becak*, called **bajaj**. Negotiating **fares** for these vehicles requires a balance of firmness and tact. Taxis are generally cheaper than a *bajaj*, and in most cities use a meter (*argo*), though *bajaj* can prove useful when in a hurry during the peak-hour mess.

ACCOMMODATION

Prices for the simplest double room start at around $4 (more in touristy areas like Bali), and in all categories are at their **most expensive** from mid-June through to August, and in December and January. Single rooms are a rarity; the best lone travellers can usually hope for is a 25 percent discount or so on a double.

Check-out time is usually noon. The most basic accommodation has shared, cold-water **bathrooms**, where you wash using a mandi (see p.35). Toilets in these places are generally squat affairs, flushed manually with water scooped from the pail that stands alongside, so you'll have to provide toilet paper yourself.

The bottom end of Indonesia's accommodation market is provided by homestays and hostels. *Penginapan*, or **homestays**, are most often simply spare bedrooms in the family home, though there's often not much difference between these and losmen, *pondok* and *wisma*, which are also family-run operations. Rooms vary from whitewashed concrete cubes to artful bamboo structures – some are even set in their own walled gardens. Hard beds and bolsters are the norm, and you may be provided with a light blanket. Most losmen rooms have fans and cold-water bathrooms.

Almost any place calling itself a **hotel** will include at least a basic breakfast in the price of a room. Most of the mid-range and top-end places add a service-and-tax surcharge of between 10 and 22 percent to your bill, and smarter establishments quote prices – and often prefer foreigners to pay – in dollars, though they accept plastic or a rupiah equivalent. In popular areas such as Bali and Tanah Toraja, it's worth booking ahead during the peak seasons. Bland and anonymous, inexpensive urban hotels are designed for local businesspeople rather than tourists, and have tiny rooms and shared squat toilets and mandi. Moderately priced hotels often have a choice of fan or a/c rooms, almost certainly with hot water.

In rural Indonesia, you may end up **staying in villages** without formal lodgings, in a bed in a family house. First ask permission from the local police or the *kepala desa* (village head). In exchange for accommodation and meals, you should offer cash or useful gifts, such as rice, salt, cigarettes or food, to the value of about $2 at the very least. The only bathroom might be the nearest river. With such readily available and inexpensive alternatives, **camping** is only necessary when trekking.

Usually, **electricity** is supplied at 220–240 volts AC, but outlying areas may still use 110 volts. Most outlets take plugs with two rounded pins.

FOOD AND DRINK

Compared to other Southeast Asian cuisines, Indonesian food lacks variety. Coconut milk and aromatic spices at first add intriguing tastes to the meats, vegetables and fruits, but after a while everything starts to taste the same – spiced, fried and served with rice. Be particularly careful about food **hygiene** in rural Indonesia, avoiding poorly cooked fish or meat.

Rice (*nasi*) is the favoured staple across much of the country, an essential, three-times-a-day fuel. Noodles are also widely popular. The seafood is often superb, and chicken, goat and beef are the main meats in this predominantly Muslim country. **Vegetarians** can eat well in Indonesia, though restaurant selections can be limited to *cap cay* – fried mixed vegetables. There's also plenty of tofu and the popular *tempe*, a fermented soya-bean cake.

INDONESIAN FOOD

Spices, the backbone of all Indonesian cooking, are ground and chopped together then fried to form a paste, which is either used as the flavour-base for curries, or rubbed over ingredients prior to frying or grilling. Chillies always feature, along with *terasi* (also known as *belacan*), a fermented shrimp paste. Meals are often served with *sambal*, a blisteringly hot blend of chillies and spices.

Light meals and snacks include various rice dishes such as **nasi goreng**, a plate of fried rice with shreds of meat and vegetables and topped with a fried egg, and **nasi campur**, boiled rice served with a small range of side dishes. Noodle equivalents are also commonly available, as are **gado-gado**, steamed vegetables dressed in a peanut sauce, and *sate*, small kebabs of meat or fish, barbecued over a fire and again served with spicy peanut sauce. Indonesian bread (*roti*) is made from sweetened dough, and usually accompanies a morning cup of coffee.

Sumatran **Padang restaurants** are found right across Indonesia, the typically fiery food pre-cooked – not the healthiest way to eat – and displayed cold on platters piled up in a pyramid shape inside a glass-fronted cabinet. There are no menus; you either select your composite meal by pointing, or wait for the staff to bring you a selection and pay just for what you consume. You may encounter boiled *kangkung* (water spinach); *tempe*; egg, vegetable, meat or seafood curry; fried whole fish; potato cakes; and even fried cow's lung.

WHERE TO EAT

The cheapest places to eat in Indonesia are at the **mobile stalls** (*kaki lima*, or "five legs"), which ply their wares around the streets and bus stations during the day, and congregate at night markets after

4

dark. You simply place your order and they cook it up on the spot. **Warung** are the bottom line in Indonesian restaurants, usually just a few tables, and offering much the same food as *kaki lima* for under a dollar a dish. **Rumah makan** are bigger, offer a wider range of dishes and comfort, and may even have a menu. Outside of major cities, most eateries labelled as **restaurants** are likely to cater to foreigners, with fully-fledged service and possibly international food. Most warung, rumah makan and restaurants are open from around 10/11am until 10pm, though few operate to strict timings. Many of the moderate and all of the expensive establishments will add up to 21 percent service tax to the bill.

DRINKS

Most tap **water** in Indonesia has had very little treatment, and can contain a whole range of bacteria and viruses. Drink only bottled, boiled or sterilized water. Boiled water (*air putih*) can be requested at accommodation and restaurants, and dozens of brands of **bottled water** (*air minum*) are sold throughout the islands. Indonesian **coffee** is among the world's best, and drunk with copious amounts of sugar and, occasionally, condensed milk.

4

Alcohol can be a touchy subject in parts of Indonesia, where public drunkenness may incur serious trouble. There's no need to be paranoid about this in cities, however, and the locally produced **beers**, Anker and Bintang, are good, and widely available at Chinese restaurants and bigger hotels. In non-Islamic regions, even small warung sell beer. **Spirits** are less publicly consumed, and may be technically illegal, so indulge with caution. Nonetheless, home-produced brews are often sold openly in villages. *Tuak* (also known as *balok*) or palm wine, made by tapping a suitable tree for its sap, comes in plain milky white or pale red varieties, and varies in strength. Far more potent are rice wine (*arak* or *brem*), and *sopi*, a distillation of *tuak*, either of which can leave you incapacitated after a heavy session.

CULTURE AND ETIQUETTE

Indonesia is the world's most populous Muslim country, but the practice of **Islam** across the archipelago has been shaped by centuries of interaction with Hinduism, Buddhism and other faiths, as well as traditional animist practices. As a result, Islam in Indonesia is far removed from the more austere practices of the Gulf

TRADITIONAL DANCE AND MUSIC

Given Indonesia's enormous cultural and ethnic mix it's hardly surprising that the range of traditional music and dance across the archipelago is so vast.

DANCE

Best known are the highly stylized and mannered **classical dance performances** in Java and Bali, accompanied by the gamelan orchestra. Every step is minutely orchestrated, and the merest wink of an eye or arch of an eyebrow has significance. Ubud on Bali and Yogyakarta on Java are the centres for these dances. Yogya is also the main place to catch a performance of **wayang kulit**, shadow puppet plays.

GAMELAN

A gamelan is an ensemble of tuned percussion, consisting mainly of gongs, metallophones and drums, made of bronze, iron, brass, wood or bamboo, with wooden frames, which are often intricately carved and painted. The full ensemble also includes vocalists and is led by the drummer in the centre. A large gamelan may be played by as many as thirty musicians, and is a communal form of music-making – there are no soloists or virtuosos.

Sundanese (West Javanese) *degung* is arguably the most accessible gamelan music for Western ears. Its musical structures are clear and well defined, and it is played by a small ensemble, but includes the usual range of gongs and metallophones found in all gamelan.

By Jenny Heaton and Simon Steptoe

states. In the capital, it's possible to find mosques situated across the street from nightclubs that would make the raunchiest bar back home seem positively prudish. Although there are regional variations in accepted social norms, with Aceh among the most conservative provinces and Bali the most liberal, there are also differences within provinces. Following your common sense is the best course of action. Outside the main tourist resorts, dress conservatively, especially if visiting religious sites, to avoid giving offence. Be especially sensitive during the Muslim fasting month of Ramadan.

Visitors to **Balinese temples** (*pura*) show respect to the shrines and dress modestly – no skimpy clothing, bare shoulders or shorts. Often you'll be required to wear a sarong and a ceremonial sash around your waist (usually provided by the most-visited temples).

Indonesia shares the same **attitudes to dress and social taboos** as other Southeast Asian cultures (see p.40). In addition, Indonesians are generally very sociable, and dislike doing anything alone. It's normal for complete strangers engaged in some common enterprise – catching a bus, for instance – to introduce themselves and start up a friendship. **Sharing cigarettes** between men is in these circumstances a way of establishing a bond, and Westerners who don't smoke should be genuinely apologetic about refusing; it's worth carrying a packet to share around even if you save your own "for later".

SPORTS AND OUTDOOR ACTIVITIES

DIVING

Indonesia has many of the world's best **diving sites**, among the finest of which are Pulau Bunaken off **Sulawesi** and **Pulau Weh** off northern Aceh in Sumatra. **Bali** has many good sites, including the famous *Liberty* wreck, and reputable tour operators at all major beach resorts. The best time for diving is between late April and early October. Most major beach resorts have dive centres, but once you get further afield you'll probably have to rely on live aboard cruises or even on having your own gear. A day's diving costs anything from $45 to upwards of $100. Ask about the reputation of the dive operators before signing up, check their PADI or equivalent accreditation and, if possible, get first-hand recommendations from other divers. Be aware that it is down to you to check your equipment, and that the purity of an air tank can be suspect, and could cause serious injury. Also check your guide's credentials carefully, and bear in mind that you may be a long way from a decompression chamber.

SURFING

Indonesia is also one of the world's premier surfing destinations, with an enormous variety of first-class waves and perfect breaks. The best-known waves are found on **Bali**, **G-Land** (Grajagan) on Java and around **Krui** in southern Sumatra; further afield, **Sumba** and the **Mentawai Islands** are also increasingly popular.

In June and July, during the best and most consistent surf, you can expect waves to be crowded, especially in Java and Bali. Several surf companies in Bali offer all-in surf safaris to other destinations in Indonesia. Try to bring your own board, though in the popular surf spots you can rent some decent boards on the beach. Most public transport charges extra for boards, but many surfers simply rent motorbikes with board-carrying attachments.

For detailed reviews of surf breaks, see the book *Indo Surf and Lingo*, available from Ⓦindosurf.com.au and from surfshops and bookshops in Bali. Good surf websites include Ⓦbaliwaves.com, Ⓦwannasurf.com and Ⓦwavehunters.com.

TREKKING

There are endless **trekking** opportunities in Indonesia. The most popular **volcano treks** include Gunung Batur on Bali and Gunung Bromo and Gunung Merapi on Java; more taxing favourites include Gunung Rinjani on Lombok and

4

Gunung Sinabung in Sumatra. Also in Sumatra, the **Gunung Leuser National Park** is Southeast Asia's largest, and includes the famous Bukit Lawang orang-utan sanctuary. The long haul to **Gunung Leuser** itself from Ketambe as well as many routes heading into the park from Bukit Lawang require **guides**, and not just to find the paths: turning up at a remote village unannounced can cause trouble, as people may mistrust outsiders, let alone Westerners. Guides are always available from local villages and tourist centres, most charging from Rp250,000 per day.

COMMUNICATIONS

Aside from the usual services, some **post offices** (*kantor pos*) offer internet facilities. Indonesia's **poste restante** system is fairly efficient, but only in the cities. In larger post offices, the parcels section is usually in a separate part of the building; sending one is expensive and time-consuming. The cheapest way of sending mail home is by surface (under 10kg only). Don't seal the parcel before staff at the post office have checked its contents; in larger towns there is usually a parcel-wrapping service nearby.

4

To **call abroad** from Indonesia, dial ☎001 or ☎008 + country code + area code (minus the first 0) + number. For international directory enquiries call ☎102; the international operator is ☎101.

Mobile phone coverage is good across most of Java, Sumatra and Bali, but elsewhere is confined largely to the main cities and populated areas only (though is improving). If you're staying longer than a week or so in Indonesia, consider purchasing an Indonesian SIM card for a few dollars. The dominant operators are Telkomsel, Three and Indosat. There's a complicated registration process, so ask the sales assistant for help to set up your phone. You shouldn't have to pay to receive calls.

Internet access is increasingly widespread, and there are internet cafés in many towns and cities; prices vary widely from Rp3000 to Rp30,000 per hour. Free wi-fi is a common feature in tourist cafés, hotels and shopping malls.

CRIME AND SAFETY

Indonesia has endured a torrid time over the past decade or so, most recently with the July 2009 bombings of the *Ritz-Carlton* and *JW Marriott* hotels in Jakarta, which killed nine and injured more than fifty people. Together with the 2002 Bali bombings which left more than 200 (mostly foreigners) dead and the violence that surrounded the political and religious upheavals of the past decade, it undermines the idea that Indonesia is a safe place to travel. Considering the scale of Indonesia and the vast number of international travellers, incidents involving Westerners are rare. **Petty theft**, however, is a fact of life, so don't flash around expensive camera equipment, jewellery or watches. Don't hesitate to check that doors and windows – including those in the bathroom – are secure before accepting **accommodation**; if the management seems offended by this, you probably don't want to stay there anyway. Some guesthouses and hotels have safe-deposit boxes.

If you're unlucky enough to get **mugged**, never resist and, if you disturb a thief, raise the alarm rather than try to take them on. Be especially aware of **pickpockets** on buses or bemos, who usually operate in pairs: one will distract you while another does the job. Afterwards, you'll need a **police report** for insurance purposes. Try to take along someone to translate, though police will generally do their best to find an English-speaker. You may also be charged "administration fees", the cost of which is open to sensitive negotiations. Have nothing to do with **drugs** in Indonesia: the penalties are extremely tough, and you won't get any sympathy from consular officials.

EMERGENCY NUMBERS

Police ☎**110**
Ambulance ☎**118**/☎**119**
Fire ☎**113**

MEDICAL CARE AND EMERGENCIES

If you have a minor ailment, head to a **pharmacy** (*apotik*), which can provide many medicines without prescription. Condoms (*kondom*) are available from pharmacists and some convenience stores. If you need an English-speaking doctor (*doktor*) or dentist (*doktor gigi*), seek advice at your accommodation or at the local tourist office. You'll find a **public hospital** (*rumah sakit*) in major cities and towns, and in some places these are supplemented by **private hospitals**, many of which operate an accident and emergency department. If you have a serious accident or illness, you will need to be evacuated home or to Singapore, which has Asia's best medical provision. It is, therefore, vital to arrange **health insurance** before you leave home.

INFORMATION AND MAPS

There's a range of **tourist offices** in Indonesia, including government-run organizations, normally called **Dinas** (or Kantor) Pariwisata (Diparda). However, many tourist information centres in Indonesia are little more than pamphlet outlets. Good hostels are often the best sources of information.

Good all-round maps include GeoCentre's 1:2,000,000 series and the Nelles Indonesia series. In the same league is the Periplus (Ⓦperiplus.com) range of user-friendly city and provincial maps.

MONEY AND BANKS

The Indonesian currency is the **rupiah** (abbreviated to "Rp"). **Notes** come in denominations of Rp500 (rare), Rp1000, Rp5000, Rp10,000, Rp20,000, Rp50,000 and even Rp100,000; **coins**, mainly used for public telephones and *bemos*, come in Rp25 (rare), Rp50, Rp100, Rp500 and Rp1000 denominations. Officially, rupiah are available outside Indonesia, but the currency's volatile value means that few banks carry it. At the time of writing, the exchange rate was Rp19,600 to £1 and Rp12,000 to US$1.

Sometimes prices for tourist services, such as diving or organized trips, are quoted in **dollars** or **euros**, but you can pay in rupiah at the exchange rate at that time.

You'll find **banks** capable of handling foreign exchange in provincial capitals and bigger cities throughout Indonesia, and most bigger places have **ATMs**, which take at least one from Visa, MasterCard or Cirrus-Maestro. There are also privately run **moneychangers** in major tourist centres. Always count your money carefully, as unscrupulous dealers can rip you off, either by folding notes over to make it look as if you're getting twice as much, or by distracting you and then whipping away a few notes from your pile.

In less-travelled regions, provincial banks won't cash travellers' cheques, but will take **dollars**. Over-the-counter **cash advances** on Visa can be used for getting the best possible exchange rate.

OPENING HOURS AND HOLIDAYS

As a rough outline, businesses such as airline offices open Monday to Friday 8am to 5pm and Saturday 8am to noon. Banking hours are Monday to Friday 8am to 3pm and Saturday 8am to 1pm, but banks may not handle foreign exchange in the afternoons or at weekends. Post offices operate roughly Monday to Thursday 8am to 2pm, Friday 8 to 11am and Saturday 8am to 1pm, though in the larger cities the hours are much longer. Muslim businesses, including **government offices**, may also close at 11.30am on Fridays, the main day of prayer, and national **public holidays** see all commerce compulsorily curtailed.

Ramadan, a month of fasting during daylight hours, falls during the ninth Muslim month, which changes from year to year. Even in non-Islamic areas, Muslim restaurants and businesses shut down during the day, and in staunchly Islamic parts of rural Lombok, Sumatra and Kalimantan's Banjarmasin, you should not eat, drink or smoke in public at this time.

BAHASA INDONESIA

Although there are also more than 250 native languages spoken throughout the archipelago, Indonesia's national language is Bahasa Indonesia, a form of Bahasa Malay. Because it's written in Roman script, has no tones and uses a fairly straightforward grammar, it's relatively easy to learn.

PRONUNCIATION

a as in a cross between father and cup
e sometimes as in along; or as in pay; or as in get; or sometimes omitted (*selamat* pronounced "slamat")
i either as in boutique; or as in pit
o either as in hot; or as in cold
u as in boot
ai as in fine
au as in how
c as in cheap
g always hard, as in girl
k hard, as in English, except at the end of the word, when you should stop just short of pronouncing it

GREETINGS AND BASIC PHRASES

Good morning	*Selamat pagi*
Good day	*Selamat siang*
Good afternoon	*Selamat sore*
Good evening	*Selamat malam*
Goodbye	*Selamat tinggal*
Please (requesting)	*Tolong*
Please (offering)	*Silakan*
Thank you (very much)	*Terima kasih (banyak)*
You're welcome	*Sama sama*
Sorry/Excuse me	*Ma'af*
No worries/Never mind	*Tidak apa apa*
Yes	*Ya*
No (with verb)	*Tidak* (sometimes pronounced "*tak*")
Do you speak English?	*Bisa bicara bahasa Inggris?*
I don't understand	*Saya tidak mengerti*
I want/would like …	*Saya mau …*
I don't want it/No thanks	*Tidak mau*
Open/Closed	*Buka/tutup*
Where is the …?	*Dimana …?*
How much/many?	*Berapa?*
What is the price for this?	*Berapa harga ini?*
Airport	*Lapangan terbang*
Bank	*Bank*
Beach	*Pantai*
bemo/bus station	*terminal*
city/city centre	*kota*
hospital	*sakit*
hotel	*losmen*
market	*pasar*
pharmacy	*apotik*
police station	*kantor polisi*
post office	*kantor pos*
shop	*toko*
telephone office	*wartel/kantor telkom*
bicycle	*sepeda*
bus	*bis*
car	*mobil*
entrance/exit	*masuk/keluar*
ferry	*ferry*
motorbike	*sepeda motor*
taxi	*taksi*
ticket	*karcis*
Stop!	*Estop!*
air conditioning	*AC*
bathroom	*kamar mandi*
breakfast	*makan pagi*
fan	*kipas*
hot water	*air panas*
mosquito net	*kelambu nyamuk*
toilet	*kamar kecil/wc* (pronounced "*way say*")

NUMBERS

Zero	*Nol/kosong*
1	*Satu*
2	*Dua*
3	*Tiga*
4	*Empat*
5	*Lima*
6	*Enam*
7	*Tujuh*
8	*Delapan*
9	*Sembilan*
10	*Sepuluh*
11, 12, 13, etc	*Sebelas, duabelas, tigabelas*
20	*Duapuluh*
21, 22, etc	*Duapuluh satu, duapuluh dua, duapuluh tiga, etc*
30, 40, etc	*Tigapuluh, Empatpuluh, Limapuluh*
100	*Seratus*
200	*Duaratus*
1000	*Seribu*

FOOD AND DRINKS GLOSSARY

Daftar makanan	Menu
Dingin	Cold
Enak	Delicious
Goreng	Fried
Makan malam	Dinner
Makan pagi	Breakfast
Makan siang	Lunch
Panas	Hot (temperature)
Pedas	Hot (spicy)
Saya ingin bayar	I want to pay
Saya seorang vegetaris	I'm a vegetarian
Saya tidak makan daging	I don't eat meat
Sayur saja	Only vegetables

Meat, fish and basic foods

Anjing	Dog
Ayam	Chicken
Babi	Pork
Bakmi	Noodles
Buiah	Fruit
Es	Ice
Ikan	Fish
Itik	Duck
Jaja	Rice cakes
Jus	Juice
Kambing	Goat
Kare	Curry
Kepiting	Crab
Nasi	Rice
Sambal	Hot chilli sauce
Sapi	Beef
Soto	Soup
Telur	Egg
Tikkus	Rat
Udang	Prawn

Everyday dishes

Ayam bakar	Fried chicken
Bakmi goreng	Fried noodles and meat
Bakso	Meat balls
Bubur ayam	Rice porridge with chicken (breakfast food)
Cap cay	Mixed fried vegetables
Gado-gado	Steamed vegetables served with a spicy peanut sauce
Kue tiaw	Singaporean stir-fry of flat rice noodles and meat
Lumpia	Spring rolls
Murtabak	Thick dough pancake, often filled with meat
Nasi ayam	Boiled rice with chicken
Nasi campur	Boiled rice served with small amounts of vegetable, meat, fish and sometimes egg
Nasi goring	Fried rice
Nasi gudeg	Rice with jackfruit and coconut-milk curry
Nasi pecel	Vegetables and rice cooked with peanut sauce
Nasi putih	Plain boiled rice
Nasi soto ayam	Chicken-and-rice soup
Pisang goring	Fried bananas
Rendang	Dry-fried beef and coconut-milk curry
Rijsttaffel	Dutch/Indonesian buffet of six to ten meat, fish and vegetable dishes with rice
Sate	Meat or fish kebabs served with a spicy peanut sauce
Tahu goring telur	Tofu omelette
Urap-urap/urap timum	Vegetables with coconut and chilli

Drinks

Jus jeruk	Orange juice
Jus jeruk nipis	Lemon juice
Air minum	Drinking water
Arak	Palm or rice spirit
Bir	Beer
Brem	Local rice beer
Kopi	Coffee
Kopi susu	Coffee (with) milk
Sopi	Palm spirit
Susu	Milk
The	Tea
Tuak	Palm wine

PUBLIC HOLIDAYS

Most of the national public holidays fall on different dates of the Western calendar each year, as they are calculated according to Islamic or local calendars.

January 1 New Year's Day (*Tahun Baru*)
Jan/Feb Chinese New Year
Muharam (usually Jan) Islamic New Year
March/April *Nyepi*, Balinese New Year
March/April Good Friday and Easter Sunday
Maulud Nabi Muhammad (usually March or April) Anniversary of the birth of Muhammed
May/June *Waisak* Day. Anniversary of the birth, death and enlightenment of Buddha
May/June Ascension Day of Jesus
Lailat al Miraj (usually between July and Sept) Ascension Day of Muhammed
August 17 Independence Day (*Hari Proklamasi Kemerdekaan*)
Idul Fitri (usually Oct or Nov) The celebration of the end of Ramadan
Idul Adha (usually between Dec and Jan) Feast of Sacrifice
4 **December 25** Christmas Day

FESTIVALS

In addition to national public holidays, there are frequent **religious festivals** throughout Indonesia's Muslim, Hindu, Chinese and indigenous communities. Each of Bali's twenty thousand temples has an anniversary celebration, for instance, and other ethnic groups may host elaborate marriages or funerals, along with more secular holidays. Many of these festivals change annually against the Western **calendar**.

Erau Festival Tenggarong, Kalimantan. September. A big display of indigenous Dayak skills and dancing.
Funerals Tanah Toraja, Sulawesi. Mostly May to September. With buffalo slaughter, bullfights and *sisemba* kick-boxing tournaments.
Galungun Bali. Takes place for ten days every 210 days to celebrate the victory of good over evil.
Kasada Bromo, East Java. Offerings are made to the gods and thrown into the crater. Held on the fourteenth day of Kasada, the twelfth month in the Tenggerese calendar year (Dec).
Krakatau Festival Lampung, Sumatra. October. Five days of events highlighting Lampung's cultural heritage, including Tuping Karnaval (Lampung Mask Carnival); part of the celebration occurs on the island of Anak Krakatau itself.
Nyepi Throughout Bali. End of March or beginning of April. The major purification ritual of the year.
Pasola West Sumba. Held four times in February and March, this festival to balance the upper sphere of the heavens culminates with a frenetic pitched battle between two villages of spear-wielding horsemen.

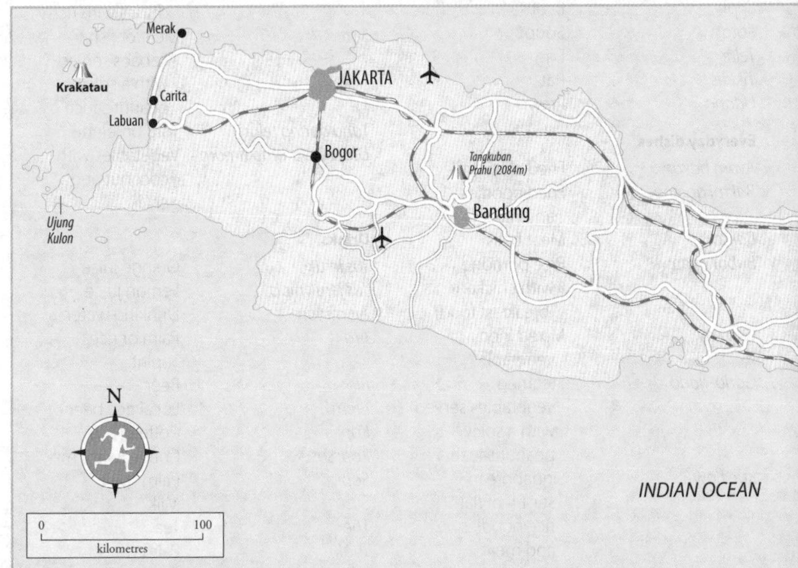

Sekaten Central Java. March or April. The celebration of the birthday of the prophet Muhammed includes a month-long festival of fairs, gamelan recitals and performances.

Java

One of the most densely populated places in all of Asia, **Java** is also characterized by great natural beauty. This island's central spine is dominated by volcanoes, over forty of which remain active, their fertile slopes supporting a landscape of glimmering rice fields dotted with countless villages. To the south of this mountainous backbone is the homeland of the ethnic Javanese and the epicentre of their arts, culture and language, epitomized by the royal courts of **Yogyakarta** and **Solo**. Still steeped in traditional dance, music and art, these two cities are the mainstay of Java's tourist industry, providing excellent bases from which to explore the sublime Buddhist temple of **Borobudur**, as well as the equally fascinating Hindu complex of **Prambanan**. To the east, the volcanic massif of **Gunung Bromo** is another major stop on most travellers' itineraries, not least for the sunrise walk to its summit. But there are plenty more volcanic landscapes to explore, including the turquoise lake of **Kawah Ijen**, the ancient temples and coloured lakes of the windswept **Dieng Plateau**, and the world's most famous – and destructive – volcano, **Krakatau**, off the west coast of Java.

Aside from Yogyakarta, Java's cities are somewhat less enticing to travellers, although **Jakarta**, the chaotic sprawl that is Indonesia's capital, boasts interesting museums, a host of gargantuan new malls, and the best nightlife on the island. Moving on to Java's neighbouring islands is easily done – Bali is just a forty-minute ferry from Banyuwangi in the east, as is Sumatra from Merak in the west.

JAKARTA

Bounded to the north by the Java Sea and to the south by the low Bogor Hills, **JAKARTA** is Indonesia's unrivalled megalopolis. Home to over ten million (almost thirty million including the greater, official metropolitan area known as Jabodetabek), it comprises almost 700 square kilometres of concrete sprawl, an amalgam of glamorous shopping malls,

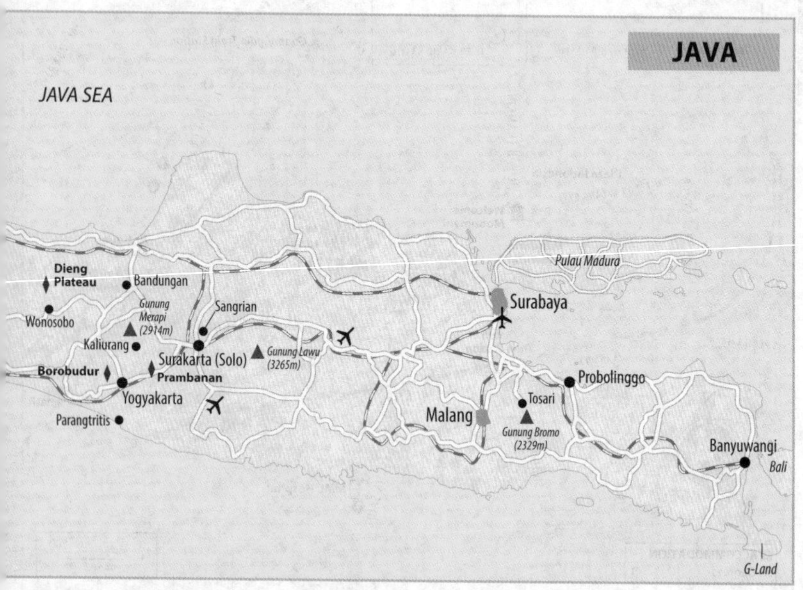

colonial-era relics, exclusive enclaves and slums spread beneath a soaring skyline. It's notorious for noise, congestion and pollution on a scale to match any city its size, and therefore many travellers don't give it a second glance – thereby missing out on the many charms of the national capital. Indeed, there's nowhere better to experience Indonesia's pulsing dynamism and its heart-rending sea of contrasts than in the "Big Durian", the modern face of Indonesia.

Among the city's highlights are **Kota** in the north, former heart of the colonial

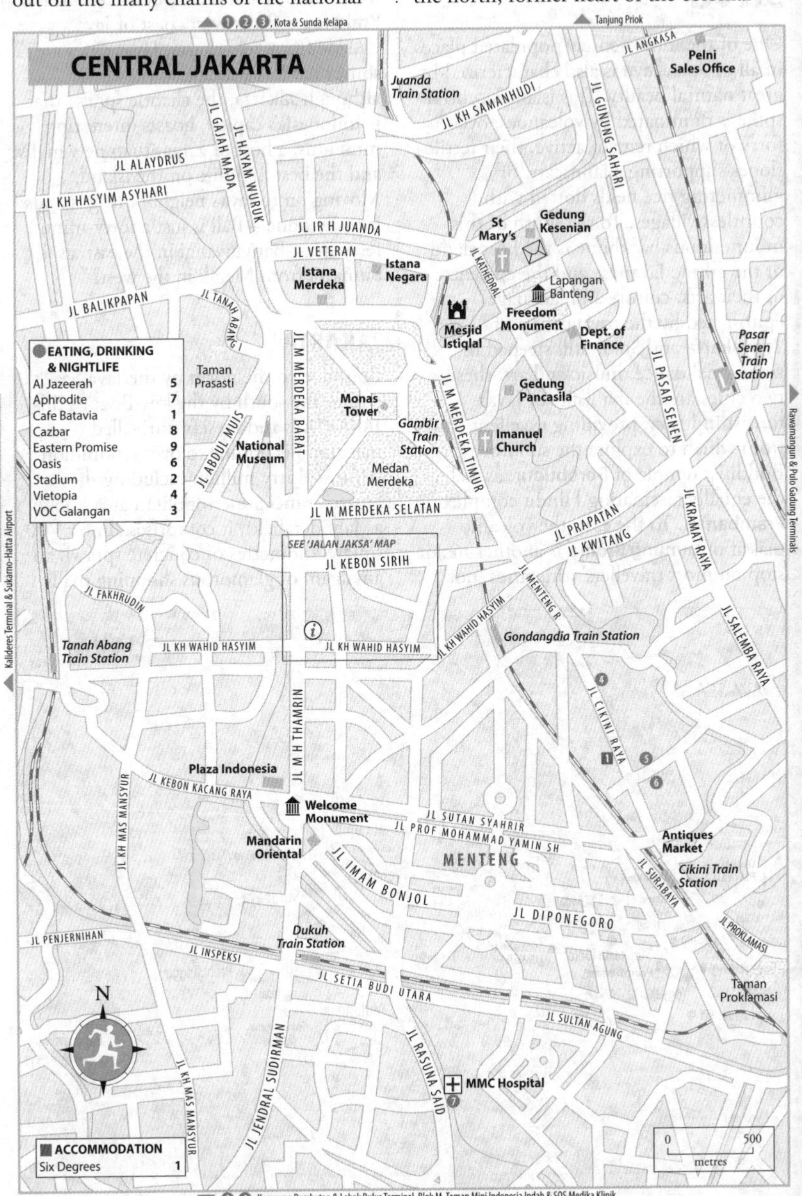

Dutch city, and the neighbouring **Sunda Kelapa**, Jakarta's bustling old port. Both districts are dotted with historic buildings, including a few of the country's finest museums, among them the **Maritime Museum**, the **Wayang Museum** and the **National Museum**.

WHAT TO SEE AND DO

To head from north to south through the centre of Jakarta is to go forward in time, from the quaint old Dutch area of **Kota** in the north to modern golf courses and amusement parks in the south. **Medan Merdeka**, a giant, threadbare patch of grass, marks the spiritual centre of Jakarta, if not exactly its geographical one, bordered to the west by the city's major north-south thoroughfare. The main commercial district and the budget accommodation enclave of **Jalan Jaksa** lie just a short distance to the south of Medan Merdeka.

Kota (Old Batavia)

Formerly known as **Batavia**, the quaint old district of Kota was once the administrative centre of the Dutch trading empire. To reach Kota, take the Trans Jakarta from Sarinah (Rp3500), which ends up in front of the Art Deco-style **Kota train station**, built in 1929. North of the station along Jalan Lada, past the Politeknik Swadharma, you enter the formerly walled city of Batavia, whose centre, **Taman Fatahillah**, an attractive cobbled square hemmed in by museums, lies 300m to the north of the train station. On the south side, the **Jakarta History Museum** (Tues–Sun 9am–3pm; Rp2000) traces the region's history back to the Stone Age; most displays are accompanied by English descriptions. The finest exhibit is the ornate **Cannon Si Jagur**, which previously stood in the square and was built by the Portuguese to defend Melaka. It is emblazoned with sexual imagery, from the clenched fist (a suggestive gesture in Southeast Asia) to the barrel itself, a potent phallic symbol in Indonesia.

To the west of the square is the small but worthwhile **Wayang Museum** (Tues–Sun 9am–3pm; Rp2000), dedicated to the Javanese art of puppetry and housed in one of the oldest buildings in the city. Although some of its exhibits are poorly maintained, the museum has puppets from right across the archipelago, and there is a free bimonthly **wayang show** (second and fourth Sunday of each month at 10am). While in the area, don't miss the chance to luxuriate in the stylish surroundings of the historic *Café Batavia*, on the northwestern corner of Taman Fatahillah. To the east of the square, the **Balai Seni Rupa** (Tues–Sun 9am–3pm; Rp3000), Jakarta's fine arts museum, and the **Ceramics Museum** house works by Indonesia's most illustrious artists.

Sunda Kelapa and around

About 1km north of Kota lies the historic harbour of **Sunda Kelapa** (Rp15,000), the most important foreign port of the entire Dutch empire. Although the bulk of the sea traffic docks at Tanjung Priok these days, a few of the smaller vessels, particularly some picturesque wooden schooners, still call in at this eight-hundred-year-old port. You can either walk here from Kota (about 20min) or hail an ojek (Rp10,000).

From Sunda Kelapa, cross over the bridge to the west (on the right as you exit the port) and turn right at the nineteenth-century watchtower, the **Uitkijk**, built to direct shipping traffic to the port. Here, buried in the chaotic Pasar Ikan (fish market) that occupies this promontory, is the entrance to the **Museum Bahari**, or **Maritime Museum** (Tues–Sun 9am–3pm; Rp2000), housed in a warehouse dating from 1652. All kinds of sea craft are on display, from the Buginese *pinisi* to the *kora-kora* war boat from the Moluccas.

Head towards the *VOC Galangan* restaurant, keeping the Kali Besar canal on your left until you come to the ornate wooden drawbridge, **Jembatan Pasar Ayam**, which is in immaculate condition. The grand Dutch terraced houses on the streets south of here were once the smartest addresses in Batavia, the most famous being the Chinese-style **Toko Merah** (Red Shop) at 11 Jalan Kali Besar Barat – the former home of the Dutch governor-general, Van Imhoff. The Batavia bus station lies on the other side

of the canal, from where frequent pale-blue minivans (Rp2000) run back to Kota and the Trans Jakarta.

Medan Merdeka

The heart and lungs of Jakarta, **Medan Merdeka** is a square kilometre of sun-scorched grass and pleasant manicured gardens in the middle of the city. At its centre stands the **Monas Tower**, a soaring 137m marble, bronze and gold torch, commissioned by Sukarno in 1962 to symbolize the indomitable spirit of the Indonesian people, and known as "Sukarno's last erection" in recognition of his world-famous philandering. You can take a lift up to its top for an impressive city view (Tues–Sun 8.30am–5pm; Rp10,000); the ticket includes entry to the **National History Museum** and the Goblet Yard at Monas' base, a series of 48 dioramas that depict the history of Jakarta and Indonesia's struggle for independence.

4

The **National Museum** (Tues–Sun 9am–3pm; Rp1500; ☎021 386 8172), on the western side of Medan Merdeka, is an interesting detour and a great introduction to Indonesia. Many of the country's top ruins have been plundered for their statues, which now sit, unmarked, in the museum courtyard. Other highlights include huge Dongson kettledrums, the skull and thighbone of Java Man, found near Solo in 1936, and the cache of golden artefacts discovered at the foot of Mount Merapi in 1990.

The dazzling white, if rather unprepossessing, **Mesjid Istiqlal** looms over the northeastern corner of Medan Merdeka. Completed in 1978, it is the largest mosque in Southeast Asia and can hold up to 250,000 people. For a small donation, and providing you're conservatively dressed, the security guards will take you on an informal tour. At the foot of the minaret sits a 2.5-tonne wooden drum from east Kalimantan, the only traditional feature in this otherwise state-of-the-art mosque.

Mini Indonesia

Eighteen kilometres south of Medan Merdeka, on the road to Bogor, is the **Taman Mini Indonesia Indah** theme park (Tues–Sun 8am–5pm; Rp10,000). This peculiar oasis is like an Indonesian Neverland celebrating the archipelago's rich ethnic and cultural diversity with gondolas offering the best view of the sprawling complex. At its centre is a man-made lake, around which are 26 houses, each built in the traditional style of Indonesia's provinces.

The park also contains a reptile garden, bird park and several museums. Among these are the **Museum of Indonesia** (daily 8am–4pm; Rp5000), which has displays on the country's people, geography, flora and fauna, and the neighbouring **Museum**

Purna Bhakti Pertiwi (daily 8am–4pm; Rp9000), which displays a fabulously opulent collection of gifts presented to President Suharto, including a whole gamelan orchestra made of old Balinese coins, a series of carved wooden panels depicting Suharto's life story, and an enormous rubber-tree root decorated with the nine gods of Balinese Hinduism. To get here from Sarinah, catch the Trans Jakarta bus south to Semanggi then switch buses to reach Garuda Taman Mini.

ARRIVAL AND DEPARTURE

BY PLANE

Jakarta's Sukarno-Hatta Airport (☎ 021 550 5000) is 13km west of the city centre and connects with virtually all of Indonesia's major cities. The airport has a small tourist office in Terminal 2D (☎ 021 550 7088) and a handful of exchange booths, most of which close at 10pm; rates at these are significantly lower than in the city centre. Terminal 1 serves domestic flights from all but Air Asia, Mandala and Garuda; Terminal 2 serves most international flights as well as domestic flights for Garuda and Merpati; and Terminal 3, the newest and most attractive terminal, is reserved for budget airlines such as Air Asia, Lion Air and Mandala. Free yellow shuttle buses connect the terminals. DAMRI buses connect the airport to Gambir train station (45min; Rp25,000), with services every 15min from 4am until the last flight, and from Gambir to the airport from 4am–8pm. Upon arrival, turn left out of the gate and walk about 200m to the bus stand. Taxis between the airport and Jl Jaksa cost about Rp150,000, including Rp35,000 in toll fees. Blue Bird (blue cabs) and Express (white cabs) are the most reliable firms. On all embarkations from Sukarno-Hatta Airport, a departure tax is required for both international (Rp150,000) and domestic flights (Rp40,000).

Destinations Banda Aceh (2 daily; 2hr 50min); Balikpapan (21 daily; 2hr); Bandung (14 daily; 40min); Bangkok (6 daily; 3hr 30min); Denpasar (40 daily; 1hr 50min); Jayapura (daily; 5hr 30min); Kota Kinabalu (3 weekly; 2hr 35min); Makassar (38 daily; 2hr 20min); Manado (5 daily; 3hr 20min); Mataram (8 daily; 2hr); Medan (5 daily; 2hr 15min); Pekanbaru (16 daily; 1hr 40min); Singapore (44 daily; 1hr 40min); Solo/Surakarta (13 daily; 1hr 10min); Surabaya (54 daily; 1hr 20min); Yogyakarta (30 daily; 1hr 5min).

BY BUS

Buses connect Jakarta to all points in Java as well as many cities on neighbouring islands. There are five major bus terminals, all serving the same destinations and all connected by Trans Jakarta buses to Jl Jaksa. From here, the closest is Rawamangun (☎ 021 489 7455), 10km east of Jaksa in East Jakarta; the others are Pulo Gadung (☎ 021 489 3742), 14km east of Jaksa, where there are the most buses heading to east Java and Bali; Kampung Rambutan (☎ 021 840 0062), 20km south, with the most frequent departures to Bogor and Bandung; Lebak Bulus (☎ 021 750 9773), 18km to the southwest; and Kalideres (☎ 021 544 5348), 17km west, from where there are the most frequent departures for all points west in both Java and Sumatra, including Labuan and Merak. Bus tickets are cheaper from the bus stations than from agencies in town, although tickets bought from agencies often include free connections to the far-flung terminals. Allow at least 1hr 30min to get from the city centre to any bus station. Due to crowds it's advisable not to attempt bus travel at the end of Ramadan.

Destinations Frequent departures for Bandung (4hr 30min); Bogor (1–2hr); Bukittinggi (30hr); Denpasar (24hr); Labuan (3hr 30min); Medan (2 days); Merak (3hr); Padang (32hr); Pangandaran (12hr); Solo (13hr); Surabaya (15hr); Yogya (12hr).

BY FERRY

All Pelni ferries dock at Tanjung Priok harbour, 500m from the bus station of the same name. Trans Jakarta buses connect the harbour with Jl Jaksa's Sarinah stop (take the #12 corridor then switch to #1 at Kota), and taxis should cost around Rp100,000 in bad traffic. The Pelni booking office (☎ 021 6385 0960) is at Jl Angkasa 18 in Kemayoran; catch the Trans Jakarta to Senen, then the red #10 or #11 buses (Rp5000) to Angkasa. Tickets can be bought from numerous agents around town.

Destinations Banda (monthly; 4 days); Jayapura (weekly; 7 days); Makassar (2 weekly; 48hr); Padang (monthly; 3 days); Pontianak (monthly; 48hr); Pulau Batam (weekly; 30hr); Surabaya (fortnightly; 24hr); Ternate (monthly; 5 days).

BY TRAIN

There are four central train stations (and dozens of minor suburban ones). Gambir (☎ 021 386 2363) is the most popular and convenient, with executive and business-class trains heading all across West and Central Java – including Yogya, Surakarta (Solo), Bogor and Bandung. The office at the north end of Gambir (daily 7.30am–7pm) sells tickets for the *Parahyangan Express* to Bandung and the *Argolawu Express* to Yogya and Solo. The walk from Gambir to Jl Jaksa takes 20min, while taxis are also available for around Rp20,000 from Gambir to Jaksa; avoid the touts and head for the Blue Bird or Express taxi ranks. Ojeks outside Gambir are especially handy during peak hour (around Rp15,000). Of the other stations, the most useful are Pasar Senen (☎ 021 421 0006), east of the city centre, serving economy-class trains heading to all points east; and Kota (☎ 021 692 8515), near old Batavia. All train stations are linked by the Trans Jakarta network to Jl Jaksa; its stop is Sarinah, a 5min walk from Jaksa. If you have a local SIM card, save the trip to the station by dialling ☎ 121 for train information and bookings, after

which you will receive a confirmation code via SMS: take this to the nearest Indomaret or Alfamart to pay and get a receipt. If you can work with Bahasa Indonesia, you may search and book tickets on the railway's official website, ⓦ tiket.kereta-api.co.id (Bahasa Indonesia); though a more user-friendly agent is ⓦ tiket.com – often worth the small commission (about Rp13,000). Be at the station at least one hour early to exchange booking receipts for boarding passes.

Destinations From Gambir station unless stated otherwise: Bandung (7 daily; 3hr); Bogor (every 20min; 1hr 30min); Purwokerto (Gambir and Pasar Senen; 12 daily; 5–6hr); Solobapan, Solo (5 daily; 7hr–10hr 25min); Surabaya (5 daily; 9hr–14hr 30min); Yogyakarta (Gambir and Pasar Senen; 9 daily; 6hr 50min–8hr 40min).

INFORMATION

Tourist office Jakarta's Visitor Information Centre is inside the Jakarta Theatre building next to *Burger King*, opposite Sarinah's department store on Jl Wahid Hasyim (Mon–Fri 9am–6pm, Sat 9am–2pm; ⓣ 021 314 2067). Useful maps and brochures covering Jakarta are available here and the English-speaking staff are friendly.

4

GETTING AROUND

BY BUS

Trans Jakarta busway system The only bus service (daily 4am–11pm) in Jakarta with designated stops and by far the easiest and most useful service for tourists. It runs from the Harmoni Central Busway to Kalideres, Ancol, Pulo Gadung, Rawamangun, Rambutan, Ragunan and Blok M. With its own designated bus lane, it's also quicker than other transport services. Buy your ticket (Rp3500 one-way; flat fare) before boarding from the ticket office at the station. Other useful stations include Sarinah (for Jl Jaksa), Kota (for Old Batavia and the Jakarta History Museum) and Monumen (for the Monas Tower and National Museum), although the latter are just a short walk from Jl Jaksa.

Other buses Most other buses operate a set-fare system, regardless of distance, but prices depend on the type of bus. The cheapest are the small, pale-blue *angkots* (minivans), which operate out of Kota bus station charging a minimum of Rp2000, while the large coaches found all over the city charge Rp3000 to Rp6000 or Rp7000 (for a/c buses). To alight from the bus, hail the driver or conductor with "*kiri!*" (left) or rap the overhead rail with a coin.

BY BAJAJ

The two-stroke motorized rickshaws, or *bajaj* (pronounced "ba-jais"), monopolize the city's backstreets. *Bajaj* are banned from major thoroughfares such as Jl Thamrin, so you might get dropped off in an inconvenient spot for your final destination. A journey from Jl Jaksa to the post office should cost Rp10,000–15,000, and from Jl Jaksa to Gambir should cost Rp8000. Bargain hard.

BY TAXI

Jakarta's taxis are numerous and, providing you know your way around the city, inexpensive. Many taxi drivers will take the "scenic route" to your destination if you seem unsure. Recommended firms are Blue Bird (ⓣ 021 798 9000) and Express (ⓣ 021 2650 9000). Most drivers speak little to no English, but will usually use the meter ("argo") without being asked; fares depend on how long you spend stuck in Jakarta's infamous traffic jams (a half-hour ride should cost about Rp80,000). Although meters begin at Rp6000 (except for Blue Bird taxis, which start at Rp7000), the minimum fare is around Rp10,000. Women should avoid travelling in taxis alone at night as there are increasing reports of assaults and robberies.

ACCOMMODATION

Jakarta's cluster of backpacker-oriented lodgings fills up fast and should be booked ahead. Most budget places are on or around Jl Jaksa, the city's travellers' enclave to the south of Medan Merdeka, though there are also good options in the Cikini Raya area, 2km southeast of Jaksa.

JALAN JAKSA AREA

Asri Jl Kebon Sirih Barat I Gang 10/18 ⓣ 021 314 7684; map p.180. Hidden down a narrow lane across from Borneo, this homestay is a quiet retreat from the noise of Jaksa. Still off the radar for travellers, it offers spotless a/c rooms at a bargain price, each with inside mandi. **Rp150,000**

Bloemsteen Jl Kebon Sirih Timur I/174 ⓣ 021 319 25389; map p.180. Although the rooms are nothing to rave about and staff seem disinterested, this is one of Jaksa's cheapest options. Both fan and a/c rooms (Rp150,000) are available, and wi-fi works in both the lobby and in the small, pleasant outdoor area. **Rp90,000**

Borneo Jl Kebon Sirih Barat 37 ⓣ 021 314 0095; map p.180. Friendly and quiet (except for the morning call from the mosque next door), this cavernous hostel looks a little frayed, but offers good-value rooms, the best of which come with private bathrooms (Rp130,000). **Rp100,000**

Delima Jl Jaksa 5 ⓣ 021 3190 4157; map p.180. The oldest of the city's homestays and it shows. All the rooms have shared bathrooms, and the single rooms are about as cheap as it gets on Jaksa (Rp75,000). There's a small library, a kitchen serving cheap food (breakfast Rp20,000), and a friendly owner who can help with onward travel. **Rp85,000**

Hostel 35 Jl Kebon Sirih Barat 35 ⓣ 021 392 0331; map p.180. This refurbished hostel has a range of attractive rooms; the nicer a/c rooms (Rp250,000) come with new fittings, widescreen TVs and renovated bathrooms. Even the cheaper ones include inside bathrooms, breakfast and free wi-fi in the lobby. **Rp150,000**

Istana Ratu Jl Jaksa 7–9 ⓣ 021 314 2472; map p.180. Although rooms in this hotel are a tad worn, all have a/c, cable TV and hot showers, while there are great city views

from the upper floors and wi-fi in the classy downstairs lobby. Worth the splurge, though it can get busy here so ring ahead. Discounts are available for longer stays. Rp260,000

KL Inn Jl Kebon Sirih Barat Gang 7/4 ⓣ 021 3193 3226; map p.180. Brand-new flashpacker hotel, launched in 2013 down the lane opposite KL Village. Rooms are spotless and come with sparkling bathrooms, flatscreen TVs and wi-fi. Breakfast is included too. Cheaper rooms on the upper floors are otherwise identical to the rest. Rp250,000

Le Margot Jl Jaksa 15 ⓣ 021 391 3830, ⓦ margotkafe.com; map p.180. This popular mid-range place is showing its age, and though a tad stuffy, the well-furnished rooms come with a/c, cable TV and hot water, and the price includes a simple breakfast and wi-fi in the lobby/popular restaurant downstairs. Street-facing rooms get noisy at night. Rp300,000

Tator Jl Jaksa 37 ⓣ 021 3192 3940; map p.180. This cool and quiet family-run hotel is a travellers' favourite and is often fully booked. Spread across three storeys, the ageing but well-kept rooms all have a/c and inside bathrooms. Breakfast is included in the price and there is a lovely seating area at the front. Rp160,000

CIKINI RAYA

Six Degrees Jl Cikini Raya 60 B–C ⓣ 021 314 1657, ⓦ jakarta-backpackers-hostel.com; map p.178. Within a short hop of the city centre, this friendly new hostel has all-a/c rooms and dorms, one of which comes with a private bathroom (Rp300,000). Designed for backpackers, it has a welcoming lounge with fast, free wi-fi and computers, a rooftop garden, a pool table and a kitchen available to guests. Simple breakfast included. Dorm Rp120,000, double Rp250,000

EATING AND DRINKING

There is more variation to the cuisine here than elsewhere in the country, from a wealth of affordable fine dining options to a thriving street food scene.

JALAN JAKSA AND JALAN HA SALIM (JALAN SABANG)

Some of the best-value street food in the city can be found at the stalls crammed along Jl HA Salim.

Beirut and Lebanon Jl HA Salim 57; map p.180. Something different in this largely generic area, this sleek establishment serves good hummus with tahini (Rp25,000), *shawarma* sandwiches (Rp30,000), grilled meats and a decent range of mezze and shisha (Rp35,000). There's an a/c section and an outdoor terrace overlooking the busy intersection. Daily 9am–2am.

KL Village Jl Jaksa 21–23; map p.180. The best value on the street and deservedly the most popular with both locals and travellers, serving cheap Indonesian food (*nasi goreng* Rp12,000) and a good range of Chinese, Indian, Malay and Thai cuisine (including *roti canai* for Rp8000 and an amazing tom yum soup for Rp17,000). Packed in the evenings, so be prepared to wait for your meal. Daily 7am–4am.

Memories Jl Jaksa 17 ⓣ 021 392 8839; map p.180. The most popular evening drinking den on Jl Jaksa and a great place to meet fellow travellers. There is a huge menu of Western and Indonesian dishes, though most patrons don't come for the food, which is on the expensive side (chicken *sate* Rp36,000). It also has one of Jaksa's largest libraries as well as some decent rooms on offer (fan or a/c Rp100,000/175,000). Daily 8am–2am.

Pappa's Jl Jaksa 41; map p.180. Great place for a curry (Rp38,000) at the quieter southern end of Jl Jaksa. *Pappa's* supplements its Indian dishes with live European football and is a popular travellers' hangout day and night. *Bintang* Rp30,000. Daily 8.30am–4am.

Warung Desa Jl HA Salim 55A; map p.180. A trendy little place that is always packed with locals and travellers. Offers a good range of seafood dishes, Chinese favourites and international cuisine (*nasi goreng* Rp9,000, *kwetiauw goreng* seafood Rp21,000). Daily 24hr.

ELSEWHERE

Al Jazeerah Jl Raden Saleh 58, Cikini ⓦ aljazeerahinjakarta.com; map p.178. Authentic Middle Eastern restaurant serving pan-Arab cuisine, a good change if you've had your fill of the *nasi goreng* and toasted sandwiches of Jl Jaksa, with a pricey but mouthwatering menu of kebabs, hummus dishes (Rp46,000), salads and good Turkish coffee. Daily 10am–3am.

Café Batavia Taman Fatahillah, Kota; map p.178. A classy café and restaurant housed in one of central Jakarta's oldest buildings, with great views across the square. The expensive and predominantly Western menu is good but not exceptional (club sandwich Rp79,000); it's the historic setting you're paying for. Mon–Thurs 8am–midnight, Fri 8am–1am, Sat 7am–1am, Sun 7am–midnight.

Eastern Promise Jl Kemang Raya 5; map p.178. Combined British pub and Indian restaurant with good pub-style food. Popular among expats, the meat pies (Rp65,000) are fantastic. There's a pool table, several LCD

★TREAT YOURSELF

Oasis Jl Raden Saleh 47 ⓣ 021 315 0646, ⓦ oasisjakarta.com; map p.178. Jakarta's finest restaurant has a fantastic old-world vibe. A large gong is sounded to greet each diner to this 1920s Dutch villa in Cikini, which is adorned with elegant colonial paintings and a crystal chandelier. The menu ranges from lobster thermidor (Rp630,000) to roasted duck (Rp342,000).

4

screens for sports fans and live music Fri & Sat in the spacious beer garden. Daily 10am–late.

Vietopia Jl Cikini Raya 33; map p.178. The first authentic Vietnamese restaurant in the capital, serving moderately priced *pho bo* (Rp50,000), *goi cuon* (Rp26,000) and other favourites in a sleek, minimalist-style venue (meals from Rp25,000). Daily 11.30am–9.30pm.

VOC Galangan Jl Kakap 1; map p.178. Set in a restored seventeenth-century Dutch warehouse a short stroll from the Maritime Museum, *VOC Galangan* serves tasty Western and Indonesian at reasonable prices (*gado gado* Rp13,500). A vintage car and horse carriage rest by the veranda. Good for a break from sightseeing in Sunda Kelapa. Daily 9am–5pm.

NIGHTLIFE AND ENTERTAINMENT

Jakarta has hundreds of nightclubs and a wide range of entertainment, but most travellers passing through don't leave Jl Jaksa in the evening, preferring to hang out in one of the low-key bars along the road.

Aphrodite Bar & Restaurant Jl HR Rasuna Said Kav 22 Ⓦ aphroditebar.com; map p.178. Featuring cold beer, finger foods, a couple of pool tables and a slew of flatscreen TVs, this sports bar near the Australian embassy draws a mixed crowd of locals and expats. Mon–Thurs 6am–2am, Fri & Sat 6am–3am, Sun 6am–12.30am.

4

Cazbar Jl Mega Kuningan Ⓦ thecazbar.com; map p.178. Very popular with expats, *Cazbar* has a sports bar upstairs with a pool table, darts and screenings of English premier league football, as well as occasional live music downstairs (check website for schedule). Free wi-fi. Daily 7am–2am.

Cocktail n Friends Jl Jaksa 10; map p.180. The most inviting spot on Jaksa, recently renovated with indoor and outdoor seating – the inside is a favourite for lighting up the sheesha pipes. A good selection of cheap cocktails (Rp30,000) and dancing till late. Daily 3pm–4am.

Dyna Pub Jl KH Wahid Hasyim 116; map p.180. One of Jakarta's most characterful venues, this old backstreet bar and pub is just a short walk from Jaksa. Kitsch to the extreme, every centimetre is covered in mismatched decor. Plenty of drinks (Bintang Rp35,000) and popcorn served. Daily 6pm–2am.

Stadium Jl Hayam Wuruk 111 Ⓦ stadiumjakarta.com; map p.178. The wildest spot in Jakarta, this is a huge, dark, four-storey nightclub where you can share the dancefloor with thousands at weekends. They've hosted plenty of renowned DJs, playing mostly techno, progressive and house beats. However, it's also known to be rife with drugs, prostitution and pickpockets. Thurs–Mon 24hr.

SHOPPING

While Jakarta has no particular indigenous craft of its own, the capital isn't a bad place to go souvenir shopping.

Books There are a couple of places in the basement of the smart Indonesia Plaza, including a branch of the excellent Periplus chain. For secondhand books, visit Jaksa Bookshop on Jl Jaksa, or *Memories Café*.

Market There's an antiques market on Jl Surabaya, Pasar Cikini, one block west of Cikini Station in Jakarta's Menteng district, and a textile market at Tanah Abang, a few blocks west of Sarinah – the oldest wholesale market in Indonesia (dating from 1735) and the largest of its kind in Southeast Asia.

Souvenirs The fourth and fifth floors of the Sarinah department store on Jl Kh Wahid Hasyim are given over to souvenirs, with wayang kulit and wayang golek puppets, leather bags and woodcarvings. Batik fabrics are sold on the fourth floor. For a similarly wide range and slightly better prices, head to the giant Mangga Dua complex near Kota.

DIRECTORY

Banks and exchange Banks with ATMs are available throughout the city. Cimb Niaga, near the northern end of Jl Jaksa on Jl Kebon Siri, offers the best exchange rates in town.

Embassies and consulates Australia, Jl H Rasuna Said Kav 15–16 (Ⓣ 021 2550 5555); Canada, World Trade Centre, 6th Floor, Jl Jend Sudirman Kav 29 (Ⓣ 021 2550 7800); Malaysia, Jl Rasuna Said Kav 1–3, Kuningan (Ⓣ 021 522 4947); New Zealand, 10th Floor, Jl Asia Afrika 8 (Ⓣ 021 2995 5800); Singapore, Jl Rasuna Said 2, Kuningan (Ⓣ 021 2995 0400); South Africa, Wisma GKBI, 7th Floor, Jl Jend Sudirman Kav 28 (Ⓣ 021 2991 2500); Thailand, Jl Imam Bonjol 74 (Ⓣ 021 390 4055); UK, Jl Patra Kuningan Raya Blok L5–6 (Ⓣ 021 2356 5200); US, Jl Medan Merdeka Selatan 5 (Ⓣ 021 3435 9000).

Hospitals and clinics The best in town are the MMC hospital on Jl Rasuna Said (Ⓣ 021 520 3435) and the SOS Medika Klinik (Ⓣ 021 5794 8600) on Jl Lingkar Mega, both in Kuningan. Any *Praktek Umum* (public clinic) will treat foreigners cheaply. Dial Ⓣ 118 for an ambulance.

Internet There are cheap internet cafés along Jl Jaksa, among them Greenet (daily 24hr; Rp6000/hr), just north of Tator. Many restaurants have free wi-fi.

MERAK AND FERRIES TO SUMATRA

Near the northwestern tip of Java, **Merak** is the port for ferries across the Sunda Straits to Bakauheni on Sumatra. Regular ferries **to Sumatra** leave every thirty minutes throughout the day and less frequently at night (2hr 30min; Rp13,000), while fast ferries depart every thirty minutes from 7.40am to 5pm (40min; Rp30,000). Crowds of buses connect with the ferries to take you on to Bandar Lampung (1hr 30min; Rp30,000), Palembang or destinations further north in Sumatra.

Post office The GPO lies to the north of Lapangan Benteng (Mon–Sat 8am–8pm, Sun 9am–5pm), northeast of Medan Merdeka.
Tourist police Jl Wahid Hasyim 9 (2nd Floor of Jakarta Theatre) ⓣ 021 526 4073. For emergencies, dial ⓣ 110.
Travel agents Good travel agencies on or near Jl Jaksa include Divalina Tour and Travel (ⓣ 021 314 9330) at Jl Jaksa 35, PT Robertur Kencana (ⓣ 021 314 2926) at Jl Jaksa 20B, and PT Bali Amanda (ⓣ 021 3193 1006) at Jl Wahid Hasyim 110A.

KRAKATAU

At 10am on August 27, 1883, an explosion equivalent to ten thousand Hiroshima atomic bombs tore apart **KRAKATAU ISLAND**; the boom was heard as far away as Sri Lanka. As the eruption column towered 40km into the atmosphere, a thick mud rain began to fall over the area and the temperature plunged by 5°C. One single **tsunami** as tall as a seven-storey building raced outwards, erasing three hundred towns and villages and killing more than 36,000 people. Once into the open sea, the waves travelled at up to 700km/h, reaching South Africa and scuttling ships in Auckland harbour. Two-thirds of Krakatau had vanished for good, and on those parts that remained, not so much as a seed or an insect survived.

Today, the crumbled caldera is clearly visible west of the beaches near Merak and Carita, its sheer northern cliff face soaring straight out of the sea to nearly 800m. But it is the glassy black cone of **Anak Krakatau**, the child of Krakatau volcano, that visitors come to see, a barren wasteland that's still growing and still very much active. It first reared its head from the seas in 1930, and now sits angrily smoking among the remains of the older peaks. To get here requires a several-hour **motorboat trip**, then a half-hour walk up to the crater, from where you can see black lava flows, sulphurous fumaroles and smoke. The most convenient way to visit the volcano is from **Carita**, although tours are slightly cheaper from Sumatra.

Carita

Boasting one of the most sheltered stretches of sea in the western reaches of Java, Carita is the island's best spot to arrange **tours to Krakatau** as well as to **Ujung Kulon National Park**. When you arrive in town, be wary of unlicensed guides. Krakatau Tour (ⓣ 0813 8666 8811, ⓦ krakatau-tour.com) is a reputable company that offers day-trips from Rp3,500,000 (per group of at least three people). **Buses** run from the Kalideres bus station in Jakarta to Labuan (3hr 30min); from here you can catch an *angkot* to Carita – don't get conned into taking transport to the *angkot* stop, which is just two minutes' walk towards the seafront and to the right. All **accommodation** in Carita is on or close to the main seaside road, known as Jalan Carita Raya or Jalan Pantai Carita. Prices shoot up at the weekend, when the town is invaded by jet-skiers. *The Sunset View* (ⓣ 0253 801075, ⓦ augusta-ind.com; Rp355,000) is one of the best-value places in town, with 40 percent discounts outside peak season. The public parts of the beach in Carita are lined with **food** carts selling *murtabak*, *sate* and *soto* (traditional soup).

BOGOR

Located 300m above sea level and just over an hour's train journey south of Jakarta, **BOGOR** is home to the famously lush Kebun Raya Bogor or **Botanical Gardens** (daily 8am–6pm; Rp26,000), founded by Sir Stamford Raffles in 1811. Worth a day-trip from Jakarta, the magnificent gardens offer respite from the congested streets of Bogor, and it is a delight to wander the shady pathways between towering bamboo stands, climbing bougainvillea, tropical rainforest and ponds full of water lilies and fountains. Near the gardens' main entrance is the **Zoological Museum** (daily 8am–4pm; included in Kebun Raya ticket), which houses some 30,000 specimens, including a complete skeleton of a blue whale, a stuffed Javan rhino and, most impressively, the remains of a huge coconut crab. Bogor is also an ideal base for hiking in **Mount Halimun Salak National Park**, as well as whitewater rafting and visiting hot springs, waterfalls and some of Java's most picturesque terraced rice paddies.

4

ARRIVAL AND DEPARTURE

By bemo The main bemo stop is behind the bus terminal, but the best place to pick up bemos is by the train station. Bemo #2 runs between the station and the Botanical Gardens; #3 runs between the station and bus terminal.

By bus The Bogor bus terminal is about 500m southeast of the gardens.

Destinations Bandung (every 20min; 3–4hr); Jakarta (every 20min; 1–2hr).

By train The train station is about 500m northwest of the Botanical Gardens, with connections to Jakarta (every 20min; 1hr 30min).

INFORMATION

Tourist office A useful tourist information centre lies about 50m to the right on Jl Kapten Muslihat 51 when exiting the train station at Taman Topi (daily 8am–5pm; ⓣ0251 836 3433). Eco-tours to Mount Halimun Salak National Park can be arranged here.

ACCOMMODATION

4

★**Abu Pensione** Jl Mayor Oking 15 ⓣ0251 832 2893 or ⓣ0815 862 65324. With friendly staff, spotless rooms, river views and excellent breakfasts (Rp35,000), this is the best budget place in Bogor. The pricier rooms have hot water and a/c (Rp300,000), and the staff can help with travel bookings. Manager Selfi leads interesting 3–4hr walking tours along the river (Rp250,000). To get here, turn right out of the station then take your first right down Jl Mayor Oking. **Rp150,000**

Mirah Sartika Jl Dewi Sartika 6A ⓣ0251 831 2343. Conveniently situated just one block east of the train station, this unremarkable hotel lacks charm but has clean, basic rooms, simple breakfasts and wi-fi in the lobby. **Rp268,000**

Pensione Firman Jl Paledang 48 ⓣ0251 832 3246. Popular with backpackers, *Firman* has simple and rather grotty rooms, the better ones with inside mandi (Rp120,000). However, there is free wi-fi, tea and coffee, a helpful owner and great views over the river. Walk 1km from the station along Jl Paledang or catch #2 and jump out by the *McDonald's* at the junction of Jl Juanda and Jl Paledang. **Rp90,000**

EATING

Night stalls along Jl Pengadillan set up after 6pm. There are also busy daytime stalls along Jl Kaptan Muslihat.

Kembang Desa Jl Pangrango 30 ⓦkembangdesaresto.com. Set in an old colonial residence, this stylish restaurant specializes in Sundanese fare, but serves dishes from throughout the archipelago. Try the *tahu gapit* (tofu stuffed with chicken and shrimp chops; Rp25,000). Daily 10am–10pm.

Salak Sunset Café Jl Paledang 38. 50m down to the left from *Pensione Firman* on Jl Paledang, with wonderful views and cheap beer. A great evening hangout and there's a good selection of pizzas (try the veg pizza; Rp45,000), as well as expensive Indonesian food. Daily from 4pm.

BANDUNG AND AROUND

Set 750m above sea level, and protected by a fortress of watchful volcanoes 190km southeast of Jakarta, **BANDUNG** is a centre of industry and traditional Sundanese arts. Sundanese culture has remained intact here since the fifth century when the first Hindu Sundanese settled in this part of West Java. Modern Bandung, although teeming with noise and traffic and certainly far removed from its quaint colonial days, remains one of the nation's cultural and intellectual hubs, bubbling with life in its myriad cafés, restaurants, bars, open markets and flashy new malls. Still, the top attraction for most visitors to the area is the nearby **Tangkuban Prahu volcano**, from where there's a pleasant two-hour forest walk that winds down to the city.

WHAT TO SEE AND DO

On Jalan Asia-Afrika, northeast of the *alun-alun* (town square), is the **Gedung Merdeka** building, host of the first Asia-Afrika Conference in 1955 and known as the Asia-Afrika or Liberty Building. Inside, a small museum (daily 8am–3pm; free) commemorates the conference. Running north from here is **Jalan Braga**, the chic shopping boulevard of 1920s Bandung. The side streets that run off Jalan Braga were notorious for their raucous bars and brothels. The seediness remains today, as this historic district comes alive each night with its slew of lively bars and pubs.

A twenty-minute walk to the northeast takes you to the impressive 1920s **Gedung Sate Building** at Jalan Diponegoro 22, which gets its name from the regular globules on its gold-leaf spire, resembling meat on a skewer. The excellent **Geographical Museum** (Mon–Thurs 9am–2pm, Fri 9–11am, Sat 9am–1pm; donation) is nearby at Jalan Diponegoro 57, and displays mountains of fossils, as well as the skeletons of dinosaurs and a 4m mammoth.

ARRIVAL AND DEPARTURE

By plane The airport is 5km northwest of the city centre (taxi Rp50,000).

Destinations Balikpapan (daily; 2hr 5min); Denpasar (10 daily; 1hr 40min); Kuala Lumpur (5 daily; 2hr 5min); Singapore (4 daily; 2hr); Solo (2 daily; 1hr 10min); Surabaya (4 daily; 1hr 25min).

By bus The main terminal is Leuwi Panjang, 5km south of the city centre, with buses heading west to Bogor and Jakarta; Cicaheum terminal on the eastern edge of town is for those heading to central and east Java. Both terminals are connected to one another and to the city centre by local DAMRI buses (Rp3000).

Destinations Frequent departures unless otherwise stated: Banyuwangi (2 daily; 24hr); Bogor (4hr); Jakarta (5hr); Pangandaran (2 daily; 5hr); Yogyakarta (9hr 30min).

By train The train station is located near the city centre, within walking distance of most budget accommodation. The *Argo Willis* (daily 8am) is recommended for the scenic ride eastward to Yogyakarta and Surabaya.

Destinations Jakarta (6 daily; 3hr); Surabaya (3 daily; 12–13hr); Yogyakarta (6 daily; 7–8hr).

INFORMATION

Tourist office The main tourist information office (daily 8am–7pm; ☎ 022 421 6648) is by the south exit of the train station. Staff are helpful, speak English and have up-to-date information on Bandung and the surrounding area.

GETTING AROUND

Buses and minibuses Bandung's white-and-blue DAMRI buses cost Rp3000 for non-a/c and Rp4500 for a/c. The buses ply routes between the bus terminals through the centre of town. Red *angkots* (minibuses) also run a useful circular route, via the train station and the *alun-alun* (town square), to the Kebun Kelapa bus terminal, which serves Cicaheum bus terminal, Dago, Ledeng and Lembang.

Becaks and taxis Becaks line the major streets and are useful for short journeys where the numerous one-way streets can make an otherwise simple taxi journey expensive. Bandung train station to Jl Braga costs around Rp20,000. Regardless of meters, the minimum taxi charge is usually Rp15,000. A recommended firm is Blue Bird (☎ 022 756 1234).

4

ACCOMMODATION

In recent years, some good backpacker accommodation has sprung up in Bandung, most of it a 10- to 15min walk from the train station.

By Moritz Jl Belakang Pasar/Luxor Permai 35 ☎ 022 420 5788. One of the longest-standing backpacker-oriented places in Bandung, this remains a great place to meet other travellers. The friendly staff can arrange tours and onward travel, and the bright rooms, combined with free breakfast and wi-fi in the lobby, are a bargain. **Rp130,000**

Chez Bon Jl Braga 45 ☎ 022 426 0600, Ⓦ chez-bon.com. Opened by culinary celebrity Bondan Winarno in 2013, this shiny but sterile hostel is set right in the heart of Braga. Along with clean beds in three a/c dorm rooms, guests enjoy free wi-fi, hot water showers, private lockers and complimentary breakfasts on the rooftop. **Rp120,000**

★ **Hunny Hostel** Kompleks Paskal Hyper Square Blok C 28 ☎ 022 860 60701 or ☎ 022 7608 0006, Ⓦ hunnyhostel.com. This super-clean, modern hostel is a 5min walk from the train station by the Pascal Food Market. Friendly owner Michael is a good source of local information. There's also free wi-fi, breakfast, coffee and tea on tap, hot showers, big lockers and a/c all around. Book ahead. Dorm **Rp100,000**, double **Rp240,000**

4

EATING

Bandung Suki Jl Braga 70. Serves an affordable selection of Chinese, Thai, Korean and seafood dishes in a welcoming setting with minimalist decor. Specializes in *dim sum* and spring rolls (Rp17,000 for three), and offers regular discounts and promotions. Daily 10am–10pm.

Braga Permai Jl Braga 58 Ⓦ bragapermai.com. Local and expat favourite, with plenty of outdoor seating right in the thick of Braga's action. Despite its popularity it remains one of the street's cheapest options, with a large Sundanese and Italian menu (margharita pizza Rp25,300). Daily 9am–midnight.

★ **Paskal Food Market** Paskal Hyper Square, Jl Pasirkaliki 25–27. Huge and pleasant open-air food court offering over a thousand dishes from Southeast Asia (meals from Rp8000). It's one of the most popular evening hangout spots in Bandung, with live music at weekends. Order from as many stalls as you like, then take a receipt from the main cashier and wait for each dish to arrive at your table. Mon–Fri 11am–11.30pm, Sat & Sun 10am–midnight.

NIGHTLIFE

Bandung's liveliest (and seediest) nightlife centres around the Jl Braga area, although dozens of other bars, pubs and entertainment venues are scattered across town.

Amnesia Pascal Hyper Square, Jl Pasirkaliki. One of Bandung's most popular venues, this flashy, spacious nightclub is often packed on weekends, with hundreds of patrons – students, businessmen, expats, and plenty of *ayam* (local parlance for working women) – sharing the dancefloor. Music ranges from house to remixed Top 40 tunes and there's karaoke upstairs. Tues–Sun 10pm–4am.

Esco Bar Jl Braga 71. A laidback islander-themed bar with a good cocktail list, a hip, younger crowd and live music from 10pm at weekends. Happy hour 6–9pm. Mon–Thurs 7pm–2am, Fri–Sun 7pm–2.30am.

King Garden Billiard Hall *King Garden Hotel*, Jl Gardujati 81–83. One of many pool halls around the city, though more welcoming than most. Beer isn't cheap (Rp50,000 for a large Bintang), but the tables are the best deal in town (Rp24,000/hr). Daily 11am–2am.

ENTERTAINMENT

Pick up the *Jakarta and Java Kini* magazine from the tourist information office to find out about special performances.

Ram fighting The most spectacular local event is the ram fighting (*adu domba*), held every other Sunday at 10am near the Sari Ater hot spring, 30km from the city. Check ahead at the tourist office, and take a Subang minibus from the train station to Ciater (Rp15,000). To the sound of Sundanese flutes and drums, the magnificently presented rams lunge at each other until one of them fades; there's no blood, just flying wool and clouds of dust.

Saung Angklung Jl Padasuka 118 ☎ 022 727 1714, Ⓦ angklung-udjo.co.id. *Angklung* (bamboo instrument) musical performances are held at this venue east of town on the way to Cicaheum bus terminal (daily 3.30–5pm; Rp80,000).

SHOPPING

Shoppers flock to Bandung from all across the region for its clothing markets and flashy malls.

Jeans Street Cihampelas, to the north of the city centre, is known to Westerners as Jeans Street. It is lined with shops and factory outlets selling cheap T-shirts, bags, shoes and jeans.

Megamalls Of Bandung's many malls, the largest is the Trans Studio Mall on Jl Gatot Subroto, complete with an indoor theme park, while a close second is the lavish Paris Van Java, named for the city's colonial-era title and set a few kilometres north of the train station on Jl Sukajadi.

DIRECTORY

Banks and exchange The two Golden Megacorp moneychangers, at Jl Juanda 89 opposite the Telkom building and at Jl Otista 180, have excellent rates.

Internet Rakha Net (Rp3000/hr), across the road from the *King Garden*, and Cyber Zone on Jl Braga (Rp5000/hr).

Police station Central Bandung Station (Polresta Bandung Tengah), Jl Jend Ahmad Yani 282 ☎ 022 720 0058. Dial ☎ 110 for emergencies.

Post office Jl Asia-Afrika 49 at Jl Banceuy (Mon–Sat 8am–9pm).

TANGKUBAN PRAHU VOLCANO AND THE DAGO TEAHOUSE WALK

The mountainous region to the north of Bandung is the heart of the Parahyangan Highlands – the "Home of the Gods" – a highly volcanic area considered by the Sundanese to be the nucleus of their spiritual world. A pleasant day out from Bandung on public transport takes you first to the 2084m-high **Tangkuban Prahu**, the most visited volcano in West Java, 29km north of Bandung. After decades of dormancy, the volcano erupted several times in October 2013, and continues to spew out vast quantities of sulphurous gases. To get there from Bandung, take a Subang **minibus** from the train station (30min; Rp15,000) and ask to be put down at the turn-off for the volcano, where there's a Rp55,000 entrance fee. From here you can either charter an ojek or minibus up the asphalt road to the summit (10min; Rp10,000) or walk up – it's about 5km up the road, or take the good footpath via the Domas Crater, which starts just over 1km up the road from the guard post, to the right by the first car park. The **information booth** at the summit car park has details about crater walks; guides will offer their services, but it's pretty obvious where you should and shouldn't go – just be sure to wear strong hiking boots. The main crater, **Kawah Ratu**, is the one you can see down into from the end of the summit road, a huge, dull, grey cauldron with a few coloured lakes. From the summit you can trek down to **Domas Crater**, site of a small working sulphur mine.

The Dago Teahouse walk

On the return journey from Tangkuban Prahu to Bandung you'll pass through Lembang (Rp6000), where you can change on to a minibus for the resort of **Maribaya** (4km; Rp4000). There are waterfalls near the entrance gate and hot springs which have been tapped into a public pool. Further down is a larger **waterfall**, which costs extra to see (Rp8000). An ugly iron bridge has been built right across the lip of the falls, and this is the starting point for an easy **walk down to the Dago Teahouse** on the edge of Bandung (6km; 2hr). The path winds downhill through a gorge and forests – just before the teahouse are World War II-era Japanese tunnels and the Dago waterfall, set amid bamboo thickets. The teahouse itself has superb views over Bandung city. From here, minibuses connect to the city centre (15min; Rp4000).

THE DIENG PLATEAU

The moody expanse of the **Dieng Plateau** northwest of Yogya lies in a volcanic caldera 2093m above sea level and holds a rewarding mix of multicoloured sulphurous **lakes**, craters that spew pungent sulphuric gases, and some of the oldest **Hindu temples** in Java. The volcano is still active – clouds of poisonous gases killed 149 people in 1979 and forced the evacuation of 1200 people in 2011 – and the landscape up on this misty, temperate plain is terraced on nearly every surface with cabbage and potato plantations clinging to the edges of impossible slopes. Dozens of homestays have sprung up in Dieng village and there is an increasing number of multilingual guides in both Dieng and nearby Wonosobo. Though many travellers arrive on day-trips from Yogya, it is worthy of an overnight visit (not least because of the four-hour journey from Yogya). The temples here are interesting and the plateau offers a different, more temperate side to Java.

WHAT TO SEE AND DO

There are numerous trekking options available on the plateau and further afield, as well as sunrise trips to **Sikunir Hill** and **Cebong Lake**. All the main attractions can be reached from the village of **Dieng**, just across the fields from the plateau's main temple complex.

The temples

It is believed that the Dieng Plateau was once a fully self-contained **retreat** for priests and pilgrims. Unfortunately, it soon became completely waterlogged, and the entire plateau was finally abandoned in the thirteenth century, only to be rediscovered, drained and restored some six hundred years later by

the Dutch. The eight temples left on Dieng today are a tiny fraction of what was once a huge complex built by the Sanjayas in the seventh and eighth centuries.

Of these temples, the five that make up the **Arjuna complex** (daily 6.15am–5.15pm; Rp20,000) standing in fields opposite Dieng village, are believed to be the oldest. The northernmost of these two-storey temples, the **Arjuna Temple**, is the oldest on Java (c.680 AD), and was dedicated to Shiva. Next to Arjuna stands **Candi Srikandi**, the exterior of which is adorned with reliefs of Vishnu (on the north wall), Shiva (east) and Brahma (south). **Candi Gatutkaca** overlooks the Arjuna complex 300m to the southwest, and twenty minutes' walk (1km) south of here stands the peculiar-looking **Candi Bima**, currently under renovation.

4

The lakes

From Candi Bima, you can continue down the road on foot for 1km or so to **Telaga Warna** (Coloured Lake; daily 8am–5pm; Rp15,000), the best example of Dieng's coloured lakes, where sulphurous deposits shade the water blue, from turquoise to azure. Adjacent to the lake is crystal-clear **Telaga Pengilon**, which makes for beautiful photos in nice weather.

The craters

Around 2km from Candi Gatutkaca is **Sikidang Crater**. This volcanic bowl has numerous hot springs that have appeared through the bubbling mud. Behind the black spring is a walking path that has a great vantage point of the area. There are no safety rails and the path can get slippery when it rains, so take care not to fall into the scalding mud ponds.

ARRIVAL AND DEPARTURE

By bus Buses connect the Dieng Plateau with Yogya, for which you'll need to change buses several times. From Yogya's Jombor terminal, first head to Magelang (Rp10,000), then to Wonosobo (Rp15,000), and finally to Dieng itself (Rp10,000). The complete journey takes roughly four to five hours. From Jakarta, head west to Purwokerto (5–6hr by train; 9hr by bus), from where frequent buses connect to Wonosobo (Rp20,000).

ACCOMMODATION AND EATING

The tiny village of Dieng skirts Jl Raya Dieng, which runs along the plateau's eastern edge.

Gunung Mas Jl Raya Dieng 42 ⓣ0813 2702 7929. Spotless, if spartan, rooms with hot water and breakfast. The shared, second-storey balcony overlooks a small courtyard removed from the noise from the main road (but not the call to prayer from the adjacent mosque). **Rp200,000**

Homestay Bougenville Jl Raya Dieng ⓣ0813 2707 2112. Friendly little place in the centre of town, near the entrance to the Arjuna temple complex. There are five well-kept rooms with comfy beds and decent hot showers on the second floor of the owner's home, tea and coffee on tap and a cosy shared sitting room and balcony. **Rp150,000**

Mbak Mien In the square behind *Hotel Bu Djono*. The best of the warung here, offering cheap Indonesian fare (*nasi goreng* Rp8000) and the hot herbal drink *purwaceng* (Rp10,000), which locals call the "Javanese Viagra". Daily 7am–9pm.

DIRECTORY

Banks There's a BNI with an ATM just north of Gunung Mas.

Internet Clinic Computer, just north of Bougenville, has an internet connection (Rp3000/hr).

YOGYAKARTA

YOGYAKARTA (pronounced "Jogjakarta" and often just shortened to Yogya, or "Jogja") ranks as one of the best-preserved and most attractive cities in Java, and is a major centre for the classical **Javanese arts** of batik, ballet, drama, music, poetry and puppet shows. It is also the perfect base from which to explore the temples of Borobudur and Prambanan, or take an early morning hike up **Gunung Merapi**. Tourists flock here, attracted not only by the city's courtly splendour, but also by the cuisine and shopping, and the various language and cultural courses on offer. As a result there are more tourist-oriented hotels in Yogya than anywhere else in Java and, unfortunately, a correspondingly high number of touts, pickpockets and con artists.

Sultan Hamengkubuwono I (also known as **Mangkubumi**) established his court here in 1755, spending the next 37 years building the new capital, with the Kraton as the centrepiece and the court at Solo as the blueprint. In 1946, the capital of the newly declared Republic of Indonesia

was moved to Yogya from Jakarta, and the **Kraton** became the unofficial headquarters for the republican movement. The royal household of Yogya continues to enjoy almost slavish devotion from its subjects, and the current sultan, Hamengkubuwono X, remains an influential politician.

WHAT TO SEE AND DO

The layout of Yogya reflects its character: frenetic, modern and brash on the outside, but with a tranquil, ancient and traditional heart in the **Kraton**, the walled city. Set in a 2km-wide strip of land between the rivers Kali Winongo and Kali Code, this is the focus of interest for

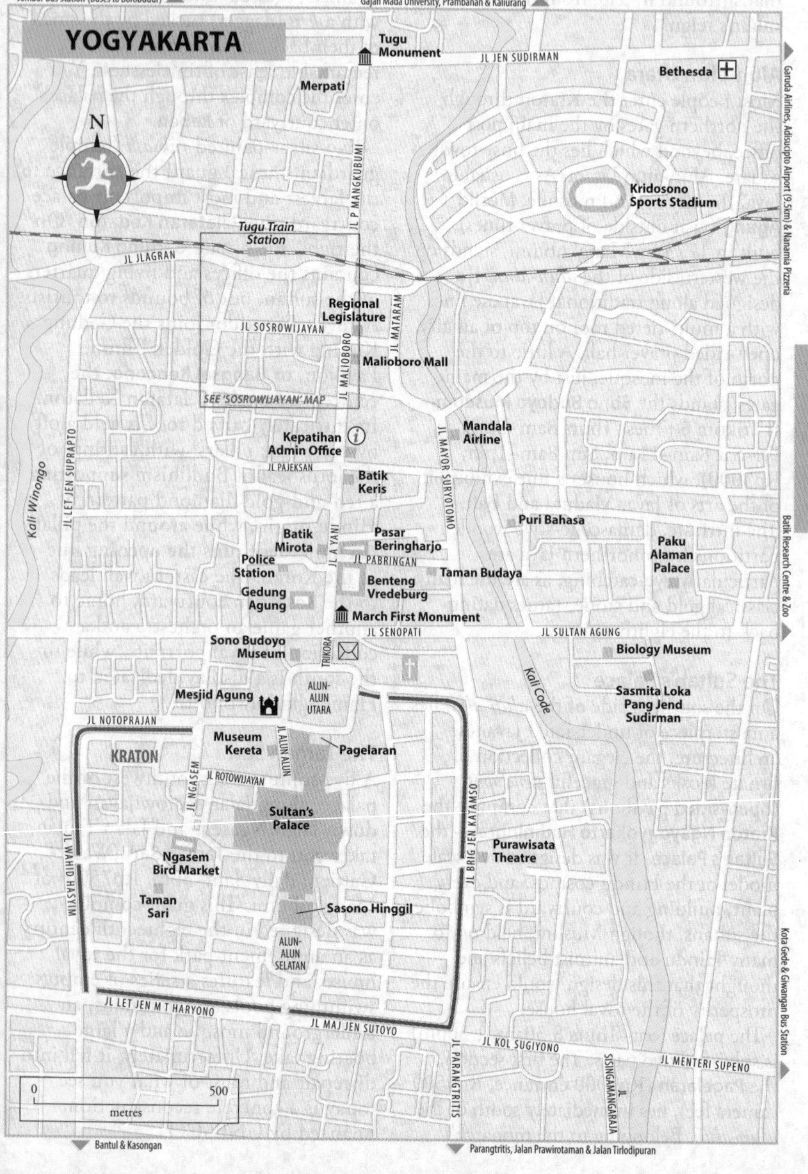

most visitors. Kraton means "royal residence" and originally referred just to the **Sultan's Palace**, but today it denotes the whole of the walled city (plus Jalan Malioboro), a town of some ten thousand people. The Kraton has changed little in two hundred years; both the palace, and the 5km of crenellated icing-sugar walls that surround it, date from the first sultan's reign.

Alun-alun Utara

Most people enter the Kraton through the northern gates by the main post office, beyond which lies the busy town square, Alun-alun Utara. As is usual in Java, the city's grand mosque, **Mesjid Agung** (visit outside of prayer times), built in 1773 by Mangkubumi, stands on the western side of the *alun-alun*. It's designed along traditional Javanese lines, with a multi-tiered roof on top of an airy, open-sided prayer hall. A little to the north of the mosque, just by the main gates, stands the **Sono Budoyo Museum**, Jl Trikora 6 (Tues–Thurs 8am–2pm, Fri–Sat 8am–11am, Sun 8am–1pm; Rp3000), which houses a fine exhibition of the arts of Java, Madura and Bali. The intricate, damascene-style wooden partitions from northern Java are particularly eye-catching, as are the many classical gold and stone statues dating back to the eighth century.

The Sultan's Palace

On the southern side of the *alun-alun* lies a masterpiece of understated Javanese architecture, the elegant collection of ornate kiosks and graceful *pendopos* (open-sided pavilions) that comprise the **Kraton Ngayogyokarto Hadiningrat** – the **Sultan's Palace**. It was designed as a scale model of the Hindu cosmos, and every plant, building and courtyard is symbolic; the sultans, though Muslim, held on to many Hindu and animist beliefs and thought that this design would ensure the prosperity of the royal house.

The palace (Sat–Thurs 8.30am–1.30pm) is split into two parts. The first section, the **Pagelaran** (Rp7000 entrance, Rp1500 camera fee), lies immediately south of the *alun-alun*. Belonging to the monarch's brother, this section is often bypassed by tourists as there is little to see.

Further south stands the entrance to the sultan's **main palace** (Rp12,500 including optional guided tour, Rp3000 camera fee). Little has changed here in 250 years: the hushed courtyards, the faint stirrings of the gamelan and the elderly palace retainers, dressed in the traditional style with a *kris* (dagger) tucked by the small of their back, all contribute to a remarkable sense of timelessness. You enter the complex through the palace's outer courtyard or **keben**.

Two silver-painted *raksasa* (temple guardian statues) guard the entrance to the largest and most important palace courtyard, the **Pelataran Kedaton**. On the right, the ornate **Gedung Kuning** contains the offices and living quarters of the sultan, out of bounds to tourists. A covered corridor joins the Gedung Kuning with the Golden Throne Pavilion, or **Bangsal Kencono**, the centrepiece of the Pelataran Kedaton. Its intricately carved roof is held aloft by hefty teak pillars, with carvings of the lotus leaf of Buddhism supporting a red-and-gold diamond pattern of Hindu origin, while around the pillar's circumference runs the opening line of the Koran. The eastern wall leads to the **Kesatrian** courtyard, home to another gamelan orchestra and a collection of royal portraits, while to the south is a display dedicated to Hamengkubuwono IX.

The Taman Sari

A five-minute walk southwest of the palace, along Jalan Rotowijayan and down Jalan Ngasem and Jalan Taman, takes you to the **Taman Sari** (Water Garden; daily 8am–3pm; Rp7500) of Mangkubumi. This giant complex was designed in the eighteenth century as an amusement park for the royal house, and features a series of empty swimming pools and fountains, an underground mosque and a large boating lake. Unfortunately, it fell into disrepair and most of what you see today is a concrete reconstruction, financed by UNESCO.

Jalan Malioboro

The 2km stretch of road heading north from the alun-alun is as replete with history as it is with batik shops and becak. It was designed as a **ceremonial boulevard** by Mangkubumi, along which the royal cavalcade would proceed on its way to Mount Merapi. Today it is a bustling stretch of old and new, with touts and jewellery sellers sitting shoulder to shoulder along the pavement that leads towards the spectacular palace. The road changes name three times along its length, beginning as Jalan A Yani in the south, continuing as Jalan Malioboro, and then finally ending as Jalan Mangkubumi. At the southern end of the street stands the **Benteng Vredeburg**, Jalan A Yani 6 (Tues–Thurs 8.30am–1pm, Fri 8.30–11am, Sat & Sun 8.30am–noon; Rp10,000), a fort ordered by the Dutch, and built by Mangkubumi in the late eighteenth century. This relic of Dutch imperialism has been restored to its former glory, and now houses a series of informative dioramas recounting the end of colonialism in Indonesia.

Pakualaman Palace

Yogyakarta's second court, **Paku Alaman Palace** (Tues, Thurs & Sat 9.30am–1.30pm; Rp7500), was built in 1813 to the northeast of the Biology Museum on the north side of Jalan Sultan Agung. As is traditional, the minor court of the city faces south as a mark of subservience to the main palace.

ARRIVAL AND DEPARTURE

By plane Adisucipto Airport (T 0274 498261) lies 10km east of the city centre, connected with Jl Malioboro in Yogya by Trans Jogja #1A and #3A (daily 6am–7.30pm; 30–45min; Rp3000); for Prawirotaman, transfer to #2A. There's also a train station near the airport, connected by underpass and linking Yogya's Tugu Station as well as Solo's Solobalapan Station.

Destinations Bandung (2 daily; 1hr 10min); Denpasar (7 daily; 1hr 15min); Jakarta (29 daily; 1hr 10min); Surabaya (9 daily; 1hr).

By bus Inter-city buses arrive and depart from Giwangan terminal, about 5km southeast of the city centre. Those arriving from Borobudur or elsewhere in the north or west can alight at Jombor terminal, around 3km north of the city centre, from where Trans Jogja #2A (Rp3000) links to the main post office. Trans Jogja buses #3A and #3B link Giwangan with Jl Malioboro and Jl Sosrowijayan, while city buses #2 and #15 (Rp2500) link Giwangan with Prawirotaman.

Destinations Frequent departures to Bandung (9hr 30min); Bogor (10hr 30min); Borobudur (2hr); Cilacap (5hr); Denpasar (15hr); Jakarta (11hr 30min); Magelang (1hr 30min); Prambanan (45min); Probolinggo (9hr); Solo (2hr); Surabaya (7hr 30min).

By train Tugu Train Station (T 0274 514270) is one block north of Jl Sosrowijayan, on Jl Pasar Kembang. A taxi to Jl Prawirotaman costs Rp25,000; or catch southbound bus #2A along Jl Malioboro from the Trans Jogya station.

Destinations Bandung (6 daily; 6hr 30min); Jakarta (12 daily; 8hr 45min); Malang (daily; 6hr 50min); Solo (12 daily; 1hr 30min); Surabaya (9 daily; 4hr 50min).

INFORMATION

Tourist information Jl Malioboro 16 (Mon–Thurs 8am–8pm, Fri & Sat 8am–7pm; T 0274 566000, E ticmalioboro@yahoo.com, W visitingjogja.com). Plenty of information on local events, language and meditation courses and up-to-date transport information. Also check W jogjatogo.com for information on Jogja events and attractions.

Intras Travel Agents Jl Malioboro 131 T 0274 561972. Probably the most respected and reliable of Yogya's travel agents, set just a few metres south of the eastern end of Jl Sosro.

TOUR OPERATORS

Yogya tour companies number in the hundreds, most offering trips to the nearby temples (from Rp100,000 for a tour of both Prambanan and Borobudur), as well as further afield. Trips to Bali with overnight stops at Bromo and Ijen are most popular (2-day/3-day tours Rp450,000/Rp650,000).

Cecko Trans Jl Sosro Gang II 63 T 0274 560966. Friendly guide offering some of the cheapest deals in the area, including interesting mountain-bike trips to Merapi (Rp175,000; minimum 3 people).

Rumah Guides Kasongan village, 7km south of city centre T 0856 285 9193. A group of young Yogya residents keen to show off their city and surrounding villages. They charge a daily rate of Rp350,000 per group of up to four people (Rp500,000 for five or more), and can arrange overnight stays with local families.

Via Via Café Jl Prawirotaman 30 T 0274 372874, W viaviajogja.com. The most innovative of Yogya's operators. Tours include cycling, motorbiking, hiking and rafting trips, as well as a five-day trip to Bali taking in Mount Bromo, the hill town of Kalibaru and the Meru Betiri National Park (€385; minimum two people).

4

GETTING AROUND

Buses Convenient Trans Jogya buses run eight set routes linking important points in the city (Rp3000). Route maps are displayed at every station or *halte* (stop).

Becak Becak are the most convenient form of transport, and there are plenty of them around. It should cost no more than Rp10,000 from Jl Sosro to the main post office (Rp15,000 from Jl Prawirotaman).

Horse-drawn carriages Known as *andong*, they tend to queue up along Jl Malioboro, and are a little pricier than becak (starting around Rp20,000 for a ride around Malioboro).

Taxis Good value (Rp5500 minimum). You can usually find them hanging around the main post office, or ring Citra/Jas Taksi (T 0274 373737).

Bike rental Try Cecko Trans on Jl Sosro Gang II (Rp15,000/day) or Satu Dunia at Jl Prawirotaman 44 (T 0851 6285 9800); motorbikes start at Rp50,000/day. Orange-suited parking attendants throughout the city will look after your bike for around Rp1000.

ACCOMMODATION

A kilometre north of the Kraton, Jl Sosrowijayan (known as Jl Sosro) is Yogyakarta's answer to the Khao San Road in Bangkok. There's a quieter, more upmarket cluster of tourist hotels and restaurants around Jl Prawirotaman, in the suburbs southeast of the Kraton.

JALAN PRAWIROTAMAN AND AROUND

Agung Guesthouse Jl Prawirotaman II MGIII/609 T 0274 375512; map opposite. Friendly, ageing guesthouse with a swimming pool to complement its decent-value doubles, some with hot water (Rp160,000) and all with breakfast options. **Rp140,000**

Agung Inn Jl Prawirotaman 30 T 0274 383577; map opposite. Bearing no connection to *Agung Guesthouse*, this sleek new spot next to *Via Via* is friendly and efficient but small, offering just three spotless rooms with balconies, wi-fi, hot showers and breakfasts, as well as coffee, tea and mineral water on tap around the clock. **Rp250,000**

Delta Homestay Jl Prawirotaman II MGIII/597A T 0274 372051, W dutagardenhotel.com; map opposite. Run by the same people as the *Duta Guesthouse* and the mid-range *Duta Garden*, this cheap homestay has basic, somewhat worn rooms, the better ones with a/c and private bathrooms (Rp200,000). Amenities include a pool out back, free wi-fi, breakfast and an evening snack with coffee or tea. **Rp125,000**

Duta Guesthouse Jl Prawirotaman 26 T 0274 372064, W dutagardenhotel.com; map opposite. Popular with groups, this big hotel has fan and a/c rooms (Rp250,000); it has a pleasant pool, breakfast buffet and workout facilities next door to the reception. Wi-fi in the lobby. **Rp200,000**

Kampoeng Djawa Guesthouse Jl Prawirotaman 40 T 0274 378318, W kampoengdjawahotel.com; map opposite.

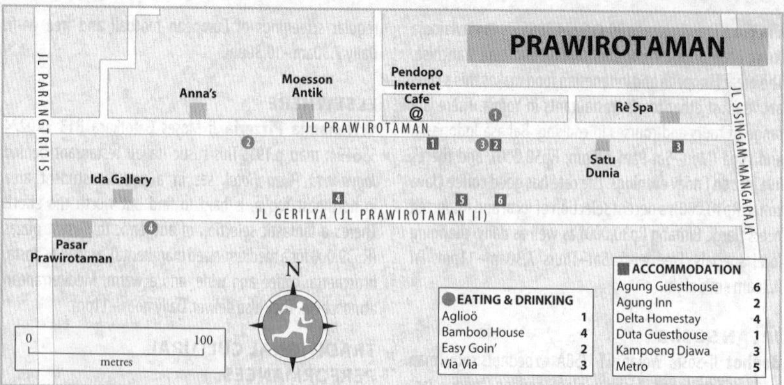

Popular among backpackers, *Kampoeng Djawa* boasts clean rooms with hot and cold water, with the option of fan or a/c (Rp200,000). Self-service tea and coffee, afternoon snacks, breakfast and wi-fi in a lush sitting area. Book ahead. **Rp100,000**

Metro Jl Prawirotaman II 71 ☎ 0274 372364, ⓦ metro-gh.com; map above. A big hotel with a pool, restaurant, pleasant sitting area and clean sheets in both the a/c (Rp250,000) rooms and the more dingy economy rooms set across the street. There's also free wi-fi and a basic breakfast. **Rp175,000**

JALAN SOSRO AND AROUND

Anda Jl Sosro Gang II; map opposite. This friendly losmen is one of the cheapest places on Jl Sosro. The simple rooms have attached mandis and a pleasant outdoor sitting area. No reservations: rooms go on a strictly first-come-first-served basis. **Rp80,000**

★ **Bladok** Jl Sosro 76 ☎ 0274 560452; map opposite. Whitewashed hotel with clean, comfortable rooms, all en suite, and a brilliant pool with a waterfall out the back. VIP rooms come with poolside terrace, hot water, a/c, fridge and TV (Rp320,000), and the open-air restaurant and café out front is one of the most popular spots on the street. **Rp100,000**

Merbabu Jl Sosro Gang I32 ☎ 0274 551421, ⓦ merapimerbabuhotel.net; map opposite. The somewhat worn rooms here all come with inside bathrooms, and the wi-fi works in the rooms on the third floor and in the breezy rooftop restaurant with views over Yogya. Deluxe rooms have a/c and TVs (Rp230,000). Simple breakfast included. **Rp130,000**

Setia Kawan Jl Sosro GT1/127 ☎ 0274 512452, ⓦ bedhots.com; map opposite. Run by the owners of the nearby *Bedhot* restaurant, this is a good-value guesthouse with spotless, brightly coloured rooms, some with a/c (Rp200,000). There's wi-fi, friendly staff and a handful of popular day-courses (batik Rp180,000/person). Book ahead. **Rp160,000**

Tiffa Jl Sosro Gang II ☎ 0274 512841, ⓔ tiffaartshop@yahoo.com; map opposite. This hidden little homestay near the mosque has coffee and tea on tap, free wi-fi and good self-service breakfasts. All rooms are bright and decorated with local artwork, and there's a shared balcony overlooking the alley. Discounts of up to 50 percent in low season. **Rp300,000**

EATING AND DRINKING

Yogya's specialities are *ayam goreng* (fried chicken) and *nasi gudeg* (rice and jackfruit), and many food stalls serve nothing else. Every evening a food market sets up on Jl Malioboro and by 8pm the entire street is thronged with diners. Yogya's nightlife is really an early-evening affair; very few places stay open beyond midnight, and most of the action happens between 7 and 11pm, when the city's cultural entertainment is in full swing.

JALAN PRAWIROTAMAN

Aglioö Jl Prawirotaman 29; map above. Cosy Italian restaurant with a warm, candlelit ambience serving delicious pizzas (Rp40,000) cooked in a wood-fired oven, as well as pasta (from Rp25,000) and a good selection of Indonesian food. Alfresco dining, with generous portions, friendly service and free wi-fi. Daily 11am–11pm.

Bamboo House Jl Prawirotaman II MGIII/616 ⓦ bamboohousecafe.com; map above. Small café with a pleasant, relaxed atmosphere, breezy upstairs deck, free wi-fi and a range of local and international food (*gado gado* Rp28,000). Fresh juices start at Rp14,000. Daily 9am–11pm.

Easy Goin' Jl Prawirotaman 12 ☎ 0274 384092, ⓦ easygoingresto.com; map above. A sleek new café, bar and restaurant with a broad menu of tasty Western, Indonesian and Mexican dishes ranging from beef burritos (Rp55,000) to *nasi tumpeng* (Rp50,000). Happy hour lasts from 2–7pm, and it's one of the cleanest and brightest spots along the street, with a pool table and wi-fi. Daily 10.30am–after midnight.

4

Via Via Jl Prawirotaman 30 ⓣ 0274 386557, ⓦ viaviajogja.com; map p.195. A popular, foreign-run café franchise. The great European and Indonesian food makes this a class above most other tourist restaurants in Yogya. There is a range of tours and courses in cooking, Bahasa Indonesia, and yoga (Mon–Sat 9am & 6pm; Rp50,000), and there's live jazz on Friday evenings. The café has good coffee (Java coffee Rp10,000), a decent selection of local and imported beers (large Bintang Rp30,000) as well as daily-changing local specials. Free wi-fi. Sat–Thurs 7.30am–11pm, Fri 7.30am–midnight.

JALAN SOSRO

Bedhot Jl Sosro Wetan GT I/58A ⓦ bedhots.com; map p.194. Central and friendly place serving Indonesian, Chinese and decent interpretations of Western food in a dimly lit, bohemian setting. Try the tasty *tempe* (soya bean) burgers (Rp28,000), arak (rice wine; Rp28,000) or *sayur lodeh* (vegetables in coconut sauce; Rp17,000), a Javan speciality. Wi-fi available. Daily 8am–11pm.

Bintang Cafe Jl Sosro 54; map p.194. Fun bar and restaurant that is the most popular venue on the street, with live music from Wednesday to Saturday nights, ranging from rock to reggae. The food is a standard mix of Indonesian and Western, and the cafe's namesake beer costs Rp33,000. Happy hour 2–7pm. Daily 8am–1am.

4

Batik Resto Jl Sosro 10; map p.194. Formerly known as *FM Resto*, this pleasant bar and restaurant has nice seating areas away from the street, a range of Indonesian and Western dishes (pizza Rp40,000), fresh juices (from Rp12,000) and free wi-fi. There's also an epic happy hour (1–8pm). Daily 6am–1am.

Legian Jl Perwakilan 9 ⓦ legianrestaurant.weebly.com; map p.194. A great location overlooking the buzzing street below. Though a little pricey (chicken *sate* Rp40,000; glass of wine Rp50,000), the selection of fresh lobster, squid and imported New Zealand tenderloin is worth the extra thousands of rupiah. Daily noon–10pm.

Lucifer Jl Suryowijayan 71; map p.194. On the corner of Jl Sosro, this attractive venue has live music every night starting at 9.30pm. It's the perfect place for a cold beer or a "Lucifer Shaker" cocktail after a day exploring the temples. Daily 5pm–1am.

Mi Casa es Tu Casa Jl Sosro Wetan GT I ⓦ micasaestucasa.mye.name; map p.194. A fairly new, laidback spot down Gang I, run by the friendly San Sebastian. On the menu are both European and Indonesian specialities from *sate tahu* (Rp16,000) to paella (from Rp90,000). If you're feeling brave, try the "devil drink" (cobra blood; Rp40,000). Daily 8am–10pm.

Superman Jl Sosro Gang I/71; map p.194. Spacious, thatched-roof restaurant down a pokey side street. It's popular for its relaxed vibe and broad international menu, with delicious pancakes (from Rp10,000), ice-cold beer, regular screenings of European football and free wi-fi. Daily 7.30am–10.30pm.

ELSEWHERE

★**Nanamia Pizzeria** Jl Moses Gatotkaca B13 ⓣ 0274 556494; map p.191. This rustic Italian restaurant behind *Jogyakarta Plaza Hotel*, set in a popular student area in northeast Yogya, is hard to find but worth the effort. There's a fantastic selection of authentic thin-crust pizzas (Rp39,000 for a medium-sized margharita), as well as pasta, bruschetta, coffee and wine, and a warm, Mediterranean atmosphere. They also deliver. Daily noon–11pm.

TRADITIONAL CULTURAL PERFORMANCES

WAYING KULIT AND WAYANG GOLEK

Wayang kulit (shadow puppetry) is the epitome of Javanese culture, and it's worth catching a show, although wayang golek, where wooden puppets are used, tends to be easier to follow, as the figures are more dynamic and expressive. With one honourable exception, all of the performances listed are aimed at tourists, and only two hours long. For more up-to-date events, check ⓦ jogjapages.com.

Sasono Hinggil Alun-alun Selatan. Yogya's only genuine, full-length wayang kulit performance runs from 9pm to 5.30am on the second Saturday of every month (Rp20,000).

Sono Budoyo Museum Jl Trikora 1. The most professional and popular abridged wayang kulit show (Mon–Sat 8–10pm; Rp20,000).

Sultan's Palace On Saturday mornings (10am–noon), there's a practice-cum-performance of wayang kulit in the Sri Minganti courtyard, and every Wednesday (10am–noon) a free wayang golek show. On Monday, Tuesday and Thursday mornings between 10am and noon there are free gamelan performances.

JAVANESE DANCING

The Ramayana dance drama is a modern extension of the court dances of the nineteenth century, which tended to use that other Indian epic, the *Mahabharata*, as the source of their story lines.

Prambanan Jl Raya Yogya-Solo km16 ⓣ 0274 497771. The indoor Trimurti Theatre at Prambanan holds seasonal Ramayana ballet performances (Nov–April; Tues, Thurs & Sat 7.30–9.30pm; ⓣ 0274 496408), while the Open Air Theatre puts on the full story during summer months (May–Oct 3–4 times weekly; 7.30–9.30pm) and individual episodes at sporadic intervals the rest of the year. Tickets for both performances (Rp75,000–250,000 depending on where you sit) are available at the door or from the tourist office in Yogya, where you can check the complete schedule.

Purawisata Theatre Jl Brig Jen Katamso ⓣ 0274 374089, ⓦ purawisatajogjakarta.com. Every night the

Purawisata Theatre puts on a 1hr 30min performance of the Ramayana (8–9.30pm; Rp250,000); the story is split into two episodes, each performed on alternate nights.

Sultan's Palace The Kraton Classical Dance School holds weekly public rehearsals (Sun 9.30am–noon). No additional fee once you've paid to get into the palace. Very worthwhile.

SHOPPING

Yogya is Java's souvenir centre, with keepsakes and mementoes from all over the archipelago finding their way into the city's shops and street stalls.

ANTIQUES, PUPPETS AND CURIOS

There are a number of cavernous antique shops near Jl Prawirotaman dealing mainly in teak furniture from Jepara and the north, but they also sell woodcarvings, wayang kulit puppets and *keris* daggers.

Ida Gallery Jl Prawirotaman III. Set in a courtyard, this shop sells puppets and *keris* daggers, among other curios. You can also walk around the furniture restoration workshop at the back.

Marco Polo Antique Jl Sosrowijayan 11. Strange little shop selling antique bicycles and vintage parts in the heart of the backpacker district.

Moesson Antik Jl Prawirotaman 27 Ⓦmoessongallery.com. This shop's collection ranges from simple tat to genuine antiques – great for a rummage even if you have no intention of buying.

BATIK

With the huge influx of tourists over recent decades, Yogya has evolved a batik style that increasingly panders to Western tastes. However, there is still plenty of the traditional indigo-and-brown batik clothing for sale, especially on Jl Malioboro and in Pasar Beringharjo. For the best-quality – and most expensive – batiks in town, head to Jl Tirtodipuran, west of Jl Prawirotaman.

Batik Plentong Jl Tirtodipuran 48. Large shop with friendly staff that stocks a wide selection of good-quality batik fabrics.

Batik Research Centre Jl Dr Sutomo 13. Puts the craft in a historical context and provides examples of the several techniques and styles.

COURSES

Batik courses Right by the entrance to the Taman Sari is the workshop of Dr Hadjir (Ⓣ0274 377835, Ⓔherry_krishnamurti@yahoo.com), who runs a three- to five-day course (US$35 including materials). The Batik Research Centre (Jl Kusumanegara 2) also has intensive three-day courses for US$55. Basic courses are also offered at many hotels, including *Via Via* (daily 9am–1pm; Rp130,000) and Setia Kawan (Rp180,000).

Cookery courses *Via Via* (see p.195) runs morning and afternoon courses (from Rp140,000).

Language courses Yogya is the place to learn Bahasa Indonesia. The two most established schools are Alam Bahasa Indonesia, Kompleks Kolombo 3, Jl Cendrawasih (Ⓣ0274 589631, Ⓦalambahasa.com); and Puri Bahasa Indonesia, Jl Purwanggan 15 (Ⓣ0274 588192, Ⓦpuribahasa.net). One-to-one tuition typically costs US$10/hr. Meanwhile, *Via Via* (see p.195) offers a daily three-hour course starting at 9am (Rp80,000).

BOOKS

The Lucky Boomerang Jl Sosro Gang I. The Lucky Boomerang stocks new and secondhand English-language novels and a good selection of multilingual books.

Periplus Lower ground floor of Malioboro Mall. Has a wide selection of English-language novels and histories of Indonesia, as well as guidebooks and maps.

LEATHER AND POTTERY

All around Yogya, and particularly in the markets, and some of the shops along Jl Malioboro, hand-stitched, good-quality leather bags, suitcases, belts and shoes are for sale extremely cheaply.

Javanese pottery is widely available throughout Yogya. The markets along Jl Malioboro sell ochre pottery, including decorative bowls, erotic statues, whistles, flutes and other pottery instruments.

SILVER

The Kota Gede suburb is the home of the silver industry in Central Java, famous for its fine filigree work. Jl Kemasan is the "silver street" of Yogya and there is a huge selection of jewellery and trinkets. If your budget is limited, note that the stallholders along Jl Malioboro sell perfectly reasonable silver jewellery, much of it from East Java or Bali. To reach Kota Gede, take the Trans Jogja 3A from Malioboro or the 2A from Prawirotaman.

MD Silver Keboan Kotagede. This workshop situated down an alley off Jl Pesegah KG has top-quality jewellery and is one of the cheaper options.

Tom's Silver Jl Ngeksi Gondo 60. This huge workshop produces great work and you can wander around and watch the smiths at work.

SOUVENIRS

The main shopping area for inexpensive souvenirs is Jl Malioboro, where you'll find batik pictures, leather bags, woodcarvings, silver rings and the traditional Yogyan batik headdresses (*blangkon*).

Batik Keris Jl A Yani 104. Reputable shop offering a huge array of souvenirs from Yogya and elsewhere in Indonesia.

Batik Mirota Jl A Yani 9. A batik specialist who will tailor clothes and also offer other souvenirs.

DIRECTORY

Banks and exchange There are many banks with ATMS in the city centre, including BNI (Jl Trikora 1, just in front of the post office). To exchange money, head to PT Gajahmas Mulyosakti, Jl A Yani 86A, or PT Dua Sisi Jogya Indah, at the southern corner of the Malioboro Mall, each offering competitive rates.

Hospitals and clinics The Gading Clinic, south of the Alun-alun Selatan at Jl Maj Jen Panjaitan 25, has English-speaking doctors (T 0274 375396).

Internet Wi-fi is available in numerous cafés across town. There are also several internet cafés in each area (Rp7000/hr), including Chaterina (daily 9am–11pm), across from *Bladok* in Sosro, and Pendopo Cafe Net (daily 8am–11pm; W pendopocafenet.com), opposite *Duta Guesthouse* in Prawirotaman.

Police station Jl Reksobayan 1, near the Benteng Vredeburg Museum T 274 512511 or T 274512940. Dial T 110 for emergencies.

Post office Jl Senopati 2, at the southern end of Jl Malioboro (Mon–Sat 6am–10pm, Sun 6am–8pm). There's a smaller branch near Bladok on Jl Sosro 55 (Mon–Fri 8am–2pm, Sat 8am–noon). The parcel office is on Jl Mayor Suryotomo (Mon–Sat 8am–3pm, Sun 9am–2pm).

4

GUNUNG MERAPI AND KALIURANG

Marking the northern limit of the Daerah Istimewa Yogyakarta, symmetrical, smoke-plumed **Gunung Merapi** (Giving Fire) is an awesome 2914m presence in the centre of Java, visible from Yogyakarta, 25km away. This is one of Indonesia's most volatile volcanoes, and some volcanologists consider it the most consistently active volcano on earth. Through the centuries its ability to annihilate has frequently been demonstrated – as recently as 2010 an entire mountain village was destroyed, killing more than 350 people.

Nearly 1km up on Merapi's southern slopes is the misty and ramshackle hill village of **KALIURANG**. Bemos here cost Rp12,000 from Jalan Simanjutak in Yogya. In Kaliurang, you can join a trekking group to reach high on the barren flanks of Merapi (organized by *Vogel's Hostel*; US$15; see below), a fairly arduous five-hour scramble, much of it through the humid jungle that beards Merapi's lower slopes. During Merapi's dormant months (usually March to Oct) it's possible to climb all the way to the top, but at other times, or when the volcano is active, you may have to settle for a distant view from the observation platform. All treks begin in the dark between 3–5am. Bring warm clothes, a torch or headlamp and a sturdy pair of shoes.

ACCOMMODATION

Hotel Muriah Jl Astya Mulya T 0274 446 4257. This clean and central hotel offers good-value rooms with TVs and hot water. Friendly staff don't speak much English, and treat guests to snacks of *roti bakar* on arrival. **Rp100,000**

★**Vogel's Hostel** Jl Astya Mulya 76, Kaliurang T 0274 895208, W vogelshostel.blogspot.com. This is a great budget hostel, split into several parts: the rooms in the newer green and white bungalows are beautiful (from Rp100,000), while those in the old building are more spartan but good value. The food is delicious (try the *paniki* Rp30,000), and there's a good travellers' library. The staff can organize various treks and the owner, Christian Awuy, a Manado-native, is a bona fide expert on Merapi. Dorm **Rp25,000**, double **Rp50,000**

BOROBUDUR

Forty kilometres west of Yogya, surrounded on three sides by volcanoes and on the fourth by jagged limestone cliffs, is the largest Buddhist monument in the southern hemisphere. This is the temple of **Borobudur**, the greatest single piece of classical architecture in the entire archipelago. The temple is actually a colossal multi-tiered Buddhist stupa lying at the western end of a 4km-long chain of temples (one of which, the nearby **Candi Mendut**, is also worth visiting), built in the ninth century by the Saliendra dynasty. At 34.5m tall, however, and covering an area of some 200 square metres, Borobudur is on a different scale altogether, dwarfing all the other *candi* in the chain. Abandoned and neglected for almost a thousand years, Borobudur was "rediscovered" by the English in 1815, though nothing much was done until 1973, when UNESCO began to take the temple apart, block by block, in order to replace the waterlogged hill with a concrete substitute.

WHAT TO SEE AND DO

Borobudur is pregnant with symbolism, and precisely oriented so that its four sides face the four points of the compass; the **ticket office** lies to the southeast (daily 6am–5.30pm; adult US$20/Rp190,000, student or child US$10/Rp95,000;

guided tour Rp75,000). You may also purchase a package ticket for both Borobudur and Prambanan (adult/ student Rp320,000/160,000).

The stupa

Unlike most temples, Borobudur was not built as a dwelling for the gods, but rather as a representation of the Buddhist cosmic mountain, Meru. Accordingly, at the base is the real, earthly world, a world of desires and passions, and at the summit is nirvana. Thus, as you make your way around the temple passages and slowly spiral to the summit, you are symbolically following the path to enlightenment.

The first five levels – the square terraces – are covered with three thousand **reliefs** representing man's earthly existence. As you might expect, the lowest, subterranean level has carvings depicting the basest desires, best seen at the southeast corner. The reliefs on the **first four levels above ground** cover the beginning of man's path to enlightenment. Each of the ten series (one on each level on the outer wall and one on the inner wall) tells a story, beginning by the eastern stairway and continuing clockwise. Follow all the stories, and you will have circled the temple ten times – a distance of almost 5km. Buddha's own path to enlightenment is told in the upper panels on the inner wall of the first gallery. As you enter the **fifth level**, the walls fall away to reveal a breathtaking view of the surrounding fields and volcanoes. You are now in the Sphere of Formlessness, the realm of enlightenment: below is the chaos of the world, above is nirvana, represented by a huge empty stupa almost 10m in diameter. Surrounding this stupa are 72 smaller ones, most of which are occupied by statues of Buddha.

Candi Mendut

Originally Borobudur was part of a chain of four temples joined by a sacred path. Two of the other three temples have been restored, and at least one, **Candi Mendut** (daily 7am–5pm; Rp3300), 3km east of Borobudur, is worth visiting. Buses between Yogya and Borobudur drive right past Mendut (Rp8000 from Yogya, 1hr 20min; Rp3000 from Borobudur, 10min). Built in 800 AD, Mendut was restored at the end of the nineteenth century. The exterior is unremarkable, but the three giant **statues** sitting inside – of Buddha and the Bodhisattvas Avalokitesvara and Vajrapani – are exquisitely carved and startling in their intricacy.

ARRIVAL AND DEPARTURE

Most choose to see the site on a day-trip from Yogya, with plenty of agencies offering all-inclusive tours (from Rp75,000); these are only slightly more expensive than reaching the sites by public transport, which involves multiple changes. Motorbike rental is a cheaper option (Rp50,000), allowing the freedom to explore the scenic countryside around Borobudur.

By bus Numerous buses depart from Yogya's Giwangan Station and call in at Jombor bus station (handy for Jl Sosro, connected by Trans Yogya 2A) before heading off to Borobudur village bus station (1hr–1hr 30min; Rp15,000, although tourists are generally asked for Rp20,000–25,000); your bus may stop briefly in Muntilan. The entrance to the temple lies about 750km southwest of the bus stop, and the last bus back to Yogya leaves Borobudur around 6pm.

ACCOMMODATION AND EATING

Most people who stay in Borobudur overnight choose to eat in their hotel, though there are a couple of inexpensive Padang places and the usual warungs opposite the entrance to the temple grounds.

Lotus II Jl Balaputradewa 54 T 0293 788845, W facebook .com/lotusguesthouse. Owned by the family that runs *Lotus Guesthouse*, the popular sequel is set slightly further from the temple and has larger rooms with hot water, some featuring patios and balconies overlooking the rice fields. Internet is available in the lobby and friendly staff provide excellent local information. Be prepared for an early wake-up call from the mosque next door. **Rp200,000**

Lotus Guesthouse Jl Medang Kamulan 2 T 0293 788281. This old stalwart, set near the temple entrance, is looking a little worse for wear, though rooms are cheap and sufficiently clean. The better ones have hot water (Rp200,000), and there are great views from the rooftop. **Rp100,000**

Rajasa Jl Badrawati 2 T 0293 788276, E ariswara_sutomo @yahoo.com. Just south of the temple, this peaceful hotel has beautiful views over the rice fields and the Menora Hills in the distance, although the beds are a little lumpy. Rooms with hot water and a/c available for Rp400,000. **Rp200,000**

THE PRAMBANAN PLAIN

Nourished by the volcanic detritus of Mount Merapi and washed by innumerable small rivers, the verdant

4

RAMAYANA BALLET PERFORMANCES

The highlights of the dancing year in Central Java are the phenomenal Ramayana ballets held each summer at **Prambanan's Open-Air Theatre**, to the west of the complex (see below). From May to October, the timeless Hindu epic is performed in its entirety with the magnificent Shiva, Vishnu and Brahma temples serving as a backdrop. Individual episodes are performed sporadically outside this time.

Prambanan Plain lies 18km east of Yogya, a patchwork blanket of sun-spangled paddy fields and vast plantations sweeping down from the southern slopes of the volcano. As well as being one of the most fertile regions in Java, the plain is home to the largest concentration of ancient ruins on the island. Over thirty **temples** and **palaces** lie scattered over a thirty-square-kilometre area, most built during the eighth and ninth centuries by two rival kingdoms, the Buddhist Saliendra and the Hindu Sanjaya dynasties.

Prambanan

Heading east from Yogya along Jalan Adisucipto, you'll catch sight of three giant, rocket-shaped temples looming up by the side of the highway, each of them smothered in intricate narrative carvings. This is the **Prambanan Archeological Park** (daily 6am–6pm; Rp125,000; package ticket including Ratu Boko Rp260,000; package ticket including Borobudur Rp320,000; guided tour Rp75,000), the largest Hindu temple compound in all of Indonesia and a worthy rival to Borobudur. The complex consists of six temples in a raised **inner courtyard**, surrounded by **224 minor temples** which now lie in ruins. The three largest temples are dedicated to the Hindu triad: Shiva, whose 47m temple is the tallest of the three, Brahma (to the south of the Shiva temple) and Vishnu (north). Facing these are three smaller temples housing the animal statues – or "chariots" – that would accompany the gods: Hamsa the swan, Nandi the bull and Garuda the sunbird respectively.

The **Shiva Temple** is decorated with exceptional carvings, including a series along the inner wall of the first terrace walkway that recounts the first half of the Ramayana epic. At the top of the steps is the temple's inner sanctuary, whose eastern chamber contains a statue of Shiva, while in the west chamber is Shiva's elephant-headed son, Ganesh. A beautiful sculpture of Nandi the Bull stands inside the temple of Shiva's chariot. Just as painstakingly decorated, the first terrace of the **Brahma Temple** takes up the Ramayana epic where the Shiva Temple left off, while the carvings on the terrace of Vishnu's temple recount stories of **Krishna**, the eighth of Vishnu's nine earthly incarnations.

North of Prambanan

Just north through the trees from the Prambanan Temple are three ancient Buddhist temples (daily 6am–6pm; entrance included in Prambanan ticket), built in the late eighth century and therefore predating Borobudur. Though not as grand as the Shiva Temple, visitors will share these sites with much thinner crowds – sometimes only the sheep that graze in the ruins' shade. After passing the crumbling ruins of **Candi Lumbung** and **Candi Bubrah**, the last temple you'll reach is **Candi Sewu** (1km north of Shiva Temple), the most intact and impressive of Prambanan's Buddhist temples. Laid out in a mandala pattern and guarded at each entrance by a pair of burly dwarapala statues, the complex includes more than 240 structures, many adorned with beautifully carved bodhisattvas.

South of Prambanan

More worthwhile ruins lie to the south of Prambanan. About 2.5km south of Prambanan and perched on a hill rising 200m over the Prambanan Plain is the ninth century **Kraton Ratu Boko** (daily 6am–6pm; entrance Rp125,000). The ruins are in two parts: the ceremonial gate that adorns most advertising posters, and, 400m to the east, a series of bathing pools. The views from the kraton are wonderful, and on a clear day the restaurant has wonderful vistas of Merapi.

To reach the palace from Prambanan, head south about 2km before turning left up the steep, signposted path that leads to the complex (1hr walk). There is also a shuttle bus linking Ratu Boko and Prambanan (15min; Rp45,000). Still less-visited is **Candi Sojiwan**, a plain, square temple, sparingly decorated with scenes from Buddhist folklore and set about 2km southeast of Prambanan village.

West of Prambanan

A short hop to the west of Prambanan are several more worthwhile temples (daily 6am–6pm; entrance Rp2,000 for each) near the village of Kalasan, reached by a short angkot ride or a half-hour walk. The first one you'll reach heading west is the eighth-century **Candi Sari** (3km), just north of the main road. With an unusual, house-like design capped with stupas resembling those of Borobudur, the temple features elaborate carvings of various goddesses and bodhisattvas. About 150m southwest amid rice fields just across the main road is the artfully crumbling spire of **Candi Kalasan**. An inscription here bears the date of 778 CE, and both of these Buddhist temples are believed to be among the very oldest of the entire Prambanan plain. Just over 2km north of the main road is the ninth-century **Candi Sambisari**, a small Shiva temple complex adorned with statues of Hindu gods. Buried in 5m of soil and volcanic ash until its excavation in the 1980s, it has sparked curiosity over how much yet remains undiscovered in the Prambanan plain.

ARRIVAL AND DEPARTURE

The Prambanan temple complex is easily visited on a day-trip from Yogya. Many tour companies offer package trips including transport and guide for around Rp90,000.

By bus Prambanan is linked to Malioboro in Yogya by Trans Yogya bus #1A (Rp3,000; 40min). Buses also link Solo's Tirtonadi terminal (Rp15,000; 1hr 30min).

By bike Some visitors cycle here from Yogya in order to then easily visit more of the plain's far-flung ruins. Fume-choked Jl Adisucipto is the most straightforward route, but there's a quieter alternative that begins by heading north along Yogya's Jl Simanjutak and Jl Kaliurang until you reach the Mataram Canal, just past the main Gajah Mada University compound. Follow the canal path east for 12km (1hr), and you'll eventually come out near Candi Sari on Jl Adisucipto. *Via Via* (see p.195) also organizes bike rides to Prambanan. By motorbike, the trip can easily be combined with a ride to Kaliurang.

SURAKARTA (SOLO)

Sixty-five kilometres northeast of Yogya stands quiet, leafy low-rise **SURAKARTA**, or, as it's more commonly known, **SOLO**. This is the older of the two royal cities in Central Java, and its ruling family can lay claim to being the rightful heirs to the Mataram dynasty.

Not long after their establishment – in 1745 and 1757 respectively – Solo's two royal houses wisely stopped fighting and instead threw their energies into the arts, developing a highly sophisticated and graceful court culture. The gamelan pavilions became the new theatres of war, with each city competing to produce the more refined court culture – a situation that continues to this day.

WHAT TO SEE AND DO

Like Yogya, Solo has two **royal palaces** and a number of museums, yet its tourist industry is nowhere near as developed. The city's main source of income is from textiles, and Solo has the biggest **batik market** on Java. Solo also makes an ideal base from which to visit the home of Java Man at Sangiran, as well as the intriguing temples Candi Ceto and Candi Sukuh, each about 35km to the northeast.

Kasunanan Palace

Brought from Kartasura by Pakubuwono II in one huge day-long procession in 1745, the **Kasunanan Palace** (Mon–Thurs & Sat 8.30am–2pm, Sun 9am–1pm; Rp15,000; T 0271 644 4946) is Solo's largest and most important royal house. It stands within the kraton, just south of the *alun-alun*; guides are available free of charge and are definitely worth using. Non-royals must enter the main body of the palace by the eastern entrance. This opens out into a large courtyard whose surrounding buildings house the palace's **kris** (dagger) collection, as well as a number of chariots, silver ornaments and

4

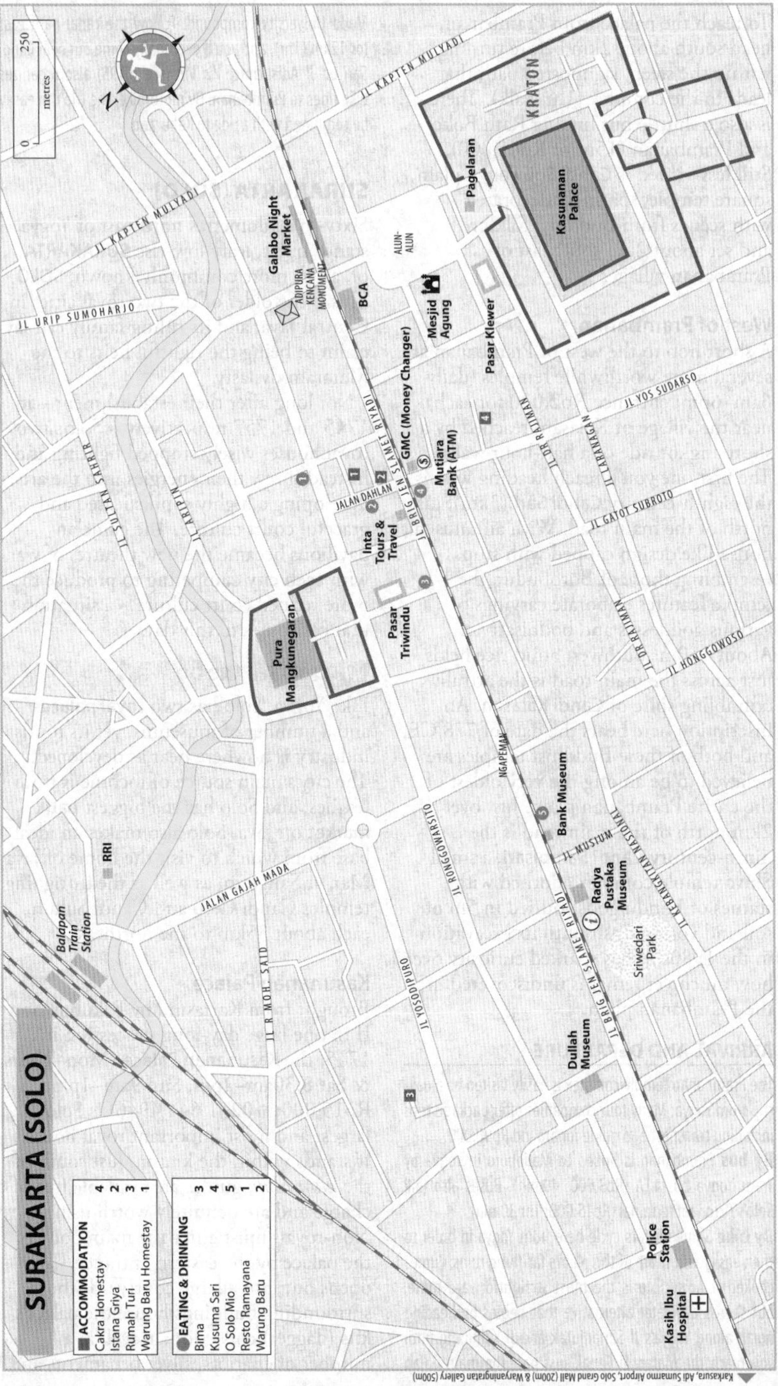

4

SURAKARTA (SOLO)

ACCOMMODATION

Cakra Homestay	4
Istana Griya	2
Rumah Turi	3
Warung Baru Homestay	1

EATING & DRINKING

Bima	3
Kusuma Sari	4
O Solo Mio	5
Resto Ramayana	1
Warung Baru	2

0 250 metres

Tirtonadi & Gilingan Bus Stations
Balapan Train Station
RRI
JL SULTAN SAHRIR
JL URIP SUMOHARJO
JL KAPTEN MULYADI
JL ARIPIN
JALAN GAJAH MADA
JL R MOH. SAID
Pura Mangkunegaran
Galabo Night Market
ADIPURA KENCANA MONUMENT
BCA
ALUN-ALUN
Inta Tours & Travel
JALAN DAHLAN
Pasar Triwindu
JL BRIG JEN SLAMET RIYADI
GMC (Money Changer)
Mutiara Bank (ATM)
Mesjid Agung
Pagelaran
Pasar Klewer
KRATON
Kasunanan Palace
JL YOSODIPURO
JL RONGGOWARSITO
NGAPEMAN
JL DR RAJIMAN
JL GATOT SUBROTO
JL LARANAGAN
JL YOS SUDARSO
JL HONGGOWOSO
Bank Museum
JL MUSIUM
Radya Pustaka Museum
Sriwedari Park
JL KEBANGKITAN NASIONAL
Dullah Museum
Police Station
Kasih Ibu Hospital
Karkasura, Adi Sumarmo Airport, Solo Grand Mall (200m) & Waryaningratan Gallery (500m)

other royal knick-knacks. An archway to the west leads into the Susuhunan's living quarters. Many of the buildings in this courtyard are modern copies, the originals having burnt down in 1985.

Pura Mangkunegaran

The second royal house in Solo, the **Pura Mangkunegaran** (Mon–Sat 9am–2pm, Sun 9am–1pm; Rp18,000; T 0271 644 4946) stands 1km west of the kraton and, like Yogya's court of Paku Alam, faces south towards the Kasunanan Palace as a mark of respect. With its fine collection of antiques and curios, in many ways the Pura Mangkunegaran is more interesting than the Kasunanan Palace. It was built in 1757 to placate the rebellious Prince Mas Said (Mangkunegara I), a nephew of Pakubuwono II, who was given a royal title, a court in Solo and leadership over four thousand of Solo's households in a peace deal. The palace hides behind a high white wall, entered through the gateway to the south. The vast **pendopo** (the largest in Indonesia) that fronts the palace shields four gamelan orchestras underneath its rafters, three of which can only be played on very special occasions. The *pendopo*'s vibrantly painted roof features Javanese zodiac figures surrounding the main batik centrepiece that took three years to complete. A portrait of the current resident, Mangkunegara IX, hangs by the entrance to the **Dalam Agung**, or living quarters, whose reception room has been turned into a good museum, displaying ancient coins, ballet masks and chastity preservers.

Radya Pustaka Museum

A kilometre west along Jalan Brig Jen Slamet Riyadi brings you to the well-kept **Radya Pustaka Museum** (Tues–Sun 9am–2pm; Rp10,000, camera charge Rp5000). Built by the Dutch in 1890, this is one of the oldest and largest museums in Java, housing an extensive Dutch and Javanese library as well as dusty collections of wayang kulit puppets, *kris*, and scale models of the mosque at Demak and the cemetery at Imogiri.

ARRIVAL AND DEPARTURE

By plane Adi Sumarmo Airport is 10km west of Solo and just 2km north of Kartasura. The Solo Batik Trans bus service links the city centre (every 15min; 1hr; Rp7000). A taxi (30min) will cost about Rp65,000 from the airport to Solo, and Rp50,000 in the opposite direction.

Destinations Jakarta (13 daily; 1hr 10min); Kuala Lumpur (3 weekly; 2hr 25min); Singapore (2 weekly; 2hr).

By bus Buses terminate at the Tirtonadi bus station in the north of the city. Just across the crossroads by the northeastern corner of Tirtonadi is the minibus terminal, Gilingan. From the front of the *Hotel Surya*, overlooking Tirtonadi, orange angkot #6 (Rp3000) departs for the town centre, stopping at Ngapeman, the junction of Jl Gajah Mada and Jl Brig Jen Slamet Riyadi. To reach the bus station from the centre, catch a #05 orange bus from Matahari dept. store.

Destinations Frequent buses to Bandung (12hr); Banyuwangi (12hr); Jakarta (13hr); Malang (7hr); Semarang (3hr); Surabaya (6hr); Yogyakarta (2hr).

By train You'll pay about Rp15,000 for a becak and Rp20,000 for a taxi from outside the Balapan train station, 300m south of Tirtonadi, to Jl Dahlan. Avoid the pre-paid taxi stand inside the station, which charges Rp30,000 for the same trip.

Destinations Bandung (5 daily; 8hr 50min); Jakarta (5 daily; 10hr 30min); Malang (daily; 6hr 25min); Purworketo (6 daily; 3hr 15min); Surabaya (6 daily; 3hr 20min); Yogya (14 daily; 1hr 30min).

4

INFORMATION AND TOURS

Tourist information Solo has two tourist offices, one located at the airport (daily 8am–4pm; T 0271 781164) and another behind the Radya Pustaka Museum at Jl Brig Jen Slamet Riyadi 275 (T 0271 711435). Only the latter (daily 8am–5pm; T 0271 711435) is of much use, with details of events, a reasonable range of brochures and maps, and, when Patrick Orlando is around, English-speaking staff.

Tours Several hotels in Solo organize a range of excursions. Cycling tours are popular, among the most rewarding run by Istana Griya (Rp120,000), Cakra Homestay (Rp125,000), *Warung Baru* (Rp100,000) and the friendly Patrick Orlando (T 081 3296 03992, E patrick.orlando@ymail.com; Rp125,000), often found at the Tourist Information Office; each includes a visit to a gamelan factory, bakery, tofu factory and even an *arak* manufacturer.

Travel agents Inta Tours & Travel, Jl Brig Jen Slamet Riyadi 96 (T 0271 655600), are recommended.

GETTING AROUND

Becak Unlike the ones in Yogya, Solo's becak do not charge a higher rate if there is more than one person in the carriage. As ever, bargain hard.

Taxis The main taxi stand is situated by the Matahari department store; they are metered. Minimum fare is Rp15,000.

Bike rental Being flat and, for a Javanese city, relatively free of traffic, cycling is an excellent way to get around. Bikes can be rented from many of the homestays for Rp20,000/day.

ACCOMMODATION

The backpacker enclave is around Jl Dahlan.

★**Cakra Homestay** Jl Cakra II/15, Kauman ⊕0271 634743, ⊕hotelcakrahomestay@yahoo.com. This place is a hidden gem, with its own pool, free wi-fi, Javanese furnishings, and even a gamelan orchestra where practices are held Mon and Thurs – all tucked away behind high walls. The very peaceful rooms are simple but comfortable, a few have a/c (Rp175,000). **Rp100,000/150,000**

Istana Griya Jl Dahlan 22 ⊕0271 632667. Highly efficient homestay with smart, good-value rooms, some with a/c and hot water (Rp175,000) and all with free wi-fi and breakfast. The friendly English-speaking owner organizes a range of tours and rents out bikes (Rp20,000) and motorbikes (Rp100,000) for the day. **Rp60,000/100,000**

4

Rumah Turi Jl Sri Gading 2 Turisari 12 ⊕0271 736606, ⊕rumahturi.com. A sleek and modern eco-hotel in a quiet back alley off Jl Yosodipuro. Worth the splurge, with elegant, spacious a/c rooms equipped with flatscreen TVs, wi-fi, minibars and hot water showers. On site there's also a fancy restaurant with an outside deck attached, as well as a spa and meditation corner. **Rp462,000**

Warung Baru Homestay Off Jl Dahlan ⊕0271 656369 or ⊕0815 6763 1000 (ask for Yant), ⊕wb_solo_1979@yahoo.com. A neat and friendly little place down a quiet alley off Jl Dahlan. There is a wonderful garden and sitting area out the front and the colourful rooms have a/c, hot water and comfy beds. **Rp150,000**

EATING AND DRINKING

Solo's warung are renowned for local specialities such as *nasi liwet* (chicken or vegetables and rice drenched in coconut milk and served on a banana leaf) and *nasi gudeg* (jackfruit curry). For dessert, try *kue putu* (coconut cakes) or *srabi*, a combination of pancake and sweet rice served with a variety of fruit toppings. Most of these are found along Jl Brig Jen Slamet Riyadi at the Galabo night market.

Bima Jl Brig Jen Slamet Riyadi 128. Welcome relief from the heat outside, *Bima* has cheap Indonesian food (*nasi gudeg* Rp20,000) as well as a smattering of Western, Japanese and Chinese dishes and ice creams (banana split Rp15,000). Daily 10am–9.30pm.

Kusuma Sari Jl Brig Jen Slamet Riyadi 111. Popular with locals, this cool, clean and spacious restaurant has grilled dishes, soups and ice creams at very affordable prices (*nasi goreng* Rp13,000). Daily 10am–9pm.

O Solo Mio Jl Brig Jen Slamet Riyadi 253 ⊕0271 727264. One of the more pricey spots in town, this smart Italian restaurant has top-rate service, a great selection of international wines (Rp78,500 for a glass of house wine), and wood-fired pizzas from an oven constructed using stones from Gunung Merapi (pizza mozzarella Rp38,500). Daily 10.30am–11pm.

Resto Ramayana Jl Imam Bonjol 49. Clean and air-conditioned, Ramayana is popular with both locals and foreigners. There's an extensive menu of seafood and *sate* dishes (*sate ayam* starts at Rp20,000). Daily 8am–9pm.

Warung Baru Jl Dahlan 23. The most popular travellers' restaurant in Solo. Delicious and very inexpensive Solonese food such as *nasi liwet* and *nasi pecel* (vegetable and peanut sauce; Rp10,000 each) plus delicious home-made bread. Bike tours and batik courses can be organized here too. Daily 8am–9pm.

PERFORMING ARTS

For the last two centuries, the royal houses of Solo have developed highly individual styles for the traditional Javanese arts of gamelan and wayang. Wayang orang, which features human performers rather than the leather shadow puppets used in wayang kulit, is something of a local speciality. It combines dance, vocal and character performances to evoke scenes from the Mahabharata and Ramayana.

Puro Mangkunegaran The practice gamelan performances are performed (Wed 10am–noon) in the beautiful surroundings of the palace.

Radio Republik Indonesia (RRI) Jl Marconi 55, just to the south of the Balapan train station, regularly records performances of Solo's traditional arts, including gamelan, wayang orang (second Tues of the month 8pm) and wayang kulit (third Sat of the month starting 9pm). Tickets for performances should be bought in advance from the RRI Building just to the south of the Balapan train station.

Sriwedari Park Two-hour performances of wayang orang (Mon–Sat 8–11pm; Rp3000).

DIRECTORY

Banks and exchange Most banks are found at and around the eastern end of Jl Riyadi, with ATMs and money changers. Just across Jl Riyadi from Jl Dahlan is GMC, at Jl Yos Sudarso 1.

Batik courses Solo is the cheapest and arguably the best place to try your hand at batik. Homestays and restaurants organize a number of courses costing around Rp75,000: the *Warung Baru* restaurant on Jl Dahlan runs an extremely popular course through Yoyo Ding (from Rp100,000/day) on Jl Toyodiningratan (⊕0271 716625 or ⊕0813 2913 8877 mobile).

Hospital Rumah Sakit Kasih Ibu on Jl Brig Jen Slamet Riyadi 404, has English-speaking doctors.

Internet Wi-fi is available in some restaurants and cafés as well as in Solo Grand Mall; internet cafés around town charge Rp6000/hr.
Police Station Jl Slamet Riyadi 376 ⓣ0271 740683 or ⓣ0271 713003. Dial ⓣ110 for emergencies.
Post office Jl Jend Sudirman (daily 6am–10pm).
Shopping Pasar Triwindu (daily 9am–4pm), an antique market set a block south of Pura Mangkunegaran, with a wide range of old trinkets, from porcelain pieces to brass batik stamps to car parts. Meanwhile, set just to the north of Kasunanan Palace is Pasar Klewer (daily 10am–4pm), one of Indonesia's largest textile markets; some of the best bargains can be found here. More upmarket batik galleries are numerous in Solo, one of the best-known being Wuryaningratan Gallery on Jl Slamet Riyadi 261 (ⓣ0271 713140; daily 9am–3pm).

SURABAYA

Chaotic, noisy and sweltering, **SURABAYA** is Indonesia's second-largest city and the major port of East Java. Although to most tourists it's little more than a place to switch buses or trains between Yogya and Bromo, Surabaya isn't without its charms. Dubbed the "City of Heroes," the city is heralded among Indonesians as the birthplace of the national independence movement, and its leafy boulevards are lined with statues and monuments honouring that heritage. Rich in contrasts and diversity, modern Surabaya boasts bazaars, mega-malls, chic cafés and ancient relics as well as some of the country's most colourful ethnic minority quarters.

WHAT TO SEE AND DO

Surabaya's **Chinese quarter** hums with activity, an abundance of traditional two-storey shophouses line its narrow streets, and minuscule red-and-gold altars glint in shops and houses. The area centres on Jalan Slompretan, Jalan Bongkaran and the part of Jalan Samudra southwest of the three-hundred-year-old **Hok Teck Hian Temple** on Jalan Dukuh. The temple itself is a vibrant place with several tiny shrines spread over two floors, and Buddhist, Confucian and Hindu effigies.

Kampung Arab

North of the Chinese quarter is the most interesting part of Surabaya – **Kampung Arab** or **Qubah**, the Arab area. Here you will find the oldest and most famous mosque in Surabaya, **Mesjid Ampel**, originally erected in 1421. The whole kampung – bounded by Jalan Nyanplungan, Jalan KH Mas Mansur, Jalan Sultan Iskandar Muda and Jalan Pabean Pasar – was originally settled by Arab traders and sailors who arrived in Kali Mas harbour more than five hundred years ago. Resembling an Arab souk, its maze of tidy, well-kept alleyways is crammed cheek by jowl with stalls selling flowers, dates, shawls, beads, perfumes, prayer caps and headscarves. Dress conservatively when visiting the area.

House of Sampoerna

Whether or not you're a fan of kreteks, the **House of Sampoerna** on Jl Taman Sampoerna 6 (daily 9am–10pm; free; ⓣ031 353 9000, ⓦhouseofsampoerna.museum), a museum near both the Chinese Quarter and the Qubah, makes a worthwhile stop. This stately Dutch compound, recently restored and opened to the public, was built in 1862 and later transformed into one of Indonesia's biggest kretek cigarette factories. It once employed 2900 workers rolling 325 cigarettes each per hour, though there are far fewer workers around today. If you come during working hours, you can glimpse the workers hand-rolling the ever-popular Dji Sam Soe.

Downtown

Near the city centre, you can take a walk through the steel belly of **Kapal Selam Monument** on Jalan Pemuda 39 (daily 8am–10pm; Rp5000; ⓣ031 549 0410), a Russian-built submarine acquired by the Indonesian Navy. Up the street is the Joko Dolog, an ancient Buddha statue of dubious origin set just south of **Taman Apsari Park**, across from the governor's residence on Jalan Pemuda.

ARRIVAL AND DEPARTURE

By plane Visas are available on arrival at Surabaya's Juanda International Airport (ⓣ031 298 6343), 18km south of the city. No public bus connects with the town centre directly, but DAMRI buses connect with Purabaya bus station (every 15min; Rp15,000), from where the #P1 service (Rp4000) connects with the city centre at the

intersection of Jl Tunjungan and Jl Pemuda. There's a rank for fixed-price taxis (Rp90,000) and DAMRI buses.

Destinations Balikpapan (20 daily; 1hr 30min); Bandung (4 daily; 1hr–2hr 30min); Denpasar (23 daily; 1hr 10min); Jakarta (58 daily; 1hr 25min); Makassar (25 daily; 1hr 30min); Manado (3 daily; 2hr 30min); Medan (3 daily; 3hr); Yogyakarta (9 daily; 1hr).

By bus The main bus station is Terminal Purabaya, 6km south of the city, better known locally as Bungurasih. All long-distance and inter-island buses start and finish here, plus many of the city buses and bemos. Local buses into the city leave from the far end of the Bungurasih terminal: follow the signs for "Kota". From the city, catch a #C (Rp2500), #P (Rp4000) or #PAC (Rp4000) bus heading

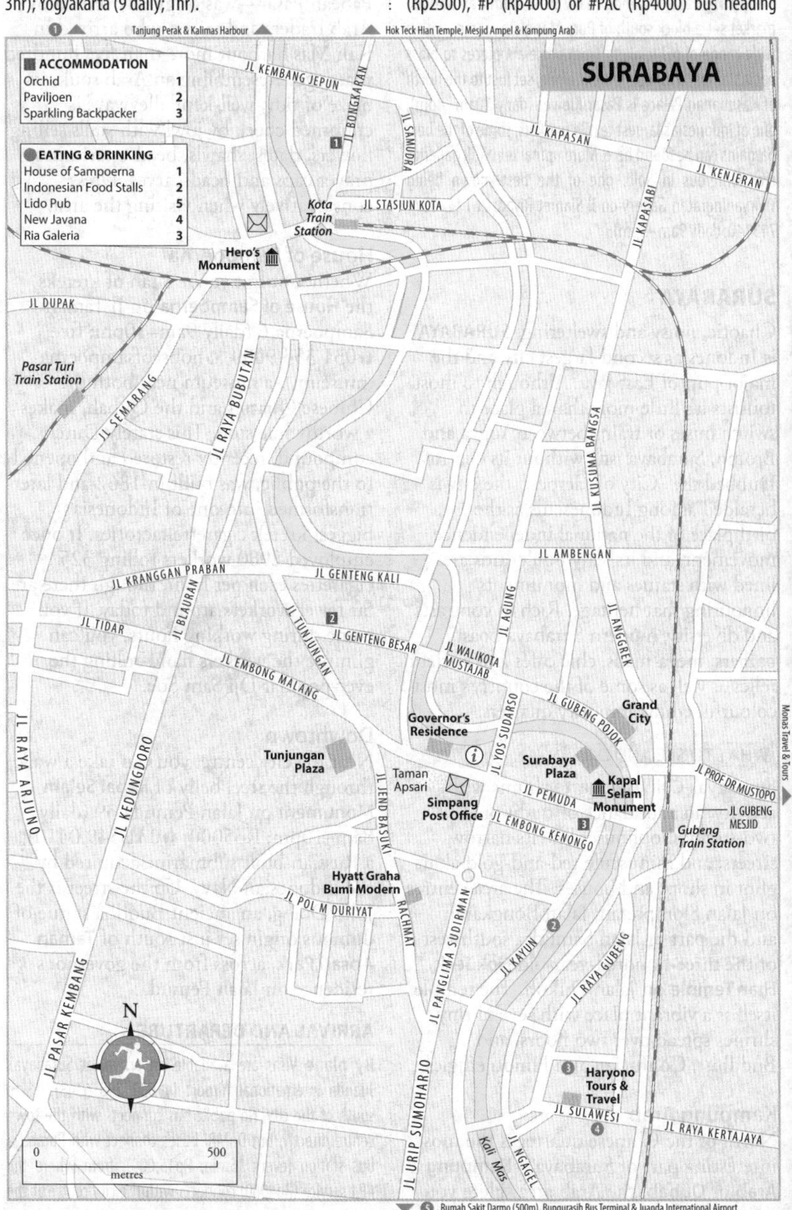

south to Bungurasih along Jl Panglima Sudirman just after the intersection with Jl Pemuda (Rp4000–5000). Bungurasih also has a huge taxi rank – minimum fare of Rp10,000; expect to pay about Rp40,000 to anywhere in town. Long-distance journeys are completed by night buses (departing 2–6pm); tickets are available from the offices within the bus station as well as from agents on Jl Basuki Rahmat in the city centre. Book ahead. For Jakarta, use Lorena and Karina (T 031 854 3328) and for Yogya take EKA (T 031 8819 8899, W ekamirabus.com).

Destinations Banyuwangi (every 30min; 6–7hr); Denpasar (4 daily; 11hr); Jakarta (20 daily; 14hr); Probolinggo (every 30min; 2hr); Solo (every 30min; 6hr); Yogyakarta (every 30min; 8hr).

By ferry Pelni ferries dock at Tanjung Perak in the far north of the city, served by #C, #P and #PAC buses. The main Pelni office is at Jl Pahlawan 112 (Mon–Thurs 9am–noon & 1–3pm, Fri & Sat 9am–noon; T 031 353 9048).

Destinations Jakarta (2 weekly; 21–24hr); Jayapura (Mon & Wed; 5–6 days); Makassar (Mon, Tues & Wed; 24hr); Nunakan (fortnightly; 4–5 days); Samarinda (fortnightly; 3 days).

By train Surabaya has three main train stations. Most useful to travellers are Gubeng, in the centre of town near most accommodation, serving the routes to Banyaungi and Yogyakarta; and Pasar Turi, west of the city centre, serving the faster, northerly route to Jakarta.

Destinations Banyuangi (2 daily; 7hr); Jakarta (3 daily; 10–12hr); Probolinggo (2 daily; 2hr); Solo (6 daily; 4hr); Yogyakarta (4 daily; 5hr).

INFORMATION

Tourist information The useful tourist office is at Jl Pemuda 15 (daily 8am–8pm; T 031 547 8853, W sparklingsurabaya.info), with English-speaking staff and good maps and brochures.

Travel agents Many agents in Surabaya offer all-inclusive tours to the sights of the region, either day-trips or longer, plus international bookings. Among the largest, best-established setups are Haryono Tours and Travel, Jl Sulawesi 27–29 (T 031 503 4000, W haryonotours.com), and Monas Tours and Travel, Jl Dharahusada Utara 6 (T 031 596 5696).

GETTING AROUND

Taxi Blue Bird is recommended (T 031 565 1234; flagfall Rp5500, minimum fare Rp10,000 when hailed on the street or Rp20,000 by phone).

ACCOMMODATION

Orchid Jl Bongkaran 49 T 031 355 0211. Situated close to the city's historic districts, this place has an attached café and clean but somewhat gloomy rooms, all with a/c, TV and friendly staff. **Rp150,000**

Paviljoen Jl Genteng Besar 94–98 T 031 534 3449. A good budget hotel, with friendly Dutch and English-speaking staff and clean rooms in a quiet but centrally located colonial bungalow. Rooms at the back have verandas set around a courtyard and all have attached cold-water mandi. Southbound buses #P1 and #P2 stop just at the end of the street on Jl Tunjungan. **Rp126,500**

Sparkling Backpacker Hotel Jl Kayun 2AB T 031 532 1388. Though not quite sparkling and somewhat less than friendly, rooms are clean and offer good value. It's also just a short walk from the train station. Room 25 (Rp155,000) with huge windows and a/c is the best. There is also a kitchen, wi-fi and a simple breakfast included. **Rp135,000**

EATING AND DRINKING

There is a huge selection of cheap food stalls by the river, past the flower market on Jl Kalun, serving Indonesian coffee, grilled fish and chicken dishes for the mainly local clientele. One of the local favourites is *rawon*, a thick, black beef soup served throughout the night at Surabaya's warungs.

House of Sampoerna Café Jl Taman Sampoerna. Set in an elegant colonial building attached to the famous cigarette factory of the same name, this posh café's menu features Western and Indonesian cuisine (barbecue beef soup Rp30,000), as well as smoking and non-smoking sections. Daily 9am–10pm.

Lido Pub Jl Mayjen Sungkono 8–9. Close to the *Shangri-La Hotel*, this is a smoky little dive bar, popular with expats for its laidback atmosphere, good live music starting around 9pm, standard pub fare (mains from Rp40,000) and cheap beer. There is a nightclub upstairs at weekends. Daily 10am–1am.

New Javana Jl Sulawesi 44. A popular seafood restaurant serving a good selection of grilled fish, crab and octopus dishes (from Rp35,000–38,000). It's set just off a noisy thoroughfare, and there's wi-fi in the sleek, spotless a/c interior. Daily 10am–10pm.

Ria Galeria Jl Bangka 2–4. This beautifully decorated Javanese restaurant offers affordable Indonesian specialities (oxtail soup Rp48,000, fried rice with chicken *sate* Rp32,500), served in elegant surroundings. Daily 11am–9.30pm.

DIRECTORY

Banks and exchange All of the main Indonesian banks have huge branches in Surabaya, with exchange facilities.

Consulates US, Jl Citra Raya Niaga 2 (T 031 297 5300); UK and Australian consulates closed.

Hospitals Rumah Sakit Darmo, Jl Raya Darmo 90 (T 031 567 6253).

Immigration office Jl Jend S Parman 58A (T 031 853 1785).

Internet All the big plazas have at least one internet café (Rp4000–8000/hr).

Police station In north Surabaya on Jl Raden Saleh (☎031 568 8099). For emergencies, call ☎031 199.

Post office The main post office (Mon–Thurs 8am–3pm, Fri & Sat 8am–1pm) is at Jl Kebonrojo 10. To get there from the city centre, take a #C, #P1, #P2, #PAC1 or #PAC2 bus from outside Tunjungan Plaza to the junction of Jl Kebonrojo and Jl Bubutan. If you're just sending letters, the Simpang post office is more central at Jl Taman Apsaril 1 (Mon–Thurs 8am–12.30pm, Fri 8–11am, Sat 8am–noon), beside Taman Apsari Park.

THE BROMO REGION

The **Bromo region** is best known for its awesome scenery. At its heart is a vast, ancient volcanic crater with sheer walls over 300m high, within which the dramatic, still-smoking Gunung Bromo (2329m) – one of three volcanoes in the crater – rises up from the Sea of Sand, a desolate plain at the crater's base. Hundreds of thousands visit each year to glimpse Bromo at sunrise.

4

WHAT TO SEE AND DO

This unique landscape now comprises the Bromo-Tengger-Semeru National Park, whose highlights are the dramatic smoking crater of **Gunung Bromo**, **Gunung Penanjakan** – on the outside crater's edge and one of the favourite sunrise spots – and **Cemoro Lawang**, with its brilliant panoramic view of the crater, at its best during the dry season. The park also contains the highest mountain in Java, **Gunung Semeru**, which can be climbed by experienced trekkers.

The most popular approach to the Bromo region is to head inland from **Probolinggo**, on the north coast, to the crater's edge at Cemoro Lawang, where most people stay in order to make the dawn trip to Gunung Bromo as easy as possible. A much less common approach involves heading inland from Pasuruan, 60km southeast of Surabaya, in order to reach the villages of Tosari and Wonokitri, also linked by road to Gunung Penanjakan.

Gunung Bromo

The climb to the top of **Gunung Bromo** (2392m) is the most popular excursion from Cemoro Lawang; if you're lucky with the clouds, there may be an absolutely spellbinding sunrise. There's a Rp75,000 per person entry fee for the park. To get to the base of Gunung Bromo, you can walk (1hr; bring a torch and follow the white pillars through the Sea of Sand), get a horse (Rp60,000), or hire a jeep for the morning to take in both Gunung Bromo and Gunung Penanjakan (Rp350,000). However you get there, you'll still have to manage the 249 concrete stairs up to the crater rim, from where there are great views down into the smoking crater and back across the Sea of Sand. Dress warmly.

Gunung Penanjakan

The best spot for postcard-perfect sunrise views, taking in the entire Bromo area, is **Gunung Penanjakan** (2770m). The whole crater area lies below, Bromo smoking and Semeru puffing up regular plumes while the sun rises dramatically in the east. You can **camp** up here if you wish, but you'll be invaded before dawn by the hordes. Most visitors take the jeep tour from Cemoro Lawang at around 4am that will then drive across the Sea of Sand to Bromo before returning to Cemoro Lawang (Rp350,000).

Gunung Semeru

Essentially a dry-season expedition (June–Sept or possibly Oct), the climb up **Gunung Semeru** (3676m), Java's highest mountain, is a three-day hike for fit, experienced trekkers only and requires good preparation and equipment. The volcano has been in a continuous state of eruption since 1967, and over twenty thousand seismic events are typically recorded each year; it's a good idea to take a guide (ask at the PHPA office or your hotel) and heed local advice. The path starts at the village of **Ranu Pane** (2117m) to the north of the mountain, accessible from Cemoro Lawang by ojek (Rp50,000) or via a four-hour path across the Sea of Sand to Jemplang, from where it's another 6km to the village. Ranu Pane has several basic homestays (Rp80,000) and the **PHPA office** (☎0335 541038) where you must register before your hike. Here you may also find porters (from Rp120,000 per day) and rent a cooking

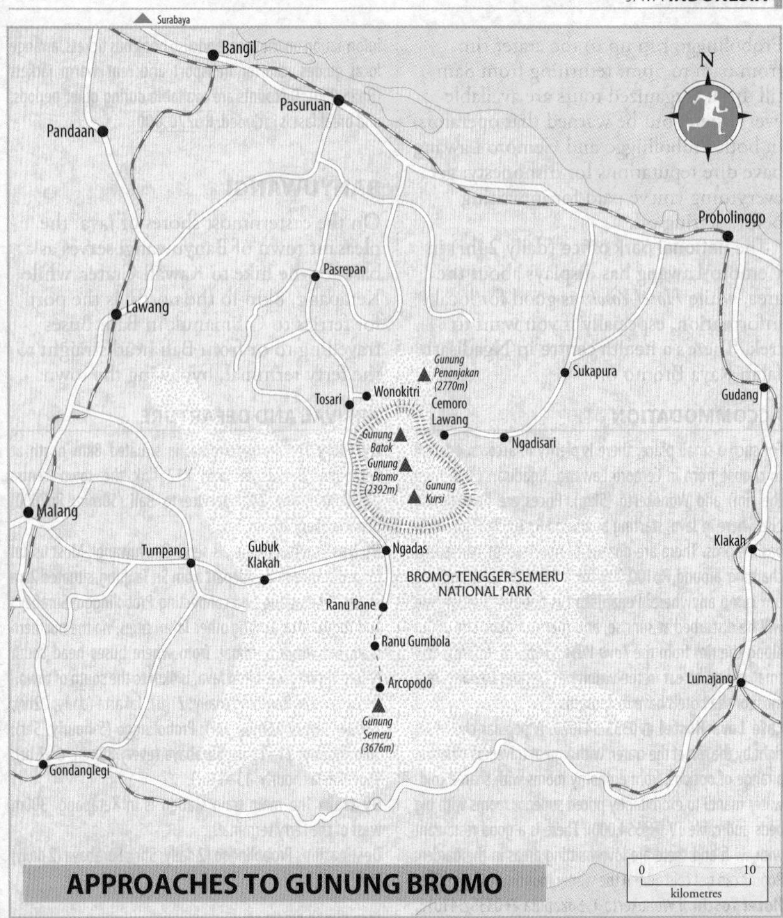

APPROACHES TO GUNUNG BROMO

stove, but bring your own sleeping gear for the hike.

Probolinggo

PROBOLINGGO, the mango capital of Indonesia and the most popular access point for Bromo, is 100km southeast of Surabaya. The **train station** is on the northern side of the *alun-alun*, while the **Bayu Angga bus terminal** is 6km southwest of the leafy town centre, connected by yellow microlets (Rp5000). From here to Cemoro Lawang are two daily buses – labelled "Sukapura" and "Ngadisari" on the front – as well as frequent minibuses from just outside the terminal, running until 4pm (Rp20,000). Regular buses also link Banyuwangi (5hr), Surabaya (2hr) and Yogyakarta (9hr). There is a helpful tourist information office at the train station (Ⓣ0335 432420), and passable budget rooms set around a small garden at *Hotel Paramita* on Jl Siaman (Ⓣ0335 421535; Rp90,000), 2km to the south.

Cemoro Lawang

The small village of **CEMORO LAWANG**, 46km from Probolinggo, sits on the crater's edge and offers the easiest launching point for the pre-dawn excursion to Gunung Bromo itself. The precipice at the end of Cemoro Lawang gives brilliant views of the entire area – best from the road in front of *Lava View Lodge*. **Minibuses** (Rp20,000) from

Probolinggo run up to the crater rim from 6am to 5pm, returning from 8am till 4pm. Organized tours are available everywhere, but be warned that operators in both Probolinggo and Cemoro Lawang have dire reputations for dishonesty; get everything you've paid for in writing before setting off.

The **national park office** (daily 24hr) in Cemoro Lawang has displays about the area, while *Hotel Yoschi* is good for local information, especially if you want to trek. There's a **health centre** in Ngadisari, Jalan Raya Bromo 6.

ACCOMMODATION

For such a small place, there is plenty of accommodation to choose from in Cemoro Lawang, Ngadisari (3km from the rim) and Wonokerto (5km). Prices are higher than elsewhere in Java, starting at around Rp100,000 for ultra-basic rooms. There are dozens of nondescript homestays charging around Rp100,000 for a basic double, and you can camp anywhere: Penanjakan is popular, though you will be disturbed at sunrise, and there's a good site 200m along the rim from the *Lava View Lodge*. There are a few small places to eat in the vicinity of Cemoro Lawang, and most of the hotels have restaurants.

Café Lava Hostel ⊕0335 541020. A popular choice set right by the rim of the crater, with a great travellers' vibe and a range of options, from economy rooms with shared cold-water mandi to exorbitantly priced superior rooms with big beds and cable TV (Rp554,000). There is a good restaurant with wi-fi and there are lovely sitting areas in the garden. Rooms can get cold during the winter months. **Rp218,000**

Hotel Yoschi Jl Wonokerto 1, Sukapura ⊕0335 541018, ⊛yoschihotel.com. A cosy place with numerous room options (from cramped economy rooms with shared bathrooms to comfortable family bungalows), eclectic decor and a great garden for relaxing. Staff provide good information on the area, and also book bus tickets, arrange local guides, charter transport and rent warm jackets (Rp25,000). Discounts are available during quiet periods, and breakfast is included. **Rp270,000**

★TREAT YOURSELF

Lava View Lodge Cemoro Lawang ⊕0335 541009. This family-run place is in high demand, largely due to the unmatched views from the restaurant and upper bungalows. Although slightly aged, the lodge has decent en-suite rooms, a great Indonesian buffet (included with room price), live music and a volleyball court. To get there, go past the drab-looking square and follow the main track towards the lip of the crater. **Rp580,000**

BANYUWANGI

On the easternmost shores of Java, the pleasant town of Banyuwangi serves as a base for the hike to Kawah Crater, while Ketapang, 8km to the north, is the port for ferries to Gilimanuk in Bali. Buses travelling to or from Bali head straight to the ferry terminal, bypassing the town.

ARRIVAL AND DEPARTURE

By ferry The ferry terminal is situated 8km north at Ketapang. Bemos #6 and #12 link the town centre (Rp10,000). The 24hr service to Bali (50min; Rp7000) departs every 20min.

By bus Two bus terminals serve Banyuwangi. Most useful long-distance routes depart from Sri Tanjung, situated 2km north of Ketapang and connecting Probolinggo, Surabaya and Yogyakarta, among other Javan cities, via the northern road. Brawijaya terminal, from where buses head south before curving west into Java, is 4km to the south of town.

Destinations Bandung (daily; 21hr); Jakarta (daily; 22hr); Jember (every 15min; 3hr); Probolinggo (5 hourly; 5hr); Solo (hourly; 11–13hr); Surabaya (every 30min; 6–7 hr); Yogyakarta (hourly; 13–14hr).

By train The main train station is in Ketapang, 300m west of the ferry terminal.

Destinations Probolinggo (2 daily; 5hr); Surabaya (2 daily; 7hr).

INFORMATION

Tourist office The friendly tourist information office (Mon–Fri 7am–4pm; ⊕0335 424172) is near the town centre at Jl A Yani 78.

ACCOMMODATION AND EATING

Street stalls and warung are plentiful in the city centre, especially along the corner of Jl Wahid Hasyim and Jl MT Haryono.

Hotel Anda Jl Jend Basuki Rachmat 34 ⊕0333 41441. Set just off a busy road 200m from the bemo station, this scruffy losmen has a helpful owner and worn rooms that are OK for a night. **Rp60,000**

Hotel Baru Jl MT Hariyono 82–84 ⊕0333 421369. Basic hotel with enthusiastic, English-speaking staff, in a quiet, central location a 10min walk from the post office. Economy rooms come with attached mandi, and the price goes up for a fan (Rp90,000) or a/c (Rp160,000), though all come with wi-fi and breakfast. **Rp75,000**

DIRECTORY

Banks and exchange For exchange, go to BCA at Jl Jend Sudirman 85–87 or BNI at Jl Banetrang 46.

Hospital Yasmin Hospital, Jl Letkol Istikqlah 80–84 ⓣ0333 424671.

Internet There are hotspots all over the city, and internet cafés charging around Rp4000/hr.

Post office Jl Diponegoro 1 (Mon–Thurs 8am–3pm, Fri 8–11am, Sat 8am–1pm, Sun & hols 8am–noon), west of the sports field.

KAWAH IJEN

The view from the rim of **Kawah Ijen** (Ijen Crater; 2386m) is among the most spectacular to be found in all of Indonesia. Set within a 20km-wide caldera and bounded by sheer cliffs, the steaming crater holds a 200m-deep, 1km-wide, turquoise lake of highly acidic waters, the sulphuric shoreline striped in bright yellow. As well as otherworldly vistas, some of the planet's toughest workers may be seen in action here, battling toxic fumes and treacherous terrain while hauling 70kg sacks brimming with sulphur deposits.

Ijen can be reached from either Banyuwangi or Bondowoso, although most choose the former route, entailing a slightly shorter drive (1hr 15min) through forests and coffee plantations to the trailhead at Pos Paltuding. There, hikers must register their names at the PHKA Office and pay the admission fee (Rp25,000) before making the one- to one-and-a-half-hour hike to the lip of the crater. Guides are not necessary during the day, but prove helpful when making the thirty-minute descent into the crater itself, which is challenging due to both toxic fumes and a steep and sometimes unclear path. Guides are certainly recommended for the increasingly popular night-time hike, where hikers reach the base of the crater in the predawn darkness in order to glimpse the **blue flames** – jets of sulphur gas that burn bright blue – before climbing back to the crater's rim for glorious sunrise views. The relatively dry months from April to October are ideal for the hike. Transportation to Pos Paltuding is easily arranged in Banyuwangi (Rp580,000 per car or Rp150,000 per ojek, including waiting time). The guides of Ijen Smile (ⓣ0821 4184 2445), some of them former mine workers, are recommended.

GRAJAGAN: G-LAND

On the borders of Alas Purwo National Park in the far southeastern corner of Java, the fishing village of **GRAJAGAN** has become famous for its world-class surf. Better known as G-Land, it boasts awesomely long right- and left-handers and many kilometres of pristine beach. The ideal surfing season here is during the dry season, roughly from April to October. Several tour operators on Bali and Lombok run all-inclusive trips. Prices start from US$510 for an all-inclusive three-day, three-night surfing package. G-Land operators based in Kuta include G-Land Bobby's Surf Camp (ⓣ0361 755588, ⓦgrajagan.com), and G-Land Surf Camp (ⓣ0361 750320, ⓦg-landsurfcamp.com).

4

Sumatra

An explorer's paradise, the vast majority of Sumatra remains undiscovered. Most off the beaten-path highlights are situated along the old Trans-Sumatra highway, which spans from Banda Aceh in the far north to Bandar Lampung at the island's southern tip. Of these, most are clustered in the north: the misty jungles of **Bukit Lawang**, offering the best chance in Indonesia to see orang-utans in the wild; the ancient crater lake of **Danau Toba**, spiritual heartland of the fascinating Batak tribe; the twin volcanoes of **Berastagi**, a charming hill town and ideal trekking base; and the top-notch dive spots of Aceh's laidback **Pulau Weh**, situated at Indonesia's kilometre zero. Meanwhile, within easy reach of steamy Padang on the west coast lies a wealth of attractions: **Bukittinggi**, the bustling, cultural capital of the stunning Minangkabau Highlands; **Danau Maninjau**, a palm-fringed lake surrounded by jungle-covered cliffs; and the remote **Mentawai**, a surfer's paradise.

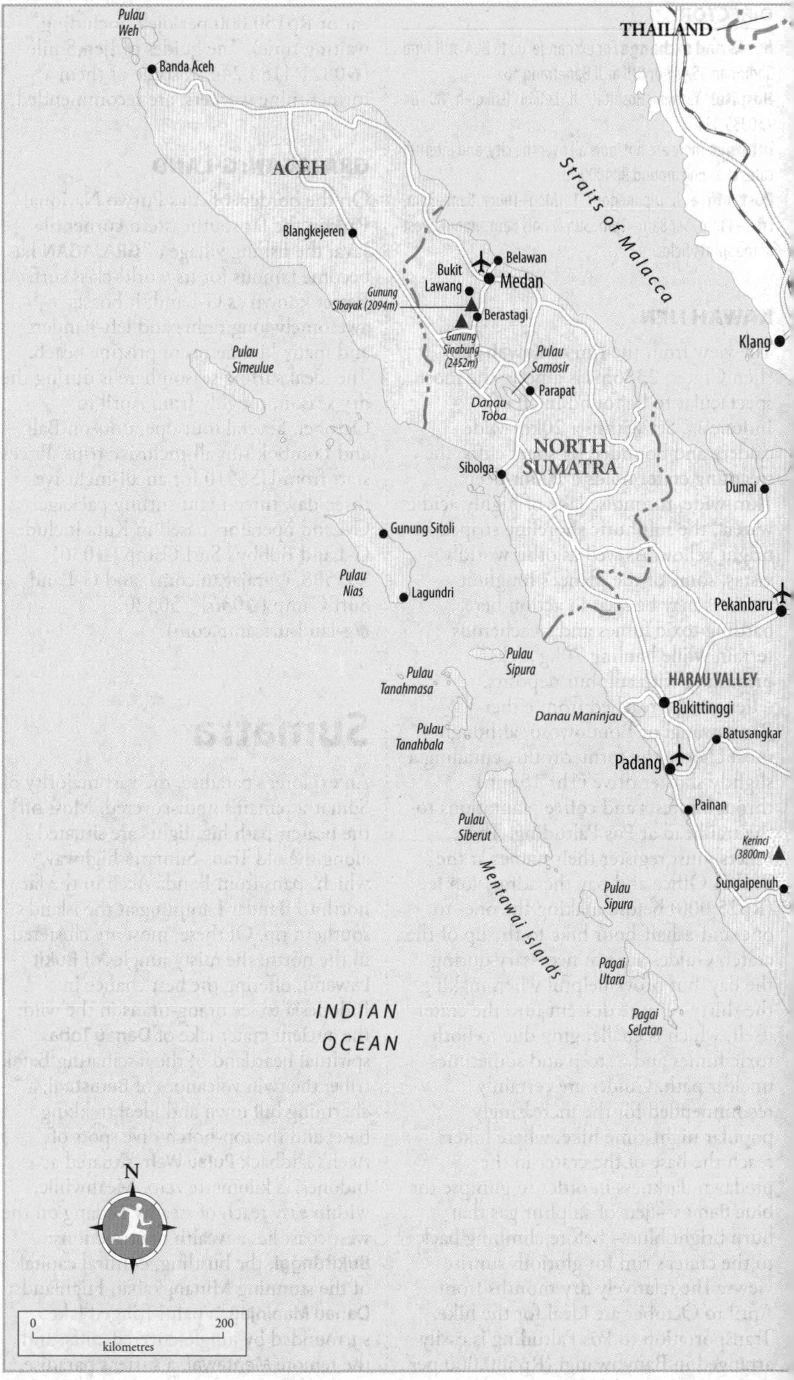

Pulau Weh
Banda Aceh
THAILAND
ACEH
Straits of Malacca
Blangkejeren
Belawan
Bukit Lawang
Medan
Gunung Sibayak (2094m)
Berastagi
Gunung Sinabung (2452m)
Klang
Pulau Simeulue
Pulau Samosir
Parapat
Danau Toba
NORTH SUMATRA
Sibolga
Dumai
Gunung Sitoli
Pulau Nias
Lagundri
Pekanbaru
Pulau Sipura
Pulau Tanahmasa
HARAU VALLEY
Bukittinggi
Danau Maninjau
Pulau Tanahbala
Batusangkar
Padang
Painan
Pulau Siberut
Kerinci (3800m)
Mentawai Islands
Sungaipenuh
Pulau Sipura
Pagai Utara
Pagai Selatan
INDIAN OCEAN
N
0
200
kilometres

4

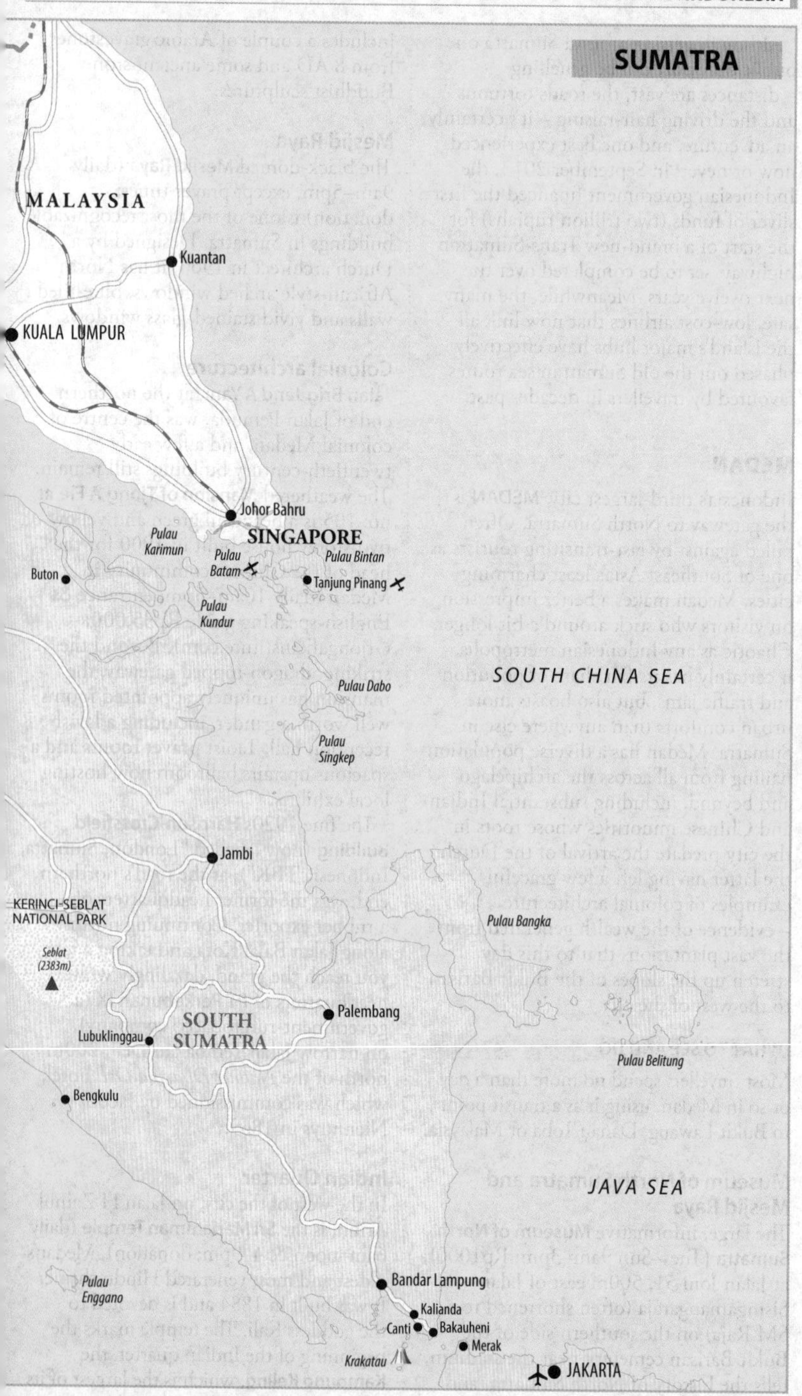
SUMATRA
MALAYSIA
Kuantan
KUALA LUMPUR
Johor Bahru
SINGAPORE
Pulau Karimun
Pulau Batam
Pulau Bintan
Tanjung Pinang
Buton
Pulau Kundur
SOUTH CHINA SEA
Pulau Dabo
Pulau Singkep
Jambi
KERINCI-SEBLAT NATIONAL PARK
Seblat (2383m)
Pulau Bangka
Palembang
SOUTH SUMATRA
Lubuklinggau
Pulau Belitung
Bengkulu
JAVA SEA
Bandar Lampung
Pulau Enggano
Kalianda
Canti
Bakauheni
Merak
Krakatau
JAKARTA

4

Although getting around Sumatra on **public transport** can be gruelling – distances are vast, the roads tortuous and the driving hair-raising – it's certainly an adventure, and one best experienced now or never: in September 2013, the Indonesian government financed the first sliver of funds (two trillion rupiahs) for the start of a brand-new Trans-Sumatran highway, set to be completed over the next twelve years. Meanwhile, the many safe, low-cost airlines that now link all the island's major hubs have effectively phased out the old Sumatran sea routes favoured by travellers in decades past.

MEDAN

Indonesia's third-largest city, **MEDAN** is the gateway to North Sumatra. Often railed against by fast-transiting tourists as one of Southeast Asia's least charming cities, Medan makes a better impression on visitors who stick around a bit longer. Chaotic as any Indonesian metropolis, it certainly has its fair share of pollution and traffic jams, but also boasts more urban comforts than anywhere else in Sumatra. Medan has a diverse population hailing from all across the archipelago and beyond, including substantial Indian and Chinese minorities whose roots in the city predate the arrival of the Dutch, the latter having left a few graceful examples of colonial architecture – evidence of the wealth generated from the vast plantations that to this day stretch up the slopes of the Bukit Barisan to the west of the city.

4

WHAT TO SEE AND DO

Most travellers spend no more than a day or so in Medan, using it as a transit point to Bukit Lawang, Danau Toba or Malaysia.

Museum of North Sumatra and Mesjid Raya

The large, informative **Museum of North Sumatra** (Tues–Sun 9am–3pm; Rp1000), at Jalan Joni 51, 500m east of Jalan Sisingamangaraja (often shortened to SM Raja) on the southern side of the Bukit Barisan cemetery near the stadium, tells the history of North Sumatra, and includes a couple of Arabic gravestones from 8 AD and some ancient stone Buddhist sculptures.

Mesjid Raya

The black-domed **Mesjid Raya** (daily 9am–5pm, except prayer times; donation) is one of the most recognizable buildings in Sumatra. Designed by a Dutch architect in 1906, it has North African-style arched windows, blue-tiled walls and vivid stained-glass windows.

Colonial architecture

Jalan Brig Jend A Yani, at the northern end of Jalan Pemuda, was the centre of colonial Medan, and a few early twentieth-century buildings still remain. The weathered **Mansion of Tjong A Fie** at no. 105 is a beautiful green and yellow two-storey house built in 1900 for the head of the Chinese community in Medan (daily 10am–5pm; entrance & English-speaking guide Rp35,000; ⓦtjongafieinstitute.com). Beyond the striking, dragon-topped gateway, the mansion has uniquely appointed rooms well worth a gander, including a lavish reception hall, Taoist prayer rooms and a spacious upstairs ballroom now hosting local exhibits.

The fine 1920s **Harrison-Crossfield Building** (now labelled "London, Sumatra, Indonesia TBK"), at the road's northern end, was the former headquarters of a rubber exporter. Continuing north along Jalan Balai Kota and taking a left, you reach the grand, dazzlingly white headquarters of **PT Perkebunan IX** (a government-run tobacco company), on narrow Jalan Tembakau Deli, 200m north of the *Natour Dharma Deli* hotel, which was commissioned by Jacob Nienhuys in 1869.

Indian Quarter

In the west of the city, on Jalan H Zainul Arifin, is the **Sri Mariamman Temple** (daily 6am–noon & 4–9pm; donation), Medan's oldest and most venerated Hindu shrine. It was built in 1884 and is devoted to the goddess Kali. The temple marks the beginning of the Indian quarter, the **Kampung Keling**, which is the largest of its

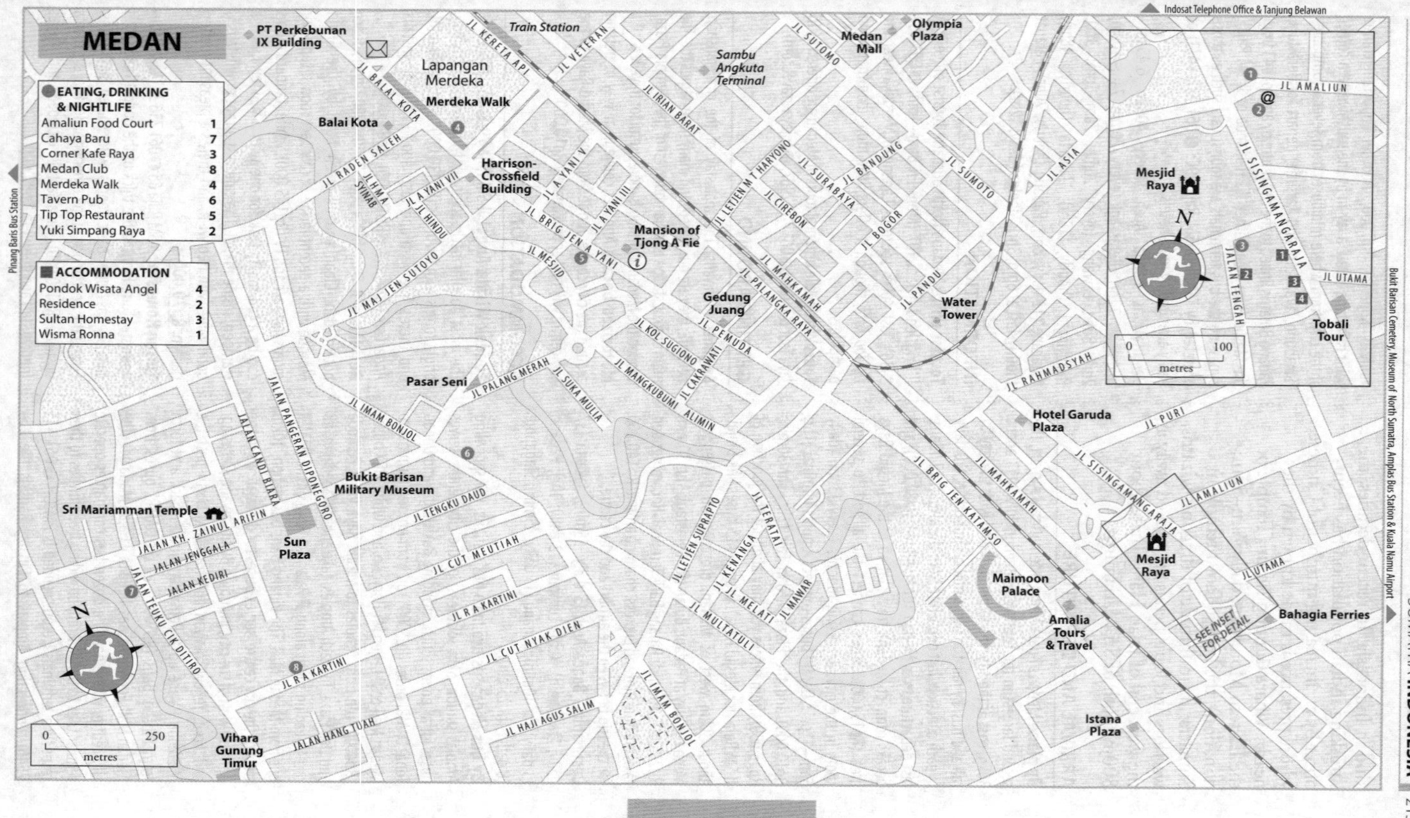
MEDAN
EATING, DRINKING & NIGHTLIFE
Amaliun Food Court 1
Cahaya Baru 7
Corner Kafe Raya 3
Medan Club 8
Merdeka Walk 4
Tavern Pub 6
Tip Top Restaurant 5
Yuki Simpang Raya 2
ACCOMMODATION
Pondok Wisata Angel 4
Residence 2
Sultan Homestay 3
Wisma Ronna 1
Indosat Telephone Office & Tanjung Belawan
Bukit Barisan Cemetery, Museum of North Sumatra, Amplas Bus Station & Kuala Namu Airport
Pinang Baris Bus Station
PT Perkebunan IX Building
Train Station
Lapangan Merdeka
Merdeka Walk
Balai Kota
Harrison-Crossfield Building
Mansion of Tjong A Fie
Sambu Angkuta Terminal
Medan Mall
Olympia Plaza
Gedung Juang
Water Tower
Pasar Seni
Hotel Garuda Plaza
Bukit Barisan Military Museum
Sri Mariamman Temple
Sun Plaza
Maimoon Palace
Amalia Tours & Travel
Mesjid Raya
Bahagia Ferries
See Inset for Detail
Istana Plaza
Vihara Gunung Timur
Tobali Tour
JL Kereta Api
JL Veteran
JL Balai Kota
JL Raden Saleh
JL H M A Syinab
JL A Yani VII
JL Hindu
JL A Yani V
JL A Yani III
JL Brig Jen A Yani
JL Mesjid
JL Maj Jen Sutoyo
JL Irian Barat
JL Sutomo
JL Letjen M T Haryono
JL Surabaya
JL Cirebon
JL Bandung
JL Sumoto
JL Asia
JL Bogor
JL Mahkamah
JL Palangka Raya
JL Pemuda
JL Pandu
JL Kol Sugiono
JL Carrawati
JL Mangkubumi
Alimin
JL Palang Merah
JL Suka Mulia
JL Imam Bonjol
JL Rahmadsyah
JL Puri
JL Sisingamangaraja
JL Amaliun
JL Utama
Jalan Tengah
JL Brig Jen Katamso
Jalan Candi Biara
Jalan Pangeran Diponegoro
Jalan Kh. Zainul Arifin
Jalan Jenggala
Jalan Kediri
Jalan Teuku Cik Ditiro
JL Tengku Daud
JL Cut Meutiah
JL R A Kartini
JL Cut Nyak Dien
JL Haji Agus Salim
Jalan Hang Tuah
JL Letjen Suprapto
JL Teratai
JL Kenanga
JL Melati
JL Mawar
JL Multatuli
N
0 250 metres
0 100 metres
4

kind in Indonesia. In recent decades, the shrinking Indian population has been offset by an increasing number of Chinese, whose presence is made known by the nearby **Vihara Gunung Timur** (Temple of the Eastern Mountain; daily 7am–5pm; donation), the largest Taoist temple in Sumatra. Its multitude of dragons, wizards, warriors and lotus petals are tucked away at the west end of Jalan Hang Tuah, about 800m south of Sri Mariamman.

ARRIVAL AND DEPARTURE

By plane Medan's Kuala Namu International Airport, the second largest in the country, opened in July 2013 about 30km east of the city. The airport is linked with the city by rail and bus. By rail, the trip is quicker but pricier (10 daily in each direction, last departure from the airport 12.15am, last departure from Medan 10pm; 40min; Rp80,000), and becaks connect Medan's train station to the Mesjid Raya area (Rp15,000). Buses connect the airport to several spots in the city: departing roughly every 15min (daily 5am–11pm), DAMRI buses connect Amplas Terminal (1hr; Rp10,000) and the Plaza Medan Fair (1hr–1hr 30min; Rp15,000), from where you may alight at the junction of Jl SM Raja (for Mesjid Raya). Orange ALS buses link Binjai, about 30km west of Medan, dropping off passengers along the way at Padang Bulan (for Berastagi; 1hr; 30min; Rp20,000), and near Pinang Baris Terminal. Recommended taxis are Blue Bird and Express, charging around Rp140,000 for the trip between the airport and city centre.

Destinations Banda Aceh (5 daily; 55min); Jakarta (37 daily; 2hr 20min); Kuala Lumpur (12 daily; 1hr); Padang (3 daily; 1hr 10min); Penang (15 daily; 45min); Singapore (8 daily; 1hr 25min).

By bus Medan has two main bus stations. The sprawling Amplas station, 5km southeast of the city centre, serves buses for all points south, including Bukittinggi and Danau Toba. DAMRI buses (Rp5000) run from Amplas terminal to Medan Mall on Jl Letjen MT Haryono, and white MRX buses (Rp4000) run from Amplas to Mesjid Raya via Jl Pemuda and Deli Plaza. To reach Amplas, take angkot "Soedarko" #3 or #4 heading south along Jl Palangka Raya or the DAMRI bus from Medan Mall. The Pinang Baris bus station, 10km west of the city centre, serves buses for destinations to the north or west of the city, including Bukit Lawang, Berastagi and Aceh. Yellow minivan #64 travelling north past the Maimoon Palace up Jl Permuda shuttles back and forth from Pinang Baris (Rp5000), as do DAMRI buses from Medan Mall. For Aceh buses, head to Jl Gajah Mada near the city centre, where nearly a dozen bus companies operate regular trips to Banda Aceh, providing free shuttles to their respective terminals (recommended is PMTOH ☎ 061 415 2546). Connecting Amplas to Pinang Baris is the #64 minivan "Koperasi" (Rp7000). Another important transit point is Padang Bulan, a lay-in by the southwestern corner of the city, from where minibuses from several companies (Sinabung Jaya, Sutra and Karsima) depart for Berastagi. Padang Bulan is linked to the city centre by angkot #41 from the Mesjid Raya area (either Jl RH Juanda or Jl SM Raja). Bypassing the bus terminals are tourist cars such as those operated by Tobali (Jl SM Raja 79C; ☎ 061 732 4471) or easily arranged by most hotels.

Destinations Banda Aceh (every 40min 6.45am–midnight; 12hr); Berastagi (every 20min 7am–10pm; 2hr); Bukit Lawang (every 20min 7am–5pm; 3hr); Bukittinggi (hourly; 18hr); Jakarta (hourly; 48hr); Kutacane (12 daily; 8hr); Padang (hourly; 20hr); Parapat (hourly, last at 6pm; 3hr); Sibolga (daily; 12hr).

INFORMATION

Tourist office Medan's North Sumatra tourist office is at Jl Brig Jend A Yani 107 (Mon–Fri 8am–4pm; ☎ 061 452 8436), just 400m south of Lapangan Merdeka near the *Tip Top Kafé*, though it offers little more than maps and pamphlets.

Tours Worthwhile historical tours of Medan are offered by Tri Jaya Tour & Travel (☎ 061 703 2967, Ⓦ trijaya-travel.com).

GETTING AROUND

Angkots (minivans) The mainstay of the city transport network; they are numbered, and many have names too. The main angkot station is at Sambu, west of the Olympia Plaza, though the Medan Mall stop is more useful for travellers.

Motorized becaks Another convenient way of getting around the city centre. A ride from the Mesjid Raya to the city centre will cost approximately Rp10,000.

ACCOMMODATION

Pondok Wisata Angel Jl SM Raja 70 ☎ 061 736 1078. The most popular backpacker spot in town, with clean, bright rooms with fan or a/c (Rp130,000). Staff are helpful, and there's free wi-fi and tasty food in the downstairs *Angel Café* (*nasi goreng* Rp10,000). **Rp80,000**

Residence Jl Tengah 1 ☎ 061 7760 0980, Ⓦ residencehotelmedan. Clean and all-green hotel by the Grand Mosque with a decent range of compact rooms: top-floor rooms have a/c and TV (Rp145,000), while standard rooms can be a tad musty (ask for one with a window) with a cramped, inside mandi. The café/restaurant downstairs is good value with free wi-fi, and there's a pleasant rooftop garden. **Rp70,000**

Sultan Homestay Jl SM Raja 66 ☎ 061 736 3311, Ⓦ sultanhomestay.com. Right in the thick of the budget hotels, this cheapie has super-basic rooms with shared bathrooms. Escape the heat in one of the otherwise identical a/c rooms upstairs (Rp100,000). Breakfast is included, and there's friendly staff and free wi-fi. **Rp80,000**

Wisma Ronna Jl SM Raja 34C. Offers simple, scruffy fan rooms that are among the cheapest in town; cheaper yet is the roof, where the friendly owner allows guests to set up camp from April–Aug (Rp20,000). Only a few of the rooms have inside bathrooms (Rp80,000). No phone bookings. **Rp70,000**

EATING

Medan has its own style of alfresco eating, where a bunch of stall-owners gather in one place and put out chairs and tables. Servers then bring around menus listing all the food available from each of the stalls.

Amaliun Food Court 3 Jl Amaliun. Lively, open-air food court just across from *Yuki Simpang Raya*, offering a wide range of Indonesian meals, from seafood to *nasi ayam* (Rp20,000), as well as fresh juices and ice-cream floats. A handful of restaurants stay open 24hr. Daily midnight–2am.

★**Cahaya Baru** Jl Cik Ditiro 12. The best of the Indian restaurants in Kampung Keling, set in clean, a/c surroundings. The menu is mostly North Indian (veg/chicken thali Rp20,000/26,000), with a handful of South Indian favourites (*masala dosa* Rp15,000) and local dishes. Authentic flavours, colourful decor and local patrons combine to make you feel as though you're in Delhi. Daily 10am–10pm.

Corner Kafé Raya Jl SM Raja & Sipisopiso 1. The closest thing Medan has to a travellers' café, serving mainly Western food, including fried breakfasts and great burgers (from Rp16,000). There's also a flatscreen TV on the wall, wi-fi and jugs of Bintang for Rp66,000. Daily 10am–midnight.

Merdeka Walk Lapangan Merdeka, Jl Balai Kota. One of Medan's most popular evening hangouts, with a lively ambience and a good selection of outdoor restaurants and fast-food joints serving everything from hamburgers to durian pancakes. Favourite spots among locals include *Nelayan* and *Jala-Jala* for their affordable seafood specialities. Daily 9am–midnight.

Tip Top Restaurant Jl Brig Jen A Yani 92 Ⓦ tiptop-medan.com. Part restaurant, part Medan institution – this is a venerable old place that's been serving European and Indonesian food since 1934. The large menu includes Western, Chinese and Indonesian dishes as well as an extensive selection of cakes (from Rp4000) and ice creams. Daily 10am–9.30pm.

NIGHTLIFE AND ENTERTAINMENT

Medan Club Jl Kartini 36 Ⓣ 061 451 6133. Also known as *MC&P*, this rambling old colonial-style place near Sun Plaza and just behind the governor's office attracts a posh crowd of wealthy locals and expats. The charming restaurant has decent food and is a good spot for a drink. Sometimes it's booked for private events, so call to check. Daily 9.30am–10pm.

Tavern Pub Hotel Danau Toba, Jl Imam Bonjol 17. A friendly pub long-favoured as an expat hangout, although these days the crowd is predominantly local. There's a relaxed atmosphere with draught beer (Rp45,000) and live music – including traditional Batak tunes – but it has become a little seedy. Daily 10pm–2am.

Yuki Simpang Raya Jl SM Raja. A popular bowling alley (Rp8000/game) in the basement of this shopping mall, situated just across from Mesjid Raya. There are also pool tables (Rp20,000/hr). Daily 9am–8pm.

DIRECTORY

Banks There are many banks at the corner of Jl Diponegoro and Jl H Zainul Arifin, including BCA, which offers the best rates in town. There is also a slew of moneychangers along Jl SM Raja near the Grand Mosque. Compare rates before exchanging.

Consulates Australia, Jl Kartini 32 (Ⓣ 061 455 4504); Malaysia, Jl P Diponegoro 43 (Ⓣ 061 453 1342); UK, Jl Kapt Pattimura 459B (Ⓣ 061 821 0559); US, 4th floor, Jl Let Jend MT Haryono A1 (Ⓣ 061 451 9000).

Hospital Gleni International Hospital, Jl Listrik 2A (Ⓣ 061 456 6368).

Immigration Office Jl Mangkubumi 2 (Mon–Fri 8am–4pm; Ⓣ 061 453 3117).

Internet Most hotels and restaurants have wi-fi, while there are many warnets around the city centre. Try Nusanet in the basement of the Yuki Simpang Raya shopping plaza opposite the Mesjid Raya (Rp4000/hr).

Post office Jl Balai Kota, on the northwest corner of Lapangan Merdeka (Mon–Fri 7.30am–6pm, Sat 7.30am–6pm).

4

BANDA ACEH

Capital of Aceh, **BANDA ACEH** is the transit point for **Pulau Weh**, and the gateway to the wonders of Sumatra's most far-flung province. As the crow flies, the city sits closer to India than to the Indonesian capital, and the relatively few foreigners who make it up this far along the spine of Sumatra are rewarded with a vastness of primate-packed rainforests, volcanic peaks, empty beaches, eye-popping dive sites and a welcoming population of predominantly devout Muslims. Since Islam's first landing in the region (see box, p.219), Aceh's proud history was shaped by the sultans of this capital city, strategically set at the entrance to the Straits of Malacca. Recent decades have been turbulent, to say the least, with deadly conflict engulfing the province as the separatist Free Aceh Movement battled with Indonesian forces from 1976 right up

until the heart-wrenching devastation of the 2004 Boxing Day tsunami. The wave (see box, p.220) changed everything, taking more than 70,000 lives in Banda Aceh alone, while bringing an end to the violence. When the waters receded, a massive influx of NGOs and an unprecedented amount of international aid money helped put the city back on its feet, and successful peace talks in 2005 brought much-needed stability. Now, a decade since the calamity, the doors to both city and province are wide open to intrepid explorers.

WHAT TO SEE AND DO

Although most travellers breeze through Banda Aceh to catch the ferry to Pulau Weh, there are numerous attractions around town and some pretty beaches nearby.

4

Mesjid Raya Baiturrahman

The most prominent survivor of the 2004 earthquake and tsunami, Banda Aceh's stunning central mosque (Sat–Thurs 7–11am & 1.30–4pm; donation) is widely held by locals as evidence of divine intervention, and has become a symbol of Acehnese resilience. Italian-designed and Dutch-built in 1881, the mosque blends Mughal and colonial styles, and has expanded over the last century to include seven black, teardrop domes that cap an ornate, whitewashed facade. The adjacent square is a great spot for people-watching, particularly during the Friday prayers. Women should don a headscarf before entering the grounds.

Tsunami Museum

Opened in 2009, Banda Aceh's controversial, ship-shaped **Tsunami Museum** (Sat–Thurs 9am–noon & 2–4.30pm, Fri 9–11.30am & 2.30–4.30pm; free) is the result of US$6.7 million from the Aceh Reconstruction Fund. Its four rambling storeys feature collections of photos and clay models, as well as an electronic simulation of the

SHARIA IN ACEH

Towards the end of the thirteenth century, Aceh became Islam's first foothold in Southeast Asia, a religious heritage of which the Acehnese remain proud. Today, Aceh maintains a reputation as the most strictly **Islamic province** – by far – in all of Indonesia. Sharia-based regulations were introduced in 2001, then greatly expanded in 2009, amounting to a widespread enforcement of Islamic laws and customs in much of the province. Travellers in Aceh should dress modestly and avoid alcohol, gambling, overt homosexuality or fraternizing with members of the opposite sex (outside of marriage) in public areas, the official penalty for which can be up to 60 lashes. The rules are much relaxed, however, in tourist areas such as Palau Weh, where bars serve alcohol, beach-goers bathe in the sun and both genders fraternize without fear of flogging or stoning.

earthquake and tsunami and an "escape hill", built for refuge in the event of another tsunami. The ambitiously designed structure is as much a symbolic monument as it is a museum, with a roof that resembles a tidal wave, walls that depict a traditional Acehnese dance, and a dark, narrow entrance corridor set between 10m-tall walls of water.

Tsunami landmarks

Around town are several prominent reminders of the tsunami. By far the largest of these is the 2,600-tonne **PLTD Apung** (Sat–Thurs 9am–noon & 2–5.30pm, Fri 2–5pm; donation), 1km east of the Tsunami Museum. Formerly an electricity generator docked in Ulee Lheue Harbour, it was swept inland by the giant wave, finally coming to rest almost 3km from the coast. It's now a tourist attraction with a monument to the victims, quaint grounds and ramps leading up to viewing decks that offer good views of the new cityscape, shared by several other (much smaller) boats that also rest on the homes they crushed. The most famous of these is a fishing boat perched directly on the roof of a house in **Lampulo** (daily 9am–5pm; donation), 3km north of the city centre.

Most Acehnese have no way of knowing which of the area's **mass graves** bears the remains of lost loved ones, so they visit them all. The largest, Lambaro, lies halfway along the road to the airport, and is the resting place of 47,781 tsunami victims. The second-largest and most famous mass grave site is Meuraxa, beside the ruins of a hospital in Ulee Lheue and just a few hundred metres from the signposted Tsunami Zero Point.

Dutch Cemetery

Stretching behind the Tsunami Museum is yet another solemn sight, known locally as **Kerkhof** (Dutch for "cemetery"; daily 7am–6pm). Here lie around 2,000 soldiers killed in the Aceh War (1873–1904), hailing from the Netherlands as well as from all across Indonesia, from Java to Ambon. It is the largest Dutch graveyard outside of the Netherlands, and worth a stroll to scan the names inscribed on whitewashed tombstones and large tablets set beside the entrance gate.

Gunongan

Like Shah Jahan's Taj Mahal, **Gunongan** (daily 7am–6pm) was built by Sultan Iskandar Muda (1607–36) to honour his beloved queen. Set near the Tsunami Museum, the small, whitewashed monument, once used as a private royal playground, has a striking design, with cascading petal-shaped walls that represent the mountains of the Pahang state of Malaysia, Kamaliah's native land. Visitors can stroll around the peaceful grounds and – provided there's someone to unlock the gate – up the monument's stairs and narrow walkways.

Lhoknga and Lampu'uk

Among the hardest-hit by the tsunami were the coastal villages of **Lhoknga** and **Lampu'uk**, about 2km apart and 15km southwest of Banda Aceh. Both have world-class waves in season (November–March), but Lampu'uk's beach, bounded to the north by cliffs, is the more attractive spot for swimming. The beaches remain blissfully quiet on weekdays and fill up with escapees from Banda Aceh on weekends. Several homestays and

4

bungalows cater to surfers, among them *Eddie's* (0812 9420 9714, eddieshomestay.com; Rp50,000) in Lhoknga and *Joel's* (0813 7528 7765; joelbungalows@gmail.com) in Lampu'uk, with quaint huts (Rp100,000) pressed right up against the cliffs.

ARRIVAL AND DEPARTURE

By plane You can purchase a visa on arrival at Banda Aceh's dome-capped Sultan Iskandar Muda International Airport, 18km east of the city centre. It is linked by taxi (to/from the airport Rp70,000/100,000), DAMRI buses (to and from Simbun supermarket, beside Mesjid Raya Rp15,000) and *labi labi* (Rp10,000).

Destinations Jakarta (2 daily; 2hr 50min); Kuala Lumpur (daily; 1hr 35min); Medan (7 daily; 1hr); Penang (4 weekly; 1hr 40min).

By bus Bathoh Terminal is 3km south of the city centre along Jl Teuku M Hasan (Rp15,000 by becak), with regular daily departures for Medan (every 40min 7am–11pm; 10hr). There are about a dozen companies; among the better ones is PMTOH (0651 21072).

4

By ferry Boats to Pulau Weh depart from Ulee Lheue Harbour, about 6km northwest of the city centre (Rp50,000 by taxi and Rp25,000 by becak). Check the schedule for further details (see p.165).

INFORMATION

Tourist information The tourist information office (Jl Sultan Iskandar Muda 4 0651 805 2019, bandaacehtourism.com) is centrally located, with helpful, English-speaking staff, as well as useful brochures and maps.

GETTING AROUND

Banda Aceh's important sites are spread out, and using local transportation can be challenging.

Labi labi Called angkots or opelets elsewhere in Indonesia, the packed minibuses of Aceh are known as labi labi. Minibuses through town stop on Jl Diponegoro, by the central Pasar Aceh, and connect the airport (30min; Rp10,000) and harbour (15–20min; Rp5000), as well as Lhoknga and Lampu'uk (both 20min; Rp20,000).

Becak The most pleasant way to get around town, becaks generally charge Rp3000/km. Negotiate a price before setting off. For a reliable English-speaking becak driver who can double as an excellent guide, call Firman (0823 6354 1712).

ACCOMMODATION

There is a dearth of good-value accommodation in Banda Aceh, and many travellers head straight for the ferry to Pulau Weh. Couples may be asked to produce proof of marriage in order to share a hotel room.

Medan Jl Ahmad Yani 17 0651 21501, hotel-medan.com. Pushed up against the river near the centre of town, this business hotel is among the better-value picks in the city centre, with clean, white-tiled a/c rooms with TVs, hot water, a breakfast buffet and wi-fi in the lobby. **Rp245,000**

Prapat Jl Ahmad Yani 19 0651 22159. Just next door to the *Medan Hotel*, this is a good budget option in the town centre. It has a motel vibe, with a pair of three-storey blocks facing each other across a parking lot, and though rooms are somewhat worn, they are kept sufficiently clean, with fans and attached bathrooms. Pricier options come with a/c and TVs (Rp200,000). **Rp100,000**

Siwah Jl Twk Muhammad Daudsyah 18–20 0651 21128. All a/c business rooms in a central location. Deluxe rooms come with shower boxes (Rp368,000), but even the cheaper ones have wi-fi, a simple breakfast, a pair of slippers and a toiletry set. **Rp252,000**

EATING

Ultra-cheap Acehnese food (*mie aceh* Rp10,000), as well as more familiar Indonesian favourites, are easily found at the food stalls that pop up each night all around the city centre. The biggest grouping is at Pasar Malam Rek, in a lot by the junction between Jl SM Raja and Jl Khairil Anwar (daily dusk–2am).

Bunda Jl Pante Pirak 7. Bright, polished restaurant in the centre of town offering friendly service and the city's best Malay and Minang (Padang) food (*nasi pakai ayam* Rp15,000). Good-value combo deals available from Rp22,000. Daily 9am–10pm.

Mie Razali Jl Panglima Polem 85. A long-standing favourite among both locals and *bule*, this unassuming

THE BOXING DAY TSUNAMI

On the peaceful Sunday morning of **December 26, 2004**, 10m-tall waves raced towards the shores of Aceh at speeds of up to 500km/h, triggered by a whopping magnitude 9.1 tremor off the Sumatran coast. The waves obliterated coastal settlements before reaching up to several kilometres inland. When the black, debris-strewn waters receded, the Acehnese were left to assess the damage: 140,000 homes destroyed, 500,000 homeless and 160,000 dead in and around Banda Aceh. The NGOs left years ago, virtually all projects are complete and just about all the aid money has finally been spent – US$7 billion – on over a hundred thousand new homes, thousands of kilometres of roads as well as bridges, schools and other infrastructural projects.

little street-side restaurant opened its doors in 1967 and is now more popular than ever for its tasty Acehnese noodles. Choose from boiled or fried noodles, served dry or in a soup with mushrooms, squid, shrimp (Rp18,000), crab (Rp30,000), or any combination. Daily 10am–10.30pm.

Rasa Baru Utama Jl T Cut Ali 42. Grubby little hole in the wall just across the street from the Mesjid Raya, popular among locals for its super-cheap, authentic Acehnese fare, such as *kari kambing* (curry goat; Rp20,000) and *gulai Aceh* (Rp10,000). Daily 11am–10pm.

DIRECTORY

Banks and exchange There are many ATMs around town, including BII (Jl Panglima Polim 50–52). Belangi at Jl T Cut Ali 68 changes money (Mon–Sat 9am–5pm).

Hospital The state-of-the-art, German-built general hospital (Rumah Sakit Umum Dr. Zainal Abidin) is 5km east of the city centre at Jl Tgk Daud Beureueh 108 (T 0651 34565).

Internet Most hotels and some restaurants have wi-fi, while there are a few internet cafés across the river on Jl Cut Meutiah charging Rp6000/hr.

Post office Near the city centre on Jl H Bendahara 33 (Mon–Thurs 8am–5pm, Fri 8am–noon & 2–5pm).

PULAU WEH

A tiny volcanic island 15km off the northern tip of Sumatra and at the very southern edge of the Andaman Sea, **PULAU WEH** is one of Southeast Asia's very best diving spots. The clear waters around Weh include a pair of protected areas, **Pulau Weh Marine Park** (26 square kilometres) and **Iboih Recreation Park** (13 square kilometres), each featuring a kaleidoscope of reef life and a plenitude of bigger fish. Among the larger pelagics easily spotted here are morays, dolphins, sharks, Napoleon (maori) wrasse, stingrays and barracuda, while in season, divers may also share the waters with manta rays and whale sharks. There are about twenty dive sites scattered around the island, with highlights including the calm, shallow **Rubiah Sea Garden**, the gorgonian-rich caves and arches of **The Canyon**, and the 134m German-built **Sophie Rickmers wreck**. Offering a refreshing respite from the noise, congestion and chaos of mainland Sumatra, Pulau Weh's slow island pace tends to keep travellers around longer than planned.

Known among foreigners as Pulau Weh, it's known locally by the same name as the principal town, Sabang, situated on the island's northeast corner. The main tourist areas are spread along the beaches of Iboih and Gapang to the northeast, as well as palm-fringed Sumur Tiga, a short hop south of the town on the east coast. Diving is year-round, although conditions are optimal during the relatively dry months from October to April.

WHAT TO SEE AND DO

The bulk of Weh's allure lies offshore, but there are a number of worthwhile excursions out of the water. Beyond relaxing on the island's handful of small beaches, popular activities include circling the island's well-kept roads by motorbike, delving into the jungle-clad interior to reach the island's small semi-active volcano, swimming at the pretty **Pria Laot waterfall**, or trekking to the remote **Kilometre Zero marker**, a whitewashed, 20m monument marking the far northwest edge of the archipelago.

Iboih

Most backpackers make a beeline for **Iboih**, the small beach on the island's northwest shore. A laidback base for both diving and snorkelling, its long, spread-out bungalow strip faces directly across from the small, jungle-covered rock of **Pulau Rubiah**, about 100m offshore. The stunning coral reefs in the turquoise waters ringing the island are known as the **Sea Garden**, and offer some of the best snorkelling around Weh.

ARRIVAL AND DEPARTURE

By ferry Fast and slow ferries connect Banda Aceh's Ulee Lheue Harbour with Weh's Balohan Harbour, on the southeast of the island. Plan to arrive at either port at least 45min before departure. Slow ferries (2hr; Rp22,000) depart in each direction on Mon, Tues, Thurs and Fri (2pm from Banda Aceh; 8am from Pulau Weh), and twice on Sat, Sun and Wed (11am & 4pm from Banda Aceh; 8am & 2pm from Pulau Weh). Fast ferries (45min) depart in each direction three times daily (9am, 10am & 4pm from Banda Aceh; 8am, 2.30pm & 4.30pm from Pulau Weh). The two fast ferry operators have ticket windows at each harbour:

4

with Kapal Bahari Express (T 0852 7054 6464) tickets are Rp65,000/75,000 (economy or ac), and with PT Pelnas (T 0852 6131 6401) tickets cost Rp70,000.

INFORMATION

Tourist office The friendly tourism office (T 0652 21513, W budpar.sabangkota.go.id), located just above the town of Sabang on Jl Diponegoro, has good maps and information on the island's attractions.

DIVE OPERATORS

There are only a handful of dive centres on Weh, the two mainstays located at Iboih and Gapang, each offering experienced instructors and PADI courses from Scuba Diver to Divemaster.

Lumba Lumba Diving Centre Gapang Beach T 0811 682787, W lumbalumba.com. Dutch-Indonesian diving outfit that offers top-notch equipment and the best reputation for safety on the island. €54 for two dives, including all gear.

Rubiah Tirta Iboih Beach T 0652 332 4555, W rubiahdivers.com. Started up in the 1970s, this family-run diving centre is the oldest on Weh, and continues to offer bargain prices and considerable discounts to experienced divers. €48 for two dives.

4

GETTING AROUND

Shared taxis connect all corners of the island, most importantly Balohan to Sabang (Rp30,000; 15min), Balohan to Gapang and Iboih (Rp50,000; 30min), Balohan to Sumur Tiga (Rp25,000; 15min) and Sabang to Gapang and Iboih (Rp50,000; 25min).

ACCOMMODATION AND EATING

Weh's most popular backpacker accommodation strip fans out along the beach at Iboih. Nearby Gapang Beach has a wider range of accommodation, from basic huts (Rp50,000) to upmarket bungalows catering to divers. Book ahead in high season.

IBOIH

Iboih Inn T 0811 841570, W iboihinn.com. Friendly place towards the end of the trail from the beach, with a good range of rooms, all with sea views. Small fan huts are situated above the main trail, while the pricier options are among the most luxurious in Iboih: waterfront cottages with hot showers and a/c (Rp400,000). The wi-fi-equipped restaurant is set on a spacious deck over the water, and there's a pier pointing out towards Pulau Rubiah. Payment at check-in. **Rp200,000**

Mama's Overlooking the sandy beach beside Rubiah Tirta, this relaxed little place serves a good mix of Indonesian and Western dishes, with tasty tempe wraps, *mie aceh* (Rp17,000) and chicken coconut soup (Rp24,000). Across from *Mama's* is the equally popular *Dee Dee's*; both are traveller hangouts. Daily 8am–10pm.

★Olala T 0852 6060 7311 or T 0852 4096 1716, W facebook.com/olalacaferestaurant. Friendly, good-value bungalows a 5min walk from the parking lot. Choose between tiny, spartan cheapies up the hill and brand-new bungalows over the water, each with private balcony and hammock (Rp150,000). There's wi-fi in the popular restauraunt, a good spot for meeting fellow travellers. **Rp50,000**

Yulia T 0821 6856 4383. The last guesthouse along the trail from the beach and the quietest spot in Iboih. There are a few ultra-basic huts and three cosy waterfront bungalows (Rp150,000) equipped with balconies, hammocks, private bathrooms and showers. Wi-fi occasionally works in the restaurant. **Rp60,000**

AROUND THE ISLAND

Lumba Lumba Gapang Beach T 0811 682787, W lumbalumba.com/staying.html. Accompanying the popular diving centre is the most comfortable place on Gapang Beach, with a range of options, from simple rooms with shared bathrooms to plush cottages with fridges, baths and broad, sea-facing verandas with hammocks (€30). There's wi-fi, computers for uploading underwater photography and books on marine life. Non-diving guests are welcome as long as there's a spare room. **€12**

> **★TREAT YOURSELF**
>
> A worthy splurge on Weh's east coast, **Freddie's** (Jl Bahagia T 0813 6025 5001, W santai-sabang.com) makes the most of its rocky, palm-strewn setting overlooking the white sand of Sumur Tiga Beach. Varnished wooden walkways connect its en-suite bungalows, each equipped with hammocks, hot showers and sea views from private balconies. Meals are prepared by friendly owner Freddie Rousseau and served buffet-style in the restaurant, which has wi-fi and a free coffee station. **Rp320,000**

DIRECTORY

Banks There are several banks with ATMs along Jl Perdagangan in Sabang, including Mandiri (no. 80), where you can also change money.

Internet There's wi-fi in most guesthouses and computers with internet access at the post office.

Motorbike Rental Available from all guesthouses for Rp100,000/day; or head to Mimi's (daily 8am–10pm; T 0812 6968 1550), in the parking lot at Iboih.

Pharmacy Bunda Farma at Jl Perdagangan 104, Sabang (daily 9am–2pm & 5–10pm).

Post office Jl Perdagangan 53, Sabang (Mon–Thurs 8am–3pm, Fri 8am–noon).

Snorkelling Gear Rental Masks and fins are available all over the island (Rp30,000/day).

BUKIT LAWANG

Tucked away on the easternmost fringes of Gunung Leuser National Park, the popular tourist resort of **BUKIT LAWANG** is home to the **Orang-utan Rehabilitation Centre**. With a wonderful selection of treks into the heart of the jungle, whitewater adventures and some of the world's best opportunities to see orang-utans in the wild, this is a destination worth visiting.

WHAT TO SEE AND DO

Bukit Lawang is in a stunning location below curtains of thick jungle on the banks of the Bohorok River. Aside from swimming in the river or relaxing at one of the many cafés and bars, the main attractions are feeding times behind the **Orang-utan Rehabilitation Centre** and treks in **Gunung Leuser National Park.**

The Bohorok Orang-utan Rehabilitation Centre

The reason for the existence of the tourist resort is the **Bukit Lawang Bohorok Orang-utan Rehabilitation Centre** (Ⓦorangutans-sos.org), founded in 1973 by two Swiss women, Monica Borner and Regina Frey, with the aim of returning captive and orphaned orang-utans into the wild after re-educating them in the art of tree climbing and nest building. Although the rehabilitation programme was suspended a while ago, the centre remains open, having become more a tourist attraction than anything else.

Visitors are allowed to watch the twice-daily (8am & 3pm), hour-long **feeding sessions** that take place on the hill behind the centre. All visitors must have a permit (Rp20,000) from the PHPA office. All being well, you should see at least one orang-utan during the session, and to witness their gymnastics is to enjoy one of the most memorable experiences in Indonesia.

Trekking

Bukit Lawang is the most popular base for organizing **treks** into the Gunung Leuser National Park, with plenty of guides based here. In the forests around Bukit Lawang, your chance of seeing monkeys, gibbons, macaques and – of course – orang-utans is high. A range of treks is on offer, from one-day walks to week-long slogs towards Ketambe in Aceh province, passing through some pristine tracts of primary forest. You may also head deeper into the jungle to reach Tangkahan, which offers elephant-mounted treks and whitewater rafting. One of the most popular and enjoyable options from Bukit Lawang remains the full-day trek, which includes lunch and finishes with a thirty-minute trip to Bukit Lawang through the rapids on an inflatable tube raft. You must have a **permit** (see p.224) for each day that you spend in the park, as well as a **guide** with IGA approval. Fees from the IGA Office (guides in hotels charge slightly more) are €20 for a three-hour trek, €25 for a day and €195 for seven days, which should include a permit for the park, food, tent and a guide. Read guest-book logs for up-to-date trek reviews. Whoever you decide to hire, they should never feed, touch or even call the orang-utans. Keep an eye out for the notorious Mina, a mischievous, semi-wild female known for intimidating visitors and occasionally descending from the trees to give chase.

Tubing

Hurtling down the Bohorok in an inflated inner tube, battered by wild currents – has become a time-honoured tradition in Bukit Lawang. Tubes can be rented from sheds along the river for about Rp15,000 per day. If you're not a strong swimmer, consider tubing on a Sunday, when the locals employ a rescue team along the more dangerous stretches of the river. The rapids can be quite extreme after heavy rain: proceed with caution, especially if you are without a guide, and avoid the section just before the town centre. There is a bridge 12km downstream of the village (2–3hr), from where you can catch a bus back (Rp10,000).

4

4

ARRIVAL AND DEPARTURE

By bus Bukit Lawang's bus terminal is about 1km from the Bohorok Visitor Centre (Rp5000 by motorized becak). The only buses are to Medan's Pinang Baris Terminal (every 20min 5.30am–3.30pm daily; 4hr). Large buses charge Rp40,000, while minibuses charge just Rp20,000.

By private minibus or car You may book a seat in a tourist car or minibus at numerous travel offices around town, among them Tobali (set near the parking area T 0813 7018 9501). These depart in the morning for Medan (4hr; Rp100,000), Berastagi (5hr; Rp135,000) and Danau Toba (7hr; Rp200,000). Some charter trips to Danau Toba take in scenic spots along the way, such as Sipisopiso waterfall at the north end of the lake. For Tangkahan (3hr), you can go by ojek (Rp200,000) or 4WD (Rp500,000). Compare prices and don't be afraid to bargain.

INFORMATION

Tourist information and permits The permit office is part of the excellent Bohorok Visitor Centre (daily 7.30am–3pm), packed with information about the park. You can get a permit (Rp20,000/day plus Rp50,000–150,000 camera fee) to watch the feeding sessions at the orang-utan centre from the PHPA Permit Office (daily 7am–4pm), which overlooks the square to the east, by the visitor centre. Separate trekking permits (Rp20,000/day; Rp25,000/two days; Rp30,000/three days) are available from the IGA (Indonesian Guide Association) Office, though this is always included in the trekking fee with organized hikes.

ACCOMMODATION AND EATING

The best accommodation in Bukit Lawang is clustered along the Bohorok's north shore, opposite to the feeding centre. The best places to eat are the restaurants attached to each guesthouse, and most have live music on Sat nights.

Garden Inn and Restaurant T 0813 9600 0571 (Ujai), W bukitlawang-garden-inn.com. Simple rooms and bungalows (Rp150,000) by the river, with an attached, cosy restaurant serving standard dishes and surrounded by gardens. It has a small library, friendly staff, a French-speaking owner and a pair of hammocks that are great for relaxing in with a cold beer. **Rp100,000**

Green Hill Café and Guest House T 0813 7034 9124 or T 0823 7061 6357, W greenhill-bukitlawang.com. In a fantastic location overlooking the water, offering a range of rooms from simple dorms to treetop bungalows with balconies, hammocks and even jungle bathrooms with sit-down toilets (Rp150,000–250,000). Cheaper rooms come with a shared squat toilet and mandi. Attached café downstairs with live acoustic music at night. **Rp60,000**

★ **Indra Inn** T 0813 9737 5818, W indravalleyinn.com. Small, laidback place right on the river with cheap, simple rooms with private balconies and hammocks, the nicest ones upstairs (Rp100,000). The attached *Valley Café* is also popular, featuring regular acoustic sing-alongs. Ask owner Obiwan or any of the friendly resident guides about the "jungle-style surfing" out back. **Rp60,000**

Jungle Inn T 0813 7016 0173. Situated near the river crossing to the rehab centre, this is the most organized and well-maintained spot in Bukit Lawang, and also offers some of the best nightlife. A wide selection of rooms, all with private bathrooms – from great-value standard doubles, complete with balconies, to a gigantic honeymoon suite with a four-poster bed (Rp450,000). **Rp50,000**

Rain Forest T 0813 6207 0656, E nora_in2003@mailyahoo.com. This cheap little guesthouse overlooking the Bohorok has some ultra-basic rooms consisting of a mattress on the floor, a mosquito net, flimsy rattan walls and shared bathrooms) as well as quite comfortable and clean doubles (Rp100,000). Fantastic meals (and cooking lessons for Rp100,000) prepared by Nora. **Rp40,000**

DIRECTORY

Internet There are a few computers at Harmony Net, near the parking area in town (Rp4000/hr).

Money The nearest ATM accepts only Mastercard and is 11km away in Bohorok village (Rp50,000 return by ojek); better to bring sufficient cash for your stay. There are exchange facilities, though rates are lower than in Medan.

BERASTAGI

Lying 1330m above sea level, 70km southwest of Medan and 25km due north of the shores of Danau Toba, **BERASTAGI** is a cold and scruffy hill station in the centre of the Karo Highlands. It was founded by the Dutch in the 1920s as a retreat from the sweltering heat of Medan, and has been popular with tourists ever since. The town is set among rolling farmland bookended by two huge but climbable **volcanoes**, Gunung Sibayak and dangerously active Gunung Sinabung (see p.227), and provides a perfect base for **trekking**. It's little more than a one-street town, with most accommodation running north of the bus station on Jalan Veteran.

WHAT TO SEE AND DO

Aside from the volcanoes, Berastagi has a handful of attractions; there are lively fresh produce markets behind the bus station and across from the war memorial, and a **Sunday market**

(8am–7pm) is held on top of Gundaling Hill, from where there are great views of Gunung Sinabung when the weather clears. There are also a handful of scenic waterfalls in the vicinity, by far the most impressive being the 120m-high **Sipisopiso**, a few minutes off the main road running south of Kabanjahe. Meanwhile, the surrounding area boasts a smattering of **Karo heritage**.

The Karo villages

During the Dutch invasion of 1904, most of the towns in the Karo Highlands were razed by the Karonese themselves to prevent the Dutch from appropriating them. But there are villages where you can still see the **traditional wooden houses** with their striking palm-frond gables.

The most accessible is **Peceren** (donation), 2km northeast of Berastagi. If you're coming from the town, take the road to Medan and turn down the lane on your right after the *Green Garden* hotel. There are three traditional houses here, though the village is probably the least picturesque example. There are three more villages to the south of Berastagi, but many of the houses are slipping into a terrible state of repair. **Lingga** (donation) is probably the best-preserved Karo village in the area, with ten traditional houses in various states of disrepair. It is possible to walk or cycle here (*Losmen Sibayak* has good maps), otherwise take a yellow Karya minibus (Rp4000) from the bus station in Berastagi to Kabenjahe, then another minibus to Lingga (Rp3000). Coming back, there are red Sigantangsira minibuses departing infrequently direct to Berastagi (Rp5000).

ARRIVAL AND DEPARTURE

By bus Buses to Padang Bulan in Medan (around every 30min 6am–8pm; Rp12,000; 3hr) leave every day from the bus station at the southern end of Jl Veteran and can be hailed from anywhere along the main street. Most hotels, including Losmen Sibayak, arrange direct tourist buses to Medan (2hr; Rp80,000), Bukit Lawang (4hr 30min; Rp120,000) and Parapat (for Danau Tobal; 4hr 30min; Rp120,000), which is also linked by public buses (5hr): from Berastagi, the first minibus gets you to Kabenjahe (Rp4000; 25min), the second to Siantar (Rp25,000; 3hr) and the third to the jetty at Parapat (Rp20,000; 1hr 15min; last departure 4pm). Less frequent buses also connect to Kutacane (Rp70,000; 5hr).

INFORMATION

Tourist office The friendly tourist office at Jl Gundaling 1 (Mon–Sat 8am–5pm; ⓣ 0628 91084) is just over the road from the post office, and offers scale-challenged maps, though information at most hotels tends to be at least as helpful.

Trekking The Losmen Sibayak and Wisma Sibayak can set you up with good guides for trekking, or call Awan, a veteran guide often found at *Talitha* (ⓣ 0813 7072 1793, ⓔ awan072@hotmail.com).

ACCOMMODATION

Losmen Sibayak Jl Veteran 119 ⓣ 0628 91122. Entered through a busy travel office in the centre of town, this friendly, no-frills hotel is set back from the noise of the main road. The rooms are a bit worn, but the best of them

4

THE KARO

Covering an area of almost five thousand square kilometres, from the northern tip of Danau Toba to the border of Aceh, the **Karo Highlands** comprise an extremely fertile volcanic plateau at the heart of the Bukit Barisan mountains. The plateau is home to more than two hundred farming villages and two main towns: the regional capital, Kabanjahe, and the popular market town and tourist resort of **Berastagi**.

According to local legend, the Karo people were the first of the Batak groups to settle in the highlands of North Sumatra and, as with all Batak groups, the strongly patrilineal Karo have their own language, customs and rituals, most of which have survived, at least in a modified form, to this day. These include convoluted wedding and funeral ceremonies, both of which can go on for days, and the **reburial ceremony**, held every few years, where deceased relatives are exhumed and their bones are washed with a mixture of water and orange juice.

Today, the vast majority of the Karo are Christian, with minorities adhering to Islam and the traditional Karo religion. However, all members of Karonese society are bound by obligations to the clan, which are seen as more important than any religious duties.

come with squat toilets and cold showers (Rp75,000). There's wi-fi in the restaurant downstairs, which serves delicious pizzas (from Rp45,000) and other travellers' favourites. **Rp60,000**

Talitha Guest House Jl Kolam Renang 60B T 0628 91480 or T 0813 7066 4252. Near the 4-star *Sinabung Hotel* (reached by yellow Karya (KT) angkots heading up past the fruit market from the war memorial; Rp2000), *Talitha* has six spotless rooms attached to the Dutch-speaking owner's home, set amid manicured lawns away from the bustle and noise of the city centre. The bigger rooms come with hot water, while tea and coffee are provided around the clock. Breakfasts Rp25,000. **Rp100,000**

Wisma Sibayak Jl Udara 1 T 0628 91104, E morina_pelawi@yahoo.co.id. One of Sumatra's longest-established hostels, with a homely feel and spacious, simple rooms with private balconies, bathrooms and hot showers (Rp100,000). There's wi-fi until 10pm, a pleasant grassy sitting area and a cosy restaurant (coconut potato curry Rp25,000). It's worthwhile perusing the worn travellers' comment books here. **Rp50,000**

4

EATING

Every evening from 7pm–3am, rows of street stalls pop up along Jl Veteran serving everything from *ikan bakar* (grilled fish) to hamburgers.

Mexico Coffee Resto Jl Veteran 18 T 0628 92707. This relatively new restaurant off the main street has a long, bright dining area with a fast-food feel. Aside from coffee, a good chunk of the menu is fried chicken (from Rp60,000) and Indonesian dishes (*gado gado* Rp18,000), while there's free wi-fi and an attached hotel with spotless but pricey rooms that have hot water (Rp250,000). Daily 7.30am–11pm.

Raymond Café Jl Trimurti. Friendly little tourist café just off Jl Veteran that doubles as a local hangout, serving a mix of Western and Indonesian dishes as well as steaks and curries (Rp15,000). There's wi-fi and computers with internet connection, and it's a good place for cheap drinks (chai tea Rp6000). Daily 7am–11pm.

DIRECTORY

Banks There's a BNI and BRI bank, each with ATM, on either side of *Losmen Sibayak*, which is the best place to change US dollars or travellers' cheques.

Internet Raymond Café (Rp3000/hr) is one of the few internet cafés not occupied by gamers.

Pharmacy There are several health centres on Jl Veteran, including Apotek Berastagi Jaya (no. 94).

Police The police station is situated by the war memorial, just off Jl Veteran.

Post office The post office (Mon–Thurs 7.30am–3pm, Fri 7.30am–noon & Sat 7.30am–1pm) is next to the police station.

VOLCANOES AROUND BERASTAGI

There are two active volcanoes more than 2000m high in the immediate vicinity of Berastagi: **Sibayak** (2094m), to the north of town, is possibly the most accessible volcano in the whole of Indonesia, and takes just two hours to climb up and two hours down, while the hike up **Sinabung** (2452m) – which has seen dramatic eruptions of late – to the southwest of town, is longer and tougher, involving a bus or taxi to the trailhead. The long lists of missing trekkers plastered all around Berastagi prove that these climbs are not as straightforward as they may at first seem. The tourist office and losmen urge climbers always to take a guide – though for Sibayak a guide is unnecessary provided there's good visibility and you're climbing with someone else. For both volcanoes, set off early in the morning. Pick up a map from *Wisma Sibayak* or *Losmen Sibayak* and bring some trail food, warm clothing, and – if you're looking to take advantage of the hot springs at the foot of Sibayak – your swimming costume and a towel, too.

Gunung Sibayak

Although it's the easier of Berastagi's volcanoes, it's wise to get an early start or else consider taking along a guide: plenty of hikers have become lost on this route. Take a Kama van (Rp3000) to the coffee shop by the trailhead, where you must register your name and pay the hiking fee (Rp4000). From here, walk past the angkot station and you'll begin the series of up-and-down dips leading to the summit. Near the top, look out for some rough steps cut into the embankment on your left. If you reach the end of the tarmac, you've gone too far.

Finding the path back down to the hot springs is the hardest part of the walk: if you're not certain of the way down, walk back down the way you came up. For those who wish to visit the hot springs, however, at the crater rim you'll see a cluster of antennae high up on a pinnacle. Facing the antennae, walk down in an anticlockwise direction to about 3 o'clock and climb up to your right from there. At the top you'll see a path running along the rim. Turn right, and after about 50m

you'll come to the first couple of broken steps – little more than concrete strips in the ground at this stage. As you follow the steps, you'll descend through a forest and pass a grove of bamboo before emerging at a geothermal plant. Below this is a series of **hot springs** (Rp5000) – a great reward for a hard trek.

Afterwards, angkots leave occasionally for Berastagi (Rp8000; last one departs 5pm); otherwise you'll have to continue along the road for several kilometres to the junction with the main road and pick one up from there (Rp4000).

Gunung Sinabung

Indonesia's latest volcanic surprise, **Gunung Sinabung** rumbled to life with a dramatic eruption in 2010 that came after several centuries of silence, killing two people and forcing 30,000 to evacuate. Several years later, beginning in September 2013, more eruptions rocked the region, forcing over 20,000 to evacuate as of January 2014, ejecting 9km-high ash plumes and causing disruption as far afield as Medan, where visibility was reduced to just 20m. At the time of writing, the highest level of alert was still in place.

The roughly eight-hour return hike to the summit begins beside a restaurant to the north of **Danau Kawar** (Rp5000 hiking fee). Continue through cabbage fields for approximately an hour before entering fairly thick jungle, after which the hike becomes relentlessly tough. Having left the jungle, you soon find yourself scrambling up some steep and treacherous rocky gullies. A couple of hours later, you'll be standing on the edge of a cliff looking down into Gunung Sinabung's pair of craters. Take care when walking around up here, as the paths are crumbling and it's a long way down. A guide is highly recommended for this trip.

To reach Danau Kawar, take either a bus (Rp10,000; hourly departures from the bus station starting 7.30am; 45min) or taxi (Rp350,000 return for up to seven people, including the driver's long wait by the lake). Unless you're super in-shape, the latter option is recommended as the last bus from Danau Kawar heads back to town at 4pm.

PARAPAT

Sprawled along the eastern shores of Danau Toba, the bustling town of **PARAPAT** offers wonderful views across the lake. It's used primarily as a stopover, with most visitors staying just long enough to catch the ferry to Samosir. Perched at a pleasant 900m above sea level, the town is divided in two – the **resort**, crammed with ageing hotels and souvenir shops by the water, and the commercial sector to the east, in the hills away from the lake.

ARRIVAL AND DEPARTURE

By bus Buses arriving in Parapat drive through the resort to Tigaraja harbour before heading back to the bus station, 2km east of town. Frequent opelets connect the harbour with the bus station (Rp3000).

Destinations Berastagi (5hr; via Siantar 1hr 15min) and Kabenjahe (3hr), from which buses link Berastagi until 8pm (25min); Bukittinggi (3 daily; Rp190,000/220,000 for a/c; 16hr); Medan (every 45min; Rp35,000; 5hr); Padang (2 daily; Rp220,000/250,000 for a/c; 18hr); Sibolga (daily; 6hr).

By private minibus or car Private tourist transport services are faster, have a/c and break down much less often. Call to book ahead during high season. The following are clustered beside Tigaraja harbour: Bagus Taxi (T 0813 6130 1344 or T 0813 6239 7309), Tobali Tour (T 0625 41103) and Raja Taxi Trans (T 0852 7005 5172). All charge roughly the same: Bukittinggi (Rp270,000; 13hr); Berastagi (Rp120,000; 4hr); Bukit Lawang (Rp160,000; 7hr); Medan (Rp80,000; 4hr 30min).

By ferry Daily ferries connect Tigaraja harbour with Tuk Tuk on Pulau Samosir (hourly in each direction, departing from Tigaraja 8.30am–7pm; departing from Tuk Tuk 7am–5.30pm; Rp10,000; 30min). Arriving in Tuk Tuk, ferries usually stop at several quays around the peninsula: name your chosen hotel and you'll be instructed where to disembark. When leaving Tuk Tuk, wave down a ferry from any hotel's quay.

ACCOMMODATION AND EATING

There are several budget hotels right around the harbour and plenty of cheap *rumah makan* along Jl Haranggaol.

Charlie's Jl Pekan Tiga Raja 7 T 0821 6622 3027. Situated on the market square next to the ferry terminal, *Charlie's* is run by a local music legend with loads of information on the area. If you're lucky he'll share his ballads of Danau Toba. Windowless rooms in the back are gloomy; the ones in front are slightly better. There's a small sitting area overlooking the market, a simple menu and wi-fi. **Rp80,000**

Hong Kong Jl Haranggaol 9–11. Still the busiest place in town, with spotless surroundings and a comprehensive

4

Chinese menu, offering everything from sweet-and-sour pork to fried pig liver (both Rp47,000). Free wi-fi. Daily 8am–10pm.

Soloh Jaya Jl Haranggaol 51 ⓣ 0625 41617. Among the best-value digs in town, with well-kept rooms, pleasant courtyards and a spacious terrace offering good views of the town. The bright, airy rooms at the top have big windows and bathrooms with cold showers, and are worth the extra rupiahs (Rp100,000). **Rp80,000**

DIRECTORY

Banks There's a BRI ATM on Jl Sisingamangaraja, a Bank Sumut on Jl Haranggaol next to *Marina*, and a Mandiri by the bus station.

Internet Several warnets are spread along Jl Haranggaol, including *Harry Net* (daily 10am–midnight; Rp3000/hr), about 50m up from the market.

Pharmacy Robika on Jl Haranggaol 83 (daily 7am–10pm) supplies basic medicines.

Post office Jl Sisingamangaraja, opposite the BRI ATM (Mon–Fri 7.30am–4pm, Sat 7.30am–2pm).

DANAU TOBA AND PULAU SAMOSIR

Lying right in the middle of the province at 525m, jewel-like **DANAU TOBA** is Southeast Asia's largest freshwater lake. It was formed about 80,000 years ago in the wake of a colossal volcanic eruption, the resulting caldera eventually buckling under massive pressure and collapsing in on itself to create the steep-walled basin now occupied by the lake. A second, smaller volcanic eruption, 50,000 years after the first, created the Singapore-sized island in the middle of the lake, **Pulau Samosir**. Connected by ferry from **Parapat** on the lake's eastern shore, this island is the cultural and spiritual heartland of the Toba Batak people and one of the most pleasant and fascinating destinations in Indonesia.

4

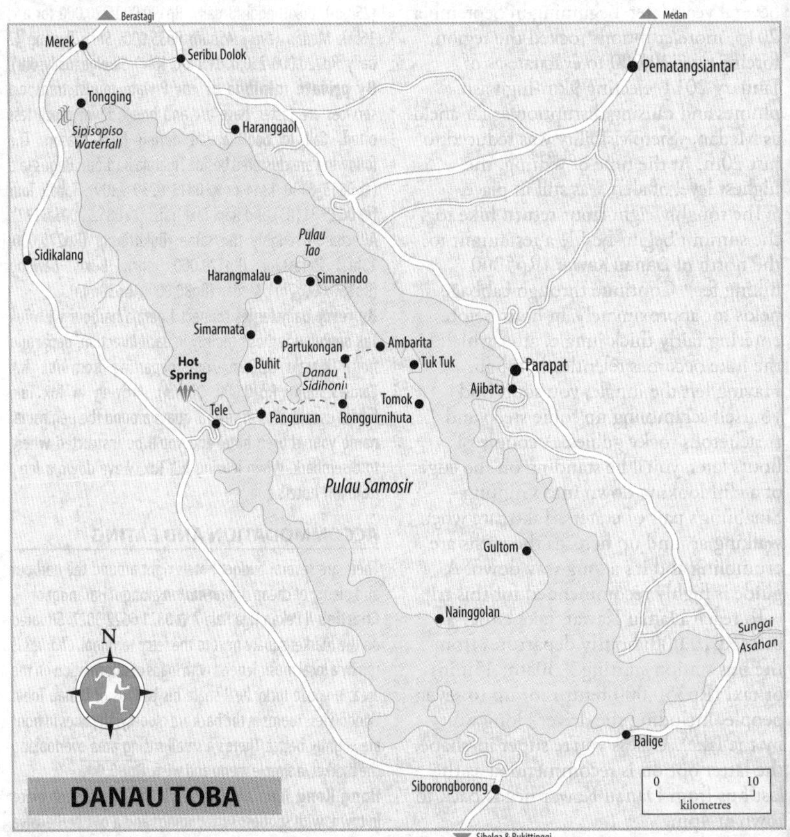

WHAT TO SEE AND DO

Pulau Samosir is arguably the best spot in Sumatra in which to relax for a few days on a hammock by the azure water. Most tourists make for the eastern shores of Samosir, directly across the lake from Parapat, where there's a string of enjoyable resorts, the main one being Tuk Tuk, with plenty of hotels, restaurants and bars. From here, you can trek into the deforested hills within the centre of Samosir or circle the island's coastline by motorbike, calling in at tiny Batak villages that have flamboyant tombs and distinctive concave-roofed houses, as well as the island's cultural centre of Simanindo, on Samosir's northern shore.

Tuk Tuk

The waters that lap the shores of **Tuk Tuk** are safe for **swimming**, though they can be dirty; the roped-off section of the lake by *Carolina's*, complete with pontoons, canoes and a diving board, is the most popular place. There are also a few activities on offer in Tuk Tuk, including guided treks through the interior of the island (Rp750,000) and speedboat trips to Tomok, Ambarita and Simanindo (Rp500,000/hr). You can also rent **bicycles** (Rp25,000/day) and **motorbikes** (Rp80,000/day), should you want to visit the more far-flung reaches of the island.

Tomok

Tomok, 3km south of Tuk Tuk, is the most southerly of the resorts on the east coast; dozens of virtually identical souvenir stalls line the main street. Tomok's most famous sight is the early nineteenth-century stone **tomb of Raja Sidabutar** (daily 7am–7pm; donation), the chief of the first tribe to migrate to the island. You'll be asked to drape an *ulos* (traditional Batak scarf) across your shoulder as a mark of respect before entering. The sarcophagus has a Singa face – a part-elephant, part-buffalo creature of Toban legend – carved into one end, and a small stone effigy of the king's wife on top of the lid. On the way to Ambarita from Tomok, due west of Tuk Tuk, is the tiny village of **Garoga**, from where you can hike to the spectacular waterfall of the same name (after rainfall). Ask locals for directions.

Ambarita

At the foot of a small banyan in **Ambarita** lies a curious collection of stone chairs (daily 6.30am–6pm; Rp6000), one of which is mysteriously occupied by a stone statue. Most of the villagers will tell you that two centuries ago, this site played host to royal conferences and the beheadings of criminals; others say the chairs are actually less than fifty years old, the work of a local mason who copied drawings of the original.

Simanindo

Simanindo lies at the northern end of the island, 15km beyond the town of Ambarita. The **Museum Huta Bolon Simanindo** (daily 9am–5pm; Rp10,000) is housed in the former longhouse of Raja Simalungun, a Batak king, and showcases a range of historic artefacts, including spears, Chinese porcelain, magical charms, a wooden *guri guri* (ashes urn) and the royal boat. There are daily Batak puppet dance performances (Mon–Sat 10.30am, Sun 11.35am; Rp50,000).

Simarmata and Pangururan

Continuing round to the western side of the island takes you to **Simarmata**, halfway between Simanindo and Pangururan, and one of the best-preserved Batak villages on Samosir. There's little to see in **Pangururan** itself, though there's a hot spring across the bridge in the village of Tele. *Rico Melati*, a restaurant at the top of the hill, has great views and the nicest hot-spring pool in the area (free for diners; Rp5000 if you just want to swim).

Trekking across Samosir

The hills in the centre of Samosir tower 700m above the lake, and at the heart of the island is a large plateau and **Danau Sidihoni**, a body of water about the size of a large village pond. It's a ten-hour walk from one side of the island to the other, but a stopover in one of the villages

4

on the plateau is usually necessary. Most begin in Ambarita on the eastern shore, on the uphill path, from where it's two to three hours' climb to the tiny hilltop village of **Partukongan** – aka Dolok or "summit" – the highest point on Samosir. There are a couple of ultra-cheap homestays here, *John's* and *Jenny's*, and *Peter's* in the next village on the trail, **Ronggurnihuta**. The villagers can be a bit vague when giving directions, so take care and check frequently with passers-by that you're on the right trail.

Ronggurnihuta is a three- or four-hour walk away, with **Pangururan** three to fours hours further on at the end of a tortuously long downhill track (18km) that passes **Danau Sidihoni** on the way. Arrive in Pangururan before 5pm to catch the last bus back to the eastern shore (Rp15,000); otherwise, stay at the *Wisata Samosir* (☎0626 20050) at Jalan Dr TB Simatupang 42 by the bus stop.

4

ACCOMMODATION AND EATING

Nearly all accommodation on Samosir is found on the Tuk Tuk peninsula. Tell the ferryman which hotel you're going to and he'll drop you off at the nearest quay.

Bagus Bay Homestay ☎0625 451287, Ⓦbagus-bay.page.tl. One of the best budget options on Tuk Tuk, with ultra-cheap boxy rooms sharing a grubby latrine (a bargain for single travellers at Rp30,000), comfortable deluxe rooms with cosy terraces and hot water (Rp200,000), and more options in between. It also has an internet café, billiards, volleyball, bike rental, in-house massage, a bar and a lengthy menu in the restaurant, which hosts Batak performances (Wed & Sat 8pm). **Rp40,000**

Carolina's ☎0625 451210, Ⓔcarolina@indosat.net.id. Classy Batak-style bungalows, each with a lakeside view and a small slice of beach (Rp120,000), while the cheapest rooms on the hill are also good value. There's a huge, breezy restaurant with wi-fi and a range of information on the island at the reception. **Rp75,000**

Liberta Homestay ☎0625 451035, Ⓔliberta_homestay@yahoo.co.id. Cheap, simple rooms in Batak-style cottages with an attached restaurant and a friendly owner. Rooms with hot water from Rp65,000. Liberta lies on the southwest side of the peninsula – get off the ferry at Bagus Bay harbour. **Rp50,000**

Merlyn Guesthouse ☎0813 6116 9130, Ⓔmerlynguesthouse@mail.com. Run by a German-Indonesian couple, this centrally located little cheapie has a great backpacker vibe. All of its smart, simple rooms come with hot water, somewhat dim bathrooms and great lake views. It's an easy swim straight out from here to a rocky little island. The attached café is also good value. **Rp70,000**

Romlan's ☎0625 451386, Ⓔromlantuktuk@yahoo.com. A wonderful isolated location gives this scruffy little guesthouse its charm. The cheapest rooms are in traditional bungalows overlooking the water to Parapat, all rooms come with hot water, and there's a pleasant open-air restaurant with free wi-fi. **Rp100,000**

Samosir Cottages ☎0625 451170, Ⓦsamosircottages.com. A long-standing favourite on the peninsula, with rooms ranging from the basic to luxury bungalows (with hot water and a bathtub; Rp200,000) overlooking the lake. It has wi-fi, satellite TV, ping-pong, a pool table and a good restaurant and bar that hosts regular Batak music and dance performances (Wed & Sat 8.30pm). **Rp80,000**

NIGHTLIFE

Brando's Blues Bar Just a 2min walk from *Samosir Cottages*, this is Tuk Tuk's most happening nightlife venue, mixing reggae beats with thumping dance music and packing its spacious dancefloor with a local crowd at weekends. Pool tables, cocktails and ice-cold Bintang (bottle Rp35,000). Daily 8am–2am.

Anju Karaoke ☎0813 9797 9757 A pair of sofa-decked karaoke rooms in a roadside annexe of *Anju Cottages*, next door to *Samosir Cottages*, along with a simple menu of bar food and drinks (Bintang Rp30,000). Book ahead on Sat nights (9am–10pm Rp50,000/hr, 10pm–midnight Rp70,000/hr). Daily 9am–midnight.

DIRECTORY

Banks Guesthouses and a handful of moneychangers offer exchange services at generally poor rates. The nearest ATM is at the BRI in Ambarita.

Bicycle and motorbike rental Available from almost all of Tuk Tuk's hotels (bikes/motorbikes Rp25,000/90,000).

Books Penny's Bookstore (daily 8am–10pm) in Tuk Tuk has a huge range of novels, DVDs, guidebooks and maps for rent, buy or exchange.

Cooking classes The friendly owner of *Juwita Café* (☎0625 451217, Ⓔkikiandrea07@yahoo.com), based just north of *Carolina's*, offers Indonesian cooking lessons (from Rp150,000).

Health centre There's a 24hr health centre near Penny's Bookstore (☎0625 451075).

Internet There is wi-fi at most cafés and guesthouses, and computers at *Bagus Bay* (Rp10,000/hr).

Massage *Bagus Bay Homestay* in Tuk Tuk has an on-site massage therapist (Rp80,000).

Post office The nearest post office is in Ambarita, but you can ask to use the postboxes at local shops.

Tours Many of the guesthouses, in particular *Samosir Cottages, Bagus Bay Homestay* and *Carolina's*, have their own travel agencies, which can book transport and tours.

PADANG

The seaside city of **PADANG** is an important transport hub for the rest of Sumatra. Famous for its spicy local cuisine, **Makanan Padang** (Padang food), the city's climate is equally extreme: hot and humid, with the highest rainfall in Indonesia at 4508mm a year. For most travellers, Padang is little more than a transit point for Bukittinggi or the nearby Mentawai Islands, especially since the devastating 7.9-magnitude earthquake in 2009, which killed 1300 people, leaving around one million temporarily homeless. Some of the damage was irreversible: more than eighty percent of

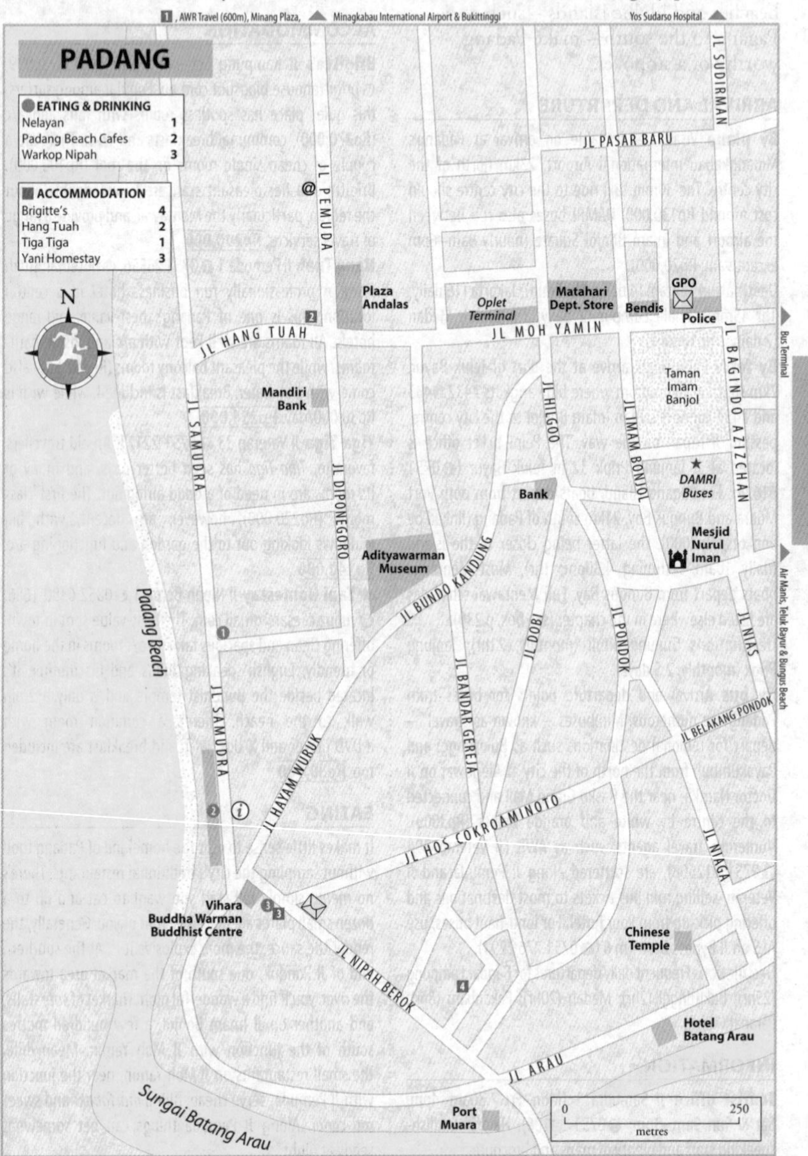

the exhibits at the **Adityawarman Museum** (Mon–Sat 8.30am–4pm; Rp2000) were destroyed. Traces of the earthquake remain scattered throughout the buzzing central market around Jalan Pasar Baru, though Padang today is as lively as ever. Its leafy boulevards, café-lined coast, attractive nearby beaches and idyllic islands – such as Pagang to the south – make Padang worthy of a stopover.

ARRIVAL AND DEPARTURE

By plane Visas are available on arrival at Padang's Minangkabau International Airport, 23km north of the city centre. The 30min taxi ride to the city centre should cost around Rp130,000. DAMRI buses also run between the airport and Imam Bonjol Square (hourly 6am–6pm except 9am; Rp20,000).

Destinations Batam (4 daily; 1hr 5min); Jakarta (16 daily; 1hr 45min); Kuala Lumpur (2 daily; 1hr 5min); Medan (2 daily; 1hr 10min).

4 **By ferry** Pelni boats arrive at the port of Teluk Bayur, 7km south of town, from where blue angkots #432, #433 and #434 connect Taman Imam Bonjol to the city centre, passing Jl Nipah on the way. The Pelni ticket office is located at Jl Tanjung Priok 32 in Teluk Bayur (T 0751 61624). For Pagang island, boats depart from both Port Muara and Bungus Bay, 21km south of Padang (linked by angkots; Rp7000), the latter being closer to the island (daily 10am, returning 4.30pm; 1hr). Most Mentawai boats depart from Bungus Bay. Full Mentawai schedules are listed elsewhere in the chapter (see box, p.239).

Destinations Gunung Sitoli (monthly; 21hr); Tanjung Priok (monthly; 2.5 days).

By bus Arrival and departure points for buses from Padang are numerous. Minibuses – known as "travel" – depart for regional destinations such as Bukittinggi and Payakumbuh from the north of the city at Aie Tawar on Jl Doctor Hamka, near the Basko Grand Mall and connected to the centre by white and orange oplets (Rp3000). Numerous travel agents, such as AWR (Jl Veteran 29A T 0751 812508), are scattered along Jl Pemuda and Jl Veteran, selling minibus tickets to most destinations and offering pick-up from your hotel. For long-haul buses, use ALS on Jl Bypass Baru Km 6 (T 0751 776 2291).

Destinations Frequent daily departures for Bandar Lampung (25hr); Bukittinggi (2hr); Medan (20hr); Pekanbaru (8hr); Parapat (18hr).

INFORMATION

Tourist office Jl Samudra 1 (Mon–Fri 7.30am–4pm, Sat & Sun 9am–3pm; T 0751 34186). Helpful English-speaking staff and plenty of maps and brochures.

GETTING AROUND

Buses and angkots Local angkots (Rp3000) run from 6am to 10pm daily. Angkots run from Jl Moh Yamin, in the market area. Look out for the route number and destination signs suspended high above the oplet waiting area.

Bendis Stacks of horse-drawn carriages hang out by the central market, just east of the oplet terminal. Short hops around town will cost around Rp10,000.

ACCOMMODATION

Brigitte's Jl Kampung Sebelah 1/14D T 0751 36099, W brigittehouse.blogspot.com.au. Popular among surfers, this quiet place has spotless rooms with fans and a/c (Rp270,000), communal breakfasts and wi-fi. There are a couple of cheap single rooms on the roof (Rp100,000). Brigitte and her pleasant staff are knowledgable about the region, particularly the Mentawai, and provide a range of travel services. **Rp200,000**

Hang Tuah Jl Pemuda 1 T 0751 26556, W hotelhangtuah.com. A professionally run business hotel in a central location, this is one of Padang's best-value mid-range hotels. All rooms are well kept with a/c and inside bathrooms, while the pleasant balcony rooms (Rp351,500) also come with hot water. Breakfast is included, while wi-fi is Rp30,000/day. **Rp254,000**

Tiga-Tiga Jl Veteran 33 T 0751 22173. An old travellers' favourite, *Tiga-Tiga* has seen better days, and many of its rooms are in need of a good airing out. The first-class rooms (Rp220,000), however, are decent, with big windows looking out to the garden and functioning a/c. **Rp140,000**

★**Yani Homestay** Jl Nipah Berok 1 T 0852 6380 1686, E yuliuz.caesar@gmail.com. The best-value spot in town, offering clean and spacious fan and a/c rooms in the home of friendly, English-speaking Julius and his mother. It's located beside the Buddhist temple and is only a 2min walk to the beach. There's a common room with a DVD player and X-box; wi-fi and breakfast are included too. **Rp80,000**

EATING

It makes little sense to visit the homeland of Padang food without sampling the city's traditional restaurants. There's no menu: simply tell staff you want to eat and up to a dozen small plates are placed in front of you. Generally, the redder the sauce, the more explosive it is. At the southern end of Jl Pondok, due south of the market area towards the river, you'll find a wonderful night market of *sate* stalls, and another on Jl Imam Bonjol, a few hundred metres south of the junction with Jl Moh Yamin. Meanwhile, the small restaurants on Jl Moh Yamin, near the junction with Jl Pemuda, serve cheap, filling *martabaks* and sweet *roti canai*. Along Jl Pemuda things can get somewhat seedy at night.

Nelayan Jl Mongonsidi 4B–E ☎ 0751 32238. A sparkling two-storey seafood restaurant with views of the beach. The top floor has a/c and nightly live music, and friendly owner Chandra is more than happy to show customers the daily catch. Mains start from about Rp40,000, and groups can order by the kilo (crab Rp250,000; lobster Rp400,000). Daily 11am–11pm.

Padang Beach Cafés Jl Samudra. The beach has a collection of nondescript cafés and restaurants serving simple Indonesian food and drinks (*nasi goreng* Rp10,000). The tables on the sand are the best spot in the city to enjoy a cold beverage and watch the sunset. Daily 8am–after midnight.

Warkop Nipah Jl Nipah Berok 1D. Bright and spacious whitewashed café next door to *Golden Homestay* and two doors down from *Yani*. A popular breakfast and lunchtime hangout, it features a range of Indonesian favourites cooked just off the roadside (*nasi goreng* Rp12,000). Daily 7am–2pm.

DIRECTORY

Banks and exchange Bank of Central Asia, Jl H Agus Salim 10A; Bank Dagang Negara, Jl Bagindo Azizchan 21; Bank Negara Indonesia, Jl Dobi 1. ATMs are everywhere.

Hospital Yos Sudarso Hospital, Jl Situjuh 1 (☎ 0751 33230).

Internet There are plenty of warnets around town, and many hotels now have wi-fi. The warnet on Jl Pemuda (Rp4000hr) has a good connection.

Post office The main post office is conveniently located at Jl Bagindo Azizchan 7, just north of the junction with Jl Moh Yamin (Mon–Fri 7.30am–6pm, Sat & Sun 9am–3pm).

BUKITTINGGI

Situated on the eastern edge of Ngarai Sianok Canyon with the conical peaks of Merapi and Singgalang rising to the south, the bustling town of **BUKITTINGGI** is a wonderful base for exploring the Minangkabau Highlands. Although chaotic and sprawling, its town centre, which is of most interest to visitors, is relatively compact and easy to negotiate. The most useful **landmark** is Djam Gadang, the clock tower at the junction of Jalan A Yani (the main thoroughfare) and Jalan Sudirman (the main road leading out of town to the south). Bukittinggi's **Pasar Atas** (Upper Market) stretches to the south of the tower, while down the hill to the north and west lies **Pasar Bawah** (Lower Market), both of which swell to bursting point on Wednesdays, Saturdays and Sundays. Jalan A Yani, 1km from north to south, is the tourist hub of Bukittinggi, and most

4

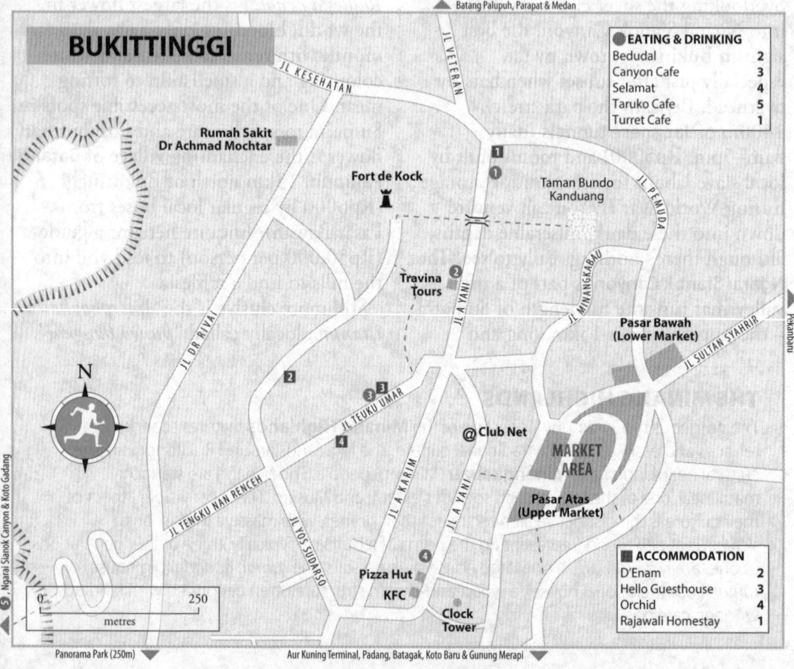

of the sights, hotels, restaurants and shops that serve the tourist trade are on this street or close by. This is one of Sumatra's most pleasant towns in which to spend a few days, boasting a range of restaurants and hotels and a plenitude of attractions in the surrounding area, which includes the rafflesia reserve at **Batang Palupah**, beautiful **Ngarai Sianok Canyon**, spectacular **Harau Valley** and the enormous palace of **Pagaruyung**.

WHAT TO SEE AND DO

A few hundred metres to the north of the clock tower, **Fort de Kock** (daily 7.30am–6pm; Rp10,000) was built by the Dutch in 1825. There's little left of the original structure but some old cannons and parts of the moats. The fort is linked by a footbridge over Jalan A Yani to the park, Taman Bundo Kanduang, which has a depressing zoo and a Minangkabau museum (same hours; Rp2500) housed in a beautiful *rumah gadang* constructed in 1934.

Much more pleasant is a stroll around **Panorama Park** (7.30am–5.30pm daily; Rp5000), perched on a lip of land overlooking the sheer cliff walls down into Ngarai Sianok Canyon, the best sight in Bukittinggi town by far, especially just after sunset when bats fly overhead. Beneath the park stretch 1400m of **Japanese tunnels** (daily 8am–5pm; Rp5000) and rooms built by local slave labour for ammunition storage during World War II. You can venture down into these dank, miserable depths, although there's nothing really to see. The **Ngarai Sianok Canyon** is part of a rift valley that runs the full length of Sumatra – the canyon here is 15km long and around 100m deep, with a glistening river wending its way along the bottom.

Koto Gadang

Just beyond the western edge of the **Ngarai Sianok Canyon** lies **Koto Gadang**, a small Minangkabau village of silversmiths. Though linked by occasional oplets (15min; Rp2000), it's a scenic walk from Bukittinggi. From Jalan Tengku Umar continue along up and over the top, passing the Japanese tunnels on your left as you descend the canyon. Continue along through the U-bend in the track and over the bridge, to where you will find a bamboo warung and a footpath that leads up the canyon. The trail crosses a suspension bridge and climbs to the opposite ridge along the **Great Wall of Koto Gadang** (free), a curious, kilometre-long miniature of China's most iconic monument, opened in 2013. After taking in the views looking back across the canyon, continue along the road another kilometre to reach Koto Gadang.

Batang Palupuh

Sometimes spanning a full metre across, *Rafflesia arnoldi* is the largest flower in the world, blooming only a few days each month with remarkable red-and-white colouring and a smell akin to rotting meat. One of the most accessible spots in Sumatra to see this rare and extraordinary flower is the enchanting village of **Batang Palupuh**, 13km north of Bukittinggi (Rp6000 by regular local buses from Pasar Bawah). Enquire here for a guide (Rp50,000 per person) to lead you into the hills to find a rafflesia.

Still more elusive is the *Amorphophallus titanum*, locally called "*bunga bangkai*",

THE MINANG HIGHLANDS

The gorgeous mountainous landscape of the **Minang Highlands** features soaring rice terraces and easily accessible traditional culture. The highlands around Bukittinggi are the cultural heartland of the **Minangkabau** (Minang) people. The Minang are staunchly matrilineal, one of the largest such societies extant, and Muslim. The most visible aspect of their culture is the distinctive architecture of their homes, with massive roofs soaring skywards at either end (representing the horns of a buffalo). Typically, three or four generations of one family would live in one large house built on stilts, the *rumah gadang* (big house) or *rumah adat* (traditional house), a wood-and-thatch structure often decorated with fabulous wooden carvings.

another rare, smelly and gigantic flower: *A. titanum*'s flowering stem often reaches two-metres-high. Its genus name describes it as "misshapen penis", and it blooms briefly just once every four years.

Yet another worthy reason to visit Batang Palupuh is kopi luwak, one of the world's rarest and most expensive brews. Made from digested coffee beans picked out from the droppings of palm civets, the coffee has an earthy, caramel taste – try it at Umul Khairi's home (T 0819 758 6874, E umulross@yahoo.com; 100g bag Rp200,000) next to the Taqwa Mosque (see box, p.236).

Tanah Datar Valley

The Minang court of the fourteenth to nineteenth centuries was based in the valley and the entire area is awash with cultural relics, megaliths and places of interest. The largest town in the valley is **Batusangkar**, 39km southeast of Bukittinggi. Just a few kilometres away is the village of Silinduang (Rp5000 by ojek), which houses the elegant **Istana Pagaruyung**, the reconstructed palace of Sultan Arifin Muning Alam Syah, last Raja Alam of the Minangkabau (daily 8am–5.30pm; Rp12,000). Sadly, the building burnt down in 2007 after being struck by lightning, but having been painstakingly restored it is again the most resplendent sight in the valley, with intricately carved and painted wood panels and five layers of giant, curved roofs with pointed eaves. In the surrounding countryside are many other examples of Minangkabau *rumah adat*, including at the scenic villages of **Rao Rao**, north of Batusangkar, and **Pariangan**, between Batusangkar and Padangpanjang, which is said to be the oldest Minangkabau village and boasts centuries-old tombs and hot springs.

Given the distances involved, most travellers visit Batusangkar on a day-trip from Bukittinggi (1hr 30min; Rp18,000), via Padangpanjang or Baso.

Harau Valley

A fertile expanse of rice paddies and palm trees hemmed in by sheer vertical cliffs of 100m, the **Harau Valley** is one of West Sumatra's most visually stunning destinations. During the rainy season there are waterfalls, some with crystal-clear pools at their base, scattered along the valley floor where tapir, boar and siamang (tailless, black-furred gibbons) are rumoured to roam. The valley (entry Rp5000) begins just over an hour along the road from Bukittinggi to Pekanbaru, and about fifteen minutes past the city of Payakumbuh. Most people still visit Harau on day-trips, though some travellers have begun to linger longer thanks to a handful of accommodation options. The most popular backpacker spot is *Abdi Homestay* (T 0852 6378 1842, E abdihomestay.blogspot.com; Rp60,000), set in a tranquil spot near a 50m waterfall and run by the ever-friendly Ikbal. There are also nine mid-range cottages at *Echo Homestay* (T 0812 6619 1501, W echohomestay.blogspot.com; Rp90,000).

Although the trip from Bukittinggi is far more convenient on your own two wheels, public transport is an option: first, take a bus to Payakumbuh (1hr; Rp10,000), an angkot to the gate (15min; Rp3000), then an ojek to Harau (10min; Rp5000). If you miss the last bus returning from Payakumbuh, wave down one of the many buses coming along the main road from Pekanbaru.

4

ARRIVAL AND DEPARTURE

By bus Long-distance buses dock at the Aur Kuning terminal, 3km southeast of the town centre. If you're coming from Padang ask the bus to stop at the Jambu Air crossing on the southern outskirts of town before turning off for the terminal; you can get a red #14 bemo (Rp2500) into the town centre from this junction. There are frequent local buses from Aur Kuning terminal (daily 7.30am–5pm) for Maninjau, Batusangkar, Payakumbuh and Padang, as well as long-distance buses (book ahead). Tourist cars, or travel, link Pekanbaru, Padang, Parapat (for Danau Toba) and Maninjau, and may be booked through travel agents around town, among them Travina (T 0752 21281).

Destinations Bandar Lampung (3 daily; 24hr); Batusangkar (hourly; 1hr 30min); Bengkulu (daily; 16hr); Maninjau (hourly 7am–4pm; 1hr 30min); Medan (16 daily; 20hr); Padang (hourly 5.30am–8pm; 3hr); Pekanbaru (8 daily; 6hr); Parapat (2 daily, including 5pm ALS [a/c]; 14hr); Sibolga (daily; 11hr).

KOPI LUWAK: THE CAT POO COFFEE

Some find it delicious and others repulsive, but all pay a pretty price for *kopi luwak*. One of the world's most expensive coffees, the unique beverage is brewed from beans fermented within the stomachs of **palm civets**, arboreal creatures that look more like weasels than cats. The palm civets tend to pick only the ripest and sweetest of red coffee cherries from the plantations of West Sumatra and their stomach enzymes go to work breaking down the proteins that give coffee its bitter taste. Following defecation, the civets' excrement strings are picked from the jungle floor bordering the plantations to be cleaned, sun-dried, roasted over cinnamon wood and finally hand-pounded into a fine powder. Thanks to the civet cats' digestive tracts, no filter is necessary when serving: simply stir in a teaspoon of the coffee powder, wait a few minutes and decide for yourself whether *kopi luwak* is worth its hefty price tag.

4

INFORMATION

Tourist Information *Rajawali Homestay* (Jl A Yani 152) is the best option for maps and local activities. Also useful are the listed tour operators (see below), as well as the ever-helpful Arman (T 0812 674 1852) at PT Maju Indosari near the clock tower.

Tours The top tour operators are based in Bukittinggi's popular hotels and cafés. Among the best of these are Lite 'n' Easy (Fikar T 813 7453 7413, W liteneasy.nl), based at *Turret Café*; Roni's Tour & Travel (T 812 675 0688, W ronistour .com), based at *Orchid*, both of which run group tours as well as individual motorbike tours. There's also Wendra Tours (T 0752 21652, W seruling-travel.com), based at *Canyon Café*; and AdvenCulture (T 0852 6513 1335) at *Bedudal*.

GETTING AROUND

Angkots scurry around town in a circular route (Rp2500). For the bus terminal, stop any red angkot heading north on Jl A Yani, which will circle to the east of town and pass the main post office before turning for Aur Kuning.

ACCOMMODATION

D'Enam Jl Yos Sudarso T 0752 32240. Simple, clean rooms in an airy bungalow on top of the ridge. There's a friendly, family atmosphere, a lounge for residents and a laundry service next door. **Rp100,000**

Hello Guesthouse Jl Teuku Umar 6B T 0752 21542, E helloguesthouse12@gmail.com. The newest addition to Bukittinggi's accommodation scene is already among the most popular. Friendly owner Ling offers simple, clean rooms with hot water. There's also wi-fi, self-service tea and coffee, as well as breakfast included. Dorm **Rp75,000**, double **Rp140,000**

Orchid Jl Teuku Umar 11 T 0752 32634. One of the best deals in town, with clean, well-kept rooms, most of which sleep three and come with balconies. Ask for a room facing west (to the right when entering), both for the sunset views and to dampen the wake-up call from Masjid Nurul Haq to the east. On the roof there are a couple of no-frills crash pads with shared mandi, and there's a café with wi-fi downstairs, where friendly owner Roni provides excellent information on local and regional activities. **Rp75,000/120,000**

Rajawali Homestay Jl A Yani 152 T 0752 31905, E ulrich.rudolph@web.de. This unassuming place on the corner has decent-value, spartan rooms upstairs with grimy inside mandi and a pleasant rooftop sitting area that's great for meeting fellow travellers. Owner Ulrich offers a veritable wealth of information on local activities, including a number of original, GPS-mapped trekking and motorbiking routes. **Rp70,000**

EATING

Dozens of nameless food stalls set up shop each night along Jl A Yani junction (7.30pm–3am), offering *sate*, *nasi goreng* and other staples.

Bedudal Cafe Jl A Yani 95 W bedudal.com. The hippest traveller hangout on Jl A Yani, featuring reggae, live music on weekends and a good selection of Western and Indonesian dishes. Roast chicken dinners for Rp150,000. Daily 8am–midnight.

Canyon Café Jl Teuku Umar 8. There's a pleasant outdoor seating area and knowledgeable staff at this quiet place just beside *Hello Homestay*. Super-cheap meals (*nasi goreng* Rp10,000; veggie taco Rp13,000; chicken sandwich Rp18,000) are delicious and come in generous portions. Fast, free wi-fi. Daily 8am–10pm.

Selamat Jl Ahmad Yani 19. One of the best Padang restaurants in town; they usually have eggs in coconut sauce, especially good for vegetarians, and staff are used to Westerners. Daily 8am–10pm.

Taruko Café Jl Taruko. Set 6km west of town along the scenic road to Koto Gadang, *Taruko* is a splendid place to while away an afternoon. Seated under a large Maningkabau-style thatched roof, you'll have a breath-taking view of Tabiang Takuruang, a lone spire projecting from a bend in Sianok Canyon, with Gunung Singgalang rising in the background. Attracting a hip, young local crowd, there's a varied menu of local, Chinese and Italian cuisine (carbonara Rp26,000). Daily 8am–7pm.

Turret Café Jl Ahmad Yani 140–142. Breezy open café and bar next door to *Rajawali* with friendly,

English-speaking staff serving modestly priced Western and Indonesian dishes. Friendly owner Harita makes the most delicious *beef rendang* in town (Rp40,000). The friendly Lite 'n' Easy crew is often found here. There's also free wi-fi and a pair of flatscreens showing football matches. Daily 8am–11.30pm.

TRADITIONAL ENTERTAINMENT

Bull-racing and bullfighting *Pacu jawi* (bull racing) is held every year on September 30 in the muddy rice fields around Batusangkar. Another Minangkabau tradition is *adu kerbau* (bullfighting), held on Wednesday in Batagak (9km south of Bukittinggi), an event which stems from the legend of an invading Javanese king whose campaign ended in defeat after he wagered the outcome on a bullfight.

DIRECTORY

Banks and exchange There are plenty of banks with ATMs along Jl A Yani, including Bank Negara Indonesia, Mandiri and BNI.

Bookshops Anyone heading into central and southern Sumatra, an English-language book desert, should stock up in the new and secondhand bookshops on Jl Teuku Umar and Jl A Yani.

Car and motorbike rental Enquire at your accommodation or any of the travel agents in town (generally Rp70,000/day).

Hospital Rumah Sakit Dr Achmad Mochtar is on Jl Dr Rivai (☎0752 21013 or 33825).

Internet Club Net, Jl A Yani 25 (daily 10am–10pm), has good machines and a fast connection (Rp3000/hr).

Pharmacy Apotek Yani Baru, Jl A Yani 87 (daily 8am–8pm), offers basic medical supplies.

Post office The main post office is inconveniently far from the town centre on Jl Sudirman.

CLIMBING GUNUNG MERAPI

Access to 2890m **Gunung Merapi** (Fire Mountain) is from the tower in Koto Baru, 12km south of Bukittinggi. Typically, the climb, which is strenuous rather than gruelling if you're reasonably fit, takes five hours up and four down; most people start at around 11pm in order to arrive for sunrise at the smoking crater on the summit plateau. You may spot bats, gibbons and squirrels in the forest, but the main draw is the view across to Gunung Singgalang. Bring sturdy footwear and warm clothes for the top. Roni's (☎0812 675 0688) in Bukittinggi provides experienced guides for the hike for Rp300,000/person.

Travel agents Try Travina Tours and Travel Service, Jl A Yani 105 (☎0752 21281 or ☎0813 7424 4560); or PT Tigo Balai, Jl A Yani 100 (☎0752 31996).

DANAU MANINJAU

A palm-fringed crater lake surrounded by 400m-high jungle-covered walls, **DANAU MANINJAU** (Lake Maninjau) lies just 15km west of Bukittinggi as the crow flies. The actual journey spans 37km through rice paddies and lush forests, and gangs of monkeys look on as you slip over the rim of the caldera and snake downwards to the lake, notching 44 hairpin turns – each one signposted. At an altitude of 500m high, the lake is 17km long and 8km wide, the area of interest for tourists stretching from the village of **MANINJAU**, where the road from Bukittinggi reaches the lakeside, to the village of **Bayur**, 4km north.

4

WHAT TO SEE AND DO

Most visitors come to Maninjau simply to relax and swim in the lake, though more energetic souls may like to hike into the jungle-clad hills behind the village. Popular activities include tracking down a **rafflesia** flower, hiking to the nearby **waterfall**, known locally as "sarasa" (20min), or all the way to Puncak Lawang, the highest vantage point above the lake (2hr). For any of these excursions, try *Bagoes Café*, which runs tours as well as trekking and Sunday pig-hunting with dogs, a traditional local activity. Cycling along the lakeside is also popular, but motorbikes are just about essential if you want to circumnavigate the entire lake.

ARRIVAL AND DEPARTURE

By bus Buses from Bukittinggi make a stop in the small square at the foot of the mountain road before continuing along the lakeside road to Bayur – ask the conductor to drop you at your hotel. For the return trip, daily buses depart from the square in Maninjau (approximately hourly 6am–5pm). There is no direct bus to Padang: either head back to Bukittinggi or board an opelet to Lubukbasung (half-hourly; 45min), from where you can hail a bus to Padang (infrequent; 2hr).

Destinations Bukittinggi (hourly; 1hr 30min); Pekanbaru (daily; 8hr).

By car Seven-seater "travel" cars to Bukittinggi are easily hailed from anywhere along the main road. Cars for Padang and Pekanbaru leave from Maninjau's main square.

Destinations Bukittinggi (every 10min; 1hr 30min; Rp25,000); Padang (4 daily; 3hr; Rp65,000); Pekanbaru (daily 8am & 5pm; 8hr; Rp100,000).

INFORMATION

Tourist information There is no official tourist information office but local information is generally available at hotels. At PT Kesuma Mekar Jaya (T 0812 6699 6610, W sumatratravelling.com), just north of the BRI Bank and across the road, the ever-present Muhammad Ali is a spring of knowledge on local activities. Another good spot is Indowisata Cipta Permai (T 0752 61418), set within *Bagoes Café*.

ACCOMMODATION AND EATING

Accommodation options are dotted along the lake's eastern shore, from about 500m south of the Bukittinggi road junction to a couple kilometres past Bayur to the north.

4

44 T 0752 61238. Bookended by fish farms, these shoreside bungalows 600m north of town are some of Maninjau's cheapest, with grimy attached mandi and simple rooms consisting of a mattress on the floor with woven-thatch walls. The family is very welcoming and the café is good value with both Western and Indonesian dishes. (*nasi goreng* Rp12,000; *Bintang* Rp27,000). **Rp50,000**

★ **Arlen Nova's Paradise** T 0813 7408 0485, W nova-maninjau.id.or.id. A couple of hundred metres along a narrow trail through the rice paddies 2km north of Bayur, *Arlen Nova's* enjoys a peaceful lakeside setting free of fish farms. There are large bungalows with mosquito nets, hot water and comfortable beds, a clean and pleasant café attached with delicious food (tempe tofu curry Rp16,000), scooters and motorbikes for rent, and one of the lake's few sandy beaches. **Rp175,000**

Bagoes Café Popular traveller's hangout near the centre of town with wi-fi, a library and a range of tours offered by Indowisata Cipta Permai. The restaurant offers some of Maninjau's highest-quality Western and Indonesian food (green veg curry Rp22,000; *beef rendang* Rp30,000). Daily 9am–10.30pm.

Beach Guest House T 0812 6626 4483. Ageing, friendly little guesthouse about 500m north of town. Simple rooms have great views from the verandas, while out front there is a small beach and a tangled banyan tree hanging over the water, handy for launching into the lake. The small café serves drinks. **Rp75,000**

Maransy Restaurant Beyond the smattering of exotic animals caged outside its entrance, this local favourite has a huge deck overlooking the lake just south of Bayur, with a decent range of local and Western dishes. A good place to have a beer or a cocktail (large Bintang Rp35,000; Irish coffee Rp50,000) while taking in the sunset. Daily 10am–10pm.

Tan Dirih T 0752 61263. Just over 1km north of town, this is the lake's romantic option, offering a bit more comfort. Room service is available and all four rooms have TV, hot water and tubs while sharing a broad porch. Unfortunately, the outlook across the water is partly obstructed by fishing platforms. Pancake breakfasts included. **Rp275,000**

DIRECTORY

Banks The BRI Bank north of the Bukittinggi junction has an ATM, although VISA cards are not accepted.

Bike Rental Bicycles can be rented from *Beach Guest House* or PT Kesuma Mekar Jaya (Rp35,000/day); the latter also rents motorbikes (manual/automatic Rp65,000/80,000 per day).

Bookshops *Bagoes Café* has the largest range of books in Maninjau.

Internet A few little warnets are found just south of the junction leading back to Bukittinggi, among them Be Love Near (Rp5000hr), while *Bagoes Café* offers free wi-fi access for customers (or use of an in-house computer Rp4000/hr).

Post office The post office is a short hop towards the lake from the junction on Jl Telaga Biru Tanjung Raya (Mon–Thurs 8am–4pm, Fri 8am–noon & 2–4pm).

PEKANBARU

The oil boom town of **PEKANBARU** used to be popular among travellers as a gateway into Indonesia from Singapore via **Pulau Batam**, as well as from Malacca in Malaysia. In recent years, however, cheap airfares have reduced ferry traffic to a trickle, and the city now sees few foreign visitors. The main street, Jalan Sudirman, runs north to south from the river through the centre of town to the airport – most hotels, restaurants and shops are within easy reach of this thoroughfare. Pekanbaru's **markets** are a reasonable diversion: Pasar Pusat is the morning food and household-goods market, and Pasar Bawah and Pasar Tengeh in the port area are a maze of stalls and alleyways, with decent Chinese goods, ceramics and carpets on offer.

ARRIVAL AND DEPARTURE

By plane All domestic and international flights touch down at Sultan Syarif Kasim II Airport, 9km south of the

THE MENTAWAI ISLANDS

A world apart from the mainland, the enticing jungle-clad **Mentawai islands** lie 150km off the west Sumatran coast from which it was separated half a million years ago. These days, the islands are at least as famous for their world-class waves as for being home to a unique tribal culture and a wealth of endemic flora and fauna – including langurs, macaques and the long-armed Mentawai (Kloss' gibbon). Both are under serious threat, from Illegal logging and a government seeking to integrate the Mentawaian tribes into the Indonesian mainstream.

The islanders' traditional culture is based on communal dwelling in longhouses (*uma*) and subsistence agriculture, while their religious beliefs centre on the importance of coexisting with the invisible spirits that inhabit the world. With the advent of Christian missionaries and the colonial administration in the early twentieth century, many of the islanders' religious practices were banned, but plenty of beliefs and rituals have survived and some villages have built new *uma*.

Generally, Mentawai people welcome tourism as a way of validating and preserving their own culture, although due to the mainland's longtime monopoly on Mentawai tours, locals have received little financial benefit from it. Fortunately, independent travel has become increasingly feasible. There is a handful of basic homestays at the port of **Siberut**, the largest island (4000 square kilometres), where local guides may be hired, and surfers may choose from numerous all-inclusive surf camps that charge as little as Rp300,000/day.

Boat schedules are subject to change, and departures are sometimes cancelled without warning. From Padang to Siberut, you can take Mentawai Express speedboats (Thurs morn, returning Fri morn; 4hr), Sumber Rezeki boats (Mon & Wed, returning Tues and Thurs), Ambu-Ambu (Thurs 7pm, returning Fri 7pm) and the brand-new KMP Gambolo (Fri & Mon, returning Sat 7pm and Tues 8pm; 10hr). More ferries link the islands' other ports, such as Tuapejat on Sipora Island and Sikakap on North Pagai Island. Get tickets from Bevys Sumatra (Jl Batang Arau ⓣ0751 781 0835), located within *Hotel Batang Arau*, and pack some anti-seasickness tablets if big waves make you queasy.

city centre. Taxis (about Rp60,000) link the airport and city centre.

Destinations Batam (4 daily; 50min); Jakarta (15 daily; 1hr 40min); Kuala Lumpur (2 daily; 50min); Medan (4 daily; 1hr); Padang (daily; 50min); Yogyakarta (2 daily; 2hr 10min).

By ferry Daily ferries to Melaka leave from Dumai, 4hr north of Pekanbaru (departs 1pm; 7hr). Daily ferries to Batam leave from Buton, 3hr east of Pekanbaru (around 8am; 6hr). From Batam's Sekupang port, daily Batam Fast boats (ⓦbatamfast.com) depart for Singapore's Harbour Front (almost hourly until 7pm; 45min).

By bus Long-distance buses to destinations throughout Sumatra and Java arrive and depart at the well-run Bandar Raya Payung Sekaki station (BRPS), 10km west of the city centre and credited with winning Pekanbaru the 2011 Adipura award as Indonesia's cleanest city. Green angkots connect the bus station with Jl Nangka.

Destinations Frequent daily departures to Bandar Lampung (24hr); Bukittinggi (5hr); Dumai (4hr); Medan (12hr); Padang (8hr).

INFORMATION

There's a tourist office at Jl Jend Sudirman 200 (Tues–Thurs 8am–2pm, Fri 8–11am, Sat 8am–12.30pm; ⓣ0761 31452).

ACCOMMODATION AND EATING

A good food market runs during the day in Pasar Pusat, just off Jl Bonjol. At night the stretch along Jl Sudirman near Jl Gatot Subroto is full of *sate* stalls, the busiest of which is *Radar Siang Malam*, with a huge menu of *sate* (from Rp12,000).

Poppie's Jl Cempedak III ⓣ0812 7553 1889. No-frills, hard-to-find homestay not too far off Sudirman with a friendly, English-speaking owner. Offers about the only backpacker accommodation in town. Ask a local for directions. Single **Rp100,000**

Tune Hotel Jl Tgk Zainal Abidin 23 ⓣ0761 851008, ⓦtunehotels.com/my/en/ourhotels/pekanbaru. This new branch of the popular Malaysian franchise, run by the CEO of Air Asia, is right in the city centre, offering sleek and spotless a/c rooms. **Rp230,000**

DIRECTORY

Banks and exchange There are plenty of banks with ATMs throughout the city centre, including BCA (Jl Sudirman 448) and BNI (Jl Sudirman 63).

Internet Jl Gadot Subroto 6 (Rp6000/hr).

Post office The main post office is at Jl Sudirman 229 (Mon–Thurs 8am–5pm, Fri 8am–noon & 2–5pm).

Travel agents PT Indah Wisata Tours and Travel, Jl Pangeran Hidayat 2 (ⓣ0761 45881), sells minibus tickets to many Sumatran destinations, including Bukittinggi.

4

BANDAR LAMPUNG

Occupying a stunning location in the hills overlooking Lampung Bay, from where you can see as far as Krakatau on a clear day, **BANDAR LAMPUNG** is an amalgamation of Teluk Betung, the traditional port, and Tanjung Karang, the administrative centre on the hills behind. Local people continue to talk about Teluk Betung and Tanjung Karang, and when you're coming here from other parts of Sumatra your destination will usually be referred to as Rajabasa, the name of the bus terminal.

Travellers rarely stay long in Lampung, instead heading south for the ferry to Java or climbing into long-haul buses to move north. However, there are numerous off-the-beaten-path activities to keep visitors around, among them jungle trekking through swampy Way Kambas, river trips in Way Kanan, boat charters to check out dolphins in Kiluan Bay and the white sandy beaches and frontal views of Krakatau in Sebuku and Sebesi islands. Meanwhile, surfers may want to head straight to **Krui** on the west coast, one of the best year-round surf spots in the country (see box below).

4

ARRIVAL AND DEPARTURE

By plane Radin Inten II Airport is 22km northwest of the city, linked by light-brown angkots to Rajabasa terminal (Rp3000), then DAMRI buses from there to the city centre (Rp3000). Fixed-price taxis from the airport into town will cost Rp110,000.

Destinations Jakarta (13 daily; 53min); Palembang (daily; 50min).

SURFING IN SOUTHERN SUMATRA

Bandar Lampung is also a base from which to access the coastal town of **Krui**, one of Indonesia's best surfing destinations. Most surf camps offer to arrange your transfer from Bandar Lampung, but you can also take the Krui Express bus (3–4hr) from Rajabasa terminal. Several local operators offer **surfing expeditions** in the area. Check out *Lovina Krui Surf* (T 0853 7780 2212, W lovinakruisurf.com), which has beautiful new cottages (built in 2012) facing the waves and starting at Rp200,000.

KRAKATAU ON A BUDGET

Although tours to **Krakatau** can be arranged easily through Bandar Lampung's Tourist Information Centre (see below), it's much cheaper to head south to Kalianda (1hr 30min; bemo Rp12,000), then 6km further south to Canti (ojek Rp10,000), the closest port to Krakatau. Here you can join other travellers in chartering a boat to Krakatau (2hr 30min; Rp1,200,000 for up to 20 people).

By bus Long-distance buses arrive and depart from the Rajabasa terminal, 7km north of the city. DAMRI buses (Rp3500) head to Pasar Bawah then down Jl Raden Intan, along Jl A Yani and up Jl Kartini before reaching Rajabasa. Buses from Bakauheni or Kalianda arrive at the Panjang terminal, about 1km east of Pasar Panjang, some continuing to Rajabasa. Orange bemos run between Panjang terminal and Sukaraja terminal in the heart of Teluk Betung; from here, you can get a purple bemo into the city (Rp3500; until 10pm) as far as Pasar Bawah, or a large orange bus direct to Rajabasa via the eastern ring road. Although pricier, private services can be worthwhile for skipping Rajabasa altogether.

Destinations Bakauheni (every 30min; 2–3hr); Bukittinggi (6 daily; 24hr); Jakarta (20 daily; 8hr); Kalianda (every 30min; 1hr 30min); Medan (10 daily; 2 days); Padang (6 daily; 24hr); Pekanbaru (6 daily; 24hr).

By train Bandar Lampung marks the southern end of southern Sumatra's modest rail network, extending north to Palembang. The train station is on Jl Kotoraja, about 100m from Pasar Bawah.

Destination Palembang (2 daily; 8–9hr).

INFORMATION

Tourist office The useful tourist office is Dinas Investasi Kebudayaan Dan Parwisata (or you could just ask for the Kantor Pariwisata), Jl Jend Sudirman 29 (T 0721 266184). There you'll find some of the best information on the region, including lesser-known attractions, from Yaman Aziz (T 081 641 0630, E yaman_lampung@yahoo.com).

GETTING AROUND

Buses and bemos DAMRI bus services (daily 6am–9pm) operate between the two major terminals or up and down Jl Randen Intan and Jl Diponegoro. Bemo routes are less fixed than buses: tell them your destination as you enter. The big green buses of the new Trans Bandar Lampung service (Rp3500) run between Rajabasa and Sukaraja in Teluk Betung.

Taxis Drivers are reluctant to use meters so negotiate a fare first (across town should cost Rp20,000–30,000).

FERRIES TO JAVA

Around 30km southeast of Kalianda, and 90km southeast of Bandar Lampung, lies the Bakauheni ferry port (ⓣ 0721 252032), the departure point for ferries to Merak (see box, p.184), on Java's northwest tip. Regular buses travel to Bandar Lampung (1hr 30min; Rp30,000) and bemos connect to Kalianda – there's no reason to stay in Bakauheni itself. Ferries from Bakauheni operate round the clock (2hr 30min; Rp13,000), leaving every thirty minutes during the day and less frequently at night. **High-speed ferries** (40min; Rp30,000) also depart half-hourly from 7.40am to 5pm.

ACCOMMODATION

Arnes Central Hotel Jl Cut Nyak 20 ⓣ 0721 263339, ⓦ arinashotel.com/our-groups/arnes-central-hotel.html. Worth the splurge, this good-value one-star hotel has big, beautiful rooms that come with a/c, cable TV, wi-fi access, mini-bar and breakfast. Across the road from the purple bemo route. **Rp295,000**

Lusy Jl Diponegoro 186 (Karang-Betung buses and pink angkots pass the door) ⓣ 0721 485695. Big place on a busy road in the town centre, with helpful staff and a range of spacious though slightly grotty a/c rooms, some with hot water (Rp200,000). **Rp120,000**

Rarem Jl Way Rarem 23 ⓣ 0721/261392. Tucked away in a quiet spot behind Jl KHA Dahlan, near the *Marcopolo Hotel* and on the green bemo route, this place has decent-value rooms, the best of which come with private bath and a/c (Rp260,000). Indonesian breakfast included. **Rp235,000**

EATING

Pasar Mambo, the night market, is at the southern end of Jl Hassanudin (dusk–midnight).

Begadang II Jl Diponegoro 164. Huge, busy Padang restaurant loved by locals that serves cheap seafood dishes (*ikan mas* Rp12,000). Due to their popularity, owner Haji Dasril has opened five of these restaurants around town, this one next to the Harley Davidson club and on the purple bemo route. Closed for Ramadan. Daily 10am–11pm.

Marcopolo Restaurant *Marcopolo Hotel*. The fantastic views over the city and Lampung Bay from the terrace of this somewhat ageing hotel make this a great choice for Indonesian, Chinese and Western food (*ayam goreng* Rp28,000). You can choose between indoor and outdoor seating, and there's free wi-fi. Daily 24hr.

DIRECTORY

Hospital Rumah Sakit Bumi Waras, Jl Wolter Moginsidi (ⓣ 0721 255032).

Immigration Jl Diponegoro 24 (ⓣ 0721 482607 or ⓣ 0721 481697).

Internet There are plenty of internet cafés along Jl Raden Intan and Jl Sudirman (Rp5000/hr).

Police station Jl WR Supratman 1 (ⓣ 0721 488477)

Post office Jl KHA Dahlan 12 and Jl Raden Intan (Mon–Thurs 8am–5pm, Fri 8am–noon & 2–5pm).

4

Bali

With its pounding surf, emerald-green rice terraces and exceptionally artistic culture, the small volcanic island of **Bali** – population around 4.2 million and Southeast Asia's only Hindu society – has

BALI: A SHORT HISTORY

Bali was a more or less independent society of Buddhists and Hindus until the fourteenth century, when it was colonized by the strictly **Hindu Majapahits** from neighbouring Java. Despite the subsequent Islamicization of nearly all her neighbours, Bali has remained firmly Hindu ever since. In 1849, the Dutch started to take an interest in Bali, and by January 1909 had wrested control of the whole island. Following a short-lived Japanese occupation in World War II, and Indonesia's subsequent declaration of independence in 1945, Bali became an autonomous state within the Republic in 1949. But tensions with Java are ongoing and there is concern about wealthy entrepreneurs from Jakarta (and the West) monopolizing the financial benefits from Bali's considerable attractions, with the Balinese fearing they may lose control of their own homeland. These tensions were horrifically highlighted when Muslim extremists from Java bombed Kuta's two most popular nightclubs on October 12, 2002, killing more than two hundred people and sending Bali's tourist-dependent economy into severe decline. A second attack, in October 2005, came just as the island was starting to recover. Reprisals and religious conflict did not ensue, however, due in part to Bali's impressively equanimous Hindu leadership; tourist numbers have since recovered, though the impact of the bombings is still felt.

long been Indonesia's premier tourist destination. Although predictably congested and commercialized, Bali's original charm is still much in evidence, its distinctive temples and elaborate festivals set off by the mountainous, river-rich landscape of the interior.

Bali's most famous and crowded resort is the **Kuta-Legian-Seminyak** strip, an 8km sweep of golden sand, with plenty of accommodation, shopping and nightlife. Surfing is fun here too, but experienced wave-riders head for the surfing beaches on the Bukit peninsula and along Bali's southwest coast. **Sanur** is a fairly sedate southern beach resort, but most backpackers prefer the tranquil island of **Nusa Lembongan**, the beaches of peaceful east-coast **Amed, Candi Dasa** and **Padang Bai**. Immensely rich sea life means that snorkelling and diving are big draws at all these resorts. Dolphin-watching is the main attraction in **Lovina** on the north coast, while Bali's major cultural

4

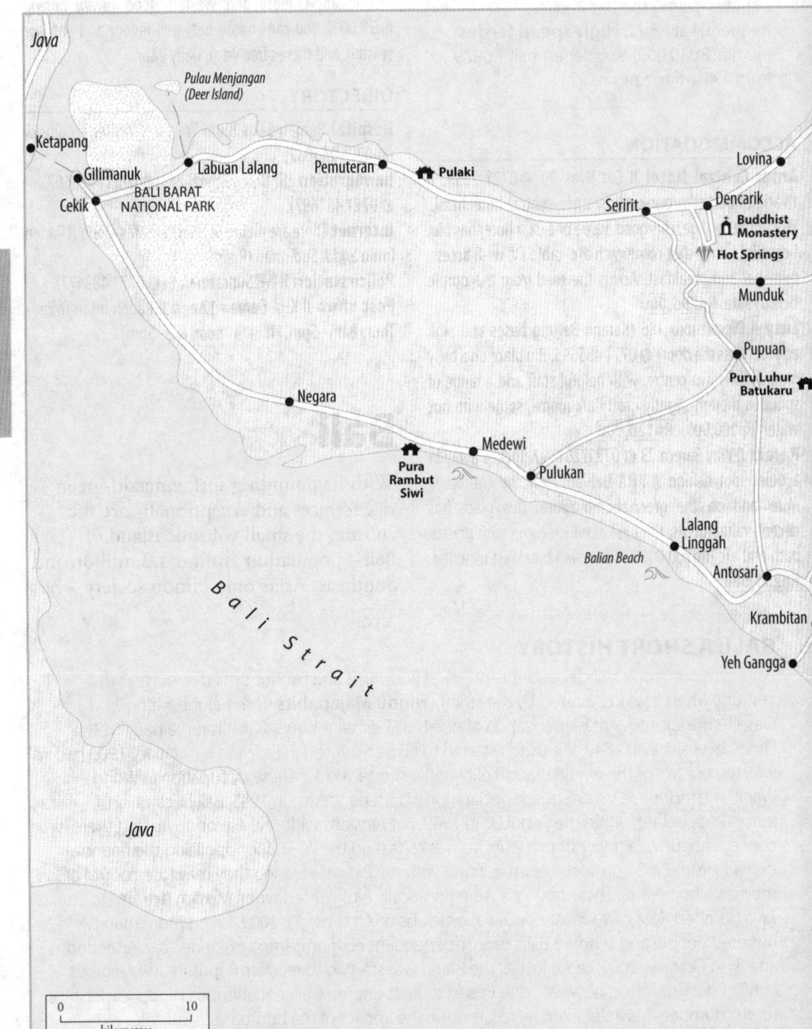

destination is **Ubud**, where traditional dances are staged every night and the streets are full of organic cafés, yoga studios and art galleries. In addition, there are numerous elegant Hindu temples to visit, particularly at **Tanah Lot** and **Besakih**, and a good number of volcano hikes: the most popular is the route up **Gunung Batur**, with **Gunung Agung** only for the very fit.

Transport to and from Bali is efficient: the island is served by scores of international and domestic flights, which all land at Ngurah Rai Airport just south of Kuta, as well as ferries from Java, west across the Bali Strait from **Gilimanuk**, and from Lombok, east of **Padang Bai**. Pelni ferries from ports across Indonesia call at Benoa harbour (see p.245).

DENPASAR

Bali's capital city, **DENPASAR** (sometimes known as Badung), has a museum and several lively markets, but lacks the

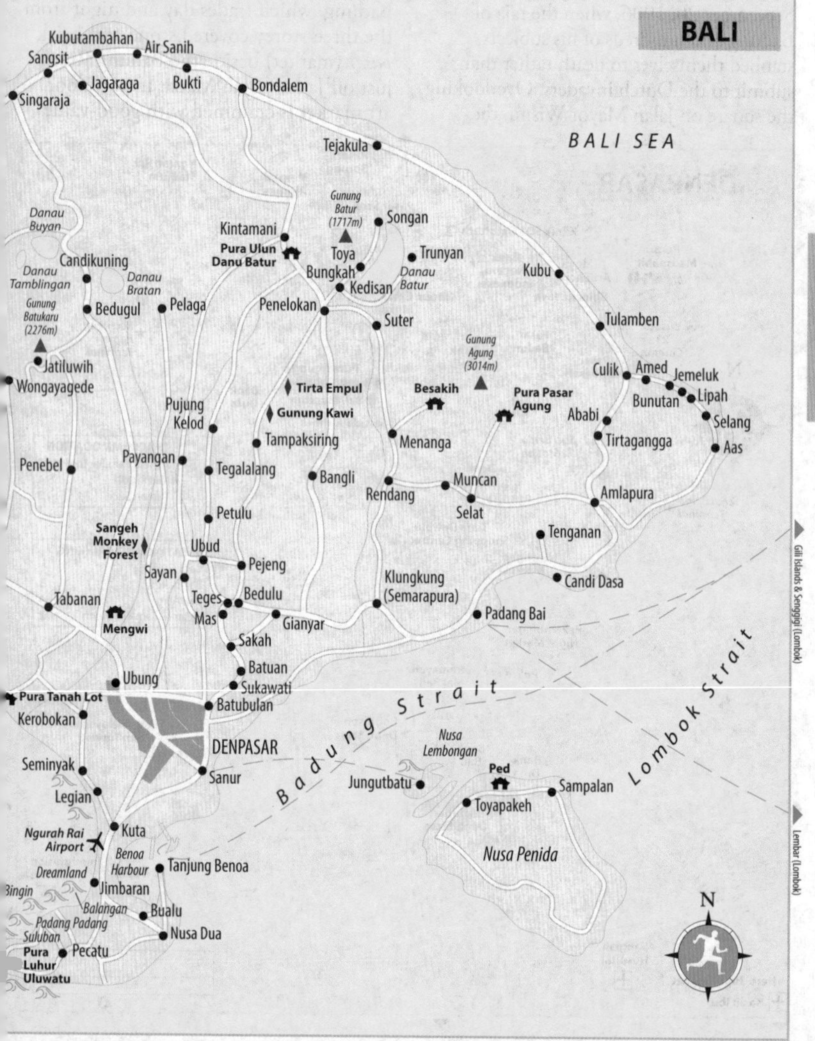

tourist accommodation and other facilities of Kuta, Legian, Seminyak and Sanur. Most visitors simply come for the day, or use it as a transport interchange, but a night in the city's traditional northern neighbourhoods offers an interesting chance to experience untouristed urban Bali.

WHAT TO SEE AND DO

Puputan Square marks the heart of the downtown area. It commemorates the ritual fight to the death (*puputan*) on September 20, 1906, when the raja of Badung and hundreds of his subjects stabbed themselves to death rather than submit to the Dutch invaders. Overlooking the square on Jalan Mayor Wisnu, the **Bali Museum** (Museum Negeri Propinsi Bali; Mon–Thurs & Sat 8am–3pm, Fri 8am–12.30pm; Rp5000; on the turquoise Kereneng–Ubung bemo route) has displays on prehistory, textiles and theatrical costumes as well as an interesting exhibit on spiritual rituals in the Gedung Karangasem building. Alongside the Bali Museum stands the modern state temple of **Pura Agung Jagatnatha**, built in 1953.

Pasar Badung and Pasar Kumbasari

The biggest of Denpasar's markets is Pasar Badung, which trades day and night from the three-storey covered stone-and-brick *pasar* (market) beside the Badung River, just off Jalan Gajah Mada. Its top-floor art market is crammed with good-value

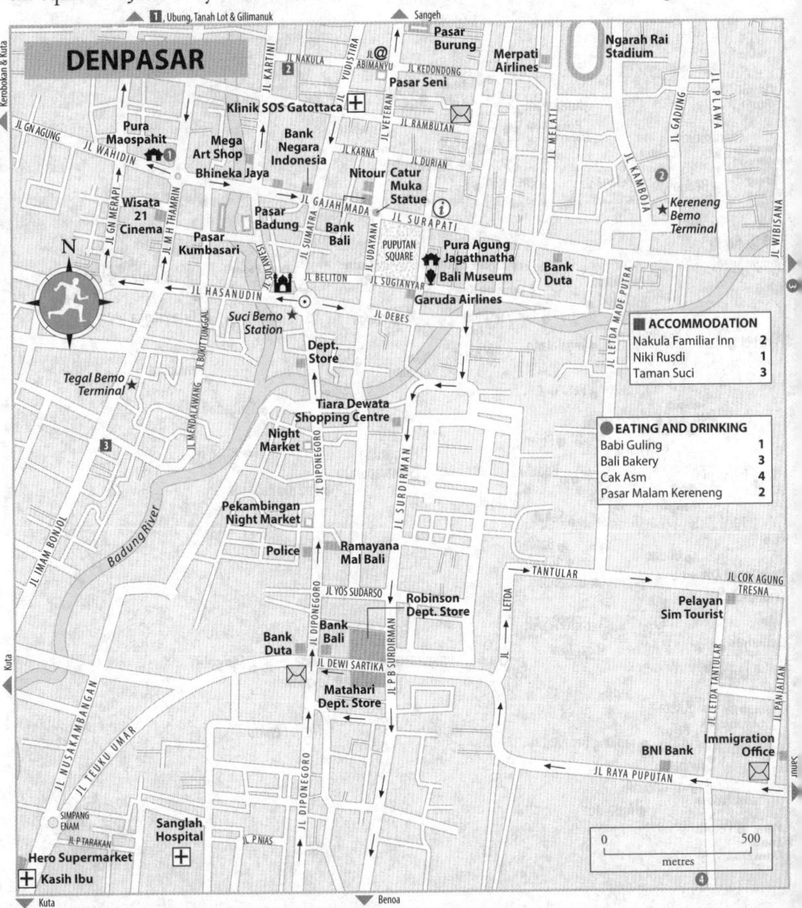

sarongs, batik cloth and ceremonial gear, but you may get landed with a self-appointed guide. The four-storey **Pasar Kumbasari** is across on the west bank of the river just south off Jalan Gajah Mada, and is another good source of inexpensive handicrafts and clothes.

ARRIVAL AND DEPARTURE

By plane All flights to Bali land at Ngurah Rai Airport, which is not in Denpasar as usually implied, but just south of Kuta (see p.246). Taxis charge Rp70,000–90,000 to/from Denpasar.

By bemo or public bus Denpasar has four main terminals, from where trans-city bemos beetle into the centre and out to the other bemo stations. Bemos from Tegal run to destinations south of Denpasar; Batubulan is for Ubud, east and north Bali; and Ubung serves north and west Bali, Padang Bai (for Lombok) and Java. No shuttle buses operate out of Denpasar. Bemo services are becoming less reliable on certain shorter routes because of the huge rise in motorbike ownership, so expect to wait for up to an hour between departures, especially in the afternoon; most don't run after 5pm.

Destinations from Batubulan terminal Candi Dasa (2hr); Gianyar (1hr); Kintamani (1hr 30min); Kuta (eastern edge; DAMRI buses; 40min); Padang Bai (for Lombok; 1hr 40min); Sanur (western edge; 20min); Semarapura (1hr 20min); Singaraja (Penarukan terminal; 3hr); Ubud (50min).

Destinations from Kereneng terminal Sanur (15–25min).

Destinations from Tegal terminal Kuta (25min); Ngurah Rai Airport (35min); Sanur (25min).

Destinations from Ubung terminal Bedugul (1hr 30min); Cekik (3hr); Gilimanuk (3hr 15min); Jakarta (24hr); Kediri (30min); Lalang Linggah (1hr 15min); Medewi (1hr 30min); Singaraja (Sukasada terminal; 3hr); Solo (15hr); Surabaya (10hr); Yogyakarta (15hr).

By boat All Pelni ships from the rest of Indonesia dock at Benoa harbour (Pelabuhan Benoa), 10km southeast. Pelni boat tickets for long-distance ferries can be bought from Pelni offices at Jl Diponegoro 165 (T 0361 234680, W pelni.co.id) and at Benoa harbour (T 0361 723689). Bemos meet the ships and take passengers into Denpasar, terminating near Sanglah hospital. A taxi from the port costs Rp35,000–50,000 to Denpasar, Kuta or Sanur.

Destinations from Benoa harbour Bima (Sumbawa; 3 fortnightly; 21–31hr); Bitung (Sulawesi; fortnightly; 5 days); Ende (Flores; fortnightly; 2 days); Kupang (West Timor; fortnightly; 26hr); Labuanbajo (Flores; 30hr); Makassar (Sulawesi; 2 fortnightly; 2–4 days); Maumere (Flores; fortnightly; 3 days); Surabaya (Java; fortnightly; 23hr); Waingapu (Sumba; fortnightly; 26hr).

By ferry Benoa harbour to the Gili Islands (1–2 daily; 2hr–2hr 30min).

INFORMATION

Tourist offce There's a (not particularly helpful) tourist office just off Puputan Square, at Jln Surapati 7 (Mon–Thurs 7.30am–3.30pm, Fri 8am–1pm; T 0361 234569).

GETTING AROUND

Bemos Colour-coded public bemos shuttle between the city's bemo terminals and cost about Rp5000, though frequencies are erratic (more common in the morning). Turquoise Kereneng–Ubung bemos go past the tourist office; both the dark blue Tegal–Sanur bemos and the beige Kereneng–Tegal bemos will take you close to the downtown department stores on Jl Dewi Sartika.

Taxis Metered taxis circulate around the city (Rp5000 flagfall, then Rp5000/km). Bali Taksi, recognizable by its distinctive blue colour, or Bluebird, with a small bird logo on its roof light, are the most reliable choices.

ACCOMMODATION

Nakula Familiar Inn Jl Nakula 4, a 10min walk from the museum or a 15min walk from Tegal bemo terminal T 0361 226446, W nakulafamiliarinn.com. Welcoming family-run losmen with plain, huge, modern fan rooms; ones with a/c or TVs cost an extra Rp50,000. **Rp175,000**

Niki Rusdi Jl Pidada, just behind Ubung bus and bemo terminal T 0361 416397, W hotelnikirusdi.com. Good clean fan and a/c rooms at this little hotel that's ideal for Ubung bus departures/arrivals, though also a bit noisy. **Rp150,000**

Taman Suci Jl Imam Bonjol 45 T 0361 485254, W tamnsuci.com. Friendly business-traveller-style hotel with smart, if character-free, rooms, in a convenient spot in the centre of town. **Rp375,000**

EATING

Babi Guling Jl Sutomo, next to Pura Maospahit, opposite Bale Banjar Gerenceng. Simple warung serving the city's best roast suckling pig. The standard plate comes with a selection of cuts including fat, offal and crispy pigs' ears served with rice and vegetables, but you can point to the leaner, more expensive bits when ordering. A good feed costs around Rp20,000–30,000. Daily 11am–10pm.

Bali Bakery Jl Hayam Wuruk 181 T 0361 243 147, W balibakery.com. Free wi-fi, decent coffee and tasty baked goods (from Rp10,000) to fulfil any craving; the cheese croissants are especially tasty. Daily 7.30am–10.30pm.

Cak Asm Jl Tukad Gangga. The setting is basic, but the food, particularly the seafood, is delicious and extremely good value (from around Rp15,000). As a result, this simple little café is always buzzing with customers. Daily 11am–9pm.

Pasar Malam Kereneng Off Jl Hayam Wuruk, next to Kereneng bemo terminal. Night market with over fifty hot-food vendors, serving from dusk to dawn. Rp20,000 will buy you several dishes. Daily sunset–dawn.

4

DIRECTORY

Banks and exchange There are ATMs on all main shopping streets and exchange at most central banks.

Embassies and consulates Most foreign embassies are in Jakarta (see p.184), but residents of Australia, Canada and New Zealand should apply for help in the first instance to Bali's Australian consulate at Jl Letda Tantular 32 in the Renon district of Denpasar (T 0361 241118, W bali.indonesia.embassy.gov.au). The US consulate is at Jl Hayam Wuruk 188 in Renon (T 0361 233605, W jakarta.usembassy.gov/bali_consular.html). The UK consulate is in Sanur (see p.254).

Hospitals Sanglah Public Hospital (Rumah Sakit Umum Propinsi Sanglah, or RSUP Sanglah) at Jl Kesehatan Selatan 1, Sanglah (T 0361 227911, W sanglahhospitalbali.com; Kereneng–Tegal bemo and Tegal–Sanur bemo) is the main provincial public hospital.

Immigration office Jl Panjaitan at Jl Raya Puputan, Renon (Mon–Thurs 8am–4pm, Fri 8–11am, Sat 8am–2pm; T 0361 227828; Sanur–Tegal bemo).

Internet There are cyber cafés inside the main shopping centres including the Ramayana Mal Bali on Jl Diponegoro.

Pharmacies Several along Jl Gajah Mada and inside all the major shopping centres.

Police There are police stations on Jl Patimura and Jl Diponegoro. The main police station is in the far west of the city on Jl Gunung Sanghiang (T 0361 424346).

Post offices The most central post office is on Jl Rambutan, north of Puputan Square. Poste restante (Mon–Fri 8am–7pm & Sat 8am–6pm; Sanur–Tegal bemo) arrives at the GPO on Jl Raya Puputan in Renon.

Shopping Good-quality crafts from Mega Art Shop, Jl Gajah Mada 36 (Mon–Sat 9am–5pm). Department stores (daily 9am–9pm): Ramayana Mal Bali, Jl Diponegoro 103 (Kereneng–Tegal and Tegal–Sanur bemos), and Matahari, Jl Dewi Sartika 4 (Tegal–Sanur bemo), with a small basement bookshop.

KUTA, LEGIAN AND SEMINYAK

Crammed with hotels, restaurants, bars, clubs, tour agencies and shops, the **KUTA-LEGIAN–SEMINYAK** conurbation, 10km southwest of Denpasar, is Bali's biggest, brashest beach resort. The beach itself is one of the finest on the island, its gentle curve of golden sand stretching for 8km, and lashed by huge breakers that bring experienced and novice surfers flocking. Be wary, however, of the strong undertow and always swim between the red- and yellow-striped flags. Everyone else comes to shop and party, fuelled by a pumping nightlife that ranges from the trashy in Kuta to the chic in Seminyak and Petitenget, though drugs, prostitution and gigolos (known as "Kuta cowboys" or "mosquitoes" because they jump from woman to woman) feature all over. Although the resort's party atmosphere was shattered in 2002, when Islamic extremists from Java bombed Kuta's two most popular clubs, and again when Kuta Square was attacked in 2005, the good-time vibe has resurfaced. **A Monument of Human Tragedy** now occupies the 2002 "Ground Zero" site.

Accommodation, shopping and restaurant options broadly fit the same geographical pattern, with Kuta the destination of party-going travellers, Legian the choice for families and couples, and Seminyak favoured by those with style and/or money. Kuta stretches north from the Matahari department store in Kuta Square to Jalan Melasti, while its southern fringes, extending south from Matahari to the airport, are defined as **Tuban**. Legian runs from Jalan Melasti as far as Jalan Double Six (Jalan Pantai Arjuna); Seminyak goes from Jalan Double Six up to the *Oberoi Hotel*, where **Petitenget** begins.

ARRIVAL AND DEPARTURE

BY PLANE

Ngurah Rai Airport All international and domestic flights use the modern Ngurah Rai Airport (T 0361 751011), which is in the Tuban district, 3km south of Kuta Square, not, as is often assumed, in Denpasar. There are ATMs, currency exchanges and hotel reservation desks here. The domestic terminal is in the adjacent building. The 24hr left-luggage office is outside, midway between international arrivals and departures (from Rp20,000/item/day).

Airport transport The easiest transport from the airport is by pre-paid taxi: rates are fixed (though you may be asked for a little more; be firm) and are payable at the counter just beyond the customs exit doors: Rp65,000–90,000 to Tuban, Kuta, Legian or Seminyak. Metered taxis are cheaper, but you have to walk out of the airport compound to hail one. Cheaper still are the infrequent dark-blue public bemos (daily 5am–6pm; around Rp10,000 to Kuta/Legian, double with luggage), whose route takes in Jl Raya Tuban, about 700m beyond the airport gates. The northbound bemos go via Kuta's Bemo Corner and Jl Pantai Kuta as far as Jl Melasti, then travel

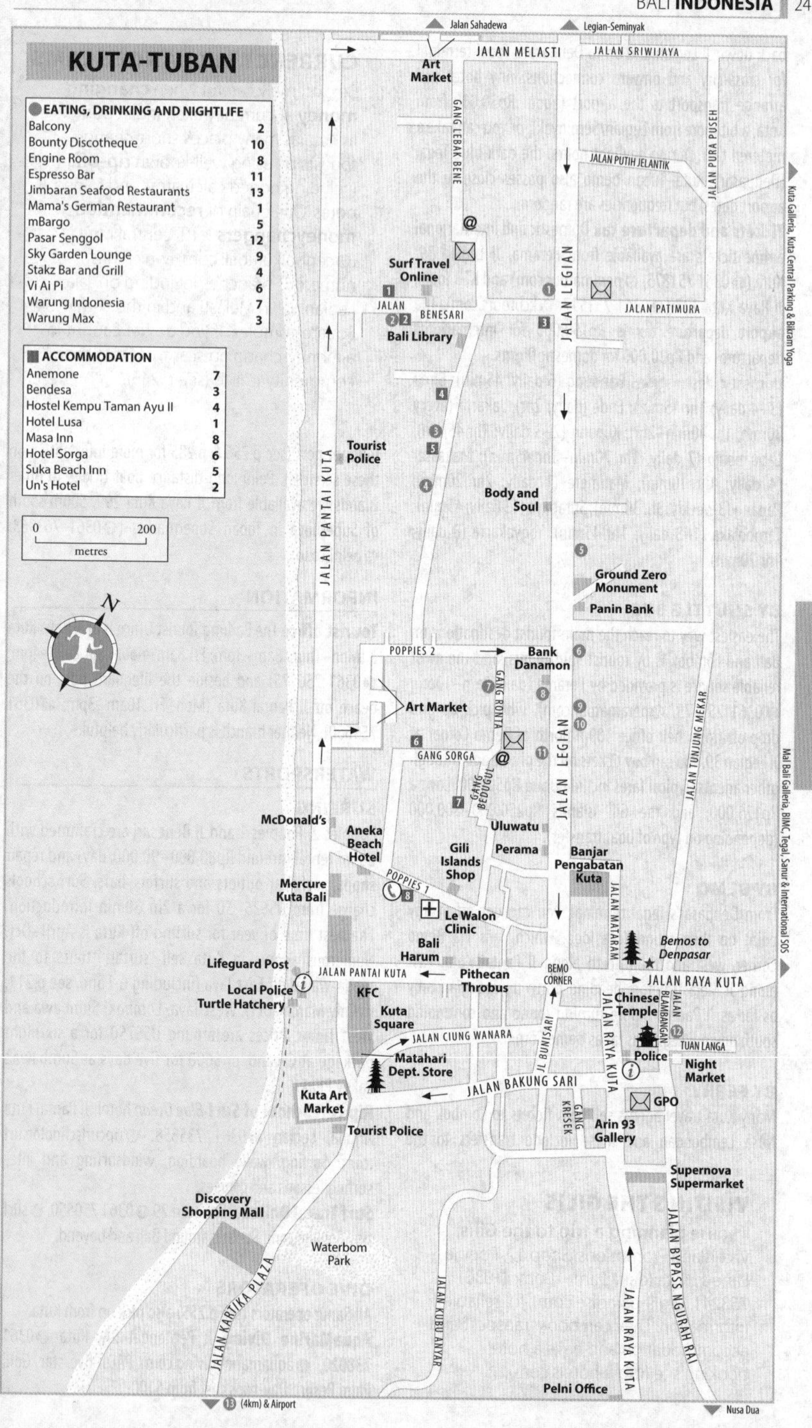

KUTA-TUBAN
EATING, DRINKING AND NIGHTLIFE
Balcony 2
Bounty Discotheque 10
Engine Room 8
Espresso Bar 11
Jimbaran Seafood Restaurants 13
Mama's German Restaurant 1
mBargo 5
Pasar Senggol 12
Sky Garden Lounge 9
Stakz Bar and Grill 4
Vi Ai Pi 6
Warung Indonesia 7
Warung Max 3
ACCOMMODATION
Anemone 7
Bendesa 3
Hostel Kempu Taman Ayu II 4
Hotel Lusa 1
Masa Inn 8
Hotel Sorga 6
Suka Beach Inn 5
Un's Hotel 2
0 200 metres
N
Jalan Sahadewa
Legian-Seminyak
JALAN MELASTI
JALAN SRIWIJAYA
Art Market
GANG LEBAK BENE
JALAN PUTIH JELANTIK
JALAN PURA PUSEH
Kuta Galleria, Kuta Central Parking & Bikram Yoga
Surf Travel Online
JALAN BENESARI
JALAN PATIMURA
JALAN LEGIAN
Bali Library
Tourist Police
Body and Soul
JALAN PANTAI KUTA
Ground Zero Monument
Panin Bank
POPPIES 2
Bank Danamon
GANG RONTA
Art Market
GANG SORGA
GANG BEDUGUL
JALAN TUNJUNG MEKAR
Mal Bali Galleria, BIMC, Tegal, Sanur & International SOS
McDonald's
Aneka Beach Hotel
Uluwatu
Perama
Gili Islands Shop
Banjar Pengabatan Kuta
Mercure Kuta Bali
POPPIES 1
Le Walon Clinic
JALAN MATARAM
Bali Harum
Bemos to Denpasar
Lifeguard Post
JALAN PANTAI KUTA
Pithecan Throbus
BEMO CORNER
JALAN RAYA KUTA
Local Police
Turtle Hatchery
KFC
Kuta Square
Chinese Temple
JALAN BLAMBANGAN
JALAN CIUNG WANARA
JL BUNISARI
TUAN LANGA
Matahari Dept. Store
Police
Night Market
JALAN BAKUNG SARI
Kuta Art Market
GPO
GANG KRESEK
Tourist Police
Arin 93 Gallery
Supernova Supermarket
Discovery Shopping Mall
Waterbom Park
JALAN KARTIKA PLAZA
JALAN KUBU ANYAR
JALAN RAYA KUTA
JALAN BYPASS NGURAH RAI
Pelni Office
(4km) & Airport
Nusa Dua
4

back down Jl Legian and on to Denpasar's Tegal terminal for cross-city and onward connections. Any hotel will arrange transport to the airport (about Rp50,000 from Kuta, a bit more from Legian/Seminyak), or you can take a metered taxi. During daylight hours, the dark-blue Tegal (Denpasar)–Kuta–Tuban bemo also passes close to the airport gates, but frequencies are random.

Tickets and departure tax Domestic and international airline tickets are available from Perama, Jl Legian 39, Kuta (T 0361 751875, W peramatour.com) and KCB Tours, Jl Raya Kuta 127 (T 0361 751517, W kcbtours.com). The airport departure tax is Rp150,000 for international departures and Rp30,000 for domestic flights.

Domestic destinations Bandung (6 daily; 45min); Bima (3–4 daily; 1hr 15min); Ende (daily; 2hr); Jakarta (every 30min; 1hr 40min–2hr); Kupang (2–3 daily; 1hr 45min); Labuanbajo (7 daily; 1hr 20min–1hr 45min); Makassar (4 daily; 1hr 10min); Maumere (1 daily; 2hr 20min); Padang (3 weekly; 3hr 30min); Surabaya (13 daily; 45min); Tambolaka (1–3 daily; 1hr 45min); Yogyakarta (8 daily; 1hr 20min).

BY SHUTTLE BUS

The easiest way to reach the main tourist destinations on Bali and Lombok is by tourist shuttle bus, and the most reliable service is provided by Perama (daily 7am–10pm; T 0361 751875, W peramatour.com), who pick up and drop off from their office 100m north of Bemo Corner at Jl Legian 39. You can buy tickets on the phone and through other agents. Typical fares include Ubud Rp50,000; Lovina Rp125,000; and the Gili Islands Rp250,000–500,000 (depending on type of boat transfer).

BY BEMO

From Denpasar's Tegal terminal, you can get off at any point on their round-Kuta loop, which runs via Bemo Corner, west and then north along Jl Pantai Kuta, east along Jl Melasti before heading north up Jl Legian only as far as Jl Padma before turning round and continuing south down Jl Legian as far as Bemo Corner.

BY FERRY

Many Kuta travel agents sell boat tickets to Lombok and Nusa Lembongan and these include transfers to the relevant port (see p.256 & p.285 for more information on these services). Pelni long-distance boat tickets to other islands are available from Jl Raya Kuta 299, 500m south of Supernova in Tuban Supermarket (T 0361 763963, W pelni.co.id).

VISITING THE GILIS

If you're **planning a trip to the Gilis**, visit Island Promotions, Shop 12, Poppies Lane 1, Kuta (daily 9am–10pm; T 0361 753241, W gili-paradise.com), for reliable information. They can book transport and accommodation and have a hotel booking site (W gili-hotels.com).

CURRENCY EXCHANGE SCAMS

Be extremely careful when **changing money** at currency exchange counters in Kuta as many places short-change tourists by using well-known **rip-offs** including rigged calculators and folded notes. One chain of **recommended moneychangers** is PT Central Kuta (W centralkutabali.com), which has numerous branches including on Jalan Legian, Jalan Melasti and in the Seminyak Square complex. If you do get caught in a money-changing scam, contact the community police (see p.246).

INFORMATION

Tourist office The Badung Tourist Office is at Jl Raya Kuta 2 (Mon–Thurs 8am–3pm, Fri 8am–noon, Sat 8am–4pm; T 0361 756175) and beside the lifeguard post on the beach off Jl Pantai Kuta (Mon–Fri 10am–3pm; T 0361 755660). Neither branch is particularly helpful.

WATERSPORTS

SURFING

Poppies 2, Poppies 1 and Jl Benesari are crammed with board rental (around Rp80,000–90,000/day) and repair shops, surfwear outlets and surfers' bars. Surf schools charge from US$35–50 for a 2hr 30min introduction. The best time of year for surfing off Kuta is April–Oct. Numerous agents in Kuta sell "surfari" tours to the mega-waves off East Java (including G-Land, see p.211; mainly March–Oct), West Java, Lombok, Sumbawa and West Timor. Prices are around US$750 for a six-night package at G-Land, or $600 for five days at Sumbawa's Lakey Peak.

Rip Curl School of Surf *Blue Ocean* hotel, Jl Pantai Kuta Arjuna, Legian T 0361 735858, W ripcurlschoolofsurf.com. Surfing, wake boarding, windsurfing and kite-surfing lessons and courses.

Surf Travel Online Jl Benesari 29 T 0361 750550, W surftravelonline.com. Surfaris around Bali and beyond.

DIVE OPERATORS

All Sanur operators (see p.255) also pick up from Kuta.

AquaMarine Diving Jl Petitenget 2A, Kuta T 0361 738020, W aquamarinediving.com. PADI five-star Gold Palm Resort. Day-trips cost from $100.

GETTING AROUND

Bemos The dark-blue Tegal–Kuta–Legian bemos (at least hourly; 5am–8.30pm) only cover a clockwise loop around Kuta, leaving out most of Legian and all of Seminyak. Flag them down at any point along this route; expect to pay around Rp5000.

Taxis and drivers The most reliable metered taxis are the light-blue Bali Taksi (T 0361 701111; note that almost all drivers turn off the meter unofficially after midnight; expect to pay at least Rp50,000 to get home from a night out no matter how short the distance). The informal taxi service offered by the ubiquitous transport touts is rarely cheaper for short trips but can be worthwhile for longer journeys and day-trips (around Rp450,000/day).

Motorbike and bicycle rental Tour agents and touts offer motorbikes (from Rp50,000) and bicycles (from Rp20,000) for rent.

ACCOMMODATION

The biggest concentration of inexpensive accommodation is in Kuta, along Poppies 1, Poppies 2 and Jl Benesari. Legian has good-value places with pools and a/c; Seminyak is more sophisticated and pricier.

KUTA

Anemone Gang Sorga T 0361 754683. Spick-and-span rooms, all with a/c and hot water, in a quiet family compound with a tiny pool. Breakfast not included. **Rp160,000**

★**Bendesa** Jl Legian T 0361 754 366, W bendesaaccommodation.com. A cut above most of the competition, with a range of decent-sized rooms in a large, leafy complex around a pleasant pool, and friendly staff. **Rp200,000**

Hostel Kempu Taman Ayu II Just off Jl Benesari T 0361 754376, W hostelkemputamanayu2.com. Solid budget choice, with plain but clean, fan-cooled rooms with fridges and hot water; some more expensive a/c options are available too. Relatively quiet, yet close to the action. **Rp150,000**

Hotel Lusa Jl Benesari T 0361 753714, W hotellusakuta.com. Large, well-run hotel with a range of rooms, including cold-water, fan-cooled "economy" options (rooms with hot water cost an extra Rp60,000 or so), and a nice garden and pool. **Rp275,000**

Masa Inn 31 Poppies 1 T 0361 758507, W masainn.com. If you're looking for a touch more comfort, but don't want to break the bank, Masa Inn has a/c, mid-range rooms, two pools and a restaurant. Good-value singles (Rp300,000) too. **Rp500,000**

Hotel Sorga Gang Sorga T 0361 751897, W hotelsorga.com. The rooms in this rather old hotel look a bit shabby, but the fan rooms in a three-storey block set around a small pool and restaurant still offer good value for the price (though the cheapest ones only have cold water). **Rp220,000**

Suka Beach Inn Jl Benesari, off Poppies 2 T 0861 752793. This backpacker favourite offers spartan fan-cooled rooms (though don't expect "luxuries" such as towels) in blocks surrounding a large pool. **Rp140,000**

Un's Hotel Jl Benesari, off Poppies 2 T 0361 757409, W unshotel.com. Popular mid-range place where the least expensive rooms come with fans, TVs and hot water. There's a pool and a good restaurant too. **Rp575,000**

LEGIAN AND SEMINYAK

Blue Ocean Jl Double Six T 0361 730289. Basic and shabby fan rooms (some with kitchens) whose real attraction is their prime location on the beachfront road. There's a surf school on the premises. Staff are laidback to the point of being horizontal. Breakfast costs extra. **Rp300,000**

Inada Losmen Gang Bima 9, off Jl Dhyana Pura and Jl Raya Seminyak T 0361 732269, E inada@eksadata.com. Top-value losmen on a quiet leafy lane, with a dozen large and clean but dark rooms set round a garden yard complete with a koi pond. **Rp150,000**

The Island Gang Abdi at Jl Legian T 0361 762662, W theislandhotelbali.com. A boutique hostel run by friendly, laidback Australians and Brits. The cool white rooms are set around an infinity pool and dorm beds have fabulous thick mattresses. Rates includes a free massage for those in the private rooms and for backpackers staying at least three nights. The perfect place to relax for a few days and meet new friends, though it's not the quietest place in town. Dorm **Rp250,000**, double **Rp600,000**

★**Raja Gardens** Jl Abimanyu, next to Santo Mikael Church T 0361 730494, E jdw@eksadata.com or E walker808id@yahoo.com. An excellent hotel well worth stretching the budget for, with large, spotless (if a little bare) rooms with fans (a/c costs Rp100,000 extra) set around a lovingly

HOT SHOPPING

Jl Oberoi (often referred to as Eat Street thanks to its plethora of trendy restaurants) is Bali's very own Rodeo Drive – though rather than established designers, this is the place to find up-and-coming design talent from all over the world. Popular designers include the French brand Magali Pascal (daily 10am–10pm; T 0361 736147, W magalipascal.com).

If you're looking for something more than the beachside market stalls in Kuta, head to the colossal, seafront **Discovery Shopping Mall** (Sun–Thurs 10am–10pm, Fri–Sat 10am–10.30pm; T 0361 755522, W discoveryshoppingmall.com) on Jl Kartika Plaza, for clothes from known labels, as well as local designers. You'll also find books, crafts and gifts here.

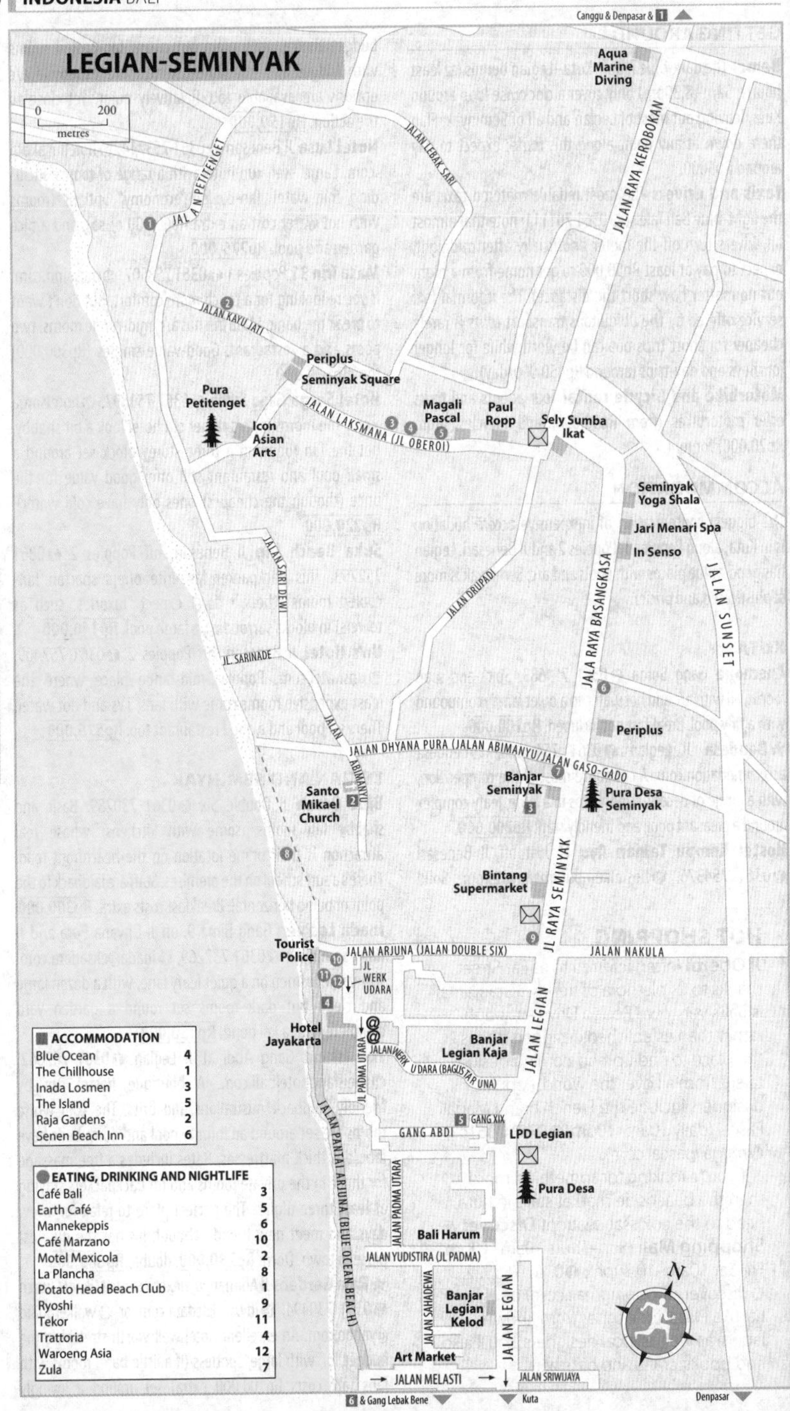
Canggu & Denpasar & 1
LEGIAN-SEMINYAK
0 200
metres
Aqua
Marine
Diving
JALAN RAYA KEROBOKAN
JALAN LEBAK SARI
JALAN PETITENGET
JALAN KAYU JATI
Periplus
Seminyak Square
Pura
Petitenget
Icon
Asian
Arts
JALAN LAKSMANA (JL OBEROI)
Magali
Pascal
Paul
Ropp
Sely Sumba
Ikat
Seminyak
Yoga Shala
Jari Menari Spa
In Senso
JALAN SUNSET
JALA RAYA BASANGKASA
JALAN DRUPADI
JALAN SARI DEWI
JL. SARINADE
JALAN ABIMANYU
Periplus
JALAN DHYANA PURA (JALAN ABIMANYU/JALAN GASO-GADO
Banjar
Seminyak
Pura Desa
Seminyak
Santo
Mikael
Church
JL RAYA SEMINYAK
Bintang
Supermarket
Tourist
Police
JALAN ARJUNA (JALAN DOUBLE SIX)
JALAN NAKULA
JL
WERK
UDARA
Hotel
Jayakarta
JALAN WERK UDARA (BAGUSTAR UNA)
Banjar
Legian Kaja
JALAN LEGIAN
JL PADMA UTARA
GANG XIX
GANG ABDI
LPD Legian
Pura Desa
JALAN PANTAI ARJUNA (BLUE OCEAN BEACH)
JALAN PADMA UTARA
Bali Harum
JALAN YUDISTIRA (JL PADMA)
JALAN SAHADEWA
Banjar
Legian
Kelod
JALAN LEGIAN
Art Market
JALAN MELASTI
JALAN SRIWIJAYA
N
6 & Gang Lebak Bene
Kuta
Denpasar
ACCOMMODATION
Blue Ocean 4
The Chillhouse 1
Inada Losmen 3
The Island 5
Raja Gardens 2
Senen Beach Inn 6
EATING, DRINKING AND NIGHTLIFE
Café Bali 3
Earth Café 5
Mannekeppis 6
Café Marzano 10
Motel Mexicola 2
La Plancha 8
Potato Head Beach Club 1
Ryoshi 9
Tekor 11
Trattoria 4
Waroeng Asia 12
Zula 7

★TREAT YOURSELF

The Chillhouse Jl Kubu Manyar 22, Br Pipitan, Canggu ⓣ081 353 130 002, ⓦthechillhouse.com. Austrian couple Alex and Sabine run this idyllic surf-focused getaway in Canggu, just away from the noise and hubbub of the main resorts. Each individual cottage is charmingly kitted out, either with outdoor terraces or bales (open-air structures) on the roof. *The Chillhouse* is just ten minutes from the beach; yoga and trips to various places on Bali are available daily, and the surf instruction's considered to be the best in Bali. Book well in advance. From €385/ week including breakfast and dinner.

tended garden. The highlight is a large pool shaded by palm trees. Breakfast costs extra. **Rp500,000**

Senen Beach Inn Gang Senen no.2, off Gang Lebak Bene ⓣ0361 755470. Situated in a tranquil little lane and run by a friendly group of young Indonesian guys, *Senen Beach Inn* has basic, cleanish rooms with outdoor bathrooms. Breakfast costs extra. **Rp130,000**

EATING

KUTA AND TUBAN

Balcony Un's Hotel, Jl Benesari 16 ⓣ0361 757409, ⓦunshotel.com. Where surfers in the know come for a giant breakfast (from Rp25,000) after their early morning surf. Browse the photos of famous surfers on the walls while enjoying a stack of pancakes, eggs done any way or a fruit salad with muesli and yoghurt. Also good for dinner and cocktails. Daily 7.30am–11.30pm.

★**Jimbaran Seafood Restaurants** Jimbaran Beach, 4km south of Kuta (about Rp50,000 by taxi). More than fifty seafood warung barbecue the day's catch at tables on the beach here (from around Rp60,000 with trimmings); they open from noon but are best by candlelight at night.

Mama's German Restaurant Jl Legian ⓦbali-mamas .com. Open all day, every day, serving all manner of German specialities, notably sausages (from Rp65,000) and Black Forest gateau, as well as cold beer (from Rp30,000). Daily 24hr.

Pasar Senggol Jl Blambangan. Kuta's main night market is busy with hot-food stalls serving inexpensive Indonesian food to locals and thrifty travellers. Daily 5pm–late.

Stakz Bar and Grill Jl Benesari ⓦstakzbarandgrill.com. Run by a pair of Australians, this joint serves the best burgers in Kuta (Rp30,000–65,000); try the chilli-spiked Portuguese chicken version. Daily 7am–1am.

Warung Indonesia Gang Ronta. Welcoming, budget warung with an inviting selection of Balinese dishes, including a tasty *nasi campur*, most for under Rp20,000. Daily noon–11pm/midnight.

Warung Max Jl Benesari ⓦfacebook.com/warungmax. Despite the name, there's nothing Indonesian about this Mexican restaurant; come here for salsa sounds, frozen margharitas, Mexican-style pizzas and sizzling beef fajitas with salsa and guacamole (mains from Rp40,000). Daily 8am–11.30pm.

LEGIAN AND SEMINYAK

★**Café Bali** Jl Oberoi ⓣ0361 736484. French-colonial-style building serving inventive dishes (Rp39,000–108,000) and catering to the chic expats of Bali – the strawberry margharitas and tuna tartare are to die for. Book ahead in the evenings. Daily 7.30am–11.30pm.

Earth Café Jl Oberoi ⓣ0361 736645. This vegetarian-, vegan-, gluten-intolerant- and raw-foodie-friendly café/ shop serves up restorative dishes such as quinoa pancakes, chickpea burgers, and fruit and granola, as well as an array of drinks. Perfect if you've over-indulged. Daily 7am–11pm.

Café Marzano Jl Double Six. Open-fronted café serving authentic and reasonably priced Italian fare, with excellent wood-oven pizzas (Rp46,000–85,000) panini and salads. Daily 10am–11pm.

4

Motel Mexicola Jl Kayu Jati ⓣ0361 736688, ⓦmotel mexicolabali.com. A colourful blast of Mexicana, this appealing taqueria-bar is full of memorabilia – from Day of the Dead icons to World Cup photos. The menu runs from tacos (Rp35,000) to ceviche; great drinks too. Daily11am–1am.

Ryoshi Jl Seminyak 17 ⓣ0361 731152. As well as serving the best Japanese food (mains Rp49,000–96,000) in Bali, Ryoshi also hosts a massively popular jazz night on Friday evening. Delivery service available. Daily noon–11pm.

Tekor Jl Double Six ⓣ0361 735268. Understated, friendly café overlooking the sea, perfect at any time of day. Equally tasty Indonesian and Western mains vie for attention on the menu, and the breakfasts (Rp36,000–57,000) are great too. Daily 7.30am–11pm.

★**Trattoria** Jl Oberoi. Outstanding home-style Italian cuisine; the pizzas (Rp53,000–74,000) and the daily specials are the best-value options. Save some room for the divine chocolate tart with orange jam. The house wines are reasonably priced for Indonesia. Daily noon–10pm.

★**Waroeng Asia** Jl Double Six 23. Shady restaurant that's an expat favourite for its palate-tingling, well-priced Thai food (mains Rp43,000–75,000). Arrive early to bag a seat – it fills up fast. Daily 11am–10.30pm.

Zula Jl Dhyana Pura ⓣ0361 732723. Under the same management as Earth Café (see above), Zula has a similar ethos, with a focus on fresh smoothies, juices, lassis, tea or tonic (there are special concoctions that claim to cure everything from anxiety to constipation). Great cakes and chocolates too. Daily 7am–11pm.

DRINKING AND NIGHTLIFE

For gigs and nightlife listings see the free fortnightly magazine *The Beat* (beatmag.com). If you're planning a big night out in Kuta, nothing really gets going until about midnight. Entrance is generally free unless there's a special event or party (when it can become pretty pricey, with some places charging up to Rp1,000,000). Check *The Beat* or look out for posters on the beach for details.

KUTA

Bounty Discotheque Jl Legian 0361 752529, bountydiscotheque.com. Infamous hub of Australian excess, housed in a replica of Captain Bligh's eighteenth-century galleon. DJs play everything from house to hip-hop, and there are eclectic events, including foam parties, drag acts, muscle shows and karaoke. Jam jars (lethal, pint-sized cocktails) are the signature drink. Daily 8pm–4am.

Engine Room Jl Legian. The place for some seriously energetic dancing to pumping R&B, hip-hop and, occasionally, tribal music. Beer around Rp20,000. Daily 9pm–3/4am.

Espresso Bar Jl Legian. Local cover bands make a decent attempt at all the classics in this small but very popular rock bar. Drinks specials include two- for-one mojitos. Cocktails around Rp50,000. Daily 7pm–3am.

mBargo Jl Legian 0361 756000, mbargonightclub.com. Thumping music from hip-hop, house and electro DJs ensures packed dancefloors at this raucous lounge bar and dance club. Daily 10pm–4am.

Sky Garden Lounge Jl Legian 61 61legian.com. Perched on the top floors of a tall glass building, Sky Garden is one of Kuta's most popular clubs, full of people up for a good time and fuelled by daily drinks specials. Daily 10pm–3/4am.

Vi Ai Pi Jl Legian 88 0361 752355, viapibali.com. Smarter and (slightly) more sedate than many of its Kuta neighbours, this trendy restaurant-bar-club is also a bit pricier than average. Still, the drinks and music (both DJs and live bands) make it well worth a look. Daily 11am–3am.

★TREAT YOURSELF

Potato Head Beach Club (Jl Petitenget, Seminyak 0361 737979, ptthead.com) is arguably Bali's hottest venue. The curved exterior, designed as a modern take on the Colosseum and clad in eighteenth-century teak shutters, shelters an oasis of beachside infinity pools. You can lounge on vintage designer furniture with a cocktail (Rp110,000–130,000) among Seminyak's most fashionable by day, or dance the night away to resident DJs and guest acts (which, in 2013, included Snoop Dogg). Daily 11am–2am.

LEGIAN AND SEMINYAK

Mannekeppis Jl Raya Seminyak 2 0361 847 5784, mannekepis-bistro.com. This restaurant-bar brings together Belgian beer (around Rp86,000; Bintang from Rp29,000), Euro-Asian cuisine, jazz and blues (live music Thurs–Sat from 9pm), and table football. It's an appealing combination. Sun–Thurs 10am–1am, Fri–Sat 10am–2am.

★ **La Plancha** A terraced beachside café with colourful beanbags and umbrellas strewn across the sand. It gets packed at sunset with people enjoying a beer or cocktail (around Rp100,000) overlooking the sea. Daily 7am–1am.

DIRECTORY

Banks and exchange There are ATMs every few hundred metres, and a Moneygram agent at Bank Danamon just south of Poppies 2 on Jl Legian.

Bookshops There are several secondhand bookshops on Poppies 1, Poppies 2, Jl Benesari and Jl Padma Utara. New books are available from Periplus (daily 10am–10pm; 0361 769757, periplus.com) at Discovery Shopping Centre, Jl Kartika Plaza.

Dentist Bali Dental Clinic 911, Mal Bali Galleria, Simpang Siur roundabout, Jl Bypass Ngurah Rai (0361 766254, bali911dentalclinic.com).

Embassies and consulates In Denpasar (see p.246).

Festivals and events The Kuta Karnival is held in early September and features parades, surfing and skateboarding competitions and gigs by local bands.

Hospitals, clinics and pharmacies The nearest hospitals are in Denpasar (see p.246). Most expats use one of two reputable small, private 24hr hospitals on the outskirts of Kuta, both of which have English-speaking staff: Bali International Medical Centre (BIMC), Jl Bypass Ngurah Rai 100X, near the Simpang Siur roundabout (0361 761263, bimcbali.com); and nearby International SOS (Klinik SOS Medika), Jl Bypass Ngurah Rai 505X (0361 710505, sosindonesia.com). Consultations cost from around Rp550,000. Smaller, less expensive clinics include La Walon Clinic at the hotel of the same name on Poppies 1 (0361 757326 or 0361 757234, lewalonclinic.com). There are pharmacies on every major shopping street.

Internet There are countless internet cafes; most charge around Rp15,000–20,000/hr.

Police The English-speaking community police, Satgas Pantai Desa Adat Kuta, have a 24hr office on the beach in front of *Inna Kuta Beach Hotel* (0361 762871). The government police station is at Jl Raya Kuta 141, south Kuta (0361 751598).

Post office Kuta's GPO and poste restante is on unsignposted Gang Selamat, between Jl Raya Kuta and Jl Blambangan (Mon–Sat 8am–5pm). There are numerous small postal agents elsewhere.

Shopping Small shops selling silver, clothing, textiles and other souvenirs are everywhere in the Kuta-Legian-Seminyak

4

area. Bargain hard. For a one-stop shop, head to the huge hypermarket-style store, Bintang Pusat Belanja on Jl Raya Seminyak 17 (daily 8am–10pm).

Spas and massage Jari Menari, Jl Raya Basangkasa 47, Seminyak, is one of the area's best spas (T 0361 736740, W jarimenari.com; massages from Rp280,000.

Yoga Several hostels and hotels offer inexpensive yoga sessions. Alternatively, try Seminyak Yoga Shala (T 0361 730498; classes Rp120,000), next to Jari Menari on Jl Raya Basangkasa, which offers daily ashtanga and hatha classes, or the friendly Bikram Yoga (Jl Patih Jelatik, Istana Kuta Galleria Block VL 12 T 0361 769100, W bikrambali.com; drop-in classes Rp145,000), Bali's only Bikram studio.

THE BUKIT

Just south of Kuta, southern Bali bulges out into **the Bukit** ("hill"), a harsh, infertile limestone plateau whose craggy coastline challenges surfers with its world-class breaks, most famously at Uluwatu and Padang Padang. Where once only hardcore wave-riders would endure the potholed tracks to get to its secluded little **surf beaches**, increasing numbers of backpackers are now following suit as the roads are improved and tiny hotels are hollowed out of the clifftops, often accessible only via steep rock-cut steps. Take local advice on where it's safe to swim as currents can be treacherous round here.

There's almost no public transport on the Bukit, so you'll need to rent a car or bike from Kuta or take a taxi (from around Rp125,000–150,000, if you bargain hard); to get to the beaches, simply follow signs for the temple, Pura Luhur Uluwatu, at Bali's southwesternmost point, until directed otherwise.

Surf beaches

The first of the main surf beaches is **Dreamland**, with its gloriously white sands; it is home to a monstrous hotel complex and condo project, popular with domestic tourists, which has replaced the warungs and surfer accommodation of the past. Access to the beach is via the ostentatious entrance to the Pecatu Indah development. Fast developing into the liveliest of the Bukit surf beaches, nearby **Bingin** enjoys the same great coastal scenery and a more laidback surfer vibe, with budget accommodation nestled into the cliff face and seafood warungs on the sand. *The Temple Lodge* (T 0857 3901 1572, W thetemplelodge.com) at the top of the cliff offers food, drink, yoga classes and massage, as well as rooms (see p.254). **Balangan Beach** to the north has a long stretch of sand, dotted with sun umbrellas and loungers for rent, with plenty of backpacker accommodation and budget restaurants. Impossibles, to the south of Bingin, is another small surf beach, while the break at **Padang Padang** is considered to be one of the most exciting in Indonesia. Accommodation lines the roadside close to both of these spots. Nearby **SULUBAN** is the location of the world-famous **Uluwatu surf breaks.**

Pura Luhur Uluwatu

Revered since the tenth century as one of Bali's most important temples, **Pura Luhur Uluwatu** (daily sunrise–sunset; Rp20,000 including sarong rental) commands a superb position on a rocky promontory 70m above the foaming surf, at the far southwestern tip of Bali, 2km south of Suluban and 18km from Kuta. As a directional temple, or *kayangan jagat*, Pura Luhur Uluwatu is the guardian of the southwest and is dedicated to the spirits of the sea; it's also a state rather than a village temple and so has influence over all the people of Bali. Despite this, the temple structure itself lacks magnificence, being relatively small, and its greyish-white coral bricks are for the most part unadorned. Most tourists come here at sunset, when the setting is at its most dramatic and there's a performance of the **Kecak and Fire Dance** (daily 6–7pm; Rp80,000).

ACCOMMODATION

There's no shortage of budget accommodation on the Bukit.

★ **Flowerbud Bungalows** Balangan T 0828 367 2772, W flowerbudbalangan.com. Rightly popular, family-run place in a great cliff-top location. The lovely bungalows sleep up to five people and are set in tranquil grounds, which also feature a pool and restaurant. **Rp300,000**

The Gong Suluban roadside T 0361 769976, E thegong acc@yahoo.com. This chilled and friendly surfers' favourite has six fan-cooled rooms, rents scooters and surfboards, and sells warung-style food and travellers' breakfasts. **Rp200,000**

4

★TREAT YOURSELF

The Temple Lodge Bingin ⓣ0857 3901 1572, ⓦthetemplelodge.com. Perched at the top of Bingin cliff, The Temple Lodge is well worth a splurge for its gorgeous suites, all with great views. Perks include an infinity pool, daily yoga classes, spa (massages from Rp120,000/hr), and a delightful restaurant serving Indian, Italian and Balinese dishes. **$70**

Kelly's Warung Bingin cliff ⓣ0813 3705 8284, ⓔricki miranda22@hotmail.com. Basic but stylish and spotless beachfront rooms above a juice bar and surf shop. It's worth paying a little extra for the rooms at the front, which have massive balconies overlooking the surf. **Rp150,000**

Leggies Bingin ⓣ0815 5890 8900, ⓦleggiesbungalows.com. Appealing place with comfortable rooms (with either fans or a/c) around a lush garden and pool. There's also a decent restaurant and TV lounge, and vehicle rental is available. **Rp250,000**

Pondok Indah Gung and Lynie Bingin clifftop ⓣ0361 847 0933. Welcoming lodge with a dozen rather tasteful fan-cooled rooms set round a garden, some of them in pretty coconut-wood-and-thatch bungalows. **Rp300,000**

4

SANUR

Nicknamed "Snore" because it lacks the clubs and all-night party venues of Kuta, **SANUR** is a sedate resort popular with older visitors, and has a distinct village atmosphere, a fairly decent, 5km-long sandy beach, and plenty of attractive budget accommodation. It's also a major centre for diving and the main departure point for boats to Nusa Lembongan, plus it's only 15km to Kuta and forty minutes' drive to Ubud.

Though the sea here is only properly swimmable at high tide (a big expanse of shore gets exposed at low tide, and the currents beyond the reef are dangerously strong), there are lots of inviting restaurants along the beach and you can walk or cycle the entire 5km from the *Inna Grand Bali Beach* in the north to *Hotel Sanur Beach* in the south along a seafront esplanade.

ARRIVAL AND DEPARTURE

By shuttle bus Perama shuttle buses stop at Warung Pojok mini-market, Jl Hang Tuah 31, north Sanur; bemos run from near here to Jl Danau Tamblingan.

Destinations Bedugul (daily; 2hr–2hr 30min); Candi Dasa (3 daily; 2hr–2hr 30min); Gili Islands (daily; 9hr); Kintamani (daily; 2hr 15min); Kuta/Ngurah Rai Airport (5 daily; 30min–1hr); Lovina (daily; 2hr 30min–3hr); Padang Bai (3 daily; 1hr 30min–2hr); Senggigi (Lombok; 2 daily; 8hr 30min); Ubud (4 daily; 30min–1hr).

By bemo or public bus There's a direct bemo between Sanur and Denpasar terminals at Kereneng (green; 15min; around Rp8000) and Tegal (blue; 30min; around Rp8000). Both routes cover north Sanur's Jl Bypass/Jl Hang Tuah junction, dropping passengers just outside the *Inna Grand Bali Beach* compound, before continuing via Jl Danau Beratan and Jl Danau Buyan and running down Jl Danau Tamblingan to the *Trophy Pub Centre* in south Sanur. From Denpasar's Batubulan terminal, white DAMRI buses bound for Nusa Dua drop Sanur passengers at the *Sanur Paradise Plaza* hotel on Jl Bypass in north Sanur (20min; around Rp10,000). Take this bus back to Batubulan for connections to Ubud.

By boat Sanur is the main departure point for boats to Nusa Lembongan, which leave from the eastern end of Jl Hang Tuah in north Sanur, 200m east of the Perama bus stop. Gili Cat, a catamaran service to Gili Trawangan and Lombok, runs free transfers to the departure point in Padang Bai from its central Sanur office at Jl Danau Tamblingan 51 (ⓣ0361 271680, ⓦgilicat.com).

By plane Flight tickets can be bought from JBA, inside the compound of the *Diwangkara Hotel* on Jl Hang Tuah 54, north Sanur (ⓣ0361 286501, ⓔjbadwkbl@denpasar.wasantara.net.id), and at Sumanindo Tour on Jl Danau Tamblingan 22, central Sanur (ⓣ0361 288570, ⓔsuman travel@dps.centrin.net.id). Official airport taxis charge Rp95,000 from Ngurah Rai Airport to Sanur. Most hotels and losmen will arrange a car for around Rp100,000, or you can hail a metered taxi; Perama shuttle buses charge Rp25,000/person.

INFORMATION

Online There's no tourist office but ⓦgotosanur.com is useful.

GETTING AROUND

Bemos The Denpasar–Sanur bemos (see above), are useful for getting around Sanur, especially for destinations along the 2km-long Jl Danau Tamblingan; a local ride costs around Rp5000.

Taxis and transport touts Ubiquitous metered light-blue Bluebird cars (ⓣ0361 701111) are most reliable. Negotiate with transport touts for longer rides and day-trips.

Car and motorbike rental Easily arranged through transport touts and tour agencies.

Bicycles Countless outlets along Jl Danau Tamblingan and the beachfront promenade (from Rp20,000/day).

WATERSPORTS AND DIVING

Four-day PADI Open Water dive courses cost about $350–550; two-dive excursions to superior reefs beyond south Bali cost from around $115.

Blue Oasis Beach Club Beachfront of Hotel Sanur Beach, south Sanur ⓣ0361 288011, ⓦblueoasisbeachclub.com. As well as diving, they offer parasailing, wake-boarding, kitesurfing, kayaking and water-skiing sessions, courses and equipment rental.

Blue Season Bali Jl Tamblingan 69XX, central Sanur ⓣ0361 282574, ⓦbaliocean.com. PADI five-star IDC dive centre.

ACCOMMODATION

Ari Homestay Jl Danau Tamblingan 40, central Sanur ⓣ0361 289673, ⓦhomestaysanur.com. Elementary but cheerful and low-cost rooms (most with shared bathrooms) set behind the family shop. Large breakfast included. **Rp100,000**

★**Flashbacks** Jl Danau Tamblingan 110, central Sanur ⓣ0361 281682, ⓦflashbacks-chb.com. Beautifully decorated rooms (the cheapest only have shared bathrooms) and bungalows, run by friendly and professional staff. The attached *Porch Café* has divine espressos. **Rp300,000**

Pondok Santi Homestay Jl Hangtuah 39, north Sanur ⓣ0361 285592. Ten simple rooms in a friendly family-run compound, down a quiet side road a few minutes' walk from the beach. **Rp150,000**

Yulia Homestay 1 Jl Danau Tamblingan 38, central Sanur ⓣ0361 288089. Attractive, terraced, fan-cooled bungalows in a homestay compound filled with the owner's prize-winning songbirds. **Rp200,000**

EATING

The night market, inside the Sindhu Market at the Jl Danau Tamblingan/Jl Danau Toba intersection, central Sanur, is good for inexpensive local eats from around 5pm through to the early hours.

Manik Organik Jl Danau Tamblingan 85, south Sanur ⓣ0361 855 3380, ⓦmanikorganik.com. Ubud-style health-food café with rejuvenating juices, smoothies, salads, soups and veg, vegan and organic mains (Rp35,000–80,000). It also hosts yoga sessions, cookery classes and Friday open-mic nights. Daily 8am–10/11pm.

★**Massimo** Jl Danau Tamblingan 228, south Sanur ⓣ0361 288942, ⓦmassimobali.com. Excellent south Italian restaurant serving more than fifty types of pizza (from Rp60,000), plus specialities from Lecce and delicious home-made *gelato* (sundaes from Rp23,000). Daily 11am–11pm.

Ryoshi Jl Danau Tamblingan 156, south Sanur ⓣ0361 288473, ⓦryoshibali.com. Cross over a cute little humpback bridge to this Balinese institution, which is perfect if you're fed up with *nasi goreng* and the like. The Japanese food here is divine – try the sashimi (from Rp21,0000) or the sushi (from Rp30,000). Daily 11am–midnight.

DRINKING AND NIGHTLIFE

Jazz Bar & Grille Komplek Pertokoan Sanur Raya 15, next to *KFC* at the Jl Bypass/Jl Hang Tuah crossroads, north Sanur ⓣ0361 285892. Some of Bali's best jazz, blues and pop bands play live sets nightly from about 9.30pm. Daily 10am–2am.

Laghawa Jl Danau Tambligan 51, central Sanur ⓣ0361 288494, ⓦlaghawa.com. Huge, popular place with regular live music events, including traditional Balinese dance on Wednesday evenings. It's also a great place to chill during the day and for drinks at night (cocktails from Rp69,000). Daily 6.30am–11pm.

Mango Beach Jl Pantai Sindhu. Decorated with flags from around the world, this reggae bar opens right out onto the beach and hosts live music events (Tues, Thurs & Sat night). There are also comfy sofas, pool tables and a surprisingly good food menu. Daily 8am–11pm.

Warung Sunrise Jl Hang Tuah. Beachside bar with chairs on the sand, live reggae and strong cocktails (from around Rp40,000). Daily 10am–late.

The Wicked Parrot Jl Danau Tamblingan 47 ⓣ0361 281814, ⓦwickedparrot.com. Raucous place with live Irish music by the Bali Leprechauns three nights a week (Mon, Wed & Fri). Daily 7.30am–late.

DIRECTORY

Banks and exchange There are ATMs and exchange facilities all over the resort, including an authorized moneychanger at Jl Danau Tamblingan 18.

Bookshops Periplus, inside Hardy's Grosir supermarket, Jl Danau Tamblingan 193, central Sanur (daily 8.30am–10pm; ⓣ0361 282790, ⓦperiplus.com); Ganesha Books, Jl Danau Tamblingan 42, central Sanur (daily 8am–10pm; ⓦganeshabooksbali.com).

Embassies and consulates UK consulate at Jl Tirta Nadi 20A, Sanur ⓣ0361 270601, ⓔbcbali@dps.centrin.net.id; US and Australian consulates in Denpasar (see p.246).

Hospitals and clinics All the big hotels provide 24hr medical service; try the *Inna Grand Bali Beach* (ⓣ0361 288511, ⓦgraninnabali.com). Expats tend to use the two international clinics on the edge of Kuta (see p.252); the nearest hospitals are in Denpasar (see p.246).

Internet Centres on all main roads.

Pharmacies Guardian Pharmacy next to Hardy's Grosir, Jl Danau Tamblingan.

Police The police station is on Jl Bypass in north Sanur, just south of the Paradise Plaza hotel (ⓣ0361 288597).

Post office The main post office is on Jl Danau Buyan, north-central Sanur. There are postal agents opposite *Respati* hotel at Jl Danau Tamblingan 66, central Sanur, and inside the Trophy Centre on Jl Cemara in south Sanur.

NUSA LEMBONGAN

Southeast across the Badung Strait, encircled by a mixture of white-sand beaches and mangrove, the tiny island of **NUSA LEMBONGAN** (4km by 3km) is an ideal escape from the bustle of the south. Seaweed farming is the major occupation here, supplemented by tourist income from surfers, snorkellers, divers and anyone seeking attractive beaches, a bit of gentle exploring and an addictive somnolent atmosphere.

WHAT TO SEE AND DO

Ranged along the west coast for over 1km, the low-key beachside village of **Jungutbatu** has plenty of losmen and restaurants. **Coconut Beach**, **Chelegimbai** and **Mushroom Bay** (Tanjung Sanghyang) to the southwest and **Dream Beach** on the south coast offer more upmarket accommodation, and Mushroom Bay is the destination for day-trippers from the mainland. This can disturb the peace in the middle of the day but does little to detract from the idyllic white sand and turquoise waters.

4

You can walk around the island in three to four hours. Motorbikes and bicycles are widely available for rent in Jungutbatu, though you will have to dismount and push the latter up some of the very steep hills.

Three **surf breaks**, aptly named Shipwrecks, Lacerations and Playground, are all reached from Jungutbatu. You can paddle out to Shipwrecks from the northern end of the beach, and to the other two from Coconut Beach around the cliffs to the south of Jungutbatu, but if you are staying further away you can charter a boat (around Rp50,000 including waiting time). There are several sites for snorkelling accessible by rented boat around the island. Further away, the Penida Wall and Crystal Bay, close to the neighbouring island of Nusa Penida, are also popular (around Rp200,000–250,000 for two hours for two people including equipment). World Diving (see below) also take snorkellers, if there's room on the boat and the site is suitable ($25, including equipment; about 4hr). The area around the islands is popular for diving, although the sea can be cold with treacherous currents so it is important to dive with operators familiar with the area. Manta Point off the south coast of Nusa Penida is renowned for *mola mola* – although sadly during high season this generally means you can't see any that do turn up, due to the huge crowds of divers surrounding them.

ARRIVAL AND DEPARTURE

By boat Several companies operate fast boats between Sanur/Padang Bai and Nusa Lembongan, including Scoot (T 0361 285522, W scootcruises.com; Rp350,000 one-way including pick-up; connections to the Gili Islands and mainland Lombok available too) and Rocky (T 0361 801 2324, W rockyfastboat.com; $28 one-way including pick-up); the crossing takes around 45min. Perama (T 0361 750808, W peramatour.com; Rp100,000 one-way) is cheaper but takes around an hour and a half. The lowest-priced options are the public ferries from Sanur, though they take about two hours and can be unnervingly crowded. Note that drop-off points for the boats to Jungutbatu and Mushroom Bay depend on the tide – you'll wade ashore wherever you land.

DIVING

World Diving Lembongan (T 0812 390 0686, W world-diving.com). The most established company on the island, this is a PADI five-star international operator, based at Pondok Baruna resort in Jungutbatu. Single dives cost $48; a one-day & two-dive package is $85.

ACCOMMODATION

JUNGUTBATU

Bunga Bungalo T 0828 9760 8691, W bleucitron.net/bunga. Little place full of eccentric touches, with chairs made of giant clam shells and a cute little garden. The restaurant overlooking the beach does great wood-fired pizzas. Rp285,000

Bungalo No. 7 T 0366 559 6363, W bungalo-no7.com. Family-run place, set up 30 years ago, with good-value rooms at the far southern end of the beach; all have balconies or verandas, though the cheapest only have cold water. There's also a pool overlooking the beach. Rp250,000

Linda Bungalows T 0812 360 0867, E bcwcchoppers@yahoo.com. Aussie-run, spotlessly clean place right next to the beach. Rooms are in well-built two-storey buildings with good-quality furnishings. Rp200,000

★**Mandara Beach Bungalows** T 0812 460 9291, E mandarabeach@hotmail.com. Excellent-value concrete cottages with private terraces surrounding a pretty tropical garden. The traditional thatched bungalows with a/c

overlooking the sea are among the best budget options in Jungutbatu. Rp200,000

Pondok Baruna ⓣ0812 390 0686, ⓦworld-diving.com. The basic fan rooms overlooking the beach are small but prettier than some of the other budget options in Jungutbatu. The more expensive a/c bungalows surrounding an inviting pool at the back are decked out with marble tiles and heavy wooden furniture, and are worth the extra splurge (Rp650,000). Rates include breakfast. World Diving Lembongan is based here. Rp250,000

Secret Garden ⓣ0813 5313 6861, ⓦbigfishdiving.com. Charming British-run hideaway with simple but comfy bungalows, a good pool, movie nights, yoga classes and a decent dive centre. Rp200,000

Suka Nusa ⓣ0878 60023778, ⓔsukanusa@yahoo.com. These simple but elegant two-storey *lumbung* (traditional thatched rice-barn) bungalows are built around a small pool and have outdoor bathrooms and huge verandas for gazing over the sea. Rp350,000

Tarci Bungalows ⓣ0812 390 6300, ⓦtarcibungalows.com. Next to Linda Bungalows, this hotel has an excellent beachfront location, pool, restaurant and two classes of room: the simple standard class overlook the garden, while the smarter deluxe options have sea views and TVs; both have a/c. Standard double Rp250,000

COCONUT BEACH

★**Morin Lembongan** ⓣ0361 746 2258. Set back on cliffs in the southern part of the island, these four quiet, sturdy bungalows offer stunning views over Coconut Beach. Glorious. Rp450,000

EATING AND DRINKING

Most hotels have restaurants (mostly open daily 8am–10pm) right on the beach; some can be pricey for what you get.

Pondok Baruna Jungutbatu. All the food (mains from around Rp40,000) here is good, but if you like it hot, their *ikan pepes* (fish with chilli, coconut and Balinese spices cooked in banana leaf) and Baruna curry are especially recommended; the excellent fruit lassis are a great accompaniment.

Scallywags Sunset Beach ⓦscallywagsresort.com. Excellent spot for drinkers and diners alike, with inventive sandwiches, authentic tapas, barbecued steaks and seafood and hard-to-get imported tipples such as draught Kilkenny (Rp70,000/pint).

DIRECTORY

Banks and exchange There are no ATMs. Several places offer cash advances for a hefty commission.

Hospitals and clinics Contact the health centre (*klinik*) in Jungutbatu through your accommodation.

Internet Most hotels and restaurants offer free wi-fi.

PURA TANAH LOT

Dramatically marooned on a craggy, wave-lashed rock just off the coast about 30km northwest of Kuta, **Pura Tanah Lot** (daily sunrise–sunset; Rp30,000) is Bali's most photographed sight. Framed by frothing white surf and glistening black sand, its elegant multi-tiered shrines have become Bali's unofficial symbol and attract huge crowds of visitors every day, particularly around sunset. Unfortunately this has brought all the joys of tourism with it, and now the temple sits against a background of stalls and overenthusiastic hawkers. The temple is said to have been founded in the sixteenth century by the wandering Hindu priest Nirartha and is one of the most holy places on Bali. Only bona fide devotees are allowed to climb the stairway carved out of the rock face and enter the compounds; everyone else is confined to the base of the rock.

Although there are occasional bright-blue bemos from Denpasar's Ubung terminal direct to Tanah Lot, you'll probably have to go via **Kediri**, 12km east of the temple on the main Denpasar–Tabanan road. All Ubung (Denpasar)–Gilimanuk bemos drop passengers at Kediri bemo terminal (about Rp5000; 30min), where you should change on to a Kediri–Tanah Lot bemo (more frequent in the morning; about Rp5000; 25min). Alternatively, join one of the numerous tours to Tanah Lot that operate out of all major tourist resorts.

SOUTHWEST SURF BEACHES

West of Tabanan, the Denpasar–Gilimanuk coast road passes a couple of appealingly low-key black-sand surf beaches, both of them served by Denpasar (Ubung)–Gilimanuk bemos. The current can be severe all along this coast, so check locally before swimming.

About 26km west of Tabanan, the village of **Lalang Linggah** gives access to the austere black sand of Balian beach, which is known for its consistent surf breaks. *Balian Segara Homestay* (ⓣ0819 1645 6147; Rp150,000) has four simple, concrete en-suite bungalows above the surf.

4

Twenty-five kilometres further west, **Medewi** beach (about 2hr by bemo from Ubung) is known for its light current and fairly benign waves, making it a popular spot for novice surfers. *Mai Malu* (0361 43897; Rp150,000) is a popular place near the highway; it has eight plain, fan-cooled rooms, plus a restaurant serving pizza. They can also organize surf trips (around $50 per day), and car and motorbike rental. About 600m east of *Mai Malu* is *CSB Beach Inn* (0813 3866 7288; Rp150,000) which has large, well-kept fan and a/c rooms overlooking the shorefront rice fields.

UBUD AND AROUND

UBUD is Bali's cultural hub, a seductive town set amid terraced rice paddies and known for its talented classical dancers and musicians, and for its prolific painters and artisans. Tradition is particularly important here and temple festivals happen almost daily. However, although it's fashionable to characterize Ubud as the real Bali, especially in contrast with Kuta, it's a major tourist destination and bears little resemblance to a typical Balinese town – there's even a Starbucks here now.

4

WHAT TO SEE AND DO

Arty, high-minded Ubud has Bali's best art museums and commercial galleries, and is also a recognized centre for **spiritual tourism**, with many opportunities to try out indigenous and imported healing therapies. Organic cafés, riverside bungalows and craft shops crowd its central marketplace, while the surrounding countryside is ideal for walks and cycle rides, and there's easy access to the northern volcanoes.

There is major (mostly tasteful) development along the central Jalan Monkey Forest, and Ubud's peripheries encompass the neighbouring hamlets of Campuhan, Sanggingan, Penestanan, Nyuhkuning, Peliatan, Pengosekan and Padang Tegal.

Central Ubud

Ubud's oldest and most central art collection is the **Museum Puri Lukisan** on Jalan Raya (daily 9am–6pm; Rp50,000; 0361 971159, museumpurilukisan.com), which, though set in prettily landscaped grounds, suffers from poor labelling and is outshone by the Neka Art Museum in nearby Sanggingan (see p.260).

A water garden fronts central Ubud's most atmospheric temple, **Pura Taman Saraswati** (generally sunrise–sunset; free). Through the red-brick temple gate, you'll find various shrines dotted around the temple courtyards, including a towering lotus throne sculpted with a riot of carvings and resting on the cosmic turtle and sacred naga serpents.

Campuhan and Penestanan

Extending west from central Ubud, the hamlet of **CAMPUHAN** is famous as the home of several charismatic expatriate painters, including the late Antonio Blanco, a flamboyant Catalan ("the Bali Dalí") whose house and gallery on Jalan Raya Campuhan has been turned into the enjoyably camp **Museum Blanco** (daily 9am–5pm; Rp50,000; blancomuseum.com).

Across the road from here, the track that runs north along the grassy spine behind Pura Gunung Lebah forms part of the very pleasant ninety-minute circular **Campuhan Ridge walk**, taking you around the rural outskirts of Campuhan via the elevated spur between the Wos Barat and Wos Timor river valleys. You leave the ridge at the northern end of the village of Bangkiang Sidem, taking a sealed road that forks left and continues through Payogan and Lungsiakan before hitting the main road about 1.5km northwest of the Neka Art Museum.

The side road that turns off southwest beside Museum Blanco leads to the charmingly old-fashioned village of **PENESTANAN**, a centre for beadwork. The more scenic approach to the village is via the steep flight of steps 400m further north along Jalan Raya Campuhan. The steps climb the hillside to a westbound track that passes several arterial paths to panoramic hilltop accommodation before dropping down into the next valley and reaching a crossroads with Penestanan's

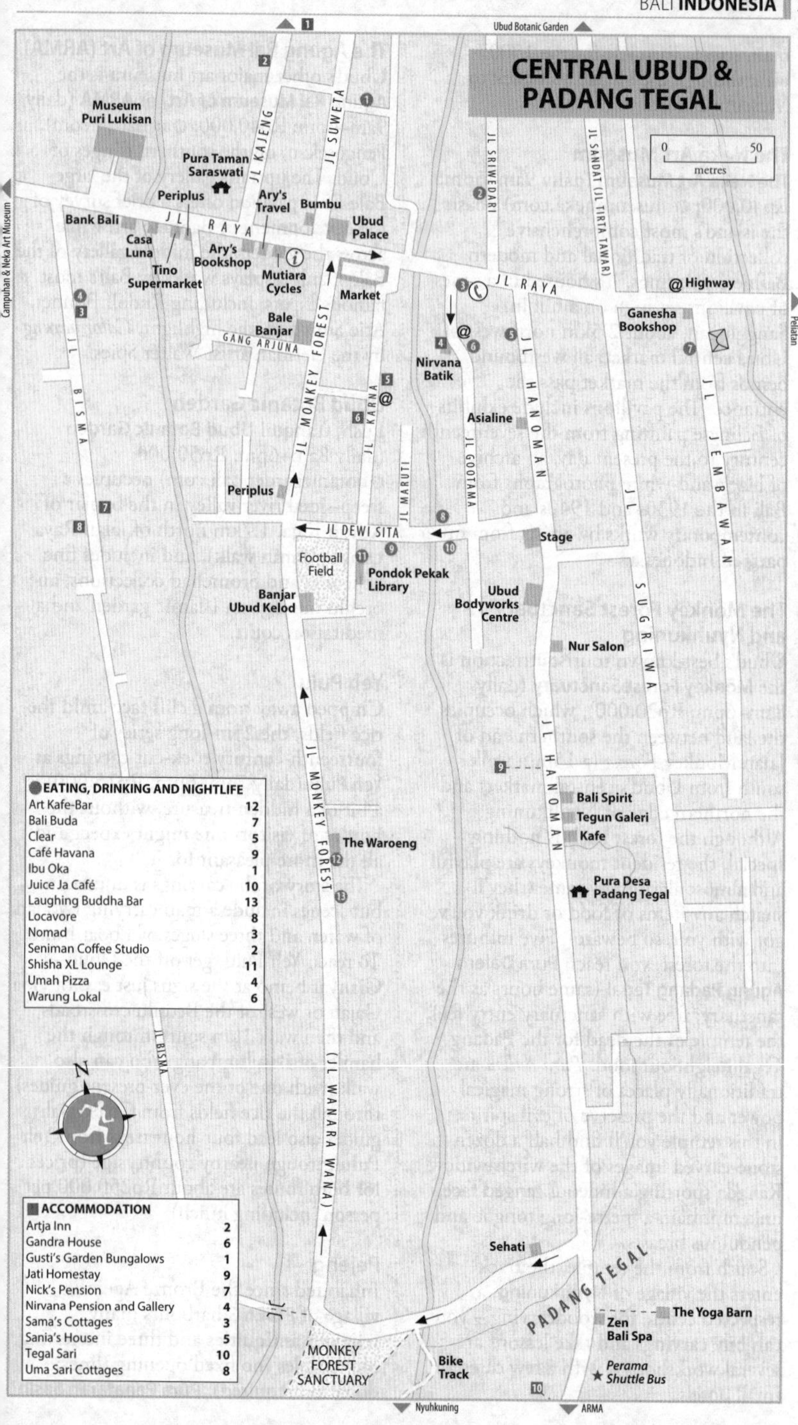
CENTRAL UBUD & PADANG TEGAL
0
50
metres
Ubud Botanic Garden
Campuhan & Neka Art Museum
Pelatan
Nyuhkuning
ARMA
Museum Puri Lukisan
Pura Taman Saraswati
Periplus
Bank Bali
Casa Luna
Tino Supermarket
Ary's Bookshop
Ary's Travel
Bumbu
Ubud Palace
Mutiara Cycles
Market
Bale Banjar
Nirvana Batik
Asialine
@ Highway
Ganesha Bookshop
Stage
Football Field
Pondok Pekak Library
Banjar Ubud Kelod
Ubud Bodyworks Centre
Nur Salon
Bali Spirit
Tegun Galeri
Kafe
Pura Desa Padang Tegal
The Waroeng
Sehati
Zen Bali Spa
The Yoga Barn
Perama Shuttle Bus
Bike Track
MONKEY FOREST SANCTUARY
PADANG TEGAL
JL RAYA
JL KAJENG
JL SUWETA
JL SRIWEDARI
JL SANDAT (JL TIRTA TAWAR)
GANG ARJUNA
JL MONKEY FOREST
JL KARNA
JL GOOTAMA
JL MARUTI
JL HANOMAN
JL JEMBAWAN
JL SUGRIWA
JL BISMA
JL DEWI SITA
JL MONKEY FOREST (JL WANARA WANA)
EATING, DRINKING AND NIGHTLIFE
Art Kafe-Bar 12
Bali Buda 7
Clear 5
Café Havana 9
Ibu Oka 1
Juice Ja Café 10
Laughing Buddha Bar 13
Locavore 8
Nomad 3
Seniman Coffee Studio 2
Shisha XL Lounge 11
Umah Pizza 4
Warung Lokal 6
ACCOMMODATION
Artja Inn 2
Gandra House 6
Gusti's Garden Bungalows 1
Jati Homestay 9
Nick's Pension 7
Nirvana Pension and Gallery 4
Sama's Cottages 3
Sania's House 5
Tegal Sari 10
Uma Sari Cottages 8

4

main street. Turn left for the 1500m walk through the village and back to Museum Blanco.

The Neka Art Museum

The Neka Art Museum (daily 9am–5pm; Rp40,000; ⓦmuseumneka.com) boasts the island's most comprehensive collection of traditional and modern Balinese paintings. It's housed in a series of pavilions set high on a hill in Sanggingan, about 2.5km northwest of Ubud central market; all westbound bemos from the market pass the entrance. The pavilions include exhibits of Balinese painting from the seventeenth century to the present day, an archive of black-and-white photographs from Bali in the 1930s and 1940s and contemporary works by artists from other parts of Indonesia.

4

The Monkey Forest Sanctuary and Nyuhkuning

Ubud's best-known tourist attraction is the **Monkey Forest Sanctuary** (daily 8am–6pm; Rp20,000), which occupies the land between the southern end of Jalan Monkey Forest (a 15min walk south from Ubud's central market) and the northern edge of Nyuhkuning. Although the forest itself is nothing special, the resident monkeys are playful and almost alarmingly tame (they'll snatch any items of food or drink you've got with you, so beware). Five minutes into the forest, you reach **Pura Dalem Agung Padang Tegal** (same hours as the sanctuary; free with sanctuary entry fee), the temple of the dead for the Padang Tegal neighbourhood. *Pura dalem* are traditionally places of strong magical power and the preserve of evil spirits; in this temple you'll find half a dozen stone-carved images of the witch-widow Rangda sporting a hideous fanged face, unkempt hair, a metre-long tongue and pendulous breasts.

South from the temple, the track enters the village of **Nyuhkuning**, a respected centre for woodcarving – you can buy carvings and take lessons at several workshops – with a few cafés and small hotels.

The Agung Rai Museum of Art (ARMA)

Ubud's other major art museum is the **Agung Rai Museum of Art**, or **ARMA** (daily 9am–6pm; Rp40,000; ⓦarmabali.com), in Pengosekan, on the southern fringes of Ubud. The upstairs gallery of the large Bale Daja pavilion offers a brief survey of the development of Balinese art, while across the garden, the middle gallery of the Bale Dauh displays works by Bali's most famous expats, including Rudolf Bonnet, Arie Smit and, the highlight, *Calonnarang* by the German artist Walter Spies.

Ubud Botanic Garden

Lush, tranquil **Ubud Botanic Garden** (daily 8am–6pm; Rp50,000; ⓦbotanicgardenbali.com) occupies a steep-sided river valley in the banjar of Kutuh Kaja, 1.7km north of Jalan Raya Ubud (30min walk), and includes fine heliconia and bromeliad collections, an orchid nursery, an Islamic garden and a meditation court.

Yeh Pulu

Chipped away from a cliff face amid the rice fields, the 25m-long series of fourteenth-century rock-cut carvings at **Yeh Pulu** (daily 7am–6pm; Rp15,000) is a bit of a hidden treasure, without the hordes of visitors one might expect and all the more pleasant for it.

The story of the carvings is uncertain, but scenes include a man carrying two jars of water, and three stages of a boar hunt. To reach Yeh Pulu, get off the Ubud–Gianyar bemo at the signs just east of Goa Gajah or west of the Bedulu crossroads, and then walk 1km south through the hamlet of Batulumbang. You can also walk (with one of the ever-present guides) through the rice fields from Goa Gajah; guides also lead four-hour treks from Yeh Pulu through nearby countryside (prices for both routes are about Rp250,000 per person including lunch).

Pejeng

Inhabited since the Bronze Age, the village of **PEJENG** harbours many religious antiquities and three interesting old temples (no fixed opening times; donation required). **Pura Penataran Sasih**

UBUD AND NEIGHBOURING VILLAGES

ACCOMMODATION	
Family Guest House	6
Gerebig Bungalows	4
Londo Bungalows	3
Santra Putra	2
Sri Sunari	5
Taman Indrakila	1

EATING AND DRINKING	
Jazz Cafe	5
Made's Warung	3
Murni's Warung	4
Naughty Nuri's	1
Sari Organik	2
Taco Casa	6
Warung Nasi Pak Sedan	7

4

(the Moon Temple) houses the Moon of Pejeng, a beautifully etched 2m-long hourglass-shaped bronze gong that probably dates from the third century BC. Nearby **Pura Pusering Jagat** is famous for its elaborately carved 1m-high fourteenth-century stone water jar, while the focus of **Pura Kebo Edan** (Crazy Buffalo Temple) is the 4m-high fertility statue of the Pejeng Giant, complete with massive lifelike phallus. To reach Pejeng from Ubud, take a Gianyar-bound bemo to the Bedulu crossroads and then either wait for a Tampaksiring-bound one, or walk 1km to the temples.

Gunung Kawi

Hewn from the rocky walls of the lush, enclosed valley of the sacred Pakrisan River, the eleventh-century royal *candi* (tomb-style memorials) at **Gunung Kawi** (daily 8am–5.30pm; Rp15,000) occupy a lovely, impressive spot and don't get many visitors. They're signed about 400m north of Tampaksiring's bemo terminus (served by Gianyar–Bedulu–Tampaksiring bemos).

4

ARRIVAL AND DEPARTURE

By plane Taxis to/from the airport charge around Rp200,000–300,000; shuttle buses cost around Rp50,000.

By bemo Bemos serving the east and south arrive and depart from the central market on Jl Raya; north- and westbound bemos leave from just round the corner on Jl Monkey Forest. Services operate at least every 30 minutes from about 6am until around 2pm (though can be sporadic at times), then every hour or so until about 5pm. For some destinations south, west and on to Java you'll need to change in Denpasar. For Padang Bai (for Lombok) and Candi Dasa change in Gianyar.

Destinations Campuhan/Sanggingan (yellow; 5–10min); Denpasar (Batubulan terminal; chocolate brown or light blue; 50min) via Peliatan (5min) and Sukawati (30min); Gianyar (turquoise or orange; 20min) via Goa Gajah (10min); Kintamani (brown or bright blue; 1hr).

By shuttle bus Perama shuttle buses stop at the incoveniently located office at the southern end of Jl Hanoman in Padang Tegal, about 750m from the bottom of Jl Monkey Forest and 2.5km from the central market (☎ 0361 973316, Ⓦ peramatour.com). There are no local bemos or metered taxis from this inconvenient spot, so you'll either have to negotiate a ride with a transport tout, or walk. Independent shuttle-bus operators (from Kuta or Lovina, for example) may drop you off more centrally. Perama runs buses to the island's main tourist destinations and Lombok. Tickets are also available from the tourist office and some travel agencies.

Destinations Bedugul (daily; 1hr 30min); Candi Dasa (3 daily; 1hr 30min–2hr); Gili Islands (daily; 8hr); Kintamani (daily; 45min); Kuta/Ngurah Rai Airport (5–6 daily; 1hr–1hr 30min); Lovina (daily; 1hr 30min–2hr); Nusa Lembongan (daily; 2hr 30min); Padang Bai (3 daily; 1hr–1hr 30min); Sanur (5 daily; 30min–1hr); Senggigi (Lombok; 2 daily; 7hr 30min–11hr 30min).

INFORMATION AND TOURS

Tourist information The office on Jl Raya (daily 8am–8pm; ☎ 0361 973285) has dance performance schedules and details of festivals, runs inexpensive day-trips and sells shuttle-bus tickets. It also dishes out the free *Ubud Community* booklet. If you're planning to do any local walks or cycle rides, buy the *Bali Pathfinder* map (Rp50,000) from any bookshop. The website Ⓦ ubud.com has news, entertainment and restaurant listings.

Walking, trekking and cycling tours Guided cultural walks and sunrise volcano treks with Keep Walking Tours, c/o Bali Spirit, Jl Hanoman 44B (☎ 0361 970581, Ⓦ balispirit.com/tours). Sunrise treks up Gunung Batur and Gunung Agung with Bali Sunrise Tours, Jl Raya Tegalalang 88 (☎ 0818 552669, Ⓦ balisunrisetours.com).

GETTING AROUND

Bemos You can use the public bemos for short hops around the area (around Rp5000): for Campuhan/Sanggingan, just flag down any bemo heading west, such as the turquoise ones going to Payangan.

Bicycle rental From Rp30,000/day from numerous street-side outlets along Jl Monkey Forest.

Car and motorbike rental Numerous places on Jl Monkey Forest rent out motorbikes (from Rp50,000/day) and cars (from Rp180,000/day). Reputable car rental, plus optional third-party insurance, from Ary's Business and Travel Service (☎ 0361 973130, Ⓦ arys_tour@yahoo.com) on Jl Raya.

Transport touts and drivers There are no metered taxis, so you need to negotiate with the ubiquitous transport touts. Expect to pay around Rp20,000–30,000 for local rides on a motorbike, a bit more in a car.

ACCOMMODATION

Accommodation on the lanes around Jl Monkey Forest is both central and peaceful. Peliatan, Penestanan, Campuhan/Sanggingan and Nyuhkuning have better views but are more remote.

CENTRAL UBUD AND PADANG TEGAL

Artja Inn Jl Kajeng 9 ☎ 0361 971876; map p.259. Classic, peaceful losmen offering a handful of rustic but pleasant

bamboo-walled rooms with fans and outside toilets and showers. **Rp150,000**

Gandra House Jl Karna 8 ⓣ0361 976529; map p.259. One of Ubud's better cheapies, Gandra House has no frills losmen-style rooms inside a quiet but central family compound. All the rooms have fans, (generally) hot-water bathrooms and small verandas. **Rp150,000**

Gusti's Garden Bungalows Jl Kajeng 27 ⓣ0812 465 1441, ⓦgustigardenbungalows.com; map p.259. Fifteen better-than-average losmen rooms, all with hot water and fans, set around a terraced garden and swimming pool. The same owners run the nearby and equally good Gusti's Garden 2. **Rp300,000**

Jati Homestay Jl Hanoman ⓣ0361 977701, ⓦjatihs.com; map p.259. Run by a family of painters, this cheerful homestay has comfortable bungalows with hot water and private terraces facing the rice paddies. They charge per person, so singles (Rp125,000) are good value. **Rp250,000**

Nick's Pension Jl Bisma ⓣ0361 975636, ⓦnickshotels-ubud.com; map p.259. A well-run, reliable choice with rooms (all with private bathrooms, verandas and plenty of space) ranged down the valley side. The same owners also run the similar, if less central, Nick's Hidden Cottages and the more economical Nick's Homestay. **Rp550,000**

Nirvana Pension and Gallery Jl Gootama 10 ⓣ0361 975415, ⓦnirvanaku.com/pension.html; map p.259. Situated next to a family compound, these simple Balinese-style rooms are artistically decorated, and benefit from a friendly atmosphere. Batik classes are on offer too. **Rp350,000**

Sania's House Jl Karna 7 ⓣ0361 975535, ⓔsania_house@yahoo.com; map p.259. Hugely popular, well-run, but densely packed backpackers' favourite. There are well-maintained fan or a/c rooms (some in multistorey buildings) close to the market, and there's even a small pool. The small compound, however, can feel a bit cramped. **Rp250,000**

★**Tegal Sari** Jl Hanoman ⓣ0361 973318, ⓦtegalsari-ubud.com; map p.259. Exceptionally appealing, tastefully furnished rooms, all with both fan and a/c, strung out alongside the paddy fields. Also has a pool, and provides free local transport. Book well in advance. **Rp330,000**

★TREAT YOURSELF

Sama's Cottages Jl Bisma ⓣ0361 973481, ⓦsamascottagesubud.weebly.com; map p.259. Tranquil hideaway, just five minutes from central Ubud but a world away from the hustle and bustle. The charming cottages are built on steep tiers in a river gully. There's a small pool, and breakfast is brought to your veranda each morning. **Rp632,500**

Uma Sari Cottages Jl Bisma ⓣ0361 972964, ⓦumasaricottages.com; map p.259. Uma Sari has comfortable rooms with fans or a/c in two-storey buildings in a quiet but convenient spot. All have terraces or verandas overlooking the rice fields, and there's a small pool. **Rp450,000**

THE OUTSKIRTS

★**Family Guest House** Tebesaya, Peliatan ⓣ0361 974054, ⓦfamilyubud.com; map p.261. Friendly place offering well-maintained, fan-cooled bungalows in the family compound, all of them with stylish furniture, hot water and large verandas. Rates include breakfast, tea/coffee and an afternoon snack. **Rp300,000**

Gerebig Bungalows Penestanan Kelod ⓣ0813 3701 9757, ⓦgerebig.com; map p.261. Appealing rooms and bungalows, all with fan, fridge and some with kitchen facilities, set a short distance from the road amid local rice fields. The swimming pool is a bit further out in the fields. **Rp350,000**

Londo Bungalows Southern ridgetop, Penestanan ⓣ0361 976548, ⓦlondobungalows.com; map p.261. Ultra-friendly, family-run little place up on the ridge offering four large two-storey west-facing cottages; each sleeps four and has a kitchenette. **Rp300,000**

Santra Putra Jl Raya Campuhan, Campuhan ⓣ0361 977810, ⓔkarjabali@yahoo.com; map p.261. A mix of traditional thatched and modern concrete bungalows, complete with kitchenettes, panoramic rice-field views and a fabulously relaxed atmosphere. The owner offers painting and drawing classes, so you can happily spend a few days just pottering around the guesthouse. **Rp250,000**

Sri Sunari Jl Gunung Sari, Peliatan ⓣ0361 970542, ⓦsunari-bali-inn.com; map p.261. Just four large, tasteful fan-cooled rooms and a saltwater swimming pool in paddyfields about 2km from Ubud market. Bicycle rental is available. **Rp450,000**

Taman Indrakila Jl Raya Sanggingan, Sanggingan/Campuhan ⓣ0361 975017, ⓦtamanindrakila.net; map p.261. Offering a top-end view at mid-range prices, this is a low-key operation with a/c rooms (which are OK but could do with a refurb) ranged along the hillside, all affording spectacular panoramas over the Campuhan ridge. **Rp450,000**

EATING

CENTRAL UBUD

Art Kafe-Bar Jl Monkey Forest; map p.259. Pretty café with white crochet tablecloths, floral cushions and lots of mirrors, serving slightly pricey but delicious juices and smoothies, coffee, and a selection of curries, salads and pizzas (from Rp44,000). Good desserts too, and regular live music. Daily 8am–11pm.

★**Bali Buda** Jl Jembawan 1 ⓣ0361 844 5935, ⓦbali buda.com; map p.259. The café that started the Ubud trend for wholesome organic food still serves reviving juices and smoothies (from Rp28,000), vegan and raw-food meals, and (less healthily) bread, cakes and pastries. There's a useful noticeboard downstairs and a bakery/store round the corner. Daily 7am–10pm.

Clear Jl Hanoman ⓣ0361 889 4437, ⓦclear-café-ubud.com; map p.259. *Clear* offers an excellent range of organic raw, vegan, vegetarian and seafood dishes, drawing culinary inspiration from across the globe. The decor is eye-catching, and with mains from around Rp50,000 it won't break the bank. Daily 8.30am–10pm.

★**Ibu Oka** Just off Jl Suweta; map p.259. This open-sided warung attracts queues of diners for its *babi guling* (roast suckling pig), which is cooked fresh every day (Rp44,000 with rice and *sambal*). There are a couple of other branches around town too. Daily 11am–5.30pm (or until the *babi guling* runs out).

Juice Ja Café Jl Dewi Sita ⓣ0361 971056; map p.259. This chilled-out café has a huge range of home-made (and generally organic) juices, lassis and smoothies (around Rp20,000–35,000), soups, bagels, salads, crepes, sandwiches and cakes. Daily 8am–10pm.

4

Nomad Jl Raya Ubud 35 ⓣ0361 977169, ⓦnomad-bali.com; map p.259. Serving good-value travellers' food (mains from Rp40,000) since 1979, including top soups, salads, pastas and Indonesian dishes – the "Balinese tapas" options are ideal for groups. Service can't be faulted either. Daily 9am–midnight.

★**Seniman Coffee Studio** Jl Sriwedari ⓣ0361 972085, ⓦsenimancoffee.com; map p.259. Coffee (Rp21,000–28,000) is elevated to an art form at this hip café/roastery/design shop, which has a range of equipment that would look more in place in a science lab. The menu features five regular, single-origin coffees, plus weekly "guest beans". A range of courses is also on offer. Daily 8am–7pm.

Umah Pizza Jl Bisma; map p.259. Although not the most authentic pizzeria in Ubud, Umah serves up large, tasty and very good-value wood-fired thin-crusts (Rp25,000–55,000), washed down with cold Bintangs (from Rp19,000). Daily 8am–10pm.

Warung Lokal Jl Gootama; map p.259. One of the best budget warungs in Ubud, with tasty *nasi* and *mie goreng* for Rp12,000 and most other dishes below Rp20,000. Daily 11am–10pm.

★TREAT YOURSELF

Locavore Jl Dewi Sita ⓣ0361 977733, ⓦfacebook.com/RestaurantLocavore; map p.259. *Locavore* serves innovative modern European dishes made from local produce, with five- and seven-course tasting menus that change every month, as well as a select à la carte menu (mains Rp144,000–173,000). Techniques such as sous-vide, textures such as foams and unusual ingredients all feature. Pricey for Bali, but not with comparable restaurants further afield. Mon–Sat 5–11pm.

THE OUTSKIRTS

Made's Warung Penestanan ridge; map p.261. Homely spot serving well-priced travellers' favourites (from Rp25,000), including inexpensive juices, good *nasi campur* and (with 24hr notice) Balinese smoked duck (Rp195,000 for two people). Daily 8am–10pm.

Murni's Warung Jl Raya Campuhan ⓦmurnis.com; map p.261. Well-established, multi-tiered restaurant built into the Wos River valley and serving curries, home-made soups and Indonesian specialities (mains from Rp30,000), as well as strawberry cheesecake. Daily 8am–10pm.

Naughty Nuri's Jl Raya Sanggingan ⓣ0361 847 6722, ⓦnaughtynurisbali.com; map p.261. Very popular grill-house serving sublime ribs (Rp105,000) and martinis (the latter highly rated by travelling gastronome Anthony Bourdain) in an understated shack with long communal tables. Daily 11am–10.30pm.

★**Sari Organik** Off Jl Abangan, about a 800m walk north along a path from the aqueduct on western Jl Raya Ubud: follow signs from Abangan Bungalows; ⓣ0361 972087, ⓦsariorganik.com; map p.261. Marooned in the rice fields, this chilled-out café grows its own organic produce and serves great veggie kebabs, delicious chicken and salads. Mains from Rp30,000. Daily 8am–8pm.

Taco Casa Jl Pengosekan ⓣ0361 212 3818, ⓦtacocasa bali.com; map p.261. Smashing little spot, popular with expats and tourists alike, serving excellent Mexican food in hearty portions (around Rp45,000–80,000). Daily 11am–10pm.

Warung Nasi Pak Sedan Jl Raya Pengosekan; map p.261. Some of the most economical food (dishes around Rp10,000) in and around Ubud is served at the low-key Warung Nasi Pak Sedan: try the tasty house speciality, *nasi campur ayam*. Daily 7.30am–5pm.

DRINKING AND NIGHTLIFE

The bar scene can be very quiet, so choose a live-music night to ensure a decent crowd. Most places outside offer a free pick-up service if you phone ahead.

CENTRAL UBUD

★**Café Havana** Jl Dewi Sita ⓣ0361 972973, ⓦcafe havanabali.com; map p.259. This is where Ubud comes to shake its booty during live Latin music and salsa class sessions. At other times this great spot just dishes up tasty Cuban and Caribbean dishes and an array of cocktails

featuring Havana Club rum, including a fine mojito (Rp86,000). Daily 10am–midnight.

Laughing Buddha Bar Jl Monkey Forest ⓣ0361 970928, ⓦlaughingbuddhabar.net; map p.259. Small, relaxed bar with a big drinks menu plus plenty of nibbles and tapas to share alongside some larger meals. Sunset Happy Hour stretches from 4pm to 7pm and there's live music every night. Daily 9am–midnight.

Shisha XL Lounge Off Jl Monkey Forest ⓦxlshishalounge.com; map p.259. This comfortable, chilled-out place overlooking the football field stays open late and features DJs and live music. The drinks menu includes sangria and ice-cold beer (around Rp25,000) and, as the name suggests, shishas. Daily 10am–2am.

THE OUTSKIRTS

Jazz Café Jl Sukma 2, Peliatan ⓣ0361 976594, ⓦjazzcafebali.com; map p.261. Excellent jazz bar-restaurant, with live acts every night of the week. Beer from Rp29,000. Daily 5pm–late.

TRADITIONAL DANCE

Up to nine different traditional dance and music shows are staged every night in the Ubud area; the tourist office publishes the weekly schedule (also available at ⓦubud.com) and arranges free transport to outlying venues. Tickets (Rp75,000–100,000) can be bought at the tourist office, from touts, or at the door. If you have only one evening to catch a show, either choose the lively Kecak (Monkey Dance), or go for whatever is playing at the Ubud Palace (Puri Saren Agung), central Ubud's most atmospheric venue.

COURSES

Batik Nirvana Batik, Jl Gavtama 10 (ⓣ0361 975415, ⓦnirvanaku.com; Rp485,000/day).

Cooking Casa Luna restaurant, Jl Raya Ubud (ⓣ0361 977409, ⓦcasalunabali.com; Rp350,000); and Tegal Sari Jl Hanoman, Padang Tegal (ⓣ0361 973318, ⓦtegalsari-ubud.com; Rp350,000/3hr 30min), offer excellent Balinese cookery courses in which you learn to prepare up to six dishes.

Crafts ARMA, JL Raya Pengosekan, Pengosekan (ⓣ0361 976659, ⓦarmabali.com) offers courses (Rp300,000–600,000) in Balinese painting, woodcarving, batik, gamelan, dance and theatre, jewellery-making, basket weaving, traditional architecture, Hinduism, astrology and making offerings.

Music and dance Sehati, Jl Monkey Forest (ⓣ0361 976341, ⓦsehati-guesthouse.com; from Rp100,000/hr).

Yoga Several daily classes at The Yoga Barn, southern Jl Hanoman (ⓣ0361 971236, ⓦtheyogabarn.com; RP110,000); arrange via the holistic information centre, Bali Spirit, at Jl Hanoman 44B (ⓣ0361 970992, ⓦbalispirit.com).

DIRECTORY

Banks and exchange There are ATMs throughout Ubud and its environs. Many tour agents offer exchange services, but there are some common scams to be aware of (see box, p.248). Western Union agents include the GPO, and Bank Mandiri on Jl Raya Ubud.

Bookshops Find new, secondhand and rare/out-of-print English-language books and maps at Ganesha Bookshop, Jl Raya (daily 8am–9pm; ⓣ0361 970320, ⓦganeshabooksbali.com). Periplus, Jl Monkey Forest, and Jl Raya Ubud (daily 9am–10pm; ⓣ0361 975178, ⓦperiplus.com), has a good range of new titles.

Hospitals and clinics Ubud Clinic at Jl Raya Campuhan 36 (ⓣ0361 974911, ⓦubudclinic.baliklik.com) is open 24hr, staffed by English-speakers and will respond to emergency call-outs; it also has a dental service. For anything serious, the nearest hospitals are in Denpasar (p.246).

Internet Highway, Jl Raya Ubud (high-speed connection and laptop hook-ups; open 24hr; Rp10,000/20min) is Ubud's best internet café.

Pharmacies There are several pharmacies on Jl Raya Ubud, Jl Monkey Forest and Jl Peliatan.

Police The main police station is on the eastern edge of town, on Jl Andong, and there is a more central police booth at the Jl Raya and Jl Monkey Forest crossroads.

Post office The GPO on Jl Jembawan (Mon–Sat 8am–5pm, Sun & hols 9am–4pm) keeps poste restante, and there are postal agents throughout Ubud.

Shopping Souvenirs at the sprawling central market, Jl Raya Ubud. Also worthwhile are Sukawati art market, 8km south of Ubud (served by Ubud–Batubulan bemos), and the handicraft outlets that line the 12km Ubud–Tegalalang–Pujung road (best with own transport).

Spas and massage At Nur Salon, Jl Hanoman 28 (ⓣ0361 975352), and Ubud Bodyworks Centre, Jl Hanoman 25 (ⓣ0361 975720, ⓦubudbodyworkscentre.com; massages from Rp90,000).

4

BESAKIH

The major tourist draw in the east of Bali is undoubtedly the **Besakih temple complex** (daily 8am–5pm; Rp10,000), situated on the slopes of Gunung Agung, the holiest and highest mountain on the island.

Besakih is the most venerated site on Bali for Balinese Hindus, who believe that the gods occasionally descend to reside in the temple, during which times worshippers don their finery and bring them elaborate offerings. The complex's sheer scale is impressive, and on a clear day, with Agung towering dramatically behind, and with ceremonies in full swing, it's beautiful.

However, Besakih has also evolved the habit of separating foreign tourists from their money as quickly as possible, which can make for a frustrating experience.

WHAT TO SEE AND DO

The complex consists of more than twenty separate temples spread over a site stretching for more than 3km. The central temple is **Pura Penataran Agung**, the largest on the island, built on seven ascending terraces, and comprising more than fifty structures. Start by following the path just outside Pura Penataran Agung's wall, and then wander at will: the *meru* (multi-tiered shrine roofs) of Pura Batu Madeg, rising among the trees to the north, are enticing. Pura Pengubengan, the most far-flung of the temples, is a couple of kilometres through the forest.

Unless you're praying or making offerings, you're forbidden to enter the temples, and most remain locked unless there's a ceremony going on. However, a lot is visible through the gateways and over walls. The rule about wearing a sarong and sash appears to be inconsistently applied, but you'll definitely need them if you're in skimpy clothing; sarong and sash rental are available, with negotiable prices, but it's much easier to take your own.

There are huge numbers of local guides at Besakih hoping to be engaged by visitors, but you don't need one to explore the complex; stick to the paths running along the walls outside the temples, wear a sarong and sash, and you'll be in no danger of causing religious offence. If you do hire a guide, you should use one who has an official guide badge and is wearing an endek shirt as uniform, and always establish the fee beforehand; around Rp20,000 is reasonable. If you're escorted into one of the temples to receive a blessing from a priest you'll be expected to make a "donation" to the priest.

ARRIVAL AND DEPARTURE

By tour Without your own transport, the easiest way of getting to Besakih is to take an organized tour, available from any of the tourist centres (from Rp200,000/person), but anything offering less than an hour at the temple isn't worth it. If you're in a group, it's more economical to charter a car and driver for the day (Rp400,000–500,000) and put together your own itinerary.

By public transport Bemos from Semarapura (also known as Klungkung) go as far as Menanga from where there are ojek to the temple car park. In Semarapura bemos pass through Jl Gunung Rinjani just north of the main road in the town centre. Bemos also run from Amlapura via Selat to Rendang, with some going on to Menanga. Most bemos run in the morning and dry up in the afternoon. There are no public bemos north of Menanga to Penelokan.

INFORMATION

Tourist office The tourist office (daily 8am–7pm), on the right just beyond the car park, is, unfortunately, staffed by guides who will pressure you to make a donation and engage their services (both are unnecessary). There's a noticeboard with a map of the complex on the left as you approach Pura Penataran Agung, beyond all the shops that line the road up to the temple from the car park.

PADANG BAI

PADANG BAI, the port for Lombok, nestles in a small white-sand cove lined with fishing boats. Many travellers stay a night or two and the tiny village has developed into a laidback resort. Jalan Silayukti is the main seafront road at the eastern end of the bay, while all the small roads leading from the seafront to the road across the top of the village are named, from west to east, Jalan Segara 1, Jalan Segara 2 and so on.

WHAT TO SEE AND DO

If you find the main beach too busy, head to the bay of **Bias Tugal** (also known as Pantai Kecil), to the west, which is quieter; follow the road past the post office and, just as it begins to climb, take the roadway to the left. East over the headland from the main beach, if you take the left fork for a couple of hundred metres beyond the beachside Topi Inn, you reach the white-sand cove of Blue Lagoon, where there's the best snorkelling in the area and a few laidback cafés. Several places in Padang Bai rent out snorkelling equipment (around Rp30,000–50,000 per day); the water in the main bay is surprisingly clear, but the currents can be strong here. There's also

CLIMBING GUNUNG AGUNG

At 3014m, **Gunung Agung** is the highest Balinese peak and visible from throughout eastern Bali. The spiritual centre of Bali, it is believed that the spirits of the ancestors of the Balinese people dwell there. Climbing is forbidden at certain times because of **religious festivals**. Weather-wise, the **dry season** (April to mid-Oct) is best; don't contemplate it during January and February, the wettest months. You'll need walking boots, a torch, water and snacks; for the descent, a stout stick is handy.

ROUTES

There are two main routes. From **Pura Pasar Agung**, it's at least a three-hour climb with an ascent of almost 2000m, so you'll need to set out at 3am or earlier to get to the top for sunrise. From Besakih, the climb is longer (5–7hr) and much more challenging; you'll need to leave between 10pm and midnight. A third, less-used, route, from **Dukuh Bujangga Sakti**, inland from Kubu on the north coast, involves starting out in the afternoon, camping on the mountain and completing the three hours to the summit pre-dawn.

GUIDES

If you want to trek at night to make it in time for sunrise, it's probably a good idea to engage a guide, but be prepared to barter (very) hard. The local organization of trekking guides has people on stand-by at Pura Pasar Agung day and night (from Rp350,000 for a guide for one or two people). At Besakih, arrange guides at the tourist office (from Rp700,000 per guide for two people).

Closest to **Pura Pasar Agung** is Gung Bawa, Jl Sri Jaya Pangus 33, Selat (Ⓣ0812 387 8168, Ⓦgb trekking.blogspot.com), which charges Rp500,000–700,000 per person.

Inevitably, prices are higher if you arrange the trek from further afield. Options include: Bali Sunrise 2001 in Ubud (Ⓣ0818 552669, Ⓦbalisunrisetours.com; from Rp1,000,000/person depending on the pick-up point), who pick up pretty much anywhere on Bali; and Perama (contact any of their offices Ⓦperamatour.com; Rp1,000,000/person, minimum two people).

a big volleyball pitch just behind the harbour, with a permanent game going on that anyone can join.

Padang Bai is a good base for diving, and the sites at Blue Lagoon attract eels, wrasses, turtles, flatheads and lion fish – plus there's a good chance of spotting sharks. The operators also arrange dive trips further afield to Nusa Penida, Amed, Tulamben, Candi Dasa and Gili Selang.

ARRIVAL AND DEPARTURE

By plane A taxi to/from Ngurah Rai Airport is around Rp315,000.

By bemo Bemos from Semarapura and Amlapura stop at the port entrance at the western end of the bay, and everything is within easy walking distance.

Destinations Amlapura (45min); Candi Dasa (20min); Denpasar (Batubulan terminal; 2hr); Semarapura (30min).

By ferry The public ferry from Lembar on Lombok arrives at the port, and departs every 90min daily (4hr–4hr 30min; Rp40,000).

By speedboat Speedboats to the Gili Islands and mainland Lombok (see p.282) arrive and depart from the jetty in the bay.

By shuttle bus Perama buses stop at their office near the port entrance (daily 7am–7pm; Ⓣ0363 41419, Ⓦperamatour.com).

Destinations Candi Dasa (3 daily; 30min); Gili Islands via ferry (daily; 5–6hr); Kuta/Ngurah Rai Airport (3 daily; 2hr 30min); Lovina (daily; 2hr 30min–3hr; Rp125,000); Sanur (3 daily; 1hr 30min–2hr); Senggigi via public ferry (daily; 5–6hr; there's also another service via Perama's fast boat); Ubud (3 daily; 2hr–2hr 30min).

INFORMATION

Tourist office The closest tourist office is in Candi Dasa (see p.268). The glossy magazine *Agung*, widely distributed across the island, is a good source of information and has an up-to-date map of the village.

DIVE OPERATORS

Dive trips from $60; PADI courses up to Divemaster are available (the PADI Open Water course is around $400).

Blue Bubble Jl Segara Ⓣ0813 858827, Ⓦbluebubble-bali.net.

Geko Dive Jl Silayukti, on the seafront Ⓣ0363 41516, Ⓦgekodive.com.

Water Worx Close to Geko on Jl Silayukti Ⓣ0363 41220, Ⓦwaterworxbali.com.

ACCOMMODATION

Kembar Inn Jl Segara 6 ⓣ0363 41364. The lowest-priced rooms in this popular budget hotel are basic and dark, but the buffet breakfast ensures value for money. **Rp150,000**

Lemon House Jl Segara 6 ⓣ0812 4637 1575, ⓦlemonhouse.me. Hike up a steep flight of steps to this welcoming guesthouse with spick-and-span rooms (the deluxe ones with sea views are a steal). Early morning noise from the temple can be an issue for some (though others find it atmospheric). Dorm **Rp85,000**, double with shared bathroom **Rp100,000**, deluxe double **Rp150,000**

Puri Rai Jl Silayukti ⓣ0363 41385, ⓦpuriraihotels.com. If you are looking for something a bit smarter, Puri Rai has fan-cooled rooms with TVs, hot water and fridges (a/c options cost around Rp120,000 extra), plus three pools and a restaurant. **Rp480,000**

Serangan Inn II JL Segara 8 ⓣ0818 0550 2124, ⓔputuadi56@yahoo.com. The rooms here are clean and keenly priced (some have hot water). Noise from the nearby bars can be an issue, however, so it's not a good option for light sleepers. **Rp150,000**

★**Topi Inn** Jl Silayukti ⓣ0363 41424, ⓦtopiinn.nl. Five nicely furnished rooms, some with shared bathrooms, plus a dorm and a restaurant (see below). The Dutch owners are extremely friendly and offer cultural and artistic workshops (from Rp180,000/person, minimum two people) including batik, dancing, cooking, and even tree-climbing. Dorm **Rp80,000**, rooms **Rp225,000**

EATING AND NIGHTLIFE

Alola Café On the square just off Jl Segara 8. Sprawling place with raised seating areas for lounging and great smoothies and eclectic dishes that range from tropical salads to goulash, as well as takeaway baguettes (around Rp30,000) for the ferry ride to Lombok. Daily 7am–late.

Babylon Reggae Bar Jl Segara 8. Perennially popular late-night drinking and music venue. Next door is the *Kinky* reggae bar, and the two meld into one big party come the evening. Daily 3pm–late.

Manggala Restaurant Jl Segara 8, opposite Babylon. A cut above most of its competitors, Manggala serves tasty Indonesian and Western food (barbecued dishes from Rp50,000) with candles, tablecloths and lilting music. Daily 5–10/11pm.

★**Ozone Café** On the main road heading to the harbour, just beyond the volleyball court. A multicoloured, chill-out venue offering tasty organic food (such as edam sandwiches made with home-made brown bread) and fruit and soya shakes and smoothies (from Rp12,000) in a hippyish atmosphere. Daily noon–10pm.

Sunshine bar Jl Segara 8. Tiny, friendly little place with only four tables, serving cocktails (around Rp50,000) with slightly off names such as the rather uncomfortable-sounding "sex on the rocks". Daily 3pm–late.

Topi Inn Jl Silayukti. The menu is several centimetres thick, with great bread, cakes, coffee and plenty of imaginative vegetarian dishes (from Rp40,000) such as wholemeal pasta with home-made pesto supplementing the more typical Western and Indonesian meals. The colourful adjoining bar is a popular night-time hangout, with live-music parties every Mon. Water refills available. Daily 8am–1am.

DIRECTORY

Banks and exchange BRI Bank on the main road into town (about 100m from the port entrance) has an ATM. There are moneychangers on the main street.

Car and motorbike rental Ask at your accommodation or any of the seafront tourist counters.

Doctor Dr Nisa (ⓣ0811 380645) is a highly regarded, English-speaking local doctor who will visit sick tourists privately. He can also be contacted at Water Worx dive centre on the seafront. The nearest hospitals are in Amlapura and Denpasar.

Internet Several internet cafés charge from Rp300/min. Most hotels and restaurants offer free wi-fi.

Police ⓣ0363 41388 Near the port entrance.

Post office 100m southwest of the port entrance.

CANDI DASA

At the eastern end of Amuk Bay is **CANDI DASA**, a relaxed resort that appeals mostly to older visitors, with a wide choice of accommodation and restaurants. A good centre for snorkelling, diving and exploring the east, it makes a nice change from some of the more frenetic resorts in the south of the island. The main beach has suffered serious erosion in recent decades due to over-construction in the area – the offshore coral reefs were harvested to provide lime for building tourist resorts in the 1980s – but there are several small pockets of white sand along the waterfront where hotels have created artificial beaches.

The pretty lagoon in the centre of Candi Dasa, just across the main road from the temple, is a useful landmark. Most of the **accommodation** in Candi Dasa is spread about 1km along the main road running just behind the beach both east and west of the lagoon. East of this central section is Forest Road, which has some quiet guesthouses.

JELLYFISH

Watch out for **jellyfish**, especially at dusk. Places that are totally harmless during the day are suddenly home to jellyfish sporting massive tentacles (3m-long tentacles, in fact, courtesy of the blue jellyfish) that whip you and leave you oozing black poison from painful lumps. Ultimately they don't do any damage, but travel with antihistamine and avoid swimming at sunset, no matter how romantic it might seem at the time. The tiny red jellyfish that float about during the day do little more than give you a weird electric-shock sensation.

WHAT TO SEE AND DO

The group of tiny islands lying just off the coast (Gili Tepekong, Gili Biaha and Gili Mimpang) offer excellent sites for experienced divers (currents can be strong), including walls, a pinnacle and the dramatic Tepekong Canyon. All the operators also arrange trips further afield to Padang Bai, Nusa Penida, Nusa Lembongan, Amed, Tulamben and Gili Selang.

For fantastic views over the coastline, follow the headland trail that forks off the road leading east in the direction of Amlapura. Beyond the headland there are some pretty beaches, with wide stretches of sand.

The reef along the coast is gradually rejuvenating and there is some decent **snorkelling** just offshore, stretching for about 1km westwards from the area in front of *Puri Bagus Candidasa* hotel. Take care not to venture too far out and be aware of your position as the currents can be hazardous. You can also go on snorkelling trips to more distant spots with local boat-owners (around Rp300,000–400,000 for two hours for up to three people including equipment), and dive operators also take snorkellers along on dive trips ($15–30); always be clear whether or not equipment is included in the price.

ARRIVAL AND DEPARTURE

By plane Taxis to/from Ngurah Rai Airport (see p.246) cost around Rp350,000 (around 2hr).

By bus and bemo Public transport services stop anywhere along the main road through Candi Dasa.

Destinations Amlapura (20min); Denpasar (Batubulan terminal; 2hr); Gianyar (1hr); Padang Bai (20min); Semarapura (40min).

By shuttle bus Perama (daily 8am–9pm; ☎ 0363 41114, ⓦ peramatour.com) stop at their office at the western end of the central area.

Destinations Amed (2 daily, min 2 people; 1hr–1hr 30min); Kuta/Ngurah Rai Airport (3 daily; 3hr); Lovina (daily; 3hr–3hr 30min); Padang Bai (3 daily; 30min); Sanur (3 daily; 2hr–2hr 30min); Tulamben (2 daily, min 2 people; 2hr); Ubud (3 daily; 1hr 30min–2hr).

INFORMATION

Tourist office The tourist office close to the lagoon has erratic opening hours and staffing. The glossy magazine *Agung*, widely distributed across the island, is a good source of information and up-to-date maps about the east including Candi Dasa.

DIVE OPERATORS

Dive trips cost from $85; PADI Open Water courses cost around $450 and are widely available. Many operators charge extra for equipment rental ($5–15/day) so check at the time of booking.

Divelite Main Rd, just west of the lagoon ☎ 0363 41660, ⓦ divelite.com. Offering fun dives and courses in Japanese, Indonesian and English.

Shangrila Scuba Divers At the Bali Shangrila Beach Club on Forest Road ☎ 0813 3733 5081, ⓦ divingatbali shangrila.com. Offers a similar range of dives.

ACCOMMODATION

CANDI DASA

★ **Ari Homestay** Near the Perama office ☎ 0817 970 7339. Excellent budget choice run by a really friendly Indonesian/Australian family. There's a kitchen, lovely roof garden and huge breakfasts, and guests have scrawled their appreciation all over the walls. As well as rooms, there's also a dorm downstairs, and several self-contained units for longer stays. The hot dogs and chilli burgers served in the café (daily 11am–8pm) are legendary. Dorm **Rp80,000**, double **Rp160,000**

Kelapa Mas 100m west of the lagoon ☎ 363 41369, ⓦ kelapamacandidasa.com. This centrally located homestay is justifiably popular, with a range of clean bungalows (each with private bathrooms and fans) in a lovely garden on the seafront. A/c is available too. **Rp400,000**

★ **Temple Café and Seaside Cottages** Just east of the Perama office ☎ 0363 41629, ⓦ balibeachfront -cottages.com. The budget rooms here are some of the best in Bali, with extras such as stylish bedspreads, heavy

4

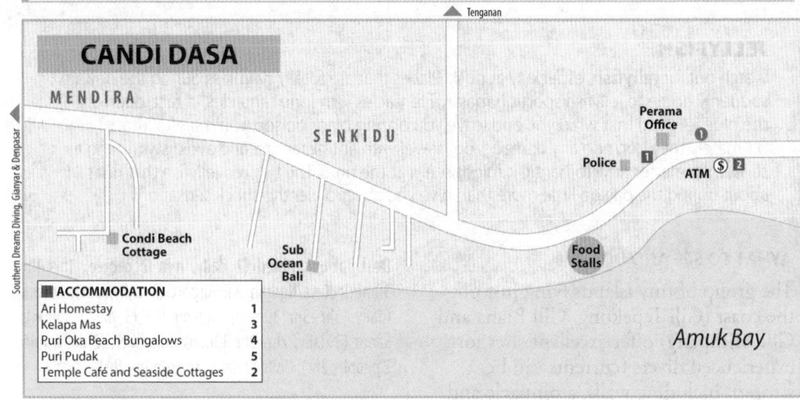

wooden furniture and bedside lamps that you won't find elsewhere for this price. The more expensive beachside bungalows with a/c and hot water have lovely views. Breakfast not included. Rp200,000

FOREST ROAD

4

Puri Oka Beach Bungalows Forest Rd ☎ 0363 41092, Ⓦ purioka.com. Accommodation at this resort ranges from simple budget rooms with ornate, colourfully painted doors to spacious beachside bungalows with four-poster beds, modern finishes and gorgeous views (Rp750,000), all set around an inviting pool. Rp335,000

Puri Pudak Forest Rd ☎ 0363 41978. The best rooms are those on top of the little two-storey pagodas. These offer gorgeous sea views and an airy aspect. All rooms have a dressing room, large verandas and sweet touches such as carved animal tiles and ornate doors. Rp250,000

EATING, DRINKING AND NIGHTLIFE

For an inexpensive meal, head to the food stalls on the waterfront opposite the police station to the north of town (11am–9pm). Candi Dasa's nightlife, such as it is, consists of live music nights at venues such as *New Queen Pub*.

Aquaria Along a side road near the junction of Forest Rd and the main road ☎ 0363 41127, Ⓦ aquariabali.com. Tiny restaurant attached to a small hotel with tables overlooking a pretty swimming pool and serving inventive fusion food. The fixed-price menu (Rp143,000 for three courses) changes daily, makes full use of local produce and offers vegetarian options. Daily noon–10pm.

Bali Bagus East of the lagoon ☎ 0363 41363. This keenly priced restaurant, also known as *Warung Astawa*, specializes in fish and seafood (from Rp47,000), and also has a great-value three-course set meal (Rp75,000). Daily 8am–10pm.

New Queen Pub Near the Perama office. One of the liveliest nightspots in Candi Dasa, with an extensive menu of well-prepared Western and Indonesian favourites, a popular happy hour (6–8pm) and live music several nights a week. Daily 9am–midnight.

★ **Vincent's** Opposite the post office, near the lagoon ☎ 0363 41368, Ⓦ vincentsbali.com. This is the classiest venue in town, with comfortable sofas, lounge jazz on the speakers and a large, candlelit garden at the back. The varied menu (mains from Rp68,000) features treats such as crab tortellini, while the drinks list offers a good range of imported beers, as well as bottled Guinness (Rp46,000). They hold popular live jazz nights on the first and third Thursday of the month. Daily 10.30am–11.30pm.

DIRECTORY

Banks and exchange There are ATMs in front of *Seaside Cottages* and next to *Kelapa Mas*, north of the lagoon.

Bike rental Sub Ocean Bali in central Candi Dasa (from Rp25,000/day). Beware of the busy traffic on the main road.

Car and motorbike rental Ask at your hotel: Cars from around Rp200,000, motorbikes from Rp50,000. There's also no shortage of touts on the street to negotiate with, though be careful what insurance is included if you rent a vehicle through one. To put together your own day-trip, you'll be looking at Rp400,000–650,000/day for vehicle, driver and petrol, depending on your itinerary.

Doctor Dr Nisa (see p.268) will visit Candi Dasa.

Internet There are a few internet cafés on the main street.

Police Just west of the Perama office.

Post office Near the lagoon (Mon–Fri 8.30am–noon). The Asri supermarket sells stamps and has a postbox.

Spa and massage The spa at the small hotel and restaurant *Aquaria* (off Forest Road; ☎ 0363 41127, Ⓦ aquariabali.com) offers massage, scrubs, hot-stone treatments, crystal massages and facials in their oceanfront spa from Rp150,000.

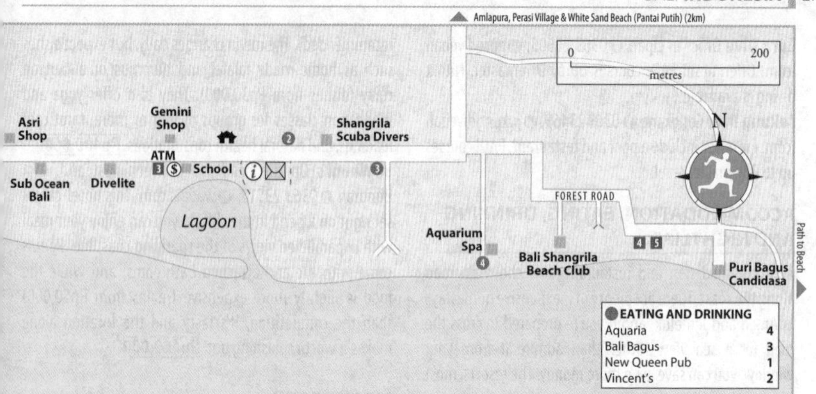

AMED, JEMELUK AND THE FAR EAST COAST

The stretch of coast in the far east of Bali from Culik to Aas is known as **AMED** although this is just one village here. Accommodation is mushrooming along the 11km stretch from Amed to Aas, as people come here to enjoy the peace and quiet, the clifftop views of the glorious coastline and black beaches, and to take in the stunning underwater attractions.

Access to Amed is from the small junction village of **Culik** just over 9km north of Tirtagangga on the Amlapura–Singaraja road. In Amed, 3km away, life centres on fishing and salt production, which you can see at close quarters. A kilometre east is the hamlet of Congkang, then **Jemeluk**, 6km from Culik, which attracts divers and snorkellers for the offshore coral terrace leading to a wall dropping to a depth of more than 40m. There's a high density of fish, with sharks, wrasses and parrotfish in the outer parts. From Jemeluk lies headland after headland: the beaches and villages of Bunutan and Lipah Beach are the most developed areas, though they remain low-key, leading on to Lehan Beach, Selang, Ibus, Banyuning and eventually Aas, almost 15km from Culik.

As well as at Jemeluk, there's excellent **diving** at a wreck at Lipah Beach and a drift dive at Bunutan, with the chance to see schools of barracuda and giant barrel sponges. Advanced divers can explore Gili Selang, the eastern tip of Bali, where a pristine reef, pelagics and exciting currents are the draw. Good **snorkelling** spots include Jemeluk, the Lipah Beach wreck and a Japanese wreck near the coast at Banyuning.

ARRIVAL AND DEPARTURE

By bemo and ojek From Culik, bemos run via Amed to Aas in the morning; hard bargaining should achieve a fare of around Rp10,000 to Lipah Beach. Later in the day you'll need to charter a bemo or ojek (aim for around Rp30,000/person).

By car or motorbike It's a picturesque 30km from Amlapura to Aas. Allow at least 90min for the trip. Take local advice before setting off; rivers cross the road, which may become impassable in the rainy season.

By shuttle bus Two daily Perama charter services run from Candi Dasa (minimum two people). Phone the Candi Dasa office to book (0363 41114, peramatour.com). *Amed Café* (0363 23473, amedcafe.com) near Jemeluk also operates shuttle buses (2–3 daily; destinations include Padang Bai, Ubud, the southern resorts, the airport and Lovina).

By boat Kuda Hitam Express (0363 23482, kudahitamexpress.com) runs daily boats between Jemeluk Beach, all three of the Gili Islands (1–2hr; Rp650,000) and mainland Lombok (2hr 30min; Rp650,000).

DIVE OPERATORS

PADI Open Water courses are around $375, and fun dives cost from $75. Most guesthouses have snorkel gear for rent (from Rp25,000/day).

Apneista Jemeluk beach 0813 3830 1158, apneista.com. This centre runs freediving courses ($200/two-day course), as well as yoga and meditation sessions.

Eco-Dive Jemeluk (between *Amed Café* and *Bamboo Bali losmen*) 0363 23482, ecodivebali.com. The staff have tremendous local knowledge and offer dives for experienced divers, as well as PADI courses up to Divemaster level in English, German and French.

4

Euro Dive Office in Lipah ⓣ0363 23605, ⓦeurodivebali.com. Offering all PADI courses up to Divemaster. Nitrox diving is available.

Jukung Dive Congkang ⓣ0363 23469, ⓦjukungdivebali.com. Premises include a pool and restaurant. PADI courses up to Divemaster level.

ACCOMMODATION, EATING, DRINKING AND NIGHTLIFE

All accommodation and restaurants line the main road along the coast. There are plenty of inexpensive homestays in Amed and Jemeluk, and if you're prepared to cross the road for a sea view rather than admire it from your window, you can save even more money. The resorts, most of which have decent restaurants, get more luxurious and spread out the further you travel from Amed.

AMED, CONGKANG AND JEMELUK

Ganesh Amed Jemeluk ⓣ0859 3516 2475, ⓦganeshamed.com. As well as economical fan-cooled rooms (and more expensive a/c rooms with private verandas), Ganesh Amed has a small pool and direct beach access. Yoga and meditation classes (Rp100,000) are available too. **Rp300,000**

4

★**Geria Giri Shanti** Jemeluk ⓣ0819 1665 4874, ⓦgeriagirishanti.com. Four spotless bungalows above the road in Congkang, all with verandas, four-poster beds, hot water and fans; two also have views of the bay. **Rp315,000**

Kadek Homestay Jemeluk ⓣ0878 6322 7487. Six spotless rooms run by friendly hosts, some opening directly onto the beach. The surrounding area looks like a construction site, but the rooms are still excellent value. **Rp120,000**

Sunrise Café and Bungalows Jemeluk ⓣ0363 23477, ⓔsunrisejem@yahoo.com. The best-kept budget rooms in town, run by a lovely family, with comfy beds, crisp white sheets and colourful embroidered tapestries on the walls. It's worth paying a little extra for the upstairs rooms, which have huge verandas for watching the sunrise over the bay. Great low-season rates and discounts for solo travellers. As the name suggests, there's a top café too. **Rp200,000**

Warung Family Beside Sunrise Café, Jemeluk. The cheapest tourist warung in the area, with fresh juices, grilled tuna with a choice of sauces, and *nasi* or *mie goreng* with barracuda or tuna for just Rp16,000. The highlight, though, is the delicious coconut satay shrimp. Most dishes are under Rp30,000. Daily 11am–10pm.

BUNUTAN

Aiona Garden of Health West end of Bunutan ⓣ0813 3816 1730, ⓦaionabali.com. This small, eco-friendly hotel has charming cottages constructed from natural materials (rates include a delicious breakfast). There's also a lovely chilled-out vegetarian/vegan restaurant, open for lunch (noon–3pm) and dinner (from 6pm; reservations recommended). The menu changes daily, but expect dishes such as home-made falafel and hummus or aubergine curry (dishes from Rp30,000). They also offer yoga and meditation classes for groups of four or more, tarot card readings, and natural health consultations. **Rp400,000**

★**Waeni's** On the headland between east and west Bunutan ⓣ0363 23515, ⓦwaenis.com. This hotel-café is set right on a bend in the cliff, so you can enjoy your meal with unparalleled views of the sparkling coastline. Rooms come with a/c and attached bathrooms, and while the food is slightly more expensive (mains from Rp50,000) than the competition, it's tasty and the location alone makes it worth splashing out. **Rp400,000**

LIPAH BEACH

Le Jardin Lipah Beach ⓣ0363 23507, ⓔlimamarie@yahoo.fr. Four spacious and stylish bungalows, each with open-air bathrooms and sleeping up to four in a lovely garden in the central part of Lipah Beach, with the beach a short walk away. The restaurant (daily 7–10pm) has vegetarian, fish and chicken dishes, plus French cakes, ice cream and yoghurt. **Rp350,000**

Wawa Wewe In the village ⓣ0363 23522, ⓦbaliwawawewe.com. The closest thing Amed has to nightlife – a large bar that gets busy for its live music nights on Wednesdays and Saturdays. The lads who run the place are cheerful and friendly, they have two large a/c rooms to rent (though don't expect much in the way of sleep) and the food is decent too. Not to be confused with *Wawa Wewe 2* (or any of their other ventures), which is much more expensive. **Rp200,000**

LEHAN, SELANG, BANYUNING AND AAS

★**Aquaterrace** Selang ⓣ0813 3791 1096, ⓔaquaterrace.amed@gmail.com. Run by a Japanese-Balinese couple, this place has just three rooms, each one immaculately minimalist, in a cool, white, chic bungalow fronted by a gorgeous pool. As it is set on the corner of the cliff at Selang, the panoramic views are spectacular and the food in the restaurant, including Japanese specialities such as wasabi-seared tuna, is excellent. Book the rooms well in advance. **Rp650,000**

Baliku Across the road from the beach at Banyuning ⓣ0828 372 2601, ⓦamedbaliku.com. This smart resort restaurant has good Western food cooked by an Australian chef (mains from Rp50,000), and free use of the showers and pretty mosaic-tiled pool if you dine. The Japanese wreck is just offshore. Daily 7am–10.30pm.

Eka Purnama Above the road between Banyuning and Aas ⓣ0828 372 2642, ⓦeka-purnama.com. Situated on a hillside, these four bamboo bungalows with tiled roofs have large verandas looking seawards, fans and attached bathrooms. The larger "Family House" (Rp896,000) is a good option for groups. **Rp336,000**

★**Komang John Café** At Blue Moon Villas on the headland beyond the beach at Selang. The amazing sea views and the setting, around a tranquil pool, make this place the perfect choice for a romantic dinner. Though not cheap by local standards, the food (Western and Indonesian) is good (mains from Rp45,000) and the welcome friendly. Daily 7am–10pm.

DIRECTORY

Banks and exchange Moneychangers in Lipah Beach, Bunutan and Jemeluk; the closest ATM is in Amlapura.
Bicycle rental Ask at your accommodation (generally around Rp35,000/day). The gradients over some of the headlands are quite extreme.
Hospital The nearest hospital is in Amlapura.
Internet Warung Telkoms with pricey internet access in Lipah and *Amed Café* near Jemeluk.
Massage and spa Beach massages for Rp60,000/hr. For more pampering, try the D and J spa, with facials from Rp60,000, across the road from *Three Brothers Bungalows* in Amed (T 0818 0555 5484).
Motorbike rental Ask at your accommodation (usually around Rp50,000 /day).

TULAMBEN

The small village of **TULAMBEN**, about 10km northwest of Culik, is mainly a destination for diving and snorkelling. It's the site of the most popular dive in Bali, the **Liberty wreck**, attracting up to a hundred divers a day. The wreck lies about 30m offshore and is encrusted with hard and soft coral, gorgonians and hydrozoans, providing a wonderful habitat for around three hundred species of fish that live on it, and more than a hundred species that visit from deeper water. The wreck is pretty broken up and there are plenty of entrances letting you explore inside. Parts of it are in shallow water, making this a good snorkelling site, too. It's worth staying in the village to avoid the rush hours (11.30am–4pm) on the wreck, enjoy a night dive and explore some of the area's other excellent sites, but if you are not diving or snorkelling there is little else to do.

ARRIVAL AND DEPARTURE

By bus Buses and minibuses between Amlapura and Singaraja pass through the village and will stop where you want.

By shuttle bus Perama services (minimum two people) run between Tulamben and destinations throughout Bali; book through the Candi Dasa office (T 0363 41114, W peramatour.com).

DIVE OPERATORS

The two dive centres below are the most established operators in Tulamben. Both offer local dives to the wreck and other Tulamben sites (from $45), trips to other sites on Bali (for example, Pulau Menjangan), PADI courses and live-aboards.
Tauch Terminal T 0363 22911, or contact in southern Bali T 0361 774504, W tauch-terminal.com.
Tulamben Wreck Divers T 0363 23400, W tulambenwreckdivers.com.

ACCOMMODATION

★**Liberty Dive Resort** T 0363 23347, W libertydiveresort.com. Solid, spacious a/c rooms (and pricier bungalows) with exceptionally comfortable beds set in charmingly landscaped surroundings. You could easily lose a few days here lounging by the gorgeous dark-blue pool and gazing at the sea. **Rp525,000**
Matahari Tulamben Resort T 0363 22916, W divetulamben.com. This dive resort has rooms for most budgets, including fan-cooled, cold-water options; they're a little dark, but acceptable. There's also a spa, tiny pool and restaurant. **Rp220,000**
Puri Madha Near the Liberty wreck T 0363 22921, W purimadhabeachotel.weebly.com. Set around a pretty courtyard garden, *Puri Madha's* lowest priced options (fan-cooled) are basic but acceptable; there are also newer and smarter options (from Rp450,000) with a/c, TVs and ocean views. There's also a restaurant. **Rp200,000**

DIRECTORY

Banks and exchange Moneychanger on the main road; the closest ATM is in Amlapura.
Hospital The nearest hospital is in Amlapura.
Internet Tulamben Wreck Divers offers internet access.

GUNUNG BATUR AND DANAU BATUR

The **BATUR** area, the most popular and dramatic volcanic scenery in Bali, was formed thirty thousand years ago when a gigantic volcano erupted. The rim of this vast crater remains clearly visible and it is the views from here that are the main draw. Confusingly, the entire area is sometimes referred to as **Kintamani**, although this is the name of just one of many villages. The highest points on the rim are **Gunung Abang** (2153m) on the

4

eastern side, the third-highest mountain in Bali, and **Gunung Penulisan** (1745m) on the northwest corner, with Pura Puncak Penulisan on its summit. Rising from the floor of this huge crater is **Gunung Batur** (1717m), an active volcano with four craters of its own and Danau Batur lake nestled beside it. Many visitors come to the area to climb Gunung Batur, usually for the sunrise.

There's an admission charge to the area (Rp11,000); the ticket offices are just south of Penelokan on the road from Bangli and at the junction of the road from Ubud and the rim road.

The crater rim

The villages of Penelokan, Batur and Kintamani are spread for 11km along the rim of the vast ancient crater and virtually merge. The views across the stark volcanic landscape from Penelokan (1450m) are majestic. Danau Batur lies far below, while Gunung Batur and Gunung Abang tower on either side of the lake. An entourage of hawkers accompanies the hordes of day-trippers who pass through Penelokan. The only way to avoid the circus is to come early or late, or stay overnight.

About 4km north of Penelokan, **Pura Ulun Danu Batur** (daily sunrise–sunset; admission by donation; sarong rental available) is the second most important temple on the island after Besakih. It's a fascinating place to visit at any time as there are usually pilgrims making offerings and praying, and the mist that frequently shrouds the area adds to the atmosphere.

Danau Batur and around

Situated at the bottom of the ancient crater, 500m below its rim, **Danau Batur** is the largest lake in Bali, 8km long and 3km wide, and one of the most glorious. Home of Dewi Danu, the goddess of the crater lake, it is especially sacred to the

CLIMBING GUNUNG BATUR

Batur remains **active** so check the current situation for climbing at Ⓦvsi.esdm.go.id – it's mostly in Indonesian but it is clear if a mountain is on alert. Climbing Batur is best in the **dry season** (April–Oct).

There's a choice of **routes up Gunung Batur**. If you have your own wheels, the easiest route is to drive to **Serongga**, off the Yehmampeh road, west of Songan. From the car park, it's from thirty minutes to an hour to reach **Batur I**, the highest peak and largest crater.

The most common walking routes up to Batur I are from **Toya Bungkah** and **Pura Jati**. The path from Pura Jati is shadeless and largely across old lava fields. From Toya Bungkah, numerous paths head up through the forest (one starts just south of *Arlina's* guesthouse) and up to the warung perched on the crater rim. Allow two to three hours to get to the top from either start and about half that time to get back down.

A **medium-length trek** involves climbing to Batur I, walking around the rim and then descending by another route (around 4hr 30min–6hr 30min return).

In **daylight**, you don't need a guide from Toya Bungkah or Pura Jati if you've a reasonable sense of direction, but you shouldn't climb alone and you should let somebody responsible know where you are going. If you climb in the **dark**, which most people do to reach the top for the fabulous sunrise views, you'll need to leave around 4am, and a guide is vital.

GUIDES AND TREKKING AGENCIES

Local guides are organized into the **Association of Mount Batur Trekking Guides**, or **HPPGB** (Ⓣ0366 52362), with offices in Toya Bungkah and at Pura Jati, and anyone who climbs Batur is under intense pressure to engage them. However, in spite of "fixed" prices supposedly displayed in the offices (from Rp400,000/group of four people), they can be confusing to use. Be absolutely sure you negotiate all details beforehand (for example, whether breakfast is included and which route you take).

All hotels and the **trekking agencies** in Toya Bungkah arrange climbs. These include Jero Wijaya Treks at *Lakeside Cottages* (Ⓣ0366 51249), who charges from around Rp400,000. Bali Sunrise (Ⓣ0818 552669, Ⓦbalisunrisetours.com) arranges treks including pick-ups throughout Bali (Rp550,000–900,000/person depending on the pick-up point, the trek and whether overnight accommodation in Toya Bungkah is included). Usually minimum of two people.

Balinese, and its waters are believed to percolate through the earth and reappear as springs in other parts of the island. Villages sit on the lake's shores – **Kedisan** is at the junction where the road from Penelokan reaches the lakeside and Toya Bungkah is further north on the western shore of the lake. Its hot springs, Toya Devasa (daily 8am–8pm; Rp150,000 including lunch), are clean and attractive, with a cold-water swimming pool and smaller hot-water pools.

ARRIVAL AND DEPARTURE

By bemo The lakeside villages of Kedisan and Toya Bungkah are linked by bemo to Ubud and Penelokan.

By bus The main road through Penelokan, Batur and Kintamani is on the bus route between Singaraja (Penarukan) and Denpasar (Batubulan). Buses pass through every 30min–1hr.

Hotel transport Some of the Kedisan accommodation offers free pick-ups in the area.

By shuttle bus A Perama (T 0361 750808, W perama tour.com) charter service (minmum two people) runs from Ubud (daily; 1hr 30min), Sanur (daily; 2hr) or Kuta (daily; 2hr 30min).

INFORMATION

Tourist information Yayasan Bintang Danu, a local organization, runs the tourist office in Penelokan (daily 10am–3pm; T 0366 51730), almost opposite the turning down to Danau Batur.

ACCOMMODATION

ON THE RIM

Lakeview T 0366 51394. Right on the edge of the crater rim in Penelokan, where the main road turns south away from the rim. All the rooms have stunning views, hot water and thick quilts. **Rp610,000**

Miranda Homestay 100m north of Kintamani market; all public transport along the rim passes the door; T 0366 52022, W mirandahomestay.com. The rooms are clean (though rather garish) and have attached mandi and squat toilet. The owner, Made Senter, is an experienced trekking guide. Good-value singles (Rp90,000) too. **Rp175,000**

BY THE LAKE

Baruna Cottages T 0366 51378, W barunacottages.com. One of the better lakeside options with spacious, well-furnished rooms in a quiet compound. Free pick-ups from Ubud (and discounted ones from further afield). **Rp400,000**

Nyoman Mawar III (also known as Under the Volcano III) T 0813 3860 0081. Simple, clean bungalows close to the lake in Toya Bungkah with fabulous views. **Rp200,000**

EATING

Most of the hotels have decent restaurants, notably Baruna Cottages.

Volcano Breeze Toya Bungkah. On a quiet track down to the lake, *Volcano Breeze* offers a selection of Western and Indonesian dishes from Rp25,000. Daily 8am–9/10pm.

DIRECTORY

Banks and exchange There's an international ATM in the car park of the Lakeview hotel, but otherwise it's difficult to change money, so bring plenty of cash.

Post office Just off the main road 2km north of Penelokan.

DANAU BRATAN AND CANDIKUNING

Neither as big nor as dramatic as the Batur region, the **Danau Bratan** (Lake Bratan) area, sometimes just known as Bedugul, has impressive mountains, beautiful lakes, quiet walks and attractive and important temples. The area generally caters for domestic rather than foreign tourists, and is pleasantly cool compared with the rest of Bali.

Situated at 1200m above sea level and thought to be 35m deep in places, Danau Bratan is surrounded by forested hills and, like Danau Batur, is revered by Balinese farmers as the source of freshwater springs across a wide area of the island. The lake (and its goddess) are worshipped in the temple of **Pura Ulun Danu Bratan** (daily 7am–5pm; Rp30,000), one of the most photographed temples in Bali, which consists of several shrines, some dramatically situated on small islands that appear to float on the surface of the lake.

The lake nestles in the lee of Gunung Catur, on the main Denpasar–Mengwi–Singaraja road 53km north of Denpasar and 30km south of Singaraja; no direct route links it to Batur. There are the smaller, quieter lakes of Buyan and Tamblingan about 5km to the northwest, both worth exploring if you have time.

Candikuning

The small village of **CANDIKUNING**, which sits above the southern shores of Danau Bratan, is home to one of the gems of central Bali, the **Bali Botanical Gardens** (Kebun Raya Eka Karya Bali; daily

4

8am–6pm; Rp18,000; ⓦkebunrayabali.com), home to more than two thousand species of plant, including trees, bamboo and orchids, and a rich area for birdwatching. The entrance is a short walk from the market area, along a small side road. Inside the gardens is the wonderful **Bali Treetop Adventure Park** (ⓣ0361 852 0680, ⓦbalitreetop.com; $19.50–24) with five circuits of ropeways, bridges, platforms and zip lines constructed up to 20m off the ground. Booking is recommended, weekends and holidays are best avoided, and packages are available from the southern resorts.

Candikuning's daily **market**, Bukit Mungsu, offers a vast range of fruit, spices and plants, including orchids.

ARRIVAL AND DEPARTURE

By bus Candikuning is on the bus route between Denpasar (Ubung; 1hr 30min) and Singaraja (Sukasada; 1hr 30min).

By shuttle bus Perama services drop you at the *Sari Artha losmen* (ⓣ0368 21011), just below Bukit Mungsu market on the main road in Candikuning. There's one daily service to the north of the island and one to the south.

Destinations Kuta (2hr 30min–3hr); Lovina (1hr 30min); Sanur (2hr–2hr 30min); Ubud (1hr 30min).

4

ACCOMMODATION

Ashram ⓣ0361 21450. There are rooms of varying standards here, set on a grassy hillside overlooking the lake. The nicest are the ones higher up, which have hot water and great views. Rp150,000

Bali Botanic Gardens ⓣ0368 203 3211, ⓦkebunrayabali.com. The budget "Researcher Guest House" rooms here are a bucolic place to stay; all come with shared, hot-water bathrooms, access to kitchen facilities and free entry to the gardens. Rp150,000

EATING

Anda Just across the road from the turning to the Botanical Gardens. This is one of the few places open in the evenings. There's tasty Indonesian and Chinese food from Rp20,000. Daily 8am–10pm.

Roti Bedugul On the main road near Bukit Mungsu market. This café-bakery makes fabulous home-baked bread, sweet buns and cookies, all for around Rp5000. Daily 8am–4pm.

Strawberry Stop 2km north of Candikuning. Attached to a strawberry farm and with a menu devoted to the red fruit. Try the strawberries with cream, ice cream, milkshakes or pancakes (all around Rp10,000–20,000). Daily 8am–4/5pm.

DIRECTORY

Banks and exchange Moneychangers in the market and the car park of Pura Ulun Danu Bratan temple.

Internet There's an internet café on the road to the Botanical Gardens.

SINGARAJA AND AROUND

The second-largest Balinese city after Denpasar, **SINGARAJA** has an airy spaciousness created by broad avenues, large monuments and colonial bungalows set in attractive gardens. It's of most interest to travellers for its transport connections: if you're visiting the north you'll probably pass through at some point.

ARRIVAL AND DEPARTURE

By bemo and bus There are three bemo and bus terminals in Singaraja.

Destinations Sukasada (locally called Sangket), to the south of the town, serves Bedugul (1hr 30min) and Denpasar (Ubung terminal; 3hr); Banyuasri, on the western edge of town, serves the west, including Lovina (20min), Seririt (40min) and Gilimanuk (2hr 30min); and Penarukan is for services eastwards along the north coast via Tulamben (1hr) to Amlapura (3hr), Culik (2hr 30min), Denpasar (Batubulan terminal; 3hr), Gianyar (2hr 20min), Penelokan (1hr 30min), Kubutambahan (20min) and Tirtagangga (2hr 30min). Small bemos (around Rp5000) ferry passengers between the terminals.

By long-distance bus All these buses leave from the offices listed; departure times are notoriously prone to change so check before you set off. Menggala, Jl Jen Achmad Yani 76 (ⓣ0362 24374), operates daily night buses to Surabaya (7pm; 8hr), arriving at Probolinggo and Pasuruan in East Java, access point for the Bromo region, in the middle of the night. Safari Dharma Raya, Jl Jen Achmad Yani 84 (ⓣ0362 23460), runs daily buses to Jakarta (3pm; 24hr). Puspa Rama, Jl Jen Achmad Yani 90 (ⓣ0362 22696), operates daily buses to Surabaya (7.30pm; 8hr) and Malang (7.30pm; 9–10hr). They also sell tickets for the daily bus that leaves Gilimanuk at 5pm for Yogyakarta (12hr).

INFORMATION

Tourist office The tourist office is south of the town centre at Jl Veteran 23 (Mon–Thurs 8am–3pm, Fri 8am–11am; ⓣ0362 25141).

ACCOMMODATION

Wijaya Jl Sudiman 74 ⓣ0362 21915. Located conveniently close to Banyuasri terminal, *Wijaya* has clean rooms, some with a/c and hot water, and a restaurant. Rp100,000

EATING

There's a night market in the Jl Durian area, between Jl Dr Sutomo and the main market, Pasar Anyar, in the city centre. Kampung Tinggi, just east of the bridge on the main road east out of Singaraja, is lined with stalls every afternoon (2–8pm).

Warung Kota Jl Ngurah Rai. A place popular with the young folk of Singaraja, with a bamboo interior and live music nights. It serves inexpensive tasty *nasi* and *mie goreng* (around Rp10,000) and other Indonesian basics. Daily 24hr.

DIRECTORY

Banks and exchange Bank Central Asia on Jl Dr Sutomo has exchange facilities and an ATM.

Hospitals Rumah Sakit Umum (the public hospital) is on Jl Ngurah Rai ⓣ 0362 41046.

Post office The main post office and poste restante is at Jl Gajah Made 156 (Mon–Thurs 8am–3pm, Fri 8am–1pm & Sat 8am–noon), and is also a Western Union agent.

LOVINA

LOVINA stretches along 8km of black-sand beach, the largest resort in Bali outside the Kuta–Legian–Seminyak conurbation. While the peak season (June–Aug & Dec) is busy, Lovina is a whole lot sleepier than the southern resorts, although there's some nightlife and activity centres on the beach, with snorkelling, diving and dolphin-watching as diversions. It's also an ideal base for exploring the whole of the north coast and the volcanic areas inland.

Beginning 6km west of Singaraja, the resort encompasses six villages, from east to west: Pemaron, Tukad Mungga, Anturan, Kalibukbuk (including a side road, to the east of the centre, known as Banyualit), Kaliasem and Temukus.

Kalibukbuk is the centre of Lovina and full of accommodation, restaurants and tourist facilities. East of here, in **Tukad Mungga** (where the beach is known as Pantai Happy), the small fishing village of Anturan and along the Banyualit side road Jalan Laviana, 1.5km from the centre, it tends to be quieter despite the development of losmen and restaurants. West of Kalibukbuk, restaurants and accommodation line the roadside in the villages of Kaliasem and Temukus. Road noise is the enemy here; only consider accommodation set far enough back to block it out.

WHAT TO SEE AND DO

Lovina is famous (or infamous) for dawn trips to see the **dolphins** that frolic off the coast; opinions are evenly split between those who think it's grossly overrated and those who consider it one of the best things on Bali. It's pretty much the luck of the draw: some days there is little to see while on others the dolphins cavort around and under the boats in a grand display. Boats leave at 6am and trips cost from around Rp70,000 per person for the two-hour trip; book directly with the skippers on the beach or through your accommodation.

The skippers also know the best spots on the local reef for snorkelling (from Rp70,000; 1hr 30min–2hr), and dive operators will take snorkellers on dive trips further afield if they have space; this is more expensive but offers greater variety.

Situated between the main north-coast diving areas, Lovina is an ideal base for diving, with fun dives in the Lovina area and further afield at Pulau Menjangan, Tulamben and Amed all available, though you will have to drive for at least 1hr 30min to reach each of these sites. The local reef, perhaps unfairly, has a reputation as being uninteresting, though there's an excellent range of fish, and tyres, an old car and a small boat have been placed on the reef to encourage coral growth.

Brahma Viahara Ashrama and hot springs

One popular outing from Lovina is to the Buddhist monastery, **Brahma Vihara Ashrama** (no fixed opening hours, but rarely closed; donation includes sarong rental), 10km southwest of Lovina, a colourful confection in a wonderful hillside setting and with a glorious gold Buddha as the centrepiece in the main temple. Catch any westbound bemo to Dencarik, where a sign points inland to the monastery, and ojek wait to take you the last steep 5km. From the temple you can walk to the hot springs (daily 8am–6pm; Rp10,000): head back downhill from the monastery and take

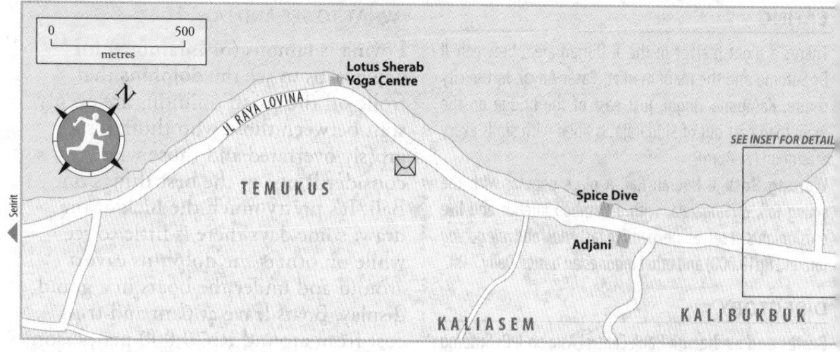

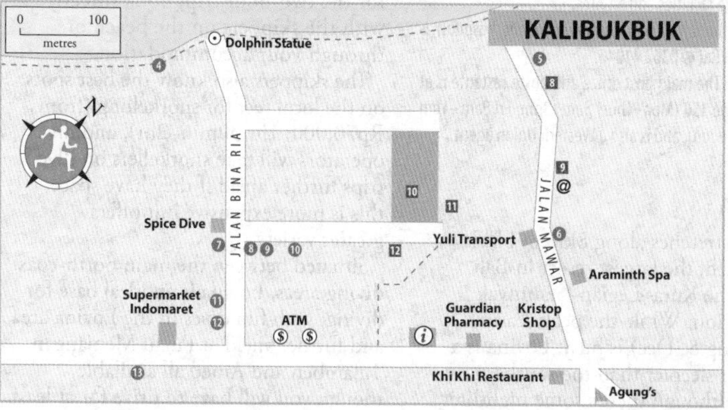

4

the first road to the left. After a few hundred metres you'll reach a major crossroads and marketplace at the village of Banjar Tega. Turn left and after about 200m you'll see a sign for the "Air Panas Holy Hot Spring", from where it's a 1km-walk.

ARRIVAL, DEPARTURE AND GETTING AROUND

By plane Taxis to/from Ngurah Rai Airport cost around Rp500,000.

By bemo To get around the resort, you can pick up the frequent bemos (daily 4am–6pm) that zip between Singaraja and Seririt.

By bus Inter-island buses from Java to Singaraja pass through Lovina, as do Gilimanuk–Singaraja and Amlapura–Gilimanuk services and all buses from the west of the island. The Denpasar (Ubung)–Singaraja services via Pupuan also stop in Lovina. Services to and from east Bali stop at Singaraja's Banyuasri terminal, a short bemo ride from Lovina. As the accommodation is so spread out, it's worth knowing where you want to be dropped off when you arrive.

Destinations Gilimanuk (2hr 30min); Pemuteran (1hr 15min); Seririt (20min); Singaraja (Banyuasri terminal; 20min).

By shuttle bus Perama buses stop at their office (daily 8am–10pm; ⓣ0362 41161, ⓦperamatour.com) in Anturan, a short walk from the Anturan accommodation. Check with other shuttle-bus operators whether they will stop more centrally. There are also long-distance buses from Singaraja (see p.276). Perama book buses to other parts of Indonesia, including Jakarta, Surabaya and Yogyakarta, as well as within Bali and Lombok.

Destinations Bedugul (daily; 1hr 30min); Candi Dasa (daily; 3hr–3hr 30min); Kuta, Bali/Ngurah Rai Airport (daily; 3hr); Padang Bai (2 daily; 2hr 45min); Sanur (daily; 2hr 30min–3hr); Senggigi (daily; 7hr 30min–8hr 30min); Ubud (daily; 3hr 30min–4hr).

INFORMATION

Tourist office Lovina's tourist office (officially Mon–Sat 8am–8pm; ⓣ0362 41910) is on the main road in Kalibukbuk, but only erratically open. The monthly tourist paper the *Lovina Pages* (ⓦlovinabali.com) is worth picking up for listings and maps. The useful community website ⓦlovina.net has travel tips and accommodation and restaurant listings.

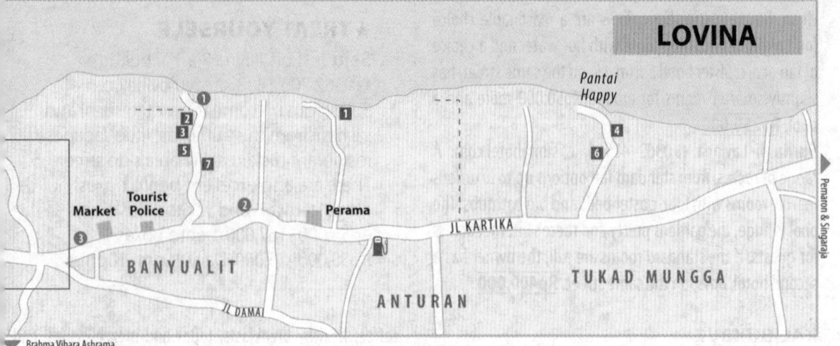

ACCOMMODATION		EATING, DRINKING AND NIGHTLIFE			
Angsoka	10	Akar	7	Poco Bar Evolution	12
Gede Homestay	1	Bakery Lovina	3	Sea Breeze	4
Harris Homestay	11	Jasmine Kitchen	9	Seju	10
Mas Bungalows	7	Kantin 21 Bar and Restaurant	13	Volcano Club	2
Padang Lovina	12	Le Madre	6	Warung Ayu	5
Puri Bedahulu	4	Papagello	8	Warung Bias	1
Puspa Rama	6			Zigiz Bar	11
Rambutan	9				
Ray Beach Inn	5				
Rini	8				
Sartaya	3				
Suma	2				

DIVE OPERATORS

Spice Dive In Kaliasem and on Jl Bina Ria, Kalibukbuk ⓣ0362 41509, ⓦbalispicedive.com. A five-star PADI dive centre and the longest-established in Lovina. PADI Open Water courses (from €195) and fun dives (from €45) in the Lovina area, Pulau Menjangan, Tulamben and Amed are all available, as are dive packages, introductory dives and refresher sessions.

ACCOMMODATION

Most of the accommodation is on side roads leading to the beach, with a few places right behind the beach. There are a few hotels on the main road, though they are best avoided due to high traffic volumes along here at all hours. Most places with a pool allow non-guests to use it for around Rp25,000/day.

TUKAD MUNGGA

Puri Bedahulu Next to the beach at Pantai Happy ⓣ0362 41731. Comfortable bungalows with elegant Balinese carvings and a low-key restaurant on the beach; more expensive options with a/c and TVs are also available. **Rp350,000**

ANTURAN

★**Gede Homestay** Just off the beach ⓣ0362 41526, ⓦgedehomestay.com. Good-quality accommodation in two rows of bungalows just behind the beach. There's a small restaurant with free wi-fi and a sunbathing area; a/c is available in the more expensive rooms. **Rp120,000**

Puspa Rama Just off Jl Raya ⓣ0362 42070, ⓔagungdayu@yahoo.com. A mix of basic but acceptable rooms (the most basic only have cold water) in a compound full of fruit trees; book ahead for the cheapest rates. **Rp150,000**

BANYUALIT

Mas Bungalows Jl Laviana ⓣ0362 41773, ⓦmasbungalows.com. The colourful rooms here are showing their age, but all come with a/c, hot water, TVs, safes and fridges. The family who run the place are lovely, and there's a large pool in a garden full of flowers. **Rp315,000**

Ray Beach Inn Jl Laviana ⓣ0362 41088. Good-value, cheerful rooms (with either fans or a/c) in a two-storey building facing a small garden a short way from the beach. **Rp180,000**

Sartaya Jl Laviana ⓣ362 42240, ⓔkembarsartaya@hotmail.com. Despite decidedly lax management, these

clean, Balinese-style bungalows are a reasonable choice for a night or two; they come with hot water and a choice of fan or a/c. Sister hotel *Sartaya II*, on the same street, has slightly smarter rooms for around Rp50,000 more and a pool. **Rp250,000**

Suma Jl Laviana 0362 41566, sumahotel.com. A range of rooms, from standard fan options up to luxurious marble rooms with four-poster beds and big bathtubs. The pool is huge, the gardens pretty and there's internet access for guests. If the standard rooms are full, the owner has a second hotel, *Rays*, on the same street. **Rp400,000**

KALIBUKBUK

Angsoka Off Jl Bina Ria 0362 41841, angsoka.com. The brown floor tiles, nylon curtains and leatherette chairs do little for the look of the basic bungalows here, but they are spacious and clean, and there's a large pool shaded by mango trees. **Rp165,000**

Harris Homestay Just off Jl Bina Ria 0362 41152. A popular budget gem with just five simple and immaculately clean rooms, all with fans and en-suite cold-water bathrooms. **Rp150,000**

Padang Lovina Just off Jl Bina Ria 0362 41302, padanglovina@yahoo.com. Central but quiet accommodation in a two-storey block, with Balinese-style wooden furniture, friendly hosts and a nice pool. **Rp310,000**

★**Rambutan** Jl Mawar 0362 41388, rambutan.org. Top hotel with a range of spick and span fan rooms (and more expensive villas) and an array of facilities including two pools, a volleyball court, ping pong and pool tables, and a dart board. **Rp410,000**

Rini Jl Mawar 0362 41386, rinihotel.com. One of the area's bigger hotels, with a range of rooms, including budget fan-cooled ones with cold water, as well as a decent pool and restaurant. **Rp230,000**

EATING

Lovina has some excellent places to eat. Restaurants are concentrated in Kalibukbuk; in the other areas, guesthouses offer meals. Opening hours vary depending on the season, but most cafés and warungs serve food from about 10/11am–9pm in the high season (at other times, many places operate restricted hours).

BANYUALIT

Warung Bias Jl Laviana. Large range of delicious international food, including schnitzel and Indian curries (mains around Rp50,000), as well as good sandwiches and cakes. Happy hour 6–8pm. Daily 11am–10.30pm.

KALIBUKBUK

★**Akar** Jl Bina Ria. A charming organic café with just a handful tables serving the finest ice cream (from Rp17,000) in Lovina (and possibly Bali), as well as Illy coffee, healthy breakfasts, tapas and mezze dishes, and delicious curries and pastas. Daily 7am–10pm.

★TREAT YOURSELF

Seju Just off Jl Bina Ria, Kalibukbuk 0362 706 1888, seyulovina.com. Splash out on some top-notch sushi and sashimi from this authentic little Japanese restaurant tucked away on a side street. There are also excellent bento boxes, gyoza, terriyaki and yakitori. Sushi sets Rp55,000–167,000, bento boxes Rp55,000–75,000. Daily 10am–10pm.

Bakery Lovina Corner of main road and Jl Kartika. If you're feeling homesick, this German-run bakery is the place to come: as well as 15 types of bread, cakes and pastries, and imported cheese, hams and salami, there are goods such as Heinz baked beans. Sandwiches from Rp40,000. Daily 7am–10pm.

Jasmine Kitchen Just off Jl Bina Ria. Outstanding restaurant serving fabulous Thai food – from zingy soups to delicately spiced curries – as well as home-made cakes and desserts, plus great coffee. Mains Rp44,000–77,000. Daily noon–10.30pm.

Le Madre Jl Mawar. Little terrace restaurant offering good-value (if rather small) thin-crust pizzas (Rp35,000–65,000) and tasty focaccia (Rp35,000–40,000; try the one with aubergine, mozzarella, tomato and basil), plus pasta and Indonesian dishes. Daily 10am–9/10pm.

Papagello Jl Bina Ria. A huge choice of wood-fired pizza (Rp40,000–85,000) in a three-storey building with book-swap shelves along the walls. The open-air third floor is best for looking out over Lovina with a beer. Daily 7am–10.30/11pm.

Sea Breeze On the beach, just off Jl Bina Ria. A great beachside spot for sunset drinks, with an excellent menu of Western, Indonesian and seafood dishes (mains from Rp30,000), plus good cakes and desserts. Acoustic music regularly accompanies the setting sun. Daily 8am–9pm.

Warung Ayu Jl Mawar. One of several budget warungs at the beach end of this strip, with great *pepes ikan* (fish cooked in banana leaf with spices and coconut) for just Rp20,000. Try the Indonesian platter for two to sample a few of their best dishes. Daily 11am–9pm.

DRINKING AND NIGHTLIFE

Kantin 21 Bar and Restaurant Main road, Kalibukbuk. A popular late-night spot, with live music every night and jugs of cocktails (from Rp80,000) to get everyone in the mood. Daily 1pm–late.

Poco Bar Evolution Jl Bina Ria, Kalibukbuk. Popular spot with live music every night (cocktails from Rp45,000). Daily noon–midnight/1am.

Volcano Club Main Road, near Banyualit. Lovina's main nightlife venue, set in what appears to be a cave, with music so loud it's basically unrecognizable, though this doesn't appear to put off the predominantly local crowd. Opening varies with the season (though it's generally open at least on Sat 6pm–3am); look out for local adverts.

Zigiz Bar Jl Bina Ria, Kalibukbuk. Two doors down from *Poco*, the tourist-oriented *Zigiz* is a similar setup with a more laidback vibe. Daily 4pm–late.

DIRECTORY

Banks and exchange There are moneychangers throughout the resort. Several ATMs accept international cards, including on the main road in Kalibukbuk.

Bicycle rental Several places on Jl Mawar (from Rp20,000/day).

Car and motorbike rental Available throughout the resort from established firms and from people who'll approach you on the street. Cars around Rp200,000/day, motorbikes from Rp50,000/day. Established companies include Yuli Transport (T 036 41184), on Jl Mawar. To charter a vehicle and driver, you'll be looking at around Rp450,000/day.

Cookery classes Adjani (T 0812 385 6802, W adjanibali.com; Rp400,000/3hr) is well established and has an office in Kaliasem.

Hospital The closest hospital is in Singaraja (see p.276).

Internet Offered by many places including *Spice Dive* on Jl Bina Ria, Kalibukbuk (Rp16,000/hr).

Pharmacy Guardian Pharmacy, on the main road in Kalibukbuk.

Police On the main road to the east of Kalibukbuk (T 0362 41010).

Post office The post office is about 1km west of Kalibukbuk. The Tip Top shop on Jl Lovina is a postal agent.

Spas and massages There are plenty of spas in addition to beach massages: Agung's (T 0362 42018, W agungs.com) on the road to *Damai Lovina Villas*; and Araminth Spa (T 0362 41901, W arunaspa.com) on Jl Mawar. Massages from Rp60,000.

Yoga Lotus Sherab Yoga Centre (next to Dolphin Beach Apartments, Jl Raya Lovina T 0339 128680, W lotus sherabyoga) runs morning and evening sessions on the beach.

BALI BARAT NATIONAL PARK

Bali's only national park, **Bali Barat National Park** (Taman Nasional Bali Barat), protects some 190 square kilometres of savannah, forest and reef 40km west of Lovina and is home to 160 species of bird, including the endangered Bali starling, Bali's one true endemic creature. A few trails are open to the public, but most visitors come to dive and snorkel the spectacular **Pulau Menjangan** reefs. All visitors must hire a guide and buy a permit (Rp25,000), either through the **National Park headquarters** (daily 8am–5pm) in **CEKIK**, 3km south of Gilimanuk, or at the Pulau Menjangan jetty (see below). Guides charge Rp250,000–350,000 to Rp600,000–750,000 for a two- to seven-hour hike. All Denpasar (Ubung)–Gilimanuk bemos pass the park headquarters, as do all Singaraja–Gilimanuk bemos.

If your main interest is birdwatching, opt for the Prapat Agung Peninsula trek (1–2hr) or the Teluk Terima trail (2hr). The Gunung Klatakan–Gunung Bakingan rainforest trail (7hr) is more strenuous but lacking in wildlife.

ACCOMMODATION

The most pleasant place to stay is the lovely little beach haven of Pemuteran, 28km east of Cekik, served by Gilimanuk–Singaraja bemos. Camping is forbidden in most of the park, but you can ask to pitch your tent on Labuan Lalang's beach or at the Cekik headquarters, though there are few facilities at either.

Jubawa Homestay Pemuteran T 0362 94745. Friendly guesthouse with bright and airy rooms, plus a decent restaurant. Staff can organize snorkelling and diving trips to Menjangan. Rp250,000

Pondok Wisata Lestari 1.5km north of the park headquarters on the road to Gilimanuk T 0365 61504. The nearest hotel and restaurant to the park, and the cheapest acceptable option in the area, with very basic rooms. Rp90,000

Pulau Menjangan (Deer Island)

By far the most popular part of Bali Barat is **Pulau Menjangan** (Deer Island), a tiny uninhabited island 8km off the north coast, whose shoreline is encircled by fabulous coral reefs, with drop-offs of up to 60m, first-class wall dives and superb visibility.

Guides, permits and boat transport should be arranged at the jetty in **Labuan Lalang**, 13km east of Cekik, on the Gilimanuk–Singaraja bemo route (30min from Gilimanuk or 2hr from Lovina). There's a small national park

4

office here (daily 8am–3pm), and several warung. Boats to Pulau Menjangan can be hired any time up to 3pm; they hold ten people and cost around Rp500,000 for a four-hour snorkelling tour – it takes thirty minutes to reach the island. You'll also have to pay about Rp70,000 for your guide (one per boat), plus Rp25,000 per person for the national park permit. There are occasional reports of thefts from the boats while snorkellers are underwater, so leave your valuables elsewhere. Pulau Menjangan also features on day and overnight tours for snorkellers (from $50) and divers (from $100) based in Pemuteran, Lovina, Kuta, Sanur or Candi Dasa.

GILIMANUK

4

Situated on the westernmost tip of Bali, about 17km west of Labuan Lalang, the small, ribbon-like port town of **GILIMANUK** is of interest only for its ferry connections to East Java less than 3km away.

ARRIVAL AND DEPARTURE

By boat The ferry terminal is a 100m walk northwest of the bus terminal to the north of town.

Destinations Ketapang, East Java (24hr service, every 20min; 45min).

By bus and bemo Buses and bemos depart when full from the transport depot across the road from the ferry terminus.

Destinations Amlapura (4hr); Cekik (10min); Denpasar (Ubung; 3hr 15min); Kediri (for Tanah Lot; 2hr 45min); Medewi (1hr 45min); Labuan Lalang (25min); Lovina (2hr 15min); Padang Bai (5hr); Pemuteran (1hr); Singaraja (Banyuasri; 2hr 30min).

ACCOMMODATION

Accommodation in Gilimanuk is grim, so avoid staying overnight unless absolutely necessary.

Hotel Sari Jl Raya Gilimanuk, about 800m south of the ferry terminal, next to the karaoke bar ⓣ 0365 61264. The best of a bad bunch, despite the wailing from the karaoke bar next door. Rooms are big and clean enough. **Rp150,000**

DIRECTORY

Banks The only ATM that accepts foreign cards is in the ferry terminal compound.

Lombok and the Gili Islands

Thirty-five kilometres east of Bali at its closest point, Islamic **Lombok** (80km by 70km) is populated by Sasak people. It differs considerably from its Hindu neighbour, with lots of wide-open spaces and unspoilt beaches, and much less traffic and pollution. Tourist facilities are less widespread (though improving) and public transport sparser. The island's northern area is dominated by the awesome bulk of **Gunung Rinjani** (3726m), and trekking at least part of the way up is the reason many tourists come to Lombok. Most base themselves in the nearby villages of Senaru or Sembalun Lawang. Other visitors enjoy the cool foothills at tiny Tetebatu and Sapit. The other big draw is the beaches. The trio of **Gili Islands**, just off the northwest coast, attracts increasing numbers of visitors, while the resort of **Senggigi** on the west coast and south-coast **Kuta**, a popular surfing centre, also offer a range of tourist facilities. Lombok's capital and main city area **Ampenan-Mataram-Cakranegara-Sweta** has good transport connections and is pleasantly user-friendly.

AMPENAN-MATARAM-CAKRANEGARA-SWETA

The **AMPENAN-MATARAM-CAKRANEGARA-SWETA** conurbation comprises four towns and stretches over 8km from west to east, but is easy to get around and offers a good opportunity to experience Indonesian city life. At the western end of the city is the bustling old port town of **Ampenan**, the jumping-off point for Senggigi a few kilometres up the coast. Merging into Ampenan to the east, **Mataram** is the capital of West Nusa Tenggara province as well as the district of West Lombok and full of offices and government buildings. East again, **Cakranegara**, usually known as Cakra (pronounced "Chakra"), is the commercial heart of the island, with shopping centres, markets and workshops. **Sweta**, on the eastern edge of the city area,

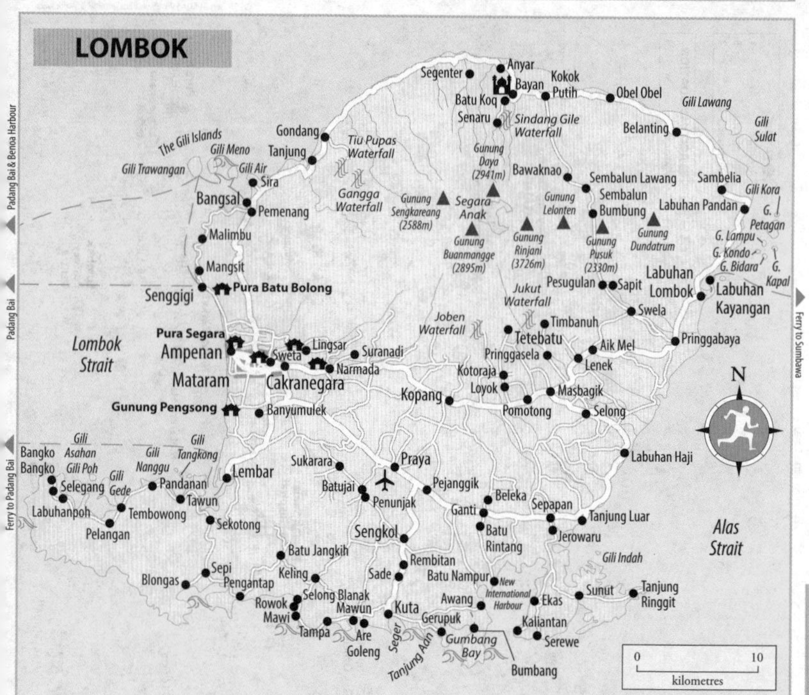

is the location of the island's main bus station. Most tourists come to the city for the day, but an overnight stay is a good chance to try the city's restaurants in the evening and visit early morning markets.

WHAT TO SEE AND DO

The vibrant **markets** offer a great chance to see local life. The Kebon Roek market in Ampenan and the market near the Bertais/Mandalika/Sweta bus terminal at Sweta are both worth wandering around, but the friendliest is Cakranegara market behind the Jalan Gede Ngurah/Jalan Pejanggik crossroads.

The best one-stop craft centre is the Sayang Sayang Art Market (daily 9am–6pm), on Jalan Jend Sudirman, with handicraft stalls ranged around a car park. It's a more lively offshoot of the Lombok Handicraft Centre, also known as Sayang Sayang, which is around the corner on Jalan Hasanudin at Rungkang Jangkok.

Lombok pottery has an international reputation, and the Lombok Pottery Centre, Jalan Sriwijaya 111A (Mon–Fri 9am–4pm; ⓣ0370 640351, ⓦlombokpotterycentre.com), is the showroom of the Lombok Craft Project, which has fuelled a renaissance of pottery on the island. The showroom stocks a small range of products (from Rp25,000).

ARRIVAL AND DEPARTURE

By plane Mataram's Selaparang Airport closed in 2011. All domestic and international flights now operate out of Lombok International Airport (Bandara Internasional Lombok) at Praya, 23km southeast of Mataram. There are ATMs and currency exchanges here, and hotel-reservation desks. The easiest transport from the airport is by taxi (there's a small departure fee to pay). Coupons are available at the counter outside the exit doors to the terminal. A metered taxi to Senggigi or Kuta will cost about Rp175,000, to Mataram around Rp100,000. Public DAMRI buses depart every 90min (3am–8pm) for the Mandalika terminal in Mataram and Senggigi.

Inter-island buses Buy tickets for inter-island departures at the Bertais/Mandalika/Sweta terminal.

Destinations Bima (Sumbawa; 1–2 daily; 12hr); Denpasar (Bali; hourly; 6–8hr); Dompu (Sumbawa; 1–2 daily; 10hr); Labuanbajo (Flores; 1–2 daily; 24hr); Sumbawa Besar (Sumbawa; 7–8 daily; 6hr).

AMPENAN–MATARAM–CAKRANEGARA

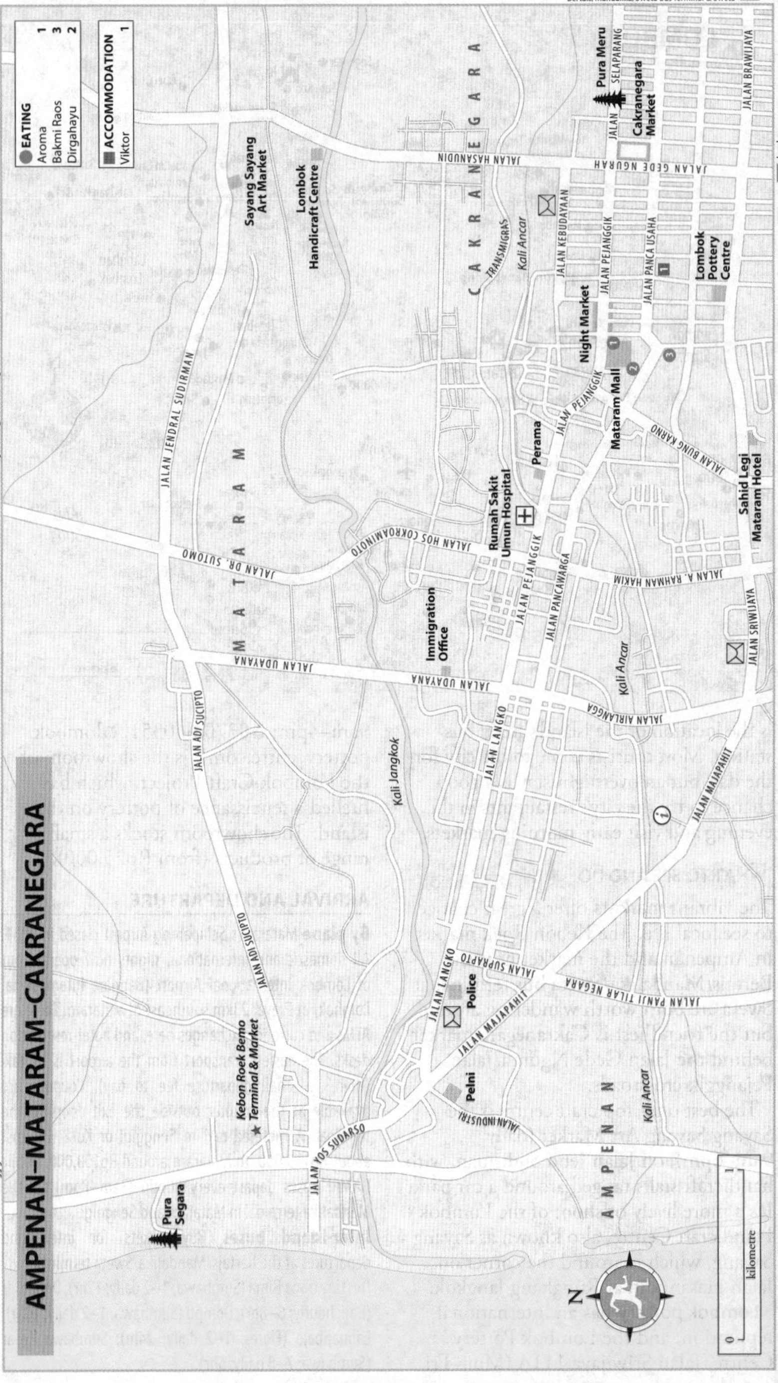

EATING
Aroma 1
Bakmi Raos 3
Dirgahayu 2

ACCOMMODATION
Viktor 1

Bertais/Mandalika/Sweta Bus Terminal & Sweta
Pemenang for Bangsal & Gunung Sari
Senggigi
Lembar

AMPENAN
MATARAM
CAKRANEGARA

Pura Segara
Kebon Roek Bemo Terminal & Market
Pelni
Police
Immigration Office
Rumah Sakit Umun Hospital
Perama
Mataram Mall
Night Market
Sahid Legi Mataram Hotel
Lombok Pottery Centre
Cakranegara Market
Pura Meru
Sayang Sayang Art Market
Lombok Handicraft Centre

Jalan Yos Sudarso
Jalan Adi Sucipto
Jalan Industri
Jalan Langko
Jalan Majapahit
Jalan Suprapto
Jalan Panji Tilar Negara
Jalan Udayana
Jalan Dr. Sutomo
Jalan Hos Cokroaminoto
Jalan Jendral Sudirman
Jalan Pejanggik
Jalan Pancawarga
Jalan Airlangga
Jalan Sriwijaya
Jalan A. Rahman Hakim
Jalan Bung Karno
Jalan Kebudayaan
Jalan Panca Usaha
Jalan Transmigrasi
Jalan Hasanuddin
Jalan Gede Ngurah
Jalan Selaparang
Jalan Brawijaya
Kali Jangkok
Kali Ancar

0 kilometre 1

By public buses and bemos Services to and from Senggigi use the Kebon Roek terminal. All other Lombok destinations depart and arrive at the Bertais/Mandalika/Sweta terminal.

Destinations Bayan (for Gunung Rinjani; 2hr 30min); Labuhan Lombok (2hr); Lembar (30min); Pemenang (for the Gili Islands; 1hr); Pomotong (for Tetebatu; 1hr 15min); Praya (for Kuta; 30min).

By ferry To find out about services and book tickets head to the Pelni office at Jl Industri 1, Ampenan (Mon–Fri 8am–3pm, Sat 8am–1pm; ⓣ 0370 637212, ⓦ pelni.co.id).

INFORMATION

Tourist office The (not particularly helpful) tourist office is on Jl Singosari 2 (Mon–Thurs 7am–2pm, Fri 7–11am & Sat 7am–2pm; reduced opening hours during Ramadan; ⓣ 0370 634800).

GETTING AROUND

Bemos Yellow bemos (around Rp5000) ply numerous routes between Kebon Roek terminal in Ampenan and Bertais/Mandalika/Sweta terminal. Most follow the Jl Langko–Jl Pejanggik–Jl Selaparang route heading west to east, and Jl Tumpang Sari–Jl Panca Usaha–Jl Pancawarga–Jl Pendidikan heading east to west, although there are many variations.

Taxis There are plenty of easily identifiable official metered taxis, or contact Lombok Taxis (ⓣ 0370 627000).

Cidomo The horse-drawn carts here have small pneumatic tyres and are called *cidomo* (or "Lombok Ferraris"); they aren't allowed on the main streets, instead covering the back routes that bemos don't work. Always negotiate a fare beforehand. Around Rp10,000 per kilometre is reasonable.

ACCOMMODATION

Viktor Jl Abimanyu 1 ⓣ 0370 633830. One of the better budget options, with a range of decent a/c rooms (some more modern than others) split between several different buildings in Cakra. Free tea and coffee. **Rp150,000**

EATING

The night market along Jl Pejanggik, just east of Mataram Mall, comes to life as darkness falls.

Aroma Jl Pejanggik 22A, Cakranegara. Delicious, packed Chinese restaurant where the decor is simple and the food (dishes around Rp40,000) is hot and fresh – try the fried squid with chilli sauce. Daily 11am–9/10pm.

Bakmi Raos Jl Panca Usaha ⓦ bakmiraos.com. This trendy new noodle bar offers the spiciest, tastiest noodle soup in town, as its popularity clearly shows (mains around Rp20,000–30,000). Daily 10am–10pm.

Dirgahayu Jl Cilinaya 10. Local restaurant on the road alongside Mataram Mall with a big Indonesian menu. Excellent for inexpensive dining, with plenty of dishes around Rp10,000. Daily 11am–9/10pm.

DIRECTORY

Banks and exchange All the large Mataram and Cakra banks change money and travellers' cheques, and have international ATMs. The most convenient are BCA, Jl Pejanggik 67 ⓣ 0370 622587; BNI, Jl Langko 64 ⓣ 0370 622788; Bank Danamon, Jl Pejanggik ⓣ 0370 622408. The main post office doubles as a Western Union agent.

Car rental The best choice and prices are in Senggigi (see p.286).

Dentist Dr Darmono, Jl Kebudayan 108, Mataram (ⓣ 081 836 7749), speaks good English.

Hospital The public hospital, Rumah Sakit Umum, (Jl Pejanggik 6, Mataram; ⓣ 0370 622254), has a tourist clinic (daily 8am–noon).

Immigration office Kantor Imigrasi, Jl Udayana 2, Mataram ⓣ 0370 632520.

Internet Elian Internet, Panca Usaha Komplek 1, Mataram Mall (open 24hr).

Police Jl Langko ⓣ 0370 631255.

Post office Lombok's main office is at Jl Sriwijaya 37, Mataram (Mon–Sat 8am–5pm, Sun 8am–noon).

LEMBAR

Boats to and from Bali and Pelni ferries dock at **LEMBAR**, 22km south of Mataram. There's little accommodation here and no advantage in staying.

ARRIVAL AND DEPARTURE

By bus/bemo Bemos (around Rp15,000) run between Ampenan-Mataram-Cakranegara-Sweta area and Lembar.

By ferry (Pelni ferries) Tickets for Pelni ferries can be bought from the Pelni office in Mataram on Jl Industri 1 (Mon–Sat 8am–noon & 1–3.30pm; ⓣ 0370 637212, ⓦ pelni.co.id).

Destinations The following are fortnightly services unless otherwise stated: Baubau (Sulawesi; 61hr); Benoa (Bali; 4hr); Bima (Flores; 15hr); Bitung (Sulawesi; every 4 days; 20hr); Kendari (Sulawesi; 73hr); Ende (Flores; 32hr); Kalabahi (Alor; 57hr); Kolonedale (Sulawesi; 92hr); Kupang (Timor; 44hr); Labuanbajo (Flores; 24hr); Lewoleba (Lembata; 64hr); Luwuk (Sulawesi; every 4 days; 1hr); Makassar (Sulawesi; weekly; 37hr or 95hr); Maumere (Flores; 72hr); Nunukan (Kalimantan; every 6 days; 20hr); Parepare (Sulawesi; every 4 days; 18hr); Raha (Sulawesi; 66hr); Tarakan (Kalimantan; every 6 days; 12hr); Waingapu (Sumba; 24hr).

By ferry (other operators)

Destinations Padang Bai (Bali; hourly, 24hr/day; 4hr–4hr 30min). Buy tickets from the office at the port.

By taxi Metered taxis are available at the port or just outside the gates 24 hours a day. Typical fares include Rp70,000 or so to Cakranegara.

SENGGIGI

Covering a lengthy stretch of coastline, **SENGGIGI**, with sweeping bays separated by towering headlands, is a sleepy beach resort built along the main road. Its plethora of smart resorts attract older visitors and families, but there are several budget hotels, homestays and traveller restaurants catering for younger backpackers, and a low-key nightlife. The beach in central Senggigi is separated into two parts by a peninsula. The southern beach, to the east of the peninsula, is much calmer than the beach

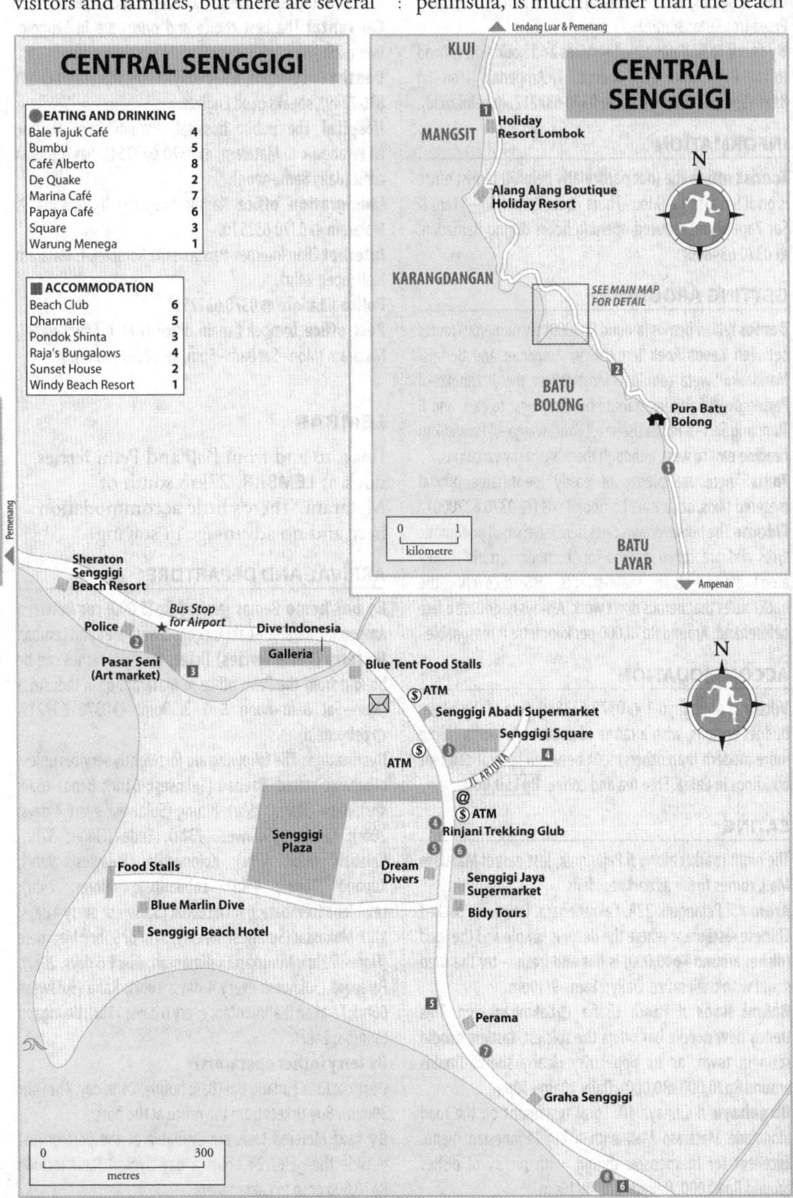

TRIPS TO SUMBAWA, KOMODO AND FLORES

Travel agencies on Lombok and the Gili Islands advertise boat trips to Flores via Sumbawa, Komodo and Rinca, including snorkelling, trekking, sightseeing and a visit to see the Komodo dragons, with some including diving. Conditions on board can be pretty basic and comforts limited. Prices vary, starting at around Rp2,750,000 per person for a three- to five-day trip. Be clear where the trip ends and how you'll move on (air transport out of Labuanbajo on Flores can be difficult to arrange). Tour operators include Perama (W peramatour.com; contact any office) and Kencana Adventure (T 0370 693432, W kencanaadventure.com) – widely available through agents in Senggigi and the Gili Islands. Dive centres in Senggigi (see below) also run live-aboard trips that call in at Sumbawa, Komodo and Flores.

to its west, which is full of locals on dates, food stalls and splashing children. Proximity to the airport makes it an ideal first- or last-night destination but it is also a good base from which to explore the island. There are, however, plenty of hawkers in the central areas – keeping your cool and getting to know them is the best approach.

Plenty of operators cater for people who want to dive in the Gili Islands, and operators also take snorkellers on trips (around Rp200,000 per half day), though if you plan to travel to the Gilis you'd be better off saving your diving for then when you won't have to pay for transport.

Tour operators along the main strip also offer cycling tours (from around Rp400,000 per day) that take you to the picturesque Sekotong Beach and Pengsong Hill.

ARRIVAL, DEPARTURE AND GETTING AROUND

By plane From the airport, a metered taxi will cost about Rp200,000–250,000. A DAMRI airport bus departs every 90min from outside the Art Market on Jl Raya Senggigi (3am–8pm).

By bemo Bemos to and from Ampenan run throughout the day (every 15–20min) along the main road as far as Lendang Luar.

By boat The speedboats from Bali to the Gili Islands drop passengers at Teluk Nara, north of Senggigi, but the majority of companies include a shuttle-bus service to central Senggigi in the price. If not, note that there's a taxi desk by the jetty where you can buy a voucher for a share taxi to central Sengiggi. Perama has an office in central Senggigi (daily 6am–10pm; T 0370 693007, W perama tour.com) which operates a daily boat to Gili Trawangan at 10am (1hr 30min; Rp200,000), which then goes on directly to Padang Bai (Rp400,000), from where there are connections to destinations across Bali.

DIVE OPERATORS

Fun dives cost around $65, while PADI Open Water courses will set you back around $370. Most operators also have offices in the Gili Islands, and offer diving instructor and live-aboard trips.

Blue Marlin Holiday Resort Hotel T 0370 693719, W blue marlindive.com.

Dive Zone Bidy Tours next to Senggigi Jaya Supermarket T 0370 660 3205, W divezone-lombok.com.

Dream Divers Jl Raya Senggigi Kau T 0370 693738, W dreamdivers.com.

ACCOMMODATION

Noise from local mosques and bars is an issue in central Senggigi, so bring earplugs.

SOUTH SENGGIGI

★ **Sunset House** Beachfront T 0370 692020, W sunset house-lombok.com. Pretty, well-maintained cottages set in an ornamental garden right on the beachfront. Breakfast is delivered directly to your private balcony/veranda. **Rp450,000**

CENTRAL SENGGIGI

★ **Beach Club** Jl Raya Senggigi T 0370 693637, W the beachclublombok.com. Australian-run beachside resort with excellent-value en-suite "backpacker rooms" close to the pool, with a common room for lounging and watching DVDs. Also much smarter bungalows (Rp650,000). **Rp185,000**

★ TREAT YOURSELF

Windy Beach Resort Mangsit, 5km north of central Senggigi T 0370 693191, W windybeach.com. Several standards of well-furnished bungalows in a great garden with a stunning beachside pool (Rp20,000 for non-residents). All rooms have hot water and a/c, and there's a restaurant. There are a couple of good spots for snorkelling nearby (you can rent equipment). **Rp550,000**

4

Dharmarie Jl Raya Senggigi ☎0370 693050. These a/c bungalows are a little frayed around the edges, but are more than acceptable. Some bungalows have sea views. **Rp350,000**

Pondok Shinta Just off Jl Raya Senggigi ☎0818 0529 1377. Centrally located, great-value place tucked away in a small garden offering clean, fan-cooled digs with private bathrooms and verandas. **Rp125,000**

Raja's Bungalows Off Jl Arjuna ☎0812 373 4171, Ⓔrajas22@yahoo.com. Raja's has four pretty and clean, budget bungalows with fans and attached cold-water bathrooms set in a lush garden. **Rp150,000**

EATING

The beach at the end of the road to *Senggigi Beach Hotel* comes alive in the afternoons with *sate* sellers. In the evenings, the roadside area next to the post office is filled with food stalls – it is known locally as the "Blue Tent".

Bale Tajuk Café Jl Raya Senggigi. Cheerful central place with a big menu of Indonesian, Sasak and Western food (most mains under Rp40,000); if you're hungry, go for the set meal for two. Daily 10am–10pm.

4

Bumbu Jl Raya Senggigi. Small, popular place in central Senggigi. The Thai food (curries around Rp50,000) is excellent, but tell the waiters if you can't cope with industrial quantities of chilli. There are plenty of other options, including steaks and sandwiches. Daily 9am–11pm.

Café Alberto Batu Bolong ☎0370 693039, Ⓦcafealbertolombok.com. In a great beachfront location, perfect for a sundowner before dinner, *Café Alberto* has delicious home-made pasta (around Rp55,000), thin-crust pizzas and limoncello (Rp20,000/glass). Daily 8.30am–midnight.

★**De Quake** Off Jl Raya Senggigi, behind the Art Market ☎0370 693694, Ⓦdequake.com. The perfect spot to enjoy a sunset margarita on their seaside terrace before digging into a barbecued steak with mashed potato and pepper sauce or one of their excellent Thai dishes (most around Rp30,000–60,000). Popular with expats. Daily 11am–11pm.

Warung Menega 3km south of Senggigi. A simple place on the coast, easily spotted by the sign on the main road, with delectable seafood sold by weight or in good-value set meals (from Rp90,000 including drinks). Daily 10am–11pm.

★TREAT YOURSELF

Square Jl Raya Senggigi ☎0370 693688, Ⓦsquarelombok.com. A sophisticated restaurant-bar, well worth splashing out in. The menu features escargots, foie gras, USDA steaks, and baby pigeon, all expertly prepared (mains under Rp100,000). Fine drinks list too. Daily 11am–11pm.

DRINKING AND NIGHTLIFE

Senggigi is the only place on mainland Lombok with any sort of nightlife, but it is extremely sedate, in keeping with local sensibilities. The following are all on the main road in central Senggigi.

Marina Café Jl Raya Senggigi ☎0370 693136, Ⓦmarinasenggigi.com. Senggigi's main club has DJs playing every night, on-stage dancers, live sport on the big screens and pool tables. Mon–Fri 7pm–2am, Sat & Sun 9pm–3am.

Papaya Café Jl Raya Senggigi. Lively, friendly bar with deafeningly loud live music from 8pm every night, plus fantastic grilled fish (whole snapper Rp50,000) if you need something to soak up the alcohol. Daily noon until late.

DIRECTORY

Banks and exchange There are several ATMs that accept international cards on the main road, as well as a few moneychangers.

Car and motorbike rental Plenty of places rent vehicles with and without drivers. Check the insurance at the time of renting. Cars from around Rp180,000/day, motorbikes from Rp50,000/day, bicycles from Rp30,000/day. Chartering a car with a driver costs around Rp450,000/day.

Doctor *Senggigi Beach Hotel* (☎0370 693210, Ⓦsenggigibeachhotel.com; 24hr) can put you in touch with one. There are also hospitals in Ampenan-Mataram-Cakranegara-Sweta (see p.282).

Internet There are several internet cafés on the main street.

Police The tourist police (☎0370 632733) are on the main road.

Post office In the centre of Senggigi (Mon–Thurs 7.30am–5pm, Fri & Sat 7.30am–4pm).

Shopping The main road has several good-quality craft shops selling items from across the island. The art market, Pasar Seni, at the north end of the main road in central Senggigi, is full of craft stalls.

THE GILI ISLANDS

Strikingly beautiful, with glorious white-sand beaches lapped by warm, brilliant-blue waters, the three **Gili Islands** just off the northwest coast of Lombok are a magnet for visitors. Of the three, **Gili Trawangan** best fits the image of "party island", with heaps of accommodation, restaurants and nightlife. The smallest of the islands, **Gili Meno**, has no nightlife and is known as the "honeymoon island" for its secluded atmosphere. Closest to the mainland is **Gili Air** which offers a mix of the two, with plenty of facilities in the south and

TRAVEL TO AND FROM THE GILI ISLANDS

Most boats to the Gili Islands anchor in the shallows and passengers wade to and fro, so expect to get your feet wet. Confusingly, ferries leaving Gili Trawangan don't usually depart from the harbour, but from wherever it's moored along the east coast, so ask for directions to their mooring site when you book.

FROM BANGSAL

The access port for the Gili Islands is **Bangsal**, 25km north of Senggigi, a *cidomo* (horse-drawn cart) ride or a shadeless 1.5km walk from **Pemenang**, 26km beyond the Ampenan-Mataram-Cakranegara-Sweta area and served by buses from Bertais/Mandalika/Sweta terminal. There is no bemo service along the coastal road north from Senggigi to Pemenang.

The ticket office (daily 8am–4.30pm) is right on the seafront; there's a printed price list covering public boats, shuttles and charters. Buy your ticket only from there; ignore anybody who tries to persuade you otherwise. Everything on sale in Bangsal is also on sale on the Gili Islands, including water, mosquito coils and return boat tickets, despite what the hawkers insist.

Public boats Between Bangsal and Gili Air, Gili Meno and Gili Trawangan, leaving when full (7.30am–4.30pm; 20–45min; Rp10,000). You can also charter a boat for up to ten people, one-way or return, or for trips to more than one island. Prices, from Rp150,000 for a one-way charter, are fixed and displayed in the ticket offices at Bangsal and on the islands.

SENGGIGI AND ELSEWHERE ON LOMBOK AND BALI

Combination tickets for tourist shuttle buses and public ferries between the Gili Islands and all main tourist destinations on Bali and Lombok are widely advertised. Perama customers can use the Perama boat between Padang Bai and Senggigi/Gili islands or public ferries and buses. Other companies use public ferries. For more information, contact Island Promotions (see box, p.248).

From Senggigi Daily Perama boat at 10am (returning 8am; Rp200,000; 2hr). Charters are also available – approach the boat captains on the beach (or they're quite likely to approach you). It's a great trip but the boats are small and weather conditions sometimes make it impossible.

From Serangan Harbour to Gili Trawangan: daily Mahi Mahi (book through Island Promotions: ⓣ 0818 0530 5632) and Blue Water Express (ⓣ 0813 3841 8988, ⓦ bwsbali.com) boats (Rp690,000 one-way; 2hr 30min).

From Benoa (Denpasar harbour, Bali) to Gili Trawangan, Gili Meno, Gili Air: daily Blue Water Express (see above) boat runs daily June to October (Rp690,000; 2hr).

From Padang Bai (Bali) to Gili Trawangan: daily Gili Cat (Rp700,000; 1hr 30min–2hr 30min; ⓣ 0361 271680, ⓦ gilicat.com), one of numerous companies.

From Nusa Lembongan/Sanur (Bali) see p.254.

From Amed (Bali) see p.271.

In addition, increasing numbers of skippers arrange charters to the islands. The boats are often small with single engines and don't carry radios. For the return trip talk to Dean on Gili Meno (see p.293) and Ozzy's Shop (see p.293) on Gili Air, who have twin-engined boats.

ISLAND HOPPING

The "**hopping island**" boat service is handy for day-trips to other islands. It does one circuit – Air–Meno–Trawangan–Meno–Air – in the morning, and one in the afternoon. It's conveniently timetabled, picking people up between 8.30 and 9.30am, and returning between 2.30 and 4pm. A return journey costs Rp25,000–35,000, depending which islands you want to travel between. Prices and times are posted in ticket offices on the islands.

4

more peace elsewhere. It's worth noting that there's no fresh water on any of the islands – showers are salinated, except in the smarter resorts which transport the water by boat from the mainland.

Accommodation prices vary dramatically depending on the season, increasing by anything up to 100 percent from June to September and in December. Reservations are essential in the high season, or you face a long, possibly fruitless, search for a bed.

Women should take care during and after the Gili Trawangan parties – don't leave these alone. You'll inevitably be offered drugs on the islands, but remember

4

Indonesia has extremely tough anti-drugs laws. There are no police; it's the role of the *kepala desa*, the headman who looks after Gili Air and Gili Meno, and the *kepala kampung* on Gili Trawangan, to deal with any problems, so report any incidents to them initially. If you need to make a police report, go to the police on the mainland (at Tanjung or Ampenan).

Gili Trawangan

Furthest from the mainland, the largest of the islands, **GILI TRAWANGAN**, attracts the greatest number of visitors (many of whom come for the island's infamous magic mushrooms) and is the most developed. The southeast of the island is wall-to-wall guesthouses, restaurants and dive shops, although it is still low-key outside the high season. For quieter surroundings, head further north.

Island transport is by *cidomo* (horse and cart), or you can rent bicycles (from Rp20,000 per day) – particularly popular at sunset for reaching the 100m hill, from which you can enjoy stunning views of the Bali volcanoes with the sky blazing behind. To get there, follow any of the

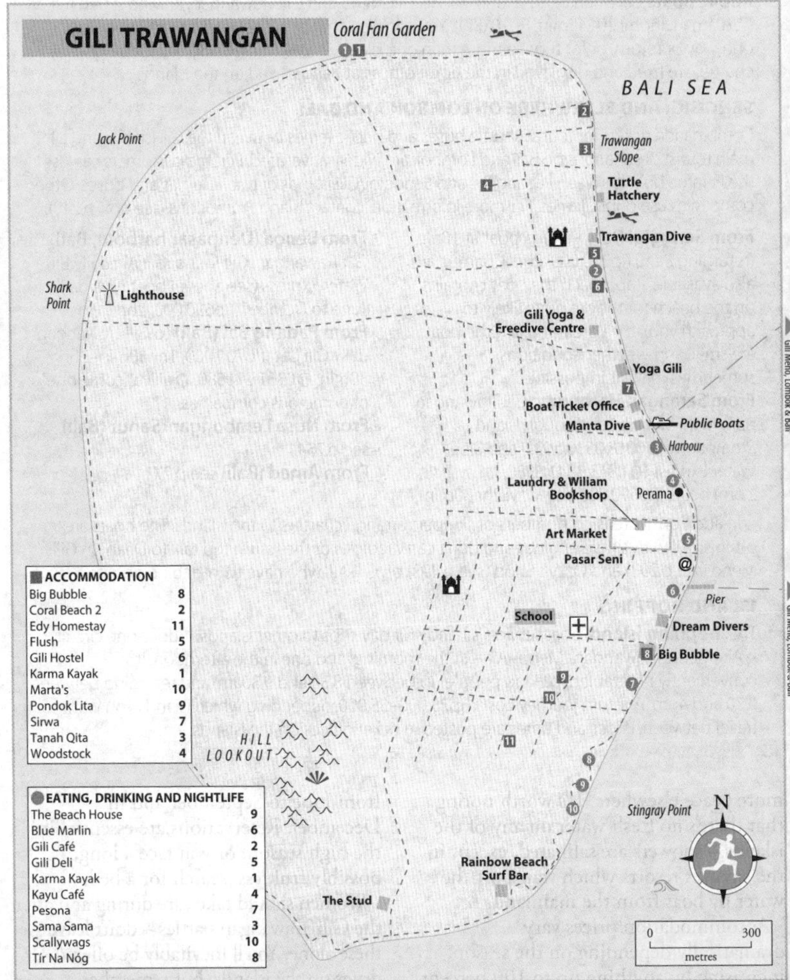

tracks from the southern end of the island, but be sure to return before dark, as riding through the sand is fairly hazardous. A walk around the island, less than 3km long by 2km at its widest part, takes four hours or less. The northern end of the east coast is popular for snorkelling: most people hang out here during the day, and there are plenty of restaurants nearby.

ACCOMMODATION

Prices are greatly reduced during low season, particularly on the coasts. If you're staying on the north of the island, and have booked ahead, it's worth asking your hotel to send a *cidomo* to pick you up from the boat.

Big Bubble East coast ⓣ0370 625020, ⓦbigbubblediving.com. Well-decorated and maintained bungalows (with either fans or a/c) in the garden behind the dive shop. There's also a pool, and you're right in the heart of the action. **Rp400,000**

Edy Homestay In the southeast, a 5min walk inland ⓣ0812 373 4469. Neat, fairly clean rooms in a tidy compound, with a/c and hot water available. Breakfast is served at any time. Look at *Maulana* (same price) across the road if they are full. **Rp150,000**

Flush East coast, near the mosque ⓣ0819 1725 1532. Unappealing name, but charming little place with presentable rooms, some with sea views. Very close to the mosque though, so not the quietest. **Rp250,000**

Gili Hostel East coast ⓣ0877 6526 7037, ⓦgilihostel.com. Funky hostel with seven-bed, a/c dorms (each bed comes with its own locker, power source and reading light). There's also a rooftop bar, volleyball court, and regular film screenings. Dorm **Rp150,000**

Pondok Lita Village ⓣ0370 648607. A fine choice, Pondok Lita has simple rooms set around a small garden; they have fans and cold-water bathrooms, and there are two with a/c. **Rp250,000**

Sirwa East coast ⓣ0819 1724 6125. A row of small, basic bungalows, some with a/c, across the track from the main sunbathing beach. If they are full, consider *Sagita* (ⓣ0812 373 1832) to the north, or *Emalia* (ⓣ0819 1713 4470) to the south, which offer similar rooms for the same price. **Rp250,000**

THE NORTH COAST

Coral Beach 2 ⓣ0813 5358 9422, ⓔcoralbeach_2@yahoo.com. Simple bungalows just behind the beach in the northeast, with a/c and hot water available in the more expensive lumbung. **Rp200,000**

★**Karma Kayak** North coast ⓣ0818 0364 0538, ⓦkarmakayak.com. Excellent bungalows with a/c which are well built, thoughtfully designed (each inspired by a different country or region) and in a fabulous location in the far north of the island. A *cidomo* here from the central area costs Rp50,000. **Rp650,000**

Tanah Qita Northeast coast ⓣ0370 639159 ⓔtanahqita@yahoo.de. A narrow limestone path winds its way among colourful overhanging flowers, leading to five modern wooden lumbung with a/c and four-poster beds, and two "backpacker" bamboo versions with basic outdoor bathrooms. **Rp300,000**

Woodstock In the northeast part of the village ⓣ0821 4765 5877, ⓦwoodstockgili.com. Eco-conscious, 1960s-focused complex of bungalows (each named after a rock-and-roll icon and powered by solar energy) set around a pool and surrounded by fruit trees. **Rp600,000**

★TREAT YOURSELF

Marta's Village ⓣ0812 377 2777, ⓦmartasgili.com. If you're looking for a touch more comfort, try this delightful place run by an Indonesian-British couple. Here you'll find comfortable, split-level rooms with a/c, minibars and private terraces. There's a pool, and if you book in advance they'll meet you off the boat. **Rp850,000**

EATING

In addition to the cafés and restaurants listed below, the night market near the pier heaves every evening with stalls serving barbecued meat and seafood; there are also numerous low-cost warungs in and around the village.

The Beach House Southeast coast. The Beach House is a great place to come for breakfasts and also a good choice for barbecued seafood in the evenings. Mains from Rp36,000. Daily 8am–10pm.

Gili Café East coast. Appealing place with breakfast options (Rp26,500–52,000) from Israel, France, Sweden, Mexico, Italy and the UK, as well as salads, sandwiches, seafood and pasta, plus a boat on the sand that has been transformed into a bar. Daily 8am–10pm.

Gili Deli East coast ⓦthegilideli.com. The service may be slow, but the coffees (Rp22,000/cup) and teas (Rp22,000/pot) – the menu features a dozen varieties of each – are worth the wait. Excellent wraps, panini, baguettes, bagels and breakfast options too. Daily 7am–7/8pm.

Karma Kayak North coast ⓦkarmakayak.com. A delightful spot on the beach with excellent, imaginative tapas and mezze (Rp15,000–33,000), plus sangria (Rp155,000/jug). From May to mid-Sept, this is the prime sunset-viewing destination. Daily 8am–10pm.

Kayu Café East Coast ⓣ0870 6547 2260, ⓦfacebook.com/kayucafe. Top spot for a fresh juice, smoothie or shot of wheatgrass, or less healthy cakes and pastries (around

4

Rp25,000), plus Illy coffee and great breakfast and lunch options. There's a/c and BBC World too. Daily 7am–7pm.

★**Scallywags** Southeast coast ⓦscallywagsresort.com. Several restaurants at the southern end of the strip have seafood barbecues (from Rp60,000, including jacket potato/rice and salad bar), but *Scallywags* is the best. The creative menu also features Basque-style tapas, hearty sandwiches, tempting desserts (such as blueberry cheesecake), and even draught Kilkenny (Rp70,000/pint). Daily 8am–10/11pm.

NIGHTLIFE

Gili Trawangan is renowned for its high-season parties, which alternate between venues depending on the day, and full-moon parties in the low season. All get going at about 11pm. Expect to pay around Rp20,000–25,000 for a small Bintang at any of the bars below.

Blue Marlin East coast ⓦbluemarlindive.com. Rather incongruously the Monday-night party venue, at the dive shop of the same name, also serves tasty barbecued seafood and hosts regular yoga sessions.

Pesona Southeast coast. One of the most laidback places on Gili T, with a sea of multicoloured beanbags and shisha pipes (Rp100,000), plus decent north Indian food. Daily noon–late.

4

Sama Sama East coast. One of the liveliest bars on the island, with parties most nights, often featuring reggae acts (check the posters and flyers around Gili T to see what's on). Daily noon–late.

Tír Na Nóg Southeast coast ⓦtirnanoggili.com. Rocking Irish bar – the Wednesday-night party venue – with beer, darts, movies and huge screens for sports events plus comfort food such as cottage pie, bangers and mash and a full Irish breakfast. The drinks list includes bottled Guinness and Irish whiskey. Daily 7am–late.

DIRECTORY

Banks and exchange There are ATMs every 100m at the southern end of the strip, including next to the *Villa Ombak Hotel*. Moneychangers are everywhere but rates are better on the mainland. Dive companies offer advances on Visa and MasterCard – useful in an emergency but you will pay ten percent for this.

Books Several places sell and exchange secondhand books, including Wiliam Bookshop (daily 8am–8pm) behind the market.

Bus tickets Perama (daily 7am–10pm) is near the jetty and many other companies also have stalls by the harbour.

Health There are several clinics, including at the Villa Ombak hotel. The nearest hospital is in Mataram (see p.282).

Internet Most hotels, restaurants and bars provide free wi-fi. There are also numerous internet cafés on the main strip.

Post There's a postal agent in the Pasar Seni area on the east coast.

Yoga Gili Yoga offers a morning and evening class in hatha and vinyasa flow (east coast; ⓣ0871 471 8710, ⓦgiliyoga.com; Rp100,000).

CLIMBING GUNUNG RINJANI

Lots of people who want to climb **Gunung Rinjani** (3726m) opt to do so from the Gilis – there are plenty of tour operators along the main strip offering transport to the volcano, a one- two- or three-day trek up it, and transport either back to the Gilis or to Senggigi. Trips start at around Rp1,000,000 for a two-day trek including all food and equipment. A good tour operator is Lombok Rinjani Trekking Adventure (ⓣ081 8036 52874, ⓦlombok-rinjanitrekking-info.com).

Gili Meno

A similar oval shape to Gili Trawangan, **GILI MENO** is much smaller, about 2km long and just over 1km wide. This is the most tranquil island of the three, with a small local population, no nightlife and arguably the best beaches, as less space is taken up by fishing boats and hawkers (although unfortunately the few hawkers there are here are even more persistent than most). It takes a couple of hours to stroll around the island. There's a bird park in the middle of the island (Taman Burung; daily 9am–5pm; Rp50,000) that's worth a visit; it houses three hundred tropical birds.

The snorkelling is good along the east coast; start at Royal Reef and drift down to Kontiki in the south. Take care – boats come in and out to the harbour along here. The other option is to start at the yellow light beacon in the north of the island; swim left and the current will take you round to the west coast over the Meno Wall and you can get out at the old Bounty jetty, part of the way down the west coast. Keep your fins on until you're in very shallow water, as there can often be quite an undertow (see box, p.295). You can venture further afield by boat: ask on the beach (about Rp250,000 per person for a minimum of two people off Gili Meno; around Rp400,000 for all three islands). Equipment is available on the island but a lot has seen (far) better

★TREAT YOURSELF

Shack 58 & 59 In the north of the island (no telephone) shack58.net. Despite the unprepossessing name, these are two charming a/c bungalows in a tranquil spot ideal for a romantic tryst: #59 is inland, and slightly cheaper (Rp720,000); #58 is right on the beach, and worth the extra (Rp800,000). Very popular, so book well in advance.

days (from around Rp30,000 per day). There are also several dive operators on the island (see box; p.295). For boat trips, search out Dean (0813 3950 9859), one of the boat captains; he's often in front of the Blue Marlin dive shop. He'll take you on fishing trips and to see dolphins (best in March–Aug & Nov) in the sea off the north coast of Lombok (around Rp400,000 per person).

ACCOMMODATION

Amber House In the north of the island 0813 3757 9728, amber_house02pm@hotmail.com. A quiet choice, Amber House has basic thatch-and-bamboo bungalows with squat toilets and salt-water bathrooms set slightly back from the beach. Options with fresh-water showers cost more. **Rp250,000**

Sunset Gecko In the northeast of the island, north of the lake 0813 5356 6774, thesunsetgecko.com. Despite the variable standards of accommodation, the low rates make this a popular option. Both the "backpacker" rooms and the A-frame bungalows have shared bathrooms; ask to see a few before making your choice. Room **Rp210,000**, bungalow **Rp310,000**

★Tao' Kombo' In the southeast of the island, 200m behind the beach; take the turn inland just south of *Mallia's Child* 0812 372 2174, tao-kombo.com. This place has a large bar (with live music in the high season), garden games and welcoming staff. The six bungalows have fans and fresh-water showers, and there's also a good-value "family room" sleeping up to four (Rp640,000). **Rp480,000**

EATING AND DRINKING

Opening hours vary depending on the season, but generally speaking most places are open daily 8/9am–9/10pm.

Bibi's Attached to Villa Nautilus just south of the harbour. Bibi's serves delicious, authentic, wood-fired pizzas (from Rp45,000) under white parasols overlooking the sea.

Diana Café In the north of the island. A great spot for a sundowner (beer around Rp25,000), especially if you bag one of the hammocks. Also excellent grilled fish and a lip-smacking coconut, chocolate and banana pancake.

Jungle Bar *Tao' Kombo'*. One of the main late-night chill-out spots, with cool music and plenty of drinks. The jungle juice cocktails (around Rp50,000) are as wild as they sound. Hosts traditional dance performances with local people in high season.

★Yaya Warung Just north of the harbour area, overlooking a sandy cove. Simple shack serving up economical juices, smoothies and warung staples (under Rp20,000) such as *nasi goreng* and *nasi campur*.

DIRECTORY

Banks and exchange No ATMs. Moneychangers at two kiosks, one south of *Mallia's Child* and one further north.

Boat tickets The office is under a tree in the harbour area of the east coast – by the red hand-painted sign nailed to the tree.

Bus tickets The Perama agent is at the *Kontiki* hotel in the south of the island.

Internet access There are numerous internet cafés on the east coast, and virtually everywhere has free wi-fi access.

4

Gili Air

GILI AIR stretches about 1.5km in each direction and takes a couple of hours to walk round. It's a pleasant cross between lively, social Gili Trawangan and peaceful Gili Meno; however, as there's no more land available on Gili Trawangan, the island is, sadly, becoming increasingly developed. Although accommodation is spread around most of the coast, it's concentrated on the southeast and northeast corners.

The beach in the southeast corner is popular, with good snorkelling. Snorkelling gear is widely available for rent; try Ozzy's Shop on the east coast (from Rp30,000 per day). For snorkelling further afield, boat trips are advertised pretty much everywhere (around Rp100,000 per person including equipment; 9.30am–2.30pm) and take in sites off all three islands. There are several dive operators (see box, p.295).

ACCOMMODATION

7Seas Backpackers Southeast corner of the island 0811 385 1212, 7seas-cottages.com. The dorms and private rooms here are good value and generally well kept, and there's a pool, though service is so-so and noise can sometimes be an issue. Accommodation-and-dive packages available. Dorm **Rp80,000**, double **Rp300,000**

Banana Cottages East coast ☎ 0181 037 0640. These cheerful fan-cooled, bright-yellow bungalows have comfy beds and lovely outdoor bathrooms (with cold water). There's a small book swap and rental bikes are available (Rp35,000/day). **Rp250,000**

★ **Biba Beach Village** On the east coast ☎ 0819 1727 4648, ⓦ bibabeach.com. A dream of a hotel, with gorgeous solid bungalows all boasting king-size beds. There's an excellent restaurant (see below), and you could opt for a private dinner served for you on the veranda or on the beach. **Rp550,000**

Coconut Cottages East coast ☎ 0370 635365, ⓦ coconuts-giliair.com. An attractive, clean, English-run place with bungalows in a garden haven set back from the east coast. All have hot water and a/c is available. The staff are lovely, and there's a great restaurant. **Rp450,000**

Gili Air Santay East coast ☎ 0818 0375 8695, ⓦ giliair-santay.com. Popular, good-quality traditional cottages, run by an Indonesian-Austrian couple, set 100m back from the east coast in a shady garden; all have cold water only and fans. There are *brugak* (wooden platforms with cushions and a low table) on the beach for relaxing. **Rp350,000**

Gita Gili East coast ☎ 0813 3955 3395. About 10min walk up the east coast from the jetty with thatch, wood and bamboo bungalows facing the sea. All have fans and attached cold-water bathrooms. **Rp200,000**

Island View Bungalows West coast ☎ 0877 6526 5737, ⓦ islandviewgiliair.com. If you're after isolation, this is the place to come. Set in a coconut grove facing the beach on the quiet western side of the island, these bungalows come with fans or a/c, private balconies and private hot-water bathrooms. **Rp400,000**

EATING AND DRINKING

Visitors flock to the northeast corner of the island to enjoy sunset cocktails on the beach. Pretty coloured lanterns are strewn along the path to guide your way between the many beachside bars and restaurants that liven up as the night goes on. Opening hours vary depending on the season, but most places serve food from 10/11am until at least 9.30pm.

Biba Beach Village On the east coast ☎ 0819 1727 4648, ⓦ bibabeach.com. Attached to the hotel of the same name, this restaurant serves quality Italian cuisine (mains

4

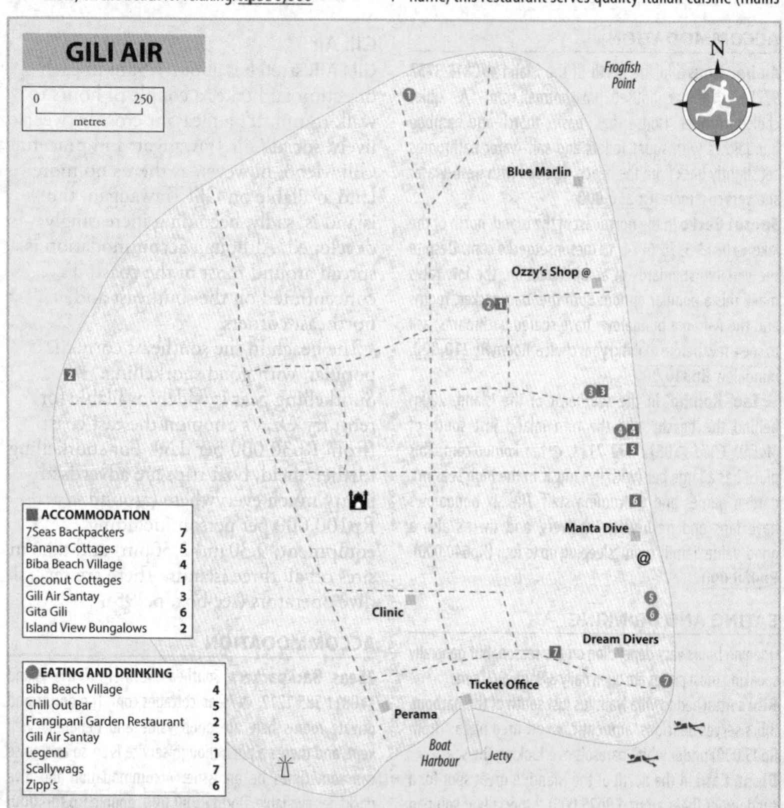

SNORKELLING AND DIVING ON THE GILI ISLANDS

The **snorkelling and diving** around the Gili Islands is some of the best and most accessible in Lombok, despite the havoc wreaked by an El Niño in 1998, which locals estimate has cut down the visible marine life to around a fifth of what it was. Despite this, and a lot of visitors, however, the reefs remain in reasonable condition. All the islands are fringed by coral reefs and visibility is generally around 15m. The fish life includes white-tip and black-tip reef sharks, sea turtles, manta rays, Napoleon wrasse and bumphead parrotfish.

There are good snorkelling spots just off all the islands' beaches. Snorkel gear is widely available from around Rp25,000 per day, but the condition does vary. Dive companies take snorkellers further afield for about $10–20, and half-day tours of the three islands in a glass-bottomed boat (around Rp100,000 per person) are commonly advertised. The **offshore currents** around the island are strong and can be seriously hazardous. Dive operators are aware of this, but if you're snorkelling or swimming off the beach it's easy to get carried out further than you intend and then be unable to get back to land. There have been drownings in recent years.

The best **dive sites** involve short boat trips. There are plenty of **dive operators** on the islands, and there's a price agreement, so they all charge the same. Prices include: $35 for a fun dive (for qualified divers), $370 for a PADI Open Water, and $295 for a PADI Advanced Open Water course.

All divers pay a one-off **reef tax** of Rp50,000 (snorkellers pay Rp25,000) to the Gili Eco Trust, which works to protect the reefs around the islands.

The nearest hospital is in Mataram, where there is also a **decompression chamber** at Jl Adi Sucipto 13B (24hr hotline ⓣ0370 660 0333).

DIVE OPERATORS

Big Bubble (see p.291) Gili Trawangan ⓣ0370 625020, ⓦbigbubblediving.com. Friendly place owned by two British women. Groups are small so dives are planned to suit guests and take advantage of quiet sites. Join them for volleyball at the end of every afternoon on the court in front of the dive shop.

Blue Marlin Gili Trawangan ⓣ0370 632424; Gili Meno ⓣ0370 639980; Gili Air ⓣ0370 634387, ⓦbluemarlindive.com. British-owned, with an expertise in technical diving and offering courses up to PADI IDC (Instructor Development Courses) and IANTD (International Association of Nitrox and Technical Divers) Instructor Training Course level.

Dream Divers Gili Trawangan ⓣ0370 603 4496; Gili Air ⓣ0370 634547, ⓦdreamdivers.com. Courses up to PADI IDC. Dive instruction offered in German and English by friendly and exceptionally helpful staff.

Manta Dive Gili Trawangan ⓣ0370 643649; Gili Air ⓣ0813 5305 0462, ⓦmanta-dive.com. British-owned company with highly respected local dive guides. Courses up to PADI Divemaster level are offered, as well as trips to the more distant Tunang Wall which has some excellent coral and is suitable for all levels.

Trawangan Dive North Gili Trawangan ⓣ0370 649220, ⓦtrawangandive.com. At the quieter part of Gili T, they pride themselves on taking good care of divers (fruit, water and towels on boats). They also offer technical diving and underwater photography courses.

from Rp40,000) such as home-made pasta, gnocchi and ravioli, plus wood-fired pizzas and focaccia.

Chill Out Bar In the southeast corner of the island ⓦchilloutbargili.com. A great spot to hang out during the day between forays into the water and to linger long into the night sipping cold beers (around Rp20,000) and cocktails.

Frangipani Garden Restaurant At *Coconut Cottages*. The most imaginative dining on the island with Western and local cuisine and seafood (mains from Rp40,000). The set menu is a feast of Sasak food and needs to be ordered the day before.

Gili Air Santay East coast. This warung is a good, low-key spot for Indonesian and Thai (or at least Thai-style) food (from around Rp30,000).

Legend North coast. Expect hearty portions and reggae music at *Legend*, which also hosts weekly parties on Wednesdays during the high season and "Dark Moon" parties in Feb and Aug – see posters around the island for details.

★**Scallywags** Southeast coast ⓦscallywagsresort.com. Scallywags has the island's best seafood barbecues (from Rp60,000, including jacket potato/rice and salad bar), plus great desserts and drinks. There's another branch on Gili T (see p.292).

Zipp's Next to the *Chill Out Bar*, *Zipp's* has a similar vibe and is a good place to hang out after dark. The food is decent too – though make sure you order from (cheaper) locals' menu.

4

DIRECTORY

Banks and exchange The island now has an ATM, on the east coast, as well as a few moneychangers near the jetty and up the east coast – rates are poor. Try to bring some cash with you.

Bicycle rental Ozzy's Shop, halfway up the road running up the east coast, rents bicycles (from Rp25,000/day).

Bus tickets The Perama office (daily 7am–1pm & 2–6pm; ⓣ0370 637816 or ⓣ0818 0527 2735) is next to *Villa Karang* hotel.

Internet *The Gili Beach Café* beside Manta Dive has a reliable connection and Skype.

Medical aid There is a clinic inland from the harbour, with a nurse in attendance most days (7–9am & 5–7pm). The closest hospital is in Mataram (see p.282).

Yoga H20 Yoga (ⓣ0877 6103 8836, ⓦh2oyogaandmeditation.com), just inland from Gili Air Santay, run daily yoga and meditation classes (Rp100,000).

GUNUNG RINJANI AND AROUND

From a distance, **Gunung Rinjani** (3726m) appears to rise in solitary glory from the plains, but in fact the entire area is a throng of bare summits, wreathed in dense forest. The climb up Rinjani, taking in Danau Segara Anak, the magnificent crater lake, with the perfect cone of Gunung Baru rising from it, is the most energetic and rewarding trek on either Bali or Lombok. Climbs start from either Senaru to the north of the mountain or Sembalun Lawang to the northeast.

Trekking on Rinjani is not for the unfit. A guide is essential (see box opposite) and you must register at the Rinjani Trek Centres at Senaru or Sembalun Lawang and pay the National Park admission fee (Rp150,000; ⓦrinjaninationalpark.com). You'll need basic equipment; bring your own walking boots, a torch and food and drink (take loads of snacks and sweets even if food is provided). If you haven't got a seriously warm, windproof jacket with you, rent one. The Rinjani Trek Centres rent out radios but increasingly mobile phones are being relied on as emergency back-up; make sure your party has one or the other.

Gunung Rinjani

There are several possible **climbs** around Rinjani, and few trekkers reach the summit – most are satisfied with shorter, less arduous trips. All treks are dependent on how active the volcano is, so check the website (see above) before planning a trip.

The shortest trek is from Senaru to the crater rim, from where there are spectacular views across Segara Anak to Gunung Baru, and back to Senaru (two days, one night). For a longer trek (three days/two nights), a path continues from the crater rim (2hr) and descends into the crater to the lake, at 2050m. It is steep and scary at the top with metal handrails and some ropes but it gets better further down. You can bathe in the lakeside hot springs, and from the lake you return the same way to Senaru.

The shortest route to the summit of Rinjani is to climb from Sembalun Lawang on the northeast side of the mountain, starting on the track next to the Rinjani Trek Centre. It takes seven to eight hours to reach the overnight campsite, *Plawangan II*, and you then attack the summit the next morning. It's an extraordinarily steep haul up to the summit (3–4hr up; 3hr back down to *Plawangan II*). You then descend to the lake to ease tired muscles in the **hot springs** and return to Sembalun Lawang (three days/two nights).

The most complete exploration of the mountain involves a one-way trip; ascending from Sembalun Lawang, taking in the summit, then the lake and descending to Senaru – this has the advantage of getting the most exhausting ascent over while you are fresh (four days/three nights).

Batu Koq and Senaru

The small villages of **BATU KOQ** and **SENARU**, south of Bayan (about 86km from Mataram), are reached by ojek from Anyar, a few kilometres north. Buses from Mandalika/Bertais/Sweta and Labuhan Lombok terminate in Bayan.

Just south of Pondok Senaru, a small path heads east to the river and **Sindang Gile waterfall** (no fixed opening times; Rp5000). The main fall is about 25m high. **Tiu Kelep** is another waterfall a further hour beyond the first, but it is essential to take a guide (around Rp60,000–80,000/3hr). You should probably take a dip here; the local belief is that you become a year younger every time you swim behind the falls. It's also the perfect way to cool off

ORGANIZING THE TREK

If you want to climb Gunung Rinjani, an extremely useful first stop is one of the **Rinjani Trek Centres**: at the top of the village at the start of the path to Gunung Rinjani in Senaru, and in the centre of Sembalun Lawang (June–Sept daily 7am–5pm; at other times opening hours are more hit and miss). They provide information about climbing routes, can arrange all-inclusive trips, and they register and collect the fee from everyone entering the National Park. If you want to put your trek together **independently**, it is possible to arrange a guide (from around Rp220,000/day) and porters (from around Rp180,000) at the Trek Centres (all guides and porters should be licensed) and rent equipment there, though you'll need to buy your own food, and food for the porter and guide. Be aware that you'll need to start trekking in the morning, so you should organize everything the day before.

Don't forget to bring warm clothes, as it's freezing at the top, particularly when you're trying to sleep, and extra water, as the guides almost invariably don't bring enough.

TOUR PRICES

Prices largely depend on your bargaining ability (though everyone quotes "published prices", you should still negotiate). They should include guide, porters, equipment (including sleeping bags and tents) and meals. Return transport should be included in treks arranged in Senggigi or from the Gilis. Most people pay from Rp1,000,000 for a budget two-day/one-night crater-rim trek including transport to and from either Senggigi or the Gilis (you can often secure cheaper deals).

QUESTIONS TO ASK

What exactly is included in the price?
How many porters and guides are included?
What is the menu? Will snacks be provided?
Will the person you are talking to be going with you?
Will your group be part of a larger group or going independently?

TREKKING COMPANIES

The number of trekking **agencies** arranging all-inclusive treks is bewildering. In Senggigi, the Rinjani Trekking Club (T 0370 693202, W info2lombok.com), which is linked to the Rinjani Trek Centres in Senaru and Sembulan, have fully trained local guides who are committed to sustainable tourism, and take all rubbish with them off the mountain.

In **Senaru and Sembalun** check out the Rinjani Trek Centres (RTC), which have a representative in most guesthouses, and other local operators, including John's Adventures (T 0817 578 8018, W rinjanimaster.com).

It is also possible to organize a trip from the Gilis (see p.288).

after a trek, and it's likely to be the best shower you'll take all trip.

If you are not up to climbing Rinjani, note that the Rinjani Trek Centres also organize a half-day panoramic walking tour of the area with a female guide, including a visit to a local village (from Rp100,000 per person; 4hr).

ACCOMMODATION AND EATING

All accommodation listed below is spread for several kilometres along the road through Batu Koq and Senaru. Bemos go all the way so you can stop outside any of them. All offer luggage storage and have small restaurants attached, serving simple food.

Gunung Baru Near the start of the trail, Senaru T 0819 0741 1211. Small set-up not far from the start of the trail, with a handful of simple, tiled bungalows. Rp100,000

Pondok Indah Senaru Cottages T 0878 653 3344. Ten basic, slightly overpriced rooms, all with attached cold-water bathrooms. A veranda provides calming views over the surrounding landscape. Rp200,000

Simar Selaran Jl Pariwisata, Senaru T 0818 540673, E sinar_selatan@hotmail.com. Basic but good-value rooms, including a decent breakfast to fuel your trek. The manager, Jul, is also a rep for the RTC so you can book treks from here, with one free night's accommodation and onward transport included in the price. Rp100,000

Sembalun Lawang and Sembalun Bumbung

Set in countryside that is unique in Lombok, the Sembalun area is a high, flat-bottomed mountain valley surrounded by hills. SEMBALUN LAWANG is accessed via a steep 16km road from

Kokok Putih (by minibuses or ojek) or an equally steep, 16km road north from Sapit on the other side of the mountains. Kokok Putih is accessible by bemo or minibus from Bayan or Labuhan Lombok.

The village of **SEMBALUN BUMBUNG** is 4km south of Sembalun Lawang with houses clustered around the mosque. Buses run through here between Sembalun Lawang and Aik Mel; all buses between Labuhan Lombok and the Bertais/Mandalika/Sweta bus terminal pass through Aik Mel.

ACCOMMODATION

Lembah Rinjani On the start of the track to Rinjani beside the Rinjani Trek Centre in Sembalun Lawang ⓣ 0818 0365 2511, ⓦ sites.google.com/site/lembahrinjani. Well-established place with simple, clean rooms with verandas facing Rinjani, as well as a restaurant; most bathrooms only have cold water, but buckets of hot water can be supplied. **Rp300,000**

TETEBATU

Set amid picturesque scenery on the southern slopes of Gunung Rinjani, 50km east of Sweta, the small village of **TETEBATU** is a cool, but not cold, quiet spot for a few days of relaxation. From here you can rent motorcycles and hire guides for local treks. Guides can also be arranged at all the accommodation; the most popular trek is through rice paddies and the local monkey forest to Jukut Waterfall (Rp125,000 per person; 4–6hr).

If you're travelling here by public transport, get off the bemo or bus at Pomotong on the main road and either take a bemo (though they are becoming less regular as motorbikes take over) or an ojek to Tetebatu.

It isn't easy to change money locally and there's currently no public telephone or internet access.

ACCOMMODATION AND EATING

Accommodation is on the main road north through the village and the road off to the east, Waterfall St. Most have restaurants attached – the best views are from those at *Cendrawasih* and *Hakiki*. *Bale Bale Café* and *Salabuse* on the main road serve Indonesian and Western dishes, plus some Sasak options. The food in the cafés is often tasty, but hygieine standards are variable. Even if you skip the food, *Bale Bale* is still a great place for live music – the owner and his mates get going on a guitar and play all night, with even more enthusiasm when the power runs out (which is often).

★ **Hakiki Inn** ⓣ 0818 0373 7407, ⓦ hakiki-Inn.com. In the middle of paddy fields at the eastern end of Waterfall St is this two-storey, traditional rice-barn-style accommodation with excellent verandas. The cheapest have squat toilets; ones with Western-style toilets cost an extra Rp100,000. The food at the attached restaurant is excellent and can be enjoyed on platforms surrounded by picturesque green rice paddies. **Rp100,000**

Pondok Bulan ⓣ 0812 3796 3422. A few simple, tiled rooms and a "family room" sleeping up to four (Rp200,000), which is in fact a two-storey house with gorgeous views over the rice paddies. **Rp120,000**

LABUHAN LOMBOK

The port town of **LABUHAN LOMBOK** runs ferries to Sumbawa (every 45min; 1hr 45min–2hr) from the terminal, Labuhan Kayangan, at the far end of the promontory, 3km around the south side of the bay (accessed by bemo or ojek). Buses run regularly along the cross-island road between Labuhan Lombok and the Bertais/Mandalika/Sweta terminal at Sweta, with some continuing on to the ferry terminal, and between Labuhan Lombok and Bayan; change at Kokok Putih for the Sembalun valley. Travelling between Kuta and Labuhan Lombok involves changing at Praya and then Kopang, on the main road. A decent place to stay is *Hotel Melati Lima Tiga*, Jl Kayangan 14 (ⓣ 0376 23316; Rp150,000), about 150m from the town centre on the road to the ferry terminal, which has rudimentary rooms. There's a local Perama office on the coast side of the road to the harbour (ⓣ 0376 292 4534 or ⓣ 0813 3991 1345, ⓦ peramatour.com), which can organize transfers to Kuta, Senggigi and beyond.

KUTA AND AROUND

The only major tourist development on the south coast is **KUTA**, 54km from Mataram and 32km from Praya, a tiny

fishing village situated behind a sweeping, white-sand beach. It's great for a few quiet days by the sea, especially if you like wild coastal scenery and turbulent surf, but you need to have your own transport (renting a motorbike is ideal) to reach surrounding beaches and make the most of the area. Apart from the Sunday and Wednesday **markets**, Kuta is a quiet and laidback place.

Kuta days revolve around the beach or pool. You can hire surfboards or book classes and tours at Kimen Surf (T 0370 655064, W kuta-lombok.net) in the village. Dive operator Dive Zone (T 0370 660 3205, W divezone-lombok.com) knows of sites for all levels of experience, and arranges snorkelling trips to Gili Sudah and Gili Poh. Mimpi Manis (see below) organizes fishing trips (Rp1,000,000/4–5hr for up to three people).

Around Kuta

The glorious beaches of **Seger** and **Tanjung Aan** to the east of Kuta are, at a push, walkable, though bicycles and scooters are a good idea (many of the roads are in a poor condition, so be prepared for a bumpy ride). Past Tanjung Aan, the small fishing village of Gerupuk, just under 8km from Kuta, perches on the western shores of Gumbang Bay. There are some good surf waves here, and boatmen will ferry you out for around Rp80,000 per boat including waiting time. From **Gerupuk**, there are fine views across the bay to **Bumbang** on the eastern shore, and you can rent a canoe or motorboat to take you across.

Along the coast west of Kuta you can explore half a dozen or more of the prettiest beaches on the island. The closest is the tiny (but lovely) **Are Goleng**, a couple of kilometres out of Kuta, and heading west you come to **Mawun**, a gorgeous curve of golden sand with calm waters which are good for swimming, **Tampa**, **Mawi** (recommended for surfing) and **Rowok**, before reaching the small village of **Selong Blanak**, 15km from Kuta, from where you can cut inland to Keling and on to Praya (24km). Selong Blanak beach is well worth the distance, as there's hardly anybody there and the white sand and gentle waves are idyllic. There's a small refreshment shack behind the beach, so you can happily spend the whole day there. Take a decent road map if you're exploring any further west from Selong Blanak and be aware that the road deteriorates badly the further west you go.

ARRIVAL AND DEPARTURE

By bemo Coming from the west, buses run to Praya from Bertais/Mandalika/Sweta terminal in Sweta. From Praya, bemos either go as far as Sengkol, where you can change, or right through to Kuta. From the east of Lombok, bemos run to Praya from Kopang on the main cross-island road. Bemos pass Mimpi Manis on their way into Kuta, then stop at the western end of the village – it's a 10min walk to the accommodation along the beach.

By charter transport Ask at your accommodation. Most people use charters for one-way drops: around Rp200,000–250,000 to Mataram, Rp250,000–300,000 to Senggigi, and Rp300,000–350,000 to Bangsal.

ACCOMMODATION

All accommodation is spread a few hundred metres along the road behind the beach at the eastern end of the village or in the village itself.

G'day Inn T 0370 655342, W gday-inn.com. Five well-kept rooms with attached cold-water bathrooms in a friendly family homestay in the village; head east at the main village crossroads that are just inland from the market area. **Rp120,000**

Mimpi Manis T 081 836 9950, W mimpimanis.com. Just over 1.5km north of the beach on the way to Sade, this spotless place is run by a Balinese–English family. Choose between fan or a/c rooms (Rp225,000), or a two-storey house (Rp250,000); all have private bathrooms, safes and DVD players (there's a big collection of films to borrow). **Rp150,000**

Segare Anak T 0370 654846. This long-standing favourite, on the road that runs behind the beach, has a wide range of rooms, some with a/c, all with cold water, set in a lovely garden with a dinky pool. **Rp200,000**

★**The Spot** T 0370 702 2100, W thespotbungalows.com. Small but lovely bamboo bungalows (each with a private deck and hammock), as well as a grassy communal area for socializing and a small bar-restaurant. **Rp280,000**

Surfers Inn T 0370 655582. Simple but sizeable and well-maintained fan rooms with communal verandas and more swish a/c bungalows set in a pretty garden surrounding a pool that's big enough to swim lengths in. **Rp220,000**

★**Yuli's Homestay** T 0819 1710 0983, W yulishomestay.com. Run by a welcoming Indonesian–Kiwi

couple, this modern take on a homestay has cheerful a/c rooms, guest kitchens, and two swimming pools. Ideal if you're looking for a bit more comfort. Rp450,000

EATING AND NIGHTLIFE

The village has plenty of pizza joints and traveller cafés to choose from. The beach road is lined with candlelit warungs that have nightly barbecues and inexpensive seafood; all serve until about 10pm.

★**Ashtari** ashtarilombok.com. At the top of the hill on the road west from Kuta – a bit of a trek but a great place to stop if you're biking around. The views are spectacular, and the superb food – a small vegetarian menu of sandwiches, salads and Indonesian, Indian and Mediterranean dishes (from Rp25,000) – is great value. Save space for the home-made cakes. Daily 8.30am–8pm.

Dwiki's Cuisine Western end of the village. Decent wood-fired oven pizzas (around Rp70,000) and Westernized versions of Indonesian dishes served on white tablecloths by friendly staff. Daily 8am–10/11pm.

Full Moon Café Eastern end of the beach. Choose between cushions on the floor at low tables, bamboo furniture on the sand, or the lofty terrace with lovely views, to enjoy great grilled chicken with spicy Sasak sauce and barbecued seafood (around Rp50,000–70,000). Daily 8am–10/11pm.

The Shore Bar 0370 653144. Regular live music in the high season at this ramshackle, laidback shack with a huge dancefloor at the far eastern end of the road that runs along the beach. Free pick-ups if you call ahead. Sun–Tues 11am–11pm, Wed 11am–12.30am, Thurs 1.15–11pm & Sat 11am–2.30am.

★**Sonya's** It's not just the heart-shaped portions of rice that set this beach warung apart from the rest on this strip; their chicken satay, fish curry and *nasi campur* (all around Rp25,000–30,000) have customers returning night after night. They also refill water bottles and have an all-you-can-eat seafood barbecue every Friday night. Daily 8am–10pm.

DIRECTORY

Banks and exchange There's an ATM at the eastern end of the beach road, close to the village. *Surfer's Inn* changes money.

Bicycle rental From Rp30,000/day from the internet café beside *Dwiki's Cuisine*.

Bus tickets *Segare Anak* (see p.299) are Perama agents.

Internet There's an internet café next door to *Dwiki's Cuisine*.

Motorcycle rental From Rp50,000/day from most guesthouses.

Post *Segare Anak* (see p.299) is a postal agent. The nearest post office is in Praya.

Yoga *Ashtari* has daily 6.30am sessions on its terrace.

Sumbawa

Most travellers crossing the scorched, mountainous island of **SUMBAWA**, east of Lombok, experience it solely through the window of a long-distance bus. But transit travel doesn't do justice to this friendly, laidback island, with its fine beaches and surfing, offshore islands and traditional villages.

Historically, Sumbawa was divided between east and west, with the western Sumbawans influenced by the Balinese and Sasaks of Lombok, while the eastern Bimans share linguistic and cultural similarities with the Makarese of Sulawesi and the peoples of Flores and Sumba. The whole island is Muslim, however, and conservative dress is recommended.

Sumbawa has been a bit unsettled in recent years, with riots in Sape in 2012 and Sumbawa Besar in 2013, so check the security situation before your trip.

SUMBAWA BESAR

SUMBAWA BESAR, usually referred to simply as Sumbawa, is the largest town on the island, although it sprawls without a real centre. The main streets run on a one-way loop, forming a convenient racetrack for ojek drivers in the evenings, although the side streets are quiet and leafy. The area around the Sultan's Palace, to the south of town, is a particularly pleasant place to wander, where luxurious modern mansions sit side by side with old wooden huts on tiny, colourful alleys. You're welcome to walk through the palace itself, an elaborate stilted wooden

GETTING TO SUMBAWA

Ferries to and from Lombok (every 45min; 1hr 45min–2hr) dock at Poto Tano; buses meet all incoming ferries and run south from the harbour to Sumbawa Besar (2hr 30min), and sometimes all the way to Bima (9hr); it's easy to change at Sumbawa Besar if not. Ferries to and **from Flores** (daily; 6–9hr) and **Sumba** (2 weekly; 9–12hr) use the port at Sape. Pelni ferries dock at Bima.

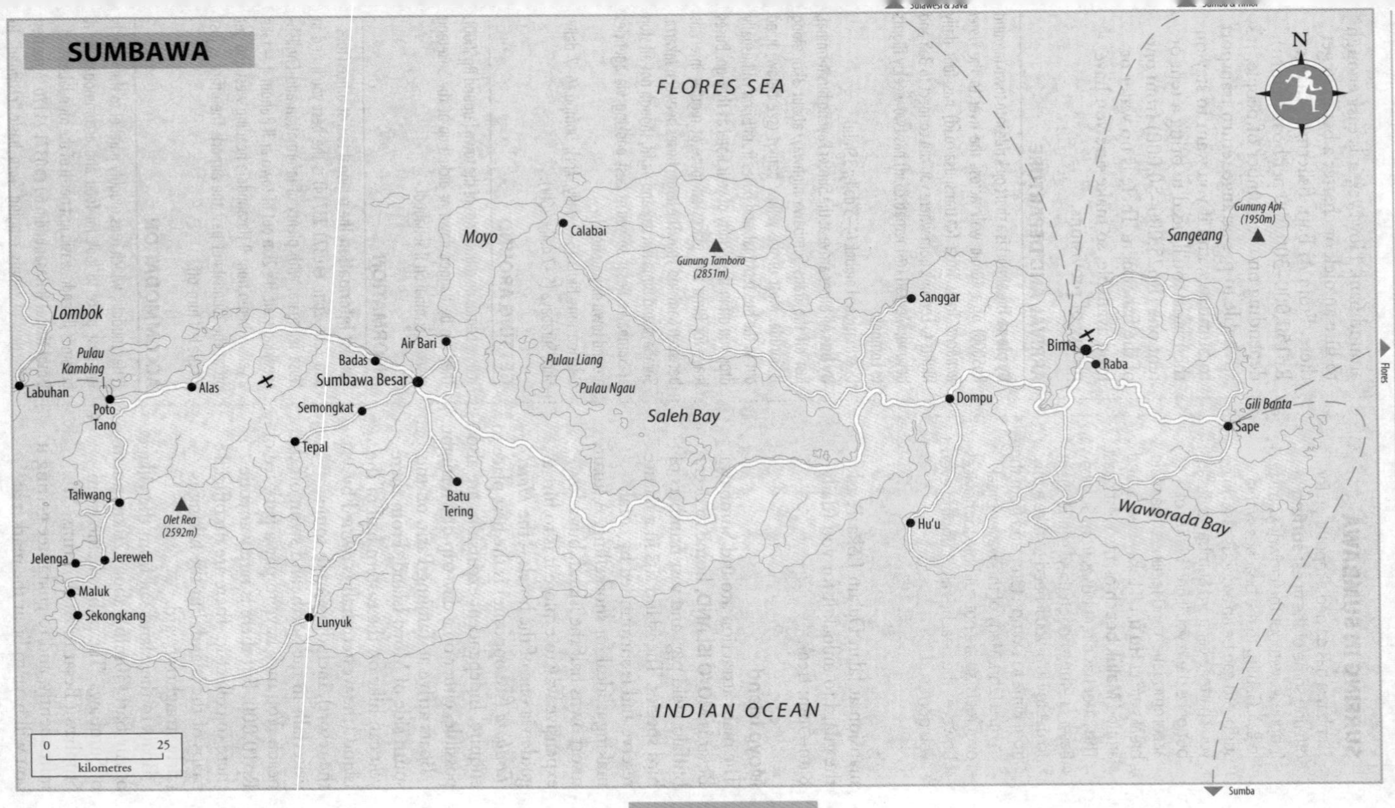
SUMBAWA
N
Sulawesi & Java
Sumba & Timor
Flores
Sumba
FLORES SEA
INDIAN OCEAN
Lombok
Labuhan
Pulau Kambing
Poto Tano
Alas
Taliwang
Jereweh
Jelenga
Maluk
Sekongkang
Olet Rea (2592m)
Tepal
Semongkat
Badas
Sumbawa Besar
Air Bari
Lunyuk
Batu Tering
Moyo
Calabai
Pulau Liang
Pulau Ngau
Saleh Bay
Gunung Tambora (2851m)
Sanggar
Dompu
Hu'u
Bima
Raba
Sangeang
Gunung Api (1950m)
Gili Banta
Sape
Waworada Bay
0
25
kilometres

4

SURFING IN SUMBAWA

Sumbawa has gained a reputation for offering some of the finest **surfing** in Indonesia, without the crowds you'll find in Bali. Getting to the beaches with a surfboard can be an arduous task unless you charter a car from Sumbawa Besar, but once there you'll find plenty of accommodation and facilities. The main breaks are at **Hu'u**, off Lakey beach, and around **Maluk beach** on the west coast. The latter has direct buses from Sumbawa Besar (3–4hr), though they're infrequent. To get to Hu'u, you'll need to take a bus from Bima to Dompu (3hr), and from there to Hu'u (2hr). Many of the waves break over reefs, so are not suitable for novices; however, the beaches are stunning even if you don't surf.

mansion at Jalan Dalam Loka 1; ask the guard to unlock it for you (daily 8am–5pm; free).

Moyo Island

The main attraction around Sumbawa Besar is **MOYO ISLAND**, home to deer, buffalo, wild pigs and vast numbers of bird species. The island sits in a nature reserve and is surrounded by coral, making it ideal for snorkelling. A luxury resort owns half the island, but a less expensive way to explore it is to hire a guide via one of the hotels – the *Hotel Tambora* (see opposite) is the best place to enquire. Independent excursions are also possible, either on a day-trip or overnight.

Boats arrive at Tanjung Pasir, on the south side of Moyo Island. From there you can hike on the eastern half of the island (the western half is owned by the resort), including up to some waterfalls in the north, and swim off the beach. You may have to pay a park fee of Rp10,000, but there is rarely anyone there to collect it. There are no official maps of the island, but the hiking is fairly straightforward.

Boats to the island sail from the village of Air Bari (30min), about 20km north of Sumbawa. The public bemo from Sumbawa Besar to Ai Bari runs infrequently, and to guarantee getting it you will have to be at the market at around 6am. However, it is easy enough to hire an ojek or charter a bemo to get there. From Ai Bari, fishermen charge Rp150,000–300,000 per boat (return), depending on the number of people. It's advisable to pre-arrange return transport to Sumbawa, and if you want to stay on the island you'll need to bring a tent or rent one (Rp25,000–50,000) from one of the fishermen. There is no water or food available, so make sure you have plenty of provisions.

ARRIVAL AND DEPARTURE

By plane The airport is a short ojek ride into town (around Rp5000) or a 10min walk across the river to the *Hotel Tambora*. Trans Nusa (ⓦ transnusa.co.id) has four daily flights to Lombok from where you can connect to Bali and beyond; Merpati (ⓦ merpati.co.id) has two weekly flights to Lombok.

Destinations Lombok (4–5 daily; 35min).

By bus All buses arrive at the Sumer Payong bus terminal, just off the Trans-Sumbawa highway, about 3km along Jl Garuda. Most of the yellow bemos (see below) head out to the bus terminal, and buses from Bima will usually drop you off in the vicinity of your hotel as they go. Buses leave for Bima and places en route at regular intervals between 6am and 1pm. The larger buses between Jakarta, Surabaya and Bima run day and night, though not all stop at Sumbawa Besar so you're best booking via agencies around town or your hotel.

Destinations Bima (6–7 daily; 7hr); Dompu (6–7 daily; 5hr); Surabaya (5–7 daily; 26hr).

GETTING AROUND

Yellow bemos do round-trips of the town (around Rp5000). They can be flagged down or picked up at the Seketeng market terminal on Jl Setiabudi.

INFORMATION

Tourist information The regional tourist office (Tues–Sun 7am–2pm; ⓣ 0371 23714) is the best you'll find in Nusa Tenggara, with plenty of information and English-speaking staff. It's 2km out of town at Jl Bungur 1 – take a yellow bemo from Jl Hasanuddin heading west and get off at the roundabout past the airport. The office is just off the left turn-off.

ACCOMMODATION

Jl Hasanuddin, which runs roughly parallel to the river, is the best place to look for food and accommodation; it becomes Jl Cendrawasih just north of the roundabout.

Dewi Hotel Jl Hasanuddin 60 ⓣ 0371 21170. A motley collection of rooms ranging from basic "*ekonomi*" to

large doubles with minibar, TV, bathtub and a/c (Rp150,000). **Rp50,000**

Hotel Cendrawasih Jl Cendrawasih 130 ⓣ 0371 24184. Slightly out of town, to the north, this smarter-than-average establishment offers excellent value for money. All but the cheapest rooms are concrete bungalows and have small balconies, and the setting is pleasant and peaceful. **Rp100,000**

★ **Hotel Tambora** Jl Kebayan ⓣ 0371 21555. The best option in town, with plenty of rooms ranging from basic to mid-range. Bizarrely, the cheapest rooms have Western toilets and a quiet location at the back, while the mid-range ones, with squat toilets, face the busy reception. The friendly staff are an excellent source of information. **Rp100,000**

EATING

Jl Hasanuddin is lined with restaurants, and you can also find plenty of warungs around town, with the main cluster next to the stadium.

Happy Jl Hasanuddin 43A. A small, simple canteen offering all the local staples at low prices (less than Rp20,000), including *nasi campur*, *bakwan* (meatball soup), and a range of fresh juices. Daily 11am–9pm.

DIRECTORY

Banks BNI bank on Jl Kartini has an ATM and is the best place to change foreign currency or travellers' cheques; it offers better rates than most banks further east in Nusa Tenggara. There are a couple of other ATMs around town, including outside the *Hotel Tambora*.

Internet Rasya Global Net, Cendrawasih 33, provides internet access.

Pharmacy Kimia Farma, Jl Cendrawasih 1.

Post office Jl Yos Sudarso 101 (Mon–Thurs 8am–3pm, Fri 8–11am & Sat 8am–1pm).

BIMA

The rather sleepy port town of **BIMA** is quiet but friendly. Its people have a strong sense of Bimanese identity, offering an insight into the patchwork of ethnicities you'll find throughout Nusa Tenggara. The town is centred around the market on Jalan Flores; most of the accommodation lies to the west of the **Sultan's Palace**, whose museum (Mon–Sat 8am–5pm; Rp5000) houses a rather shabby collection of traditional costumes. The area around Bima, Wawo, boasts a distinct style of traditional thatched house; examples can be seen at Maria and Sambori, both on the Bima–Sape bus route. If you need to relax on the beach after a hard day's travel, charter a boat (15min; a negotiable Rp50,000–75,000 return) from the harbour out to the island of **Pulau Kambing**, where you'll find relative seclusion.

ARRIVAL AND DEPARTURE

By plane The airport is 20km away on the main road to Sumbawa Besar. Buses stop in both directions, and taxis meet arrivals. Merpati (Jl Sukarno Hatta 58; ⓣ 0374 42857, ⓦ merpati.co.id) and Trans Nusa (Jl Sulawesi 26; ⓣ 0374 647251, ⓦ transnusa.co.id) have regular flights to Bali; the latter also has daily flights to Lombok.

Destinations Bali; (3–4 daily; 1hr 15min) Lombok (daily; 30min).

By bus Most buses to Bima arrive at the bus terminal just south of town, a short walk or bemo ride to the centre. There are several night-bus agents on Jl Pasar that offer a/c and standard buses to all major destinations, including Mataram and Sumbawa Besar. Buses to Sape leave roughly hourly from the main bus terminal.

Destinations Mataram via Sumbawa Besar (1–2 daily; 12hr); Sape (hourly; 1hr 30min); Sumbawa Besar (6–7 daily; 7hr).

By ferry Pelni ferries dock at the harbour, 2km west of Bima and served by dokar and bemo. The Pelni office is about 1.5km out of the centre at Jl Kesatria 2 (ⓣ 0374 42046, ⓦ pelni.co.id), by the port, though you can also book tickets in town through the agent at Jl Kaharuddin 36. If you need to catch one of the early-morning ferries from Sape to Labuanbajo, tell your hotel the night before and the bus to Sape should pick you up at 4am.

Destinations Makassar (Sun; 28hr); Surabaya (Wed; 34hr); Waingapu (Fri; 13hr); Kupang (Fri; 27hr).

INFORMATION

Tourist office Jl Gajah Mada, about 2km east of town just before the bridge (Mon–Sat 8am–2pm; ⓣ 0374 44331). English-speaking and helpful; to get here, catch a blue bemo heading east from the BNI Bank on Jl Hasanuddin.

ACCOMMODATION AND EATING

Bima is distinctly lacking in proper restaurants, but there are plenty of warungs and padang places, especially around the market.

Hotel Favorit Jl Pahlawan Dara ⓣ 0374 45285. Conveniently if noisily located next to the bus station, with clean rooms at very low rates – even the cheapest have showers. **Rp70,000**

Hotel La'mbitu Jl Sumbawa 4 ⓣ 0374 42222. The best option in town, with large clean rooms in a cool, airy building, and small suites available from Rp280,000. **Rp150,000**

4

Lila Graha Jl Lombok 20 ☎ 0374 42740. Friendly place near the market with two entrances and a labyrinth of rooms inside, though it's quite gloomy; it's worth spending a bit extra to get one of the a/c rooms with TVs. Decent restaurant too. **Rp120,000**

DIRECTORY

Banks The BNI on Jl Hasanuddin changes foreign currency and travellers' cheques; it has an ATM, as does the BRI next to the sports field.
Internet There's a 24hr internet café across from the bus station.
Pharmacy Jl Kaharuddin.
Post office Jl Hasanuddin, at the corner of Jl Datuk Dibanta (Mon–Sat 8am–3pm).

SAPE

SAPE, where you'll find the port of Bugis, is a quiet, dusty town where livestock wander the streets and local fishermen ply the harbour at dusk. There isn't much to see, but it is a pleasant enough place to stay the night. Nearby **Gili Banta** makes a good day-trip, with nice beaches and a burgeoning turtle population; if you get a group together, you can charter a boat there from the harbour for around Rp100,000–150,000 per person. Otherwise, there's the dark-sand Papa Beach, 10km out of town, which is a peaceful spot for a picnic; take an ojek. Most of the town's facilities, including the post office and an ATM, are on the main road down to the port.

4

ARRIVAL AND DEPARTURE

By bus Buses to and from Bima (1hr 30min) operate from Sape harbour, from where they leave every hour or so until 3pm; from Bima it's easy enough to catch onward transport to Sumbawa Besar or Lombok.
By ferry The ASDP ferry office is at the harbour, about 2km east of the centre (☎ 0374 71075). There is a daily ferry service to Labuanbajo on Flores (8am; 6–9hr), and two weekly services to Waikelo on Sumba (Fri & Mon 10pm; 9–12hr).

ACCOMMODATION AND EATING

Arema Right next to the port. The best place to eat, with rice and noodle dishes for around Rp20,000 and internet access.
Losmen Mutiara Near Arema ☎ 0374 71337. The best-established hotel in town and the one that most travellers head to, but rooms are average and staff can be apathetic. **Rp50,000**

Komodo and Rinca

Off the east coast of Sumbawa lies **Komodo National Park**, a group of parched but majestic islands, home to the Komodo dragon, or *ora* as it is known locally, which lives nowhere else. The south coast of the main island is lined with impressive, mostly dormant volcanoes, the north with mainly dusty plains, irrigated to create rice paddies around the major settlements. The two most-visited islands in the national park are **Komodo** and **Rinca**.

KOMODO

Most visitors to **Komodo Island** offload at the PHPA (park service) camp at **LOH LIANG**, where you'll find all the facilities. Although the practice of feeding live goats to the dragons stopped a long time ago, you may still feel as if you've stepped straight into *Jurassic Park* if your visit coincides with big tour groups. That said, the longer treks around the island, especially out of high season, should guarantee you some peace and quiet, and with a good guide you can enjoy the full primordial experience.

Treks and excursions

The full-day's walk from the PHPA camp to the top of **Gunung Ara**, the highest

THE KOMODO DRAGON

Varanus komodoensis, the **Komodo dragon**, is the largest extant lizard in the world. The biggest recorded specimen was well over 3m long and weighed a mammoth 150kg, but most fully grown males are around 2m and 60kg. The dragon usually strikes down prey with its immensely powerful tail or slices the leg tendons with scalpel-sharp fangs. Once the animal is incapacitated, the dragon eviscerates it, feeding on its intestines while it slowly dies. With larger prey, the dragon may simply bite the animal, then trail it until the wound becomes fatally infected from the reptile's toxic saliva.

VISITING KOMODO AND RINCA

The best way to reach Komodo and Rinca is by organizing a trip **from Labuanbajo on Flores** (see p.306), although there are also cruises to Sumbawa, Komodo and Flores **from Lombok** (see box, p.287). A host of agencies compete for tourists, so it's worth shopping around or asking for recommendations. Most people are content with a **day-trip** to Rinca, which costs from Rp400,000 per person. A multi-day trip that includes both Komodo and Rinca is worth it if only to see for yourself just how different, scenically, the two islands are. A **two-day trip** including both islands, snorkelling, meals and a night on the boat costs from Rp800,000 per person. It's also possible to visit both islands independently by chartering a boat from Labuanbajo (around Rp800,000 return), though rough waters can make small fishing boats a bit risky.

The PHPA charges Rp50,000 for **entry** to the park (both islands; valid for three days); in addition, there are conservation (Rp20,000), camera (Rp50,000) and, if you want to explore beyond the short, free guided tour, guide (Rp50,000 per person, extra if you want to trek for more than one hour) fees. These fees are rarely included in the price negotiated with the boat owner/travel agent, so bring enough money and plenty of small change. On all excursions around the islands a guide is necessary. Treks around the national park should reward you with sightings of wild horses, deer, wild pigs and, on Rinca, macaques, but trekking on both islands can be hot and tiring, so bring decent footwear and plenty of water.

There is a handful of simple rooms (Rp150,000) on Rinca and a reasonable lodge (Rp450,000) on Komodo; both are overpriced. Some people bring their own food (which the cafés will cook for you), but the island's cafés serve noodles, omelettes and pancakes.

point on the island, doesn't promise dragon sightings, but it is absolutely extraordinary. It's an arduous, excruciatingly hot march, but you'll see scores of unusual plants, animals and birdlife, such as sulphur-crested cockatoos, brush turkeys and the **megapode bird**, which builds huge ground nests where its eggs are incubated in warm dung. Bring water and wear decent boots.

There are also regular guided walks from the PHPA camp to the **Banunggulung** river bed and to **Sebita**, one of the mangrove forests that are vital for providing shelter and food for the island's populations of bats, birds, crabs and fish.

The seas around Komodo, though home to spectacular coral reefs and an abundance of fish, are laced with riptides, whirlpools, sea snakes, sea-wasp jellyfish and a healthy shark population, so stick to recommended snorkelling locations such as the excellent **Pantai Merah**. Many boat operators will include at least one snorkelling stop on visits to the island. If you visit between October and January, you may be lucky enough to catch sight of migrating whales.

RINCA

With its proximity to Labuanbajo, **Rinca** receives as many visitors as Komodo, if not more, and given that the dragon populations are denser and there's less cover, you're much more likely to catch sight of them here. Rinca consists mostly of parched grassland covering steep slopes, drought-resistant lontar palms and huge patches of flowering cacti and other hardy shrubs. The PHPA camp at **LOH BUAYA** has just four rooms and a small café. There are a couple of well-trodden treks and at the right time (mornings and late afternoons) you shouldn't have any problems spotting dragons, monkeys, buffalo, deer and wild pigs.

Flores

A fertile, mountainous barrier between the Savu and Flores seas, **Flores** comprises one of the most alluring landscapes in the archipelago. The volcanic spine of the island soars to 2500m, and torrential wet seasons result in a lushness that marks Flores apart from its scorched neighbours. It also differs religiously – 95 percent of

islanders are Catholic. The most spectacular sight in Flores is magnificent **Kelimutu**, near Moni, northeast of **Ende**. The three craters of this extinct volcano each contain a lake of different, vibrant and gradually changing colours. In the east of Flores, high-quality **ikat weaving** still thrives. At the extreme west end of the island, **Labuanbajo** has some fine **coral gardens** and is also the port for ferries to and **from Sumbawa**. All of Flores's major towns are linked by bus, but these can be slow, crowded and unpleasant. A number of private operators, including the recommended Gunung Mas, run faster, more comfortable *travels* (cars and minibuses) around the island, to strictly observed schedules, with hotel pick-ups – well worth the few extra rupiah.

A useful source of info on Flores is Ⓦflorestourism.com.

4

LABUANBAJO

The port town of **LABUANBAJO** is experiencing a boom in tourism, serving as the gateway to Flores and the main departure point for trips to **Komodo National Park** (see box, p.305), but it nevertheless retains a laidback village feel. You can stay in town or at one of the nearby island hotels – a pleasant option, as most of these places offer a quiet getaway with unspoilt beaches and decent snorkelling, although they tend to be pricey. You can also easily organize **dive trips** from one of the many dive shops in town.

ARRIVAL AND DEPARTURE

By plane The airport is about 2km away from the waterfront; bemos run into town. Trans Nusa (Ⓣ0385 41800, Ⓦtransnusa.co.id), Lion Air/Wings Air (Ⓣ0385 41709, Ⓦlionair.co.id) and Merpati (Ⓣ0804 162 1621, Ⓦmerpati.co.id) have direct daily flights to Bali, and fluctuating services to other destinations.

Destinations Bali (7 daily; 1hr–1hr 45min; Ende (3 weekly; 40min); Maumere 1–2 daily; 1hr 5min).

By bus Your hotel can reserve you a place in a *travel*, which will come and pick you up. Public buses drop off along Jl Sokarno on their way into town; they leave from the bus station next to the harbour.

Destinations Bajawa (2 daily; 10hr); Ende (daily; 14hr); Ruteng (2 daily, 4–5hr).

By ferry Ferries from Sumbawa dock at the passenger harbour near the northern end of main Jl Sokarno, on which almost all of the town's tourist shops and restaurants are situated. The Pelni agent (Ⓣ0385 41141, Ⓦpelni.co.id) is up a dirt track behind the sports field; the ASDP office (Ⓣ0385 41396) is at the harbour. Timetables change frequently, so make sure you check the latest info on the ground.

Destinations Benoa (3 monthly; 36hr); Bima (fortnightly; 10hr); Makassar (fortnightly; 20hr); Sape (daily 8am; 6–9hr).

INFORMATION

Tourist office Jl Gabriel Gampur (Ⓣ0385 41170; Mon–Fri 8am–2pm). A 15min walk out of town but they're friendly and helpful. To get here, head up the hill opposite the supermarket.

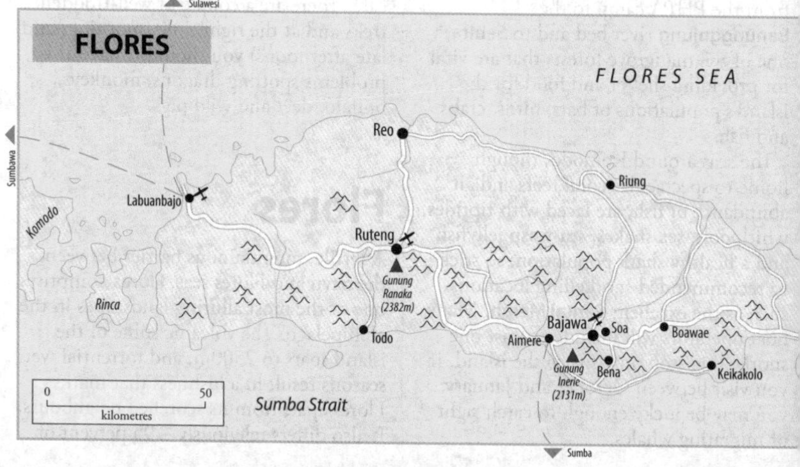

ACCOMMODATION

IN TOWN

In addition to the accommodation listed below, there are also a couple of small homestays just south of the harbour on Jl Sokarno (around Rp50,000/person).

Bayview Gardens Jl Ande Bole ⓣ0385 41549, ⓦbayview-gardens.com. Run by a Dutch-Indonesian family, this charming hotel has a lush, tropical feel, with beautiful grounds, great views and well-appointed a/c rooms. Rp500,000

Gardena Hotel Jl Sokarno ⓣ0385 41258, ⓦgardenaflores.com. With its pretty bamboo bungalows climbing the hillside, this remains the most popular place to stay in town, though the management has got a bit complacent as a result. Many of the rooms boast super views over the bay – the better ones are those higher up. Rp200,000

★**Golo Hilltop** Up a dirt road at the northern end of town ⓣ0385 41337, ⓦgolohilltop.com. Heavenly Dutch-run place, with spacious, immaculate rooms, a swimming pool and a small restaurant; perks include free wi-fi, coffee and tea. Well worth the walk or ojek ride up the hill, if only for the views. They also run the nearby *Paradise Bar*, a romantic spot with intimate tables spread across a slope below. Rp325,000

Losmen Diaz At the northeast corner of the sports field, just inland from the harbour. ⓣ0813 3048 7795. Small family-run place offering basic en-suite rooms around a dusty courtyard, each with its own porch. Rp100,000

ON THE BEACH

There are various island beach resorts available, though they're relatively expensive given that running water and electricity may not always be available, and only breakfast is included so you're stuck with their (rather pricey) restaurants. Rates include transport from Labuanbajo.

Kanawa Hotel Office on Jl Sokarno ⓣ0385 42089, ⓦkanawaislandresort.com. Standing on its own island north of Labuanbajo (1hr by boat), this hotel has reasonable bungalows, *bales* and tents (if you bring your own, there's a Rp25,000 discount on the rates) set back from the beach. Bungalow Rp400,000, *bale* Rp250,000, tent Rp175,000

Seraya Island Bungalows North of Labuanbajo ⓣ0813 3949 5244, ⓦserayaisland.com. Under the same ownership as the *Gardena* (see above), this is another bungalow resort that can boast its own island just north of Labuanbajo (1hr by boat). Slightly cheaper than the *Kanawa*, but similar quality. Rp350,000

EATING

Bajo Bakery Jl Sokarno. A cosy little café serving delicious home-baked bread, sandwiches, brownies, muffins, pastries, cakes and ice cream, plus fine coffee. Snacks from Rp10,000. Daily 8am–6/7pm.

Lounge Jl Sokarno. A swanky retreat from the heat of Labuanbajo, serving a range of pizzas and other Western dishes (from around Rp50,000), as well as Indonesian options. There's also a small book exchange, and shisha pipes available if you're hankering for a smoke. Daily 8am–late.

Made in Italy Jl Sokarno. Labuanbajo's top Italian restaurant serves authentic wood-fired, thin-crust pizzas, superior risotto and pasta dishes, as well as great coffee. Daily 9am–11pm.

Mediterraneo Jl Sokarno ⓦmediterraneoinn.com. Sink into one of the beanbags strewn across the waterfront deck and while away the hours with a cold beer (around Rp25,000) and some grilled seafood, pizza or pasta. Daily 9am–11pm.

4

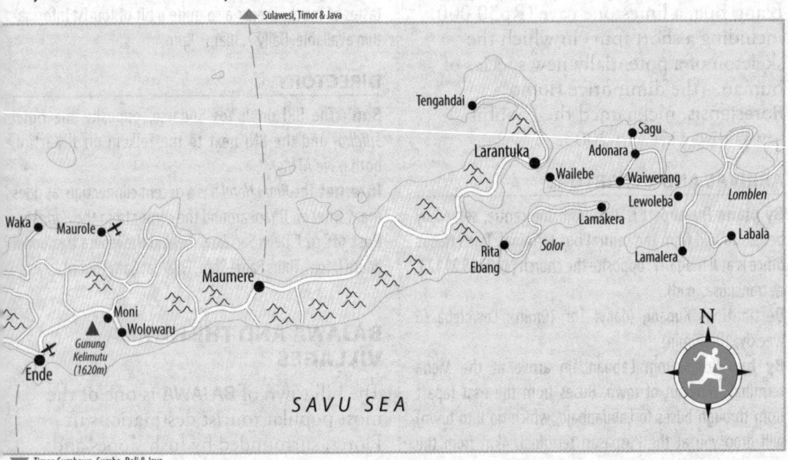

DIRECTORY

Banks BNI and BRI banks at the south end of town both have ATMs; the BRI next to the post office changes most common currencies.
Diving Blue Marlin Komodo, Jl Sokarno (T 0812 3775 7892, W bluemarlinkomodo.com).
Internet There are several internet cafés on Jl Sokarno. Most hotels and restaurants provide free wi-fi.
Pharmacy Several on Jl Sokarno, past the post office.
Post office Jl Sokarno (Mon–Thurs 8am–3pm, Fri & Sat 8am–noon).

RUTENG

4

The first large town after Labuanbajo is **RUTENG**, 140km to the east. Surrounded by forested volcanic hills and rolling rice-paddy plains, it's a cool, relaxing place. The market just to the south is the central meeting point for the local **Manggarai** people, as Ruteng is their district capital. They speak their own language and have a distinctive culture most in evidence in villages on the south coast. Their traditional houses are conical and arranged in concentric circles around a circular sacrificial arena; even the rice paddies are round, divided up like spiders' webs, with each clan receiving a slice. Most of these formations are no longer used, but a good example can still be seen at **Golo Cara**, thirty minutes by bemo from the central bus station, and traces of them are visible from the bus to Bajawa.

Around 15km north of Ruteng is Liang Bua, a limestone cave (Rp30,000, including a short tour) in which the skeleton of a potentially new species of human – the diminutive **Homo floresiensis**, nicknamed the "hobbit" – was discovered in 2003.

ARRIVAL AND DEPARTURE

By plane The airport is 2km from the centre, served by bemos to and from the central bus terminal. Trans Nusa's office is at Jl Niaga 17, opposite the church (T 0385 21123, W transnusa.co.id).
Destinations Kupang (daily; 1hr 10min); Lewoleba (6 weekly; 1hr 40min).
By bus Buses from Labuanbajo arrive at the Mena terminal, 3km out of town. Buses from the east (apart from through buses to Labuanbajo, which go into town) will drop you at the Puspasari terminal, 4km from the centre. Bemos will take you into town from either station. When you leave Ruteng, your hotel can arrange for the bus to pick you up to save you the hassle of getting back out to the terminal.
Destinations Bajawa (several daily; 5hr); Ende (1–2 daily; 9hr); Labuanbajo (several daily; 4–5hr); Maumere (1–2 daily; 14hr).
By shared taxi The *Rima Hotel* runs a travel service to Bajawa, Ende, Labuanbajo and Maumere.

ACCOMMODATION

Hotel Susteran Jl Ahmed Yani T 0385 22834. A ray of light amid Ruteng's dismal accommodation offerings, this guesthouse (also known as "MBC") is actually part of a convent. Rooms are simple, but immaculate. The convent choir starts early, a strange but not unpleasant way to wake up in the morning. **Rp200,000**
Ranaka Jl Yos Sudarso 2 T 0385 21353. Tiny place in the town centre, with just a few rudimentary rooms, the cheapest of which share a bathroom. Prices are low and the staff are friendly enough. **Rp75,000**
Hotel Sindha Jl Yos Sudarso 26 T 0385 21197. The standard rooms here, clustered around a garden courtyard, are basic, but all come with Western toilets and showers; there's also a newer wing of smarter options (Rp300,000). **Rp100,000**

EATING

Ruteng shuts down at 9pm, so eat well before then.
Agape Coffee House & Café Jl Bhayangkara 8. A reasonable attempt at a Western-style café, with a wide selection of hot drinks and sweet snacks (from Rp10,000), as well as main dishes. Daily 9am–8pm.
Merlin Jl Bhanyangkara, across from *Agape*. The intriguingly named Merlin has a wide range of Chinese food for around Rp40,000–50,000, though none of it tastes of much. There's also quite a bit of tourist information available. Daily 7.30am–8pm.

DIRECTORY

Bank The BRI on Jl Yos Sudarso, opposite the *Hotel Sindha*, and the BNI next to the Telkom on Jl Kartini, both have ATMs.
Internet The *Rima Hotel* has a decent connection, as does the warnet on Jl Yani around the corner from the *Ranaka*.
Post office Jl Dewi Sartika 6, behind the replica traditional house (Mon–Thurs 8am–3pm, Fri & Sat 8am–noon).

BAJAWA AND THE NGADA VILLAGES

The hill town of **BAJAWA** is one of the most popular tourist destinations in Flores, surrounded by lush slopes and

NGADA ARCHITECTURE

In the centre of most villages in this district stand several **ceremonial edifices**, which represent the ancestral protection of, and presence in, the village. These include the **Ngadhu**, which resembles a man in a huge hula skirt, the thatched skirt sitting atop a crudely carved, phallic forked tree trunk, which is imbued with the power of a male ancestor. The female part of the pairing, the **Bhaga**, is a symbol of the womb, a miniature house. The symbolic coupling is supplemented by a carved stake called a **Peo**, to which animals are tied before being sacrificed.

striking volcanoes. **Gunung Inerie** (2131m) is just one of the active volcanoes near Bajawa: it's an arduous but rewarding hike, and if it's clear you can see all the way to Sumba from the summit.

Bajawa is the largest town in the **Ngada district**, an area that maintains its status as the spiritual heartland of Flores. Here, despite the growing encroachment of tour groups, indigenous animist religions flourish and the villages maintain traditional houses, megalithic stones and interesting totemic structures. Up to sixty thousand people in the Ngada district speak the distinct Ngada language, and a good proportion of the older generation don't understand basic Bahasa Indonesian.

Not for the faint-hearted are the local specialities of **moke**, a type of wine that tastes like methylated spirits, and **raerate** or "**rw**" (pronounced "air-vay"), dog meat marinated in coconut milk and then boiled in its own blood.

WHAT TO SEE AND DO

The influx of tourists to the Ngada region has led to a booming **guide** industry in Bajawa, with a corresponding hike in prices. For around Rp250,000–350,000 a day per person, a guide will arrange transport, entrance to all the villages and often a traditional Bajawan meal; for mountain treks, guides charge from Rp500,000 a day per group. A day-tour should cover at least **Bena** and **Wogo**, as well as the hot springs at **Soa**, but many also include a trip to **Wawo Muda**, one of Indonesia's newest volcanoes. If you don't get approached by a licensed guide at your hotel, try the guide association which operates an information office opposite the *Hotel Eidelweis*, though it's only open sporadically.

Soa, Wogo and Bena are all accessible by public transport from Bajawa (though Bena only has one bemo a day); it can be hard to find accurate information about this, and guides will often inflate prices to discourage you from independent visits, so ask bemo drivers directly. Alternatively, you can **rent a motorbike** and explore the region for yourself. The market is a good place to look for people willing to hire out their wheels; expect to pay from Rp150,000 per day. An ojek (motorbike with driver) will be around the same price. Female travellers should be careful of the latter, though, as there have been several reports of indecent behaviour by ojek drivers in the area.

4

Ngada villages

BENA is the prettiest and most traditional of the Ngada villages, lying about 13km south of Bajawa. To reach it, take the turn-off past the large church at Mangulewa, 5km east of Bajawa. Here they have nine different clans, in a village built on nine levels with nine Ngadhu/ Bhaga couplings (see box above). It's the central village for the local area's religions and traditions, and one of the best places to see **festivals** such as weddings, planting and harvest celebrations.

Some of the finest megaliths and Ngadhu are at the twin villages of **WOGO BARU** and **WOGO LAMA**, the former lying 1km south of Mataloko (30min by bemo from Bajawa). Wogo Baru is a typically charming Ngada village, but the main attraction lies about 1.5km further down the road at Wogo Lama, where some apparently neglected megaliths sit in a clearing. All of the above villages ask visitors to give a donation, but the amount is up to you; Rp20,000 per person is reasonable, although more is always appreciated.

Hot springs and Wawo Muda

The most popular destination near Bajawa is the **hot springs** at **SOA** (Rp20,000). The springs are set in peaceful surroundings, and a small but powerful waterfall provides the cheapest hot shower on Flores. **Bemos** from Bajawa market run to Soa village, from where you can pick up an ojek for the remaining 6km to the springs – you'll need to ask your driver to wait if you don't want to walk back. There are some quieter, though equally seductive, hot springs at Malanage, 3km south of Bena.

In the first few months of 2001 a new **volcano** erupted above the small village of Ngoranale, about 10km to the north of Bajawa, leaving a blackened crater. There are currently five small red lakes in the bottom of the crater, though they shrink to nothing in the dry season. There are no bemos to **Wawo Muda**, so you'll need private transport to Ngoranale, where you can ask a villager to show you the start of the wide and easy-to-follow trail, which takes about an hour and a half to meander up to the summit.

4

ARRIVAL AND DEPARTURE

By plane Bajawa airport is around 20km out of town. If you're lucky there may be a bemo to Bajawa waiting, otherwise you'll have to walk to the main road (turn right as you leave the terminal) and catch one there. If you're going to the airport, either catch a bemo from Bajawa, or take one to Soa and walk the last 2km. Trans Nusa (T 0384 222 3666, W transnusa.co.id) has regular flights to Kupang (5 weekly; 1hr).

By bus The bus terminal is 3km out of town at Watujaji. Regular bemos connect the terminal with the town. Some buses come into town to look for passengers who are leaving Bajawa, but it's best to be on the safe side and go out to the terminal to pick them up.

Destinations Ende (several daily; 4hr); Labuanbajo (2 daily; 10hr); Moni (daily; 6hr); Ruteng (several daily; 5hr).

By shared taxi *Travels* cluster outside the *Hotel Virgo* to the north of the market, running daily services to Ende (4hr) and Ruteng (4hr).

ACCOMMODATION

The increase in tourism means, unfortunately, that almost every option in Bajawa is overpriced. It is also possible to stay in some of the villages around Bajawa; contact the guide association (see p.309) for information about two-day treks including an overnight in Bena, or you can ask directly at the village (around Rp250,000/person including meals).

Elizabeth Jl Inerie 4 T 0384 21223. A cosy little place in a quiet neighbourhood, with simple en-suite rooms set around a small garden – very good value by Bajawa standards. **Rp125,000**

★ **Hotel Happy Happy** Jl Sudirman T 0384 21763, W hotelhappyhappy.com. This small, Dutch-run hotel is a clear step up from Bajada's underwhelming accommodation options. Rooms are simple, clean and comfortable. Tours (from Rp600,000) of the surrounding area are on offer too. **Rp300,000**

Villa Silverin 4km outside town T 0852 5345 3298, W silverin-villa.blogspot.com. In a quiet location outside Bajada (a 30min walk), Villa Silverin has scruffy but acceptable rooms with hot water. **Rp350,000**

EATING

Restaurants have not suffered from the tour groups, and you'll find three good options on Jl Yani. Most places serve until around 9pm.

Camellia Jl Yani. Live music every night, and some of the tastiest Indonesian and Western food in Bajawa served in large portions by friendly staff. Plenty of options from Rp20,000.

Dito's Jl Yani. Not much more than a large bamboo-walled hut, but the food is flavoursome and there are plenty of Indonesian, Chinese and Western options, including schnitzel, from Rp20,000.

Lucas Jl Yani. Another little cabin of a place serving good food including a variety of *sates* (around Rp25,000), beer and locally distilled *arak*.

DIRECTORY

Banks BNI off Jl Basoeki Rahmat and BRI on Jl Sukarno-Hatta both have ATMs; the former also changes money.

Internet There's an internet café at Jl Yani 12.

Post office The main post office is up on the hill at the Jl Sukarno-Hatta crossroads (Mon–Thurs 8am–3pm, Fri 8–11.30am & Sat 8am–1pm).

ENDE

Situated on a narrow peninsula with flat-topped Gunung Meja and the active volcano Gunung Ipi at its sea end, the port of **ENDE** is the largest town on Flores and provides access to Kelimutu and Moni (see opposite), though there is little in town to attract tourists other than banks and **ferries** to other destinations. Black-sand **beaches** stretch down both east and west coasts: the Bajawa road runs right along the seafront, so just catch a bemo out to Ndao bus terminal and the beach begins right there. The area around Ende is known for its

ikat weaving. **NGELLA** is a weaving village about 30km east from Wolowana bus terminal in Ende, near the coast.

The cheaper losmen and some restaurants are spread out along Jalan Yani and around the airport roundabout, while the rest are down in the old town; travelling between the two areas is easily done by bemo or ojek.

ARRIVAL AND DEPARTURE

By plane The airport is just north of the town, on Jl Yani; you can walk into town, or catch an ojek. Trans Nusa (T 0381 24333 or T 24222, W transnusa.co.id) is at Jl Kelimutu 39 and the airport; Lion Air/Wings Air (T 0381 22896, W lionair.co.id) is at the airport.

Destinations include Kupang (daily; 50min); Labuanbajo (3 weekly; 40min); Tambolaka (3 weekly; 45min).

By bus Buses from the east arrive 4km further on from the airport at the Wolowana bus terminal, where you'll be mobbed by ojek drivers who will take you to town. Buses from the west arrive at Ndao bus terminal, about 2km west of town; bemos are in plentiful supply.

Destinations Bajawa (several daily; 4hr); Labuanbajo (daily; 14hr); Maumere (several daily; 5hr); Moni (several daily; 1hr 30min); Ruteng (several daily; 9hr).

By ferry Ipi harbour in the old town is used for all long-distance boats; the ferry and harbour masters' offices are on the road that leads down to the harbour. Pelni ferries stop here, and there are also ASDP ferries serving Sumba and Kupang once a week. The Pelni office at Jl Kathedral 2 (T 0381 21043, W pelni.co.id) can help with Pelni and ASDP tickets.

Destinations Bima (fortnightly; 23hr); Denpasar (fortnightly; 44hr); Kupang (Mon; 20hr); Surabaya (fortnightly; 58hr); Waingapu (Sat; 10–12hr).

INFORMATION

Tourist information Jl Soekarno 4 (Mon–Thurs & Sat 7am–2pm, Fri 7–11am; T 0381 21303).

ACCOMMODATION

Grand Hotel Wisata Jl Kelimutu 32 T 0381 22974, W grandhotelwisatahotel-ende.com. Located close to the aiport, Wisata has variable rooms with mid-range pretensions (TVs, fridges and so on), a decent restaurant and a pool. **Rp500,000**

Ikhlas Jl Yani 69 T 0381 21695. A reasonable budget option, with rooms to suit most budgets and plenty of information, though the staff aren't terribly responsive. **Rp120,000**

Safari Jl Yani 65 T 0381 21997. Next to *Ikhlas* and offering rooms around an airy courtyard, including some smarter options with mod cons such as a/c, showers and TV. **Rp75,000**

EATING

Bangkalan II Jl Yani. Up near the airport roundabout and offering inexpensive and tasty chicken and goat *sates* (around Rp20,000), along with the usual padang food. Daily 8am–9pm.

Iklhas Jl Yani. The restaurant of the hotel (see above), serving cheap Indonesian staples as well as Western dishes such as fish and chips; mains around Rp15,000. Daily 8am–9pm.

DIRECTORY

Bank BRI and Danamon banks – two blocks up from the sea on Jl Soekarno – have ATMs, as does the BNI just east of the airport roundabout.

Internet There's an internet café opposite *Hotel Safari* on Jl Yani, but the connection can be slow.

Pharmacy Jl Sudirman 6.

Post office Up the hill on Jl Basuki Rahmat (Mon–Thurs 8am–3pm, Fri 8–11.30am, & Sat 8am–1pm).

KELIMUTU AND MONI

Stunning **Kelimutu** volcano, with its three strangely coloured crater lakes, is without doubt one of the most startling natural phenomena in Indonesia. The picturesque village of **Moni**, 40km northeast of Ende, stretches along the road from the lower slopes of the volcano down to the valley floor, and makes a great base from which to hike up to Kelimutu and around.

Kelimutu

The summit of **Kelimutu** (1620m) forms a barren lunar landscape with, to the east, two vast turquoise pools separated by a narrow ridge. A few hundred metres to the west, settled in a deep depression, lies a dark khaki lake. The lakes' colours are due partly to the levels of certain **minerals** that dissolve in them. As the sulphurous waters erode the caldera they lie in, they uncover bands of different compounds and, as the levels of these compounds are in constant flux, so are the colours. Just as important, however, is the level of oxygen dissolved in the water. When their supply is low, the lakes look green. Conversely, when they are rich in oxygen, they range from deep red to black. In the 1960s, the lakes were red, white and blue.

Every morning at around 4am tourists ride by ojek (around Rp70,000 return)

4

from their hotel in Moni to Kelimutu, making it to the top in time to see the sun rise hazily over the mountains; make sure you organize this early departure the night before, though you can also go later if you prefer. Just before the car park near the summit you need to pay a park fee of Rp20,000, plus Rp50,000 for a camera. There are two vantage points – you can only see two lakes from the first one, so most tourists and all the local coffee-sellers head to the second. The **walk** back down to Moni, which takes about two and a half hours, is a joy, especially in fine weather, providing views over rolling hills down to the sea. There's a path to the right at the two white pillars around the 6km mark, which cuts a good 4km off the road route, taking you through some charming local villages and past the **waterfall** (*air terjun*) on the edge of Moni – a great spot for a dip. If you take this route you'll need good shoes, as it gets very narrow and steep. Following the road, you'll pass some hot springs in which to soak your tired feet. Be sure to take plenty of water, as even going downhill you'll warm up quickly.

4

Moni

Nestling among lush rice paddies, the village of **MONI** exudes a lazy charm. Full of homestays and little family-run cafés, it's a relaxed place to spend a few days, with great walking in the surrounding hills. There is no bank or post office in Moni, despite the increasing number of tourists; but you can make phone calls at the tiny **wartel** off the main road, and the *Bintang Restaurant* offers internet access. There's a small book exchange in the nearby village of Woloara, off the road to Maumere.

ARRIVAL AND DEPARTURE

By bus Buses from Ende (1hr 30min) and Maumere (3hr 30min) stop here regularly throughout the day, and there's one bus daily to Bajawa, though you should ask your homestay to book it, otherwise it may be full by the time it gets to Moni.

ACCOMMODATION

There is only one road through Moni, and many of the homestays offer very similar rates and rooms.

Bintang Lodge and Restaurant On the main road ⓣ0852 3916 8310. This friendly restaurant has a few rooms of varying size, all with showers and mosquito nets; the newer, slightly more expensive options are the best bets. **Rp150,000**

Maria Inn Opposite the market ⓣ0821 4607 0423. The most basic rooms in the back of this small homestay are dingy, but the three bamboo bungalows up front (Rp150,000) are quite pretty. **Rp100,000**

Sao Ria Wisata A 10min walk uphill from the village ⓣ0852 39256119. The bungalows here are showing their age but nonetheless represent excellent value, with great views over the valley. There's also a reasonably priced restaurant on site, saving you the walk back into town. **Rp100,000**

EATING

There are more cafés than you'd think a town this size could merit, though very little stands out.

Bambu Set-menu evening meals in a local house. You'll need to book in advance, but the owner will probably accost you as you walk through town anyway. The local specialities he serves are delicious, and a good deal at Rp60,000 for three courses. Daily 6–11pm.

Rainbow Café At the top of the village. The menu is limited to Indonesian staples and some Western-style pasta dishes (around Rp40,000), but it's tasty, and there's plenty of it. Daily 9/10am–9/10pm.

MAUMERE

On the north coast of Flores, roughly equidistant between Ende and Larantuka, **MAUMERE** was once the tourism centre of the island and its best diving resort. In 1992, a devastating earthquake and tsunami destroyed most of the town, as well as the coral, though this is slowly recovering. Improved transport links and regular air services are steadily making it one of the main stops on trips around Nusa Tenggara; from here, you can organize tours that take in all of Flores's attractions. Maumere is the capital of the Sikka district, especially renowned for its **weaving**, which incorporates maroon, white and blue geometric patterns in horizontal rows on a black or dark-blue background.

ARRIVAL AND DEPARTURE

By plane The airport is 15min outside town; taxis from here cost Rp50,000, or take an ojek from the main road. Trans Nusa (ⓣ0382 21393, ⓦtransnusa.co.id) flies

to/from Kupang, Merpati (0382 21342, merpati.co.id) to/from Bali, Labuanbajo and Merauke, Lion Air/Wings Air (0382 22993, lionair.co.id) to/from Bali.

Destinations Bali (1–2 daily; 2hr); Kupang (3 weekly; 50min); Labuanbajo (1–2 daily; 1hr 5min); Merauke (daily; 1hr).

By bus Buses to and from Ende, Moni and other destinations in the west are served by the Ende bus terminal, several kilometres down Jl Gajah Mada southwest of town. Bemos run from here to the centre. For onward travel, note that buses depart from the terminal but meander around town before leaving.

Destinations Bajawa (daily; 9hr); Ende (several daily; 5hr); Moni (several daily; 3hr 30min); Ruteng (daily; 14hr).

By ferry The harbour is at the northern end of town, a 15min walk or quick ojek ride to the centre. Tickets for Pelni services to Kupang and Makassar can be bought at the office at Jl Sikokoru 2 by the harbour (0382 21013, pelni.co.id). A private ferry, the *KM Mahkota*, runs passengers every Monday to Surabaya (36hr); tickets can be bought from the *Hotel Benggoan* (0382 21041), just up from the market at Jl Moa Toda 49.

Destinations Kupang (Wed; 12hr); Makassar (Wed; 17hr).

By shared taxi *Travels* can be arranged by your hotel and cost around Rp50,000 to Moni.

INFORMATION

Tourist information Located south of the stadium on Jl Wairklau (0382 21652; Mon–Thurs 8am–2pm, Fri 8–11am), they can provide a map and some local information.

ACCOMMODATION

Maumere itself offers a selection of decent accommodation, but you may prefer to take advantage of the beaches and stay out of town, from where you can also go snorkelling or diving.

MAUMERE

Gardena Jl Patirangga 28 0382 22644. The backpacker's stalwart, with good-value if rather frayed rooms (with fans or a/c) and friendly staff. They may have a representative at the airport but you'll still have to pay for transport into town. **Rp100,000**

Maiwali Jl Don Thomas 6 0382 21220. The cheapest and top-end rooms here are good, and all are en suite; the mid-range rooms are getting a bit tired, but do come with pleasant porches. **Rp110,000**

Wini Rai I Jl Gajah Mada 50 0382 21388. Efficiently run and friendly, offering a wide range of options for all budgets. The *Wini Rai II*, near the market at Jl Soetomo 7 (0382 21362), has cheaper rooms at only Rp50,000/person, but they're pretty basic. **Rp110,000**

ON THE COAST

There are a few pleasant beachside options outside Maumere, all of which offer diving.

Gading Beach Hotel Around 7km outside Maumere 0852 3900 4490. These peaceful bungalows are owned by the same people as the *Gardena* (see above). Room rates include transport from Maumere, and they can organize diving and snorkelling trips. **Rp150,000**

Sea-World Club Jl Sawista, Waiara 0382 21570, sea-world-club.com. Smart bungalows on a lovely stretch of beach, about 9km from Maumere. There's a dive centre (two-dive day-trip $75), numerous tours on offer and a good restaurant. Rates include an airport pick-up/drop-off. **$45**

EATING

The harbour is the best place to find seafood, with a number of places offering grilled fish, priced by weight, for around Rp40,000/person. There are also some warungs along the dry riverbed near the harbour, and a supermarket east of the sports field.

Suroboyo Jl Gajah Mada, opposite the *Hotel Wini Rai I*. Serves a wide variety of chicken, beef and seafood dishes, including some unusual options (around Rp20,000–30,000) such as lemon chicken. Daily 11am–10pm.

Surya Indah Jl Raja Centis. This padang joint near the market serves the best beef *rendang* in town, as well as good *sate soto*. Dishes cost Rp10,000–20,000. Daily 11am–10pm.

DIRECTORY

Banks BRI on Jl A Yani and BNI on Jl Sukarno Hatta both change money and have ATMs.

Internet Flobamora on Jl Sukarno Hatta is open 24hr.

Post office Jl A Yani, near the sports field (Mon–Thurs 8am–3pm, Fri & Sat 8am–1pm).

Sumba

Sumba is a land of contrasts. The east of the island is made up of arid grasslands and limestone plateaux, while the west is fertile and green, with rolling hills and a long rainy season. **Waingapu**, the capital, is well known for producing the finest *ikat* fabric in Indonesia. A little further out at **Rende** and **Melolo** sit stone tombs with bizarre carvings, and in other villages on the east coast you'll find quality weaving, traditional structures and deserted beaches. The main town in the west is **Waikabubak**,

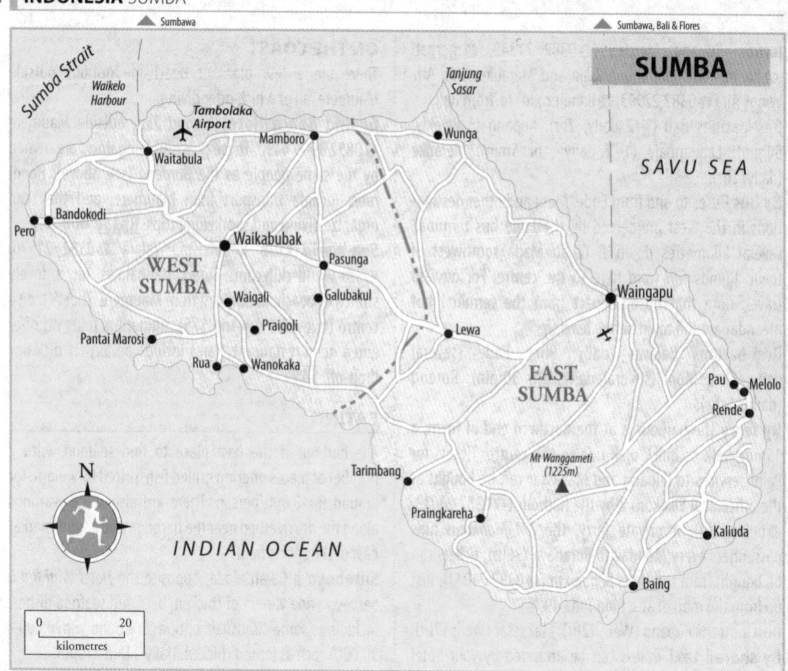

4

where characteristic houses with thatched roofs soar to an apex over 15m above the ground.

Access to Sumba is either by **ferry** from Ende in Flores to Waingapu or from Sape in Sumbawa to Waikelo, or by **air** to either Waingapu or Waikabubak. Most people choose to fly out of **Waingapu** rather than Waikabubak, which has a very chequered record for reliability and cancellations.

WAINGAPU

It may be the largest port and town on Sumba, but **WAINGAPU** is far from a modern metropolis. Goats wander along the main road, horses are stabled in front porches, and locals still walk around barefoot, with *ikat* tied around their heads and waists. The older half of the hourglass-shaped town is centred around the port, the newer part around the market. It's only a fifteen-minute walk between the two, but every passing ojek will assume you need a lift. The bay to the west of town has a harbour at the extreme point of either shore; all ferries dock at the **western harbour**, requiring an 8km journey around the bay to town. The eastern harbour in the old town is now just used for fishing boats, and can be picturesque, especially at sunset.

WHAT TO SEE AND DO

PRAILU is the most visited of the local **ikat-weaving villages**, and is an easy walk from the hotels near the market. After signing in at the large, traditional house (no fixed opening hours but generally daily 10/11am–5/6pm; Rp10,000), you can inspect weavings that weren't good enough to be bought by the traders. The **ikat** blankets of east Sumba are ablaze with symbolic dragons, animals, gods and head-hunting images. The cloth worn by men is called the **hinggi**, and is made from two identical panels sewn together into a symmetrical blanket. These are the most popular souvenirs, as they make great wall hangings. Small blankets of medium quality usually retail for under $50, but will mainly use only chemical dye. For larger, high-quality pieces, you can pay

anything from $100 to $1000. A tight weave, clean precise motifs and sharp edges between different colours are all signs of a good piece. Dealers in the towns will often give you better prices and more choice than those in the villages.

ARRIVAL AND DEPARTURE

By plane The airport is about 10km to the southeast on the road to Rende. Representatives from the main hotels are usually on hand to ferry tourists into town – as long as you agree to look at their hotel first; if they're not there, take a taxi (Rp50,000), or step outside and flag down an ojek. Lion Air/Wings Air (lionair.co.id) and Merpati (0804 162 1612, merpati.co.id) have flights to/from Bali, and Trans Nusa (0387 62427, transnusa.co.id) to/from Kupang.

Destinations Bali (1–2 daily; 1hr 35min); Kupang (4 weekly; 50min).

By bus All buses will stop at the terminal west of town, but most also drive into and around town to pick up passengers for the return journey, so you should get dropped off at the market if not right at your hotel.

Destinations Melolo and Rende (several daily; 2hr); Waikabubak (several daily; 4hr 30min).

By ferry Passengers arriving at the main western harbour can get any bemo to drop them at the hotel of their choice. The Pelni office (0387 61665, pelni.co.id) is down at the bottom of the hill near the old harbour. Ferries leave from the western harbour; an ojek will take you there. Head to the harbour for information about ASDP ferries.

Destinations (Pelni) Bima (fortnightly; 13hr); Denpasar (fortnightly; 30hr); Ende (fortnightly; 10hr).

Destinations (other) Aimere (Tues; 10hr); Ende (Sun; 10–12hr); Kupang (Tues & Sun; 24hr).

ACCOMMODATION

All the accommodation below is in the newer part of town near the market. Hotels can arrange transport to the airport if required.

Elvin Jl A Yani 73 0387 61462. Friendly staff and the cheapest rooms in Waingapu – large, clean and en suite – though there are lots of mosquitoes and no nets. **Rp90,000**

Merlin Jl Dil Panjaitan 25 0387 61300. Rooms are tiled and clean, and some open onto a big wrap-around balcony; but the road outside is very, very noisy. **Rp154,000**

Sandalwood Jl Dil Panjaitan 23 0387 61887. Homely place right by the market, pleasantly quiet and good value for money. The English-speaking staff are full of helpful information, and there's also a decent restaurant. Single rooms are only Rp66,000. **Rp99,000**

EATING

You're almost spoilt for choice for food, with warungs lining the main road linking the old and new towns.

Nazareth Jl Lalamentik. Popular Chinese restaurant, with a good choice of food at reasonable prices (mains from Rp15,000). Daily except Sun 11am–10pm.

4

SUMBA'S TRADITIONS AND CUSTOMS

One of the main reasons to visit Sumba is to experience the extraordinary agrarian **animist cultures** in the villages. These villages, or kampung, comprise huge clan houses set on fortified hills, centred around megalithic graves and topped by a totem made from a petrified tree, from which villagers would hang the heads of conquered enemies. The national government insisted that all totems be removed back in the 1970s, and though some do remain, many have disappeared.

The most important part of life for the Sumbanese is death, when the mortal soul makes the journey into the spirit world. Sumbanese **funerals** can be extremely impressive spectacles, inspiring several days of slaughter and feasting, the corpse wrapped in hundreds of exquisite *ikat* cloths.

Ostensibly, visiting the villages often involves nothing more than renting a motorbike (available from town from around Rp70,000/day; your hotel is the best place to ask), but the difficulty for **Western visitors** to Sumba is that traditions and taboos in Sumbanese village life are still very powerful and sit ill at ease with the demands of modern tourism. A visitor to a Sumbanese village should first take the time to share *sirih pinang* (**betel nut**) with both the *kepala desa* (village headman) and his hosts. Bringing betel nut is seen as a peace offering (enemies would rarely turn up brandishing gifts), while its use is a sign of unity; Sumbanese ritual culture sets great store by returning blood to the earth, and the bright-red gobs of saliva produced by chewing *sirih* represent this. (The central purpose of the Pasola festivals is similarly to return blood to the soil; see box, p.317.) Many villages that are on the regular trail for tourists have supplanted the tradition of sharing betel with a simple request for money, but if you come with gifts (betel nuts, cigarettes, or anything else that can be shared) you'll be far more welcome.

Restu Ibu Jl Juanda 1. Long-established restaurant with a fine reputation, on the way into the old town and serving Indonesian staples (Rp10,000–20,000). Daily except Sun 11am–10pm.

★**Warung** Jl Lalmentik ends at a T-junction just beyond *Nazareth*. Immediately opposite the junction, hidden behind trees, is a warung serving the best *sate* and soups on Sumba, at low prices (less than Rp20,000). Daily 11am–10pm.

DIRECTORY

Banks BRI on Jl A Yani and BNI on Jl Palapa have ATMs that accept foreign cards; the latter also has the best rates for cash and travellers' cheques.

Internet There's a 24hr warnet in the market on Jl Palapa.

Pharmacy Jl Yani, across from the *Elvin*.

Post office Jl Dr Sutomo, in the old town (Mon–Thurs 8am–3pm, Fri 8–11.30am & Sat 8am–1pm).

WAIKABUBAK

4

Surrounded by lush green meadows and forested hills, tiny **WAIKABUBAK** encloses several kampung with slanting thatched roofs and megalithic **stone graves**, where life proceeds according to the laws of the spirits. Kampung **Tarung**, on a hilltop just west of the main street, has some excellent megalithic graves and is regarded as one of the most significant spiritual centres on the island. The **ratu** (king) of Tarung is responsible for the annual **wula padu** ceremony, which lasts for a month at the beginning of the Merapu New Year in November. The ceremony commemorates the visiting spirits of important ancestors, who are honoured with animal sacrifices and entertained by singing and dancing. Kampung **Praijiang** is a fine five-tiered village on a hilltop surrounded by rice paddies, several kilometres east of town. You can catch a bemo (around Rp5000) to the bottom of the hill. Waikabubak enjoys an extended rainy season lasting well into May, with daily downpours and chilly nights. Most things you need in Waikabubak are either on the main street of Jalan Sudirman, which becomes Jalan Bhayangkara, or not far from it. Ikat traders come from all over the island to Waikabubak's daily market.

ARRIVAL AND DEPARTURE

By plane Tambolaka Airport is a good 1hr 30min north of town, though like many of Indonesia's smaller airports, it has a patchy safety record; buses (around Rp15,000) meet arriving planes. In Pasola season (see box opposite), flights are more reliable than at other times, but you'll need to book months in advance. Merpati (Jl Bhayangkara 20; ⓣ0387 21051, ⓦmerpati.co.id) has services to Denpasar and Kupang, and Trans Nusa (Hotel Aloha; ⓣ0387 22563, ⓦtransnusa.co.id) to Ende and Kupang.

Destinations Denpasar (1–3 daily; 1hr 30min); Ende (3 weekly; 45min); Kupang (1–2 daily; 1hr 30min).

By bus The bus terminal is in the southwest of the town; bemos also stop here.

Destinations Waingapu (several daily; 4hr 30min); Waitabula (several daily; 1hr).

By ferry The twice-weekly ferry from Sape in Sumbawa arrives in Waikelo harbour; buses run to Waikabubak (1hr 15min). The ferry runs to Sape on Saturdays and Tuesdays (9–12hr).

INFORMATION

Tourist information Jl Teratai 1 (ⓣ0387 21880). Opening hours are decidedly erratic, but turn up in the morning and you've got a good chance of getting some useful information.

ACCOMMODATION

For such a small town, the choice of places to stay is pretty good.

Hotel Aloha Jl Sudirman 26 ⓣ0387 21245. Spotless rooms, some with a/c, and a friendly welcome at this laidback family-run hotel. **Rp125,000**

★**Artha** Jl Veteran 11 ⓣ0387 21112. Large rooms set around a garden courtyard and very helpful, friendly staff, though they don't speak much English. The best-value and most popular place in town. **Rp170,000**

Pelita Jl A Yani 2 ⓣ0387 21104. Renovation and extension work here means some parts resemble a building site, but the rooms themselves are quiet and comfortable, and they're the cheapest option in town. **Rp100,000**

EATING

As well as those listed below, there are a handful of warungs scattered around town.

★**Gloria** Jl Bhayangkara 46, opposite the petrol station. Offers an extensive menu of very tasty Indonesian and Chinese dishes served in generous portions; even the basics (around Rp20,000–40,000) such as *nasi goreng* and *soto ayam* are full of flavour. Daily 11am–10pm.

Rumah Maken & Café Jl Gajah Mada 35. Something of a misnomer on both counts as this is really just a large warung, but the fish is excellent and inexpensive (from Rp15,000). Daily 11am–10pm.

THE PASOLA

By far the best-known and most dazzling festival in Nusa Tenggara, the **Pasola** is one of those rare spectacles that actually surpasses all expectations. It takes place in **Kodi** and **Lamboya** in February and in **Wanokaka** and **Gaura** in March; most hotels can give you a rough idea of the date. This brilliant pageant of several hundred colourfully attired, spear-wielding horsemen in a frenetic and lethal pitched battle is truly unforgettable. It occurs within the first two moons of the year, and is set off by the mass appearance of a type of sea worm which, for two days a year, turns the shores into a maelstrom of luminous red, yellow and blue. The event is a rite to balance the upper sphere of the heavens and the lower sphere of the seas. The Pasola places the men of each village into two teams in direct opposition; the spilling of their blood placates the spirits and restores balance between the two spheres. The proceedings begin several weeks before the main event, with villagers hurling abuse and insults at their neighbours in order to get their blood up. The actual fighting takes place on special Pasola fields where the battle has been fought for centuries.

DIRECTORY

Banks The BNI bank at the junction of Jl A Yani and Jl Sudirman and the BRI bank on Jl Gajah Mada both change money and have ATMs.

Internet In the Telkom office, a few hundred metres south of the bus station.

Post office Jl Bhayangkara 1, just west of the BNI bank (Mon–Thurs 8am–2pm, Fri 8–11.30am & Sat 8am–1pm).

KODI AND PERO

In the extreme west of Sumba lies the increasingly popular Kodi district. Its centre is the village of **Bandokodi**, well known for the towering roofs that top its traditional houses. It is also one of the main **Pasola** venues in west Sumba (see box above). With your own transport, you can explore the area from Waikabubak, or you can stay in Pero (see below). There are direct buses from Waikabubak to Bandokodi, but they can be hard to find; it's easy enough to take a bus to **Waitabula** in the north and then connect to a Kodi service, which should take you all the way to Pero – check the price with a local, as drivers optimistically overcharge travellers. Direct buses back to Waikabubak leave Pero around 6am – you should be able to connect back to Waingapu the same day if necessary.

Pero

The only place to stay in Kodi is **PERO**, a seaside village with a solitary losmen. The village is not constructed in traditional Sumbanese style, but has a quiet charm. Numerous kampung with teetering high roofs and mossy stone tombs dot the surrounding countryside, some only a short walk away. The *Homestay Stori* (no tel; full-board only, Rp150,000) offers basic rooms, which can get stuffy at night. There are a lot of mosquitoes and no nets are provided, so come prepared. The main surfers' beach, a desolate long stretch where high waves crash onto the steeply sloping sand, is to the right, but the currents and undertow are ferocious. There's a more sheltered beach to the left over the river, with a vantage point above for local crowds to gather and gawp as you swim.

Kalimantan

Dense tropical jungle, murky village-lined rivers teeming with traffic and with wildlife so abundant it becomes the norm, jungle-cloaked Kalimantan appeals to those looking to venture into undiscovered territory. Occupying the southern two-thirds of the island of Borneo, Kalimantan remains largely untouched by tourism. With few roads, the interior's **great rivers** are its highways and a trip up one of them will give you a taste of traditional Dayak life and introduce you to lush areas of dense jungle. More intrepid explorers can spend weeks on end navigating their way through seldom-ventured parts, and a visit to one of the national parks could bring you face to face with wild **orang-utans** (see box, p.321). The urban

4

centres of **Pontianak**, **Balikpapan**, **Banjarmasin** and **Samarinda** are sprawling, dusty towns which offer little aside from their services. However, once out of the crowded, populated areas Kalimantan's character starts to unfold.

For the independent traveller, Kalimantan can be expensive and a bit of a mission; time, patience, knowledge of Bahasa and effort are certainly required. But if you're looking for a true sense of Borneo, then these obstacles are a small price to pay.

PONTIANAK

The capital of West Kalimantan, or Kalbar (short for "Kalimantan Barat"), **PONTIANAK** is a sprawling, grey industrial city of more than half a million people. Lying right at the equator on the confluence of the Landak and Kapuas Kecil rivers, it is a hot and noisy place, often smoky from the vast forest fires that recurrently rage inland. The most interesting thing about the city is its name, which translates roughly as "the vampire ghost of a woman who dies in childbirth." Most travellers stay just long enough to stock up on supplies before moving on to Kuching (see p.476) in Malaysia, Tanjung Puting or Putussibau to explore the upper reaches of the **Sungai Kapuas**, Indonesia's longest river.

WHAT TO SEE AND DO

To get your bearings, take a **boat** up the river (around Rp150,000 per hour) from the Seng Hie harbour or from behind the BNI building on Jalan Rahadi Usman,

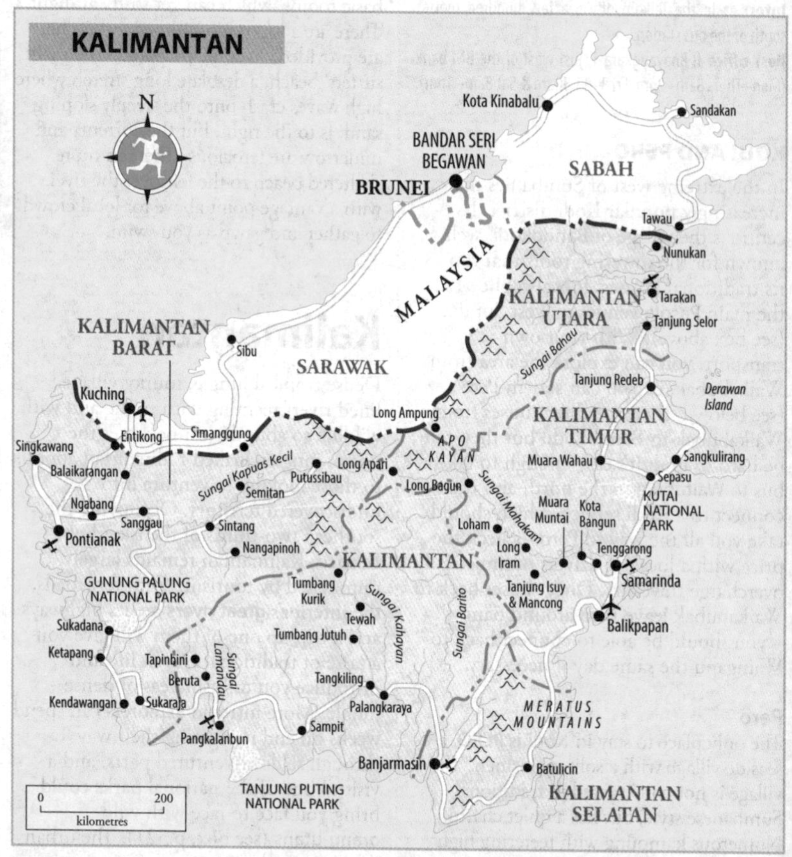

> **VISAS**
>
> If you're visiting Kalimantan from outside of Indonesia you must make sure you have a valid visa before entering. **Balikpapan** and **Pontianak** are the only airports in Kalimantan offering visas on arrival. At the time of writing, those travelling overland from Kuching to Pontianak could pick up a thirty-day visa at the border; in Sabah, the visa is available from the consulates in **Kota Kinabalu** and **Tawau**; sixty-day visas are at the discretion of the consulates.

near the ferry terminal. Along the river, there are still several old buildings of interest: the eye-catching **Istana Kadriyah**, built in 1771, and the traditional Javanese four-tiered roof of **Mesjid Jami** stand near each other on the eastern side of the Kapuas Kecil, just over the Kapuas bridge from the main part of town.

On Jalan Jend A Yani, 1.5km south of the town centre (Rp2500 by opelet), is the worthwhile **Museum Negeri** (Tues–Sun 8am–3pm; Rp2500), which contains a comprehensive collection of Dayak tribal masks, tattoo blocks, weapons and musical instruments. Just round the corner from the museum, on Jalan Sutoyo, is an impressive replica of a **Dayak longhouse**.

ARRIVAL AND DEPARTURE

By plane Supadio Airport lies 20km south of the city centre, linked by taxi (Rp90,000). For most destinations in Kalimantan you'll have to transit through Jakarta.

Destinations Balikpapan (several daily via Jakarta; 3hr with transit); Jakarta (20 daily; 1hr 25min); Ketapang (2 daily; 35min); Kuching (at least 1 daily; 45min); Pangkalan Bun (2 daily; 1hr); Putussibau (daily; 1hr).

By bus International buses arrive and depart from Ambawang bus terminal. Reliable companies include DAMRI (Jl Pahlawan 226/3; ⓣ0561 744859) and Bintang Jaya (Jl Tanjung Pura 310A; ⓣ0561 659 7402). The intercity bus terminal is Batu Lawang, north of the city, serving destinations across West Kalimantan.

Destinations Bandar Seri Begawan (2 daily; 26hr); Kota Kinabalu (daily; 38hr); Kuching (several daily; 9hr); Putussibau (daily 4pm; 19hr).

By ferry The main ferry port where Pelni and other passenger boats arrive is a few hundred metres north of the *Kartika Hotel* on Jl P Kasih. For Pelni ferries, you can buy tickets at their office at Jl Sultan Abdul Rahman 17 (ⓣ0561 748124). Agents on Jl Gajah Mada and Jl Diponegoro can arrange tickets for express boats to Jakarta and Surabaya; PT Indo Pacific Jasaprataura at Jl Gajah Mada 2A is one of the better ones. Comfortable a/c express boats run regularly to Ketapang on the west coast.

Destinations Jakarta (weekly; 36hr); Katapang (daily 7am; 6hr); Surubaya (fortnightly; 48hr); Tanjung Priok (fortnightly; 38hr).

INFORMATION

Tourist information The tourist information office is largely useless for foreigners. For in-depth information contact experienced local English-speaking guide Alex Afdhal (ⓣ0812 576 8066, ⓔalexafdhal@yahoo.com) of Borneo Access Adventurer on Jl Tanjung Harapan Gang HD Usman 46 (ⓦborneoaccessadventurer.com), who arranges numerous adventure-based tours, from Dayak Longhouse visits to 19-day trans-Borneo expeditions.

ACCOMMODATION

Ateng House 201 Jl Gajah Mada (above Ateng Tours) ⓣ0561 732683, ⓦatengtravel.com. Bright, clean a/c rooms with free wi-fi characterize this central budget option; the twin rooms are on the small side. Single **Rp150,000**, twin **Rp175,000**

★**Hosanna Inn** Jl Pahlawan 224 ⓣ0561 735052, ⓦhosannainn.com. Although tiny, this bright boutique hostel is the best budget option in town. Friendly staff, tidy a/c rooms and great location; it's right above the DAMRI ticket office where buses stop for Kuching. Rates include a simple breakfast and wi-fi. Single **Rp115,000**, twin **Rp155,000**

EATING

There are plenty of street stalls around town, especially near the market and harbour.

Beringin Jl Diponegoro 113. This is the largest of four locations around town. The friendly owner offers good West Sumatran food at low prices; the *sate* Pedang and *sambal sotong* (squid in chilli sauce) really stand out. Mains from Rp20,000. Daily 9am–10pm.

Gajah Mada Jl Gaja Madah 202. Large, upmarket Chinese restaurant famous for its excellent seafood and freshwater fish dishes. Try the crab *fu yung* (Rp35,000) or the *jelawat* (West Kalimantan river fish; Rp40,000). Daily 10am–10pm.

> **TAXI OR TAKSI?**
>
> In Kalimantan there are two forms of transport; a **taxi** is a traditional taxi cab, while a **taksi**, which is often an overcrowded minibus known as an angkot, an opelet or a bemo elsewhere in Indonesia, has different colours, numbers or letters to indicate its route.

4

THE DAYAK

Dayak is an umbrella name for all of Borneo's indigenous peoples. In Dayak religions, evil is kept at bay by attracting the presence of helpful spirits, or scared away by protective tattoos, carved spirit posts (*patong*) and lavish funerals. Shamans also intercede with spirits on behalf of the living. Although now you'll often find ostensibly Christian communities with inhabitants clutching mobile phones and watching satellite TV, the Dayak are still well respected for their jungle skills and deep-rooted traditions.

Traditionally, **head-hunting** was an important method of exerting power and settling disputes. It was believed that when cutting off someone's head the victim's soul was forced into the service of its captor. It is not practised now, but in 1997, West Kalimantan's Dayak exacted fearsome revenge against Madurese transmigrants. An estimated 1400 people were killed in a horrific purge of ethnic cleansing which involved head-hunting and cannibalism. Similar violence reoccurred between the Malays and the Madurese in the Sampit region of South Kalimantan in 2001. The situation is relatively peaceful now, and head-hunting has once again been relegated to the past.

DIRECTORY

Banks and exchange The bigger banks and moneychangers have branches near the junction of Jl Tanjungpura and Jl Diponegoro. There are ATMs all over the centre.
Hospital Dr Sudarso Hospital, Jl Adisucipto (☎0561 732077).
Immigration office Jl Sutoyo 122 (☎0561 767655).
Post office Jl Sultan Abdul Rahman 49 (Mon–Fri 7.30am–7pm, Sat 7.30am–6pm).

BALIKPAPAN

Built around a huge petroleum complex, **BALIKPAPAN** is Kalimantan's wealthiest city, its residents enjoying a high standard of living thanks to massive offshore oil reserves that shed a dim orange glow on the surrounding waters at night. For the traveller, Balikpapan is the transit point en route to Samarinda, Banjarmasin or the Mahakam River. The intersection of the main roads Jalan Ahmed Yani and Jalan Sudirman serves as the city's core, where you'll find hotels, restaurants and the best shops, but, as almost everything is imported from Java or Sumatra, prices are generally much higher here than in the rest of Kalimantan.

ARRIVAL AND DEPARTURE

By plane Sepinggang Airport (☎0542 766886), 10km east of the city centre, is linked by taxi (15min; Rp55,000) and taksi (from the airport, take green #7, and switch at the Damai taksi terminal to a blue #5 or #6 into town; each Rp4000). VOA (Visa On Arrival) available at the airport.
Destinations Jakarta (21 daily; 2hr); Makassar (6 daily; 1hr 5min); Manado (2 daily; 1hr 40min); Pontianak (via Jakarta; 3hr including transit); Singapore (1–2 daily; 2hr 15min); Surabaya (20 daily; 1hr 30min); Tarakan (13 daily; 1hr 5min).
By ferry Boats from Java, Sumatra and Sulawesi berth at the Pelni docks, 2.5km west of the centre on Jl Sudirman. Taksis #3 and #6 both go here. Tickets are available from the Pelni office (Jl Yos Sudarso 1; ☎0542 424171) at the harbour or from one of the many travel agents in the centre.
Destinations Makassar (1–2 weekly; 22hr); Nunukan (1–2 weekly; 32hr); Tarakan (weekly; 24hr).
By bus Terminal Batu Ampar, 6km north of the centre, serves long-distance destinations such as Samarinda (daily every 20min from 6am–7pm; 2hr 30min) and

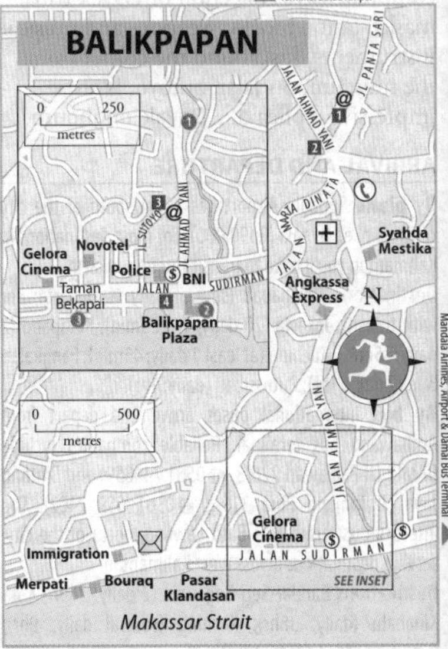

ACCOMMODATION		EATING & DRINKING	
Aida	2	Balikpapan Plaza	2
Aiqo	3	Bondy	1
Ayu	1	Zeuss	3
Gajah Mada	4		

Banjarmasin (several daily; 14hr). Take blue taksi #3 (Rp5000) to get into town.

INFORMATION AND TOURS

Balikpapan's tourist office (T 0542 876033) is on Jl MR Iswahyudi 121, near the airport, offering little more than maps and brochures. It's easier to organize tours in Samarinda.

ACCOMMODATION

Accommodation is mainly clustered into two groups: at the central intersection of Jl Jend A Yani and Jl Sudirman, and a few kilometres north up Jl A Yani. Decent budget accommodation is scarce.

Aida Jl Jend A Yani 12 T 0542 421006. At the north end of the street, this sprawling yet friendly place has clean, decent-sized rooms, though some are dark. All rooms have cable TV and inside mandi, and some have a/c (Rp205,000). Breakfast and wi-fi included. **Rp150,000**

Aiqo Jl APT Pranoto 9 T 0542 750288, W aiqohotel.com. Snazzy, bright place with compact spick-and-span rooms, with a/c, cable TV, reliable hot water, and wi-fi in the lobby. Avoid the rooms without windows. Breakfast included. **Rp268,000**

Ayu Jl P Antasari 18. T 0542 425290. Offers some of the best value in town, with small but clean fan and a/c rooms (Rp190,000) upstairs, all with attached bathrooms, set

AT HOME WITH THE ORANG-UTANS

Over the past few decades, Indonesia has lost about eighty percent of its original forest habitat. Illegal logging is still the number one culprit but expanding palm-oil plantations are a huge problem as well. This means the loss of the natural habitat of the stunning redhead of the simian world, the **orang-utan**. Kalimantan is one of the few areas where orang-utans still roam free; **Tanjung Puting National Park** in southern Kalimantan, **Gunung Palung National Park** in West Kalimantan, and **Kutai National Park** in East Kalimantan offer the best opportunities for seeing them in the wild. Although time, money, knowledge of Bahasa and determination are definite requirements for independent visitors, it's worth the effort.

GUNUNG PALUNG NATIONAL PARK

This national park is thought to be home to over 2000 wild orang-utans, and is also the site of an established research centre, the Gunung Palung Orang-utan Project (T people.bu.edu). At the time of writing, the only tour company allowed in the park was Nasalis Tour & Travel (Jl Gajah Mada 24, Kalinilam, Ketapang T 0534 772 2701, W gunungpalung.net). They organize multi-day stays in the park, with starting points in either Ketapang or Sukadana, each accessible from Pontianak. Packages start from Rp1,350,000 for two days and one night; bring your own sleeping bag, waterproof gear, mosquito net and torch.

KUTAI NATIONAL PARK

East Kalimantan suffered from prolific logging back in the 1970s, and the 3000-square-kilometre Kutai National Park was established in 1982 to try and prevent further decline, but fires then destroyed sixty percent of the protected area. Nowadays the forest is recovering and reasonably accessible. **From Samarinda**, signing up for a tour is currently the only way of visiting the park. A recommended operator is DeGiant Tours (Jl Martadinata 21 T 0541 709 1536, W borneotourgiant.com), run by Dutchman Lucas who has more than two decades of tour-leading experience in the region.

TANJUNG PUTING NATIONAL PARK

The 4000-square-kilometre Tanjung Puting National Park, comprising swamp forest, lowland rainforest and heath forest, is home to proboscis monkeys, clouded leopards, gharials and 6000 wild orang-utans. It was founded in the early 1970s by the legendary Dr Biruté Mary Galdikas. Part of the park, Camp Leakey (W orangutan.org/our-projects/research/camp-leakey), is less touristy than similar establishments in Sarawak and Sabah but shares their goal of rehabilitating orphaned or rescued orang-utans before reintroducing them to the wild. All-inclusive three-days and two-nights klotok (riverboat) tours can be arranged for around Rp1,750,000 per person from Kumai, easily accessible from Pangkalan Bun, which has daily flights to and from Pontianak, Jakarta and Surabaya with Kal Star and Trigana Air. Although more expensive, an easier route is through Borneo Eco Adventure (T 0517 551 6064, W borneoecoadventure.com), which leads tours for five days and four nights (Rp6,000,000 per person), taking care of everything once you've arrived in Pangkalan Bun.

4

about 100m off busy Jl A Yani. Free wi-fi reaches to the second floor. **Rp150,000**

Gajah Mada Jl Jend Sudirman 328 ⓣ 0542 734634. A more upmarket hotel in a central location, with friendly staff and spacious, tidy rooms, the pricier ones with a/c and hot water (Rp315,000). Free wi-fi and buffet breakfast. **Rp270,000**

EATING

There are cheap warung along the coastal road, at the Pelni harbour, next to the post office west on Jl Sudirman, and on the north side of Taman Bakapai.

Balikpapan Plaza Pacifica Foodcourt Jl Sudirman. On the upper floor of the giant Balikpapan Plaza. Great for those who struggle with Bahasa, this food court has pretty pictures of the food on offer. It's cheap and serves great *gado-gado* (Rp22,000). Daily 10am–10pm.

Bondy Jl Jend A Yani 1. Long popular among both locals and expats, this rambling restaurant has indoor and outdoor seating on a pleasant terrace, and offers seafood, burgers (from Rp28,000) and steaks imported from New Zealand (Rp100,000). Home-made ice cream and pastries in the attached confectionery shop. Daily 11am–10pm.

4

Zeuss Jl Jend Sudirman. Sleek new seafood restaurant next door to the equally popular *Ocean's*, with seating in a plush, a/c lounge or outdoors on a breezy wooden deck overlooking the sea. There's wi-fi and live music in the upstairs bar (daily 8–11pm). Daily 10am–midnight.

DIRECTORY

Banks and exchange There are scores of ATMs, and big branches of BNI, BCA and BRI on Jl Sudirman and Jl A Yani. For exchange, use PT Marazavalas (Jl A Yani 5).

Hospital International SOS Jl Papuk Raya 54 (ⓣ 0542 765966).

Immigration Office Jl Sudirman 23 (ⓣ 0542 421175).

Internet There are internet cafés across the city, including several on Jl Ahmad Yani and one on Jl P Antasari to the north. Rates are around Rp6000/hr.

Pharmacies The Kimia Farma has two 24hr pharmacies, one on Jl Sudirman near the Terminal Rasa, the other at Jl A Yani 95.

Post office The main post office with EMS counters is at Jl Sudirman 31 (Mon–Sat 8am–8pm, Sun 9am–5pm).

SAMARINDA

Some 120km north of Balikpapan, the tropical port town of **SAMARINDA** is 50km upstream from the sea, where the Sungai Mahakam is 1km wide and deep enough to be navigable by ocean-going ships. It has become increasingly prosperous since large-scale logging of Kalimantan Timur's interior began in the 1970s, its western riverfront abuzz with mills. The town is not particularly attractive, but it is the gateway to the interior and a convenient place to stock up for trips up the Mahakam.

ARRIVAL AND DEPARTURE

By plane Until the long-promised opening of the new Sungai Siring airport north of town, Samarinda is served by Temindung Airport, linked to the city centre by taxi (Rp40,000), ojek (Rp30,000) and red-brown B taksi (Rp3500).

Destinations Balikpapan (4 daily; 25min); Berau (with Kal Star; daily; 45min); Nunukan (with Kal Star; daily; 1hr 10min); Tarakan (daily; 1hr 20min).

By ferry The Mahakam river ferries use the Terminal Feri on Jl Sungai Kunjang, connected to the town by green taksis (Rp3500). All ocean-going vessels use the docks east of the centre along Jl Sudarso. Pelni runs twice monthly from here to Surabaya via Sulawesi. You can get tickets at their office at Jl Yos Sudarso 76 (ⓣ 0541 741402). For boats upriver, it's best to be in the harbour by 6am. Journey times vary widely depending on the state of the river, while downstream journeys are much faster.

Destinations Daily boats upstream to Kota Bangun (7hr); Long Bagun (water levels permitting; 40hr–3 days); Long Iram (30hr); Melak (24hr); Muara Muntai (10hr); Surabaya (fortnightly; 3 days); Tenggarong (3hr).

By bus Buses serving Balikpapan, Kota Bangun and destinations further upriver use Terminal Sungai Kunjang, on the north side of the river and 5km west of the centre – take a green taksi A into town (Rp5000). Buses for destinations to the north (Berau and Kutai) use Terminal Lampake, 5km northeast of the city, from where brown taksis link Jl Bhavangkara in the city centre (Rp5000). Taksis to Tenggarong (Rp10,000) use Terminal Banjarmasin on the south bank of the Mahakam.

Destinations Balikpapan (every 15min 5.30am–8pm; 2hr 30min); Kota Bangun (every 30min 6.30am–4pm; 3hr); Kuyung (downriver of Muara Muntai; daily 7.30am; 5hr); Melak (about hourly until 1.30pm; 8hr); Tenggarong (hourly; 1hr 30min).

INFORMATION AND TOURS

Tourist information The Dinas Pariwisata, or provincial tourist office, is on the corner of Jl Awang Long and Jl Sudirman (Mon–Fri 7.30am–5pm), where you'll usually find helpful, English-speaking Dennis (ⓣ 0821 5454 7600).

Tours There are several reputable companies in town which organize trips up the Mahakam and to other parts of Kalimantan, such as Kutai National Park (see box, p.321).

ALONG THE SUNGAI MAHAKAM

Borneo's second-longest river, the **Mahakam**, winds southeast for over 900km from its source far inside the central ranges on the Malaysian border, before emptying into the Makassar Straits through a multi-channelled delta. An established three-day circuit takes in the historic town of **Tenggarong** and the Benuaq Dayak settlements at **Tanjung Isuy** and adjacent **Mancong**. With a week to spare, scanty forest and communities inland from the Middle Mahakam townships of **Melak** and **Long Iram** are within range; ten days is enough to include a host of Kenyah and Benuaq villages, as you venture up the changing Mahakam through the rapids towards **Long Iram** and **Long Bagun**.

Unlike in Sarawak, less than a week on the Mahakam won't get you as far as the traditional Dayak longhouses, and this experience does not come cheap – expect to pay around US$125 per day if travelling as part of a group; solo travel can also be prohibitively expensive. If you don't go with one of the recommended tour companies in Samarinda (see opposite) it's easy enough to find freelance guides there, but the quality varies dramatically. The best guides are contracted to work for the tour companies. Beyond Long Bagun – the end of the line for *kapal biasa* (river ferries) – guides are essential if you don't speak the language. Expect to pay around Rp200,000 per day for a guide.

KOTA BANGUN TO TANJUNG ISUY

Where the trip begins in Samarinda or Tenggarong, the river is almost 1km wide, but narrows perceptibly as you reach the one-street town of **Kota Bangun** (also linked by buses departing from Samarinda's Terminal Sungai Kunjang (every 30min 6.30am–4pm; 3hr). Market stalls and warung line the street either side of the main pier, and there are plenty of opportunities to charter private boats from the town to explore villages upstream. It's essential to arrive by 3pm if you want to reach the river villages before dark, otherwise there are spartan rooms at *Penginapan Mukjizat* (Jl Mesjid Raya 46 ⓣ 0541 666 8586) that come with shared mandi (Rp50,000), set just across the road from an ATM.

Beyond Kota Bangun, there's a definite thickening of the forest along the banks as the river enters the marshy lakelands – though sadly, even here the effect of years of logging is evident. Around two hours from Kota Bangun by *ces* (motorized one-person-wide canoe; Rp250,000) is the 3km boardwalk, candy-coloured stilt village of **Muara Muntai**. Complete with convenience stores, a hospital and several losmen (among them Penginapan Adi Guna, to the right coming up the jetty; Rp50,000), Muara Muntai is the last place along the Mahakam to buy supplies. There's one daily bus at 7.30am from Kuyung (a 20min ces ride downstream; Rp70,000) to Samarinda (5hr).

The boat ride towards Tanjung Isuy (chartered ces Rp450,000 return; 2hr depending on water level), the first Dayak village on the Mahakam, takes you further into the jungle, passing hornbills, sweeping kingfishers and pot-bellied proboscis monkeys along the way. The villagers of Tanjung Isuy – a small township of gravel lanes, timber houses and fruit trees – live in kampung houses rather than traditional longhouses, but it's still a good place to catch a traditional dance performance in full costume. Accommodation is available at the museum-like *Losmen Louu Taman Jamrout* (Rp90,000), a restored Dayak longhouse surrounded by carved wooden patong posts (spirit posts). Moving on from Tanjung Isuy, you can either return to Muara Muntai, or hire a *ces* to take you across the northwest towards Mancong (Rp220,000).

THE MIDDLE AND UPPER MAHAKAM

Along the Mahakam to the northwest of Muara Muntai, you'll pass a number of Dayak villages that still practise the traditional Kaharingan religion; funerals here involve the sacrifice of water buffalo. You can access some traditional villages via motorbike from the town of Melak. From the small community of Barong Tongkok, 18km west of Melak, you can travel southwest to Mancimai, worth visiting for its museum showcasing traditional farming methods, and Eheng, the site of a fantastic traditional longhouse and a good place to buy local handicrafts.

Further northwest of Melak along the river, the villages have a more traditional character, though the missionaries have done a thorough job and some of the groups are Christian converts. It's challenging to travel by public transport beyond Long Iram – an attractive little town with some remnants of colonial Dutch architecture – since there is little demand for it and the water is not high enough during dry season. However, if you do continue towards Long Bagun, you will pass through increasingly dramatic scenery dotted with Kenyah villages.

4

The best of these is DeGigant Tours, Jl Martadinata 21 (0541 777 8648, borneotourgigant.com). You can also hire a local guide for a cheaper rate if you'd rather use less pricey public boats up the Mahakam, as opposed to the more comfortable houseboats provided by tour companies. Guides tend to congregate around *Hidayah 1*, *Hidayah 2* and *Aida* hotels.

ACCOMMODATION

As you're only likely to stop here for a night or two before heading up the Sungai Mahakam, you're better off staying near the centre, within easy reach of all Samarinda's services.

Aida Jl KHM Temenggung 0541 742572. Next to the *pasar pagi*, this spot, which is decent enough, has clean rooms with cable TV and attached bathrooms, though many rooms are dark; some have a/c (Rp225,000). It's popular, so arrive early in the day. **Rp180,000**

Gelora Jl Niaga Selatan 62 0541 742024, hotel_gelora@telkom.net. Overlooking a busy market just east of the mosque, this is one of the cheapest spots in town. Rooms are a bit worn, though some have a/c (Rp185,000) and all have inside mandi. There's wi-fi and breakfast (included) in the downstairs café. **Rp121,000**

4

Hayani Jl Pirus 31 0541 742653. A more upmarket choice opposite *Pirus Hotel*, with good-sized, spotless rooms that have showers, a/c, TVs and wi-fi access. Staff are friendly and there's a simple breakfast buffet. **Rp275,000**

EATING

There's a bounty of cheap warung around Jl Awang Long and the Mesra Indah store.

Daisaku *Bumi Senyiur Hotel*, Jl Diponegoro 17–19. Smart Japanese restaurant offering good sushi, *teppanyaki* dishes and even some Korean options, washed down with large bottles of sake. Mains from Rp30,000. Daily 10am–10pm.

Lezat Baru Chinese Restaurant Jl Mulawarman 56, near the Ramayana shopping mall. A popular place serving simple rice dishes – fans of Samarinda's famous giant river prawn (*udang galah*) won't go hungry. Take red taksi B from pasar pagi. Mains from Rp30,000. Daily 10am–3pm, 6am–9pm.

DIRECTORY

Banks and exchange Banks with ATMs such as BCA are found along Jl Sudirman.

Internet Kaltimnet on the ground floor of the *MJ Hotel* (Jl KH Khalid 1) is open 24hr (Rp9000/hr).

Pharmacies Rumah Sakit Bhakti Nugraha on Jl Basuki Rachmat 50.

Post office Jl Gajah Mada at Jl Awang Long, near the tourist office.

TENGGARONG

On from Samarinda, the Mahakam River is broad and slow, with sawmills and villages peppering the banks. **TENGGARONG** is 45km and three hours upstream by ferry – or just an hour by road. This small, neat and very prosperous country town was, until 1959, the seat of the Kutai Sultanate, whose territory encompassed the entire Mahakam basin and adjacent coastline. It's a good place to stay if you want to escape big cities and a convenient location to start trips up the river.

The former palace, just opposite the **ferry dock** on Jalan Diponegoro, is now the **Museum Negeri Mulawarman** (Sat–Thurs 9am–4pm, Fri 9–11am; Rp5000), which includes statuary from Mahakam's Hindu period (pre-fifteenth century), with replicas of fourth-century conical stone *yupa*, Indonesia's oldest written records. Dayak pieces include Benuaq weaving, Kenyah beadwork and Bahau *hudoq* masks.

ARRIVAL AND DEPARTURE

By ferry Boats arrive at the pier on the southern end of Jl Sudirman. Be there at 6am for the daily boats heading upstream.

Destinations Kota Bangun (5hr); Long Bagun (36hr); Long Iram (30hr); Melak (21hr); Muara Muntai (10hr).

By bus Terminal Timbau is 5km south of town beyond the huge road bridge, linked by blue taksis (Rp5000). Until 5pm, there are regular buses to Samarinda (1hr; Rp10,000) and Kota Bangun (2hr; Rp20,000); for Balikpapan, ask to be dropped at the junction with the main Balikpapan road in Loa Janan (1hr), just before Samarinda: there you can easily flag down a bus to Balikpapan (2hr 30min).

INFORMATION AND TOURS

Tourist office The tourist information centre is at the back of the marketplace on Jl Dioponegoro (Sun–Fri 9am–4pm).

Guides Rio (0821 5684 9766) at the *Hotel Anda Dua* speaks excellent English and is a good contact for finding a local guide.

ACCOMMODATION AND EATING

Tenggarong is a cheaper, more relaxed and quieter place to stay than Samarinda. Tasty warungs are spread along Jl Cut Nya Din and Jl Diponegoro (at night).

Anda Dua Jl Sudirman 52 (set back from the road) 0541 661409. Welcoming place with spacious rooms, some equipped with a/c (Rp200,000), in an old wooden

family home. Friendly, English-speaking owner Rio can arrange tours or provide plenty of advice on how to get further upriver. Breakfast included. **Rp150,000**

Tepian Pandan Opposite the museum. Highly recommended *rumah makan* with a great location right on the river and excellent Kutai food. Fresh grilled prawns are a speciality (from Rp40,000). Daily 8am–10pm.

TARAKAN

A 24km spread of low hills just off the coast northeast of Tanjung Selor, Pulau Tarakan floats above extensive oil reserves: offshore rigs dot the horizon, while the west-coast town of **TARAKAN** is surrounded by smaller-scale "nodding donkey" pumps. An island still physically scarred by World War II battles between the Japanese and Australian forces, this is a convenient hopping-off point for Sabah in Malaysian Borneo, just a stone's throw from **Pulau Nunukan** and the open **border with Malaysia.**

ARRIVAL AND DEPARTURE

By plane The airport is 2km north of town, Rp35,000 by taxi or Rp3000 by taksi from the main road.

Destinations Balikpapan (11 daily; 1hr 5min); Jakarta (daily; 2hr 50min); Tawau (daily; 40min).

By ferry The port is 2km south of the town centre (taksi Rp3000). Ferries to and from Berau and Nunukan use the Tengkayu jetty, while Mulundung harbour, 500m further down, is served by Pelni ferries to Balikpapan, Nunukan, Sulawesi and Java as well as ferries to Tawau in Malaysia. The Pelni office is here too (T 0551 21529).

Destinations Balikpapan (1–2 weekly; 34hr); Berau (2 weekly; 10hr); Nunukan (3 daily; 2hr); Tanjung Selor (10 daily; 1hr 30min); Tawau, Malaysia (daily except Sun; 4hr).

INTO MALAYSIA: TARAKAN TO TAWAU

The border crossing into Malaysia lies between **Nunukan** and the Malaysian town of **Tawau** in Sabah (see p.513). Ferries link Tarakan with Nunukan (several daily; 2hr; Rp85,000), from where you can continue to Tawau (several daily; 1hr Rp110,000). More conveniently, there are direct ferries from Tarakan to Tawau (Mon–Sat 10am; 4hr; Rp300,000), run by Indomaya Express and Tawindo ferries, and a daily flight for the same trip run by Malaysian Air (40min).

ACCOMMODATION AND EATING

Most accommodation is to the east down Jl Sudirman, within 150m of the centre.

Makmur Jl Yos Sudarso 1 T 0821 4879 9014, W hotelmakmur.com. Clean rooms with TV, fridge and city views for Rp330,000. Rates include local in-room breakfast and good wi-fi. If it's full, take a room (windowless) over the road at the cheaper sister property, *Sakura*. **Rp250,000**

Rumah Makan Cahaya Jl Sudirman. A popular Chinese restaurant, serving large portions of spicy seafood (Rp18,000), *nasi goreng* (Rp12,000) and more. Daily 8am–10pm.

Taufiq Grand Jl Yos Sudarso 7 T 0551 22402. Friendly business hotel in the centre of town; rooms are clean and come with a/c and good views of town from the upper floors. Breakfast in the small café downstairs is included. **Rp225,000**

DIRECTORY

Banks and exchange The BNI bank on Jl Sudarso has good exchange rates and ATMs.

Internet Starnet beside the *Hotel Makmur* on Jl Sudirman 17 (Rp9000/hr).

Pharmacies Tarakan Plaza, Jl Sudirman.

Post office Jl Yos Sudarso (Mon–Fri 7.30am–6pm, Sat 7.30am–2pm).

Travel agents Panjung Harapan, Jl Sudarso 38 (T 0551 21572), for ferry tickets to Nunukan and Tawau.

Sulawesi

Sulawesi sprawls in the centre of the Indonesian archipelago, a tortuous outline resembling a 1000km letter "K", and one of the country's most compelling regions. Nowhere in Sulawesi is much more than 100km from the sea, though an almost complete covering of mountains isolates its four separate peninsulas from one another and from the outside world. Invaders were hard pushed to colonize beyond the coast, and a unique blend of cultures and habitats developed. The south is split between the highland **Torajans** and the lowland **Bugis**, there are various isolated tribes in the central highlands, and the Filipino-descended **Minahasans** reside in the far north.

The most settled part of the island, the south, is home to most of Sulawesi's fifteen million inhabitants. This is also

where you'll find the capital, the busy port of **Makassar**. The southern plains rise to the mountains of **Tanah Toraja**, whose beautiful scenery, unusual architecture and vibrant festivals are the island's chief tourist attractions. Those after a more languid experience can soak up tropical sunshine on the **Togian Islands**, and there's fabulous diving at **Pulau Bunaken**, out from the northern city of **Manado**. In most areas, Sulawesi's roads are well covered by **public transport**, though freelance *kijang* (shared taxis) and minibuses are often faster and

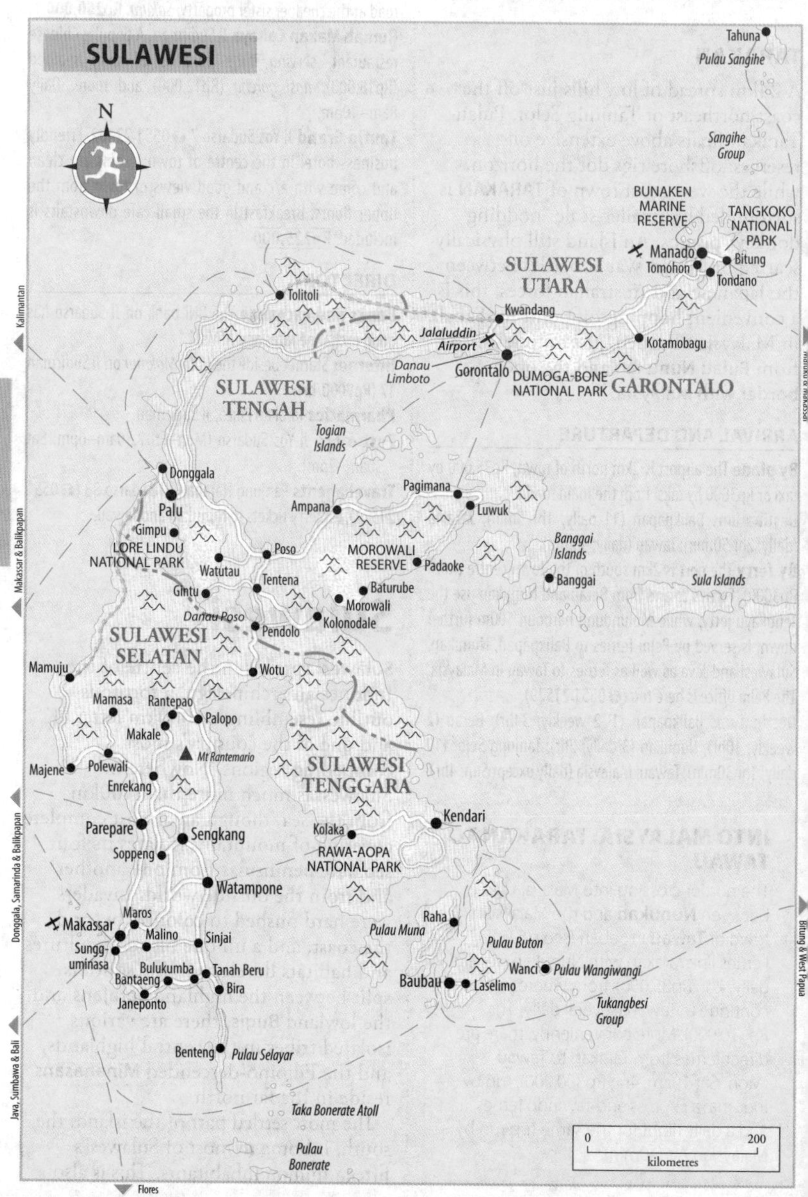

TROUBLE IN SULAWESI

Between 1998 and 2001, violent unrest and bloody fighting between Christians and Muslims in and around the town of **Poso** claimed more than two thousand lives. A 2001 peace deal has largely stabilized the region and tourism is finally on the rise, though sporadic attacks continue, most recently with a suicide bomber driving into the Poso police station in June 2013. A degree of caution is still advised for travellers wishing to remain in Poso beyond the time it takes to switch buses. Check with your government advisory website (see box, p.44) for up-to-date information about the safety of the area.

better value than public buses. Where these fail you'll find ferries, even if services are unreliable.

MAKASSAR

At Sulawesi's southwestern corner, facing Java and Kalimantan, **MAKASSAR** (also known as Ujung Pandang) is a large, hot and crowded port city with good transport links between eastern and western Indonesia. More than anything, Makassar offers an introduction to Sulawesi's largest ethnic group, the **Bugis**, who continue to export their goods well beyond Sulawesi in *prahu*, distinctive vessels with steep, upcurved prows. The city has a long and distinguished history as a crucial trading port and coastal defence.

WHAT TO SEE AND DO

A monument to Sulawesi's colonial era, **Fort Rotterdam** on Jalan Ujung Pandang (daily 7.30am–6pm; Rp10,000) was established as a defensive position in 1545 and enlarged a century later when the Dutch commander Cornelius Speelman rechristened it in memory of his home town. A wander round the thick stone walls lets you peer out to sea on one side and down onto backstreets on the other. Located on the northwest side is Speelman's House, the oldest surviving building, standing next to one half of **La Galigo Museum** (same times; entry included in fort ticket), which houses a fairly interesting collection of ethnographic and historic items, including models of local boat types.

The **Pasar Sentral** (Central Market), freshly rebuilt after a devastating fire in 2011, was once the city's main shopping district, and although the mega malls now steal much of its custom, it remains a thriving place and the best spot to find *pete-petes* (local bemos). From here you can pick up a becak (Rp25,000) or an ojek (Rp20,000) to take you 3km north up Jalan Sudarso to **Paotere harbour** (Rp5,000 admission), where Bugis *prahu* from all over Indonesia unload and embark cargo each morning; it's quite a spectacle when the harbour is crowded, the red, white and green *prahu* lined up along the dock.

ARRIVAL AND DEPARTURE

By plane Hasanuddin Airport, 20km northeast of the city, is linked by taxi (Rp100,000) and DAMRI buses, which run every 30min from the arrivals hall to the city, ending near the fort at the junction of Jl A Yani and Jl Riburane (daily 6am–10pm, departing from Medan Karebosi in the city 7am–8pm; Rp25,000). If you're going directly to the bus station, take the free airport shuttle (daily 5am–11pm) to just outside the gates, then catch a *pete-pete* to Terminal Daya (Rp4500).

Destinations Balikpapan (6 daily; 1hr); Denpasar (6 daily; 1hr 20min); Gorontalo (4 daily; 1hr 30min); Jakarta (47 daily; 2hr 20min); Manado (4 daily; 1hr 40min); Palu (6 daily; 1hr 10min); Surabaya (26 daily; 1hr 30min); Yogyakarta (daily; 2hr).

By bus Both day and night buses for Rantepao dock at the huge Terminal Daya, 14km to the east on the way to the airport, from where you can catch a metred taxi (around Rp50,000) or *pete-pete* (Rp4500) into the centre; in the other direction, *pete-petes* depart from Medan Karebosi. Buses heading south use Terminal Malengkeri, 7km south of the centre, or Sungguminasa, another 4km southeast of Malengkeri; both are linked by red *pete-pete* to Jl Jend Sudirman in the city (Rp45000). Relatively comfortable a/c bus operators such as Litha (Jl Gunung Merapi 135 ⓣ0411 442263) and Bintang Prima (Jl Perintis Kemerdekaan Ruko 22 ⓣ0411 4772888), each charging around Rp140,000 per seat, will pick you up in town.

Destinations Daily departures for Ampana (28hr); Manado (2–3 days); Rantepao (8hr); Tentena (19hr).

4

By ferry The Pelni harbour, Pelabuhan Makassar, is less than 1km northwest of Pasar Sentral on Jl Nusantara, with ferries running to ports all around Sulawesi, as well as Java, Sumatra, Kalimantan, Bali and Nusa Tenggara. The Pelni office is at Jl Jend Sudirman 38 (Mon–Fri 9am–3pm, Sat 9am–noon ☎0411 331401). Other boats dock at Paotere harbour, 3km north of the centre; their ticket offices are across from the harbour on Jl Nusantara. Ojeks will take you into town for around Rp20,000.

Destinations Balikpapan (1–2 weekly; 22hr); Denpasar (weekly; 2 days); Jakarta (1–2 weekly; 48hr); Jayapura (1–2 weekly; 4 days); Kupang (weekly; 34hr); Nunukan (1–2 weekly; 2–3 days); Larantuka (monthly; 27hr); Surabaya (2–3 weekly; 24hr); Tarakan (weekly; 48hr).

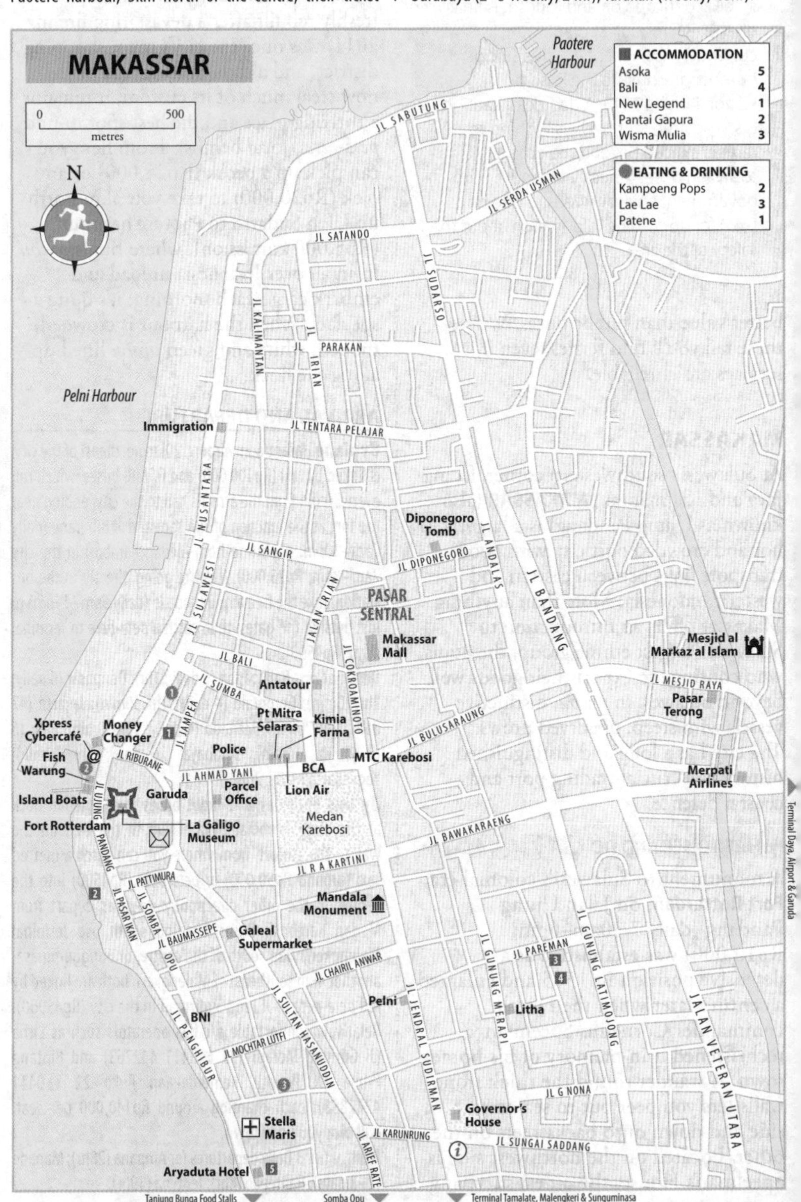

4

INFORMATION

Tourist Office Jl Jend Sudirman 23 (T 0411 831800 or 878912, W celebes-tourism.com). The Sulawesi Tourist Information Centre has helpful staff and useful maps and brochures (Sun–Fri 8am–5pm).

GETTING AROUND

Becaks Makassar's becak drivers are annoyingly persistent, and there's a good chance of ending up somewhere completely unexpected; a fare of Rp8000/km is reasonable. Bargain hard. Rp20,000 to Paotere.

Pete-petes Makassar's blue *pete-petes* (bemos) charge Rp4500, and most terminate at or near Karebosi. They have their routes written on the windscreen, colour-coded for different destinations; the most useful is the purple one to Terminal Daya.

Taxis Bosowa (T 0411 454545) is the recommended firm.

ACCOMMODATION

Asoka Jl Latumahina 21/38 T 0411 873476. The friendly owners rent out five lovely a/c rooms in a huge, elegant house just around the corner from the seafront *Aryaduta Hotel*. Price includes wi-fi and breakfast. **Rp300,000**

Bali Jl Sungai Pareman III 15–17 T 0411 362 0071. Although large and anonymous, this is a good option if *Wisma Mulia* just down the road is full, and even the cheapest rooms have windows. Breakfast and wi-fi are included, and guests pay a Rp100,000 deposit upon check-in. **Rp165,000**

New Legend Jl Jampea 5G T 0411 361 3777, W newlegendhostel.com. The backpacker favourite, with a common room, dorm and restaurant serving free breakfasts on the top floor. Though cheaper than elsewhere, basic rooms are windowless and stuffy. A more upmarket version of the same name sits next door. Dorm **Rp75,000**, double **Rp125,000**

Wisma Mulia Jl Sungai Pareman III 1 T 0411 365 0967. Friendly and immaculate, this is the best value for money in town. The cheaper rooms lack windows, but are large, with cable television, a/c and en-suite bathrooms. Breakfast included. **Rp150,000**

EATING AND DRINKING

Wander past Fort Rotterdam of an evening, and the shabby patch of concrete opposite will have woken up and filled with warungs, mostly serving fish.

Kampoeng Pops Jl Ujung Pandang 4. Pleasant waterfront patio just opposite Fort Rotterdam, surrounded by Indonesian, Western and Japanese fast-food stalls (dishes from Rp20,000), featuring live rock music on weekends. Daily 10am–midnight.

Lae Lae Jl Datamuseng 8. Popular yet friendly seafood restaurant, with staff who will make recommendations if you look confused; a one-person fish comes to about Rp30,000. The main doors are permanently closed, but follow the painted fish to the side entrance. Daily 9.30am–midnight.

Patene Jl Sulawesi 48. In the centre of the Chinese quarter, this large, clean and colourful place offers decent portions of Indonesian food (*nasi campur* Rp25,000, *gado gado* Rp15,000). Daily 9am–10pm.

★TREAT YOURSELF

Even if you can't afford to stay for the night, the **Hotel Pantai Gapura** on Jl Pasar Ikan 10 (T 0411 368 0222, W pantaigapura.com) provides an excellent shelter from the heat and hurly-burly outside. Wend your way through the maze of bungalows, perched on stilts above the sea, to the sunset bar in the far right corner, where you can enjoy a drink, cool breeze and sea view. There's also a lovely pool available to non-guests for Rp30,000. Rooms are cheaper Sun–Thurs. **Rp640,000**

DIRECTORY

Banks and exchange Most banks have ATMs, with many located along Jl Jend A Yani and at the northeast corner of Medan Karebosi. The best moneychanger in town is Haji La Tunrung, by the seafront at the southern end of Jl Nusantara.

Hospitals Stella Maris, Jl Penghibur (T 0411 873346), is your best chance in southern Sulawesi for correct diagnosis and treatment by English-speaking staff.

Immigration Jl Perintis Kemerdekaan Km 13, Tamalanrea (T 0411 584559). Set northeast of town towards the airport; not the easiest place in Indonesia for a visa extension.

Internet There's wi-fi in many hotels and restaurants, while Xpress Cybercafe at Jl Ujung Pandang 12A has terminals (Rp5000/hr).

Pharmacy Kimia Farma on Jl Ahmad Yani.

Police Jl Ahmad Yani.

Post office Jl Slamet Riyadi near Fort Rotterdam (Mon–Sat 8am–9pm).

Shopping The huge MTC Karebosi on the northeast corner of Medan Karebosi is a good place to cool off and shop for bargains.

Travel agents The most efficient agent is Antatour on Jl Dr Wahidin Sudirohusodo 34A (T 0411 361 8648, W antatour.com).

TANAH TORAJA

Some 250km north of Makassar, a steep wall of mountains marks the limits of Bugis territory and the start of **Tanah Toraja's highlands**, a beautiful spread of hills and valleys where sleek buffalo wallow in lush green paddy fields. Known as **Tator** in the local idiom, Tanah Toraja is home to one of Indonesia's most confident and vivid cultures, and is planted firmly on the agenda of every visitor to Sulawesi. There's a morbid attraction to many of the region's sights, which feature ceremonial animal slaughter, decaying coffins and dank mausoleums spilling bones. Tour groups tend to concentrate on key sites, so it's not hard to find more secluded corners. Each spot charges an entry fee of Rp20,000.

Tanah Toraja's main town, at least as far as tourists are concerned, is **Rantepao**, 18km north of the regional capital, Makale. It's a popular base for travellers, most of whom descend for the major **festival season** between July and September. Expect hot days and cool nights; there is a "dry" season between April and October, but this is relative only to the amount of rain at other times, so bring non-slip walking boots and rainwear.

Rantepao

A prosperous market town on the rocky banks of **Sungai Sadan Valley**, **RANTEPAO**

4

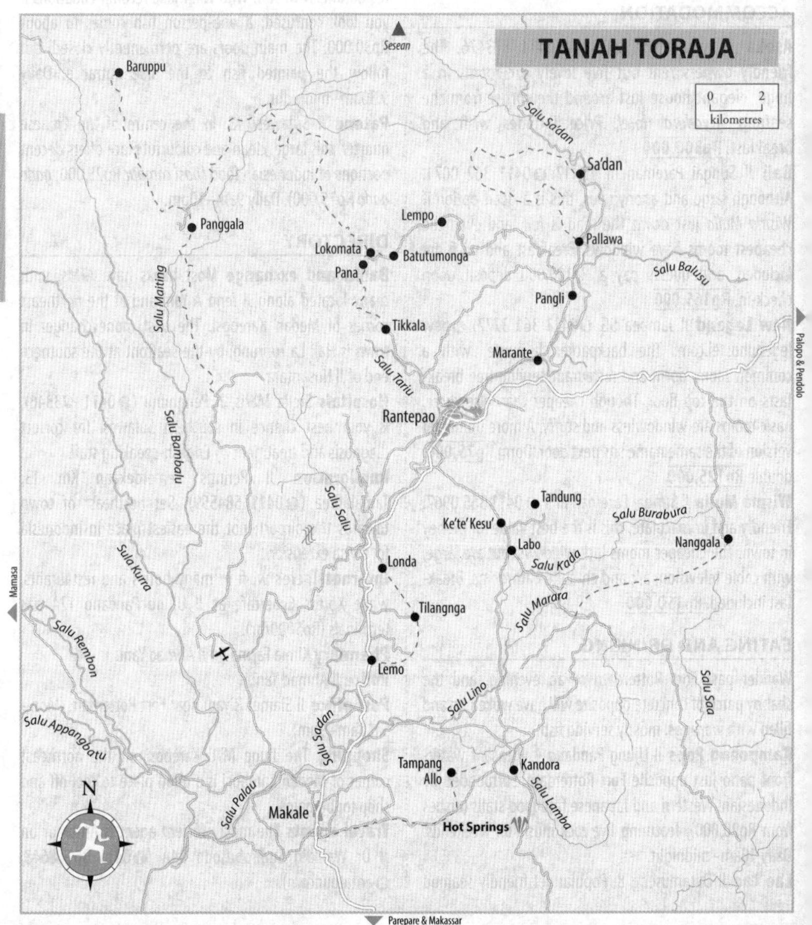

is home to the Sadan Toraja. With an abundance of good-value accommodation and worthwhile excursions in every direction, it makes an ideal base for exploring Tanah Toraja. And though it's perfectly possible to visit much of the area independently, Rantepao also offers a whole host of experienced guides who can be found at almost any hotel, travel agent or restaurant in town; if you'd prefer to pick your own, drop by *Pia's Poppies* (see p.333) in the morning or evening. Prices start at around Rp300,000 a day per guide, but you will need to pay for transport and, for attending a ceremony, gifts on top of this.

The town itself stretches just over 1km along the eastern bank of the Sadan, the central **crossroads** marked by a miniature *tongkonan* (see box, p.332) on a pedestal. North from here is Jalan Mappanyuki, a short run of souvenir shops, bus agents and restaurants; Jalan Ahmad Yani points south towards Makale before becoming Jalan Pong Tiku; east is Jalan Diponegoro and the Palopo road, while westerly Jalan Landorundun leads to the riverside past a small fresh-produce market.

Rantepao's main **market** – the biggest in Tanah Toraja, 2.5km northeast of the centre at Terminal Bolu – is a must: where else could you pick up a bargain buffalo then celebrate your purchase with a litre or two of palm wine? Large markets are held every six days, though you'll find some traders in the marketplace every day of the week. You can walk there in half an hour by following Jalan Mappanyuki over the river, passing a few impressive *tongkonan* before crossing the river again to the market. A bemo back costs Rp4000.

South of Rantepao

Makale is the administrative capital of Tanah Toraja, and the most famous sites lie off the road running south from Rantepao to Makale. The route is plied all day long by bemos running in both directions (20min; Rp7000). Just south of Rantepao, a concrete statue of a buffalo marks the turn-off to four much-restored tongkonan at Ke'te' Kesu' (4km), the central of which is said to be the oldest in the district. An adjacent *rante* (ceremonial ground) sports a dozen megaliths, the tallest about 3m high. A path leads up the hill past hanging and no-longer-hanging coffins mortised into the side of the truncated peak.

Some of the other sights to the south of Rantepao can be combined to form a pleasant day's stroll. The walk begins 9km from Rantepao at the turn-off to Lemo. One kilometre from the road, **Lemo** is famous for its much-photographed tau-tau, set 10m up a cliff face and mutely staring over the fields with arms outstretched. Turn left in the centre of Lemo, then follow the road to **Tilangnga**, where you'll find a pleasant rocky pool to swim in, but watch out for the resident eels. From here, **Londa** is about an hour's walk: continue through Tilangnga, bearing left when the road forks. Turn right just before the school, then left when you hit the paved road. After about twenty minutes you'll emerge from the forest and see a large red-roofed church on your right, at which point strike off to the left across the paddy fields to reach Londa. Set in a shaded green glen underneath tall cliffs, overhung with a few coffins and a fantastic collection of very lifelike tau-tau, Londa boasts two caves whose entrances are strewn with bones and offerings of tobacco. You'll need a guide with pressure lamps (Rp25,000 for the lamp, plus a tip for the guide) to venture inside. From Londa, either follow the tarmac for twenty minutes or ask villagers to point out the short cut through rice paddies to the main road for a bemo back to Rantepao.

East of Rantepao

Six kilometres east of Rantepao on the Palopo road is the spread-out village of **Marante**, which contains almost all the main features of Tanah Toraja. Close to the road is a fine row of tongkonan; behind, a path leads to where tau-tau and weathered coffins face out over a river. A few kilometres further on, look out for a group of megaliths in a field at **Tondon**. **Nanggala**, about another 6km along the Palopo road from Marante,

4

then 2km south, is a stately village with a dozen brilliantly finished tongkonan, and a large flying-fox colony in the neighbouring trees.

There's a very pleasant five-hour walk due west to **Ke'te' Kesu** from here, though the network of paths around Nanggala means you really need a map or, better still, a guide.

North of Rantepao

If you're more interested in the living than the dead, it's worth wandering north from Terminal Bolu in Rantepao to Sa'dan. Bemos along this road are reasonably frequent, or you can walk between sites. Seven kilometres from Rantepao you reach **Pangli**, famed for its *balok* (palm wine). Not much further, a signed road off to the left leads past some megaliths to **Pallawa**, whose tongkonan are embellished with scores of buffalo horns. For the more active, it's possible to walk a large loop from here to Sa'dan, though again you'll need a map. Back on the main road, another 4km brings you to a fork in the road: east is **Sa'dan** itself, with a bizarre array of mausoleums and an *ikat* market every six days; west is **Sangkombong**, where local women will demonstrate their weaving skills before making their sales pitch.

TORAJAN CULTURE AND FESTIVALS

Anthropologists place Torajan **origins** as part of the Bronze Age exodus from Vietnam; Torajans say that their ancestors descended from heaven by way of a stone staircase, which was later angrily smashed by the creator Puang Matua after his laws were broken. These laws became the root of **aluk todolo**, the way of the ancestors. Only a fraction of Torajans now follow the old religion, the strict practice of which was prohibited after head-hunting and raunchy life-rites proved unacceptable to colonial and nationalist administrations. But its trappings remain: everywhere you'll see extraordinary **tongkonan** and **alang**, traditional houses and rice-barns, and the Torajan social calendar remains ringed with exuberant ceremonies involving pig and buffalo sacrifices. Torajans are masters at promoting their culture; positively encouraging outsiders to experience their way of life.

TORAJAN FESTIVALS

Ceremonies are divided into *rambu tuka*, or smoke ascending (associated with the east and life), and *rambu solo*, smoke descending (associated with the west and death). A typical *rambu tuka* ceremony is the **dedication of a new tongkonan**.

The biggest of all Torajan ceremonies are **funerals**, the epitome of a *rambu solo* occasion. Held over several days, it begins with the parading of the oval coffin, and traditionally, the first afternoon ends with **buffalo fights**. The following day – or days, if it's a big funeral – is spent welcoming guests, who troop village by village into the ceremonial field, led by a noblewoman dressed in orange and gold, bearing gifts of *balok* (palm wine), pigs trussed on poles and buffalo. The next day, the **major sacrifice** takes place: the nobility must sacrifice at least 24 buffalo, with one hundred needed to see a high-ranking chieftain on his way. Finally, the coffin is laid to rest in a west-oriented house-grave or rock-face mausoleum, with a **tau-tau**, a life-sized wooden effigy of the deceased, positioned in a nearby gallery facing outwards, and – for the highest-ranking nobles – a megalith raised in the village ground.

ATTENDING TORAJAN CEREMONIES

Witnessing a traditional ceremony is what draws most visitors to Tanah Toraja, particularly during the "peak festival season" in the agriculturally quiet period from June to September. To visit a ceremony outsiders should really have an **invitation**, via a guide. As more participants means greater honour, however, it's also possible to turn up at an event and hang around the sidelines until somebody offers to act as your host. You are highly unlikely to be the only foreigner attending; snap-happy tourists are part of the scenery, with each sacrifice a photographic feeding frenzy. Make sure you take a **gift** for your hosts – a carton of cigarettes, or a jerry can of *balok* – and hand it over when they invite you to sit down with them. Do not sit down uninvited; dress modestly and wear **dark clothing** for funerals – a black T-shirt with blue jeans is perfectly acceptable, as are thong sandals.

ARRIVAL AND DEPARTURE

By bus Terminal Bolu is 2.5km northeast of town and linked by bemos (Rp4000), though buses from Makassar can drop you off at your accommodation or in the vicinity of the crossroads. Bus companies are set along Jl Andi Mappanyuki in the town centre, and buses leave from just outside their offices. Buses to Makassar run day and night, with luxury a/c options available from a number of companies (Rp100,000–150,000). For Tentena and Poso, the best companies are Ketty (Jl Andi Mappanyuki 49 ⓣ 0853 4215 4747) and Rappan Marannu (Jl Andi Mappanyuki 52 ⓣ 0423 25193), each with daily departures at 8am (Rp150,000).

Destinations Makassar (8hr); Pendolo (10hr); Poso (14hr); Tentena (12hr).

By bemo Bemos leave Jl Ahmad Yani every few minutes for Makale (Rp7000), and just as often from Jl Diponegoro for Terminal Bolu.

INFORMATION

Tourist information The government tourist office (Mon–Thurs 7.30am–2pm, Fri 7.30–11.30am, Sat 7.30am–12.30pm; ⓣ 0423 25455) is just past the hospital at Jl Ahmad Yani 62A; however, the friendly tourist services at the Tora Tora gallery, Jl Mappanyuki 64, are open longer hours (daily 9am–6.30pm).

ACCOMMODATION

Accommodation is scattered across town, with some offering excellent value for money.

Duta 88 Jl Sawerigading 12, signposted off Jl Mappanyuki ⓣ 0423 23477. Seven beautiful, tightly packed traditional-style bungalows, all with hot water, in an atmospheric garden. Very central, but the road outside is noisy. **Rp250,000**

★Pia's Poppies Jl Lorong Merpati 4, off Jl Pong Tiku ⓣ 0423 21121. This backpacker stalwart remains a beautiful and tranquil place to stay, with a small garden and creatively decorated rooms featuring rock-pool bathtubs with hot water. Good value for solo travellers (Rp100,000). Breakfast is extra (Rp25,000), but the food is fantastic. If full, check across the street at *Pison*, which has basic, good-value rooms. **Rp154,000**

Wisma Maria I Jl Dr Ratulangi 23 ⓣ 0423 21165. Central and good value, this friendly place offers a range of prices (up to Rp220,000) according to room size, location and water temperature. Everything is kept immaculate, though the cheapest rooms suffer slightly from damp. **Rp132,000**

Wisma Monton Jl Abdul Gani 14A ⓣ 0423 21675. Hidden away down a quiet side street, this homely family-run guesthouse offers en-suite rooms with bathtubs; slightly more money (Rp250,000) gets you hot water. Breakfast is on the rooftop terrace, and the upstairs rooms boast mountain views. **Rp100,000**

EATING AND DRINKING

Most restaurants offer local Torajan dishes such as *piong* (chicken, fish, pork or buffalo cooked over an open fire in bamboo shoots with coconut, herbs and spices) and *pamarassan* (again chicken, fish, pork or buffalo cooked in black Torajan spice), though you should give at least two hours' notice.

Riman Jl Andi Mappanyuki 113. Serving a wide range of local dishes, this is a good place to stock up on vitamins, with excellent fruit juices, fried vegetables and an assortment of Torajan specialities (Rp45,000). Daily 8am–10pm.

Saruran Jl Diponegoro 19. Popular restaurant, just before the banks on Jl Diponegoro if you're coming from town; serves large portions of tasty Indonesian food with a Chinese twist (sweet-and-sour chicken Rp28,000), and there's wi-fi. Daily 8am–10pm.

DIRECTORY

Banks and exchange The BNI and Danamon banks, next to each other on Jl Diponegoro, and the BRI on Jl Ahmad Yani, all have ATMs.

Hospital The best doctors are at Elim Hospital, Jl Ahmad Yani (ⓣ 0423 21258).

Internet There are many internet cafés around town, including several on Jl Mappanyukki; all charge Rp4000–6000/hr.

Motorbike Rental Lebonna, Jl Monginsidi (ⓣ 0423 23520), rents out motorbikes, as do most hotels and tour agents in town, for Rp70,000/day.

Pharmacy Jl Mappanyukki 92.

Post office Jl Ahmad Yani 111, just south of the main crossroads (Mon–Thurs 8am–3.30pm, Fri 8am–4pm, Sat 8am–12.30pm).

Travel agencies Metro Permai, at Jl Mappanyuki 15 (ⓣ 0423 21785).

TENTENA

Straddling the northern shores of Danau Poso, Indonesia's third-deepest lake, the charming Christian town of Tentena offers a welcome rest on the road between the Togians and Tanah Toraja. It's also a decent base for excursions to the pristine forests and mystifying megaliths of Lore Lindu National Park. A pleasant motorbike ride through Tentena's countryside passes dozens of churches, cacao plantations and wonderful vistas across the lake, eventually reaching **Saluopa** (Rp10,000), a spectacular set of falls set in the jungle 14km west of town.

ARRIVAL, DEPARTURE AND INFORMATION

By bus The bus terminal is 4km northeast of the town's accommodation hub (ojeks cost Rp5000). There are daily bemos to Poso (10am; 2hr; Rp25,000), from where buses connect Ampana (2 daily; 5hr); and night buses to Rantepao (daily 6pm; 12hr) run by Ketty and Rappan Marannu.

Information The friendly tourist office (daily 7.30am–9pm 0852 4200 3420, 0458 215111) is just east of the new bridge, offering maps and arranging tours. Good maps and information are also available from *Hotel Victory*.

ACCOMMODATION AND EATING

The warungs near the bridges serve the local speciality, *sogili bakar* (grilled freshwater eel).

Tandolala Cottages Jl Poros Tentena-Peura Km 3 0812 4527 3438, tandolala-cottages.com. 3km south of town, this newly built set of private (Rp300,000) and duplex cottages sits on stilts over the lake, each equipped with a mosquito net and balcony. Further out on the water, the restaurant serves set lunches and dinners (Rp55,000/60,000). Friendly owner Simon has plenty of helpful advice and can pick you up from the bus station with advance notice. **Rp200,000**

Victory Jl Diponegoro 18 0458 21392, victorytentena.com. The most popular spot in town, set on a quiet street not far from the pair of bridges. Rooms are basic and clean, some with hot water (Rp250,000) and all set around a small garden. Friendly, English-speaking staff double as excellent guides, leading treks in Lore Lindu. **Rp100,000**

DIRECTORY

Banks There's a Mandiri Bank ATM just northeast of town on the road to Poso.

Internet Shiawase Café on Jl Diponegoro (daily 8am–9.30pm) near *Hotel Victory*, with free wi-fi for customers, and computers for Rp5000/hr.

AMPANA

Small but reasonably tourist-friendly **AMPANA** is the southern access point for the Togian Islands. There are plenty of warung spread along the coastal road and a handful of decent accommodation options for those awaiting ferries, as well as most services lacking in the islands. Internet cafés are scattered around town, and there's an ATM at the BRI Bank two blocks west of *Oasis*, though the one at the Mandiri Bank, just over 1km east along the main road to Labuhan, is more useful. Boats to Wakai (for Kadidiri) leave from the main port, just north of Oasis, while boats to Bomba depart from the port of Labuhan, 3km east near Marina Cottages.

ACCOMMODATION

Irama Jl RA Kartini 11 0464 21055. Just up the road from *Oasis*, this losmen is among the cheapest in town, with friendly staff and basic, somewhat ageing rooms that come with TVs and are adequate for a night. **Rp100,000**

Marina Cottages Jl Tanjung Api 33 Labuhan 0464 21280. Handy for the boats to Bomba, *Marina* is in Labuhan, 3km east of the town centre (Rp7000 by ojek). It has spotless private bungalows, some with a/c (Rp220,000) and all with terraces facing a black pebble beach. Staff are helpful, there's wi-fi in the spacious restaurant and breakfast is included. **Rp150,000**

Oasis Jl RA Kartini 5 0464 21058. Set just 100m from the port and run by the same management as that of *Kadidiri Paradise*, this is the most popular backpacker hotel in town, with clean, simple rooms set around a pleasant courtyard. Unfortunately, all but the a/c deluxe rooms (Rp180,000) suffer from karaoke noise late into the night. There's wi-fi in the lobby, and breakfast included. **Rp120,000**

THE TOGIAN ISLANDS

The **TOGIAN ISLANDS** form a fragmented, 120km-long crescent across the shallow blue waters of Tomini Bay, their steep grey sides weathered into sharp ridges capped by coconut palms and hardwoods. The exceptional **snorkelling and diving** around the islands features turtles, sharks, octopus, garden eels, and a mixed bag of reef and pelagic fish species. On the downside, there are also nine depots in the Togians dealing in the live export of seafood to restaurants in Asia; many of these operations employ cyanide sprays, which stun large fish but kill everything else – including coral.

From west to east, **Batu Daka**, **Togian** and **Talata Koh** are the Togians' three main islands, with **Walea Kodi** and **Walea Bahi** further east. The main settlements are **Bomba** and **Wakai** on Batu Daka, and **Katupat** on Togian. Wakai is something of a regional hub, with transport out to smaller islands. There are no vehicle roads or widespread electricity in the Togians and you'll find it pays not to be on too

tight a schedule; most accommodation places offer day-trips and shared transfers. Tourism in the islands is budget-oriented but good, and prices include meals. July through to September are the coolest months, when winds can interrupt ferries. Diving is usually good all year round, though visibility in December can be variable.

Bomba

Four hours from Ampana and at the western end of Batu Daka, **BOMBA** comprises a few dozen houses and a mosque facing north across a pleasant bay. There's a long beach 5km west of town, but it's the sea that warrants a visit here, with the Togians' best snorkelling an hour away at **Catherine reef**. The coast near here is interesting, too, offering the possibility of seeing crocodiles in remote inlets; some islets east of Bomba are completely covered by villages, their boundaries reinforced with hand-cut coral ramparts.

Wakai and Kadidiri

At the eastern end of Batu Daka, about five hours from Ampana and two from Bomba, **WAKAI** is only of interest as a transport hub. Half an hour by motorized outrigger from Wakai, 3km-long **Kadidiri**, with its fine beaches, is one of the nicest of the islands.

ARRIVAL AND DEPARTURE

FROM THE SOUTH

Boats from Ampana to Wakai (for Kadidiri) depart daily except Fri (10am; 5hr; Rp60,000 one-way), and return from Wakai to Ampana daily except Mon & Fri (10am; 5hr). On Mon, Tues, Wed & Sat, boats continue from Wakai to Katupat (for Bolilanga; 1hr; Rp60,000 from Ampana), returning Sun, Tues & Thurs at 7am. Boats from Ampana to Bomba depart Sun, Tues & Fri (9am; 3hr; Rp25,000), returning from Bomba to Ampana on Mon, Thurs & Sat (9am; 3hr). Boats to Wakai leave from the main port, just north of *Oasis Hotel*, while boats to Bomba depart from 3km to the east near Marina Cottages.

FROM THE NORTH

From the port of Gorontalo, the KM Tuna Tomini departs for Wakai every Tues & Fri (8pm; 12–13hr), returning from Wakai on Thur & Sun (4.30pm; 12–13hr; Rp75,000/Rp90,000 a/c).

GETTING AROUND

Getting around the Togians is a slow process, and schedules are constantly changing. Your best bet is to get to Wakai, Bomba or Kadidiri, and assess your options from there, as even in Ampana and Gorontalo everyone's schedules tend to differ slightly. If time is of the essence, or if you're in a group, there is always the option of chartering local boats, though make sure you see the vessel first. The hotels on Kadidiri will pick you up from Wakai, and the hotels on Bomba can hail the passing public boats that head between Wakai and Ampana five days of the week.

ACCOMMODATION

Phone reception on the islands is notoriously bad, so the numbers below might not always work. All prices include meals.

BOMBA

★Island Retreat ⓣ0852 4115 8853, ⓦtogianislandretreat.com. This smart American-run place to the south of Bomba boasts one of the longest beaches in the Togians, most of its basic cottages only a few metres from the water. The food is fantastic, and they run a competitively priced diving operation as well (from $31/dive, plus $6 for equipment rental). Contact them at least two weeks in advance to arrange for a pick-up. **$35**

Poya Lisa Cottages ⓣ0464 21592, ⓔpoyalisaisland@gmail.com. A handful of very basic cottages set on their own idyllic island just off Bomba, a location that makes up for the lack of facilities. Friendly staff organize snorkelling trips, but for diving and equipment hire you'll need to go through *Island Retreat* (see above). **Rp125,000**

KADIDIRI

Three sets of cottages share a single beach, though only *Black Marlin* and *Paradise* organize diving.

Black Marlin ⓣ0856 5720 2004, ⓦblackmarlindiving.com. Efficient, friendly dive centre, with smart, clean and well-equipped bungalows that all face the sea. Diving costs €28/dive. **€16/person**

Kadidiri Paradise contact the *Oasis* in Ampana ⓣ0464 21058, ⓦkadidiriparadise.com. A friendly, laidback place that takes up most of the beach. Their basic bungalows aren't as modern as *Black Marlin*'s but they do offer more privacy, and the luxury bungalows over the water (Rp450,0000) are very elegant. €30/dive. **Rp200,000**

Lestari ⓣ0821 9144 4503, ⓔteteng.lestari@yahoo.com. This friendly, rustic retreat offers some of the cheapest board in the Togians, and is the most popular place to stay on Kadidiri. Basic rooms have shared mandi, while larger bungalows come with private bathrooms (Rp150,000). Free boats for snorkelling excursions. **Rp100,000**

BOLILANGA

About an hour away from Kadidiri, tiny Bolilanga Island is relatively un-touristy, the perfect spot if you're after complete seclusion. There's only one place to stay, and the owners can arrange a free pick-up from Katupat on Togian Island if you call ahead. From Wakai, they'll charter a boat for you for Rp300,000.

Bolilanga Island Resort ⊕0852 4100 3685, ⓦbolilangaresort.com. An intimate place offering fourteen beachfront bungalows with a wonderfully relaxing, end-of-the-world feel and good food. Inexpensive snorkelling and fishing trips are available, and guests can paddle a small boat around the island for free. **Rp200,000/person**

GORONTALO

GORONTALO is a quiet but well-equipped town, not an unpleasant place to get stranded should you be unlucky with Togian boat schedules. Its streets are laid out on a grid system, making it easy to navigate. The main north–south road is Jalan A Yani, where you'll find ATMs at the BNI and Danamon banks. Crossing it east–west is Jalan 23 Januari, with the post office at the junction and the Pelni office a short way further along. Wi-fi is available at the *New Melati Hotel* next to the sportsground. There are plenty of warungs around, and a lively night market.

4

ARRIVAL AND DEPARTURE

By plane Jalaluddin Airport is 32km north of town. A seat in a shared taxi costs around Rp60,000.

Destinations Makassar (4 daily; 1hr 30min); Manado (2 daily; 40min).

By bus Terminal Andalas is 3km to the north of town, Rp10,000 by bentur (motorized rickshaw), with buses to Manado (daily 6am; 10hr) and Palu (17hr).

By car Faster and more comfortable for the trip to Manado, kijangs meet ferries arriving from the Togians. You can also book these at their offices north past the bus terminal on Jl Andalas, among them PO Garuda (⊕0435 828343). Tickets are priced according to your seat (back/front Rp125,000/Rp175,000), and they can pick you up at your hotel.

By ferry The harbour is a 15min bentur ride from town (Rp10,000). The Pelni office is in town on Jl 23 Januari 31 (⊕0435 21089).

Destinations Bitung (monthly; 15hr); Denpasar (monthly; 5 days); Makassar (2 monthly; 72hr).

ACCOMMODATION

Karina Jl A Yani 28 ⊕0435 828411. The best-value accommodation in town, in a conveniently central position. Smart, sparkling clean and very friendly, it offers a/c, hot-water showers, TV and Western-style toilets in all rooms. **Rp150,000**

New Melati Jl A Yani ⊕0435 822934, ⓦnewmelatihotel.com. Remains a favourite among backpackers, with decent budget rooms set around a pleasant garden beyond the posh new entrance. All rooms come with worn bathrooms, and some have a/c (Rp180,000) and hot water (Rp325,000). Friendly staff are expert at helping with onward travel. Wi-fi and breakfast included. **Rp130,000**

EATING

There are plenty of warungs around town, including in the park in front of the *New Melati*.

Magic Pan Pizzeria Jl A Yani 55 ⊕0435 829619. Opened in 2012, this offers a welcome change for those freshly arrived from the Togians. Set in attractive, a/c surroundings, it serves a range of thin-crust pizzas (medium Rp50,000), pastas (from Rp35,000) and a few Indonesian favourites. There's wi-fi, and they deliver (Rp7000). Daily 7am–10pm.

MANADO

Capital of Sulawesi Utara, **MANADO** is mainly used by travellers as a launching point for spectacular **diving and snorkelling** in the Bunaken Marine Reserve. You can either base yourself in Manado and do day-trips to the reefs, or stay on the island itself, where there are plenty of accommodation and dive operators to choose from.

Manado is busy, noisy, hot and in a permanent state of near-gridlock, but it also exudes a bustling energy, which can be refreshing for those feeling deprived of civilization after a trip to the Togians. The town's old hub lies in the north, where you'll find the harbour and the fresh produce market, Pasar Bersehati, although in recent years the area's popularity has been overtaken by the vast strip of new shopping centres known collectively as the Manado Boulevard, stretching south between Jalan Pierre Tendean and the rapidly expanding coastline. Microlets, many of which turn into mobile discos at night – complete with flashing lights, thumping bass and sometimes even LCD TVs – swarm along

both this road and parallel Jalan Sam Ratulangi to the east.

Manado was flattened in 1844 by a devastating **earthquake**, and tremors measuring up to 5.0 on the Richter scale continue to rattle the town for a few seconds every three months or so.

ARRIVAL AND DEPARTURE

By plane Sam Ratulangi Airport is 12km northeast of the centre. Taxis to town cost around Rp80,000, and microlets connect terminal Paal Dua (Rp4000). Some of the bigger dive centres have representatives on hand to answer questions and help book trips.

Destinations Jakarta (several daily; 2hr 10min); Makassar

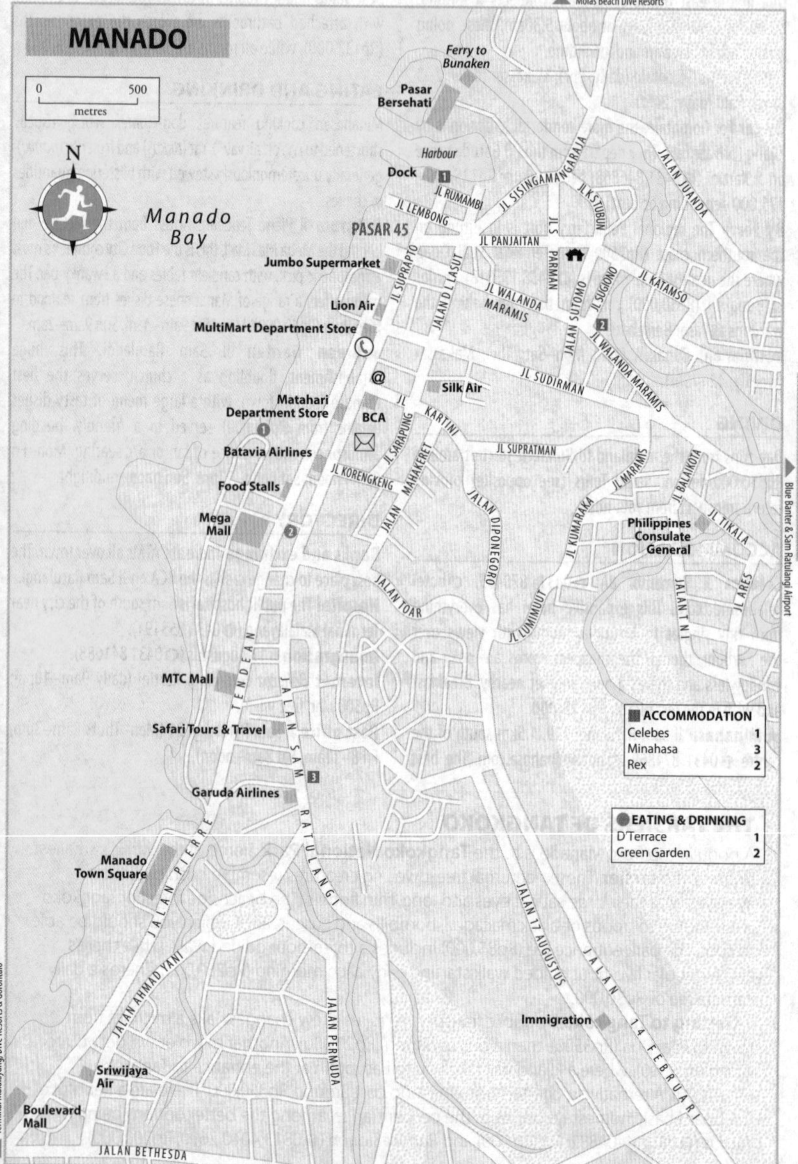

4

(several daily; 1hr 35min); Singapore (5 weekly; 3hr 30min); Surabaya (daily; 1hr 35min).

By bus Long-distance buses serving Gorontalo, Palu and Makassar use Terminal Malalayang, about 6km south along the coast, linked by microlets to the centre (Rp5000). Buses for the Minahasa Highlands use Terminal Karombasan, also to the south (microlets Rp5000). Paal Dua in the east (microlet Rp3500) connects to Bitung. Buses for Gorontalo leave at about 5.30am; those going further afield leave around lunchtime.

Destinations Gorontalo (daily; 8hr); Makassar (daily; 2–3 days); Palu (daily; 24hr).

By car For Gorontalo, the more comfortable option is by kijang (private car). They depart from the PO Garuda office on Jl Kartini (T 0431 846868; before 10am; Rp125,000–175,000 depending on seat).

By ferry The regional Pelni ferry port is in Bitung on the southern coast (Rp7500 from Terminal Paal Dua), where the nearest Pelni office is (T 0438 135818). Ferries to Bunaken (Rp50,000) run from the river behind the warungs at Pasar Bersehati.

Destinations Bunaken (2pm Mon–Sat; 1hr); Makassar (weekly; 42–78hr).

4

DIVING

Day-trips from the mainland to Bunaken start at around Rp650,000/person. Safari Tours (see opposite) provide return transport from your hotel.

ACCOMMODATION

Celebes Jl Rumambi 8A T 0431 870425, W hotelcelebesmdo.com. This expansive hotel has everything from tiny singles to luxurious rooms with views over the harbour, though the cheapest rooms are poky and windowless and there's a noisy market nearby. Breakfast and wi-fi in the restaurant. **Rp125,000**

★**Minahasa** Jl Sam Ratulangi 199, 1.5km south of the centre T 0431 874869, W hotelminahasa.com. The best place in town by a long shot. Most rooms are set along a pretty garden path leading up to the swimming pool, which offers superb views over Manado Bay. All rooms have hot water and a/c, while there's wi-fi and a good breakfast buffet in the restaurant. **Rp282,000**

Rex Jl Sugiono 3 T 0431 851136, W hotelrexmanado.com. Although it isn't saying much, *Rex* offers about the best-value budget rooms in town. The larger, a/c rooms with attached bathrooms are worth the extra rupiahs (Rp137,000), while all rooms are very noisy. **Rp115,000**

EATING AND DRINKING

Minahasan cooking features dog (*rintek wuuk*, usually shortened to *rw*, or "airvay"), rat (*tikkus*) and fruit bat (*paniki*), generally unceremoniously stewed with blistering quantities of chillies.

D'Terrace Jl Pierre Tendean. Across from the McCafe and behind the Mega Mas Mall, this is the Food City complex's most atmospheric pick, with candlelit tables and a swanky bar. The menu offers a range of Manadonese dishes from seafood to fried duck (Rp40,000). Mon–Sat 9am–4am, Sun 9am–2am.

★**Green Garden** Jl Sam Ratulangi. This huge establishment, doubling as a church, serves the best Chinese food in town, with a large menu of tasty dishes (mains from Rp30,000) served in a friendly, bustling atmosphere with a choice of fan or a/c seating. Mon–Fri 8am–noon, Sat noon–11pm, Sun noon–midnight.

DIRECTORY

Banks and exchange There are ATMs all over town. The best place to change cash is the BCA on Jl Sam Ratulangi.

Hospital The public hospital is 6km south of the city near Terminal Malalayang (T 0431 853191).

Immigration Jl 17 Augustus (T 0431 841688).

Internet *Ballecoz Café* on Jl Kartini (daily 9am–10pm; Rp5000/hr, free wi-fi).

Post office Jl Sam Ratulangi 21 (Mon–Thurs 8am–3pm, Fri 8–11am, Sat 8am–noon).

THE TARSIERS OF TANGKOKO

A popular trip from Manado is to the **Tangkoko National Park**, home of the world's smallest primate, the **tarsier**. These nocturnal tree-dwelling creatures resemble bush babies or aye-ayes with their large saucer eyes and long, thin fingers. The beachside forest of Tangkoko is also home to troops of black macaque, hornbills and cuscus, all of which you should be able to spot. The park entrance fee (Rp85,000) includes a three-hour guided walk, while there's also a popular five-hour guided walk starting early each morning (Rp250,000). There's a daily camera fee of Rp30,000.

Getting to Tangkoko by public transport requires a few changes. Take a microlet from town to Paal Dua (Rp3500), then a bus to Bitung (Rp20,000). Another microlet will get you to Girian (Rp5000), where a kijang will take you to Batuputih at the entrance to Tangkoko (Rp20,000). Alternatively, charters from Manado cost around Rp350,000. There are a handful of full-board basic homestays opposite the park entrance, among the better options being *Tarsius* (T 0812 4404882; Rp200,000) and *Ranger Station* (T 0813 4040 7690; Rp200,000).

Travel agents Safari Tours and Travel (Ⓣ0431 857637, Ⓦmanadosafaris.com) offer flights and tours; their office is at Jl Sam Ratulangi 178, almost opposite the *Minahasa*.

BUNAKEN MARINE RESERVE

Indonesia's official scuba centre is **Bunaken Marine Reserve**, a 75-square-kilometre patch of sea northwest of Manado. Coral reefs around the reserve's four major islands drop to a 40m shelf before plunging to depths of 200m and more, creating stupendous reef walls abounding with Napoleon (maori) wrasse, barracuda, trevally, tuna, turtles, manta rays, whales and dolphin. Set aside concerns about snakes and sharks and avoid instead the 1m-long Titan triggerfish, sharp beaked and notoriously pugnacious when guarding its nest; and small, fluorescent-red anemone fish, which are apt to give divers a painful nip.

Diving is well established in Bunaken, with high-quality operators both in Manado and within the reserve on Pulau Bunaken. The island makes for an infinitely more pleasant base, with a wide range of accommodation. Experienced divers will also find plenty of budget operators on the island, though you must check the **reliability** of rental gear and **air quality**, the two biggest causes for concern here.

Off the island's west beach, between Bunaken village and Liang beach, are **Lekuan 1**, **2** and **3**, exceptionally steep deep walls, where you'll find everything from gobies and moray eels to black-tip reef sharks. There are giant clams and stingrays at Fukui, on the far western end of the island, while **Mandolin** is good for turtles and occasional mantas, and **Mike's Point** attracts sharks and sea snakes. Non-divers can snorkel straight from the beach, or ask to join a diving boat.

The best **weather conditions** are between June and November, with light breezes, calm seas and visibility underwater averaging 25m and peaking beyond 50m. Try to avoid the westerly storms between December and February and less severe, easterly winds from March until June.

Pulau Bunaken

About an hour by ferry out from Manado, **Pulau Bunaken** is a low-backed, 5km-long comma covered in coconut trees and ringed by sand and mangroves. Entry into the national park costs Rp150,000, which buys a tag valid for one year, or Rp50,000 for a day. The cheaper hotels often don't bother charging you, but do ask as the money goes toward maintaining the park. If you book in advance your homestay will usually arrange your transport. The main alternative is to take a **public ferry** to Bunaken village from the river behind the warungs at Pasar Bersehati in Manado (Mon–Sat at 2pm but get there a good hour early; return 8am; Rp50,000). A wander round the main harbour will also get you a plethora of offers, usually from homestays who will charge around Rp35,000 if you stay with them, or Rp50,000 if you don't.

DIVE OPERATORS

All operators below are part of the North Sulawesi Water-sports Association (Ⓦdivenorthsulawesi.com), which promotes environmentally responsible diving in Bunaken.

★**Froggies** (see p.340). Popular place with high standards and a good reputation with experienced divers. €65 for two dives.

Immanuel's Part of *Daniel's Homestay* on Pangalisang Beach. Friendly and popular with budget divers. €60 for two dives.

Living Colours Pangalisang Beach Ⓣ0812 430 6063, Ⓦlivingcoloursdiving.com. Large, efficient operator with a good reputation for both equipment and environmental awareness. €65 for two dives.

Two Fish Divers (see p.340). Pangalisang-based, UK-run outfit with good equipment and high standards. €60 for two dives.

ACCOMMODATION

There is plenty of accommodation on the island, though with the exception of *Daniel's* all the places listed are a fair walk from the village – ask anyone with a scooter to take you (Rp5000–10,000). All rates include three meals a day.

PANGALISANG

★**Daniel's** Ⓣ0852 4096 1716 or Ⓣ5612 7448, Ⓦimmanueldivers.com. One of the first you come to from the village, though it can be hard to spot – look for the *Immanuel Divers* sign. Friendly, social, justifiably

4

popular and the best value on the island. Wi-fi connection available. **€20/person**

Lorenso's Beach Garden Cottages ⓣ 0852 5697 3345, ⓦ lorensobunaken.com Friendly place with basic bungalows made of bamboo, palm bark or gleaming wood, all set in a tropical garden. Lorenzo and his family of musicians serenade guests in the restaurant with guitars and a drum set of tin cans. Sizeable off-season discounts. **€25/person**

Two Fish Divers ⓣ 0813 5687 0384, ⓦ twofishdivers.com. Efficient, friendly place set in pleasant sandy gardens. There is a range of rooms, some with attached bathrooms (€30 per person), and a swimming pool, library and wi-fi connection in the lounge/restaurant. **€20/person**

LIANG BEACH

On the other side of the island from Bunaken village, Liang fronts a beach rather than mangroves.

Cicak Senang ⓣ 0852 9806 4906, ⓦ happygeckoresort.com. This little gem has five spacious, two-room wooden bungalows equipped with fans, tastefully furnished and all looking out towards Manado. Run by a Dutch-Indonesian couple, it also offers some of the island's most affordable diving at Gecko Dive Centre. **€22/person**

Froggies ⓣ 0812 4301356, ⓦ divefroggies.com. Comfortable rooms in beautiful bungalows with showers, hot water and Western bathrooms throughout. It's a bit of a climb to the upper bungalows, but the sea views are worth it. Free wi-fi and laundry. **€30/person**

MONK, LUANG PRABANG

Laos

HIGHLIGHTS

❶ **Vang Vieng** Enjoy a great range of outdoor activities at this spectacular natural playground. **See p.364**

❷ **Luang Prabang** A fabulous UNESCO World Heritage Site: a great place to explore. **See p.368**

❸ **Nong Khiaw** Soak up the stunning limestone karsts from a riverside bungalow. **See p.380**

❹ **Slow boat on the Mekong** Chug down the vast river on a wooden cargo boat. **See p.386**

❺ **Wat Phou** Seek serenity among sun-warmed Khmer ruins. **See p.396**

❻ **Si Phan Don** Kick back with a Beerlao on these sandy Mekong islands. **See p.397**

HIGHLIGHTS ARE MARKED ON THE MAP ON P.343

ROUGH COSTS

Daily budget Basic US$20/Occasional treat US$25–30

Drink Beerlao US$1.25

Food Noodle soup US$1.25

Hostel/budget hotel US$3–6

Travel Bus: Vientiane–Luang Prabang (390km; 10–12hr, US$14); Slow boat: Houayxai–Luang Prabang (300km; 2 days, US$28)

FACT FILE

Population 6.7 million

Language Lao

Religion Theravada Buddhism

Currency Kip (K)

Capital Vientiane

International phone code ☎ 856

Time zone GMT + 7hr

5

Introduction

Until the 1990s, Laos remained shut off from the outside world, and largely unknown to Western travellers. Since then, more and more visitors have come to discover that this landlocked country – ruled by the same communist regime since 1975 – offers some of Southeast Asia's most enchanting natural landscapes and a fascinating diversity of cultures. Although still much less developed than neighbouring Thailand, traveller-oriented services have expanded considerably in recent years. For many travellers a journey through Laos consists of a whistle-stop tour through the two main towns of Vientiane and Luang Prabang, with a stop in Vang Vieng, and perhaps a brief detour to the mysterious Plain of Jars or idyllic Si Phan Don. But those willing to explore further and brave bumpy, often frustratingly long, bus journeys and basic tourist facilities will still find the Laos of old, where people lead traditional, rural lifestyles not much changed over the centuries.

Laos's lifeline is the **Mekong River**, which runs the length of the landlocked country and in places serves as a boundary with Thailand. Set on a broad curve of the Mekong, **Vientiane** is Southeast Asia's most modest capital city and provides an easy, if unexciting, introduction to Laos, offering a string of cosmopolitan cafés to compensate for a relative lack of sights. From here, most travellers dash north to the notorious tubing capital **Vang Vieng**, set in a striking position among limestone karsts, for a few days of cycling, climbing, caving and – despite attempts to reinvent the town's image – partying. From here, one of the most dramatic roads in the country curves through mountains to cultured **Luang Prabang**, once the heart and soul of the ancient kingdom of Lane Xang and now the country's most enticing cityscape, with its spellbinding panoply of gilded temples and weathered shophouses.

The wild highlands of the **far north** are the best for trekking: **Luang Namtha** remains the most popular base from which to arrange treks to nearby hill-tribe villages. From here, you can travel by bus to **Houayxai**, an entry point popular with travellers arriving from Thailand in search of a slow boat for the picturesque journey south to Luang Prabang. Some of the most dramatic scenery in Laos is in the northeast, especially round the towns of **Nong Khiaw** and **Muang Ngoi.** Following routes 6 and 7 south brings you to the **Plain of Jars**, a grassy, war-scarred plateau that's dotted with ancient funerary urns. In the south, the vast majority of travellers zip down Route 13, stopping off in the major southern towns: genial **Savannakhet**, and the important transport hub of **Pakse**. Further south, near the charming small town of **Champasak**, lie the atmospheric ruins of **Wat Phou**, one of the most important Khmer temples outside Cambodia. South again, the lazy river islands of **Si Phan Don** lie scattered across the Mekong, home to traditional fishing communities, thunderous waterfalls and rare Irrawaddy dolphins.

WHEN TO GO

November to February are the most pleasant months to travel in lowland Laos, when daytime temperatures are agreeably warm and evenings slightly chilly; at higher elevations, temperatures can drop to freezing point. In March, temperatures begin to climb, peaking in April, when the lowlands are baking hot and humid. The rains begin in May and last until September.

CHRONOLOGY

Iron Age The Plain of Jars in the northeast dates from around 2000 years ago, and is the earliest known indigenous culture in Laos.

First century AD Indian traders introduce Buddhism to Southeast Asia; between the sixth and ninth centuries, upper Laos is dominated by the Theravada Buddhist culture of the Mon people, known as Dvaravati.

Ninth century The Hindu Khmer Empire of Angkor expands across the whole region, building dozens of Angkor-style temples.

1353 With Khmer support, exiled prince Fa Ngum takes Luang Prabang (then called Xieng Dong Xieng Thong). He establishes the Lane Xang Hom Khao Empire, the "Kingdom of a Million Elephants and the White Parasol", and extends its borders.

1512 The golden Buddha image, the Pha Bang, is brought to Xieng Dong Xieng Thong from Vientiane by King Visoun (1500–20), establishing it as the symbol of a unified Buddhist kingdom.

1563 With the Burmese Empire encroaching, the capital is moved to Vientiane, but the Pha Bang statue is left, and

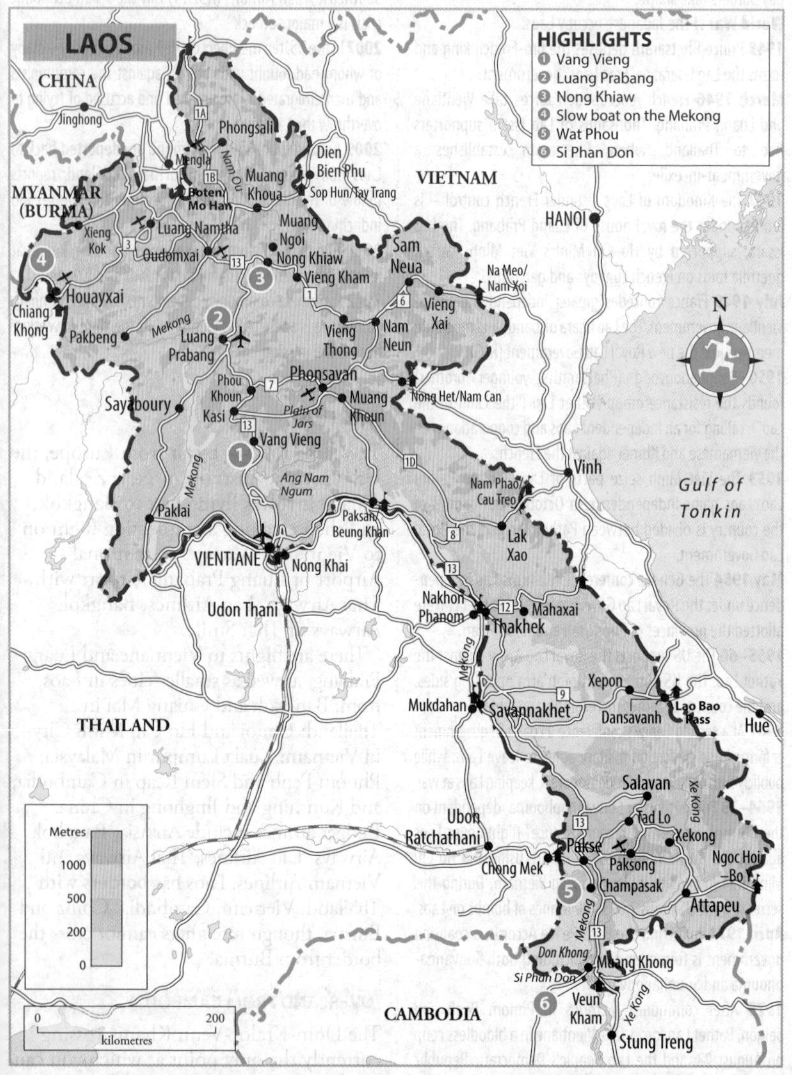

5

Luang Prabang is renamed after it. Burmese warrior-kings reduce the kingdom of Lane Xang to vassalage.

1637–94 The reign of Sourinyavongsa, and the Golden Age of Lane Xang. After his death the region divides into three principalities.

1778 The kingdom of Siam takes Vientiane, capturing the precious Pha Bang statue. Over the next century, Siam and Vietnam compete to control fragmented Lao principalities.

1893 The French vice-consul in Luang Prabang persuades the northern kingdom to pay tribute to France. For half a century, Laos is a French colony, and the country's present-day borders take shape.

World War II The Japanese occupy Laos.

1945 Prince Phetsarath deposes the pro-French king and forms the Lao Issara, or "Free Laos" government.

March 1946 French reoccupation forces take Vientiane and Luang Prabang. Thousands of Lao Issara supporters flee to Thailand, where Phetsarath establishes a government-in-exile.

1947 The Kingdom of Laos – under French control – is unified under the royal house of Luang Prabang. The Lao Issara, supported by Ho Chi Minh's Viet Minh, launch guerrilla raids on French convoys and garrisons.

July 1949 France concedes greater independence to the Vientiane government. The Lao Issara disbands and moderate members join the new Royal Lao Government (RLG).

1950 Souphanouvong (Phetsarath's younger brother) founds the resistance group Pathet Lao ("the Land of the Lao"), calling for an independent Laos and cooperation with the Vietnamese and Khmer against the French.

1953 The Viet Minh seize parts of Laos for the Pathet Lao. Laos gains independence in October, but control of the country is divided between Pathet Lao and the Royal Lao Government.

May 1954 The Geneva conference reaffirms Lao independence under the Royal Lao Government; the Pathet Lao are allotted the provinces of Phongsali and Houa Phan.

1955–60 The US supports the Royal Lao Army against the Pathet Lao. The US and Soviet Union arm opposing sides, and the country becomes increasingly unstable.

1961 At a second Geneva conference a coalition government is formed and all foreign military agree to leave Laos; while publicly supporting this, all sides ignore it, keeping Laos at war.

1964–73 Prime minister Souvannaphouma, dependent on the US, permits "armed reconnaissance" flights over Laos against the North Vietnamese, who are using the Ho Chi Minh Trail in Laos to infiltrate South Vietnam. During this secret war the US drops 2,093,100 tonnes of bombs on Laos.

April 1974 Following the Paris Peace Accords, a coalition government is formed in Laos, including both Souvannaphouma and Souphanouvong.

1975 After communist victories in Phnom Penh and Saigon, Pathet Lao forces take Vientiane in a bloodless coup on August 23, and the Lao People's Democratic Republic (PDR) is proclaimed on December 2. A rigid, socialist regime is established and up to fifty thousand royalists are sent to malaria-ridden labour camps.

1977 The royal family are arrested and exiled to Houa Phan province, ending the centuries-old Lao monarchy.

1986 Prime minister Kaysone Phomvihane implements the New Economic Mechanism, essentially a market economy, though there are no political reforms and dissenters are still arrested.

1992 Diplomatic relations are re-established with the US.

1997 Laos becomes a member of the Association of Southeast Asian Nations (ASEAN) but the Asian economic crisis is a major setback.

2007 In the US, ten members of the Hmong minority – many of whom had fought with the US against the communists and then emigrated – are arrested and accused of trying to overthrow the Lao government.

2009 Around four thousand Hmong are deported back to Laos from refugee camps in northern Thailand; reports follow of retribution for their involvement in the second Indochina War.

2011 Two tropical storms cause severe flooding, killing at least 27 people and washing away roads and villages.

2012 Prominent community development worker Sombath Somphone is abducted in Vientiane. At the time of writing, he was still missing.

ARRIVAL

Travelling to Laos **by air** from Europe, the US, Canada, Australia or New Zealand usually involves flying first to Bangkok, and then catching a connecting flight on to Vientiane's Wattay International Airport or Luang Prabang Airport with Thai Airways, Lao Airlines, Bangkok Airways or Thai Smile.

There are flights to Vientiane and Luang Prabang, as well as smaller cities in Laos, from: Bangkok and Chiang Mai in Thailand; Hanoi and Ho Chi Minh City in Vietnam; Kuala Lumpur in Malaysia; Phnom Penh and Siem Reap in Cambodia; and Kunming and Jinghong in China. Budget airlines include AirAsia, Bangkok Airways, Lao Airlines, Thai Airways and Vietnam Airlines. Laos has **borders** with Thailand, Vietnam, Cambodia, China and Burma, though foreigners cannot cross the border from Burma.

OVERLAND FROM CAMBODIA

The Dom-Kralor-Veun Kham crossing is currently the only point at which you can

cross overland from Cambodia. You can get a visa on arrival here (see below), and may have to pay a small fee of a dollar or two to immigration officials, as well as the visa fee.

OVERLAND FROM CHINA

From the town of Jinghong in China's southwestern Yunnan province, daily buses travel to and from Oudomxai and Luang Namtha. The last town on the Chinese side is the village of Mo Han and the first Lao village you come to is Boten. It's not currently possible to cross into Laos on the river.

OVERLAND FROM THAILAND

There are six main points along the Thai border where Westerners can cross into Laos: Chiang Khong (see box, p.764) to Houayxai; Nong Khai (see box, p.77) to Vientiane; Nakhon Phanom (see p.770) to Thakhek; Mukdahan (see box, p.770) to Savannakhet; Chong Mek (see box, p.769) to Pakse; and Beung Khan to Paksan. At the time of writing, visas on arrival were available at all except the last crossing (see below); check locally for the most up-to-date information before you travel. It's also possible to get a visa in advance from the Lao embassy in Bangkok.

OVERLAND FROM VIETNAM

From Vietnam, it's possible to travel overland into Laos at six main border points: Tay Trang–Sop Hun (see box, p.863); Nam Xoi–Na Meo (see box, p.377); Nam Khan–Nam Can (see box, p.868); Cau Treo–Nam Phao (see box, p.868); Lao Bao–Dansavanh (see box, p.868); Ngoc Hoi–Bo Y (see box, p.889). Lao visas on arrival are available at all of these crossings.

VISAS

Unless you hold a passport from Japan, Russia, Switzerland or one of the ASEAN member states, you'll need a **visa** to enter Laos. The good news is that you probably won't need to arrange it in advance; thirty-day visas are now available on arrival at most international borders. Note that all visitors must hold a passport that is valid for at least six months from the time of entry into Laos. For a visa longer than thirty days, you will have to apply in advance at a Lao embassy (see p.49) or through a travel agency.

Visas on arrival take just a few minutes to process, cost around $35 (prices vary according to nationality), and are available to passengers flying into Luang Prabang Airport, Pakse Airport and Wattay Airport in Vientiane. Those travelling to Laos from Thailand can pick up visas on arrival at any of the border crossings open to foreign tourists (except the border at Paksan), as can those entering from Vietnam (at Nam Khan, Na Meo, Bo Y, Tay Trang, Cau Treo and Lao Bao), Cambodia (Dom Kralor) and China (Mo Han). Only US dollars are accepted as payment and a passport-sized photo is required. If you forget the photo, border officials will usually turn a blind eye for an extra $1.

Officially, only the immigration office in Vientiane can issue **visa extensions**, but a number of travel agents in other towns (particularly Luang Prabang and Vientiane) can arrange it for you. The extension charge is $2 per day; the maximum length of a visa extension is sixty days. If you overstay your visa, you'll generally have to pay around $10 for each extra day you spend in the country when you exit Laos; this is paid (in cash) to immigration when you leave the country.

GETTING AROUND

Boats, the traditional means of travel in Laos, still ply the Mekong and its tributaries, but **buses** are now the predominant form of transport in most areas. Regardless of whether you go by road or river, you only need to travel for a week or two in Laos before realizing that timetables are flexible and estimated times of arrival pointless. It is also possible to fly, although this is obviously not the most economic mode of transport. Considering the scenery you'd be missing and the chances for interaction with locals, it's usually worth taking the time to travel by road or river instead.

5

PLANES

The government-owned **Lao Airlines** (laoairlines.com) is the country's main domestic carrier. Its safety record is patchy, to say the least; in October 2013, a Lao Airlines turboprop travelling from Vientiane hit bad weather, plunging into the Mekong as it approached Pakse, killing all 49 people on board. Since the accident the airline has continued to operate as normal, and it still has the most comprehensive domestic schedule by far, with flights from Vientiane to Oudomxai, Luang Namtha, Luang Prabang, Houayxai, Pakse and Xieng Khuang (for the Plain of Jars). Laos' first private airline, **Lao Central Airlines** (flylaocentral.com), has a small fleet flying between Vientiane, Luang Prabang and Bangkok, and has now been joined by **Lao Skyway** (laoskyway.com), who operate flights between Vientiane and several northern destinations including Luang Prabang, Houayxai, Luang Namtha and Oudomxai.

BOATS

The main boat **route** is along the Mekong River between Houayxai and Luang Prabang; smaller passenger **boats** normally also cruise up the Nam Ou River, linking Luang Prabang to Nong Khiaw, Muang Ngoi and points north, though at the time of writing the Luang Prabang–Nong Khiaw service had been suspended. As infrastructure improves and ambitious dam projects block traditional river routes, more and more Lao are opting to travel by road.

The **slow boats** (*heua sa*) that ply the Houayxai to Luang Prabang route are fitted with seats for passengers – these can be anything from cushioned wooden benches to seats that appear to have been lifted from a minibus. Some boats are kitted out with a small shop selling basic provisions like crisps and Beerlao. An overnight stop is made (in both directions) at Pakbeng (see p.387), where you can stock up on supplies.

Parts of the Mekong are also plied by a dwindling number of **speedboats** (*heua wai*), which are a more costly but faster alternative to the slow boats. Connecting towns along the river all the way to the Chinese border, these 5m terrors accommodate up to eight passengers and can shave hours off a river journey. Fares for speedboats cost two to three times the slow-boat fare. Crash helmets are handed out before journeys and life jackets are occasionally available. Think twice about taking a speedboat, however: the Mekong has some tricky stretches, and can be particularly rough late in the rainy season. Fatal accidents occur with an alarming frequency. You should insist on a life jacket and helmet.

BUSES

Buses in Laos range from air-conditioned coaches to rattling wrecks; cramped, overloaded and extremely slow, the latter can be profound tests of endurance and patience – however, until you get on the bus, there's often no way to tell in advance which you're likely to get.

Scheduled toilet stops are few and far between, so it's usual to ask the driver to stop when nature calls; passengers usually relieve themselves by the side of the road. Keep in mind that some areas are still littered with unexploded ordnance (see box, p.379), so although you may want privacy, it's not a good idea to go too far off the road.

Ordinary buses run between major towns, and often link provincial hubs with their surrounding areas. In most cases, tickets should be bought from the bus station before boarding; if you're picking up a bus in the middle of its route, however, you pay on board. It's a good idea to turn up at the bus station at least half an hour before your bus's scheduled departure, especially in major transport centres where buses may leave as soon as they're full. **Timetables** are usually posted above or next to the ticket office, though published times should be taken with a pinch of salt. Most buses leave in the morning – usually between 7am and 9am – but popular routes may have a lunchtime departure, and some tourist-focused nightbuses run between major towns and on long-distance routes (for example, Vientiane to Pakse). Despite road improvements, travelling around Laos by bus is often still painfully slow – your bus might only depart when

there are enough passengers, it may stop numerous times to pick up people (and food) along the road, and you'll often find yourself crammed in with more people (and animals) than you would normally think could fit into the space. Be patient and good-humoured, however, and the experience will be more than worthwhile.

MINIBUSES

In major tourist centres – most of the places listed in this chapter, in fact – it's also possible to travel to your next destination by **minibus**. These are popular with locals and tourists, though depending on the number of people on board (drivers love to fill their seats), they may not actually be any more comfortable than travelling by local bus. Tickets can be bought from guesthouses, travel agents and minibus stations, and usually include pick-up from your accommodation. Travelling by minibus is generally a little quicker (and more dangerous) than travelling by local bus, and you will normally have to pay a small premium for the privilege – usually 10,000–50,000K extra per journey.

SAWNGTHAEWS

In most provinces, the local bus network is complemented by **sawngthaews** – converted pick-up trucks – into which drivers cram as many passengers as they can get onto two benches in the back. They usually depart from the regular bus station and, though they will have scheduled hours, often only leave when there are enough passengers to make the trip worthwhile. Sometimes the fare is paid towards the end of the ride, but if you get on at a bus station you will often be asked to pay before you leave. To catch a sawngthaew in remote areas simply flag it down from the side of the road and tell the driver where you're headed.

JUMBOS AND TUK-TUKS

Transport within Lao towns is by motorized samlors (literally "three wheels"), which function as shared taxis for up to four or five passengers. There are two types of samlor: **jumbos** and **tuk-tuks**. Jumbos are home-made three-wheelers consisting of a two-wheeled carriage welded to the side of a motorcycle; these days, they're seen rather infrequently outside Pakse. Tuk-tuks are just bigger, sturdier jumbos, with up to eight passengers crammed into the back. To catch one, flag it down and tell the driver where you're going. You pay at the end of the ride, but make sure you agree the fare before you get in. Rates vary according to the number of passengers, the distance travelled and your bargaining skills.

VEHICLE RENTAL

Renting a car can be prohibitively expensive, and though self-drive car rental is possible in Laos, it's easier (and safer) to hire a **car and driver**. In most major towns, tour agencies have air-conditioned vans and 4WD pick-up trucks, and can provide drivers as well. Prices can be as much as $80 to $100 per day, plus fuel. Always clarify who pays for petrol and repairs, as well as the driver's food and lodging, and be sure to ask what happens in case of a major breakdown or accident. A much cheaper alternative for short distances or day-trips is to charter a tuk-tuk or sawngthaew.

Renting a **motorbike** costs 50,000–100,000K per day. 250cc dirt bikes are available in larger cities, but elsewhere you'll be limited to 100cc step-throughs such as the Honda Dream. A licence is not required and insurance is not available, so make sure you have travel insurance coverage. Before zooming off, check the bike thoroughly for any damage and take it for a test run. Few rental places will have a helmet on offer, but it doesn't hurt to ask. **Bicycles** can be rented from guesthouses and tourist-oriented shops in most towns for around 10,000–15,000K per day, depending on the quality.

ACCOMMODATION

Inexpensive **accommodation** can be found all over Laos. For a basic double room, prices start at around 40,000K in smaller towns, but in Vientiane and Luang Prabang you can expect to pay

5

> **STREET NAMES**
> Only a handful of cities in Laos actually have street names, signs are rare, and many roads change names from block to block. Use street names to find a hotel on a map in the guide text, but when asking directions or telling a tuk-tuk driver where to go, it's usually best to refer to a landmark, monastery or prominent hotel.

around 70,000K. Thankfully, large Lao cities have an increasing number of **dorm beds**, going for as little as 30,000K per night. Elsewhere, a very simple double or single room with a shared bathroom will be the cheapest option.

Standards and room types can vary widely within the same establishment so it's worth looking at several rooms before choosing one. **Electricity** is supplied at 220 volts AC; two-pin sockets are the norm. En-suite showers and flush toilets are now found in almost every hotel, though a dying breed of very cheap places still have communal facilities and squat toilets. Note that most guesthouses and hotels will advertise hot water, but "hot" can often be less than lukewarm, and may depend on the time of day and how many other people are showering at the same time.

The distinction between a **guesthouse** and a **hotel** is blurred in Laos. Either can denote anything ranging from a bamboo-and-thatch hut to a multistorey concrete building. An increasing number of guesthouses take advance bookings through sites like Ⓦagoda.com and Ⓦbooking.com, though few have their own website.

Mid-range hotels are common in medium-sized towns and are mostly four- or five-storey affairs, offering large rooms with tiled floors and en-suite bathrooms from around 120,000K. The beds are usually hard but the sheets and quilts are clean, and often you'll get TV, wi-fi and air conditioning thrown in too.

FOOD AND DRINK

Fiery and fragrant, with a touch of sour, **Lao food** owes its distinctive taste to fermented fish sauces, lemongrass, coriander leaves, chillies and lime juice and is closely related to Thai cuisine. Eaten with the hands along with the staple sticky rice, much of traditional Lao cuisine is roasted over an open fire and served with fresh herbs and vegetables. Pork, chicken, duck and water buffalo all end up in the kitchen, but freshwater fish is the main source of protein. An ingredient in many recipes is *nâm pa*, or fish sauce, which is used like salt. Most Lao cooking includes fish sauce so you may want to order "*baw sai nâm pa*" ("without fish sauce") if you are a vegetarian.

Vientiane and Luang Prabang have the country's best food, with excellent Lao food and international cuisine, but in remote towns you'll be faced with trying some of the more daring local dishes, such as ant egg soup, or sticking to noodle soups and fried rice. Although Laos is a Buddhist country, very few Lao are **vegetarian**. It's fairly easy, however, to get a vegetable dish or vegetable fried rice. As for **hygiene**, Laos kitchens are often nothing more than shacks without proper lighting or even running water. Sticking to well-frequented places is the safest bet, but it is by no means a guarantee that you won't get an upset stomach. In any case, do not drink tap water, try to avoid cooked food that has been left standing, and only eat fruit that you can peel.

WHERE TO EAT

The **cheapest** places for food are markets, street stalls and noodle shops. Despite their name, **morning markets** (*talat sâo*) remain open all day and provide a focal point for noodle stalls (*hân khãi fõe*), coffee vendors, fruit stands and sellers of crusty French loaves. In Luang Prabang and Vientiane, vendors hawking pre-made dishes gather in **evening markets** (*talat láeng*) towards late afternoon. Takeaways such as grilled chicken (*pîng kai*), spicy papaya salad (*tam màk hung*) and minced pork salad (*larp mu*) are commonly available.

Some **noodle shops** and street stalls feature a makeshift kitchen surrounded by a handful of tables and stools. Most stalls will specialize in only one general

food type, or even only one dish; for example a stall with a mortar and pestle, unripe papayas and plastic bags full of pork rinds will only offer spicy papaya salads. Similarly, a noodle shop will generally only prepare noodles with or without broth. A step up from street stalls and noodle shops are *hân kin deum*, literally "eat-drink shops", where you'll find a somewhat greater variety of dishes along with beer and whisky.

The concept of eating out is relatively new in Laos, so the majority of **restaurants** (*hân ahăn*) are aimed at tourists; for a more local experience, it's best to head to the places mentioned above. Most proper restaurants that are frequented by locals are usually run by ethnic Vietnamese and Chinese, and may have a limited (or no) English-language menu.

LAO FOOD

Most Lao meals feature **sticky rice** (*khào niaw*), which is served in a lidded wicker basket (*típ khào*) and eaten with the hands. Typically, the rice will be accompanied by a fish or meat dish and soup, with a plate of fresh vegetables, such as string beans, lettuce, basil and mint, served on the side. Grab a small chunk of rice from the basket, squeeze it into a firm wad and then dip it into one of the dishes. It's thought to be bad luck not to replace the lid at the end of your meal. Plain, steamed, white rice (*khào jâo*) is eaten with a fork and spoon; chopsticks (*mâi thu*) are reserved for noodles.

So that a variety of tastes can be enjoyed during the course of a meal, Lao meals are eaten **communally**, with each dish, including the soup, being served at once rather than in courses. For two of you, order two or three dishes, plus rice.

If Laos were to nominate a **national dish**, a strong contender would be *larp*, a "salad" of minced meat mixed with garlic, chillies, shallots, galangal, fish sauce and ground sticky rice. Another quintessentially Lao dish is *tam màk hung* (or *tam sòm*), a spicy salad made with shredded green papaya, garlic, chillies, lime juice and fish paste (*pa dàek*). Usually not too far away from any *tam màk hung* vendor, you'll find someone selling *pîng kai* (basted grilled chicken). Grilled fish (*pîng pa*) is another favourite, with the whole fish skewered and barbecued.

Fõe, the ubiquitous **noodle soup**, is primarily eaten for breakfast, though usually found in markets throughout the day. The basic bowl of *fõe* consists of a light broth, to which is added thin rice noodles and slices of meat (usually beef or water buffalo). It is usually served with a plate of lettuce, mint, coriander leaves and bean sprouts, which you add to your dish alongside table condiments like fish- and chilli sauce. Also on offer at many noodle shops is *mi*, a yellow wheat noodle served in broth with slices of meat and a few vegetables.

The best way to round off a meal is with **fresh fruit** (*màk mâi*), as the country offers a wide variety including guava, lychee, rambutan, mangosteen and pomelo. Markets often have a food stall specializing in inexpensive **coconut-milk desserts,** generally called *nâm wān* – look for a stall displaying a dozen bowls containing everything from water chestnuts to fluorescent green and pink jellies.

DRINKS

The Lao don't drink **water** straight from the tap and nor should you; contaminated water is a major cause of sickness. Plastic bottles of drinking water (*nâm deum*) are sold countrywide for 2000–5000K. Noodle shops and inexpensive restaurants generally serve free pitchers of weak tea or boiled water (*nâm tóm*), which is fine, although perhaps not as foolproof. Most of the **ice** you'll encounter in Laos is produced in large blocks under hygienic conditions, but it can become less pure in transit or storage, so be wary. Brand-name soft drinks are widely available; more refreshing are the **fruit shakes** (*màk mâi pan*) available in larger towns, which consist of your choice of fruit blended with ice, liquid sugar and sweetened condensed milk.

The Lao drink very strong **coffee**, or *kafeh hâwn*, which is served with sweetened condensed milk and sugar. If you prefer your coffee black and without sugar, ask

for *kafeh dam baw sai nâm tan*. Black **tea** is available at most coffee vendors and is mixed with sweetened condensed milk, when you request *sá hâwn*.

Alcohol

Beerlao (*Bia Lao*) is a very enjoyable, cheap brew sold throughout the country for around 10,000K for a large bottle. In Vientiane and Luang Prabang, draught Beerlao known as *bia sót* is often available at bargain prices by the litre. Drunk with equal gusto is *lào-láo*, a clear **rice alcohol** with the fire of a blinding Mississippi moonshine. *Lào-láo* is usually sold in whatever bottle the distiller had around at the time (look twice before you buy that bottle of Pepsi) and is sold at drink shops and general stores for around 5000K per 750ml.

CULTURE AND ETIQUETTE

Laos by and large shares the same attitudes to dress and **social taboos** as other Theravada Buddhist Southeast Asian cultures (see p.40). The lowland Lao traditionally **greet** each other with a *nop* – bringing their hands together in a prayer-like gesture. The status of the persons giving and returning the *nop* determines how they will execute it, so most Lao prefer to shake hands with Westerners. If you do receive a *nop* as a gesture of greeting or thank you, it is best to reply with a smile and nod of the head.

Take care to respect Lao attitudes to religion by sticking to basic temple etiquette; don't dress too provocatively, and always remove your shoes before entering the temple. It can also cause offence to photograph monks and images of the Buddha. It's important that women should never touch Buddhist monks, novices, or their clothes, and should also not hand objects directly to them.

SPORTS AND OUTDOOR ACTIVITIES

Laos's landscape is a sports haven: mountainous highlands and ethnic villages for trekkers; well-paved, relatively traffic-free routes for bike enthusiasts; and rivers for rafters and kayakers. Outdoor activities and adventure companies include **Green Discovery** (T 021 264 528, W greendiscovery.org) and **Tiger Trail** (T 071 252655, W laos-adventures.com), which organize kayaking, rafting, trekking and cycling trips.

TREKKING

Trekking is gaining popularity in Laos, especially in the northern part of the country, though in recent years there has been an increase in trekking opportunities in the south. The main centres are Luang Prabang (see p.368) and Luang Namtha (see p.383), where it's easy to arrange a few days' hiking through forests and sleeping at village homestays, offering the opportunity to experience authentic Lao life.

Companies like Green Discovery will lead you through spectacular wildlife on ecotours that cross through national parks called **National Biodiversity Conservation Areas (NBCA)**, which are host to a wealth of diverse flora and fauna. Despite these areas being officially protected, poaching remains a problem and habitats continue to be destroyed.

CYCLING

Cycling is an increasingly popular way to explore Laos. Organized trips are provided by companies such as London-based Red Spokes (T 0207 502 7252, W redspokes .co.uk), which runs a popular two-week tour that takes in Luang Prabang, Vang Vieng and Vientiane, as well as some rural stretches with spectacular scenery. It's also possible to rent fairly good mountain bikes in towns like Vang Vieng (see p.364) and set off on your own adventure around the countryside.

WATERSPORTS

Watersports fans can opt for **whitewater rafting** trips out of Luang Prabang on the northern rivers such as the Nam Ou, the Nam Xeuang and the Nam Ming. Those who prefer a more relaxed paddle can **kayak** downriver at a slower pace while taking in the lovely views of Vang Vieng (see p.364), Muang Ngoi (see p.381) and Si Phan Don (see p.397), among others.

Tubing on the Nam Song in Vang Vieng (see p.364) is still the most popular watersport in Laos, as much for the bars along the route as for the afternoon spent floating along the river.

CAVING AND ROCK CLIMBING

Caving and **rock climbing** are best at Vang Vieng, where Laos's first bolted cliff face has several routes available for all abilities. With so many limestone karsts, Laos offers plenty of opportunities for caving, from Vang Vieng to the area just east of Thakhek in South Central Laos. For any caving excursion, remember to take a head torch and some good footwear.

COMMUNICATIONS

Most mobile phones and smartphones bought in recent years can be used in Laos, though call, text and data charges will be high, so if you're planning on using your phone it's worth buying a local SIM card. These are readily available from shops and markets, and for around 35,000K you'll be able to buy a package with enough data to last you several weeks of daily use. Local network Unitel has excellent 3G coverage in even mid-sized towns. Top-up cards can be purchased in villages across Laos that have even the most basic shop – just look for the flag displaying the network's name. **Regional codes** are given throughout the chapter: the "0" must be dialled before all long-distance calls.

Internet cafés are found all over the country; charges range from around 5000–10,000K an hour. In tourist areas especially, **free wi-fi** is widespread.

LAOS ONLINE

ecotourismlaos.com An informative website by the Lao National Tourism Administration that features helpful tips on exploring Laos's national parks.

laoembassy.com Website of the Lao embassy to the United States features tourist info and the latest visa regulations.

laos-guide-999.com Good, locally made website with information on transport, visas and Lao culture.

vientianetimes.com News, accommodation listings and links to hundreds of other websites on Laos.

CRIME AND SAFETY

Laos is a relatively **safe country** for travellers. For the most part, if you keep your wits about you, you shouldn't have any problems. Theft – especially among travellers – is likely to be your greatest worry (aside from UXO, see box, p.379). If you have anything stolen, you'll need to get the police to write up a report for your insurance; bring along a translator if you can.

UNEXPLODED ORDNANCE

The Second Indochina War left Laos with a legacy of **bombs**, **land mines** and **mortar shells** that will haunt the country for decades to come, despite the efforts of de-mining organizations. Round, tennis-ball-sized anti-personnel bomblets, known as "bombies", are the most common type of **unexploded ordnance** (UXO). Larger bombs, ranging in size from 100kg to 1000kg, also abound.

Although most towns and tourist sites are free of UXO, 25 percent of villages remain contaminated. As accidents often occur while people are tending their fields, the risk faced by the average visitor is extremely limited. Nonetheless, the number-one rule is: don't be a trailblazer. When in rural areas, always stay on well-worn paths, even when passing through a village, and don't pick up or kick at anything if you don't know what it is.

DRUGS

It is **illegal** to smoke ganja and opium in Laos, although these and other drugs (including magic mushrooms) are still available in some places. Tourists who use illegal drugs risk substantial "fines" if caught by police, who do not need a warrant to search you or your room. Wide-scale government crackdowns on drug tourism have been effective, especially in Vang Vieng, but other areas such as the touristy islands of Si Phan Don have found ways to sell drugs openly.

LAO

The main language of Laos is Lao. The spoken Lao of Vientiane is very similar to the Thai spoken in Bangkok, though there are pockets of Laos where no dialect of Lao, much less the Vientiane version, will be heard. Since economic liberalization, English has become the preferred foreign tongue, and it's quite possible to get by without Lao in the towns. Out in the countryside, you will need some Lao phrases.

PRONUNCIATION

The dialect of Lao spoken in Vientiane, which has been deemed the official language of Laos, has six tones. Thus, depending on its tone, the word *"sang"* can mean either "elephant", "craftsman", "granary", "laryngitis", a species of bamboo, or "to build".

a as the "ah" in "autobahn"
ae as the "a" in "cat"
ai as in "Thai"
aw as in "jaw"
ao as in "Lao"
e as in "pen"
eu as in French "fleur"
i as in "mimi"
ia as in "India"
o as in "flow"
oe as in "Goethe"
u (or ou) as the "ou" in "you"
ua (or oua) as the "ua" in "truant"
b as in "big"
d as in "dog"
f as in "fun"
h as in "hello"
j (or ch) as in "jar"
k as in "skin" (unaspirated)
kh as the "k" in "kiss"
l as in "luck"
m as in "more"
n as in "now"
ng as in "singer" (this combination sometimes appears at the beginning of a word)
ny as in the Russian "nyet"
p as in "speak" (unaspirated)
ph as the "p" in "pill"
s (or x) as in "same"
t as in "stop" (unaspirated)
th as the "t" in "tin"
w (or v) as in "wish"
y as in "yes"

WORDS AND PHRASES IN LAO

Questions in Lao are not normally answered with a yes or no. Instead the verb used in the question is repeated for the answer. For example: "Do you have a room?" (*"mí hàwng wàng baw"*), would be answered "Have" (*"mí"*) in the affirmative or "No have" (*"baw mí"*) in the negative.

GREETINGS AND BASIC PHRASES

Hello	*Sabai di*
Goodbye	*Lá kawn*
Goodbye (in reply)	*Sok di*
How are you?	*Sabai di baw*
I'm fine	*Sabai di*
Please (rarely used)	*Kaluna*
Thank you (very much)	*Khop jai (lai lai)*
Do you speak English?	*Jâo wâo phasã angkit dâi baw*
I don't understand	*Khói baw khào jai*
Yes	*Lâew*
No	*Baw*
Right/Left	*Khwã/Sâi*
Where are you from?	*Jâo má tae sãi*
Hospital	*Dae*
I need a doctor	*Khói tâwng kan hã mãw*
Where is the …?	*… yu sãi*
Can you help me?	*Jâo suay khói dâi baw*
Police station	*Sathani tamluat*
Do you have any rooms?	*Mí hàwng wàng baw*
Can I have the bill?	*Khãw sek dae*
How much is this?	*An nî thao dai?*
Foreigner	*Falang*

NUMBERS

0	*sun*
1	*neung*
2	*sãwng*
3	*sãm*
4	*si*
5	*hà*
6	*hók*
7	*jét*
8	*pàet*
9	*kâo*
10	*síp*
11, 12, etc	*síp ét, síp sãwng*

20	*sao*
21, 22, 23, etc	*sao ét, sao sãwng, sao sãm*

FOOD AND DRINKS GLOSSARY

I can't eat meat	*khói kin sîn baw dâi*
No ice	*baw sai nâm kâwn*

Meat, fish and basic foods

jeun khai	omelette
kai	chicken
khào jâo	rice, steamed
khào ji	bread
khào niaw	rice, sticky
kûng	shrimp
màk phét	chilli
mu	pork
nâm kat	coconut milk
nâm pa	fish sauce
nâm tan	sugar
nóm sòm	yoghurt
pa	fish
pa dàek	fish paste
pét	duck
phák	vegetables
pu	crab
sìn ngúa	beef
tâo hû	bean curd

Fruit

màk kûay	banana
màk mî	jackfruit
màk mo	watermelon
màk muang	mango
màk náo	lime/lemon
màk nat	pineapple
màk phom	apple

Noodles

fõe	rice noodle soup
fõe hàeng	rice noodle soup without broth
fõe khùa	fried rice noodles
khào piak sèn	rice noodle soup, served in chicken broth
khào pûn	flour noodles with sauce
mi hàeng	yellow wheat noodles without broth
mi nâm	yellow wheat noodle soup

30, 40, 50, etc	*sãm síp, si síp, hà síp*
100	*hôi*
1000	*phán*

Everyday dishes

khào ji pateh	bread with Lao-style pâté and vegetables
khào khùa or khào phát	fried rice
khào khùa sai kai	fried rice with chicken
khùa khing kai	chicken with ginger
khùa phák baw sai sìn	stir-fried vegetables
larp mu	minced pork
mu phát bai hólapha	pork with basil over rice
pîng kai	grilled chicken
pîng pa or jeun pa	grilled fish
tam màk hung	spicy papaya salad
tôm yam pa	spicy fish soup with lemon grass
yam sìn ngúa	spicy beef salad
yáw díp	spring rolls, fresh
yáw jeun	spring rolls, fried

Desserts

khào lãm	sticky rice in coconut milk cooked in bamboo
khào niaw màk muang	sticky rice with mango

Drinks

bia	beer
bia sót	beer, draught
kafeh	coffee
kafeh dam	black coffee
kafeh nóm hawn	hot Lao coffee (with milk and sugar)
kafeh nóm yén	iced coffee (with milk and sugar)
lào-láo	rice whisky
màk kûay pan	banana shake
màk mai pan	fruit shake
nâm deum	water
nâm kâwn	ice
nâm sá	tea
nóm	milk, usually sweetened condensed
sá jin	tea, Chinese

EMERGENCY NUMBERS

In **Vientiane** dial the following numbers: Dial T **190** in case of fire, T **195** for an ambulance, or T **1191** for police.

MEDICAL CARE AND EMERGENCIES

You'll find **pharmacies** in all the major towns and cities. Pharmacists in Vientiane and Luang Prabang are quite knowledgeable and have a decent supply of medicines.

Otherwise, healthcare in Laos is so poor as to be virtually nonexistent. The nearest **medical care** of any competence is in neighbouring Thailand, and if you find yourself afflicted by anything more serious than travellers' diarrhoea, it's best to head for the closest Thai border crossing and check into a hospital. If you're in Vientiane and the problem is not urgent, you could also try the Alliance International Medical Centre (T 021 513095 W aimclao.com) at the Honda Complex on Souphanuvong Road.

INFORMATION AND MAPS

The **Lao National Tourism Administration** (LNTA; W tourismlaos.org) operates offices in most major towns, and the staff are generally well trained and knowledgeable, though the level of English spoken varies from office to office. Green Discovery and Diethelm Travel (W diethelmtravel.com), two privately owned companies with offices in most major towns, can also provide reliable information. Word-of-mouth information from other travellers is often the best source, as conditions in Laos change with astonishing rapidity.

Good **maps** for Laos are difficult to find. The best road map of the country is the *Laos PDR Map* published by Golden Triangle Rider and available in Vientiane or online at W gt-rider.com. Other detailed maps of the country are also available from bookshops in Vientiane (see p.363). For town maps, in addition to those in this book, Hobo Maps (W hobomaps.com) provide easy-to-use maps of various tourist towns, which are available online or from local bookshops.

MONEY AND BANKS

Lao currency is the **kip** and is available in 100,000K, 50,000K, 20,000K, 10,000K, 5000K, 2000K, 1000K and 500K notes. There are no coins in circulation. Although a 1990 law technically forbids the use of foreign currencies to pay for local goods and services, some hotels, restaurants and tour operators (usually when the price is over 200,000K) actually quote their prices in dollars and accept payment in either **baht**, **dollars** or **kip**.

At the time of writing, the official **exchange rate** was around 8000 kip to the US dollar, 13,500 kip to the pound sterling and 240 kip to the Thai baht.

You can find ATMs in almost every large Lao town, and most will accept both Visa and MasterCard. Withdrawals usually incur a local charge of 20,000K, though there are machines that will dispense money without charging (your bank may still charge you). It's a good idea to have a decent supply of US dollars or Thai baht in **cash** if you intend to spend time in the remoter parts of the country, or if you wish to leave Laos and re-enter (the visa on arrival fee is only payable in dollars). Major **credit cards** are accepted at many hotels, upmarket restaurants and shops in Vientiane and Luang Prabang, and most tour operators will accept card payments. **Cash advances** on Visa cards and, less frequently, MasterCard are possible in most major towns. Bear in mind that you cannot change kip back into dollars or baht once you have left the country. Travellers' cheques are no longer accepted by any banks in Laos.

COSTS

Given the potential volatility of the kip, some mid-range hotels and tour agencies have opted to fix their rates to the dollar. However, prices for guesthouses, transport and entrance fees will almost always be quoted in kip. Some of these places will also accept dollars and Thai baht, but the rate will always be more favourable if you pay in kip, and most local businesses prefer it.

While restaurants and some shops have fixed prices, you should always **bargain** in

markets and when chartering transport (fares on long-distance passenger vehicles are fixed). Room rates can often be bargained for in low season. **Price tiering** does exist in Laos, with foreigners paying more than locals for entry to museums and famous sites.

OPENING HOURS AND HOLIDAYS

While official hours for **government offices** are 8am to noon and 1 to 5pm Monday to Friday, very little gets done between 11am and 2pm. **Post office** hours are variable, but they are generally open 8am to 4pm Monday to Friday, often with a lunch break of an hour or two in the middle. **Banking hours** are usually 8.30am to noon and 1 to 3.30pm, Monday to Friday nationwide; exchange kiosks often keep longer hours. All government businesses close on public holidays (see below), though some shops and restaurants may stay open. The only time when many private businesses do close – for three to seven days – is during Chinese New Year (new moon in late Jan to mid-Feb), when the ethnic-Vietnamese and Chinese populations of Vientiane, Thakhek, Savannakhet and Pakse celebrate with parties and temple visits.

Morning food and drink **stalls** are up and running at about 7am, while night stalls are usually open from 6 to 9pm. Most **restaurants** are open daily until about 10pm.

PUBLIC HOLIDAYS

January 1 New Year's Day
January 6 Pathet Lao Day
January 20 Army Day
March 8 Women's Day
March 22 Lao People's Party Day
April 13–15 Lao New Year
May 1 International Labour Day
June 1 Children's Day
August 13 Lao Issara
August 23 Liberation Day
October 12 Freedom from France Day
December 2 National Day

PEOPLE

The **Lao Loum** (or lowland Lao) make up the majority in Laos: between fifty percent and sixty percent of the population. They prefer to inhabit river valleys and practise Theravada Buddhism as well as some animist rituals. Of all the ethnicities found in Laos, the culture of the lowland Lao is dominant, mainly because it is they who hold political power. Their language is the official language, their religion is the state religion and their holy days are the official holidays.

MON-KHMER GROUPS

The **Khamu** of northern Laos, speakers of a Mon-Khmer language, are the most numerous of the indigenes, and have assimilated to a high degree.

Another Mon-Khmer-speaking group that inhabits the north are the **Htin**. Owing to a partial cultural ban on the use of any kind of metal, the Htin excel at fashioning bamboo baskets and fish traps.

HIGHLAND GROUPS

The **Lao Soung** (literally the "high Lao") live at the highest elevations and include the Hmong, Mien, Lahu and Akha.

The **Hmong** are the most numerous, with a population of approximately 200,000. Hmong apparel is among the most colourful to be found in Laos and their silver jewellery is prized by collectors. Their written language uses Roman letters and was devised by Western missionaries.

SOUTHERN PEOPLES

The Bolaven Plateau in southern Laos is named for the **Laven** people, a Mon-Khmer-speaking group whose presence pre-dates that of the Lao. The Laven were very quick to assimilate the ways of the southern Lao. Other Mon-Khmer-speaking minorities found in the south, particularly in Savannakhet and Salavan, include the **Bru**, who are skilled builders of animal traps; the **Gie-Trieng**, who are expert basket weavers; the **Nge**, who produce textiles featuring stylized bombs and fighter planes; and the **Katu**, a very warlike people.

5

FESTIVALS

All major **festivals**, whether Buddhist or animist, feature parades, music and dancing, not to mention the copious consumption of *lào-láo*. Because the Lao calendar is dictated by both solar and lunar rhythms, the dates of festivals change from year to year. Tourists are usually welcome to participate in the more public Buddhist festivals, but at hill-tribe festivals you should only watch from a distance.

Festivals of most interest to tourists include:

February The Makkha Busa Buddhist holy day, observed under a full moon in February, commemorates a legendary sermon given by the Buddha.

April Lao New Year, or Pi Mai Lao, is celebrated all over Laos in mid-April, most stunningly in Luang Prabang, where the town's namesake Buddha image is ritually bathed.

May During Bun Bang Fai, also known as the rocket festival, crude projectiles are made from stout bamboo poles stuffed with gunpowder and fired skywards. It's hoped the thunderous noise will encourage the spirits to make it rain after months of dry weather.

October Lai Heau Fai, on the full moon in October, is a festival of lights most magically celebrated in Luang Prabang. Residents build large floats and festoon them with lights.

November That Luang Festival, which takes place in Vientiane in the days leading up to the full moon, kicks off with a colourful procession around the country's most famous stupa as locals seek to make merit.

December–January Bun Pha Wet, which commemorates the Jataka tale of the Buddha's second-to-last incarnation as Pha Wet, or Prince Vessantara, takes place at local monasteries on various dates throughout December or January. In larger towns, expect live bands and dancing.

Vientiane and around

Hugging a bend of the Mekong River, the low-rise capital of Laos is a quaint and easy-going place. Arriving in **VIENTIANE** from other cities in the region, your first impression is likely to be of a small, fairly quiet, dusty town; arriving from elsewhere in Laos, however, the city feels very much like a buzzing metropolis. In the twenty-odd years since Laos reopened its doors to foreign visitors, Vientiane has changed with dizzying rapidity. Today, with foreign investment continuing to pour in, the city is growing fast, and swish black Range Rovers easily outnumber rusting tuk-tuks. Along with new shopping malls and luxurious high-rise developments, the city has a thriving tourist economy and some excellent places to stay. That said, it remains one of Southeast Asia's quietest and easily navigable capital cities, and the people have managed to retain their hospitality and sense of humour.

A few hours north of the capital is **Vang Vieng**, a notorious backpacker hangout set amid spectacular scenery on the road to Luang Prabang. Despite attempts to reinvent the town as an outdoor destination, it remains a favourite stop on the backpacker route through Laos, and for many, tubing (and drinking) on the scenic Nam Song River is still the biggest draw.

VIENTIANE

Two days is sufficient to see Vientiane's main sights, though those who stick around longer will find plenty to keep them occupied. The impressive collection of Lao art at **Haw Pha Kaew** should be high on any visitor's list, as should the placid Buddhist monastery known as **Wat Sisaket**. At sunset, it's worth taking a ride out to **That Luang**, Laos's most important religious building, to admire the shimmer of warm sunrays across its golden surface. The city's most eye-opening attraction is the **COPE Visitor Centre**, which highlights some of the challenges faced by ordinary Lao people whose lives continue to be affected by ordnance dropped during the Second Indochina War. A more light-hearted day-trip destination is **Xieng Khuan** or the "**Buddha Park**", a Hindu-Buddhist fantasy in ferro-concrete on the banks of the Mekong.

WHAT TO SEE AND DO

The plaza surrounding **Nam Phou Fountain** marks the heart of tourist-friendly Vientiane, near which you'll

find the greatest concentration of accommodation, restaurants and shops catering to visitors. The fountain, which once created a pleasant public space for locals and foreigners to cool off after the sun goes down, has now been converted into a tacky outdoor food court with live music most evenings.

The Lao National Museum

North of Nam Phou, on Samsenthai Road, the dingy **Lao National Museum** (daily 8am–noon & 1–4pm; 10,000K) deals primarily with the events, both ancient and recent, that led to the "inevitable victory" of the proletariat in 1975. Inside, scenes portray Lao patriots liberating the motherland from Thai and Burmese feudalists, and French colonialists bull-whipping villagers. Black-and-white photographs tell the story of the struggle against "the Japanese fascists" and "American imperialists".

Wat Sisaket

Towards the southeastern end of Setthathilat Road, the street running parallel to and just south of Samsenthai Road, stands **Wat Sisaket** (daily 8am–noon & 1–4pm; 5000K), the oldest wat in Vientiane. Constructed by King Anouvong (Chao Anou) in 1818, it was the only monastery to survive the Siamese sacking ten years later. Surrounded by a tile-roofed cloister, the *sim* (building housing the main Buddha image) contains some charming, though badly deteriorating, murals. A splendidly ornate candle-holder of carved wood situated before the altar is a fine example of nineteenth-century Lao woodcarving. Outside, the cloister holds countless niches with diminutive Buddhas peering out from them.

The Presidential Palace and Haw Pha Kaew

Opposite Wat Sisaket stands the **Presidential Palace**, an impressive French Beaux Arts-style building built to house the French colonial governor, now used mainly for government ceremonies. Next to the palace, **Haw Pha Kaew** (daily 8am–noon & 1–4pm; 5000K), once the king's personal Buddhist temple, now functions as a **museum of art and antiquities**. The temple is named for the Emerald Buddha, or Pha Kaew, which was pilfered by the Siamese in 1779 and carried off to their capital where it remains to this day. The museum houses the finest collection of Lao art in the country, one of the most striking works being a Buddha in the "Beckoning Rain" pose (standing with arms to the sides and fingers pointing to the ground) and sporting a jewel-encrusted navel.

Lane Xang Avenue and Patouxai

Lane Xang Avenue, leading off north from Setthathilat Road, is reputedly modelled on France's Champs Élysées and **Patouxai**, standing at one end, on the Arc de Triomphe. Popularly known as *anusawali* (Lao for "monument"), this massive concrete victory gate (daily 8am–4.30pm; 3000K), 1km from the Presidential Palace, was built in the late 1950s to commemorate casualties of war on the side of the Royal Lao Government. The view of Vientiane from the top is worth the climb. A handful of hawkers shelter by a ceiling adorned with reliefs of the Hindu deities; the walls depict characters from the Ramayana, the epic Hindu story of battles between good and evil.

COPE Visitor Centre

Around 1km southeast of the Talat Sao bus station is the superb **COPE Visitor Centre** (daily 9am–6pm; donations appreciated), set up by a non-profit organization to document the devastating effects of unexploded ordnance (UXO) left over from the Second Indochina War. The main exhibition, housed in an old store room, starts by describing how America's secret bombing campaigns during the Vietnam War left Laos littered with unexploded "bombies". But the centre isn't only about looking back; here you can find out how prosthetic limbs and rehabilitation programmes are giving victims another chance at life, and see how those advances are helping other people too, including those injured in motorbike accidents.

That Luang

One and a half kilometres northeast of Patouxai stands the Buddhist stupa, **That Luang** (Tues–Sun 8am–noon & 1–4pm; 5000K), Laos's most important religious building, and its national symbol. The original That Luang is thought to have been built in the mid-sixteenth century by King Setthathilat, whose statue stands in front, and was reported to have looked like a gold-covered "pyramid". Today's structure dates from the 1930s: the tapering golden spire of the main stupa is 45m tall and rests on a plinth of stylized lotus petals; it's surrounded on all sides by thirty short, spiky stupas. Within the cloisters is kept a collection of very worn Buddha images, some of which may have

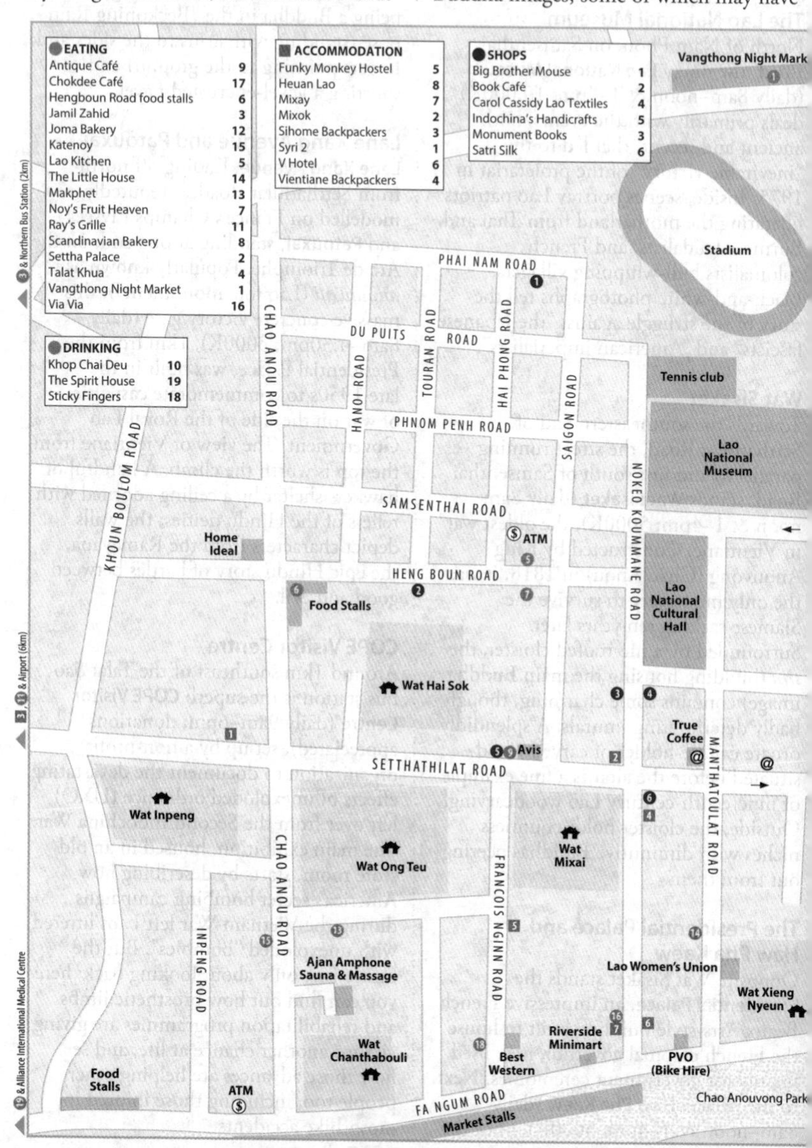

been enshrined in the original Khmer temple that once occupied the site.

ARRIVAL AND DEPARTURE

By air Wattay International Airport is 6km northwest of downtown Vientiane. Airport facilities include visa-on-arrival (around $35 plus one photo; see p.345) and exchange services. The only official way to get into town from the airport itself is to take a taxi (car $7, minivan $8). To save cash, walk out to Luang Prabang Avenue, a few hundred metres from the terminal, and hail an eastbound sawngthaew (10,000K). These usually stop at the Talat Sao bus station, but will drop you off anywhere along the route if requested.

Destinations Bangkok, Thailand (3–4 daily; 1hr 5min); Hanoi, Vietnam (2 daily; 1hr 10min); Houayxai (1–2 daily; 55min); Kunming, China (2 daily; 1hr 20min); Luang Namtha (daily; 55min); Luang Prabang (4 daily; 50min); Oudomxai (1–2 daily; 50min); Pakse (2 daily; 1hr 15min); Phnom Penh,

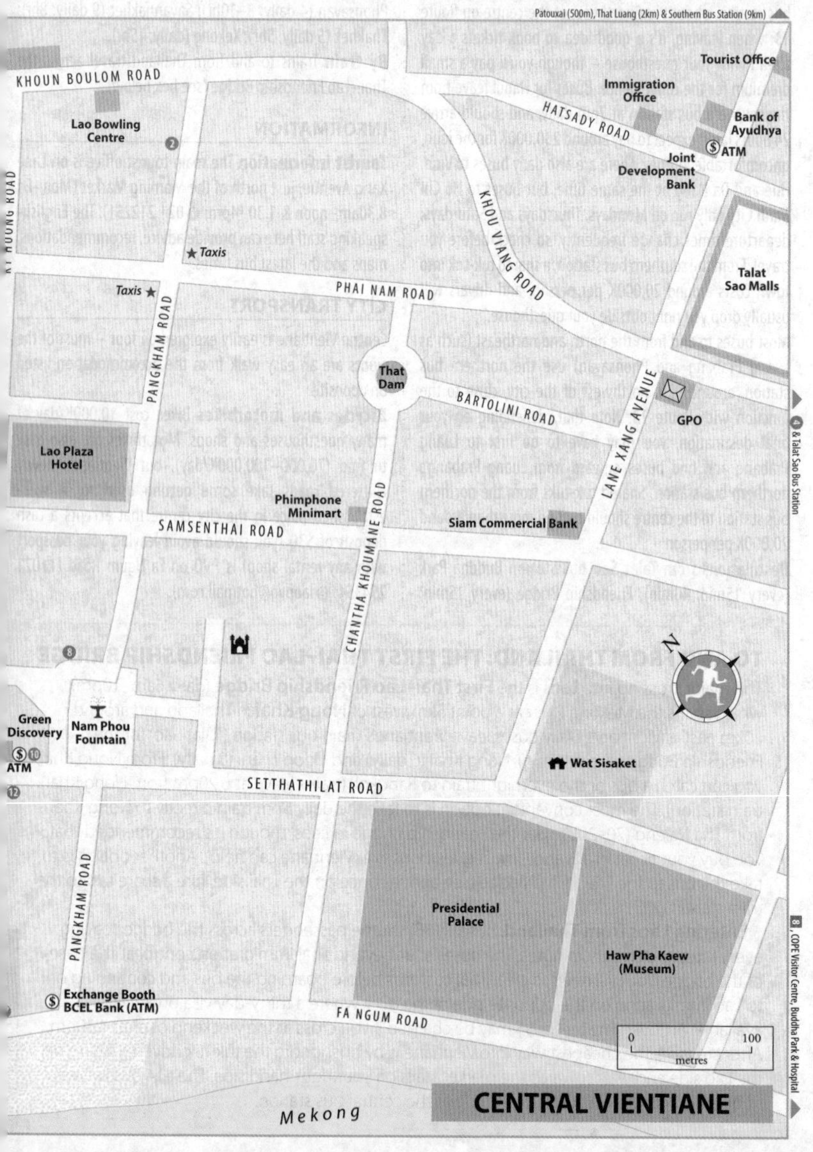

5

Cambodia (daily; 1hr 30min); Phonsavan/Xieng Khuang (daily; 30min); Savannakhet (1–3 daily; 55min).

By bus Public buses to destinations around Vientiane (including the Thai–Lao Friendship Bridge near Nong Khai) use the Talat Sao bus station, next to the Talat Sao Malls on Khou Vieng Road, about 1500m from Nam Phou fountain. From here, it's only a short tuk-tuk ride to all the central hotels and guesthouses.

Buses to and from the south tend to use the southern bus station, about 9km northeast of the centre on Route 13; when leaving, it's a good idea to book tickets a day ahead with your guesthouse – though you'll pay a small premium for the convenience. Buses for Hanoi leave from the southern bus station at 7pm daily, and should arrive 24 hours later; expect to pay around 230,000K for the long, uncomfortable journey. There are also daily buses to Vinh, Hue and Da Nang at the same time, but buses to Ho Chi Minh City only run on Mondays, Thursdays and Saturdays; departure times change frequently, so check before you travel. From the southern bus station, a shared tuk-tuk into town costs around 20,000K per person, and drivers will usually drop you right outside your guesthouse.

Most buses to and from the north and northeast (such as Luang Prabang and Phonsavan) use the northern bus station, around 9km northwest of the city, close to the junction with Route 13. Note that, depending on your final destination, you may have to go first to Luang Prabang and find buses onward from Luang Prabang's northern bus station. Shared tuk-tuks from the northern bus station to the centre should cost no more than around 20,000K per person.

Destinations from Talat Sao bus station Buddha Park (every 15min; 40min); Friendship Bridge (every 15min; 30min); Kasi (daily; 6hr); Thalat (hourly; 2hr); Vang Vieng (7 daily; 4hr).

Destinations from northern bus station Bokeo (3 daily; 30hr); Luang Prabang (11 daily; 9–11hr); Luang Namtha (2 daily; 24hr); Oudomxai (4 daily; 12–17hr); Phonsavan (6 daily; 8–10hr); Phongsali (1 daily; 26hr).

Destinations from southern bus station Attapeu (3 daily; 16hr); Don Khong, Si Phan Don (daily; 17hr); Pakse (15 daily; 8–13hr); Paksan (every 30min; 1–2hr); Phonsavan (4 daily; 8–10hr); Savannakhet (9 daily; 8hr); Thakhek (5 daily; 5hr); Xekong (daily; 15hr).

By train Trains to and from Thailand travel across the Thai–Lao Friendship Bridge (see box below).

INFORMATION

Tourist information The main tourist office is on Lane Xang Avenue, just north of the Morning Market (Mon–Fri 8.30am–noon & 1.30–4pm; T 021 212251). The English-speaking staff here can provide advice, recommendations, maps and the latest bus times.

CITY TRANSPORT

Central Vientiane is easily explored on foot – most of the sights are an easy walk from the accommodation listed on opposite.

Bicycles and motorbikes Bikes cost 10,000K/day at many guesthouses and shops. Motorbikes are also easy to find (70,000–100,000K/day), but Vientiane's newly cluttered roads take some getting used to. A well-established place in the city centre that accepts a cash deposit of $30 (you should avoid leaving your passport with any rental shop) is PVO on Fa Ngum Road (T 021 254354; E laopvo@hotmail.com).

TO AND FROM THAILAND: THE FIRST THAI–LAO FRIENDSHIP BRIDGE

The major crossing into Laos is the **First Thai–Lao Friendship Bridge** (daily 6am–10pm), which spans the Mekong River at a point 5km west of **Nong Khai** in Thailand and around 20km east of Vientiane. Daily buses leave Vientiane's main bus station (Talat Sao) for the Friendship Bridge (every 15min), Nong Khai (6 daily) and Udon Thani (8 daily). From Nong Khai, you can catch a bus or the overnight train to Bangkok (trains leave at 6.20pm from Nong Khai's train station). The most convenient option is to take the daily 5pm train directly to Nong Khai from Tha Naleng (20–30B), near the Friendship Bridge in Laos, though it's recommended that you buy your ticket in advance (most guesthouses in Vientiane can help). Another option is to take the bus to the Friendship Bridge (see above); once on the Thai side, hire a share taxi to the train station (20B).

Entering Laos from Thailand, buses (15B) shuttle passengers across the bridge, leaving every fifteen to twenty minutes. The buses start beyond Thai immigration control at the base of the bridge. You will need to clear Thai customs before boarding the bus and continuing on to Lao immigration on the opposite side of the river, where a thirty-day visa on arrival is available. An "overtime fee" of $1 may be charged if you cross at the weekend or after 4.30pm. After crossing, the cheapest way into Vientiane is by bus. Ignore the tuk-tuk drivers waiting on the Lao side and walk towards the market stalls on your right-hand side. The #14 bus leaves frequently from here (6000K), pulling up at the central bus station.

Tuk-tuks Shared tuk-tuks generally ply frequently travelled routes, such as Lane Xang Avenue between the Morning Market and That Luang, and along Setthathilat and Fa Ngum roads, and charge around 10,000K/person for destinations within the city. There are usually a few tuk-tuks parked and waiting for foreign passengers near Nam Phou; note that the prices the drivers have listed on laminated sheets are inflated for tourists.

Taxis Expensive, metered yellow taxis tend to congregate outside Day Inn on Pangkham Rd, just north of the *Lao Plaza* hotel.

ACCOMMODATION

Funky Monkey Hostel François Ngin Rd ⓣ 021 254181, ⓦ funkymonkeyhostel.com. Very simple rooms and dorms in a tired-looking building a quick stroll up from the Mekong. Low prices attract young backpackers and solo travellers, who wind up drinking around the lobby's pool table most evenings. Dorm 40,000K, double 120,000K

Heuan Lao Off Samsenthai Rd, near Wat Simuang ⓣ 021 216258. This friendly, rambling guesthouse run by an older couple is located on a quiet lane opposite a park. Around the peaceful courtyard, where cats and dogs relax in the sun, you'll find singles, doubles and triples, all en suite. Double 120,000K

Mixay 39 Nokeo Koummane Rd ⓣ 021 217023. One of the cheapest places in town, with spartan rooms ranging from fan singles to triples rented out bed-by-bed like dorms, with either attached bathrooms or shared facilities. The double rooms seem better maintained. Two rooms have balconies overlooking the street. Dorm 35,000K, double 100,000K

Mixok 189 Setthathilat Rd ⓣ 021 251606. Cheap and central backpacker digs similar to *Mixay*, with singles, triples and dorms. A/c doubles are also available. Expect some noise from the busy road outside. Double 130,000K

★ **Sihome Backpackers** 056 Sihom Rd, halfway between the two petrol stations ⓣ 020 9551 2668, ⓦ sihome backpackershostel.com. The most popular place for young backpackers, with super-cheap bunks, walls covered in murals and a sociable bar area out front. Dorms here are quite cramped, but there's a TV room to stretch out in and doubles are available. Dorm 60,000K, double 280,000K

Syri 2 63/67 Setthathirat Rd ⓣ 021 241345, ⓔ syri2 @hotmail.com. Aquariums, sculptures and vases clutter the reception area of this rather odd place with a Chinese-Lao owner. The rooms are gloomy, but the location is good and the rates are low. Choose a/c over a fan and you'll pay an extra 50,000K per night. Double 60,000K

Vientiane Backpackers Nokeo Koummane Rd ⓣ 020 9748 4227, ⓦ vientianebackpackershostel.com. Big, shabby dorms in a very central location, with all the usual services on offer, from laundry to bike rental. The rate includes a simple breakfast, free wi-fi and access to a computer in the lobby. Dorm 40,000K

V Hotel Opposite *Via Via* on Nokeo Koummane Rd ⓣ 021 255999. A tall modern block near the river, with good-value rooms and decent hot showers. The echoing corridors tend to amplify even the smallest sounds, so noise can be a problem. Double 200,000K

EATING

The culinary scene in Vientiane caters to virtually every taste, from sausage and sauerkraut to Korean BBQ. In addition to authentically Lao markets and noodle stands, Vientiane also has a large concentration of Western restaurants.

MARKETS

Hengboun Road food stalls Hengboun Rd, between Khoun Boulom Rd and Chao Anou Rd, near Home Ideal. For cheap, tasty snacks throughout the day and into late evening, the food carts here serve up good Lao-style *khào pûn* (noodles with sauce), *tam màk hung* and excellent shakes.

Talat Khua Din Just east of the Talat Sao bus station. This dusty, partially covered market is Vientiane's cheapest place to buy fruit, vegetables and the like. Come early to watch locals buying fish and meat. Daily sunrise–sunset.

Vangthong Night Market Along Khoun Boulom Road, north of the National Stadium. This narrow, food-focused night market sets up near the bowling alley on Khoun Boulom Rd in the early evening and stays open till about 10pm, selling fresh fruit, sweet coconut desserts and *ping kai* (grilled chicken). Daily sunset to around 10pm.

BREAKFAST, BAKERIES AND CAFÉS

Antique Café Upstairs at Indochina's Handicrafts on Setthathilat Rd ⓣ 021 223528. Above an antique shop, this tiny café has space for just four or five customers at a time. With cuckoo clocks, medals and paintings cluttering the walls, it's an atmospheric spot for an iced Lao coffee (20,000K). Daily 8.30am–10.30pm.

Joma Bakery Setthathilat Rd, just west of Nam Phou ⓣ 021 215265, ⓦ joma.biz. This Canadian-owned café is Vientiane's answer to the big Western coffee chains – right down to the free wi-fi – and its decent breakfasts (from 27,000K) will set you up nicely for a day of tramping around town. The salads are good too, if a little pricey. Daily 7am–9pm.

★ **The Little House** Midway along Manthatoulat Rd ⓣ 020 5540 6036, ⓔ cafelao66@yahoo.co.jp. It's hard to spot this cute, Japanese-run coffee house, but your effort will be rewarded with sublime Lao coffee from the Bolaven Plateau (from 19,000K). Be sure to also order a couple of the divine home-made chocolate truffles. Daily 8.30am–6.30pm.

Scandinavian Bakery On the northern edge of Nam Phou Place ⓣ 021 215199, ⓦ scandinavianbakerylaos.com. Vientiane's first European bakery is still going strong, selling huge sandwiches, traditional Swedish cakes and refreshing

5

lemonade (11,000K). Views of the fountain have been all but obscured by new buildings, but the coffee makes up for it. Daily 7am–9pm.

ASIAN FOOD

Jamil Zahid Off Khoun Boulom Rd ⓣ030 9909456. Tucked down an alley near the western end of Heng Boun Rd, this shed-like Indian place does superb Punjabi curries, plus tandoor-cooked naans and tasty dhals. The eccentric owner is a camera fanatic, so expect to have your picture taken and shown on the restaurant's dusty TV screen. Daily 11am–10.30pm.

★**Lao Kitchen** Hengboun Rd ⓣ021 254332, ⓦlao-kitchen.com. Excellent, reasonably priced option for first-time visitors who want to experiment with Lao food and know exactly what they're ordering. The house special is a fresh-tasting chicken *larp* (34,000K), but the menu also extends to regional dishes like spicy, Pakse-style sausage, with a good selection of dips. Daily 11am–10pm.

Katenoy Chao Anou Rd, opp *Nazim* restaurant ⓣ020 5539 4290. Simple Lao place with plastic tables and chairs set outside on a dusty plot of land, doing cheap fruit shakes (10,000K), draught beer by the jug, and an excellent spicy rice salad with holy basil (20,000K). Daily 6pm–late.

★**Makphet** Behind Wat Ong Teu, south of Setthathilat Rd ⓣ021 260587. Upscale, not-for-profit restaurant on a quiet backstreet in the centre of town offering a modern take on classic Lao dishes. The place is run by former street kids who were trained up for the job. Hugely popular, especially with business crowds. Bookings advised. Mon–Sat 11am–9pm.

WESTERN FOOD

Chokdee Café Fa Ngum Rd ⓦchokdeecafe.com. A statue of Tintin points travellers and expats into this sociable Belgian bar/restaurant on Fa Ngum Rd. The drinks list features dozens of strong imported beers (from 40,000K) and on Friday and Saturday evenings, *moules* (cooked in local or Belgian beer) are added to the extensive menu. Mon 4.30–11pm, Tues–Sun 8am–11pm.

Noy's Fruit Heaven Heng Boun Rd ⓣ030 9960913. Need a fresh fruit fix? This relaxed smoothie bar makes great shakes for 15,000K, blending in plenty of sweet coconuts and bananas. Also does decent Western breakfasts. Daily 7am–7pm.

Ray's Grille 17/1 Sihom Rd, west of the petrol station ⓣ020 5896 6866. There isn't a proper sign outside this no-frills American burger joint, so keep your eyes peeled for the little whiteboard, which has the menu scrawled on it. The house special – a whopping philly cheese steak dripping with gooey cheddar (39,000K) – has tourists and expats coming back for multiple visits. Daily except Sat 11.30am–2pm & 6–9pm.

Via Via Opposite *V Hotel* on Nokeo Koummane Rd ⓣ020 7749 2776. Hugely popular with tourists, Via Via manages to pull off decent Lao dishes alongside its selection of Western staples, including good, Italian-style pizzas (around 55,000K). Jugs of wine and well-made mojitos get solo travellers chatting. Daily 10am–10pm.

★TREAT YOURSELF

The stunning colonial-era hotel, **Settha Palace** (6 Pangkham Rd ⓣ021 217581, ⓦsetthapalace.com), is undeniably the most atmospheric place to stay in town. Though the room rates are rather out of the reach of most backpackers ($207), the unstuffy *belle époque* restaurant is much more achievable, serving delicious, high-end Lao food using the best local ingredients. Particularly recommended are the fragrant *mok pa* ($9) and the spicy Lao sausage ($9.50). Alternatively, pop by the hotel for a dip in its gorgeous blue pool ($28/day).

NIGHTLIFE

Vientiane is not a great city for partying. Frequent government crackdowns have hamstrung the development of Vientiane's clubbing scene, especially when it comes to late-night places that appeal to Western visitors. The locals' favourite spots for drinking and dancing are a quick tuk-tuk ride west of the town centre along Luang Prabang Avenue.

BARS

Khop Chai Deu Setthathirat Rd. This big, French-period house is by far the most popular hangout for foreign tourists. Downstairs in the patio bar you can get cheap glasses of draught beer (10,000K); up the big spiral staircase you'll find another very pleasant bar on the roof. You can eat here, too – the mixed menu has reasonable Lao and Indian dishes, though the *falang* food (and service) is a bit hit and miss. Daily 9am–11pm.

The Spirit House Fa Ngum Rd, next to *Beau Rivage Mekong* ⓣ021 243795, ⓦthespirithouselaos.com, Travellers flock to *The Spirit House* for delectable cocktails (from 20,000K) and views over the river, broken only by a narrow road. One of the best places to watch the sun set over Thailand. Daily 7am–midnight.

Sticky Fingers François Nginn Rd ⓣ021 215 972. With a pleasant outdoor seating area opposite the *Best Western* hotel, this small Australian-run bar has picked up a loyal following among expats. A good crowd is almost guaranteed 6–8pm on Wed and Fri, when the famously good cocktails (from 15,000K) are half price. Tues–Sun 10am–11pm.

5

SHOPPING

The Talat Sao area just off Lane Xang Avenue is the best place to begin a shopping tour of the capital. Although there are still covered market stalls here selling Chinese electronics and cheap consumer goods, most of these have been swallowed up by the imposing Talat Sao Malls (daily 8am–5pm), which are merging into one big shopping outlet, each housing a variety of jewellery shops, clothing outlets and banks.

At some stage, most tourists end up browsing the market stalls that occupy the new riverbank area just west of Chao Anouvong Park, marked by dozens of red gazebos. T-shirts, toys, paintings, shoes and gadgets are available, though nearly everything is mass-produced and plasticky, and true bargains are impossible to find. The more interesting textile, souvenir and antique shops are found on Samsenthai and Setthathilat roads and along the lanes running between them.

ANTIQUES

Indochina's Handicrafts Setthathilat Rd ⓣ021 223528. Beautiful antique shop selling watches, paintings, coins, medals and Buddhist amulets. There's also a cosy café upstairs (see p.361). Daily 8.30am–10pm.

BOOKS

Big Brother Mouse Phai Nam Rd, just west of the National Stadium ⓣ021 264513, ⓦbigbrothermouse.com. The Vientiane branch of Big Brother Mouse is run with the same idea as the main shop in Luang Prabang. Here you can buy colourful, lightweight children's books in Lao and English (prices start at 10,000K) and then give them away to Lao children when you visit remote villages. Mon–Sat 8am–4pm.

Book Café Heng Boun Rd. Small but well-organized shop with a whole section devoted to learning Lao, plus plenty of English-language novels set in Laos. Daily 8am–8pm.

Monument Books Nokeo Koummane Rd ⓣ021 243708, ⓦmonument-books.com. Vientiane's largest selection of English-language books. Mon–Fri 9am–8pm, Sat & Sun 9am–6pm.

TEXTILES AND SILK

Shops specializing in traditional textiles and authentic silk include Satri Silk on Setthathilat Rd (ⓣ021 219295) and Carol Cassidy Lao Textiles on Nokeo Koummane Rd (ⓣ021 212123).

DIRECTORY

Banks and exchange Banks throughout town, especially on Lane Xang Avenue, can organize cash advances on Visa and MasterCard; a few local banks and independent moneychangers also maintain exchange booths around the city centre. ATMs are found on street corners throughout the city.

Bowling The Lao Bowling Centre on Khoun Boulom Rd (ⓣ021 223219) is one of the few places where late-night drinking is possible. Each game costs 11,000K (13,000K after 7pm). Open daily 8am–late.

Embassies and consulates Australia, Thadua Rd ⓣ021 353800; Britain, J. Nehru Rd ⓣ030 770 0000; Canada, c/o embassy in Bangkok ⓣ+66 2 636 0540; Cambodia, near That Khao, Thadua Rd ⓣ021 314952; China, near Wat Nak Noi, Wat Nak Noi Rd ⓣ 021 315100; Indonesia, Kaysone Phomvihane Ave ⓣ021 413909 or 413910; Ireland, c/o embassy in Kuala Lumpur ⓣ+60 3 2161 2963; Malaysia, Singha Rd ⓣ021 414205 or 414206; Myanmar (Burma), Lao-Thai Rd, Ban Wat Nak ⓣ021 314910; New Zealand, c/o embassy in Bangkok ⓣ +66 2 254 2530; Philippines, Phonthan Rd ⓣ021 452490; Singapore, Thadua Rd ⓣ021 353939; Thailand, Kaysone Phomvihane Ave ⓣ021 214580; United States, Thadua Rd ⓣ021 267000; Vietnam, near Wat Phaxai, That Luang Rd ⓣ021 413400–4.

Hospitals and clinics Alliance International Medical Centre, Honda Complex, Souphanuvong Rd ⓣ021 513095; Mahosot Hospital, Mahosot Rd ⓣ021 214018.

Immigration department Hatsady Rd, not far from the tourist office (ⓣ021 212520; daily 8am–noon & 1–4pm). Here you can extend your visa for $2/day. Travel agents in town tend to charge $3/day for the same service.

Internet *True Coffee* has the fastest computers in town (8000K/hr), but there are dozens of smaller internet cafés dotted all around the city, each charging around 200K/min and closing at about 10pm. Wi-fi is widespread.

Laundry Most hotels and guesthouses will wash clothes for you. The going rate across town is 10,000K/kg, though some places try to charge considerably more.

Massage and herbal sauna Ajan Amphone, tucked away behind Wat Chanthabouli on Fa Ngum Rd, offers Lao massage (55,000K/hr) plus a soothing herbal sauna. Daily noon–9pm.

Pharmacies The best pharmacies are on Mahosot Rd.

Swimming The *Best Western* on François Ngin Rd ($7.50/day, including access to the gym).

BUDDHA PARK

Located on the Mekong River 25km from downtown Vientiane, **Xieng Khouan** or the "**Buddha Park**" (daily 8am–5pm; 5000K, additional 3000K for cameras) is Laos's quirkiest attraction. This collection of massive ferro-concrete sculptures, which lie dotted around a wide riverside meadow, was created under the direction of Luang Phu Boonlua Surirat, a self-styled holy man who claimed to have been the disciple of a cave-dwelling Hindu hermit in Vietnam. Upon

returning to Laos, Boonlua began the sculpture garden in the late 1950s as a means of spreading his philosophy of life and his ideas about the cosmos. Besides the brontosaurian reclining Buddha that dominates the park, there are concrete statues of every conceivable deity in the Hindu-Buddhist pantheon. After the revolution, Boonlua was forced to flee across the Mekong to Nong Khai in Thailand, where he established an even more elaborate version of his philosophy in concrete at Sala Kaeo Kou (also known as Wat Khaek). The cheapest way to **get to the park** is to take a bus #14 from Vientiane's central bus station (every 15min; 6000K). Although the bus is scheduled to run all the way to the Buddha Park, we've had reports of the bus stopping at the Friendship Bridge, only for tourists to be coaxed into buying an (overpriced) tuk-tuk ride for the last part of the journey. If this happens, walk back to the main road and flag down a shared tuk-tuk heading east; it shouldn't cost more than 5000K/person.

VANG VIENG

Just 155km north of the capital among spectacular limestone karsts sits **VANG VIENG**, the once-sleepy town now synonymous with tubing. Within a few short years, what started as a peaceful activity – floating down the Nam Song River in an inflated tractor inner tube, stopping for a beer or two along the way – developed into one of Southeast Asia's biggest parties, with thousands of bare-chested backpackers descending on the place. The Lao government found itself struggling to control an inland version of Thailand's Ko Pha Ngan, complete with the drugs and drunken revelry. Only after dozens of tourists died (through drink, drugs, drowning, or a combination of all three) did the authorities take action, tearing down all of the riverside bars. Some of these have now been rebuilt, but tubing – and the town itself – is now definitely more restrained.

Needless to say, Vang Vieng is no hub of Lao culture. However, the town's jaw-dropping riverside setting, with a whole host of ethnic villages, waterfalls and caves nearby, makes it the perfect rest stop en route to or from the north. You could easily spend a week or more here cycling, caving, rafting or hiking. And, if you know where to look, there are still parties too.

WHAT TO SEE AND DO

Vang Vieng itself is a small town that would be unremarkable except for its beautiful riverside position. As such, there's little to see and do in the town itself; the real attraction lies beyond the town, on the river and in the caves.

Tubing

Love or hate what it's done to the place, tubing remains Vang Vieng's premier attraction. Following a government crackdown (see p.367), only a few bars now dot the river, and illegal drugs (once sold openly on menus) are seldom seen. For many, drinking is still a big part of the experience, with bars offering free shots of *lào-láo* and buy-one-get-one-free deals on whisky. While the rope swings and slides that claimed lives have now disappeared, drinking on the river is still risky, so take care and, if you're a weak swimmer, ask for a life jacket.

To avoid getting back after dark, it's best to start tubing early. Tubes are available from the lock-up near the post office. There's no need to book so just turn up, pay the fee (55,000K, plus a 60,000K deposit) and a tuk-tuk will drive you to the start point, 3km north of town near the Organic Mulberry Farm. Tuk-tuks will only depart with at least four people on board, so on quiet days you may have to wait for others to arrive.

A float back into town should take two or three hours, but you could easily spend the whole day dancing, drinking and playing mud volleyball at the bars along the way. It's important to leave enough time to get back before dark, as it gets cold and it becomes almost impossible to see where you're going in the fast-flowing water. Arrive back late and you will lose your deposit. A good sunblock is essential if you don't want to come out looking like a lobster.

5

Phou Kham Cave and the Blue Lagoon

Six kilometres west of Vang Vieng, **Phou Kham Cave** (10,000K) makes a rewarding half-day trip that takes in some fine scenery and affords the chance to visit a cave and enjoy a good swim along the way. To reach the cave and lagoon, cross the toll bridge next to Riverside Boutique Resort and follow the road to Na Thong, 4km west. Signs will lead you to the car park, where the admission fee is collected. The fish-filled **Blue Lagoon** here is a great spot for a swim, with a rope swing dangling over the water; you can buy snacks, beer and fruit shakes nearby. From the far side of the small lagoon it's a

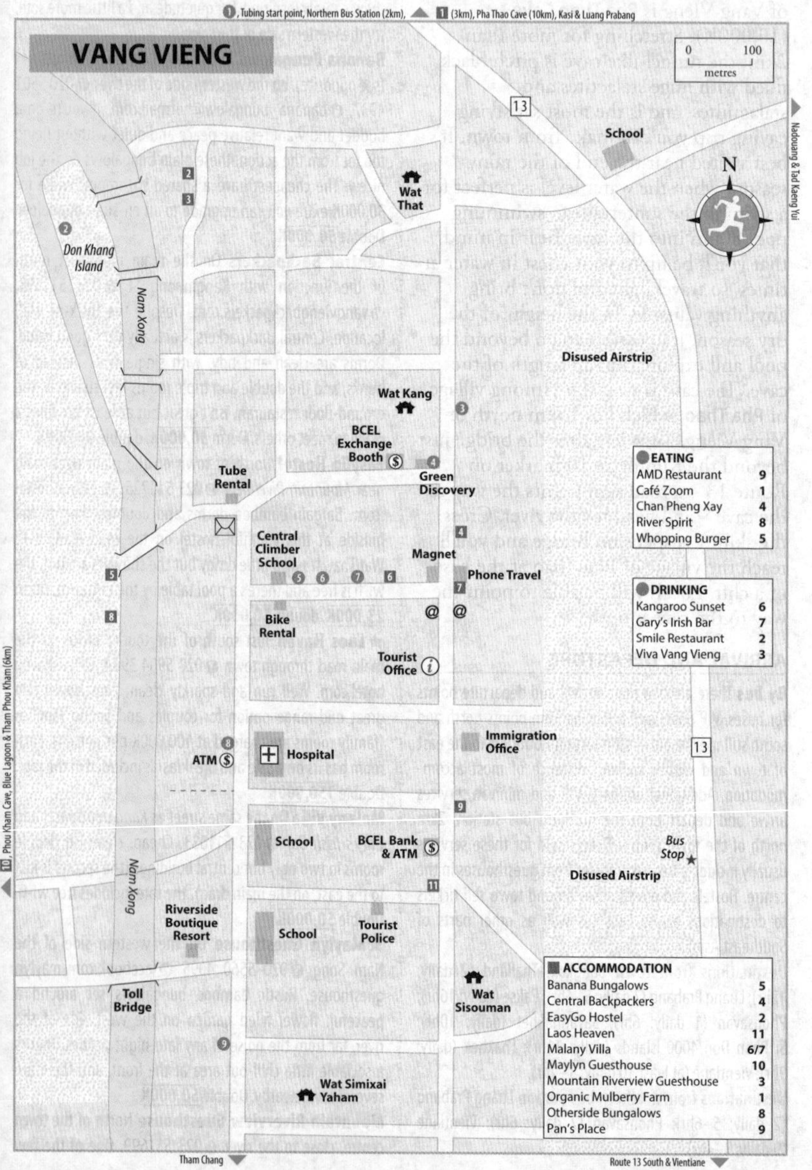

5

short, steep climb to the cave's entrance. In the main cavern reclines a bronze Buddha; bring a torch if you want to explore the tunnels branching off the main gallery.

Pha Thao Cave

A short motorbike or tuk-tuk ride north of Vang Vieng is **Pha Thao Cave** (10,000K). Stretching for more than 2km, the tunnel-like cave is pitch black, filled with huge stalactites and stalagmites, and is the most satisfying caving trip you can make from town. It's best visited near the end of the rainy season, when the water level is perfect for a swim in the subterranean swimming pool 800m into the cave. Bear in mind that you'll be up to your chest in water at times, so travel light and don't bring anything valuable. In the height of the dry season, it's possible to go beyond the pool and explore the full length of the cave. The cave is near the Hmong village of **Pha Thao**, which lies 13km north of Vang Vieng. Turn left after the bridge just beyond the Kilometre 10 marker on Route 13 – a road sign points the way to the cave – and head for the river. Cross the skinny suspension bridge and you'll reach the village of Pha Thao at the base of a cliff. Locals will be able to point the way to the cave mouth.

ARRIVAL AND DEPARTURE

By bus There are two main arrival and departure points for buses. VIP buses and minivans from points north and south still use the old airstrip just off Route 13, to the east of town and within walking distance of most accommodation. Additional ordinary, VIP and minivan services arrive and depart from the northern bus station, 2km north of the town centre. Tickets sold for these services usually include a tuk-tuk transfer from guesthouses in the centre. Hostels and guesthouses around town sell tickets to destinations across Laos (as well as other parts of Southeast Asia).

Destinations from town Bangkok, Thailand (2 daily; 12hr); Luang Prabang (7 daily; 5–6hr); Pakse (daily; 16hr); Phonsavan (1 daily; 6hr); Savannakhet (daily; 10hr); Si Phan Don/4000 islands (daily; 11hr); Thakhek (daily; 9hr); Vientiane (at least 10 daily; 3–4hr).

Destinations from northern bus station Luang Prabang (2 daily; 5–6hr); Phonsavan (2 daily; 6hr); Vientiane (9 daily; 3–4hr).

By sawngthaew If you're heading to Vientiane, sawngthaews are a reasonable option, leaving the northern bus station every 20min throughout the day. Though as they take around four hours to reach the capital you'd do just as well to take a quicker, similarly priced minivan instead.

ACCOMMODATION

Cheap rooms are in abundance in Vang Vieng, though they're rarely inspiring. For quietude and a little more soul, try the western side of the river.

Banana Bungalows Just north of *Otherside Bungalows* (see opposite), on the western side of the river T 020 5501 4937, E banana_bungalow@hotmail.com. If you're on a budget and want relative peace and quiet without being too far from the action, these plain bungalows do the job nicely. The cheapest have a shared bathroom, while for 30,000K extra you can upgrade to an en-suite bungalow. Double **50,000K**

Central Backpackers On the main road, just north of the junction with Kangmuong St T 023 511593, W vangviengbackpackers.com. Despite the thick-of-it-all location, Central Backpackers is actually very good value. Dorms are clean and tidy, with single beds instead of bunks, and the double and triple rooms feel spacious. The ground-floor restaurant isn't great but at least provides a place to meet others. Dorm **30,000K**, double **80,000K**

EasyGo Hostel North of town on the main river road, near *Mountain Riverview* T 023 511725, W easygohostel.com. Bargain bamboo dorms and doubles cling to the hillside at this youthful hostel on the road leading to Wat That. It's all a little dingy but the showers are hot, the wi-fi is free and there's a pool table by the entrance. Dorm **23,000K**, double **50,000K**

★ **Laos Haven** Just south of the tourist office on the main road through town T 020 5904 3944, W laoshavenhotel.com. Well run and sparkly clean, *Laos Haven* is a great mid-range option for couples and young families (family rooms are charged at 100,000K per person). Each room has its own safe and breakfast is included in the rate. Double **150,000K**

Malany Villa On the same street as *Kangaroo Sunset* and *Gary's Irish Bar* T 023 511083. Cheap, clean-ish double rooms in two ugly but central buildings (the second is just to the east, on the main drag). The rate includes free wi-fi. Double **50,000K**

★ **Maylyn Guesthouse** On the western side of the Nam Song T 020 5560 4095 W facebook.com/maylynguesthouse. Rustic bamboo bungalows set around a peaceful, flower-filled garden on the west side of the river, far from the noise of any late-night parties. There's a sociable little chill-out area at the front, and there are several caves nearby. Double **50,000K**

Mountain Riverview Guesthouse North of the town centre, close to the river T 023 511699. One of the few

DRUGS IN VANG VIENG

Just a few years ago, buying **drugs** in Vang Vieng was as easy as buying lunch – literally. Many of the town's restaurants kept whole sections of their menus reserved for pizzas and shakes made using opium or mushrooms, plus pre-rolled joints of all shapes and sizes.

When backpackers began to die with alarming regularity (not so much through the drugs, but what they did when they were on them), the government could no longer turn a blind eye. Nowadays drugs are harder to spot, although nitrous oxide balloons are sold openly in bars and weed still does the rounds. Having a smoke may be tempting, especially given the tranquil setting, but consider the consequences of getting caught. Plain-clothes police officers routinely issue heavy fines ($500 is not unheard of) if they catch a whiff of anything suspicious.

guesthouses built in the boom years to retain a little bit of character, this place has clean, fan-cooled rooms. Some, like the name suggests, have excellent views of the distant mountains – though you'll pay 20,000K extra for the privilege. Double **60,000K**

Organic Mulberry Farm 3km north of town ⓣ 023 511220, ⓦ laofarm.org. This working organic farm offers dorms, simple doubles and the chance to help out with farm chores and teaching in the nearby village. The attached café serves tasty home-grown organic food. Dorm **30,000K**, double **50,000K**

Otherside Bungalows Just south of *Banana Bungalows* (see opposite), on the western side of the river ⓣ 020 5610 6070. The en-suite rooms here are slightly cheaper than those next door at *Banana Bungalows*, but feel a little damp and drab. Even so, the staff are friendly, and free tea and coffee helps to sweeten the deal. Double **60,000K**

Pan's Place At the southern end of the main road ⓣ 023 511484, ⓦ pansplacelaos.com. A popular budget pick, *Pan's Place* has a relaxed TV room and a selection of single, double and triple rooms with shared facilities. For 20,000K more, you can bag yourself a room with an en-suite bathroom. Double **50,000K**

EATING

The selection of restaurants in Vang Vieng is particularly uninspired, with most places offering the same mix of international and local dishes. The sandwich and pancake stalls around town (most items 10,000K) are a good, cheap alternative.

★ **AMD Restaurant** South of the hospital along the main river road ⓣ 020 5530 1238. Pint-sized, family-run restaurant serving some of the best food in town. The tangy *tom yam* soup (35,000K) is reason enough to make the walk south from the centre, but the tiny open kitchen also turns out good curries, stir-fries and steaks. Daily 7.30am–10pm.

Café Zoom Sun 3km north of town on the road leading to the *Organic Mulberry Farm* ⓣ 020 5610 6536. Quiet café near the tubing start point, which was set up to help local kids get involved with wholesome activities like traditional dancing and weaving. For $3, you can get a coffee and a guided tour of the centre to find out more about the centre's programmes. Tues–Sun 2–7pm.

Chan Pheng Xay Just east of the Green Discovery office on Kangmuong St ⓣ 020 2889 0860. One of the more reliable street-side restaurants in the very centre of town, with reasonable red curries (meat and veggie versions available) for 25,000K. Daily 7am–11pm.

River Spirit South of town along the river road at *Ban Sabai Bungalows*. Good Lao and Thai dishes in an excellent waterfront setting. The expansive menu includes spring rolls with pork (35,000K) and a vegetable *larp* (28,000K), plus a few Western dishes like burgers and steaks. Daily 7.30am–10pm.

Whopping Burger Next door to the Central Climber School in the middle of town. Funky, Japanese-run restaurant serving tasty burgers (with extraordinarily large buns) while 60s and 70s music blares out. Try the samurai chicken burger, which comes with chunky chips and bundles of fresh coriander (50,000K). Daily 6–11pm.

DRINKING

Now that the clubs on the island in the Nam Song have been torn down, parties tend to happen in the centre of town. There are two main late-night venues: *Viva Vang Vieng* (see p.368) and *Room 101*. They're opposite each other on the main drag, and host cheesy club nights on alternate days. Regardless of which club's night it is, things get lively at around midnight when the other bars close.

Kangaroo Sunset Just west of *Gary's Irish Bar* in the middle of town. The post-tubing bar du jour, with beer pong, free pool and cheap drinks (a large Beerlao costs 10,000K 7–8pm every night) helping to pull in a young *falang* crowd. Daily 8am–midnight.

Gary's Irish Bar Just east of *Kangaroo Sunset* in the middle of town ⓣ 030 9407039, ⓦ garysirishbar.com. Chirpy Irish bar staff and regular live music sessions make *Gary's* stand out among the cookie-cutter bars in the centre of town. There's also a good pool table, a dartboard, and live football on the TV. Daily 9am–midnight.

Smile Restaurant Towards the north of Don Khang Island. Known as *Smile Bar* until the government cleared all "bars" from along the river, *Smile Restaurant* is one of

5

the few surviving spots in the middle of the river where you can swing in a hammock drinking beer (15,000K) or a fruit shake (8,000K). As the name of his bar implies, the owner is a happy chappy. Daily 10am–8pm.

Viva Vang Vieng On the main drag. There's little in it between Vang Vieng's two late-night clubs, both of which play loud chart hits from the past couple of years. Of the two, Viva is bigger and tends to fill up more quickly. Open until around 2am every other night.

Luang Prabang and around

Nestling in a slim valley shaped by lofty, green mountains and cut by the swift Mekong and Khan rivers, **LUANG PRABANG** is northern Laos's major tourist

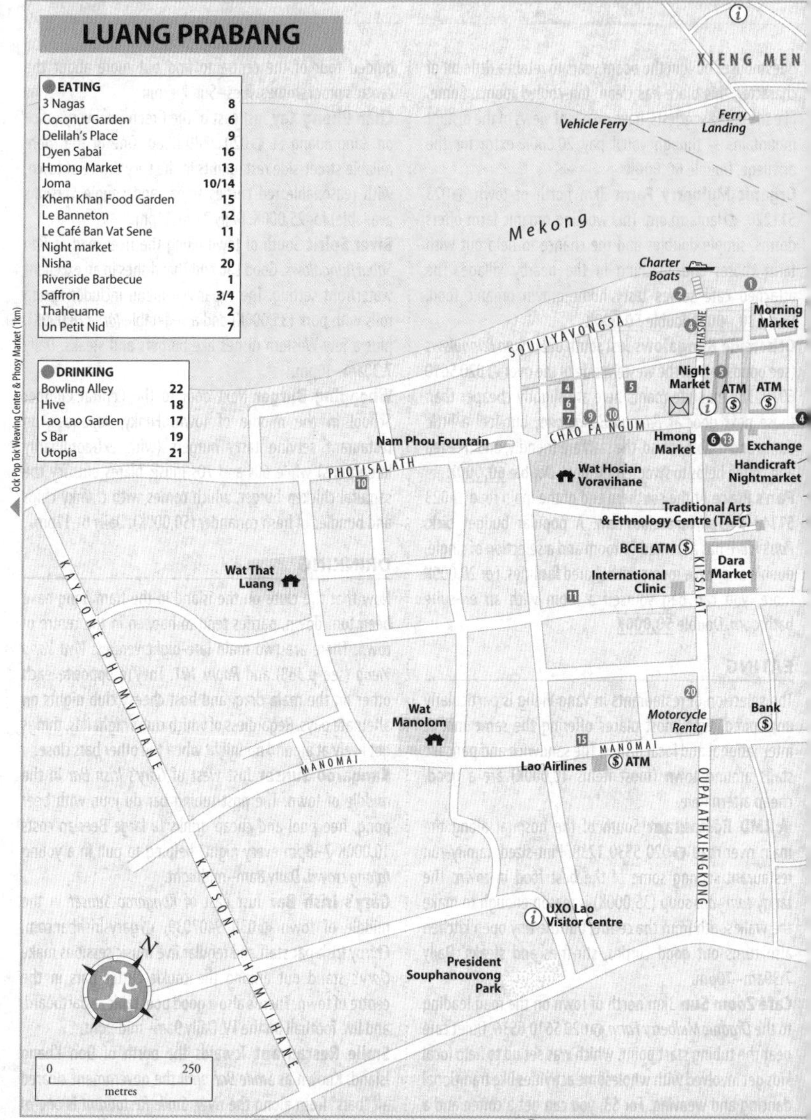

Southern Bus Station and Naluang Tourist Bus (Minibus) Station (1km), 22 (2.5km), Provincial Hospital (2.5km) & Kouang Si Waterfall (23km)

draw. Designated a World Heritage Site in 1995, the city is endowed with a legacy of ancient, red-roofed temples and French-Indochinese architecture, not to mention some of the country's most refined cuisine, its richest culture and most sacred Buddha image. Yet for all its undeniable beauty and charm, there's no doubt that Luang Prabang has been transformed by its ever-growing popularity with Western visitors, with almost every property in the historic centre now serving the travel industry in some form or another, and foreigners now outnumbering locals across much of the old city. All the more reason, once you've had your fill of the good life, to strike out on foot, by bike or by

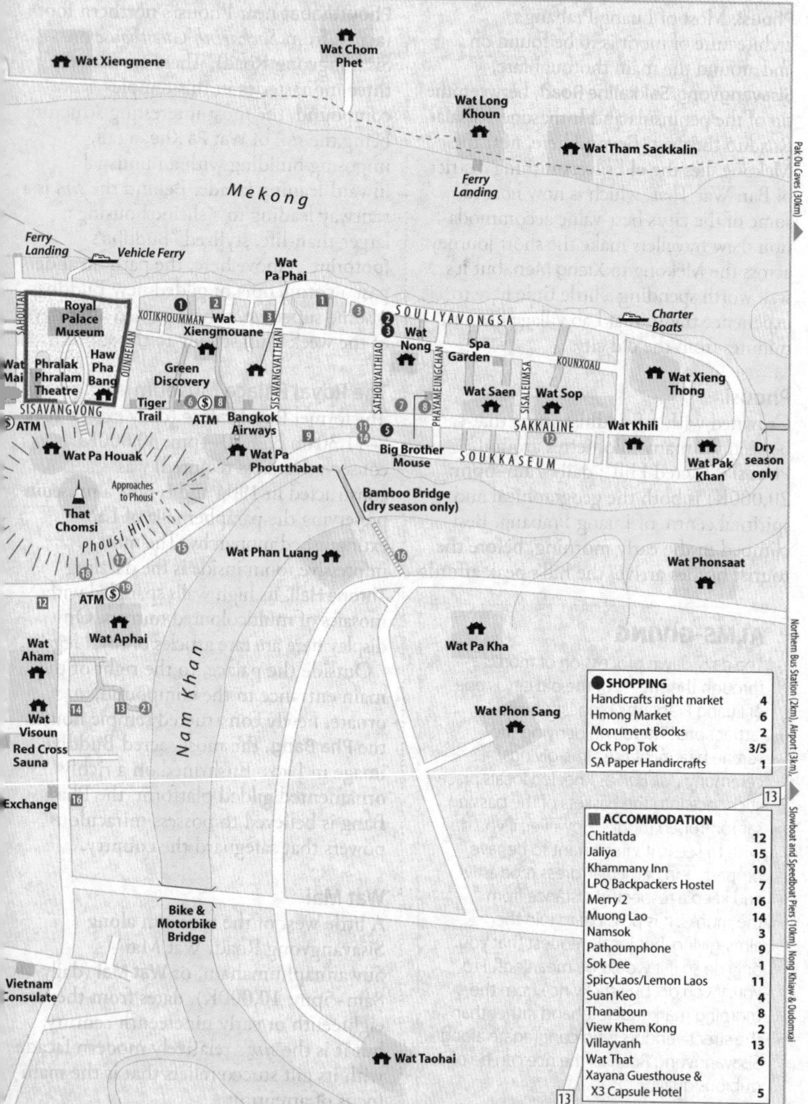

boat to the city's outlying sights and beautiful hinterland.

WHAT TO SEE AND DO

Luang Prabang's **old city** is largely concentrated on a tongue of land, approximately 1km long and 250m wide, with the confluence of the Mekong and Nam Khan rivers at its tip. This peninsula is dominated by a steep and forested hill, **Phousi**. Most of Luang Prabang's architecture of merit is to be found on and around the main thoroughfare, **Sisavangvong/Sakkaline Road**, between the tip of the peninsula and Inthasone/Kitsalat Road to the west. Beyond here, near the Mekong, lies the old silversmithing district of Ban Wat That, which is now host to some of the city's best-value accommodation. Few travellers make the short journey across the Mekong to **Xieng Men**, but it's well worth spending a little time here to experience traditional Lao village life, just minutes from the old city.

Phousi

Crowned with a Buddhist stupa that can be seen for many kilometres around, **Phousi** ("Sacred Hill"; daily 7am–6pm; 20,000K) is both the geographical and spiritual centre of Luang Prabang. Best climbed in the early morning, before the tourist hordes arrive, the hill's peak affords a stunning panorama of the city, and can be reached by several different routes. The most straightforward is via the stairway directly opposite the main gate of the Royal Palace Museum. It's worth stopping first at the adjacent *sim* (main temple building) of **Wat Pa Houak** (donation recommended), a fine little temple that contains some fascinating murals.

An alternative approach is via **Wat Pa Phoutthabat** near Phousi's northern foot (across from *Sackarinh Guesthouse* on Sisavangvong Road). There are actually three monasteries in this temple compound, the most interesting structure being the *sim* of **Wat Pa Khe**, a tall, imposing building with an unusual inward-leaning facade. Behind the *sim* is a stairway leading to a shrine housing a larger-than-life, stylized "**Buddha's footprint**". Above here, the path meanders past a cornucopia of gilded new Buddhas – some supersize, others named after days of the week – up steeply to the summit.

ALMS-GIVING

The daily dawn procession of monks through the streets of the old city is one of Luang Prabang's biggest tourist "attractions". There's no denying the serene beauty of the alms-giving ceremony (*Tak Bat*) as kneeled locals place sticky rice into the baskets of the passing saffron-robed monks. However, if you do wish to see it, it's important to behave properly – in particular, dress modestly and keep a respectful distance from the monks. It is possible to join the alms-giving, but locals request that you only do so if it would be meaningful to you. If you do, buy sticky rice from the morning market beforehand rather than the street vendors who congregate along Sisavangvong Road as the rice can be of dubious quality.

The Royal Palace Museum

The former **Royal Palace** (daily except Tues 8–11.30am & 1.30–4pm; 30,000K; conservative dress required) was constructed in 1904 and is now a museum preserving the paraphernalia of Laos's extinguished monarchy. The most impressive room inside is the dazzling **Throne Hall**, its high walls spangled with mosaics of multicoloured mirrors. On display here are rare articles of royal regalia.

Outside the palace, to the right of the main entrance to the compound, an ornate, newly constructed temple houses the **Pha Bang**, the most sacred Buddha image in Laos. Enshrined on a richly ornamented gilded platform, the Pha Bang is believed to possess miraculous powers that safeguard the country.

Wat Mai

A little west of the museum along Sisavangvong Road, Wat Mai Suwannaphumaham, or **Wat Mai** (daily 8am–5pm; 10,000K), dates from the late eighteenth or early nineteenth century, but it is the *sim*'s relatively modern facade with its gilt stucco reliefs that is the main focus of attention.

Wat Pa Phai and Wat Saen

Lined with restaurants and travel agents, the commercial neighbourhood just east of the Royal Palace Museum along Sisavangvong Road contains some fine examples of traditional Chinese shophouse architecture, given a Franco–Lao treatment. A left turn down Sisavangvatthani Road will take you to **Wat Pa Phai**, the "Bamboo Forest Monastery", whose *sim* is painted and lavishly embellished with stylized *naga* (water serpents) and peacocks.

Doubling back up to the corner, turn left to continue down Sakkaline Road as far as **Wat Saen**, where an ornate boat shed houses the monastery's two longboats used in the annual boat race festival. Held at the end of the rainy season, the boat races are believed to lure Luang Prabang's guardian *naga* back into the rivers after high waters and flooded rice paddies have allowed them to escape.

Wat Xieng Thong

Probably the most historic and enchanting Buddhist monastery in the entire country, **Wat Xieng Thong** (daily 6am–6pm; 20,000K), near the northernmost tip of the peninsula, is unmissable. The wonderful, graceful main *sim* was built in 1560 and a recent, extensive US-funded project has vividly restored much of its intricate gold stencilling and mosaic work. You'll need to stand at a distance to get a view of the roof, the *sim*'s most outstanding feature. Elegant lines curve and overlap, sweeping nearly to the ground, and evoke a bird with outstretched wings or, as the locals say, a mother hen sheltering her brood.

Across the monastery grounds is the **Funerary Carriage Hall**. The hall's wide teakwood panels are deeply carved with depictions of characters from the Lao version of the Ramayana. Inside, the principal article on display is the *latsalot*, the royal funerary carriage, used to transport the mortal remains of King Sisavong Vong, the penultimate monarch of Laos, to cremation. The vehicle is built in the form of several bodies of parallel *naga*, with jagged fangs and dripping tongues.

Traditional Arts and Ethnology Centre (TAEC)

Situated up a steep road off Kitsalat Road, the small **Traditional Arts and Ethnology Centre** (Tues–Sun 9am–6pm; 25,000K; Ⓦ taeclaos.org) offers a fascinating insight into Laos's hill tribes and their customs. Exhibits include numerous items of clothing, such as an amazing Akha Pouly Nyai woman's headdress made up of over three hundred silver ornaments, as well as household objects and religious artefacts. There's also an excellent shop and café here.

Wat Visoun and Wat Aham

The older parts of the city may have a higher concentration of monasteries and historic buildings, but there is plenty to see beyond its confines. **Wat Visoun** and **Wat Aham** (20,000K for both) share a parcel of land on the opposite side of Phousi from the Royal Palace Museum. Wat Visoun has a bulbous, finial-topped stupa, while half-hidden behind a pair of huge banyan trees, neighbouring Wat Aham features a delightfully diminutive *sim* and a couple of mould-blackened *that* (stupa).

UXO Lao Visitor Centre

Behind the large President Souphanouvong Park, 1km south of the old city, the **UXO Lao Visitor Centre** (Mon–Fri 8am–noon & 1–4pm; donations welcome) addresses the devastating impact on Laos of the US's nine-year bombing campaign during the Second Indochina War. The small exhibition lays out the shocking statistics – more ordnance was dropped on the country than was used during the whole of World War II – and outlines the uphill task facing UXO Lao.

Phosy Market and Ock Pop Tok

Around 2km southwest of the centre along Photisalath Road (20,000K by tuk-tuk), **Phosy Market** (daily 7am–5pm) provides a welcome taste of real daily life in Luang Prabang away from the tourists. This huge, largely covered market sells almost everything you can think of, from machetes to mobiles to giant Miffys.

5

Tucked down a bumpy lane opposite the market on the banks of the Mekong, **Ock Pop Tok** ("East Meets West"; ⓦockpoptok.com) offers fascinating guided tours of its Living Crafts Centre (every 30min: daily 8.30am–5pm; free), which employs thirty expert weavers from local villages. They also run excellent classes and workshops.

Xieng Men

The village of **Xieng Men**, just across the Mekong from the old city, feels a world away from the crowds of Sisavangvong Road. Head uphill from the ferry landing and you'll find a narrow lane to the right, which will lead you past traditional wooden houses to the first of the temples, **Wat Xiengmene** (10,000K), built in 1592. Much of what you now see dates from modern times, though its *sim* retains its beautifully carved doors. Further on, a short but steep climb up steps to the left brings you to the timeworn *sim* and stupas of **Wat Chom Phet** (10,000K), a disused monastery best visited at dusk when the views of the sunset are spectacular. Continuing along the path will lead you to **Wat Long Khoun** (10,000K). Check out the two Chinese door guardians painted either side of the main entrance to the *sim* and the finely drawn, colourful murals within. Your ticket includes a guided visit to nearby **Wat Tham Sackkalin**, a cave repository for old and damaged Buddha images.

A frequent vehicle ferry (10,000K) operates between Luang Prabang and Xieng Men, leaving from the landing northwest of the Royal Palace Museum, or arrange with one of the boatmen to be dropped at the main Xieng Men ferry landing and picked up below Wat Long Khoun (around 20,000K).

ARRIVAL AND DEPARTURE

By air The airport is 4km northeast of the old city. If you're arriving on an international flight, you can get a thirty-day visa on arrival here (see p.345). There is also a foreign exchange booth and a couple of ATMs. Minivans (buy a ticket at the counter just after the exit; 50,000K/600B for up to three people) shuttle tourists to the centre, and will take you straight to your accommodation. Heading out to the airport, tuk-tuks charge a flat fare of 50,000K from the centre – it's worth booking one in advance through your guesthouse or arranging with a tuk-tuk driver to pick you up.

Airlines Bangkok Airways, Sisavangvong Rd (ⓣ071 253334); Lao Airlines, Manomai Rd (ⓣ071 212172); Lao Central Airlines, Airport (ⓣ071 410215); Thai Smile (ⓦthaismileair.com); Vietnam Airlines, Airport (ⓣ071 213048).

Destinations Bangkok, Thailand (3–4 daily; 1hr 40min); Chiang Mai, Thailand (daily; 1hr); Hanoi, Vietnam (2 daily; 1hr); Jinghong, China (2 weekly; 1hr); Pakse (daily; 1hr 40min); Siem Reap, Cambodia (daily; 1hr 40min); Vientiane (4 daily; 40min).

By boat In 2012, the slow boat pier for services to/from Houayxai and Pakbeng was moved to Ban Don, 10km east of the old city, in a move to benefit the local tuk-tuk drivers; speedboats arrive at the same place. Sawngthaews to town (20,000K/person) will drop you at your accommodation once you've bought a ticket at the booth at the top of the landing. At the time of writing, there were no boat services running on the Nam Ou to Nong Khiaw (8hr), though these were rumoured to restart by mid-2014; until they were suspended, they ran from the old slow boat pier behind the Royal Palace in the old city. Slow boats depart daily for Pakbeng (for Houayxai; 110,000K) at 8.30am. While you can buy tickets at the pier (arrive at least 30min early), it's much easier to pick one up from a travel agent in town. Prices are much higher (190,000K to Pakbeng is typical) but will include pick-up from your accommodation; otherwise, a sawngthaew to the pier will cost around 60,000K. The eight-seater speedboats to Pakbeng (190,000K) and Houayxai (320,000K) theoretically depart at 9am (again, arrive early to be sure of a seat), though as they'll only set off when full they often leave (much) later; since there's no guarantee they'll run, some travel agents are reluctant to sell tickets in advance.

Destinations Houayxai (speedboat 6–7hr); Pakbeng (slow boat 8hr, speedboat 3–4hr).

By bus Luang Prabang has two public bus stations, plus a third for faster and pricier tourist minibuses and "VIP" international coaches; tuk-tuks to any of the stations from town cost around 20,000K. Buses from points north arrive at the Northern bus station, 3km northeast of town, near the airport. Buses from Vang Vieng, Vientiane and other points south along Route 13 stop at the Southern bus station, 3km south of the centre. Naluang tourist bus station (aka minibus station) is opposite the Southern bus station. Tourist buses will normally drop you centrally – often at a guesthouse that the driver has links to, though you're not obliged to stay there. You can buy tickets at the bus stations, but it's usually easier (if more expensive) to get them from one of the tour agencies on Sisavangvong Road, which will include a transfer from your guesthouse. For tourist buses, you'll save money if you book direct with the bus station itself (ⓣ071 212979, ⓦnaluangstation.com); their tickets are cheaper than the agencies in town but still include transfer.

Destinations from Northern bus station Houayxai

(Borkeo; 2–3 daily; 14hr); Luang Namtha (daily; 9hr); Nong Khiaw (3 daily; 4hr); Oudomxai (3 daily; 6hr).

Destinations from Southern bus station Phonsavan (daily; 10hr); Vang Vieng (2 daily; 6–7hr); Vientiane (10 daily; 10–12hr); Vinh, Vietnam (daily; 22hr).

Destinations from Naluang tourist bus station Chiang Mai, Thailand (daily; 16hr); Hanoi, Vietnam (6 weekly; 24hr); Kunming, China (daily; 26hr); Loei, Thailand (daily; 9hr); Luang Namtha (daily; 9hr); Nong Khiaw (daily; 3hr 30min); Oudomxai (daily; 5hr); Phonsavan (daily; 7hr); Vang Vieng (3–5 daily; 5–6hr); Vientiane (2 daily; 10hr); Vinh, Vietnam (6 weekly; 24hr).

INFORMATION AND TOURS

Tourist information Lao National Tourism Administration, Sisavangvong Rd (Mon–Fri 8–11.30am & 1.30–4pm, Sat & Sun 9–11.30am & 1–3.30pm; ⓣ 071 212487, ⓦ tourismluangprabang.org); Ban Natha, Chomphet, a 5min walk north of the Xieng Men boat landing (Mon–Fri 8–11.30am & 1.30–4pm).

Tour agencies Sisavangvong Road is lined with tour agencies (including those listed here) offering day and overnight treks, mountain biking, kayaking, white-water rafting (in season), elephant rides – and myriad combinations thereof. Though they're a little pricier than the competition, Green Discovery (ⓣ 071 212093, ⓦ greendiscoverylaos.com) and Tiger Trail (ⓣ 071 252655, ⓦ laos-adventures.com) can be relied on for both the quality and ethics of their tours.

CITY TRANSPORT

Bicycles Many guesthouses, and various shops along Sakkaline/Sisavangvong Road, rent bicycles for 20,000K/day, and you can also find motorbikes for rent on Sisavangvong Rd (from 100,000K/day).

Tuk-tuks Tuk-tuks can be surprisingly hard to find when you need one; there are always congregations outside the tourist office and above the vehicle ferry pier. A ride anywhere in town should cost around 15,000–20,000K but you'll need to haggle.

ACCOMMODATION

Accommodation in Luang Prabang is significantly more expensive than elsewhere in the country, and it can be hard to find much below 100,000K in high season. While the old city is still home to a dwindling number of budget options, the nicest area to stay for travellers on a budget is in the narrow lanes behind *Joma* café a short stroll west from the old city between Chao Fa Ngum Rd and the Mekong, though for a bit more nightlife (such as it is) you may prefer one of the guesthouses around *Lao Lao Garden* and *Utopia*, southeast of Phousi. Prices tend to rise around November but you can get good discounts in low season (May–Sept). Almost all places have free wi-fi.

THE OLD CITY

★**Namsok** Sisavangvatthani Rd ⓣ 020 2235 4747, ⓔ taetotam@hotmail.com. On one of the few streets in the old city where you can still get a room for $10, this friendly place is excellent value, with big and spotless, if rather sparse, wood-floored rooms. For a bit more style (and cash), the ones in the block behind have TVs and snazzy black bathrooms. Double **80,000K**

Pathoumphone Soukkaseum Rd ⓣ 071 212946. A real bargain, especially considering its location right opposite the Nam Khan, with very friendly owners. Rooms have shared bathrooms and verge on dingy, but you won't find cheaper. Ask for room two, which has a small balcony and views over the river. Double **60,000K**

Sok Dee Off Souliyavongsa Rd ⓣ 071 252555. Tucked off the Mekong Road, this popular guesthouse is a great choice for somewhere a little quieter but still central. Go for one of the rooms upstairs in the main building – bright and welcoming, though the trade-offs are thin walls and periodic lapses in cleanliness. Very handy for breakfast at *Saffron*. Double **140,000K**

Thanaboun Sisavangvong Rd ⓣ 071 260606, ⓔ thanaboun.gh@gmail.com. Rooms here are set back from the main drag and are plain but attractive. The most atmospheric, yet also the smallest and cheapest, are those off the small courtyard at the back. Double **150,000K**

View Khem Khong Souliyavongsa Rd ⓣ 071 213032, ⓔ ericsensaoui@msn.com. The cheapest rooms here may be rather cramped and without a view, but you won't find many better priced on the Mekong road. The attached restaurant (see p.375) is good. Double **140,000K**

SOUTHWEST OF THE OLD CITY

★**Khammany Inn** Photisalath Rd ⓣ 020 9529 3925, ⓔ khammanyhostel@gmail.com. Professionally run and immaculately kept, this sociable place a 10min walk from the old city is hugely popular with backpackers and justifiably so. Ask for one of the smaller basement dorms – from the first-floor 16-bedder there's a two-storey hop down to the bathroom. Breakfast included. Dorm **45,000K**, double **160,000K**

LPQ Backpackers Hostel Off Chao Fa Ngum Rd ⓣ 020 9113 8686. On the nicest and leafiest of the little lanes leading to the river, with slightly squished dorms but smart bathrooms with top-notch showers, and a chilled-out movies room. Avoid the overpriced, box-like private rooms, though. Dorm **50,000K**, double **120,000K**

SpicyLaos/Lemon Laos ⓣ 020 2255 5539. Prone to periodic identity crises (hence the twin names), this long-established backpacker joint has cheap but not hugely cheerful accommodation in very dark dorms – so great for escaping the heat, or recovering from a Beerlao hangover. There's a large patio and a great communal vibe. Dorm **30,000K**, double **70,000K**

5

Suan Keo Off Chao Fa Ngum Rd ⓣ 071 254404. Flowery bedspreads enliven the good-sized rooms at this peaceful, ever-popular guesthouse in Ban Wat That. You'll have to be quick to nab one of the two lovely wooden rooms upstairs. Good value. Double **100,000K**

Wat That Off Chao Fa Ngum Rd ⓣ 071 212913, ⓦ watthat guesthouse.net. Very pleasant guesthouse set across two buildings on either side of a pretty lane. Ask for the big, wooden room upstairs at the back of the lovely traditional Lao house next to *LPQ*; the bigger building opposite is more expensive (double 150,000K) but has a gorgeous wooden balcony. Big discounts off-season. Double **100,000K**

Xayana Guesthouse & X3 Capsule Hotel Off Chao Fa Ngum Rd ⓣ 071 260680, ⓦ mylaohome.com. The doubles at this modern guesthouse are disappointingly basic and cramped; come here instead for the "capsule" dorms, which have surprisingly large beds. Dorm **40,000K**, double **100,000K**

SOUTHEAST OF PHOUSI

Chitlatda Ban Aphai ⓣ 071 212227. Behind a bank of internet terminals, the cheapest rooms at this friendly, popular guesthouse are windowless and cell-like but clean and en-suite. The wood-floored rooms upstairs are bigger (with TVs) but almost twice the price. Double **60,000K**

Jaliya Manomai Rd ⓣ 071 252154. Facing onto a lovely private garden and tucked well away from the road, the rooms at this old-fashioned, peaceful place are all very clean and comfortable, with TVs. Good value. Double **120,000K**

Merry 2 Ban Visoun ⓣ 071 254445. Popular guesthouse at the start of a little lane leading down the Nam Khan. The cheapest rooms are slightly dingy but clean enough – much better to head upstairs where an extra 20,000K will get you a bathroom, gleaming wood floors and a shared balcony. Double **60,000K**

Muong Lao Ban Visoun ⓣ 071 252741, ⓔ thavone9 @gmail.com. The rooms at this good-value, friendly guesthouse opposite Wat Visoun are simple but very pleasant, and the old-fashioned, all-wood rooms upstairs have a nice shared balcony overlooking the temple. There's also an attractive outside restaurant. Double **140,000K**

Villayvanh Ban Aphai ⓣ 071 252757. Nestling among coconut palms down the warren of lanes leading to *Utopia*, this welcoming little guesthouse is a real find. Rooms (with TV) are immaculately maintained; the wood-floored ones at the back feel slightly newer. Free tea and coffee all day. Double **120,000K**

EATING

Luang Prabang prides itself on its food, and the city boasts more restaurants than anywhere in the country outside of Vientiane. Many of the city's tourist restaurants are located along a 500m strip of Sisavangvong Road that expats sarcastically call "Thang Falang" ("white man's way"), and they tend to be fairly pricey by Lao standards. Much cheaper meals can be found at the delightful riverside restaurants along Souliyavongsa Road.

> **LOCAL SPECIALITIES**
>
> You shouldn't miss out on having a traditional Lao meal in Luang Prabang. At the top of the list should be **or lam**, a bittersweet soup, heavy on aubergines and mushrooms. Other local specialities include **jaew bong**, a condiment of red chillies, shallots, garlic and dried buffalo skin, and **phak nâm**, a type of watercress particular to the area and widely used in salads.

STREET FOOD

Hmong Market Sisavangvong Rd/Kitsalat Rd. Baguettes and fresh fruit shakes are sold throughout the day at the Hmong Market, and during the evenings you'll also find someone selling delicious *kanom krok* (little coconut and rice pancakes) here. Daily 9am–9pm.

Night market Off Sisavangvong Rd. The best way to dine for next to nothing is to head to the buffet stalls set up down the narrow side street next to *Ancient Luang Prabang* and join the communal tables, sampling local treats in a casual, buzzing atmosphere. Just 10,000K will buy you as much rice and veg as you can cram onto a plate, then order tasty meat grills and beer separately. Daily 5–10pm.

CAFÉS

Delilah's Place Chao Fa Ngum Rd. A chilled-out place with ethnic cushion-strewn benches and a couple of candlelit roadside tables out front. Come for a pancake (20,000K) and cup of strong Lao coffee at breakfast time, and choose from the Lao menu later on. Daily 7am–10pm.

Joma Branches on Chao Fa Ngum and Soukkaseum roads. Perennially popular, though really you could be anywhere in the world. A good choice if you're craving a Western breakfast or lunch, with bagels (18,000K), sandwiches and cakes on offer, plus a range of coffees and fruit juices. Daily 7am–9pm.

★ **Le Banneton** Sakkaline Rd. Situated a little up from Wat Saen, this superb café-boulangerie feels decidedly French, with an excellent choice of patisseries, including the best croissants in town, plus delicious baguettes and good coffee. Breakfast sets from 40,000K. Daily 6.30am–6pm.

Le Café Ban Vat Sene Sakkaline Rd. A fan-spun café-restaurant that's full of colonial charm and a good choice throughout the day. Though there's an extensive menu, with a range of Lao and European options (baguettes around 40,000K), it's the cakes that are the standout here – including a heavenly banana tatin (24,000K). Daily 6.30–10pm.

★**Saffron** Branches on Souliyavongsa and Inthasone roads. The best place in town for a pulse-quickening espresso, either inside among sepia photos and jazz music, or (at the Souliyavongsa branch) outside on the terrace overlooking the Mekong. There's a good range of breakfasts, including a delicious granola bowl (20,000K), and you can also buy their own locally grown coffee here. Daily 7am–9pm.

RESTAURANTS

Coconut Garden Sisavangvong Rd. One of the most atmospheric choices along this over-populated stretch, with seats under lanterns in the courtyard, and a strong Lao menu that includes *kranab pa* (grilled river fish stuffed with pork and herbs, wrapped in a banana leaf; 48,000K), though portions can be a little small. Daily 8am–11.30pm.

★**Dyen Sabai** Ban Phan Luang, across the Nam Khan from the old city. Eating and drinking in Luang Prabang doesn't get much more atmospheric than *Dyen Sabai*, reached by bamboo bridge (5000K from 8am to 6pm) in dry season, and by boat in wet season. Cushions are scattered around the low bamboo "huts" here, creating a really relaxing place from which to make the most of the two-for-one cocktails (25,000K) during happy hour (noon–7pm), and specialities like *sin dad* (Lao barbecue; from 70,000K for two). Daily 8am–11pm.

Khem Khan Food Garden High on the bank of the Nam Khan River behind Phousi, this is a great venue for traditional Lao food, with lovely views of the Nam Kham. The *keng kai màk nao*, a soup served with chicken, and the *sai oua* sausages (both 40,000K) are standouts. Daily 8am–10pm.

Nisha Kitsalat Rd. No-frills Indian that dishes up Luang Prabang's best south Indian veg curries – try the *malai kofta* (16,000K) or *aloo baingan* (13,000K) – though there's also the obligatory *chicken tikka masala* for the meaty-minded. Daily 9am–11pm.

Riverside Barbecue Souliyavongsa Rd. By far the most popular spot by the Mekong, this big, bustling *sin dad* joint packs in hundreds every night, especially in winter when you can huddle around the smouldering pits for warmth. Obliging waiters are on hand to help you perfect your barbecue technique. All-inclusive buffet (excluding alcohol) 60,000K. Daily 6–10pm.

Thaheuame Souliyavongsa Rd. One of the most popular riverside restaurants, with both locals and tourists, serving an extensive, predominantly Lao menu that includes a spicy papaya salad for 15,000K. Daily 6am–9pm.

Un Petit Nid Sakkaline Rd. This cute "biblio-bistro" set slightly back from the main road makes a nice retreat throughout the day; try the *kao pun* (noodle soup with coconut milk, potatoes and galangal; 25,000K). Daily 7.30am–9.30pm.

★TREAT YOURSELF

3 Nagas Sakkaline Rd ⓣ 071 253888, ⓦ 3-nagas.com. If you can afford to splash out on one meal, it should be at the atmospheric dining room of this gorgeous hotel. The Lao dishes are beautifully prepared and presented – try the exquisite *larp* with sliced Mekong fish (56,000K) or the lemongrass stuffed with pork (60,000K). The wine list is excellent, and the boozy cocktails (Lao sling 50,000K) to die for. Daily 6.30am–10.30pm.

DRINKING AND NIGHTLIFE

The main bar area is southeast of the old city, between Phousi and the Nam Khan. Don't expect amazing nightlife – a town curfew has the bars closing at 11.30pm.

Bowling Alley 4km southwest of town, past the Southern bus station. Believe it or not, the place to be after the bars close is the ten-pin bowling alley. A game costs 20,000K/person, though judging by the quality of play it's the Beerlao (15,000K) that's the bigger attraction. Tuk-tuks wait outside *Lao Lao Garden* and *Utopia* at chucking-out time to take you there. Daily noon–2am.

Hive Popular if rather brash bar that runs a hip-hop and "Ethnik" fashion show (Tues–Sun from 7pm), though happy hour (noon–7pm) is arguably the biggest draw, offering two-for-one deals on classic cocktails (25,000K each). Daily 7am–11.30pm.

Lao Lao Garden Large, hugely atmospheric garden bar – a great place to chill out over a Lao barbecue (49,000K) under the lanterns, before things pick up later on. The huge drinks menu includes a range of rather potent two-for-one cocktails from 20,000K, and large Beerlao for 14,000K. Daily 8am–11.30pm.

S Bar With a drinks menu printed on 12" vinyl, this new kid on the block thinks of itself as a cooler, classier alternative to the competition along the main bar strip. It's quickly become famous for its burgers (55,000K), and there are occasional themed nights and gigs (check ⓦ facebook.com/sbarlaos). Daily noon–11.30pm.

★**Utopia** On the river south of Wat Aham; follow the signs from the main road. "Zen by day, groovy by night" is *Utopia*'s philosophy – and it's a real winner. With stunning river views, rustic-tropical decor, and a good menu of food and booze, not to mention early morning yoga, "beach" volleyball, DJ evenings and BBQ-in-a-bomb nights, there's enough to make your visit last all day. Daily 8am–11.30pm.

ENTERTAINMENT

L'Etranger Books & Tea, just west of the *Hive* bar, shows quality films nightly at 7pm; there's no charge, but you are expected to buy food (see opposite) or a drink. Movies are also shown most nights at *Xayana* and *LPQ Backpackers* (see p.373).

5

Phralak Phralam Theatre Royal Palace Museum. Demonstrations of classical Lao dance are given four times a week (Mon, Wed, Fri & Sat 6pm) at the Royal Ballet Theatre. Performances include excerpts from the Lao version of the Ramayana and cost 100,000–150,000K/person depending on the seat.

SHOPPING

Many of the town's souvenir shops are on Sisavangvong Road, especially in Ban Jek, near the museum. Textiles are one of the best buys, sold by shops throughout town; the nicest are of high quality and thus will have corresponding prices.

MARKETS

Handicrafts night market Sisavangvong Road. The city's biggest draw is undoubtedly the handicrafts night-market, between the post office and the Royal Palace Museum, which sells, among other things, silk scarves, bags, lamps, Beerlao T-shirts and Hmong silver. Haggling is expected, but do be reasonable (and friendly) throughout, and don't enter into a discussion about price unless you're prepared to buy. Daily 5–10pm.

Hmong Market The small Hmong Market, on the corner of Sisavangvong and Kitsalat roads, sells much of the same produce as the night market, usually with less pressure from the sellers. Daily 9am–9pm.

SHOPS

Monument Books Sathouyaithiao Rd. Great little bookshop stocking a good range of magazines, local and international fiction and non-fiction, travel guides, maps and children's books. Mon–Fri 9am–9pm, Sat 9am–7pm.

Ock Pop Tok Branches on Sakkaline and Sathouyaithiao roads. Though the textiles here are a little pricey, there's no denying the superb quality of the craftsmanship. All of the products have been made in Laos – either in the shop's Living Crafts Centre (see p.372) or through their Village Weaver Projects which support local communities. Daily 8am–8pm.

SA Paper Handicrafts Off Souliyavongsa Rd. Tucked down a tiny lane opposite Wat Xieng Mouane, this is one of a number of shops selling colourful traditional mulberry-paper lanterns, including collapsible models, plus books and cards. Daily 9am–9pm.

DIRECTORY

Banks and exchange 24hr ATMs are dotted around all the main tourist areas, and there are several exchange places along Sisavangvong Road, most of which are open till 9 or 10pm.

Hospital The provincial hospital is 4km southwest of town.

Internet Internet cafés can be found along Sisavangvong Rd east of the Royal Palace Museum, as well as on Kitsalat Rd. Most places charge 100K/min.

Massage and herbal sauna The Red Cross Sauna on Visounalat Rd (daily 8am–8pm; T 071 252856) has traditional Lao massage at 40,000K/hr and an excellent sauna for 10,000K. For a wider choice of massages in less spartan surroundings, Spa Garden, Ban Phonheuang (daily 9am–9.30pm; T 071 212325), is highly recommended.

Post office GPO, Chao Fa Ngum Rd (Mon–Fri 8am–noon & 1–5pm, Sat 8am–noon).

Volunteering Big Brother Mouse, Phayameungchan Rd (T 071 254937, W bigbrothermouse.com), is a project that runs programmes to teach and encourage Lao children to read and write. You can go and visit the centre, help the children with their English (daily 9am & 5pm; 2hr), and buy books and donate them to the cause.

DAY-TRIPS FROM LUANG PRABANG

Luang Prabang's most popular excursions are to the **Pak Ou Caves**, 30km north of the city, and **Kouang Si waterfall**, around 25km to the southwest – both are typically half-day trips. In addition, tour agencies in town offer a wide variety of trips and activities out of the city (see p.373).

Kouang Si

The best day-trip from Luang Prabang is the picturesque, multi-level **Kouang Si waterfall** (daily 8am–5.30pm; 20,000K), tumbling 60m before spilling through a series of crystal-blue pools ideal for swimming; there are basic changing facilities at the lower pools. The steep path on the opposite side of the falls leads to the top in about thirty minutes, though it can get quite slippery, so be very careful – and don't attempt it in the wet season. Numerous simple restaurants and food stalls crowd around the entrance to the falls and there are a couple of basic places to eat inside; better still, bring a picnic.

There are several ways to reach Kouang Si. The cheapest option is by **minibus**, booked via a tour agency or direct with Naluang bus station (see p.372; daily 11.30am & 1.30pm; 45min; 60,000K). Taking a **tuk-tuk** can also be an economical way to go if you can assemble a group – drivers charge a flat fee of 200,000K (for up to five people), though you can usually pay a bit less if there's just one or two of you. The slowest but most scenic

route is by **boat** down the Mekong River – boatmen congregate at the bottom of Inthasone Road and at the tip of the peninsula near Wat Xieng Thong, and charge 100,000K per person return (for six people), which should include the final portion of the journey by tuk-tuk.

The Pak Ou Caves and around

Numerous caves punctuate the limestone cliffs around Pak Ou – the confluence of the Mekong and Nam Ou rivers. The best-known caves are the "**Buddha Caves**", Tham Ting and Tham Phoum (daily 8am–sunset; 20,000K). They have been used for centuries as a repository for old and unwanted Buddha images that can no longer be venerated on an altar, and the hundreds upon hundreds of serenely smiling images covered in dust and cobwebs make an eerie scene. **Tham Ting**, the lower cave, just above the water's surface, is light enough to explore without artificial light, but the upper cave is unlit, so bring a torch.

Boat trips (70,000K/person) can be arranged with the boatmen at the bottom of Inthasone Road – most boats leave around 8.30am. Later in the day you'll need to charter one yourself (300,000K per six-person boat, but be prepared to haggle). It's possible to make the journey by road, but there's little point as the boat journey is at least half the fun.

Boatmen usually combine a visit to the caves with a stop at Ban Xang Hai, the so-called **Whisky Village**, some 6km back downriver towards the city. It's a bit of a tourist trap, but once you've seen a cave full of Buddhas you may be ready for a good, stiff drink.

The northeast

Once difficult to reach and still short on proper tourist sites, the remote **northeast** is one of the least-visited parts of Laos. This area was heavily bombed during the Second Indochina War, particularly at the strategic **Plain of Jars**, which takes its name from the fields of ancient, giant funerary urns which are now the northeast's main tourist draw. Few travellers make it here, unless en route to or from Vietnam – either at the crossing near Ban Nong Het, near Phonsavan, or at Na Meo, near Sam Neua.

PHONSAVAN

The capital of **Xieng Khuang province**, **PHONSAVAN** has emerged as the most important town on the Plain of Jars since the total devastation of the region in the Second Indochina War. Hastily rebuilt in the aftermath of decades of fighting, Phonsavan is only now beginning to recover economically, thanks in large part to international interest in the world-famous **jar sites** scattered around the perimeter of the plain. Although most visitors come only to see these,

INTO VIETNAM FROM THE NORTHEAST

There are two official border crossings into Vietnam from northeastern Laos, though both can be long and slow-going.

NONG HET TO NAM CAN

The easiest way to cross in to Vietnam from Phonsavan is on the direct bus to **Vinh**, which leaves Phonsavan's inter-provincial bus station at 6.30am each morning (except Tues), taking around 10 hours to reach Vinh (150,000K), from where connections to Hanoi are available. The border is open 6am–6pm daily, and to enter Vietnam you'll need to have arranged your visa in advance.

NA MEO CROSSING FOR THANH HOA PROVINCE

To get to Na Meo from Sam Neua, the nearest big town, catch the daily sawngthaew (3hr; 50,000K) from Sam Neua's Nathong bus station. There's also a daily bus service to Thanh Hoa from Sam Neua's main bus station, which takes nine hours (180,000K). Make sure you have obtained your Vietnamese visa in advance.

5

the Xieng Khuang Plateau is a place of great natural beauty and its back roads are well worth exploring.

ARRIVAL AND DEPARTURE

By air Tuk-tuks cost 20,000K/person for the 5km ride from the airport into town. You may even be able to get a free lift with one of the hotel reps. Note that Phonsavan is marked as Xieng Khuang on flight schedules. Currently Lao Airlines only flies to Phonsavan from Vientiane (daily; 30min).

By bus Buses arrive and depart from several stations across town. When leaving Phonsavan, you may prefer to book your ticket a day in advance at the *Lao Falang Restaurant* (see below). The owner takes a cut of around 20,000K on each booking, but will arrange tuk-tuk transport to the bus station for you, or even have the bus pull up outside your guesthouse.

The main inter-provincial bus station, handling arrivals from Vientiane, Luang Prabang and Vang Vieng, is 4km west of the centre on route 7; tuk-tuks (10,000–15,000K per person) will ferry you into town. The Bounmixay bus station, south of the tourist office on route 1D, is where the majority of buses travelling from Vientiane come to a stop – tuk-tuks are on hand to meet buses.

Minibuses connecting Phonsavan with Laos' three main tourist centres depart early in the morning from a lot in the centre of town, just off route 7.

Destinations from inter-provincial bus station Luang Prabang (daily; 8hr); Sam Neua (daily; 10hr); Vang Vieng (daily; 6hr); Vientiane (5 daily; 9hr); Vinh, Vietnam (daily except Tues; 10hr).

Destinations from Bounmixay bus station Pakse (daily; 16hr); Vientiane (7 daily; 8hr).

Destination from minibus station Luang Prabang (daily; 7hr); Vang Vieng (daily; 5hr); Vientiane (daily; 8hr).

INFORMATION AND TOURS

Banks There's a BCEL ATM on Route 7, close to the centre; the main branch, which has a currency exchange, is about 1km west of here, on the same road. Most travel agents, and some guesthouses, will change currency.

Internet There's an internet café next to *Simmalay Restaurant* (daily 7am–10pm), charging 10,000K/hr.

Mines Advisory Group office (MAG) On Route 7 W maginternational.org; free. This team of de-miners has been working in the fields to stop the bombs from ruining more lives. The office is a good place to learn about the effects and devastation of the war. Mon–Fri 8am–8pm, Sat & Sun 4–8pm.

Tours There are a number of tour agencies in town that will organize trips around the jar sites for around 150,000–200,000K, depending on the number of people. The tours run by Sousath Travel (T 020 296 7213, E rasapet_lao @yahoo.com) are particularly recommended.

ACCOMMODATION

Dokkhoune Hotel Just west of *White Orchid* along Route 7 T 020 234 2555. With a lobby full of decorative UXO and good views of the mountains from the hallways, this four-floor block is in a good central location. The large but dull rooms are a bit of a disappointment, but not bad value. Double 80,000K

★ **Kong Keo Guesthouse** 200m north of Route 7 (follow the dirt track that starts just north of the *Lao Falang Restaurant*) T 055 211354, E kongkeojar @hotmail.com. The best and most quirky choice for budget travellers. Rooms are rather small, beds are lumpy and the bathrooms pretty poky, but the overall vibe of the place more than makes up for it, with a cool bar-restaurant and a garden littered with UXO. In addition to tours, they can also arrange visas for Cambodia, China and Vietnam. Double 60,000K

Kounsy At the far eastern end of the main drag, near the junction T 061 211170. This guesthouse, a short stroll from the main drag, has a number of basic, rather dark rooms, though they're cosier than many others on Route 7. Double 70,000K

Lao Falang Above *Lao Falang Restaurant*, just north of the *White Orchid* hotel T 020 2221 2456. The cheapest place to crash for the night, with basic dorm beds above a restaurant that serves food and beer to a mostly Western crowd. Automatic motorbikes are available here for 100,000K/day. Dorm 30,000K

Nice Directly opposite *White Orchid* on Route 7 T 061 312454. Comfortable little en-suite rooms off a lantern-strung outdoor hallway. The staff are helpful and the place is in a good location close to the best restaurants, but the place gets chilly during the winter. Double 70,000K

EATING

Eating options aren't great in Phonsavan, though there are a few places to choose from on the main road.

Bamboozle! Route 7, just west of *Nisha* T 030 9523913. Bamboo-bedecked, *falang*-friendly restaurant with a menu that mixes Western dishes with cheaper Asian staples (the Lao noodle soup is just 15,000K). Daily 7am–11pm.

Craters East of *Simmaly* on route 7 T 020 780 5775. A relaxed place with UXO lined up outside and old weaponry decorating the interior. The menu offers everything you would expect from a travellers' café, including Western breakfasts (from 14,000K), club sandwiches (32,000K) and a few good Asian dishes. Daily 6.30am–10pm.

Lao Falang Restaurant Just north of the *White Orchid* hotel T 554 06868. Not really recommended for its food (mains around 30,000K) as service is so slow, but this is still a good place to grab a Beerlao and mingle with other travellers. Each night at 6pm the owner screens a film about the American bombing of Laos. Daily 6.30am–11.30pm.

UXO IN XIENG KHUANG PROVINCE

The countless **mines**, **bombies** (round bomblets) and **bombs** littering Xieng Khuang province remain a huge danger to the local people; when travelling in the province (as elsewhere in Laos), be sure to stick to well-trodden paths. The three main jar sites have been cleared of unexploded ordnance (UXO), but even so it's advisable to stick to the paths. For more information about UXO, visit the Mines Advisory Group in Phonsavan (see opposite), or the COPE Visitor Centre in Vientiane (see p.356).

Nisha Just east of *Bamboozle!* on route 7 ☎ 020 9826 6023. Bare-bones Indian place serving great dosa, alongside the usual assortment of curries. In the mornings it's popular with backpackers, who come for the good banana roti (12,000K). Daily 6am–9.30pm.

Simmaly Opposite the Mines Advisory Group on route 7 ☎ 030 5727430. This Chinese-run restaurant is always full of a good mix of locals and tourists. Portions are large and prices cheap, with great spicy soups and fried rice dishes going for 10,000K. Daily 7am–10pm.

THE PLAIN OF JARS

The 15km-wide stretch of grassy meadows and low rolling hills around Phonsavan takes its name from the clusters of chest-high urns found here. Scattered across the **Plain of Jars** and on the hills beyond, the ancient jars, which are thought to be around two thousand years old, testify to the fact that Xieng Khuang province, with its access to key regional trade routes, its wide, flat spaces and temperate climate, has been considered prime real estate in Southeast Asia for centuries. The largest jars measure 2m in height and weigh as much as ten tonnes. Little is known about the Iron Age megalithic civilization that created them, but in the 1930s, bronze and iron tools as well as coloured glass beads, bronze bracelets and cowrie shells were found at the sites, leading to the theory that the jars were funerary urns, originally holding cremated remains. More recent discoveries have also revealed underground burial chambers. During the **Second Indochina War**, the region was bombed extensively. American planes levelled towns and forced villagers to take to the forest, as the two sides waged a bitter battle for control of the Plain of Jars, which represented a back door to northern Vietnam. The plain was transformed into a wasteland, the treeless flatlands and low rolling brown hills dramatically pockmarked with craters.

WHAT TO SEE AND DO

Of the dozens of jar sites that give the Plain of Jars its name, three groups have become tourist attractions, largely because they are accessible and have a greater concentration of jars. All three of these sites can be seen in a day, with hotels and tour companies pitching them as a **package** (see opposite). If you're on a tour, check in advance if the entry fee for each site is included in the price. It's also possible to visit independently; you can charter a tuk-tuk (around 150,000K for a half day), or rent a bike or motorcycle (around 20,000K and 80,000K respectively).

Site 1

Of the three main groups, the closest one, **Thong Hai Hin** ("Stone Jar Plain") – known as Site 1 (15,000K) – just 2km southwest of Phonsavan, has over two hundred jars and is the most visited. From here, a path leads up to **Hai Cheaum** ("Cheaum Jar"), a massive 2m-high jar named after a Tai Lau hero. Nearby is another group of jars, one of which has a crude human shape carved onto it. In the hill off to the left is a large cave that the Pathet Lao used during the war – and which, according to local legend, was used as a kiln to cast the jars. Erosion has carved two holes in the roof of the cave – natural chimneys that add weight to the kiln theory. It may also have been used as a crematorium.

Site 2

Site 2 (10,000K) is located about 10km southwest of the village of Lat Houang, which is on the road to Muang Khoun. The site is based on two adjacent hills

called Phou Salato. Nearly a hundred jars are scattered across the twin hills here, lending the site the name **Hai Hin Phou Salato** ("Salato Hill Stone Jar").

Site 3

Site 3 (10,000K), the most atmospheric of the three sites, lies 4km up the road from Site 2, just beyond the village of Ban Xieng Di. Here you'll see Wat Xieng Di, a simple wooden monastery that holds a bomb-damaged Buddha. A path at the back of the monastery leads up a hill through several fields to the site, **Hai Hin Lat Khai**, where there are more than a hundred jars on a hillside with sweeping views of the plain below.

The far north

Until recently, decades of war and neglect had kept Laos's isolated **far north** from developing, unwittingly preserving a way of life that has virtually vanished in neighbouring countries. Although inward investment from China is beginning to transform the landscape with large-scale agriculture and dam projects, the hills and mountains up here remain the domain of a scattering of **animist tribal peoples**, including the Hmong, Mien and Akha. It is largely the chance to experience first-hand these near-pristine cultures that draws visitors to the region today.

By far the most popular route out of Luang Prabang is by road or (if services are running) by river to **Nong Khiaw**, perhaps with a side-trip to tiny **Muang Ngoi**, then through **Oudomxai** to **Luang Namtha**, a popular base for trekking, owing to decent accommodation and easy access to Akha, Mien and Tai Dam villages. Travellers en route to **Vietnam** are able to cross at Tay Trang, accessible by bus from Muang Khoua (see box, p.382), and those bound for **China** are able to cross at Boten, reached by bus from Luang Namtha or Oudomxai. From Luang Namtha, it's just a few hours on a fast road to **Houayxai**, a major border crossing with Thailand. Many travellers entering from Thailand travel straight to Luang Prabang from here, via **slow boat along the Mekong**, but if you've got time, the north rewards further exploration.

NONG KHIAW

Resting at the foot of a striking red-faced cliff, amid towering blue-green limestone escarpments, the dusty town of **NONG KHIAW** on the banks of the Nam Ou River lies smack in the middle of some of the most dramatic scenery in Indochina. Part of Nong Khiaw's attraction has always lain in reaching the town itself – the eight-hour journey up the picturesque Nam Ou from Luang Prabang is one of the best river journeys in Laos. Unfortunately, boat trips were suspended in late 2013 owing to work on a Chinese-constructed dam, one of seven that will radically change life along the Nam Ou over the next decade; services were rumoured to resume by mid-2014.

Although the old town stretches for 1km parallel to the main highway, most of Nong Khiaw's tourist facilities are located by the big bridge over the Nam Ou. At the northern end of the bridge, you'll find the boat mooring, a few guesthouses and the more local side of town. Across the bridge, on the opposite bank, are the majority of guesthouses and restaurants.

A five-minute walk south of the bridge, a path leads off the main road up through thick jungle to the stunning **Nong Khiaw View Point** (daily 6.30am–3.30pm; 20,000K) atop Phou Phadeng, a tough but rewarding ninety-minute climb; bring suitable footwear. A further 2.5km walk or cycle will take you to the atmospheric **Pathok Caves** (daily 7am–5pm; 5000K), where villagers hid during the Second Indochina War – take a torch, as they are very dark.

ARRIVAL AND DEPARTURE

By bus The bus station is a 15min walk from the bridge, on the northwestern edge of town. All buses depart from here, though a minibus comes down to the boat landing to meet boats from Muang Ngoi, and will take passengers up to the bus station. Most guesthouses also offer minibus services, which include pick-up from where you're staying.

Destinations Luang Prabang (3 daily; 3–4hr); Oudomxai (daily; 4hr).

By boat Boats leave for Muang Ngoi at 11am and 2pm (1hr; 25,000K); one of the morning boats will sometimes continue to Muang Khoua (see box, p.382; 6hr; 120,000K) if there's enough demand (usually five people). Tickets should be bought at least 30min beforehand.

INFORMATION AND TOURS

Bicycles Mountain bikes for exploring the beautiful surrounding countryside can be rented next to *Coco Home* (daily 7am–6pm; 30,000K).

Internet Most of the guesthouses and some of the restaurants have wi-fi, and *Deen* restaurant, on the south side of the bridge, has a computer terminal available for 250K/min.

Massage Sabai Sabai, opposite Sophdun Temple on the southern side of town, is the perfect place to revive yourself after a long bus journey or a day of exploring. Use of the herbal sauna costs 20,000K (5–9pm) and massages start from 50,000K (9am–10pm).

Tours There are three excellent tour operators. Run by forward-thinking local guide Home, ★NK Adventures (T 020 5868 6068, E bounhome68@hotmail.com), next to Sabai Sabai, runs good-value cycling, trekking, kayaking and bamboo-rafting trips; Green Discovery (W greendiscoverylaos.com), on the main street, offer all these and more, while opposite, in the same building as *Delilah's*, Tiger Trail (T 020 5439 5686, W laos-adventures.com) run an excellent 100 Waterfalls trek that involves clambering over the eponymous waterfalls and through paddy fields.

ACCOMMODATION

Bamboo Paradise On the southern side of the bridge, first path to the right T 020 5554 5286. The original bamboo-thatch rooms (60,000K) here each have cute hammock-slung private balconies at right angles to the river. Rooms in the newer building above enjoy better views, though balconies are shared, while the cheapest, viewless rooms at the back are plainest but largest. Double **50,000K**

Delilah's North side of the bridge, on the main street T 020 5439 5686. Nong Khiaw's cheapest accommodation, with a six-bed dorm and a couple of small doubles. The popular travellers' café downstairs is a choice spot for breakfast and offers takeaway lunches and good cakes and desserts, too. Dorm **35,000K**, double **55,000K**

Sengdao Chittavong T 030 9237089. Conveniently located at the northern end of the bridge, this tranquil place has big bamboo huts, each with a balcony, neatly arranged around a long, pretty garden. There's also a nice, breezy restaurant that looks over the river. Double **80,000K**

Sunrise On the southern side of the bridge T 030 9853899. A collection of simple, clean, bamboo-thatch bungalows on the river, all with hammocks and balconies (shared in the cheapest rooms, which also have squat toilets). Double **60,000K**

★TREAT YOURSELF

Nong Kiau Riverside Follow the signs to the left after crossing the bridge from the western side of town T 071 810004, W nongkiau.com. These huge wood-and-thatch bungalows, set a little away from the main road, have incredible views of the karsts and the bridge, and are beautifully decorated with dark wood furniture. Each bungalow has a wide private balcony that you could easily lose days on, and the large, cool restaurant serves excellent Lao food. Rates include breakfast. **$56**

EATING AND DRINKING

Most of the guesthouses have restaurants, offering a fairly standard menu of local and Western dishes.

Alex South side of the bridge, on the same lane as *Bamboo Paradise*. Rustic, bamboo-walled place that's widely agreed to provide the best Thai–Lao cooking in town (*larp* 25,000K), though the care they show in preparation tends to show in painfully slow service. Daily 6am–10pm.

Coco Home Main street, just up from the boat landing. This leafy beer garden has a pool table, good sounds and lots of hideaway corners in which to chill. The cute little movie room upstairs is usually full of supine travellers catching the twice-nightly film showings. Daily 7am–10.30pm.

MUANG NGOI

Hidden away on a peninsula on the Nam Ou about an hour's boat ride from Nong Khiaw, tiny **MUANG NGOI** is the perfect place for a few days' peace and quiet among beautiful scenery. Most visitors tend to just while away their days sleeping, eating, reading and relaxing by the river, though there are options for the more energetic: excursions to local caves, kayaking down the river, trekking through buffalo-ridden rice fields, and fishing with the locals at sunset.

ARRIVAL AND DEPARTURE

By boat Boats from Nong Khiaw arrive at the landing at the north end of the village, which is strung out along a single dirt track that runs parallel to the river. Boats

leave Muang Ngoi around 9.30am for both Nong Khiaw (25,000K; 1hr) and, if there's enough demand, Muang Khoua (for Vietnam, see box below; 100,000K; 5hr). Boats to Nong Khiaw arrive in time for you to catch the bus to Luang Prabang.

INFORMATION AND TOURS

Bicycles Mountain bikes can be rented from the shop in front of *Phonevaly Guesthouse* (60,000K/day).

Services Note that there's nowhere to change money in Muang Ngoi and, for the time being, no internet – though this was likely to change in 2014.

Tours Lao Youth Travel (T 030 2005385, W laoyouthtravel.com), near the boat landing, can organize treks and kayaking tours.

ACCOMMODATION AND EATING

Muang Ngoi has lots of cheap wood and bamboo bungalows built on stilts, most of which line the strip along the riverbank. Sleepy by day, the village is positively supine by nightfall, and on a quiet night many restaurants will have packed up for bed by 8.30pm.

Bee Tree Right at the bottom end of the village, this attractive, lantern-lit restaurant with seating on bamboo sofas offers the village's best Lao food – well spiced and freshly made, with mains around 35,000K. Daily 11.30am–11.30pm.

Lattanavongsa T 020 2236 2444. Up from the boat landing, on the left. A very popular guesthouse, with four very clean and large rooms in a low wooden bungalow plus a few newer bungalows in a flower-filled compound at the top of the road. Also has one of the nicest restaurants in town, on a breezy balcony overlooking the boat landing. Double **80,000K**

Lertkeo T 020 7730 5041. With fantastic views across the river, this is as upmarket as Muang Ngoi gets, offering five sturdily built concrete bungalows with immaculate bathrooms – though they're a little packed together. Double **100,000K**

Riverside Bungalows T 020 2214 8777, E pdvbungalows@gmail.com. Though it's a bit pricier than similar ramshackle bungalows along the strip, what you lose in pennies you gain in genuinely hot showers, *two* hammocks per balcony (so no squabbling…) and the best mattresses in town. The same owners sometimes have "beach" barbecues up at the *Riverbeach Bar*, north of the boat landing. **80,000K**

INTO VIETNAM: TAY TRANG

Travellers bound for Vietnam can take a direct bus to **Dien Bien Phu**, via the border at Sop Hun/Tay Trang, from the workaday crossroads town of **Muang Khoua**, reached by bus from Oudomxai (see below) or on a spectacular boat journey up the Nam Ou through primeval jungle from Nong Khiaw or Muang Ngoi (see p.381). The most convenient service leaves around 10.30am from outside Muang Khoua's tourist office, arriving in Dien Bien Phu around 3pm. Note that you will need to already have your Vietnamese visa to make this crossing. You can also reach Dien Bien Phu direct from Oudomxai and even Houayxai.

For **accommodation** in Muang Khoua, the most popular backpacker choice is the *Nam Ou Guesthouse* (T 088 210844; 40,000K), with a sociable terrace restaurant right above the boat landing, though the cell-like rooms are a little flimsy.

OUDOMXAI

North of Luang Prabang, the bustling administrative town of **OUDOMXAI** is an important transport hub at the junction of Route 1 and Route 4; if you spend any time travelling in the north, you'll most likely need to spend a night here. Though it's not the most exciting of towns, it has an energy about it that you don't often find in Laos. The **fresh market**, 1.5km northwest of the bus station (daily 7am–6pm), is a fascinating place to spend half an hour, though the meat and fish section is not for the faint-hearted.

ARRIVAL AND DEPARTURE

By air There are 1–2 flights daily from Vientiane to Oudomxai's airport, 1km southeast of town (50min). Tuk-tuks run into the centre (10,000K), though you could easily walk.

By bus Buses from all destinations arrive at the bus station, a 5–10min walk from most of the guesthouses (turn left up the main road out of the bus station). Arrive 30min–1hr early when catching a bus out of Oudomxai, as it's not unknown for them to set off early if they're full.

Destinations Dien Bien Phu, Vietnam (daily; 7hr); Houayxai (Bokeo; daily; 7hr); Luang Namtha (3 daily; 4hr); Luang Prabang (3 daily; 5hr); Mengla, China (via Boten; daily; 6hr); Muang Khoua (3 daily; 3hr); Nong Khiaw (daily; 4hr); Pakbeng (2 daily; 3hr 30min); Vientiane (4 daily; 15hr).

INFORMATION

Bicycles Bikes (from 30,000K) and motorbikes (from 80,000K) can be rented from Xaiya Service, 300m east off the main road (turn right just south of *Litthavixay*).

5

Internet There are a number of computers available at *Litthavixay* (see below) for 8000K/hr. For a dose of free wi-fi, your best bet is the coffee shop at *Charming Lao Hotel*, the town's poshest, about 200m north of the tourist office.

Tourist information There is a very helpful provincial tourism office (Mon–Fri 8am–noon & 1.30–5pm; T 081 212483, W oudomxay.info) just beyond the bridge 1km north of the bus station, with information about treks in the area and more.

ACCOMMODATION

Litthavixay Main road, 500m north of the bus station T 081 212175, E litthavixay@yahoo.com. Arguably the best deal in town, with bright, very clean rooms, all with TV and en suite. Internet access is available in the large reception area. Double 80,000K

Vivanh Just south of the bridge, 900m north of the bus station T 081 212219. A really sweet little guesthouse offering big, sparkling rooms with TV and brightly coloured bedspreads; the female staff are very welcoming and friendly. Double 60,000K

Xaysana Left off the main road, 400m north of the bus station T 020 251 5737. An attractive, scrupulously well-maintained hotel tucked up a quiet street. The big, bright rooms, up a rather grand wooden staircase, have high ceilings and pretty curtains. Excellent value. Double 80,000K

EATING

For breakfast, the bus station is the best option, with women selling baguettes, *kao larm* (bamboo filled with sticky rice and coconut) and bags of fruit for 2000K each.

Mrs Kanya's Right off the main road, 800m north of the bus station. Locals swear this big, bustling restaurant is Oudomxai's top choice for authentic Lao food. Grab a seat at one of the shared tables and choose one of the wonderfully sour soups (30,000K) and *larp*, though bear in mind that anything with beef is likely to come with big slabs of tripe. Huge portions. Daily 6am–10pm.

Souphailins Just off the main road, 400m north of the tourist office. Half concealed behind thick vegetation, this gorgeous little thatched restaurant feels a world away from the busy Oudomxai traffic. The *falang*-friendly northern Lao menu encompasses a good selection of vegetarian dishes, though food can be bland unless you ask for spice. Mains around 30,000K. Daily 6am–9pm.

LUANG NAMTHA

Surrounded by forested hills that remain lush even when the rest of the countryside is a dusty brown in the hot season, **LUANG NAMTHA** is the north's most touristy town after Luang Prabang, though it still has a quiet local charm, away from the travellers' cafés and tour operators. The town is a popular base from which to access the beautiful **Nam Ha NBCA**, with a whole range of activities available, from rafting and kayaking on the Nam Tha to exploring the surrounding area by bike and trekking to hill-tribe villages.

ARRIVAL AND DEPARTURE

By air The tiny airport is located 7km south of the main town, with flights to Vientiane (5 weekly; 1hr); a shared tuk-tuk will cost around 10,000K/person.

By bus The main bus station is 11km southeast of town; a shared tuk-tuk should cost 10,000K/person. Buses from within the province (including Boten) arrive at the local bus station, just south of the centre, from where it's a short walk to most guesthouses.

Destinations Boten, for Chinese border (6 daily; 2hr); Dien Bien Phu, Vietnam (daily; 11hr); Houayxai (2 daily; 4hr); Jinghong, China (daily; 8hr); Luang Prabang (daily; 9hr); Oudomxai (3 daily; 5hr); Vientiane (2 daily; 19hr).

INFORMATION AND TOURS

Tourist information The tourist office (T 086 211534, W luangnamtha-tourism-laos.org; Mon–Fri 8am–11.30am & 1.30–4pm) is situated one street east of the main road, behind the night market.

Bike and motorbike rental Bicycles (from 10,000K/day), mountain bikes (from 15,000K/day) and motorbikes (from 40,000K/day) can be rented from Vehicle Rental Service, just north of *Manychan* on the main street.

Internet There are various internet cafés on the main road, including Green Mountain and Smile Internet, which has Skype facilities (12,000K/hr). All the guesthouses have free wi-fi.

INTO CHINA: BOTEN

The easiest way for travellers with a valid visa to cross into China is to take the 8am direct bus all the way to Jinghong (daily; 8hr), via Mengla (5hr), from Luang Namtha's main bus station. Services also run throughout the morning (every 90min from 8.30am; 2hr) from the local bus station to the border crossing at Boten (open daily 7am–4pm), but you'll need to change buses both here and at Mengla to reach Jinghong this way. Those coming down from China can get a thirty-day Lao visa on arrival.

5

TREKKING, RAFTING AND KAYAKING AROUND LUANG NAMTHA

Trekking in the National Biodiversity Conservation Area must be booked through a licensed agent, or via the tourist office (see p.383). Though Luang Namtha has a few cowboys, there are some excellent outfits (all operating from offices on the main strip) running reliably well-organized treks with a strong ethical stance, as well as kayaking, rafting (July–Oct only) and mountain-biking trips. Not all the trips leave daily, and you'll probably find that your choice is limited by those that have already been signed up for by other travellers – be sure to arrange one as soon as you arrive, or better still, book in advance. Note that for all treks and activities, the price you pay is dependent on the number of people on it, and you should make sure that if you're visiting a local village, a percentage of the money you pay goes towards supporting the community.

★**Green Discovery** Ⓣ086 211484, Ⓦgreendiscoverylaos.com. Undoubtedly one of the best set up operations in town (and also the priciest), offering an excellent range of trips and treks, from a two-day kayaking adventure on the Nam Tha (from $69) to overnight treks into beautiful Nam Ha NBCA, staying at hill-tribe villages (from $62).

★**Jungle Eco-Guide Services** Ⓣ020 9551 8889, Ⓦthejungle-ecotour-laos.com. The best locally run outfit, with a network of nine well-maintained trails through the NBCA. Their tough but rewarding three-day Jungle Camp Adventure Trek tramps through wildlife-rich primary forest, with stops for fishing and swimming en route (from $70).

Massage Herbal Sauna and Massage, on the road leading to *Tai Dam* (15,000K sauna; 50,000K massage).

Post office Main street (daily 8am–noon & 1–4pm).

ACCOMMODATION

Adounsiri One street west of the main road Ⓣ020 299 1898. In a leafy plot, this popular guesthouse has simple but very pleasant rooms, some of which are off a sweet communal terrace. Double **60,000K**

Manychan Main road Ⓣ020 2292 7878. Simple en-suite rooms in a tall building just behind the popular restaurant of the same name. Double **60,000K**

Tai Dam 200m east of the main market Ⓣ020 2239 0552, Ⓦtai-dam-guesthouse.com. A lovely little place tucked down a dirt track well off the main drag, with rustic, round-roofed, wood-and-thatch bungalows overlooking paddy fields. Check the website for directions. Double **50,000K**

★TREAT YOURSELF

Northern Laos's most famous eco-style resort is the **Boat Landing** (Ⓣ086 312398, Ⓦtheboatlanding.com), situated 6km south of the centre on the banks of the Nam Tha River. It's fantastic value at $47 for a beautiful bungalow overlooking the river, and treks and kayaking can also be arranged here. The restaurant serves the best food in the area, with a wide choice of northern specialities – the spicy Lao dips (from 12,000K) and Akha ginger chicken soup (38,000K) are particularly worth trying. A tuk-tuk from town is 20,000K for two.

★**Thavyxai** Two streets west of the main road Ⓣ030 5110292. In a giant-columned building with airy, high-ceilinged rooms, *Thavyxai* both looks and feels grander than its rates suggest. The terrace at the back is a lovely place to gaze over the rooftops and soak up the sun. Good English spoken and excellent value. Double **60,000K**

★**Thoulasith** Just off the main street Ⓣ086 212166, Ⓦthoulasith-guesthouse.com. Set in a graceful building facing onto a garden, with large, bright rooms and arguably the best bathrooms in town. The pick of the rooms are upstairs, which face onto a lovely balcony. Double **80,000K**

Zuela Opposite the night market Ⓣ020 5588 6694, Ⓔzuelaguesthouse@gmail.com. One of the most atmospheric places to stay, with large rooms in two gorgeous wooden buildings, set back from the main drag, and a lovely restaurant. Double **80,000K**

EATING AND DRINKING

A small night market (daily 5–10pm) sets up in the compound next to the BCEL bank at dusk each evening, where you can pick up grilled meat and cold Beerlao here and enjoy it at the tables in the middle.

★**Bamboo Lounge** Opposite the entrance to *Thoulasith*. Attached to the well-regarded Forest Retreat trekking office, this Kiwi-run, eco-themed bar-restaurant is always the busiest place on the strip, with excellent wood-fired pizzas (50,000–90,000K), daily specials and a decent range of booze (Lao daiquiri 15,000K). Daily 6.30am–11.30pm.

★**Manikong Bakery** Opposite the night market. With its cute gingham tablecloths and friendly welcome, this efficient new bakery-café is a great breakfast choice, with fresh croissants and muffins, plus sets from 35,000K.

TREKKING ETIQUETTE

Always trek in **groups**, as there have been assaults on Western tourists in rural areas. If you are approached by armed men and robbery is clearly their intent, do NOT resist. Most hill-tribe peoples are **animists**. Offerings to the spirits, often bits of food left in what may seem like an odd place, should never be touched or tampered with. The Akha are known for the elaborate gates they construct at the entrances to their villages. These gates have special meaning to the Akha and should also be left alone. Many hill folk are willing to be photographed, but old women, particularly of the Hmong and Mien tribes, are not always keen, so ask first. Passing out sweets to village kids is a sure way to generate mobs of young beggars.

The ham, egg and cheese bagel (25,000K) will set you up for the day. Daily 6.30am–10pm.

Minority Just off the main road. Run by a Tai Dam family who collect traditional recipes from different tribes in the region, including the Khamu and Akha. Some dishes are better than others, but all are interesting and worth a try. Rattan shoot and banana-flower soup 25,000K. Daily 7am–10.30pm.

Two Sisters Local bus station. This sweet place, decorated with birds' nests, antlers and local basketry, is a good lunch stop, especially if you're hanging around for a bus. The beef noodle soup (10,000K) is lovely, and there's a good variety of other dishes including *larp* (40,000K). Daily 8am–11pm.

HOUAYXAI

The town of **HOUAYXAI**, situated on a hilly stretch of the Mekong River, has long been a favourite crossing point for people moving between Laos and Thailand. Travellers arriving in Houayxai can cruise down the Mekong by boat to Luang Prabang (see box, p.386), or take a bus overland up Route 3 to Luang Namtha and beyond. Despite its border-town status, Houayxai is not completely devoid of charm, though the main reason to pause here is to take part in the acclaimed Gibbon Experience (see box, p.387).

Most accommodation and travel services are clustered around the old ferry landing for (now locals-only) boats from Chiang Khong.

WHAT TO SEE AND DO

Opposite the old ferry landing, Houayxai's main sight is the hilltop **Wat Chom Khao Manilat**, with a tall, Shan-style drum tower and, to the left of the *sim*, a picturesquely weathered teakwood building now used as a classroom for novice monks. A 1km (signposted) walk south from the temple are the weather-beaten remains of **Fort Carnot**, where you can climb one of the two watchtowers for a fine view across to Thailand.

ARRIVAL AND DEPARTURE

By air Houayxai's airport is 9km south of the centre, with daily flights with Lao Airlines and twice-weekly services with Lao Skyway to Vientiane (55min). Chances are you'll need to charter a sawngthaew to town (50,000K).

By bus Houayxai currently has two bus stations, around 1km apart. Domestic VIP and international buses, including services from Chiang Rai, arrive at the swish new private bus (Phetarloun) station, 6km south of the centre. At the time of writing, normal buses were still arriving at the old (Keo Champa) bus station, 5km south of the centre. Sawngthaews from either bus station cost 10,000K/person to the centre of town. You can buy tickets for onward travel through tour agencies in Houayxai; these cost a bit more than buying direct from the bus station as a transfer is included. Note that most buses to Houayxai are marked "Bokeo" or "Borkeo".

INTO THAILAND

With the opening in 2013 of the grand **Fourth Thai–Lao Friendship Bridge** (daily 6am–10pm), 11km south of Houayxai's ferry landing, foreigners are no longer permitted to use the river crossing to Chiang Khong. The easiest way to cross the border is to take a sawngthaew to the new bus station and pick up one of the direct VIP services to Chiang Rai (57,000K), via Chiang Khong (8000K), which leave at 8am, 9am, 4pm and 5pm. Alternatively, take a sawngthaew to the bridge (20,000K), from which (after Lao immigration) buses shuttle across (7000K) to Thai immigration (visas are available on arrival), then a tuk-tuk to Chiang Khong (B150–200). There are banks and an information point at the bridge.

5

Destinations from new bus station Chiang Khong, Thailand (4 daily; 30min); Chiang Rai, Thailand (4 daily; 4hr); Dien Bien Phu, Vietnam (6 weekly; 15hr); Jinghong, China (6 weekly; 12hr); Kunming, China (daily; 17hr); Luang Namtha (daily; 3hr 30min); Luang Prabang (daily; 12hr); Mengla, China (6 weekly; 8hr); Vang Vieng (daily; 17hr); Vientiane (daily; 21hr).

Destinations from old bus station Luang Namtha (2 daily; 4hr); Luang Prabang (daily; 13hr); Oudomxai (daily; 8hr); Vientiane (daily; 23hr).

By boat The slow-boat pier is about 1km north of the centre; there's a daily departure for Pakbeng, midway to Luang Prabang, at 11.30am (110,000K), but arrive at least 30min early to ensure a seat. The speedboat pier is 4km downriver of the centre (tuk-tuk 15,000K). Boats for Pakbeng (170,000K) and Luang Prabang (340,000K) theoretically depart at 9.30am but leave when full – get there well in advance (and conversely be prepared for a wait), or to be safe book via an agent in town.

Destinations Luang Prabang (speedboat: daily; 6–7hr); Pakbeng (slow boat: daily 7hr; speedboat: daily 3–4hr).

INFORMATION

Tourist information The tourist office (Mon–Fri 8.30am–noon & 1.30–4pm), in the centre just south of the old ferry landing, is mainly interested in pointing customers towards its tours.

Internet The *Gateway* hotel, at the top of the old ferry landing, has internet terminals (10,000K/hr).

Massage and sauna The Red Cross Sauna (Mon–Fri 1.30–9pm, Sat & Sun 10.30am–9pm) offers traditional massage (from 35,000K/hr) and herbal sauna (10,000K). It is just beyond the wooden bridge towards the slow boat pier.

ACCOMMODATION

Arimid Just south of the slow boat landing ⓣ 084 211040. A collection of a dozen basic but attractive two-room bungalows, with a very cheap restaurant. If you're looking for something with Lao flavour, this is a good choice. Double **80,000K**

Phonetip At the top of the old ferry landing ⓣ 084 211084. The cheapest rooms here are rather cramped, with shared bathrooms, but an extra 20,000K will buy you a bit more space and an en suite. Double **40,000K**

Phonevichith Above the slowboat pier ⓣ 084 211765, ⓦ houayxairiverside.com. Set in a striking ochre-orange building (next to swisher sister property, *Houayxai Riverside*), with good-value rooms that demonstrate a touch more class than down in town. The wooden terrace restaurant right on the water offers all kinds of soups, salads and fried dishes. Also organizes bus travel to Thailand. Double **100,000K**

★ **River View** Behind the *Meuang Neu* restaurant, 100m north of the old ferry landing ⓣ 030 9030993. Spacious rooms in a long, three-story block leading down to the river. Shaded by tall palm trees, the garden terrace at the back is one of the loveliest places to contemplate the sunset with a Beerlao. Double **80,000K**

★ **Sabaydee** 200m north of the old ferry landing ⓣ 020 5692 9458. This modern hotel boasts big, spotlessly clean rooms, with a terrace at the top that offers terrific views of the Mekong. A friendly welcome and the best deal in town. Double **90,000K**

EATING AND DRINKING

Bar How? 100m north of the old ferry landing. Relaxed restaurant and lounge with good music and ambient

DOWN THE MEKONG

Although it's now a well-worn tourist route, many travellers agree that the two-day journey by **slow boat** (*heua sa*) along the Mekong from Houayxai to the old royal capital of Luang Prabang, stopping overnight at the village of Pakbeng, is one of those definitive Southeast Asian experiences. Originally, these antiquated diesel-powered boats were primarily for cargo and the occasional Lao passengers who relied on them for trade and transport. These days it's a fairly comfortable journey, the boats fully converted for fat Western bottoms, with seating generally on cushioned wooden benches or reclinable "airline" seating, and enough space to wander around, play cards, read Kindles and so on. Drinks and a few snacks are on sale on board – though you'd do better to bring your own provisions – and there are Western loos. Big bags are normally stored down in the hold at the back. It can be chilly on board, so bring warm clothing.

Whether you consider taking one of the **speedboats** (*heua wai*) between Houayxai and Luang Prabang, which stop in Pakbeng for lunch, depends on how risk-averse you are. Skimming across the water at speeds of up to 60km/hr, or even faster, these cramped eight-seater crafts cut hours off journey times, but there's no doubt that the exhilarating ride is a great deal less comfortable and more dangerous – deaths have been reported, though the vast majority of journeys pass off incident-free. Life vests and crash helmets are provided – the latter most useful as protection against the wind and engine noise.

THE GIBBON EXPERIENCE

An ecotourism project 83km from Houayxai, **The Gibbon Experience** (T 084 212021, W gibbonexperience.org) offers both spectacular treehouse accommodation and a unique way to explore the Bokeo Nature Reserve – via zip line through the forest canopy. All food and transportation are provided, as well as guides, who will help you spot wildlife including black gibbons and elephants. At $190 for one night or $310 for two, it's expensive but worth the splurge. Be sure to reserve a place well in advance. The Houayxai office is on the main road, just north of the old ferry landing.

lighting. Serves a range of reasonably priced Lao, Thai and *falang* food, plus mojitos for 30,000K. Daily 6am–11pm.

Dream Bakery 100m south of the old ferry landing. Cheerful and inviting bakery-café with big wooden chairs and colourful tablecloths. Coffee comes from the Bolaven plateau and the cakes and pastries (pecan pie 10,000K) are more than passable. Daily 7am–8pm.

Meuang Neu 100m north of the old ferry landing. Travellers' favourite with a rustic feel, which serves a largely Western menu, including pizzas (from 55,000K) and desserts like fried banana in chocolate sauce. Also a good place to pick up a sandwich before a long boat or bus journey south. Daily 6am–11pm.

Phongdao Buffet Just up from the slow boat landing, on the right. Westerners normally pass straight by this unassuming locals' place, but it does the best *sin dad* (Lao barbecue) in town, the buffet table groaning under the weight of fresh meat, veg, fish and seafood. Daily 5–10pm.

PAKBENG

Following kilometre after kilometre of lush jungle-clad hills, the river approach to Pakbeng, the only sizeable town or roadhead between Houayxai and Luang Prabang, feels rather welcome, even if the town has little more than a ramshackle charm about it. Perched above the water on the hill that rises through the town, Pakbeng may not be a particularly glamorous start to your travels in Laos, but it does have a distinctly northern Laos feel about it, and for all its touts and travellers' cafés, beyond the main guesthouse area it still feels very much like somewhere where local people live.

ARRIVAL AND DEPARTURE

By boat From the (separate) slowboat and speedboat landings it's a short (uphill) walk to most of the town's guesthouses and restaurants, and a further 1km into the centre of town. Slow boats usually depart around 9.30am to Luang Prabang, and about 8.30am to Houayxai – it's best to check times locally the night before. Heading to Luang Prabang, arrive at least 30min before departure to ensure a seat. Tickets are bought onboard. Some captains stop briefly at the caves at Pak Ou (see p.377) before Luang Prabang, charging each passenger who disembarks for a look a few thousand kip extra. Speedboats in either direction normally depart around 9am, though will only leave when full; buy tickets from the booth at the top of the speedboat landing.

Destinations Houayxai (daily: slow boat 8hr; speedboat 3hr); Luang Prabang (daily: slow boat 7hr; speedboat 3hr).

By bus Buses run twice daily to Oudomxai (4hr) from the bus station, 2km east of the boat landings (5000K in a shared tuk-tuk).

ACCOMMODATION AND EATING

Travellers arriving off the slow boat are usually greeted by countless touts for the town's guesthouses. In the morning, a few stalls lining the road just up from the landings put steaks, sausages and chicken on to grill – a tastier sandwich option for the boat journey than the baguettes sold by the numerous guesthouse bakeries.

Dockhoun 100m east at the top of the landings T 081 212540. Good-sized rooms with colourful bedspreads in a vivid green building, but the real advantage is the lovely restaurant, bedecked with hanging baskets and boasting superlative river views. Double **100,000K**

Duangpasert 20m east at the top of the landings T 081 212624. Friendly place that's more clued up than most along the strip. For river views go for one of the upstairs rooms, though those downstairs have a big shared terrace; all have high ceilings and hot showers. Also has a bakery. Double **100,000K**

Sarika T 081 212306. One of the best options, in a plumb position at the top of the speedboat landing, with smallish but well-maintained, whitewashed rooms. Some have views of the Mekong. Double **100,000K**

Vassana 300m east of the boat landings T 081 212302. Despite its unassuming exterior, this is actually the best deal in town. For once, some thought has gone into the colour scheme, and rooms have big, comfy beds, sparkling bathrooms and (very Lao this) reclining chairs ripped straight out of vans. No views, though. Double **80,000K**

5

South central Laos

Many travellers see very little of **south central Laos**, spending just a night or two in the town of Savannakhet before pressing on to the far south or **crossing the border** into Vietnam. The two principal settlements of the region – Thakhek and Savannakhet – both lie on the Mekong River, and both offer straightforward border crossings into Thailand. Route 8 between Vientiane and Thakhek is the best and easiest overland route to Vietnam, the paved road snaking through mountains, rainforests and the Phu Pha Man "stone forest" before winding down to the city of Vinh. **Savannakhet** has been described as southern Laos's Luang Prabang, its inhabitants living comfortably among the architectural heirlooms handed down by the French, and is a pleasant enough place. East from Savannakhet, Route 9 climbs steadily until it eventually bisects another route of more recent vintage: the **Ho Chi Minh Trail**. The trail was used by the North Vietnamese Army to infiltrate and finally subdue its southern neighbour, and is still littered with lots of war junk, some of it highly dangerous. The best way to view these rusting relics is to use the town of **Xepon** as a base. Journeying further east leads to the **Vietnam border crossing** at Dansavanh, popularly known as "Lao Bao".

SAVANNAKHET

The town of **SAVANNAKHET**, known locally as "Savan", is south central Laos's most-visited provincial capital. Its popularity is due in part to its central location on the overland routes between Vientiane and Pakse, and Thailand and Vietnam. Travellers doing the "Indochina loop" – through Cambodia, Vietnam, Laos and Thailand – have the option of taking the 240km-long Route 9 on their way between Laos's two neighbours, hence the presence of both a **Thai** and a **Vietnamese consulate.** But Savannakhet also has its own appeal, with impressive architecture inherited from the French colonial period and narrow streets and shophouses of ochre-coloured stucco reminiscent of parts of Hanoi. A large percentage of the town's population is ethnic Vietnamese, though most have been living here for generations and consider themselves to be Lao in habit and temperament.

WHAT TO SEE AND DO

The town square is dominated by the octagonal spire of **St Teresa Catholic Church** built in 1930. Check out the old teakwood confessional and, high up on

INTO VIETNAM: NAM PHAO/CAU TREO BORDER CROSSING

Roughly halfway between Paksan and Thakhek at the junction town of **Ban Vieng Kham**, Route 8 heads across central Laos to the Kaew Nua Pass, which marks the border with Vietnam, before switchbacking down to the city of Vinh on the coast of Vietnam.

The **buses** that make the trip to the frontier town of Lak Xao from Thakhek and Vientiane (daily; 8hr) stop at its market. The **Vietnamese border** at Nam Phao/Cau Treo, is 35km from Lak Xao and best reached by joining a shared tuk-tuk (20,000K per person) from the market. However, you may have to charter it outright (around 100,000K).

Crossing the border (daily, roughly 8am–5pm) can be a hassle, so it's best to start your journey early to ensure you don't end up stuck at the border. On the Vietnamese side there's usually a small army of touts ready to pull you into a van headed for Vinh. Neither immigration post is near a town of any size; the settlement on the Vietnamese side of the border is **Cau Treo**, 105km west of Vinh on Highway 8.

A relatively stress-free way to get across this border is by taking one of the nightly Vinh-bound buses from Vientiane (160,000K).

Lao visas on arrival are available at this border, but you'll need to arrange your Vietnamese visa in advance.

the walls, a set of hardwood plaques with Vietnamese mother-of-pearl inlay work depicting the fourteen Stations of the Cross.

Roads laid out on a neat grid surrounding the square constitute the **Old French Quarter**, and are lined with some fine examples of European-inspired architecture. Aside from wandering about admiring the crumbling buildings and the town's pleasant wats and Chinese temples, there's not much more to do in Savannakhet but watch the sun set over the Mekong.

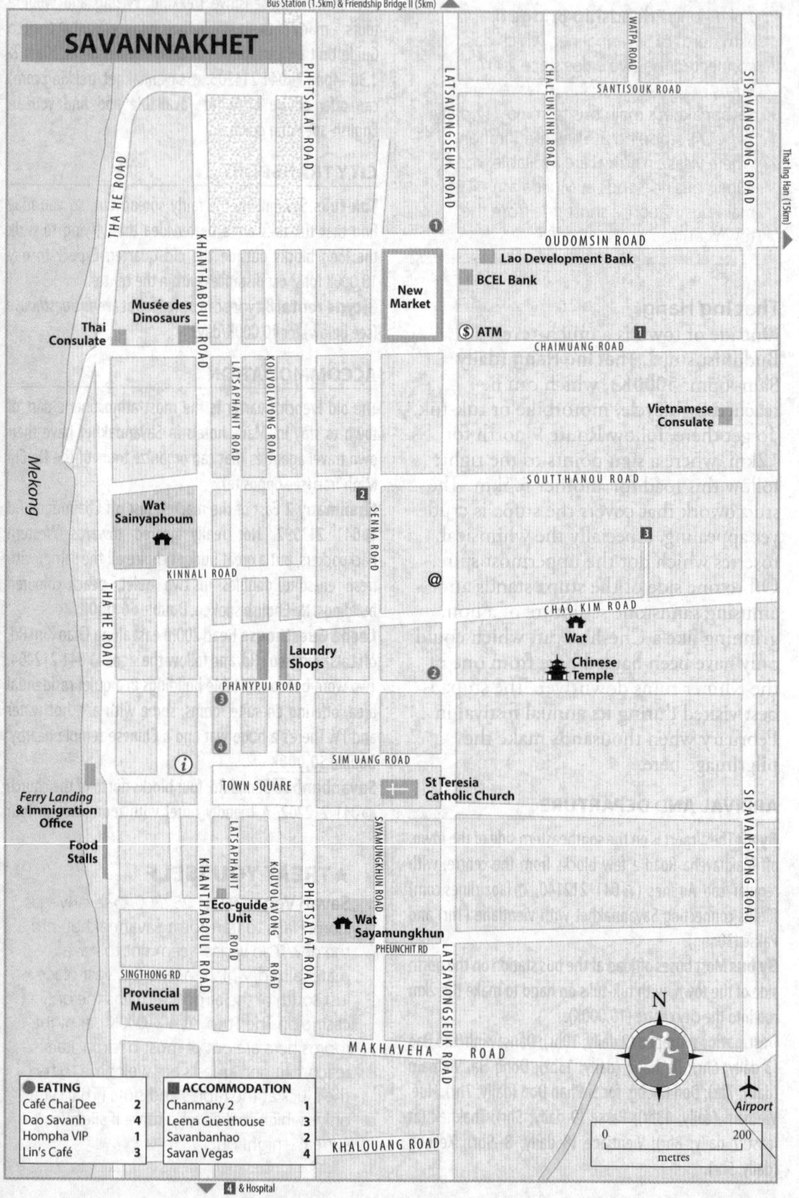

5

INTO THAILAND: SAVANNAKHET TO MUKDAHAN

Passenger ferries still operate between Savannakhet and Mukdahan in Thailand, but these are for locals only; tourists crossing into Thailand must use the 1.6km-long **Friendship Bridge II**, 5km north of Savannakhet, which has connected the two cities since 2007. Buses bound for Mukdahan leave Savannakhet's main bus terminal (12 daily; 14,000K), stopping at Thai immigration, where visas on arrival are available. The 40min bus ride ends at Mukdahan's main bus station, a short ride from the town centre.

That Ing Hang

Outside of town is a much-revered Buddhist stupa, **That Ing Hang** (daily 8am–6pm; 5000K), which can be reached by bicycle, motorbike or tuk-tuk. To get there, follow Route 9 north for 12km, where a sign points to the right; follow this road for another 3.5km. The stuccowork that covers the stupa is crude yet appealing, especially the whimsical rosettes which dot the uppermost spire. Off to one side of the stupa stands an amusing sandstone sculpture of a lion, grinning like a Cheshire cat, which could only have been hauled here from one of the Khmer ruins downriver. The stupa is best visited during its annual festival in February when thousands make the pilgrimage here.

ARRIVAL AND DEPARTURE

By air The airport is on the southeastern side of the town, off Makhaveha Road a few blocks from the centre, with regular Lao Airlines (T 041 212140, W laoairlines.com) flights connecting Savannakhet with Vientiane (1hr) and Pakse (30min).

By bus Most buses offload at the bus station on the north side of the town, with tuk-tuks on hand to make the 2km run into the city centre (10,000K).

Destinations Attapeu (2 daily; 10hr); Dansavanh/Lao Bao (3 daily; 6hr); Da Nang (daily; 13hr); Dong Ha, Vietnam (daily; 7hr); Don Khong, for Si Phan Don (daily; 7hr); Hué, Vietnam (daily; 13hr); Pakse (9 daily; 5hr); Thakhek (at least 7 daily; 8hr); Vientiane (8 daily; 8–9hr); Xekong (daily; 5hr).

INFORMATION

Tourist information The very well-equipped tourist office, west of the main square (Mon–Fri 8–11.30am & 1.30–4pm; T 041 212755), can help with general enquiries, but if you want to go trekking make a beeline for the Eco Guide Unit (see below).

Tours Savannakhet province is packed with options for environmentally sensitive trekking, cycling and wildlife tours – many of them still in their infancy. Staff at the Eco Guide Unit on Latsaphanit Road (Mon–Fri 8–11.30am & 1.30–4pm; T 041 214203; W savannakhet-trekking.com) can offer advice on what's available and find you an English-speaking guide.

CITY TRANSPORT

Tuk-tuks Savannakhet is fairly spread out, so you may find that tuk-tuks are a better idea than trying to walk the long blocks outside the old quarter. Expect to pay 10,000K for short distances within the centre.

Bicycle rental Bicycles can be rented at *Leena Guesthouse* (see below) for 10,000K/day.

ACCOMMODATION

The old French quarter is the most atmospheric part of town to stay in. Many hotels in Savannakhet have their own travel agencies that can organize tours of the Ho Chi Minh Trail (see opposite).

Chanmany 2 East of the market, just off Chaimuang Rd T 041 213992. Not really geared towards Western backpackers, but a great budget choice all the same, with fresh en-suite doubles in two quiet, peach-coloured buildings. No English spoken. Double **60,000K**

Leena Guesthouse Head 200m east along Chao Kim Rd, off Latsavongseuk Rd, and follow the signs T 041 212404. Two worn but comfortable buildings in a quiet residential area, offering en-suite rooms, some with a/c, hot water and TV. There's a huge wat and a Chinese temple nearby. Double **50,000K**

Savanbanhao Senna Rd, four blocks north of the church T 041 212202. A friendly hotel with rooms set in four

★TREAT YOURSELF

Savan Vegas T 041 252200, W savanvegas .com. Plans to transform Savannakhet into the new "Lao Vegas" seem not to have materialized, which means this vast place just south of the airport remains the only casino on The Strip. At 400,000K per night, rooms here are out of most backpackers' reach, but non-guests are welcome to try their luck at the tables and slots (Thai baht only), which makes for a fun – if slightly surreal – night out.

rather austere blocks. There are four room types available – some of the cheapest are actually brighter and larger than others. Double **60,000K**

EATING AND DRINKING

One famous local noodle dish worth seeking out is *baw bun* (Vietnamese rice noodles served with chopped-up spring rolls and beef).

Café Chai Dee Latsavongseuk Rd ⓣ 020 5988 6767, ⓦ cafechaidee.com. Chilled café-restaurant turning out a mix of Western and Japanese dishes, plus *lào-láo* mojitos (24,000K) and red wine by the glass (20,000K). There's also a book exchange, and handmade local crafts for sale. Daily except Fri 8.30am–9pm.

Dao Savanh On the northwestern side of the town square ⓣ 041 260888. This excellent French place is a bit pricey (the three-course set menu is 65,000K), but choose wisely and you can enjoy the delightful ambience on the cheap. The croque monsieur, for example, costs just 35,000K. Daily except Tues 10am–9.30pm.

Hompha VIP Latsavongseuk Rd, on the northern edge of the New Market. Few Westerners venture into this busy beer garden, which often has live music, but those who do tend to end up chatting and drinking with the locals. The papaya salad (15,000K) is brutally spicy. Daily 11am–11pm.

★ **Lin's Café** Latsaphanit Rd, just north of the town square ⓣ 020 9988 1630. Ideal spot for a coffee or coconut milkshake (10,000K), with free wi-fi and a wide selection of books about Laos. The food menu runs from organic salads to home-made veggie curries. Daily except Wed 8.30am–8pm.

DIRECTORY

Banks and exchange The Lao Development Bank and the BCEL are near the intersection of Latsavongseuk and Oudomsin roads, the former facing Oudomsin Rd and the latter facing Latsavongseuk Rd. You'll find ATMs at both.

Consulates Thailand, Tha He Rd, opposite Lao Derm restaurant (Mon–Fri 8am–noon & 1–4pm; ⓣ 041 212373); Vietnam, Sisavangvong Rd (Mon–Fri 7.30–11am & 1.30–4pm; ⓣ 041 212418).

Hospital The biggest hospital is located on Khanthabouli Rd, near the provincial museum.

Internet access A handful of internet places can be found around town. The gaming shop on Latsavongseuk Rd, just across from the turn-off to *Leena Guesthouse*, has computers available for 4000K/hr (daily 7am–11pm). Otherwise, most guesthouses and Western-style cafés have free wi-fi.

Laundry You'll get a fast and cheap service at the laundry shops along Kouvolavong Rd, north of the town square.

ROUTE 9: THE HO CHI MINH TRAIL AND THE VIETNAMESE BORDER

Route 9 weaves east through a series of drab towns from Savannakhet to the **Lao Bao border crossing** into Vietnam. While most travellers barrel through on the direct buses, the frontier is not without points of interest, and there are **Ho Chi Minh Trail** sites open for tourism on both sides of the border.

Xepon

A dusty village in the foothills of the Annamite Mountains, 45km from the Vietnamese border, **XEPON** is a pleasant rural stopover between Vietnam and

OPERATION LAM SON 719

In 1971, US President Richard Nixon ordered an attack on the **Ho Chi Minh Trail** in order to cut off supplies to communist forces. US ground troops were prohibited by law from crossing the border from Vietnam into Laos and Cambodia, but US command saw this as a chance to test the policy of turning the ground war over to the South Vietnamese ("Vietnamization"). During the operation, code-named **Lam Son 719**, ARVN (Army of the Republic of Vietnam) troops were to invade Laos and block the trail with US air support. The objective was **Xepon**, a town straddled by the Trail, which was 30–40km wide at this point. In early February, ARVN troops and tanks pushed across the border into Laos. Like a caterpillar trying to ford a column of red ants, the South Vietnamese troops were soon engulfed by superior numbers of North Vietnamese (NVA) regulars. Halfway to Xepon, the ARVN stopped and engaged the NVA in a **series of battles** that lasted over a month. US air support proved ineffectual, and by mid-March scenes of frightened ARVN troops retreating were being broadcast around the world.

The most tangible relics of Operation Lam Son 719 are two rusting **American tanks** that sit on the outskirts of Ban Dong, on Route 9. Ban Dong is said to have been cleared of UXO, but it's still a good idea to ask a villager to show you the way to any war relics, rather than blazing your own trail.

Savannakhet. The old town of Xepon was obliterated during the Second Indochina War – along with every house in the district's two hundred villages – and was later rebuilt here, 6km west of its original location. The old city had become an important outpost on the Ho Chi Minh Trail, and was the target of a joint South Vietnamese and American invasion in 1971, Operation Lam Son 719 (see box, p.391).

Buses and sawngthaews arriving from Savannakhet or the Lao Bao border stop at the market. Frequent sawngthaews head west towards Savannakhet (40,000K), and east towards Ban Dong (see below) and the border with Vietnam (20,000K). There are **guesthouses** along Route 9 a short walk east from here, including the central *Vieng Xay*, which has doubles for 50,000K. If you need to **exchange money**, there's a Western Union branch at the eastern end of Xepon's main drag (Mon–Fri 8am–3.30pm).

Halfway between Xepon and the Vietnam border is the town of **BAN DONG**, the site of one of America's most ignominious defeats during the war and a popular stop on tours of the **Ho Chi Minh Trail**. It is situated in the foothills of the Annamite Mountains, where bomb craters and unexploded ordnance still litter the landscape more than 35 years after the end of the war. If you're travelling by public transport, it's best to visit Ban Dong in the early morning; few late-afternoon sawngthaews ply this stretch of Route 9 and facilities for tourists in Ban Dong are extremely limited.

Dansavanh

Route 9 ends its journey through Laos in the village of **DANSAVANH**, 1km from the Lao immigration office. For a remote border town, Dansavanh is relatively tourist-friendly, with food, accommodation and exchange services. There's a Lao Development Bank in town, as well as a branch at the Lao immigration office on the border. From Dansavanh, you can hire a motorcycle taxi for the final 1km ride to the Lao immigration office, or walk. If you've entered Laos from Vietnam, note that there are four buses a day to Savannakhet (4hr) from Dansavanh, and four daily (1hr) buses to Xepon. These buses are supported by much more frequent sawngthaews, which leave when full – or simply at the whim of the driver.

The far south

Bordered by Thailand, Cambodia and Vietnam, the far south conveniently divides into two regions, with **Pakse** – the most important market town and the access point for the Chong Mek **border crossing** into Thailand – as the hub. In the west, the Mekong River corridor is scattered with dozens of ancient Khmer temples, including **Wat Phou**, one of the most important Angkorian ruins outside Cambodia. From the nearby town of **Champasak**, it makes sense to go with the flow of the river south to **Si Phan Don**, where the Mekong's 1993km journey through Laos rushes to a thundering conclusion in a series of tiny riverine islands at the Cambodian border; the waters here are home to a dwindling number of very rare Irrawaddy **dolphins**. In the east of the region, the fertile highlands of the **Bolaven Plateau** separate the Mekong

INTO VIETNAM: LAO BAO BORDER CROSSING

Crossing the **Dansavanh/Lao Bao border** (7am–10pm) can take time, so it pays to head for the Lao immigration post early in the morning if possible. Remember, **travellers wanting to enter Vietnam** must arrange a visa in advance.

On the Vietnamese side, there are motorcycle taxis to take you down the hill to Lao Bao town where buses leave for Khe Sanh and Dong Ha, where bus or train connections can be made to Hanoi and Hué.

This border is 255km from Savannakhet, from where you can catch direct buses to Da Nang (daily; 13hr) or Hue (daily; 13hr), which stop at immigration, or four daily buses that go as far as Dansavanh.

corridor from the Annamite Mountains that form Laos's border with Vietnam. Much of the area east of the Mekong lies off the beaten track and involves hard journeys on bumpy roads. One city well worth making the effort to see, though, is **Attapeu**, known as the garden city for its pleasant atmosphere and laidback pace.

PAKSE

Located at the confluence of the Xe Don and Mekong rivers, roughly halfway between the Thai border and the Bolaven Plateau, **PAKSE** is the far south's biggest city and its commercial and transport hub. For travellers, it is usually a stopover en route to Si Phan Don and Cambodia, and it makes a comfortable base for exploring the Bolaven Plateau (see p.402), with its excellent waterfalls. There is also a border crossing to Thailand just west of Pakse at Chong Mek, making it a logical entry or exit point for travellers doing a north–south tour of Laos.

WHAT TO SEE AND DO

Pakse is short on proper tourist attractions. The two main sights are both just east of the town centre on Route 13 and easily reachable by bicycle or tuk-tuk. The first is the **Champasak Palace Hotel**, a majestic eyesore resembling a giant cement wedding cake. Legend has it that the late Prince Boun Oum na Champasak, a colourful character who was the heir to the Champasak kingdom and one of the most influential southerners of the twentieth century, needed a palace this size so that he could accommodate his many concubines. It is now a hotel.

The second attraction, 500m further along Route 13, is the **Champasak Provincial Museum** (Mon–Fri 8am–11.30am & 1.30–4pm; 10,000K), which houses some fine examples of ornately carved pre-Angkorian sandstone lintels taken from sites around the province.

Also worth a visit is the huge **New Market** (Talat Dao Heuang), south of the museum. Along with the usual array of mounds of

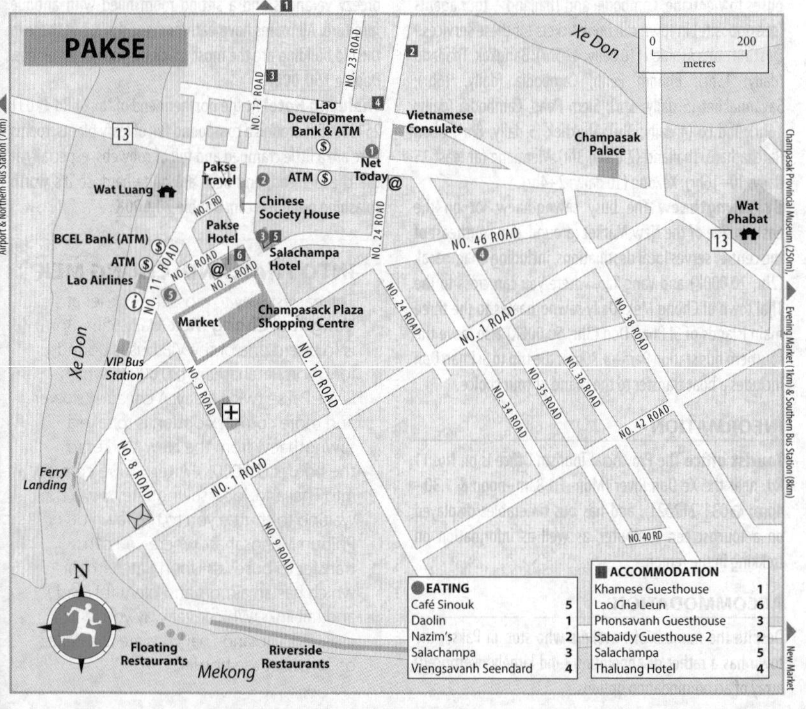

5

tobacco, plastic ware and live chickens, specialities available at the market include tea, coffee and a variety of fruit and vegetables, many of which are from the bountiful Bolaven Plateau.

ARRIVAL AND DEPARTURE

By air The airport lies 2km northwest of the city on Route 13, and is served by tuk-tuks (20,000–30,000K). The Lao Airlines office is on No. 11 Rd, near the BCEL Bank (Mon–Fri 8–11.30am & 1.30–4.30pm; ☎ 031 212152).

Destinations Luang Prabang (daily; 1hr 40min); Ho Chi Minh City, Vietnam (3 weekly; 1hr 25min); Savannakhet (daily; 30min); Siem Reap, Cambodia (2 daily; 1hr); Vientiane (2 daily; 50min).

By boat Tourist boats (60,000K each way) run between Pakse and Champasak when demand is strong enough. To book, contact *Sabaidy Guesthouse 2* (see below).

By bus Long-distance buses pull in at stations around the city. Generally speaking, services to and from the north use the Northern Bus Station, 7km north of the city on Route 13, while those to and from the south and east pull up at the Southern Bus Station, 8km southeast of town on Route 13 at the big T-junction; tuk-tuks from either bus station into town cost around 20,000K. The VIP Bus Station, just south of the tourist office on No. 11 Rd, is for buses to Vientiane, Cambodia and Thailand – tour agents (see opposite) in town can book tickets for these services.

Destinations Attapeu (10 daily; 4–5hr); Bangkok, Thailand (daily; 15hr); Phnom Penh, Cambodia (daily; 16hr); Savannakhet (5 daily; 5hr); Siem Reap, Cambodia (daily; 16hr); Tad Lo (4 daily; 3hr); Thakhek (5 daily; 8hr); Ubon Ratchathani, Thailand (2 daily; 3hr); Vientiane (at least 15 daily; 10–16hr); Xekong (10 daily; 2–4hr).

By sawngthaew The busy sawngthaew lot on the eastern side of the New Market (around 2km southeast of the centre) serves local destinations, including Champasak (2hr; 20,000K) and Vang Tao, where you can cross to the Thai town of Chong Mek. Daily sawngthaews to the three main islands of Si Phan Don (3hr; 50,000K) also leave the southern bus station 9am–3.30pm; the trip to Si Phan Don includes a boat transfer to the island of your choice.

INFORMATION

Tourist office The Provincial Tourism Office is on No. 11 Rd, near the Xe Don River (Mon–Fri 8am–noon & 1.30–4pm; ☎ 031 212021), and has bus timetables displayed on a touchscreen computer, as well as information on trekking in the region.

ACCOMMODATION

Despite the number of travellers who stop in Pakse, the town has a rather disappointing (and largely overpriced) array of accommodation options.

Khamese Guesthouse Up a narrow track off No. 21 Rd, north of the school ☎ 030 5712963. The cheapest double rooms in town can be found at this very basic riverside guesthouse, which has lovely views over the Xe Don. For 30,000K you get a mattress on the floor of a box room, plus access to a shared (cold) shower. More expensive en-suite rooms (60,000K) are available. Double **30,000K**

Lao Cha Leun No. 10 Rd, opposite the *Salachampa* ☎ 031 251333. The large rooms in this hotel are a touch on the overpriced side, offering just a little more comfort than other budget options. Light sleepers should ask for a room away from the main road. Double **135,000K**

Phonsavanh Guesthouse No. 12 Rd ☎ 031 212842. A concrete block without much charm, but comfortable and relatively good value nonetheless. All rooms are en suite, and the more expensive ones (100,000K) come with a/c, hot water and TV. Double **80,000K**

Sabaidy Guesthouse 2 No. 24 Rd ☎ 031 212992. All budget travellers seem to head straight to this guesthouse, sited in an old residential area and hence quieter than those in the middle of town. Rooms (with shared bathroom) are clean if spartan, and the dorm is the best in town. Dorm **40,000K**, double **80,000K**

Salachampa No. 10 Rd, near Champasak Plaza ☎ 031 212273. An elegant restored French villa, with teak floors, breezy verandas and a sitting room filled with antique furniture. All rooms have bathrooms and a/c, but those in the old building are the most spacious, with high ceilings. Double **150,000K**

Thaluang Hotel At the northern end of No.24 Rd ☎ 031 251399. Set around a compound full of leafy plants, rooms here are a little cramped and full of cobwebs, especially at the cheaper end, and beds are quite hard, so it's worth splashing out if you can. Double **70,000K**

INTO THAILAND: CHONG MEK

The easiest way to cross the border at **Vang Tao/Chong Mek** (daily 5am–8pm) is to board one of the VIP buses bound for Ubon Ratchathani (80,000K), which leave Pakse twice a day. A cheaper, slower and more complex option is to take a sawngthaew from the New Market to the border (20,000K). After you've crossed into Thailand, local sawngthaews will be waiting to shuttle you to the town of Phibun Mangsahan, where you can transfer to buses to Ubon Ratchathani, which has an airport and plentiful road and rail links. Whichever way you're crossing, Lao and Thai visas are available on arrival at the border.

EATING AND DRINKING

Café Sinouk No 11 Rd. A lovely, relaxed café, perfect for whiling away a few hours, though not especially cheap. Drinks 15,000–30,000K. Daily 6.30am–8.30pm.

Daolin At the junction of Route 13 and No. 24 Rd ⓣ 020 5573 3199. Positively bustling most of the day, *Daolin* lures people in with low prices and reliable backpacker food that's prepared in an open kitchen. Apart from the usual noodle dishes and cheese baguettes (15,000K), there's decent local coffee and gooey ice-cream sundaes (20,000K). Daily 6.30am–9pm.

★**Nazim's** No.12 Rd, just south of Route 13 ⓣ 031 254059. A very well-managed branch of Laos's most popular Indian restaurant chain, serving affordable meat and veggie curries (from 9000K). Wash down the chillies with an ice-cold mango lassi. Daily 7.30am–10pm.

Salachampa Attached to the *Salachampa* hotel (the entrance is on No. 12 Rd) ⓣ 031 254059. Sip draught Beerlao (8000K/glass) in the shade of tall palm and papaya trees. The food isn't anything special, but there are some reasonably priced Lao dishes (watered down for Western tastebuds) to accompany the beer. Mon–Sat 6–10pm.

Viengsavanh Seendard Just south of No. 46 Rd ⓣ 031 212388. No nonsense place that wins over locals with very tasty, inexpensive, barbecued meat that's fantastic with cold beer. The beef set, including lime, salad, dips and instant noodles, costs 50,000K. Daily 5–10pm.

DIRECTORY

Banks and exchange BCEL, on No. 11 Rd, and Lao Development Bank on Route 13, both with ATMs.

Consulates Vietnam, on No. 24 Rd (Mon–Fri 8–11am & 2–4.30pm; ⓣ 031 212058).

Hospital South of the shopping centre on No. 9 Rd.

Internet Internet cafés come and go; your best bet is Sedone (daily 8am–6pm; 5000K/hr), just south of *Pakse Hotel*. Otherwise, most hotels and tourist-oriented restaurants have free wi-fi.

Tour agencies Green Discovery (ⓦ greendiscovery.org) on No. 10 Rd; Pakse Travel (ⓣ 020 227 7277) on No. 12 Rd.

CHAMPASAK

An increasingly popular backpacker destination, **CHAMPASAK** serves as the gateway to **Wat Phou** and the **Khmer** ruins, although it is also possible to visit Wat Phou as a day-trip from Pakse. Meandering for 4km along the right bank of the Mekong, Champasak is an unassuming town, but was once the capital of a Lao kingdom whose territory stretched from the Annamite Mountains into present-day Thailand. A former **palace of Prince Boun Oum na Champasak**, the scion of the royal family of Champasak and one-time prime minister, can be seen in the town itself – the first of two pale, old French mansions, if you're coming from the north.

ARRIVAL AND DEPARTURE

By boat Two or three Pakse-bound tourist boats leave town each day (the first is at 1pm). These services take around two hours in either direction (70,000K). Travelling to and from Si Phan Don by boat is an altogether more complicated process. Unless lots of other travellers have the same idea, you'll need to hire the entire boat for the six-hour journey, and stump up around $250. To get yourself on a boat, call in at the tourist office (see below).

By bus Sawngthaews from Pakse should let you off at Champasak's tiny roundabout, towards the north of town. Three sawngthaews run through Champasak each morning (between 6.30am and 9am), charging 20,000K for the journey to Pakse.

For bus connections to and from Si Phan Don, you'll need to cross the river to Ban Muang (7000K). Tickets to Si Phan Don sold at the tourist office in Champasak (70,000K) include a pick-up from your hotel, the ferry crossing, and a minibus ride to either Ban Hat Xai Khoun or Nakasang, where you can catch a boat to the islands. Note that you'll have to pay for the final boat ride.

INFORMATION

Tourist information The tourist office (Mon–Fri 8–11am & 2–4.30pm) is situated near the post office. They can organize a small number of tours around the region and provide the latest information on chartering boats to Pakse or Si Phan Don.

Bank Lao Development Bank (Mon–Fri 8.30am–3.30pm) is just west of the roundabout, with an exchange desk and ATM.

Internet Wi-fi is available at the restaurant at *Inthira* (see p.396), among other places.

ACCOMMODATION

Khamphouy Just south of the roundabout ⓣ 020 2227 9922, ⓔ gnesthouse@hotmail.com. All of the furniture is mismatched, but this very welcoming, old-school guesthouse has good-value double and twin rooms in two separate buildings. Free wi-fi, free tea, and a little lobby lounge full of books. Double **40,000K**

Siamphone Hotel West of the roundabout, near the bank ⓣ 031 920128. Plain, tiled and very clean en-suite rooms in a large and soulless block. Double **100,000K**

5

★TREAT YOURSELF

Inthira On the main road, south of the roundabout ⓣ 031 511011, ⓦ inthirahotels.com. The spacious rooms in this boutique hotel feel like they should cost a lot more, and are full of dark wood and Lao touches, creating a romantic feel. Tucked off the main road, they're undoubtedly the nicest in the centre of town, and some of the rooms have a private outdoor shower. The attached restaurant is also worth a visit (see below). Doubles from $49

Vongpaseud Just south of *Inthira* ⓣ 031 920038. Super-low prices make this place the top choice among budget travellers. Rooms here are dingy but en suite, with hot water costing 20,000K extra per night. Cheap breakfasts are available on the creaking deck out back, which has splendid Mekong views. Double 30,000K

EATING

Champasak With Love North of the roundabout ⓣ 030 9265926. Fresh and funky with its own terrace and a tree swing, *Champasak With Love* stands out among the town's riverside restaurants. The iced coffee (15,000K) is very good. Free wi-fi. Daily 7am–10pm.

★**Inthira** On the main road, south of the roundabout. The best, and smartest, restaurant in town, but unpretentious and very relaxed. The menu covers a good range of dishes, from *larp* to barbecue chicken baguettes and fresh lime juice. Cocktails are 25,000K 6–8pm each evening. Daily 7am–10pm.

WAT PHOU

The most evocative Khmer ruin outside Cambodia, the UNESCO World Heritage Site of **Wat Phou** (daily 8am–4.30pm; 35,000K), 8km southwest of Champasak, should be at the top of your southern Laos must-see list. A romantic and rambling complex of pre-Angkorian temples dating from the sixth to the twelfth centuries, Wat Phou occupies a setting of unparalleled beauty in a lush river valley. Unlike ancient Khmer sites of equal size or importance found in neighbouring Thailand, Wat Phou has yet to be over-enthusiastically restored, so walking among the half-buried pieces of sculpted sandstone gives a good idea of what these sites once looked like.

Wat Phou, which in Lao means "Mountain Monastery", is actually a series of ruined temples and shrines at the foot of Lingaparvata Mountain. Although the site is now associated with Theravada Buddhism, sandstone reliefs indicate that the ruins were once a **Hindu place of worship**. When viewed from the Mekong, it's clear why the site was chosen. A phallic stone outcropping is easily seen among the range's line of forested peaks: this would have made the site especially auspicious to worshippers of Shiva, a Hindu god often symbolized by a phallus.

Archeologists tend to disagree on who the original founders of the site were and when it was first consecrated. The oldest parts of the ruins are thought to date back to the sixth century and were most likely built by the ancient Khmer. The site is highly sacred to the ethnic Lao, and is the focus of an annual festival (in February) that attracts thousands of pilgrims.

WHAT TO SEE AND DO

As you approach from the east, a **stone causeway** – once lined with low stone pillars – leads up to the first set of ruins. On either side of the causeway there would have been reservoirs, which probably represented the oceans that surrounded the mythical Mount Meru, home of the gods of the Hindu pantheon. Just beyond the causeway, on either side of the path, stand two megalithic structures of sandstone and laterite. They may have served as segregated **palaces**, one for men and the other for women.

Continuing up the steep stairs, you come upon a ruined temple containing the finest examples of decorative **stone lintels** in Laos. Although much has been damaged or is missing, sketches done at the end of the nineteenth century show that the temple has changed little since then.

Up the hill behind the temple is a **shallow cave** with a constant drip of water from its ceiling collecting below. This water is considered highly sacred, as it has trickled down from the peak of

Lingaparvata. Foreign visitors should resist the temptation to wash with this water, which would be akin to having a bath in the baptismal font.

If you follow the base of the cliff in a northerly direction, a bit of sleuthing will lead you to the enigmatic **crocodile stone** that may have been used as an altar for pre-Angkor-period human sacrifices.

ARRIVAL AND DEPARTURE

Tuk-tuks from Champasak can be hired for the 8km journey to Wat Phou. The drivers charge around 80,000K for up to three passengers, and will wait for you while you visit the ruins. A much more interesting approach to the ruins is by bike – bikes can be rented from a number of places along Champasak's main road (15,000K) – the route is flat and straightforward (just follow the road south through town until you reach Wat Phou, at the end of the road).

SI PHAN DON

In Laos's deepest south, just above the border with Cambodia, the muddy stream of the Mekong is carved into a 14km-wide web of rivulets, creating a landlocked archipelago ripe for exploration. Known as **Si Phan Don**, or "Four Thousand Islands", this labyrinth of islets, rocks and sandbars has acted as a kind of bell jar, preserving traditional southern-lowland Lao culture from outside influences. Local life unravels slowly and peacefully: fishermen head out at sunset silhouetted against the sky's colourful backdrop and cast their nets out across the water, and children play and run about the villages while their parents and grandparents sit and watch the world go by. The archipelago is home to rare flora and fauna, including a species of **freshwater dolphin**.

5

Southeast Asia's largest **waterfalls** are also located here.

Don Khong

The largest of the Four Thousand Islands group, **Don Khong** draws a steady stream of visitors, but has a more laidback feel than popular Don Det (see opposite). It boasts a venerable collection of Buddhist temples, good-value accommodation and interesting fresh-fish cuisine.

Don Khong has only two settlements of any size: the port town of **Muang Sen** on the island's west coast, and the east-coast town of **Muang Khong**, where the best accommodation and restaurants are. Like all Si Phan Don settlements, both Muang Sen's and Muang Khong's homes and shops cling to the bank of the Mekong for kilometres but barely penetrate the interior, which is reserved for rice fields.

WHAT TO SEE AND DO

The best way to explore the island is to rent a bicycle (10,000K/day) or motorbike (50,000K/day) – the flat terrain and lack of heavy traffic makes it relatively easy to get about.

Excursion 1

Follow the river road south from Muang Khong, and cross the wooden bridge: stick to the narrow path along the river, not the road that parallels it slightly inland. A couple of kilometres south of Muang Khong lies the village of **BAN NA**, where the real scenery begins. The trail snakes between thickets of bamboo, past traditional southern-Lao wooden houses. Approaching the tail of the island you'll emerge onto a paved road. The vast bridge you see on your left-hand side stretches for more than 700m, and cost nearly US$35 million to complete. Follow the road around to the far end of the bridge, and continue west along the road, passing rice paddies and the swishing tails of dusty water buffalos. Tall trees provide welcome shade as you pass through **BAN SIW**. The village monastery, Wat Silananthalangsy, is worth a look. The number of houses lining the road continues to grow until you reach Muang Sen, a sleepy port with a popular floating restaurant. While there is nothing much to see in the town, it's a recommended stop for rest and refreshment before heading east via the shade-stingy 8km stretch of very potholed road that leads back to Muang Khong.

Excursion 2

For another interesting trip, head due west from Muang Khong, on the road that bisects the island. Just before reaching the town of **MUANG SEN** on the western side of the island, turn right at the crossroads and head north. Follow this road up and over a low grade and after about 4km you'll cross a bridge-like hump in the road. Keep going another 1.5km and you'll notice large black boulders beginning to appear off to the left. Keeping your eyes left, you'll see a narrow trail leading up to a ridge of the same black stone, along with a large reclining Buddha. Park your bike at the foot of the ridge, and, following the trail up another 200m to the right, you'll spot the teak buildings of **Wat Phou Khao Kaew**, an evocative little forest monastery situated atop a stone bluff overlooking the Mekong. The centrepiece is a **brick stupa**; a fractured pre-Angkorian stone lintel found at the base of the stupa would, assuming it was once fixed to it, date the structure to the middle of the seventh century. Sadly, large parts of the original stupa have been haphazardly covered over with concrete and painted red and gold.

ARRIVAL AND DEPARTURE

By boat Taking the boat from Pakse or Champasak sounds romantic but is very expensive to arrange these days. Boats from other parts of Si Phan Don dock in the middle of Muang Khong, near Done Khong Guesthouse. Boats to Don Khon and Don Det depart from the same spot daily at 8.30am (1hr 30min) and cost 40,000K; arrange through the guesthouses the day before.

By bus and sawngthaew Minibuses from Pakse (70,000K including boat transfer; 3hr; buy tickets from tour agents) run daily and drop you at the passenger ferry at Ban Hat Xai Khoun (you can choose which of the three main islands you go to from here). Identical packages run in the opposite direction, with boat and bus tickets to

Champasak also available (70,000K). Alternatively, take the ferry across the Mekong and flag down a bus heading north along Route 13 – be aware that buses may be very full. Minibuses can also be arranged to Thailand and Cambodia. Sawngthaews for Pakse and Champasak depart from in front of the tourist office in Muang Khong at around 8am each morning (2–3hr; 50,000K).

INFORMATION

Bank The Agricultural Promotion Bank (daily 8am–3.30pm), at the south end of Muang Khong, past the wat, exchanges dollars and baht and has an ATM.

Bikes and motorbikes Several of the guesthouses and shops facing the Mekong in Muang Khong offer bicycles for rent (10,000K/day). Motorbikes are available for 50,000K/day.

Internet Most guesthouses offer free wi-fi. Otherwise, try the internet café just north of V Mala (200K/minute).

ACCOMMODATION

Don Khong's accommodation is concentrated in Muang Khong, which provides a good launching point for excursions around the Si Phan Don area.

Done Khong Guesthouse Just across the road from the ferry landing ⓣ031 214010. This long-established place in a very handy location near the dock has basic en-suite rooms (those at the front share a little terrace) and very friendly staff who speak English and French. Double 70,000K

★**Pon's River Guesthouse** 150m north of the ferry landing ⓣ020 2227 0037, ⓦponsriverguesthouse-donkhong.com. A great place to stay, with tidy en-suite rooms, and a very popular restaurant downstairs. TV and a/c are available for an extra 20,000K. The manager is well connected locally and can arrange a variety of tours. Double 60,000K

Souk Sabay Along the waterfront ⓣ031 214122. Modern, en-suite rooms around a family compound, set back from the river road. The rooms downstairs are a bit dark and musty – it's worth paying 10,000K more for one upstairs. Double 50,000K

V Mala Just north of the ATM on the main north–south road ⓣ020 9754 5787. Simple but surprisingly stylish, these timber-floored rooms are located in a rust-red wooden house one street back from the river. Bathrooms are shared, but there are separate facilities for men and women. Good value. Double 50,000K

EATING AND DRINKING

Most of the guesthouses have restaurants attached, serving the usual array of Western and Asian dishes from near-identical menus.

Done Khong At the guesthouse of the same name (see above). Breezy restaurant on a deck overlooking the water, with a fish-focused menu (mains around 40,000K) and decent coffee shakes. Daily 6.30am–10pm.

Pon's River Guesthouse Attached to the guesthouse of the same name (see above). Ideally situated with a river view and popular with travellers, Pon's does cheap beer (10,000K) and fried rice (15,000K). Daily 6am–10pm.

Ratana Riverside Close to the boat pier. A relaxed restaurant under a thatched roof, with *falang*-friendly versions of Lao dishes (don't be afraid to ask for more chilli), plus Western favourites. Daily 6.30am–10pm.

Don Khon and Don Det

The tropical islands of **Don Khon** and **Don Det**, 15km downstream from Don Khong, are fringed with swaying coconut palms and planted with jade- and emerald-coloured rice paddies. Besides being a picturesque little haven for backpackers, who come here in ever-increasing numbers, they also offer some leisurely walks and bike rides.

The more popular island for backpackers to stay on is the rapidly developing island of Don Det, with Don Khon catering for more mid-range budgets. Despite the explosion of travellers' cafés, many of which openly sell happy shakes and joints, parts of Don Det still maintain a rustic charm, though if you're looking for something a bit quieter, it's best to head for Don Khon. Simple wooden bungalows with hammocks out front line the coastlines of both islands, coaxing people into staying here for days (and, in many cases, weeks).

FISH AND WHISKY

Fish is a staple in Si Phan Don. Recipes range from the traditional **larp pa** (a salad of minced fish mixed with garlic, chillies, shallots and fish sauce) to tropical fish steamed in coconut milk. Be sure to try the island speciality **mók pa**, fish steamed in banana leaves, which has the consistency of custard and takes an hour to prepare.

The local **lào-láo** has gained a reputation as one of the best **rice whiskies** in Laos. For those who haven't taken a shine to Lao white lightning, Muang Khong has devised a gentler blend known as the "Lao cocktail", a mix of wild honey and *lào-láo* served over ice.

5

WHAT TO SEE AND DO

A delightfully sleepy place with a timeless feel about it, **BAN KHON**, at the northern end of Don Khon, is the islands' largest settlement. To explore the remnants of Laos's old French railway, head just south of the bridge back behind some houses. There you'll find the rusty remains of the locomotive that once hauled French goods and passengers between piers on Don Khon and Don Det, bypassing the rapids that block this stretch of the river.

Ban Hua Det

Most budget travellers head straight for the busy backpacker enclave of **Ban Hua Det**, at the northern end of Don Det. Here, dozens of tourist-friendly **guesthouses**, **bungalows** and **restaurants** have sprung up just a stone's throw from an incongruous industrial structure once used for hoisting cargo from the train onto awaiting boats; it's all that remains of the railroad's northern terminus. In just a few short years the place has grown from a sleepy island community into something resembling Thailand's party islands, and construction continues apace to keep up with the influx of visitors. Needless to say, if you'd rather be woken up by a crowing rooster than the screech of a band saw, stay further south.

Walking

Linked by a bridge and traversed by a trail, Don Khon and Don Det can be easily explored on foot. The fee to cross the railway bridge is 25,000K per day; there's a ticket booth at the southern end of the bridge. A short walk west of the bridge on Don Khon stands the village monastery, Wat Khon Tai. Taking the southerly path behind the wat for 1.5km, you'll come to a ticket checkpoint, and then a cliff overlooking **Somphamit Falls**, a series of high rapids crashing through a jagged gorge.

Dolphin-spotting from Ban Hang Khon

From Ban Khon, follow the path that turns inland near *Chanthounma's Restaurant* through rice paddies and thick forest and eventually, after 4km, you'll reach the village of **BAN HANG KHON**, the jumping-off point for **dolphin-spotting** excursions. The April to May dry season, when the Mekong is at its lowest, is the optimum time of year to catch a glimpse of this highly endangered species (early mornings and late afternoons are best), and boats can be hired out from the village to see them. Boats cost 60,000K for a one-hour trip, depending on the number of people, and you're obliged to pay for the boat regardless of whether you see any dolphins.

The bluish-grey freshwater **Irrawaddy dolphins** (*Orcaella brevirostris*), known as *pa kha*, are rare in Lao waters, as most are unable to swim beyond the Khon Phapheng Falls near the Laos–Cambodia border. Over the past century their numbers in the Mekong have dwindled dramatically, from thousands to around one hundred today. Gill-net fishing and, across the border, the use of poison, electricity and explosives, are to blame. A more pressing threat to the dolphins' survival is the vast Don Sahong dam, currently being built south of Don Khon, which scientists believe could change the river's hydrological balance forever.

Khon Phapheng Falls

Despite technically being the largest waterfall in Southeast Asia, **Khon Phapheng** (30,000K), to the east of Don Khon, is not all that spectacular. Indeed, it's best described as a low but wide cliff that just happens to have a huge volume of water running over it. The vertical drop is highest during the March-to-April dry season, and a tourist pavilion above the falls provides an ideal place to sit and enjoy the view. Most tourists do the falls as a package from Don Khon or Don Det, but it is also possible to get there by motorbike – get a boat to Ban Hat Xai Khoun (opposite Muang Khong) and head south along Route 13.

ARRIVAL AND DEPARTURE

By boat Boats between Don Khong and Don Det/Don Khon run daily at around 8.30am (1hr 30min; 40,000K) in both directions. It's possible to get a boat from either of the islands to Nakasang (15min; 15,000K) for onward connections, though the easiest option is to arrange the whole journey through your guesthouse.

5

By bus Buses from Pakse and elsewhere in Laos, plus those coming over the Cambodian border, stop at Nakasang, from where boatmen will ferry you across to the islands. To move on from Don Det and Don Khon, it's best to book your bus through your guesthouse or a local tour operator; the price will include a boat to Nakasang, and once there, the boatman will direct you to the correct place to pick up your bus. Though bus departure times are advertised as 11am, this is usually the time of the boat pick-ups from the islands. Alternatively, you could hire a boat to Nakasang yourself and pay for a bus once you're across, but aim to be there by at least 11am to make sure you can get on your desired service. Buses run to Champasak, Pakse, Vientiane and beyond, plus Siem Reap and other destinations in Cambodia and Thailand.

Destinations Champasak (daily; 2hr 30min); Pakse (daily; 3hr); Savannakhet (daily; 7hr 30min); Thakhek (daily; 10hr); Vientiane (daily; 19hr).

INFORMATION

Banks and exchange There are no banks on either island but dollars and baht are exchangable at some guesthouses and tour agencies.

Bike rental Bicycles are for rent at many guesthouses on each island for 10,000K/day.

Internet On Don Det, there are a number of internet cafés along the main "road", at the tip of the island, all charging 400K/min.

Tours The tour agents on Don Det and Don Khon are all much of a muchness, and most are run by guesthouses. In addition to kayaking and boat trips around the islands, they can all organize and book onward transport to Thailand, Cambodia and Vietnam.

ACCOMMODATION

DON DET

Bountip's Eastside Guesthouse On the east coast of the island, south of the *Crazy Gecko* restaurant ⓣ 054 813900. Exceptionally cheap bungalows that just happen to be located in a very peaceful coconut grove by the water's edge. It's a bit of a walk from the centre of Ban Hua Det, however, and you'll have to share a tatty cold-water bathroom. Double 30,000K

Don Det Bungalows On the east coast of the island, around 1.2km south of the centre of Ban Hua Det ⓣ 020 2300 4959. For something quiet and relatively classy, try these comfy bungalows, which have swooping Lao-style rooflines and cocoon-like hammocks. There's a reasonable restaurant on the other side of the path. Double 130,000K

Keo Inpeng Towards the northern end of the island, off Ban Hua Det's main drag. Hard to spot off the main drag (look for the small sign on the right as you walk south from the beach), Keo Inpeng has good-value en-suite rooms in a modern block that's surrounded by marigolds. Double 60,000K

The Last Resort On the west side of the island, around 750m south of Ban Hua Det ⓦ facebook.com/lastresortdondet. This self-styled travellers' community was started by a former banker from the UK. Thatched wigwams sleeping two to four people are set around a sociable garden that's home to a fire pit and an open-air cinema. Organic herbs grown onsite are used in communal meals. Double 60,000K

Santiphab Right next to the railroad bridge. Decent en-suite bungalows are available at this long-running place at the northern end of the old French bridge, with views across to Don Khon on the other side of the babbling river. Double 40,000K

Saeng Chanh At the eastern end of the main road through town ⓣ 020 9738 8727. A little run-down (some of the raised riverside bungalows have holes in the floor), but very cheap and handy for the centre. Double 35,000K

DON KHON

Somphamit Just west of the *Sala Done Khong* hotel on the main river road ⓣ 020 526 2491. Comfortable riverside bamboo bungalows equipped with fans and wide, shared terraces with decent hammocks. All rooms are en suite, and some are a little musty. Double 60,000K

Sunset Paradise Guesthouse The easternmost guesthouse on the main riverside path in Ban Khon. Spacious and solid, these wooden bungalows face one another across a peaceful garden, just back from the river. The helpful staff speak English and French, and there's good food at the waterfront restaurant. Double 100,000K

> **★TREAT YOURSELF**
>
> **Seng Ahloune** Don Khon, to the right of the bridge as you cross from Don Det ⓦ sengahloune.com. Ten charming rooms in wooden bungalows right by the water, with lovely touches like handcrafted decorations on the door and windows. A really peaceful spot from which to watch the Mekong rushing past. $40

EATING AND DRINKING

Most places on the islands serve a fairly predictable mix of Lao and Western dishes, and Mekong fish is always on the menu – though if you want to try *mok pa* (fish cooked in coconut milk), you'll generally need to order an hour or so in advance.

DON DET

Crazy Gecko Sunrise side, south of *Don Det Bungalows*. This laidback riverfront restaurant, its terrace strewn with swinging lanterns and tropical plants, stands out for its

5

INTO CAMBODIA: VEUN KHAM

Although buses run to the border, the easiest way to get into Cambodia via the **Veun Kham** crossing is to take a direct bus (daily; 5hr; $17–18) that leaves either from the islands or from Pakse to Stung Treng (see p.392) – minibuses are usually your best option, and direct tickets are also available to Siem Reap and Phnom Penh. Cambodian and Lao **visas** are available on arrival. Immigration officials on both sides ask for a $1–2 fee to stamp your passport, in addition to a visa fee.

varied menu, which dares to deviate from fried rice and pancakes. Dishes include a lightly spiced pumpkin burger (20,000K). Daily 7am–9.30pm.

Reggae Bar A short walk south of the beach, at the northern end of the island. Joints are passed around at this lazy, sit-down bar, where empty crates of Beerlao prop up the long and sociable tables. The "hangover breakfast" here includes fruit, Coke, and – oddly – garlic bread (35,000K). Daily 8am–11pm.

Rib Shack Ban Hua Det. Friendly streetside place run by a man from Tennessee, USA, who's been living on the island for a few years. His pork ribs, which sell for 10,000K a piece, are great with beer. Daily 6pm–late.

DON KHON

Sunset Paradise Guesthouse The easternmost guesthouse on the main riverside path in Ban Khon. Of the many riverside terraces facing Don Det, this one (see p.401) has the most appealing. Bar stools face out over the water, providing the perfect spot for fresh spring rolls (20,000K) or an ice cream. Daily 7am–10.30pm.

Seng Ahloune At the guesthouse of the same name (see box, p.401). As long as you avoid it when the tour groups descend for lunch, this large, friendly restaurant is a good choice, offering a predominantly Lao menu, with dishes such as fish *larp* (50,000K), served right by the river. Daily 7am–10pm.

THE BOLAVEN PLATEAU AND TAD LO

High above the hot Mekong River valley stands the natural citadel of the **Bolaven Plateau** – hilly, roughly circular in shape, and with an average altitude of 600m – dominating eastern Champasak province and overlooking the provinces of Salavan, Xekong and Attapeu to the east. Rivers flow off the high plateau in all directions and then plunge out of lush forests along the Bolaven's edges in a series of spectacular waterfalls, some more than 100m high.

Tad Lo

In the past few years the area around **Tad Lo**, a 10m-high waterfall on the banks of the Xe Set, has been attracting a growing stream of backpackers. The cheap guesthouses and restaurants in the village just downstream of the main waterfall (there are three along this section of the river) provide everything visitors need for a few days' relaxation. In the hot season, the pools surrounding **Tad Hang**, the falls closest to the guesthouses, are a refreshing escape from the heat. For a long, scenic walk that takes in all three falls, follow the well-marked trail that runs around the back of the Tad Lo Lodge. The tourist office on the road to the falls can hook you up with a guide for this walk if you'd prefer not to do it alone. If you do decide to swim, take care and be sure to clear the water before darkness, when the floodgates of a dam upstream sometimes unleash a torrent of water without warning.

ARRIVAL AND DEPARTURE

By bus The Tad Lo Falls are 88km northeast of Pakse by bus (about 2hr) and about 30km southwest of Salavan. The turn-off for Tad Lo is just beyond the village of Lao Ngam; buses will drop you at the turn-off, from where it's a 1.5km tuk-tuk ride (10,000K/person) along a dirt road to Tad Hang. Moving on, ask your guesthouse for a lift back to the main road (10,000K), where you can pick up a morning bus to Salavan or Pakse.

ACCOMMODATION AND EATING

★**Café Em** Next door to the tourist office on the road to the falls ⓣ 020 5633 4637, ⓔ ema.g@gmx.at. Wonderful little outdoor coffee shop using organic, freshly roasted Arabica beans from the Bolaven Plateau. The breakfast, with Austrian-style coffee and honey-smothered pancakes (25,000K), is a great way to start the day. Daily 6am–7pm.

★**Palamei Guesthouse** At the T-junction in the middle of the village, just east of the tourist office ⓣ 030 9620192. The superb-value rooms at this family-run garden guesthouse are very clean and well looked after. Cheaper rooms share a bathroom, while more expensive ones (60,000K) have en-suite facilities. If you want the chance to chat with

locals, join the family for dinner (they charge 30,000K/person, and you can help with the cooking if you prefer). Double **40,000K**

Sabai Sabai Just west of the tourist office ⓣ 020 9858 9266. Bamboo-built, backpacker-friendly guesthouse, which has some of the cheapest – and simplest – dorm beds in Laos. Downstairs there's a restaurant serving cheap food (grilled chicken and chips 15,000K), and a shop selling local handicrafts. Also motorbike rental, BBQ parties, and free wi-fi for customers. No set opening hours. Dorm **15,000K**, double **35,000K**

Tim Opposite the school library on the road to the falls ⓣ 034 211885, ⓔ soulidet@gmail.com. This long-running place has reasonable doubles and twins with shared facilities, but compared with others nearby they feel poor value. Downstairs there's a restaurant serving simple backpacker grub (fried rice 15,000K). Double **50,000K**. Restaurant open daily 7am–10pm.

THE XE KONG RIVER VALLEY

The **Xe Kong** is one of Laos's great rivers, starting high in the Annamite Mountains from the eastern flanks of 2500m-high Mount Atouat and flowing southwestward around the southern edge of the Bolaven Plateau and then across the plains of Cambodia to join the Mekong at Stung Treng. The main towns along the Xe Kong in Laos are **Xekong** and **Attapeu**, which are linked by a paved road. Roads into the vast forest interior are still poor, but various tributaries link the Xe Kong to no fewer than four of Laos's most pristine National Biodiversity Conservation Areas.

Xekong

In 1984, a wide expanse of jungle was cleared of trees and flattened, heralding the birth of **XEKONG**. There's little to see or do in the town itself, which sits alongside the meandering Xe Kong River, and for some of the intrepid travellers that make it here, that's where the appeal lies. Xekong is a small, working town, without any of the usual tourist trappings. Three major branches of the Ho Chi Minh Trail snaked through the jungle surrounding Xekong, making this area one of the most heavily bombed in Laos. An astonishing amount of UXO still blankets this province, so exploring solo is a definite no-no.

ARRIVAL AND DEPARTURE

By bus Buses to and from Pakse and other towns around the Bolaven Plateau operate from the bus station, about 4km out of town; a handful of tuk-tuks await arriving buses and will ferry you into the centre for 10,000K.

Destinations Attapeu (2 daily; 2hr); Pakse (8 daily; 2–4hr); Vientiane (8 daily; 15hr).

ACCOMMODATION AND EATING

Phathip Restaurant Near the post office. The best place for delicious Vietnamese food, including vegetable-packed (but very salty) noodle soups (10,000K). The menu – in English, Swedish, French and Lao – has plenty of info on exploring the surrounding area. Daily 7am–7pm.

Sekong Hotel Just across from *Phathip Restaurant*, on the road nearest the river ⓣ 038 211039. Get past the grumpy dogs guarding the yard out front and this hotel has reasonably comfortable en-suite doubles, as well as more expensive "VIP" rooms (100,000K). The walls are nicotine stained, but otherwise it's not bad value. Double **50,000K**

Woman Fever Kosment Center Guest House Just across from *Phathip Restaurant*, on the road nearest the river ⓣ 020 563 8286. There's little English spoken at this rickety old guesthouse (which might explain the barmy name), though the rooms – which share squat toilets at the end of the building – are very cheap. Double **40,000K**

Attapeu

Despite its name literally translating as "buffalo shit", Attapeu is a cosy settlement of almost twenty thousand

INTO VIETNAM: BO Y

There's a border crossing with Vietnam at the end of Route 18B, 113km east of Attapeu. Five minibuses leave Attapeu for Vietnam each morning (hourly from 6am), crossing the border at **Bo Y** after a winding, three-hour drive. You can buy tickets in advance from the *Dúc Lôc* **hotel** (see p.404). By the time you read this, direct shuttle buses to the border may well be running from Attapeu's main bus station, but, for now, you'll have to buy a ticket that takes you all the way to Vietnam (80,000K to Kon Tum, though tickets to Ngoc Hoi and Gia Lai are also available). Tickets to other Vietnamese destinations via Bo Y, including Da Nang and Hue, can be bought in Pakse (see p.390). To cross into Vietnam, you must have arranged your visa before arrival at the border.

5

people, most of whom are Vietnamese, Chinese or Lao. Occupying a bend in the Xe Kong River, with coconut palms and banana trees shading spacious wooden houses with generous balconies, the town is known throughout southern Laos as the "Garden City." Although it was near this distant outpost that the Ho Chi Minh Trail diverged, with one artery running south towards Cambodia and the other into South Vietnam, Attapeu somehow eluded the grave effects of war and remains an easy-going place that's ideal for leisurely wandering. This region of Laos has one of the country's highest rates of malaria, so heed the advice on p.37.

ARRIVAL AND DEPARTURE

By bus Arriving by bus, you'll find yourself on the northwestern outskirts of the city, 4km from the centre. The bus station is served by frequent buses from Pakse, with shared tuk-tuks on hand for the run into town (10,000K per person).

Destinations Pakse (at least 5 daily; 4–7hr); Vientiane (4 daily; 16hr); Xekong (2 daily; 2hr).

SERVICES

Bank There's a branch of the Lao Viet Bank, along with an ATM, right outside the *Hoang Anh Attapeu Hotel*. You can change money at a couple of places within 20m or so of the *Dúc Lôc* hotel.

Market Near the bridge. Mostly household goods and food, best in the morning (daily 7am–4pm).

ACCOMMODATION AND EATING

Eating well in Attapeu isn't especially easy: try the market, the downstairs restaurant at *Dúc Lôc* (see below), or head to one of the bars near the riverfront – though these are more about beer and karaoke than decent dinners.

Dúc Lôc In the city centre, on the south side of Route 18 ☎ 020 9982 2334. Very well-run Vietnamese place close to the market, and convenient for those heading to the Bo Y border crossing. The wood-panelled rooms feel very fresh, with TV and a/c to boot. Downstairs there's a restaurant serving good Vietnamese pho for 10,000K. Double **80,000K**

Sokpaseud Riverside Guesthouse South of the centre along the main river road ☎ 030 9990773. Slightly twee, this mansion-like guesthouse just across the road from the Xe Kong is an excellent budget choice. Chandeliers hang from the wooden ceilings and rooms are unexpectedly good for the money. Double **80,000K**

SARAWAK CULTURAL VILLAGE

Malaysia

HIGHLIGHTS

❶ **Georgetown** Sample local cuisine at its best in Malaysia's food capital. **See p.437**

❷ **Pulau Perhentian** An earthly paradise of palm-fringed white sand and crystal-clear waters. **See p.457**

❸ **Malacca** Explore this colonial city rich in heritage buildings. **See p.465**

❹ **Longhouse stay** Explore Sarawak's rich cultural heritage by staying with indigenous tribes. **See p.484**

❺ **Mount Kinabalu** Watch the sunrise from the summit of Borneo's highest mountain. **See p.502**

❻ **Sipadan** Swim with sharks and turtles at one of the world's top diving spots. **See p.513**

HIGHLIGHTS ARE MARKED ON THE MAP ON PP.408–409

ROUGH COSTS

Daily budget Basic RM55/Occasional treat RM80

Drink Beer US$1.50 (pricier in stricter Muslim areas)

Food *Mee goreng* (noodles) US$1.50

Budget hotel US$6.50–18

Travel Bus: Kuala Lumpur–Malacca (144km) US$7; Ferry: Mersing–Pulau Tioman (50km) US$11; Train: Kota Bharu–Jerantut (131km) US$8

FACT FILE

Population 29.2 million

Language Bahasa Malaysia (also English, Tamil, Hokkien, Cantonese and Mandarin)

Currency Malaysian Ringgit (RM)

Capital Kuala Lumpur

International phone code ☎ + 60

Time zone GMT + 8hr

Introduction

Malaysia has something to offer every traveller – from heady bar- and club-hopping in the capital, historical buildings in towns rich in colonial history and countless regional delicacies, to trekking and wildlife-watching in the world's oldest tropical rainforest and diving at some of the world's best sites off the white-sand beaches of its many islands. The country is full of charm and beauty, and its rich cultural heritage is apparent in both traditional village areas and in its commitment to religious plurality. The dominant cultural force is undoubtedly Islam, but the country's diverse population of Malays, Chinese, Indians and Borneo's indigenous tribes has created a fabulous juxtaposition of mosques, temples and churches, a panoply of festivals, and a wonderful mixture of cuisines. The Malays insist that their food combines the best flavours and dishes of the surrounding countries – and after a few meals from a sizzling street stall, you're likely to agree.

First impressions of Malaysia's high-tech, fast-growing capital, **Kuala Lumpur (KL)**, are likely to be of a vibrant and colourful modern metropolis with gleaming skyscrapers. Less than three hours' journey south lies the birthplace of Malay civilization, **Malacca**. Further up the coast is the first British settlement, the island of **Penang**, and its fascinating historical capital, **Georgetown.** For a taste of Old England and walks through emerald-green tea plantations, head for the **Cameron Highlands**.

WHEN TO GO

Temperatures in Malaysia constantly hover around 30°C (22°C in highland areas), and humidity is high all year round. The monsoon season brings heavy and prolonged downpours to the east coast of Peninsular Malaysia, the northeastern part of Sabah and the western end of Sarawak from November to February; boats to most of the islands stop running. For tropical heat and a buzzing atmosphere, May to September is the time to go, with July and August being the busiest months due to holidays in Europe and the States. For those prepared to risk a few showers, the months bordering the monsoon, March–April and October–November, are good options.

Pulau Langkawi is a popular, palm-fringed, duty-free island north of Penang, while routes down the Peninsula's east coast include stops at the truly stunning islands of **Pulau Perhentian** and **Pulau Tioman**. The state capitals of **Kota Bharu**, in the northeast, and **Kuala Terengganu**, further south, are great stops for soaking up Islam-infused Malay culture, while the unsullied tropical rainforests of **Taman Negara National Park** offer innumerable trails, animal hides, a high canopy walkway and rushing waterfalls.

Across the sea, East Malaysia comprises the Bornean states of **Sarawak** and **Sabah**. **Kuching**, Sarawak's attractive colonial capital, beckons with its mix of the old and the new, but the real attraction lies in the interior: in staying in the **traditional longhouses** of the Iban communities of the Batang Ai and Batang Lupar river systems, or the Bidayuh and Orang-Ulu communities closer to the Kalimantan border. The best time to visit is in late May to early June during the rice harvest festival celebrations. **Sibu**, further to the north, is another starting point for longhouse visits. In the north of the state, **Gunung Mulu National Park** beckons with its extraordinary razor-sharp limestone needles providing demanding climbing and its caves among the largest in the world.

There are many reasons for a trip to Sabah: to conquer the 4095m granite peak of **Mount Kinabalu**; to visit the lively modern capital of **Kota Kinabalu**; and to **watch the wildlife**, such as wild orang-utans, proboscis monkeys and hornbills along the Kinabatangan River, not to mention diving at the world-class island destination of **Pulau Sipadan** with its host of sharks, fish and turtles.

CHRONOLOGY

38,000 BC Evidence of earliest human habitation in Malaysia, based on a 40,000-year-old skull found in the Niah Caves, Sarawak (see p.487).

200 AD onwards Indian traders arrive in the region, bringing Hindu and Buddhist practices. Hindu-Malay kingdom established in what is now Kedah.

Seventh to thirteenth centuries Sumatra-based Buddhist Srivijaya Empire dominates Malaysia, Indonesia and Borneo.

c.1390 Sumatran prince Paramesvara founds the Malacca Sultanate.

Fifteenth century Malacca flourishes as a trading centre. Islam is adopted as the dominant religion, and the Malacca Sultanate expands along the west coast of the Peninsula to Singapore and east-coast Sumatra.

1511 The Portuguese take Malacca and Sultan Mahmud Shah flees.

1526 The Portuguese raze the Sultan's court of Johor on Pulau Bentam. Johor's court moves frequently during a century of assaults by Portugal and Aceh.

1641 The Dutch East India Company take Malacca, which goes into decline. The Johor court ally becomes the predominant Malay kingdom.

Sixteenth to nineteenth centuries Trade with China grows; many Chinese merchants come to Malacca and marry Malay women, creating the unique Baba-Nyonya culture.

1786 The British establish a trading fort at Penang (Georgetown).

1819 Sir Stamford Raffles establishes a British trading station in Singapore, which weakens both Malacca and Penang, forcing the Dutch to relinquish the former to the British.

1823 The British and Dutch split the territories between them, giving the Dutch Indonesia, and leaving Malaysia to Britain.

1826 The British unify Malacca, Penang and Singapore into one administration, the Straits Settlements, with Singapore replacing Penang as its capital in 1832.

1839 British explorer James Brooke arrives in Kuching, helps the Sultan of Brunei suppress a rebellion and becomes the first White Rajah.

1874 Struggles between Chinese clan groups are rife and Malay factions frequently become involved, causing a string of civil wars. The British sign the Pangkor Treaty with the Perak Malay chief, Rajah Abdullah, formalizing the control of the British Empire over Peninsular Malaysia.

1880s The name British Malaya comes into use. The Malay sultans' powers are gradually eroded, while the introduction of rubber estates makes British Malaya one of the most productive colonies in the world.

1888 Sarawak, Sabah and Brunei are made British protectorates.

1896 The Peninsula states under British control are given the title the Federated Malay States, with Kuala Lumpur the regional capital.

1909–19 British control in the Peninsula expands to the northern Malay states of Kedah and Perlis (1909), Johor (1914) and Terengganu (1919).

1930s Chinese–Malay tensions increase with Chinese immigration. The Malayan Communist Party is founded in 1930, with significant support in the Chinese community, demanding an end to British rule and the perceived privileges of the Malays. The Singapore Malay Union, formed in response, advocates a Malay supremacist line.

1942–45 Japanese occupation. The British shamefully flee and up to fifty thousand people – mainly Chinese – are killed in the two weeks following the British surrender of Singapore. Chinese activists in the MCP organize much of the resistance.

1946 The British introduce the Malayan Union, which gives Chinese and Indian inhabitants equal rights to Malays. In response, Malayan nationalists form the United Malays National Organization (UMNO), arguing that Malays should retain special privileges.

1948 The Federation of Malaya replaces the Malay Union. It re-establishes the power of the Malay sultans, and Chinese and Indians only qualify as citizens if they have lived there for fifteen years and speak Malay or English. Sarawak and North Borneo made British Crown Colonies.

1948–60 "The Emergency", with the predominantly Chinese Malayan Communist Party members taking to the jungle and striking at economic targets and at the British in a bid to loosen state control. The violence peaks in 1950–51.

1955 UMNO's leader, Tunku Abdul Rahman, wins the first federal elections by cooperating with moderate Chinese and Indian parties and campaigning for *merdeka* (freedom) – an independent Malaya.

August 31, 1957 Britain grants independence to Malaya, and Rahman becomes the first prime minister. Under the new constitution nine Malay sultans alternate as king.

September 1963 North Borneo (renamed Sabah), Sarawak and Singapore join Malaya to form the Federation of Malaysia. Brunei refuses to join.

6

6

August 1965 Following tensions between the Malay-dominated UMNO Alliance Party in KL and Lee Kuan Yew in Singapore, Singapore leaves the Federation.

1969 When the UMNO Alliance loses parliamentary elections, rioting breaks out in major cities. Hundreds of Chinese are killed. The country remains under a state of emergency for nearly two years.

1970 Rahman resigns, handing over to Tun Abdul Razak, also from UMNO, who introduces positive discrimination for ethnic Malays, known as *bumiputra*, which gives them favoured positions in business and professions. This remains a major cause of ethnic tension within Malaysia today.

1981 UMNO leader Dr Mahathir Mohammed becomes prime minister.

2003 Mahathir hands over the premiership to Abdullah Badawi.

2007 Malaysia celebrates fifty years of independence.

March 2008 Badawi and the UMNO scrape to victory in elections.

April 2008 Pakatan Rakyat, an informal Malaysian political coalition party, is formed by the former Deputy Prime Minister, Anwar Ibrahim. It is comprised and collectively managed by the People's Justice Party (PKR), Democratic Action Party (DAP) and Pan-Malaysian Islamic Party (PAS), following their success in a number of states in the March general election.

July 2009 Thousands of people protest on the streets of Kuala Lumpur against the Internal Security Act, which allows for the arrest and detention without trial of any individual deemed a threat to national security.

2010 A Malaysian court rules that a Roman Catholic newspaper could use the world "Allah" to describe the Christian God in its Malay-language edition. Churches are attacked by protest Muslim groups in Kuala Lumpur, Perak and Sarawak.

2013 The ruling National Front retains power in the national elections.

ARRIVAL AND DEPARTURE

Malaysia's main **airport** is Kuala Lumpur International Airport (KLIA; ⓦklia.com.my), to which there are international flights from most countries. **Domestic** and **low-cost flights** to other Southeast Asian destinations (and beyond) depart from The Low Cost Carrier Terminal (LCCT; ⓦlcct.com.my), dominated by AirAsia, situated nearby. Between them, these terminals handle almost all international flights, and are well

connected to KL's main transport hub – KL Sentral train station. Penang, Langkawi, Kuching and Kota Kinabalu also receive some international flights. From KL, AirAsia covers a number of domestic routes, and prices are spectacularly low, especially if booked in advance. Malaysia's bus and train routes are extremely efficient, and crossing the entire length of the Peninsula can be done overnight.

Malaysia has **land borders** with Thailand, Singapore, Brunei and Kalimantan (Indonesian territory), with frequent long-distance buses crossing all of them.

FROM INDONESIA

A variety of ferries and speedboats depart from **Indonesia** to Malaysia: from Medan (see p.214), in north Sumatra, to Penang; from Dumai (see p.239), south of Medan, to Malacca; from Pulau Batam, near Pe Kan baru (see p.238), to Johor Bahru; from Satun, Thailand, to Langkawi; and from Tanjung Balai, in Sumatra, to Port Klang; between Zamboanga, Philippines, and Sandakan; and from Tarakan (see box, p.325) in northeastern Kalimantan to Tawau in Sabah.

There is a **land border** at Entikong, 100km south of Kuching in Sarawak; buses run from Pontianak in southern Kalimantan through here to Kuching (see p.476).

FROM THAILAND

Recent political unrest and the threat of terrorism has made travelling from Thailand to Malaysia more dangerous and visitors are strongly advised against venturing into the provinces of Pattani, Yala, Narathiwat and Songkhla on the Thai–Malaysia border. This makes the city and transport hub of **Hat Yai** and several of the main border crossings to Malaysia essentially out of bounds for the time being: it includes travelling by rail from Hat Yai (and Bangkok) to Butterworth via Padang Besar, and

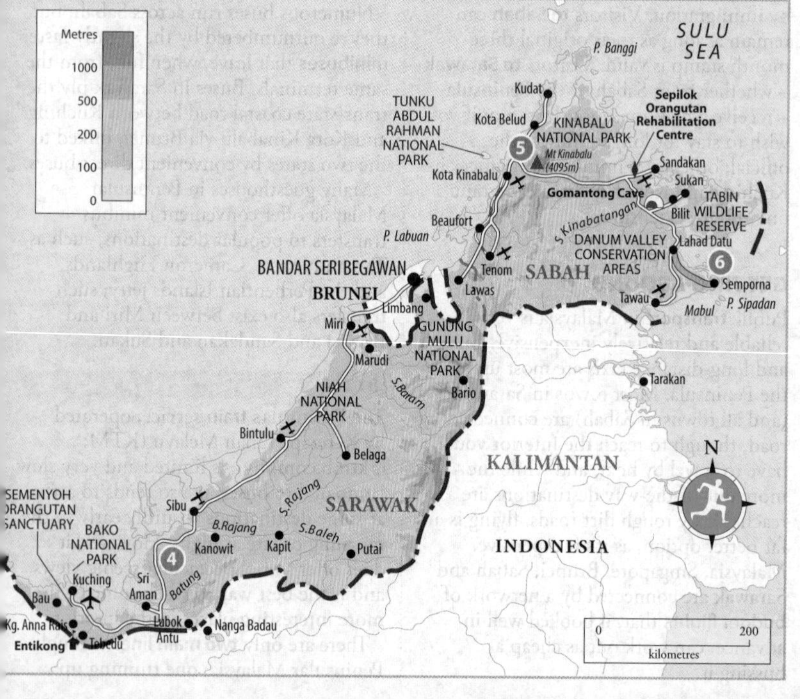

down the east coast to Kota Bharu. If you plan on taking any of these routes, check official advice, such as that of the Foreign & Commonwealth Office (fco.gov.uk), and ask locals before going. The safest routes are those from **Satun** and **Ko Lipe** (see box, p.819). From Satun, there is local transport to Kuala Perlis and Pulau Langkawi or Alor Setar, and the ferry from Koh Lipe to Pulau Langkawi is a relatively straightforward route.

VISAS

Citizens of the UK, the US, Australia, New Zealand, Ireland, Canada and most other European countries do not need a **visa** for stays of up to three months in Malaysia. To **extend your visa**, go to a local immigration department office or simply cross into Singapore (or Thailand) and back. Two-month extensions are possible. Citizens of Israel are forbidden to enter Malaysia.

Tourists travelling from the Peninsula to Sarawak and Sabah must be cleared again by immigration. Visitors **to Sabah** can remain as long as their original three-month stamp is valid. Visitors **to Sarawak** – whether from Sabah or the Peninsula – receive a new, one-month stamp; if you wish to stay for longer, inform the official; otherwise, immigration offices in Kuching and Kota Kinabalu can grant one-month extensions.

GETTING AROUND

Public **transport** in Malaysia is very reliable and relatively inexpensive. Buses and long-distance taxis are most useful on the Peninsula. Most towns in Sarawak (and all towns in Sabah) are connected by road, though to reach the interior you'll have to travel by boat, and while the more out-of-the-way destinations are reachable by rough dirt roads, flying is a far better option, as it's inexpensive. Malaysia, Singapore, Brunei, Sabah and Sarawak are connected by a network of **budget flights** that, if booked well in advance, can work out as cheap as bussing it.

BY BUS

Interstate destinations are covered by comfortable, air-conditioned **express buses**, operated either by the government's Transnasional (ktb.com.my), or by state or private bus companies; each company has an office at the bus station and prices are very competitive. In many larger cities, long-distance bus terminals tend to be inconveniently located outside city centres, but are connected to a central (local) bus station by a shuttle bus.

Buses for long-distance routes (over 3hr) typically leave in clusters in the early morning and late evening, while shorter routes are served throughout the day. In most cases, you can just turn up, though on popular routes like KL to Penang (8hr), overnight buses from KK to Semporna, or during public and school holidays, reserve ahead. **Local buses** usually operate from a separate station, serve routes within the state and are cheaper, but also slower, less comfortable and without air conditioning; buy your ticket on the bus.

Numerous buses run across Sabah, but they're outnumbered by the slightly faster **minibuses** that leave, when full, from the same terminals. Buses in Sarawak ply the trans-state coastal road between Kuching and Kota Kinabalu via Brunei, linked to the two states by convenient direct buses.

Many guesthouses in Peninsular Malaysia offer convenient minibus transfers to popular destinations, such as Taman Negara, Cameron Highlands, and the Perhentian Islands jetty; such transfers also exist between Miri and Brunei and Sandakan and Sukau.

BY TRAIN

The Peninsula's **train** service, operated by Keretapi Tanah Melayu (KTM; ktmb.com.my), is limited and very slow compared to buses; it also tends to arrive at some destinations absurdly early in the morning or late at night. However, it does offer some spectacular scenic views and is the best way to reach some of the more interesting places in the interior.

There are only **two main lines** through Peninsular Malaysia: one running up

from Singapore along the west coast via KL, Ipoh, Tapah Road (for the Cameron Highlands) and Butterworth to Padang Besar, connecting with Thai Railways which then continue to Hat Yai and north to Bangkok. You may have to change trains in KL before continuing up north. The second train line splits off between KL and Singapore at Gemas, 58km northeast of Malacca, running north through the mountainous interior covered in lush vegetation – a section known as the **Jungle Railway** – via Kuala Lipis and skirting Kota Bharu to the northeastern border town of Tumpat. The north-bound train from Gemas is a night train, so for the jungle views, do this stretch from north to south. East Malaysia's only rail line is the bone-shaking 55km link between Kota Kinabalu and Tenom in Sabah.

Express trains (*Ekspres Rakyat* or *Ekspres Sinaran*) stop at principal stations only; ordinary trains, labelled *M* on timetables, stop at most stations and are only slightly cheaper. Trains offer first-, second- and sometimes third-class carriages; the first two have air conditioning. On overnight sleepers, only first- and second-class fares are available and the air conditioning tends to be on full-blast. From KL to Butterworth costs RM67/34/23 for first/second/third-class travel on an overnight express train. Train fares from Singapore cost double what you'd pay in Malaysia, so if travelling north from Singapore, buy a ticket to Johor Bahru and then purchase a separate ticket there. Tickets can be booked at Ⓦktmb.com.my.

BY FERRY AND BOAT

Boats sail to all the major islands off Malaysia's coasts, but during the monsoon (Nov–Feb), east-coast services are almost nonexistent. West-coast islands such as Penang and Langkawi are served by passenger/car ferries; reaching the Perhentian Islands requires a bumpy speedboat ride.

In **Sarawak**, regular turbo-charged "flying coffin" express boats ply the mighty Rejang and Baram rivers.

On the smaller tributaries, or during dry season, travel is by **longboat**, which you may have to charter. This mode of travel can get very expensive, as diesel prices multiply alarmingly the further into the interior you travel. Many inland destinations are becoming reachable by 4WD and truck along rough logging tracks, though it's slower and pricier than going by river. **Sabah** has no express boats, but ferries **to Indonesia** from Tawau are increasingly used by travellers, given the absence of direct flights.

BY PLANE

The cheapest airline with the most domestic flight routes is **AirAsia** (Ⓦairasia.com). Flights are quick and efficient – it is just 55 minutes from KL to Langkawi as opposed to an eleven-hour bus and ferry journey. Other airlines with domestic and Southeast Asian flights include: Malaysia Airlines (Ⓦmalaysiaairlines.com); Firefly (Ⓦfireflyz.com.my) – a budget subsidiary of Malaysia Airlines with flights to Alor Star, Malacca, Langkawi, Kota Bharu, JB, Penang and Singapore; and Silk Air (Ⓦsilkair.com) and Berjaya Air (Ⓦberjaya-air.com), who operate flights to Pulau Tioman, Pulau Pangkor and Singapore from KL.

Flights to East Malaysia operate mainly out of Kuala Lumpur, with Johor Bahru providing additional services to Kuching and Kota Kinabalu. Within Sarawak and Sabah, MASwings (Ⓦmaswings.com.my) is a subsidiary of Malaysian Airlines, serving Kuching, Miri, Bintulu, KK, Sandakan, Sibu, Bario, Tawau, Lahad Datu and more. AirAsia also flies to all of these destinations, barring Mulu and Bario, which are only reachable by small aircraft.

VEHICLE RENTAL

Malaysia's main roads tend to be in good condition, though many drivers rarely give way or signal and sometimes don't obey traffic lights or signs. Drivers flash their headlights when they are claiming the right of way, *not* the other way around.

Malaysians drive on the left, and wearing seat belts in the front is compulsory. To rent a vehicle, you must be 23 or over and have held a clean international driving licence for at least

6

a year. Avis, Budget, Hertz and National have offices in major towns and at the airports; **rates** start at RM170 per day or RM800 per week. **Motorbike and scooter rental** is offered by guesthouses and shops in touristy areas (around RM30 per day). You may need to leave a deposit, but it's unlikely you'll have to show any proof of eligibility – officially, you must be over 21 and have an appropriate driving licence. Wearing helmets is compulsory. **Bicycles** can be rented for about RM10 per day.

ACCOMMODATION

Malaysia offers inexpensive **accommodation** to suit all budgets. Besides high season and low season prices, many lodgings have three tariffs: weekday, weekend and holiday, the former being the cheapest and the last the most expensive. Many places offer special deals, particularly in the off-season. Fans of colonial-era architecture will find an abundance of mid-range options with all the amenities but without the shockingly high tariffs.

Room rates rise dramatically during the major holiday periods – Christmas, Easter, Chinese New Year and Hari Raya Haji – but as a general rule it's always worth bargaining.

The mainstays of the travellers' scene in Malaysia are **guesthouses**, located in popular tourist areas. They can range from simple beachside A-frame huts and simple chalets to modern multistorey apartment buildings. Most offer dormitory beds (from RM20) and basic double rooms (from RM50, depending on area). At the budget end of the market, you're likely to get a choice of rooms; the cheaper ones will be fan-equipped and share bathrooms, whereas the pricier ones will be en suite with air conditioning.

The larger, more popular city destinations such as KL and Georgetown in Penang will have international-standard **youth hostels** with all the amenities that globetrotters on a budget have come to expect: clean dorms with lockers and air conditioning, free wi-fi and a plethora of tours. The most atmospheric accommodation in Malaysia is in stilted **longhouses**, found on the rivers of Sarawak and Sabah. These can house dozens of families, and usually consist of three elevated sections reached by a simple ladder. The snag is that it's difficult to stay in them as an independent traveller as you need to have contacts within the community, but it is possible to stay at longhouses as part of an organized tour or with the help of a local guide.

Electricity in Malaysia is supplied at 220 volts, and plugs have three prongs like British ones.

FOOD AND DRINK

The **cuisine** in Peninsular Malaysia is inspired by the three main communities: Malay, Chinese and Indian, whereas in Borneo, you'll also find many delicious indigenous dishes. Food everywhere is remarkably good value – basic noodle or rice-based meals at a street stall can be had from around RM5, and a full meal with drinks in a decent restaurant will seldom cost more than RM55 a head. Food hygiene standards are generally quite high; if you're eating from street stalls, it's best to go for the ones with the most customers.

THE CUISINES

Malay cuisine is based on rice, often enriched with *santan* (coconut milk), which is served with a dazzling variety of curries, vegetable stir-fries and sambals, a condiment of chillies and *belacan* (shrimp paste).

The most famous dish is satay – which comprises skewers of barbecued meat dipped in spicy peanut sauce. The classic way to sample Malay curries is to eat *nasi campur*, a buffet (usually served at lunchtime) of steamed rice – supplemented by up to two dozen accompanying dishes, including *lembu* (beef), *kangkong* (greens), fried chicken, fish steaks and curry sauce, and various vegetables. Another popular dish is *nasi goreng* (mixed fried rice with meat, seafood and vegetables). For breakfast, the most popular dishes are *nasi lemak*

– rice cooked in coconut milk and served with *sambal ikan bilis* (tiny fried anchovies in hot chilli paste).

In **Sabah**, there's the Murut speciality of *jaruk* – raw wild boar fermented in a bamboo tube (other meats cooked in bamboo tubes are also delicious), and also *hinava*, raw fish pickled in lime juice. Indonesian and Filipino influences are present in places with large immigrant populations, which only enhances the local cuisine. In **Sarawak**, Iban cuisine features many pork dishes, wild boar, *midin* – a curly, crunchy jungle fern commonly found in restaurants (known as "Sabah vegetable" in Sabah) – and sticky rice. A particular favourite in Kuching is bamboo clams – small, pencil-shaped, slivery delicacies that only grow in the wild in mangrove-dense riverine locations.

Typical **Nyonya dishes** (the distinctive fusion cuisine formed by the descendants of Chinese and Malay intermarriage) incorporate elements from Chinese, Malay and Indonesian cooking. Chicken, fish and seafood form the backbone of the cuisine, and, unlike Malay food, pork is used. Noodles (*mee*) flavoured with chillies, and rich curries made from rice flour and coconut cream, are common. A popular breakfast dish is *laksa*, noodles in spicy coconut soup served with seafood and bean sprouts, lemon grass, pineapple, pepper, lime leaves and chilli. Other popular Nyonya dishes include *ayam buah keluak*, chicken cooked with Indonesian "black" nuts; and *otak-otak*, fish mashed with coconut milk and chilli and steamed in a banana leaf.

Chinese food dominates in Malaysia – fish and seafood is nearly always outstanding, with prawns, crab, squid and a variety of fish on offer almost everywhere. Noodles, too, are ubiquitous, and come in wonderful variations – thin, flat, round, served in soup (wet) or fried (dry). Particular favourites include *hokkien mee*: fat white noodles with *tempe* (a cheese-like food made of the soy residue from tofu-making) in a rich soy sauce, and *kuey teow goreng*, flat rice noodles fried with chicken or seafood and local greens. *Dim sum* make a regular appearance, as does **steamboat**, with thinly sliced meat, fish and vegetables cooked to the desired consistency in a bubbling pot in the middle of the table, with titbits then dunked in soy and chilli sauce.

North Indian food tends to rely more on meat, especially mutton and chicken, and breads – *naan*, *chapatis*, *parathas* and *rotis* – rather than rice. A favourite breakfast is *roti canai* (delicious flaky flat bread) and *dhal*. **Southern Indian food** tends to be spicier and more reliant on vegetables. Its staple is the *dosa* (rice-flour pancake), often served at breakfast as a *masala dosa*, stuffed with onions, vegetables and chutney. Indian Muslims serve *murtabak*, a grilled *roti* stuffed with egg and minced meat. Many South Indian cafés serve *daun pisang* at lunchtime, usually a vegetarian meal where rice is served on banana leaves with vegetable curries.

As for **desserts**, try *ais kacang*, shaved ice with fruit syrup, and often served with sweet red beans and condensed milk. It's deliciously refreshing, particularly in the heat.

WHERE TO EAT

The cheapest places to eat are the ubiquitous **hawker stalls**, often found on the roadside or in hawker centres, and serving standard Malay noodle and rice dishes, satay, Indian fast food such as *roti canai*, plus regional delicacies. Most are scrupulously clean, and the food is cooked in front of you. Some hawker stalls don't have menus and you don't have to sit close to the stall you're patronizing: find a free table, and the vendor will track you down when your food is ready. You may find that the meal should be paid for when it reaches your table, but the usual form is to pay when you're finished. Most outdoor stalls open at around 11am and often stay open late – the early ones close around 10pm, while some continue until 2 or 3am.

There are few streets without a *kedai kopi*, a **coffee house** or **café**, usually run by Chinese or Indians. Most open at 7am or 8am; closing times vary from 6pm to midnight. These places offer more than coffee; basic Chinese coffee houses serve noodle and rice dishes all day, as well as

6

cakes. The culinary standard might not be very high, but a filling one-plate meal only costs a couple of dollars.

Inexpensive **restaurants** are found in all cities. Many offer cheap lunchtime deals. In larger cities – and particularly in Kuala Lumpur – you can find excellent Thai, Italian and other international food.

DRINKING

Tap water is said to be safe to drink in Malaysia, though it's wise to stick to bottled water. Using ice for drinks is generally fine. Sweet condensed milk is usually added to tea and coffee unless you ask for it without. In city centres, look out for the sweetened soy milk, coconut milk and sugar-cane juice touted on street corners.

Malays are big **tea** and **coffee** drinkers; tea is locally grown in the Cameron Highlands (see p.433), while most of the coffee comes from Indonesia. Coffee tends to be strong and sweetened with condensed milk, but you can specify *kurang manis* (less sugar), *tak mahu manis*

PEOPLES OF MALAYSIA

With a pivotal position on the maritime trade routes between the Middle East, India and China, Malaysia has always attracted immigration. The region also had many **indigenous tribes**, *Orang Asli* ("the first people"). On the Peninsula, the Malays form just over fifty percent of the population, the Chinese nearly 38 percent, Indians ten percent and the Orang Asli around one percent; in Sarawak and Sabah, the indigenous tribes account for around fifty percent of the population, the Chinese 28 percent, with the other 22 percent divided among Malays, Indians and Eurasians. Although many of Malaysia's ethnic groups are now nominally Christian or Muslim, many of their old **animist** beliefs and ceremonies still survive.

THE MALAYS

The **Malays** first moved to the west coast of the Malaysian Peninsula from Sumatra in early times, but the growth in power of the Malay sultanates from the fifteenth century onwards – coinciding with the arrival of Islam – established Malays as a significant force. They developed an aristocratic tradition, courtly rituals and a social hierarchy that still has an influence today. The main contemporary change for Malays in Malaysia was the introduction after independence of the *bumiputra* policy, which was designed to make it easier for the Malays, the Orang Asli of the Peninsula and other indigenous groups to compete in economic and educational fields against the high-achieving Chinese and Indians. Malays now hold most of the top positions in government and in state companies.

THE CHINESE AND STRAITS CHINESE

The first significant **Chinese** community established itself in Malacca in the fifteenth century. However, the ancestors of the majority of Chinese now living in Peninsular Malaysia emigrated from southern China in the nineteenth century to work in the tin-mining industry. In Sarawak and Sabah, the Chinese played an important part in opening up the interior. Chinatowns developed throughout the region, and Chinese traditions became an integral part of a wider Malayan culture. The Malaysian Chinese are well represented in parliament. One of the few examples of regional intermarrying is displayed in the Peranakan or "Straits-born Chinese" heritage of Malacca and Penang. When male Chinese immigrants married local Malay women, their male offspring were termed "Baba" and the females "Nyonya" (or Nonya). **Baba–Nyonya** society adapted elements from both cultures: the descendants of these sixteenth-century liaisons have a unique culinary and architectural style.

THE INDIANS

The first large wave of **Tamil** labourers arrived in the nineteenth century. But an embryonic entrepreneurial class from **North India** soon followed and set up businesses in Penang. Although Indians comprise only ten percent of Malaysia's population, their impact is felt everywhere.

THE ORANG ASLI

The **Orang Asli** are the indigenous peoples of Peninsular Malaysia, thought to have migrated here around fifty thousand years ago. They mostly belong to three distinct

(no sugar) or *kopi kosong* (black, no sugar). Black tea/coffee is *teh/kopi o kosong*.

Drinking alcohol is only outlawed in certain places on the east coast of the Malaysian Peninsula, but there are numerous places where the sale and consumption of alcohol is frowned upon. Elsewhere, alcohol is available in bars, restaurants, Chinese *kedai kopi*, supermarkets and sometimes at hawkers' stalls. Anchor and Tiger **beer** (lager) are locally produced and are probably the best choices. **Wine** is becoming more common and competitively priced, too. Sarawak and Sabah offer their own lethal tipple in the form of *tuak* (fermented rice wine); the young, milky wine isn't particularly strong, but the clear, overproof stuff packs a punch.

There is a thriving bar scene in KL, Penang and Langkawi; less so in other towns. Fierce competition keeps happy hours a regular feature (usually 5–7pm), bringing beer down to around RM5 a glass. Some bars open all day (11am–11pm), but many double as clubs, opening in the evenings until 2 or 3am.

6

groups, of which there are various tribes. Though most tribes retain some cultural traditions, government drives have encouraged many tribespeople to integrate. The largest group is the **Senoi** (with a population of 40,000), who live in the forested interior of Perak, Pahang and Kelantan states and are divided into two main tribes, the Semiar and the Temiar. They follow animist customs and practise shifting cultivation. The dark-skinned **Semang** (or Negritos; pop. 2000) live in the **northern** areas of the Peninsula and share a traditional nomadic, hunter-gatherer culture. The so-called **Aboriginal Malays** live south of the Kuala Lumpur–Kuantan road.

SARAWAK'S PEOPLES

Nearly fifty percent of **Sarawak's population** is made up of various indigenous Dyak and Orang Ulu groups – including the Iban, Bidayuh, Kayan, Kenyah, Kelabit and Penan tribes, many of whom live in longhouses and maintain a rich cultural legacy. The **Iban**, a stocky, rugged people, make up nearly one-third of Sarawak's population. Iban longhouse communities are found in the Batang Ai river system in the southwest, and along the Rajang, Katibas and Baleh rivers. These communities are quite accessible, their inhabitants always hospitable and keen to show off their traditional dance, music, textile-weaving, blow-piping, fishing and game-playing. In their time, the Iban were infamous head-hunters, but this tradition has been replaced by that of *berjelai*, or "journey", whereby a young man leaves the community to prove himself in the outside world – returning to his longhouse with television sets, generators and outboard motors, rather than heads. The Iban are also famous for their intricate tattoos, each signifying a particular achievement in an individual's life. The southernmost of Sarawak's indigenous groups are the **Bidayuh**, who traditionally lived away from the rivers, building their longhouses on the sides of hills. Most of the other groups in Sarawak are classed as **Orang Ulu** (people of the interior). They inhabit the more remote inland areas, on the upper Rajang, Balui, Baram and Linau rivers, and their most striking features are the elongated earlobes, achieved by wearing exceptional weighty earrings – a privilege granted only to prominent members of the community. The most numerous, the **Kayan** and the **Kenyah**, are longhouse-dwellers, animists and shifting cultivators. The **Kelabit** live in longhouses on the highland plateau that separates north Sarawak from Kalimantan, and are Christian. The nomadic **Penan** live in the upper Rajang and Limbang areas and rely on hunting and gathering, though the number of true nomads has decreased to a few hundred with government pressure on them to settle.

SABAH'S PEOPLES

The **Dusun**, or Kadazan/Dusun, account for around a third of Sabah's population. Traditionally agriculturists, they inhabit the western coastal plains and the interior. Although most Dusun are now Christians, remnants of their animist past are still evident. The mainly Muslim **Bajau** tribe drifted over from the southern Philippines some two hundred years ago, and now constitute ten percent of Sabah's population, living in the northwest. They are agriculturists and fishermen, noted for their horsemanship and their rearing of buffalo. The **Murut** inhabit the area between Keningau and the Sarawak border, in the southwest.

CULTURE AND ETIQUETTE

The Malays like to please and in general are likely to be some of the friendliest and most helpful people you'll come across. The flipside, however, can be that they don't necessarily furnish you with negative information.

6

The vast majority of Malaysians are Muslims, but there are also significant numbers of Hindus, Buddhists, Confucianists and animists (see p.40) among the population.

Islam in Malaysia today is relatively liberal. Although most Muslim women don headscarves, few wear a veil, and some taboos, like not drinking alcohol, are ignored by a growing number of Malays. There are stricter, more fundamentalist Muslims – in Kelantan the local government is dominated by them – and there's a constant push for replacing state law with sharia law in that province, but in general, Islam here has a moderate and modern outlook. There are clear hints of other religions within Malaysian tradition as well – the traditional Malay wedding ceremony, for example, has clear **Hindu** influences, and talking to people about their day-to-day beliefs and superstitions often suggests the influence of **Chinese animistic religions**. Just like the cultures, religions tend to overlap fairly easily in Malaysia. That said, visitors belonging to the Jewish faith should not advertise that fact, as anti-Semitism is widespread.

Malaysia shares the same attitudes to dress and social taboos as other Southeast Asian cultures (see p.40).

SPORTS AND OUTDOOR ACTIVITIES

The varied terrain of Malaysia means activities such as **cycling** and **horseriding** are possible across the country. Cycling in towns isn't all that advisable as traffic is fairly unpredictable, but in more regional areas it's a great way to explore. On the islands, **kayaking** is also a great way to go from cove to cove, and kayak rental is usually available from guesthouses for RM15–20 per day.

SNORKELLING AND DIVING

The crystal-clear waters of Malaysia and its abundance of tropical fish and coral make **snorkelling and diving** a must for any underwater enthusiast. This is particularly true of East Sabah's islands, which include Sipadan and Mabul, and the Peninsula's east-coast islands of Perhentian, Kapas and Tioman. Pulau Tioman offers the most choice for schools and dive sites, while the Perhentians offer superb snorkelling, with frequent turtle and shark sightings. Make sure that the dive operator you go with is registered with PADI (Professional Association of Diving Instructors) or equivalent; dive courses cost from around RM900 for a four-day PADI Open Water course to RM2200 for a Divemaster course. If you're already certified, it's possible to rent all the necessary equipment for a day's worth of diving for RM100–120.

TREKKING

If **trekking** either on the Malaysian Peninsula or in Sarawak and Sabah, you should be prepared for heat, humidity and leeches; also, trails and rivers become much more difficult to negotiate when it rains. That said, although the rainy season (Nov–Feb) undoubtedly slows your progress on some of the trails, conditions are less humid and the parks and adventure tours not oversubscribed. Most visitors trek in the large **national parks** to experience the remaining primary jungle and rainforest at first hand. For these, you often need to be accompanied by a guide, which can either be arranged through tour operators in KL, Kuching, Miri and Kota Kinabalu, or at the parks themselves. For less experienced trekkers, the Cameron Highlands (see p.433) and Taman Negara National Park (see p.450) are probably the best places to start, while Sarawak's Gunung Mulu National Park (see p.490) offers sufficient challenges for most tastes. Few people who make it across to Sabah forego the chance of climbing **Mount Kinabalu** (see p.502).

COMMUNICATIONS

Malaysia's postal service is inexpensive and generally reliable; postcards to Europe and the US take ten to fourteen days. Packages are expensive to send, with surface/sea mail taking two months to Europe, longer to the US.

By far the easiest and cheapest way to call home is by using **Skype**; most internet cafés in Malaysia offer facilities for this. Local SIM cards cost around RM20; DiGi, Maxis and Celcom networks offer the widest coverage (Celcom is best for Borneo) and inexpensive international calls. Telecom Malaysia (TM) iTalk cards can be used to make international calls on your mobile.

There are **TM payphones** in most towns in Malaysia; they take coins or prepaid TM cards which you can buy at 7-Elevens, post offices and TM offices.

To call **abroad** from Malaysia, dial ⓣ00 + IDD country code + area code minus first 0 + subscriber number.

Internet cafés are plentiful and most hostels, hotels and guesthouses offer free wi-fi; many offer internet access, too – mostly for free.

CRIME AND SAFETY

The most common crimes are perpetrated by **pickpockets** and snatch thieves on motorbikes, who grab handbags. Watch your bag in most cities, especially in KL, as motorbike theft is a common occurrence there. **Theft** from dormitories by other tourists is also a relatively common complaint. In the more remote parts of Sarawak or Sabah there is little crime.

If you do need to report a crime in Malaysia, head for the nearest **police station**, where there'll be someone who speaks English – you'll need a copy of the police report for insurance purposes. **Violent crime** against tourists is rare but muggings do occasionally happen after hours in Kuala Lumpur, Penang and in run-down neighbourhoods in general.

Women travelling alone can expect a certain amount of male attention, particularly on the more conservative east coast of Malaysia, so dressing modestly and treating overly friendly strangers with caution is a must.

The penalty for **drug trafficking** is death – foreigners have been executed in the past – and even carrying a small amount on you will earn you a lengthy prison sentence and a caning.

EMERGENCY NUMBERS

Fire Brigade ⓣ**994**
Police/Ambulance ⓣ**999**

MEDICAL CARE AND EMERGENCIES

Levels of hygiene and **medical care** in Malaysia's larger cities are higher than in much of the rest of Southeast Asia; staff almost everywhere speak good English and use up-to-date techniques. There's always a well-stocked pharmacy in main towns. Oral contraceptives and condoms are sold over the counter, but you won't find tampons outside KL, so bring your own. Opening hours are usually Monday to Saturday 9.30am to 7pm; pharmacies in shopping malls stay open later. **Private clinics** are found even in the smallest towns; a visit costs around RM30, excluding medication. The **emergency department** of each town's general hospital will see foreigners for the token fee of RM5, though costs rise rapidly if continued treatment or overnight stays are necessary.

Recommended **vaccinations** for Malaysia include Hepatatis A, rabies, tetanus and diphtheria; if you're planning on spending time in the jungle in Peninsular Malaysia's interior or in Sarawak or Sabah, you will require appropriate anti-malarial prophylactics.

INFORMATION AND MAPS

Tourism Malaysia (ⓦtourism.gov.my) operates a **tourist office** in most major towns, but it's not that useful for areas off the beaten track. Their website, however, is a good source of information. Locally run **visitor centres**, found in most major towns, are more geared up to independent travellers' needs. You can

BAHASA MALAYSIA

Although you'll be able to get by with English in all but the most remote areas, the national language of Malaysia, **Bahasa Malaysia**, is simple enough to learn. Nouns have no genders and don't require an article, while the plural form is constructed just by saying the word twice; thus "child" is *anak*, while "children" is *anak anak*. Doubling a word can also indicate "doing"; for example, *jalan jalan* is used to mean "walking". Verbs have no tenses either, so you qualify the verb by saying when you did something. Sentence order is the same as in English, though adjectives usually follow the noun.

PRONUNCIATION

The **pronunciation** of Bahasa Malaysia is broadly the same as the English reading of Roman script, with a few exceptions:

a as in c**u**p
c as in **ch**eap
e as in **e**nd
g as in **g**irl
i as in bout**i**que
j as in **j**oy
k hard, as in English, except at the end of the word, when you should stop just short of pronouncing it.
o as in g**o**t
u as in b**oo**t
ai as in f**i**ne
au as in **how**
sy as in **sh**ut

GREETINGS AND BASIC PHRASES

Selamat is the all-purpose greeting derived from Arabic, which communicates general goodwill.

Good morning	*Selamat pagi*
Good afternoon	*Selamat petang*
Good evening	*Selamat malam*
Goodnight	*Selamat tidur*
Goodbye	*Selamat jalan*
Welcome	*Selamat datang*
Bon appetit	*Selamat makan*
Please	*Tolong*
Thank you	*Terima kasih*
You're welcome	*Sama sama*
Sorry/excuse me	*Maaf*
Yes	*Ya*
No	*Tidak*
Do you speak English?	*Bisa bercakap bahasa Inggris?*
I don't understand	*Saya tidak mengerti*
Can you help me, please?	*Bolekah anda tolong saya?*
Where is the ...?	*Di manakah ...?*
Bus stop	*Perhentian bas*
Train station	*Stesen keratapi*
Bus station	*Stesen bas*
Airport	*Lapangan terbang*
Hotel	*Hotel*
Post office	*Pejabat pos*
Restaurant	*Restoran*
Shop	*Kedai*
Market	*Pasar*
Taxi	*Teksi*
How much is ...?	*Berapa banyak ...?*
Cheap/expensive	*Murah/mahal*
Good	*Bagus*
Closed	*Tutup*
Ill/sick	*Sakit*
Toilet	*Tandas*
Water	*Air*
Food	*Makan*
Drink	*Minum*

NUMBERS

0	*Kosong*
1	*Satu*
2	*Dua*
3	*Tiga*
4	*Empat*
5	*Lima*
6	*Enam*
7	*Tujuh*
8	*Lapan*
9	*Sembilan*
10	*Sepuluh*
11, 12, 13, etc	*Sebelas, duabelas, tigabelas*
20	*Dua-puluh*
21, 22, etc	*Dua-puluh satu, dua-puluh dua*
30, 40, 50, etc	*Tiga-puluh, empat-puluh, lima-puluh*
100, 200, 300, etc	*Seratus, dua ratus, tiga ratus*
1000	*Seribu*

FOOD AND DRINK GLOSSARY

menu	menu
sejuk	cold
panas	hot (temperature)
pedas	hot (spicy)
saya vegetarain	I am a vegetarian
saya tak makan daging	I don't eat meat or fish

Noodles (*mee*) and noodle dishes

bee hoon	thin rice noodles
char kuey teow	flat rice noodles with prawns, sausage, fishcake, egg, vegetables or chilli
foochow noodles	steamed and served in soy and oyster sauce
hokkien fried mee	yellow noodles fried with pork, prawn and vegetables
kuey teow	flat rice noodles
laksa	noodles, bean sprouts, fishcakes and prawns in a spicy coconut broth
mee	round yellow wheat-flour noodles
mee goreng	spicy fried noodles
mee suah	noodles served dry and crispy
wan ton mee	roast pork, noodles and vegetable soup with dumplings

Rice (*nasi*) dishes

claypot	rice topped with meat, cooked in an earthenware pot over a fire
daun pisang	banana-leaf curry
nasi campur	rice served with several meat, fish and vegetable dishes
nasi goreng	fried rice with diced meat and veg
nasi puteh	plain boiled rice

Meat, fish and basics

syam	chicken
babi	pork
daging	beef
garam	salt
lada hitam	pepper
gula	sugar
ikan	fish
kambing	mutton
kepiting	crab
sup	soup
tahu	tofu (beancurd)
telor	egg
udang	prawn
sotong	squid

Desserts

ais kacang	shaved ice with red beans, rose syrup and evaporated milk
bubor cha cha	sweetened coconut milk with pieces of sweet potato, yam and tapioca balls
cendol	coconut milk, palm syrup and pea-flour noodles poured over shaved ice

Drinks (*minum*)

air minum	water
bir	beer
jus	fruit juice
kopi	coffee
kopi-o	black coffee
kopi susu	coffee with milk
lassi	sweet or sour yoghurt
teh	tea
teh susu	tea with milk
teh tarik	sweet, frothy, milky tea

MALAYSIA ONLINE

tourism.gov.my The Malaysian Tourist Board's website provides excellent information.

virtualmalaysia.com Another official website, which provides good information.

visitorsguide.com.my A visitors' guide to the country.

also book permits and accommodation for the **national parks** at these centres.

The best general **maps** of Malaysia are Macmillan's 1:2,000,000 *Malaysia Traveller's Map* and the more detailed Nelles 1:650,000 *West Malaysia* (not including Sabah and Sarawak). The best coverage of Sabah is on maps produced by Nelles. **City maps** can usually be picked up in the visitor centres.

MONEY AND BANKS

Malaysia's unit of **currency** is the ringgit, divided into 100 sen. You'll see the ringgit written as "RM" (as it is throughout this chapter), or simply as "$" (M$), and often hear it called a "dollar". Notes come in RM1, RM5, RM10, RM20, RM50, RM100, RM500 and RM1000 denominations; coins are minted in 5 sen, 10 sen, 20 sen, 50 sen and M$1 denominations. At the time of writing, the **exchange rate** was around RM5 to £1, RM4.56 to E1 and around RM3.2 to $1.

Sterling and US dollar **travellers' cheques** can be cashed at Malaysian banks, licensed moneychangers and some hotels. Licensed moneychangers' kiosks in bigger towns tend to open until around 6pm, and sometimes at weekends. It's not difficult to change money in Sabah or Sarawak, though if travelling by river in the interior or outside the larger cities, you should carry a fair bit of cash in small denominations. If travelling to the islands off the coast of Malaysia, a surplus of cash is a necessity, since most of them don't have banks.

Major **credit cards** are accepted in many hotels and large shops, but beware of illegal surcharges. Banks will advance cash against major credit cards, and with American Express, Visa and MasterCard as well as Cirrus, Plus and Maestrobank (debit) cards, you can withdraw money from ATMs in big cities and many towns.

OPENING HOURS AND PUBLIC HOLIDAYS

Shops are open daily 9am to 6pm, Monday to Saturday, and shopping centres 10am to 11pm. **Government office** hours are Monday to Thursday 8am to 12.45pm and 2pm to 4.15pm, Friday 8am to 12.15pm and 2.45pm to 4.15pm, Saturday 8am to 12.45pm; however, in the states of Kedah, Kelantan and Terengganu, on Thursday the hours are 8am to 12.45pm; they're closed on Friday and are open with full working hours on Sunday. **Banking hours** are generally Monday to Friday 10am to 3pm and Saturday 9.30am to 11.30am. **Post offices** are open Monday to Saturday 8am to 6pm, while on the east coast they're closed on Fridays but open on Sundays.

PUBLIC HOLIDAYS

The Muslim holidays of Hari Raya Haji, which celebrates the end of the annual Muslim pilgrimage to Mecca, and Hari Raya Puasa, which celebrates the end of the Ramadan fast, change from year to year according to the lunar calendar.

January 1 New Year's Day
January/February Chinese New Year (two days)
January/February Thaipusam (depending on the full moon)
February/March Birthday of the Prophet Muhammed
March/April Maal Hijrah (the Muslim New Year)
April Good Friday (Sarawak and Sabah only)
May Pesta Kaamatan – Harvest festival (Sabah only)
May 1 Labour Day
June 1 & 2 Gawai Dayak – Harvest festival (Sarawak only)
June 4 Yang di-Pertuan Agong's (King's) birthday
August 31 National Day
September 16 Malaysia Day (Sabah only)
September/October Hari Raya Puasa (end of Ramadan; two days)
November Deepavali (the Hindu festival more commonly known as Diwali, the Festival of Light)
December 25 Christmas Day

FESTIVALS

Three religions – Islam, Buddhism and Hinduism – are represented in Malaysia, and they play a vital role in the everyday lives of the population. Some religious festivals are celebrated at home or in the mosque or temple. During Ramadan, Muslims fast during the daytime for a whole month, while other festivals are marked with great spectacle. Most of the festivals change annually according to the lunar calendar.

Chinese New Year Jan–Feb. Chinese operas and lion and dragon dance troupes perform in the streets. The festival is actually fifteen days long, but in general only the first two and the last are observed with actual events – throughout the rest of the time, a general holiday atmosphere abounds but life continues as normal (though in places with a large Chinese population, many services may shut down).

Thaipusam Jan/Feb. Entranced Hindu penitents carry elaborate steel arches, attached to their skin by hooks and skewers (especially at KL's Batu Caves) in honour of Muruga, the god of war.

Gawai Dayak June. Sarawak's Iban and Bidayuk people hold extravagant feasts to mark the end of the rice harvest, best experienced at the Iban longhouses on the Ai, Skrang and Lemanak rivers near Kuching (June) and in Bidayuh communities around Bau.

Dragon Boat Festival June/July in Penang, Malacca and Kota Kinabalu, where the traditional dragon boats race.

Rainforest Music Festival July/Aug at the Cultural Village near Kuching, Sarawak. Three-day music and art extravaganza with artists from around the world and an emphasis on the indigenous music of Borneo.

Festival of the Hungry Ghosts Late Aug. Known locally as Yue Lan, this is a festival for appeasing both ancestors and homeless spirits, by providing them with essentials such as food and drink. The best festivities are held in Penang.

Navarathiri Sept–Oct. Hindu temples devote nine nights to classical dance and music in honour of the deities, and young girls dress as the goddess Kali.

Kuala Lumpur and around

Founded in the mid-nineteenth century, **KUALA LUMPUR**, or KL, is a vast modern metropolis, a fast-changing super-city, an impressive mix of architectural styles, the most iconic structures being the twin Petronas Towers, which dwarf most other gleaming skyscrapers. As a mix of cultures, KL manages to combine the best of all worlds, being less frenetic than most Indian cities and friendlier and more laidback than a lot of Chinese ones. With a population of nearly two million, it has undeniable energy, but still manages to retain a relaxed old-world charm – and the inhabitants' warmth is hard to beat. There are certainly enough interesting monuments, galleries, markets and museums to keep visitors busy for a while, and its shopping and dining scenes are second to none.

6

WHAT TO SEE AND DO

The city centre is quite compact, with the **Colonial District** centred on Merdeka Square; close by, across the river and to the north, **Chinatown** and **Little India** are the two main traditional commercial districts. One of the most prominent (and busiest) of KL's central streets, Jalan Tuanku Abdul Rahman, or **Jalan TAR** as it's often known, runs due north from Merdeka Square for 2km to Chow Kit Market; west of the square are the **Lake Gardens**, while to the south lie the **Masjid Negara** (National Mosque), the **Islamic Arts Museum**, the landmark **Old KL train station** and the **Muzium Negara** (National Museum).

Merdeka Square and the National Textiles Museum

The small **Colonial District** is centred on the beautifully tended **Merdeka Square** on the west bank of the Klang River: Malaysian Independence (*merdeka*, or freedom) from the British was proclaimed here on August 31, 1957. On the same square is the **National Textiles Museum** (daily 9am–6pm; free; Ⓦjmm.gov.my/en/museum/national-textiles-museum) showcasing the origins of textiles from prehistoric times. Also exhibited are the traditional techniques of textile making, with a focus on Malaysia's most common textiles.

Masjid Negara

South, down Jalan Sultan Hishamuddin, is the impressive 70m-high minaret and

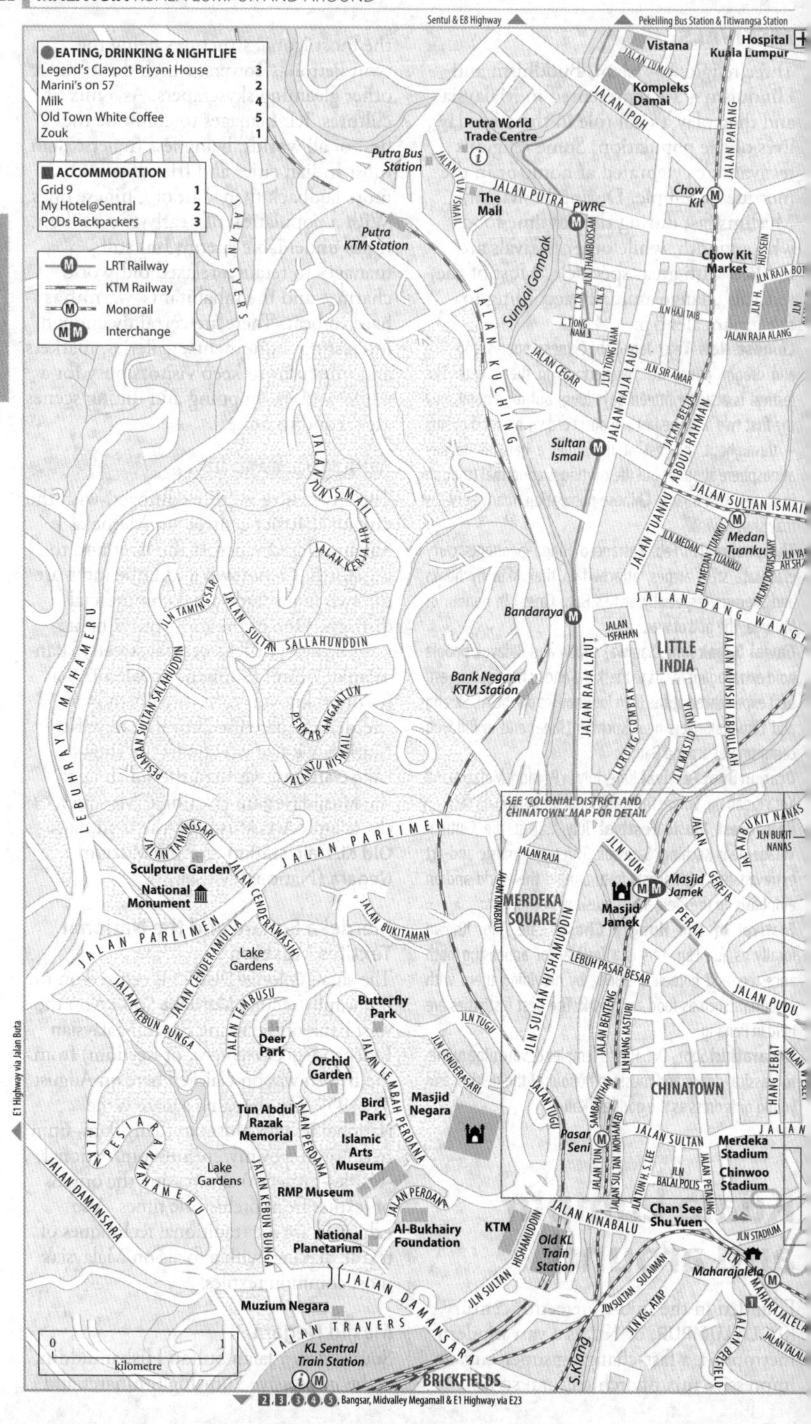
EATING, DRINKING & NIGHTLIFE
Legend's Claypot Briyani House 3
Marini's on 57 2
Milk 4
Old Town White Coffee 5
Zouk 1
ACCOMMODATION
Grid 9 1
My Hotel@Sentral 2
PODs Backpackers 3
LRT Railway
KTM Railway
Monorail
Interchange
Sentul & E8 Highway
Pekeliling Bus Station & Titiwangsa Station
Vistana
Hospital Kuala Lumpur
Kompleks Damai
JALAN IPOH
JALAN PAHANG
Putra World Trade Centre
Putra Bus Station
JALAN PUTRA
PWRC
The Mall
Chow Kit
Chow Kit Market
Putra KTM Station
JALAN SYERS
JALAN KUCHING
Sungai Gombak
JALAN RAJA ALANG
JALAN CEGAR
JALAN RAJA LAUT
JLN SIR AMAR
JALAN TUANKU ABDUL RAHMAN
Sultan Ismail
JALAN SULTAN ISMAIL
Medan Tuanku
JALAN TUN ISMAIL
JALAN KERJA AIR
JALAN DANG WANGI
Bandaraya
LITTLE INDIA
JALAN MUNSHI ABDULLAH
JALAN SULTAN SALLAHUDDIN
LEBUHRAYA MAHAMERU
Bank Negara KTM Station
PERKAR ANGANTUN
LORONG GOMBAK
SEE 'COLONIAL DISTRICT AND CHINATOWN' MAP FOR DETAIL
JALAN PARLIMEN
JALAN TAMINGSARI
Sculpture Garden
National Monument
JALAN RAJA
JLN TUN PERAK
Masjid Jamek
MERDEKA SQUARE
JALAN CENDERAWASIH
JALAN BUKITAMAN
Lake Gardens
LEBUH PASAR BESAR
JALAN PUDU
JLN SULTAN HISHAMUDDIN
JALAN KEBUN BUNGA
JALAN TEMBUSU
Butterfly Park
Deer Park
Orchid Garden
JLN TUGU
JLN CENDERASARI
CHINATOWN
Masjid Negara
Bird Park
Tun Abdul Razak Memorial
Islamic Arts Museum
JALAN PERDANA
JALAN LEMBAH PERDANA
Pasar Seni
JALAN SULTAN
Merdeka Stadium
Chinwoo Stadium
JALAN PESIARAN MAHAMERU
JALAN DAMANSARA
RMP Museum
Lake Gardens
JALAN KINABALU
Chan See Shu Yuen
National Planetarium
Al-Bukhairy Foundation
KTM
Old KL Train Station
Maharajalela
JLN MAHARAJALELA
Muzium Negara
JALAN TRAVERS
KL Sentral Train Station
BRICKFIELDS
S.Klang
JALAN BELFIELD
0 1 kilometre
E1 Highway via Jalan Buta
Bangsar, Midvalley Megamall & E1 Highway via E23

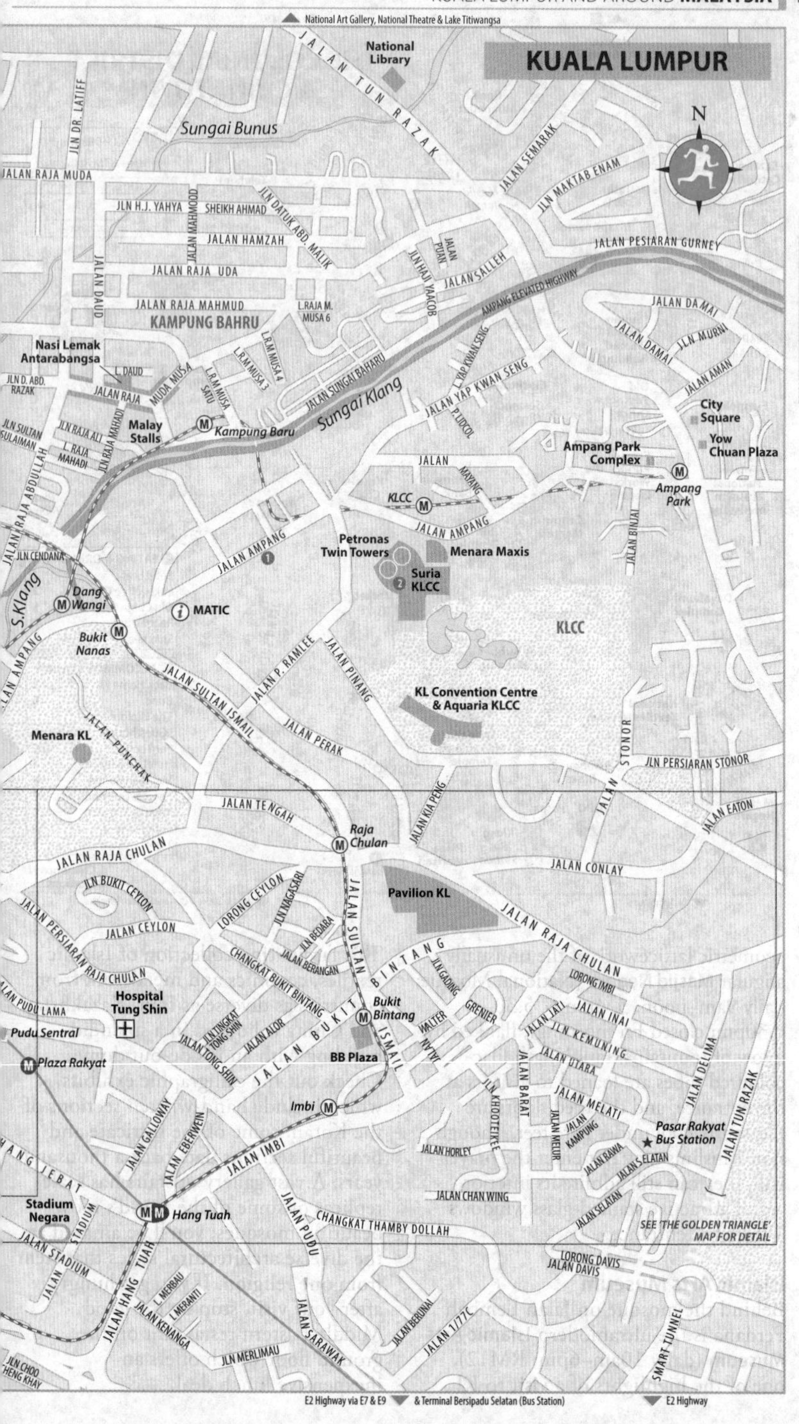
KUALA LUMPUR
N
National Art Gallery, National Theatre & Lake Titiwangsa
National Library
Sungai Bunus
Kampung Bahru
Nasi Lemak Antarabangsa
Malay Stalls
Kampung Baru
Sungai Klang
City Square
Yow Chuan Plaza
Ampang Park Complex
Ampang Park
KLCC
Petronas Twin Towers
Menara Maxis
Suria KLCC
Dang Wangi
Bukit Nanas
MATIC
Menara KL
KL Convention Centre & Aquaria KLCC
Raja Chulan
Pavilion KL
Hospital Tung Shin
Pudu Sentral
Plaza Rakyat
Bukit Bintang
BB Plaza
Imbi
Pasar Rakyat Bus Station
Stadium Negara
Hang Tuah
SEE 'THE GOLDEN TRIANGLE' MAP FOR DETAIL
E2 Highway via E7 & E9
& Terminal Bersipadu Selatan (Bus Station)
E2 Highway

6

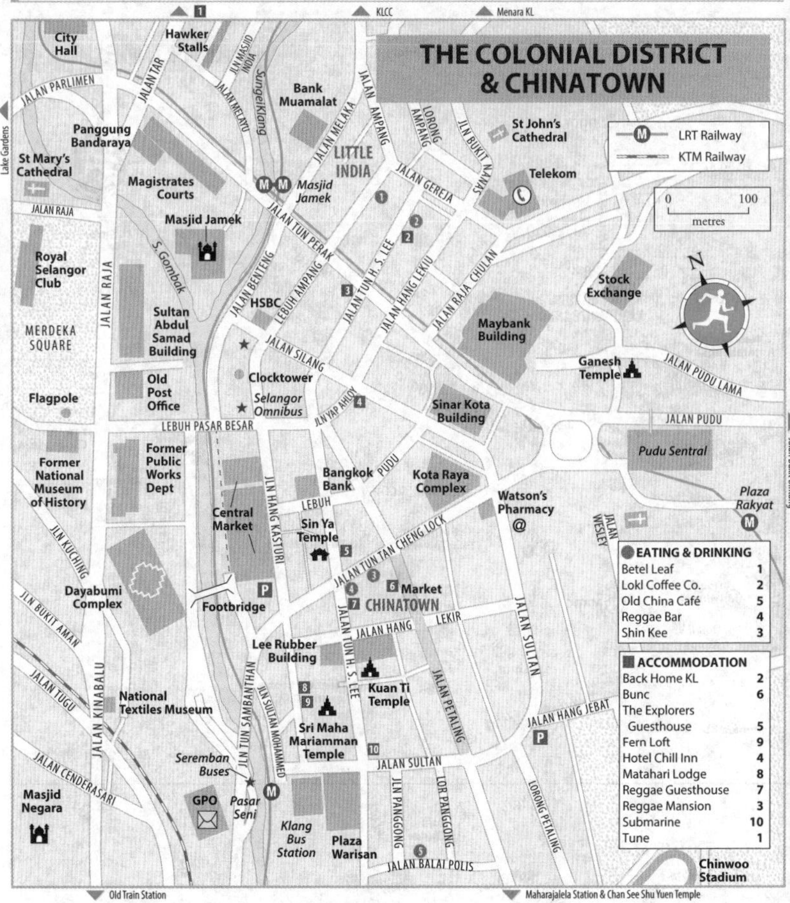

geometric latticework of the unusually angular **Masjid Negara** (National Mosque; daily 9am–noon, 3–4pm & 5.30–6.30pm; closed Fri morning), flanked by a row of fountains. Full-length lilac-coloured robes are loaned to visitors at the entrance, and the tiled floors are pleasantly cool under bare feet. Though non-Muslims may not enter the prayer hall, they can still admire its interior – and attractive stained-glass windows – from the entrance.

Islamic Arts Museum

Behind the mosque on Jalan Lembah Perdana is the ultramodern **Islamic Arts Museum** (daily 10am–6pm; RM12), one of the highlights of a visit to KL. This fascinating collection of Islamic textiles, ceramics and metalwork from countries as diverse as Iran, Kazakhstan and China is housed in a splendid building with an inside-out dome. Check out the calligraphic exhibits, which include hand-written sections of the Koran; some of the intricate and beautiful sections date back a thousand years. A vast gallery upstairs has scale replicas of some of the world's most beautiful mosques; you'll be amazed at the diverse architectural styles that stem from one religion. If you get hungry after your visit, stop by the good Middle Eastern restaurant on the ground floor which offers an inexpensive lunch deal.

The old KL train station and National Museum

One kilometre southeast of the Islamic Arts Museum is the 1911 Moorish-style **KL train station** (the KTM Komuter Railway's Kuala Lumpur station), with its spires, minarets, domes and arches. Similar in concept to the British-era train station in Yangon, Kuala Lumpur's old train station was a successful blend of European and culturally indigenous architectural motifs. Of all the European (and American) colonial-era structures in Southeast Asia, this is quite possibly the most memorable, though few trains leave from here these days.

Ten minutes' walk west along Jalan Damansara brings you to the extensive ethnographic and archeological exhibits of the **Muzium Negara** (National Museum; daily 9am–6pm; RM5; Ⓦmuziumnegara.gov.my). The museum traces the country's early history and displays dioramas of traditional Malaysian life. The upstairs floor recounts the history and administration of the Colonial era and the domination of the Portuguese, Dutch, British and Japanese, and guides visitors through the struggle for independence and the formation of Malaysia.

Lake Gardens

The extensive **Lake Gardens** stretch between the National Museum and the Museum of Islamic Art and are a pleasant sprawl of green, dotted with small lakes. The main attraction here is the **Bird Park** (daily 9am–6pm; RM48), the largest of its kind and home to a wealth of tropical birds. It has a number of walking trails leading you past the enclosures.

Masjid Jamek

East of Merdeka Square, on a promontory at the confluence of the Klang and Gombak rivers, stands KL's most attractive devotional building, the **Masjid Jamek** (open to visitors outside prayer time; observe conservative dress code – wear long trousers and cover your shoulders and head if female; free). The mosque was completed in 1909, and its pink brick walls, arched colonnades, oval cupolas and squat minarets are inspired by Moghul architecture.

Chinatown

Bordered by **Jalan Tun Perak** to the north and **Jalan Petaling** to the east, **Chinatown**'s narrow lanes are home to the rowdy hubbub of permanent street markets, as well as revealing dilapidated shophouses and Chinese pharmacies. The area's largest temple, **Chan See Shu Yuen**, stands at the far southern end of Jalan Petaling, and displays an ornately painted inner shrine covered in scenes of mythical creatures battling with warriors.

KL's main Hindu place of worship, **Sri Maha Mariamman Temple**, is also located in the heart of Chinatown, on **Jalan Tun H.S. Lee**, between the two main Buddhist temples. Built in 1873, it was radically renovated in the 1960s with a profusion of statues on and around the five-tiered gate tower. On display inside is the silver chariot which makes an annual journey through the street of KL all the way to the Batu Caves during Thaipusam, followed by crowds of the faithful.

One hundred metres west of Jalan Tun H.S. Lee lies the **Central Market** (daily 10am–10pm). Over a hundred stalls here sell everything from textiles to stationery, fine art to batik clothing and T-shirts, as well as a large array of food on the first floor.

Little India

Just to the north of Chinatown is compact **Little India**, the commercial centre for the city's Indian community. As you turn into Jalan Masjid India from Jalan Tun Perak, it's soon clear that you've entered the Tamil part of the city, with *poori* and *samosa* vendors and cloth salesmen vying for positions on the crowded streets.

Chow Kit

Two kilometres due north of Central Market along Jalan TAR lies **Chow Kit**, a daily market that sells anything and everything. There are excellent hawker stalls here, a great variety of textiles and clothes, as well as fish, meat and vegetables.

6

The Golden Triangle and Aquaria KLCC

KL's fashionable consumer sector is known as the **Golden Triangle**. Many of the city's expensive hotels, nightclubs and modern malls line the three main boulevards of Jalan Bukit Bintang, Jalan Imbi and Jalan Sultan Ismail, and a visit here is a must.

Apart from some flash shopping and dining in the Golden Triangle's many malls, there's also the impressive **Aquaria KLCC** (daily 10.30am–8pm, last admission 7pm; RM50), a state-of-the-art aquarium showcasing more than 5000 denizens of the sea, including sharks, a giant octopus and a touch pool for a closer encounter with rays; it's situated in the Kuala Lumpur Convention Centre on the other side of the park. Highlights include a moving walkway inside a 90m tunnel, where you can watch sharks and rays swimming around, a hidden shipwreck slowly becoming part of the artificial coral reef, and feeding time, when divers hand-feed sharks, turtles and giant catfish.

The Petronas Towers and the Menara KL Tower

Among the Golden Triangle's main landmarks are the lofty **Petronas Twin Towers**, which, at just over 452m high, were the tallest structures in the world until 2004. They are now the tallest twin structure in the world (quite a few metres shy of the world's tallest building – the 830m-high Burj Khalifa in Dubai) and form part of the **KLCC** (Kuala Lumpur City Centre) development on the northeast of the Golden Triangle. A limited number of tickets are issued daily for the **Skybridge** (170m) connecting the two towers and observation deck (370m) on the 86th floor (Tues–Sun 9am–9pm; last entry 8.15pm; closed 1–2.30pm on Fri; RM80; Ⓦpetronastwintowers.com.my). Tickets are issued on a first come first served basis at the counter in the basement (daily 8.30am–8pm), although the queue forms well before that at around 6.30am – particularly on weekends. The easiest approach is to buy a ticket online (Ⓦpetronastwintowers.com.my).

Though 69m shorter than the Petronas Towers, the **Menara KL Tower** offers an observation deck (daily 9am–9.30pm; RM49; Ⓦmenarakl.com.my) at 276m, giving you a great overview of the city; sunset is the best time to visit. The tower is situated to the west of the Petronas Towers, on the other side of Jalan Sultan Ismail.

ARRIVAL AND DEPARTURE

BY PLANE

Kuala Lumpur International Airport (KLIA), the hub for international flights and domestic flights with Malaysia Airlines, is 70km southwest of the centre. The fastest and most efficient way into the city is by KLIA express trains (every 20–30min; 30min; RM35), which terminate at Kuala Lumpur's transportation hub, KL Sentral station, which conveniently connects with LRT and Monorail lines. If you want to halve your fare, take the non-express train (45min) to Putrakaya and then buy a separate ticket to KL Sentral from there. KLIA express coaches connect the international airport to Sentral station (every 30min, 3am–midnight; 1hr; RM10). Domestic and low-cost airlines use the AirAsia-dominated Low Cost Carrier Terminal (LCCT), 20km from KLIA. Skybus and Aerobus Airport coaches (6am–midnight, every 30min; RM8–9) take roughly 1hr 15min to KL Sentral. KLIA and LCCT are connected by a short shuttle ride (every 20min; RM4). Flights with the tiny Berjaya Air (for Pulau Tioman, Pulau Redang, Pulau Langkawi or Pulau Pangkor), Malindo Air and Firefly Airways depart from KL Subang, 20km west of the city centre. Taxi is the quickest option (45min; RM50), or take bus #U81 from outside KL Sentral (hourly, 6am–11pm; 1hr; RM2.50).

Destinations Bandar Seri Begawan, Brunei (daily; 2hr 20min); Ipoh (2 daily; 35min); Johor Bahru (4 daily; 45min); Kota Bharu (4 daily; 50min); Kota Kinabalu (10 daily; 1hr 45min); Kuala Terengganu (3 daily; 45min); Kuantan (4 daily; 40min); Kuching (10 daily; 1hr 45min); Miri (4 daily; 2hr 15min); Penang (11 daily; 45min); Pulau Langkawi (4 daily; 55min); Pulau Tioman (daily; 1hr); Sibu (daily; 2hr); Singapore (10 daily; 55min).

BY BOAT

The closest port to Kuala Lumpur is Port Klang, 38km southwest of KL, with ferries to Dumai or Tanjung Balai, both in Sumatra, Indonesia. Tickets are available at the jetty, or from Aero Speed (for Tanjung Balai; Ⓣ03 3165 2545 or Ⓣ03 3165 3073) or Indomal Express (for Dumai; Ⓣ03 3167 1058). You can get a visa on arrival at Dumai, but you must arrange an Indonesian visa in advance if entering at Tanjung Balai. The best way to get to Port Klang is by Komuter train (every 30min; 1hr 10min; RM4.80) from KL's train station, which stops opposite the main jetty.

Destinations Dumai (10am on Tues, Thurs & Sat; 4hr); Tanjung Balai (daily except Sun; 3hr 30min).

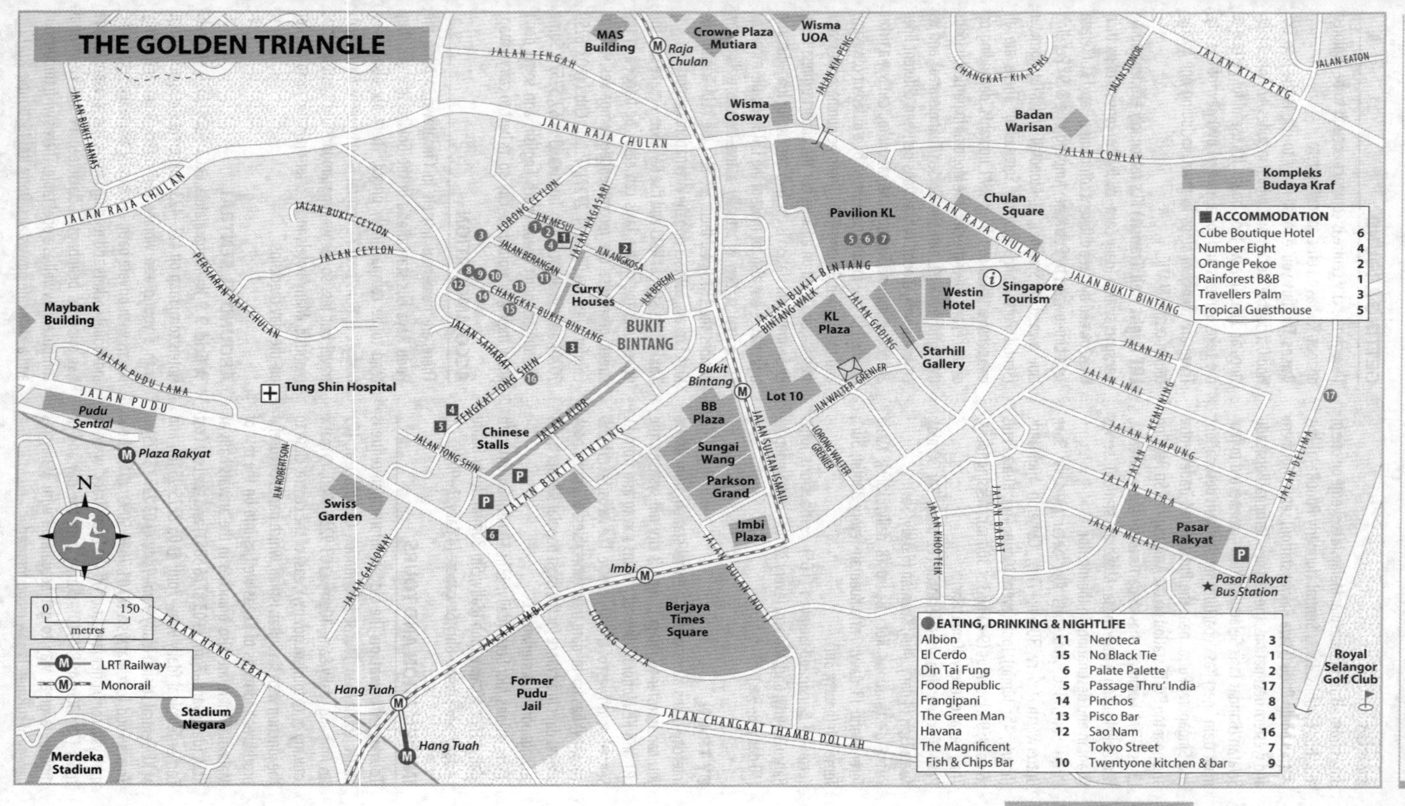
THE GOLDEN TRIANGLE
ACCOMMODATION
Cube Boutique Hotel 6
Number Eight 4
Orange Pekoe 2
Rainforest B&B 1
Travellers Palm 3
Tropical Guesthouse 5
EATING, DRINKING & NIGHTLIFE
Albion 11
El Cerdo 15
Din Tai Fung 6
Food Republic 5
Frangipani 14
The Green Man 13
Havana 12
The Magnificent Fish & Chips Bar 10
Neroteca 3
No Black Tie 1
Palate Palette 2
Passage Thru' India 17
Pinchos 8
Pisco Bar 4
Sao Nam 16
Tokyo Street 7
Twentyone kitchen & bar 9
LRT Railway
Monorail
0 150 metres
N
MAS Building
Raja Chulan
Crowne Plaza Mutiara
Wisma UOA
Wisma Cosway
Badan Warisan
Kompleks Budaya Kraf
Chulan Square
Pavilion KL
Westin Hotel
Singapore Tourism
KL Plaza
Starhill Gallery
Maybank Building
Curry Houses
BUKIT BINTANG
Bukit Bintang
Lot 10
BB Plaza
Sungai Wang
Parkson Grand
Imbi Plaza
Tung Shin Hospital
Pudu Sentral
Plaza Rakyat
Chinese Stalls
Swiss Garden
Imbi
Berjaya Times Square
Former Pudu Jail
Hang Tuah
Stadium Negara
Merdeka Stadium
Pasar Rakyat
Pasar Rakyat Bus Station
Royal Selangor Golf Club
JALAN TENGAH
JALAN KIA PENG
CHANGKAT KIA PENG
JALAN STONOR
JALAN EATON
JALAN RAJA CHULAN
JALAN CONLAY
JALAN BUKIT NANAS
LORONG CEYLON
JLN MESUI
JALAN NAGASARI
JLN ANGKOSA
JLN BEREMI
JALAN BUKIT CEYLON
JALAN CEYLON
JALAN BERANGAN
CHANGKAT BUKIT BINTANG
PERSIARAN RAJA CHULAN
JALAN SAHABAT
TENGKAT TONG SHIN
JALAN ALOR
JALAN TONG SHIN
JALAN PUDU LAMA
JALAN PUDU
JLN ROBERTSON
JALAN GALLOWAY
JALAN HANG JEBAT
JALAN IMBI
LORONG 1/77A
JALAN BULAN (NO 1)
JALAN CHANGKAT THAMBI DOLLAH
JALAN BUKIT BINTANG
BINTANG WALK
JALAN GADING
JLN WALTER GRENIER
LORONG WALTER GRENIER
JALAN SULTAN ISMAIL
JALAN KHOO TEIK
JALAN BARAT
JALAN JATI
JALAN INAI
JALAN KEMUNING
JALAN KAMPUNG
JALAN UTRA
JALAN MELATI
JALAN DELIMA

6

BY BUS

Buses from all over Peninsular Malaysia converge on one of four bus stations. Pudu Sentral (formerly PuduRaya) bus station on Jln Pudu (Plaza Rakyat station) serves northern and western destinations; the vast new Terminal Bersipadu Selatan (Bandar Tasik Selatan station – connected to four main train lines) has departures for southern destinations and Singapore; Putra, near the Putra World Trade Centre and near the PWTC station on the Ampang and Sri Petaling Lines (KTM Komuter), has departures for the east coast, while Pekeliling (Titiwangsa Monorail station) serves Kuantan and destinations in the interior.

Pudu Sentral destinations Alor Setar (9 daily; 9hr); Butterworth (every 30min; 7hr); Cameron Highlands (hourly; 4hr 30min); Ipoh (every 30min; 4hr); Kuala Perlis (6 daily; 9hr); Lumut (9 daily; 3hr 30min); Mersing (daily; 7hr); Penang (every 30min; 8hr).

Pekeliling destinations Jerantut (12 daily; 3hr 30min); Kuala Lipis (4 daily; 4hr); Kuantan (5 daily; 5hr).

Putra destinations Kota Bharu (8 daily; 10hr); Kuala Terengganu (3 daily; 7hr); Kuantan (every 30min; 5hr); Temerloh (hourly; 3hr).

Terminal Bersipadu Selatan (TBS) destinations Johor Bahru (hourly; 6hr); Malacca (every 30min; 2hr); Singapore (10 daily; 8–9hr).

BY TRAIN

Intercity trains all stop at KL Sentral station, from where you can transfer to Kuala Lumpur's city rail systems: the LRT and KL Monorail. Intercity trains run to and from KL Sentral, southwest of the city centre. The website (W ktmb.com.my) has up-to-date train timetables. You must book several days in advance for the most popular sleeper trains to Singapore or Butterworth.

Destinations Alor Setar (daily; 13hr 10min); Butterworth (daily; 10hr 40min); Ipoh (daily; 5hr 30min); Johor Bahru (4 daily; 5hr 30min–8hr); Singapore (4 daily; 7–9hr).

INFORMATION AND TOURS

Tourist information The biggest information centre is MATIC (Malaysian Tourist Information Complex) at 109 Jln Ampang (daily 8am–10pm; T 03 9235 4800, W matic.gov.my or W tourism.gov.my), east of the centre, close to the junction with Jln Sultan Ismail, which hands out useful brochures and maps of KL, as well as info on the rest of Malaysia. There are also branches in the arrivals halls at KLIA (daily 9am–7pm; T 03 8776 5651) and the Low Cost Carrier Terminal (daily 9am–7pm; T 03 8775 2518), and at KL Sentral station (daily 9am–7pm; T 03 2272 5823).

Tours Food Tour Malaysia (T 01 7616 5090, W foodtourmalaysia.com) offer fantastic "Off the Eaten Track" walking tours (3hr 30min; RM110), during both the day and at night – a great way to get acquainted with Malaysia's variety of cuisines. Highly recommended.

GETTING AROUND

Though the city centre is compact enough to be explored on foot, KL has an efficient rail system.

Buses The bus you're most likely to use is the Hop On, Hop Off double-decker bus, which includes 42 sightseeing stops and has free wi-fi on board. It's useful for getting to the Lake Gardens and for a general overview of the city. There are plenty of stops in town, including one by the tourist centre MATIC.

LRT (Light Rail Transit) KL's reasonably efficient public transport system (daily 6am–midnight) consists of six train lines, owned by three different companies: Rapid KL (Kelana Jaya Line owned by Putraline; Ampang Line & Sri Petaling Line owned by Starline), KL Monorail and KTM Komuter (Sentul Port Klang, Rawang Seremban). These are all inexpensive (fares cost from RM1 upwards, depending on distance) and cover the city (the Monorail in particular loops through central KL and the Golden Triangle area) and its environs well, though connections between different lines are poor due to inadequate integration. You can buy a ticket on one LRT line for another owned by a different company, and the Touch'n Go card (RM10) can be purchased at major stations and used on all lines bar the airport express train. KL Sentral train station is the hub not just for long-distance train travel, but also for most of the LRT lines; the monorail KL Sentral station is actually a five-minute walk away. Besides the LRT lines, there are also the KLIA Transit and KLIA Express, both serving the international airport.

Taxis Fares start at RM3 and rise RM1/km – make sure the driver uses the meter. Taxis can easily be flagged in the street, otherwise use recommended companies such as Comfort Taxi (T 03 8024 2727), Public Cab (T 03 6259 2020) and Sunlight Radio Taxi (T 03 9057 5757). Some taxi drivers don't speak much English, and some don't know their way around the city, so it's best to carry a map.

ACCOMMODATION

There are numerous hostels in Chinatown, around the Pudu Raya bus station and in the Golden Triangle; they tend to be comparatively priced. There are also a few budget options near KL Sentral – convenient for onward travel but less so for walking around and sampling the nightlife. Many hotels in KL offer dramatic discounts for on-the-day check-ins.

AROUND KL SENTRAL

★ **Grid 9** 9 Jln Maharajalela T 03 9226 2629, W grid9hotels.com; map pp.422–423. This great flashpacker joint with a young and vibrant feel offers clean and comfy rooms with private bath, a/c and TV, while dorms all have individual sockets and reading lamps. The pleasant lounge has colourful beanbags, a flatscreen TV and communal computers, as well as a pool table. There's wi-fi throughout and a little café downstairs. Dorm RM45, double RM129

My Hotel@Sentral 1, 4 Jln Tun Sanbanthan, Brickfields ⓣ 03 2273 8000, ⓦ myhotels.com.my; map pp.422–423. A great place to overnight before catching a train or flight the next day, this budget hotel offers clean, neat and tidy rooms, all with a/c, wi-fi, TV and coffee-making facilities. Double RM110

PODs Backpackers Unit 1–6, 30 Jln Thambipillay, Brickfields ⓣ 03 2260 1434, ⓦ podsbackpacker.com; map pp.422–423. Decked out in pea green, *PODs* offers small but comfy rooms, all with shared bath; there's a chill-out "platform" with beanbags and TV, and a minimart right downstairs. Dorm RM30, double RM75

CHINATOWN AND LITTLE INDIA

★ **Back Home KL** 30 Jln Tun H. S. Lee ⓣ 03 2022 0788, ⓦ backhome.com.my; map p.424. This leafy hostel has parquet floors, exposed brick walls and comfy modern rooms, all with sink and wardrobe. Staff are friendly and guests' names are creatively jotted on each door upon arrival. Dorm RM46, double RM135

Bunc 37 Jln Petaling ⓣ 03 2026 8899, ⓦ bunchostel.com .my; map p.424. This large new arrival in Chinatown is set over five floors, and offers clean modern dorms with lockers, personal reading lamps and individual plug sockets. All rooms, including dorms, have private bath and a/c, and there's also a spacious rooftop terrace. Dorm RM35, double RM110

The Explorers Guesthouse 128 & 130 Jln Tun H.S. Lee ⓣ 03 2022 2928, ⓦ theexplorersguesthouse.com; map p.424. This calm little oasis in bustling Chinatown features exposed brick walls, recycled wooden furniture and pebble tiles in the bathroom. Rooms are kept neat and tidy, and beds are sturdy. Dorm RM30, double RM88

Fern Loft 60A Jln Hang Kasturi ⓣ 03 2022 0688, ⓦ fernloft .com; map p.424. The female and mixed dorms here are on the cramped side, but there's a spacious rooftop terrace with kitchenette that makes up for it. Wi-fi, TV area, laundry facilities and pub crawls too. Double RM80, dorm RM20

Hotel Chill Inn 5 Jln Yap Ah Loy ⓣ 03 2031 0611, ⓦ hotel chillinn.com; map p.424. This budget hotel with brightly painted red and green hallways offers spacious, comfortable a/c rooms with flatscreen TVs and wi-fi throughout. Double RM55

Matahari Lodge 58–1 Jln Hang Kasturi ⓣ 03 2070 5570, ⓦ mataharilodge.com; map p.424. This is a well-located cheapie with a plant-filled roof terrace to relax on, a cosy guest lounge and colourful rooms. Simple breakfast included. Dorm RM25, double RM70

Reggae Guesthouse 1st Floor, 156 Jln Tun H.S. Lee ⓣ 03 2078 8163, ⓦ reggaehostelsmalaysia.com; map p.424. This laidback hostel appeals to the sedate backpacker, with its relaxed quiet vibe, all-day TV and coffee and chill-out area with rugs and wicker chairs. Dorm RM35, double RM90

★ **Reggae Mansion** 53 Jln Tun H. S. Lee ⓣ 03 2072 6877, ⓦ reggaehostelsmalaysia.com; map p.424. This funky three-storey white mansion attracts scores of travellers for its cool, welcoming vibe and safe setting. Premises are kept spic-and-span and each dorm bed is fully equipped with privacy curtain, plug, reading light, mirror, shelves and personal locker. There's even a cinema here and the bar on the rooftop terrace is a great spot to mingle. Dorm RM40, double RM140

Submarine 1st Floor, 206 Jln Tun H.S. Lee ⓣ 03 2022 2259, ⓦ submarinehotels.com; map p.424. This little guesthouse offers small simple rooms that open on to the small communal area, all with shared bath. Dorm RM30, double RM70

Tune 316 Jln Tunku Abdul Rahman ⓣ 03 7962 5888, ⓦ tunehotels.com; map p.424. Following AirAsia's success in flying budget travellers from A to B, they have now ventured into budget accommodation. Rooms are spotlessly clean, coolly decorated and have en-suite power showers. Additional extras (such as a/c, hairdryer etc) are charged according to requirements. Best value when booked in advance. Double RM45

THE GOLDEN TRIANGLE

Cube Boutique Hotel 180 Jln Pudu ⓣ 03 2145 1180, ⓦ cubehotel.com.my; map p.427. With funky furnishings and TVs, these compact, individually decorated rooms are some of the best value in town. Each comes with coffee/tea-making facilities. Double RM110

Number Eight 8–10 Jln Tengkat Tong Shin ⓣ 03 2144 2050, ⓦ numbereight.com.my; map p.427. Not as well looked after as it used to be, with some rooms in need of a splash of paint and a revamp, although there are plans to refurbish. The showers are solar powered, there's a/c and some rooms have private bath. Dorm RM40, double RM100

★ **Orange Pekoe** 1–1 Jln Angsoka ⓣ 03 2110 2000, ⓦ orangepekoe.com.my; map p.427. This welcoming place has clean and tidy rooms with wooden wicker boxes as bedside tables, a/c, wi-fi and private bath. There are splashes of greenery throughout the premises and a lounge area with cable TV and DVDs. Double RM99

★ **Rainforest B&B** 27 Jln Mesui, off Jln Nagasari ⓣ 03 2145 3525, ⓦ rainforestbnbhotel.com; map p.427. This guesthouse does a good job of creating a jungle-lodge ambience with plants everywhere and funky wooden decor in the a/c rooms. There are a couple of single-sex dorms sleeping three. Perks include a library and free breakfast. Dorm RM39, double RM115

Travellers Palm 10 Jln Rembia, off Tengkat Tong Shin ⓣ 03 2145 4745, ⓦ travellerspalm-kl.com; map p.427. Staying here is more like staying with a favourite auntie than in a hostel. The lovely owner encourages mingling in the shaded courtyard and is full of helpful advice; inevitably, many backpackers linger longer than originally intended. Dorm RM30, double RM80

Tropical Guesthouse 2 Tengkat Tong Shin 03 2141 1168, tropicalguesthousekl.com; map p.427. This pleasant guesthouse is decorated with leafy bamboo and pebble walkways; rooms are on the smallish side but are kept clean and tidy. Couples can opt for the interestingly named "sexy room" or the "horny room". Double RM79

EATING

6

The best-value Chinese food in KL is to be found at the rowdy, chaotic outdoor food stalls of Jln Alor, a couple of streets behind Jln Bukit Bintang. At the top of Jln Alor, Changkat Bukit Bintang serves every national cuisine imaginable, from Thai and Japanese to Russian. A roaring Indian food market can be found on Jln Masjid India. All of the shopping malls have extensive food courts, which serve all manner of cuisine – a good choice for a cheap meal throughout the day. The trendiest area to eat and drink is the expat area of Bangsar, around 4km west of the centre; take the Putra LRT line from KL Sentral to Bangsar and then walk for ten minutes.

AROUND KL SENTRAL

Legend's Claypot Briyani House 50 Jln Vivekananda; map pp.422–423. Half a block up the street from *PODs*, this canteen-style local favourite specializes in delicious claypot biriyanis (from RM14.90) as well as inexpensive banana-leaf meals (RM7.50), with lots of vegetarian dishes. Daily 7am–10.30pm.

Old Town White Coffee Jln Tun Sambanthan at Jln Thambipillay; map pp.422–423. Right near *My Hotel*, this popular chain attracts plenty of locals who come here to socialize over the sought-after coffees (RM3.80) and decent grub that includes *nasi lemak* (RM10.50). Daily 24hr.

CHINATOWN AND LITTLE INDIA

Betel Leaf 77A Leboh Ampang; map p.424. This authentic Indian restaurant serves wonderful curries (RM12) and kebabs (RM15) in an a/c setting. There's plenty on offer for vegetarians, too. Daily 11am–11pm.

Lokl Coffee Co. 30 Jln Tun H.S. Lee; map p.424. This cute welcoming café offers a range of savoury dishes, such as chicken chops (RM21.90) and beef burgers (RM20.90), as well as a selection of cakes and pastries (RM9). Mon–Sat 7.30am–5pm.

Old China Café 11 Jln Balai Polis; map p.424. Step back into the Chinese community's former social life at this old-world café serving traditional dishes such as *nasi lemak* (RM10.90). Daily 11.30am–10.30pm.

Shin Kee 9 Jln Tun Tan Cheng Lock; map p.424. This great little place specializes in superb bowls of mixed beef noodles (RM7). Thurs–Tues 10.30am–8.30pm.

> **★TREAT YOURSELF**
>
> **Marini's on 57** 57th Floor, Menara 3 Petronas Tower marinis57com; map pp.422–423. Instead of paying to go up to Sky Bridge at KLCC, head up to *Marini's* at sunset and soak in the spectacular views, cocktail in hand (from RM30), from this chic 57th-floor bar with floor-to-ceiling glass windows. Dress up or you may be refused entry. Daily 5pm–late.

GOLDEN TRIANGLE

Jln Alor is lined with garrulous Chinese restaurants specializing largely in seafood, and you're guaranteed a good meal at any one that looks popular.

Albion 31 Jln Berangan; map p.427. Exceptional authentic Sunday roasts with Yorkshire pudding and all the trimmings at this Modern British restaurant also serving great slow-roast pork belly (RM41). The weekday Express lunch menu (RM22–28) is great value. Tues–Sat noon–3pm & 5–11pm, Sun noon–10.30pm.

Din Tai Fung Level 6, Pavilion KL; map p.427. Watch the chefs at work as your dumplings (RM10–15) are rolled out and stuffed, then steamed in front of your very eyes. Daily 10am–10pm.

El Cerdo 43 & 45 Changkat Bukit Bintang; map p.427. Make sure you head to this hugely popular restaurant with a hungry belly; it specializes in pork dishes (their motto is "nose to tail eating") and the half piglet (RM188) goes down a treat (mains from RM42). Mon–Sat noon–2.30pm & 6–10.30pm. Sun dinner only.

Food Republic Pavilion KL; map p.427. One of the best food courts you'll find in a KL mall, with a huge range of cuisines, from Korean and Sarawakian to *dim sum* and steak, as well as a fresh fruit-juice stall doing a roaring business. Daily 10am–10pm.

Havana Changkat Bukit Bintang; map p.427. A great place for meat lovers, with an outdoor courtyard and an open-plan steak and grill bar offering juicy burgers (RM28), tender steaks (RM46) and racks of beef ribs (RM45). The upstairs bar and club really kicks off on weekends (see opposite). Mon–Fri 4pm–3am, Sat & Sun 4pm–2am.

The Magnificent Fish & Chips Bar 28 Changkat Bukit Bintang; map p.427. This authentic chippie serves excellent fish & chips wrapped in newspaper (RM27) and Sunday roasts (beef, lamb or chicken; RM48) in a cool and stylish setting. Upstairs, there's a balcony and bar with British memorabilia. Daily 9.30am–2am.

Neroteca 8 Lorong Ceylon; map p.427. This stylish restaurant and wine bar has floor-to-ceiling shelves stacked with wine bottles and offers popular Italian dishes. The deli counter displays meats and cheeses, while the home-made pasta (RM26) is served with exquisite sauces. Daily 11.30am–11.30pm.

Passage Thru' India 4 Jln Delima; map p.427. An Indian

experience through and through, with the colourful, kitsch decor matching the fire and flavour of the dishes. The banana-leaf curries stand out and the home-made chutneys are a treat to the palate. Mains from RM15. Daily 11.30am–2.45pm & 6.30–10.30pm.

Pinchos 18 Changkat Bukit Bintang; map p.427. This bustling Spanish tapas place is always packed with customers who come for great wine and delicious tapas (RM11–26). Tues–Sun 6am–1am.

Sao Nam 25 Tengkat Tong Shin; map p.427. Authentic, beautifully presented Vietnamese dishes, with standout mains such as *ga nuong mat ong* (grilled chicken with honey; RM30) and crisp, flavourful spring rolls (RM20). Daily 12.30–2pm & 7–10.30pm.

Tokyo Street Level 6, Pavilion KL; map p.427. Experience Japanese ambience at Tokyo Street, packed with little shops selling Japanese trinkets and places serving great sushi. Mains from RM25. Daily 10am–10pm.

BANGSAR

Alexis 29 Jln Telawi 3. This smart coffee shop serves wonderful cakes (RM13), as well as mains (RM24), in an upmarket setting. Mon–Thurs 10am–1am, Fri & Sat 8am–2am, Sun 8am–1am.

Bangsar Fish Head Corner Lorong Ara Kiri 3. Malays of all backgrounds stand in line at this hugely popular street-food joint serving great fish head curry, fried fish, and chicken and beansprouts. A meal will set you back RM25–30. Mon–Sat 7am–7pm.

Devi's Corner Jln Telawi 2 at Jln Telawi 4. This laidback bustling place attracts scores of locals and expats who flock here to feast on all manner of bargain south Indian dishes including great *thosai* (RM1.70). Daily 24hr.

La Bodega 16 Jln Telawi 2. The Catalan chef at one of Bangsar's most sought-after restaurants rustles up some great tapas (RM10–28) and paella (RM35). Daily 8am–midnight.

Sri Nirwana 43 Jln Telawi 3. A popular local hangout serving excellent banana-leaf meals for just RM8. Daily 10am–2am.

Yeast 24G Jln Telawi 2. This pleasant restaurant-bakery offers a selection of cakes and pastries (RM4–13), as well as light mains (RM20–32). There's 30 percent off takeaway breads and pastries daily between 5–7pm. Sun–Thurs 8am–10pm, Fri & Sat 8am–10.30pm.

NIGHTLIFE AND ENTERTAINMENT

Most bars are open from noon until midnight. The music played at clubs ranges from house and techno to hip-hop and R&B. Entrance charges are around RM25 including a drink.

CHINATOWN AND LITTLE INDIA

Reggae Bar 158 Jln Tun H.S. Lee; map p.424. A popular place attracting backpackers and international school students for its laidback atmosphere, Bob Marley and R&B tracks and pool tables.

GOLDEN TRIANGLE

Frangipani 25 Changkat Bukit Bintang; map p.427. Ditch the trainers and dress up for this snazzy bar. It attracts KL's socialites who mingle over great cocktails (RM29) to the sounds of R&B and house. Daily 5pm–1am, Fri & Sat until 3am.

The Green Man 40 Changkat Bukit Bintang; map p.427. The congenial atmosphere at one of KL's most popular pubs will ensure a leisurely evening, especially if you linger over the good pub grub. Daily 11am–midnight.

Havana Changkat Bukit Bintang; map p.427. This retro nightclub above a bustling steak-and-grill restaurant gets packed at weekends, as expats and locals alike stomp around to 70s, 80s and 90s classics. Fri & Sat 10am–2am.

No Black Tie 17 Jln Mesui, off Jln Nagasari; map p.427. This intimate little venue hosts regular jazz, classical and acoustic sessions, as well as occasional comedy shows and poetry readings. Pricey Japanese food (set menu RM98) and cocktails (RM25) can be enjoyed as you watch the show. Daily 5pm–2am.

Palate Palette 21 Jln Mesui; map p.427. This quirky bar with mismatched furniture and colourful wall designs has a lively atmosphere and is a great place for pre- or post-dinner drinks (from RM20). Mon–Fri noon–midnight, Sat & Sun until 2am.

Pisco Bar 29 Jln Mesui; map p.427. As the name suggests, pisco sours (RM26) are the drink of choice at this popular bar with exposed brick walls, wooden planks lining the ceiling and upside-down buckets serving as bar lamps. Live bands and open mic on Wed at 9.30pm, while Fri & Sat DJs spin an eclectic selection of tracks from 10pm. Tues–Thurs 5pm–1am, Fri & Sat 5pm–3am.

Twentyone kitchen & bar 20-1 Changkat Bukit Bintang; map p.427. Stylish bar and club with delicious modern European food with an Asian touch to complement the excellent cocktails and an open-air area for skyline gazing. Cocktails from RM24. Sun–Tues noon–1.30am, Wed–Sat until 3am.

FURTHER AFIELD

MILK 18 Jln Liku, Bangsar; map pp.422–423. Swanky offshoot of the popular *Mist Club*, featuring hip-hop, R&B and cutting-edge DJs. Their MILKshake really does bring all the boys (and girls) to the yard. Mon–Sat 9pm–3am.

Zouk 113 Jln Ampang; map pp.422–423. A complete clubbing complex to suit all tastes, this is also the biggest nightclub in Malaysia. The KL branch of this Singapore-based megaclub comprises a two-level beach-themed venue, divided into seven sections, featuring such genres as trance, hip-hop, R&B and pop. Entry RM20–50. Tues–Sun 10pm–5am.

6

SHOPPING

KL is full of shopping malls, particularly in the Golden Triangle; most are open daily from 10am to 10pm. A wander around KL's many and varied markets is also a great way to soak up some of the atmosphere of the city and perhaps even pick up some bargains.

ENGLISH-LANGUAGE BOOKS

Kinokuniya Level 4, Suria KLCC. Great selection of fiction and travel guidebooks.

Times Books Level 6, Pavilion KL. Besides a good fiction and non-fiction selection, there's an extensive array of English-language magazines.

HANDICRAFTS AND BATIK

Central Market Jln Hang Kasturi. There are numerous batik stalls on the first floor in particular, selling sarongs, colourful shirts and scarves.

Peter Hoe 2nd Floor, Old Lee Rubber Building, Jln Tun H.S. Lee. A stone's throw from Central Market, this is a more upmarket outlet specializing in beautiful bags, batik shirts and sarongs, as well as locally made and Indonesian crafts.

MARKETS

Chow Kit Market Jln Haji Hussein, off Jln TAR. Quite an experience, with its warren of stalls selling everything from animals' brains to quality batik textiles. Daily 9am–5pm.

Jalan Petaling Market Near Central Market. The covered walkways here are crowded and lively and you can pick up anything from an Angry Birds backpack to knock-off designer gear and the usual "I Heart MY" T-shirts. Bargaining is a must. Daily 9am–10pm.

SHOPPING MALLS

Bangsar Village 1 Jln Telawi, Bangsar. Chic and shiny, with marble floors and a host of stores that stock international designer labels and draw a yuppie crowd.

BB Plaza Jln Bukit Bintang. Offering excellent deals on cameras, electronic equipment, shoes and much else besides.

> **★TREAT YOURSELF**
>
> Kuala Lumpur is teeming with **masseurs** and Jalan Bukit Bintang is home to a whole host of them, all waiting to soothe your aching muscles. There's usually an assortment of relaxing treatments on offer, including traditional reflexology treatments, body massages, fish spas (where little fish nibble on the dead skin of your feet), body scrubs and facials, all from the comfort of a reclining chair. Prices start from RM40 for a half-hour foot massage.

Pavilion KL Jln Bukit Bintang. Award-winning shopping venue with an excellent selection of designer stores and high-street outlets, pampering spas, restaurants and in *Food Republic*, one of the city's best food courts (see p.430).

Suria KLCC Golden Mile. If you're on a mission to shop, then this is the place to head to. An awesomely large complex set across six floors, there are plentiful Western brands from designers such as Louis Vuitton to more affordable high-street brands such as Quiksilver and Marks & Spencer, as well as an art gallery and a science discovery centre.

DIRECTORY

Banks and exchange ATMs and banks can be found throughout the city centre. Major branches include: HSBC, 2 Lebuh Ampang, Little India, and Standard Chartered Bank, 2 Jln Ampang. Official moneychangers, of which there are scores in the main city areas, give better exchange rates than banks.

Embassies and consulates Australia, Jln Yap Kwan Seng (T 03 2146 5555); Brunei, 19th Floor, Menara Tan & Tan, 207 Jln Tun Razak (T 03 2161 2800); Cambodia, 46 Jln U Thant (T 03 4257 3711); Canada, 17th Floor, Menara Tan & Tan, 207 Jln Tun Razak (T 03 2718 3333); China, 1st Floor, Plaza OSK, 25 Jln Ampang (T 03 2163 6815); Indonesia, 233 Jln Tun Razak (T 03 2116 4000); Laos, 25 Jln Damai (T 03 2148 7059); New Zealand, Menara IMC, 8 Jln Sultan Ismail (T 03 2078 2533); Philippines, 1 Jln Changkat Kia Peng (T 03 2148 4233); Singapore, 209 Jln Tun Razak (T 03 2161 6404); Thailand, 206 Jln Ampang (T 03 2148 8222); UK, 185 Jln Ampang (T 03 2170 2200); US, 376 Jln Tun Razak (T 03 2168 5000); Vietnam, 4 Persiaran Stonor (T 03 2148 4036).

Emergencies T 999 for ambulance, police or fire.

Hospitals and clinics Hospital Kuala Lumpur, Jln Pahang (T 03 2615 5555, W hkl.gov.my); Tung Shin Hospital, 102 Jln Pudu (T 03 2037 2288). For less serious ailments, try the Twin Towers Medical Clinic, Level 4, Suria KLCC (Mon–Sat 8.30am–6pm T 03 2382 3500, W ttmcklcc.com.my; consultation from RM35).

Immigration Level 1–7, 15 Persiaran Perdana (Mon–Fri 8am–5pm; T 03 8000 8000, W imi.gov.my). This office deals with visa extensions.

Internet The tourist office MATIC offers computers with free internet access; Yoshi Connection, Concourse Level of Suria KLCC (daily 10am–10pm; RM8/hr).

Pharmacies Pharmacies can be found in every shopping mall.

Post office The GPO is on Jln Tun Sambanthan (Mon–Fri 8.30am–8pm, Sat 8.30am–5pm).

Tourist police The tourist police station (daily 24hr), where you must report stolen property and claim your insurance form, is within the same complex as the tourist office MATIC at 109 Jln Ampang (T 03 2163 4422).

DAY-TRIPS FROM KL

The biggest attractions **around KL** are north of the city, where limestone peaks rise up out of the forest and the roads narrow as you pass through small kampungs (villages). Amid dramatic scenery just 13km from the city, the vast Hindu shrine at the **Batu Caves** is one of Malaysia's main tourist attractions. Southwest of KL, **Kuala Selangor Nature Park** and the fireflies at **Village Kuantan** appeal to nature lovers.

The Batu Caves

The **Batu Caves**, dark openings in the vast limestone hills, are said to be over 400 million years old, and were once used as shelters by the Orang Asli. Since 1891, the caves have sheltered Hindu shrines, and it is now one of the biggest shrines outside India. The caves are always packed with visitors, never more so than during the three-day Thaipusam festival held in late January, when more than a million faithful gather here, the skin of many pierced with metal hooks with ropes attached to them; the most devout follow the silver chariot that is taken from the Sri MahaMarianman temple in the centre of KL (see p.425). If you're lucky enough to be here during Thaipusam, arrive at dawn to have any chance of a place to stand.

Coming out of the train station, you pass a giant statue of the monkey god Hanuman, vendors selling all manner of little trinkets, and the entrance to **Cave Villa** (daily 9am–6.30pm; RM15); the complex here incorporates an Art Gallery Cave, home to dozens of multicoloured deity statues, a bird and a reptile sanctuary. Just beyond is the bottom of the steep 272-step staircase leading up to the main cave, dwarfed by the enormous golden statue of Lord Subramaniam, otherwise known as Muruga, the god of war.

At the top of the main staircase is **Subramaniam Swamy Temple** (daily 7am–9pm; free), set deep in a huge cave, its walls lined with idols representing the six lives of Lord Subramaniam and its interior crowded with the faithful, their shaved heads covered with yellow chalk. The whole place is swarming with macaques who are not afraid of humans – thanks to those who feed them. Just before the entrance to the main temple, a short path leads to the **Dark Cave** (Tues–Fri 10am–5pm; Sat & Sun 10.30am–5.30pm; RM35); guided excursions are organized at the entrance (45min) and you may see bats and trapdoor spiders.

To get to the caves, take a direct train on the KMT Komuter Line from KL Sentral to the Batu Caves stop (every 15min; 30min).

Kuala Selangor Nature Park and the fireflies

North of Klang is the small **Taman Alam Kuala Selangor Nature Park** (daily 9am–6pm; RM4; ❶ 03 289 2294, Ⓦ mns.org.my), set in partial primary rainforest; the trails are short (taking between 15min and 2hr to walk) but lead to hides that make perfect **birdwatching** spots. The park is accessible by bus #141 from behind the Central Market (every 30min 6.30am–7.30pm; 2hr; RM7.30; the last bus back is at 7.45pm).

To view the **fireflies** for which the area is so famous, join one of the tours organized by many of the hostels or take a taxi (RM20 return from Kuala Selangor – there's no bus) to **Kuantan** 10km away. It costs RM10 to take a ride in a battery-powered *sampan* (small boat), RM15 in a fibreglass boat, along the river, Sungei Kuantan, at around 8pm, to see the thousands of fireflies glowing on the riverbank.

The west coast

The west coast of the Malaysian Peninsula, from Kuala Lumpur north to the Thai border, is the most industrialized and densely populated part of the country. This is also the area in which the British held most sway, attracted by the political prestige of controlling such a strategic trading region.

The hill stations of the **Cameron Highlands** are a perfect place to relax and escape the heat and humidity, while **Georgetown** on the island of Penang gives another taste of colonial life with its charming old shophouses and fantastic food. From here, it's not too far to the pretty white-sand shores of popular

Pulau Langkawi or tiny **Pulau Pangkor** for a few lazy days on the beach.

CAMERON HIGHLANDS

Amid the lofty peaks of Banjaran Titiwangsa, the various outposts of the **Cameron Highlands** (1524m) form Malaysia's most extensive hill station, and have been used as a weekend retreat since the 1920s. The rolling hills are lush and tranquil, and the bright, pure colour of the sky and tea plantations alone is enough to make anybody feel considerably rejuvenated (though during rainy season you may face torrential rains all day long). While **Brinchang** is the principal settlement for locals, **Tanah Rata** is the backpackers' centre, boasting budget accommodation, travel information, plenty of cheap places to eat and a plethora of tours. Be aware that it's considerably colder here than in the lowlands, so it might be wise to bring a sleeping bag as nights get chilly. There are direct buses to Tanah Rata from Georgetown, KL and Taman Negara, and guesthouses in other towns can often arrange minibus transfers.

WHAT TO SEE AND DO

There's plenty to keep you occupied in the Highlands, and activities can either be embarked on alone, armed with the maps and information available at all guest-houses, or as part of a tour – the easiest way to take in all the highlights in one day if you don't have your own transport. There are **strawberry farms** (daily 8.30am–6pm), where you can pick your own (at a price); the **butterfly farm** (daily 8am–6pm; RM5), where you can see leaf insects and cobras; **honey bee farms** (daily 8am–7pm), the BOH (Best Of the Highlands) **tea plantation** and the Buddhist temple **Sam Poh** (daily 7am–7pm).

You can also go **jungle trekking**, taking in some of the most spectacular scenery in Malaysia; day tours of the Cameron Highlands can also include a jungle hike through the mossy forest.

Otherwise, there are a number of trails from Tanah Rata itself; most guesthouses provide rudimentary trail maps with numbered routes, though some of the trails are poorly maintained and are sometimes badly signposted. Always inform someone at your guesthouse where you are going and what time you expect to be back. Take plenty of water, food, a whistle, a torch, a lighter and a jacket; it's advisable to take a guide if you want to do any extensive trekking.

Tanah Rata

Meaning "Flat Land" in Malay, **TANAH RATA** is the one-street travellers' hangout – the location of most hotels, banks and restaurants – and a comfortable base for exploring the highlands. Many walks originate here, and a couple of waterfalls and three reasonably high mountain peaks are all within hiking distance.

ARRIVAL AND DEPARTURE

By bus Local buses go from the bus station, about halfway along the main road. Most guesthouses can arrange direct minibus transfers to popular spots.

Bus destinations Ipoh (10 daily; 2hr); Kuala Lumpur (12 daily; 4hr); Penang (3 daily; 5hr); Singapore (daily at 10am; 10hr).

Minibus destinations Taman Negara (2 daily; 3hr 30min & 2hr boat journey) and the Perhentians (3 daily; 6hr & 1hr ferry).

ACCOMMODATION

Cameronian Inn 16 Jln Mentigi ⓣ05 491 1327, ⓦthecameronianinn.com. The tidy rooms here are set at

TOURS FROM THE CAMERON HIGHLANDS

Cameron Secrets at *Father's Guesthouse* ⓣ016 566 1111, ⓦcameronsecrets.com. An established, recommended outfit offering jungle walks, country-side tours, tea plantation trips and Rafflesia tours.

Kang Tours & Travel 38 Jln Besar ⓣ05 491 5828, ⓦkangholiday.com. Not only do these guys arrange daily transfers to Georgetown, Taman Negara, KL and the Perhentian Islands, but they also have a host of well-organized tours on offer – from the full-day Rainforest Adventure (RM98) and whitewater rafting (RM155) to the less demanding Agro Farm Adventure (RM90).

the back of a leafy courtyard with a plethora of potted plants; there's a little garden area with seating, an annexe with TV lounge and a hair salon for adventurous types in need of a makeover. Dorm RM20, double RM45

Father's Guest House 4 Jln Mentigi ☎016 566 1111, @fathersguesthouse.net. A friendly welcoming place that buzzes with travellers who come here for the laidback family atmosphere. Rooms are simple but clean, there's all-day tea and coffee, wi-fi and board games. Dorm RM20, double RM90

Gerard's Place Carnation Block C9, C10 & C17, Greenhill Resort ☎012 588 5454, @fathersguesthouse.net. Under the same management as *Father's Guest House*, *Gerard's* offers clean, pleasant rooms in a welcoming setting where guests socialize in the comfortable lounge and around the outdoor seating area. Double RM70

Hillview Inn 17 Jln Mentigi ☎05 491 2915, @hillview-inn.com. This mock Tudor building with a pleasant garden offers spacious carpeted rooms, most with balcony. There's wi-fi throughout and an on-site café serving freshly baked scones. Double RM45

Kang Travellers Lodge 9 Lorong Perdah ☎05 491 5823, @kangholiday.com. This longstanding favourite has a popular, rustic bar that makes for many a sociable night. There are two small attic dorms at the top of a tiny staircase and simple doubles with tacky pictures as decor. Dorm RM12, double RM45

EATING AND DRINKING

At night, food stalls set up on Main Road, chiefly opposite the post office; the food is mostly Malay and you're unlikely to spend more than RM10 on a meal. Many restaurants serve steamboat, which involves dipping raw fish, meat, noodles and vegetables in a steaming broth until cooked.

The Jungle Bar Located behind *Kang Travellers Lodge*. Travellers congregate nightly at this laidback, rustic bar made of pine and bamboo. Guests can enjoy drinks (RM6.50) by the crackling bonfire or over a game of pool. Daily 7.30pm–midnight.

Kumar 26 Main Road. This great Indian place specializes in claypot rice (RM6), tandoori (RM7) and banana-leaf meals (RM7). The combination set is great value at just RM9. *Sri Brinchang* next door offers similar grub. Daily 7am–10.30pm.

May Flower 81A Persiaran Camelli 4. This well-liked restaurant offers a selection of steamboat dishes (including vegetarian; RM12), noodles and fried rice (RM6). Those feeling more adventurous can try the ostrich and deer meat (RM12). Daily 8.30am–3pm & 5.30–10pm.

Ferm Nyonya 78 Persiaran Camellia 4. By the *May Flower*, this restaurant specializes in Chinese and Nyonya dishes; the beef *rending* (RM13) is among their bestsellers, and there are also Western dishes for those wanting familiar comfort food. Daily 11am–10pm.

IPOH

Eighty kilometres northwest of Tapah in the Kinta Valley, **IPOH** grew rich on the tin trade and is now the third-largest city in Malaysia. The muddy **Sungai Kinta** River cuts the centre of Ipoh neatly in two; most of the hotels are situated east of the river, while the **old town** is on the opposite side between Jalan Sultan Idris Shah and Jalan Sultan Iskander. Many Ipoh buildings show the influence of colonial and Straits-Chinese architecture, with the Moorish-style **railway station** being a particularly impressive example. Ipoh's main attractions, however, lie outside the city, and include **Sam Poh Tong**, a large and impressive cave temple (daily 8.30am–4pm) reachable by the Kampar bus, and **Perak Tong**, one of the largest and most striking Chinese temples in Malaysia (daily 8am–5pm). The temple, 6km north of the city, dates back to 1926 and is home to over forty Buddha statues and wonderful cave paintings. Follow the steps up and through the cave from where there are views over Ipoh. To get here take the Kuala Kangsar bus from the local bus terminal.

ARRIVAL AND DEPARTURE

By bus The local bus station, 200m south of the train station, is at the junction with Jln Tun Abdul Razak. It is connected by frequent shuttle buses to Amanjaya – the long-distance bus hub 15km out of town, which serves all main destinations along the west coast. Buses from the Cameron Highlands serve both stations (check which when purchasing your ticket).

Destinations Butterworth (hourly; 3hr); Cameron Highlands (several daily; 2hr); Georgetown (hourly; 3hr); Kuala Lumpur (hourly; 4hr); Lumut (the departure point for Pulau Pangkor; several daily; 1hr 30min); Singapore (4 daily; 10–11hr).

By train The train station is on Jln Panglima Bukit, west of the old town, next to the GPO.

Destinations Hat Yai (Thailand; daily at 1.30am; 10hr); KL (4 daily; 3hr).

INFORMATION

Tourist office The tourist office is on Jln Bandar (Mon–Fri 8am–5pm, closed for lunch Mon–Thurs 1–2pm & Fri 12.15–2.45pm; ☎05 208 3151, @mbi.gov.my).

ACCOMMODATION AND EATING

The area of Little India has scores of Indian restaurants, while Malay and Chinese food can be enjoyed at the night hawker stalls (daily 8pm–2am) on Jln Sultan Abdul Jalil.

6

★**French Hotel** 60-62 Jln Dato Onn Jaafar. The spick-and-span rooms here all have modern private bathrooms, fridges, TVs and a/c. Staff are welcoming and helpful, and there's a superb, cosy café serving Western dishes on the first floor. Double RM138

★**Jose & Deli** 2nd Floor, 60–62 Jln Dato Onn Jaafar. This wonderful café-deli within *French Hotel* has rustic wooden tables, comfy wicker armchairs and soothing background music. The menu embraces great Western cuisine, including soups (RM10), Caesar salads (RM25) and a selection of sandwiches and burgers (RM20), as well as fish and chips (RM28). Daily 7.30am–10.30pm.

Sun Yuan Foong White Coffee 15A Jln Bandar Timah. A local institution, this no-frills place is packed with Chinese customers who come here for the great white coffee (RM1.50) to be enjoyed with sponge cake (RM1.30) or toasted bread with butter and local jam (RM1.60). Mon–Sat 6.30am–5.30pm, Sun 6.30am–1pm.

PULAU PANGKOR

At only 3km by 9km, **PULAU PANGKOR** is one of the most minute of the west coast's islands, with some pleasant stretches of beach. It's only a forty-minute ferry ride from the port of Lumut (85km southwest of Ipoh).

Most villages lie along the east coast, while tourist accommodation and the best beaches are on the west side of the island, at Pasir Bogak and Teluk Nipah. A sealed road runs right round the island, and if you're exploring Pulau Pangkor by motorbike, you do have to be a confident rider, as there are some **steep hairpin bends** between Teluk Dalam on the north coast by the airstrip and the east coast, as well as the stretch between Pasir Bogak and Tekuk Nipah.

The west coast

Down the south end of the west coast is **Pasir Bogak**, a beach popular with locals. Halfway along the west coast is **Teluk Nipah**, the most popular place for visitors, with an attractive beach fringed with shade-providing palm trees. Just north of Teluk Nipah is **Coral Beach**, a perfect cove with crystal-clear sea and smooth white sand, reachable by road; at its north end you'll find the decidedly strange **Lin Je Kong Temple** featuring two devotional figures of Donald Duck and Mickey Mouse. Up from Coral Beach is a lovely stretch of road running through the jungle, passing the airstrip and emerging at the less-than-clean Teluk Datam Beach.

There are plenty of independent outfits offering activities and watersports, from kayaking (RM20/hr) to jet skiing (RM70/20min), as well as island-hopping (RM20) and snorkelling trips (RM15).

The east coast

While the east coast's main settlement, pungent-smelling Pangkor Town, is unlikely to detain you for long, just north of the centre is a turn-off for the colourful **Foo Lin Kong Temple**, featuring fearsome deities and a miniature version of the Great Wall of China. Three kilometres south of Pangkor Town you'll come across **Kota Belanda**, the Dutch fort originally built in 1670, which looks new because it was rebuilt in the 1980s.

ARRIVAL AND DEPARTURE

By boat Pulau Pangkor is served by frequent ferries from Lumut (every 30min, 6.30am–8.30pm; 30min; RM10 one-way), calling at Sungei Pinang Kecil before reaching the main jetty at Pangkor Town.

By plane Berjaya Air (berjaya-air.com) flies between Pulau Pangkor and Kuala Lumpur's Subang Airport (3 weekly; 45min).

By bus In Lumut, buses depart from the town's bus station, a 3min walk from the jetty.

Destinations Butterworth (8 daily; 4hr); KL (hourly; 6hr); Kota Bharu (2 daily; 10hr); Malacca (2 daily; 8hr); Ipoh (hourly; 1hr 30min).

GETTING AROUND

Minibus taxis These pink vehicles meet the ferries from Lumut and charge RM15 from Pangkor Town to Pasir Bogak, RM20 to Teluk Nipah and RM80 for a round-island trip.

Motorbike and bicycle rental The best way to explore is by motorbike (RM30 for manual or RM50 for a scooter/day) or bicycle (RM20/day), available from guesthouses in Telik Nipah.

ACCOMMODATION

Nazri Nipah Camp 05 685 2014. This well-established backpacker favourite offers tiny A-framed huts sleeping two for a bargain RM30, as well as larger, more comfortable rooms with private bath. There's a leafy chill-out area with benches and hammocks, and a kitchen for guests' use. Dorm RM15, double RM50

Nipah Bay Villa 05 685 2198, nipahbay.com. The larger rooms here are located in comfy wooden chalets,

★TREAT YOURSELF

Tiger Rock ⓣ04 264 3580, ⓦtigerrock.info. This tropical paradise has inviting rooms decorated with local furniture and beautiful art dotted around lush, verdant grounds. You can while away your afternoons by the inviting swimming pool as you refuel with exquisite Malay food served at the laidback dining area. Full board from RM550 per person per day.

while the smaller budget rooms are at the back. All are clean, neat and tidy, and there's a spacious rooftop terrace to unwind. Great single rates, and good discounts in low season. Double RM100

★Nipah Guesthouse ⓣ017 506 9259, ⓦpangkorbeachchalet.com. This wonderful guesthouse has four neat A-framed huts surrounding a pleasant pool area with loungers. Breakfast consists of a continental buffet in the breezy dining area, where guests are encouraged to rustle up their own eggs and pancakes. Double RM180

Sunset View Chalet ⓣ05 685 5448, ⓦsunsetviewchalet.com. Clean rooms with little balconies opening out onto an avenue charmingly shaded by bougainvillea. There are hammocks to chill out in by the outdoor TV and seating area. Double RM60

EATING

Most guesthouses have an attached restaurant serving a mix of seafood and international dishes.

Daddy's Café On the southern end of Coral Beach. This beachside restaurant serves fresh Pangkor seafood and local specialities including fish head curry (RM19) and Malaysian crab curry (RM25). Daily 11am–11pm.

Food stalls The northern end of Teluk Nipah beach comes alive in the evening with informal stalls all doing a roaring trade in inexpensive fresh seafood and noodles. It's one of the best places to eat on the island. Seafood mains RM14; noodles RM5.

Yee Lin 195 Jln Pasir Bogak. Locals from all over the island head to this popular place for the excellent fish and seafood dishes. Daily 7pm–midnight.

PENANG AND GEORGETOWN

On Malaysia's northwestern coast is **PENANG**, a large island of 285 square kilometres, connected to the mainland by a bridge and frequent ferry services from Butterworth. It became the first British settlement in the Malay Peninsula in 1791, and a major colonial administrative centre, only declining after the foundation of Singapore in 1819. Its capital, **GEORGETOWN**, was declared a UNESCO World Heritage Site in 2008, lined with beautiful pastel-coloured buildings that were once townhouses and shophouses. The city is known as the "Food Capital of Malaysia", offering a tantalizing range of cuisines that incorporate the very best of Malay, Chinese and Indian elements. In recent years, Georgetown has also witnessed a growing arts scene, with quirky works of art and wrought-iron caricatures hidden along the street's quaint alleyways. The city is a perfect base to explore nearby sights, including the island's commercialized north-coast beach of **Batu Ferringhi** where it's possible to stay overnight.

WHAT TO SEE AND DO

Georgetown retains more of its cultural history than virtually anywhere else in the country, with a host of beautiful colonial buildings to admire and explore.

Fort Cornwallis and around

The site of **Fort Cornwallis** (Mon–Sat 9am–7pm; RM2), on the northeastern tip of Pulau Penang, marks the spot where the British fleet under Captain Francis Light disembarked on July 16, 1786. For all its significance, however, it holds little of interest save a history gallery, the outer walls of the fort and historic cannons facing the sea. Southwest from the fort is **Lebuh Pantai**, which holds some fine colonial buildings. West of Lebuh Pantai, on Jalan Masjid Kapitan Kling (or Lebuh Pitt), stands the Anglican **St George's Church** (Mon–Fri 10am–noon & 2–4pm, Sat 10am–noon, Sun open for services only at 8.30 & 10.30am; free); construction here started in 1817, making it one of the oldest buildings in Penang. Next to the church on Lebuh Farquhar, **Penang State Museum** (daily except Fri 9am–5pm; RM1) has an excellent collection of rickshaws, as well as period objects, press cuttings and black-and-white photographs charting the city's history.

Little India

The area enclosed by parallel Lebuh King and Lebuh Queen forms Georgetown's

6

6

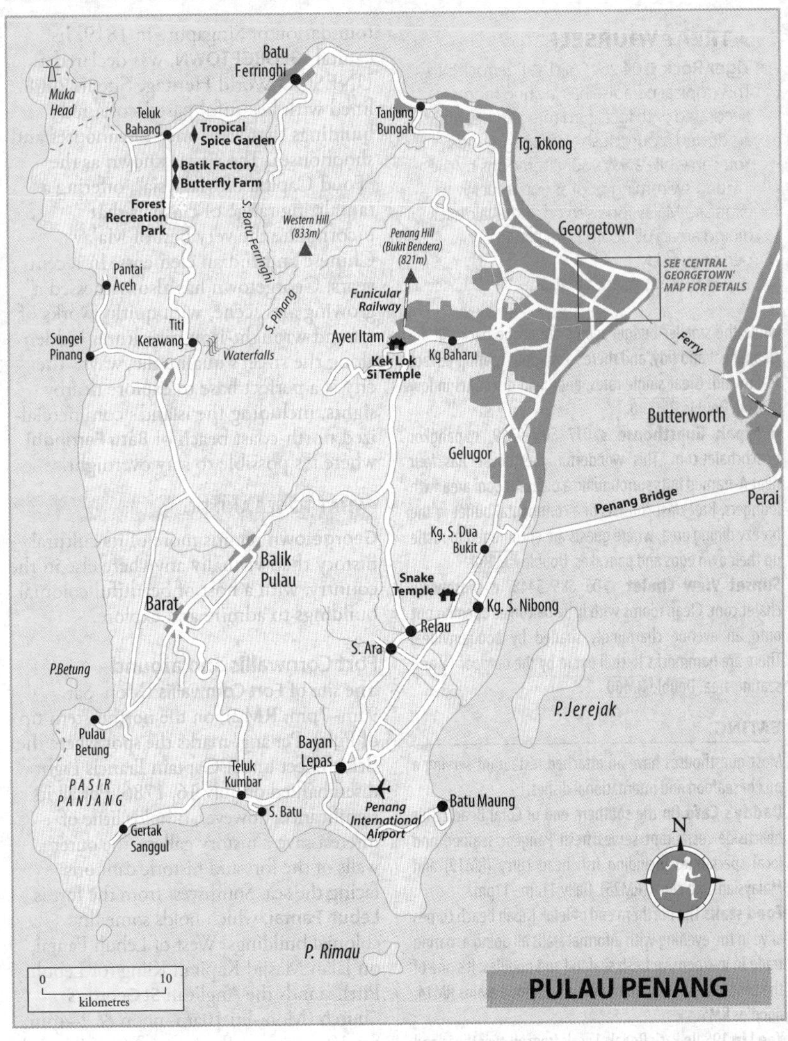

compact **Little India** district, full of sari and incense shops as well as banana-leaf-curry houses. It is also home to the towering Hindu **Sri Mahamariamman Temple** (daily 7.30am–noon & 5–9pm) on Lebuh Queen, the city's oldest Hindu temple, built in 1833, and one of the starting points for the *kavadi* dance procession during the Thaipusam festival.

Khoo Kongsi

To the south, accessed through an archway via Cannon Square, stands the **Khoo Kongsi** (daily 9am–6pm; RM10), also known as Dragon Mountain Hall – one of many *kongsi*, or traditional "clan-houses", in Penang where Chinese families gather to worship their ancestors, look after the welfare of family members, and settle clan affairs. The original building was started in 1894 and meticulously crafted by experts from China. Its central hall is dark with heavy, intricately carved beams and pillars and bulky mother-of-pearl inlaid furniture. The hall on the left is a richly decorated

shrine to Tua Peh Kong, the god of prosperity; the right-hand hall contains the gilded ancestral tablets. Connecting all three halls is a balcony minutely decorated in carvings of folk tales, with dragons and immortals an important part of the cast. The clan house is currently overseen by the 29th generation of the original Leongs who settled in Georgetown.

Pinang Peranakan Mansion

This wonderful mansion, at 29 Lebuh Gereja (daily 9.30am–5pm; RM20; Ⓦpinangperanakanmansion.com.my), re-creates the sumptuous lifestyle of a wealthy Peranakan family, also referred to as Baba and Nyonya, descendants of Chinese migrants who intermarried with Malays. The Peranakans adopted Malay customs while living in line with British colonial traditions. The nineteenth-century stately home displays over a hundred antiques and collectables that embrace a variety of styles, from Chinese carved wooden panels to Scottish ironworks.

Cheong Fatt Tze Mansion

On the western edge of Georgetown, at 14 Lebuh Leith, is the stunning **Cheong Fatt Tze Mansion** (guided tours Mon–Fri 11am, 1.30 & 3pm, Sat & Sun 11am; 1hr; RM12), whose outer walls are painted a striking, rich blue. It's the best example of nineteenth-century Chinese architecture in Penang, and was commissioned by Cheong Fatt Tze, a Hakka businessman, in 1880. The elaborate halls of ceremony, bedrooms and libraries, separated by courtyards and gardens, have been restored, and tours of the interior give you a fascinating glimpse into the life of the wealthy Straits Chinese at the time.

Kek Lok Si Temple

Bedecked with flags, lanterns, statues and pagodas, the sprawling and exuberant **Kek Lok Si Temple** (daily 9am–6pm; free), also known as the "Temple of Supreme Bliss", to the west of the city, is the largest Buddhist temple complex in Malaysia. The "Pagoda of its Thousand Buddhas" is the most prominent feature of the compound, with its tower of simple Chinese saddle-shaped eaves and more elaborate Thai arched windows, topped by a golden Burmese stupa. It costs RM5 to climb the 193 steps to the top for a great view of Georgetown and the bay.

Visit in the evening and find Kek Lok brightly lit with multicoloured fairy lights and flashing neon. Getting there involves a thirty-minute bus ride west on bus #201, #203, #204 or #502; ask to be let off at Air Item for the temple. Buses leave around every half an hour after 8pm; the last bus is at about 9.30pm.

Penang Hill (Bukit Bendera)

A trip up to the highest point in Penang (833m) is very worthwhile for the commanding view of the island and the mainland beyond – particularly impressive at sunset. Asia's longest **funicular railway**, with the steepest tunnel track in the world, runs from the base of

TRANSPORT FROM BUTTERWORTH

The industrial town of **Butterworth** is the main port for the island of Penang and its capital, Georgetown, and a major transport hub. The **bus station**, port complex, taxi stand and **train station** are all next door to each other on the quayside.

By bus to: Bangkok, Thailand (2 daily; 18hr); Hat Yai, Thailand (2 daily; 5hr 30min); Ipoh (hourly; 3hr); Kota Bharu (2 daily; 6hr); Kuala Lumpur (every 30min; 7hr); Kuala Terengganu (2 daily; 8hr); Kuantan (3 daily; 12hr); Lumut (4 daily; 4hr); Malacca (daily; 6–10hr); Singapore (3 daily; 9hr); Surat Thani, Thailand (2 daily; 10hr 30min).

By ferry The passenger and car ferry service (6am–1am; 20min; RM2 return) runs three times an hour from the port complex to Pengkalan Weld in Georgetown.

By train to: Alor Setar (2 daily; 2hr); Bangkok, Thailand (daily; 23hr 30min); Hat Yai, Thailand (2 daily; 4hr 45min–6hr); Ipoh (daily; 5hr); Kuala Lumpur (daily; 10hr 25min).

the hill to the top from near the Kek Lok Si Temple (every 30min between 6.30am and 8am, every 15min between 8am–6pm, every 30min between 6pm and 10pm; until 11pm on weekends; RM30 return). There are several walking trails crisscrossing the hill, including the well-signposted 8km hike down to the Moon Gate at the Botanical Gardens. To get here, take bus #204 from Komtar. The last bus back to Georgetown leaves at 10.40pm.

6

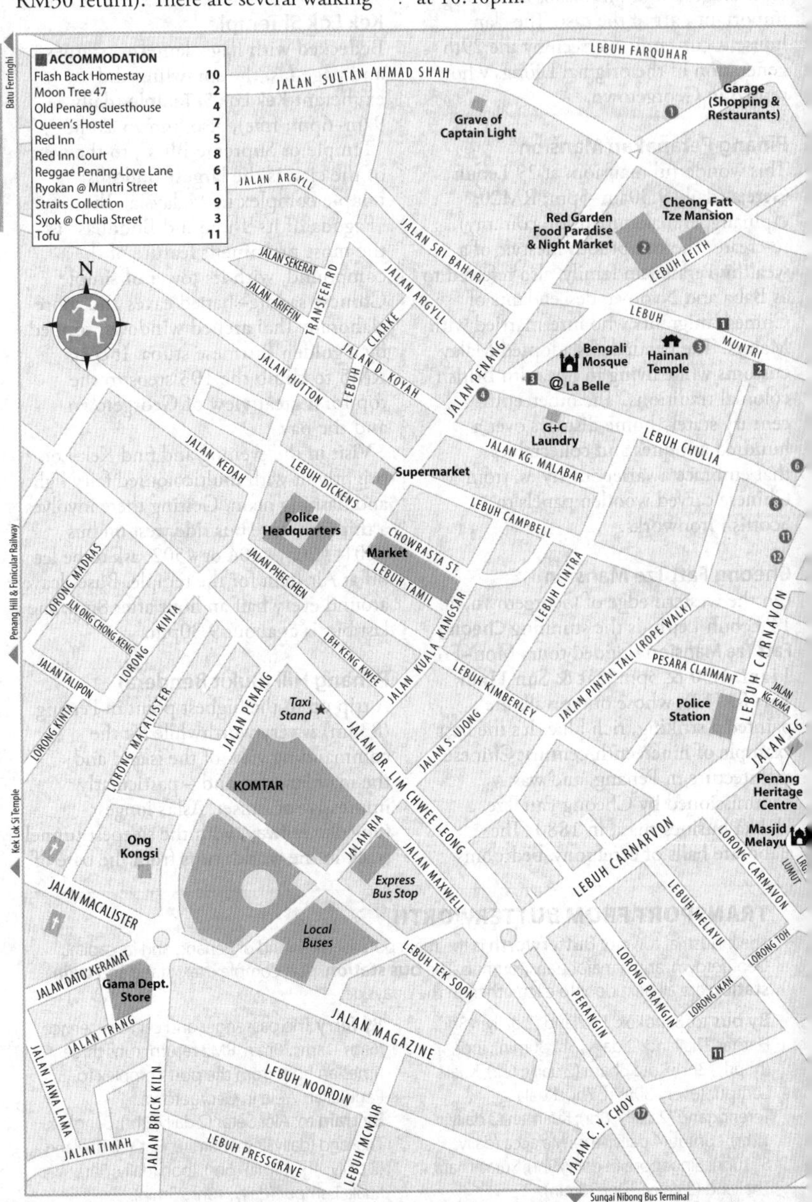

ARRIVAL AND DEPARTURE

Arriving at either the bus station, taxi stand or ferry terminal on Pengkalan Weld or nearby Swettenham Pier puts you at the eastern edge of Georgetown, a 15min walk from the hotels.

By plane Penang International Airport (ⓣ 04 643 0811) is on the southeastern tip of the island, reachable by buses #401, #305, #401E from the Pengkalan Weld or the KOMTAR complex (every 30min 6am–10pm; 40min), or else by taxi (30min; RM45). From Batu Ferringhi catch bus #102. The airport is served by Malaysia Airlines, AirAsia, Cathay Pacific, Firefly, Thai Airline and Singapore Airlines.

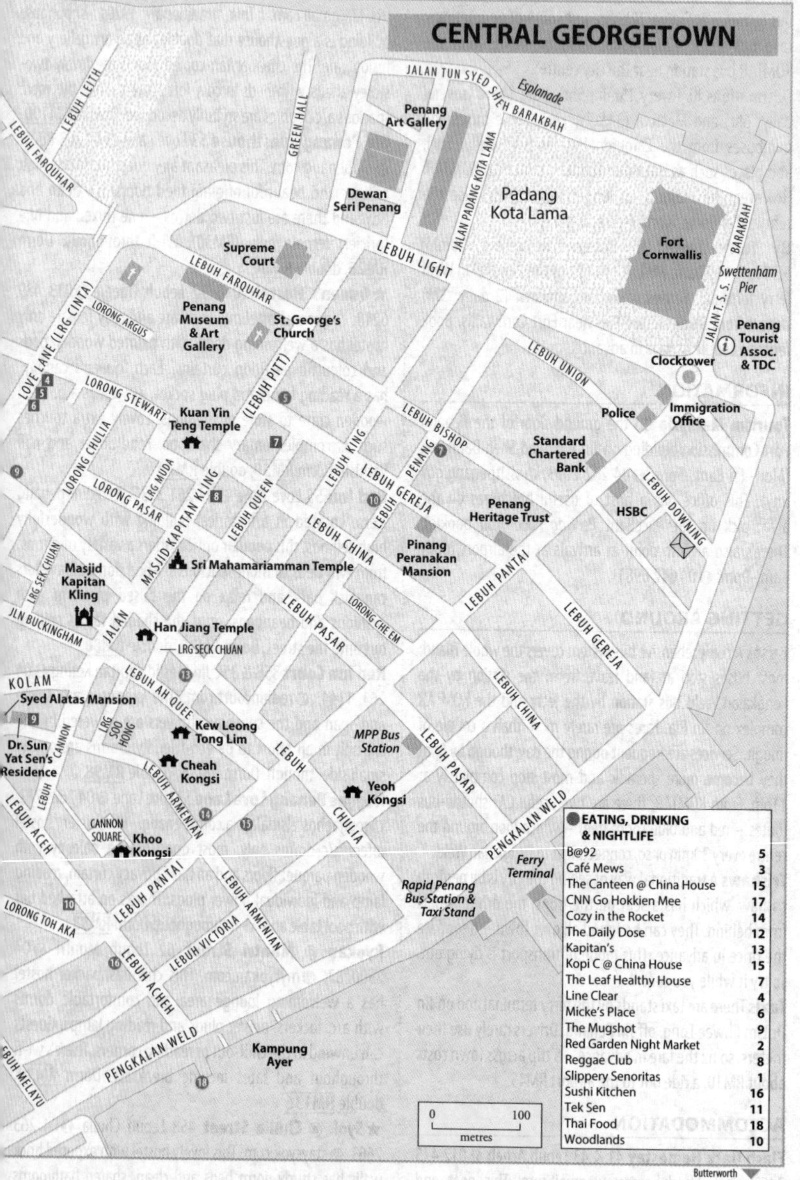

6

Destinations Bangkok, Thailand (3 daily; 1hr 40min); KL (14 daily; 45min); Langkawi (2 daily; 30min); Medan, Indonesia (daily; 20min); Phuket, Thailand (3 weekly; 30min); Singapore (4 daily; 1hr 10min).

By bus Although some buses to destinations on the Peninsula depart from Pengkalan Weld in Georgetown, most long-distance buses depart from the long-distance bus terminal at Sungai Nibong, just south of Georgetown; take bus #303, #305, #306, #401 or #401E from the KOMTAR bus station near the city centre.

Destinations KL (every 15min; 5hr), Kota Bharu (several daily; 6hr) and Malacca (3 daily; 7hr). Some buses and minibuses from the Cameron Highlands (5 daily; 5hr), and places such as Hat Yai in Thailand stop near KOMTAR. However, the majority of long-distance buses use the terminal at Butterworth (see box, p.439).

By ferry Ferries to Butterworth (every 20min; 5.30am–11.30am; RM1.40) run from the Pengkalan Weld ferry terminal. Ferries to Pulau Langkawi (2 daily; 3hr) depart from Swettenham Pier near Fort Cornwallis. Book ferries a couple of days in advance.

INFORMATION

Tourism Malaysia On the ground floor of the Penang Port Commission building on Jln Tun Syed Sheh Barakbah (Mon–Fri 8am–5pm; ⓣ04 262 2093, ⓦvisitpenang.gov.my). This office has a host of useful brochures on the area; pick up the excellent *Penang Food Trail* booklet. There's also an info point at arrivals at the airport (daily 8am–9pm; ⓣ04 642 6981).

GETTING AROUND

Buses A comprehensive bus system covers the whole island; most buses stop at (and leave from) the station by the Pengkalan Weld bus station by the jetty and the KOMTAR complex on Jln Ria. Fares are rarely more than a couple of ringgit. Services are frequent during the day, though by 8pm they become more sporadic and most stop completely at 11pm. From KOMTAR, there are two useful CAT shuttle-bus routes – red and blue (both free) – which loop around the centre every 30min or so, connecting it to Pengkalan Weld.

Trishaws A traditional way of seeing the city is by pedicab trishaw, which has a seat on the front; the driver pedals from behind. They can be found all over town – negotiate the price in advance. This mode of transport is dying out, so try it while you can.

Taxis There are taxi stands by the ferry terminal and on Jln Dr Lim Chwee Long, off Jln Penang. Drivers rarely use their meters, so fix the fare in advance – a trip across town costs about RM10, a ride out to the airport RM45.

ACCOMMODATION

Flash Back Homestay 41 & 43 Lebuh Acheh ⓣ012 475 2453, ⓔflashback.homestay@gmail.com. This neat and simple hostel, managed by friendly and accommodating staff, offers private singles, two-, three- and four-bed rooms. There's a small lounge area with cable TV and DVDs, as well as decent showers. The downside is that rooms are a bit of a squeeze and do not have a fully partitioned ceiling, which means guests can overhear one another. Double RM88

Moon Tree 47 47 Muntri St ⓣ04 264 4021, ⓔmoontree47@gmail.com. This traditional 1920s shophouse building is a guesthouse that doubles as an art gallery and fusion café. The cheaper fan-cooled rooms are lovely two-storey affairs with beds in cosy loft spaces, while the more spacious a/c doubles are stylishly decorated. Double RM100

Old Penang Guesthouse 53 Love Lane ⓣ04 263 8805, ⓦoldpenang.com. This pleasant airy guesthouse has high ceilings and beautiful original tiled floors. It's clean and tidy, and there are just two dorms – one mixed and one (pricier) female only (RM30). Wi-fi throughout. Dorm RM26, double RM80

★**Queen's Hostel** 20 & 22 Lebuh Queen ⓣ013 489 6218, ⓦqueenshostel.my. This cute and cosy female only hostel has a welcoming dorm with painted wooden pods and colourful partition curtains. Each "queen's canopy" has a reading lamp and plug socket, as well as a painted wooden crate to store possessions. Lovely extra touches such as complementary shampoo, conditioner and nail varnish. Dorm RM59, double RM99

Red Inn 55 Love Lane ⓣ04 261 3931, ⓦredinnpenang.com. Located in a historical building with wonderfully high ceilings, this popular option offers a variety of dorms, from two beds to more spacious six-bed dorms. Travellers can kick back and relax on the raised platform with cushions and beanbags, or at the shaded tables spilling out onto the street. Dorm RM30, double RM80

Red Inn Court 35B & 35C Jln Mesjid Kapitan Keling ⓣ04 261 1144, ⓦredinncourt.com. The premises are spick-and-span and the spa-type showers are powered by the a/c unit in an effort to be eco-friendly. Dorms are on the small side, though. Dorm RM35, double RM98

Reggae Penang Love Lane 57 Love Lane ⓣ04 262 6772, ⓦreggaehostelsmalaysia.com/penang. KL's sister hostel offers a/c dorms only; most open onto a balcony with wooden parquet floors and all have privacy curtain, reading lamp and individual power plugs. There's an attached bar with pool table and wi-fi throughout. Dorm RM33

Ryokan @ Muntri Street 62 Lebuh Muntri ⓣ04 2500287, ⓦmyryokan.com. This chic flashpacker hostel has a welcoming lounge area and comfortable dorms with a/c, lockers, power plugs and reading lamps. Guests can unwind in the chill-out or reading corners. There's wi-fi throughout and rates include breakfast. Dorm RM30, double RM136

★**Syok @ Chulia Street** 458 Lebuh Chulia ⓣ04 263 2663, ⓦstaysyok.com. This lovely hostel with exposed brick walls has sturdy dorm beds and clean, shared bathrooms

★TREAT YOURSELF

Straits Collection Armenian Street Ⓣ04 263 7299, Ⓦstraitscollection.com.my. Make yourself at home at one of these wonderful apartments located in pastel-coloured colonial buildings along Armenian Street. They have all been fully renovated to reflect the town's historical past and are equipped with fridges, TVs, wi-fi, rain showers and a/c. Some apartments can sleep up to five. **RM450**

with pretty painted wooden doors. There's a pleasant a/c lounge area with beanbags, table footie and DVDs, as well as a sunny terrace with outdoor seating. Guests are encouraged to disclose their deepest darkest secrets on the "confession wall". Dorm **RM58**, double **RM110**

★**Tofu** 484 Lebuh Pantai Ⓣ016 486 1850, Ⓦtofuhostel .wix.com/tofucafebedsnbikes. The cosy "super single" (RM55) and "double bed" (RM99; sleeps two) cubicles – all with privacy curtain, reading lamp, towel rail and plug socket – look just like soft squares of tofu. The welcoming eco-friendly owners encourage recycling and rent out bikes for the day. There's also a wonderful café serving great scones and home-made muffins. Breakfast included. Mixed dorm **RM55**, female only dorm **RM59**

EATING

Penang is all about hawker food. There are hawker stalls on most street corners, serving cheap and tasty dishes including the local favourite, *Penang laksa* – noodles in thick fish soup garnished with vegetables, pineapple and *belacan* (shrimp paste). There's a choice of hawker stalls on Lebuh Kimberley and Lebuh Cintra, and a fantastic food court on Lebuh Leith.

Café Mews 77 Lebuh Muntri. A pleasant escape from the city's stifling heat, this café has indoor seating as well as a secluded outdoor area. The menu mainly consists of local dishes (try the *nyonya laksa lemak*; coconut and fish based soup RM18). Live music performances on Sat at 9pm, from jazz to R&B. Daily 8am–11pm.

CNN Go Hokkien Mee Lebuh Pantai at Jln Perangin. This truly local hawker joint seems to have adopted this name following a CNN report on its much sought-after *hokkien mee*, shrimp noodles (RM3.50) – make sure you get here early. Tues–Sun 7am–1pm.

Cozy in the Rocket 262 & 264 Lebuh Pantai. This arty café has an eclectic choice of furniture and a pleasant outdoor garden with little potted plants. The changing menu is scribbled on the board; breakfasts (RM15), great coffees (RM6) and pasta dishes (RM23). Tues–Sun 10am–5pm.

The Daily Dose 80 Lebuh Carnarvon. The New Mexican owner, artist and chef at this chilled café with laidback jazzy tunes rustles up great Mexican dishes using healthy fresh ingredients. The changing menu also embraces great takes on French, Spanish and Vietnamese cuisines. Mains RM20. Daily 10am–7pm.

Kapitan's 93 Lebuh Chulia. This Penang institution is open virtually all night, just in case you get a post-midnight craving for tandoori chicken, claypot biryani or curry. Perpetually popular. Mains RM8. Daily 7.30am–4am.

Kopi C @ China House 153 & 155 Lebuh Pantai. Housed within the China House arts space, this pleasant café is a sweet tooth's delight, harbouring recipes to over 100 delectable cakes, all lovingly prepared by the pastry chefs. The bread (RM10) is home-made too, and there's all-day breakfast (from RM14) as well as international dishes with fusion and Middle Eastern flavours. Daily 9am–midnight, Fri & Sat until 1am.

The Leaf Healthy House 5 Lebuh Penang. Laidback Chinese veggie café perfect for a healthy pit stop as you explore town; there are *nyonya* dishes, noodles, high-fibre rice and spaghetti (RM5.90), as well as exceptional fresh juices. Weekdays there's a set lunch menu for only RM6.90. Mon–Fri 11.30am–2.30pm & 5.30–8.45pm, Sat 11.30am–8.45pm.

★**Line Clear** Lebuh Chulia at Jln Penang. Hands down one of Georgetown's best *nasi kandar* (rice with curry) at this no-frills hawker stall where an exceptionally tasty meal will set you back no more than RM10. Daily 24hr.

Micke's Place 94 Love Lane. Travellers scribble their musings all over the walls of this itty-bitty café serving local and Western dishes, from pancakes (RM9) to pastas (RM13). Mon–Sat 4–11pm.

★**The Mugshot** 302 Lebuh Chulia. This friendly café offers freshly made yoghurt served in cute glass jars with imaginative toppings, from kiwi and honey to walnuts and raisins, and tasty home-made bagels prepared in the little wood-fired oven. There's a great bakery attached, too, and free wi-fi. Daily 8am–9pm.

Red Garden Night Market 20 Lebuh Leith. Penangites' favourite food court boasts an array of scrumptious dishes: grilled seafood, claypot noodles, *hokkien mee* (prawn noodles), Indian curries and Thai food. Mains from RM6.

Sushi Kitchen 12 Gat Lebuh Acheh. The vegan dishes at this small Japanese restaurant are served at low tables where barefooted customers sit on tatami mats. All the ingredients are fresh, with no artificial colouring, preservatives or MSG. Sushi (RM8.80), udon noodles (RM7.80) and plenty more on offer. Wed–Fri 11.30am–9.30pm, Sat & Sun 11.30am–2.30pm & 6–10pm.

Tek Sen 18–20 Lebuh Carnarvon. This hugely popular place gets packed at lunch and dinner with hungry customers who flock here for the sought-after Chinese grub. Try the double-roasted pork (RM14); the home-made tofu (RM10) also goes down a treat. Wed–Mon noon–2.30pm & 6–9pm.

6

Thai Food 97A Tan Jetty Weld Quay. A short walk along Tan Jetty is this hidden place that attracts plenty of custom for its great Thai dishes (mains from RM20). Daily 11am–2.30pm & 5–10pm; closed 1st & 3rd Tues of the month.

Woodlands 60 Lebuh Penang. This simple vegetarian restaurant fills up rapidly at mealtimes, attracting plenty of custom for its "tongue tickling dishes", as the menu clearly states. Try the *chenna batura*, large bread served with chickpea stew (RM4.40), or the *appam* (available Fri–Sun only; RM1.20), a bowl-shaped salty bread with curried vegetables and coconut milk. Daily 8.30am–10pm.

DRINKING AND NIGHTLIFE

Most of Georgetown's bars are comfortable places to hang out, but when the fleet arrives, a good many turn into rowdy meat markets, so choose carefully. Usual opening hours are 6pm–2am. Upper Jln Penang is lined with buzzing night venues. The cover charge for clubs is around RM25.

B@92 92 Lebuh Gereja. This laidback bar serves great food, nibbles and drinks – the owners make you feel right at home and are keen to share stories over an ice-cold beer or two. Daily 12.30am–1am.

The Canteen @ China House 153 & 155 Lebuh Pantai. Enjoy a cocktail (RM22) or two at this artsy bar and performance venue hosting great live music bands, from jazz to folk, on Fri, Sat & Sun at 9.30pm. Daily 6pm–midnight, Fri & Sat until 1am.

Reggae Club 483 Lebuh Chulia. This reggae venue decked out in bright Rastafarian colours and Bob Marley memorabilia attracts plenty of backpackers from nearby hostels who come here to sway to reggae beats with a chilled beer in hand. Daily 6pm–3am.

Slippery Senoritas 2 Jln Penang. It may sound like a sleazy strip club, but it's actually one of Georgetown's most popular venues, attracting young Penangites from the island over for the salsa club within, as well as live music and house and R&B tracks that keep the dance floor packed until the wee hours. On weekends, entry is RM25 before midnight, RM35 thereafter. Daily 5pm–3am.

DIRECTORY

Banks and exchange Major banks (Mon–Fri 10am–3pm, Sat 9.30–11.30am) with ATMs are along Lebuh Pantai. Licensed moneychangers are on Lebuh Pantai, Lebuh Chulia and Jln Kapitan Kling (daily 8.30am–6pm).

Hospital Penang General Hospital, Jln Residensi (T 04 222 5333).

Immigration office Pejabat Imigresen, Lebuh Pantai at Lebuh Light (Mon–Fri 8am–5pm; T 04 250 3413).

Internet La Belle, 440B Lebuh Chulia (daily 9am–11pm; RM3/hr).

Laundry G&C Laundry, 461 Lebuh Chulia (Mon–Sat 9am–8pm; RM5/kg).

Pharmacy There are several pharmacies along Jln Penang, as well as in the KOMTAR complex.

Police station The tourist police is at Lebuh Dickens, just off Jln Penang (T 04 899 3222).

Post office The GPO is on Lebuh Downing (Mon–Fri 8.30am–5.30pm, Sat 8.30am–1pm).

Batu Ferringhi

BATU FERRINGHI, a 45-minute bus ride west of Georgetown on bus #101, is a spread-out one-street village largely populated by flash resorts, but with a decent enough beach and several guesthouses. The road runs more or less straight along the coast for 3km, with all the hotels and restaurants lined up side by side.

Nearby is the peaceful **Tropical Spice Garden** (daily 9am–6pm; RM15), with a range of spices growing among five hundred species of tropical flora and fauna. A few kilometres west is a **batik factory** (daily 9am–5.30pm; free), where you can watch Malaysian-style batik being made and buy the finished product. One kilometre further up the road is the **Butterfly Farm** (daily 9am–6pm; last entry at 5pm; RM27), which boasts over a hundred species of tropical butterflies, with up to 7000 fluttering around at any one time. There are also resident reptiles and amphibians, and there are daily talks and entertaining shows on the life of butterflies and other insects.

TRAVEL TO THAILAND

There are regular **minibus services** to Thailand, including Bangkok (3 daily; 18hr), Hat Yai (4 daily; 4hr), Krabi (3 daily; 8hr), Koh Lanta (daily; 8hr), Koh Phi Phi (daily; 11hr), Koh Li Pe (daily; 11hr), Koh Samui (3 daily; 12hr), Kho Phangan (3 daily; 16hr), Koh Tao (3 daily; 18hr), Phuket (2 daily; 13hr), Surathani (3 daily; 9hr) and Trang (3 daily; 6hr). There's likely to be a change of vehicle in Hat Yai while you go through the immigration procedures, sometimes with a fair amount of waiting around, but booking it all as one trip from Penang does at least save you the hassle of having to organize the different legs of the journey yourself.

ACCOMMODATION AND EATING

The budget guesthouses face the beach and are all on the same street.

Ali's ⓣ 04 881 1316. A welcoming guesthouse with simple rooms set over two floors that open on to a leafy courtyard. Some have private bath and there's a shaded lounge area perfect for a short afternoon kip. Double **RM80**

Baba Guesthouse ⓣ 04 881 1686, ⓔ babaguesthouse2000@yahoo.com. Friendly, budget family-run guesthouse with clean rooms and a welcoming owner who can organize onward domestic travel, as well as buses to Thailand and Singapore. Double **RM45**

Bora Bora This laidback beachside bar with fairy lights and a jungle-like ambience is a popular spot to enjoy a sundowner. There's Western food too, and beach boys lighten up the scene with fire shows. Mains RM15.90, beer RM10. Mon–Fri noon–1am, Sat & Sun noon–3am.

PULAU LANGKAWI

Situated 30km off the coast at the very northwestern tip of the Peninsula is a cluster of 104 tropical islands, the largest of which is **PULAU LANGKAWI**, a resort island popular with travellers and locals alike. Here it's easy to while away a good few days, snorkelling, beach-hopping, taking trips to the mangrove areas and exploring the waters around the island by boat. The name Langkawi combines the Malay words *helang* (eagle) and *kawi* (strong) – hence the eagle is the symbol for the island. Langkawi's principal town is **Kuah**, on the southeastern side of the island, but the main tourist developments have been on the west of the island, at **Pantai Tengah** and **Pantai Cenang**.

Langkawi is a large island – almost 500 square kilometres – and to explore it properly you'll need to rent a car or scooter. There is basically one circular road around the island, with the other main road running north and south along with some minor roads branching off from it.

Kuah

Located in the southeastern corner of the island, **Kuah** is the largest town on Langkawi and has a ferry terminal, hotels and duty-free shopping complexes. You'll be passing through here if taking a boat to Penang or Thailand.

Pantai Tengah and Pantai Cenang

A clearly signed junction 18km west from Kuah points you to the popular beaches of **Pantai Cenang** and **Pantai Tengah**. Within walking distance of each other, these two main strips are the best places for cheap accommodation. Pantai Cenang has numerous bars and restaurants with Malaysia's largest aquarium, the soulless concrete **Underwater World** (daily 10am–6pm; RM38), lying about half way down.

The bay itself forms a large sweep of wide, white beach with crisp, sugary sand, and is hugely popular with travellers and revellers. Plenty of places offer **watersports** such as jet skiing (RM120 per 30min), waterskiing (RM120 per 15min) and parasailing (RM100). **Boat trips** are also easy to arrange (see box, p.448).

Gunung Machinchang

Head north along the coast past the airport and you'll eventually reach **Mount Machinchang**, the vertiginous hilly jungle (708m high at its peak) scaled by the **Langkawi Cable Car** (daily 10am–7pm, Wed from noon; 15min; RM30) from the touristy shopping complex below. It is allegedly the steepest in the world, and the journey up is pretty spectacular, with the cable cars wobbling up a sheer cliff at an angle of 42 degrees. From the Skybridge and the two viewing stations at the top you can see the entirety of the island, as well as some Thai islands. If it's windy, the cable cars won't run.

Telaga Tujuh (Seven Wells)

Shortly before the turn-off for the cable car, a side road leads to **Seven Wells**, a series of natural rock pools connected by a stream gliding over smooth rock, making natural water slides – great, refreshing fun. It's reached via a ten-minute climb up a long staircase leading up from the car park; there is also a signposted 2.5km trail that runs up to the top of Gunung Machinchang, from which you can descend by cable car.

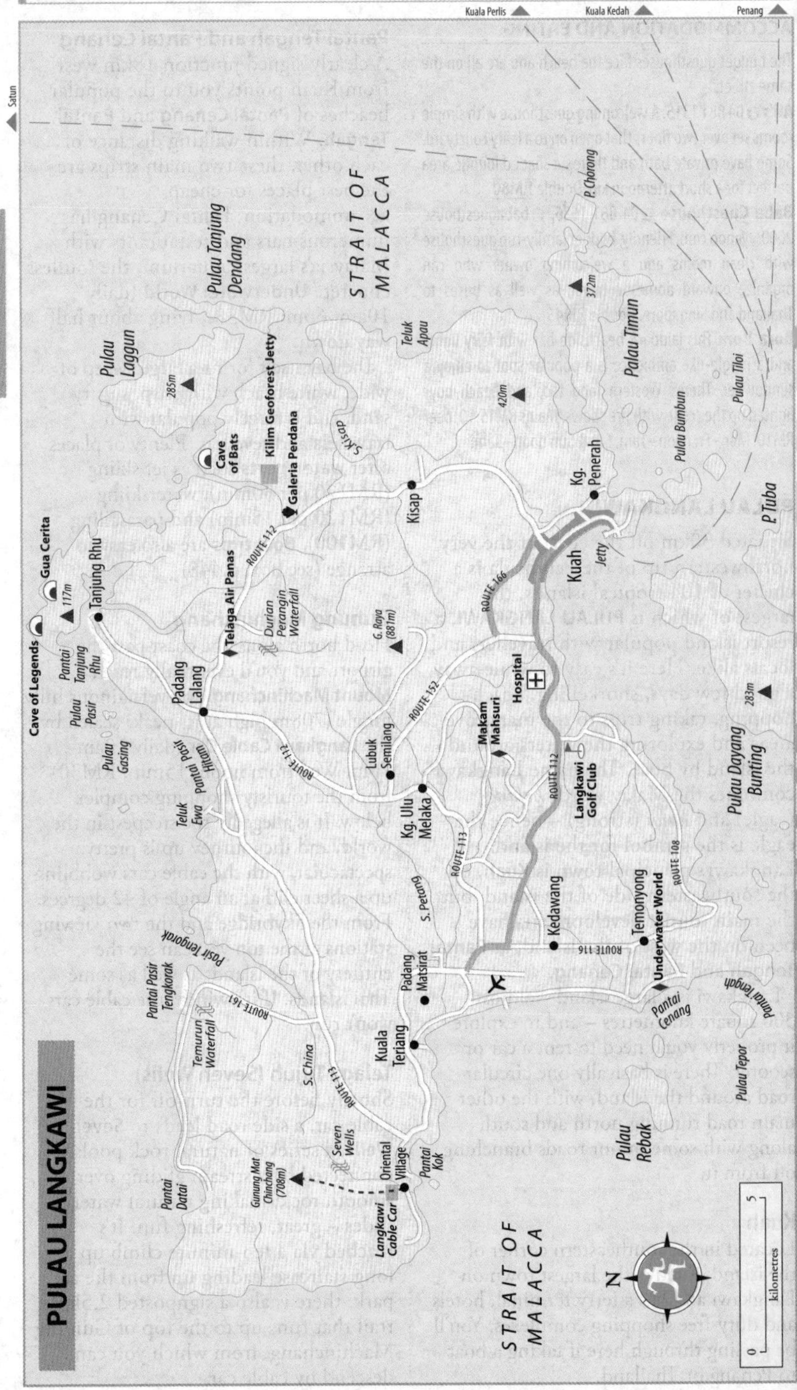

6

Satun
Kuala Perlis
Kuala Kedah
Penang
PULAU LANGKAWI
STRAIT OF MALACCA
STRAIT OF MALACCA
Pulau Laggun
285m
Pulau Tanjung Dendang
P. Chorong
Teluk Apau
372m
420m
Pulau Timun
Cave of Bats
Kilim Geoforest Jetty
Galeria Perdana
S. Kisap
Kisap
Kg. Penerah
Pulau Bumbun
Pulau Tiloi
P. Tuba
Gua Cerita
117m
Tanjung Rhu
Telaga Air Panas
ROUTE 112
Durian Perangin Waterfall
Kuah
Jetty
ROUTE 166
Cave of Legends
Pantai Tanjung Rhu
Pulau Pasir
Pulau Gasing
Padang Lalang
G. Raya (881m)
Hospital
283m
Pantai Pasir Hitam
Teluk Ewa
Lubuk Semilang
ROUTE 152
Makam Mahsuri
Langkawi Golf Club
Pulau Dayang Bunting
Kg. Ulu Melaka
ROUTE 113
Kedawang
ROUTE 108
Pasir Tengkorak
Pantai Pasir Tengkorak
S. Petang
Padang Matsirat
ROUTE 116
Temonyong
Underwater World
Temurun Waterfall
ROUTE 161
Pantai Cenang
Pantai Tengah
Kuala Teriang
S. China
Pulau Tepor
Seven Wells
Pulau Rebak
Pantai Datai
Gunung Mat Chinchang (708m)
Oriental Village
Langkawi Cable Car
Pantai Kok
N
0
5
kilometres

BEWARE THE JELLYFISH!

In **jellyfish season** (Feb and March) it's advised not to go swimming, as the **deadly box jellyfish**, responsible for at least three deaths since the 1990s, has been sighted in Langkawi waters, particularly near the mangroves. If you do go for a dip, you're likely to experience a sort of electric shock sensation when you're in the water, which can be a little uncomfortable while swimming. If you notice that you have a visible or particularly painful sting, a splash of vinegar or alcohol (NOT fresh water!) should help alleviate it.

The beaches

The north coast has several attractive **beaches**. Langkawi's loveliest, cleanest beach at **Datai**, reachable by signposted turn-off from Route 113, is accessible only to hotel guests, but on the way you pass a small crescent of white sand with some picnic tables, popular with locals and holidaying Russians, just before the path to the **Temurun waterfall** on the opposite side of the road. With its gorgeous white sand and stunning aquamarine water, Langkawi's northernmost beach – **Tanjung Rhu** – is another attractive option, though it lacks any shade. Though it's known for its sunsets, due to its location on the west side of the island, the views from Pantai Cenang are actually almost as good.

Gunung Raya

Route 112, which cuts across the middle of the island from Tanjung Rhu to the airport and beyond, has a turn-off to the east halfway along for **Gunung Raya** (881m), Langkawi's tallest mountain. A long, winding and somewhat potholed road leads up to the summit, from where you can enjoy all-encompassing views of the island and beyond.

Galeria Perdana

If you take Route 112 between Padang Lalang and Kuah, you will pass the vastly entertaining **Galeria Perdana** (daily 8.30am–5.30pm; RM15), a private museum dedicated to the splendid gifts that former Malay prime minister, Dr Mohathir Mohammed, received from various heads of state.

ARRIVAL AND DEPARTURE

By plane The airport is 6km north of Pantai Cenang, to which a taxi will cost RM36 from the prepaid taxi counter in the airport.

Destinations Kuala Lumpur (hourly; 1hr); Singapore (4 weekly; 2hr); Penang (2 daily; 20min).

By boat Destinations from the Kuah jetty (reachable by taxi only; RM25): Kuala Perlis (hourly; 1hr 15min); Kuala Kedah (hourly; 1hr 45min); Penang (2 daily; 3hr); Satun, Thailand (4 daily; 1hr 15min). In high season (Oct–April) there are also boats to Kho Lipe, Thailand (2 daily; 45min), leaving from Telaga Harbour, on the western coast of the island.

INFORMATION

Tourist information There is an information point at the airport (daily 7am–11pm; ⓣ 04 955 1311).

GETTING AROUND

Car and motorbike rental Many of the chalets and motels offer motorbike and scooter rental (from RM30/day) – the cheapest and most convenient way to explore the island. Take a map, water and plenty of sunscreen. Renting a car will set you back about RM80/day, plus fuel.

Taxis A journey to Pantai Cenang from both the Kuah jetty and from the airport will cost you around RM25/person; from Pantai Cenang to Tanjung Rhu it costs around RM60.

ACCOMMODATION

PANTAI TENGAH

★**Pondok Keladi** Lot 1011, Kg. Padang Putih ⓣ 04 955 1648, ⓦ pondok-keladi.com. This wonderful guesthouse has six neat and pleasant a/c, en-suite rooms decked out in Malay and Indonesian furnishings and opening onto the

★TREAT YOURSELF

Bon Ton Resort Pantai Cenang ⓣ 04 955 3643, ⓦ bontonresort.com. The lush green paddy fields that surround *Bon Ton*, a five-minute drive from Cenang, create the perfect location if you're looking for tranquillity and a little luxury. The resort consists of eight luxurious Malay stilt houses surrounding a pool and decorated with traditional craftwork (from RM700). The *Nam restaurant* here serves a tantalizing range of Asian and Western fusion dishes (mains around RM40).

well-manicured garden. There's a lovely chill-out area with kitchenette and plenty of complimentary food, from noodles to eggs. The owner also rents out a fully equipped house sleeping five close to the beach (RM150). Double **RM140**

Zackry Guest House 735 Jln Teluk Baru. Three dogs plod the premises of this family-run place, which has a slightly grubby feel; there's a laidback family vibe, with plenty of day-trips organized with other travellers, frequent communal meals and fun drinking games. A good option for solo travellers. Double **RM45**

6

PANTAI CENANG

Gecko Guesthouse ⓣ019 428 3801, ⓔrebeccafiott@hotmail.com. This verdant guesthouse has a series of rooms set around a leafy communal area. There's a bar with cheap drinks that stays open until midnight, and a café serving breakfast too. Double **RM40**

Rainbow Lodge Kampung Haji Maidin ⓣ04 955 8103, ⓦrainbowlangkawi.com. As the name suggests, this large place with over fifty rooms is decked out in a myriad of bright colours; there are 15 fully furnished houses each sleeping four, as well as a selection of doubles and a large 20-bed dorm by the communal area with pool table and café. Dorm **RM25**, double **RM45**

Rumours ⓣ04 955 2585, ⓔwans.rumoursguesthouse@gmail.com. Set back off the main road, opposite Underwater World, friendly *Rumours* has an open-fronted communal area with a pool table that is a great place to mingle. Clean, spacious rooms are surrounded by a lovely garden, and there's even a tiny fish spa for the ladies, and wi-fi, too. Dorm **RM25**, double **Rm70**

Sweet Inn Lot 792, Mukim Kedawang ⓣ04 955 8864, ⓦsweetinns.net. Off the main road, near *Gecko Guesthouse*, this motel-like setup in a salmon pink concrete block offers clean, tiled rooms and an inclusive buffet breakfast. Double **RM90**

White Lodge Mukim Kedawang ⓣ04 955 3072, ⓦwhitelodgechalet.com. On the southern end of Cenang, just after *Red Tomato*, this is undoubtedly one of the best budget options on the island. The spotless tiled rooms give onto a pristine garden lit up at night by spotlights. All are spacious and have fridge, a/c, TV and private bath. Double **RM148**

EATING AND DRINKING

PANTAI TENGAH

★ **La Chocolatine** On the northern end of Tengah. All ingredients are imported from France at this French-run café and bakery serving delectable home-baked pastries (RM8), from flaky croissants to warm *pain au chocolat*. There's even goat's cheese salad (RM28) and crêpes (RM10) for a light lunch. Daily 8.30am–7pm.

Sagar Closer to the northern end of the beach, this airy Indian restaurant has attentive service and a range of tasty curries (mains from RM20). Daily noon–4pm & 6–11pm; closed Mon lunchtime.

Sunba On the northern end of Tengah. Located in a large complex, this bar with wooden interiors is set out to resemble a dwelling in a traditional Malay village. There's an in-house band as well as DJs spinning retro tracks from the '60s to '80s. You can belt your heart out at the karaoke rooms within the same building, or try your hand at snooker. Daily 9pm–2am.

PANTAI CENANG

There are a few places along the beach at Pantai Cenang that are great for a sundowner or after-dinner cocktails. The area's only club is further south at Pantai Tengah.

Brasserie By *Best Star Resort*. This stylish Italian-owned place is a popular spot for a sundowner (happy hour daily 4–6pm). The Mediterranean cuisine includes grilled meats and fish, and there's a light lunch menu featuring pastas, salads and sandwiches. Mains from RM22. Daily noon–11pm.

Champor Champor By *Best Star Resort*. Wooden masks, potted plants, Thai mats and all manner of memorabilia

LANGKAWI TOURS

The most popular activities on Langkawi are **speedboat trips** to the nearby islands, **diving and snorkelling trips** and **mangrove tours** on the north coast. Most guesthouses can arrange pick-up.

A whole plethora of companies offer half-day speedboat island-hopping tours (RM45), which usually consist of landing on one of the nearby islands for a swim in the freshwater lake, and a stop to feed the sea eagles – not a particularly environmentally sound practice as it can result in food poisoning and makes the birds dependent on handouts.

Dev's Adventure Tours ⓦlangkawi-nature.com. Highly recommended operator leading mangrove kayaking tours (RM220), jungle treks (RM120), bird-watching (RM200) and nature cycling tours (RM120) around the island.

East Marine ⓣ04 966 3966, ⓦeastmarine.com.my. Specializes in diving and snorkelling ventures to Pulau Payar, halfway between Langkawi and Penang; day-trips depart at 9.30am, returning around 4pm; snorkelling RM250, diving RM350.

from as far away as Africa decorate this welcoming restaurant. The calming sounds of the water fountain and ethnic music add to the therapeutic atmosphere. Creative dishes include *bumbu bali* duck with coriander, turmeric and chilli (RM39). Mon–Sat 6–11.30pm.

Little Lylia's Halfway down the beach. This welcoming place with rustic candlelit tables is a great place for a sundowner – try the Langkawi sunset (mango juice and red wine on ice; RM12) as you nibble on chicken satay (RM10). They also offer great fish and seafood barbecues, and there's live music nightly at 9pm. Daily 10am–3am.

Rafii's Halfway down the beach. Laidback beachside restaurant with a bar and tables spilling onto the sand. It offers great Western and Malay dishes (mains RM15). Thurs–Tues noon–midnight.

★ **Red Tomato** Opposite *McDonald's*. This hugely popular German-owned place attracts expats and travellers alike for generous, tasty dishes of Western grub such as leafy salads, thin-crust pizzas, saucy pastas and wonderful desserts. Coeliacs will rejoice too – all the above also come gluten free. Mains from RM20. Daily 9am–11pm.

Yellow Café Towards the south end of Cenang, commanding a great spot on the beach, this French-owned restaurant offers great steaks, kebabs, salads and seafood barbecue. The cocktails (RM20) complement the sunset very nicely indeed and there are occasional live bands. Mains from RM20. Tues–Sun noon–1am.

DIRECTORY

Banks Langkawi's banks are on three parallel streets behind the MAYA shopping complex in Kuah. In Pantai Cenang there is a Maybank with ATM at Cenang Mall; there's also a Maybank ATM at Underwater World and a couple of ATMs and moneychangers at the airport.

Hospital The Langkawi District Hospital is at Jln Bukit Teguh (☎ 04 966 3333).

Laundry On the northern end of Pantai Tengah. Two Seasons Laundry (daily 9am–7pm; RM4.50/kg).

Post office The GPO is at Jln Kisap in Kuah town; there's also a branch at Padang Matsirat near the airport (daily except Fri 8am–5pm).

The interior

Banjaran Titiwangsa (Main Range) forms the western boundary of the interior; to its east is an H-shaped range of steep, sandstone mountains and luxuriant valleys where small towns and villages nestle. The rivers that flow from these mountains – Pahang, Tembeling, Lebir, Nenggiri and Galas – provide the northern interior's indigenous peoples, the Negritos and Senoi, with their main means of transport. Visitors, too, can travel by boat to perhaps the most stunning of all Peninsular Malaysia's delights, **Taman Negara National Park**, with its numerous jungle trails. And what better way to get from the coasts to these wilderness places than by the **Jungle Railway**, which chugs leisurely through the lush green interior to **Kota Bharu** on the northwest coast.

THE JUNGLE RAILWAY

The **Jungle Railway** winds through the valleys and round the sandstone hills from Mentakab in southern Pahang to Kota Bharu, 500km to the northeast. It also offers useful stops at Jerantut and Kuala Tembeling, both access points for Taman Negara. The line was completed in 1931 and runs at a snail's pace along valley floors where trees and plants almost envelop the track.

It's a great way to encounter rural life, and for the Malays, Tamils and Orang Asli who live in these remote areas, the railway is the only alternative to walking. Many people do this trip from south to north, but going in the opposite direction, from north to south, gives you many more hours of daylight in the jungle. Since the trains (even the express ones) tend to be slow, it's best to take a bus from KL to Jerantut, and then take the 2pm train from there to Kota Bharu; if travelling from Kota Bharu, take the 6.30am train south, scheduled to arrive in Jerantut at 1.30pm. Check ⓦktmb.com.my for updated schedules.

JERANTUT

JERANTUT, a small grid of streets surrounded by jungle, with only one major street, Jalan Besar, is the gateway to Taman Negara National Park. It also has useful transport links to the Perhentian Islands, Kota Bharu and Kuantan.

ARRIVAL AND DEPARTURE

By bus The bus station is located along Jln Diwangsa, in the town centre and a couple of blocks south of the main Jln Besar.

6

6

Local buses Take a local bus towards Kuala Lipis (daily 6am, 10.30am & 3.30pm; 40min; RM5) and ask the driver to let you off at the Tembeling jetty if you want to approach Taman Negara by river, or else all the way to Kuala Tahan, the village opposite the park headquarters (daily 8am & 1pm; 2hr; RM7), if you prefer to get there quicker. Alternatively, note that both *NKS Hotel & Travel* and *Greenleaf Travellers Inn* offer a convenient minibus service both to the jetty (daily 8.30am & 1.30pm; 30min; RM5) and the village itself (daily 6.30am, 8.30am & 4.30pm; 1hr; RM25).

Long-distance buses Buses to Kuala Lumpur (hourly; 3hr), Kuantan (3 daily; 3hr 30min), Ipoh (every other day; 6hr 30min), Butterworth (every other day; 10hr) and Kuala Perlis (every other day; 12hr 30min) leave from Jengka Bus Station, a 30min taxi ride from Jerantut. *NKS Hotel & Travel* arranges transport to the Perhentian Islands (9hr), the Cameron Highlands (3hr 30min), Kota Bharu (9hr), Penang (6hr 30min), and Kuala Lumpur (2hr 30min) according to demand.

By train The train station is off Jln Besar, just behind *Hotel Sri Emas*. Some of the trains from Jerantut leave for various destinations in the middle of the night. Get to the train station half an hour before the scheduled departure time.

Destinations Kota Bharu (3 daily at 2pm, 3am & 5am; 8hr); Kuala Lumpur (daily at 1am; 8hr); Singapore (2 daily at 2pm & 3am; 8hr). Check ⓦ ktmb.com.my for the latest schedules.

ACCOMMODATION AND EATING

Food Court Jln Pasar Besar. Between the train and bus stations there are several open-air no-frills restaurants clustered along the side of the road. They're very popular with locals and travellers alike, and serve a mix of Thai, Malay and Chinese food, the special being *tom yam* soup, though there's excellent *roti*, *nasi goreng* and *kuey teow* too. Mains RM5. Daily 6pm–2am.

Hotel Sri Emas 46 Jln Besar ⓣ 09 266 4499. A 5min walk from the train station, this basic hotel has rooms decked out in purple paint; beds are pretty spindly and the rooms are quite poky. The "dorm" just has two beds. Dorm **RM8**, double **RM15**

NKS Hotel & Travel 21–22 Jln Besar ⓣ 09 260 1770, ⓦ taman-negara-nks.com. A backpacker favourite, this place is your one-stop shop for organizing your trip to Taman Negara – from transport to accommodation and activity packages. Rooms are pretty spartan and toilet facilities basic, but they are kept clean enough. Double **RM15**

TAMAN NEGARA NATIONAL PARK

Taman Negara is Peninsular Malaysia's largest and most popular national park and contains perhaps some of the most spectacular jungle scenery in West Malaysia. Trails ranging from short, sunlit strolls to hardcore tropical treks snake through some of the oldest rainforest in the world. Accommodation ranges from luxury resorts and rustic guesthouses to hides and campsites. To catch sight of some of the more impressive mammals, you probably need to do a three- or four-day trek, staying in hides along the way.

The most popular and convenient location to base yourself from is **Kuala Tahan**, the village across the river from the park headquarters. The best time to **visit** the park is between February and October, during the "dry" season, although it still rains even then. In the wet season (mid-Oct to Feb), there may be restrictions on the trails and boat trips.

WHAT TO SEE AND DO

While many come to Taman Negara for intense **trekking** and **wildlife-spotting**, there are plenty of others who just fancy a meander through the jungle. There are options galore for both, with multi-day treks, waterfalls to explore, off-the-beaten-track jungle camps, a man-made canopy walkway and plenty of short hikes. Other attractions include the bat caves of Gua Telinga, the river rapids of Trenggan River, night jungle walks, night boat safaris and a lazy boat ride down the Sungei Tahan itself.

The hides

Spending a night in one of the park's **hides** (*bumbun*), situated beside salt licks, doesn't guarantee sightings of large mammals, but the sound of the jungle at night does guarantee that it'll be a memorable experience, and you may catch sight of deer, tapir, elephant, leopard or wild ox. The hides offer very (very) basic bunk accommodation in concrete huts for six to eight people and must be booked at the wildlife office in the resort (RM5 per person, depending on the hide). They are sturdily built and sufficiently raised up that you don't have to worry about things creeping up on you during the night, and they do have very basic washing and toilet facilities (except Bumbun Tahan), but no electricity, so bring a torch. Take all the food and drink

you will need, a sleeping bag, rain gear and hat – and don't forget to bring your rubbish back.

The closest hide to the park headquarters is the **Bumbun Tahan**, just south of the junction with the Bukit Teresek trail. There's also the **Bumbun Tabing**, on the east bank of Sungei Tahan, about 3km from the start of the trail, and **Bumbun Cegar Anjing**, an hour from the Tabing, across the river on the west bank of Sungei Tahan. The most distant hide to the north of the resort is the six-bed **Bumbun Kumbang**, an 11km walk from Kuala Tahan and the best place to catch sight of animals, since the number of visitors to the park scare the wildlife at the hides closer to the park headquarters.

The canopy walkway

The **canopy walkway** (Sat–Thurs 9.30am–3.30pm, Fri 9am–noon; RM5) located about thirty minutes' walk east from the park headquarters, gives you the opportunity to rise above the jungle and spot animals and birds you wouldn't otherwise see. Only a small group of people can gain access to the walkway at any one time. The walkway is a swaying bridge made from aluminium ladders bound by rope and set 40m above the ground, reachable by climbing a sturdy wooden tower. At 530m, it's one of the longest walkways of its kind in the world, taking around 30 minutes to cross, with gorgeous views and frequent sightings of grey-banded leaf monkeys and

6

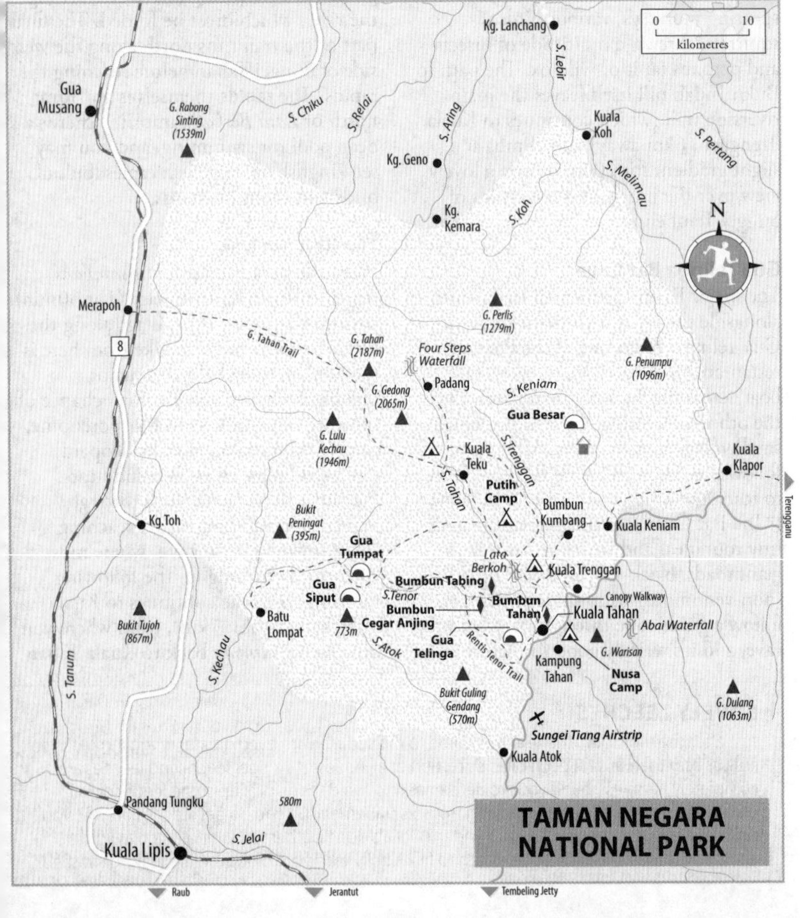

6

white-eyed dusky leaf monkeys swinging determinedly among the branches – particularly in the mornings, as in the middle of the day the wildlife tends to be hiding from the heat. From the walkway, you can climb up to the two viewpoints of Bukit Teresek; from the first you can enjoy panoramic views over the surrounding jungle and Tembeling River, while from the second you can soak in views of Peninsular Malaysia's highest mountain, Gunung Tahan.

The Bukit Indah trail

This is a steep but lovely hill climb, meandering northeast past the canopy. It's a three-hour round trip from the park headquarters. Initially, this follows the riverbank, and you stand a chance of spotting monkeys, various birds, squirrels, shrews, a multitude of insects and perhaps tapir or wild ox. The path to Bukit Indah hill itself leaves the main riverside trail (which continues to Kuala Trenggan, 6km away) and climbs at a slight gradient for 200m to give a lovely view over the jungle and the rapids of Sungei Tembeling.

Gua Telinga Bat Cave

The major Rentis Tenor trail leads south alongside the river, with branches to Gua Telinga. From one of the floating restaurants in Kuala Tahan, take a taxi boat across the Sungei Tahan River. On the other side, follow the trail through a small village into the trees. After 3km, follow the sign north for a further 200m to reach the limestone cave of **Gua Telinga** ("The Bat Cave"), which is teeming with tiny roundleaf and fruit bats, as well as giant toads, black-striped frogs and (non-venomous) whip spiders. You can follow a guide rope through the 80m-long cave, and it's weirdly good fun, even though fitting through some of the cavities requires some contortionist action (wear clothes you don't mind ruining).

At the time of research the cave was temporarily closed due to structural problems. Check with the park headquarters for further information.

The rapids of Lata Berkoh

Most people visit the rapids of **Lata Berkoh** by boat, but you could walk the trail there and arrange for a boat to pick you up for the return journey. **Sampans** from Kuala Tahan cost around RM90 for four people and take half an hour. The **trail** from the park headquarters (8.5km; 4hr) starts at the campsite and leads through dense rainforest, then crosses gullies and steep ridges, before reaching the river, which must be forded. The final part of the trail runs north along the west side of Sungei Tahan before reaching the rapids. The **rapids** themselves are 50m north of *Lata Berkoh* campsite. There's a deep pool for swimming, and you may see kingfishers, large fish eagles, bulbul birds and monitor lizards.

The Keniam trail

From the park headquarters *sampans* travel to Kuala Keniam jetty (1hr 30min), passing Kampong Pagi village along the way. The most popular hike from here is the **Keniam trail** (14km), a major highlight, where there's a small chance of spotting elephants, as well as porcupine, gaur (wild buffalo), clouded leopard, tapir, wild pigs, civets and sun bears. From the jetty a path leads through jungle (5–6hr; 7km) before reaching **Gua Kepayang Besar cave**, where most visitors stay overnight. The following morning, the hike continues to Kuala Trenggan (5–6hr; 7km), from where you can catch a *sampan* back to Kuala Tahan

LOVELY LEECHES

Just after the monsoon, the **leeches** come to the surface with even greater wriggling enthusiasm than usual. Leech bites don't hurt at all (unless it's a tiger leech) and leeches are completely harmless, but if you are determined to avoid them, pick up some leech socks before you leave home and wear long trousers underneath. If you do get leeches on you, you can just gently ease them off; you'll find that locals don't bother with things such as lighters and salt; they tend to wait for the leech to fill its belly with your blood, before leaving satisfied.

(30min). Alternatively, you can spend an extra night at *Bumbun Kumbang* campsite, about five hours south of the cave, from where you can then trek to Kuala Trenggan).

Gunung Tahan

The park's most rugged trek takes you to Gunung Tahan, Peninsular Malaysia's **highest mountain** (2187m). The mountain is 55km from the park headquarters and the trek is doable in seven or nine days, depending on the route you take. There are some steep scrambles en route and you have to take everything with you – from a tent, able to withstand torrential rain, to food and water. There are a number of campsites along the way (RM1 per person). For this hike, a guide is mandatory (around RM1200 for seven days, RM150 for every additional night on top of that). The park headquarters can help you organize the hike; get in touch several days in advance.

Other activities

The park headquarters and tour operators such as NKS organize the popular **night jungle walk** (1hr 30min; RM35), with the guide pointing out nocturnal insects and fauna; a **night safari** is similar but involves a 4WD (RM40). It's also possible to ride the **river rapids** on the Trenggan River and combine that with a visit to one of the local Orang Asli communities (both combined RM60), where the tribal elders demonstrate traditional skills such as fire-starting and blowpipe shooting. Most of the fee for visiting the community goes to the tour company, so purchasing some handicrafts ensures that the community benefits directly.

ARRIVAL AND DEPARTURE

Kuala Than is tiny and everything is within easy walking distance.

By bus/minibus Buses and minibuses pull up opposite the car park just in front of the primary school.

Destinations There are four local buses daily back to Jerantut (7.30am, 10am, 3pm & 7pm; 2hr; RM7), from where there are connections to Kuala Lumpur, Kuantan and Kota Bharu. *NKS* runs three minibuses daily to Jerantut (8am, 10am & 7pm; 1hr 30min; RM25), with onwards minibus connections (see p.449).

By boat Most visitors approach the park by taking a scenic longboat ride from the Tembeling jetty (daily 9am & 2pm, except Fri 9am & 2.45pm; 3hr; RM35) along the Sengei Tahan River to the village of Kuala Tahan; you may well spot monkeys leaping through trees along the way or hornbills sitting on the tallest branches. Boats from the Tembeling jetty dock at the Kuala Tahan jetty just below the village. Regular boats transport ferry passengers across the river to the park headquarters (RM1). Longboats make the return journey to the Tembling jetty (2hr 30min) at 9am and 2pm (double-check times in advance).

INFORMATION

The Taman Negara Park Information Centre At the Park Headquarters (Sat–Thurs 8am–6pm, Fri 8am–noon & 3–6pm; ☎09 266 1122), located at the *Mutiara Taman Negara Resort*, on the opposite bank of the Sungei Tahan River from Kuala Tahan, easily reachable by *sampan*, which ferry people across all day (RM1). It deals with all park queries, books you into hides and offers an excellent free site and park map. You can also obtain park entry (RM1) and camera permits (RM5) here; if you come to the park by boat, you pay for the two at the jetty. Hold on to your permit at all times; the penalty for not having a permit is a fine of up to RM10,000 and three years' imprisonment. The park headquarters screen introductory videos on Taman Negara (daily 9.30am, 3pm & 5pm; 25min). There are shops in Kuala Tahan that rent sleeping bags and mats (RM10–15) – though it's best to bring your own. Reliable internet is found at IDD Internet, opposite *Teresek View Motel*.

Trekking in the park The trails are well signposted and most do not require guides, though you will get more out of your hikes if accompanied by someone who really knows the jungle and who can point out medicinal and edible plants or spot well-camouflaged wildlife. Guides are licensed by the Ministry of Tourism; the park headquarters can help you to arrange a guide for the day (RM250).

ACCOMMODATION

Most accommodation options besides *Mutiara Taman Negara Resort* are located across the river in Kuala Tahan village. The village has only a few actual roads; the rest of the accommodation options are connected by dirt paths.

Julie's Hostel ☎017 904 0344. This friendly, brightly painted place has just three spotless rooms – all decked out in purple, with private bath and a/c. Towels are provided, including in the seven-bed dorm, while the more expensive private has a fridge and TV. A great option. Dorm **RM25**, double **RM90**

Mahseer Chalet ☎019 383 2633. The neat and tidy wooden chalets here are kept clean; rooms have private bath and a/c, and there's wi-fi too. Dorm **RM15**, double **RM100**

6

Mutiara Taman Negara 09 266 2200, mutiarahotels.com. This luxurious resort is by far the best place to camp; you can pitch a tent in the lush grounds shaded by large trees for a very reasonable price (RM15; RM10 if you have your own tent). The location is handy too, as all the park's trails start from here. There are also pricey eight-bed dorms with mosquito nets, ceiling fans, lockers and communal bathrooms. There's a kitchen for campers too, and wi-fi in the lobby area. Dorm RM80, double RM320

6

Rainbow 09 266 6601. This laidback little place has clean, freshly painted rooms facing one another; all have a/c and private bath and there's wi-fi too. Double RM70

Yellow Guest House 09 266 4243 or 017 946 3357, mat_kepau@yahoo.com. Run by the warm and welcoming Mohamad, this friendly guesthouse has very spacious tiled rooms with a/c and private bath. There's just one cheap room with shared bath (RM40), while the pricier ones have private balcony. There's all-day tea and coffee, computers for guests' use and free wi-fi. Double RM70

EATING AND DRINKING

Floating Restaurants The riverside is lined with floating restaurants serving a samey mix of Malay, Indian and pseudo-Western dishes (mains RM5).

Mutiara Taman Negara Resort Besides being one of the very few places that serves alcohol, this fairly pricey restaurant at the park headquarters offers international dishes, such as pasta, steaks and burgers, welcome to those who've overdosed on noodles and rice. Mains from RM30. Daily noon–10pm.

The east coast

The 400km stretch from the northeastern corner of the Peninsula to Kuantan, roughly halfway down the east coast, is the most "Malay" region in Malaysia, with strong cultural traditions – particularly in conservative **Kota Bharu**, the last major town before the Thai border, and one of the few towns in Malaysia with a Muslim majority. The food on the east coast is some of the most imaginative in Malaysia and Islamic traditions are strictly followed – the call to prayer will wake you up before sunrise, and there are fewer buses on Fridays. There are some good beaches along the east coast, including laidback **Cherating**. The most beautiful beaches, however, are on **Pulau Perhentian** in the north, with its stunningly clear azure waters and white sands fringed with palm trees. Further south is **Pulau Kapas**, which also boasts fantastic coral reefs and wildlife in idyllic settings. The annual monsoon affects the east coast between November and February (see box, p.406).

KOTA BHARU

At the very northeastern corner of the Peninsula, close to the Thai border, **KOTA BHARU** is the capital of Kelantan State and one of the few **Muslim-governed** states in Malaysia. The town itself is rather drab, although there are a few interesting sights that will keep you busy for an afternoon. There's an impressive Cultural Centre, lots of craft workshops, museums and a bustling night market. During the holy month of **Ramadan**, strongly Muslim Kota Bharu virtually shuts up shop.

WHAT TO SEE AND DO

Small Padang Merdeka in the north part of town is Kota Bharu's historical heart. There's a cluster of museums here (all open daily except Fri 8.30am–4.45pm), the best of which is the **Istana Jahar** (RM4). It houses the Royal Customs Museum, whose ground floor is given over to a display of exquisite *ikat* and *songket* textiles and ornate gold jewellery. Upstairs, you'll see life-size reconstructions of various traditional royal ceremonies, from weddings to circumcisions.

Around the corner to your left is the sky-blue **Istana Batu** (RM2), now the **Kelantan Royal Museum**, in which the sultan's family's rooms have been left in their original state including photographs of the royal family.

Inside the impressive 1912 Bank Kerapu building, the **War Museum** (RM3) tells the story of World War II in Southeast Asia and the effects of the Japanese occupation on Malaysia.

The octagonal **central market** is one of the most vibrant in Malaysia; from the first floor there's an extremely photogenic view of the produce stalls below, while the Buluh Kubu complex next door has several floors devoted to **batik** – an

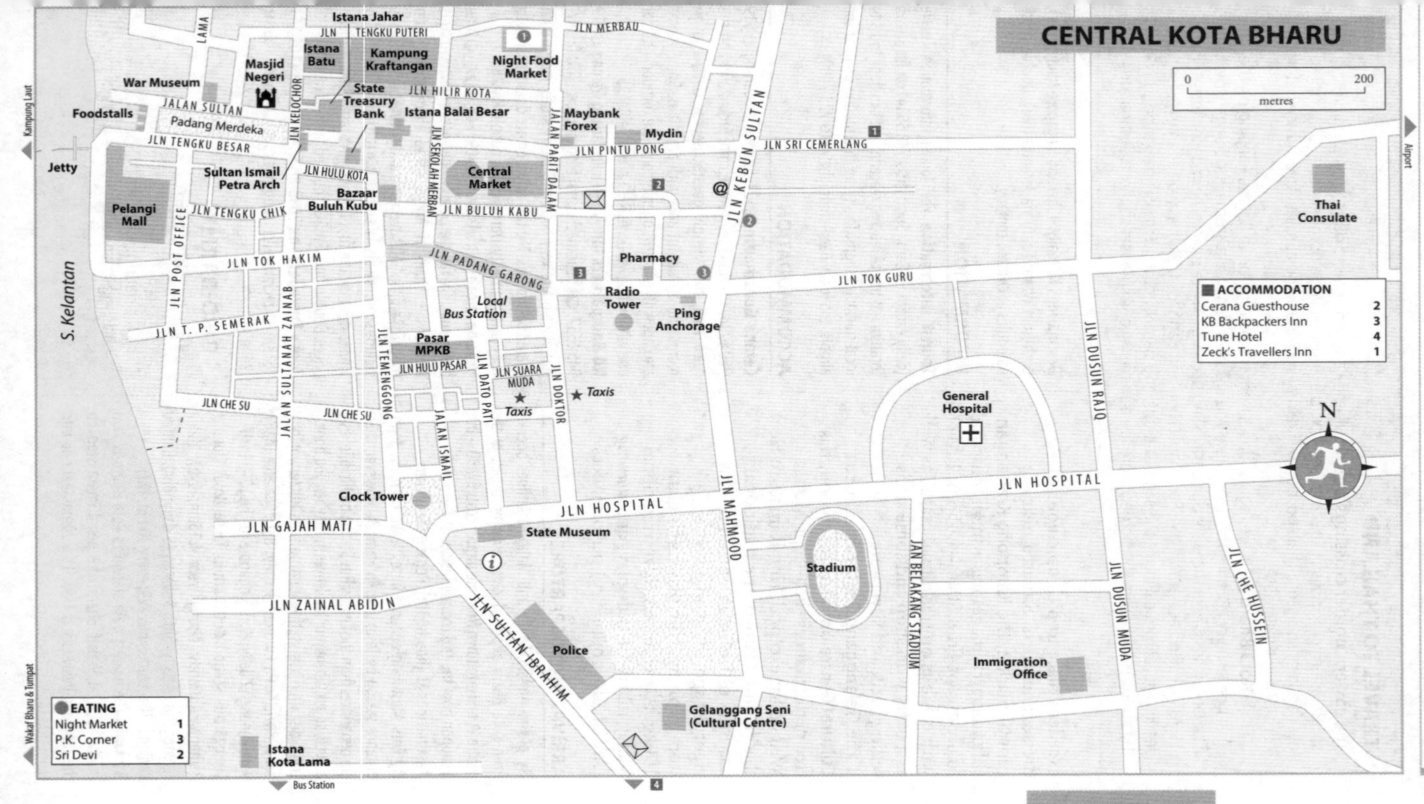
CENTRAL KOTA BHARU
0
200
metres
ACCOMMODATION
Cerana Guesthouse 2
KB Backpackers Inn 3
Tune Hotel 4
Zeck's Travellers Inn 1
EATING
Night Market 1
P.K. Corner 3
Sri Devi 2
Kampung Laut
Airport
Wakaf Bharu & Tumpat
Bus Station
Istana Jahar
JLN TENGKU PUTERI
LAMA
Istana Batu
Kampung Kraftangan
Masjid Negeri
War Museum
JALAN SULTAN
Foodstalls
Padang Merdeka
JLN TENGKU BESAR
JLN KELOCHOR
State Treasury Bank
JLN HILIR KOTA
Istana Balai Besar
Night Food Market
JLN MERBAU
Maybank Forex
Mydin
JALAN PARIT DALAM
JLN PINTU PONG
JLN KEBUN SULTAN
JLN SRI CEMERLANG
Jetty
Sultan Ismail Petra Arch
JLN HULU KOTA
Bazaar Buluh Kubu
JLN SEKOLAH MERBAN
Central Market
JLN BULUH KABU
Pelangi Mall
JLN TENGKU CHIK
JLN POST OFFICE
JLN TOK HAKIM
JLN PADANG GARONG
Pharmacy
Radio Tower
Ping Anchorage
JLN TOK GURU
Thai Consulate
S. Kelantan
JLN T. P. SEMERAK
JALAN SULTANAH ZAINAB
Local Bus Station
Pasar MPKB
JLN TEMENGGONG
JLN HULU PASAR
JLN DATO PATI
JLN SUARA MUDA
JLN DOKTOR
Taxis
Taxis
JLN CHE SU
JLN CHE SU
JALAN ISMAIL
General Hospital
JLN DUSUN RAJQ
N
Clock Tower
JLN HOSPITAL
JLN HOSPITAL
JLN GAJAH MATI
State Museum
JLN MAHMOOD
Stadium
JAN BELAKANG STADIUM
JLN DUSUN MUDA
JLN CHE HUSSEIN
JLN ZAINAL ABIDIN
JLN SULTAN IBRAHIM
Police
Immigration Office
Gelanggang Seni (Cultural Centre)
Istana Kota Lama

TRAVEL TO THAILAND

The **eastern border crossings** are still currently advised against, due to political unrest in the southeastern provinces of Thailand (see box, p.819). However, a number of travellers opt to use overland transport into Thailand, but ensure that you check the current travel advice before considering these routes.

From **Kota Bharu** there are regular buses from the bus station to Rantau Panjang on the Thai border (every 30min; 1hr). From here you will pass through customs into Sungai Kolok in Thailand, from where there are trains travelling up north. There is a morning departure at 11.30am calling at Hat Yai (4hr), Sarathani (10hr) and Bangkok (22hr), as well as an express train leaving at 2.20pm calling at the same stations, and partially cutting travel time (although only by about 1–2hr). From the border, there are also plenty of minibuses to these destinations.

excellent place to pick up colourful dresses and shirts. Situated near the central market, the **Kampong Kraftangan** (Handicraft Village) has a small museum (daily except Fri 8.30am–4.45pm; RM1) with exhibits on traditional crafts, as well as a batik workshop and some stalls selling batik and silverware.

The **Gelanggang Seni**, Kota Bharu's **Cultural Centre** on Jalan Mahmood, has free performances (Feb–Sept Mon, Wed & Sat except during Ramadan; free) that feature many of the traditional pastimes of Kelantan, including the vigorous sport of *gasing uri* (top-spinning), the playing of giant 100kg *rebana* drums, *silat* (traditional Malay martial art) displays and *wayang kilit* (shadow puppetry) performances.

ARRIVAL AND DEPARTURE

By plane AirAsia, Firefly and Malaysia Airlines operate from Kota Bharu airport, located 9km northeast of the centre. A taxi into town from the airport costs RM30 – buy a coupon from the taxi counter inside.

Destinations KL (hourly; 1hr); Penang (daily; 1hr).

By bus Most long-distance buses leave from the long-distance station by Tesco's on Jln Hamzah. However, there are departures from the Central Bus Station on Jln Hilir Pasar as well, so ask where your bus leaves from when you book.

Long-distance bus station destinations Butterworth (2 daily; 8hr); Kuala Lumpur (3 daily; 8hr); Malacca (daily; 9hr); Penang (2 daily; 8hr); Singapore (daily; 10–11hr).

Central bus station destinations Kuala Besut (for the Perhentian Islands; hourly from 6.15am; 2hr); Kuala Terengganu (3 daily; 3hr); Kuantan (5 daily; 8hr); Rantau Panjang (Thai border; bus #29; every 30min; 1hr).

By train The nearest train station to Kota Bharu is 7km to the west at Wakaf Bharu, the penultimate stop on the Jungle Railway (see p.449). It's a 20min taxi ride into town (RM30).

Destinations KL (daily; 13hr) and Singapore (daily; 16hr), both from Wakaf Bharu via Jerantut (6hr). Double-check schedules at ktmb.com.my.

INFORMATION

Tourist information The Tourist Information Centre (daily except Fri 8am–5pm; 09 748 5534) on Jln Sultan Ibrahim has useful reading material and can book tours to local craft workshops. There's an information point at the airport, too (daily 6am–midnight; 09 773 7400).

ACCOMMODATION

Cerana Guesthouse 39521 Jln Padang Garong 019 960 6734, ceranaguesthouse.com. Tucked away off the main road, this friendly guesthouse has clean enough rooms and a chill-out area with armchairs. Some rooms are dark with windows opening onto the corridor – ask for one with windows. Dorm RM12, double RM35

KB Backpackers Inn 171–81 Jln Padang Garong 019 945 6557, kbbackpackersinn.blogspot.com. This family-run place offers very basic and pretty stuffy rooms with shared bathrooms. The taxi driver owner does transfers to the Perhentian jetty. Dorm RM10, double RM28

★Tune Hotel Jln Hamzah 09 744 3822, tunehotels.com. By far the best budget option in town, this inexpensive chain of hotels offers clean rooms with modern facilities. All have a safe and private bath; add-ons include soap, towels, TV and wi-fi in the rooms. There's also a restaurant on the first floor serving tasty food at cheap prices. Double from RM28 if booked far in advance

Zeck's Travellers Inn 7088 Jln Sri Cemerlang 09 743 1613, zecktravellers.blogspot.com. Located about

BIRD-BARMY

If you hear **birdsong** outside your window at midnight, you're not hallucinating: residents of Kota Bharu are birdsong-crazy, and in some parts of town, birdsong is piped through loudspeakers to attract and encourage birds to nest.

10min walk from the centre, this guesthouse/homestay offers cheap basic rooms, most with shared bath. The owners are friendly and welcoming, and can point you in the right direction with onward travel. Double **RM30**

EATING

Night market Jln Pintu Pong. Easily the most exciting place to eat, with a large variety of local dishes. Try the local speciality *ayam percik* (barbecued chicken with a creamy coconut sauce) or the delicious *nasi kerabu* (purple, green or blue rice with a dash of vegetables, seaweed and grated coconut); finish off with a filling *pisang murtabak* (banana pancake) and you won't have parted with much more than RM7. Daily 6–10pm.

P.K. Corner 1069C Jln Kebun Sultan. It's often hard to get a table at this hugely popular outdoor place featuring local dishes from *tom yam* (RM6) to tempura (RM10), as well as more substantial mains such as crispy sea bass with mango salad (RM30). Daily 1pm–midnight.

Sri Devi 421 Jln Kebun Sultan. No-frills local Indian joint serving banana-leaf curries (RM8.50), as well as a few veggie options (RM4.50). Daily 7.30am–9pm.

DIRECTORY

Banks and exchange HSBC Bank, Jln Padong Garong; Standard Chartered Bank, Jln Tok Hakim.

Hospital Hospital Kota Bharu, Jln Hospital (☎ 09 748 5533).

Internet There's a Cyber Café on Jln Kebun Sultan, diagonally opposite the road from *Sri Devi* (Sat–Thurs 9.30am–10pm, Fri 3–10pm; RM2/hr).

Post office On Jln Sultan Ibrahim.

Thai visas From the Royal Thai Consulate, 4426 Jln Tok Guru (Mon–Thurs & Sun 9am–noon & 2–3.30pm; ☎ 09 744 5266). Two-month tourist visas are issued within 24 hours.

PULAU PERHENTIAN

Pulau Perhentian, just over 20km off the northeastern coast, is actually two islands – **Perhentian Kecil** (Small Island) and **Perhentian Besar** (Big Island). Both have turquoise waters and some of the most attractive white-sand beaches in Malaysia. Each is less than 4km in length and neither has roads; in cheaper lodgings, there's little or no electricity during daylight hours and internet is offered at a premium (usually RM10/hr), although a number of resorts and cafés have free wi-fi. During the beginning or end of the monsoon season, prices are exceptionally low, you'll have the islands practically to yourself and the rains are few and far between.

There's an excellent choice of budget accommodation, a good range of cafés and restaurants and a few laidback bars. The Perhentians are also a great place either to learn to **dive** or to enjoy some breathtaking "fun dives". Dives include **The Three Brothers** (Terumbu Tiga), where you go through three seriously impressive rock formations; **Temple of the Sea**, popular on account of its good visibility which enables divers to see an incredible variety of fish; and the **Sugar Wreck**, one of the few wreck dives in the world suitable for relative beginners. But you don't have to dip far below the waves to see some spectacular marine life; most guesthouses offer **snorkelling trips** which take in different points around the islands where you can see reef sharks, turtles and more (around RM45 per person; 4hr).

There are no banks in Kuala Besut or on the islands, so **change money** before you go.

Perhentian Kecil

This is generally considered to be the livelier of the two islands and it is very popular with backpackers, having a slightly more ramshackle atmosphere than its larger neighbour. On the southeastern corner of **Perhentian Kecil** lies the island's only village, **Kampung Pasir Hantu**, with a jetty, police station, school, clinic and littered beach. **Coral Bay** is the most popular west-facing cove on the island, lined with friendly guesthouses and shack restaurants. East-facing **Long Beach** has a wide stretch of white beach and a laidback atmosphere, though litter management is currently a problem. The beach is much more exposed to the elements, and the crashing surf forces many of the chalet owners to close up from the end of October through to March.

Coral Bay is usually the first drop-off point when coming from the mainland.

Perhentian Besar

Perhentian Besar is more sedate than its neighbour and more popular with families and a slightly older crowd than with the just-out-of-uni backpacking set. The pace of life is even more laidback than on Kecil, but Besar's got plenty of budget

6

accommodation and better beaches than its neighbour. The best place on the islands for turtle-watching is undoubtedly **Three Coves Bay** on the north coast. A stunning conglomeration of three beaches, it is separated from the main area of accommodation by rocky outcrops and is reached only by speedboat. The bay provides a secluded haven between May and September for green and hawksbill turtles to come ashore and lay their eggs, though sadly, dwindling numbers mean the chances of spotting any are slim.

ARRIVAL AND DEPARTURE

By boat A whole slew of companies run speedboats (30min; RM70 return) from the town of Kuala Besut, the departure point for Pulau Perhentian, to the islands every hour or so between 8am and 5pm, weather permitting. Tell the boatman which bay you want to be dropped off at when you board the boat; boats from the mainland can't dock at Perhentian Kecil's Long Beach, but stop 50m from shore; from here, you'll have to transfer to a smaller taxi boat (RM2) to take you to the shore. Boat travel is very weather-dependent, so services between the islands and Kuala Besut are virtually nonexistent during the November–February monsoon season. Boats leave the islands at 8am, noon and 4pm; let your guesthouse know the day before which boat you intend to take. There is a RM5 entrance fee to the islands that is paid upon boarding the boat.

By bus From Kota Bharu's central bus station catch bus #629 to Kuala Besut (hourly; 2hr).

Destinations From Kuala Besut: KL (3 daily; 8hr), Penang (3 daily; 7–8hr), Kuala Polis (for Langkawi; daily; 8hr), Cameron Highlands (3 daily; 7hr) and Kuala Terengganu (every 2hr; 2hr). From Jerteh, 16km away: Cherating (every 2hr; 5hr), Mersing (for Tioman; every 2hr; 8hr), Singapore (daily; 9hr) and Johor Bahru (2 daily; 8hr).

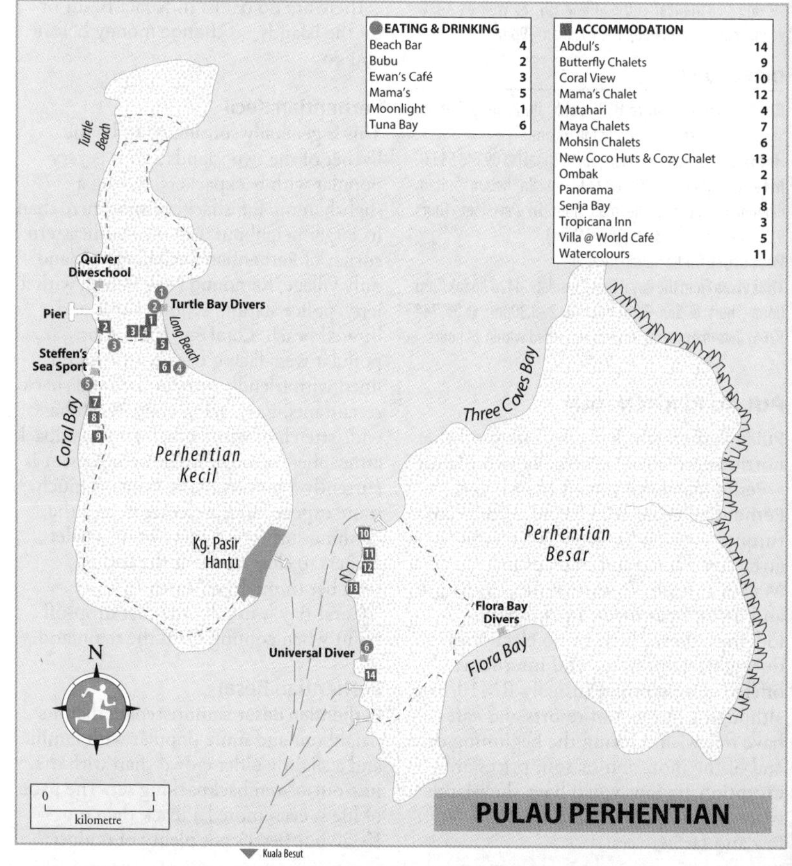

By taxi Most guesthouses in Kota Bharu organize shared taxis (1hr 30min; RM80) direct to Kuala Besut.

GETTING AROUND

Boats Taxi boats shuttle visitors between the beaches and two islands. Each bay has at least one clearly signposted taxi-boat point. Prices vary from RM5 to beaches on the same island, RM10 between the Fisherman's Village on Kecil and the point directly opposite on Besar, to RM25 to remoter coves on either island.

DIVE OPERATORS

The Perhentians are a good place to get your PADI Open Water certificate.

PERHENTIAN KECIL

Quiver Diveschool Coral Bay ⓣ 012 213 8855, ⓦ quiver-perhentian.com. This brilliant dive school only operates with small groups and is probably the best bet on either island for friendliness and personal attention. PADI Open Water RM1000, fun dive (3–4 hr) RM70.

Turtle Bay Divers Long Beach ⓣ 09 691 1630, ⓦ turtlebaydivers.com. A large, well-kitted-out dive school with friendly staff. They also have a sister outfit at *Mama's Chalets* on Perhentian Besar. PADI Open Water RM1050, "'discover scuba" (one day) RM200.

PERHENTIAN BESAR

Flora Bay Divers ⓣ 09 691 1661, ⓦ florabaydivers.com. A popular dive outfit that operates dives in small groups. Prices are slightly more expensive than others on the island, but the service and attention from the instructors is exceptional. PADI Open Water RM1200, fun dive RM160.

Universal Diver ⓣ 09 691 1621, ⓦ universaldiver.net. A well-organized dive centre run by a group of friendly enthusiasts. PADI Open Water RM980, fun dive RM90.

ACCOMMODATION

PERHENTIAN KECIL: CORAL BAY

Butterfly Chalets No phone. This place is so laidback that travellers just stroll in, poke their heads in a few rooms, see which tickles their fancy and scribble how many nights they'll be staying on the whiteboard. Staff seem to be away more often than not, but things somehow fall into place. The rustic chalets, all with balconies, perch off the southern end of the beach and have great views. Double **RM50**

Maya Chalets ⓣ 09 691 1037. All the chalets here have wooden floors and a little balcony, and there are hammocks slung between palm trees to have a little kip in. You can also pitch your own tent in the garden (RM10), or rent one (RM20). Double **RM80**

Ombak ⓣ 09 691 1021, ⓦ ombak.my. One of the priciest resorts along the beach, but justifiably so – the rooms are welcoming and clean, and there's electricity 24/7. The two dorms with lockers are by far the nicest on the island. There's also a restaurant with comfy cushioned seating and movies screened on the outdoor projector, although the service and food here are pretty mediocre. Dorm **RM40**, double **RM200**

Senja Bay ⓣ 09 691 1799, ⓦ senjabay.com. On the southern end of the bay, this popular resort consists of several rows of chalets, all pretty clean and with a/c. The walls are paper-thin though and sadly staff aren't the most welcoming around, but there are nice views of the beach from the restaurant. Double **RM100**

> **★TREAT YOURSELF**
>
> **Villa @ World Café** ⓦ theworldcafe.com.my. On the southern end of Long Beach, these six lovely, secluded villas boast huge windows, lots of natural light and beautifully designed interiors, with king-sized beds dominating the spacious rooms. It also has outside power showers set amid sprouting bamboo shoots. Ideal for a romantic getaway. **RM750**

PERHENTIAN KECIL: LONG BEACH

Matahari ⓣ 09 691 1740, ⓦ mataharichalet.com. Slightly back from the beach, this place has a large cluster of chalets and bungalows set around a pleasant garden. There is a new concrete block with clean a/c rooms, while the cheaper A-frame huts towards the front can get quite loud due to the nearby shop's generator. Double **RM60**

Mohsin Chalets ⓣ 09 691 1363, ⓦ mohsinchalet.my. Nestled on the hillside overlooking Long Beach, the chalets here are basic but functional; the 22-bed dorm has a ward-like feel to it, but the wonderful views over the beach from the breezy restaurant area compensate. You can also try your hand at *takraw*, a Malay version of volleyball played with your feet. Dorm **RM40**, double **RM150**

Panorama ⓣ 09 691 1590. Possibly the most popular choice for backpackers, with rustic chalets and A-frame huts set around a large, verdant area. The vibe is laidback, and there's a pool and nightly films at the welcoming restaurant. Plenty of diving package deals, too. Double **RM60**

Tropicana Inn ⓣ 016 266 1333, ⓦ perhentiantropicana.com. Halfway between Coral Bay and Long Beach, this guesthouse has a peaceful jungle location and spotless, freshly painted private rooms and dorms, all with en suite and comfortable beds. There's a café with wi-fi, too. Bring a torch for walking up from either beach in the dark. Dorm **RM30**, double **RM120**

6

6

PERHENTIAN BESAR

Abdul's 019 912 7303, abdulchalet.com. Located on one of the best strips of beach, these cute green-roofed chalets range from basic A-frames to more sophisticated a/c rooms with sea views. The restaurant is right on the sand and open until 11pm, after which it's extremely peaceful here. Double RM80

★**Coral View** 09 697 4943, coralview.com.my. This wonderful resort has attractive a/c chalets with private terrace and sun loungers, mostly overlooking the sea. A pathway leads to the slightly more economical chalets (twin RM140) at the back, set around a cascading little waterfall. The restaurant serves a good seafood barbecue, there's wi-fi, and the nicest beach on the island lies just a 2min walk away. Double RM190

Mama's Chalet 013 984 0232 or 019 985 3359, mamaschalet.com. Run by the friendly Aziz and Jimie, a source of local knowledge, *Mama's* has well-kept chalets, all spotless with wooden floorboards, set around a leafy garden. The more upmarket chalets with a/c and private bath open up onto the beachfront. Double RM70

New Coco Huts & Cozy Chalet 09 691 1810, perhentianislandcocohut.com. The spacious green-roofed wooden chalets here with sea views are built on a headland that separates the beach north and south, while the cheaper rooms with garden views are set back from the beach. All rooms have a balcony, cable TV and a fridge. RM220

Watercolours 09 691 1850, watercoloursworld.com. Next door to *Mama's* and connected with the Watercolours Dive Centre, this place offers welcoming rooms set around a pleasant garden with a volleyball court. The downside is that the cheaper rooms don't have power sockets. Double RM120

EATING AND DRINKING

Most of the guesthouses on both islands have a restaurant attached, which are mentioned if they're noteworthy; on Besar, there aren't any stand-alone restaurants, just those at guesthouses. Several places serve alcohol, while others don't mind if you bring your own. Though there aren't many bars on the islands, Perhentian Kecil does have a couple that stay open late and have a bit of a party atmosphere.

PERHENTIAN KECIL: CORAL BAY

Ewan's Café Just at the start of the trail from Coral Bay to Long Beach, this laidback restaurant bustles with hungry people dropping by for the inexpensive rice and noodle dishes (RM9). There are also more substantial mains such as fresh fish curry (RM13), and free wi-fi, too. Daily 8am–10pm.

Mama's The smell of grilled fish wafts down the beach from this laidback place where the day's catch is barbecued before your very eyes. You can feast away for just RM18. Daily 8.30am–11pm.

PERHENTIAN KECIL: LONG BEACH

Beach Bar This laidback bar seems to close shop more often than not, but when it is open it attracts quite a crowd for the cheap drinks and fire shows on the beach. Opening hours vary.

★**Bubu** It may be a tad pricy but it's well worth it: the top-notch Western and Malay dishes here are the best on the island and the beach setting is lovely. The menu includes large salads (RM30), pastas (RM25), burgers and sandwiches (both RM30). Daily 7.30–10.30am & noon–10.30pm.

Moonlight On the northern end of the beach, things here kick off at moonlight, when reggae and island music bands take centre stage Thurs–Sun. Beers RM9. Daily 8am–10.30pm.

PERHENTIAN BESAR

Tuna Bay The service here is disorganized, but it's a popular hangout serving good Western and Asian dishes, as well as fresh fish and seafood. There are also plenty of decadent desserts, such as home-made apple pie and tiramisu (both RM15). Daily 7.15–10am & 11.30am–9.45pm.

DIRECTORY

Clinic There's a very basic clinic at Village Pasir Hantu on Perhentian Kecil; the dive centres can offer limited medical care, but you're better off returning to the mainland.

KUALA TERENGGANU

The tiny Muslim metropolis of **KUALA TERENGGANU**, 160km south of Kota Bharu, is a traditional town set on an estuary and a pleasant place for a quick stopover.

At the western end of Kuala Terengganu, Jalan Bandar forms the centre of **Chinatown**, where you'll find the excellent Teratai, at no. 151, selling local arts and crafts. Kuala Terengganu's **Central Market** (daily 7am–6pm), a little further down on the right, close to the junction with Jalan Kota, also deals in batik, *songkets* and brassware. Located on the same road, it's also worth taking a peek inside the lavish **Ho Ann Kong Temple** (daily 7.50am–7.45pm), which was built by Taoist devotees in 1801.

The newly opened **State Museum** (Sat–Thurs 9am–5pm, Fri 9am–noon & 3–5pm; RM15) is the largest in Malaysia, covering an area of 270,000 square metres. The museum consists of a number of galleries dedicated to textiles,

crafts, Islam, fisheries, and even petroleum. Among the objects on display are Chinese potteries, traditional garments used in wedding and circumcision ceremonies, daggers, weapons, and fishing equipment used by local fishermen. To get here, catch Heritage bus #C02 from the bus station.

ARRIVAL AND DEPARTURE

By plane Sultan Mohammed Airport is located 13km northeast of the centre, a RM25 taxi ride into town. Kuala Terengganu is served by Malaysia Airlines, Firefly and AirAsia, with daily flights to KL (3 daily; 55min).

By bus The bus station is off Jln Tok Lam in the centre of town.

Destinations Butterworth (2 daily; 9–10hr); Ipoh (2 daily; 7hr); Johor Bahru (4 daily; 10hr); Kota Bharu (2 daily; 4hr); Kuala Besut (every 2hr; 2hr); KL (6 daily; 8–9hr); Kuala Perlis (for Langkawi; 3 daily; 10hr); Kuantan (10 daily; 4hr); Malacca (3 daily; 7hr); Marang (hourly; 30min); Mersing (2 daily; 7hr); Singapore (daily; 10hr).

INFORMATION

Tourist Information Centre Jln Sultan Zainal Abdin, on the seafront near the GPO (Sun–Thurs 8am–5pm, Fri 9am–1pm, Sat 9am–5pm; closed for lunch break 1–2pm; T 09 622 1553, W tourism.terengganu.gov.my). Helpful staff can provide brochures on the area.

ACCOMMODATION

Awi's Yellow House 3576 Kampong Duyong Besar T 017 984 0337. This rickety complex of basic stilted huts (not yellow, incidentally), built over the water on the tiny island of Duyung, gives you a taste of relaxing village life from years past, though it's a little out of the way. There's a kitchen for self-caterers and a fabulous night market right on the doorstep. From the bus station, take bus Bandar to Pulau Duyong, and get off at the base of the Sultan Mahmud Bridge, from where *Awi's* is a short walk. After 6pm, you'll probably have to take a taxi (RM15). Dorm **RM15**, chalet **RM35**

Ping Anchorage 77A Jln Sultan Sulaiman T 09 626 2020, W pinganchorage.com.my. The rooms here are basic and pretty spartan, with shared bathrooms that will just about do for a night or two. The leafy rooftop café decorated with traditional vases makes up for it though, and there's a well-organized travel agency downstairs who can help with onward travel. Double **RM38**

EATING

Batu Buruk Food Court Along Batu Buruk Beach. One of the best food courts along Malaysia's east coast, this one is famous for local dishes such as *keropok* (deep-fried fish and seafood rolls with sago flour and pandan leaves with chilli sauce for dipping; RM8) and the incredible fried ice cream. Daily 4pm–midnight.

Madam Bee's Kitchen 177 Jln Kampung Cina. This welcoming little restaurant keeps Peranakan culture and traditions alive – it's allegedly the only place in Terengganu state that serves traditional home-cooked Pernakan dishes. Popular choices include *nasi lemak* (RM6) and *laksa Terengganu* (RM5.80). Thurs–Tues 9.30am–5.30pm.

The Vinum XChange 221 Jln Bandar. This little drinking hole is a truly unusual sight on Malaysia's conservative eastern coast. This café and bar serves beers (RM8), wines from the world over (bottles only; from RM37) and spirits (bottles only; from RM118). Teetotallers can settle for a coffee (RM5) and little pastries (RM1.30). Daily 11am–11pm.

PULAU KAPAS

A thirty-minute ride by speedboat from Marang takes you to the lovely island of **PULAU KAPAS**, less than 2km in length, where all accommodation options are

TRAVEL TO AND FROM MARANG

The small coastal town of **Marang**, 18km south of Kuala Terengganu, is the jumping-off point for nearby Pulau Kapas, 6km offshore (see above). You'll find a couple of banks here, as well as onward connections to other east-coast destinations. Any Dungun or Rhu Muda-bound **bus** (every 30min) from Kuala Terengganu, or Kuala Terengganu-bound bus from Cherating, will drop you on the main road at Marang, from where the centre is a short walk downhill towards the sea. The bus ticket kiosk is on Jln Tanjung Sulong Musa. To get to Cherating by local bus, catch a Kuala Dungun-bound bus and change there, or take a local bus to Kuala Terengganu's long-distance bus station.

Ferry company offices are all located by the jetty and there are regular departures for Pulau Kapas – Suria Link is a reliable option, dropping you off right in front of your resort (RM40 return) – most companies do three runs daily to the island from around 8.30am to 4pm; the boats leave before their scheduled departure if full. There's practically no service during the monsoon season (Nov–Feb).

6

clustered along the sandy coves along its western side. Kapas is a designated marine park; its white-sand beaches are some of the cleanest in Malaysia, and the aquamarine waters are ideal for sea kayaking and snorkelling. The best snorkelling is around tiny Pulau Raja, just off Kapas and rocky Pulau Gemia, off the northwestern shore, home to a resort and a turtle sanctuary. The northernmost cove is good for **turtle-spotting** and turtles and reef sharks have also been spotted at the south side of the island at *Turtle Valley* resort. Besides snorkelling, Kapas has a few good diving sites; set on the main beach, Aqua Sport (T 019 983 5879, W aquasportdiver.com.my) charge RM110 for a regular dive and RM150 for a night dive. A couple of **jungle trails** cross the island – one from behind *Kapas Island* resort and the other branching off from the trail leading over the promontory to *Turtle Valley* resort; this one is more demanding and there's a certain amount of hauling yourself up using ropes; both trails end up pretty much at the same spot on the east side of the island.

ACCOMMODATION AND EATING

Accommodation is arranged along four coves along the west side of the island; all accommodation options have their own restaurant.

SAVE THE TURTLES

Marang is one of the remaining places in Malaysia where you can see turtles. However, with turtle numbers dwindling, sanctuaries such as the **Ma'Daerah Turtle Sanctuary** (W madaerah.org) are becoming increasingly important. Volunteering here is a truly rewarding and worthwhile experience, and can be done for as short a time as a single weekend, or even an afternoon. In April, the beaches are cleaned up ready for the nesting season and any willing hands for this task are gratefully received. A donation of at least RM250 is required, but meals and accommodation are included for your stay, and your money will be going towards the work of the sanctuary. Alternatively, you can adopt a turtle (RM150), or a nest (RM100).

Captain's Longhouse T 012 377 0214. At the southern end of the main beach, this longhouse has a spacious dorm with colourful mosquito nets, local fabrics and clean communal bathrooms. Couples can make use of the darkish doubles, or opt for a double bed within the shared dorm (RM60). There's a chill-out area with hammocks, and nipah carpets are strewn over the wooden floors. Dorm RM30, double RM70

★ **Kapas Beach Chalet (KBC)** T 019 343 5606, E hans.keune@gmail.com. The friendly and laidback vibe at this Dutch-Malay owned place might tempt you to stay for longer than planned, whiling away your afternoons swinging in a hammock and swimming. The little A-frame chalets with private bath are dotted around a garden and there's a kitchen for guests' use, chill-out areas for rainy days and a sociable restaurant. Dorm RM15, double RM40

★ **Koko's** This welcoming English-Malay-run beachside place with coconut beams and rustic wooden furniture serves outstanding Malay dishes – the fresh fish/prawns/squid cooked in a yellow coconut sauce (RM20) is an absolute must. Daily 9am–4pm & 7.30–10.30pm.

Pak Ya Sea View T 019 960 3130. Run by the welcoming, smiley Zai, who will go out of his way to help you and make you feel right at home, this place has seven rustic chalets that line the beach, all with private bath and fan. A great option for those seeking a laidback, quiet time. Double RM70

Turtle Valley This intimate, slightly more upmarket, Dutch-owned place is a popular spot for a wonderful lunch or dinner – the chef rustles up excellent takes on various cuisines, from Indonesian to Mexican. The chocolate fondant is also a winner. Dinner reservations required. Mains RM35. Daily noon–1.30pm & 6–8.30pm.

CHERATING

CHERATING, 47km north of Kuantan, hugs the northern end of a windswept bay, protected from the breeze by the shelter of a rocky cliff. **Surfers**, kitesurfers and windsurfers love this travellers' hangout while many others find the village a bit lacklustre. These days the town has lost some of its laidback kampung vibe due to large resorts popping up all over the place.

The main drag is a tiny surfaced road that runs roughly parallel to the beach; this is where you'll find most of the restaurants and bars, as well as convenience stores and arts and craft shops selling batik, T-shirts

and other trinkets. Limbong Art, in particular, has an excellent range of woodcarvings upstairs, and also offers batik classes.

You can rent surfboards from several places from around RM40 per hour; most offer surfing lessons. Windsurfing (RM60/hr), kitesurfing (RM100/hr) and X Sail (RM100/hr) equipment can be rented right on the beach from Kam's Surf Shack (T 019 923 8558, E kamsurf007@gmail.com), who also offer surf lessons (RM120/hr), windsurfing lessons (RM100/hr) and kite surfing lessons (RM250/hr).

For non-surfers, there are plenty of activities on offer, including firefly and mangrove tours, snorkelling trips, turtle watching (March–Sept), and visiting the local turtle sanctuary.

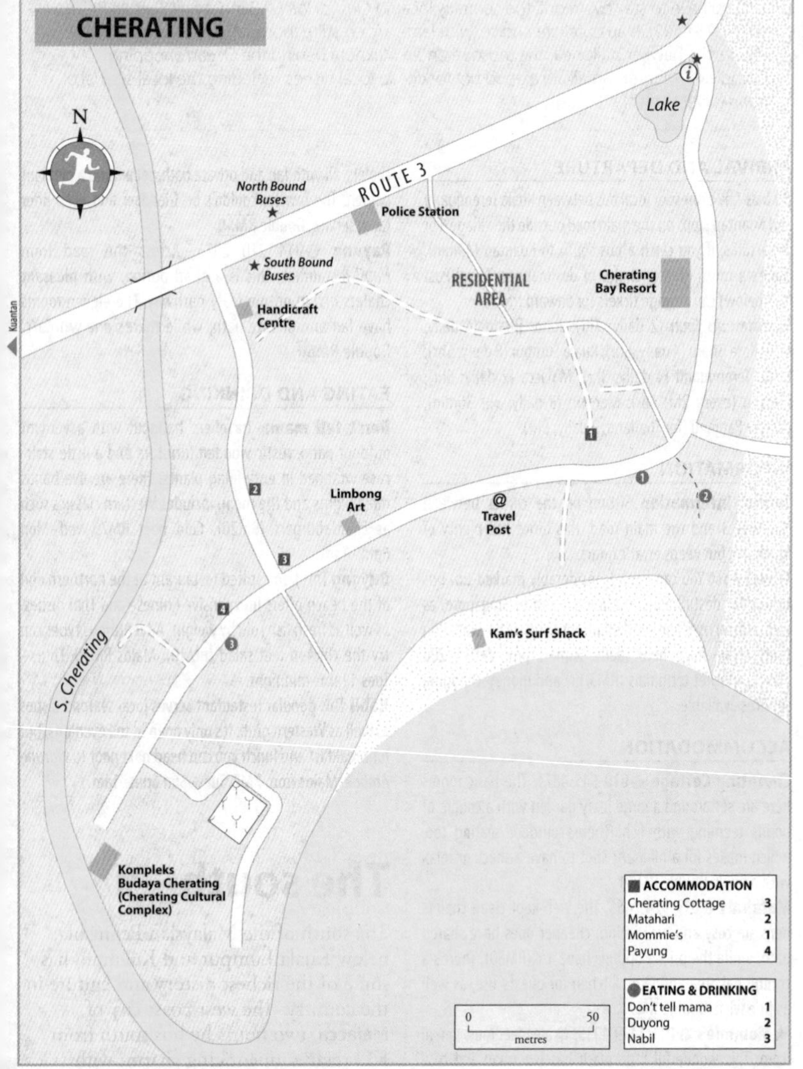

6

TRAVEL TO AND FROM KUANTAN

Kuantan is the region's transport hub, lying at the junction of routes 2 (which runs across the Peninsula to KL), 3 and 14.

By plane Kuantan Airport, 15km west of town, is served by several daily Malaysia Airline flights to KL (3 daily; 40min), while Firefly connects it to Singapore (4 weekly; 45min) and KL's Subang airport.

By bus The Terminal Sentral is fifteen minutes out of town, serving Butterworth (2 daily; 8hr); Jerantut, for Taman Negara National Park (3 daily; 3hr 30min); Kota Bharu (5 daily; 5hr); Kuala Lipis (2 daily; 5hr); Kuala Lumpur (hourly; 4hr); Kuala Terengganu (5 daily; 3hr 30min); Malacca (2 daily; 5hr); Mersing (6 daily; 3hr); Singapore (2 daily; 6hr). Note that buses to Cherating (every 2–3hr; 1hr) leave from the local bus station in Kuantan itself. To get here, catch a taxi.

If you have to stay overnight, the centrally located *Classic Hotel*, 7 Bangunan LKNP, Jln Besar (T 09 516 4599), is an excellent choice, with large a/c en-suite rooms and wi-fi access. As for eating, the hawker stalls near the mosque on Jln Makhota behind the Ocean Shopping Complex on Jln Tun Ismail are a good bet for cheap local dishes, including the local special of *patin* (silver catfish).

ARRIVAL AND DEPARTURE

By bus Any express or local bus between Kuala Terengganu and Kuantan stops on the main road outside the village. For departures, if you catch a bus south to Kuantan (45min), there's a much greater choice of destinations. Travel Post (see below) can arrange tickets for onward travel.

Destinations Ipoh (2 daily; 7hr); Johor Bharu (4 daily; 6hr); Kota Bharu (4 daily; 5hr); Kuala Lumpur (8 daily; 5hr); Kuala Terengganu (4 daily; 3hr); Malacca (2 daily; 6hr); Marang (every 2hr; 4hr); Mersing (3 daily; 3hr 30min); Rantau Panjang (for Thailand; 2 daily; 6hr).

INFORMATION

Tourist information Sitting on the corner between Highway 3 and the main road, this office has plenty of brochures but keeps erratic hours.

Travel Post You can book (considerably marked-up) bus tickets for destinations in Malaysia and to Singapore, as well as local river and snorkelling trips and turtle-watching tours (May–Aug) here (daily 9am–11pm; T 014 206 5054). Internet terminals (RM3/hr) and money-changing services available.

ACCOMMODATION

Cherating Cottage T 010 545 4874. The basic rooms here are set around a large leafy garden with a couple of ponds teeming with fish. There's outdoor seating too, which makes for a pleasant spot to have a snack or relax with a book. Double **RM50**

Matahari T 017 924 7465. The well-kept clean chalets here are cosy and welcoming; cheaper ones have shared bath, while the pricier options have a/c (RM80). There's a communal area and large kitchen for guests' use, as well as free wi-fi. Double **RM25**

★ **Mommie's** T 011 1499 4035, E afeedaedrous@gmail.com. This wonderful little place has ten small and cosy chalets, all with fan and private bath, set around a pleasant garden. The owners couldn't be friendlier and even offer room service. Double **RM50**

Payung T 014 210 2973. Across the road from *Nabil* restaurant, this is a good option, with pleasant chalets giving onto a leafy pathway. The eleven rooms have fan and private bath, while there's one with a/c. Double **RM60**

EATING AND DRINKING

Don't tell mama Travellers' hangout with a verdant outdoor patio, rustic wooden furniture and a little staircase wrapped in entwining plants. There are live bands most nights and the menu includes Western classics such as cheeseburgers (RM20). Cold beer RM7. Wed–Mon 6pm–1am.

Duyong This large stilted restaurant at the northern end of the beach offers inexpensive Chinese and Thai dishes, as well as fresh fish sold by weight. Adventurous types can try the chicken feet salad (RM10). Mains RM10. Thurs–Tues 11am–midnight.

Nabil This popular restaurant serves local seafood dishes as well as Western grub. It's only open in the evenings, but for breakfast and lunch you can head next door to *Warung Ambak*. Mains from RM7. Tues–Sun 6pm–1am.

The south

The south of the Malaysian Peninsula, below Kuala Lumpur and Kuantan, has some of the richest history and culture in the country. The west-coast city of **Malacca**, two hours by bus south from KL, retains an enticing charm, with

waterside walkways and a stunning mixture of architecture from its Portuguese, Dutch and British colonial days. The relaxed island of **Pulau Tioman** is located on the opposite coast and boasts numerous sandy beaches and good diving opportunities.

MALACCA

When Penang was known only for its oysters and Singapore was just a fishing village, **MALACCA** had already achieved worldwide fame. Under the auspices of the Malacca Sultanate, founded in the early fifteenth century, political and

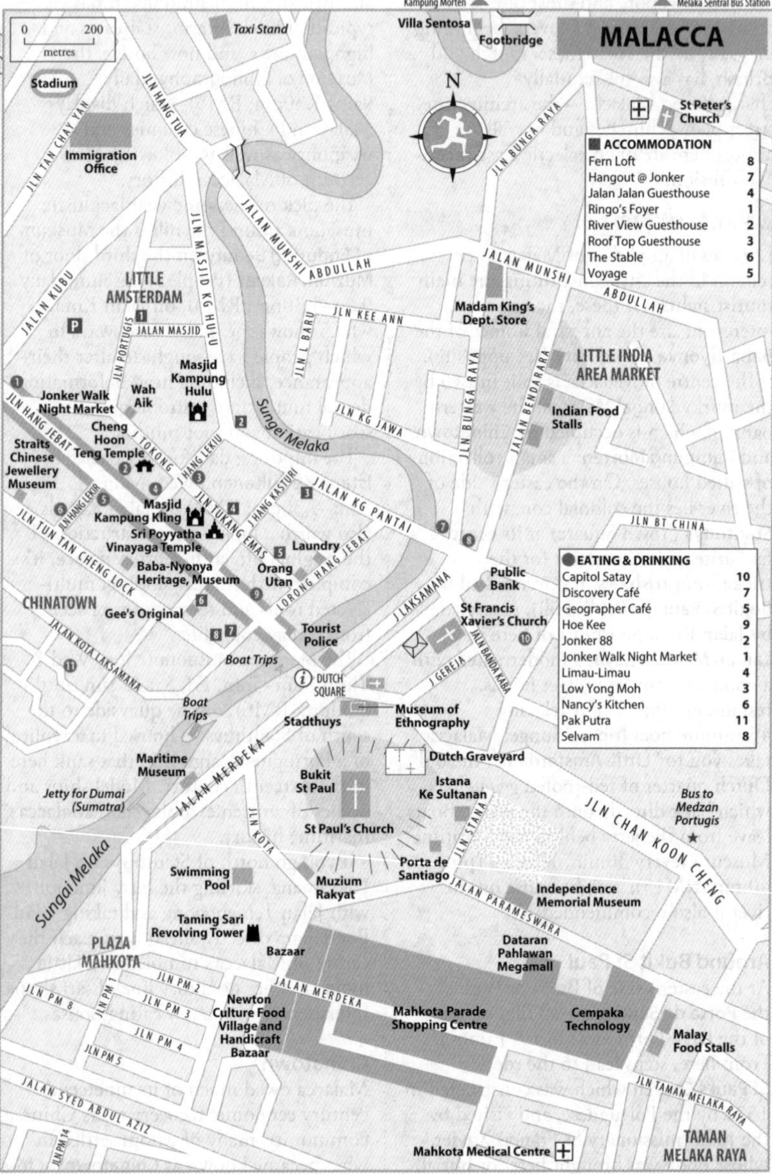

6

cultural life flourished. The town grew rich by **trading spices** from the Moluccas in the Indonesian archipelago and textiles from Gujarat in northwest India. A levy on all imported goods made it one of the wealthiest kingdoms in the world, and it gradually expanded its territory to include Singapore and most of east-coast Sumatra. A series of takeovers, beginning in 1511, by the Portuguese, Dutch and British, has also substantially characterized Malacca – the architecture, street plans, churches and overall atmosphere are of an eclectic East-meets-West fusion.

WHAT TO SEE AND DO

Legacies of all phases of Malacca's past remain in the city, constituting the main tourist sights. Of these, the most interesting are the ancestral homes of the **Baba-Nyonya community** (see opposite).

The centre of Malacca is split in two by the murky **Sungai Malacca**, the western bank of which is occupied by **Chinatown** and **Kampung Morten**, a small collection of stilted houses. On the eastern side of the river lies the colonial core with **Stadthuys** (Town Square) at its centre – a favourite gathering point for the tricked-out trishaws. It's overlooked by **Bukit St Paul** (St Paul's Hill), encircled by Jalan Kota. Southeast of here is **Taman Malacca Raya**, a modern area with a good selection of budget hotels, restaurants and bars. A relaxing 45-minute **boat trip** up Sungei Malacca takes you to "**Little Amsterdam**", the old Dutch quarter of red-roofed *godowns*, which back directly onto the water. Boats leave from the jetty behind the Maritime Museum (every 30min, 10am–11pm; 40min; RM15); a night cruise on the river is also recommended.

Around Bukit St Paul

At the eastern side of Bukit St Paul is the **Porta de Santiago** – all that remains of the large Portuguese fort A Famosa. From here, steps lead to the roofless **St Paul's Church** which was constructed in 1521 by the Portuguese, and visited by the Jesuit missionary St Francis Xavier, whose body was brought here for burial, and later moved to Goa in India. Commemorative brass plaques for Dutch and Portuguese dignitaries rest against the church's inner walls. Down a winding path is the sturdy **Stadthuys**, a collection of buildings that dates from 1660 and was used as a town hall during the Dutch and British administrations. It has typically Dutch interior staircases and high windows, and now houses the **Museum of Ethnography** (daily 9am–5.30pm; RM5), which displays Malay and Chinese ceramics and weaponry as well as a blow-by-blow account of Malaccan history.

The pick of the somewhat lacklustre museums around the hill is the **Museum of Enduring Beauty** on the third floor of **Muzium Rakyat** (People's Museum; daily 9am–5.30pm; RM3), on Jalan Kota, which shows the many novel ways in which people have sought to alter their appearance, including head deformation, dental mutilations, tattooing, scarification and foot-binding.

The imposing dark timber palace of **Istana Ke Sultanan** (Wed–Mon 9am–5.30pm; RM2) on Jalan Kota is also worth a look – a reconstruction of the original fifteenth-century palace, it's complete with sharply sloping, multi-layered roofs and re-creations of scenes from Malay court life.

The **Maritime Museum** (Mon, Wed & Thurs 9am–5pm, Fri, Sat & Sun until 8.30pm; RM6), on the quayside to the south of Stadthuys, is housed in a replica of a Portuguese cargo ship that sank here in the sixteenth century. Model ships and oodles of written exhibits chart Malacca's maritime history.

If you go north of Stadthuys up Jalan Laksamana, skirting the busy junction with Jalan Temenggong and taking Jalan Bendahara directly ahead, you reach the centre of Malacca's tumbledown **Little India**, a rather desultory line of sari shops, interspersed with a few eating houses.

Chinatown

Malacca owed much of its nineteenth-century economic recovery to its Chinese community, many of whom settled in what became known as **Chinatown**, across

Sungai Malacca from the colonial district. This is one of the most lively, compact areas in Malacca, popular for wandering around during the day and enjoying a few drinks come evening. The traffic-clogged narrow streets are full of quaint and unexpected cafés and trinket shops at every corner, all housed within the elegant townhouses that were the ancestral homes of the Baba-Nyonya community. The wealthiest and most successful built long, narrow-fronted houses, and minimized the "window tax" by incorporating several internal courtyards. Chinatown's central street, **Jalan Hang Jebat**, known as **Jonker Walk**, famous for its antique shops and weekend night market, looks particularly striking lit up with red lanterns in the evening.

The **Baba-Nyonya Heritage Museum** at 48–50 Jalan Tun Tan Cheng Lock (Mon–Thurs 10am–1pm & 2–4.30pm; Fri–Sun 9.45am–4.30pm; RM12) is an amalgam of three adjacent houses belonging to one family, and an excellent, atmospheric example of the Chinese Palladian style. Typically connected by a common covered footway, decorated with hand-painted tiles, each front entrance has an outer swing door of elaborately carved teak, with two red lanterns hanging either side of the doorway and a canopy of Chinese tiles around the shuttered windows. Inside, the homes are filled with gold-leaf fittings, splendid blackwood furniture inlaid with mother-of-pearl (look for the opium bed) and delicately carved lacquer screens.

A few doors down at 108 Jalan Tun Tan Cheng Lock is the **Straits Chinese Jewellery Museum** (daily 10am–5pm; RM15), which displays a wonderful collection of skilfully crafted Peranakan jewellery embracing Chinese, Malay and Indo-European designs and motifs. Among the elaborate pieces on display are gold ankle bangles, gold, silver and diamond hairpins, embroidered velvet slippers and tobacco boxes.

At 25 Jalan Tokong you'll find the **Cheng Hoon Teng Temple** (daily 7am–7pm), the oldest Chinese temple in Malaysia dedicated to Kuan Yin, the goddess of mercy. Busy with worshippers during the day and awash with incense smoke, its roofs are intricately decorated with mythological figures and creatures, made of broken porcelain pieces from ceramics originally brought over from Chinese traders.

Kampong Chitty

Northwest of Chinatown, around 1.5km along Jalan Gajah Berang, is the traditional Straits-born Indian community, **Kampung Chitty**. The Chitties pre-date the Baba-Nyonya community, their ancestors having arrived in Malaysia in the 1400s, and the neighbourhood is fun to wander around; look for the archway decorated with elephant sculptures.

ARRIVAL AND DEPARTURE

The compact city centre is best explored on foot.

By bus The Malacca Sentral bus station is located a 15min bus ride out of town at Meleka Sentral. Bus #17 connects the station to Dutch Square (30min; RM1.50); taxis cost RM20.

Destinations Butterworth (5 daily; 6hr 30min); Ipoh (6 daily; 4hr); Hat Yai (Thailand; 2 daily; 10hr); Johor Bahru (8 daily; 3hr); Kota Bharu (daily; 9hr); Kuala Lumpur (8 daily; 2hr); Kuala Perlis (for Langkawi; 2 daily; 8hr); Kuala Terengganu (2 daily; 8hr); Kuantan (7 daily; 5hr); Mersing (3 daily; 5hr); Penang (3 daily; 7hr); Singapore (6 daily; 4hr).

By ferry The Tunas Rupat ferry (T 06 283 2506) to Dumai in Sumatra docks at the ICQX Complex, close to the historical centre (daily 10am; 2hr 30min; RM130).

INFORMATION AND GETTING AROUND

Tourist information centre On Jln Kota (daily 9am–6pm; T 06 283 6220, W melaka.gov.my), just across the roundabout from the Stadthuys. Staff are helpful and there are plenty of brochures on the town's attractions. Free historical walking tours on Tues, Thurs & Sat (9.30am; 2hr 30min) leave from the tourist office.

Trishaws There are trishaws at Padang Pahlawan Square and outside the Mahkota Parade Shopping Centre. A sightseeing tour costs RM40 for one hour.

ACCOMMODATION

Fern Loft 24 Jln Tun Tan Cheng Lock T 011 1288 3334, W fernloft.com. Sister hostel to *Fern Loft* in KL, this new little addition to Malacca has just three rooms, all with shared bath – a large 16-bed dorm with lockers and clothes racks, a little twin and a family room. There's wi-fi throughout and a/c in the rooms 7pm–9am. Dorm **RM25**, twin **RM70**

6

Hangout @ Jonker 19 & 21 Lorong Hang Jebat ☎ 06 282 8318, ⓦ hangouthotels.com. This secure flashpackers' place with magnetic swipe cards offers a selection of modern rooms with cable TV, a/c and private bath, set over four floors. There's a kitchen, a lounge area with computers and wi-fi throughout. Double **RM210**

★ **Jalan Jalan Guesthouse** 8 Jln Tukang Emas ☎ 06 283 3937, ⓦ jalanjalanguesthouse.com. Run by helpful owner Sam, this quiet, laidback guesthouse has a selection of cosy rooms set in two "old" and "new" buildings – both equally charming with sociable communal areas. If you stay in the "new" guesthouse, make sure to choose room five, an airy spacious double. Dorms are welcoming and all have lockers. There's wi-fi throughout and bikes for RM5 per stay. Dorm **RM15**, double **RM38**

Ringo's Foyer 46A Jln Portugis ☎ 06 281 6393, ⓦ ringosfoyer.com.my. This welcoming guesthouse has simple darkish rooms giving off a maze of hallways. The congenial owner Howard takes his guests on educational bike tours around the city. There's a funky rooftop terrace that is a great spot to socialize over an evening beer. Dorm **RM17**, double **RM40**

★ **River View Guesthouse** 94 & 96 Jln Kampong Pantai ☎ 012 327 7746, ⓔ riverviewguesthouse@yahoo.com. Set in a 200-year-old house, this lovely guesthouse with high ceilings and beautiful wooden floorboards has a leafy terrace looking over the river – the views at night are particularly spectacular. There's only one three-bed dorm, while the rest of the rooms are privates. Dorm **RM25**, double **RM68**

Roof Top Guest House Malacca 39 Jln Kampong Pantai ☎ 012 327 7746, ⓔ rooftopguesthouse@yahoo.com. Under the same management as *River View Guesthouse*, this friendly place has a couple of breezy rooftop terraces; most rooms face the interior courtyard and as a result are a bit on the darkish side, but are livened up with a splash of colourful paint. There's a kitchen, living area, book exchange and wi-fi throughout. Dorm **RM30**, double **RM68**

★ TREAT YOURSELF

The Stable Jln Hang Kasturi ☎ 012 623 4459, ⓦ thestablemalacca.com. If you've ever been accused of having been raised in a barn, how about sleeping in a stable? Malacca's quirkiest boutique lodgings are indeed in a converted sixteenth-century stable and consist of just one room: all exposed brick walls, original wooden beams, raised bed with crisp linens and ultra-modern touches such as plasma-screen TV. Unique. **RM380**

Voyage 40 Lorong Hang Jebat ☎ 06 281 5216, ⓦ voyagetogether.com. This laidback place has a lounge area with TV and pool table downstairs, while the first floor has a large 15-bed dorm with mosquito nets. The staff seem rather inattentive though, and anyone can just stroll in and out, as the reception is a few doors down at their sister guesthouse *Sama-Sama*. Dorm **RM15**, double **RM40**

EATING AND DRINKING

Sampling the spicy dishes of Nyonya cuisine – with its emphasis on sour herbs such as tamarind, tempered by creamy coconut milk – is a must in Malacca.

Capitol Satay 41 Lorong Bukit Cina. The queue at this local institution starts as soon as the shutters are pulled up mid-afternoon – hungry bellies wait in line for satay (RM0.90 each) of skewered meat and fish, from pork liver to fish balls, cooked in the sizzling peanut sauce pots found at the centre of each table. Daily 5pm–midnight.

Discovery Café 3 Jln Bunga Raya. Three-litre towers of beer (RM57.90) are on offer for the thirsty at this travellers' hangout; the interior is decorated with old curios, while local and Filipino pop bands take centre stage in the outdoor seating area each day. Daily 9am–1am.

Geographer Café 83 Jln Hang Jebat. A backpacker favourite, this leafy café, restaurant and bar offers a large selection of veggie dishes, as well as Asian and Western grub. There are live R&B bands on Fri, Sat & Sun, while on Mon the musical flavour is jazz. Daily 10am–midnight.

Hoe Kee 4, 6 & 8 Jln Hong Jebat. This popular place specializes in one of Malacca's traditional eats: tasty chicken rice balls (RM4.50) that go down a treat. Daily 11am–3pm.

★ **Jonker Walk Night Market** On Friday, Saturday and Sunday evenings, Jonker Walk becomes a pedestrian street, lined with all manner of food stalls – a great way to sample local specialities such as *otak-otak* (spicy fish paste grilled in banana leaf), *popiah* (mega spring roll stuffed with prawns, garlic, carrot, palm sugar and chilli), *cendol* (shaved ice topped with flavoured syrups, coconut milk and jelly) and much more. Snacks from RM3.

Jonker 88 88 Jln Hang Jebat. A sweet tooth's delight serving all manner of refreshing desserts including *baba cendol* (RM3). There are plenty of hearty savoury portions too – try the *baba laksa* (noodles with egg, prawn and tuna; RM5). Mon–Thurs 10am–6pm, Fri & Sat 10am–9pm, Sun 10am–6.30pm.

Limau-Limau 9 Jln Hang Lekiu. Cosy little café set on two floors and dotted with little knick-knacks and mismatched furniture. The light menu includes soups (RM7.90), sandwiches (RM11.90) and focaccia cheese melts (RM18.90), as well as freshly squeezed juices, milkshakes and lassis (RM8). Thurs–Tues 9am–6pm.

Low Yong Moh 32 Jln Tukang Emas. A great local hangout to refuel with a pork, shrimp or chicken *dim sum* (RM2) as you explore the city. Wed–Mon 5.30am–noon.

Nancy's Kitchen 7 Jln Hang Lekir. This little Nyonya restaurant has been the hottest table in town for quite some time; it's still going strong – try their signature chicken candlenut (RM18), which is cooked in a macademia nut sauce, or the prawns cooked with spices and coconut milk (RM27). Mon–Thurs & Sun 11.30am–3pm, 4–5.30pm; Fri & Sat until 9.30pm. Occasionally closed on Tues.

★ **Pak Putra** 56 & 58 Jln Laksamana. This hugely popular North Indian place with outdoor seating attracts a crowd for its superb chicken tandoori: spicy, crispy and succulent. Mains RM7. Tues–Sun 5.30pm–1am.

Selvam 3 Jln Temenggong. This welcoming Indian place serves excellent banana-leaf curries (RM4), all carefully prepared at your table. On weekends there are lunch specials, including tasty biryanis (RM6) and tandoori sets (RM6). Daily 7am–10pm; closed Tues every fortnight.

SHOPPING

Antiques Malacca is famed for its antiques, and there are many specialist outlets along Jln Hang Jebat and Jln Tun Tan Cheng Lock, though they are by no means cheap. If it's a genuine antique, check that it can be exported legally and fill in an official clearance form. A number of shops charge RM3 just to browse.

Crafts and souvenirs Wah Aik at 56 Jln Tokong is a third-generation shoemaker selling bound feet silk shoes, while Gee's Original on Jln Hang Kasturi has a shopful of handcrafted wooden clogs. For modern souvenirs, try Orang Utan, 59 Lorong Hang Jebat – it's the outlet for local artist Charles Cham's witty cartoon T-shirts and paintings.

DIRECTORY

Banks and exchange The most central bank is Public Bank on Jln Laksamana; HSBC, Jln Hang Tuah, has a 24hr ATM, as does OCBC bank, in Dataran Pahlawan Megamall. Moneychangers are often more convenient and offer as good rates as the banks: there are a few around town, including on Jonker Street.

Hospital Mahkota Medical Centre, 3 Makhota Malacca, Jln Merdeka (T 06 285 2999).

Immigration The Immigration Office is in the Urban Transformation Centre (UTC) on Jln Hang Tuah (T 06 333 3333), for on-the-spot visa renewals.

Internet All accommodation options reviewed offer free wi-fi; most offer free internet too.

Laundry Clean Clean, Jln Hang Jabat at Jln Kampung Kuli (Mon–Sat 10.30am–12.30pm & 1.30–5.30pm; RM4/kg).

Police The Tourist Police Office (T 06 288 3732; open 24hr) is on Jln Kota.

Post office On Jln Laksama (Mon–Fri 8.30am–5.30pm, Sat 8.30am–1pm).

MERSING

The small fishing town of **MERSING**, between Kuantan and Johor Bahru, is the gateway both to Pulau Tioman and to the Endau-Rompin National Park and, as such, gets a steady stream of visitors outside the monsoon season. The town centre is grouped around two main streets, Jalan Abu Bakar and Jalan Ismail, both branching off from the main roundabout. You'll most likely find yourself staying here overnight on the way to the island, as boats are far more frequent in the mornings.

ARRIVAL AND DEPARTURE

By bus Both long-distance and local buses arrive at the bus station not far from the bridge across the river, a couple of minutes from the roundabout. Mersing is well connected to a number of destinations. You can also get to Singapore by taking a bus to Johor Bahru and changing to one of the frequent connections there.

Destinations Johor Bahru (5 daily; 20hr 30min); Kota Bharu (2 daily; 10hr); Kota Terrenganu (2 daily; 6hr); Kuala Lumpur (4 daily; 5hr 30min); Kuantan (2 daily; 3hr); Malacca (daily; 3hr 30min); Singapore (daily at 1.30pm; 3hr).

By ferry The jetty is about 10min walk from the roundabout along Jln Abu Bakar. The boat companies that ply the route between Mersing and Tioman have offices inside the R&R Plaza near the jetty; in peak season, get your ticket the day before. Boats for Tioman depart between 7am and 4.30pm, with far more departures in the morning; the journey takes 1hr 30min–2hr. Expect to pay around RM70 for a round trip plus the additional RM5 marine conservation fee. There's very little service during the monsoon season (Nov–Feb).

INFORMATION

Tourist information The Mersing Tourist Information Centre along Jln Abu Bakar (T 07 799 5212) keeps erratic opening hours, but has some helpful brochures and photocopied maps of Tioman.

ACCOMMODATION AND EATING

Embassy Hotel 2 Jln Ismail T 09 798 2864. This large concrete hotel with a central location right near the roundabout offers spacious clean rooms with a/c and cable TV. Boat departure times are posted by the reception and there's wi-fi throughout (though not great on the top floor). Double RM55

Ee Lo Tepi Jln Dato' Mohd Ali. This no-frills restaurant serves tasty Chinese dishes, with mains from S$5. Daily 10.30am–3pm & 6.30–10pm.

PULAU TIOMAN

PULAU TIOMAN, 30km east of Mersing, is a popular holiday island scattered with small palm-fringed beach coves. Express boats travel here in less than two hours, and several daily flights arrive from Singapore and Kuala Lumpur.

Damage has unfortunately been inflicted on the surrounding coral and marine life, but Tioman still has some breathtaking natural scenery. Most of the island's facilities are at industrial **Tekek**, on the west coast, and the popular budget places are in the bay of **Ayer Batang** or **Salang**. The east coast's attractive sole settlement, **Juara**, is less developed. One road wide enough for cars spans the length of Tekek, and another stretches along Juara, with a steep, pitted, narrow road connecting the two. Apart from these, the island is crossed by dirt roads and jungle tracks.

Many of Tioman's nearby islets provide excellent opportunities for snorkelling and diving, with numerous dive centres around Tioman. Most of the chalet operations offer day-trips to nearby reefs and around the island, taking in the Asah waterfall on the south coast.

Tekek

TEKEK is the main settlement on Pulau Tioman, with the main jetty and airport

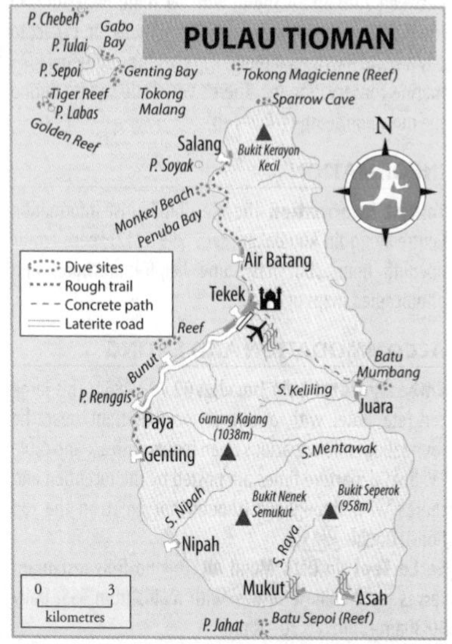

both located here as well as most of the island's shops. It's also one of the least attractive places to visit on the island, but this is where you'll find essential services. Situated north of the main jetty at the very end of the bay, the **Marine Centre** (daily 8.30am–4pm; free), set up to protect the coral and marine life around the island, and to patrol the fishing taking place in its waters, contains engaging interactive displays on the marine fauna.

Ayer Batang

AYER BATANG, commonly referred to as ABC, the next beach north of Tekek (jetty to jetty), is the most popular choice for backpackers, and essentially a single concrete track running along the long stretch of beachfront, with guesthouses and restaurants spread out along it amid the greenery. There's a good stretch of beach at the southern end, near *Nazri's* (see p.473), a charming series of bridges linking the chalets at the northern end and a pleasant, laidback atmosphere to the whole area. When walking around, you do have to watch out for locals who cruise up and down the concrete path on motorbikes and trundling three-wheelers. It's a twenty-minute walk to here from Tekek, or hitch a ride for RM5.

Salang

North of Ayer Batang, **SALANG** is a pleasant backpacker option with a handful of guesthouses lining the seafront. It's smaller than ABC, although things can get quite lively here too. The northern rocky end of the beach is not ideal for swimming, while the southern end is the more scenic, and Pulau Soyok, the small island off the southern headland, has a pretty reef for snorkelling.

Juara

At **JUARA**, situated across two quiet, spread-out stretches of beach on the east coast, the only entertainments are diving, surfing and sunbathing, and the vibe is friendly and more relaxed than on the other side of the island. As the northern (more populated) bay faces out to open sea, it's more susceptible to bad weather

but lovely when the weather is good. The southern bay is more secluded, but does have a couple of chalets.

Hikes around the island

Tioman has a good number of enjoyable and challenging hikes, both along the coast and in the interior. It's very easy to get from ABC to Tekek; there's a ten-minute path running up and over the promontory. Also from ABC, a fifteen-minute **jungle trail** leads over the headland to the north, which – after an initial scramble – flattens out into an easy walk, ending up at secluded **Penuba Bay**. From here, it's around an hour and a quarter to gorgeous, secluded Monkey Beach, and then another hour and a half to Salang. This trail involves scrambling over rocky outcrops and is not always easy to follow (follow the power lines overhead).

Another tricky trail is the cross-island one from Tekek to Juara, taking around two or three hours and quite steep in some places. The start of the trail in Tekek (a five-minute walk from the airstrip) is the only signposted concrete path that heads off in the direction of the local mosque before hitting virgin jungle after about fifteen minutes; from Juara, the trail starts opposite the jetty. There's no danger of losing your way: cement steps climb steeply through the greenery, tapering off into a smooth, downhill path once you're over the ridge. After an hour or so, there is a **waterfall** – it's forbidden to bathe here, since it supplies Tekek with water. From the waterfall, it's another hour or so to Juara village.

ARRIVAL AND DEPARTURE

Transport on the island is somewhat limited. In favourable weather, walking and kayaking are good ways to explore the island.

By plane Berjaya Air (berjaya-air.com) flights from Kuala Lumpur and Singapore land at the airstrip in Tekek, from where you'll have to take a boat taxi to the bay of your choice (unless you're staying in ABC, in which case the distance is easily walkable). During monsoon season, flying is the only reliable way of getting on and off the island. The baggage allowance limit is 10kg, unless you purchase the most expensive Flexi ticket option, in which case it's 20kg. **Destinations** KL (3 weekly; 1hr) and Singapore (5 weekly; 50hr).

By boat You'll have to decide in advance which bay you want to stay in since the boats generally make stops only at the major resorts of Genting, Paya, Tekek, Ayer Batang and Salang (in that order); there are only occasional boats from Mersing to Juara on the east coast. If you book a return boat ticket in Mersing, you have to specify your return time at the time of booking. If you booked a one-way ticket in Mersing,

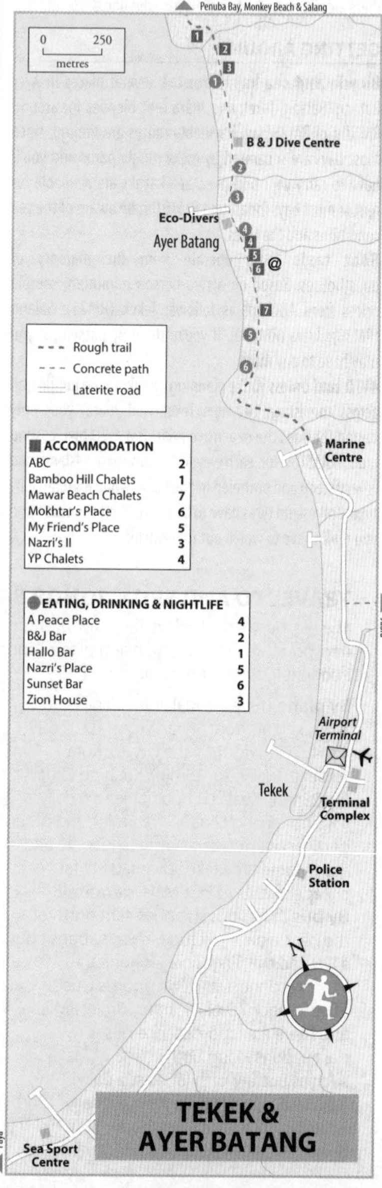

6

ask at your guesthouse for the departure times from the particular bay you're staying in – the first boat leaves Salang at 7am, stopping at each jetty in turn, and the last is at mid-afternoon (around 4pm). Bad weather causes delays and the unscrupulous boat companies often pick up more passengers than the boat is designed for, meaning that some end up standing all the way back to Mersing (and it also mean that there are not enough life jackets for everyone).

GETTING AROUND

Bicycle and sea-kayak rental Several places in Ayer Batang, Salang, Tekek and Juara rent bicycles for around RM5/hr or RM25/day. Navigable routes are limited, since most bays are separated by rocky jungle paths and you'll have to carry your bike over. Sea kayaks are available for rent in most bays for around RM10/hr; be aware of the sea conditions and the tides.

Boat taxis These operate from the majority of guesthouses. Based on a two-person minimum, sample prices from ABC are as follows: Tekek (RM25); Salang (RM30); Juara (RM150). If you're the only passenger, you may have to pay more.

4WD taxi Unless you're planning on taking the jungle trail across the island between Tekek and Juara, your only option (besides the expensive boat) is a 4WD taxi, costing around R35/person each way. The narrow cross-island road is very steep and potholed in places, so while it's doable by bike, brakes and tyres have to be in excellent condition and you really have to watch out for vehicles.

DIVE OPERATORS

Many dive centres on Tioman offer the range of PADI certificates, from the four-day Open Water course (usually around RM1000) through to the fourteen-day Divemaster (RM2000); always check that qualified English-speaking instructors are employed, and that the cost includes equipment.

WEST COAST

B & J Dive Centre T 09 419 5555, W divetioman.com. This friendly, long-standing outfit on Ayer Batang is a good choice, with the advantage of an open-air pool, so skills don't have to be practised in the unpredictable sea currents. Four-day/three-night PADI Open Water courses from RM1250, including accommodation. They have a sister outfit at Salang beach.

Eco-Divers T 09 419 1794, W eco-divers.net. Also on Ayer Batang, this is a slightly smaller centre than B & J, with friendly staff. Half-day Discover Scuba courses from RM200; Open Water RM1050.

EAST COAST

1511 Asia T 09 419 3101, W 1511asia.com. This resort on Juara offers a range of activities, including windsurfing, kitesurfing, island hopping, snorkelling and scuba diving.

ACCOMMODATION

AYER BATANG

ABC T 013 922 0263, E abcbeachtioman@hotmail.com. At the far northern end of the bay, with pretty, inexpensive chalets set in a well-tended garden by a nice stretch of beach.

TRAVEL TO AND FROM JOHOR BAHRU

The big, busy city of Johor Bahru (or JB), right across the border from Singapore, is an excellent transport hub with bus, train and plane connections to all main destinations in Malaysia and frequent ferries to Indonesia.

By plane There are Malaysia Airlines and AirAsia flights from Senai Airport (T 07 599 4500), 20km north of the city, to: Kota Kinabalu (daily; 2hr 15min); Kuching (3 daily; 1hr 25min); Kuala Lumpur (at least 6 daily; 45min); Penang (2 daily; 1hr 5min); and other destinations. You can stay in Singapore and at the same time take advantage of far cheaper flights to East Malaysia from JB.

By bus Larkin bus station is 4km north of the centre on Jln Geruda. The city transit bus #170 and the Singapore–Johor Bahru Express connect it to Singapore's Queen Street station (every 15min; 30min; RM2.20) and there are long-distance buses to destinations along both coasts of Malaysia, such as Butterworth (at least 2 daily; 14hr); Ipoh (4 daily; 9hr); Kota Bharu (2 daily; 12hr); Kuala Lumpur (every 30min; 4hr 30min); Kuala Terengganu (2 daily; 8hr); Kuantan (6 daily; 5hr); Malacca (5 daily; 2hr 30min); Mersing (at least 5 daily; 2hr 30min).

By train JB Sentral is slightly east of the city centre, off Jln Tun Abdul Razak, with regular connections to Singapore, destinations along Malaysia's west coast and some towns in the interior: Gemas (4 daily; 3–4hr); Kuala Lumpur (4 daily; 5hr 30min–7hr 10min); Singapore (6 daily; 1hr). There are no direct trains from JB to Kota Bharu along the Jungle Railway (see p.449), but you can travel north as far as Gemas and change trains there. Check W ktmb.com.my for the latest schedules.

By ferry The Zon Ferry Terminal (T 07 221 1677) is 2km east of the Causeway, with departures to the Indonesian destinations of Tanjung Pinang (6 daily; 1hr 30min) and Pulau Batam (hourly; 1hr 30min). There are also boats departing from Kukup, southwest of JB, which go to Tanjung Balai, Sumatra.

All come with mosquito nets and their own bathroom, while the more pricey ones have a/c and tea- and coffee-making facilities. Double RM50

Bamboo Hill Chalets 09 419 1339, bamboohillchalets.com. Nestled on the northernmost tip of the beach, the six wooden chalets here perch on the headland and enjoy great views over the bay. Chalets range from basic with fan to more sophisticated choices with a/c and pretty verandas. Double RM90

Mawar Beach Chalets 09 419 1153. Simple A-frame huts line the beachfront, the cheapest of which are an absolute steal. The attached restaurant is a popular spot, serving tasty yet inexpensive food. Double RM30

Mokhtar's Place 09 419 1148. Two regimental rows of clean and airy chalets with little porches, *Mokhtar's* offers booking services for buses on the mainland, water-taxis, fishing and snorkelling trips, for non-guests as well as guests. There is also internet at RM10/hr. Double RM60

My Friend's Place 09 419 1150. A small budget resort, made up of simple chalets in two prim rows, facing each other across a garden, all of which have a fan and attached bathroom. Double RM45

Nazri's II 09 419 1375, nazrisplace.com. The little chalets here are nestled on a pretty leafy hillside amid twisting tree roots and rocks. The small budget huts are at the very top, while the pricier a/c rooms are dotted around the sloping grounds. Double RM100

YP Chalets One of ABC's cheaper options, *YP* has rows of simple chalets, all with little verandas, just inland from a decent stretch of beach. Double RM50

SALANG

Ella's Place 09 419 5004. This welcoming, quiet place at the northern end of the beach is dotted with colourful potted plants and hammocks slung between palm trees, perfect to while the afternoon away. Rooms range from simple huts with private bath to larger a/c rooms facing the beach. Staff are friendly and can organize snorkelling trips too. Double RM60

Salang Indah Resort 09 419 5015, salangindah.com. This large catch-all resort has rooms catering to all budgets, from simple fan huts in various stages of disrepair (have a look at a few) to more upmarket a/c rooms. Double RM50

JUARA

Beach Shack 09 419 3148, timstormsurf@yahoo.au. This laidback Malay-Ozzie owned place oozes a mellow vibe, with surfers lounging around waiting to catch a good wave. There are tiny A-frame huts with shared bath lining the beach, as well as more spacious doubles all made of recycled timber. The restaurant includes Western and Malay dishes, and there are rumours that the owner may even feature Ozzie kangaroo steak on the menu. Double RM40

Bushman Square Chalets 09 419 3109, matbushman@hotmail.com. This friendly place offers clean and well-kept chalets on the beach, with sun loungers shaded by palm trees at your very doorstep. The attached restaurant serves good food, and they also rent out snorkelling equipment for RM10/day. Double RM60

Juara Beach The chalets here are set around a large garden that is pleasantly lit up at night. The a/c rooms are spacious and kept clean, and there are tea- and coffee-making facilities too. Double RM120

EATING, DRINKING AND NIGHTLIFE

Most guesthouses and resorts have their own restaurants and usually offer fantastic barbecued seafood. Juara is the quietest of them all; Ayer Batang and Salang keep their nightlife low-key, although at times things can get pretty lively on both.

AYER BATANG

A Peace Place This friendly and laidback bar prepares sizzling fish and squid barbecues to be washed down with an ice-cold beer. There's unplugged music and open jams, too. Happy hour 4.30–7pm. Tues–Sun 2pm–2am.

B&J Bar This diver hangout opens its doors as divers return to shore, ready to share their underwater tales over a cold beer or two. In the evenings travellers socialize around the beach bonfire, where there are fire poi performances. Happy hour 5–7pm. Daily 2pm–midnight.

Hallo Bar A wonderfully laidback place where you can enjoy a sundowner in one of the open-fronted lime tree cabañas that stretch out into the sea. Beer RM5. Daily 5pm–2am.

Nazri's Place This large, newly renovated restaurant with wooden floors and ceilings offers Western, Malaysian and Indian dishes. Daily 7.30am–3pm & 7–11pm.

Sunset Bar As the name suggests, this bar at the southernmost end of the beach attracts thirsty travellers who come here to watch the last rays disappear over the horizon. Thurs–Tues 2pm–midnight.

Zion House Right by the jetty, this chilled place with low tables spread below a shading tree is a good spot to enjoy some live reggae and island music. There are nightly chicken and fish barbecues and the Western menu includes fish and chips and burgers (RM12). Daily noon–1am.

SALANG

Mini White House Café Confusingly decked out in yellow, this place is where it's at for nightly barbecues (RM15). They also serve pancakes, omelettes and meat dishes. Daily 7pm–10.30pm.

Salang Beach Restaurant Consistently good Chinese dishes of fish, prawn, chicken, mutton and beef, at one of Salang's best restaurants. Mains RM17. Daily 8am–3pm & 6–10pm.

6

Salang Indah Restaurant This large restaurant with sea views offers an extensive menu; breakfast includes *roti canai* (RM1.20), while for lunch and dinner the emphasis is on Thai food (RM8). Daily 7.30am–3.30pm & 6.30–10.30pm.

JUARA

Juara Beach Located north of the jetty, this restaurant along the seafront serves quality Chinese food; the extensive menu includes fish, prawn, squid, chicken and beef dishes. Mains RM15. Daily 8am–10pm.

Paradise Point There's exquisite food at this popular restaurant serving local dishes, from *roti canai* (RM2) to noodles and curries (RM5). The fresh fish comes grilled, steamed or fried and can be accompanied by all manner of sauces, from sweet and sour to spicy curry. Daily 8am–10pm.

Santai Bistro Right on the waterfront, *Santai* serves refreshing fruit juices and tasty Malaysian and Western dishes – try the garlic prawns (RM19). There are nightly barbecues at 7pm, and there's free wi-fi too. Daily 9am–11pm.

DIRECTORY

Banks and exchange There are moneychangers in the Terminal Complex (though rates are lousy). *Bank Simpanan Nasional* has an ATM and is located opposite the airport.

Clinic Poliklinik Komuniti Tekek (Mon–Fri 8am–5pm; ⓣ 09

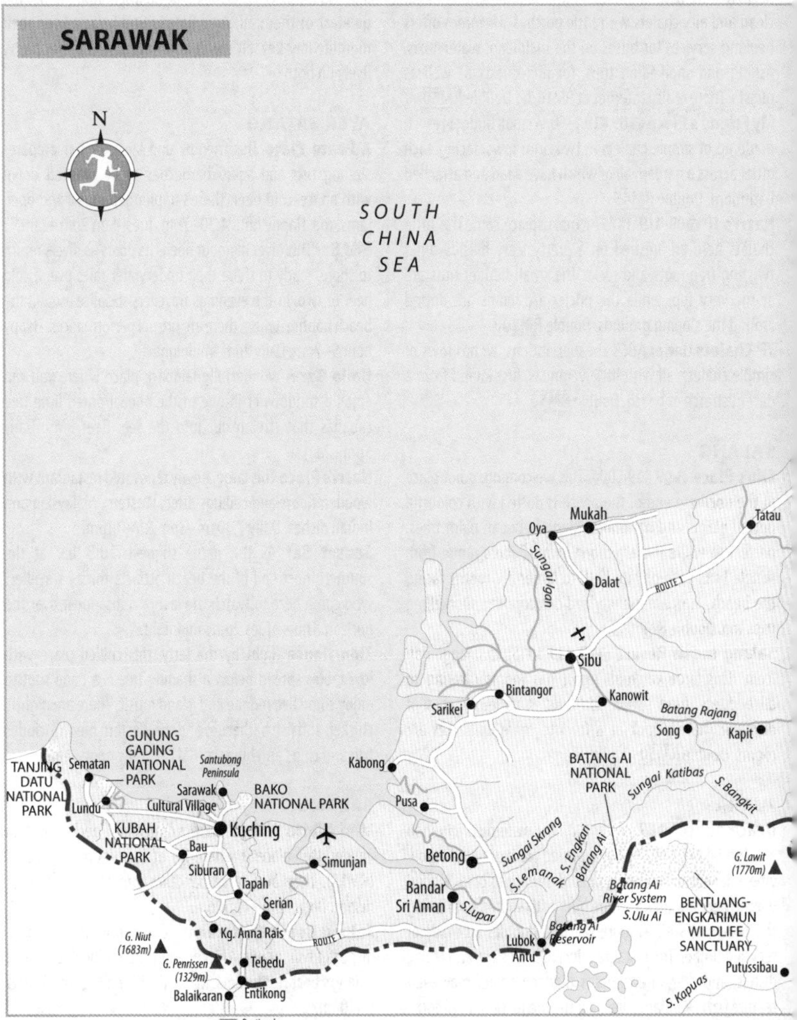

419 1800). Situated in a small gated compound 100m south of the jetty in Tekek and deals with minor ailments.

Internet Usually expensive and slow. Try *Featherlight Café* on the first floor of the Terminal Complex by the airport (daily 9am–5pm; RM10; wi-fi RM5); *Mokhtar's Place* on ABC (Sat–Thurs 8am–1pm & 2–5pm, Fri 8am–12.45pm & 2.45–5pm; RM10). There are no internet cafés at either Salang or Juara, but plenty of restaurants and guesthouses offer wi-fi, sometimes for a fee.

Police station A 10min walk south of the main jetty in Tekek (daily 24hr; ⓣ 09 419 1167).

Post office By the ATM opposite the airport (Mon–Fri 9am–4.30pm).

Sarawak

Separated from Peninsular Malaysia by the South China Sea, the two East Malaysian states of Sarawak and Sabah lie on the northern side of the island of Borneo. If Sabah is all about natural attractions, then **SARAWAK** is steeped in indigenous culture, with a large chunk of its population still living in traditional longhouses along Borneo's mighty rivers (even if the legendary head-hunting is no

6

6

longer practised). Sarawak is the larger of the two states, and, though well developed, is a good deal wilder than its mainland counterpart. Clear rivers spill down the jungle-covered mountains, and the surviving rainforest, plateaux and river communities are inhabited by indigenous peoples – traditionally grouped as Land Dyaks, Sea Dyaks and Orang Ulu.

Most people start their exploration of Sarawak in the capital **Kuching**, from where you can visit Iban longhouses and Bidayuh traditional dwellings. **Bako National Park** is a short day-trip away from Kuching and is the best place in Sarawak to spot the pot-bellied proboscis monkeys. A four-hour boat ride northeast of Kuching, **Sibu** marks the start of the popular route along **Batang Rajang**, Sarawak's longest river. Most people stop at **Kapit** and from there visit longhouses on the Katibas and Baleh tributaries, before making their way up to **Belaga** to explore more of the interior; Belaga can also be accessed directly from the coast from **Bintulu**. Northwest of Bintulu is **Niah National Park**, which boasts a vast cave system and accessible forest hikes. On its way north to the Brunei border, the road goes to Miri, from where you can fly to the spectacular **Gunung Mulu National Park**, Sarawak's chief natural attraction, which features astonishing limestone pinnacles, some of the world's largest caves and a swathe of pristine rainforest for challenging multi-day treks. Also accessible from Miri are the remote **Kelabit Highlands** and their main village of **Bario**, where you can opt for homestays with the Kelabit people and head further into the interior to meet the nomadic Penan.

KUCHING

Sprawled along a lazy waterfront, **KUCHING** has a magnetic charm, brought alive by its waterside stalls, antique and trinket markets and some lively bars. Exploring the town's streets on foot is one of the greatest pleasures, and Kuching also makes a great base for trips out into the surrounding area. Kuching's courthouse and fort hark back to the days of the White Rajahs, lending the town a historic air, while the commercial district in the old town is a warren of crowded lanes.

At weekends, the market off Jalan Satok comes alive with vendors selling mounds of fruit and fresh chillies, pungent dried fish, handicrafts, orchids and all kinds of snacks. Saturday afternoon is the best time to get there.

WHAT TO SEE AND DO

The city sprawls along the banks of the Sungai Sarawak, making the waterfront its main focus. The southern side of the river is flanked by a waterfront promenade, appealing green spaces and numerous food stalls. Facing the waterfront is the **Main Bazaar**, lined with antique and indigenous handicraft shops and still sporting the remains of its original wooden *godowns* (river warehouses). Heading eastwards along the waterfront takes you past Kuching's columned **nineteenth-century courthouse** – now preserved as a tourist centre – with its colonial-Baroque clock tower and Charles Brooke memorial, to the Grand Margherita area, which is full of bars, restaurants and plazas.

The Sarawak museums

The excellent **Sarawak Museums** (Mon–Fri 9am–4.45pm, Sat & Sun 10am–4pm; free; Ⓦmuseum.sarawak.gov.my), spread across opposite sides of Jalan Tun Haji Openg, depict Sarawak in a nutshell. The main building dates from the 1890s and is set in the grounds of the botanical gardens. The ground floor of the museum is a taxidermist's dream, displaying a range of stuffed and pickled Sarawak wildlife. Upstairs, the exceptional ethnographic section includes an authentic wooden Iban longhouse, a Penan hut, traditional tools, musical instruments and weapons. In the same grounds, the **Art Museum** (same hours; free) houses some interesting tribal carvings and hit-and-miss local exhibitions.

Across the bridge is the **Islamic Museum** (Mon–Fri 9am–4.45pm, Sat & Sun 10am–4pm; free), which exhibits aspects

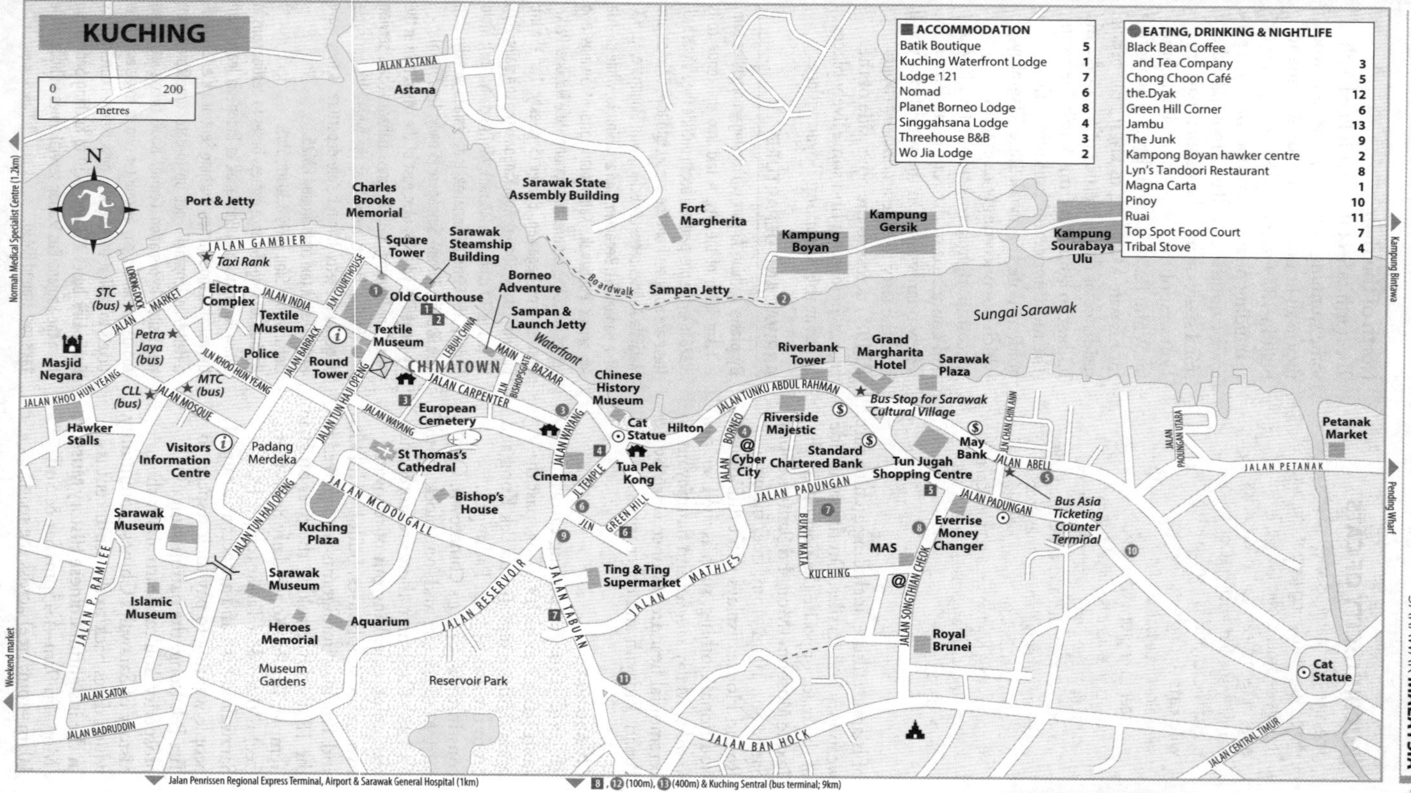
KUCHING
0
200
metres
N
ACCOMMODATION
Batik Boutique 5
Kuching Waterfront Lodge 1
Lodge 121 7
Nomad 6
Planet Borneo Lodge 8
Singgahsana Lodge 4
Threehouse B&B 3
Wo Jia Lodge 2
EATING, DRINKING & NIGHTLIFE
Black Bean Coffee and Tea Company 3
Chong Choon Café 5
the.Dyak 12
Green Hill Corner 6
Jambu 13
The Junk 9
Kampong Boyan hawker centre 2
Lyn's Tandoori Restaurant 8
Magna Carta 1
Pinoy 10
Ruai 11
Top Spot Food Court 7
Tribal Stove 4
Kampung Bintawa
Pending Wharf
Normah Medical Specialist Centre (1.2km)
Weekend market
Jalan Penrissen Regional Express Terminal, Airport & Sarawak General Hospital (1km)
8, 12 (100m), 13 (400m) & Kuching Sentral (bus terminal; 9km)
JALAN ASTANA
Astana
Sarawak State Assembly Building
Fort Margherita
Kampung Boyan
Kampung Gersik
Kampung Sourabaya Ulu
Port & Jetty
Charles Brooke Memorial
Square Tower
Sarawak Steamship Building
Borneo Adventure
Sampan & Launch Jetty
Waterfront
Boardwalk
Sampan Jetty
Sungai Sarawak
JALAN GAMBIER
Taxi Rank
STC (bus)
LORONG DOCK
JALAN MARKET
Petra Jaya (bus)
Masjid Negara
Electra Complex
JALAN INDIA
Textile Museum
JLN COURTHOUSE
Old Courthouse
Police
JALAN BARRACK
Round Tower
Textile Museum
LEBUH CHINA
MAIN BAZAAR
JLN BISHOPSGATE
CHINATOWN
JALAN CARPENTER
JLN KHOO HUN YEANG
MTC (bus)
CLL (bus)
JALAN MOSQUE
JALAN KHOO HUN YEANG
Hawker Stalls
Visitors Information Centre
Padang Merdeka
JALAN TUN HAJI OPENG
JALAN WAYANG
European Cemetery
St Thomas's Cathedral
Chinese History Museum
Cat Statue
Hilton
Tua Pek Kong
Cinema
JL TEMPLE
JLN GREEN HILL
Riverbank Tower
Grand Margharita Hotel
Sarawak Plaza
JALAN TUNKU ABDUL RAHMAN
Bus Stop for Sarawak Cultural Village
JALAN BORNEO
Riverside Majestic
Cyber City
Standard Chartered Bank
Tun Jugah Shopping Centre
May Bank
JLN CHAN CHIN ANN
JALAN ABELL
JALAN PADUNGAN
Bus Asia Ticketing Counter Terminal
Everrise Money Changer
MAS
BUKIT MATA KUCHING
JALAN SONGTHIAN CHEOK
Royal Brunei
JALAN PADUNGAN UTARA
JALAN PETANAK
Petanak Market
Cat Statue
JALAN CENTRAL TIMUR
JALAN BAN HOCK
JALAN MATHIES
Ting & Ting Supermarket
JALAN TABUAN
JALAN RESERVOIR
Reservoir Park
JALAN MCDOUGALL
Bishop's House
Kuching Plaza
Sarawak Museum
Sarawak Museum
Islamic Museum
Heroes Memorial
Aquarium
Museum Gardens
JALAN P. RAMLEE
JALAN SATOK
JALAN BADRUDDIN

6

KUCHING: CITY OF CATS

The many cat statues scattered around the centre of Kuching hint at the origin of the city's name, though while "kuching" does indeed mean "cat" in Malay, it's normally spelled "kucing". One theory is that the town was named after the **wild cats** (*kucing hatan*) which were seen along the banks of the river in the nineteenth century, while another suggests that it's a result of James Brooke pointing at the original settlement and asking "What's that?" and the person being asked mistakenly thinking that Brooke was pointing at a cat. The most likely theory is that Kuching is a corruption of Cochin (port). In any case, the cats are here to stay.

of Islamic culture, including architecture, weaponry and textiles. On the same side of the road, opposite the post office, the **Textile Museum** (Mon–Fri 9am–4.45pm, Sat & Sun 10am–4pm; free) in the Round House displays rich exhibitions of traditional clothing, such as the Iban *pua kumbu*, Malay *songket* and flamboyant ceremonial headdresses once worn by the Penan, Bidayuh and other tribes.

Chinatown

The grid of streets running eastwards from Jalan Tun Haji Openg, past the main Chinese temple Tua Pek Kong and on to the end of Jalan Padungan, constitutes Kuching's **Chinatown**. On busy Main Bazaar and, one block south, on Jalan Carpenter, there are stores and restaurants operating out of renovated two-storey shophouses, built by Hokkien and Teochew immigrants who arrived in the 1890s. Overlooking the river on Jalan Temple, **Tua Pek Kong** (daily 8am–6pm; free) is the oldest Taoist temple in Sarawak (1876) and attracts a stream of people wanting to pay their respects to Tua Pek Kong, the patron saint of prosperity. You can learn about the history of Sarawak's Chinese community, which dates back to the tenth century, in the insightful **Chinese History Museum** (Mon–Fri 9am–4.45pm, Sat & Sun 10am–4pm; free) across the road.

North of the river

The north side of the river is lined with some stunning buildings, especially when they're all lit up at night. **Fort Margherita**, built in 1879 to protect Kuching from marauding pirates, has good views over the town from the crenellated roof; take the spiral staircase up. The **Astana** (palace), 1km west of the fort, was originally built by White Rajah Charles Brooke as a gift for his wife Margaret; today, it's the official residence of the Governor of Sarawak, and it's best to admire it from across the river. The most noticeable building is the golden-roofed **Sarawak State Assembly**, which disconcertingly resembles a spaceship, right across from Main Bazaar and connected to the Kampong Boyan by a new boardwalk. On the waterfront you'll find the jetty to take a *tambang* (boat; RM0.5) across to the other side of the river, where you'll find some lively places to eat at the Kampong Boyan village.

ARRIVAL AND DEPARTURE

By plane Kuching Airport (kuchingairportonline.com) is 11km south of the city. A taxi into the centre costs RM26 from the pre-paid taxi booth outside the arrivals hall. There are no buses from the airport into town. AirAsia and Malaysia Airlines connect Kuching with Singapore, KL, KK, Sibu, Bandar Seri Begawan, Miri and Bintulu, while Batavia Air serves Pontianak, Kalimantan, and MASwings also serves Miri, Sibu, Bintulu and Gunung Mulu National Park.
Destinations Begawan, Brunei (5 weekly; 1hr 15min); Bintulu (2 daily; 30min); Kota Kinabalu (up to 4 daily; 2hr); KL (up to 10 daily; 1hr 40min); Miri (6 daily; 1hr); Mulu (2 daily; 1hr 15min); Pontianak, Indonesia (3 weekly; 1hr); Sibu (8 daily; 40min); Singapore (5 daily; 1hr 25min).
By boat The wharf is 6km east of the city centre in the suburb of Pending, with Ekspress Bahagia boats serving Sibu (RM45). Tickets are sold at the wharf. It's advisable to get to the jetty 30min before departure as they leave early if full. A taxi costs around RM25.
Destinations Sibu (daily 8.30am; 5hr).
By bus All long-distance express buses to destinations in Sarawak, Brunei and Pontianak in Indonesia leave from the massive, modern new Kuching Sentral a.k.a. "Six-and-a-Half-Mile-Terminal"; get up-to-date timetables from the Visitor Information Centre. Book tickets at a bus company counter, pay at counter two or three and show tickets to staff at the check-in desk before boarding. City Public Link buses #K3 and #K10 to Kuching Sentral run from the Saujana Bus Station several times an hour, while taxis cost around RM30.

TRAVEL TO INDONESIA

You can travel across the border into Indonesian Kalimantan directly from Kuching. A nine-hour bus ride (from the Kuching Sentral bus station) will take you as far as **Pontianak** (several buses leave either early in the morning or late at night). The border crossing at Entikong issues 30-day visas on arrival to citizens of various countries, but since the visa situation in Indonesia is volatile, check the **Indonesian embassy website** (W embassyofindonesia.org/consular/voa.html).

Destinations Bandar Seri Begawan (daily; 20hr); Bintulu (10 daily; 12hr); Miri (8 daily; 10–15hr); Pontianak, Indonesia (6 daily; 9hr); Sibu (10 daily; 8–10hr).

INFORMATION

Tourist information The excellent Kuching Visitor Information Centre (Mon–Fri 8am–5pm; T 082 410944, W sarawaktourism.com) is in the Old Courthouse on Jln Tun Abang Haji Openg. Grab the *Kuching Visitor's Guide*, which has plenty of information on accommodation, transport and local attractions (though it is a little outdated). The booking desk of the National Parks and Wildlife Office (Mon–Fri 8am–5pm; T 082 248088, W sarawakforestry.com), which issues permits and makes bookings for overnight stays at Bako, Gunung Gading and Kubah national parks, is next door.

ACCOMMODATION

Kuching Waterfront Lodge 15 Main Bazaar T 082 231111, W kuchingwaterfrontlodge.com. This is located inside one of the historical houses along the waterfront. It has a beautiful lobby with carved wooden staircase, simple, tastefully decorated rooms, an attractive roof terrace and welcome touches of greenery throughout. Breakfast included. Dorm RM40, double RM125

Lodge 121 Lot 121, Jln Tabuan T 082 428121, W lodge121.com. Though there's a bit of an industrial feel to this spotless hostel, – rooms are sparse and some lack windows – it gets consistently good reviews from backpackers for the helpfulness of its owners and little touches such as unlimited free tea and coffee. Dorm RM30, double RM79

Nomad 1st Floor, 3 Jln Green Hill T 082 237831, W borneobnb.com. Some rooms are windowless; there's an outdoor terrace, two guest lounges and kitchen. The owners' knowledge is invaluable, and they're happy to impart their wisdom over a beer or two. Prices include a pancake breakfast. Dorm RM30, double RM80

Planet Borneo Lodge 10 Lorong Park T 082 4121000, W planetborneolodge.com. Particularly good if you're travelling with friends or love to socialize, this detached lodge features mostly multi-person rooms with beds rather than bunks. There's a dipping pool in the garden, and Bryan, the manager, gets rave reviews for his in-depth local knowledge. Room RM60 per person

★**Singgahsana Lodge** 1 Temple St T 082 429277, W singgahsana.com. *Singgahsana* has a beautiful lounge and on-site café, a lively rooftop bar and walls decorated with vivid photos from the owners' travels. Though downstairs rooms lack natural light, the rest are bright and have comfy beds. If you want to retreat from Kuching's hustle and bustle, ask about *Village House*, the owners' other property out of town. Dorm RM30, double RM88

Threehouse B&B 51 Upper China St T 082 424229, W bedsguesthouse.com. A beautifully decorated hostel with a comfy common area with plenty of books and DVDs. There's a fan-cooled dorm, doubles (some with a/c) and multi-person rooms. The only downside is that the toilets are practically in the kitchen. Dorm RM38, double RM88

Wo Jia Lodge 17 Main Bazaar T 082 251776, W wojialodge.com. This waterfront guesthouse, run by laidback and helpful guys, and featuring a large common area strewn with cushions, has large, sparsely furnished rooms and is great value for money. One of the few places to offer single rooms. Double RM48

EATING

For awesome desserts, keep an eye out for branches of *Secret Recipe* around town; there's one along Jln Song Thian Cheok.

★**Black Bean Coffee and Tea Company** Jln Carpenter. You smell this tiny coffee shop before you arrive, thanks to its wide selection of freshly ground beans from Java, Sumatra and Sarawak itself. The tea list is extensive, too. Mon–Sat 7am–6pm; closed Sun.

Chong Choon Café Lot 121, Section 3, Jln Abell. Considered by many to be Sarawak's best *laksa* (which is different from mainland *laksa*; RM5) outlet. Get there early before it's all sold out. Mon & Wed–Sun 7–11am; closed Tues.

★TREAT YOURSELF

Batik Boutique 38 Jln Padungan T 082 422845, W batikboutiquehotel.com. With just 15 rooms – each with a king-sized bed and rain shower – all individually decorated with a batik-style pattern on the wall, this boutique hotel is a splendid central choice. Sip a beer in the courtyard, surrounded by green bamboo shoots, or soak in the jacuzzi. RM250

6

Green Hill Corner Jln Temple at Jln Green Hill. This Chinese *kopitiam* is legendary among locals for its beef noodle soup. The noodles are handmade, and chicken rice, *laksa* and savoury rice porridge are also on offer. Mains from RM3. Daily 7am–11pm.

Kampong Boyan hawker centre Take one of the regular boats across the river in the evening (RM0.50) and choose anything from curry to noodles to *tom yam* from the hawker stalls. Behind the food court, there's a restaurant that specializes in fantastic grilled chicken served on a banana leaf.

Lyn's Tandoori Restaurant Lot 267, Jln Song Thian Cheok. Not only does Lyn cook up the best *tandoori roti* in town, but the tandoori dishes, curries and freshly baked naan are excellent, too. Lots of veggie options. Mains from RM15. Daily 11.30am–10.30pm.

Magna Carta The Courthouse, Jln Tun Abang Haji Openg. Breezy veranda setting by one of Kuching's most venerable colonial buildings; the menu is international fusion and the seafood pasta deserves a prize. Lunch RM20; dinner mains RM25. Daily noon–2.30pm & 6–11pm. Similar menu at *Magenta*, also at the Courthouse. Daily 6–11pm.

Pinoy 143 Jln Padungan. If you like pork, you'll love this popular Filipino restaurant with its emphasis on the likes of barbecued three-layered pork, pork stew and pork *asado* with black vinegar. Accompaniments include veggies such as *midin* (jungle fern) and imaginative fruit juices. Mains from RM16. Daily noon–10pm.

★**Top Spot Food Court** Jln Bukit Mata. The best food court in town for seafood, located on the roof of a multi-storey car park. Fish and seafood is priced according to weight and includes delicious bamboo clams as well as giant prawns, squid and soft-shell crab. Mains come in small, medium and large; from RM12. Daily noon–11pm.

★**Tribal Stove** Jln Borneo, opposite the *Hilton*. Decorated with photos of the Kelabit people, this compact restaurant serves dishes from the Kelabit highlands, such as *ab'eng* (shredded river fish), tapioca fritters and bamboo chicken, to the accompaniment of string melodies on the stereo. The lunch buffet (RM18) is good value. Mon–Sat 11.30am–10.30pm.

★TREAT YOURSELF

the.Dyak Jln Simpang Tiga ☎082 234068. Kuching's best restaurant gives you a chance to sample authentic Iban cooking in a refined setting, surrounded by photographs of the Iban owner's ancestors, mirrors and framed indigenous artefacts. From the steamed fish with wild ginger, the three-layered pork with sambal and the traditional fermented pork to the numerous vegetable dishes (such as jungle ferns and sweet potato leaves), everything is beautifully presented and the flavours are superb. Finish off with the only fusion item on the menu – fermented rice topped with ice cream and *tuak* (rice wine) – and don't shy away from a glass of the stuff, brewed according to an old family recipe. Mains from RM20; reservations suggested on Friday and Saturday nights. Daily noon–11pm.

DRINKING AND NIGHTLIFE

Jambu 32 Jln Crookshank. Head for the tapas bar at this Mediterranean restaurant that's 1.5km south of the waterfront; here you can shoot some pool, have a beer while watching sports on TV or indulge in the likes of Spanish meatballs and tortilla (potato omelette). Tues–Sun 6–10.30pm.

The Junk 80 Jln Wayang. With an antique-shop-meets-bar vibe, this local institution is as much fun to look around as to drink in, with two bars and a signature cocktail (the "555")which packs a real punch. Also good for Italian food. Mon & Wed–Sun 6–11pm; closed Tues.

Ruai 7 Jln Ban Hock. Sip your drinks on the *ruai* (covered longhouse veranda) of this Iban-owned bar, decorated with Orang Ulu art and popular with locals and expats. Daily 5pm–1am.

DIRECTORY

Banks and exchange HSBC, Bangunan Binamus, off Jln Padungan; Standard Chartered Bank, Jln Tunku Abdul Rahman. Everise Moneychanger, 199 Jln Pandungan, offers good rates.

Embassies and consulates Australian Honorary Consul, E39, Level 2, Taman Sri Sarawak Mall, Jln Tunku Abdul Rahman (☎082 230777); British Honorary Consul (☎082 250950); Brunei, No. 325 Lorong Seladah 10, Jln Seladah (☎082 456515); Indonesia, No. 21, Lot 16557, Block 11, Jln Stutong (☎082 421734); New Zealand, Lot 8679, Section 64, Pending Commercial Centre (☎082 482177).

Hospitals Sarawak General Hospital, Jln Hospital (☎082 276666), has an excellent A&E department and inexpensive consultations, though it can be crowded. For private treatment, go to Normah Medical Specialist Centre, Jln Tun Abdul Rahman (☎082 440055; emergency ☎082 311999).

Immigration Bahagian Visa, 2nd floor, Bangunan Sultan Iskandar, Kompleks Pejabat Persecutuan, Jln Tun Razak at Jln Simpang Tiga (Mon–Thurs 8am–5pm, Fri 8–11.45am & 2.15–5pm; ☎082 245661) for visa extensions; take STC bus #K8 or #K11 from outside Kuching Mosque.

Internet All accommodation options reviewed offer free wi-fi; some offer free internet as well.

Laundry Easy Wash on Jln Ban Hock at Jln Song Thian Cheok.

6

SHOPPING IN KUCHING

If you're after **tribal handicrafts**, textiles and more, Kuching is hands down the best place to shop for them. This pleasure does not come cheap, though you can strike reasonable bargains. It's possible to buy tribal artefacts elsewhere at a slightly cheaper rate, but Kuching offers by far the best selection. **Main Bazaar** along the waterfront is lined with shops selling a mix of mass-produced touristy tat and genuine gems – usually found towards the back of the shops. If you know what you're after, don't be afraid to bargain, but be prepared to pay accordingly for genuine Penan blowpipes, carved Iban shields, longhouse charms and rice paddy guardians. Remember that shipping any part of an endangered animal or bird – hornbill, sun bear, clouded leopard – carries a prison sentence and hefty fine if caught. Not all items you find in the shops are from Sarawak, or, indeed, Borneo; Sarawak crafts are being pushed out of the market by far cheaper Indonesian ones, so if you want to know more about an item's age or origin, ask the sellers and they'll be happy to oblige. Be prepared to spend hours (or even days) just browsing.

The most reputable shops to look out for along Main Bazaar are Kelvin Gallery, Nelson's Antiques and Jewellery, John's Gallery, Bong Gallery and Borneo Tribal Arts.

If you're after some presents to take home, Main Bazaar is also a good spot to pick up Iban *pua kumbu* textiles, Sarawak pepper, sago biscuits, and the ubiquitous *kek lapiz* – colourful, multi-flavoured layer cakes that will survive the journey if you're heading straight home from Kuching.

Pharmacies Several around the Electra House shopping centre on Jln Power.

Police There is a Tourist Police unit at Kuching Waterfront (T 082 250522); most speak English.

Post office Jln Tun Haji Openg (Mon–Sat 8am–6pm, Sun 10am–1pm).

THE SARAWAK CULTURAL VILLAGE

The **Sarawak Cultural Village** (daily 9am–5pm; RM60; T 082 846411, W scv.com.my) is picturesquely located on the Santubong Peninsula 35km north of Kuching, and is very much a show for tourists, but a great educational experience nonetheless. A walkway loops around a small lake, passing replicas of traditional dwellings belonging to the Penan, Iban, Malanau, Bidayuh and other indigenous peoples of Sarawak. You can visit all the dwellings, take part in activities such as baking biscuits from sago flour and blowpipe shooting, and shop for traditional crafts such as batik shirts and sarongs. There's an excellent 45-minute dance show at 11.30am and 4pm, featuring dancers in traditional Iban, Malanau and Bidayuh costumes, a hunter demonstrating blowpipe shooting and those five minutes of non-obligatory audience participation. The SCV also hosts the renowned **Sarawak Rainforest World Music Festival** (W rainforestmusic-borneo.com), held during three days in July and featuring acts from around the globe. To get here, take the shuttle from the *Singgahsana Lodge* at Jln Wayang (four daily from 9.15am; 45min; RM20 return).

SEMENGOH NATURE RESERVE

Semengoh Nature Reserve (daily 8am–5pm; feeding times 9am & 3pm; RM5; W sarawakforestry.com) is home to 25 semi-wild **orang-utans** that have been orphaned or rescued from captivity. Here they are trained in the vital skills to survive in the wild and fend for themselves. Although the main programme has been transferred to Matang Wildlife Centre, Semengoh still has some younger orang-utans which you can see swinging through the trees. They generally spend most of their time roaming the surrounding forest, but some usually come to the main platform for feeding time (though a sighting is not guaranteed during the wet season, when there is plenty of fruit in the forest).

Most hostels offer transfers to and from the nature reserve for RM35, entry included. To get here by public transport, catch bus #K6 to "Semenggok" (at 7.15am, 10.15am, 1pm and 3.30pm,

6

TOURS FROM KUCHING

Kuching tour operators run trips to the longhouses for upwards of RM200 per person per day; reductions are available depending on the size of the group. They can also arrange trips to other parts of the state, including Gunung Mulu National Park.

Adventure Alternative Borneo Danny Voon ⓣ016 810 5614, ⓦaaborneo.com. Tom of *Lupa Masa* (see p.505) and Kuching-based Danny arrange offbeat, sustainable trips all over Borneo. They can help you put together an independent trip into less-trodden areas and put you in touch with another Kuching-based agency that organizes homestays at a traditional Malay fishing village.

Borneo Adventure 55 Main Bazaar ⓣ082 245175, ⓦborneoadventure.com. Award-winning, professional tour agency with another branch in KK. Can arrange anything from informative tours of Kuching to multi-day wildlife-watching tours and stays in their own Nanga Sampa jungle lodge in Ulu Ai, by the border with Kalimantan, which has links to the traditional Iban community next door and jungle treks.

Borneo Experiences Jln Temple ⓣ082 241346, ⓦborneoexperiences.com. Apart from quirky city tours and cycling trips to the Damai peninsula, this *Singgahsana Lodge*-based tour agency also offers a couple of adventurous options – a three-day/two-night stay in a traditional Bidayu village in the Bungu range, reachable only on foot, and homestays in Bario, in the remote Kelabit Highlands (see p.494).

returning at 8.30am, 11.15am, 2.15pm and 4.30pm; 45min; RM4 one-way) from Jalan Masjid. This will drop you at the entrance to the park where you buy your ticket; it's then a 1.3km clearly signed walk through pretty botanical gardens along a tarmac pathway to the feeding area. Taxis cost around RM100 return, including waiting time.

BAKO NATIONAL PARK

BAKO NATIONAL PARK was established in 1957 and is the best place to see wildlife in the state. The rare proboscis monkey, found only in Borneo, is resident here, and most visitors are treated to a sight of its unmistakeable hooter, which has earned it the native nickname "Dutchman". You'll definitely catch sight of cheeky macaques that hang around the visitor centre, and it's not uncommon to see vipers, wild pigs, giant monitor lizards and silver leaf monkeys. Bako can easily be visited as a day-trip from Kuching, but since wildlife is at its most active early in the morning and late in the afternoon, it's far more rewarding to stay overnight.

To get to the park, catch the red bus #1 (hourly 7am–5pm; 45min; RM3.50) from 6 Jln Khoo Hun Yeang, across from the Open-Air Market to the jetty at Kampung Bako. From here, you must pay the park fee (RM10), sign in and then take a motorized boat that bounces along the surf all the way to the park headquarters (RM94 return per boat of up to five people, or four people during rainy season when seas are rough; 20min), where you must register. Maps are available from the park HQ.

The park boasts seventeen **trails**, which all start from park headquarters and are colour-coded with paint splashes every 20m. The trails vary in difficulty and length of time. The easiest and shortest walk (and the best to see proboscis monkeys) is the Telok Paku trail. There's a hike to **Tajor Waterfall** (3.5km; about 2hr), which involves climbing the forested cliff through *kerangas*, with plentiful pitcher plants and peat bogs. As you leave the main trail at the wooden hut you'll see a path that descends to two beautiful beaches, **Telok Pandan Kecil** and **Telok Pandan Besar** (30min), with dramatic karst jutting out of the sea. The longest and most demanding trail is the 13km **Telok Limau** (8hr 30min one-way), which ends on a remote beach where you can camp. You can agree to get picked up by boat at an assigned time (RM165), and you can generally get a mobile phone signal on the slopes above the beach.

Get a **permit** and reserve your lodgings at the visitor centre in Kuching or online at ⓦebooking.com.my before you go (see p.479), especially on weekends, as

the park is very popular. At the park headquarters, you can camp (RM5), stay in a four-bed dorm (RM15.90 per person or RM42 per room) or in one of the lodges (RM50 for a room with shared bathroom; RM106 for a three-bed room with private bathroom or a two-room chalet for RM159), all of which provide bed linen but no cooking facilities. Some hikers prefer to camp on the trails and others have been known to sling a hammock up on the beach somewhere; you must inform the park office of your plans. There's a good cafeteria at headquarters serving rice and noodle dishes (buffet meal RM9) and a provisions shop.

SIBU

SIBU, 60km from the coast up Batang Rajang, is Sarawak's second-largest city and the state's biggest port. If Kuching's symbol is the cat, then Sibu's is the swan, and you'll see plenty of those about. Most of the local population is Foochow Chinese, and its remarkable growth is largely attributed to these enterprising immigrants who came here in the early twentieth century. Sibu is the jump-off point for trips up the Batang Rajang River.

WHAT TO SEE AND DO

The town's most striking landmark is the towering, seven-storey **pagoda** at the back of Tua Pek Kong Temple (daily 6am–8pm) – the oldest Chinese temple in Sibu – beyond the western, waterfront end of Jalan Khoo Peng Loong. The roof and columns are decorated with traditional dragon and holy bird statues, and murals depict the signs of the Chinese zodiac; the view from the top is particularly splendid at sunset. Across the way, in the network of streets between Jalan Market, Jalan Channel and Jalan Central, is **Chinatown**. The central artery, **Jalan Market**, runs from Jalan Pulau beside the temple, and forms the hub of possibly the most vibrant and exotic *pasar malam* (night market) in Sarawak. Beside Jalan Channel, the daily **Sibu Central Market** opens before dawn and closes around 5pm; there are hundreds of stalls here, selling anything from mounds of fruit and jungle ferns to rattan baskets, beadwork and charm bracelets.

Along Jalan Central you'll find the **Sibu Heritage Centre**, with an excellent museum (Tues–Sun 9am–5pm; free) on the first floor charting the history of Sibu and Sarawak through a series of photographs and objects associated with each ethnic group – from the Iban and Penan to the Chinese immigrants. Shrunken heads in a wicker harness is a standout exhibit.

NAUGHTY MONKEYS

Campers may only put up their tents after 6pm and remove them during the day due to marauding macaques; wherever you stay, make sure your belongings and food are stored away securely or the monkeys will wreak havoc.

ARRIVAL AND DEPARTURE

By plane The airport is 23km east of the city centre. Taxis cost RM35 (via pre-paid coupon at the taxi counter) into the centre. Between them, MASwings and AirAsia connect Sibu to Kuching, KK, Bintulu, Miri and KL.

Destinations Bintulu (2 daily; 35min); Kota Kinabalu (3 daily; 1hr 35min); Kuala Lumpur (2 daily; 2hr); Kuching; (2 daily; 40min); Miri (2 daily; 55min).

By boat Boats dock at the River Express Terminal, across the road from the local bus station. The "flying coffin" express boats (named because of their shape) to Kapit (some via Kanowit and Song; RM20–25) depart once or twice an hour between 5.45am and 2.30pm from the Regional Ferry Terminal, in the same building as the River Express Terminal. If water levels allow, the 5.45am boat continues to Belaga (most regular during the rainy season Oct–April; RM70). Large clocks display the departure time for each boat company; arrive 30min early and, during holidays, buy tickets a day in advance. Express Bahagia (☎ 084 319228) runs a daily service to Kuching at 11.30am.

Destinations Belaga (daily; 11hr); Kapit (12 daily; 3hr 30min–4hr); Kuching (daily; 5hr).

By bus The local bus and taxi station is on Jln Khoo Peng Loong, opposite the boat terminal. Long-distance buses depart from the Sibu Bus Terminal on Jln Pahlawan, 3.5km northeast of the centre along Jln Pedada. To get there, take the #21 Lanang bus from the city bus station.

Destinations Bintulu (11 daily; 3hr 15min); Kuching (15 daily; 7–8hr); Miri (10 daily; 6hr 30min).

6

INFORMATION

Tourist information The helpful Sibu Visitors' Information Centre (Mon–Fri 8am–5pm; ⓣ084 340980, ⓦsarawaktourism.com) at 32 Jln Tukang Besi has plenty of information on how to get upriver and to access the Rajang longhouses, along with a list of recommended local guides which is by no means definitive.

ACCOMMODATION

Eden Inn 1 Jln Lanang, next to the Sacred Heart Church ⓣ084 337277. The large en-suite rooms at this Catholic association-run guesthouse come with a/c and TVs. Double RM70

★**Li Hua Hotel** 2 Jln Lanang ⓣ084 324000, ⓦlihua.com.my. Close to the bus and ferry terminals to the west of town, rooms in this friendly hotel are spotless, spacious and come with river or city views. Free wi-fi. Double RM65

River Park Hotel 51–53 Jln Maju ⓣ084 316688. Comfortable riverfront hotel with friendly staff and river views from some of the a/c rooms (the cheapest are windowless). Wi-fi available. Double RM60

EATING AND DRINKING

Jln Maju, by the waterfront, is lined with cheap Chinese *kopitiams*.

★**Café Café** 10 Jln Chew Geok Lyn. Trendy spot serving wonderful fusion dishes (mains from RM18), oodles of noodles and the likes of tiramisu and black sesame ice cream for dessert. Tues–Sun noon–4pm & 6–11.30pm.

Emas Corner Jln Morshidi Sidek. Located underneath the *Plaza Inn*, this is a popular local spot. It has the usual *nasi goreng* dishes as well as *kam pua mee*, a Foochow speciality of thin noodles tossed in pork lard and served with roast pork (mains from RM5). Daily 10am–9pm.

★**Night market** Jln Market. Night-time stalls selling everything from Chinese pork and rice to satay, BBQ chicken, grilled fish balls, curry, steam buns and a variety of wonderful unidentifiable fried things (from RM4). Extremely popular with locals. Daily 6–10pm.

Sibu Central Market Pasar Sentral Sibu. Hawker stalls at the Lembangan produce market are the busiest place in the morning, serving mostly Chinese specialities, such as *kam pua mee* and chicken porridge (mains from RM3). Daily from 5am to midnight; different stalls open at different times.

LONGHOUSE VISITS

The interior of Sarawak is home to many tribal groups who still live in their **longhouse communities**, and a visit to one of these longhouses is a true highlight of any trip to this region. With the exception of the more remote communities in the Kelabit Highlands and by the Indonesian border, these longhouse communities no longer live a picturesquely "primitive" lifestyle: many longhouses have electricity, radios and TVs. Modern ones are built of brick rather than wood.

There are many tour operators in Kuching who arrange either day- or overnight trips, but some can be very touristy, with "traditional" dances put on for the visitors, while others are traditional farming and hunting communities which let you absorb the atmosphere and enjoy the hosts' hospitality. Before you book any tour, make sure you establish exactly what the longhouse visit entails and whether the rates cover transport, meals and activities. A good longhouse visit should provide a mix of cultural interaction, traditional food and activities such as jungle trekking. During the **Gawai harvest festival** in June, all longhouses welcome visitors and non-stop revelry continues for several days, fuelled by copious amounts of fairly lethal *tuak* (rice wine). If you don't want any, touching your lips with your fingers and then the rim of the glass will suffice.

A stay with the gregarious Iban and Bidayuh will make a trip at any time of year an enjoyable one, and you may even be offered some local delicacies to try – just watch out for that boiled monkey. Taking **presents** for the community is the norm – things that they can use, such as schoolbooks and pencils for the children, are best. Try to find out how many families live in the longhouse, as gifts will get divided equally. When walking through the communal areas, be careful not to walk across any of the mats that are laid out on the floor. It's considered rude to turn up at a longhouse without an invitation, so you either have to go with a tour company or find a local guide with a particular longhouse connection.

The reviewed **tour companies** in Kuching (see box, p.482) are recommended for a longhouse visit. If you can only spare a day, many companies run day-trips to the splendid nineteenth-century **Annah Rais Longhouse** near Tebedu, where you'll notice some shrunken heads in the rafters, left over from the head-hunting days. Here you can stay overnight at the community-run homestay project (ⓦlonghouseadventure.com).

RIDING THE "FLYING COFFINS"

The long, swift, closed-top boats that ply the Batang Rejang's waters are a unique experience. Choose between riding in the (mostly) air-conditioned interior, or riding on the roof (hold on tight) to watch nimble-footed boat attendants and passengers disembark at various longhouses carrying anything from roofing material to live chickens in cages. The boats have a reinforced steel walkway along the sides, so you can hang on to the rails and loiter outside. Boating from **Kapit to Belaga** used to be a hair-raising experience during the river stretch encompassing the Pelagus Rapids, as it involved expert manoeuvring in a strong current in between large rocks. Many of those rocks have since been dynamited and the journey is a lot smoother. During dry season, the low water levels sometimes make the Pelagus Rapids section impassible for weeks.

6

THE BATANG RAJANG

The mighty 560km-long **BATANG RAJANG RIVER** lies at the very heart of Sarawak and a trip into the interior along its cappuccino-coloured waters is still Borneo's great river journey. This is a semi-isolated world where the jungle encroaches on both sides, and where people still live in traditional longhouses, though the area has changed greatly since Redmond O'Hanlon's trip, described in *Into the Heart of Borneo*. The communities here are used to visitors, and travel along the river is fairly straightforward. Express "flying coffin" speedboats from Sibu head to **Kapit**, a busy indigenous market town, while further upriver lies little **Belaga**; both of these can be used as springboards for local longhouse visits as well as trips further inland.

Kapit

KAPIT is a busy little trading town with a frontier atmosphere and streets flooded with brand-new SUVs, hinting at the extent of illegal logging in the area, lots of cheap cafés, an excellent night market and ATMs. It's also the main place to organize trips to local Iban communities with one of the tour operators based in town. Close to the jetty is Kapit's main landmark, **Fort Sylvia**, which houses a small museum (Tues–Sun 10am–noon & 2–5pm; free) of tribal artefacts and rice wine jars. It was built in 1880 in an attempt to prevent the warring Iban attacking smaller groups such as the upriver Ukit and Bukitan. The walk west along Jalan Temenggong, which forms the northern edge of Kapit's main square, leads to the daily market (around 7am–5pm), which sells some tribal artefacts.

LONGHOUSES AROUND KAPIT

These longhouses can be visited from Kapit:

Rumah Bundong Traditional Iban longhouse on the Sumgai Kapit; 45min by minibus.

Rumah Jandok Another traditional Iban longhouse downriver along the Batang Rejang; some English-speakers live here.

Rumah Lulut Tisa Longhouses with official homestays; first take the road to Rumah Masam and then a boat for 1hr 30min or so.

ARRIVAL AND DEPARTURE

BY BOAT

Express boats from Sibu dock at the eastern wharf while those Belaga-bound dock 100m away at the western wharf, just off the Kapit town square; both flank the tiny town centre.

Permits Theoretically, you need a (free) permit from the Resident's Office, 9th Floor, Jln Bleteh (T 084 796230) to travel beyond Kapit up the Batang Rajang to Belaga and beyond. However, since permits are never checked and since you don't need one to access Belaga from Bintulu, most travellers don't bother getting one.

Destinations Belaga (daily at around 9.30am; 5–6hr; RM45); Sibu (hourly from 6.40am–3.15pm; 3hr; RM20–25).

ACCOMMODATION

Ark Hill Inn Jln Penghulu Gerinang T 084 796168. Located near the square, with twenty clean en-suite rooms (the singles are tiny) and free wi-fi. Double RM85

Greenland Inn Lot 463-464 Jln Teo Chow Beng T 084 796388. A block from the waterfront, this 19-room hotel offers clean lodgings with a/c and wi-fi, though you may have to open a window to let the stale smoke smell out. Double RM120

6

VISITING A LONGHOUSE FROM KAPIT AND BELAGA

The tourist office in Sibu keeps a list of recommended local guides in Sarawak's interior. In **Kapit**, the only licensed guide is Alice Chua (T 019 8593126, E atta_kpt@yahoo.com), but her tours tend to be rather expensive and receive mixed reviews. There are plenty of unlicensed guides who are perfectly knowledgeable, but finding one can be pot luck. It's best to talk to other travellers and local accommodation owners to see whom they recommend. In **Belaga**, *Belaga Hotel* can contact guides for upriver longhouse visits, and local guide Daniel Levoh from *Daniel Levoh's Guesthouse* has lots of contacts in the area. Try also Hasbie (T 013 8429767) from *Belaga B&B* or Hamdani Louis (T 019 8865770), both recommended by Sarawak Tourism. Tour charges tend to be from around RM85 per person for day-trips and around RM125 for overnight stays in a longhouse.

TRANSPORT & ARRIVAL

It's possible to visit longhouses on your own. In Kapit, some are reachable by **minibus** that departs from Kapit Town Square, while for others you'll have to negotiate a **longboat** price at the Jeti RC Kubu – the jetty facing Fort Sylvia. In Belaga, it's also possible to get a ride on a **boat**. Independent travellers are typically charged around RM20 for a day visit to a longhouse or RM60 for an overnight stay; bring your own food. Speak to the headman first (some may expect a tip) and take useful gifts. It's best to speak some Malay as few longhouses have English-speakers, and unless you're coming with a guide/interpreter, there may not be much in the way of activities, as the residents will be busy with their daily lives.

New Rajang Inn 104 Jln Teo Chow Beng T 084 796600. This is a real bargain with tiled en-suite a/c rooms with TV, fridge, wi-fi and a Bible for your spiritual needs. Double RM85

EATING

At the covered market off Jln Penghulu Nyanggau there are a dozen stalls serving Chinese, Malay and Dyak dishes (breakfast and lunch only).

Night market Between Jln Teo Chow Beng and Jln Penghulu Berjaya. Mostly Malay dishes, such as satay and *nasi goreng*; also curry and a few Dyak dishes. Mains from RM4. Daily 5–11pm.

Public Café Across the street from the night market, this spot serves the likes of squid sambal and *mee hoon* with jungle fern (mains from RM7). Picture menu. Daily: breakfast and lunch only.

Soon Kit Café 13 Jln Tan Sit Liong. Informal place that's locally famous for its chicken rice (RM5) and laksa (RM4). Daily 6am–5pm.

Belaga

Further up the Batang Rajang is **BELAGA**, a small, remote village with a laidback atmosphere, filled with crowing roosters and backed by mist-covered mountains. There is one notoriously unreliable ATM, so bring all the cash you need with you. The rivers around Belaga have a good few Kayan, Kenyah and Orang Ulu **longhouses**, making this one of the better places for a more authentic longhouse visit. Independent travel to the longhouses depends on a certain amount of luck and, ultimately, chatting to someone who will invite you over – try asking around on the boat from Kapit or at one of the cafés, where you're sure to find someone who can help, or else try one of the recommended local guides (see box above). There are also various treks that take you further into the jungle, past the Bakun Dam area and into the villages beyond; again, a guide is a very good idea.

LONGHOUSES AROUND BELAGA

These longhouses are in order of distance from Belaga.

Dong Daah Easily visited Kayan longhouse that's a 10min boat ride upstream.

Lirong Amo Kayan longhouse that's reachable by a 30min walk.

Long Liten Traditional Kejaman longhouse that's around 30min upriver.

Sekapan Pajang Traditional Sekapan longhouse 30min downriver.

Sihan Penan settlement a two-hour walk from the opposite bank of the river.

ARRIVAL AND DEPARTURE

By boat Express boats from Belaga to Kapit leave from the main jetty by the village (daily around 7.30am; RM45). During dry season, boats can't bypass the Pelagus Rapids en route to Kapit and Sibu, but it's still possible to travel upriver to various longhouses.

By 4WD For those who want to travel on to Bintulu (or who are travelling during dry season), there are daily 4WD trips (7.30am departure; 4hr; RM60) using the newly paved logging road. Ask Daniel Levoh (see box opposite) to book transport for you.

ACCOMMODATION AND EATING

Belaga is tiny, with just a few roads and places to stay, all of which are cheap and rather shabby. Basic Chinese and Malay restaurants tend to be open from early morning until around 7pm at the latest; the most reliable is the Malay joint that's second from the left along Main Bazaar (mains from RM4).

Belaga B&B Main Bazaar ⓣ 013 8429767. Clean, spartan rooms with shared bathrooms and some with a/c, run by recommended local guide Hasbie. Double **RM25**

Belaga Hotel 14 Main Bazaar ⓣ 086 461244. Right on the main drag, this cheapie has 15 rather battered rooms, all but two of which are fitted out with a/c. No hot water. Double **RM35**

Daniel Levoh's Guesthouse Jln The Ah Kiong ⓣ 086 461997 or ⓣ 013 848 6351. Two blocks behind the Main Bazaar, off the main road that runs straight from the dock, this guesthouse, run by local guide Daniel Levoh (see box opposite), has four simple, fan-cooled rooms (a couple without windows) and shared facilities. Kayan guide Daniel is knowledgeable and helpful. Wi-fi comes and goes. Dorm **RM15**, double **RM30**

BINTULU

BINTULU is a coastal boom town grown rich on offshore gas, used as a jumping-off point for the Niah National Park (see below) and Belaga; it's also the only place with transport to Belaga (see opposite) during dry season. There are a couple of sights worth visiting, the main one being **Tua Pek Kong** (daily 9am–5pm; free), the large and colourful Chinese temple right on the Main Bazaar. Behind the temple a couple of dozen fighting cocks are tethered and fill the air with their crowing. The **daily market** (around 7am–5pm) at the west end of Main Bazaar is filled with colourful mounds of fresh produce; you can also buy bowls of writhing sago grubs – a local speciality.

ARRIVAL AND DEPARTURE

By plane The airport (ⓣ 086 339163), served by AirAsia, Malaysia Airlines and MASwings, is 23km out of town. There are no public buses and a taxi to the centre costs around RM35.

Destinations Kota Kinabalu (daily; 1hr 15min); Kuala Lumpur (3 daily; 3hr); Kuching (3 daily; 1hr); Miri (2 daily; 35min); Sibu (2 daily; 35min).

By bus The long-distance bus station is 5km out of town at Medan Jaya. A taxi to the centre from here will cost RM15, or you can take bus #29 from the local bus station on Lebuh Ray Abang Galau (RM1), which becomes Jln Sri Dagang as it enters town. The long-distance bus station serves Batu Niah, Kuching, Sibu and Miri.

Destinations Kuching (10 daily; 7–10hr); Miri via Niah Junction (every 30min; 4hr); Sibu (10 daily; 3hr 30min).

By 4WD A Belaga resident makes the trip from Belaga to Bintulu and back every day along the newly paved logging road (4hr). Call Daniel Levoh (see box opposite) to make arrangements to be picked up from Bintulu. The 4WD tends to head back to Belaga daily at around 2.30pm.

ACCOMMODATION AND EATING

Kintown Inn 93 Jln Keppel ⓣ 086 333666. Excellent-value budget hotel with a good view from the upper floors, though the carpeted a/c rooms could do with renovating and wi-fi access. Double **RM85**

Night market Located beside Jln Kampung Dadang, off Jln Abanng Galau. The night market is a great place for fresh, delicious local dishes and is a good way to mix with locals. Mains from RM4. Daily 4–10pm.

Pasar Utama Main Bazaar, next to the produce market. New Market has a few informal stalls on the first floor, serving the likes of *nasi goreng* and *kueh tiaow* noodles. Mains from RM6. Daily 7am–5pm.

Riverfront Inn 256 Taman Sri Dagang ⓣ 086 333111. Cheerful cheapie on the waterfront with clean, serviceable rooms. Some rooms have no windows; others have river views. Double **RM90**

NIAH NATIONAL PARK

Visiting **NIAH NATIONAL PARK** is a highly rewarding experience – in less than a day you can see one of the largest caves in the world, as well as prehistoric rock graffiti in the remarkable **Painted Cave**, and hike along primary forest trails. This is one of Sarawak's smaller national parks, but it is recognized as one of the most important archeological sites in the world. In the outer area of the present park, deep excavations have revealed human remains and flake stone tools, mortars and shell

6

ornaments that date back forty thousand years – the first evidence that people lived in Southeast Asia that long ago. The park is roughly halfway between Bintulu and Miri, 11km off the main road and 3km north of Batu Niah, reached either by a half-hour walk or by taxi.

WHAT TO SEE AND DO

Niah National Park is spread over around 31 square kilometres of peat swamp, forests and gigantic limestone outcrops. The caves are joined by a wooden walkway which takes you through the lowland forest along to all the caves. The marked route takes you into the depths of the cave system; a torch is mandatory (bring your own) and good footwear is a bonus, since the walkway can be slippery; you may also want to wear a hat and poncho to protect you from the bat guano. There are a couple of trails and a 400m limestone ridge which you can scale, all of which are clearly signposted from park headquarters.

A small **museum** (daily 9am–5pm; free) just across the river from the park headquarters covers the geology of the caves and the history of the extremely dangerous profession of collecting birds' nests – a few locals still practise it (see box below).

From the park headquarters, it's a thirty-minute walk to the **caves**: take a *sampan* across the river (RM1; on demand) and then follow a wooden walkway through dense rainforest where you may see monkeys, hornbills, birdwing butterflies, tree squirrels and flying lizards. Inside the caves themselves, you will see bats, swiftlets, cockroaches that feed on the bat guano, and carnivorous crickets.

The caves

The main walkway heads up through the **Traders Cave** (so-called because early nest- and guano-gatherers would congregate here to sell their harvests) to the vast west mouth of the **Great Cave**, its walls stained different shades of green and the small temporary shelters of the birds'-nest collectors dwarfed by the cave's size. From within the immense, draughty darkness, and if you're there during nest-collecting season, you'll hear the voices of the bird's-nest collectors who gather swiftlet nests, and you'll see their tiny lights near the cave ceiling; their thin beanstalk poles snake up from the cave floor like ultra-fragile scaffolding. Once inside, the walkway continues via **Burnt Cave** and then **Moon Cave** for 600m or so in the pitch black before exiting into the jungle again to follow a pathway up to the **Painted Cave**, thirty minutes' walk away. Here, early Sarawak communities buried their dead in boat-shaped coffins, known as "death ships" and arranged around the cave walls; dating of the contents (which have been relocated to the Sarawak Museum) has proved that the caves have been used as a cemetery for tens of thousands of years. The red hematite figures of the wall paintings are fenced off for preservation.

The trails

There are two other colour-coded **trails** in the park. Jalan Madu splits off the main walkway around 800m from the park

THE PERILOUS LIVES OF BIRDS'-NEST COLLECTORS

The long *belian* (ironwood) wooden poles hanging down from the vast 60m ceiling of the Great Cave are part of the scaffolding used by birds'-nest collectors – men who risk their lives during the short harvesting periods to shimmy up these poles, armed with bamboo sticks with an attached *penyulok* (scraper) to prize **swiftlets' nests** from the ceiling. Men fall to their deaths every year, as no safety equipment is used. Their prize is a delicacy highly valued by the Chinese who consider birds'-nest soup to be an aphrodisiac, and it is the most expensive foodstuff on earth. The male swiftlets make their nests by regurgitating long threads of glutinous saliva that hardens when attached to the cave wall. The nests of the white-nest swiftlets are the most highly prized of all, fetching up to US$2000/kg; black-nest swiftlets' nests are collected as well but require removing dirt and feathers. When cooked, the nests have a gelatinous texture but little taste, making you wonder what all the fuss is about.

headquarters and cuts first east then south across a peat swamp forest, where you can see wild orchids, mushrooms and pandani. The trail crosses Sungai Subis and then follows its south bank to its confluence with Sungai Niah, from where you'll have to hail a passing boat to cross over to Batu Niah.

The more spectacular trail to Bukit Kasut starts at the confluence of these two rivers. After crossing the Niah River, the clearly marked trail winds through freshwater swamp forest, round the foothills of Bukit Kasut and up to the summit – a hard one-hour slog, at the end of which there's a view both of the forest canopy and Batu Niah.

ARRIVAL AND DEPARTURE

By bus In Miri take bus #33A to the Pujut Bus Terminal, and then any express bus heading towards Bintulu, Sibu or Sarikei. Ask to get off at Niah Junction (2hr; RM15), where taxis wait to take you to park headquarters (30min; RM30–40), 15km away. From Bintulu bus station there are several buses to Batu Niah (3hr; RM15). The park office is 3km from Batu Niah, either a taxi ride from the bus station (RM30), or a 30min stroll. The easiest way to reach the caves from Miri is by transfer (RM60) from the *Dillenia Guesthouse* (see p.490).

By taxi Taxis from Miri (1hr 20min) cost around RM150 one-way. A taxi from Bintulu (1hr 40min) costs around RM160.

INFORMATION

Park Headquarters Niah National Park HQ (T 085 737454) is the place to register on arrival. The trails are well signposted.

ACCOMMODATION AND EATING

The park can be visited as a day-trip, but stay overnight if you want to see the "changing of the guard" – swiftlets returning to the cave at sunset and bats flying out (notify park HQ first). Accommodation at the park HQ should be booked in advance through the National Park Booking Office (T 085 434184).

Camping There is a campsite with enough pitches for thirty tents. RM7 per person

Canteen There's a café at the park which serves rice and noodle dishes. Mains from RM8. Daily 9am–6pm.

Forrest Hostel Four simple rooms, each with four beds and attached bathrooms. Bedding provided. RM45

Forrest Lodge Seven chalets, some with fan, some with a/c, consisting of two en-suite rooms with two single beds/room. Bedding provided. From RM115

MIRI

MIRI is a booming oil town with a significant expat community and a strong Chinese character. For tourists, it's the main departure point for independent and organized trips into Gunung Mulu National Park (see p.490), and more local national parks, such as the Niah Caves and Lambir Hills National Park, and the route northeast to Brunei and Sabah.

WHAT TO SEE AND DO

Miri's old town around Jalan China in the west of town has a cluster of cafés, shops and a few cheap hotels. The fish market occupies the top of Jalan China, along with the Tua Pek Kong Chinese Temple, dedicated to a deity well loved by overseas Chinese. **Jalan Brooke** is the main artery through town, with a couple of markets selling fresh fruit and veg, pigs' heads and more. The wide road running east from here and parallel to the river, **Jalan Bendahara**, is the simplest route into the new town area. Directly south of the local bus station is the Padang, on whose border lies **Tamu Muhibbah** (daily 6am–4pm), the town's produce market. There's a better market on Lutong Rd, 3km from the centre (Thurs–Sat 5–10pm), where the Orang Ulu come to sell crafts and jungle produce. Take bus #1, #1A, #31, #42 or #62.

For a great **view** of Miri, you can take a taxi up **Canada Hill**. At the top you'll find a lively bar with an outdoor terrace, the well-designed **Petroleum Museum** (daily 9am–5pm; free), detailing the history of oil in Malaysia, and the **Grand Old Lady** – the remnants of the 1910 Shell oil well – the first in the region.

ARRIVAL AND DEPARTURE

By plane The airport (W miriairport.com) is 8km west of the town centre; bus #28 (every 90min between 5.45am and 6.40pm; RM3) runs from outside the terminal to the bus station (look for the 'Bas' sign; a taxi costs RM20. Between them, Malaysia Airlines and AirAsia cover major destinations such as KL, KK, Kuching and Sibu, while MASwings serves smaller destinations such as Mulu (for Gunung Mulu National Park) and Bario, the latter with eight-person Twin Otters (10km luggage maximum); flights to Bario are very weather-dependent.

6

6

Destinations Bario (daily; 40min); Bintulu (2 daily; 35min); Mulu (2 daily; 30min); Kota Kinabalu (4 daily; 40min); Kuala Lumpur (5 daily; 2hr 15min); Kuching (4 daily; 1hr); Sibu (3 daily; 1hr).

By bus Long-distance buses depart from the Pujut Bus Terminal, 4km northeast of the city centre; take bus #33A from the local bus station (10min; RM2.60) or a taxi (RM15). Pujut Bus operates services to Bintulu (RM27), Sibu (RM22) and Kuching (RM90), while Bintang Jaya Express (T 085 432178) and Borneo Express (T 085 430420) have services to Kota Kinabalu, Sabah (RM90), and PHLS bus (T 085 407175) serves Bandar Seri Begawan, Brunei (RM40).

Destinations Bandar Seri Begawan (2 daily at 8.15am & 3.45pm; 4hr 30min); Bintulu (10 daily; 4hr 30min); Kota Kinabalu (daily at 7.45am except Wed & 8.30am; 12hr); Kuching (8 daily; 14hr); Sibu (13 daily; 8hr).

INFORMATION AND TOURS

Tourist information The ultra-helpful visitor information centre (Mon–Fri 8am–5pm, Sat & Sun 10am–3pm; T 085 434181) is next to the local bus station, just off Jln Brooke. Besides reams of info on Miri and the region, there are up-to-date long-distance bus timetables.

Tours Borneo Jungle Safari, 1st Floor, Centrepoint Commercial Centre, Jln Kubu (T 085 422595), runs caving and climbing trips, as well as excursions to the Kelabit Highlands.

ACCOMMODATION

★ **Dillenia Guesthouse** 1st floor, 846 Jln Sida T 085 434204, E dillenia.guesthoouse@gmail.com. Cheerful lime-green a/c rooms presided over by the helpful and friendly Mrs Lee, who is brilliant at anticipating her guests' wishes and has detailed information on all regional attractions. Breakfast includes fresh fruit. Airport pick-up and transfers to Bandar Seri Begawan, Brunei and Niah Caves can be arranged. Dorm **RM30**, double **RM90**

Highlands Backpackers 2nd floor, Lot 839, Jln Merpati T 085 422327, W highlandsmiri.com. In a new central location, this established backpacker favourite, owned by a Kiwi Twin Otter pilot, offers simple, clean rooms with a/c (some without windows), a guest lounge with satellite TV and a dorm with too many beds in it. Dorm **RM22**, double **RM50**

Minda's Guesthouse 1st & 2nd floor, 637 Jln North Yu Seng T 085 411422. Budget B&B smack-bang in the centre of town, opposite the popular *Ming Café*. Rooms are spacious and colourful, though they could be cleaner. There's unlimited tea and coffee, a notice-board for travellers and a cool roof terrace. Dorm **RM30**, double **RM60**

EATING

Apollo Seafood Centre 4 Jln South Yu Seng. Local institution specializing in very fresh seafood (just pick your meal from a tank); the crab and prawn dishes stand out (mains from RM16). Accompaniments include *midin belacan*, a delicious, crunchy jungle fern cooked with shrimp paste. Daily noon–10pm.

Bilal Islamic Restaurant Taman Jade Manis, behind the *Mega Hotel*. Informal Indian joint with plastic chairs, some of the best curry in town and a great selection of vegetarian dishes – the okra ones are particularly good. Dishes RM6–17. Daily 10am–10pm.

★ **Ming Café** Jln North Yu Seng. This corner establishment is popular both with locals and travellers due to a catch-all mix of Malay and Indian food as well as Chinese and Western dishes and barbecued seafood (from RM10), washed down with cold beer or fresh juices. Doubles as a sports bar. Daily 9am–11pm.

Summit Café Centre Point Commercial Centre, Jln Melayu. Canteen-style café serving delicious dishes from the Kelabit Highlands, such as jungle fern and shredded fish (mains from RM3). No English spoken, so just point to whatever looks good on display. It's a couple of minutes' walk southwest from the Visitors' Information Centre. Mon–Sat 6am–2pm; get here early.

SHOPPING

Miri Handicraft Centre Jln Brooke at Jln Merbau. Indoor craft centre consisting of numerous stalls selling a mix of touristy tat and genuine indigenous craft; the beadwork from the Kelabit Highlands and woven rattan items are particularly good.

DIRECTORY

Banks Maybank, Jln Bendahara; ATMs at the airport. There are also moneychangers and ATMs along Jln China and Jln Melayu.

Hospital Columbia Asia Hospital, Jln Bulan Sabit (T 085 437755, W columbiaasia.com/miri), 4km northeast of *Mega Hotel*, is a private hospital with a 24hr emergency ward favoured by expats.

Immigration (Jabatan Imigresen) 2nd floor, Yu Lan Plaza, Jln Brooke (Mon–Thurs 8am–5pm, Fri 8–11.45pm & 2.15–5pm; T 085 442117, W imi.gov.my); opposite the police station. Does visa extensions.

Post office Jln Poste (Mon–Sat 8am–4.30pm).

GUNUNG MULU NATIONAL PARK

GUNUNG MULU NATIONAL PARK is Sarawak's premier natural attraction and home to the second-largest cave on earth was showcased in a David Attenborough documentary. At the last count, Gunung

Mulu featured more than three hundred animal species and nearly three thousand plant species, adding incredible natural diversity to the stunning landscape. The park comprises primary rainforest, and is characterized by clear rivers and high-altitude vegetation, supremely accessible caves and three dramatic mountains, including Gunung Mulu itself and 50m-high, razor-sharp limestone spikes known as the **Pinnacles**, which offer some of the best (and most challenging) hiking in all of Borneo.

WHAT TO SEE AND DO

It is quite possible to see the four main caves in a day, but if you're considering caving, or one of the treks as well, you'll need to allow three or four days extra. The park is covered in rich primary rainforest

6

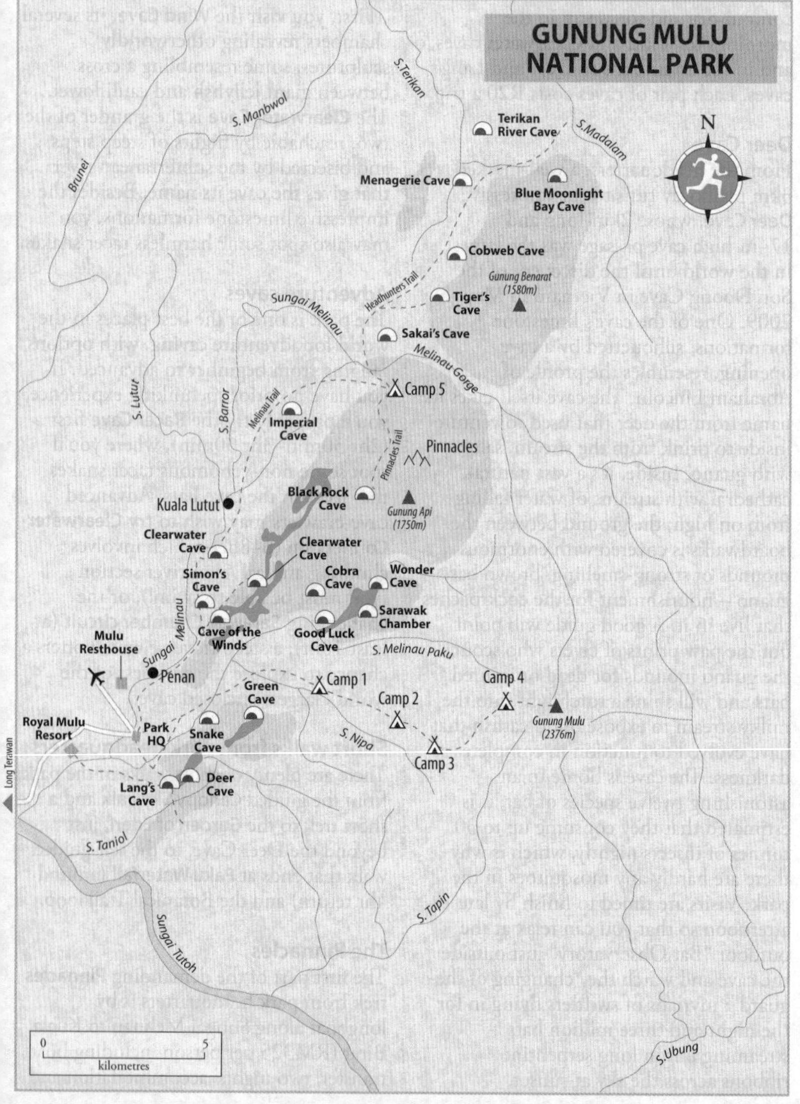

and offers a whole range of excellent multi-day **jungle treks** and **mountain hikes**, including the challenging Pinnacles Trail. There are also short, gentle walks along well-marked trails.

The show caves

6

Only four of the 25 caves so far explored in Mulu are open to casual visitors; they're known as "show caves" and can get quite crowded. Guides are compulsory and tours run in the mornings to Wind and Clearwater caves, and in the afternoons to Deer and Lang's caves. Each pair of caves costs R20 a trip.

Deer Cave

From the headquarters, a well-marked 3km plankway runs to the impressive **Deer Cave**, whose 2km-long and 174m-high cave passage was the largest in the world until the discovery of the Son Doong Cave in Vietnam in May 2009. One of the cave's limestone formations, silhouetted by a cave opening, resembles the profile of Abraham Lincoln. The cave itself takes its name from the deer that used to venture inside to drink from the stream, salty with guano. Inside, it's a vast natural cathedral with streams of water falling from on high; the ground between the boardwalks is covered with enormous mounds of strong-smelling, brown bat guano – nourishment for the cockroaches that live in it. A good guide will point out the paw prints of civets who scour the guano mounds for dead or injured bats and will shine a torchlight into the milky stream to expose blind catfish that have evolved to function in complete darkness. The cave is home to an astonishing twelve species of bat; it is estimated that they consume up to 30 tonnes of insects nightly, which is why there are hardly any mosquitoes in the park. Visits are timed to finish by late afternoon so that you can relax at the outdoor "Bat Observatory" just outside the cave and watch the "changing of the guard": myriads of swiftlets flying in for the night and three million bats streaming out in long serpentine ribbons across the sky at sunset.

Clearwater Cave and Wind Cave

Probing some 107km through Mulu's substratum, **Clearwater Cave**, thought to be the longest in Southeast Asia, is reached by a fifteen-minute longboat journey (RM30) along Sungai Melinau from park headquarters. On the way there's the obligatory stop at the small Penan village where you can buy some beautiful rattan weavings, jungle jewellery and Kelabit beadwork.

First, you visit the **Wind Cave**, its several chambers revealing otherworldly sculptures, some resembling a cross between giant jellyfish and cauliflower. The **Clearwater Cave** is the grander of the two, reachable by flights of steep steps and bisected by the subterranean river that gives the cave its name. Besides the impressive limestone formations, you may also spot some harmless racer snakes.

Adventure caves

The park is one of the best places in the world for adventure caving, with options ranging from beginner to advanced. If you have no prior spelunking experience, you'll probably try the **Racer Cave** first (2hr 30min–3hr 30min), where you'll spot some non-venomous racer snakes that feed on the cave bats. Advanced cave-crawlers may wish to try **Clearwater Connection** (6–8hr), which involves climbing and a 1.5km river section (you must be able to swim!), or the challenging **Sarawak Chamber circuit** (at least 10hr), a steep traverse which offers a chance to explore the darkness of the world's largest enclosed cave.

Short walks from park headquarters

There are plenty of short walks in the park, from the guided **Canopy Skywalk** and a short trek to the **Garden of Eden**, just beyond the Deer Cave, to the self-guided walk that ends at **Paku Waterfall** (around 4hr return) and the Botanical Trail loop.

The Pinnacles

The first part of the demanding **Pinnacles** trek from park headquarters is by longboat along Sungai Melinau to Kuala Birar (RM325 per person including boat transfer, two nights' accommodation and

guide fee). From here, it's an easy 9km walk to *Camp 5*, which nestles under Gunung Api (1750m) and Gunung Benarat (1580m). Most climbers spend two nights at *Camp 5*, where there's a large hostel (RM40); bring a sleeping bag.

The ascent up the south face of Gunung Api is only 2.4km, but the climb is unrelentingly steep and the vertical final section requires an actual climb involving ladders and ropes. Climbers make it to the top in two to five hours and the descent also takes up to five hours. If you fail to reach the mini-Pinnacles within one hour, you are not fit enough and will be sent back to *Camp 5*. Bring at least two litres of water, lunch, footwear with good traction and sturdy biking gloves, as you'll be using your hands to scramble up the sharp rock.

Headhunters' Trail

It's possible to hike from *Camp 5* to Limbang along the so-called **Headhunter's Trail**, a route once traced by Kayan war parties. Cross the bridge, turn left and walk along a wide trail passing a large rock (around 4km). From here, a clearly marked flat trail to **Kuala Terikan**, a small Berawan settlement on the banks of Sungai Terikan, takes four hours (11km). To get from Kuala Terikan to Medamit or Limbang Cina, you'll need to organize a guide or boatman in advance via Limbang-based Borneo Touch Ecotour (RM500 for a boat and van in either direction for up to five people; walk2mulu.com). Boats run frequently from Limbang to Bandar Seri Begawan, Brunei (hourly until 4.30pm).

Gunung Mulu

The route to the summit of **Gunung Mulu** (2376m) is a straightforward, though very steep and relentless, climb that takes four days and three nights. Park regulations require that you hire a guide (RM475 per person). The first stage is from park headquarters to *Camp 1*, an easy three-hour walk on a flat trail. The first night is at the open hut at *Camp 1*, which has cooking facilities. Day two comprises a hard, ten-hour uphill slog, some of it along the southwest ridge, a series of small hills negotiated by a narrow, twisting path. The hut at *Camp 4* is at 1800m; it can be cool here, so bring a sleeping bag. Most climbers set off well before dawn for the hard ninety-minute trek to the summit, to arrive at sunrise. Near the top you have to haul yourself up by ropes onto the cold, windswept, craggy peak. From here, the view, looking down on Gunung Api, is exhilarating.

ARRIVAL AND DEPARTURE

By plane The tiny airport is 2km west of park headquarters; taxis (RM5) meet the planes to take you to the headquarters or accommodation.

Destinations Flights to Miri with MASWings (maswings.com.my) leave the park twice daily (30min), to Kuching daily (1hr 40min) and to Kota Kinabalu daily (1hr 30min).

INFORMATION

Park Headquarters The Park Headquarters office (daily 8am–5pm; 085 792305, mulupark.com) is the place

TREKKING IN THE PARK

If you're trekking independently, it makes sense to get a group of at least four together to spread the high cost of boat and guide fees in the park; if you're travelling on your own or simply want to get more people together you can post up a note on the board at headquarters. Upon arriving, you need to register at the **park headquarters** (if it's after 5.30pm, register for the following day), and pay the RM30 park fee. Arranging one of the longer treks with the park office itself (in advance) is considerably cheaper than coming as part of a tour group from KL, Kuching or Miri, though out of peak season you may have trouble making up the numbers (minimum of four people required).

Take plenty of water, decent walking shoes, a sun hat and swimming gear, a poncho or rain sheet, a torch, mosquito repellent, ointment for bites and a basic first-aid kit. Mats and sleeping bags (should you want one) can usually be rented from the park headquarters. Wear shorts and T-shirts on the trails (it'll be easier to spot leeches), and bring long trousers and long-sleeved shirts for the insect assault at dusk.

to sign up for walks, and there are colourful, detailed displays on the park's history, flora and fauna.

ACCOMMODATION

There are several types of accommodation here: a dorm, chalets and bungalows belonging to the park and basic guesthouses along the road from the airport and just outside the park entrance. Reserve accommodation inside the park in advance as it fills up fast; prices include a decent breakfast. *Camp 5* is only for hikers doing the Pinnacles (RM160 including boat ride).

6

PARK ACCOMMODATION

Chalets Two chalets with two spacious rooms each, a/c and hot showers. From RM180

Garden Bungalows The swishest option in the park, with room for up to three people; spacious, attractive a/c rooms and shaded porches. RM230

Hostel There's a large twenty-bed dorm in the hostel with ceiling fans, shared bathrooms and lockers at extra cost. RM45

Longhouse Rooms Ten rooms that can sleep up to four people, with ceiling fans and attached bathrooms. From RM180

ACCOMMODATION OUTSIDE THE PARK

D'Cave Homestay ⓣ 012 872 9752. The last guesthouse before the turn-off for the park, this homestay gets rave reviews thanks to the warmth and hospitality of its owners, Robert and Dina, and the excellent home-cooked meals. Dorm RM35, room RM60

Mulu River Lodge ⓣ 012 852 7471. Family-run accommodation consisting of a 30-bed, fan-cooled dorm and a couple of basic rooms. Electricity from 5.30–11.30pm. Right outside the park entrance. RM40 per person

EATING

Café Mulu The on-site park café serves a good mixture of Malay and international food; mains from RM10. Daily 7.30am–9pm.

Sweetwater Bar & Restaurant Part of the *Mulu River Lodge*, this unpretentious place serves basic Malay dishes of noodles and rice (RM10) washed down with cans of beer (RM10). The local *paku* (edible fiddlehead fern), lightly sautéed with garlic and fish sauce, is an excellent accompaniment to any meal. Daily 8am–10pm.

KELABIT HIGHLANDS

Sitting between the Indonesian border and the Gunung Mulu National Park, the **KELABIT HIGHLANDS** are inhabited by the Kelabits and the main attraction of this still-remote park of Sarawak is hiking from longhouse to longhouse along mountain trails and enjoying Kelabit hospitality as part of homestays. There are no banks here, so bring plenty of cash in small denominations.

Bario

Bario is the main settlement, consisting of around a dozen small villages spread out all over the valley. You can visit the **Bario Asai longhouse**, a traditional dwelling where some of its older residents have earlobes distended down to their shoulders due to wearing heavy brass earrings. Not far from the longhouse is a **monument** dedicated to British Major Tom Harrisson who did a parachute drop here behind the Japanese enemy lines in 1945 and lived in Bario after the war. It's also possible to hike up nearby **Prayer Mountain** (2hrs each way) for wonderful views of the valley. Jungle treks can be arranged through your accommodation.

ARRIVAL AND DEPARTURE

By plane The tiny airport is linked to Miri by twice-daily MASWings Twin Otter flights (though these flights are very weather-dependent). The eight-person planes have a checked luggage allowance of 10kg and 5kg carry-on. Passengers are weighed before departure.

ACCOMMODATION AND EATING

Guesthouses and longhouses offer room and board. The options below have patchy wi-fi.

Bario Asal Lembaa Longhouse ⓣ 014 590 7500 or ⓣ 014 893 1139, ⓔ jenetteulun@yahoo.com. Longhouse

PICNIC WITH THE PENAN

If even the Kelabit Highlands are not remote enough for you, you have the option of staying with the last of Borneo's nomadic **Penan** who live near the Indonesian border and can be reached from the Kelabit Highlands by jungle trek and boat. The website ⓦ picnicwiththepenan.wordpress.com caters to those interested in learning about traditional Penan culture, with jungle treks, camping and survival training thrown in. This can be arranged via Alternative Adventure Borneo (see box, p.482); it helps if you speak some Malay to get the most out of the experience.

cooperative, with some families renting out rooms to guests, and others providing meals. Provides excellent immersion in Kelabit culture. Transport from airport can be arranged. RM65 per person

Junglebluesdream T 019 8849892, W junglebluesdream.weebly.com. Combined lodge and art gallery run by local artist Stephen and his Danish wife Tine, with excellent home-cooked food and individually decorated rooms. Trekking maps available and kayaking excursions possible. Airport pickup can be arranged. RM70 per person per day

Libal Paradise T 019 8071640. Run by a Canadian-Kelabit couple, this rural farm is a wonderfully laidback place to stay. Stu runs kayaking trips and the farm is a short walk eastwards from the airport strip. Dorm RM30, room RM65

Sabah

Bordering Sarawak on the northeastern flank of Borneo, **SABAH**'s beauty lies in its wealth of natural resources and abundant wildlife. You can watch turtles hatch on **Libaran Turtle Island**, see orang-utans at the **Sepilok Orang-utan Rehabilitation Centre**, observe the antics of sun bears at the **Bornean Sun Bear Conservation Centre** and marvel at forest-dwelling proboscis monkeys, macaques and wild orang-utans along the lower reaches of the **Kinabatangan River**. The diving is incredible: **Pulau Sipadan** is rated one of the world's top dive destinations. Sabah's other major attraction is climbing the granite shelves of 4095m-high **Mount Kinabalu**: it's certainly challenging, but the rewards are spectacular.

As well as its natural beauty, Sabah also has a diverse ethnic heritage. Until European powers gained a foothold here in the nineteenth century, the northern tip of this remote land mass was inhabited by **tribal groups** who had only minimal contact with the outside world. The peoples of the Kadazan and Dusun tribes constitute the largest indigenous racial group, along with the Murut of the southwest and Sabah's so-called "sea gypsies", the Bajau. Recently economic migrants from the Philippines and neighbouring Kalimantan have added to the state's rich ethnic mix.

As in Sarawak, travel is more expensive in Sabah than in Peninsular Malaysia. While there are plenty of tour operators, independent travel is completely achievable and a breeze compared to other parts of Borneo.

6

KOTA KINABALU

Settled on the South China Sea, **KOTA KINABALU** is the thoroughly modern capital of Sabah and the main entry point to the region. Stretching along the waterfront and sporting several large shopping malls, KK offers a range of budget accommodation and plenty of restaurants and bars. Lacking in architectural charm, it's nevertheless pleasant enough to amble around on foot, exploring the various markets, trying local delicacies and soaking up the waterfront atmosphere. KK is also the gateway to the ultra-popular **Kinabalu National Park**, and there's good snorkelling and diving to be had off the **Tunku Abdul Rahman Islands**, a short hop by speedboat from KK's jetty.

WHAT TO SEE AND DO

Downtown KK was almost obliterated by World War II bombs, and only in the northeastern corner of the city centre – an area known as KK Lama, or old KK – are there even the faintest remains of its colonial past, with three notable old buildings: the old **General Post Office**, **Atkinson's Clock Tower** and the **Lands and Surveys building**, now home to the Sabah Tourism Board. Jalan Gaya is the most attractive of the central streets, lined with colourful and popular Chinese *kedai kopis*.

The markets

On Sundays, the length of Jalan Gaya comes alive with the **Gaya street market** (6am–2pm) – a great place to buy anything from souvenirs to jungle produce. Along the waterfront you'll find three markets. The **Filipino market** (daily 10am–6pm) on Jalan Tun Fuad Stephens is the best place to buy Sabahan ethnic wares, such as textiles, cultured pearls, bamboo goods and more, as well as Filipino baskets, kampong-wood salad

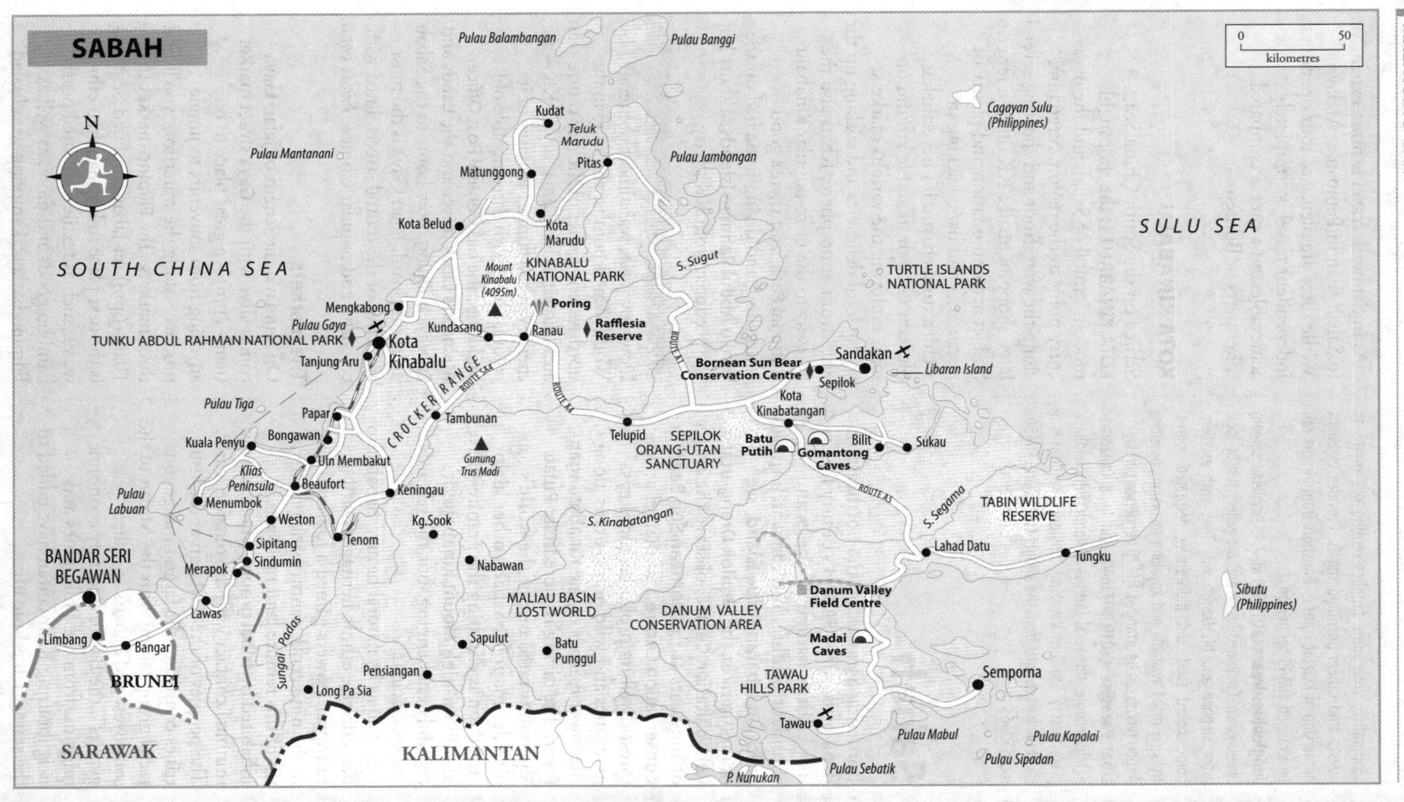
SABAH
N
SOUTH CHINA SEA
SULU SEA
0
50
kilometres
Pulau Balambangan
Pulau Banggi
Cagayan Sulu (Philippines)
Kudat
Teluk Marudu
Pulau Mantanani
Pitas
Pulau Jambongan
Matunggong
Kota Belud
Kota Marudu
S. Sugut
TURTLE ISLANDS NATIONAL PARK
Mount Kinabalu (4095m)
KINABALU NATIONAL PARK
Mengkabong
Poring
Rafflesia Reserve
Pulau Gaya
TUNKU ABDUL RAHMAN NATIONAL PARK
Kota Kinabalu
Kundasang
Ranau
ROUTE A1
Sandakan
Libaran Island
Bornean Sun Bear Conservation Centre
Sepilok
Tanjung Aru
CROCKER RANGE
ROUTE SA4
ROUTE A4
Kota Kinabatangan
Pulau Tiga
Papar
Tambunan
Telupid
SEPILOK ORANG-UTAN SANCTUARY
Batu Putih
Gomantong Caves
Bilit
Sukau
Kuala Penyu
Bongawan
Uln Membakut
Gunung Trus Madi
Klias Peninsula
Beaufort
Keningau
ROUTE A5
Pulau Labuan
Menumbok
Weston
Tenom
Kg.Sook
S. Kinabatangan
S. Segama
TABIN WILDLIFE RESERVE
Sipitang
Sindumin
Lahad Datu
Tungku
BANDAR SERI BEGAWAN
Merapok
Nabawan
Lawas
MALIAU BASIN LOST WORLD
DANUM VALLEY CONSERVATION AREA
Danum Valley Field Centre
Sibutu (Philippines)
Limbang
Bangar
Sungai Padas
Sapulut
Batu Punggul
Madai Caves
Pensiangan
BRUNEI
Long Pa Sia
TAWAU HILLS PARK
Semporna
Tawau
Pulau Mabul
Pulau Kapalai
SARAWAK
KALIMANTAN
Pulau Sipadan
Pulau Sebatik
P. Nunukan

bowls and bags (don't forget to bargain). Next door is the dark and labyrinthine **general market**, selling fresh fruit and vegetables, and behind that is the manic waterfront **fish market**. At the northern end of the central market is the **night market** (daily 5–11pm) – hands down the best place in KK for seafood (see p.500).

Sabah State Museum and Heritage Garden

The **Sabah State Museum** on Jalan Muzium (Sat–Thurs 9am–5pm; RM20; ⓦmuseum.sabah.gov.my) is twenty minutes' walk west of the town centre along Jalan Tunku Abdul Rahman. In the main building, its highlight is the **ethnographic collection**, which includes human skulls from Sabah's head-hunting days, Penan blowpipes, traditional costume and musical instruments, carved totem poles and photos of Murut hunters. The **natural history** section showcases a fairly complete collection of stuffed, pickled or pinned examples of Borneo wildlife, but the **Art Museum** is rather hit and miss. Outside, the **Heritage Village** features authentic replicas of Murut- and Rungus-style longhouses and a Chinese farmhouse.

From the museum, a signposted path leads to the rather bland **Museum of Islamic Civilization**, though there are some beautiful ornate swords and Qu'ran pages. If you're heading to Sandakan, you can use the same **entrance ticket** to enter the **Agnes Keith House** (see p.506).

Mari Mari Cultural Village

Even if you've already visited Sarawak's Cultural Village (see p.481), it's still more than worth your while to pay a visit to the **Mari Mari Cultural Village** (ⓦmarimariculturalvillage.com), its counterpart in Sabah, which showcases the traditional dwellings and crafts of Sabah's ethnic groups. It's a very interactive experience; the three-hour tour involves your group being led around by a traditionally attired guide who takes you through the jungle between the Dusun, Lundai, Kajan and other houses, stopping at each one. At each stop, there's an activity for you to try – from cooking in a bamboo tube (you'll get to sample your own efforts after the tour) to blowpipe shooting, *tuak-* (rice wine) making and tasting, fire starting, and jumping on a bamboo trampoline – followed by a spirited traditional dance show and delicious meal. There are three scheduled visits per day, and the price (RM160) includes transport there and back; you can organize the tour directly through Mari Mari, most hostels and the tourist office.

Around 400m beyond the Cultural Village is the **Kiansom Waterfall**, with an appealing swimming hole.

KK Heritage Walk

Those interested in the historical and cultural side of the city should take the informative and highly entertaining **KK Heritage Walk** (Tues & Thurs 9–11.30am; RM200; ⓦkkheritagewalk.com), which can be booked through several tour operators and consists of a walking tour that includes visits to the North Borneo War Memorial, the Atkinson Clock Tower, Chinese herbal shops and *kopitiam* (coffee shops), and culminates in a treasure hunt at the *Jesselton Hotel.*

ARRIVAL AND DEPARTURE

By plane KK's airport, served by numerous national and international flights, is 6.5km southwest of the centre in Tanjung Aru. The two terminals are completely separate from each other; most airlines land at Terminal 1, with the exception of AirAsia and Tiger Airways, which land at Terminal 2. Minibuses (RM3) and city bus #1 connect Terminal 1 with the central bus station, whereas Terminal 2 is served by buses #2 and #16A (RM1.50) from the City Park bus station downtown. Taxis from the airport cost RM35; buy a voucher at the pre-paid taxi counter. KK has good connections within Sabah and Sarawak, as well as regular flights to Brunei, mainland Malaysia, Indonesia, the Philippines, Thailand, China and Australia.

Destinations Bandar Seri Begawan (3 daily; 20min); Bintulu (5 weekly; 1hr 15min); Kuala Lumpur (6 daily; 3hr); Kuching (4 daily; 2hr 15min); Manila (daily; 3hr); Miri (6 daily; 40min); Penang (daily; 3hr); Sandakan (6 daily; 50min); Sibu (3 daily; 1hr 35min); Sydney (4 weekly; 11hr); Tawau (4 daily; 45min).

By bus Most long-distance buses operate from the bus terminal at Inanam, 9km north of the centre, reachable by local buses from Wawasan central bus station (RM2; 30min) or by taxi (RM25). Buses to Brunei leave from across the

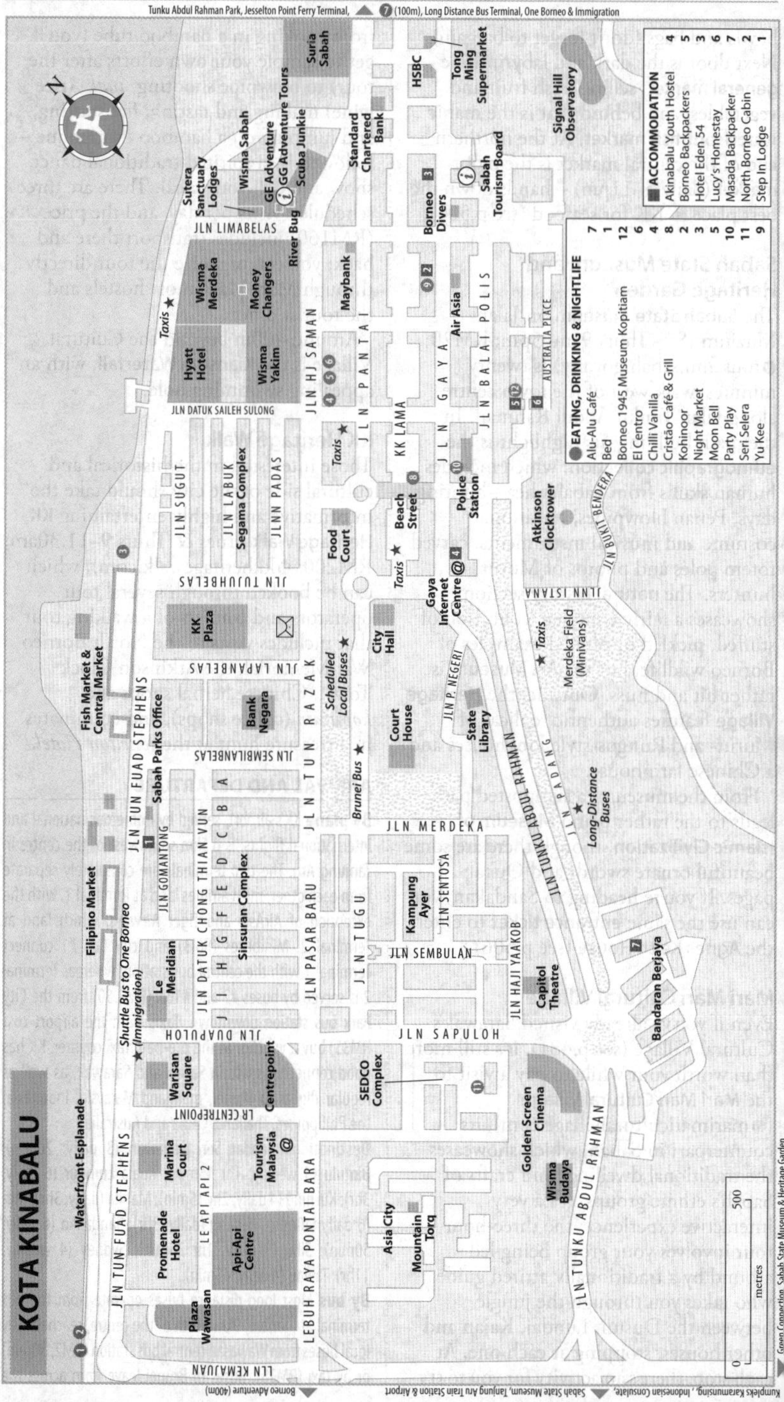

6

KOTA KINABALU

Tunku Abdul Rahman Park, Jesselton Point Ferry Terminal, 7 (100m), Long Distance Bus Terminal, One Borneo & Immigration

Borneo Adventure (400m)

Sabah State Museum, Tanjung Aru Train Station & Airport

Kumpleks Karamunsing, , Indonesian Consulate, Green Connection, Sabah State Museum & Heritage Garden

Waterfront Esplanade
Filipino Market
Fish Market & Central Market
JLN TUN FUAD STEPHENS
Shuttle Bus to One Borneo (Immigration)
Sabah Parks Office
JLN GOMANTONG
Promenade Hotel
Marina Court
Warisan Square
Le Meridian
Plaza Wawasan
LE API API 2
LR CENTREPOINT
JLN DUAPULOH
JLN DATUK CHONG THIAN VUN
J I H G F E D C B A
Sinsuran Complex
JLN SEMBILANBELAS
JLN LAPANBELAS
KK Plaza
JLN TUJUHBELAS
JLN SUGUT
JLN LABUK
Segama Complex
JLNN PADAS
JLN DATUK SAILEH SULONG
Hyatt Hotel
Wisma Merdeka
Wisma Yakim
Money Changers
Taxis
JLN LIMABELAS
Sutera Sanctuary Lodges
Wisma Sabah
GE Adventure
GG Adventure Tours
Scuba Junkie
River Bug
Suria Sabah
LLN KEMAJUAN
Api-Api Centre
Tourism Malaysia
Centrepoint
Bank Negara
LEBUH RAYA PONTAI BARA
JLN PASAR BARU
JLN TUN RAZAK
JLN HJ SAMAN
Scheduled Local Buses
Brunei Bus
Food Court
Maybank
Standard Chartered Bank
JLN TUGU
JLN PANTAI
City Hall
Court House
Beach Street
KK LAMA
HSBC
Tong Ming Supermarket
Borneo Divers
Asia City
Mountain Torq
SEDCO Complex
JLN SAPULOH
JLN SEMBULAN
Kampung Ayer
JLN SENTOSA
JLN MERDEKA
JLN P. NEGERI
Gaya Internet Centre
Police Station
JLN GAYA
Air Asia
JLN BALAI POLIS
Sabah Tourism Board
State Library
JLN HAJI YAAKOB
Capitol Theatre
Golden Screen Cinema
Wisma Budaya
JLN TUNKU ABDUL RAHMAN
JLN PADANG
Long-Distance Buses
Merdeka Field (Minivans)
JLN ISTANA
Atkinson Clocktower
AUSTRALIA PLACE
JLN BUKIT BENDERA
Signal Hill Observatory
Bandaran Berjaya
0 500 metres

EATING, DRINKING & NIGHTLIFE	
Alu-Alu Café	7
Bed	1
Borneo 1945 Museum Kopitiam	12
El Centro	6
Chilli Vanilla	4
Cristão Café & Grill	8
Kohinoor	2
Night Market	3
Moon Bell	5
Party Play	10
Seri Selera	11
Yu Kee	9

ACCOMMODATION	
Akinabalu Youth Hostel	4
Borneo Backpackers	5
Hotel Eden 54	3
Lucy's Homestay	6
Masada Backpacker	7
North Borneo Cabin	2
Step In Lodge	1

street from the courthouse on Jln Pantai. Minivans to take you to Mount Kinabalu National Park congregate around the Merdeka Field area, just off Jln Tunku Abdul Rahman. Generally, buses leave when full; turn up by 7am to ensure a seat. Buses and shared taxis for Kudat leave from the Padang Merdeka bus terminal on Jln Padang.

Destinations Bandar Seri Begawan, Brunei (daily; 9hr); Kinabalu National Park (8 daily; 2hr 30min); Kudat (3 daily, 3hr 30min–4hr); Sandakan (15 daily; 6hr); Semporna (4 daily; 9hr); Tawau (3 daily; 9hr).

INFORMATION AND TOURS

TOURIST INFORMATION

The Sabah Tourism Board (Mon–Fri 8am–5pm, Sat & Sun 9am–4pm; ☎ 088 212121, ⓦ sabahtourism.com) is at 51 Jln Gaya and has a range of information on the top tourist destinations in Sabah. Staff are very helpful and provide you with a good map of KK.

TOURS

Borneo Adventure Block E-27-3A, Signature Office, KK Times Square ☎ 088 486800, ⓦ borneoadventure.com. Award-winning operator that organizes anything from multi-day wildlife safaris and trips to Mt Kinabalu to longhouse visits on the northern tip of Sabah. Three-day/two-night MT Kinabalu tour RM1868.

GG Adventure Tours Lot F-105b, 1st floor, Wisma Sabah ☎ 088 316385, ⓦ gogosabah.com. Very helpful operator that can create pretty much any itinerary you want, depending on your interests, as well as organizing offbeat dirt-bike tours and renting motorbikes. Scooter rental RM45/day.

River Bug Lot 227-229, 2nd Floor, Wisma Sabah ☎ 088 260501, ⓦ traversetours.com. Whitewater rafting on the Klias River and Padas River (RM235/day-trip).

Scuba Junkie Lot G23, ground floor, Wisma Sabah ☎ 088 255816, ⓦ scubajunkiekk.com. A reputable and affordable diving operator offering underwater adventure in the Tunku Abdul Rahman Marine Park. Open Water course RM980.

ACCOMMODATION

Akinabalu Youth Hostel Lot 133 Jln Gaya ☎ 088 272188, ⓦ akinabaluyh.com. Green is the dominant colour here – the lime green of walls and the deep green of plants that make the breezy common area look like an indoor garden. The rooms are a little on the dark side, but the staff are cheerful and helpful. Dorm RM25, double RM70; a/c rooms cost more.

Borneo Backpackers 24 Lorong Dewan, Australia Place ☎ 088 234009, ⓦ borneobackpackers.com. A guest lounge perfect for socializing, friendly staff on hand for booking travel, clean rooms and dorms (singles available), free breakfast and a great café downstairs. What more can one ask for? Dorm from RM25, double RM60

Lucy's Homestay 25 Lorong Dewan, Australia Place ☎ 088 261495, ⓦ lucyhomestay.go-2.net. Like the home of a favourite auntie, hospitable Lucy's place, complete with her cherished cats, has been a traveller favourite – particularly with solo female backpackers – for years. The rooms are simple and clean, there's a cosy library nook and Lucy goes out of her way to help you. Walk-ins preferred. Dorm RM23, double RM58

★ **Masada Backpacker** Jln Masjid Lama, Pusat Bandar ☎ 088 238494, ⓦ masadabackpacker.com. Besides the massive cityscapes superimposed on its walls and maps and Mt Kinabalu photos galore, this hostel is ahead of the pack thanks to its good, bed-sized bunks with proper mattresses, super-helpful staff running the lounge and other nice touches, such as all the coffee you can guzzle. Dorm RM35, double RM80

North Borneo Cabin 74 Jln Gaya ☎ 088 272800, ⓦ northborneocabin.com. The rather spartan a/c or fan-cooled rooms and dorms at this super-central hostel are popular with a mix of local and international backpackers, and the staff are some of the nicest in town. Breakfast included. Dorm RM20, double RM56; a/c rooms pricier.

Step In Lodge Block L, Kompleks Sinsuran, Jln Tun Fuad Stephens ☎ 088 233519, ⓦ stepinlodge.com. A bright exterior hides prim rooms with colourful bed linen and large, comfortable mattresses; the staff are helpful and fellow backpackers congregate around the satellite TV in the lounge, fuelled by the complimentary (real) coffee. Dorm RM28, double RM70

EATING

Self-caterers will find many Western foods that they've been missing at the pricey Tong Hing Supermarket on Jln Gaya. Cheaper supermarkets are found at KK Plaza and Centre Point. Keep an eye out for good, popular chains such as *Secret Recipe* and *Old Town White Coffee*.

Alu-Alu Café Jesselton Point. Feast on marine dishes such as fish in creamy buttermilk sauce, made from ecologically sourced fish at this bright and breezy spot. Plenty of vegetable dishes here, including Sabah vegetables in oyster sauce. Mains from RM12. Daily 11am–2.30pm & 6.30–10pm.

Borneo 1945 Museum Kopitiam 24 Jln Bewan, Australia Place. Both a memorial to the Australian soldiers

★ TREAT YOURSELF

Hotel Eden54 54 Jln Gaya ☎ 088 266054, ⓦ eden54.com. At this stylish boutique hotel – an absolute bargain at the price – you can expect beds with crisp linen, great showers, urban-chic decor and satellite TV, though the cheapest rooms lack windows. The staff are extremely helpful, too. RM149

6

who died and one of the most sociable cafés in town, this friendly joint offers a great *nasi lemak*, among other Malay dishes – the "special" comes with delicious chicken, cooked in a pandan leaf (RM14); Anzac biscuits also on offer. Daily 7.30am–midnight.

★**Chilli Vanilla** 35 Jln Haji Saman. This great little fusion spot serves veggie dishes – lentil soup, chunky Mediterranean sandwiches with grilled aubergine – as well as home-made chicken liver pâté, washed down with fresh fruit juice, organic coffees, shakes and smoothies. Mains from RM16. Mon–Sat 11am–10pm.

★**Cristão Café & Grill** 1 Jln Jati Ⓦ cristaokk.com. Come here for Malaysian Portuguese soul food, from melt-in-your-mouth pulled pork burgers with 'slaw to fiery devil chicken curry and pork vindaloo. Decadent desserts also available. Mains from RM15. Tues–Sun 11.30am–3pm & 6–9.30pm.

Kohinoor Waterfront Esplanade. Large portions of tandoori dishes and curries are on offer at KK's best Indian restaurant. Plenty of dishes for vegetarians, including okra masala (mains from RM12). Daily 11.30am–2.30pm & 5.30–11pm.

★**Night Market** Jln Tun Fuad Stephens. Easily the best place for inexpensive seafood, this waterfront market kicks off after 5pm. Pick a stall, order fresh fish and seafood by weight, and specify how you want it prepared (mains from RM13). Accompaniments include rice and "Sabah vegetable" (jungle fern), and sellers from drinks stalls will come by to take your drinks orders.

Moon Bell 33 Jln Haji Saman. Xinjiang dishes from northwest China, ranging from the signature caramelized aubergine to twice-cooked pork and lamb dishes. Mains from RM15. Tues–Sun 11am–9pm.

Seri Selera SEDCO Complex, off Jln Sapuloh. A restaurant-lined square with outdoor tables; one of the best places in town for fish and seafood – barbecued and Chinese-style. Pick your fresh victims and get some "Sabah vegetable" (*midin* – jungle fern) on the side. Mains from RM14. Daily 5.30–10.30pm.

Yu Kee 74 Jln Gaya. This unpretentious Chinese spot serves the versatile meat in many delicious forms, from crisp pork belly and pork intestine – an acquired taste – to ribs and barbecue pork and rice (mains from RM7). Daily 10am–10pm.

DRINKING AND NIGHTLIFE

Bed Waterfront Esplanade. Go to *Bed* to see live Filipino bands lip-synching to the latest hits (from 9pm onwards) and DJs spinning their stuff in between sets. Raucous and best enjoyed in a group, though it's not the place for an intimate conversation. Daily from 9pm until the wee hours.

★**El Centro** 32 Jln Haji Saman Ⓦ elcentro.my. Buzzing with expats and travellers, this subtly lit, lively bar pulls in the punters with a mixture of strong drinks and fusion food – from big salads to hummus and tapas. Friday is Open Mic night from 9pm, so if you want to sing or recite something, here's your chance. Wednesday is popular pub quiz night. Tues–Sun 5pm–midnight.

Party Play Jln Gaya. This self-proclaimed "lifestyle café" may well be the spot for you if your lifestyle involves margarita fishbowls to share, occasional karaoke and fusion Western-Asian food. Daily from 5pm until late.

DIRECTORY

Banks and exchange Among the various money-changers (Mon–Sat 10am–7pm) in Wisma Merdeka are Ban Loong Money Changer and Travellers' Money Changer, both on the ground floor. ATMs are easy to find throughout the centre of KK – HSBC, Jln Gaya; Maybank, Jln Pantai.

Books Times The Bookshop, Ground Floor, Warisan Square, sells an excellent selection of English books, novels and travel guides. Borneo Books 2 on the second floor of Wisma Merdeka is a secondhand bookshop with an excellent range of reference books on Sabah.

Embassies and consulates Australian Honorary Consul, Suite 10.1, Level 10, Wisma Great Eastern Life, 65 Jln Gaya (Ⓣ 088 267151); British Honorary Consul (Ⓣ 08 251755) – contact the High Commission in Kuala Lumpur (see p.432) for emergency travel documents; Brunei, Lot 8–4, 8th Floor, Api-Api Centre (Ⓣ 088 236113); Indonesia, Lorong Kemajuan, Karamunsing, Peti Surat 11595 (Ⓣ 088 218600).

Hospital Sabah Medical Centre, Lorong Bersatu, off Jln Damai, 6km southeast of the city centre (Ⓣ 088 211333, Ⓦ sabahmedicalcentre.com), offers decent private care.

Immigration office Kompleks Persekutuan Pentadbiran Kerajaan, Jln UMS, 9km south of the centre (Mon–Fri 7am–1pm & 2–5.30pm; Ⓣ 088 488700). Take bus #5A from Warisan Square and ask them to drop you off there.

Internet All accommodation options reviewed offer free wi-fi and some have free internet too. Otherwise, try Gaya Internet Centre on Jln Tinku Abdul Rahman (daily 9am–10pm).

Pharmacy Apex Pharmacy, 2 Jln Pantai, or UMH Pharmacy, 80 Jln Gaya.

Police Balai Polis KK (Ⓣ 088 241161) is on Jln Dewan.

Post office The general post office (Mon–Sat 8am–4.30pm) is on Jln Tun Razak.

Shopping Borneo Handicraft (1st Floor, Wisma Merdeka) has a good choice of woodwork, basketry and gongs; Borneo Handicraft & Ceramic Shop (Ground Floor, Centrepoint) stocks ceramics, antiques and primitive sculptures. The Filipino market (daily 8am–5pm) is a good place to bargain for cultured pearls and handicrafts from Borneo, the Philippines and elsewhere. Gaya Street Sunday Market (around 7am–3pm) is pure kitsch.

TUNKU ABDUL RAHMAN PARK

Situated within an 8km radius of downtown KK, the five islands of **TUNKU ABDUL RAHMAN PARK (TAR Park)** represent the most westerly ripples of the undulating Crocker mountain range. The largest of the park's islands is **Pulau Gaya**, where a 20km system of trails snakes across the lowland rainforest. Most of these trails start on the southern side of the island at Camp Bay, which also offers pleasant enough swimming, but a more alluring alternative is Police Beach, on the north coast. Boatmen demand extra for circling round to this side of Gaya (RM30 return), but it's money well spent: the white-sand bay is pretty idyllic. Wildlife on Gaya includes hornbills, wild pigs, lizards, snakes and macaques, which have been known to swim over to nearby **Pulau Sapi**, a 25-acre islet off the northwestern coast of Gaya that's linked by a sand bar at low tide. Pulau Sapi has several short hiking trails, a kiosk selling snacks, and decent snorkelling.

The park's other islands cluster together 2.5km west of Gaya. The largest of the three, banana-shaped **Pulau Manukan**, is the most popular island with KK residents and offers a number of hiking trails, as well as good snorkelling, a couple of restaurants and a snack joint – it's the best choice for lunch. Across a channel to the southeast is tiny **Pulau Mamutik**, which can be crossed on foot in fifteen minutes and has excellent sands on either side of its jetty, not to mention the best snorkelling of all the islands and a small café/snack bar.

On Manukan, Mamutik and Sapi it's possible to organize water activities such as banana-boat rides and parasailing. It's cheaper to rent snorkelling equipment at Jesselton Point, though.

THE RAFFLESIA RESERVE

Southeast from Kota Kinabalu, paddy fields give way to the rolling foothills of the Crocker mountain range. A 58km ride up to the 1649m-high Sinsuron Pass takes you onto the **Rafflesia Reserve** (daily 8am–3pm; free; T 088 898500). In the reserve you can see the world's largest flower, the cabbage-like rafflesia: a smelly, parasitic plant whose rubbery, orange-red blooms can reach up to 1m in diameter. It was first catalogued in Sumatra in 1818, by Sir Stamford Raffles and the naturalist Dr Joseph Arnold. Phone the visitor centre before leaving KK, as the flowers bloom unpredictably and each flower only lasts a few days before dying. To get here, take any Tembunan-bound bus (regular services from 7am to 4pm daily from the long-distance bus station in KK; 2hr; RM15).

THE NORTHWEST COAST

Sabah's northwest coast which ends in the beaches and headland of the picturesque northernmost tip of Borneo, is one of the few parts of Sabah that is not firmly on the backpacker trail. The coastal **Rungus villages** around **Tampat do Aman**, connected by dirt-and-gravel tracks, are

VISITING TUNKU ABDUL RAHMAN PARK

Several boat companies ply the route between KK's Jesselton Ferry Terminal and the islands. Choose which company you're going to go with and decide if you want to visit just one island (RM30 return) or whether you want to sign up for multi-island hopping (RM42/48 for two/three islands). **Boats** leave from 8.30am until 4pm, returning between 1pm and 5pm. Since they depart when full, it's better to go earlier in the day when there are more people going. Choose which island you want to go to first, and, once you get there, tell the representative of your boat company when you wish to go on to your next island and they'll arrange pick-up (boats tend to leave hourly). You have to pay a RM7.20 departure tax when leaving Jesselton Point, and a RM10 Environmental Conservation Fee is payable upon arrival at your first island (hold on to your receipt). All boat companies can arrange snorkel-rental at Jesselton Point (RM10), which is cheaper than renting the gear on the islands.

It is possible to **camp** on Gaya, Manukan and Mamutik for RM5 (bring your own tent); it's worth it to enjoy the islands without the crowds.

still low-key and friendly, the beaches are largely deserted, but word about this Shangri-La is beginning to get out, and since the main road has recently been paved, it's only a matter of time before development follows, so the time to go is now. The closest town to the tip of Borneo is drowsy **Kudat**, its main feature being the colourful Chinese temple near the main square.

Tampat do Aman

On the outskirts of one of the Rungus villages, this secluded eco-lodge has become a destination in itself. It's run by Howard the Brit and his Rungus wife and there's a wonderfully friendly feel to this rustic place that's hidden amid lush greenery, enhanced by a veritable menagerie of cats, ducks and local wildlife, such as civets that often appear on the electricity lines during hours of darkness. Howard runs transfers to his beachside café near the tip of Borneo several times a day, though you can easily walk the 4km yourself. At the café you can rent bicycles and motorbikes to explore the surrounding beaches and Rungus villages. Howard is an absolute treasure trove of local information and there's a museum devoted to Rungus culture on the property itself. Contact Howard in advance to arrange pickup from *Ria Hotel* in Kudat.

ARRIVAL AND DEPARTURE

By bus There are three daily buses from KK to Kudat (3hr 30min–4hr), but it's quicker to take a shared taxi. Shared taxis depart Kudat for KK (3hr; RM15) whenever they fill up and it's easier to get a ride in the mornings. To get to the tip of Borneo, you'll either need your own wheels or to stay at *Tampat Do Aman* (see below).

ACCOMMODATION AND EATING

In Kudat, there are several inexpensive Indian and Malay joints around the main square. Near the tip of Borneo, the Tampan Do Aman beach café is pretty much the only option for eating.

★**Tampat Do Aman** ⓣ013 8808395, ⓦtampatdoaman.com. Wonderful eco-lodge, consisting of a backpacker longhouse with tiny individual rooms with mosquito nets, thatched huts and a chill-out area, set amid lush greenery. There's electricity and running water in the showers, though be prepared to share them with local wildlife. Longhouse rooms **RM40**

KINABALU NATIONAL PARK

There are few sights more impressive in Borneo than the cloud-encased summit of **Mount Kinabalu**. Standing at 4095m, Kinabalu's jagged peaks look impossibly daunting from a distance, but the mountain is a relatively straightforward – if somewhat exhausting – climb. The well-defined, 8.7km path weaves up the mountain's southern side to the bare granite of the summit, where a 1.6km-deep gully known as Low's Gully cleaves the peak in two. The view from the top is awe-inspiring and the blanket of stars which envelops you until sunrise (not to mention the altitude) will leave you breathless. The aching muscles and creaking joints are well worth the sense of exhilaration you'll achieve at the top.

WHAT TO SEE AND DO

For many, climbing Mount Kinabalu is the main attraction of a visit to Sabah. However, for those not so keen on ascending the 4095m, there are other trails that you can take in the park leading through rich lowland forest to mountain rivers and waterfalls and bringing ample opportunity for birdwatching and nature walks. The park also has its own **botanical garden** and **Poring Hot Springs** – the perfect remedy for aching muscles, post-ascent. Details of all the various walks and trails are available from the park headquarters.

The climb: day one

Climbing to your first night's accommodation brings you to a height of around 3350m, and takes from three to five hours, depending on your fitness. Take your time, as it'll give you a better chance to acclimatize to the high altitude.

The trail is marked out with encouraging signboards every 500m and there are seven rest shelters with toilets and containers of untreated (but drinkable) water along the Timpohon Trail (five along the Mesilau Trail) spread out at regular intervals up until Laban Rata, your stop for the night. It's possible to do the climb in a day, but you have to be supremely fit to do so and you have to pass the control point at Laban Rata by noon to be allowed to proceed.

The trail is a combination of steep wooden stairs, uneven rock-and-dirt steps and relatively flat sections in between, so it's not all relentlessly uphill. Two or three hours into the climb, incredible views of the hills, sea and clouds below you start to unfold and the trail changes from lowland forest to dense foliage. After about 5km, the surrounding jungle becomes sparse and you have to cross some steep, exposed rocky ground, where you're most likely to be caught in the rain. The resthouses are located just after 6km at the foot of Panar Laban, from where views of the sun setting over the South China Sea are exquisite.

The climb: day two

Most climbers get up at 2am the next morning in order to make it to the top for sunrise. At 2.30am, the gate to the trail is opened and hikers join the procession snaking their way to the top by the light of their headlamps. This last section is only 2.7km but can seem interminable; the first part consists of an endless climb up steep wooden steps which then give way to exposed rock with ropes strung along it to help you haul yourself up; using your arms will give your legs a bit of a break. The last section is a short, steep scramble to the summit up some large, uneven boulders. If you make it to the summit just before sunrise, you'll have the satisfaction of watching a long line of headlamps making their way up towards you and knowing that when you're heading back down towards a well-deserved hot breakfast, they'll still be struggling up to the summit.

On a clear day, you get a splendid view of the whole valley below, illuminated by the first rays of the sun, as well as the lights of Kota Kinabalu along the coast. On the way down, you'll be able to appreciate the different peaks that you scrambled past in the darkness. If you've chosen to do the *via ferrata* (see box below), you have to descend to your assigned meeting point before beginning your vertigo-inducing adventure.

After breakfast at Laban Rata, descend at your leisure.

ARRIVAL AND DEPARTURE

By bus A/c express buses from KK to Sandakan (4hr) pass park headquarters, leaving KK hourly on the hour between 7am and 10am and then at 12.30pm, 2pm and 3pm. There are return buses going back to KK (usually before 6.30pm), which can be flagged down outside the park entrance, and a shuttle bus that heads back to KK at 3.30pm (RM40). Shared jeeps depart when full from the park gates and cost RM150 to KK (for up to five people). For Poring Hot Springs you can take a minivan or taxi for RM55 from park headquarters, hop on the daily shuttle bus from the park HQ at noon, or walk out of the main gate and hail any passing Sandakan-bound bus. They'll drop you off at Ranau (RM8), from where you can take a minibus (RM10) to the springs.

ACCOMMODATION AND EATING

It's worth spending a night at the base of Mt Kinabalu, if only to avoid getting up at an insane hour in KK before catching a bus or a taxi to the park. Most lodging options in the park include meals. Staying at the park headquarters and in Laban Rata is vastly overpriced for what it is, as

THE VIA FERRATA

If the precipitous climb to the summit of Mount Kinabalu is not enough of a challenge, you may consider taking the road less travelled and sign up for Mountain Torq's **via ferrata** – the highest in the world. Consisting of metal rungs, bars, steel cables and suspension bridges bolted to the sheer rock face, the *via ferrata* is an adventure playground for adrenalin junkies. While no prior experience is required, a good level of physical fitness is a must; the enthusiastic English-speaking guides talk you through everything else. You can take part in two circuits: **Low's Peak Circuit** (RM600) or the shorter **Walk the Torq** (RM440; Low's Peak Circuit incorporates Walk the Torq). The former requires a fair amount of abseiling or climbing down a sheer rock face and the views of the valley from up high are second to none; the latter is far shorter and easier, but still requires traversing a cliff face and wire bridge.

Mountain Torq (T 088 268126, W mountaintorq.com) now also offer **sports climbing courses** that start from RM1640/person for a three-days and two-nights itinerary, with professional instruction and accommodation at the Pendant Hut.

Sutera Sanctuary Lodges have a monopoly on it. At the park headquarters there are a couple of restaurants (daily 6am–10pm, Sat until 11pm) that serve both buffet and à la carte meals, and there's also a (pricey) provisions shop beside reception.

D'Villa Rina Ria Lodge ⓣ 088 889282, ⓦ dvillalodge .com. Just 500m outside the park headquarters, you'll find cosy-bordering-on-cramped dorms and more spacious doubles at this rather wallet-friendly lodge, presided over by super-helpful staff. The mountain views from the dining room are just splendid. Dorm **RM30**, double **RM120**

Laban Rata Resthouse Laban Rata ⓣ 088 308916, ⓦ suteraharbour.com. The place where most hikers will stay at the halfway-up-the-mountain point, this rather ordinary lodge offers heated dorms, hot showers and simple twin rooms. Prices include all meals and the cafeteria is the only place to eat on the mountain. The Gunting Lagadan, Panar Laban and Waras huts around the main lodge have somewhat cheaper (RM415) unheated dorms (and it gets very cold at night). Dorm **RM485**, double **RM920**

Mountain Resthouse ⓣ 088 771109. A budget option 200m from the park entrance, this hostel's four-bed dorms feel a lot less institutionalized than the pack-'em-in 20-bedders at the park headquarters but can be damp and cold. Wi-fi is intermittent. Dorm **RM35**

Pendant Hut Laban Rata ⓣ 088 268126, ⓦ mountain torq.com. The one non-*Sutera* option at Laban Rata belongs to Mountain Torq and consists of unheated (though you do get warm sleeping bags) but tidy dorms with superb views. Though the *Pendant Hut* accepts non-*via ferrata* guests, prices do include the *via ferrata* experience; meals are taken at the *Laban Rata Resthouse* cafeteria below. From **RM830** for two days and one night

Sutera Sanctuary Lodge Park Headquarters ⓣ 088 308914, ⓦ suteraharbour.com. If you want to stay at the park headquarters at the base of the mountain, this is the only option, a veritable catch-all consisting of two virtually identical 20-bed hostels – *Rock and Grace* and *Hill Lodge* which have semi-detached cabins; hotel rooms at the *Liwagu Suites*; semi-detached two-bedroom units at *Peak Lodge*; and two-storey, two-bedroom units at the priciest *Nepenthes Villa*. Dorm **RM192**, double from **RM580**

Poring Hot Springs

The sulphurous waters of **Poring Hot Springs** (some call them "Boring Hot Springs") are situated on the park's southeastern border. It's a place where ailing bones will be glad of a rejuvenating soak, but if you're expecting a beautiful

CLIMBING MOUNT KINABALU

There are various **tour operators** in KK who can organize trips to the summit, but it's possible to make your own way there and sort out guides and accommodation yourself. Accommodation at Laban Rata, the overnight stop halfway up the mountain, is limited and fills up fast, so you need to organize it several weeks in advance in peak season. In KK, visit the Sutera Sanctuary Lodges office (Lot G15, Ground Floor, Wisma Sabah; ⓣ 088 308914, ⓦ suteraharbour.com) to book a bed on the mountain for the night of the climb. If going with Mountain Torq (see box, p.503), you'll be staying at their own *Pendant Hut* (see below).

Buses stop about 50m from the park reception office (daily 7am–8pm), which is the check-in point for accommodation and obtaining guides. On arrival you'll need to pay the trail fee (RM10), get a climbing permit (RM100/person), mandatory insurance (RM14) and pay for an **obligatory guide** (RM42.50 per person for up to three people, RM50 per person for up to six). It's usually easy to join with others to share the guide fee at reception. The guides do not try to keep everyone walking at the same pace; they walk behind the slowest member, so it's fine if you strike out on your own, as long as you stay on the trail. To lighten your load, you can hire a porter (R40 one-way for no more than 10kg). The above guide and porter fees apply to the Timpohon route; if you want to take the longer Mesilau route, or go up one and come down the other, fees go up accordingly.

Aim to be at the park reception by 9am to make it up to the overnight resthouse before nightfall; if going with Mountain Torq, 8am is better, as you'll need to be up at *Pendant Hut* by 3pm for the briefing; also, by 9am, the headquarters become crowded with hikers.

Transport from the park headquarters to either the Timpohon Gate or the Mesilau Gate costs R35/R40 return; car sharing is cost-effective. Most hikers take the main, shorter Timpohon Trail (6km). The Mesilau Trail (8km), though longer, is partly downhill and you see a greater variety of flora along the way, such as pitcher plants. The Mesilau Trail joins the main trail at around the 4km marker.

6

WHAT TO BRING

You mustn't underestimate the rigours of the climb. There are a few essentials you should not leave KK without, all of which should fit in a small waterproof backpack:

Headlamp (with spare batteries) Essential for lighting your way during the early-morning scramble to the top on the second day.

Footwear with good traction The trail is more often slippery than not.

Plenty of cash You'll be amazed how much the entrance/guide/miscellaneous fees add up to and you can't pay with your credit card.

Fleece or warm jumper It gets very cold both at Laban Rata at night and at the top of the mountain in the pre-dawn.

Lightweight windproof and waterproof jacket To protect you from the rain and wind during the higher part of the ascent. It's also good to have a cheap plastic poncho and to save the jacket for the top of the mountain.

Water bottle Or, better still, a CamelBak water container.

Camera To record your triumph.

Long johns To wear at night and/or under your outer trousers when you get cold.

Lightweight, breathable trousers For the upper part of the ascent; up to Laban Rata, a pair of shorts will do.

At least two T-shirts One to wear for the ascent, and one dry one to change into.

Gloves For holding onto the cold, sodden ropes during the early-morning scramble to the top.

High-energy snacks Snacks sold at the park are extortionate. Bring a packed lunch from KK if you don't wish to fork out for one prepared by *Sutera Lodge*.

Collapsible hiking poles Useful for tackling the knee-popping descent.

natural spa location then you'll be disappointed: the springs are man-made and have been designed with purpose rather than luxury or comfort in mind. There are shared open-air baths (RM15) where you simply slip into a tub and just turn on the tap. There are also a couple of "private" baths that are little more than a sunken plastic tub, many with broken jacuzzis (RM20/hr). The park itself is in a beautiful location with some lovely **trails** through natural forest. A fifteen-minute trail beyond the baths brings you to Poring's **canopy walk** (daily 9am–4pm; RM15), where five tree huts connected by suspended walkways 40m above ground afford you a monkey's-eye view of the surrounding lowland rainforest. A trail strikes off uphill to the right of the baths, reaching 150m-high Langanan Waterfall about one and a half hours later. On its way, around ten minutes' walk from Poring, it passes smaller Kepungit Waterfall, where the refreshing pool is ideal for swimming. There is also an educational **butterfly farm** in the grounds (daily 9am–4pm; RM5), with a garden, nursery and hatchery, which houses some spectacular species.

Lupa Masa

Meaning "forget time" – an appropriate name for a place where people come for a few days and end up staying for weeks, **Lupa Masa** (ⓦlupamasa.wix.com) is much more than rustic accommodation in the middle of the jungle. The jungle camp, a thirty- to forty-minute hike through lush rainforest from Poring Hot Springs, is beautifully situated, overlooking a clear river with swimming holes, nearby waterfalls to frolic in and trails through the jungle used during guided night walks, longer day hikes and jungle survival training courses. The place has a very friendly vibe; there are usually a couple of volunteers living on-site and travellers who've ended up lingering here. This is a properly rustic experience: expect giant spiders in the showers and toilets (with flushing water), and the occasional snake in the waterfalls, so this place attracts laidback adventurers rather than travellers in need of creature comforts. Call in advance to be met at *Ernah Lodge* on the road to Poring Hot Springs; guests are usually collected at around 2–3pm.

ARRIVAL AND DEPARTURE

By bus Regular buses run between KK and nearby Ranau; Ranau is a short taxi ride from Poring (RM35). You can also flag down Ranau- and KK-bound buses by the entrance to Kinabalu National Park.

ACCOMMODATION AND EATING

6

At Poring itself, the accommodation scene is limited to overpriced options, so you're better off visiting Poring en route to or from Mt Kinabalu or else staying at *Lupa Masa* (see p.505). There's a café with a limited menu at the springs, and a couple of restaurants just outside the gates serving Malay food from RM10.

★**Lupa Masa** ⓣ01 820 8981 or ⓣ012 845 1987. The eco-camp features a covered lounge and open-air kitchen; sleeping arrangements range from tents on a raised platform with a roof, a mattress on a raised platform overlooking the river, with mosquito netting, or a rustic two-person *pondok* (hut) with mattress on the floor for couples. Besides generating its own electricity using a nearby river, *Lupa Masa* also composts organic waste and meals incorporate organic, locally sourced produce (including various jungle plants). Don't expect wi-fi, and bring a torch to light your way at night. RM85–100 per person per day, including food.

SANDAKAN

Sandwiched between sea and cliffs on the northern lip of Sandakan Bay, **SANDAKAN** is a gritty port, founded in 1878 by Englishman William Pryer and spread out around the bay. There's little left of the attractive architecture from its colonial heyday, as it was destroyed by Japanese bombing. During the Japanese occupation between 1942 and 1945, Sandakan was the site of a large prisoner of war camp, and more Australian prisoners died during the death march to Ranau than during the construction of the Burma Railway. Every year on ANZAC Day (April 24), former servicemen and their descendants come to visit the **Australian war memorial** at Mile Seven on Labuk Rd, towards Sepilok (take buses #8, #12 or #14, get off at the "Taman Rimba" signpost and then take Jln Rimba; taxis cost around RM35).

The **Sandakan Heritage Trail** (pick up a brochure from the tourist office) loops around the town centre, taking in Sandakan's historical buildings, such as the William Pryer monument, the St Michael and All Angels Church, the Chinese World War II memorial and the "100 steps", up to **Agnes Keith's house** (daily 9am–5pm; RM15 – free with KK Sabah State Museum ticket). This beautiful two-storey colonial residence was built on the site of the home of the American author who lived in Sandakan with her English husband between the 1930s and the 1950s. Her first book, *The Land Below The Wind*, gave Sabah an endearing epithet that stuck, while *Three Came Home* told the story of the family's internment in Japanese prisoner of war camps.

Just to the east of Sandakan is **Kampung Buli Sim-Sim**, the water village around which Sandakan expanded in the nineteenth century, its countless photogenic shacks spread like lilies out into the bay – a colourful place to wander around, with some great seafood restaurants.

Most travellers use Sandakan as a base from which to visit or a brief stopover en route to the **Sepilok Orang-utan Rehabilitation Centre** and **Bornean Sun Bear Conservation Centre**, or as a jumping-off point for **wildlife-watching** along the Kinabatangan River and the **Gomantong Caves**, connected to Sandakan by handy transfers.

ARRIVAL AND DEPARTURE

By plane The airport serving Sandakan is 11km north of town and connected by taxis (RM35) to the centre. You can also take bus #7 which stops around 500m from the airport along the main road.

Destinations Kota Kinabalu (4 daily; 1hr 45min); Kuala Lumpur (6 daily; 3hr 30min).

By bus Sandakan's local bus station is situated on the waterfront at Jln Pryer. Local buses run along Jln Utara from 6am to 6pm, their number, Batu 7 (Mile 7), telling you the distance they travel from town. A short walk west along Jln Pryer brings you to the minibus area. Most Kinabatangan nature lodges arrange daily pick-ups from Sandakan.

Destinations From the long-distance bus station at Batu 2.5 (taxis cost RM15) there are buses to and from KK (approximately hourly 7am–2pm with an evening departure around 8pm; 7hr); Lahad Datu (several daily; 2hr 30min); Ranau (3 daily; 4hr); Semporna (daily at 7.30am; 5hr 30min); Tawau (several daily; 5hr 30min).

By long-distance taxi Long-distance taxis operate from the area around the local bus station.

INFORMATION

Tourist information The tourist office (Mon–Thurs 8am–12.30pm & 1.30–4.30pm, Fri 8–11.30am & 2–4.30pm; ⓣ089 229751) at Wisma Warisan, up the stairs from Lebuh Tiga, is a mine of local and regional information; pick up your Sandakan Heritage Trail booklet here.

ACCOMMODATION

Harbourside Backpackers Lot 43, 1st floor, block HS-4, Sandakan Harbour Square ⓣ089 217072, ⓦharboursidebackpackers.com. A great central location, super-nice staff, a/c-cooled rooms and a good bathroom-to-guest ratio make this a top backpacker choice. Breakfast included. Dorm RM25, double RM80

★ **Nak Hotel** Jln Pelabuhan Lama at Jln Pryer ⓣ089 272988, ⓦnakhotel.com. Refurbished, super-central hotel with friendly, helpful staff, spacious rooms with cable TV and sparkling bathrooms, as well as a superb roof lounge, *Balin* (see below). Wi-fi only in lobby or in *Balin*. Breakfast included and singles available. RM118

Sandakan Backpackers Lot 108, Block SH-11, Sandakan Harbour Square ⓣ089 221104, ⓦsandakanbackpackers.com. Located right on the waterfront, this hostel features large, bright dorms and rooms, as well as a rooftop garden and lounge with pool table. Price also includes breakfast. Dorm RM25, double RM70

EATING AND DRINKING

There are numerous inexpensive restaurants along the waterfront, serving Malay, Chinese and Indian dishes. Central Sandakan is quiet in the evenings; Batu (Mile) 4 is a good place to head for local nightlife and a plethora of restaurants.

★ **Balin Roof Garden** At the top of *Nak Hotel*. A chic Balinese-inspired roof lounge with loads of cushions to recline on and a good restaurant and a bar overlooking the sea from the open-air section. The menu is mostly fusion, the thin-and-crispy pizzas are excellent, the fresh fruit juices are better than the cocktails on offer and the staff are just lovely (mains from RM15). Get there early for incredible sunsets over the sea. Daily 8am–11pm.

The English Tea House and Restaurant Jln Istana. Set up high on a hill overlooking the town, this attractive colonial building is home to an English teahouse. Come for the setting, the views and the scones, clotted cream and tea, but skip the rest of the menu. Also has a good wine list for those in need of more than cake. Daily 10am–midnight.

New Market Jln Pryor. Behind the waterfront Marriott, this market resembles a multi-storey car park. Head upstairs for the halal food stalls serving an excellent mix of Filipino, Chinese, Malay and Indonesian specials (mains from RM4). Daily from 7am until early afternoon.

Sim Sim Seafood Restaurant Sim Sim 8. Located at the Sim Sim stilt village, this recently spruced up joint rightly lives up to its reputation and serves some of the best seafood for miles around. Pick your fresh meal from a fish tank and they'll do the rest. Take a taxi to Sim Sim Bridge 8. Daily 8am–2pm.

SEPILOK

Twenty-five kilometres west of Sandakan lies **SEPILOK**, an area known primarily for the **Sepilok Orang-utan Rehabilitation Centre (SORC)** – the most reliable place in Borneo to see the stunning redhead of the simian world. Nearby is the **Rainforest Discovery Centre**, with nature trails through the jungle and canopy towers for wildlife-watching. A new attraction, the **Bornean Sun Bear Conservation Centre (BSBCC)**, has opened right next door to SORC, so you can see two of Borneo's most beguiling mammals during an easy day-trip.

Sepilok Orang-utan Rehabilitation Centre

One of only four orang-utan sanctuaries in the world, the **Sepilok Orang-utan Rehabilitation Centre** (daily 9–11am & 2–4pm; trails 9am–4.15pm; feeding times 10am & 3pm; RM30; camera fee RM10; ⓣ089 531180) is home to semi-wild orang-utans that have been orphaned or rescued from captivity. Young orang-utans learn essential skills – climbing, nesting, finding food – in the "Nursery" before they're allowed into the jungle and their dependence on humans is decreased until they're ready to be integrated into the wild orang-utan population of Borneo once more. The 20-minute video screening at the centre (daily at 9am, 10.30am, 11am, noon, 2.10pm and 3.30pm) shows the rescue and rehabilitation of orang-utans.

The orang-utans generally roam the surrounding jungle, but know exactly when **feeding time** is and have their body clocks well tuned to free fruit, so a sighting is pretty much guaranteed. A short boardwalk leads to feeding station A, which is linked to the trees with taut ropes that allow you to see them coming long before they reach the platform,

6

scaring off the long-tail macaques that lurk nearby, waiting to snatch their fill of fruit.

Visitors must leave all their possessions (bar cameras) in the lockers provided, as macaques and orang-utans have been known to snatch items that tickle their fancy.

6

There are also a number of **pleasant walks** throughout the park ranging from 250m to 4km in length; to gain access, you need to register at the on-site visitor reception centre.

Bornean Sun Bear Conservation Centre

The **sun bear**, named for a vaguely sun-like white crescent on its black chest, is the smallest and least studied of the world's bears (in spite of the fact that it easily rivals the panda for cuteness). An omnivore and an expert climber native to Borneo and other parts of Southeast Asia, it's increasingly under threat due to massive destruction of its natural habitat, competition from other predators, such as leopards, tigers and other bears, illegal hunting for body parts such as the gall bladder, bones and claws used in traditional Chinese medicine, and the illegal pet trade.

The **Bornean Sun Bear Conservation Centre** (Ⓦbsbcc.org.my), now open to the public (daily 9am–4pm; RM30), has made it its mission to rescue and rehabilitate orphaned and ex-captive sun bears and to raise awareness both locally and worldwide regarding their plight. Currently home to 28 sun bears and due to increase capacity to 50 once the new bear house is completed, the conservation centre has a visitor information centre and several boardwalks (including wheelchair-friendly ramps) leading to viewpoints overlooking the reserve where the bears roam, giving visitors a chance to observe these remarkable mammals in their natural habitat.

For more information on sun bears, see Ⓦsunbears.wildlifedirect.org. To help protect them, never buy bear products in markets, and if you see them on sale, report the sellers to the local authorities.

Rainforest Discovery Centre

The **Rainforest Discovery Centre** (daily 8am–5pm; RM10; Ⓣ089 533780, Ⓦforest.sabah.gov.my/rdc) – a small nature reserve that's home to flying foxes, gliding lizards, orang-utans and more – is a 1.5km walk back towards the entrance to Sepilok from SORC. There is a visitor centre by a small lake, from which nature trails branch off into the jungle. One of the longer loops leads you past the Sepilok Giant, an enormous hardwood tree, while just beyond the lake you reach the first of three canopy towers, linked by a metal canopy walk. Each tower is named after a bird you're likely to see from it (such as Hornbill Tower and Trogon Tower); the best time to see wildlife is early in the morning or later in the afternoon, so it's worth spending a night in the park.

Just behind the visitor centre is the **Plant Discovery Garden**, with a maze of short trails showcasing pitcher plants, the ginger family, giant orchids, medicinal plants and cacti.

ARRIVAL AND DEPARTURE

By bus To get to Sepilok from Sandakan take any bus from the central bus station numbering #14 or higher, since Sepilok is located just off "Batu 14" (hourly 9am–4.30pm; 45min; RM3). From Batu 14 it's 2.5km to SORC along a road lined with accommodation options; walk or take one of the taxis that shuttle to and from SORC (RM3 per person). A taxi from Sandakan to the park costs around RM45. To move on to other parts of Sabah, note that the long-distance bus station is en route to Sandakan, so ask the driver to drop you there. Many lodging options along the Kinabatangan River can pick you up from Sepilok if notified in advance.

By taxi Most of the accommodation lodges can arrange taxis to Sandakan. The journey (25min) should cost around RM45.

ACCOMMODATION AND EATING

Most lodging options include breakfast in the price and some offer full board. Otherwise, use the cafeteria at SORC which has inexpensive rice and noodle dishes.

★**Paganakan Dii** Ⓣ012 8681005, Ⓦpaganakandii.com. Beautifully situated on a ridge overlooking the jungle below, this is the only lodging option in Sepilok that's off the other side of the highway from SORC. The dorms have "breathable" walls that keep them cool; the en-suite duplex hut rooms and ridge duplexes have

open-air bathrooms and balconies, and there's an on-site café serving simple meals. Two scheduled daily transfers to SORC are included in the price. Dorm RM30, double RM135

Sepilok B&B 089 534050, sepilokbedandbreakfast.com. Opposite the Rainforest Discovery Centre, this unpretentious option offers four lodges with various configurations of basic dorms and a/c private rooms, with a communal vibe that draws the backpacker crowd. Dorm RM31, double RM68

Sepilok Forest Edge Resort 089 533190, sepilokforestedgeresort.com. Spick-and-span en-suite a/c chalets and fan-cooled dorm and rooms in a wooden longhouse, set amid lush grounds, just 500m away from SORC, with a jungle trail and jacuzzi for guests (RM8). Birdwatching trips and stays along the Kinabatangan River can be arranged. Dorm RM45, doubles RM95, chalets from RM250

Sepilok Jungle Resort 089 533031, sepilokjungleresort.com. Great location just a 5min walk from the orang-utan centre, set in the jungle in a lovely lakeside location. Try to nab one of the renovated rooms with a/c; the older rooms are a bit shabby and institutional-looking. Dorms lead off from a small living area behind the restaurant. Dorm RM28, double RM105

Uncle Tan's Mile 14, Jln Sepilok 089 535784, uncletan.com. Run by one of the oldest adventure operators in Sabah, this sociable guesthouse is located 300m from Sepilok Junction and is a firm favourite with backpackers. Although the huts are pretty basic, full board can be arranged for a reasonable price. They also arrange cheap wildlife-spotting trips to their jungle camp at Kinabatangan (see below). Dorm RM38, double RM100

LIBARAN TURTLE ISLAND

Off the northwest coast of Sabah and part of the Sandakan Archipelago, **LIBARAN** is one of the larger islands, easily accessible by boat from Sandakan. The island has a small community of fishermen at one end and a turtle conservation hatchery – part of the new Turtle Conservation Programme designed to protect endangered green turtles – on the other side of the island. Visitors can stay overnight on the island at beachside accommodation run by *Trekkers Lodge* and Nasalis Larvatus Tours, affiliated with *Nature Lodge* (see p.510). At night, wildlife guides watch for turtles coming ashore to lay eggs and lead visitors to a nearby spot where they may observe the turtle without disturbing it (flashlights and photography forbidden). The conservation programme works together with locals, discouraging them from poaching turtle eggs by offering them more money for leading them to a nesting turtle (as opposed to RM2–3 per poached turtle egg). Visitors may also participate in setting baby turtles loose from the hatchery. This new conservation programme is a better and more affordable way of seeing turtles than the nearby Turtle Islands National Park, visits to which are both hugely expensive and mismanaged.

ARRIVAL AND DEPARTURE

By boat Stays on Libaran Island include boat transfers (by arrangement) from downtown Sandakan (daily in peak season; 45min). During rainy season (Nov–Feb) the *Walai Penyu Resort* on the island may shut down as the seas are too rough for safe passage there and back.

ACCOMMODATION AND EATING

Walai Penyu Resort Booked through Nasalis Larvatus Tours 088 230534, insabah.com. This glamping resort consists of luxury tents with beds inside on a raised platform right by the beach, the best outdoorsy bathrooms you'll ever see, and a shaded veranda where you're served delicious, mostly Malay, meals. Book at least a week in advance as there's only space for 16 guests. Two days and one night all-inclusive RM445

SUNGAI KINABATANGAN

The wide cappuccino-coloured ribbon that is the Kinabatangan River cuts a long path into the jungle of east Sabah – 560km long, to be precise. The area around, hemmed in by ever-encroaching palm-oil plantations, is one of the best – and most accessible – places to see **wildlife** in Sabah. Pygmy elephants are spotted on the riverbanks during dry season. and you're likely to see wild orang-utans, proboscis monkeys, gibbons, macaques, wild boar, and huge monitor lizards in the forest flanking the river. Swimming is not a good idea, particularly in the river's tributaries, as they're favoured by crocodiles. The resident bird life – four species of hornbill, Brahmin kites, crested serpent eagles, egrets, stork-billed kingfishers and oriental darters – is equally impressive. It's much

more difficult to spot the nocturnal dwellers of the forest such as the clouded leopard, slow loris and saucer-eyed tarsier – one of the oldest mammals on earth, though with the tarsiers, you might have better luck in August, the fruit season, when they come to feed on the insects that feed on the fruit.

The best way to appreciate the river is to stay in one of the several jungle camps or lodges on its banks.

ARRIVAL AND DEPARTURE

By bus There are no direct buses from Sabah's bigger towns to Sukau and Bilit, but most jungle lodges can arrange pick-up from Sandakan or from the Sukau Junction. All buses running from KK and Sandakan to Lahad Datu, Semporna and Tawau pass by the junction, so just ask to be let off there. From Sandakan, the junction is around a 1hr 30min drive. All operators can arrange for you to be dropped off at the junction in time for the next bus north or south.

ACCOMMODATION AND EATING

Most jungle lodges are based either around the small village of Bilit, closest to the Sukau Junction, or at the spread-out village of Sukau, further east along the river. There's no public transport to or between the villages. Accommodation prices include all meals; pick-up from Sandakan or Sepilok can be arranged. Most riverside lodges offer two longboat river cruises each day – at dawn and at sunset. Depending on the location of the lodge, most also offer short jungle treks and have rubber boots and leech socks for rent. If trekking in the evening, a hand-held torch is better than a headlamp.

Barefoot Sukau Lodge Sukau ⓣ 089 237725, ⓦ barefootsukau.com. Excellent budget option with an attractive waterfront café, helpful staff and compact, whitewashed rooms. RM90

★**The Last Frontier Resort** Bilit ⓣ 016 676 5922, ⓦ thelastfrontierresort.com. Run by two friendly, knowledgeable guys – one from KL and the other from Belgium – this intimate lodge has just four en-suite doubles. Leech-free jungle treks are guaranteed due to its unique location high up on a ridge, reachable by around 600 steps. The owners can organize a dawn cruise for enthusiastic birdwatchers, and the delicious food is a cut above the rest. Two-days/one-night RM450/person; three-days/two-nights RM580/person

Nature Lodge Kinabatangan Bilit ⓣ 013 863 6263, ⓦ naturelodgekinabatangan.com. Diagonally across the river from Bilit, this lodge consists of the budget Civet Wing with dorm-style jungle huts and the pricier a/c-cooled twin-bed en-suite chalets in the Agamid Wing. Their three-days/two-nights packages, with all meals and excursions included, are very good value and their guides are knowledgeable and friendly. Double RM380, chalet RM415

★**Sukau Greenview B&B** Sukau ⓣ 089 565266, ⓦ sukaugreenviewbnb.zxq.net. Popular with backpackers, this efficient riverside lodge run by a welcoming family consists of nine raised cottage-type en-suite rooms with fans and a wi-fi-equipped dining area that serves very good buffet meals. There's also a small library for those who want to read up on the local wildlife and a daily minivan to/from Sandakan. Two-days/one-night RM190

Uncle Tan's Jungle Camp ⓣ 089 535784, ⓦ uncletan.com. Runs great tours for backpackers from a proper jungle camp consisting of raised huts with mattresses and mosquito nets. Showers are rustic and will appeal to exhibitionists. Their accommodation in Sepilok can arrange a three-days, two-nights tour for RM440 per person

GOMANTONG CAVES

The **Gomantong Caves** (daily 8am–noon & 2–4.30pm; RM30, camera RM30), 32km south of Sandakan Bay, just off the road to Sukau, are impressive enough at any time of the year, though you'll get most out of the trip when the edible nests of their resident swiftlets are being harvested (Feb–April & July–Sept). Bird's-nest soup has long been a Chinese culinary delicacy (see box, p.488) and Chinese merchants have been coming to Borneo to trade for birds' nests for at least twelve centuries.

Of the two major caves, **Simud Hitam** is the one you can visit without a guide: follow the trail from behind the staff quarters to the right of the reception building, taking a right fork after five minutes, and continue for a further ten minutes. It may not be the largest of Borneo's caves, though the ceiling is up to 90m high, but it's certainly the most impressive in terms of the amount of life it supports, and by "life", we mean **cockroaches**. They feed on the mounds of bat guano in the centre of the cave and are absolutely everywhere: on the boardwalk in front of you and on the handrails, so this visit is not for the squeamish. Bring a torch and wear long trousers, boots and a long-sleeved shirt; gloves are a great idea, since the handrails are covered in bat guano as well as roaches. The slippery boardwalk loops

around the cave and past the flimsy shelters where the birds'-nest collectors sleep, and you'll see a wealth of freshwater crabs in the stream near the exit from the cave. Simud Hitam supports a colony of black-nest swiftlets, whose nests – a mixture of saliva and feathers – sell for around US$100 a kilogram.

Above Simud Hitam, the smaller but less accessible **Simud Putih** is home to the white-nest swiftlet, whose nests are of pure, dried saliva and can fetch prices of over US$2000 a kilogram. During the harvesting season, the birds'-nest collectors live up here for ten days at a time in complete darkness, with supplies lifted up by rope pulley. To reach Simud Putih, you take the left fork, five minutes along the trail behind reception, and start climbing (45min); it's also reachable via a steep and somewhat perilous scramble along some rocks from inside Simud Hitam; ask for a guide at the park headquarters.

You can come to the caves by arranged tour from Sandakan, but many lodges along the Kinabatangan River offer a stopover here as part of their package, or will drop you off here for free at the end of your stay.

SEMPORNA

The Bajau fishing town of **SEMPORNA**, 108km east of Tawau, is the departure point for diving trips to Pulau Sipadan and other neighbouring islands. Semporna's notable feature is the huge water village stretching southwards along the coast from the centre, which incorporates mosques, shops and hundreds of dwellings. Divers and snorkellers tend to stay in Semporna overnight on their way to and from **Mabul** (see p.512).

ARRIVAL AND DEPARTURE

By bus Minivans stop in front of USNO HQ, a couple of blocks from the waterfront, while buses stop across the road from the waterfront mosque. It's a 7min walk to the waterfront accommodation options along Jln Simunul; when the mosque is in front of you, head right, then left towards the market stalls, then right again. If taking the overnight bus to KK, buy your ticket a day in advance or a few hours before departure, and remember that it gets into KK around 5.30am.

Destinations Kota Kinabalu (daily at 7.30am and 7.30pm; 10hr); Lahad Datu (4–5 daily; 3hr); Sandakan (daily; 6hr); Tawau (4–5 daily; 1hr 30min).

INFORMATION

All diving outfitters, accommodation options and restaurants are clustered along a couple of blocks of waterfront streets. If heading out to Mabul, get some cash out at Maybank along Jln Jakarullah.

ACCOMMODATION AND EATING

Bismillah Semporna Seafront. Curries and *roti canai* go for a song at this Indian cheapie. Mains from RM4. Daily 9am–11pm.

Borneo Global Backpackers Jln Causeway ⓣ 088 270976, ⓦ bgbackpackers.com. Located opposite the jetty, this clean, friendly guesthouse offers a/c dorms and simple twins and doubles (some windowless). Nab a room at the front for the best views of the bay. Dorm **RM20**, double **RM60**

Dragon Inn Jln Custom ⓣ 089 781088, ⓦ dragoninnfloating.com.my. Atmospheric wooden longhouses that extend into the not-too-clean sea, with enormous dorms and en-suite a/c rooms with tropical decor and cable TV. The attached restaurant serves decent seafood and Malay noodle dishes. Dorm **RM25**, double **RM130**

Mabul Steak House Semporna Seafront. Steak is not the best thing at this lively upstairs restaurant-cum-internet café: the seafood of your choice, cooked thirteen different ways, is a better bet, and the fresh fruit juices are enormous. Mains from RM9; count your change carefully. Daily noon–11pm.

Scuba Junkie Backpacker 36 Semporna Seafront ⓣ 089 782372, ⓦ scubajunkie.com. A lively hostel with colourful a/c-cooled dorms and rooms, some with own bathrooms. Accommodation for non-divers is twice as expensive. Dorm **RM25**, double **RM65**

★ **Scuba Junkie Bar** 36 Semporna Seafront. The most happening place on the strip, this Kiwi-run restaurant/bar has karaoke nights, excellent pizza (with imported ingredients such as feta cheese and olives) and New Zealand steak on the menu. Mains from RM20. Daily noon–midnight.

SEMPORNA ARCHIPELAGO

The waters south of Semporna are littered with tiny volcanic islands, which make up the **Semporna Archipelago**. The largest ones are Mabul, Kapalai, Si Amil, Danawan and **Sipadan** – the world-famous diving destination, though the

6

6

DIVING IN SIPADAN AND THE SEMPORNA ARCHIPELAGO

There are twelve operators who arrange dives in Sipadan and the Semporna archipelago, all of which have offices in Semporna and which also have their own accommodation on Mabul (see below). Once you have chosen an operator, they will take you out to Mabul by boat; you will stay with them, eat with them and go diving with them. Reputable operators include:

Borneo Speedy Dive Next to *Sipadan Inn Hotel*, ⓣ 089 781399, ⓦ borneospeedydive.com. Inexpensive outfit doing a lot of business with backpackers and affiliated with *Mabul Backpackers*. Three dives off Mabul/Kapalai RM300; night dive RM160; three-day PADI Open Water course RM950.

★ **Scuba Junkie** 36 Semporna Seafront ⓣ 089 785372, ⓦ scuba-junkie.com. Some of the best-value diving at Sipadan (two-day/three-night packages from RM1640) and the surrounding islands of Mabul and Kapalai (three dives RM300); booking is essential. If you've never dived before, their excellent "Discover Scuba" (RM300) day package introduces you to the underwater world courtesy of their patient, professional diving instructors.

Seaventures 4th floor, Waisma Sabah, Kota Kinabalu ⓣ 089 261669, ⓦ seaventuresdive.com. Highly regarded outfit for experienced divers, offering the most unusual lodging option on Mabul. Four-day/three-night PADI Open Water course RM3110.

Uncle Chang's 36 Semporna Seafront, entrance to *Dragon Inn* ⓣ 089 785372, ⓦ ucsipadan.com. Inexpensive dives and snorkelling trips departing from the backpacker-tastic "lodge" on Mabul (two dives Mabul, one dive Kapalai RM270; one-day snorkelling trip RM180). The diving instructors are a bit hit-and-miss, though. Uncle Chang has a reputation for being able to secure a Sipadan permit if other companies are fully booked.

other islands don't lack for diving spots themselves, which range from sunken man-made structures to caves, wrecks and reef walls, the reefs rivalling the Great Barrier Reef for diversity and home to over 200 species of fish (including sharks), as well as rays and turtles.

Mabul

MABUL is an attractive little island, bristling with jetties, where you will be based for your diving and snorkelling. The waters around the island offer the best muck-diving in the archipelago (it involves looking for small marine creatures in shallow waters and the term was coined here). There are a couple of white sandy beaches and two water villages, one Filipino and the one next to the *Scuba Junkie* resort that's home to the Bajau Sea Gypsies, most of whom are stateless and have no rights under Malay law. You'll spot their colourful houseboats and their young children paddling their own sea canoes. It takes twenty minutes or so to walk around the island; the dirt path takes you through the two villages and the expensive *Sipadan Mabul Resort* (you can wander through it, in spite of the "Non-guests Keep Out" sign, as they don't own the beach).

ARRIVAL AND DEPARTURE

By boat Each diving company operates its own speedboats, which tend to leave Semporna every day around 8am, arriving in Mabul around 9am. Afternoon boats head back to Semporna around 4pm.

DIVING AND SNORKELLING

Each resort tends to offer packages that include three dives per day, with two before lunch and one after, as well as night dives at extra cost; Sipadan day-trips include four dives. Even if you don't dive at Sipadan, there's some spectacular diving to be done off Mabul itself; the man-made structures in front of the *Scuba Junkie* resort attract numerous turtles, the reef at Kapalai Island is home to a great variety of colourful tropical fish, and there are numerous drift dives and wall dives to be done. Snorkellers go out with the diving boats; there's also great snorkelling right off the jetties in Mabul itself.

ACCOMMODATION AND EATING

There are no banks on the island; upmarket resorts accept cards but budget digs don't. All resorts have wi-fi and meals are usually included in the room price. You can buy snacks from shops in the two villages. Rates below are diver rates; non-diver rates are considerably higher.

Mabul Backpackers ⓣ 089 782334, ⓦ mabulbackpackers.com. This friendly longhouse is affiliated with *Dragon Inn* in Semporna. Rooms and facilities could be cleaner and the food is rather monotonous, but you live right over the water and the diving staff are friendly, funny and informative. **RM110**

★ **Mabul Beach Resort** ⓣ 089 782 372, ⓦ scuba-junkie.com. *Scuba Junkie's* attractive launch pad offers

lodging in the form of two rows of appealing a/c or fan-cooled chalets with porches amid sculpted grounds and beach access. The lounge/bar above the dining room has occasional live music. Dorm RM125, double RM150

Seaventures ⓣ 088 251669, ⓦ seaventuresdive.com. A little way out to sea, this brightly painted, refurbished oil rig is for serious divers only. There are lifts that go right down into the sea, and diving below the rig is amazing. The accommodation is less so, with compact, dated rooms. Four-days/three-nights RM2480

Uncle Chang's ⓣ 089 782002, ⓦ ucsipadan.com. This lively budget spot, located in the Filipino village, is always popular with backpackers in spite of rarely cleaned rooms, an indifferent proprietor and occasionally surly diving instructors, but because of its chilled-out vibe, alcohol-fuelled camaraderie and inexpensive dives. Boat transfer RM100; dorm RM75, double RM110

Pulau Sipadan

SIPADAN is a name spoken with reverence by divers worldwide, and with good cause. The waters around the tiny island, 36km south of Semporna in the Celebes Sea, which so impressed the venerable marine biologist Jacques Cousteau, teem with green turtles, sharks, barracuda, vast schools of tropical fish, and a huge diversity of coral.

Twenty metres from the shore, the bottom plunges to over 180m, delving to a vast wall of coral. Divers will find themselves face to face with moray eels, large schools of jacks, batfish, parrotfish, and white-tipped and grey reef sharks. The luckiest may catch a glimpse of a hammerhead or two; Sipadan is one of the last strongholds of the scalloped hammerhead and a large school lives around 60m deep.

The reef surrounds nearly ninety percent of the island and the ledges are a common resting point for turtles. **Barracuda Point** is a popular site on the dive circuit and is so called for the vortex of chevron barracuda that lurk in these waters. **South Point** – on the opposite side of the island from Barracuda Point – attracts large pelagic (open sea) species, such as grey reef sharks and (very rarely) manta rays and whale sharks.

Snorkellers accompanying divers to the island can expect to see everything that the divers see (barring hammerheads) without having to leave the surface; in fact, they are more likely than divers to swim among schools of giant parrotfish and jackfish as they tend to congregate in the shallows.

The island is a fully protected conservation zone; numbers are limited to 120 visitors per day, and the dive operators (see box opposite) are responsible for sorting out who gets to go and when according to their stipulated number of daily permits; some diving companies are allocated more permits than others. Make reservations several weeks in advance in low season and six months in advance for high season (July & August).

TAWAU

TAWAU, Sabah's southernmost town of any size, is a busy commercial centre and timber port and you're only likely to stop here en route to or from Semporna (if flying in) or on your way to Kalimantan.

THE PLIGHT OF SHARKS

If you've come from KK, you may have seen posters around town campaigning against shark's fin soup. In Mabul, *Scuba Junkie* takes the lead in the campaign, pushing for **shark fishing** to be banned altogether and for the Malay government to extend protected marine park status beyond Sipadan – one of the world's last strongholds of the scalloped hammerhead shark – to the rest of Semporna Archipelago. The plan is to work together with the local fishing community to ensure that they get alternative sources of income that don't involve shark fishing. Though **shark's fin soup** is a pricey delicacy on the menus of many Chinese restaurants, many consumers don't realize that when the shark is caught, the fin is chopped off straightaway and the shark, still alive, is tossed back into the sea to drown, because it cannot swim, or to bleed to death on the ocean floor, torn apart by other predators. Not only are all shark species now endangered, but since the shark is one of the biggest marine predators, its fin contains a toxic amount of mercury which is detrimental to your health.

6

TRAVEL TO INDONESIA

Tawau is the main stepping stone for onward travel to Kalimantan; your only option is to go by boat. **Ferries** to Indonesia with Tawindo Express and Indomaya Express depart from the customs wharf, 150m south of Jalan Dunlop's Shell station (taxi RM5–7). At the time of writing there were two departures a day (apart from Sundays) – at 11.30am on Mon, Wed & Fri and 10.30am on Tues, Thurs & Sat for the Indonesian island of Tarakan (RM140), and 10am & 3pm for the island of Nunukan (RM65). There is no service on Sundays. Get to the jetty at least an hour before the sailing time to guarantee a ticket. Nunukan is the less convenient of the two destinations as you'll need to reach Tarakan for onward travel; it's an hour from Tawau, after which it's a further two hours to Tarakan. While certain Indonesian airports and seaports issue visas on arrival to citizens of 64 countries (see list: Ⓦembassyofindonesia.org/consular/voa.html), neither Tarakan nor Nunukan can do so, so you must obtain an **Indonesian visa** before heading into Kalimantan.

The Indonesian consulate in Tawau (Wisma Fuji Building, Jln Sin Onn Ⓣ089 772052; Mon–Fri 9.30am–2pm) can issue 60-day visas (RM170) in one day; you need proof of onward travel, sufficient funds, a copy of your passport and two photographs. To get to the consulate, take a taxi (RM10) or a bus from the central bus station (RM1); ask the driver to drop you off in front of "Indonesia consulate".

ARRIVAL AND DEPARTURE

By plane The airport (Ⓣ089 950777) is 31km outside of town and served by frequent flights from Kuala Lumpur and Kota Kinabalu with Malaysian Airlines and AirAsia, and from Sandakan with MASwings. It can be reached by a shuttle bus from the local bus station (6 daily, 45min; RM15) or taxi (RM50) or by transfer from Semporna (RM90).

Destinations Kota Kinabalu (3 daily; 50min); Kuala Lumpur (3 daily; 3hr 15min); Sandakan (2 daily; 40min).

By bus Most long-distance buses and minibuses terminate at Sabindo Square bus station on the eastern end of Jln Dunlop (which runs parallel to the shore). Buses from KK arrive in front of the public library on Jln Chen Fook. The local bus station, serving the airport, is on Jln Stephen Tan (several blocks west of Sabindo).

Destinations Kota Kinabalu (2 daily at 8am and 8pm; 10hr); Lahad Datu (6 daily; 3hr); Sandakan (hourly between 7am and 2pm; 5hr); Semporna (approximately hourly; 2hr).

ACCOMMODATION AND EATING

The eating scene is the only thing that puts the "wow" in Tawau, with such Indonesian specialities as *soto makassar* (beef soup with cow blood, spices and offal), *gado-gado* (vegetable salad with peanut sauce) and *nasi kuning* (rice cooked with turmeric and coconut milk, served on a banana leaf).

Monaco Hotel Jln Haji Karim at Jln Bunga Ⓣ089 769911. A bright-yellow lodging option that has little in common with the glitz of its namesake country, but the spacious, carpeted rooms have a/c, cable TV and private bathrooms. Good location, great value. **RM80**

Soon Yee Jln Stephen Tan Ⓣ089 772447. This friendly cheapie is very welcoming despite its less-than-inviting exterior. Fan or a/c rooms, most of which have shared bathrooms. **RM35**

Taman Selera Jln Waterfront. A 200m stretch of open-air restaurants and hawker stalls, collectively known as Taman Selera, sets up daily two blocks below Jln Dunlop in the Sabindo Complex, with local specials competing with Chinese seafood emporiums. Daily 11am–10pm.

Yassin 1 Sabindo Square. This Indian restaurant serves a delicious range of curries (from RM6), kebabs and vegetable dishes, making it a great choice for vegetarians. Daily 11.30am–9pm.

FISHERMAN AT INLE LAKE

Myanmar (Burma)

HIGHLIGHTS

❶ **Yangon** Seek out colonial architecture and the country's most stunning temple. **See p.531**

❷ **Hpa-an** Ride through fields and villages to find Buddhist cave art. **See p.549**

❸ **Bagan** Watch sunset over a plain dotted with thousands of temples. **See p.552**

❹ **Inle Lake** Visit crumbling stupas, traditional markets, workshops and stilt villages. **See p.565**

❺ **Ayeyarwady River** Join locals on a multi-day ferry trip south from Bhamo. **See p.577**

❻ **Kyaukme and Hsipaw** Trek through beautiful valleys and sleep in remote ethnic-minority villages. **See p.581**

HIGHLIGHTS ARE MARKED ON THE MAP ON PP.518–519

ROUGH COSTS

Daily budget Basic $25/occasional treat $30–40

Drink Beer 70¢ (draught), $1.70 (bottle)

Food Chicken curry with rice $2.50

Budget hotel $10

Travel Yangon–Mandalay (691km): bus 8–10hr, $12–20; train 16hr 30min, $11–33

FACT FILE

Population 55 million

Language Burmese (Myanmar)

Religions Majority Buddhist, with Christian and Muslim minorities

Currency Kyat (K)

Capital Nay Pyi Taw

International phone code ⓣ +95

Time zone GMT + 6hr 30min

Introduction

A beautiful and culturally rich country cursed for decades with a brutally oppressive regime, Myanmar (Burma) has in recent years been making headlines for its tentative steps towards democracy. Following the softening and then removal of a fifteen-year tourism boycott led by the National League for Democracy – Myanmar's leading political opposition party – tourist numbers have swollen, but the infrastructure has not yet grown to accommodate them all. Although finding a cheap bed is harder than before, it does make this a fascinating time to discover Myanmar's glittering golden stupas, bountiful rice fields, enigmatic ruined temples and picturesque mountain paths. Most memorable of all, though, are the encounters with people eager to introduce foreigners to their country and their culture. What remains to be seen is whether today's modest political reforms translate into lasting change.

Although there are affordable flights from Bangkok to **Mandalay**, and overland arrivals became possible in 2013 with the opening of four Thai border crossings, most people still start their visit in **Yangon**. This former capital makes a great introduction to the country, with evocative colonial-era buildings, some of the country's best restaurants and the unmissable Shwedagon Paya – the holiest Buddhist site in the country.

Highlights of the southeast include the precariously balanced Golden Rock at **Kyaiktiyo**, and the limestone scenery around **Hpa-an**. Until recently it wasn't feasible to go much beyond **Mawlamyine**, but now towns such as **Dawei**, further south, have opened up for adventurous visitors.

West of Yangon is a handful of beaches, with **Ngapali** the most highly regarded, but **Chaung Tha** and **Ngwe Saung** much more affordable. Most travellers instead hasten north to Mandalay, the hub for "Upper Burma" and the base for visiting the remains of several former capital cities, or to **Bagan** further west for its stunning temple-strewn plains. East of Mandalay is **Kalaw**, the starting point for some great walks. A trek from Kalaw is one way to reach the magnificent **Inle Lake**, with its stilt villages and famous leg-rowing fishermen. If time allows, a trip on the **Ayeyarwady River** around Katha and Bhamo offers a great chance to meet locals, as do the hiking routes around **Kyaukme** and **Hsipaw** in Shan State, which pass through ethnic minority villages.

WHEN TO GO

Myanmar has a tropical **climate**, with the southwest monsoon bringing rain from May to October. Roads can become impassable, particularly from July to September. The central plains, however, receive only a fraction of the rain seen on the coast and in the Ayeyarwady delta. From October onwards the rains subside; **the best time to visit** most of the country is from November to February, when temperatures are relatively manageable. From March to May, the country becomes very hot, particularly the dry zone of the central plains where Bagan and Mandalay often see temperatures in excess of 40°C.

CHRONOLOGY

Around 11,000 BC The earliest known inhabitants settle in the central plains, around the Ayeyarwady River.

2nd century BC City-states are founded in the central plains by the Pyu, who came from present-day Yunnan (China) and convert to Buddhism in the fourth century AD.

9th century AD The Mon, who originally migrated to Burma from the east, establish a kingdom with Thaton as its capital. The Bamar, more recent arrivals from Yunnan, establish Pagan (now known as Bagan).

1044 King Anawrahta ascends to the Pagan throne. He converts to Theravada Buddhism in 1056 and defeats the Mon a year later, creating the first unified Burmese state.
1287 The Pagan Empire collapses after a Mongol invasion. A complicated succession of smaller kingdoms arises in the empire's wake, including a Shan kingdom based first at Sagaing and then at Inwa.
1540–99 Lower Burma is united under the Toungoo dynasty.
1767 Burmese armies sack the Siamese capital Ayutthaya.
1824–26 Clashes in northeastern India, along with Britain's desire for new markets and raw materials, lead to the First Anglo-Burmese War. Burma cedes Rakhine and Tenasserim.
1852 Britain provokes a naval confrontation, leading to the Second Anglo-Burmese War and the annexing of Lower Burma.
1885–86 Claiming that King Thibaw is a tyrant in league with the French, Britain takes Mandalay after the Third Anglo-Burmese War. The whole of Burma becomes a province of British India, although only the central plains are directly controlled.
1937 Burma becomes a separate crown colony.
January 1942 Japan invades Burma, assisted by Aung San and the Burma Independence Army.
August 1943 Aung San becomes Commander-in-Chief of the Burma National Army (BNA) and War Minister of a nominally independent Burma.
March 1945 The BNA rises up against Japanese occupation in association with the Anti-Fascist Organisation, which later becomes the Anti-Fascist People's Freedom League (AFPFL).
January 27, 1947 Aung San and the British prime minister Clement Attlee sign an agreement guaranteeing Burma's independence. A separate agreement later gives ethnic minority states the right to secede after ten years.
July 19, 1947 Aung San and six cabinet members are assassinated by men believed to be linked to nationalist rival U Saw. U Nu, foreign minister during the Japanese occupation, is asked to head the AFPFL and the government.
January 4, 1948 Burma gains independence and quickly plunges into chaos, as rival factions take up arms.
1958 General Ne Win forms a caretaker government following a split in the ruling AFPFL.
1960 U Nu wins an election victory, partly due to making Buddhism the state religion.
1962 U Nu is ousted in a military coup led by General Ne Win. The Socialist Programme Party becomes the sole political party, most private businesses are nationalized and the country becomes internationally isolated.
1981 Ne Win gives up the presidency to San Yu, a former general, but remains the chairman of the Socialist Programme Party.
1987 Students take to the streets to protest about currency devaluation.
1988 Pro-democracy protests start in March and reach their peak in August, following the resignation of Ne Win. A general strike begins on August 8 and the army kills thousands of protestors. Aung San Suu Kyi, daughter of Aung San, makes a speech on August 26 at Yangon's Shwedagon Paya on behalf of the newly formed National League for Democracy (NLD). The military forms the State Law and Order Restoration Council (SLORC), which abandons socialism, declares martial law and arrests democracy campaigners.
1989 SLORC renames Burma as Myanmar. Aung San Suu Kyi is placed under house arrest.
1990 The NLD wins 82 percent of seats at the general election, but the government ignores the result. Western nations begin sanctions against Myanmar.
1991 Aung San Suu Kyi is awarded the Nobel Peace Prize.
1992 Than Shwe takes over as SLORC chairman, prime minister and head of the armed forces.
July 1995 Aung San Suu Kyi is released from house arrest. She is re-arrested in September 2000, and spends nine of the following ten years under house arrest.
August 2003 Khin Nyunt becomes prime minister and announces a "road map" to democracy. In October 2004 he is placed under house arrest.
November 2005 The capital is moved to Nay Pyi Taw.
August–September 2007 Huge increases in fuel prices spark public protests.
April 2008 A proposed new constitution guarantees a quarter of parliamentary seats to the military.
May 2008 The Ayeyarwady delta is hit by Cyclone Nargis, killing around 140,000 people. The regime initially blocks international aid and presses on with a referendum on the new constitution, claiming that 92 percent voted in favour.
November 2010 The general election – boycotted by the NLD – is won by the Union Solidarity and Development Party (USDP), nominally civilian but dominated by members of the former military junta. Aung San Suu Kyi is released from house arrest.
March 2011 Thein Sein becomes president of the quasi-civilian parliament. In the following months he legalizes peaceful demonstrations, officially ends conflicts with Shan and Kachin groups, and frees selected political prisoners.
April 2012 The NLD wins 43 of 45 by-election seats, with Aung San Suu Kyi taking one. The US and EU begin to ease sanctions.
June 2012 Violence erupts in Rakhine State (see box, p.540), most of it carried out by Buddhists against Muslims of the Rohingya minority. Trouble flares again in October, and sporadically during 2013 and into 2014.
November 2012 US President Barack Obama visits Myanmar.
December 2013 A presidential spokesperson announces that all political prisoners have now been freed under conditional amnesties. Activists welcome progress but deny that it is complete.

7

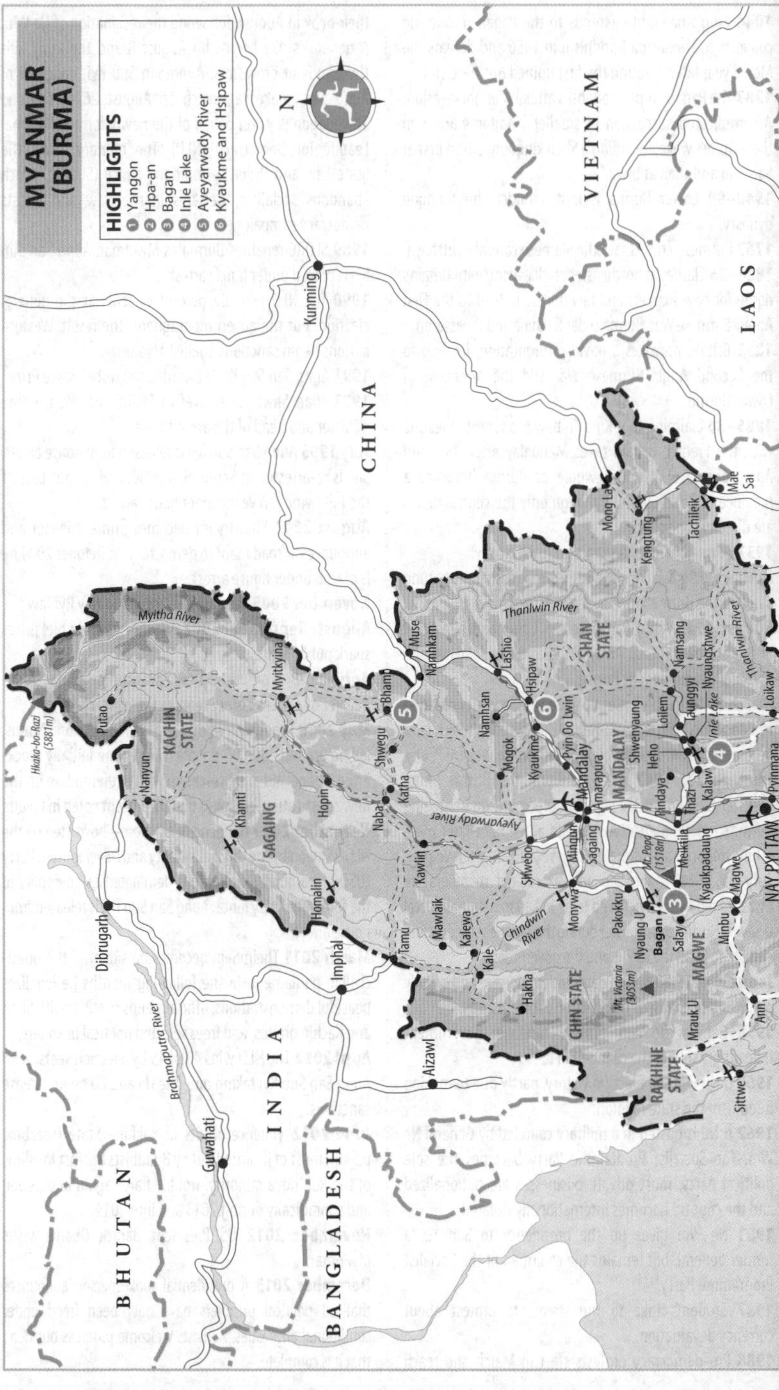

MYANMAR (BURMA)

HIGHLIGHTS

1. Yangon
2. Hpa-an
3. Bagan
4. Inle Lake
5. Ayeyarwady River
6. Kyaukme and Hsipaw

N

CHINA
VIETNAM
LAOS
INDIA
BHUTAN
BANGLADESH
KACHIN STATE
SAGAING
SHAN STATE
MANDALAY
CHIN STATE
MAGWE
RAKHINE STATE
NAY PYI TAW
Kunming
Hkaka-bo-Razi (5881m)
Putao
Nanyun
Khamti
Myitkyina
Bhamo
Muse
Namhkam
Lashio
Hsipaw
Namhsan
Mogok
Kyaukme
Pyin Oo Lwin
Mandalay
Amarapura
Sagaing
Mingun
Shwebo
Monywa
Hopin
Shwegu
Katha
Naba
Kawlin
Homalin
Tamu
Mawlaik
Kalewa
Kale
Hakha
Pakokku
Nyaung U
Bagan
Salay
Mt Popa (1518m)
Meiktila
Kyaukpadaung
Thazi
Kalaw
Pindaya
Heho
Shwenyaung
Loilem
Taunggyi
Nyaungshwe
Inle Lake
Namsang
Loikaw
Pyinmana
Magwe
Minbu
Mt Victoria (3053m)
Mrauk U
Ann
Sittwe
Kengtung
Mong La
Tachileik
Mae Sai
Myitha River
Thanlwin River
Ayeyarwady River
Chindwin River
Brahmaputra River
Dibrugarh
Imphal
Aizawl
Guwahati

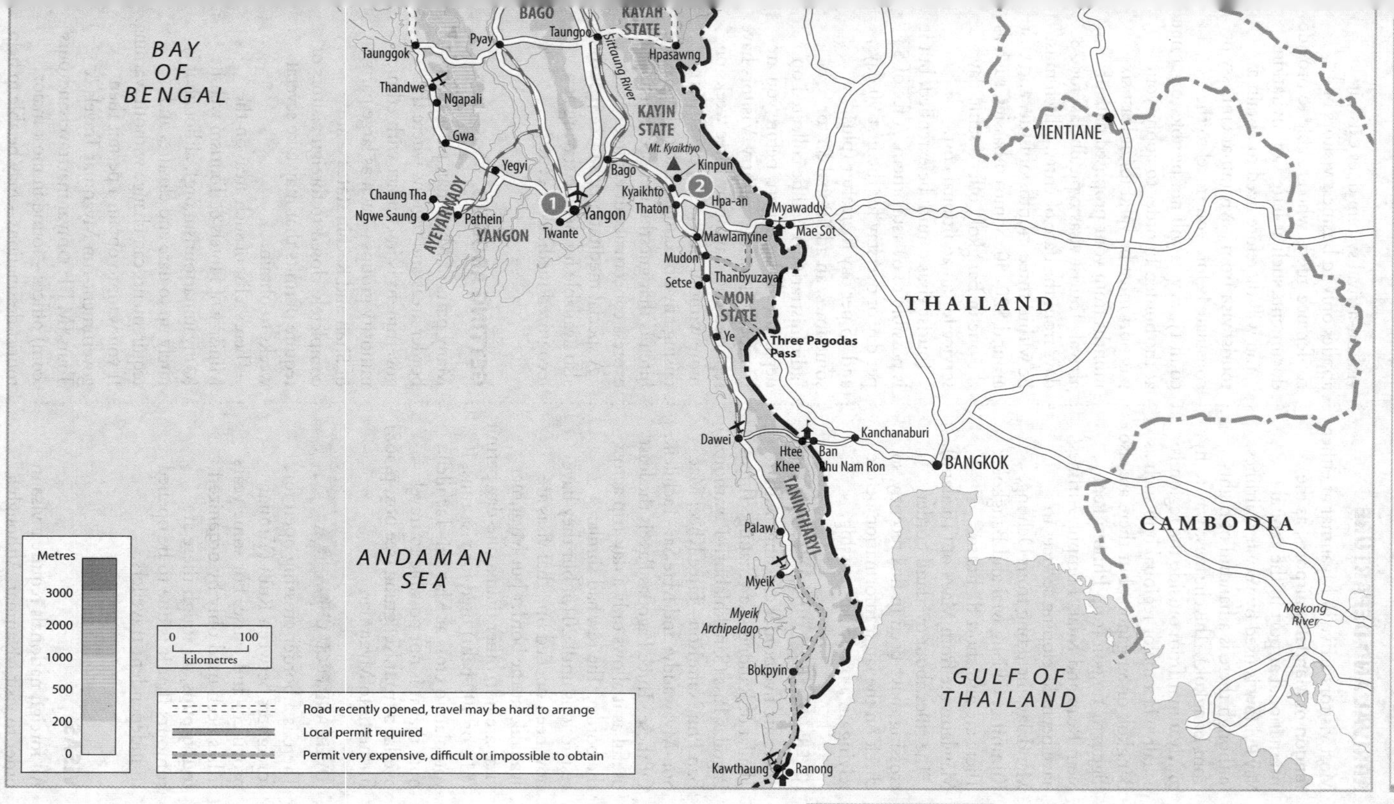

BAY OF BENGAL
BAGO
KAYAH STATE
Taungoo
Pyay
Taunggok
Hpasawng
Sittaung River
Thandwe
Ngapali
KAYIN STATE
Gwa
Mt. Kyaiktiyo
Kinpun
Yegyi
Bago
VIENTIANE
Chaung Tha
Kyaikhto
Ngwe Saung
Pathein
Yangon
Thaton
Hpa-an
Myawaddy
AYEYARWADY
YANGON
Twante
Mawlamyine
Mae Sot
Mudon
Thanbyuzayat
Setse
MON STATE
THAILAND
Ye
Three Pagodas Pass
Dawei
Kanchanaburi
Htee Khee
Ban Phu Nam Ron
BANGKOK
TANINTHARYI
CAMBODIA
Palaw
ANDAMAN SEA
Myeik
Myeik Archipelago
Mekong River
Bokpyin
GULF OF THAILAND
Kawthaung
Ranong
Metres
3000
2000
1000
500
200
0
0
100
kilometres
Road recently opened, travel may be hard to arrange
Local permit required
Permit very expensive, difficult or impossible to obtain
7

ARRIVAL AND DEPARTURE

Most visitors arrive in Myanmar at either **Yangon** or **Mandalay** airports, as the international airport in the capital **Nay Pyi Taw** is used by very few airlines (although there is a handful of flights from Bangkok). The cheapest way to fly to Myanmar from outside the region is usually via a major regional hub such as Bangkok or Singapore, but there are also flights to Yangon from Phnom Penh, Siem Reap and Kuala Lumpur. Airlines have been developing services to Mandalay, including from Dehong, Kunming, Chiang Mai and Bangkok. There are also short flights to Mawlamyine from Mae Sot (Thailand).

The rules about overland border crossings have been in flux recently, so check on the latest information before relying on a particular crossing.

OVERLAND FROM THAILAND

There are five border crossings with Thailand: Ranong–Kawthaung; Three Pagodas Pass (Sangkhlaburi–Payathonzu); Ban Phu Nam Ron– Htee Khee; Mae Sot–Myawaddy; and Mae Sai–Tachileik. Of these, Three Pagodas Pass is the least useful as it allows only a day-trip across the border. The rest had similar restrictions until 2013, but they have now been opened up. Thai visas are available at the border but Myanmar visas are not, other than a one-day permit ($10 or 500 baht) used for visa runs. If you plan to cross at Mae Sai–Tachileik, note that it is not possible to travel overland from Kengtung (see box, p.568) further into Myanmar.

OVERLAND FROM CHINA

There is a border crossing open for foreigners between Ruili (Yunnan province) and Muse. For some years it has been used only by **organized tour groups**, although there are rumours that it is due to be opened to independent travellers.

VISAS

All foreign nationals require a **visa** in order to visit Myanmar. Although a visa-on-arrival system does exist, it applies only to business visitors or conference guests who are able to provide documents such as letters of invitation.

You will therefore need to obtain a **tourist visa** from a Myanmar embassy or consulate before you travel to the country, as you will not be able to get one at the border. In order to apply, your passport must be valid for at least six months from your proposed date of arrival. Tourist visas typically last for 28 days from the date of entry, which must be within three months of issue, and cost around $20–30. Some embassies, such as the one in Bangkok, offer a same-day service for an additional cost.

Tourist visas cannot be extended, but it is possible to overstay them. A fee of $3 per day of overstay for the first 90 days, and $5 per day thereafter (plus, sometimes, an additional $3 for "administration") will be collected on departure at the airport, before you are stamped out of the country. Visitors have reported overstaying by three weeks or more without officials at the airport raising any objections. The only possible hitch is that guesthouses occasionally express concern about expired visas.

A special **meditation visa** (see p.526) is also available for people staying at a recognized meditation centre.

GETTING AROUND

Many parts of Myanmar, particularly border areas and regions where the government is in conflict with ethnic minority groups – such as large parts of **Shan** and **Kachin states** – are completely closed to foreign visitors or require **permits** that may take several weeks to obtain.

There's a list of such areas on the Ministry of Hotels & Tourism website (ⓦmyanmartourism.org), although it is rarely up to date and closures and requirements can change without warning. If you want to obtain a permit then government-run Myanmar Travels & Tours (MTT; ⓦmyanmartravelsandtours.com) offices – found in most major tourist destinations – may be able to help.

BY PLANE

In addition to state-owned Myanma Airways (myanmaairways.aero), which has a poor reputation for the condition of its aircraft, an array of **private airlines** – among them Air KBZ, Air Mandalay, Air Bagan, Asian Wings, Yangon Airways and Golden Myanmar Airlines – run services on domestic routes and have offices in major towns and cities. Given the long journey times overland, and the relatively low prices of flight tickets, travelling by plane can be an attractive choice. In a few cases it is the only option as overland routes are closed to foreigners. Many services fly on **circular routes**, stopping at several airports on the way, and it may therefore be easier to make a journey one way than the other way.

There are a number of downsides to domestic air travel. For one thing, it may not save you much time as schedules are subject to change at short notice and delays are common. For another, most

7

THE ETHICS OF VISITING MYANMAR

For many years, the official position of the **National League for Democracy** (NLD), the opposition political party of which Aung San Suu Kyi is the Chairperson and General Secretary, was to urge foreigners not to visit the country as it legitimized and enriched the regime and its cronies. Still, some tourists did visit each year and many people within Myanmar welcomed foreigners – both for the income they generated and for the opportunity to remain in contact with the outside world. In 2010, the NLD softened its stance, saying that it only opposed package and cruise tourism, and in 2012 it effectively dropped the boycott. Combined with a weakening of international economic sanctions, this has contributed to rocketing tourist numbers.

Nevertheless, the **ethical dilemma** has not simply disappeared. Although the new government is nominally civilian, in reality the same military figures are still largely in charge. In addition the prominent business leaders widely described as "cronies" – who became rich through dealing with the regime, and in some cases allegedly through trading in arms or drugs – still own many of the country's largest businesses, including hotel groups, banks and airlines. And although the government is praised internationally for reforms such as the release of political prisoners and a reduction in censorship, some people within the country see these as superficial changes intended to please foreigners – particularly the US, which hopes to lure Myanmar away from its main trading partner, China – rather than anything more fundamental.

In the meantime, the military is still fighting the world's longest-running **civil war**. For decades the regime has followed policies that have amounted to ethnic cleansing and – in the eyes of some observers – attempted genocide. Although ceasefires have now been signed with some of the ethnic militias, vast swathes of the country – particularly in northern Kachin State – remain off-limits to tourists while the military continues to fight with rebel armies. When it comes to the recent violence in Rakhine State (see box, p.540), the authorities have not only failed to protect the Rohingya Muslims, or to hold perpetrators to account, but also themselves directly contributed to the humanitarian crisis.

If free and fair elections are held in 2015 then the NLD is expected to win a landslide victory, but it remains to be seen how they propose to keep the peace with ethnic minority groups who consider the NLD to represent only the Bamar majority. Already the party has been accused of becoming too close to the generals and their cronies, but some compromise is inevitable not least because the military can veto a proposed change to the constitution to allow Aung San Suu Kyi (as someone who married a foreign national) to run for president.

Bearing all this in mind, travellers should consider limiting the amount of their money that makes it to the government and its associates. Some expenses are unavoidable, including visa fees, while others are hard to avoid if you want to see the main tourist attractions. Many banks, including AGD and KBZ, have ties with figures who have been subject to international sanctions. On the other hand, by staying in budget accommodation your money is more likely to go to ordinary individuals or families than to companies with strong government links (and we have tried to avoid recommending such places). There are also plenty of opportunities to use small companies and freelancers for services such as trekking guides. Some visitors also consider avoiding planes and even trains, which are operated by the government.

For more information, see tourismconcern.org.uk/burma.htm.

domestic airlines still do not sell tickets online – although they may allow you to make an online reservation and then pay once in the country. In addition, travellers should avoid flying if they are trying to limit the amount of their money that ends up with the government or its cronies (see box, p.521).

BY BUS

Buses are usually faster and cheaper than trains, and are generally the best way to get around on a budget. There are many different bus companies and most are privately owned. Taking buses can be quite tiring, however, since most long-distance services run through the night, stop roughly every three hours for toilet or food breaks and arrive before dawn.

Most long-distance buses are reasonably comfortable, but make sure you bring warm clothes as they tend to crank up the air conditioning. On major routes, such as Yangon to Mandalay, it's possible to take a more modern and spacious "VIP" bus for a small additional fee. There are also local buses running segments of longer routes, such as Taungoo to Mandalay (rather than the full Yangon to Mandalay trip); these are usually in worse condition but are cheaper for shorter trips, as on long-distance buses you pay the fare for the full journey even if you get on or off partway through. You'll also find smaller, 32-seat buses that should be avoided if possible for long trips, as they tend to be jam-packed with luggage.

It's a good idea to book a day or two ahead for busy routes (such as Bagan to Nyaungshwe), routes where only a few buses run (such as Ngwe Saung to Yangon) or where you're joining a bus partway through its route (such as in Kalaw). Guesthouses can often help book tickets for a small fee, or you can buy them either from bus stations (which in some cases are outside of town) or from in-town bus company offices.

BY TRAIN

The **railway system** in Myanmar is antiquated, slow and generally uncomfortable. On most routes a bus is faster and more reliable, as it is not uncommon for trains to be delayed by several hours. Trains are also more expensive than buses, and since they are state-run, the money goes to the government. All that said, there are reasons why you might want to take a train at least once during your trip. One is that on a few routes, such as from Mandalay up to Naba and Katha, road transport is closed to foreigners. Another is for the experience itself: many routes run through areas of great beauty, for example the Goteik viaduct between Pyin Oo Lwin and Kyaukme, and there is the chance to interact with local people.

All express trains have upper- and ordinary-class carriages. The former have reservable reclining seats, although the mechanism is often broken, while the latter have hard seats and no reservations. Some trains also have first-class carriages, which fall somewhere between upper and ordinary. Sleeper carriages, when available, accommodate four passengers and come with blankets and linen.

Long-distance trains may have **restaurant cars**, and food vendors either come on board or carry out transactions through the windows whenever the train stops. The bathrooms on-board are basic and often unclean.

Fares are payable only in US dollars. Try to reserve a day or so in advance, or more for sleepers.

BY SHARED TAXI AND VAN

Shared taxis and **shared vans** are available on some routes, and can be arranged either through accommodation or at shared-taxi stands. These vehicles charge separately for each seat, typically around fifty percent more than a seat on an air-conditioned bus. They will usually drop you wherever you like, however, which saves on transfer costs in towns where the bus station is inconveniently located.

CAR, BIKE AND MOTORCYCLE RENTAL

Renting a car is not a realistic option in Myanmar as there is too much red tape involved, but it's easy to arrange a **car and driver** (from around $40 per day) through your accommodation or travel agencies.

MYANMAR OR BURMA?

Arguing that **Burma** was a colonial name, the government renamed the country **Myanmar** in 1989, and that is the name used by the United Nations. Yet some governments – including those of the US and the UK – still officially call it Burma. Just to confuse things, the US has recently been using Myanmar on occasion as a "diplomatic courtesy".

So which of these is right? The usual argument is that the unelected military regime had no right to change the name, and this is why Burma is preferred by the National League for Democracy (the main opposition party). On the other hand, many members of ethnic minorities prefer Myanmar because they see Burma as referring to the dominant Bamar ethnic group. This isn't really true, since Burma and Myanmar actually both come from the same etymological roots. If anything, Burma is historically more informal and Myanmar more literary.

The fact is, though, that in everyday usage most people you're likely to meet in the country will call it Myanmar. In this chapter the default name used is Myanmar, with Burma used in a historical context and Burmese used to describe the food and the language.

7

Bicycles are available in many places for around K2000 per day. In some parts of the country you can also rent a **motorcycle**, typically for K8000–10,000 a day plus fuel. Before renting a motorbike, check that your travel insurance covers you for riding one.

There are numerous hazards for cyclists and motorcyclists: traffic can be very heavy in the cities, while in rural areas the roads are often in poor condition. Adding to these dangers is the fact that most cars are right-hand drive even though people drive on the right, meaning that cars have large blind spots.

LOCAL TRANSPORT

Local transport in Myanmar is usually some mix of public buses, taxis, pick-ups (adapted pick-up trucks with seating in the covered back portion), motorcycle taxis (where the passenger rides pillion) and cycle rickshaws. **Public buses** run only in the largest cities, including Yangon and Mandalay, and are very cheap. It can be hard to work out the routes, but if you aren't in a rush, then riding on the buses is certainly an experience. The same can be said of **pick-ups**, which cover set routes and pick up and drop people off on the way; they usually depart when full – which may include passengers riding on the roof. If you want the most comfortable seats, in the cabin, then you can pay a little extra.

Taxis are available in large towns and cities, and range from 1970s Toyotas to occasional new left-hand-drive Chinese imports. There are no meters but drivers tend not to overcharge as outrageously as in many other Southeast Asian countries. Expect to pay around K1000–1500 for a decent trip, such as from a bus station on the edge of town to a hotel.

Tricycles are still in use in many towns, although they are being edged out by **motorcycle taxis**, which are much faster and normally around the same price (around K500–1000 for a short ride).

Most of these forms of transport can also be hired for a day including a **driver**, which can be arranged direct, through accommodation or via travel agents; you'll need to bargain to get a good price. Motorcycle taxis may not work out much more expensive than renting a self-drive motorcycle.

In small towns, **horse carts** are used as a key form of transportation, and they also ferry tourists around in a number of places, notably Bagan, Inwa and Pyin Oo Lwin. The horses are not always well looked after.

ACCOMMODATION

Just a few years ago, **accommodation** in Myanmar was considered among the most affordable in Southeast Asia. This is no longer the case, thanks largely to a combination of steeply rising tourist numbers and a lack of new budget and mid-range places to stay. While international companies are rushing to build luxury hotels, things are stagnant at the lower end of the scale where profits are smaller and getting a permit to accommodate foreigners is still a hassle.

The upshot is that it's difficult these days to get a double room in a guesthouse for less than $15, or $20 in the main tourist areas; this will usually include a shared bathroom, although you might get an old air-conditioning unit rather than a fan. If you're looking for hotel facilities then the prices quickly rise to more than $30 (which, in general, is the cut-off point in this chapter). There are very few **dormitories** open to foreigners in Myanmar, although this is beginning to change, while you'll pay fifty to eighty percent of the cost of a double for single occupancy. Almost all accommodation includes breakfast, and it is almost always unadventurous by default – toast, egg, banana and instant coffee are the norm – but if you ask at reception the night before, many places can provide a **local breakfast**.

With demand exceeding supply when it comes to budget rooms in places such as Yangon, Mandalay, Nyaungshwe (Inle Lake) and Nyaung U (Bagan), it's wise to **book ahead**, particularly in peak season (November to February). It is not uncommon to see backpackers trudging around looking for an affordable room, and in a few cases having to settle for a mattress on a restaurant floor or in reception. **Monasteries** may also take in travellers looking for a bed, although they expect a donation in return.

Power cuts are commonplace in Myanmar, even in Yangon and Mandalay, and many places will have a generator to ensure that fans and air conditioners work through the night. Avoid leaving gadgets plugged in during a power cut, as there may be a surge when the supply is restored.

FOOD AND DRINK

While people in Myanmar take great pride in their cuisine, if you ask someone for a **restaurant** recommendation then there's a good chance that they will suggest a place serving Chinese food. This is partly because they worry that foreign stomachs can't cope with Burmese food, but also because most people rarely eat at restaurants, so when they do they eat Chinese as a treat. Most towns will have at least a couple of Chinese restaurants, typically with large menus covering unadventurous basics such as sweet-and-sour chicken. Dishes start at around K1000 (vegetables) or K1500 (meat). **Indian restaurants** are also popular, particularly in Yangon, which had a very large Indian population during the British colonial era. In tourist hotspots you'll also find restaurants serving Thai and Italian dishes.

A visit to a **teahouse** is an unmissable experience: they are hugely popular places to meet friends, family or business associates over tea and affordable snacks, which, depending on the owners, might be Burmese noodles, Indian samosas or Chinese steamed buns. Some teahouses open for breakfast, while others stay open late into the night.

BURMESE FOOD

As in other Southeast Asian countries, in **Burmese food** it's considered important to balance sour, spicy, bitter and salty flavours; this is generally done across a series of dishes rather than within a single dish. A mild curry, for example, might be accompanied by bitter leaves, dried chilli and a salty condiment such as fish paste.

The typical local **breakfast** is noodle soup, such as the national dish *mohingar* (catfish soup with rice vermicelli, onions, lemongrass, garlic, chilli and lime, with some cooks adding things such as boiled eggs, courgette fritters and fried bean crackers). Alternatives include *oùn-nó k'auq-s'wèh* (coconut chicken soup with noodles, raw onions, coriander and chilli) and *pèh byouq* (fried, boiled beans) served with sticky rice or naan bread. All of these dishes are served in teahouses or available to take away from markets.

Noodles also feature strongly at lunchtime: many locals will have a small bowl at a street café or teahouse. Various Shan noodle dishes are popular, including *mi-she* (rice noodles in a meat sauce accompanied by pickle). Other common dishes include various *ăthouq*, which translates to "salad" but rarely includes vegetables; they are cold dishes, usually with noodles, raw onions, gram flour,

chilli and coriander, served with a watery vegetable or bone soup. One variety worth trying is *nàn-gyì thouq*, made with thick rice noodles that look like spaghetti.

Lunchtime is also when you should try **Burmese curries** if you're worried about hygiene, since they are usually cooked in the morning then left in pots all day. Local people, however, would typically have curry in the evening at home. A meat, fish or prawn curry will be accompanied by rice (*t'ămìn*), a watery soup and fried vegetables. A great deal of oil is added to Burmese curries, supposedly to keep bacteria out, but, like locals, you can skim the oil off. At the best restaurants, the meal will also include a selection of up to a dozen small side-dishes, plus fresh vegetables and herbs with a dip (such as *ngăpí-ye*, a watery fish sauce). Green tea will usually be thrown in, and sometimes you'll get a dessert such as tasty *lăp'eq* (fermented tea leaves with fried garlic, peanuts, toasted sesame and dried shrimp). You may also get *t'ănyeq* (jaggery, unrefined cane sugar).

There are plenty of **regional variations** to discover as you travel: the food of Rakhine State, for example, is influenced by its proximity to Bangladesh, so curries are spicier. They also tend to include fish paste as an ingredient, rather than on the side as a condiment.

Vegetarians should find it reasonably easy to find suitable food throughout the country, since some Buddhists are restrained in their consumption of meat.

DRINKS

Tap water isn't safe to drink in Myanmar; bottled water is available throughout the country for around K300. In many restaurants, free **green tea** (*ye-nwè-gyàn*) is left in jugs on tables and is safe to drink. In teahouses, black tea is usually drunk with plenty of milk and sugar, while coffee is almost always instant, other than in expensive Western-style cafés.

Although there are few places resembling Western bars or pubs outside of Yangon and Mandalay, most towns will have a couple of **beer stations** which look like simple restaurants but with beer adverts on display and a predominantly male clientele. These places usually serve draught beer (around K700 for a glass) as well as bottles (from K1700 for 640ml), with the former usually restricted to the most popular brew, Myanmar Beer (produced by a government joint venture) and sometimes its rival Dagon. Both beers are also available in bottles, as are Mandalay Beer and several Thai and Singaporean beers, including Tiger, Singha and ABC Stout.

Mid-range and upmarket restaurants will often have a list of imported **wines**. There are a couple of vineyards making wine in Shan State, and it's better than you might expect: look out for Red Mountain (see p.567) and Aythaya. Fruit wines are produced around Pyin Oo Lwin, while local spirits include *t'àn-ye* (toddy or palm wine).

7

CULTURE AND ETIQUETTE

As in other Southeast Asian countries, **clothing** in Myanmar is usually modest. In some ethnic minority villages it's still the norm to wear traditional dress, and even in cities many men and women wear a skirt-like garment called a *longyi*. These days, though, it is also common for locals to wear Western-style clothes and you'll very occasionally see men in shorts. People will be too polite to say anything, but they may be offended by the sight of tourists wearing revealing clothes. This would include shorts cut above the knee, and – particularly for women – tops that are tight or show the shoulders. It's especially important to **dress conservatively** when visiting temples, and some travellers carry a *longyi* for such situations.

Most women and girls, as well as some men and boys, use *thănăk'à* (a paste made from ground bark) on their faces; traditionally thought to improve the skin and act as a sunblock, it is often applied as a circle or stripe on each cheek.

Avoid touching another person's head, as it is considered the most sacred part of the body; feet are unclean, and so when sitting don't point them at anyone or towards images of the Buddha. Remove your **shoes** before entering a Buddhist site or a home. Always use your right hand when shaking

hands or passing something to someone, as the left hand is traditionally used for toilet ablutions; however, locals do use their left hand to "support" their right arm when shaking hands.

Most people in the country are **Buddhist**, although there are significant Muslim and Christian minorities. Buddhist men are expected to experience life in a monastery at least once, usually as a child and certainly before they get married. It may only be for a week, although poorer children in particular may become novices and be educated at the monastery. Most Buddhists also believe in *nats*, spirits rooted in older animist traditions, which take an interest in the actions of humans and may need to be propitiated.

Considering the social conservatism of Myanmar's society it is interesting to note that while in the past most *nat kădaws* (spirit mediums) were women, today most are gay men and many are either transgendered or transvestites. A *nat-pwèh* (spirit festival) held, for example, at the start of a new business enterprise is an occasion on which people have licence to sing, cheer and show emotions which would otherwise be repressed in public. **Homosexuality** is, however, technically illegal in Myanmar – for tourists as well as locals – and punishable by fines or imprisonment. This is rarely enforced in practice and there is a discreet gay scene in Yangon, but little elsewhere. See Ⓦutopia-asia.com/tipsburm.htm for information and advice.

SPORTS AND ACTIVITIES

Outdoor pursuits and **adventure sports** are not yet well developed in Myanmar. With the notable exception of trekking, most activities tend to be arranged through travel agents and are prohibitively expensive.

TREKKING

Opportunities for **treks** are limited by two main factors. One is that many of the most appealing areas are in the mountainous border regions, which tend to be closed to tourists or require expensive permits. The other is that foreigners are generally expected to stay in licensed accommodation for every night of their visit. This means that camping is illegal, as is staying in local houses, in most parts of the country.

As a result, **day-hikes** are the limit in many places. There are exceptions, however, with the most notable all being in Shan State: around Kalaw (see p.562), Inle Lake (see p.565), Pindaya (see p.564), Kyaukme (see p.581) and Hsipaw (see p.581). In these areas it's possible to stay in either homes or monasteries, by prior arrangement through a tour agency, and therefore do **multi-day treks**. A guide is either obligatory or strongly recommended for most hiking, but the trails around Hsipaw are sometimes undertaken without one.

BIKING AND MOTORBIKING

Both **mountain biking** and **motorbiking tours** are available in Myanmar, through specialist agencies. There are many advantages to getting around in this way, not least the chance to interact with people in villages and rural areas; disadvantages include the poor state of many roads, plus the requirement to sleep in licensed accommodation. Some cyclists have used camping as a back-up, but it is, strictly speaking, illegal and should not be relied upon. If you cycle off the beaten path, you may be questioned about your plans and even accompanied by immigration or police officers.

SCUBA DIVING

For affordable scuba diving in Myanmar's waters, you're better off booking a live-aboard trip from Ranong in Thailand.

MEDITATION

With a strong Buddhist tradition, Myanmar is a good place to learn to **meditate**. There's even a special **meditation visa** available if you have a letter of support from a meditation centre, which lasts for three months and is extendable. Some centres will only take foreigners who commit to staying for several weeks, but one shorter option is a ten-day course in Vipassana meditation (Ⓣ01 549290, Ⓦjoti.dhamma.org;

donation) at a centre in Yangon on Nga Htat Gyi Pagoda Road, close to Shwedagon Paya. The Kyunpin Meditation Centre (T 099 1026653 or T 096 1026653; W kyunpin.com) in Sagaing, near Mandalay, also has good reports from foreign visitors.

COMMUNICATIONS

The **postal service** in Myanmar is not known for its efficiency, but many post offices have an EMS (Express Mail Service) counter offering faster and more reliable international delivery.

There are **internet cafés** in most towns and cities, typically charging K300–500 per hour. In addition some hotels and guesthouses have wi-fi access, although connections are unreliable and can be frustratingly slow. Unsurprisingly, high-end hotels and their cafés tend to be the best bet.

Many guesthouses will let you make **local calls** from reception (check the price first), or may make the call for you if you're trying to book accommodation for later in your trip. There are also local call stands – often just a table with a telephone – in the streets and in some shops. The cheapest and easiest way to call internationally is through a **VOIP** (Voice Over Internet Protocol) service such as Skype or Voipfone. Some internet cafés offer such calls for a per-minute fee if you don't have your own account.

Mobile phone numbers start with 09. International roaming is in its infancy in Myanmar, and currently works only with some Asian SIM cards. At the time of research foreigners could not buy Myanmar SIM cards, and the only (expensive) option was to rent one together with a phone at the international airports.

MYANMAR ONLINE

W **burmalibrary.org** A huge collection of text from books and articles about Myanmar, plus relevant links, organized into categories.

W **irrawaddy.org** One of the most reliable sources of up-to-the-minute news on the country.

W **myanmartourism.org** This official tourism website has hotel and tour company telephone numbers, plus a list of places that are off-limits or require permits (although this may be out of date).

CRIME AND SAFETY

Very few foreign tourists are victims of **crime** in Myanmar, possibly because the penalties for stealing are severe. There are, however, occasional reports of opportunistic theft such as of cameras left charging on ferries while the owners wander the decks. Although the government is engaged in conflict with **ethnic resistance groups** in several parts of the country, if there's any danger in an area then it will be closed to foreigners both for their protection and to keep the violence hidden away from international attention. In October 2013 a series of **explosions** in different towns and cities left three local people dead; one tourist was injured in Yangon. The government blamed the Karen National Union, but other theories suggested that the attacks were linked to the violence in Rakhine State (see box, p.540) or were carried out by the military as a way to forestall political reforms.

Although the quasi-civilian government inaugurated in 2011 has taken steps to reduce **censorship** and released many political prisoners, Myanmar is still far from being a place where freedom of speech can be taken for granted, and violence is still regularly used against dissenters and protesters. It is still therefore wise to avoid raising political topics in conversation, as local people can be nervous about finding themselves in trouble. Let them take the lead.

MEDICAL CARE AND EMERGENCIES

The quality of **health care** in Myanmar is generally poor. Routine advice and treatment are available in Yangon and Mandalay but elsewhere the hospitals often lack basic supplies, and some suffer under corrupt administrations. Avoid surgery and dental work, as hygiene standards cannot be relied upon; if you

BURMESE

Burmese, or Myanmar as it is now officially called, is the country's official language and also the native language of the country's Bamar majority. Burmese is a tonal language that is difficult for Westerners to learn, but local people tend to appreciate even a modest effort.

PRONUNCIATION

There is no universally approved way to Romanize the Burmese language. The system used here is based on the *Burmese By Ear* audio course by John Okell, available as a free download from Ⓦ www.soas.ac.uk/bbe. In the text we give place names and some very common words in their most widely recognized forms. Items on specific restaurant menus are given as printed.

There are five tones which change the meaning of a word: the low tone (syllables with no marker), the plain high tone (spoken with a relaxed throat, marked **à**), the creaky high tone (spoken with a tightened throat, marked **á**), the stopped syllable (high pitch followed by a glottal stop, marked **aq**) and the weak syllable (unstressed, marked **ă**). Aspirated consonants have a short puff of breath expelled after the consonant is pronounced and before the vowel begins; those marked as "whispered" begin with a sound similar to the start of the English "hmm".

ă	as in "about"
a	as in "car"
a in aq and an	as in "cat"
ai in aiq and ain	as in "site"
au in auq and aun	"ou" as in "lounge"
aw	as in "saw"
e	as in French "café"
e in eh	as in "sell"
e in eq	as in "set"
ei in eiq and ein	"a" as in "late"
i	as in "ravine"
i in iq and in	as in "sit"
o	"eau" as in French "peau"
ou in ouq and oun	"o" as in "tone"
u	as in "Susan"
u in uq and un	"oo" as in "foot"
b	as in "bore"
ch	same as "ky" but aspirated
d	as in "door"
dh	"th" as in "this"
g	as in "gore"
gy	as in "judge"
h	as in "hot"
hl	same as "l" but whispered
hm	same as "m" but whispered
hn	same as "n" but whispered
hng	same as "ng" but whispered
hny	same as "ny" but aspirated
hw	same as "w" but aspirated
k	as in French "corps"
k'	as in "core" (aspirated)
ky	as in "cello"
l	as in "law"
m	as in "more"
n	as in "nor"
ng	as in "long"
ny	"gn" as in Italian "gnocchi"
p	as in French "port"
p'	as in "pore" (aspirated)
q	glottal stop
r	as in "raw"
s	as in "soar"
s'	same as "s" but aspirated
sh	as in "shore"
t	as in French "tort"
t'	as in "tore" (aspirated)
th	as in "thaw"
w	as in "war"
y	as in "your"
z	as in "zone"

GREETINGS AND BASIC PHRASES

There is no word for a simple "hello" – rather, greetings are nonverbal or based on the situation (e.g. "Where have you been?"). Locals greet foreigners with the very formal *min-găla-ba*.

Goodbye	*thwà-meh-naw?*
Excuse me (to get past)	*nèh-nèh-lauq*
Sorry	*sàw-ri-naw*
Please	*kyè-zù pyú-bì*
Thank you	*kyè-zù tin-ba-deh*
Yes	*houq-kéh*
No	*hín-ìn*
Do you speak English?	*Ìn-găleiq sagà pyàw-daq-thălà?*

I don't understand	*nà măleh-ba-bù*
Can you help me?	*k'ăná-lauq louq-pè-ba*
Hospital	*s'è-youn*
Police station	*yèh-t'a-ná*
Where is the…?	*…beh-hma-lèh?*
…toilet?	*ein dha…*
Ticket	*leq-hmaq*
Airport	*le-zeiq*
Boat (ferry)	*thìn-bàw*
Bus	*baq-săkà*
Bus station	*kà-geiq*
Train station	*bu-da*
Taxi	*teq-si*
Car	*kà*
Bicycle	*seq-beìn*
Bank	*ban*
Post office	*sa-daiq*
Passport	*paq-săpó*
Hotel	*ho-teh*
Restaurant	*sà-thauq-s'ain*
open/closed	*pwín-deh/peiq-teh*
Left/right	*beh-beq/nya-beq*
Do you have any rooms?	*ăk'àn à-là*
How much is it?	*beh-lauq kyá-dhălèh?*
Cheap/expensive	*zè cho-deh/zè kyì-deh*
Air conditioner	*èh-kun*
Fan (electric)	*pan-ka*

NUMBERS

0	*thoun-nyá*
1	*tiq*
2	*hniq*
3	*thoùn*
4	*lè*
5	*ngà*
6	*chauq*
7	*k'un(-hniq)*
8	*shiq*
9	*kò*
10	*tăs'eh*
11, 12, 13, etc	*s'éh-tiq, s'éh-hniq, s'éh-thoùn…*
20, 30, 40, etc	*hnăs'eh, thoùn-zeh, lè-zeh*
100, 200, 300, etc	*tăya, hnăya, thoùn-ya*
1000, 2000, etc	*tăt'aun, hnăt'aun…*
10,000	*tăthaùn*
100,000	*tătheìn*
1,000,000	*tăthàn*

FOOD AND DRINK

Cheers!	*Chì-yà!*
Delicious	*kaùn-laiq-ta*
Vegetarian (food)	*theq-thaq-luq*
I don't eat meat or fish	*thà-gyì ngà-gyì shaun-deh*

Rice and noodles

kya-zan	vermicelli
k'auq-s'wèh	noodles
nàn-gyì	thick noodles
t'ămìn	rice
t'ămìn-gyaw	fried rice

Meat, fish and basics

ăthà	meat
ngăshín	eel
pyi-jì-ngà	squid
bèh-ú	duck's egg
ceq-ú	hen's egg
ămèh-dhà	beef
băzun	prawns
bèh-dhà	duck
kyeq-thà	chicken
hìn-dhì-hìn-yweq	vegetables
ngà	fish
s'eiq-thà	mutton
weq-thà	pork
chís	cheese
hìn	curry
ngăpí	fish paste
ngăyouq	chilli
paun-moún	bread
nan-byà	Indian naan bread
pèh-byà	tofu
s'à	salt
s'ì	oil
t'àw-baq	butter
thăgyà	sugar
thiq-thì	fruit

Drinks

ăè	soft drink
bi-ya	beer
kaw-p'ì	coffee (with milk and sugar)
kaw-p'ì nwà-nó-néh	coffee with milk
lăp'eq-ye	tea
p'yaw-ye	fruit juice
t'àn-ye	toddy
thauq-ye	drinking water
ye-nwè-gyàn	green tea
ye-thán	purified water
ye-thán-bù	bottle of purified water
nó măt'éh-néh	don't put milk in
thăgyà măt'éh-néh	don't put sugar in
ye-gèh măt'éh-néh	don't put ice in

EMERGENCY NUMBERS

Police ☎ **199**
Ambulance ☎ **192**
Fire ☎ **191**

are seriously ill then contact your embassy for advice, and expect international-quality care to be expensive (and possibly to require payment up front). As always, it is important to travel with **insurance** covering medical care, including emergency evacuation.

Minor injuries and ailments can be dealt with by pharmacists, particularly in major tourist areas where they are more likely to speak English. Pharmacists offer many things over the counter without prescription, although there are serious issues with fake and out-of-date medication.

INFORMATION AND MAPS

The best sources of **information**, besides other travellers and some online resources, are generally the staff at guesthouses. The **state tourist offices**, operated by Myanmar Travels & Tours (MTT), are rarely very helpful, although you will need to visit one if you want to apply for a **permit** to travel to a restricted area. They also give out free copies of **maps** published by Design Printing Services (Ⓦ dpsmap.com). Outside of Myanmar, you can buy a number of maps of the country, including the *Reise Know How* 1:1,500,000 and *Globetrotter* 1:1,700,000 (the latter also includes some city maps).

MONEY AND BANKS

Myanmar's **currency** is the kyat (pronounced "chat"), usually abbreviated as K, Ks or MMK. Notes are available in denominations of K1, K5, K10, K20, K50, K100, K200, K500, K1000, K5000 and K10,000, although the lowest value you are likely to encounter is the K50 note. At the time of writing the exchange rate was roughly K985 to $1, K1650 to £1, and K1355 to €1; high-value notes (particularly $100 bills) attract the best exchange rates, so bring those to change. Banks generally offer good exchange rates, and it is never a good idea to change money in the street as scams are common. Note also that kyat cannot be bought or sold overseas, so you should change any leftover currency before leaving the country.

Kyat are used to pay for food, bus tickets, taxi journeys and items in ordinary shops or markets, but **US dollars** must be used for government services including train tickets and entrance to some tourist attractions (although others have switched to requiring kyat). There are also some circumstances in which US dollars are preferred but not required, notably at hotels and guesthouses but also in some tourist-oriented shops. In these cases, prices are quoted in dollars, and if payment is made in kyat then it is usually at a poorer rate than you'd get in a bank – typically K1000 to $1. It's a good idea to bring plenty of low-denomination dollar notes for these situations.

For many years, Myanmar had a cash-only economy as far as tourists were concerned. With a relaxing of international sanctions, however, at the end of 2012 some **ATMs** – specifically those operated by CB Bank and KBZ Bank – began to accept overseas debit and credit cards, as did a handful of hotels.

It looks like this trend will continue, but at the time of writing it was still hard to recommend arriving in Myanmar without enough cash – in euros, Singapore dollars or (preferably) US dollars – to cover your entire trip. For one thing, only kyat are available from ATMs. For another, if your card doesn't

THE IMPORTANCE OF PERFECT NOTES

It is essential that any **currency** which you intend to change within Myanmar is pristine, and that US dollars were issued in 2006 or later. Notes that are creased, torn or marked in any way – however minor – may not be accepted by banks, hotels or any other outlets; if they do take them then it is likely to be at a reduced rate. Reject US dollar change unless it is in perfect condition.

work then other alternatives (such as Western Union and MoneyGram, which started to operate during 2013) are expensive and inconvenient.

OPENING HOURS AND HOLIDAYS

Standard **business hours** are Monday to Friday 9am to 5pm, with shops staying open a little later (and normally opening on Saturdays). Post office opening times vary but are generally Monday to Friday 9.30am to 4.30pm, with some opening on Saturday mornings. Banks typically open Monday to Friday 9am to 3pm, although some close earlier and currency exchange counters may not open until 11am. Museums operated by the government are open from Wednesday to Sunday 10am to 4pm. Some major pagodas are open 24 hours a day, while others tend to open from early morning until late in the evening. Restaurants are typically open daily from around 9am to 9pm, while many teahouses open much earlier for breakfast, and places aimed at tourists might close at 10pm.

PUBLIC HOLIDAYS

Several holidays are based upon the lunar calendar and therefore change date each year.

January 4 Independence Day
February 12 Union Day
March 2 Peasants' Day
March/April Tabaung full moon
March 27 Armed Forces Day
April 13–16 Thingyan (water festival)
April 17 New Year
May 1 Labour Day
July 19 Martyrs' Day
July Waso full moon (beginning of Buddhist "Lent")
October Thadingyut full moon (end of Buddhist "Lent")
November Tazaungmone full moon
December 8 National Day
December 25 Christmas

FESTIVALS

Most **festivals** in Myanmar are based on the lunar calendar; check the official Ministry of Hotels & Tourism site for a more extensive list (Ⓦ myanmartourism .org/festivals.htm).

Shwedagon Festival Feb/March. The country's biggest *paya pwèh* (temple festival) takes place at Shwedagon Paya in Yangon.

Thingyan April 13–16. The water festival is the most popular in the calendar, marking New Year with a good soaking as temperatures soar. It also has a spiritual side, as it's when the *nat* king visits the human world to record good and bad deeds. Hotels and transport are often booked solid.

Balloon Festival Nov. Daytime parades at this three-day event in Taunggyi, east of Inle Lake, include impressive animal-shaped hot-air balloons. At night, balloons are released with huge gondolas full of fireworks strapped underneath them, sometimes with predictably explosive results.

Shan New Year Dec. Keep an eye open for the different ethnic groups' new year celebrations around Dec and Jan. This one rotates between different Shan towns, and includes live bands, traditional dancing and – on Shan New Year's Eve itself – fireworks and an inclusive party atmosphere.

Ananda Pahto festival Dec/Jan. The *paya pwèh* at Ananda Pahto is the biggest in Bagan, running for the fortnight leading up to the full moon of Pyatho. For the last three days, hundreds of monks chant scriptures day and night.

7

Yangon

Though no longer the capital, **YANGON** remains Myanmar's commercial heart and also the core of its spiritual life, thanks to the glorious **Shwedagon Paya** (Pagoda), while its colonial-era buildings give the downtown area a historical charm which new capital Nay Pyi Taw – and Mandalay for that matter – will never possess. Whether you get lost in the city's animated **markets**, seek out beer and barbecue in **Chinatown**, visit Hindu **temples** or take an eye-opening ride on a commuter train, Yangon provides an engaging introduction to the country.

There is a long history of settlement in this part of the delta, but the Mon village of Dagon only grew in size and importance – and was renamed Yangon – after the area was conquered by King Alaungpaya in 1755. In 1852 it was seriously damaged by the invading British, who called the city Rangoon and rebuilt it to their own plans; in 1885 the British made Rangoon their capital.

The city was occupied by the Japanese during World War II, but bomb damage

was relatively limited. The decades of international isolation which followed meant that most of the city's heritage buildings were neglected, but international developers have now moved in following the easing of international sanctions. It remains to be seen how sensitively the planned restoration, for example of the landmark Secretariat building, will be carried out in the rush for profit.

WHAT TO SEE AND DO

Most travellers on a budget spend most of their time downtown, in the grid of streets north of the Yangon River that has **Sule Paya** at its heart. The main reason to head out of the downtown area is **Shwedagon Paya**, although there a number of other attractions further north including scenic **Kandawgyi Lake**, busy (but almost tourist-free) **Hledan Market** and the enormous marble Buddha at **Kyauk Taw Gyi**.

Sule Paya and Mahabandoola Garden

When the British drew up a plan for the city's streets, they put **Sule Paya** (daily 5am–9pm; K2000 or $2) at the heart; today its golden central stupa, 45m tall and forming a busy roundabout, is still one of the most striking landmarks in downtown Yangon. The inside of the pagoda is surprisingly peaceful, although freelance guides tend to approach tourists here. You'll also be pestered by unlicensed

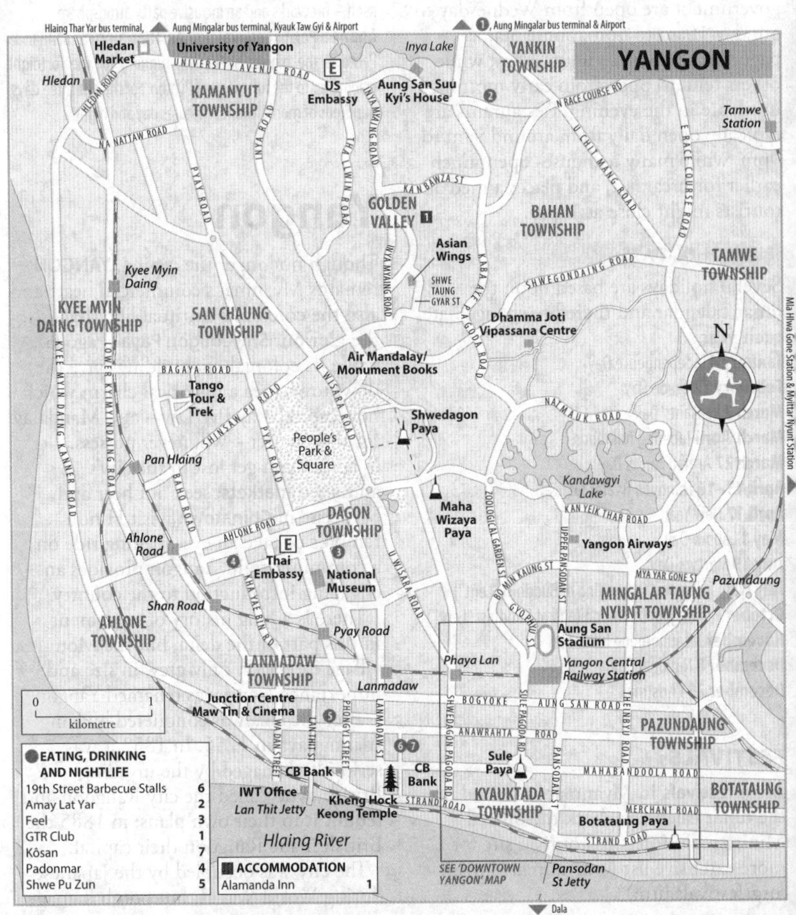

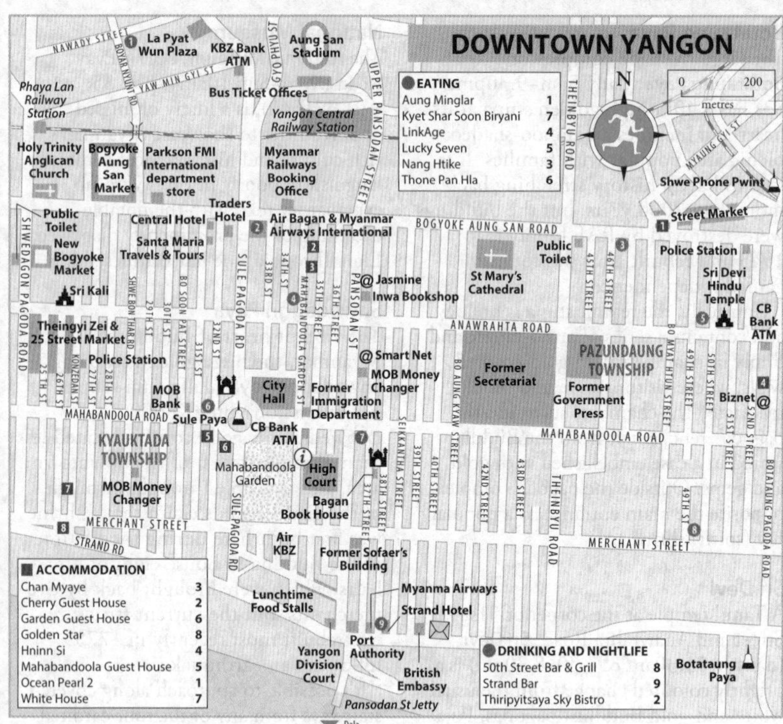

moneychangers in the streets around the pagoda, but don't be tempted – they're notorious for scamming the unwary.

Just southeast of Sule Paya is **Mahabandoola Garden** (daily 6am–6pm; free), which has been tidied up recently and is a good place to escape the downtown bustle.

The colonial core

The streets around Sule Paya contain many of Yangon's most interesting colonial-era buildings, including several abandoned by the government when it moved to Nay Pyi Taw. On the northeast of the roundabout is the imposing and still active **City Hall**, based on a British design but with ornamentation inspired by Bagan's temples. Just east of this is the former **Immigration Department**, originally built as a department store and under renovation at the time of research. Further east still is the former **Secretariat**, seat of the government and the place where General Aung San was assassinated in 1947. Abandoned and overgrown with vegetation, it is due to be redeveloped.

Back towards Sule Paya, bookstall-lined **Pansodan Street** is a treasure-trove of colonial buildings including the still-functioning **High Court**, built from 1905–11 in a style typical of the British Empire in India. The southern end of Pansodan Street was once home to the most prestigious businesses in Yangon including several in the old **Sofaer's Building** at no. 62, which was built by a Baghdadi Jew and housed legal and financial offices as well as shops selling imported luxury goods. It now contains the **Lokanat Art Gallery** (daily 9am–5pm; ⓣ01 382269, ⓦlokanatgalleries.com), which provides an interesting excuse to look inside the building.

At the corner with Strand Road are the **Port Authority** and **Yangon Division Court** buildings. A left turn leads to the **Strand Hotel**, built in 1901 and – post-restoration – once again one of the city's best hotels.

Botataung Paya

The large riverside complex of **Botataung Paya** (daily 5am–9.30pm; $3) has a 40m-high golden stupa at its heart and includes a bamboo-shaded picnic area popular with families. It is said to have a history stretching back more than 2000 years, but the buildings were destroyed by RAF bombers in 1943 and rebuilt after the country gained independence.

Unusually, the rebuilt stupa is hollow and contains a series of atmospheric and dimly lit chambers with gold-covered walls, where visitors roam and monks meditate. The chambers surround the pagoda's relic, a hair from the Buddha stored in a case embellished with gold and gems. Outside the pagoda complex, opposite the main entrance, is a popular *nat* (spirit) shrine.

Sri Devi

A Tamil temple at the corner of 51st Street and Anawrahta Road, **Sri Devi** (daily 6–11.30am & 4.30–8.30pm) is a brightly coloured change from the usual white-and-gold Buddhist pagodas. Puja (ritual offerings to the deities) usually takes place at 8am and 6pm, while the temple's biggest annual festival is on June 10. The priests prefer you not to take photos of the statues of gods.

Bogyoke Aung San Market and around

Also known as Scott Market, the huge **Bogyoke Aung San Market** (Tues–Sun 10am–5pm), on Bogyoke Aung San Road, is popular with tourists looking for souvenirs such as paintings, puppets, lacquerware and jewellery. It's also a decent place for lunch – look out for *kyeq k'auq-s'wèh* (noodles in garlic oil, with pork and a watery soup), *nàn-gyì thouq* (cold rice-noodle "salad") and avocado shakes.

The streets to the south of the market are arguably even more interesting, particularly **Theingyi Zei** (between 27th Street and Shwedagon Pagoda Road) and the street market on **26th Street**. Both are aimed purely at locals, with lower prices than Bogyoke Aung San Market.

National Museum

The **National Museum**, 66/74 Pyay Road (Wed–Sun 10am–4pm; $5; ⊕01 371540), is a litany of missed opportunities to showcase Myanmar's rich culture and history. Most exhibits languish in poorly lit cases with no explanatory text, with the notable exception of the prominently displayed Lion Throne of the last Burmese king.

Shwedagon Paya

The vibrant heart of Buddhist Myanmar, the huge golden stupa of **Shwedagon Paya** (daily 4am–10pm, last admission 9pm; K8000; ⓦshwedagonpagoda.com) is located less than 3km northwest of the downtown area, and is visible throughout much of the city. Legends claim that a shrine was first built here during the lifetime of the Buddha to house eight of his hairs, which were brought back by two merchants, but the current structure was rebuilt most recently in 1775 following an earthquake.

It's possible to approach along covered stairways from any of the four cardinal directions, or a wheelchair-accessible lift in the south. The main stupa may dominate the 14-acre platform at the top, but there's a whole host of smaller shrines, stupas and Buddha images surrounding it. For many locals a visit to the pagoda is a social event as well as a religious one, and it's particularly atmospheric in the evenings. This is also when novice monks visit to practise their English with foreigners.

As at all Buddhist holy places, you should walk clockwise around Shwedagon. The first thing many Buddhists do is visit the appropriate shrine for the day of their birth, offering flowers, lighting a candle and pouring water on the image. Next they will visit each of the four large Buddhas, one facing each entry point.

Look out also for a Buddha on the south side which has been carved from a single piece of jade, and the damaged Singu Min Bell on the west side – the British looted it in 1825, but when they got it to the river their ship sank.

Kandawgyi and Inya lakes

Boasting great views of Shwedagon Paya to the west, the boardwalk (K2000) around **Kandawgyi Lake** is a good place for a walk. The best sunset views of Shwedagon are from the Karaweik complex (K300) on the eastern side of the lake, which includes several restaurants. There's less shade at the much larger **Inya Lake** to the north, but the southern shore is the site of Aung San Suu Kyi's home. The road was off-limits when she was under house arrest but there is little to see other than the entrance gate, which has a couple of National League for Democracy flags and a picture of her father, General Aung San.

Hledan Market

Hledan produce market (daily 6am–11pm), southwest of Inya Lake and close to Hledan stop on the Circle Line train route (see p.536), is a great place to experience daily life well off the tourist trail. Hundreds of food stalls set up each day in the surrounding streets (6–11am & 3–11pm), particularly "50ft Street" behind the market, which is really buzzing in the evenings as it's a popular student hangout.

Kyauk Taw Gyi

A huge seated Buddha makes **Kyauk Taw Gyi** pagoda (daily 6am–6pm; free), situated around 14km northwest of the centre – close to the airport and infamous Insein prison – one of Yangon's most impressive Buddhist sites. It was carved from a single piece of marble near Mandalay in 1999, then brought to Yangon by boat and train. You can reach it by train yourself (it's close to Insein station on the Circle Line; see p.536) or by taxi (around K6000).

Dala

The easiest way to get a taste of small-town life in the Ayeyarwady delta is to take a ten-minute ferry ride from the Pansodan Street jetty on Strand Road, straight across the river to **Dala** township (daily 5.30am–9pm; K2000 or $2 each way). Motorbike drivers wait on the other side and offer half-day tours, but make sure that you negotiate very carefully as some of them are less than honest; a fair price is K5000 for 1hr 30min.

ARRIVAL AND DEPARTURE

By plane The airport is around 15km north of downtown Yangon, and has separate domestic and international terminals which are a 5min walk apart. Taxis into town cost K7000 from the taxi counter in the international terminal; independent drivers offer cheaper seats in shared vehicles. The taxi counter at the domestic terminal charges K9000. Crowded buses to Sule Paya (1hr; K200), in downtown Yangon, run during the day but don't stop very close to the airport: turn right out of the international terminal, walk for around 20min to the junction, take a right and then cross the road to catch a south-bound bus. Buses back to the airport leave from one block south of Sule Paya.

Destinations Bhamo (6 weekly; 2hr 40min–3hr 35min); Heho (16–17 daily; 1hr 10min–3hr 5min); Mandalay (22 daily; 55min–2hr 10min); Nyaung U (13 daily; 55min–2hr 55min); Pathein (2 weekly; 35min); Sittwe (3–4 daily; 1hr 20min–3hr); Tachileik (4–5 daily; 3hr 20min); Thandwe (4–5 daily; 50min–3hr 30min).

By bus Yangon has two major bus terminals: Hlaing Thar Yar in the northwest (for the delta region) and Aung Mingalar in the north (for most other destinations). Both are around 20km out of the city centre and should take about an hour to reach by taxi (K6000–7000). Local buses run from Sule Paya to both Aung Mingalar (at least 1hr; K300) and Hlaing Thar Yar (at least 1hr 30min; K300). Allow plenty of time however you travel though, as the traffic can be terrible. Most bus companies have offices on Kun Chan Rd, near the Aung San Stadium (daily 7am–7pm), and some offer transport (around K1000) to the appropriate bus station.

Destinations Bagan (2 daily; 11hr); Bago (6 daily; 2hr); Chaung Tha (daily; 9hr); Hpa-an (daily; 11hr 30min); Hsipaw (daily; 14hr); Kalaw (daily; 10hr); Kinpun for Kyaiktiyo (daily; 5–6hr); Mandalay (7 daily; 8–10hr); Mawlamyine (2 daily; 8hr); Meiktila (daily; 9hr 30min); Nay Pyi Taw (10 daily; 5hr 30min); Ngwe Saung (1–2 daily; 8hr 30min); Pyay (3 daily; 6hr); Pyin Oo Lwin (daily; 12hr); Sagaing (daily; 11hr); Shwenyaung for Inle Lake (daily; 11hr); Thandwe for Ngapali Beach (daily; 18hr).

By train Yangon Central Railway Station is to the north of the main grid of downtown streets, most easily reached from Sule Pagoda Rd. Advance tickets must be booked at the Myanmar Railways Booking Office on Bogyoke Aung San Rd.

Destinations Bagan (daily; 17hr 30min); Bago (8 daily; 2hr); Dawei (daily; 23hr 30min); Kyaikhto for Kyaiktiyo (3 daily; 4hr 30min); Mandalay (3 daily; 16hr 30min); Mawlamyine (3 daily; 9hr); Nay Pyi Taw (5 daily; 9hr 15min–10hr); Pyay (daily; 8hr 30min); Shwenyaung (daily;

27hr); Taungoo (5 daily; 6hr 30min–7hr); Thanbyuzayat (daily; 12hr 15min).

By boat Government-run boats to Pathein (4 weekly), from where you can take a bus to Ngwe Saung or Chaung Tha beaches, depart from Lan Thit jetty, 2.5km west of the Strand Hotel on Strand Rd. At the time of writing, however, they were running only as far as Myaunmya (22hr; $7 deck, $35 cabin) with buses (K1500) making the final 1hr journey to Pathein. Ferry tickets are available from the IWT office at the jetty – it's next to building number 64.

INFORMATION

Tourist information The official MTT office is centrally located at 118 Mahabandoola Garden St (daily 9am–5.30pm). There is also a tourist information desk at the airport.

Travel agencies Recommended agencies include: Myanmar Delight, 899 Kyaung Lane, Insein Township (ⓣ01 651833, ⓦmyanmardelight.com); Santa Maria Travels & Tours, 2nd Floor, 233–235 32nd St (ⓣ01 256178, ⓦmyanmartravels.net); Seven Diamond Express, Corner of U Wi Zar Ya & Damazedi Rd, Kamaryut Township (ⓦsevendiamondtravels.com); Tango Tour & Trek, 41 Sizone St, Sanchaung Township (ⓣ09 73109637, ⓔtango travels.info@gmail.com).

GETTING AROUND

Motorbikes are banned from the city centre.

By bus The bus network covers much of the city, and is very cheap to use, but it is hopelessly complex for those who do not speak Burmese.

By taxi Taxis are plentiful and very good value. Expect to pay K1000 for a short journey, and K1500 upwards to travel between different parts of town.

By train The Circle Line (6 daily in each direction between 8am and 2.25pm; 3hr to complete the circuit; $1) carries commuters between central Yangon and the suburbs, stopping at 39 stations as it completes the loop. It's a great way to see daily life, both on and off the train, and the easiest place to get on is platforms 6 and 7 at Yangon Central Railway Station.

ACCOMMODATION

Finding a budget room in Yangon is getting harder and harder, and it's best to book ahead to stand a chance of finding anything affordable (particularly at weekends or during holidays).

★**Chan Myaye** 256/276 Mahabandoola Garden St ⓣ01 382022 or ⓣ09 73027373, ⓔchanmyaye.gh@gmail.com; map p.533. Friendly staff and impeccable rooms combine to make this a great choice, particularly now that they've opened dorms. These are unusual in that each dorm bed is surrounded by a curtain and has its own a/c unit; more unusual still, there's a double bed dorm ($18). You'll need to be fit since reception is on the fourth floor and most bedrooms are higher still (there's no lift). Double **$24**, dorm **$10**

Cherry Guest House 278/300 Mahabandoola Garden St ⓣ01 255946 or ⓣ09 5340623; map p.533. As Yangon hotels at this price go, this is pretty good. It's situated on the fourth floor but there's a lift, and the carpeted rooms have a/c, wi-fi and flat-screen TVs. **$25**

Garden Guest House 441/445 Mahabandoola St ⓣ01 253779 or ⓣ09 73046837; map p.533. Located right on the Sule Paya roundabout, this is a reliable if unexceptional cheapie. Rooms are uninspiring but generally clean; all doubles come with a/c and attached bathrooms, while the cheapest singles ($8) have fans and shared facilities. They don't take reservations, which means they may be worth trying when everywhere else is full. **$18**

Golden Star 2nd Floor, 711–719 Merchant Rd ⓣ01 374182 or ⓣ09 73202920; map p.533. The entrance, up a dirty staircase in a residential building, isn't exactly promising, but the eight air-conditioned rooms – including triples for $35 – are surprisingly clean and tidy. There's wi-fi, but no breakfast and no discount for single occupancy. **$25**

Hninn Si 213–215 Botataung Pagoda Rd ⓣ01 299941, ⓦhninnsibudgetinn.com; map p.533. The price may edge it into mid-range territory, but the fifteen spotless new a/c rooms, including a six-bed family room ($72), do make a pleasant change from the more established and run-down budget options elsewhere. There's wi-fi access, and free snacks are served between 3–5pm. **$35**

Mahabandoola Guest House 453/459 Mahabandoola St ⓣ01 248104 or ⓣ09 5411368; map p.533. Notable mainly for being one of the cheapest places in town – it's only $6 for a single – this guesthouse is neglected and the shared bathrooms aren't particularly clean. Breakfast isn't included, but there's wi-fi in reception. **$12**

★TREAT YOURSELF

Alamanda Inn 60B Shwe Taung Kyar Road ⓣ01 534513 or ⓣ09 420283170, ⓦhotel-alamanda.com; map p.532. It may not be big and flashy like the *Strand* or the *Savoy*, but this French-owned boutique hotel – a 25min walk from Shwedagon Paya or a K2000 taxi ride from downtown – carries a much lower price tag and the colonial-era building has bags of charm. The wi-fi-equipped bedrooms make extensive use of natural materials and are decorated with wall hangings, while the buildings are set in shady gardens with parasols and loungers which give the whole place an aura of calm. The two deluxe rooms cost $120; one has a balcony and the other boasts a small private garden. **$100**

Ocean Pearl 2 100 Bogyoke Aung San St ⓣ01 299874, ⓦoceanpearlinn.com; map p.533. Formerly known as *Aung Si*, and with a sign still bearing that name, this place has wi-fi and decent-value en-suite rooms including tiny singles ($20). One major bonus is that they offer free airport pick-up by arrangement, for international flights arriving between 8am and 6.45pm. $25

White House 69–71 Konzedan St ⓣ01 240780, ⓔwhitehouse.mm@gmail.com; map p.533. One of the long-standing backpacker places around Sule Paya, with odd decor in the common areas (slate tiles with white mortar, on both walls and floors) and rooms that are too run-down to be considered truly good value. You also have to pay $8 extra for a/c. The large breakfasts are, however, a cut above most of the competition. They impose a curfew from 11pm–5am. $22

EATING

One of the most popular places for an outdoor meal is the lively collection of barbecue stalls on 19th St in Chinatown (map p.532), which set up daily from around 5–9pm. Sticks start at around K150 for veg, K300 for meat or K2500 for a whole fish. There's street food available throughout the downtown area, including Indian stalls around Shwe Bon Tha Street.

Amay Lat Yar University Ave Rd; map p.532. Keep an eye out for this place (pronounced "Amelia") if you're passing along the south side of Inya Lake – there are a couple of elephant statues at the front. Choose from around twenty curries (veg from K500–1500, meat K2500–3000) and the attentive staff will also bring over three side dishes, two pickles, jaggery, watermelon, laphet, nuts and even some lime and liquorice antacid to finish. Mon 9am–6pm, Tues–Sun 9am–9pm.

Aung Minglar Bo Yar Nyunt St; map p.533. A popular no-frills Shan noodle restaurant, serving variations including *mishay* (rice noodle soup with pork, K1500), pork rib noodles and noodles served in an earthen pot. They also make excellent dumplings. Daily 7am–9pm.

★ **Feel** 124 Pyihtaungsu Ave ⓣ09 73208132; map p.532. Ask a local to recommend a place for Burmese food and there's a good chance they'll send you here; you won't feel like you're forging a new path but you will get some of the best food in Yangon. Waiters will help you choose from a huge array of curries served with numerous side dishes (around K3000 for a meal), or you can order from the table if you know what you want (the *mohingar* is excellent). Daily 6am–10pm.

Kyet Shar Soon Biryani Corner of Mahabandoola St and Pansodan St; map p.533. Part of a small chain that started as a single Indian-run restaurant in 1947, this place cooks up mouthwatering (albeit oily) biryani in huge pots. The chicken (K1700) is the standard and comes with a side dish, lime pickle, green chillis and a bowl of soup. Daily 6am–7pm.

LinkAge 1st Floor, 221 Mahabandoola Garden St; map p.533. Also functioning as an art gallery, this restaurant can be tricky to find as the sign is on the first floor not on the ground level. It's well worth the effort as the food is very good (curries K2500) and it runs a programme to teach street children how to cook and serve food. Daily lunch and dinner.

Lucky Seven 49th St; map p.533. One of the best teahouses in the city, with service that has been described as "Formula One style" – as soon as you sit down a team of well-practised uniformed boys will swoop down to deal with your table and your order. It has both indoor and outdoor seating, serving tea (K300), snacks and noodle dishes from around K1000. Daily 6am–8pm.

Nang Htike Bogyoke Aung San Rd, between 46th and 47th sts; map p.533. The Shan noodles (K1000) in this no-frills restaurant are often said to be the best in town, while other dishes such as *ngà t'ămìn* (fish rice; K2500) and *myee-shay* (hotpot; K1500) are also highly rated. Daily 7am–11pm.

Padonmar 105–107 Kha-Yae-Bin Rd ⓣ01 538895 or ⓣ09 73029973; map p.532. Set in a 50-year-old former home, *Padonmar* serves excellent Burmese food in pleasant surroundings within the embassy district. It's popular with tour groups, so it's worth reserving a table, particularly if you want to sit out in the garden (only open in high season). Daily 10am–10.30pm.

Shwe Pu Zun 246–248 Anawrahta Rd; map p.532. There's no English sign at this busy bakery, which occupies two buildings (a café and a takeaway deli), so look out for the golden prawn logo. They serve real coffee from K1000, plus cakes and savoury pastries, but locals rave about the *faluda* (K1200), a super-sweet Indian dessert/drink of jelly and ice cream. Daily 8am–9pm.

Thone Pan Hla 454 Mahabandoola Rd; map p.533. A convenient place for breakfast if you can't bear more bread and jam at the cheap guesthouses around Sule Paya. Arrive by around 10am and you can order *mohingar* (K400), but otherwise there's a full range of affordable teahouse standards such as Shan noodles (K700). Daily 6am–7pm.

DRINKING AND NIGHTLIFE

Yangon's nightlife is getting livelier, but it still has a long way to go before it's anything close to that of somewhere like Bangkok. Check out the Myanmore website (ⓦmyanmore.com) for events listings. If you're just looking for a drink then there are plenty of simple "beer stations" around, with those in Chinatown (roughly 18th to 24th sts, and particularly 19th St) typically staying open latest. More upmarket bars are clustered in the Shwe Taung Gyar (Golden Valley) neighbourhood north of the downtown area. With a few exceptions, nightclubs in Yangon tend to involve little dancing; many have nightly "fashion shows" (in which fully clothed young women walk up and down on a stage) or karaoke.

7

50th Street Bar & Grill 01 397060, 50thstreetyangon.com; map p.533. This a/c expat haven is a bit of a surprise coming in from the scorching streets of the Botataung district. It's a US-style bar where you can sit back with a beer (happy hour 3–7pm, all day Sun) or play a game of pool. It has various deals such as 2-for-1 pasta from 5pm on Mondays and there's live music on Friday nights. Mon–Fri 11am–late, Sat & Sun 10.30am–late.

GTR Club 37 Kaba Aye Pagoda Rd, within the *Inya Lake Hotel* complex 09 73090680; map p.532. Aimed mainly at wealthy young locals, this is one of the most fashionable clubs in the city and plays mostly electro house. Although entry is free, even soft drinks cost K3000. Daily 10pm–3am.

Kôsan 108 19th St; map p.532. Although it serves food, most people come here for a drink before or after eating at one of the 19th St barbecue restaurants. It's best known for its mojitos (K800) and is popular with groups of young locals and expats. Daily noon–midnight.

7

Strand Bar *Strand Hotel*, 92 Strand Rd; map p.533. It's worth going for a drink in the bar at the classy *Strand Hotel*, which opened in 1901, if only for its colonial-era vibe. Drinks are pricey, typically $5–7, so the Friday happy hour (5–11pm) is unsurprisingly popular. There's wi-fi in the lobby and bar. Daily 11am–11pm.

Thiripyitsaya Sky Bistro 20th floor, Sakura Tower, corner of Sule Paya Rd and Bogyoke Aung San Rd 01 255277; map p.533. The prices here are steep, but during happy hour (6–9pm) a draught beer is "just" K1500 (down from K2500). It's worth it for the views of Shwedagon Paya and the downtown area. Daily 9am–10.30pm.

SHOPPING

Books Bagan Book House, 100 37th St (daily 9am–6pm; 01 377277), has the best collection of books about Myanmar. Innwa Bookstore, 246 Pansodan St (daily 8.30am–5.30pm; 01 389838), stocks a smaller selection plus international magazines. Monument Books has branches at 150 Dhamazedi Rd (01 537805) and in Junction Centre Maw Tin.

Handicrafts Pomelo, above *Monsoon* restaurant, 85–87 Thein Byu Road (pomeloyangon.com), sells fair-trade products with an emphasis on helping disadvantaged producers to improve their social and economic positions. There are a couple of handicraft shops in the National Museum, which also stock CDs of traditional music (from $5) and books.

Shopping malls and department stores Junction Centre Maw Tin, corner of Anawrahta Rd and Lan Thit St; Parkson FMI International department store, Bogyoke Aung San Road (daily 9am–9pm).

DIRECTORY

Cinema Junction Centre Maw Tin, corner of Anawrahta Rd and Lan Thit St, has a cinema showing films in English.

Embassies Thailand, 94 Pyay Rd (Mon–Fri 9am–noon & 1–5pm; 01 222784; thaiembassy.org/yangon/en); UK, 80 Strand Rd (Mon–Thurs 8am–4.30pm, Fri 8am–1pm; 01 380322, gov.uk/government/world/organisations/british-embassy-rangoon); US, 110 University Ave (Mon–Fri 8am–4.30pm; 01 536509, burma.usembassy.gov).

Internet Internet cafés include Jasmine, Pansodan St (daily 7am–midnight); BizNet, Botataung Pagoda Rd (daily 8am–11pm); Smart Net, 37th St (daily 9am–10pm).

Money The exchange booths at the international terminal of the airport generally offer very good rates, particularly the ones before you exit through customs. Many banks change dollars and euros, including MOB on Mahabandoola Rd, Shwe Bon Thar Rd and Pansodan St, and CB Bank on Mahabandoola Rd and Strand Rd. CB Bank also has ATMs (including one in the international terminal of the airport). There are moneychangers in Bogyoke Aung San Market, but there's no need to use them unless you're stuck outside of banking hours.

Post office Strand Rd (Mon–Fri 9am–3.30pm).

Swimming There's a small pool on the roof of Junction Centre Maw Tin (5th floor; Mon–Sat 6am–9pm, Sun 6am–8pm; K8000/day).

The delta region and western Myanmar

The fertile **delta region** south and west of Yangon has long been of great importance, due to its abundant agricultural production and strategic location for trading. It made news headlines around the world in 2008 after being devastated by Cyclone Nargis, when the military regime blocked foreign aid claiming that they had the situation under control. This worsened an already appalling situation and the official final death toll was 138,000 people, although in reality it was probably much higher.

Most people rush straight through the region's lush green rice fields and sleepy towns on their way to the beaches at **Chaung Tha** and **Ngwe Saung**. If you don't mind roughing it a bit, and spending a night on the river, then one good way to see more of the delta is to travel by **public ferry** from Yangon via Myaunmya and Pathein.

North of the delta region is the long and thin stretch of Rakhine State, which is separated from the plains to the east by mountains. The most touted destination here is **Ngapali Beach**, but it's a long, hard journey by bus and rising hotel prices have squeezed out anyone on a strict budget. Of more interest to most budget travellers is temple-dotted **Mrauk U**, capital of Rakhine when it was a separate kingdom.

CHAUNG THA BEACH

The sand isn't the whitest you'll see, but **Chaung Tha Beach** isn't a bad place to hang out. It gets pretty busy at the weekend and during holidays, but joining the locals at play is a cultural experience in itself. Many young children cannot swim and run into the sea clutching huge inner tubes as flotation devices. Meanwhile, teenagers play football around the food vendors who cross the beach selling grilled crabs and prawns on skewers.

ARRIVAL AND DEPARTURE

Transport can be arranged through either accommodation or Mr George (see below). The closest large city, and transport hub, is Pathein.

By boat A day-trip to Ngwe Saung costs K60,000 for up to five people. A government ferry runs from Myaunmya – a 1hr bus ride from Pathein – to Yangon (4 weekly; 22hr).

By bus The bus station is towards the southern end of the beach, opposite *Lai Lai Resort*. Tickets should be reserved at least a day in advance, particularly in peak season. There are minibuses to Pathein (5 daily; 2hr 30min) and buses to Yangon (2 daily; 6hr).

By motorbike The motorbike trip between Chaung Tha and Ngwe Saung beaches (2hr; K15,000 one-way, K17,000 day return) is one of the highlights of a visit to this part of the coast. A motorbike to Pathein costs K15,000.

INFORMATION AND TOURS

Tourist information The official tourist information office is opposite the bus station. Much more helpful is the private information office (daily 7am–10pm) run by Mr George, on the main road close to *Shwe Hin Tha* hotel. Services include bus ticket sales, bike rental (K2000/day), snorkelling equipment rental (K1500/day) and massage (K5000/hr). Mr George also arranges day-trips, as do some hotels, including snorkelling from shore (K5000) or from a boat (K30,000 for five people).

Internet There's internet and wi-fi at *Shwe Hin Tha* hotel.

ACCOMMODATION AND EATING

Hill Garden Hotel 10min bike ride away from the main beach ⓣ 09 49576072, ⓦ hillgardenhotel.com. A real find if you're after a bit of peace and quiet, with the same owner as the also-recommended *Shwe Hin Tha* hotel on the main beach. It's set amid fields, and you'll probably want to rent a bike (K1500/day), but there's a small beach nearby. $25

Shwe Ya Minn Main Rd ⓣ 042 42126. It's on the other side of the road from the beach, but the rooms are clean and manager Ma Ei provides a warm welcome. The price includes a better-than-average breakfast (available to non-guests for K1500). $12

William Restaurant Main Rd between *Ayeyarwady Hotel* and the bus station. It's further south than the bulk of the accommodation, but this friendly open-sided place dishes up some great seafood priced according to the main ingredient (fish is K3500). If you can't decide, try the fantastic hot and sour prawns. There's also a small, cheap guesthouse here (double $15). Daily 6am–10pm.

7

NGWE SAUNG

The 15km-long stretch of pale, fine sand at **Ngwe Saung** is more appealing than the beach at Chaung Tha, not least because its length means that it is much less densely developed. There are still plenty of resorts but the beach is cleaner and more laidback; it also has clearer water. The flipside is that Ngwe Saung attracts a lot more foreigners and wealthy locals, meaning that prices are higher and that it's arguably a less interesting experience.

There's a small village with a main street almost entirely devoted to fulfilling tourist needs; generally speaking, the priciest resorts are north of the village and the cheapest are strung out to the south. If you fancy a wander, then **Lover's Island**, just offshore around 500m south of the two hotels listed here, is an easy destination at low tide.

ARRIVAL AND DEPARTURE

Each of the transport options listed here can be arranged through accommodation or with Tom Tom (see p.540). The main transport hub is the city of Pathein.

By boat There's a government ferry from Myaunmya to Yangon (4 weekly; 22hr); Myaunmya is a 1hr bus ride from Pathein.

By bus Some buses pick up and drop off at hotels, others stop near the Best mini-store in the village.

Destinations Pathein (4 daily; 2hr); Yangon (2 daily; 8hr 30min).

By motorbike The motorbike ride to Chaung Tha (2hr; K15,000 one-way, K17,000 day-return) is an attraction in its own right.

GETTING AROUND AND TOURS

By motorbike or bike Motorbike taxis (from K1000) and bike- (K2000/day) and motorbike rental (K10,000/day plus fuel) can be arranged with hotels or through the helpful Tom Tom (T 09 422 462904, E tom.tunlin@gmail.com). He runs an unofficial tourist office at *Sandalwood Café* (daily 5am–10.30pm) on the main road in the village and is usually there in the evenings, while from 9am to 5pm he's more often at the *Shwe Hin Tha* hotel. Tom Tom can also arrange various day-trips, including snorkelling at Bird Island (K65,000 for 5–7 people), visits to an elephant camp (K10,000/person plus $5 entrance and $10 to ride an elephant) and trips to Simna fishing village (K12,000/person).

7

ACCOMMODATION

The two places listed here are next to each other.

Shwe Hin Tha 4km south of the village T 042 40340 or T 09 4224 62904. The best value on the beach, with options ranging from fan-cooled bamboo bungalows to rooms with a/c and satellite TV ($50). It's on a great stretch of sand with plenty of parasols and loungers, plus there's a restaurant serving decent food. $30

Silver Coast 4km south of the village T 042 40324 or T 09 520 0575. An acceptable alternative just south of *Shwe Hin Tha*. Some of the cheaper, fan-cooled rooms are a bit musty but they are clean and have small verandas. For $40 you can get a room right on the beach. The separately run *Beach Point* restaurant, overlooking the sand, is one of the best in Ngwe Saung. $30

EATING

Most resorts and hotels have their own restaurant, but it's worth heading into the village where there's much more choice.

Ngwe Hline Si Main road. Serves some of the best dishes you'll find in Ngwe Saung including a tasty spaghetti with seafood (K3500). Daily 6.30am–10.30pm.

Royal Flower Main road. Although this restaurant is aimed partly at foreign tourists, it also attracts locals and the atmosphere is all the better for it. The menu is pretty standard though, with plenty of seafood options – either grilled or in various Chinese styles – all for around K4000. Daily 7am–10pm.

NGAPALI BEACH

If you're looking for pristine white sand, clear blue sea and little to do other than kick back with a cocktail and fresh

RECENT VIOLENCE IN RAKHINE STATE

The **Rohingya**, a Muslim minority in **Rakhine State**, have been described as one of the most heavily oppressed groups in the world. Stripped of their citizenship in 1982, the Rohingya have long been discriminated against by members of the state's majority Buddhist ethnic group, the Rakhine, and tensions have simmered for decades. They boiled over in June 2012 following the rape of a Buddhist woman, allegedly by three Muslim men. As homes and public buildings in northern Rakhine State were burned by Buddhists, dozens of Muslims were killed and around 75,000 people – the vast majority of them Rohingya – were driven into refugee camps. Further violence in October 2012 saw another 36,000 displaced, and tens of thousands more being cut off from essential services such as health care.

One result was that most of the state – including Sittwe and Mrauk U but not the money-spinning Ngapali Beach – was closed to tourism. The government subsequently dropped the restrictions, but anti-Muslim violence spread beyond Rakhine in 2013, with mob violence in towns including Meiktila (Mandalay division). In October 2013 a mosque and homes were burned in Thandwe, only 14km from Ngapali.

Many Buddhists in Myanmar, including some pro-democracy campaigners and religious leaders, are vehemently anti-Rohingya and reject the use of the word Rohingya itself. They argue that the community has only a relatively short history of settlement in Myanmar, and that they are in fact Bengalis who belong in Bangladesh (which does not wish to take them). Outsiders who have tried to work with the Rohingya refugees have faced opposition and intimidation from Buddhists, including monks, and the presence of NGOs such as Médecins Sans Frontières is resented by some Rakhine people who – counter to all evidence – see themselves as the oppressed group.

Many international observers have expressed disappointment that Aung San Suu Kyi has refused to speak out in defence of the Rohingya, a stance that would be unpopular with many voters. The topic is certainly extremely emotive within Rakhine State, and it can be alarming to hear ordinary people repeating vehement anti-Rohingya propaganda.

seafood, then **Ngapali Beach** is your kind of place. Unfortunately the cost of accommodation has spiralled in recent years, plus to get to Ngapali from Yangon requires either a fifty-minute flight or a gruelling eighteen-hour bus journey.

Most of the hotels are strung out between Lintha village in the north and Jade Taw further south, with Myabin village lying in between. Several places on the beach offer **massages** from K7000 per hour, while if you're feeling more active then you can rent a bicycle in Lintha (K3000 per day) and ride down to Gyeikthaw fishing village – the market is best around 6.30am. You can also arrange **snorkelling** through hotels, although to get to the best sites you need to take a day-trip (K40,000 including barbecue lunch).

ARRIVAL AND DEPARTURE

The nearest town is Thandwe, located 7km northeast of the beach. Hire of a tuk-tuk between them costs around K7000. Caravan travel agent at Ngapali Junction (043 42404; K400 from the beach by tuk-tuk) sells plane and boat tickets.

By plane Thandwe airport – which has a currency exchange counter – is 6km north of Ngapali Beach; most accommodation will pick you up from the airport by prior arrangement.

Destinations Sittwe (1–2 daily; 40min); Yangon (5 daily; 40–55min).

By bus Hotels on Ngapali Beach sell bus tickets, and also act as drop-off and pick-up points.

Destinations Pyay (2 daily; 10hr); Yangon (daily; 17hr).

By boat Buses (frequent until 3pm; 4hr) make the 80km journey from Thandwe to Taunggok, where you can get a boat to Sittwe (Mon, Tues, Wed, Fri & Sat; 9hr).

ACCOMMODATION

Most of the accommodation in Ngapali is startlingly overpriced, so it's essential to book ahead. There's internet access at *Bayview* and *Sandoway* resorts, or more cheaply at an internet café in Jade Taw.

Laguna Lodge Between Myabin and Jade Taw 043 42312, lagunalodge-myanmar.com. Although the standard rooms here start at $50, they also have a couple of "backpacker rooms" which lack sea views. The management and staff here have created the most backpacker-friendly atmosphere in Ngapali, and arrange mountain-biking trips from K8000. $35

Memento Between Lintha and Myabin 043 42441 or 09 851 5190, ngapalimementoresort@gmail.com. The four cheapest rooms here are set back from the beach, and are fan-cooled with electricity from 5pm–7am. You can get sea views and a nicer room for $5 extra. Either way you can use the loungers on a deck overlooking the beach. $35

EATING AND DRINKING

There are a few shacks on the beach, close to Myabin, typically open from breakfast until 9pm (happy hour usually 4–6pm).

Htay Htay's Kitchen Main road, near Lintha. Customers at this welcoming, family-run restaurant rave about the great seafood – crab curry (K4000) is a favourite – and cocktails (rum sour K1500). Daily 7am–11pm.

Pleasant View Islet On a causeway in the sea, near Jade Taw village. The great location is the immediate draw, but the food here is good and the service is attentive. Daily lunch and dinner.

SITTWE

Located at the picturesque point where the Kaladan River meets the Bay of Bengal, **Sittwe** is the main transport hub for visiting Mrauk U (see p.542). The city was off-limits for much of 2012–13 and, although open to tourists again, it has been profoundly changed as Rohingya Muslims – who once formed close to half of the city's population – have almost all been driven into refugee camps.

WHAT TO SEE AND DO

The town centre is built on a grid pattern, with three main north-south roads: from east to west they are Minbargyi Rd, Main Rd and Strand Rd (along the shore). Most shops and travel agents are located on Main Rd, as are the rather dry **Cultural Museum** (Tues–Sun 9.30am–4.30pm; K2000) and the more interesting small museum further north at **Maka Kuthala Kyaungtawgyi monastery** (daily 6am–6pm).

The most rewarding place for a walk is **Strand Rd**, which has a fish market (daily 6am–5pm) at the junction with Merchant St. It's at its best early in the morning. Around 3km south of here, K2000 return by trishaw, is the View Point – a great place to appreciate Sittwe's location on the Bay of Bengal, with a café open from 6am–9pm.

7

7

ARRIVAL AND DEPARTURE

By plane The airport is 2.5km west of the town, a K3000 ride by tuk-tuk or K5000 by taxi.

By boat Boats to Mrauk U or Taunggok (for Ngapali Beach) leave from a jetty 3km north of the town. Transport to the jetty costs K3000 (tuk-tuk) or K5000 (taxi).

To Mrauk U The government ferry (6–7hr; $6 plus K500 for a seat; ⓣ 043 23382) leaves at 7am on Tues and Fri; buy tickets at the jetty from 6am. Two companies run more comfortable private ferries: Shwe Pyi Tan (2hr 30min; $20) at 7am on Wed, and Aung Kyaw Moe (5hr; $10) at 7am on Mon, Thurs and Sat. The former company has an office on Main Rd (daily 7.30am–8pm; ⓣ 043 22719 or ⓣ 09 49592709), the latter at the jetty (ⓣ 09 49676706). You can arrange a private boat for up to four people (5–6hr; K150,000 return) at the airport and leave the same day, as long as you arrive by about 2.30pm. Make sure you agree on how many days they will wait for you in Mrauk U.

To Taunggok Shwe Pyi Tan has tickets to Taunggok ($35; 9hr) on Sat, Sun and Wed.

By bus The bus station is 4km west of town. The road to Mrauk U was opened to foreigners in 2013 but taking a bus (rather than an expensive taxi) is still almost unheard of – try booking tickets through your guesthouse a couple of days ahead.

Destinations Mrauk U (3 daily; 4hr 30min; K10,000).

INFORMATION AND TOURS

Freelance guides wait at the airport; reliable guides include Than Tun (ⓣ 09 250242844; ⓔ jimes.htun@gmail.com). Agencies include Gissipandi (ⓣ 09 49662207; ⓔ smileaung09@gmail.com) and Khine Pyi Soe (25 Mill Rd; ⓣ 09 8516162).

ACCOMMODATION

Most budget guesthouses in Sittwe have either closed down or stopped taking foreign guests. Book ahead.

Mya 51/6 Bowdhi Rd ⓣ 043 23315. This is the closest you'll get to a bargain in Sittwe. Set in the same gardens as a teahouse of the same name, it has twenty spacious, simple rooms each with a cold-water bathroom. **$30**

EATING

River Valley River Rd & Beach Rd. Set in a wooden building with a garden at the side, this is the most atmospheric place to eat around sunset. The menu covers standard Chinese food from around K3500. There's also a branch on Main Rd close to *Shwe Thazin* hotel. Daily 7.30am–10pm.

DIRECTORY

Internet Kiss, Main Rd (daily 9am–9pm).

Money KBZ Bank, Main Road (Mon–Fri 9.30am–3pm), has the town's only ATM and currency exchange desk.

MRAUK U

The many sixteenth- and seventeenth-century temples of **MRAUK U**, some of them as sturdily built as fortresses, make it one of the country's most significant historical sites. Yet it receives only a fraction of the number of tourists who visit Bagan. Certainly Mrauk U is not on the same scale, but it has its own appeal, not least because the temples are located within the town itself – although it is rumoured that, as happened in Old Bagan, the government plans to force inhabitants out of the centre to develop it as a tourist attraction. There's also a new airport in the works.

It wasn't the first Rakhine capital, but from 1430 onwards Mrauk U was a centre for trade with merchants from as far away as Europe. It was at the height of its powers under King Minbin (who ruled from 1531–53), when many of the temples were built, and fell in 1784 when the Konbaung dynasty – which would later go on to found Mandalay – conquered the territory. Many Rakhine people hark back to the glory days of the kingdom, and resent what they see as continued Bamar dominance as well as the unwelcome presence of the Rohingya minority (see box, p.540).

WHAT TO SEE AND DO

The heart of modern Mrauk U is its **market** and immediately to its east lie the remains of the old royal **palace**. The two main concentrations of **temples** are to the north and east of the palace; most are open daily 7am–5.30pm. Entry to them is covered by a K5000 entry fee, which is usually collected at Shittaung Paya.

There are great views from temples including Sakya Shwegu, Rathay Thaung and Myan Daw Mu, while for Mrauk U's fabulous **sunsets** the most impressive panorama is the one from the **Discovery Viewpoint** (sunrise to sunset; K500).

The palace and around

The fifteenth-century palace was sacked when the city was conquered. The site was partially excavated in 1999, and locals claim that the work stalled because the

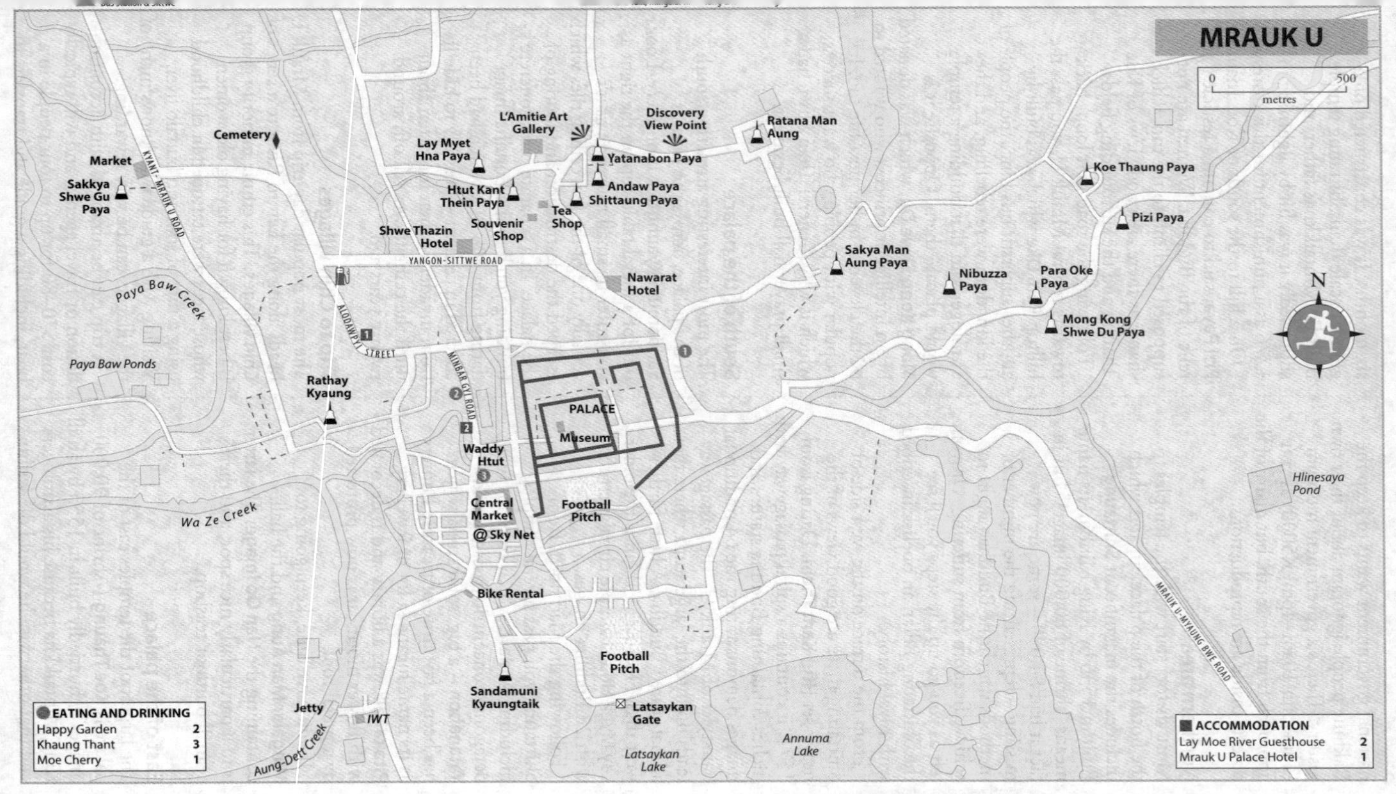
MRAUK U
0
500
metres
N
Cemetery
Market
Sakkya Shwe Gu Paya
KYANT- MRAUK U ROAD
L'Amitie Art Gallery
Lay Myet Hna Paya
Discovery View Point
Ratana Man Aung
Yatanabon Paya
Andaw Paya
Shittaung Paya
Htut Kant Thein Paya
Tea Shop
Souvenir Shop
Shwe Thazin Hotel
YANGON-SITTWE ROAD
Nawarat Hotel
Koe Thaung Paya
Pizi Paya
Sakya Man Aung Paya
Nibuzza Paya
Para Oke Paya
Mong Kong Shwe Du Paya
Paya Baw Creek
Paya Baw Ponds
ALODAWPYI STREET
MINBAR GYI ROAD
Rathay Kyaung
PALACE
Museum
Waddy Htut
Central Market
@ Sky Net
Football Pitch
Wa Ze Creek
Hlinesaya Pond
Bike Rental
MRAUK U-MYAUNG BWE ROAD
Football Pitch
Sandamuni Kyaungtaik
Latsaykan Gate
Latsaykan Lake
Annuma Lake
Jetty
IWT
Aung-Dett Creek
EATING AND DRINKING
Happy Garden 2
Khaung Thant 3
Moe Cherry 1
ACCOMMODATION
Lay Moe River Guesthouse 2
Mrauk U Palace Hotel 1

national government wants to keep the Rakhine people ignorant about their own history. There's a government **museum** (Tues–Sun 10am–4pm; K5000) as you approach from the south, but many of the objects inside are reproductions.

Northern area

Most visitors start with the temples to the north of the palace, an area which includes the magnificent **Shittaung**. Built in 1536 by King Minbin, its name means "shrine of 80,000 images" but in fact it had 84,000 – some are now missing – representing the number of methods which the Buddha taught to achieve freedom from suffering. On your left as you go up the steps you'll see the Shittaung Pillar, an obelisk inscribed with royal history.

From the terrace on the west side of Shittaung there are good views of the heavy-set **Htut Kant Thein**. Dating from 1571, it contains a spiral passageway with niches containing Buddha statues and images demonstrating the 64 traditional hairstyles of Mrauk U. The passageway leads up into the large stupa where there's a final seated Buddha. A little further west than Htut Kant Thein is the older **Lay Myek Hna**, a simple circular structure with 28 Buddha images.

Following the road north from Shittaung you pass several temples, including **Andaw**, which contains two octagonal concentric passages, and **Yatanabon** – a big, solid stupa which has been a favourite of treasure hunters as its name means "a lot of jewellery". **Pitaka Taik** was a library and is decorated with flower motifs; it is now protected by a metal roof.

If you have time, keep going to **Mingalar Man Aung** and the hall containing the **Nan Oo Image**. The latter is in a particularly nice spot, and there's a small outdoor teashop.

East of the palace

The largest of the temples east of the palace is **Koe Thaung** ("shrine of 90,000 images"), hurriedly built in 1553 by an ill King Mintaikkha because his astrologers said that otherwise he would die within six months. It was constructed on a grander scale than Shittaung temple, built by Mintaikkha's father, and supposedly it was hit by lightning in 1776 as a punishment for this disrespect.

On a hill to the south of Koe Thaung is **Pizi Paya**, said to contain a testicle ('*pizi*') relic of the Buddha. Women are not supposed to climb to the top, which is a shame as there are good views of Koe Thaung and the surrounding fields.

Following the road as it loops back towards central Mrauk U, you pass the hilltop **Para Oke** which was built by another superstitious king: the people of the kingdom were rebelling, and the astrologer said that building a temple would placate them. Opposite it is **Mong Kong Shwe Du**, which was donated by an intelligent princess who wanted to be the cleverest in her next life too. It's popular with people who want success, which is why General Than Shwe had a small prayer hall built beside it.

South of the palace

The most interesting attraction south of the palace, across the river, is **Sandamuni Kyaungtaik** monastery. Look out for a metal table-top on the right as you enter its small museum, as it's actually one of the few ceiling tiles which escaped the destruction and looting of the palace. In a separate pink concrete building you'll find a Buddha image dating from 308 BC, which had been covered in cement – possibly to hide it from invaders – then forgotten about until the cement eyes fell off, around twenty years ago.

Trip to Chin villages

The most popular day-trip from Mrauk U heads along the Lemro River to a series of **Chin villages**. This ethnic minority group is best known for having old women whose faces were tattooed in childhood using a mix of soot and buffalo liver. Visiting with a guide who knows many of the villagers can be very rewarding.

A trip can be arranged with accommodation or travel agents, and will typically cost $70–80 for up to four people in a boat, including a guide and transfers to

the jetty. In some villages you will be asked to donate to community projects such as school buildings.

ARRIVAL AND DEPARTURE

By boat The jetty is 1km south of the market. Services to Sittwe all leave at 7am. These are: the government ferry on Wed & Sat (6–7hr; $6 plus K500 for a chair), the Shwe Pyi Tan ferry on Thurs (2hr; $20) and the Aung Kyaw Moe ferry on Tues, Fri & Sun (5hr; $10). An office (T 043 50127, T 09 421733776) marked Inland Water Transport sells tickets for government ferries and also Aung Kyaw Moe boats. Buy tickets for Shwe Pyi Tan at the jetty teashop.

By bus The small bus station is just northwest of town, on the road to Sittwe. Until recently foreigners were banned from taking buses to or from Mrauk U, and at the time of research few people had successfully done so. It's easiest to get tickets through accommodation or from the bus company office next to Wady Htut guesthouse. It's theoretically possible to get to Bagan by changing at Magwe.

Destinations Magwe (3 daily; 14hr); Pyay (3 daily; 8hr 30min); Sittwe (3 daily; 4hr 30min); Yangon (3 daily; 26hr).

ACCOMMODATION

Lay Moe River Guesthouse Minbar Gyi Rd, T 043 50255 or T 09 8522139. The 12 rooms here are all the same, with wooden floors, small desk fans, mosquito nets and bathrooms with cold showers. Some rooms are in more urgent need of repainting than others, though, so it's worth looking at more than one. Staff can arrange bike rental (K2000/day), guides ($25/day) and car rental (K25,000/day). **$15**

Mrauk U Palace Resort Alodawpyi Street, T 043 50262 or T 09 250327705, W mraukupalaceresort.com. It's a stretch to call it palatial but this new hotel, in easy reach of the market and the northern temples, is the best you'll get for this price. Rooms in the duplex bungalows have wooden floors, satellite TV, a minibar and a comfortable bed – a/c is an extra $15 – although the bathrooms haven't been brilliantly finished. **$25**

EATING AND DRINKING

There are several teashops and restaurants around the market.

Happy Garden Minbar Gyi Rd. You don't have to eat in the garden here – there's also a building at the top of the slope – but it's a peaceful (if not particularly green) spot for a bite to eat or just a beer. It's run by a friendly family and serves dishes such as Rakhine curries and grilled fish (K3000 each). Daily 7am–11pm or later.

Khaung Thant Junction of Taung Rat Rd & Myinn Saing Pyin Rd. A simple and cheap place to fill up on Rakhine food, with a curry, rice and side dishes costing around K1500. Daily 8am–11pm.

Moe Cherry Just east of the palace. A backpacker favourite, family-run and with quite a homely feel considering that the decor is brick walls and concrete floors. Curries start at K4000. They can also arrange guides ($20–25/day) and transport. Daily 7am–10pm.

DIRECTORY

Internet Sky Net, close to the market on Minbar Gyi Rd (daily 8am–9pm).

Money There are no banks or ATMs in Mrauk U. You can change money (US$, euros and £) in the *Nawarat* hotel for a rate a little worse than you'd get in a bank.

Shopping L'Amitie art gallery (daily 7am–after sunset; E artsmtmu@yahoo.com) exhibits the work of Shwe Maung Tha, who has had his work shown overseas, as well as his son Khine Minn Tun. You're likely to see one or the other of them around.

7

Southeastern Myanmar

Easily overlooked by tourists in the rush to head north from Yangon, **southeastern Myanmar** more than justifies a diversion and is likely to attract many more visitors now that border crossings with Thailand have opened to foreigners (see p.551). If nothing else, it's worth seeing the holy sites of **Bago** before heading up to Mandalay, but further south you'll find more riches in store.

The most iconic attraction in Mon State is the boulder-and-pagoda balancing act at **Kyaiktiyo**, although the experience of being among believers is likely to be just as memorable as the Golden Rock itself. Further south, you can search out old colonial buildings and a ridge packed with pagodas in the former British capital of **Mawlamyine**.

The mountainous eastern part of the region, which stretches along the border with Thailand, has long been a refuge for **ethnic minority resistance groups**. Kayin State, in particular, has seen a great deal of bloodshed since the country gained independence, although the Karen National Union signed a temporary ceasefire with the government at the start of 2012. Many Karen, however, complain that the government has now started

granting their land to foreign investors such as mining companies. The state remains largely off-limits apart from **Hpa-an**, a town that makes a great base for day-trips into rice fields overlooked by imposing Mount Zwegabin, and also provides access to the border crossing at Myawaddy.

Other than the opening of the Myawaddy crossing, the other big news for tourism here has been the opening up of the **Tanintharyi Region** further south: until 2013, it wasn't possible to travel overland to **Dawei**, **Myeik** or **Kawthaung**. Some restrictions are still in place but it is now possible to take a little-travelled route south all the way to the Thai border and beyond.

BAGO

A plethora of pagodas, outsized Buddha statues and monasteries attest to the historical importance of **BAGO**, which was at the height of its influence following the decline of Bagan's empire in the thirteenth century. Its location at a major junction, 80km northeast of Yangon, helps to make it a convenient stopover or day-trip destination.

WHAT TO SEE AND DO

Most of Bago's sights are covered by a $10 government-imposed entrance fee. It's a long walk between them, so ask at accommodation about bicycle rental (around K3000 per day) or motorbike tours (around 5hr; K8000) which include the attractions listed here – plus the missable reconstructed palace and a monastery where busloads of tourists intrude on the monks' mealtime. Motorbike drivers also wait for arriving buses, and may suggest ways to avoid the $10 fee (although this might mean missing some of the main sights).

Shwemawdaw Paya and Hintha Gon

The holiest site in Bago, **Shwemawdaw Paya**, around 2km east of the centre, is the tallest pagoda in the country at 114m. It's said that the original stupa was built here during the lifetime of Gautama Buddha, but it has been destroyed many times and the current one dates back only to the 1950s.

A five-minute walk east from Shwemawdaw is a smaller pagoda, **Hintha Gon**, most notable for its *nat* (spirit) shrine in which ceremonies are often performed to bring good luck to worshippers.

Shwethalyaung reclining Buddha and around

To the west of the centre is the elegant **Shwethalyaung reclining Buddha**, over 54m in length and said to have been built by King Miga Depa in 994 to mark his conversion to Buddhism. A ten-minute walk further west is the **Mahazedi Paya**, completed in 1560 under King Bayinnaung, a reformer who is said to have put an end to human and animal sacrifices by animists. It was reconstructed in the 1980s.

Kyaik Pun Paya

The **Kyaik Pun Paya**, located down a road off the main highway, 3.5km south of the centre, consists of four large back-to-back statues representing the four Buddhas who have appeared so far in the current era. This back-to-back arrangement seems to have originated among the Mon before spreading to Bagan and Thailand.

ARRIVAL AND DEPARTURE

By bus You can buy tickets at the bus station, around 1km west of the town centre (K500 by motorbike), at your accommodation, or from the offices on the main road close to the two listed hotels. Daytime buses stop at the bus station only, while from around 6pm they may also stop close to the ticket offices.

Destinations Hpa-an (3 daily; 6–7hr); Kinpun for Kyaiktyo (hourly until 4pm; 2hr 30min); Mandalay (4 daily; 12hr); Mawlyamine (5 daily; 6hr); Nyaungshwe for Inle Lake (2 daily; 14hr); Taungoo (2 daily; 6hr); Yangon (very frequent until 5pm; 1hr 30min).

By train The station is centrally located, just north of the main road and most of the cheaper hotels. For Inle Lake (via Shwenyaung), change at Thazi.

Destinations Dawei (daily; 22hr 40min); Kyaikhto for Kyaiktiyo (3 daily; 3hr); Mandalay (3 daily; 14hr 30min); Mawlamyine (3 daily; 9hr); Nay Pyi Taw (5 daily; 7hr 30min); Taungoo (5 daily; 5hr); Thanbyuzayat (daily; 10hr 40min); Thazi (3 daily; 10–11hr); Yangon (8 daily; 2hr).

ACCOMMODATION

Mya Nan Dar 10 Main Rd ☎ 052 22275 or ☎ 09 31755255. The cheapest rooms here are simple boxes without their own bathrooms, but they're nevertheless the best budget deal in Bago, not least because they are all equipped with a/c. You also get breakfast, hot water and wi-fi in the rooms. $16

EATING

Shwe Li Kannar St. Many locals reckon that this place serves the best Chinese food in town. It's on a side street a little away from the frantic main road, and serves a standard set of dishes – such as fried prawn chilli for K4600 – in a clean dining room. Daily 10am–9pm.

Three Five Hotel Main Rd. A large and gloomy – but conveniently located – restaurant serving decent Chinese dishes. They start at around K1800 for noodles. Daily 7am–10pm.

DIRECTORY

Internet KMD, Main Rd (daily 7am–11pm).

Money CB Bank, Main Rd (currency exchange daily 11am–2pm).

KYAIKTIYO

One of the holiest Buddhist sites in the country, **Kyaiktiyo Paya** draws large numbers of non-believers among its throngs of pilgrims, primarily thanks to its spectacular location. The small pagoda was built atop the Golden Rock, a boulder 15m in circumference and coated in gold leaf, which is itself perched on a larger rock; it's a precarious-looking setup which is supposedly kept in place by one of the Buddha's hairs.

The starting point to get up to the rock is the town of **Kinpun** and the full 11km hike takes at least four hours, but almost everyone shortens the walk by cramming into the back of the open trucks (daily 6am–6pm) which depart when full – they are less frequent as the day goes on. Some trucks run only to the old Yathetaung terminal (45min; K1500 each way) from which it's an hour's walk to the top. Most, though, now run all the way to the top (1hr; K2500 each way) so that it's only a ten- to fifteen-minute walk to the rock.

A government fee of K6000 is collected at the top, shortly before the main complex; men can join the pilgrims beside the **Golden Rock** itself, and even add to its lustre (five sheets of gold leaf K1700), while women must stay a short distance away. Women are not supposed to wear trousers, shorts or miniskirts; men should also dress appropriately.

It's worth pressing on past the rock and the *Yoe Yoe Lay* hotel for fifteen minutes to reach **Kyi Kann Pa Sat**, where you can join locals throwing coins up onto a ledge for good luck. There's also a cave shrine with a very narrow entrance.

ARRIVAL AND DEPARTURE

The transport hub is the town of Kyaikhto – not to be confused with Kyaiktiyo (the name of the mountain and the pagoda) – on the main highway, with Kinpun around 14km to the northeast. Motorbike taxis (K1500) and pick-ups (K500) run between Kyaikhto and Kinpun.

By bus Some buses go right into Kinpun and stop outside *Sea Sar Restaurant*; others stop at Kyaikhto and passengers are transferred to Kinpun by truck (usually included in the bus ticket price).

Destinations Bago (4 daily; 3hr); Hpa-an (daily; 5hr); Mawlamyine (5 daily; 4hr); Yangon (4 daily; 5hr).

By train The train station is in Kyaikhto.

Destinations Mawlamyine (3 daily; 4hr 30min–5hr); Yangon (3 daily; 5hr).

By pick-up Pick-ups to Hpa-an (5hr) run from 6am until 1pm, most of them starting in Kyaikhto rather than Kinpun.

By motorbike It's possible to visit Kyaiktiyo as a day-trip from Bago; a motorbike and driver costs around K20,000 return, including waiting.

ACCOMMODATION

Most travellers on a budget stay in Kinpun, since all the hotels at the top are expensive.

Sea Sar Just off the main road, Kinpun ☎ 09 8723288. The quiet main compound here – a short way behind the restaurant of the same name – has pleasant bungalows, and there are cheaper rooms in a block very close to the starting point for trucks to the Golden Rock. No discount for single occupancy. $12

EATING

There are plenty of Chinese and Burmese restaurants on the main road in Kinpun.

Mya Yeik Nya Overlooking the truck terminal. More inviting than most restaurants in Kinpun, mainly thanks to its subdued lighting, although the friendly staff also help. Chinese or Burmese dishes cost around K3000. Daily 4am–9pm.

7

DIRECTORY

Internet You'll see locals taking advantage of the free wi-fi in the truck terminal.

Money There is a branch of KBZ Bank just southwest of the truck terminal.

MAWLAMYINE

The capital of British Lower Burma from 1827–52, when it was known as Moulmein, **Mawlamyine** remains a busy port. Visitors looking for vestiges of colonial atmosphere may initially be disappointed by Myanmar's third-largest city, but a wander around reveals many old buildings in various states of neglect. The city is also the base for day-trips to attractions ranging from a colossal Buddha – big enough to walk into – to a sobering war cemetery.

7

WHAT TO SEE AND DO

The waterside **Strand Road** is the city's most important thoroughfare, and towards its northern end are three busy markets. For colonial-era buildings, however, a better bet is **Upper Main Road**, running inland parallel to Strand Road.

Dotted with pagodas, the **central ridge of hills** makes for a great sunset trip. Start at Uzina Paya at the southern end, head north to nearby U Khanti Paya and then continue for about half an hour to the impressive Kyaikthanlan Paya. A covered walkway runs back towards town, but it's worth pressing on to see the mirrored interior of Mahamuni Paya.

Quiet little **Shampoo Island** (Gaungse Kyun), just a few minutes by boat from the city, makes an easy escape from the busy streets. The island is home to a collection of small stupas and is inhabited only by monks, nuns, and their dogs. The boat (K2000 return) runs from a shack beyond the abandoned *Mawylamyine Hotel* at the northern end of town.

Ogre Island

Around an hour out of town by ferry, **Ogre Island** is home to 200,000 people, most of whom are Mon. *Breeze Guest House* (see opposite) organizes trips to the island, charging K15000–19,000 per person, where you visit small workshops making things such as coconut-fibre doormats, rubber bands and walking sticks.

Win Sein Taw Ya

The 170m-long reclining Buddha, **Win Sein Taw Ya**, situated 24km south of Mawlamyine near Mudon, is remarkable both for its scale and for the fact that you can wander around inside it. Still a work in progress, and with an even larger counterpart being constructed opposite, it contains dozens of chambers with sculptures depicting scenes from the life of Buddha and grisly images from Buddhist hell. There are also several other shrines in the area. A motorbike taxi here will cost K6000 return, while a pick-up from the Zeigyo bus station is K700. It's a twenty-minute walk to the Buddha from the highway, or you could try to hop onto a pick-up.

Thanbyuzayat and around

Thanbyuzayat, 64km south of Mawlamyine, was the end point of the Burma–Siam "death railway", built under appalling conditions for the Japanese army by forced labour, including Allied prisoners of war. There's a locomotive and piece of track on display to commemorate it, and also a well-kept and soberingly low-key war cemetery. Buses run to Thanbyuzayat from Mawlamyine's main market (hourly 6am–4pm; 2hr).

The seaside town of **Kyaikkimi**, 9km northwest of Thanbyuzayat, is visited by locals for Yele Paya – a pagoda which is set on stilts over the sea. It can be reached by bus from Mawlamyine, or by pick-up from Thanbyuzayat. There's also a minibus from Mawlamyine market at 7am daily which visits Kyaikkami and then spends an hour or so at the grubby **Setse beach** before returning to Mawlamyine.

ARRIVAL AND INFORMATION

By plane The airport is 8km southeast of town, and can be reached by motorbike (K1500) or taxi (K3000).

Destinations Mae Sot, Thailand (daily; 30min); Yangon (weekly; 40min).

By boat There is no public ferry to Hpa-an, but private boats (4hr) run according to demand – often daily in peak season – at around K70,000 for the whole boat (up to ten passengers). Contact *Breeze Guest House* to book a seat.

By bus There are two bus stations: Myeinigone on the eastern side of the ridge that runs through the city, and Zeigyo to the south of town; buses to Hpa-an also depart from beside the football ground on the western side of the ridge. For connections to Inle Lake, take the Mandalay bus as far as Meiktila.

Destinations Dawei (daily; 10hr); Hpa-an (hourly; 2hr); Kinpun (2 daily; 4hr); Mandalay (2 daily; 12hr); Myeik (daily; 18hr); Nay Pyi Taw (daily; 10hr); Taungoo (2 daily; 7hr); Yangon (5 daily; 6hr 30min).

By shared taxi Vehicles depart for Myawaddy (6hr; K12,000), on the Thai border, between 8–10am every other day (as traffic can only run one way at a time along the road). Arrange a seat through your accommodation.

By train The train station is close to the bus station in the east of the city. Officials may be reluctant to sell you a ticket to Dawei.

Destinations Dawei (daily; 14hr); Yangon (3 daily; 8hr).

ACCOMMODATION

Aurora 277 Lower Main Rd, Mawlamyine ⓣ 057 227 85. The staff at this guesthouse one street back from the river aren't the most welcoming in town, but the rooms are a cut above their rivals at this price – they're brighter, larger, cleaner and have a little natural light. The cheapest rooms have shared bathrooms with squat toilets. **$12**

Breeze Guest House 6 Strand Rd, Mawlamyine ⓣ 057 21450 or ⓣ 09 8701180, ⓔ breeze.guesthouse@gmail.com. Still the unchallenged centre of Mawlamyine's backpacker scene, despite the resemblance of the cheapest rooms to prison cells. Even those who aren't staying drift in to arrange day-trips or pick up a town map. They take Visa and MasterCard for a charge of $3. **$16**

Family World Thanbyuzayat ⓣ 09 49820399. Hidden away in a residential district a short drive from the war cemetery, from which it's signposted, this concrete complex is a bit scruffy but it has views of the surrounding fields and the rooms are fine. Staff can help to arrange a tour of the area for around K8000. **K15,000**

EATING

A series of barbecue stalls set up in the evening on Strand Rd north of Dawei Jetty in Mawlamyine, selling affordable sticks of chicken and various innards.

Bone Gyi Strand Rd, opposite the first jetty north of *Breeze Guest House*. Considered by many locals to serve the best Chinese food in town. The menu is in English, but without prices; hot and sour fried squid costs K3500. Daily 8am–9pm.

YKKO Dawei Jetty ⓦ ykkomyanmar.com. Part of a chain with numerous branches in Yangon, this was a hot opening in a town short on good eating options. There's an extensive Chinese menu but the specialities are *kyay-oh* (variations on noodles and meatballs, some with *sichet* – fried garlic in garlic oil). Free wi-fi. Daily 10am–10pm.

DIRECTORY

Internet Unity, Lower Main Rd close to junction with Dawei Jetty Rd (daily 8.30am–9pm).

Money CB Bank, Strand Rd (currency exchange and ATM Mon–Fri 11am–3pm).

Motorbike rental *Breeze Guest House*, Strand Rd (K10,000/day); Kyaw pool club, one block north of *Breeze* (K8000/day).

7

HPA-AN

The riverside town of **Hpa-an** (pronounced "Pa-an") is small and welcoming enough to become familiar quickly, and the limestone hills surrounding it make for a very impressive backdrop to trips taking in pretty villages and caves full of Buddha statues. Many of the sights listed here can be combined into a day-trip or two, and the *Soe Brothers Guest House* provides maps and advice (as well as motorbike rental).

WHAT TO SEE AND DO

Good sunrise views can be enjoyed at serene **Kan Thar Yar Lake**, a twenty-minute walk south down Ohn Taw St; at sunset, the riverside **Shweyinhmyaw Paya**, a pagoda in the northwest of town, is particularly popular. Fabulous views of the Thanlwin River and its surrounding fields and limestone hills can also be enjoyed from the pagoda on **Mount Hpa-pu**, reached by taking the ferry (daily 6am–6pm; K500 each way) across the river from near Shweyinhmyaw Paya. Once across, head into the village and follow the sign for the mountain; the path swings right towards the river before curving back around. It's fifteen minutes to the start of the steps up, then thirty minutes to the top.

Mount Zwegabin

In the past, a stay at the monastery on top of **Mount Zwegabin** (725m) was one of southeastern Myanmar's highlights.

At the time of research, however, the immigration department had banned tourists from staying overnight. If you are interested, then check on the current situation at *Soe Brothers Guest House*.

Saddan Cave

The vast and atmospheric **Saddan Cave**, to the south of Mount Zwegabin, requires a torch to explore (or donate K3000 and they will switch on the lights) – it's a fifteen-minute walk through the cave, and slippery in places, so carry your shoes past the pagodas at the entrance then put them back on. There's a lake on the other side, and for K1000 local fishermen take visitors for a short ride. A motorbike taxi to Saddan costs K8000 return.

7

Kawgun and Yathaypyan caves

Over on the other side of the Thanlwin River from Hpa-an and Mount Zwegabin, the **Kawgun and Yathaypyan caves** are notable for their Buddhist art, some of which dates back to the seventh century. The most impressive art is at Kawgun (aka Kawthon; K3000), 13km southwest of Hpa-an, where thousands of gold-painted Buddha figures are attached to the walls. Yathaypyan (free), a couple of kilometres further west, is deeper and requires a torch if you want to reach the viewpoint at the far end. A motorbike taxi will charge K8000 to visit the two caves.

Lakkana village and Kawka Thawng cave

Scenically located **Lakkana village**, on the eastern side of Mount Zwegabin, is a delightful place to wander, while at nearby **Kawka Thawng cave** there is a cool spring-fed outdoor pool where locals swim (with women keeping well covered). There's also a cave where you can swim, although you'll probably need a torch to get down to the water.

A motorbike taxi will charge K5000 to visit both, or you can take a pick-up from the market in Hpa-an in the direction of Eindu and get off at Lakkana; it's a fifteen-minute walk from the village to the cave.

ARRIVAL AND DEPARTURE

By bus Most buses stop at the ticket offices (daily 6.30am–7pm) around the clock tower in the centre of town.
Destinations Dawei (3 daily; 10hr); Kinpun for Kyaiktiyo (daily; 3hr); Mandalay (daily; 12hr); Mawlamyine (6 daily; 2hr); Nay Pyi Taw (daily; 11hr); Taungoo (daily; 8hr); Yangon (6 daily; 7hr).

By boat Private boats to Mawlamyine (3hr; K8000) run when there is demand, and can be arranged through *Soe Brothers Guest House*.

By minibus The road to Myawaddy on the Thai border is narrow and traffic can only run in one direction each day; it is therefore possible to cross only on alternate days. Minibuses to the border (5hr; K10,000) depart at around 7am.

By pick-up The daily pick-up to Kinpun (for Kyaiktiyo) leaves at 7am.

ACCOMMODATION

Only a handful of places take foreigners and at peak times they can fill up, so consider calling ahead.

★**Soe Brothers Guest House** 2/146 Thitsa Rd Ⓣ058 21372 or Ⓣ09 49771823, Ⓔsoebrothers05821372@gmail.com. The rooms are decent in this well-established budget favourite, but more importantly the staff are expert at dealing with backpackers' needs. No breakfast, though. They can arrange tours combining various sights outside of town (day-trip K30,000 per group) and also rent out motorbikes (K8000/day plus petrol). **$12**

Than Lwin Oo Thida Rd Ⓣ058 21513. Little English is spoken and the sign simply reads "Guest House", but it's worth checking out this new place if you're on a tight budget. The a/c rooms (double K10,000) don't have their own units but instead have vents letting in cold air from the corridor. It's odd but it works. No breakfast and no towels provided. **K8000**

EATING AND DRINKING

San Ma Tau 1/290 Bogyoke Rd. This place has a well-deserved reputation for great Burmese food, though that does mean that it's often packed with foreigners. Pick from a wide variety of curries – most K500 (veg) or K1500 (meat/fish) – and it will be served with ten tasty side-dishes and soup. Rice is another K500. Daily 10am–9pm.

Shwe Htone Maung Thitsa St. This teahouse is extremely popular with locals, with an energizing if chaotic vibe. It serves a better than average range of breakfast options such as potato purée (two purées with curry and spicy sauce, K500), as well as the usual *mohingar* and Shan noodles. Daily breakfast to dinner.

DIRECTORY

Internet Cyber Café, just southeast of the clock tower (daily 8am–10pm).

Money CB Bank, 2/154, Thitsa St, has currency exchange (Mon–Fri 11am–2.30pm).

Post office School St (Mon–Fri 9.30am–3pm).

DAWEI

Only recently opened to overland travel, **Dawei** is set to be transformed as the site of a $50bn deep sea port from which goods will be transported to Bangkok and beyond. Although there have been severe setbacks, changes are already under way including new hotels built in town and a shopping mall under construction. It has also meant the opening of a **border crossing** for foreigners at Htee Khee, 160km east and providing access to Kanchanaburi in Thailand. This should see Dawei firmly established on the backpacker trail over the next few years.

WHAT TO SEE AND DO

It's a pleasant place to wander but there isn't much to do in Dawei town itself, other than visit the **Shwe Taung Za** pagoda, which has a large Buddha with a polished face. The town is a good base for day-trips, though, and your accommodation should be able to help arrange a motorbike and driver (K10,000 per day). Sights include the very large **Shwe That Layan** reclining Buddha and **Saba Taung Hill**, which was used as a base by Japanese forces during World War II. There's a monastery on the hill, as well as a few wartime buildings and a network of tunnels. The latter are hidden beneath vegetation and are not safe to explore without a guide.

Dawei also provides access to **Maungmakan Beach**, a thirty-minute (K2000) motorbike ride away. It's an attractive sweep of sand, once you get away from the litter which blights the main stretch of restaurants. With a rental motorbike (K5000 per day from *Coconut Guesthouse*) you can strike out and find your own immaculate spot, or visit nearby hot springs.

ARRIVAL AND DEPARTURE

By bus The bus station is north of the town. Minibuses to the Thai border (4hr; K30,000) run daily 7–11am, getting you there in time to cross and continue travel in Thailand – the bus to Kanchanaburi takes 3hr.

Destinations Hpa-an (3 daily; 10hr); Mawlamyine (3 daily; 10hr); Myeik (4 daily; 7–8hr); Yangon (3 daily; 15hr).

By train The main train station is just east of the town; there's also another station to the south but it's less convenient.

Destinations Mawlamyine (daily; 14hr); Yangon (3 daily; 23hr 30min).

ACCOMMODATION

There are two places licensed for tourists on Maungmakan Beach itself but they are both pricey and have strong government links.

★**Coconut Guesthouse** Maungmakan village ⓣ 09 8752293. A 10min walk from the beach, this relaxing Burmese–French-owned place has ten rooms. There are two singles for $20, but if they're full there's unfortunately no single occupancy discount for the eight doubles. Nevertheless it's a backpacker favourite in the making. **$25**

Shwe Moung Than 665 Pakaukku Kyaung St, Dawei ⓣ 059 23763. The ordinary doubles in this bright pink hotel are nothing special for K35,000 but the top-floor "cheap rooms" are the best bargain in town. You get all the important facilities – a/c, hot water and wi-fi in the lobby – but with simpler decor and no TV. **K15,000**

EATING AND DRINKING

Palé Eikari 572 Ye Yeik Tha St ⓣ 059 21780. In the evening they put out chairs and tables in the garden of this hotel restaurant, which specializes in seafood dishes such as hot and sour prawns (K4500) although there are also simple noodle dishes (K1800). Daily 7am–10pm.

DIRECTORY

Money CB Bank, 54 Rzarni Road, has currency exchange (Mon–Fri 9am–2.30pm).

THE FAR SOUTH

The town of **Myeik** (Mergui) was previously visited only by high-spending tourists en route to the very expensive, and very beautiful, Myeik Archipelago. There is still no affordable way to visit the islands, but now that Tanintharyi Region has been opened up for overland travel a steady trickle of foreigners is passing through Myeik on the way to or from **Kawthaung** (which has a border crossing with Ranong in Thailand). The road between Kawthaung and Myeik is closed to foreigners, but boats run along the coast when the weather allows.

Bagan and the central plains

The **central plains** – the arid lands between the Ayeyarwady River in the west and the Shan hills to the east – have seen many kingdoms rise and fall, including that of the Pyu who were the earliest inhabitants of Myanmar for whom records exist. The ruins of Thayekhittaya, close to the busy trading town of **Pyay**, still hint at the grandeur of the Pyu dynasty, which was at its peak from the fifth to ninth centuries. The mighty sixteenth-century dynasty based further east in **Taungoo**, on the other hand, left fewer tangible traces, but the town is still a rewarding place to spend a day or two exploring off the tourist trail. The same cannot be said of the military junta's twenty-first-century stab at a "royal capital", which is the literal translation of **Nay Pyi Taw**.

Certainly the new capital has nothing to compare to **Bagan**, but then again few places in the world can offer a spectacle as breathtaking as its vast stupa- and temple-strewn plain. In the eleventh century, King Anawrahta of Bagan became the first to unite the lands that now form Myanmar, and today the legacy of his embrace of Theravada Buddhism exerts a stronger influence on tourist imaginations than anywhere else in the country.

BAGAN

The sheer scale of **BAGAN** (formerly known as Pagan), which covers 67 square kilometres and includes more than two thousand Buddhist structures, is almost impossible to take in. Individual temples, stupas and monasteries impress in different ways – for their evocative frescoes, their imposing bulk or their graceful simplicity – but it's the broader sweep that tends to stay etched in visitors' memories: the spectacle of hot-air balloons rising from behind stupas at dawn, the cool, calm relief of temple interiors in the heat of the day, or grand sunset vistas viewed from terraces.

This stretch of the Ayeyarwady River has a long history of settlement, only rising to prominence in its own right with its 42nd king, Anawrahta, who came to the throne in 1044. He also kick-started the building activity, but it really picked up pace under King Kyansittha (who ruled from 1084–1112): formerly Anawrahta's general, he was exiled for falling in love with a princess who was supposed to marry the king, but he later returned to claim the throne.

By the end of the thirteenth century, most of the building had been finished. An earthquake in 1975 destroyed or damaged many of the temples, and overenthusiastic reconstruction is widely evident, yet collectively they remain magnificently evocative of Bagan's golden age.

ARCHITECTURE AND DECORATION IN BAGAN

Although there are a few exceptions, most of the ancient structures in Bagan are either stupas (**paya**) or temples (**pahto**). The former are usually placed over relics or Buddha images, and are solid spires or cylinders with pointed or domed tops. The latter are square or rectangular structures that can be entered. The earliest buildings bear evidence of being designed by Mon architects, brought back by Anawrahta after he conquered Thaton: early stupas are simple elongated cylinders while later ones are more elaborate and bell-like; later temples tend to be larger and more complex.

The exterior walls of temples are often decorated with **stucco**; one popular image is the *bălù pàn-zwèh*, the face of an ogre holding garlands of flowers in its mouth. The interior walls of many temples bear **murals** based on the Jataka, stories of the previous reincarnations of the Buddha. Other murals depict mythical creatures such as the *kein-năra* bird-man, a symbol of fidelity. The earliest paintings reflect Indian artistic styles, as many artists were Brahmin. Writing on the walls ranges from records of donations to curses on anyone desecrating the temples.

WHAT TO SEE AND DO

The main transport hub is **Nyaung U**, which is the nearest thing here to a large town, although once you get off the main roads it quickly feels like a village. It's where most budget travellers base themselves, and has by far the largest range of restaurants.

Southwest from here is **Old Bagan**, an area that includes the site of the old walled palace and has the greatest concentration of must-see temples and pagodas – they're packed in to the extent that you can walk between them, unlike in other parts of Bagan. The government expelled the residents of Old Bagan in 1990 partly so that it could be converted into a tourist zone.

New Bagan, a largely unengaging grid of streets to the south, is where the residents were relocated. It's worth passing through even if you aren't staying in one of its mid-range hotels, though, as there are a few impressive temples in the area.

In addition to these larger settlements, there are a number of smaller villages dotted around the area. The most notable are **Myinkaba**, on the main Old Bagan–New Bagan road and home to many lacquerware shops, and **Wet Kyi Inn**, a village immediately west of Nyaung U which has several hotels and guesthouses.

Foreign visitors are required to pay a $15 fee on arrival in Bagan, covering entry to all the temples, although the ticket is usually only checked in selected larger ones. Those buildings which can be entered or climbed are normally open during daylight hours, although you may need to locate the keyholder for smaller temples.

A large part of the pleasure of Bagan lies in exploring and visiting buildings as they catch your eye, but if time really is limited, then don't miss Shwezigon Paya, Ananda Pahto, Shwesandaw Paya and Dhammayangyi Pahto. At sunset everyone rushes to find temples which can be climbed for good views: Shwesandaw Paya and Pyathada Paya are particularly popular, while slightly quieter options include Buledi. The upper parts of some temples are off-limits.

Nyaung U

Nyaung U's most important stupa is the early twelfth-century **Shwezigon Paya**. Still an active place of worship, it's said to contain three different relics of the Buddha: a tooth, a collarbone and a frontlet (headband). The design of Shwezigon was a prototype for many later pagodas within Myanmar: the circular stupa sits on three square terraces, each level bearing clay plaques decorated with *Jataka* scenes, and an octagonal base. On each of the four sides is a shrine containing a 4m standing Buddha made of *pyin-zá-làw-ha* (an alloy of gold, silver, lead, tin and bronze).

There are also a few "cave" sites around Nyaung U, including **Thamiwhet Umin** and **Hmyatha Umin**, which are tunnels designed for meditation and carved into the sandstone hills about 1km southeast of the town. There's another similar complex, **Kyansittha Umin**, just north of the main road as you head towards Wet Kyi Inn village. Bring a torch.

Between Nyaung U and Old Bagan

There are some very good murals, dating back to 1794 but in an older style, in the **Upali Thein** ordination hall (one of only a handful still to be found in Bagan), about halfway between Wet Kyi Inn village and Old Bagan.

Htilominlo Pahto, on the other side of the road, is one of the largest temples in the area, supposedly built on the spot where a prince called Htilominlo was chosen as successor to King Narapati Sithu (who ruled from 1173–1210). The murals inside include horoscopes, possibly indicating auspicious times for events taking place at the temple.

Shortly before Tharaba Gate (see p.556), you reach the white-and-gold **Ananda Pahto**. Built at the end of the eleventh century in the shape of a cross, with all arms the same length and a square chamber at the centre, it has been described as the crowning achievement of early-period Bagan architecture. A 9.5m teak standing Buddha faces out on each side, representing the four Buddhas who have so far achieved enlightenment in the current era (Gautama Buddha was the

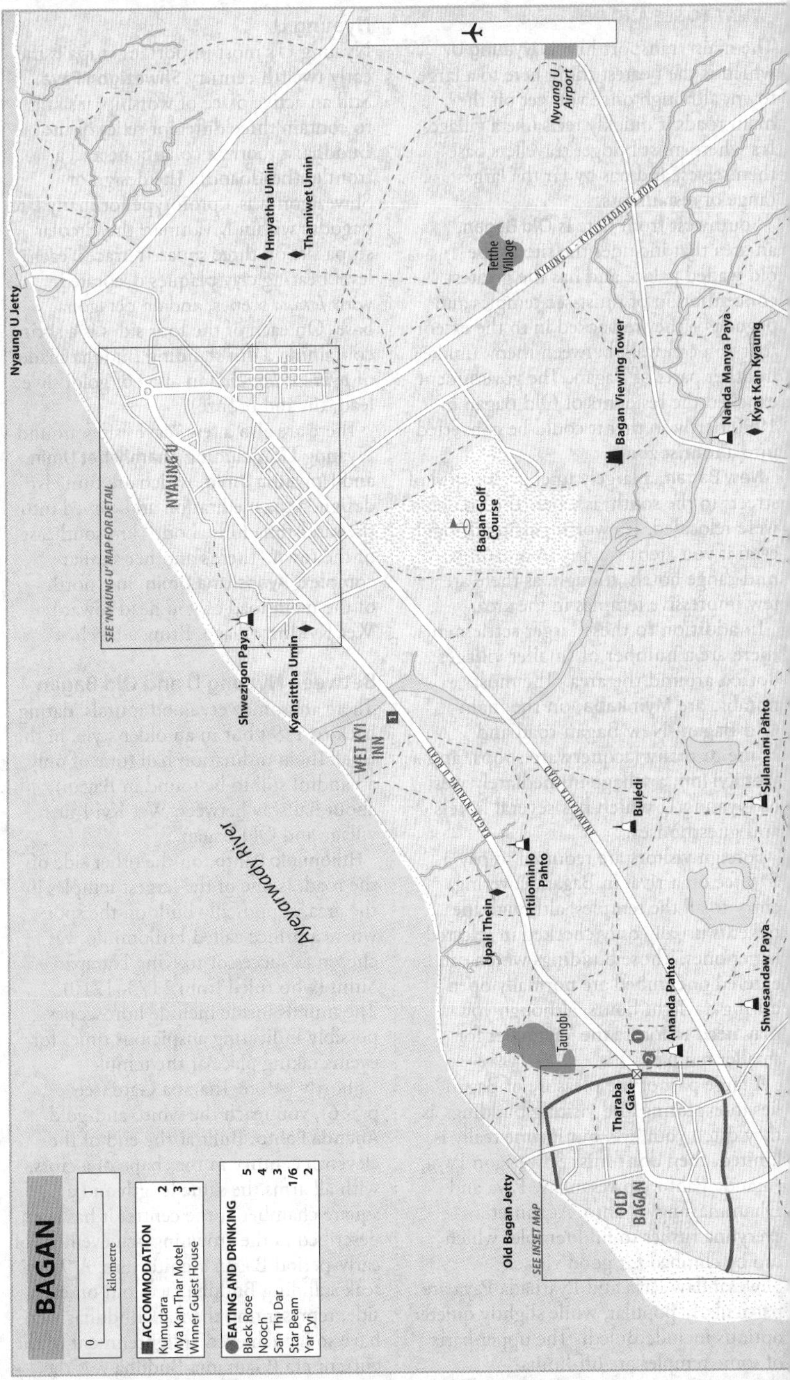

BAGAN
0
1
kilometre
ACCOMMODATION
Kumudara 2
Mya Kan Thar Motel 3
Winner Guest House 1
EATING AND DRINKING
Black Rose 5
Nooch 4
San Thi Dar 3
Star Beam 1/6
Yar Pyi 2
Nyaung U Jetty
SEE 'NYAUNG U' MAP FOR DETAIL
NYAUNG U
Shwezigon Paya
Kyansittha Umin
Hmyatha Umin
Thamiwet Umin
Ayeyarwady River
WET KYI INN
BAGAN-NYAUNG U ROAD
ANAWRAHTA ROAD
NYAUNG U - KYAUKPADAUNG ROAD
Bagan Golf Course
Tetthe Village
Nyuang U Airport
Upali Thein
Htilominlo Pahto
Old Bagan Jetty
SEE INSET MAP
Taungbi
OLD BAGAN
Tharaba Gate
Buledi
Ananda Pahto
Bagan Viewing Tower
Nanda Manya Paya
Kyat Kan Kyaung
Shwesandaw Paya
Sulamani Pahto

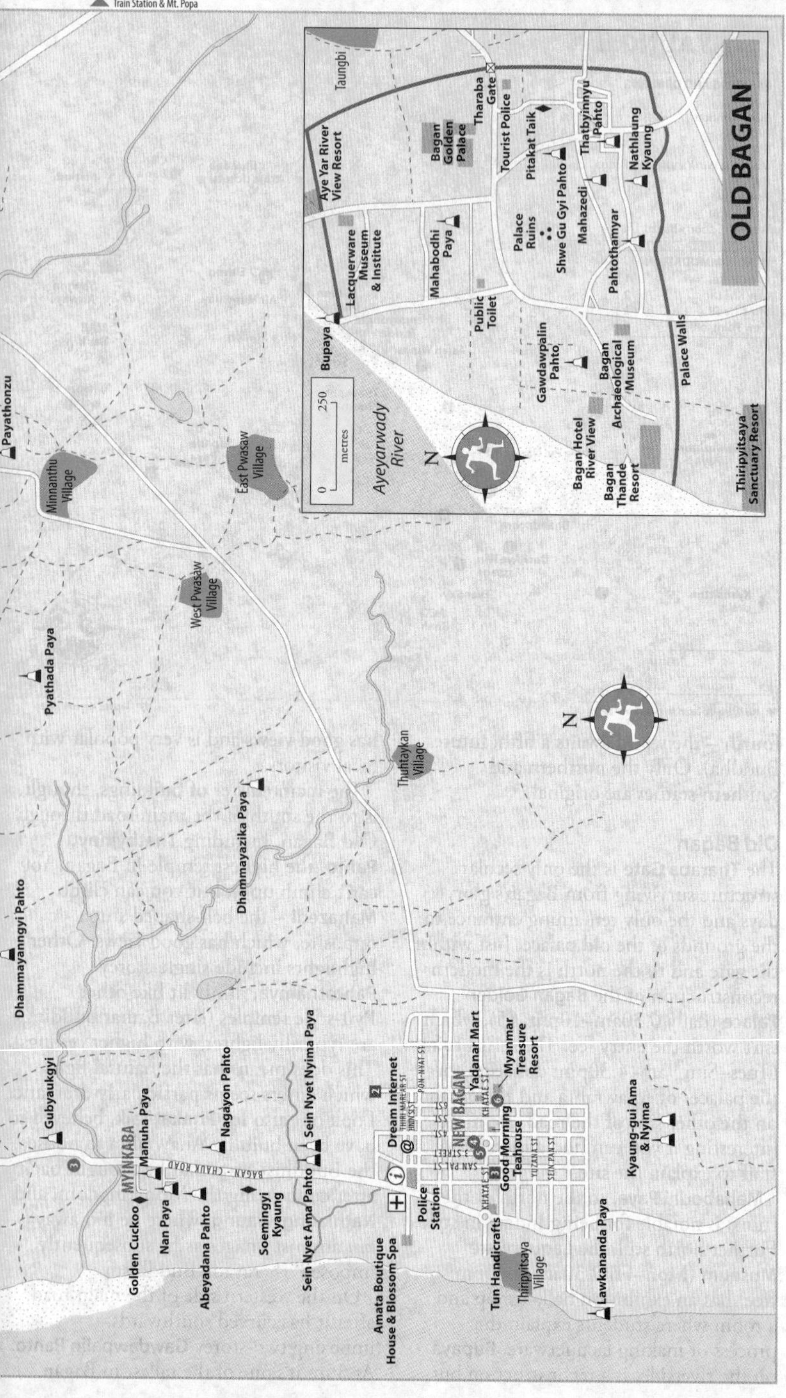

Train Station & Mt. Popa
Payathonzu
Minnanthu Village
East Pwasaw Village
West Pwasaw Village
Pyathada Paya
Thuhtaykan Village
Dhammayazika Paya
Dhammayanngyi Pahto
Gubyaukgyi
MYINKABA
Manuha Paya
Nagayon Pahto
Sein Nyet Nyima Paya
Golden Cuckoo
Nan Paya
Abeyadana Pahto
Soemingyi Kyaung
Sein Nyet Ama Pahto
BAGAN - CHAUK ROAD
Amata Boutique House & Blossom Spa
Police Station
Dream Internet
NEW BAGAN
Yadanar Mart
Myanmar Treasure Resort
Good Morning Teahouse
Tun Handicrafts
Thiripyitsaya Village
Lawkananda Paya
Kyaung-gui Ama & Nyima
N

OLD BAGAN
Taungbi
Aye Yar River View Resort
Bagan Golden Palace
Tharaba Gate
Tourist Police
Pitakat Taik
Thatbyinnyu Pahto
Nathlaung Kyaung
Lacquerware Museum & Institute
Mahabodhi Paya
Palace Ruins
Shwe Gu Gyi Pahto
Mahazedi
Pahtothamyar
Bupaya
Public Toilet
Gawdawpalin Pahto
Bagan Archaeological Museum
Palace Walls
Ayeyarwady River
Bagan Hotel River View
Bagan Thande Resort
Thiripyitsaya Sanctuary Resort
0 250 metres
N

7

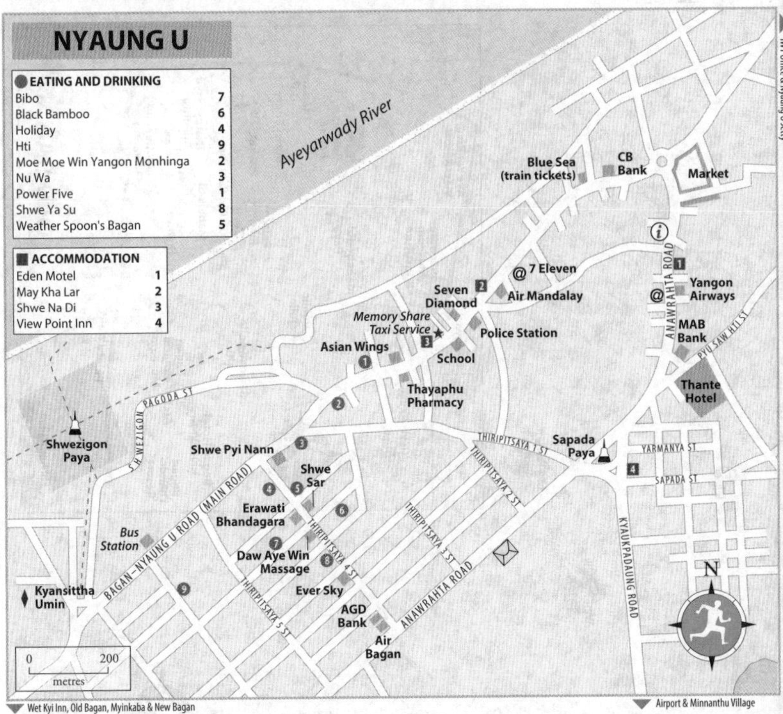

fourth – the world awaits a fifth, future Buddha). Only the northern and southern statues are original.

Old Bagan

The **Tharaba Gate** is the only secular structure surviving from Bagan's glory days and the only remaining entrance to the grounds of the old palace. Just within the gate and to the north is the modern reconstruction of the **Bagan Golden Palace** (daily 6.30am–10pm; $5), which isn't worth the entry fee. The actual **ruins** (Tues–Sun 9am–4.30pm; donation) of the palaces of Anawrahta and Kyansittha, on the other side of the road, are more interesting if you can find a member of staff to explain the site.

Mahabodhi Paya, to the north of the ruins, is notable for being Indian in style. Further north still, the **Laquerware Museum** (Mon–Fri 9.30am–4.30pm; free) has an exhibition hall, a shop and a room where students explain the process of making lacquerware. **Bupaya**, on the riverside, is a reconstruction but has good views and is very popular with local visitors.

The main cluster of buildings, though, is to the south of the main road through Old Bagan, including **Thatbyinnyu Pahto**, the highest temple in Bagan. You can't climb up it, but you can climb **Mahazedi** – the bell-shaped stupa opposite, which has good views. Other highlights include single-storey **Pahtothamya**, dimly lit like other Pyu-style temples (later Bamar buildings are typically lighter, with higher ceilings). This does mean that the natural light which enters seems particularly dramatic. Look out also for **Pitakat Taik**, believed to have been built by Anawrahta to house the Buddhist texts that he brought back after conquering the Mon kingdom, and **Nathlaung Kyaung**, where he hid away *nat* animist images as he subsequently imposed Theravada Buddhism.

On the western side of the main road, after it has curved southwards, is imposing two-storey **Gawdawpalin Pahto**. At 55m it's one of the tallest in Bagan.

South of Old Bagan

Not far south of Old Bagan are two of the most popular temples. **Shwesandaw Paya**, just south of Anawrahta Road, is particularly inundated with tour buses at sunset; the five-terraced temple has been over-restored but the views of surrounding temples are very good. The sharply tapered spire was a prototype for many others in Bagan and elsewhere in the country.

About 500m east of Shwesandaw Paya is the huge **Dhammayangyi**, said to have been started by King Narathu in 1166 but left unfinished after he died four years later. He was renowned as a particularly cruel king and it is said that he had one of his wives – an Indian princess – executed, but paid for it when her father sent assassins to kill him. The interior decoration is minimal, and nobody really knows why (or when) the inner passageways were bricked up.

Around Myinkaba

To the north of Myinkaba village, **Gubyaukgyi** has some of the best stucco work to be found in Bagan. Further along, **Manuha Paya** is notable for squeezing three large seated Buddhas and one reclining figure into rooms barely big enough to contain them. This sense of confinement is said – with a bit of poetic licence – to reflect the fact that King Manuha of Thaton commissioned the temple while he was imprisoned by Anawrahta.

There are further temples just south of Myinkaba. **Nagayon Pahto** is said to be built on the spot where Kyansittha, who later became king, was protected from his brother Sawlu by a huge *naga* (a serpent – one shelters the largest of the standing Buddha figures). The decorations reflect Theravada Buddhism, while nearby **Abeyadana Pahto** – built at the same time – is said to have been constructed for Kyansittha's wife Abeyadana, who adhered to Mahayana Buddhism. Its murals include deities borrowed from Hinduism, as well as Bodhisattvas.

Soemingyi Kyaung, just a little further along the main road, is the only surviving example in Bagan of a courtyard surrounded by meditation cells.

New Bagan

At the northern edge of New Bagan sit the thirteenth-century **Sein Nyet Ama Pahto** and **Sein Nyet Nyima Paya**. The temple has some fine stucco work, while the stupa has an unusual ribbed finial. West of the town and with good river views, in a spot which was once an important port, is **Lawkananda Paya**. Built by Anawrahta in the eleventh century to enshrine a replica of a Buddha tooth relic, its bell-shaped dome is more elongated than on later buildings.

Around Minnanthu

The village of Minnanthu is close to the road that runs inland from New Bagan to Nyaung U and the airport. En route to it, the majestic **Dhammayazaka Paya** is visible from the road, although set back from it. Unusually it has pentagonal terraces rather than square ones, and they provide very good sunset views of the temples dotted across the plain.

To the north of Minnanthu lie a number of interesting temples, including **Payathonzu**, which has a distinctive triple-stupa design and some unfinished sketches among the murals inside. Close by is an underground monastery called **Kyat Kan Kyaung**, which is still in use but is pretty bare other than for a small shrine. Back above ground, **Nanda Manya Paya** has well-preserved murals, including images of half-naked women tempting the Buddha to abandon his meditation.

ARRIVAL AND DEPARTURE

Buses will usually stop at a government post so that foreign passengers can pay the $15 Bagan entry fee. It is also collected at the airport and jetties.

By plane Nyaung U airport is around 4km southeast of town. A taxi to or from the airport costs K5000 (Nyaung U), K6000 (Old Bagan) or K7000 (New Bagan).

Destinations Heho (6 daily; 40min–1hr 30min); Mandalay (5 daily; 30min); Thandwe (2–3 daily; 1hr 55min); Yangon (11 daily; 1hr 15min–4hr 25min).

By bus The bus station is on the Main Rd in Nyaung U. It may be possible to reach Mrauk U via Magwe, although at the time of research few people had done so without a permit and private car.

Destinations Kalaw (2 daily; 8hr); Magwe (2 daily; 4hr); Mandalay (5 daily; 7–8hr); Nay Pyi Taw (1–2 daily; 5hr); Nyaungshwe for Inle Lake (3 daily; 10hr); Pakkoku

(4 daily; 1hr); Pyay (daily; 10hr 30min); Yangon (5–6 daily; 10hr).

By train The station is around 5.5km southeast of Nyaung U, and a taxi between the two costs K7000. You can buy tickets from Blue Sea (T 061 60949 or T 09 2040135), a frozen food retailer on the main road in Nyaung U.

Destinations Mandalay (daily; 8hr); Pyay (2–3 weekly; 9–10hr); Yangon (daily; 17hr).

By boat All services leave from the jetties in either Nyaung U (northeast of the market) or Old Bagan (outside the old walls, to the north), with the departure point depending on water levels. Three private operators, N Mai Hka, Malikha 2 and Mayanmar Golden River Group (MGRG), run tourist boats to Mandalay ($35 including breakfast; MGRG also include lunch). All services depart at 6am and arrive at 4.30–5.30pm, although be prepared for a late arrival. It's easiest to buy tickets through tour agencies (see below). The government agency, IWT, which has an office selling tickets close to the Nyaung U jetty, runs slow boats to Mandalay (Mon & Thurs 7am; 34hr; $10).

7

INFORMATION

Guides Licensed guides can be hired for $30/day from tour agencies or through accommodation.

Tourist information There are official tourist offices (daily 9.30am–4.30pm) on Anawrahta Rd in Nyaung U and on Main Rd in New Bagan.

Tour agencies Ever Sky, Thiripyitsaya 4 St, Nyaung U (daily 7.30am–9.30pm; T 061 60895 or T 09 43008170, E everskynanda@gmail.com); Seven Diamond, Main Rd, Nyaung U (daily 8.30am–5pm; T 061 60883).

GETTING AROUND

By bicycle Many places rent out bikes, including most accommodation. Expect to pay up to K4000/day in Old or New Bagan, or K1500/day in Nyaung U. Get a bike with a light, or bring a head torch, if you plan to stay out for sunset – there are few street lights and the main roads can be busy as night falls.

By boat Sunset sightseeing boats depart from Old Bagan jetty around 4.30pm (K10,000 per boat for up to four people; 1hr).

By electric bicycle Foreigners are not allowed to rent motorbikes in Bagan, but enterprising shops and restaurants get around this by renting imported Chinese e-bikes to tourists for K8000/day. It's a fun way to travel, but they aren't especially robust and are very heavy to pedal if you run out of juice.

By horse and cart A popular option for getting around the temples, although it's generally slower than cycling. From Nyaung U, expect to pay around K18,000/day, going no further than Myinkaba (heading to New Bagan would cost K3000–4000 extra).

By pick-up Vehicles run roughly hourly between Nyaung U and New Bagan (K1000; 45min), via Old Bagan and Myinkaba, until 4pm and less frequently after that. They stop at the main junction in New Bagan, Tharabar Gate in Old Bagan, and at the roundabout by the main market in Nyaung U.

ACCOMMODATION

Most travellers on a tight budget stay in Nyaung U or Wet Kyi Inn. There are no budget hotels in Old Bagan, and if you do feel like treating yourself then there's better value in New Bagan's mid-range accommodation.

NYAUNG U

Eden Motel Anawrahta Rd T 061 60639; map p.556. Split into two parts on opposite sides of the road; some rooms in *Eden Motel I* have bamboo-covered walls and wooden floors, while *Eden Motel II* goes for concrete, although at least the newest rooms are brightly painted. **$25**

May Kha Lar Main Rd T 061 60304; map p.556. A reliable and popular budget choice, even if some of the rooms are rough around the edges. All have a/c and some have wi-fi; a private bathroom costs $10 extra. **$20**

Shwe Na Di Main Rd T 061 60409 or T 09 402510138; map p.556. The cheapest rooms here have shared bathrooms, while a few more dollars will get you slightly shabby en-suite facilities. The newer, very pink, block at the back has the nicest rooms ($30). All have a/c. **$15**

View Point Inn Anawrahta Rd T 061 61070 or T 09 2043096; map p.556. The bare-bones fan rooms (with shared bathroom) at this family-run guesthouse are the cheapest you're likely to find in Bagan, and they also have a/c rooms for $15 or $17 (en suite). There's even a small and very basic dorm with beds for $5, although you don't get breakfast. **$13**

WET KYI INN

Winner Guest House Main Rd T 061 61069 or T 09 402501091; map pp.554–555. The cheapest rooms here are concrete-floored boxes with shared bathrooms, but at least they're cheap by Bagan standards and the place has

★TREAT YOURSELF

Kumudara Corner of 5th & Daw Na St, New Bagan T 061 65142 or T 09 6505221, W kumudara-bagan.com; map pp.554–555. This hotel benefits from the best temple views of any establishment outside of Old Bagan, particularly around dawn when hot-air balloon flights take off. The rooms are getting a little dated, but still represent good value (unlike wi-fi at $10 per day, although there's limited free access on their computers). There's a swimming pool and restaurant. **$45**

wi-fi. Rooms with a/c ($20) and private bathroom ($25) are also available. **$18**

NEW BAGAN

Mya Kan Thar Motel Main Rd ☎ 061 65014 or ☎ 09 2042005, ✉ uzawweikbgn@gmail.com; map pp.554–555. Two rows of concrete buildings located on the main road (so try to get a room at the back). The plain but comfortable rooms are equipped with new a/c units, and are good value in New Bagan terms. **$30**

EATING AND DRINKING

NYAUNG U

Thiripitsaya 4 St is lined with restaurants aimed at tourists, typically cooking many cuisines adequately rather than specializing in one. Main Rd has more restaurants frequented by locals. As for nightlife, there are a few places serving draught beer, including *Holiday* (daily 7am–10pm) and *Shwe Ya Su* (daily 10am–10.30pm) on Thiripitsaya 4 St, *Power Five* (daily 8am–midnight) on the Main Rd and *Hti* (daily 9am–midnight) close to the bus station.

Bibo Just off Thiripitsaya 4 St; map p.556. Relocated to larger premises in 2014, *Bibo* is run by a hospitable young couple offering superior versions of the usual Thai, Burmese and Italian dishes, such as river prawn curry for K4000. It's also a good place for an early-evening drink: cocktails are already cheap at K1500, making happy hour (5.30–7pm) a steal. Daily 8.30am–9pm or later.

Black Bamboo Just off Thiripitsaya 4 St ☎ 061 60782 or ☎ 09 6501444; map p.556. The perfect place to hide from the midday sun, this garden restaurant serves Asian and European dishes – the former around K3500, the latter K5000–6000. Check the blackboards for desserts, cakes and specials such as *granita* (crushed ice drinks, K2000). Daily 8.30am–10pm.

Moe Moe Win Yangon Monhinga Main Rd; map p.556. As the name suggests, this small restaurant specializes in the breakfast dish *mohingar* (K1000) and does a great job of it. It also serves other dishes such as *ohno khao swe* (K1000) and, for the adventurous, the mysteriously named "mythical dish" (also K1000). Daily 6am–9pm.

Nu Wa Main Rd; map p.556. If you're sick of the tourist-oriented restaurants around the corner on Thiripisaya 4 St, try this simple place serving Burmese curries. For K2500 you can choose one meat curry, along with rice and around ten side dishes; an extra K1000 lets you sample several meat dishes. Daily 10am–10pm.

★Weather Spoon's Bagan Thiripitsaya 4 St; map p.556. The name may amuse UK visitors (ask owner Win Tun about where it came from) but the food is seriously good – and the graffiti on the walls from satisfied customers is testament to this. The menu covers mostly Thai and Italian dishes, although the burger (K3500) is surprisingly authentic. Free wi-fi. Daily 7/8am–10pm.

OLD BAGAN

There is a clutch of restaurants just outside the Tharabar Gate, north of Ananda Paya.

★Star Beam North of Ananda Paya; map pp.554–555. Not only is this one of the best restaurants in Bagan, it's also one of the best in the country. Owner and chef Tin Myint has many years of experience in luxury hotels, and it shows in his cooking but – crucially – not in the very reasonable prices. Start with free baguettes baked on the premises, then move on to dishes such as *kyet that thoke* (chicken salad with peanut, lime juice, fish sauce and sesame seed, K3000) or exquisite grilled river fish with lemon butter sauce (K4500). End with a decadent chocolate fondant (K2500). Daily 10am–10pm.

Yar Pyi North of Ananda Paya; map pp.554–555. A rival to the more established *The Moon* vegetarian restaurant nearby, this friendly family-run place arguably has better food. The veggie curries are tasty – the owners recommend the hot-and-sour bamboo shoots (K2000) – and the guacamole with pappadom (K2500) is highly rated too. Daily 7am–11pm.

MYNKABA

San Thi Dar Main Rd; map pp.554–555. A couple of things set this simple restaurant apart from many of its competitors. One is the unusually extensive selection of vegetarian options (around K1200) alongside the usual meat dishes. The other is the friendliness of the famlly which runs it, who help to make a meal here a genuine pleasure. Daily 8am–9pm.

NEW BAGAN

There are a number of restaurants and tea shops on Khayae St, plus a few tucked away in the backstreets. Look out for the new *Star Beam* offshoot (see Old Bagan), due to open here during 2014.

Black Rose Khayae St; map pp.554–555. A family-run restaurant serving mostly Chinese and Burmese cuisine from around K2000, where you'll find very good food and a warm welcome (even if they do sometimes get very busy with tour groups). After the meal they give you tasty tamarind flakes – sweet and sour, these are supposedly an aid to digestion. Daily 10am–10.30pm.

Nooch Khayae St; map pp.554–555. At lunchtime Chinese, Burmese and Thai dishes (from around K2500) are served in the purple-themed a/c dining room, while in the evening the staff fire up a barbecue and set up outdoor seating. Daily 7am–late.

SHOPPING

Books There are two book stalls on the western approach to Ananda Temple.

General handicrafts Shwe Pyi Nann, junction of Thiripitsaya 4 St and Main Rd, Nyaung U (daily 9am–9pm; ☎ 061 60179); Amata Boutique House, Bagan–Chauk Road, New Bagan (daily 10am–10pm; ☎ 061 65099, 🌐 amatabtqhouse.com). The latter also has a café, spa and restaurant.

7

Groceries Yadanar Mart, Khayae St, New Bagan (daily 7am–9pm).

Lacquerware Lacquerware production has a long history here and there are many workshops and showrooms, particularly in Myinkaba. Golden Cuckoo, Myinkaba (daily 7.30am–10pm; ☎061 65156 or ☎09 5142421); Tun Handicrafts, 6/1 Khanlaung Quarter, New Bagan (daily 8am–9pm; ☎061 65063 or ☎09 2042295).

Parasols Pathein parasols (K5000–K11,000) from Shwe Sar, Thiripitsaya 4 St, Nyaung U (daily 8am–11pm).

Photographs Erawati Bhandagara, Thiripitsaya 4 St (daily 8am–10pm), sells good photos of Bagan and beyond, mostly for around $25–45.

DIRECTORY

7

Banks AGD Bank money change kiosk, Thiripitsaya 4 St (Mon–Fri 9.30am–3pm); MAB Bank with money change and ATM, Anawrahta Rd (Mon–Fri 10.30am–2pm); CB Bank, Anawrahta Rd (Mon–Fri 9.30am–3pm).

Internet Shwe Pyi Nann complex, junction of Thiripitsaya 4 St and Main Rd, Nyaung U (daily 9am–10pm); 7 Eleven, Main Rd, Nyaung U (daily 7am–11pm); Perfect, *Pyi Sone* restaurant, Main Rd, Wet Kyi Inn (daily 7am–9.30pm); Dream Internet Access, 3rd St, New Bagan.

Massage and spa Daw Aye Win, Thiripitsaya 4 St, Nyaung U (daily 8am–10pm; K7000/hr).

Pharmacy Thayaphu, Main Rd, Nyaung U (daily 7am–10pm).

Post office Anawrahta Rd, Nyaung U (Mon–Fri 9am–5pm, Sat 9am–noon).

Swimming pool There are pools open to the public at *Thante Hotel*, Nyaung U ($6), and *Thande Hotel*, Old Bagan ($5).

MOUNT POPA

The most popular side-trip from Bagan, **MOUNT POPA** volcano rises 1518m above sea level and is considered to be the home of the 37 *nats* (animist spirits; see p.43). Although a handful of pilgrims do ascend the main peak, most people instead visit a temple on top of a volcanic plug known as **Taungkalat** (737m) on the southwestern flank. There are almost eight hundred steps to climb, and the tiring walk is not helped by the many monkeys.

Views from the top are good, but opinions are divided on whether it's a worthwhile half-day visit. It helps to arrange a guide from Bagan (around $30) who will be able to explain the mountain's religious significance.

ARRIVAL AND DEPARTURE

By pick-up A pick-up to Mount Popa (2hr 30min; K6000 return) leaves Nyaung U bus station at 8am, returning at 1pm. If there are too few passengers for Mount Popa, the pick-up will go only as far as Kyaukpadaung (1hr 30min), where you'll need to change for the final 1hr journey to Mount Popa.

By taxi Most people visit by taxi from Bagan arranged through their accommodation or a travel agent, either a private vehicle (K35,000–45,000) or a shared taxi (K10,000 per person). The latter can also be arranged at Memory shared taxi service (Main Rd, Nyaung U; ☎09 2043579, Ⓔkohtaybgn@gmail.com).

TAUNGOO

TAUNGOO was the centre of a sizeable sixteenth-century empire that defeated Siam and brought the Shan lands under its control. Its king, Bayinnaung, has been much loved by the military junta and the current government. Today the town is a pleasant place to spend a day on the journey between Yangon and Mandalay.

WHAT TO SEE AND DO

The forests around Taungoo are key logging areas and the town's **central market** (daily 8am–4pm) is the only one in the country selling off-the-shelf items used by elephant handlers.

The grandest pagoda in town is **Shwesandaw Paya**, just west of the market, which dates back to 1597. Further west still beyond Kandawgyi Lake, whose shores are a popular leisure spot, is **Kaungmudaw Paya** – a much smaller pagoda with pleasant views over the surrounding fields.

ARRIVAL AND DEPARTURE

Taungoo is located just off the old National Highway 1 that runs between Yangon and Mandalay, and only 10km east of the newer (and faster) Yangon–Mandalay Expressway. The town centre is surrounded by a moat and the remains of the old city walls.

By bus Buses stop at ticket offices either on National Highway 1 or on the Expressway. A motorbike taxi to *Myanmar Beauty II–IV* should cost K1500 from the former, K4000 from the latter.

Destinations Bagan (daily; 5hr 30min); Kalaw (daily; 7hr); Mandalay (2 daily; 7hr); Nay Pyi Taw (5 daily; 2hr); Shwenyaung for Inle Lake (daily; 9hr); Yangon (6 daily; 4hr).

By train The train station is on the edge of town, around

1km west of National Highway 1 and the same distance southeast of the centre of town.

Destinations Bago (3 daily; 4hr 30min); Mandalay (3 daily; 8–10hr); Nay Pyi Taw (frequent; 3–4hr); Thazi (2 daily; 5hr–5hr 30min); Yangon (3 daily; 7hr).

ACCOMMODATION

★**Myanmar Beauty II–IV** Pauk Hla Gyi St ⊕054 25073. This gem of a guesthouse was built in four stages, with parts II–IV located together on the edge of a village a short way off the highway (around 3km south of the turning for Taungoo town centre). The higher the number, the nicer the accommodation: rooms in IV ($50) have a/c, heirloom furniture and rice-field views. The breakfasts are truly fabulous and bicycles are available to rent. $20

EATING

Yangon Food Villa 185 Bo Hmu Po Kun Rd. An a/c restaurant serving Burmese, Chinese, Thai and Korean dishes, most of them variations on noodles or rice (Thai red curry K2700). Daily 8.30am–9.30pm.

NAY PYI TAW

It seems strange to say that a country's capital has little to offer visitors, but then **NAY PYI TAW** is not an ordinary capital. Its construction was started from scratch in a largely rural area in 2002, with the purpose kept secret until an announcement in 2005 that government offices would move to the new site because Yangon was (supposedly) getting too congested.

WHAT TO SEE AND DO

The main reason to visit Nay Pyi Taw is to get a sense of the city's oddness. Its eight-lane highways are almost empty and link a series of grandiose government buildings and vanity projects. The most visible of these is **Uppatasanti Paya**, a huge pagoda paid for by General Than Shwe to atone for his sins.

ARRIVAL AND DEPARTURE

Nay Pyi Taw is very spread out and you're likely to need a taxi or motorcycle taxi if you want to explore. Expect to pay around K10,000 for a half-day tour by motorcycle.

By plane The airport is 16km southeast of the city.

Destinations Bangkok, Thailand (3 weekly; 2hr 30min); Mandalay (2 weekly; 40min); Yangon (2 daily; 1hr).

By bus The main Myoma Bus Station is on Yan Myo Thant Sin Rd, around 6km northwest of the hotel zone and 11km west of Uppatasanti Paya.

Destinations Hsipaw (daily; 12hr 30min); Kalaw (daily; 5hr); Mandalay (7 daily; 4hr); Pyin Oo Lwin (2 daily; 6hr); Shwenyaung for Inle Lake (daily; 7hr); Taungoo (5 daily; 2hr); Yangon (10 daily; 6hr).

By train The train station is 14km north of Uppatasanti Paya.

Destinations Bago (3 daily; 6hr 30min–7hr); Mandalay (2 daily; 6hr–6hr 30min); Taungoo (3 daily; 2hr–2hr 30min); Thazi (2 daily; 3hr–3hr 30min); Yangon (3 daily; 9hr–9hr 30min).

ACCOMMODATION AND EATING

With plenty of bus and train services there's little reason to stay overnight in Nay Pyi Taw, which is a good thing since accommodation is very expensive.

Kyauk Me Yazahtarni Rd. Serving Shan and Yunnan Chinese dishes, mostly for around K3000, this is one of several restaurants all located on the same stretch of road. Open breakfast to dinner.

7

PYAY

The lively port town of **PYAY** (pronounced "pea") boasts an impressive pagoda and provides access to ancient ruins at Thayekhittaya. Pyay sees relatively few tourists, since most people rush north on the expressway from Yangon to Mandalay rather than take the more attractive (but longer) western route via Pyay and Magwe.

WHAT TO SEE AND DO

The most obvious attraction in Pyay itself is the hilltop **Shwesandaw Paya**, which is said to contain strands of the Buddha's hair and one of his teeth. It's also worth heading south down Strand Road towards the bridge across the river, a pleasant walk past boat jetties and a 1950s Baptist church.

The most interesting day-trip is to **Thayekhittaya** (also known as Sri Ksetra; daily 8am–5pm; K5000), an archeological site 8km east of Pyay. It was the capital of a Pyu kingdom from the fifth to the ninth centuries, but its importance had faded by the time it was sacked by Bagan's King Anawrahta in 1057. There's a small government **museum** (Tues–Sat 9.30am–4.30pm; K5000) and an 11km path through the site which includes three pagodas which doubled as watchtowers. You can arrange a day-trip to Thayekhittaya from Pyay, including

transport around the site, by motorbike (K8000–10,000) or tuk-tuk (K25,000).

ARRIVAL AND DEPARTURE

By bus The bus station is around 3km east of the centre. For Ngapali Beach, avoid the very uncomfortable and slow buses which only go as far as Taunggok (12hr).
Destinations Magwe (6 daily; 5hr); Mandalay (2 daily; 13hr); Nyaung U for Bagan (daily; 10hr 30min); Thandwe for Ngapali Beach (daily; 12hr); Yangon (daily; 7hr).
By train Trains to Yangon (3 daily; 11hr) depart from the station in central Pyay, just a few metres east of the main roundabout with its statue of Aung San, although only the overnight service terminates in the central Yangon station – the others end up in Kyemyindine, northwest of the centre. Trains to Bagan (daily; 11hr) depart from Shwethekar station, around 5km east of Pyay.

ACCOMMODATION AND EATING

There is a night market between the main roundabout and the waterfront, where you can fill up on barbecue and noodle dishes for around K1000 per person.
Hline Ayar Strand Rd. A large restaurant on the river, serving Chinese dishes from around K3000. It's a popular place for a beer (draught K750) and there's a singing/fashion show in the evenings. Daily 10am–11pm.
Myat 222 Bazaar St ⓣ 053 25695. The best-value budget guesthouse in town, although the rooms aren't in great shape – expect lino floors patched up with parcel tape – and the owner is a bit too keen to sell day-trips and other services. The cheapest rooms have fans, shared bathrooms and no breakfast. $15

DIRECTORY

Bank MOB bank with currency exchange and 24hr ATM, 40 Bogyoke Rd (Mon–Fri 9.30am–3pm).
Internet Cosmic, Kan St (daily 8am–11pm).

Inle Lake and the east

With Kayah and Kayin states mostly off-limits to tourists, it's the large Shan State (a good deal of which is itself closed) which epitomizes the appeal of the hilly **east of the country**. A day-trip on **Inle Lake**, visiting stilt villages and colourful markets, is top of the list, although for many travellers the trekking opportunities around **Kalaw** are equally appealing.

KALAW

When it got too hot in the lowlands for the British during the colonial era, they retreated to hill stations such as **KALAW**. Today the climate is still part of the appeal, even if it can get a bit chilly at night in winter, and the town is a base for some excellent treks to ethnic minority villages.

WHAT TO SEE AND DO

Other than the market, which is open every day but spills out into the streets when it's Kalaw's turn to host the rotating market (see box, p.564), there isn't a lot to do in the town itself besides visit its pagodas. These include the mirrored **Aung Chan Tha Zedi** in the centre and small **Thein Taung Paya**, uphill from the Union Highway and notable mainly for the views back towards the town.

Trekking

There are many options for one- or two-day treks around Kalaw, following trails through the hills to villages inhabited by Palaung, Danu, Pa-O, Taung Yoe and other ethnic groups. There has been significant deforestation in the area, and the routes mostly run past fields and plantations, but nonetheless these hikes are a great way to get a glimpse of rural life. Prices start at around K10,000 per person per day; the trails can get very muddy during the rainy season (June to October).

The most popular longer trek is to Inle Lake (see p.565), which normally takes three days, although it's possible to shorten it to two (skipping some of the route by car) or lengthen it to four. There are many different routes and finishing points on the western side of the lake, including Khaung Dine and Indein (see p.565). Usually one night is spent in a village home and another in a monastery; the popularity of the trek means you're likely to see several other groups, particularly on the last day as the routes converge on Inle Lake. A typical three-day price is K30,000–45,000 per person, depending on group size, plus K15,000 per group for a boat from the finishing point to Nyaungshwe. Your luggage can be transported separately for K3000–5000 per bag.

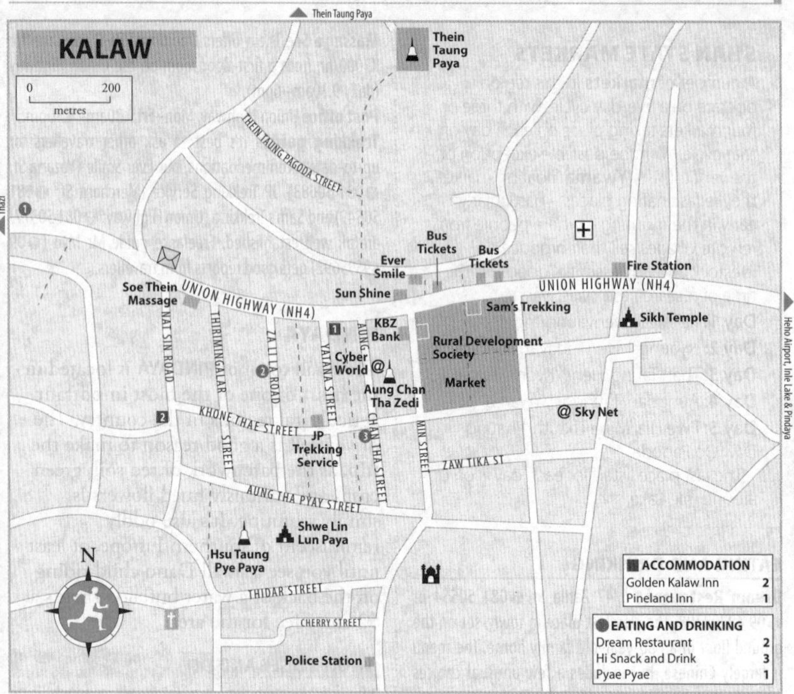

7

ARRIVAL AND DEPARTURE

By plane A taxi to Heho airport, around 35km northeast of Kalaw, costs K22,000 and takes an hour. Plane tickets are available from *Winner Hotel* on the Union Highway.

Destinations Mandalay (10 daily; 25min–1hr); Nyaung U for Bagan (10 weekly; 1hr–1hr 15min); Thandwe (2–3 daily; 1hr); Yangon (17 daily; 1hr 10min–3hr).

By bus Tickets are sold from outlets on the main road including the helpful Sun Shine (daily 8.30am–8.30pm; ⓣ081 50294 or ⓣ09 36201202), and buses arrive and depart from the same area.

Destinations Aungban (3 daily; 20min); Bagan (2 daily; 6–8hr); Bago (2 daily; 10hr); Hsipaw (daily; 12hr 30min); Mandalay (daily; 6–8hr); Nay Pyi Taw (daily; 7hr); Shwenyaung for Inle Lake (3 daily; 2hr); Taungoo (daily; 8hr); Thazi (3 daily; 4hr); Yangon (frequent from 4.30–9.30pm; 10–11hr).

By pick-up or tuk-tuk Vehicles run regularly to Aungban junction, for connections to Pindaya, daily from 7am–6pm.

By train The train station is less than 1km south of the town centre and is on a line running from Thazi to Shwenyaung (the station for Inle Lake), which is very scenic, particularly on the Thazi–Kalaw stretch. There are connections to Yangon and Mandalay from Thazi.

Destinations Shwenyaung (daily; 3hr 30min); Thazi (daily; 11hr).

By taxi A taxi to Pindaya takes 1hr 30min and costs K30,000 one-way, K35,000 return, or K55,000 to visit the caves then carry on to Nyaungshwe. Arrange this through guesthouses or travel agents.

ACCOMMODATION

While it's still possible to find a cheap room in Kalaw, most of the newer places cater to the growing number of tour groups that come here to trek.

Golden Kalaw Inn 5/92 Nat Sin Rd ⓣ081 50311 or ⓣ09 5210635, ⓔgoldenkalawinn@gmail.com. The rooms are small and need more than a lick of paint, and a private bathroom costs an extra $3, but they're clean and the price includes a choice of five local breakfasts and a warm welcome from the owners. It's a better bet than the *Golden Lily* nearby. **$9**

Pineland Inn 5/36 Union Highway ⓣ081 50020 or ⓣ09 5280662, ⓔpineland.inn@gmail.com. Often overlooked by backpackers, despite offering decent value, perhaps because the reception area is less inviting than the rooms themselves. Economy rooms have lino floors and share clean bathrooms; you get wooden floors and basic en-suite facilities for an extra $2, while upstairs rooms ($18) are in better condition and warmer at night. Try to get a room at the back as the highway is noisy. **$12**

SHAN STATE MARKETS

A number of **markets** in this region operate on a five-day cycle, with three or four markets taking place on each day of that cycle. With the possible exception of the very touristy **Ywama** "floating market", they're fascinating places – particularly early in the morning – where people from remote villages sell their produce or livestock and buy essential goods. At the time of research the cycle was:

Day 1: Kalaw/Shwenyaung/Indein
Day 2: Nyaungshwe/Pindaya/Nampan
Day 3: Than Taung/Heho/Kyone/Taung To
Day 4: Aungban/Taunggyi/Ywama
Day 5: Pwe Hla/Mine Thauth/Phaung Daw Oo Pagoda

The last place listed for each day is on or around Inle Lake.

EATING AND DRINKING

Dream Restaurant 5/47 Zatila St ⓣ 081 50554 or ⓣ 09 49298398. The classiest place in town, set on the ground floor of an 80-year-old family home. The menu is largely Chinese, but includes a few unusual choices such as mutton or beef *cabbab* (cooked with onion, tomato and paprika, served with rice; K4500). Daily 10am–10pm.

★ **Hi Snack & Drink** Khone Thae St. A genuine (if tiny) Western-style bar. It might be rough around the edges, but it has cheap whisky sours (K1000) and on most nights a battered guitar is passed around for entertainment. Daily 4.30–11pm.

Pyae Pyae Union Highway. There are plenty of cheap places to eat in the centre of Kalaw, but it's well worth a short walk west to this popular restaurant. The Shan noodle soup (K500) in particular is excellent. Daily breakfast to dinner.

SHOPPING

Handicrafts The Rural Development Society shop, on the west side of the market, is run by a non-profit organization working with local communities. Daily 9am–5.30pm.

DIRECTORY

Bank The only bank in town is a branch of KBZ Bank (Mon–Fri 9am–3pm) on Min St. It has an ATM and currency exchange.

Bicycle rental Ever Smile (Yuzana St; ⓣ 081 50683) has bikes for K2000/day.

Internet Cyber World, Aung Chan Tha St (daily 8.30am–10pm; K1000/hr); Sky Net, Kone Thae St (daily 8am–midnight; K500/hr).

Massage Soe Thein offers traditional Pa-O massage for K7000/hr, from a first-floor room on the Union Highway (daily 9.30am–6pm).

Post office Union Highway, Mon–Fri 9.30am–4.30pm.

Trekking guides It's best to ask other travellers for up-to-date recommendations, but Ever Smile (Yuzana St; ⓣ 081 50683), JP Trekking Service (Merchant St; ⓣ 081 50549) and Sam's Trekking (Union Highway; ⓣ 081 50377) are all well established. Freelance guide Mr Myo (ⓣ 09 49595692) gets good reports from travellers.

PINDAYA

The small town of **PINDAYA** is located in the heart of one of the most important agricultural regions in the country. The drive itself is a good reason to make the trip, as the patchwork of red soil, green crops and variously hued flowers is simply stunning. It's also oddly reminiscent of southern Europe, at least until you see a small Danu child riding on the back of a water buffalo. There's a $2 entry fee for the area.

WHAT TO SEE AND DO

The main attraction in the town is **Shwe Oo Min** (daily 6am–6pm; $3), an atmospheric series of caves crammed full of Buddha statues – some date back centuries, but the collection is still expanding. It's possible to continue north from here along the hillside via other shrines and a monastery; one path comes down close to the *Golden Cave* hotel.

ARRIVAL AND DEPARTURE

By bus Buses to Shwenyaung for Inle Lake (2 daily; 3hr) depart from close to the town's market.

By pick-up Pick-ups run from the market to Aungban (daily; 1hr 30min), from where you can take a taxi or pick-up on to Kalaw.

By taxi Visiting by taxi makes Pindaya a feasible day-trip from either Nyaungshwe (2hr 30min) or Kalaw (1hr 30min), or a stopover on a trip between the two.

TOURS

Guides The hills and villages around Pindaya are visited far less often than those near Kalaw. Hotels and guesthouses can arrange guides, as can U Myint Thaung at the Old Home Tour Information Centre on the crossroads beside the market. He charges $15 per person per day including food, plus a small donation for accommodation at a monastery.

ACCOMMODATION AND EATING

Public transport timetables mean that you'll need to spend a night here unless you come by taxi.

Kyan Lite Close to the market. Service is disorderly and the concrete-floored room is a bit shabby, but the Chinese standards cooked here – such as chicken cashew nut (K3500) – are tasty and popular with locals. Daily breakfast to dinner.

Myit Phyar Zaw Gyi 106 Zaytan Quarter. This hotel is centrally located close to the market, lake and several restaurants, but the rooms facing the lake can get quite noisy. **$20**

INLE LAKE

Vast and serene **Inle Lake** is one of the undoubted highlights of most trips to Myanmar. Its attractions are not just in its considerable natural beauty, however, but also in the stilt villages of the Intha ("Sons of the Lake", descendants of Mon people from the far southeast), for whom it is home.

While the lake is very firmly on the beaten path, it's big enough that you only truly notice just how many other foreigners are around when your boat pulls up at one of the stops. Even now most of the markets are aimed more at villagers of the various ethnic groups that live in the area – among them Shan, Pa-O, Kayah and Danu – than they are at tourists.

Most resorts on the lake cost at least $100 per night, so travellers on a budget usually stay in nearby Nyaungshwe.

WHAT TO SEE AND DO

A typical **day-trip**, taken in a long, narrow boat with a noisy outboard motor, will stick to the northern reaches of the lake. It will include visits to small workshops in stilt villages, such as cheroot making in Tha Lay and lotus fibre weaving in In Paw Khone, plus one or more pagodas and probably a market (see box opposite). You are also likely to see fishermen using traditional conical nets, propelling their boats using a distinctive leg-rowing technique, and other Intha residents of the lake tending to fruit and vegetables on floating gardens.

You may be offered the chance to see "long-necked" **Padaung women**, so called because they wear metal rings around their necks (which actually push their collarbones down rather than elongating their necks). These women are often exploited by those within the tourist industry and it's something which some visitors choose to avoid.

Phaung Daw Oo Paya

Boats converge on the tiered lakeside **Phaung Daw Oo Paya**, south of Ywama on the western side of the lake, to the extent that you'll probably need to climb over a log-jam of them in order to reach the shore. The pagoda building is nothing special, but men (only) crowd around to add gold leaf to five Buddha figures that are already so coated that they are no longer recognizably human in shape.

Indein

The ride west from Ywama to **Indein**, starting among reed beds before continuing

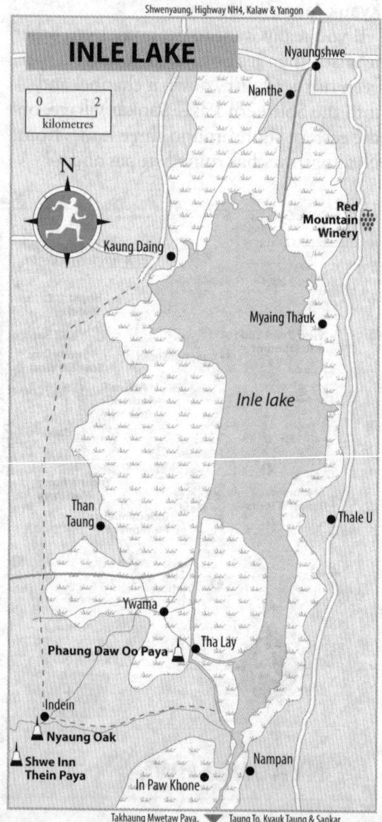

7

between tree-lined banks, is a striking contrast to the wide-open space of the lake. Just behind Indein village, at the base of a hill, is **Nyaung Oak**, a set of picturesquely overgrown stupas with carvings of Buddhas, *chin-thé* (guardian lions), *devas* (female deities), elephants and peacocks. Head uphill along a covered walkway to reach **Shwe Inn Thein Paya**, a collection of seventeenth- and eighteenth-century stupas which is being slowly and heavy-handedly restored. On the way down, look out for a path on the left which runs through a bamboo forest back to the riverside.

Further south

For an additional charge, it's possible to go down to the village of **Thaung Tho**, which is left off most tourist itineraries. It has a pagoda but is particularly worth visiting on market day (see box, p.564). You can also see potters at work in nearby **Kyauk Taung** village.

If you really want to get away from other tourists, then it's possible to arrange a trip even further south, down a channel and into the Southern Lake. **Sankar** village, on the eastern shore around three hours from Nyaungshwe, has ruined stupas and a monastery. On the other side of the lake is **Takhaung Mwetaw** pagoda, a tiered building with dozens of white stupas.

ARRIVAL AND DEPARTURE

By boat The main entry point to the lake is Nyaungshwe (see below), from which dozens of boats run during the tourist season – either depositing tourists in resorts on the lake, or taking them on day-trips. Bring a jumper for the cold morning start, and suntan lotion, since the boats have no cover.

NYAUNGSHWE

As the most convenient base for trips on Inle Lake, the once-quiet town of **Nyaungshwe** has developed into a flourishing tourist town. Those hoping for idyllic canal-side lodging and cafés will be disappointed, but the town has enough to keep you occupied when you aren't exploring the lake itself.

Nyaungshwe is particularly busy during the Balloon Festival in nearby Taunggyi (see p.531), which takes place in November, and during the Phaung Daw Oo Pagoda Festival (September/October). At these times, boatmen tend to increase their prices.

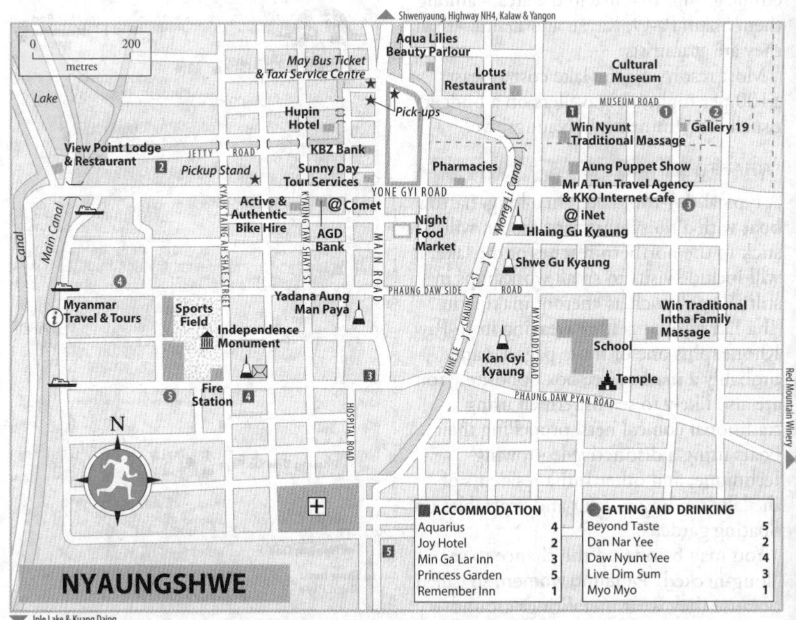

WHAT TO SEE AND DO

Boats to Inle Lake leave from the Main Canal on the western edge of town. Another much quieter canal, Mong Li, runs through the centre of Nyaungshwe and a wander alongside it is a good way to get a sense of local life. There are three sizeable monasteries – **Hlaing Gu Kyaung**, **Shwe Gu Kyaung** and **Kan Gyi Kyaung** – on its eastern bank.

The most holy pagoda in Nyaungshwe is **Yadana Man Aung Paya**, on Phaung Daw Side Road, which has an unusual stepped golden stupa. In the northeast of town is the **Cultural Museum** (Tues–Sun 10am–4pm; $2), although it's more interesting for its brick and teak building (an old Shan palace) than for its exhibits of Buddha statues.

There are many one- and two-day **treks** around the town, through rice fields, hills and villages, as well as a popular three-day route to Kalaw (see p.562). The roads around the lake are also great for **cycling**, and you can rent a bike through accommodation and travel agencies (see below). They should be able to suggest destinations, but one good bet is the **Red Mountain Winery** (daily 9am–6pm; 081 209366, redmountain-estate.com), around 4km southeast of town and signposted from the main road. It's possible to sample the wines (K2000 for four) and to have lunch in the restaurant.

ARRIVAL AND DEPARTURE

Trains arrive at Shwenyaung, a town 12km north on the highway, and many buses also stop there instead of heading into Nyaungshwe. From Shwenyaung it's 30min to Nyaungshwe by tuk-tuk (K1000/person or K5000 to hire) or taxi (K10,000). A government fee of $10 to enter the Inle Lake area is charged at a permit booth on the northern edge of Nyaungshwe. Leaving Nyaungshwe, tuk-tuks to Shwenyaung depart from north of the market on the Main Rd.

By plane For Heho airport (1hr; see p.563) take a tuk-tuk (K12,000) or taxi (K20,000).

By bus You can buy tickets from the May Bus Ticket & Taxi Services Centre (081 209176 or 09 428326117) on the Main Rd in Nyaungshwe.

Destinations Bagan (2 daily; 8hr); Bago (2 daily; 10–11hr); Hsipaw (daily; 12hr); Kalaw (6 daily; 2hr); Mandalay (2 daily; 8hr); Yangon (2 daily; 12hr).

By train The train line between Shwenyaung and Thazi (which has connections to Yangon and Mandalay) is exceptionally scenic, particularly the final Kalaw–Thazi stretch.

Destinations Kalaw (daily; 3hr 30min); Thazi (daily; 11hr 30min).

INFORMATION AND TOURS

Tourist information The official Myanmar Travel & Tours office is on Strand Rd (daily 8.30am–5pm).

Bicycle rental Guesthouses and tour agents have bikes for around K1500/day. Active & Authentic, Kyaunn Taw Shayt St (aat.toursmyanmar@gmail.com) has mountain bikes for $12/day.

Boat trips Trips on the lake can be arranged through your accommodation, with freelance boatmen (who congregate on the Main Canal), guesthouses or travel agents – prices generally start around K15,000 (or K22,000 during festivals); it's well worth an extra K5000 to include Indein in the itinerary. A trip down to Thaung Tho costs K30,000, while visiting the Southern Lake will set you back K50,000.

Travel agents Numerous offices in town offer boat trips, trekking and transport services, including Sunny Day Tour Services, Main Rd (daily 7am–8pm; 09 428315116; htwe.sunny@yahoo.com), and Mr A Tun Travel Agency, Yone Gyi Rd (09 43197443, nanmyasein1985@gmail.com). Freelance operators include Joseph Aung Tha (083 40092 or 09 49403388, thaungjoe@gmail.com).

Trekking guides Most travel agents offer trekking, charging around K7000 (half-day) or K10,000 (one day). Prices vary more for the popular three-day trek to Kalaw, with Pyone Cho from *Lotus Restaurant* (09 428313717, pyonecholotus@gmail.com) offering one of the lowest prices at K40,000 per person plus K8000 for boat transfer. Bags can be transferred to Kalaw for K5000 each. Trekking prices typically apply to two or more people; solo travellers pay more.

ACCOMMODATION

There is a lot of pressure on the accommodation in Nyaungshwe, with some former budget favourites increasing their prices by 50 percent or more from 2012 to 2013. In high season some travellers have slept in monasteries or even hotel restaurants after arriving without reservations.

Aquarius 2 Phaung Daw Pyan Rd 081 209352, aquarius352@gmail.com. An understandably popular option, as much for its friendly welcome as for its rooms (although the garden and the knick-knacks decorating the place add character). The cheapest use fans and have shared bathrooms; for $5 more you can get en-suite facilities. **$20**

★TREAT YOURSELF

Princess Garden Mine Li Quarter ☎081 209214 or ☎09 5148418. Set in delightful gardens with a small swimming pool, this is a restful and friendly little retreat that books up well in advance during peak season – hardly surprising given that the prices, particularly for bungalows, remain very reasonable. Breakfast is served on a terrace with views of the surrounding fields. $40

7

Joy Hotel Jetty Rd ☎081 209083 or ☎09 43110067, ⓔjoyhotelinle@gmail.com. This cheap and cheerful guesthouse is set beside a canal used by traders, which makes for great people-watching from the terrace where breakfast is served. The rooms are comfortable, albeit a little tired. $22

Min Ga Lar Inn Phaung Daw Pyan Rd ☎081 209198 or ☎09 5216278, ⓦmingalarinn.blogspot.co.uk. Business is obviously good at this self-proclaimed "home away from home", as they opened a slew of new rooms in 2012. It's a shame that they're so pricey – an eye-watering $85 – but four of the cheaper, and perfectly decent, older rooms remain. $28

Remember Inn Haw St ☎081 209257 or ☎09 5214070, ⓦrememberinn.jimdo.com. The forty rooms here are well kept and decent value – paying extra for a superior room gets you a fridge, TV and a/c. The best reason to stay, though, is the wealth of assistance provided by the owners. Wi-fi in reception. Visa cards accepted for a four-percent charge. $25.

EATING AND DRINKING

Beyond Taste 10 Phaung Daw Pyan St ☎09 428358111. Reflecting the tourist boom of recent years, this is one of a handful of places aiming for more sophistication. The food, such as a popular Shan fish curry (K3500), is well made and the upstairs balcony is an appealing place to sit. The K700 tax added to the bill is less welcome. Daily breakfast to dinner.

Dan Nar Yee Museum Rd. This popular beer garden – a set of simple open-sided huts in a yard – also serves some basic food, such as noodle dishes and barbecue (K200/stick). Daily 8am–late.

Daw Nyunt Yee Phaung Daw Side Rd. Locals rate this no-frills place as serving some of the best Chinese food in town. Most main dishes cost K3000–3500, though there are simple noodle or rice-based meals from K1500. Daily 6am–9pm.

★ Live Dim Sum Yone Gyi Rd. Not only are the *dim sum* here a change from standard Chinese food, but they're tasty in their own right – the chef has years of experience in international restaurants, and it shows. If you can't decide what to get then try the platters (eight pieces for K2500). They also do Peking duck, good for two people (K12,000). Daily 7am–9pm.

Myo Myo Museum Rd. Traditional Burmese dishes from the family that also owns the long-standing *Linn Htett* restaurant on the edge of the market. This newer offshoot has the same great dishes (curries K2500), and its enthusiastic owners help to make it stand out from the crowd. Daily 9am–9pm or later.

TRADITIONAL ENTERTAINMENT

Aung Puppet Show Ahletaung Kyaung Rd. The current puppeteer has been performing for 27 years; he learnt from his grandfather and is now teaching his son. They also sell puppets for $10–20 (daily 7am–9pm). Shows nightly 7pm & 8.30pm (30min; K3000).

DIRECTORY

Bank AGD Bank, Yone Gyi Rd (Mon–Fri 9am–3pm), has a money change counter. KBZ Bank, Main Rd, also has an ATM.

Internet Comet, Yone Gyi Rd (daily 8am–10pm); iNet, Ahletaung Kyaung Rd (daily 6.30am–10pm); KKO, Yone Gyi Rd (daily 7.30am–10pm).

Spa and massage Places offering massage are popping up all over Nyaungshwe. Aqua Lilies, Museum Rd (daily 9am–9pm; ☎09 428363584), is one of the most established; treatments include a traditional *anaite* massage (K11,000/hr). Win Nyunt Traditional Burmese Massage (daily 8am–8pm; K7000/hr) and Win Traditional Intha Family Massage, Shwe Chan Thar St (daily 7am–10pm; K5000/hr), are more basic setups in family homes.

Shopping Gallery 19, Shwe Chan Thar St (Tues–Sun 9am–8pm), sells work by Taunggyi-based photographer Kyaw Kyaw Win, with prices starting at $10 for a 12x8-inch print.

VISITING KENGTUNG

Reaching **Kengtung** from within Myanmar is expensive, as the road in from the west is closed to foreigners and flying is the only option. The town can, however, be reached by road from Thailand via the Mae Sai–Tachileik border (see p.763). Kengtung is a pleasant town with a lake at its heart, and provides access to many **ethnic minority villages**. It isn't possible to stay overnight in them, however, and the trailheads can only be reached by taxi. This makes hiking relatively pricey.

Mandalay and around

Thanks partly to Rudyard Kipling's evocative poem *Mandalay*, the name of Myanmar's second city suggests – for many Western visitors at least – images of a bygone Asia. Arriving in downtown **Mandalay** tends quickly to dispel such thoughts, however, as visitors find themselves in a grid of congested streets dominated by the walls of the **palace** compound (most of which is taken up by a huge military base).

Despite this, it would be a shame to rush through too quickly without giving the place a chance to grow on you. There's **Mandalay Hill** to climb, memorable both for its views and for the experience of joining throngs of locals doing the same. Then there are day-trips to former Burmese capitals such as the once-mighty **Inwa**, now a sleepy backwater scattered with stupas that you can visit by horse and cart.

MANDALAY

MANDALAY is a surprisingly young city, founded in 1857 by King Mindon partly to show the British, who were ruling Lower Burma from Rangoon, that his kingdom was still mighty. After being taken by the British in 1885, the city prospered until the Japanese occupation during World War II, which saw many of the old buildings levelled by Allied bombing. Today Mandalay is the commercial hub of northern Myanmar, particularly important for trade with China and with a large Chinese community.

MANDALAY COMBINED ATTRACTION TICKETS

Several of the city's main attractions are covered by a **K10,000 government ticket**, which is valid for a week and can be bought from any of the relevant attractions. There is a separate **K3000 government ticket** for Sagaing and Mingun, although the money is not always collected.

ADDRESSES IN MANDALAY

The **grid system** makes it easy to find your way around Mandalay. Where **addresses** are given in this section, first comes the street on which the place sits (81st St, for example), and then the cross streets between which it lies (29/30, for example).

Much of the **downtown area**, including the zone south and southwest of the old royal palace where many budget guesthouses are located, is constantly traffic-choked and first impressions are rarely positive. Yet even here the backstreets can hold surprises, such as the huddle of mosques and Hindu temples on 82nd and 83rd streets, between 26th and 29th streets. The streets further west, towards the river, are significantly quieter and a popular area for exploring by bicycle.

Mandalay Palace

Built as the residence for King Mindon and the Burmese aristocracy, **Mandalay Palace** is protected by walls and a moat more than 2km long on each side. After the British took the city they used it as a fort, and most of the huge site is still an off-limits military base.

The palace complex itself is right at the centre (daily 7.30am–4.30pm; K10,000 Mandalay ticket), although the wooden buildings all burnt down towards the end of World War II. What you see today is a 1990s reconstruction, which is impressive from a distance – such as from the helter-skelter-like watchtower – but less so up close. Foreigners can only enter the walls through the east gate.

Mandalay Hill

The 45-minute walk up **Mandalay Hill** for sunset is one of the highlights of a visit to the city. The usual starting point is the staircase between a large pair of *chin-thé* (lion-dogs) on 10th Street; there is another entrance a little further east. Whichever route you choose, the

concrete steps run uphill beneath a corrugated iron roof, lined with stalls selling drinks and souvenirs. The two routes meet just before **Byar Deik Paya**, from which a large standing Buddha points back towards the city. The story goes that the Buddha visited the hill and foretold that a great city would be built at its foot.

There are numerous other shrines on the way up the hill. As you get higher the crowds become thicker, particularly

7

GOLD LEAF WORKSHOPS

Pretty much all of the **gold leaf** applied to Buddha images by devotees in Myanmar comes from a small area of Mandalay. There are about fifty gold leaf **workshops**, many of them based in homes, in the blocks around 36th Street, just east of the railway line.

Among these, Gold Rose (36th St 78/79; daily 6am–6pm; T 02 30218) and King Galon (36th St 77/78; daily 7am–7pm; T 09 47143078) are larger businesses which are used to visits from tourists. At both, it's possible to watch the hammerers at work while a member of staff explains the process of turning a 12g piece of gold into 1200 sheets, each just 0.0003mm thick. The shops sell gold leaf and other souvenirs, but there's no pressure to buy.

around sunset, but the wide terrace of **Sutaungpyi Paya** ("wish-granting pagoda") at the top accommodates the mixture of pilgrims, tourists and novice monks, who are there to practise their English.

It's also possible to take a pick-up (K500), motorbike (K4500 return) or taxi (K12,000 return) to the top of the hill.

Around Mandalay Hill

There are several other temples and monasteries at the base of Mandalay Hill. The most impressive is probably **Shwenandaw Kyaung** (daily 8am–5pm; K10,000 Mandalay ticket), a teak structure built within the palace walls as a residence for King Mindon. The building was converted to a monastery and moved to its current site east of the palace after Mindon died in it, as it was considered bad luck by his son, Thibaw; this later saved it from burning alongside the palace's other buildings.

Close by is **Atumashi Kyaung** (daily 8am–5pm; K10,000 Mandalay ticket), originally built in the 1850s to house a Buddha statue that went missing – complete with the diamond in its forehead – when the British took the city. The current building is a 1990s reconstruction.

Kuthodaw Paya (daily 24hr), just north of Atumashi Kyaung, is home to a set of 729 marble slabs inscribed with the *Tipitaka* (the canon of Theravada Buddhist scriptures), each kept in its own small stupa. Together they have been described as the world's largest book. The nearby **Sandamuni Paya** (daily 6am–9pm) has marble slabs with commentaries on the same scriptures, while the centrepiece of the **Kyauktawgyi Paya** (daily 24hr) just to the west is a huge Buddha carved from a single piece of marble. It's the site of the city's biggest festival every October.

Jade Market

The stalls in the large **Jade Market** (daily 8–11am & 2–4pm; $1), located in an appealing canal-side district southwest of downtown, sell mostly to dealers. It probably isn't a good idea to make a purchase unless you know what you're looking for, but it's a fascinating place to visit. The main trading in the market takes place in the morning, but it's possible to see jade being cut, shaped and polished at any time. You can also see the same being done outside the market itself, on the east side.

While in the area, take a look at **Shwe In Bin Kyaung**, a peaceful, late nineteenth-century teak monastery (junction of 89th & 38th sts; free).

Mahamuni Paya

The most important Buddhist site in the city, **Mahamuni Paya** is a large complex south of the centre. At the heart of the pagoda is a 3.8m-tall Buddha figure, taken in 1784 from Mrauk U by King Bodawpaya's army. Male devotees visit to apply gold leaf to the figure, while women are not allowed within the inner area and instead hand their gold leaf to a male assistant. The figure itself is said to weigh six tonnes, and the gold leaf covering it adds another two tonnes. At 4am each day crowds gather while the face, pretty much the only part not covered in gold leaf, is washed.

Northwest of the main shrine is a cream concrete building containing Hindu figures taken originally from

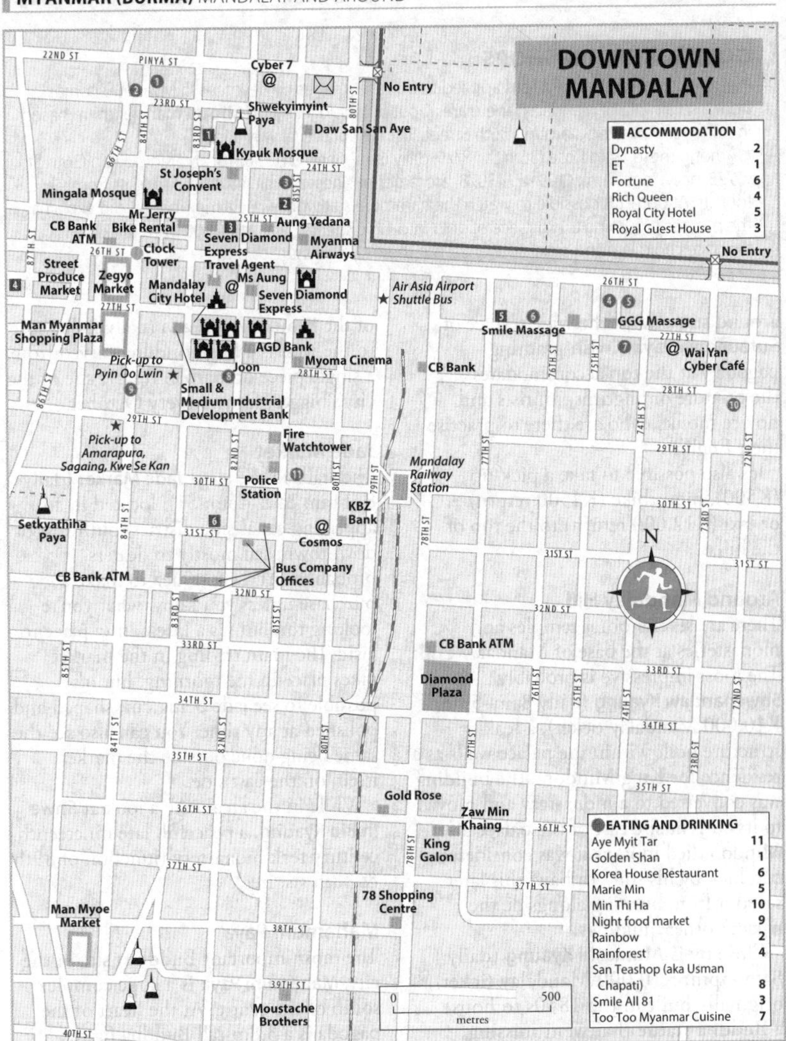

Angkor Wat by the Rakhine, before being appropriated by Bodawpaya at the same time as the large Buddha. Outside the complex, to the southwest, is a dusty and noisy district of stone-carving workshops.

ARRIVAL AND DEPARTURE

By plane The airport is 45km south of Mandalay. If you're flying with AirAsia then you can take their free shuttle buses at 9am and 9.15am from 79th St 26/27; the buses into the city are at 12.45pm and 1pm. Otherwise most guesthouses, hotels and tour agencies can arrange a taxi to the airport (shared K4000, private K12,000) – it's best to book the day before. There's a desk at the airport offering the same prices into the city.

Destinations Bhamo (4 weekly; 1hr 55min); Heho (9 daily; 25min–3hr); Nyaung U (6 daily; 30min); Yangon (19 daily; 50min–2hr 5min).

By bus Mandalay has three main bus stations, of which the most useful, Kwe Se Kan, is also the furthest away at around 10km south of town (25min; motorbike K2000, taxi K4000). The most central bus station is Thiri Mandalar, 89th St 22/24, although it's of little use to most travellers. Pyi Gyi Myat Shin bus station is on 37th St 60/62 (motorbike from downtown K2000, taxi K4000),

and has buses running east to Pyin Oo Lwin and Hsipaw. Hotels and tour agents can often arrange tickets for a small fee, and there are also many bus-company offices and ticket agents in the blocks between 80th to 83rd sts and 30th to 33rd sts. Some bus companies offer transport from the centre to the appropriate bus station.

Destinations Bago (2 daily; 10hr); Hsipaw (2 daily; 6–8hr); Kalaw (3 daily; 6hr 30min); Nay Pyi Taw (5 daily; 4hr); Nyaungshwe for Inle Lake (2 daily; 9hr); Nyaung U for Bagan (6 daily; 7–8hr); Pyay (2 daily; 13hr); Shwenyaung for Inle Lake (3 daily; 8hr 30min); Taungoo (2 daily; 7–8hr); Yangon (6 daily; 7–10hr).

By train The train station is centrally located on 30th St 78/79. If you don't want to queue upstairs, you can buy tickets from the government tourist information office on the ground floor, for a commission of around fifteen percent.

Destinations Hsipaw (daily; 10hr); Myitkyina (3 daily; 20hr); Naba for Katha (3 daily; 8–12hr); Nyaung U for Bagan (daily; 8hr); Yangon (3 daily; 15hr–16hr 30min).

By boat Government services to Mingun depart from a pier at the western end of 26th St (daily 9am; K5000 return). Most other boats leave from Gawain Jetty, at the western end of 35th St.

To Bagan Three private companies run tourist services (9hr), departing at 7am but not running every day: N Mai Hka (upper floor of railway station, 30th St 78/79; T 09 6813472, W nmaihka.com; $40), Malikha 2 (between 77th/78th & 32nd/33rd sts; T 02 72279, W malikha-rivercruises.com; $42); Myanmar Golden River Group (MGRG) (38th St 79/80, W mgrgexpress.com; T 011 202734; $45). All include breakfast, and MGRG includes lunch. The government slow boat (at least 13hr; $18) leaves at 5.30am on Wed and Sun; the service is run by IWT (35th St; daily 9.30am–4.30pm; T 02 36035).

To the north N Mai Hka services run daily to Katha (14hr; deck $20, cabin $40) and Bhamo (18–22hr; deck $30, cabin $60), but during high season they may use the boat on the Bagan route instead. An IWT slow ferry runs to Bhamo (at least 3 days; deck $12, cabin $54) via Katha at 6am on Mon, Thurs and Sat.

By pick-up Pick-ups to Pyin Oo Lwin (K2500) run daily from 5am–5pm, departing when full from the corner of 28th and 83rd sts. They are most frequent early in the morning and scarce after 3pm.

By shared taxi Duhtawadi bus company runs shared taxis to Hsipaw (K15,000; 5–6hr) from its office in town (31st St 81/82; T 01 61938). Aung Yedana (25th St 81/82; T 01 24850) has shared taxis to Kalaw and Inle Lake (around K25,000) and will pick you up from your hotel. Several operators have services to Pyin Oo Lwin (K7000; 2hr), collecting passengers from their hotels, plus there are morning departures from the corner of 27th and 83rd sts. Try Seven Diamond (see Information and Tours) for shared taxis to various destinations.

INFORMATION AND TOURS

Tour agents Daw San San Aye, 81st St 23/24 (daily 8am–8pm; T 02 31799); Seven Diamond Express, 25th St 82/83 (daily 8.30am–8pm; T 02 65865) and 82nd St 26/27 (daily 8.30am–8pm; T 02 30128; E mdl.sdm.marketing@gmail.com).

Tourist information The MTT office (daily 8am–9pm; T 02 60356) is on the corner of 68th and 27th sts.

GETTING AROUND

Bicycle or motorbike rental Several places rent out bikes and motorbikes, including Mr Lim, just outside *ET Hotel*, 83rd St 23/24 (daily 7.30am–7.30pm), and Mr Jerry, 83rd St 25/26 (daily 7am–7pm). Both charge K2000/day for a bike, and from K10,000/day for a motorbike. A ride around downtown Mandalay is not for the faint-hearted, but it's quieter further west.

By bus or pick-up Mandalay's public transport system is very confusing and it's best to ask locally for advice on which bus to take. The junction of 26th and 84th sts is a good spot to pick up a bus.

By trishaw This traditional form of transport has not yet been entirely superseded by motorbike taxis. Expect to pay around K1000 for a trip within the centre.

By taxi It isn't hard to find taxis, whether motorbikes or cars. There are small motorbike taxi stands at many street corners, and if you stay in the main budget accommodation district you'll be inundated with offers. As a guide, a short trip on a motorbike taxi should cost around K1000.

ACCOMMODATION

There is a lot of pressure on budget accommodation in Mandalay these days, so book ahead in high season.

Dynasty 81st St 24/25 T 02 35801, E hoteldynasty@myanmar.com.mm; map p.572. The 22 rooms in this hotel aren't bad by Mandalay's budget standards: the windows are small and some of the bathroom grouting needs attention, but the bedrooms are clean and you get a/c plus a fridge and small TV. **$20**

★ **ET** 83rd St 23/24 T 02 65006, E ethotel129a@gmail.com; map p.572. This guesthouse deserves kudos for renovating its rooms in 2013 without putting up the price (the exact opposite of some rivals). The cheapest fan rooms have shared bathrooms and are on the rooftop, while for $25 you can get a/c and a bathroom; the $20 singles are particularly good. There's wi-fi throughout. **$18**

Fortune 31st St 82/83 T 02 66 548; map p.572. The decor is stuck in a time warp, but the rooms here are actually decent enough. You don't get a bathroom at the cheaper end, but you do get a/c. Some rooms lack curtains, others lack windows. **$25**

7

Peacock Lodge 61st St T 02 61429 or T 09 204 2059, E peacocklodge@gmail.com; map p.570. You can be sure of a warm welcome at this family-run guesthouse, located away from the main backpacker zone. It's a popular place, and they recently added five smart new rooms with wooden floors and flat-screen TVs ($45) to the original five. All rooms, old and new, have a/c. Lunch and dinner by prior arrangement. **$30**

★ **Rich Queen** 87th St 26/27 T 02 60172 or T 09 9102 8348; map p.572. One of the best-value places you'll find in downtown Mandalay, this new guesthouse has helpful staff, clean rooms and wi-fi on the lower floors. It's tucked away on a side street – look out for the red LED display. **$25**

Royal City Hotel 27th St 76/77 T 02 31805; map p.572. All of the rooms in this affordable mid-range hotel have a/c, plus free wi-fi. Even the standard rooms are large and well-kept, but the highlight is the rooftop where you can have breakfast. **$30**

7

Royal Guest House 25th St 82/83 T 02 31400; map p.572. A long-standing budget favourite that is a definite step up from most of the nearby competition, with clean and comfortable rooms at a fair price, plus staff who can help with anything you need. The very cheapest rooms are small and windowless, but you don't need to spend much more to get something better. The only downside is that it fills up quickly. **$17**

EATING AND DRINKING

One very cheap dinner option, popular with locals, is the night market on 84th St, north of 29th St. There isn't much nightlife to speak of in Mandalay, beyond the beer stations and a handful of cultural performances put on for tourists (see below).

Aye Myit Tar 81st St 29/30; map p.572. An old favourite for Burmese food, which is still very popular with locals. There's an English menu with pictures, although you'll have to ask for the prices – expect to pay around K3000 for a curry. Daily 10am–9pm.

Central Park 27th St 68/69; map p.570. Looking a bit like a beach bar without the sand, this place draws a crowd of young locals and expats. They tend to show up in time for happy hour (6.30–7.30pm), when draught beer is three-for-two and cocktails (such as margharitas at K2800) are two-for-one. The soundtrack is Western and chilled out, and the food includes burgers (K2000), pizzas and barbecue. Daily 11am–11.30pm.

Golden Shan 84th St 22/23; map p.572. If you're feeling hungry, try this barn-like Shan restaurant: from 11am they have a buffet where you can take your pick from up to 35 dishes, including some veggie options, for a set price of K3500. Daily 6am–9.30pm.

Korea House Restaurant 27th St 76/77; map p.572. Good Korean dishes served in a plain setting. The menu includes favourites such as *bibimbap* (rice topped with beef, vegetables, egg and chilli paste, which you mix together before eating) for K3000. Daily 9am–9pm.

Marie Min 27th St 74/75 T 02 36234; map p.572. Run by an affable Tamil Catholic, Gilly Aung San, who has been serving up great vegetarian grub (such as guacamole or samosas, K2000) down a quiet alleyway since 1994. There's an antique shop in the building and Gilly also runs a small travel agency: he rents out motorbikes (K8000/day) and sells tickets for transportation. The *Rainforest Restaurant* opposite is owned by the same family and serves Thai dishes such as chicken *kaeng pa* (jungle curry) for K3500. Daily 9am–9pm.

Min Thi Ha Corner of 72nd and 28th St; map p.572. An exceptionally popular teahouse, part of a small chain known for its mutton curry puffs, where boys in claret short-sleeved shirts tend to a constant flow of locals. There's free wi-fi, or you could sit and ponder the quote from Samuel Johnson on the wall: "Great works are performed not by strength but by perseverance." Daily 5am–4pm.

Rainbow 84th St 22/23; map p.572. Set over three floors, the uppermost on the roof, this corner restaurant is a popular spot for a draught Myanmar beer (K600). They also have a menu of snacks and a few Chinese basics for K3500. Daily 9am–10pm.

San Teashop (aka Usman Chapati) Corner of 82nd and 28th St; map p.572. Every evening this teashop sets up on the pavement and serves cheap grub to eager patrons: biryani costs K1600 (chicken) or K1800 (beef), or for K1500 you can get a chicken curry, two chapatis and some daal (lentils). Daily 4–11pm.

Smile All 81 81st St 24/25; map p.572. A fine place to sit on the roadside and enjoy a beer (K600) – served in chilled glasses – with barbecued fish (K1700), chicken (K800) or fish balls (K400). The interior is a little less appealing. Daily 8am–10pm.

Too Too Myanmar Cuisine 27th St 74/75; map p.572. As the name suggests, this restaurant specializes in local dishes, served in several different rooms – some open and some with a/c. Locals attest to the quality and authenticity of the curries, which start at around K2500. Daily 9am–9pm.

TRADITIONAL ENTERTAINMENT

Mandalay is considered to be Myanmar's cultural capital, and a handful of regular shows offer foreigners a glimpse into traditional performing arts. Each of the following takes place daily at 8.30pm and lasts for one hour.

Mandalay Marionettes 66th St 26/27 T 02 34446. The performance starts with music and dancing, before telling traditional stories using marionettes. It's an entertaining show but without much explanation, so try to read the programme before the lights go down. $8.

Mintha Theater 27th St 65/66 ⓣ09 680 3607, ⓦminthatheater.com. A great opportunity to see traditional dance with extravagant costumes, accompanied by live music, with ten different performances packed into the show. K8000.

Moustache Brothers 39th St 80/81 ⓣ09 4303 4220, ⓔbosoeoo@gmail.com. The only chance you're likely to get to experience *ănyein*, a traditional form of comedy combining political satire and broad slapstick. Two of the performers, Lu Maw and Par Par Lay (who died in 2013), served six years' hard labour after making jokes about the regime in 1996, and this context is reason enough to attend even if the jokes don't always hit the mark. K8000.

SHOPPING

Books Myanmar Book Centre, Diamond Plaza, between 77th/78th sts and 33rd/34th sts (daily 9am–9pm).

Handicrafts There are several craft shops and workshops in the gold-pounding district on 36th St (see box, p.571), including Zaw Min Khaing (between 77th and 78th sts; daily 7am–6pm) for parasols.

Markets The biggest market is the Zegyo, 84th St 26/28, selling a huge range of everyday goods. The Man Myanmar Shopping Plaza to the south, 84th St 27/28, is more of the same but even more hectic. Immediately to the west of these are more interesting street markets. Man Myoe market, at 84th St 38/39, has many gold dealers at the front and is rarely visited by tourists.

Shopping centres Diamond Plaza (between 77th/78th sts and 33rd/34th sts) is the biggest in the city. The 78 Shopping Center, corner of 78th and 38th sts, includes a City Mart supermarket (daily 9am–9pm).

DIRECTORY

Cinemas Some films are shown in English at Myoma Cinema, 81st St 27/28 (K1000–1600).

Internet Cosmos, 31st St 80/81 (daily 9am–10pm); MS Aung, 82nd St 26/27 (daily 10am–10.30pm); Wai Yan, 27th St 73/74 (daily 8am–10pm).

Massage Smile (with blind masseurs), corner of 27th & 75th sts (daily 9am–11pm; K6000/hr; ⓣ09 9100 9487); GGG, 27th St 74/75 (daily 9am–11pm; K6000/hr; ⓣ09 4025 77711).

Money There are foreign exchange counters and ATMs in the arrivals section at the airport. Centrally located banks with currency exchange include AGD, 82nd St 27/28 (Mon–Fri 9.30am–3pm), and Small & Medium Industrial Development Bank (SMIDB), 83rd St 27/28 (Mon–Fri 9am–5pm). CB Bank, 78th St 27/28, also has an ATM. Diamond Plaza has a UAB bank plus several ATMs.

Post office 22nd St 80/81 (Mon–Fri 9.30am–4.30pm).

Swimming Outside guests can use the pool at *Mandalay City Hotel*, 26th St 82/83 (daily 6am–10pm; $5).

AROUND MANDALAY

Mandalay makes a good base for **day-trips** exploring the surrounding area. Each of the sites listed here has its own appeal, and most people opt to combine two or more into a day-trip by taxi or self-drive motorbike (with **Mingun** more usually visited by boat as a half-day trip). Accommodation in Mandalay will be able to help with transport, and drivers are likely to approach you in the street. Expect to pay K13,000–16,000 for a motorbike taxi tour of Amarapura, Sagaing and Inwa.

Amarapura

Amarapura was the capital of Burma from 1783–1823 and again from 1841–57, after which King Mindon moved the seat of power 11km north to the newly founded Mandalay. Although tour buses pull up each morning at Mahaganayon Kyaung monastery so that tourists can watch the monks eat lunch, the real reason to visit Amarapura is for **U Bein's Bridge** – at 1.2km, the longest teak bridge in the world. In theory you need to have a K10,000 Mandalay ticket (see box, p.569) to cross, but nobody seems to check it. The bridge gets particularly busy at sunset, with many tourists hiring boats (45min; K8000–10,000) in order to get views of the sun setting behind the bridge. It's arguably more atmospheric – and there are certainly fewer tourists – at dawn.

Sagaing

The main reason to visit the town of **Sagaing**, the fourteenth-century capital of a Shan kingdom, is for **Sagaing Hill**, which is dotted with white-and-gold pagodas. It's around 21km from Mandalay, across the Ayeyarwady River; there are two bridges side by side, and if you cross the older one (which also carries the railway) then you're likely to be charged the Mingun–Sagaing K3000 entry fee (see box, p.569).

You can drive up the hill but it's really worth making the 25-minute walk. The most common approach on foot is from the south side; the first temple you come

7

to at the top is **Soon U Ponya Shin Paya**, which has fantastic views of the Ayeyarwady River and the surrounding temple-dotted hills. There are several other religious structures on the hill, the most interesting of which is **Umin Thounzeh**, a curved chamber containing 43 seated and two standing Buddha images, a 20-minute walk from Soon U Ponya Shin.

Inwa

Today it may be a sleepy rural area, but **Inwa** – formerly known as Ava – was the site of the Burmese capital for more than 300 years, across three separate periods.

Most people take a tour of Inwa by horse and cart (2hr; K6000), covering the four main sights in a 5km circuit. The closest to the start is the bulky brick **Maha Aungmye Bonzan** monastery (K10,000 Mandalay ticket), where you should take a look in the bat-filled undercroft. The second attraction, nearby, is the "leaning tower" **Nanmyint**, one of the only structures remaining from King Bagyidaw's palace. Further west you'll find **Yedanasini Paya**, a collection of stupas situated photogenically in fields, and then **Bagaya Kyaung** (K10,000 Mandalay ticket). The highlight of Inwa, this is a wonderfully atmospheric working monastery built from teak in 1834.

You can visit Inwa as part of a tour, or by public transport: pick-ups from Mandalay (corner of 29th St and 84th St; 30min) can drop you at a junction from which it's a ten-minute walk southwest down a tree-lined road to the jetty. From there, it's a very short ferry ride (daily 6am–6pm; K1000 return, K1500 with a motorbike) to the place where horse and cart drivers wait.

Mingun

The village of **Mingun** (K3000 entry), 8km northwest (1hr) from Mandalay by boat, would not be visited today if it were not for King Bodawpaya, who in 1790 decided to build a gigantic temple here. All that was completed by the time of his death – 29 years later – was the bottom portion, an imposing 70m cube of bricks on top of a huge terrace.

To get an idea of the intended shape for **Mingun Paya**, check out the small **Pondaw Paya** to the southeast of it. The other main attraction in Mingun village is the bronze **Mingun Bell**, also commissioned by Bodawpaya and found just north of Mingun Paya. With a circumference of almost 5m, it is said to be the largest intact bell in the world. Don't miss **Hsinbyume Paya** a little further north. Its wavy design represents Mount Sumeru, the mountain at the centre of the Buddhist cosmos, and the mountains that surround it.

Unfortunately Mingun gets unpleasantly packed with tour groups and touts, so you might want to stick to the backstreets. You may also find that taking the government boat gives you too much time in Mingun; the service (1hr; K5000) leaves from the pier on 26th Street in Mandalay at 9am and returns at 1pm. The alternatives are to take the private service from Gawain jetty (depart 8am, return 11am; K6000 return), or to visit by road in conjunction with the area's other ancient city sites.

Northern Myanmar

Most of **northern Myanmar** is closed to foreigners, largely due to the history of conflict between the army and ethnic militias in Kachin State. It most recently flared up in 2011 and the army has been accused, with good evidence, of atrocities including the torture and extrajudicial killing of civilians. A preliminary ceasefire was signed in May 2013, but fighting broke out again later in the year.

For tourists, this has meant some additional travel restrictions. Those parts of the north that can be visited, however, are safe and offer some of the country's best opportunities to spend time with local people. One way to do this is to take a boat trip on the **Ayeyarwady River** north of Mandalay around **Katha** and **Bhamo** (see box above), where long journey times and a scarcity of foreigners

AYEYARWADY RIVER TRIPS

The stretch of the Ayeyarwady River north of Mandalay is much less frequently travelled by foreigners than the route to Bagan (see p.552). Although the scenery is no more spectacular, other than in the brief "second defile" (a narrowing of the river) between Bhamo and Katha, it's more rewarding for the scope it offers for interacting with local people. The route can also provide access to rarely visited villages: in addition to Bhamo and Katha, boats typically stop at Shwegu (between Bhamo and Katha) and Kyaukmyaung (between Katha and Mandalay), both of which have simple guesthouses.

The government has closed the river **north of Bhamo** to foreigners. This means that although you can take a train to Myitkina, for example, you can't start a river trip from there. Since the road to Bhamo is also closed, the easiest way to do the whole available route is to fly into Bhamo then take the boat south; the cheapest is to take a train to Katha (via Naba), travel upriver to Bhamo by boat, and then take the boat south again. Upriver travel is, of course, slower than downriver and all travel times depend on the season due to varying water levels (times given here are for November or December). On overnight trips, passengers sleep on the boat, almost always on the deck, although cabins are available on some services.

There are two travel options open to foreigners: government-run IWT ferries, and boats operated by the private company N Mai Hka. The former are much cheaper but also much slower – for example, it takes at least 30 hours to travel from Bhamo to Mandalay on the IWT ferry (deck ticket $12), but as little as 22 hours with N Mai Hka (deck ticket $30). The N Mai Hka services may not run in peak season, though, as the boats are sometimes used on the Bagan–Mandalay route instead.

Affordable meals are served onboard, or you can buy a curry for around K1000 when the boat stops at a village. Bring warm clothes as it can be cold in the mornings, plus a sleeping mat and blanket if you will be sleeping on the boat.

make it easy to get a sense of provincial life. Heading northeast from Mandalay instead, towards the Chinese border, treks from **Kyaukme** or **Hsipaw** offer the opportunity to stay in ethnic minority homes in traditional mountain villages.

KATHA

An engagingly low-key place to hang around for a day or two, the small riverside town of **Katha** was the model for Kyauktada in George Orwell's novel *Burmese Days* (see box, p.578). Although Orwell modified the plan of the town a little, it's possible to seek out several of the colonial buildings that played a part either in the novel or in Orwell's life in the town.

WHAT TO SEE AND DO

At the southern end of the town centre is the British-era **jail**, which is still in use. North of the centre, on the east side of 5th Street, is the former **British Club**, which was central to *Burmese Days*. It now functions as an association office and is closed to the public, but the **Tennis Club** beside it is still active. Further north on 5th Street is the **District Commissioner's House**, a large brick and wood building, and close by is the red half-timbered **Police Commissioner's House** where Orwell lived, which is still used by the police today.

ARRIVAL AND DEPARTURE

Foreigners are not allowed to travel by road between Mandalay and Katha.

By train The nearest mainline train station is at Naba, 30km northwest of Katha. Shuttle buses between the two take 1hr; in Katha they leave from near the fire station. There are four trains daily from Naba to Mandalay (8–12hr); the fastest and most reliable departs at 1pm.

By boat The IWT office on Strand Rd, opposite the main jetty, sells tickets for ferries to Bhamo (3 weekly; 10hr; $4) and Mandalay (3 weekly; 21hr; $9). The small N Mai Hka counter (☎075 25413 or ☎09 6813472), also on Strand Rd, sells tickets for their fast boat upriver to Bhamo (daily; 8hr; $20). If you're heading downriver, in theory you can join the N Mai Hka boat to Mandalay (daily 6pm; 17hr; $30) which begins at Bhamo, but staff are often reluctant to sell tickets. The N Mai Kha services may not run in peak season (see box, p.577).

7

ACCOMMODATION

Ayarwady Guest House Strand Rd ⓣ 075 25140. It may not be much, but this makeshift affair is the best of the two guesthouses open to foreigners and the staff can give you a handy sketch map of the town. For K15,000 you can get a/c; either way you'll have to share a bathroom and use a bucket shower. No breakfast. K5000

EATING AND DRINKING

The cheapest and most interesting dinner option is the night street market. To get there, take a right out of the *Ayarwady Guest House* and then the first right.

Shwe Sisa Strand Rd. This otherwise run-of-the-mill beer station has a riverside location ideal for whiling away some time reading *Burmese Days*, perhaps with a draught beer (K600). They also serve dishes including barbecued fish. Daily 9am–10pm.

7

BHAMO

The busy town of **Bhamo** has long profited from its position close to a Chinese border crossing (closed to foreigners). There isn't much to see in the town other than the market and waterfront, plus a few old teak buildings, but the surrounding area is worth exploring.

WHAT TO SEE AND DO

The most rewarding destination nearby is **Tain Pha Hill**, topped by a stupa and two meditation halls. It has good views but really a visit is all about the journey there: it's an hour's ride by bicycle, and if you're travelling by bike between December and June/July, you'll cross the 470m-long bamboo bridge from Wa Thatar village. Each year the bridge is destroyed by monsoon flooding, and rebuilt by two hundred villagers; a ferry (K500) runs at other times.

Though it's possible to do the trip independently, it's certain to be more interesting and enjoyable if you engage the services of Sein Win (contact through your accommodation; K10,000 per person). He's a fascinating character, and you should make sure you ask him about the helicopter that he built in his front room. He can also arrange a boat to Tain Pha Hill (1hr; K20,000), which from November to January gives you a chance of seeing dolphins. Alternatively, he offers trips to an elephant camp or a three-hour bike ride to a Kachin village called Aung Tha.

ARRIVAL AND DEPARTURE

Foreigners are not allowed to travel to Bhamo by bus.

By plane The airport is less than 3km east of town.

Destinations Mandalay (4 weekly; 55min); Yangon (4 weekly; 2hr 35min).

By boat All boats use a jetty 4km south of town for most of the year, or a jetty in the town centre in the rainy season. The government IWT office (daily 6am–8pm; ⓣ 074 50117) is in a colonial-era building just north of the main riverfront area. Their slow boat to Mandalay (30hr; deck $12, cabin $54) departs at 7am on Mon, Wed and Fri, stopping at Shwegu (4hr), Katha (9hr) and Kyaukmyaung (26hr). The N Mai Hka office (daily 6am–6pm; ⓣ 074 51258 or ⓣ 09 401595672) is just north of the clock tower. When they run (see box, p.577), their fast boats depart for Mandalay (25hr; deck $30, cabin $60) on Thurs and Sun at 10am and stop in Shwegu (4hr), Katha (8hr) and Kyaukmyaung (22hr). There's also a daily service going only as far as Katha (9hr), departing at 7am.

ACCOMMODATION

Friendship Hotel Letwet Thondaya Rd ⓣ 074 50095. Popular with the few tourists who pass through Bhamo, offering decent if slightly dated rooms plus helpful staff (ask for a copy of their town map). Wi-fi in lobby. $14

GEORGE ORWELL IN BURMA

Eric Blair (1903–50), who would later find fame under his pen name **George Orwell**, arrived in Burma in November 1922 as a youthful member of the Imperial Police. Sent first to Maymyo (now Pyin Oo Lwin), he spent time in the Ayeyarwady delta and Moulmein (now Mawlamyine, the home town of his maternal grandmother) before being posted to Katha.

Orwell's experiences in Burma convinced him of the wrongs of imperialism, and he gained a reputation as an outsider more interested in spending time with the Burmese than in more "pukka" (appropriate) pursuits for a British officer. In this he resembled **Flory**, the protagonist of his first novel *Burmese Days* (1934), which was set in a thinly disguised Katha. Orwell also wrote about Burma in his essays *A Hanging* (1931) and *Shooting an Elephant* (1936).

EATING AND DRINKING

Shamie Tiyet Rd. A typical Muslim restaurant serving up tasty biryani and curries, just around the corner from the *Friendship Hotel*. Daily 7am–9pm.

Sky Beer Bar Tiyet Rd. Young locals pack out this bar in the evenings, which isn't surprising given that it serves draught beer and cheap barbecue. There are also standard Chinese dishes for around K2500. Daily lunch & dinner.

PYIN OO LWIN

Founded in 1896 as a British hill station known as Maymyo, **Pyin Oo Lwin** remains a popular escape from the heat of Mandalay. These days, though, most visitors are well-off Burmese who stay in comfortable hotels or holiday homes south of the centre. The town is also an important military training centre and a sign as you approach from Mandalay hails "the triumphant elite of the future".

WHAT TO SEE AND DO

The commercial centre of town, marked by the **Purcell Tower**, is rather more down-to-earth than the southern suburbs and has a flavour of South Asia thanks to the descendants of Indian and Nepalese workers brought here by the British. Further east, the daily **Shan Market** on Circular Road attracts farmers from surrounding areas and is at its best from 6.30–8am.

Circular Road is also one of the richest hunting grounds for the town's **colonial architecture**. Some of the buildings have retained their old function, such as the grand *Croxton Hotel* (now the *Gandamar Myaing Hotel*) and the No. 4 Basic Education High School, both on Circular Road. Others have changed function: the British Club on Anawrahta Road is now

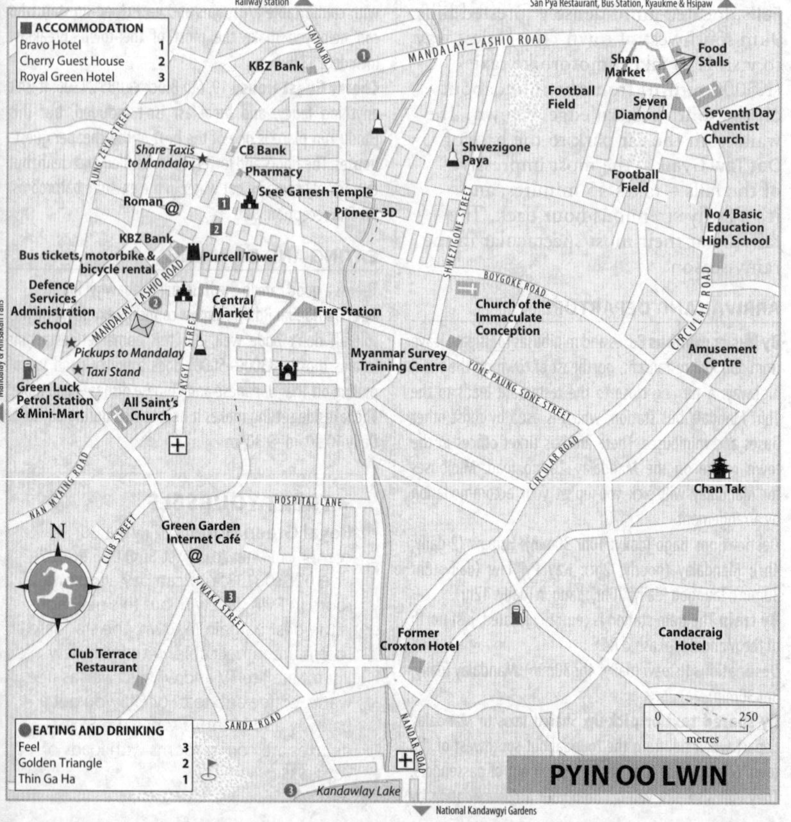

the government-owned *Candacraig Hotel*, worth popping inside for its hunting-lodge vibe.

The town's most popular attraction is the **National Kandawgyi Gardens** on Nandar Road (daily 8am–5.30pm; $5; ⓣ 085 22497), 2.5km south of the centre. Founded in 1915, this large botanical garden includes a short swamp walkway and an aviary that is a hit with children. Close to the main entrance there's an outdoor swimming pool (K1000; bring your own towel), while views from the Nan Myint tower on the northwest side give a good sense of the affluent part of town in which the gardens are set. Note that the gardens are owned by Htoo Group, which has been subject to international sanctions (see box, p.521).

7

The most rewarding half-day trip out of Pyin Oo Lwin is to the **Anisakan Falls**, located amid densely forested hills 9km southwest of town. The easiest way to visit is to take a motorbike taxi (K5000 return) from the roundabout on the southwestern edge of town. The walk from the car park to the base of **Dat Taw Gyaik** – the most impressive of the falls – takes 45 minutes, and it's a fairly strenuous hour back. The falls are at their most spectacular in the rainy season.

ARRIVAL AND DEPARTURE

By bus or minibus Buses and minibuses to Hsipaw leave from *San Pya* restaurant, northeast of town on the main highway. A turning close to the restaurant leads to the Thiri Mandala bus station, which is used by most other buses and minibuses. There are bus ticket offices in the town centre on the Mandalay–Lashio road. Minibuses for Mandalay will pick you up at your accommodation by arrangement.

Destinations Bago (daily; 10hr 30min); Hsipaw (2 daily; 4hr); Mandalay (hourly; 2hr); Nay Pyi Taw (daily; 8hr 30min); Taungoo (daily; 10hr); Yangon (daily; 12hr).

By train The train station is centrally located, just north of the Mandalay–Lashio Rd.

Destinations Hsipaw (daily; 4hr 30min); Mandalay (daily; 3hr 30min).

By shared taxi or pick-up Shared taxis to Mandalay depart when full from the roundabout southwest of the town centre, from 6am until they run out of passengers. They will also pick you up from your accommodation by arrangement, as will shared taxis to Hsipaw (3hr). Pick-ups to Mandalay (3hr) run 6am to 6pm, but more frequently early on, from Bogyoke Rd and from the train station when a service arrives. They stop at the Zegyo (main market) in Mandalay.

INFORMATION AND TOURS

Tour agents Seven Diamond Express, Circular Rd (Mon–Sat 8am–8pm, Sun 8am–6pm; ⓣ 085 33333622).

GETTING AROUND

You can get around the town's sights on foot, or rent a motorbike (K8,000/day) or bicycle (K2000/day) from guesthouses or rental shops (daily 9am–7pm) on the Mandalay–Lashio road. Alternatively, you could take one of the town's iconic horse-carts on a short tour for K6000/hr. They wait for customers around Purcell Tower and the Central Market.

ACCOMMODATION

Bravo Hotel Mandalay–Lashio Rd ⓣ 085 21223 or ⓣ 09 2044249. An understandably popular mid-range option, with comfortable a/c rooms and very clued-up staff who can help you make the most of the town. Breakfast included. **$30**

Cherry Guest House 19, 6th Block ⓣ 085 21306. It isn't anything fancy, and breakfast isn't included, but this Hindu-run place is one of the best of the cheaper guesthouses. The floors and lower walls are tiled and clean, but there's only sporadic hot water in the en-suite bathrooms. Wi-fi in reception. **$20**

EATING AND DRINKING

There's a good café in the National Kandawgyi Gardens.

Feel Off Nandar Rd. The almost comically extensive menus (plural) don't bode well, but this upmarket restaurant (mains mostly K3000–5000) does a pretty good job of pulling off Thai, Japanese and Chinese dishes – and more. The lakeside setting makes it best to visit during daylight. Daily 10.30am–9.30pm.

★TREAT YOURSELF

Royal Green Hotel 17 Ziwaka Rd, corner of Pyitawthar 1st St ⓣ 085 28422 or ⓣ 096506133. You can pay a lot for a room in Pyin Oo Lwin, but this new hotel is the best bargain in town. The standard rooms are impeccable, with fresh new linen, satellite TV and wi-fi, as well as free water, coffee and tea. For $45 you get a balcony and bathtub, while the $55 deluxes are corner rooms with loads of light. **$35**

Golden Triangle Mandalay–Lashio Rd. Pretty much the centre of tourist life in Pyin Oo Lwin, this café is lacking in local atmosphere but brews up its own-brand coffee (cappuccino K2200) and serves it with decent cakes. You can also get a few main courses, like pizza (K3000) and fried noodles (K1800). Daily 8am–9pm.

Thin Ga Ha Mandalay–Lashio Rd. There's no English sign but you can't miss this place: bamboo trellis arches have been covered with plastic sheeting to make a large tunnel, with plants among the wooden tables. There's an *á la carte* menu, plus a good-value Shan buffet at lunchtime – you get two meat dishes, two veg and soup for K1500. Daily 9am–midnight.

DIRECTORY

Bank CB Bank with ATM, Mandalay–Lashio Rd (Mon–Fri 9.30am–3pm).

Cinema Pioneer 3D (daily 10am–10pm; K2000) has only twenty seats and shows 3D blu-rays in English.

Internet Green Garden Internet Café, Ziwaka St; Roman, off the Mandalay–Lashio Rd (daily 8am–10pm).

Post office Just off the Mandalay–Lashio Rd (Mon–Fri 9.30am–4.30pm).

KYAUKME

A larger town than nearby Hsipaw, **KYAUKME** (pronounced "chow-may") is less well known, and has fewer facilities for foreign tourists, but it provides access to hiking which is arguably even better.

WHAT TO SEE AND DO

Kaukme's busy **morning market** is a few blocks west of *A Yone Oo* guesthouse, and open every day. The primary reason to visit Kyaukme, though, is for the fantastic **trekking**. You need to take a motorbike or tuk-tuk to the trailheads, which makes it more expensive than trekking around Hsipaw, but the ride itself is one of the highlights. The town's handful of guides all charge the same price of $30 per person per day. The guesthouse can put you in contact with them; Moe Set (T 09 403725869, E asiaboy.myanmar@gmail.com) comes recommended.

ARRIVAL AND DEPARTURE

By bus or minibus There are a handful of bus ticket offices opposite the morning market.

Destinations Hsipaw (3 daily; 1hr); Mandalay (4 daily; 5hr 30min).

By train The train station is northeast of the morning market. The Goteik viaduct, between Kyaukme and Pyin Oo Lwin, is a tourist attraction in its own right.

Destinations Hsipaw (daily; 1hr 15min); Mandalay (daily; 11hr 15min); Pyin Oo Lwin (daily; 6hr 15min).

ACCOMMODATION

The only guesthouse licensed for foreigners is owned by a city councillor, who is also building a more upmarket place.

A Yone Oo Shwe Phi Oo Rd T 082 40669. If it wasn't the only option in town, it would be hard to recommend this guesthouse. There are some decent rooms if you're willing to pay extra, but the basic ones are disappointing. More importantly, some staff members are unhelpful and the management take issue with simple things such as guests leaving their bags while trekking. $12

7

EATING AND DRINKING

Yu Nam Aung San Rd. A very standard Chinese restaurant, with a concrete floor and the TV usually blaring. The menu covers all the usual bases, with dishes like sweet-and-sour pork balls (K2000). Daily 7am–7pm.

DIRECTORY

Internet There's an internet café next door to *A Yone Oo* guesthouse (8am–10pm).

HSIPAW

Once considered something of a hidden gem, **Hsipaw** (pronounced as either "see-paw" or "tee-bor") is transforming from a sleepy little backwater into a bustling town, thanks both to trade with China and to a burgeoning tourist industry.

WHAT TO SEE AND DO

Most people visit to go trekking, but Hsipaw itself is an engaging place to wander around. If you can get up early enough then the daily **produce market** is particularly interesting when candlelit before dawn.

To learn more about the town and its history, a visit to the **Shan Palace** on the northeastern edge of town (daily 9am–noon & 3–6pm; donation) is a must. The last Shan *saopha* (prince) vanished in 1962, with the military implicated but denying responsibility, and his nephew Sao Oo Kya – aka Mr Donald – was arrested in 2005 on trumped-up charges. Although released

7

in 2009, he no longer lives in Hsipaw, but his wife Mrs Fern talks visitors through the history of the palace and answers questions.

There are several attractions further north on the edge of town, including **Sao Pu Sao Nai nat shrine**, which is signposted on the left-hand side of Namtu Road. West of the shrine – not far from *Mrs Popcorn's Garden* (see p.584) – is an area known as **Little Bagan**. It's a tongue-in-cheek name, but the decaying stupas are photogenic.

The most popular spot for sunset is **Thein Daung Pagoda**, on a hill 2.5km south of town across the Dokhtawady River. Take a left just after the bridge, then a right at the signposted temple gateway; it's a fifteen-minute walk to the top.

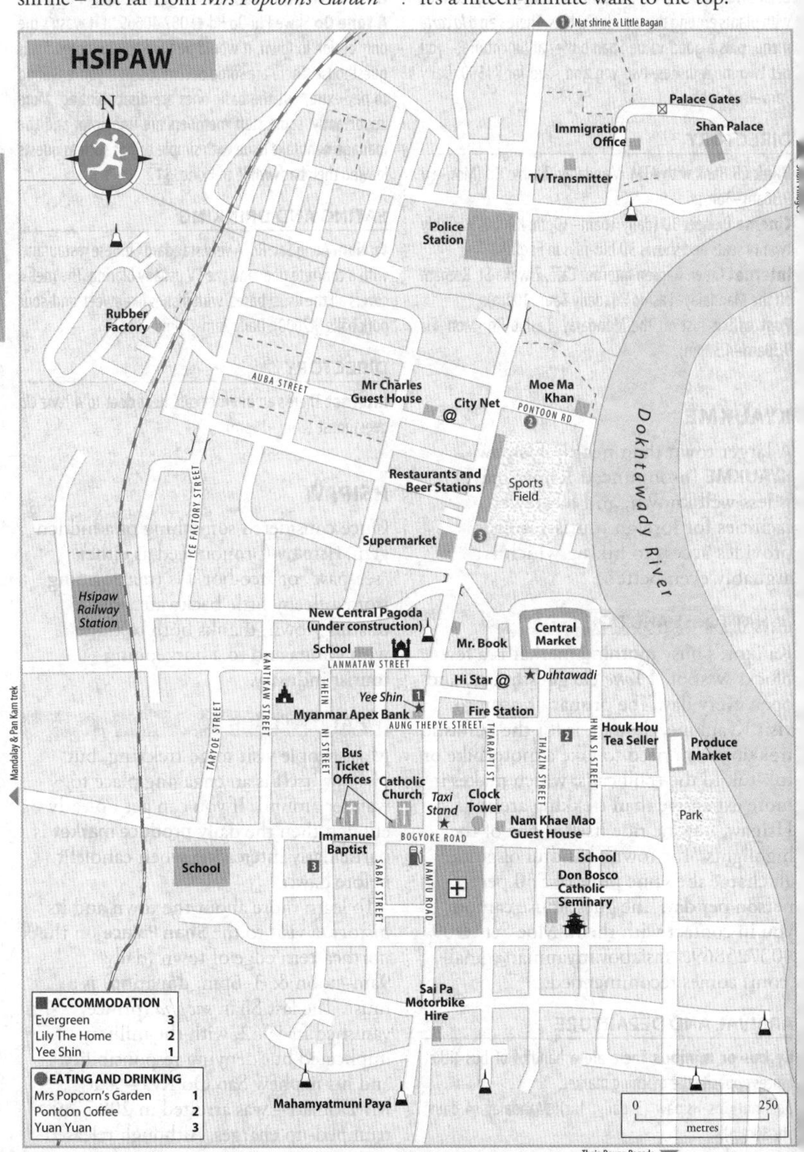

TREKKING AROUND HSIPAW

The most popular trekking route from Hsipaw is to a Palaung village called **Pan Kam**, usually as an overnight trip. It's a 4–5-hour walk through fields and then uphill, starting at a Muslim cemetery on the western edge of Hsipaw and continuing through the villages of Nar Loy, Par Pheit, Nar Moon and Man Pyit.

The headman at Pan Kam, O Maung, works closely with the *Mr Charles Guest House* in Hsipaw so the village can get busy. Some people prefer, therefore, to sleep at **Htan Sant** around 1hr 15min further along. You might want to stop in Pan Kam for lunch at O Maung's home, then ask for advice about the onward route. The main route to Htan Sant is the left path at a fork just after you leave Pan Kam, but the right path has exceptional views of the valley. Make sure you have plenty of time to reach Htan Sant before dark, particularly if you take the less-travelled right-hand path.

Accommodation in Htan Sant can be arranged with the headman, Khao San Aye; the next day you can either retrace your steps or press on through Paw Ka, Ohn Mu and Sar Maw. The latter takes around eight hours and comes out at **Baw Gyo Pagoda** on the main highway, from where you can find a pick-up or hitch back the 8km to Hsipaw.

If you get directions from your guesthouse, and don't mind asking regularly once walking, then it's possible to do these hikes without a guide. Dinner, bed and breakfast cost around K5000 per person. It's worth considering supporting independent local guides, however, such as Than Htike (T 09 36186646, E lionmanhpw@gmail.com) who charges K10,000 per person per day including accommodation.

The most popular three-day hike starts from the hilltop village of **Namhsan**, a 6hr pick-up ride from Hsipaw, but the area has been off-limits following fighting between the army and a Palaung militia. Another option is to hike to **Kyaukme**, which takes three days – it's possible to have your bags sent along. Guides can also arrange longer, more adventurous treks.

If you rent a motorbike then several other options open up. One is to ride east out of town to a series of peaceful riverside **Shan villages**. Another is to head towards Lashio, through the village of Su Plan – where the Song Pinong restaurant does wonderful barbecue fish with tamarind sauce (K1500) – and on to an **ice factory** in Pan Hsao which uses ingenious home-made equipment. A little further along is a dragon fruit plantation with a picturesque viewing platform.

Another way to explore the area is by **river**. Moe Ma Khan, on Pontoon Rd (T 09 47310166), charges K25,000 per boat for a four- to five-hour trip including visits to a monastery and a Shan village.

ARRIVAL AND DEPARTURE

By bus or minibus Buses pick up and set down passengers at the bus company offices in town, including Duhtawadi, Lanmataw St (who run an a/c bus at 2.30pm), and Yee Shin, Namtu St. There are also several companies on Bogoke Rd including Khaing Dhabyay, who also arrange minibuses to Mandalay.

Destinations Kalaw (3 daily; 12hr 30min); Kyaukme (3 daily; 1hr); Lashio (2 daily; 2hr); Mandalay (7 daily; 5hr); Nay Pyi Taw (3 daily; 11hr 30min); Nyaungshwe for Inle Lake (3 daily; 11hr 30min); Pyin Oo Lwin (6 daily; 3hr 30min); Yangon (3 daily; 13hr 30min).

By shared taxi Vehicles to Mandalay (5hr 30min) or Pyin Oo Lwin (3hr 30min) run at around 6.30am and 2.30pm. Book through your guesthouse or through Khaing Dhabyay, Bogyoke Rd.

By train The train station is on the western side of the town centre, and tickets are only sold on the day of travel. If you're heading for Mandalay it's much quicker to get off at Pyin Oo Lwin and take a bus. This still allows you to see the spectacular Goteik viaduct (see p.581).

Destinations Kyaukme (daily; 1hr 15min); Lashio (daily; 4hr); Mandalay (daily; 13hr 15min); Pyin Oo Lwin (daily; 6hr 40min).

ACCOMMODATION

By far the most successful place in town is *Mr Charles Guest House*, but some people are uncomfortable with the extent of the owner's influence over tourism in Hsipaw.

Evergreen Thein Ni St T 082 80670 or T 09 5278274. This large white concrete building has 26 rooms, with a/c available for $25 as well as en-suite fan rooms for $20; both of these have TVs and DVD players. Some of the rooms smell of cigarette smoke so you may want to see a few before choosing. There's wi-fi at reception. **$10**

Lily the Home 108 Aung Thepye St T 082 80318 or T 09 5133900, E namkhaemaoguesthouse@gmail.com. An excellent choice, with a range of rooms – the cheapest

with shared bathrooms – plus good breakfast and wi-fi. There was a lot of construction during the time of writing; it remains to be seen what impact this will have on the feel of the place. You're still sure to get a friendly welcome from Lily, the sister of Mr Charles, who along with her husband also owns the older *Nam Khae Mao Guest House*. $20

Yee Shin Namtu Rd ☎ 082 80711. This neat and tidy guesthouse has 14 tiny rooms, so small that they have little furniture other than the beds. Most of them don't have private bathrooms; for $25 you can get a/c. Wi-fi in rooms. $15

EATING AND DRINKING

There are several cheap food stalls in the central market and simple restaurants on Namtu Rd.

7

★**Mrs Popcorn's Garden** Off Namtu Rd – take the turning for the *nat* shrine (see p.582), turn left before the shrine then right at the crossroads. It may be a little out of the way, but the garden is a fantastic place for coffee, fruit juice (K600) or a snack (but not popcorn – the charming owner Khin Myint Htay doesn't make it any more). If you want lunch then she can prepare a rice or noodle dish (K1500–2500), but it may take a little while. Daily 9am–around 7pm.

Pontoon Coffee Pontoon Rd. Run by Australian expat Maureen – who has spent many years in Hsipaw – this café serves proper coffee from a shiny new Italian machine (K1000–2000) and a range of snacks such as pancakes (K1000). Daily 9am–9pm.

Yuan Yuan Namtu Rd. This street-side café is known for its excellent chicken rice (K1500) made by Ayeyong and for the drinks (K800) prepared by her husband Atha (aka Mr Shake). They also do steamed buns (K250) in the morning. Daily 11.30am–10pm.

SHOPPING

Books The stall on Namtu Rd run by Ko Zaw Tun, aka Mr Book (daily 6am–9pm), has a small but interesting selection of books in English. He also knows everything you could wish to know about the town and its citizens.

Tea Houk Hou sells Shan State tea, grown around 70km away. A kilo of the best-quality tea costs K3000, and it's possible to see it being sorted and packed.

DIRECTORY

Bicycle rental Guesthouses, including *Lily the Home*, rent out bicycles for K2000/day.

Internet Hi Star, Theraphi St (daily 9am–10.30pm); City Net, Auba St (daily 8am–11pm).

Money Myanmar Apex bank (Mon–Fri 10am–3pm) has an ATM and currency exchange.

Motorbike rental Sai Pa, Namtu Rd (daily 7am–7pm; K8000/day).

PALAWAN ISLAND, BACUIT ARCHIPELAGO

The Philippines

HIGHLIGHTS

❶ **Vigan** Travel back in time wandering along Vigan's cobbled streets. **See p.613**

❷ **The Cordilleras** Home to Sagada's hanging coffins and Banaue's 2000-year-old rice terraces. **See p.615**

❸ **Malapascua Island** Dive among magnificent thresher sharks at Monad Shoal. **See p.641**

❹ **Boracay** First stop for sun-worshippers and partygoers is White Beach. **See p.651**

❺ **Bacuit Archipelago** Turquoise waters and hidden beaches amid breathtaking limestone cliffs. **See p.663**

HIGHLIGHTS ARE MARKED ON THE MAP ON P.587

ROUGH COSTS

Daily budget Basic US$25/Occasional treat US$35

Drink San Miguel beer US$1

Food *Adobo* US$3

Hostel/budget hotel US$10/US$15

Travel Bus: Banaue–Manila (9hr) $121; Fast ferry: Dumaguete–Tagbilaran (2hr) $17; Flight: Manila–Puerto Princesa (1hr 15min) $50

FACT FILE

Population 97 million

Languages Filipino (Tagalog), Visayan, English, with nine other languages and 87 dialects

Currency Peso (P)

Capital Manila

International phone code ☎ + 63

Time zone GMT + 8hr

Introduction

Backpackers on the traditional Asian trails have tended to ignore the Philippines because it involves an extra flight, albeit a short one, across the South China Sea. You won't find the kind of travellers' scene that has come to dominate areas like southern Thailand in recent years, though the beaches and islands certainly give Thailand a run for its money. It's this very lack of mass tourism that makes the Philippines such an attractive destination. The world's second-largest archipelago (after Indonesia), with 7107 islands – sixty percent of them uninhabited – and over 36,000km of coastline, it nonetheless has a landmass only roughly the size of Italy. If you're ready to cope with some eccentric infrastructure, a distinctly laidback attitude towards time, and a national obsession with karaoke, the Philippines has plenty to offer.

Most international flights land in the capital, **Manila**, which, though dilapidated and traffic-choked, also has some of the ritziest shopping malls and liveliest nightlife in Asia. For beach connoisseurs, the central **Visayan region** is an island-hopper's paradise. Though Boracay remains the most popular island destination, travellers are discovering quiet islands around Cebu and Bohol; if you're willing to leave the beaten track, it's not hard to find your own deserted tropical beach. **Palawan** is an unforgettable wilderness of diamond-blue lagoons, volcanic lakes and first-rate scuba diving, while the **Cordillera Mountains** of northern Luzon are the country's tribal heartland, populated by the same groups that settled here around 500 BC.

Centuries of **colonial rule** have resulted in a delightfully mixed-up country of potent but conflicting influences. Spain brought Catholicism, European architecture and the *mañana* ethic, while America gave the Philippines its constitution and its passion for basketball, beauty pageants and pizza. In 1946 the Philippines became Asia's first real democracy, a fact most Filipinos remain fiercely proud of.

Despite the political intrigues and the poverty, Filipinos themselves remain enviably optimistic and gregarious. Graciousness and warmth seem to be built into their genes, though they are also passionate, sometimes hot-headedly so. They love food, music and romance; and the hundreds of **fiestas** and religious

WHEN TO GO

The Philippines has a tropical marine climate characterized by two distinct seasons: the **wet season** (southwest monsoon, or *habagat*) from May to October and the **dry season** (northeast monsoon, or *amihan*) from November to April. Between May and December the country is hit directly by at least five or six typhoons. This doesn't necessarily mean the wet season is a bad time to travel, though flights are sometimes cancelled and roads are made impassable by flood waters, even in the capital – but generally this only lasts a few days. The first typhoon can hit as early as May, although typically it is June or July before the rains really start, with August the wettest month. The southern Visayas and Palawan are less prone to typhoons.

Temperatures are fairly constant throughout the year. November through to February are the coolest months, with daytime highs of around 28°C. March, April and May are very hot: expect temperatures to peak at 36°C.

At **Christmas** and **Easter**, the whole of the Philippines hits the road and getting a seat on a bus or plane can be difficult.

ceremonies that are held throughout the year are an integral part of Filipino life. English is widely spoken and you will be greeted with the honorific "ma'am" or "sir".

The Philippines is a passion play writ large, a country that will turn every notion you ever had of Asia on its head. Even when typhoons devastate entire islands, or when volcanoes erupt, Filipinos remain stoically and passively fatalistic. When dealing with the trials and tribulations of life in the Philippines, Filipinos' usual reaction is to smile, throw up their hands, and say *bahala-na* – a

8

phrase that loosely translates to "what will be, will be".

CHRONOLOGY

500 BC Trade develops with the archipelago's neighbours – the powerful Hindu empires in Java and Sumatra, and with China.

1380 Arab scholar Makdam arrives in the Sulu Islands.

1475 Muslim leader Sharif Mohammed Kabungsuwan, from Johore, marries a local princess and declares himself the first sultan of Mindanao. Islam becomes established in Mindanao, and influential as far as Luzon.

April 24, 1521 Ferdinand Magellan arrives in Cebu and claims the islands for Spain. He is killed in a skirmish with warriors led by chief Lapu-Lapu.

1565 Miguel Lopez de Legaspi, under orders from King Philip II, establishes a colony in Bohol and erects the first Spanish fort in the Philippines on Cebu.

1571 Legaspi conquers Manila, and a year later the whole country, except the Islamic Sulu Islands and Mindanao. Spanish friars zealously spread Catholicism.

1762 The British occupy Manila for a few months, but hand it back to Spain under the conditions of the Treaty of Paris, signed in 1763.

1892 José Rizal, a lawyer, novelist and poet whose anti-colonial writings portray Spanish friars as unscrupulous and depraved, returns to Manila and founds the reform movement Liga Filipina. He is arrested and exiled to Mindanao. Andres Bonifacio takes over and establishes the revolutionary group Katipunan.

1896 Armed struggle for independence breaks out, and Rizal is arrested and then executed on December 30, in what is now Rizal Park in Manila.

1897 Allied with a young firebrand general, Emilio Aguinaldo, Bonifacio supports violent opposition. Facing all-out insurrection, the Spanish negotiate a truce with Aguinaldo, and Bonifacio is executed.

1898 The US and Spain are at war over Cuba, and the US attack and defeat the Spanish fleet in Manila Bay. The Filipinos fight with the US, and General Aguinaldo declares the Philippines independent. However, the US pays Spain US$20 million for the Philippines, and takes over as a colonizing power.

1898–1902 The Filipino–American War lasts for three years (with skirmishes for another seven), and more than 600,000 Filipinos are killed.

1935 Washington recognizes a new Philippine constitution, making the Philippines a commonwealth of the US. Manuel Quezon wins the country's first presidential elections.

1942 Japanese troops land on Luzon and conquer Manila on January 2. US General MacArthur and Quezon leave the American base on Corregidor, which the Japanese overrun in days; during the Bataan Death March that follows, 10,000 Americans and Filipinos die.

October 1944 MacArthur returns, wading ashore at Leyte and recapturing the archipelago from retreating Japanese forces.

July 4, 1946 The Philippines is granted full independence and Manuel Roxas is sworn in as the first president of the republic.

1965 Ferdinand Edralin Marcos, a brilliant young lawyer and member of the Senate, is elected president, portraying himself as a force for reform. In his first term he embarks on a huge infrastructure programme.

1969 Marcos is re-elected. Poverty and social inequality are still rife, and there is student, labour and peasant unrest, much of it stoked by communists, which Marcos (backed by the US) uses to perpetuate his hold on power.

September 21, 1972 Marcos declares martial law, arresting Senator Ninoy Aquino and other opposition leaders.

August 21, 1983 Aquino, who had been in exile in the US for three years, returns to the Philippines. He is assassinated as he leaves his plane at Manila Airport.

February 7, 1986 At a snap election, the opposition unites behind Aquino's widow, Cory. On February 25, both Marcos and Cory claim victory and are sworn in at separate ceremonies. Archbishop Jaime Sin urges the people to take to the streets and Ferdinand and Imelda Marcos flee into exile in Hawaii; Ferdinand dies in 1989. Conservative estimates of their plunder are around $10 billion.

1986–92 Cory Aquino's presidency is plagued by problems. She backtracks on promises for land reforms, survives seven coup attempts and makes little headway in tackling the widespread poverty.

July 1, 1992 Fidel Ramos is elected president.

1998 Former vice-president Joseph Estrada (known as Erap, a play on the Filipino word for friend, *pare*), a former tough-guy film actor, becomes president.

2000 Estrada is accused of receiving P500 million in illegal gambling payoffs. He is impeached, but the trial falls apart. Following protests of half a million people, the military withdraws its support and Estrada is evicted from Malacañang.

January 20, 2001 Vice-president Gloria Macapagal-Arroyo is sworn in as president.

2004 Macapagal-Arroyo wins the presidential elections against Fernando Poe Jr, a movie star and friend of Estrada. Poe's supporters claim election fraud.

November 2007 An attempted coup in Manila is put down. It is similar to one in 2003, and around a dozen others in the past twenty years.

August 2008 Separatist violence in Mindanao surges after peace talks break down, leaving at least 30 people dead.

November 2009 The slaughter of 57 civilians (at least 34 of them journalists) sends shock waves around the world in what becomes known as the Maguindinao massacre. Already ranked second only to Iraq as the deadliest country for journalists by the CPJ, the massacre underlines the Arroyo administration's tolerance of extra-judicial killings

and human rights abuses. The Ampatuan clan, accused of masterminding the slayings as part of a strike against an upcoming political rival, have long been supporters of President Arroyo, who subsequently declares a state of emergency. Peace talks resume between the government and the MILF.

May 2010 Scheduled elections use computerized voting for the first time in an attempt to limit vote rigging, though political violence is still widespread. Benigno (Noynoy) Aquino, son of democracy icons Cory and Ninoy, wins the presidency by a landslide, promising to fight corruption.

August 2013 A spate of bombings in Cagayan de Oro and Cotabato City puts Mindanao back in the spotlight. In September separatists occupy the southern city of Zamboanga. As a result of the three-week standoff thousands flee to seek safety and work, away from the troubled province.

November 2013 Typhoon Haiyan (known locally as "Yolanda") is recognized as the strongest typhoon to make landfall since records began, with windspeeds in excess of 300km/h. The total death toll is over 6000, while millions are left without food, shelter, electricity or access to clean drinking water. Aquino is criticized for a slow response, but international aid pours in, although distribution is hindered by the complete destruction of infrastructure. Full recovery will take decades in the worst hit areas (see box, p.631).

ARRIVAL

Most major Southeast Asian airlines have regular **flights** to Manila and Cebu, with a few also flying to Clark, north of Manila. **Hong Kong** is one of the most convenient gateways; there are also regular flights from many major Asian cities, including Bangkok, Tokyo, Seoul, Shanghai, Beijing, Taipei, Singapore and Kuala Lumpur.

Weesam Express offers a twice-weekly **ferry service** between Sandakan and Sabah in Malaysia and Zamboanga in Mindanao (20hr). A number of smaller, unlicensed boats also ply this route, though check the current situation in Mindanao before considering this (see box, p.656).

VISAS

Most tourists do not need a visa to enter the Philippines for up to **thirty days**, though you need a passport valid for at least six months and an onward ticket to another country. You can apply for longer visas in advance from a Philippine embassy or consulate. A single-entry visa, valid for **three months** from the date of issue, costs £22/$30 and a multiple-entry visa, valid for **one year** from the date of issue, around £65/$90, though you can only get the latter if you have previously been issued a visa for the Philippines. Apart from a valid passport and a completed application form (downloadable from some Philippine embassy websites; see p.49) you will have to present proof that you have enough money for the duration of your stay in the Philippines.

Without a visa in advance, the thirty-day stay you're granted on arrival can be extended at immigration offices in major cities and some key tourist destinations, or through many travel agents. You'll only be granted a month extension the first time, then two months the second time, at which point you'll also have to purchase an **I-Card** (an ID card which should facilitate immigration procedures and allows you to open a bank account in the Philippines). Further extensions of two months will then be granted up to a maximum of sixteen months. Extension fees generally cost P3000 for the first month extension, then P7000 for the next two months (including a one-off I-Card fee). See Ⓦimmigration.gov.ph for information on visa requirements.

GETTING AROUND

The number of **flights** and **ferry services** between major destinations makes it easy to cover the archipelago, even when you're on a budget. One essential, however, is a flexible itinerary. Local road transport is mostly limited to **buses** and **jeepneys**, although in cities such as Manila and Cebu it's still relatively cheap to get around by taxi.

BY PLANE

Air travel is a godsend for island-hoppers, with a number of airlines both large and small linking Manila to most of the country's major destinations. However, while getting from Manila or Cebu to almost any island is straightforward, it

8

AIRLINE DETAILS

Not all routes appear on the websites, so it's worth phoning to check.

Air Asia ⓣ 02 742 2742, ⓦ airasia.com
Cebu Pacific ⓣ 02 702 0888, ⓦ cebupacificair.com
PAL Express ⓣ 02 855 9000, ⓦ flyalexpress.com
Philippine Airlines (PAL) ⓣ 02 855 8888, ⓦ philippineairlines.com
SEAIR ⓣ 02 849 0101, ⓦ flyseair.com

can be difficult to fly between islands, meaning some backtracking is hard to avoid. Philippine Airlines (PAL), their budget division PAL Express and Cebu Pacific have the most comprehensive schedules, while Air Asia's buyout of Zest Air has increased competition on some key routes; Southeast Asian Airlines (SEAIR) is a competitive small airline offering regular flights to major resort areas and also to interesting destinations often not served by larger airlines. **Airfares** in the Philippines are generally inexpensive, especially if you book more than three days in advance: most flights shouldn't cost more than $75, and are often considerably less. Budget carriers' base fares are without check-in luggage, but this is a comparatively cheap add-on. Routes to minor airports which can only take small planes often have maximum **luggage restrictions** of 10kg.

BY BUS

For Filipinos, the journey is as much a part of the experience as the destination. Nowhere is this truer than on the **buses**. Dilapidated contraptions with no air conditioning compete with bigger bus lines with all mod cons (even wi-fi) on hundreds of routes that span out from Manila. Fares are cheap, but journeys can be long. Manila to Banaue, for instance, costs P450 on an air-conditioned bus, but takes nine hours. You might want to make this type of trip overnight, when traffic is lighter and delays less likely, although night drives can be scary, especially through mountain regions. For longer trips, advance booking is recommended.

BY FERRY

Boats are the bread and butter of Philippine travel, with wooden outrigger boats (*bangkas*) and ferries ready to take you from one destination to the next in varying degrees of comfort and safety. Remember that even in the dry season, the open ocean can get rough, so think carefully about using small boats that look ill equipped or overcrowded. If it looks a bit dodgy, it probably is. Ferry disasters occur with depressing regularity, often with great loss of life. Since the Chinese government 2012 buyout and amalgamation of Negros Navigation, Cebu Ferries, Supercat and Superferry, 2GO Travel (ⓦ travel.2go.com.ph) is the country's biggest ferry company. You will still see the old names used on occasion, but all routes are now operated under the 2GO banner. The companies have daily sailings throughout the country, but even these have not been accident-free. Ferries are cheap but often crowded, although on overnight journeys you can always keep away from the dormitory crowds by sleeping on the deck, or paying extra for a cabin. For an idea of **fares**: Manila to Cagayan de Oro will set you back about P1600, to Cebu City around P1300. Given that airfares are so cheap, there's little appeal in taking long-distance ferries.

LOCAL TRANSPORT

The stalwart of the transport system is the fabled **jeepney**, a legacy of World War II, when American soldiers left behind army jeeps; these were converted by ingenious locals into factotum vehicles, carrying everything from produce to livestock and people. Over the years, they evolved into today's colourful workhorses of the road, with fairy lights and cheesy decor. Provincial jeepneys charge about P9 a ride, while in Manila prices range from P8 for a short hop to P20 for longer distances. Jeepneys ply particular routes, indicated on the side of the vehicle, and stop anywhere, so simply flag one down and hop on. When you want to get off, bang on the roof or shout "*para*!"

In many cities old jeepneys are now being replaced with modern vans or "FXs", cheaper than taxis and more

comfortable than jeepneys or buses though still decorated in the same ostentatious manner. The fare is usually P20 for a short trip.

Tricycles are the Filipino equivalent of the Thai tuk-tuk, and while they are not allowed on major roads they can be useful for getting from a bus station to a beach and back again. Most tricycles carry three (or more) passengers, and fares tend to increase dramatically when a tourist approaches, so always reach agreement beforehand. The regular fare is P10 for a quick hop, and fares are lower if you are willing to share the tricycle with anyone else who flags it down and can fit on board. To hire the tricycle exclusively for yourself – or for a small group – P50 is a reasonable fare for a ten-minute journey, or you can charter one for a half day for P300–400.

TAXIS

By international standards, **taxis** in the Philippines are dirt-cheap, making them a viable option for getting around on a daily basis. In larger cities, the flag-down rate is P40 and P2 per 100m. Before you get in, make sure the driver will use his meter or that you have negotiated a reasonable fare. Never use a taxi if the driver has companions and never use one that isn't clearly marked as a taxi. All taxi registration plates have black letters on a yellow background.

ACCOMMODATION

As a budget traveller, this is likely to be your biggest expense. Accommodation is a little more expensive than in other Southeast Asian countries, with quality varying quite dramatically. On the outlying islands the budget rooms are often in the form of a **nipa hut**, made from woven palms, ranging in price from P400 for a simple room with communal bath to P1200 for something a bit more refined with private bath, air conditioning and TV. In Manila, Cebu and Boracay you can expect to pay up to P1400 at "budget" level.

Electricity is usually supplied at 220V. Plugs have two flat and rectangular pins. Power cuts ("brownouts") are common, especially in the more rural areas. Almost all budget places offer both fan and more expensive air-conditioned rooms.

ADDRESSES

It's common in the Philippines for buildings to give an **address** as 122 Legaspi cnr. Velasco streets. This means the place you are looking for is at (or near) the junction of Legaspi Street and Velasco Street. Streets are sometimes renamed in honour of new heroes but are often still referred to by their original name. The ground floor of multistorey buildings is referred to as the first floor and the first floor as the second.

FOOD AND DRINK

The high esteem in which Filipinos hold their **food** is encapsulated by the common greeting "*kain na tayo*" ("Let's eat!"). Filipino food has not been embraced worldwide because it has an unwarranted reputation for being one of Asia's less adventurous cuisines, offering a relatively bland meat and rice diet with little variety or spice. But those willing to experiment will find even the simplest rural dishes can offer an intriguing blend of the familiar and the exotic. Sampling *balut* (boiled duck embryo in the shell), a popular type of *merienda*, and reputed aphrodisiac, will practically make you an honorary *Pinoy* (Filipino), but whether the admiration of the locals is enough of an incentive is up to you! Food is something of a comfort blanket for Filipinos and to be without it is cause for panic. Any Filipino who eats only three meals a day is usually considered unwell because that's simply not thought to be sufficient. A healthy appetite is seen as a sign of a robust constitution, and sundry smaller meals and snacks – **merienda** – are eaten in between every meal. Not to partake when offered can be considered rude.

Meat dishes, notably of chicken and pork (both cheap and easily available), form the bulk of the Filipino diet. The **national dish** is *adobo*, which is chicken or pork (or both) cooked in soy sauce and vinegar, with pepper and garlic.

Baboy (pig) is the basis of many coveted dishes such as *pata* (pig's knuckle) and *sisig* (fried chopped pork, liver and onions). At special celebrations, Filipinos are passionate about their *lechon*, roasted pig stuffed with *pandan* (screwpine) leaves and cooked so the skin turns to crackling. *Lechon de leche* is roasted suckling pig. Pork is also the basis of spicy *Bicol Express*, consisting of pork cooked in coconut milk, soy sauce and vinegar, with chillies (a vegetable version is also available). Coconut, soy sauce, vinegar and *patis* (a brown fish sauce, more watery than *bagoong*, a smelly, salty fish paste) are widely used to add flavour. Sweets and desserts are popular throughout the archipelago and make use of a host of local products including cane sugar, coconut and and rice. Colonization and migration have resulted in Malay, Chinese, Spanish and American culinary influences, sometimes all within the same meal.

The **beers** of choice in the Philippines are San Miguel and San Miguel Light (SML), both very decent and, at P30–50 per bottle, some of the world's cheapest. Red Horse beer, at seven percent, is another favourite. There are also plenty of cheap Philippine-made spirits such as Tanduay rum and San Miguel *ginebra* (gin), and don't leave without trying the strong and pungent *tapuy* (rice wine). Fresh *buko* (coconut) or *calamansi* (lime) juice are refreshing on a hot day.

CULTURE AND ETIQUETTE

Filipinos tend to be outgoing people who are not afraid to ask **personal questions** and certainly don't consider it rude; prepare to be interrogated by everyone you meet. They will want to know where you are from, why you are in the Philippines, how old you are, whether you are married – if not, why not – and so on. Solo travellers are a puzzle to Filipinos, and will be asked with concern why they are alone. They pride themselves on their hospitality and are always ready to share a meal or a few drinks. Don't offend by refusing outright.

A sense of *delicadeza* is also important to Filipinos. This is what you might refer to as propriety, a simple sense of good behaviour, particularly in the presence of elders or women. Filipinos who don't speak good English will often answer any question you ask them with a smile and a nod. Be careful: a smile and a nod doesn't always mean "yes". It can also mean "no", "maybe" or "I have no idea what you are talking about". It's not advisable to **lose your temper** – Filipinos hate to be embarrassed in front of others and so don't respond well to being shouted at. The general rule is to behave in a manner conducive to what the locals refer to as "SIR", or smooth interpersonal relationships. To act otherwise is to invite the worst thing a Filipino can say about another person, that they are *walang hiya* (without shame/propriety).

Filipinos share the same attitudes to **dress** as other Southeast Asian countries (see p.40).

GOOD TO KNOW

Toilets are referred to as CRs (comfort rooms) and more often than not won't have toilet paper, so carry some tissues wherever you go.

Tampons are not displayed on pharmacy shelves; you have to ask for them at the counter.

To ask for **the bill** in a restaurant, make the sign of a rectangle in the air with your thumb and index finger.

DIVING

Of the four million tourists who visit the Philippines every year, many come for the diving alone. It's hardly surprising that in a nation made up of 7107 islands there are dive sites all over the place, with the exception perhaps of the far north. An hour from Batangas City by ferry is the hugely popular area around **Puerto Galera**, home to many dive schools and fine beaches (see p.625). The **Visayas** has dive sites in Boracay, Apo Island (near Dumaguete), Cebu and Bohol. A one-hour flight or twelve-hour ferry journey from the capital takes you to the "last frontier" of **Palawan**, where

COCKFIGHTING

Along with basketball, cockfighting (*sabong*), in its legal and illegal forms, is probably the closest thing to a national pastime in the Philippines. It's a bloody business, with knives used and thousands of pesos changing hands on larger fights. If you insist on checking it out for yourself, you're best off going with a Filipino friend.

you can dive at World War II Japanese wrecks in the company of dolphins and manta rays (see p.660). In short, you can slip into a wet suit just about anywhere.

PADI organizes most scuba tuition in the Philippines. Always pick a PADI dive centre and ask to see their certification. If you haven't been diving before, you can start with a "Discovery Dive" to see if you like it. The full PADI Open Water Diver course takes around four days and costs at least US$350. You might want to consider doing a referral course with PADI at home, which involves doing the pool sessions and written tests before you travel, then doing the final checkout dives with a PADI resort in the Philippines. You'll need to bring your PADI referral documents with you, as your instructor in the Philippines will want to see them.

COMMUNICATIONS

Letters from the Philippines take at least five days to reach other countries by air, sometimes significantly longer. If you have to post anything valuable, use a courier or registered mail. Major post offices in Manila and elsewhere have a counter for **poste restante**. International phonecards are sold in convenient stores such as 7-Eleven in P100, P200, P300 and P500 denominations, but when you can find an internet café with headsets, mainly in the larger towns, you can use Skype (Ⓦskype.com), a cheaper way to call home.

Filipinos love their cellphones (sending more than 500 million texts daily) and cell networks provide coverage in areas where landlines are limited. Using them costs next to nothing. If you're planning to be in the country even for a short time, buying a **local SIM card** (P40, including a bundle of free texts) is well worth it, being especially convenient for texting reservations to hotels and dive operators. Make sure that your phone is unlocked before you travel, though buying a handset is also pretty cheap. Packages for the country's two largest networks, Smart and Globe, are widely available in malls, and even the tiniest *sari-sari* store (small hut stores selling everything from crackers to shampoo sachets) sells phone credit – look out for the ubiquitous "*Load na dito*" signs. Prepaid cards come in units from P100 to P1000 ("loads"), or more often you'll just give your number to the stallowner, pay the amount and then instantly receive a load balance from the network supplier. Many places listed in this book only have mobile phone contact numbers, and as such are more likely to change.

Internet cafés are all over Manila, Cebu and the provincial cities (about P15–60 an hour), and many establishments now offer wi-fi. In rural areas internet access is becoming more readily available all the time.

CRIME AND SAFETY

The Philippines has something of an unfair reputation as a dangerous place, often reinforced by Filipinos themselves who are sometimes overzealous in their warnings to travellers. As long as you exercise discretion and common sense, it's no worse than anywhere else. There are a number of insurgent groups in the country fighting for causes that range from an independent Muslim homeland

THE PHILIPPINES ONLINE

Ⓦ**divephil.com** An online guide listing the country's best dive spots.
Ⓦ**tourism.gov.ph** The Department of Tourism's official website.
Ⓦ**visitmyphilippines.com** Latest news and events from around the country.
Ⓦ**itsmorefuninthephilippines.com** The DOT's marketing domain showcases the country's most sought-after activities and destinations.

in Mindanao to communist rule, and there have been numerous bombings and military stand-offs, as well as isolated cases of tourists being kidnapped in the west and far southwest areas of Mindanao and the Sulu archipelago, which is why we don't cover those areas. For updates on the situation, you can check foreign ministry, state department and embassy websites.

You'll find the same **con artists** and hustlers here that you'd find anywhere else, but most Filipinos are amazingly friendly and helpful. The most frequent scams involve changing money on the street (you'd have to be stupid to do this),

TAGALOG

There are more than 150 languages and dialects in the Philippines. Tagalog, also known as Filipino or Pilipino, is spoken as a first language by 25 million people – mostly on Luzon – and is the national language. Many English words have been adopted by Filipinos, giving rise to a slang known affectionately as Taglish.

Tagalog has formal and informal **forms of address**, the formal usually reserved for people who are significantly older. Honorifics are important to Filipinos; for your elders, use Mr or Mrs/Miss before the surname, or just use Sir/Ma'am/Miss if you don't know their name. It's common to use *kuya/ate* (elder brother/sister) to address people informally. The suffix "po" indicates respect and can be added to almost any word or phrase. The informal form of "I'm fine" is *mabuti* and the formal *mabuti-po*; *o-po* is a respectful "yes" and it's common to hear Filipinos say *sorry-po* for "sorry".

STRESSES

Tagalog sounds staccato to the foreign ear, with clipped vowels and consonants. It has no tones, and most words are spoken as they are written, though working out which syllable to **stress** is tricky. In words of two syllables, the first syllable tends to be stressed, while in words of three or more syllables the stress is almost always on the final or penultimate syllable; thus Boracay is pronounced Bo-**ra**-kay or sometimes Bo-ra-**kay**, but never **Bo**-ra-kay. Sometimes a change in the stress can drastically alter the meaning. Vowels that fall consecutively in a word are always pronounced individually, as is every syllable; for example, *tao* meaning person or people is pronounced ta-o, while *oo* for yes is pronounced oh-oh (with each vowel closer to the "o" in "show" than in "bore").

PRONUNCIATION

a as in "**a**pple"
e as in "m**e**ss"
i as in "d**i**tto", though a little more elongated
o as in "b**o**re"
u as in "p**u**t"
ay as in "b**uy**"
aw as in "m**ou**nt"
iw is the sound **ee** continued into the **u** sound of "p**u**t"
oy as in "n**oi**se"
uw as in "q**ua**rter"
uy produced making the sound **oo** and continuing it to the **i** sound in d**i**tto
c as in "s**k**in"
g as in "**g**et"
k as in "s**k**in" (unaspirated)
mga is pronounced ma**ng**
ng as in "si**nging**"
p as in "s**p**eak" (unaspirated)
t as in "s**t**op" (unaspirated)

GREETINGS AND BASIC PHRASES

Hello/how are you?	*Ka**mu**sta*
Fine, thanks	*Ma**bu**ti, salamat*
Goodbye	Pa**al**am, or *Bye*
Good evening	*Magandang ga**bi***
Excuse me	*Iskyus* (to get past)
Please	Use the word *paki* before a verb. For example, *upo* means sit, so "please sit" is *paki-upo paki*
Thank you	*Sa**la**mat*
Yes	*oo (oh-oh)*
No	*Hindi*
My name is …	*Ako si …*

FOOD AND DRINK GLOSSARY

Vegetarian ako	I'm vegetarian

Main dishes

Adobo	Chicken and/or pork simmered in soy sauce and vinegar, with pepper and garlic

or an overly keen new pal, often well dressed, buying you a drugged coffee or beer and relieving you of your belongings. Most tourists who find themselves in sticky situations are foreign men looking for local "girlfriends" and falling into honey-trap scams. It has to be said that the country's prostitution scene can be disturbingly overt, especially in certain areas of Manila, and places such as Clark and Puerto Galera, popular with older Western men. The Philippines, sadly, retains its sordid reputation for child prostitution. If you see something suspicious, contact ECPAT Philippines in Manila (T 02 920 8151, W ecpat.net).

Beef tapa	Beef marinated in vinegar, sugar and garlic, then dried in the sun, and fried
Bicol Express	Pork ribs cooked in coconut milk, soy sauce, vinegar, *bagoong* and hot chillies
Bistek tagalog	Beef tenderloin with *calamansi* (lime) and onion
Daing na bangus	*Bangus* (milkfish) marinated in vinegar and spices, then fried
Dinuguan	Pork cubes simmered in pig's blood, with garlic, onion and laurel leaves
Lechon (de leche)	Roast whole (suckling) pig, dipped in a liver-paste sauce
Longganisa/longganiza	Small beef or pork sausages, with lots of garlic
Longsilog	*Longganisa* with garlic rice and fried egg
Pinakbet	Vegetable stew with *bagoong*, often with small pieces of meat
Sisig	Fried, chopped pork, liver and onions
Tapsilog	Beef *tapa* with garlic rice and fried egg
Tocino	Marinated fried pork
Tosilog	Marinated fried pork with garlic rice and fried egg

Snacks (*merienda*) and street food

Arroz caldo	Rice porridge with chicken
Chicharon	Fried pork skin, served with a vinegar and chilli dip
Pancit	Noodles
Kanin	Rice (cooked)

Fruit (*fruitas*)

Buko	Coconut
Calamansi	Small lime
Lanzones	Outside, the size and colour of a small potato; inside, sweet translucent flesh with a bitter seed
Mangga	Mango (available in sweet and sour varieties)
Saging	Banana

Desserts

Bibingka	Cake made of ground rice, sugar and coconut milk, baked in a clay stove and served hot, with fresh, salted duck eggs
Halo-halo	Ube ice cream, crushed ice, jelly, beans or sweetcorn and condensed milk
Leche flan	Caramel custard

Drinks (*inumin*)

Buko juice	Coconut water
Chocolate-eh	Thick hot chocolate
Tapuy	Rice wine
Tubig	Water

Police in the Philippines are not Asia's finest. Successive governments have made some headway in cleaning up the force, but it is still plagued by accusations of corruption, collusion and an alleged willingness to shoot first and ask questions later. If you do get into trouble, contact your embassy immediately (see p.48).

MEDICAL CARE AND EMERGENCIES

There are pharmacies everywhere in the Philippines, so if you have a minor ailment and need to buy medicine over the counter, finding one should not be a problem. The biggest chain is Mercury, which has branches all over the place, but even the smallest village tends to have some sort of store.

In Manila and other major tourist centres, **hospitals** are reasonably well equipped and staffed by English-speaking doctors. Elsewhere your hotels can point you in the direction of a local clinic. Make sure you have arranged **health insurance** before you leave home – if you are hospitalized, you won't be allowed to leave the hospital until the bill is settled.

8

The 24-hour number for **emergency services** (police, fire and ambulance) throughout the Philippines is ⓣ117.

INFORMATION AND MAPS

The Philippine **Department of Tourism** (ⓦtourism.gov.ph) has offices throughout the Philippines, but outside of the big cities these mostly have small budgets, poorly trained staff and very little in the way of reliable information or brochures. The best sources of information are often guesthouses and hotels that cater to backpackers. Another good source is blogs; Filipinos are enthusiastic tourists of their own country, and you'll find tons more information online, especially about trekking and diving on a budget, than you will from the tourist offices. A range of maps called *E-Z Map*, covering cities, individual islands and regions, is sold in branches of the National Bookstore (P99) and hotels, and is eminently useful.

MONEY AND BANKS

The Philippine **currency** is the peso (P). It is divided into 100 centavos, with bills in denominations of P20, P50, P100, P200, P500 and P1000. Coins come in 5, 10 and 25 centavos, P1, P5 and P10. Most banks will change sterling, euros and dollars, though the last is preferred, especially outside the cities. Changing travellers' cheques requires jumping through several hoops, and should only be carried as a backup. If you're likely to be going off the beaten track, you should take a ready supply of cash, and keep small denominations of pesos handy for transport and tips. Breaking anything bigger than a P100 note can be tricky anywhere other than large businesses, so stock up on change. At the time of writing the **exchange rate** was P43 to US$1, P62 to €1 and P65 to £1.

Visa, MasterCard and, to a lesser extent, American Express are widely accepted throughout Manila and other major cities, and also in popular tourist destinations such as Boracay. You can withdraw cash from 24-hour **ATMs** (in the Visa, Plus, MasterCard and Cirrus networks) in all cities and even many smaller towns. Most banks will advance cash against cards for a commission.

OPENING HOURS AND PUBLIC HOLIDAYS

Most **government offices** including **post offices** are open Monday to Friday 8am to 5pm. Businesses generally keep the same hours, with some also open for half a day on Saturday from 9am until noon. Off the beaten track, hours are less regular. **Banks** open Monday to Friday 9am to 3pm, while **shops** in major shopping centres are usually open 10am to 8pm, seven days a week. **Restaurants** and **cafés** are generally open from early morning until 11pm, seven days a week, although they often close earlier outside of the big cities.

PUBLIC HOLIDAYS

January 1 New Year's Day
February 25 Anniversary of the overthrow of Marcos
March/April Holy Week

April 9 Bataan Day
May 1 Labour Day
June 12 Independence Day
November 1 All Saints' Day
November 30 Bonifacio Day
November/December Eid-ul-Fitr
December 25 Christmas Day
December 26 Public holiday
December 30 Rizal Day

FESTIVALS

It's at the fiestas that you get a chance to see legendary Filipino hospitality at its best. Religious fiestas are a more solemn mixture of devotion, drama and passion.

Feast of the Black Nazarene (Jan 9) Quiapo, Manila. Devotees gather in the plaza outside Quiapo Church to touch a miraculous image of Christ.

Sinulog (Third Sun in Jan) Cebu City. The second city's biggest annual event, in honour of its patron saint, Santo Niño. Huge street parade, live music and plenty of food and drink.

Ati-Atihan (Third week of Jan) Kalibo, Aklan province. Street dancing and wild costumes at arguably the biggest festival in the country.

Dinagyang (Fourth week of Jan) Iloilo, Panay. Relatively modern festival based on Ati-Atihan and including a parade on the Iloilo River.

Baguio Flower Festival (Third week in Feb) Baguio. The summer capital's largest annual event includes parades of floats beautifully decorated with flowers from the Cordillera region.

Lanzones festival (Third week of Oct) Mambajao, Camiguin. Vibrant, good-natured outdoor party giving thanks for the island's *lanzone* crop.

Masskara (Third week of Oct) Bacolod, Negros. Modern festival conceived in 1980 to promote the city. Festivities kick off with food fairs, mask-making contests, brass-band competitions, beauty and talent pageants and so forth.

Manila

The capital of the Philippines, an ever-expanding sprawl of nearly twenty million people, **MANILA** offers an introduction to the country akin to a baptism by fire. Plagued by traffic and pollution, and an infrastructure stretched almost to breaking point, it's not exactly the most traveller-friendly of cities. Many people fly in, spend a day and then get the hell out, only to venture back at the end of their trip. However, once you've acclimatized to the chaos, you'll discover that Manila has a certain shambolic charm. Considering its forbidding reputation, many are surprised by how unthreatening it feels to walk around, how friendly the people are and how (relatively) manageable it all is. Add nightlife unequalled in Asia, cavernous shopping malls and a few historical sights that are worth battling it out with the sea of jeepneys to visit, and you might find yourself lingering.

WHAT TO SEE AND DO

Manila's apparent disorder and relentless growth have been fed by unchecked urban development and an influx of *provincianos* looking for work, most of whom live in shanties on the periphery. To see the major sights you'll have to sweat it out in heavy traffic and be prepared for delays, but at least the main attractions are close to one another, grouped mostly along the crescent sweep of Manila Bay and Roxas Boulevard, taking in the neighbourhoods of **Ermita** and **Malate**, where budget visitors are most likely to want to base themselves. From here it's a relatively short hop to **Rizal Park** and the old town of **Intramuros**. Beyond **Chinatown** (Binondo), the gargantuan **Chinese Cemetery** is morbidly interesting. **Makati**, the Central Business District (CBD), is built around the main thoroughfare of Ayala Avenue and is best known for malls and restaurants. It's now rapidly overtaking Malate as the place to hang out at night.

Intramuros

Intramuros, the old Spanish capital of Manila, is the one part of the city where you get a real sense of history. Built in 1571, it remains a monumental relic of the Spanish occupation, separated from the rest of Manila by its crumbling walls. Once famous throughout Asia, it featured well-planned streets, plazas, the Governor's Palace, fifteen churches and six monasteries as well as dozens of cannons that were used to keep the natives in their place. Much of this "city within a city" was destroyed in World

8

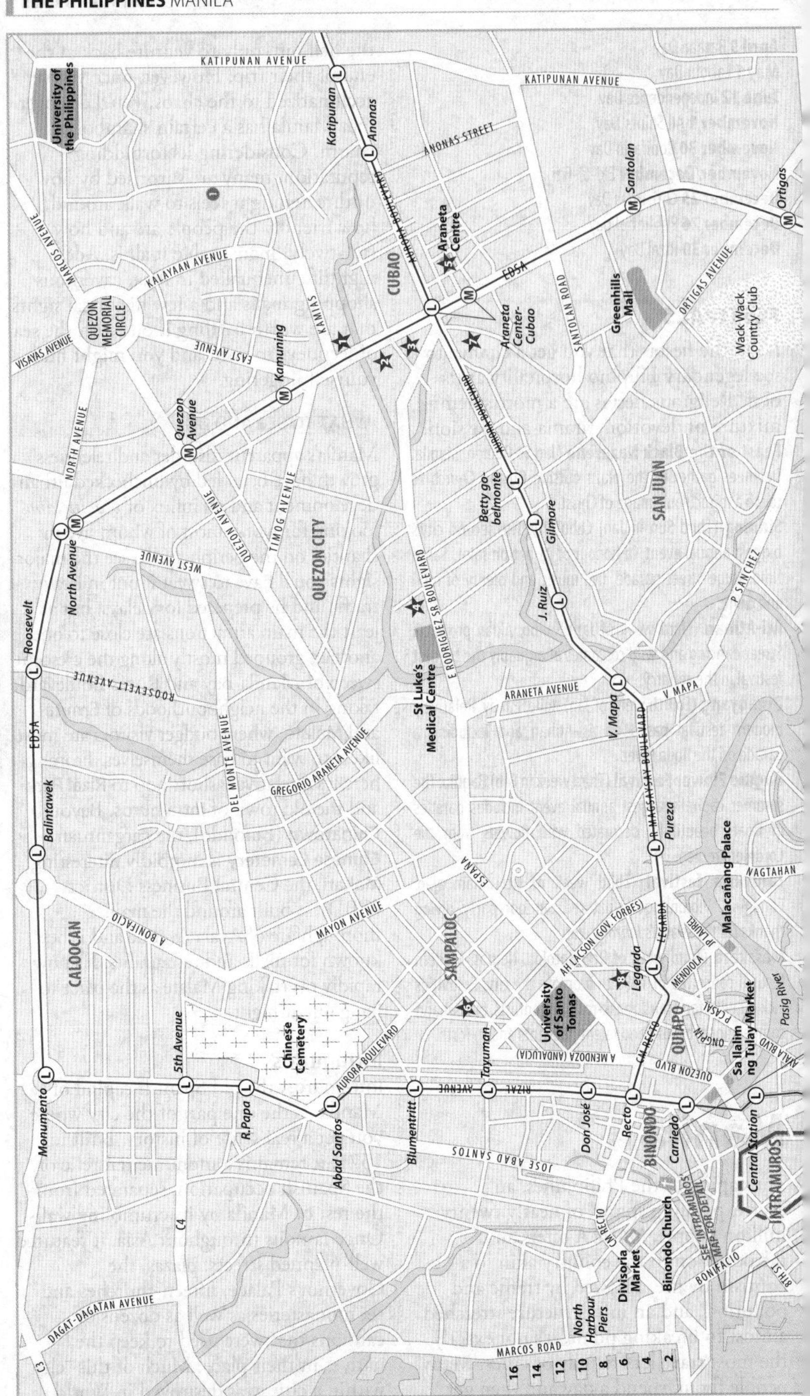
KATIPUNAN AVENUE
University of the Philippines
Katipunan
Anonas
ANONAS STREET
AURORA BOULEVARD
Santolan
Ortigas
Araneta Centre
CUBAO
EDSA
MARCOS AVENUE
KALAYAAN AVENUE
QUEZON MEMORIAL CIRCLE
VISAYAS AVENUE
EAST AVENUE
Kamuning
KAMIAS
Araneta Center-Cubao
SANTOLAN ROAD
Greenhills Mall
ORTIGAS AVENUE
Wack Wack Country Club
Quezon Avenue
NORTH AVENUE
QUEZON AVENUE
TIMOG AVENUE
QUEZON CITY
Betty go-belmonte
Gilmore
SAN JUAN
North Avenue
WEST AVENUE
Roosevelt
J. Ruiz
P SANCHEZ
St Luke's Medical Centre
E RODRIGUEZ SR BOULEVARD
ARANETA AVENUE
V. Mapa
V MAPA
R MAGSAYSAY BOULEVARD
ROOSEVELT AVENUE
DEL MONTE AVENUE
GREGORIO ARANETA AVENUE
Balintawek
Pureza
Malacañang Palace
NAGTAHAN
ESPANA
MAYON AVENUE
A BONIFACIO
CALOOCAN
SAMPALOC
AH LACSON (GOV. FORBES)
LEGARDA
Legarda
JP LAUREL
MENDIOLA
University of Santo Tomas
Pasig River
Chinese Cemetery
5th Avenue
Tayuman
QUIAPO
P CASAL
ONGPIN
A MENDOZA (ANDALUCIA)
CM RECTO
QUEZON BLVD
AYALA BLVD
Sa Ilalim ng Tulay Market
Monumento
R.Papa
Abad Santos
AURORA BOULEVARD
Blumentritt
RIZAL AVENUE
Don José
Recto
Carriedo
Central Station
INTRAMUROS
JOSE ABAD SANTOS
BINONDO
C4
Divisoria Market
Binondo Church
SEE 'INTRAMUROS' MAP FOR DETAIL
BONIFACIO
8TH ST
DAGAT-DAGATAN AVENUE
C3
MARCOS ROAD
North Harbour Piers
16
14
12
10
8
6
4
2

8

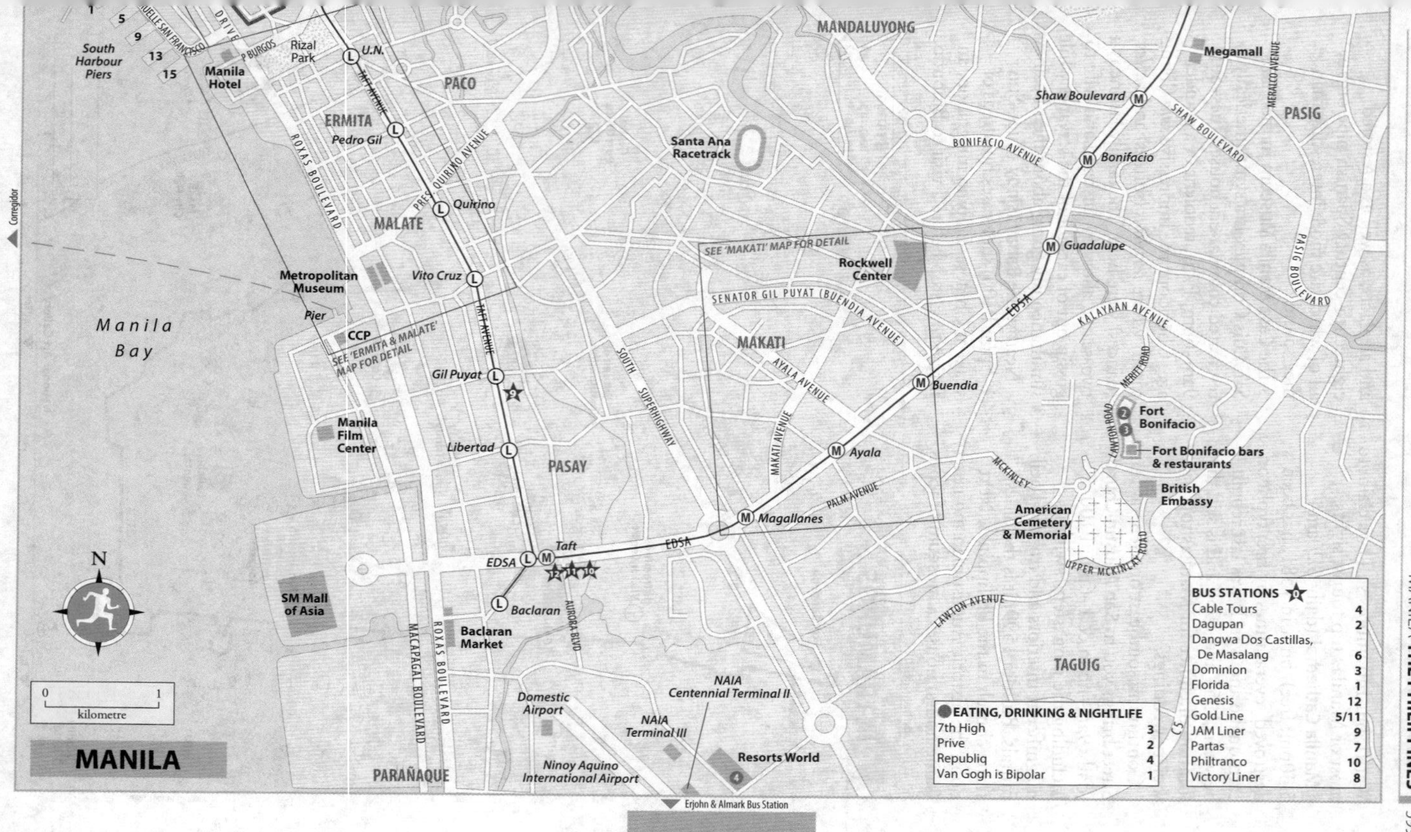
MANILA
0
1
kilometre
N
Manila Bay
Corregidor
South Harbour Piers
1
5
9
13
15
MUELLE SAN FRANCISCO
P BURGOS
DRIVE
Manila Hotel
Rizal Park
U.N.
TAFT AVENUE
ERMITA
Pedro Gil
ROXAS BOULEVARD
Metropolitan Museum
Pier
CCP
SEE 'ERMITA & MALATE' MAP FOR DETAIL
Manila Film Center
MALATE
Quirino
PRES. QUIRINO AVENUE
PACO
Vito Cruz
Gil Puyat
Libertad
PASAY
EDSA
Taft
Baclaran
Baclaran Market
AURORA BLVD
MACAPAGAL BOULEVARD
PARAÑAQUE
SM Mall of Asia
Domestic Airport
Ninoy Aquino International Airport
NAIA Terminal III
NAIA Centennial Terminal II
Erjohn & Almark Bus Station
Resorts World
SOUTH SUPERHIGHWAY
Santa Ana Racetrack
SEE 'MAKATI' MAP FOR DETAIL
Rockwell Center
SENATOR GIL PUYAT (BUENDIA AVENUE)
MAKATI
AYALA AVENUE
MAKATI AVENUE
PALM AVENUE
Magallanes
Ayala
Buendia
MANDALUYONG
BONIFACIO AVENUE
Guadalupe
Bonifacio
Shaw Boulevard
SHAW BOULEVARD
Megamall
MERALCO AVENUE
PASIG
PASIG BOULEVARD
KALAYAAN AVENUE
MERRITT ROAD
LAWTON ROAD
Fort Bonifacio
Fort Bonifacio bars & restaurants
British Embassy
UPPER MCKINLEY ROAD
MCKINLEY
American Cemetery & Memorial
LAWTON AVENUE
TAGUIG
C5
EATING, DRINKING & NIGHTLIFE
7th High 3
Prive 2
Republiq 4
Van Gogh is Bipolar 1
BUS STATIONS
Cable Tours 4
Dagupan 2
Dangwa Dos Castillas, De Masalang 6
Dominion 3
Florida 1
Genesis 12
Gold Line 5/11
JAM Liner 9
Partas 7
Philtranco 10
Victory Liner 8
8

War II, but Intramuros still lays claim to most of Manila's top tourist sights.

Manila Cathedral (daily 6.20am–5.30pm; free), built in 1581, has been destroyed several times by fire, typhoon, earthquake and war. It was last rebuilt between 1954 and 1958 and is still the location of choice for Manila's top society weddings.

Continuing southeast on General Luna Street brings you to **San Agustin Church** (daily 9am–noon & 1–6pm; P100 including the monastery), with its magnificent interiors and trompe-l'oeil murals. Built in 1599, it is the oldest stone church in the Philippines. Next door, the historic Augustinian monastery (same hours) houses a **museum** of icons and artefacts, as well as a restored eighteenth-century Spanish pipe organ, all of which are more interesting than they sound.

The **Casa Manila Museum** in the Plaza San Luis Complex is a sympathetically re-created colonial-era house (Tues–Sun 9am–6pm; P75), redolent of a grander age. Check out the impressive *sala* (living room) where *tertulias* (soirees) and *bailes* (dances) were held. The family latrine is a two-seater, allowing husband and wife to gossip out of earshot of the servants while simultaneously going about their business.

Nearby, the **Bahay Tsinoy** (Tues–Sun 1–5pm; P100) showcases hundreds of years of Chinese–Filipino integration, an interesting stop before a visit to Binondo.

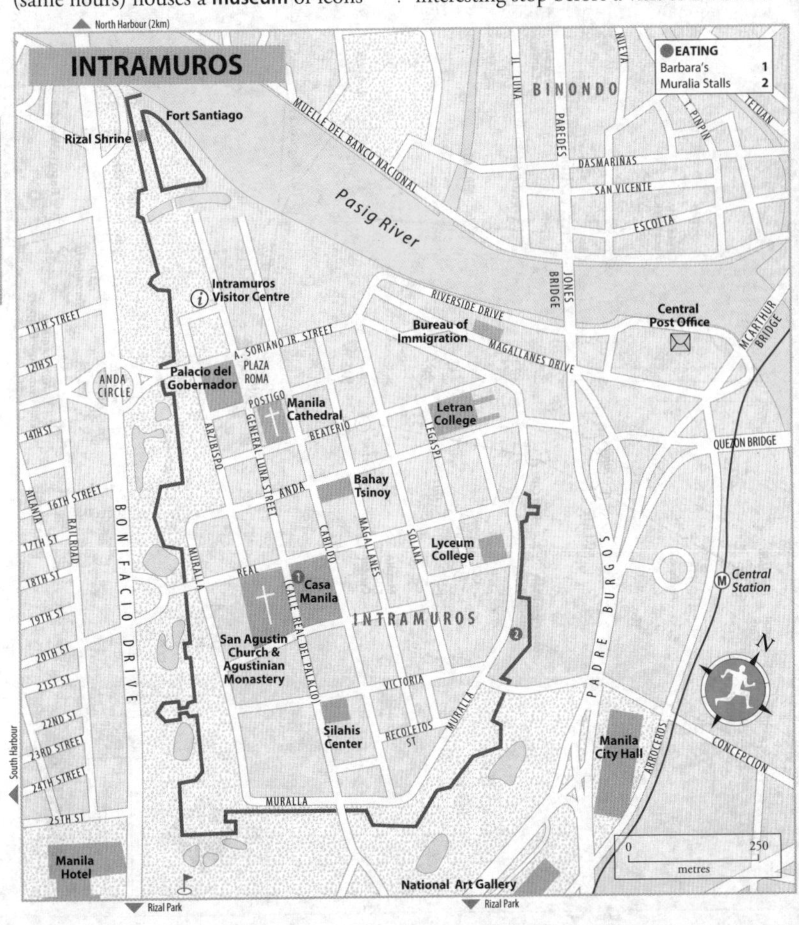

The **Silahis Center** on General Luna (daily 10am–7pm; free) is an exhibition space and craft emporium that's worth a wander. Through a pretty courtyard at the rear is the elegant *Ilustrado* restaurant and its more affordable café, *Kuatro Kantos*.

For more information on the sights or to arrange a walking tour, call into the **Intramuros Visitor Center** (**T** 02 527 2961), which has a small office in the grounds of Fort Santiago, or take one of Carlos Celdran's Intramuros walking tours (see p.606).

Fort Santiago

The ruins of **Fort Santiago** (daily 8am–6pm; P75) stand at the northernmost end of Intramuros, a five-minute walk from the cathedral. Formerly the seat of the colonial powers of both Spain and the US, it was also a dreaded prison under the Spanish regime and the scene of countless military police atrocities during the Japanese occupation. Inside is the **Rizal Shrine**, which houses the room where José Rizal spent the hours before his infamous execution and the original copy of one of the country's most significant historical documents – Rizal's valedictory poem, *Mi Ultimo Adios*, which was secreted in an oil lamp and smuggled to his family hours before his death.

Rizal Park

Rizal Park (popularly known as the Luneta) was where the colonial-era glitterati used to promenade after church every Sunday. These days, in a city notoriously short of greenery, the park is a refuge for couples and families trying to escape the burning haze of pollution that hangs over much of Manila. People take picnics and lounge under trees, though the park's sundry attractions also include a recently refurbished **planetarium** (Tues–Sat 8am–4.30pm; P50; shows must be booked in advance by calling **T** 02 527 7889), an amphitheatre where open-air concerts are held every Sunday at 5pm, a giant relief map of the Philippines, and Chinese and Japanese gardens. At the bay end of the park, close to the *Manila Hotel*, is the **Rizal Memorial** and the flagpole where Manuel Roxas, first President of the third Republic, was sworn in on July 4, 1946. Rizal's execution site is also near here, close to a memorial commemorating three priests garrotted by the Spanish for alleged complicity in the Cavite uprising of 1872.

The National Museum

At the eastern end of the park lie two branches of the **National Museum of the Philippines**, both housed in buildings designed by the American architect Daniel Burnham and well worth a visit. The **National Art Gallery**, in what used to be the Congress Building, houses a comprehensive range of Filipino paintings. Directly opposite is the **National Museum of the Filipino People** (both Tues–Sun 10am–5pm; P150, free on Sun), housed in the former Government Finance Building with displays covering geology, zoology, botany, crafts and weapons.

Manila Bay

When the capital was in its heyday, **Manila Bay** must have been a sight to behold, with its sweeping panorama across the South China Sea and its dreamy sunsets. The sunsets are perhaps more vivid than ever, thanks to the ever-present blanket of smog, and Manileños still watch them from the harbour wall, but much of the bay feels as if it's trading on its romantic past. A trip north along the boulevard from its southern end in Pasay takes you past the **Cultural Center of the Philippines** (CCP) and some of Imelda Marcos's other follies from the same era, including the **Coconut Palace**, an insane structure made entirely from coconut products (free tours Tues–Thurs at 9am, 10.30am & 2pm; reserve in advance at **T** 02 832 6791 or **E** drcomia@ovp.gov.ph. No sandals or shorts). She had it built for the pope's visit in 1981 but he refused to stay there, denouncing her for wasting such vast sums of money while people were starving. Nearby is the **Manila Film Center**, which she hoped would turn the city into the Cannes of the East. Construction was rushed to beat tight deadlines and as a result the building collapsed, allegedly

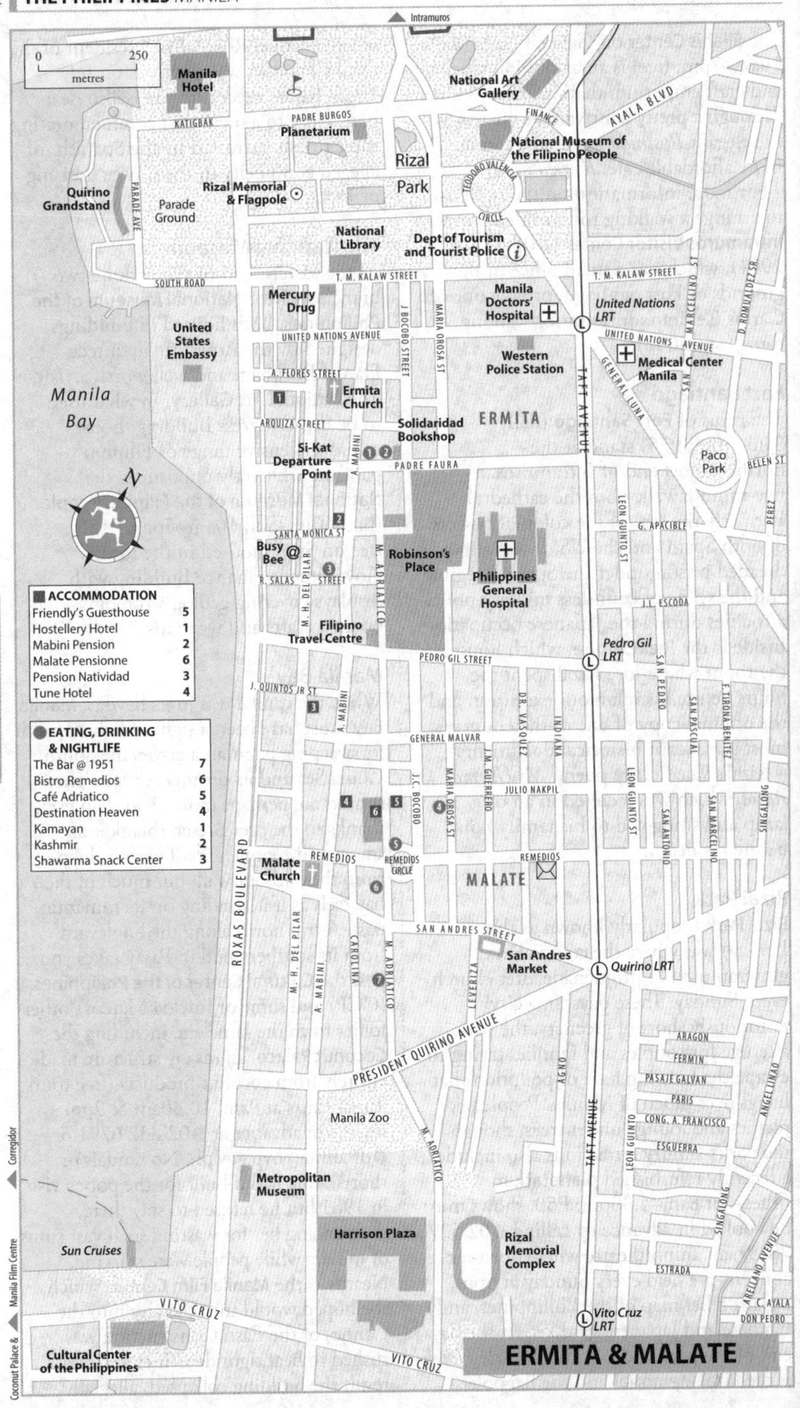
ERMITA & MALATE
Intramuros
0
250
metres
Manila Hotel
KATIGBAK
PADRE BURGOS
Planetarium
National Art Gallery
FINANCE
AYALA BLVD
National Museum of the Filipino People
Rizal Park
TEODORO VALENCIA CIRCLE
Quirino Grandstand
PARADE AVE
Parade Ground
Rizal Memorial & Flagpole
National Library
Dept of Tourism and Tourist Police
SOUTH ROAD
T. M. KALAW STREET
Mercury Drug
Manila Doctors' Hospital
United Nations LRT
MARCELINO ST
D. ROMUALDEZ SR.
United States Embassy
UNITED NATIONS AVENUE
J BOCOBO STREET
MARIA OROSA ST
Western Police Station
Medical Center Manila
GENERAL LUNA
SAN
A. FLORES STREET
Manila Bay
Ermita Church
ERMITA
TAFT AVENUE
ARQUIZA STREET
Solidaridad Bookshop
Si-Kat Departure Point
A. MABINI
PADRE FAURA
Paco Park
BELEN ST
N
LEON GUINTO ST
G. APACIBLE
PEREZ
SANTA MONICA ST
Busy Bee
Robinson's Place
Philippines General Hospital
R. SALAS
STREET
M. H. DEL PILAR
M. ADRIATICO
J.L. ESCODA
ACCOMMODATION
Friendly's Guesthouse 5
Hostellery Hotel 1
Mabini Pension 2
Malate Pensionne 6
Pension Natividad 3
Tune Hotel 4
Filipino Travel Centre
Pedro Gil LRT
PEDRO GIL STREET
J. QUINTOS JR ST
SAN PEDRO
SAN PASCUAL
F. TIRONA BENITEZ
DR. VASQUEZ
INDIANA
EATING, DRINKING & NIGHTLIFE
The Bar @ 1951 7
Bistro Remedios 6
Café Adriatico 5
Destination Heaven 4
Kamayan 1
Kashmir 2
Shawarma Snack Center 3
GENERAL MALVAR
J.M. GUERRERO
J.C. BOCOBO
MARIA OROSA ST
JULIO NAKPIL
SAN ANTONIO
SAN MARCELINO
SINGALONG
ROXAS BOULEVARD
Malate Church
REMEDIOS
REMEDIOS CIRCLE
MALATE
SAN ANDRES STREET
San Andres Market
Quirino LRT
CAROLINA
LEVERIZA
PRESIDENT QUIRINO AVENUE
AGNO
ARAGON
FERMIN
PASAJE GALVAN
PARIS
CONG. A. FRANCISCO
ESGUERRA
ANGEL LINAO
Manila Zoo
M. ADRIATICO
Corregidor
Metropolitan Museum
Harrison Plaza
Rizal Memorial Complex
ESTRADA
ARELLANO AVENUE
Sun Cruises
Manila Film Centre
VITO CRUZ
Vito Cruz LRT
C. AYALA
DON PEDRO
Coconut Palace &
Cultural Center of the Philippines

trapping an unknown number of workers inside – an incident that has now passed into local folklore. A great way to see this area is on Carlos Celdran's "Living La Vida Imelda" tour (see p.606).

The Met and the Manila Hotel

Just north of the CCP is the **Metropolitan Museum**, usually known as the Met, at the Bangko Sentral ng Pilipinas Complex, Roxas Boulevard (Mon–Sat 10am–5.30pm; P100). This fine arts museum, a Filipino mini-Guggenheim, also houses the Central Bank's collection (Mon–Fri 10am–4.30pm only) of prehistoric jewellery and coins. Roxas Boulevard ends at the atmospheric **Manila Hotel**, home from home over the years for the likes of General Douglas MacArthur (who has a suite named after him), Michael Jackson and Bill Clinton.

Ermita and Malate

Two of the city's oldest neighbourhoods, **Ermita** and **Malate**, are tucked behind Roxas Boulevard, ten minutes' walk east of Manila Bay, and are pretty much the tourist centre for backpackers. Until the late 1980s Ermita was infamous for its go-go bars and massage parlours but today it's a ragbag of budget hotels, choked streets and fast-food outlets, though convenient for Intramuros and Malate, and the services and restaurants of Robinson's Place mall. Walking southeast along **M. Adriatico Street** brings you into Malate, where things get livelier and a little less seedy, with better cafés and bars, centred along Adriatico, Nakpil, Maria Orosa and Remedios streets. A three-minute walk towards the sea from Remedios Circle brings you to **Malate Church**, on M.H. del Pilar Street, where British soldiers took refuge during their ill-advised occupation of the Philippines from 1762 to 1763.

Chinatown (Binondo)

The Chinese–Filipino (Tsinoy) community have created their own niche in **Chinatown** (Binondo), centred around the teeming hubbub of Ongpin Street, where the restaurants serve Soup Number Five, said to cure everything from colds to impotence, and containing who knows what. **Binondo Church**, at the west end of Ongpin, was built in 1614 by the Dominicans, and quickly became the hub of the Catholic Chinese community.

At the eastern end of Chinatown, across Rizal Street, you reach **Quiapo Church**, the nucleus of the Feast of the Black Nazarene on January 9, when crowds of up to three million barefooted faithful crush together to try to touch a crucifix bearing a black figure of Christ.

Two kilometres north is the morbidly impressive **Chinese Cemetery** (Abad Santos LRT station; daily 7.30am–7pm; free). The mausoleums resemble mini-houses, with fountains, balconies, bathrooms and, for at least one, a small swimming pool. It has become a sobering joke that this necropolis, now numbering more than thirty thousand tombs, is packed with amenities that millions in Manila go without. You'll get more out of a visit with one of the guides, who hang around the gates and offer their services for a negotiable fee, usually around P300.

Makati

Makati is Manila's business district, home to most of the city's expats and chock-full of plush hotels, expensive condos and monolithic air-conditioned malls. Though it can feel a bit sterile, in recent years it's begun to seriously rival Malate for nightlife. The main triangle of Makati is delineated by Ayala Avenue, Paseo de Roxas and Makati Avenue, and this is where most of the banks and multinationals are located. In terms of sights, Makati is something of a wasteland, but if all that's on your agenda is shopping, eating and drinking, it's the place to be. The biggest mall by far is the **Ayala Center**, comprising Glorietta and Greenbelt malls and a couple of more downmarket centres such as Landmark (see p.609). Next door, the **Ayala Museum**, on Makati Avenue at the corner of Dela Rosa St (Tues–Sun 9am–6pm; P425), houses original works by Filipino painters and a multimedia "People Power" room that documents the turmoil of the Marcos dictatorship and the restoration of democracy – not to be missed.

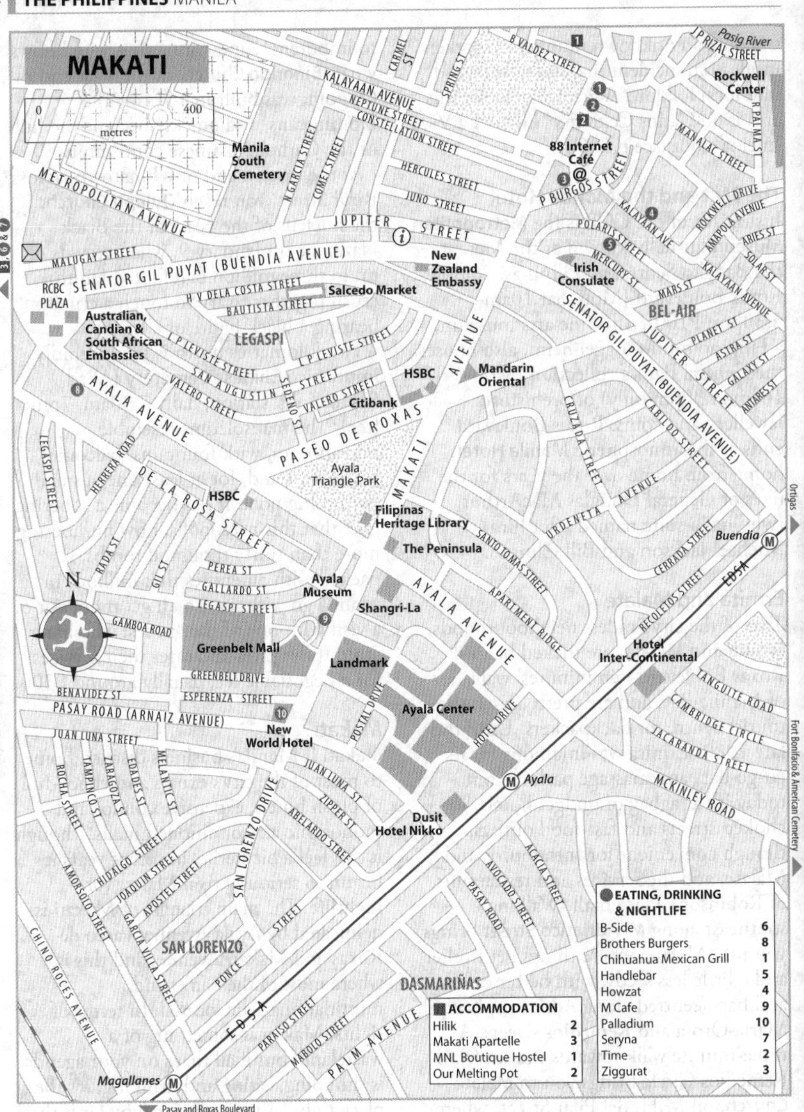

On the eastern edge of Makati on McKinley Avenue is the **American Cemetery and Memorial** (daily 9am–5pm; free). Covering a vast area, it contains 17,206 graves of the American military dead of World War II.

Corregidor

The small tadpole-shaped island of **Corregidor** lies in the mouth of Manila Bay and makes a fascinating side trip from the city. A visit to the island, which was fought over bitterly during World War II – the fall of Corregidor was to prove instrumental to the success of the Japanese occupation – offers a unique perspective on the Philippine resistance. It's worth making time for a visit to the **Malinta tunnels** (daily sound and light show at 9.30am; P150), where

General Douglas MacArthur set up temporary headquarters, and which was the site of vicious hand-to-hand combat. You can walk the island's trails, rent mountain bikes or explore the gun batteries and other ghostly reminders of the horrors of war. There is also a Japanese cemetery, a sobering museum and a memorial to the thousands who died here.

Sun Cruises at CCP Terminal A, Pedro Bukaneg St, near the Cultural Center (T 02 527 5555, W corregidorphilippines.com), organizes day- and overnight trips every morning at 7am. Packages start at P2200.

ARRIVAL AND DEPARTURE

BY PLANE

Ninoy Aquino International Airport (NAIA) is in Parañaque, on the southern fringes of the city. Most international flights arrive at Terminal 1; Terminal 2, relatively nearby, serves only Philippine Airlines (international and domestic); the tiny Domestic Passenger Airport Terminal (aka Terminal 4) is 3km away on the other side of the airport and serves AirAsia Zest, Fil-Asian Airways, SkyJet and Tigerair Philippines flights; further around is Terminal 3, serving Cebu Pacific and PAL Express (international and domestic). Terminal 3 is the best equipped and has a small Department of Tourism (DOT) reception desk, several currency exchanges, ATMs, left luggage, and stalls selling local SIM cards. A shuttle bus connects all the terminals, running frequently throughout the day, but traffic congestion means transfers can take over one hour in some cases – leave plenty of time.

Transport To get into town join the queue to take a yellow airport taxi (P70 flagfall, then P4 per 300m) from outside the arrivals hall, which will set you back about P300–400, rather than the white fixed-price taxis, which usually have no line, but cost nearly double. Taking a non-official taxi from the airport guarantees you'll be ripped off, and you should never get into a taxi that is unmarked or has other people in it. Domestic departure tax from Manila (P200) is now included in the ticket price; international departure tax is P550.

Destinations Bacolod (8 daily; 1hr 10min); Busuanga (3 daily; 1hr); Cagayan de Oro (10 daily; 1hr 25min); Caticlan (16 daily; 1hr); Cebu City (16 daily; 1hr 10min); Davao (up to 5 daily; 1hr 50min); Dumaguete (up to 5 daily; 1hr 15min); Iloilo (up to 11 daily; 1hr); Kalibo (6 daily; 50min); Laoag: (2–3 daily; 50min); Legaspi: (2–4 daily; 1hr 10min); Puerto Princesa (5 daily; 1hr 10min); San José (daily; 50min); Surigao (2 daily; 1hr 40min); Tacloban (5 daily; 1hr 10min); Tagbilaran (4 daily; 2hr).

BY BUS

There's no single bus station for Manila, and timetables are hard to come by and in a constant state of flux, which can make departing Manila by bus a bit of a headache. Often, if you tell your taxi driver your destination, he'll bring you to the right station. An up-to-date resource is the "getting around" section of W philippines-travel-guide.com.

Bus stations The majority of Manila's plethora of bus stations are located in and around Epifanio de los Santos Avenue (EDSA), in two rough groupings: Pasay (south) and Cubao (north). The MRT runs northeast along EDSA from Pasay to Quezon City, where it joins the LRT which runs west and south through Malate to Pasay, closing the loop. The closest LRT station to the tourist belt in Malate is Quirino. There are regular daily departures to most destinations.

BUS COMPANIES COVERING THE SOUTH

Erjohn & Almark Kilometre 46, Aguinaldo Highway, Silang, Cavite (T 02 529 6148). Frequent services to the Batangas region, including Tagaytay.

Gold Line Pasay Terminal (T 02 851 9737). Regular afternoon departures to Sorsogon.

JAM Liner Buendia LRT, Taft Avenue, Pasay (T 02 831 8264). Hourly to Batangas and various destinations in Laguna.

Philtranco EDSA, Apelo Cruz St, Pasay (T 02 851 8078, W philtranco.com.ph). Daily runs to Iloilo via Mindoro, and as far afield as Leyte, Samar and Davao, as well as Legaspi and Sorsogon.

Destinations south Batangas City (every 40min; 3hr); Legaspi (8–10 daily; 10hr); Sorsogon (2–3 daily; 12hr); Tagaytay (12–14 daily; 2hr).

BUS COMPANIES COVERING THE NORTH

Cable Tours 276 E. Rodriguez Ave, Quezon City (T 02 257 3582 or T 0918 521 6790). Nightly to Bontoc and Banaue.

Dagupan New York St cnr. EDSA, Cubao (T 02 727 2330 or T 928 5639). Hourly to Baguio.

Dangwa Dos Castillas, De Masalang Sampaloc (T 02 731 2879). Overnight services to Baguio and Kalinga.

Dominion New York St, Cubao (T 02 741 4146). Daily to Vigan.

Florida A.H. Lacson Ave cnr. M. Earnshaw, Sampaloc (T 02 743 3809, W gvfloridatransport.com). Direct nightly services to Banaue.

Genesis 101–A Giselle Park Plaza, EDSA cnr. Rotonda, Pasay (T 02 853 3115). Hourly to Baguio 11am–8pm.

Partas 816 Aurora Blvd at EDSA, Cubao Terminal (T 02 851 4025, W partas.com.ph). Regular services to Baguio, Laoag, San Fernando (La Union) and Vigan.

Victory Liner W victoryliner.com. From 683 EDSA, Cubao Terminal (T 02 727 4534), and 651 EDSA, Pasay Terminal (T 02 833 5019). Hourly services to Baguio.

8

TRAVELLING SAFELY IN MANILA

Manileños take every opportunity to warn visitors about travelling around their city, but as long as you exercise common sense, there's little to worry about. Armed security guards patrol MRT and LRT platforms, and there are separate waiting areas for female passengers, minimizing opportunities for muggers, though of course it pays to remain alert. Official taxis are perfectly safe, but take the precaution of sitting in the back, and lock your doors, as you are likely to sit in traffic for long stretches of any journey. For complaints about taxis in Manila, contact LTFRB, the Land Transportation Board (02 426 2526), or fill in the form at taxikick.com. Taking the bus in Manila is a potentially risky business, however, bus drivers are reckless, and some take drugs to stay awake.

Destinations north Baguio (hourly; 6–8hr); Banaue (6 daily; 9hr); Laoag (6–8 daily; 10hr); San Fernando (La Union; 4–6 daily; 6hr); Vigan (6–8 daily; 10hr).

BY FERRY

There are two main passenger dock areas in Manila: the North Harbor along Marcos Rd, a few kilometres north of Intramuros, and the South Harbor near the Manila Hotel. Almost all 2GO Travel ferries (travel.2go.com.ph) use the new terminal at Pier 4, North Harbor, but make sure to check with your ticketing agent before travelling. Taxis from North Harbor to Ermita cost about P150.

Destinations Bacolod (3 weekly; 20hr); Cagayan de Oro (weekly; 32hr); Cebu City (4 weekly; 21hr); Coron (weekly; 14hr); Iloilo (2 weekly; 20hr); Puerto Princesa (weekly; 30hr).

8

INFORMATION AND TOURS

Tourist information The tourist information centre (Mon–Fri 7am–6.30pm, Sat 8am–5pm; 02 890 0189 or 02 525 2000, visitmyphilippines.com) is at 351 Senator Gil Puyat Ave in Makati, across from the Pacific Star Building. A useful source of information on Manila is clickthecity.com.

Walking tours For something different, try Walk This Way, run by the highly entertaining Carlos Celdran (0920 909 2021 or 02 484 4945, carlosceldran.com). Carlos leads weekly history-lesson-cum-magical-mystery tours around the old city (P1100; 3hr). Also recommended is Ivan Man Dy of Old Manila Walks (0917 329 1622, oldmanilawalks.com), who conducts fun tours of Binondo and the Malacañang Palace.

GETTING AROUND

Manila's roads are in a perpetual state of chaos bordering on anarchy. There are so many vehicles fighting for every centimetre of road space that at peak times it can be a sweaty battle of nerves just to travel a few hundred metres.

MRT (MetroStar Express; daily 5.30am–11pm; dotcmrt3.weebly.com). Runs the length of EDSA from Taft Ave in the south to North Ave, Quezon City. Key stations are Taft, from where you can get a taxi, a jeepney or the LRT to Malate; Ayala, which is close to Makati's malls and hotels; and Cubao for bus stations heading north. A one-way journey ticket ranges from P10 to P15, and a prepaid ticket costs P100 and is valid for three months.

LRT (Light Rail Transit; daily 5am–9.30pm; lrta.gov.ph). An elevated railway that runs from Baclaran in the south (near the airport) to North Ave MRT terminus, creating a loop between the MRT and the LRT. Trains run frequently and journeys cost P12–20. You can use it to get to places in the north of Manila, such as Rizal Park (exit at United Nations station), Intramuros (Central station) and the Chinese Cemetery (Abad Santos station). Pedro Gil station is a 10min walk from Ermita, while Quirino station is closest to Malate.

Jeepneys Jeepneys go back and forth all over the city. Fares start at P10 for the shorter journeys and increase by P1.75 for each kilometre after. Pass your fare to the passenger sitting closest to the driver. A useful route runs the length of Taft Avenue from Baclaran in the south to Binondo in the north. From Baclaran, you can get jeepneys to the bus terminals in Pasay. Jeepneys heading to Cubao will take you past a number of bus terminals at the northern end of EDSA, where you can get buses to northern destinations.

Taxis It's extremely cheap and easy to get around Manila by taxi. Many taxi drivers are happy to turn on their meters, while others start even the shortest journey with a long negotiation. Most taxis are a/c and charge an initial P40, then P2.50 for every 300m.

Buses Local buses in Manila grind their way along all major thoroughfares. The destination is written on a sign in the front window, and fares start at P14, but they are the least reliable form of city transport (see box above).

ACCOMMODATION

Most of Manila's budget accommodation is in Ermita and Malate, which also have a high density of restaurants, bars and tourist services. They are, however, rather insalubrious areas, so make sure you remain vigilant, especially at night. Makati, the modern expat area, is a much safer option, although budget accommodation is less prevalent.

ERMITA AND MALATE

Friendly's Guesthouse 1750 Adriatico cnr. Nakpil streets, Malate ☎02 474 0742, ⓦfriendlysguesthouse.com; map p.602. The small, darkish rooms at this friendly place give off a maze of little narrow corridors. Most have shared bathrooms and there's a chilled-out balcony area to sip your free tea or coffee. Free wi-fi, too. Dorm P450, double P695

Hostellery Hotel 416 Plaza Nuestra Senyora de Guiua, Ermita ☎02 521 6545, ⓔhostellery@gmail.com; map p.602. New budget option just off the bay, with 4- and 8-bed a/c dorms, plus well-priced, clean doubles with cable TV. Dorm P500, double P2000

Mabini Pension 1337 A Mabini St, Ermita ☎02 523 3930; map p.602. Convenient, friendly and well established, with fan and a/c rooms, though in rather close proximity to a number of karaoke joints; get a room at the back. Also offers internet access, tourist information, visa extensions and flight reservations. P680

★**Malate Pensionne** 1771 M Adriatico St, Malate ☎02 523 8304, ⓦmpensionne.com.ph; map p.602. Cosy rooms delightfully furnished in Spanish-colonial style; there are beautiful parquet floors throughout and the cute little breakfast area is a good spot to start the day. Paid wi-fi. Dorm P475, double P950

★**Pension Natividad** 1690 MH del Pilar St, Malate ☎02 521 0524, ⓦpensionnatividad.multiply.com; map p.602. A well-liked guesthouse in a quiet old family home with a popular 24hr outdoor terrace café where backpackers mingle. Rooms are clean and spacious and there's free wi-fi. It's one of the best budget places in the area. Single-sex dorm P400, double P1000

Tune Hotel 1740 Mabini St, Malate ☎02 519 0888, ⓦtunehotels.com; map p.602. Air Asia hotel chain's Malate branch enjoys a good location close to the dining and nightlife scene, and its add-on price structure means you only pay for the facilities you need. Deals are available from as little as P788 if you book early. Rooms are bright, white and clean; add-ons include a/c, cable TV, wi-fi, early check-in and luggage storage. The full package costs P420 in advance. Double (walk-in rate) P2000

MAKATI

More and more options are popping up to cater for budget travellers keen to be close to Makati's dining and nightlife scene.

Hilik 2nd Floor, Mavenue Building, Makati Ave 7844 cnr. Guerrero St ☎02 519 5821 or ☎0932 950 0255, ⓦhilikbouiquehostel.ph; map p.604. Less popular but equally as good as *Our Melting Pot* in the same building, *Hilik* has clean, comfortable dorms in a great location. Free breakfast, wi-fi, lockers and use of kitchen. Dorm P550, double P1500

Makati Apartelle 4411 Montojo St, Brgy. Tejeros ☎02 897 4219, ⓦmakatiapartelle.com; map p.604. This welcoming hotel is decorated with beautiful Chinese artefacts and the odd piece of intricately decorated furniture; all rooms have a/c, kitchenette, living area, private bathroom and cable TV. Great value. P1085

MNL Boutique Hostel 4688 Valdez St ☎02 511 7514, ⓦMNLBoutiqueHostel.com; map p.604. Handy for the nightlife scene, this small new hostel has tiny, brightly painted (but windowless) rooms. Dorm P545, double P1750

★**Our Melting Pot** 4th Floor, Mavenue Building, Makati Ave 7844 cnr; map p.604. Guerrero St ☎02 659 5443 or ☎0932 950 0255, ⓦourmeltingpotbackpackers@gmail.com. Friendly hostel a stone's throw away from Makati's malls and nightlife with mixed as well as female-only dorms and a/c throughout. Dorm beds have curtains, perfect for those who value their privacy. Free breakfast, wi-fi, lockers and use of kitchen. Dorm P550, double P1500

EATING

QUEZON CITY

★**Van Gogh is Bipolar** 154H Maginhawa St, Sikatuna Village Quezon City ☎0922 824 3051, ⓦfacebook.com/vgibipolar; map pp.598–599. Cook and travel photographer Jetro lovingly prepares the dishes at this unique place by carefully selecting ingredients, such as honey and black mountain rice, that activate neurotransmitters in the brain to calm and uplift one's mood. Help out with service and get your meal for free. Only 12 diners per night, so bookings are essential. Wed–Sun 6–11pm.

INTRAMUROS

Barbara's Plaza San Luis Complex, Gen. Luna St ☎02 527 4086, ⓦbarbarasheritagerestaurant.com; map p.600. Elegant dining in a colonial setting, with wooden interiors and rich Filipino and Spanish food. Best known for its touristy buffets (around P245 for lunch; P710 for dinner) and the Kultura Filipina traditional music and dance show from 7.15pm on Tues and Thurs. À la carte dishes average P250–400. Daily 11am–2pm & 6.30–9pm.

Muralia Stalls Lining the Intramuros walls; map p.600. The eastern walls of the old Spanish capital are lined with in-built stalls attracting crowds of students for cheap eats. A meal will set you back about P70.

ERMITA AND MALATE

Bistro Remedios 1911 M. Adriatico Street, Malate; map p.602. One of the city's best restaurants for authentic Filipino food (mains P300); the welcoming interior is simple but attractive, and there are occasionally live bands wandering from table to table. Daily 11am–3pm & 6–11pm.

Kamayan 532 Padre Faura cnr. M. Adriatico streets, Ermita; map p.602. The word *kamayan* means "with your hands", which is how you eat the lovingly prepared Filipino

8

dishes here. Lunch and dinner buffets include choices of Filipino (P435) and Japanese food (including sushi and sashimi; P625), or free range of both (P725). Daily 11.30am–2.30pm & 6–10pm.

Kashmir Merchants Center Building, Padre Faura, Ermita; map p.602. Great spot in the middle of Ermita for Indian, Malaysian and Middle Eastern cuisine; all the meat here is halal and there are plenty of dishes on offer, from kebabs (P250) to tandoori specialities (from P450). Great vegetarian choices (P260) too. There's another branch at 816 Arnaiz Ave in Makati. Daily 11am–11pm.

★**Shawarma Snack Center** 485 Salas St, Malate; map p.602. This place offers great hummus (P105), *shakshouka* (P135), *tabouleh* (P175) and other Middle Eastern delicacies to be washed down with a zesty fruit shake (P75). There's another branch directly opposite. Free wi-fi. Mains P200–300. Daily 24hr.

MAKATI

Makati is fast becoming the culinary capital of the country, with a dazzling range of world food on offer in the malls and beyond.

8

Brothers Burger Unit A, Convergys Building, Ayala Avenue; map p.604. Head here to regain your senses after a big night out. If you've really had one too many, note that Manila's best burger joint even delivers (T 02 756 5656). Several other branches including at Greenhills Mall. Burgers from P165. Mon–Fri 8am–midnight, Sat 8am–9pm & Sun 11am–9pm.

Chihuahua Mexican Grill 7838 Makati Ave; map p.604. A haven for spicy food lovers with a hot sauce library of over 60 bottles, this great little Mexican place serves large and delicious portions of burritos, tacos (P295) and nachos (P245), as well as great margharitas (P195). Daily 10am–3am, Fri & Sat until 5am.

Howzat 8471 Kalayaan Ave cnr. Fermina St; map p.604. British pub serving good ol' grub such as fish & chips (P398) and steak and kidney pie (P310); there are plenty of TV screens to catch up on the latest sports from around the world. Sunday roast buffet (P545) and a great Indian curry lunch buffet (P425). Sun–Thurs 9am–2am, Fri & Sat 24hr.

Seryna 2277 Chino Roces Ave; map p.604. Well-liked Japanese place among a set of many in Little Tokyo; order your sushi inside and enjoy it in the pleasant courtyard with lanterns at the back. A huge range of other choices from P180 including udon, tempura teppenyaki, and yakiniku. Great set-menu lunches P350. Daily 11.30am–2pm & 6–11pm.

★**Ziggurat** Durban St, between Makati Ave and Burgos St; map p.604. Kick off your shoes, sit back on silky cushions and tuck into exotic curries (P120–380) at this superb restaurant serving delights from India, Africa and the Middle East. Plenty for vegetarians, including gluten-free veggie curry (P250). Not to be missed. Daily 24hr.

NIGHTLIFE

Manila's nightlife scene is centred around three main areas: Fort Bonifacio, Greenbelt in Makati and the Resorts World by the NAIA airport terminal, all home to scores of trendy bars and clubs. The area around the intersection of Nakpil and Maria Orosa streets in Malate is the centre of Manila's gay club scene. Leave your T-shirts and flip-flops at home; all the big clubs have strict dress codes. For more of a casual night out sign up for Manila's famous Thursnight pub crawl (T 0905 553 9541, W pubcrawl.ph), which takes in five bars and costs P890 on the spot, or from P590 for women, and P690 for men if you sign up in advance; free T-shirt, shot glass and hangover included!

FORT BONIFACIO AND PASAY

One of Manila's best nightlife spots, Fort Bonifacio is home to scores of restaurants, bars and clubs. Most clubs get going at around midnight and the party continues until the early hours of the morning.

7th High Fort Bonifacio W 7thhigh.com; map pp.598–599. To get a real taster of a moneyed Manileño's night out, head to this swanky club with a plush interior divided into three main areas, including a snazzy bar lounge. Wed–Sat 10pm–4am. Entry P500.

Prive Luxury Club, The Fort Strip, Bonifacio; map pp.598–599. Opened in 2011, *Prive* has fast become one of the city's most popular clubs catering to a variety of musical tastes; the crowd stomp around to house and electro on Wed and Thurs, with an open format/ mash-up on other nights. Tues–Sat 10pm–4am. Entry P600; free Tues.

Republiq Resorts World, Pasay City W republiqclub.com; map pp.598–599. This wild club is one of the city's largest and most popular, with lively crowds dancing until the early hours. Wed, Fri & Sat 9.30pm–5.30am. Entry P600.

ERMITA AND MALATE

★**The Bar @ 1951** (ex-*Penguin Café*) 1951 M; map p.602. Adriatico St, Malate. Legendary 1980s bohemian bar *Penguin Café* has been reborn as this two-floor artsy and congenial space (with a cosy loft upstairs), though locals still refer to it by the old name. Live indie bands play most nights and work from local artists adorns the walls. Tues–Sat 6pm–2am.

Café Adriatico 1790 M. Adriatico St, Malate; map p.602. Under the same ownership as *Bistro Remedios*, this great little place has been going since 1979, serving Spanish-influenced dishes (mains P300–400) and inventive cocktails (P140–168). It occupies prime people-watching real estate. There's another branch in SM Mall of Asia. Sun & Mon 7am–2am, Tues–Sat 7am–5am.

Destination Heaven Courtyard J. Nakpil St, Malate; map p.602. This collection of four bar-clubs has quickly reasserted the address of former favourite *Bed* as the heart of Malate's gay scene. Each bar has a different focus – *Red*

Banana is a good old-fashioned disco-bar (P250 cover), *Mint* is a lounge-bar, *Zinc* features karaoke and comedy acts, while *Assul* offers fine dining. Daily 7pm–4am.

MAKATI

★B-Side Suite B, The Collective, 7274 Malugay St Ⓦbsidemanila.com; map p.604. This hipster joint in a converted warehouse hosts local and foreign indie gigs and attracts a studenty crowd. Big reggae/ragga sessions on "Irie Sundays". Cover usually P200–300. It's hard to find, so check their website for details. Wed–Sat 9pm–4am, Sun 7pm–2am.

Handlebar 31 Polaris St; map p.604. Friendly biker bar with masculine trimmings and live music, sports on TV, draught beer (P72) and some of the best steaks (P545) in Makati. Daily 24hr.

★M Cafe Ayala Museum, Makati Ave; map p.604. Nibble at modern Asian tapas and *dim sum* (P195–295) as you sip an exquisite cocktail (P225; try "The M" – melon vodka, pineapple and calimansi syrup) at this swish place, which attracts big crowds on Thurs. Cool interior and atmospheric outdoor seating. Daily 8am–midnight; Thurs and Fri till 3am with DJs.

Palladium In the *New World Hotel,* Makati; map p.604. This large club set on two floors plays house, r'n'b and club tunes. The top floor has a more loungy feel to it, while the basement is where the party goes wild; it fills up around 1am. Fri & Sat 10pm–5am. Entry P500.

Time 7840 Makati Ave; map p.604. The epicentre of the electronic music scene with Filipino and international DJs performing live sets, from deep house to dubstep. Mon–Sat 9pm–4am. Mon–Thurs P200, Fri & Sat P500–800.

SHOPPING

MARKETS

Baclaran Market Southern end of Roxas Blvd. The delights on offer at this rough-round-the-edges market include clothes, puppies, quail eggs, caged finches and ubiquitous pirate DVDs. Daily from 6am, but busiest on Wed and weekends. Take the LRT to Baclaran and allow plenty of time.

Divisoria Market C.M. Recto St, Binondo. The grand-daddy of flea markets, where haggling is the order of the day. Fake Converse trainers, pirated DVDs, bags, wallets and household paraphernalia crowd the stalls at this immense and sometimes overwhelming Chinatown market. Dress down and leave valuables at your hotel. Daily from dawn until late.

★Salcedo Community Market Jaime Velasquez Park, Bel-Air, Makati. One of Manila's culinary highlights, Salcedo features a dazzling display of gastronomic delights from all corners of the Philippines and further afield to take away or enjoy at one of the communal tables. Sat 7am–2pm.

San Andres Market San Andres cnr. Guerrero streets, close to Quirino Ave LRT station. Offering a wide selection of fruit, this labyrinthine market is home to hundreds of stalls groaning under the weight of mango, pomelo, jackfruit, cantaloupe, watermelon, rambutan and more. Daily 24hr.

"Under the Bridge" Market (*Sa Ilalim ng Tulay*) Quezon Bridge, Quiapo. Mainly handicrafts and secondhand clothes, as well as meat, fish, fruit and vegetables. Daily 5am–10pm.

BOOKS

Fully Booked Branches in Greenbelt and Rockwell (Ⓦfullybookedonline.com). The country's best bookshop has a broad range of titles and also sells magazines and stationery.

National Bookstore Branches in Greenbelt, Rockwell and Robinson's Place malls. A chainstore found in almost every mall in the country, selling books, maps and stationery.

Power Books Greenbelt 4. A decent selection of books in a cosy ambience.

Solidaridad Bookshop 531 Padre Faura. Owned by celebrated Filipino novelist F. Sionil José, this place is a hidden gem, stocking more unusual Filipino titles. Mon–Sat 9am–6pm.

8

MALLS

Manila's malls loom large in the entertainment of the city, with many of the best restaurants, bars and cinemas found inside. You can also do your banking, book travel tickets and stock up on picnic supplies. Opening hours are usually Mon–Fri 10am–9pm, Sat & Sun 10am–10pm. The main malls are:

Ayala Center Makati Ave Ⓦayalamalls.com.ph. Restaurants, boutiques, bars, theatres, cinemas and so on, spread across Greenbelt malls 1–5 (in ascending order of exclusivity). Glorietta, opposite the *Shangri-La Makati*, has a seven-screen cinema complex (Ⓣ02 752 7880), including one dedicated to arthouse films, and Landmark has a well-stocked basement supermarket good for self-caterers. There are also plenty of snack chain counters here.

Robinson's Place Adriatico cnr. Padre Fauna streets, Ermita Ⓦrobinsonsmalls.com. Some great restaurants, a multiplex cinema and free wi-fi.

Rockwell Center Rockwell Drive, Makati Ⓦpowerplant mall.com Officially called the Power Plant mall, but everyone just refers to it as Rockwell.

SM Mall of Asia Bay Blvd cnr. EDSA extension, Pasay Ⓦsmmallofasia.com. The second-largest mall in the Philippines, and the fourth largest in the world. Has everything you'd expect and more that you wouldn't, including an Olympic-sized ice-skating rink.

DIRECTORY

Banks and exchange Most major banks have 24hr ATMs. If you need other services try BPI, 1792 Mabini St, Malate; American Express, 1810 A Mabini St, Malate; Citibank, 8741 Paseo de Roxas, Makati; HSBC, Ayala Ave, Makati and 648 Remedios St, Malate.

Embassies and consulates Australia, Level 23, Tower 2, RCBC Plaza, 6819 Ayala Ave, Makati (T 02 757 8100, W philippines.embassy.gov.au); Canada, Levels 6–8, Tower 2, RCBC Plaza, 6819 Ayala Ave, Makati (T 02 857 9000, W philippines.gc.ca); China, 2nd & 3rd Floors, World Center, 330 Sen Gil Puyat Ave, Makati (T 02 844 3148); Indonesia, 185 Salcedo St, Makati (T 02 892 5061); Ireland, 3/F, 70 Jupiter St, Bel-Air 1, Makati (T 02 896 4668); Laos, 34 Lapu-Lapu St, Magallanes, Makati (T 02 852 5759); Malaysia, 10th & 11th Floors, World Center, 330 Sen Gil Puyat Ave, Makati (T 02 864 0761); New Zealand, 23/F, BPI Buendia Center, 360 Gil Puyat Ave, Makati (T 02 891 5358, W nzembassy.com/philippines); Singapore, 505 Rizal Drive, Bonifacio Global City, Taguig (T 02 856 9922); South Africa, 29th Floor, Yuchengco Tower, RCBC Plaza, 6819 Ayala Ave, Makati (T 02 889 9383); Thailand, 107 Rada St, Makati (T 02 815 4220); UK, 120 Upper McKinley Rd, McKinley Hill, Taguig City (T 02 858 2200); US, 1201 Roxas Blvd (T 02 301 2000, W manila.usembassy.gov); Vietnam, 670 Pablo Ocampo, Malate (T 02 525 2837).

Hospitals and clinics Makati Medical Center, 2 Amorsolo St, Makati (T 02 888 8999, W makatimed.net.ph), is the largest and one of the most modern hospitals in Manila. In the Manila Bay area, there's the Manila Doctor's Hospital, 667 United Nations Ave, Ermita (T 02 524 3011, W maniladoctors.com.ph). In Ermita, there is the Philippines General Hospital on Taft Ave (T 02 554 8400, W stluke.com.ph), while St Luke's Medical Center, 279 E. Rodriguez Sr Blvd in Quezon City (T 02 723 0101, W stluke.com.ph), is also highly regarded.

Immigration For visa extensions, head to the Immigration Building, Magellanes Dr, Intramuros (Mon–Fri 8am–noon & 1–5pm; T 02 527 3257 or 3280).

Internet Internet access is very easy to find in all tourist areas and there are internet cafés in all malls. Most malls are free wi-fi zones, too. Busy Bee Internet Café at 1417 M.H. del Pilar St, Ermita, and 88 Internet Café, Durban St, Makati, both charge P45/hr.

Laundry Let's Talk Dirty Laundry, 4877 Durban St, Makati (daily 7am–10pm; T 02 899 0811; P45/kg).

Pharmacies You're never far from a Mercury Drug outlet. There are 24hr stores at Taft Ave cnr. Apacible St, Ermita and Makati Ave.

Police Tourist Police, Department of Tourism Compound, TM Kalaw cnr. Maria Orosa streets, Ermita (daily 7am–11pm; T 0908 894 2001). For emergencies, dial T 117.

Post office The main post office is in Intramuros, between Jones Bridge and MacArthur Bridge. In Makati, there is a post office at the junction of Malugay and Ayala avenues. In Malate, there's one at the junction of Remedios and Hidalgo streets. Opening hours are generally Mon–Fri, 8am–5pm.

Travel agents There are plenty of travel agents around Malate and Ermita. The Filipino Travel Center, 1555 M Adriatico St (T 02 528 4507, W filipinotravel.com.ph), is one of the best, and particularly strong on organizing tours. There are branches on Boracay, Panglao, and in Sabang, Puerto Galera.

Northern Luzon

The provinces of Luzon that lie immediately **northwest of Manila** are so diverse in geographical character that you can go from the volcanic landscape of **Zambales** to the tropical beaches and islands of the **Lingayen Gulf** in a single day. Major attractions of the region include **Mount Pinatubo**, the island-hopper's heaven of **Hundred Islands National Park**, and the chance to surf the breaks of **San Fernando** and **San Juan** on the La Union coast. Further north, the old Spanish-colonial outpost of **Vigan** is a reminder of how much was lost elsewhere in the bombs of World War II.

MOUNT PINATUBO

On April 2, 1991, people on the lower slopes of **Mount Pinatubo** (1780m) saw small explosions followed by steaming and the smell of rotten eggs coming from the upper slopes of the supposedly dormant volcano, whose last known eruption was six hundred years ago. Much worse was to follow, and on June 12, the first of several major explosions took place, an eruption so violent that shock waves could be felt in the Visayas. A giant ash cloud rose 35km into the sky, red-hot blasts seared the countryside and nearly twenty million tonnes of sulphur dioxide were blasted into the atmosphere, causing red skies for months afterwards. Ash paralysed Manila, closing the airport for days and turning the capital's streets into an eerie post-apocalyptic landscape. More than 350 people were killed.

Until August 2009, the one- or two-day trek through the resultant moon-like lahar landscape of Pinatubo was one of the country's top activity highlights. However, due to heavy landslides that caused the deaths of seven individuals, the trail was closed. Currently you can either take a vehicle to just below the summit and then walk for half an hour up to view the Crater Lake, or preferably drive along Crow Valley to the start of a 5.5km trail which begins with a flat hike, followed by a 300m climb to the crater lake. The lake itself is stunning, with

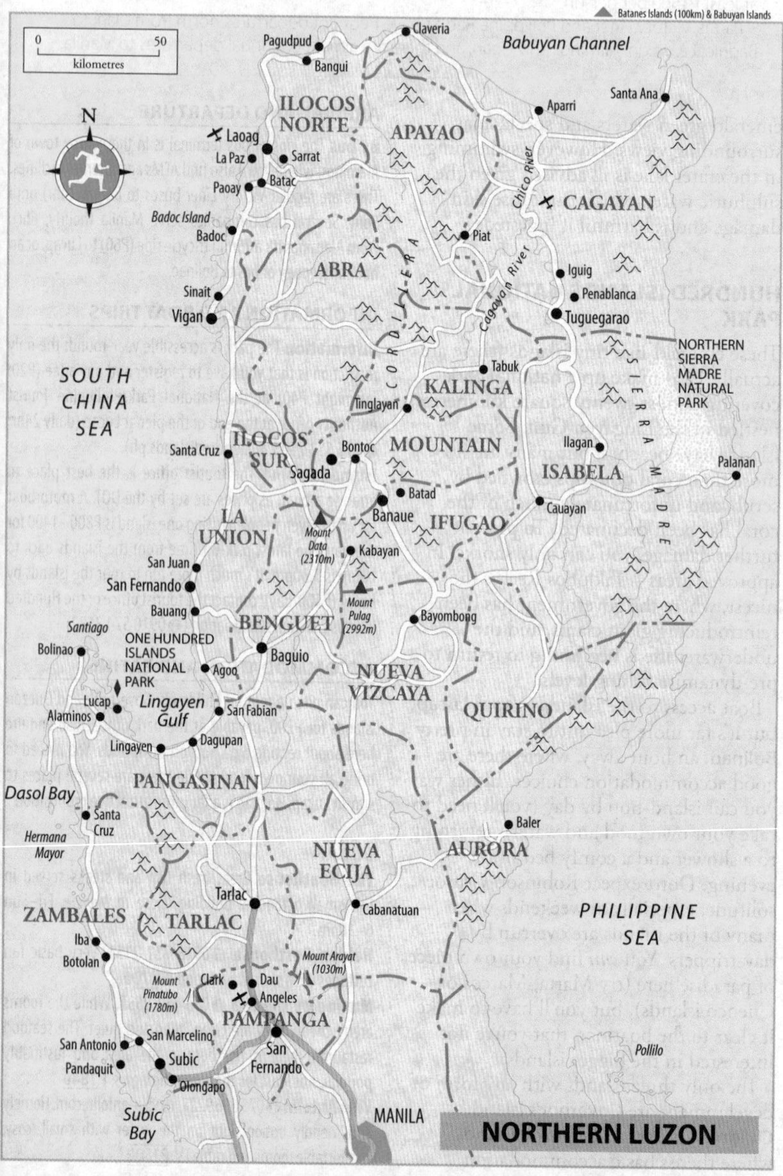

8

PINATUBO PRACTICALITIES

The **SCTEX highway** has made getting to Pinatubo much easier, and it's now more feasible as a day-trip from Manila. Trekking Pinatubo (T 02 310 5036; W trekkingpinatubo.com) has day-trips for P3750 per person (minimum of four people), which include return transport from Manila, all entrance fees, and a local guide. It's far cheaper to organize trips with the Capas Municipal Tourism Office at MacArthur Highway, Capas, Tarlac (Mon–Fri 9am–5pm; T 045 925 0112 ext 109, E capastourism@yahoo.com). Prices are dependent on group size, but count on at least P1500 per person.

Partas, Victory Liner and Philippine Rabbit have frequent departures north from Clark to Baguio, La Union, Aliminos and Vigan, and there are almost continual departures to Manila.

emerald green waters and spectacular surrounding views. However, swimming in the crater lake is ill advised given the sulphuric water, which can cause skin damage and is harmful if ingested.

HUNDRED ISLANDS NATIONAL PARK

8

These emerald-like tiny islands (there are actually 123) make up a **national park** covering almost twenty square kilometres, nestled in the Lingayen Gulf. Some islands have beaches, but many are no more than coral outcrops crowned by scrub, and unfortunately much of the coral has been decimated. To prevent further damage, you can only snorkel in approved areas – Taklobos Reef is the nicest, where the government has been reintroducing giant clams, and the underwater life is beginning to return to pre-dynamite fishing levels.

Boat access to the islands is from **Lucap**, but it's far more pleasant to stay in pretty **Bolinao**, an hour away, where there are good accommodation choices. Either way you can island-hop by day (you'll need to take your own food and water), returning to a shower and a comfy bed in the evening. Don't expect Robinson Crusoe solitude, especially at weekends when many of the islands are overrun by day-trippers. You *can* find your own piece of paradise here (try Marta, Marcos or Cuenco islands), but you'll have to make it clear to the boatman that you're not interested in the bigger islands.

The only three islands with any form of development are **Governor's Island**, **Children's Island** and **Quezon Island**, where there's basic accommodation.

ARRIVAL AND DEPARTURE

By bus The closest bus terminal is in the nearby town of Alaminos, where you'll also find ATMs and internet facilities. There are regular Victory Liner buses to Baguio (4hr) until 5pm. Several bus companies serve Manila (hourly; 6hr). From Alaminos it's a 15min tricycle ride (P60) to Lucap, or an hour by jeepney or bus to Bolinao.

INFORMATION AND BOAT TRIPS

Information The park is accessible year-round: the only restriction is that you have to register and pay a fee (P20; overnight P40) at the National Park/Philippine Tourist Authority office at the end of the pier at Lucap (daily 24hr; T 075 551 2505, W hundredislands.ph).

Island-hopping The tourist office is the best place to arrange a boat, as prices are set by the DOT. A motorboat for up to seven people visiting one island is P800–1400 for the day. The latest pick-up time from the islands back to Lucap is 5.30pm. It's much more fun to tour the islands by kayak (P500/day); contact the tourist office or the Hundred Islands Eco-Tours Association (T 0910 574 3582).

ACCOMMODATION AND EATING

You can pitch a tent on Children's, Governor's and Quezon islands for P200, payable at the park office. Also enquire here about renting nipa huts on the islands. You'll need to bring all your own food. While there are several places to stay in Lucap, Bolinao is a far more attractive proposition.

LUCAP

The Boathouse Great fresh fish and steaks served in this small octagonal building, close to *Maxine*. Fri–Sun 6–10pm.

Helden Resthouse T 0918 731 2151. Very basic fan cottages with shared bathrooms. **P700**

Maxine by the Sea T 075 551 2537. While the rooms aren't cheap, they are clean, tiled and quiet. The seafood restaurant here is the best in the area and justifiably popular, not least for the romantic views. **P1840**

Villa Antolin T 075 696 9227, W villa-antolin.com. Homely and friendly option right on the water with small, cosy, comfortable rooms and cable TV. **P1800**

BOLINAO

Punta Riviera 075 696 9227, villa-antolin.com. Lovely resort right on the beach run by a friendly Scot and Filipina couple. Clean, airy rooms and a pool. P1800

Rockview Beach 0919 8966 907. Simple bamboo and nipa huts right on the beach, close to some picturesque coastal rock formations. P1200

SAN FERNANDO (LA UNION) AND SAN JUAN

SAN FERNANDO, the capital of La Union province, is a shortish hop up the coast from Hundred Islands. Quezon Avenue runs through San Fernando from south to north, and has a number of internet cafés and ATMs. Outside the city limits, Quezon Avenue becomes the National Highway. The city itself is nothing out of the ordinary, but in nearby **San Juan**, 7km to the north, there are some laidback little beach resorts stretched along a marvellous crescent of a beach at Urbiztondo. The pounding waves here mean that from October to March this is a prime destination on the Philippines' surf scene; it's especially popular with rookies, as it's an easy, and cheap, place to learn – lessons average P400 per hour.

ARRIVAL AND DEPARTURE

By bus Partas buses from Manila heading north to Vigan stop along Quezon Ave, from where you can pick up a jeepney to San Juan (20min; P18). Alternatively, stay on the bus northbound and ask the driver to let you off at one of the resorts, which are all signposted along the road. Frequent buses to and from Baguio (1hr 30min) operate from San Fernando Plaza.

INFORMATION

Tourist information DOT office (daily 8am–5pm; 072 888 2411, dotregion1.com), *Oasis Country Resort*, 3km south of San Fernando.

ACCOMMODATION AND EATING

Circle Hostel Urbiztondo 0917 832 6253, launion .thecirclehostel.com. Hip budget surf hostel offering basic, cheap accommodation (including breakfast), just 200m back from the beach. You sleep in one huge "dorm", or in hammocks or cushions on the floor of the communal living area. A sign informs "No Strangers Here" and the relaxed nighttime vibe makes this a great place to meet travellers. P350

El Union Coffee Opposite Seabay Surf Resort, Urbiztondo. Cool little café serving an excellent variety of coffees and drinks, plus Jack Daniels cupcakes! Wed–Mon 8am–3pm & 6–9pm.

Lola Nanny's Urbiztondo 0915 725 9453, l_nanny @yahoo.com. The staff are friendly and welcoming at this backpacker place with cute green nipa huts on the terrace and a great restaurant giving onto the beach. Discounts for longer stays. P500

Monaliza Urbiztondo 072 888 4892. This surfer hang-out offering basic accommodation in fan and a/c concrete cottages (P1200), some with sea views, has been going strong since the 1980s. Board rental (P500/half-day) and lessons (P200/hr) available. P900

Seanymph Café Urbiztondo. Sit back and watch the surfers ride the waves at this beach restaurant serving a selection of Western dishes, curries and stir-fries (P150). Daily 6am–10pm.

VIGAN

About 135km north of San Fernando in La Union lies the old Spanish town of **VIGAN**, an unmissable stop on a trip through the far north for old-world charm and a flavour of the pre-war Philippines. It has become a bit of a cliché to describe Vigan as a living museum, but it does do some justice to the tag. One of the country's oldest towns, it was called Nueva Segovia in Spanish times and was an important political, military, cultural and religious centre. Having narrowly escaped bombing in World War II, it has retained its pavements of cobbled stones and some of the finest **Spanish colonial architecture** in the country, including impressive homes that once belonged to friars, merchants and colonial officials, now preserved as "Heritage Homes". Inscribed onto the UNESCO World Heritage list in 1999, it remains the best example of a planned Spanish colonial city in Asia.

WHAT TO SEE AND DO

Vigan's time-capsule ambience is enhanced by the decision to allow only pedestrians and **calesas** (one-pony, two-seat traps) on some streets. A ride in a *calesa* makes for a romantic tour of the town (P150/hr). Vigan is one of the easier Philippine towns to negotiate because its streets follow a fairly regular grid. Crisologo Street runs south from Plaza Burgos and is lined with antique

shops and cafés; running parallel to it is the main thoroughfare, Governor A. Reyes Street. On Plaza Salcedo stands **St Paul's Metropolitan Cathedral** (daily 5am–6pm; free), built here in 1790 in "earthquake baroque" style, following the tectonic destruction of the original building on the banks of the river. Across the square is the **Father José Burgos Museum** (Tues–Sun 8.30–11.30am & 1.30–4.30pm; P10), a captivating old colonial house that was once home to one of the town's most famous residents, Padre José Burgos, whose martyrdom in 1872 galvanized the revolutionary movement. It houses Burgos memorabilia, as well as fourteen paintings by the artist Villanueva, depicting the violent 1807 Basi Revolt, prompted by a Spanish effort to control the production of *basi* (sugar-cane wine).

Two **Heritage Houses** worth popping into are the Syquia Mansion on Quirino Boulevard (daily 9am–noon & 2–5pm; P20) and the Crisologo Museum on Liberation Boulevard (daily 8.30–11.30am & 1.30–4.30pm; free), which house various colonial artefacts and exhibits on the area. Vigan is also known for its **pottery**. The massive wood-fired kilns at the Pagburnayan Potteries in Rizal Street, at the junction with Liberation Boulevard, turn out huge jars, known as *burnay*, in which northerners store everything from vinegar to fish paste. Carabao (water buffalo) are still used to squash the clay under hoof.

★TREAT YOURSELF

Villa Angela Heritage House Quirino Blvd 077 722 2914, villangela.com. The most colonial of all the colonial hotels, this beautiful old Heritage House built in 1870 is a real Vigan landmark, and the place to wallow in history under the canopy of a four-poster bed. The house is chock-full of old photos and antiques; if you like your history a bit more modern, ask for the room Tom Cruise slept in: he stayed here for a few weeks in 1989 when filming *Born on the Fourth of July* on the sand dunes in nearby Laoag. Dorm beds available from P550. **P2000**

The first week of May is the **Viva Vigan Arts Festival**, one of the biggest cultural events in North Luzon, when the usually staid town lets down its hair with a *calesa* parade and lots of street dancing.

ARRIVAL AND DEPARTURE

By plane The airport is 6km west of the city centre. A tricycle into town is P20.

Destinations SEAAIR fly between Manila (departing 2.30pm; 1hr) and Vigan (departing 4.30pm; 1hr) every Fri & Sun. More flights (Cebu Pacific, PAL Express) can be found to Laoag, a 2hr (P180) bus ride from Vigan.

By bus Partas buses use their terminal near the Vigan Public Market in Alcantara St at the southern end of town. Dominion buses arrive and depart from the corner of Quezon Ave (the main street running south to north) and Liberation Blvd. Viron Trans use their terminal in Barangay Ayusan Norte. For the long trip back to Manila, Partas buses offer the most comfort, and three nightly express services. You can also catch a/c buses from the Caltex station on the highway to Laoag Airport. A tricycle between any of the bus terminals and the town centre is P30.

Destinations Baguio (hourly; 5hr); Laoag (hourly; 2hr); Manila (hourly; 9hr); San Fernando (hourly; 3hr).

INFORMATION

Tourist information Vigan City Tourism (Mon–Fri 8am–5pm; 077 622 8776, vigancity.gov.ph) is in the City Hall; they have an information centre open on Calle Crisologo (daily 8am–5pm). The Provincial Tourism Centre (daily 8am–noon & 1–5pm; 077 722 8520) is right by *Café Leona* in Plaza Burgos.

ACCOMMODATION

Grandpa's Inn 1 Bonifacio St 077 722 2118. This cosy heritage house full of old knick-knacks has welcoming rooms, all with lovely wooden floors and most with brick walls. The communal bathrooms are a bit grimy; it's worth paying a little extra for a private bathroom (P980). Free wi-fi. **P730**

HEM Apartelle 32 Gov. A. Reyes St 077 722 2173. This new hotel has six sparkling rooms, all with private bath; staff are helpful and there is free wi-fi. **P1000**

Vigan Hotel Burgos St 077 722 1906. Located in a colonial building, this hotel epitomizes the city's culture and Spanish heritage, although the cheaper fan rooms with shared bathrooms (P595) are run-down. Free wi-fi. **P995**

EATING AND DRINKING

One of Vigan's specialities is *empanada*, a type of tortilla that you can pick up for a few pesos from one of the many street stalls and small bakeries – try *Irene's* on Salcedo Street.

Café Leona Plaza Burgos. Named after the mother of the Philippines' first labour movement, *Café Leona* is Vigan's most popular restaurant, serving native Ilocano dishes as well as wood-fired pizzas (P250) and Japanese dishes (from P150). Daily 10am–10pm.

Uno Grille 2 Bonifacio St. Owned by and next to *Grandpa's*, this airy outdoor restaurant offers a variety of sizzling barbecued meats, as well as classic Filipino and European dishes. Grandpa's also runs *Café Uno*, an itty-bitty café serving light meals (pastas from P60), cakes (P65), cookies (P15), teas and coffees (P40). Free wi-fi. Daily 9am–11pm.

DIRECTORY

Banks and exchange BDO is in Plaza Maestro Mall near Plaza Burgos, and there are several ATMs along Quezon Ave.

Internet There's an internet café in Mart One on Plaza Salcedo (daily 9am–8pm; P25/hr); *Café Uno* (see above) has free wi-fi.

Police Rivero Street, east of the city centre (T 077 722 0890).

Post office Governor A. Reyes cnr. Bonifacio streets. (Mon–Fri 8am–noon & 1–5pm).

The Cordilleras

To Filipino lowlanders, brought up on sunshine and beaches, the mountainous north is still seen as a mysterious Shangri-La full of enigmatic tribes and their unfamiliar gods. **Baguio**, the traditional mountain retreat for Manileños during the fierce heat of Easter week, is about as far north as many southerners get. But it's not until you get beyond Baguio into Benguet, Ifugao and Mountain provinces, the **tribal heartlands** of the northern Philippines, that the adventure really begins. There are still towns and valleys where life has changed little in hundreds of years, with traditional customs and values still very much in evidence, but increasingly paved roads are transforming both the physical and cultural landscape.

A swing through the north shouldn't miss out the mountain village of **Sagada**, with its caves, hanging coffins and backpacker-friendly hostels, and the magnificent **rice terraces at Banaue**. A slightly longer trip might take in **Kabayan**, an Ibaloi village north of Baguio. In the early twentieth century a group of mummies, possibly dating as far back as 2000 BC, was discovered in the caves here, and it's also a base for scaling **Mount Pulag** (2922m), the highest mountain in Luzon.

BAGUIO AND AROUND

BAGUIO is known as "City of Pines", but unchecked development and chronic traffic congestion have greatly diminished its appeal. Lying on a plateau 1400m above sea level, Baguio was built in 1900 by the Americans as a recreational and administrative centre, from where they could preside over their tropical colony without working up too much of a sweat. Baguio is also etched on the Filipino consciousness as the site of one of the country's worst natural disasters, the earthquake of July 16, 1990, which caused terrible devastation and claimed hundreds of lives.

Although little more than a stopping-off point en route to Sagada and the mountain provinces, Baguio has a few

8

TRIBES OF THE CORDILLERAS

The Cordilleras are home to six main indigenous Filipino tribes: the Ibaloi, the Kankana-ey, the Ifugao, the Kalinga, the Apayao and the Bontoc, collectively known as **Igorots**. There are also smaller sub-tribes among these six.

Tribes began to gather in small, isolated communities in the archipelago during pre-Spanish times when lowland Filipinos expanded into the interiors of Luzon, isolating upland tribes into pockets in which they still exist today. Like other Filipinos, these **upland tribes** were a blend of various ethnic origins, ranging from the highly skilled Bontoc and Ifugao to more primitive groups. Some have intermarried with lowlanders for more than a century, but others, like the **Kalinga**, choose to remain isolated from lowland influences. The **Ifugao**, creators of the famous rice terraces, mostly live in and around Banaue and are the tribe that visitors to the north are most likely to come into contact with.

secrets worth discovering, such as its parks, arts enclaves and lovely bohemian cafés.

WHAT TO SEE AND DO

Burnham Park is the city's centrepiece and a nice place for a stroll, with a boating lake and strange little three-wheeled bicycles for rent. The park area was designed by Daniel Burnham, who was also responsible for parts of Chicago, Washington DC, and much of colonial American Manila. On the eastern edge of the park is Harrison Road, and behind that and running almost parallel to it is the city's congested main artery, Session Road, lined with shops and restaurants. Standing hidden above it all, and reached by a flight of a hundred steep steps, is **Baguio Cathedral** (daily 6am–6pm; free), an example of "wedding-cake gothic" in an eye-catching shade of rose pink.

The northern end of Session Road leading to Magsaysay Avenue is the least appealing area, the smoky congestion only partly redeemed by the **City Market** (dawn to dusk), one of the liveliest and most colourful in the country, which sells strawberries, peanut brittle, sweet wine, honey, textiles, handicrafts and jewellery, all produced in the Cordilleras. A huge *ukay-ukay* nightmarket also sets up along Harrison Road.

The **Baguio Museum** (Mon–Sat 10am–5pm; P40) on Governor Pack Road showcases hundreds of fascinating

artefacts from the region, as well as a Kabayan mummy.

Tam-awan Village

On the northwest outskirts of Baguio, **Tam-awan Village** (daily 8am–6pm; P50; T 074 446 2949, W tam-awanvillage.com) is a replica tribal village comprised of eight Ifugao houses and two Kalinga huts where you can stay and drink rice wine around a traditional Bontoc *dap-ay*, an outdoor meeting place with a fire at its centre. There is also a variety of native craft workshops on offer. Cordilleran food is prepared on site, work by local artists is available to buy, and staff will often perform ceremonies, songs and dances for visitors. An overnight stay here is an experience (P1000 for a small hut for two people with shared toilets and showers). Take a jacket because it can get surprisingly cold. You can reach Tam-awan Village by taxi for less than P100, or take a Tam-awan jeepney (P11) from Kayang Street.

The BenCab Museum

In February 2009, National Artist for the visual arts and longtime Baguio resident Benedicto Cabrera (universally known as BenCab), the driving force behind the Tam-awan Village, opened the **BenCab Museum** (Tues–Sun 9am–6pm; P100). About fifteen minutes outside Baguio, it's home to a mix of contemporary Filipino art and indigenous Cordilleran crafts in a beautiful setting – on a clear day you can even see the South China Sea. The tranquil café is also worth a stop. To get here, catch a jeepney (P11) bound for Asin from beside the market, and let the driver know where you're going.

ARRIVAL AND DEPARTURE

By bus Buses including Victory Liner, Partas, Dagupan, Genesis and Philippine Rabbit drop passengers on the eastern edge of the city on Governor Pack Rd. KMS and Ohayami buses arrive at the western end of Burnham Park.
Destinations For Sagada: GL Lizardo has hourly trips from the Dangwa terminal on Magsayasay Ave (6hr). Buses for Bontoc: D'Rising Sun from the Slaughterhouse Terminal on the hour 5am–4pm (5–6hr). Several morning A-Liner buses also leave from here for Kabayan (4hr 30min). Buses for Banaue: KMS (Chanum Street) has two departures daily (8am & 9.30pm; 8hr); various companies travel to San Fernando, La Union (hourly; 2hr 30min), leaving from the terminal on Shagem St. Buses for all other destinations leave from the terminal in Governor Pack Rd near Session Rd: Manila (hourly until 11pm; 6hr); Vigan (hourly; 5hr).

INFORMATION

Tourist information The DOT office (Mon–Fri 8am–5pm; T 074 442 7014, E dot_cordillera@yahoo.com) is in the Tourism Complex on Governor Pack Rd, while the Baguio Tourism Council (Mon–Sat 8am–5pm, Sun 8am–noon; T 074 446 3434) is on Lake Rd. You can pick up an *EZ Baguio* map at the National Bookstore in the SM Mall.

ACCOMMODATION

Baguio Village Inn 355 Magsaysay Ave T 074 442 3901 or T 0917 570 9675. This spotless place, a 10min walk to the bottom of Session Road, has plain smallish rooms and hardwood floors throughout; there's a pleasant coffee shop in the foyer. **P850**

La Brea Inn 23 Lower Session Rd T 074 446 6061, E la_brea_inn@yahoo.com. Clean and tidy rooms right in the centre of Baguio and just a short stroll from many cafés and restaurants; all rooms have private bath and cable TV. Free wi-fi. **P1100**

Oyana Lodge 118 Villalon St T 074 244 1235. All the rooms are decked out in princess pink at this clean little guesthouse with hot water, cable TV and free wi-fi. **P1500**

8

EATING

★ **Café by the Ruins** 25 Chuntug St. In a wonderful airy setting with rustic tables set around ruins, this café serves hearty soups (P100), organic vegetarian dishes and local favourites including *pinikpikan*, a tribal delicacy that's also known as "killing me softly" because the chicken is whipped slowly to death to make the meat bloody and tender (P180). Fresh bread, home-made jams and cookies, too. Wi-fi available. Daily 7am–9pm.

Ebai's Upper Session Rd. The home-made carrot cake (P53) here was designed for President Ramos himself; there are plenty of other options for those with a sweet tooth including chocolate, apple and almond cakes, and there's great freshly brewed Cordillera coffee (P35), too. Mains for less than P200. Daily 7am–10pm.

★ **Oh My Gulay** 5th Floor, La Azotea Building, 108 Session Rd. This unique vegetarian café-cum-art gallery translates as "Oh my vegetable" – dishes are light, including salads, sandwiches and pastas (P120). The impressive native-wood interior designed by local artist and film-maker Kidlat Tahimik features half a ship's hull and a stream with goldfish. A must-see. Daily 11am–8pm, Sun until 7pm.

DRINKING AND NIGHTLIFE

The hub of the action for the city's college students is centred around the bars of Nevada Square, a short taxi ride (P45) from the city centre; Baguio's yuppies tend to frequent the bars along Legarda Rd.

18BC Music Lounge Legarda Rd. Fun bar with nightly local bands and happy-hour weekdays 4–7pm. Mondays attract a slightly older clientele than the usual college devotees. Beer P50, cocktails P70. Mon–Fri 4pm–2.30am, Sat & Sun from 6.30pm.

Padi's Point Rizal Park. This is one of the most popular places in town, with daily bands playing an eclectic mix of tunes from R&B to rock; the DJ then takes over and spins some disco tunes as groups of students gulp "cocktail towers" (three litres). Daily 5pm–late; cover charge up to P200.

SHOPPING

Easter Weaving Room 2 Easter Rd in Guisad. A huge selection of beautifully crafted woven goods. It's quite touristy but offers the chance to see intricate designs being woven on tablecloths and rugs in the "factory". It's not too far from Tama-awan Village, and can easily be combined with a (taxi) visit. Daily 8am–5pm.

8

Narda's 151 Upper Sessions Rd. Fantastic Igorot woven accessories and housewares. Daily 8am–6pm.

SM Mall Luneta Hill, Upper Sessions Rd. There is a supermarket on the lower ground floor, ATMs, a cinema and numerous cafés and restaurants. Daily 10am–10pm.

DIRECTORY

Banks PNB branches at the northern end of Session Rd and on Abanao St both have an ATM. BPI has a number of branches, including one at the top of Session Rd, and there's another directly opposite *18BC* on Legarda.

Internet Horayzen Internet, Rizal Park (daily 9am–9pm; P20/hr), and several along Session Road; SM Mall has free wi-fi.

Laundry Laba Ever laundry by *18BC* on Legarda Rd (Mon–Sat 9am–9pm; Sun 9am–2pm; P35/kg).

Police The station (☎ 074 442 7944) is located next to the fire station off Abanao St.

Post office At the eastern end of Session Rd.

KABAYAN

The isolated mountain village of **KABAYAN**, 50km or five hours by bus north of Baguio, gained some notoriety in the early twentieth century when a group of mummies was discovered in surrounding caves. The mummies are believed by some scientists to date back as far as 2000 BC. When the Spanish arrived, mummification was discouraged and the practice died out. Controversy still surrounds the Kabayan mummies, some of which have "disappeared" to overseas collectors. Several mummies remain, however, and you can see them in their mountaintop caves and also in the small **Kabayan National Museum** (Mon–Fri 8am–5pm; P30).

You can hire a guide to trek up to some of the mummy caves (P1500): ask at the museum or your accommodation for details. **Timbak Cave** (P100) is one of the best, but it's high on a mountaintop and a strenuous four- to five-hour climb. The best place to stay is the new *Pine Cone Lodge* (☎ 0929 327 77 49; P250 per person). As the name suggests, this lodge is decked out in pine and the clean tiled rooms are spacious and all have private bath, plus there's a cosy living area with fireplace. *Kabayan Coop Lodge* is also clean and friendly, and has simple double rooms for P400. It's also the place to enquire about guides for Mount Pulag (see below). There are half a dozen *sari-sari* stores in Kabayan where you can get snacks and basic meals. Access to Kabayan is easiest from Baguio (there are several morning buses; see p.617). If you're continuing north from here, you'll have to hire a vehicle to take you to the Halsema Highway to catch a Bontoc-bound bus.

MOUNT PULAG

Standing 2992m above sea level, **Mount Pulag** is the highest mountain in Luzon and a Level III strenuous climb. Pulag is a challenge: the terrain is steep, there are gorges and ravines and, in the heat of the valleys, it's easy to forget it's bitterly cold on top.

The best **trail** for first-timers starts from nearby Ambangeg, a stop on the Baguio–Kabayan bus route. The DENR Visitors' Centre (Mon–Fri 9am–5pm; ☎ 0919 631 5402) is close to the start of a number of trails, where you must **register** and pay the park entrance fee (P800), plus organize the mandatory guide (P500 per group for the easier trails). The Akiki or Killer Trail starts 2km south of Kabayan on the Baguio–Kabayan road

and takes at least two days (P1800 per group). Talk to guides in Kabayan before you attempt any assault on the mountain. The Visitors' Centre can arrange accommodation for P100, but the best way is to take a tent (P50 per person) and expect to spend the night on top. The next morning, wake early to watch the sunrise and marvel at the whole of Luzon at your feet.

SAGADA

In spite of its increasing popularity, the village of **SAGADA**, 151km north of Baguio, at an elevation of over 1500m, still has charm and mystery to spare, much of it connected with the **hanging coffins** that can be seen perched high in the surrounding limestone cliffs. Sagada began to open up as a destination with the arrival of electricity in the early 1970s, and intellectuals flocked here to write and paint. They didn't produce much, perhaps because they are said to have spent much of their time drinking *tapuy*, the local rice wine. European hippies followed and the artistic influence has left its mark in the form of little boho cafés and inns and a distinctly laidback atmosphere, enhanced by the ready availability of locally grown weed, although a major bust in 2013 may have put paid to this scene for a while. More guesthouses and souvenir shops are springing up as improved roads increase the tourist influx, but for now, Sagada remains one of the country's genuine backpacker enclaves.

It can get very chilly, especially at night, and the streets are poorly lit; bring a sweater, scarf and torch.

WHAT TO SEE AND DO

For insight into Cordilleran culture, call into the small **Ganduyan Museum** (daily 8am–6pm; entry by donation), next to the new town hall where owner Christina Aben will talk you through her fascinating collection of Igorot artefacts, some of which were still being used in daily life into the 1990s. The museum has sporadic opening hours. It's also worth taking the time to visit the house of Eduardo Masferre a short way off the Bontoc Road, past Sagada Weaving. Of Spanish heritage, Masferre married a local woman and was one of the earliest photographers to document the people and culture of villages throughout the province in the 1930s and 1940s. He passed away in 1995 but his wife still lives in the house and animatedly tells stories of the old days as she guides you through the collection of photographs on display in the small "gallery". There are also original prints, copies and photo-books for sale. Ask at the Masferre Inn in town (which also has his works for sale) to arrange a visit.

A five-minute walk past the hospital on the road to Bontoc takes you to **Sagada Weaving** (Mon–Sat 7am–6pm), where you can watch distinctive coloured fabrics being produced using tribal designs, and buy souvenirs.

Activities

Sagada's main draw is the outdoors. The area's cool forest paths and extensive cave network make for some great **treks** (it's possible to hire guides; see p.620).

One of the most popular hikes, taking two to three hours in all, is a loop around the **hanging coffins** in **Echo Valley**, high on the surrounding limestone cliffs. There are dozens of sinuous paths leading off through deep foliage in all directions, so a guide is essential. A typical trek costs P500–600 for a group of up to ten people.

Caving in Sagada's labyrinth network of channels and caverns is an exhilarating but potentially risky activity. A small number of tourists have died in these caves, so don't risk going alone. The highlight is **Sumaging Cave**, an old burial cave whose chambers and rock formations are an eerie sight, a 45-minute walk south of town. The set price for a guided tour for up to four people is P500. A more challenging underground adventure is provided by the **Cave Connection**, linking Sumaging and Lumiang, but this is not for the faint of heart or claustrophobic and involves three to four hours of squeezing through narrow crevices and swimming, often to emerge in enormous caverns eerily lit by the glow of the guide's paraffin lamp. Other outdoors

options include a visit to pretty nearby waterfalls, rice terraces, and kayaking on the Chico River: see ⓦluzonoutdoors.com, affiliated with SEGA.

ARRIVAL AND DEPARTURE

By bus Buses and jeepneys terminate by the new town hall on the main street. The Halsema Highway to Sagada traverses the highest point on the Philippine highway system (2339m), so bring warm clothing for the trip from Baguio, and don't look down. GL Lizardo runs buses to Baguio (7 daily; 5am–1pm; 5–6hr).

By jeepney Jeepneys leave Sagada every 30min from 6.30am–9pm, then hourly from 9am–1pm for Bontoc (45min), where you can change for Banaue or Manila.

INFORMATION

Tourist information It is strongly advised that all visitors register (P20) upon arrival at the Tourist Information Center (daily 6am–5pm; ⓣ0905 137 626, ⓦsagada.org/tourism) inside the old municipal hall. They can also help organize tours.

8

Tours The Sagada Environmental Guides Association (SEGA; daily 6am–6pm; ⓦsega.sagada.org) are the longest established and fix all guiding prices in the region; Sagada Genuine Guides Association (SaGGAs; daily 8am–7pm) also provide guides.

ACCOMMODATION

Reservations are advised over holiday periods.

Masferre Inn ⓣ0918 341 6164. Just below the public market. Owned by the Masferre family, this friendly place has clean, simple rooms, some with balconies and views. The restaurant is decent and the walls are adorned with pictures by Eduardo Masferre (see p.619). **P1500**

★**Sagada Homestay** On the road to Besao ⓣ0919 702 8380, ⓔsagadahomestay@yahoo.com.ph. The smell of fresh pinewood permeates this wonderful family-run guesthouse with an alpine feel. Rooms are clean and cosy and the welcoming family do their utmost to make guests feel at home. Hot water, free wi-fi and outstanding massages. **P500**

St Joseph's Resthouse ⓣ0918 559 5934. This friendly place, with great views of the surrounding countryside, has cheap rooms in the main building, and more expensive cottages (P1700) all decked out in local wood in the attractive hilltop garden. Great restaurant, too. **P500**

EATING AND DRINKING

Bana's Café & Restaurant Sagada's best Arabica and Civet coffees (P30) at this simple café with a terrace, the perfect place to stock up before a long trek. Daily 7am–7pm.

Lemon Pie House At the bottom of the village, past *George Guesthouse*. This laidback café with pillows set around cute pine tables is a great spot for a coffee (P30) and a slice of lemon pie (P25), made with juicy local lemons. Free wi-fi. Daily 6am–9pm.

★**Log Cabin Café** ⓣ0920 520 0463. Very popular restaurant which rustles up tasty dishes using different market-fresh produce each day. The setting is cosy, with a crackling fire, and there's a great Saturday-night buffet (P390) whipped up by their French chef at 7pm. Dinner only. Essential to book in advance. Daily 6–10pm.

Yoghurt House Great place in which to soak up the surrounding views from the first-floor balcony and tuck into a creamy home-made yoghurt (P70). Excellent breakfasts and hearty dinners. The chocolate chip cookies are a must. Daily 7.30am–9pm.

DIRECTORY

Banks and exchange The Rural Bank of Sagada has an ATM, although it's inside the bank and thereby only works in line with the bank's opening hours (Tues–Sat 8.30am–4.30pm); it's much safer to stock up on pesos in Baguio. The bank will change dollars and travellers' cheques at an unfavourable rate. There's also a Western Union here.

Internet Try Golinsan, behind the new municipal hall (daily 7.30am–8pm; P30/hr).

BONTOC

The capital of Mountain province, **BONTOC**, is the first major town in the north beyond Baguio. It lies on the banks of the Chico River, 45 minutes east of Sagada by jeepney.

Bontoc is primarily a commercial town used by tourists as a rest-stop on the circuit to Banaue. It is, however, gaining a reputation as a good place for **trekking**; contact the tourism information centre (Mon–Fri 8am–5pm) in the municipal hall, or get in touch directly with local guide Francis Degay (ⓣ0948 678 7290, ⓔf_degay@yahoo.com). Guides for up to four people cost around P1500 per day. Don't miss the small but excellent **Bontoc Museum** (daily 8am–noon & 1–5pm; P50) behind *Pines Kitchenette and Inn*. It features fascinating black-and-white photos and various artefacts of tribal life in the Cordilleras, plus a decent shop downstairs. Check out the replica village built in the grounds.

ARRIVAL AND DEPARTURE

By bus Hourly to Baguio 5am–4pm (6–7hr) on D'Rising Sun, GL Lizardo, and Dangwa. Cable Tours buses for Manila

(10hr), via Banaue (2 hr), usually leave daily at 3pm from outside *Cable Café*. However, at the time of writing Cable buses were suspended following a terrible bus crash near Bontoc in which 14 passengers died.

By jeepney Departures for Banaue from outside the tourism information centre, officially at 8am and 11am, but in reality they leave when they're full (2hr; P150).

ACCOMMODATION AND EATING

Cable Café Main St. Daily bands playing an eclectic mix of music hit the little stage at 8pm, keeping Bontoc's liveliest joint up and running. The grub is Filipino, with mains such as chicken *adobo* (P95–130). Daily 8am–3pm & 6–10pm.

Churya-a Hotel Main St T 0999 994 6726, E darwin_churyaa@yahoo.com. Unremarkable doubles and cold-water showers only, but there's a nice balcony eating area with a view over the mountains and it's right in the centre of town. P400

Pines Kitchenette and Inn Behind the market T 074 602 1408. This large family house was originally built to put up adopted World War II war orphans; there's even a mini-museum within the premises showcasing old artefacts dating back to that time. Rooms are simple and the bathrooms just about pass muster, but the management is friendly and welcoming. P400

DIRECTORY

Banks and exchange PNB and Landbank both have ATMs. There's a Western Union on the main street.

Internet Cable Internet Café is directly above *Cable Café* (daily 7.30am–10pm; P20/hr).

Post office Near the Bontoc Museum.

BANAUE

It's a rugged but spectacular two-and-a-half-hour trip south from Bontoc to **BANAUE** in Ifugao province, along a winding road that leads up into the misty Cordilleras, across a high mountain pass, then down precipitous mountainside. It may only be 300km north of Manila, but Banaue is a world away, 1300m above sea level and far removed in spirit and topography from the beaches and palm trees of the south. This is the heart of **rice-terrace** country: the terraces in Banaue itself are some of the most impressive and well known, although there are hundreds of others in the area, some of the best of which are at nearby **BATAD**, where there are a couple of guesthouses, so you can stay overnight and hike back the next morning.

Banaue itself is a small town centred on a marketplace, with a clutch of guesthouses and some souvenir shops. Two kilometres up the road from the marketplace are the four main **lookout points** for the rice terraces. Tricycle drivers angle constantly to take you there, which can be irritating, but the views are truly superb. A tricycle will cost around P200, but be sure to agree the price beforehand. Ifugao in traditional costume will ask for a small fee if you want to take their photograph, and there's a handful of souvenir stalls surrounding the lookouts selling carved wooden bowls and woven blankets. Don't miss the remarkable little **museum** (daily 8am–5pm; P50) at the *Banaue View Inn*, which documents the extraordinary life of Henry Otley Beyer, an American anthropologist who came to study Ifugao tribes at the beginning of the twentieth century and, after marrying

8

THE STAIRWAYS TO HEAVEN

The "Stairway to Heaven" **rice terraces** at Banaue are one of the great icons of the Philippines. They were hewn from the land over two thousand years ago by Ifugao tribespeople using primitive tools, an achievement in engineering terms that ranks alongside the building of the pyramids.

The survival of the terraces, added to the United Nations' World Heritage list in 1995, is closely tied to the future of the tribespeople themselves. Part of the problem, it must be said, is tourism, but you can't blame locals, who would otherwise have been toiling on the terraces, for making a much easier buck selling reproduction tribal artefacts. The problem is compounded by the mass migration of many younger tribespeople to the big cities. The result is that the region now only meets a third of its rice requirements, and as you tour the region you'll notice areas where the terraces are clearly in disrepair. Given that the main reason travellers come to the region is to see the terraces, if they disappear then so will the tourist dollars. For now they remain spectacular and are at their most impressive around March, April and May, right before the rice harvest.

an Ifugao woman, settled and died in the region. The **Museum of Cordilleran Sculpture** (daily 8am–5pm; P100), further up past the *Banaue Hotel*, houses more than two thousand fascinating Ifugao artefacts, including trophy heads and erotic rice baskets.

ARRIVAL AND DEPARTURE

By bus Buses terminate at the main road above the marketplace, reached by a flight of steep stone stairs.
Destinations For Manila, Ohayami has two daily departures (6.45am & 7pm; 9hr); for Baguio KMS runs two daily services (7am & 6pm; 8hr); for Bontoc there are three daily services (2hr).
By jeepney Jeepneys stop opposite the tourist information office.
Destinations Bontoc (change for Sagada; daily 8.30am; P150).

INFORMATION

8

Tourist information The tourist information office is near the town hall (daily 7am–7pm; T 074 386 4010), where you can get maps of the area for trekking (P15). They'll also help you find a guide for half-day treks to local Ifugao communities or longer treks through the rice terraces to Batad (P700–1200/group).

ACCOMMODATION AND EATING

Banaue View Inn T 074 916 694 4551, E banaueviewinn_1984@yahoo.com. Friendly, family-run place overlooking town and the terraces beyond, and home to the Banaue Museum. Clean rooms with private hot-water bathrooms; there's also an attic dorm (P300). **P800**
People's Lodge and Restaurant Next door to the *Greenview* T 074 386 4014, E jerwin_t@yahoo.com. Only the pricier rooms here have the luxury of hot water, while the simple ones have cold showers and communal facilities. There's internet access on the ground floor (P50) and a decent enough restaurant. **P500**
★**Sanafe Lodge and Restaurant** T 0918 947 7226, W sanafelodge.com. The doubles here are clean and cosy, all with hot water and most with incredible views, while the dorms are quite stuffy with no windows. The fantastic terrace restaurant serves great international food and the views over the terraces are unbeatable. Free speedy wi-fi. Dorm **P200**, double **P800**
Uyami's Greenview Lodge and Restaurant T 0920 540 4225, W ugreenview.wordpress.com. The homely doubles here have parquet floors and pine interiors, while the cheaper concrete rooms on the bottom floor aren't as snug. The restaurant has wonderful rice-terrace views and wi-fi, and rustles up appetizing local dishes using fresh market produce. **P900**

DIRECTORY

Banks and exchange W&L moneychangers are opposite the information office, but there's no ATM.
Internet *People's Lodge and Restaurant* has an internet café (daily 7am–9pm; P50/hr).
Police Opposite the information centre.
Post office The main post office (where you can also make long-distance phone calls) is near the *Banaue Hotel & Youth Hostel*. There's another post office in the municipal town hall.

BATAD

The 19km trek from Banaue to the remote little village of **BATAD** has become something of a pilgrimage for visitors looking for rural isolation and unforgettable rice-terrace scenery. You'll need to take a tricycle (P700) from Banaue for the first (bumpy) 12km before starting a tiring walk up a steep trail, but the spectacular views more than compensate for any discomfort. A cheaper and less tiring option is to take a public jeepney (P100) to Saddle, one hour's walk from Batad. You will have to stay overnight in Batad as there is only one afternoon departure from Banaue at 3pm; you can then catch the 8.30am jeepney back to Banaue. Alternatively, you can hire a private jeepney (P2500); a guide will set you back a further P1200. The tourist information centre can give you more detail on the many different hikes in the area, or contact Robert's Trekking Adventure (T 0908 308 2316, E robert.immotna@yahoo.com) who organize great hikes of the area.

Batad nestles in a natural amphitheatre, a one-hour hike from the glorious 30m-high **Tappia Waterfall**, which has a deep, bracing pool for swimming. Village life in Batad was virtually unchanged for centuries until the development of tourism, but its influence hasn't yet been too insidious; there are just half a dozen basic **guesthouses**. Rooms in Batad, while not as dirt-cheap as they once were, are still very reasonable. Prices and quality are similar (all P200 per person), but *Simon's Inn* has a particularly good restaurant offering the widest choice of dishes in town, including fantastic home-made pitta bread. Rooms fill up quickly in summertime.

South of Manila and Mindoro

Leaving the sprawl of Manila behind and heading south takes you along the South Luzon Expressway (known to Filipinos as the South Luzon Distressway) and into the provinces of Cavite, Laguna and Batangas. Traffic can be grim, particularly on weekends and holidays, so try to time your journey for a weekday if at all possible. The province of **Batangas** is Manila's weekend playground, with some nice (but rather expensive) beach resorts around Nasugbu and Matabungkay, and alluring **Taal Volcano** to climb. The provincial capital, **Batangas City**, is a polluted port town but its ferry pier offers escape to the island of **Mindoro** and the diving resorts of **Puerto Galera**.

PAGSANJAN FALLS

Francis Ford Coppola chose **PAGSANJAN**, 90km southeast of Manila, as the shooting location for the harrowing final scenes of *Apocalypse Now*, and the sheer drama of the scenery is undeniable. Faded Hollywood associations aside, the real draw here is the chance to shoot down the fourteen rapids of the Bombongan River from **Pagsanjan Falls**. Proceed first of all to the Pagsanjan Municipal Tourism Office (daily 8am–5pm; ⓣ049 501 3544) located by the Catholic Church in the town proper, who will brief you and get you to the boating stations. The local *bangkeros* are skilled at manoeuvring their canoes between the boulders. The cost of shooting the rapids is P1250 per person, which includes a round-trip boat ride and a bamboo raft to the main falls (cushion and life vest included). There have been incidences of boatmen demanding tips of as much as P1000, but P100 per person is adequate. To get to Pagsanjan from

8

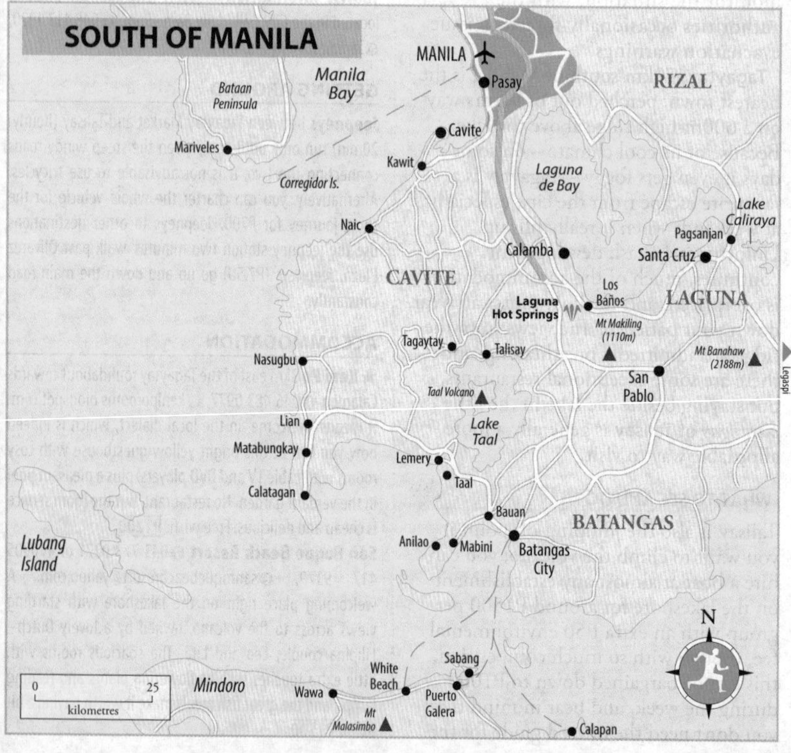

Manila, catch a DLTB or HM bus marked "Santa Cruz" from the corner of Buendia and Taft Avenue and get off at Barangay Pagsawitan from where you can get a jeepney (P10) to Pagsanjan town.

Staying overnight allows you to beat the crowds, but choices aren't great – try *Willy Flores Guesthouse* (821 Garcia St, Santa Cruz; ⓣ0909 992 1218; P500), a simple, but clean and friendly place.

TAAL VOLCANO

Rising majestically from the centre of picturesque Taal lake and perennially popular with day-trippers from Manila, **Taal Volcano** offers gentle trekking, stunning views, and a refreshing change of temperature from the city. **Taal** has had several major eruptions over the centuries and was showing signs of increased activity in 2012. A team of seismologists is permanently based on the lakeshore and continues to monitor the situation, with the authorities occasionally forced to issue evacuation warnings.

8

Tagaytay, 70km south of Manila, is the nearest town, perched out of harm's way on a 600m-high ridge above the lake. Because of its cool climate – on some days it even gets foggy – Tagaytay is a favourite escape from the city, especially at weekends when it really fills up. Unfortunately, rash development continues, much of the accommodation is overpriced, and the boat touts can wear down your patience. The views from the ridge are admittedly breathtaking, and there are some exceptional restaurants, but staying beside the lake in the little *barangay* of **Talisay** is generally a more affordable way to visit.

WHAT TO SEE AND DO

Talisay is also the jumping-off point if you want to climb the volcano; you can hire a boat at almost any establishment on the lakeshore for around P1500 per group with an extra P50 environmental fee, though with so much competition, this can be bargained down to P1000 during the week, and bear in mind that you don't need the offered guide for the hour-long walk. There's not much shade on the volcano and it can get hot, so don't go without sunblock, a good hat, food and plenty of water. There are horses for hire (P250) for the trek if you feel like enjoying the view without expending any energy. According to levels of tectonic activity climbing is sometimes prohibited. Further information can be found at the **Philippine Institute of Volcanology and Seismology** (PHILVOLCS; Mon–Fri 8am–5pm; ⓣ043 773 0293, ⓦphivolcs.dost.gov.ph) by the San Roque Beach Resort.

ARRIVAL AND DEPARTURE

By bus Erjohn & Almark buses run from Manila (Pasay) to Tagaytay (hourly; 1hr 30min) from where you can catch a jeepney to Talisay (P10; 20min). Buses for Manila leave throughout the day from outside Olivarez Plaza near the roundabout. Tagaytay is a stop on the Manila–Taal–Leery route (for Anilao).

INFORMATION

Tourist information Tagaytay City Tourism Office is located in the City Hall (daily 8am–5pm; ⓣ046 413 1220, ⓔlanidiesta@yahoo.com).

GETTING AROUND

Jeepneys between Tagaytay Market and Talisay (hourly; 20min) run only until 4pm; given the steep windy roads connecting the two, it is not advisable to use tricycles. Alternatively, you can charter the whole vehicle for the short journey for P700. Jeepneys to other destinations use the jeepney station two minutes' walk past Olivarez Plaza. Jeepneys (P7.50) go up and down the main road constantly.

ACCOMMODATION

★ **Keni Po** 3km east of the Tagaytay roundabout towards Calamba ⓣ046 483 0977, ⓦkeniporooms.blogspot.com. It means "welcome" in the local dialect, which is indeed how you feel at this bright yellow guesthouse with cosy rooms with cable TV and DVD players, plus a pleasant pool in the verdant garden. No restaurant, but the room service is cheap and delicious. Free wi-fi. **P1200**

San Roque Beach Resort ⓣ043 773 0271 or ⓣ0905 417 9179, ⓔsanroquebeachresort@yahoo.com. A welcoming place right on the lakeshore with startling views across to the volcano, owned by a lovely Dutch–Filipina couple, Leo and Lita. The spacious rooms with little extra touches such as flowering plants and reading lamps, and the great fish meals make it worth paying a bit extra. **P1500**

EATING

The Summit Ridge development opposite *Josephine's* in Tagaytay has several inexpensive chain restaurants, a *Starbucks* with wi-fi, a couple of ATMs and a Robinson's supermarket.

Gourmet Café Aguinaldo Highway, a short drive out of town ⓣ 046 414 1049, ⓦ gourmet.com.ph. This pretty little café is merely the window into the wonderful organic world of Gourmet Farms. Great salads, sandwiches, shakes, teas and coffees, plus an excellent farm shop selling everything from *polvoron* to peanut brittle. Daily 7am–10pm.

Josephine's On the Manila road, main ridge road in Tagaytay. A local legend, *Josephine's* has won scores of awards for its culinary delights, such as *kilawin* (pickled shrimps, oysters or fish) and baked shellfish, topped with garlic, butter and cheese. The views overlooking the lake and volcano are astounding. Mains P250–400. Free wi-fi. Mon–Fri 9am–9pm, Sat 7am–10pm, Sun 7am–9pm.

DIRECTORY

Banks and exchange There's a BPI and a BDO, both with ATMs, at the Tagaytay roundabout.

Internet Several internet cafés (P40/hr) around Olivarez Plaza in Tagaytay, and many cafés offer wi-fi, including *Josephine's*.

PUERTO GALERA

PUERTO GALERA, on the northern coast of **Mindoro**, is one of the Philippines' top destinations for travellers, and rightly so, though backpackers on a very tight budget will notice that some prices can be on the high side. Easily accessible from Manila (via Batangas City), it has a stunning natural harbour, countless coves and beaches, a good range of affordable accommodation and excellent diving, with around thirty listed **dive sites**. As well as being the name of a small town, "Puerto Galera" is generally used to refer to the area between Sabang, 5km to the east, and White Beach, 8km to the west.

The area's extensive and diverse coral reefs have been declared a UNESCO Man and the Biosphere Reserve – a marine environment of global importance. The direct protection that comes from such a declaration is minimal, but the reefs remain intact thanks to the efforts of local people, hotel owners and dive operators, who all cooperate to ensure that the undersea riches are not ruined.

Boats and yachts lie at anchor in Muelle Bay, and in the background looms the brooding hulk of **Mount Malasimbo** (1122m), invariably crowned with a ring of cumulus. There's plenty on offer in addition to diving, including dazzling snorkelling, trekking into the mountains and beach-hopping by Bangka. As if all this weren't enough, thrill-seekers can get their fix at **Puerto Galera X-Treme Sports Adventure Park** (ⓣ 043 287 3436, ⓦ extremesportsphilippines.com), where exhilarating activities including paint-balling, go-karting, zorbing and ziplining are on offer.

Sabang is by far the busiest area, with plenty of good restaurants and divers' bars, but as the evening progresses the

8

THE PHILIPPINES UNDERWATER

With more than 7000 tropical islands and 40,000 square kilometres of coral reefs, it is no surprise that the Philippines is one of the world's top diving destinations. The archipelago, part of the Coral Triangle, has one of the most productive marine ecosystems on the planet, with an outstanding diversity of marine life. Its waters, enriched by currents from Japan, the South China Sea, the Indian Ocean and the Celebes Sea, abound with rare species of fish, marine invertebrates and more than 500 coral species and organisms. Divers will be overwhelmed by the variety of underwater activity. **Dugongs**, found in Palawan, are more closely related to elephants than any other sea animals. They are the only herbivorous marine mammal and can consume up to 50kg of sea grass daily. Those seeking an adrenaline rush can dive at Malapascua, where **thresher sharks** are common. Their large upper caudal fin is used to stun prey and can reach the same length as the shark's body itself. Docile **whale sharks**, meanwhile, are the world's largest fish and mainly feed on plankton and microscopic plants. Donsol provides the best opportunity to swim with these curious giants. For those wanting to immerse themselves in a bit of history, the renowned Japanese World War II **shipwrecks** off the coast of Coron provide just the opportunity.

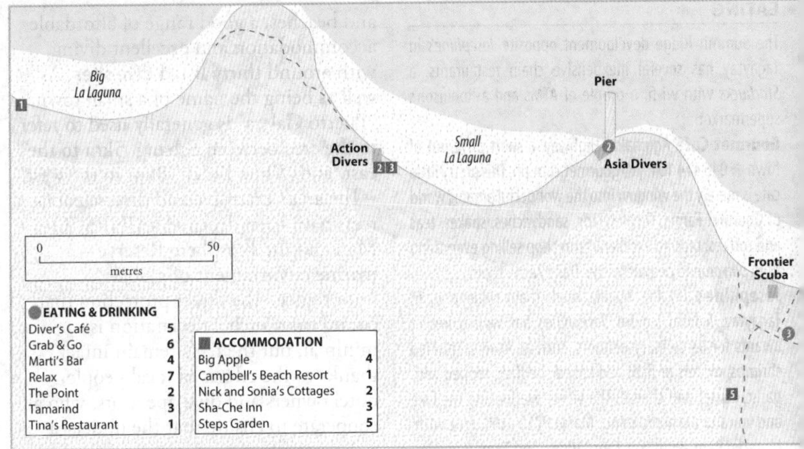

nightlife becomes increasingly sleazy, with girlie bars and "discos" taking centre stage.

Neighbouring **Small La Laguna** and **Big La Laguna** are rather more laidback and have better beaches for sunbathing. Twenty minutes by jeepney on the other side of Puerto Galera town is **White Beach**, which has fewer boorish scuba divers than Sabang, but an equal number of hawkers. It gets busy with weekenders from Manila, and also at peak times, especially Easter, when rates shoot up. Five minutes past White Beach by tricycle is quieter **Talipanan Beach**. Between the two, Aninuan has the plushest resorts in the area.

8

ARRIVAL AND DEPARTURE

By ferry There are numerous competitive ferry departures for Puerto Galera town (Muelle Pier; 1hr), Sabang and White Beach until 5pm. To return, departures begin at 6.30am and the last boat from Puerto Galera leaves at 3.30pm. The last boat from Sabang leaves at 1pm, and on high-season weekends there are also departures from White Beach. Fares are around P270 plus a P30 terminal fee and a P50 environmental user fee.

By bus and ferry The most convenient way to reach Puerto Galera from Manila is a combined bus-and-ferry service (2hr to Batangas pier, then 2hr by boat; P700 one-way). Si-Kat (T 02 708 9628, W sikatferrybus.com) leaves at 8.30am sharp from the *CityState Tower Hotel* at 1315A Mabini St, Ermita, arriving in Sabang at 12.15pm and Muelle Pier at 1pm. Coming back, the service leaves Puerto Galera at 8.15am, stopping in Sabang at 9am and arriving in Manila at 1.15pm.

INFORMATION

Information and tours There's a tourist information point at Muelle Pier in Puerto Galera (daily 7.30am–5pm; T 043 287 3051). In Sabang, GPLP Tours (T 0927 326 0535, E adventures172001@yahoo.com) provide info on the area and can arrange island-hopping (from P1000), trekking, kayaking tours or overnight trips into the tribal hinterlands (P1200). Islands Destination Travel & Tours in Puerto Galera (T 043 287 3145) can book local day-trips and plane and ferry tickets.

GETTING AROUND

Travelling between the tourist areas is relatively easy. From Sabang and White Beach, jeepneys leave regularly throughout the day for Puerto Galera town (6am–6pm; 15min; P20). A tricycle should cost P30 per person, but you'll be doing well to get this ride for less than P100. A pump boat from Big/Small La Laguna to Sabang costs P200 during the day, P400 at night.

DIVE OPERATORS

There are dozens of dive operators in the area, so take time to shop around and get the best deal. You'll find an incredible range of dives to suit all abilities. A single dive is in the region of $30, an Open Water course is about $420.

Action Divers Next to *Deep Blue Sea Inn* on Small La Laguna (T 043 287 3320, W actiondivers.com).

Asia Divers Next door to *El Galleon*, Small La Laguna (T 043 287 3205, W asiadivers.com).

Badladz Adventure Divers In the hotel of the same name at Muelle pier (T 0927 268 9095, W badladz.com/diving).

Frontier Scuba Near *Angelyn Beach Resort* in Sabang (T 043 287 3077, W frontierscuba.com).

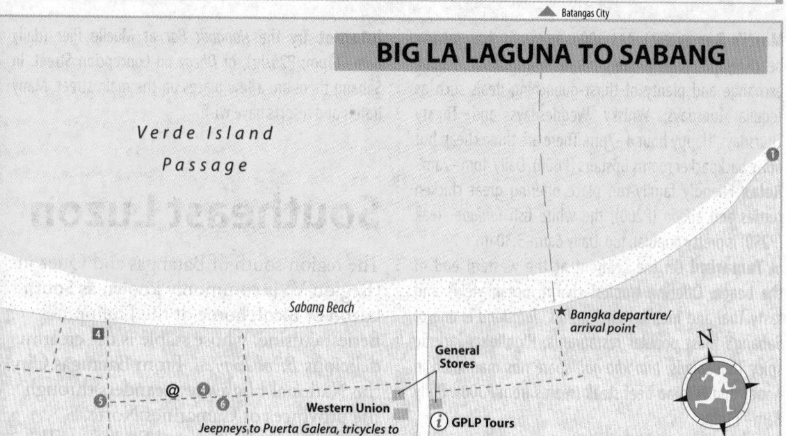

ACCOMMODATION

SABANG

Big Apple Middle of the beach ⓣ043 287 3134, ⓦdivebigapple.com. One of Sabang's most popular resorts, with a dive centre, swimming pool and 24hr bar, perfect if you're looking for plenty of action. The two budget rooms can get quite noisy, though – better to spend extra for the a/c rooms (P1100). **P500**

★**Steps Garden** Almost at the far western end of the beach ⓣ043 287 3046, ⓦstepsgarden.com. Discreetly tucked into the western end of the cove, Swedish-owned *Steps* has a wide variety of comfortable huts spread through the lovely hillside gardens, many of which have great balcony views. There's also an attractive pool, a good restaurant with wi-fi, and friendly staff. **P1600**

PUERTO GALERA

Badladz Right beside Muelle Pier ⓣ043 287 3693, ⓦbadladz.com. Still a longtime favourite despite its prices steadily going up, this place also does fantastic Mexican food and offers diving and a host of other activities. **P1738**

Bahay Pilipino Hotel-Pension In the centre of the *poblacion* opposite Candava Supermarket ⓣ043 442 0266. Cheap and friendly place run by Bavarian Dr Fritz and his Filipina wife Jasmin. The fan rooms are small and well kept, with shared bathrooms. **P550**

SMALL LA LAGUNA

Nick and Sonia's Cottages ⓣ0917 803 8156. A few simple clean rooms with their own kitchens and hot water. Easy to miss; ask at Action Divers. **P700**

Sha-Che Inn ⓣ0928 411 3748, ⓔshacheinn@yahoo.com.ph. The ten tiled rooms all have hot water, kitchen and TV, and the upstairs ones have great views. **P1200**

BIG LA LAGUNA

Campbell's Beach Resort At the far end of the beach ⓣ043 287 3466, ⓦcampbellsbeachresort.com. The simple rooms are a/c with hot water and cable, although they're a bit pricey for what you get. It has its own lively bar, *Fat Bastards*, and the café does hearty breakfasts. **P1500**

WHITE BEACH

Coco Aroma ⓣ0916 616 7337, ⓦcocoaromawhitebeach.com. At the quieter western end of the beach, this is one of the few remaining simple beachside places and has basic fan nipa huts, a couple of nicely styled a/c cottages, a laidback café and lots of ambience. **P1650**

Pacific Divers ⓣ0919 888 6763, ⓦphilippines-diving.com. This friendly dive shop has great-value rooms right in the middle of the action. Good food too. **P500**

Summer Connection At the western edge of the beach ⓣ043 287 3688 or ⓣ0920 230 5098, ⓦsummerconnection.net. The accommodation here is on the seafront and there are breezy chill-out nipa huts in which to enjoy a cold beer as you watch your fresh catch grill on the communal barbecue. Standard rooms (P2200) are clean and functional, but there are still a few simple nipa huts at the back. Table tennis and free wi-fi. **P800**

EATING, DRINKING AND NIGHTLIFE

SABANG

Diver's Café Fun bar mainly serving German food (the menu has its fair share of sausages: P125) and inventive cocktails (P185). Daily 8am–3am.

Grab & Go Cheap little place to refuel after a night out, with local favourites (P50–90) and pretty mean burgers (P140). Try the Giant Burger (P499) if you've worked up an appetite. Daily 9am–3am.

8

Martí's Bar ☎0921 723 3006, ✉martis_bar_sabangbeach@yahoo.com. A lively bar with armchairs, a book exchange and plenty of thirst-quenching deals such as Tequila Tuesdays, Whisky Wednesdays and Thirsty Thursdays. Happy hour 4–7pm. There are three cheap but noisy backpacker rooms upstairs (P600). Daily 4pm–2am.

Relax Friendly family-run place offering great chicken curries and *adobo* (P200); the white fish *tanigue* steak (P250) is pretty popular, too. Daily 6am–3.30am.

★**Tamarind** On the seafront at the western end of the beach. Offering tropical charm, ocean views and tasty Thai and international dishes, *Tamarind* is one of Sabang's most popular restaurants. Highlights include spicy Thai salads, *tom kha gai*, spare ribs marinated in honey and Filipino beef steak (mains from P300). Daily 8am–11pm.

Tina's Restaurant Pleasant little restaurant with chequered tablecloths, bamboo chairs and nice sea views. It serves a range of international dishes at reasonable prices. (P150–300). Daily 7.30am–10.30pm.

PUERTO GALERA

Sharkeez Pizza By Muelle Pier. Internet access and adequate Western food such as pizzas (P310), pastas (P235) and pie and chips (P250). Daily 8am–10pm.

8

SMALL LA LAGUNA

The Point Eastern end of the beach. The wonderful views of Small La Laguna and Sabang make this the best spot for a sundowner. Cocktails start at P120. Daily 10am–midnight.

WHITE BEACH

Ciao Italia Western end of the beach. This pricey Italian perched on the side of the cliff is well worth the splurge. There are home-made pastas (P320) and plenty of mains, from pork escalope to grilled prawns. Wonderful views, too. Try the *spaghetti del pirata* (P380). Daily 8am–11pm.

Coco Aroma Next to *Summer Connection* ☎0919 4728 882. Laidback hipster dive with live reggae, rock and blues bands on Fri & Sat evenings; good food (P170–470) and plenty of choice for vegetarians. Happy hour 5–9pm. Daily 6am–2am.

★**Pacific Divers** Great friendly spot for hearty, reasonably priced mains (P200), as well as sandwiches and pancakes. The welcoming seating area on the beach is perfect for a sundowner or a chilled beer in the evenings. Free wi-fi. Daily 8am–midnight.

DIRECTORY

Banks and exchange In Sabang there's a Western Union and an Allied Savings bank with ATM near the Muelle Pier turn-off. *John and Jayne's* at Muelle Pier changes cash and travellers' cheques, and offers long-distance phone calls.

Internet Try the *Hangout Bar* at Muelle Pier (daily 8am–11pm; P25/hr), or *Dhegz* on Concepcion Street. In Sabang there are a few places on the main street. Many hotels and resorts have wi-fi.

Southeast Luzon

The region south of Batangas and Quezon (Region V) is commonly known as **South Luzon** or **Bicol**, home of the Philippines' fieriest cuisine, whose staple is the creamy, delicious *Bicol Express*. From Batangas City the National Highway meanders through the provinces of Camarines Norte, Camarines Sur, Albay and Sorsogon. The main towns of **Daet**, **Naga** and **Legaspi** are typically provincial, with their jumbled traffic, concrete malls and occasional Spanish-era relics – Legaspi, as the jumping-off point for the active volcano **Mount Mayon**, is the only one we cover. Continuing further south, you reach the coastal village of **Donsol**, which has grown famous for the concentration of plankton-eating whale sharks that congregate here. The opportunity to swim with these gentle giants is the single biggest draw for visitors to this area of the country, though there are also some wonderfully untouched beaches around **Sorsogon**. From **Matnog** at the very tip of Luzon, you can take a ferry across the Bernardino Strait to Samar, the gateway to the Visayas.

LEGASPI

The port city of **LEGASPI** (often spelt Legazpi), two hours south of Naga and ten hours from Manila, is the place to base yourself if you fancy climbing **Mount Mayon** (2463m). Legaspi is a fairly charmless provincial town with one main thoroughfare, Peñaranda Street, which connects the port area (Legaspi city proper) with the district of Albay, where most of the hotels and restaurants are. One sight worth seeing is the nearby **Cagsawa Ruins** (daily 8am–6pm; P10), the chilling remains of a church that was buried in the devastating eruption of Mayon in 1814. The best time to visit is at dawn before the vendors stake their

claim and the clouds roll in and obscure the view of the volcano. Take a jeepney bound for Camalig and ask the driver to let you off near the ruins.

ARRIVAL AND DEPARTURE

By plane The airport is in the Albay district, about 3km west of the town centre; a tricycle will take you into town for P30.

Destinations Cebu Pacific flies to Cebu (3 weekly, Thurs, Sat and Sun; 1hr 5min); PAL and Cebu Pacific fly to Manila (daily; 55min).

By bus The bus terminal on Tahao Road, which minivans also use, is 1.5km west of the town centre.

Destinations Donsol (every 30mins; 1hr); Naga (every 30min; 2hr); Sorsogon (every 30mins; 1hr 30min). Most Manila-bound buses depart in the evening (daily; 10hr). Philtranco goes all the way from Manila to Davao, using ferries where it has to. It stops at Daet, Naga and Legaspi, before heading on to the port of Matnog, at the southernmost tip of South Luzon, for the Samar ferry.

INFORMATION

Tourist information The Legaspi City Tourism Office is in the City Hall (daily 7am–7pm; ⓣ 052 481 0250, ⓔ legazpitourismservices@gmail.com). Enquire here about arranging a guide for Mount Mayon. Call the Regional Tourism Office in Rawis (Mon–Fri 8am–5pm; ⓣ 052 482 5593) to check conditions before you set off to see the whale sharks.

Tour operators Bicol Adventure and Tours, second floor, V&O Bldg, downstairs from the *Legaspi Tourist Inn*, Quezon Ave (ⓣ 0918 910 2185, ⓦ bicoladventure.com), is the best company to organize a trip up Mayon.

ACCOMMODATION

Legazpi Tourist Inn 3rd Floor, V&O Bldg, Quezon Ave cnr. Lapu-Lapu St, Legazpi Port District ⓣ 052 480 6147, ⓔ legazpitouristinn@yahoo.com.ph. Friendly staff and a secure central location; rooms have cable TV although only those with a/c have hot water. **P700**

Magayon Hotel Peñaranda St, Legazpi Port District ⓣ 052 480 7770, ⓔ vicky_uy_ong@yahoo.com. There are helpful staff at this hotel which has 74 pretty, clean rooms; all doubles have a/c and cable TV, and the rates for single travellers (P200) don't get much better. Free wi-fi. **P800**

Mayon Backpackers Hostel Barangay Maoyod ⓣ 052 480 0365, ⓦ mayonbackpackers.wordpress.com. Legaspi's only hostel offers a decent collection of brightly painted fan and a/c dorms (P250–350) and doubles. There's a small selection of books and board games, and the rooftop terrace café has Mt Mayon views. The hostel can also arrange local tours, including ATV rides to the lava front. **P1000**

EATING AND DRINKING

Cheap street stalls line Rosario Street in Albany District. The studenty *Green Leaf* bar on Rizal Street and *Silver Bucks* and *Chick 'In* at the Capitol Annex Building form the bulk of Legaspi nightlife.

La Mia Tazza Rizal St, Albay District. Cosy little café with delicious cakes (P45), muffins (P80) and cookies (P45) to enjoy with a cup of *pili* coffee or with one of the exotic teas (P90), such as peach ginger or ginseng peppermint. Free wi-fi. There's a second branch in the Embarcadero. Daily 8am–midnight.

★**Small Talk Café 51** D. Aurora St, Albay District. Homely café with old curios and 1950s Bicol photos, serving an exotic range of fusion dishes such as their famous Bicol-inspired pastas (P105). Try the *pili* pie (P50) and *buco pandana* (coconut) smoothie (P60). Daily 11am–10pm.

Waway Peñaranda St, Albay District. Renowned for its tasty seafood and native Bicol specialities served in a large dining room. Allow enough time for dinner as it closes early. A meal will set you back P150–200. Daily 7am–8pm.

DIRECTORY

Banks and exchange There are a number of banks with ATMs on Quezon Ave and upper Rizal St.

Internet All three malls have internet cafés (daily 10am–9pm; P30/hr).

Post office At the northern end of Lapu-Lapu St cnr. Quezon Ave.

Shopping LCC Mall is on Lapu-Lapu St cnr. Quezon Ave. Gaisano Mall and Embarcadero are in the harbour area.

8

MOUNT MAYON

The perfectly triangular cone of **Mount Mayon** (2421m) in Albay province makes it look, from a distance, like a child's drawing of a mountain, but don't be deceived, Mayon has claimed many lives over the years. It is the most active volcano in the country and has erupted more than 47 times in the last four centuries – 1984 and 1993 saw significant eruptions, and in 2006 hundreds were killed by mudslides of volcanic ash loosened by typhoon Durian. In December 2009 ash and incandescent lava shot for weeks from the crater and the alert level crept up to 4. After a mass evacuation, thousands spent Christmas and the New Year in emergency shelters, but the expected devastating full-scale eruption didn't happen. Most recently, in May 2013, a minute-long eruption caused

the death of four German tourists and their guide – no wonder the locals still spin fearful stories around it. Legend has it that Mayon was formed when a beautiful princess eloped with a brave warrior and was pursued by her uncle, Magayon. They prayed to the gods who answered with a terrible landslide that buried Magayon alive. He's said to still be inside the mountain, his irrepressible anger bursting forth in the form of volcanic eruptions.

The only window of opportunity for an ascent is **March to May**, but that's only when the alert level is low. Be prepared for cold nights at altitude and showers, and even if there's no imminent volcanic threat, climbers won't be allowed past 2000m. A **guide** is essential, arranged at the tourist offices in Legaspi, or through Bicol Adventures and Tours (see p.629). Expect to pay at least P3500 per person (minimum two people). See phivolcs.dost.gov.ph for the latest updates on the status of the volcano.

SORSOGON TOWN AND GUBAT

Near the southeastern tip of the Bicol peninsula, the provincial capital of **SORSOGON TOWN** makes a good base for visiting Donsol and exploring the beaches of the eastern seaboard, where waves hammer in from the Pacific and surfing is a burgeoning industry. One gem waiting to be discovered is **Rizal Beach**, a short trike ride from the barrio of **GUBAT**, half an hour by jeepney (P10) from Sorsogon. There's little development here; you won't find loungers, sunset cocktails and other trappings of beach life, but it is wildly beautiful, and there are a couple of basic places to stay. In Sorsogon there are a number of ATMs and internet cafés stretched along Rizal Street.

ARRIVAL AND DEPARTURE

By bus and jeepney Buses, jeepneys and minivans leave from the new Grand Terminal 1km from town along the Maharlika Highway in Balogo. Tricycles can take you into town from here for P10.

Destinations Donsol (every 30min; 1hr); Gubat (every 30min; 30min); Legaspi (every 30min; 1hr 30min); Manila (hourly; 12hr).

INFORMATION

Tourist information *Fernando's Hotel* is the headquarters of the provincial tourism council and can arrange local tours, including hikes and excursions to see the whale sharks. The owners are a mine of information on the area.

ACCOMMODATION

Fernando's Hotel N. Pareja St 056 211 1357. Attractive accommodation with a quaint, old-world ambience; the small patio restaurant is easily the best place to eat in town. You can organize tours here, too. Free wi-fi. P1000

Rizal Beach Resort Hotel Gubat 0922 883 1032 or 0917 418 8233. Ageing but adequate rooms, with fan or a/c, by the beach. P850

DONSOL

The area around the peaceful fishing community of **DONSOL**, two hours from either Legaspi or Sorsogon, is best known for one of the greatest concentrations of **whale sharks** (*butanding*) in the world. Your first stop should be the **Donsol Municipal Toursim Office** (daily 7.30am–4pm; 0917 868 1626) where they'll organize everything for your whale-shark-watching trip. It's best to arrive early in the morning to secure a place (limited to 500 people per day). The number of sightings varies: during peak season (Feb–May), there's a good chance of seeing ten or fifteen whale sharks a day, but you might be unlucky and see none. In April the town holds its annual *Butanding* festival.

After watching a short video, visitors are briefed by a **Butanding Interaction Officer** (BIO), who explains how to behave in the water near one of these huge creatures. The number of snorkellers around any one whale shark is limited to six; flash photography is not permitted, nor is scuba gear, and don't get anywhere near the animal's tail because it's powerful enough to do you some serious damage. Once a whale shark has been sighted you'll need to get your mask, snorkel and flippers on and get in the water before it dives too deep to be seen – they can move pretty quickly despite their bulk. Boats **cost**

★TREAT YOURSELF

Donsoleña Capobres St ⓣ 0928 508 3415, ⓦ donsolena.com. Rest up in comfort in between boat trips at this wonderful ancestral home, decked out in native narra wood. The five spacious rooms are tastefully styled, and there's a terrace overlooking the rice paddies, plus a kitchen for guests' use. **P2000**

P3500 for up to six people, and there's also a registration fee of P300 per person for foreigners and P100 for Filipinos. Each boat has a crew of three – the captain, the BIO and the spotter – each of whom will expect a token of your appreciation (at least P100 to each person) at the end of a successful day (and even an unsuccessful one). Renting snorkelling equipment costs P300. All this makes it an expensive day out by Philippine standards, but take heart from the fact that your money is helping the conservation effort. Hour-long firefly-spotting boat trips can also be arranged along the mangroves of the Donsol River from 6.30pm (P1250 per boat of five).

If you want to stay overnight in Donsol, try the cozy *Aguluz Homestay* (P700) on San Jose Street, or the *Santiago Tourist Inn*, a P15 tricycle ride from the Visitors' Center which has decent rooms starting at P500. There's a clutch of internet places but no ATM so bring enough cash.

The Visayas

No one seems entirely sure how many islands there are in **the Visayas**, but it certainly runs into the thousands. Everywhere you turn there's a patch of tropical sand or coral reef, with a ferry or bangka to take you there. There are nine main islands – Cebu, Bohol, Guimaras, Samar, Leyte, Panay, Negros, Romblon and Siquijor – but it's the hundreds of others in between that make this part of the archipelago so irresistible. Even on the main islands, vast areas are relatively undiscovered.

No one can accuse the Visayans of being a uniform lot, and a huge variety of dialects are spoken, including Cebuano, Ilonggo, Waray Waray and Aklan. While English is less readily understood in some places, visitors won't find a warmer welcome anywhere.

Getting around is fairly easy. The major islands are accessible by air from Manila, and, increasingly, from Cebu City, but the **ferry network** is also extensive. The beauty of the Visayas is that there's no need to make formal plans. There's always another beach, another place to stay, another island lost in its own little world.

8

TYPHOON YOLANDA

On November 8, 2013 Typhoon Yolanda (internationally known as "Haiyan") hit the southeastern tip of Samar with windspeeds of up to 315km/h. The superstorm left a broad band of destruction through northern Leyte, northern Cebu, northeastern Panay and finally Busuanga before leaving the archipelago. Yolanda made landfall near **Guiuan**, and the town was almost completely destroyed, while storm surges of more then 2m wreaked havoc in **Tacloban**. In spite of a huge international relief effort, many of the worst affected areas remained without power, clean water and supplies for weeks. Looting became a major problem, while in unaffected regions local businesses and individuals rallied to raise funds and support.

Economically and aesthetically the **recovery period** will be counted in years, but for the families of the 6000 dead the losses are clearly irreparable. Aid groups are camped out in Tacloban until at least 2014, but sustained support is needed to help rebuild. Tourism can have a role here, and in popular areas (Malapascua, for example), tourist dollars have catalysed recovery. However, the worst hit areas in Samar and Leyte are still reeling from the effects of Yolanda and principal tourist sights including Sohoton National Park remain closed. We have removed Samar and Leyte from this edition of the guide, but hope to be able to include full details in the next edition.

8

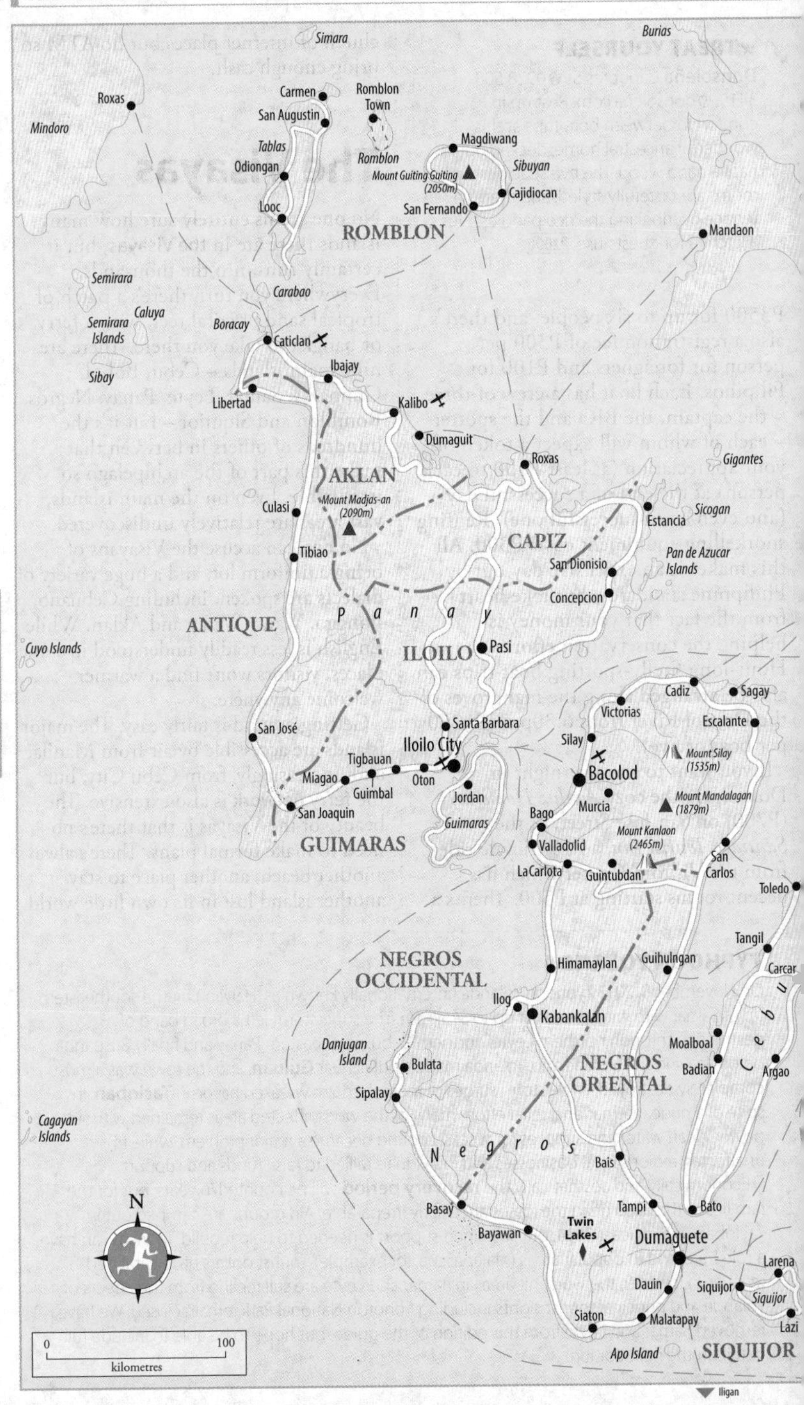

Simara
Burias
Roxas
Mindoro
Carmen
San Augustin
Romblon Town
Tablas
Romblon
Odiongan
Magdiwang
Mount Guiting Guiting (2050m)
Sibuyan
Cajidiocan
San Fernando
Looc
ROMBLON
Mandaon
Semirara
Carabao
Caluya
Semirara Islands
Boracay
Caticlan
Sibay
Ibajay
Libertad
Kalibo
Dumaguit
Roxas
Gigantes
AKLAN
Culasi
Mount Madjas-an (2090m)
Estancia
Sicogan
CAPIZ
Tibiao
San Dionisio
Pan de Azucar Islands
Concepcion
P a n a y
ANTIQUE
Cuyo Islands
ILOILO
Pasi
Cadiz
Sagay
Victorias
Escalante
San José
Santa Barbara
Silay
Iloilo City
Mount Silay (1535m)
Tigbauan
Bacolod
Miagao
Oton
Guimbal
Mount Mandalagan (1879m)
Jordan
Murcia
San Joaquin
Guimaras
Bago
Mount Kanlaon (2465m)
GUIMARAS
Valladolid
San Carlos
La Carlota
Guintubdan
Toledo
Tangil
NEGROS OCCIDENTAL
Himamaylan
Guihulngan
Carcar
Ilog
Kabankalan
Cebu
Moalboal
Danjugan Island
NEGROS ORIENTAL
Bulata
Badian
Argao
Sipalay
Cagayan Islands
N e g r o s
Bais
N
Basay
Tampi
Bato
Twin Lakes
Bayawan
Dumaguete
Larena
Dauin
Siquijor
Siquijor
Siaton
Malatapay
Lazi
0
100
kilometres
Apo Island
SIQUIJOR
Iligan

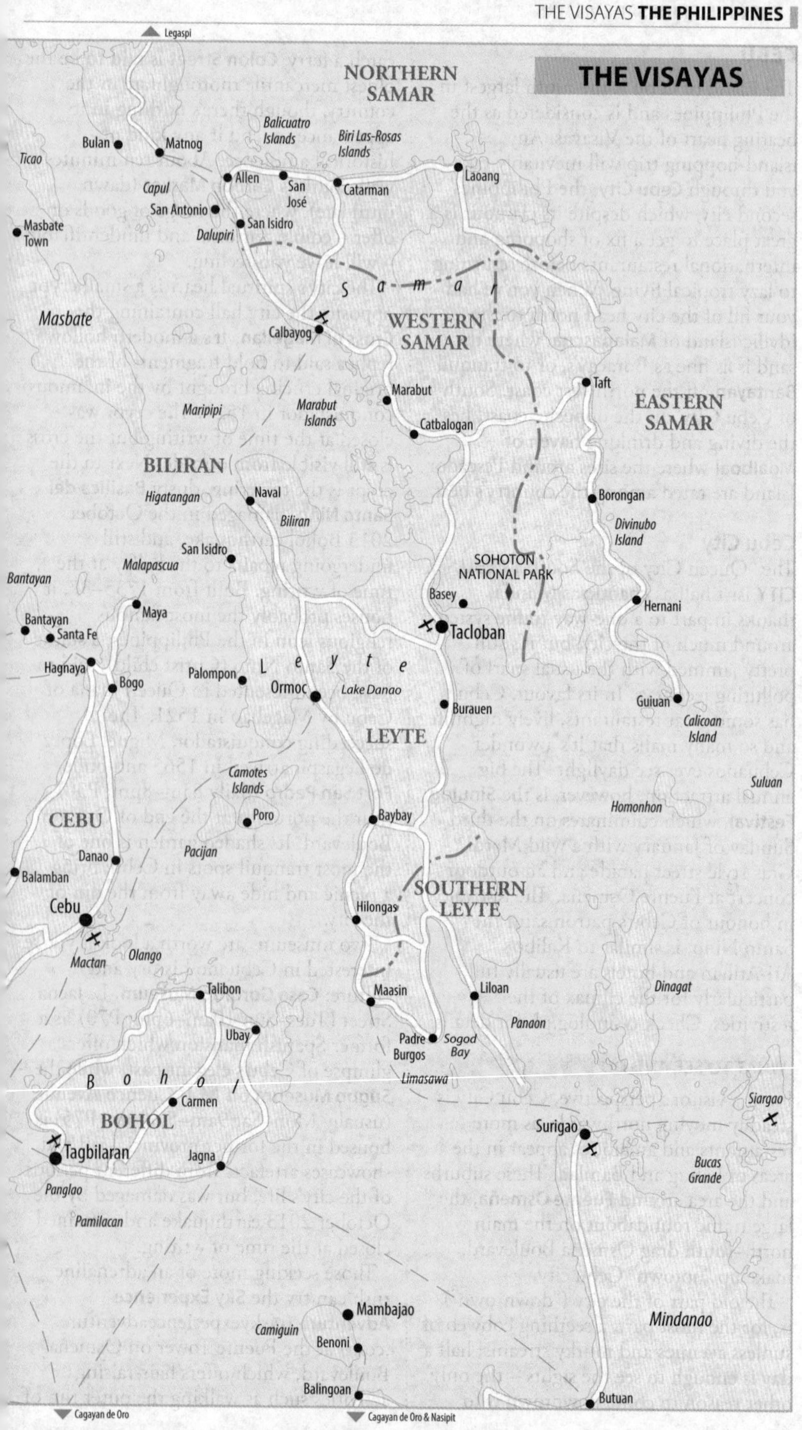
THE VISAYAS
Legaspi
NORTHERN SAMAR
Balicuatro Islands
Biri Las-Rosas Islands
Bulan
Matnog
Ticao
Capul
Allen
San José
Catarman
Laoang
San Antonio
San Isidro
Masbate Town
Dalupiri
Samar
Masbate
Calbayog
WESTERN SAMAR
Taft
EASTERN SAMAR
Marabut
Maripipi
Marabut Islands
Catbalogan
BILIRAN
Higatangan
Naval
Borongan
Biliran
Divinubo Island
San Isidro
Malapascua
SOHOTON NATIONAL PARK
Bantayan
Basey
Maya
Hernani
Bantayan
Santa Fe
Tacloban
Leyte
Hagnaya
Bogo
Palompon
Ormoc
Lake Danao
Burauen
Guiuan
Calicoan Island
LEYTE
Camotes Islands
Suluan
Homonhon
CEBU
Poro
Baybay
Pacijan
Danao
Balamban
SOUTHERN LEYTE
Cebu
Hilongas
Mactan
Olango
Talibon
Maasin
Liloan
Dinagat
Ubay
Panaon
Padre Burgos
Sogod Bay
Bohol
Limasawa
Carmen
Siargao
BOHOL
Surigao
Tagbilaran
Jagna
Bucas Grande
Panglao
Pamilacan
Mambajao
Mindanao
Camiguin
Benoni
Balingoan
Butuan
Cagayan de Oro
Cagayan de Oro & Nasipit
8

CEBU

The island of **Cebu** is the ninth largest in the Philippines and is considered as the beating heart of the Visayas. Any island-hopping trip will inevitably take you through **Cebu City**, the Philippines' second city, which despite its clamour is a great place to get a fix of shopping and international restaurants before returning to lazy tropical living. When you've had your fill of the city head north to the idyllic island of **Malapascua**, where the sand is as fine as Boracay's, or to tranquil **Bantayan** off the northwest coast. South of Cebu City, on the opposite coast, lies the diving and drinking haven of **Moalboal** where the sites around Pescador Island are rated among the country's best.

Cebu City

The "Queen City of the South", **CEBU CITY** isn't half as chaotic as Manila, thanks in part to a one-way traffic system around much of the city, but it's still pretty jammed with the usual snarl of polluting jeepneys. In its favour, Cebu has some great restaurants, lively nightlife and so many malls that it's a wonder Cebuanos ever see daylight. The big annual attraction, however, is the **Sinulog Festival**, which culminates on the third Sunday of January with a wild Mardi Gras-style street parade and an outdoor concert at Fuente Osmeña. The festival, in honour of Cebu's patron saint the Santo Niño, is similar to Kalibo's Ati-Atihan and hotels are usually full, particularly for the climax of the festivities. Check Ⓦsinulog.ph for details.

8

WHAT TO SEE AND DO

From a visitor's perspective, Cebu City is steadily moving northwards, as more restaurants and amenities appear in the areas of Lahug and Banilad. These suburbs and the area around **Fuente Osmeña**, the large traffic roundabout on the main north–south drag Osmeña Boulevard, make up "uptown" Cebu city.

The old part of the city ("downtown") is, for the most part, a seething cobweb of sunless avenues and murky streams; half a day is enough to see the sights – the only other reason to come downtown is to catch a ferry. **Colon Street** is said to be the oldest mercantile thoroughfare in the country, though there's nothing in its appearance to lend it any kind of historical ambience. About ten minutes' walk south is **Carbon Market** (dawn until late), where the range of goods on offer – edible, sartorial and unidentifiable – will leave you reeling.

The city's spiritual heart is a small crypt opposite the city hall containing the **Cross of Magellan**. It's a modern hollow replica said to hold fragments of the original crucifix brought by the infamous conquistador in 1521. The crypt was closed at the time of writing but the cross is still visible from outside. Next to the crypt is the towering, dusty **Basilica del Santo Niño**, damaged in the October 2013 Bohol earthquake, and still undergoing repairs to the belfry at the time of writing. Built from 1735–37, it houses probably the most famous religious icon in the Philippines, a statue of the Santo Niño (Christ child), said to have been presented to Queen Juana of Cebu by Magellan in 1521. The succeeding conquistador, Miguel Lopez de Legaspi, arrived in 1565 and built **Fort San Pedro** (daily 8am–8pm; P30) near the port area at the end of Quezon Boulevard. Its shaded garden is one of the most tranquil spots in Cebu; bring a picnic and hide away from the din of the city.

Two museums are worth a look if you're interested in Cebuano history and culture: **Casa Gorordo Museum**, L. Jaena Street (Tues–Sun 10am–6pm; P70), is a former Spanish mansion which offers a glimpse of Cebu's elegant past, while the **Sugbo Museum** on M.J. Cuenco Avenue (usually Mon–Sat 9am–5.30pm; P75) is housed in the former provincial jail and showcases artefacts from different periods of the city's life, but was damaged by the October 2013 earthquake and remained closed at the time of writing.

Those seeking more of an adrenaline rush can try the **Sky Experience Adventure** (Ⓦskyexperienceadventure.com) at the Fuente Tower on Osmeña Boulevard, which offers hair-raising activities such as walking the outer rim of

the 37th floor with no handrails. Alternatively, try the fun **Cebu Zipline** (032 344 3028, docepares.com.ph) in Doce Pares Mountain Training Park north of the city, which also offers Filipino martial art classes.

ARRIVAL AND DEPARTURE

By plane Mactan Cebu International Airport (MCIA) is 8km from the city, across the suspension bridges that link Mactan Island to the main island of Cebu. There's a tourist information counter (daily 5am–9pm; 032 340 2486) in the arrivals hall; outside there are white fixed-fare taxis which work out expensive for in-town destinations (P475 to Fuente Osmena for example), but offer reasonable rates for other destinations in Cebu (Hagnaya for Bantayan P2300). Alternatively, cross the road and take a metered yellow taxi into town (around P250–350, depending on your destination). Air Asia Zest, Cebu Pacific, SEAIR, PAL and Tiger Air have ticket offices at the airport, as well as in the malls.

Destinations Bacolod (3 daily; 45min); Cagayan de Oro (5 daily; 50min); Camiguin (4 weekly; 50min); Caticlan (3–5 daily; 1hr); Clark (3 weekly; 1hr 20min); Iloilo City (4–6 daily; 50min); Kalibo (daily; 50min); Manila (36 daily; 1hr 10min); Puerto Princesa (2–3 daily; 1hr 15min).

By bus The northern bus terminal (for destinations north) is in Mandaue, not far from SM City mall; the southern bus terminal, for all points south, is on Bacalso Ave, west of President Osmeña Blvd. Both are well served by jeepneys and there are usually taxis waiting, although at busy times the "queue" becomes a free-for-all.

Destinations north (departing from the northern bus terminal): Hagnaya, for Bantayan (7 daily; 3hr 30min); Maya, for Malapascua (up to 24 daily; 4hr).

Destinations south (departing from the southern bus terminal): Bato (every 30min; 4–5hr) via Moalboal (3hr); Lilo-An, via Carcar and Oslob (every 20min; 3–4hr).

By ferry Jeepneys line up at Pier 3 for the short journey into the city. Look for one marked Osmeña Blvd (uptown) or Colon St (downtown). Touts will try to usher you into a "special fare" taxi, but there are plenty of metered ones. Cebu taxi fares start at P40 and go up by P2.50 every km thereafter. A great place to get up-to-date ferry information (schedules and pier numbers often change) is at the travellers' lounge in SM City mall (032 232 4890), which has schedules and booking facilities, as well as showers and left luggage. Local papers also carry daily schedules.

Fast boats: Delta (032 232 1356), OceanJet (032 255 7560), 2GO (032 233 7000), and Weesam Express (032 231 7737) serve the following daily: Dumaguete (4hr); Ormoc (3hr); Siquijor (5hr); Tagbilaran (2hr).

Slow boats: Cokaliong (032 232 7211), George & Peter Lines (032 254 5154), Trans-Asia Shipping (032 254 6491) serve destinations including Banyatan (2 weekly; 9hr), Cagayan de Oro (4 weekly; 10hr) and Manila (1–2 daily; 21hr).

INFORMATION

Tourist information The extremely helpful main tourist information office is in the LDM Building at Lapu-Lapu cnr. Legaspi streets, near Fort San Pedro (Mon–Fri 8am–5pm; 032 254 2811, dotregion7@gmail.com).

ACCOMMODATION

With the exception of *Sugbutel*, all the following are uptown. Many places put up their prices by around thirty percent around Sinulog.

Fuente Pension House 0175 Don Julio Llorente St 032 412 4989, fuentepensionhouse.com. Well-run place in an excellent and surprisingly quiet location behind Fuente Osmeña. The newly renovated lobby makes the *Fuente* seem like a trendy boutique hotel from the outside, but inside rooms are simple, clean and good value. All have hot water and cable TV, and the rooftop restaurant offers free wi-fi. 24hr rates regardless of when you check in and single rates available too (P945). **P1145**

Gran Prix Pacific Coast Building, Mango Avenue 032 254 9169, granprixhotels.com. This modern budget hotel enjoys a great location near Fuente Osmeña and has small, presentable rooms (though many lack windows), free wi-fi and *Jollibee* vouchers for breakfast! **P1399**

Pacific Pensionne 313 A. Osmeña Blvd 032 2535271, pacificpensionne.com. Green is the colour of choice at this friendly hotel tucked into a quiet cul-de-sac behind Osmeña Blvd. The windows are on the small side so rooms are quite dark, but the cheerful coffee shop in the lobby makes up for it. **P1040**

★ **Pensionne La Florentina** 18 Acacia St 032 231 3318. This *pensionne* has been a long-standing Cebu favourite thanks to its cosy atmosphere and prime location on a quiet side street close to the Ayala Center. The little breakfast area with the odd bric-a-brac is warm and welcoming, and the rooms are excellent value. **P850**

★ **Sugbutel** South Osmeña Blvd cnr. Road East, north reclamation area 032 232 8888, sugbutel.com. The only place recommended downtown, this hostel with 88 beds has well-equipped modern dorm compartments just a short walk from SM Mall and is handy for the port. Free wi-fi. Dorm **P250–300**, double **P1200**

Vacation Hotel Juana Osmeña 032 2532766, vacationhotelcebu.com. North of Fuente Osmeña this is the cheapest place with a pool in the city centre. The best rooms are on the second floor, with balconies overlooking the small pool, although the beds are very soft. Downstairs some of the rooms at the front have little verandas, but others are darker and less enticing. **P1600**

8

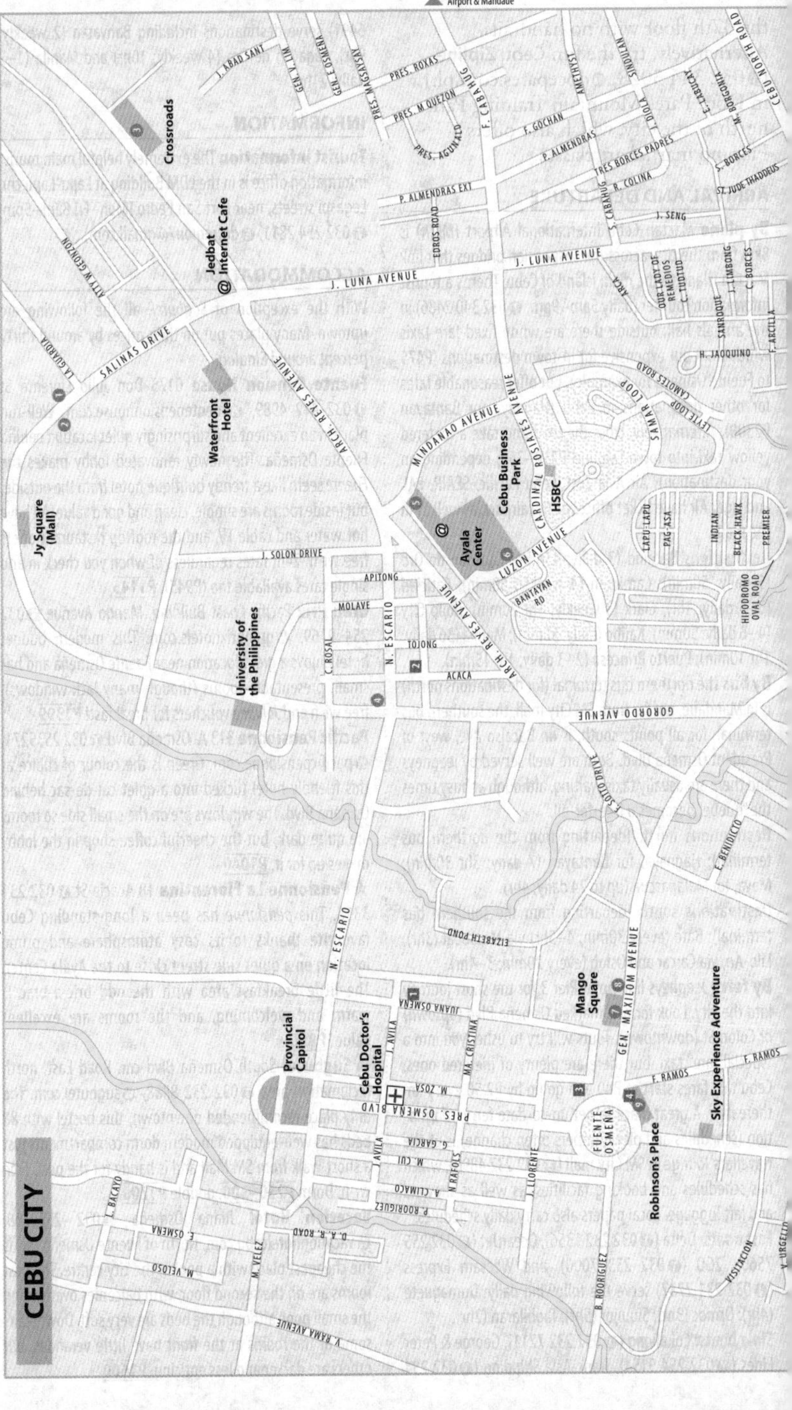

8

CEBU CITY

Airport & Mandaue
Gaisano Country Mall & Banilad
Cebu Zipline & Busay
Lahug

Crossroads
Jedbat @ Internet Cafe
Waterfront Hotel
Jy Square (Mall)
University of the Philippines
Ayala Center
Cebu Business Park
HSBC
Mango Square
Provincial Capitol
Cebu Doctor's Hospital
Robinson's Place
Sky Experience Adventure
Fuente Osmeña

J. Luna Avenue
Salinas Drive
Arch. Reyes Avenue
Mindanao Avenue
Cardinal Rosales Avenue
Luzon Avenue
Samar Loop
Leyte Loop
Camotes Road
Gorordo Avenue
Gen. Maxilom Avenue
N. Escario
J. Solon Drive
Apitong
Molave
Tojong
Acaca
C. Rosal
F. Sotto Drive
E. Benedicto
Elizabeth Pond
Bantayan Rd
Hipodromo Oval Road
Lapu-Lapu
Pag-Asa
Indian
Black Hawk
Premier
H. Jaoquino
F. Arcilla
Sanroque
C. Borces
J. Limbong
C. Tudtud
Our Lady of Remedios
Arca
J. Seng
Edros Road
P. Almendras Ext
P. Almendras
F. Gochan
F. Cabahug
S. Cabahug
R. Colina
Tres Borces Padres
S. Borces
St. Jude Thaddeus
J. Diola
E. Labucay
M. Borgonia
Cebu North Road
Sindulan
Amethyst
Pres. Aguinaldo
Pres. M Quezon
Pres. Roxas
Pres. Magsaysay
Gen. E. Osmeña
Gen. V. Lim
J. Abad Sant
Atty. W. Geonzon
La Guardia
Juana Osmeña
J. Avila
Ma. Cristina
M. Zosa
Pres. Osmeña Blvd
G. Garcia
M. Cui
A. Climaco
P. Rodriguez
N. Rafols
J. Llorente
B. Rodriguez
F. Ramos
Vistacion
V. Urgello
L. Bacayo
E. Osmeña
D.A.R. Road
M. Veloso
M. Velez
V. Rama Avenue

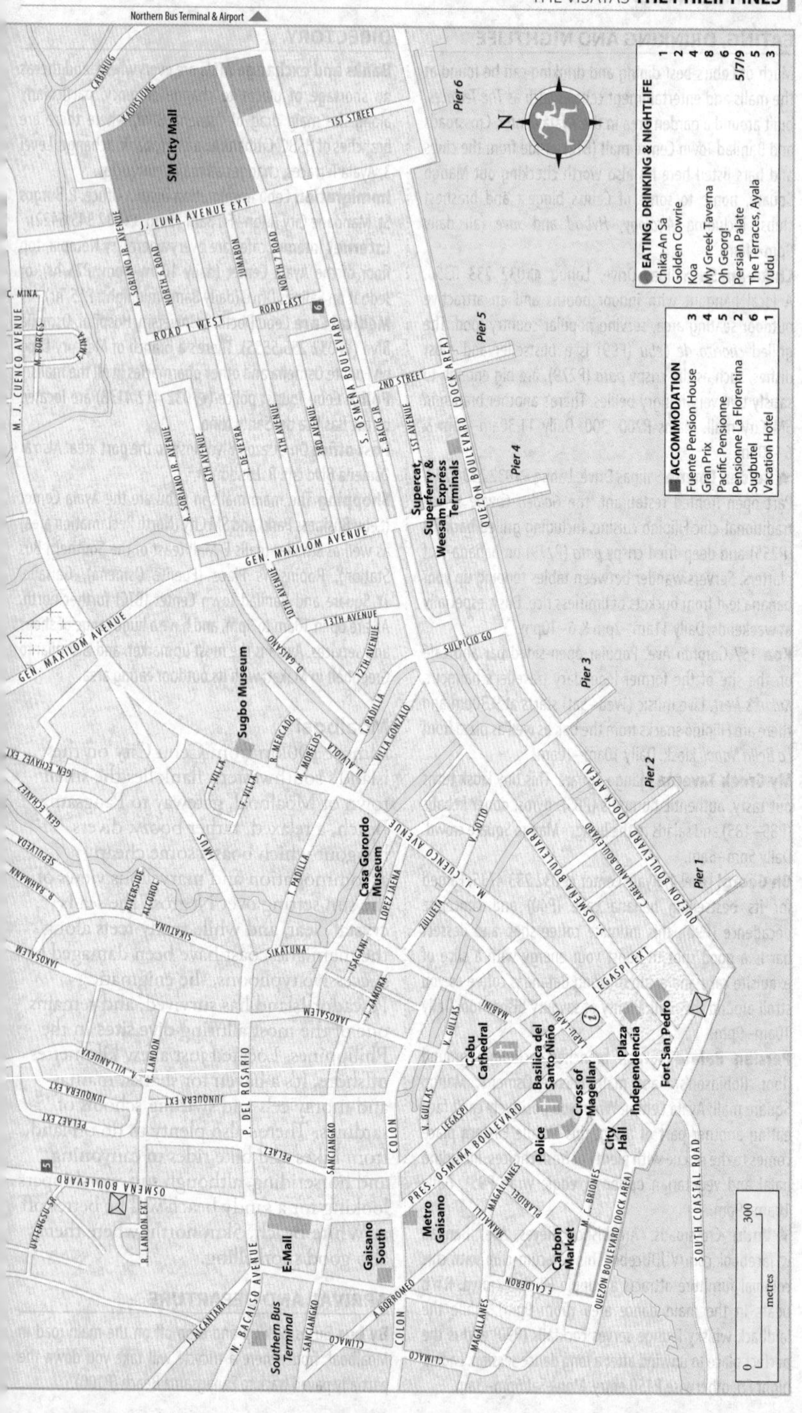
Northern Bus Terminal & Airport
ACCOMMODATION
Fuente Pension House 3
Gran Prix 4
Pacific Pensionne 5
Pensionne La Florentina 2
Sugbutel 6
Vacation Hotel 1
EATING, DRINKING & NIGHTLIFE
Chika-An Sa 1
Golden Cowrie 2
Koa 4
My Greek Taverna 8
Oh Georgi 6
Persian Palate 5/7/9
The Terraces, Ayala 5
Vudu 3
N
0
300
metres
SM City Mall
Pier 6
Pier 5
Pier 4
Pier 3
Pier 2
Pier 1
Supercat, Superferry & Weesam Express Terminals
Sugbo Museum
Casa Gorordo Museum
Cebu Cathedral
Basilica del Santo Niño
Cross of Magellan
Plaza Independencia
Fort San Pedro
Police
City Hall
Metro Gaisano
Carbon Market
Gaisano South
E-Mall
Southern Bus Terminal
J. LUNA AVENUE EXT
GEN. MAXILOM AVENUE
M. J. CUENCO AVENUE
QUEZON BOULEVARD (DOCK AREA)
S. OSMEÑA BOULEVARD
OSMEÑA BOULEVARD
PRES. OSMEÑA BOULEVARD
N. BACALSO AVENUE
SOUTH COASTAL ROAD
P. DEL ROSARIO
COLON
LEGASPI EXT
SIKATUNA
JAKOSALEM
IMUS

8

EATING, DRINKING AND NIGHTLIFE

Much of Cebu's best dining and drinking can be found at the malls and entertainment centres such as *The Terraces*, built around a garden area in the Ayala Center, Crossroads and Banilad Town Centre mall (BTC). Aside from the clubs and bars listed here it's also worth checking out Mango Square, home to some of Cebu's biggest and brashest clubs, including *Alcology*, *Hybrid* and *Jave* (all daily 9pm–4am).

Chika-An Sa Salinas Drive, Lahug T 032 233 0350. A local hangout with indoor booths and an attractive outdoor seating area, serving popular country food. The grilled *chorizo de Cebu* (P99) is a bestseller and most dishes, such as the crispy *pata* (P279), are big enough to satisfy two very hungry bellies. There's another branch in SM City mall. Mains P200–300. Daily 11.30am–2pm & 6–10pm.

★**Golden Cowrie** Salinas Drive, Lahug T 032 233 4243. Part open-fronted restaurant, the *Golden Cowrie* serves traditional-chic Filipino cuisine, including grilled backribs (P255) and deep-fried crispy *pata* (P279) on banana-leaf platters. Servers wander between tables topping up your banana leaf from buckets of limitless rice. Busy, especially at weekends. Daily 11am–2pm & 6–10pm.

Koa 157 Gorordo Ave. Popular open-sided bar and café on the site of the former legendary traveller's hangout, *Kukuk's Nest*. Live music (Wed–Sat) starts at 9.30pm and there are Filipino snacks from the bar, as well as pizza from *La Bella Napoli* kiosk. Daily 10am–10am.

My Greek Taverna Mango Square. This tiny kiosk turns out tasty, authentic hummus (P85), gyros, doner kebabs (P85–185) and salads to the hungry Mango Square crowd. Daily 5pm–5am.

Oh Georg! Level 1, Ayala Center T 032 233 4735. Famed for its bestselling banana cake (P40) and chocolate decadence (P90), this intimate coffee shop and dessert bar is a good spot to boost your energy with a slice of exquisite cake and a cup of stong Batangas coffee as you stroll around the mall. Plenty of savoury dishes too. Daily 10am–9pm.

Persian Palate Several branches including: ground floor, Robinson's Place mall; Fuente Osmeña, Mango Square mall; Ayala Center. When you positively can't face eating another part of a pig, this Middle Eastern place comes to the rescue with plenty of fresh choices, including halal and vegetarian options (veggie wrap P95). Daily 10am–9pm.

★**Vudu** Crossroads, Archbishop Reyes Ave, Banilad W facebook.com/VUDUcebu. This bar-cum-club with chic colonial furniture attracts a yuppie Filipino crowd. R'n'b beats in the main dance area (from 9pm), while the laidback whisky lounge serves cocktails (P90) and is the perfect place to unwind after a long dance session. Ladies' night Fri, otherwise P150 entry. Mon–Sat 6pm–3am.

DIRECTORY

Banks and exchange ATMs are everywhere, and there's no shortage of places to change currency, particularly along the main drag of Osmeña Blvd, where there are branches of HSBC, Citibank and Metrobank. Xchange, Level 3, Ayala Terraces, changes all major currencies.

Immigration Cebu Immigration District Office, P. Burgos St, Mandaue City (Mon–Fri 8am–5pm; T 032 345 6422).

Internet Internet cafés are everywhere. Try Netopia, top floor of the Ayala Center (daily 10am–9pm; P25/hr), or Jedbat on Salinas Drive (daily 8am–midnight; P15/hr).

Medical Care Cebu Doctor's University Hospital, Osmeña Blvd (T 032 255 5555). There's a branch of Mercury Drug on Fuente Osmeña and other pharmacies in all the malls.

Police Cebu Tourist police (T 032 412 4138) are located by the Basilica del Santo Niño.

Post office On Quezon Blvd close to the port area. Also at Osmeña Blvd cnr. R. Landon St.

Shopping The main malls in Cebu are the Ayala Center (Cebu Business Park) and SM City (North Reclamation area) as well as smaller malls E-Mall (east of the Southern Bus Station), Robinson's Place (Fuente Osmeña), Gaisano, JY Square and Banilad Town Center (BTC) further north. All are open 10am to 9pm, and have a huge range of shops and services. Ayala is the most upmarket, and is similar to Greenbelt in Makati with its outdoor eating area.

Moalboal

Almost 100km from Cebu City on the island's southwestern flank lies the small town of Moalboal, gateway to Pangsama Beach, a relaxed, rather boozy, divers' hangout which boasts some cheap accommodation and marvellous views of the sun setting over Negros. The sea is crystal clear, and while many reefs along the mainland coast have been damaged by successive typhoons, the enigmatic Pescador Island has survived, and remains one of the most alluring **dive sites** in the Philippines. Located just a few kilometres offshore, it's a haven for sharks, mantas and moray eels and swirling schools of sardines. There's also plenty to do on land, from hikes and bike rides to canyoning and horseriding, although sun-worshippers looking for a sandy beach will be better off at White Beach, 5km north, where there's also good snorkelling.

ARRIVAL AND DEPARTURE

By bus Buses pick up and drop off on the main road in Moalboal, from where a tricycle will take you down the partially paved track to Panagsama Beach (P100).

Destinations Bato (every 30min; 2hr); Cebu City (every 30min; 3hr).

DIVE OPERATORS

Dive operators are stretched along the beach and most are connected to resorts; shop around before you commit.

Freediving Philippines ⊤ 0928 263 4646, ⓦ freediving-philippines.com. One of the few freediving centres in the country; teacher Wolfgang will train you to hold your breath for 2–3 minutes at a time and dive without equipment. Prices start at US$125/day.

Savedra Dive Center ⊤ 032 474 3132, ⓦ savedra.com. This five-star operation offers plenty of choice for all levels of ability and has the only instructor development centre in Moalboal. They also arrange dive safaris to Apo Island, Bohol and Sipalay.

Visaya Divers *Quo Vadis* resort ⊤ 032 4743068, ⓦ quovadisresort.com. Swedish-Filipino owned and operated since 1997.

ACCOMMODATION

It's best to book accommodation in advance, especially at weekends.

Eve's Kiosk ⊤ 0917 950 5249 or ⊤ 0917 719 3388, ⓔ eveskiosk@live.com.ph. Just to the left of the path to the main road. Run by friendly Eve, this place has clean fan and a/c rooms (p1500) set around a garden area, as well as a decent-sized pool and terrace restaurant. Staff can arrange transport to the airport in Cebu. **P500**

Moalboal Backpacker's Lodge ⊤ 0908 607 6240, ⓦ moalboal-backpackerlodge.com. Along the main beach path. The eight dorm beds are in the foyer area so not ideal for those who value their privacy. There are also a few doubles, one of which has a private bathroom (P650). Amenities are basic, but staff are friendly, and there's a guest kitchen, sun deck and free wi-fi. Dorm **P275**, double **P480**

Nido's Garden Resort ⊤ 032 474 3068, ⓦ quovadisresort.com. Back from the beach on the road leading past *Marcosas Cottages Resort*. *Quo Vadis*' budget wing gives preference to those diving at the resort but, if available, the simple fan huts are a decent deal and offer use of the resort pool. **P980**

Pacita's Beach Resort ⊤ 0910 858 7222. Towards the southern end of the beach, just past where the path begins to break up. Nice enough spot with a range of well-kitted-out cottages set in gardens leading to the seafront. Avoid Saturday nights here unless you plan to spend the night at the disco next door which booms music through the grounds until the wee hours. **P1000**

★**Tipolo Beach Resort** ⊤ 0917 583 0062, ⓦ tipoloresort.com. A slightly pricier option but well worth the splurge with beautifully built bamboo a/c chalets, all with private balcony and sea views. There's also a small private beach for sun-worshippers. Owned by the same Filipino-German couple as *The Last Filling Station* and Planet Action Adventure. If Tipolo is fully booked ask about their new budget property, *Bamboo Inn* (from P750), a 10min walk back towards Moalboal. Free wi-fi. **P1800**

EATING, DRINKING AND NIGHTLIFE

Chili's Bar Midway along the beach path. Lively place with great sea views and two pool tables where you can get a Jaegerbeer for just P99. Snacks and meals are also on offer. Daily 9am–1.30am.

★**The Coffee Shop** North end of the beach path ⊤ 0906 353 4315. A fantastic new café, *The Coffee Shop* offers great breakfasts (try the Parisienne, P180), French crepes (P220), good coffee (P60–80) and daily specials. The owner, Sebastien, is as friendly as the vibe, right down to the sand on the floor. Free wi-fi. Daily 7am–10pm.

Hannah's Place Just to the right of the main road to Moalboal. In spite of Hannah's passing, this lovely little hideaway continues to serve the best seafood in town (P350). Daily 8am–10pm.

★**The Last Filling Station** Just south of *Pacita's*. Friendly, laidback place rustling up tasty international dishes and great wood-oven pizzas (P245), as well as freshly baked bread and home-made yoghurt (P125) for breakfast. Free wi-fi. Daily 6.30am–10pm.

DIRECTORY

Internet There are several internet cafés (P25/hr) in Moalboal town; many hotels and cafés offer free wi-fi.

Money There is now an ATM which accepts foreign cards in the 360 Pharmacy in Moalboal, though it's still best to bring enough cash with you. There's a moneychanger by the police station.

Tour operators Apart from diving, one of the best things about Moalboal is Planet Action Adventure (⊤ 032 474 3016, ⓦ action-philippines.com), next to *The Last Filling Station*, where you can arrange caving, trekking, canyoning and mountain-biking trips, as well as renting mountain bikes P300–700/day). Adventure day-trips start from P2200.

BANTAYAN ISLAND

Just off Cebu's northwestern coast, low-lying **Bantayan Island** was badly hit by typhoon Yolanda. At the time of writing boat services to the island were limited and many hotels were still closed or only partially open. The lack of diving (and therefore diving clientele) means that it may take Bantayan longer to get back on its feet than Malapascua, but it

certainly shouldn't be written off, and visitors are more welcome than ever. Partial electricity returned to the island in February 2013, but check facebook.com/choosebantayan for the latest. The Back to Sea Project (facebook.com/backtoseaproject) is a great initiative offering visitors the chance to help out financially and physically with the repair projects including boatbuilding and fishing implement construction (P3500 per project). Typhoon damage is unlikely to deter the crowds of Filipino tourists who descend on the island every Easter, when rooms are booked out for weeks in advance. For the rest of the year it's one of the most blissful spots in the Visayas. Most of the island's resorts stretch north and south of the pier in the formerly attractive little town and main port of **SANTA FE** on Bantayan's southeast coast – the beach remains exquisite, in parts rivalling Bounty Beach on Malapascua (see opposite). Prior to the typhoon there were money exchanges and a couple of internet places here, and it is presumed these will reopen. No ATMs on the island accept foreign cards however. A good way to explore is to make like the locals and hop on a bike; almost all the resorts rent bikes (P200/day) and motorbikes (P300/day), or try Santa Fe Adventures on the main street who also offer quad bikes (P495/day). Scoot off to the **Bantayan Island Nature Park** (P75) where you can take a swim in the two caves (or the pool) before proceeding to explore the rest of the island. An excellent resource on all things Bantayan is wowbantayan.com.

8

ARRIVAL AND DEPARTURE

By bus Several bus companies including White Stallion Lines, Auto Bus and Ceres Liner compete for business from Cebu's north terminal to the northern port town of Hagnaya (7 daily; 3hr 30min) where you can catch a ferry to Bantayan Island. Ceres is the most reliable and comfortable.

By ferry There are seven scheduled daily crossings to Santa Fe (1hr); the last departures are 4.30pm from Hagnaya and 6pm from Santa Fe. Palacio Shipping has twice-weekly overnight ferry services from Cebu at 9pm arriving in Santa Fe at 6am. Days of departure are seasonal. From further afield, there are several weekly ferries to Bantayan town on the west coast from Cadiz and Sagay on Negros. You can also hire a bangka to take you directly to Bantayan from Malapascua (upwards of P3500).

ACCOMMODATION

Following the destruction caused by typhoon Yolanda, all of the hotels listed below were at least partially open at the time of writing.

Beach Placid North of the pier, Santa Fe 032 406 5686, beachplacidresort.com. The cheaper accommodation here is in the five huts with bamboo floors and walls made of woven coconut, all immaculately clean and with free breakfast in low season (June–Oct). Use of kitchen, free wi-fi and an excellent restaurant, too. **P1500**

Budyong Beach Resort Santa Fe Beach 0921 314 5275, budyong.byethehost7.com. Palm trees provide some welcoming shade at this popular place with great-value nipa huts just on the seafront. Economy rooms are in demand, so book ahead. **P500**

Hard Kock Kafe 'n' Kiwi Kottages Main St (public market road), Santa Fe 032 438 9013 or 0920 668 1268, kiwikottages@yahoo.com.ph. Although you may not feel too comfortable asking for directions to get here, this popular café/restaurant is renowned for its chicken vindaloo (P180) and also offers accommodation in pleasant huts at the back. Right in the centre of town but a 10min walk to the beach. Free wi-fi. **P550**

★ **St Bernard Beach Resort** North of the pier, Santa Fe 0917 963 6162, bantayan.dk. Norwegian-Filipino-owned place 5min from the pier, with cosy and quaint little circular cottages right on the beach. Free wi-fi. **P950**

EATING AND DRINKING

The following are all on or just off the Public Market road in Santa Fe. In addition, almost all the resorts have their own restaurants.

Blue Ice Popular Swedish-owned place with Swedish music and dancing in the evenings. Quieter types can settle for a game of chess on the big wooden board. Salads include "Nick the Greek", and there's an extensive selection of mains including steaks, seafood and pizza (P200). Daily 8am–late.

CouCou A few tables are sprinkled around the front garden area at this popular restaurant serving excellent seafood and stir-fries (beef P180). For dessert try the Fiesta Halo Halo. There's a decent drinks menu including wine by the glass (P110), as well as a pool table and free wi-fi. Daily 7am–11pm.

D'Jungle If you can't face another bowl of rice or pork, head here for comfort food; there's good old shepherd's pie (P95) and fish and chips (P165), as well as delicious chilli crab. Backpacker rooms available to rent for a bargain P200–250. Daily 7am–midnight.

Khel's BBQ Stall Without a doubt the cheapest joint in town, this well-liked stall draws crowds for sticks of

chicken (P30), pork (P35) and hot dogs (P8). The more adventurous can go for chicken ovaries (P28), intestines or blood, both for a bargain P5. Daily 8am–midnight.

MALAPASCUA ISLAND

Eight kilometres off the northern tip of Cebu, the tiny island of **Malapascua** is one of Southeast Asia's finest diving destinations and was just hitting the big time when typhoon Yolanda struck. Almost every roof on the island was destroyed, and most of the local population was left without shelter. Substantial private contributions have helped the island to begin to find its feet, but at the time of writing only the bigger, more established resorts were operational. Repair work on boats, roofs, houses and hotels was taking place all around, and by the time you read this the vital tourist economy should be up and running and will hopefully facilitate the community's recovery.

At 2.5km long and about 1km wide, and with some of the warmest, most welcoming people you'll meet in the Philippines, Malapascua has been touted as a potential baby brother to Boracay, largely because of the charms of **Bounty Beach**, a blindingly white stretch of sand on the south coast.

Though Boracay-style development has yet to transpire, it is on its way. The new pier is finally complete (although currently only used by a few dive boats) and visitor numbers are already recovering post-Yolanda. While the island may not be quite as picture perfect as it once was, it remains a wonderful low-key divers' and travellers' paradise, and the friendly locals are as happy to see you as ever!

ARRIVAL AND DEPARTURE

By boat There are frequent bangkas from Maya to Malapascua from dawn until 6pm (40min; P80, subject to enough passengers on board), though there are more in the morning. Until the new pier is fully operational you'll often have to transfer to a smaller boat for the last 50m to shore (P10). On the way back the first bangka of the day leaves Malapascua at 6.30am. Travelling to or from Bantayan, you'll have to hire a bangka.

By bus Buses run between Cebu City's northern bus terminal and Maya (every 30min; 4hr). Buses run every 30min from 6am and it's best to set off early to avoid traffic and the heat.

ACCOMMODATION

All the places listed below are on Bounty Beach, and rates include breakfast. Early booking for the limited economy rooms is advised.

Blue Water Beach Resort ⓣ0917 627 2951, ⓦmalapascuabeachresort.com. Badly damaged by Yolanda, *Blue Water* was closed at the time of writing, but was planning to reopen soon. When they do, plans are for the same clean nipa chalets around a pleasant garden area. Rates include breakfast and there's also free wi-fi. **P1000**

★**Evolution** ⓣ0915 666 1584, ⓦevolution.com.ph. At the end of Dano Beach. Friendly English-Irish owned place with pleasant huts set around the garden area. Rates include delicious breakfasts (see *The Craic House*). If you're on a tight budget the neighbour (*Mr Kwiz*) at the back rents cheap rooms for just P500 – ask at reception. **P1800**

★**Hippocampus** Eastern end of the beach ⓣ0917 860 8439, ⓦhippocampus-online.com. Bamboo huts decorated with mahogany wood furniture, all with mosquito nets and private tiled bathrooms. Staff are very helpful and friendly, and there's a cosy little bar and restaurant with happy hour 5–7pm. Free wi-fi. Ask about "walk-in discounts" if you haven't booked, otherwise **P1500**

White Sands Bungalows Logon Beach ⓣ0927 318 7471, ⓦwhitesand.dk. Karl's three simple huts have had an upgrade and now feature a simple upper mezzanine level with a double mattress (P100 per extra person) as

8

DIVING MALAPASCUA

Some shallower dive sites were damaged by Yolanda, but the major drawcard – thresher sharks – remain in residence and anyone staying more than a few days is almost guaranteed a sighting. Long-established dive operators on the island are Thresher Shark Divers (ⓣ0927 612 3359, ⓦmalapascua-diving.com), Malapascua Exotic Island Dive and Beach Resort (ⓣ032 406 5428, ⓦmalapascua.net) and Sea Explorers (ⓣ032 234 0248, ⓦsea-explorers.com).

Nearby **Gato Island** is a marine sanctuary and a breeding place for black-and-white banded sea snakes, and overnight trips can be arranged to the tiny volcanic island of Maripipi, where reef sharks and dolphins are common.

★TREAT YOURSELF

Angelina (☎0915 340 4906). Replete with checkered blue and white tablecloths in a plush dining room overlooking pretty Logon Beach, *Angelina's* turns out some of the best (and most expensive) food on the island. Beef carpaccio (P320), tartar di tonno (P345) and squid-ink spaghetti (P315) are all on the menu, but there's no shame in ordering a good old-fashioned pizza (P350–410). Quality coffee and *crèma catalana* round off the meal perfectly. Daily 8am–10pm.

well as the main downstairs room. Many of the palms in the garden were damaged by Yolanda, but *White Sand* is open for business, and the beachside location is as appealing as ever. **P1000**

EATING AND DRINKING

The Craic House In *Evolution* (see p.641). The new double-sized restaurant had just opened when Yolanda arrived and destroyed the roof. This hasn't stopped the kitchen from turning out the island's best breakfasts (P200) and some of the tastiest grub around including Guinness beef stew (P400), and a pork and apple burger with red onion relish. Daily 7am–11pm.

Ging-Ging's Flower Garden Behind *Cocobana*. Obliterated by typhoon Yolanda, old backpacker favourite *Ging-Ging's* was serving food again in a makeshift dining room at the time of writing and planned to rebuild fully. The menu still holds a host of mains for less than P100, plus outstanding chocolate-and-banana pancakes (P75). Daily 6.30am–10pm.

8

BOHOL

It's hard to imagine that sleepy **Bohol**, a two-hour hop south of Cebu by fast ferry, has a bloody past. The only reminder is a memorial stone in the barrio of **Bool**, marking the spot where Rajah Sikatuna and Miguel Lopez de Legaspi concluded hostilities in 1565 by signing a compact in blood. These days, away from a few tourist hotspots, Bohol is largely a dozy sort of place, although the whole island was shaken up by the magnitude 7.2 earthquake that struck on October 15, 2013. Over 200 people died, and thousands of homes and buildings were destroyed, including some of the island's beloved Spanish-era churches. A few of the famed **Chocolate Hills** were also damaged by the quake, as was the viewing complex, but they are still as gorgeous as ever. The main transit hub is the capital, **Tagbilaran**, somewhere you may well pass through at some stage, though there's not a whole lot of reason to base yourself here when you could be on Panglao Island's **Alona Beach** in twenty minutes. This powdery strip of sand 1.5km long, with world-class diving and boozy nightlife, is quickly moving upmarket, but there are still a few places catering to backpackers. Aside from the diving and sights on offer on the main island of Bohol, Alona itself will appeal to some as a sort of mini-Boracay. **Panglao Island** is connected to the main island by a bridge from the capital and another from Bool.

WHAT TO SEE AND DO

The island's most iconic tourist attraction is the **Chocolate Hills**, which legend says are the calcified tears of a giant, whose heart was broken by the death of a mortal lover. The best time to see the Chocolate Hills – there are allegedly 1268 of them – is at dawn, at the end of the dry season when the grass has turned brown, and, with a short stretch of the imagination, the hills really do resemble chocolate drops. The original Chocolate Hills Tourist Complex was badly damaged by the quake, but in the meantime the nearby **Chocolate Hills Adventure Park** (☎0932 667 7098; P60) offers vistas, plus a host of activities, including a canopy walkway, a high-rope challenge course, and even a bike zipline. Other attractions in the interior include the **Philippine tarsier**, one of the world's tiniest primates. The tarsier is simultaneously heart-meltingly cute, with its big eyes, and terrifyingly alien; those eyes are fixed: instead it rotates its head 180 degrees. Sadly now endangered, its continued survival is thanks in part to the efforts of the **Tarsier Foundation** (@tarsierfoundation.org), and a visit to their sanctuary near Corella (daily 8am–5pm; P50), about half an hour from Tagbilaran, is a great way to experience some of Bohol's jungle

interior. Most people see the interior as part of an organized countryside tour, which also includes lunch on a floating restaurant along the lush banks of the Loboc River. Adrenaline-seekers may want to head to the **Loboc Ecotourism Adventure Park** (T 038 37 9292) where you can zipline (P350) or ride a rickety cable car (P250) above the river at a height of 100m. You can arrange tours of the interior through your accommodation or the tourist office. Otherwise, you can catch a bus to Carmen from the Dao terminal (hourly; P60) and tell the driver you're going to the Chocolate Hills Adventure Park. There are also frequent jeepneys to Sikatuna (40min; P30) from the Dao bus terminal, which stop at the Tarsier sanctuary. Another great way to see the island's highlights is to rent a motorbike in Panglao and explore at leisure.

Other than visiting the interior, the main activities are **beach-based**. There's world-class diving around Panglao; experienced divers shouldn't miss a trip to either the exquisite little island of **Balicasag**, or to **Pamilacan Island**, where it's possible to see short-finned pilot whales, long-snouted spinner, spotted, bottlenose and melon-headed dolphins. Any resort or dive operator on Alona Beach can arrange this. As with all diving spots in the Philippines, it pays to shop around before committing.

ARRIVAL AND DEPARTURE

By plane Tagbilaran Airport is under 1km from the city. A tricycle will cost P100 to the centre of town. Private taxis will take you to Alona Beach for P500–600.

Destinations Air Asia, Cebu Pacific and PAL all fly from Tagbilaran to Manila (daily; 1hr 15min).

By bus Dao integrated bus terminal is 10min north of Tagbilaran along Clarin Ave by tricycle (P25) and is the departure point for all other destinations on Bohol. Buses and jeepneys heading for Panglao are marked for Alona. For the Chocolate Hills, catch a bus to Carmen (hourly; 1hr 30min). Buses from Alona to Tagbilaran pick up on the main road, but aren't particularly frequent. Sharing a taxi/private transfer between Alona and Tagbilaran can be a good-value option (P500–600).

By ferry The pier is in the northwest of Tagbilaran off Gallares St, a 10min tricycle ride (P30) to the centre. The terminal fee is P11.25.

Destinations Daily fast ferries to Cebu City (hourly; 2hr) and Siquijor (3hr 30min) via Dumaguete (2 daily; 2hr)

INFORMATION

Facilities at Alona revolve around the tourist centre and Seashine Travel (see below) next door, although you can also make most bookings at your resort.

Tourist information Tagbilaran: The tourist office (Mon–Fri 8am–5pm; T 038 411 3666, W bohol.gov.ph) is located in the New Capitol Commercial Complex, Marapao St, and, while not terribly helpful, can organize countryside tours (P2500). There's also a small tourist office at the ferry dock (daily 8am–7pm) and at the airport (daily 8am–5pm). Most resorts are well geared up for tourists and can offer better information.

Tourist Information Panglao: Seashine Travel (daily 9am–8pm; T 038 502 9038), where the beach path meets the road, can arrange transport to Tagbilaran pier and day-trips to the Chocolate Hills. The tourist centre (daily 9am–9pm; T 038 502 9100), next door to Seashine Travel, has a postal service, currency exchange and internet access.

ACCOMMODATION

ALONA BEACH

Chillout Guesthouse T 038 502 4480, W chillout-panglao.com. French-run guesthouse with seven spic-and-span rooms, all with spacious private terraces. There's also a chill-out lounge and bar serving authentic French crêpes and home-made yoghurt. **P1000**

Citadel Alona T 038 502 9424, W citadelalona.com. Rooms at this British-owned place are located in an airy and cosy house, all with shared bathroom. Good option for self-caterers, with communal kitchen and barbecue facilities. There's a self-contained unit at the back for those wanting more privacy. Free wi-fi. **P750**

Coco Farm 5km south of Alona Beach T 0917 304 9801. Enjoy a taster of authentic Filipino life at this welcoming coco farm with accommodation in native huts. All greens served at the restaurant are freshly picked from the herbal garden and there are giant hammock swings to while the afternoon away. Call for pick-up (P100 from Alona Beach). Find them on Facebook. Dorm **P300**, double **P600**

Paragayo T 038 502 4043, W paragayoresort.com. On the edge of Alona, a 5min walk back from the beach, this English-owned budget place has well-equipped rooms set around a pleasant garden with wi-fi. Pay P300 extra for a/c. **P900**

Reggae Guesthouse T 0949 319 1946, W reggaeguesthousephilippines.com. Run by a chilled-out French couple, this guesthouse, with hemp flags and Bob Marley memorabilia decorating the communal area, has six cosy, spotless bungalows set around a pleasant garden area. **P1000**

8

EATING, DRINKING AND NIGHTLIFE

TAGBILARAN

Buzzz Café Upper Ground Floor, Island City Mall, opposite Dao bus terminal. Don't miss a stop at this offshoot of the organic Bohol Bee Farm in Dauis (boholbeefarm.com), which sells delicious home-grown treats as well as spreads, bee products and little pots of honey. Home-made muffins (P15) and ice cream (P40), too. Another branch is set to open on Alona Beach. Daily 8am–9pm.

ALONA BEACH

There's no shortage of restaurants, mainly offering good seafood, along the beach and the path leading towards the road inland.

Hayahay The superb Thai dishes (P180–300) at this beachfront restaurant are rustled up by the experienced Thai chef and the pizzas are also excellent – try the salmon- and tuna-laden "Balicasag" (P240). Daily 7am–11pm.

★ **Jugali's Bistro** This small, pleasant restaurant a few minutes from the beachfront offers excellent European dishes, and serves Alona's best fish and seafood (P380–500). The mango chicken with chutney and rice (P270) is another standout. Freshly baked bread and croissants, too. Daily 7am–11pm.

8

Pinerella By far the most popular bar in Alona, playing fun 70s, 80s and 90s classics; it doesn't kick off until at least 10pm and goes on until the early hours. Daily 6pm–4am.

DIRECTORY

Banks PNB is at the junction of Garcia Ave cnr. Clarin St, and BPI is on Garcia Ave cnr. Visarra St. There's also a BPI with ATM at Alona Beach.

Police Behind St Joseph's Cathedral.

Post office Behind St Joseph's Cathedral. Same complex as the police station.

Internet There are a number of cheap internet cafés near the market in Grupo St, as well as in both BQ and ICM malls (daily 10am–9pm; P30/hr).

NEGROS

The island of **Negros** lies at the heart of the Visayas, between Panay to the west and Cebu to the east. Shaped like a boot, it is split diagonally into Negros Occidental and Negros Oriental. The demarcation came when early missionaries decided the central mountain range was too formidable to cross, even in the name of God. It's an island that many tourists skip, yet it has many kilometres of untouched coastline, some relaxed towns – **Dumaguete**, the capital of Negros Oriental, is one of the stateliest in the Philippines – and dormant **volcanoes**. It also has a couple of superb beaches, such as Sugar Beach near Sipilay, whose relative inaccessibility means they have yet to be incorporated into the tourist trail. Negros is known as "Sugarlandia", and produces fifty percent of the country's **sugar**, an industry that has defined its history in sometimes bloody ways. Around **Bacolod**, the capital of Negros Occidental, well-preserved Spanish ancestral homes serve as reminders of the rich sugar barons of the past.

Bacolod

The city of **BACOLOD**, the provincial capital and an important transport hub for the Western Visayas, is big, hot, noisy and lacking much to see or do, although it offers first-rate dining.

The main street is Lacson, which runs almost the entire length of the city. Jeepneys marked "Bata–Libertad" constantly run north–south along Lacson. Backpackers will want to base themselves uptown, in the numbered streets, which benefit from their proximity to the university quarter. The third week of October sees everybody who is anybody joining in with Bacolod's flamboyant **Masskara Festival** (see p.597).

WHAT TO SEE AND DO

Though damaged by a storm in 2012, the Old Capitol Building remains one of the few architectural highlights, and is home to the **Negros Museum** (Tues–Sun 9am–noon & 1–6pm; P10), which details five thousand years of local history. Nearby the **Negros Forest and Ecological Foundation** (Mon–Sat 9am–noon & 1.30–4pm; P20) has a selection of Negros' indigenous wildlife including the Visayan warty pig and the bleeding-heart pigeon. In Talisay on the edge of town, **The Ruins** (daily 10am–8pm; P50; 034 476 4334) are the remnants of a monumental memorial mansion built by the Lacsons, one of nineteenth-century Negros' pre-eminent sugar families. There is also a restaurant here which makes a wonderful spot for dinner. The easiest way to visit is to hire a round-trip taxi (P200–300 depending on how long you stay).

ARRIVAL AND DEPARTURE

By plane The airport is 15km northeast of the city. A taxi to the centre of town costs around P500. Regular shuttles (P150) to SM and Robinson's malls.

Destinations Cebu Pacific and PAL fly daily to Cebu City (30min), Davao (1hr 10min) and Manila (1hr).

By bus and jeepney Ceres Liner, which dominates transport in the area, has two bus terminals, one for northern destinations (T 034 433 4993) located at Barangay Bata and one for southern destinations, located on Lopez Jaena St (T 034 434 287). Jeepneys run regularly to city plaza, from where you can catch a jeepney uptown (P7).

Destinations Cebu City (hourly; 10hr including ferry); Dumaguete (every 40min; 5hr 30min); Sipalay (hourly; 5hr). For destinations north, including Cadiz (1hr) and Sagay, from where you can take a boat to Bantayan, buses run every 40min from 6am–6pm.

By ferry Bredco Port, 500m west of the plaza, is the arrival and departure point for most major ferries. Frequent Jeepneys into town from Bangko (P8).

Destinations Iloilo City (24 daily; 1hr); Manila (3 weekly; 20hr).

INFORMATION

Tourist information Negros Occidental Tourism Center, Provincial Capitol Building (Mon–Fri 9am–5pm; T 034 432 2881, W negrosoccidentaltourism.com), is a good source of information on exploring the region's sights.

ACCOMMODATION

11th Street Bed and Breakfast 11th St T 034 433 9191 or T 0922 843 3919, W bb11st.webeden.co.uk. Rooms at this friendly little pension are set around a leafy garden and parking area; shaded glass windows make the rooms a little dark, but they all have cable TV and rates include free wi-fi and breakfast. **P550**

Pension Bacolod 11th St T 034 433 3377 or T 034 434 7065. Not as welcoming as the *11th Street B&B* along the road, this popular cheapie feels secure and is great value, though both the walls and mattresses are thin. **P250**

★TREAT YOURSELF

L'Fisher Chalet 14th Lacson St T 034 433 3791, W lfisherhotelbacolod.com. You don't have to spend too much extra to buy a little sophisticated urban living at *L'Fisher's* budget wing, *Chalet*. The cheapest "budget" and "economy" rooms are windowless, but the stylish standard twins and doubles (P1795) have all mod cons and balconies looking out over the city. The real reason to stay though is for free use of the hotel's trendy rooftop pool with swim-up bar, plus there's a small but well-equipped gym and a decent restaurant. **P1195**

EATING, DRINKING AND NIGHTLIFE

Bacolod has a well-developed culinary scene and Lacson Street is lined with top-notch restaurants serving local and international food. It's also worth heading out to the *The Ruins* (see opposite) for a meal. The city's main nightlife entertainment zone, Goldenfields, is in the far south of the city, and has a few decent clubs, along with a strip of girlie bars. Lacson Street has a more sophisticated selection; the best option is artsy lounge-bar *Mushu* near 20th Street.

Café Uma 15th Street & Lacson Street, next to *L'Fisher*. This trendy little café serves delicious but expensive drinks, snacks and meals including eggs Benedict (P450), fish and chips (P450), and lemon-herb roasted chicken (P400). There's free wi-fi for customers. Daily 10.30am–9.30pm.

Calea 14th St and also in Robinson's Place mall. Hugely popular with a young clientele, this café, decorated in mellow blue and yellow tones, puts all the Negros sugar to good use; dozens of cakes and sandwiches (P115–155) as well as delectable coffees (P60–90). Mon–Thurs 8am–10pm, Fri–Sun 9am–11pm.

Imay's 6th Lacson St. Traditional Filipino food in a large outdoor aquarium-themed gazebo, popular for weekend family lunch but also open for dinner. Probably Bacolod's best seafood. Extensive menu with mains at around P200. Daily 11am–2pm & 5.30–11pm.

Manokan Country Just outside SM Mall. The name roughly translates as "where you find chicken" and so it is – the dozens of chicken restaurants here are funded by the city government, keeping the locals happy. A meal here will set you back less than P100. Daily 10am–late.

Organic Market Restaurant Behind the Provincial Capitol Building. Fruit and veg market with a great organic restaurant serving all sorts of health foods from organic rice meals (P40) to shakes (P35) and coffee. Meals for less than P100. Daily 6am–6pm.

DIRECTORY

Banks PNB on Lacson St has an ATM and foreign exchange.

Internet There's no shortage of cheap internet cafés around the university and in the malls. For a little more comfort try Le Cafenet in Mayfair Plaza at 12th Lacson St (Mon–Fri 8am–8pm, Sat 9am–7pm; P25/hr).

Post office Gatuslao cnr. Burgos streets.

Mount Kanlaon National Park

Mount Kanlaon, two hours from Bacolod by jeepney, is the tallest peak and most active volcano in the central Philippines. Climbers have died scaling it, so don't

underestimate its fury, especially considering that it has been rumbling ominously since 2006. The surrounding forest helped keep President Manuel Quezon hidden from invading Japanese forces during World War II and contains all manner of wonderful wildlife, including pythons, monitor lizards, tube-nosed bats and the *dahoy pulay*, a venomous green tree snake. The best way to get here is by jeepney via Murcia, southeast of Bacolod.

There are several routes up the volcano; one of the best is from the village of **Guintubdan** on the western slopes, and most involve three tough days of walking and two nights of camping. Before you set out you must visit the Park Superintendent's office in Bacolod (Penro compound, Abad Santos Street, Barangay 39; ⓣ034 433 3813) to put your name down for a park permit (P500) and a compulsory guide (P700). If required, porters cost P500 per day. Local guide and biologist Angelo (ⓣ0917 301 1410) can arrange everything for you, and tailor the climb to the level of difficulty you're looking for. For up-to-date information about the safety of climbing Kanlaon, contact the tourist office in Bacolod (see p.645).

8

Sipalay

About halfway between Bacolod and Dumaguete on the island's west coast, the remote town of **SIPALAY** is surrounded by a scattering of islands and some wild and wonderful beaches. Chief among these is **Sugar Beach**, a long stretch of powdery sand that still feels like one of the Philippines' best-kept secrets. Sipalay's historical focal point is the plaza and the church, but these days most activity centres on the main road, where there are numerous canteens, bakeries and a couple of convenience stores. **Buses** will leave you close to *Driftwood* restaurant (affiliated with the resort of the same name on Sugar Beach) on Poblacion Beach, which has the best **food** in town and is the de facto pick-up point for boats to Sugar Beach. The nearest ATM is a long way north at Kabankalan, so make sure that you have enough cash to keep you going.

Sugar Beach

The long and lovely **Sugar Beach** has a backdrop of coconut groves and mountains and faces due west, with wonderful sunsets. Though beginning to be discovered by tourists, it's still at its busiest when the kids get out of school and gather there to play in the relative cool of the late afternoon. Nothing more strenuous than sunbathing and beach volleyball are the order of the day here, though a favourite excursion is to the nearby wildlife sanctuary of Danjugan Island, which you'll need to reserve in advance (see ⓦprrcf.org for more information). Better diving is to be had at **Punta Ballo**, another clean, quiet and beautiful beach fifteen minutes from Sipalay by tricycle (P150). You can stay here at the *Artistic Diving Beach Resort* (ⓣ034 453 2710, ⓦartisticdiving.com; P1280), which has beachfront accommodation in fan or air-conditioned rooms and a good Swiss/Filipino restaurant.

ACCOMMODATION

Driftwood Village ⓣ0920 900 3663, ⓦdriftwood-village.com. This welcoming place with 18 cottages,

GETTING TO AND FROM SUGAR BEACH

The easiest thing to do is to arrange a boat transfer with your resort; they'll send their boatman over to pick you up from Poblacion Beach in Sipilay town, directly where the bus from Bacolod or Dumaguete will drop you. Rates are about P300 per boat (4 to 6 people). A cheaper and more roundabout way of getting to Sugar Beach involves taking a tricycle to Nauhang (P150), where you take a small paddle boat across the creek (P20), and walk around the headland. If you decide to take this route, ask to be let off the bus in Montilla rather than Sipalay, which is closer to Nauhang. Coming from Dumaguete the quickest bus route follows the coast south around the toe of the island and then north through Hinoba-an, but an equally scenic option is to head north and then across the mountains to Kabanklan before travelling south for Sipalay.

including one dorm, dotted amid jungle greenery has an atmospheric chill-out area and restaurant serving great Thai food. Boat transfers are P300. Dorm **P250**, double **P450**

Sulu Sunset Beach Resort 0919 716 7182, sulusunset.com. The simple nipa huts right on the beach are good value, and there's table tennis, table football, darts, billiards and hammocks to while away the afternoons. The restaurant is superb, with plenty of veggie dishes (P180), freshly baked wood-oven bread and pizzas (P190). Boat transfers P300. **P550**

★**Takatuka Lodge** 0920 230 9174, takatuka-lodge.com. The wacky world of *Takatuka* has to be seen to be believed. Rooms all feature verandas and one-of-a-kind furnishings, from the pink Cadillac bed in the Superstar room, to the stereo-controlled microphone lights in Rockadelic. For a/c or hot showers add P200–300 per night. The restaurant serves some of the best food on the beach and the *Salamizza* (salami *rösti*) is recommended. Wi-fi costs P50 per 30min. **P1050**

Dumaguete and around

DUMAGUETE, the elegant capital of Negros Oriental, lives up to its reputation as "The City of Gentle People". Lying on the southeast coast of Negros, within sight of the most southerly tip of Cebu Island, it's a nicer-than-average port town and the perfect jumping-off point for **Siquijor** and the marine sanctuary of **Apo Island**, where the diving is superb, plus there are plenty of adventurous pursuits to be found in the mountainous hinterlands, from lakes and waterfalls to hot springs and traditional markets. The main street is Perdices Street, which runs north–south, and where you can find plentiful ATMs, travel agents and pharmacies.

ARRIVAL AND DEPARTURE

By plane The airport is a few kilometres northwest of the city centre. Tricycles make the trip for P120. A taxi-van will set you back P250.

Destinations PAL and Cebu Pacific fly to Cebu (daily; 30min) and Manila (5 daily; 1hr 15min).

By bus The Ceres Liner terminal is on Governor Perdices St near Robinson's Place mall. A tricycle costs P20. For departures to the north of the island, it's worth making sure that you get on an express bus, shaving a few painful hours from journey times.

Destinations Hourly buses to Sipalay (45hr) via Kabankalan or Hinoba-an, and Bacolod (6hr). For Cebu island, take a van (P11, or tricycle P100) north to Sibulan (or Tampi for Bato on Cebu) from where there are boats (every 30min; 30min; P35–70) to Lilo-An. From Lilo-An there are buses up the east coast to Cebu City, while from Bato buses go north to Moalboal (and then on to Cebu City).

By ferry The pier is near the northern end of Rizal Blvd, within easy walking distance of the centre. A tricycle costs P20.

Destinations Cagayan de Oro (weekly; 7hr); Cebu City (1–2 daily; 4hr); Dapitan (on Mindanao; daily; 3hr); Manila (weekly; 19hr); Siquijor (6 daily; 45min); Tagbilaran (1–2 daily; 2hr).

INFORMATION

Tourist information The tourist office has a kiosk in Quezon Park (Mon–Fri 8am–5pm; 035 225 0549, tourismdgte@gmail.com) on Santa Catalina Street. However, *Harold's Mansion* (see p.648) is a better source of information for backpackers.

Internet The internet cafés around the Silliman University complex, at the northern end of Hibbard St, are plentiful and cheap (P25/hr). There's also free wi-fi in many hotels.

8

APO ISLAND

The **Apo Island Marine Reserve and Fish Sanctuary** is said by those in the know to be one of the world's top ten diving sites. There are two "resorts" on the island, plus a few budget lodgings. The plush *Apo Island Beach Resort* (035 321 1038 or 0939 915 5122 3359, apoislandresort.com; double from P2700, dorm P800) stands on an isolated sandy cove hemmed in by rocks, while cheaper *Liberty's Lodge* (0920 2385 704, apoisland.com; double P1950 including all meals for two) is on the main beach. To get to Apo, take a bus going to Bayawan and ask to get off at Malatapay, where the boats leave, and which also has a fascinating Wednesday-morning market. Small bangkas (good for four people) cost P2000 round-trip, while the next size up is P3000 (up to ten people), or alternatively you can arrange a place on one of the four daily *Liberty Lodge* shuttles (P300 per person). General admission to the marine sanctuary is P100. To get the most out of your trip, talk to the guys at *Harold's Mansion* (see p.648) before you go.

ACCOMMODATION

DUMAGUETE

★**Harold's Mansion** 205 Hibbard Ave ⓣ035 225 8000, ⓦharoldsmansion.com. Dumaguete's only true hostel has immaculate male and female dorms, plus simple rooms with common or private (P600) bathroom, plus a roof-deck coffee shop perfect for meeting other travellers. *Harold's* also has its own dive shop and there's an invaluable information centre from where you can organize excursions. If you want to enjoy some fresh air without venturing too far from the city, ask about their very simple eco-lodge up in Valencia (P500). Dorm **P250**, double **P500**

Hotel Palwa Locsin St ⓣ035 422 8995, ⓦhotelpalwa.com. Excellent budget option with small but nicely styled a/c rooms with flat-screen TV. There's a pleasant café with free wi-fi in the lobby. **P969**

SOUTH OF DUMAGUETE

The beach resorts of Dauin are only a 20min drive south of town, and make a pleasant alternative to staying in the centre.

8

★**Liquid Barangay** Bulak, Dauin ⓣ0917 314 1778, ⓦliquiddumaguete.com. Run by a friendly British-Canadian couple, this low-key dive resort has eight attractive beach huts, all with sea views. There's wi-fi, a pool, and the roof-top café serves tasty meals, good cocktails and has a small bakery. There are also a few super-cheap rooms (P350) at the back, though these are exclusively for dive instructors and students. **P1450**

EATING, DRINKING AND NIGHTLIFE

Happy hour (4–6pm) is a nice time to watch the promenaders on Rizal Blvd, though the bars get sleazier as the night wears on.

The Blue Monkey Grill Silliman Ave cnr. Rizal Blvd. Set in a pretty torch-lit garden in a prime location for people-watching, its tasty food (P135) is popular with college students. Mon–Sat 4pm–2am, Sun 4–11.30pm.

★TREAT YOURSELF

Casablanca Rizal Blvd ⓣ035422 4080. The best steaks in town (and probably all of Negros) are worth splashing out for, even if you opt for the local beef (P50–600), rather than imported. The intimate inside is lined with movie posters and has a decent deli, but it's more atmospheric (and noisy) to sit outdoors and watch the world wandering by, to the backdrop of Siquijor across the water. Daily 11am–9pm.

Coco Amigos Rizal Blvd. Popular Mexican along the seafront, with favourites such as chilli con carne (P160), and mouthwatering enchiladas (P200), as well as international dishes. It can attract a seedy crowd in the evenings. Daily 7am–midnight.

Sans Rival Rizal Blvd. The original little cake shop on San Jose Street still turns out delicious cakes and coffee, while its larger sister round the corner on Rizal serves tasty but inexpensive meals (P120–250), including lasagne, salads, burgers and sandwiches. Daily 9am–9pm.

Santa Teresa Restaurant Hibbard Avenue. Clean and great value – just point at whatever tickles your fancy (fish and meat mains around P100) and take it through to the pleasant seating area. Daily 7am–10pm.

SIQUIJOR

Siquijor, a laidback little island where life is simple and backpackers are made very welcome, lies slightly apart from the rest of the Visayas off the southern tip of Cebu and about 22km east of Negros. The Spanish sailors nicknamed Siquijor the Isla del Fuego ("Island of Fire") because of eerie luminescence generated by swarms of fireflies at night. Even today, the island is suffused with a lingering sense of mystery, with many Filipinos refusing to visit, believing Siquijor to be a centre of witchcraft and black magic, a superstition reinforced by the staging of the Folk Healing Festival in the mountain village of San Antonio every Easter on Black Saturday. You can circumnavigate Siquijor by tricycle and jeepney along the coastal road, and most resorts can also arrange motorbike rental or guided tours to the lush, jungled interior.

SIQUIJOR TOWN is the capital and main port, where you'll find a couple of internet spots, including 3JK on the main street (daily 24hr; P15/hr). Nearby is a tricycle terminal that the locals use, a better bet than using the touts around the pier. The town lies twenty minutes by tricycle (P20) southwest of Larena, where the island's only (temperamental) ATM is located, along with a Western Union and another smattering of internet cafés. The tourist office (Mon–Fri 8am–5pm) is in the provincial capital building near Siquijor Town, but can't do much more than give you a map of the island (handy for motorbike travel).

The most popular beaches on Siquijor are **Sandugan**, where there's also fantastic diving, half an hour north of Larena, and **Paliton** and **San Juan** beaches on the west coast. Multi-cabs and jeepneys run around the island, but stop services early, so if you plan on using them to circumnavigate Siquijor make sure you start in the morning. It's not much more expensive, and far more liberating, to rent a motorbike, or even a mountain bike (both P350 per day) to explore the island at leisure.

ARRIVAL AND DEPARTURE

By ferry Up to six fast ferries run daily between Siquijor Town and Dumaguete (6am–3pm; 45min).

ACCOMMODATION

★ **Coral Cay Resort** San Juan Beach ⓣ 0908 896 5263 or ⓣ 0919 269 1269, ⓦ coralcayresort.com. The excellent-value seafront cottages here are well worth the extra cost; the budget rooms are set slightly inland. There's a pool, kayaks, gym, pool table, book exchange and a floating raft for those wanting to catch some rays. The laidback restaurant is a good place to mingle over tasty international food. **P1050**

Hambilica San Juan Beach ⓣ 0917 700 0467, ⓦ hambilicasiquijor.com. Birds flock to the garden sanctuary at dawn and the firefly hatchery glitters at night at this little place with seven rooms. There's great diving off the shore, but no beach for sun-worshippers. **P900**

Kiwi Dive Resort Sandugan, next to *Islanders* ⓣ 0908 889 2283, ⓦ kiwidiveresort.com. Relaxed, laidback Kiwi-owned place with rustic nipa cottages. There's a pleasant terrace restaurant with a book swap, and they also rent motorbikes and run island tours. Free wi-fi. **P450**

★TREAT YOURSELF

Coco Grove ⓣ 035 225 5490, ⓦ cocogrovebeachresort.com. Towering coconut trees line the 800m stretch of beach at this welcoming family-run resort with tropical gardens. The 41 cottages and villas are dotted around the 15 acres of luscious property and there are plenty of activities on offer from Hobie cat sailing to island hopping. The two pools have natural chlorination and there are energy-saving lamps in an effort to go green. What's more, the resort supports the rehabilitation of Tubod Marine Sanctuary. **P2400**

PANAY

The big heart-shaped island of **Panay** has been largely bypassed by tourism, perhaps because everyone seems to get sucked towards Boracay off its northern tip instead. Panay comprises four provinces: Antique on the west coast, Aklan in the north, Capiz in the northeast and Iloilo along the east coast to **Iloilo City** in the south. The province of most interest to tourists is Aklan, whose capital **Kalibo** is the home of the big and brash **Ati-Atihan Festival**, held every year in mid-January.

Iloilo City

ILOILO CITY is a useful transit point for Guimaras and other Visayan islands, as well as Kalibo and Boracay if you're coming from the south, but is otherwise of little interest. Apart from some graceful old houses in its side streets and a handful of interesting churches, the city has little to distinguish it from other port cities throughout the archipelago.

West of the city in Molo district is **Molo Church** (daily 8am–7pm except for Mass), a splendid nineteenth-century Gothic Renaissance structure made of coral and egg whites. If you have an hour to spare, the **Museo Iloilo** (Mon–Sat 9.30am–5pm; P25) next door to the tourist office is well worth a browse; it covers the history of Panay through displays of fossils, Stone Age tools, pottery, shells and teeth. The Dinagyang Festival on the fourth weekend in January adds some extra frenzy to the city. Iloilo is known for a number of delicacies, including **pancit Molo soup**, a garlicky concoction of pork dumplings and noodles in rich broth, sold at numerous street stalls. **Batchoy**, an artery-hardening combination of liver, pork and beef with thin noodles, is also available everywhere.

The long, traffic-choked artery of General Luna Street is home to banks with ATMs, travel agents, pharmacies, the police and the hospital.

ARRIVAL AND DEPARTURE

By plane Iloilo International Airport is 19km northwest of the city; a taxi to the centre will cost P350–400; a cheaper option is to take one of the frequent shuttles (P80) to SM City mall, and then a taxi from there (P100).

8

Destinations Cebu Pacific and PAL Express have several daily fights to Cebu (45min) and Manila (1hr). The former also flies to Davao (daily; 1hr 5min) and Puerto Princesa (3 weekly; 1hr 5min).

By bus and jeepney The bus terminal is at Tagbac, 5km north of the centre. Jeepneys marked "Jaro Liko", "Legares" or "Zarraga" all serve the centre of town (P12).

Destinations The terminal serves northern destinations, including Caticlan (hourly; 6hr) and Kalibo (hourly; 5hr) via Concepcion and Roxas. Non-stop minivans from here are slightly quicker, but more expensive. Both services are most frequent until 1pm. Note that early-morning Ceres buses (until 6am) leave from Tanza Street. Plenty of companies also serve Manila, using the roll-on, roll-off (RoRo) ferries.

By ferry Three terminals serve Iloilo. Ferries to Guimaras are served by Ortiz wharf; ferries serving Bacolod arrive at the Iloilo-Bacolod ferry terminal on Muelle Loney Street, while other domestic services use the nearby wharf off Fort San Pedro Drive, at the eastern end of the city. From Ortiz, walk to the main street and catch a "Baluuarte" or "SM City" jeepney into town; from Fort San Pedro, walk to the main street and catch a "Jaro CPU" jeepney; there are jeepneys just outside the Iloilo-Bacolod terminal.

8

Destinations Cebu City (7 weekly; 12–14hr); Manila (weekly; 20hr).

INFORMATION

Tourist information The city's tourist information office is on Bonifacio Drive (Mon–Fri 8am–5pm; ⓣ033 337 5411 or ⓣ335 0245, ⓦwesternvisayastourism.com.ph)

ACCOMMODATION

★**Highway 21** General Luna St ⓣ033 335 1220 or ⓣ0917 722 4321, ⓦhighway21hoteliloilo.com. One of three "21" lodgings in Iloilo, this wonderfully efficient hotel is centrally located and has helpful staff. Rooms are modern and spotless, and all have a/c and cable; those in the annexe are slightly smaller and plainer, though cheaper. Wi-fi available. **P900**

Sarabia Charter Pension House General Luna St ⓣ033 508 1853 or ⓣ0920 6149 263. Tucked behind the faded grandeur of the *Sarabia Manor Hotel*, this budget pension has small, simple and attractive rooms set around a small garden, and benefits from use of the *Sarabia's* pool. **P720**

EATING, DRINKING AND NIGHTLIFE

Butot Balat Solis St. A haven of tropical tranquillity and greenery in the midst of the downtown mayhem, this popular restaurant offers candlelit dining under thatched cabanas surrounding a small pond. Try chilli shrimps (P245), pork Bicol Express (P175), beef *kare-kare* (P285) or fish by weight.

★**Freska** Smallville Boardwalk, Diversion Rd. *Freska* continues to make Ilonggo dining easy with its mouth-wateringly good-value daily lunch and dinner buffets. Over 40 dishes are on offer, including green mango salad, chicken Inasal, BBQ pork and a delicious dessert line-up. Your thirst can be quenched by the huge selection of imported beers and staff are impressively upbeat. Daily 11.30am–2.30pm & 5.30–10.30pm.

Smallville Complex Diversion Rd, just north of the river. This outdoor complex is pretty much the centre of Iloilo nightlife. Popular bars/clubs to look for include *Aura* and *Ice.* All have live bands and/or DJs nightly, usually with a P100 entry fee, and don't get going till about 11pm. Daily 11am–5am.

DIRECTORY

Banks Plenty with ATMs along General Luna St, including BDO.

Internet Netopia at SM City Mall or at Robinson's Mall (both Mon–Fri 9am–8pm, Sat & Sun 10am–8pm; P20/hr); Taven Cyber Café at Riverside Inn (daily 9am–7pm; P15/hr).

Police Opposite the University of San Agustin on General Luna Street.

Post office On Muelle Loney Street by the Iloilo-Bacolod terminal.

Kalibo

KALIBO lies on the well-trodden path to Boracay and for most of the year is an uninteresting town, but every third Sunday of January it becomes the epicentre of probably the biggest street party in the country, **Ati-Atihan** (see box opposite).

Kalibo is a compact place with most amenities within walking distance of each other. The major thoroughfare is Roxas Avenue, which runs into town from the **airport** in the southeast, with most streets leading off it to the southwest.

ARRIVAL AND DEPARTURE

By plane The 10min tricycle ride into town from the airport costs P10/person, or P30 for private hire. There are direct vans and buses from the airport to Caticlan (P200).

Destinations Cebu (2 daily; 55min); Manila (15 daily; 1hr).

By bus Regular buses and vans serving Caticlan (the jumping-off point for Boracay) arrive and depart directly from the airport (P200; 2hr); cheaper buses and vans (P100) to Caticlan leave from the terminal on Osmeña Ave, from where there are regular buses to Iloilo (5hr).

By ferry Dumaguit port is 50min away. There are several 2GO and Moreta Shipping Lines ferries weekly to Manila (16–20hr); Moreta's office is at 19 Martyr's St. Jeepneys run between the port and the town centre.

ATI-ATIHAN FESTIVAL

Every January (exact dates change slightly each year), the Filipino town of **Kalibo** on the island of Panay erupts into Southeast Asia's biggest street party, **Ati-Atihan**. This exuberant festival celebrates the original inhabitants of the area, the Atis, and culminates with choreographed dances through the streets by locals daubed in black paint (Ati-Atihan means "to make like the Atis"). Thousands dress up in outrageous outfits, blacken their faces with soot (in honour of the aboriginal Ati, whose descendants still live on Panay), and salsa through the streets amid cries of "*hala bira, puera pasma*" ("keep on going, no tiring"). It is said that the festival originated when ten Malay chieftains chanced upon the island and persuaded the Ati to sell it to them; the deal was naturally sealed with a party, where the Malays darkened their faces to emulate their new neighbours. Centuries later, the Spanish incorporated Catholic elements into Ati-Atihan and the modern festival is now dedicated to the Santo Niño (Holy Infant Jesus). The event comes to a climax with a huge Mass in the cathedral, and the three-day party ends with a masquerade ball and prizes for the best dressed.

Good accommodation can be hard to find during the Ati-Atihan and prices increase by up to a hundred percent. Direct flights to Kalibo from Manila are often fully booked.

INFORMATION

Tourist information Kalibo Tourism Office, Kalibo Tourism Centre, Magsaysay Park (Mon–Fri 8am–5pm; ⓣ 036 262 1020).

ACCOMMODATION

Garcia Legaspi Mansion 159 Roxas Ave ⓣ 036 262 5588. The clean fan rooms, all with shared bathrooms, and friendly staff, make this the most popular budget place in Kalibo. **P700**

RB Lodge N Roldan St ⓣ 036 268 5200. The new branch of this hotel offers clean and simple but stylish rooms with wi-fi and cable TV in the heart of town. The old wing on Pastrana is nearly as nice and also has an internet café and coffee shop. **P1150**

EATING AND DRINKING

Kalibo's culinary scene is gradually expanding beyond *Andok's*, *Chowking* and *Jollibee* to include a few decent coffee shops.

Latte Café Coffee Archbishop Reyes cnr. Santa Monica streets. There are two branches of this pleasant coffee shop in Kalibo, both of which sell sandwiches and light meals (P140–350), alongside Havaiana flip-flops. Great coffee and free wi-fi make this place a favourite with students. Daily 9am–7pm.

Kitty's Kitchen Rizal Street, near the police station. Friendly Kitty rustles up some pretty tasty meals; the speciality is barbecue ribs with salad and rice (P110). The vast menu is a mix of sandwiches, pasta, curries and noodles. Daily 9am–9pm.

DIRECTORY

Banks Several, including BPI and Allied Banking, on Martelino St close to Kalibo Cathedral. There's also a BNP on Pastrana St.

Internet Plenty of internet cafés along Roxas Ave, including *Ed's Video Place* at the junction with Pastrana. There's wi-fi access at both branches of *Latte Coffee Café* (daily 9am–7pm).

Post office In the Provincial Capitol Building, on Fernandez St.

BORACAY

It may be only 7km long and 1km wide at its narrowest point, but **BORACAY**, 350km south of Manila off the northeastern tip of Panay, is a big tropical island in a small package. **White Beach** grows more commercial and upmarket every year, and caters more and more to Asian package tourists to the point where it's now almost unrecognizable from its backpacker origins, but the beauty of Boracay is that there really is room for everybody. Budget travellers might have to hunt a bit harder for accommodation but there are plenty of compensations, chief among them some of the country's most chilled-out nightlife and its most genuinely breathtaking stretch of beach. The scene around White Beach is what it is, and while some complain about the vendors and the fact that there's hardly a patch of sand not appropriated by the resorts, it's also great fun – and the only place of its kind in the Philippines. Besides, with thirty other beaches and coves to discover around the island and offshore, it's never too difficult to escape the crowds.

Boracay is a thrill-seekers' paradise, with horseriding, kiteboarding, beach volleyball, mountain biking, motorcycling, kayaking and diving all on offer. There are 24 official **dive sites** in and around the island, and because of the calm waters near the shore outside the rainy season it's a good place to learn. That said, probably the most popular activity here is simply sitting on the beach at dusk with a cocktail watching the sun drift towards the horizon, or having a massage by the sea (P350 per hour).

White Beach

The jewel in the crown of the Philippine Tourist Board, White Beach, on the island's western shore, is 4km of the kind of powder-white sand that you thought only existed in Martini ads. It really does merit the hype. The word Boracay is said to have come from the local word *borac*, meaning cotton, a reference to the sand's colour and texture. **Main Road** runs the western length of Boracay, from Yapak in the north, through White Beach and down to Angol on its southern tip. Not surprisingly, most of the development on the island is here, and for the majority of visitors, White Beach is Boracay. Before the present ferry system came into place, bangkas from Caticlan used to dock directly onto the beach, in three "stations", still used to indicate the south (3), middle (2) and north (1) of the beach. The northern end, beyond the old boat station 1, is the quietest area and home to the more expensive resorts. **D'Talipapa Market** is just north of the tourist centre, while **D'Mall** is a little south of station 1. As a general rule, accommodation at the southern end is cheapest, increasing in price as you move north.

The rest of the island

A good way to get around the island is to hire a bangka from local boatmen on White Beach (subject to sea conditons); you should pay around P1500 for half a day per group. An underused alternative is to rent a bike (ask around on the beach path). To the north of White Beach, accessible via a path carved out of the cliffs, sits the little village of **Diniwid** with its tranquil, snorkeller-friendly seashore. At the end of a steep path over the next hill is tiny **Balinghai Beach**, enclosed by walls of rock, while on the north coast, quiet **Puka Beach**, the second longest on the island, gives an idea of what White Beach must have been like back in the day. A tricycle here will cost P150. On the northeast side of the island, Ilig-Iligan Beach has caves and coves to explore, as well as jungle full of fruit bats. From here, a path leads a short way up the hill to **Bat Cave**, a fantastic place to be at dusk when the indigenous flying foxes emerge in immense flocks.

Mount Luho in the north of the island is an easy ascent (P60 entry fee), and the reward is terrific: 360-degree views of the island and neighbouring Romblon. One of the nicest stretches of island to cycle is from **Punta Bunga** to **Tambisaan Beach**, where the shoreline is dotted with installation art, including the famous Boracay Sandcastle.

Nearby **Carabao Island**, part of the **Romblon** group, makes a nice side trip from Boracay, with wonderful beaches, affordable seafront accommodation at Inobahan on the island's east coast (where the bangkas arrive), and a few simple restaurants.

ARRIVAL AND DEPARTURE

By plane The two closest airports to Boracay are Kalibo and Caticlan. Kalibo is an easy 90min drive (P200), while Caticlan is only an expensive 5min tricycle ride (P50) from the pier; flights to Caticlan are usually more expensive than those to Kalibo.

Destinations (from Caticlan) Cebu (3 daily; 1hr); Manila (30 plus daily; 1hr).

By bus Ceres Liner buses and a/c vans travel between Caticlan and Iloilo's Tagbac terminal to Caticlan (5–7hr). There are regular Ceres buses plying the Manila–Caticlan route (12hr) using RoRo. From Puerto Galera you can take a bus to Calapan, then change for Roxas from where you can get a boat to Caticlan (10hr).

By ferry It's a 20min boat journey to Boracay from the ferry terminal at Caticlan (every 10min 5.30am–6pm, limited service 6–10pm). Tickets are P25 in the day, or P30 at night, plus a P100 terminal fee, and another P75

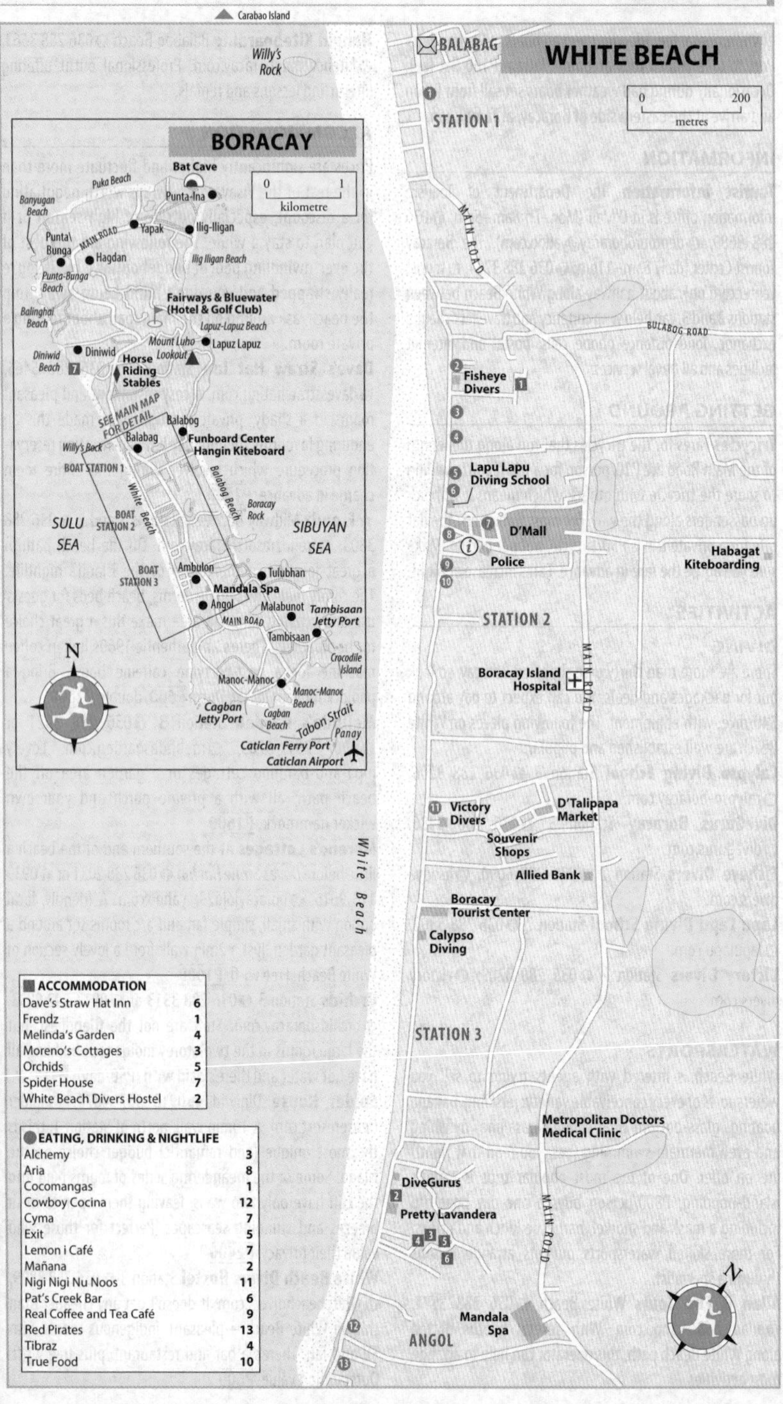

WHITE BEACH
0 200 metres
BOREACAY
0 1 kilometre
Carabao Island
Willy's Rock
BALABAG
STATION 1
MAIN ROAD
BULABOG ROAD
Fisheye Divers
Lapu Lapu Diving School
D'Mall
Police
Habagat Kiteboarding
STATION 2
Boracay Island Hospital
Victory Divers
D'Talipapa Market
Souvenir Shops
Allied Bank
Boracay Tourist Center
Calypso Diving
STATION 3
Metropolitan Doctors Medical Clinic
DiveGurus
Pretty Lavandera
Mandala Spa
ANGOL
White Beach
Bat Cave
Puka Beach
Banyugan Beach
Punta-Ina
Punta Bunga
Yapak
Ilig-Iligan
Hagdan
Ilig Iligan Beach
Punta-Bunga Beach
Fairways & Bluewater (Hotel & Golf Club)
Balinghai Beach
Lapuz-Lapuz Beach
Mount Luho Lookout
Lapuz Lapuz
Diniwid Beach
Diniwid
Horse Riding Stables
SEE MAIN MAP FOR DETAIL
Balabog
Balabag
Funboard Center Hangin Kiteboard
Willy's Rock
BOAT STATION 1
Balabog Beach
White Beach
Boracay Rock
SULU SEA
BOAT STATION 2
SIBUYAN SEA
BOAT STATION 3
Ambulon
Tulubhan
Mandala Spa
Angol
Malabunot
Tambisaan Jetty Port
MAIN ROAD
Tambisaan
Crocodile Island
Manoc-Manoc
Manoc-Manoc Beach
Cagban Jetty Port
Cagban Beach
Tabon Strait
Panay
Caticlan Ferry Port
Caticlan Airport
N
ACCOMMODATION
Dave's Straw Hat Inn 6
Frendz 1
Melinda's Garden 4
Moreno's Cottages 3
Orchids 5
Spider House 7
White Beach Divers Hostel 2
EATING, DRINKING & NIGHTLIFE
Alchemy 3
Aria 8
Cocomangas 1
Cowboy Cocina 12
Cyma 7
Exit 5
Lemon i Café 7
Mañana 2
Nigi Nigi Nu Noos 11
Pat's Creek Bar 6
Real Coffee and Tea Café 9
Red Pirates 13
Tibraz 4
True Food 10

8

environmental fee. Tricycles meet all boats at Cagban Jetty Port to take you to your accommodation (P100 flat fee). Occasionally during bad weather boats set sail from Tabon and arrive at the eastern side of Boracay, at Tambisaan.

INFORMATION

Tourist information The Department of Tourism information office is in D'Mall (Mon–Fri 8am–5pm; Ⓣ036 288 3689, Ⓔdeptour6boracay@yahoo.com). The Boracay Tourist Center (daily 8am–11pm; Ⓣ036 288 3704, Ⓦtouristcenter.com.ph), about halfway along White Beach between stations 2 and 3, can help with currency and travellers' cheque exchange, long-distance phone calls, postal and internet facilities and all travel services.

GETTING AROUND

Tricycles Fares for the tricycles that run along the length of the Main Road are P10/person for a trip if you're willing to share the tricycle with others, which means it will pick up passengers along the way. For most foreigners, the flat rate for a private trip is P50/tricycle, not per person. Make sure you agree the fare in advance. Fares increase at night.

8

ACTIVITIES

DIVING

There are more than thirty dive shops on Boracay, so look out for packages and deals. You can expect to pay around $40/dive, with equipment. The following places on White Beach are well established and popular:

Calypso Diving School Station 3 Ⓣ036 288 3206, Ⓦcalypso-boracay.com.

DiveGurus Boracay Station 3 Ⓣ036 288 5486, Ⓦdivegurus.com.

Fisheye Divers Station 2 Ⓣ036 288 6090, Ⓦfisheyedivers.com.

Lapu Lapu Diving School Station 2 Ⓣ036 288 3302, Ⓦlapulapu.com.

Victory Divers Station 2 Ⓣ036 288 3209, Ⓦvictorydivers.com.

WATERSPORTS

White Beach is littered with agents trying to sell you watersports of every conceivable variety: jetskiing, banana boating, glass-bottom boat rides, parasailing, flyfishing and even mermaid swimming (yes, you read that right!) are on offer. One of the most popular trips is a day's island-hopping; P800/person buys a one-day boat trip including a mask and snorkel, barbecue lunch and drinks. For more skilled watersports pursuits arrange lessons through a specialist.

Allan B Fun Tours White Beach Ⓣ036 288 5577, Ⓔallan_b68@yahoo.com. With several booths dotted along White Beach path, this operator can help to arrange most activities.

Hangin Kiteboarding Balabog Beach Ⓣ036 288 3663, Ⓦkiteboardingboracay.com. Professional outfit offering kitesurfing lessons and rentals.

ACCOMMODATION

Prices are significantly higher and fluctuate more than in the rest of the Visayas; it's always worth negotiating for a discount, especially outside of high season or if you plan to stay a while. The following are the best of the ever-dwindling pool of budget options, but if you're really strapped and you don't mind being away from the beach, ask around on the main road about renting a private room.

Dave's Straw Hat Inn Station 3 Ⓣ036 288 5465, Ⓦdavesstrawhatinn.com. A cosy restaurant and pleasant rooms in a shady, private location have made this an enduring favourite, though they have an irritating reservation procedure which involves wiring the entire room charge in advance. **P1500**

★**Frendz** Midway between stations 1 and 2 Ⓣ036 288 3803, Ⓦfrendzresortboracay.com. Off the beach path in a great location in the centre of the island's nightlife. The comfy male and female dorms, beach beds for guests' use and buzzing common area make this a great choice for backpackers. There's an authentic 1960s Italian coffee machine for a post-partying caffeine boost. Bring a padlock for your locker. Dorm **P600**, double **P2000**

Melinda's Garden Station 3 Ⓣ036 288 3021 or Ⓣ0907 261 6703, Ⓦmelindasgarden.com. Lovely nipa-and-bamboo cottages in a garden area off the beach path, all with a private porch and your own wicker hammock. **P1600**

Moreno's Cottages At the southern end of the beach a little before *Dave's Straw Hat Inn* Ⓣ036 288 2031 or Ⓣ0939 118 9616, Ⓔboracayjojo29@yahoo.com. A friendly, local option with small, simple fan and a/c rooms set around a pleasant garden, just a 2min walk from a lovely section of White Beach. Free wi-fi. **P1000**

Orchids Station 3 Ⓣ036 288 3313 or Ⓣ0917 242 0833, Ⓦorchidsboracay.com. Staff are not the friendliest, but the large rooms in the two-storey indigenous building all have hot water and there's paid wi-fi (P50/day). **P915**

Spider House Diniwid Ⓣ0918 557 4874, Ⓦspiderhouseresort.com. A 10min walk north of Station 1, this is the most unique (and romantic) budget choice on the island. Some of the meandering series of rooms built into the cliff have only two walls, leaving them open to fresh breezes and stunning seascapes. Perfect for those who value their privacy. **P2400**

White Beach Divers Hostel Station 3 Ⓣ036 288 3809, Ⓦwhitebeachdivers.com. It doesn't get any cheaper than this on White Beach – pleasant, indigenous rooms with TV and fan. There's a bar and restaurant, plus free wi-fi. Outstanding value. **P600**

EATING

Restaurants and bars come and go in Boracay, but the best ones stand the test of time. Choices are so extensive and diverse that you can eat and drink your way up and down White Beach almost 24 hours a day. For a more traditional experience head to D'Talipapa Market where you can buy fresh fish and seafood and get one of the restaurants to prepare it (from P120).

Alchemy North of D'Mall. New-world cuisine at a welcoming restaurant serving dishes prepared with local produce. The emphasis is on flavour and presentation, but the service is hit and miss. Mains from P270. Daily 8am–11pm.

Aria Station 2. Decent pizzas at this popular D'Mall place which fronts the beach. Great affiliated *gelateria* next door, too. Daily 11am–midnight.

Cowboy Cocina Station 3. Great place for some good old comfort food, with Sunday roasts (P370), fish and chips (P320), gammon steak (P350), bangers and mash (P290) and good pizzas. Pub quiz every Monday. Daily 7am–10.30pm.

Cyma D'Mall. *Cyma's* Boracay branch is smaller and more initimate than in other locations, but the food is every bit as tasty and authentic. Try the *saganaki* (flamed cheese; P225), chicken *souvlaki* (P365) or *horiatiki* (Greek salad; P265) and save some room for the desserts which include baklava (P200). It's very popular and there's limited seating so reserve a table during peak periods. Daily 10am–11pm.

★ **Lemon i Café** D'Mall. Mellow decor creates a soothing ambience at this café-cum-restaurant which continues to turn out some of Boracay's best food. The pan-fried mahi mahi is a stand-out, as are many of the lemon desserts (P60–180) and cocktails. Free wi-fi. Daily 7am–11pm.

Mañana Northern end of Station 2. Colourful interior with sombreros and bright tablecloths at this Mexican place serving good fajitas (P363) and exquisite margharitas (P155). Daily 10am–10pm.

★ **Real Coffee and Tea Café** Station 1. *Real Coffee* has moved back to the heart of the action, a stone's throw from D'Mall, yet its second-floor location overlooking the beach is somehow removed from the hubbub. The bamboo interior harks back to a simpler time when this was the first "real" coffee (P80–160) on the beach. Good breakfasts (P175–350), as well as a great selection of teas (punchy ginger tea, P90) and cookies (P25). Daily 7am–7pm.

Tibraz North of D'Mall. Great French café-cum-bar serving tasty panini (P225–290), croque monsieur (P225) and madame (P240), and fantastic cocktails. Daily 7am–11.30pm.

True Food South of D'Mall. Sit back on puffy yellow cushions and tuck into some of the island's best Indian food – the mouthwatering curries are big enough for two (P300–400) and there are plenty of meat-free options to keep vegetarians happy (P225). Daily noon–10.30pm.

DRINKING AND NIGHTLIFE

Nightlife on Boracay starts with drinks at sunset and carries on well into the following morning. You'll find everything from swanky resort bars and chilled-out beach shacks to downright raucous dives.

Cocomangas Raucous bar on the main road behind *Guilly's Island*, Station 1. Infamous for drinking games involving potent cocktails, it gets rowdier as the night wears on. P100 cover charge on Saturdays. Daily 7pm–3am.

Exit Station 2. Little expat bar on the beach, attracting quite a crowd for its P50–100 drinks; a lively drinking hole to end the evening. There's a pool table too. Daily 4pm–2am.

Nigi Nigi Nu Noos Southern end of Station 2. Hang around at the bar and socialize pub-style at this enduringly popular hangout serving bar food. Happy hour 5–7pm. Daily 6am–1am.

★ **Pat's Creek Bar** Just north of D'Mall. At the very southern end of Station 3. A laidback bar with nightly live bands; it's mainly reggae, to be enjoyed with a chilled beer (P65) or a cocktail (P150) in hand. They share bands with *Bom Bom* next door. Happy hour 5–8pm. Shisha pipes, too. Daily 5pm–2am.

★ **Red Pirates** At the southern end of the beach. Enjoy the beats and the sounds of the sea at this chilled-out place with little beach tables in leafy surroundings. Cheap cocktails (P100) and happy hour 4–7pm. Daily 10am–4am.

DIRECTORY

Banks and exchange Allied Bank on the main road near the access path to the Tourist Center changes travellers' cheques, and has an ATM. Many resorts also change money. In D'Mall, there's a small branch of BPI with an ATM. Credit cards are widely accepted.

Hospitals and clinics The main facility is the Boracay Island Hospital, Main Rd (☎ 036 288 3041). Metropolitan Doctors Medical Clinic is also on Main Rd (☎ 036 288 6357) and is open 24hr. In the event of serious injury, treatment in Kalibo is recommended.

Internet There are dozens of internet cafés on Boracay, most with fast connections (around P70/hr) – such as the Boracay Tourist Center. Plenty of hotels and restaurants offer wi-fi.

Laundry Pretty Lavandera, Station 3 (daily 9am–7pm; P60/kg).

Pharmacies There are pharmacies selling most necessities in D'Mall, Boracay Tourist Center and D'Talipapa Market.

Police The Philippine National Police (☎ 036 288 3066) are immediately behind the Tourism Information Office in D'Mall.

Post office The post office in Balabag, the small community halfway along White Beach, is open Mon–Fri 8am–5pm. The Boracay Tourist Center on White Beach has full postal services although they charge a small surcharge.

8

Shopping Dozens of small *sari-sari* stores line White Beach selling the usual range of drinks and snacks, plus beachwear, T-shirts and souvenirs, while at D'Talipapa Market you can buy fruit and fish. D'Mall has an ever-expanding range of shops selling clothes, souvenirs and handicrafts. Boracay Budget Mart at the back of D'Mall is an inexpensive supermarket (by Boracay standards); Heidiland deli in D'Mall is another good, if expensive, option for self-caterers.

Mindanao

The signals **Mindanao** sends to the rest of the Philippines and the wider world are nothing if not mixed. This massive island at the foot of the archipelago is a place where tribalism and capitalism clash head on, and a refuge for those fleeing Manila in search of cleaner air and greener pastures. All of this has led to something of a cultural and economic boom in cities such as **Davao**, Mindanao's de facto capital and gateway to the southern half of the region, but Mindanao is also a troubled island, with various indigenous Islamic groups agitating, sometimes violently, for autonomy (see box below). Following renewed tensions and violence in 2013, at the time of writing the entire island was considered unsafe for visitors and all travel to the area is strongly advised against. However, the situation may change and visiting this area may be possible at the time of reading. Pay attention to the news and seek local advice before considering a trip to Mindanao. For this edition we have focused on the islands of **Camiguin** and **Siargao** and provided information on **Cagayan de Oro** as a transit hub.

8

CAGAYAN DE ORO

CAGAYAN DE ORO (CDO) on the north coast of Mindanao is the starting point for many travellers for a trip to dazzling Camiguin Island. The only reason to linger in CDO is to go **whitewater rafting**. Rafting Adventure Philippines on Hayes Street (T 088 856 3514, W raftingadventurephilippines.com) can organize everything from beginners' courses to night rafting trips.

ARRIVAL AND DEPARTURE

By plane The new Laguindingan International Airport, 46km southwest of the city, finally opened in June 2013, but has been plagued by problems, with many cancellations, in part due to the absence of landing lights. The airport is accessible by jeepney (P40 to Laguindingan turn-off, then P20 shuttle to the airport), shuttle vans (Magnum Express leave from Magnum Radio in CM Recto hourly from 4am to 3pm for P199) or taxi (P1200).

Destinations Air Asia, Cebu Pacific and PAL fly to Cebu City (5 daily; 50min); Davao (daily; 1hr); and Manila (15 daily; 1hr 30min).

THE MINDANAO PROBLEM

Mindanao has been a nagging thorn in the side of successive governments, with repeated attempts by the island's Muslims (*Moros*) to establish autonomy on the island, while the indigenous Lumad peoples also assert rights to their traditional lands. The Communist New People's Army (NPA) has also been resurgent in recent years.

The **Moro National Liberation Front** (MNLF) started a war for independence in the 1970s. Meanwhile, a communist-led rebellion spread from the northern Philippines to Mindanao, drawing in many Filipinos. In 1996 the MNLF were recognized by Manila, when they co-signed a peace pact granting a certain degree of autonomy to four provinces. This led to the formation of several splinter groups including the MILF and **Abu Sayyaf** ("Bearer of the Sword"), whose centre of operations is largely Basilan Island, part of the Sulu archipelago off Mindanao's southern coast. Abu Sayyaf is widely believed to have ties to al-Qaeda and to have been responsible for the Philippines' deadliest terrorist attack, the bombing of the WG&A *Superferry 14* in February 2004, which claimed 116 lives. Since the **Maguindanao massacre** (see p.588) of November 2009, which led to the president declaring a state of emergency, numerous ceasefires have come and gone, but at the time of writing the whole province was on high alert following a spate of bombings in Cagayan de Oro and Cotabato City, and the month-long separatist occupation of Zamboanga city.

By bus There are two major integrated bus terminals in the city, eastbound and westbound. A jeepney ride to either of these from the town centre is P10–12, or you can take a taxi for around P50.

Destinations Butuan (for Surigao; every 45min until 5pm; 4hr); Davao (every 30min; 8hr). The Butuan buses also pass through Balingoan (1hr 30min), the departure point for Camiguin.

By ferry Macabalan Wharf is 5km north of the centre, with regular jeepneys back and forth. 2GO runs the majority of services from CDO, with a few routes also served by Transa Asia.

Destinations Bacolod (weekly; 21hr); Cebu City (3 weekly; 8hr); Dumaguete (weekly; 7hr); Iloilo (3 weekly; 14hr) Manila (weekly; 32hr); and Tagbilaran (3 weekly; 8hr).

INFORMATION

Tourist office The regional tourist office (Mon–Fri 8.30am–5.30pm; ⓣ 088 856 4048, ⓔ dotr10_nm@yahoo.com) is in the Pelaez Sports Centre on Velez St, a short walk north of the city centre. The detailed website ⓦ cdoguide.com is also helpful.

Amenities Besides a supermarket and the usual stores, the Limketkai mall (ⓦ limketkaicenter.com) is home to several banks, internet cafés and a cinema.

ACCOMMODATION

★**Budgetel** Coralles Extension St ⓣ 088 856 4200 or ⓣ 0917 794 1010, ⓔ thebudgetel@gmail.com. Gleaming modern backpacker facility with 34 rooms and several dorms, all with a/c. Dorms have clean communal bathrooms with hot water, while the private rooms also have flat-screen cable TV. Close to the wharf, the bus station and Gaisano mall. Free wi-fi in the restaurant. Dorm **P250**, double (with breakfast included) **P900**

Hotel Ramon Burgos St ⓣ 088 857 4804. The cheapest rooms have private bathrooms, a/c and TV, but it's worth paying extra for a garden or river view (P900). Free in-room wi-fi. **P700**

Loft Inn Velez cnr. J.R. Borja streets ⓣ 088 2274 5010. All rooms here have a/c, TVs, clean bathrooms and free wi-fi. Look at a couple before you decide. **P600**

EATING, DRINKING AND NIGHTLIFE

The centre of the action in town is around where Velez crosses Hayes and Chavez streets. A couple of kilometres east, the Limketkai mall has a good mix of restaurants, the most bustling area being the Rosario Arcade outside the main entrance. Catch a jeepney here from Velez St.

Bigby's Café Rosario Arcade, Limketkai mall. Bright, deli-type place serving great coffee (P75) and light lunches P200–300. Free wi-fi. Daily 11am–10pm, Fri & Sat until midnight.

BrewBerry Café Velez cnr. T. Chavez streets. Filipino favourites including *adobo*, plus grills, sizzlers, sandwiches and pastas mostly under P150, as well as real coffee and free wi-fi. Mon–Sat 7am–10pm, Sun noon–8pm.

Club Mojo Hayes St. The main nightspot in the area, which has regular live bands and gets going late. *Ralf's Bar*, upstairs, has pool tables. Tues–Sun 9pm–2am.

★**Divisoria Market** Golden Friendship Park. The best place to hang out on weekend evenings, with buzzing outdoor food stalls, cheap beer, live music and communal tables. Fri & Sat nights 6pm–2am.

CAMIGUIN ISLAND

Sitting about 90km north of Cagayan de Oro, the pear-shaped volcanic island of **Camiguin** is one of the country's little gems, offering ivory beaches, iridescent lagoons and undulating scenery. It's a peaceful, almost spiritual island, where people are proud of their faith, though there's no shortage of adventure either, with reasonable scuba diving and tremendous trekking and climbing in the rugged interior, especially on volcanic **Mount Hibok-Hibok**. Camiguin is home to six other volcanoes, a multitude of hot springs, a carbonated spring, and a submerged cemetery for divers to explore near the coastal town of **Bonbon**. Another major draw is the hugely welcoming **Lanzones Festival**, held in the third week of October when everyone stomps and dances in the streets as a tribute to this humble fruit, one of Camiguin's major sources of income.

Mambajao is the bustling little capital on the north coast of Camiguin, 17km north of the port at Benoni.

It doesn't really matter where you stay on the island because you can reach all the sights from anywhere. The **coastal road** is almost 70km long, making it feasible to circle the island in a day, most easily on a motorbike, which are widely available to rent. Jeepneys and trikes also pass frequently along the coastal road in both directions. Most resorts can arrange climbing, trekking, diving and other adventurous excursions, but there are also two good operators in Mambajao, **FunTrips** (ⓣ 0917 702 2278, ⓦ funtripstravelandtours.com) on Rizal Street, and **Wow Camiguin** (ⓣ 088 310 0698, ⓦ wowcamiguintandt.blogspot.com), both of which can also organize ferry and air tickets.

ARRIVAL AND DEPARTURE

By plane Cebu Pacific fly from to and from Cebu (daily; 50min).

By ferry Ferries depart roughly hourly between 5am–6pm (1hr) from Balingoan, about 80km northeast, for Benoni on Camiguin's southeast coast. From here, jeepneys run frequently to and from Mambajao. Transport rates to everywhere on the island are fixed by the tourist office and displayed on a board at the pier in Benoni.

INFORMATION

Tourist information The tourist office (Mon–Fri 8am–5pm; ⊤ 088 387 1097, Ⓔ camiguin.tourism@gmail.com) is in the Provincial Capitol building a short tricycle ride from the centre of Mambajao.

Amenities In Mambajao there's a branch of PNB, an ATM, a couple of internet cafés and a cluster of cheap places to eat around the market area.

ACCOMMODATION, EATING AND DRINKING

8

Most of the best beach accommodation is west of Mambajao between the *barangays* of Bug-ong and Yumbing, though the beach itself is coarse dark sand. This stretch also gives quickest access to White Island, a dazzling serpentine ribbon of sand that makes a fun, early morning boat excursion (since there's no shade on the island it can be too hot later in the day). All of the listings below, except *GV*, have their own restaurants.

★**Camiguin Action Geckos** Bug-ong ⊤ 088 387 9146, Ⓦ camiguin.ph. Welcoming, well-run resort on a spectacular stretch of beach, and one of the best places on the island to organize activities. Free wi-fi. Fan rooms **P900**

Enigmata 2km inland, east of Mambajao ⊤ 088 387 0273 or ⊤ 0918 230 4184, Ⓦ camiguinecolodge.com. This place is something different: an eco-lodge built around a giant acacia tree in the middle of a sculpture garden, and managed by an artists' collective. There's also a great restaurant serving budget meals. Hippy heaven, if you don't mind being inland. Dorm **P250**, double **P1050**

GV Hotel Burgos St, Mambajao ⊤ 088 387 1041. Located in the town itself, *GV* has fan and a/c rooms (P580) with bathrooms and TVs. **P330**

Jasmin by the Sea Bug-ong ⊤ 088 387 9015, Ⓔ melindawidmer@yahoo.com. The basic rooms are excellent value, though there's not much beach here. *Jasmin* offers motorbike rental (P300/day) and excursions (White Island, P500) at a cheaper rate than many of the other resorts. **P800**

SURIGAO

The busy capital of the province of Surigao del Norte, **SURIGAO** provides nothing more than a jumping-off point for the picture-postcard island of **Siargao**. It's a compact place and easy to negotiate on foot: the main street, Rizal, runs from north to south; at the northern end is the central plaza, where you'll find a couple of banks with ATMs and a handful of fast-food restaurants. The *Leomondee Hotel* (Borromeo St; ⊤ 086 232 7334; P650), a block inland from the sea, is a good place to try if you get stuck here, with small but decent air-conditioned rooms and free wi-fi. The city tourism office (Mon–Fri 8am–5pm; ⊤ 086 826 8064, Ⓔ tourism_surigaocity@yahoo.com) is at the southern end of Rizal Street at the Luneta Park, where you can get the latest information about transport to Siargao.

ARRIVAL AND DEPARTURE

By plane The airport is 5km out of town. There are daily flights to Cebu (2 daily; 55min) with Cebu Pacific and to Manila with PAL Express (1hr 40min).

By bus The bus terminal is 4km west of the city, where there's a helpful traveller's lodge with timetables (⊤ 086 826 3488). Buses run hourly between 6am and 10pm to Butuan (3hr) where you can connect to Cagayan de Oro or Balingoan (for Camiguin). There are also frequent a/c minibuses until 7pm, which make fewer stops.

By ferry The wharf is at the southern edge of Navarro Street; take a tricycle from here to the city centre. There are daily ferries (4hr) between Surigao and Dapa on Siargao, as well as daily fast crafts (2hr 30min).

SIARGAO

Off the northeastern tip of Mindanao lies the teardrop-shaped and largely undeveloped island of **Siargao**, with its secluded white-sand beaches and dramatic coves and lagoons. Siargao has got everything, with a typically tropical coastal landscape of palm trees and dazzling seas, and a lush hinterland of small *barangays* and coconut groves. Some of the first tourists here were **surfers**, who discovered a break at Tuason Point that was so good they called it Cloud 9. Over the years, word of mouth brought an increasing number of surfers from around the world, and today it's the centre of surfing in the Philippines. There's a handful of seaside resorts around the island's friendly little capital of **GENERAL LUNA**, known as GL,

ON CLOUD 9

The Philippines is not a destination at the forefront of most surfers' minds, although enthusiasts have been riding waves here since the 1960s. Thanks to its location on the Pacific typhoon belt, the country is home to some of the world's greatest swells. The acclaimed reef break **Cloud 9**, with its famed hollow barrel, gained fame in the late 1980s and is today considered one of the world's top surfing waves. It is the site of the annual **Siargao Cup**, a domestic and international surfing competition that draws crowds of avid followers from all over the globe. The east coast is blessed with some of the country's best surf, with a number of destinations still rarely accessed because of their remote location. Among the country's other popular surfing destinations is San Juan in Northern Luzon, a laidback surfing village with some good reef breaks on the South China Sea.

which feels more like a village, being little more than a couple of streets with some *sari-sari* stores. For **surfers**, the area to stay is by the Cloud 9 break (see box above), less than 2km north of GL.

WHAT TO SEE AND DO

Kayaking is a great way to explore, paddling through mangrove swamps or into hidden coral bays (P250–400/hr). You can also hire a bangka to do some serious **island-hopping**, or rent a motorbike for the day and tootle up the dusty coastal road to Alegria and Burgos at the island's northernmost tip, visiting beaches that few travellers see. Don't miss a trip out to Dako and Naked islands (access is easiest from GL), both with superb snorkelling. *Patrick's* (see below) is the best place to organize things, or just ask around.

Surfing remains the main draw, however; you can rent equipment (board rental P750–1000/day) from the resorts, and lessons cost about P400 an hour. The annual **surfing cup**, held every year in late September or early October, has risen in profile over the past few years and attracts competitors from Australia, the US and Europe, as well as from around the Philippines.

ARRIVAL AND DEPARTURE

By plane Cebu Pacific flies between Siargao and Cebu (daily; 1hr).

By ferry There are daily ferries (4hr) between Surigao and Dapa, as well as daily fast crafts (2hr 30min).

GETTING AROUND

There are sporadic jeepneys between Dapa and GL, but you're much better off getting a ride on a *habal-habal* (motorbike taxi; P100) or arranging pier/airport pick-up through your accommodation (P200–300). The bumpy roads here mean motorbikes are the best way of getting around, and they're widely available for rent (P500/day).

ACCOMMODATION, EATING AND DRINKING

Room prices increase exponentially during the surfing competitions; ask about long-term discounts. The best places to hang out at night are *Nine Bar* in GL and *Bar 101* at Cloud 9, both full of laidback surf dudes talking about the day's swells.

Kesa Cloud 9 Resort T 0921 281 2960, W cloud9philippines.com. A decent budget option overlooking the Cloud 9 break, though you're better off going down the road to *101* to arrange surfing. The restaurant has views over the lagoon and specializes in fresh seafood dishes. Sometimes closed for a few weeks in Dec and Jan so phone ahead. A/c rooms (P1500) have their own bathroom, while fan rooms have shared bathrooms. **P500**

Ocean 101 T 0919 826 8837, W ocean101cloud9.com. Catering to surfers, with a wide range of accommodation from smaller rooms with communal bathrooms at the back of the resort to a/c doubles with sea views and private bathrooms (P2000). There's a good restaurant serving international and local dishes and they accept credit cards. **P750**

★ **Patrick's on the Beach** T 0918 481 6483, W patrickonthebeach.com. This is the centre of the action in GL, with comfortable beach hut accommodation, right on a lovely swimming beach. Helpful staff can arrange everything from travel and tours to surfing and island excursions. There's a sister resort at Cloud 9 itself, open seasonally. A bit steep if you're on a tight budget, although there's tent accommodation for P400–800 (depending on size). The restaurant offers dishes from fifteen different countries. Free wi-fi. **P1500**

DIRECTORY

Banks and exchange There is an ATM in Dapa and several places accept credit cards; *Patrick's* (see above) will advance cash.

Internet access There's internet access in Dapa, GL and Cloud 9 (P30/hr); wi-fi is also increasingly common.

8

Palawan

If you believe the travel agent clichés, **Palawan** is the Philippines' last frontier. For once, it's almost true. Tourism is making inroads into this long, sword-shaped island to the southwest of Luzon, and travellers willing to take the rough with the smooth will find a Jurassic landscape of coves, beaches, lagoons and razor-sharp limestone cliffs that rise from crystal-clear water. Palawan province encompasses 1780 islands and islets, many of which are surrounded by a coral shelf that acts as an enormous feeding ground and nursery for marine life. It is sometimes said that Palawan's **Tubbataha Reef** is so ecologically important that if it dies, the Philippines will perish too. If you're looking for varied and challenging diving, you won't find better anywhere in the world, but there's also plenty to keep non-divers happy.

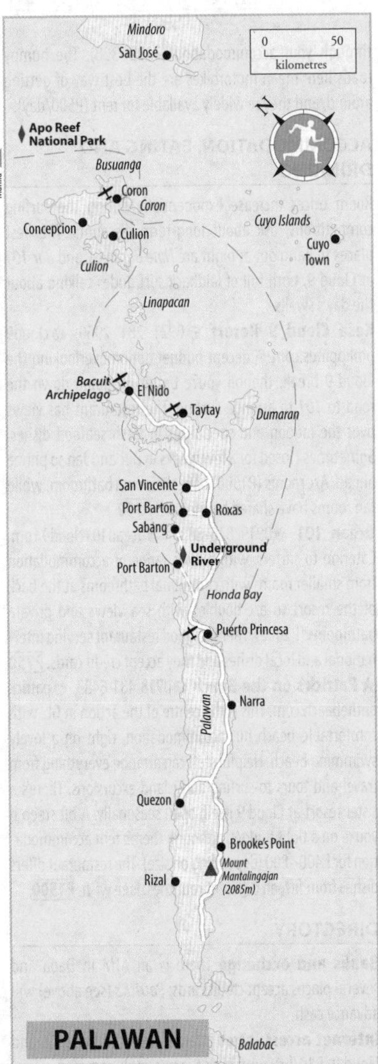

The capital and main gateway, **Puerto Princesa**, makes a good starting point for exploring the northern half of the island, which is where all the tourist attractions are. A typical journey through Palawan might take you from Puerto Princesa, north to **Honda Bay** and the **Underground River at Sabang**, then onwards up the coast to **Port Barton**, and **El Nido**, before heading across to **Busuanga** and the rest of the Calamian Islands. The southern half of Palawan, from Puerto Princesa downwards, is relatively unexplored, one reason being that during the wet season the southern roads become almost impassable.

PUERTO PRINCESA

Most visitors treat **PUERTO PRINCESA**, the provincial capital and only major town in Palawan, as a one-night stop on the way to the beaches, islands and coral reefs of the north. It does, however, have a handful of exceptionally good **restaurants**, and is the administrative centre of the island – stock up on cash and arrange Underground River permits while you're here. It also prides itself on being clean and green, with enforced fines for littering.

ARRIVAL AND DEPARTURE

By plane The airport is at the eastern end of Rizal Ave, the main drag, within walking distance of most accommodation. Though there are always tricycles waiting (P50), it's cheaper to flag one down on the road outside.

Destinations Air Asia, Cebu Pacific and PAL Express fly to Manila (11 daily; 1hr 20min). Air Asia and Cebu Pacific also fly to Cebu (2 daily; 1hr 10min).

By bus, van and jeepney Buses, vans and jeepneys depart from the San José terminal 7km north of the centre. A multi-cab to the centre of town will set you back P15, a

tricycle P120. Departures to all points north are most frequent in the early mornings; the times here are guidelines only. Vans are typically 25 percent quicker than buses, but are correspondingly more expensive, and often less comfortable. Daytripper Palawan (T 0917 848 8755, W daytripperpalawan.com) is a notable exception, and is well worth the extra money. They have one daily service from Puerto Princesa to El Nido in each direction at 9am (P900).

Destinations El Nido (10 daily, mornings; 6–8hr); Port Barton (daily at 9am; 3hr); Sabang (8 daily, 6.30am–3pm; 2hr 30min).

By ferry The pier is at the eastern end of Malvar St, a short walk to Rizal Ave.

Destinations 2GO operates a Puerto Princesa–Coron–Manila service (Sat midnight; 14hr to Coron, 30hr to Manila).

INFORMATION

Tourist information The tourist office (Mon–Fri 9am–5pm; T 048 433 2968, W visitpuertoprincesa.com) is in the Provincial Capitol Building on Rizal Ave. They also have information on the rest of Palawan. A good place to plug into the travellers' grapevine is the *Casa Linda Inn* (see below), where the staff are helpful. There is also a tourist office at the airport arrivals area (T 048 434 4211), which is open for inbound flights.

Tours Plenty of tour companies on Rizal Ave offer day-trips to Honda Bay (P1300); the standard rate for a day-trip to the Underground River is P1500/person.

ACCOMMODATION

★**Banwa Art House Pension** Liwanag cnr. Mendoza streets T 048 434 8963 or T 0912 797 5863, W banwa.com. A bohemian oasis set back from the road and decorated with local artwork and tapestry. Rooms are spick-and-span (no hot water though unless you take the most expensive room at P900) and the bamboo chill-out lounge area at the back is the perfect place to meet other backpackers. Free wi-fi. Dorm **P350**, double **P800**

Casa Linda Inn Behind *Badjao Inn*, down a narrow road off Rizal Ave T 048 433 2606, E casalindainn@gmail.com. The large rooms, all with private bath (and some with a/c P999), are arranged around a tranquil garden area with a few loungers; arching coconut trees provide some respite from the sun. The staff are helpful and there's wi-fi. **P650**

Lola Itang Roxas St T 048 433 2990 or T 0916 233 3652, W lolaitang.com. Located in a quiet downtown area near the port, the rooms here are all equipped with cable TV, private bathroom and a/c. Rates include breakfast and there's free wi-fi in the garden restaurant. **P1350**

★**Moana Hotel** Rizal Ave Ext T 048 434 4753, W moanahotelpalawan.com. The cosy fan rooms here come with beautiful parquet flooring and *amakan* (bamboo) ceilings which open onto an interior courtyard with a pool. There are also a/c rooms (P1250–1450). In fact the only downside is the rumbling planes overhead, although there's free airport pick-up for those not willing to walk the 200m to the terminal! They offer diving packages and rent snorkelling equipment too. Free wi-fi. **P1000**

EATING, DRINKING AND NIGHTLIFE

Catabom Rizal Ave. Laidback vibe at this boho bar which is sister to *Bom Bom* on Boracay. There's a chill-out lounge upstairs with cushions and coconut-leaf mats, live acoustic reggae nightly and bands on Wed, Fri & Sat. Happy hour 5–8pm. Daily 5pm–2am.

Ima's Gulay Bar 46 Fernandez Street. Ima rustles up tasty dishes in the little kitchen at the back of this healthy vegetarian place with vegan options. The tofu and broccoli with sweet and sour sauce is a bestseller (P90); healthy shakes (P60), too. Sun–Thurs 11am–9pm, Fri 11am–3pm, Sat 6.30–9pm.

★**KaLui** 369 Rizal Ave. Almost opposite the entrance to *Casa Linda*, this atmospheric restaurant where everyone goes barefoot is one of the best in the city and is deservedly popular (reservations essential for dinner). Daily set meals (P435 for two) are built around either seafood or meat and come with salad, sweet potato fries and a small portion of fresh, raw seaweed, all topped off by a tropical fruit salad served in a coconut shell. Mon–Sat 11am–2pm & 6–11pm.

Kinabuch's Bar and Grill 348 Rizal Ave. Owned by a five-times national motocross champion, this restaurant/sports bar in a large garden has plenty of racing mementos on show. Tasty grills from tuna belly (P160) to spare ribs (P195); more adventurous types can settle for the spicy *Crocodile a la Bicol Express* (P345). Draught beers (P45), pool tables and a big screen. Daily 4pm–1am.

DIRECTORY

Banks All major banks are at the heart of Rizal Ave. Puerto Princesa is more or less the only place on the island with ATMs.

Internet There are plenty of cheap internet spots along Rizal Ave and Manalo Extension – try Czarwinx Internet (P13/hr) near the *Hibiscus Garden Inn* on Manalo Ext. *Itoy's Coffee House*, on Rizal Ave near the corner of Baltan St, also has internet access (Mon–Thurs & Sun 6am–11pm, Fri–Sat till midnight; P40/hr), wi-fi and good coffees.

Post office Burgos St cnr. Rizal Ave.

HONDA BAY

Beautiful **Honda Bay** sits 10km north of Puerto Princesa by road and makes a lovely relaxed day-trip of island-hopping and snorkelling. There are twelve islands in the bay, although only six are open to

8

visitors. Most tours (which can be arranged through any travel agent in Puerto for about P1300) will cover three, including **Snake Island**, which has a good reef for snorkelling, and is the only place with simple provisions. **Pandan Island** has the finest white sand, and, on **Bat Island** in the late afternoon, look out for the scores of bats that suddenly fly away on their nocturnal hunting trips.

If you want to go independently, catch a multi-cab (P25) from Rizal Avenue at the corner of Burgos Street to **Santa Lourdes wharf**. Sign in at the little tourist office and arrange a bangka (last departure at 2.30pm), which will cost P1300–1500. There's a P21 terminal fee and all islands, except Snake Island, ask visitors to pay a small fee (P25–50).

SABANG AND THE UNDERGROUND RIVER

The **Underground River**, or to give it its proper name, Puerto Princesa Subterranean River National Park, is another UNESCO World Heritage Site and top of the list of wonders for most visitors to central Palawan. One of the longest underground rivers in the world, it meanders for more than 8km through a bewildering array of caverns, chambers and pools passing stalactites, stalagmites, columns and thousands of bats. The formations are made even more eerie on your ride through by the shadows cast by the boatmen's lamp, though their somewhat inane running commentary detracts from the atmosphere.

Boat trips from Sabang wharf start daily from 8am and the last boat leaves at 3.30pm. Since the site was recognized as one of the "new Seven Wonders of Nature" in 2012 it has become more popular than ever and the daily quota of 900 visitors is reached every day during peak season. In order to help control visitor numbers you now have to arrange your permit (P250) in Puerto Princessa at least one day in advance of your visit. If you join an organized tour this will be done for you, but if not it's easy enough to arrange by visiting the park office in the City Coliseum in San Pedro, Puerto Princesa (☎048 723 0904). Even if you don't pre-organize a permit, local agents in Sabang (try Green Verde travel centre) can arrange for a visit up until 8pm the day before you want to go. The permit will specify the time you need to report to Sabang wharf for the twenty-minute bangka ride (P700 for up to six guests) to the cave. It's easiest to secure a permit for 8am–9am (before the day-trippers arrive), but even if you are issued a different time you can just turn up at the wharf with your permit, pay the P40 terminal fee, and they'll put you on the next boat with space.

Afterwards, if you're feeling energetic, you can hike back from the mouth of the river to **Sabang**, a 5km trip through lush scenery. When you arrive at the park, look out for the famous resident monitor lizards (*bayawak*), and monkeys. The wonders of the Underground River aside, Sabang has a beautiful stretch of beach and is becoming an increasingly popular beach resort in its own right. As well as sunbathing and swimming (pay attention to the flags, though, as currents can be strong), there's an 800m zipline at the far eastern end of the beach (plus another one 30 minutes away at Ugong Rock), ATV rides (P800/hr), mangrove boat trips (P200; 45min) and even jungle trekking (P500 per person). Ask at Green Verde travel centre (☎0926 230 9137) for more information. Or if this all sounds like too much, there are numerous massage shacks (P350/hr) dotted along the beach.

ARRIVAL AND DEPARTURE

Buses, vans and jeepneys make daily morning trips (2–3hr) from the San José terminal in Puerto to Sabang, the jumping-off point for the Underground River. The last departure from Sabang to Puerto is at 6pm (with Lexus vans), although the majority of services leave in the mornings. For El Nido, catch a jeepney to the junction at Salvacion (7am, 10am, noon and 2pm) from where you can change for El Nido services. You can expedite this connection by pre-purchasing a van seat through *Green Verde* travel centre, or Lexus vans.

Bangkas Unscheduled bangkas sometimes do the Sabang–Port Barton route (2hr 30min; P1200/person or P7200 for the whole boat), and might even continue on to El Nido (9hr) if there's demand – ask at the *Green Verde* travel centre.

ACCOMMODATION AND EATING

There are a growing number of places to stay on Sabang, most of which are aimed at backpackers. With the exception of the two upmarket resorts and *Green Verde*, all of the cheapies only have electricity from 6–11pm and cold-water showers.

Blue Bamboo A 10min walk west from the wharf ⊤0910 797 0038. Owned by a friendly local, Lorena, this place has cottages set up the hillside and is perfect for those looking to escape it all (if you don't mind not being on the beach). The budget backpacker rooms are very simple, but great value, while the family rooms (P1000) are some of the most luxurious in Sabang (aside from the resorts) and have great views over the bay. **P350**

★ **Green Verde** Towards the middle of the beach ⊤0910 978 4539. Small, clean and simple fan rooms with 24hr electricity and cold-water showers. The popular restaurant has the best budget meals on the strip, including decent breakfasts (P90–160) and tasty curries (P155). The helpful travel service is run by the owner's brother Miguel and can help with everything from Underground River permits to Port Barton boats. **P840**

Paregosan Cottages (formerly *Taraw Lodge* and that's still what the sign says) East of *Green Verde* ⊤0917 701 9034. Plain bamboo cottages with shared or private bathroom (P700) on a nice broad stretch of beach. **P500**

PORT BARTON AND AROUND

On the northwest coast of Palawan, roughly halfway between Puerto Princesa and El Nido, **Port Barton** has become something of a travellers' rest stop in recent years. There are several white-sand islands in the bay and Port Barton itself has a glorious stretch of beach that is home to half a dozen resorts. **Jeepneys** from Puerto Princesa arrive on Rizal Street, very close to the beach and the town centre. Internet access is available at *Greenviews Resort, Summer Homes* and *Jambalaya*, all along the beach, but is dependent on the town's electricity supply, which can be sporadic. About 15km north along a rough coastal road from Port Barton is the sleepy fishing village of **San Vicente**, which has a market and a pier where bangkas can be chartered to **Long Beach**, an undeveloped (for now) 14km stretch of stunning sand that ranks as one of the most extraordinary beaches in the country – you can see both ends only on a brilliantly clear day. The marvellous beaches around here make a fantastic day-trip from Port Barton. There's a tourist assistance centre (daily 8am–5pm) midway along the beach that can provide more local information.

ARRIVAL AND DEPARTURE

By jeepney Jeepneys leave by *Ayette's Bamboo House*. You can change at Roxas for El Nido. Roxas (daily 7.30am; 1hr); Nido; Puerto Princesa (daily 9am; 5hr).

ACCOMMODATION

Ayette's Bamboo House Rizal St ⊤0928 408 1551. Friendly place with a couple of budget rooms and nipa huts with private bathrooms set back from the beach; if they're full, the owner's mum can put you up at hers. Fantastic rates for single travellers (P200) and a great restaurant, too. **P500**

Greenviews Resort ⊤0929 268 5333, ⓦpalawandg.clara.net. The rooms here are set around a tranquil garden area with two little gazebos and a few hammocks; the cosy restaurant serves good Western and local food. There's free wi-fi and they accept credit cards. **P1700**

El Dorado Sunset Resort ⊤0920 329 9049, ⓦeldoradosunsetresort.webs.com. This beachfront place has two itty-bitty budget huts (P300) as well as a range of traditional nipa rooms with private bathrooms and funny egg-shaped toilet bowls. **P700**

EATING

Barton Bistro At the southern end of the beach. Serves an eclectic mix of comfort food from fish and chips (P250) to chilli con carne (P260); the little nursery with herbs and veggies provides the greens for the day. Daily 7am–midnight.

Jambalaya This welcoming café serves Cajun-style cooking halfway up the beach. The eponymous dish (P220), a Louisiana-style mix of spicy rice, fresh fish and veg, is a bestseller, and the Mega Mix Cornflakes (P250) go down a treat for early birds. Freshly baked bread, too. Daily 7am–9pm.

EL NIDO AND THE BACUIT ARCHIPELAGO

In the far northwest of Palawan is the small coastal town of **EL NIDO**, departure point for excursions to the innumerable islands of the **BACUIT ARCHIPELAGO**, undoubtedly one of the highlights of any trip to the Philippines. This is spectacular limestone-island country, with jaw-dropping formations rising from the sea everywhere you look. These iconic

karst cliffs with their fearsomely jagged rocky outcrops are believed to have been formed over sixty million years ago, emerging from the sea as a result of India colliding with mainland Asia. Weathering and erosion have produced deep crevices, caves, underground rivers and sinkholes in endlessly strange and wonderful permutations that were allegedly the inspiration for Alex Garland's novel *The Beach*. The result is one of the most beautiful island seascapes on earth.

El Nido itself is a laidback, backpacker-friendly place where electricity is sometimes only available from 2pm to 6am, but it's changing fast. Advance reservations are essential if you're on a budget, and especially at Christmas, New Year and Chinese New Year. Prices for all-day island-hopping bangka trips are set by the local government and now cost P1200–1400 per person depending on the islands visited, plus a P200 ecotourism development fee valid for ten days. There are numerous places offering trips; one of the best is the *El Nido Boutique and Artcafé*.

ARRIVAL AND DEPARTURE

By plane The town is a 6km tricycle ride (P200) from the airport. Island Transvoyager (ⓦ islandtransvoyager.com) flies between Manila and El Nido three times daily (1hr 15min), and tickets (P6750) can now be booked long in advance through Manila booking agents or the *El Nido Artcafé* (see below). There's a strict 10kg luggage allowance (including hand luggage), but excess baggage is available at P100/kg.

By bangka Daily morning bangkas to Coron leave at 8am and cost P1800 including lunch for the 7–8hr trip. Arrange your ticket at the *El Nido Boutique and Artcafé*.

By bus and van The bus and van "terminal" is in Corong Corong, a 10min walk or P20 tricycle ride from El Nido town. There's a local market here where you can stock up on supplies for your journey. There are regular (P294) and a/c (P465) buses to Puerto Princesa (via Taytay and Roxas) with Roro and Cherry (more comfortable), which take around eight hours. Faster and more expensive, but often more cramped vans (6hr; P700) also leave throughout the day. Palawan Daytripper (ⓣ 0917 848 8755, ⓦ daytripperpalawan.com; P900) is the comfortable alternative, although they currently only have one daily service at 9am. There are more bus and van services in the mornings and last trips leave at 10pm. For Port Barton change in Roxas, and for Sabang jump off at the Salvacion turn-off.

INFORMATION

Tourist information The Municipal Tourist Office (daily 8am–5pm; ⓣ 0917 841 7771, ⓦ elnidotourism.com) is near the church; they provide maps, info on the local area and accommodation. *El Nido Boutique and Artcafé* (ⓦ elnidoboutiqueandartcafe.com) on Calle Serena is a better resource for tourist information and you can make travel arrangements here.

ACCOMMODATION

The Alternative Calle Serona ⓣ 0917 595 5952, ⓔ beckycea@yahoo.com. The waves literally break under the rooms and the top-floor restaurant has original beanbag "nests" which you can sink into over some great vegetarian food. Free wi-fi. **P600**

La Banane ⓣ 0921 544 7868, ⓔ chelgravino@yahoo.com. Decent backpacker accommodation with two dorm rooms and a few doubles named after fruit. Once you settle into the beanbags on the beach you may never get up again. Free computer access and wi-fi too. Dorm **P350**, double **P800**

Relucio Pension ⓣ 0926 219 6640, ⓔ reluciopension@yahoo.com. Three tame dogs plod the premises of this welcoming family home with great-value rooms; there's a balcony upstairs to soak in the wonderful sea views. **P700**

★ **Spider Pension House** ⓣ 0917 541 2885 or ⓣ 0929 572 2887. A warm welcome from a very friendly family who will make you feel at home; ask for room one (P1000), which has incredible sea views. The *Spider* is affiliated with the popular Tuba Tours (ⓦ tuba-tours.com). Owner Trecel gives fantastic massages too. Dorm **P400**, double **P500**

EATING AND DRINKING

There's an increasing array of places to eat, serving everything from simple Pinoy classics to fresh seafood and a range of international cuisine.

Balay Tubay Real St. Great little joint for daily live music, with local bands hitting the stage at 7.30pm. Check out owner Bong's impressive drawings of those who have made a mark, from musicians to politicians. Happy hour 5–7pm. Daily 5pm–1am.

El Nido Boutique and Artcafé Calle Serena. A real travellers' hangout and popular for hearty breakfasts before an island-hopping trip, *El Nido* fills up again in the evening for the live music (every night except Tues) and cocktails. Meals (P200–400) are efficiently rustled up with vegetables from their farm 7km out of town. Free wi-fi. Daily 6.30am–11pm.

Lonesome Carabao Lounge Calle Hama. This homely American-owned Mexican café-bar is popular for its burritos, tacos and quesdillas (P250–290), plus its good tunes and hard-hitting cocktails. They also feature a few Middle Eastern dishes including *shakshouka* (P190). Free wi-fi. Daily 7.30am–10.30pm.

Marber's At the southern end of the beachfront. Head to this old favourite beachfront bar-restaurant with a pool table for the coldest beers (P50) in town. The food is home-made, with a strict no MSG policy; they do great burgers, schnitzels (P330) and veggie dishes. Mains P100–450. Daily 7.30am–10pm.

Pukka Bar In the middle of the beach. Next door to *Spider Pension House*. This reggae café is the perfect place to watch the sky turn pink over the astounding view; good meat and fish dishes (P180–350), though portions are on the small side. Daily 3pm–2am.

Sea Slugs At the southern end of the beachfront. Popular place with candlelit tables spilling onto the beach and a loyal crowd who come to see their favourite local band play nightly. Seafood dishes are the speciality here; try the chilli crab in coconut milk (P350). Free wi-fi. Daily 6am–midnight.

DIRECTORY

Banks El Nido's one and only bank doesn't accept international cards; make sure you bring plenty of cash. Some of the smarter resorts accept credit cards, or there is a Western Union near the church.

Internet There are plenty of internet places around town, though the connection only works when there's electricity (from 2pm); numerous cafés and resorts also have free wi-fi.

Police Calle Hama (daily 24hr; ☎ 0921 255 6368).

THE CALAMIAN ISLANDS

Access to the beautiful Calamian Islands, the largest of which is **Busuanga**, followed in size by **Culion** (where there's spectacular snorkelling) and **Coron**, is through the increasingly popular little fishing port of **CORON TOWN**, which, confusingly, is on Busuanga, not Coron.

The Calamian group was badly affected by Typhoon Yolanda, and though the landscapes and diving remain largely intact, many houses and buildings (including resorts) were damaged and electricity supply remains sketchy. All of the accommodation options listed in this book were at least partially open at the time of writing, and it is certainly still worth the long journey here to see the spectacular limestone cliffs of **Coron Island**, regardless of whether you also plan to dive the famous wrecks. Coron Island is twenty minutes by boat from Coron Town, and it's only when you get close to the cliffs in a kayak (P250 per day) or bangka that they reveal dozens of perfect little coves, hidden in the folds of the mountains. Tribes, including the Tagbanua, still live in the interior, where a short, steep climb takes you to the island's volcanic **Kayangan Lake**, a great place to swim and one of the area's favourite dive sites. You could spend a lifetime on Coron and still not get to see every hot spring, hidden lake or pristine cove.

Busuanga Island (Coron Town)

Coron Town is home to Busuanga's most backpacker-friendly resorts, and is the place to arrange bangkas for island trips (there's no beach in town). Apart from a couple of more expensive resorts dotted around the island, the rest of Busuanga is very rural, with limited electricity and, occasionally, patchy cell-phone coverage. For breathtaking views of the area climb the 722 steps up to Mount Tapyas in time for sunset, before heading to the 36°C **Maquinit Hot Springs** (daily 8am–8pm; P150), which were damaged by Typhoon Yolanda but are now open again. A fun way to explore the region is to rent a motorbike or hop on a bus from the market to take you west along the **south Busuanga coast** to the villages of Concepcion, Salvacion and Old Busuanga. The presence of several sunken Japanese World War II ships in the bays near Coron Town has made it a point of pilgrimage for **wreck divers**, and the rest of the Calamians have plenty to occupy island-hoppers and regular divers. Plenty of places in town offer island-hopping trips (P1500, depending on what you want to do), although *SeaDive* are the most reliable. They also offer scuba packages and more adventurous itineraries, including overnight safaris.

ARRIVAL AND DEPARTURE

By plane The airport is 30min by van/jeepney (P150) from Coron Town. All the airlines have offices in town, and there are also several travel agencies, including Calamian Islands Travel and Tours on Rosario St.

Destinations Cebu Pacific and PAL Express fly to Manila (3 daily; 1hr). Cebu Pacific also has a flight to Cebu (daily; 1hr 40min).

8

By bangka There is one daily scheduled bangka to El Nido (9am; 8hr; P1800 including lunch), bookable through any resort. *SeaDive Resort* is the arrival and departure point. This service is especially prone to timetable changes, and is weather dependent.

By ferry The 2GO Manila–Coron ferry service leaves Manila at 4pm on Fri, arriving in Coron at 6am on Sat morning; it departs one hour later for Puerto Princesa arriving at 9pm on Sat. On the way back, it leaves Puerto at midnight on Sat night/Sun morning, stopping off in Coron at 2pm on Sun, leaving at 3.30pm, and arrives in Manila at 5.30am on Mon morning.

ACCOMMODATION

In spite of damage from Typhoon Yolanda and ongoing repairs, all of the options below were at least partially open at the time of writing.

KokusNuss Resort T 0919 776 9544 or T 0919 448 7879, W kokosnuss.info. The first accommodation as you approach Coron Town from the airport, 1km before the town. Accommodation is set around a lovely garden area with hammocks and a small pool. Rooms range from basic with shared bath to privates with a/c, hot showers, mosquito nets and flatscreen TVs. Free wi-fi. Repair was under way at the time of writing and plans are for a concrete dorm room (P600) in place of the old nipa huts. **P1680**

Krystal Lodge T 0949 333 0429 or T 0926 723 1212, E pretty_kryz23@yahoo.com. A unique place, with traditional huts on stilts connected by a number of passages made of misshapen wooden planks and wonky bamboo sticks, which somehow seem to support the entire structure. *Krystal* was hit hard by Yolanda, and only a few rooms were operational at the time of writing. Free wi-fi. Dorm **P400**, double **P600**

SeaDive Resort T 0920 945 8714 or T 0918 400 0448, W seadiveresort.com. This five-star PADI resort right on the seafront offers budget accommodation with shared bath facilities (all with hot water), plus some en-suite fan rooms (P900), while some of the a/c rooms (P1300) have sea views (P1600). It also has a fantastically popular restaurant and is a reliable place from which to organize trips or rent kayaks (P250). Free wi-fi in bar and restaurant. **P450**

EATING AND DRINKING

The Bistro Don Pedro St. Easily the best restaurant in Coron; the appetizing smell of sizzling dishes wafts into the street. Mouthwatering fish and seafood dishes (from P145), and there's plenty for meat-lovers too (P170–470). Daily 8am–11pm.

Helldiver Bar inside *SeaDive Resort*. This lively bar with fascinating World War II memorabilia, such as a shot-down American plane propeller, offers the widest range of alcoholic drinks in town at great prices (beer P50). You can also order food from the restaurant at *Sea Dive*. Daily 4pm–midnight.

DIRECTORY

Banks BPI, Allied Bank and Landbank all have ATMs. There's also a Western Union on Real St. You can change US$ at Bonito Money Changer on Rizal Ave near the junction with Valencia St.

Internet XTE and SinTech are along National Highway, Barangay Poblacion 1 (both daily 8am–8pm; P25/hr); many hotels offer wi-fi.

GARDENS BY THE BAY

Singapore

HIGHLIGHTS

❶ **Ku dé ta, Marina Bay Sands** Soak in 360-degree city views as you sip a cocktail. **See p.675**

❷ **Chinatown** Traditional shophouses, fiery red temples and venerable restaurants. **See p.679**

❸ **Little India** Ornate temples, manic markets and fine restaurants. **See p.682**

❹ **Singapore night safari** Experience a close encounter with nocturnal primates at this incredible zoo. **See p.692**

❺ **Sentosa** A theme-park island with beaches and an historic fort. **See p.693**

HIGHLIGHTS ARE MARKED ON THE MAP ON P.669

ROUGH COSTS

Daily budget Basic US$70/Occasional treat US$95

Drink Tiger beer US$5/pint

Food Chicken rice US$5

Hostel/budget hotel US$20–40/US$90

Travel Bus and MRT: across whole island US$2.20; Taxi: airport to downtown US$30

FACT FILE

Population 5.3 million

Languages English, Malay, Mandarin and Tamil

Religions Buddhism, Islam, Christianity, Taoism, Hinduism

Currency Singapore dollar (S$)

International phone code ☎ + 65

Time zone GMT + 8hr

9

Introduction

Conveniently linked by a kilometre-long causeway to the southern tip of Malaysia, the vibrant city-state of Singapore makes a gentle gateway for many first-time travellers to Asia, providing Western standards of comfort alongside traditional Chinese, Malay and Indian enclaves. Its downtown areas are dense with towering skyscrapers and gleaming shopping malls, yet the island retains an abundance of nature reserves and lush, tropical greenery.

Singapore is a wealthy nation compared to the rest of Southeast Asia. Outsiders have traditionally bridled at the country's somewhat extreme regulations (neglecting to flush a public toilet carries a sizeable fine), but there are suggestions that the government is starting to loosen its grip on the population, and as Singapore begins to change, it has transformed into the social hub of Southeast Asia. The conscious effort to liberalize the island has led to a growing **arts scene** and a vibrant **nightlife.**

Although the city is a beacon of modernization, it is still possible to get lost in the diverse districts – **Chinatown, Little India** and the **Colonial District** – that make up the leafy island. Much of the country's appeal springs from its multicultural population: of the five million residents, 74 percent are Chinese (a figure reflected in the predominance of Chinese shops, restaurants and temples across the island), sixteen percent are Malay, and nine percent are Indian, while the remaining one percent comprise other ethnic groups.

WHEN TO GO

Singapore is just 136km north of the equator, which means that you should be prepared for a hot and sticky time whenever you go; **temperatures** hover around 30°C throughout the year. November, December and January are usually the coolest and wettest months, but rain can fall all year round. July usually records the lowest annual rainfall.

CHRONOLOGY

Third century AD The earliest known mention of Singapore is a Chinese reference to Pu-luo-chung, or "island at the end of a peninsula".

Eleventh century The tiny island is known as "Singa Pura" (Lion City) – according to legend because a prince mistook a local animal for a lion.

Late thirteenth century Marco Polo reports seeing a place called Chiamassie, possibly Singapore, which was known locally as Temasek – "sea town" – and was a minor trading outpost of the Sumatran Srivijaya Empire.

c.1390 A Sumatran prince, Paramesvara, flees to present-day Singapore, murders his host and rules the island until a Javanese offensive forces him to flee north to the Peninsula. He and his son, Iskandar Shah, found the Melaka Sultanate.

1613 A Portuguese account describes the razing of an unnamed Malay outpost at the mouth of Sungei Johor, an event that marks the beginning of two centuries of historical limbo for Singapore.

1819 Thomas Stamford Raffles, lieutenant-governor of Bencoolen (in Sumatra), arrives in Singapore to establish a British trading station.

1822 Raffles draws up the demarcation lines that divide present-day Singapore. South of the Singapore River is earmarked for the Chinese; the commercial district is established on a filled-in swamp at the mouth of the river; and Muslims settle around the Sultan's Palace in today's Arab Quarter.

1824 Singapore is ceded outright to the British, and the island's population reaches ten thousand as Malays, Chinese, Indians and Europeans arrive in search of work.

1826 The fledgling state unites with Penang and Melaka (now under British rule) to form the Straits Settlements.

1860 The population reaches eighty thousand. Arabs, Indians, Javanese and Bugis arrive, but most populous of all are the Chinese from the southern provinces of China.

1877 Henry Ridley introduces the rubber plant into Southeast Asia; Singapore becomes the world centre of rubber exporting, helped as British control of the Malay Peninsula expands, completed in 1913.

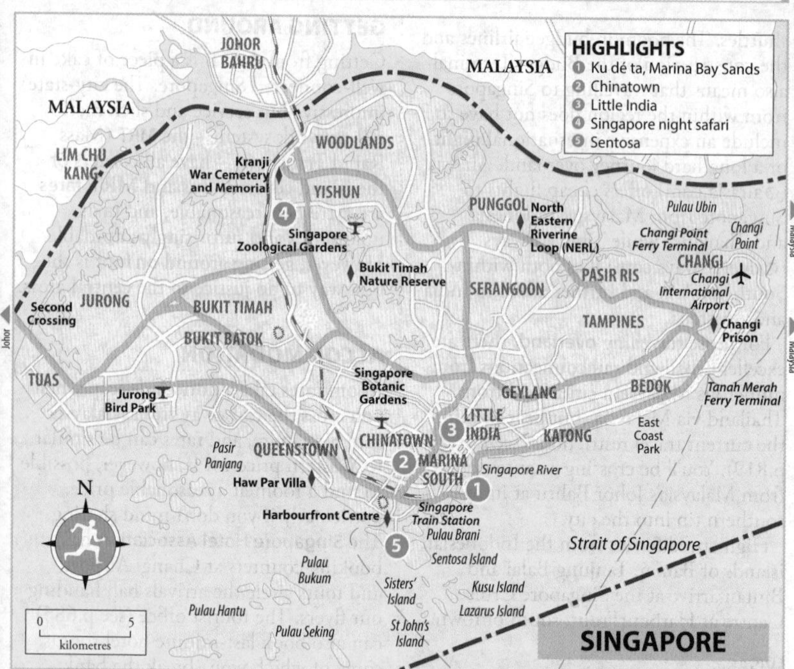

1887 The Armenian Sarkies brothers open the *Raffles Hotel*. It becomes the social hub of a booming and cosmopolitan Singapore.

1926 The pro-independence Singapore Malay Union is established, but grumblings of independence are no more than a faint whisper.

1942–45 Singapore is occupied by the Japanese during World War II. Thousands of civilians are executed in vicious anti-Chinese purges and Europeans are either herded into Changi Prison, or marched up the Peninsula to work on Thailand's infamous "Death Railway".

1945 Singapore returns to British control.

May 1959 The People's Action Party (PAP), led by Cambridge law graduate Lee Kuan Yew, wins 43 of the 51 seats for the new legislative assembly, which Britain had agreed to two years earlier. Lee becomes Singapore's first prime minister.

1963 Singapore, Malaya, Sarawak and British North Borneo (modern-day Sabah) form the Federation of Malaysia, but within two years Singapore falls out with Kuala Lumpur and leaves the federation.

August 9, 1965 Independence for Singapore, described by Lee Kuan Yew as "a moment of anguish".

1970s Under Lee, Singapore is transformed into an Asian economic heavyweight, but at a price: in an apparent trade-off between freedoms and economic efficiency, media is censored and political opponents suppressed.

1990 Lee retires and is succeeded as prime minister by Goh Chok Tong; Lee remains senior minister.

1997 The Asian economic crisis hits Singapore.

2004 Lee Hsien Loong, son of Lee Kuan Yew, becomes prime minister.

March 2008 Twelve people, including the leader of the opposition Singapore Democratic Party (SDP), Chee Soon Juan, are arrested for protesting outside parliament against fast-rising prices.

September 2008 Singapore hosts its first Formula One night-time Grand Prix.

February 2010 The city-state's first casino opens on Sentosa Island.

June 2013 Singapore calls for urgent action in Indonesia after forest fires envelop the state in a cloud of smoke.

ARRIVAL AND DEPARTURE

Singapore is one of the major gateways into Southeast Asia, serviced by 80 airlines from 59 different countries, including much of Europe, the US and Australia – all touching down at the impressive **Changi International Airport,** regularly voted the best in the world and connected to the city centre with frequent trains, buses and minibus

9

shuttles. The boom in budget airlines and the construction of the Budget Terminal also means that travelling to Singapore from within the region does not have to include an expensive international flight or a long hard journey over land. AirAsia (ⓦairasia.com) offers cheap flights to Singapore from Malaysia, Indonesia and Thailand, while Tiger Airways (ⓦtigerairways.com) flies both within Southeast Asia and further afield to India and Australia.

For those travelling **overland**, there are excellent road and rail connections from numerous Malaysian cities, and from Thailand via Malaysia (but bear in mind the current travel restrictions; see box, p.819). You'll be crossing a causeway from Malaysia's Johor Bahru at its southern tip into the city.

High-speed **ferries** from the Indonesian islands of Batam, Tanjung Balai and Bintan arrive at the Singapore Cruise Centre at HarbourFront, south of town.

VISAS

Citizens of Western Europe, the US and Commonwealth countries are automatically granted a visa upon arrival in Singapore by air. Arriving by land or sea, you will be given a **fourteen-day visa**; arriving by air, you will receive a **thirty-day visa**. Check with the "Visa Requirements" section of the Singapore Immigration and Registration Department (Mon–Fri 8am–5pm, Sat 8am–1pm; ⓣ6391 6100, ⓦica.gov.sg) for a list of nationals who need to obtain a visa before entering Singapore.

You can **extend your visa** online at the immigration department's website for up to three months, giving you an extra thirty days, though there are several restrictions to this, all listed on the website, which should be referred to before submitting an application. The Singapore immigration department is not particularly forgiving of transgressions. An alternative option is to take a bus up to **Johor Bahru**, the Malaysian border town, and return on the same bus – which can be completed in a morning (although bear in mind it's only a fourteen-day extension).

GETTING AROUND

Getting from A to B is a piece of cake in well-connected Singapore. The city-state's impressive bus service and slick metro rail network system – the **MRT** (Mass Rapid Transport) – have all corners of the island covered. Bus and MRT **fares** are extremely reasonable, and **taxis** ubiquitous and surprisingly affordable. However, getting around **on foot** is the best way to do justice to the central areas.

ACCOMMODATION

Room rates take a noticeable leap when you cross the causeway from Malaysia into Singapore, and rates can be similar to Western prices. It is, however, possible to find a room at a reasonable price, particularly if you don't mind sharing. The **Singapore Hotel Association** has booking counters at Changi Airport, and touts circle the arrivals hall handing out flyers. The tourist office (see p.685) can also book last-minute hotel rooms, some of which won't break the bank.

An increasing number of **hostels** are opening up in Singapore, catering for travellers in funky, stylish surroundings. Most offer a choice of dorm beds (from S$25) and doubles (from S$90) and have air conditioning, free wi-fi and internet, private lockers, laundry and cooking facilities, as well as free breakfast.

Decent guesthouses and more upmarket "flashpacker" hostels are opening all the time, meaning that budget travellers no longer need limit themselves to places with paper-thin walls and spartan rooms; expect to pay around S$45–55 per double. All over Singapore you'll find branches of **Hotel 81**, a predictable but well-equipped budget option, often near main attractions.

ADDRESSES

With so many of Singapore's shops, restaurants and offices located in vast high-rise buildings and shopping centres, deciphering **addresses** can sometimes be tricky; an address containing 10-08 refers to room 8 on the 10th floor (ground level is denoted #01).

In more modern, **mid-range hotels**, an en-suite room for two with air conditioning and TV will cost around S$90–140.

Electricity is supplied at 220 volts.

FOOD AND DRINK

Eating is one of the most profound pleasures that Singapore affords its visitors, and ranks alongside shopping as one of the two main national pastimes. An enormous number of food outlets cater for this obsession, and strict government regulations ensure that they are consistently hygienic. By far the cheapest and most fun place to dine is in a **hawker centre** or **food court**, where scores of stalls let you mix and match Asian dishes, fast-food style, at really low prices; it's possible to eat like a king for S$8. Otherwise, there's a whole range of **restaurants** to visit, ranging from no-frills, open-fronted eating-houses and coffee shops to swanky establishments serving any cuisine you can think of. Even in restaurants, you'll be hard-pressed to spend more than S$40–50 a head, including drinks, unless you opt for one of the island's more exclusive addresses.

All types of cuisine can be found here, from North and South Indian to Malay, Indonesian, Korean, Japanese and Vietnamese. Chinese restaurants are some of the most popular, which reflects the fact that three-quarters of the population is Chinese. The closest Singapore comes to an indigenous cuisine is **Nonya**, a hybrid of Chinese and Malay food developed by the Peranakan community, formed as a result of the intermarrying of nineteenth-century Chinese immigrants and Malay women. However, there are a few quintessentially Singaporean dishes to look out for, such as **chilli crab** (wok-fried crabs cooked in a chilli and tomato sauce) and **Hainanese chicken rice** (boiled chicken served on rice cooked with chicken stock). For other dishes, see "Food and drink" in the Malaysia chapter (see p.412).

Vegetarians need to tread carefully, as chicken and seafood will appear in a whole host of dishes unless you make it perfectly clear that you don't want them. The best bets for vegetarians are specialist Chinese and Indian restaurants, as well as international fusion ones; a few stalls at hawker centres serve **vegetarian food** too.

Most restaurants are open daily between 11.30am and 2.30pm and 6 to 10.30pm, though cheaper places tend to open longer hours. Tap **water** is drinkable throughout Singapore.

CULTURE AND ETIQUETTE

Singapore is a young and vibrant country and Singaporeans are easy-going, friendly and generally liberal in outlook. The state itself, however, is still synonymous with strict rules.

Sexual activity between men is illegal, though the authorities tend to turn a

CHINESE FOOD

The majority of the **Chinese** restaurants in Singapore are Cantonese, from Guangdong in southern China, though you'll also come across northern Beijing (or Peking) and western Szechuan cuisines, as well as the Hokkien specialities of the southeastern province of Fujian, and Teochew dishes from the area east of Canton. Whatever the region, it's undoubtedly the real thing – Chinese food as eaten by the Chinese – which means it won't always be particularly appealing to foreigners: the Chinese eat all parts of an animal, from its lips to its undercarriage, and dishes such as "frog porridge" may be an acquired taste.

Fish and seafood are nearly always outstanding, but for something a little more unusual, try a **steamboat**, a Chinese-style fondue filled with boiling stock in which you cook meat, fish, shellfish, eggs and vegetables; or a **claypot** – meat, fish or shellfish cooked over a fire in an earthenware pot. In many Cantonese restaurants (and in other regional restaurants, too), lunch consists of **dim sum** – steamed and fried dumplings served in little bamboo baskets.

9

blind eye to the gay scene. All citizens of Singapore are guaranteed housing, but the government enforces strict ethnic quotas per apartment building to prevent the forming of ethnic enclaves or ghettoes. Although undoubtedly authoritarian, this approach does mean that Singapore doesn't suffer from the ethnic tensions which plague Malaysia.

SPORTS AND OUTDOOR ACTIVITIES

Despite its urban reputation, Singapore is a great spot to enjoy the outdoors. Head down to the East Coast for some beachfront **cycling** or **rollerblading** (rental S$3–6/hr). Also situated on the East Coast is Singapore's first cable **ski park**, Ski360 (1206A East Coast Parkway; Ⓦ ski360degree.com), which offers an affordable way to have a go at **wakeboarding** or **waterskiing** (1hr from S$35), while being dragged by an overhead cable instead of a boat. Try to get down there midweek as the weekends tend to be crowded and more expensive. The Bukit Timah Nature Reserve offers several good **running routes**.

Singapore's recent boom has paved the way for several new international sporting events. In 2008, it became an addition to the **F1 Grand Prix** circuit, with events being held every September. The route weaves between the Central Business District and some of the country's major attractions. Other major events include the Barclays Golf Open (November) and the Singapore Airlines International Horse Riding Cup (May).

COMMUNICATIONS

Singapore's postal system is predictably efficient (even during Christmas), with letters and cards often reaching international destinations in as little as a week. There is an abundance of **post offices** across the state, with usual hours of Monday to Friday 8.30am to 5pm and Saturday 8.30am to 1pm, though postal services are available until 9pm at the Singapore Telecom Comcentre Complex, on Killiney Road.

SINGAPORE ONLINE

Ⓦ **timeout.com/sg** A great guide to the city's bars and clubs.
Ⓦ **yoursingapore.com** The official tourism website with general details on Singapore's major sights.

The easiest way to make **local calls** is to pick up an inexpensive SIM card for your mobile phone; SingTel, StarHub and M1 cards cost around S$10. Changi Airport has free courtesy phones.

International calls (IDD) can be made from all public cardphones, but the cheapest and easiest way is to use internet-based **Skype**. All accommodation options reviewed in this chapter offer **free wi-fi** and **internet**. Travellers can also enjoy limited free wi-fi in certain malls.

CRIME AND SAFETY

Singapore is the cleanest, safest city in Southeast Asia for travellers, including single women, though you shouldn't become complacent – muggings have been known to occur and theft from dormitories by other tourists is a common complaint.

It's with some irony that Singaporeans refer to the place as a "**fine city**". There's a fine of S$500 for smoking in public places such as cinemas, trains, lifts, air-conditioned restaurants and shopping malls, as well as eating or drinking on public transport, and one of S$50 for jaywalking – here defined as crossing a main road within 50m of a pedestrian crossing or bridge. It's worth bearing all these offences in mind, since foreigners are not exempt from the various Singaporean punishments. Contrary to rumour, chewing gum isn't illegal in Singapore, but you won't find it on sale. As in other Southeast Asian countries, the possession of **drugs** in Singapore – hard or soft – carries a hefty prison sentence

EMERGENCY NUMBERS

Police Ⓣ **999**
Ambulance and Fire Brigade Ⓣ **995**

and caning with a rattan cane. Trafficking is punishable by the death penalty. If you are caught smuggling drugs into or out of the country, at the very best you are facing a long stretch in a foreign prison; at worst, you could be hanged.

Singapore's **police**, who wear dark blue, are generally polite and helpful when approached.

MEDICAL CARE AND EMERGENCIES

Medical services in Singapore are some of the best in the world, with hospital staff almost everywhere speaking good English and offering modern services and facilities.

Pharmacies (daily 9am–6pm) are well stocked and pharmacists can recommend a range of treatments for minor problems. If you're in any doubt you should contact a local doctor.

Larger hotels have doctors on call at all times. Dentists are listed in the *Singapore Buying Guide* (equivalent to the *Yellow Pages*) under "Dental Surgeons", and "Dentist Emergency Service".

MONEY AND BANKS

The **currency** is Singapore dollars, usually written simply as $, though throughout the chapter we have used S$. The Singapore dollar is divided into 100 cents. Notes are issued in denominations of S$2, S$5, S$10, S$50, S$100, S$500, S$1000 and S$10,000; coins are in denominations of 5, 10, 20 and 50 cents, and S$1. At the time of writing, the exchange rate was around S$2.04 to £1 and S$1.25 to US$1.

Sterling or US-dollar **travellers' cheques** can be cashed at Singaporean banks, licensed moneychangers and some hotels. Major **credit cards** (preferably MasterCard and Visa over American Express) are widely accepted in shops and restaurants. There are also moneychangers in shopping centres and at hotels. No black market operates in Singapore, nor are there any restrictions on carrying currency in or out of the state. This means that rates at moneychangers are as good as you'll find at the banks.

OPENING HOURS AND PUBLIC HOLIDAYS

Shopping centres officially open daily from 10.30am to 9pm but opening times are far from set in stone. Banks open at least Monday to Friday 10am to 3pm, Saturday 9.30am to 1pm; while offices generally work Monday to Friday 8.30am to 5.30pm and sometimes on Saturday mornings. In general, Chinese temples open daily from 7am to around 6pm, Hindu temples from 6am to noon and 5 to 9pm, and mosques from 8.30am to noon and 2.30 to 4pm.

PUBLIC HOLIDAYS

January 1 New Year's Day
January/February Chinese New Year (two days)
March/April Good Friday
May 1 Labour Day
May Vesak Day
August 9 National Day
October/November Deepavali
November/December Hari Raya Puasa
December 25 Christmas Day
December/January Hari Raya Haji

FESTIVALS

With so many ethnic groups and religions represented in Singapore, you'll be unlucky if your trip doesn't coincide with some sort of **festival**, secular or religious. Most of the festivals have no fixed dates, but change annually according to the lunar calendar; check with the tourist office (see p.685).

LANGUAGE

English, Mandarin, Malay and Tamil all have the status of official languages, and you should have no problem getting by in English. One intriguing by-product of Singapore's ethnic melting pot is **singlish**, or Singaporean English, a patois that blends English with the speech patterns, exclamations and vocabulary of Chinese and Malay. Look out for the word "lah" when conversing with Singapore locals – it was originally used to add emphasis to the point being made; now it is just used to round off a sentence.

9

Chinese New Year (Jan/Feb; two days) Chinese operas and dragon dances in Chinatown.

Thaipusam (Jan/Feb) Watch Hindu devotees pierce their own flesh with elaborate steel cages and walk from the Sri Srinivasa Perumal Temple to the Chettiar Hindu Temple.

Singapore Food Festival (July) Singapore celebrates its oldest pastime.

Festival of the Hungry Ghosts (July) Catch a free performance of a Chinese opera, or wayang, in which characters act out classic Chinese legends.

Moon Cake Festival or Mid-Autumn Festival (July–Aug). Celebrate with children's lantern parades after dark in the Chinese Gardens.

Birthday of the Monkey God (Sept) Similar to Thaipusam but on a smaller scale. Best witnessed at the Monkey God Temple on Seng Poh Rd.

Navarathiri (Oct) The Chettiar and Sri Mariamman Hindu Temples stage classical dance and music.

Thimithi (Oct) Watch Hindu devotees running across a pit of hot coals.

Deepavali/Diwali (Oct/Nov) The Hindu festival celebrating the victory of Light over Dark is marked by the lighting of oil lamps outside homes.

Downtown Singapore

Ever since Sir Stamford Raffles first landed on its northern bank, in 1819, the area around the Singapore River, which strikes into the heart of the island from the south coast, has formed the hub of Singapore. All the city's central districts lie within a 3km radius of the mouth of the river – which makes **Downtown Singapore** an extremely convenient place to wander around.

WHAT TO SEE AND DO

The entire state is compact enough to be explored exhaustively in just a few days. Forming the core of downtown Singapore is the **Colonial District**, around whose public buildings and lofty cathedral the island's British residents used to promenade. Each surrounding enclave has its own distinct flavour, from the aromatic spice stores of **Little India** to the tumbledown backstreets of **Chinatown**, where it's still possible to find calligraphers and fortune-tellers, or the **Arab Quarter**, whose cluttered shops sell fine cloths and perfumes.

SINGAPORE RIVER, ISLAND AND HARBOUR CRUISES

Fleets of **cruise boats** ply Singapore's southern waters every day and night. The best of these, the **Singapore River Cruises** (T 6336 6111, W rivercruise.com.sg), cast off from a number of jetties around the city, including Clarke Quay, Boat Quay, Esplanade and Merlion Park (daily 9am–10pm; every 10min). Cruises on a traditional bumboat (S$20 for 40min) take you past the old *godowns* upriver where traders once stored their merchandise. A boat cruise by night is particularly spectacular.

The Colonial District

As the colony's trade grew, the **Singapore River** became its main artery, clogged with traditional cargo "bumboats", which ferried coffee, sugar and rice to the *godowns*, or warehouses. A handful still remain, offering trips downriver and around Marina Bay (see box above). The lower end of North Boat Quay is marked with a statue of Stamford Raffles, Singapore's founder. Singapore River cruise boats depart from a tiny jetty a few steps along from the statue. North of the statue is the dignified white Victorian building of the Old Parliament House, formerly a private dwelling for a rich merchant and now a centre for the arts, The Arts House (see p.691).

Asian Civilisations Museum and around

At the **Asian Civilisations Museum** (daily10am–7pm, Sun until 9pm; S$8; W acm.org.sg), housed in a robust Neoclassical building, each of the ten themed galleries is devoted to the art and culture of a particular region of Asia, including China and the Islamic World. It's a fascinating introduction to the region, from its prehistory to the advent of its Islamic civilization and beyond, with interactive exhibits and exquisite items, such as a sensuously modelled Thai Walking Buddha, Islamic calligraphy,

ancient Chinese writing implements and Southeast Asian textiles.

The smaller **Peranakan Museum** (daily 10am–7pm, Fri until 9pm; S$6; Ⓦperanakanmuseum.org.sg), at 39 Armenian St, features a wonderful collection of Peranakan art and objects, including a gallery dedicated to traditional wedding ceremonies.

The nearby **Philatelic Museum** (Mon 1–7pm, Tues–Sun 9.30am–7pm; S$6; Ⓦspm.org.sg) at 23B Coleman Street showcases a fascinating collection of stamps tracing Singapore's history.

The Esplanade

In a city obsessed with high-rises, the spiky **Esplanade Theatres** (Ⓦesplanade.com), dubbed "the durians" by the locals due to their resemblance in shape to the stinking fruit, look like nothing else in Asia and are a popular venue for plays and classical music.

Across the river is the popular **Merlion Park**, where the 8.6m-tall Merlion – a lion's head atop a scaly body with a fish tail – spews water into the bay. On the eastern side of the bay, an ambitious building reminiscent of a lotus flower houses the cutting-edge **ArtScience Museum** (daily 10am–10pm; S$25; Ⓦmarinabaysands.com/Singapore-Museum/), which explores the boundary where art and science meet through its interactive exhibits and fantastic temporary exhibitions.

Raffles Hotel

The lofty halls, restaurants, bars and peaceful gardens of the legendary **Raffles Hotel** at 1 Beach Rd (Ⓦraffles.com) all conspire to evoke a sense of the bygone colonial era. The hotel opened for business on December 1, 1887, and quickly began to attract some impressive guests, including Joseph Conrad, Rudyard Kipling and Hermann Hesse. During World War II, the hotel became Japanese officers' quarters, then a transit camp for liberated Allied prisoners. Postwar deterioration ended with a S$160-million facelift in 1991, which retained much of the building's colonial grace. A visit to the hotel's legendary

THREE-DAY MUSEUM PASS

The three-day **museum pass** (Ⓦnhb.gov.sg) costs S$20 and grants access to the National Museum of Singapore, Peranakan Museum, Singapore Art Museum, Asian Civilisations Museum, Singapore Philatelic Museum and several lesser venues, guaranteeing you a saving of at least S$19.

GETTING HIGH IN SINGAPORE

This is by no means an encouragement to partake in the consumption of illegal substances, since Singapore carries some of the world's stiffest penalties; here are other ways to feel on top of the world.

The Singapore Flyer 30 Raffles Avenue (daily 8.30am–10.30pm; S$33). This 165m-high observation wheel offers 360-degree views of everything from the bustling business district to the surrounding Indonesian and Malaysian islands. The best way to reserve a spot in one of the pods is to book online (Ⓦsingaporeflyer.com); the tourist office also offers discounted attraction combos which include the Flyer (see p.685).

G-max the Ultimate Bungee Jump & GX-5 Xtreme Swing Clarke Quay (daily 2pm–late; S$50; Ⓦgmax.com.sg). Want to see the lights of the big city while upside down at a height of 60m, having left your stomach somewhere below? Now you can. Next to the bungee catapult is the five-seater swing that catapults you above the Singapore River.

1-Altitude 1 Raffles Place Ⓣ6438 0410, Ⓦ1-altitude.com. Sip a cocktail in Singapore's highest alfresco gastrobar while enjoying fantastic views of the city.

Ku dé ta Marina Bay Sands, North Tower, 1 Bayfront Ave Ⓣ 6688 7688, Ⓦkudeta.com.sg. Perched at the top of the futuristic *Marina Bay Sands* hotel, 200m above the city, this rooftop bar and restaurant boasts unparalleled 360-degree views of Singapore.

Long Bar – a favourite watering hole for the likes of Noël Coward and Ernest Hemingway – is a highlight for many travellers, and you don't have to dress up to the nines to sip the signature Singapore Sling (S$32) and shell your peanuts on the floor.

Singapore Art Museum (SAM) & SAM AT 8Q

Located in the Bras Basah Bugis Precinct at 71 Bras Basah Rd, the **Singapore Art Museum** (daily 10am–7pm, Fri until 9pm; S$10, free 6–9pm Fri; Ⓦ singaporeartmuseum.sg) is housed in

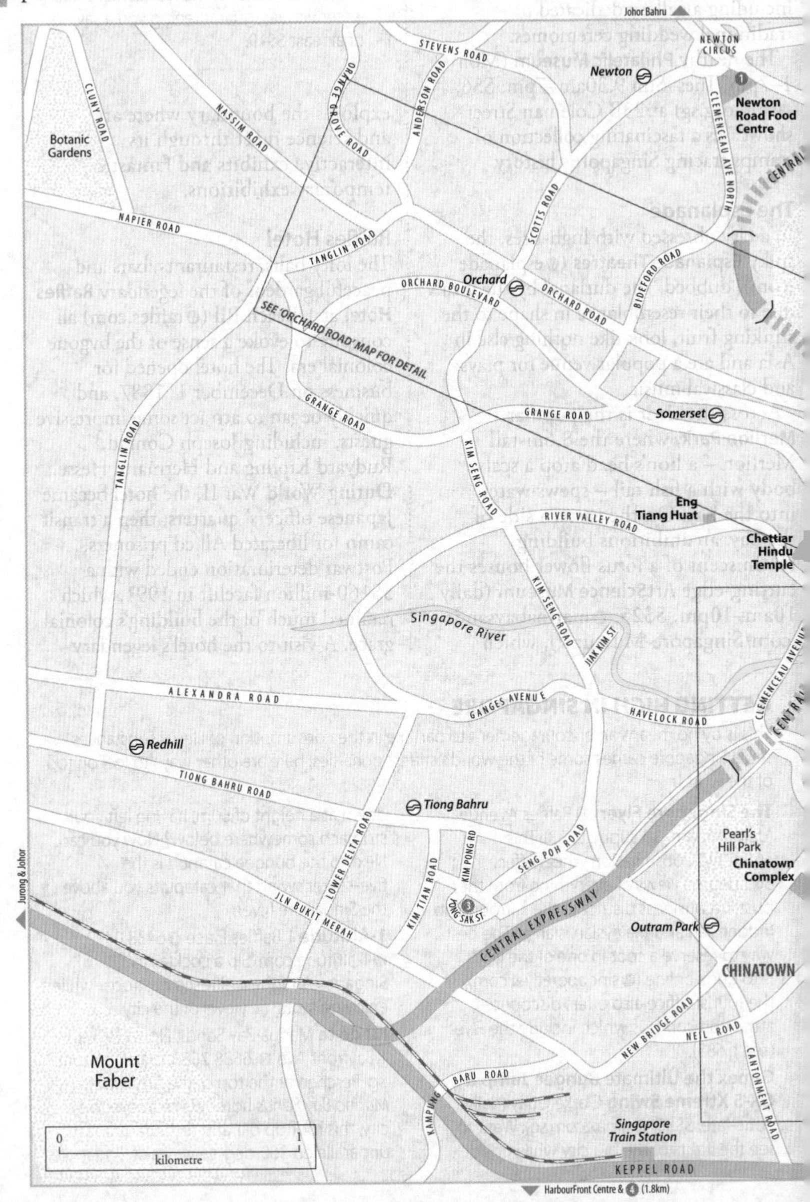

9

the venerable St Joseph's Institution, one of Singapore's oldest Catholic schools. SAM's strength lies in presenting contemporary art from Singapore and the Southeast Asian region. Guides conduct free **tours** around the museum's major works.

SAM at 8Q, an extension of SAM just around the corner, houses interactive art, thought-provoking installations, and contemporary works by local and international artists. SAM also organized the Singapore Biennale in both 2011 and 2013 (Ⓦ singaporebiennale.org).

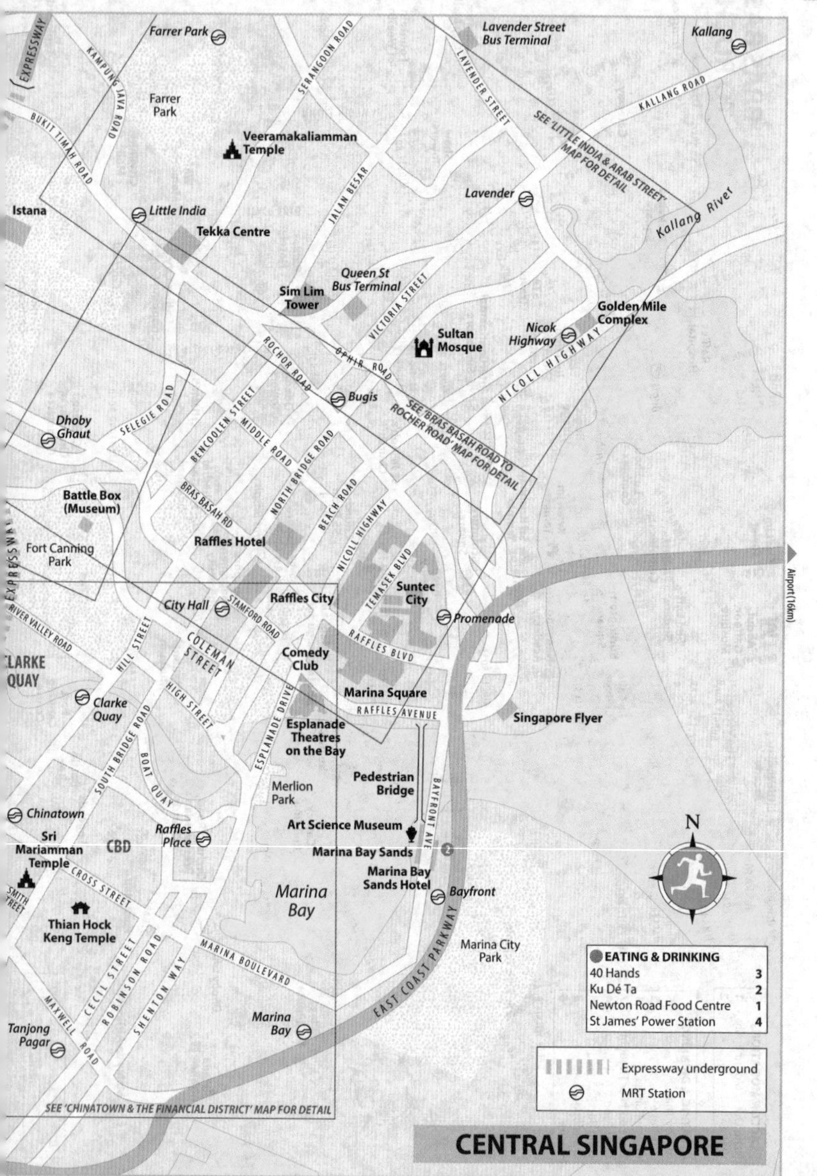

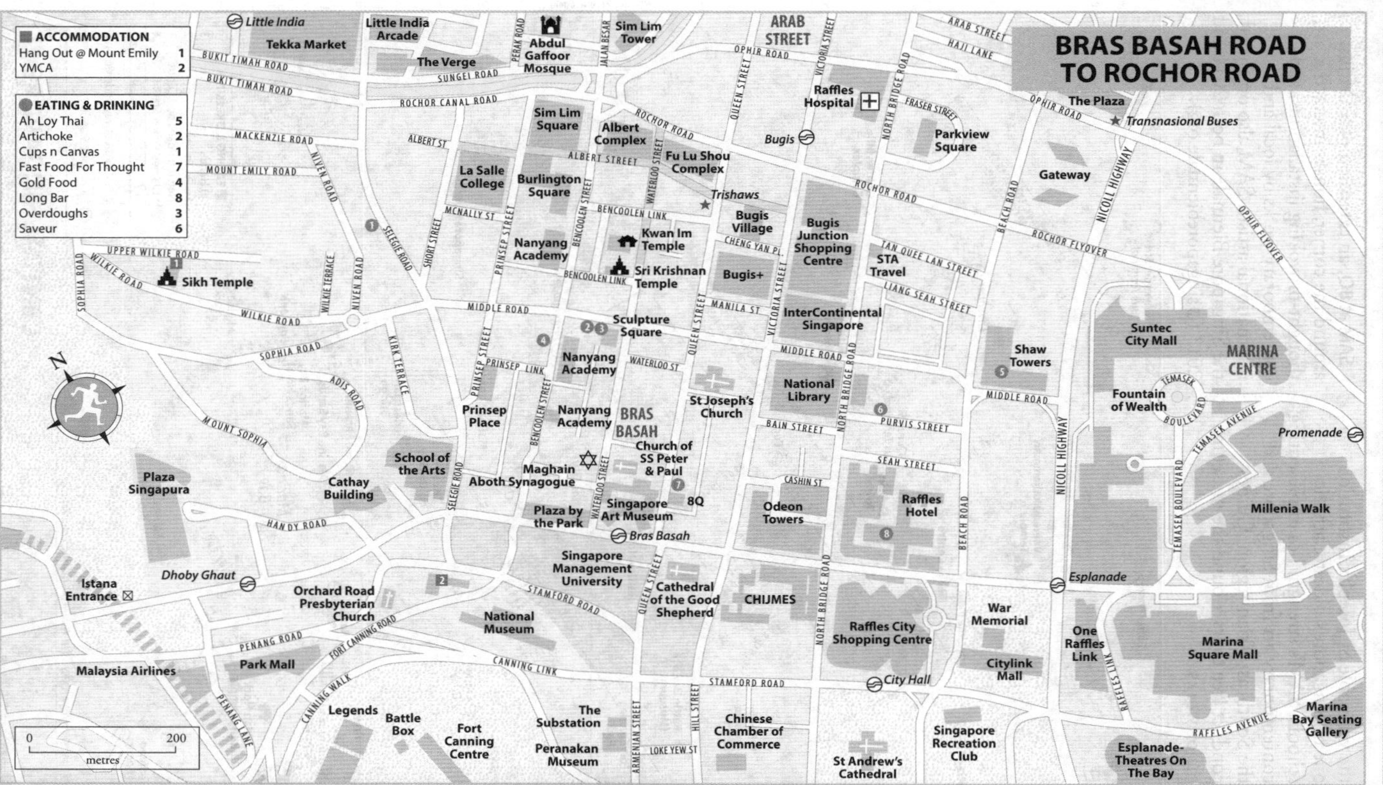
BRAS BASAH ROAD TO ROCHOR ROAD
ACCOMMODATION
Hang Out @ Mount Emily 1
YMCA 2
EATING & DRINKING
Ah Loy Thai 5
Artichoke 2
Cups n Canvas 1
Fast Food For Thought 7
Gold Food 4
Long Bar 8
Overdoughs 3
Saveur 6
Little India
Tekka Market
Little India Arcade
The Verge
Abdul Gaffoor Mosque
Sim Lim Tower
ARAB STREET
Raffles Hospital
The Plaza
Transnasional Buses
Parkview Square
Gateway
Sim Lim Square
Albert Complex
Fu Lu Shou Complex
La Salle College
Burlington Square
Trishaws
Bugis
Bugis Village
Bugis Junction Shopping Centre
STA Travel
Nanyang Academy
Kwan Im Temple
Sri Krishnan Temple
Bugis+
Sikh Temple
Sculpture Square
InterContinental Singapore
Suntec City Mall
MARINA CENTRE
Shaw Towers
National Library
St Joseph's Church
Fountain of Wealth
Prinsep Place
BRAS BASAH
Church of SS Peter & Paul
Promenade
School of the Arts
Maghain Aboth Synagogue
Plaza Singapura
Cathay Building
Singapore Art Museum
8Q
Odeon Towers
Raffles Hotel
Millenia Walk
Plaza by the Park
Bras Basah
Singapore Management University
Dhoby Ghaut
Istana Entrance
Orchard Road Presbyterian Church
Cathedral of the Good Shepherd
CHIJMES
Esplanade
War Memorial
National Museum
Raffles City Shopping Centre
One Raffles Link
Marina Square Mall
Park Mall
Malaysia Airlines
Citylink Mall
City Hall
Legends
Battle Box
Fort Canning Centre
The Substation
Peranakan Museum
Chinese Chamber of Commerce
St Andrew's Cathedral
Singapore Recreation Club
Esplanade-Theatres On The Bay
Marina Bay Seating Gallery
0 200
metres
BUKIT TIMAH ROAD
SUNGEI ROAD
ROCHOR CANAL ROAD
PERAK ROAD
JALAN BESAR
OPHIR ROAD
VICTORIA STREET
QUEEN STREET
NORTH BRIDGE ROAD
ARAB STREET
HAJI LANE
FRASER STREET
ROCHOR ROAD
MACKENZIE ROAD
MOUNT EMILY ROAD
NIVEN ROAD
ALBERT ST
ALBERT STREET
WATERLOO STREET
BENCOOLEN STREET
BENCOOLEN LINK
MCNALLY ST
PRINSEP STREET
SHORT STREET
SELEGIE ROAD
BEACH ROAD
NICOLL HIGHWAY
ROCHOR FLYOVER
OPHIR FLYOVER
TAN QUEE LAN STREET
LIANG SEAH STREET
CHENG YAN PL
MANILA ST
UPPER WILKIE ROAD
WILKIE ROAD
WILKIE TERRACE
SOPHIA ROAD
MIDDLE ROAD
KIRK TERRACE
PRINSEP LINK
WATERLOO ST
ADIS ROAD
MOUNT SOPHIA
PURVIS STREET
BAIN STREET
TEMASEK BOULEVARD
TEMASEK AVENUE
SEAH STREET
CASHIN ST
HANDY ROAD
STAMFORD ROAD
PENANG ROAD
FORT CANNING ROAD
CANNING LINK
CANNING WALK
PENANG LANE
RAFFLES LINK
RAFFLES AVENUE
ARMENIAN STREET
HILL STREET
LOKE YEW ST

National Museum of Singapore

The **National Museum of Singapore** at 93 Stamford Rd (Singapore History Gallery: daily 10am–6pm; Singapore Living Galleries: until 8pm; Living Galleries free 6–8pm; S$10; ⓦnationalmuseum.sg) is housed in one of Singapore's most distinguished colonial buildings. One of the highlights is the permanent Singapore History Gallery, best accompanied by the free audioguide. It charts the city's humble beginnings through to the harrowing World War II occupation by Japanese forces, then to independence and the present day, using artefacts, visual presentations and audio footage. The Living Galleries showcase interactive exhibits which explore Singapore's complex society through food, fashion, photography, film and wayang.

Fort Canning Park and Clarke Quay

When Raffles first caught sight of Singapore, **Fort Canning Park** was known locally as *Bukit Larangan* (Forbidden Hill). Singapore's first British Resident, William Farquhar – a political officer appointed by London – displayed typical colonial tact by promptly having the hill cleared and building a bungalow on the summit. The bungalow was replaced by a fort in 1859. An early European **cemetery** still survives, however, on whose stones are engraved intriguing epitaphs to nineteenth-century sailors, traders and residents.

There's a back entrance to the park which involves climbing an exhausting flight of steps that runs next to the Hill Street Food Centre on Hill Street. Once you reach the top, you're greeted by a brilliant view along High Street towards the Merlion monument at the mouth of the Singapore River. The highlight of Fort Canning, however, is the **Battle Box** (daily 10am–6pm, last admission 5pm; S$10), an underground bunker museum which uses audio and video effects and animations to bring to life the last hours before the Japanese occupation began in February 1942.

On the other side of River Valley Road, which skirts the southwestern slope of Fort Canning Park, lies a chain of nineteenth-century *godowns* (warehouses) which have been renovated into one of the most popular nightspots in town, **Clarke Quay** – a buzzing hive of clubs, bars and restaurants. Nearby **Boat Quay** and **Robertson Quay** are almost equally lively, lined with restaurants and bars.

Chinatown

The two square kilometres of **Chinatown**, located just south of the Singapore River, once constituted the focal point of Chinese life and culture in Singapore. Although nowadays the traditional aspects of the area are on their last legs, a wander through the surviving nineteenth-century streets unearths historic craft shops and restaurant buildings.

The **Chinatown Heritage Centre** (daily 9am–7.30pm; S$10), at 48 Pagoda St, is located in a row of restored shophouses which give visitors an idea of what the whole neighbourhood once looked like. The five-tiered, Tang Dynasty-inspired **Buddha Tooth Relic Temple** (daily 7am–7pm; free) at 288 South Bridge Street houses what is reputedly the sacred tooth of the Buddha, kept in a gold stupa and only brought out on the first day of the Chinese New Year. The multilevel museum and rooftop garden are worth lingering in. The enormous **Thian Hock Keng Temple** (the "Temple of Heavenly Happiness"; daily 7.30am–5.30pm) at 158 Telok Ayer Street, a hugely impressive Hokkien building, is one of Singapore's oldest; dragons stalk its broad roofs, while the temple compound's entrance bristles with ceramic flowers, foliage and sculpted figures.

Amoy Street is another Hokkien enclave from the colony's early days. Long terraces of shophouses flank the street, all featuring characteristic **five-foot ways**, simply covered verandas that were so called because they jut five feet out.

Turn right out of Ann Siang Hill and you'll see **Eu Yan Sang** at 269 South Bridge Road (Mon–Sat 8.30am–7pm), opened in 1910 and geared up, to an extent, for the tourist trade. The shop has been beautifully renovated and sells a weird assortment of ingredients, from herbs and roots to various dubious remedies derived from endangered species.

9

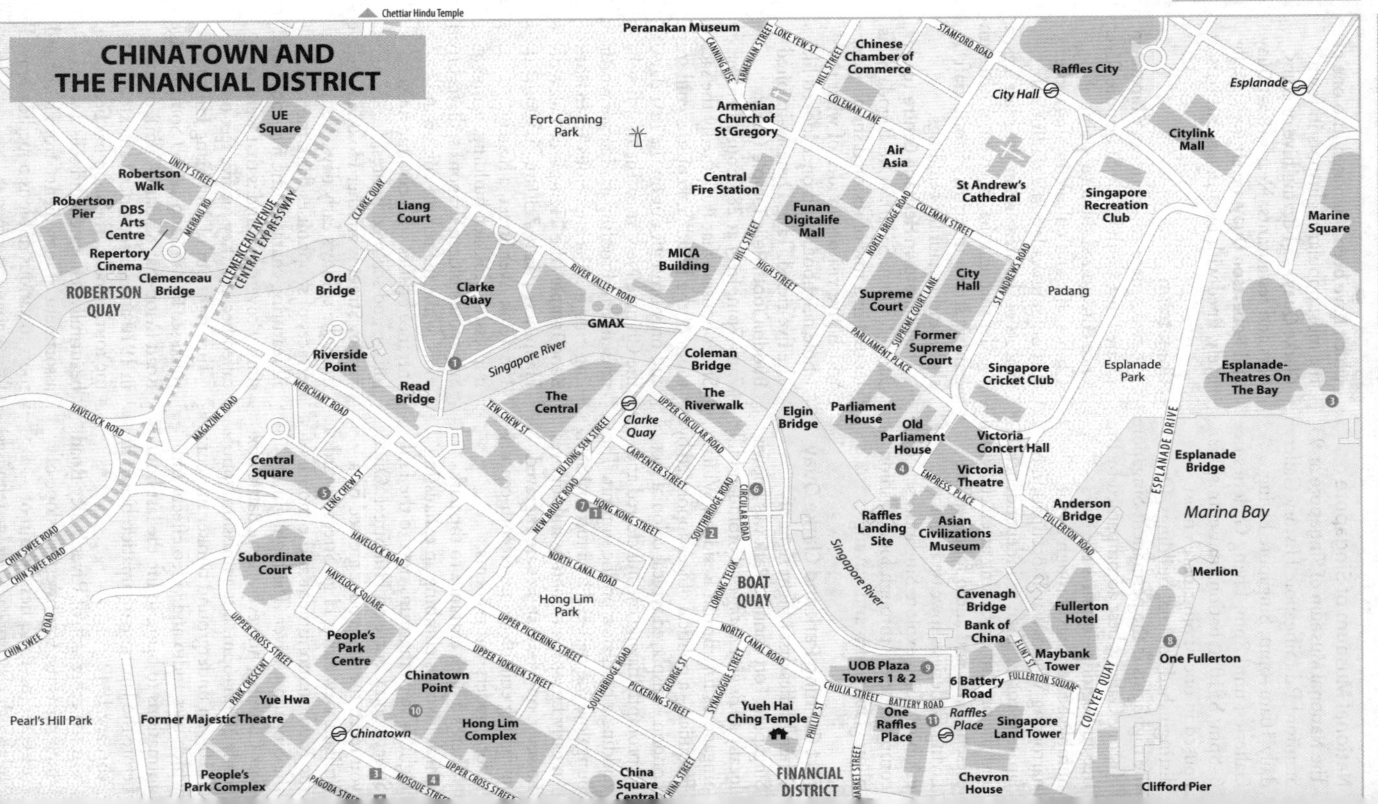
CHINATOWN AND
THE FINANCIAL DISTRICT
Chettiar Hindu Temple
Peranakan Museum
CANNING RISE
ARMENIAN STREET
LOKE YEW ST
HILL STREET
Chinese Chamber of Commerce
STAMFORD ROAD
Raffles City
City Hall
Esplanade
UE Square
Fort Canning Park
Armenian Church of St Gregory
COLEMAN LANE
Air Asia
Citylink Mall
Robertson Walk
UNITY STREET
Robertson Pier
DBS Arts Centre
MERBAU RD
Repertory Cinema
Clemenceau Bridge
ROBERTSON QUAY
CLEMENCEAU AVENUE
CENTRAL EXPRESSWAY
Central Fire Station
St Andrew's Cathedral
Singapore Recreation Club
Marine Square
CLARKE QUAY
Liang Court
Funan Digitalife Mall
NORTH BRIDGE ROAD
COLEMAN STREET
MICA Building
HILL STREET
HIGH STREET
ST ANDREWS ROAD
City Hall
Padang
Ord Bridge
Clarke Quay
RIVER VALLEY ROAD
Supreme Court
SUPREME COURT LANE
GMAX
Former Supreme Court
PARLIAMENT PLACE
Riverside Point
Singapore River
Coleman Bridge
Singapore Cricket Club
Esplanade Park
Esplanade-Theatres On The Bay
Read Bridge
The Central
The Riverwalk
Elgin Bridge
Parliament House
Old Parliament House
Victoria Concert Hall
HAVELOCK ROAD
MERCHANT ROAD
MAGAZINE ROAD
TEW CHEW ST
Clarke Quay
UPPER CIRCULAR ROAD
EU TONG SEN STREET
Central Square
LENG CHEW ST
CARPENTER STREET
Victoria Theatre
EMPRESS PLACE
Esplanade Bridge
ESPLANADE DRIVE
NEW BRIDGE ROAD
HONG KONG STREET
SOUTHBRIDGE ROAD
CIRCULAR ROAD
Raffles Landing Site
Asian Civilizations Museum
Anderson Bridge
FULLERTON ROAD
Marina Bay
CHIN SWEE ROAD
Subordinate Court
HAVELOCK ROAD
NORTH CANAL ROAD
Singapore River
Merlion
HAVELOCK SQUARE
Hong Lim Park
LORONG TELOK
BOAT QUAY
Cavenagh Bridge
Fullerton Hotel
UPPER CROSS STREET
People's Park Centre
UPPER PICKERING STREET
NORTH CANAL ROAD
Bank of China
FLINT ST
Maybank Tower
One Fullerton
PARK CRESCENT
Chinatown Point
UPPER HOKKIEN STREET
SOUTHBRIDGE ROAD
GEORGE ST
SYNAGOGUE STREET
UOB Plaza Towers 1 & 2
6 Battery Road
FULLERTON SQUARE
COLLYER QUAY
Yue Hwa
PICKERING STREET
CHULIA STREET
BATTERY ROAD
Pearl's Hill Park
Former Majestic Theatre
Hong Lim Complex
Yueh Hai Ching Temple
PHILLIP ST
One Raffles Place
Raffles Place
Singapore Land Tower
Chinatown
People's Park Complex
PAGODA STREET
MOSQUE STREET
UPPER CROSS STREET
China Square Central
CHINA STREET
FINANCIAL DISTRICT
MARKET STREET
Chevron House
Clifford Pier

9

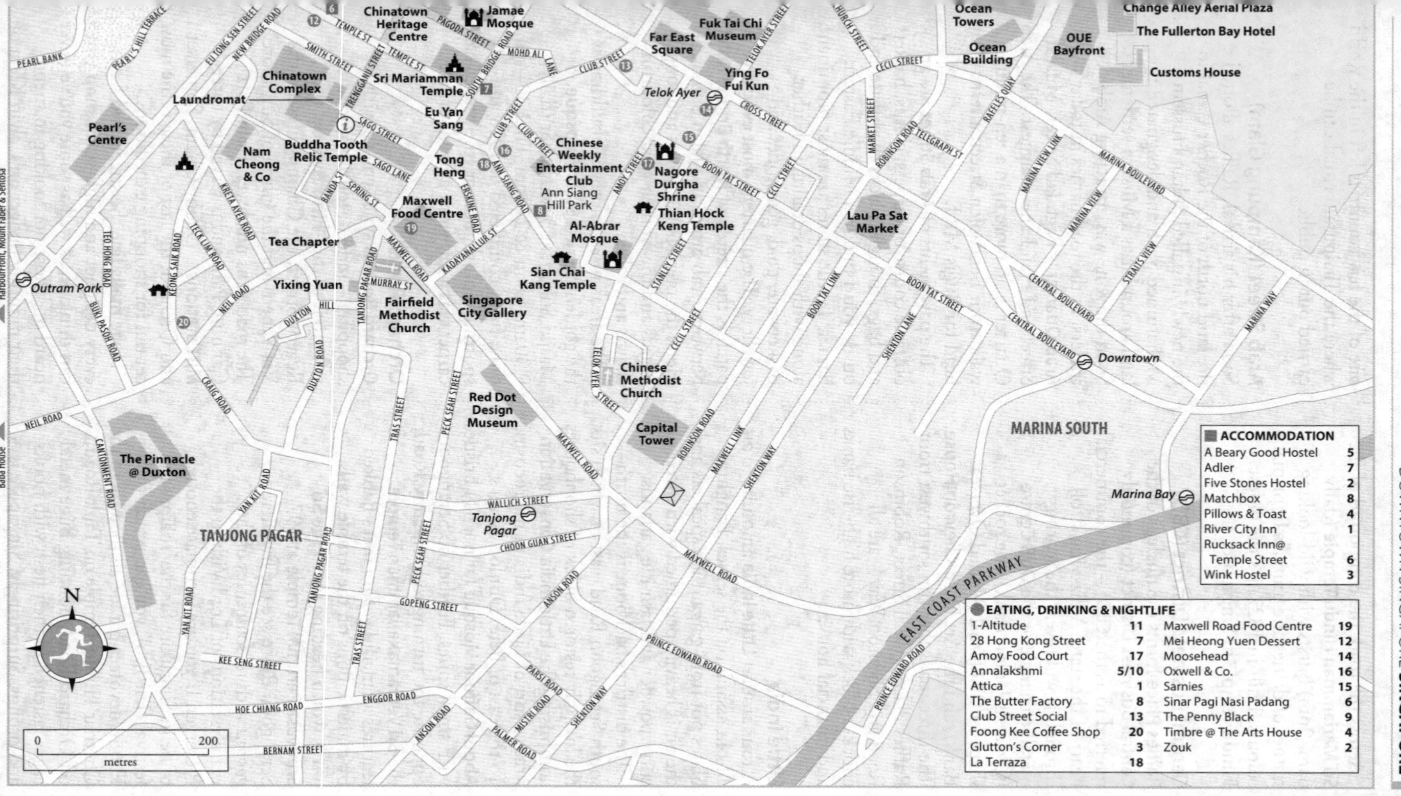
ACCOMMODATION
A Beary Good Hostel 5
Adler 7
Five Stones Hostel 2
Matchbox 8
Pillows & Toast 4
River City Inn 1
Rucksack Inn@ Temple Street 6
Wink Hostel 3
EATING, DRINKING & NIGHTLIFE
1-Altitude 11
28 Hong Kong Street 7
Amoy Food Court 17
Annalakshmi 5/10
Attica 1
The Butter Factory 8
Club Street Social 13
Foong Kee Coffee Shop 20
Glutton's Corner 3
La Terraza 18
Maxwell Road Food Centre 19
Mei Heong Yuen Dessert 12
Moosehead 14
Oxwell & Co. 16
Sarnies 15
Sinar Pagi Nasi Padang 6
The Penny Black 9
Timbre @ The Arts House 4
Zouk 2
Change Alley Aerial Plaza
The Fullerton Bay Hotel
Customs House
OUE Bayfront
Ocean Towers
Ocean Building
Downtown
Marina Bay
MARINA SOUTH
EAST COAST PARKWAY
Lau Pa Sat Market
Fuk Tai Chi Museum
Far East Square
Ying Fo Fui Kun
Telok Ayer
Nagore Durgha Shrine
Thian Hock Keng Temple
Chinese Methodist Church
Capital Tower
Chinese Weekly Entertainment Club
Ann Siang Hill Park
Al-Abrar Mosque
Sian Chai Kang Temple
Jamae Mosque
Singapore City Gallery
Red Dot Design Museum
Tanjong Pagar
Chinatown Heritage Centre
Sri Mariamman Temple
Eu Yan Sang
Tong Heng
Maxwell Food Centre
Fairfield Methodist Church
Buddha Tooth Relic Temple
Chinatown Complex
Tea Chapter
Yixing Yuan
Nam Cheong & Co
Laundromat
TANJONG PAGAR
The Pinnacle @ Duxton
Pearl's Centre
Outram Park
Harbourfront, Mount Faber & Sentosa
Baba House
0
200
metres
N

Across the road, the compound of the **Sri Mariamman Hindu Temple** (daily 6am–9pm) bursts with wild-looking statues of deities and animals in primary colours. Built in 1827, it's the oldest Hindu temple in Singapore.

Central Business District (CBD)

Raffles Place forms the nucleus of the **Central Business District** (commonly referred to as the **CBD**) – the commercial heart of the state. A dizzying stroll through it will reveal the soaring metallic triangle of the **OUB Centre** (Overseas Union Bank), the rocket-shaped **UOB Plaza 2** (United Overseas Bank), and the Art Deco **Chevron House**. The three roads that run southwest from Raffles Place – Cecil Street, Robinson Road and Shenton Way – are all chock-a-block with more high-rise banks and financial houses.

Little India

A tour around **Little India** amounts to an all-out assault on the senses. Banghra blares out from gargantuan speakers and the air is heavily perfumed with incense, curry powder and jasmine garlands.

The district's backbone is the north–south Serangoon Road, east of which sits the lovingly restored block of shophouses comprising the **Little India Conservation Area**, a sort of Little India in microcosm. To the east of here, Dunlop Street's **Abdul Gaffoor Mosque** (at no. 41) bristles with small spires. Further up Serangoon, opposite the turning to Veerasamy Road, the **Sri Veeramakaliamman Temple** features a fanciful *gopura* that's flanked by majestic lions on the temple walls.

It is worth heading up to the **Sri Srinivasa Perumal Temple** at 397 Serangoon Rd to see the five-tiered *gopura* with its sculptures of the manifestations of Lord Vishnu the Preserver. If you are fortunate enough to be in Singapore for the Thaipusam festival (Jan/Feb), you can watch the Hindu devotees parade all the way to the Chettiar Hindu Temple on Tank Road, off Orchard Road, donning huge metal cages fastened to their flesh with hooks and prongs. Surprisingly, Singapore is one of the few countries left in the world where the Thaipusam ritual can be carried out in public.

Arab Street (Kampung Glam)

Soon after his arrival, Raffles allotted the land north of the Rocher Canal to the newly installed Sultan Hussein Mohammed Shah and designated the land around it as a Muslim settlement. Soon the zone was attracting Arab traders, as the road names in today's **Arab Quarter** – Baghdad Street, Muscat Street and Haji Lane – suggest. The Arab Quarter is no more than a ten-minute walk from Bencoolen Street; alternatively, head for Bugis MRT.

The pavements of **Arab Street** are an obstacle course of carpets, cloths, baskets and bags, though it lacks the hustle and bustle you'd find in a Middle Eastern bazaar. Textile stores are most prominent, along with shops dealing in leather, basketware, gold, gemstones and jewellery. The quarter's most evocative patch is the stretch of **North Bridge Road** between Arab Street and Jalan Sultan. Here, the men sport sarongs and long beards and the women wear colourful shawls and robes.

The area's most impressive building is the golden-domed **Sultan Mosque**, or Masjid Sultan, at 3 Muscat St (daily 9.30am–noon & 2–4pm, Fri 2.30–4pm only; free), completed in 1928 and sporting a plush interior (the prayer-hall carpet was a gift from a Saudi prince).

Orchard Road

Orchard Road is synonymous with shopping – indeed, tourist brochures refer to it as the "Fifth Avenue, the Regent Street, the Champs Elysées, the Via Veneto and the Ginza of Singapore". The road runs northwest from Fort Canning Park and is served by three **MRT stations** – Dhoby Ghaut, Somerset and Orchard; the last of these is the most central for shopping expeditions.

Huge **malls** line the streets and feature every designer and high-street shop you can think of, as well as some you've never heard of. Those not looking to spend their monthly budget on Calvin Klein or

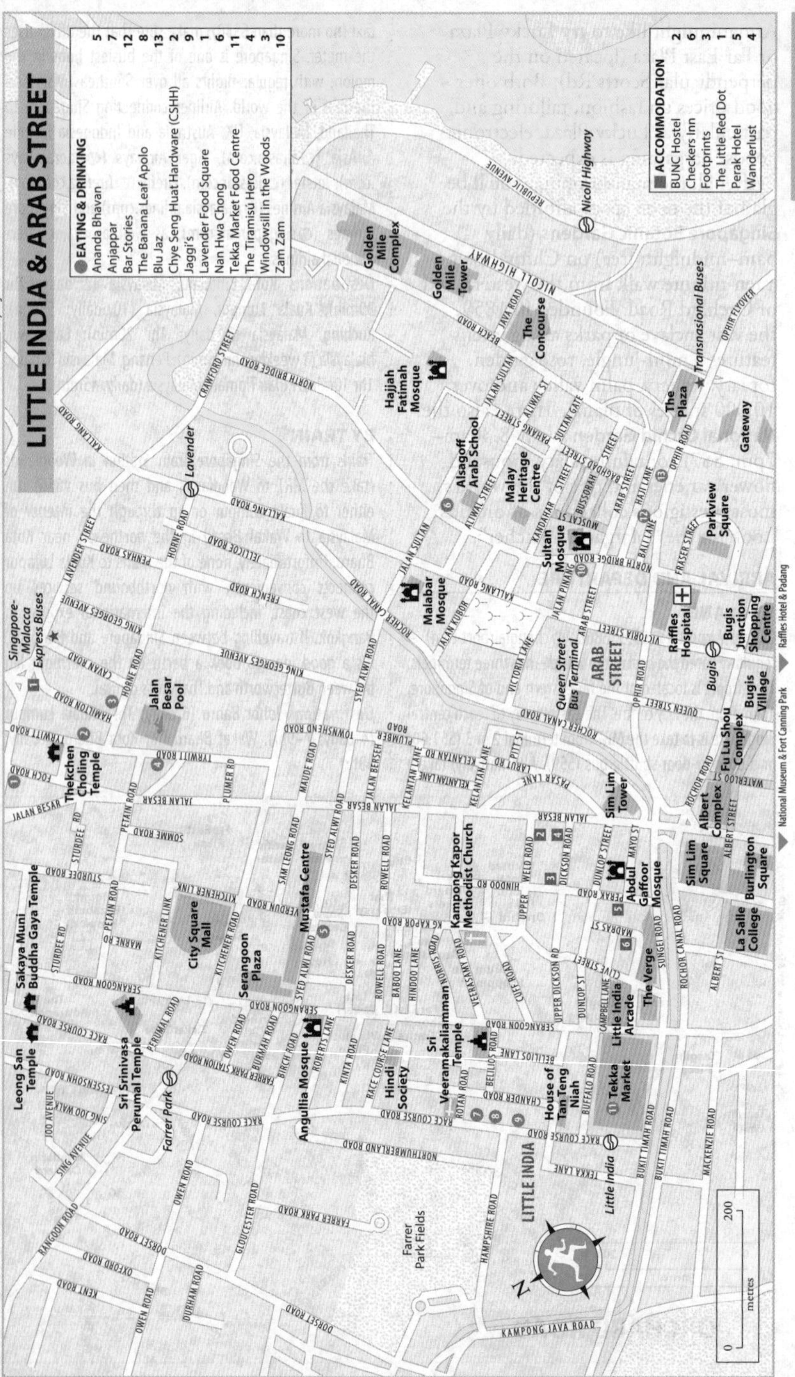
LITTLE INDIA & ARAB STREET
EATING & DRINKING
Ananda Bhavan 5
Anjappar 7
Bar Stories 12
The Banana Leaf Apolo 8
Blu Jaz 13
Chye Seng Huat Hardware (CSHH) 2
Jaggi's 9
Lavender Food Square 1
Nan Hwa Chong 6
Tekka Market Food Centre 11
The Tiramisù Hero 3
Windowsill in the Woods 4
Zam Zam 10
ACCOMMODATION
BUNC Hostel 2
Checkers Inn 6
Footprints 3
The Little Red Dot 1
Perak Hotel 5
Wanderlust 4
LITTLE INDIA
ARAB STREET
Geylang
Newton Circus
National Museum & Fort Canning Park
Raffles Hotel & Padang
0 200 metres

Armani might like to try Lucky Plaza or Far East Plaza (located on the perpendicular Scotts Rd). Both offer good prices on fashion, tailoring and, particularly at Lucky Plaza, electronic goods. Bargaining is expected.

After all the mall-hopping, you'll be glad of the open space afforded by the **Singapore Botanic Gardens** (daily 5am–midnight; free) on Cluny Road, a ten-minute walk from the western end of Orchard Road. Founded in 1859, the vast enclave of parks and gardens features a mini-jungle, rose garden, topiary, fernery, palm valley and over 10,000 species of plants. There's also the **National Orchid Garden** (daily 8.30am–7pm; S$7) containing sixty thousand flower varieties and one of the world's most prestigious collections of orchids. Look for the "Margaret Thatcher".

ARRIVAL AND DEPARTURE

BY PLANE

Changi Airport (☎6595 6868, ⓦchangiairport.com) – regularly voted the best in the world – has three terminals. The airport is located at the far eastern end of Singapore, 16km from the city centre. The easiest way to reach central Singapore is to take the MRT from terminal 2 or 3 (S$1.60) or a door-to-door shuttle bus (S$9). Alternatively, take a taxi (no more than S$30); make sure that the driver uses the meter. Singapore is one of the busiest hubs in the region, with regular flights all over Southeast Asia and the rest of the world. Airlines connecting Singapore to Thailand, Malaysia, UK, Australia and Indonesia include AirAsia (ⓦairasia.com), Tiger Airways (ⓦtigerairways.com), Jetstar (ⓦjetstar.com), Firefly (ⓦfireflyz.com.my), Malaysia Airlines (ⓦmalaysiaairlines.com) and Singapore Airlines (ⓦsingaporeair.com), as well as major international airlines.

Destinations Kota Kinabalu, Malaysia (2 daily; 2hr 30min); Kuala Lumpur, Malaysia (10 daily; 55min); Kuching, Malaysia (2 daily; 1hr 20min); Langkawi, Malaysia (3 weekly; 1hr 25min); Penang, Malaysia (6 daily; 1hr 10min); Pulau Tioman, Malaysia (daily; 45min).

BY TRAIN

Trains from the Singapore Train Station in Woodlands (take the MRT to Woodlands and then bus #856) run either to Kuala Lumpur or up through the interior of Malaysia to Wakaf Bharu in the northeast, near Kota Bharu. Unfortunately, none of the trains to Kuala Lumpur connects conveniently with northbound services up the west coast, including the international express to Bangkok. If travelling between Singapore and Bangkok, it's a good idea to book a berth on the overnight leg between Butterworth and Thailand's capital.

Destinations Johor Bahru (6 daily; 1hr); Kuala Lumpur (4 daily; 7–9hr); Wakaf Bharu (for Kota Bharu: 1 daily; 13hr).

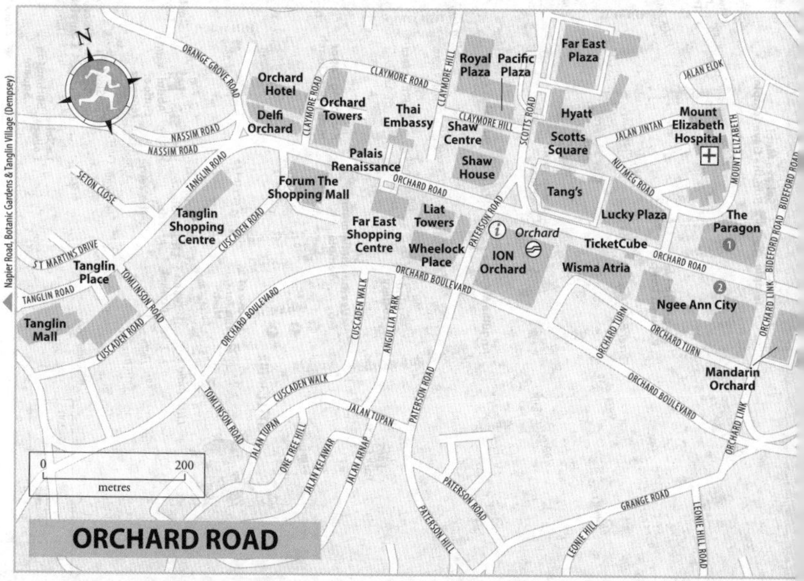

BY BUS

Singapore has two bus terminals, serving numerous destinations in Malaysia. There is no need to change buses as they will ferry you across the causeway, through passport control and on to your destination. Buses to Johor Bahru leave from Queen St terminal at the junction of Queen and Arab streets, while the Golden Mile Complex at 5001 Beach Rd serves all other destinations such as Penang, Butterworth and Ipoh.

Destinations Butterworth, Malaysia (3 daily; 16hr); Ipoh, Malaysia (4 daily; 10–11hr); Johor Bahru, Malaysia (every 30min; 1hr); Kota Bharu, Malaysia (at least 1 daily; 10hr); Kuala Lumpur, Malaysia (15 daily; 7hr); Kuantan, Malaysia (3 daily; 7hr); Melaka, Malaysia (9 daily; 5hr); Mersing, Malaysia (2 daily; 3hr 30min).

BY BOAT

Boats to and from the Indonesian Riau archipelago dock at the HarbourFront Centre, near the MRT of the same name. Boats to Pulau Batam sail to Sekupang (daily 7.30am–7pm; 30min; S$40 one-way), from where you can take a taxi to Hangnadim Airport for internal Indonesian flights or another boat to Tanjung Buton on the Sumatran mainland. Ferries to Bintan in Indonesia depart from Tanah Mera Ferry Terminal (take the MRT to Tanah Mera, then bus #35 to the ferry terminal). It's also possible to travel between Singapore and Malaysia by boat. Ferries depart from Changi Point ferry terminal to Pengerang in Johor (take the MRT to Tanah Mera, then bus #2 to Changi Village); check in one hour before departure.

INFORMATION AND TOURS

Tourist offices The Singapore Tourism Board (STB) is at the intersection of Orchard and Cairnhill roads (daily 9.30am–10.30pm; hotline ⓣ 1800 736 2000, ⓦ yoursingapore.com); staff have a host of brochures and can give advice on attraction combination tickets. There's also a visitor centre in Chinatown at 2 Banda St (Mon–Fri 9am–9pm, Sat & Sun 9am–10pm; ⓣ 6221 5115, ⓦ chinatown.sg).

The Original Singapore Walks ⓣ 6325 1631, ⓦ singaporewalks.com. Fantastic walking tours of the city's unique neighbourhoods (S$35; 2–3hr). There's a different tour each day bar Sunday; choose from the likes of "Secrets of the Red Lantern", "End of Empire" and "Sultans of Spice".

GETTING AROUND

A one-way journey on the MRT costs between S$1.20 and S$2.20. Alternatively, a 24hr Singapore Tourist Pass (ⓦ thesingaporetouristpass.com; available from Changi Airport, Orchard, Chinatown, City Hall, Raffles Place, Harbour Front and Bugis MRT stations) will allow you unlimited travel for 24 hours on the bus and MRT for just S$10.

By MRT (Mass Rapid Transit) Singapore's clean, efficient and good-value MRT system (Transitlink Hotline ⓣ 1800 767 4333, ⓦ smrtcorp.com) runs on four main lines threading the island together (map p.686), with more lines in the works. Trains run every five minutes or so, daily 6am–midnight. Eating and drinking are both prohibited on the MRT – punishable with a fine of S$500.

By bus For information about fares and routes and to plan journeys around the city, check out ⓦ sbstransit.com.sg or

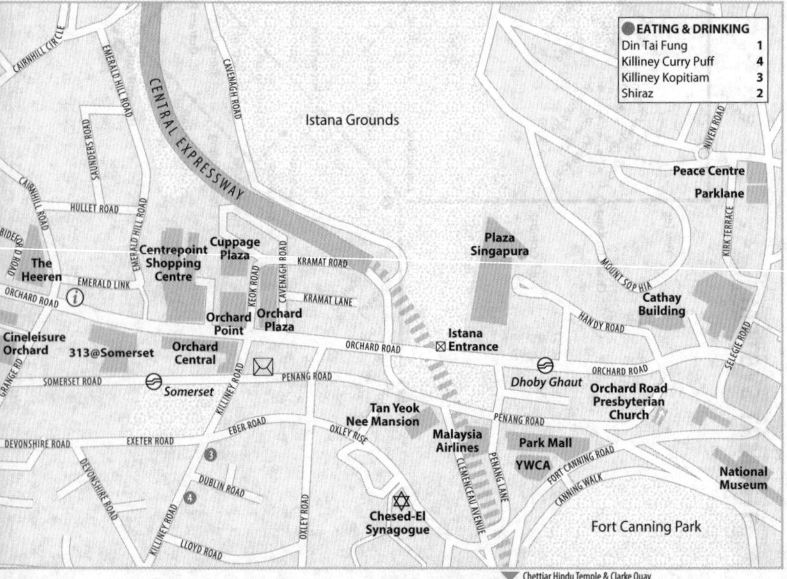

9

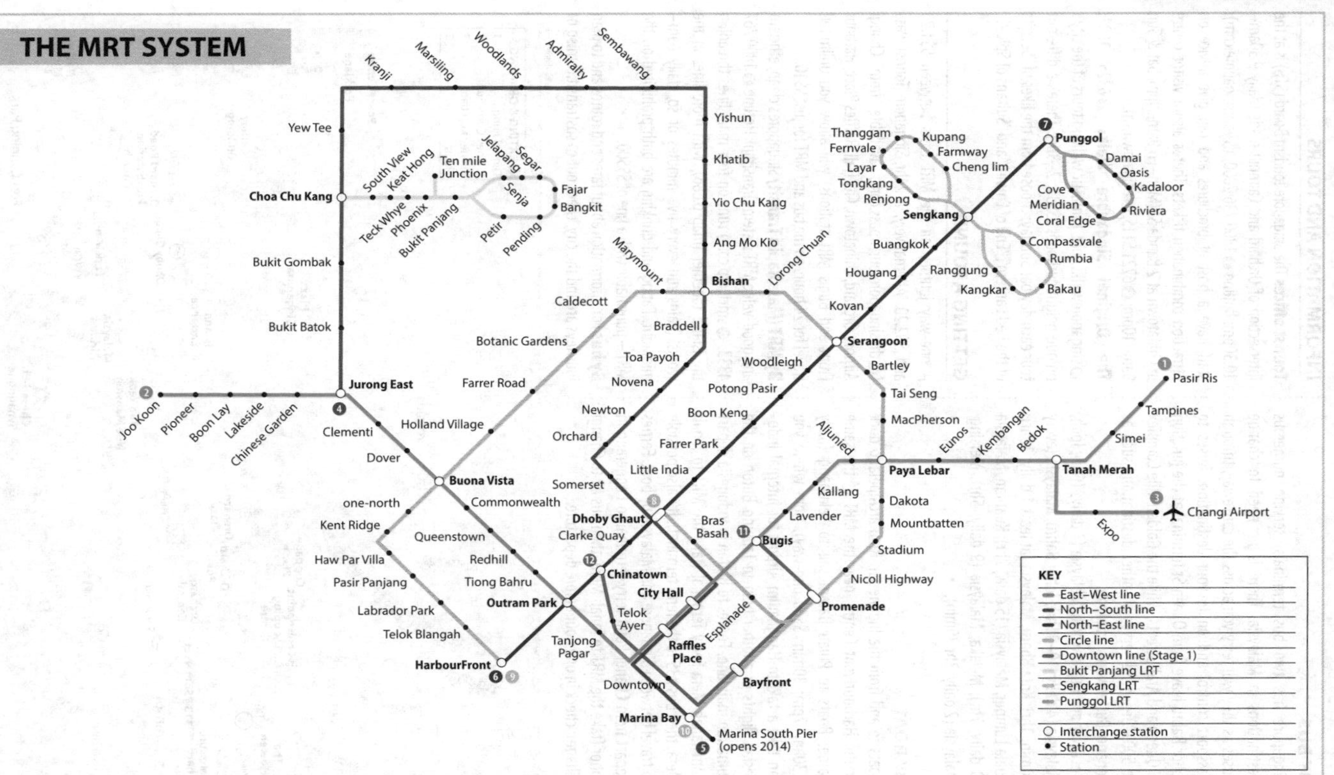
THE MRT SYSTEM
Kranji
Marsiling
Woodlands
Admiralty
Sembawang
Yishun
Khatib
Yio Chu Kang
Ang Mo Kio
Bishan
Braddell
Toa Payoh
Novena
Newton
Orchard
Somerset
Dhoby Ghaut
City Hall
Raffles Place
Marina Bay
Marina South Pier (opens 2014)
Yew Tee
Choa Chu Kang
Bukit Gombak
Bukit Batok
Jurong East
Joo Koon
Pioneer
Boon Lay
Lakeside
Chinese Garden
Clementi
Dover
Buona Vista
Commonwealth
Queenstown
Redhill
Tiong Bahru
Outram Park
Tanjong Pagar
South View
Keat Hong
Teck Whye
Phoenix
Bukit Panjang
Ten mile Junction
Jelapang
Segar
Senja
Fajar
Bangkit
Petir
Pending
Marymount
Caldecott
Botanic Gardens
Farrer Road
Holland Village
one-north
Kent Ridge
Haw Par Villa
Pasir Panjang
Labrador Park
Telok Blangah
HarbourFront
Lorong Chuan
Serangoon
Bartley
Tai Seng
MacPherson
Paya Lebar
Dakota
Mountbatten
Stadium
Nicoll Highway
Promenade
Bayfront
Esplanade
Bras Basah
Bugis
Lavender
Kallang
Aljunied
Eunos
Kembangan
Bedok
Tanah Merah
Simei
Tampines
Pasir Ris
Expo
Changi Airport
Kovan
Hougang
Buangkok
Sengkang
Punggol
Woodleigh
Potong Pasir
Boon Keng
Farrer Park
Little India
Clarke Quay
Chinatown
Telok Ayer
Downtown
Thanggam
Fernvale
Layar
Tongkang
Renjong
Kupang
Farmway
Cheng lim
Compassvale
Rumbia
Bakau
Kangkar
Ranggung
Damai
Oasis
Kadaloor
Riviera
Coral Edge
Meridian
Cove
KEY
East–West line
North–South line
North–East line
Circle line
Downtown line (Stage 1)
Bukit Panjang LRT
Sengkang LRT
Punggol LRT
Interchange station
Station

ⓦ transitlink.com.sg. Most buses charge distance-related fares, ranging from S$0.90 to S$1.80. If you don't have an EZ-Link Card, a contactless value card used for public buses and train fares that can be topped up at stations island-wide (ⓦ ezlink.com.sg); tell the driver where you want to go, and he'll tell you how much money to drop into the metal chute. Change isn't given, so make sure you have enough coins.

By taxi Singapore's taxis are relatively affordable. They are all metered, with a starting fare of S$3.20 for the first kilometre, then rising 20 cents for every 225m thereafter. However, once the MRT stops at midnight there's a fifty percent surcharge.

By bicycle Renting a bike (S$6–10/hr, with ID) is possible along the East Coast Parkway, where a cycle track skirts the seashore. The dirt tracks on Pulau Ubin, off Changi Point, are ideal for cycling, and there's a range of bikes available for rent next to the ferry terminal on Sentosa Island (S$5–10/hr).

ACCOMMODATION

CHINATOWN & THE FINANCIAL DISTRICT

Adler 259 South Bridge Rd ⓣ 6226 0173, ⓦ adlerhostel.com; map pp.680–681. This luxury hostel has wonderful antique furniture. The dorms have swanky pods with crisp linen, privacy curtain, reading lamp and individual plugs. Towels, earplugs and drinking water are also provided, and there's wi-fi throughout. Dorm S$65

A Beary Good Hostel 668A Pagoda St ⓣ 6222 4955, ⓦ abearygoodhostel.com; map pp.680–681. As the name suggests, all three "beary" hostels in Chinatown have cuddly toys scattered around, giving a cosy feel. The Pagoda St location is small and welcoming, with a kitchenette and comfy dorms. Dorm S$27

Five Stones Hostel 61 South Bridge Rd ⓣ 6535 5607, ⓦ fivestoneshostel.com; map pp.680–681. The themed rooms here offer a little glimpse into Singaporean life, from the history of rickshaws to the traditional game of *chaptah*. Polaroid snaps line the hallway and there's a wii in the chill-out area. Dorm S$31, double S$113

Matchbox 39 Ann Siang Rd ⓣ 6423 0237, ⓦ matchbox.sg; map pp.680–681. In an enviable location in the heart of Singapore's nightlife, this welcoming hostel offers capsule beds with thick walls and little hatch windows to communicate with your neighbour. There's a large attic lounge with parquet floors and TV, as well as wi-fi throughout. Dorm S$35

Pillows & Toast 40 Mosque St ⓣ 6220 4653, ⓦ pillowsntoast.com; map pp.680–681. Decked out in quirky orange and white murals, this friendly hostel has clean smallish dorms with bunks and metal lockers. There's a spacious attic lounge too. Dorm S$30

River City Inn 33C Hong Kong St ⓣ 6532 6091, ⓦ rivercityinn.com; map pp.680–681. The largest dorms here are a bit regimental, with rows of bunks, but very clean. Staff are friendly and there's wi-fi throughout. Dorm S$26

Rucksack Inn@Temple Street 52 Temple St ⓣ 6438 5146, ⓦ rucksackinn.com; map pp.680–681. The narrow dorms here are a bit of a squeeze, most don't have windows and the lounge is very small, although it remains a backpacker favourite thanks to the friendly staff, warm atmosphere and great location in the heart of Chinatown. Dorm S$33

Wink Hostel 8A Mosque St ⓣ 6222 2940, ⓦ winkhostel.com; map pp.680–681. The original pod hostel in the heart of Chinatown, with spotless dorms named after heritage trees and livened up with a splash of paint. There are also double pods for couples (S$90) – each with a reading light, socket and thick walls for privacy. A relaxed vibe prevails and the staff are among the friendliest in town. Dorm S$50

BRAS BASAH ROAD TO ROCHOR ROAD

Hang Out @ Mount Emily 10A Upper Wilkie Rd ⓣ 6438 5588, ⓦ hangouthotels.com; map p.678. Popular with flashpackers, this central budget hotel has bright, stylish rooms, a rooftop patio, a trendy lounge with a pool table and terrace. Pricier than a hostel, but the facilities are top-notch. Men-only dorm S$60, double S$285

YMCA 1 Orchard Rd ⓣ 6336 6000, ⓦ ymcaih.com.sg; map p.678. With over 100 rooms, this great hostel with modern amenities feels more like a hotel. Rooms are clean and all have private bath, flat-screen TVs and a/c, and wi-fi throughout. There's a fully equipped gym and an awesome rooftop terrace with a large swimming pool and incredible city views. Check the website for promotional deals. Dorm S$40, double S$180

LITTLE INDIA & ARAB STREET

★ **BUNC Hostel** 15 Upper Weld Rd ⓣ 6262 2862, ⓦ bunchostel.com; map p.683. This bright and airy hostel has it all, from Apple Macs for guests' use to fully equipped dorms with clothes racks, reading lamps, individual sockets, lockers and wi-fi. Guests can make use of the BBQ set by the breezy kitchen, and chill out in the outdoor lounge area with colourful beanbags, an Xbox, a mini football table and even a piano. The hostel regularly hosts local musicians, too. Dorm S$29, double S$140

★ TREAT YOURSELF

Wanderlust 2 Dickson Rd ⓣ 6396 3322, ⓦ wanderlusthotel.com; map p.683. Its lobby decked out in industrial glam chic, this award-winning boutique hotel entices travellers with unique interiors – from Origami-inspired doubles to whimsical rooms on the top floor with "Space", "Bling" and "Typewriter" themes. Doubles from S$301

Checkers Inn 46 Campbell Lane ⓣ 8533 4793, ⓦ checkersinn-backpackers.com; map p.683. This sought-after hostel right in the heart of Little India has an open-plan kitchen and a welcoming chill-out area with quirky ceiling decor. The bright, spacious dorms are spotless and staff are friendly. Dorm S$22, double S$98

Footprints 25A Perak Rd ⓣ 6295 5134, ⓦ footprintshostel.com; map p.683. This welcoming hostel has a lounge area with DVDs and a massage chair to soothe aching muscles. Dorms have lockers, individual plugs and reading lamps, and some have private bath. It's worth paying a bit extra for the freshly painted private rooms on the ground floor. Wi-fi throughout. Dorm S$24, double S$120

The Little Red Dot 125 Lavender St ⓣ 6294 7098, ⓦ atthelittlereddot.com; map p.683. The friendly staff at this dorm only hostel will make you feel right at home. There are dorms with bunks, as well as larger mixed and female dorms with "capsule beds" – each pod has a privacy curtain, locker and reading lamp. There's also a laidback lounge area with beanbags and sofas, a book exchange, Xbox, and free walking tours, pub crawls and gourmet safaris. S$22

Perak Hotel 12 Perak Rd ⓣ 6299 7733, ⓦ peraklodge.net; map p.683. This pleasant lodge in the heart of Little India offers private rooms with tea and coffee makers, TV, a/c and private bath. The hallways are decorated with paintings depicting the hustle and bustle of old Singapore. Double S$150

EATING

CENTRAL SINGAPORE

40 Hands 78 Yong Siak St (Tong Bahru MRT) ⓦ 40handscoffee.com; map pp.676–677. It's well worth travelling to this superb café hidden in a quiet residential area for coffees (S$4) made by award-winning baristas and imaginative cakes and pastries (S$2.50–7). There's a brunch menu Fri–Sun and gourmet hotdogs (S$12) and beers (S$10) in the evenings. Tues–Sun 8am–7pm, Fri & Sat until 10pm.

Newton Road Food Centre; map pp.676–677. Widely known as Newton Circus, this hawker centre by Newton MRT is a good spot for people watching as you tuck into some chilli crab and barbequed seafood. Mains from S$5. Daily noon–2am.

CHINATOWN & THE FINANCIAL DISTRICT

Amoy Food Court Telok Ayer St, at Amoy St; map pp.680–681. A huge range of noodle, rice and porridge dishes, all cheap and delicious. Mains from S$3. Mon–Fri 7am–4pm.

Annalakshmi 20 Havelock Rd; map pp.680–681. The profits at this terrific Indian veggie place go to an Indian cultural association. There's no set menu with prices – customers donate what they can. Daily 11am–3pm & 6.15–9.30pm.

Club Street Social 5 Gemmill Lane; map pp.680–681. This New York-style café and bar with bare brick walls serves all-day breakfasts (S$12), salads (S$15) and tasty panini (S$20). Mon–Fri 11am–10.30pm, Sat 9am–10.30pm, Sun 9am–9pm.

Foong Kee Coffee Shop 6 Keong Saik Rd; map pp.680–681. No-frills hawker restaurant serving award-winning roast pork, chicken noodles and roasted duck noodles – all for less than S$5. Mon–Sat 9am–6pm.

Glutton's Corner Next to Esplanade Mall (MRT); map pp.680–681. A great open-air hawker centre in an enviable waterside location serving chilli crab, satay, BBQ chicken wings, oyster omelettes and more (mains S$10). Mon–Thurs 5pm–2am, Fri 5am–3pm, Sun 4pm–1am.

Maxwell Road Food Centre Maxwell Rd, at Neil Rd; map pp.680–681. Open-sided food hall with over 100 stalls serving a variety of local and regional dishes including *tian tian* chicken rice, *char kway teow* and congee with pork and century egg. Daily 8am–10pm.

Mei Heong Yuen Dessert 65–67 Temple St; map pp.680–681. Cool down with a refreshing traditional dessert at this local café as you explore Chinatown. The large snow ice desserts (S$5) are creatively presented, and are big enough to share. Daily 10.30am–10pm.

Moosehead 110 Telok Ayer St; map pp.680–681. A friendly, cosy restaurant serving Mediterranean food to share, as well as lunchtime salads and sandwiches. Service is a bit lethargic but it's well worth the wait – the grilled sea bass (S$28) is outstanding. Mon–Fri noon–midnight, Sat 5pm–midnight.

★**Sarnies** 136 Telok Ayer St; map pp.680–681. This welcoming little café, with the menu casually scribbled on the walls in colourful chalk, serves hearty sandwiches with sourdough or rye bread (S$13.50). The freshly roasted coffee (S$5) is great too, and there's all-day brunch at the weekend. Mon & Tues 7.30am–7pm, Wed–Fri 7.30am–10pm, Sat & Sun 9am–4pm.

Sinar Pagi Nasi Padang 13 Circular Rd; map pp.680–681. Join the queue of hungry business workers from the nearby offices in Boat Quay who head here for the flavourful authentic Padang food. A meal will set you back no more than S$10. Mon–Fri 11am–9pm.

BRAS BASAH ROAD TO ROCHOR ROAD

Ah Loy Thai 100 Beach Rd; map p.678. Located within the Shaw Tower, the service here may be leisurely but the inexpensive Thai food is well worth the wait – the dishes here are among the city's very best. Mains from S$8. Mon–Fri noon–8.15pm, Sat 1–7.15pm.

★**Artichoke** 161 Middle Rd; map p.678. Tucked away in a little courtyard just off Middle Rd, this gem of a place attracts expats and locals alike for its creative Middle Eastern food, prepared using local ingredients. The award-winning chef rustles up succulent lamb dishes, and there are sharing plates and home-made mezze too. Evenings only during the week. Mains S$20. Tues–Fri 6.30–9.45pm, Sat & Sun 11.30am–2.45pm & 6.30–9.45pm.

Cups n Canvas 139 Selegie Rd; map p.678. This cosy café-art studio with mismatched furniture and colourful artworks on display offers soups (S$6.90), salads (S$9.90), nibbles (S$5.90) and sandwiches (S$9.90). There are weekend art jamming sessions with tutors. Tues–Thurs 10.30am–10pm, Fri & Sat 10.30am–11pm, Sun 10am–8pm.

Fast Food For Thought 8 Queen St; map p.678. This great café and burger (S$8.50) joint doubles up as a community art museum. Part of the profits support social causes – check out the empty glass jars with orphans' notes and drawings that decorate the ceiling. Tues–Sun 10am–10pm.

Gold Food 91 Bencoolen St; map p.678. A popular Thai Chinese restaurant serving great *pad thai* (S$10) – make sure you get here early before the long queue forms. Daily 11.30am–4pm & 5–11pm.

Overdoughs 161 Middle Rd; map p.678. This tiny bakery under the same management as *Artichoke* displays a delectable selection of sweet pastries including exquisite baklava, which come in a variety of flavours including fig chutney and pistachio and apricot. Tues–Sat 10am–6pm, Sun 10am–4pm.

Saveur 5 Purvis St; map p.678. The queue at this casual-chic French bistro with minimalist decor forms way before the doors even open. Hearty dishes are prepared using local ingredients – try the tasty duck leg confit (S$10.90). Mon–Sat noon–2.15pm & 6–9.30pm, Sun 6–9pm.

ORCHARD ROAD

Din Tai Fung The Paragon, Orchard Rd; map pp.684–685. Watch the chefs at work in the glass-panelled kitchen as they skilfully wrap juicy meat dumplings (S$7.30) in soft, thin dough and steam them on bamboo racks. Mon–Fri 11am–10pm, Sat & Sun 10am–10pm.

Killiney Curry Puff 93 Killiney Rd; map pp.684–685. A simple place to refuel with a curry puff (S$1.40) or two. Different fillings include potato and beef. Mon–Fri 7am–7.30pm, Sat & Sun 7am–6pm.

Killiney Kopitiam 67 Killiney Rd; map pp.684–685. It doesn't get any cheaper than this at this well-established no-frills café – a *nasi lemak* will set you back just S$2, while a chicken curry is just S$6.50. Bargain. Daily 6.30am–11pm, Tues & Sun until 6pm.

Shiraz 391 Orchard Rd; map pp.684–685. This kebab joint right outside Ngee Ann City Mall is the best spot to grab a kebab (S$9.20) as you shop. Daily 11am–11pm.

LITTLE INDIA & ARAB STREET

Ananda Bhavan 95 Syed Alwi Rd; map p.683. This outstanding Indian restaurant is known throughout Little India for its superb vegetarian dishes, from tandoori (S$7.35) to biryani sets (S$9.60). Open 24hr.

Anjappar 76–78 Race Course Rd; map p.683. This a/c restaurant exclusively serves dishes from Chennai. The excellent chicken biryani (S$10) sells like hot cakes – or try the *chettinad* chicken masala (S$8.50). Daily 11.30am–10.30pm.

The Banana Leaf Apolo 54 Race Course Rd; map p.683. This place has been going strong since 1974, specializing in tenderly cooked red snapper fish head curry (S$22). There's plenty else on offer, including a smattering of veggie dishes. Daily 10.30am–10.30pm.

★ **Chye Seng Huat Hardware (CSHH)** 150 Tyrwhitt Rd; map p.683. Set in a former metal and hardware store, this little gem of a café is a coffee lover's paradise: the island bar has a 360-degree view of baristas brewing coffee (S$5), a wall displaying coffee products and a little shop selling quirky accessories and equipment. There are "tummy fillers" too, from scrambled eggs (S$11) to tuna melts (S$12). Tues–Fri 9am–7pm, Sat & Sun 9am–10pm.

★ **Jaggi's** 34–36 Race Course Rd; map p.683. The wonderful smell of mouth-watering curry reaches you as soon as you open the doors of this superb Punjabi restaurant. Line up, point at what tickles your fancy and enjoy (dishes from S$2.70). Mon–Fri 11.30am–3pm & 5.30–10.30pm; Sat & Sun 11–3.30pm & 5.30–10.30pm.

Lavender Food Square 195 Lavender St; map p.683. This popular food court serves inexpensive dishes –the *Kok Kee Wanton* stall rustles up particularly good noodles (S$4). Open 24hr.

WHERE TO EAT

The city's chain **coffee shops**, serving lattes and bagels, are the cheapest choice for a Western breakfast. The classic Chinese breakfast is congee, a watery rice porridge augmented with strips of meat, though *dim sum* is available to those with less exotic tastes. As for good **chains**, you'll spot *Bread Talk* (delicious cakes and other baked goodies) and *Mr Bean*, a soymilk drink outlet all over Singapore, which also serves coffee, muffins and waffles.

Hawker centres are by far the best places for an inexpensive lunch or dinner; they are open either from lunchtime through to dinner or from around 5pm until late. Also, pretty much every mall has its own **food court** (generally open from noon to 10pm) featuring numerous cuisines. Don't know what to get at a hawker centre? Look for the stalls with the long queues and join them; the locals know what's good. Avoid the peak lunch (12.30–1.30pm) and dining (6–7pm) periods, and watch for reserved seats, often indicated by something as easy to miss as a packet of tissues.

9

Nan Hwa Chong 812 North Bridge Rd; map p.683. Hugely popular Teochew Chinese place serving fish head steamboat soup heated over charcoals. The secret here is the tipoh, dried sole fish, which is added to the broth for flavour. A meal will set you back about S$20. Daily 4.30pm–12.30am.

Tekka Market Food Centre Bukit Bimah at Serangoon Rd (MRT); map p.683. One of the best and cheapest spots in town to grab a quick meal – there's plenty of choice, from Indian to Chinese dishes (mains from S$3). Daily 7.30am–11pm.

The Tiramisú Hero 121 Tyrwhitt Rd; map p.683. This mellow café with fairy lights and mismatched furniture is a sweet tooth's delight, offering ten different flavours of tiramisu, from oreo to cinnamon, served in cute glass jars (S$7.30). There are also mini portions (S$3.50) for those just wanting to tickle their tastebuds while enjoying a refreshing iced coffee (S$6.50). Thurs–Tues 11am–10pm.

Windowsill in the Woods 78 Horne Rd; map p.683. With over fifteen creatively made sweet pies (S$7) including banana almond brittle, lime vodka coconut and strawberry lemon, this is the place for an energetic sugar kick as you explore Little India. There are light dishes too, such as roast beef sandwiches (S$14). Tues–Thurs 11am–9.30pm, Fri 11am–10.30pm, Sat & Sun 10am–10.30pm.

Zam Zam 697–699 North Bridge Rd; map p.683. This friendly place has been making great murtabak (S$5) since 1908; the biryani (S$6) is wonderful too. Daily 7am–11pm.

NIGHTLIFE

The lively area around Club Street, to the east of China Town, is home to trendy restaurants and bars, and really comes alive on the weekends. There are also a number of bars and clubs in nearby Boat Quay.

BARS AND PUBS

It's possible to buy a small glass of beer in most bars and pubs for around S$10, but prices can be double or treble that, especially around Orchard Road or on the Quays. During happy hour in the early evening, bars offer local beers and house wine either at half price, or "one for one" – you get two of whatever you order, but one is held back for later. Most places close around 2am.

28 Hong Kong Street 28 Hong Kong St; map pp.680–681. This inconspicuous "secret" bar with just a beige door and no sign is well worth looking for. The atmosphere is bustling and the wonderfully innovative cocktails (S$18) will ensure you stay for more than one. Book ahead. Mon–Wed 5.30pm–1am, Thurs until 2am, Fri & Sat until 3am.

Bar Stories 57A Haji Lane; map p.683. Sit at the bar and watch the bartenders creatively mix colourful concoctions of cocktails (S$25) with all the necessary love and care. There's no menu so just wait and be surprised. Sun–Thurs 3pm–1am, Fri & Sat 3pm–2am.

Long Bar 1 Beach Rd; map p.678. Though the *Long Bar* has become a tourist trap in recent years, it is the birthplace of the Singapore Sling (S$32) after all… Sip away at the bar and shell your peanuts on the floor at this iconic drinking hole in the swanky *Raffles Hotel*. Sun–Thurs 11am–12.30am, Fri & Sat 11am–1.30am.

Oxwell & Co. 5 Ann Siang Rd; map pp.680–681. Welcoming bar with eclectic interiors featuring wooden and vintage furniture. Sample all manner of house-distilled spirits, or try the excellent home-made gin and tonics (S$12) available on tap. Tues–Sat 10am–1am.

The Penny Black 26–27 Boat Quay; map pp.680–681. Named after the world's oldest stamp, this Victorian London pub was built in Britain and painstakingly reassembled on the busy waterfront. The outdoor area is a great spot for people-watching over an Old Speckled Hen or for watching a Premiership game. Mon–Thurs 11.30am–1am, Fri & Sat 11.30am–2am, Sun 11.30am–midnight.

La Terraza 12 Ann Siang Rd; map pp.680–681. The fourth-floor breezy rooftop terrace of The Screening Room is a great spot for drinks – soak in the city views as you sip on a cocktail or two. Mon–Thurs 6pm–1am, Fri & Sat until 3am.

CLUBS

Singapore's clubs have become increasingly sophisticated in recent years: European and American dance music dominates and many feature live cover bands. Clubs tend to open around 9pm, and can stay open until 5 or 6am. Most clubs have a cover charge of S$15–35, though this is usually less for women.

Attica 3A River Valley Rd, #01–03, Clarke Quay; Clarke Quay MRT; map pp.680–681. One of Singapore's most popular clubs with professionals, expats and fashionistas. The outside bar offers a welcome alternative to the energetic dancefloor. A place to see and be seen, *Attica* is generally still pumping in the wee hours. Fri & Sat S$32 entrance fee, including two free drinks. Wed–Sat 10.30pm–4am.

The Butter Factory 1 Fullerton Road; Raffles City MRT; map pp.680–681. This club is a bit of a local legend, with a loyal Singaporean clientele, DJs-of-the-moment dishing out urban grooves, r'n'b and EDM, while trendies and creatives check each other out in the Art Bar. Wed 11pm–4am, Fri & Sat 11pm–6am.

St James' Power Station 3 Sentosa Gateway ☎ 6270 7676; HarbourFront MRT; map pp.676–677. The refurbished power station has been converted into an insomniac's dream; with more than six bars and clubs under one roof, punters can move between salsa, karaoke rooms and r'n'b without getting wet. One cover charge (S$20 women, S$25 men); free Sun–Thurs. Daily 6am–6pm.

Zouk 17 Jiak Kim St ⓦzoukclub.com; Tiong Bahru MRT; map pp.680–681. Still going strong after 22 years and one of Singapore's trendiest venues, *Zouk* features different-themed sub-clubs. DJs from Europe and the US often appear here, as well as other local live acts. Cover charge from S$25 (includes 2 drinks). Happy hour 11pm–midnight. Tues–Sat 10pm–3am.

LIVE MUSIC

Check out the latest live music gigs on ⓦsideshow.sg, the website of an events company who organize parties at a number of offbeat venues around town.

Blu Jaz 12 Bali Lane ⓦblujaz.net; map p.683. Mellow jazz café serving reasonably priced beer. There's live music most nights – check the website for listings. Mon–Thurs noon–1am, Fri noon–2am, Sat 4pm–2am.

Timbre @ The Arts House 1 Old Parliament Lane #01-04 ⓦtimbregroup.asia; map pp.680–681. Set in a historical building by Boat Quay and the Singapore River, this popular joint is a good spot to sit back and enjoy some live tunes. There are nightly bands – check the website for what's on. Mon–Thurs 6pm–1am, Fri & Sat 6pm–2am.

ENTERTAINMENT

CINEMA

Singapore has more than fifty cinemas so you should have no trouble finding one if you're in need of a movie fix. The following cinemas show films in English:

Cathay Cineplex Cineleisure Orchard 8 Grange Rd ⓦcathaycineplexes.com.sg; S$11.

Screening Room 12 Ang Siang Rd ⓦscreeningroom.com.sg; free although there's a minimum spend of S$15 on food and drink at the bar.

THEATRE

Esplanade Theatres on the Bay 1 Esplanade Drive ⓣ6828 8377, ⓦesplanade.com. With more than eight venues within the two domes, there is something going on every night, including plays from Europe, Australia and other parts of Asia.

Repertory Theatre DBS Arts Centre, 20 Merbau Rd, near Clarke Quay ⓦsrt.com.sg. This understated, refurbished warehouse shows some of the best international and local plays in Singapore.

SHOPPING

Singapore is synonymous with shopping, though prices aren't rock bottom across the board. Good deals can be found on watches, cameras, electrical equipment, fabrics and antiques; however, many other items offer no substantial savings. The free monthly *Where Singapore* (available in coffee shops, large hotels and MRT stations), has plenty of suggestions as to what you can buy and where. Note that there is a goods and services tax (GST) of seven percent, but tourists can claim a refund on purchases at retailers displaying a blue and grey Tax-Free Shopping sticker.

Books Kinokuniya, #03-10/15 Ngee Ann City, 391 Orchard Rd, is the island's biggest bookshop.

Clothes Here you're spoiled for choice, since you can find any designer you want in Orchard Street's malls. For something quirkier, try the local designers along Haji Lane in the Arab Street area. Also, check out bYSI at #B1-33 Citylink Mall for affordable luxury for women, or Frü Frü & Tigerlily at 19 Jalan Pisang (Bugis MRT) for playful jewellery and creative items of clothing.

Electronic equipment The intersection of Bencoolen St and Rochor Rd is known for electrical goods; Sim Lim Square at 1 Rocher Canal Rd is a gadget nerd's wonderland.

Fabrics and silk On Arab St (see p.682), you'll find exquisite textiles and batiks, and some good deals on jewellery. From here, make a beeline for the silk stores and goldsmiths of Little India (see p.682).

Music Singapore's biggest music retailer is That CD Shop, #01–01 Pacific Plaza, 9 Scotts Rd.

Souvenirs Eng Tiang Huat, 284 River Valley Rd, for Oriental musical instruments, wayang costumes and props. Singapore Handicraft Centre, Chinatown Point, 133 New Bridge Rd, has around fifty souvenir shops under one roof. If you're looking for something unique, purple gold creations are available from Aspial, Lee Hwa Jewellery and Goldheart Jewellery at #01–37 41 Wisma Atria. TWG Tea Company at ION Orchard, 2 Orchard Turn, specializes in more than 800 brands of tea, including the rare-as-gold-dust Sakura! Sakura!

CHINESE OPERA

If you walk around Singapore's streets for long enough, you're likely to come across a **wayang**, or Chinese opera, played out on tumbledown outdoor stages that spring up overnight next to temples and markets, or just at the side of the road. Wayangs are highly dramatic and stylized affairs, in which garishly made-up and costumed characters enact popular Chinese legends to the accompaniment of the crashes of cymbals and gongs. They take place throughout the year, but the best time to catch one is during the Festival of the Hungry Ghosts (see p.674) when they are held to entertain passing spooks. An alternative is to pop along to the **Chinese opera teahouse** at 5 Smith St, near the Chinatown Complex (ⓣ6323 4862, ⓦctcopera.com), where S$25 buys you Chinese tea, snacks, desserts and an opera performance with English subtitles.

9

DIRECTORY

Banks and exchange There are banks and ATMs throughout central Singapore. All of Singapore's banks change travellers' cheques. Licensed moneychangers abound on Arab Street, at the Serangoon Road's Mustafa Centre, and in Orchard Road's shopping centres.

Embassies and consulates Australia, 25 Napier Rd (☎6836 4100); Brunei, 325 Tanglin Road (☎6733 9055); Canada, 1 George St (☎6854 5900); Indonesia, 7 Chatsworth Rd (☎6737 7442); Ireland, 541 Orchard Road, Liat Towers, 8th floor (☎6238 7616); Laos, 51 Goldhill Plaza (☎6250 6044); Malaysia, 301 Jervois Rd (☎6235 0111); New Zealand, 1 George St (☎6235 9966); Philippines, 20 Nassim Rd (☎6737 3977); South Africa, 331 North Bridge Rd, Odeon Towers, 15th floor (☎6339 3319); Thailand, 370 Orchard Rd (☎6737 2644); UK, 100 Tanglin Rd (☎6424 4200); US, 27 Napier Rd (☎6476 9100); Vietnam, 10 Leedon Park (☎6462 5994).

Hospitals Singapore General Hospital, Outram Rd (☎6222 3322); Raffles Hospital, 585 North Bridge Rd (☎6311 1111).

Internet All accommodation options reviewed have free wi-fi; most offer free internet too.

Laundry EasyWash Laundromat (S$5; 24hr) Block 4 Sago Lane #01-105, Chinatown, and at Block 17 Beach Road #01-4709. Check the Yellow Pages for laundry nearest to your guesthouse/hostel.

Pharmacy Guardian Pharmacy has more than forty outlets, including ones at Centrepoint Shopping Centre, 176 Orchard Rd, and Raffles City, 252 North Bridge Rd.

Police Report thefts at Orchard Neighbourhood Police Station, 51 Killiney Rd, off Orchard Rd (☎1800 735 9999); in an emergency, dial ☎999.

Post office 2 Orchard Turn, #B2-62 ION (daily 11am–7pm); 79 Robinson Rd (Mon–Fri 8.30am–6pm, Sat 8.30am–1pm).

Day-trips

Beyond the downtown area, Singapore still retains pockets of greenery in between its sprawling new towns. Most rewarding is the justifiably world-famous **Singapore Zoo** – one of the world's finest. In the east, not too far from Changi Airport, is **Changi Village**, in whose prison the Japanese interned Allied troops and civilians during World War II. It's preceded by **East Coast Park**, a favourite with rollerbladers, waterskiers and seafood lovers. **Sentosa Island**, south of HarbourFront, attracts beachgoers and thrill-seekers with its white sand crescents and 4-D amusement park rides.

SINGAPORE ZOO AND NIGHT SAFARI

The award-winning **Singapore Zoo** (daily 8.30am–6pm; S$22) on Mandai Lake Road is an open zoo, where moats are used to separate the animals instead of cages. Though leopards and pumas are kept behind glass-fronted enclosures, this is a more thoughtful and humane place than conventional zoos and it manages to approximate the natural habitats of the animals it holds. There are more than 2800 animals here, representing more than 300 species, so it's best to allow a whole day for your visit.

Highlights include free-ranging orang-utans, the new Frozen Tundra exhibit which features Inuka, the first polar bear to be born in the tropics, wolverines and raccoon dogs, and Fragile Forest, a 20,000-cubic-metre flight area which immerses visitors in the richness and diversity of a rainforest.

Even more spectacular than the daytime zoo, and one of Singapore's highlights, is undoubtedly the **Night Safari** (daily 7.30pm–midnight; S$35 inclusive of tram ride), where you take the night tram and walk the jungle trails of the park to watch over 2500 animals including giant fruit bats, Asian elephants, Indian rhinos, giraffes, leopards, hyenas, otters, pangolins and incredibly cute (but shy) fishing cats play out their nocturnal routines. Don't forget to watch the impressive "Creatures of the Night" show. The zoo and Night Safari combined ticket is S$49.

To get to the zoo, take **bus** #171 from either Stamford Road or Orchard Road to Mandai Road, then transfer to #927. Alternatively, take the MRT to Ang Mo Kio and connect with bus #138, or take the MRT to Chua Chu Kang and connect with bus #927.

EAST COAST PARK

While the beach at this vast waterfront park, stretching for 10km along the East Coast Parkway, is not the prettiest, this shaded park itself is a favourite with Singaporeans for rollerblading, biking, windsurfing and eating – this is where

you find the fabled **East Coast Seafood Centre**, famous for its chilli crab and other sea bounty (1202 East Coast Parkway; dinner only). You can rent bikes (S$5–10/hr) and inline skates from the kiosks in the park, or else try your hand at cable skiing (waterskiing while pulled around the lake along a wire cable; SG$32 for one hour).

Take bus #401 from Bedok MRT.

NORTH EASTERN RIVERINE LOOP (NERL)

The North Eastern Riverine Loop (Ⓦnparks.gov.sg) is a system of connected scenic pathways offering a stunning view of Singapore's waterways and reservoirs. The 26km loop links four parks – Punggol Park, Punggol Point Park, Punggol Waterway Park and Sengkang Riverside Park – home to rich biodiversity and birds such as collared kingfishers, herons and egrets.

Visitors can cycle (S$8/hr) the entire 26km, or opt for a shorter 13km loop. There are places to eat and a riding school (S$65/30min) along the way.

CHANGI MUSEUM

Bus #2 from Tanah Merah MRT drops you right outside the **Changi Museum**, near the infamous site of a World War II POW camp in which Allied prisoners were subjected to the harshest of treatment by their Japanese jailers. The hugely moving prison **museum** (daily 9.30am–5pm; free) has sketches and photographs that plot the Japanese invasion of Singapore and the fate of the soldiers and civilians subsequently incarcerated here and in nearby camps. There's a replica of a simple wooden chapel, its north wall inscribed with poignant messages penned by former POWs, their friends and relatives.

SENTOSA ISLAND

The theme-park island of **Sentosa Island**, occupying five square kilometres, is a contrived but enjoyable place, linked to the southern shore of downtown Singapore by a 710m causeway and by a necklace of cable cars. Avoid coming at the weekend and don't even think about visiting on public holidays.

At the **Underwater World** (daily 10am–7pm; S$29.90), located near Siloso Point, a moving walkway carries you along a tunnel between two large tanks: sharks lurk menacingly on all sides, huge stingrays drape themselves languidly above you and immense shoals of gaily coloured fish dart to and fro; you can also feed rays by hand in a separate tank. Admission to the dolphin shows at **Dolphin Lagoon** is included in the price.

Those wanting a bit more action can take part in the **Gogreen Segway Eco Adventure** (daily 10am–8.30pm; S$38), learn to surf on the artificial waves of **Wave House Sentosa** (daily 10.30am–10.30pm; S$40/hr), race down a paved track on the **Sentosa Luge** (daily 10am–9.30pm; S$13), live out your circus dreams on the **Flying Trapeze** (Mon–Fri 2.30–6.30pm, Sat & Sun 2.30–7pm; S$10 per swing), or take part in the **4-D rides** (daily 10am–9pm; S$38.90 per ride) and virtual roller

VISITING SENTOSA

The easiest way to get to Sentosa is to catch the MRT to HarbourFront Station; from there, you can either hop onto the Sentosa Express (S$4) or take a stroll down the Sentosa Boardwalk (S$1). The most spectacular way there, however, is by cable car (daily 8.45am–10pm; S$26) from HarbourFront Tower II.

Sentosa has an efficient **monorail** and **bus** system (daily 7am–10.30pm, Sat until midnight) – there's a colour-coded system of three bus lines and a beach tram that link the island's attractions, although the best way to get about is to **rent a bike** for the day (S$12/hr; tandem bike S$18) from Go Green Cycle & Island Explorer (Ⓦgogreencycle.sg). With over 60 food and beverage outlets, there are plenty of options for **eating**. Sentosa's many attractions add up, so it's really worth looking into **ticket packages** (visit Ⓦsentosa.com.sg for details).

coaster at Singapore's branch of **Universal Studios** (daily 10am–7pm; S$74).

Fort Siloso (Bus #1, #2 or #3 from Beach Station; daily 10am–6pm; S$8; free guided tours Fri, Sat & Sun at 12.30pm & 3.30pm), on the far western tip of the island, is actually a cluster of buildings and gun emplacements above a series of tunnels bored into the island – it guarded Singapore's western approaches from the 1880s until 1956, but was rendered obsolete in 1942, when the Japanese invaded Singapore from the north. Today, the recorded voice of Battery Sergeant Major Cooper talks you through a mock-up of a nineteenth-century barracks, complete with living quarters, laundry and assault course.

Sentosa also boasts a trio of nice **beaches** (free trams connect the beaches) on its southwestern coast, with a cluster of restaurants nearby.

AYUTTHAYA

Thailand

HIGHLIGHTS

❶ **The Grand Palace, Bangkok** Home of the country's holiest temple. **See p.711**

❷ **Ayutthaya** Crumbling relics of an ancient kingdom. **See p.732**

❸ **Chiang Mai** Thailand's adventure tourism capital. **See p.744**

❹ **Ko Pha Ngan** Choose between quiet island beaches and the infamous full-moon parties. **See p.790**

❺ **Khao Sok National Park** Mist-clad cliffs and whooping gibbons make for a memorable stay. **See p.801**

❻ **Krabi region** Home to stunning islands, lovely beaches and great diving. **See p.808**

HIGHLIGHTS ARE MARKED ON THE MAP ON PP.698–699

ROUGH COSTS

Daily budget Basic US$20, occasional treat US$50

Drink Singha beer (large) US$2.50

Food *Pad Thai* US$1

Hostel/Budget hotel US$6–15

Travel Bangkok–Chiang Mai (713km): bus 10hr, US$15–29; train 12hr, US$8–48

FACT FILE

Population 67 million

Language Thai

Religions Buddhism and Islam

Currency Baht (B)

Capital Bangkok

International phone code ☎ 66

Time zone GMT + 7hr

10

Introduction

With sixteen million foreigners flying into the country each year, Thailand is Asia's primary holiday destination and a useful and popular first stop on any overland journey through Southeast Asia. Despite the influx of tourist cash and influence, Thailand's cultural integrity remains largely undamaged. Some ninety percent of Thais practise Theravada Buddhism, and King Bhumibol is a revered figure. The country is still mainly traditional and rural, and though some cities boast modern high-rises and neon lights, tiered temple rooftops and saffron-robed monks still predominate.

Most journeys start in **Bangkok**, which can be an overwhelming introduction to Southeast Asia, but there are traveller-oriented guesthouses aplenty, as well as heaps of spectacular temples to visit. A popular side-trip is to **Kanchanaburi**, home of the infamous Bridge over the River Kwai. After Bangkok, most travellers head north, sometimes via the ancient capitals of **Ayutthaya** and **Sukhothai**, to the enjoyably laidback city of **Chiang Mai**, where they organize all manner of outdoor activities. To the northwest of Chiang Mai, the beautiful highlands around **Mae Hong Son** and **Pai** are idyllic, while Thailand's **northeast** (Isaan), its least-visited region, offers ancient Khmer ruins at **Phimai** and **Phanom Rung** and is home to the country's most accessible national park, **Khao Yai**.

WHEN TO GO

The **climate** of most of Thailand is governed by three seasons: rainy (roughly June–Oct), caused by the southwest monsoon; cool (Nov–Feb); and hot (March–May). The cool season is the most pleasant time to visit and the most popular; during the hot season, temperatures can rise to 40°C. The rainy season hits the Andaman coast harder than anywhere else in the country – heavy rainfall often starts in May and persists until November. The Gulf coast gets much less rain from the southwest monsoon, but is also hit by the northeast monsoon, which brings rain between October and December.

After trekking and temples in the north, most visitors head for the **beach**. Thailand's **eastern and southern coasts** are lined with gorgeous white-sand shores, aquamarine seas and kaleidoscopic reefs. The most popular resorts for backpackers are the east-coast islands of **Ko Samet** and **Ko Chang**, the **Gulf coast islands** of Ko Samui, Ko Pha Ngan and Ko Tao, and the **Andaman coast** centres of Laem Phra Nang, Ko Phi Phi, Ko Lanta and Ko Lipe; on this coast, Ko Chang and Ko Phayam offer quieter scenes.

CHRONOLOGY

c. Third or second century BC Buddhism is introduced to the region by Indian missionaries.

c. Sixth century AD The Theravada Buddhist Dvaravati civilization emerges in central Thailand.

Eighth century Peninsular Thailand comes under the sway of the Srivijaya Empire, a Mahayana Buddhist state centred on Sumatra.

Ninth century The Khmer Empire, based at Angkor, takes control of much of Thailand. Their administrative centre is at modern-day Lopburi.

1238 The Thais capture the Khmer outpost at Sukhothai.

1278–99 The reign of King Ramkhamhaeng. He seizes control of the Chao Phraya Valley and develops Sukhothai as the capital of the first major Thai kingdom. Following his death the empire declines.

1351 King Ramathibodi founds the city of Ayutthaya and adopts Angkor's elaborate court rituals. Ayutthaya prospers and by 1540 it rules most of the area of modern-day Thailand.

1568 The Burmese occupy for twenty years.

Seventeenth century Ayutthaya makes a spectacular comeback, as its foreign trade booms, first with Portugal, then Spain, England, France and Holland.

1767 Ayutthaya is recaptured by the Burmese, who raze it to the ground, take tens of thousands of prisoners and abandon the city to the jungle.

1768 Phraya Taksin, a charismatic general, emerges out of the lawless mess, and is crowned king at Thonburi, on the opposite bank to modern-day Bangkok. He conquers all of Ayutthaya's territories, plus Cambodia and Laos.

1782 Taksin is ousted in a coup led by his military commander, Chao Phraya Chakri.

1782–1809 Chakri – reigning as Rama I – moves the capital across the river to Bangkok and builds a new royal palace in Ratanakosin.

1809 Rama I's son, Rama II, succeeds the throne, securing the Chakri dynasty, still in place today.

1851–68 The reign of Rama IV, known as Mongkut. Signs trade treaties with the British, French and the US. By avoiding a close relationship with one power, he protects Thailand from annexation.

1868 Mongkut's son, fifteen-year-old Chulalongkorn (who had been educated by Mrs Anna Leonowens, subject of *The King and I*), takes the throne as Rama V.

1893 Thailand comes under pressure from Western powers, most notably during the Franco–Siamese Crisis when the French send gunboats as far as Bangkok. Chulalongkorn cedes Laos and parts of Cambodia to France.

June 24, 1932 Lawyer Pridi Phanomyong and an army major, Luang Phibunsongkhram (Phibun), lead a coup. Siam's absolute monarchy comes to an end as King Rama VII is sidelined to a symbolic position.

1938 Phibun is elected prime minister. A year later he renames the country Thailand.

December 8, 1941 The Japanese invade, and, after initially resisting, Phibun's government allies with Japan. Pridi secretly coordinates the resistance movement. More than 100,000 people (POWs and Asian labourers) die constructing the notorious Death Railway linking Thailand and Burma.

January 1946 Pridi is elected prime minister.

June 9, 1946 Rama VII's successor, King Ananda, is shot dead in his bed. Three palace servants are convicted, but the murder has never been satisfactorily explained. He is succeeded by King Bhumibol, the current king (Rama IX).

April 1948 Phibun becomes prime minister, and allies with the US against the communist threat.

1957 Phibun narrowly wins a general election, but only by vote-rigging and coercion. He is overthrown by army chief General Sarit, who encourages the monarchy into a more active role.

1963 Sarit dies and is succeeded by General Thanom. The Thais, with US backing, conduct covert military operations in Laos. By 1968, around 45,000 US military personnel are in Thailand, and the economy swells with dollars. Prostitution proliferates, especially in Bangkok's Patpong district.

October 1973 Bloody student demonstrations bring the downfall of Thanom.

October 1976 Students demonstrate again, and hundreds are beaten by police; the military take control and suspend the constitution.

1980 General Prem Tinsulanonda becomes prime minister, with broad popular and parliamentary support, and rules with a unique mixture of dictatorship and democracy. He stands down in 1988 to allow for a democratic prime minister.

February 23, 1991 Prem's successor, Chatichai Choonhavan, is overthrown in a coup. General Suchinda becomes premier.

May 1992 Mass demonstrations against Suchinda are brutally crushed, with hundreds killed or injured, but Suchinda is forced to resign when King Bhumibol expresses his disapproval.

1997 Foreign-exchange dealers mount speculative attacks on the baht and the currency collapses, causing a currency crisis across the region.

2001 One of Thailand's wealthiest men, telecoms tycoon Thaksin Shinawatra, and his new party, Thai Rak Thai (Thai Loves Thai), win the elections.

2004 Violence in the Islamic southern provinces escalates sharply, with frequent attacks on police, soldiers, and also Buddhist monks.

September 2006 Thaksin's government is overthrown in a bloodless army coup.

December 2007 The pro-Thaksin People Power Party wins parliamentary elections.

October 2008 Pro-royalist "Yellow Shirts" escalate their protests, blockading Bangkok Airport.

December 2008 The Democrat Party's Abhisit Vejjajiva becomes prime minister.

March 2010 Thousands of "Red Shirts" or pro-Thaksin supporters seize a part of central Bangkok, demanding the resignation of Abhisit, who sends in the troops in May, resulting in 91 deaths.

May 2011 Thaksin's sister, Yingluck, wins a general election and begins to work on a pardon for her brother, who, convicted of corruption, has been living in exile.

January 2014 Royalist, nationalist protesters attempt to shut Bangkok down and postpone elections indefinitely.

ARRIVAL

Thailand has **land borders** with Myanmar (Burma), Laos, Cambodia and Malaysia, and all these countries have embassies in Bangkok. Bangkok is a major transport hub in Southeast Asia and there are **flights** in from all over the world. There are also international airports at Phuket, Chiang Mai, Ko Samui and Krabi with flights from regional hubs, including Kuala Lumpur and Singapore.

10

10

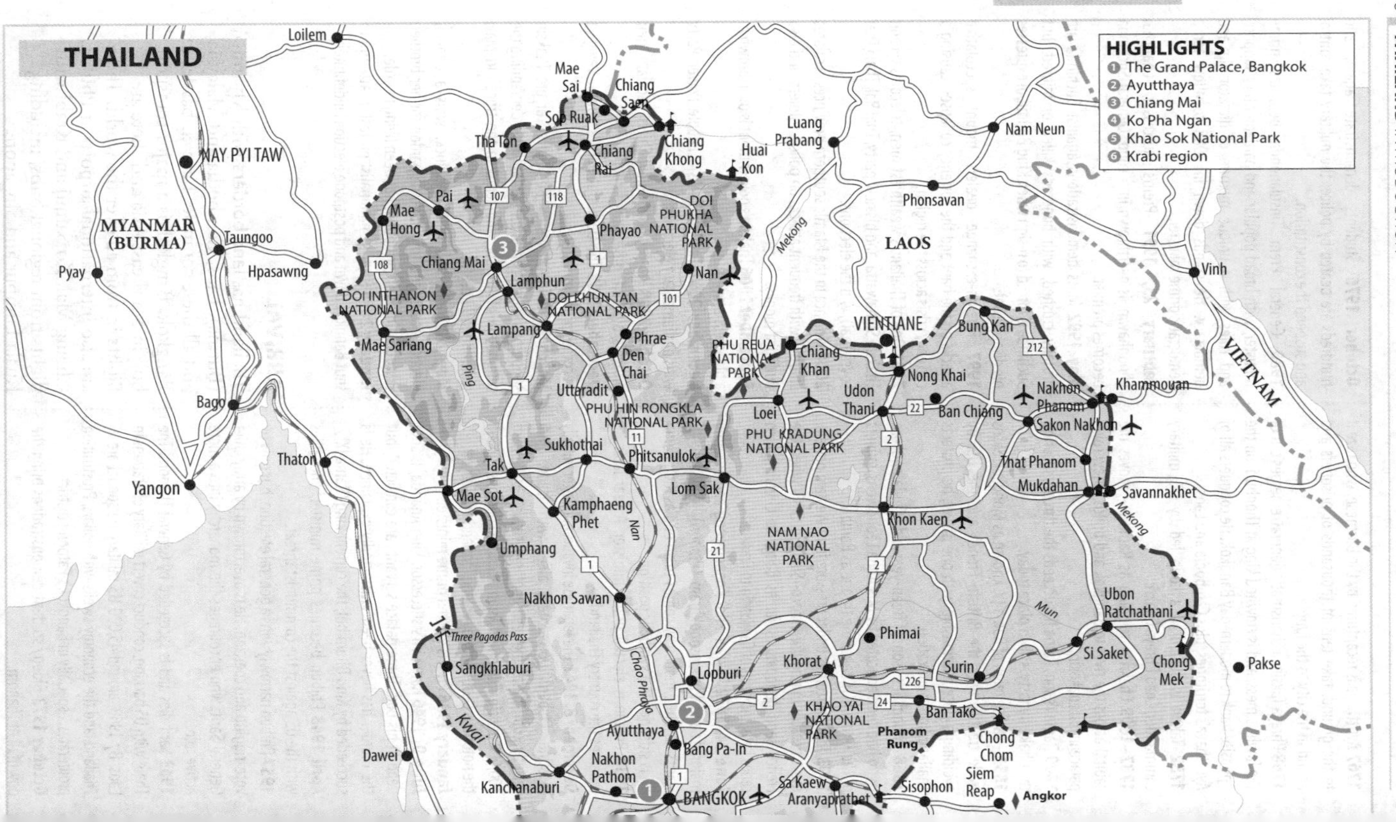
THAILAND
HIGHLIGHTS
1 The Grand Palace, Bangkok
2 Ayutthaya
3 Chiang Mai
4 Ko Pha Ngan
5 Khao Sok National Park
6 Krabi region
MYANMAR (BURMA)
NAY PYI TAW
LAOS
VIETNAM
VIENTIANE
BANGKOK
Loilem
Pyay
Taungoo
Hpasawng
Bago
Thaton
Yangon
Dawei
Mae Sai
Chiang Saen
Sop Ruak
Tha Ton
Chiang Rai
Chiang Khong
Huai Kon
Luang Prabang
Nam Neun
Phonsavan
Vinh
Mekong
Pai
Mae Hong Son
Chiang Mai
Lamphun
Phayao
DOI PHUKHA NATIONAL PARK
Nan
DOI INTHANON NATIONAL PARK
DOI KHUN TAN NATIONAL PARK
Lampang
Mae Sariang
Ping
Phrae
Den Chai
Uttaradit
PHU HIN RONGKLA NATIONAL PARK
PHU REUA NATIONAL PARK
Chiang Khan
Loei
Nong Khai
Udon Thani
Bung Kan
Ban Chiang
Nakhon Phanom
Khammouan
Sakon Nakhon
PHU KRADUNG NATIONAL PARK
That Phanom
Mukdahan
Savannakhet
Sukhothai
Phitsanulok
Tak
Lom Sak
Mae Sot
Kamphaeng Phet
Nan
Khon Kaen
NAM NAO NATIONAL PARK
Umphang
Nakhon Sawan
Mun
Ubon Ratchathani
Phimai
Three Pagodas Pass
Sangkhlaburi
Chao Phraya
Lopburi
Khorat
Surin
Si Saket
Chong Mek
Pakse
KHAO YAI NATIONAL PARK
Ban Tako
Phanom Rung
Ayutthaya
Bang Pa-In
Chong Chom
Kwai
Nakhon Pathom
Siem Reap
Kanchanaburi
Sa Kaew
Aranyaprathet
Sisophon
Angkor
1
2
11
21
22
24
101
107
108
118
212
226

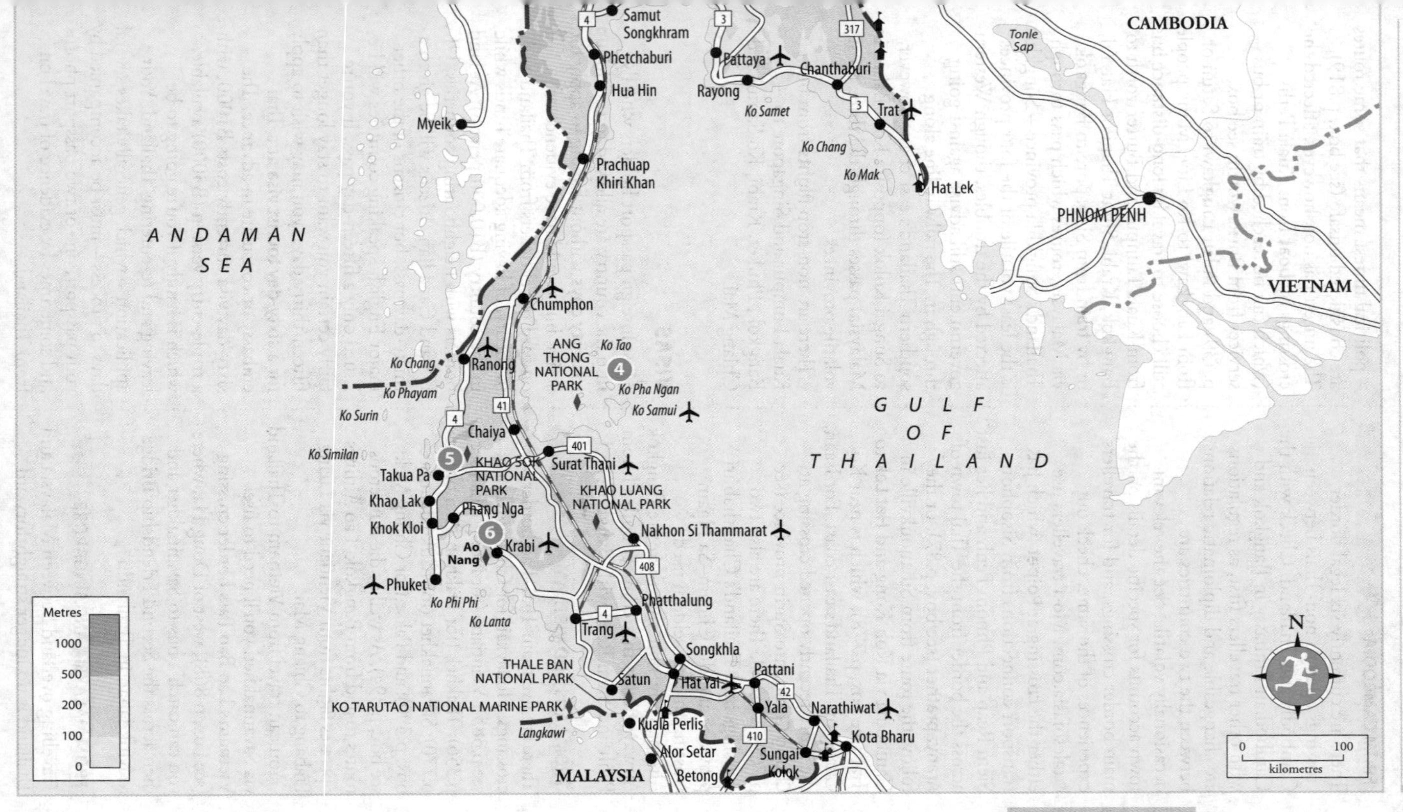

CAMBODIA
VIETNAM
PHNOM PENH
Tonle Sap
GULF OF THAILAND
ANDAMAN SEA
MALAYSIA
Samut Songkhram
Phetchaburi
Hua Hin
Prachuap Khiri Khan
Chumphon
Ranong
Myeik
Ko Chang
Ko Phayam
Ko Surin
Ko Similan
Takua Pa
Khao Lak
Khok Kloi
Phuket
Ko Phi Phi
Phang Nga
Ao Nang
Krabi
Ko Lanta
Chaiya
KHAO SOK NATIONAL PARK
ANG THONG NATIONAL PARK
Ko Tao
Ko Pha Ngan
Ko Samui
Surat Thani
KHAO LUANG NATIONAL PARK
Nakhon Si Thammarat
Trang
Phatthalung
Songkhla
Hat Yai
Satun
THALE BAN NATIONAL PARK
KO TARUTAO NATIONAL MARINE PARK
Langkawi
Kuala Perlis
Alor Setar
Betong
Pattani
Yala
Narathiwat
Sungai Kolok
Kota Bharu
Pattaya
Rayong
Ko Samet
Chanthaburi
Trat
Ko Chang
Ko Mak
Hat Lek
4
5
6
3
317
41
401
408
42
410
N
0
100
kilometres
Metres
1000
500
200
100
0

10

FROM CAMBODIA

There are currently six legal border crossings open to non-Thais between Cambodia and Thailand. Check with the Cambodian Embassy in Bangkok and with other travellers first, as regulations are changeable and diplomatic relations between the two countries are occasionally volatile. See the relevant town accounts for specific details on the main border crossings, and for travellers' experiences of the same, check out Ⓦtalesofasia.com. Most travellers use either the crossing at **Poipet**, which has transport connections from Sisophon, Siem Reap and Phnom Penh and lies just across the border from the Thai town of **Aranyaprathet** (see box, p.87); or they follow the route from Sihanoukville in Cambodia via Koh Kong and **Hat Lek** to Trat (see box, p.778), which is near Ko Chang on Thailand's east coast. For Isaan, the more recently opened crossing at **Chong Chom** into Surin province (see p.769) is useful. There are also two crossings into Thailand's Chanthaburi province and the Choam–Sa Ngam crossing that are seldom used. Alternatively, note that there are Bangkok Airways **flights** that connect both Phnom Penh and Siem Reap with Bangkok.

FROM LAOS AND VIETNAM

There are five main Thai–Lao border crossings: Houayxai (for Chiang Khong; see p.385); Vientiane (for Nong Khai; see p.356); Thakhek (for Nakhon Phanom; see p.770); Savannakhet (for Mukdahan; see box, p.390); and Pakse (for Chong Mek; see box, p.394). As well as the numerous routes to and from Bangkok, Lao Airlines operates **flights** from Vientiane via Luang Prabang to Chiang Mai.

You can travel from **Vietnam** to Thailand via Savannakhet; you'll need to use Vietnam's Lao Bao Pass border crossing (see box, p.868), west of Dong Ha, where you can catch a bus to Savannakhet and then across the Second Friendship Bridge to Mukdahan in Thailand.

FROM MALAYSIA AND SINGAPORE

Travelling overland between Malaysia and Thailand is no longer straightforward – political unrest means that some routes are considered unsafe (see box, p.819). The unrest has not, however, affected the crossings by **boat** from Kuala Perlis (which can be reached by train or bus services from Butterworth; see box, p.439) and Pulau Langkawi to Satun or from Langkawi to Ko Lipe. Many people still choose to travel by **long-distance bus** from Kuala Lumpur and Butterworth to Bangkok, Krabi, Surat Thani or Hat Yai, or by **train** from Singapore to Bangkok via Malaysia, routes which pass through Thailand's Songkhla province – Songkhla is the least volatile of the four provinces affected by the troubles, though Western governments still advise against going through it. The railway line along southern Thailand's east coast, however, to Sungai Kolok (opposite Kota Bahru in Malaysia) passes through the three most volatile provinces.

There are non-stop **flights** from both Kuala Lumpur and Singapore to Bangkok, Phuket, Krabi, Ko Samui and Chiang Mai.

VISAS

Most foreign passport holders who fly into the country are allowed to stay **for up to thirty days** without having to apply for a visa, but should have evidence of onward travel tickets from Thailand and, in theory, of having adequate funds while in the country (B10,000/person). At land borders with neighbouring countries, UK, US and Canadian citizens will be given a thirty-day pass, but citizens of the other major English-speaking countries will be issued only a fifteen-day pass. If you're fairly certain you want to stay longer than fifteen/thirty days, you may wish to apply for a **sixty-day tourist visa** at a Thai embassy or consulate in advance. The sixty-day visa currently costs B1000, with a triple-entry version (B3000) available, which is handy if you're going to be leaving and re-entering Thailand. Your application – which generally takes several days to process – must be accompanied by your passport, one or two passport photos and sometimes by evidence of travel on from Thailand.

It's not a good idea to **overstay** your visa limits. Once at the airport or the border, you'll be required to pay a fine of B500 per day before you leave. And if you get involved with police or immigration officials while in possession of an expired visa, they're obliged to take you to court, possibly imprison you, and deport you.

Sixty-day tourist visas can be **extended** in Thailand for a further thirty days, and fifteen- and thirty-day stays for seven to ten days, at the discretion of officials; extensions cost B1900 and are issued within the hour over the counter at immigration offices (*kaan khao muang*) in nearly every provincial capital – most offices ask for one or two photos as well, plus one or two photocopies of the main pages of your passport, including your Thai arrival card and arrival stamp or visa. Many tour agents on Bangkok's Thanon Khao San offer to get visa extensions for you, but beware: they are reputedly faking the stamps.

For the latest information, see the Thai Ministry of Foreign Affairs' **website** at Ⓦmfa.go.th; for further, unofficial details, such as the perils of overstaying your visa, see Ⓦthaivisa.com.

If you need a visa for China or India, you might want to apply at the consulates in Chiang Mai. Laos and Vietnam have consulates in Khon Kaen as well as in Bangkok.

GETTING AROUND

The wide range of efficient **transport** options makes travelling around Thailand very easy and inexpensive.

BUSES, SONGTHAEWS AND MINIBUSES

Ordinary (ie not air-conditioned) orange buses (*rot thammadaa*) are now found mostly in more remote areas, covering short distances between towns. They've generally been replaced as the workhorses of the bus system by blue, **second-class** (*baw sawng*), air-conditioned buses (*rot air*), which are state-run and inexpensive, but can get packed and are usually quite slow because they stop fairly frequently.

The state-run, blue, **first-class** (*baw neung*), air-conditioned buses are faster and more comfortable, but tend to depart less frequently and don't cover as many routes. In a lot of cases they're indistinguishable from **privately owned air-conditioned buses** (often known as *rot thua*), which ply the most popular long-distance routes and often operate out of government bus terminals.

On some longer routes, there are also more expensive **VIP buses**, with fewer seats and more legroom. Major private companies, such as Nakorn Chai and Win Tour, are generally reliable, but many smaller companies on the main travellers' routes, especially from Thanon Khao San to Chiang Mai and Surat Thani, have a poor reputation for service and comfort despite attracting customers with bargain fares and convenient timetables. Travellers have reported a frightening lack of safety awareness and frequent thefts from luggage on these routes, too (see p.707).

Tickets for all buses can be bought from the departure terminals and from major post offices (see also Ⓦthaiticketmajor.com for information about buying by phone or online), but for second-class buses it's normal to buy them onboard. First-class and VIP buses may operate from a separate station, and tickets for the more popular routes should be booked a day in advance. As a rough indication of **prices**, a trip from Bangkok to Chiang Mai (713km) costs up to B900 VIP, B500–600 first-class and B438 second-class.

In rural areas, the bus network is supplemented or replaced by **songthaews** (see p.702). Usually cramped, crazily fast and uncomfortable, **air-conditioned minibuses** (*rot tuu*), which sometimes operate like share taxis, only leaving when they are full, increasingly feature on popular inter-town routes all over the country.

TRAINS

Managed by the State Railway of Thailand (SRT; Ⓦrailway.co.th), the **rail network** consists of four main lines and a few branch lines. **Fares** depend on the class of seat, whether or not you want air conditioning and on the speed of the train – always slow, and usually late. Hard,

10

wooden, third-class seats are very cheap (Bangkok–Chiang Mai B231); in second class, you can often choose between reclining seats or berths, with or without air conditioning, on long journeys (Bangkok–Chiang Mai B391–881); and in first class (B1253–1453) you'll be in a one- or two-person air-conditioned sleeping compartment. Nearly all long-distance trains have dining cars. **Advance booking** of at least one day is strongly recommended for second-class seats on all lengthy journeys, and for sleepers, book as far in advance as possible. Make bookings at the station in any major town, or through a Thai travel agent such as Thailand Train Ticket (Ⓦthailandtrainticket.com). The SRT has a 24-hour hotline (Ⓣ1690) and publishes free **timetables**; the best place to get hold of one is over the counter at Bangkok's Hualamphong Station (see p.719), or from their website.

BOATS

Plenty of **boats**, in all shapes and sizes, connect the islands of southern Thailand to the mainland and each other. Large **ferries** with interior seating and decks often jammed with sunbathers serve the bigger islands, and vehicle ferries, catamarans and speedboats are also common. The most pleasurable water vessels to travel in, however, are the traditional **longtail boats**, so named for their long-stick propellers that make shallow coastal navigation a doddle. Longtails cover mainland coastal or coast-to-island hops and short inter-island journeys.

PLANES

Thai Airways (Ⓦthaiair.com) and Bangkok Airways (Ⓦbangkokair.com) are the major full-service airlines on the internal **flight** network, which extends to all parts of the country, using some two dozen airports; Thai Smile (Ⓦthaismileair.com) is Thai Airways' low-cost but often barely distinguishable arm. AirAsia (Ⓦairasia.com) and Nok Air (Ⓦnokair.com) provide the main low-cost competition; look out also for Orient Thai (Ⓦflyorientthai.com), Thai Lion Air (Ⓦlionairthai.com) and, mostly out of Chiang Mai, Kan Airlines (Ⓦkanairlines.com). Book early if possible – you can reserve online with all companies – as fares fluctuate wildly on all of these airlines. For a fully flexible economy ticket, Bangkok to Chiang Mai costs around B4000 with Thai Airways, but you'll find flights on the same route with the low-cost carriers for less than B1000 (with restrictions on changes), if you book far enough in advance.

CAR AND MOTORBIKE RENTAL

Nearly all tourist centres rent **cars** (B800–1500/day) and **motorbikes** (B150–400/day), for which a national driver's licence is usually acceptable; helmets are obligatory on bikes. Thais drive on the left, and the speed limit is 60km per hour within built-up areas and 90km per hour outside them; in practice, a major road doesn't necessarily have right of way over a minor, but the bigger vehicle always has right of way. Avoid driving at night, which can be very dangerous.

LOCAL TRANSPORT

Most sizeable towns have some kind of fixed-fare transport network of **local buses, songthaews** or even **longtail boats**, often with set routes, but never with rigid timetabling; within towns songthaews tend to act as communal taxis, picking up people heading in the same direction and usually taking them to their destination, with set prices (around B10–30). It's possible to charter a whole songthaew as a private taxi (notably in Chiang Mai), though this makes it much more expensive. In most towns, you'll find the songthaew "terminal" near the market; to pick one up between destinations, just flag it down, and to indicate to the driver that you want to get out, press the bell, shout, or rap hard with a coin on the ceiling.

Named after the noise of its excruciatingly unsilenced engine, the three-wheeled open-sided **tuk-tuk** is the classic Thai vehicle. They are fast and fun, with fares starting at around B40 (B60 or more in Bangkok), regardless of

the number of passengers. Even faster and more precarious than tuk-tuks, **motorbike taxis** feature both in big towns and out-of-the-way places; prices are lower than tuk-tuks and they can halve journey times during rush hour. Motorbike taxis should come with helmets for the pillion passenger. Around the country, these are supplemented by a wonderful variety of jerry-built, hybrid vehicles, including a dwindling band of tricycle rickshaws (*samlor*).

With all types of taxi, bar Bangkok's metered taxis, always establish the fare before you get in.

ACCOMMODATION

It is possible in most places to find simple double rooms with shared bathrooms for B150–350. If you're travelling on your own, expect to pay anything between sixty and one hundred percent of the double-room price. Checkout time is usually noon, so during high season (roughly Nov–Feb, July & Aug) you should try to arrive to check in at about 11.30am.

With private rooms so cheap and just thirty officially registered **youth hostels** in the whole country (@tyha.org), it's not worth becoming a YHA member just for your trip to Thailand. There's little point in lugging a tent around either, unless you're planning an extensive tour of national parks (which, in any case, often rent out fully equipped tents). Many **national parks** offer basic bungalow accommodation: they aren't always cheap, but advance booking is usually unnecessary except on weekends and holidays; book online at @thaiforestbooking.com.

Most of Thailand's **budget accommodation** is in traveller-friendly **guesthouses** and, at the beach, **bungalows**, which nearly always include an inexpensive restaurant and often also have internet access and a tour desk. Many offer a spread of options: their cheapest rooms will often be furnished with nothing more than a double bed, a blanket and a fan (window optional, private bathroom extra) and might cost around B150–300 for two people. For a room with air conditioning and a hot shower, and perhaps a TV and fridge as well, you're looking at B350–1500.

Few Thais use guesthouses, opting instead for Chinese–Thai-run **budget hotels**, often located near bus stations, with rooms in the B200–600 range. They're generally clean and en suite, but usually lack any communal area. Beds are usually large enough for a couple, and it's quite acceptable for two people to ask and pay for a single room (*hong diaw*). **Mid-range hotels** (B600–1200) are often much more comfortable and come equipped with extras such as TV, fridge, air conditioning, hot showers and pool; they generally work out to be good value.

Electricity is supplied at 220 volts AC and available at all but the most remote and basic beach huts. Several **plug** types are commonly in use, most usually with two round pins, but also with two flat-blade pins, and sometimes with both options.

FOOD AND DRINK

Thai **food** is renowned for its fiery but fragrant dishes, flavoured with lemongrass, holy basil and chilli, and you can eat well and cheaply even in the smallest provincial towns. **Hygiene** is a consideration when eating anywhere in Thailand, but there's no need to be too cautious: wean your stomach gently by avoiding excessive amounts of chilli and too much fresh fruit in the first few days and always drink bottled (or boiled) water. You can be pretty sure that any noodle stall or curry shop that's permanently packed with customers is a safe bet.

WHERE TO EAT

Throughout the country most inexpensive Thai **restaurants** specialize in one type of food – a "noodle shop" might do fried noodles and noodle soups plus a basic fried rice, but nothing else; a restaurant displaying whole roast chickens and ducks will offer these sliced or with chillies and sauces served over rice; and "curry shops" serve just that. The best and most entertaining places to

eat are the local **night markets** (*talaat yen*), where pushcart kitchens congregate from about 6pm (sometimes until 6am), often close to the fruit and vegetable market or the bus station. Each stall is fronted by tables and stools, and you can choose your food from wherever you like.

At a cheap café, you'll get a main course for less than B60, while upmarket restaurants can charge more than B130. Nearly all restaurants open every day for lunch and dinner, often closing around 9pm.

WHAT TO EAT AND DRINK

Thais eat **noodles** when Westerners would dig into a sandwich – for lunch or as a late-night snack – and at around B30 they're the cheapest hot meal you'll find anywhere. They come in assorted varieties (wide and flat, thin and transparent, made with eggs, soy-bean flour or rice flour) and get boiled up as soups, doused in sauces, or stir-fried. The most popular noodle dish is *pad thai*, a delicious combination of fried noodles, spring onions and egg, sprinkled with ground peanuts and lime juice, and often spiked with dried shrimps. Fried **rice** is the other faithful standby. Although very few Thais are **vegetarian** (*mangsàwirat*), you can nearly always ask for a vegetable-only fried rice or noodle dish – though many places will routinely add fish sauce as a salt substitute. All traveller-oriented restaurants are veggie-friendly.

Aside from fiery **curries** and **stir-fries**, restaurant menus often include spicy Thai **soup**, which is eaten with other dishes, not as a starter. Two favourites are *tôm khàa kài*, a creamy coconut chicken soup, and *tôm yam kûng*, a prawn soup without coconut milk. Food from the northeastern **Isaan** region is popular throughout the country, particularly sticky rice, which is rolled up into balls and dipped into chilli sauces, and *sôm tam*, a spicy green-papaya salad with garlic, raw chillies, green beans, tomatoes, peanuts and dried shrimps. Barbecued chicken on a stick (*kai yaang*) is the classic accompaniment. Raw minced pork is the basis for *larb*, subtly flavoured with mint and served with vegetables.

Sweets (*khanom*) don't really figure on most restaurant menus, but a few places offer bowls of *luk taan cheum*, a jellied concoction of lotus seeds floating in syrup, and coconut custard (*sangkaya*) often cooked inside a small pumpkin. Sweets are more likely to be sold on the street, alongside sticky cakes made from glutinous rice and coconut cream pressed into squares and wrapped in banana leaves.

Thais don't drink **water** straight from the tap, and nor should you: plastic bottles of drinking water are sold countrywide, and in some towns you'll find blue- and-white roadside machines that dispense drinking water at B1 for 1 or 2 litres (bring your own bottle). Night markets, guesthouses and restaurants do a good line in freshly squeezed **fruit juices** and shakes, as well as fresh coconut water and freshly squeezed sugar-cane juice, which is sickeningly sweet.

Beer costs around B35 for a 330ml bottle in a shop, more in a restaurant or bar; the most famous beer is the locally brewed Singha, though many people prefer Leo or Heineken. At about B60 for a 375ml bottle, the local **whisky** is a lot better value and Thais think nothing of consuming a bottle a night. The most drinkable of these is the 35 percent proof Mekhong. Sang Som is an even stronger **rum**. Bars aren't an indigenous feature, as Thais rarely drink out without eating, but you'll find a fair number in Bangkok and the tourist centres.

CULTURE AND ETIQUETTE

Tourist literature has so successfully marketed Thailand as the "Land of Smiles" that a lot of tourists arrive in the country expecting to be forgiven any outrageous behaviour. This is just not the case: there are some things so universally sacred in Thailand that even a hint of disrespect will cause deep offence. The worst thing you can possibly do is to bad-mouth the universally revered **royal family**. The king's anthem is always played before every film screening in the cinema, during which the audience is expected to stand up.

Thais rarely shake hands, using the **wai**, a prayer-like gesture made with raised hands, to greet and say goodbye and to acknowledge respect, gratitude or apology. The *wai* changes according to the relative status of the two people involved, and as a *farang* (foreigner) it's best to wait for the other person to initiate before responding: raise your hands close to your chest, bow your head and place your fingertips by your nose. Although all Thais have a first name and a family name, everyone is addressed by their first name – even when meeting strangers – prefixed by the title **Khun** (Mr/Ms).

Thailand shares the same attitudes to dress and social taboos as other Southeast Asian cultures (see p.40).

SPORTS AND OUTDOOR ACTIVITIES

Thailand's natural environment is well exploited by numerous tour agencies cashing in on the tourist dollar. While this can sometimes lead to dodgy, often dangerous, practices, the range of outdoor activities available – from snorkelling and scuba diving, river rafting and inner-tube riding, sea kayaking, jet skiing, whitewater rafting, waterskiing and parasailing to rock climbing, caving, bungee jumping, elephant trekking, jungle trekking and bike riding – is astonishing. Always choose your tour operator carefully, however, and ask for advice from other travellers.

THAI BOXING

Thai boxing (*muay thai*) enjoys a following similar to football in Europe: every province has a stadium, and whenever it's shown on TV you can be sure that large noisy crowds will gather round the sets in streetside restaurants and noodle shops. The best place to see live Thai boxing is at one of Bangkok's two stadiums (see box, p.725). There's a strong spiritual and ritualistic dimension to *muay thai*, adding grace to an otherwise brutal sport. Any part of the body except the head may be used as an offensive weapon, and all parts except the groin are fair targets. Kicks to the head are the blows that cause most knockouts.

TREKKING

Trekking is concentrated in the north around Chiang Mai (see p.744) and Chiang Rai (see p.761) but there are smaller, less touristy trekking operations in Kanchanaburi (see p.727), Mae Hong Son (see p.756), Pai (see p.758) and Umphang (see p.743), all of which are worth considering. Treks in the north usually include overnight stays in hill-tribe villages (see box, pp.750–751), a visit to a hot spring or waterfall, elephant riding and bamboo or whitewater rafting, plus around three hours' walking per day (see box, p.745). A few **national parks**, such as Khao Yai (see p.765) and Khao Sok (see p.801), offer shorter trails for unguided walks; most national parks charge a B200–400 entrance fee.

DIVING

You can **dive** all year round in Thailand, as the coasts are subject to different monsoon seasons: the diving seasons are from November to April along the Andaman coast, from December or January to October on the Gulf coast, and all year round on the east coast.

Major dive centres include Ko Chang (see p.799) on the east coast; Phuket (see p.804), Ao Nang near Krabi (see p.810), Ko Phi Phi (see p.811) and Ko Lanta (see p.813) on the Andaman coast; and Ko Tao (see p.794), Ko Samui (see p.785) and Ko Pha Ngan (see p.790) on the Gulf coast. The diving off the Similan islands, which are accessible from Khao Lak (see p.802), is widely considered to be the most spectacular in the country, and the seas around Ko Tarutao National Marine Park (see p.817) are also impressive. You can organize dive expeditions and undertake a certificated diving course at all these places; Ko Tao dive centres offer the cheapest courses, charging B9000–10,500 for a four-day PADI Open Water course. For beginners with not much cash or time, Discover Scuba dives, which involve diving with Dive Master, who regulates your

10

MEDITATION CENTRES AND RETREATS

Of the hundreds of **meditation** temples in Thailand, a few cater specifically for foreigners by holding meditation sessions and retreats in English. The meditation is mostly Vipassana, or "insight", which emphasizes the minute observation of internal physical sensation. Novices and practised meditators alike are welcome. Longer retreats are for the serious-minded only: there's usually around eight hours of meditation per day; tobacco, alcohol, drugs and sex are forbidden; there's generally no eating after midday and no talking; and conditions are spartan. In the south, the most famous retreat centre for foreigners is at Wat Suan Mokkh (Ⓦ suanmokkh-idh.org), an hour north of Surat Thani, with a branch on Ko Samui (Ⓦ dipabhavan.org), while frequent ten-day retreats are held at Wat Khao Tham on Ko Pha Ngan (see p.790). For options in the north, head to the Northern Insight Meditation Centre at Wat Ram Poeng or the International Buddhism Centre at Doi Suthep, both just outside Chiang Mai (see p.750).

equipment (leaving you to focus on breathing steadily and equalizing), are a wonderful introduction to the underwater world. Always verify the dive instructors' PADI or equivalent credentials, as this guarantees a certain level of professionalism. There are currently **recompression chambers** in Bangkok, Pattaya, on Ko Samui and on Phuket.

OTHER OUTDOOR ACTIVITIES

Thailand's other major outdoor activities are **snorkelling**, which is so widespread that you may want to buy your own equipment rather than rent the often-ropey local gear; and **sea kayaking** – most famous are the guided tours among Krabi and Phang Nga's lagoon caves (see box, p.809), but you'll find kayaks to rent (or sometimes free at your resort) on scores of beaches. **Mountain-bike** rental is sometimes available, but most islands are considerably mountainous, so be prepared for a workout and bring lots of water. At Railay, in the south, you will find one of the best **rock-climbing** destinations in the world, with towering limestone cliffs. **Sailing**, **windsurfing** and **kiteboarding** courses and rental are offered on most of the main islands, and **fishing tours** are also plentiful. But to truly appreciate your surroundings while working up a sweat there's **beach volleyball** and **football**, a sunset phenomenon on most island beaches and great way to make new friends; there's truly nothing like freshening up after a big game with a sunset swim in the ocean.

COMMUNICATIONS

International **mail** takes around a week from Bangkok, longer (up to two weeks) from more isolated areas. Almost all main post offices across the country operate a **poste restante** service and will hold letters for two to three months. Surface packages take three months.

Internet access is available at private outlets almost everywhere in Thailand, averaging B2 per minute in tourist centres, and as little as B20 per hour upcountry, especially in Bangkok. **Wi-fi** has made rapid inroads and is now offered free at nearly all guesthouses, as well as at many cafés and restaurants.

Most foreign **mobile-phone** networks have links with Thai networks, but you might want to check roaming rates, which are often exorbitant, before you leave home. To get round this, most travellers purchase a Thai pre-paid SIM card (1-2-Call is the biggest network with the best coverage). Available for as little as B50 (sometimes free at airports) and refillable at 7-Elevens around the country, they offer very cheap calls, both domestically and internationally (especially if you use low-cost international prefixes such as 1-2-Call's 003). The cheapest option, of course, is to find a guesthouse or café with free wi-fi and **Skype** from your own device; Skype is also available on the computers in most internet cafés.

Note that Thai area codes have been incorporated into the subscriber number so even when phoning from the same city, you must dial the entire number.

CRIME AND SAFETY

As long as you keep your wits about you and follow the usual precautions, you shouldn't encounter much trouble in Thailand. **Theft** and **pickpocketing** are two of the main problems, but the most common cause for concern is the **con-artists** who dupe gullible tourists into parting with their cash: be suspicious of anyone who makes an unnatural effort to befriend you, never buy anything from a tout, and heed specific warnings given throughout this chapter. The most notorious scam entails flogging low-grade **gems** at vastly inflated prices: don't be tempted to get involved in gem-dealing unless you know a lot about precious stones.

Theft from some long-distance **overnight buses** is also a problem, with the majority of reported incidents taking place on the temptingly cheap buses run by private companies direct from Bangkok's Khao San Road (as opposed to those that depart from the government bus stations) to destinations such as Chiang Mai and the southern beach resorts. The best solution is to travel direct from the bus stations. On any bus or train, be wary of accepting food or drink from strangers, especially on long overnight journeys: it may be drugged so as to knock you out while your bags are stolen. Violent crime against tourists is not common but it does occur.

There have been several serious attacks on **women travellers** in the past few years, but bearing in mind the millions of tourists visiting the country every year, the statistical likelihood of becoming a victim is extremely small. Unfortunately, it's also necessary for female tourists to think twice about spending time alone with a monk, as there have been rapes and murders committed by men wearing the saffron robes of the monkhood.

Drug smuggling carries a maximum penalty of death in Thailand, **dealing** will get you anything from four years to life in a Thai prison, and **possession** of Category 1 drugs (heroin, amphetamines, LSD and ecstasy) for personal use can result in a life sentence; travellers caught with even the smallest amount of drugs at airports and international borders are prosecuted for trafficking. Away from international borders, most foreigners arrested in possession of small amounts of cannabis are fined and deported, but the law is complex and prison sentences are possible.

EMERGENCY NUMBERS

In any emergency, contact the English-speaking **tourist police** who maintain a 24-hour toll-free nationwide line (**T 1155**) and have offices in most tourist centres.

10

MEDICAL CARE AND EMERGENCIES

Thai **pharmacies** (*raan khai yaa*; typically open daily 8.30am–8pm) are well stocked with local and international branded medicaments, and most pharmacists speak English. All provincial capitals have at least one **hospital** (*rong phayaabahn*). Cleanliness and efficiency vary, but generally hygiene and healthcare standards are good; most doctors speak English. In the event of a major health crisis, get someone to contact your embassy or insurance company – it may be best to get yourself flown to Bangkok or even home.

INFORMATION AND MAPS

For impartial but often limited **information** on local attractions and transport, call in at the **Tourism Authority of Thailand** (TAT; W tourismthailand.org), which has offices in Bangkok and dozens of regional towns, all open daily 8.30am to 4.30pm, except where noted in the text. You can also contact the TAT Call Centre from anywhere in the country on T 1672 (daily 8am–8pm). For a decent **map** of the country, try the 1:1,500,000 maps produced by Nelles and Bartholomew. In addition, Nancy Chandler's maps of Bangkok and Chiang Mai are interesting and quirky; they are available from bookshops.

MONEY AND BANKS

Thailand's unit of **currency** is the baht (abbreviated to "B"), which is divided

THAI LANGUAGE

Most Thais who deal with tourists speak some English, but off the beaten track you'll probably need a few words of **Thai**. Thai is extremely tonal and difficult for Westerners to master. Five different tones are used – low (syllables marked ˋ), middle (unmarked), high (marked ˊ), falling (marked ^), and rising (marked ~). Thus, using four of the five tones, you can make a sentence from just one syllable: mái mài mâi mãi – "New wood burns, doesn't it?"

Street signs in tourist areas are nearly always written in Roman script as well as Thai. Because there's no standard system of transliteration of Thai script into Roman, Thai words and names in this book will not always match the versions written elsewhere. Ubon Ratchathani, for example, could come out as Ubol Rajatani, while Ayutthaya is synonymous with Ayudhia.

PRONUNCIATION

a as in "dad"
aa is pronounced as it looks, with the vowel elongated
ae as in "there"
ai as in "buy"
ao as in "now"
aw as in "awe"
ay as in "pay"
e as in "pen"
eu as in "sir", but heavily nasalized
i as in "tip"
ii as in "feet"
o as in "knock"
oe as in "hurt", but more closed
oh as in "toe"
u as in "loot"
uu as in "pool"
r as in "rip"; often pronounced like "l"
kh as in "keep"
ph as in "put"
th as in "time"
k is unaspirated and unvoiced, and closer to "g"
p is also unaspirated and unvoiced, and closer to "b"
t is also unaspirated and unvoiced, and closer to "d"

GREETINGS AND BASIC PHRASES

Whenever you speak to a stranger in Thailand, it's polite to end your sentence in *khráp* if you're a man, *khâ* if you're a woman. *Khráp* and *khâ* are also often used to answer "yes" to a question, though the most common way is to repeat the verb of the question (preceded by *mâi* for "no").

Hello	*sawàt dii*
Where are you?	*pai nãi?* (used as a general greeting)
I'm out having fun/I'm travelling	*pai thîaw* (answer to *pai nãi*)
Goodbye	*sawàt dii/la kàwn*
Excuse me	*khãw thâwt*
Thank you	*khàwp khun*
What's your name?	*khun chêu arai?*
My name is…	*phõm* (men)/ *diichãn* (women) *chêu…*
I don't understand	*mâi khâo jai*
Do you speak English?	*khun phûut hasãa angkrìt dâi mãi?*
Can you help me?	*chûay phõm/ diichãn dâi mãi?*

GETTING AROUND

Where is the …?	*… yùu thîi nãi?*
How far?	*klai thâo rai?*
I would like to go to …	*yàak jà pai …*
When will the bus leave?	*rót jà àwk mêua rai?*
Train station	*sathàanii rót fai*
Bus station	*sathàanii rót meh*
Airport	*sanãam bin*
Ticket	*tũa*
Hotel	*rohng raem*
Restaurant	*raan ahãan*
Market	*talàat*
Hospital	*rohng pha-yaabaan*
Motorbike	*rót mohtoesai*
Taxi	*rót táksîi*
Boat	*reua*
How much is … ?	*… thâo rai?/kìi bàat?*
Cheap/expensive	*thùuk/phaeng*
A/c room	*hãwng ae*
Bathroom/toilet	*hãwng nám*
Telephone	*thohrásàp*
Today	*wan níi*
Tomorrow	*phrûng níi*
Yesterday	*mêua wan*
Now	*diãw níi*
Morning	*cháo*
Afternoon	*bài*
Evening	*yen*
Night	*kheun*

NUMBERS

0	*sũn*
1	*nèung*
2	*sãwng*
3	*sãam*
4	*sìi*
5	*hâa*
6	*hòk*
7	*jèt*
8	*pàet*
9	*kâo*
10	*sìp*
11	*sìp èt*
12, 13, etc	*sìp sãwng, sìp sãam*
20	*yîi sìp/yiip*
21, 22, etc	*yîi sìp èt, yîi sìp sãwng*
30, 40, etc	*sãam sìp, sìi sìp*
100, 200, etc	*nèung rói, sãwng rói*
1000	*nèung phan*

FOOD AND DRINK GLOSSARY

Khãw…	I would like …
Khãw check bin?	Can I have the bill please?
kin ahãan/mangsàwirát/jeh	I am vegetarian/vegan

Basic ingredients

kài	chicken
mũu	pork
néua	beef, meat
pèt	duck
ahãan thalay	seafood
plaa	fish
kûng	prawn, shrimp
puu	crab
khài	egg
phàk	vegetables

Noodle dishes

ba mìi	egg noodles
ba mìi kràwp	crisp fried egg noodles
kwáy tiãw	white rice noodles
… haêng	… fried with egg, meat and vegetables
… nám (mũu)	… with chicken broth (and pork balls) …
… rât nâ (mũu)	… fried in sauce with vegetables (and pork)
pad thai	thin noodles fried with egg and spring onions, topped with ground peanuts

Rice (khâo) dishes

… màn kài	… with chicken
… nâ kài/pèt	… with chicken/duck with sauce
… rât kaeng	… with curry
khâo niãw	sticky rice
khâo pàt kài/muũ/kûng/néua/phàk	fried rice with chicken/pork/shrimp/beef/vegetables
Khâo tôm	rice soup

Curries, soups and other dishes

kaeng phèt	hot, red curry
kaeng phánaeng	thick, savoury curry
kaeng khiãw wan	green curry
kài pàt nàw mái	chicken with bamboo shoots
kài pàt mét mámûang	chicken with cashew nuts
kài pàt khi˜ng	chicken with ginger
mũu prîaw wãan	sweet and sour pork
néua pàt krathiam phrík thai	beef fried with garlic and pepper
néua pàt nám man hõy	beef in oyster sauce
pàt phàk lãi yang	stir-fried vegetables
plaa rât phrík	whole fish cooked with chillies
plaa thâwt	fried whole fish
sôm tam	spicy papaya salad
tôm khàa kài	chicken coconut soup
tôm yam kûng	hot and sour prawn soup
yam néua	spicy beef salad

Drinks (khreûang deùm)

bia	beer
chaa ráwn	hot tea
chaa yen	iced tea
kaafae ráwn	hot coffee
nám klûay	banana shake
nám maprao	fresh coconut water
nám awy	fresh sugar-cane juice
nám plaò	drinking water

into 100 satang. Notes come in B20, B50, B100, B500 and B1000 denominations. At the time of writing, the **exchange rate** was B54 to £1 and B33 to US$1. You should be able to withdraw cash from hundreds of **ATMs**, though you'll be charged a fee of B150 at most of them.

OPENING HOURS AND HOLIDAYS

Most **shops** open at least Monday to Saturday from about 8am to 8pm. **Banking hours** are Monday to Friday 8.30am to 3.30 or 4.30pm, though bank exchange booths in tourist areas will stay open much later. **Post offices** are generally open Monday to Friday 8.30am to 4.30pm, Saturday 9am to noon. **Private office** hours are generally Monday to Friday 8am to 5pm and Saturday 8am to noon, though in tourist areas these hours are longer, with weekends worked like any other day. **Government offices** work Monday to Friday 8.30am to noon and 1pm to 4.30pm, and national **museums** tend to stick to these hours, too, but some close on Mondays and Tuesdays rather than at weekends. Most shops and tourist-oriented businesses, including TAT, stay open on national holidays. The only time an inconvenient number of shops, restaurants and hotels do close is during **Chinese New Year**, which, though not marked as an official national holiday, brings many businesses to a standstill for several days in late January or early February.

PUBLIC HOLIDAYS

January 1 International New Year's Day.
February/March (day of full moon) Maha Puja.
April 6 Chakri Day.
April (usually 13–15) Songkhran. Thai New Year.
May 1 Labour Day.
May 5 Coronation Day.
May/June (day of full moon) Visakha Puja. The holiest of all Buddhist holidays, celebrating the birth, enlightenment and death of the Buddha.
July/August (day of full moon) Asanha Puja.
August 12 Queen's Birthday/Mothers' Day
October 23 Chulalongkorn Day. The anniversary of Rama V's death.
December 5 King's Birthday/National Day.
December 10 Constitution Day.
December 31 Western New Year's Eve.

FESTIVALS

Thais use both the Western Gregorian **calendar** and a Buddhist calendar – the Buddha is said to have died (or entered Nirvana) in the year 543 BC, so Thai dates start from that point: thus 2014 AD becomes 2557 BE (Buddhist Era). The most spectacular festivals include:

Songkhran (usually April 13–15) Thai New Year is welcomed in with massive public water fights in the street, at their most exuberant in Chiang Mai and on Bangkok's Th Khao San.
Candle Festival (July/Aug) For three days around the full moon, enormous wax sculptures are paraded through Ubon Ratchathani to mark the beginning of the annual Buddhist retreat period.
Vegetarian Festival (Oct/Nov) Chinese devotees in Phuket and Trang become vegetarian for a nine-day period and then parade through town performing acts of self-mortification.
Loy Krathong (late Oct or early Nov) Baskets of flowers and lighted candles are floated on rivers and ponds to celebrate the end of the rainy season. Best in Sukhothai and Chiang Mai.
Elephant Roundup (third weekend of Nov) The main tourist-oriented festival is in Surin: two hundred elephants play team games, and parade in battle dress.

Bangkok and around

Manic, thrilling, dynamic, exhausting, overpowering, titillating – the one thing **BANGKOK** (Krung Thep in Thai; the "City of Angels") is not, is boring. Whether you spend two days here or two weeks you'll always find something to invigorate your senses, kick-start your enthusiasm and drive you crazy: frenetic markets and bustling temples, zinging curries and cutting-edge clubs. Bring patience, a sense of adventure and comfy shoes; leave your Western expectation of aesthetics behind and you'll not be disappointed.

Bangkok began life as a largely amphibious city in 1782 after the Burmese sacked the former capital of Ayutthaya. The first king of the new dynasty, Rama I, built his palace at Ratanakosin, which remains the city's spiritual heart. The capital was

modernized along European lines in the late nineteenth century, and since World War II has undergone a dramatic transformation. Most of the city's waterways have been concreted over, its citizens no longer live on floating bamboo rafts and the charmless urban sprawl is spiked by skyscrapers. Yet in among the chaotic jumble of modern Bangkok there remains a city fiercely proud of its traditions. As such it is a perfect microcosm of Southeast Asia, and the perfect place to begin your adventures.

WHAT TO SEE AND DO

Bangkok's traveller heart is **Banglamphu**, with its myriad guesthouses, bars and restaurants. From here, it's a short walk to **Ratanakosin**, the royal island on the east bank of the Chao Phraya that is home to the **Grand Palace**, **Wat Pho** and the **National Museum.** To the east, **Chinatown** is noteworthy for its markets and street food, while across the river **Thonburi**'s appeal lies in its traditional canal-side life and boat rides. The amorphous sprawl of **downtown** Bangkok offers several impressive historical residences among its rampant commercialism, though it's primarily a shopper's paradise. At weekends, don't miss the enormous **Chatuchak Weekend Market**, on the city's outskirts, which sells just about everything under the sun.

Wat Phra Kaeo and the Grand Palace

Built as a private royal temple in 1782, the dazzling and sumptuous **Wat Phra Kaeo** is the holiest site in the country and houses its most important icon, the Emerald Buddha. The temple is located within the eighteenth-century **Grand Palace**, now used solely for state functions. The main entrance is on Thanon Na Phra Lan, near to Banglamphu and Tha Chang express-boat pier. Admission is B500 (daily 8.30am–4pm, last admission 3.30pm; 2hr personal audioguide B200, with passport or credit card as deposit), and includes entry to the new Queen Sirikit Textiles Museum, just to the right of the main gate (daily 9am–4.30pm), and to Vimanmek Palace (see p.716). There's a strict dress code (legs and shoulders must be covered) but suitable garments and shoes are available just inside the main entrance (free, B200 deposit).

Most visitors head straight for the bot (main sanctuary), which contains the sacred Emerald Buddha, a tiny, jadeite Buddha image, which is just 75cm high. The Crown Prince ceremonially changes the statue's costume and jewellery seasonally. At the western end of the upper terrace, the eye-boggling gold Phra Si Ratana Chedi enshrines a piece of the Buddha's breastbone. Worth looking out for here are the well-preserved murals of the Ramayana, which stretch for more than 1km inside the wat walls and depict every blow of this ancient Hindu story of the triumph of good over evil in 178 panels.

Wat Pho

Lying south of the Grand Palace, close to the Tha Thien express-boat pier, the seventeenth-century **Wat Pho** (daily 8am–5pm; B100), Bangkok's oldest temple, is most famous for housing an enormous statue of the **reclining Buddha.** In 1832, Rama turned the temple into "Thailand's first university" by decorating the walls with diagrams on history, literature and animal husbandry. The wat is still a centre for traditional medicine,

A WORD OF WARNING

If you're heading for the major sights, beware of **scams**. Tuk-tuk drivers or well-dressed people pretending to be students or officials may lie and tell you that the sight is closed, because they want to lead you on a shopping trip, invariably to purchase gems or silk that are often fake or on sale at vastly inflated prices (for which they'll receive a hefty commission). Major sights are rarely closed for national holidays or state occasions, so play it safe and check it out for yourself (you can check closing days for the Grand Palace, for example, at Ⓦ palaces.thai.net). Similarly, steer clear of tuk-tuk or taxi drivers who offer to take you on a ridiculously cheap tour of the city; gem shops are often in the itinerary.

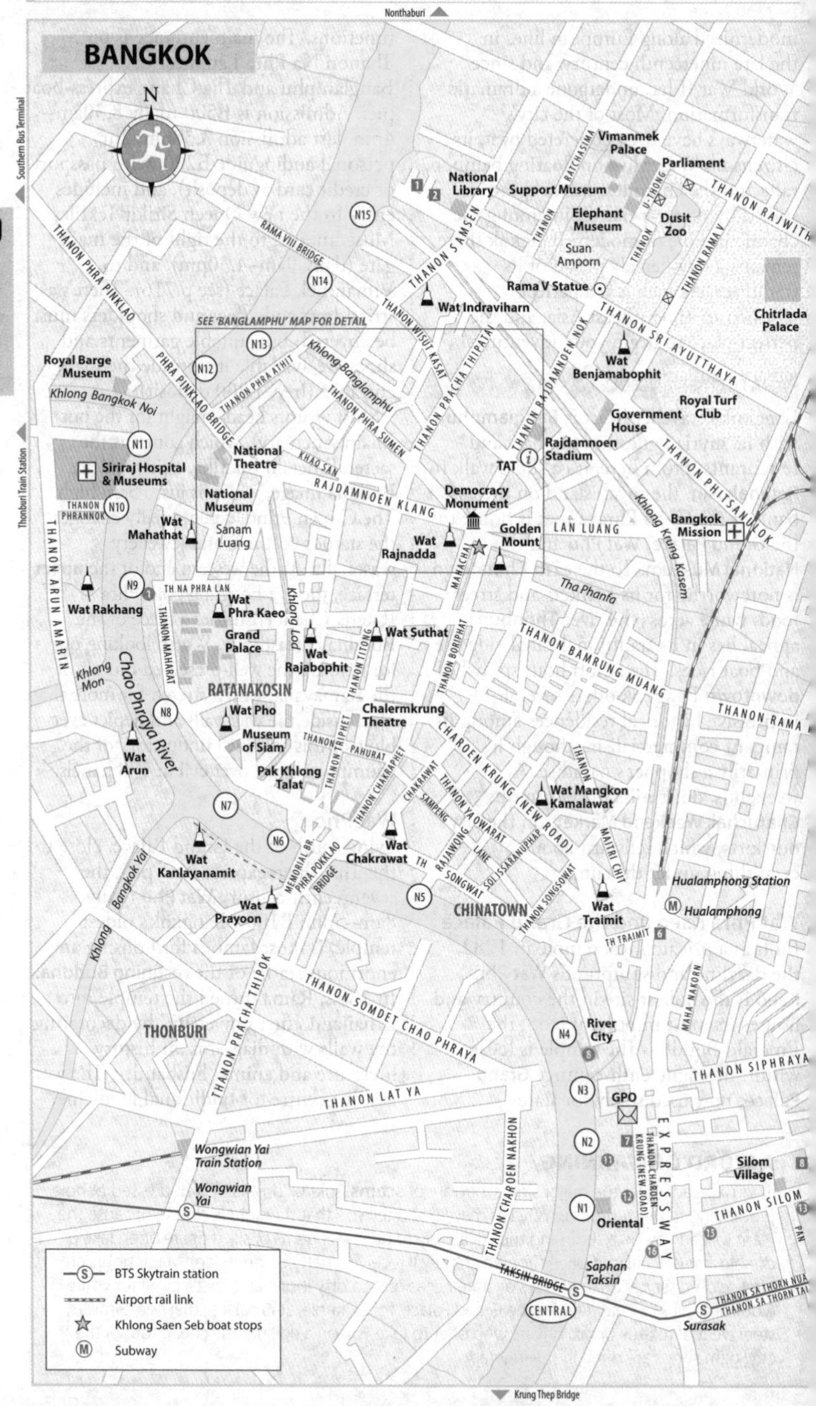
BANGKOK
N
Nonthaburi
Southern Bus Terminal
Thonburi Train Station
Krung Thep Bridge
SEE 'BANGLAMPHU' MAP FOR DETAIL
National Library
Support Museum
Vimanmek Palace
Parliament
Elephant Museum
Suan Amporn
Dusit Zoo
Rama V Statue
Chitrlada Palace
Wat Indraviharn
Wat Benjamabophit
Royal Turf Club
Government House
Rajdamnoen Stadium
TAT
Democracy Monument
Golden Mount
Wat Rajnadda
Bangkok Mission
Royal Barge Museum
Khlong Bangkok Noi
Siriraj Hospital & Museums
National Theatre
National Museum
Sanam Luang
Wat Mahathat
Wat Rakhang
Wat Phra Kaeo
Grand Palace
Wat Rajabophit
Wat Suthat
Khlong Lod
Khlong Banglamphu
Tha Phanfa
Khlong Krung Kasem
RATANAKOSIN
Wat Pho
Museum of Siam
Chalermkrung Theatre
Pak Khlong Talat
Wat Arun
Chao Phraya River
Khlong Mon
Wat Kanlayanamit
Wat Prayoon
Wat Chakrawat
Wat Mangkon Kamalawat
Wat Traimit
Hualamphong Station
Hualamphong
CHINATOWN
THONBURI
River City
GPO
Oriental
Silom Village
Saphan Taksin
Surasak
CENTRAL
Wongwian Yai Train Station
Wongwian Yai
Khlong Bangkok Yai
Khlong
EXPRESSWAY
THANON RAJWITHI
THANON RAMA V
U-THONG
THANON RATCHASIMA
THANON SAMSEN
THANON WISUT KASAT
THANON PRACHA THIPATAI
THANON RAJDAMNOEN NOK
THANON SRI AYUTTHAYA
THANON PHITSANULOK
THANON PHRA PINKLAO
PHRA PINKLAO BRIDGE
RAMA VIII BRIDGE
THANON PHRA ATHIT
THANON PHRA SUMEN
KHAO SAN
RAJDAMNOEN KLANG
LAN LUANG
MAHACHAI
THANON PHRANNOK
THANON ARUN AMARIN
TH NA PHRA LAN
THANON MAHARAT
THANON TITONG
THANON BORIPHAT
THANON BAMRUNG MUANG
THANON RAMA
THANON TRIPHET
THANON PAHURAT
THANON CHAKRAPHET
CHAKRAWAT
SAMPENG
THANON YAOWARAT
CHAROEN KRUNG (NEW ROAD)
RAJAWONG
LANE
SOI ISSARANUPHAP
TH SONGWAT
THANON SONGSOWAT
MAITRI CHIT
TH TRAIMIT
MAHA NAKORN
MEMORIAL BR.
PHRA POKKLAO BRIDGE
THANON PRACHA THIPOK
THANON SOMDET CHAO PHRAYA
THANON LAT YA
THANON CHAROEN NAKHON
THANON SIPHRAYA
THANON CHAROEN KRUNG (NEW ROAD)
THANON SILOM
PAN
TAKSIN BRIDGE
THANON SA THORN NUA
THANON SA THORN TAI
N1
N2
N3
N4
N5
N6
N7
N8
N9
N10
N11
N12
N13
N14
N15
BTS Skytrain station
Airport rail link
Khlong Saen Seb boat stops
Subway

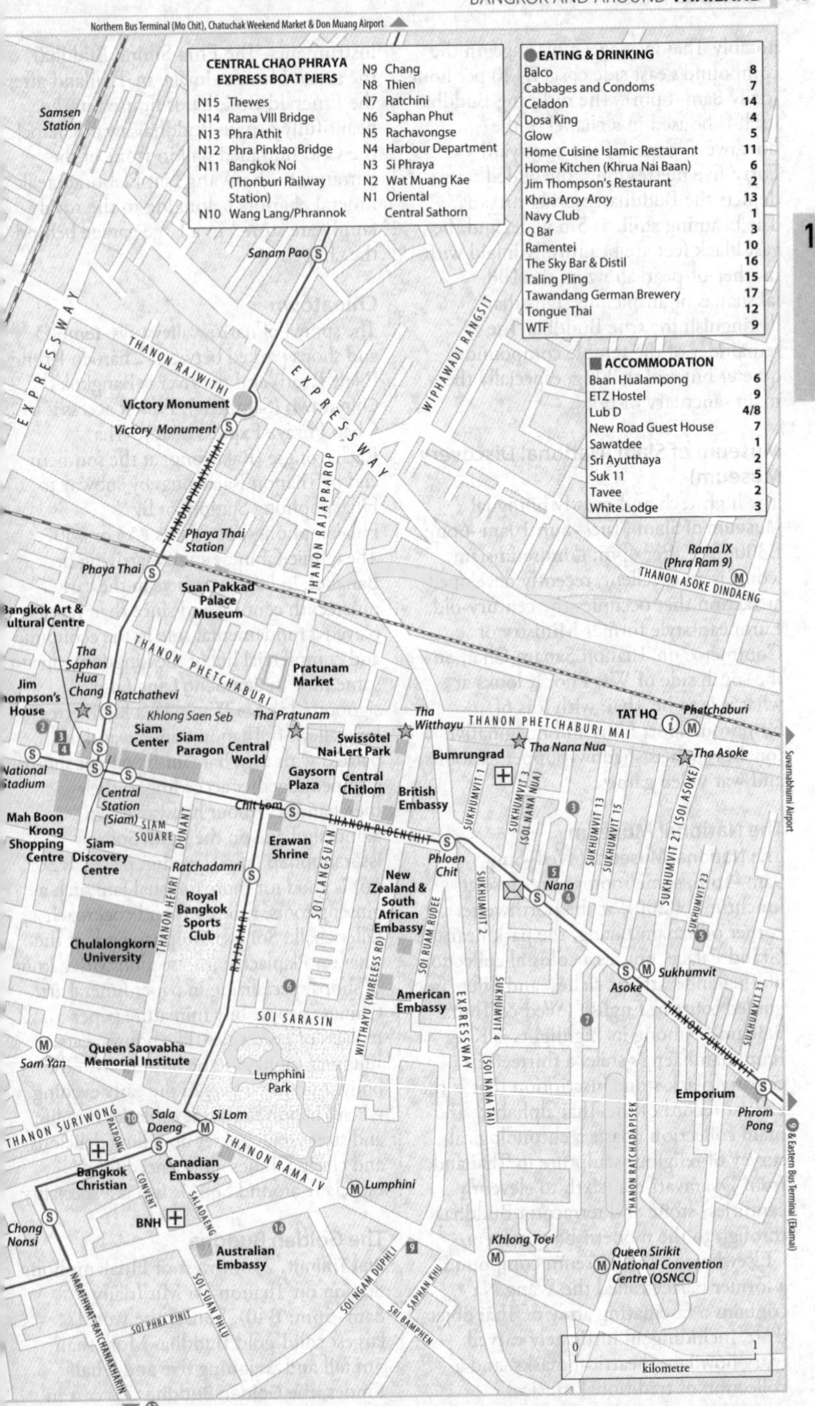
Northern Bus Terminal (Mo Chit), Chatuchak Weekend Market & Don Muang Airport
CENTRAL CHAO PHRAYA EXPRESS BOAT PIERS
N15 Thewes
N14 Rama VIII Bridge
N13 Phra Athit
N12 Phra Pinklao Bridge
N11 Bangkok Noi (Thonburi Railway Station)
N10 Wang Lang/Phrannok
N9 Chang
N8 Thien
N7 Ratchini
N6 Saphan Phut
N5 Rachavongse
N4 Harbour Department
N3 Si Phraya
N2 Wat Muang Kae
N1 Oriental
Central Sathorn
EATING & DRINKING
Balco 8
Cabbages and Condoms 7
Celadon 14
Dosa King 4
Glow 5
Home Cuisine Islamic Restaurant 11
Home Kitchen (Khrua Nai Baan) 6
Jim Thompson's Restaurant 2
Khrua Aroy Aroy 13
Navy Club 1
Q Bar 3
Ramentei 10
The Sky Bar & Distil 16
Taling Pling 15
Tawandang German Brewery 17
Tongue Thai 12
WTF 9
ACCOMMODATION
Baan Hualampong 6
ETZ Hostel 9
Lub D 4/8
New Road Guest House 7
Sawatdee 1
Sri Ayutthaya 2
Suk 11 5
Tavee 2
White Lodge 3
10
Samsen Station
Sanam Pao
EXPRESSWAY
THANON RAJWITHI
Victory Monument
WIPHAWADI RANGSIT
THANON PHAYATHAI
THANON RAJAPRAROP
Phaya Thai Station
Phaya Thai
Suan Pakkad Palace Museum
Rama IX (Phra Ram 9)
THANON ASOKE DINDAENG
Bangkok Art & Cultural Centre
THANON PHETCHABURI
Pratunam Market
Tha Saphan Hua Chang
Ratchathevi
Jim Thompson's House
Khlong Saen Seb
Tha Pratunam
Tha Witthayu
THANON PHETCHABURI MAI
TAT HQ
Phetchaburi
Siam Center
Siam Paragon
Central World
Swissôtel Nai Lert Park
Tha Nana Nua
Tha Asoke
Bumrungrad
Suvarnabhumi Airport
National Stadium
Gaysorn Plaza
Central Chitlom
British Embassy
Central Station (Siam)
Chit Lom
THANON PLOENCHIT
SUKHUMVIT 1
SUKHUMVIT 3 (SOI NANA NUA)
SUKHUMVIT 13
SUKHUMVIT 15
SUKHUMVIT 21 (SOI ASOKE)
SUKHUMVIT 23
Mah Boon Krong Shopping Centre
Siam Discovery Centre
SIAM SQUARE
DUNANT
Erawan Shrine
SOI LANGSUAN
Phloen Chit
Ratchadamri
New Zealand & South African Embassy
SUKHUMVIT 2
Nana
THANON HENRI
Royal Bangkok Sports Club
RAJDAMRI
SOI RUAM RUDEE
Chulalongkorn University
WITTHAYU (WIRELESS RD)
Sukhumvit
Asoke
SUKHUMVIT 31
American Embassy
EXPRESSWAY
SUKHUMVIT 4 (SOI NANA TAI)
SOI SARASIN
THANON SUKHUMVIT
Sam Yan
Queen Saovabha Memorial Institute
Lumphini Park
Emporium
Phrom Pong
& Eastern Bus Terminal (Ekamai)
THANON SURIWONG
PATPONG
Sala Daeng
Si Lom
THANON RAMA IV
Bangkok Christian
Canadian Embassy
CONVENT
Lumphini
THANON RATCHADAPISEK
Chong Nonsi
BNH
SALADAENG
Australian Embassy
Khlong Toei
Queen Sirikit National Convention Centre (QSNCC)
SOI NGAM DUPHLI
SAPHAN KHU
SOI SUAN PHLU
SRI BAMPHEN
SOI PHRA PINIT
NARATHIWAT-RATCHANAKHARIN
0
1
kilometre
17

notably Thai massage: a massage on the compound's east side costs B420 per hour (daily 8am–6pm). The reclining Buddha itself is housed in a chapel in the northwest corner of the courtyard. Forty-five metres long, the gilded statue depicts the Buddha entering nirvana. The beaming smile is 5m wide, and the vast black feet are beautifully inlaid with mother-of-pearl showing the 108 lakshanas or auspicious signs that distinguish the true Buddha. The remainder of the temple compound is quieter but still striking, especially the main sanctuary or bot.

Museum of Siam (National Discovery Museum)

The high-tech and mostly bilingual **Museum of Siam** (Tues–Sun 10am–6pm; B300, free after 4pm; Ⓦmuseumsiam .com) is an excellent, recently developed attraction that occupies the century-old, European-style former Ministry of Commerce on Thanon Sanam Chai, on the south side of Wat Pho. It looks at what it is to be Thai, with lots of humorous short films and imaginative touches such as shadow-puppet cartoons and war video games.

The National Museum

The **National Museum** (Wed–Sun 9am–4pm, some rooms may close at lunchtime; B200), at the northwestern corner of Sanam Luang, the park near the Grand Palace, houses a colossal collection of Thailand's artistic riches, and offers free guided tours in English (Wed & Thurs 9.30am). Among its highlights is King Ramkhamhaeng's stele, a thirteenth-century black stone inscription that is the earliest record of the Thai alphabet. The main collection boasts a chronological survey of religious sculpture in Thailand, from Dvaravati-era (sixth to eleventh centuries) stone and terracotta Buddhas through to the modern Bangkok era.

Elsewhere in the museum compound, a former palace called the Wang Na contains a fascinating array of Thai objets d'art, including an intricately carved ivory howdah, theatrical masks, and a collection of traditional musical instruments. The Phra Sihing Buddha, the second holiest image in Thailand after the Emerald Buddha, is housed in the beautifully ornate Buddhaisawan Chapel, the vast, muralled hall in front of the entrance to the Wang Na. Elaborate teak funeral chariots belonging to the royal family are stored in a large garage behind the chapel.

Chinatown

The sprawl of narrow alleyways, temples and shops packed between Charoen Krung (New Road) and the river is Bangkok's **Chinatown** (Sampeng). Easiest access is by Chao Phraya Express boat to Tha Rachavongse (Rajawong) at the southern end of Thanon Rajawong, by subway to Hualamphong Station, or by Hualamphong-bound bus #53 or #507. The ethnic Chinese started arriving in Bangkok in large numbers in the early nineteenth century and since then have played a fundamental role in the economic and commercial life of the kingdom. Spend some time in **Sampeng Lane** (also signposted as Soi Wanit 1), a kilometre-long alley off Thanon Songsawat that's packed with tiny, bargain-basement shops grouped together according to their merchandise. About halfway down Sampeng Lane on the right, **Soi Issaranuphap** (also signed in places as Soi 16) is good for more unusual fare such as ginseng roots, fish heads and cockroach-killer chalk. Soi Issaranuphap ends at the Thanon Plaplachai intersection with a knot of shops specializing in paper funeral art: Chinese people buy miniature paper replicas of necessities (like houses, cars, suits and money) to be burned with the body. Aim to be here in the early evening when **Thanon Yaowarat** explodes into life and street stalls are set up selling delicious and cheap Chinese-influenced food, especially around Soi 11; fish is a speciality.

The Golden Buddha

Wat Traimit, 250m west of Hualamphong Station on Thanon Tri Mit (daily 8am–5pm; B40), houses the world's largest solid-gold Buddha. More than 3m tall and weighing five and a half tonnes, the **Golden Buddha** was cast in

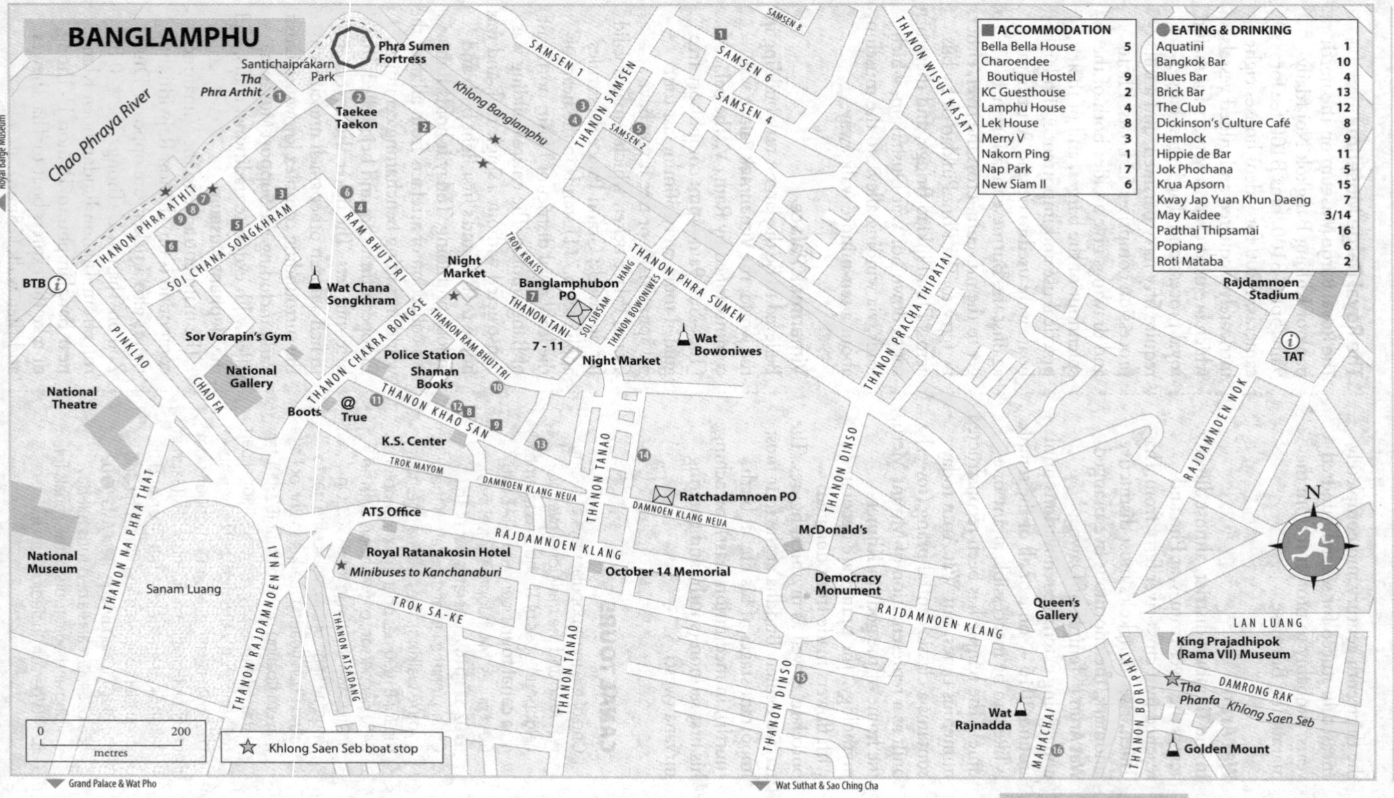
BANGLAMPHU
ACCOMMODATION
Bella Bella House 5
Charoendee Boutique Hostel 9
KC Guesthouse 2
Lamphu House 4
Lek House 8
Merry V 3
Nakorn Ping 1
Nap Park 7
New Siam II 6
EATING & DRINKING
Aquatini 1
Bangkok Bar 10
Blues Bar 4
Brick Bar 13
The Club 12
Dickinson's Culture Café 8
Hemlock 9
Hippie de Bar 11
Jok Phochana 5
Krua Apsorn 15
Kway Jap Yuan Khun Daeng 7
May Kaidee 3/14
Padthai Thipsamai 16
Popiang 6
Roti Mataba 2
Chao Phraya River
Santichaiprákarn Park
Tha Phra Arthit
Phra Sumen Fortress
Taekee Taekon
Khlong Banglamphu
Wat Chana Songkhram
Sor Vorapin's Gym
National Gallery
National Theatre
National Museum
Sanam Luang
BTB
Night Market
Banglamphubon PO
7 - 11
Night Market
Wat Bowoniwes
Police Station
Shaman Books
@ True
Boots
K.S. Center
ATS Office
Royal Ratanakosin Hotel
Minibuses to Kanchanaburi
October 14 Memorial
Ratchadamnoen PO
McDonald's
Democracy Monument
Queen's Gallery
Wat Rajnadda
King Prajadhipok (Rama VII) Museum
Tha Phanfa
Khlong Saen Seb
Golden Mount
Rajdamnoen Stadium
TAT
N
SAMSEN 1
SAMSEN 2
SAMSEN 4
SAMSEN 6
SAMSEN 8
THANON SAMSEN
THANON WISUT KASAT
THANON PRACHA THIPATAI
THANON PHRA SUMEN
THANON BOWONIWES
SOI SIBSAM HANG
THANON TANI
TROK KRAISI
RAM BHUTTRI
THANON RAM BHUTTRI
THANON CHAKRA BONGSE
THANON KHAO SAN
SOI CHANA SONGKHRAM
THANON PHRA ATHIT
PINKLAO
CHAD FA
TROK MAYOM
DAMNOEN KLANG NEUA
RAJDAMNOEN KLANG
THANON TANAO
THANON DINSO
TROK SA-KE
THANON ATSADANG
THANON RAJDAMNOEN NAI
THANON NA PHRA THAT
RAJDAMNOEN NOK
THANON BORIPHAT
MAHACHAI
LAN LUANG
DAMRONG RAK
0 200 metres
Khlong Saen Seb boat stop
Royal Barge Museum
Grand Palace & Wat Pho
Wat Suthat & Sao Ching Cha

the thirteenth century and completely encased in stucco for several hundred years, probably to protect it from the marauding Burmese.

Wat Arun

In the **Thonburi** district, almost directly across the river from Wat Pho and reached by a cross-river ferry from Tha Thien, rises Bangkok's most distinctive landmark, the enormous five-pranged **Wat Arun** ("Temple of Dawn"; undergoing extensive renovations until around 2016 – some or all of the temple is likely to be inaccessible at any one time). The temple has been reconstructed numerous times, but Wat Arun today contains a classic central prang (tower) built as a representation of Mount Meru, the home of the gods in Khmer mythology. The prangs are decorated with flowers made from donated porcelain as well as mythical figures. The terrace depicts Buddha at the four most important stages of his life: at birth (north), in meditation (east), preaching his first sermon (south) and entering nirvana (west).

CANAL TOURS

One of the most popular ways of seeing Wat Arun and the traditional riverine neighbourhoods of Thonburi is to embark on a **canal tour**. Licensed by TAT, with fixed prices, Mitchaopaya Travel Service (T 02 623 6169) operates out of Tha Chang (on the left at the start of the pier, if you're walking). They offer a one-hour trip for B1000 per boat (max 6 people) or B450 per person, or two hours with an orchid farm thrown in for B1500. On Saturday and Sunday, you could get to Taling Chan floating market in 2hr, or Lat Mayom floating market in 3hr (B2500), far to the west in a leafy, more traditional part of Thonburi. It's also possible to organize your own boat trip around Thonburi from other piers, including Central Pier (Saphan Taksin Skytrain station), Tha Thien and the small piers between Tha Phra Athit and the Phra Pinklao Bridge. Real Asia (T 02 665 6364, W realasia.net) runs full-day walking and boat tours of the canals for B2140/person, including lunch.

The Royal Barge Museum

The Royal Barge Museum on the north bank of Khlong Bangkok Noi (daily 9am–5pm; B100, plus B100 fee for cameras, B200 for video) houses eight intricately lacquered and gilded vessels which are used every few years for major royal processions. The largest barges require fifty navy oarsmen, and a full procession comprises 52 boats. Photos and drawings give an idea both of the splendour of the barges, and of their practical use and importance; similar boats were used to defend Ayutthaya against the Burmese invasion in 1767. To get to the museum, cross the river, either by ferry to Tha Phra Pinklao or by bus across Phra Pinklao Bridge, and then turn south down Soi Wat Dusitaram, which leads, via winding alleys, to the museum, about a ten-minute walk away.

Vimanmek Palace

Believed to be the largest teak building in the world, the **Vimanmek Palace** was commissioned by Rama V. The palace (Tues–Sun 9am–4pm; compulsory free guided tours every 30min, last tour 3.15pm; B100, or free if you have a Grand Palace ticket, which remains valid for one week; Grand Palace dress rules apply; see p.711) stands in the heart of the leafy royal district of Dusit, northeast of Banglamphu. The entire building was constructed without a single nail, and was home to Thailand's first light bulb and indoor plumbing. Today it holds Rama V's collection of artefacts from all over the world including bencharong ceramics, European furniture and bejewelled Thai betel-nut sets. The ticket also covers entry to half a dozen other small museums in the surrounding complex known as Dusit Park, including the **Support Museum**, filled with exquisite traditional crafts, and the **Elephant Museum**.

The main entrance to the Vimanmek compound is on Thanon Rajwithi, but there's also a ticket gate opposite Dusit Zoo on Thanon U-Thong. The #70 bus runs from Thanon Rajdamnoen Klang near Banglamphu to Thanon U-Thong, or take the express boat to Tha Thewes and then walk (15min).

Wat Benjamabophit

Located on Thanon Sri Ayutthaya, about 600m southeast from Vimanmek's U-Thong gate, **Wat Benjamabophit** (daily 8.30am–6pm; B20) was commissioned by Rama V in the early 1900s. The style blends classical Thai and nineteenth-century European design – the Carrara-marble walls, which gleam in the midday sun, are complemented by unusual stained-glass windows. The courtyard behind the bot houses a gallery of Buddha images from all over Asia. Wat Ben is also the best place to see the daily early-morning ritual alms-giving ceremony (between about 6am and 7.30am); in contrast to the usual parade of monks around the locality, the temple's monks line up and await donations from local citizens.

Wat Indraviharn

The temple complex of **Wat Indraviharn** is dominated by an enormous standing Buddha, 32m high. The striking image, commissioned in the mid-nineteenth century and covered in gold mirror-mosaic, is the tallest representation in the world of the Buddha holding an alms bowl from beneath his robes. His toes peep out through flower garlands, and you can climb the stairs supporting the statue to get a decent view over the area. The temple compound is an interesting amalgam of religious architectural styles and includes a Chinese shrine. Wat In is an easy ten-minute walk north of Banglamphu, along Thanon Samsen; bus #53 stops nearby on Thanon Samsen. Be aware that the complex has become a favourite hangout for con-artists (see box, p.711).

Jim Thompson's House

Decades after his death, Jim Thompson remains Thailand's most famous *farang* (foreigner). A former agent of the OSS (later to become the CIA), Thompson moved to Bangkok after World War II and later disappeared mysteriously in Malaysia's Cameron Highlands in 1967. He is most famous for introducing Thai silk to the world and for his collection of traditional art, much of which is now displayed at his former home, **Jim Thompson's House**, which can be seen by compulsory guided tour (daily from 9am, last tour 5pm; B100; National Stadium or Siam Central Skytrain stations or on the Khlong Saen Seb canal boat), near Siam Square at 6 Soi Kasemsan 2, Thanon Rama I. The grand, rambling house was constructed – without nails – from six two-hundred-year-old teak houses that Thompson shipped to Bangkok from around the kingdom. The tasteful interior has been left as it was during Thompson's life. There's an appealing restaurant (see p.723) on site.

Bangkok Art and Cultural Centre

A striking, white hunk of modernity at the junction of Rama I and Phrayathai roads, the prestigious **Bangkok Art and Cultural Centre** (Tues–Sun 10am–9pm; free; Ⓦbacc.or.th) houses several galleries on its upper floors, connected by spiralling ramps like New York's Guggenheim, as well as performance spaces. There's always something interesting among its temporary shows, which are by contemporary artists from Thailand and abroad across all media. To get here, catch the Skytrain to National Stadium or Siam (Central).

Erawan Shrine

Located on the congested corner of Ploenchit and Rajdamri roads, sitting conspicuously next to the *Grand Hyatt Erawan*, the garishly ornate **Erawan Shrine** is well worth a visit. It is dedicated to Brahma, the Hindu creation god, and Erawan, his elephant. Buddhists, including many from Singapore, Hong Kong and Taiwan, come in droves to pray and offer thanks to each of Brahma's heads – luckily for the flower and incense hawkers. Thai dance troops can be hired to perform thanksgiving routines here when a prayer has been answered; the number of dancers depends on the magnitude of the wish fulfilled.

Suan Pakkad Palace Museum

The **Suan Pakkad Palace Museum** (daily 9am–4pm; B100), five minutes' walk

10

from Phaya Thai Skytrain station at 352–4 Thanon Sri Ayutthaya, is the former palace of Prince and Princess Chumbhot, and visitors can view their private collection of antiquities. The palace is constructed of groups of individual buildings clustered around a garden. Highlights include four-thousand-year-old pottery and jewellery, and the interior of the Lacquer Pavilion, which is decorated with Ramayana panels in gilt on black lacquer. Elsewhere you'll find Thai and Khmer sculptures, ceramics and some fine theatrical *khon* masks.

Chatuchak Weekend Market

With eight thousand open-air stalls to peruse, the enormous **Chatuchak Weekend Market** (Sat & Sun 7am–6pm), about 5km north of Banglamphu, is Bangkok's most enjoyable shopping experience. It's the place to make for if you want to get handicrafts and cheap northern and northeastern textiles and products, including axe pillows, silk, farmers' shirts, musical instruments, jeans, jewellery and designer T-shirts. The market occupies a huge patch of ground adjacent to Mo Chit Skytrain station and Chatuchak Park and Kamphaeng Phet subway stations, and can also be reached by air-conditioned bus #509 from Rajdamnoen Klang in Banglamphu (1hr). By far the best map of the market is on Nancy Chandler's *Map of Bangkok* (see p.707), but boards with maps are also posted at various points around the market, including in the subway stations. You can change money in the market building, and there are ATMs here, too.

ARRIVAL AND DEPARTURE

BY PLANE

Suvarnabhumi Airport Bangkok's main airport (pronounced su-wan-na-poom; BKK; ⓣ 02 132 3888) is 30km east of central Bangkok. Tourist information desks, currency exchange booths and accommodation desks (all 24hr) are located in the arrivals hall on Level 2, and ATMs are found throughout the airport. There's an airport rail link from here to the city centre, where the most useful stop is Phraya Thai, which is connected to Phraya Thai Skytrain station; non-stop Express Line trains from the airport to Phraya Thai (hourly; 18min) cost B150, while stopping City Line trains to Phraya Thai (every 12–15min; 30min) cost B45. An air-conditioned, metered public taxi to central Bangkok, from clearly signposted counters outside Gates 4 and 7 on Level 1, should cost around B300–400 (depending on traffic), including expressway tolls and B50 airport fee. Never take an unlicensed taxi, as robberies are not unknown. To get back out to the airport, guesthouses and travel agents in Banglamphu can book tickets on hourly private minibuses for around B140.

Don Muang Airport Don Muang Airport (DMK), 25km and a B350 taxi ride north of the city, handles mostly domestic flights operated by Air Asia, Nok Air and Orient Thai. Shuttle buses from outside Arrivals run roughly every 15min to Suvarnabhumi (free with a boarding pass) or to Mo Chit Skytrain and Chatuchak Park subway stations (B30).

Destinations Chiang Mai (30 daily; 1hr); Chiang Rai (11 daily; 1hr 20min); Chumphon (2–3 daily; 1hr); Khon Kaen (7 daily; 55min); Ko Samui (20 daily; 1hr 20min); Krabi (18 daily; 1hr 20min); Lampang (3 daily; 1hr); Mae Sot (4 daily; 1hr 15min); Nakhon Phanom (2 daily; 1hr 5min); Nakhon Si Thammarat (10 daily; 1hr 15min); Nan (3 daily; 1hr 40min); Phitsanulok (6 daily; 45min); Phuket (30 daily; 1hr 25min); Ranong (2–4 daily; 1hr 35min); Sukhothai (2 daily; 1hr 10min); Surat Thani (9 daily; 1hr 15min); Trang (6 daily; 1hr 30min); Trat (3 daily; 50min); Ubon Ratchathani (10 daily; 1hr 5min).

BY BUS

Bangkok has three long-distance bus terminals. Most services from Malaysia and the south, and from places west of Bangkok, come in at the Sai Tai Mai (Southern) Bus Terminal, about 10km into Thonburi (a few of these services also use the Northern Bus Terminal). City buses serving this terminal include #124 for Banglamphu, #511 for Banglamphu and Th Sukhumvit, and #516 for Thewet and Banglamphu. Services from the north and northeast use the Mo Chit (Northern and Northeastern) Bus Terminal on Th Kamphaeng Phet 2, near Chatuchak Weekend Market; either take a short taxi or motorbike taxi ride to Mo Chit Skytrain station or Kamphaeng Phet subway station, or use buses #3, #509 or #512 to Banglamphu. Most buses from the east coast pull into the Ekamai (Eastern) Bus Terminal at Soi 40, Th Sukhumvit (a few east-coast services also use the Northern and Southern Bus Terminal), which is right next to Ekamai Skytrain Station. On departure, seats on long-distance a/c bus services should be reserved ahead, either at the relevant bus station, at major post offices or at the ATS (Advance Technology System; Mon–Fri 9am–5pm) office near the *Royal Ratanakosin Hotel* on Th Rajdamnoen Klang in Banglamphu, the official seller of government a/c bus tickets; see also ⓦ thaiticketmajor.com for details on booking by phone and online.

Eastern Bus Terminal Ban Phe (for Ko Samet; hourly; 3hr); Rayong (every 30min; 2hr 30min–3hr); Trat (roughly hourly; 5–6hr).

Northern Bus Terminal Aranyaprathet (10 daily; 4hr 30min); Ayutthaya (every 20–30min; 2hr); Chiang Khong (10 daily; 13–14hr); Chiang Mai (30 daily; 9–11hr); Chiang Rai (at least 20 daily; 12hr); Chong Mek (daily; 11hr); Kanchanaburi (hourly; 2hr 30min); Khon Kaen (hourly; 6–7hr); Khorat (every 20min; 3hr); Lampang (at least hourly; 8hr); Lopburi (every 30min; 3hr); Mae Hong Son (3 daily; 16hr); Mae Sai (13 daily; 13hr); Mae Sot (12 daily; 8hr 30min); Mukdahan (20 daily; 11hr); Nakhon Phanom (20 daily; 12hr); Nong Khai (20 daily; 10hr); Pak Chong (every 15min; 3hr); Phitsanulok (more than 50 daily; 5–6hr); Sukhothai (more than 30 daily; 6–7hr); Surin (up to 20 daily; 8–9hr); Trat (9 daily; 4–5hr); Ubon Ratchathani (19 daily; 10–12hr).

Southern Bus Terminal Chumphon (roughly hourly; 7–9hr); Damnoen Saduak (every 30min; 2hr); Kanchanaburi (every 15min; 2–3hr); Ko Pha Ngan (2 daily 14hr); Ko Samui (9–10 daily; 13hr); Krabi (12 daily; 12–14hr); Nakhon Pathom (every 10min; 40min–1hr 20min); Nakhon Si Thammarat (19 daily; 12hr); Phang Nga (8 daily; 11hr–12hr 30min); Phetchaburi (4–7 daily; 2hr); Phuket (20 daily; 14hr); Ranong (10 daily; 8hr); Surat Thani (12 daily; 10–12hr).

BY BUDGET TRANSPORT

Many Bangkok outfits offer budget transport on small and large buses to Chiang Mai, Surat Thani, Krabi, Ko Samet and Ko Chang. This often works out cheaper than a public a/c bus, and is often handier as departures are usually from Th Khao San. However, many of the buses are cramped and airless, drivers often race, and drop-off points can be far from the town centre, despite adverts to the contrary. Security on large buses is also a big problem, so keep everything of value on your person at all times and lock other luggage. If you're heading for an island, check whether your bus ticket covers the ferry ride. Consult other travellers before booking any budget transport – all in all, it's better to take the train or a public a/c bus instead.

BY TRAIN

All trains use centrally placed Hualamphong Station except services to Kanchanaburi (plus a few, very slow trains to the south), which leave from Thonburi Station, about an 850m walk west of the Bangkok Noi express-boat pier. Hualamphong is on the subway line and served by buses #53 to Banglamphu and Thewes, #159 which runs between the Southern and Northern bus terminals, and #507 to Banglamphu and the Southern Bus Terminal. See p.701 for general information about train timetables and booking tickets. The 24-hour State Railways (SRT) information booth in the main concourse at Hualamphong Station keeps English-language timetables. Between 8.30am and 4pm, advance tickets can be bought from the clearly signed Advance Booking counters #15–20 under the main departures board; at other times, check availability at the SRT information booth, then buy your ticket at any ticket counter (daily 4.30am–midnight).

Hualamphong Station to: Aranyaprathet (2 daily; 5hr 30min); Ayutthaya (20 daily; 1hr 30min); Butterworth, Malaysia (daily; 23hr); Chiang Mai (5 daily; 12–15hr); Chumphon (12 daily; 7hr–9hr 30min); Khon Kaen (4 daily; 7hr 30min–10hr 20min); Khorat (12 daily; 4–5hr); Lampang (6 daily; 11–13hr); Lopburi (14 daily; 2hr 30min–3hr); Nakhon Pathom (13 daily; 1hr 30min); Nakhon Si Thammarat (2 daily; 15–16hr); Nong Khai (3 daily; 11–12hr); Pak Chong (11 daily; 3hr 30min–4hr 45min); Phetchaburi (10 daily; 2hr 45min–3hr 45min); Phitsanulok (11 daily; 5hr 40min–8hr); Surat Thani (10 daily; 9–12hr); Surin (10 daily; 7–10hr); Trang (2 daily; 16hr); Ubon Ratchathani (7 daily; 8hr 30min–14hr).

Thonburi (Bangkok Noi) Station to: Kanchanaburi (2 daily; 3hr); Nakhon Pathom (2 daily; 1hr 10min); Nam Tok (2 daily; 5hr).

10

CENTRAL STOPS FOR THE CHAO PHRAYA EXPRESS BOAT

N15 Thewes (all express boats) – for Thewes guesthouses.
N14 Rama VIII Bridge (no flag) – for Samsen Soi 5.
N13 Phra Athit (no flag and orange flag) – for Th Khao San and Banglamphu.
N12 Phra Pinklao Bridge (all boats) – for Royal Barge Museum.
N11 Bangkok Noi (Thonburi Railway Station; no flag) – for Kanchanaburi trains.
N10 Wang Lang (or Prannok; all boats) – for Siriraj Hospital.
N9 Tha Chang (no flag, green flag and orange flag) – for the Grand Palace.
N8 Thien (no flag and orange flag) – for Wat Pho, and the ferry to Wat Arun.
N7 Ratchini (no flag).
N6 Saphan Phut (Memorial Bridge; no flag and orange flag) – for Pak Khlong Talat.
N5 Rachavongse (all boats) – for Chinatown.
N4 Harbour Department (no flag and orange flag).
N3 Si Phraya (all boats) – for River City.
N2 Wat Muang Kae (no flag) – for GPO.
N1 Oriental (no flag and orange flag) – for Th Silom.
Central Sathorn (all boats) – for the Skytrain and Th Sathorn.

10

GETTING AROUND

BY BOAT

Bangkok's network of waterways is the most interesting means of getting around the city.

Express boats The Chao Phraya Express (ⓦ chaophraya expressboat.com) runs large river buses in daylight hours between Krung Thep Bridge in the south and Nonthaburi in the north, stopping at numbered piers (*tha*) all along its course. "Local" boats with no flag stop at every landing, but only operate during rush hours (Mon–Fri 6.20–8am & 3–5.30pm; every 20–25min; B10–14). The only boats to run all day (6am–7pm) every day are on the limited-stop orange-flag service (every 5–20min; B15). Other limited-stop, express services run only during rush hours, flying either a yellow (B20–29) or green (B13–32) flag; a sign on each pier shows which service stops there. The important central Chao Phraya Express stops are outlined in the box on p.719 and marked on our city map (see pp.712–713).

Tourist boats Chao Phraya Express tourist boats, distinguished by light-blue flags, with on-board guides, run between Phra Athit (every 30min; 9.30/10am–4/4.30pm; currently experimenting with running till 9/9.30pm, though this may not last) and Sathorn, stopping at all piers close to tourist attractions, on both sides of the river. A one-day ticket with unlimited stops costs B150; one-way tickets are also available, costing B40.

Khlong saen seb boats Passenger boats run every fifteen minutes during daylight hours along Khlong Saen Seb canal from Tha Phanfa, near Democracy Monument (handy for Banglamphu, Ratanakosin and Chinatown), and head way out east, with useful stops at Th Phrayathai, aka Saphan Hua Chang (for Jim Thompson's House and Ratchathevi Skytrain stop), Pratunam (for the Erawan Shrine) and Soi Asoke (Soi 21, for Phetchaburi subway stop) off Th Sukhumvit. This is your quickest and most interesting way of getting across town, if you can stand the stench of the canal; fares cost B12–20.

BY BUS

There are two main types of bus services in the city: ordinary (non-a/c; currently free), which come in various colours and run either from around 5am to 10pm or 24hr; and blue, yellow or orange a/c buses (B10–23), most of which stop at around 8.30pm. The box below highlights the most useful routes. Of the several bus maps sold at bookshops and hotels, the best and most useful is Bangkok Guide's Bus Routes & Map.

BY SKYTRAIN

Although their networks are limited, the BTS Skytrain and the subway provide much faster alternatives to the bus. There are two Skytrain lines (ⓦ bts.co.th), both running daily every few minutes from 6am to midnight, with fares B15–52/trip depending on distance travelled. The Silom Line's Saphan Taksin station links up with express boats at Central pier.

BY SUBWAY

The single-line subway runs frequently (up to every 2min in rush hour) from 6am to midnight each day. Fares are B16–40. Work is under way (scheduled to complete in 2015) to continue the line from Hualamphong, through Chinatown and Ratanakosin, to Thonburi.

BY TAXI

Fares in Bangkok's metered, a/c taxi cabs start at B35 (look out for the "TAXI METER" sign on the roof, and a red light in the windscreen by the passenger seat, which means that the cab is free). Insist that the taxi use its meter; some taxis

USEFUL BUS ROUTES

#3 (ordinary and a/c): Northern Bus Terminal–Chatuchak Weekend Market–Th Samsen–Th Phra Athit–Th Sanam Chai–Th Triphet–Memorial Bridge–Wat Suwan.

#25 (ordinary and a/c, 24hr): Eastern Bus Terminal–Th Sukhumvit–Siam Square–Hualamphong Station–Th Yaowarat (for Chinatown and Wat Traimit)–Wat Pho–Tha Chang (for the Grand Palace).

#53 circular (also anticlockwise; ordinary): Thewes–Th Krung Kasem–Hualamphong Station–Th Yaowarat–Th Maharat (for Wat Pho and the Grand Palace)–Sanam Luang–Th Phra Athit and Th Samsen (for Banglamphu guesthouses)–Thewes.

#159 (ordinary): Southern Bus Terminal–Phra Pinklao Bridge–Democracy Monument–Hualamphong Station–MBK Shopping Centre–Th Ratchaprarop–Victory Monument–Chatuchak Weekend Market–Northern Bus Terminal.

#511 (a/c, 24hr): Southern Bus Terminal–Phra Pinklao Bridge–Rajdamnoen Klang–Democracy Monument–Th Lan Luang–Th Phetchaburi–Th Sukhumvit–Eastern Bus Terminal–Pak Nam (for Muang Boran Ancient City buses). Note, however, that some #511 buses take the expressway, missing out the Eastern Bus Terminal.

#512 (a/c): Northern Bus Terminal–Chatuchak Weekend Market–Th Phetchaburi–Th Lan Luang–Democracy Monument (for Banglamphu guesthouses)–Sanam Luang–Tha Chang (for Grand Palace)–Pak Khlong Talat.

refuse especially for late-night or inconvenient journeys. Try to have change with you as cabs tend not to carry a lot of money or will pretend not to.

BY TUK-TUK

The unmetered buggies known as tuk-tuks have very little to recommend them (see p.702). The drivers prey on rookie tourists and often overcharge; always agree a price before you set off, and don't forget to barter. Also, there have been cases of robberies and attacks on solo women in tuk-tuks late at night. It's always cheaper (and more pleasant) to use a taxi.

BY MOTORBIKE TAXI

Motorbike taxis, which can only carry one passenger, generally do short local journeys down into the side streets (from B10) but can also be hired to go out onto the main streets (around B40 from Th Samsen to the National Museum). The riders wear numbered, coloured vests; crash helmets are now compulsory. Always agree a price before you set off.

INFORMATION

Tourist information Bangkok Tourism Division, 17/1 Th Phra Athit next to Phra Pinklao Bridge in Banglamphu (Mon–Fri 8am–7pm, Sat & Sun 9am–5pm; ⓣ02 225 7612, ⓦbangkoktourist.com), provides a decent information service and has twenty or so booths around the capital. Tourism Authority of Thailand (TAT), 4 Th Rajdamnoen Nok (daily 8.30am–4.30pm; ⓣ02 356 0650; national tourist hotline daily 8am–8pm ⓣ1672), covers destinations further afield.

ACCOMMODATION

Banglamphu, with Th Khao San (better known as Khao San Rd) at its heart, remains the city's travellers' ghetto and subsequently is home to most of its cheapest accommodation. Downtown accommodation is well placed for Bangkok's shopping districts and nightlife.

THANON KHAO SAN AND BANGLAMPHU

Th Khao San itself has become progressively more upmarket and really cheap accommodation is no longer plentiful. The cheapest places share cold-water bathrooms.

Bella Bella House 74 Soi Chana Songkhram ⓣ02 629 3090; map p.715. Above an attractive, plant-strewn café, the pastel-coloured rooms here are no frills but well priced, and a few boast lovely views over Wat Chana Songkhram. The cheapest share cold-water bathrooms, a notch up gets you an en-suite hot shower, while the most expensive have a/c. In-room wi-fi available throughout. Double **B350**

Charoendee Boutique Hostel 189 Th Khao San ⓣ02 629 1980, ⓔcharoendeehotel@gmail.com; map p.715. Pretty, colonial-style edifices around a small courtyard. Fan rooms share hot-water bathrooms, but it's well worth paying B200 extra for an a/c, en-suite room in the airy original building; good rates for singles. Free coffee and toast for breakfast. At the bottom of a narrow alley, so quieter than many. Double **B450**

KC Guesthouse 64 Trok Kai Chae, corner of Th Phra Sumen ⓣ02 282 0618, ⓦkc64guesthouse.com; map p.715. Friendly, family-run guesthouse offering exceptionally clean, colourful fan and a/c rooms, with or without private bathrooms. Double **B350**

Lamphu House 75 Soi Ram Bhuttri ⓣ02 629 5861–2, ⓦlamphuhouse.com; map p.715. With smart bamboo beds, coconut-wood clothes rails, and elegant rattan lamps, this travellers' hotel set round a quiet courtyard has a calm, modern feel. The cheapest fan rooms share facilities and have no outside view. Double **B440**

Lek House 125 Th Khao San ⓣ02 281 8441; map p.715. Old-style guesthouse, where most of the small, basic rooms with shared bathrooms have windows; go for one on the front with a balcony, if you want the full Khao San blast. Can get noisy at night. Double **B240**

Merry V Soi Ram Bhuttri ⓣ02 282 9267; map p.715. Large, efficiently run guesthouse offering some of the cheapest accommodation in Banglamphu (small, with shared bathrooms). Better en-suites with hot showers and a/c also available. Decent rates for singles. Double **B240**

Nakorn Ping 9/1 Soi 6, Th Samsen ⓣ02 281 6574, ⓦnakornpinghotel.com; map p.715. In a low-rise, orange building dotted with plants on a fairly quiet soi, this classic Thai-Chinese hotel is efficiently run and good value, offering fridges, cable TV and bathrooms in all rooms. Double **B460**

Nap Park 5 Th Tani ⓣ02 282 2324, ⓦnappark.com; map p.715. On a surprisingly untouristed street just north of Th Khao San, this lively new hostel shelters smart dorm beds with free wi-fi, personal TVs, lockers and hot showers, as well as plenty of space for lounging, either inside in front of the TV or outside in the tamarind-shaded front yard. Women-only dorm and laundry available. Dorm **B440**

New Siam II 50 Trok Rong Mai, off Th Phra Athit ⓣ02 282 2795, ⓦnewsiam.net; map p.715. Tastefully decorated fan or a/c rooms in a quiet, clean, modern guesthouse, with a small swimming pool. Double **B740**

THEWES

The guesthouses clustered behind the National Library on Th Sri Ayutthaya, close to the lively Thewes market, are more charming than their Banglamphu counterparts, appealing to a mixed crowd of travellers and families.

Sawatdee 71 Th Sri Ayutthaya, cnr Soi 16 ⓣ02 281 0757; map pp.712–713. Cheap and basic, but friendlier than many in the Thewes area, this long-running old-style guesthouse offers no-frills fan rooms with partition walls. Double **B250**

10

Sri Ayutthaya Soi 14, 23/11 Th Sri Ayutthaya ⓣ02 282 5942, ⓔsriayuttaya@yahoo.com; map pp.712–713. The most attractive guesthouse in Thewes, with elegant, wood-panelled rooms, some of them en-suite with a/c. There's a great restaurant downstairs which serves delicious vegetarian food. Double **B500**

★Tavee 83 Soi 14, Th Sri Ayutthaya ⓣ02 280 1447, ⓔtaveethai@yahoo.com; map pp.712–713. Down a pedestrian alley behind *Sri Ayutthaya Guesthouse* and owned by the same family, but quieter and friendlier. Fan rooms sport attractive wood floors and share hot-water bathrooms, while the a/c options are en-suite. Double **B450**

10

DOWNTOWN

The following are away from the main sights of Ratanakosin, but handy for nightlife and shopping.

Baan Hualampong 336/20 Soi Chalongkrung, off Th Rama IV ⓣ02 639 8054, ⓦbaanhualampong.com; map pp.712–713. Convenient for Hualamphong Station, stylish, wooden twin rooms that are spacious and have a traditional feel. Staff are friendly, and dorms and good-value singles are also available; most rooms share facilities. Dorm **B250**, double **B520**

ETZ Hostel 5/3 Soi Ngam Duphli, off Th Rama IV ⓣ02 286 9424, ⓦetzhostel.com; map pp.712–713. Above a branch of the recommended ETC travel agent, and handy for Lumphini subway. Helpful, modern and clean, with a roof terrace and a lounge with free computers. A/c dorms share hot showers; free wi-fi throughout. Dorm **B200**, double **B900**

★TREAT YOURSELF

A great way to see Bangkok's beautifully illuminated riverside temples at night is on a dinner cruise. Chomping on Thai green curry while gliding past the Grand Palace is an experience you'll never forget. Cruises usually last two hours. Always book in advance; some cruises may not run during the rainy season.

Loy Nava ⓣ02 437 4932, ⓦloynava.com. The original, forty-year-old converted rice-barge service still departs Si Phraya pier twice nightly, at 6pm and 8.10pm, with pick-ups at Tha Sathorn possible. Live traditional music and dancing. B1400, including hotel pick-up in central Bangkok.

Manohra Beautiful converted rice-barge operated by the *Anantara Riverside Resort*, south of Taksin Bridge in Thonburi (ⓣ02 476 0022 ext 1416, ⓦmanohra cruises.com). Departs hotel at 7.30pm, with pick-ups at Tha Sathorn possible. From B1750.

Lub D 4 Th Decho ⓣ02 634 7999 & 925/9 Th Rama I ⓣ02 612 4999, ⓦlubd.com; map pp.712–713. Great hostel with a chilled-out vibe, big, funky, a/c dorms and bedrooms with swish, hot-water bathrooms. The communal areas have an open layout and a friendly feel. Free wi-fi. Dorm **B450**, double **B1100**

★New Road Guest House 1216/1 Th Charoen Krung, between sois 34 and 36 ⓣ02 630 9371, ⓦvisitbeyond.com/thailand; map pp.712–713. Thai headquarters of a Danish backpacker tour operator, with a helpful travel agent and interesting Thailand tours. On offer are comfortable a/c dorms, fan doubles with hot-water bathrooms and attractive a/c rooms, set around a quiet courtyard off New Rd. Free wi-fi. Dorm **B250**, double **B550**

Suk 11 1/33 Soi 11, Th Sukhumvit ⓣ02 253 5927, ⓦsuk11.com; map pp.712–713. The most backpacker-oriented guesthouse on Sukhumvit Rd, whose interior resembles a village of traditional wooden houses, with a wide variety of guest rooms, terraces and lounging areas. The rooms themselves are simple but comfortable, all with a/c and some are en-suite; all showers are hot. Good rates for singles. **B749**

White Lodge 36/8 Soi Kasemsan 1, Th Rama I ⓣ02 216 8867; map pp.712–713. The cheapest guesthouse among several on this soi, with plain white a/c cubicles with hot showers and a lively, welcoming atmosphere – the best rooms, bright and quiet, are on the upper floors. **B600**

EATING

Bangkok boasts an astonishing fifty thousand places to eat, ranging from chicken on a stick to world-class haute cuisine. There are food stalls on almost every corner (expect to pay B30–50), so you could easily spend a week here without setting foot inside a restaurant.

BANGLAMPHU AND RATANAKOSIN

Aquatini Navalai River Resort, 45/1 Th Phra Arthit ⓣ02 280 9955; map p.715. Occupying a nice wooden deck in a breezy riverfront spot, this hotel restaurant does exceptionally good Thai food at quite reasonable prices. Seafood's the speciality, with most mains B200–300. Daily 6.30am–11pm.

Hemlock 56 Th Phra Athit ⓣ02 282 7507; map p.715. Small, stylish restaurant that offers a long, mid-priced menu, including delicious green curry (B100). Good veggie selection. Mon–Sat 4–11pm; worth reserving on Fri and Sat nights.

Jok Phochana Soi 2, Th Samsen; map p.715. This bare-basics, forty-year-old restaurant, which has featured on national TV, is about as real as you're going to get near Th Khao San (green curry B70). The day's ingredients are colourfully displayed at the front of the shop, and the quiet pavement tables get more crowded as the night wears on. Daily 5pm–2am.

Krua Apsorn Th Dinso ⓣ02 685 4531; map p.715. Very good, spicy and authentic food and a genteel welcome.

Try the green fish-ball curry (B100) and put the fire in your mouth out with home-made coconut sorbet. Mon–Sat 10.30am–8pm.

Kway Jap Yuan Khun Daeng Th Phra Athit ☎ 085 246 0111; map p.715. Bustling canteen serving delicious *kway jap yuan* (noodle soup) – go for the "extra" version with egg (B57) and you're set up for the day. Find it in an historic shophouse, unmistakeably painted white and green. Mon–Sat 11am–9.30pm.

★**May Kaidee** Ⓦ maykaidee.com. May Kaidee is something of a Bangkok institution and now serves her excellent Thai vegetarian food at two locations, as well as running cookery courses (from B600). One streetside restaurant sits on a lane off the east side of Th Tanao (map p.715), while a/c *May Kaidee 2* is at 33 Th Samsen (opposite Soi 2; map p.715). Most dishes B70–90. Both daily 9am–10pm.

Navy Club (Krua Khun Kung) Tha Chang ☎ 02 222 0081; map pp.712–713. The real draw here is the shaded terrace built right over the river, immediately on the south side of the express-boat pier (though you have to walk around, through the navy compound to get to it), where you can enjoy excellent dried prawn and lemongrass salad (B120) and other marine delights. Mon–Fri 11am–2pm & 4–10pm, Sat & Sun 11am–10pm.

Padthai Thipsamai 313 Th Mahachai (no English sign) ☎ 02 221 6280; map p.715. The most famous *phat thai* in Bangkok, flash-fried by the same husband-and-wife team since 1966. The "special" option is huge, comes with especially juicy prawns, and is wrapped in a translucent, paper-thin omelette. Daily except alternate Wed, 5.30pm–1am.

Popiang Soi Ram Bhuttri; map p.715. Very popular place serving freshly cooked seafood for rock-bottom prices (plates of BBQ mussels B80, squid B140). Testament to the rule that the worse the decor is, the better the food. Claims to open 24hr.

Roti Mataba 136 Th Phra Athit; map p.715. Famous outlet for very cheap fried Indian breads, or rotis, served here in lots of sweet and savoury varieties, including with vegetable and meat curries (from B51), and with bananas and condensed milk (B35). A good place to watch the world go by. Tues–Thurs 10am–9pm, Fri–Sun 9.30am–9.30pm.

DOWNTOWN

Cabbages and Condoms 6–8 Soi 12, Th Sukhumvit ☎ 02 229 4610; map pp.712–713. The Population and Community Development Association of Thailand runs this relaxing restaurant, decorated with condoms from around the world and the slogan "our food is guaranteed not to cause pregnancy". Try the pomelo salad with chicken and shrimp (B170); there's also a varied vegetarian menu. Daily 11am–10pm.

Celadon Sukhothai Hotel, 13/3 Th Sathorn Tai ☎ 02 344 8888; map pp.712–713. Consistently rated as the best Thai hotel restaurant in Bangkok, in an elegant setting among lotus ponds; well worth a splurge (dishes from around B350). Try the pomelo salad and the red curry with duck and apple. Daily noon–3pm & 6.30–11pm.

Dosa King Soi 11/1, Th Sukhumvit ☎ 02 651 1700; map pp.712–713. Usually busy with expat Indian diners, this vegetarian Indian restaurant serves delicious food from both north and south, including more than a dozen different dosa (southern pancake) dishes, tandooris and the like. Most dishes B100–200. Daily 11am–11pm.

10

Home Cuisine Islamic Restaurant 186 Soi 36, Th Charoen Krung; map pp.712–713. A short, cheap menu of very good Indian and southern Thai dishes, including delicious *khao mok kai* (B85), a kind of chicken biryani, served with pickled aubergine. Mon–Sat 11am–10pm, Sun 6–10pm.

Home Kitchen (Khrua Nai Baan) 94 Soi Lang Suan; map pp.712–713. Congenial, unpretentious restaurant on whose inexpensive Thai and Chinese picture menu you're bound to find something delicious, such as *kaeng som*, a curried soup with shrimp and acacia-shoot omelette (B150). Daily 8am–midnight.

Jim Thompson's Restaurant Jim Thompson's House, 6 Soi Kasemsan 2, Th Rama I ☎ 02 612 3601; map pp.712–713. A civilized, moderately priced haven with delicious Thai dishes (around B200) such as grilled mushroom salad as well as desserts, cakes and other Western food. Daily noon–5pm & 7–11pm.

Khrua Aroy Aroy 3/1 Th Pan; map pp.712–713. In a fruitful area for street food (there's also a night market across Th Silom on Soi 20), this simple shophouse stands out for its choice of cheap, tasty dishes such as chicken massaman curry (B90). Daily 8am till about 7pm, or when the food runs out.

★**Ramentei** 23/8–9 Soi Thaniya, Th Silom; map pp.712–713. Excellent Japanese noodle café: bright, clean and welcoming. The open kitchen turns out especially good, huge bowls of miso ramen (B200), which goes very well with the gyoza dumplings (B130). Daily 11am–2am.

★**Taling Pling** Baan Silom Arcade, corner of Th Silom and Soi 19 ☎ 02 236 4829; map pp.712–713. One of the best Thai restaurants in the city outside of the big hotels. The house deep-fried fish salad (B145) and the green beef curry (B145) with roti are both delicious and the atmosphere's relaxing, too. Branches in Siam Paragon and Central World shopping centres. Daily 11am–10pm.

Tongue Thai 18–20 Soi 38, Th Charoen Krung, in front of the Oriental Place shopping mall ☎ 02 630 9918–9; map pp.712–713. Very high standards of food and service, in a hundred-year-old shophouse elegantly decorated with Thai and Chinese antiques. Veggies are well catered for, while carnivores should try the beef green curry (B170). Set lunch for B80 is currently on special offer. Daily 10.30am–2.30pm & 5.30–10.30pm.

DRINKING AND NIGHTLIFE

The lively, teeming venues of backpacker-oriented Banglamphu are a great place to meet other travellers and enjoy live music. Elsewhere, Silom 2 (Soi 2, at the east end of Th Silom) and Silom 4 are the focus of the city's gay scene. Venues such as Q Bar are over-20s only and will want photocopies of your passport to prove it. Ask at *Dickinson's* about the same owners' *Café Democ* and *Club Culture*, which are currently looking for new venues.

10

BANGLAMPHU

Bangkok Bar 100 Th Ram Bhuttri; map p.715. This multi-tiered bar-restaurant around a fountain courtyard hosts live indie bands and local DJs and draws capacity crowds of drinkers and clubbers. Daily 6pm–late.

Blues Bar (aka Ad Here the 13th) 13 Th Samsen; map p.715. Small, chilled-out bar where you can relax with musos and enjoy popular live jazz and blues from about 9.30pm onwards. Good cocktails too. Daily 6pm–midnight.

Brick Bar Buddy Village complex, 265 Th Khao San; map p.715. Funky live-music bar that offers reggae, ska, rock'n'roll and Thai pop. Popular with locals and gets rammed at weekends, when there's sometimes an entry charge, depending on who's on. Daily 8pm–2am.

The Club Th Khao San; map p.715. If all the Chang beer's gone straight to your feet, grab your dancing shoes and head to *The Club*. Resident DJs pump thumping house tunes through the two bars and relatively spacious dance-floor until late. Daily 10pm–3am.

Dickinson's Culture Café 64 Th Phra Athit; map p.715. Grungy shophouse café decorated with a mess of empty picture frames and traffic cones, which hosts some great DJs at the weekends (Fri, Sat, sometimes on Sun, & Mon). Sip on cocktails (including dozens of martinis) or buckets. Daily 9am–2pm.

★**Hippie de Bar** 46 Th Khao San; map p.715. Inviting courtyard bar set away from the main fray, attracting a mixed studenty/arty/high-society, mostly Thai crowd, to drink at its wrought-iron tables and park benches. Indoors is totally kitsch. Daily 4pm–2am, till 3am Fri & Sat.

RED-LIGHT BANGKOK

More than a thousand sex-related businesses operate in Bangkok: they dominate Thanon Sukhumvit's Soi Cowboy (between sois 21 and 23) and Soi Nana (Soi 4), but the city's most notorious zone is **Patpong**, between the eastern ends of Silom and Suriwong roads. If you do end up at a sex show, be warned that you'll be charged exorbitant prices for drinks, and will have to face a menacing bouncer if you refuse to pay.

★TREAT YOURSELF

Bangkok can be monstrously ugly by day, but as the sun sets and the smog dissolves, the city can reveal a magical charm. The best way to take advantage of this is to treat yourself to a pricey drink at one of the enormously tall skyscraper hotels that have rooftop bars.

Balco 5th floor, River City shopping centre; map pp.712–713. Welcoming rooftop bar, whose armchairs and sofas provide a great view of the river up towards Chinatown and down to Saphan Taksin. Nothing like as stunning as the lofty hotel bars, but then again the drinks are about a quarter of the price. Tues–Sun 6.30pm–midnight.

The Sky Bar & Distil Floor 63, State Tower, 1055 Th Silom, corner of Th Charoen Krung; map pp.712–713. Come around 5.30pm to enjoy the stunning panoramas in both the light and the dark. It's standing-only at the circular *Sky Bar*, on the edge of the building with almost 360° views, but for the sunset itself, you're better off on the outside terrace of *Distil* on the other side of the building, which has huge couches to recline on. Daily 5pm–1am.

DOWNTOWN

Glow 96/4–5 Soi 23, Th Sukhumvit; map pp.712–713. This small, three-storey venue is one of the clubs of the moment, attracting an interesting roster of Thai and international DJs to play house, techno and drum'n'bass – see Ⓦbk.asia-city.com for details of who's on. Daily 6pm–1am.

Q Bar 34 Soi 11, Th Sukhumvit Ⓦqbarbangkok.com; map pp.712–713. Very dark, very trendy, New York-style bar-club, famous for its wide choice of chilled vodkas, and for its music from local and international DJs. Admission price depends on who's on, but count on B300 including one free drink. Daily 8pm–late.

★**Tawandang German Brewery** 462/61 Th Rama III Ⓣ02 678 1114–6, Ⓦtawandang.com; map pp.712–713. A taxi ride south of Chong Nonsi Skytrain down Th Narathiwat Ratchanakharin – and best to book a table in advance – but this vast, good-time all-rounder is well worth the effort: good food, great microbrewed German beer and a hugely entertaining cabaret, featuring Thai and Western music, magic shows and ballet. Daily 5pm–1am.

WTF 7 Soi 51, Th Sukhumvit, 5min walk west of BTS Thong Lo Ⓣ02 662 6246, Ⓦwtfbangkok.com; map pp.712–713. Small, hip, Spanish-influenced bar-café and art gallery, which hosts occasional poetry nights, left-field DJs and

gigs. It offers tapas, a tempting variety of cocktails and wines, and a great soundtrack. Tues–Sun 6pm–1am.

SHOPPING

Department stores, shopping malls and tourist-oriented shops in the city open at 10 or 11am and close at about 9pm.

BOOKS

Asia Books Ⓦ asiabooks.com. English-language bookshop with many branches including: on Th Sukhumvit between sois 15 and 19; in Siam Discovery Centre and Siam Paragon, both on Th Rama I; and in Thaniya Plaza on Soi Thaniya off Th Silom.

Bookazine Huge range of foreign newspapers and magazines plus a decent selection of English-language books and maps: Hualamphong train station; Gaysorn Plaza, Th Ploenchit.

Shaman Books 71 Th Khao San. One of Banglamphu's main outlets for secondhand books. Daily 9am–10pm.

MALLS

Mah Boon Krong (MBK) Rama I/Phrayathai intersection; National Stadium Skytrain stop. Labyrinthine shopping centre that houses hundreds of small, mostly inexpensive outlets. It's great for cheap flip-flops, handbags and clothes, and there are numerous opticians as well as stalls selling cut-price beauty products. Floor 3 is the best place to buy anything to do with mobile phones; floors 5 and 6 have extensive food courts and floor 7 has a cinema with daily English-language film showings.

Siam Square The area around Siam Square is packed full of malls; check out Siam Centre and Siam Discovery Centre, the former of which is especially good for trendy local labels. In Siam Square, head to what's styled as the area's "Centerpoint" between sois 3 and 4, around which hundreds of inexpensive boutiques sell colourful streetgear. Siam Paragon houses the most expensive shops in Bangkok in a luxurious mall and has an incredible food centre in the basement.

Ploenchit Around Ploenchit you'll find yet more upmarket malls, including the unclassifiably huge Central World and the small but ever so chi-chi Gaysorn Plaza, as well as Central Chitlom, the city's best department store.

MARKETS

Chatuchak Weekend Market See p.718.

Pak Khlong Talat Sprawling 24hr flower and vegetable market in Chinatown that's been in business since the nineteenth century.

Talat Saphan Phut Night bazaar around the base of Memorial Bridge, Chinatown, purveying cheap and idiosyncratic fashions. Tues–Sun 8pm–midnight.

10

DIRECTORY

Embassies and consulates Australia, 37 Th Sathorn Tai (Ⓣ 02 344 6300, Ⓦ thailand.embassy.gov.au); Cambodia, 518/4 Th Pracha Uthit (Ⓣ 02 957 5851–2); Canada, 15th floor, Abdulrahim Place, 990 Th Rama IV (Ⓣ 02 646 4300, Ⓦ thailand.gc.ca); Ireland (honorary consul), Room 407, Thaniya Building, 62 Th Silom (Ⓣ 02 632 6720, Ⓦ irelandinthailand.com); Laos, 502 1–3 Soi Sahakarnpramoon, Th Pracha Uthit (Ⓣ 02 539 6667–8, Ⓦ laoembassybkk.com); Myanmar (Burma), 132 Th Sathorn Nua (Ⓣ 02 234 4789); New Zealand, 14th Floor, M Thai Tower, All Seasons Place, 87 Th Witthayu (Ⓣ 02 254 2530); South Africa, Floor 12A, M Thai Tower, All Seasons Place, 87 Th Witthayu (Ⓣ 02 659 2900, Ⓦ saembbangkok.com); UK, 14 Th Witthayu (Ⓣ 02 305 8333); US, 120 Th Witthayu (Ⓣ 02 205 4000); Vietnam, 83/1 Th Witthayu (Ⓣ 02 650 8979).

Emergencies For English-speaking help in any emergency, call the tourist police on their free 24hr phoneline Ⓣ 1155. The tourist police headquarters is on the eastern edge of town at 2107 Bangkok Tower, Th Phetchaburi Mai (east of Phetchaburi subway station), or drop in at the more convenient Chana Songkhram Police Station at the west end of Th Khao San in Banglamphu (Ⓣ 02 282 3166). In the evenings, you'll also find tourist police at the Silom end of Patpong 1.

Exchange The Suvarnabhumi Airport exchange desks are open 24hr, while many other exchange booths stay open till 8pm or later, especially along Khao San, Sukhumvit and Silom roads and in the major shopping malls. You can withdraw cash from hundreds of ATMs around the city and at the airports.

Hospitals, clinics and dentists Most expats rate the private Bumrungrad Hospital, 33 Soi 3, Th Sukhumvit (Ⓣ 02 667 1000, emergency Ⓣ 02 667 2999, Ⓦ bumrungrad.com),

THAI BOXING

Thai boxing (*muay thai*) can be very violent, but also very entertaining. Sessions usually feature ten bouts of five three-minute rounds and are held at Rajdamnoen Stadium, next to the TAT office on Thanon Rajdamnoen Nok (Ⓦ rajadamnern.com; Mon, Wed & Thurs 6.30pm, Sun 5pm & 8.30pm), and Lumphini Stadium, in its new location on Thanon Ram Intra way out near Don Muang Airport (Ⓦ muaythailumpinee.net; Tues & Fri 6pm, Sat 4pm & 8.30pm). Tickets range from B1000 to B2000. To partake in *muay thai* yourself, head to Sor Vorapin's Gym at 13 Trok Kasap, off Thanon Chakrabongse in Banglamphu (B500 per session; Ⓣ 02 282 3551, Ⓦ thaiboxings.com).

10

as the best and most comfortable in the city; also has a dental department (02 667 2300).

Immigration office North of the centre off Th Wiphawadi Rangsit at Floor 2, B Building, Government Complex, Soi 7, Th Chaengwattana (Mon–Fri 8.30am–noon & 1–4.30pm; 02 141 9889, bangkok.immigration.go.th). Be very wary of any Khao San tour agents who offer to organize a visa extension for you: some are reportedly faking the relevant stamps.

Internet There's a whole host of internet cafés dotted all around Bangkok, especially on Th Khao San. Expect to pay B30–40 an hour. To surf in style, head for *True*, housed in an early twentieth-century villa in a courtyard off the western end of Th Khao San, where you can also sip coffee (daily 9.30am–8pm).

Laundry Nearly all guesthouses offer a one-day turnaround laundry service for around B40/kg (including ironing).

Left luggage At Suvarnabhumi Airport (B100/day); Don Muang Airport (B75/day); Hualamphong Station (B30–100/day); the bus terminals, and at most hotels and guesthouses.

Pharmacies There are English-speaking staff at most pharmacies, including the citywide branches of Boots the Chemist (most usefully on Th Khao San and in the Mah Boon Krong Centre on Th Rama I), which are also the easiest places to buy tampons.

Post office The GPO is at 1160 Th Charoen Krung, a few hundred metres left of the exit for Wat Muang Kae express-boat pier.

Telephones SIM cards can be bought at all 7-Elevens, starting from around B100 for connection and credit. International cardphones are dotted all over the city. Skype, with headphones, is widely available at internet cafés.

Travel agents Banglamphu is a notorious centre of fly-by-night operations, some of which have indeed been known to flee with travellers' money overnight. Try Lampoo Travel, *Viengtai Hotel*, 42 Th Rambuttri (02 281 9303), or Olavi Travel, opposite the west end of Th Khao San at 53 Th Chakrabongse (02 629 4710, olavi.com). Recommended agents elsewhere in the city include: *New Road Guesthouse* (see p.722); and STA Travel, 14th Floor, Wall Street Tower, 33/70 Th Suriwong (02 236 0262, statravel.co.th), the Bangkok branch of the worldwide travel agent.

DAY-TRIPS FROM BANGKOK

There are a few day-trips out of Bangkok that provide a happy respite from the smog and mayhem.

Muang Boran Ancient City

A day-trip out to the **Muang Boran Ancient City** open-air museum (daily 8am–5pm; B500), 33km southeast of Bangkok, is a great way to explore Thailand's history and architecture. There are 116 immaculately reproduced or restored traditional Thai buildings dotted around the Thailand-shaped 320 acres of landscaped grounds, ranging from a copy of the Grand Palace and a reconstruction of the lost palace of Ayutthaya to a rare and original scripture library from Samut Songkhram. The best way to do the site justice is to rent a bike (B50).

ARRIVAL AND DEPARTURE

To get here, take (a/c) bus #511 from Banglamphu or Th Sukhumvit to Samut Prakan on the edge of Greater Bangkok (about 1hr 30min), then change onto songthaew (pick-up) #36 for Muang Boran.

Damnoen Saduak floating markets

To get an idea of what shopping in Bangkok used to be like before all the canals were tarmacked over, many people take an early-morning trip to the floating markets of **Damnoen Saduak** (daily 6–11am), 109km southwest. Vineyards and orchards back onto a labyrinth of narrow canals thick with paddle boats, and floating farmers in traditional dress sell fresh fruit and vegetables as well as touristy souvenirs. It's picturesque but feels increasingly manufactured; there are hordes of tour groups and some visitors have complained of seeing more tourists than vendors. The target for most groups is the main **Talat Khlong Ton Kem**, 2km west of the tiny town centre at the intersection of Khlong Damnoen Saduak and Khlong Thong Lang. However, **Talat Khlong Hia Kui** (a little further south down Khlong Thong Lang) should be a little less crowded. Touts congregate at the Ton Kem pier to sell boat trips (hourly rates from B300/person) or you can explore on foot along the canalside walkways and bridges.

ARRIVAL AND DEPARTURE

By bus To make a trip worthwhile you'll need to catch an early bus from Bangkok's Southern Bus Terminal (every 30min from 5am; 2hr). Frequent yellow songthaews will carry you the 2km to Ton Kem.

On an organized tour Nearly all Bangkok travel agents (see above) run half-day tours to Damnoen Saduak, usually leaving at 7am (B350, B150 extra for a boat ride).

Nakhon Pathom

NAKHON PATHOM, 56km west of Bangkok, has little of interest to most travellers, but if you're into temple chedis, this is the *crème de la crème*. Measuring a staggering 120m – the same height as St Paul's Cathedral in London – **Phra Pathom Chedi** (daily dawn–dusk; B40) is the tallest in the world. Legend has it that the Buddha rested in Nakhon Pathom, and the original Indian-style chedi may have been erected to commemorate this. It was rebuilt with a Khmer prang (tower) between the eighth and twelfth centuries, which was later encased in the enormous plunger-shaped chedi that exists today. The inner and outer chambers at the cardinal points each contain a tableau of the life of the Buddha, and there are two **museums** within the chedi compound: the newer Phra Pathom Chedi National Museum (Wed–Sun 9am–noon & 1–4pm; B100), which is clearly signposted from the bottom of the chedi's south staircase, displays historical artefacts excavated nearby, while the Phra Pathom Chedi Museum (same hours; free), halfway up the steps near the east viharn, contains a beguiling selection of curios.

For inexpensive Thai food, head for the market in front of the train station, where you'll find some of the tastiest *khao laam* (bamboo cylinders filled with steamed rice and coconut) in Thailand.

ARRIVAL AND DEPARTURE

By train If you arrive at Nakhon Pathom's train station (13 daily from Bangkok Hualumphong, 2 daily from Thonburi Station; 1hr 30min), a 200m walk south across the canal and past the market will get you to the chedi's north gate.

By bus Buses from Bangkok's Southern Bus Terminal (every 10min; 40min–1hr 20min) stop at the bus station, 1km east of the town centre, but most will drop you off near the chedi first.

The central plains

North and west of the capital, the unwieldy urban mass of Greater Bangkok peters out into the vast, well-watered **central plains**, a region that for centuries has grown the bulk of the nation's food and been an irresistible temptation for neighbouring power-mongers. The riverside town of **Kanchanaburi** has long attracted visitors to the notorious Bridge over the River Kwai and is now well established as a budget travellers' hangout. Few tourists venture further west except to travel on the Death Railway, but the tiny hilltop town of **Sangkhlaburi** is worth the trip for its idyllic remoteness. On the plains north of Bangkok, the historic heartland of the country, the major sites are the ruined ancient cities of **Ayutthaya**, **Lopburi** and **Sukhothai. Mae Sot** makes a therapeutic change from old monuments and is the departure point for **Umphang**, a remote border region that's becoming increasingly popular for trekking and rafting.

KANCHANABURI AND AROUND

Nestled among limestone hills 121km northwest of Bangkok, the peaceful riverside guesthouses of **KANCHANABURI** make it a popular and pleasant travellers' hangout. Aside from the main historical sights – the Bridge over the River Kwai

THE DEATH RAILWAY

In spite of the almost impenetrable terrain, Japanese military leaders chose the River Kwai basin as the route for the construction of the 415km **Thailand–Burma Railway**, which was to be a crucial link between Japan's newly acquired territories in Singapore and Burma. Work began in June 1942, and Kanchanaburi became a POW camp and base for construction work on the railway. About sixty thousand Allied POWs and 200,000 conscripted Asian labourers worked on the line. With little else but picks and shovels, dynamite and pulleys, they shifted three million cubic metres of rock and built more than 14km of bridges. By the time the line was completed, fifteen months later, it had more than earned its nickname, the Death Railway: an estimated sixteen thousand POWs and 100,000 Asian labourers died while working on it.

10

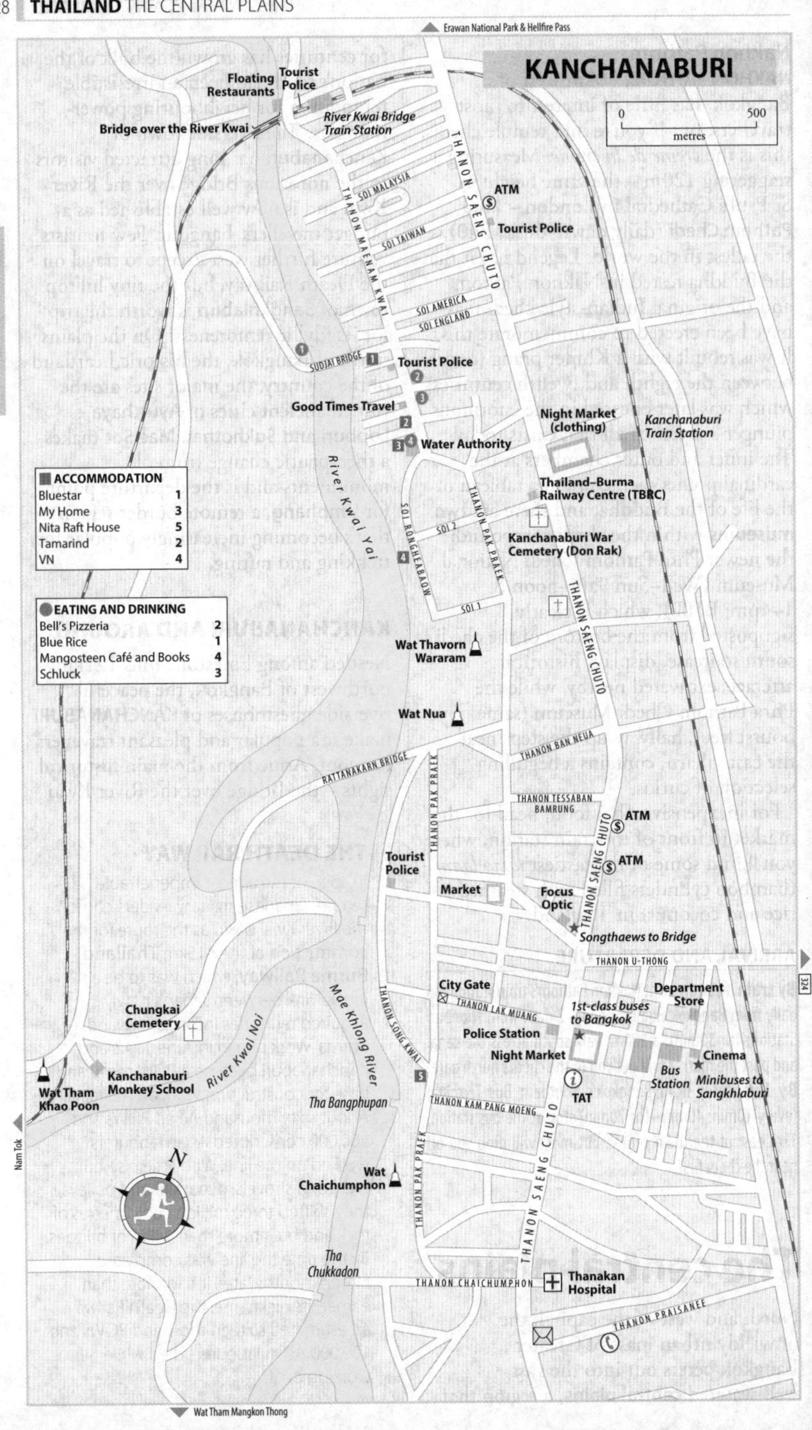
KANCHANABURI
Erawan National Park & Hellfire Pass
0
500
metres
Floating Restaurants
Tourist Police
Bridge over the River Kwai
River Kwai Bridge Train Station
THANON SAENG CHUTO
THANON MAENAM KWAI
SOI MALAYSIA
SOI TAIWAN
SOI AMERICA
SOI ENGLAND
ATM
Tourist Police
SUDJAI BRIDGE
Tourist Police
Good Times Travel
Water Authority
Night Market (clothing)
Kanchanaburi Train Station
Thailand–Burma Railway Centre (TBRC)
River Kwai Yai
ACCOMMODATION
Bluestar 1
My Home 3
Nita Raft House 5
Tamarind 2
VN 4
THANON PAK PRAEK
SOI RONGHEABAOW
SOI 2
Kanchanaburi War Cemetery (Don Rak)
EATING AND DRINKING
Bell's Pizzeria 2
Blue Rice 1
Mangosteen Café and Books 4
Schluck 3
SOI 1
Wat Thavorn Wararam
Wat Nua
RATTANAKARN BRIDGE
THANON BAN NEUA
THANON TESSABAN BAMRUNG
ATM
ATM
Tourist Police
Market
Focus Optic
Songthaews to Bridge
THANON U-THONG
324
City Gate
THANON LAK MUANG
THANON SONG KWAI
Department Store
1st-class buses to Bangkok
Police Station
Night Market
Cinema
Bus Station
Minibuses to Sangkhlaburi
TAT
Mae Khlong River
Chungkai Cemetery
River Kwai Noi
Wat Tham Khao Poon
Kanchanaburi Monkey School
Tha Bangphupan
THANON KAM PANG MOENG
Nam Tok
N
Wat Chaichumphon
Tha Chukkadon
THANON CHAICHUMPHON
Thanakan Hospital
THANON PRAISANEE
Wat Tham Mangkon Thong

and several moving memorials to the area's role in World War II – there are caves and waterfalls to explore. A very popular commemorative *son-et-lumière* River Kwai Bridge Festival is held here for ten days every November or December.

WHAT TO SEE AND DO

Kanchanaburi's commercial heart is a dusty, frenetic place, while the northern part of town is full of package tourists snapping photos of the bridge. The main tourist street, Thanon Maenam Kwai, is lined with guesthouses and expat bars, and, despite the tragic history, there's an upbeat feel to the place. But Kanchanaburi's real charm lies in the natural sights out of town, especially the seven-tiered Erawan Falls, and the unusual cave temples across the river. The Death Railway itself makes a fascinating day-trip as it winds through rugged terrain towards the tiny town of Nam Tok.

The museum and cemeteries

The excellent **Thailand–Burma Railway Centre** (daily 9am–5pm; B120), west of the train station, gives a clear and successfully impartial introduction to the horrifying history of this line, and features some extraordinary original photographs and film footage shot by Japanese engineers, as well as interviews with surviving labourers and POWs.

Thirty-eight POWs died for each kilometre of track laid on the Death Railway, and many of them are buried in Kanchanaburi's two war cemeteries. Next to the Thailand–Burma Railway Centre, the **Kanchanaburi War Cemetery**, also known as Don Rak (daily 8.30am–6pm; free), is the bigger of the two, with 6982 POW graves laid out in straight lines amid immaculately kept lawns.

The Bridge over the River Kwai

For most people the plain steel arches of the **Bridge over the River Kwai** come as a disappointment: it's commercialized and looks nothing like as awesome as it appears in David Lean's famous 1957 film, *The Bridge on the River Kwai* (which was actually filmed in Sri Lanka). The Bridge was severely damaged by Allied bombers in 1944 and 1945, but has since been repaired and is still in use today. In fact, the best way to see the bridge is by walking gingerly across the tracks, or taking the train right over it: the Kanchanaburi–Nam Tok service crosses it three times a day.

Sights across the river

Several of Kanchanaburi's sights lie **across the river**, and are best reached by bike. For Chungkai Cemetery and Wat Tham Khao Poon, both on the west bank of the Kwai Noi, it's best to cycle over Rattanakarn Bridge, just south of Wat Nua. After about 2km you'll reach **Chungkai Cemetery**, built on the banks of the Kwai Noi at the site of a former POW camp, and final resting place for some 1750 POWs. One kilometre on from Chungkai Cemetery, at the top of the road's only hill, sits the cave temple **Wat Tham Khao Poon** (daily 8am–6pm; B20), a fascinating labyrinthine grotto presided over by a medley of religious icons.

Luscious greenery and craggy limestone cliffs make a trip across to the east bank of the River Kwai Noi an equally worthwhile bike trip, but the main attraction at **Wat Tham Mangkon Thong** ("show" times and prices dependent on number of tourists), otherwise known as the "Floating Nun Temple", is fairly tacky: a nun will get into the temple pond and float there, meditating – if tourists give her enough money to make it worth her while. To get here by bicycle or motorbike, take the ferry across the Mae Khlong River at Tha Chukkadon and then follow the road on the other side for about 4km.

MONKEY BUSINESS

If you're given the opportunity to visit Kanchanaburi's "**Monkey School**" as part of a tour around Kanchanaburi, you're strongly advised to turn it down. The monkeys here are said to have been rescued from abusive owners, but now they spend their days chained up by the neck until they are coerced into performing circus tricks like shooting hoops and riding children's bicycles.

The Death Railway and Hellfire Pass

The scenic two-hour-plus rail journey from Kanchanaburi to **Nam Tok** (three trains daily in each direction) travels the POW-built **Death Railway**. Highlights include crossing the Bridge over the River Kwai, squeezing through 30m solid rock cuttings at Wang Sing (Arrow Hill), and the Wang Po viaduct, where a 300m trestle bridge clings to the cliff face as it curves with the Kwai Noi.

Starting 18km beyond Nam Tok, seven separate cuttings were dug over a 3km stretch, which has now been turned into a memorial walk. The longest and most brutal of these cuttings was Hellfire Pass, which got its name from the hellish lights of the fires the POWs used when working at night. At the trailhead, the beautifully designed **Hellfire Pass Memorial Museum** (daily 9am–4pm; donation), the best and most informative of Kanchanaburi's World War II museums, movingly documents the POWs' story. Most Kanchanaburi tour operators feature visits to Hellfire Pass, or any bus from Kanchanaburi (1hr 15min) or Nam Tok (20min) that's bound for Thong Pha Phum or Sangkhlaburi will drop you outside; the last bus back to Kanchanaburi passes the museum at about 4.45pm.

Erawan National Park

Chances are that when you see a poster of a waterfall in Thailand, you'll be looking at a picture of the seven-tiered falls in **Erawan National Park** (daily 8am–4pm; B200), 65km northwest of Kanchanaburi. The falls really are astonishingly lovely, with clear, glacial-blue waters gushing through the forest. From the entrance there's a fairly easy trail up to the fifth tier (2km), beyond which you have to scramble (wear strong shoes); the best pools for swimming are at levels two, five and, during the rainy season, seven.

Buses run from Kanchanaburi's bus station to the national park visitor centre near the base of the falls (#8170; roughly every hour; 1hr 30min; the last bus back to Kanchanaburi departs at around 4pm). However, the vast majority of foreign tourists charter return transport from Kanchanaburi (from B1300 per car) through the guesthouses. The falls are about 40km from Nam Tok so are also commonly combined with a ride on the Death Railway.

ARRIVAL AND DEPARTURE

By train Trains are the most scenic way to get to Kanchanaburi from Bangkok (daily 7.50am and 1.55pm).

Destinations Bangkok Thonburi (2 daily; 3hr); Nakhon Pathom (2 daily; 1hr 40min–2hr); Nam Tok (3 daily; 2hr 20min).

By bus and minibus As well as the buses detailed here, there's a useful a/c minibus service from outside the *Royal Ratanakosin Hotel* on Th Rajdamnoen Klang in Bangkok's Banglamphu, which will drop wherever you want in Kanchanaburi (hourly; 2hr). Tourist minibuses to Ayutthaya can be booked through guesthouses.

Destinations Bangkok (Northern Bus Terminal; hourly; 2hr 30min); Bangkok (Southern Bus Terminal; every 15min; 2hr); Erawan (hourly; 1hr 30min); Nakhon Pathom (every 15min; 2hr); Nam Tok (every 30min; 1hr 30min); Sangkhlaburi (roughly hourly; 4hr).

GETTING AROUND

As well as songthaews and tuk-tuks (about B50/journey in town), there are bicycles (B50/day) and motorbikes (about B200/day) available for rent from guesthouses and tour agencies.

By songthaews Orange songthaews run along Th Saeng Chuto, originating from outside the Focus Optic optician's, three blocks north of the bus station, and travelling north via the Kanchanaburi War Cemetery, Thai-Burma Railway Centre, train station and access road to the bridge (#2; every 15min until 6pm; B10).

INFORMATION AND TOURS

Tourist information The TAT office (daily 8.30am–4.30pm; T 034 511200, E tatkan@tat.or.th) is on Th Saeng Chuto near the bus station and keeps up-to-date bus timetables.

Tour operators Many tour operators offer reasonably priced day-trips and overnight excursions to local caves, waterfalls and sights, plus elephant-riding, trekking and rafting. Operators include: Good Times Travel, 63/1 Th Maenam Kwai (T 034 624441, W good-times-travel.com), which does all the standard trips plus cycle tours; and Safarine, outside of town in Ban Puksakan (T 086 049 1662, W safarine.com), a kayaking specialist.

ACCOMMODATION

The stretch of river along Soi Rongheabaow and Th Maenam Kwai is the most popular area for backpacker accommodation. Many of the guesthouses have cheaper

floating raft rooms, though boat noise can be a problem during the day.

Bluestar 241 Th Maenam Kwai ⊕034 512161, ⊕bluestar-guesthouse.com. Popular and clued-up, with a wide range of good-value accommodation, including very cheap, basic, en-suite fan rooms, in a quiet garden that runs down to the riverside. Double B150

My Home 18/1 Th Maenam Kwai, signposted down an unnamed soi just north of the Water Authority building ⊕034 625555, ⊕myhomekan.com. Central, modern, good-value guesthouse where the spacious, tile-floored rooms have TV, hot showers and free wi-fi. Double B350

Nita Raft House Th Pak Praek ⊕034 514521, ⊕nita_rafthouse@yahoo.com. Away from the Th Maenam Kwai fray, a friendly, laidback, old-school guesthouse, whose simple, woven-bamboo floating rooms (some en-suite) are among the cheapest in town. Also does great food. Double B200

Tamarind 29/1 Th Maenam Kwai ⊕034 518790, ⊕tamarind_guesthouse@yahoo.co.th. At this very clean, friendly place, sleep either in the two-storey house or in one of the spacious rafthouse rooms (all en-suite), which share a breezy, orchid-strewn terrace. Double B350

VN 44 Soi Rongheabaow ⊕034 514082, ⊕vnguesthouse.net. A quiet, pretty place just south of the Maenam Kwai hub, with good food and decent raft-house rooms: they're large, en-suite and come with terraces and either fan or a/c. Double B275

EATING AND DRINKING

At dusk, the ever-reliable night market sets up alongside Th Saeng Chuto on the edge of the bus station; its range of choices will satisfy even the pickiest eater. Drinking haunts are not hard to come by either, with plenty of bars along Th Maenam Kwai, many of which show sport and serve basic Western food.

Bell's Pizzeria 24/5 Th Maenam Kwai. Swiss-run place with pavement tables that's justly popular for its great pizzas (from B160). Also offers pasta and a handful of Thai dishes (*tom yam* soup B80). Daily 5–11pm or later.

Blue Rice *Apple's Retreat*, on the west bank of the Kwai Yai, across Sudjai Bridge ⊕034 512017. In a lovely riverside guesthouse restaurant, delicious mid-priced Thai food, including veggie options and mouthwatering curries – *massaman* is the signature dish (B95). Cookery classes available (B1550 for a one-day course). Daily 7.30–10am, 11.30am–2pm & 6–9pm.

★**Mangosteen Café and Books** 13 Th Maenam Kwai ⊕mangosteencafe.net. Hard to spot among the bustle of the main drag, yet still peaceful, this bright, cheery café has a brilliant Thai and Western menu (most dishes B60–100) and serves great smoothies and coffee. There is also an array of reading material to peruse or buy. Daily 8am–9pm; closed first and third Mon of every month.

Schluck Th Maenam Kwai. Cosy a/c restaurant serving salads, pizzas and steaks (from B150) as well as Thai food, but what really makes it stand out are its mouthwatering, home-made cakes such as vanilla choux buns and lemon meringue tart. Tues–Sun 4–10pm.

DIRECTORY

Banks and exchange There are several banks with ATMs and money-changing facilities on Th Saeng Chuto and Th Maenam Kwai.

Hospitals The private Thanakan Hospital is at 20/20 Th Saeng Chuto (⊕034 622366).

Internet If you're looking for an internet café, your best bet is Th Maenam Kwai.

Tourist police Main office on Th Saeng Chuto (⊕1155 or ⊕034 512668), with a handy booth by the bridge.

SANGKHLABURI

Located right at the northernmost tip of the 73km-long Vajiralongkorn Reservoir, the tiny hilltop town of **SANGKHLABURI**, 220km north of Kanchanaburi, is a charming if uneventful hangout. It lies close to the border with Myanmar, though at the time of writing the crossing at the Three Pagodas Pass was closed to foreign tourists (this may change to allow day-trips to the Burmese town of Payathonzu).

WHAT TO SEE AND DO

You can boat across the reservoir in search of the submerged temple **Wat Sam Phrasop** in canoes rented from *P* guesthouse (see p.732); during the dry season it's possible to swim through the temple's windows. Alternatively, join a sunset longtail boat trip (B350–500/boat).

Across the reservoir stands the Mon village of Ban Waeng Ka, which grew up in the late 1940s after the outbreak of civil war in Myanmar forced the country's ethnic minorities to flee across the border. To reach it, people normally walk across the lake via what's said to be the longest handmade wooden bridge in the world, at nearly 400m, which is reputedly visible from space. However, a 2013 flood washed away 70m of its length, though it's likely to be repaired fairly quickly and, in the meantime, a bamboo bridge has been built alongside.

10

BAAN UNRAK

Baan Unrak ("House of Joy"; ⓦbaanunrak.org) is a local charity that supports destitute women and children in the community, many of whom are Burmese refugees. The charity runs a children's home, primary school, organic farm and a project that encompasses a weaving and sewing centre to help women learn skills that enable them to earn money. If you want to make a worthwhile contribution while on your travels, note that Baan Unrak offers a number of volunteering opportunities, including teaching English.

Dramatic **Wat Wang Wiwekaram** stands 2km from the bridge at the edge of Ban Waeng Ka; its massive, golden chedi is modelled on the centrepiece of India's Bodh Gaya, the sacred site of the Buddha's enlightenment.

ARRIVAL AND DEPARTURE

By bus Frequent a/c minibuses from Kanchanaburi terminate about 100m east of the market, about 2km or more from the accommodation listed here; less frequent, larger buses stop directly in front of the market. Motorbike taxis will take you to the guesthouses for B20–30.

Destinations Bangkok (Northern Bus Terminal; 4 daily; 7hr); Kanchanaburi (14 daily; 3–4hr).

ACCOMMODATION AND EATING

The food stalls at the market are great for cheap eats, but otherwise the restaurant at *P* guesthouse, with fine lake views from its large terrace, is your best bet for a full Thai (or Burmese) meal.

Graph Café Opposite *P* guesthouse. A neatly manicured lawn leads the way to this chilled modern café serving a wide range of teas, chais and speciality coffees (from B40), as well as smoothies, cocktails and pizza. Free wi-fi. Daily 8am–9pm.

J Family 17/1 Soi 2 ⓣ034 595511. A genuine homestay offering five big rooms with fan and shared cold-water bathroom in the large family home of the Mon woman, Kumsai Soonploy, who runs the Baan Unrak shop. She speaks good English and is very welcoming. **B150**/person

P ⓣ034 595061, ⓦp-guesthouse.com. Spacious rooms, a garden leading down to the lake and stunning views across the water make this a worthwhile choice. The fan rooms have great shared bathrooms (cold showers); the a/c rooms are en-suite (hot showers; B950), but unless it's really hot, they're not worth splashing out on. Motorbikes (B200/day) and canoes (B150/half-day) can be rented. Also offers good-value packages with trekking, boat rides, bamboo rafting and elephant rides. Double **B250**

DIRECTORY

Bank The bank behind the market has an ATM and exchange facilities.

Internet Wi-fi and computers at Baan Unrak's Bakery.

Post office Just south of the bus station.

AYUTTHAYA

The city of **AYUTTHAYA**, 80km north of Bangkok, was founded in 1351 by King U-Thong and rapidly became the pre-eminent city-state in Thailand. By 1685 it had a population of one million people – roughly double the population of London at the same time – living largely on houseboats in a 140km network of waterways. In 1767, the city was sacked by the Burmese and today its ruins are a designated UNESCO World Heritage Site. Over a week in mid-December, this status is celebrated with nightly *son-et-lumière* shows.

WHAT TO SEE AND DO

The heart of this ancient city was a 4km-wide river island, and the majority of the ancient remains are spread among the grassy spaces of its western half; the hub of the modern town occupies its northeast corner. The only way to do justice to the ruins is to rent a bicycle (B40–60/day) or motorbike (B250/day), available from guesthouses. Otherwise, there are plenty of tuk-tuks around (about B50 for short journeys on the island).

Wat Phra Mahathat and Wat Ratburana

Built in the fourteenth century to enshrine relics of the Buddha himself, the overgrown **Wat Phra Mahathat** (daily 8am–6pm; B50) is the epitome of Ayutthaya's atmospheric decay, and the home of an oft-photographed Buddha head serenely trapped in gnarled tree roots. Across the road is towering, fifteenth-century **Wat Ratburana** (daily 8am–6pm; B50), which retains some original stuccowork, including fine

statues of garudas (large, mythical birds) swooping down on nagas. It's possible to go down steep steps inside the prang (central tower) to the crypt, where you can make out fragmentary murals of the early Ayutthaya period.

Wat Phra Si Sanphet and Viharn Phra Mongkol Bopit

Further west is the grand, well-preserved **Wat Phra Si Sanphet** (daily 8am–6pm; B50), which was built in 1448 as a private royal chapel; its three grey chedis have become the most hackneyed image of Ayutthaya. Save for a few bricks in the grass, the wat is all that remains of the huge walled complex of the royal palace that extended north as far as the Lopburi River.

Viharn Phra Mongkol Bopit (Mon–Fri 8am–4.30pm, Sat & Sun 8am–5pm), on the south side of Wat Phra Si Sanphet, is a replica of a typical Ayutthayan viharn (assembly hall), complete with characteristic chunky lotus-capped columns. It was built in 1956, with help from the Burmese to atone for their flattening of the city two centuries earlier, in order to shelter the still-much-revered Phra Mongkol Bopit. This powerfully austere bronze statue, with its flashing mother-of-pearl eyes, was cast in the fifteenth century, then sat exposed to the elements from the time of the Burmese invasion until its new home was built.

Wat Na Phra Mane

Across on the north bank of the Lopburi River, **Wat Na Phra Mane** (daily 8am–6pm; B20) is Ayutthaya's most rewarding temple, as it's the only one from the town's golden age that survived the ravages of the Burmese. The main bot (ordination hall), built in 1503, is typically Ayutthayan: its outside columns are topped with lotus cups, and there are slits in the walls instead of windows to let the wind pass through. Inside, underneath a rich red-and-gold coffered ceiling representing the stars around the moon, sits a powerful 6m-high Buddha in the disdainful, overdecorated style characteristic of the later Ayutthaya period.

Museums

Ten minutes' walk south of Viharn Phra Mongkol Bopit, the large **Chao Sam Phraya National Museum** (Wed–Sun 9am–4pm; B150) holds numerous Ayutthaya-era Buddhas, some fine woodcarving and gold treasures such as the original relic casket from Wat Mahathat. The **Historical Study Centre** (daily 9am–5pm; B100), a few minutes' walk away along Thanon Rojana, dramatically presents a broad social history of Ayutthaya with the help of videos and reconstructions.

Wat Yai Chai Mongkol and Wat Phanan Choeng

The colossal and celebrated chedi of the ancient but still functioning **Wat Yai Chai Mongkol** (daily 8am–5pm; B20), across the bridge to the southeast of the island, was built by the greatest Ayutthayan king, Naresuan, to mark his decisive victory over the Burmese in 1593. By the entrance, a reclining Buddha, gleamingly restored in toothpaste white, dates from the same time.

To the west of Wat Yai Chai Mongkol, at the confluence of the Chao Phraya and Pasak rivers, stands the city's oldest and liveliest working temple, **Wat Phanan Choeng** (daily 8am–5pm; B20), whose main Buddha image has survived since 1324, and is said to have wept when Ayutthaya was sacked by the Burmese. The stunning murals in the ordination hall have been beautifully restored.

ARRIVAL AND DEPARTURE

By bus and minibus Most buses to and from Bangkok's Northern Bus Terminal use the bus stop on Th Naresuan, near the main accommodation area, though some only stop at Ayutthaya's Northern Bus Terminal, 5km to the east of the centre, from where you'll need a tuk-tuk (B100–150). Licensed, a/c minibuses to and from Bangkok's Victory Monument and Southern Bus Terminal can also be found on Th Naresuan (both about every 20min; 1–2hr depending on traffic). Tourist minibuses to Kanchanaburi can be booked through guesthouses.

Destinations Bangkok (every 20–30min; 2hr); Chiang Mai (15 daily; 10hr); Chiang Rai (13 daily; 12hr); Lampang (17 daily; 8hr); Lopburi (every 20min; 2hr); Phitsanulok (15 daily; 5hr); Sukhothai (10 daily; 6hr).

10

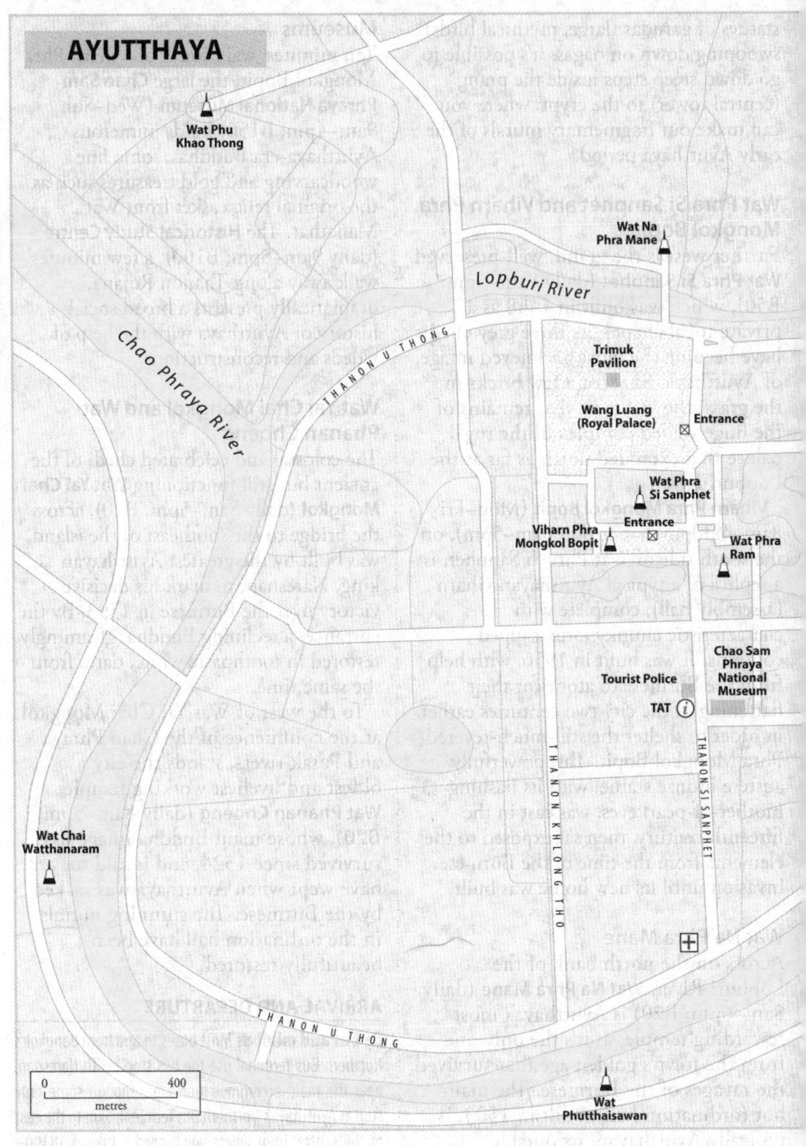

By train From the pier 100m west of the train station, take the ferry (B3; last ferry around 8pm) up to Chao Phrom pier, then walk five minutes to the junction of U-Thong and Naresuan (Chao Phrom) roads, to reach the centre. (If you're staying at *Bann Kun Pra*, however, take the ferry from the neighbouring jetty, which runs directly across the river.) The station has a left-luggage service (24hr; B20/piece/day).

Destinations Bangkok Hualamphong (around 20 daily; 1hr 30min–2hr); Chiang Mai (5 daily; 10–13hr); Lopburi (20 daily; 45min–1hr 30min); Nong Khai (3 daily; 9hr 30min); Phitsanulok (11 daily; 3hr 30min–6hr 20min); Ubon Ratchathani (6 daily; 7hr 20min–10hr 30min).

INFORMATION

Tourist information TAT, in the former city hall, Th Si Sanphet (☎035 246076–7, ✉tatyutya@tat.or.th; daily 8.30am–4.30pm); it's well worth heading upstairs to the

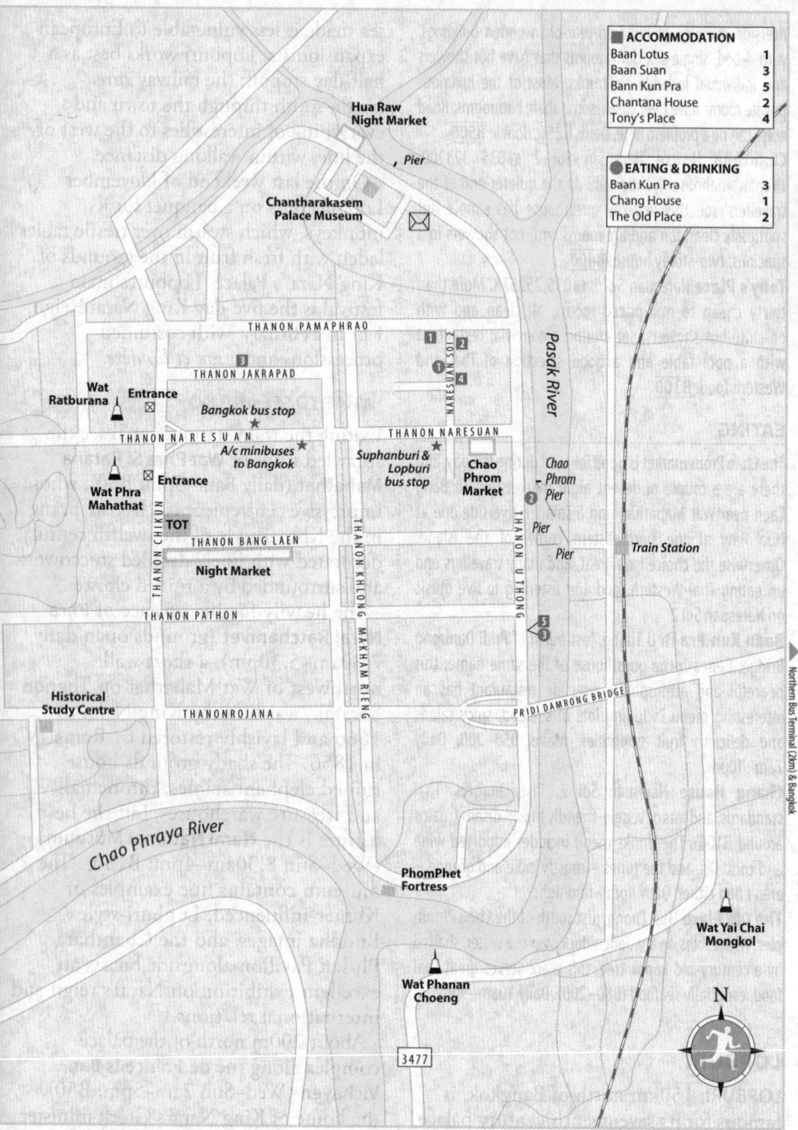

free, smartly presented multimedia exhibition on Ayutthaya (daily except Wed 8.30am–4.30pm).

ACCOMMODATION

Most of the guesthouses and tourist amenities are crowded into an area that's become known as "Soi Farang" (Naresuan Soi 2), which runs north from Chao Prom market.

Baan Lotus Th Pamaprao ⓣ 035 251988. Two tranquil old houses with polished wooden floors and large, plain, but clean rooms, some with shared hot showers, at the end of a long garden with a lotus pond at the back. Double **B350**

Baan Suan 23/1 Th Jakraprad ⓣ 089 797 6397, ⓦ baansuanguesthouse.com. Resort-style, a/c bungalows with hot showers (B500) set in a neat little garden, plus bright, simple rooms in the airy main building, in a quiet spot near Wat Ratchaburana. Singles B150. Double **B250**

Bann Kun Pra Th U Thong, just north of Pridi Damrong Bridge ⓣ 035 241978, ⓦ bannkunpra.com. A gorgeous

riverside complex of hundred-year-old wooden buildings, with 4-bed, single-sex dorm rooms that have hot showers and individual lockable tin trunks. Most of the luxurious private rooms have river views, some share bathrooms. Road noise can be a problem here. Dorm B250, double B500

Chantana House Naresuan Soi 2 ⓣ035 323200, ⓔchantanahouse@yahoo.com. At the quieter end of the travellers' soi, this low-key guesthouse has simple but spotlessly clean fan and a/c rooms with hot showers in a spacious, two-storey house. B400

10

Tony's Place Naresuan Soi 2 ⓣ035 252578. More than thirty cheap to mid-priced rooms, all clean and with en-suite hot showers, set around a convivial restaurant with a pool table and a good selection of Thai and Western food. B300

EATING

The Chao Prom market is good for food during the day, and there are a couple of decent night markets: on Th Bang Laen near Wat Mahathat, and a smaller, riverside one at Hua Raw at the northeastern corner of the island. Otherwise the choice isn't great, and many travellers end up eating Thai-Western food and listening to live music on Naresuan Soi 2.

Baan Kun Pra Th U Thong, just north of Pridi Damrong Bridge. Beneath the guesthouse of the same name, this peaceful and atmospheric riverside restaurant has an interesting menu including lots of seafood, spicy salads and delicious fruit smoothies. Mains B50–200. Daily 7am–10pm.

Chang House Naresuan Soi 2. Tasty burgers, Thai standards, and lots of veggie-friendly Indian dishes (mains around B100). The drinks menu includes imported wine and cocktails, and the tunes – mostly indie and grunge – aren't bad either. Daily 4pm– midnight.

The Old Place Th U Thong, just south of the Chao Phrom pier. With tables on a wooden deck over the water, shaded by a century-old kapok tree, this place serves great Thai food, especially seafood (B80–200). Daily 10am–9pm.

LOPBURI

LOPBURI, 150km north of Bangkok, is famous for its seventeenth-century palace, its historically important but rather unimpressive Khmer ruins – and the large pack of tourist-baiting monkeys that swarm all over them. Many of the ruins date back to the eleventh century, when Lopburi was the local capital for the extensive Khmer Empire. The town was later used as a second capital both by King Narai of Ayutthaya and Rama IV of Bangkok because its remoteness from the sea made it less vulnerable to European expansionists. Lopburi works best as a half-day stopoff; the railway runs north–south through the town and everything of interest lies to the west of the line, within walking distance.

On the last weekend of November Lopburi puts on a banquet for its monkeys, which swarm over trestle tables laden with fresh fruit in the grounds of King Narai's Palace. Lopburi's main festival is the five-day King Narai Reign Fair in February, with costumed processions and a *son et lumière*.

WHAT TO SEE AND DO

Exiting the train station, you'll see the sprawled ruins of **Wat Phra Si Ratana Mahathat** (daily 8am–5pm; B50), whose impressive centrepiece is a laterite prang in the Khmer style of the twelfth century, decorated with finely detailed stuccowork and surrounded by a ruined cloister.

The heavily fortified palace of **Phra Narai Ratchanivet** (grounds open daily 7.30am–5.30pm), a short walk northwest of Wat Mahathat on Thanon Sorasak, was built by King Narai in 1666 and lavishly restored by Rama IV in 1856. The shady grounds house ruined elephant stables, throne halls and treasure warehouses, but the best feature is the **Narai National Museum** (Wed–Sun 8.30am–4pm; B150). The museum contains fine examples of Khmer-influenced, Lopburi-style Buddha images, and the Chanthara Phisan Pavilion alongside boasts an excellent exhibition on Narai's reign and international relations.

About 200m north of the palace complex along rue de France is **Ban Vichayen** (Wed–Sun 7am–5pm; B50), the home of King Narai's Greek minister (*vichayen*), Constantine Phaulkon. Originally built as a residence for foreign ambassadors, its Christian chapel is incongruously stuccoed with Buddhist motifs. Around 150m east along Thanon Vichayen, past the three red-brick towers of Prang Khaek, an eighth-century shrine to Shiva sitting on a traffic island, is the striking **Phra Prang Sam Yod** (daily 8am–6pm; B50), a Hindu temple later

converted to Buddhism under the Khmers. The three chunky prangs, made of dark laterite with some restored stuccowork, are a favourite haunt of Lopburi's fierce monkeys. Just east at San Phra Karn, there's even a monkeys' adventure playground beside the ruins of a huge Khmer prang.

ARRIVAL AND INFORMATION

By bus and minibus The bus station is 2km east of the town centre: a blue city bus or red songthaew will save you the walk. Fast a/c minibuses between Bangkok's Victory Monument and Lopburi are based on Th Na Phra Karn, 200m north of the train station near Phra Prang Sam Yod.
Destinations Ayutthaya (every 20min; 2hr); Bangkok (every 30min; 3hr); Chiang Mai (5 daily; 9hr); Khorat (hourly; 3hr 30min); Phitsanulok (6 daily; 4hr).

By train The train station is directly opposite Wat Phra Si Ratana Mahathat; there are left-luggage facilities.
Destinations Ayutthaya (20 daily; 45min–1hr 30min); Bangkok Hualamphong (14 daily; 2hr 30min–3hr); Chiang Mai (5 daily; 9–11hr); Phitsanulok (12 daily; 3hr–5hr 15min).

Tourist information TAT's office (T 036 770096, E tatlobri@tat.or.th; daily 8.30am–4.30pm) is 5km east of San Phra Karn on Highway 311 in the provincial hall.

ACCOMMODATION AND EATING

There are food stalls dotted around the centre of Lopburi, especially on Th Ratchadamnern between the northeast corner of Phra Narai Ratchanivet and the railway. A good night market sets up along the west side of the tracks on Th Na Phra Karn; this is the best place for dinner, with a wide variety of dishes from B30, and it is a great place to sit and people-watch.

Coffee House Th Ratchadamnern. A comfortable a/c café serving cheap snacks and a good range of espresso coffees (from B25). Daily 8am–5pm.

Nett Hotel One block east of Phra Narai Ratchanivet at 17/1–2 Soi 2, Th Ratchadamnern T 036 411738. Slightly sterile but clean and friendly, with plain en-suite rooms. Double B250

Noom Guest House Two blocks east of Phra Narai Ratchanivet on Th Praya Kumjud T 036 427693, W noomguesthouse.com. Teak-floored rooms with shared hot showers (and good rates for singles), above a bar-restaurant in the main house, or en-suite bungalows in the back garden. The friendly staff can organize rock climbing and motorbike rental. Double B250

Thai Sawang Th Sorasak. This a/c café opposite Phra Narai Ratchanivet serves tasty Vietnamese food, including roll-your-own fresh spring rolls stuffed with salad leaves and sausage. Most dishes B60–80. Daily 9am–8pm.

PHITSANULOK

Pleasantly located on the banks of the Nan River, **PHITSANULOK** (locally called "Phitlok") is a major transport hub and a handy base for exploring the Sukhothai area (see p.739), but only holds a couple of sights itself.

10

WHAT TO SEE AND DO

Dating from the fourteenth century, **Wat Phra Si Ratana Mahathat** (aka Wat Mahathat or Wat Yai; dress conservatively) draws a constant stream of worshippers to view the country's second most important Buddha image. The holy statue itself, Phra Buddha Chinnarat, is a lovely example of late Sukhothai style, and boasts an unusual flame-like halo around its upper body; it is said to have wept tears of blood when Ayutthayan princes arrived to oust the last Sukhothai king in the fifteenth century.

Across town on Thanon Wisut Kasat, southeast of the train station (bus #8 will drop you close by), is the small **Sergeant Major Thawee Folklore Museum** (daily 8am–4.30pm; B50), one of the best ethnology museums in the country; it includes a reconstruction of a typical village house, as well as traditional toys and animal traps. About 50m south of the museum, at 26/43 Th Wisut Kasat, is the **Buranathai Buddha Bronze-Casting Foundry** (daily roughly 8am–5pm; free). The foundry gives you a rare chance to see Buddha images being forged; anyone can drop in to watch the stages involved in moulding and casting an image.

ARRIVAL AND INFORMATION

By plane Nok Air and Air Asia run flights to Bangkok (Don Muang; 6 daily; 50min) from Phitsanulok Airport, 7km south of the centre and about B150 by tuk-tuk.

By bus Buses for Sukhothai and other adjacent provinces use the old bus station, 2km east of the city centre; Sukhothai buses also make useful stops in the centre near Topland Plaza, as marked on our map. Long-distance buses now use the new bus station, which is about 7km east of the centre at Indochina Junction, where highways 11 and 12 meet. Shared songthaews (B20) shuttle between old and new bus stations; the former is linked to the centre by many city buses, including #1, #6 and #8. A tuk-tuk to the new bus station should cost about B120.
Destinations Bangkok (50 daily; 5–6hr); Chiang Mai (40 daily; 5–6hr); Chiang Rai (30 daily; 7–8hr); Khon Kaen

10

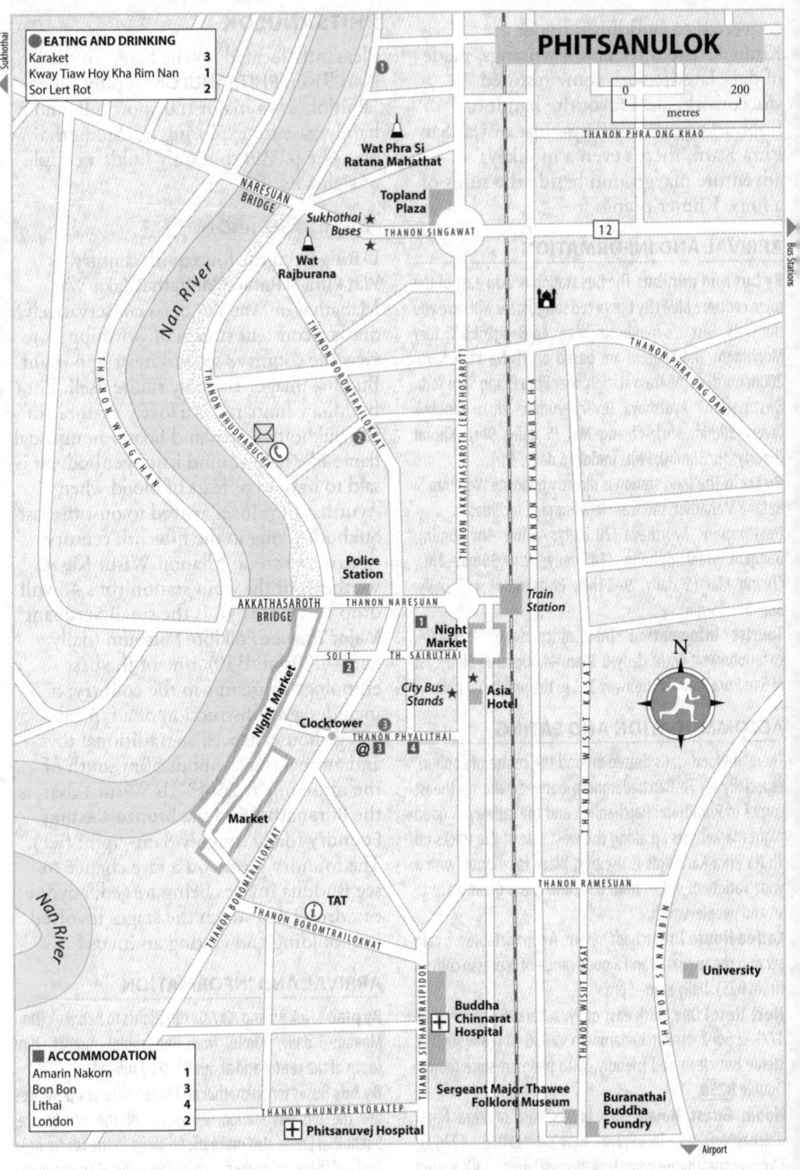

(16 daily; 6hr); Khorat (14 daily; 6–7hr); Mae Sot (8 daily; 4hr); Nan (5 daily; 6hr); Sukhothai (at least every 40min; 1hr–1hr 30min).

By train The train station is in the town centre, less than 500m from the accommodation listed below. Left-luggage costs B20 (daily 7am–11pm).

Destinations Ayutthaya (11 daily; 4hr 30min–6hr 20min); Bangkok Hualamphong (11 daily; 5hr 30min–8hr); Chiang Mai (7 daily; 6–8hr); Lopburi (11 daily; 3hr–5hr 15min).

Tourist information The TAT office is on the eastern arm of Th Boromtrailoknat (T 055 252742–3, E tatphlok@tat.or.th; daily 8.30am–4.30pm).

GETTING AROUND

By bus Many city buses (mostly B10–13) start their routes at the bus stops 150m south of the train station, where

southbound buses pick up outside the *Asia Hotel*, and northbound ones from across the road. Useful routes include: #1, from the old bus station to the train station and Wat Mahathat; #8, from the old bus station to the Folklore Museum, train station, Topland Plaza and Wat Mahathat; and #11, via the train station, Topland Plaza and Wat Mahathat.

ACCOMMODATION

Amarin Nakorn 3/1 Th Chao Phraya ⓣ055 219069. Very central, good value but dated, this hotel has compact a/c rooms, all with hot showers; the upper floors enjoy panoramic views of the city. Double **B430**

Bon Bon 77 Th Phayalithai ⓣ055 219058 or ⓣ081 707 7649. The only genuine guesthouse in town, set back from the road around a small yard. The rooms are kept nice and clean and have en-suite hot showers and TVs; pay B100 extra for a/c. Double **B350**

Lithai Guesthouse 73/1–5 Th Phayalithai ⓣ055 219629, ⓔlithaiphs@yahoo.com. Good but bland option, used mainly by salespeople so not especially cosy and much more of a hotel than a guesthouse. The clean, bright rooms come with hot shower, TV and either fan or a/c. Double **B350**

London 21–22 Soi Bhudhabucha 1 ⓣ055 225145. Very cheap and very basic, with shabby rooms (shared cold-water bathroom) in a converted family home. Double **B100**

EATING AND DRINKING

Along the east bank of the river, south of Akkathasaroth Bridge, there's a good night market, where the most famous dish is "flying vegetables" – morning glory is stir-fried before being tossed flamboyantly in the air to the plate-wielding waiter.

Karaket Th Phayalithai. Tasty Thai curry shop, popular in the early evening, where you make your selection from the trays on the pavement table (around B40/serving), then eat in a/c comfort inside. Daily 3.30–8pm.

Kway Tiaw Hoy Kha Rim Nan 100m north of Wat Mahathat. The Sukhothai noodles here – rice noodles with red pork in a sweet and spicy broth (B35) – are so famously tasty they've been on all the local TV channels. You sit on the raised floor with legs dangling (*hoy kha*) under the table (with some river views). There's no English sign, but it's got a brown awning and is always packed. Daily 9am–4pm.

Sor Lert Rot Th Boromtrailoknat, immediately south of the *Pailyn Hotel*. It doesn't look much, but this basic, rather untidy, Thai-Chinese restaurant cooks up some of the best food in town. Try the fried chicken (B100) and the salted fish with Chinese kale (*khana pla khem*; B50). Mon–Sat 8am–10pm.

DIRECTORY

Hospital Buddha Chinnarat Hospital, Th Sithamtraipidok (ⓣ055 219844–52).

Internet There are internet cafés across town, including one just west of *Bon Bon Guest House*.

Tourist police In the far northern suburbs near the stadium (ⓣ1155).

SUKHOTHAI

For a brief but brilliant hundred and forty years (1238–1376), the walled city of **SUKHOTHAI** presided as the capital of Thailand. Now an impressive assembly of elegant ruins, Muang Kao Sukhothai (Old Sukhothai), 58km northwest of Phitsanulok, has been designated a historical park. It's one of Thailand's most visited sites and is the most famous place to celebrate the **Loy Krathong Festival** in October/November. Most travellers stay in lively "New" Sukhothai, 12km to the east, which has good travel links and a broader range of accommodation and restaurants.

10

WHAT TO SEE AND DO

Cycling around **Old Sukhothai** is a great way to spend a day; its collapsed ruins are evocative of a glorious time gone by. Some of its temples are exquisitely restored, while others have been left to crumble. In its prime, Old Sukhothai boasted some forty separate temple complexes and covered an area of about seventy square kilometres. At its heart stood the walled royal city, protected by a series of moats and ramparts. **Sukhothai Historical Park** covers all this area and is divided into five zones, with all the most important temples in the central zone. There's free access to the east and south zones, but the central (daily 6.30am–7pm, until 9pm on Sat, when it's floodlit), north (daily 7.30am–5.30pm) and west zones (daily 8am–4pm) each charge B100/person, plus B10–50/vehicle.

The central zone

Just outside the entrance to the central zone is the well-presented **Ramkhamhaeng National Museum** (daily 9am–4pm; B150), named after Sukhothai's most important king. As well as several illuminating exhibitions and some of the finest sculptures and reliefs

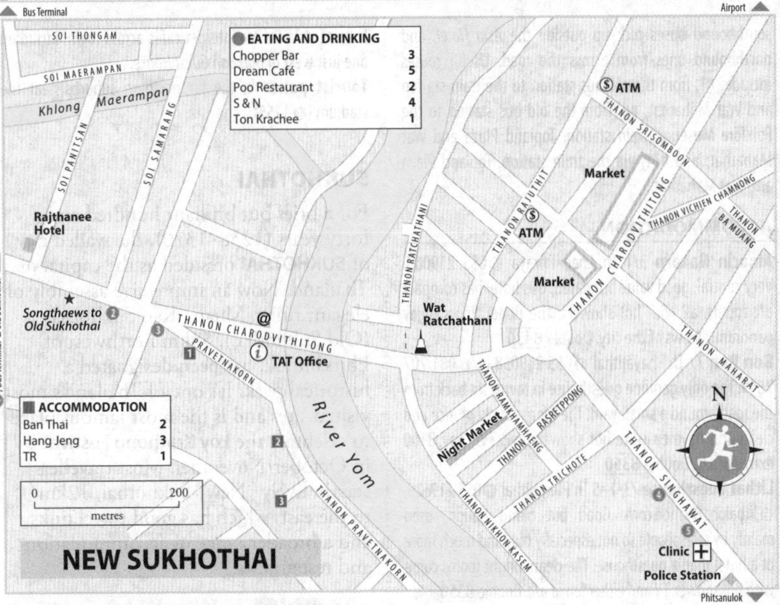

NEW SUKHOTHAI

EATING AND DRINKING

Chopper Bar	3
Dream Café	5
Poo Restaurant	2
S & N	4
Ton Krachee	1

ACCOMMODATION

Ban Thai	2
Hang Jeng	3
TR	1

Bus Terminal
Airport
Soi Thongam
Soi Maerampan
Khlong Maerampan
Soi Panitsan
Soi Samarang
Rajthanee Hotel
Songthaews to Old Sukhothai
Thanon Charodvithitong
Pravetnakorn
TAT Office
River Yom
Thanon Pravetnakorn
Thanon Ratchathani
Wat Ratchathani
ATM
Thanon Srisomboon
Market
Thanon Rajuthit
Thanon Vichien Chamnong
Thanon Ba Muang
Thanon Maharat
Thanon Ramkhamhaeng
Rasretppong
Night Market
Thanon Trichote
Thanon Nikhon Kasem
Thanon Singhawat
Clinic
Police Station
Phitsanulok
1, Bus Terminal & Old Sukhothai
0 200 metres

found among the ruins, it contains a copy of Ramkhamhaeng's famous stele – essentially an advertisement for a utopian land of plenty, aimed at prospective traders and settlers. Turn left inside the gate to the central zone for Sukhothai's most important site, the enormous **Wat Mahathat** compound, packed with the remains of scores of monuments and surrounded, like a city within a city, by a moat. It was the spiritual epicentre of the city, the king's temple and symbol of his power.

A few hundred metres southwest, the triple corn-cob-shaped prangs of **Wat Sri Sawai** indicate that this was a pre-Sukhothai Hindu shrine for the Khmers, which was later pressed into Buddhist service; the square base inside the central prang originally supported the Shiva lingam (phallus). Just west, the ordination hall of **Wat Trapang Ngoen** rises gracefully from an island in the middle of the eponymous "silver pond". On the pond's west bank, north of the graceful lotus-bud chedi, notice the fluid lines of the walking Buddha mounted onto a brick wall – a classic example of Sukhothai sculpture. Taking the water feature one step further, **Wat Sra Sri** commands a fine position on two connecting islands north of Wat Trapang Ngoen; its bell-shaped chedi with a tapering spire and square base shows a strong Sri Lankan influence.

The outer zones

There are also interesting outlying temples in the north, west and east zones, but there's little worth seeing in the south zone. Continuing north of Wat Sra Sri, cross the city walls into the north zone and you'll find **Wat Sri Chum**, which boasts Sukhothai's largest surviving Buddha image. The enormous brick-and-stucco seated Buddha, measuring over 11m from knee to knee and almost 15m high, peers through the slit in its tightly fitting, custom-made building.

Around 5km west of the city walls, lonely **Wat Saphan Hin** sits atop a hill, affording decent views of the surrounding countryside and the distant ruins. About 1km east of the city walls, the best temple in the east zone is **Wat Chang Lom**, by a canal just off the road to New Sukhothai. Chang Lom translates as "surrounded by elephants": the main feature here is a large, Sri Lankan-style, bell-shaped chedi encircled by a frieze of pachyderms.

10

ARRIVAL AND INFORMATION

By plane You can fly between Bangkok's Suvarnabhumi Airport and Sukhothai with Bangkok Airways (2 daily; 1hr 15min), although fares are quite high. The airport is about 15km north of New Sukhothai; flights are met by shuttle buses that head into the centre (B180/person).

By bus Buses use the terminal 3km northwest of New Sukhothai's town centre on the bypass. A tuk-tuk from here to the centre costs B60–80.

Destinations Ayutthaya (30 daily; 6hr); Bangkok (30 daily; 6–7hr); Chiang Mai (up to 22 daily; 5–6hr); Chiang Rai (3–4 daily; 8–9hr); Khon Kaen (10–11 daily; 6–7hr); Lampang (20 daily; 4hr); Mae Sot (6 daily; 2hr 30min–3hr); Nan (1 daily; 6hr); Phitsanulok (at least every 40min; 1hr–1hr 30min).

Tourist information The TAT office is on Th Charodvithitong (T 055 616228–9, E tatsukho@tat.or.th; daily 8.30am–4.30pm).

GETTING AROUND

By songthaew Big songthaews (every 30min; roughly 30min) run between New Sukhothai and the historical park; they leave from 200m west of TAT on Th Charodvithitong, and some also stop at the main bus station. They pull into Old Sukhothai near the central zone entrance point and several bicycle rental outlets (B30/day).

By bike Most guesthouses in New Sukhothai rent out bicycles (B30/day) and motorcycles (B250/day).

ACCOMMODATION

OLD SUKOTHAI

Old Sukhothai only has a handful of restaurants, but it is laidback and staying here allows you to take your time with the sights – and catch them deserted at sunrise and sunset when the light's at its most spectacular.

Old City Guest House Th Charodvithitong, opposite the museum T 055 697515. Within spitting distance of the ruins, a wide range of options mostly in two-storey wooden buildings around a yard, set back from the road. The cheapest are small, rather dark rooms with shared bathrooms. Double B200

NEW SUKHOTHAI

Ban Thai 38 Th Pravetnakorn T 055 610163, E banthai_gueshouse@yahoo.com. A great choice: clean, comfortable, wood-floored rooms sharing hot-water bathrooms set in a small garden, which also has some smart wooden en-suite bungalows (from B400). The restaurant is a good place to meet people and does tasty Thai food tamed for the *farang* palate. *Ban Thai* is also a friendly and reliable source of local information. Double B250

Hang Jeng Soi Meakaphut, signposted off Th Pravetnakorn just beyond *Ban Thai Guesthouse* T 055 610585 or T 081 972 4345. Down a short, quiet lane, this sprawling concrete house with big balconies offers bright rooms with parquet floors and hot showers, sharing plentiful toilets. Double B250

★ **TR** 27/5 Pravetnakorn Rd T 055 611663, W sukhothaibudgetguesthouse.com. This friendly family-run guesthouse with en-suite hot showers throughout offers free wi-fi, a little restaurant, neat rooms in a hotel-style building, plus some slightly more expensive, charming wooden bungalows (B450) with verandas overlooking the small back garden. Double B300

EATING AND DRINKING

OLD SUKHOTHAI

The Coffee Cup Th Charodvithitong, opposite the museum. At this clean and airy café, the menu of Thai, Western and fusion dishes is huge, with photos to help: try the massaman chicken curry (B100) and perhaps round it off with an Irish coffee or a delicious fruit shake. Daily 6am–10pm.

NEW SUKHOTHAI

One of the best places to eat in New Sukhothai is the covered night market on the soi between Th Ramkhamhaeng and Th Nikhon Kasem. Food carts also set up every evening in front of Wat Ratchathani on Th Charodvithitong.

Chopper Bar Th Pravetnakorn. This popular balcony bar with nightly live acoustic music, cheap beer and a vague biker theme is a great place to watch the world go by. Daily 4pm–midnight.

Dream Café 88/1 Th Singhawat. Cosy, wood-panelled restaurant with an artsy atmosphere and walls full of curios. It has a great mid-priced menu (most dishes above B100) of fiery Thai curries, fresh Vietnamese-style spring rolls, deep-fried banana-flower fritters – and gin and tonics. Daily 5–11pm.

Poo Restaurant 26 Th Charodvithitong. Although the surroundings aren't up to much, the cheap curries are tasty (around B50), while a nice Belgian beer will set you back around B150. See how many toilet humour fans you see snapping pictures by the sign. Daily 6.30am–11pm.

S & N (Sun & Night) Coffee House Th Singhawat, next to *Sawasdipong Hotel*. As well as excellent espresso coffees (from B30), smoothies and ice cream, this friendly a/c café offers interesting, varied Thai dishes such as green curry with roti pancakes (B89) and Western breakfasts (from B59). Daily 9am–8pm.

Ton Krachee Th Charodvithitong, about 500m west of the bridge. One of the best places to try the very more-ish Sukhothai noodle soup – laced with palm sugar, it's sour, spicy and sweet (B30). English menu but no English sign – it's the old one-storey wooden building next to Saijo Denki a/c shop. Daily 8am–4pm.

DIRECTORY

Hospital Sukhothai Hospital (☎ 055 611782) is west of New Sukhothai on the road to Old Sukhothai.

Post office Th Nikhon Kasem, about 1km south of the bridge (Mon–Fri 8.30am–4.30pm, Sat & Sun 9am–noon).

MAE SOT

10

Located only 6km from the Burmese border, **MAE SOT** boasts a thriving trade in gems and teak and a rich ethnic mix of Burmese, Karen, Hmong and Thai, plus a lively injection of committed NGO expats working with the thousands of refugees from Myanmar. It's a relaxed place to hang out before heading down to Umphang for some trekking (see box opposite) – treks can be arranged from Mae Sot – and chances are you'll meet some interesting people at one of the many excellent places to eat.

WHAT TO SEE AND DO

There's little to see in the small town apart from several glittering Burmese-style temples, an ornate Chinese temple and a bustling, Burmese-influenced day market with interesting delicacies such as eels, live toads, tiny tortoises and a range of insects. Frequent songthaews (B20) run from Thanon Banthung near the south end of the market to the Burmese border at **Rim Moei**, 6km from Mae Sot, where a large, slightly tacky market for Burmese handicrafts and other goods crowds the banks of the River Moei. Look out for shops selling exquisite woodcarvings to the east of the market. At the time of writing, access to the Burmese village of Myawaddy on the opposite bank of the River Moei is only open to *farangs* for a day's shopping (B500 entry); visitors are allowed no further into Myanmar. When coming back through Thai immigration (6.30am–6pm) you will automatically be given a new fifteen-day Thai stamp (thirty days for British, US and Canadian citizens).

> Most of the aid organizations that work in the Burmese refugee camps welcome donations, and some are happy to receive visitors and even short-term volunteers; ask at Borderline or *Krua Canadian* restaurant (see opposite).

ARRIVAL AND DEPARTURE

By plane Nok Air (ⓦ nokair.com) operates flights from Bangkok (Don Muang; 4 daily; 1hr 15min) and Chiang Mai (1 daily; 50min), as well as Yangon and Mawlamyine in Myanmar, to Mae Sot's airport, 3km west of town. Motorbike taxis await arrivals.

By bus, songthaew and a/c minibus The government bus station is about 2km west of town at the intersection of Highway 105 and the main east–west street, Th Indharakiri, with motorbike taxis shuttling passengers to the guesthouses. A/c minibuses to and from Phitsanulok and Sukhothai arrive at a terminus on Th Banthung, near the south end of the market, while songthaews to Umphang can be found about 300m to the east on the same street.

Destinations Bangkok (12 daily; 8hr 30min); Chiang Mai (2 daily; 6hr 30min); Chiang Rai (2 daily; 10hr); Lampang (2 daily; 4–5hr); Mae Sai (2 daily; 12hr); Phitsanulok (8 daily; 4hr); Sukhothai (9 daily; 2hr 30min–3hr); Umphang (hourly 7.30am–3.30pm; 4–5hr).

ACCOMMODATION

Bai Fern 660 Th Indharakiri ☎ 055 531349, ⓦ bai-fern.com. A popular, well-run and helpful guesthouse in the centre of town, offering simple rooms with shared bathrooms, and very good rates for singles. Double B250

Ban Pruksa Th Indharakiri, beyond Wat Arunyaket on the west side of town ☎ 055 532656, ⓦ banpruksa.com. Comfortably furnished rooms, some with shared hot-water bathrooms, in a spacious modern building with a nice garden area. Double B300

Duang Kamol (DK) Hotel 298/2 Th Indharakiri, near the post office ☎ 055 531699. Great-value town-centre hotel offering huge, clean rooms, many of them with little balconies and some with a/c and hot showers. The entrance is on the first floor, above a series of shops. Double B250

EATING AND DRINKING

Borderline Tea Garden Th Indharakiri, behind the Borderline crafts shop. Cheap Burmese dishes (mostly B30–40), including tea-leaf salad and potato curry, Burmese tea, lemon-grass juice and other healthy drinks, are sold at this simple, relaxed tea garden. Also runs cookery classes (B450–1000 depending on group size). Tues–Sun 10am–6pm.

Casa Mia Th Don Kaew, off Th Indharakiri west of *Ban Pruksa Guest House*. Delicious home-made pastas and pizzas (from B130), as well as Thai food, veggie options and great cakes. Daily except Sat 7.30am–10pm.

Krua Canadian 3 Th Sriponit, off Th Indharakiri diagonally across from the police station. Huge menu of tasty dishes (mostly around B100), including Thai, Mexican, vegetarian, Western breakfasts and deli sandwiches. Also a good source of local information. Daily 7am–9.30pm.

DIRECTORY

Banks There are banks dotted all about Mae Sot, especially on Th Indharakiri and Th Prasat Vithi.
Internet Internet is available at many places around Mae Sot, especially on Th Indharakiri.
Motorbike rental Available at most guesthouses (around B200/day).
Post office To the east of the police station on Th Indharakiri.

UMPHANG

Even if you don't fancy joining a trek, it's worth considering making the spectacular 164km trip south from Mae Sot to the village of **UMPHANG**, both for the fine mountain scenery and for the buzz of being in such an isolated part of Thailand. Chances are your songthaew will be crammed full of people from varied ethnic and tribal backgrounds. About halfway, the road goes past Umpiem Mai, a refugee camp for fifteen thousand or so Burmese.

Surrounded by mountains and sited at the confluence of the Mae Khlong and Umphang rivers, Umphang itself is small and quiet; it takes no more than twenty minutes to walk from one end to the other. It has few signposted roads, but the two main points of orientation are the River Umphang at the far western end of the village, and the wat – about 500m east of the river bridge – that marks its centre.

ARRIVAL AND DEPARTURE

By songthaew Songthaews drop people at the bus station, just east of the village centre; most places are within walking distance, though there are also motorbike taxis. In terms of public transport, Umphang is effectively a dead end, so you'll need to return to Mae Sot (at least hourly until noon; 4–5hr) before continuing on to other destinations.

ACCOMMODATION

Most trekking companies (see box below) have their own accommodation. As Umphang accommodation is geared towards trekkers in transit, charges are per person rather than per room.

Phu Doi Campsite Resort North side of the bus station ⓣ 055 561049, ⓦ phudoi.com. Dark wood-panelled fan rooms with spotless hot-water bathrooms and verandas, in log buildings overlooking a lotus pond. Also has a popular restaurant with an English-language menu. **B300** per person

Suan Boonyaporn Garden Huts 106 Th Umphang-Palata, by the river bridge ⓣ 055 561093, ⓦ boonyaporn resort.com. Simple wooden huts and bungalows, the cheapest with shared hot showers, set around a pretty garden with partial river views. **B200** per person

TREKKING AROUND UMPHANG

The focus of most treks from Umphang is the three-tiered **Tee Lor Su Waterfall**. It's at its most thunderous just after the rainy season in November, when you can also swim in the beautifully blue lower pool, though trails can still be muddy at this time. During the dry season (Dec–April), you can get close to the falls by road and it's usually possible to climb up to one of the upper tiers. A typical trek lasts three days and features rafting, hot springs, three or four hours' walking per day, a night in a Karen village and an elephant ride. Bring a fleece as nights can get chilly. Most itineraries now include transport from and to Mae Sot (and sometimes accommodation in Umphang), with prices starting at around B5200 for a three-day trek. From June to October, trips focus on whitewater rafting.

TREKKING OPERATORS

Max One Tour In the DK Hotel plaza, 296/2 Th Indharakiri, Mae Sot ⓣ 055 542942, ⓦ maxonetour .com. Outlet for Umphang Hill (see below).

Mr Boonchuay 360 Th Pravitpaiwan, northwest of Umphang bus station ⓣ 055 561020, ⓦ boonchuaytour .com. Umphang-born and bred, Mr Boonchuay knows the area well and has a good reputation; his English is not perfect, but he has English-speaking guides.

Umphang Hill Resort By the bridge in Umphang ⓣ 055 561063, ⓦ umphanghill.com. The biggest outfit in the area is efficiently run and offers eleven different itineraries.

The north

Beyond the northern plains, the climate becomes more temperate, nurturing the fertile land that gave the old kingdom of **the north** the name of **Lanna**, "the land of a million rice fields". Until the beginning of the last century, Lanna was a largely independent region, with its own styles of art and architecture. Its capital, the pleasant, 700-year-old city of **Chiang Mai**, is now a major centre for travellers' activities and courses and the most popular base from which to organize treks to nearby hill-tribe villages. Another great way of exploring the scenic countryside up here is to rent a jeep or motorbike and make the 600km loop over the forested western mountains, via the backpackers' honeypot of **Pai**, to **Mae Hong Son** and back. Heading north from Chiang Mai towards the Burmese border brings you to the smaller town of **Chiang Rai**, a base for trekking and river trips, and then on to the frontier settlement of **Mae Sai**, the so-called "**Golden Triangle**" at Sop Ruak, and the atmospheric ruined temples of **Chiang Saen**. **Chiang Khong**, on the Mekong River, is an important crossing point to Laos.

CHIANG MAI

Despite becoming a fixture on the package-tourist itinerary, **CHIANG MAI** – Thailand's second city – manages to preserve a little of the atmosphere of an overgrown village and a laidback traveller vibe, especially in the traditional old quarter, set within a two-kilometre-square moat. Chiang Mai is a fun and historic city, packed with culture and bustling markets, but its real charm lies in the staggering range of tours, treks, courses and activities available. You can easily spend a week in Chiang Mai and do something completely different every day: elephant riding, walking to hill-tribe villages, waterfalls, massage, cooking classes, mountain biking, rock climbing, bungee jumping, river cruises, unlimited shopping experiences and national parks. On top of that, there are fabulous temples, delicious food, unparalleled evening markets and an energetic nightlife that caters to everyone. It's impossible to get bored here.

WHAT TO SEE AND DO

The main sights are mostly situated within the ancient city walls, which are surrounded by a moat, and intersected at the cardinal points by elaborate gates. Tha Pae Gate, on the east side of old Chiang Mai, leads out to the town's commercial centre and the river. Just 16km west of town, the striking Wat Phra That Doi Suthep is set on a mist-shrouded mountain.

Wat Phra Singh

If you see only one temple in Chiang Mai it should be **Wat Phra Singh**, at the far western end of Thanon Ratchdamnoen in the old town. Just inside the gate to the right, the recently restored wooden library is the best example of its kind in the north, inlaid with glass mosaic and set high on a base decorated with stucco angels. The temple's largest structure, a colourful modern viharn (congregation hall) fronted by naga (serpent) balustrades, hides from view the beautiful Viharn Lai Kam, a wooden gem of early nineteenth-century Lanna architecture, with its squat, multi-tiered roof and exquisitely carved and gilded pediment. Inside sits the Phra Singh Buddha image, a portly, radiant and much-revered bronze in fifteenth-century Lanna style. The walls are enlivened by murals depicting daily life in the north a hundred years ago.

Wat Chedi Luang

The nearby **Chedi Luang** (main entrance on Thanon Phra Pokklao) is an enormous crumbling pink-brick chedi, which was reduced to its present height of 60m by an earthquake in 1545. It once housed the Emerald Buddha in the niche on its eastern side (now in Bangkok's Wat Phra Kaeo), but now has to make do with an oversized replica. On the northeast side of the chedi,

TREKKING

Trekking in the mountains of northern Thailand differs from trekking in most other parts of the world, in that the emphasis is not primarily on the scenery but on the region's inhabitants. More than a hundred thousand travellers now trek each year, most heading to well-trodden areas such as the Mae Tang Valley, 40km northwest of Chiang Mai, and the hills around the Kok River west of Chiang Rai. This steady flow of trekkers creates pressures for the traditionally insular hill tribes. Foreigners unfamiliar with hill-tribe customs can easily cause grave offence, especially those who go looking for drugs. Most tribespeople are genuinely welcoming to foreigners; nonetheless, it is important to take a responsible attitude.

The hill tribes are big business in northern Thailand. **Chiang Rai** is the second-biggest trekking centre after Chiang Mai, and agencies can also be found in Nan, **Mae Hong Son** and **Pai**, although these usually arrange treks only to the villages in their immediate area. Guided trekking on a much smaller scale than in the north is available in **Umphang** (see p.743).

THE BASICS

On any trek, you'll need walking boots or training shoes, long trousers (against thorns and wet-season leeches), a hat, a sarong or towel, a sweater or fleece, plus insect repellent and, if possible, a mosquito net. On an organized trek, water, blankets or a sleeping bag, and possibly a small backpack, should be supplied. It's wise not to take anything valuable with you; most guesthouses in Chiang Mai have safes, but check their reputation with other travellers, and sign an inventory – theft and credit-card abuse are not uncommon.

TREKKING ETIQUETTE

As guests, it's up to *farangs* to adapt to the customs of the hill tribes and not to make a nuisance of themselves.

- Dress modestly and wear a sarong when showering; no bikinis or swim suits.
- Before entering a hill-tribe village, look out for taboo signs of woven bamboo strips on the ground outside the village entrance, which mean a special ceremony is taking place and that you should not enter. Be careful about what you touch. In Akha villages, keep your hands off cult structures such as the entrance gates and the giant swing. Do not touch or photograph any shrines, or sit underneath them. You'll have to pay a fine for any violation of local customs.
- Most villagers do not like to be photographed, in keeping with their spiritualist and animist beliefs. Be particularly careful with pregnant women and babies – most tribes believe cameras affect the soul of the foetus or newborn. Always ask first, and accept that you may have to offer a "donation" for any photos taken.
- Offering gifts is dubious practice: ask your guide what the village actually *needs* and follow their advice; clothes are always useful but avoid sweets and cigarettes, as they may encourage begging.

ORGANIZED TREKS

Organized treks usually last for three days, have six to twelve people in the group, and follow a route regularly used by the agency. There will be a few hours' walking every day, plus the possibility of an elephant ride and a trip on a bamboo raft. The group usually sleeps on the floor of the village headman's hut, and the guide cooks communal meals. A typical three-day trek costs B1500–3000 in Chiang Mai, sometimes less in other towns, and much less without rafting and elephant rides.

Word of mouth is often the best way to choose a trekking agency. If you want to trek with a small group, get an assurance that you won't be tagged onto a larger group. Meet the guides, who should speak reasonable English, know about hill-tribe culture and have a certificate from the Tourism Authority of Thailand (TAT). Check how much walking is involved per day, and ask about the menu. Also enquire about transport from base at the beginning and end of the trek, which sometimes entails a long public bus ride. Before setting off, each trek should be registered with the tourist police.

"Monk Chat" is advertised (daily 9am–6pm), giving you a chance to meet and talk to the monks in English. An impressive new building in traditional Lanna style to the left of the main entrance enshrines the Sao Inthakin, Chiang Mai's city pillar, which is celebrated with a major festival in late May or early June.

The city museums

Three adjacent museums provide an informative overview of the history, customs and culture of the city and

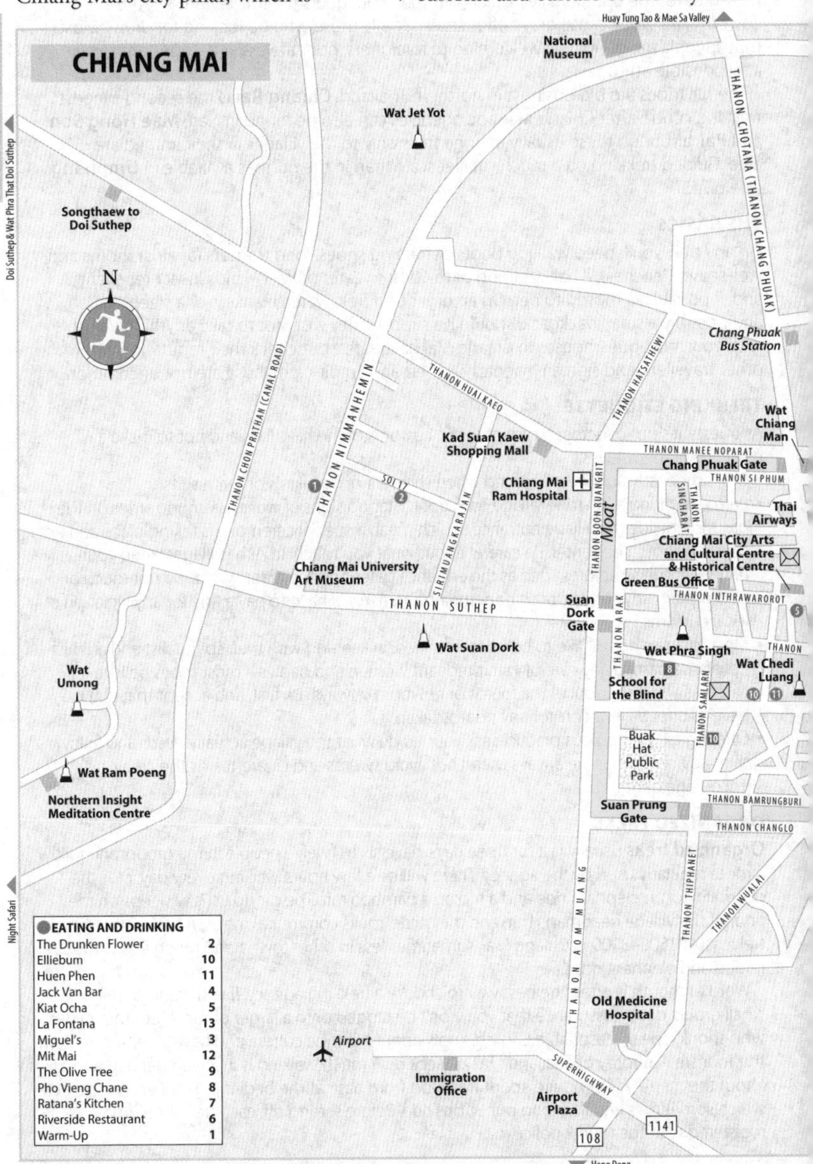

the region and are well worth a visit (Tues–Sun 8.30am–5pm; B90 each, or B180 for all 3). Housed in an elegant 1920s former provincial office on Thanon Phra Pokklao, the main **Chiang Mai City Arts and Cultural Centre** focuses on the city's identity and culture. Behind it, you'll find the **Chiang Mai Historical Centre**, where you can see the excavated walls of the chapel of the old Chiang Mai royal palace, while the **Lanna Folklife Museum** occupies the 1920s former courthouse opposite.

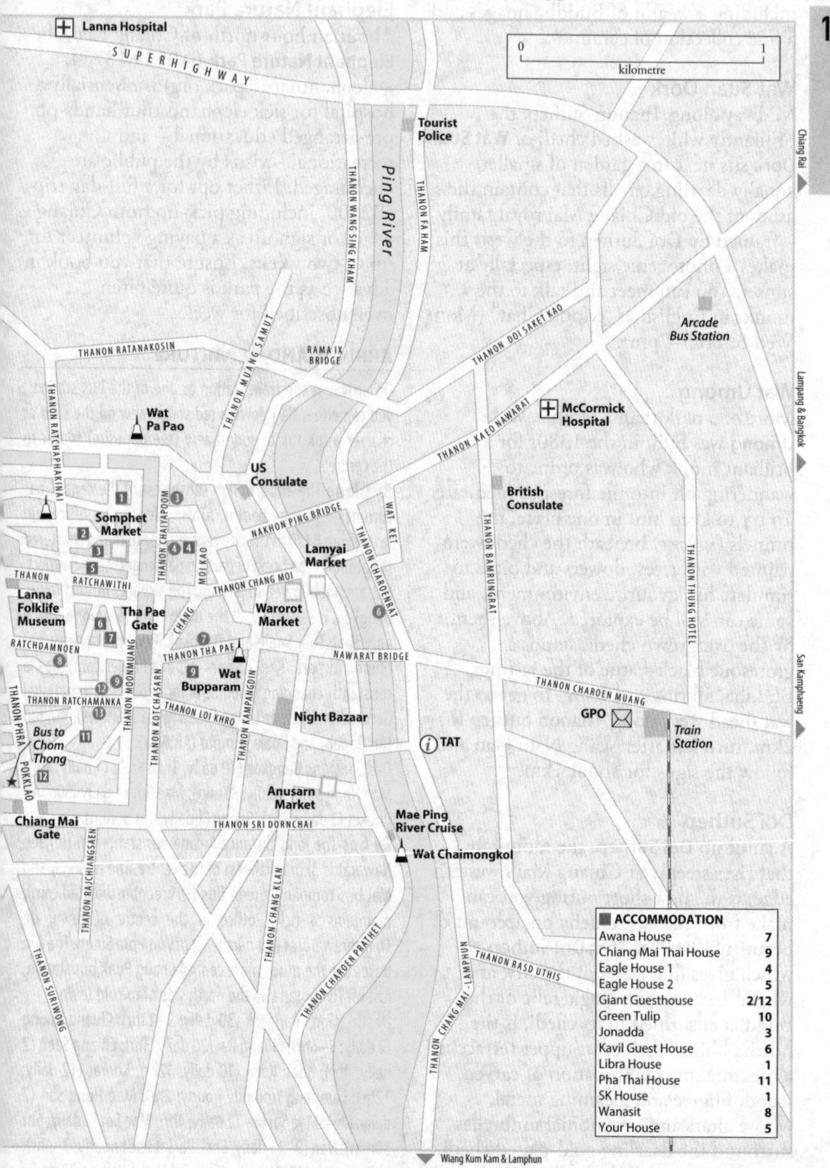

10

National Museum

Chiang Mai's branch of the **National Museum** (Wed–Sun 9am–4pm; B100), on the northwestern outskirts of town, doesn't tell its story as well as the City Arts and Cultural Centre, but has a much more interesting array of artefacts, including a wealth of Buddha images and a fine collection of ceramics.

Wat Suan Dork

Midway along Thanon Suthep, the brilliantly whitewashed chedi of **Wat Suan Dork** sits next to a garden of smaller, equally dazzling chedis that contain the ashes of the old Chiang Mai royal family – framed by Doi Suthep to the west, this makes a photogenic sight, especially at sunset. You can meet and talk to the monks in English at "Monk Chat" (Mon, Wed & Fri 5–7pm).

Wat Umong

More of a park than a temple, **Wat Umong** was built in the 1380s for a brilliant monk who was prone to wandering off into the forest to meditate. To try to keep him in one place, the tunnels (*umong*) beneath the chedi were painted with trees, flowers and birds to simulate his favourite environment, and some can still be explored. Above them, by the overgrown chedi, stands a grotesque black statue of the fasting Buddha, all ribs and veins. To get to the wat, head west along Thanon Suthep for 2km, turn left after Wang Nam Gan and follow the signs for about 1km.

Doi Suthep

A jaunt up **Doi Suthep**, the mountain that rises steeply at Chiang Mai's western edge, is the best short outing you can make from the city, chiefly on account of beautiful **Wat Phra That Doi Suthep**, which gives fine views of the city, and which, because of a magic relic of the Buddha enshrined in its chedi, is the north's holiest shrine. Its upper terrace is a breathtaking combination of carved wood, filigree and gleaming metal, whose altars and ceremonial umbrellas surround the dazzling gold-plated chedi. **Songthaews** leave when full from the northwest end of Thanon Huai Kaeo, in front of the zoo and the university, for the 16km trip up the mountain (B40–50 each way per person). The road, although steep in places, is paved all the way and well suited for motorbikes.

Elephant Nature Park

About an hour north of Chiang Mai, the **Elephant Nature Park** (T 053 818754, W elephantnaturepark.org) is essentially a hospital for sick elephants, but hands-on pre-arranged educational – and recreational – visits by the public are encouraged. Either opt for a full-day trip (B2500, including pick-up from Chiang Mai), or sign up as a paying volunteer for up to two weeks. Ensure that you book in advance as the park is quite often oversubscribed for weeks.

ARRIVAL AND DEPARTURE

On arrival at the train station or one of the bus stations, you can either flag down a red songthaew on the road or charter a tuk-tuk or songthaew (see opposite) to get to the centre.

By plane The airport, 3km southwest of the centre, has currency exchange booths, ATMs, cafés, a post office and taxis (from B120 to the city centre); tuk-tuks and chartered songthaews can bring departing passengers to the airport, but are not allowed to pick up. The airport's busiest route, Bangkok, is served by all the main carriers, among which only Thai, Thai Smile and Bangkok Airways use Suvarnabhumi Airport. Kan Airlines (W kanairlines.com) has a constantly changing schedule of local routes. International destinations include Luang Prabang (Lao Airlines), Yangon (Air Bagan) and Kuala Lumpur (Air Asia).

Destinations Bangkok (30 daily; 1hr); Krabi (1 daily; 2hr); Mae Hong Son (3 daily; 35min); Mae Sot (1 daily; 50min); Phuket (3 daily; 2hr); Samui (1 daily; 1hr 50min).

By bus The long-distance Arcade bus station on Th Kaeo Nawarat is 3km northeast of the centre. The main Chiang Mai bus company, Green Bus (W greenbusthailand.com), maintains a ticket office in the centre of town, on Th Inthrawarorot just northeast of Wat Phra Singh. Tha Ton buses use the much more central Chang Puak bus station, just off Th Chotana on the north side of the old town.

Destinations Bangkok (30 daily; 9–11hr); Chiang Khong (2 daily; 5–6hr); Chiang Rai (20 daily; 3hr); Chiang Saen (2 daily; 4hr); Khon Kaen (10 daily; 12hr); Khorat (12 daily; 12hr); Lampang (roughly hourly; 2hr); Mae Hong Son (7 daily; 8hr); Mae Sai (8–11 daily; 4hr); Mae Sot (2 daily; 6hr 30min); Nan (9–11 daily; 6hr); Pai (at least hourly; 3–4hr); Phitsanulok (40 daily; 5–6hr); Sukhothai (up to 22 daily;

5–6hr); Tha Ton (4 daily; 4hr); Ubon Ratchathani (6 daily; 17hr); Udon Thani (for Nong Khai; 4 daily; 12hr).

By train The train station is on Th Charoen Muang, just over 2km east of Tha Pae Gate, and has a left-luggage office.

Destinations Ayutthaya (5 daily; 10–13hr); Bangkok (5 daily; 12–14hr); Lampang (7 daily; 2hr 30min); Lopburi (5 daily; 9–11hr); Phitsanulok (7 daily; 6–8hr).

GETTING AROUND

By bike Some guesthouses rent bicycles for around B50/day, and you can also pick them up around Tha Pae Gate.

By car or motorbike Many places around Tha Pae Gate rent out motorbikes (from B150) and cars (from B800). The latter should come with insurance included: check before you set off.

By songthaew Red trucks (songthaews) act as shared taxis within the city, picking up people heading in roughly the same direction and taking each to their specific destination; fares to most places should cost B20 during the day. They sometimes also operate as chartered taxis for about the same price as tuk-tuks.

By tuk-tuk The city is stuffed with tuk-tuks, ready to take advantage of tourists – haggle hard. Expect to pay around B60 for a short journey from the Night Bazaar to Tha Pae Gate.

INFORMATION

Tourist information The TAT office (daily 8.30am–4.30pm; ⓣ 053 248604) is at 105/1 Th Chiang Mai–Lamphun on the east bank of the river near Nawarat Bridge. It's not to be confused with TAD Travel and Tours on Th Ratchaphakinai, which pretends to be a government information office but is in fact a private travel agent.

Maps Nancy Chandler's *Map of Chiang Mai* (B250) is very handy for a detailed exploration.

TREKKING AND ADVENTURE TOURS

In Chiang Mai, treks (see box, p.745) are usually arranged through one of the guesthouses, among which *Eagle House*, which passes on a proportion of its revenue towards funding projects in hill-tribe villages, and *Your House* have particularly good reputations. The choice of other adventure activities on offer is staggering.

TOUR OPERATORS

Chiang Mai Mountain Biking 1 Th Samlarn, 50m south of Wat Phra Singh ⓣ 081 024 7046, ⓦ mountainbikingchiangmai.com. A wide range of routes for all levels of fitness and experience, ranging from single-track downhill rides, mostly on Doi Suthep, to cross-country leisure trips.

Chiang Mai Rock Climbing Adventures 55/3 Th Ratchapakhinai ⓣ 053 207102, ⓦ thailandclimbing.com. Climbing trips based at the striking "Crazy Horse Buttress" 35km from Chiang Mai. Runs climbing and caving courses, with extensive equipment for rent or to buy, and a partner-finding service. Its in-town bouldering wall is a good place to meet and train.

Click and Travel 158/40 Th Chiang Mai–Hod ⓣ 053 281553, ⓦ clickandtravelonline.com. Belgian-Thai company that runs cycling tours of Chiang Mai and the north, lasting from a few hours to four days, and maintains a useful website, ⓦ chiangmaicycling.org, full of all manner of information for cyclists.

Contact Travel Based at Tasala, east of Chiang Mai ⓣ 053 850160, ⓦ activethailand.com. Offers treks, river- and lake-kayaking, cycling and whitewater rafting.

Flight of the Gibbon ⓣ 053 010660, ⓦ treetopasia.com. Zoom through the tropical rainforest on zip wires and sky bridges in this exhilarating trip high above the jungle floor.

Jungle Bungy Jump ⓣ 053 297700, ⓦ junglebungy.com. Experienced bungee-jump specialists offering 50m jumps over water.

The Peak 302 4 Th Chiang Mai–Lamphun ⓣ 053 800567, ⓦ thepeakadventure.com. Out-of-town combination trips with rock climbing, quad-biking and whitewater rafting.

COURSES

The courses listed below are only a taster of the huge range on offer.

COOKERY

Baan Thai Cookery School 11 Soi 5, Th Ratchadamnoen ⓣ 053 357339, ⓦ cookinthai.com. Based in central Chiang Mai, Baan Thai has interesting menu choices and offers both full-day (B1000) and evening courses (B800).

★ **Chiang Mai Thai Farm Cooking School** 38 Soi 9, Th Moonmuang ⓣ 081 288 5989, ⓦ thaifarmcooking.com. A good way to escape the city: you can pick your own organic vegetables, herbs and fruits for cooking on their farm, a 30min drive from town (B1100/day, transport provided).

CHIANG MAI BOAT TRIPS

One of the most leisurely ways to explore the surrounding countryside is to take a river cruise with **Mae Ping River Cruise** (Wat Chaimongkol, Th Chareonprathet; ⓣ 053 274822, ⓦ maepingrivercruise.com; minimum two people; transfers from your accommodation included), who offer two-hour cruises through lush countryside, with a stop at a local farmer's house and herbal drink and snack included (B550 per person), as well as popular trips to the ruined city of Wiang Kum Kam, by boat and horse-and-carriage (B700). They also offer evening dinner cruises (6.45pm; B650).

10

THE HILL TRIBES

There are at least ten different **hill tribes** in northern Thailand, many of them divided into distinct subgroups. Migrating from various parts of China and Southeast Asia, most arrived in Thailand in the twentieth century and many have tribal relatives in other parts of Southeast Asia. The tribes have sophisticated systems of customs, laws and beliefs, and are predominantly animists. They often have exquisitely crafted costumes, though many men and children now adopt Western clothes for everyday wear. To learn more about the tribes, visit the hill tribe museum in Chiang Rai (see p.762).

KAREN

The largest hill-tribe group (pop.500,000), the **Karen** began to arrive in the seventeenth century, though many are recent refugees from Myanmar. Most of them live west of Chiang Mai, stretching all the way down to Kanchanaburi. Unmarried Karen women wear loose V-necked shift dresses, often decorated with grass seeds at the seams. Married women wear blouses and skirts in bold red or blue. Perhaps the most famous of all hill-tribe groups are the **Padaung**, a small subgroup of the Karen. Padaung women wear columns of heavy brass rings around their necks (see p.756).

HMONG

The **Hmong** (or Meo; pop.110,000) are found widely in northern Thailand, and are also the most widespread minority group in south China. The Blue Hmong subgroup live to the west of Chiang Mai, while the White Hmong are found to the east. Most Hmong live in extended families in traditional houses with a roof descending almost to ground level. Blue Hmong women wear intricately embroidered pleated skirts decorated with bands of red, pink, blue and white. White Hmong women wear white skirts for special occasions and black baggy trousers for everyday use. All the Hmong are famous for their chunky silver jewellery.

LAHU

The **Lahu** (pop.80,000) originated in the Tibetan highlands. The Lahu language has become the lingua franca of the hill tribes, since the Lahu often hire out their labour. About one-third of Lahu have been converted to Christianity. The remaining animist Lahu believe in a village guardian spirit, who is often worshipped at a central temple. Houses are built on high stilts and

MASSAGE

Massages in Thailand are considered a healthy part of daily life rather than a luxurious pampering treat so they're readily available all over Chiang Mai, with prices starting around B150/hr.

Old Medicine Hospital 78/1 Soi Mo Shivagakomarpaj, off Th Wualai ☎053 201633, ⓦthaimassageschool.ac.th. Highly respected week-long courses (B5000) with dorm accommodation available; foot, oil and herbal compress courses are also available. Also the best place in Chiang Mai to get a massage (B250/90min).

Thai Massage School of Chiang Mai 203/6 Th Mae Jo ☎053 854330, ⓦtmcschool.com. Five-day courses (B7500) fully accredited by the Ministry of Education, as well as longer professional courses.

MEDITATION

Most meditation courses are serious undertakings: conditions are sparse, the routine is strict and there's often no reading or music, and speaking must be kept to a minimum.

Wat Phra That Doi Suthep (see p.748) International Buddhist Meditation Centre ☎053 295012, ⓦfivethousandyears.org. A variety of meditation courses for beginners and experienced students, from 4 to 21 days. Registration must be made in advance (courses are often full).

Wat Ram Poeng Northern Insight Meditation Centre, off Th Chon Prathan near Wat Umong ☎053 278620, ⓦpalikanon.com/vipassana/tapotaram/tapotaram.htm. Disciplined courses (with a rule of no food after noon and respectful silence), taught by Thai monks with translators. The basic course is 26 days but the meditation practice can be "tried out" for ten days with special permission.

Wat Suan Dork (see p.748) ⓦmonkchat.net. Introductory retreat course to meditation and Thai Buddhist culture, including chanting and alms-giving. Courses begin at 1pm Tues, before departure to the training centre on Doi Suthep, returning on Wed afternoon (B500). Participants need to wear white clothes, available for B300.

ACCOMMODATION

The main concentrations of guesthouses are in the surprisingly quiet sois around the eastern side of the moat, close to all the sights and amid a proliferation of

10

thatched with grass. Some Lahu women wear a distinctive black cloak with diagonal white stripes, decorated in bold red and yellow on the sleeve, but many now wear ordinary clothes. The tribe is famous for its richly embroidered shoulder bags.

AKHA

The poorest of the hill tribes is the **Akha** (pop.50,000). Every Akha village is entered through ceremonial gates decorated with carvings of human attributes – even cars and aeroplanes – to indicate to the spirit world that only humans should pass. Akha houses are recognizable by their low stilts and steeply pitched roofs. Women wear elaborate headgear consisting of a conical wedge of white beads interspersed with silver coins, topped with plumes of red taffeta and framed by dangling silver balls.

MIEN

The **Mien** (or Yao; pop.42,000) consider themselves the aristocrats of the hill tribes. Originating in central China, and widely scattered throughout the north, they are the only people to have a written language, and a codified religion, based on medieval Chinese Taoism, although many have converted to Christianity and Buddhism. Mien women wear long black jackets with bright scarlet lapels, and heavily embroidered, loose trousers and turbans.

LISU

The **Lisu** (pop.30,000), who originated in eastern Tibet, are found mostly in the west, particularly between Chiang Mai and Mae Hong Son. They are organized into patriarchal clans, and their strong sense of clan rivalry often results in public violence. The Lisu live in extended families in bamboo houses. The women wear a blue or green knee-length tunic, with a wide black belt and blue or green trousers. Men wear green, pink or yellow baggy trousers and a blue jacket.

LAWA

The **Lawa** people (pop.17,000) have inhabited Thailand since at least the eighth century and most Lawa villages look no different from Thai settlements. But between Hot, Mae Sariang and Mae Hong Son, the Lawa still live a largely traditional life. Unmarried Lawa women wear strings of orange and yellow beads, white blouses edged with pink, and tight skirts in parallel bands of blue, black, yellow and pink. All the women wear their hair tied in a turban.

restaurants. Many guesthouses make their bread and butter from trekking and will encourage you to use their service; though this can be convenient, it's always worth shopping around. None of the places listed should hassle you to trek.

Awana House 7 Soi 1, Th Ratchdamnoen ⊕053 419005, ⓦawanahouse.com. This helpful, Thai-Dutch guesthouse has a tiny pool, fan rooms sharing hot-water bathrooms and large, nicely furnished, en-suite, a/c rooms. Internet access and free wi-fi. Double B375

Chiang Mai Thai House 5/1 Soi 5, Th Tha Pae ⊕053 904110, ⓦchiangmaithaihouse.com. There's a choice of smallish but well-furnished rooms with fan, hot shower and TV or bigger ones with a/c in this centrally located place, which also has a tiny pool. Wi-fi and internet. Double B500

Eagle House 1 16 Soi 3, Th Chang Moi Kao ⊕053 235387, ⓦeaglehouse.com. Friendly, well-maintained Thai-Irish guesthouse with a good garden café and en-suite doubles with cold or hot showers; well-organized treks are on offer, plus free pick-ups from train or bus stations or airport. Double B220

Eagle House 2 26 Soi 2, Th Ratchawithi ⊕053 418494, ⓦeaglehouse.com. Under the same management as *Eagle House 1*, a decent guesthouse with garden café and en-suite double rooms with hot showers, plus two- or three-bed dorms; cookery courses are on offer, as well as treks and free pick-ups. Dorm B150, double B300

★**Giant Guesthouse** Soi 6, Th Moonmuang ⊕053 227338, ⓦgiantguesthouse.com. This popular option is right next to the market and has its own kitchen – ideal if you fancy practising your Thai cooking. The staff are helpful and offer free pick-ups from airport or bus station, free bicycles and free internet, and also put on films in their comfortable lounge. Rooms, all with wi-fi, come with fan (shared or en-suite bathrooms) or a/c. There's another branch at the bottom of Th Ratchaphakinai with three- or four-bed dorms (B120). Double B180

Green Tulip 85 Th Samlarn ⊕053 275858, ⓦgreentuliphouse.com. In a handy location near Wat Phra Singh, with vivid colour scheme and a bar-restaurant downstairs offering good food. Clean, bright, basic rooms with fan or a/c and en-suite hot showers. Internet access. Dorm B150, double B500

10

Jonadda Guest House 23/1 Soi 2, Th Ratchawithi ☎ 053 227281, ✉ jonadda@hotmail.com. Quiet and friendly Thai–Australian place with a variety of bright, clean, comfortable fan rooms with hot showers, in a modern, multistorey building. Good prices for singles. Double **B350**

Kavil Guest House 10/1 Soi 5, Th Ratchdamnoen, near Somphet Market ☎ 053 224740. Smallish, friendly, well-run place in a quiet soi with fan and a/c rooms; all have hot-water bathrooms. Double **B300**

Libra House 28 Soi 9, Th Moonmuang ☎ 053 210687, ⓦ librahousechiangmai.com. Excellent, family-run, trekking-oriented guesthouse with 24hr check-in. All of the fifty-plus rooms are en suite, some with hot water, some with a/c, and all with free wi-fi. Free pick-ups during the day. Double **B250**

Pha Thai House 48/1 Th Ratchaphakinai ☎ 053 278013 or ☎ 081 998 6933, ⓦ phathaihouse.com. A wide variety of rooms, all en suite with hot showers and wi-fi, in a leafy, garden setting. Double **B400**

SK House 30 Soi 9, Th Moonmuang ☎ 053 210690, ⓦ theskhouse.com. Efficient, brick-built high-rise with internet access and a small, shaded swimming pool. Fan and fancier a/c rooms come with hot-water bathrooms. Double **B250**

Wanasit 6 Soi 8, Th Ratchamanka ☎ 053 814042. Tranquil and popular for longer stays, this three-storey guesthouse by the south wall of Wat Phra Singh is showing its age a little but offers bright, clean rooms with small, hot-water bathrooms, most with balconies, and a roof terrace. Double **B400**

Your House 8 Soi 2, Th Ratchawithi ☎ 053 217492, ⓦ yourhouseguesthouse.com. Welcoming old-town teak house. Big rooms with shared hot-water bathrooms, plus some smarter en-suite ones in two modern annexes; optional a/c in most. Fabulous, inexpensive breakfasts. Good for treks and day-trips; free pick-ups are sometimes possible from train and bus stations or the airport. Double **B250**

EATING AND DRINKING

There are several night markets with good street-food stalls, including Somphet on Th Moonmuang, and by Chiang Mai Gate on Th Bamrungburi.

NORTHERN FOOD

Northern food has been strongly influenced by Burmese cuisine, especially in curries such as the spicy **kaeng hang lay**, made with pork, ginger and tamarind. Another favourite local dish, especially for lunch, is **khao soi**, a thick broth of curry and coconut cream, with meat and both soft and crispy egg noodles.

CAFÉS AND RESTAURANTS

Elliebum 114/3 Th Ratchamanka. A good spot to refuel while looking around the old town: great coffee, delicious fruit smoothies (B50) and top-notch breakfasts, sandwiches and Thai lunches (B60). Mon–Sat 8am–5.30pm, Sun 8am–12.30pm.

Huen Phen 112 Th Ratchamanka. Probably Chiang Mai's most authentic northern restaurant. Try local specialities such as *sai oua* (sausage), *kaeng hang lay* (pork curry) and *khao soi* (noodle curry; B40). The more attractive evening restaurant around the back is pricier but also serves good northern Thai food. Daily 8am–4pm & 5–10pm.

Kiat Ocha 41–43 Th Inthrawarorot, off Th Phra Pokklao (the English sign says "Hainanese chicken"). Delicious and very popular satay and *khao man kai* – boiled chicken breast served with dipping sauces, broth and rice – at around B40 a dish. Daily 6am–3pm, or until the food runs out.

La Fontana 39/7–8 Th Ratchamanka. Chiang Mai's best Italian, dishing up great home-made pastas (B150–200), authentic pizzas and delicious Italian desserts. Daily 11am–11pm; sometimes closed Tues and at lunchtimes in low season.

Miguel's Th Chaiyapoom. Warm welcome, a relaxing terrace and great Mexican food: feast on the nachos grande for B160. Daily 10am–11pm.

Mit Mai 42/2 Th Ratchamanka. Excellent food in good-sized portions from Yunnan province in southwest China, including a zesty chicken salad and delicious snow peas with Yunnanese ham (B90). Daily 10am–10pm.

The Olive Tree 29/7 Th Moonmuang. Small a/c café serving Middle Eastern food, including pitta bread, hummus (B100), home-made cheeses and yoghurts, right near Tha Pae Gate. Daily except Fri 11am–3pm & 5–11pm.

Pho Vieng Chane Kad Klang Wieng, Th Ratchdamnoen, cnr of Ratchaphakinai. Specializes in pho (pronounced "fur"; from B30), a tasty noodle soup, but serves all manner of excellent, cheap Vietnamese food. At the shared outside tables in the grassy courtyard, you can also order good Italian dishes from the neighbouring restaurant. Daily 8am–9pm.

Ratana's Kitchen 320–322 Th Tha Pae. A favourite among locals both for northern specialities, such as *kaeng hang lay* and *khao soi*, and for tasty Western breakfasts, sandwiches and steaks, all at good prices (B50–150). Daily 7.30am–11.30pm.

Riverside Restaurant 9 Th Charoenrat ☎ 053 243239. Candlelit terraces by the water and an often heaving, lively bar for gigs, and, on the other side of the road, a spacious complex of rooms, terraces and a stage. Various soloists and bands perform nightly on the two stages, with the tempo increasing as the night wears on. Long, high-quality menu of Western, Thai and northern Thai food and drinks on offer (*tom yam kung* B160). For an extra B150, you can eat on their boat, which cruises up the Ping River each evening at 8pm (boarding 7.15pm). Daily 10am–1am.

10

BARS

Chiang Mai has a huge number of bars, most of which serve food; *Riverside* (see opposite) is also a great place just for a drink. There's a clutch of hostess bars along Th Loi Khro, but the town generally avoids Bangkok's sexual excesses.

The Drunken Flower Soi 17, Th Nimmanhaemin. Laidback and congenial, this quirky venue is a favourite among twenty-somethings, both Thai and *farang*. Reasonable prices for drink and an eclectic range of background music. Tues–Sun 5pm–midnight.

Jack Van Bar Th Chaiyapoom. Favourite late-late hang-out, where you sit at outdoor tables on a large forecourt and order up mean cocktails from a Jack Daniels-sponsored camper van. Hours are temperamental: usually around 10pm–very late.

Warm-Up Th Nimmanhemin. Hugely popular bar-club hosting both DJs and live bands, where girls in short skirts dance around their handbags to pulsating techno beats. Either chill out at the tables out front or tackle the madness of the masses within. Daily 6pm–2am.

SHOPPING

Chiang Mai is a shopper's paradise, selling everything from touristy slogan T-shirts to unique hill-tribe handicrafts. It's worth shopping around as quality and prices vary, and don't forget to haggle in the night market, but be prepared to pay out for quality handmade products.

BOOKS

Backstreet Books Th Chang Moi Kao (just off Th Tha Pae). The main, equally well-stocked rival to Gecko Books, right next door.

Gecko Books 2/6 Th Chang Moi Kao (just off Th Tha Pae). Sells a huge range of secondhand books in a well-organized display.

Suriwong 54/1 Th Sri Dornchai. The best place for new books, and also sells maps.

CRAFTS AND FABRICS

The road to San Kamphaeng, which extends due east for 13km from the end of Th Charoen Muang, is lined with craft shops and factories, including silverware, lacquerware, ceramics, woodcarving and jade. The biggest concentrations are at Bo Sang, the "umbrella village", 9km from town, and at San Kamphaeng itself, dedicated chiefly to silk-weaving. Frequent white songthaews to San Kamphaeng leave Chiang Mai from the central Lamyai market. In Chiang Mai itself, the biggest selections of local crafts are at the Night Bazaar and the Walking Streets. There are several stylish outlets for clothes and interior design around Sop Moei Arts on Th Charoenrat, and at the northern end of Th Nimmanhaemin around Soi 1.

Kritiya 46 Th Khwang Men. In the atmospheric lanes to the south of Warorot Market, this small shop is probably the best place in town to buy bolts of high-quality local silk at competitive prices. Closed Sun.

Sop Moei Arts 150/10 Th Charoenrat ⓦsopmoeiarts.com. Gorgeous fabrics – scarves, wall-hangings, bags and cushion covers – and stylish basketware, with part of the profits going back to the Karen refugee camp where they're made.

Thai Tribal Crafts (Fair Trade Shop) 25/9 Th Moon-muang, near Th Ratchamanka. Non-profit shop with a wide range of products made by seven hill tribes, from bags and silverware to musical instruments. Closed Sun.

MARKETS

Chiang Mai Night Bazaar Spread expansively around the junction of Chang Klan and Loi Khro roads, this is the main shopper's playground, where bumper-to-bumper street stalls and shops sell just about anything produced in Chiang Mai. Highlights are the hill-tribe jewellery and bags, and buffalo-hide shadow puppets. Daily from 5pm.

Walking Streets Th Ratchdamnoen turns into a huge, pedestrianized market on Sunday evenings, spreading west from Tha Pae Gate as far as Wat Phra Singh; on offer are typical northern Thai items such as clothes and musical instruments, lots of cheap street food and music. There's a smaller version on Saturday night on Th Wualai.

Warorot Market Bustling daytime market selling food, cheap cotton, linen and ceramics; there's a pungent and colourful flower market on its east side.

DIRECTORY

Banks and exchange There are banks all over Chiang Mai, most of which offer exchange facilities and ATMs.

Consulates UK, 198 Th Bumrungrat (ⓣ053 263015); US, 387 Th Witchayanon (ⓣ053 107700).

Hospitals 24hr emergency service (and dentistry) at Lanna Hospital, 103 Superhighway (ⓣ053 999777, ⓦlanna-hospital.com), east of Th Chotana.

Immigration office 300m east of the airport (ⓣ053 201755–6).

Laundry Laundry is available at most guesthouses (around B35/kg) or at small shops and hairdressers across town.

Post office Probably the most convenient is on Th Samlarn near Wat Phra Singh (Mon–Fri 8.30am–4.30pm, Sat 9am–noon).

Tourist police They have a base at the end of Th Huai Kaeo at the start of the road up Doi Suthep, but in emergencies it's best to phone them on ⓣ1155.

LAMPANG

The north's second-largest town and an important transport hub, **LAMPANG**,

100km southeast of Chiang Mai, has a sedate, traditional charm and a few key attractions, such as temples and an elephant conservation centre.

The majority of the town is south of the river, which curls west to east; the clock tower is considered the central point, while Thanon Tipchang and Thanon Talat Kao run along the south bank just northeast of here. Lampang is unique in Thailand for its horse-drawn carriages, which act as charming, if bumpy, taxis (from B200 for a 3km ride).

Wat Phra Kaeo Don Tao

The imposing, Burmese-influenced **Wat Phra Kaeo Don Tao** on Thanon Phra Kaeo, northeast of the river, about 3km from the clock tower, is noteworthy for its bronze Mandalay Buddha, housed in a Burmese-style building with a high, gilded roof. From 1436 to 1468 it was the home for the Emerald Buddha, now housed in Bangkok at Wat Phra Kaeo (see p.711).

Wat Si Rong Muang

West of the clock tower on Thanon Takrao Noi, **Wat Si Rong Muang** is a Burmese-style temple built in 1905. Its wooden viharn has a beautifully tiered roof, and its interior is elaborately decorated with coloured glass in patterns of animals, flowers, leaves and guardian angels. The nine spires represent the nine families who donated generously for the building of the temple.

Wat Phra That Lampang Luang

It's also well worth heading 18km southwest of town to **Wat Phra That Lampang Luang**, a grand and well-preserved capsule of beautiful Lanna art and architecture. Its main, open-sided, wooden viharn is one of the oldest in Thailand, dating back to 1486, and features attractive nineteenth-century painted panels. To get here, take a blue songthaew from Thanon Robwiang and be sure to ask for Wat Phra That Lampang Luang (roughly hourly; 45min); or rent a motorbike from Pornpitak Tour, Th Thipchang, near the *Riverside* restaurant (B250/day).

Thai Elephant Conservation Centre

The **Thai Elephant Conservation Centre** (shows daily 10am, 11am & 1.30pm; bathing at 9.40am and 1.10pm; B200; ⓣ054 228034, ⓦthailandelephant.org), 30km northwest of Lampang on Highway 11 towards Chiang Mai, is the most authentic place to see elephants displaying their skills; it also cares for abandoned and sick elephants in its elephant hospital. The interpretive centre has exhibits on the history of the elephant in Thailand, elephant rides are available and there is a full-day package on offer combining a show, bathing your elephant and bareback riding with the chance to meet the staff and see the hospital, plus lunch (B4000). The centre is best visited en route between Chiang Mai and Lampang: any Chiang Mai-bound bus will drop you off on Highway 11 at the main entrance to the centre; from the gates there are regular shuttle buses to the elephant showground 2km away.

ARRIVAL AND INFORMATION

By plane Bangkok Airways runs flights from Bangkok's Suvarnabhumi Airport (3 daily; 1hr 30min). The airport is just south of town, and songthaews are on hand for the short ride to the centre (about B100).

By bus The bus station is around 1km southwest of the city, though many buses also stop on Th Phaholyothin in the centre. Shared yellow-and-green songthaews will drop you off at your destination (B20).

Destinations Bangkok (at least hourly; 8hr); Chiang Mai (every 30min; 1hr 30min); Chiang Rai (every 30min; 4hr); Mae Sot (2 daily; 4–5hr); Nan (9–11 daily; 4hr).

By train The train station is about 500m further west than the bus station, on Th Prasaanmaitri, and is also served by shared songthaews (B20).

Destinations Bangkok (6 daily; 10–12hr); Chiang Mai (7 daily; 2–3hr).

Information There's a small tourist information centre (Mon–Fri 9am–5pm, plus Sat in high season 10am–4pm; ⓣ054 237229 ⓦlampangcity.go.th), just west of the clocktower, next to the fire station on Th Takrao Noi.

ACCOMMODATION AND EATING

The stretch of Th Takrao Noi west of the clocktower is lively after dark, featuring many simple restaurants and the Atsawin night market running off it to the south, as well as pubs and karaoke bars. On Saturday and Sunday evenings, Th Talat Kao comes to life as a "walking street", similar to

though not as interesting as those in Chiang Mai, with food and crafts for sale.

★**Aroy One Baht** Th Tipchang ☎ 089 700 9444. Cheap eats in a nice old wooden house staffed by happy young Thais. The spicy snakehead fish soup, served in coconut milk, is a bargain at B40. Highly recommended. Daily 4pm–midnight.

Grandma's Café Th Tipchang. Central coffee hangout for artsy young Lampangers, which serves good espresso and simple dishes (fried rice B35). Mon–Sat 10am–7pm.

R Lampang Th Talat Kao, just east of *Riverside Guest House* ☎ 054 225278, ⓦ r-lampang.com. Part guesthouse, part doll's house, with shades of green and pink providing the backdrop for a weird and wonderful collection of curios. Occupying a prime spot on the riverfront, its cheapest offerings are small fan rooms with mattresses on the floor. Bicycles for rent. Double **B350**

Riverside Guest House 286 Th Talat Kao ☎ 054 227005, ⓦ theriverside-lampang.com. Traditional garden compound of elegant, mostly en-suite rooms in two teak houses; the helpful owner also rents out bikes and motorbikes. Double **B350**

Riverside Restaurant 328 Th Tipchang. This relaxing bar-restaurant-bakery on rustic wooden terraces overlooking the water offers a wide variety of excellent Thai dishes, including northern specialities (from B70) and Western food, live music, and fresh pizzas Tues, Thurs, Sat & Sun evenings. Daily 11am–midnight.

NAN

Ringed by high mountains, the small but prosperous provincial capital of **NAN**, 225km northeast of Lampang, rests on the grassy west bank of the Wang River. Few visitors make it out this far, but it's a likeable place with a thriving handicraft tradition, a good museum and some superb temple murals at Wat Phumin.

The National Museum

The best place to start a tour of Nan is at the **National Museum**, just off Thanon Phakong in the southwest part of town (Wed–Sun 9am–4pm; B100), which occupies the century-old palace of the former lords of Nan with its superb teak floors. Its informative, user-friendly displays give a bite-sized introduction to Nan, its history and its peoples, the prize exhibit being a talismanic elephant tusk with a bad case of brown tooth decay, which is claimed to be magic black ivory.

Wat Phumin

With a five-hundred-year-old cruciform building as its centrepiece, bisected by two giant nagas, **Wat Phumin**, a five-minute walk south of the museum down Thanon Phakong, will please even the most over-templed traveller. What really sets this temple apart are its murals, the bright, simple colours of which seem to jump off the walls of the bot. Executed in the late nineteenth century – though retouched in recent years – the paintings take you on a whirlwind tour of heaven, hell, the Buddha's previous incarnations, local legends and incidents from Nan's history, and include stacks of vivacious, sometimes bawdy, detail, which provides a valuable pictorial record of that era.

ARRIVAL AND DEPARTURE

By plane The airport is 2km northwest of town, served by Nok Air flights from Bangkok (3 daily; 1hr 40min) and Kan Airlines from Chiang Mai (2 weekly; 45min). A/c minibuses run between here and the *Dhevaraj Hotel*, in the centre of town.

By bus The bus station is in the southwest corner of town, off the main road to Phrae; songthaews to the centre cost B20.

Destinations Bangkok (10 daily; 12hr); Chiang Mai (9–11 daily; 6hr); Chiang Rai (daily; 6–7hr); Den Chai (on the Bangkok–Chiang Mai railway; hourly; 2hr 30min); Phitsanulok (5 daily; 6hr).

ACCOMMODATION AND EATING

When it comes to eating, there's a good night market, about 500m north of the museum on Th Phakong.

TOURS AROUND NAN

★**Fhu Travel** 453/4 Th Sumondhevaraj ☎ 054 710636, ⓦ fhutravel.com. Owner Fhu and his wife can organize two- to three-day treks (around B3700/person, based on two sharing) which head west, through tough terrain of thick jungle and high mountains, visiting Mrabri, Htin, Hmong and Mien villages. Other options include cycling tours around town, one- or two-day whitewater-rafting excursions, kayaking, and trips to Luang Prabang in Laos, via the border crossing at Huai Kon in the north of Nan province, which is open to foreigners.

10

Poom 3 Around the corner from the night market on Th Anantaworarichides. Simple streetside restaurant serving excellent, inexpensive Thai and Chinese food. Daily 5pm–late.

SP Guest House On a narrow alley off the main street, Th Sumondhevaraj ⓣ054 774897. Among a handful of cheap places in the centre, this is the pick of the bunch. It's well maintained, friendly and quiet, and has spacious rooms, all with hot-water bathrooms. The owners are extremely helpful, and there's internet and wi-fi, too. Double B400

10

DOI INTHANON NATIONAL PARK

Covering a huge area to the southwest of Chiang Mai, **Doi Inthanon National Park** (B200, plus B20–30 per vehicle), with its hill-tribe villages, dramatic waterfalls and fine panoramas, is a popular destination for naturalists and trekkers. The park supports about 380 bird species and, near the summit of Doi Inthanon itself, the highest mountain in Thailand, the only red rhododendrons in the country (in bloom Dec–Feb). Night-time temperatures occasionally drop below freezing, so bring warm clothing. The park is best explored as a day-trip from Chiang Mai using private transport, but set out early because there's a lot to see and the distances are deceptive.

WHAT TO SEE AND DO

Three sets of **waterfalls** provide the main roadside attractions on the way to the park headquarters: overrated and overcrowded Mae Klang Falls, 8km from Chom Thong; Vachiratharn Falls, a long misty drop 11km beyond; and the twin cascades of Siriphum Falls, behind the park headquarters. The more beautiful **Mae Ya Falls**, believed to be the highest in Thailand, are accessed by a road that heads west off the main park road 3km north of Chom Thong.

Beyond headquarters, the paved road to Mae Chaem skirts yet more waterfalls: 7km after the turn-off from the summit road, look for a steep, unpaved road to the right, leading down to a ranger station and, just to the east, the dramatic long drop of **Huai Sai Luaeng Falls**. A circular 2.5km **walking trail** from the ranger station takes in some smaller waterfalls, such as Mae Pan Falls.

For the most spectacular views in the park, head for the twin chedis on the summit road. Just above the chedis lies the trailhead of **Kew Mae Pan Trail**, an easy two-hour circular walk (closed June–Oct) through beautiful forest and savanna – home of the red rhododendrons – around the steep, western edge of **Doi Inthanon**; you need to hire a guide at the trailhead (B200/guide). Doi Inthanon's summit (2565m), 6km beyond the chedis, is a disappointment.

ARRIVAL AND INFORMATION

By private transport The best way to access Doi Inthanon is by using private transport rented in Chiang Mai; the roads, though winding, are well paved and the views are stunning.

By bus and songthaew If you want to use public transport, however, you'll need to get to the village of Chom Thong, 58km southwest of Chiang Mai on Highway 108. Frequent buses run from Chang Puak bus station, via Chiang Mai Gate, in Chiang Mai to Chom Thong, from where you can catch a songthaew towards Mae Chaem through the park, leaving you to hitch the last 10km to the summit, or you can charter a whole songthaew from Chom Thong's temple (from B1000 round trip). The main road through the park leaves Highway 108 1km north of Chong Thong, winding northwestwards for 48km to the top of Doi Inthanon.

Information The park's visitor centre is 9km up the main park road from Chom Thong, while the park headquarters are 22km further on. Both sell park maps.

ACCOMMODATION AND EATING

You can stay in the national park bungalows (ⓣ053 286728–9, ⓦdnp.go.th; from B1000) near the headquarters, or camp near the headquarters and at Huai Sai Luaeng Falls (B30/person). Two- to three-person tents (B225, bedding extra) can be rented at the headquarters. Food stalls operate at Mae Klang, Vachiratharn and Mae Ya Falls (daytime only) and at the park headquarters, and there's a daytime canteen by the twin chedis.

MAE HONG SON AND AROUND

Set deep in a mountain valley, **MAE HONG SON** is often billed as the "Switzerland of Thailand", and has enjoyed a boost in tourism due in part to the zoo-like villages of "long-necked" Padaung women nearby. Most travellers come here to trek in the beautiful countryside and cool climate, but crowds are also drawn

here over the first weekend in April for the spectacular parades of the **Poy Sang Long Festival**, which celebrates local Thai Yai/Shan boys' temporary ordination into the monkhood.

WHAT TO SEE AND DO

Mae Hong Son's main Thanon Khunlumprapas, lined with shops and businesses, runs north–south and is intersected by Singhanat Bamrung at the traffic lights in the centre of town.

To the southeast of the traffic lights, the town's classic picture-postcard view is of its twin nineteenth-century Burmese-style temples, **Wat Chong Kham** and **Wat Chong Klang**, from the opposite bank of Jong Kham Lake. The latter temple is famous for its paintings on glass, depicting stories from the lives of the Buddha.

The town's vibrant, smelly **morning market** is a magnet for hill-tribe traders and worth getting up at dawn for. Next door, the many-gabled viharn of **Wat Hua Wiang** shelters the beautiful bronze Burmese-style Buddha image, Chao Palakeng. For a godlike overview of the area, especially at sunset, climb up to **Wat Doi Kong Mu** on the steep hill to the west.

Local treks

Trekking up and down Mae Hong Son's steep inclines is tough, but the hill-tribe villages are generally unspoilt and the scenery is magnificent. To the west, trekking routes tend to snake along the Burmese border and can sometimes get a little crowded; the villages to the east are more traditional. Plenty of guesthouses and travel agencies run treks out of Mae Hong Son (see below).

Pha Sua Falls and Mae Aw

North of Mae Hong Son, a trip to **Pha Sua Falls** and the border village of Mae Aw takes in some spectacular and varied countryside, best visited by motorbike (around B200/day from guesthouses) or on a tour (around B900–1200/person). Head north for 17km on Highway 1095 (ignore the first signpost for Pha Sua, after 10km) and then, after a long, steep descent, turn left onto a side road, paved at first, which passes through the village of Ban Bok Shampae. About 9km from the turn-off, you'll reach the wild, untidy Pha Sua Falls; take care when swimming, as several people have been swept to their deaths here.

Above the falls, the paved road climbs 11km to the village of Naphapak, from where it's another 7km to **Mae Aw** (aka Ban Ruk Thai), a settlement of Kuomintang (anti-communist Chinese) refugees. It's the highest point on the Burmese border that visitors can reach, and provides a fascinating window on Kuomintang life. Bright-green tea bushes line the slopes, and Chinese ponies wander the streets of long bamboo houses. In the marketplace on the north side of the village reservoir, shops sell Oolong and Chian Chian tea, and dried mushrooms.

ARRIVAL AND DEPARTURE

By plane Mae Hong Son airport is towards the northeast of town. Nok Air and Kan Airlines run direct flights to and from Chiang Mai (6 daily; 35min). From the airport terminal tuk-tuks (about B80) run into the centre.

By bus and minibus Buses to Mae Hong Son depart from Chiang Mai's Arcade bus station, travelling via Mae Sariang or Pai. To meet tourist demand, there are also hourly a/c minibuses between Pai's bus station and Mae Hong Son. Minibuses go past the Khunlumprapas–Singhanat Bamrung crossroads, so ask the driver to stop there if you're staying in town. From the bus station, south of the centre, tuk-tuks (about B80) run into the centre.

Destinations Bangkok (3 daily; 16hr); Chiang Mai via Mae Sariang (5 daily; 8–9hr); Chiang Mai via Pai (1 daily; 8hr); Pai (hourly; 3hr).

INFORMATION AND TOURS

Information TAT, Th Ratchathumpitak, towards the northeast of the city centre (daily 8.30am–4.30pm; ⓣ 053 612982–3, ⓔ tatmhs@tat.or.th).

Tour operators There are more than thirty registered tour agencies in Mae Hong Son, each of which can arrange local treks. Day tours might include elephant riding and boating or bamboo rafting on the babbling Pai River. Rose Garden Tours at 86/4 Th Khunlumprapas (ⓣ 053 611681, ⓦ rosegarden-tours.com) has day-long excursions starting from B900. For treks and tours, try *Sunflower Café* (see p.758) or Tour Merng Tai at 89 Th Khunlumprapas (ⓣ 053 611979, ⓦ tourmerngtai.com), which offers community-based tourism programmes including homestays, employing village guides and cooks and contributing part of the profits to local communities.

10

ACCOMMODATION

Friend House 20 Th Praditjongkham ⓣ053 620119. Decent, clean, teak-and-concrete house at the northwest corner of the lake, where the cheapest rooms have shared hot-water bathrooms and mattresses on the floor. Double **B200**

Jonnie House 5/1 Th U-Domchaonitesh ⓣ053 611667. In a small compound on the north side of the lake, this clean, friendly place has airy rooms, sharing hot showers, in a nice, old, wooden house, as well as bright, concrete affairs with en-suite hot-water bathrooms. Double **B200**

Romtai House 22 Th Chamnansathit ⓣ053 612437, ⓦmaehongson-romtai.com. Southeast of the lake, beyond the twin temples, this tranquil place offers a wide choice of spacious, well-kept rooms and bungalows with hot showers, set around a rambling garden. Double **B400**

EATING AND DRINKING

Fern 87 Th Khunlumprapas, south of the central traffic lights. Justly popular restaurant, with a nice terrace and a good reputation for its varied Thai and Western food (from B80). Daily 10.30am–10pm.

★**Salween River** 23 Th Praditjongkham ⓣ053 613421, ⓦsalweenriver.com. English- and Thai-run restaurant and bar, on the west side of the lake, with wi-fi and a book exchange. There's a big selection of Western grub (main dishes from B100), plus Thai and Burmese dishes including a delicious green tea salad (B40). Daily 8am–10pm.

Sunflower Café Th Praditjongkham ⓣ089 950 1798. A good place for breakfast, lunch, dinner or just a drink, on a terrace overlooking the west side of the lake. Espresso coffees, home-made bread and pizzas, and some tasty Thai dishes (around B80). Daily 8am–10pm.

PAI

Once just a stopover on the tiring journey to Mae Hong Son, **PAI**, set in a broad, lush, upland valley 135km from Chiang Mai, is now a major tourist hub. It has retained some of the laidback, New Age feel that draws certain travellers in for weeks, but has also become a honeypot for Thai tourists. There's all manner of **outdoor activities** to tempt you, plus courses and therapies – including retail therapy at the art studios, leather and jewellery shops. It's very pleasant to stroll through the stalls that set up along the "walking street" of Thanon Chaisongkhram every evening.

WHAT TO SEE AND DO

Pai itself is a cute but rambling town. Most points of interest lie west of the Pai River, although the most tranquil guesthouses are east of the river.

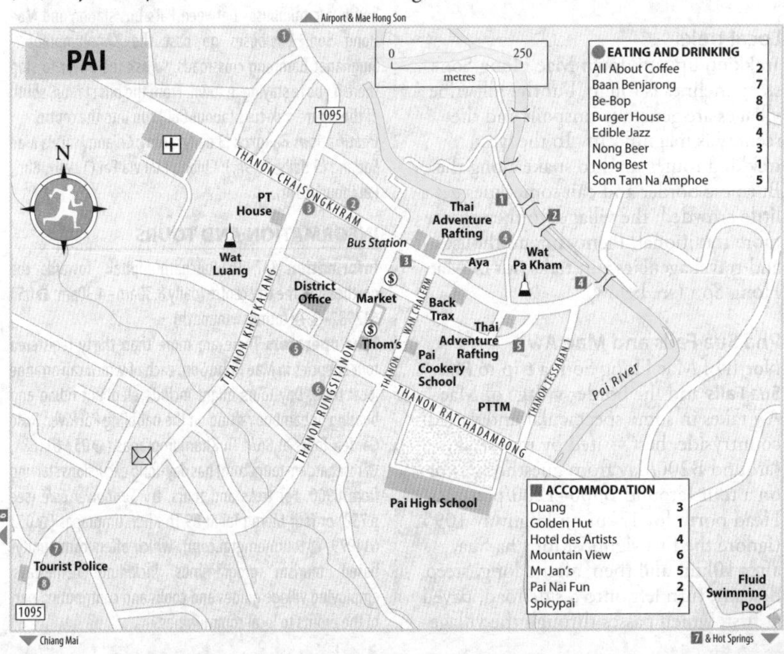

Swimming and hot springs

On the east side of town is Fluid, a large open-air **swimming pool** with a gym, restaurant and free wi-fi (daily 9am–sunset; B60; fluidswimmingpool.com). About 7km southeast of town, down the minor road beyond the swimming pool, the **hot springs** (200B) aren't up to much, but nearby spas put the piped hot water to much better use. *Pai Hotsprings Spa Resort* (053 065748, paihotspringssparesort .com), down a side road about 1km north of the springs, has a large pool (B100) and offers massages and other treatments.

Trekking, elephants and rafting

Pai is a centre both for undemanding valley walks and for **trekking** (around B800/day, plus extra for rafting and elephant-riding) through varied terrain to Karen, Lisu and Lahu villages. These can be arranged either through guesthouses such as *Duang* or via Back Trax at 17 Thanon Chaisongkhram (053 699739, backtraxinpai@yahoo .com). Among several **elephant camps** about 5km south of town on the hot springs road, Thom's maintains an office in town on Th Runsiyanon (053 065778, thomelephant.com). Here you can arrange rides that include going into the river with the elephants, as well as one-day mahout training courses. From early June to early February you can take an impressive two-day **rubber-raft trip** down the Pai River to Mae Hong Son with Thai Adventure Rafting, Thanon Rungsiyanon(053 699111, thairafting .com; B2900), who also run treks and mountain-biking trips. Agencies in town can also arrange bamboo-rafting, kayaking and tubing on the Pai River.

ARRIVAL AND DEPARTURE

By plane Domestic airline Kan Airlines (kanairlines .com) flies to Pai from Chiang Mai (3 weekly; 25min), landing at the airstrip on the north side of town.

By bus and minibus There's now only one bus a day (non-a/c) between Chiang Mai and Mae Hong Son via Pai. A/c minibuses cover the route at least hourly, through either Prempracha at the bus station or Aya, a nearby travel agent which also organizes minibuses to Chiang Khong, Chiang Rai and Mae Sai.

Destinations Chiang Mai (hourly; 3–4hr); Mae Hong Son (hourly; 3–4hr).

COURSES

Cookery classes Pai Cookery School, Th Wan Chalerm (081 706 3799), holds Thai cooking courses of two hours (B500), four hours (B750) or up to three days, including a trip to the market to learn about ingredients; vegetarians catered for.

Massage and massage courses Mr Jan's is famous for its Thai and Burmese/Shan massages (from B150/hr; see below). Pai Traditional Thai Massage on Th Wangtai (PTTM; 053 699121) teaches a three-day massage course (B2500) and gives excellent massages (B180/1hr).

ACCOMMODATION

Duang 5 Th Rungsiyanon 053 699101. Opposite the bus station, this is a clean and reliable place to stay, with hot showers throughout, whether shared or en suite, though it all feels a little cramped. Double **B200**

Golden Hut North of Edible Jazz, next to the river 053 699949. Very cheap bamboo fan rooms with shared hot showers, in a quiet garden set back from the river, or riverside bungalows on stilts. Double **B200**

Mountain View 500m up a side road by the tourist police at the south end of town 086 180 5998, themountain viewpai.com. Laidback resort of wood and woven bamboo bungalows, most with private bathrooms, on ten acres of land. Free pick-ups if you call, and free access to Fluid swimming pool (see above). Double **B160**

Mr Jan's 3 Th Sukhaphibun 053 699554. In a mess of alleys behind Th Chaisongkhram, *Mr Jan's* offers quiet, double rooms with hot showers set in a medicinal herb garden. Double **B250**

Pai Nai Fun 081 641 5493, painaifun.com. Meaning "Pai in a Dream", this spot has prime position among several resorts with bamboo bathing platforms that line the east bank of the river here. The cheapest rooms are

★TREAT YOURSELF

Hotel des Artists (Rose of Pai)
Th Chaisongkhram 053 699539, hotelartists.com. On a corner plot near the river and centred around an attractive glass-sided living room, this stylish new hotel has just fourteen bedrooms, the best of which have fantastic terraces that face out across the water. In the spacious rooms, bell-shaped lanterns illuminate the beds (which are raised off the ground on platforms made from local wood) while facilities include a/c, TVs, DVD players, minibars and artfully tiled en-suite bathrooms. Rates, which include breakfast, are significantly lower between April and mid-October. Double **B3600**

simple, thatched, bamboo A-frames sharing hot showers in the scrappy garden at the back (you'll have to fork out B900 for an A-frame on the riverbank). Double **B200**

★**Spicypai** Around 700m east of the bridge; keep right at the junctions you pass along the way and then follow the signs to the hostel ⓣ 085 715 9627, ⓦ spicyhostels.com. Ultra-cheap and ultra-sociable dorm beds with mosquito nets in a series of lofty, thatched, bamboo huts surrounded by vivid green paddy fields. Breakfast, hot showers and wi-fi included. Dorm **B150**

10

EATING AND DRINKING

Because of the thriving international expat community in Pai it's easy to get food from all over the world, including Mexican, German and French. Pai is no Khao San Rd, however; its nightlife scene is more laidback and music-oriented, so don't expect too much drunken revelry.

All About Coffee Th Chaisongkhram. A tantalizing array of coffee (from B45) and cakes in an atmospheric art gallery/café. Daily 8am–5pm.

Baan Benjarong Th Rungsiyanon, to the south of town. An understandably popular restaurant that serves some of the best Thai food in town, on a varied and imaginative menu (dishes around B100). Daily 11am–1.30pm & from 5pm until they get "tired", about 7.30pm.

Be-Bop Th Rungsiyanon, at the south end of town. A popular travellers' bar that hosts live jazz, funk, blues and rock in the evenings (from about 10pm). Open mike Wed. Daily 8pm–1am.

Burger House Th Rungsiyanon. Tasty burgers using imported beef, plus breakfasts and other Western dishes. For something different, try the delicious chicken and avocado burger (B89). Daily 8.30am–9pm.

★**Edible Jazz** Just off Th Chaisongkhram near Wat Pa Kham. This ramshackle and laid-way-back garden café-bar on a quiet, leafy lane is a mellow spot for a cheap beer (B50). It offers an acoustic set roughly 8.30–10.30pm and an open mike night on Sun. Daily roughly noon–midnight.

Nong Beer Cnr Chaisongkhram and Khetkalang. One of Pai's longest-standing and most popular places for cheap eats, dishing up great *khao soi* (northern curry noodle soup; B40), pork satay and a wide array of buffet stir-fries and curries. Daily 8am–10pm.

Nong Best Th Khetkalang, just south of *Pai Flora Resort*. Bare-bones restaurant with an open streetside kitchen that's very popular with locals, and you can taste why – excellent pork with basil and chillies (B50) and crispy pork with snow peas (B60). Daily 9am–9pm.

Som Tam Na Amphoe Th Ratchadamrong ⓣ 053 698087. The papaya salad here (B30) is a must-eat for Thai visitors to Pai, served with grilled chicken (B70), or available in the Khorat version, *tam sua*, with rice noodles and crab (B60). The sign's in Thai, but includes the phone number. Daily 10am–4.30pm.

DIRECTORY

Banks There are a few banks dotted along Th Chaisongkhram and Th Rungsiyanon with ATM and exchange facilities.

Bicycles These can be rented from PT House on Th Khetkalang (B50/day).

Internet There are several shops near the intersection of Th Rungsiyanon and Th Ratchadamrong.

Local info The free, monthly, English-language *Pai Events Planner* has news about what's on.

Motorbikes These can be rented from Aya Service on Th Chaisongkhram (ⓣ 053 699940; B100/day).

Post office At the southern end of Th Khetkalang.

Tourist police South end of town on the road to Chiang Mai (ⓣ 1155).

THA TON AND THE KOK RIVER

Leafy **THA TON**, 176km north of Chiang Mai, sits clustered either side of the **Kok River**, which flows out of Myanmar, 4km upstream. The main attractions here are boat and raft rides, which offer a novel way of getting to Chiang Rai. There are also magnificent panoramic views of the river and the surrounding landscape from the top of the hill on the west bank where you'll find **Wat Tha Ton**, with its over-the-top ornamental gardens and colossal Buddha statue.

Travelling down the 100km stretch of the Kok River to Chiang Rai gives you the chance to soak up a rich diversity of typical northern landscapes, through rice fields and orchards, past riverside wats and over rapids. Noisy, canopied longtail boats leave from the south side of the bridge in Tha Ton every day at 12.30pm for the four-hour trip (B350). Return boats from Chiang Rai leave at 10.30am (ⓣ 053 750009). If you have more time, choose the peaceful bamboo rafts, which glide downriver to Chiang Rai in two or three days. These can be organized via *Garden Home Nature Resort* (B7000/raft for 2 days, B8500 for 3 days, for 2 people, including food and soft drinks), visiting hill-tribe villages and the hot springs on the way.

ARRIVAL AND DEPARTURE

By bus Regular buses (roughly every 2hr) between Chiang Mai's Chang Phuak bus station and Tha Ton take about four hours. Otherwise, take one of the more

frequent buses or a/c minibuses to Fang and change onto a yellow songthaew for the last 40min to Tha Ton.

ACCOMMODATION

Garden Home Nature Resort 300m north of the bridge on the east bank of the river ⓣ 053 373015, ⓦ thatonaccommodation.com. By far the best accommodation option in town is *Garden Home Nature Resort*, with attractive bungalows and rooms, all with en-suite hot showers, in a lychee orchard. They also rent out motorbikes. Double B200

CHIANG RAI

CHIANG RAI lives in the shadow of the local capital, Chiang Mai, but offers a good choice of accommodation, some splendid temples and a variety of treks and tours in the surrounding countryside.

WHAT TO SEE AND DO

Sprawled untidily over the south bank of the Kok River, the town's main daytime focus is the bustling market on Thanon Tanalai, where you can watch elaborately dressed tribal people selling their wares.

Doi Tong

A walk up to **Doi Tong**, the hill to the northwest of the centre, offers a fine view up the Kok River. On the highest part of the hill stands a kind of phallic Stonehenge centred on the town's new **Lak Muang** (the city pillar) representing the Buddhist layout of the universe. The old wooden Lak Muang can be seen in the viharn of **Wat Phra That Doi Tong**, the city's first temple, which sprawls shambolically over the eastern side of the hill.

10

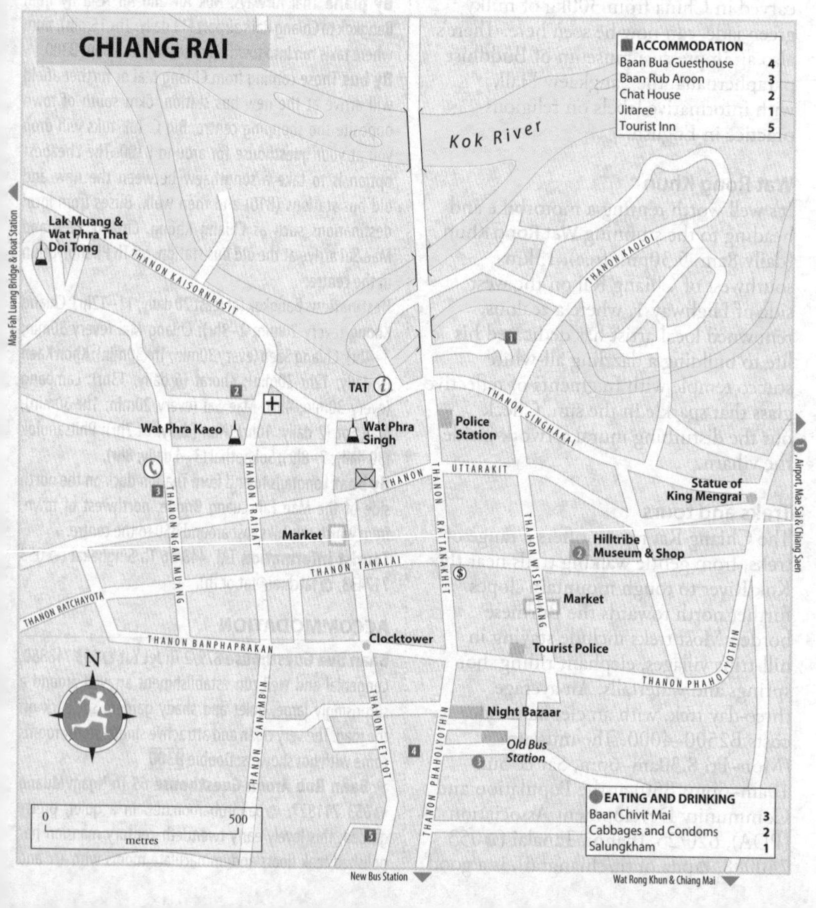

AKHA HILL HOUSE

An authentic and rewarding way of spending time in a hill-tribe village is offered by the *Akha Hill House* (☎ 089 997 5505, akhahill.com; B250), situated just 23km from Chiang Rai (with free pick-up) among stunning mountain scenery and within walking distance of waterfalls, hot springs and other hill-tribe villages. There's a wide variety of bamboo, wooden and adobe-style bungalows, most with view-filled balconies and some with charming open-air bathrooms; all have access to hot showers, whether en suite or shared. From here you can either trek independently or take an organized tour. It's also possible to get here from the Tha Ton–Chiang Rai boat (see below), disembarking at the hot springs on the south bank of the river near Huai Kaeo waterfall and walking for 3km.

Wat Phra Kaeo

The Emerald Buddha, Thailand's most important image (now housed in Bangkok; see p.711), resided at **Wat Phra Kaeo** on Thanon Trairat for 44 years from 1390. A beautiful replica, millimetres smaller than the actual statue, which was carved in China from 300kg of milky green jade, can now be seen here. There's also an impressive museum of Buddhist paraphernalia, the Sangkaew Hall, with informative labels on religious practice in English.

Wat Rong Khun

It's well worth renting a motorbike and heading to the stunning **Wat Rong Khun** (daily 8am–5.30pm; free), 13km southwest of Chiang Rai on the west side of Highway 1, where a zealous, renowned local artist has dedicated his life to building a dazzling all-white stucco temple with fragments of reflective glass that sparkle in the sun. Check out the disturbing mural artwork inside the viharn.

Treks and tours

The Chiang Rai region offers a range of **treks**, from gentle walking trails near the Kok River to tough mountain slopes further north towards the Burmese border. Most treks include staying in hill-tribe villages, elephant riding, hot springs and waterfalls. An average three-day trek, with an elephant ride, costs B2500–4000. The museum (Mon–Fri 8.30am–6pm, Sat & Sun 10am–6pm; B50) at the Population and Community Development Association (PDA), 620/25 Thanon Tanalai (☎ 053 740088, pda.or.th/chiangrai), is a good place to find out about the local hill tribes before going on a trek; there's a non-profit-making handicrafts shop here, too. The PDA also offers treks and tours, as does *Chat House* (see opposite).

ARRIVAL AND INFORMATION

By plane Thai Airways, Nok Air and Air Asia fly from Bangkok to Chiang Rai's airport (11 daily; 1hr 15min), from where taxis run into town (8km south), for about B300.

By bus Those coming from Chiang Mai or further afield will arrive at the new bus station, 6km south of town opposite the shopping centre, Big C. Tuk-tuks will drop you at your guesthouse for around B100. The cheapest option is to take a songthaew between the new and old bus stations (B10) and then walk. Buses from local destinations such as Chiang Khong, Chiang Saen and Mae Sai arrive at the old bus station, off Th Phaholyothin in the centre.

Destinations Bangkok (at least 20 daily; 11–12hr); Chiang Khong (every 20min; 2–3hr); Chiang Mai (every 30min; 3–4hr); Chiang Saen (every 30min; 1hr 30min); Khon Kaen (6 daily; 12hr 30min); Khorat (6 daily; 13hr); Lampang (every 30min; 4hr); Mae Sai (every 20min; 1hr 30min); Mae Sot (2 daily; 10hr); Nan (daily; 6–7hr); Phitsanulok (30 daily; 7–8hr); Sukhothai (3–4 daily; 8hr).

By boat Longtails to and from Tha Ton dock on the north side of the Mae Fah Luang Bridge, northwest of town, from which tuk-tuks cost around B50 to the centre.

Tourist information TAT, 448/16 Th Singhakai (☎ 053 717433, tatchrai@tat.or.th).

ACCOMMODATION

Baan Bua Guesthouse 879/2 Th Jet Yot ☎ 053 718880. Congenial and well-run establishment arrayed around a surprisingly large, quiet and shady garden, set back off the road. The very clean and attractive single-storey rooms come with hot showers. Double **B300**

★ **Baan Rub Aroon Guesthouse** 65 Th Ngam Muang ☎ 053 711827, baanrubaroon.net. In a quiet, pretty garden, this lovely early twentieth-century mansion has polished teak floors and immaculate rooms with a/c and

shared hot showers. Breakfast included. Dorm B300, double B550

Chat House 3/2 Soi Sangkaew, Th Trairat ☎053 711481, chatguesthouse.com. Behind its own garden café-bakery on a quiet soi, Chiang Rai's longest-running travellers' hangout has a laidback atmosphere and fantastic staff. The cheaper rooms are in an old, mostly wooden house with shared hot showers. Dorm B100, double B200

Jitaree 246/3 Soi Santirat, Th Singhaklai ☎053 719348. Welcoming place offering big, clean rooms with hot showers in a concrete block with hanging plants, set around a large courtyard. Double B300

Tourist Inn 1004/4–6 Th Jet Yot ☎053 752094, touristinnhotel.com. Clean guesthouse with its own European-style bakery, serving good breakfasts, and rooms with hot-water bathrooms, both shared and private. Free wi-fi in the main building. Double B200

EATING AND DRINKING

There's a wide selection of food stalls in the night bazaar off Th Phaholyothin selling everything from roasted crickets to *tom yam kung*. You need never go without a good coffee fix in Chiang Rai: the stuff grown on the nearby mountains of Doi Wawee, Doi Chaang and Doi Salong is served up at eponymous cafés around the main Rattanakhet–Phaholyothin junction.

Baan Chivit Mai 172 Th Prasobsuk, opposite the old bus station baanchivitmai.com. Bakery run by a Swedish charity that helps children in Chiang Rai and Bangkok slums. Very clean a/c café, serving excellent sandwiches, cakes (chocolate cake B45) and coffees, plus pastas and simple Thai dishes. Internet access. Mon–Sat 8am–8.30pm.

Cabbages and Condoms 620/25 Th Tanalai. Proclaiming "our food is guaranteed not to cause pregnancy", this popular restaurant run by the Population and Community Development Association serves traditional northern and veggie dishes (B70–200) and hosts regular live music. Daily 10am–midnight.

Salungkham 834/3 Th Phaholyothin, between King Mengrai's statue and the river ☎053 717192. By far the best Thai and northern Thai food in town (mains from B80), with a garden for evening dining; try the superb banana-flower salad with fresh prawns. There's no sign in English, but look out for the Cosmo petrol station opposite. Daily 10.30am–10pm.

DIRECTORY

Cooking classes *Chat House* runs one-day cookery classes (B950) including transfers from your accommodation and a trip to the local market.

Motorbike and bicycle rental Guesthouses rent out motorbikes (around B200/day) and bicycles (B70–100).

Tourist police Th Phaholyothin (☎1155).

MAE SAI

MAE SAI, with its bustling border crossing, is Thailand's northernmost town, 61km from Chiang Rai. Thanon Phaholyothin is the town's single north–south street, which ends at a pedestrianized bridge over the Mae Sai River, the frontier with Myanmar.

It's possible to make a day-trip across to **Tachileik** in Myanmar (6am–6pm; note that Myanmar is 30min behind Thailand), though the frontier is occasionally closed during disputes. Thai immigration on the bridge will exit-stamp your passport; on the Burmese side it costs B500 or US$10 for a one-day stay. On return to Thailand you'll automatically be given a new fifteen-day visa (thirty days for British, US and Canadian citizens).

ARRIVAL AND INFORMATION

By bus Buses to Mae Sai stop 4km south of the frontier at the bus station, from where frequent songthaews (B20) run into town.

Information There's a tourist police booth (☎1155) at the frontier bridge.

ACCOMMODATION

Yeesun Guest House ☎053 733455. There's no reason to stay in Mae Sai; if you get stuck, head for *Yeesun Guest House*, which offers a/c rooms with hot showers a 5min walk west of the frontier bridge on the riverbank. Double B500

SOP RUAK

For the benefit of tourists, the "**Golden Triangle**" (see box, p.765) has been artificially concentrated into the precise spot where the Thai, Lao and Burmese borders meet, at the confluence of the Ruak and Mekong rivers, 70km northeast of Chiang Rai: **SOP RUAK**. Don't expect to run into sinister drug-runners, addicts or even poppy fields here – instead, you'll find souvenir stalls and much-photographed "Golden Triangle" signs. The ambitious **Hall of Opium**, about 2km out of the village towards Mae Sai (Tues–Sun 8.30am–5.30pm, last entry 4pm; B300), gives an imaginatively presented, balanced picture of the use and abuse of opium, and its history over

five thousand years. For uninterrupted views of the meeting of the rivers and of Myanmar and Laos beyond, climb up to **Wat Phra That Phu Khao**, a 1200-year-old temple perched on a small hill above the village.

ARRIVAL AND DEPARTURE

To get to Sop Ruak you'll have to go via Chiang Saen or Mae Sai first. From Chiang Saen, you have a choice of regular blue songthaew or rented bicycle (an easy 10km ride on a paved road). From Mae Sai, blue songthaews make the 45min trip from Th Phaholyothin, about 300m south of the bridge.

CHIANG SAEN

Combining the tumbledown ruins of an ancient trading post with sweeping Mekong River scenery, **CHIANG SAEN**, 60km northeast of Chiang Rai, makes a relaxing base camp for the border region east of Mae Sai. Armed with a Chinese visa, it should also be possible to move on from here to Jing Hong, by either cargo boat or irregular passenger boat – ask at *Gin's Guesthouse* (see below).

WHAT TO SEE AND DO

The informative **National Museum** on the main east–west street, Thanon Phaholyothin (Wed–Sun 9am–4pm; B100), houses some impressive, locally cast Buddha images and architectural features rescued from the ruins. Originally the town's main temple, **Wat Phra That Chedi Luang** next door is worth looking in on for its imposing, overgrown octagonal chedi, said to contain a relic of the Buddha's breastbone. Outside the town's ramparts just to the northwest, **Wat Pa Sak** (daily 8am–5pm; B50) is the most impressive of Chiang Saen's many temple ruins. Enshrining relics of the Buddha's right ankle, the central, square-based chedi owes its eclectic shape largely to the grand temples of Pagan in Myanmar and displays some beautiful carved stucco decoration.

ARRIVAL AND DEPARTURE

Buses from Chiang Rai and Chiang Mai and songthaews from Sop Ruak and Mae Sai stop just west of the T-junction of the main Th Phaholyothin and the river road. Songthaews from Chiang Khong stop on the river road to the south of the T-junction.

ACCOMMODATION AND EATING

At night, street stalls specializing in *suki* (Thai hot pot) set up on the illuminated riverfront north of the T-junction. Throughout the day, and in the evenings, a range of street stalls set up on Th Phaholyothin.

Gin's On the riverside road to Sop Ruak, 2km north of the T-junction ⓣ053 650847. Chiang Saen's best budget option by far, an attractive, helpful guesthouse, which also serves good food. Choose between A-frame bungalows in a lychee orchard and spacious rooms with polished wood floors in the main house, all en suite, most with hot

INTO LAOS AT CHIANG KHONG

Chiang Khong, 70km downriver from Chiang Saen, is the only crossing point into Laos in this part of Thailand. The journey from Chiang Saen is convoluted and time-consuming: green songthaews run when they're full and you usually have to change to a red songthaew halfway at the village of Ban Hat Bai. The journey can take up to four hours. Regular buses run to Chiang Khong from Chiang Rai (every 20min; 2–3hr), and there are direct a/c minibuses from Chiang Mai, available through travel agents, or from the bus station. Chiang Khong's best guesthouse is the helpful, easy-going *Ban Tam-Mi-La*, down a riverside lane off the main street 1km north of the bus station (ⓣ053 791234, ⓦbaantammila.com; B400; farm homestays also available). It has an excellent restaurant (daily 7am–7pm) with awesome views across into Laos.

Tourists cross the border via the new Fourth Thai-Lao Friendship Bridge, 8km downstream from Chiang Khong (daily 6am–10pm), where thirty-day **visas for Laos** (see p.345) are available on arrival. From the Lao town opposite Chiang Khong, Houayxai (see p.385), you can get passenger boats down the Mekong to Luang Prabang, and buses to elsewhere in northern Laos.

From Chiang Khong, catch a tuk-tuk to the bridge (B150–200; Ban Tam-Mi-La are currently offering free lifts once a day to guests, at 8.30am). Then there are shuttle buses across the bridge (B25/person), and songthaews on the Lao side to the piers for Luang Prabang boats (B60–100/person).

THE GOLDEN TRIANGLE

Opium growing has been illegal in Thailand since 1959, but during the 1960s and 70s, rampant production and refining of the crop in the lawless region on the borders of Thailand, Myanmar and Laos earned the area the nickname "the **Golden Triangle**". Two "armies" operated most of the trade within this area: the Shan United Army from Myanmar, led by the notorious warlord Khun Sa, and the Kuomintang (KMT) refugees from communist China. The Thai government's concerted attempt to eliminate opium growing within its borders has been successful, but Thailand still has a vital role to play as a conduit for heroin; most of the production and refinement of opium has simply moved over the borders into Myanmar and Laos. More worryingly for the Thai authorities, factories just across the Burmese border are now also producing vast quantities of methamphetamines, either **ya baa** or "ice" (crystal meth), destined for consumption in Thailand itself.

showers. They offer local tours and rent out motorbikes (B200/day). Double **B300**

The northeast: Isaan

Bordered by Laos and Cambodia on three sides, the tableland of **northeast** Thailand, known as **Isaan**, is the least-visited region of the kingdom and the poorest, but also its most traditional. Most northeasterners speak a dialect that's more comprehensible to residents of Vientiane than Bangkok, and Isaan's historic allegiances have tied it more closely to Laos and Cambodia than to Thailand. Between the eleventh and thirteenth centuries, the all-powerful Khmers covered the northeast in magnificent stone temple complexes, which can still be admired at **Phimai** and **Phanom Rung**. The mighty **Mekong River** forms 750km of the border between Isaan and Laos, and there are four main points along it where foreigners can cross the border (there's also a little-used border crossing into Cambodia from Isaan; see box, p.769). The river makes a popular backpackers' trail, not least because of the laidback waterfront guesthouses in towns such as **Nong Khai**. Inland scenery is rewarding too, with good hiking trails at **Khao Yai National Park**.

KHAO YAI NATIONAL PARK

Only 120km northeast of Bangkok, **Khao Yai** is Thailand's most popular national park. It offers a realistic chance of seeing wild elephants, white-handed (lar) gibbons, pig-tailed macaques, hornbills, civets and barking deer, plus the very slim possibility of sighting a tiger. The park has lots of waterfalls and several undemanding walking trails. The best way to see Khao Yai is to stay in the park, or in the nearby town of **Pak Chong**. You have the choice of exploring the trails yourself or joining a backpackers' tour; bring warm clothes as it gets cool at night.

WHAT TO SEE AND DO

You're most likely to spot the animals if you join a tour with an expert guide, but if you're short on time or money you can always take your chances and follow the trails. Several **trails** radiate from the area around the park's visitor centre and headquarters (at kilometre stone 37), and a few more branch off from the roads that cross the park. The most popular include the paths to Nong Pak Chee observation tower (4.5km one-way; 2hr 30min); and to Haew Suwat Falls (8.3km one-way; 3–4hr), which featured in the 1999 film, *The Beach*. Brochures with maps are available at the visitor centre.

ARRIVAL AND DEPARTURE

There are two access roads to the park – one from the south and another from the north – with checkpoints on both. Everyone travelling by public transport approaches the park from Pak Chong, about 25km north of the northern entrance, and around 4hr from Bangkok by train, 2–3hr by bus or a/c minibus.

By songthaew Public songthaews leave from outside the 7-Eleven shop in Pak Chong, 200m west of the footbridge on the north side of the main road near Soi 21 (Mon–Sat every 30min 6.30am–4pm, less frequently on Sun; 30–45min; B40). Songthaews cannot enter the park itself, so you'll be dropped at the park checkpoint, about

14km short of the Khao Yai visitor centre. At the checkpoint (where you pay the B400 national park entrance fee) park rangers will flag down passing cars and get them to give you a ride up to the visitor centre; this is common practice here. A quicker but more expensive option is to charter a songthaew from the corner of Soi 19 in Pak Chong (B1500 for a return trip, including several hours in the park).

10

GUIDED TOURS

The good thing about joining a tour of Khao Yai is that you're accompanied by an expert wildlife-spotter, and you have transport between the major sights of the park; book ahead if possible. Beware, however, that Khao Yai has problems with unscrupulous, fly-by-night tour operators. Our recommended companies run the standard tours lasting for a day and a half, with the middle night spent outside the park; national park fees are included in the prices, but accommodation is extra.

Green Leaf Tour At kilometre stone 7.5 on the park road, 12.5km out of Pak Chong ⓣ 044 365073, ⓦ greenleaftour.com. The staff here go out of their way to make sure your stay runs smoothly, and will pick you up from Pak Chong. As well as specialist birding trips, they offer tours ranging from half a day (B500/person) to one and a half days (B1500/person). Sparse though brightly decorated en-suite rooms (B300) and decent Thai meals.

Wildlife Safari 2km north of Pak Chong ⓣ 089 628 8224, ⓔ jayjungletrek@gmail.com. This friendly family-run business offers jungle trekking and birdwatching, as well as smart en-suite rooms with hot showers in the garden of the family home (B400 including breakfast). Bespoke tours as well as the standard one-and-a-half-day tour, which is priced according to the size of the group (from B1500/person). Call for free transfer from Pak Chong.

NIGHT SAFARIS

A much-touted park attraction is the hour-long night safaris that take truckloads of tourists round Khao Yai's main roads in the hope of sighting wildlife in the glare of specially fitted searchlights. You can book a place on one of the trucks at the national park headquarters; they leave from here every night at 7pm and 8pm and cost B500 for up to ten people.

ACCOMMODATION AND EATING

INSIDE THE PARK

To stay at the national park lodges in high season, you'll probably need to reserve ahead through the Royal Forestry Department office in Bangkok (ⓣ 02 562 0760, ⓦ dnp.go.th), though there may be availability for walk-ins on weekdays. Advance booking is not usually necessary if camping, but is advisable at weekends. Tents and bedding can be rented for around B250 for two people. There's a cafeteria complex opposite the HQ and visitor centre.

PAK CHONG

Pak Chong's exceptionally good night market sets up on the edge of the main road, between Tesaban sois 17 and 19.

Pak Chong Hotel 650/1 Th Mittraphap, near the main bus stop ⓣ 044 279082. This plain white block just off the main road has friendly staff and clean, en-suite, good-value rooms with hot showers. Breakfast included. Double **B460**

KHORAT (NAKHON RATCHASIMA)

Ninety kilometres from Pak Chong, bustling and non-touristy **KHORAT** (officially known as Nakhon Ratchasima) is Isaan's largest city and a major transport hub, where you may have to change buses. It can be used as a base for exploring Phimai and Phanom Rung, though you'll be better off for budget accommodation in Phimai itself and in Surin (for Phanom Rung).

The town's most important statue is of **Thao Suranari** (Ya Mo), the deputy governor's feisty wife whose bravery and cunning were an inspiration to the people of Khorat when it was attacked by Laos in 1826. People come in their droves in the evening to lay flowers at her feet, and some even dance around her. From March 23 to April 3, the town holds a festival in her honour.

ARRIVAL AND INFORMATION

By bus Most buses from other provinces arrive at the main Bus Terminal 2, north of the city on Highway 2 and connected to it by tuk-tuks and metered taxis (around B60). Bus Terminal 1, just off Th Suranari, is closer to the town centre and runs local services as well as a few buses to Bangkok.

Destinations Bangkok (every 20min; 3hr); Ban Tako (for Phanom Rung; every 30min; 2hr); Chanthaburi (7 daily; 6hr); Chiang Mai (12 daily; 12hr); Chiang Rai (6 daily; 13hr); Khon Kaen (at least hourly; 2hr 30min–3hr); Lopburi (hourly; 3hr 30min); Nakhon Phanom (3 daily; 8hr); Nong Khai (11 daily; 6–8hr); Phimai (every 30min; 1hr–1hr 30min); Phitsanulok (14 daily; 6–7hr); Rayong (for Ko Samet; at least 8 daily; 6–8hr); Surin (every 30min; 4–5hr); Ubon Ratchathani (hourly; 5–7hr).

By train The train station on Th Mukkhamontri, towards the west of town, is served by city bus routes #2 and #3.

Destinations Ayutthaya (12 daily; 3hr 30min); Bangkok (12 daily; 4hr–6hr 40min); Khon Kaen (5 daily; 3hr 20min); Surin (13 daily; 2hr–3hr 20min); Ubon Ratchathani (10 daily; 4hr–6hr 10min); Udon Thani (4 daily; 5hr–5hr 40min).

Tourist information The TAT office (daily 8.30am–4.30pm; 044 213666, tatsima@tat.or.th) is on the western edge of town on Th Mitraphap. Take city bus #2 or #3 to reach it.

GETTING AROUND

Khorat is sprawling and clogged with traffic, so walking is rarely the best option.

By bus and songthaew Local buses and songthaews (B8–15) travel most of Khorat's main roads. The most useful routes are #2, which runs between the TAT office in the west, via the train station, and Suranari and Assadang roads to the east; and #3, which also runs right across the city, via Mahathai and Jomsurangyat roads, past the train station.

By tuk-tuk and taxi Tuk-tuks and metered taxis swarm the streets.

ACCOMMODATION AND EATING

There are night markets about 400m east of *Siri Hotel* on Th Pho Klang (corner of Th Yota) and on the east side of the centre near the *Iyara Hotel* on Th Chumphon.

Cabbages and Condoms 6/1 Th Suebsiri (north–south road just east of TAT). Excellent Thai and Isaan food at this cosy, mid-priced restaurant (most dishes around B100), with all proceeds going to the Population and Community Development Association. Daily 10am–10pm.

De Bus Café Th Suranari, 5min walk northeast of the train station. Bright a/c café serving lattes, mochas and cappuccinos for B45, plus an interesting range of breakfast choices. Daily 7am–10pm.

Siri Hotel 688 Th Pho Klang, 500m northeast of the train station 044 242831, sirihotelkorat.com. A modern and comfortable choice with very smart, spacious and quiet rooms, all with a/c, hot showers and cable TV. Breakfast included. Double B650

Tokyo Hotel 256 Th Suranari 044 242788. A 5min walk southwest of Bus Terminal 1, or 15min northeast of the train station. Conveniently located with large, fairly clean rooms with hot showers and the choice of fan or a/c. Double B300

DIRECTORY

Hospital Expats favour the private Bangkok Hospital at 1308/9 Th Mittraphap (Highway 2; 044 429999, bangkokhospital.com/ratchasima).

Internet There's a cluster of internet cafés in the area around the post office and Klang Plaza II on Th Jomsurangyat, charging from B20/hr.

Tourist police Opposite Bus Terminal 2 044 341778 or 1155.

PHIMAI

A more appealing overnight stop than Khorat is tiny **PHIMAI**, 60km to the northeast. It's particularly attractive during its four-day festival in early November, which includes longboat races, *son-et-lumière* and classical dance performances.

Prasat Hin Phimai

The town is dominated by the exquisitely restored eleventh-century Khmer temple complex of **Prasat Hin Phimai** (daily 7.30am–6pm; B100), considered by many to be the blueprint for Angkor Wat. Built mainly of dusky pink and greyish-white sandstone, it was connected by a direct road to the Khmer capital of Angkor and follows the classic symbolic precepts of Khmer temple design: the moat represented the cosmic ocean, the surrounding walls the mountains, and the main prang (sanctuary tower) Mount Meru, the mythological axis of the world according to Hindu cosmology.

Phimai's magnificent main prang has been restored to its original cruciform groundplan, complete with an almost full set of carvings, mostly picking out episodes from the Ramayana. Those around the outside of the prang depict predominantly Hindu themes: Shiva – the Destroyer – dances above the main entrance to the southeast antechamber heralding the end of the world and the creation of a new order. By the early thirteenth century, Phimai had been turned into a Buddhist temple, and the main prang now houses Phimai's most important image – the Buddha sheltered by a seven-headed naga (snake).

Phimai National Museum

Many other stonecarvings, notably an exceptionally fine sandstone statue of Khmer king Jayavarman VII rescued from the main prang, can be seen at the well-presented **Phimai National Museum** (Wed–Sun 9am–4pm; B100), 10min walk north of the ruins by the river.

ARRIVAL AND DEPARTURE

By bus Buses to and from Khorat's Bus Terminal 2 (every 30min; 1hr–1hr 30min) stop near the ruins and the museum; the last return bus departs Phimai around 7pm. If coming from the north (for example, Khon Kaen), take any bus towards Bangkok and get off at the Highway 2–Highway 206 junction, where you can change to the Khorat–Phimai service for the last 10km.

ACCOMMODATION AND EATING

The cheapest place to eat is the night market just east of the entrance to the ruins on Th Anantajinda.

Baiteiy On the main road, about 4km northwest of the town centre ⓣ 081 065 8714. This huge indoor restaurant is very popular with locals and has a worthy reputation for duck dishes, spicy salads and fresh fish. You'll need to take a tuk-tuk or taxi to get here. Daily 9.30am–9pm.

10

Boonsiri Guest House 228 Th Chomsudasadet, 50m south of the ruins ⓣ 044 471159, ⓦ boonsiri.net. Clean, ten-bed dorms at great prices, plus private rooms with hot showers and a nice planted roof terrace with seating. Bicycle rental and wi-fi. Dorm B150, double B400

PHANOM RUNG AND MUANG TAM

Built during the same period as Phimai, the temple complexes of **Prasat Hin Khao Phanom Rung** (often shortened to just Phanom Rung) and **Prasat Muang Tam** form two more links in the chain that once connected the Khmer capital with the limits of its empire. It's best to visit the ruins as a day-trip from either Khorat (see p.766) or Surin (see below).

Prasat Hin Khao Phanom Rung

Prasat Hin Khao Phanom Rung (daily 6am–6pm; B100, or B150 for a joint ticket with Muang Tam) dates back to the tenth century and stands as the finest example of Khmer architecture in Thailand, its every surface ornamented with exquisite carvings and its buildings so perfectly aligned that on the morning of the full-moon day of the fifth lunar month (usually April) you can stand at the westernmost gateway and see the rising sun through all fifteen doors. This event is celebrated here with a day-long festival of huge parades.

Before entering the temple, it's well worth visiting the excellent, museum-like **Phanom Rung Tourist Information Centre** (daily 9am–4.30pm; free) by the main entrance to learn more about its symbolism and background. You approach the temple compound along a dramatic 200m-long avenue flanked with lotus-bud pillars, going over the first of three naga bridges, and past four small purification ponds. This constitutes the symbolic crossing of the abyss between earth and heaven. Part of the gallery that runs right round the inner compound has been restored to its original covered design, with arched roofs, small chambers inside and false windows. Above the entrance to the main prang are carvings of a dancing ten-armed Shiva, and of a reclining Vishnu, who is dreaming up a new universe.

Prasat Muang Tam

Down on the well-watered plains 8km to the southeast of Phanom Rung, and accessed via a scenic minor road that cuts through a swathe of rice fields, lies the small but elegant temple complex of **Prasat Muang Tam** (daily 7.30am–6pm; B100, or B150 for a joint ticket with Phanom Rung). It sits behind a huge kilometre-long *baray* (Khmer reservoir), which was probably constructed at the same time as the main part of the temple, in the early eleventh century. Like Phanom Rung, Muang Tam is based on the classic Khmer design of a central prang, flanked by minor prangs and encircled by a gallery punctuated with gateways. The four stone-rimmed L-shaped ponds between the gallery and the outer wall may have been used to purify worshippers as they entered the complex.

ARRIVAL AND DEPARTURE

To get to the ruins, you first need to take a bus to the small town of Ban Tako, located on Highway 24, 115km southeast of Khorat or 83km southwest of Surin; bus #274 travels between the two provincial capitals (every 30min). From Ban Tako, it's 12km south to Phanom Rung and another 8km south to Muang Tham, so you'll either have to hitch or rent a motorbike taxi (B300–400/person round trip). The last bus back to Khorat from Ban Tako leaves around 5pm.

SURIN

The quiet, typically northeastern town of **SURIN** is best known for the much-hyped elephant roundup held here every year on the third weekend of November when hundreds of elephants congregate from the surrounding countryside (contact TAT for details and tickets). Situated about 150km east of Khorat, Surin makes a good base for Phanom Rung and has a

INTO CAMBODIA: CHONG CHOM–O'SMACH

A/c minibuses (every 30min; 1hr 30min) travel to the **Chong Chom border pass**, 70km south of Surin, mostly to service the casino on the Cambodian side. Cambodian visas are issued on arrival at the Chong Chom–O'Smach checkpoint (daily 6am–10pm; US$20, although you may be asked for B1000), from where you can get taxis to Siem Reap,150km from the border crossing (reckon on B1500 per car).

fine guesthouse. It's also an excellent place to buy silk, either from the women around the Tannasarn–Krungsrinai intersection, or from one of the town's silk shops.

ARRIVAL AND INFORMATION

By bus Buses stop one block east of the train station.

Destinations Bangkok (at least hourly; 8–11hr), Khon Kaen (hourly; 4hr–5hr 30min) and Khorat (at least hourly; 4–5hr).

By train Trains from Bangkok (7 daily) and Ubon (11 daily) pull in at the northern edge of town.

Tourist information The TAT office is just east of the centre at 355/3–6 Th Tessaban 1 (daily 8.30am–4.30pm; T 044 514447–8, E tatsurin@tat.or.th).

ACCOMMODATION AND EATING

For fiery Isaan food, you can't beat Surin's lively night market, which occupies the eastern end of Th Krungsrinai.

Pirom's Guest House 55-326 Soi Arunee, Th Thung Poh, about 1.5km northwest of the train station T 089 355 4140. Quiet, laidback and super-clean guesthouse run by Pirom, a knowledgeable ex-social worker and his friendly wife Aree; they also serve food. Their fascinating tours give tourists an unusual glimpse into rural northeastern life; most itineraries feature the Ban Ta Klang elephant trainers' village. Double B200

UBON RATCHATHANI

Almost always referred to simply as Ubon, **UBON RATCHATHANI**, 168km east of Surin, is Thailand's fifth-largest city, but only really worth stopping at en route to the Lao border. If you're here in early July, though, drop by for the **Ubon Candle Festival**, when huge beeswax sculptures are paraded through the streets.

Wat Thung Si Muang, 200m east of the central Thung Si Muang Park along Thanon Sri Narong, is noteworthy for its well-preserved teak library – raised on stilts over an artificial pond to keep book-devouring insects at bay – and its murals in the bot, to the left of the library, which display lively scenes of nineteenth-century life. The Ubon Ratchathani National Museum (Wed–Sun 9am–4pm; B100), south from the park across Thanon Sri Narong, has decent displays on the region's geology, history and folk crafts.

ARRIVAL AND INFORMATION

By plane Ubon Airport is just north of the town centre, with frequent flights to and from Bangkok; a metered taxi to the centre costs about B60.

By bus The main long-distance bus terminal is about 3km north of Ubon city centre on Th Chayangkun, from where songthaews #2 and #3 run into town.

Destinations Bangkok (hourly; 10hr); Chiang Mai (6 daily; 17hr); Chong Mek (17 daily; 1hr); Khon Kaen (at least hourly; 4–6hr); Khorat (hourly; 5–7hr); Mukdahan (every 30min; 3hr); Pakse, Laos (2 daily; 3hr); Rayong (10 daily; 13hr); Surin (hourly; 3hr).

By train The train station is in Warinchamrab, south across the Mun River. Songthaew #2 (B10) runs from the train station across the river into central Ubon; a taxi costs around B60.

Destinations Ayutthaya (7 daily; 7hr–10hr 40min); Bangkok (7 daily; 8hr 30min–12hr 15min); Khorat (9 daily; 3hr 45min–6hr); Surin (11 daily; 1hr 50min–2hr 40min).

Tourist information The TAT office is on Th Khuenthani (daily 8.30am–4.30pm; T 045 243770–1, E tatubon @tat.or.th).

INTO LAOS: CHONG MEK

Ninety-nine kilometres east of Ubon, Highway 217 hits the **Lao border** at **Chong Mek**, site of a Thai–Lao market, and one of the legal border crossings for foreigners.

There are a/c minibuses roughly hourly to Chong Mek from the main bus terminal, but the fastest and easiest way to get across is to take the a/c bus all the way to Pakse, the main town on the other side of the border (2 daily, currently 9am & 3pm; 4hr); the bus will wait at Vongtao, on the Lao side of the border, while you get a visa on arrival for Laos (see p.345).

10

10

ACCOMMODATION AND EATING

Ubon's night market on Th Khuenthani, just west of TAT, is a great place to eat, selling a wide variety of food, including the Isaan classics, grilled chicken, sticky rice and *som tam* (papaya salad).

Chiokee 307–317 Th Khuenthani. Long Thai and Western menu across from the museum, especially popular for breakfast (rice soup and Chinese doughnut B43). Daily 6am–6pm.

Phadaeng Mansion & Gallery 167 Th Pha Daeng, 5min walk north from the northeast corner of Thung Si Muang park ⓣ 045 254600, ⓦ thephadaeng.blogspot.com. Behind an extravagant colonnaded portico in a quiet part of town, clean, good-sized rooms, all with a/c, hot shower, TV and fridge. Free wi-fi. Double B500

Sakhon 66 Th Pha Daeng, 2min walk north of the northeast corner of Thung Si Muang park. One of the best places in Ubon to sample Isaan food, particularly recommended for its more unusual seasonal dishes, like *tom yam* soup with fish eggs. Most dishes around B80. Daily 10am–10pm.

Tokyo Hotel 178 Th Upparat ⓣ 045 241739. Basic but acceptable and welcoming hotel, where fan rooms have hot showers and TV, and it's only an extra B90 if you want a/c. It's about a 5min walk north of the museum. Double B360

DIRECTORY

Hospital Ubonrak-Thonburi Hospital, Th Burapanai (ⓣ 045 260300), to the east of the town centre.

Tourist police Th Suriyat (ⓣ 1155).

NAKHON PHANOM

NAKHON PHANOM, 100km north of Mukdahan and 313km east of Nong Khai, affords stunning views of the Mekong and the mountains behind but is chiefly of interest as a point of access to Laos. Every two hours during the day, buses from Nakhon Phanom's bus station run across the third Thai–Lao Friendship Bridge, 8km north of the town centre, to Khammouan (Thakhek) in Laos; they'll wait while you get a Lao visa on arrival (see p.345). The passenger ferry across the Mekong is now for Lao and Thai people only.

INTO LAOS: MUKDAHAN

Buses run to **Mukdahan**, 170km north of Ubon Ratchathani, from Bangkok (20 daily; 11hr), Khon Kaen (every 30min; 3hr), Nakhon Phanom (hourly; 2hr) and Ubon (roughly hourly; 4hr). Tourists can cross to Laos here by catching one of the Savannakhet buses from Mukdahan bus station over the Second Friendship Bridge, 7km north of town (roughly hourly from 8.30am to 7pm); you can get a thirty-day Lao visa on arrival (see p.345).

ARRIVAL AND INFORMATION

By plane AirAsia and Nok Air each have a daily route flying from Bangkok (Don Muang) to Nakhon Phanom; the airport is 15km from town, and served by a/c minibuses (B100/person).

By bus The bus station is about 2km west of the centre; buses arrive here from Nong Khai (6 daily; 6hr), Mukdahan (hourly; 2hr) and Bangkok (20 daily; 12hr).

Tourist information There's a TAT office 700m north of the ferry pier at 184/1 Th Sunthon Vichit, on the corner with Th Salaklang (daily 8.30am–4.30pm; ⓣ 042 513490, ⓔ tatphnom@tat.or.th).

ACCOMMODATION

Grand Hotel 210 Th Sri Thep ⓣ 042 513788. The best budget place to stay is the central *Grand Hotel*, a block back from the river just south of the ferry pier and market, with fan or a/c rooms all with en-suite hot showers. Double B280

NONG KHAI

The major border town in these parts is **NONG KHAI**, the terminus of the rail line from Bangkok and the easiest place to cross overland into Laos, whose capital Vientiane is just 24km away. The town is reasonably tranquil and still retains a backwater charm, but has been developing fast since the construction of the huge First Thai–Lao Friendship Bridge over the Mekong to its west. As with most of the towns along this part of the Mekong, the thing to do in Nong Khai is just to take it easy, enjoying the peaceful atmosphere and the stunning sunsets.

WHAT TO SEE AND DO

Nong Khai stretches 4km along the south bank of the Mekong. Running from east to west, Thanon Meechai dominates activity, with the main shops and businesses plumb in the middle around the post office and the main pier and Thai-Lao market at Tha Sadet. The town

is famous for the **Bang Fai Phaya Nak (naga fireballs)**: pink balls of light that rise noiselessly from the river after dusk on the last day of Buddhist Lent on October's full-moon night. Despite eager attempts to disprove it as a hoax, no evidence of misdoing has been found and thousands of people amass every year to gawp at this mysterious phenomenon. One of the best ways to see Nong Khai's famous sunset is on a cruise run by *Mut Mee Guest House* (daily 5pm; about 1hr 30min; B100) on their floating restaurant, *Nagarina*, which docks at the pier beneath (food is available at extra cost).

Just off the main highway, 5km east of Nong Khai, **Sala Kaeo Kou** (daily 7am–5pm; B20) is best known for its bizarre sculpture garden, which looks like the work of a giant artist on acid. The temple was founded by the unconventional and charismatic holy man, Luang Phu Boonlua Surirat, who believed, somewhat controversially, in a fusion of the teachings from all religions. The garden bristles with Buddhist, Hindu, Christian and secular figures, all executed in concrete with imaginative abandon by unskilled followers under Luang Phu's direction, and continued after his death in 1996. He also established a similarly weird "Buddha Park" (Xieng Khouan) across the Mekong near Vientiane in Laos (see p.363). The best way to get here is to rent a bike (from B30/day) or motorbike (around B200) from your guesthouse, but return trips in a tuk-tuk (around B150) are also possible.

ARRIVAL AND INFORMATION

By bus The bus terminal is on the east side of the centre off Th Prajak; tuk-tuks abound, and guideline rates for common trips are posted within the terminal. You could easily walk from here to *Sawasdee* but not the other guesthouses listed here.

Destinations Bangkok (20 daily; 11hr); Khon Kaen (20 daily; 3hr 30min); Khorat (20 daily; 6hr 30min); Nakhon Phanom (6 daily; 6hr); Rayong (19 daily; 12hr); Vientiane (Laos; 6 daily; 1hr–1hr 30min).

By train The train station is 3km west of the town centre towards the Friendship Bridge; tuk-tuks wait around to ferry passengers into town.

Destinations Ayutthaya (3 daily; 9hr 30min–11hr); Bangkok (3 daily; 11–13hr); Khon Kaen (4 daily; 2hr 45min); Khorat (4 daily; 6hr); Tha Naleng, Laos (2 daily; 15min).

Tourist information The TAT office is 1.5km south of the centre on the west side of Highway 2 (daily 8.30am–4.30pm; ⓣ 042 421326). *Mut Mee Guest House* is also a good source of information.

ACCOMMODATION

Janhom Apartment 479 Soi Srichumchuen, between Th Meechai and Th Prajak ⓣ 042 460293. A modern, lime-green block on a quiet, central soi with a pleasant sitting area at the front. Not really apartments, but large, clean rooms with TVs and hot showers. Double **B250**

★**Mut Mee** 1111 Th Kaeworawut, on the west side of town ⓣ 042 460717, ⓦ mutmee.com. A magnet for travellers with its huge range of well-kept rooms in an attractive riverside garden, friendly, informative staff, yoga, meditation and massage sessions, and mountain bikes. It's always busy, so aim to arrive early. Double **B230**

Sawasdee Guest House 402 Th Meechai ⓣ 042 420259, ⓦ sawasdeeguesthouse.com. A grand old wooden shophouse set around a pleasant courtyard east of the centre, with cheap fan rooms that share bathrooms (try to avoid those overlooking the noisy main road). A/c rooms

INTO LAOS: NONG KHAI

The border crossing at Nong Khai is the **First Friendship Bridge** (daily 6am–10pm, although the shuttle buses across the bridge stop around 9pm, sometimes earlier), where you can get a thirty-day Lao visa on arrival (see p.345; expect to pay $1 extra if you arrive after 6pm or at the weekend). It's possible to pay in baht for your visa, rather than dollars, though their exchange rate is very poor, at B50/dollar. From Nong Khai's bus station, you can take one of the six daily buses that run all the way through to Vientiane (B55), but only if you have arranged your Lao visa in advance. If you need a visa on arrival, take a tuk-tuk to the foot of the bridge (about B30–40 from the railway station), then a shuttle bus (B20) across the span itself; on the other side you can catch a shared a/c minibus (B100–150/person), tuk-tuk (about B300/vehicle) or infrequent bus (B20) to Vientiane, 24km away.

At Nong Khai railway station it is possible to switch to the international train for the quick hop across to Tha Naleng (2 daily), but as the tracks stop here (around 20km from downtown Vientiane) you'll need to charter a tuk-tuk, car or minibus for the rest of the journey.

10

with en-suite hot-water bathrooms also available, plus wi-fi. Double **B200**

EATING AND DRINKING

★**Daeng Namnuang** Th Rimkhong, near Tha Sadet. Delicious, inexpensive Vietnamese food at this stupendously popular place with a lovely riverside terrace. For B180, you can try all their specialities on a set meal, which include *naem nuang*, make-them-yourself fresh spring rolls with sausage. Daily 8.30am–8pm.

10

Nagarina As well as cruising on the river (see p.771), *Mut Mee*'s floating restaurant serves tasty authentic Thai food in an atmospheric setting, specializing in seafood and Isaan dishes (main dishes B50–1200. There's also a floating bar, *Gaia*, with live music and a laidback atmosphere. Meanwhile, under bamboo shelters back on dry land, the main guesthouse restaurant offers lots of Thai vegetarian dishes and apple pie. Daily 10am–9pm.

SHOPPING

Hornbill Bookshop Th Kaeworawut, on the access road to *Mut Mee Guest House*. Stocks new and secondhand books and offers internet access and an international phone service. Mon–Sat 10am–7pm.

KHON KAEN

The lively, studenty city of **KHON KAEN**, 213km south of Nong Khai, makes a decent resting point on the

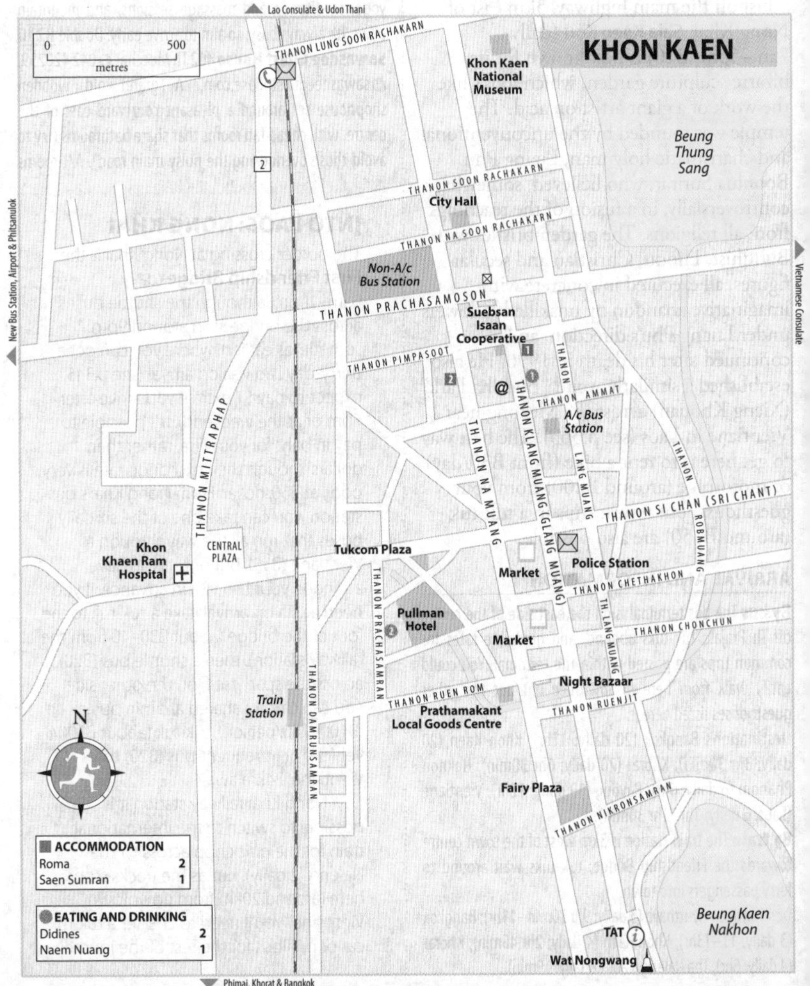

Bangkok–Nong Khai rail line and has both a Lao and a Vietnamese consulate, the only ones outside Bangkok.

In keeping with its status as a university town, the **Khon Kaen National Museum**, on Thanon Lung Soon Rachakarn (Wed–Sun 9am–4pm; B100), boasts several fine collections including Bronze Age pots, Buddha images and local folk art. South of the centre, the striking, modern, nine-tiered pagoda at **Wat Nongwang**, resplendent in red, white and gold, is also well worth a visit. It offers good views of Beung Kaen Nakhon, the adjacent lake in a park.

ARRIVAL AND INFORMATION

By plane The airport, 10km west of the city centre, has flights to Bangkok (6 daily; 55min) with Thai (Suvarnabhumi Airport) and Air Asia (Don Muang). Many hotels send a/c minibuses out to pick up guests; otherwise, a taxi will cost around B200.

By bus The a/c bus station is right in the city centre off Th Klang Muang, while the non-a/c bus station is on Th Prachasamoson. It's planned to use these stations for minibus services only, while bus services are meant to move to the recently built bus station, way out of town on the western bypass. However, the bus companies are reluctant to shift out to the distant new bus station, and at the time of writing very few services are using it.

Destinations Bangkok (hourly; 6–7hr); Chiang Mai (12 daily; 10–12hr); Khorat (every 30min; 3hr); Nong Khai (10 daily; 3hr 30min); Phitsanulok (16 daily; 6hr); Sukhothai (10 daily; 6–7hr); Surin (hourly; 5hr); Ubon Ratchathani (at least hourly; 4hr 30min).

By train Khon Kaen's train station is on the southwest edge of the centre.

Destinations Ayutthaya (4 daily; 7hr–7hr 30min); Bangkok (4 daily; 8hr 30min–9hr 45min); Khorat (5 daily; 3hr–3hr 30min); Nong Khai (3 daily; 2hr 25min–3hr 30min).

Tourist information The TAT office is south of the centre on Th Klang Muang (daily 8.30am–4.30pm; T 043 227144–6, E tatkhkn@tat.or.th).

ACCOMMODATION AND EATING

Khon Kaen has a reputation for very spicy food, particularly sausages (*sai krog isaan*), served at stalls along Th Klang Muang (around *Saen Sumran*). Food stalls pop up across town at dusk, with a particular concentration at the night bazaar on Th Ruen Rom. Nightlife is focused on Th Prachasamran, behind the *Pullman Hotel*.

Didines Th Prachasamran. Welcoming American-run bar-restaurant offering tasty Thai and Western food, including pizzas (from B190) and Mexican, as well as craft beers and a wide selection of wines. Mon–Thurs & Sun 4pm–midnight, Fri & Sat 4pm–2am.

Naem Nuang Next door but one to the *Saen Sumran Hotel* at 87/14–15 Th Klang Muang. Very popular a/c place that serves good Vietnamese food, including *naem nuang*, do-it-yourself fresh spring rolls with pork sausage (sets from B130). Daily 6.30am–11pm.

★**Roma** 50/2 Th Klang Muang T 043 334444. Newly renovated, with some of the cheeriest rooms in town. Some feature Warhol-style pop-art prints, while others have funky bird-shaped stickers on the walls. Ask to see a few rooms before settling in as they vary in quality, though all have hot showers. Free wi-fi. Double **B230**

Saen Sumran 55 Th Klang Muang T 043 239611. The most traveller-oriented hotel in town, with clued-up managers. Its spacious wooden-floored en-suite rooms are good value, if slightly dilapidated. Double **B220**

DIRECTORY

Consulates The Lao consulate is on the east side of Highway 2 towards Udon Thani, 8km north of town and accessible on most #4 city songthaews (Mon–Fri 8am–noon & 1–4pm; T 043 393402). The Vietnamese consulate is off the east end of Th Prachasamoson at 65/6 Th Chataphadung (Mon–Fri 8–11.30am & 1.30–4.30pm; T 043 242190; city songthaew #10 can save you a long walk).

Hospital Khon Kaen Ram Hospital, on the far western end of Th Si Chan (T 043/333800, W khonkaenram.com).

Internet is available at various locations on Th Klang Muang.

Tourist police Southwest of town on Th Mittraphap (T 043 235095 or T 1155)

The east coast

Thailand's **east coast** is a 500km string of fairly dull beaches and over-packaged resorts, the largest and most notorious of which is eminently missable Pattaya. Offshore, the tiny island of **Ko Samet** with its pretty white-sand beaches attracts weekending Bangkokians and an increasing number of package-holiday-makers. Further east are the much larger, forested island of **Ko Chang**, whose long, fine beaches have made it Thailand's latest resort destination; and the small, much less developed **Ko Mak**. East of Ko Chang lies the Cambodian border post of Hat Lek, one of two points in this region – the other being Aranyaprathet, a little

INTO CAMBODIA: ARANYAPRATHET

The most commonly used overland crossing into Cambodia from Thailand is at **Poipet**, which lies just across the border from the Thai town of **Aranyaprathet**, 210km due east of Bangkok. It's best to arm yourself in advance with an e-visa for Cambodia (see p.67) and to make the journey to Aranyaprathet by regular public transport, but it's also possible to buy a ticket all the way through to Siem Reap and to get a thirty-day visa on arrival at the border, though both of the latter options are more likely to open you up to the many **scams on this route**, including a fake "Cambodian Consulate/Immigration" in Aranyaprathet and rip-off currency exchange (it's not compulsory to buy riel before entering Cambodia, despite what some touts may say).

Once you've walked across the border and entered Cambodia, it's about two hours in a taxi or bus to Siem Reap, 150km away. If you have the deep misfortune of getting stuck in dusty, dirty Aranyaprathet, where local transport comes in the form of tuk-tuks, try the comfortable fan and a/c rooms at *Inter Hotel* at 108/7 Th Chatasingh (T 037 231291, W ourweb.info/interhotel; B300).

From **Bangkok**, you can travel to Aranyaprathet Station, 4km from the border post, by **train** (2 daily; at least 6hr); you'll need to catch the 5.55am if you want to get across the border the same day. Alternatively, take a **bus** from Bangkok's Northern (Mo Chit) Bus Terminal to Aranyaprathet (at least hourly; 4hr 30min), or a faster, more expensive a/c minibus from Victory Monument. There is now also a regular public bus from Bangkok's Northern Bus Terminal through to Siem Reap (1 daily; 7hr).

To reach Aranyaprathet from east-coast towns, the easiest route is to take a bus from **Chanthaburi** to the town of **Sa Kaew**, 130km to the northeast, and then change to one of the frequent buses for the 55km ride east to Aranyaprathet.

way north – where it's possible to **cross overland into Cambodia** (see box, p.778).

KO SAMET

Pretty little **Ko Samet** attracts big crowds these days, drawn mostly from Bangkok's middle classes and expats, especially at weekends and on national holidays. Despite being declared a national park in 1981 (B200; payable at the checkpoint near Hat Sai Kaew or at Ao Wong Duan pier), a building ban has had little effect and the island is now weighed down with more than fifty sprawling, albeit low-rise, resorts. The shady beaches, however, are still blessed with squeaky white sand, and there's plentiful plant and animal life.

At just 6km long, the island's size means you can easily walk to most destinations, along the mostly well-marked paths that link the east-coast beaches. There are also motorbikes and quad bikes for rent on every beach, though be warned that the dirt road down the spine of the island, joined by tracks to the beaches, is very rough in places. Fleets of green songthaews wait for fares at the pier in the main village of Na Dan and half-a-dozen other stands around the island. You'll generally be charged for chartering the whole vehicle (around B350, say, to go from Na Dan pier to Ao Sang Thian). Only if there's a large group of people travelling, for example when boats dock at Na Dan, will you get the "shared" rates (B20–40/person).

The beaches

Hat Sai Kaew (Diamond Beach), so called after its beautiful long stretch of luxuriant sand, lies on the south side of Na Dan village, ten minutes' walk down the village high street from the main pier. It's the busiest beach on Samet, packed with resorts and restaurants.

Separated from Hat Sai Kaew by a low promontory, **Ao Hin Kok** has equally fine sand. It's much smaller than its neighbour and has more of a travellers' vibe, with some backpacker-oriented budget choices for accommodation.

Past the next rocky divide is **Ao Phai**, one of the livelier places to stay on the island. By day, a relaxed beach-life atmosphere pervades, but by night sleep in the central part of the strand is elusive

as *Silver Sand*'s nightly parties thump out bland dance music until the small hours of the morning.

Further south is **Ao Tub Tim**, also known as Ao Pudsa, a small white-sand bay sandwiched between rocky promontories. It has just two bungalow operations, shaded by plentiful trees.

Clamber up over the headland from Ao Tub Tim (which gives you a fine panorama over Hat Sai Kaew) to reach Samet's smallest and most laidback beach, the secluded **Ao Nuan**, effectively the private domain of *Ao Nuan Bungalows*. Because it's some way off the main track, the beach gets hardly

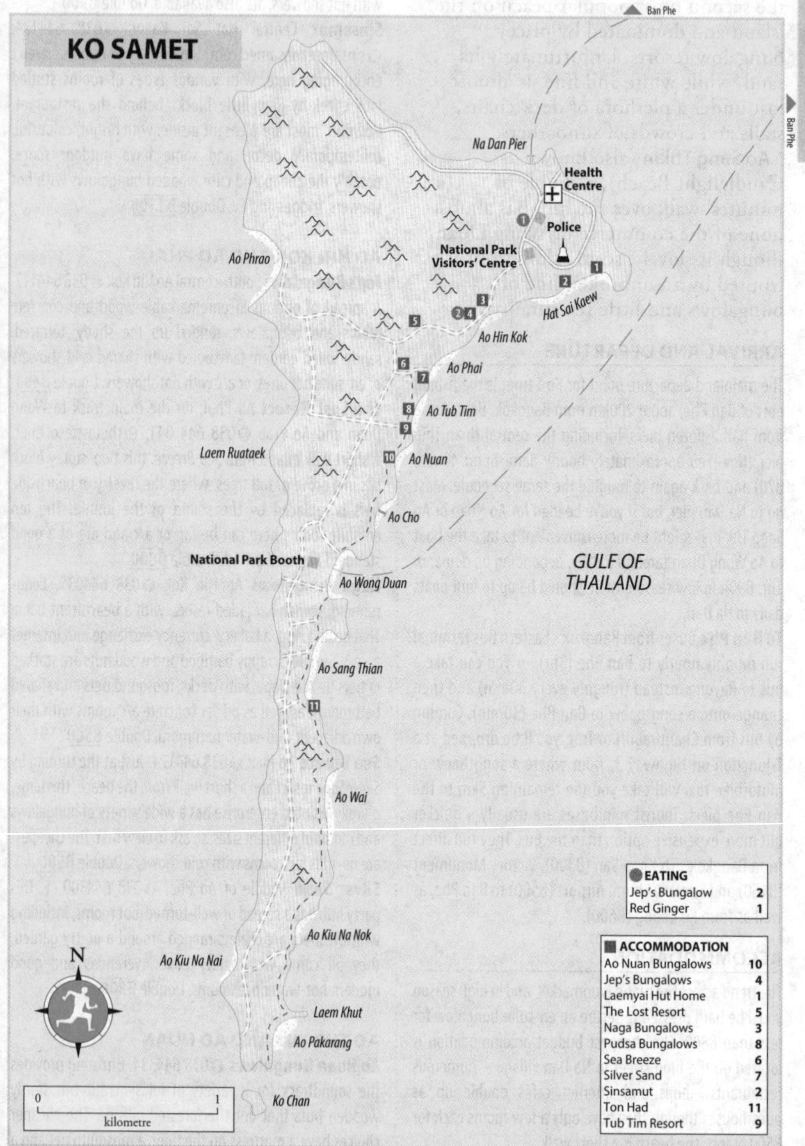

10

any through-traffic and feels quiet and private. Although not brilliant for swimming, the rocky shore reveals a good patch of sand when the tide withdraws.

A ten-minute walk south along the track from Ao Nuan brings you to the horseshoe bay of **Ao Wong Duan**, the second most popular beach on the island and dominated by pricey bungalow resorts. Unfortunately its sand, while white and fine, is almost lost under a plethora of deck chairs, stalls and crowds of sunbathers.

Ao Sang Thian (also known as Candlelight Beach), a couple of minutes' walk over the hill, has almost none of the commerce of Wong Duan, though its lovely, scenic shorefront is fronted by an unbroken line of bungalows and little restaurants.

ARRIVAL AND DEPARTURE

The mainland departure point for Ko Samet is the fishing port of Ban Phe, about 200km from Bangkok. Boats leave from half a dozen piers, including the central Nuan Thip pier (Nov–Feb approximately hourly 8am–6pm; 40min; B70) and back again to roughly the same schedule. Most go to Na Dan pier, but if you're headed for Ao Nuan or Ao Sang Thian, it might be more convenient to take the boat to Ao Wong Duan (around 3 daily, depending on demand; 1hr; B90). In low season, there should be up to four boats daily to Na Dan.

To Ban Phe Buses from Bangkok's Eastern Bus Terminal run roughly hourly to Ban Phe (3hr), or you can take a bus to Rayong instead (roughly every 30min) and then change onto a songthaew to Ban Phe (30min). Coming by bus from Chanthaburi or Trat, you'll be dropped at a T-junction on Highway 3, from where a songthaew or motorbike taxi will take you the remaining 5km to the Ban Phe piers. Tourist minibuses are usually a quicker but more expensive option than the bus. They run direct from Bangkok's Th Khao San (B300), Victory Monument (B160) and Suvarnabhumi Airport (B500) to Ban Phe, as well as from Ko Chang (B600).

ACCOMMODATION

The trend across the island is upmarket, and in high season you'll be hard pressed to secure an en-suite bungalow for less than B800. The cheapest budget accommodation is located on the high street in Na Dan village – numerous restaurants, shops and internet cafés double up as guesthouses though they have only a few rooms each for B500 or less; the beach is a short walk.

HAT SAI KAEW

Laemyai Hut Home North end of Hat Sai Kaew ⓣ 038 644282. The fan bungalows here are the best of the budget options on this beach, not least because they're dotted widely around a shaded, sandy, plant-filled garden in one of the prettiest spots, under the Laem Yai headland at the quieter northern end. Fan bungalows are simple but en suite and colourfully painted; a/c versions, some with hot showers, are also available. Double **B900**

Sinsamut Central Hat Sai Kaew ⓣ 038 644134, ⓦ sinsamutkohsamed.com. Initial appearances aren't encouraging here, with various types of rooms stuffed into cheek-by-jowl little blocks behind the restaurant. However, most are pleasant inside, with bright, colourful, contemporary decor, and some have outdoor space, notably the cheap and cute wooden bungalows with hot showers, fridges and TV. Double **B1100**

AO HIN KOK AND AO PHAI

Jep's Bungalows South-central Ao Hin Kok ⓣ 038 644112. A spread of options in unremarkable wood and concrete rooms and bungalows, ranged up the shady, terraced, sandy-soiled garden: fan-cooled with shared cold showers or en-suite hot ones, or a/c with hot showers. Double **B400**

The Lost Resort Ao Phai, on the main track to Wong Duan and Ao Prao ⓣ 038 644 041, ⓦ thelostresort.net. A short way inland from *Sea Breeze*, this two-storey block sits in a grove of tall trees, where the revelry of beachside bars is replaced by the sound of the jungle. The ten en-suite rooms here can be fan or a/c and are of a good standard and well priced. Double **B800**

Naga Bungalows Ao Hin Kok ⓣ 038 644035. Long-running, somewhat jaded resort, with a beachfront bar, a Thai boxing ring, a bakery, currency exchange and internet access. Simple, scrappy bamboo and wood huts are stacked in tiers up the slope, with decks, mosquito nets and shared bathrooms, as well as pricier concrete a/c rooms with their own adjacent cold-water bathroom. Double **B500**

Sea Breeze Ao Phai ⓣ 038 644124. Just at the turning by *Silver Sand* resort and a short walk from the beach, this large, gaudily-painted enterprise has a wide variety of bungalows and rooms of different sizes, so ask to view first. The cheapest are no-frills fan rooms with cold showers. Double **B500**

Silver Sand Middle of Ao Phai ⓣ 038 644300–1. This party hub has a spread of well-turned-out rooms, including whitewashed, a/c chalets ranged around a pretty garden; they all come with safety boxes, verandas and good modern hot-water bathrooms. Double **B800**

AO TUB TIM AND AO NUAN

Ao Nuan Bungalows ⓣ 038 644334. Birdsong provides the soundtrack for a variety of idiosyncratic but sturdy wooden huts that dot the forested hillside. The cheaper choices have a mattress on the floor, a mosquito net and a

shared cold-water bathroom, but the view of the beach from the balconies is great. Double B800

Pudsa Bungalows Ao Tub Tim 038 644030. Smallish place offering a range of large, sturdy but rather battered huts, all en suite, but most with cold-water shower only. There's a beachside restaurant that does BBQs. Double B800

Tub Tim Resort Ao Tub Tim 038 644025, tubtimresort.com. The most popular place to stay here is a sprawling, well-run resort with over a hundred handsome chalet-style wooden bungalows of various sizes and designs, plus a good restaurant. The cheapest bungalows sport cold showers, ceiling fans and small verandas. Double B800

AO SANG THIAN

Ton Had At the very southern end of Ao Sang Thian 081 435 8900. Welcoming, laidback place offering slightly battered old-school wooden bungalows, with hot showers and large verandas on the beachfront. Double B800

EATING

Most visitors to Ko Samet just eat at their resorts, and in truth there are few restaurants worth making an effort to get to.

Jep's Bungalow Ao Hin Kok. Popular all-rounder serving a great menu of authentic Thai dishes (from around B100), as well as Indian and other international food, at its tables on the sand, set under trees strung with fairylights and given extra atmosphere by mellow music. Also does cappuccino and cakes. Daily 6.30am–10pm.

Red Ginger Diagonally opposite the police sub-station on the high street in Na Dan village. This cosy and welcoming Thai-Canadian place serves popular Western dishes such as oven-baked ribs (B285) as well as much cheaper Thai dishes. Daily noon–around 10pm, depending on who's in.

DIRECTORY

Banks and exchange There are ATMs in the village and on most of the main beaches, and the island's bigger resorts will change money.

Emergencies Ko Samet's health centre and police station (038 644111) are on Na Dan high street, but for anything serious you should go to the Bangkok-Rayong hospital in Rayong (038 921999, bangkokrayong.com).

Post office At *Naga Bungalows* on Ao Hin Kok (generally 9am–4pm).

CHANTHABURI

There's not a lot to see in **CHANTHABURI**, a provincial capital 80km east of Ban Phe that's famous for its gem trade and its high-quality fruit, but you may find yourself stranded here, as this is a transit point for many Rayong–Trat buses and a handy terminus for services to and from the northeast.

ARRIVAL AND DEPARTURE

By bus Seven daily buses make the scenic six-hour Chanthaburi–Sa Kaew–Khorat journey in both directions, with Sa Kaew (3hr) being a useful interchange for buses to Aranyaprathet and the Cambodian border (see box, p.774). Buses to and from all these places, as well as Bangkok's Eastern and Northern bus terminals, use the Chanthaburi bus station on Th Saritdidech, a 10min walk northwest of the town centre.

ACCOMMODATION

River Guest House 3/5–8 Th Srichan 039 328211. In the centre, by one of the main river bridges at, you'll find the traveller-oriented *River Guest House*, which has fan and air-conditioned rooms with private or shared facilities, some with hot showers and river-view balconies. Double B190

TRAT

The small, engaging market town of **TRAT**, 68km east of Chanthaburi, with its charming historic neighbourhood of narrow lanes, old wooden shophouses and lively bars, cafés and restaurants, is a good place to while away time and stock up on essentials before heading, via local ports, to Ko Chang and the outer islands, or moving on to Cambodia.

ARRIVAL AND INFORMATION

By plane The airport is 16km from the centre; a taxi will cost B500/person.

Destinations Bangkok (Suvarnabhumi; 3 daily with Bangkok Airways; 1hr).

By bus The bus station is 1.5km northeast of Trat centre. Songthaews charge B20 (or B60/vehicle) into Trat's centre and around B50 (B250–300/vehicle) to the island ferry ports near Laem Ngop.

Destinations Bangkok Eastern Bus Terminal (10 daily; 5hr); Bangkok Northern Bus Terminal (9 daily; 5hr); Bangkok Suvarnabhumi Airport (6 daily; 4hr 10min); Chanthaburi (hourly; 1hr–1hr 30min); Hat Lek (roughly every 45min; 1hr 30min).

Information The best sources of local information are Tratosphere, a good secondhand bookshop, 200m east along Th Lak Muang from the main Th Sukhumvit, at 23 Soi Kluarimklong, which also has a useful website, tratmap.com; and *Cool Corner* restaurant, with its travellers' comments books (see p.778).

10

10

INTO CAMBODIA: HAT LEK

Many travellers use the **Hat Lek–Koh Kong border crossing** for overland travel into Cambodia. It's best to arm yourself in advance with an e-visa for Cambodia (see p.67) and to make the journey by regular public transport, but it's also possible to buy a package all the way through to Sihanoukville and Phnom Penh and to get a thirty-day visa on arrival at the border, though both of the latter options are more likely to open you up to the many **scams on this route**.

The only way to get to **Hat Lek** under your own steam is by minibus from Trat bus station, 91km northwest (roughly every 45min; 1hr–1hr 30min). Hat Lek (on the Thai side) and Koh Kong (in Cambodia) are on opposite sides of the Dong Tong River estuary, but a bridge connects the two banks. Once through immigration, taxis ferry you into **Koh Kong** town for onward transport to Sihanoukville and Phnom Penh or for guesthouses should you arrive too late for connections (mid-afternoon onwards). **Vans, buses and share-taxis** to Phnom Penh and Sihanoukville should take around 4–5hr.

ACCOMMODATION AND EATING

The day market, on the ground floor of the Th Sukhumvit shopping centre, and the atmospheric night market, north of the historic centre, between Soi Vichidanya and Soi Kasemsan (east of Th Sukhumvit), are good places to eat.

★**Ban Jaidee** 67–69 Th Chaimongkon, about 200m southeast of the market ⓣ083 589 0839. Very calm, inviting and rather stylish guesthouse with a pleasant seating area downstairs and simple bedrooms sharing hot-water bathrooms. The nicest rooms are in the original building and have polished wood floors. Double **B200**

★**Cool Corner** 49–51 Th Thoncharoen, about 200m southeast off the main Th Sukhumvit. An enjoyably arty spot to chill out over real coffee, quality breakfasts, veggie specials and great Thai food, such as chicken and cashew nuts (B90). Daily 7.30am–9/10pm, usually with an hour-long break in the afternoon.

Residang House 87/1–2 Th Thoncharoen, about 500m southeast off the main Th Sukhumvit ⓣ039 530103, ⓦtrat-guesthouse.com. Comfortably appointed, good-value German–Thai-managed guesthouse. Rooms are large, light and clean and all have thick mattresses, hot-water bathrooms and wi-fi. Double **B350**

KO CHANG

The focal point of a national marine park archipelago of 52 islands, **Ko Chang** is Thailand's second-largest island (after Phuket) and an increasingly popular destination, drawing crowds to its beautiful white-sand beaches, which are backed by a mountainous interior of dense jungle. During peak season, accommodation on the west coast fills up very fast, but it gets quieter (and cheaper) from May to October, when fierce storms can make the sea too rough for swimming.

Hat Sai Khao (White Sand Beach)

Framed by a broad band of fine white sand at low tide, **Hat Sai Khao** (White Sand Beach) is the island's longest beach but also its most commercial, with scores of unattractive hotel-style developments and bungalow operations squashed in between the road and the shore. The atmosphere is more laidback and traveller-oriented at the northern end of the beach, however, where through a maze of haphazard boardwalks (a high-tide necessity) you'll find the most budget-priced accommodation. Currents can get very strong on Hat Sai Khao, so be careful when swimming.

Hat Khlong Phrao and Hat Kai Bae

Just south of the khlong fed by **Khlong Phu Waterfall** (B200 entry) is the long sandy beach of central **Hat Khlong Prao**, which remains a beauty. Behind a thin line of casuarinas there's a scattering of cheap and charming bungalow operations nestled in a huge coconut grove. About 5km further south, the narrow, once-beautiful beach at **Hat Kai Bae**, while almost ruined by breakneck development, remains quaint at its southern extremity.

Hat Tha Nam (Lonely Beach)

Around the southern headland from Hat Kai Bae is the long curve of white-sand bay at **Hat Tha Nam** – dubbed **Lonely Beach** before it became the backpackers' haven – which is lovely, if slightly sullied by a few ugly developments. There's a youthful atmosphere, cheapish accommodation and raucous parties

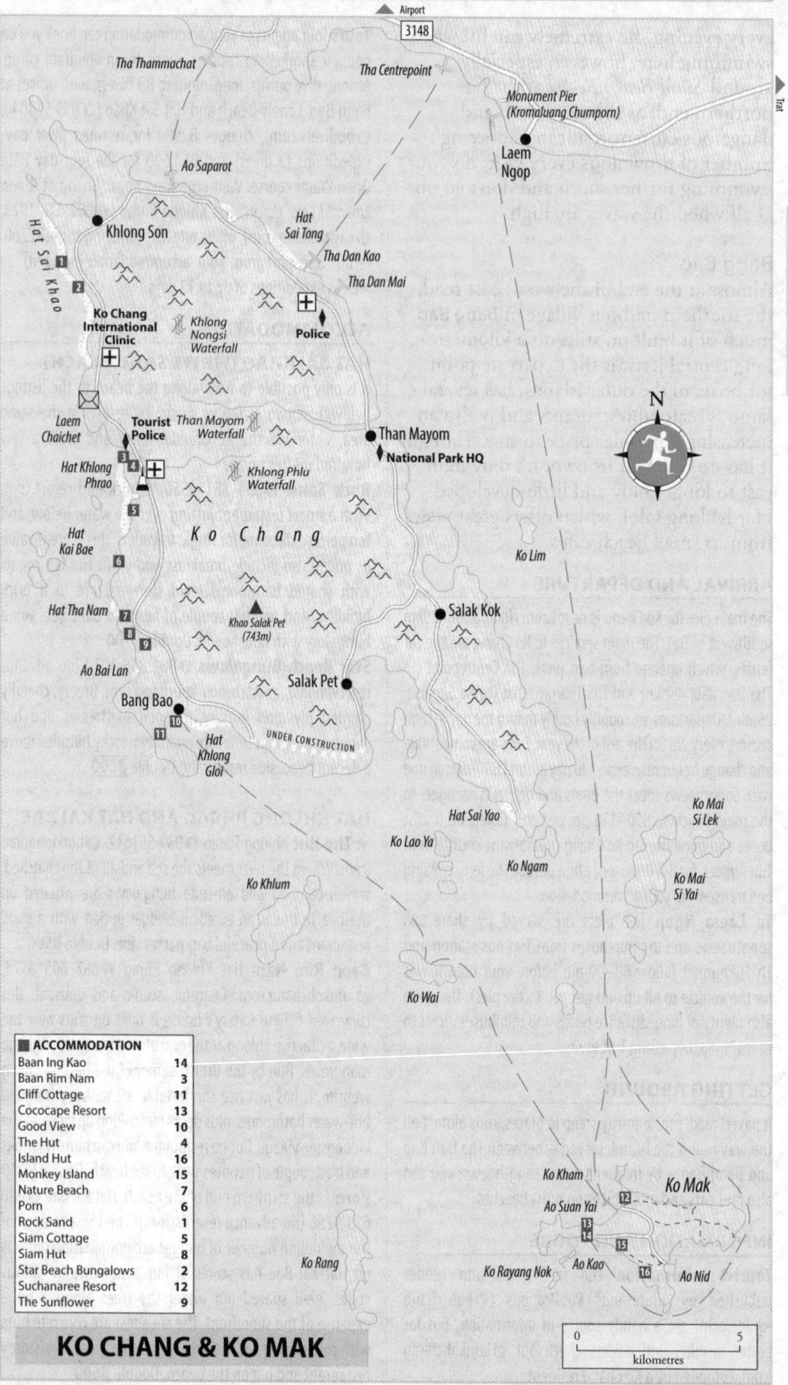
KO CHANG & KO MAK
Airport
3148
Tha Thammachat
Tha Centrepoint
Monument Pier
(Kromaluang Chumporn)
Trat
Laem Ngop
Ao Saparot
Hat Sai Khao
Khlong Son
Hat Sai Tong
Tha Dan Kao
Tha Dan Mai
Ko Chang International Clinic
Khlong Nongsi Waterfall
Police
Laem Chaichet
Tourist Police
Than Mayom Waterfall
Than Mayom
National Park HQ
Hat Khlong Phrao
Khlong Phlu Waterfall
Hat Kai Bae
Ko Chang
Ko Lim
Hat Tha Nam
Khao Salak Pet (743m)
Salak Kok
Ao Bai Lan
Salak Pet
Bang Bao
Hat Khlong Gloi
UNDER CONSTRUCTION
Hat Sai Yao
Ko Lao Ya
Ko Ngam
Ko Mai Si Lek
Ko Mai Si Yai
Ko Khlum
Ko Wai
Ko Kham
Ko Mak
Ao Suan Yai
Ko Rang
Ko Rayang Nok
Ao Kao
Ao Nid
N
0
5
kilometres
ACCOMMODATION
Baan Ing Kao 14
Baan Rim Nam 3
Cliff Cottage 11
Cococape Resort 13
Good View 10
The Hut 4
Island Hut 16
Monkey Island 15
Nature Beach 7
Porn 6
Rock Sand 1
Siam Cottage 5
Siam Hut 8
Star Beach Bungalows 2
Suchanaree Resort 12
The Sunflower 9

every evening. Be extremely careful when swimming here, however, especially around *Siam Beach Resort* at the far northern end, as the steep shelf and dangerous current result in a sobering number of **drownings** every year; do your swimming further south and don't go out at all when the waves are high.

Bang Bao

Almost at the end of the west-coast road, the southern harbour village of **Bang Bao**, much of it built on stilts off a kilometre-long central jetty, is the departure point for boats to the outer islands, has several famous seafood restaurants and is also an increasingly popular place to stay. Though it has no beach of its own, it's only 2km east to long, sandy and little-developed Hat Khlong Gloi, which offers great views from its small beach cafés.

ARRIVAL AND DEPARTURE

The main pier for Ko Chang is near Laem Ngop, about 20km southwest of Trat. The main services to Ko Chang are the car ferries, which operate from two piers, Tha Centrepoint (to Tha Dan Kao; 45min) and Tha Thammachat (to Ao Saparot; 25min). Departures are roughly hourly during the day in high season, every 2hr for the rest of the year. Fares are competitive and change frequently: expect to pay around B80/person one way. Songthaews meet the boats and deliver passengers to the main beaches (B50–150 per person). Tickets on tourist buses and minibuses to Ko Chang (notably the shuttle from Trat Airport, for B470/person) often include the ferry crossing and transport to your accommodation.

To Laem Ngop The piers are served by share-taxi songthaews and a/c minibuses from Trat bus station and Th Sukhumvit (allow 60–90min before your boat leaves for the vehicle to fill up and get you to the pier). There are also plenty of long-distance buses and minibuses direct to Laem Ngop, bypassing Trat town.

GETTING AROUND

A paved road, precipitously steep in places, runs almost all the way round the island, served – between Tha Dan Kao and Bang Bao – by frequent public songthaews; you can also rent cars and motorbikes on most beaches.

INFORMATION AND TOURS

Tourist information The free maps and guides published by Whitesands Publications (Ⓦ koh-chang-guide.com) are a handy source of information, but for better insights and advice, check out Ⓦ iamkohchang.com, compiled by a Ko Chang resident.

Tours Tour agents or your accommodation can book you on popular snorkelling trips or a visit to an elephant camp. Among dive outfits, long-running BB Divers, with offices at Bang Bao, Lonely Beach and Hat Sai Khao (Ⓣ 039 558040, Ⓦ bbdivers.com), charges B2900 for certified diver day-expeditions (2 dives) and B14,500 for the four-day PADI Open Water course. Well-organized Kayak Chang at *Amari Emerald Cove Resort*, Hat Khlong Phrao (Ⓣ 087 673 1923, Ⓦ kayakchang.com), offers one-day kayaking trips (B2200, return transport from your accommodation included), as well as expeditions of up to 12 days.

ACCOMMODATION

HAT SAI KHAO (WHITE SAND BEACH)

It is only possible to walk along the beach to the listings below, just two of ten or so similar resorts in the same area; enter via the *KC Grande Resort* and walk a few hundred metres north.

Rock Sand Ⓣ 084 781 0550, Ⓦ rocksand-resort.com. With a smart restaurant jutting over the water below, and ten percent discount for single travellers, this is great value as prices also include breakfast and wi-fi. The fan rooms with shared bathrooms (cold showers) are in a brick building, and another couple of hundred baht gets you a bungalow with hot shower. Double **B700**

Star Beach Bungalows Ⓣ 084 345 1079 (no advance reservations), Ⓦ starbeach-kohchang.com. Breezy, cheerily painted plywood huts, with good mattresses and hot showers, perch precariously on a steep rocky hillside, above a decent beachside restaurant. Double **B600**

HAT KHLONG PHRAO AND HAT KAI BAE

★**The Hut** Khlong Phrao Ⓣ 039 551632, Ⓦ hutklongprao.com. Where the river meets the sea and all of the thatched, woven-bamboo and en-suite bungalows are situated on the beach; this is an excellent budget option with a good restaurant and a peaceful backpacker vibe. Double **B500**

Baan Rim Nam Hat Khlong Phrao Ⓣ 087 005 8575, Ⓦ iamkohchang.com. Peaceful, scenic and unusual, this converted fishing family's house is built on stilts over the wide, attractive khlong at the end of a walkway through the mangroves. Run by the British author of the best Ko Chang website, it has just five comfortable a/c rooms with good hot-water bathrooms, plus decks for soaking up views of the khlongside village, but no restaurant. You can borrow kayaks and it's a couple of minutes' walk to the beach. Double **B900**

Porn At the southern end of the beach, Hat Kai Bae Ⓣ 080 613 9266 (no advance reservations). The most famous of the dwindling number of budget accommodation options on Hat Kai Bae has scores of fan bungalows in various styles, well spaced out under the trees along a huge expanse of the shorefront. The cheapest are concrete huts with cold showers at the back. Also has a great two-storey restaurant and bar on the beach. Double **B600**

Siam Cottage Northern Hat Kai Bae 089 153 6664. With cheerily painted interiors, partly outdoor bathrooms and decks, the wooden bungalows here face each other across a narrow but well-watered, flowery lot that runs down to the sea and a cute restaurant. Double **B500**

HAT THA NAM (LONELY BEACH)

Nature Beach Central Lonely Beach 081 803 8933. Responsible for Lonely Beach's party reputation, this place's rooms, bar-restaurant (with built-in DJ station) and the beach out front are all hugely popular. The cheapest of its shady, closely set bungalows are attractive, polished-concrete en-suite abodes with verandas at the back by the road. Double **B500**

Siam Hut Central Lonely Beach 086 609 7772. Row upon row of flimsy, primitive, bamboo huts, all of which are en suite. It is, however, one of the few remaining budget options on the beach. There's a big restaurant/bar deck that's great for watching the sunset and hosts barbecues, movies and parties. Double **B480**

The Sunflower Soi Sunset 084 017 9960. Run by a genial German and his Thai family, the bungalows here are set under palm and banana trees 200m or so from the roadside village and equidistant from the rocky coast at *Sunset Hut*, a 5min walk south of the sandy beach. Choose between wooden fan bungalows with mosquito nets and open-roofed, hot-water bathrooms, and concrete bungalows with a/c; all have good thick mattresses and are kept very clean. The restaurant is also good. Double **B500**

BANG BAO

★**Cliff Cottage** West side of Bang Bao bay 085 904 6706, cliff-cottage.com. British-run resort with a nice deck restaurant on a west-facing cove, and kayaks and snorkels for rent. Basic, thatched, bare-wood huts with decent mattresses, mosquito nets, shared bathrooms and good sunset views sit up on a small, dusty, shady rise; there's also a rowhouse of a/c rooms, all with hot showers, facing in on Bang Bao bay. Double **B400**

Good View Bang Bao jetty 089 108 0429, goodview bangbao.wordpress.com. Built over the water halfway down the east side of the jetty, the good views from this guest-house take in the shoreline opposite. Lovely, clean, bright, large, wooden-floored bedrooms come with huge hot-water bathrooms, big balconies and a/c – it's worth paying B200 extra for an upstairs room. There's a very large, attractive ground-floor deck with a book corner. Double **B800**

DIRECTORY

Most beaches offer ATMs, currency exchange and internet access.

Clinic The 24hr Ko Chang International Clinic (1719 or 039 551155, bangkoktrathospital.com) is beyond the south end of White Sand Beach.

Post office On the road between Sai Khao and Khlong Phrao (Mon–Fri 10am–noon & 1–6pm, Sat 10am–1pm).

Tourist police At the north end of Hat Klong Phrao (1155).

KO MAK

Tiny **Ko Mak** (sometimes spelt "Maak") is 20km southeast of Ko Chang and offers a slow-paced, peaceful alternative. An interior of palm and rubber plantations makes road journeys a pleasure, and the colourful reefs and fishes of nearby islands are a treat for scuba divers and snorkellers (contact Koh Mak Divers, 083 297 7724, kohmakdivers.com). The palm-fringed, white-sand and shallow **Ao Kao** on the southwest coast is the most developed beach, with plush resorts and a couple of budget options. Long, curvy **Ao Suan Yai**, on the northwest coast, also has fine sand and a pretty outlook. Most bungalows offer, or can arrange, motorbike (B300–350/day) or mountain-bike (B150/day) rental, and there's a small clinic off the Ao Nid road, though no banks or ATMs.

ARRIVAL AND DEPARTURE

From Trat/Laem Ngop In high season, up to five speedboats a day run from Kromaluang (Monument) pier in Laem Ngop, to either Ao Kao or Ao Suan Yai on Ko Mak (45min; B450). A/c minibuses to Laem Ngop from Bangkok, for example, will sometimes only go as far as the Thammachat or Centrepoint Ko Chang piers, however – check exactly which piers are served when you buy your minibus ticket, or you may be able to pay the driver a little extra to go on to Kromaluang.

From Ko Chang The main company is Bang Bao Boat (087 054 4300), which in high season runs a slow boat once daily (2hr; B400) and a speedboat twice daily (1hr; B550) from Bang Bao pier in the south of Ko Chang to Ao Suan Yai on Ko Mak. Prices include transfers to or from the west coast of Ko Chang.

ACCOMMODATION

It is best to book accommodation in advance for free pick-up transfers from the piers.

Baan Ing Kao Ao Kao 087 053 9553. Located over a steep hill at the western end of the beach, this secluded resort of thatched bamboo bungalows exudes a quaint, village-like atmosphere. The beach is rocky and kayaks can be rented to explore the islands close by. Double **B350**

Island Hut Ao Kao 087 139 5537. The cheapest option on the island, offering en-suite rough-hewn timber huts,

10

10

★TREAT YOURSELF

Cocoape Resort (T 039 501003, W kohmakcococape.com). Southern end of Ao Suan Yai. Individually designed rooms, bungalows and converted boats situated on a rocky cliffside offering stunning views over the bay or around a lotus pond. *Cococape* has direct access to good snorkelling via a small, wooden pier with a sun deck and a cocktail bar as well as easy access to the lovely Ko Pee across the water. The beach is a short walk away and there is a pool and two restaurants serving Thai and Western food. Double **B900**

many with idiosyncratic driftwood artwork, on a quiet stretch of beach. Double **B250**

Monkey Island Ao Kao T 089 501 6030, W monkeyislandkohmak.com. A laidback, monkey-themed resort which has a wide range of accommodation, starting with nice, thatched wooden huts with shared facilities and hammocks. There's also a beach bar with live reggae and Thai folk every evening. Double **B350**

★**Suchanaree Resort** Ao Suan Yai T 081 983 2629. Friendly little place in a lush garden, set by a stream with tables and deckchairs on the shady, beachfront lawn. The small, basic but good-quality, shaggy-thatched wooden bungalows all have fan, mozzie nets and bathrooms. The island post office service, internet access, money-change and transport bookings are all offered at *Koh Mak Resort* next door. B650.

Southern Thailand: the Gulf coast

Southern Thailand's Gulf coast is famous chiefly for the three fine islands of the Samui archipelago: large and increasingly upmarket **Ko Samui**, laidback **Ko Pha Ngan**, site of monthly full-moon parties at **Hat Rin**, and tiny **Ko Tao**, which is encircled by some of Thailand's best dive sites. Other attractions seem minor by comparison, but the historic town of **Phetchaburi** has a certain charm, and the grand old temples in **Nakhon Si Thammarat** are worth a detour.

The Gulf coast has a slightly different **climate** from the rest of Thailand, being hit heavily by the northeast monsoon's rains, especially in November, when it's best to avoid this part of the country altogether. Most times during the rest of the year should see pleasant, if changeable, weather, with some effects of the southwest monsoon felt between May and October.

PHETCHABURI

Straddling the River Phet about 120km south of Bangkok, the provincial capital of **PHETCHABURI** flourished as a seventeenth-century trading post. Now a centre for sweet manufacturing, it retains much of its old-world charm, with fine historic wats, wooden shophouses and a nineteenth-century hilltop palace.

WHAT TO SEE AND DO

The town's central sights cluster around Chomrut Bridge (**Saphaan Chomrut**) and the River Phet. About 700m east of the bridge is the still-functioning seventeenth-century **Wat Yai Suwannaram** which contains a remarkable set of faded old murals, depicting divinities ranged in rows of ascending importance, in its ordination hall and a well-preserved scripture library built on stilts over a pond. A further five minutes' walk east, and then ten minutes' walk south, takes you to the five crumbling stone prangs of **Wat Kamphaeng Laeng**, elegant structures of weathered earth-tone beauty. Built to enshrine Hindu deities, they were later adapted for Buddhist use. A short way southwest of Chomrut Bridge stands Phetchaburi's most fully restored and important temple, **Wat Mahathat**, probably founded in the fourteenth century. The five landmark prangs at its heart are adorned with stucco figures of mythical creatures, while miniature angels and gods embellish the roofs of the main viharn and bot.

About thirty minutes' walk west of Chomrut Bridge is **Khao Wang**, the hill on which stands Rama IV's palace – a great place to explore. Quaint brick paths wind through a forest of gnarled frangipanis, some covered in brilliant

flowering vines, to reveal whitewashed – now peeling and pleasingly mottled – chedis and gazebos, as well as the king's summer house, Phra Nakhon Khiri, and observatory, now a museum (daily 8.30am–4pm; B150). It's reached on foot from near the western end of Thanon Rajwithi or by cable car from the western base of the hill off Highway 4 (daily 8.30am–4.30pm; B40); songthaews from Chomrut Bridge should drop you close to either access point. The hill is populated by a large number of monkeys, who can be aggressive, so keep your distance and don't carry food.

ARRIVAL AND DEPARTURE

By bus Phetchaburi is served mostly by through-buses on their way to or from Bangkok. Highway 4 passes right through the west side of town – ask to get off at "Sii Yaek Phetcharat", the crossroads by Phetcharat Hospital, about 2km southwest of Chomrut Bridge (catch a songthaew or motorbike taxi). The station for dedicated Phetchaburi–Bangkok buses is close to the night market, and there are a/c minibuses to Bangkok's Victory Monument just east of here across the river; from the night market, it's an easy 10min walk south to Chomrut Bridge.

Destinations Bangkok (4–7 daily; 2hr 15min); Chumphon (roughly hourly; 5hr); Nakhon Si Thammarat (2 daily; 12–13hr); Surat Thani (10 daily; 7hr).

By train The train station is about 1km northwest of Chomrut Bridge.

Destinations Bangkok (Hualamphong 10 daily, Thonburi Station 3 daily; 3hr); Chumphon (10 daily; 4hr–6hr 30min); Surat Thani (8 daily; 6hr 45min–9hr).

ACCOMMODATION AND EATING

Decent, cheap accommodation is in short supply in Phetchaburi.

Rabieng Rimnum Guest House Beside Chomrut Bridge at 1 Th Chisa-in ⊕032 425707. Situated in a century-old teak house, this guesthouse offers basic rooms with hard mattresses and shared facilities; it can get noisy, so ask for a room away from the road. The staff are helpful and can provide a town map, and the riverside restaurant serves a range of excellent Thai food (from B60) accompanied by a blues and Americana soundtrack. Double B240

CHUMPHON

CHUMPHON is the main departure point for Ko Tao, and can also give access to the more distant islands of Ko Pha Ngan and Ko Samui, but is otherwise of little interest. Thanon Sala Daeng, running north–south, is the city's main stem, a good place to orient yourself, and the place to head to for most amenities. If you do find yourself stuck here and hungry, then follow the smells to the night market on east–west Thanon Kromluang Chumphon.

ARRIVAL AND DEPARTURE

BY PLANE

Nok Air (2 daily; 1hr 10min) flies from Don Muang to Chumphon Airport, which is 40km north of town, and sells through-tickets to Ko Tao with Lomprayah. Happy Air flies once daily (except Tues; 1hr; ⓦhappyair.co.th) from Suvarnabhumi. A/c minibuses to hotels in Chumphon will cost B150/person (B600/vehicle).

BY BOAT

Tickets for all boats are sold by travel agents and guesthouses in town. As well as the services below, there are several different night boats (B200–400 depending on quality; pick-ups from town extra), which take about 6hr to reach Ko Tao. Lomprayah and Songserm tickets include transport to the pier from town, with pick-ups available even from guesthouses and from the station, including off the overnight train from Bangkok that arrives around 4am.

Lomprayah Catamaran Office at the train station ⊕077 558212–3, ⓦlomprayah.com. Twice daily from Ao Thung Makham Noi, 27km south of Chumphon; 1hr 45min to Ko Tao (B600); around 3hr 30min to Ko Pha Ngan (B1000); around 4hr to Maenam, Ko Samui (B1100).

Songserm Express Office at the train station ⊕077 506205, ⓦsongserm-expressboat.com. Daily from Pak Nam, about 20km south of Chumphon; 3hr to Ko Tao (B500); around 5hr to Ko Pha Ngan (B900).

BY BUS AND MINIBUS

The government bus station is 11km south of town on Highway 4, where buses to all points north and south will call in; it's connected to the centre by songthaews (B50/person). Long-distance services will sometimes drop in town; two Bangkok a/c buses a day drop off and pick up on Th Tawee Sinka, west of TAT. Among private bus services, Chokeanan Tour buses to Bangkok (4 daily; 8hr) and some Rungkit buses to Phuket (5 daily; 7hr), via Ranong and Khao Lak, start from Th Pracha Uthit, which runs southeast from Th Sala Daeng. Ask at TAT or your guesthouse about a/c minibuses from Chumphon to places such as Krabi and Ko Lanta, most of which are tourist services organized by travel agents.

BY TRAIN

The train station is 100m west of Th Sala Daeng on Th Kromluang Chumphon.

Destinations Bangkok (12 daily; 7hr–9hr 30min); Phetchaburi (10 daily; 4hr–6hr 30min); Surat Thani (11 daily; 2–4hr).

INFORMATION

The TAT office is down a short soi at 111 Th Tawee Sinka, which runs northwest off Th Sala Daeng (daily 8.30am–4.30pm; ☎ 077 501831, ✉ tatchumphon@tat.or.th).

10

ACCOMMODATION

Fame 188/20–21 Th Sala Daeng ☎ 077 571077, ⓦ chumphon-kohtao.com. Above a good travellers' restaurant, specializing in Italian food, and a reliable tour agency, both of the same name, this place has good-sized and very clean rooms (some with mattresses on the floor), with fans and hot water in either shared or en-suite bathrooms. Double B150

Suda Guest House Th Sala Daeng Soi 3 (aka Soi Bangkok Bank), 30m off Th Tha Tapao ☎ 077 504366. Welcoming guesthouse and travel agent, offering clean, well-maintained rooms, some with shared hot-water bathrooms, and plenty of information. Double B250

SURAT THANI

Uninspiring **SURAT THANI** is of use only as a jumping-off point for trips to Ko Samui, Ko Pha Ngan and, at a pinch, more distant Ko Tao. On Thanon Ban Don, which hugs the River Tapi on the northwest side of the town centre, you'll find Ban Don pier and an atmospheric night market. To the south, east–west Thanon Namuang bustles with retail trade, while multi-laned Thanon Taladmai, the next block south, is the town's main thoroughfare; the bus terminals, Talat Kaset I and Talat Kaset II, are here, a few hundred metres east of the main post office.

ARRIVAL AND DEPARTURE

BY PLANE

Air Asia, Nok Air and Thai Smile serve Surat Airport, 27km northwest of town. A minibus (B100) connects with the town centre, or you can buy a bus-boat combination ticket to Ko Samui (B350) or Ko Pha Ngan (B550).

Destinations Bangkok (9 daily; 1hr 15min); Kuala Lumpur, Malaysia (3 weekly; 1hr 35min).

BY BOAT

Details of boats to Ko Samui, Ko Pha Ngan and Ko Tao, most of which leave from Don Sak pier, 68km east of Surat, are given in the account of each island. Phunphin and the bus stations are teeming with touts, with transport waiting to escort you to their employer's boat service to the islands – they're generally reliable, but make sure you don't get talked onto the wrong boat.

Lomprayah Th Taladmai, just east of Taksin Hospital ☎ 077 288732–3, ⓦ lomprayah.com. Catamarans to Samui and Pha Ngan, with their own connecting buses to Don Sak and connections on to Ko Tao.

Samui Tour Th Sriwichai ☎ 077 372806. Handles buses to Ko Samui and Ko Pha Ngan via the Raja vehicle ferries from Don Sak.

Seatran In the petrol station on Th Taladmai opposite Wat Thammabucha ☎ 077 275063, ⓦ seatranferry.com. Vehicle ferries to Samui (with their own connecting buses), from Don Sak.

Night boats The night boats to Samui, Pha Ngan and Tao, which are barely glorified cargo boats, line up during the day at Ban Don Pier in the centre of Surat; turn up and buy a ticket as early as you can to snag a bed.

BY BUS

Buses use three different locations, two of which are on Th Taladmai in the centre of town: Talat Kaset I on the north side of the road (Phunphin train station, non-a/c Nakhon Si Thammarat services and other local buses) and opposite at Talat Kaset II (a/c minibuses and most long-distance buses, including those for Krabi, Phuket and Ranong, and Nakhon Si Thammarat a/c services). The new BKS (Baw Khaw Saw) terminal, 2km southwest of the centre on the road towards Phunphin, handles mostly Bangkok services. Many buses heading west out of Surat also make a stop at Phunphin train station.

Destinations Bangkok (12 daily; 10–12hr); Chumphon (roughly hourly; 3hr 30min); Khao Sok (10 daily; 2hr 30min); Krabi (roughly hourly; 3–4hr); Nakhon Si Thammarat (21 daily; 2hr 30min); Phuket (8 daily; 5–6hr); Ranong (10 daily; 4hr 30min).

BY TRAIN

The train station is at Phunphin, 13km to the west. Here you can buy a boat ticket to Ko Samui and Ko Pha Ngan, including a connecting bus to the relevant pier. Otherwise, buses run into town every 40min or so during the day.

Destinations Bangkok (10 daily; 9–12hr); Butterworth, Malaysia (1 daily; 10hr 30min); Nakhon Si Thammarat (2 daily; 4hr); Trang (2 daily; 4hr 30min).

GETTING AROUND

Small share-songthaews buzz around town, charging around B15–20/person for most journeys.

INFORMATION

Tourist information TAT (daily 8.30am–4.30pm; ☎ 077 288818, ✉ tatsurat@tat.or.th) is at the western end of

town at 5 Th Taladmai. Surat's best travel agency is the reliable Phantip, in front of Talat Kaset I at 293/6–8 Th Taladmai (T 077 272230 or T 077 272906), where you can book bus-and-boat, train and plane tickets.

ACCOMMODATION AND EATING

There's a large night market on Th Ton Pho between Th Si Namuang and Th Ban Don, which displays an eye-catching range of dishes; a smaller offshoot by Ban Don pier offers less choice but is handy if you're taking a night boat.

Ban Don Hotel 268/2 Th Namuang T 077 272167. Set above a basic but good Thai-Chinese restaurant, most of the very clean rooms here, with en-suite cold-water bathrooms, TV and fans or a/c, are set back from the noise of the main road. Double B250

Milano Opposite the night-boat piers on Th Ban Don. This place has an authentic oven turning out very tasty and reasonably priced pizzas, though its home-made pasta is less successful. Also serves breakfasts and espresso coffee. Daily 10am–11pm.

My Place 247/5 Th Namuang T 077 272288, W myplacesurat.com. A recently renovated spot near the night market in the town centre with wi-fi. The cheapest rooms have shared facilities and plusher en-suite options are available for B120 more. Double B199

KO SAMUI

An ever-widening cross section of visitors, from globetrotting backpackers to suitcase-toting fortnighters, comes to southern Thailand just for the beautiful beaches of **Ko Samui**, 80km from Surat Thani. At 15km across and down, Samui is generally large enough to cope with this diversity, except during the Christmas and New Year rush. The island was once *the* destination for paradise sands fringed with palm trees, but development behind the beaches is extensive and often thoughtless, with girly bars by the main beaches beginning to rival those of Phuket. At least there's a local bylaw limiting construction to the height of a coconut palm (about three storeys), and there are still a few pockets of bungalows for backpackers.

Na Thon

The island capital, **NA THON** is a frenetic half-built town that most travellers use only for stocking up with supplies en route to the beaches. The three piers come to land at the promenade, Thanon Chonvithi, which is paralleled by Thanon Taweeratpakdee (or Route 4169), the round-island road.

Maenam

The 4km bay of **Maenam**, 13km from Na Thon, with its leafy, relatively unadulterated beachfront set well away from the ugly round-island road, is an attractive location for a day or two of swimming and relaxation. Here, a number of quiet, cheap beachside accommodations, offering great views, make Maenam a popular destination for budget travellers. On Thursday evenings, the pier road at the centre of Ban Maenam village becomes a pleasant **walking street**, with performances, cheap souvenirs and lots of food stalls.

10

Bophut, Bangrak and Choeng Mon

The next beach east of Maenam is 2km-long **Bophut**. The beach here is wider and has welcoming clear water, but the area is becoming steadily more upmarket and now has hardly any budget accommodation. Its narrow beach road is surprisingly quaint, however, with a number of attractive, traditional Thai wooden buildings in what's now tagged "**Fisherman's Village**". At night, the village is a pleasant place for a stroll, with a concentration of good restaurants; on Friday evenings, it hosts a **walking street** very similar to Maenam's.

Bangrak is also known as Big Buddha Beach, after the huge **Big Buddha** statue on a small island at the east end of the bay, which gazes down on the sunbathers populating its less-than-perfect beach. A short causeway leads to a clump of souvenir shops and food stalls in front of the temple, and ceremonial dragon-steps take you to the terrace around the statue, from where there's a fine view of the sweeping north coast.

After Bangrak comes the northeastern cape and beautiful, laidback **Choeng Mon**, whose white sandy beach is lined with casuarina trees.

Chaweng

For sheer natural beauty, none of the other beaches can match **Chaweng**,

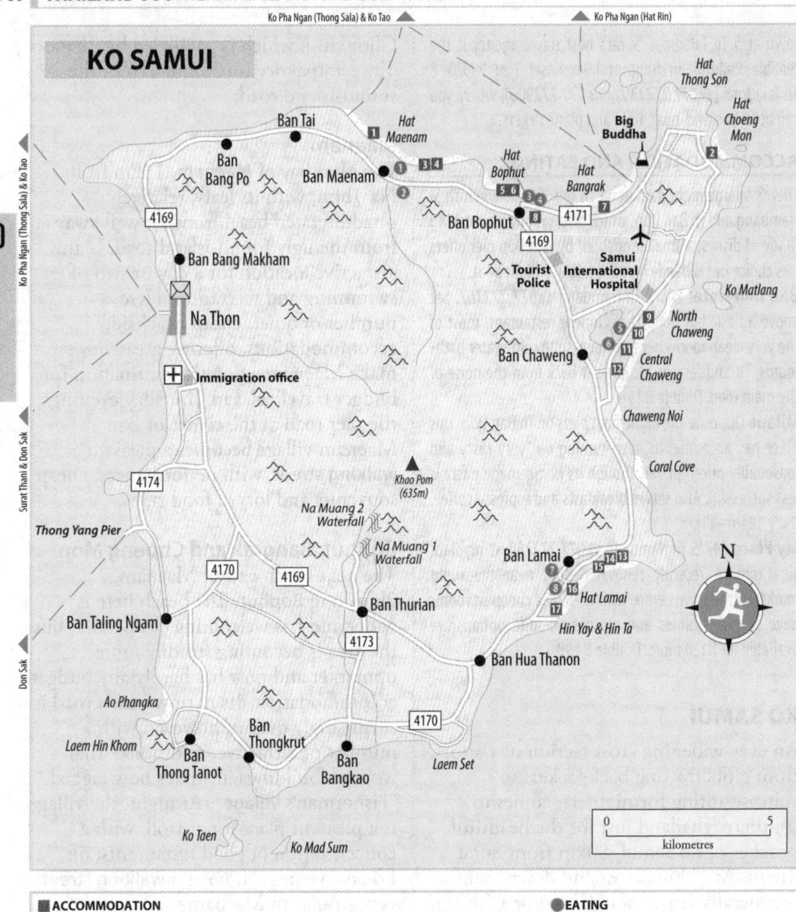

10

ACCOMMODATION

Akwa Guesthouse	12	Green Villa	17	The Scent	7
Amity Bungalows	16	Khunthai Guesthouse	6	Shangrilah	1
Baan Kluaymai Guesthouse	11	The Loft Samui	10	The Wave	9
Beer House	15	Moonhut	3		
Bophut Mansion	8	New Hut	14		
Cactus	5	New Lapaz Villa	4		
Flower Paradise	13	Ô Soleil	2		

EATING

Angela's Bakery	2	La Fabrique	7
Eldorado	8	Ninja Crepes	6
Juzz'a Pizza 2	3	Noori	5
Ko Seng	1	Satsuman	4

with its gently sloping 6km strip of white sand framed between the small island of Ko Matlang at the north end and the headland above Coral Cove in the south. However, there has been heavy development and resorts are piled side to side along the stretch of road. There are numerous tacky bars with thumping nightlife set just a few steps back from the beach, and diverse watersports are also on offer here. An ugly sprawl of amenities stretches for 2km behind the central section to the round-island road and the original village of Ban Chaweng.

Lamai and around

Lamai is almost as heavily developed as Chaweng and its nightlife is just as tawdry, with planeloads of European tourists sinking buckets of booze at women's Thai boxing, mud-wrestling shows and hostess bars. Running roughly north–south for 4km, the white palm-fringed beach is, fortunately, still a picture. It's possible to avoid the mayhem

by staying at the quiet extremities of the bay, where there's still a decent selection of beachside backpackers' resorts. The nightlife action is concentrated behind the centre of the beach, where you'll also find supermarkets, banks, ATMs, clinics, internet outlets and vehicle rental. The small rock formations on the bay's southern promontory, Hin Yay ("Grandmother Rock") and Hin Ta ("Grandfather Rock"), never fail to raise a giggle with their resemblance to the male and female sexual organs.

Na Muang Falls

About 10km inland of Lamai, off the round-island road, lie **Na Muang Falls**. Each of the two main falls has its own kilometre-long paved access road off Route 4169: the lower falls splash down a 20m wall of rock into a large pool, while Na Muang 2, upstream, is a more spectacular cascade that requires a bit of foot-slogging from the car park (about 15min uphill); alternatively, you can walk up there from Na Muang 1, by taking the 1.5km trail that begins 300m back along the access road from the lower fall.

ARRIVAL AND DEPARTURE

BY PLANE

Flights to Samui are among the most expensive in Thailand, so you might want to consider flying from Bangkok to Surat Thani or Nakhon Si Thammarat; Nok Air and Air Asia offer good-value through-tickets via either of these airports, including flight, bus and boat to Samui. You can get to Ko Samui direct from Suvarnabhumi Airport with Thai Airways (2 daily), or with Bangkok Airways (about 20 daily), which also operates flights from Chiang Mai, Hong Kong, Krabi, Kuala Lumpur, Phuket and Singapore. A/c minibuses meet incoming flights (and connect with departures, bookable through your accommodation), charging B130 to Chaweng for example.

BY BOAT

The most obvious way of getting to Ko Samui is on a boat from the Surat Thani area, the main piers being at Don Sak, 68km east of Surat. The main port on Samui is Na Thon; Thong Yang pier is 9km south of Na Thon. Buses leave about 1hr 30min before boat departure from Surat Thani centre and 1hr 45min before from the train station. The night boat leaves Ban Don pier in Surat Thani for Na Thon at 11pm daily (6hr); tickets (B250) are sold at the pier on the day of departure. Boats to Ko Pha Ngan (see p.790), Ko Tao (see p.794) and from Chumphon (see p.783) all offer the same service in the return direction.

Lomprayah Catamaran to Na Thon (Na Thon **T** 077 950028, **W** lomprayah.com): twice daily; 45min; B450 including bus from Surat Thani, B500 from Phunphin. Both continue to Ko Pha Ngan.

Seatran vehicle ferries to Na Thon (Samui **T** 077 426000–2, **W** seatranferry.com): hourly; 1hr 30min; B270 including bus from Surat Thani, B320 from Phunphin.

Raja vehicle ferries to Lipa Noi aka Thong Yang (Samui **T** 077 415230–3, **W** rajaferryport.com): hourly; 1hr 30min; B270 including bus from Surat Thani, B320 from Phunphin.

10

BY LONG-DISTANCE BUS

Ko Samui's government bus terminal (Baw Khaw Saw) is on Th Taweeratpakdee towards the north end of Na Thon (**T** 077 421125 or **T** 077 420765). It handles bus-and-boat services (via Don Sak and Lipa Noi), for example from Bangkok's Southern Terminal (some also stopping at Mo Chit bus terminal; 9–10 daily; 13hr), which cost from B608 on a basic a/c bus to B1066 on a VIP bus – these are far preferable to the cheap deals offered by dodgy travel agents on Th Khao San, as the vehicles used on the latter services are often substandard and many thefts have been reported. The Baw Khaw Saw also sells through-tickets to Nakhon Si Thammarat (roughly hourly; 4hr), which involve catching the ferry to Don Sak, then changing on to an a/c minibus.

GETTING AROUND

By car and motorbike You can rent motorbikes (from B200/day) at all the main beaches, though note that dozens are killed on Samui's roads each year, so go with extreme caution and wear a helmet. You can also rent four-wheel drives (from B800).

By songthaew Songthaews, which congregate at the car park near the southerly pier in Na Thon, cover a variety of set routes during the daytime, either heading off clockwise or anticlockwise on Route 4169, to serve all the beaches; destinations are marked in English and fares range from B40–50 to Maenam to B80–100 to Chaweng or Lamai. In the evening, they tend to operate more like taxis and you'll have to negotiate a fare to get them to take you exactly where you want to go.

By taxi Ko Samui sports dozens of a/c taxis. Although they all have meters, you'd be wasting your breath trying to persuade any driver to use his; instead, you're looking at a flat fare of around B500 from Na Thon to Chaweng, for example.

INFORMATION

Tourist information TAT runs a small but helpful office (daily 8.30am–noon & 1–4.30pm; **T** 077 420504,

tatsamui@tat.or.th), tucked away on an unnamed side road in Na Thon, north of the pier and inland from the post office. Another useful source of information is samui.sawadee.com, which allows direct booking at a range of hotels on the island.

DIVING

10

Samui has around a dozen scuba-diving companies, offering trips for divers and snorkellers and courses throughout the year, and there's a decompression chamber at Bangrak (081 081 9555, sssnetwork.com). Most trips for experienced divers, however, head for the waters around Ko Tao (see p.794); a day's outing costs around B4000–5500, but of course if you can make your own way to Ko Tao you'll save money.

Easy Divers Head office on Highway 4269 opposite *Sandsea Resort*, Lamai 077 231190, easydivers-thailand.com. PADI Five-Star dive centre, with several branches around the island.

Planet Scuba Head office next to the Seatran pier on Bangrak 077 413050, planetscuba.net. PADI Five-Star dive centre, with a branch on Chaweng.

ACCOMMODATION

Budget accommodation is increasingly scarce on Ko Samui, with very little left for less than B400. All the accommodation prices given below are for high season, but dramatic reductions are possible out of season (roughly April–June, Oct & Nov).

MAENAM

Moonhut On the east side of the village 077 425247, moonhutsamui.com. Welcoming English-run place on a large, sandy, shady plot, with wi-fi and a lively restaurant and beach bar. The colourful, substantial and very clean bungalows all have en-suite bathrooms, and some have hot water and a/c. Kayaking, water-skiing and wake-boarding available. Double B600

New Lapaz Villa Down a 1km access road, east of the village centre but just west of the post office 077 425296, newlapaz.com. Enjoying plenty of shade, the lush, spacious grounds here shelter a small swimming pool and fifty diverse bungalows on stilts, with verandas and hot showers, many in bright pastel colours – maintenance could be better but they're clean enough. Double B600

Shangrilah On an access road 500m west of the village 077 425189, shangrilah.net. In this huge compound that sprawls onto the nicest, widest stretch of sand along Maenam, the main area of shoulder-to-shoulder bungalows sports beautiful flowers, trees and carefully tended topiary. All rooms are well maintained and en-suite, with verandas on stilts, ceiling fans and sturdy furniture. The restaurant serves good Thai food. Double B500

BOPHUT, BANGRAK AND CHOENG MON

Bophut Mansion Signposted down a short lane that runs south off the Bangrak road, on the east side of Bophut village 077 245933 or 081 719 4629. Mostly for long-stayers, this quiet mansion block also does a good-value nightly rate. Rooms have a/c, hot showers, fridges, cable TV and small sitting rooms. Double B500

Cactus Access from the highway, west Bophut 077 245565, cactusbung@hotmail.com. Ochre cottages with attractive bed platforms, large French windows and stylish, earth-tone bathrooms stand in two shady rows, running down to the inviting beachfront restaurant with a pool table. Choose either fan and cold shower or a/c and hot shower. Double B650

Khunthai Guesthouse West of the pier, 30m behind *The Shack* restaurant, Bophut village 077 245118 or 086 686 2960. Friendly spot set back from the beach in an orange, two-storey concrete house, offering basic, clean rooms with wall fans or a/c, hot showers, TVs, fridges and free wi-fi. Double B500

Ô Soleil Choeng Mon 077 425232, osoleilbungalow.com. Lovely, orderly, Belgian-run place in a tranquil, pretty garden dotted with ponds. Among the well-built, clean bungalows, the cheapest are fan-cooled, with cold showers, at the back, while the elegant beachside restaurant has a nice shaded deck area and serves 600 cocktails. Double B400

CHAWENG

Budget travellers have been priced off Chaweng beachfront – all of the following are a short walk from the beach.

★ **Akwa Guesthouse** South Chaweng 084 660 0551, akwaguesthouse.com. This colourful guesthouse has imaginatively designed rooms with quirky pop art and an excellent range of amenities: a/c, hot showers, wi-fi, king-sized beds, duvets, TV and DVD players (and a DVD library), safety boxes and fridges. Double B950

★ TREAT YOURSELF

The Scent Bangrak 077 962198, thescenthotel.com. The nostalgic powers of scent provide the excuse for retro, colonial styling at this small beachfront hotel set around an attractive pool. So, amid bottles of spices and pungent dried flowers, you can expect lots of dark wood, wicker chairs, prints of old Siam and huge baths with brass fittings. There's a small, aromatic spa and a beachside, mostly French, restaurant where you can indulge in afternoon tea. Double B5800

Baan Kluaymai Guesthouse Soi Colibri, central Chaweng ☎077 413836, Ⓦbaankluaymaiguesthouse.com. Excellent-value rooms in a brick building above a pleasant Chinese restaurant. All have large beds, hot shower, a/c and satellite TV. Double **B700**

The Loft Samui Central Chaweng ☎077 413420, Ⓦtheloftsamui.com. Swanky place with a raised wooden bar and restaurant area full of nooks and crannies; a great place to watch the world go by on the street below. The cheapest rooms have fans and all have hot showers. Breakfast is included. Double **B790**

The Wave Central Chaweng ☎077 230803, Ⓦthewavesamui.com. Located above a popular bar-restaurant of the same name, *The Wave* offers good fan-cooled rooms, all with shared cold-water shower. If you manage to bag the room at the top of the building (B1650) you'll be rewarded with a/c, hot water and your own roof terrace. Double **B400**

LAMAI

Lamai's budget accommodation is concentrated around the beach's northern and southern ends.

Amity Bungalows Southern end of the bay ☎077 424084, Ⓦamity-bungalow.com. A huge range of accommodation in a welcoming, organized place. Tightly packed near the beach, the cheapest wooden bungalows are battered but clean enough, with fan, veranda and small bathroom. Double **B400**

Beer House In the central section of the northern part of the beach ☎077 230467, Ⓦbeerhousebungalow.com. A hidden, single-storey cement building at the back holds a row of down-at-heel but very cheap rooms. Facilities are basic, with cold shower and bucket-flush toilets. Pay more for the very appealing bungalows in its lush, shaded compound (from B600). Double **B300**

Flower Paradise On the bay's northern headland ☎077 418059, Ⓦsamuiroestiland.com. Just a short walk from the beach, a friendly, well-run German-Swiss place in a small but beautiful garden. All the attractive, well-tended bungalows of varying sizes have verandas and hot water. Double **B350**

Green Villa Southern end of the bay ☎077 424296 or ☎081 893 7227, Ⓔgreenvillasamui@hotmail.com. Though set back from the beach towards the main road, this resort enjoys a spacious, leafy garden among palm trees, and a small swimming pool. Clean, simple, en-suite, wooden bungalows with fans (some with hot water), or grand, a/c villas. Double **B450**

New Hut *Beer House*'s northern neighbour ☎077 230437, Ⓔnewhutlamai@yahoo.co.th. These rustic A-frames are close together, but cheap, attractive and located right on the beach. They consist of nothing more than a mattress, fan and mosquito net, and have shared cold-water bathrooms, but there's a good restaurant attached and you can't beat the location. More expensive en suites (B600–800), some with hot showers, are also available. Double **B400**

EATING

MAENAM

Angela's Bakery Almost opposite the police station on the main through-road, east of the pier ☎077 427396. American-style, a/c diner, offering great breakfasts (French toast B100) and a wide choice of sandwiches, salads, soups and Western main courses, as well as home-made cakes and apple pie (B100 with ice cream). Daily 8am–4pm.

Ko Seng On the road parallel to and just east of the pier road ☎077 425365. At this locally famous seafood restaurant that's been on national TV, you buy your seafood according to weight, or plump for noodles (B80) or dishes such as *kaeng som plaa* (B200), a thin fish curry with tamarind paste that can be spiced to order. Daily 10am–10pm.

BOPHUT

Juzz'a Pizza 2 Bophut village, 100m east of the pier ☎077 245663. Friendly, small, elegant restaurant with a beachside terrace, serving excellent, authentic pizzas (from B230), with vegetarian and seafood options, as well as pastas, sandwiches and Thai and Western main courses. Tues–Sun 4–11pm.

Satsuman *Elysia Resort*, Bophut village, 100m east of the pier ☎077 425029, Ⓦsatsumansamui.com. Great Japanese food, good service and killer cocktails; the breaded chicken with fried onion, egg and rice is tasty and hearty (B160), or treat yourself to a mixed sushi plate (B390). Daily 4–11pm.

CHAWENG

For cheap Thai food, join local workers at the evening food stalls of Laem Din market, on the road between the heart of central Chaweng and Ban Chaweng.

Ninja Crepes Central/south Chaweng. This un-atmospheric place is a popular option for cheap, good-quality Western and Thai meals along with breakfasts and sweet and savoury crepes. Main dishes around B70. Daily noon–11pm.

Noori Opposite *Chaweng Buri Resort* towards the north end of central Chaweng. Superior Indian food (around B200/dish) in relatively basic surroundings, including all the old favourites such as chicken tikka masala, as well as plenty of seafood and vegetarian options. Daily 11am–11.30pm.

LAMAI

Eldorado Just west of the central crossroads. Good-value Swedish restaurant, serving a few Thai favourites and all manner of tasty international mains. All-you-can-eat barbecue on Wed (B260). Daily 3–10.30pm.

La Fabrique Route 4169, just south of the temple in Lamai village. Authentic French patisserie-café, a civilized retreat from the busy road. Superb custard cakes (B80), quiches (B60), omelettes, pizzas, salads and sandwiches. Daily 7am–8pm.

DRINKING AND NIGHTLIFE

All of the beaches have relaxing places to drink on the sands, but the main bars and clubs are on Chaweng.

Ark Bar North-central Chaweng. Hosts popular beach parties with international and Thai house DJs, fire shows, a bucket bar and a pool bar. Parties Wed & Fri 2pm–2am.

Green Mango Soi Green Mango North-central Chaweng. Now surrounded by bars, a long-standing megaclub in a massive multi-zoned shed with tropical-garden touches. Daily 10pm–3am.

Q Bar North off the Ban Chaweng road. Sleek, futuristic decor, great views over the lake from high on its north shore and cutting-edge music from local and international DJs, at this branch of the famous Bangkok bar-club. Daily 6pm–late.

Reggae Pub Inland from Central Chaweng across the lake. Chaweng's oldest nightclub is a venerable Samui institution – with a memorabilia shop to prove it. It does time now as an unpretentious, good-time party venue, with pool tables, big-screen sports and live reggae bands every night. Daily 6pm–3am.

DIRECTORY

Books Bookazine sells English-language books, newspapers and magazines at two stores in central Chaweng and one in Lamai. Nathon Book Stores on Th Na Amphoe, Na Thon, is a good secondhand bookshop.

Hospitals The state hospital (T 077 421230–2), 3km south of Na Thon off Route 4169, plus several private ones.

Immigration office Located 2km south of Na Thon down Route 4169 (T 077 421069)

Post office At the northern end of the promenade, Na Thon (Mon–Fri 8.30am–4.30pm, Sat & Sun 9am–noon), with international telephones upstairs (closed Sat & Sun). Dotted along Route 4169, there are further post offices at Maenam, Chaweng and Lamai.

Tourist police On the Route 4169 ring road between Bophut and Chaweng, north of Big C supermarket on the same side of the road (T 1155 or T 077 430016).

ANG THONG NATIONAL MARINE PARK

It's possible to buy tickets at any of the beaches on Samui for boat trips to **Ang Thong National Marine Park** (B1300 including entry to the national park, snorkelling, lunch), a gorgeous group of 42 small islands, 30km west of Samui. Boats generally leave Na Thon at 8.30am and return at 4.30–5pm; there are also fairly regular trips from Ko Pha Ngan. First stop on any boat tour is usually **Ko Wua Talab**, site of the park headquarters, from where it's a steep 430m climb (at least 1hr return; bring walking sandals or shoes) to the island's peak and fine panoramic views. The feature that gives the park the name Ang Thong, meaning "Golden Bowl", is a steep-sided lake, 250m in diameter, on Ko Mae Ko to the north of Ko Wua Talab; it was the inspiration for the setting of Alex Garland's cult bestseller, *The Beach*. Steps (30min return) lead up from the beach tunnels to the rim of the cliff wall encircling the lake, which is connected to the sea by an underground tunnel. If you want to get away from it all, you could rent a bungalow (from B500) or tent (around B200) at park headquarters (W dnp.go.th) and catch a return boat to Samui on another day.

KO PHA NGAN

In recent years, backpackers have tended to move over to Ko Samui's fun-loving little sibling, **Ko Pha Ngan**, 20km to the north, which generally has a simpler atmosphere, mostly because the poor road system has been an impediment to the developers. With dense jungle covering its inland mountains and rugged granite outcrops along the coast, Pha Ngan lacks sweeping beaches, but it does have some coral and a few beautiful, sheltered bays. The legendary pilgrimage site for ravers, Hat Rin, is where the infamous full-moon parties are held, which see swarms of visitors descend upon the island.

Thong Sala and Wat Khao Tham

THONG SALA is a port of entrance and little more. In front of the piers, transport to the rest of the island (songthaews, jeeps, a/c minibuses and motorbike taxis) congregates by an assortment of banks, restaurants, supermarkets, dive centres, and motorbike and jeep rental places.

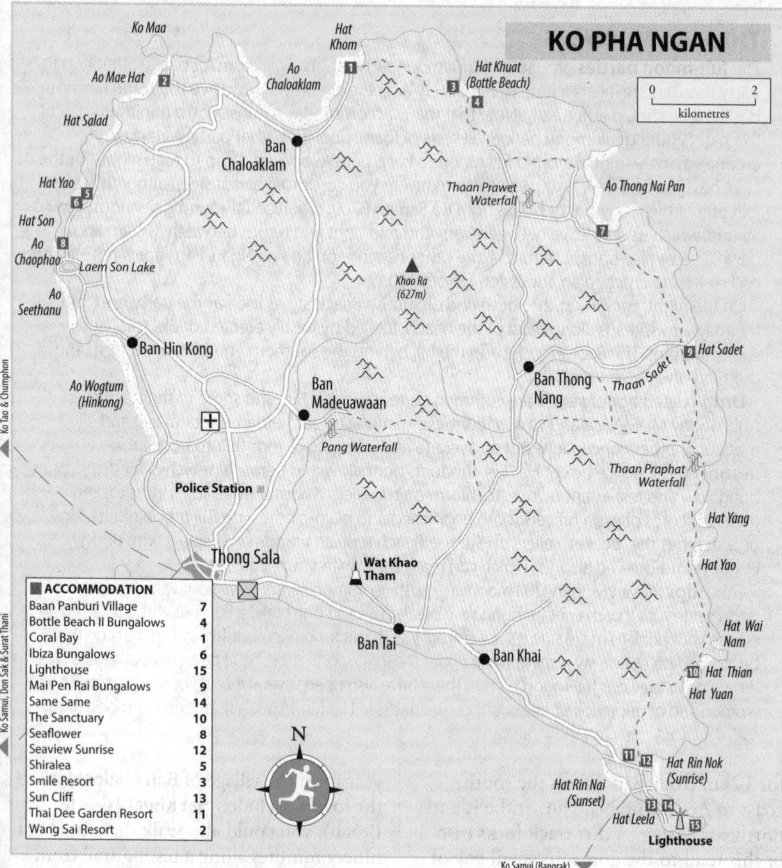

The island's south coast is lined with bungalows, but it's hard to recommend staying here as the beaches are mediocre by Thai standards. But if you're interested in meditation note that **Wat Khao Tham** holds silent retreats, starting on the 10th of every month (Ⓦnunamornpun-kohphangan.com).

Hat Rin

Hat Rin's **full-moon parties** (see box, p.792) have established it as the major party venue in Southeast Asia. Comprising two back-to-back beaches, joined by transverse roads at the north and south ends and a whole mess of chaotic development, Hat Rin's geography is ideally suited to an intense party town. The main, eastern beach, usually referred to as **Sunrise** or Hat Rin Nok, is a classic curve of fine sand between two rocky slopes, but with so much boat traffic and its disturbing role as a public urinal at full-moon time, these days its waters are far from limpid. **Sunset Beach** (Hat Rin Nai) is often littered with flotsam, but has plenty of quieter accommodation.

The east coast

North of Hat Rin, no roads run along the rocky, exposed **east coast**. Accessible in ten to fifteen minutes by longtail boats from Sunrise are the picturesque bays of Hat Yuan and the small, sandy **Hat Thian**, which make a quiet alternative to Hat Rin.

Inland, a bumpy dirt track, slowly developing into a concrete road, winds

10

THE FULL MOONERS

The **full-moon parties** on Hat Rin (Ⓦfullmoonpartykohphangan.com for dates) attract up to thirty thousand revellers a time to the beach. As there are only around five thousand rooms in Hat Rin, you should arrive early. Note that many accommodations insist on a minimum stay of five nights during full-moon period (all sorts of foam, pool and other parties are now organized on the nights around full moon to keep people occupied), up to nine nights for the big Christmas and New Year parties. Alternatively, you can forget about sleep altogether and join one of the many **party boats** from Ko Samui (B700; organized through guesthouses in Ko Samui), which usually leave between 9pm and midnight and return between 3.30am and dawn. There's also transport from all the other beaches on Ko Pha Ngan. Partygoers not staying on Hat Rin are charged an admission fee of B100.

On the night, *Paradise* at the south end of Sunrise Beach styles itself as the party host, but the mayhem spreads along most of the beach, fuelled by hastily erected drinks stalls and sound systems. The *Back Yard* club, up the hill behind the southern end of Sunrise, hosts the morning-after.

Drug-related horror stories are common currency in Hat Rin, and some of them are even true: dodgy MDMA, ice and *ya baa* (Burmese-manufactured methamphetamines) and all manner of other concoctions put an average of two *farangs* a month into hospital for treatment. The police box at Hat Rin conducts bungalow and personal searches for drugs, pays bungalow and restaurant owners to inform on travellers whom they've sold drugs to, and drafts in scores of extra officers (both uniformed and plain-clothes) on full moon nights. Not only that but the "bucket" sellers on Sunrise Beach replace brand-name spirits with dodgy, illegal, home-brewed alcohol, which can really mess with your head.

Other **tips** for surviving the full moon are mostly common sense: leave your valuables in your resort's safe – it's a bad night for bungalow break-ins – and don't take a bag out with you; keep an eye on your drink to make sure it's not spiked; watch out for broken bottles and anchors on the beach; and do not go swimming while under the influence – there have been several deaths by drowning at previous full-moon parties. There have also been several reports of sexual assaults on women and of unprovoked, late-night gang attacks in Hat Rin, especially around full-moon night.

for 12km from Ban Tai on the south coast to Ao Thong Nai Pan, at the island's northeast corner. A dirt track forks east of this road to the gorgeous small bay of **Hat Sadet**, which is framed by large boulders and within walking distance of the beautiful Thaan Sadet waterfall, a favourite of King Rama V and a great place to unwind.

Ao Thong Nai Pan is a beautiful, two-part sandy bay, good for swimming and backed by steep, green hills; it has decent budget accommodation, a few shops, dive outfits and restaurants. Songthaews connect with boats at Thong Sala every day.

The north coast

Ao Chaloaklam, the largest bay on the **north coast** with a vibrant fishing village, can easily be reached by songthaew or motorbike taxi from Thong Sala, 10km away. If the sea is not too rough, longtail boats run three times a day for most of the year from the village of **Ban Chaloaklam** to the lovely, secluded **Hat Khuat** (Bottle Beach); you could also walk there in about ninety minutes along a testing trail from Hat Khom.

The west coast

Pha Ngan's **west coast** is lush and hilly with good sunset views over the islands to the west; reefs, enclosing most of the bays, keep the sea too shallow for a decent swim, however, especially between May and October.

Ao Chaophao, with its narrow strand and densely foliaged beachfront, is a nice place to relax. Beyond, the long, gently curved beach of **Hat Yao** boasts soft white sand and clear waters, and is becoming deservedly busier and more popular. On the northwest tip of the island, the broad, coarse-sand bay of **Ao Mae Hat** is good for swimming and snorkelling among the coral that lines the sandy causeway to the islet of **Ko Maa**.

ARRIVAL AND DEPARTURE

BY PLANE

Kan Airlines (ⓦ kanairlines.com) are building an airport on the island, currently scheduled to open in late 2014.

BY BOAT

From Surat Thani A basic overnight boat, with mattresses on the floor, leaves Ban Don pier in Surat Thani at 11pm every night for Thong Sala (7hr; B450); tickets are available from the pier on the day of departure. It returns at 10pm from Thong Sala.

From Don Sak There are five Raja vehicle ferries daily (at least 2hr 45min; B350, including transfer from Surat Thani) and two Lomprayah catamaran sailings (via Ko Samui; 3hr; B550, including transfer from Surat Thani).

From Ko Samui Lomprayah catamarans sail both from Na Thon and from Wat Na Phra Larn at the west end of Maenam to Thong Sala (both 2 daily 30min; B300). From Bangrak (Big Buddha Beach), the Had Rin Queen has four sailings a day to Hat Rin (50min; B200), while Seatran Discovery sails twice a day to Thong Sala (30min; B300).

From Ko Tao Two Lomprayah catamarans a day (1hr 15min; B450) and two Seatran Discovery ferries (1hr 30min; B400) sail to Thong Sala.

From Chumphon Boat services also run from Chumphon (see p.783).

INFORMATION

The free, regularly updated *Phangan Info* guide is available at the pier and most travel agents. It has a good website, ⓦ phangan.info, on which you can book accommodation. The excellent English-Thai travel agency, Backpackers Information Centre, towards the south end of Hat Rin Sunrise (ⓣ 085 784 0019) also has a very useful website (ⓦ backpackersthailand.com).

ACCOMMODATION

HAT RIN

Beachside budget accommodation is gradually being replaced by more upmarket resorts, but dormitory guesthouses – most open only during full moon – are found in the road network between the two beaches (as well as in the village of Ban Tai to the west).

Lighthouse On the tip of the Hat Rin peninsula, beyond Leela Beach ⓣ 077 375075, ⓦ lighthousebungalows.com. At this friendly haven, fan-cooled wooden and concrete en-suite bungalows, sturdily built into the rock to withstand the wind, are priced according to size and comfort; all have good-sized balconies with hammocks. The restaurant food is varied and tasty. Phone for a pick-up from Hat Rin or Thong Sala, or do the 30min walk from *Chicken Corner* in the centre of Hat Rin, the last section along a wooden walkway over the rocky shoreline. Double **B600**

Same Same Above the south end of Sunrise at the start of the road to Leela Beach ⓣ 077 375200, ⓦ same-same.com A sociable and well-run Scandinavian guesthouse offering good-value rooms, all en suite, colourful and clean, some with a/c. There's a decent restaurant downstairs with a bar and a long list of excuses to party to a mainstream soundtrack. Dorm **B500**, double **B550**

Seaview Sunrise Northern end of Sunrise ⓣ 077 375160, ⓦ seaviewsunrise.com. On a big plot of shady, flower-strewn land at the quieter end of the beach, this clean, friendly, orderly old-timer with a good restaurant offers more than forty bungalows and rooms. The bungalows on the beachfront are all fan-cooled with hot showers. Further back are a/c versions, as well as the cheapest rooms with cold showers. Double **B500**

Sun Cliff High up on the tree-lined slope above the south end of Sunset Beach ⓣ 077 375134 or ⓣ 077 375463, ⓔ rsvnsuncliff@hotmail.com. Friendly, spacious place with great views of the south coast and Ko Samui, especially from its heart-shaped pool by the restaurant. Among a wide range of bungalows that are a bit rough around the edges, you'll find some quirky architectural features such as rock-built bathrooms and fountains; some have huge decks for partying. The more expensive a/c rooms all have hot showers, fridges and TVs. Double **B500**

Thai Dee Garden Resort Northern transverse ⓣ 082 275 6199, ⓦ thaideegarden.com. Pleasant staff and a range of smart concrete and white clapboard bungalows, on a broad, grassy slope strewn with trees and plants and set back from the road. Choose either fan and cold water or a/c and hot. Not on the beach, so one of the last places to fill at full moon. Double **B400**

THE EAST COAST

Many of the resorts here provide shuttles at B200/person from or to Thong Sala Pier.

Baan Panburi Village Southern end of Thong Nai Pan ⓣ 077 238599, ⓦ baanpanburivillage.com. Two rows of well-designed bungalows with verandas and deckchairs run down a slope dotted with wicker hammocks, either side of a small, artificial waterfall. Choose between old-style, thatched, wood-and-bamboo huts with mosquito nets, fans and cold showers, and pricier, large, wooden, a/c affairs with hot water and tiled floors. Double **B500**

★ **Mai Pen Rai Bungalows** Hat Sadet ⓣ 080 719 0700, ⓦ thansadet.com. On the beach within a short walk of the waterfalls, these basic but attractive fan bungalows, some with big upstairs terraces, have a bohemian vibe. An easy place to lose time. There's a 1pm taxi from the piers in Thong Sala (B200/person). Double **B500**

★ **The Sanctuary** Hat Thian ⓣ 081 271 3614, ⓦ thesanctuarythailand.com. This magical fairyland, connected by a labyrinth of dirt paths, offers a huge range of basic and luxury en-suite bungalows built into the

lush promontory. It also hosts courses in yoga and meditation, and has a spa and a wellness and detox centre. The beautiful timber restaurant serves up healthy plates with a great selection of vegetarian food. Dorm **B250**, double **B770**

THE NORTH COAST

Bottle Beach II Bungalows Eastern end of Bottle Beach T 085 654 4770. Two rows of old-school, bamboo-clad huts with fans, cold showers and mosquito nets. This is where to head for if you want total relaxation on a quiet and beautiful stretch of beach. Double **B400**

Coral Bay On a grassy promontory that divides Ao Chaloaklam from Hat Khom T 077 374245. Friendly, laidback outfit with plenty of space and great views. The sturdy bungalows range from simple wooden affairs to large pads with a/c and hot showers, some with funky bathrooms built into the rock; snorkelling equipment can be rented to make the most of Hat Khom's reef. Phone ahead to ask about their daily transfers from Thong Sala. Double **B400**

Smile Resort Western end of Bottle Beach T 085 429 4995, W smilebungalows.com. Set on a rocky slope strewn with flowers and trees on the western side of the beach, with fun owners and a sociable bar-restaurant area. The basic bungalows come with wall fans and mosquito nets. Double **B450**

THE WEST COAST

Ibiza Bungalows Hat Yao T 077 349121. Friendly, central spot on a spacious lawn that's shaded by mature trees, with a good restaurant. The thirty airy bungalows run the full gamut, from fan and cold-water offerings near the beach to a/c, hot-shower affairs. Double **B400**

★**Seaflower** Ao Chaophao T 077 349090, W seaflowerbungalows.com. Quiet spot, set in a lush garden, with good veggie and non-veggie food. En-suite bungalows with their own hot-water bathrooms vary in price according to their size and age. Kayaks are available, as well as fishing and snorkelling day-trips and occasional overnighters to Ang Thong National Marine Park (see p.790). Free pick-ups from Thong Sala with advance notice. Double **B600**

Shiralea Hat Yao T 077 349217, W shiralea.com. On a broad, grassy bank beneath coconut trees behind the north end of the beach, the spacious, very attractive thatched bungalows here all come with hot water, safety boxes and hammocks, and there's a seductive pool and a dive school. Double **B600**

Wang Sai Resort Ao Mae Hat T 077 374238, W wangsairesort.com. Popular, friendly spot by a shady creek at the south end of the bay. On a huge plot of land, most of the en-suite bungalows are set back from the beach, with fans and cold showers – pay B200 extra for those that are up the slope, with great sunset views. The best and most expensive are across the creek on the beach, all with a/c, some with hot water. On-site dive school and kayaks and snorkels for rent. Double **B600**

DIRECTORY

In the dense tourist village of Hat Rin you will easily find supermarkets, travel agents, motorbike rental places (from B200/day), overseas phone facilities, dozens of internet outlets and plenty of ATMs and currency exchange booths.

Books Bookazine on the southern transverse in Hat Rin.

Diving **Lotus Diving** has a dive resort on Ao Chaloaklam (T 077 374142, W lotusdiving.net), plus an office at Backpackers Information Centre in Hat Rin. A PADI Five-Star centre, it offers frequent courses and trips to Sail Rock, halfway between Pha Ngan and Tao.

Hospital 3km north of Thong Sala, on the road towards Mae Hat; in Hat Rin, the Bandon International Hospital operates a small clinic on the southern transverse, near the pier (T 077 375471–2).

Kitesurfing Cuttlebone, Holiday Beach Resort, about 2km southeast of Thong Sala (T 081 940 1902; W cuttlebone.net), runs great kitesurfing classes.

Police The main station is 2km up the Ban Chaloaklam road from Thong Sala (T 077 377114), and there's a tourist police office at the main pier in Thong Sala (T 1155).

Post office About 500m southeast of the piers on Thong Sala's old main street (Mon–Fri 8.30am–noon & 1–4.30pm, Sat 9am–noon).

KO TAO

Forty kilometres north of Ko Pha Ngan, small, forested **Ko Tao** is the last and most remote island of the archipelago, with a long curve of classic beach on its west side, **Hat Sai Ree**, and secluded rocky coves along its east coast. It's a popular travellers' destination, especially from December to March. Ko Tao feels the southwest monsoon more than Samui and Pha Ngan, so June to October can have strong winds and rain.

Blessed with clear seas (visibility up to 35m), a wide range of coral species and other marine life, and deep water relatively close to shore, Ko Tao is one of Thailand's premier **diving** locations. Diving is possible year-round, but visibility is best from April to July, and in September (usually best of all) and October; November is the worst time.

If you're just arriving and want to stay on one of the less accessible beaches, it might be a good idea to hook up with

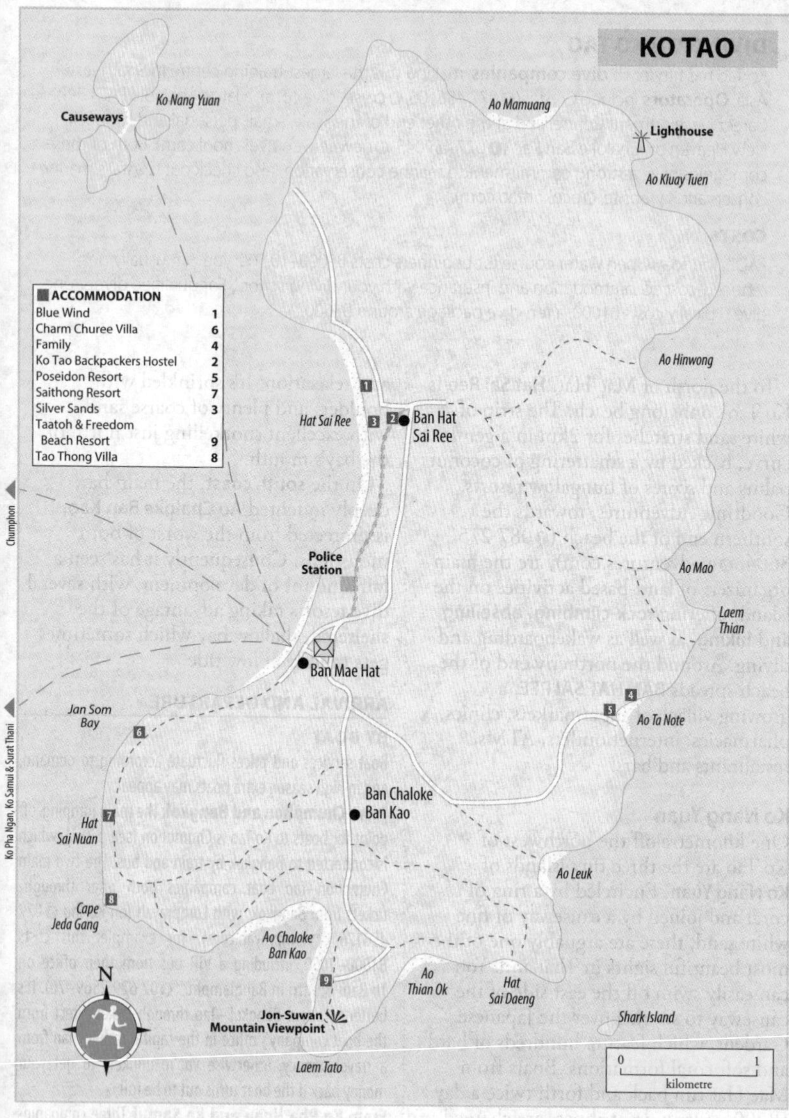

one of the touts who meet the ferries at **Mae Hat**, the island's main village, with pick-up or longtail boat on hand; otherwise call ahead, as most bungalow owners come to market once a day (pick-ups are either free or B50–150/person). Note that some resorts with attached scuba-diving operations have been known to refuse guests who don't sign up for diving trips or courses.

The west coast

All boats to the island dock at **BAN MAE HAT**, a small, lively village with the most facilities on the island. On the roads leading inland from the main pier and the neighbouring Seatran pier, and on the narrow coastal road that extends north and south of them, you'll find bars, restaurants, bakeries, internet, motorbike rental, banks and more.

10

DIVING ON KO TAO

Ko Tao has fifty or so **dive companies**, making this the largest training centre in Southeast Asia. **Operators** include Crystal (T 077 456106, W crystaldive.com), a large, sociable PADI 5-Star Career Development Centre; and at the other end of the scale, small, personal and laidback New Heaven on Chaloke Ban Kao (T 077 457045, W newheavendiveschool.com). Both of these companies have a strong commitment to marine conservation (also check out Crystal's marine conservation website, W ecokohtao.com).

COSTS

PADI's four-day Open Water course for beginners costs B9000–10,500; you can usually get reduced-cost accommodation and insurance with your diving school. For qualified divers, one dive typically costs B1000, a ten-dive package around B7000.

To the north of Mae Hat, **Hat Sai Ree** is Ko Tao's only long beach. The strip of white sand stretches for 2km in a gentle curve, backed by a smattering of coconut palms and scores of bungalow resorts. Goodtime Adventures, towards the southern end of the beach (T 087 275 3604, W gtadventures.com), are the main organizers of land-based activities on the island, offering **rock-climbing**, **abseiling** and **hiking**, as well as wakeboarding and diving. Around the northerly end of the beach spreads **BAN HAT SAI REE**, a growing village of supermarkets, clinics, pharmacies, internet outlets, ATMs, restaurants and bars.

Ko Nang Yuan

One kilometre off the northwest of Ko Tao are the three tiny islands of **Ko Nang Yuan**. Encircled by a ring of coral and joined by a causeway of fine white sand, these are arguably one of the most beautiful sights in Thailand. You can easily swim off the east side of the causeway to snorkel over the Japanese Gardens, which feature hundreds of hard and soft coral formations. Boats from Mae Hat run back and forth twice a day (B200 return); day-trippers are charged B100 to land on the island, and cans, plastic bottles and fins are banned.

The east and south coasts

The sheltered inlets of the **east coast**, most of them containing at least one or two sets of bungalows, can be reached by boat, pick-up or four-wheel-drive. **Ao Ta Note**, a horseshoe inlet with half-a-dozen resorts, is a good option for watersports and relaxation. It's sprinkled with boulders and plenty of coarse sand, with excellent snorkelling just north of the bay's mouth.

On the **south coast**, the main bay, deeply indented **Ao Chaloke Ban Kao**, is protected from the worst of both monsoons. Consequently it has seen a fair amount of development, with several dive resorts taking advantage of the sheltered, shallow bay which sometimes gets muddy at low tide.

ARRIVAL AND DEPARTURE

BY BOAT

Boat services and prices fluctuate according to demand, and in high season extra boats may appear.

From Chumphon and Bangkok The main jumping-off point for boats to Ko Tao is Chumphon (see p.783), which is connected to Bangkok by train and bus. The two main Chumphon–Tao boat companies both offer through-tickets from Bangkok; with Lomprayah (on Ko Tao T 077 456176, W lomprayah.com), for example, this costs B1000–1050, including a VIP bus from their office on Th Ram Bhuttri in Banglamphu (T 02 629 2569–70). It's better to buy a Bangkok–Tao through-ticket direct from the boat company's office in the capital rather than from a travel agency, otherwise you're unlikely to get your money back if the boat turns out to be full.

From Ko Pha Ngan and Ko Samui Three companies currently operate daily scheduled boats between Thong Sala on Ko Pha Ngan and Ko Tao. Songserm (on Ko Tao T 077 456274, W songserm-expressboat.com) does the voyage in around 2hr (1 daily; B350). Lomprayah (see p.787) and Seatran (on Ko Tao T 077 456907, W seatrandiscovery.com) cover the ground in about 1hr 15min (both 2 daily; B430–450). The Lomprayah catamaran originates at Maenam, Seatran at Bangrak, on Ko Samui (total journey time to Ko Tao on either about 2hr; B600).

From Surat Thani If you're coming from Surat Thani, you could take Lomprayah's Don Sak–Na Thon (Samui)–Thong Sala catamaran all the way to Ko Pha Ngan, then change onto its Maenam (Samui)–Thong Sala–Ko Tao service (total journey time from Surat about 6hr; B700). There's a night boat from Ban Don pier in Surat Thani town, departing at around 11pm (T 077 284928; 8hr; B500); in the opposite direction, this leaves Ko Tao at around 9pm.

GETTING AROUND

You can get around easily enough on foot, but there are roads of sorts now to most of the resorts, though many are still very rough, steep tracks, suitable for four-wheel-drive only. A paved road extends down the west coast from north to south (ending at Ao Chaloke), and one is being built eastwards to Ao Ta Note.

By taxi Pick-up taxis are available in Mae Hat (B100/ person to Chaloke Ban Kao, for example, minimum 2 people; rates are higher at night, or for a 4WD to somewhere more remote), as are motorbike taxis (B100 to Chaloke Ban Kao, for example).

By motorbike Rental motorbikes are available from B150/day. If you can, resist the temptation to rent a quad bike, or ATV – not only do they have a disproportionate number of accidents, but they're also very polluting. There have been lots of reports of travellers being charged exorbitant amounts if they bring the vehicle back with even the most minor damage – avoid the outfits in front of the main pier in Mae Hat, and rent from your bungalow or someone reliable like Save Shop, on the front street, just south of the piers.

By boat Round-island boat tours are available at Mae Hat or through your bungalow, with stops for snorkelling and swimming (B650/person, including lunch and pick-ups, or around B2000 to rent your own longtail boat for the day).

INFORMATION

Tourist information The regularly updated and widely available free booklet, *Ko Tao Info*, is a useful source of information, along with its associated website, W kohtaoonline.com, which features online accommodation booking.

ACCOMMODATION AND EATING

WEST COAST

Blue Wind Just north of Sai Ree village T 077 456116. This popular old-timer offers a variety of well-kept, en-suite rooms and bungalows scattered about a shady compound. It also has a very good, relaxing bakery-restaurant on the beach, serving Thai, Indian and Western food. Double **B450**

Ko Tao Backpackers Hostel Middle of Sai Ree village, inland from *Silver Sands Resort* T 088 447 7921, W kohtaobackpackers.com. A popular choice offering eight-bed dormitories with a/c and hot showers in good, shared facilities. There are security lockers, a swimming pool and a bar/restaurant hosting regular parties. Dorm **B300**

Saithong Resort Sai Nuan beach, 1hr walk south of Mae Hat pier T 077 456868. An isolated, shady place, with soft sand on two small beaches, offering various types of en-suite bungalows either in gardens or perched on the rocks – the latter with stunning sea views. Kayaks and snorkels for rent. Double **B600**

Silver Sands Ban Hat Sai Ree T 077 456606, W silver-sands-resort.com. Clean, well-kept bungalows and rooms on a narrow but lush and shady plot. Among its bungalows, the cheapest are simple wooden affairs with cold showers well off the beach. Guests can use the adjacent pool at the affiliated dive company, Davy Jones' Locker. Snorkels to rent. Double **B900**

Tao Thong Villa 1hr walk south of Mae Hat T 077 456078. Sturdy, en-suite bungalows dotted around the rocky outcrop of Cape Jeda Gang and the slope behind, with a breezy restaurant on the tiny, grassy isthmus with two small beaches in between. Plenty of shady seclusion, great views and good snorkelling and swimming. Double **B500**

EAST COAST

Family (Ta Note Bay Resort) Ao Ta Note T 077 456757–8, E tanotebay@hotmail.com. The pick of the half-dozen resorts here, with plenty of well-designed en-suite wooden and concrete bungalows, set among thick bougainvillea, some enjoying large view-filled verandas. Snorkelling equipment available. Double **B800**

Poseidon Resort Ao Ta Note T 077 456734–5, W poseidontao.atspace.com. Basic en-suite bungalows with balconies and hammocks, set back a little from the beach on the flower-strewn, rocky slopes. There is a traveller vibe, a stargazing cocktail bar above a restaurant and kayaks and snorkels for rent. Double **B400**

SOUTH COAST

Taatoh & Freedom Beach Resort Ao Chaloke Ban Kao T 077 456596, W taatoh.com. Two combined resorts with

★TREAT YOURSELF

Charm Churee Villa Jan Som Bay, about a 30-minute walk south from the southern end of Ban Mae Hat T 077 456394, W charmchureevilla.com. A certain rustic charm blended perfectly with exquisite linen, Thai and Balinese decor and its own private beach, where the coral is protected with a ban on longtails. There are two restaurants, one with a fabulous ocean view, a dive centre and a spa. Double **B3600**

10

their own private beaches; white-sand Freedom Beach is a particularly lovely spot for snorkelling. The en-suite, balconied bungalows are perched on the hillside – some offering beautiful views – and are great value. Double **B800**

DIRECTORY

10

Health Mae Hat has a small government health centre (halfway up the high street from the main pier, turn right), plus several private clinics, pharmacies and diving medicine clinics.

Police A 5min walk on the narrow coast path heading north from Mae Hat (T 077 456631).

Post office At the top of the road leading inland from the Seatran pier (Mon–Fri 9am–5pm, Sat 9am–noon).

NAKHON SI THAMMARAT

NAKHON SI THAMMARAT, a seldom-visited but bustling town, is the south's religious capital. A major Buddhist pilgrimage site, it is also well known for its traditional handicrafts, shadow plays and especially its festivals. The biggest of these is Tamboon Deuan Sip every September/October, which is marked by a ten-day fair at Thung Talaat park on the north side of town, as well as processions, shadow plays and other theatrical shows.

WHAT TO SEE AND DO

The town runs 7km from north to south, to either side of Thanon Ratchadamnoen (the third parallel street, east of the rail line), which is served by frequent blue share-songthaews. The south's most important temple, **Wat Mahathat**, is on this road, about 2km south of the town centre. Its courtyard is dominated by the huge Sri Lankan-style chedi enshrining relics of the Buddha, around which are arrayed row upon row of smaller chedis, an Aladdin's cave of a temple museum, and local handicraft stalls. A few minutes' walk south of Wat Mahathat on the same road is the **National Museum** (Wed–Sun 9am–noon & 1–4pm; B150), which houses a small but diverse collection covering prehistoric finds, Buddha images and ceramics.

For the best possible introduction to southern Thailand's **shadow puppet theatre**, head for 110/18 Soi 3, Th Si Thammasok (T 075 346394), ten minutes' walk and two blocks east of Wat Mahathat – the easiest way is to walk north, turn right along Thanon Panyom (past *Khanom Jiin Muangkon*, where you can get a great lunch of rice noodles topped with curry sauce), turn right again onto Thanon Si Thammasok, then left into Soi 3. Here, Suchart Subsin, one of the south's leading exponents of shadow puppet theatre, and his sons have opened their workshop to the public and will show you scenes from a shadow play, for which you might want to leave a tip or donation. You can also buy puppets here and see them being made.

ARRIVAL AND INFORMATION

By plane The airport is around 20km northwest of Nakhon, costing around B300 in a taxi. There are six flights daily from Bangkok (1hr 10min) with Nok Air, four with AirAsia; both airlines offer through-tickets to Ko Samui and Ko Pha Ngan, via the nearby piers at Don Sak.

By bus Nakhon's bus terminal, southwest of the train station on the other side of the river, is a cheap songthaew or motorbike taxi ride from town. A/c minibuses leave from at least half a dozen points around the town; hotels and the TAT office can advise on the exact locations.

Destinations Bangkok (19 daily; 12hr); Krabi (7 daily; 4hr); Phuket (7 daily; 6hr); Ranong (1 daily; 7hr); Surat Thani (21 daily; 2hr 30min).

By train Nakhon's train station is on the west side of the town centre. There are two trains to Bangkok daily (14–16hr).

Tourist information The very helpful TAT office is south of the centre, just off Th Ratchadamnoen in Sanam Na Muang park (daily 8.30am–4.30pm; T 075 346515–6, E tatnksri@tat.or.th).

ACCOMMODATION AND EATING

There's a busy, colourful night market on Th Chamroenwithi near the *Bue Loung Hotel*.

Bue Loung (Bua Luang) Hotel 1487/19 Soi Luang Muang, Th Chamroenwithi (the second parallel street, east of the rail line) T 075 341518. Friendly and central, about 200m south of the station, but reasonably quiet; gets the thumbs-up from visiting sales reps, with a choice of fan and cold water or a/c and hot water in basic double or twin rooms with cable TV. Double **B250**

Hao Coffee In Bovorn Bazaar, a courtyard off the east side of Th Ratchadamnoen, just south of Th Pak Nakorn. Modelled on an old Chinese-style coffee shop and packed full of antiques, *Hao* offers a wide selection of inexpensive Thai dishes, Western breakfasts, cakes and Thai filter coffee. Daily 7am–5pm.

★**Krua Thale** Th Pak Nakhon, opposite the *Nakorn Garden Inn* (no English sign – look for the Coke sign).

The town's best restaurant, renowned among locals for its excellent, varied and inexpensive seafood. Plain and very clean, with an open kitchen and the day's catch displayed out front, and relaxing patio tables at the back. Recommended dishes include very good *yam plaa duk foo*, shredded and deep-fried catfish with a mango salad dip (B80). Daily 4–10pm.

★**Nakorn Garden Inn** 1/4 Th Pak Nakhon (the road running east from the train station, about 500m along) ☎ 075 313333. Large, nicely appointed rooms set on three floors in red-brick buildings overlooking a tree-shaded courtyard. All have a/c, hot water, cable TV and minibars. Double B445

The Andaman coast

The landscape along the Andaman coast is lushly tropical and spiked with dramatic limestone crags, best appreciated by staying in **Khao Sok National Park** or taking a boat trip around the bizarre **Ao Phang Nga Bay**. Most people, however, come here for the beaches and the coral reefs. **Phuket** is Thailand's largest island, though it's overdeveloped and hugely commercial. **Ko Phi Phi** and **Ao Nang** are heading the same way, but retain their great natural beauty. The **Similan Islands**, located further north, are among the best dive sites in Thailand. Meanwhile, **Ko Chang**, **Ko Phayam**, **Laem Phra Nang** and **Ko Lanta** have great beaches and a laidback vibe where you can kick back for weeks on end. The Andaman coast is hit by the southwest monsoon from May to October, when the rain and high seas render some of the outer islands inaccessible and litter many beaches with debris, so prices drop significantly during this period.

RANONG

The multi-ethnic provincial capital of **RANONG** is chiefly of interest as a stepping-off point for boats to Ko Chang and Ko Phayam. It's well linked to major towns, being on the bus route from Bangkok to Phuket.

ARRIVAL AND INFORMATION

By plane Happy Air fly to Ranong from Bangkok's Suvarnabhumi Airport (2 daily, except Tues; 1hr 45min), Nok Air from Don Muang (2 daily; 1hr 35min). *Pon's Place* (see below) have a counter at the airport and organize a/c minibuses to town or the pier (B200/person).

By bus Most services between Bangkok (15 daily) and Phuket (7 daily) or other points south stop at the bus terminal, 1.5km southeast of the centre on Highway 4, Th Phetkasem. Hourly a/c minibuses to and from Chumphon and Surat Thani also use the bus terminal. Songthaew #2 or #6 can take you to the main street, Th Ruangrat (B15).

By boat To get to the islands pier, take songthaew #3 or #6 (B15) from the market on Th Ruangrat, or #6 from the bus station, to Saphan Pla 5km southwest, then it's a 500m walk south from the main road to the pier.

Tourist information There is no official TAT office in town, but *Pon's Place* restaurant and travel agency (see below) offers good information on the islands, organizes visa runs to Myanmar and sells transport tickets.

ACCOMMODATION AND EATING

Th Ruangrat is the place to head for a bed and cheap eats.

Asia Hotel 39/9 Th Ruangrat ☎ 077 811113. Very basic traditional Chinese hotel, though all en suite, very central and passable for one night. Double B250

Luang Poj Further north beyond Pon's Place at 225 Th Ruangrat ☎ 077 833377. An attractive conversion of a colonial-style mansion, preserving its polished wooden floors. Smart, modern bedrooms, hot showers and wi-fi throughout. Double B500

Pon's Place North of the market at 92/1 Th Ruangrat ☎ 081 597 4549, ⓦ ponplace-ranong.com. The obvious place to eat while you plan your next move, offering Western breakfasts, Thai food, traditional coffee and free wi-fi. Daily 7.30am–9pm.

KO CHANG

Not to be confused with the much larger Ko Chang on Thailand's east coast (see p.778), Ranong's **Ko Chang** is an ultra-laidback forested island about 5km offshore, with a charmingly low-key atmosphere and many long-stay Europeans. The beaches are connected by tracks through the trees; there are only a couple of cars on the island and sporadic electricity. At the moment, there's barely any commercial activity on Ko Chang save for a couple of local mini-markets and a dive operator, Aladdin, at *Cashew Resort* on Ao Yai (also at the islands pier in Saphan Pla; ☎ 087 274 7601,

10

aladdindivesafari.com), who organize Surin, Similan Islands and Myanmar live-aboards and PADI courses. The prettiest (and longest) beach on the island is **Ao Yai**, which arches its way along the mid-west coast.

ARRIVAL AND DEPARTURE

10

By boat A daily boat service runs from the islands pier in Saphan Pla (see p.799) to the pier on Ko Chang's east coast (1hr; B200; sometimes cancelled in the rainy season). You should be able to arrange some kind of a pick-up from the pier through your resort; otherwise it's a 3km walk to Ao Yai. From about early November to late April, there are also two daily boat departures to Ko Chang's west coast, stopping at most resorts, from Saphan Pla (1hr 30min; B200).

ACCOMMODATION

The dozen or so family-run bungalow operations are mostly scattered along the west coast, many of them hidden among the shore-front trees on Ao Yai; they nearly all close June–Oct. Most of them are simple constructions with mosquito nets on the beds; you shouldn't necessarily expect flush toilets (buckets and dippers are provided). Though the bungalow resorts nearly all have their own generators (which usually only operate in the evenings), some stick to candles and paraffin lamps so it's best to bring a torch; very few bungalows have fans.

Cashew Resort North end of Ao Yai 081 485 6002, my.cashew.resort@gmail.com. The largest outfit, *Cashew* feels like a small village, with its forty en-suite, sea-view bungalows spread among the cashew trees along 700m of prime beachfront. The resort offers the most facilities on the island, including internet and foreign exchange, and its restaurant bakes bread and serves Thai and a few German dishes. Double **B300**

★**Crocodile Rock** 081 370 1434, tonn1970@yahoo.com. In a shady, elevated position at the start of Ao Yai's southern headland, with great views of the whole bay, on which the friendly owners have capitalized, with attractive decks at the restaurant and picture windows in some of the bathrooms. Bungalows, some of which have nice pebbledash bathrooms, have a touch more style than the Ko Chang average. The restaurant bakes its own bread, and serves espresso coffee. Internet access. Double **B350**

Sawasdee Resort By a stream at the far southern end of Ao Yai 084 846 5828, sawasdeekohchang.com. This welcoming place has twelve thoughtfully designed, even stylish wooden bungalows with big decks and good bathrooms. There's a good, attractive restaurant, serving a wide variety of Thai dishes and plenty of vegetarian options, with decks and terraces under the shady trees. Double **B350**

Sunset Bungalows Towards the far north end of Ao Yai 084 339 5224. Homely and friendly family-run place with wooden bungalows and a lovely rustic restaurant blending into the beach surroundings. There's also a raised deck with a well-stocked library (loan only) in English and German. Double **B350**

KO PHAYAM

Diminutive **KO PHAYAM**, measuring just 5 by 8km, is home to some fine white-sand beaches and relaxing beachfront bungalows connected by a network of winding concrete paths. Behind the beaches, the island is covered in rubber, cashew and palm plantations. Slightly more developed than Ko Chang, it has electricity evenings only at most places, a fledgling though still very low-key bar scene, and a **village** at the port comprising several small shops, restaurants, a clinic, and a dive shop (081 891 5510, a-one-diving.com; live-aboards to Surin, Similan and Myanmar, and PADI courses). Motorbike rental (from B200) is available in the village or at the bungalows, many of which close down during the wet season (June–Oct).

Ko Phayam's nicest beach is the 3km-long **Ao Yai** on the southwest coast, a beautiful sweep of soft white sand that occasionally gets pounded by large waves. Across on the northwest coast, the prettiest stretch of beach is the northern part of **Ao Kao Kwai** (also known as Ao Kao Fai, or Buffalo Horn Bay).

ARRIVAL AND DEPARTURE

By boat There are two daily slow boats to Ko Phayam from Saphan Pla (2hr; B200). From November to May, there are also up to five daily speedboat services (45min; B350). Motorbike taxis meet incoming boats from Ranong's port Saphan Pla (see p.799) at the pier in Ko Phayam village and charge B80 to most bungalows.

ACCOMMODATION

Most bungalows only provide electricity from around 6 to 11pm and the cheapest rooms often don't have a fan. There is now internet access at many places.

Aow Yai Bungalow Southern end of Ao Yai 083 389 8688, aowyai.com. French-Thai resort with more than twenty good-quality en-suite bungalows of various styles, dotted around an extensive garden of flowers, fruit trees

and palms. There's wi-fi and internet access, plus snorkels, boogie boards and kayaks. Double B300

Bamboo Bungalows Central Ao Yai 077 820012, bamboo-bungalows.com. Israeli-Thai managed and very traveller-savvy, with free wi-fi and kayaks, plus snorkels, surf- and boogie-boards, and currency exchange. Its en-suite bungalows are set under the trees in a well-tended flower garden and all have fans (electricity 24hr in high season). Double B550

Coconut Beach Resort Ao Yai 089 920 8145, koh-phayam.com. Occupying a great spot in the centre of the bay and run by a Ko Phayam family, the good-value, en-suite bungalows here are of a high standard, each set in its own tiny garden. Kayaks, motorbikes and mountain bikes for rent, free snorkels. Double B300

Smile Hut Central Ao Yai 077 820335, smilehutthai.com. At this popular spot, the 35 thatched, split-bamboo and wooden huts are simple but en suite and are spread among the shorefront trees, with the slightly cheaper versions set one row behind. Double B400

★**Starlight Bungalows** Northern end of Ao Kao Kwai 081 978 5301, phayambooking.com. Not the cheapest on Kao Kwai, but very laidback and peaceful at the best stretch of beach. There is a restaurant with a fabulous stargazing deck, tasty food and bamboo en-suite bungalows or more expensive wooden ones. Double B300

Vijit 077 834082, kohpayam-vijit.com. This long-running outfit in a lush garden is very popular, offering en-suite, clapboard bungalows with fans. Free wi-fi. Double B400

EATING AND DRINKING

Several laidback little beach-bars, including *Rasta Baby* at the north end of Ao Yai and *Hippie Bar* at the north end of Ao Kao Khwai, put on fireshows and occasional parties.

Bamboo Bungalows Central Ao Yai 077 820012, bamboo-bungalows.com. Tasty pasta, schnitzels, sandwiches and breakfasts at this beachfront restaurant (Western dishes around B150), as well as lots of Thai standards, including seafood priced by weight. Daily 7.45am–10pm.

★**Oscar's** Village, just north of the pier-head 084 842 5070. Breakfasts, including home-baked bread, Thai standards such as *tom yam kung* (B90), Indian curries and lasagne at this sociable open-air bar-restaurant. Also a good source of information, offering currency exchange and transport tickets. Daily 7am–late.

KHAO SOK NATIONAL PARK

Whether you're heading down the Andaman or the Gulf coast, the stunning jungle-clad limestone crags of **Khao Sok National Park** (B200, valid for 24hr) are well worth veering inland for.

WHAT TO SEE AND DO

Much of the park is carpeted in impenetrable rainforest, home to gaurs, leopard cats and tigers among others – and up to 155 species of bird – but it offers a number of easy trails. The park has two centres: the **tourist village** that has grown up on the access road to the park headquarters, which offers ATMs and currency exchange; and the dam, 65km further east, at the head of **Cheow Lan Lake**, which has some scenic rafthouse accommodation. Most visitors stay in the tourist village and organize their lake trips from there.

The trails

Seven of the park's nine attractions (waterfalls, pools, gorges and viewpoints) branch off the clearly signed main **trail** that runs west of the park headquarters, along the Sok River (sketch map available from the park checkpoint). Most people walk to **Ton Kloi waterfall**, 7km from headquarters (allow 3hr each way), which tumbles into a pool that's good for swimming.

Cheow Lan Lake

With photogenic karst islands and mist-clad mountains encircling jade-coloured waters, the vast **Cheow Lan Lake** (aka **Ratchabrapa Dam**) is Khao Sok's most famous feature. Tours generally combine a longtail trip on the lake with a trek through the nearby flooded cave system and a night on a floating rafthouse.

For many people, the highlight of the park is the three-hour hike through **Nam Talu cave**. The **trek** is not for everyone, however, as the cave section entails an hour-long wade through the river and there will be at least one 20m section where you have to swim. Never attempt the cave without an authorized park guide; in October 2007 a flash flood caused nine fatalities here. Wear sandals with decent grip and take a torch.

ARRIVAL AND DEPARTURE

Khao Sok Track & Trail in the tourist village (081 958 0629, khaosoktrackandtrail.com) sells bus (including a VIP bus to Bangkok), boat, plane and train tickets, as well as tickets for a/c minibuses to destinations that include

10

GUIDED TREKS AND TOURS OF KHAO SOK

Most visitors join one of their guesthouse's **guided treks** at some point during their stay, as they're fun, informative and inexpensive. The usual **day trek** (B700–900) goes to Ton Kloi waterfall, and from about December to March there's a special route that takes in the blooming of the world's second-biggest flower, the **rafflesia kerrii meier**; it's also known as "stinking corpse lily" because of its smell. **Night safaris** along the main park trails (B600–800 for 2–4hr) are also popular. You get to stay out in the jungle on the **overnight camping trips** (about B2500), usually around Tan Sawan falls. Khao Sok guesthouses charge around B1500 for a day-trip to Cheow Lan Lake and B2500 for two-day, one-night trips.

Krabi (2hr) and Surat Thani via the train station at Phunphin (1hr 45min).

By bus All buses between the west-coast junction town of Takua Pa and Surat Thani pass the main park entrance, including some Surat Thani services to and from Khao Lak and Phuket. If you're coming by bus from Bangkok or Chumphon, take a Surat Thani-bound bus, but ask to be dropped off at the junction with the Takua Pa road, about 20km before Surat Thani, and then change onto a Takua Pa bus. At the start of the access road to the tourist village and headquarters, guest-house staff meet bus passengers and offer free lifts to their accommodation.

Destinations Bangkok (1 daily; 11hr); Khao Lak (3 daily; 1hr 30min); Surat Thani (every 90min; 2hr); Takua Pa (every 90min; 50min).

ACCOMMODATION

As well as guided treks and trips to Cheow Lan Lake, guesthouses can arrange elephant rides and fix you up with equipment and transfers for tubing and canoeing trips along the Sok River. Just north of the river, a side road leads east off the north–south access road to many guesthouses, including *Bamboo House* and *Nung House*.

Bamboo House T 081 787 7484, W krabidir.com/bamboohouse. Welcoming place, known for its treks, set in a grassy orchard. The simple, stilted, en-suite, wooden huts with mosquito nets here are the cheapest in this part of the park and there's a good riverside restaurant. Double B200

Khao Sok Green View Resort On the north–south access road, 150m south of the river T 086 271 0526, E lekkhaosokbungalow@hotmail.com. Attractive bamboo bungalows with hot showers set in a lovely garden, full of orchids, flowering shrubs and quaint timber bridges. Double B500

★ **Morning Mist Resort** On the north–south access road, just south of the river T 089 971 8794, W khaosokmorningmistresort.com. Built within a profuse riverside garden, this well-run place offers large, immaculate rooms in variously styled wooden and concrete bungalows, all with hot water. Small swimming pool and excellent restaurant. Double B550

Nung House T 077 395147, W nunghouse.com. Friendly place known for good trekking, with very good huts set around an attractive grassy garden full of rambutan trees. Choose either simple but sturdy bamboo and wood constructions with en-suite facilities, or brick and concrete bungalows; some have hot showers. Attached are a good Thai and Western restaurant and the chilled *Nirvana Bar*. Double B300

KHAO LAK

Just an hour north of Phuket International Airport, **KHAO LAK** has established itself as a mid-market beach resort, with opportunities for diving and snorkelling at the supreme national park reefs of **Ko Similan**, and a style that is determinedly unseedy. It is mostly a bit pricey for backpackers, but is extremely popular with northern European tourists.

The area usually referred to as Khao Lak is in fact a string of beaches west off Highway 4. **Khao Lak** proper is the southernmost and least developed, 5km from the most commercial part of the resort, **Nang Thong** (aka Bang La On), which throngs with restaurants, dive centres, banks, ATMs, clinics, a post office (at its north end) and countless places to stay, both on the beachfront and inland from Highway 4. North again about 3km is lower-key, slightly more youthful **Bang Niang**, a lovely long stretch of golden sand that's backed by a developing tourist village with a network of sois.

There is little obvious evidence these days of the December 2004 **tsunami**, when the undersea earthquake off Sumatra sent a series of waves on to Khao Lak's shores, vaporizing almost every shorefront home and hotel here and killing thousands.

ARRIVAL AND DEPARTURE

By bus All buses running from Phuket to Takua Pa and Ranong (and vice versa) pass through Khao Lak and can drop you anywhere along Highway 4; coming from Krabi or Phang Nga you'll generally need to change buses in

TSUNAMI MEMORIALS

In Bang Niang, on Highway 4, the small **International Tsunami Museum** (daily 9am–7pm; B100) traces the geographical cause and aftermath of the tsunami. In a vacant lot, 100m north of here, a **beached police boat** stands as a memorial to the tsunami's power – it was propelled up here, 2km inland, while patrolling the waters in front of *La Flora* resort, where Princess Ubolrat and her children, one of whom perished in the disaster, were staying.

The main local tsunami memorial is on the beach at **Ban Nam Khem**, the worst-hit village in Thailand, where half of the four thousand inhabitants died in the waves; it lies 25km north of Bang Niang up Highway 4, then left for a signposted 3km. Built by the Thai army, it's an evocative installation: you walk down a path between a curling, 4m-high, concrete "wave" and a grassy bank, representing the land, on which plaques commemorate individual victims. Through a window in the concrete wave, a fishing boat looms over you – this "miracle boat" was swept inland but stopped just short of devastating a house and its occupants.

Khokkloi, from Khao Sok, in Takua Pa. On departure, you can flag down most buses on the main road, but the Bangkok services use a bus station at the far north end of Bang Niang. A/c tourist minibuses to Krabi, Surat Thani and elsewhere, can be arranged with any local tour company.

Destinations Bangkok (3 daily; 12hr); Phuket (20 daily; 2hr 30min); Ranong (8 daily; 2hr 30min–3hr); Takua Pa (18 daily; 30min).

GETTING AROUND

By songthaew A few public songthaews shuttle between Nang Thong and Bang Niang (where they have a base in front of the market), charging B10–20, but mostly they act as private taxis instead and charge B100 or more.

By motorbike Motorbikes are available for rent on all beaches and through guesthouses (from B250/day).

DIVING AND SNORKELLING

There are plenty of snorkelling and diving trips to the spectacular reefs off Ko Similan (Nov–April), 2hr away by speedboat. This archipelago of nine islands offers visibility of up to 30m and an enormous diversity of underwater species. The prices here include the national park fees.

IQ Dive Nang Thong, opposite *McDonald's* ⊤076 485614, ⓦiq-dive.com. Swiss–Thai-run PADI Five-Star Centre that specializes in one-day dive trips to the Similans, on a big dive boat (B5100; B3100 for snorkellers). Their Openwater courses cost from B14,500 with one day spent diving the Similans.

Sea Dragon Dive Center Across from Nang Thong supermarket ⊤076 485420, ⓦseadragondivecenter.com. Highly regarded and the longest-running Khao Lak dive operator, Sea Dragon operate both budget and deluxe live-aboard dive trips to the islands (3 days from B11,900). PADI Openwater B9800, or B13,200 with one day spent diving the Similans.

Similan Tour At *Poseidon Bungalows*, 7km south of central Nang Thong, in Khao Lak ⊤087 895 9204, ⓦsimilantour.com. Highly recommended three-day live-aboard snorkelling trips to the Similans (B8500).

ACCOMMODATION

BANG NIANG

Amsterdam Resort Soi 3 ⊤081 857 5881, ⓦamsterdamresortkhaolak.com. Just 200m inland from the beach, this helpful Dutch-run little complex offers some of the cheapest accommodation in Bang Niang and serves good food. The rooms and red-brick bungalows of varying size have either fans or a/c; most have hot water. Also has internet and free wi-fi, cycle and motorbike rental and a tour desk. Double **B600**

NANG THONG

Jai Bungalows Towards the north end, on Highway 4 ⊤076 485390, ⓔjai_bungalow@hotmail.com. A busy, family-run place that offers some of the cheapest accommodation in Khao Lak. The good-quality, decent-sized, en-suite concrete bungalows are set around a lawn dotted with trees behind the popular restaurant, quite close to the highway and about 600m from the beach. Double **B450**

Phu Khao Lak Resort Towards the south end, east side of Highway 4 ⊤076 485141, ⓦphukhaolak.com. There's a luxurious amount of space at this well-run place with a swimming pool, where the large, spotlessly clean bungalows sit prettily amid a grassy park-style coconut plantation. Fan rooms have tiled floors and most have hot-water bathrooms. About 500m walk from the beach. Double **B600**

★**Walkers Inn** South end, on Highway 4 ⊤084 840 2689, ⓔwalkers.inn@gmail.com. The dorm beds with hot showers at this Thai–Australian place are the best budget option in town. Very friendly, free wi-fi, a good bar-restaurant with a pool table, sports on TV and a decent cup of tea. Dorm **B200**, double **B500**

KHAO LAK

★**Poseidon Bungalows** 7km south of central Nang Thong ⊤087 895 9204, ⓦsimilantour.com. Surrounded by rubber plantations and set above a partly sandy, partly

rocky shore, the fifteen bungalows at this Swedish–Thai-run guesthouse have generous amounts of space, hot showers and balconies, some enjoying sea views; there's also a swimming pool, internet access, free wi-fi and motorbike rental. Get off the bus at the *Poseidon* sign between kilometre-stones 53 and 54, then phone for a pick-up or walk 1km. Double **B950**

10

EATING AND DRINKING

BANG NIANG

Khao Niau In front of the market. Rustic, open-sided restaurant dishing up very good northeastern Thai food, including loads of salads (from B60) such as *som tam* (green papaya salad). Daily 1–10pm; closed 9th and 23rd of each month.

NANG THONG

Happy Snapper North of *Jai*, east side of road. Khao Lak's most famous dive-staff hangout has a folksy lounge ambience and a drinks menu that runs to over a hundred cocktails. There's live music Mon–Sat from around 10.30pm, and a chill-out DJ on Sun – plus the occasional open-mike session. Daily 8.30pm–1am.

O Rendezvous Next to Sea Dragon Dive Centre, east side of road ⓣ 084 325 8106. Highly regarded, indoor-outdoor, French-Thai bar-restaurant, where you can feast on duck in orange and wine sauce (B400) or Thai specialities like chicken *matsaman* curry (B140). Daily 5pm–midnight (kitchen closes 10pm). Closed May–Oct.

PHUKET

Thailand's largest island and a province in its own right, **Phuket** (pronounced "Poo-ket") ranks second in tourist popularity only to Pattaya. Thoughtless developments have scarred much of the island, particularly along the central west coast, and the trend on all the beaches is to cater very much for package tours, with very few budget resorts left.

WHAT TO SEE AND DO

Phuket is Thailand's most important **diving** centre, offering access to some of the most spectacular reefs in the world. The sea gets quite rough during monsoon season (May–Oct), when diving is less rewarding and swimming can be dangerous. Aside from the beaches and the reefs, the island's main attractions include the dramatic headland of **Laem Promthep** at Phuket's southernmost tip – a popular coach-tour stop for sunset – and the **Gibbon Rehabilitation Centre** (daily 9am–4.30pm; B200 national park admission fee; ⓦgibbonproject.org), which is in Phra Taew National Park, 10km northeast of the Heroines' Monument, off Route 4027. It's accessible by songthaew from Phuket Town heading towards Bang Rong or Ao Po (most frequent in the mornings; about 40min; B40); ask for Bang Pae, then it's a 1km walk.

Phuket's west-coast beaches are connected by road; however, to get from one beach to another by public transport (songthaew) you have to go back into Phuket Town, or take an exorbitantly priced taxi or tuk-tuk. **Motorbikes** can be rented on all the beaches but be sure to wear a helmet, as the compulsory helmet law is strictly enforced on Phuket and the driving is probably the worst in Thailand.

Phuket Town

Most visitors only remain in **PHUKET TOWN** long enough to jump on a beach-bound songthaew; they run regularly throughout the day from Thanon Ranong by the market in the town centre to all the main beaches (B25–40). However, it's a good place to base yourself to explore the island, as all songthaews connect here, and the town has the best-value budget accommodation and restaurants on the island. With some fine colonial-style (so-called Sino-Portuguese) architecture, this is an authentic Thai town, in striking contrast to the tailor-made tourist settlements that make up the rest of the island, and it has a few art galleries, handicrafts shops and a decent used-book shop on its central east–west road, Thanon Phang Nga. The next road up, Thanon Thalang, is pedestrianized for strolling and shopping as a "**walking street**" every Sunday evening. Every evening, the **night market** materializes around 6pm near Robinson department store on the southeast side of the centre. The town hosts the spectacular **Vegetarian Festival** over nine days in October or November, which features mind-blowing acts of self-mortification (ⓦphuketvegetarian.com).

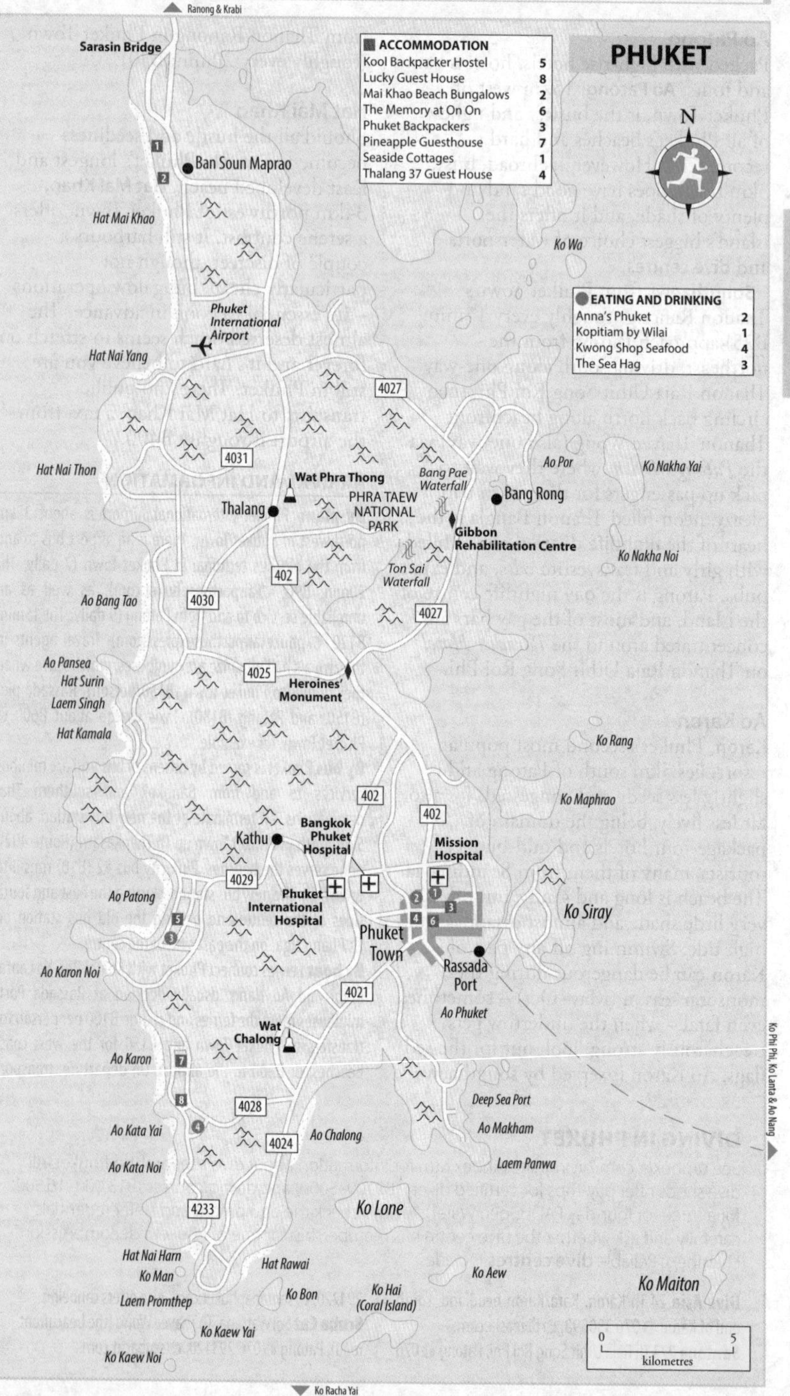
PHUKET
ACCOMMODATION
Kool Backpacker Hostel 5
Lucky Guest House 8
Mai Khao Beach Bungalows 2
The Memory at On On 6
Phuket Backpackers 3
Pineapple Guesthouse 7
Seaside Cottages 1
Thalang 37 Guest House 4
EATING AND DRINKING
Anna's Phuket 2
Kopitiam by Wilai 1
Kwong Shop Seafood 4
The Sea Hag 3
Ranong & Krabi
Sarasin Bridge
Ban Soun Maprao
Hat Mai Khao
Phuket International Airport
Hat Nai Yang
Hat Nai Thon
Wat Phra Thong
Thalang
PHRA TAEW NATIONAL PARK
Bang Pae Waterfall
Bang Rong
Gibbon Rehabilitation Centre
Ton Sai Waterfall
Ko Wa
Ao Por
Ko Nakha Yai
Ko Nakha Noi
Ao Bang Tao
Ao Pansea
Hat Surin
Laem Singh
Hat Kamala
Heroines' Monument
Ko Rang
Ko Maphrao
Bangkok Phuket Hospital
Mission Hospital
Kathu
Phuket International Hospital
Ao Patong
Phuket Town
Rassada Port
Ko Siray
Ao Karon Noi
Ao Phuket
Wat Chalong
Ao Karon
Deep Sea Port
Ao Makham
Ao Kata Yai
Ao Chalong
Laem Panwa
Ao Kata Noi
Ko Lone
Hat Nai Harn
Ko Man
Hat Rawai
Ko Aew
Ko Maiton
Laem Promthep
Ko Bon
Ko Hai (Coral Island)
Ko Kaew Yai
Ko Kaew Noi
Ko Racha Yai
Ko Phi Phi, Ko Lanta & Ao Nang
4027
4031
402
4030
4025
4029
4021
4028
4024
4233
0
5
kilometres

10

Ao Patong

Packed with high-rise hotels, hostess bars and touts, **Ao Patong**, 15km west of Phuket Town, is the busiest and ugliest of all Phuket's beaches and hard to recommend. However, its broad, busy, 3km beach does have good sand and plenty of shade, and it offers the island's biggest choice of watersports and **dive centres**.

Songthaews from Phuket Town's Thanon Ranong (roughly every 15min; B25) approach Patong from the northeast, driving south along one-way Thanon Raja Uthit Song Roi Phi, then circling back north along beachfront Thanon Thavee Wong (also one-way) via the *Patong Merlin*, where they wait to pick up passengers for the return trip. Sleazy, neon-filled Thanon Bangla is the heart of the **nightlife** district, and is filled with girly and transvestite bars, and expat pubs. Patong is the **gay** nightlife centre of the island, and most of the gay bars are concentrated around the *Paradise Hotel* on Thanon Raja Uthit Song Roi Phi.

Ao Karon

Karon, Phuket's second most popular resort, lies 5km south of Patong and is slightly less seedy and congested. It's also far less lively, being the domain of package-tour hotels and mid-budget tourists, many of them from Scandinavia. The beach is long and sandy, but offers very little shade and almost disappears at high tide. Swimming off any part of Karon can be dangerous during the monsoon season (May–Oct) – sometimes even fatal – when the undertow gets treacherously strong; look out for the red flags. Ao Karon is served by songthaews from Thanon Ranong in Phuket Town (roughly every 20min; B30).

Hat Mai Khao

Should all the hustle and seediness become too much, Phuket's longest and least developed beach, **Hat Mai Khao**, 34km northwest of Phuket Town, offers a serene contrast. It still harbours a couple of discreet, though not particularly cheap, bungalow operations – it's essential to book in advance. The almost deserted beach seems to stretch on forever and it's hard to believe you are still in Phuket. There's no public transport to Hat Mai Khao; a taxi from the airport is roughly B400.

ARRIVAL AND INFORMATION

By plane Phuket International Airport is about 32km northwest of Phuket Town. There is an airport bus to and from the old bus terminal in Phuket Town (7 daily; 1hr 20min; B90; ⓦ airportbusphuket.com), as well as an unreliable service to and from Patong (9 daily; 1hr 15min; B120; ⓦ phuketairportbusexpress.com). Travel agents in the arrivals hall organize a/c minibuses, which leave when they're full, to Phuket town (B150/person), Rassada pier (B150) and Patong (B180). Taxis charge about B600 to Phuket Town, for example.

By bus Phuket is served by dozens of bus and a/c minibus services to and from Bangkok and southern Thai destinations. All terminate at the new bus station, about 5km north of Phuket Town up Th Thepkasatri (Route 402); none serves the beaches. Pink city bus #2 (B10) runs into town from the new bus station, skirting the east and south sides of the centre and passing the old bus station on Th Phang Nga, on the east side of the centre.

By boat Ferries connect Phuket with Ko Phi Phi, Ko Lanta, Krabi and Ao Nang, usually docking at Rassada Port; minibuses meet the ferries and charge B100 per person for transfers to Phuket Town and B150 for the west-coast beaches, or B200 to the airport. On departure, transport

DIVING IN PHUKET

See ⓦ phuket.com/diving/sites/index.htm for information about dive sites around Phuket. All dive shops offer day-trips for certified divers (B2700–5000) and diving courses (B13,000–16,500 for a three- or four-day PADI Open Water). Always check the equipment and staff credentials carefully and ask whether the dive centre has membership for one of Phuket's decompression chambers. Reliable **dive centres** include:

Dive Asia 24 Th Karon, Kata/Karon headland, south end of Karon ⓣ 076 330598, ⓦ diveasia.com.

Santana 273 Th Raja Uthit Song Roi Phi, Patong ⓣ 076 294220, ⓦ santanaphuket.com. Also offers canoeing.

Scuba Cat Soi Wattana, Th Thavee Wong (the beachfront road), Patong ⓣ 076 293120, ⓦ scubacat.com.

from Phuket Town or beaches to the port is usually included in your ferry ticket.

Tourist information TAT, 191 Th Thalang, Phuket Town (daily 8.30am–4.30pm; ⓣ076 212213, ⓔtatphket@tat.or.th).

ACCOMMODATION

PHUKET TOWN

The Memory at On On 19 Th Phang Nga Rd ⓣ076 216161, ⓦthememoryhotel.com. Phuket's atmospheric first hotel (circa 1929) in Sino-Portuguese style has just been tastefully renovated, opening up the light wells and communal sitting areas and putting in traditional dark-wood furniture. The a/c 4- and 6-bed dorms are good value, with curtains for privacy, comfy mattresses, free wi-fi and lots of other facilities. Dorm B500, double B1750

Phuket Backpackers 167 Th Ranong Rd ⓣ076 256680, ⓦphuketbackpacker.com. Probably the best-value budget option in Phuket, with a lively bar-restaurant downstairs and lots of tours and information available. The hostel has a kitchen available for use, a huge TV with a well-stocked DVD library, and a nice little garden; wi-fi is free. Dorm B250, double B800

Thalang 37 Guest House 37 Th Thalang ⓣ076 214225. Housed in a 1940s, Sino-Portuguese, wood-floored shop-house in one of the Old Town's most attractive streets, this place is fairly simple but full of character, traveller-friendly and good value. The twelve fan and a/c rooms are large and en suite; rates include a simple breakfast. Double B400

AO PATONG

Kool Backpacker Hostel 3rd floor, Ocean department store, 31 Th Bangla, the main east–west road in central Patong ⓣ076 340739. A strange location for this new, modern hostel, but it's lively, colourful and well equipped: a/c rooms (including a women-only dorm), hot showers, free wi-fi, free lockers and locks, and a lounge with TV and DVD. Dorm B400

AO KARON

Lucky Guest House 110/44–45 Th Taina ⓣ076 330572, ⓔluckyguesthousekata@hotmail.com. Good-value place offering unusually large, bright en-suite rooms in a low-rise block and some rather plain semi-detached bungalows on land further back; set back a bit down a small soi, this guest house has a refreshing sense of space that's at a premium on this road packed with shops, bars and restaurants (Th Taina runs east–west at the far south end of Ao Karon and is sometimes known as "Kata Centre"). Double B600

Pineapple Guesthouse Karon Plaza, off Patak and Luang Pho Chuan rds ⓣ076 396223, ⓦpineapplephuket.com. Good-value British-Thai guest house offering sprucely kept, tiled-floor rooms, all with fridges, TV and hot water, most with a/c, plus a ten-bed mixed dorm, with lockers and a/c. Free internet access and free wi-fi throughout. Dorm B250, double B500

HAT MAI KHAO

Mai Khao Beach Bungalows ⓣ081 895 1233, ⓦmaikhaobeach.wordpress.com. Sturdy but simple en-suite bungalows sit in spacious, grassy grounds just behind the shore, beneath coconut palms hung with hammocks, next door to the *Holiday Inn*. There's a nice restaurant and a massage *sala* here too, but not much else. Closed Aug, sometimes longer, during the rainy season. Double B1000

Seaside Cottages ⓣ094 805 9318, ⓦmai-khao-beach.com. A peaceful spot in a large and colourful beachfront garden with thatched bamboo and wooden huts with shared facilities, as well as expensive en-suite cottages (B2000) and a decent restaurant. There are directions in English and Thai on the website to print out. Double B600

EATING AND DRINKING

PHUKET TOWN

Anna's Phuket Th Ratsada (1 street south of Th Phang Nga), by the fountain roundabout ⓣ076 210535. Cool, artfully un-designed bar-restaurant in a Sino-Portuguese mansion, with a careful mish-mash of furniture. Lots of specialist beers and good Thai and Western food – it's hard to resist the very comforting roast chicken and mashed potato (B250). Live bands nightly at 8.30pm. Tues–Sun 6pm–midnight.

Kopitiam by Wilai 14 & 18 Th Thalang ⓣ083 606 9776. Traditional coffee shop (plus an a/c room two doors away) that's been cleverly updated and made accessible to foreigners by broadening its menu. Alongside tasty Phuket specialities such as pork belly simmered with Chinese spices (B100), you can get sandwiches, salads and afternoon tea with plates of Phuket sweets (B150). Mon–Sat 11am–10pm.

PATONG AND KARON

Kwong Shop Seafood 114 Th Taina, Karon. Unassuming but very popular, family-run institution sporting gingham tablecloths that's famous for its well-priced fresh fish (around B40/100gm) and seafood cooked to order. Daily 8am–midnight.

The Sea Hag Soi Wattana, Th Tavee Wong (the seafront road), Patong ⓣ076 341111. The same chef has been cooking great seafood here for two decades and this is where expat hoteliers come for a good Patong feed. Fish and seafood cooked any number of Thai-style ways for B200–400. Daily noon–4pm & 6pm–midnight.

10

10

DIRECTORY

Banks, ATMs and exchange These are plentiful in Phuket Town, Patong and Karon.

Books South Wind Books, Th Phang Nga, Phuket Town, has a big, sprawling range of secondhand books (Mon–Sat 9am–5pm, Sun 10am–3pm).

Hospital Phuket International Hospital (T 076 249400, emergencies T 076 210935, W phuketinternational hospital.com), north of Central Festival shopping centre on Highway 402, just west of Phuket town, is considered to have the best facilities.

Immigration office At the southern end of Th Phuket, Phuket Town, near Ao Makham (T 076 221905; Mon–Fri 8.30am–4.30pm).

Post office On Th Montri, near the corner of Th Phang Nga, Phuket Town; on Th Patak, just south of Th Taina, in Karon; and on beachfront Th Thavee Wong, south of its intersection with Th Bang La, in Patong.

Tourist police For all emergencies, contact the tourist police, either on the free, 24hr phone line (T 1155) or at their main office at 327 Th Yaowarat on the north side of Phuket town (T 076 223891).

AO PHANG NGA

Covering some four hundred square kilometres of coast between Phuket and Krabi, the mangrove-lined bay of **Ao Phang Nga** is dotted with dramatic limestone karst formations of up to 300m in height.

WHAT TO SEE AND DO

The best, and most affordable, way of seeing the bay is to join one of the longtail **boat trips** arranged from the nearby town of **Phang Nga**. There are half-day tours (daily at about 8.30am & 2pm; 3–4hr; B500) and full-day tours (B800). Overnight trips with a stay in the Muslim stilt village of Ko Panyi cost an extra B500–650. **Kayaks** can be rented along the way for an extra B350. The standard itinerary follows a circular or figure-of-eight route around the bay, passing weirdly shaped karst silhouettes including "James Bond Island" which was Scaramanga's hideaway in *The Man With the Golden Gun*. Most boats return to the mainland via Ko Panyi.

ARRIVAL AND DEPARTURE

By bus The bus station is centrally placed on Th Phetkasem, a few minutes' walk from the hotels, banks (with ATMs and exchange) and restaurants along the same road. Phang Nga town has bus connections to Phuket, Krabi and Trang at least hourly, and five daily to Surat Thani.

TOURS

Sayan Tour (T 076 430348, W sayantour.com) and Mr Kean Tour (T 076 430619 or T 089 871 6092) in Phang Nga town both have offices inside the bus station and offer similar waterborne itineraries. They will also store your baggage for a few hours and sell bus and boat tickets to Ko Phi Phi and Ko Samui, for example.

ACCOMMODATION AND EATING

Baan Phang Nga 100/2 Th Phetkasem T 076 413276. Friendly new guesthouse, offering a/c rooms with TVs, free wi-fi, hot-water bathrooms and a few touches of kitsch contemporary decor. The popular ground-floor restaurant and bakery does everything from Western breakfasts to massaman curry. Double **B650**

Phang-nga Guest House 99/1 Th Phetkasem T 076 411358. Opposite *Baan Phang Nga*, offering clean, en-suite fan rooms with cold showers and cable TV. Double **B380**

KRABI

The small estuary town of **KRABI** is a major transport hub for the islands of Ko Phi Phi and Ko Lanta and makes a nice spot to stay for a night. Although the town has no beaches of its own, Ao Nang and Laem Phra Nang (Railay) are only 45 minutes away. Every Krabi travel agent sells **sea-kayaking** expeditions (see box opposite) and snorkelling trips, and many also offer tours of Krabi's mangrove swamps and trips to Wat Tham Seua, dramatically sited inland amid limestone cliffs. Krabi River runs north to south on the eastern flank of the town. North–south Thanon Utrakit provides a lot of the town's restaurants and tourist facilities; the longtail-boat pier and night market are just off it to the east.

ARRIVAL AND DEPARTURE

From Bangkok, one of the most comfortable options is to get an overnight sleeper train to Surat Thani and then pick up a Krabi bus.

By plane Krabi Airport is 18km east of town, just off Highway 4. Flights are met by shuttle buses to Krabi (B90) and Ao Nang (B150). AirAsia, Bangkok Airways, Nok Air and Thai Airways supply numerous hour-long flights to Bangkok each day. Bangkok Airways also has flights to Samui (1 daily), while AirAsia flies to Chiang Mai (1 daily) as well as to Kuala Lumpur (2 daily).

By bus and minibus The bus station is on Highway 4, 5km north of Krabi town at Talat Kao, from where there's a frequent songthaew service (B30) to the town centre. Private a/c minibus services (all roughly hourly) run from various offices in Krabi town to Surat Thani, Nakhon Si Thammarat, Trang and Ko Lanta – ask at a travel agent or your guesthouse. A/c minibuses to Phuket and Ko Lanta use the Talat Kao bus station.

Destinations Bangkok (12 daily; 12hr); Phang Nga (every 30min; 2hr); Phuket (every hour; 3–5hr); Ranong (2 daily; 5hr); Satun (4 daily; 5hr); Surat Thani (5 daily; 3hr); Trang (hourly; 3hr).

By boat There are boats to Ko Phi Phi (year-round; 2–4 daily; 2hr) and Ko Lanta (roughly mid-Nov to mid-April; 1–2 daily; 2hr 30min) from Krabi Passenger Port (Tha Khlong Jilad), 2km southwest of Krabi town. Ferry tickets bought from tour operators in town should include a free transfer from central Krabi. There are also boat services from Hat Nopparat Thara, next to Ao Nang, some of which call at Railay, to Ko Phi Phi Don (1 daily; 2hr) and to Phuket (1–2 daily; 2hr 30min), both year-round in theory though they sometimes don't run in the monsoon season; and to Ko Lanta (2hr 30min) from roughly November to April. Transfers from Ao Nang hotels are included in the ticket price.

INFORMATION

Tourist information The unhelpful TAT office (daily 8.30am–4.30pm; ⓣ 075 622163, ⓔ tatkrabi@tat.or.th) is 3km north of the centre on Maharat Rd.

ACCOMMODATION

★**Chan-Cha-Lay** 55 Th Utrakit ⓣ 075 620952, ⓦ chanchalay.com. With its stylish blue-and-white theme throughout, this is the most charming and arty place to stay in Krabi. The en suites in the garden are by far the nicest option; rooms in the main building share bathrooms and some don't have windows. Wi-fi available. Double **B300**

K Guest House 15–25 Th Chao Fa, just southwest off Th Utrakit ⓣ 075 623166, ⓔ kguesthouse@yahoo.com. Deservedly popular and well run, this long, timber-clad row house sits in a peaceful but central spot. The nicest bedrooms are upstairs with wooden floors, streetside balconies and hot showers, but there are also cheaper rooms with shared bathroom downstairs. Free wi-fi. Double **B250**

Pak-up Hostel 87 Th Utrakit ⓣ 075 611955. Colourful, modern hostel in a short tower block on Krabi's busiest corner, with smart, a/c, ten-bed dorms. Lots of tours available, as well as free wi-fi throughout. This is the place to come to meet people, with lots of common areas, a rooftop bar and an adjacent garden bar. Dorm **B270**

EATING

Try either the riverside night market near the longtail-boat pier on Th Kong Ka, or the inland night market on Soi 10, Th Maharat, off the northern end of Th Utrakit. At weekends, the pedestrianized night bazaar on Soi 8 offers cheap eats in a lively atmosphere.

Ko Tung 36 Th Kong Ka, opposite the longtail pier. Though it looks nothing much, this little Thai restaurant is always packed with locals savouring the excellent seafood. Special highlights include the sweet mussels and baked crab. Most dishes around B80. Mon–Sat 11am–10pm.

Pizzeria Firenze Th Kong Ka, north of the longtailboat pier. Authentic Italian dishes, including great thin-crust pizzas (around B200) and home-made pastas, espresso coffee and Italian wines. Daily 9am–9.30pm.

DIRECTORY

Hospital Krabi Hospital is about 1km north of the town centre at 325 Th Utrakit (ⓣ 075 611212).

Immigration office In the compound of government offices on the way to Krabi Passenger Port (Mon–Fri 8.30am–4.30pm; ⓣ 075 611097).

SEA-KAYAKING IN THE KRABI AREA

By far the most enjoyable way of exploring the glories of the Krabi coastline is by **sea kayak**. Paddling into the mangrove swamps and secret tidal lagoons, or **hongs**, hidden inside the limestone karsts is a fantastic experience and gives you close-up views of birds, animals and plants that would be impossible from a roaring longtail.

The most popular kayaking destination is **Ao Thalen** (also called Ao Talin or Talane), about 25km northwest of Krabi Town, where you can paddle out to the *hongs* and beaches of Ko Hong and Ko Bileh. Another 25km north up the Krabi coast, the Ban Bor Tor (aka Ban Bho Tho) area of **Ao Luk** bay is famous for its caves, in particular Tham Lod, which has a long tunnel hung with stalactites, and Tham Phi Hua Toe, whose walls display around a hundred prehistoric cave paintings.

Kayaking **trips** usually cost about B2000–2500 for a full day or B1000 for half a day. Trips can be arranged through any tour operator in Krabi Town, Laem Phra Nang or Ao Nang, or with reputable, though more expensive, kayaking operators such as John Gray Sea Canoe (ⓣ 076 254505, ⓦ johngray-seacanoe.com) in Phuket Town.

Post office About 100m south of *Chan-Cha-Lay* on Th Utrakit (Mon–Fri 8.30am–4.30pm, Sat 9am–noon).

AO NANG AND HAT NOPPARAT THARA

10

AO NANG, 22km west of Krabi town, is a busy, commercial resort that has seen mass development over the years and caters mainly for package tourists. Most travellers who stop here do so in order to take a longtail boat to nearby Laem Phra Nang (Railay). Though the beach in Ao Nang is no great shakes, the less-developed western beach, **Hat Nopparat Thara**, part of which comes under the protection of a marine national park, is prettier and more peaceful.

Ao Nang is Krabi's main hub for snorkelling trips and **dive shops** – most diving expeditions head to the reefs around Ko Phi Phi and Ko Ha (near Ko Lanta). A reputable firm is Poseidon, a few hundred metres from the beach up the main access road in front of *Paradise Resort* (T 075 637263, W poseidon-diving.com), who offer local two-dive trips for B2600, and Openwater courses for B14,900.

ARRIVAL AND DEPARTURE

By songthaew To reach Ao Nang, take a white songthaew from Krabi bus station or town centre, passing eastern Nopparat Thara en route (roughly 45min; B50–60).

ACCOMMODATION AND EATING

With package holidays taking over, budget accommodation is becoming increasingly hard to find. There's a small night market in front of *Krabi Resort*, on the main road about 200m from the main beachfront, heading towards Nopparat Thara. Locals eat at the seafood restaurants in the national park visitors' centre car park, which is at the west end of Nopparat Thara's eastern beach.

AusThai Hotel 1km from the beach up the main access road, Ao Nang T 081 719 1748. This friendly, recently built place has a variety of options with a/c and hot showers (the more expensive rooms with balconies) and can rent motorbikes. Free wi-fi. Dorm B350, double B800

Laughing Gecko Soi Hat Nopparat Thara 13 T 081 270 5028, E laughinggecko99@hotmail.com. Perhaps the last of the old-style bungalows left in the Ao Nang area, this is an easy-going and exceptionally traveller-friendly haven run by a Thai-Canadian couple, with nightly all-you-can-eat Thai buffets. Choose from a range of simple, thatched, fan-cooled, en-suite bamboo huts set around a garden dotted with cashew trees, including four-person dorms. It's about a 10min walk from the beach at Hat Nopparat Thara East. Dorm B200, double B500

Wang Sai Beside the bridge at the far eastern end of Hat Nopparat Thara T 075 638128. There are no reasonably priced, authentic Thai restaurants left on Ao Nang proper, but fortunately this place is just around the corner on the main road, where you can get fried rice for as little as B80. It offers good sunset views from its beachfront tables, an enormous range of the freshest seafood and lots of southern Thai specialities. Daily 10.30am–10pm.

LAEM PHRA NANG (RAILAY)

The stunning headland of **Laem Phra Nang** is accessible only by boat, so staying on one of its four beaches feels like being on an island. The sheer limestone cliffs, pure-white sand and emerald waters make it a spectacular spot, though bungalows have now been built in all the prime spots so the whole place feels a little congested.

Furthest out on the headland, **Ao Phra Nang** is the prettiest beach, with luxuriously soft sand, reefs close to shore, and luxury hotels. It's reached by a short path from the southern end of **East Railay**, which is not suitable for swimming because of its fairly dense mangrove growth and a tide that goes out for miles, but has cheap accommodation. Five minutes' walk away on the opposite side of the headland, **West Railay** enjoys impressive karst scenery, crystal-clear water and a much longer stretch of good sand. On the other side of a rocky promontory from northern West Railay (take a longtail or walk along the path from East Railay in 20min), the beach at **Ao Ton Sai** is coarse and littered with rocks that make it impossible to swim at low tide. Leafy and wedged between towering limestone cliffs, this is the travellers' beach, with budget bungalows set among the palms several hundred metres back from the shore, and regular all-night beach parties at the beachfront *Freedom Bar* and *Chillout Bar*.

ARRIVAL AND DEPARTURE

By boat Longtail boats to the cape depart when full from the pier on Th Kong Ka in Krabi town and dock at East Railay (roughly 45min), from where it's easy to cut across

to West Railay along any of the through-tracks. Krabi boats do run during the rainy season, but it's safer to go via Ao Nang instead. Ao Nang is much closer to Laem Phra Nang, and longtails run from the beachfront here to West Railay and Ao Ton Sai (10min) year-round.

ACTIVITIES

Laem Phra Nang is Thailand's premier rock-climbing centre, with seven hundred bolted sport-climbing routes around Ton Sai and Railay (see railay.com for a full rundown). Of the many climbing schools that rent out equipment and lead guided climbs, the most established include King Climbers, just behind *Flame Tree* restaurant on West Railay (railay.com/railay/climbing/climbing_king_climbers.shtml), and Basecamp Tonsai on Ton Sai (081 149 9745, basecamptonsai.com). A typical half-day introduction costs from B800.

ACCOMMODATION

During high season (Nov–Feb), it's essential to arrive on the beaches as early in the morning as possible to get a room. Most accommodation options have attached restaurants.

Pasook Resort Ao Ton Sai, on the inland road above and parallel to the beach 089 645 3013. Friendly, welcoming spot, set on sloping lawns amid flowers and small trees, offering en-suite, fan-cooled concrete rooms and clapboard bungalows. Prices change frequently, according to demand. Double **B400**

Railay Cabana 075 621733. In a spacious, grassy, tree-filled amphitheatre of majestic karst cliffs, a 5min walk from East Railay beach on the track to Ton Sai, this friendly and quiet family-run place offers simple bungalows with mosquito nets, fans, cold-water bathrooms and big verandas. Double **B500**

Rapala Rock Wood Resort East Railay, north end. Climb a steep flight of stairs to reach the thirty rough-hewn, fan-cooled huts and rooms here, which are among the cheapest on Railay, set around a scruffy, breezy garden high above the beach, with some enjoying dramatic karst views from their verandas. The restaurant serves Indian food and bakes its own tasty biscuits and bread. No advance bookings, walk-ins only. Double **B400**

Sai Tong Resort Ton Sai, 400m along the track to East Railay 081 079 6583. This friendly, good-value little place offers cheap, bare-basics, woven-bamboo huts with nets, fans and bathrooms. Double **B250**

KO PHI PHI

One of southern Thailand's most famous destinations, the two spectacular **Ko Phi Phi** islands, 40km south of Krabi and 48km east of southern Phuket, leapt to international notoriety as the location for the 1999 film, *The Beach*. Then, in December 2004, they became headline news again as the tsunami wreaked inconceivable destruction on the two main beaches of the larger island, **Ko Phi Phi Don**, and on the densely packed tourist village connecting them. The island made a fast recovery, however, and Ko Phi Phi is very much a thriving tourist hub, perhaps too crowded for its own good; budget accommodation is sparse, particularly in peak season. Phi Phi Don's sister island, **Ko Phi Phi Leh**, home to the magnificent Maya Bay, is an uninhabited national marine park and can only be visited on day-trips.

Detailed **maps** are available at travel agents and dive shops in the village.

Ao Ton Sai, Laem Hin and Ao Loh Dalum

Ko Phi Phi Don would itself be two islands were it not for the narrow isthmus that connects the hilly expanses to the east and west, separating the stunningly symmetrical double bays of **Ao Ton Sai** to the south and Ao Loh Dalum to the north. The land between the two bays is occupied by a commercial tourist village, crammed with guesthouses, tour operators, restaurants, bars, internet cafés and dive centres.

East along the coast from the pier, about ten minutes' walk down the main track is the **Laem Hin** promontory which overlooks a quieter patch of swimmable beach. Just a few minutes' walk north through Ton Sai village, seductively curvaceous **Ao Loh Dalum** is much better for swimming and sunbathing, though the tide here goes out for miles. The **viewpoint** that overlooks eastern Ao Loh Dalum affords a magnificent panorama over the twin bays, and every evening a stream of people makes the steep fifteen-minute climb up the steps for sunset shots.

Hat Yao (Long Beach)

With its luxurious white sand and large reefs just 20m offshore, **Hat Yao** (Long Beach), east along the coast from Ao Ton Sai, is the best of Phi Phi's main beaches, though it is extremely crowded. Longtail

boats do the ten-minute shuttle from Hat Yao to Ao Ton Sai between 8am to 8pm (B100 per person, minimum 2 people), and from Ao Ton Sai to Hat Yao till all hours of the morning, but it's also possible to walk between the two in half an hour. At low tide you can get to Hat Yao along the rocky shore, from Laem Hin, past many quaint secluded beaches. The island's single road follows an inland route to the east end of Hat Yao from *The Rock* junction in the village; it's a hot, hilly and unshaded forty-minute walk.

10

Hat Rantee and Ao Toh Koh

For those wishing to escape the maddening crowds, the small, east-coast bays of **Hat Rantee** and **Ao Toh Koh** offer affordable tranquillity. Transfers from Ao Ton Sai cost B800 by longtail boat.

ARRIVAL AND DEPARTURE

By boat Scheduled ferries connect Ko Phi Phi Don with Ao Nang and Railay (1 daily; 2hr; B350–450); Ko Lanta (1–4 daily; 1hr 30min; B300–350); Krabi (4 daily; 1hr 30min–2hr; B300); and Phuket (3–5 daily; 1hr 30min–2hr 30min; B300). All boats dock at Ao Ton Sai, where there's a B20 entry fee.

DIVING

Ko Phi Phi is an exceptionally good diving and snorkelling site, and you can arrange day-dives (from B2500) and four-day Openwater courses (B12,900) through Viking Divers, east of the pier in Ao Ton Sai (T 081 719 3375, W vikingdiversthailand.com). As well as responsible, small-group dive trips and courses, Phi Phi Adventure Club in Ao Ton Sai (T 081 895 1334, W phi-phi-adventures.com) offers half-day snorkelling trips to swim with sharks or to Phi Phi Leh (B800).

ACCOMMODATION

Ko Phi Phi is one of Thailand's most expensive locations, with Hat Yao the most exorbitant.

AO TON SAI

Coco's Close to the base of the viewpoint access steps T 075 601400, W facebook.com/ppcoco1. Reminiscent of a city guesthouse, with a main two-storey block and diverse other rooms, all painted bright white, clean and well organized. All rooms are en suite, some have a/c. Double B600

Oasis Ton Sai village (no phone, walk-in only). Behind a travel agent, almost opposite and just south of *The Rock*, the basic rooms here are cheap and decent enough crashpads, some with shared bathrooms. Minimum 2 nights. Double B300

The Rock T 081 607 3897. Traveller-oriented hangout behind a landmark boat-shaped bar-restaurant, offering some of the cheapest beds on the island, in large mixed-sex dorms; up to seventeen bunk beds are crammed in each, but there are fans and lockers. Also has a few singles (B350) and doubles with shared, cold-water bathrooms. Dorm B250, double B500

Tara Inn Ton Sai village T 075 601021. A budget favourite for many years; fan rooms are spacious if a little on the tired side. Most bungalows have large balconies and views over the bay with more expensive a/c options (B1200) having the better views. Double B450

Tee House East end of Ton Sai village, just north of the mosque T 084 851 5721. Small but clean rooms (with even smaller, hot-water bathrooms) decorated in earth tones, some with driftwood balconies, some with a/c. Crepes, baguettes and detox shakes for breakfast. Double B700

HAT YAO

Long Beach Bungalows Central Hat Yao T 089 973 6425. The least expensive place to stay on Long Beach, on a great stretch of beach with an attached dive shop (W longbeachdivers.com). The cheapest of the tightly packed but recently renovated rooms have fans and cold-water bathrooms. Double B800

Phi Phi Hill Resort On the southeastern tip of Ko Phi Phi, up a very steep stairway T 075 618203, W phiphihill.com. This quiet place occupying a large headland plateau is a real no-frills affair, with sturdy, simply furnished, wooden bungalows on stilts. The cheapest have fans and cold showers and no view. The restaurant, with ample decking, looks across to Phi Phi Leh. Closes for some of the rainy season. Double B750

AO TOH KO AND HAT RANTEE

Ao Toh Ko Beach Resort T 081 537 0528, W tohkobeachresort.com. The exceptionally welcoming family who run this place keep people staying and returning – and they're great cooks too. The comfortable range of accommodation kicks off with attractive, breezy, en-suite, bamboo huts with mossie nets, some sitting right over the sea on the rocks. Double B1800

Rantee Sunrise Hat Rantee T 080 696 2711. A cluster of unimpressive huts dotted along the hillside. All have fans and cold showers, and the bathrooms have certainly seen better days. However, the staff are friendly and the location is good. Call in advance for free pick-up from Ao Ton Sai. Double B800

EATING

Ao Ton Sai is the best place to eat on the island and offers the most choice.

Lemongrass East of the pier, on the first north–south alley. Friendly, basic restaurant with an open kitchen,

serving very tasty Thai standards, starting with chicken fried rice for B100. Daily 10am–8pm.

Patcharee Bakery On the main alley running east from the pier. This place and *Pee Pee Bakery* square up to each other across the narrow alley, vying for trade. Croissants – plain, chocolate (B30), almond or savoury – are the thing here, washed down with espresso, but it also does delicious grilled baguettes with mozzarella, tomato and ham (B80), as well as rice and noodle dishes. Daily 7am–8pm (closes 5pm in low season).

NIGHTLIFE

Ko Phi Phi is a major party island. In high season, Ao Ton Sai and Ao Loh Dolum teem with young Westerners out for a good time.

Reggae Bar East of the pier in Ao Ton Sai, on the main route heading towards *The Rock*. A Phi Phi institution in the heart of the village that's been running for years in various incarnations. These days it arranges regular amateur *muay thai* bouts in its boxing ring at around 9.30pm – "beat up your friend and win free buckets" – and has pool tables and a bar around the sides. Daily roughly 8.30am–2am.

Slinky Towards the east end of Loh Dalum, where the left fork just before *The Rock* hits the beach. The messy, throbbing heart of Phi Phi nightlife, with a booming sound system, fire shows, and buckets and buckets of booze. Daily roughly 9pm–2am.

Stones Bar On the beach at the east end of Loh Dalum. One of the bars of the moment, with dozens of nifty red, gold and green axe cushions scattered on the beach and on platforms under the trees, and a DJ station in a treehouse. Claims to be open 24hr.

KO LANTA

At 25km long, **Ko Lanta** (actually two islands, Ko Lanta Yai and adjacent, untouristed Ko Lanta Noi) offers plenty of fine sandy beaches all along its west coast and is a deservedly popular destination. It's also within easy day-tripping distance of the stunning beaches and reefs of Ko Rok Nai and Ko Rok Nok, 47km south (B1200 through any tour agent).

Though Lanta has plenty of boat connections, its main form of access is by air-conditioned minibus on two short car ferry routes from the mainland; a bridge between Ko Lanta Noi and Ko Lanta Yai is planned. A road runs the entire length of Ko Lanta's west coast, serviced by plenty of tuk-tuks; many bungalows rent out **motorbikes** (B250). Most beaches have some facilities, but to be sure of getting what you want, head to the commercial centre and port at the north end of the island, **Ban Sala Dan**, which is jammed full of clothing stalls, banks, restaurants, travel agents, and arts and crafts shops.

10

Hat Khlong Dao and Ao Phra-Ae (Long Beach)

Ko Lanta's most developed beach, **Hat Khlong Dao**, is broad and nice, but no longer has any decent budget accommodation. A couple of kilometres south of Khlong Dao, **Ao Phra-Ae** (also known as **Long Beach**) boasts a beautiful long strip of white sand and an enjoyably youthful ambience. Traveller-oriented bamboo huts are fairly plentiful here, as are beach-shack **bars** with mats on the sand.

Hat Khlong Khong, Hat Khlong Nin and Ao Kantiang

The lovely long beach at **Hat Khlong Khong**, south of Ao Phra-Ae, is peppered with rocks and you can only really swim at high tide. There are lots of beautiful places to stay and a number of colourful beachfront bars that host regular parties.

About 4km south of Hat Khlong Khong, the road forks, with the left-hand, east-bound arm running across to Ko Lanta Yai's east coast, via Tham Mai Kaew caves and Viewpoint Hill, and the right-hand fork running south to long, sandy, laidback **Hat Khlong Nin**, a great spot for swimming. About 8km further south, **Ao Kantiang** has a lovely beach in a sheltered bay, where swimming is possible year-round.

ARRIVAL AND DEPARTURE

Bungalow touts meet the boats at Ban Sala Dan and will usually transport you to the beach of your choice. If you need to use the motorbike sidecar taxi or white songthaew services instead, be warned that drivers will try and charge arrivals way over the normal fares; walk 250m from the pier head to the main road to get a ride at more reasonable rates. For the a/c minibuses listed below, the price often depends on how far south on Ko Lanta you want to go.

From Krabi Ferries run from Krabi Passenger Port (roughly mid-Nov to mid-April 1–2 daily; 2hr 30min; B400). There are also year-round a/c minibuses from Krabi bus station (hourly; 2hr 30min–4hr; B250–350). On

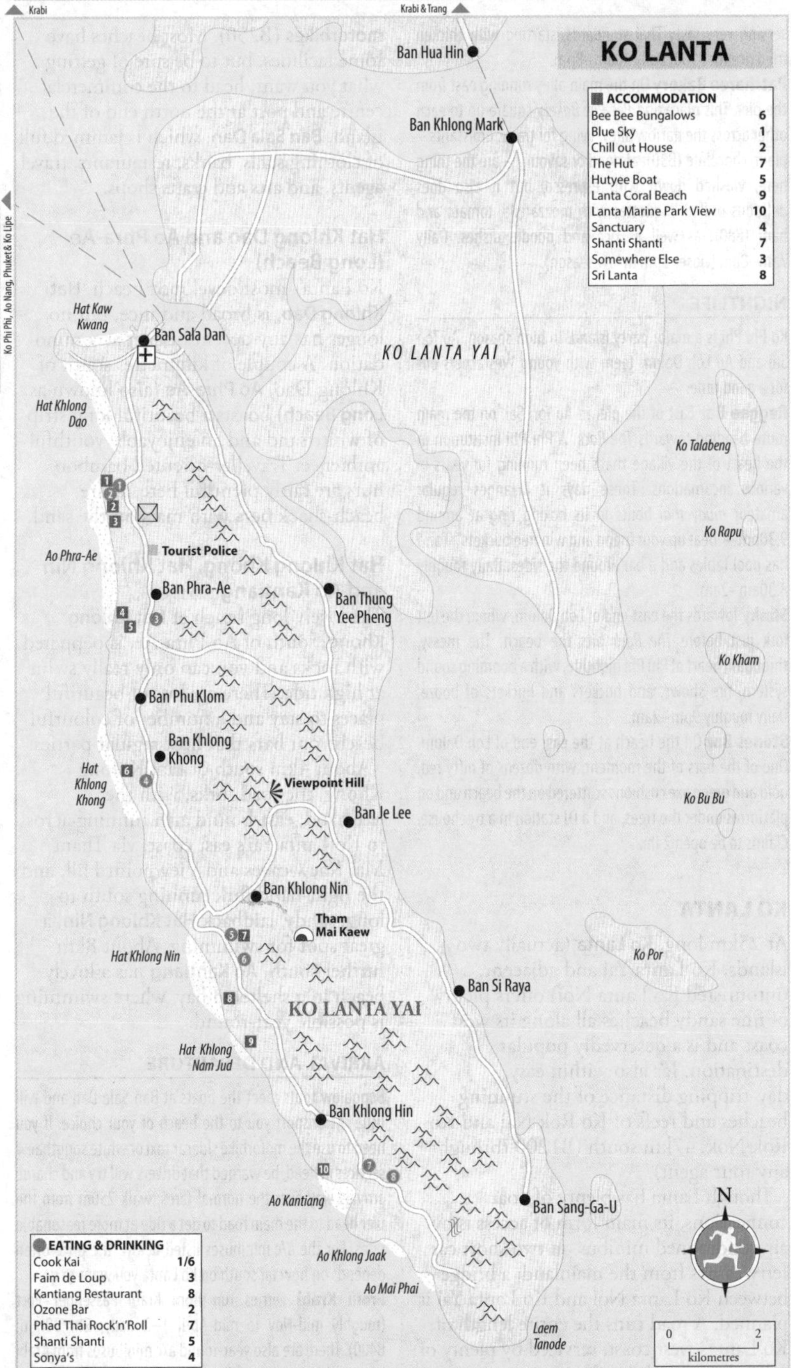

Krabi
Krabi & Trang
KO LANTA
ACCOMMODATION
Bee Bee Bungalows 6
Blue Sky 1
Chill out House 2
The Hut 7
Hutyee Boat 5
Lanta Coral Beach 9
Lanta Marine Park View 10
Sanctuary 4
Shanti Shanti 7
Somewhere Else 3
Sri Lanta 8
EATING & DRINKING
Cook Kai 1/6
Faim de Loup 3
Kantiang Restaurant 8
Ozone Bar 2
Phad Thai Rock'n'Roll 7
Shanti Shanti 5
Sonya's 4
Ban Hua Hin
Ban Khlong Mark
Hat Kaw Kwang
Ban Sala Dan
KO LANTA YAI
Hat Khlong Dao
Tourist Police
Ao Phra-Ae
Ban Phra-Ae
Ban Thung Yee Pheng
Ban Phu Klom
Ban Khlong Khong
Hat Khlong Khong
Viewpoint Hill
Ban Je Lee
Ban Khlong Nin
Tham Mai Kaew
Hat Khlong Nin
Ban Si Raya
KO LANTA YAI
Hat Khlong Nam Jud
Ban Khlong Hin
Ao Kantiang
Ban Sang-Ga-U
Ao Khlong Jaak
Ao Mai Phai
Laem Tanode
Ko Talabeng
Ko Rapu
Ko Kham
Ko Bu Bu
Ko Por
N
0
2
kilometres

10
Ko Phi Phi, Ao Nang, Phuket & Ko Lipe

departure from Lanta, the Krabi minibuses will drop you off at Krabi Airport; on arrival, you'll need to call ☎ 081 606 3591 to ask them to pick you up at the airport.

From Phuket Ferries run from Rassada Port (at least 1 daily; 4hr; B800–900), via Ko Phi Phi (1hr 30min; B300–400). There are also a/c minibuses from Phuket (at least 1 daily; 5hr; B550–600).

From Hat Nopparat Thara (near Ao Nang) Ferries usually travel via Laem Phra Nang (1 daily; 2hr 15min; B470).

From Ko Lipe In high season, there's one daily ferry (5hr; B1700) and two daily speedboat services (3–4hr; B1900).

From Trang A/c minibuses run year-round (6 daily; 3hr; B320–400).

ACTIVITIES

Cooking classes Cooking classes are provided by Time for Lime (next door to Lanta Paddlesports; ☎ 075 684590, Ⓦ timeforlime.net).

Diving Among reliable diving centres, Lanta Diver, on the main road into Ban Sala Dan (☎ 075 668058, Ⓦ lantadiver.com), is a Swedish-owned, PADI Five-star Instructor Development Centre, charging from B2900 for two dives, excluding equipment, and B13,900 for the Openwater course.

Watersports Lanta Paddlesports, at the south end of Hat Khlong Dao (☎ 094 316 2159, Ⓦ lantapaddlesports.com), offers paddleboard lessons and rental, as well as windsurfing, kayaking and surfing.

ACCOMMODATION

Accommodation prices listed here are for high season; many places increase their rates for "peak season", usually between mid-December and mid-January, while in the rainy season (May–Oct) rates are vastly discounted and some bungalows close down.

AO PHRA-AE (LONG BEACH)

Blue Sky North Long Beach ☎ 081 906 7577, Ⓦ blueskylanta.com. This place has it all: decent, cheap, en-suite, fan bungalows, free wi-fi, beachside restaurant and bar, massage platform, coffee bar and a bookshop. Double **B500**

★**Chill out House** North Long Beach, same road as to *Ozone* ☎ 082 183 2258, Ⓦ chillouthouselanta.com. Hand-built using recycled materials, bamboo and driftwood, this is a fabulous place with a relaxed bar and free wi-fi. The dorm beds share hot and cold showers and some of the rooms and bungalows have en-suite cold showers. There's a relaxing common area with big-screen TV. Dorm **B140**, double **B250**

Hutyee Boat South Long Beach, behind *Red Snapper* restaurant ☎ 083 633 9723. These large, sturdy, stilted bungalows stand in a grove of tall, shady trees less than 50m from the beach, have en-suite bathrooms and fridges – and the owner's a real character. Double **B400**

> **★TREAT YOURSELF**
>
> **Sri Lanta** Hat Khlong Nin ☎ 075 662688, Ⓦ srilanta.com. On a lengthy beachfront here, the restaurant, bar, pool and attractive spa sit in beautiful gardens, adorned with ponds, fountains and a huge lawn. Meanwhile, running up the lush slope across the road, the large cottages enjoy plenty of space, as well as all the facilities you need; they're decorated with dark wood and some nice artsy touches. Book in advance for the best rates. Double **B3600**

Sanctuary Southern Long Beach ☎ 081 891 3055, Ⓦ sanctuarykohlanta.com. Cheap A-frames with shared facilities at the back and elegant bamboo-clad bungalows with pretty interiors and open-air bathrooms at the front. The restaurant serves Indian and vegetarian food and home-made bread, and there's a cute bar hut on the beachfront. Double **B250**

Somewhere Else North Long Beach ☎ 081 536 0858. Located in the heart of the liveliest part of Ao Phra-Ae, with bars to the left and right, this cheap, congenial place on a beachside lawn is one of the main travellers' centres on the beach. Its spacious, unusually designed hexagonal bungalows made of tightly woven bamboo come with pretty bathrooms with hot showers. Double **B500**

HAT KHLONG KHONG, HAT KHLONG NIN AND AO KANTIANG

★**Bee Bee Bungalows** Hat Khlong Khong ☎ 081 537 9932, Ⓔ beebeepiya02@hotmail.com. This place stands out for its highly individual huts, each one a charming experiment in bamboo architecture. All are simple but comfortably furnished, given style with batik fabric flourishes, and have fans, mosquito nets and partially open-air bathrooms. There's a good bar-restaurant, too, with similarly experimental but lovely wood and thatch salas. Double **B550**

The Hut Hat Khlong Nin ☎ 084 446 5585. A small, laidback and friendly place, just across the road from *Otto's Bar & Grill*, with clean, simple bungalows packed tightly together in a small garden, and a tasty restaurant (mains from B90). Double **B350**

Lanta Coral Beach Hat Khlong Nam Jud, a tiny bay between Hat Khlong Nin and Ao Kantiang ☎ 075 662535, Ⓦ lantacoralresort.com. Friendly resort with a lovely, lofty restaurant – especially nice at sunset – up on the rocky point. The plain but very clean and en-suite bamboo and concrete huts are scattered over a lawn among the palms (some of which are hung with hammocks); the concrete options, whether fan or a/c, boast hot showers. Double **B500**

Lanta Marine Park View Ao Kantiang ⓣ075 665063, ⓦlantamarine.com. The bungalows here are ranged up the slope at the northern end of the beach, with steps leading down to the shore. The best of them are on stilts and enjoy glorious bay views, while the plain, cheap fan-cooled wood and bamboo bungalows sit further back. There's also a small cliffside bar affording great views. Double B500

10

Shanti Shanti Hat Khlong Nin ⓣ089 044 2298, ⓔshantishantikohlanta@yahoo.com. Behind the same owners' restaurant and set back from the beach in an attractive small garden, simple, well-designed bungalows, the cheapest of which have platform beds and cold showers. Double B300

EATING, DRINKING AND NIGHTLIFE

AO PHRA-AE (LONG BEACH)

On Long Beach, bars take turns putting on parties so there's usually something going on somewhere, as advertised on posters and fliers. On the road towards the north end of the beach, there's a branch of the good Hat Khlong Nin restaurant, *Cook Kai* (see below).

★**Faim de Loup** On the main road towards the south end of the bay. Very good French bakery, where the croissants, pains au chocolat, fruit tarts and excellent espressos just hit the spot. Also does sandwiches, quiches (B250 for a big one with salad) and savoury croissants. Daily 7.30am–5pm.

Ozone Bar On the beach, north of *Somewhere Else* bungalows. One of the most famous bars on the beach, especially for its weekly DJ parties (currently Thurs), which usually draw a lively crowd. Daily roughly 10am–2am.

HAT KHLONG KHONG, HAT KHLONG NIN AND AO KANTIANG

On Hat Khlong Nin, you can get delicious coffee, cakes and snacks at the travel agent Monkey Biziness (see below).

Cook Kai Hat Khlong Nin. Friendly restaurant hung with shell mobiles and lamps, dishing up hearty portions of all the Thai classics, including a good seafood salad (B150) and a few Western dishes including breakfast. Daily 8am–10pm.

★**Kantiang Restaurant** Inland Kantiang, 100m south of the 7-Eleven. A simple, rustic place with individual tables in cute, thatched cabanas serving authentic Thai food, including a huge selection of salads. The massaman curry (B120) and the spicy mango salad with crispy catfish are both delicious (B120). Daily 10am–10pm.

Phad Thai Rock'n'Roll North end of Ao Kantiang. Simple but stunning combination, almost as good as rock and roll: delicious *pat thai* (B90) and espresso coffees (B50). Daily 9am–4.30pm & 6–9pm.

Shanti Shanti Hat Khlong Nin. This unpretentious, roadside, French-Thai restaurant dishes up very good pasta dishes (around B200), simple French main courses and Western breakfasts, as well as superb home-made ice creams and espresso coffees. Nov–March daily 8.30am–10pm; April, May, Sept & Oct Tues–Sun 8.30am–10pm.

Sonya's On the main road in Hat Khlong Khong, just north of 7-Eleven and 50m south of *Bee Bee's* ⓣ089 471 5014. Very popular, cheap, garden restaurant, where you can "build your own" pasta from a wide choice of pastas, sauces, meats and extras. Also has a big selection of Thai food (from B60), Western breakfasts, sandwiches, and espresso coffees; plus cheap, functional dorms and rooms. Daily 8.30am–9pm.

DIRECTORY

Health centre Just south of the town centre is Sala Dan Health Centre (ⓣ075 668170).

Post office On the main road towards the north end of Ao Phra Ae, just north of *Peaceful Resort*.

Tourist police On the main road in central Ao Phra Ae (ⓣ1155).

Travel agent As well as being a cool gift shop and café, Monkey Biziness on Hat Khlong Nin is a friendly and clued-up agent for transport tickets, tours, motorbike and car rental (ⓣ087 033 5325, ⓔmonkey-biziness@hotmail.com).

The deep south

As Thailand drops down to meet Malaysia, the cultures of the two countries begin to merge. Many inhabitants of the **deep south** are ethnically more akin to the Malaysians, and a significant proportion of the 1,500,000 followers of Islam here speak a dialect of Malay. Some also yearn for secession from Thailand; since 2004 there has been continuing violence in the region, leading the Thai government to introduce special security measures in certain parts of Pattani, Yala and Narathiwat provinces – currently all but essential travel is advised against. For up-to-the-minute advice, consult your government travel advisory. The safest border crossings to Malaysia are detailed below.

TRANG AND AROUND

TRANG hosts a **vegetarian festival** every October that's similar to but smaller than Phuket's (see p.804), but is chiefly of interest for the string of gorgeous **beaches and islands** nearby. Travel agents

offer snorkelling day-trips to the islands of Ko Hai, Ko Mook and Ko Kradan, which provide a perfect getaway and also have some accommodation. Trang province's coastline, from Ban Pak Meng down to Ban Chao Mai, offers some exceptional beaches, well worth exploring on motorbike, by car or as a part of a tour. Trang town's main thoroughfare is Thanon Rama VI, where you'll find restaurants, bars, accommodation, banks and travel agents – most cluster near the train station at its western extremity.

ARRIVAL AND INFORMATION

By plane Trang Airport, around 3km south of town, is served by 1hr 30min flights from Bangkok's Don Muang Airport with Air Asia and Nok Air (both 3 daily). BB Tour on Th Rama VI, 50m from the train station (T 075 219054), offers a flight-correlated minibus service to and from the airport (B90/person).

By bus and minibus All buses arrive at the terminal on Th Phatthalung (Highway 4), about 3km northeast of the centre; take a tuk-tuk (B80 or B20/person) into town. Travel agents sell tickets for a/c minibus services to Ko Lanta (6 daily; 3hr) and Pak Bara (at least 1 daily; 1hr 30min) in high season.

Destinations Bangkok (11 daily; 12–14hr); Krabi (hourly; 2–3hr); Nakhon Si Thammarat (hourly; 3hr); Phuket (hourly; 5hr); Satun (hourly; 3hr).

By train From the train station at the western end of Th Rama VI, two trains depart for Bangkok daily (14–16hr).

Tourist information TAT have a helpful office on Th Wisetkul, 200m south of the clocktower on Th Rama VI (daily 8.30am–4.30pm, sometimes closed for lunch on Sat & Sun; T 075 215867, E tattrang@tat.or.th). The best travel agent in town is Trang Island Hopping Tour, directly opposite the station at 28/2 Th Sathanee (T 082 804 0583, W trang-island-hopping.com), a great source of impartial information on the area. *Wunderbar*, just around the corner (see below), also acts as a helpful and clued-up travel agent.

ACCOMMODATION AND EATING

For a cheap feed, try the night market on Th Ruenrom (100m up Th Rama VI from the clocktower, turn left).

Koh Teng Hotel 77–79 Th Rama VI T 075 218622. This characterful 1940s Chinese hotel is a little battered and dusty but offers large, mostly clean en-suite rooms, some with cable TV and a/c, above a popular restaurant and coffee shop that serves southern Thai and Chinese food and Western breakfasts. Double B200

See Far Lifestyle 37 Th Phattalung, by the entrance to Soi 3 (100m north up Th Wisetkul from the clocktower, turn right). Good, inexpensive restaurant with a varied menu of carefully prepared dishes, specializing in healthy cuisine and local food, such as *kao yook* (B150), a Chinese-style dish of steamed pork with taro. Daily 10.30am–8.30pm.

Wunderbar Th Rama VI T 075 214563, W wunderbar-trang.com. Multi-purpose *farang* bar-restaurant with free wi-fi that serves a wide selection of drinks (including wine and espressos), Thai food, and burgers (B60), salads, pizzas, breakfasts and other Western standards, as well as cheese platters (B270). Daily 7.30am–10pm.

Yamawa 94 Th Visetkul, north from the clocktower on Th Rama VI T 086 685 4987, W yamawaguesthouse.com. Around a stairwell decorated with hanging vines and pot plants, the rooms are en suite with cable TV, and some have a/c and hot shower. Free wi-fi. Double B350

KO TARUTAO NATIONAL MARINE PARK

Ko Tarutao National Marine Park is perhaps the most beautiful of all Thailand's accessible beach destinations. The park covers 51 mostly uninhabited islands, of which three – Tarutao, Adang and Lipe – are easy to reach and have accommodation. The port of **Pak Bara**, towards the north end of Satun province, is the main jumping-off point for the park, and houses the main **national park visitor centre** (T 074 783485, W dnp.go.th), near the pier. There are ATMs in Pak Bara, but none on the islands. The park admission fee (B200, valid for 5 days) is collected on the islands of Tarutao or Adang; it's not collected for Lipe which, though technically part of the park, is now heavily developed. The park's forests and seas support a fascinating array of wildlife, including about 25 percent of the world's tropical fish species, as well as dugongs, sperm whales, dolphins and a dwindling population of turtles. Snorkelling gear can be rented on Tarutao or Adang for B50 per day, and is widely available from the private bungalow outfits or dive shops on Ko Lipe. The park amenities on Tarutao and Adang are closed to tourists from early May to mid-October or mid-November (depending on the weather), while getting to Lipe at the height of the monsoon in September and early October is an unlikely – or at the very least unappealing – proposition.

10

10

Ko Tarutao

Hilly **Ko Tarutao**, the largest of the islands, is wild and covered in rainforest and has perfect beaches all along its 26km west coast. Boats dock at **Ao Pante**, on the northwestern side, where you'll find the park headquarters, a visitor centre, restaurant and a small shop, all of which have a slightly institutional feel; there is, in fact, an old prison on the island, now being reclaimed by the jungle. You can stay in the national park bungalows (B600–1200), more basic longhouses (B500, sleeps four), or tents (B225; bedding and pillows B50/person), or pitch your own tent (B30/person/night); kayaks and mountain bikes are available. Behind the settlement, the steep, half-hour Tolkienesque climb to **To-Boo Cliff** is a must, especially at sunset, for its fine views. Boat trips, arranged at the park headquarters (1hr; B500/boat; fits 10 people), venture up a bird-filled, mangrove-lined canal to Crocodile Cave. A half-hour walk south from Ao Pante brings you to the quiet, white-sand bays of **Ao Jak** and **Ao Molae**, the latter with bungalows (B600) and a good restaurant; beyond (2hr from Ao Pante; look out for the road behind the house at the south end of Ao Molae) lies **Ao Sone**, a timeless, all-natural beach environment, backed by a steep forested escarpment. The Ao Pante visitor centre can arrange transport by road, usually in an open truck, to several of the island's beaches, charging B50/person to Ao Molae and around B400/vehicle to Ao Sone.

Ko Adang

Ko Adang, an untamed island covered in rainforest where you really can get away from it all, has a **national park station** at Laem Sone beach, the luxurious white-sand curve of its southeast coast. Facilities include an inexpensive cafeteria-style restaurant, a visitor centre, great-value en-suite bungalows overlooking the sea (from B600) and simpler longhouses (B400 sleeps three). There are also tents for rent (B225; bedding and pillows B50/person), which can be pitched in a pleasant casuarina grove fronting the beach (pitch your own for B30/person). Should you wish to venture further afield, the visitor centre can give information on forest trails and waterfalls, and can organize excellent snorkelling trips to nearby islands (from B1500 for up to 8 people).

Ko Lipe

Home to around a thousand *chao ley* or sea gypsies (a traditionally nomadic group, with animistic beliefs and their own language), tiny **Ko Lipe**, just 2km south of Ko Adang, is something of a frontier maverick. It attracts ever more travellers with one dazzling beach – **Hat Pattaya**, a southwesterly crescent of squeaky-soft white sand, though sometimes clogged with longtails – a relaxed, anything-goes atmosphere and mellow nightlife.

Lipe's main drag is **Walking Street**, a paved path lined with tourist businesses between the eastern end of Hat Pattaya and the south end of the island village, which lies on east-facing **Sunrise**, an exposed, largely featureless beach that gives access to some good snorkelling around Ko Gra. Paved tracks run both from here and from the far west end of Pattaya across to **Sunset** beach, a shady, attractive spot with good views northwest to Ko Adang.

ARRIVAL AND INFORMATION

By boat From Pak Bara, boats (mostly speedboats; 1hr 30min; B650) leave for Lipe twice daily in high season, once daily in low season. Generally, they'll call in at Tarutao upon request (B400 from Pak Bara, B500 from Lipe). In high season, there's one daily ferry (5hr; B1700) and two daily speedboat services (3–4hr; B1900) to Lipe from Ko Lanta, as well as boats from Langkawi (see p.445). At Ko Lipe, you are usually transferred onto a longtail: B50 to Ko Lipe shore, up to B200 to Ko Adang. To get to Pak Bara from Trang, either take the direct high-season a/c minibus opposite the train station (1hr 30min), or catch a Satun-bound bus (2hr–2hr 30min) to Langu and change to a red songthaew for the 10km hop to the port. From Satun, frequent buses and a/c minibuses travel the 50km to Langu.

Tourist information The best travel agent and source of information on the island is Koh Lipe Thailand (Boi's Travel; ⓣ089 464 5854, ⓦkohlipethailand.com), which has two outlets on Walking Street, with the main one hard by Hat Pattaya.

ACTIVITIES

The prime diving and snorkelling sites around Ko Lipe are around Ko Adang, Ko Rawi and Ko Dong, just to the north and west in Ko Tarutao National Marine Park, where encounters with reef and even whale sharks, dolphins and stingrays are not uncommon. Koh Lipe Thailand (T 089 464 5854, W kohlipethailand.com) run snorkelling day-trips for B550–650 per person, including lunch. The Canadian-run dive shop Sabye Sports (on the east side of *Porn Resort*, behind *Flour Power Bakery*, on Sunset beach; T 089 464 5884, W sabyesports.com), Lipe's oldest, offers daily trips (from B1950 for two dives) and PADI courses (from B11,900 for the Openwater). Also has kayaks, paddle-boards and windsurfers.

ACCOMMODATION

PATTAYA BEACH

Café Lipe West of Walking Street, central Pattaya T 086 969 9472, W cafe-lipe.com. Eco-conscious place in a great location, offering large, old-style bamboo bungalows that are nicely spaced out under a thick canopy of teak and fruit trees. Each has a partly outdoor, cold-water bathroom, fan and mosquito net. Three-night minimum stay. Good Western and Thai daytime restaurant. Double **B700**

Daya West end T 081 542 9866, W aneelipe.com. More than thirty colourful, en-suite rooms and bungalows in a large, shady, flower-strewn garden behind a popular restaurant on the beach, ranging from simple concrete rooms to clapboard bungalows in a great position on the beach. Kayaks and snorkels available. Double **B600**

Koh Lipe Backpackers Just east of *Daya* W kohlipebackpackers.com. Part of Davy Jones' Locker diving centre, this place offers two eight-bed dorms in plain concrete rooms with thick mattresses, free wi-fi, hot showers and lockers; a/c 6pm–10am. Dorm **B500**

Pattaya Song Far west end T 086 960 0418, W pattayasongresort.com. Rough-and-ready Italian-run resort, the oldest on the beach (the name means "Pattaya no. 2"), where plain, en-suite clapboard or concrete bungalows are strung out away from the beach or in a lovely location up on a steep promontory; kayaks for rent. Good Italian (including home-made pizzas) and Thai restaurant. Double **B500**

10

INTO MALAYSIA FROM SOUTHERN THAILAND

Because of ongoing violence in parts of the deep south, all major Western governments are currently advising **against all but essential travel** through the Thai provinces of **Songkhla, Pattani, Yala and Narathiwat**. With violent attacks happening almost on a daily basis, it's important to check your country's foreign office advice (see box, p.44) for up-to-date information. The city and transport hub of **Hat Yai** and several of the main border crossings to Malaysia are included in the no-go zones, though trains do still run from Hat Yai (and Bangkok) to Butterworth via Padang Besar. Unaffected by the troubles, the safest routes into Malaysia are the border crossings from Satun and Ko Lipe.

FROM SATUN

Remote Satun, in the last wedge of Thailand's west coast, has boat and overland passages to Malaysia. Satun's bus terminal is at the town's southeastern periphery, but many buses also make a detour through the town centre. Should you need to stay here, try *Ang Yees Guesthouse* (T 080 534 0057; B350), 21–23 Th Tirasathit, opposite Kasikorn Bank on the main street. Songthaews (B40) to Thammalang pier, 10km south of Satun, leave from near the 7-Eleven on Th Sulakanukul. From Thammalang pier, longtail boats leave, when full, to Kuala Perlis (45min; B150) on the northwest tip of Malaysia, from where there are plentiful transport connections down the west coast; 9am is usually a good time to turn up at Thammalang for these boats, but they need a minimum of ten passengers (or B1500), which means that on some days they don't run. Ferries to the Malaysian island of Langkawi also depart from Thammalang (2–4 daily; 1hr 15min; B300).

FROM KO LIPE

In high season, there are two speedboats a day between Langkawi and Lipe (1hr; B1200), serviced by an immigration office box on Lipe's Pattaya Beach.

FROM HAT YAI

It is not recommended to travel to Hat Yai, but being a major transport hub and stop-off point to or from Malaysia, you might find yourself stuck here. If so, make your way to *Cathay Guest House* (93/1 Th Niphat Uthit 2; T 074 243815; B240), a short walk east of the train station, which has a small café, basic en-suite rooms and a useful travel agency downstairs.

10

★TREAT YOURSELF

Castaway Beach Resort Sunrise beach, south of the village ⓣ083 138 7472, ⓦcastaway-resorts.com. The perfect place to splurge. The thatched, hardwood two-storey bungalows are spacious and elegant, with large decks and hammocks, and the multi-tiered bar-restaurant fronting the beach is charming. There's also a dive shop and massage spa. Double B3300

Seaside Near the midpoint ⓣ087 398 7932. Basic but sturdy woven-bamboo bungalows with large bathrooms and mosquito nets, in plenty of space on a grassy patch and mostly under shade, behind the popular *Family* restaurant. Double B600

SUNRISE BEACH

Varin Village Central beachfront ⓣ085 079 9145. No-frills, thatched bamboo bungalows with fans, mosquito nets and en-suite, cold-water bathrooms. Set in rows, they're well spaced out though on a scrappy stretch of lawn with little shade. Double B600

SUNSET BEACH

Porn Resort ⓣ084 691 8743. Popular spot in a pleasant, spacious, sloping setting under the trees, with the beach to itself. Wood or bamboo bungalows come with verandas, mosquito nets and en-suite bathrooms. Snorkelling equipment for rent. Double B500

EATING AND DRINKING

The east end of Pattaya has Lipe's biggest concentration of bars, with low candlelit tables and cushions sprawled on the sand, fire shows and names like *Peace and Love*.

Elephant Walking Street, 100m inland from Pattaya ⓣ088 046 8234. Mellow restaurant and secondhand bookshop, where you can tuck into delicious chicken sandwiches (B180) and burgers made with Australian beef, as well as salads, breakfasts and espressos. Daily 8am–8pm.

Jack's Jungle Resort About 400m south of *Flour Power* on Sunset, on the paved track towards the village and Sunrise. It's well worth the walk out to this appealing wooden deck set among trees, for some very tasty Thai food in huge portions and spiced to order, such as chicken massaman curry with rice (B170). Also does wine by the glass, pasta and a few other simple Western dishes. Daily 8am–9.30pm (last orders).

FLOATING MARKET NEAR CAN THO

Vietnam

HIGHLIGHTS

❶ **Hanoi** Sample the street food of the captivating capital city. **See p.837**

❷ **Sa Pa** Hike amid rice terraces and stay overnight in minority tribe villages. **See p.857**

❸ **Phong Nha–Ke Bang National Park** Go caving or jungle trekking. **See p.864**

❹ **Hoi An** Admire beautifully preserved historical houses and feast on great food. **See p.877**

❺ **Nha Trang** Vietnam's beach central is perfect for diving and snorkelling. **See p.883**

❻ **HCMC** Eat, drink and party in Vietnam's liveliest city. **See p.896**

❼ **Mekong Delta** Cycle through the lush countryside and cruise the waterways. **See p.906**

HIGHLIGHTS ARE MARKED ON THE MAP ON P.823

ROUGH COSTS

Daily budget Basic US$30–35/Occasional treat US$50
Drink Bottle of beer US$1.50
Food Pho (noodle soup) US$2
Budget hotel US$8–20
Travel Hanoi to Hue (660km): train 14hr, US$52; tourist bus 12hr, US$25

FACT FILE

Population 90.4 million
Language Vietnamese
Religion Mahayana Buddhism, Catholicism, animism, Protestantism, Hoa Hao, Cao Dai
Currency Vietnamese dong (VND) or US$
Capital Hanoi
International phone code ☎ 084
Time Zone GMT + 7hr

Introduction

History weighs heavily on Vietnam, but nearly forty years after the end of its infamous war, this incredibly resilient nation has certainly emerged from its shadows. Travellers find that this is a land not of bomb craters and army ordnance, but of shimmering paddy fields and white-sand beaches, historical cities and venerable pagodas, vast caves, craggy mountains and friendly minority tribes. The speed with which Vietnam's population has been able to transcend the recent past comes as a surprise to visitors, who are generally met with warmth, curiosity and a seemingly irrepressible desire to connect.

For many visitors, venerable **Hanoi** – Vietnam's capital for close on a thousand years – provides a full-on introduction to Vietnam, its mad traffic clashing with its colonial buildings, pagodas and dynastic temples. From here, many strike out east to the labyrinth of limestone outcrops and karst jutting out of the azure **Ha Long Bay**. The market town of **Sa Pa**, set in spectacular uplands close to the Chinese border in the far northwest, makes a good base for exploring nearby ethnic minority villages. Heading south, **Phang Nha Ke Banh National Park** is home to the world's largest cave, with one of the most picturesque parts of the **Ho Chi Minh Trail** winding its way through the beautiful countryside. Further south still, beyond the wartime memorials of the **DMZ**, is aristocratic **Hue**, with its temples, palaces and imperial mausoleums. Next up comes the most beautiful city in Vietnam: **Hoi An**, its city centre full of beautifully preserved wooden shophouses and some of the best food in the country. If you then head further south, the quaint hill-station of **Da Lat** provides a good place to cool down, but some travellers eschew the highlands for the **beaches** of **Mui Ne** or **Nha Trang**. The southern gateway to Vietnam is the furiously commercial city of **Ho Chi Minh City** (**HCMC**, formerly Saigon), where memories of the Vietnam War are immortalized in one of the country's best museums. In contrast, the southernmost part of the country, the **Mekong Delta** – rice fields and orchards bisected by canals and the slow-moving river – provides an antidote to the high-octane cities, with its slow pace of life and **cycling trails** running through the lush greenery.

CHRONOLOGY

2789 BC Vang Lang kingdom – the first independent Vietnamese state – is founded by the Hung Vuong kings.
111 BC The Chinese Han emperors take over the Red River Delta; they introduce Confucianism, a rigid, feudalistic hierarchy, and a millennium of occupation.
938 AD Vietnamese forces defeat the Chinese at the battle of the Bach Dang River, heralding nearly ten centuries of Vietnamese independence (in the north) under a series of dynasties.
1010 AD Thanh Long (City of the Soaring Dragon) – present-day Hanoi – becomes Vietnam's new capital.
c. Third century onwards The kingdom of Champa dominates the south, and builds numerous temples, including My Son.
1288 AD Mongol invasion repelled by General Tran Hung Dao's forces.
1377 & 1383 AD Thanh Long besieged by Cham forces who kill Viet emperor Tran Due.
1428 AD Le Loi defeats the Chinese and becomes the first emperor of the Le dynasty.
1516 AD Portuguese traders introduce Catholicism via Faifo (present-day Hoi An) trading post.
1524 AD Two powerful clans split the country in two: the Trinh lords in Hanoi and the north, and the Nguyen in Hue down to the Mekong Delta.
17th century Ethnic Vietnamese settle in the Mekong Delta, taking advantage of Khmer weaknesses.
1771 The Tay Son rebellion, led by three brothers with a message of equal rights, justice and liberty, gains broad support. By 1788 they have overthrown both the Trinh and Nguyen lords.
1802 Vietnam comes under a single authority when Emperor Gia Long captures the throne and establishes his capital at Hue, building its magnificent citadel and reimposing feudal order.

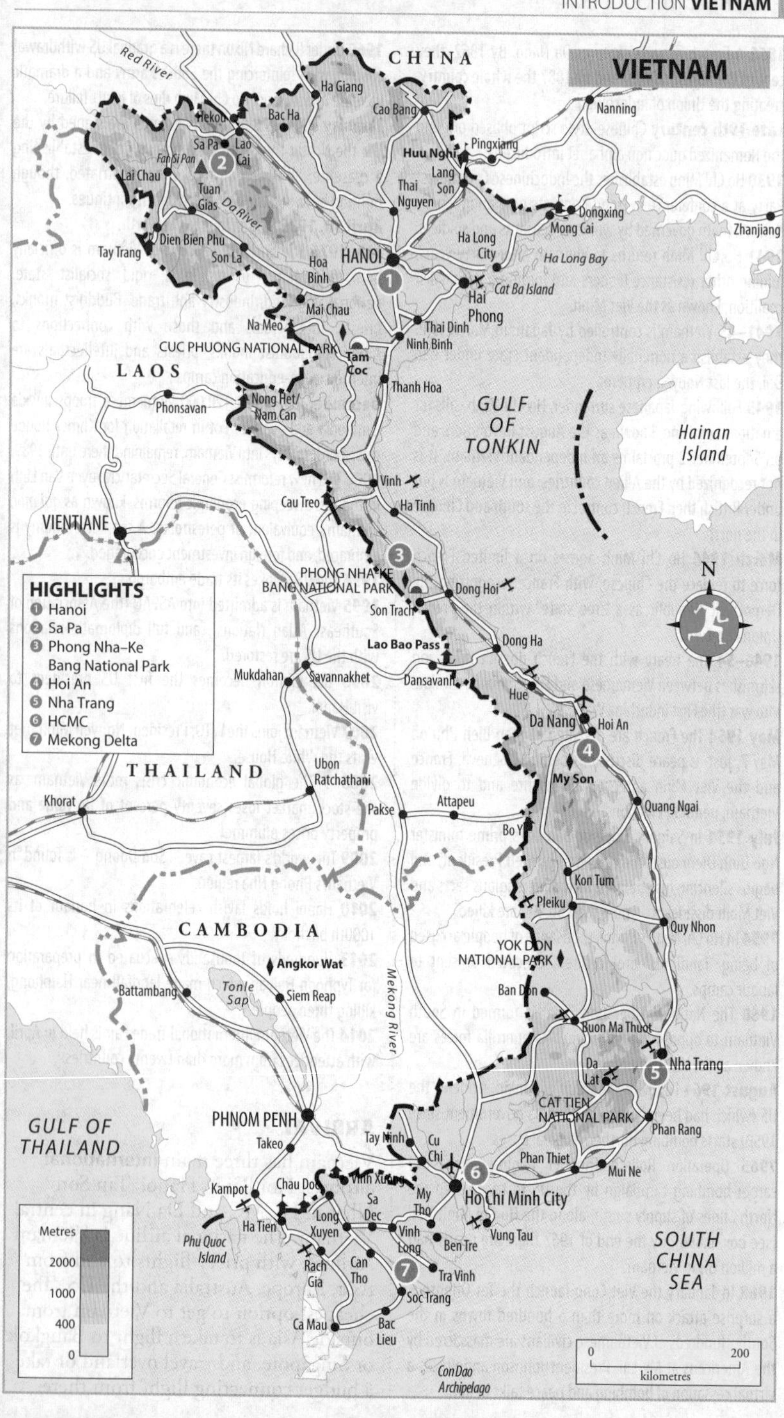
VIETNAM
CHINA
LAOS
THAILAND
CAMBODIA
GULF OF TONKIN
GULF OF THAILAND
SOUTH CHINA SEA
Hainan Island
Red River
Da River
Mekong River
Tonle Sap
Ha Giang
Bac Ha
Cao Bang
Nanning
Hekou
Sa Pa
Lao Cai
Fan Si Pan
Pingxiang
Huu Nghi
Lai Chau
Tuan Gias
Lang Son
Thai Nguyen
Dongxing
Mong Cai
Zhanjiang
Dien Bien Phu
Tay Trang
Son La
Ha Long City
Ha Long Bay
HANOI
Hoa Binh
Cat Ba Island
Hai Phong
Mai Chau
Na Meo
Thai Dinh
Ninh Binh
CUC PHUONG NATIONAL PARK
Tam Coc
Thanh Hoa
Phonsavan
Nong Het/ Nam Can
Vinh
Cau Treo
Ha Tinh
VIENTIANE
PHONG NHA-KE BANG NATIONAL PARK
Dong Hoi
Son Trach
Dong Ha
Lao Bao Pass
Mukdahan
Savannakhet
Dansavanh
Hue
Da Nang
Hoi An
My Son
Ubon Ratchathani
Khorat
Pakse
Attapeu
Bo Y
Quang Ngai
Kon Tum
Pleiku
Quy Nhon
YOK DON NATIONAL PARK
Angkor Wat
Battambang
Siem Reap
Ban Don
Buon Ma Thuot
Nha Trang
Da Lat
CAT TIEN NATIONAL PARK
PHNOM PENH
Phan Rang
Takeo
Tay Ninh
Cu Chi
Phan Thiet
Mui Ne
Kampot
Chau Doc
Vinh Xuong
Sa Dec
My Tho
Ho Chi Minh City
Vung Tau
Ha Tien
Long Xuyen
Vinh Long
Ben Tre
Phu Quoc Island
Rach Gia
Can Tho
Tra Vinh
Soc Trang
Ca Mau
Bac Lieu
Con Dao Archipelago
HIGHLIGHTS
1 Hanoi
2 Sa Pa
3 Phong Nha–Ke Bang National Park
4 Hoi An
5 Nha Trang
6 HCMC
7 Mekong Delta
Metres
2000
1000
400
0
0
200
kilometres
N

1858 A French armada captures Da Nang. By 1862, they control the Mekong Delta, and by 1887 the whole country, creating the Union of Indochina.

Late 19th century Chinese-style script phased out and the Romanized quoc ngu alphabet introduced.

1930 Ho Chi Minh establishes the Indochinese Communist Party at a conference in Hong Kong, its goal an independent Vietnam governed by workers, peasants and soldiers.

1941 Ho Chi Minh returns to Vietnam after thirty years, joining other resistance leaders and forging a nationalist coalition, known as the Viet Minh.

1941–45 Vietnam is controlled by Japan; in March 1945 they establish a nominally independent state under Bao Dai, the last Nguyen emperor.

1945 Following Japanese surrender, Ho Chi Minh calls for a national uprising, known as the August Revolution, and on September 2 proclaims an independent Vietnam. It is not recognized by the Allied countries, and Vietnam is put under British then French control in the south and Chinese in the north.

March 1946 Ho Chi Minh agrees on a limited French force to replace the Chinese, with France recognizing the Democratic Republic as a "free state" within the French Union in return.

1946–54 The treaty with the French doesn't hold, and skirmishes between Vietnamese and French troops escalate into war (the First Indochina War).

May 1954 The French are defeated at Dien Bien Phu on May 7, just as peace discussions begin in Geneva. France and the Viet Minh agree to a ceasefire and to divide Vietnam, pending elections.

July 1954 In Saigon, Emperor Bao Dai's prime minister Ngo Dinh Diem ousts him, declares himself President, and begins silencing his enemies, including religious sects and Viet Minh dissidents – more than 50,000 are killed.

1954 In Ho Chi Minh's Hanoi, thousands of people accused of being "landlords" are tortured, executed or sent to labour camps.

1960 The National Liberation Front is formed in South Vietnam to oppose Diem's regime; its guerrilla forces are known as the Viet Cong.

August 1964 Following the Gulf of Tonkin incident, the US (which had been bankrolling Diem's government since 1950) starts bombing northern coastal bases.

1965 Operation Rolling Thunder begins, a massive carpet-bombing campaign by the US to try to stop the North's lines of supply south, along the Ho Chi Minh Trail (see box, p.896). By the end of 1967 there are nearly half a million GIs in Vietnam.

1968 In January the Viet Cong launch the Tet Offensive, a surprise attack on more than a hundred towns in the South. Hundreds of Vietnamese civilians are massacred by the Americans at My Lai. President Johnson announces a virtual cessation of bombing and peace talks begin.

1969 Under Richard Nixon there is a gradual US withdrawal coupled with reinforcing the South's army and a dramatic increase in bombing. Ho Chi Minh dies of heart failure.

January 27, 1973 The Paris Accords are signed by the US, the North, the South and the Viet Cong, establishing a ceasefire; all American troops are repatriated, though fighting between the North and South continues.

April 30, 1975 Saigon falls to the North.

July 1976 The Socialist Republic of Vietnam is officially born, and Hanoi ushers in a rigid socialist state, nationalizing land, industry and trade. Buddhist monks, priests, intellectuals and those with connections to America, Buddhist monks, priests and intellectuals are interned in "re-education camps".

December 25, 1978 120,000 Vietnamese troops invade Cambodia and oust Pol Pot in retaliation for Khmer Rouge cross-border forays into Vietnam, remaining there until 1989.

1986 The new reformist General Secretary Nguyen Van Linh introduces sweeping economic reforms, known as *doi moi*, Vietnam's equivalent of perestroika. A market economy is embraced, and foreign investment encouraged.

1994 The US revokes its trade embargo.

1995 Vietnam is admitted into ASEAN (the Association of Southeast Asian Nations), and full diplomatic relations with the US are restored.

2000 Bill Clinton becomes the first US president to visit Hanoi.

2007 Vietnam joins the WTO; President Nguyen Minh Triet visits the White House.

2008–9 The global economic crisis rocks Vietnam, as the stock market loses seventy percent of its value and property prices plummet.

2009 The world's largest cave – Son Doong – is found in Vietnam's Phong Nha region.

2010 Hanoi holds lavish celebrations in honour of its 1000th birthday.

2013 Hundreds of thousands evacuated in preparation for Typhoon Haiyan which made landfall near Haiphong, killing three people.

2014 The Vietnam International Trade Fair is held in April, with attendees from more than twenty countries.

ARRIVAL

Vietnam has three main **international airports:** Noi Bai in Hanoi, Tan Son Nhat in HCMC and Da Nang in central Vietnam. The national airline is Vietnam Airlines, with pricey flights to and from Asia, Europe, Australia and the US. The cheapest option to get to Vietnam from outside Asia is to take a flight to Bangkok or Singapore, and travel overland or take a budget connecting flight from there.

WHEN TO GO

Vietnam has a tropical **monsoon climate**, dominated by the south or southwesterly monsoon from May to September and the northeast monsoon from October to April. Overall, late September to December and March and April are the best times if you're covering the whole country, but there are distinct regional variations. In **southern Vietnam and the Central Highlands** the dry season lasts from December to April, and daytime temperatures rarely drop below 20°C in the lowlands, averaging 30°C during March, April and May. Along the **Central Coast** the wet season runs from September to February, though even the dry season brings a fair quantity of rain; temperatures average 30°C from June to August. Typhoons can hit the coast around Hue in April and May and the northern coast from July to November, when flooding is a regular occurrence. **Hanoi and northern Vietnam** are generally hot (30°C) and very wet during the summer, warm and sunny from October to December, then cool and misty until March.

Current routes within Asia include Hanoi to Kunming, Beijing, Hong Kong, Tokyo, Luang Prabang, Vientiane and Bangkok; and HCMC to Phnom Penh, Singapore, Kuala Lumpur and Bangkok. Low-cost airfares are offered by Tiger Air, AirAsia, Jetstar and VietJet Air.

A large number of travellers, especially backpackers, arrive overland through one of Vietnam's **borders** with Cambodia, Laos and China. **Visas** for Vietnam must be arranged in advance (see below).

OVERLAND FROM CAMBODIA

Tourist buses ply the route between Phnom Penh and **HCMC**, via the **Moc Bai–Bavet** border crossing (see box, p.85). Foreigners can also cross at a popular border crossing at **Vinh Xuong–Kaam Samnor**, near Chau Doc in the Mekong Delta; some tour operators run boats from Phnom Penh down the Mekong River through to Chau Doc in Vietnam (see box, p.85). There is another border checkpoint near Chau Doc at **Tinh Bien–Phnom Den** (see box, p.910), or at **Xa Xia–Prek Chang** (see box, p.111) near Kep and Kampot on the Cambodian side and just 10km from Ha Tien in Vietnam.

OVERLAND FROM LAOS

There are seven border points between **Laos** and Vietnam where tourists can cross overland. **Lao Bao–Dansavanh** (see box, p.392), roughly 240km from Savannakhet, is the most popular, though the international bus link between Savannakhet and Da Nang can take up to 24 hours (see p.389).

There are also border crossings open at **Bo Y–Pho Keau** near Kon Tum in the Central Highlands (see box, p.403) and **Tay Trang–Sop Hun** near Dien Bien Phu in the far northwest (see box, p.382), which offer two interesting but challenging routes. There are additional crossings close to the Vietnamese city of Vinh at **Cau Treo–Nam Phao** (see box, p.388) and **Nong Het–Nam Can**, east of Phonsavan in Laos (see box, p.377).

OVERLAND FROM CHINA

At the time of writing, the Chinese border was open to foreigners at three points: **Lao Cai–Hekou** from Kunming (see box, p.857), the little-used **Mong Cai – Dongxing** from Guangzhou (see box, p.853) and, busiest of all, at **Youyl Guan–Huu Nghi Quan** from Pingxiang or Nanning (see box, p.849). There is one **direct train service** between China and Vietnam from Beijing to Hanoi (see box, p.849). The Kunming–Hanoi service was suspended in 2004; you can take the bus to Lao Cai, and then take the train from there to Hanoi.

VISAS

All foreign nationals need a **visa** to enter Vietnam. **Tourist visas** are generally valid for **thirty days** from your specified arrival date and cost $40–80, depending on where you apply. **Three-month visas** are also available for $100 to $145; both types take three to ten days to process, though some agencies and consulates (see p.49) offer an express one-day service. In Southeast Asia, Bangkok and Phnom

Penh are the cheapest, quickest and most popular places to apply for a Vietnamese visa (1–5 working days).

There are a growing number of **authorized agents** in Vietnam – including Ann Tours and STA in HCMC and Hanoi – who can issue **visas on arrival** (contact the agent five days before to secure paperwork; costs start at $15 plus $20 "stamp fee"); this is especially helpful for people with no Vietnamese consulate in their home country, or those strapped for time. The agent will email you a special clearance fax to show upon arrival in Vietnam which you'll need to print out in order to hand it in upon arrival at one of Vietnam's international airports, along with a passport-sized photo and a completed application form (available at the airport) in order to be granted a visa. A number of online agencies offer visa on arrival; some are scams while others are reliable; the latter include Vietnam Evisa (ⓦvietnam-evisa.org). Visas on arrival may only be picked up at designated international airports not land border crossings.

At the time of writing, **thirty-day visa extensions** were being issued through tour agents and travellers' cafés in HCMC, Da Lat, Nha Trang, Hoi An, Hue, Da Nang and Hanoi (from $25; 1–5 working days, depending on where you apply), but the situation changes frequently, so check with the embassy before you leave. The **fine** for overstaying your visa can also vary; fines cannot be paid at the airport, so if you do overstay make sure to visit an immigration office before trying to board your plane.

GETTING AROUND

Vietnam's main thoroughfare is Highway 1, which runs from Hanoi to HCMC and is shadowed by the country's main rail line. **Public transport** is comprehensive and inexpensive, with many upgraded trains and state-run buses, fleets of "open-tour" buses run by travellers' cafés, an increasing number of high-quality, privately owned sleeping buses and minibuses plying popular routes, and cheap domestic flights crisscrossing the country. In the Mekong Delta, passenger boats ply the rivers between towns and fast passenger ferries connect the mainland to outlying islands such as Phu Quoc in the south and Cat Ba in the north. There's still room for improvement, however: local bus timetables are often unreliable and all buses are at the mercy of slow traffic that clogs up Vietnam's main roads. Trains get booked up weeks in advance before Tet New Year celebrations in January/February. Many tourists opt for internal flights in order to avoid these hassles, but nothing beats terrestrial transport as a way to see the country and interact with locals.

PLANES

There are five airlines offering **domestic flights**; Vietnam Airlines (ⓦvietnamairlines.com.vn) has the most comprehensive network. Jetstar (ⓦjetstar.com), the budget branch of Qantas, offers flights to Vietnam's major cities, as well as destinations in Australia, New Zealand, China, Thailand, Cambodia, Singapore, Hong Kong, Japan, Malaysia, Myanmar and the Philippines; budget airline VietJet Air (ⓦvietjetair.com) has flights to all major cities in Vietnam, as well as Bangkok, while Air Mekong (ⓦairmekong.com.vn) serves Hanoi and destinations in southern Vietnam and Vasco (ⓦvasco.com.vn) links Ho Chi Minh City with the Mekong Delta. A flight between Hanoi and HCMC, for instance, can cost as little as $50. Book as far ahead as you can.

BUSES, MINIBUSES AND OPEN-TOUR BUSES

Vietnam's **national bus network** offers daily services between all major towns, served by a mixture of ancient, jam-packed local buses and minibuses that leave when full, deluxe air-conditioned buses and "open-tour" buses that originally catered to foreign budget travellers but are now used also by savvy locals.

Most towns and cities have at least two bus stations, the location dependent on the destination (north or south of the city) and type of service (local, long-distance, express, etc). Local buses tend to depart early, from 5am through

mid-morning, while local minibuses tend to run until early afternoon; both pick up passengers en route and can be flagged down along roads. For longer journeys, tickets are best bought a day in advance, since many routes are heavily oversubscribed. Most bus stations have boards displaying timetables and departures.

There are also an increasing number of privately owned "high-quality" **air-conditioned buses**, **minibuses** and **sleeping buses** (with fully reclined seats) run by private transport companies, including the recognizable white-and-green Mai Linh Express (Ⓦmailinh.vn) that operate from their own offices as well as some bus stations and the bright orange Futa Express (Ⓦfutaexpress.com.vn) buses that serve destinations around the Mekong Delta. These run according to timetables, and fares are not much higher than those charged on public buses.

Special "**open-tour**" **buses** shuttling two or three times daily between major tourist destinations are the most popular and comfortable way for foreigners to travel in Vietnam. If you have a good idea of your route, the best thing to do is buy a one-way open ticket, for example from HCMC to Hue ($32) or Hanoi ($45), which enables you to stop off at specified destinations en route: Mui Ne, Da Lat, Nha Trang, Hoi An, Da Nang and Hue. Sinh Tourist (Ⓦthesinhtourist.vn) is the original company to offer this service and still the best. You can also buy separate sector tickets between destinations. Tickets and onward reservations are available from agents in each town; book a day in advance. Longer overnight journeys are covered by sleeper buses, with three rows of double-decker sleeping berths; if you're of compact stature, they are reasonably comfortable, though toilet stops are few and far between.

Watch your luggage at stops and don't accept drinks from strangers as there's a chance of being drugged and robbed.

BOATS

In the Mekong Delta, boats are a bona fide means of transport between towns, as well as vehicles for recreational river tours. Frequent ferries and boats run between the mainland and Phu Quoc Island, as well as between Nha Trang and outlying islands and Hoi An and the Cham Islands.

TRAINS

Though Vietnamese **trains** (Ⓦvr.com.vn) can be slow on some services, they generally provide the most comfortable and pleasant way to travel the country. The website Ⓦseat61.com is a useful resource.

The main line shadows Highway 1 on its way from **HCMC to Hanoi** (1726km), passing through Nha Trang, Da Nang and Hue en route. **From Hanoi**, one branch goes northwest to Lao Cai; another runs north to Dong Dang, which is the route taken by the two weekly trains from **Hanoi to Beijing**; and the third goes to **Hai Phong**.

The most popular lines with tourists are the shuttle from Da Nang to Hue, which offers some of the most stunning views in the country, and the overnighters from Hue to Hanoi and from Hanoi up to Lao Cai, for Sa Pa. Five "**Reunification Express**" trains, labelled SE1 to SE8, depart each day from Hanoi to HCMC and vice versa, taking 33–37 hours. There are also two cheaper daily trains in each direction, labelled TN1–TN4, that act as commuter trains and stop at nearly every station.

There are four main ticket **classes** of travel: hard seat, soft seat, hard sleeper and soft sleeper; only faster express trains have air conditioning. When choosing which class to travel in, it's worth paying extra for more comfort. Hard seats are packed wooden benches in smoky carriages with trash on the floor (and can make for interesting encounters with local people). Soft seats are regular coach-style seats. On overnight journeys, you should go for a **berth**: cramped hard-sleeper berth compartments have three tiers of bunks (six bunks in total, the cheapest at the top), while soft-sleeper berths have only four bunks. Bed linen is provided, but you may have to ask the carriage attendant for fresh sheets if you get on anywhere besides the initial boarding station, as they don't get changed automatically.

Several private companies have designated first-class "tourist carriages" attached to the night trains between Hanoi and Lao Cai (for Sa Pa). S3–S8 trains have a choice of soft-sleeper berths and soft seats with air conditioning or fan; hard-sleeper berths and hard seats have fan only. On the modern S1 and S2 trains, all compartments, even hard-sleeper, have air conditioning, and reclining soft seats are located in new double-decker carriages. Booking ahead for sleeper berths is essential; you may need your passport if you buy a ticket at the station.

11

Fares vary according to class and speed of the train. On S3 and S4 express trains, a hard seat from Hanoi to HCMC costs 625,000VND, a soft seat is 745,000VND, a hard sleeper is 1,230,000VND and a soft-sleeper costs 1,586,000VND. Fares on slower trains tend to be cheaper; fares can go up considerably just before, during or after Tet.

VEHICLE RENTAL

Bicycles are available from hotels and tour agencies in most towns for $2 to $3 per day. Small **motorbike** rental ($6–10/day) is possible in most major destinations, but you have to be confident to cope with the hazardous conditions on Vietnam's roads and be aware that the risk of an accident is very real (see box above). Organized motorbike tours can be a better option (see p.832); trail bikes rent for around US$20/day and comprehensive travel insurance is essential. If you go it alone, check everything carefully, especially brakes, lights, horn and the small print on your **insurance** policy, and carry a repair kit. **Repair shops** are ubiquitous – look for a Honda sign or ask for *sua chua xe may* (motorbike repairs). Fuel (*xang*) is around $1 (21,000VND) per litre and widely available.

The theory is that you **drive on the right**, though in practice motorists and cyclists swerve and dodge wherever they want, using no signals and their **horn** as a surrogate brake. **Right of way** invariably goes to the biggest vehicle on the road; pull over onto the hard shoulder to avoid them. Road conditions can be extremely poor in rural areas; watch out for livestock, giant potholes, children and landslides. Police frequently fine motorists for real and imagined offences, including speeding. If you are involved in an **accident** and it is deemed to be your fault, the penalties can involve major fines.

WEAR A HELMET

A shocking eleven thousand people or so die every year on Vietnamese roads, and a further thirty thousand are seriously injured. Traffic accidents are the leading cause of death, severe injury and evacuation for foreigners. Insist on a helmet before renting a motorbike or getting on the back of a *xe om*, and check that the chin straps are properly adjusted and fastened before taking off. Wearing a helmet is compulsory, though the law doesn't specify the type of helmet, as a result of which many wear nothing more than glorified eggshells. Cheap plastic helmets can be bought in nearly every town for as little as 50,000VND; for more serious protection, you can pick up an imported sturdier helmet in Hanoi and HCMC for $25–35.

LOCAL TRANSPORT

Taxis are common in big cities, and inexpensive by Western standards, charging around 10,000–15,000VND per kilometre. Use a reputable company, such as Mai Linh, as some taxis have been known to use rigged meters that run at lightning pace. Be wary of drivers insisting that your hotel is "closed" or "full", and taking you to another one; this is usually part of a commission scam – always be firm with your directions. Real shoestring travellers may use some city **bus** services, which can be handy for transport between major bus stations and shuttling to and from the airports, though travelling by local bus can be extremely time-consuming. Other modes of transport include the ubiquitous *xe om* (pronounced: zay-ohm) or motorbike taxi. Drivers loiter at bus stations and cruise along the roads to solicit custom. Negotiate the price before getting on; a short ride should cost around

10,000–15,000VND, a longer (more than 2km) ride or night ride 20,000–25,000VND and the per hour rate is around 45,000VND.

Cyclos – three-wheeled bicycle rickshaws – are found in major cities, though they are dying out; they can carry one person (two at a push) and the costs are similar to that of a *xe om*; bargain hard. The motorized version of the cyclo, found in the south, is known as the **cyclo mai**. In the Mekong Delta, the **xe dap loi** is also a variation on the cyclo, and the motorized version is known as a **Honda loi**.

After dark, stick to taxis from reputable companies and avoid cyclos and *xe om*.

ACCOMMODATION

Compared to some Southeast Asian countries, such as Indonesia, **accommodation** in Vietnam is more expensive but generally of good quality. Free wi-fi is pretty much ubiquitous in budget accommodation. The cheapest option is a bed in a **dormitory**; an increasing number of budget guesthouses (*nha khach* or *nha nghi*) and rooms for rent in Hanoi, HCMC, and other tourist centres offer dorms at around $5–9 per bed per night. Genuine youth hostels (mostly foreign-run) exist only in a few cities, such as Hanoi, HCMC, Mui Ne and Hue, and a full range of services is on offer – tours, guest lounge, book exchange, free internet. Next up is a simple en-suite fan room in either a **state-run hotel** (*khach san*) or (usually family-run) **guesthouse** for around $8–12. In the main tourist destinations, **mini-hotels** (a modest, privately owned hotel) and **hotels** offer decent en-suite rooms with fans, hot water and phone, for around $8–12; add air conditioning and satellite TV and they can range from $12–35; both are very good value and some throw in a free breakfast. **Rates** are sometimes negotiable in budget hotels in rural areas, and during low season prices can drop by up to fifty percent.

Hotel **security** can be a problem as elsewhere in the world, so never leave valuables in your room.

ADDRESSES

Where two numbers are separated by a slash, such as 110/5, you simply make for number 110, where an alley will lead off to a further batch of buildings – you want the fifth one. Where a number is followed by a letter, as in 117a, you're looking for a single block encompassing several addresses, of which one will be 117a.

On the whole there's little need to book ahead, not even during the festival of Tet (Jan/Feb), as most destinations have plentiful budget accommodation.

Upon check-in, you're required to hand in your passport; lodgings tend to hold on to it until your departure as they need to register all guests with the authorities.

FOOD AND DRINK

The cheapest and most fun places to eat are the **street kitchens**, which range from makeshift food stalls set up on the street to open-fronted eating houses. They are permanent, with an address if not a name, and most serve one type of local speciality, generally indicated on a signboard. **Com binh dan**, "people's meals", comprise an array of prepared dishes like stuffed tomatoes, fried fish, tofu, pickles and eggs, plus rice; expect to pay around 30,000VND for a good plateful. Outside the major cities, street kitchens rarely stay open beyond 8pm.

Western-style **Vietnamese restaurants** (*nha hang*) serve a wide range of meat and fish dishes; some menus don't show prices, resulting in overcharging. Most restaurants aimed at tourists serve a range of Vietnamese and Western dishes; large cities and tourist hotspots such as Hanoi, HCMC and Nha Trang also have good Indian, French and Italian restaurants. A modest meal for two will cost roughly $10–15. Catering primarily to budget travellers, **travellers' cafés** tend to serve reasonably priced Western and Vietnamese dishes – from banana pancakes to steak and chips or fried noodles – and usually open from 7am to 11pm.

VIETNAMESE FOOD

Vietnamese food is very distinct, using plenty of fresh herbs, though flavours and dishes vary depending on the region. The cuisine relies on a balance of salty, sweet, sour and hot flavours, achieved through use of *nuoc mam*, a fermented **fish sauce**, cane sugar, the juice of kalamansi citrus fruit or tamarind and chilli peppers. Vietnamese food tends not to be overly spicy, as chilli sauces are served separately, but pepper is used liberally; Vietnamese pepper is some of the most flavourful in the world.

The staple of Vietnamese meals is **rice** (*com*), with **noodles** a popular alternative, and potatoes eaten in the northern highlands. Typically, rice will be accompanied by a fish or meat dish, a vegetable dish and soup. The other great staple is **pho** (pronounced "fur"), a noodle soup eaten at any time of day but primarily at breakfast. The basic bowl of pho consists of a light beef or chicken broth flavoured with ginger and coriander, to which are added broad, flat rice noodles, spring onions and slivers of chicken, pork or beef; there are regional variations.

Spring rolls or *nems* are ubiquitous throughout Vietnam. Various combinations of minced pork, shrimp or crab, rice vermicelli, onions, straw mushroom, catfish and dill, bean sprouts and fragrant herbs are rolled in rice-paper wrappers, and then eaten fresh or deep-fried, usually dipped in the ubiquitous chilli-fish sauce, or a dark peanut sauce. **Lau** or **steamboat** is the Vietnamese take on the Chinese hotpot, with groups of diners cooking slices of meat and seafood in the communal pot, and then afterwards drinking the flavourful liquid that's left.

Vietnam is a great country for **seafood**, with clams, crab, prawns, squid, and all manner of fish (including the snake-head fish in the Mekong Delta). Meats consumed include beef, chicken, pork; less conventional sources of protein include freshwater snails, rat, dog, snake and frogs.

Most restaurants offer a few **meat-free dishes**, such as stewed spinach or similar greens, or a mix of onion, tomato, bean sprouts, various mushrooms and peppers (*rau xao cac loai*); places used to foreigners may do **vegetarian** spring rolls (*nem an chay* or *nem khong co thit*). The phrase to remember is *nguoi an chay* (vegetarian), or seek out a vegetarian rice-shop (*tiem com chay*) – Buddhist restaurants that serve faux-meat dishes.

Regional specialities not to miss in the south include: *bahn mi* (baguette sandwiches with sausage, pâté and mayo, *canh chua ca* (a hearty Mekong Delta soup with snakehead fish, pineapple and taro in a tamarind broth), and *bahn xeo* (chewy rice crepe with pork, shrimp and mung bean filling). Central Vietnam is famous for *bun bo hue* (rice noodle soup with chilli, lemongrass, beef, pork and herbs), *com hen* (rice served with tiny clams and broth, garnished with rice crackers, pork crackling, herbs and vegetables), and *bahn khoai* (crepes filled with shrimp, pork, bean sprouts, star fruit and green banana, dunked in a fermented soybean sauce). In Hoi An and further north you'll find claypot dishes featuring smoky charred aubergine, while northern dishes include *bahn cuon* (steamed rice rolls filled with pork, mushrooms and dried shrimp, garnished with crispy shallots), *bun cha* (barbecued pork patties with rice, vermicelli and fresh herbs, dipped in fish sauce with pickled vegetables) and *pho bo* (beef noodle soup made with shallot, black cardamom, star anise and fish sauce).

Vietnam is blessed with dozens of tropical and temperate **fruits**. Pineapple, coconut, papaya, mango, longan and mangosteen flourish in the south. A fruit that people either love or hate is the **durian**, a spiky, yellow-green football-sized fruit with an unmistakeably pungent odour and a strong taste. Vegetables such as aubergines and potatoes are widely used, particularly in northern cooking; look out also for wonderful salads that use banana blossoms and green papaya.

DRINKS

Don't drink the **tap water** in Vietnam; bottled water and carbonated drinks are ubiquitous throughout the country.

Good thirst-quenchers include fresh coconut milk, orange, lime and other fruit **juices**, and sugar-cane juice (*mia da*). Somewhere between a drink and a snack is **chè**, sold in glasses at the markets. Made from taro flour and green bean, it's served over ice with chunks of fruit, coloured jellies and even sweetcorn or potato.

Vietnam is one of the world's leading exporters of **coffee**, which is very high-quality, served strong and in small quantities, black with sugar (*ca phé den*), iced (*ca phé da*) or with a dollop of condensed milk (*ca phé sua*). Green tea is also widely available.

Several foreign **beers** are brewed under licence in Vietnam, but good local brews include 333 (*Ba Ba Ba*), Halida and Saigon. **Bia hoi** ("fresh" or draught beer) is super-cheap, served warm from the keg and then poured over ice. *Bia hoi* has a 24-hour shelf life, so the better places sell out by early evening; there is at least one in every town; most offer snacks of some sort. You'll also come across rice wine (*ruou*), 80 percent proof and often flavoured with herbs, fruit and spices. In the northern part of the country, locals drink it through long bamboo straws from communal clay vessels. Avoid buying *ruou ran* (snake wine with pickled cobras inside); this elixir is allegedly good for male virility but bad news for the endangered cobra population.

CULTURE AND ETIQUETTE

Vietnam shares similar **attitudes to dress and social taboos** (see p.40) as other Southeast Asian cultures. In a pagoda or temple you are also expected to leave a small **donation**; taking photos inside a temple is a sign of disrespect. If you have been invited to dinner, always wait for your host to be seated first, and never refuse food that is placed in your bowl during the meal; it will be taken as a sign of ingratitude.

Tipping is not expected, but greatly appreciated; some upmarket restaurants will automatically add a service charge. It's good practice to tip good tour guides; $5 for a day's work is a reasonable amount.

Although officially deemed a "social evil" on a par with drug use and prostitution, **homosexuality** is largely ignored in Vietnam, though discretion is advised. The gay scene is slowly emerging in Hanoi and HCMC. Visit ⓦutopia-asia.com for more information and advice.

SPORTS AND ACTIVITIES

Outdoor pursuits and adventure sports have taken off in Vietnam over the past few years, and specialist tour agencies now offer a wide range of options for adventurous travellers.

TREKKING AND ROCK CLIMBING

Compared to other countries in Asia, **trekking** in Vietnam remains relatively

VIETNAM'S MINORITY TRIBES

Vietnam's culture is far from homogeneous and the Vietnamese government recognizes 54 different minority tribes that number around 11 million people. Each tribe has its own language, culture, spiritual beliefs and elaborate, beautifully embroidered traditional dress, though the latter is largely worn by tribes in the northern highlands, while many others have reverted to wearing regular, mass-produced clothing, at least outside special events. Most make a living from subsistence agriculture, though enterprising tribeswomen act as guides in the mountains around Sa Pa (see p.857) or sell traditional embroidery to visitors; many practise animism and ancestor worship. The relationship of the hill tribes with the government has always been fraught with tension; during the war with the French, many tribesmen fought on the French side, and were then recruited as US Special Forces during the Vietnam War, for which the tribes have paid dearly since, their languages, customs and clamours for religious freedom reportedly violently suppressed. Though the Vietnamese government limits contact between foreigners and tribes people by placing visiting restrictions on certain villages and regions, you can visit Dao and H'mong villages in the valleys around Sa Pa (p.857), see the Flower H'mong in Bac Ha (p.862), meet the White Tay in Mai Chau (p.889) and stay in Bahnar villages around Kon Tum (p.863), among other places.

low-key, but one-day hikes and longer treks incorporating overnight stays in minority villages are a popular way to explore the countryside. Sa Pa and Mai Chau in the north, and to a lesser extent Da Lat and Kon Tum in the Central Highlands, provide good bases for treks. A guide is essential for longer treks into more remote areas, especially if you intend to stay the night, as many places are sensitive to the presence of foreigners, and some require a permit or may even be out of bounds altogether: unexploded ordnance still litters Vietnam (see box, p.867). As the tallest mountain in the country, Mount Fansipan (see p.859) offers one of the most challenging hikes, but easier, very pleasant treks can be taken around the country's national parks, including Cat Ba (see p.853), Cuc Phuong (see p.851) and Yok Don. Multi-day hikes that incorporate jungle trekking, caving (and camping in caves) and crossing rivers are available in Phong Nha–Ke Bang National Park (see p.864)

The rivers and waterfalls around Da Lat provide good conditions for **canyoning** and **rock climbing**, and the limestone karsts and caves around Ha Long Bay are attracting international attention for their climbing, deep-water soloing and bouldering opportunities.

11

CYCLING, MOUNTAIN BIKING AND MOTORBIKING

Cycling, **mountain biking** and **motorbiking** have become very popular means of travel for tourists visiting Vietnam. The most popular motorbiking routes include Hanoi to HCMC through the Central Highlands along the scenic Ho Chi Minh Highway, and the Northwestern circuit (see p.856), while the pancake-flat Mekong Delta, and numerous mountain-to-coast routes starting in Da Lat and ending in Mui Ne, Nha Trang or Hoi An are particularly popular with cyclists. You can rent your own bike or motorbike, but make sure you have adequate insurance cover; a guide is highly recommended but not essential, as main roads are generally well signposted. Motorbike **tours** can be booked with independent guides, travel agencies or outfits such as the legendary Easy Riders in Da Lat (see p.895) or Flamingo in Hanoi (see p.844).

DIVING AND WATERSPORTS

A number of **watersports** operators have opened up along Vietnam's 3000km coastline, though classes and equipment rental aren't cheap. Mui Ne is the country's premier **kitesurfing** and **windsurfing** destination, hosting an international kitesurfing competition every spring (usually February); paddle-boarding and surfing are also on offer. Several operators in Nha Trang and Hoi An can organize **wakeboarding**, **waterskiing**, **kitesurfing** and **sea kayaking**, while the surf is up on China Beach near Da Nang from September to December. **Sea kayaking** between the karsts around Cat Ba Island is one of the most rewarding ways to experience Ha Long Bay.

The waters around Phu Quoc, Nha Trang and Hoi An are popular places for **scuba diving** and **snorkelling**; Nha Trang is the undisputed top diving destination, and established outfits in all three locations offer certified courses to suit all levels as well as discovery dives.

COMMUNICATIONS

Regular mail can take anywhere from four days to four weeks in or out of Vietnam; from major towns, eight to ten days is the norm, though express mail service (EMS), available in larger cities, is twice as fast and everything is sent recorded delivery.

When **sending a parcel** take it unwrapped to the post office parcel counter (often open mornings only; take your passport as well). After inspection, and a good deal of form-filling, the parcel will be wrapped for you.

Internet cafés are still found in most towns and cities, although they are becoming obsolete with the ever-increasing number of free wi-fi hotspots. The vast majority of hotels and guesthouses provide free wi-fi; some also have computers for guest use.

The cheapest way to make **international calls** is via Skype. Alternatively, it's well

VIETNAM ONLINE

vietnamtourism.com Government tourist information site, listing basic background information about the country and its main tourist attractions, and also offering an expensive hotel and tour-booking service.

vietnamnews.vnagency.com.vn Online version of the national English-language daily newspaper, with brief snippets of local, regional and international news.

diadiem.com Vietnamese online mapping service, which works better than anything else when it comes to finding obscure streets in Vietnamese towns.

worth getting a local SIM card from Viettel, Vinaphone or Mobifone. SIM cards can be purchased at the airports and from company stores; these cost around 160,000VND per package and a prepaid package typically includes an hour's worth of local calls, eight minutes of international calls and 600MB of internet data. Top-up packages are available in 20,000–100,000VND, and international calls are charged at between 7000VND and 14,000VND per minute.

The general enquiries numbers are: International Operator T 110; Directory Enquiries T 116.

CRIME AND SAFETY

Violent **crime** against tourists in Vietnam is extremely rare, but there are a few things to be wary of. Some tourist destinations, such as HCMC, Hanoi and Nha Trang, have more than their fair share of pickpockets and con artists, and some cases of **bag snatching** – day or night – are occasionally reported. Always take care when carrying valuables and money, and wherever possible leave them in a hotel safe. You should also be careful with taxis and cyclos.

Penalties for buying and using drugs are severe.

Vietnam is generally a safe country for **women** to travel around alone; that said, it pays to take the normal precautions, especially late at night, when you should avoid taking a *xe om* or cyclo by yourself – take a taxi instead.

If you have anything valuable **stolen**, go to the nearest **police** station and ask for a report for your insurance company; try to recruit an English-speaker to come with you – and be prepared to pay a few dollars (usually around $20) as a "fee".

Photographing **military installations**, border regions, military camps, bridges, airports and train stations is never a good idea, as you may be stopped and fined by the police.

Undetonated explosives still pose a serious threat throughout Vietnam (see box, p.867): the problem is most acute in the Demilitarized Zone. Always stick to well-trodden paths and never touch any shells or half-buried chunks of metal.

MEDICAL CARE AND EMERGENCIES

Pharmacies can generally help with minor injuries or ailments, and provide some medication without prescription, though fake medicines and out-of-date drugs are common, so it pays to bring anything you know you're likely to need from home.

Local **hospitals** will treat minor problems, but are overcrowded and not many have a licence to treat foreigners. In a real emergency head for Hanoi, Da Nang or HCMC, where excellent international medical centres can provide diagnosis and treatment.

INFORMATION AND MAPS

There is no such thing as an impartial tourist office in Vietnam; government-owned enterprises such as Vietnam Tourist are travel agencies looking to make a profit, so your best bet for **information** is the many **travellers' cafés** and your fellow travellers.

EMERGENCY NUMBERS

Try to get a Vietnamese-speaker to phone for you.

Police T **113**

Fire T **114**

Ambulance T **115**

VIETNAMESE

Vietnamese is tonal and is extremely tricky for Westerners to master – luckily the script is Romanized, and English is increasingly spoken in tourist areas. Vietnam's minority peoples have their own languages, and may not understand standard Vietnamese.

PRONUNCIATION

Six tones are used, which change the meaning of a word: the mid-level tone (syllables with no marker), the low falling tone (marked ă), the low rising tone (marked à), the high broken tone (marked ã), the high rising tone (marked á) and the low broken tone (marked ạ).

a "a" as in father
ă "u" as in hut (slight "u" as in unstressed English "a")
â "uh" sound as above only longer
e "e" as in bed
ê "ay" as in pay
I "i" as in -ing
o "o" as in hot
ô "aw" as in awe
o' "ur" as in fur
u "oo" as in boo
u' "oo" closest to French "u"
y "i" as in -ing
ai "ai" as in Thai
ao "ao" as in Mao
au "a-oo"
âu "oh" as in oh!
ay "ay" as in hay
ây "ay-i" (as in "ay" above but longer)
eo "eh-ao"
êu "ay-oo"
iu "ew" as in few
iêu "i-yoh"
oa "wa"
oe "weh"
ôi "oy"
o'l "uh-i"
ua "waw"
uê "weh"
uô "waw"
uy "wee"
u'a "oo-a"
u.u "er-oo"
u'o'l "oo-uh-i"
c "g"
ch "j" as in jar
d "y" as in young
v "d" as in day
g "g" as in goat
gh "g" as in goat
gi "y" as in young
k "g" as in goat
kh "k" as in keep
ng/ngh "ng" as in sing
nh "n-y" as in canyon
ph "f"
q "g" as in goat
t "d" as in day
th "t"
tr "j" as in jar
x "s"

GREETINGS AND BASIC PHRASES

How you speak to somebody depends on their gender, age and social standing. Addressing a man as *ông*, and a woman as *bà*, is being polite. With someone of about your age, you can use *anh* (for a man) and *chi* (for a woman).

Hello	*Chào ông/bà*
Goodbye	*Chào, tạm biêt*
Excuse me	*Xin lôi*
Excuse me (to get past)	*Xin ông/bà hú' lôi*
Please	*Làm o'n*
Thank you	*Cám o'n ông/bà*
Do you speak English?	*Ông/bà biê't nói tiê'ng không?*
I don't understand	*Tôi không hiê'u*
Yes	*Vâng (N); da (S)*
No	*Không*
Can you help me?	*Ông/bà có thê' giúp tôi không?*
hospital	*bê'nh viê'n*
police station	*don cong an*
Where is the…?	*…ò' đâu?*
ticket	*vé*
aeroplane	*máy bay*
airport	*sân bay*
boat	*tàu bè*
bus	*xe buýt*
bus station	*bê'n xe buýt*
train station	*bê'n xe lù'a*
taxi	*tăc xi*
car	*xe hoĭ*
bicycle	*xe đap*
bank	*nhà băng*
post office	*sô bu' điên*
passport	*hô chiê'u*
hotel	*khách san*
restaurant	*nhà hàng*

left/right	*bên trái/bên phài*
Do you have any rooms?	*Ông/bà có phòng không?*
How much is it?	*Bao nhiêu tiên?*
cheap/expensive	*rè/đàt*
air conditioner	*máy lanh*
fan (electric)	*quat máy*
open/closed	*mò cù'a/vóng cù'a*

NUMBERS

For numbers ending in 5, from 15 onwards, *lăm* is used in the north and *nhăm* in the south, rather than the written *nam*. An alternative for numbers that are multiples of 10 is *chaục* – so, 10 can be *môt chục* etc.

0	*không*
1	*môt*
2	*hai*
3	*ba*
4	*bốn*
5	*năm*
6	*sáu*
7	*bày*
8	*tám*
9	*chín*
10	*mùòi*
11, 12, 13 etc	*mu'òi môt, mu'òi hai, mu'òi ba*
20, 30 etc	*hai mu'òi, ba mu'òi*
100	*mot trăm*
1000	*mot ngàn*

FOOD AND DRINK GLOSSARY

Some names differ in the north (N) and south (S).

Useful phrases

bát (N); chén (S)	bowl
can chén (N); can ly (S)	cheers!
đá	ice
đũa	chopsticks
chay	vegetarian
tôi không ăn thit	I don't eat meat

Rice and noodles

bún	round rice noodles
bún bò	beef with bun noodles
bún cha	vermicelli noodles with pork and vegetables
bún gà	chicken with bun noodles
com	cooked rice
com rang (N); com chiên (S)	fried rice
com trang	boiled rice
cháo	rice porridge
mì xào	fried noodles
pho	flat rice noodle soup
pho bò	noodle soup with beef

Fish, meat and vegetables

cá	fish
cá rán (N); cá chiên (S)	fried fish
cua	crab
con luon	eel
muc	squid
tôm	shrimp or prawn
tôm hùm	lobster
bò	beef
gà	chicken
lon (N); heo (S)	pork
vit	duck
rau co or rau các loai	vegetables
xà lách	salad
trái cây	fruit

Miscellaneous

bánh	cake (sweet or savoury)
bánh mì	bread
bo	butter
pho mát	cheese
lac (N); đau phong (S)	peanuts (groundnuts)
muoi	salt
ot	chilli
tiêu	pepper
tàu hũ (N); đau phu (S)	tofu
trung	egg

Drinks

bia	beer
cà phê	coffee
cà phê đá	iced coffee
cà phê đen	black coffee
cà phê sua	coffee with milk
trà	tea
trà voi chanh	tea with lemon
trà voi sua	tea with milk
không đá	no ice
nuoc	water
nuoc khoáng	mineral water
nuoc cam	orange juice
nuoc chanh	lime juice
nuoc dua	coconut milk
ruou ran	snake wine

The best **maps** of Vietnam are the International 1:1,000,000 *Travel Map of Vietnam*, and several covering Vietnam, Laos and Cambodia, including Nelles (1:1,500,000); cyclists and bikers may wish to track down the *Viet Nam Administrative Atlas* by Ban Do.

MONEY AND BANKS

11

Vietnam's **currency** is the **dong**, usually abbreviated as "VND" or "d". Notes come in denominations of 1000VND, 2000VND, 5000VND, 10,000VND, 20,000VND, 50,000VND, 100,000VND, 200,000VND and 500,000VND. Dong are not available outside the country, but the **US dollar** is used as unofficial tender throughout Vietnam (with the exception of rural areas, where dong is the preferred currency). If you pay in dollars, the exchange rate is 20,000VND to the dollar, but if you actually exchange dollars for dong at a money exchange, you get a better rate of around 21,000–22,000VND to the dollar; large denomination bills (US$50 and $100 get better rates than if you exchange $1, $5, $10 or $20). At the end of your trip, try to use up your dong, as few countries outside Vietnam will exchange their own currencies for it. At the time of writing, the exact **exchange rate** was 21,090VND to $1; 34,626VND to £1; and 28,822VND to €1.

Major **credit cards** are accepted in many hotels and upmarket restaurants and shops throughout the country. twenty-four-hour ATMs (on the Visa, Plus, MasterCard, Maestro and Cirrus networks) are ubiquitous in larger cities, and even smaller ones will have a couple (dong only).

DOLLARS OR DONG?

In Vietnam, most of the larger costs (such as accommodation and transport) are quoted in **US dollars**, but can be paid for in either currency; smaller amounts (for a street meal or a museum entrance ticket) change hands in **dong**, but both currencies are used interchangeably throughout the country. We've given prices in the currency quoted in each case.

US dollar travellers' cheques can be cashed at major banks for 0.5–2 percent commission (Vietcombank usually charges the lowest rates for Amex travellers' cheques), but often not at banks in smaller towns.

PRICES AND BARGAINING

Vietnam's **two-tier pricing** system, whereby foreigners pay more than locals for transport and accommodation, is still unofficially in place; even the national train system quotes different prices to locals and foreigners so it pays to ask a local to buy your ticket. The Vietnamese have a reputation for a particularly voracious attitude to making money, so be mindful of constant overcharging. Many private transport companies charge you twice the local fare, some *xe om* and taxi drivers take you on circuitous routes, taxis may have tampered meters or take you to places where they can glean a commission, street vendors and market stalls increase the price of goods up to tenfold when they see a foreigner approaching, and we have even heard of some shop owners becoming verbally aggressive if a prospective buyer comes in to browse but decides not to buy anything. The good thing is that most prices are negotiable, even for things like accommodation; ask for a "discount" when checking in. If shopping, **bargain** hard but with a smile and good humour, as anger and unpleasantness constitutes a major loss of face. The idea is to agree on a price that both you and seller are happy with. Don't make your interest obvious, shop around to see how much other sellers are asking and decide on a reasonable price that you're happy to pay; if you can't get it, then walk away, and in most cases the seller will chase after you.

OPENING HOURS AND HOLIDAYS

State-run **banks** and government offices usually open Monday to Friday, closing at weekends. **Banking hours** are usually Monday to Friday 7.30 to 11.30am and 1 to 4pm, though cash exchanges keep longer hours. Most main **post offices** are open daily from 6.30am to 8pm or 9pm.

Travellers' cafés and tour agents tend to open early to late every day. **Museums** are open daily from 7 or 8am to 5pm; some Hanoi museums tend to close on Monday or Friday. Temples and pagodas tend to be open from 5 or 6am until 8 or 9pm. **Restaurants** tend to open around 8am and stay open right through until 10pm. Bars are generally open until 11pm, with later opening hours common in the bigger cities and tourist hotspots.

PUBLIC HOLIDAYS

January 1 New Year's Day
Late January/mid-February (dates vary each year). Tet, Vietnamese New Year (three days, though businesses and restaurants tend to close down for a full week)
February 3 Founding of the Vietnamese Communist Party.
March/April (tenth day of the third lunar month) Commemoration of the Hung Kings (celebration of modern Vietnam)
April 30 Liberation of Saigon, 1975
May 1 International Labour Day
May 19 Ho Chi Minh's birthday
June Buddha's birthday (Phat Dan); eighth day of the fourth lunar month
September 2 National Day

FESTIVALS

Most Vietnamese **festivals** are fixed by the lunar calendar. On the eve of the full moon, every month, Hoi An celebrates a **Full-Moon Festival**. Electricity is switched off, silk lanterns light up traffic-free streets, and traditional games, dance and music are performed in the streets.

Tet Nguyen Dan Or simply Tet ("festival"). Seven days between the last week of January and the third week of February, when families get together to celebrate the New Year. Ancestral spirits are welcomed back to the household, offerings are made to Ong Tau, the Taoist god of the hearth, and everyone in Vietnam becomes a year older. The eve of Tet explodes into a cacophony of drums and percussion, and the subsequent week is marked by feasting on special foods. Tet can be a great time to visit Vietnam's villages, as towns tend to be dead; bear in mind that just before, after and during Tet local transport is reduced to a skeletal service and tickets get booked up weeks in advance.

Water Puppet Festival At Thay Pagoda, west of Hanoi, as part of Tet.

Buddhist full-moon festival (March–April). Two-week festival at the Perfume Pagoda, west of Hanoi (see box, p.848).

Buon Ma Thuot Coffee Festival (March). A great time for caffeine addicts to head for the highlands.

Tet Doan Ngo (late May to early June). Summer solstice, marked by offerings to spirits and dragon boat races.

Hue Festival (June 2014, 2016, 2018). This biennial festival is the biggest cultural event in Vietnam, held in Hue every two years.

Trung Nguyen (Wandering Souls Day) Huge food offerings are made to spirits on the fifteenth day of the seventh lunar month.

Children's or Mid-Autumn Festival (Sept–Oct). Dragon dances take place in Hoi An and children are given lanterns in the shape of stars, carp or dragons.

Hanoi

Vietnam's elegant capital, **Hanoi**, lies in the heart of the northern delta. Given the political and historical importance of this thousand-year-old city and its burgeoning population of more than six million, parts of it are surprisingly low-key. Its narrow streets and colonial buildings of the Old Quarter are steeped in history, while the parks and pagodas around its many lakes are still an oasis of calm. In the evenings, locals gather at the *bia hoi*, while countless street stalls churn out delicious dishes from dawn to night. The pace of life is becoming ever more frenetic, but, for the moment at least, Hanoi remains a beguiling mix of tradition and modernity.

WHAT TO SEE AND DO

At the heart of Hanoi lies **Hoan Kiem Lake**, around which you'll find the banks, post office, hotels, restaurants, shopping streets and markets. The lake lies between the compact but endlessly diverting **Old Quarter** in the north, and the tree-lined boulevards of the **French Quarter** to the south. West of this central district, across the rail tracks, some of Hanoi's most impressive monuments occupy the wide, open spaces of the former **Imperial City**, grouped around Ho Chi Minh's Mausoleum on Ba Dinh Square and extending south to the ancient, walled gardens of the Temple of Literature. The large **West Lake** sits north of the city, harbouring a number of appealing temples and pagodas.

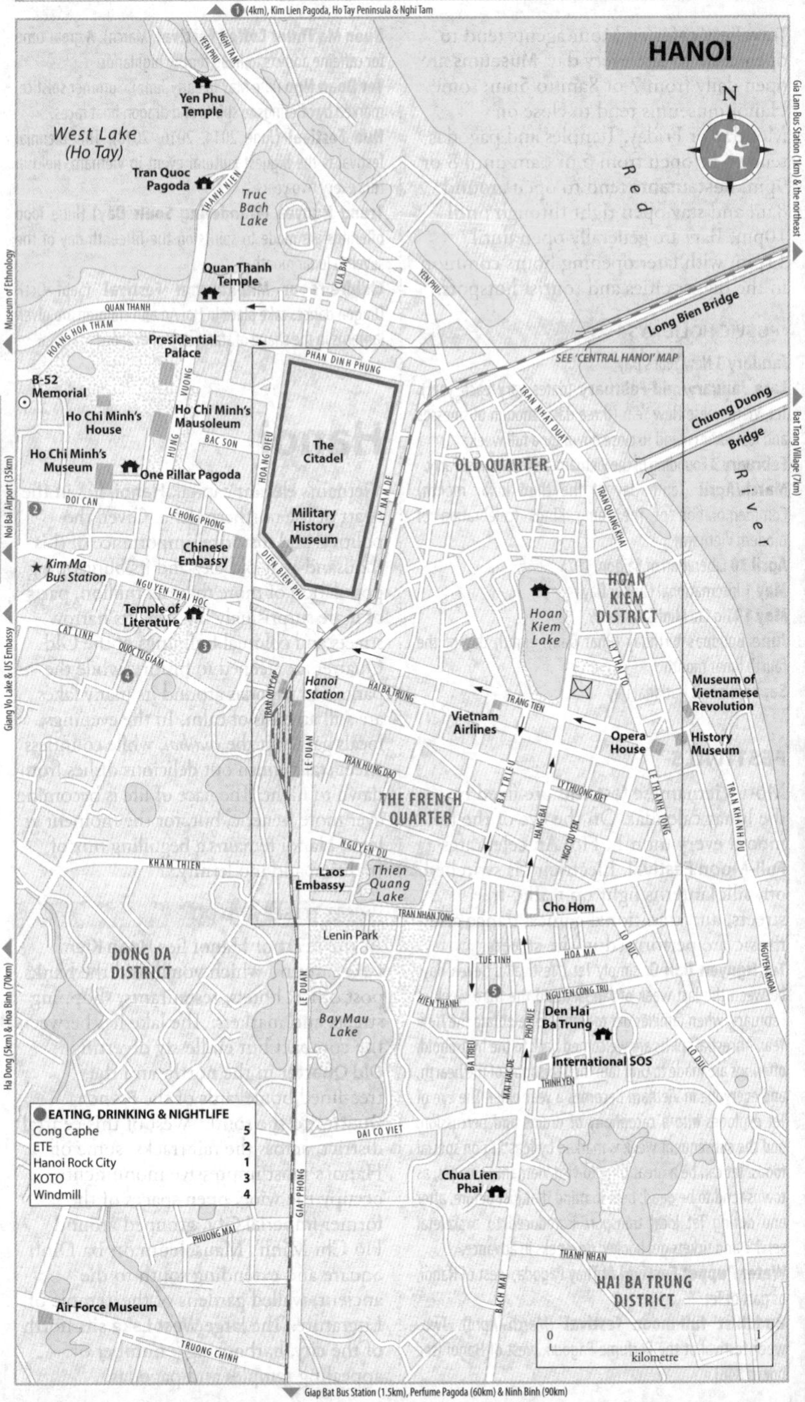

HANOI

(4km), Kim Lien Pagoda, Ho Tay Peninsula & Nghi Tam

Gia Lam Bus Station (1km) & the northeast

Bat Trang Village (7km)

Museum of Ethnology

Noi Bai Airport (35km)

Giang Vo Lake & US Embassy

Ha Dong (5km) & Hoa Binh (70km)

Giap Bat Bus Station (1.5km), Perfume Pagoda (60km) & Ninh Binh (90km)

SEE 'CENTRAL HANOI' MAP

Yen Phu Temple
West Lake (Ho Tay)
Tran Quoc Pagoda
Truc Bach Lake
Quan Thanh Temple
Presidential Palace
B-52 Memorial
Ho Chi Minh's House
Ho Chi Minh's Mausoleum
Ho Chi Minh's Museum
One Pillar Pagoda
Chinese Embassy
Kim Ma Bus Station
Temple of Literature
The Citadel
Military History Museum
Long Bien Bridge
Chuong Duong Bridge
Red River
OLD QUARTER
HOAN KIEM DISTRICT
Hoan Kiem Lake
Hanoi Station
Vietnam Airlines
Opera House
Museum of Vietnamese Revolution
History Museum
THE FRENCH QUARTER
Laos Embassy
Thien Quang Lake
Cho Hom
Lenin Park
DONG DA DISTRICT
Bay Mau Lake
Den Hai Ba Trung
International SOS
Chua Lien Phai
HAI BA TRUNG DISTRICT
Air Force Museum

YEN PHU, NGHI TAM, THANH NIEN, CUA BAC, QUAN THANH, HOANG HOA THAM, PHAN DINH PHUNG, HUNG VUONG, BAC SON, HOANG DIEU, DOI CAN, LE HONG PHONG, DIEN BIEN PHU, LY NAM DE, TRAN NHAT DUAT, TRAN QUANG KHAI, NGUYEN THAI HOC, CAT LINH, QUOC TU GIAM, TRAN QUY CAP, HAI BA TRUNG, TRANG TIEN, LY THAI TO, LE DUAN, TRAN HUNG DAO, BA TRIEU, HANG BAI, NGO QUYEN, LY THUONG KIET, LE THANH TONG, TRAN KHANH DU, NGUYEN DU, KHAM THIEN, TRAN NHAN TONG, TUE TINH, HOA MA, LO DUC, NGUYEN KHOAI, NGUYEN CONG TRU, HIEN THANH, PHO HUE, MAI HAC DE, THINH YEN, DAI CO VIET, GIAI PHONG, PHUONG MAI, THANH NHAN, BACH MAI, TRUONG CHINH

EATING, DRINKING & NIGHTLIFE	
Cong Caphe	5
ETE	2
Hanoi Rock City	1
KOTO	3
Windmill	4

0 — 1 kilometre

11

Hoan Kiem Lake

Hoan Kiem Lake itself is small – you can walk round it in thirty minutes – but to Hanoians this is the soul of their city, a point of social convergence for groups of power-walkers, families, older folk practising Tai Chi and young courting couples; it's particularly attractive when lit up at night. A squat, three-tiered pavilion known as the **Turtle Tower** ornaments a tiny island in the middle of Hoan Kiem, "Lake of the Restored Sword". The names refer to a legend of the great fifteenth-century Vietnamese hero, Le Loi, whose miraculous sword, used to drive the Chinese out of Vietnam, was snatched by a golden turtle that restored the sword to its divine owners. Cross the red-lacquered Huc Bridge to a second island on which stands **Den Ngoc Son** temple (daily 7am–5pm; 15,000VND), founded in the fourteenth century and rebuilt in the 1800s in typical Nguyen dynasty style. National hero General Tran Hung Dao, who defeated the Mongols in 1288, is depicted on the principal altar, while a giant stuffed turtle, found in the lake, sits in a glass box in a side room.

St Joseph's Cathedral

The neo-Gothic **St Joseph's Cathedral** (daily 5am–noon & 2–7.30pm) at the far end of Nha Tho Street, was constructed in the early 1880s, and boasts an impressive interior featuring an ornate altar and French stained-glass windows. Sunday-evening Mass is a good time to dawdle outside and listen to the singing.

The Old Quarter

At the northern end of Hoan Kiem Lake lies the congested square kilometre known as the **Old Quarter**. Hanoi is the only city in Vietnam to retain its ancient merchants' quarter, and its street names date back five centuries to when the area was divided among 36 artisans' guilds, each gathered around a temple or a *dinh* (communal house) dedicated to the guild's patron spirit. Even today, a surprising number of streets are still dedicated to the original craft or its modern equivalent: Hang Quat remains full of bright red banners and lacquerware for funerals and festivals, and at Hang Ma, paper votive objects have been made for at least five hundred years.

The aptly named fifteenth-century **tube-houses**, most of which still remain today, evolved from market stalls into narrow single-storey shops. Some are just 2m wide, the result of taxes levied on street-frontages and of subdivision for inheritance, while behind stretches a succession of storerooms, living quarters and courtyards up to 60m in length. The range of building styles along Hang Bac and Ma May is typical, and Ma May even retains its own **dinh** (no. 64).

The quarter's oldest and most revered place of worship is **Bach Ma Temple** on Hang Buom (White Horse Temple; daily 8–11am & 2–5pm; free), dating from the eighteenth century and featuring an ornate wooden chariot carved with dragons.

The city's largest covered market, **Cho Dong Xuan** (open daily from 7am), occupies a whole block behind its original 1889 facade, and is packed with stalls selling cheap clothing, souvenirs and fresh and dried food.

The French Quarter

The first French concession was granted in 1874, and gradually elegant villas filled plots along the grid of tree-lined avenues to the south and east of Hoan Kiem Lake. The jewel in the crown was the stately **Opera House** (now known as the Municipal Theatre), at the eastern end of Trang Tien, which was based on the neo-Baroque Paris Opéra, complete with Ionic columns and tiles imported from France.

Stretching west from the Opera House, **Trang Tien** is the main artery of the French Quarter. South of Trang Tien you enter French Hanoi's principal residential district, whose distinguished villas run the gamut of styles from elegant Neoclassical through to 1930s Modernism and Art Deco.

French Quarter museums

The **National Museum of Vietnamese History**, at 1 Pham Ngu Lao, inside an elegant 1920s colonial building (Mon–Fri 8am–noon & 1.30–5pm; 20,000VND;

ⓦnmvnh.org.vn), houses exhibits that include arrowheads and ceremonial bronze drums from the Dong Son culture, a sophisticated Bronze Age civilization that flourished in the Red River Delta from 1200 to 200 BC. Upstairs, there are eye-catching ink-washes depicting Hue's Imperial Court in the 1890s, along with sobering evidence of royal decadence and French brutality. The story continues at the **Museum of Vietnamese Revolution**, just opposite at 216 Tran Quang Khai (Tues–Sun 8–11.30am & 2–4.15pm; 15,000VND), which catalogues the

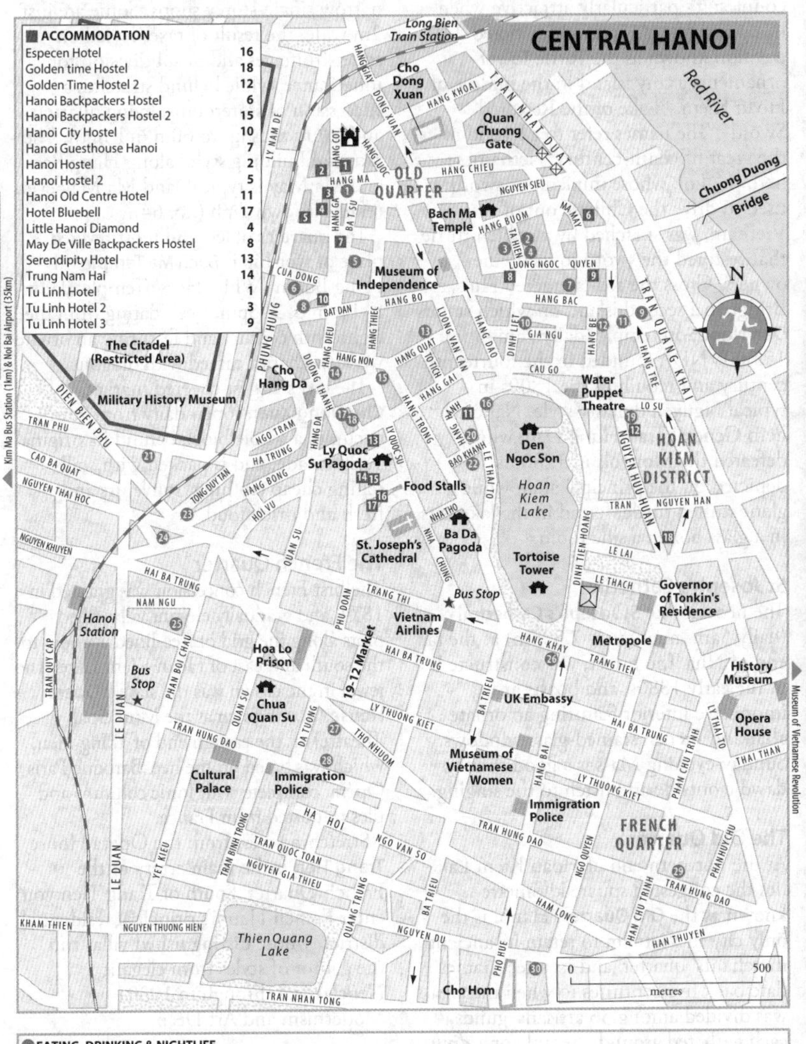

EATING, DRINKING & NIGHTLIFE

Bahn Cuan	1	Chay Nang Tam	28	Highway 4	5/9	Nha Hang Ngon	29
Bia Hoi	6	Face Club	26	International		Pho Gia Truyen	8
Bun Bo Nam Bo	14	Factory	22	Bia Hoi Corner	4	Le Pub	12
Bun Ca	18	Fanny Ice Cream	16	Kinh Do Café	24	Quan An Ngon	25
Bun Cha Dac Kim	15	Funky Buddha	2	Luna d'autunno	27	Quan Ly	30
Bun Cha Nem		GC Pub	20	Mao's Red Lounge	2	Tamarind Café	7
Cua Be Doc Kim	17	Goldmalt Brewery	21	Namaste Hanoi	19	Tet Bar	3
Café Giang	11	Green mango	13	Net Hue	23	Thanh Hop	10

WATER PUPPETRY

Traditional **water puppetry**, *mua roi nuoc* – literally, puppets that dance on the water – is a northern Vietnamese art form that originated in the Red River Delta over one thousand years ago. Traditional performances consist of short scenes depicting rural life or historic events accompanied by musical narration. Puppeteers stand waist-deep in murky water, behind a bamboo screen, manipulating the heavy, colourfully painted wooden puppets (that only last for three months of continuous use, hence the puppet-making villages outside Hanoi), attached to long underwater poles, to the accompaniment of a single-stringed zither, bamboo xylophones, drums, wooden flutes and gongs. The Thang Long Water Puppet Troupe give tourist-oriented performances at **Kim Dong Theatre** in Hanoi, 57b Dinh Tien Hoang (6 daily, first performance 2.15pm; last performance 9.15pm; 70,000–120,000VND). It's an entertaining spectacle; front row seats occasionally get splashed.

"Vietnamese people's patriotic and revolutionary struggle" from the first anti-French movements of the late nineteenth century to post-1975 reconstruction. The **Vietnamese Women's Museum**, at 36 Ly Thuong Kiet (Tues–Sun 8am–4.30pm; 40,000VND; ⓦwomenmuseum.org.vn), is a moving tribute to the wartime contribution of heroic individuals and their role in the national struggle, as well as an introduction to women's role in Vietnamese society. Besides extensive jewellery displays and propaganda posters, there is also a display of ethnic minority dress and craftwork, and excellent temporary exhibitions focus on topics such as human trafficking and single mothers.

Further west, the yellow stone colonial building at 1 Hoa Lo, dating back to 1896, is the **Hoa Lo Prison** (daily 8am–5pm; 20,000VND). Its displays deal with the pre-1954 period when the French incarcerated and tortured thousands of patriots and revolutionaries here. The exhibition includes the French guillotine used, and mock-ups of the appalling conditions here, prisoners shackled to the ground in tiny, cramped cells. Following the liberation of the North in October 1954, Hoa Lo became a state prison, and from 1964 to 1973 it was used to detain American prisoners of war, who nicknamed it the **Hanoi Hilton**; several displays are dedicated to American pilots held prisoner here, including John McCain. The photographs of American POWs playing volleyball, designed to convey a holiday camp atmosphere, should be taken with a pinch of salt; the experience of McCain and others included torture.

Ho Chi Minh Mausoleum complex

The wide, open spaces of **Ba Dinh Square**, their multiple flagpoles flying the red banners festooned with hammer-and-sickle, 2km west of Hoan Kiem Lake, are the nation's ceremonial epicentre. It was here that Ho Chi Minh read out the Declaration of Independence to half a million people on September 2, 1945, and here that independence is commemorated each National Day with military parades. Cyclos and *xe om* will bring you to Ba Dinh Square from the centre for 20,000–25,000VND. The square's west side is dominated by **Ho Chi Minh's Mausoleum** (year-round Tues–Thurs 8–11am, Dec–Sept Sat & Sun 8–11.30am also; free). In the tradition of great communist leaders, Ho Chi Minh's compact, embalmed body is displayed under glass in a cold, dark room, with four guards of honour in crisp white standing to attention around the glass sarcophagus. Huge crowds come here to pay their respects to "Uncle Ho", especially at weekends: sober behaviour and appropriate dress are required (no shorts or vests, preferably full-length skirts or trousers) and nothing can be taken inside; storage is provided for your belongings. Note that "Uncle Ho" takes a two-month "holiday" to Russia each year to be touched up by those responsible for Lenin's upkeep.

Nearby is **Ho Chi Minh's house**, 3 Ngoc Ha (Tues–Thurs, Sat & Sun 7.30–11am & 2–4pm, Fri 7.30–11am;

25,000VND), built by the president in 1954 and modelled on an ethnic minority stilt house. The ground-level meeting area was used by Ho and the politburo; upstairs, his study and bedroom are austere, with a simple bed, desk and bookcase on display. Ho Chi Minh's cars, including a Soviet ZIL, are parked nearby and the rather orange Presidential Palace – a restored colonial building – stands in stark contrast to the leader's humble lodgings. **Ho Chi Minh's Museum** (Mon–Thurs, Sat & Sun 8–11.30am & 2–4pm, Fri 8–11.30am; 25,000VND) contains many photographic displays, a collection of "feudal and imperialist" objects and symbolic art installations celebrating Ho Chi Minh's life and the pivotal role he played in the nation's history.

11

Close by the mausoleum is the tiny **One Pillar Pagoda**, which rivals the Tortoise Tower as a symbol of Hanoi and represents a flowering of Vietnamese art. Founded in the eleventh century (and reconstructed in 1954), it is supported on a single column rising from the middle of a lake; the whole structure is designed to resemble a lotus blossom, the Buddhist symbol of enlightenment.

Vietnam Military History Museum

The **Vietnam Military History Museum**, 28 Dien Bien Phu (Tues–Thurs, Sat & Sun 8–11.30am & 1–4.30pm; 30,000VND; Ⓦbtlsqsvn.org.vn), chronicles military history from the 1930s to the present day, a period dominated by the French and American wars, well documented in two separate halls, and with a supporting cast of weaponry from both wars as well as a Soviet-built MiG-21 jet fighter. Unlike HCMC's War Remnants Museum, the captions here are still clogged with outdated communist rhetoric – "spies", "bandits" and "puppet-regime soldiers" are everywhere. Speaking of outdated relics, there is a Lenin statue in the small park opposite the museum.

Temple of Literature

The **Temple of Literature**, or **Van Mieu**, west of the centre in a park off Nguyen Thai Hoc, is Vietnam's principal Confucian sanctuary and its historical centre of learning (daily: mid-April to mid-Oct 7.30am–5.30pm; mid-Oct to mid-April 8am–5pm; 20,000VND). The temple is one of the few remnants of Thang Long, the Ly kings' original eleventh-century city, and consists of five walled courtyards, modelled on that of Confucius's birthplace in Qufu, China. As you enter the third courtyard, via an imposing double-roofed gateway, you'll see the central Well of Heavenly Clarity (a walled pond), flanked by the temple's most valuable relics: 82 stone **stelae** mounted on tortoises. Each stele records the results of a state examination held at the National Academy between 1442 and 1779, and gives biographical details of successful candidates. The fourth courtyard leads to the **ceremonial hall**, a long, low building whose sweeping, tiled roof is crowned by two lithe dragons bracketing a full moon. Here, the king and his mandarins would make sacrifices before the altar of Confucius. Directly behind the ceremonial hall lies the temple sanctuary, where Confucius sits with his four principal disciples. The fifth courtyard was formerly the site of the National Academy, Vietnam's first university, which was destroyed by French bombs in 1947.

Ho Tay (West Lake)

North of the city, cool breezes drift off **Ho Tay (West Lake)**. In the seventeenth century, villagers built a causeway across the lake's southeast corner, creating a small fishing lake still in use today and now called **Truc Bach**. The eleventh-century **Quan Thanh Temple** (daily 8am–5pm; 5000VND) stands on the lake's southeast bank, and is dedicated to the Guardian of the North, Tran Vo, whose statue, cast in black bronze in 1677, is nearly 4m high and weighs 4 tonnes. The shrine room also boasts a valuable collection of seventeenth- and eighteenth-century poems and parallel sentences (boards inscribed with wise maxims and hung in pairs). The gate of Quan Thanh is just a few paces south of the causeway, Thanh Nien, which leads to Hanoi's oldest religious foundation,

Tran Quoc Pagoda, occupying a tiny island in West Lake (daily 7.30–11.30am & 1.30–6.30pm). The pagoda probably dates back to the sixth century, and the sanctuary's restrained interior, part of which was under renovation at the time of writing, is typical of northern Vietnamese pagodas. West of Quan Thanh in Ngoc Ha (Flower Village), down the alley next to 55 Hoang Hoa Tham, lies the **B-52 Memorial**. The remains of the downed bomber, half-submerged in a lake, form a poignant memorial to the victims of the 1972 "Christmas Bombing" raids.

Museum of Ethnology

The highly recommended **Museum of Ethnology**, or Bao Tang Toc Hoc Viet Nam, situated on the western outskirts of Hanoi in the Cau Giay district along Nguyen Van Huyen (Tues–Sun 8.30am–5.30pm; 40,000VND; ⓦvme .org.vn), is a bit of a trek out of town, but worth the effort for its fantastic exhibitions on all the country's major ethnic groups. Musical instruments, games, traditional dress and other items of daily life fill the showcases, alongside excellent life-size displays on funerary ceremonies, conical-hat production and traditional sacrificial spears. Outside in the museum grounds there are detailed replicas of various ethnic dwellings and burial statues; standout exhibits include a thatch-roofed Giarai tomb and stilt village houses. The museum is 7km from the centre, signposted left off Hoang Quoc Viet. A taxi from the Old Quarter will set you back around 130,000VND, or hop on city bus #14 (4000VND) from the west side of Hoan Kiem Lake to the Hoang Quoc Viet stop, from where it's a 500m walk.

ARRIVAL AND DEPARTURE

By plane It's a 45min ride into central Hanoi from Noi Bai Airport (ⓦhanoiairportonline.com), 35km away. The cheapest option upon arrival is to take public bus #17 to Long Bien station (5000VND), and take a *xe om* to your hotel from there (20,000VND). Just outside the international and domestic arrival terminals, you'll find Vietnam Airlines minibuses (32,000VND) that bring you to their office at the corner of Trang Phi and Quang Trung. Airport Taxi charges a flat fee of 190,000VND for a door-to-door ride and it's $18 if you've booked transport with your accommodation. In the airport arrivals hall, there are ATMs and exchange bureaux. To get to the airport, you can take the Vietnam Airlines minibus from their office (daily 6am–7pm), which leaves every half-hour from 4.30am–11.30am and every hour from noon–6pm. Alternatively, sign up at one of the travellers' cafés for a shared car or bus ($5/person).

Destinations Da Lat (4 daily; 1hr 40min); Da Nang (14 daily; 1hr 15min); Dien Bien Phu (daily; 1hr); HCMC (36 daily; 2hr); Hue (4 daily; 1hr 10min); Nha Trang (4 daily; 1hr 40min); Phu Quoc (daily; 2hr 15min).

By open-tour bus For tickets and information on long-distance open-tour buses that stop at popular cities between Hanoi and HCMC, contact reliable operators such as Sinh Tourist (see p.844). Direct one-way (and hugely uncomfortable) overnight buses run to Vientiane (daily; 16hr; $30), departing from Hanoi at 7pm, crossing the border at Cau Treo.

11

SCAMS IN HANOI

Hanoi plays host to a large number of hotel racketeers, phoney tour operators and con artists determined to part you from your cash. Check the authenticity of any establishment before booking a tour (check the real address using a guidebook or the internet), as names of genuinely good and popular hotels, taxi companies and tour agencies are shamelessly copied, and be very sceptical of taxi drivers telling you that a hotel or restaurant has closed down or relocated. Many taxis that loiter outside the bus and train stations have rigged meters, so try and get a taxi with a reputable company (see p.844) or be aware how far you're travelling and how much you should be paying (prices per km are displayed on the sides of taxis). If you take a cyclo, firmly agree on a price and be aware that some cyclo drivers try to add an extra zero when you come to pay ("I said 200,000, not 20,000") or try to charge double for two people. Also be wary of "students" who approach you around Hoan Kiem Lake wishing to practise their English – it is a renowned scam that could land you with a restaurant or bar bill of a few hundred dollars. Such incidents should be reported to the Vietnam National Administration of Tourism, 3 Tran Phu (ⓣ04 33560789, ⓦhanoitourism.gov.vn).

11

By public bus Hanoi has three main bus stations. Luong Yen bus station (Tran Quang Khai at Nguyen Khoai), 3km southeast of the Old Quarter, serves the south and the east, including Ninh Binh, Hue, Da Lat, Nha Trang and HCMC, as well as Cat Ba Island. Northeast services to Hai Phong and Bai Chay/Ha Long Bay and Lao Cai operate from Gia Lam station (Ngoc Lam), 3km northeast of the centre on the east bank of the Red River. My Dinh bus station (Pham Hung), 7km west of the city, serves northern and western destinations, such as Dien Bien Phu and Mai Chau, with onwards sleeper buses to Laos from Dien Bien Phu (see p.863). *Xe om* rides from these bus stations to the centre vary between 40,000–70,000VND. For popular destinations, it's best to buy tickets the day before.

Destinations Bai Chay (2 hourly; 3hr 30min); Da Lat (daily at 11am & 6pm; 24hr); Da Nang (hourly between 2pm & 6pm; 13hr); Hai Phong (2 hourly; 2hr); HCMC (daily at 11am, 3pm & 6pm; 36hr); Hue (hourly between 2pm & 6pm; 12hr); Lao Cai (daily at 1 & 7pm; 9hr); Mai Chau (daily at 6.30am & 2.30pm; 2hr); Nha Trang (daily at 10am & 6pm; 22hr); Ninh Binh (2 hourly; 2hr 30min).

By train Trains to and from the south use the main station (Ga Hang Co) at 120 Le Duan, 1km southwest of the Old Quarter. If you're arriving by train, you'll exit onto Le Duan (exit A). Trains for Lao Cai (for Sa Pa) and China leave from the separate Tran Quy Cap station, just behind the main train station (exit B). Eastbound trains to Hai Phong run either from the Gia Lam station, on the east side of Song Hong River, or from Lon Bien, on the west side of the river. A taxi from the main train station to the Old Quarter should be no more than 40,000VND, and a *xe om* 25,000VND. Book tickets early, especially for sleeping berths to Hue and HCMC.

Destinations Beijing (Tues & Fri at 6.30pm; 42hr); Da Nang (5 daily; 14–18hr); Hai Phong (daily; 2hr 30min); HCMC (5 daily; 30–41hr); Hue (6 daily; 13–15hr); Lao Cai (5 daily; 8hr 30min–10hr 15min); Nha Trang (5 daily; 23–31hr); Ninh Binh (4 daily; 2hr–2hr 30min); Vinh (7 daily; 5hr–6hr 40min).

GETTING AROUND

By cyclo Cyclos are banned from some roads in central Hanoi, notably around Hoan Kiem Lake and in some parts of the Old Quarter, so don't be surprised if you seem to be taking a circuitous route; city authorities are threatening to ban them altogether. Always agree on a price in advance (about 30,000VND for a short journey) and avoid using cyclos at night.

By taxi Metered taxis wait outside the more upmarket hotels and at the north end of Hoan Kiem Lake and cost about 15,000VND/km; prices are displayed on the side of the taxi. Reputable companies include Mai Linh Taxis ☎ 04 38616161 and Thang Nga Taxis ☎ 04 38215215.

By bike Bicycles can be rented for around $3/day from many hotels and travellers' cafés in the Old Quarter. It's best to pay the minuscule charge at a supervised bike park (*gui xe dap*), located on most main roads. Parking is banned on Trang Tien and Hang Khay; elsewhere, it's only allowed within designated areas. Motorbikes are available from guesthouses and small tour agencies for about $7–10/day. Park in supervised motorbike parks (*gui xe may*).

By bus Hanoi's a/c city buses are little-used by tourists and only useful for transport between the long-distance bus stations (every 15min 5am–5.30pm; 5000VND one-way). *Xe Buyt Hanoi* is a bus route map on sale at the Thang Long Bookshop (see p.847) or see Ⓦ hanoibus.com.vn.

INFORMATION AND TOURS

It's best to go to one of the reliable travellers' cafés for information on visas, tours and transport. State-run "tourist offices" such as Vietnam Tourism are only interested in selling substandard tours, as are the batch of duplicate-name travel agencies, such as the plethora of fake "Sinh Cafés" in the Old Quarter, trading on the reputation of the original.

Travellers' cafés Most travellers' cafés organize bargain-basement tours to the Perfume Pagoda ($20), Ha Long Bay (2 days; $55–110) and the Sa Pa area (3–4 days; $100–150), though for the last two, it's far better to organize tours from Cat Ba Island (see p.853) and Sa Pa (see p.857), respectively. *Sinh Tourist*, at 52 Luong Ngoc Quyen (☎ 04 39261568, Ⓦ thesinhtourist.vn) and 64 Tran Nhat Duat (☎ 04 39290394), is the pick of the bunch.

Specialized tour agencies Hidden Hanoi, 137 Nghi Tam (☎ 091 2254045, Ⓦ hiddenhanoi.com.vn), organizes several excellent walking tours ($20–25/hr), among others in the French Quarter and Kim Lien district, as well as hands-on cooking lessons ($50). Hanoi Street Foods (Ⓦ hanoistreetfoods.com), at 137 Hang Bac, organize enjoyable daily tours (11am & 5pm; 2hr 30min) of local street food venues for $20/person; you get to sample five or so local dishes and finish off with a strong Vietnamese coffee as your guide explains each dish. Free Wheelin' Tours (☎ 091 39262743, Ⓦ freewheelin-tours.com) at 9 Hang Vai, above *Tet* bar (see p.847), organize motorbike tours around the north of Vietnam, ranging from four to fourteen days. The reputable Flamingo Travel (☎ 091 92214554, Ⓦ flamingotravel.com.vn), at 66 Dao Duy Tu, also get rave reviews for their inexpensive motorcycle tours of the country. Handspan Adventure Travel ☎ 091 39262828, Ⓦ handspan.com), at 78 ma May, specialize in community-based tourism in northern Vietnam, sea kayaking in Ha Long Bay, mountain biking and trekking tours, while Ethnic Travel (☎ 091 39261951, Ⓦ ethnic travel.com.vn), at 35 Hang Giay, has a good reputation for small-group, off-the-beaten-track tours of the north, trekking, cycling and also cooking tours.

ACCOMMODATION

Have the exact address of your lodgings written down for taxi drivers and insist on being taken to the hotel of your choice.

Especen Hotel 28 Tho Xuong and 41 Ngo Huyen ⓣ 04 38244401, ⓦ especen.vn; map p.840. Both branches of this well-run operation are located just a stone's throw from St Joseph's Cathedral. The rooms are spacious and bright, some have balconies, and all come with satellite TV, wi-fi and a/c. Double **$25**

Golden Time Hostel 2 8 Ly Thai To ⓣ 04 38259654, ⓦ goldentimehostel.com; map p.840. Huge rooms with flat-screen TVs, welcome drinks for guests and other nice touches, such as the huge breakfast, earn this hostel rave reviews, as does the helpfulness of Tony the manager. Original sister hostel at 43 Ly Thai To (ⓣ 04 93351091) has smaller rooms but equally friendly service and enormous breakfasts. Double **$18**

★ **Hanoi Backpackers Hostel** 48 Ngo Huyen ⓣ 04 38285372, ⓦ hanoibackpackershostel.com; map p.840. Australian-run, standard-setting hostel west of Hoan Kiem Lake, offering bunks in mixed or women-only dorms and private doubles. Lockers, breakfast and internet access are included, and the rooftop bar hosts regular barbecues and parties. The sociable vibe makes it a great place for solo travellers, and their tour service runs high-octane trips to Ha Long Bay that include tubing and paddleboarding. The second branch at 9 Ma May (ⓣ 04 39351890) is particularly well located, had a lively on-site bar and spacious dorms and rooms. Dorm **$7.50**, double **$25**

Hanoi City Hostel 95B Hang Ga ⓣ 04 38281379, ⓦ hanoicityhostel.com; map p.840. Efficient, well-located and well-run place with a/c rooms, decked out in pastel shades. Some staff members go out of their way to make you feel welcome. **$16**

Hanoi Guesthouse 14 Bat Su ⓣ 04 38245732, ⓦ hanoiguesthouse.com; map p.840. Wonderfully welcoming family-run guesthouse popular among travellers. The rooms are clean, comfortable and quiet, with heavy wooden furniture; satellite TV and breakfast are included; the deluxe rooms have balconies. **$26**

Hanoi Hostel 91C Hang Ma ⓣ 04 62700006, ⓦ vietnam-hostel.com; map p.840. Peaceful lilac rooms with crisp sheets, comfortable dorm beds and sweet, helpful staff make this a great backpacker choice. Friendly vibe without it being a party hostel. Dorm **$5.50**, double **$18**

Hotel Bluebell 41 Ngo Huyen ⓣ 04 36345123, ⓦ hanoibluebellhotel.com; map p.840. This hotel has a great central location near the cathedral, helpful owner and decent-sized rooms, plus free tea, coffee and bananas are left out for guests. **$12**

Little Hanoi Diamond 48 Hang Ga ⓣ 04 38284461, ⓦ littlehanoihostel.com; map p.840. This friendly mini-hotel has modern superior rooms with baths and balconies, and cheaper, windowless doubles. The six-bed a/c dormitory is excellent value, including breakfast and free coffee all day long. Dorm **$6**, double **$20**

★ **May De Ville Backpackers Hostel** 1 Hai Tuong ⓣ 04 39352468, ⓦ maydevillebackpackershostel.com; map p.840. Luxury for a budget price, this is more like a hotel than a hostel, with spacious rooms (private ones come with laptops you can borrow and plasma-screen TVs), well-furnished dorms and a vast buffet breakfast. Dorm **$5**, double **$30**

Serendipity Hotel 14 Chan Cam ⓣ 04 38289868, ⓦ hanoiserendipityhotel.com; map p.840. Central, friendly guesthouse, with austere, mid-sized rooms and very helpful reception staff. Breakfast included. Sister hotel, *Trung Nam Hai*, at 27 Phu Doan (ⓣ 04 39288228 ⓦ trungnamhaihotel.com), has equally top-notch service, mid-sized rooms with all mod cons and good showers. Double **$21**

Tu Linh Hotel 58 Hang Cot ⓣ 04 38282626, ⓦ tulinhpalacehotels.com; map p.840. Not quite a palace, but neither a hovel: large, sparklingly clean rooms come with mod cons such as satellite TV, electronic safes and comfortable beds, and the staff's attitude gets rave reviews also. Equally popular sister hotels at 2B Hang Ga and 86 Ma May have virtually identical decor, facilities and equally congenial staff. Double **$28**

11

EATING

Bun Bo Nam Bo 67 Hang Dieu; map p.840. Deservedly popular place serving generous portions of rice noodles topped with lean beef, mint, roasted peanuts and garlic, all swimming in a delicious broth, for 55,000VND. Daily 7am–9pm.

Bun Cha Dac Kim 1 Hang Manh; map p.840. This local restaurant draws crowds of locals for its excellent *bun cha* (grilled port over flat rice noodles) and *nem cua be* (crabmeat spring rolls), from 20,000VND. Daily noon–10pm.

Café Giang 39 Nguyen Huu Huang; map p.840. Pop down a narrow lane to this very local café, and perch on a stool to sample some of Hanoi's best coffee. Go for

★ TREAT YOURSELF

Green Mango 18 Hang Quat, 1a Xuan Dieu ⓦ greenmango.vn; map p.840. Stylish, subtly lit restaurant reminiscent of an opium den, offering innovative Western and Asian-fusion dishes, like blackened sea bass with turmeric vinaigrette or spicy lamb sausage with gnocchi. There's an extensive wine and cocktail menu, and several dining areas to choose from, with plush nooks for romantic occasions, an alfresco terrace for balmy evenings, and large tables for group celebrations. They also run a recommended boutique hotel upstairs. Mains from 200,000VND. Daily noon–11pm.

caphe trung da – coffee topped with a frothy beaten egg white. Daily 10am–10pm.

Chay Nang Tam 79a Tran Hung Dao; map p.840. Small Buddhist vegetarian restaurant down a quiet alleyway off Tran Hung Dao, which specializes in making veggie dishes that look like meat. *Nom hoa chuoi*, a salad of banana flower, star fruit and pineapple, is recommended, or try one of the well-priced set menus (from 80,000VND). Daily 11am–11pm.

Cong Caphe 152; map p.838 Trieu Viet Vuong. Decorated with communist memorabilia, this is a popular hangout for trendy young locals. The iced coffee with condensed milk really hits the spot. Daily 8am–9pm.

Fanny Ice Cream 48 Le Thai To; map p.840. Snigger at the name if you must, but this is the best place in town for French-style local ice cream, and the more unusual flavours include *com* (young sticky rice). One scoop 20,000VND. Daily 10am–8pm.

11

★**Highway 4** 3 Hang Tre; map p.840. The Old Quarter's most atmospheric bar-restaurant, with a warren of rooms on three floors culminating in a great rooftop terrace. Known for its excellent array of northern Vietnamese dishes (mains from 80,000VND), such as catfish and dill spring rolls, glass noodles with crab and jicama salad, as well as liquor made from glutinous rice. Another branch at 25 Bat Su. Daily 8am–midnight.

Kinh Do Café 252 Hang Bong; map p.840. Follow in Catherine Deneuve's footsteps and have a strong coffee at this landmark café, like she did during the filming of *Indochine*. The French pastries and toasted sandwiches are delicious, too. Mains from 40,000VND. Daily 8am–8pm.

KOTO 59 Van Mieu; map p.840. *"Know One Teach One"* restaurant, overlooking the Temple of Literature, has bright seating areas strewn with cushions and the menu runs the gamut from expertly prepared Vietnamese dishes (snakehead fish soup, fresh spring rolls and honey prawns) to Western offerings, such as cheeseburgers, fettucine and fish and chips. The staff are disadvantaged children and former street kids being trained by an Australian-run charity. Mains from 115,000VND. Daily 7am–10.30pm, closed Mon eve.

Luna d'autunno 78 Tho Nhuom; map p.840. Decent pizzas and home-made pasta make this classy Italian restaurant a good option. Mains from 160,000VND. Daily 10am–11pm.

Namaste Hanoi 47 Lo Su; map p.840. One of the best Indian restaurants in the country, this reasonably priced place serves up a huge range of dishes from across the Subcontinent, with an emphasis on northern Indian (mains from 70,000VND), along with ample options for vegetarians. The fantastic ice cream is the one non-Indian item on the dessert menu, but we're not complaining. Daily 11am–2.30pm & 6–10.30pm.

Net Hue Cam Chi at Hang Bong; map p.840. If you don't make it to Hue, there's no reason why you should miss out on its exceptional cuisine. This family-run restaurant serves great takes on the likes of *banh nam* (steamed rice pancake with minced shrimp filling) and *bun bo hue* (noodle dish with a multitude of toppings). Mains from 40,000VND. Daily 11am–10pm.

Nha Hang Ngon 26A Tran Hung Dao; map p.840. The courtyard of this restored French villa plays host to excellent street food from all over Vietnam, just like the sister restaurant, *Quan An Ngon* (below). Choose from a vast array of spring rolls, filled pancakes, soups, noodle dishes, steamed fish and seafood. Mains from 40,000VND. Daily 11am–11pm.

★**Quan An Ngon** 18 Phan Boi Chau; map p.840. Semi-enclosed food court known as *the* place to sample traditional Vietnamese street food in more salubrious surroundings; choose from the likes of steamed clams with lemongrass, shrimp paste on sugarcane stalks, papaya salad with dried beef, all manner of fresh and fried spring rolls and more. Mains 35,000–80,000VND. Daily 11am–11pm.

Tamarind 80 Ma May; map p.840. A cut above most vegetarian restaurants, serving innovative food with a Japanese-Vietnamese slant; dishes such as the *baba ganoush* burger and aubergine claypot are excellent. Wash it all down with fresh juices or a selection of lassis. Daily 7am–11pm.

STREET EATS

Hanoi's street food scene is legendary, and for sheer value for money and atmosphere it's hard to beat the rock-bottom, stove-and-stool **food stalls** or the slightly more upmarket **street kitchens**. Pho Cam Chi is a narrow lane around 500m northeast of the main train station, packed with cheap eateries; streets such as Mai Hac De, Hang Dieu and Duong Thanh are also a good bet. If you're after specific Hanoi specialities, pop into *Thanh Hop* at 12 Dinh Liet for chicken noodle soup (daily noon–10pm; 40,000VND). The street stall at 52 Ly Quoc Su is excellent for Vietnamese-style empanadas filled with minced pork and glass noodles, as well as deep-fried spring rolls. *Banh Cuon* (daily 4–11pm) at 14 Hang Ga is an excellent spot for just that: thin steamed rice crepes filled with mushrooms, minced pork and ground shrimp and topped with crispy shallots) while *Bun Ca* (daily noon–10pm) at 77 Duong Thanh serves bowls of spicy soup with flat wheat noodles. For the ubiquitous pho noodle soup, one of the best places is *Pho Gia Truyen*, 49 Bat Dan (daily 7am–10am), while for *bun cha*, barbecued pork served over a bowl of rice noodles and minty greens, head for *Bun Cha Nem Cua Be Doc Kim*, 67 Duong Thanh (daily 11am–3pm).

DRINKING AND NIGHTLIFE

Venues open and close quickly and popularity wavers, so check the English-language press such as *Vietnam Pathfinder* (ⓦ pathfinder.com.vn) for the latest information and consult ⓦ beervn.com for the best beer and microbreweries in Hanoi (and elsewhere in Vietnam). Legally, all bars should close by 11pm, but many host nightly lock-ins – the shutters go down and the drinking continues late into the night. Police raids are common. Ta Hien is home to most of the bars catering to expats and backpackers.

BARS

ETE 95 Giang Van Minh; map p.838. Microbrewery serving its "special" beer in unmarked bottles. This spot is popular with expats in the know, has friendly English-speaking staff and excellent hamburgers. Daily noon–11pm.

Funky Buddha 2 Ta Hien; map p.840. Crowded bar-cum-club, with a small dancefloor, drinks specials and trippy disco lights. Backpackers tend to haunt the L-shaped bar. Daily 5pm–late.

GC Pub 3 Bao Khanh; map p.840. Friendly gay bar with a good mix of locals and foreigners; a good place to make enquiries about other gay venues. Daily noon–late.

Goldmalt Brewery 34 Tran Phu; map p.840. Microbrewery popular with locals, with drinking space spread over two floors and frat-house atmosphere. Blond and dark beer on tap. There's another branch at 9 Hoang Cau. Daily noon–11pm.

Le Pub 25 Hang Be; map p.840. Relaxed and welcoming by day, atmospheric and crowded by night, this tavern-like bar with streetside seating draws a regular crowd of backpackers and expats, with nightly drinks specials and the coldest beer in the capital. You can pick your own music too. Daily noon–late.

Mao's Red Lounge 7 Ta Hien; map p.840. Wonderfully chilled, friendly little dive bar in the heart of the Old Quarter, with cheap beer, eclectic music, and comfortable couches to lounge about on. Daily 5pm–late.

Quan Ly 82 Le Van Hu; map p.840. This traditional *ruou* (Vietnamese liquor) bar has been around for a long time, and the English menu can help you get acquainted with the many varieties on offer – from ginseng to ones with life forms in them. If that's too exotic for you, stick to the *bia hoi* and the good Vietnamese bar food. Daily 5pm–late.

Tet Bar 2a Ta Hien; map p.840. Multi-level yet intimate and smoky bar, popular with expats and doubling as a very small dance venue as the night drags on. Daily 5pm–late.

CLUBS AND LIVE MUSIC

The clubs below are open daily from around 8pm till late, unless noted.

Face Club 6 Hang Bai; map p.840. The city's trendiest late-night spot, popular with well-heeled Hanoians, has a decent sound system thumping out loud electro and house music. Drinks here are pricey, though.

Factory 11a Bao Khanh; map p.840. This funky multi-level drinking venue has an appealing roof terrace, decorated with socialist art; sit back with a hookah and enjoy the live music or snack on the edible goodies at the bar. Daily noon–late.

Hanoi Rock City 27/52 To Ngoc Van ⓦ hanoirockcity.com; map p.838. The 7km journey north of the centre is worth making for the excellent live music – from hip-hop and punk to electronica and DJ mixes.

BIA HOI

Serious beer-drinking tends to be an all-male preserve in Vietnam, but the local **bia hoi** outlets are fun, friendly and extremely cheap. The four small *bia hoi* joints at the crossroads of Ta Hien and Luong Ngoc Quyen are known as **International Bia Hoi Corner**, and draw crowds of backpackers, expats and locals for their glasses of 10,000VND beer and convivial atmosphere. Popular with foreigners and locals alike, **Windmill** (daily noon–10pm), near the Temple of Literature at 31 Dang Tran Con (map p.838), serves Czech beers and Vietnamese dishes in a shady courtyard.

SHOPPING AND MARKETS

Hanoi has perhaps the best value, quality and choice when shopping for traditional silk clothes, accessories and souvenirs in Vietnam. The best areas to browse are Hang Gai in the Old Quarter, and around the southeastern edge of Hoan Kiem Lake.

Art The Apricot Gallery, 40b Hang Bong, is a well-established gallery with a range of works by local artists. Viet Art Centre at 42 Yet Kieu is good for contemporary Vietnamese art and photography.

Books The best for English-language books are the Bookworm, 44 Chau Long (daily 9am–7pm; ⓦ bookwormhanoi.com), and Thang Long, 53–55 Trang Tien, with a good selection of books on Vietnam's history as well as maps of the country.

Clothing For vintage clothing and one-off pieces try the boutiques at the eastern end of Ly Thuong Kiet. Things of Substance, 5 Nha Tho, stocks both tailored fashions and off-the-rack items. Look out for the Made in Vietnam stores, which stock end-of-the-line designer gear at rock-bottom prices.

Communist memorabilia Several small shops on Hang Bong supply Communist Party banners and badges and Vietnamese flags, while Old Propaganda Posters at 122 Hang Bac sells original and replica propaganda posters.

Handicrafts The non-profit Craft Link, 43–45 Van Mieu, sells traditional crafts made by ethnic minorities, including lacquerware, paper goods, baskets and clothes. Indigenous, at 36 Au Trieu, sells Fair Trade coffee as well as ethnic-style gifts.

Markets Hanoi has more than fifty markets, selling predominantly foodstuffs: Cho Dong Xuan on Dong Xuan Street is a good place to buy cheap bags, shoes, hats and materials; also try Cho Hom, 81 Pho Hue, which has clothing upstairs and is good for purchasing fabrics if you're looking to get some clothes tailored. All around Cho Hom are specialist shopping streets: Tran Nhan Tong focuses on shirts and jackets, while Phung Khac Khoan, off Tran Xuan Soan, is a riot of colourful fabrics.

11

Silk Compared with Thailand, Vietnamese silk is of slightly inferior quality, but prices are lower and the tailoring is great value. So many silk shops are concentrated on Hang Gai, at the southern edge of the Old Quarter, that it's now known as "Silk Street". One of the best known is Silk Road at 96 Hang Gai, but try also Kenly Silk at no. 108. For a large selection of exquisite silk bags and shoes, go to Ha Dong Silk at 102 Hang Gai. The Tailoring Shop Co, 18 Nha Tho, has some of the best handmade clothes in town.

DIRECTORY

Banks and exchange Vietcombank's main branch is at 198 Tran Quang Khai; there's another branch at 78 Nguyen Du. 24hr ATMs are widespread.

Embassies and consulates Australia, 8 Dao Tan, Ba Dinh Ⓣ 04 37740100; Canada, 31 Hung Vuong Ⓣ 04 37345000; China, 46 Hoang Dieu Ⓣ 04 38453736; Ireland, Vincom City Towers, 8th floor, 191 Ba Trieu Ⓣ 04 39743291; New Zealand, 5th floor, 63 Ly Thai To Ⓣ 04 38241481; UK, 5th Floor, 31 Hai Ba Trung Ⓣ 04 39360500; USA, The American Center, 1st floor, Rose Garden Tower, 170 Ngoc Khanh Ⓣ 04 38505000.

Hospitals and clinics Hanoi Family Medical Practice and Dental Surgery in Van Phuc, 109–112 Kim Ma (Mon–Fri 8.30am–5.30pm, Sat 8.30am–noon; Ⓣ 04 38430748, Ⓦ vietnammedicalpractice.com), and SOS International Clinic, 51 Xuan Dieu (Ⓣ 04 39340666, Ⓦ internationalsos.com), both have international English-speaking doctors, and provide 24hr emergency care. Make sure your travel insurance will cover the high costs.

Pharmacies 119 Hang Gai and 3 Trang Thi. There's also a 24hr pharmacy at 87 Phu Doan.

Post office The main post office occupies a whole block at 75 Dinh Tien Hoang (Mon–Sat 8am–7pm, Sun 9am–6pm).

WHAT'S ON IN HANOI

A number of resources carry **listings** information for Hanoi and the surrounding area, including *Hanoi Grapevine* (Ⓦ hanoigrapevine.com), which has info about art exhibitions and concerts. Others include the *New Hanoian* Ⓦ newhanoian.com) – with a wealth of info for visitors and expats, including restaurant and bar reviews; *The Word* (Ⓦ wordhanoi.com) – the online version of the free monthly expat magazine filled with local lifestyle articles and restaurant listings. *Sticky Rice* (Ⓦ stickyrice.typepad.com) is a great resource for foodies. The excellent **website** for expats in Hanoi, Ⓦ tnhvietnam.xemzi.com, carries reliable restaurant and bar reviews, as well as listings and upcoming events.

Around Hanoi

The fertile and densely populated landscape of the Red River Delta that surrounds Hanoi is crisscrossed by massive ancient dykes and studded with temples and pagodas, including the **Perfume Pagoda** – the city's most popular day-trip. The magnificent karst scenery at **Tam Coc**, 90km south of Hanoi, can also be visited as a day-trip from the capital, but many travellers choose to explore the area at a more leisurely pace: the sleepy town of **Ninh Binh** makes an excellent base for Tam Coc, the nearby ancient capital of **Hoa Lu** and trips to **Cuc Phuong National Park.**

THE PERFUME PAGODA

Sixty kilometres southwest of Hanoi, a forested spur shelters north Vietnam's most famous Buddhist pilgrimage site, the **Perfume Pagoda** (Chua Huong) – a pagoda and shrine complex built into the cliffs of Huong Tich Mountain, and said to be named after spring blossoms that scent the air.

The pagoda occupies a grotto more than 50m high; the journey there begins with a pleasant, hour-long sampan ride up a flooded valley among karst hills, then a path brings you to the seventeenth-century Chua Thien Chu ("Pagoda Leading to Heaven"), in front of which stands a magnificent, triple-roofed bell pavilion. Quan Am, Goddess of Mercy, takes pride of place on the pagoda's main

INTO CHINA

THE TRAIN TO CHINA

Tickets should be booked well in advance for the direct train service from Hanoi to China, and you'll need your passport with a valid China visa when you buy them. The **Hanoi–Beijing** service (42hr; around 7,000,000VND) leaves Hanoi main station on Tuesdays and Fridays at 6.30pm and cannot be boarded anywhere other than Hanoi; it stops in Dong Dang, Nanning, Guilin, Zhengzhou and Beijing. The Hanoi–Kunming service was suspended in 2004 due to landslide damage on the Chinese side, and works on the tracks were still in progress at the time of writing, but services may resume in early 2015. Meantime, you can take the train to Lao Cai, and take a bus from there to Kunming (see box, p.857). See Ⓦ seat61.com for up-to-date details of train journeys between Vietnam and China.

HUU NGHI AND ON TO NANNING

The road crossing known as the **Huu Nghi ("Friendship") Gate** is 164km northeast of Hanoi at the end of Highway 1 and is the most popular border crossing in the north. Local trains from Hanoi (hard seat only) terminate at Dong Dang station, 800m south of the main town, from where you can take a *xe om* up to the border (40,000VND). The Huu Nghi border (daily 7am–5.30pm) has no exchange facilities; there's a walk of less than 1km between the two checkpoints. On the Chinese side, shared taxis and buses (from ¥20–40) will take you to **Pingxiang**, 15km away, for the nearest accommodation and the trains to **Nanning** (3 daily; 4hr–5hr 30min; $7). If entering Vietnam here, ignore the touts and get on a minibus at the Dong Dang minibus terminal, with frequent services to Hanoi (2 hourly; 3hr 15min).

altar. To the right, a slippery 3km path leads steeply uphill (1–2hr), at the end of which a gaping cavern is revealed beneath the inscription "supreme cave under the southern sky". The Perfume Pagoda is also dedicated to Quan Am and a flight of 120 steps descends into the dragon's-mouth-like entrance, where gilded Buddhas emerge from dark recesses wreathed in clouds of incense (bring a torch). You must wear long trousers and long-sleeve shirts to visit Chua Thien Chu, and shoes with good grip are highly recommended. If you don't want to hike to the top, you can take the **cable car** (one-way/return 60,000/100,000VND) to the summit.

This is a popular destination for Vietnamese tourists, day-trippers from Hanoi and Buddhist pilgrims; to avoid the worst of the crowds, don't come on the even dates of the third lunar month (March or April), avoid weekends and expect to be pursued by hawkers throughout the experience. The easiest way to visit the pagoda is on an all-inclusive tour from Hanoi (approx $15–20).

NINH BINH AND AROUND

The dusty provincial capital of **Ninh Binh**, 90km from Hanoi, has little to detain you, but serves as a good base for exploring the beautiful countryside that surrounds it. Two radio masts provide convenient landmarks in town: the taller stands over the post office in the south, while the shorter signals the northern extremity 2km away up Highway 1 (Tran Hung Dao).

WHAT TO SEE AND DO

The most rewarding way to see the area is by **renting a bicycle**; the surrounding landscape, with giant limestone karsts dramatically rising from glistening rice paddies, makes the journey to **Tam Coc** worthwhile; it can be combined with the temples of **Hoa Lu** in a day-trip.

Tam Coc

It's hard not to be won over by the mystical, watery beauty of the Tam Coc region, a miniature, landlocked version of Ha Long Bay. Journey's end for the three-hour sampan ride through the flooded landscape is **Tam Coc**, three long, dark tunnel-caves eroded through the limestone hills with, in places, barely sufficient clearance for the sampan.

The starting point is the dock in Van Lam village. **Boats** leave here between 7am and 5pm, as they fill up (go early or late to avoid the crowds), and cost

90,000VND per boat; each boat carries two people. However, many tourists complain of constant hassle to buy refreshments and handicrafts; be firm from the outset.

Follow the road another 2km beyond the boat dock to visit the cave-pagoda of **Bich Dong** (free), where stone-cut steps lead up a cliff face peppered with shrines to the cave entrance. Three Buddhas sit unperturbed on their lotus thrones beside a head-shaped rock, which bestows longevity if touched.

The most enjoyable way to reach Tam Coc is to rent a **bicycle** ($2–3/day) or **motorbike** ($7–10/day) from a Ninh Binh guesthouse, which should also be able to provide a photocopied map. The turning, marked by four large pillars, is 4km south of the town centre on Highway 1. A *xe om* from Ninh Binh will cost about 100,000VND all-in. If your next stop is Hoa Lu, you can take a back road for a spectacular 10km ride through rice fields, karst scenery and villages; the 30km round trip is easily done in a day. This route starts in the village halfway down the road between Highway 1 and the boat landing; follow the signs for Troung Yen village to reach Hoa Lu.

Hoa Lu

Thirteen kilometres northwest of Ninh Binh stands **Hoa Lu** (15,000VND), site of the tenth-century capital of an early, independent Vietnamese kingdom called Dai Co Viet. The fortified royal palaces of the Dinh and Le kings are now in ruins, but their dynastic temples, seventeenth-century copies of eleventh-century originals, still rest quietly in a narrow valley surrounded by hills. Opposite the temples, steps lead up "Saddle Mountain" for a panoramic view of Hoa Lu.

The quickest way out to Hoa Lu is by *xe om* (260,000VND or so round trip), but going by **bicycle** is another option. Follow Highway 1 for 6km; then it's a pleasant ride on paved back roads west of the highway, following signs to Truong Yen village and Hoa Lu (13km in total). You can then cycle back along the Sao Khe River: take the paved road heading east directly in front of the temples, turn right over the bridge and follow the dirt track for about 4km to the first village. Here, a left turn leading to a concrete bridge will take you back to Ninh Binh, while the road straight ahead continues for another 6km to Tam Coc.

ARRIVAL AND INFORMATION

By bus The bus station is on Le Dai Hanh, east of the Van River, less than 1km by *xe om* from Tran Hung Dao. From here, public buses depart every 20min for Hanoi's Giap Bat and Luong Yen stations. Open-tour buses en route to and from Hanoi and points south, including Hue, Da Nang, Hoi An and HCMC (all 2 daily), pick up and drop off at their associated hotels.

Destinations Hai Phong (several daily; 3hr); Hanoi (every 20min; 2hr 30min).

By train The station is east of the Van River at the western end of Hang Hoa Tham, a short *xe om* ride from Tran Hung Dao.

Destinations Da Nang (5 daily; 14hr); Hanoi (4 daily; 2hr 30min); HCMC (5 daily; 40hr); Hue (5 daily; 12hr 30min); Nha Trang (5 daily; 24hr).

Information The Vietcombank, on the main strip on Tran Hung Dao, has an ATM.

ACCOMMODATION AND EATING

There are very few good independent restaurants in Ninh Binh, but the hotels listed here all offer decent food. A string of goat meat (*thit de*) restaurants line the road 3km out of town; this local speciality is served with rice paper and herbs. Atmospheric *bia hoi* stands line the riverside just north of Hong Phong. All these hotels can assist with tours, car and motorbike rental, as well as onward transport.

Canh Dieu Hotel 74 Nguyen Van Cu ⓣ 030 3888278, ⓦ canhdieuhotel.com.vn. Efficiently run budget hotel with helpful staff who arrange tours of the area. The a/c units double as a heater and there are nice little extras, such as welcome drinks and map of the area. Double **$20**

Kim Lien Guest House 54 Van Thanh Phuc Thinh ⓣ 030 6250800, ⓦ guesthousekimlien.com. Friendly, family-run guesthouse that makes a great base due to the owner's knowledge of the area (a book's been compiled for the guests' perusal). Rooms are clean and perfectly comfortable. Double **$17**

Thanh Binh Hotel 31 Luong Van Tuy ⓣ 030 3872439, ⓦ thanhbinhhotelnb.com.vn. Clean and spacious accommodation with breakfast and internet included; the rooms in the new wing ($20) boast great views from the top floors. Good-quality mountain bikes for rent ($2/day), as well as motorbikes. Double **$15**

Than Thuy's Guesthouse 53 Le Hong Phong ⓣ 030 3871811, ⓦ hotelthanhthuy.com. Good spot for meeting

other travellers, with decent older rooms in the guesthouse ($15), and spacious, fully equipped rooms in the newer hotel at the back ($30). Their tailor-made motorbike tours to outlying villages are popular. Double **$10**

Trung Tuyet 14 Hoang Hoa Tham. Quite possibly the best restaurant in town, with large portions of inexpensive Vietnamese dishes such as vegetable spring rolls and fried noodle with egg. A "small" is plenty for one person; only go for "large" if there's a ravenous group of you. Mains from 60,000 VND. Daily 11.30am–9pm.

CUC PHUONG NATIONAL PARK

Established as Vietnam's first national park in 1962, **Cuc Phuong**, 200 square kilometres of tropical evergreen forest surrounded by limestone mountains, spreads over three provinces and two mountain ranges. The myriad species of wildlife that live among the forest's ancient trees – some of which are more than a thousand years old – include more than three hundred bird and ninety mammal species, including bats, bears, leopards, rare butterflies, and one of the world's most endangered monkeys, Delacour's langur. At the entrance gate (30,000VND), the **visitors' centre** (daily 9–11am & 1.30–4pm; Ⓦ cucphuongtourism.com) can organize biking, hiking, birdwatching, night-spotting and overnight accommodation either in the park headquarters, bamboo bungalows or stilt houses in a Muong village in the park ($7–15 per person).

Beyond the visitors' centre stands the **Endangered Primate Rescue Center** (daily 9–11am & 1.30–4pm), where you can see the park's research, conservation and breeding programmes to save endangered langurs, lorises and gibbons and learn about the threats to this unique environment in the form of illegal logging and poaching. There's also good hiking to be done here; a popular 3km walk leads to a 1000-year-old tree, and there's a tougher 11km walk to Silver Cloud Peak, as well as a fairly tough 15km (5hr) hike to the Muong village of Kanh; park staff can provide basic maps, but it's worth hiring a guide for longer hikes ($25 or so for a hike up to Silver Cloud Peak).

ARRIVAL AND DEPARTURE

On a tour Tourist agencies in Hanoi arrange day-trips to Cuc Phuong for about $35 per person (not including entrance fees).

By bus A morning bus runs from Giap Bat bus station in Hanoi directly to the park at 9am, returning at 3pm. If coming from Ninh Binh, take the public bus (20,000VND).

By bike From Ninh Binh you can rent a motorbike or hire a *xe om* (about 250,000VND return including waiting time). Head north along Highway 1 for about 10km, and take the left at the sign for Cuc Phuong. From here it's another 18km to the park entrance.

Ha Long Bay

11

Nearly two thousand bizarrely shaped limestone outcrops jut out of the emerald **Ha Long Bay**, its hidden coves, echoing caves and needle-sharp ridges providing the inspiration for dozens of local legends and poems. Navigating the watery channels and scrambling through caves is a hugely popular activity, justifiably so, but some may be put off by the numerous boats that congregate in the bay and the floating garbage left in their wake. If you want to go off the beaten track and experience true beauty without the crowds, it's well worth taking a small-group tour with Cat Ba Ventures (see p.855) on Cat Ba Island or heading out to the remote Bai Tu Long Bay (see box, p.852). Bear in mind also that the weather from January to March can be overcast and even cold.

The vast majority of visitors to Ha Long Bay come on **organized tours** from Hanoi (two days/one night; from $110); the same can be organized from Cat Ba Island. It's well worth staying overnight on the boat for the chance of a midnight dip in the phosphorescent waters.

The gateway to Ha Long Bay is **Ha Long City**, an amalgamation of two towns – Hong Gai and Bai Chay – but unless you're a Chinese or Korean tourist, staying in Bai Chay resort is neither appealing nor necessary, as the better tour agencies from Hanoi use the nicer boats from Cat Ba, rather than the large, poorly maintained ones from Ha Long City.

If you're planning on visiting Ha Long Bay from Cat Ba Island and are travelling up from the south, it's possible to bypass Hanoi and go via the port city of Hai Phong instead.

HA LONG BAY AND BAI TU LONG BAY

Ha Long Bay and Bai Tu Long Bay, to the northeast, are separated by a wide channel running north–south: the larger, western portion contains dramatic scenery and most of the caves, while to the northeast lies an even more attractive collection of smaller islands, known as Bai Tu Long and part of the Bai Tu Long National Park; this bay is still relatively untouristy and unpolluted, making for a more laidback experience than Ha Long Bay.

The bay's most famous cave is **Hang Dau Go** ("Grotto of the Wooden Stakes"). In 1288, General Tran Hung Dao amassed hundreds of wooden stakes here; these were driven into the Bach Dang River estuary mud, skewering the boats of Kublai Khan's Mongol army as the tide went out. The same island also boasts the beautiful **Hang Thien Cung** cave, whose rectangular chamber, 250m long and 20m high, holds a textbook display of sparkling stalactites and stalagmites. To the south, you should single out **Ho Dong Tien** ("Grotto of the Fairy Lake") and the enchanting **Dong Me Cung** ("Grotto of the Labyrinth").

Of the far-flung sights, **Hang Hanh** is one of the more adventurous day-trips from Cat Ba Island: the tide must be exactly right (at half-tide) to allow a coracle ($15 extra, or $2 per person) access to the 2km-long tunnel-cave; a powerful torch is very useful. Dau Bo Island, on the southeastern edge of Ha Long Bay, encloses **Ho Ba Ham** ("Three Tunnel Lake"), a shallow lagoon wrapped round with limestone walls and connected to the sea by three low-ceilinged tunnels that are only navigable by sampan or kayak at low tide. This cave can be included in a one- or two-day excursion from Cat Ba Island.

HAI PHONG

Located 100km east of Hanoi, **HAI PHONG** is north Vietnam's principal port – a small, orderly city of broad avenues, with hydrofoil and ferry links to Cat Ba Island (for Ha Long Bay). Given the frequency of transport

HA LONG BAY CRUISES

Cruises around Ha Long Bay are peddled by every hotel and travel agency in Hanoi, but despite the undeniable beauty of the karst-studded bay, complaints abound about the tours and the service provided, particularly on budget tours. You tend to get what you pay for so, if you're only being charged $50 for a two-day-one-night trip, expect a dirty, unsafe boat and being shuttled from one commission-paying place to another. That said, even paying doesn't always help; travel agencies seldom own their own boats, merely acting as agents for boat operators in Ha Long and Cat Ba (white boats are from Ha Long, brown from Cat Ba), who shift passengers mid-tour from boat to boat to cram as many on board as possible. Day-trips from Hanoi to Ha Long Bay are not worth it, as you spend a great deal of time on the bus; overnight trips that throw in some kayaking and swimming are a better way to go, and if you can spare three days and venture as far as the remote Bai Tu Long Bay, even better. A great way to see Ha Long Bay is to base yourself on Cat Ba Island and do an unhurried small-group tour with the highly professional Cat Ba Ventures (see p.855) who take you kayaking to more remote lagoons where you're not constantly paddling through floating garbage left in the wake of numerous tour boats. If booking from Hanoi, the high-octane adventure that includes tubing and waterboarding as well as cruising is organized by Hanoi Backpackers (see p.845). Otherwise, ask as many questions as you can about what's included before booking, and request a written itinerary detailing the size of the group, standard of accommodation, and planned activities, so you have some comeback at the end if the tour fails to live up to what was promised. Report any unsatisfactory experiences to the Administration of Tourism in Hanoi (see box, p.843). There are several recommended tour companies in Hanoi (see p.844).

INTO CHINA: MONG CAI

Buses from Hanoi (8hr; 230,000VND) arrive at Mong Cai bus station, 500m west of the centre. The blue, space-age building northwest of the roundabout identifies Mong Cai's focal point, the covered market. The **Chinese border** is 1km away: walk north along Tran Phu and turn left at the end of the road to reach the border gate (daily 7am–7pm; visas must be arranged in advance). Once in Dongxing on the Chinese side, take a *xe om* to the bus station, from where regular buses depart for Nanning and Guilin.

For somewhere to stay in Mong Cai, try *Truong Minh*, 36 Trieu Duong (T 033 3883368), or *Thanh Tam* down the street at no. 71 (T 033 3770181); both have clean, pleasant rooms for around 300,000VND. Streets near the market turn into open-air food stalls in the evening. Vietcombank has a branch with a 24hr ATM north of the market, on Van Don.

For those arriving **in Mong Cai**, there are numerous buses to Hai Phong (every 2 hours; 4hr); Hanoi (at least hourly; 8hr) and Ha Long City (2 hourly; 4hr).

connections to and from Hai Phong, there's little reason to linger en route either to Hanoi or the south.

ARRIVAL AND DEPARTURE

By plane Cat Bi airport is 6km southeast of the city, around 130,000VND by taxi.

Destinations Da Nang (3 daily; 1hr 20min); HCMC (5 daily; 2hr).

By boat Ben Binh harbour is on the Cua Cam River, a short walk from the Lac Long bus station. A fast boat runs from Ben Binh to Cat Ba's Cai Vieng harbour at 7am and 10am, with a bus connection waiting in Cat Ba to take you to Cat Ba Town; return buses leave Cat Ba Town at 2pm and 4pm (1hr 30min one-way). Another option is to take a bus from Haiphong's Ben Binh harbour to Dinh Vu port to catch another hydrofoil to Cat Ba's Cai Vieng harbour, as departures from Dinh Vu are more frequent (6 daily; 2hr).

Destinations Cat Ba Island (hydrofoils 8 daily; 45min–1hr).

By bus Buses serving the south and west operate from Niem Nghia bus station, 3km from the centre on Tran Nguyen Han. Some Hanoi services use Tam Bac bus station, near the west end of Tam Bac Lake, though Hanoi-bound minibuses also hang around the Ben Binh harbour and can be flagged down on the riverfront south of Dien Bien Phu. The Hoang Long bus-boat-bus combo from Hanoi to Cat Ba Town (see below) connects in Haiphong with Hoang Long sleeper buses from the south at around 10am and 12.30pm; if you're heading south from Cat Ba Town, you can take the return bus to Hanoi at 9.15am and 1.15pm and change to a south-bound sleeper bus in Haiphong; these head all the way to HCMC via Hanoi, Vinh, Hue, Da Nang and Nha Trang.

Destinations Da Nang (15hr); Hanoi (2hr 30min); HCMC (38hr); Hue (14hr); Nha Trang (10hr); Ninh Binh (3hr).

By train Hai Phong train station is on the southeast side of town on Luong Khanh Thien.

Destinations Hanoi (2 daily; 2hr 30min).

CAT BA ISLAND

11

Dragon-back mountain ranges loom on the horizon 20km out of Hai Phong as boats approach **Cat Ba Island**, the largest member of an archipelago sitting to the west of Ha Long Bay.

WHAT TO SEE AND DO

The island's main settlement is **Cat Ba Town**, an old fishing village, but the main strip along the waterfront is now lined with countless budget hotels, restaurants, and massage parlours. Eight hundred metres to the east across a small headland is the main ferry pier, Ben Ca, where floating seafood restaurants bob around just offshore. A fifteen-minute walk along a steep road just east of the waterfront leads to a small, sandy **beach**, **Cat Co 1**; from here, a ten-minute walk north leads you to a second, quieter and more secluded beach, **Cat Co 2**, where it is also possible to stay overnight (see p.856). From Cat Co 2, follow a scenic, cliff-hugging boardwalk south to reach a third beach, **Cat Co 3**. Overlooking the Cat Co 1 and Cat Co 2 beaches is **Fort Cannon**, (sunrise–sunset; 20,000VND), its guns and underground tunnels first used by the Japanese in World War II, and later by the French and the Vietnamese. The sunsets from this spot are fantastic and the entrance is a steep ten-minute walk from Cat Ba Town. A tourist train (40,000VND) saves you twenty minutes' legwork if you don't want to trudge uphill from the gate.

Almost half the island and adjacent waters are part of **Cat Ba National Park**

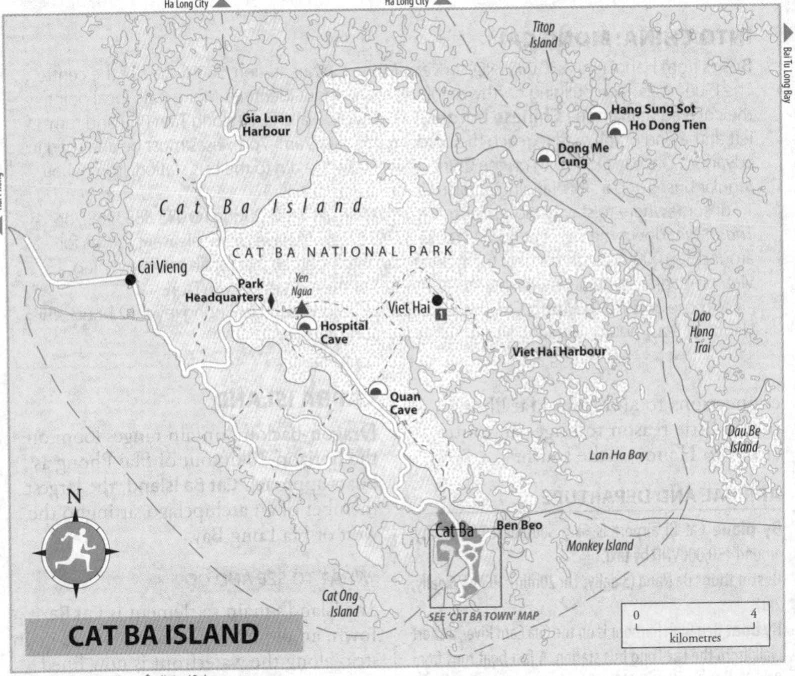

CAT BA ISLAND

Ha Long City
Ha Long City
Bai Tu Long Bay
Hai Phong
Titop Island
Hang Sung Sot
Ho Dong Tien
Dong Me Cung
Gia Luan Harbour
Cat Ba Island
CAT BA NATIONAL PARK
Cai Vieng
Park Headquarters
Yen Ngua
Hospital Cave
Viet Hai
1
Viet Hai Harbour
Dao Hong Trai
Quan Cave
Dau Be Island
Lan Ha Bay
Cat Ba
Ben Beo
Monkey Island
Cat Ong Island
SEE 'CAT BA TOWN' MAP
0 4 kilometres
N

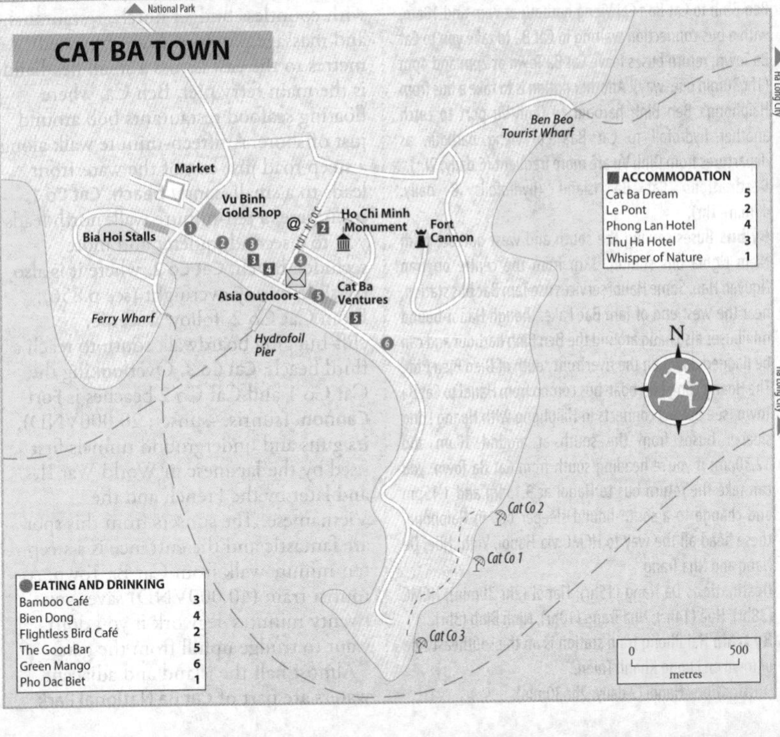

CAT BA TOWN

National Park
Ha Long City
Ha Long City
Hai Phong
Ben Beo Tourist Wharf
Market
Vu Binh Gold Shop
Bia Hoi Stalls
NUI NGOC
Ho Chi Minh Monument
Fort Cannon
Asia Outdoors
Cat Ba Ventures
Ferry Wharf
Hydrofoil Pier
Cat Co 2
Cat Co 1
Cat Co 3
N
0 500 metres

ACCOMMODATION

Cat Ba Dream	5
Le Pont	2
Phong Lan Hotel	4
Thu Ha Hotel	3
Whisper of Nature	1

EATING AND DRINKING

Bamboo Café	3
Bien Dong	4
Flightless Bird Café	2
The Good Bar	5
Green Mango	6
Pho Dac Biet	1

11

(30,000VND), home to over seventy species of bird, and mammals such as civets, deer, wild boar and the world's most endangered primate – the golden-headed or Cat Ba langur – with only sixty or so remaining. The park entrance is 13km along the road from Cat Ba Town. Companies such as Cat Ba Ventures and Asia Outdoors (see below) run half- and full-day hiking tours of the park; otherwise it's worth hiring an experienced and English-speaking guide to explore the park (around 270,000VND for a full day) from the ranger station to point out the wildlife. There are several short hikes in the park, including one to **Trung Trang Cave** and a rewarding 18km hike up one of the peaks. Many guided hikes either finish at or stop for lunch at the remote minority village of **Viet Hai**, where *Whisper of Nature* (see p.856) is located. You'll need good boots, lots of water and mosquito repellent. The going can be quite tough, and trekking should be avoided after heavy rains, when the paths can be slippery and treacherous. You can reach the park independently via the green QH public buses that depart from the hydrofoil dock in Cat Ba Town (at 5am, 8.10am, 11.10am and 4pm; 20min; 20,000VND) or by your own rented motorbike or scooter.

En route to the park, 10km north of Cat Ba Town, is the **Hospital Cave** (daily 7am–4.30pm, 15,000VND), a three-storey construction within a natural cave that served as a hospital and shelter for Viet Cong leaders from 1965 to 1975. It's well worth paying the extra 30,000VND for a guide who'll point out where the cinema and swimming pool used to be and explain what each of the seventeen spartan bunker rooms was used for.

ARRIVAL AND INFORMATION

By boat Coming from Hai Phong, fast boats pull in at Cai Vieng harbour at the island's western point, about 20km from town, and are met by a bus that whisks passengers off to Cat Ba Town. Ferries from Tuan Chau (accessed from Ha Long City) and tourist boats from Bai Chay (Ha Long City) land at the Gia Luan pier, in the north of the island, 40km from Cat Ba Town. Public QH Green Buses leave Gia Luan at 6am, 1.10pm, 4pm and 5pm (25,000VND) for Cat Ba Town, and despite what some unscrupulous locals might tell you, foreigners are very much allowed to take the bus. Tourist boats from Bai Chay dock too late to take the last bus, leaving you at the mercy of *xe om* and taxi drivers, who've been known to charge as much as $50 to take you to Cat Ba Town, though onward bus transport from the pier can be arranged via Cat Ba Ventures (see below).

Destinations Fast boats to Hai Phong (4 daily; 45min); ferries to Bai Chay (hourly May–Sept, 3 daily rest of year; 1hr); ferries to Tuan Chau, Ha Long City (5 daily; 1hr); boat and bus to Hanoi (4 daily; 4hr 30min).

Information There are several ATMs in town, including an Agribank at no. 209 on the waterfront.

GETTING AROUND

By bus QH Green Buses run between Cat Ba Town and Gia Luan pier (5 daily; 25,000VND); for the latest timetables, check with Cat Ba Ventures (see below).

By motorbike The most efficient way to get around is by renting a motorbike or scooter from most hotels; rental is around US$5 per day and Cat Ba's roads have very little traffic.

TOURS AND ACTIVITIES

Tours and treks Popular tours include full-day treks through the national park, with lunch in Viet Hai village, and a boat trip back to Cat Ba Town via Lan Ha Bay ($18 including lunch and kayaking). A day venture into Lan Ha and Ha Long Bay, including kayaking, swimming and a visit to one of the bay's most dramatic caves, Ho Ba Ham, costs $28–31, food included. Cat Ba Ventures (daily 7.30am–8pm; ⓣ 0313 3688237, ⓦ catbaventures.com), no. 223 along the main waterfront, is hands down the best operator when it comes to small-group cruises, with their highly professional management, English-speaking guides and well-organized tours that don't feel rushed or whisk you off to commission-paying pearl farms. Asia Outdoors (see below) also offer recommended tours for small numbers, but they are particularly well known for rock climbing. The website ⓦ catba.com.vn has information on sights, activities and accommodation.

Sea kayaking Some shops and hotels near the seafront can rent out two-person sea kayaks ($10/day) for self-powered paddling around the bay.

Rock climbing The limestone outcrops at Ba Island, Lan Ha Bay and Ha Long Bay are internationally renowned sites for amateur and professional climbers. Asia Outdoors, no. 222 (daily 9am–8pm; ⓣ 091 3688450; ⓦ asiaoutdoors.com.vn), is run by two experienced American climbers, who have developed an extensive network of rock-climbing routes and bouldering sites in the area suitable for all skill levels. They can also incorporate boat trips (necessary to access some of the climbing sites), deep-water soloing, kayaking, trekking, and the occasional beach party into their highly recommended, tailor-made packages.

ACCOMMODATION

The summer months can get very busy with domestic tourists, so it's best to book in advance. For hotels located along the main waterfront strip, we give the street number in brackets. We've had complaints from travellers that many budget hotels pressure their guests to take poor-quality tours and can restrict hot water access, but accommodation reviewed here was exempt from these problems at the time of writing.

Cat Ba Dream (226) ⓣ 031 3888274, ⓦ catbadream.com.vn. A central location, good sea views from the top floors of this seven-storey building, and friendly management make this hotel a solid bet. Double $15

Le Pont 64 Nui Ngoc ⓣ 031 3888353. Budget hotel with a French-speaking manager and largely indifferent staff. Rooms are comfortable enough and good value during the week (doubles rise to $30 at weekends). There's also a cheap, fourteen-bed rooftop dorm. Dorm $5, double $17

Phong Lan Hotel (214) ⓣ 31 3888605. Excellent central location overlooking the harbour and a friendly, English-speaking owner are bonuses here. The rooms are comfortable but unremarkable. Boat tours with this hotel are not recommended. Double $12

Thu Ha Hotel (205) ⓣ 031 3888343. Refurbished waterfront hotel (try to nab a room with a balcony) with efficient service and comfortable, if not terribly memorable, rooms. Double $15

★ **Whisper of Nature** Viet Hai Village ⓣ 04 39233706, ⓦ vietbungalow.com. Located in the tiny village of Viet Hai, in the Cat Ba National Park, this cluster of thatch-roofed bungalows sits by a stream on the edge of the forest; most house private en-suite rooms, with one large bungalow acting as a dorm room. The setting is unbeatable and getting there is part of the fun; contact the management before you set off. Dorm $15, double $28

EATING AND DRINKING

At night, you'll find a cluster of *bia hoi* stands at the western end of the strip and in front of the pier – an atmospheric place for a cheap beer (25,000VND) or a sugar-cane juice. The floating restaurants at Ben Ca harbour are best avoided as they are renowned for ripping tourists off.

Bamboo Café (199). Delicious, reasonably priced fresh seafood, including crab spring rolls (70,000VND) and mains such as steamed clams with lemongrass (90,000VND) or garlic prawns (125,000VND). Daily 8am–10pm.

Bien Dong 8 Nui Ngoc. Pick your dinner from the seafood tanks at this local favourite and say how you want it done; it doesn't come fresher than this. Mains from 120,000VND. Daily noon–10pm.

Flightless Bird Café (189). Friendly Kiwi-run bar serving a good range of international drinks, accompanied by great stone-baked pizza (from 120,000VND). Daily 5pm–midnight.

The Good Bar (231). The most popular place with visitors due to its laidback vibe and sizeable portions of Western and Vietnamese mains. The banana and pineapple pancakes (40,000VND) make a great breakfast, too. Daily 7.30am–11pm.

Green Mango (231). The ambitious menu of Western and Asian dishes at this trendy restaurant fails to live up to expectations, but the coffee is excellent and it's a good spot for a happy-hour cocktail. Daily noon–11pm.

Pho Dac Biet (184) Busy local joint with plastic chairs and sticky menus, serving ample portions of pho (from 30,000VND), deep-fried spring rolls (50,000VND) and noodle dishes (30,000–60,000VND). Daily 7am–10pm.

The far north

Vietnam fans out above Hanoi, the majority of it a mountainous zone wrapped around the Red River Delta. The region is mostly wild and inaccessible, sparsely populated by a fascinating mosaic of **minority tribes** whose presence is the chief tourist attraction in the area. The popular hill station of **Sa Pa** is the main departure point for treks to minority villages. **Mai Chau** and **Bac Ha** are less-visited centres, Bac Ha famous for its Sunday market; those on Vietnam's war trail or en route to Laos will want to stop in **Dien Bien Phu**, while the **northwestern circuit** is a difficult but rewarding trip that takes you far off the beaten track.

THE NORTHWESTERN CIRCUIT

Highway 6 loops around Vietnam's northwest, skimming the borders of Laos and China, and passing through some of the country's most dramatic landscapes. The journey from Hanoi typically passes through **Mai Chau**, **Moc Chau**, **Son La**, **Dien Bien Phu** and **Muong Lay** before finishing in **Sa Pa** or Lao Cai. Terraced rice paddies, tropical rainforests, stilt-house minority villages and markets bursting with colour make a journey around the northwestern circuit one of the most spectacular in Southeast Asia. However, there is a reason why the route attracts so few tourists: the bumpy, unpaved road swerves around hairpin

bends, and landslides are common, causing serious delays even after a short spell of rain. Public transport takes the form of rickety old minivans crowded to twice their capacity, so the best way to travel is by motorbike. You can then detour off Highway 6 and on to smaller back roads, with even more stunning scenery and many Hmong, Black and White Thai, Dao and Muong villages, where it is usually possible to stay overnight in a local house. It takes at least a week to make the journey, and ten days to do so comfortably. **Guided motorbike** and **mountain-bike tours** of the region are offered by agents in Hanoi (see p.844) for between $100 and $125 per day all-inclusive. Northern Vietnam's final frontier is the **Ha Giang province** that borders China, with remote, spectacular mountain scenery; travel here requires permits due to to its proximity to the border.

LAO CAI

The Red River Valley runs northwest from Hanoi, and after 300km, pushing ever deeper into the mountains, you eventually reach the border town of **LAO CAI**, renowned for cross-border trade and all manner of illegal smuggling. Travellers tend to pass through en route to Sa Pa or if catching the bus **into China** en route to Kunming.

ARRIVAL AND DEPARTURE

By train Most people arrive on the night train from Hanoi; the train station is on the east bank of the Red River, just 3km south of the Chinese border. Several travel agents hook their own air-conditioned, soft-berth carriages up to the three nightly trains between Hanoi and Lao Cai (ⓦet-pumpkin.com, ⓦfansipantrain.com or ⓦlivitrans.com; from $30/berth). Vietnam Railways' (VR) carriages are almost as good; buy your tickets (hard a/c sleeper 290,000VND, soft a/c sleeper 350,000VND) in Hanoi, purchasing the return ticket at Sa Pa's VR office, or the train station in Lao Cai.

By bus Minibuses to Sa Pa (1hr; 50,000VND) meet the morning Hanoi trains; bear in mind that drivers have been known to overcharge foreign tourists, so if possible, double check with a local how much they're paying. Many hotels in Sa Pa offer pick-up if you've booked a room with them.

INTO CHINA: LAO CAI

The border crossing from Lao Cai into China is via the **Hekou border gate** (daily 7am–10pm), on the east bank of the Red River, 3km from the train station (around 25,000VND by *xe om*). Queues at immigration are longest in the early morning. Inside the Vietnamese border post building, there's an exchange desk that deals in dong, dollars and yuan. There's a bank across the street, and plenty of women hanging around eager to change cash. Across on the Chinese side, several high-quality a/c buses depart for **Kunming**, 520km away, from Hekou bus station, 100m from the border crossing (three in the morning, two sleeper services in the evening around 7pm; 12hr; $25). Visas for both countries must be arranged in advance. China is one hour ahead of Vietnam.

ACCOMMODATION AND EATING

Unless you arrive in the evening there's no need to stay in Lao Cai. The road outside the train station is lined with mediocre, overpriced restaurants.

Hotel Terminus (Hiep Van) 342 Nguyen Hue ⓣ020 3835470. Clean, spacious rooms opposite the train station. Rate includes breakfast. Double **300,000VND**

Peter Chef By the main train station building. A reasonably priced Vietnamese joint serving a mix of noodle, rice, meat and fish dishes. Mains from 70,000VND. Daily noon–10pm.

SA PA AND AROUND

Forty kilometres from Lao Cai, the small market town of **SA PA** perches dramatically on the western edge of a high plateau, overshadowed by imposing **Fansipan**, Vietnam's highest peak. A former hilltop retreat for French rulers, Sa Pa enjoys a refreshing climate and magnificent scenery, with vertiginous mountains plunging into lush green valleys terraced with rice paddies. From here it is possible to visit the outlying **minority villages** of H'mong, Dao, Tay and Giay peoples. Sa Pa is loveliest between July and September, when the rice terraces are green with crops, but is also busiest at that time; winter can be cold, but at least the town doesn't feel overcrowded. Weekdays throughout the year are quieter than weekends.

11

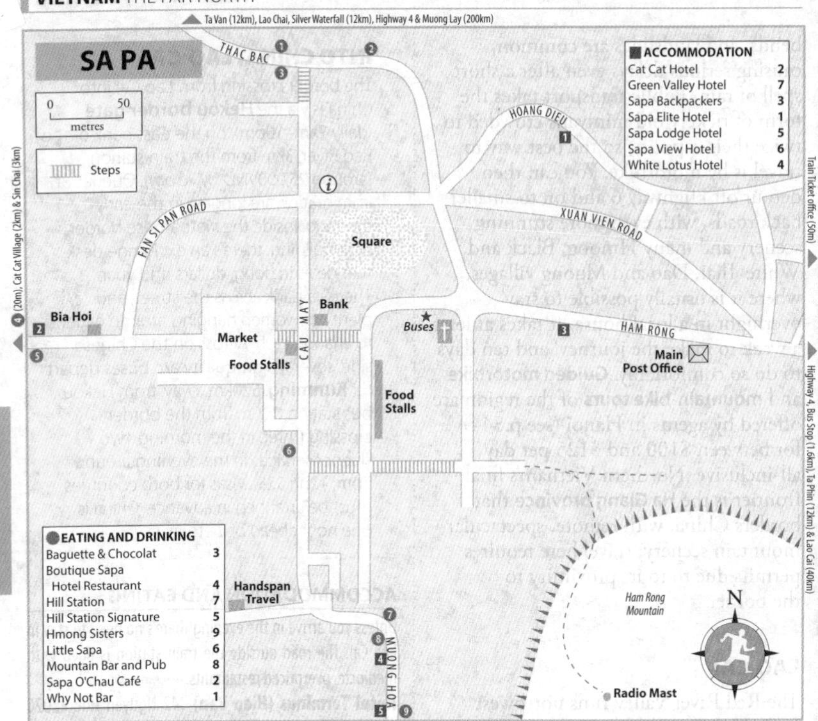

11

WHAT TO SEE AND DO

As part of the Vietnamese government's policy is to limit the minority tribes' contact with outsiders in order to isolate them, tourists are only allowed to visit the area around Sa Pa (including Ta Phin, Hoang Lien valley and Fansipan) with a **permit and guide**; only Cat Cat village can be explored solo. Permits are free and arranged by licensed tour agents for guided hikes in the area (see p.860).

Sa Pa market

In Sa Pa, the Hmong minority are a majority, and the **market**, busiest on Saturdays, draws in villagers from all around, with the women clad in their colourful finery. The evening "love market" sees local youths come to Sa Pa to try and find a love interest. However, tourists often outnumber locals and the market is more modest than those in Can Cau (see p.862) and Bac Ha (see p.862). It is, however, a good place to pick up pre-packed herbs if you want to try to re-create the spectacular Red Dao baths (see opposite) at home.

Cat Cat village

A steep, lovely 3km walk leads down into the valley from the western end of Fansipan road, reaching **CAT CAT** village (30,000VND entrance fee), a huddle of wooden houses hidden among fruit trees and bamboo. The hike offers spectacular views over the valley's terraced rice paddies. Look out for tubs of indigo dye outside the houses, used to colour the hemp cloth typical of Hmong dress. **Cat Cat waterfall** is just below the village. Bear in mind that the 30,000VND entrance fee is charged by a private company and none of the money goes to the community.

Ta Phin

Some of the most enjoyable guided treks in the area take you into the valley north of Sa Pa. The most popular is a gentle hike that skirts rice terraces and small

villages, with pot-bellied pigs rooting around in the dirt. You get great views of the valley during the walk, which culminates in a homestay in the Red Dao village of **TA PHIN**. Sapa O'Chau (see box, p.860) work with a particularly welcoming family who live in a traditional house with earthen floors and with smoked meat hanging above the fire. Don't miss the chance to try a traditional herbal bath, which involves soaking in a wooden tub; the fumes make you feel wonderfully relaxed and a little light-headed. From Ta Phin, treks take you to the Hmong village of **TRUNG CHAI** where hikers get picked up and taken back to Sa Pa.

Ta Van and Lao Chai

The most spectacular scenery in the area is in the Muong Hoa valley south of Sa Pa, with expansive views of rice terraces and villages below. The best of the guided treks takes you down into the valley into the Hmong village of **LAO CHAI**, from where you follow the road that meanders through the fields to **TA VAN**, a Dao village uphill from a Giay community. From here, treks either cross the river and join the main road for a pick-up back to Sa Pa, or carry on down the valley to stay overnight in the Tay village of **BAN HO**. Note that some tour groups do the well-trodden hike to Ta Van along the main road, where they have to contend with traffic.

Fansipan

Rising dramatically above the rest of the Hoang Lien Son mountain range is **Mount Fansipan**, Vietnam's highest peak at 3143m. The mountain lies within Hoang Lien Son Nature Reserve, a thirty-square-kilometre national park established in 1986 to protect the forest habitat. Fansipan's summit is 19km from Sa Pa and it is recommended to do the climb in one day, as the rudimentary camps along the way have been adversely affected by trash which attracts rats. An experienced **local guide** is essential; organized group excursions with all equipment can be arranged by reputable operators such as Sapa O'Chau (see box, p.860). There are no facilities on the mountain, so you will need to bring your own sleeping bag, tent and food supplies for overnight treks. It is not a technical climb, but a strenuous one, and day-trippers have to get up before sunrise to make it to the summit and back before dark. The view from the summit on a clear day rewards those who make it to the top, taking in the whole mountain

HIKING AROUND SA PA

Historically, all the peoples of northern Vietnam migrated from southern China at various times throughout history: those who arrived first, notably the Tay and Thai, settled in the fertile valleys, where they now lead a relatively prosperous existence, whereas late arrivals, such as groups of Hmong and Dao, were left to eke out a living on the inhospitable higher slopes. More than five million minority people (nearly two-thirds of Vietnam's total minority population) now live in the northern uplands, mostly in isolated villages. The largest ethnic groups are **Thai** and **Muong** in the northwest, **Tay** and **Nung** in the northeast, and **Hmong** and **Dao** dispersed throughout the region. Despite government efforts to forcibly integrate them into the Vietnamese community, many of the minorities in these remote areas continue to follow a way of life little changed over the centuries.

It is easy to arrive in Sa Pa independently and organize a local guide from there, rather than in Hanoi; it's of greater benefit to the local community and yourself if you have a guide from one of the surrounding villages. While throngs of Hmong women wait outside Sa Pa guesthouses to escort visitors to the surrounding villages, they only speak a smattering of English, and while all hotels can also arrange guides, many pay them poorly and send guests on the well-trodden trek along a main road to Ta Van (see above). Your best option is to join a small-group tour with Sapa O'Chau, Sapa Sisters, or Topas Travel – reputable operators that take you off the beaten track, have English-speaking guides and pay them fairly. Expect to pay from \$25 per person for a day hike, from \$60 for 2D1N, and from \$100 from 2D3N. If you have four days to spare, you can stay with three different minority tribes during the course of your hike. Meals and accommodation are included; bring sunblock and plenty of water.

SAPA O'CHAU

The brainchild of local Hmong girl, Shu Tan, **Sapa O'Chau** (8 Thac Bac, ⓣ 091 5351479, ⓦ sapaochau.com) was created to empower and educate the local Hmong youth, an endeavour in which Shu is ably assisted by expat Yorkshireman Peter Gilbert. Shu Tan herself started out by selling handicrafts to tourists as a child – many local children are kept out of school so that they can earn a living that way, or as tour guides. Alcoholism, domestic violence, marriage at a very young age and virtual illiteracy are also commonplace. Sapa O'Chau aims to educate the young Hmong generation to reduce the prevalence of such practices, providing education at the Sapa O'Chau Learning Centre – a live-in school where children learn English and Vietnamese to improve employment opportunities. Sapa O'Chau welcome volunteers and do some of the best trek-and-homestay combos in the region.

11

range of northwest Vietnam, south to Son La province, and north to the peaks of Yunnan in China.

ARRIVAL AND DEPARTURE

By bus Minibuses from Lao Cai (connecting from the Hanoi train) drop you along the main street, Cau May. To return to Lao Cai, minibuses congregate all day from near the church on the main square; your hotel can also arrange for you to be picked up from your lodgings. Tickets for the night trains from Lao Cai to Hanoi are in short supply, so book as far ahead as possible, either at the Lao Cai Railway Station Office in Sa Pa across from the bus station off Ngu Chi Son (daily 7am–4pm; ⓣ 020 3871480), or (more expensively) through your guesthouse. Vietbus (ⓣ 04 36272727) runs two daily sleeper buses directly to Hanoi (7.30am and 5.30pm; 10hr) from the Sa Pa bus station, a 30,000VND *xe om* ride from the centre. Minibuses also run from Sa Pa to Dien Bien Phu (7.30am; 9hr; from 190,000VND).

INFORMATION AND TOURS

Information The Tourism Information Centre of Sa Pa, 2 Fansipan (daily 7.30am–7.30pm; ⓣ 020 3871975, ⓦ SaPa-tourism.com), is unusually helpful, with good maps for sale (20,000VND), and free internet.

Tours Sapa O'Chau (see box above) are one of the best tour operators in and around Sa Pa. The Sapa Sisters – four Hmong girls who speak excellent English (as well as some French and Spanish) – offer guided day treks, longer treks with overnight stays in surrounding villages and the trek up Fansipan (ⓦ sapasisters.webs.com); email them in advance. Sa Pa-based Topas Travel at 24 Muong Hoa (ⓣ 091 387 1331, ⓦ topastravel.vn) offer hiking, biking and homestays, as well as sojourns at their highly regarded *Topas Eco Lodge*.

Motorbike rental Can be arranged through most hotels for around US$10/day. Keep in mind that roads around Sa Pa are narrow and winding, landslides are common, fog can make visibility extremely poor and alcohol-induced accidents are also common.

Services The Agribank at 1 Cau May can exchange cash and travellers' cheques. There are a few ATMs in town. There are several pharmacies on Cau May and the Post Office is at 6 Ham Rang (daily 7am–9pm).

ACCOMMODATION

Sa Pa is generally busy all year round, especially at weekends. Rooms can be in short supply in high season (March, April & Sept–Nov).

Cat Cat Hotel 46 Fansipan ⓣ 020 3502681. A popular terraced guesthouse just below the market, offering budget and mid-range rooms with fireplaces and panoramic views of Fansipan from the spacious balconies. There's also a decent restaurant. Double **$25**

Green Valley Hotel 45 Muong Hoa ⓣ 020 3871449. Somewhat grungy dorm rooms that have electric blankets and good showers in spite of being the cheapest beds in town, plus decent private rooms with stunning views of the valley below. Dorm **$6**, double **$14**

Sa Pa Backpackers Ham Rong ⓣ 016 44225438. Part hostel, part community centre for homeless children, run by a friendly family. Rooms could be a tad cleaner, and there's a 10pm curfew, but it's one of the cheapest spots in town. Dorm **$6**, double **$15**

Sa Pa Elite Hotel 12 Hoang Dieu ⓣ 020 3888368, ⓦ sapaelitehotel.com. Great central location, spacious rooms with

★TREAT YOURSELF

Sa Pa View Hotel Muong Hoa 41, ⓣ 020 3872388, ⓦ sapaview-hotel.com. Overlooking the valley below at the southern end of Muong Hoa, *Sa Pa View Hotel* offers more than just spectacular views: each of the five floors has a local minority tribe theme and the luxurious rooms have timber floors, old-style fireplaces and rain showers. The dining room serves delicious meals prepared from locally sourced ingredients and the hotel supports the local school for orphans. Double **$30**

ETIQUETTE

There's a whole debate about the **ethics of cultural tourism** and its negative impact on traditional ways of life. Most villagers are genuinely welcoming, appreciating contact with Westerners. Nonetheless, it's important to take a responsible attitude, and try not to cause offence. It's preferable to visit the minority villages as part of a **small group**, ideally four people or fewer, as this causes least disruption and allows for greater communication. Dress modestly (no shorts or vests), never take photographs without asking and only enter a house when invited, removing your shoes first and carrying your backpack in your hands; don't ever enter homes with leaves, bones or feathers hanging above the entrance. If you're staying overnight, remember that your hosts go to bed early and get up early. Respect religious rituals and symbols. To avoid fostering a culture of begging, rather than bringing gifts, see if you can contribute to the community in a meaningful way by donating to a local school, hiring a local guide and purchasing local crafts. Take all your litter with you.

king-sized beds, wooden floors, electric blankets and a choice of breakfasts make this a good option. On the downside, the staff don't speak much English. Double $25

Sa Pa Lodge Hotel 18A Muong Hoa ⓣ020 3772885, ⓦsapalodge.net. Though only some have incredible views of the valley below ($20), all rooms here are spacious and have a/c that doubles as a heater. Staff are very helpful. Double $10

White Lotus Hotel 8 Muong Hoa ⓣ020 3658668, ⓔthansapa@hotmail.com. A cheapie that's great value for money, with comfortable beds, attentive staff and good food at the on-site restaurant. If you're pinching your pennies, go for the cheapest rooms without views. Double $10

EATING AND DRINKING

For local barbecued meat, pho and rice dishes, try the food stalls on Pham Xuan Huan, parallel to Cau May. Stalls also pop up in the evenings by the market and along Ngu Chi Son, by Sa Pa Lake. There's a *bia hoi* on the corner of Cau May and Fansipan.

Baguette & Chocolat Thac Bac. For delicious breakfasts, bakery snacks, pizzas and Vietnamese favourites, look no further than this cosy branch of a Hanoian-based training school for disadvantaged youth. They also sell lunch packets for gourmet hikers. Mains 75,000VND. Daily 7.30am–9pm.

Boutique Sa Pa Hotel Restaurant 41 Fansipan. Beautifully presented dishes made from local ingredients – try the buffalo steak with pepper sauce (160,000VND) and other Hmong-themed delights. Daily 11.30am–10pm.

★Hill Station Signature 37 Phan Si Pan ⓦthehillstation.com/signature-restaurant. This former hill station, flooded with natural light and boasting unusual decor, specializes in traditional cuisine from the region, so expect the likes of sweet potato cooked over hot coals, dried buffalo meat, fresh spring rolls with raw trout and smoked pork belly. The only non-local item is Häagen-Dazs ice cream. Not to be confused with *Hill Station* on Muong Hoa, which is a deli. Mains from 75,000VND. Daily 12.30–10pm.

Hmong Sisters 31 Muong Hoa. Cosy little bar with thumping music, a good mix of locals and visitors, and a pool table to while away the evening. Daily 4pm–late.

Little Sa Pa 18 Cau May. The best bet for Vietnamese food, right in the middle of Sa Pa, the menu running the gamut from curries, pho and spring rolls to filled pancakes, enormous hotpots and mulled wine – perfect for warming your cockles on a cold evening. Mains from 60,000VND. Daily 11am–10pm.

Mountain Bar and Pub 2 Muong Hoa. Very popular night spot with lethal cocktails, raucous games of table football, shishas, massive hamburgers and pick-me-up warm apple wine. Daily 5pm–1am.

Sapa O'Chau Café 8 Thac Bac. A gathering point for hikers and homesick travellers, this cheerful café, part of the Sapa O'Chau tour agency, serves scrumptious beer-battered fish and chips, full English breakfasts, and a range of Vietnamese dishes. Great coffee, too. Mains from 60,000VND. Daily 8am–6pm.

Why Not Bar 2 Thac Bac. Tucked away a block from the main square, this friendly bar, run by a graduate of Hanoi's KOTO school for disadvantaged youths, has a free pool table, cheap beer (20,000VND) and cocktails for just 50,000VND, making it a great place to unwind after days of hiking. Daily noon–11pm.

SHOPPING

Sa Pa and the surrounding villages are a great place to pick up Hmong or Dao embroidered items – from clothing to bags and more; however, many sellers also peddle mass-produced Chinese items, so you need to be able to tell the difference. The lovely but very persistent Red Dao and Hmong ladies will find you the minute you set foot on Cau May, and they do have some quality items for sale (if you don't mind the hard sell). For more sedate browsing, check out the Indigo Cat shop at 46 Phan Xi Pang, which sells quality Hmong items. Finally, if you wish to try and re-create the Red Dao herbal bath (see p.859) at home, you can buy pre-packed bags of herbs at the market.

BAC HA AND AROUND

The small, untouristy town of **BAC HA**, nestling in a high valley 40km northeast of Highway 7, is a good base for exploring nearby minority villages. Numerous travellers also come here on a long day-excursion from Sa Pa, especially on Sunday for the lively and colourful local market.

WHAT TO SEE AND DO

Bac Ha is a far less commercial town than Sa Pa, and makes for a peaceful alternative, if you're looking to interact with local minority tribes without the hard sell employed by some of Sa Pa's tour agencies. Guided treks and trips around Bac Ha can be arranged through one indefatigable, knowledgeable local (see below).

Bac Ha Sunday Market

Bac Ha's **Sunday market** (6am–2pm) sees villagers of the Tay, Dao, Thai, Thulao, Xa Fang, Lachi, Fula, Nung, Giay and Flower Hmong ethnic minorities converging on the town, transforming the otherwise rather drab centre into a mass of colour and activity. Everything – from haircuts to suits, vats of rice wine and corn liquor to bundles of incense, and of course the usual vegetables, meat and dried fish – is on sale. The stunningly adorned Flower Hmong women trade embroidery, cloth and silver, and there's a large livestock fair to the rear of the market. Hotels in Sa Pa can organize a long day-trip to the Sunday market for about $15 per person, but it's far better to stay overnight in Bac Ha and visit the market early to avoid the Sunday crowds.

Hiking around Bac Ha

The picturesque Flower Hmong hamlet of **BAN PHO**, 3km from town, makes a pleasant stroll. Take the road half left at the hammer-and-sickle sign and head down past the *Sao Mai Hotel*, turning left immediately after the next big building, which is the local hospital. The road continues up the hill for 2km after the village, and affords good views of the valley; you can carry on to the nearby village of **Na Kheo**. Other good day hikes include an 8km return walk to the village of **Tireu Cai** and a 6km return walk to **Na Ang** village; both are best done with a local guide.

Can Cau market

The village of **CAN CAU**, 19km north of Bac Ha, hosts a market each Saturday, which is well worth visiting. The emphasis is on livestock, especially buffalo, with traders trekking in from as far afield as China in search of bargains. Relatively few visitors get here, and the fair retains much of its authenticity; you may well be invited to drink some *ruou* with the locals. It's possible to arrange guided trips from Bac Ha that take in the market and include an afternoon trek to the nearby Fula village.

ARRIVAL AND INFORMATION

By bus Local buses terminate at Bac Ha's bus station, near the market's south entrance in the centre of town. Tourist buses running directly to Sa Pa depart from the main square outside the post office between 1pm and 2pm on Sundays; and regular minibuses depart for Sa Pa from Lao Cai. To get to Bac Ha from Sa Pa, it's easier and quicker to join a tour ($15), which will include the market and a short trek, with the option of being dropped off at Lao Cai on the way back if catching a night train to Hanoi. A motorbike from Sa Pa takes three hours and costs $30–35, from Lao Cai $25.

Information Operating out of *Hoang Vu Guesthouse*, Mr Nghe is by far the best source of information on the area, and his website ⓦ bachatouurist.com is a great starting point for planning your trip.

ACCOMMODATION AND EATING

The town's hotels and restaurants are clustered around the square near the post office.

Cong Fu Hotel ⓣ 020 3880254. Smart mini-hotel offering the most modern accommodation in Bac Ha; some rooms have huge windows overlooking the livestock market. The restaurant (daily 11am–9pm) is popular with the Sunday tourists for its cheap rice and noodle dishes (from 50,0000VND). Double $25

★ **Hoang Vu Hotel** ⓣ 020 880264, ⓦ bachatouurist.com. Basic but friendly hotel with ten large en-suite rooms. The owner, Mr Nghe, knows everything there is to know about the surrounding area and can arrange all manner of tours and transport, and rent out motorbikes. Double $10

Ngan Nga Bac Ha Hotel 115–117 Ngoc Uyen ⓣ 020 3880286, ⓦ nganngabachahotel.com. The rooms are spacious though a little worn, and the family that runs this place is friendly and helpful; you can even sweet-talk

them into making you a picnic lunch for your hike. The restaurant fills with day-trippers on Sundays, with an enormous selection of Vietnamese food and set menus for 115,000VND. Double $20

Sao Mai Hotel Restaurant A more sophisticated menu than most places in town, serving decent European and Vietnamese dishes at reasonable prices (mains around 80,000VND, rice and noodle dishes 40,000VND). Daily 11.30am–10pm.

MAI CHAU

The minority villages of the fertile **Mai Chau Valley**, inhabited mainly by White Thai people, related to tribes in Thailand, Laos and China, are close enough to Hanoi (150km) to make this a popular destination, particularly at weekends. The valley is still largely unspoilt, a peaceful scene of rice fields and jagged mountains. **MAI CHAU** is the valley's main village, a friendly, quiet place that suddenly bursts into life for its **Sunday market** (7am–3pm), when minority people – who, unlike in Sa Pa, have largely forsaken their traditional dress (though the women still produce beautifully-embroidered clothing) – trek in. Polite bargaining is the norm here, rather than the hard sell. You can overnight in Mai Chau, but it's more interesting to head for the outlying villages.

The most accessible village in the Mai Chau Valley is **BAN LAC**, a White Thai settlement where you can buy hand-woven textiles, watch performances of traditional dancing and sleep overnight in a stilt house; expect to pay around 160,000VND per person per night, plus breakfast. There is a good trek between Ban Lac and the Hmong **Xa Linh village**, 18km away; an overnight stay in a village en route is the norm, as it's quite a tough trek for one day, with 600m elevation.

ARRIVAL AND INFORMATION

By bus You can either come to the Mai Chau Valley on an organized tour from Hanoi or take a bus from Hanoi's My Dinh bus station (several between 8am and 2pm; 3hr 45min); a fee of 5000VND may be required to enter the village.

Accommodation Stilt house accommodation (split-level thatched-roof houses with bamboo floors, electricity and Western toilets) is easy to find and needn't be booked in advance.

INTO LAOS: TAY TRANG

A relatively straightforward border crossing operates at **Tay Trang** (daily 7am–7pm), 31km from Dien Bien Phu. Local buses depart from the bus station in **Dien Bien Phu** (daily 5.30am; 8hr; 100,000VND; buy ticket the day before) to the town of Muang Khoua on the Laos side, from where you can catch a boat down the Nam Ou River to Muang Ngoi or Nong Khiaw. Several daily buses depart from Muang Khoua for elsewhere in the region; for onward travel to Luang Prabang, take a bus to Oudomxai and from there a bus to Luang Prabang. One-month Lao visas are available on arrival for $40–50; you'll need two passport photos. If you need to stay in Dien Bien Phu, the *Viet Hoang Hotel* opposite the bus station (67 Tran Dang Ninh; ☎ 020 3735046; 200,000VND) will do in a pinch.

11

The central provinces

Vietnam's narrow waist comprises a string of provinces squeezed between the long, sandy coastline and the formidable barrier of the Truong Son Mountains, which mark the border between Vietnam and Laos. The most heavily bombed during the war, this is also one of the most beautiful parts of Vietnam. The **Phong Nha–Ke Bang National Park** is as yet an unspoilt part of the country, with the world's largest cave, lush green countryside, friendly village life and dramatic karst its main attractions. In 1954, Vietnam was divided at the Seventeenth Parallel, only 100km or so south of here, where the **Demilitarized Zone** (**DMZ**) marked the border between North and South Vietnam until reunification in 1975. The desolate battlefields of the DMZ and the extraordinary complex of residential tunnels at nearby **Vinh Moc** are a poignant memorial to those who fought here on both sides, and to the civilians who lost their lives in the bitter conflict. Further south lies the city of **Hue**, its central role

in imperial Vietnam evident in an immense citadel and wealth of royal tombs. The coastal city of **Da Nang** boasts some spectacular cave temples, while further south still, the riverside town of **Hoi An** is one of Vietnam's most charming destinations and a highlight of the region. Renowned for its hundreds of tailor shops, crafts, traditional Chinese merchants' houses and temples, and some of the best food in the country, it also makes a good base for exploring the fine ruins of the Cham temple complex at nearby **My Son**.

PHONG NHA–KE BANG NATIONAL PARK

Consisting of 885 square kilometres of unspoilt jungle, the mountainous **PHONG NHA–KE BANG NATIONAL PARK** stretches up to the border with Laos and is an area of incredible biodiversity. A UNESCO World Heritage Site since 2003, its ancient karst mountains hide extensive cave systems, many of which haven't yet been explored properly, and are home to more than one hundred species of mammal, including tigers, elephants and monkeys, as well as more than three hundred species of bird. The subterranean highlights are Phong Nha Cave, one of the longest in the world, and, Son Doong, the world's largest cave, properly explored for the first time in 2009 (see box opposite).

WHAT TO SEE AND DO

As this was the most heavily shelled region of Vietnam during the Vietnam War, there is no question of solo treks into the jungle, though guided jungle treks combined with caving are available (see p.866). A beautiful stretch of the Ho Chi Minh Trail also passes through the park.

Son Trach

The largest village in the park is **SON TRACH** (or Phong Nha Town), a spread-out, mostly one-street settlement that sits along the slow-flowing Song Con River, surrounded by karst mountains covered in lush vegetation. This is where you find the boat dock, a smattering of budget hotels and restaurants and other amenities. Life here runs at a sedate pace, apart from during the raucous celebrations for the Tet festival (see p.837). It's an easy bicycle or motorbike ride 10km through the countryside toward Dong Hoi to reach **Khuong Ha**, a smaller village with some of the best accommodation.

Phong Nha Cave

Discovered in 2005, **Phong Nha Cave** is the park's most popular attraction, reached via a 45-minute sedate ride in a dragon boat from Son Trach dock. "Phong Nha" means "cave of teeth", and the "teeth", or stalagmites, are indeed numerous, illuminated by multicoloured lights along with the turrets and stony cascades of myriad other rock formations. Visitors may only access a 1km section of the cave, though the cave is actually a staggering 55km long. As the boat enters the cave mouth, the boatman turns off the engine and switches to oars, rowing silently as you watch the subtly lit rock formations pass by in the semi-gloom. You're then deposited on a sandy beach, from where you make your way out of the cave on foot to the boat landing.

Outside, a steep flight of 330 steps leads up to the smaller **Tien Son Cave**, used as a makeshift hospital by the Viet Cong during the Vietnam War. Even if you don't enter the cave, the climb is worth it for the expansive views over the countryside; the pools of water in the fields are former bomb craters.

You'll need to purchase tickets for the two caves (60,000VND each) and for the boat (320,000VND) at the jetty in Son Trach; if you can get other people to share your boat, it works out significantly cheaper per person. Seasonal flooding means that Phong Nha Cave may be closed in November and December, and on weekends, especially in summer, both caves tend to be mobbed by Vietnamese tourists.

Paradise Cave

The third-largest cave in the park, and reputedly the world's biggest cave without any water source, **Paradise Cave** (daily 7.30am–4.30pm; 150,000VND) is greater than 31km in length, though

THE WORLD'S LARGEST CAVE

Found by local hunter Ho Khanh in 1991 and explored for the first time by British cavers, led by Howard Limbert, in 2009, **Son Doong cave** (ⓦ sondoongcave.org) is a natural phenomenon. It is the world's largest cave – almost double the size of Malaysia's Deer Cave, the world's second largest. It is 449m tall at its highest point, its caverns are big enough to accommodate an entire city, and where the roof has collapsed, enormous skylights have allowed two separate jungles to flourish, with 50m-tall trees home to monkeys, eagles, hornbills and other wildlife.

Access to the cave is very limited, with a view to preserving the pristine environment. Oxalis Adventure Tours (see p.866) have permission to take a total of 224 visitors into the cave during the course of a year in small groups. The ultimate caving adventure, the six-day expedition involves more than two dozen porters and expert guides. Everything is carried back out of the cave, even the composting toilets. At the time of writing, the cost of this expedition was $3000 per person, with at least $1000 going to the national park; tickets are snapped up almost instantly on release.

visitors are only allowed access to a small part of it. To reach the cave, which is fairly high up, you either have to take a steep set of steps or else a more circuitous trail up the side of the small mountain. Uneven steps lead down into the deceptively small entrance, but as soon as you enter, you immediately feel like the Hobbit in the lair of Smaug – tiny and insignificant compared to the sheer size of the cavern, its twisted and sculpted rock formations glimmering with quartz fragments in the subtle light. A boardwalk takes you into the bowels of the earth, with numerous viewpoints along the way.

Paradise Cave lies around 14km southwest of Son Trach. There are a couple of restaurants at the car park and buggies will ferry you the 1.5km to the steps that lead up to the cave ($5 return per buggy; buy ticket along with entry ticket).

Ho Chi Minh Trail Loop

A spectacular and sometimes steep section of the Ho Chi Minh Trail ribbons its way through the park. The **Eight Ladies' Cave**, in which eight young locals died when they took shelter during an American bombing, makes a poignant stop. The bombs dislodged a rock that sealed the cave, making it their tomb.

The road running back towards Son Trach passes the **Nuoc Mooc Eco-trail** (daily 7am–5pm; 60,000VND), a set of wooden walkways next to a turquoise waterhole fed by a subterranean river, and a wonderful place to swim and sunbathe.

Near Son Trach, you pass a **cemetery** filled with tombs sporting multicoloured towers; most villagers still practise kin worship and come to tend the ancestral graves. Almost directly opposite is a brand-new Catholic church; many villagers have converted to Catholicism over the last couple of years in return for financial incentives provided by American missionaries.

ARRIVAL AND DEPARTURE

By plane The airport is 6km north of Son Trach; taxis cost around 90,000VND.

Destinations Hanoi (4 weekly; 1hr 20min); HCMC (4 weekly; 1hr 45min).

By bus There are no public buses to Son Trach. The nearest town on the public bus route is Dong Hoi, 50km southeast; open-tour buses can drop you off here on request. Transfers can be arranged between Dong Hoi and Son Trach through *Phong Nha Farmstay* (see p.866). A convenient daily shuttle minibus runs between *Easy Tiger* (see p.866) in Son Trach and *Hue Backpackers* (see p.873) in Hue, departing at 7.30am and stopping at the Vinh Moc tunnels at the DMZ along the way (500,000VND).

Destinations (from Dong Hoi) Hanoi (9hr–12hr 30min); Hue (2hr 30min–6hr).

By train North- and south-bound trains pass through Dong Hoi; the train station is 3km west of the centre.

Destinations (from Dong Hoi) Hanoi (7 daily; 9hr–12hr 30min); Hue (9 daily, 2hr 30min–6hr), HCMC (5 daily; 22hr –25hr 30min).

INFORMATION AND TOURS

Services The cash machine in Son Trach works most of the time, but bring plenty of cash just in case. Bicycles ($3–5/day), and motorbikes ($7–10/day) can be rented from guesthouses and hotels.

Tour operators Oxalis Adventure Tours, (@oxalis.com.vn) run extremely professional, well-organized caving and trekking tours to the Tu Lan cave system and Hang En cave. Oxalis is also the only operator that has permission to lead seven-day adventure tours into Son Doong cave (see box, p.865); beware of dodgy operators in Dong Hoi who fleece travellers by charging them $1000, promising to take them to Son Doong and taking them to another cave altogether.

ACCOMMODATION

Easy Tiger Son Trach 052 3677844, easytigerphongnha@gmail.com. Orange, Aussie-run multistorey backpacker magnet, with clean, comfortable dorms and staff who know their stuff. All manner of local adventures organized. Dorm $8

11

Ho Khanh's Homestay Son Trach 091 6794506, phong-nha-homestay.com. At the western end of the village, 2km from the centre, this delightful homestay run by Khanh – the hunter who originally discovered the world's biggest cave – and his welcoming family consists of three cosy, fan-cooled doubles overlooking the river. Happy puppies scamper about the property and you're greeted in the morning with strong, sweet coffee and views of the mist-shrouded karst across the river. Double $30

★**Pepperhouse** Kuong Ha pepperhouse-homestay.com. Sitting amid tranquil countryside and surrounded by pepper trees, this is the home of loquacious Aussie "Multi", a fount of local knowledge, and his wife Diem. The dorm and doubles are basic but comfortable, the home-cooked food is delicious and the communal nature of the meals encourages socializing. Dorm 200,000VND, double 400,000VND

Phong Nha Lakeside Resort Kuong Ha, Hung Trach 012 64746876, phongnhalakehouse.com. Besides the most luxurious dorms that you're likely to see in Vietnam, with proper two-tiered beds and mosquito nets, this Australian-run guesthouse, owned by Tony and his wife Tham, has expansive views over a lake from the terrace, a lively bar and restaurant and spacious en-suite "rustic chic" villas and bungalows, the latter with own garden areas. Tony has motorbikes for rent ($10/day). Dorm $8, double $35

Thang Dat Hotel 052 3677328. The pick of the budget hotels along Son Trach's only street, this centrally-located option is friendly, comes with comfortable beds, clean rooms and reliable wi-fi. Double $12

★TREAT YOURSELF

Phong Nha Farmstay 094 4759864, phong-nha-cave.com. Phong Nha's most luxurious accommodation is this lodge, with its tall ceilings and dark wood accents, delicious Asian and Western food, a pool table and bar, and motorbikes and bicycles for rent. Cosy en-suite rooms offer great sunset views over the rice paddies and there's a swimming pool for dipping. Helpful owners Ben and Bich can not only advise you on the surrounding attractions, but also arrange excellent tours of the park. 600,000VND

EATING AND DRINKING

The guesthouses listed here all offer good food.

Cavern Bar Son Trach. Friendly bar serving a good mix of Western and Vietnamese dishes. The owner goes out of his way to be helpful and is full of useful info about the area. Daily noon–10pm.

Easy Tiger Son Trach. *Easy Tiger's* on-site restaurant dishes out shepherd's pie, burgers and other Western comfort food, as well as hefty breakfasts, Vietnamese fried rice, spring rolls and noodle dishes. Mains from 60,000VND. Daily 7.30am–10pm.

Pub with Cold Beer Kuong Ha. Cycle south down a dirt road from Kuong Ha (arm yourself with a map from your homestay), haul your bike across the river, fling yourself into a hammock and enjoy a cold beer. If you're hungry and there's several of you, the friendly proprietress will kill and cook a chicken. Daily 7am–8.30pm.

Viet Binh Son Trach. Though it looks nondescript, this is the best spot in town for Vietnamese food, with tofu dishes, sticky ribs, stir-fried morning glory, steamed fish and excellent French fries. Mains from 40,000VND. Daily 11.30am–9.30pm.

THE DMZ

Under the terms of the 1954 Geneva Accords, Vietnam was split in two along the Seventeenth Parallel. The demarcation line ran along the Ben Hai River and was sealed by a strip of no-man's-land 5km wide on each side known as the **Demilitarized Zone**, or **DMZ**. The two provinces either side of the DMZ were the most heavily bombed and saw the highest casualties, civilian and military, American and Vietnamese, during the American War. So much firepower was unleashed over this area, including napalm and herbicides, that for years nothing would grow in the chemical-laden soil, but the region's low, rolling hills are now mostly reforested and green. There's not that much to see here nowadays, besides the museums at Ben Hai, Vinh Moc and Khe Sanh, but Quang

UNEXPLODED ORDNANCE

Casualties of the Vietnam War persist to this day, due to an estimated 350,000 to 800,000 tonnes of unexploded ordnance and more than 3 million mines that still remain uncleared. From 1975 to the present day, unexploded ordnance in Vietnam has resulted in more than 100,000 injuries and 45,000 deaths. Each year, around 1000 people die and almost twice as many are injured, mainly in the countryside; the number of children and members of minority tribes is disproportionately high. Don't stray from marked paths when hiking and check out the work of such NGOs as Mines Advisory Group (maginternational.org) and Clear Path International (learpathinternational.org); the former work to dispose of the ordnance and the latter help survivors of landmine and UXO accidents through various community projects.

Tri, Hamburger Hill and other names live in infamy due to the bloody battles fought there, so visiting the locations alone is meaningful enough to those interested in the country's recent history.

WHAT TO SEE AND DO

You can explore the DMZ independently, but it's highly recommended to take a local **guide** who will be able to show you the unmarked sites and will know which paths are free from **unexploded mines** (see box above). The daily **DMZ bus** day-trip starting in Hue (from 6am–6pm; $18 including entrance fees and breakfast) is the easiest way to see the most important places and can be booked at most travel agents. As well as the sights detailed below (barring Hamburger Hill), the day-trip takes in the **Rockpile**, a 230m-high karst used by the US as an artillery base and lookout, a section of the **Ho Chi Minh Trail** and the touristy **Van Kieu Bru minority village**. This tour involves a lot of driving, with short stops for photographs, and your understanding of the area depends a great deal on how good the guide is. For an in-depth tour, it's better to spend a few dollars more and hire a car or motorbike and guide from Hue or Dong Ha.

Vinh Moc tunnels

The creation of the **Vinh Moc** tunnels was an impressive feat and they're the highlight of the DMZ. To provide shelter from constant American air raids, from 1966 villagers spent two years digging more than fifty tunnels. All were constructed on three levels at 10, 15 and 20–23m deep, with freshwater wells, a generator and lights. The underground village had a school, clinics, and a maternity room where seventeen children were born. Families of up to five people were each allocated a tiny cavern, and were only able to emerge at night; the lack of fresh air and the smoke from the kerosene lamps and cooking caused respiratory problems, and the lack of sunlight also impacted on the villagers' health. In 1972, the villagers finally abandoned their tunnels and rebuilt their homes above ground. A section of the tunnels has been restored and opened to visitors, with a small museum at the entrance (daily 7am–5pm; 40,000VND).

11

Doc Mieu Firebase

The American front line comprised a string of firebases looking north across the DMZ. The most accessible of these is **Doc Mieu Firebase**, where a number of bunkers built by the North Vietnamese Army (NVA) still stand amid a landscape pocked with craters. Before the NVA overran Doc Mieu in 1972, the base played a pivotal role in the South's defence, and for a while, this was the command post for calling in airstrikes along the Ho Chi Minh Trail.

Con Thien Firebase

The largest American installation along the DMZ was **Con Thien Firebase**, which, in the lead-up to the 1968 Tet Offensive, became the target of prolonged shelling. The Americans replied with everything in their arsenal, but the NVA finally overran the base in the summer of 1972. From the single remaining US-built bunker in the ruined lookout post on Con Thien's highest point you get a great view over the DMZ and directly north to former enemy positions on the opposite bank of the Ben Hai River.

INTO LAOS: LAO BAO, CAU TREO AND NAM CAN

It's possible to cross into Laos at three border crossings in the central provinces. Long-distance tourist buses depart from Da Nang, Hue and Hanoi. Thirty-day tourist visas for Laos are available at all three crossings (about $35, depending on your nationality).

THE LAO BAO BORDER CROSSING

The **Lao Bao** border crossing (daily 7am–6pm) is the most popular of Vietnam's overland routes into Laos. There are daily buses from Hue to **Savannakhet** in Laos, leaving between 6am and 8am, arriving at around 5pm, and you can also opt for Sinh Tourist (see p.873) buses (from 300,000VND), which leave Hue on odd days at 7am and arrive in **Savannakhet** in Laos at around 5pm; in Hue, you can also buy tickets for sleeper buses all the way to Vientiane (around 700,000VND), which arrive at around 9am the following day.

THE CAU TREO BORDER CROSSING

It is also possible to cross the border at **Cau Treo** (daily 7am–6pm), 95km west of the city of **Vinh** on Highway 8, though overcharging and delays are common. From Vinh's provincial bus station (Ben Xe Cho Vinh), about 500m from Vinh's market, several morning buses depart for Tay Son (formerly Trung Tam) from 6am, the last settlement of any size before the border. There are morning buses from Tay Son to Lak Sao but you have to get there mid-morning in order to make the connection. From here, you'll either have to pick up a motorbike taxi for the last 35km to Cau Treo, or catch one of the regular shuttle buses that ferry locals to the border. Alternatively, hotels in Vinh can arrange a share taxi all the way to the border for around $50, or a *xe om* for $25. An easier option are the Laos-bound buses, booked in Hanoi (see p.844), that trundle through this border en route to Vientiane. Facilities at Cau Treo amount to about half a dozen pho stalls, so sort out money (carrying dollars is best) and anything else you need before leaving.

THE NAM CAN–NONG HET BORDER CROSSING

The **Nam Can** border crossing (daily 7am–5pm) is also accessible from Vinh, and near Nong Het in Laos, convenient for Phonsavan and the Plain of Jars (see p.379). Direct buses depart from Vinh to Phonsavan on Wed, Fri, Sat and Sun at 6am (300,000VND; 13hr); going the other way, buses that claim to take passengers all the way to Hanoi can leave them in Vinh.

The Ben Hai River

Right next to Highway 1, a bridge lined with Vietnam's flags spans the Ben Hai River. On the south bank there is a grandiose reunification monument, the heroic figure holding stylized palm leaves. On the north bank, there's a reconstructed flag tower with Socialist mosaics around its base. The museum (daily 7am–5pm; 20,000VND) across the road features wartime photos and mementoes.

The Truong Son Cemetery

The **Truong Son War Martyr Cemetery** is dedicated to the estimated 25,000 men, women and children – some soldiers were as young as twelve – who died on the Truong Son Trail, better known in the West as the Ho Chi Minh Trail. Around 300,000 North Vietnamese soldiers were missing in action – far, far more than a total of 10,036 graves lie in this cemetery; each simple headstone announces *liet si* ("martyr").

Khe Sanh

The **battle of Khe Sanh** attracted worldwide media attention and, along with the simultaneous Tet Offensive, demonstrated the futility of the US's efforts to contain its enemy. The North Vietnam Army's (NVA) attack on the US base at Khe Sanh began in the early hours of January 21, 1968, and the battle lasted nine weeks, during which time the US pounded the area with nearly 100,000 tonnes of bombs, averaging one airstrike every five minutes, backed up by napalm and defoliants. The NVA were so well dug in that they continued to return fire, despite horrendous casualties. By the middle of March, the NVA had all but gone, having successfully diverted American resources away from southern

cities prior to the Tet Offensive. The battle cost 500 American lives, 10,000 North Vietnamese lives and uncounted civilian lives. Three months later, the Americans also withdrew, leaving a plateau that resembled a lunar landscape, contaminated for years to come with chemicals and explosives; gazing at the lush greenery and coffee plantations that cover the place now, it's difficult to imagine.

Hamburger Hill

Right near the border with Laos, **Hamburger Hill** is where a massive infantry battle (immortalized in a film of the same name) took place in May 1969, resulting in the deaths of 72 Americans and more than 600 Vietnamese. It's possible to visit the bunkers, trenches and war memorial by first obtaining a permit in the nearby town of Aluoi.

HUE

A UNESCO World Heritage Site since 1993, **HUE** is the city of the Nguyen emperors. The city has suffered extensive damage, both when the French destroyed much of the once-magnificent Imperial City, and during the 1968 **Tet Offensive**, when the North Vietnamese Army (NVA) held Hue for 25 days, and the city was all but levelled in the ensuing counter-assault.

Nevertheless, some magnificent historical sights remain – including the nineteenth-century walled citadel, and seven palatial royal mausoleums in the city's outskirts.

Hue is the main starting point for day-tours of the DMZ, as well as a springboard for buses to Savannakhet in Laos, via the Lao Bao border (see box opposite) and a handy connection to Phong Nha National Park.

WHAT TO SEE AND DO

Built astride the wide, slow-flowing **Perfume River**, with its pleasant, tree-lined boulevards, abundance of historic sights, beautiful buildings and picturesque surrounding countryside, Hue repays exploration at a leisurely pace. The imperial **citadel** stands on the northern bank of the river, while the southern bank hosts the majority of the city's hotels and restaurants. The city is easily navigated on foot, while the best way to visit outlying **temples** and **mausoleums** and enjoy the surrounding countryside is by renting a bicycle or motorbike, or on the back of a *xe om*.

The citadel

Hue's days of glory kicked off in the early nineteenth century when Emperor Gia Long, founder of the **Nguyen dynasty**, moved the capital here and laid out a vast **citadel**, comprising three concentric enclosures. The city must have been truly awe-inspiring in its heyday; today, only twenty of the original 148 buildings survive, though the citadel is as imposing as ever, with a large chunk of Hue's residents still living within its 10km-long, 2m-thick walls.

Ten gates pierce the citadel wall: you enter through Ngan Gate, east of the flag tower. A second moat and defensive wall inside the citadel guard the **Imperial City** (daily 7am–5.30pm; 100,000VND), which follows the same symmetrical layout along a north–south axis as Beijing's Forbidden City, though on a much smaller scale. By far the most impressive of its four gates is south-facing **Ngo Mon**, the Imperial City's principal entrance and a masterpiece of Nguyen architecture. The gate itself has five entrances: the central one for the emperor, two for civil and military mandarins, and two for the royal elephants. Perched on top is an elegant pavilion called the **Five Phoenix Watchtower** as its nine roofs are said to resemble five birds in flight. Facing Ngo Mon, **Thai Hoa Palace**, dating from 1883, boasts a spectacular interior glowing with sumptuous red and gold lacquers. This was where major imperial ceremonies were held; it's well worth watching the introduction video for the digital reconstruction of the Citadel.

The **Forbidden Purple City**, enclosed by a low wall, was the personal domain of the emperor; only eunuch servants and concubines were allowed in. Many of the residential palaces are nothing but

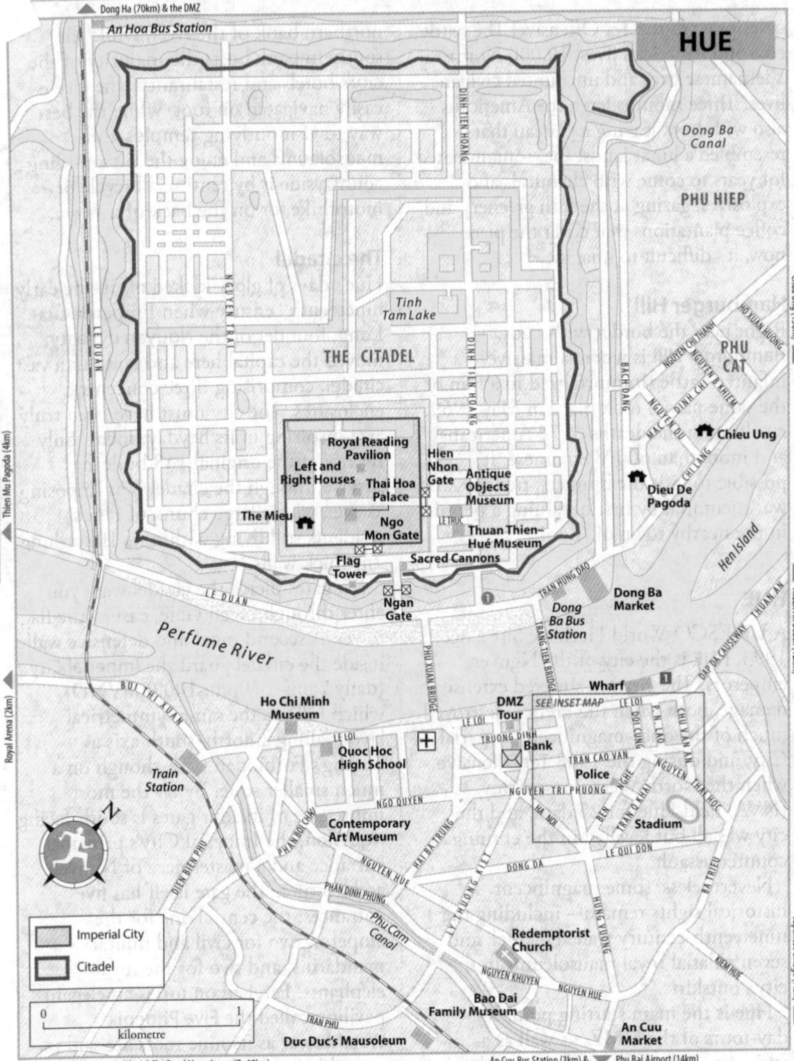

HUE

Dong Ha (70km) & the DMZ

An Hoa Bus Station

Dong Ba Canal

PHU HIEP

Chua Ong (150m)

PHU CAT

Chieu Ung

Dieu De Pagoda

Hen Island

Thuan An Beach (12km)

Tinh Tam Lake

THE CITADEL

Royal Reading Pavilion

Left and Right Houses

Thai Hoa Palace

Hien Nhon Gate

Antique Objects Museum

The Mieu

Ngo Mon Gate

Thuan Thien–Hué Museum

Flag Tower

Sacred Cannons

Ngan Gate

Dong Ba Market

Dong Ba Bus Station

Perfume River

Wharf

Ho Chi Minh Museum

DMZ Tour

Bank

Quoc Hoc High School

Police

Train Station

Contemporary Art Museum

Stadium

Redemptorist Church

Phu Cam Canal

Bao Dai Family Museum

Duc Duc's Mausoleum

An Cuu Market

Thien Mu Pagoda (4km)

Royal Arena (2km)

Japanese Bridge (7km)

Imperial City

Citadel

0 1 kilometre

Hon Chen Temple (9km) & The Royal Mausoleums (7–10km)

An Cuu Bus Station (3km) & Phu Bai Airport (14km)

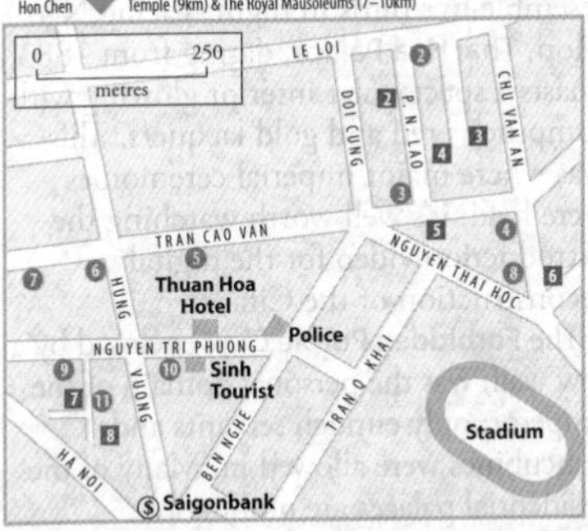

SEE INSET MAP

Streets: Le Duan, Nguyen Trai, Dinh Tien Hoang, Le Truc, Bach Dang, Nguyen Chi Thanh, Ho Xuan Huong, Nguyen B Khiem, Dinh Chi, Mac Dinh Chi, Nguyen Du, Chi Lang, Tran Hung Dao, Trang Tien Bridge, Phu Xuan Bridge, Dap Da Causeway, Thuan An, Bui Thi Xuan, Le Loi, Truong Dinh, Doi Cung, P. N. Lao, Chu Van An, Tran Cao Van, Nguyen Thai Hoc, Nguyen Tri Phuong, Ha Noi, Ben Nghe, Tran Q Khai, Ngo Quyen, Phan Boi Chau, Dien Bien Phu, Hai Ba Trung, Nguyen Hue, Phan Dinh Phung, Ly Thuong Kiet, Dong Da, Le Qui Don, Hung Vuong, Ba Trieu, Kiem Hue, Nguyen Khuyen, Nguyen Hue, Tran Phu

Inset map: 0 250 metres; Le Loi, Doi Cung, P. N. Lao, Chu Van An, Tran Cao Van, Nguyen Thai Hoc, Hung Vuong, Thuan Hoa Hotel, Police, Nguyen Tri Phuong, Sinh Tourist, Ha Noi, Ben Nghe, Tran Q Khai, Stadium, Saigonbank

EATING, DRINKING & NIGHTLIFE

La Boulangerie Française	10
Brown Eyes	8
Café on Thu Wheels	11
DMZ Bar	2
Lac Thien	1
Mandarin Café	7
Omar Khayyam's Indian Restaurant	9
Phuong Nam	5
Take	6
Xuan Trang	3
Why Not Bar	4

ACCOMMODATION

Canh Tien	3
Hue Backpackers Hostel	2
Jade Hotel	6
Phoenix Hotel Hue	1
Phong Lan (Wild Orchid)	4
Star City Hotel	5
Sunny A Hotel	8
Sunny C Hotel	7

grass-covered stone outlines today, thanks to the damage inflicted by the French as they attempted to retake the city in 1947. The **Royal Reading Pavilion**, an appealing, two-tier structure surrounded by bonsai, and the nearby Royal Theatre are all that remain intact; the latter holds music performances (9am, 10am, 2.30pm, 3.30pm; 100,000VND). The beautifully restored dynastic **Mieu temple**, a decorous low, red-lacquerwork building in the south corner of the citadel complex, has a row of thirteen altar tables dedicated to the Nguyen royal emperors. Behind it is the partially ruined **Dien Tho Residence** where the queen mothers resided, followed by the **Truong San Residence** with its splendid dragon-and-phoenix gate.

Thien Mu Pagoda

Founded in 1601 by Nguyen Hoang, **Thien Mu Pagoda** (daily 7am–5pm; free), 4km from Hue, is the oldest in **Hue** and has long been a hotbed of Buddhist protest against repression. In 1963, it hit international headlines when one of its monks, Thich Quang Duc, immolated himself in Saigon in protest at the excesses of President Diem's repressive regime. The monk's powder-blue Austin car is now on display here, with a copy of the famous photograph that shocked the world. The seven tiers of the octagonal, brick stupa each represent one of Buddha's incarnations on earth. Thien Mu Pagoda is included on most boat trips along the river (see box above), but is also within **cycling** distance of Hue (30min). Follow Le Duan (Highway 1) west along the river.

The Mausoleum of Tu Duc

Emperor Tu Duc was a romantic poet and a weak king, who ruled Vietnam from 1847 to 1883. His mausoleum is the most harmonious of all those in Hue. It took only three years to complete (1864–67), allowing Tu Duc a full sixteen years here for boating and fishing, meditation, and composing some of the four thousand poems he is said to have written, while sitting with his concubines in a lakeside pavilion. From the southern gate, brick paths lead alongside a lake and a couple of waterside pavilions, from where steps head up through a triple-arched gateway to a second enclosure containing the **Hoa Khiem temple**, which Tu Duc used as a palace. Behind the temple stands the colourful royal theatre, where you can now play dress-up in traditional Vietnamese clothing, and the austere, dark wood **Luong Khiem temple** dedicated to Tu Duc's mother, Tu Du. The second group of buildings, to the north, is centred on the **emperor's tomb**, preceded by the salutation court and stele-house. The imperial remains are actually buried in an unknown location to prevent grave robbing; the two hundred servants who buried him were beheaded to (literally) take the secret to the grave. Tu Duc's Mausoleum is around 5km from central Hue by road. From the boat jetty, it's a 2km walk or *xe om* ride (30,000VND return).

The Mausoleum of Khai Dinh

The **Mausoleum of Khai Dinh** is a monumental confection of European Baroque and ornamental Sino-Vietnamese style, set high up on a wooded hill. Khai Dinh was the penultimate Nguyen emperor and his mausoleum has neither gardens nor living quarters. Though he only reigned for nine years (1916–25),

PERFUME RIVER BOAT TRIPS

A boat trip on the **Perfume River** is in theory one of the city's highlights, puttering in front of the citadel, past row boats heading for Dong Ba market. The standard **boat trip** takes you to Thien Mu Pagoda, Hon Chen Temple and the most rewarding royal mausoleums. You can enquire directly at the wharf east of the Trang Tien Bridge, rather than going through middleman tour agents; be clear as to what the tour involves and whether lunch and motorbike fees from the moorings to the tombs are included or extra. Hotels, travellers' cafés and tour agents offer group tours that tend to last from around 8am to 4pm and cost around US$10 per person (this does not include entrance to the tombs or Hon Chen Temple). Agents can also arrange charter boats at $25–30 for the day.

11

VISITING THE ROYAL MAUSOLEUMS

The Nguyens built magnificent **royal mausoleums** in the valley of the Perfume River among low, forested hills to the south of Hue. Each one is a unique expression of the monarch's personality, usually planned in detail during his lifetime to serve as his palace in death. Though details vary, all the mausoleums consist of three elements: the **main temple** is dedicated to the worship of the deceased emperor and his queen, and houses their funeral tablets and possessions; a large, stone **stele** records details of his reign, in front of which spreads a paved courtyard, where ranks of stone mandarins line up to honour their emperor; and the royal **tomb** itself is enclosed within a wall.

The contrasting mausoleums of Tu Duc, Khai Dinh and Minh Mang are the most attractive and well preserved, and are easily accessible, though they can be crowded – particularly Tu Duc, which is the most popular. **Entry** to the mausoleums (daily 7am–5.30pm) is 80,000VND each for the main three; most of the others are free. To **get to the mausoleums** you can either rent a bicycle or motorbike, or take a Perfume River boat trip (see box, p.871), which entails a couple of longish walks or *xe om* rides; the best way to avoid the crowds, go early in the morning by *xe om*; you can negotiate your custom tour stops with the likes of *Café on Thu Wheels* (see opposite). If cycling, take plenty of water and a good map.

it took eleven (1920–31) to complete his mausoleum. The approach is via a series of dragon-ornamented stairways leading through an imposing gate first to the **Honour Courtyard**, watched over by stone mandarin honour guards, and the stele-house. Climbing up a further four terraces brings you to the main **Thien Dinh temple**, with a jaw-droppingly splendid interior, decorated to the hilt in glass and porcelain mosaic that writhes with dragons and is peppered with symbolic references; the ceilings are covered in dragon murals. A life-size statue of the emperor holding his sceptre sits under the canopy, his remains interred 18m under. Khai Dinh's Mausoleum is 10km from Hue by road, or a 1.5km walk or *xe om* ride from the boat jetty.

The Mausoleum of Minh Mang

Court officials took fourteen years to find the location for the **Mausoleum of Minh Mang** and then only three years to build it (1841–43), using ten thousand workmen. Minh Mang, the second Nguyen emperor (1820–41), was a capable, authoritarian monarch who was passionate about architecture, and he designed his mausoleum along traditional Chinese lines, in a beautiful wooded location, with 37 acres of superb landscaped gardens and plentiful lakes to reflect the red-roofed pavilions. Inside the mausoleum, a processional way links the series of low mounds bearing all the main buildings. After the salutation courtyard and stele-house comes the crumbling **Sung An temple** where Minh Mang and his queen are worshipped. Continuing west you reach **Minh Lau**, the elegant, two-storey "Pavilion of Pure Light" standing among frangipani trees, symbols of longevity. A stone bridge leads across the Tan Nguyet Lake to the gate of the emperor's sepulchre, opened only on the anniversary of his death.

You can reach Minh Mang's Mausoleum from Khai Dinh's by following the **road** west for 1.5km and crossing the bridge over the Perfume River. The entrance is then 200m away on the other side.

ARRIVAL AND DEPARTURE

By plane Flights into Hue's Phu Bai Airport, 15km southeast of the city, are met by an airport bus run by Vietnam Airlines (70,000VND), which goes to central hotels, and by metered taxis (about 200,000VND). Going to the airport, the bus departs from the Vietnam Airlines branch office at 23 Nguyen Van Cu (☎ 054 3824709), or you can arrange a pick-up from your hotel reception.

Destinations Hanoi (3 daily; 2hr); HCMC (8 daily; 1hr 20min).

By bus Hue is one of the stops on the open-tour bus routes; buses stop at the cluster of travel agents and hotels along Hung Vuong or the northern end of Le Loi. *Hue Backpackers* (see opposite) run a convenient daily minibus service at 1pm straight to Phong Nha National Park, stopping at the Vinh Moc tunnels at the DMZ along the way (500,000VND). Southbound bus services operate from An Cuu station (sometimes called Phai Nam station),

4km southeast of the centre along Highway 1; northbound buses for Hanoi and other destinations run from An Hoa station, 4km northwest on Highway 1.

Destinations Da Nang (3hr); Dong Ha (1hr 30min); Hanoi (16–17hr); HCMC (22hr).

By train The train station lies 1.5km from the centre at the far western end of Le Loi.

Destinations Da Nang (8 daily; 2hr 30min–4hr); Dong Hoi (8 daily; 3hr–5hr 30min); Hanoi (5 daily; 12hr–16hr 30min); HCMC (4 daily; 19–22hr); Nha Trang (4 daily; 11hr–15hr 30min); Ninh Binh (5 daily; 10–13hr).

TOURS

Tour operators Sinh Tourist, 7 Nguyen Tri Phuong (daily 6.30am–10pm; T 054 3823309, W thesinhtourist.vn), arranges Perfume River boat trips and DMZ tours, as well as tickets for buses to Savannakhet in Laos. The *Café on Thu Wheels* (see below) and the *Stop & Go Café* at 3 Hung Vuong (T 054 3827051, W stopandgo-hue.com) are recommended for their motorcycle tours around the area ($10–20) as well as car tours of the DMZ (around $45 per person).

ACCOMMODATION

Canh Tien 9/66 Le Loi T 054 3822772. One of several budget guesthouses on an alley leading off northern Le Loi, this family-run place offers simply decorated, spotlessly clean rooms with all the amenities and free breakfast. Double $15

Hue Backpackers Hostel 10 Pham Ngu Lao T 054 3826567, W hanoibackpackershostel.com. Branch of the perennially popular Hanoian hostel (see p.845), with simple yet smart a/c dorms, doubles and lots of activities on offer – from the Top Gear motorbike tour to cooking classes. Rates include breakfast, and the perpetually busy bar downstairs is a good spot for happy hour (5–6pm). Dorm $8, double $20

Jade Hotel 17 Nguyen Thai Hoc T 054 3938849, W jadehotelhue.com. Renovated by an artist, this hotel combines classic architecture with modern features and its rooms are spacious and clean as a whistle, presided over by attentive staff. Double $20

Phoenix Hotel Hue 66 Le Loi T 054 3826736. Overlooking the Perfume River, this friendly spot has thirty rooms in various configurations – good news for single travellers and groups of friends. Double $16, triple $18

★ **Phong Lan (Wild Orchid)** 12/66 Le Loi T 054 3826255, E phonglanhue@gmail.com. Tucked away at the end of a quiet cul-de-sac, this cheerful guesthouse offers pleasant, warmly decorated rooms, has the friendliest, most helpful staff and pretty balconies hung with orchids. Breakfast included. Double $15

Star City Hotel 2/36 Vo Thi Sau T 054 3831358, W starcityhotelhue.com. Centrally located hotel with clean, spacious rooms spread over seven floors. Rates included breakfast and the a/c doubles as a heater in winter. Double $22.50

Sunny A Hotel 17/34 Nguyen Tri Phuong T 054 3829990, W binhduonghotel.com. The budget rooms in this bright and friendly mini-hotel are outstanding value, equipped with satellite TV and a/c, and all but the cheapest have their own computer with internet access. The *Sunny C Hotel* (4/34 Nguyen Tri Phuong; T 054 3830145; $15) has larger rooms, also equipped with all mod cons. Double $12

EATING

Hue is renowned for its imperial cuisine, thanks to the fussy Emperor Tu Duc, and local specialities to try include *bun bo hue* (a spicy rice noodle soup with lemongrass, shrimp paste and plenty of fresh herbs), *banh hoai* (a small, crispy yellow pancake, fried up with shrimp, pork and bean sprouts, and served with peanut and sesame sauce, star fruit, green banana, lettuce and mint), *bahn nam* and *bahn beo* (steamed royal rice cakes), *com hen* (rice with steamed clams, green banana, salted shredded meat and chilli), and *che* (a sweet dessert soup). Find these (from 7000VND) and more at the *Dong Ba Market* on Tran Hung Dao (daily 6.30am–8pm), just north of the Trang Tien Bridge.

Café on Thu Wheels 10/2 Nguyen Tri Phuong. This tiny bar-café, run by the charmingly nutty Mrs Thu, has friendly staff who run excellent motorbike tours – attested to by the recommendations scribbled on the walls – and serves a mix of Vietnamese and Western dishes. Daily 7.30am–10pm.

La Boulangerie Française 46 Nguyen Tri Phuong. Sells fresh croissants, brown bread, pastries and cakes for 8000–30,000VND – perfect for that early bus departure. Profits go to local charities. Daily 7am–8.30pm.

★ **Lac Thien** 6 Dinh Tien Hoang. This is one of Hue's more interesting restaurants, run by a family with several deaf members and popular both with locals and visitors. The food is excellent, taking in the Hue staples, including steamed fish (mains from 20,000VND). Order a beer to get a special bottle opener made by the owner. The two other similarly named restaurants along this street are owned by the proprietor's brothers. Daily 11am–9pm.

Mandarin Café 24 Tran Cau Van. Popular backpacker café serving Western breakfasts and Vietnamese dishes (set menus from 120,000VND), and offering good travel advice. The owner, Mr Cu, is an accomplished photographer, and prints of his photos depicting daily life around Hue are on sale. Daily 8am–8pm.

Omar Khayyam's Indian Restaurant 34 Nguyen Tri Phuong. This restaurant is deservedly popular for its north Indian menu, which includes numerous vegetarian dishes, biryanis, curries, naan and thali. Mains from 90,000VND, thalis from 140,000VND. Daily noon–10pm.

...ong Nam 38 Tran Cao Van. Perch yourself on a plastic chair at this friendly, family-run spot and order deep-fried spring rolls with mushrooms (from 30,000VND), Vietnamese mains (from 40,000VND), salads and delectable fruit shakes (15,000VND). Daily 10.30am–8pm.

Take 34 Tran Cao Van. Austere Japanese restaurant with traditional seating and wonderfully affordable sushi sets (from 50,000VND), as well as tonkatsu, gyoza, noodle dishes and more. Wash it down with an avocado shake or sweetened cucumber juice. Daily 11.30am–9.30pm.

Xuan Trang 42 Chu Van An. Above-average Vietnamese place serving a mix of Western and Hue speciality dishes – try the *nem lui*, grilled pork with peanut sauce, fresh veg and rice paper (60,000VND) or the banana flower salad. Daily 11.30am–9.30pm.

DRINKING AND NIGHTLIFE

Brown Eyes 56 Chu Van An. Late-night bar-club playing rock and punk, with a pool table and happy crowds comprising mostly inebriated backpackers. Cocktails are two-for-one from 5–10pm. Daily 5pm–late.

DMZ Bar 44 Le Loi. The hottest spot in town, crowded with a mix of locals and backpackers on any given night, with a free pool table, nightly drinks specials and an extensive food selection, including pizza (from 70,000VND). Cocktails from 55,000VND. Daily noon–midnight.

Why Not Bar 21 Vo Thi Sau. Western food (including some good veggie pizzas), football on the big screen, a pool table, good deals on beer and streetside seating are the draws here. Daily 5pm–late.

DIRECTORY

Bank Saigon Bank, 50 Hung Vuong; Vietcombank, 30 Le Loi.
Bike rental Bicycles ($2–3/day) and motorbikes ($5–7/day) can be rented from most hotels, guesthouses and cafés.
Hospital Hue Central Hospital, 16 Le Loi ⓣ 054 3822325.
Pharmacies 33 and 36 Hung Vuong.
Post office 8 Hoang Hoa Tham.

DA NANG

Da Nang is Central Vietnam's dominant port and its fifth-largest city. Though there are few sights in the city itself beyond the exceptional Cham Museum, greater attractions lie just outside. Da Nang is also a major transport hub with air connections as well as road and rail links, and it's the main access point for China Beach. During the American War it served as a massive South Vietnamese airbase and played host to thousands of US troops, as well as refugees searching for work.

WHAT TO SEE AND DO

Besides exploring the **Cham Museum**, it's possible to organize tours to **Nam O Beach**, where American troops first landed in Vietnam, **My Khe**, a long, narrow strip of golden sand, **Monkey Mountain** with its giant Buddha statue and some truly remarkable temples inside the **Marble Mountains** to the south of the city. To reach the outlying sights, rent a motorbike or hire a *xe om* or an Easy Rider via *Sinh Tourist* (see p.873) to take you around.

The Cham Museum

The Cham Museum, at the end of Bach Dang (daily 7am–5pm; 40,000VND; ⓦ chammuseum.danang.vn), is the most comprehensive exhibit of Cham art in the world, giving a tantalizing glimpse of the artistically inspired culture that ruled most of southern Vietnam for a thousand years. The terracotta and sandstone figures of the Hindu pantheon are on display here, from Shiva, Vishnu and Lakshmi to Ganesh and Brahma, as well as stylized animal figures, garudas and graceful apsuras (nymphs). There is also a scale model of My Son (see p.882) and exhibits on Cham culture today. Exhibits are grouped according to their place of origin: My Son (4–11C), Tra Kieu (Simhapura; 4–10C), Dong Duong (Indrapura; 8–10C) and Binh Dinh (11–15C).

Nam O Beach

Fifteen kilometres northwest of the city is the palm-fringed **Nam O Beach**, where American troops first landed in Vietnam in 1965. Residents of Nam O village are famous for their *goi ca* – Vietnamese sashimi that consists of raw fish marinated in a special sauce and rolled in a spicy powder.

My Khe (China Beach) and Non Nuoc Beach

Thirty kilometres of white sand stretches from the Son Tra Peninsula to Cua Dai Beach in Hoi An. The most well-known section of the beach is **My Khe** (China Beach), where American servicemen from all over Vietnam were sent for R&R

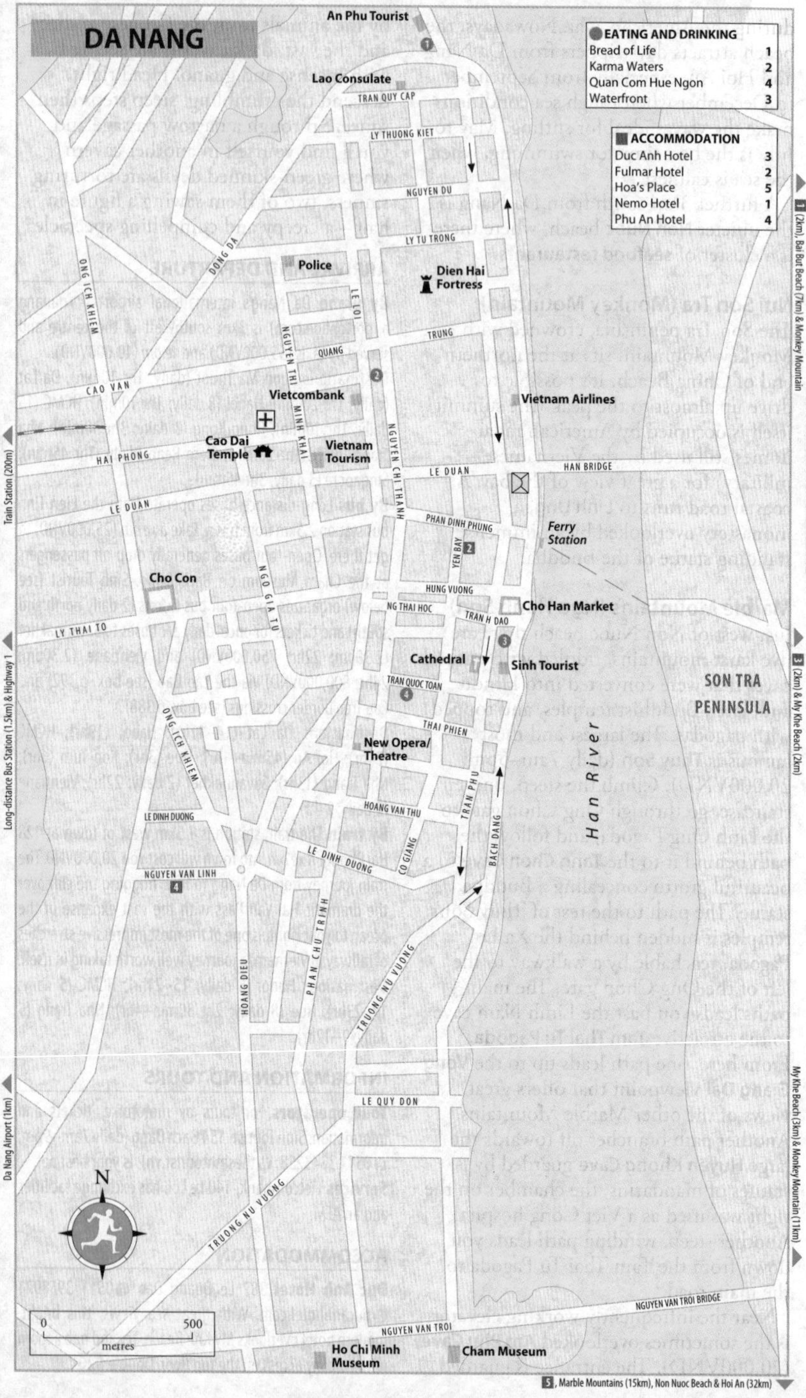

DA NANG

EATING AND DRINKING

Bread of Life	1
Karma Waters	2
Quan Com Hue Ngon	4
Waterfront	3

ACCOMMODATION

Duc Anh Hotel	3
Fulmar Hotel	2
Hoa's Place	5
Nemo Hotel	1
Phu An Hotel	4

An Phu Tourist
Lao Consulate
TRAN QUY CAP
LY THUONG KIET
NGUYEN DU
LY TU TRONG
DONG DA
ONG ICH KHIEM
Police
Dien Hai Fortress
LE LOI
NGUYEN THI MINH KHAI
TRUNG
QUANG
CAO VAN
Vietcombank
Vietnam Airlines
NGUYEN CHI THANH
Cao Dai Temple
Vietnam Tourism
HAI PHONG
LE DUAN
HAN BRIDGE
PHAN DINH PHUNG
YEN BAY
Ferry Station
NGO GIA TU
Cho Con
HUNG VUONG
Cho Han Market
NG THAI HOC
TRAN H DAO
LY THAI TO
Cathedral
Sinh Tourist
TRAN QUOC TOAN
SON TRA PENINSULA
THAI PHIEN
New Opera/ Theatre
Han River
TRAN PHU
HOANG VAN THU
LE DINH DUONG
BACH DANG
CO GIANG
NGUYEN VAN LINH
PHAN CHU TRINH
HOANG DIEU
TRUONG NU VUONG
LE QUY DON
N
NGUYEN VAN TROI BRIDGE
NGUYEN VAN TROI
0 500 metres
Ho Chi Minh Museum
Cham Museum

Train Station (200m)
Long-distance Bus Station (1.5km) & Highway 1
Da Nang Airport (1km)
1 (2km), Bai But Beach (7km) & Monkey Mountain
3 (2km) & My Khe Beach (2km)
My Khe Beach (3km) & Monkey Mountain (11km)
5, Marble Mountains (15km), Non Nuoc Beach & Hoi An (32km)

…g the American War. Nowadays, the …each attracts day-trippers from Da Nang and Hoi An, especially from September to December when rough sea conditions make the waves ideal for surfing. May to July is the best time for swimming, when the sea is calmest.

A further 3km south from Da Nang is the quieter **Non Nuoc** beach, where there is a cluster of **seafood restaurants**.

Nui Son Tra (Monkey Mountain)

The Son Tra peninsula, crowned with Monkey Mountain, sits at the northern end of China Beach. It's possible to drive up almost to the peak (the summit itself is occupied by American radar domes still used by the Vietnamese military) for a great view of the bay. A coastal road runs to **Linh Ung**, a monastery overlooked by an immense standing statue of the Buddha.

Marble Mountains (Ngu Hanh Son)

Just west of Non Nuoc beach there are five karst mountains, riddled with natural caves that were converted into Hindu and, later, Buddhist temples, and topped with pagodas. The largest and most famous is **Thuy Son** (daily 7am–5pm; 20,000VND). Climb the steep, uneven staircase, go through Ong Chon gate to the Linh Ong Pagoda, and follow the path behind it to the **Tang Chon Cave** to a beautiful grotto concealing a Buddha statue. The path to the rest of Thuy Son's temples is hidden behind the Xa Loi Pagoda, reachable by a walkway to the left of the Ong Chon gate. The main paths leads you past the Limh Nam cave to the attractive **Tam Thai Tu Pagoda**. From here, one path leads up to the **Vong Giang Dai** viewpoint that offers great views of the other Marble Mountains. Another path branches off towards the large **Huyen Khong Cave** guarded by statues of mandarins; the chamber on the right was used as a Viet Cong hospital. Another steep, winding path leads you down from the Tam Thai Tu Pagoda to the main road.

Near the infrequently working elevator is the sometimes overlooked **Am Phu Cave** (20,000VND). The entrance is guarded by the animals from the Chinese zodiac and the vast, dark caverns are scented with incense and guano. Head right, descend the crumbling, steep steps then squeeze through a narrow passage and you'll find yourself in another cavern where green-skinned devils are torturing sinners, two of them sawing a figure in half – a creepy and compelling spectacle.

ARRIVAL AND DEPARTURE

By plane Da Nang's international airport (ⓦdanangairportonline.com) is 3km southwest of the centre and served by taxis (55,000VND) and *xe om* (40,000VND).

Destinations Buon Ma Thuot (daily; 1hr 10min); Da Lat (daily; 1hr 20min); Hanoi (8 daily; 1hr 10min); HCMC (15 daily; 1hr 10min); Hong Kong (3 daily; 3hr 30min); Nha Trang (daily; 1hr 20min); Siem Reap (daily; 1hr 45min); Singapore (3 daily; 3hr 45min).

By bus Long-distance buses operate from the Lien Tinh bus station 2.5km from town. Take a *xe om* (25,000VND) to get there. Open-tour buses generally drop off passengers at the Cham Museum on Bach Dang. Sinh Tourist (see below) organizes open-tour bus tickets (2 daily north and south) and tickets for once-daily a/c buses to Savannakhet (2.30pm; 22hr; 750,000VND) and Vientiane (2.30pm; 24hr; 800,000VND) via the Lao Bao (see box, p.392) and Cau Treo border crossings (see box, p.388).

Destinations Da Lat (14–17hr); Hanoi (19hr); HCMC (24hr); Hoi An (45min–1hr); Hue (3hr); Kon Tum (6hr); Nha Trang (13hr); Savannakhet (2 daily; 22hr); Vientiane (2 daily; 24hr).

By train The train station is 1.5km west of town at 128 Hai Phong. A *xe om* into town will cost you 20,000VND. The train journey from Da Nang to Hue, hugging the cliff over the dramatic Hai Van Pass with the vast expanse of the ocean to your right, is one of the most impressive stretches of railway in Vietnam, a journey well worth taking in itself.

Destinations Hanoi (5 daily; 15–21hr); HCMC (5 daily; 17–23hr); Hue (8 daily; 2hr 30min–4hr); Nha Trang (5 daily; 9–12hr).

INFORMATION AND TOURS

Tour operators For tours by motorbike, tickets and information, Sinh Tourist, 154 Bach Dang (daily 7am–9pm; ⓣ0511 3843258, ⓦthesinhtourist.vn), is your best bet.

Services Vietcombank, 140 Le Loi, has exchange facilities and an ATM.

ACCOMMODATION

Duc Anh Hotel 387 Le Quang Dao ⓣ0511 3958971 ⓦducanhhotel.com. With great sea views, this bright, modern hotel overlooks My Khe Beach. Try and nab a room with balcony access on the top floor. Double **$20**

Fulmar Hotel 11 Yen Bai ⓣ 054 3810808, ⓦ fulmarhotel.com. Friendly four-storey hotel with compact, bright rooms and helpful management. Central location is a boon and there are plenty of single rooms for solo travellers. Double $20

★**Hoa's Place** 215/14 Huyen Tran Cong Chua ⓣ 0511 3969216, ⓔ hoasplace@gmail.com. The genial Hoa and his wife offer renowned backpacker accommodation just a stone's throw from Non Nuoc Beach; nightly communal dinners (80,000VND), cheap beer and friendly conversation make it the kind of place where days slip leisurely into weeks. There are surfboards and bodyboards for rent. Dorm $8

Nemo Hotel 100/2 Nguyen Van Thoai ⓣ 0511 3951951, ⓦ Da Nangnemohotel.com. Quiet hotel near China Beach and some great seafood restaurants. Expect spacious doubles and helpful owners. Double 400,000VND

Phu An Hotel 29 Nguyen Van Linh ⓣ 0511 3825708. Spacious, somewhat dark rooms, a short walk from the Cham Museum. If you're a light sleeper, avoid the rooms at the front. Double $15

EATING AND DRINKING

Bread of Life 4 Dong Da. Excellent bakery and café employing members of the deaf community, where you can enjoy cakes, gourmet sandwiches and Italian coffee. The home-made baked beans and bacon on wholegrain toast (40,000VND) will set you up for the day, and the pizzas are also good. Mon–Sat 8.30am–9.30pm.

Karma Waters 113/10 Nguyen Chi Thanh. Vegetarians and vegans, rejoice, for this Indian restaurant prides itself on the best vegetable dishes in town and fresh juices, as well as bakery items. Daily 8am–9pm.

Quan Com Hue Ngon 65 Tran Quoc Toan. This is a friendly and very local spot that does some of the best Vietnamese barbecue in town as well as rice and noodle dishes. Mains from 50,000VND. Daily 3–9.30pm.

★**Waterfront** 150–152 Bach Dang. Choose between the trendy open bar downstairs or the chic restaurant upstairs; either way, you're in for gastronomic treats in the form of seared seabass, Vietnamese spring rolls, deluxe burgers and chunky, imaginative sandwiches (100,000VND). Don't skip the equally fabulous desserts. Daily 10am–11pm.

HOI AN

The ancient core of seductive, charming **HOI AN** – recognized as a UNESCO World Cultural Heritage Site in 1999 – is a rich architectural fusion of Chinese, Japanese, Vietnamese and European influences dating back to the sixteenth century. In its heyday the port town attracted vessels from the world's great trading nations, and many Chinese merchants stayed on. Today its charming two-hundred-year-old wooden-fronted shophouses are among its chief attractions, as is the city's dining scene.

WHAT TO SEE AND DO

The **historic core** of Hoi An consists of just three short parallel streets: Tran Phu is the oldest and, even today, the principal commercial street, with plenty of crafts shops and galleries; one block south, Nguyen Thai Hoc has many wooden townhouses and some galleries, while riverfront Bach Dang holds the market and several waterside cafés. There are also a couple of attractive **beaches** nearby, and a cluster of **islands** that make for excellent day-trips from the town.

Japanese Covered Bridge

The western end of Tran Phu is marked by a small arched bridge known as the **Japanese Covered Bridge**, which used to connect the Japanese community to the Chinese one in the sixteenth century and has been adopted as Hoi An's emblem since. It has been reconstructed several times throughout its existence to the same simple design. Inside the bridge's narrow span are a collection of stelae and four statues, two dogs and two monkeys, usually said to record that work began in the year of the monkey and ended in that of the dog. You need a ticket to access the chapel in which a monster called Cu is said to have lived.

The Chinese Assembly Halls

Historically, Hoi An's ethnic Chinese population organized themselves

TICKETS FOR SIGHTS IN THE OLD TOWN

More than eight hundred historical buildings have been preserved in Hoi An, thanks to UNESCO, and you'll need to buy a ticket to access the most important sights (ⓦ hoianworldheritage.org.vn). There are several ticket booths (daily 7am–5pm) scattered throughout the Old Town where you can buy strips of five tickets (120,000VND), each one valid for a UNESCO site of your choice.

HOI AN

ACCOMMODATION

An Hoi Hotel	9
Hoang Trinh	7
Hoi Pho	5
Hop Yen	2
Nguyen Phuong	3
Starfruit Homestay	1
Thanh Binh I	8
Thanh Binh III	4
Thanh Van Hotel	6

EATING, DRINKING & NIGHTLIFE

Before & Now	6
Blue Dragon	12
Cargo Club	10
Dive Bar	9
Fusion Café	13
Miss Ly Cafeteria	3
Morning Glory Street Food Restaurant	7
Q Bar	8
Quan An	11
Reaching Out Café	5
Secret Garden	4
Sleepy Gecko	14
Streets	2
Zero Seamile Beach Club	1

Bus Station (700m) & An Banh Beach (3km)
Chua Chuc Thanh (120m), 1 (600m), & Da Nang (30km)
1 (4km) & Cua Dai Beach (4km)
My Son (40km)
Cam Kim
Cam Nam Island
Nguyen Tat Thanh
Ly Thuong Kiet
Thai Phien
Nguyen Truong To
Tran Cao Van
Hai Ba Trung
Ba Trieu
Sinh Travel
Tran Hung Dao
Phan Dinh Phung
Le Quy Don
Le Loi
Tran Family Chapel
Bi Bi SilK
Ticket Office
Nguyen Hue
Hoang Dieu
Police
Museum of History of Culture
Trieu Chau Assembly Hall
Nguyen Duy Hieu
Phan Chu Trinh
Phuoc Kien Assembly Hall
Quong Cong
Museum of Trading Ceramics
Truong Family Working House
Phung Hung House
Cantonese Assembly Hall
Nguyen Thi Minh Khai
Tran Phu
Quan Thang House
Food Stalls
Hoang Van Thu
Tran Quy Cap
Market
Phan Boi Chau
Tran Duong House
Japanese Covered Bridge
Museum of Sa Huynh Culture
Mr Xe's Ship
Nguyen Thai Hoc
Museum of Folklore
Tan Ky House
Bach Dang
Performance House of Traditional Art
Ferry Station
Fish Market
Thu Bon River
Cam Nam Bridge
Randy's Book Exchange
Nguyen Phuc Chu
An Hoi Island
N
0 200 metres

according to their place of origin (Fujian, Guangdong, Chaozhou or Hainan), and each group maintained its own assembly hall as both community centre and house of worship. The most populous group hails from Fujian, and their **Phuoc Kien Assembly Hall**, at 46 Tran Phu (daily 7am–5.30pm), is an imposing edifice with an ostentatious, triple-arched gateway. The hall is dedicated to Thien Hau, Goddess of the Sea and protector of sailors. She stands, fashioned in 200-year-old papier-mâché, on the main altar flanked by her green- and red-faced assistants. It is said that they can see or hear any boat in distress over a range of 1600km.

Trieu Chau Assembly Hall, on the far eastern edge of town at 157 Nguyen Duy Hieu (daily 7.30am–5.30pm), was built in 1776 by Chinese from Chaozhou and has a remarkable display of woodcarving. In the altar-niche sits Ong Bon, a general in the Chinese Navy, surrounded by a frieze teeming with bird, animal and insect life; the altar table also depicts life on land and in the ocean.

The merchants' houses

Most of Hoi An's original wooden buildings are on Tran Phu and south towards the river, which is where you'll see the best-known merchants' house, at 101 Nguyen Thai Hoc. The **Tan Ky House** (daily 8am–noon & 2–4.30pm) is a beautifully preserved example of a two-storey, late eighteenth-century shophouse, all dark wood and dimly lit, with shop space at the front, a tiny central courtyard, and access to the river at the back. It is wonderfully cluttered with the property of seven generations grown wealthy from trading silk, tea and rice, and boasts two exceptionally fine hanging poem-boards and a wall devoted to photos of Hoi An's floods. The house gets very crowded and is best visited early or late in the day.

Just up from the covered bridge, at 4 Nguyen Minh Khai, **Phung Hung House** (daily 8am–7pm) has been home to the same family for eight generations since they moved from **Hue** in about 1780. The large two-storey house is Vietnamese in style although its eighty ironwood columns and small glass skylights denote Japanese influence, and it's decorated with beautiful embroidery and elaborate lanterns.

Museums

Housed in a traditional timber residence-cum-warehouse, the **Museum of Trading Ceramics** (daily 7am–5.30pm) at 80 Tran Phu showcases the history of Hoi An's ceramics trade, which peaked in the fifteenth and sixteenth centuries. The smaller **Museum of Sa Huynh Culture** at 149 Tran Phu displays artefacts found in Sa Huynh, 130km south of Hoi An, which flourished between the second century BC and the second century AD, while the **Museum of History and Culture** (daily 7am–5.30pm), behind the seventeenth-century Quang Cong Temple at 7 Nguyen Hue, features ceramics, burial jars, and bronze and gold jewellery from the early Dong Son civilization.

Markets

The produce **market** at the east end of Tran Phu retains the atmosphere of a typical, traditional country market despite the tourist contingent.

The bustling riverside **fish market** (6–7am), opposite the southern end of the market, is worth setting the alarm clock for; it's a hive of early-morning activity, as dozens of fishwives gather to sell the catch of the night.

The beaches

The 30km of coastline between Hoi An and Da Nang boast some of Vietnam's finest beaches. **Cua Dai Beach** – a 3km stretch of golden palm-lined sand – lies a pleasant 5km bike ride east of Hoi An along Cua Dai Road (30,000VND by *xe om*). It's becoming rather built-up, and the vendors go for the hard sell here, but a number of restaurants near the road are a worthwhile stop for seafood. Windsurfers, bodyboards and surfboards are available for rent from the five-star *Palm Gardens Beach Resort*.

An Banh Beach, 3km from town along Hai Ba Trung, is much quieter and more beautiful – a wide stretch of sand as yet

unspoilt by development, though small restaurants have been springing up along the beach.

The islands

Touring the outlying islands on a rented bicycle makes a good day out. **Cam Nam Island** lies over the Cam Nam Bridge, offering a great view of Hoi An across the water. The waterfront restaurants to the south of the island specialize in *hen tron* (fried fresh clams).

From Hoi An ferry station on Bach Dang, you can take a ferry (20,000VND) to **Cam Kim**, a large island famous for its specialist craft villages. The island's woodcarving workshops are a popular stopover for tourist boats returning from My Son, but the maze of sandy tracks, bamboo "monkey" bridges and picturesque little villages makes the island a beautiful place to explore independently. A main road bisects the island from the western to eastern shore, where there is a small jetty with boats to ferry you back to Hoi An.

The mountainous **Cham Islands**, 10km offshore from Cua Dai Beach, are renowned for their swallows' nests, a culinary delicacy that can fetch up to $2500 per kilo. The islands' main attraction for tourists, however, is the coral reefs and marine life in the surrounding waters; diving and snorkelling (see below) are possible mainly between April and September as the seas get too rough out of season.

ARRIVAL AND DEPARTURE

By bus Once-daily open-tour buses drop off at central hotels. They provide the easiest and quickest way out of Hoi An, stopping at all major destinations north and south. There are also once-daily buses departing for Savannakhet and Vientiane in Laos. Tickets can be booked from Sinh Tourist or in your hotel. Local buses stop at the main bus station about 1km northwest of the town centre at 96 Hung Vuong; these are notorious for overcharging tourists.
Destinations Da Lat (18hr); Da Nang (1hr); Hanoi (21hr); HCMC (22hr); Hue (4hr); Mui Ne (17hr).

INFORMATION AND ACTIVITIES

Tours Hoi An has plenty of agencies offering tours, visas, open-tour bus, train and air tickets, Sinh Tourist, 587 Hai Ba Trung (daily 6am–10pm; T 0510 3863948, W thesinhtourist.vn), being a particularly reliable option.

Cooking Many restaurants teach you how to make Hoi An specialities during their half-day (around $30) and full-day (around $50) cooking courses. The Morning Glory Cooking School (106 Nguyen Thai Hoc; T 0510 2241555, W restaurant-hoian.com) comes highly recommended, with a visit to the market, and professional kitchen, but large groups. Red Bridge Cooking School (T 0510 3933222, W visithoian.com/redbridge) teaches small groups at their school, reachable by 4km boat cruise down the river; the full-day course is particularly worthwhile.

Diving Blue Coral Diving (77 Nguyen Thai Hoc; T 0090 5939291, W divehoian.com) is run by experienced dive masters and offers snorkelling and diving trips around the Cham Islands; a one-day trip including two dives costs $87 (PADI certification required); snorkelling day-trips cost $40.

ACCOMMODATION

An Hoi Hotel 69 Nguyen Phuc Chu T 0510 3911888, W anhoihotel.com.vn. Decent a/c rooms in a perfect location for the Old Town, on Hoi An Island. Perks include a swimming pool and breakfast. Double $25

Hoang Trinh 45 Le Quy Don T 0510 3916579, W hoianhoangtrinhhotel.com. All rooms in this friendly place have a bath and a balcony, and even the cheapest are given the sorts of personal touches you'd expect from a much more expensive hotel. Rooms at the front ($30) have views of the Confucius Temple, and the communal rooftop terrace is a great spot for breakfast. Double $20

Hoi Pho 627 Hai Ba Trung T 0510 3916382, E hoiphohotel@yahoo.com. The bright, unfussy rooms in this quiet little hotel are good value, the staff are helpful and there's a good book exchange in the lobby. Double $15

Hop Yen 103 Ba Trieu T 0510 3863153, E hopyenhotel@yahoo.com. Basic hostel offering simple doubles and twins and two three-bed dorms in the attic. The rooms are nothing to write home about, but they're clean, and one of the cheapest options in town. Dorm $6, double $15

Nguyen Phuong 109 Ba Trieu T 0510 3916588, E nguyenphuonghotel1@gmail.com. Polished, spotlessly clean little a/c rooms, a short walk from the Old Town. Double $20

★**Starfruit Homestay** 26A Dinh Tien Hoang T 0510 6260026, W starfruithomestay.com. Run by a wonderfully friendly family, this beautiful guesthouse, a 20min walk from the Old Town, offers luxurious rooms with starfruit-green accents, proper bathtubs and a filling breakfast. Free bicycles available for guest use. Double $25

Thanh Binh III 98 Ba Trieu T 0510 3916777. One of several similar hotels in the Hai Ba Trung cluster, with spacious a/c rooms and a swimming pool. All rooms have a private balcony or patio, and there's an on-site spa as well. Double $30

Thanh Van Hotel 78 Tran Hung Dao ⊕0510 3916916, ⊕thanhvanhotel.com. Great location on the fringe of the Old Town, rooms are comfortable, there's a pool to lounge around and breakfast is included. Double $25

EATING

Blue Dragon 46 Bach Dang. A percentage of the profits made at this restaurant goes to the Blue Dragon Foundation, assisting street kids in Hoi An. There are more than a hundred inexpensive dishes to choose from, including Hoi An specialities such as *banh bao vac* (30,000VND). Cookery classes are also available ($15). Mains 40,000–80,000VND. Daily 11am–10pm.

Cargo Club 107 Nguyen Thai Hoc. A colonial-style Vietnamese and international restaurant, executing Western breakfasts, speciality dumplings, grilled seabass and gnocchi with equal ease. Next door the bakery section serves delicious home-made cakes, ice cream and pastries (from 30,000VND). Mains from 90,000VND. Daily 7.30am–11pm.

Fusion Café 96 Bach Dang. With a pretty terrace overlooking the river, this popular family-run restaurant delights the tastebuds with barbecue, fresh spring rolls, burgers with bacon and blue cheese, muesli trifle and more. Wash it down with chilli lemonade. Mains from 70,000VND. Daily 9am–10pm.

Miss Ly Cafeteria 22 Nguyen Hue. This refined, well-established restaurant is run by a delightful family who take great pride in the Hoi An specialities they serve, such as *cao lau* (50,000VND). The taster plate (160,000VND) is a great intro to four local dishes. Daily 11.30am–10pm.

★Morning Glory Street Food Restaurant 106 Nguyen Thai Hoc. The king of the dining scene, featuring an incredible array of street-food dishes – from squid stuffed with pork and a smoky aubergine claypot dish, to fragrant spring rolls and mackerel steamed in banana leaf. Cooking classes also on offer. Mains 70,000–120,000VND. Daily 11am–11pm.

Quan An 19 Hoang Van Thu. The guestbook testifies to the popularity of this little restaurant, with outside seating, friendly service and cold *bia hoi* for just 5000VND/glass. The chilli duck (70,000VND), prawn spring rolls, vegetarian *cao lao* and pork hotpot all get rave reviews. Daily 11.30am–11pm.

Reaching Out Café 131 Tran Phu. A wonderfully tranquil spot for tea and coffee (they've got quite a selection), this café is dedicated to providing fair treatment and wages to servers who are hearing- and speech-impaired. Daily 9am–7pm.

Secret Garden 132/2 Tran Phu. Hidden away down an alley off Le Loi (turn at no. 60), this restaurant is a gem. Dine on high-quality, thoughtfully prepared Vietnamese cuisine in a romantic candlelit garden, with live traditional music every night and excellent service. Mains 120,000–160,000VND. Daily noon–11pm.

Streets 17 Le Loi. This beautifully restored shophouse provides a wonderful setting for the equally wonderful food: try the squid salad with tamarind or the crispy rice pancake with shrimp and pork, or grab a sandwich with pear and grilled cheese. Mains from 65,000VND. Daily 11am–10pm.

DRINKING AND NIGHTLIFE

Before & Now 51 Le Loi. Popular traveller hangout, with colourful pop-art portraits of rock legends adorning the walls, and suitably loud music to match. They serve good cocktails. Daily 5–11pm.

Dive Bar 88 Nguyen Thai Hoc. British-run bar that's also home to the Cham Islands Diving Center, with a lovely cocktail garden, great mix of tunes and extensive cocktail list. Learn to make your own in their mixology classes. Daily 4–11.30pm.

Sleepy Gecko Cam Nam Island. The upstairs balcony facing Hoi An from across the river is a great vantage point from which to watch the sun go down, while the downstairs bar attracts expats with a good mix of music and Vietnamese and Western food. Daily noon–11pm.

Q Bar 94 Nguyen Thai Hoc. Trendy, gay-friendly bar that's always packed with a good mix of locals and travellers, thanks to its expertly-mixed cocktails and chilled-out electronica on the stereo. Daily 5–11.30pm.

Zero Seamile Beach Club Cua Dai Beach. A popular late-night backpacker hangout with themed party nights, happy-hour cocktail specials (cocktail buckets 80,000VND), beach bonfires, a swimming pool and a sweaty dancefloor for bopping to cheesy pop. After 11pm, a free hourly shuttle bus runs from *Before & Now* to the *Zero Seamile*. Daily 7am–4am.

SHOPPING

Books Randy's Book Exchange (daily 8am–7pm) on Cam Nam Island has by far the largest selection in English, and the owner is a good source of local information.

Handicrafts The trio of streets running parallel to the river – Bach Dang, Nguyen Thai Hoc and Tran Phu – are the best places to search for lacquerware, original and copied artwork, pottery and ceramics, and shops selling colourful silk lanterns, a Hoi An speciality. Reaching Out (⊕reachingout vietnam.com) at 103 Nguyen Thai Hoc is a particularly good fair-trade shop that employs artisans with disabilities.

Tailors Tailors are a dime a dozen in Hoi An and some will approach you as soon as you set foot in town. Those who offer to make your clothes in 24 hours are ones to avoid, as it allows no time for alterations and presumably involves sweatshop labour to carry out your order in such a short space of time. Recommended places include: Thu Thuy (⊕thuthuysilk.com) at 60 Le Loi and Yaly (⊕yalycouture .com) at 47 Nguyen Thai Hoc. It's possible to arrange for your clothing order to be shipped to your country.

DIRECTORY

Bank Agribank, 12 Tran Hung Dao, has an ATM. The post office has a Vietcombank ATM.

Bike rental Bicycles (30,000VND/day) and motorbikes ($7–10/day) are available for rent from most guesthouses.

Hospital Dr Ho Huu Phuoc Practice, 74 Le Loi ☎ 0510 3861419; daily 11am–12.30pm & 5–9.30pm. Local doctor who speaks English.

Pharmacy Bac Ali, 68 Nguyen Thai Hoc.

Post office 4b Tran Hung Dao (daily 6.30am–9pm).

MY SON

11

The mouldering, overgrown World Heritage-listed ruins of Vietnam's most evocative Cham site, **MY SON** (daily 6.30am–4pm; 70,000VND), lie 40km southwest of Hoi An in a bowl of lushly wooded hills.

The kingdom of Champa existed between the second and fifteenth centuries, and Cham kings were buried here as early as the fourth century, but the ruined sanctuaries you see today were erected between the seventh and thirteenth centuries. My Son was considered the domain of gods and god-kings, and, in its prime, comprised some seventy buildings, which weathered well until the 1960s when the Viet Cong based themselves here and were pounded by American B52s. There are **unexploded mines** in the area, so don't stray from main paths.

Archeologists regard **Group B** as the spiritual epicentre of My Son. Of the eleventh-century central *kalan* (sanctuary), **B1**, only the base remains; stone epitaphs reveal that it was dedicated to the god-king Bhadresvara, a hybrid of Shiva and King Bhadravarman. **B5**, the impressive **repository room**, boasts a bowed, boat-shaped roof still in reasonably good shape. The outer walls support ornate columns and statues of deities, and, on the western side, a crumbling bas-relief depicting two elephants with their trunks entwined around a coconut tree. Next door in **Group C**, the central *kalan*, **C1**, is fairly well preserved; statues of gods stand around the walls and a carved lintel runs across the entrance.

East of B and C, the two long, windowed meditation halls that comprise **Group D** now house modest galleries: **D1** contains a lingam, the remains of a carving of Shiva and a statue of Nandi, Shiva's Bull; **D2** houses a fine frieze depicting many-armed Shiva dancing, and, below the steps up to its eastern entrance, stands a statue of Garuda. Bomb damage was particularly cruel near **Group A**, reducing the once-spectacular *kalan*, **A1**, to a heap of toppled columns and lintels. Within, a huge lingam base is ringed by a number of detailed, small figures at prayer. Group A is reached by a stairway up the small hillock; Group A, immediately to the south, is mostly overgrown rubble.

The path loops past Groups G, E and F, finally passing the stand-alone, vegetation-covered temple at K before reaching the car park.

ARRIVAL AND DEPARTURE

On a tour Most visitors come on tours from Hoi An; there's a choice of sunrise tours (departing at 5am, returning at 11am; 180,000VND) and regular tours (departing at 9am, returning at 1pm; 120,000VND); for both tours there's the option to return by boat, visiting traditional villages along the river; allow a couple of extra hours and around 40,000VND more.

The south-central coast

Extending from the central provinces all the way down to the wetlands of the Mekong Delta, Vietnam's south-central coast was, from the seventh to the twelfth century, the domain of the Indianized trading empire of Champa. A few communities of Cham people still live in the area, and there are some fine relics of their ancestors' temple complexes near the seaside city of **Nha Trang**. The other beach resort along this stretch of coast is the one-street **Mui Ne**, a 21km-long arc of fine sand lapped by aquamarine waters that's a big destination for kitesurfers. At both resorts the majority of tourists are sun-seeking Russians.

NHA TRANG

Some 508km south of Hoi An, **NHA TRANG's** main features are its fine municipal beach, some excellent examples of **Cham architecture** and the plentiful marine life and coral reefs of the outlying islands that make it the top **diving** destination in Vietnam. The nascent party vibe and glut of beachfront high-rise hotels are not to everyone's taste, however, and the region has a **rainy season** lasting from November through to early January when the sea becomes choppy, the beach windy and rather dirty, and the waters too murky to dive.

WHAT TO SEE AND DO

Most new arrivals make a beeline for the **municipal beach**, a grand 6km scythe of soft yellow sand lined with some decent restaurants and high-end resorts. If the sea is too rough for swimming, you can rent a bodyboard on the beach instead.

The Pasteur Institute at the top of Tran Phu, which runs parallel to the beach, houses the **Alexandre Yersin Museum** (Mon–Fri 7.30–11am & 2–4.30pm, Sat 8–11am; 30,000VND). It profiles the Swiss-French scientist who settled in Nha Trang in 1893, discovered the cause of the bubonic plague in 1894, and became a local hero, thanks to his educational work and his ability to predict typhoons. The work of internationally acclaimed photographer Long Thanh is on display at **Long Thanh Gallery**, 126 Hoang Van Thu (Mon–Sat 8am–5.30pm; free; Ⓦlongthanhart.com). Mr Thanh, whose black-and-white photographs capture poignant vignettes of Vietnamese life, is often on-hand to talk to visitors, and prints are available for purchase.

The Po Nagar Cham towers

Nha Trang's most gripping attraction, the **Po Nagar Cham towers** (daily 6am–6pm; 20,000VND), stand 1.5km north of the city centre along Duong 2/4 (a 30,000VND *xe om* ride). The Hindu Cham probably built ten towers, or *kalan*, here on Cu Lao Hill between the seventh and twelfth centuries, but only four remain. The largest and most impressive is the 23m-high northern tower, built in 817 and dedicated to Yang Ino Po Nagar, Goddess Mother of the Kingdom and a manifestation of Uma, Shiva's consort. Time has taken its toll on this square-shaped tower, but the lotus-petal and spearhead motifs are still intact, as is the lintel over the outer door, on which four-armed Shiva dances. Inside, the dark and smoky main chamber holds a black stone statue of ten-armed Uma. To go inside the towers, scented with incense and used as places of worship, you need to don one of the "lab coats" provided if you're not appropriately attired.

11

The islands

Perhaps the single greatest pleasure of a stay in Nha Trang is an excursion to one of the nearby **islands**, easiest reached on one of the popular day-trips for around $8/person (see p.885). Morning trips include a tour of the islands, snorkelling and lunch on board, while in the afternoon the booze-cruise party boats come out.

The closest island, **Hon Mieu**, is also served by a local ferry from Cau Da wharf 5km south of the centre (irregular service on demand; 15min; 40,000VND return), which docks at the fishing village of Tri Nguyen. From here it's a few minutes' walk to Tri Nguyen Aquarium (daily 9am–4.30pm; 60,000VND), a series of saltwater ponds constructed for breeding and research purposes, and a small indoor aquarium.

★TREAT YOURSELF

Soak yourself in organic mud and mineral-water baths at the **Thap Ba Hot Springs** (4km north of town, phone or ask your hotel for their 30,000VND pick-up service; daily 7am–7.30pm; Ⓣ058 3835335, Ⓦthapbahotspring.com.vn). Treatments cost from 60,000VND for a soak in a communal mineral pool to 120,000VND for a communal mud bath, and 2,300,000VND for a full-day's pampering in the "VIP Spa", including oil massage, sauna, mud and mineral baths, and a full health check.

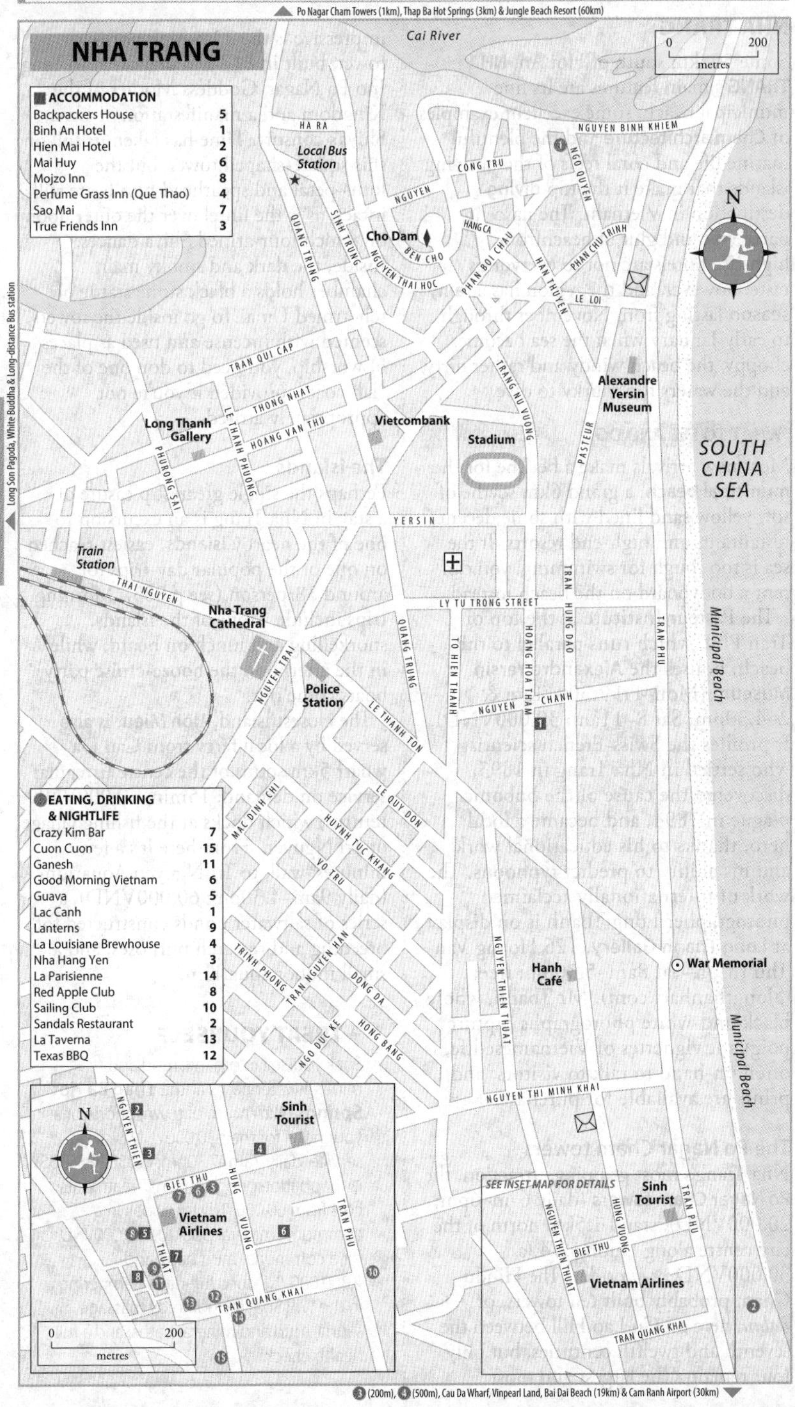

Po Nagar Cham Towers (1km), Thap Ba Hot Springs (3km) & Jungle Beach Resort (60km)

NHA TRANG

ACCOMMODATION

Backpackers House	5
Binh An Hotel	1
Hien Mai Hotel	2
Mai Huy	6
Mojzo Inn	8
Perfume Grass Inn (Que Thao)	4
Sao Mai	7
True Friends Inn	3

EATING, DRINKING & NIGHTLIFE

Crazy Kim Bar	7
Cuon Cuon	15
Ganesh	11
Good Morning Vietnam	6
Guava	5
Lac Canh	1
Lanterns	9
La Louisiane Brewhouse	4
Nha Hang Yen	3
La Parisienne	14
Red Apple Club	8
Sailing Club	10
Sandals Restaurant	2
La Taverna	13
Texas BBQ	12

Cai River
0 200 metres
Ha Ra
Local Bus Station
Nguyen Binh Khiem
Cong Tru
Ngo Quyen
Nguyen
Hang Ca
Cho Dam
Ben Cho
Quang Trung
Sinh Trung
Nguyen Thai Hoc
Phan Boi Chau
Han Thuyen
Phan Chu Trinh
Le Loi
Tran Qui Cap
Thong Nhat
Hoang Van Thu
Le Thanh Phuong
Phuong Sai
Long Thanh Gallery
Vietcombank
Stadium
Trang Nu Vuong
Pasteur
Alexandre Yersin Museum
SOUTH CHINA SEA
Long Son Pagoda, White Buddha & Long-distance Bus station
Yersin
Train Station
Thai Nguyen
Nha Trang Cathedral
Ly Tu Trong Street
Tran Hung Dao
Tran Phu
Municipal Beach
Quang Trung
To Hien Thanh
Hoang Hoa Tham
Nguyen Chanh
Nguyen Trai
Police Station
Le Thanh Ton
Le Quy Don
Mac Dinh Chi
Huynh Tuc Khang
Vo Tru
Nguyen Thien Thuat
Hanh Café
War Memorial
Trinh Phong
Tran Nguyen Han
Dong Da
Hong Bang
Ngo Duc Ke
Nguyen Thi Minh Khai
SEE INSET MAP FOR DETAILS
Sinh Tourist
Biet Thu
Hung Vuong
Vietnam Airlines
Tran Quang Khai

Inset: Nguyen Thien Thuat, Biet Thu, Hung Vuong, Tran Phu, Tran Quang Khai, Sinh Tourist, Vietnam Airlines, 0 200 metres

3 (200m), 4 (500m), Cau Da Wharf, Vinpearl Land, Bai Dai Beach (19km) & Cam Ranh Airport (30km)

11

The shallows that ring **Hon Tam**, 2km southeast of Mieu, are good for snorkelling. **Hon Tre** is the largest of Nha Trang's islands, endowed with dramatic cliffs and a fine, white-sand beach, Bai Tru – perhaps the best beach in the area. Two smaller isles hover off Hon Tre's southern coast: **Hon Mot** has a stony beach which is popular with snorkellers, and while there's no beach to speak of on **Hon Mun**, there's some great coral.

ARRIVAL AND DEPARTURE

By plane Cam Ranh Airport (ⓦ nhatrangairport.com) is 28km south of town; Vietnam Airlines runs buses to and from its pick-up point at 86 Tran Phu (60,000VND) two hours before scheduled departure times; metered taxis costs about 320,000VND.

Destinations Da Nang (2 daily; 1hr 20min); Hanoi (5 daily; 2hr); HCMC (9 daily; 55min).

By bus Nha Trang is a major stop for open-tour buses which terminate at their respective agencies' offices in the centre. They run twice a day to HCMC (9hr) and Mui Ne (6hr), and once a day to Da Lat (5hr), Da Nang (12hr), Hanoi (32hr) and Hue (17hr). Open-tour buses are the only way to reach Mui Ne, which is not served by local buses. The Phia Nam Nha Trang long-distance bus station is 500m west of the train station on Thai Nguyen. The recommended Mai Linh company (book through your lodgings) runs buses to Buon Ma Thuot (several daily; 4hr), Da Lat (several daily; 5hr) and HCMC (hourly; 9hr) from the bus station; hotel pick-up available.

By train Nha Trang's train station is just west of the centre along Thai Nguyen. The ticket office is open daily 7–11.30am, 1.30–6pm & 7–9pm.

Destinations Da Nang (5 daily; 12–15hr); Hanoi (5 daily; 26–33hr); HCMC (5 daily; 9–12hr); Hue (5 daily; 11hr 30min–16hr).

INFORMATION AND TOURS

Services Vietcombank is at 17 Quang Trung. There are pharmacies at 23d Biet Thu & 21 Quang Trung and the post office is at 24 Hung Vuong.

Tour operators Tour operators can arrange motorbike tours ($20–60/day, depending on distance), open-tour buses, tours of the region, and boat trips to nearby islands. Reputable operators include Sinh Tourist, 2a Biet Thu (ⓣ 058 3522982, ⓦ thesinhtourist.vn).

ACTIVITIES

Diving During the rainy season, visibility can be low, and dives are often cancelled. The most reliable and professional operators are Rainbow Divers, 90a Hung Vuong (ⓣ 090 8781756, ⓦ divevietnam.com); Mark Scott's Diving, 22/4 Hung Vuong (ⓣ 012 29037795, ⓦ divingvietnam.com); and Oceans 5 Dive, 78 Tue Tinh (ⓣ 058 3522012, ⓦ oceans5.co). Expect to pay $75 for two fun dives for certified divers, including lunch on the boat. All offer PADI Open Water beginner and advanced courses ($395).

Watersports Waves Watersports, based at *La Louisiane Brewhouse* (see p.887), organize wakeboarding, water-skiing, windsurfing, catamaran sailing, kitesurfing and kayaking. They also offer surfing courses in the winter ($100/day).

CRIME IN NHA TRANG

Nha Trang seems to have more **petty crime** than elsewhere, so leave surplus cash in the hotel safe when heading out. There have been reports of attacks on young men coming back alone late at night, as well as drive-by bag snatchings and laced drinks in nightclubs. Check prices on tickets to avoid being overcharged at tourist sites.

ACCOMMODATION

Backpackers House 54g Nguyen Thien Thuat ⓣ 058 3524500, ⓦ backpackershouse.net. Very popular hostel with spacious a/c dorms and private double rooms, one with a private garden. Wi-fi is patchy and bathrooms could be cleaner. Breakfast included. Dorm $7, double $12

Binh An Hotel 28H Hoang Hoa Tham ⓣ 058 3524858, ⓦ binhanhotel.com. Hotel run by a congenial old couple, with spotless, tiled rooms, some with balconies, fresh fruit for guests, and a quiet location just outside the main backpacker area. Double $15

Hien Mai Hotel 55/6 Nguyen Thien Thuat ⓣ 058 3526745. Family-owned hotel with considerate staff, clean and secure rooms featuring cable TV and a/c. Breakfast included. Double $25

Mai Huy 7h Hung Vuong ⓣ 058 3527553, ⓦ maihuyhotel.com. Appealing guesthouse in a quiet but central alley-way, offering warmly decorated fan and a/c rooms with wooden furniture and pretty bedspreads. Double $15

★ **Mojzo Inn** 120/36 Nguyen Thien Thuat ⓣ 058 6255568, ⓦ mojzo-inn.com. The staff here are a lot of fun, plus the good location, free breakfasts, particularly comfortable bunk beds and thoughtful touches such as storage cages and individual power sockets make this a top backpacker choice. Dorm $8, double $18

Perfume Grass Inn (Que Thao) 4a Biet Thu ⓣ 058 3524286, ⓦ perfume-grass.com. Thoughtful employees, a good café, and compact, tastefully furnished en-suite rooms equipped with cable TV and a/c or fan. The upper rooms have sea views, and all rates include breakfast. Double $17

Sao Mai 99 Nguyen Thien Thuat 058 3526412, saomai2ht@yahoo.com. Small, welcoming, family-run hotel with basic, clean en-suite rooms, a small rooftop terrace and a dorm; don't leave any valuables in your room, though. The owner Mr Mai Loc is an accomplished photographer and sells beautiful postcards. Dorm $5, double $10

True Friends Inn 79 Nguyen Thien Thuat 090 6424266. This hostel's facilities are fairly standard, but it's the receptionists who go out of their way to be helpful that make the difference. Full breakfast included and good social area to meet fellow travellers. Dorms $5, doubles $14

EATING

11

★**Cuon Cuon** 3/9 Trang Quang Khai. Tucked away down a side street, this friendly restaurant, decorated with colourful prints and carnival masks, serves roll-your-own fresh spring rolls (75,000VND), fragrant curries (105,000VND), pho and other delicious Vietnamese dishes. Daily 11.30am–10pm.

Ganesh T82 Nguyen Thien Thuat. Arguably the best Indian restaurant in Nha Trang, *Ganesh* serves authentic northern Indian dishes, accompanied by superb lassis. The thalis – vegetarian or seafood (159,000–179,000VND) – make a great complete meal. Mains from 75,000VND. Daily noon–11pm.

Good Morning Vietnam 19D Biet Thu. Clichéd name aside, this is a good stop for lasagne, pasta and pizza, and the strong Vietnamese coffees make for a very good morning indeed. Mains from 90,000VND. Daily 7.30am–11pm.

La Parisienne 3/2 Tran Quang Khai. Come here for breakfast (American, continental or French toast), cakes (50,000VND) and coffee. Daily 7am–7pm.

La Taverna 115 Nguyen Thien Thuat. Excellent pizza, pasta, steaks and Vietnamese dishes made using imported ingredients are served up by the Italian-Swiss owner in an atmospheric, trattoria-style setting. Pizzas from 100,000VND. Daily 11.30am–11pm.

Lac Canh 44 Nguyen Binh Khiem. Set in the quiet streets east of Cho Dam, *Lac Canh* is locally renowned for its mouth- and eye-watering cooked-at-table barbecues from 47,000VND/person. Daily 11.30am–11pm.

Lanterns 72 Nguyen Thien Thuat. Pleasant little restaurant offering a range of Vietnamese and Western dishes; the claypot dishes are particularly good (from 80,000VND). Some of the profits go to a local orphanage, and cookery classes are also available. Daily noon–11pm.

Nha Hang Yen 3/2A Tran Quang Khai. Expertly prepared Vietnamese dishes are the name of the game here; standout choices include claypot dishes, imperial pork spring rolls and zesty papaya salad. Mains from 70,000VND. Daily 11am–10pm.

★**Texas BBQ** 26a Tran Quang Khai. American-run, with American music, American service and meat imported from the United States. This popular steak-house serves up excellent flame-grilled burgers (100,000VND) and huge plates of melt-in-your-mouth ribs with home-made coleslaw and baked potatoes (195,000VND). Daily noon–11pm.

DRINKING AND NIGHTLIFE

Crazy Kim Bar 19 Biet Thu. Enjoy the huge cocktails during the 4.30–10.30pm happy "hour", or drop by for a hangover breakfast (60,000VND). A percentage of the profits goes towards Kim's campaign to assist vulnerable street children, and accommodation is offered to

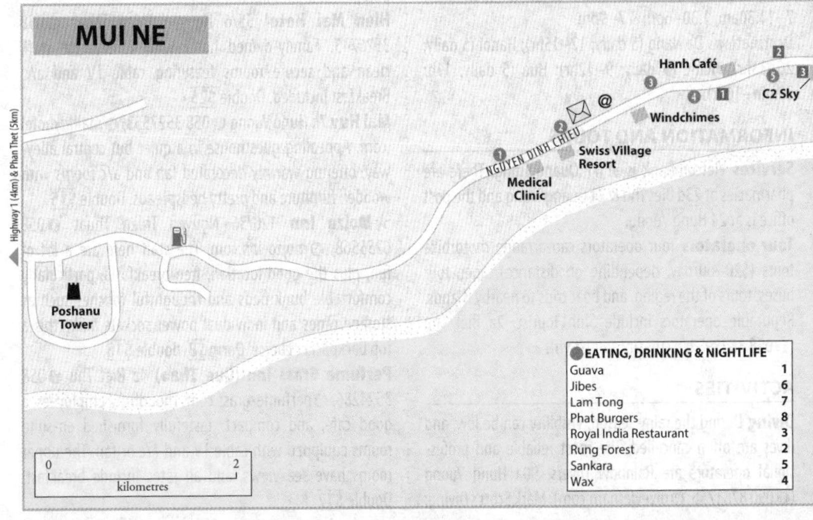

volunteers who wish to teach English in her free education scheme. Daily 10am–1am.

Guava 17 Biet Thu. Stylish cocktail bar with comfortable couches, afternoon movies and themed drinks specials in the evenings (happy hour 5–9pm), as well as Bloody Marys to go with your breakfast. Daily 10am–midnight.

La Louisiane Brewhouse 29 Tran Phu. Beach club with a free pool and private beach; the microbrewery offers a range of beers (large beer 75,000VND) made with all natural ingredients, and there's an eclectic menu of Japanese, Vietnamese, Thai and international dishes. Daily 7am–1am.

Red Apple Club 54b Nguyen Thien Thuat. Adjoining *Backpackers House*, this wildly popular nightspot caters to the party crowd that favours the afternoon booze cruise boats. Guzzle from a cocktail bucket (60,000VND) or a beer funnel. Daily 2pm–late.

Sailing Club 7 Tran Phu. Draws a well-heeled expat crowd and hordes of tourists to its refined beachfront bar and dancefloor. Rowdy travellers and drunks not welcome. Monthly full-moon parties are held on the beach with live DJ sets. Admission 90,000VND including one drink. Daily 7am–2am.

MUI NE

What started out as a pristine 10km-long stretch of sand with a small fishing village at the end of it is now lined cheek-by-jowl with budget beachside accommodation and an increasing number of upmarket resorts. Low-key **Mui Ne** is a prime place for adrenaline junkies: the waves between August and December attract surfers, while the strong, consistent winds and relatively low rainfall mean that kitesurfers and windsurfers thrive year-round, particularly from late October to late April.

WHAT TO SEE AND DO

Mui Ne is justifiably famous for its impressive Sahara-esque red and white **sand dunes**, best seen in late afternoon, which can be visited as part of a guided tour or independently by bicycle or motorbike. The white-sand dunes are quite far out and neither the white nor the red is pristine, unfortunately; a steady stream of visitors brings a steady stream of rubbish and quad bikes erode the fragile landscape. En route to the dunes, it is worth a stop at **Mui Ne village** for a scenic vantage point from the road, high over the bevy of blue fishing boats jostling in the harbour, as the fishmongers prepare their wares on the sand below. Another worthy stop is the **Fairy Springs**, 5km east of the centre of Mui Ne, a shallow stream that runs through a beautiful red rock and sand dune canyon. Ignore the young men who offer to be guides; you can hardly get lost here.

ARRIVAL AND DEPARTURE

By bus Open-tour buses from both north and south pass through around noon and, less conveniently, around 2am.

11

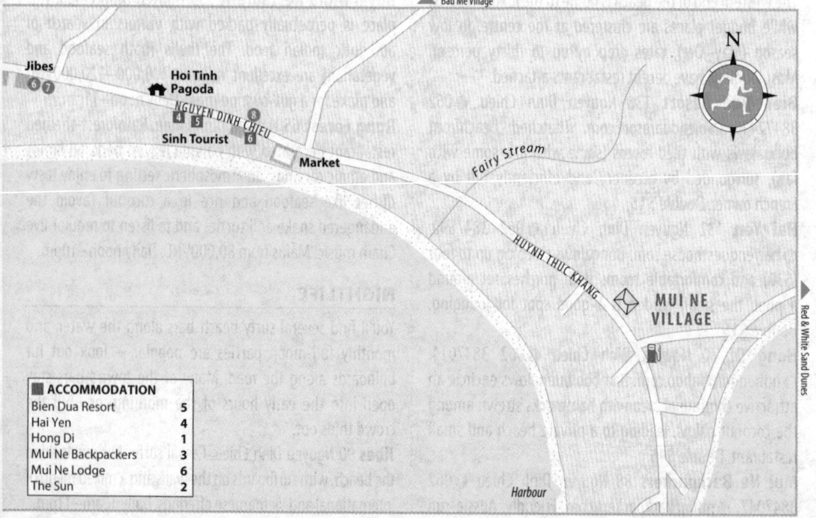

Sinh Tourist buses operate from their office at *Mui Ne Resort*, 144 Nguyen Dinh Chieu (T 062 847542) near Mui Ne village.

Destinations Da Lat (5hr); HCMC (5hr); Nha Trang (5hr).

INFORMATION

Tourist information The website W muinebeach.net has independent information on hotels, activities and local events.

Tours Sinh Tourist, all other tour operators on the strip and lodgings offer almost identical sunset tours to the red and white dunes ($7–10) that also tend to take in the Fairy Springs.

Services There are numerous ATMs scattered along the length of Nguyen Dinh Chieu. The area is best seen independently by bicycle ($2–4/day) or motorbike ($10/day), rentable from numerous lodgings and tour operators.

11

ACTIVITIES

Watersports C2Sky (82 Nguyen Dinh Chieu; T 091 6655241, W c2skykitecenter.com) offer a two-hour taster kitesurfing course for $100, and their seven-hour beginner course costs $385. Jibes (90 Nguyen Dinh Chieu; T 062 3847008, W windsurf-vietnam.com) rent windsurfers, surfboards, kitesurf equipment, paddleboards and kayaks and offer lessons ($60–70/hr). Vietnam Kitesurfing Tours (T 090 9469803, W vietnamkitesurfingtours.com) specialize in kitesurfing only, with a team of expat and local riders as instructors, taking you to great spots further out of Mui Ne; day-trips from $90.

ACCOMMODATION

The western end of the beach is home to the luxury resorts, while budget places are clustered at the centre. In low season (May–Oct), rates drop by up to thirty percent. Most lodgings have decent restaurants attached.

Bien Dua Resort 136 Nguyen Dinh Chieu T 062 3847241, W bienduaresort.com. Thatched beachfront bungalows with tiled rooms (some with a/c, some with fan), surrounded by greenery and efficiently run by a French owner. Double $15

Hai Yen 132 Nguyen Dinh Chieu T 062 3847890, W haiyenguesthouse.com. Bungalows sleeping up to four ($30) and comfortable rooms with porches set around a pool; the small garden is a good spot for lounging. Double $15

Hong Di 70 Nguyen Dinh Chieu T 062 3847014, E hdhongdi@yahoo.com. Bamboo bungalows encircle an attractive communal area with hammocks strewn among the coconut palms, leading to a private beach and small restaurant. Double $15

Mui Ne Backpackers 88 Nguyen Dinh Chieu T 062 3847047, W muinebackpackers.com. Friendly, Aussie-run backpacker favourite with beach loungers, comfortable a/c dorms and even a small pool. Great for organizing tours and helpful when it comes to local info. Dorm $8, double $35

Mui Ne Lodge 150 Nguyen Dinh Chieu T 062 3847327, W muinelodge.com. Popular resort with bungalows in a range of sizes with fan or a/c, all tastefully decorated, very clean and well equipped. The most expensive rooms ($25) have two double beds and glass fronts facing onto a private beach. Double $17

The Sun 117C Nguyen Dinh Chieu T 062 3743086. A laidback compound of ten simple thatched-roof bungalows with spacious, somewhat dark, fan-cooled rooms sit around a tranquil garden space full of lush greenery. Double $15

EATING

Guava 55 Nguyen Dinh Chieu. More sophisticated than the surfer joints on the beach, this open terrace bar is a pleasant place for a quiet (if slightly pricey) evening cocktail and some sizzling seafood. Mains from 80,000VND. Daily noon–11pm.

★ **Lam Tong** 92 Nguyen Dinh Chieu. Great-value fresh seafood and other local specialities served on a simple, extremely popular open-air terrace right on the beach. Try the fried fish with lemon grass and chilli (60,000VND) or their flavourful take on *pho bo*, with tiny peppery meatballs (27,000VND). Daily 7.30am–10pm.

Phat Burgers 253 Nguyen Dinh Chieu. This bright little place serves some of the best burgers in the country; choose from "phat phish", "baby phat" (if not too hungry) or the enormous, 1.25kg "king of Mui Ne" (if ravenous). Burgers 70,000–300,000VND. Daily 11.30am–11pm.

Royal India Restaurant 253 Nguyen Dinh Chieu. This place is perpetually packed with visitors in search of authentic Indian food. The thalis (both seafood and vegetarian) are excellent value at 100,000–120,000VND and make for a gut-busting meal. Daily noon–11pm.

Rung Forest 65 Nguyen Dinh Chieu. Rainforest-themed restaurant decorated with banana leaves, bark, oil lamps and ethnic carvings; an atmospheric setting to enjoy tasty dishes like seafood and rice in a coconut (avoid the endangered snake and turtle) and to listen to regular live Cham music. Mains from 80,000VND. Daily noon–10pm.

NIGHTLIFE

You'll find several surfy beach-bars along the water, and monthly full-moon parties are popular – look out for billboards along the road. Many of the town's bars stay open into the early hours of the morning, or until the crowd thins out.

Jibes 90 Nguyen Dinh Chieu. Casual surfer bar overlooking the beach, with surfboards on the walls and a mixed menu of international and Vietnamese offerings. Daily 10am–11pm.

Sankara 78 Nguyen Dinh Chieu. Sankara does its best to promote itself as "Swankara", with its intimate gazebos and chillout couches around a tiny beachside pool, upmarket international bar snacks, extensive cocktail list and DJs spinning tunes into the small hours. Daily noon–late.

Wax 68 Nguyen Dinh Chieu. A popular little beach bar whose dancefloor and serious sound system can make for a rowdy night out. Their beach bonfire is particularly popular with revellers. Daily 5pm–late.

The southern and central highlands

After a hot and sticky stint in the Delta or by the coast, you'll find that the **southern and central highlands**, with their host of ethnic minorities, mist-laden mountains, vast plantations and trickling waterfalls, provide an enjoyable contrast. Many of the highlands' inhabitants are *montagnards* ("mountain folk") from Bah Nar, E De, Jarai, Sedang, Koho and Mnong **ethnic minorities**, but visiting their villages independently can be difficult and is best done by basing yourself in the highland towns of **Buon Ma Thuot** and **Kon Tum**. For most tourists, the main target is the former French mountain retreat of **Da Lat**, with its refreshingly cool climate, an abundance of fruit and veg, and its prime setting for motorcycle tours of the region and visits to one of Vietnam's biggest natural treasures – **Cat Tien National Park.**

KON TUM

Some 174km south of Hoi An as the crow flies, southbound Highway 14 runs into the northern limits of diminutive **KON TUM**, a sleepy, friendly town that serves as a springboard for jaunts to its outlying **Bah Nar villages**, or as a brief stop en route to Laos.

WHAT TO SEE AND DO

Phan Dinh Phung forms the western edge of town; running east above the river is Nguyen Hue, and between these two axes lies the town centre. Scrap-metal yards piled high with bomb shells and rusting weapons betray the hardships endured during the American War; a major battle was fought here between the North and South Vietnamese in 1972, which ended in defeat for the South, the soldiers joined by many civilians in the "Convoy of Tears". Going back further in time, a stroll along Nguyen Hue still reveals red-tile terraces of shophouses left over from the French era. At the base of Tran Phu stands the grand, whitewashed bulk of Tan Huong Church. Further east is the so-called **Wooden Church**, built by the French in 1913. In the grounds, there's a scale model of a communal house.

11

Kon Ko Tu

There are dozens of Bah Nar villages encircling Kon Tum, but one of the most accessible is **KON KO TU**, a relatively timeless community 5km east of town. Follow Tran Hung Dao east, crossing Duong Dao Duy Tu and passing an impressive high-roofed *rong* (communal house) just before you cross Dakbla River over the suspension bridge. Turn left at the first crossing after the bridge and continue for 3 to 4km to reach the village. Many of the dwellings are still made of bamboo and secured with rattan string, but it's the village's immaculate *rong*, with its impossibly tall thatch roof, that commands the most attention. Constructed with wood and bamboo, and without the use of any nails, the *rong* is used for festivals and village meetings, and as a village court at which anyone found guilty of a tribal offence must

INTO LAOS: BO Y

The easiest option to reach the border crossing at **Bo Y**, 86km northwest of Kon Tum, is to catch a direct bus to Attapeu in Laos, which passes through Kon Tum daily at 9.30am (7hr; 260,000VND). From Attapeu, the bus continues on to Pakse (12hr; 350,000VND). Alternatively, Mai Linh Express (Ⓦ mailinh.vn) also run more comfortable daily buses to Attapeu. One-month Lao visas are available at the border for about $40, depending on your nationality.

apologize and ritually kill a pig and a chicken. Kon Tum Tourist (see below) can organize homestays in local villages as well as day-trips to those further out (from $25 per person).

ARRIVAL AND DEPARTURE

By bus Kon Tum's bus station is 3km north of the main bridge along Phan Dinh Phung. Take a *xe om* back into the centre (around 40,000VND), or ask the driver to let you off at the bridge, from where it's a 250m walk east along riverside Nguyen Hue to the foot of Le Hong Phong, and another 150m to Tran Phu; both run up into the town centre. Destinations Buon Ma Thuot (5 daily; 5hr); Da Lat (2 daily at 4.30am & 5.30am; 8hr); Da Nang (15 daily; 4hr); Nha Trang (daily; 9hr).

INFORMATION

Tours Kon Tum Tourist (T 060 3861626, W kontumtourist.com), in the *Dakbla Hotel*, 2 Phan Dinh Phung, offers tailor-made tours and homestays in nearby villages. A popular two-day tour combines a jungle trek with a night in a Bah Nar village stilt house and a riverboat trip.
Services BIDV bank is at 1 Tran Phu.

ACCOMMODATION AND EATING

Dakbla 620 Nguyen Hue. Friendly restaurant serving surprisingly sophisticated local and Western dishes alongside wild game in ambient surroundings with tribal artefacts on walls. Mains from 40,000VND. Daily 8am–10pm.
★ **Eva Cafe** 1 Phan Chu Trinh. Designed and built by the owner, this treehouse-like café is a wonderfully relaxed spot to munch on inexpensive local dishes that use locally grown vegetables, and try a speciality drink, such as coffee with whipped egg. Mains from 60,000VND. Daily 10.30am–9pm.
Family Hotel 235 Tran Hung Dao T 060 3862448, E phongminhkt@yahoo.com. Family-run hotel with fairly rustic rooms set around a pretty garden courtyard. The wi-fi is iffy and some travellers have been met with indifferent and not terribly helpful staff. Double **$12**
Thing Vuong Hotel 16B Nguyen Trai T 060 3914729. Arguably Kon Tum's best lodgings, this friendly mini hotel is clean, and conveniently located down a side street in the centre. Rooms are large and airy. Double **$12**

BUON MA THUOT

In recent years coffee production in the highlands has grown rapidly, making Vietnam the second-largest coffee producer in the world after Brazil. The highland town of **BUON MA THUOT** holds a deserved reputation for the best (and strongest) coffee in Vietnam, and the town boasts many **streetside cafés** serving cups of the syrupy brew. Though the town is not terribly appealing in itself, it makes a good base for visiting Yok Don National Park and the outlying **minority villages** – the province is home to 44 different tribes. However, following protests by local ethnic minority groups in 2004 against oppressive government policies, restrictions were put in place, and tourists may be forbidden from visiting some of the surrounding villages; you need a permit to visit those to which you're allowed access. How stringently these restrictions are enforced depends on the current political climate, so it's worth checking with Dak Lak Tourist Office (see opposite).

WHAT TO SEE AND DO

The one ethnic minority village you can easily visit from Buon Ma Thuot is the E De village of **Ban Don**. It's very touristy, though you can witness gong performances and participate in drinking rice wine through long bamboo straws from communal jars.

If you need to while away a few hours in town, try the **Ethnographic Museum** on Le Duan (entrance 4 Y Ngong (daily 9am–5pm), with its exhibits about local minority peoples, including a scale model of an E De longhouse, rice-wine jars and instruments for taming elephants.

The Dray Sap and Trinh Nu Falls

The splendid crescent-shaped **Dray Sap Falls** (7am–5pm; 25,000VND) and neighbouring Dray Nur Falls lie 30km from Buon Ma Thuot, and can be reached by heading southwest out of town along Chu Jut. A local bus plies the route hourly, leaving from Nguyen Tat Thanh near the Victory Monument (30,000VND); otherwise a *xe om* return trip will cost around 240,000VND. Almost 15m high and more than 100m wide, the "waterfall of smoke" can be reached by clambering through bamboo groves, across suspension bridges and over rocks to the right of the pool formed by the falls. From here, a 5km walk through the jungle and past a good swimming

hole brings you to Trinh Nu Falls, smaller than the other two but quite pretty nonetheless. To get there, turn left off the road to Dray Sap at the sign for "Trinh Nu" and continue along a dirt track for about 2km.

Yok Don National Park

The entrance to Vietnam's largest wildlife reserve – the 1155-square-kilometre **Yok Don National Park** (yokdonnationalpark.vn) – lies 45km west of Buon Ma Thuot. More than sixty species of animals, including tigers, leopards and red wolves, and around two hundred types of birds, from peacocks to hornbills, populate the park, but many are visitor-shy; you're likely to spot some monkeys, though. Four minority villages, populated by the Mnong, Lao and Ede people, are found within the park boundaries; the Mnong are renowned for their skill at capturing wild elephants.

One-day walking tours, overnight safaris, elephant rides (240,000VND per hour) and boat tours down the Serepok River are available, as are longer tours penetrating deeper into the forest. The park is best visited in the dry season (Aug–March) when wildlife is more visible. For enquiries, check the park website, or arrange through a tour operator (see below), who can organize transport and combined day-tours to visit the park and Ban Don. There's also a range of basic **accommodation** available by the park entrance (doubles 200,000VND), and it's possible to stay overnight in the park at the forest stations (basic wooden huts; $5).

Ban Don

The three sub-hamlets that comprise the much-visited village of **BAN DON** lie 2km beyond Yok Don's Park HQ on the bank of the crocodile-infested Serepok River. Khmer, Thai, Lao, Jarai and Mnong live in the vicinity, as do the **E De**, who adhere to a matriarchal social system and build their houses on stilts. As you explore, you may be invited to share tea or rice wine. The two Buon Ma Thuot travel agents (see below) arrange tours here, but you could just as well hire a *xe om* (around 350,000VND return). Hourly local buses also run here from Ly Thuong Kiet in Buon Ma Thuot (25,000VND).

Both the Ban Don Tourist Centre (daily 7am–5pm; 0500 3783082), in the centre of the village, and the Yok Don park HQ (see above) can organize an overnight stay in a nearby longhouse ($10).

ARRIVAL AND DEPARTURE

By plane The airport is 8km east of town; a taxi costs around 140,000VND.

Destinations Da Nang (4 weekly; 1hr 10min); Hanoi (daily; 1hr 40min); HCMC (3 daily; 55min).

By bus Buon Ma Thuot's bus station is 4km north of town at 71 Nguyen Tat Thanh. Regular local buses run to elsewhere in the Highlands, Nha Trang and HCMC. Buses to and from Lak Lake and Dray Sap Falls stop near the Victory Monument in the centre of town.

Destinations Da Lat (4hr); Da Nang (12hr); Kon Tum (5hr); Lak Lake (1hr 30min); HCMC (9hr); Nha Trang (5hr).

INFORMATION

Travel agents Dak Lak Tourist, 51 Ly Thuong Kiet (0500 3858243, daklaktourist.com.vn), and Vietnam Highland Travel, 24 Ly Thuong Kiet (0500 3855009, vietnamhighlandtravel.com), can arrange tours and treks in the surrounding hills and jungles.

Services Agribank is at 37 Phan Boi Chau.

ACCOMMODATION

Ngoc Mai Guesthouse 14B Dien Bien Phu 0500 3853406. The owner at this pleasant, centrally located guesthouse speaks both English and French and is happy to share his knowledge of the area. Rooms come with firm beds and balconies; wi-fi comes and goes. Double **280,000VND**

Thanh Binh 24 Ly Thuong Kiet 0500 3853812. Rooms are basic and a little worn, but clean. The rooms in the centre of the building are cheaper but smaller and windowless; all come with a/c. Double **260,000VND**

Tuan Vu Hotel 135/1 Tan An 0500 6252252, tuanvuhotel.com.vn. This hotel is good value, and while its decor is nothing out of the ordinary, rooms are comfortable, staff are friendly and the food is decent. Double **300,000VND**

EATING AND DRINKING

A popular local dish on offer in the street kitchens lining the western end of Ly Thuong Kiet is *com tam* (broken rice) served with barbecued pork or chicken and fresh vegetables.

An Thai Café 18 Hai Ba Trung. Pleasant and popular café, where you can sample the region's finest brew (12,000VND) on a leafy terrace. Daily noon–10pm.

11

Pho Nuong 150 Hung Vuong. Apart from large helpings of pho, this popular local spot, set back from the street, serves great seafood dishes and the likes of deep-fried fish in honey sauce. Mains from 60,000VND. Daily 7.30am–9pm.

Thanh Tram 22 Ly Thuong Kiet. One of several friendly family-run restaurants on Ly Thuong Kiet serving excellent *nems* (fresh spring rolls) for 35,000VND in spotless, bright surroundings. Daily 11.30am–9.30pm.

LAK LAKE AND AROUND

Fifty-two kilometres south of Buon Ma Thuot, Highway 27 passes **Lak Lake**, a beautiful and peaceful spot. Along the lake's shoreline, Emperor Bao Dai's palace, which has been converted into a three-star resort, enjoys a prime vantage point. Beyond this sits **JUN VILLAGE**, a thriving Mnong community, whose impressive longhouses clustered on the shore have remained practically unchanged, although numerous tourists visiting detract slightly from the tableau.

Dak Lak Tourist (see p.891) has one branch by the lake and one inside the village gate, both of which organize homestays with a family at a Jun longhouse in the village ($12), gong shows and rice-wine feasts ($60/group), guided treks or elephant rides around the lake ($30/hr for two).

On the southwestern shore is a Mlieng village, which can be reachable by boat or by elephant; consult Dak Lak Tourist.

ARRIVAL AND DEPARTURE

By xe om It's possible to get to Lak Lake independently by *xe om* (around 220,000VND for a day-trip).

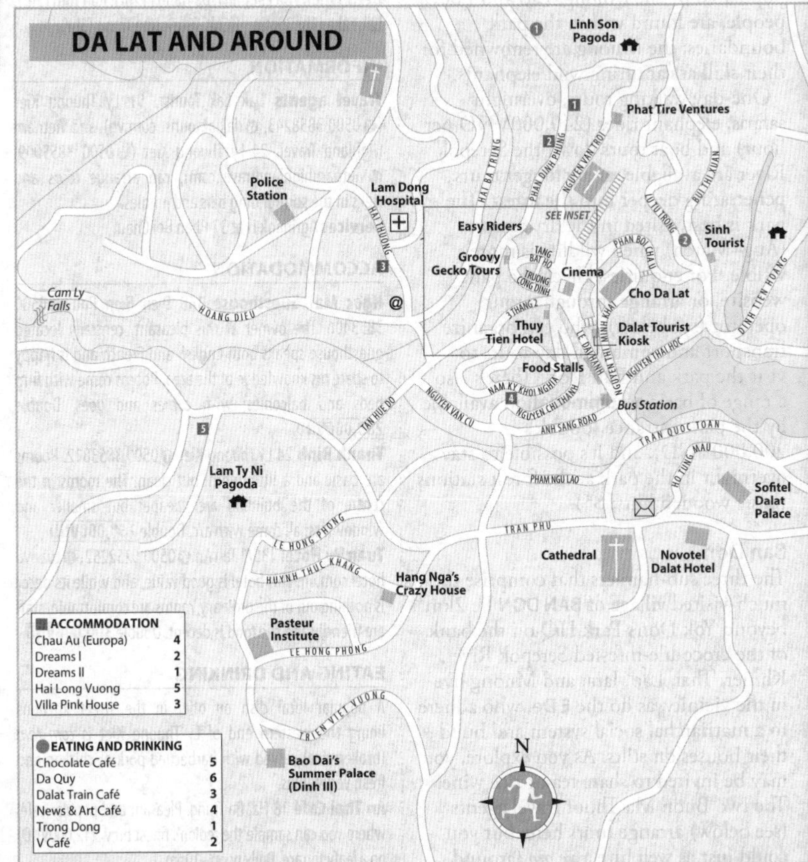

On a tour Lak Lake is part of many Easy Rider (see p.895) tours of the region.

DA LAT AND AROUND

Standing at an elevation of around 1500m, the city of **DA LAT** is Vietnam's premier hill station, an amalgam of maze-like streets and picturesque churches, and French colonial buildings spliced with less appealing new constructions. In 1897, the governor-general of Indochina ordered the founding of a convalescent hill station here, where Saigon's hot-under-the-collar *colons* could recharge their batteries. By tacit agreement during the American War, both Hanoi and Saigon refrained from bombing the city and many of the old buildings remain.

WHAT TO SEE AND DO

Da Lat's major attractions can all easily be seen in one day by bicycle. **Day-trips** to outlying attractions, best seen on the back of a *xe om* with a good guide (see p.895), usually take in a minority village, silk-worm hamlet and factory, Lien Khuong and Prenn waterfalls, a rice-wine factory and a cut-flower farm. It's well worth making Da Lat your base for an extra day to do a motorbike tour to Cat Tien National Park – great for hiking, birdwatching and mountain biking.

Hang Nga's Crazy House

One of Vietnam's more unusual attractions, *Hang Nga's Crazy House* (3 Huynh Thuc Khang; daily 8.30am–7pm; 40,000VND) is the brainchild of

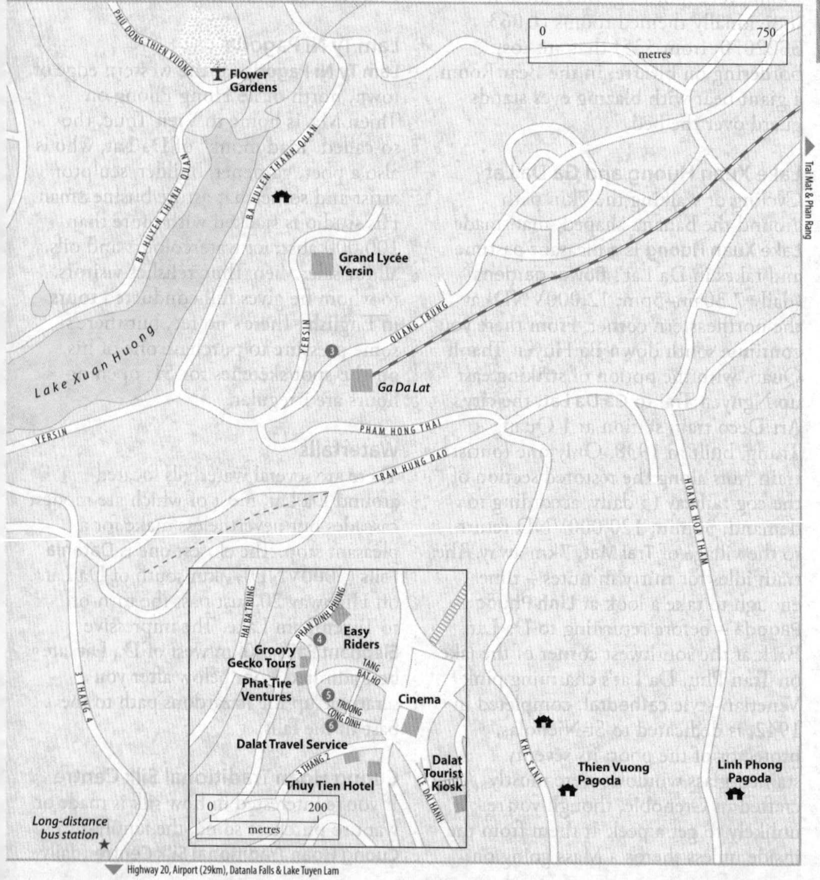

a local architect – Mra Dang Viet Nga, the daughter of Ho Chi Minh's right-hand man who studied architecture in Soviet Moscow. Not that that's evident in her creation – a bizarre, Gaudí-meets-Lord-of-the-Rings construction of intertwining buildings joined by seemingly organic, tangled walkways and drowning in bougainvillea, with the gingerbread cottage in the little garden peeking from behind giant cobwebs and oversized mushrooms. It's a wonderful adventure playground for adults and children alike, though you have to watch your step on the higher walkways, as there's little to stop you from plummeting to your doom. If you want to stay here and don't mind crowds tramping past your room every morning, there are ten individually themed rooms (T 063 3822070; from $35) that are cosy bordering on bizarre; in the Bear Room, a giant bear with blazing eyes stands guard over the bed.

Lake Xuan Huong and Ga Da Lat

Cycling or walking the 7km path around the banana-shaped, man-made **Lake Xuan Huong** is a pleasant pastime and takes in Da Lat's **flower gardens** (daily 7.30am–5pm; 12,000VND) at the northeastern corner. From there you continue south down Ba Huyen Thanh Quan, with the option of striking east up Nguyen Trai to **Ga Da Lat**, the city's Art Deco train station at 1 Quang Trung, built in 1938. Only one tourist train runs along the restored section of the cog railway (5 daily, according to demand; 30min; 120,000VND return) to the village of **Trai Mat**, 7km away. The train idles for thirty minutes – time enough to take a look at **Linh Phuoc Pagoda** – before returning to Da Lat. Back at the southwest corner of the lake on Tran Phu, Da Lat's charming pink Venetian-style **cathedral**, completed in 1942, is dedicated to St Nicholas, protector of the poor; its seventy stained-glass windows were mostly crafted in Grenoble, though you're unlikely to get a peek at them from the inside unless there's a Mass going on.

Dinh III

On a wooded hillock just off Le Hong Phong sits the oddly shaped **Dinh III** (daily 7am–5pm; 15,000VND), erstwhile summer palace of Emperor Bao Dai, erected between 1933 and 1938 to provide him with a bolt hole between elephant-slaughtering sessions. The palace has nautical portholes punched into its walls and a mast-like pole sprouting from its roof, giving it the distinct look of a ship's bridge. Inside, you have the chance to peek into the emperor's working room, festivities room and imperial bedrooms, which are surprisingly modest and reminiscent of a dated budget hotel. Photos above the fireplace are those of the crown prince, Bao Long, and his wife, Empress Nam Phuong.

Lam Ty Ni Pagoda

Lam Ty Ni Pagoda, at the western edge of town, north of Le Hong Phong on Thien My, is home to Vien Thuc, the so-called "mad monk" of Da Lat, who is also a poet, gardener, builder, sculptor, artist and somewhat astute businessman. His studio is stacked with more than 100,000 abstract watercolours and oils, all for sale; Vien Thuc relishes visitors, to whom he gives full conducted tours in English. There's no fee, but there's some pressure to purchase one of his on-the-spot sketches for $1; opening hours are irregular.

Waterfalls

There are several waterfalls located around Da Lat, most of which are modest cascades but nevertheless make for a pleasant stop. The closest one is **Datanla Falls** (5000VND), 7km south of Da Lat, off Highway 20, just past the turn-off to Tuyen Lam Lake. The impressive **Elephant Falls**, 30km west of Da Lat, are best admired from below after you scramble up the hazardous path to the base of the falls.

Cuong Hoan Traditional Silk Centre

If you're interested in how silk is made or want to purchase some, the family-run **Cuong Hoan Traditional Silk Centre** (daily

7.30am–5pm) is a great place to watch the entire process – from the sorting of the cocoons to weaving them into beautiful fabrics. A local snack of cooked silk-worm grubs, which have a nutty and not entirely unpleasant flavour, is provided.

ARRIVAL AND DEPARTURE

By plane Lien Khuong Airport is 29km south of the city, off the road to HCMC: Vietnam Airlines shuttles (45,000VND) run from here to their office at 2 Ho Tung Mau two hours before scheduled flights; a taxi or *xe om* will cost about 340,000VND or 240,000VND, respectively.

Destinations Da Nang (daily; 1hr 20min); Hanoi (2 daily; 2hr 15min); HCMC (4 daily; 50min).

By bus Buses arrive at Da Lat's long-distance bus station, about 2km south of the centre, and most public buses leave early in the morning from here. Open-tour buses will drop you off at their respective offices. You can buy tickets for daily open-tour bus departures to HCMC, Mui Ne and Nha Trang from Sinh Tourist inside the *Trung Cang Hotel* at 4a Bui Thi Xuan (T 063 3822663, W thesinhtourist.vn) or most hotels.

Destinations Buon Ma Thuot (5hr); HCMC (7–8hr); Hoi An (16hr); Mui Ne (5hr); Nha Trang (4hr).

INFORMATION AND TOURS

Motorbike tours *Xe om* drivers charge $20–25 for a day-long tour to local pagodas, waterfalls and ethnic villages. If they don't find you first, look for the Easy Riders (70 Phan Dinh Phung; W dalat-easyrider.com.), a group of war veterans who have been conducting highly rated tours of the area for the past twenty years. English-, French- and German-speaking guides are available, and their local knowledge is unrivalled. Each Easy Rider carries identification and wears a black-and-blue jacket to distinguish them from the many impersonators in town, but membership is not as exclusive as it once was and some say standards have dropped. Many other *xe om* drivers are decent too – discuss your itinerary before you set off to ensure that your guide is knowledgeable and speaks good English. Trips through the Central Highlands, ending up in Hoi An, HCMC, Nha Trang, Mui Ne or even Hanoi, are all possible (approx $80/day, including accommodation).

Activities Phat Tire Ventures at 109 Nguyen Van Troi (T 063 3829422, W phattireventures.com) and Groovy Gecko Tours at 65 Trong Cong Dinh (T 063 3836521; W groovygeckotours.net) both organize recommended adventure trips including hiking, mountain biking, climbing and canyoning; prices start at $30 for a day's hike to $170 for a two-day all-included off-road mountain-bike trip.

ACCOMMODATION

Check that you're accommodation has hot water and heating – necessities in Da Lat during the colder months.

Chau Au (Europa) 76 Nguyen Chi Thanh T 063 3822870. Popular, well-run mid-range hotel, with an English- and French-speaking owner. Rooms are simply decorated but homely and clean; some come with balconies ($20). Double **$15**

Dreams 1 and 2 151 and 164b Phan Dinh Phung T 063 3833748, W dreamshoteldalat.com. Two neighbouring mini-hotels with well-equipped and spotlessly clean en-suite rooms, all with massaging power-showers and some with jacuzzi bathtubs. Generous free breakfasts (complete with Marmite and peanut butter) and friendly staff have made these a hit with travellers. *Dreams 1* has smaller rooms, but has a sauna, steam room and communal jacuzzi on the upper level. Call to reserve. Double **$25**

★ **Hai Long Vuong** Log 6, Tran Le T 090 9862901, E phuonghanhhotel@gmail.com. The friendliest guest-house in town, a 10min walk from the centre. The English-speaking owner is always on hand to advise and most rooms have great views over Da Lat. Double **350,000VND**

Villa Pink House 7 Hai Thuong T 090 5883224. So pink that you can't miss it, this welcoming, family-run guesthouse has spacious, modern rooms, some with balcony. Mr Rot's "secret tour" of the area is worthwhile. Double **$18**

EATING AND DRINKING

Pho and *com* are cooked up on the second level of the central market during the day, and in the surrounding streets at night. There are also one or two vegetarian stalls, signposted as *com chay*.

★ **Chocolate Café** 40 Trunh Cong Dinh. Super-friendly service and an eclectic menu distinguish this little place. You can't go wrong with the spring rolls, aubergine mains or fried ice cream; in season, try the avocado milkshake. Mains from 75,000VND. Daily 8am–10pm.

Da Quy 49 Truong Cong Dinh. Popular restaurant with French bistro-style decor, offering decent Western dishes and local specialities such as fish stewed in a clay pot. Mains 55,000–100,000VND. Daily noon–10pm.

Dalat Train Café 1 Quang Trung. Take the first left after Ga Da Lat for this converted train carriage-cum-café. The menu is mixed Western and Vietnamese but the ambience is the biggest attraction here. Mains from 80,000VND. Daily 8am–10pm.

News & Art Café 70 Truong Cong Dinh. A stylish, bamboo-clad restaurant serving delicious Vietnamese dishes, such as fresh spring rolls and caramelized claypot fish. The restaurant doubles as a gallery displaying the owner's artwork. Mains 75,000–85,000VND. Daily 11.30am–10pm.

THE HO CHI MINH TRAIL

Conceived in 1959, the **Ho Chi Minh Trail** was a vital supply route from North Vietnam into the South during the American War. By the end of its "working" life the trail had grown from a rough assemblage of jungle paths to a highly effective logistical network stretching from near Vinh, north of the Seventeenth Parallel, to Tay Ninh province on the edge of the Mekong Delta. For much of its southerly route the trail ran through **Laos** and **Cambodia**, always through the most difficult, mountainous terrain.

Initially, it took up to six months to walk from north to south, travelling mostly by night, but by 1975, the Ho Chi Minh Trail – comprising at least three main arteries plus several feeder roads and totalling more than **15,000km** – was wide enough to take tanks and heavy trucks, and could be driven in just one week. It was protected by anti-aircraft emplacements and supported by fuel depots, ammunition dumps, food stores and hospitals, often located underground.

By early 1965, **aerial bombardment** by American planes had begun in earnest, using napalm and defoliants as well as conventional bombs. In eight years the US Air Force dropped more than two million tonnes of bombs, mostly over Laos and the Central Highlands, in an effort to cut the flow. But the trail was never completely severed, and you can ride parts of it today. The Ho Chi Minh Highway is a stunning road that runs from south of Hanoi and passes through some of the country's most picturesque mountain scenery along the way. Motorbike tours can be arranged with Easy Riders in Da Lat (see p.895) and Flamingo in Hanoi (see p.844).

Trong Dong 220 Phan Dinh Phung. Feast on eel and rabbit dishes – this restaurant's specialities – as well as noodles, rice and soups at this bistro-type spot. Mains from 50,000VND. Daily noon–10pm.

V Café 1/1 Bui Thi Xuan. This American-run restaurant is decked out with pictures of trains and musicians and the menu features such comfort food as home-made macaroni cheese, spinach cannelloni, pizza, and chewy, chocolatey brownies. Live music most nights. Mains from 80,000VND. Daily noon–11.30pm.

DIRECTORY

Banks Vietin Bank, 1 Le Dai Hanh, and Agribank at 36 Hoa Binh. There are Vietcombank ATMs south of the market.

Bike rental Hotels and tourist offices rent bicycles and mountain bikes ($3–5/day).

Hospital Lam Dong hospital, 4 Pham Ngoc Thach (T 063 3821369).

Pharmacies 34 Khu Hoa Binh.

Post office 14 Tran Phu.

Ho Chi Minh City

Above the Mekong Delta, some 40km north of the South China Sea, **HO CHI MINH CITY (HCMC)** is Vietnam at its frenetic best, with the city's colonial villas and elegant pagodas sitting alongside glitzy malls, stylish restaurants and towering skyscrapers, and never-ceasing ribbons of crazy traffic lubricating the city's veins. Perched on the west bank of the Saigon River, HCMC has gone through many changes – serving first as the capital of French Indochina as Saigon, and then as the capital of the Republic of Vietnam before it fell to the northern Vietnamese forces in 1975. It was renamed Ho Chi Minh City in 1976, a year after the communists rolled through the gates of the Presidential Palace and took control of the city, but the evocative old name lives on.

WHAT TO SEE AND DO

Ho Chi Minh City is divided into eighteen districts, though tourists rarely travel beyond districts 1, 3 and 5. The city proper hugs the west bank of the Saigon River, and its central area, District 1, nestles in the hinge formed by the confluence of the river with the silty Ben Nghe Channel; traditionally the French Quarter of the city, this area is still widely known as **Saigon**. Dong Khoi is its backbone, and around the T-shape it forms with Le Duan are scattered most of the city's museums and colonial remnants. Except for **Cho Lon**, HCMC's frenetic Chinatown, the city doesn't carve up into homogeneous districts, so visitors have to do a dot-to-dot between sights. These are almost invariably places that relate to the American War, but there are

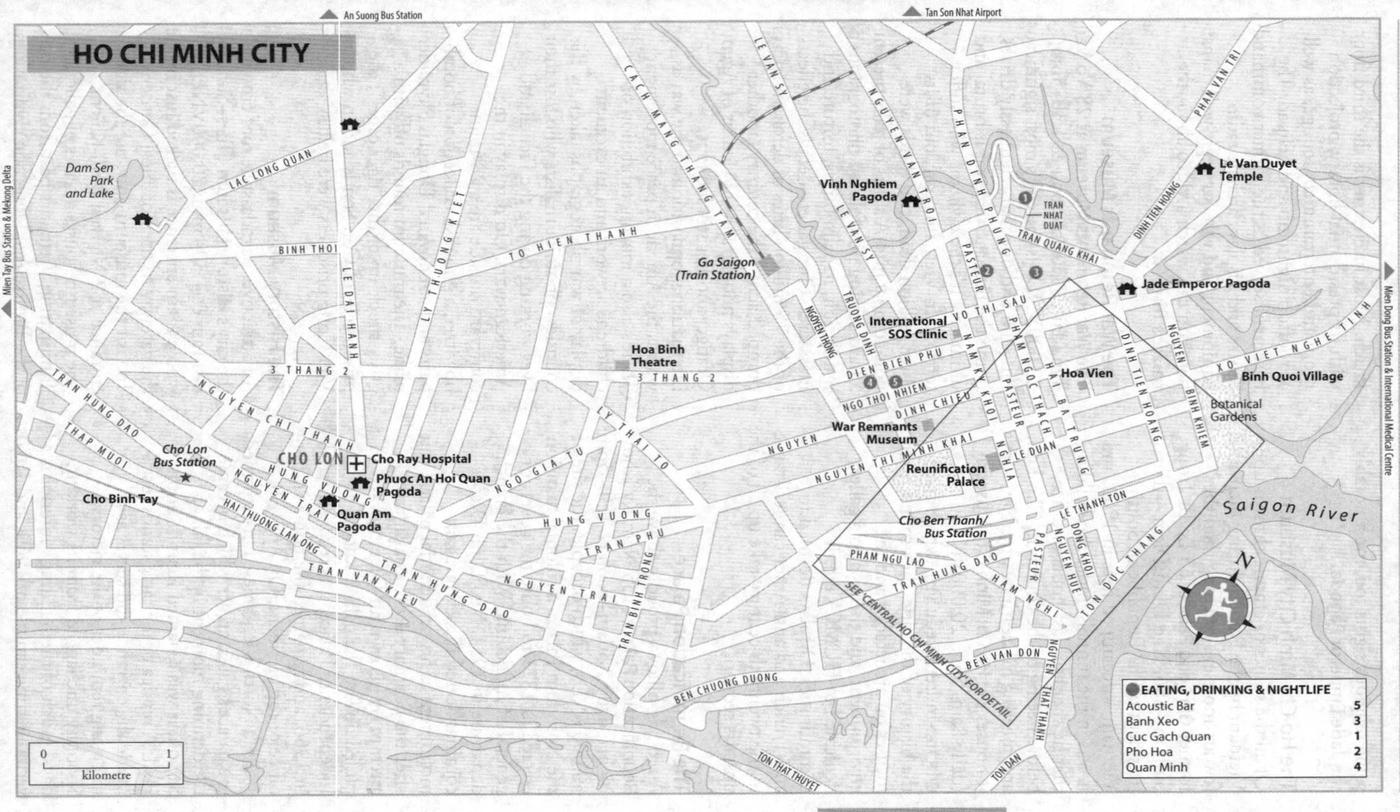
HO CHI MINH CITY
An Suong Bus Station
Tan Son Nhat Airport
Mien Tay Bus Station & Mekong Delta
Mien Dong Bus Station & International Medical Centre
Dam Sen Park and Lake
LAC LONG QUAN
BINH THOI
LE DAI HANH
LY THUONG KIET
TO HIEN THANH
CACH MANG THANG TAM
LE VAN SY
NGUYEN VAN TROI
PHAN DINH PHUNG
TRAN NHAT DUAT
TRAN QUANG KHAI
DINH TIEN HOANG
PHAN VAN TRI
Le Van Duyet Temple
Vinh Nghiem Pagoda
Ga Saigon (Train Station)
Jade Emperor Pagoda
International SOS Clinic
VO THI SAU
NGUYEN THONG
TRUONG DINH
PASTEUR
DIEN BIEN PHU
NGO THOI NHIEM
DINH CHIEU
NAM KY KHOI NGHIA
PHAM NGOC THACH
HAI BA TRUNG
Hoa Vien
NGUYEN BINH KHIEM
XO VIET NGHE TINH
Binh Quoi Village
Botanical Gardens
War Remnants Museum
NGUYEN THI MINH KHAI
LE DUAN
Reunification Palace
Hoa Binh Theatre
3 THANG 2
TRAN HUNG DAO
THAP MUOI
NGUYEN CHI THANH
Cho Lon Bus Station
CHO LON
Cho Ray Hospital
Phuoc An Hoi Quan Pagoda
HUNG VUONG
NGUYEN TRAI
Quan Am Pagoda
Cho Binh Tay
HAI THUONG LAN ONG
TRAN VAN KIEU
NGO GIA TU
LY THAI TO
TRAN PHU
TRAN BINH TRONG
Cho Ben Thanh/ Bus Station
PHAM NGU LAO
LE THANH TON
DONG KHOI
NGUYEN HUE
HAM NGHI
TON DUC THANG
Saigon River
SEE 'CENTRAL HO CHI MINH CITY' FOR DETAIL
BEN VAN DON
NGUYEN THAT THANH
BEN CHUONG DUONG
TON THAT THUYET
TON DAN
N
0
1
kilometre
EATING, DRINKING & NIGHTLIFE
Acoustic Bar 5
Banh Xeo 3
Cuc Gach Quan 1
Pho Hoa 2
Quan Minh 4

some religious sights too, most notably the **Jade Emperor Pagoda**.

The Ho Chi Minh City Museum

Of all the stones of empire thrown up in Vietnam by the French during their rule, few are more eye-catching than the former **Gia Long Palace**, 65 Ly Tu Trong, built in 1886. Ngo Dinh Diem – the president of the Republic of South Vietnam – decamped here in 1962, and it was in the tunnels under the building that he spent his last hours of office, before fleeing to the church in Cho Lon, and meeting his death nearby. Nowadays, it houses the **Ho Chi Minh City Museum** (daily 8am–5pm; 20,000VND; ⓦhcmc-museum.edu.vn), which traces the history of the city. The ground floor focuses on archeology and the environment, and there's also a gallery dedicated to HCMC's ethnic communities. Displays devoted to anti-French and anti-American resistance in the twentieth century take up all of the upstairs section.

The Reunification Palace

A red flag billows proudly above the **Reunification Palace** (135 Nam Ky Khoi Nghia; daily 7.30am–noon & 1.30–5pm; 30,000VND), which occupies the site of the Norodom Palace, a colonial mansion erected in 1871 to house the governor-general of Indochina. With the French departure in 1954, Ngo Dinh Diem commandeered this extravagant monument as his presidential palace, but after the February 1962 assassination attempt by his own air force, it was pulled down. The palace, known as Independence Palace, was reconstructed in 1966, and remained the home and office of the president. On April 30, 1975, a North Vietnamese tank stormed the palace's gates, an act which became the defining moment in the fall of Saigon; it was renamed Reunification Hall. A replica of the tank stands just inside the entrance and serves as an imposing reminder of the victory. Spookily unchanged from its working days, much of the building's interior is a veritable time capsule of 1960s and 1970s kitsch. Most interesting is the third floor, with its presidential library, projection room and entertainment lounge, as well as rooftop nightclub and helipad. The basement served as the former command centre and displays archaic radio equipment and vast, strategic wall maps; here you can watch a video about the palace's history.

The War Remnants Museum

The **War Remnants Museum** at 28 Vo Van Tan (daily 7.30am–noon & 1.30–5pm; 20,000VND) is the city's most significant museum and one that relentlessly drives home the message that war is brutal and ultimately it's the civilians who suffer terribly. In Vietnam's case, out of its three million dead, two thirds were non-combatants. A series of halls present a hard-hitting portfolio of photographs of mutilation, napalm burns, torture and massacres. One gallery details the effects of the 75 million litres of defoliant sprays dumped across the country; another displays photographs of victims of Agent Orange; another still looks at international opposition to the war as well as the American peace movement. There's also a moving exhibition of children's artwork and an excellent display of war photographs taken by the countless photojournalists who lost their lives working during the French and American wars. On display in the courtyard outside are a 28-tonne howitzer, a ghoulish collection of bomb parts and a renovated Douglas Skyraider plane. The museum rounds off with a grisly mock-up of the "tiger cages", the prison cells of Con Son Island in which Viet Cong prisoners were held.

The History Museum

An attractive, pagoda-style roof crowns the city's **History Museum** (Tues–Sun 8–11am & 1.30–5pm; 20,000VND), whose main entrance is tucked just inside the gateway to the Botanical Gardens. To visit the museum only, use the side entrance at 2 Nguyen Binh Khiem. The museum houses a series of galleries illuminating Vietnam's past from the rise of the Bronze Age Dong Son civilization,

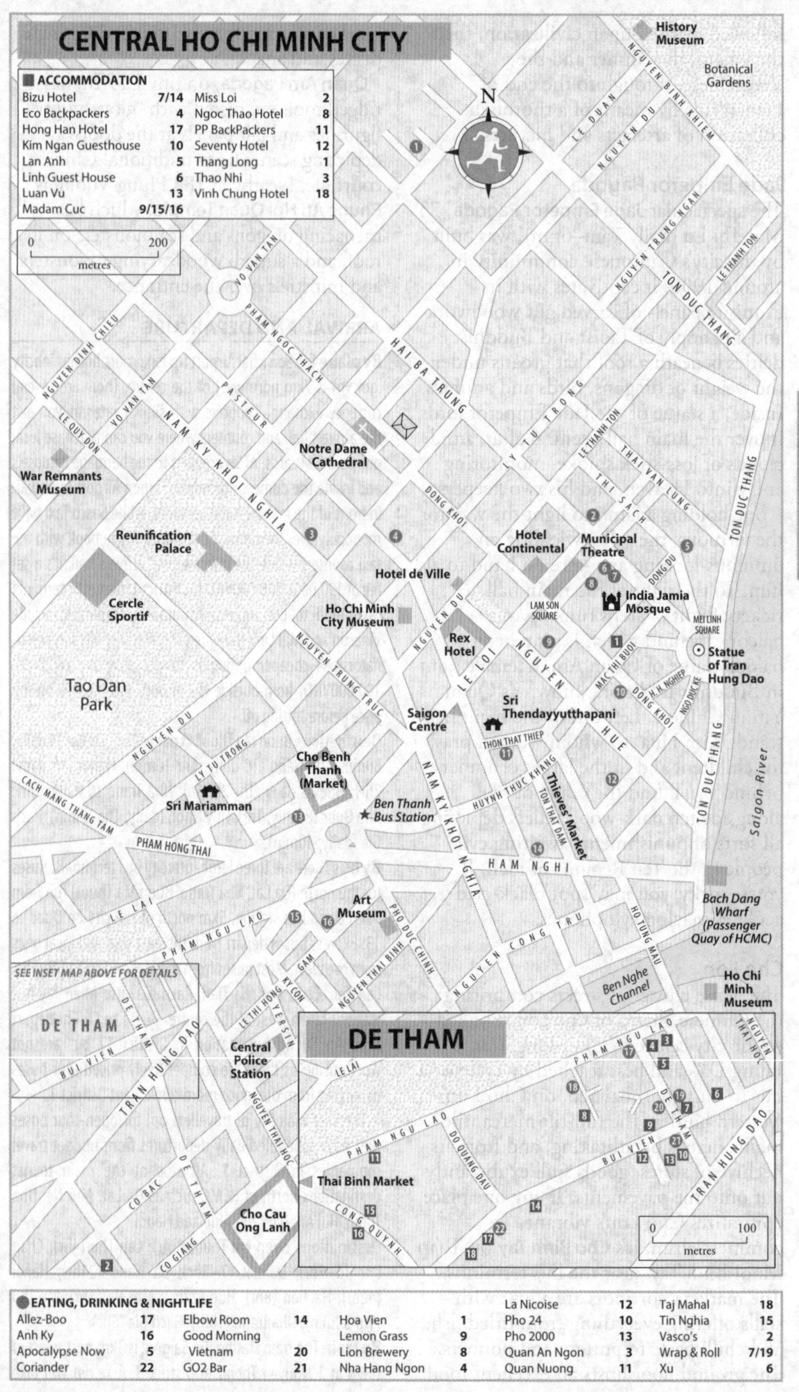

EATING, DRINKING & NIGHTLIFE

Allez-Boo	17	Elbow Room	14	Hoa Vien	1	La Nicoise	12	Taj Mahal	18
Anh Ky	16	Good Morning Vietnam	20	Lemon Grass	9	Pho 24	10	Tin Nghia	15
Apocalypse Now	5	GO2 Bar	21	Lion Brewery	8	Pho 2000	13	Vasco's	2
Coriander	22			Nha Hang Ngon	4	Quan An Ngon	3	Wrap & Roll	7/19
						Quan Nuong	11	Xu	6

followed by the Funan civilization, then the Cham, the Khmer and the Vietnamese, through to the end of French rule by means of a thorough collection of artefacts and pictures.

Jade Emperor Pagoda

The spectacular **Jade Emperor Pagoda**, 73 Mai Thi Lu (daily 7am–6pm), was built by the city's Cantonese community in around 1900. It captivates with its exquisite panels of carved gilt woodwork and a panoply of Taoist and Buddhist deities beneath a roof that groans under the weight of dragons, birds and animals.

Inside, a statue of the Jade Emperor lords it over the main hall's central altar, amid clouds of joss-stick smoke, monitoring entry into Heaven, and his two keepers – one holding a lamp to light the way for the virtuous, the other wielding an ominous-looking axe – are on hand to aid him. To the right of the main hall, a rickety flight of steps runs up to a balcony, behind which is set a neon-haloed statue of Quan Am, a female saint in Buddhist tradition, known as Quan Yin in Chinese. Left out of the main hall stands Kim Hua, to whom women pray for children, and in the larger chamber behind you'll find the Chief of Hell alongside ten dark-wood reliefs depicting all sorts of punishments awaiting evil people in the Ten Regions of Hell. If you're lucky, you may spot black-clad acolytes playing xylophones.

Cho Lon

The dense cluster of streets comprising the Chinese ghetto of **Cho Lon** is linked to the city centre by 5km-long Tran Hung Dao and best reached by cyclo or a bus to Huynh Thoai Yen, on Cho Lon's western border. The full-tilt mercantile mania here is breathtaking, and from its beehive of stores, goods spill exuberantly out onto the pavements. If any one place epitomizes Cho Lon's vibrant commercialism, it's **Cho Binh Tay** on Thap Muoi Binh Tay, near the bus terminus. The market's corridors are abuzz with stalls offering everything from dried fish and chilli paste to pottery and bonnets. The ground floor hosts an excellent food market offering freshly prepared Chinese dishes and snacks.

Quan Am Pagoda, on tiny Lao Tu, has ridged roofs encrusted with "glove-puppet" figurines and gilt panels at the doorway depicting scenes from traditional Chinese court life. Nearby at 184 Hung Vuong is **Phuoc An Hoi Quan Temple**, which has menacing dragons and sea monsters on its roof, and a superb woodcarving of jousters and minstrels over the entrance.

ARRIVAL AND DEPARTURE

By plane Tan Son Nhat Airport (ⓦ tsnairport.hochiminhcity.gov.vn) is 7km northwest of the centre. There are several currency exchange counters with similar rates as you exit the arrivals hall and counters where you can purchase local pre-paid SIM cards. ATMs are next to the baggage carousels and inside the domestic terminal. Saigon Airport Taxis wait in front of the international terminal, while Sasco Taxi have monopoly over the domestic terminal; if you book with the taxi counters inside the international arrivals hall, it's a set fee of 190,000–200,000VND to District 1; domestic terminal taxis tend to use meters. Reputable companies include Vinasun and Mai Linh (beware of similarly-spelled impersonators). A cheaper option is to get a *xe om* (80,000–100,000VND) from outside the airport gates; agree on the price before setting off.

Destinations Buon Ma Thuot (3 daily; 1hr); Da Lat (4 daily; 50min); Da Nang (10 daily; 1hr 10min); Hanoi (10 daily; 2hr); Hue (6 daily; 1hr 20min); Nha Trang (6 daily; 1hr); Phu Quoc (8 daily; 1hr); Quy Nhon (daily; 1hr 25min); Rach Gia (daily; 40min).

By bus There are three large intercity bus terminals. Buses for the north (Da Lat, Nha Trang, Buon Ma Thuot) run from Mien Dong bus station, 5km north of the city on Quoc Lo 13. Express buses depart from the east side and local ones from the west. Most buses from the Mekong Delta (My Tho, Can Tho, Chau Doc, Ha Tien, Rach Gia) use Mien Tay bus station, 10km west of the centre. Buses to Cu Chi depart from An Suong bus station in District 12 but are not worth using as there are competitively priced tour buses departing from the much more convenient District 1.

The vast majority of travellers opt for open-tour buses that have scheduled daily departures from budget travel companies in District 1. All stop at the main tourist destinations north of HCMC such as Da Lat, Mui Ne, Nha Trang, Hoi An, Da Nang, Hue and Hanoi.

Destinations Buon Ma Thuot (9hr); Can Tho (4hr); Chau Doc (6–7hr); Da Lat (7–8hr); Da Nang (21hr); Hanoi (42hr); Ha Tien (8hr); Hue (27hr); Mui Ne (5hr); My Tho (1hr 30min); Nha Trang (10hr); Rach Gia (6hr).

By train The train station, Ga Saigon, is 3km northwest of town at 1 Nguyen Thong in District 3. A *xe om* will take

CRIME IN HCMC

HCMC has more than its fair share of people for whom progress hasn't yet translated into food, lodgings and employment, so begging, stealing and prostitution are all facts of life here. Petty crime is a fairly regular occurrence and drive-by bag snatching can occur. Keep a tight grip on your belongings while walking the streets, or travelling on cyclos and motorbikes – especially after dark and around tourist nightspots.

you to or from District 1 for around 40,000VND (10min); a taxi is about 60,000VND. Always book train tickets as far ahead as possible, through a travel agent or in person at counters no. 9–16 on the first floor of the train station (daily 7am–9pm).

Destinations Da Nang (5 daily; 15–20hr); Hanoi (5 daily; 30–41hr); Hue (5 daily; 18–24hr); Nha Trang (5 daily; 6hr 20min–8hr 30min).

GETTING AROUND

Cyclo Cyclos are nowhere as plentiful as they once were and are banned from many streets, having to take circuitous routes as a result. Some drivers were South Vietnamese soldiers and speak fluent English as a result. You should always agree a price before setting off, writing down numbers or holding up the exact number of bills to avoid frequent "misunderstandings". Short hops coast around 20,000–30,000VND; cyclos can also be rented per hour (around 55,000VND).

Xe om Motorbike taxis (*xe om*) are ubiquitous, with drivers hanging around street corners. Agree on a price before setting off; short hops are around 30,000VND. Keep a close grip on your bag.

Taxis Get your lodgings to call Mai Linh taxis (T 08 38383838) or Vinasun taxis (T 08 38272727) to avoid dodgy taxis with rigged super-fast meters. Rates should be approximately 15,000VND/km.

Bike and motorbike Most rental places are around Pham Ngu Lao; prices per day average around $3–4 for a bicycle and $7–12 for a moped or medium-sized motorbike. Traffic in HCMC is chaotic and road accidents are common.

INFORMATION AND TOURS

The best sources of information are hotels, tour agencies and travellers' cafés, which also offer open-tour buses, motorbike and car rental, guide services and day-trips; some also do longer tours and visa services.

Tour agencies Recommended agencies include: Sinh Tourist, 246–248 De Tham (T 08 38389593, W thesinhtourist.vn); Sinhbalo, 283/20 Pham Ngu Lao (T 08 38376766, W sinhbalo.com); and Handspan, 7th floor, Titan Building, 18 nam Quoc Cang, District 1 (T 08 39257605, W handspan.com).

ACCOMMODATION

HCMC's budget enclave centres are Pham Ngu Lao, Bui Vien and De Tham, 1km west of the city centre. The charming alleyways between Co Giang and Co Bac offer excellent family-run budget options a 10min walk away. The most pleasant (though pricey) area to stay in is around Dong Khoi. Staying in Cho Lon leaves you marooned in the bustle of the city's Chinatown, but there are a few bargains.

DE THAM AND AROUND

Bizu Hotel 183 De Tham T 08 39208986, W bizuhotel .com; map p.899. Spotless, spacious, tiled rooms with crisp sheets in a fantastic central location. The receptionists are particularly helpful. Double **$32**

Eco Backpackers 264 De Tham W hostelworld.com; map p.899. We're not sure where the "eco" bit comes in, but the individual pods in the dorms give some measure of privacy, the location is as central as can be and the private rooms, though dark, are clean and spacious. Dorm **$6**, double **$20**

Hong Han Hotel 238 Bui Vien T 08 38361927, W honghanhotelhcm.com; map p.899. Huge, well-furnished rooms, a great central location, helpful staff and good view of the city from the top floor are all pros. On the downside, there's no lift, so woe betide you if you're on the top floor and out of shape. Double **$25**

Kim Ngan Guesthouse 217/29 De Tham T 08 38368801, E hotel97buivien@yahoo.com; map p.899. The staff are on the ball here, the fan rooms are spacious and clean with quirky chequered floor tiles, there's a homey, relaxed vibe and an extra $4 will get you a/c. Singles ($13) are a boon for solo travellers. Double **$18**

Lan Anh 252 De Tham T 08 38365197; map p.899. A popular budget option run by a congenial family, with bright a/c and fan rooms, and friendly hosts; breakfast included. Double **$22**

Luan Vu 35/2 Bui Vien T 08 38377185, W luanvuhotel .com; map p.899. Located down an alley away from the traffic, this hotel has pleasantly furnished rooms, free breakfast and helpful staff. Double **$22**

Madam Cuc 64 Bui Vien T 08 38365073; 127 Cong Quynh T 08 38368761; 184 Cong Quynh T 08 38361679; W madamcuchotels.com; map p.899. Hugely popular, this trio of guesthouses offers a range of comfortable rooms, some sleeping up to four ($35), with satellite TV and fridges, plus free breakfast and airport transfers. Staff can be less than polite. Double **$20**

Ngoc Thao Hotel 241/4 Pham Ngu Lao T 08 38370273, E ngocthaohotel@yahoo.com; map p.899. Family-run hotel, offering quiet and smart double, triple and family rooms with all the amenities. The owner, Mr Tuan, runs

tours to the Mekong Delta and the staff are friendly and helpful. Dorms $10, doubles $20

PP BackPackers 283/41 Pham Ngu Lao ⓣ012 62501823; map p.899. Great location in the heart of the backpacker district and a super-friendly manager make this a welcoming backpacker haven. The mid-sized dorms and rooms are comfortable and the triples and quads are good value if travelling with friends. Dorm $7, double $19

Seventy Hotel 70 Bui Vien ⓣ09 05870087, ⓦseventyhotel.com; map p.899. A popular and expanding veteran, offering a choice of tidy and tastefully decorated a/c rooms, most of them airy and pleasant. Hot drinks and good breakfast are included. Double $25

Thao Nhi 185/20 Pham Ngu Lao ⓣ08 39201262, ⓔthaonhihotel@hcm.vnn.vn; map p.899. Reminiscent of the *Premier Inn* chain, this hotel, located down an alleyway, offers clean, spacious rooms with all amenities and excellent breakfast. Double $17

11

★Vinh Chung Hotel 283/26 Pham Ngu Lao ⓣ09 09113312, ⓦvinhchunghotel.com; map p.899. The owner of this hotel bends over backwards to accommodate her guests, some rooms come with balcony, some come with cable TV and the beds are a tad softer than the usual hard-as-rock variety. Double $20

CO GIANG AREA

Miss Loi 178/20 Co Giang ⓣ08 38379589, ⓔmissloi@hcm.fpt.vn; map p.899. This charmingly old-fashioned multistorey guesthouse, with a communal dining area complete with colourful statuettes and welcoming staff, is a local institution. However, lack of lift is a disadvantage for those with heavy luggage, and the breakfast is nothing to write home about. Double $16

DONG KHOI AND AROUND

Linh Guest House 40/10 Bui Vien ⓣ08 38369641; map p.899. Down a quiet side street in the backpacker district, this immaculate spot is excellent value; doubles come with a/c, fridges and cable TV. Double $12

★TREAT YOURSELF

Xu 75 Hai Ba Trung ⓣ08 38248468, ⓦxusaigon.com; map p.899. Its name meaning "coin", this dark and stylish resto-lounge with impeccable service specializes in Vietnamese fusion. Delight your senses with the likes of dragon-fruit salad with crab, seabass spring rolls, braised pork belly and chicken rice and save some room for durian tiramisu. Dinner dishes are designed for sharing. Mains from 200,000VND. Daily 11.30am–2.30pm & 6.30–11pm.

Thang Long 48 Mac Thi Buoi ⓣ08 38222595, ⓦthanglonghotel.com.vn; map p.899. Mini-hotel in mock-traditional style, with dark-panelled rooms of varying sizes, all with a/c, breakfast and satellite TV. Double $27

EATING

The culinary capital of Vietnam, HCMC offers everything from fine French cuisine in the Dong Khoi area, to noodle soups and fresh spring rolls at the makeshift street kitchens scattered around the city. Cho Lon has the best Chinese restaurants, and average but reasonably priced backpacker cafés predominate around Pham Ngu Lao. Where phone numbers are given, it's best to book ahead.

DE THAM AND AROUND

Coriander 185 Bui Vien; map p.899. Flavoursome Thai favourites at reasonable prices, with two streetside tables from which to watch the world go by. The curries and the pad thai are particularly good; mains from 80,000VND. Daily 10am–11.30pm.

★Cuc Gach Quan 10 Dang Tat ⓦcucgachquan.com; map p.897. The food at this French colonial house is beautiful Vietnamese, with an emphasis on local and organic ingredients and eco-friendly practices. Try sea bass in passion-fruit sauce, aubergine sautéed with pork, lotus-shoot salad or clams steamed with lemongrass, and don't run off without trying the home-made durian or black bean ice cream. Mains from 80,000VND. Daily noon–10.30pm.

Good Morning Vietnam 197 De Tham; map p.899. One of several branches of this Italian-run pizza chain, serving authentic pizza and pasta (from 85,000VND) in a trattoria-style setting using imported ingredients. Daily 9am–midnight.

Pho 2000 1–3 Phan Chu Trinh, next to Ben Thanh; map p.899. Tuck into big bowls of delicious noodle soup for 60,000VND at the spot visited by President Clinton. Daily 7am–11pm.

Taj Mahal 241/1 Pham Ngu Lao; map p.899. An unfussy little snug with just six tables tucked down an alley. They offer delicious northern Indian dishes (mains from 55,000VND), such as tandoori, biryani and plenty of vegetarian options. Daily noon–10.30pm.

Tin Nghia 9 Tran Hung Dao; map p.899. Mushrooms, tofu and home-made soups (35,000VND) provide the backbone to the inventive menu in this genial Buddhist "pure vegetarian" restaurant, established over eighty years ago. Daily 7am–2pm & 4–9pm.

Wrap & Roll 62 Hai ba Trung; map p.899. Excellent chain that specializes in different types of rolls (steamed rice with minced pork, mustard lettuce rolls with prawns, fresh and fried spring rolls), as well as hotpots, claypot dishes, salads and noodle dishes, all served in cheerful yellow-and-white surroundings. Also at 226 De Tham. Mains from 68,000VND. Daily 11.30am–10.30pm.

STREET FOOD

Informal local eating-houses, makeshift **street kitchens** and market **food stalls** offer the cheapest, most authentic dining experience; those packed with locals are your best bet. At night, the stalls around Ben Thanh Market buzz with life, as locals and foreigners alike tuck into steaming bowls of soup, barbecued meat skewers and delectable seafood dishes. For street food in more refined surroundings, Nha Hang Ngon (160 Pasteur; mains 55,000–100,000VND) is the perfect place to sample local specialities; pick and choose your dishes from the dozens of food stalls scattered through the leafy courtyard of this lovely old colonial villa, and they'll be delivered to your table; alternatively, you can order off the extensive menu. The nearby *Quan An Ngon* (138 Nam Ky Khoi Nghia; mains 45,000–115,000VND) has a similar setup.

AROUND DONG KHOI AND THI SACH

Anh Ky 80 Le Thi Hong Gam; map p.899. This roadside eatery is a local favourite for wonton noodle soup (40,000VND), which is all it serves. Daily 6.30am–midnight.

Elbow Room 52 Pasteur; map p.899. Elbow room can be difficult to find at this popular American-style bistro, serving ample breakfasts of pancakes, bacon, eggs and more. If you're homesick, the giant burritos, hot dogs, pizza and burgers may dull your pain. Mains from 120,000VND. Mon–Sat 8am–10pm, to 5pm Sun.

La Nicoise 56 Ngo Duc Ke; map p.899. Cosy French restaurant that serves well-executed dishes such as steak au poivre, *moules mariniéres* and French onion soup; the lunchtime *plat du jour* is particularly good value. Mains from 100,000VND. Daily 8am–11pm.

Lemon Grass 4 Nguyen Thiep; map p.899. Located off Dong Khoi, this stylish three-floor restaurant serves highly rated southern Vietnamese food (mains from 80,000VND) to the strains of traditional music recitals every night. Daily 11am–10.30pm.

Pho 24 71–73 Dong Khoi; map p.899. Leading pho chain in Vietnam, serving large bowls of flavourful beef or chicken noodle soup for 45,000VND. Daily 7am–late.

Quan Nuong 29–31 Thon That Thiep; map p.899. Convivial rooftop restaurant, where groups of locals, expats and visitors alike barbecue their own shrimp, beef, pork and vegetables on individual tabletop grills (120,000–180,000VND/person). Round off your meal with a sundae from *Fanny* on the ground floor. Daily 5–11pm.

AROUND DIEN BIEN PHU

Banh Xeo 46a Dinh Cong Trang; map p.897. Enormous, cheap and filling Vietnamese pancakes stuffed with shrimp, pork, beans and egg for around 60,000VND are the speciality at this streetside place off Hai Ba Trung. Daily 10am–9pm.

Pho Hoa 260c Pasteur; map p.897. Heaving with locals and decorated with striking bamboo murals, this restaurant serves up generous portions of pho (55,000VND) with slivers of beef or chicken and piles of fresh greens. Daily 7am–10pm.

Quan Minh Bo Minh 107/P Truong Dinh; map p.897. *Lau* (steamboat) and pho (30,000VND) are the staples at this streetside, no-frills restaurant. Daily 6am–11pm.

DRINKING AND NIGHTLIFE

The area around Pham Ngu Lao is lined with lively, cheap bars, while Dong Khoi and around plays host to most of the city's nightclubs, which shut in the early hours of the morning; take care of your bag when leaving, and be aware that quite a few bars have upfront prostitution.

Acoustic Café 6E1 Ngo Thoi Nhiem; map p.897. Leave the backpackers behind and join Saigon's student population to see the seriously un-acoustic local rock bands performing predominantly American covers every night in this heaving live music hub at the end of a narrow alleyway. Daily 7pm–midnight.

Allez-Boo 187 Pham Ngu Lao; map p.899. Pham Ngu Lao's busiest bar, popular for its classic tunes, Thai food and selection of cocktails; there's seating on the street outside and backpackers show what they're made of on the dancefloor upstairs. Daily 7am–late.

Apocalypse Now 2c Thi Sach; map p.899. One of the original Saigon nightspots, attracting travellers, locals, expats and a few "nymphs of the pavement" with its party atmosphere and eclectic mix of music. Always heaving and apocalyptically busy on weekends. Daily 9pm–late.

GO2 Bar 187 De Tham; map p.899. Fabulously cheesy backpacker hangout, with Vietnamese and Western snacks served late into the night in the neon-lit downstairs bar to a soundtrack of classic pop tunes. The upstairs dancefloor hosts a nightly DJ and you can chill out with a hookah on the roof terrace. Open 24hr.

★ **Hoa Vien** 18bis/28 Nguyen Thi Minh Kai; map p.899. The best microbrewery in town, with a spacious yet cosy interior and an attractive garden, three kinds of beer on tap (the dark is particularly good) and Czech-inspired food. Daily noon–late.

Lion Brewery 11C Lam Son Square; map p.899. This large, German-style beer is centrally located, serves numerous bottled beers as well as two of its own to a good mix of expats and locals, and the menu features some German exotica, as well as Vietnamese dishes. Daily noon–late.

Vasco's 74/7D Hai Ba Trung; map p.899. One of several bars hidden away in a secluded courtyard, this refined little place is a long-time favourite with the expat crowd. With happy hour from 4–7pm, downstairs is a good spot

to enjoy a pre-dinner cocktail and pizza; head upstairs for the live music and DJ sets. Daily 4pm–midnight.

TRADITIONAL ENTERTAINMENT

Hoa Binh Theatre 3 Thang 2 ⓣ 08 38653353, ⓦ nhahathoabinh.com.vn. Regular performances of modern and traditional Vietnamese music, as well as traditional theatre and dance.

Saigon Water Puppet Theatre History Museum, Nguyen Binh Khiem. This very Vietnamese form of entertainment is way more fun than Punch and Judy, with the watery stage adding a measure of magic to the show performed with beautifully carved wooden puppets (daily at 9am, 10am, 11am, noon, 2pm, 3pm and 4pm; 20min).

11

SHOPPING

Art Galleries specializing in replicas of famous originals abound in HCMC, especially along Nguyen Hue. You can buy prints of vintage communist propaganda posters at the Hanoi Gallery, 79 Bui Vien.

Books HCMC's best bookshop is Fahasa, at 40 Nguyen Hue and 60–62 Le Loi, which has a good range of new English-language titles. Binh Anh (147–149 Bui Vien) and Thai Nhi (40/4 Bui Vien) both have a decent selection of second-hand books.

Clothes For quirky Vietnam-themed T-shirts, check out Ginko (Life's Too Shirt) at 54–56 Bui Vien and 10 Le Loi. For tailoring, try Zakka at 134 Pasteur. Mai's at 132–134 Dong Khoi does hand-stitched designer clothing and accessories.

Handicrafts For lacquerware, ceramics, hand-embroidered household goods and other souvenirs, try the Ben Thanh Market or Mai Handicrafts at 298 Nguyen Trong Tuyen – a fair trade shop selling ethnic fabrics, and other gifts, the proceeds from which support street children.

Markets The city's biggest market is Cho Ben Thanh, at the junction of Tran Hung Dao, Le Loi and Ham Nghi, with everything from conical hats, basket-ware bags, Da Lat coffee and Vietnam T-shirts to buckets of eels and pigs' ears and snouts. Dan Sinh Market at 104 Yersin sells army surplus gear, so pick up rain ponchos and mosquito nets here, as well as combat boots.

WHAT'S ON IN HCMC

Several publications carry listings information: try the monthly *Vietnam Economic Times*' supplement *The Guide*, *The Word HCMC* (ⓦ wordhcmc.com), the weekly *Vietnam Investment Review*'s supplement *Time Out* ($2.50) and *Asia Life HCMC* (ⓦ asialifehcmc.com). These feature HCMC listings, reviews and useful travel tips, and are widely available in bars, hotels and backpacker cafés around the city.

DIRECTORY

Banks and exchange ANZ, 11 Me Linh Square; HSBC, 235 Dong Khoi; Vietcombank, 29 Chuong Duong and 17 Chuong Duong. Outside normal banking hours, try the Donga Bank exchange bureau at 187 Pham Ngu Lao (Mon–Sat 7.30am–1pm & 1.30–7.30pm) or the exchange bureau at 1A Nguyen An Ninh (daily 8am–8pm).

Embassies and consulates Australia, Landmark Building, 5b Ton Duc Thanh ⓣ 08 35218100; Canada, 9th floor, The Metropolitan, 235 Dong Khoi ⓣ 08 38279899; China, 39 Nguyen Thi Minh Khai ⓣ 08 38292457; USA, 4 Le Duan ⓣ 08 35204200.

Hospitals and clinics International SOS Clinic, 65 Nguyen Du (ⓣ 08 38298520; ⓦ internationalsos.com), has a 24hr emergency service, and international doctors who speak English; they also have a dental clinic. International Medical Centre, 1 Han Thuyen (ⓣ 08 38272366, ⓦ cmi-vietnam.com), is a non-profit hospitalization centre staffed by English-speaking French doctors, with a 24hr emergency service and profits subsidizing operations for underprivileged children.

Pharmacies Several around the Pham Ngu Lao area, including at 65 Bui Vien. Also at 156 Pasteur and 105 Nguyen Hue.

DAY-TRIPS FROM HO CHI MINH CITY

The single most popular trip out of the city takes in two of Vietnam's most memorable sights: the **Cu Chi tunnels**, for twenty years a bolt hole, first for Viet Minh agents, and later for Viet Cong cadres; and the weird and wonderful **Cao Dai Holy See** at Tay Ninh, the fulcrum of the country's most charismatic indigenous religion. Most HCMC travel agents combine these two sights, with tours costing $12–17 (not including entrance to the tunnels); the two attractions combined take a whole day to visit.

The Cu Chi tunnels

During the American War, the villages around the district of Cu Chi supported a substantial Viet Cong (VC) presence. Faced with American attempts to neutralize them, they quite literally dug themselves out of harm's way, and the legendary **Cu Chi tunnels** were the result.

By 1965, 250km of tunnels crisscrossed Cu Chi and the surrounding areas. The tunnels could be as small as 80cm wide

and 80cm high, and were sometimes four levels deep; there were latrines, wells, meeting rooms and dorms here, as well as rudimentary hospitals, where operations were carried out by torchlight using instruments fashioned from shards of ordnance. At times inhabitants stayed below ground for weeks on end, and they often had to lie on the floor to get enough oxygen to breathe. American attempts to flush out the tunnels proved ineffective. They evacuated villagers into strategic hamlets and then used defoliant sprays and bulldozers to rob the VC of cover, in "scorched earth" operations. A special GI unit known as tunnel rats was faced with the task of infiltrating the tunnels themselves, which involved crawling in complete darkness with a partner, facing all manner of booby traps, as well as bombs and fire from the Viet Cong. Some sections of tunnels were deliberately flooded and the casualty rate was very high.

Today, the tunnels have been widened to allow passage for tourists, but it's still a dark, claustrophobic experience, as it's very warm inside the tunnels and you can go down as far as the third level during the 50m stretch of tunnel that visitors are allowed to access. To unwittingly add a touch of authenticity, there are occasional power cuts that leave you briefly in complete darkness. Before entering the tunnel, you are led around by guides in army greens who demonstrate various crude but effective pit traps used by the Viet Cong, as well as a bomb crater and an M-41 tank. There are two sites – Ben Duoc and Ben Dinh, the most popular being **Ben Dinh** (daily 7.30am–4.30pm; 80,000VND), around 50km from HCMC and easiest visited on a tour organized through your lodgings.

The Cao Dai Holy See

Northwest of Cu Chi at Tay Ninh lies the fantastical confection of styles that is the **Cao Dai Holy See** (open 24hr; free). The Cao Dai religion was founded in October 1926 as a fusion of oriental and occidental religions. Though its beliefs centre on a universal god and it borrows the structure and terminology of the Catholic Church, Cao Dai is primarily influenced by Buddhism, Taoism and Confucianism, and looks to hasten the evolution of the soul through reincarnation.

The cathedral's central portico is topped by a bowed, first-floor balcony and a Divine Eye, the most recurrent motif in the building. Two figures in semi-relief emerge from either side of the towers: Cao Dai's first female cardinal, Lam Huong Thanh, on the left; and on the right, Le Van Trung, Cao Dai's first pope. Men enter through an entrance in the right wall, women by a door to the left. Tourists can wander through the nave as long as they remain in the aisles and don't stray between the rows of pink pillars, entwined by green dragons. The papal chair stands at the head of the chamber, its arms carved into dragons. Dominating the chamber, though, and guarded by eight silver dragons, a vast, duck-egg-blue sphere, speckled with stars, rests on a polished, eight-sided dais. **Services** are held daily at 6am, noon, 6pm and midnight, and tours usually arrive in time

INTO CAMBODIA: MOC BAI

At present, the main overland entry and exit point between Cambodia and Vietnam for foreigners is at **Moc Bai**, northwest of HCMC. The Moc Bai border is open daily 7am–5pm. Sinh Tourist, Kim Travel (see p.901) and a number of other operators around Pham Ngu Lao run daily a/c buses **to Phnom Penh** from their offices, leaving hourly from 6am–2pm ($14; 6–7hr). Some, such as Mekong Express at 275F Pham Ngu Lao (Ⓦcatmekongexpress.com), also have direct daily services to Sihanoukville ($26; 10–11hr) and Siem Reap ($26; 13–14hr). Bus tickets can be bought in advance or on the day. Another option is to sign up with a tour operator for a **share taxi** in Pham Ngu Lao ($30–40 for a full car); this will take you as far as the Moc Bai border crossing, from where you can walk over the border into the duty-free shopping zone and negotiate onward transport to Phnom Penh. One-month Cambodian visas are available on the border for $25 including the "processing fee".

11

to catch the noon service. A traditional band plays as robed worshippers chant, pray and sing. Dressing modestly is a must and photographing worshippers without their permission is a no-no; however, it's possible to photograph the colourfully robed adherents from the balconies above.

The Mekong Delta

11

The orchards, paddy fields and swamplands of the **Mekong Delta** stretch from Ho Chi Minh City's limits southwest to the Gulf of Thailand, crisscrossed by nine channels of the Mekong River – Asia's third-longest river after the Yangtse and Yellow rivers. Here in the delta, not only does the Mekong water "Vietnam's rice bowl", but it also serves as a crucial transportation artery, teeming with rowing boats, sampans, ferries and floating markets.

The most enjoyable way to experience delta life is by boat: most travellers come by tour from HCMC, with boat trips organized for them, taking in laidback **Ben Tre** and the delta's most famous floating markets near **Can Tho**. From here, a road runs to the Cambodian border towns of **Chau Doc** and **Ha Tien**, the latter also a gateway to French-prison-cum-beach-resort Phu Quoc island, as is the port town of **Rach Gia**.

BEN TRE

The travellers who head into river-locked **Ben Tre province** – nearly all of whom do so as part of organized tours – are rewarded with breathtaking scenery of fruit orchards and coconut groves. Ben Tre Town itself is a pleasant place, famous for its *keo dua* (coconut candy); stop at a riverside candy workshop to watch the sticky mixture swirled around in a cauldron, the hardened sweets then wrapped in rice paper.

Beyond the buzzing **market** in the centre of town, there's little to see in Ben Tre itself. From the channel's more rustic south bank, where scores of boats moor in front of thatch houses, you can explore the maze of dirt tracks and visit the riverside **wine factory**, 450m west of the bridge, where *ruou trang* (rice wine) fizzes away in earthenware jars; bicycles are available for rent at the *Hung Vuong* hotel or at Ben Tre Tourist. Further afield are the **fruit orchards of Cai Mon**, reachable as part of a three-hour tour by *xe om* from Ben Tre (around 250,000VND) or as part of a Sinh Tourist tour (see box below).

ARRIVAL AND INFORMATION

By bus Long-distance buses terminate at the bus station 4km north of town (30,000VND to the centre by *xe om*). Buses leave from early in the morning until early afternoon.

Destinations Can Tho (1hr 30min); Ha Tien (4hr 30min); HCMC (1hr 30min).

Tourist information Ben Tre Tourist, 65 Dong Khoi (daily 8–11.30am & 1.30–5pm; ⓣ 075 3829618, ⓦ bentretourist.vn), can help with local tours and also rents bikes and canoes.

TOURS OF THE DELTA

If you have little time and you wish to see as much of the Mekong Delta as possible – particularly the Ben Tre/Can Tho/floating markets area, then tours with Sinh Tourist (see p.901) are extremely worthwhile, as they provide hassle-free transport between destinations, quality accommodation, excellent food and English-speaking tour guides. It's possible to reach all of the sights under your own steam, but it'll take much longer and work out as more expensive as you'll have to charter your own boats. The two-day-one-night Delta tour takes in Ben Tre's canals, a coconut candy workshop, rowing boats and motorcarts for passengers through the countryside, a visit to fruit orchards, an overnight stay and free time in Can Tho, a morning visit to the Cai Rang floating market and a stop at the Vinh Long market en route back to HCMC.

Since the back roads of the Delta lend themselves to cycling, it's also very rewarding to explore at a slower pace on two wheels. Sinhbalo Adventures in HCMC (see p.901) organize multi-day tours of the green, sleepy countryside and its friendly villages.

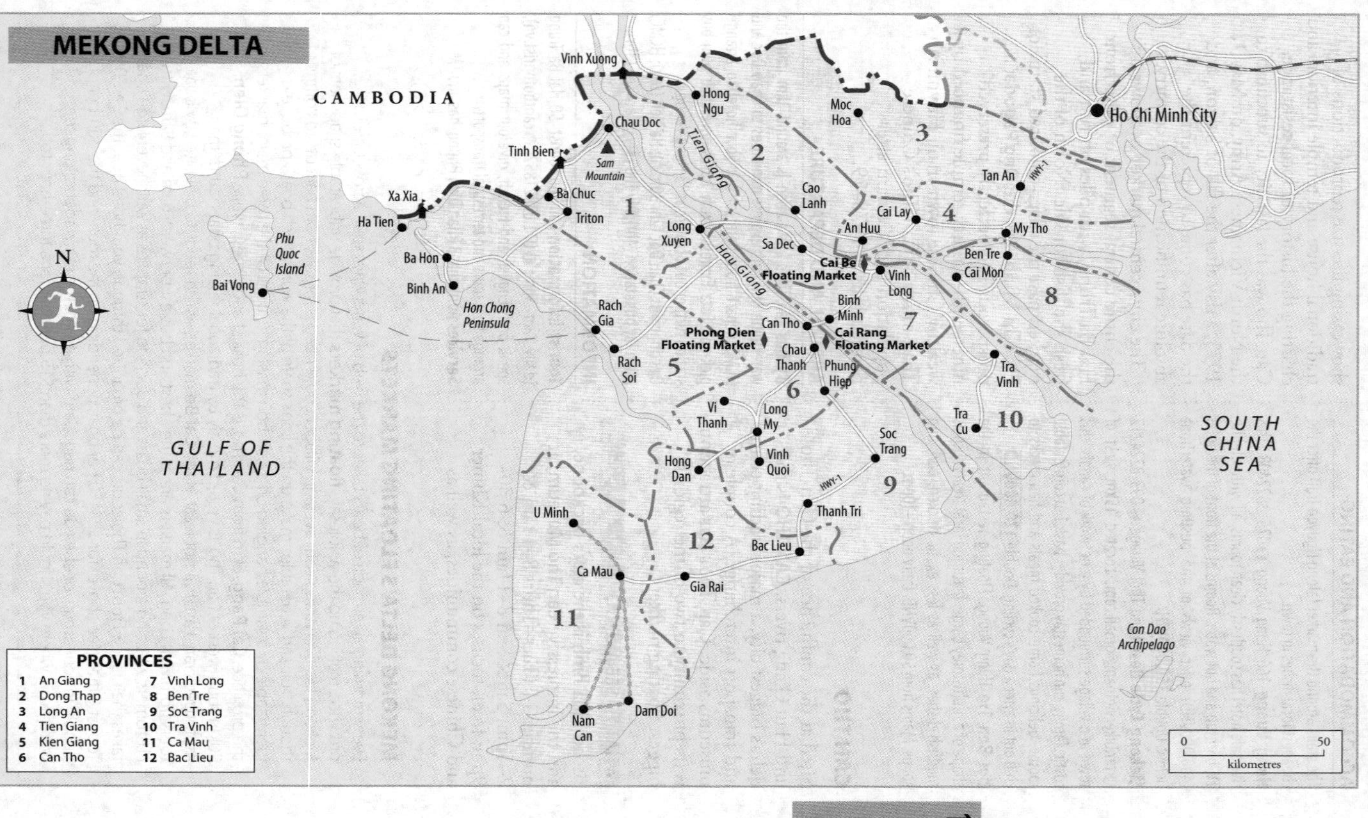
MEKONG DELTA
CAMBODIA
Vinh Xuong
Hong Ngu
Moc Hoa
Ho Chi Minh City
Chau Doc
Tinh Bien
Sam Mountain
Tien Giang
2
3
Tan An
HWY-1
Xa Xia
Ba Chuc
Triton
1
Cao Lanh
Cai Lay
4
Ha Tien
Long Xuyen
An Huu
My Tho
Phu Quoc Island
Sa Dec
Ben Tre
N
Ba Hon
Hau Giang
Cai Be Floating Market
Vinh Long
Cai Mon
Bai Vong
Binh An
Hon Chong Peninsula
Rach Gia
Binh Minh
8
Can Tho
7
Phong Dien Floating Market
Cai Rang Floating Market
Chau Thanh
Tra Vinh
Rach Soi
5
Phung Hiep
6
Vi Thanh
Long My
Tra Cu
10
SOUTH CHINA SEA
GULF OF THAILAND
Soc Trang
Hong Dan
Vinh Quoi
9
Thanh Tri
U Minh
12
Bac Lieu
Ca Mau
Gia Rai
11
Con Dao Archipelago
Nam Can
Dam Doi
PROVINCES
1 An Giang
2 Dong Thap
3 Long An
4 Tien Giang
5 Kien Giang
6 Can Tho
7 Vinh Long
8 Ben Tre
9 Soc Trang
10 Tra Vinh
11 Ca Mau
12 Bac Lieu
0 50
kilometres

11

ACCOMMODATION AND EATING

The stalls around the market (along Nguyen Trai) offer the cheapest local dishes in town.

Hung Vuong 166 Hung Vuong 075 3822408. This riverside hotel has spotlessly clean rooms, all with satellite TV, bathtub and hot water. Rooms at the front of the hotel (400,000VND) offer views of the bustling waterfront below. Double 350,000VND

Mekong Cycle Rest Long Thoi Village 093 8224212 tanbikervietnam@gmail.com. Located 15km west of town in a village surrounded by a network of canals, this rustic, family-run homestay provides basic but comfortable rooms, delicious home-cooked meals and hammocks to chill out in after a day's cycling. Double 120,000VND

Noi Ben Tre Hung Vuong. Floating restaurant in the shape of a multistorey barge, featuring local treats such as mudfish dishes, as well as less exotic chicken, pork and soups. Mains from 50,000VND. Daily noon–10pm.

11

CAN THO

Sited at the confluence of the Can Tho and Hau Giang rivers, **CAN THO** is the delta's biggest city, a major trading centre and transport interchange. A couple of museums aside, Can Tho's star attraction is its proximity to two of the region's biggest floating markets.

WHAT TO SEE AND DO

Broad Hoa Binh is the city's backbone, and the impressive **Can Tho Museum**, at number 11 (Tues–Thurs 8–11am & 2–5pm, Sat & Sun 8–11am & 6.30–9pm; free), focuses on the local Khmer and Chinese communities, as well as showcasing life-size reproductions of traditional house and temple interiors and charting the history of local resistance. Can Tho was the last city to succumb to the North Vietnamese Army, on May 1, 1975, a day after the fall of Saigon, and the date has come to represent the absolute reunification of the country.

The city's **central market** swallows up the entire central segment of waterfront Hai Ba Trung, with piles of fruit and fresh shellfish for sale. North of the market, past the silver-coloured statue of Ho Chi Minh, lies the **Ong Pagoda**, a prosperous and perfectly preserved nineteenth-century temple financed by a wealthy Chinese townsman, Huynh An Thai; much of Can Tho's Chinese population fled Vietnam after persecutions in 1978–79.

ARRIVAL AND DEPARTURE

By bus Can Tho's bus station is around 1km from the waterfront. Mai Linh express minibuses to Chau Doc and HCMC depart from here (or ask your hotel to arrange pick-up). Futa Express luxury buses have their own bus station further out of town, at 13 Hung Vuong.

Destinations Chau Doc (2hr 30min); Ha Tien (6hr); HCMC, Mien Tay bus station (4hr); My Tho (3hr); Rach Gia (3hr).

INFORMATION

Tourist information Can Tho Tourist, 50 Hai Ba Trung (daily 7am–5pm; 071 03821852, canthotourist.vn), speak both English and French, give out maps and can arrange boat tours and terrestrial transport.

Services Agribank, 3 Phan Dinh Phung, has an ATM.

MEKONG DELTA'S FLOATING MARKETS

Every morning an armada of boats takes to the web of waterways spun across Can Tho province, making up the wholesale **floating markets** that provide unbeatable snapshots of Mekong life. Everything your average villager could need is for sale, from haircuts to coffins, though fruit and vegetables make up the lion's share of the wares. Each boat's produce is identifiable by a sample hanging off a bamboo mast in its bow. Of the three major markets in the province, **Cai Rang**, 6km from Can Tho, is the busiest and largest, while **Phong Dien**, 20km southwest of Can Tho, is visited mostly by traditional rowing boats rather than motorized craft. Last, but not least, is the **Cai Be** market, which tends to be visited by boat tours from Vinh Long. All markets are at their best and busiest between 6am and 8am, with customers whizzing around in small boats and docking for supplies at whichever large boat takes their fancy. From Can Tho, tours can be organized through your hotel or at the Can Tho Tourist Office (see above) for $25–50 per boat, depending on the route and the number of people in your group, or else you can negotiate with any of the many touts along the waterfront, where you should pay no more than $15 per boat for a three-hour tour.

ACCOMMODATION

Chambres D'Hotes Mekong Logis 142 May Than 071 03834685, mekonglogis.com. A hotel run by a wonderfully helpful family; the parents speak French and the daughter speaks English. They can help organize all manner of local outings and the meals are delicious, too. Double **$15**

Huy Hoang 35 Ngo Duc Ke 071 03825833, huyhoang hotel.com. A pleasant small hotel with clean and bright rooms, all with satellite TV, and helpful staff. Double **200,000VND**

Kim Tho Hotel 1 Ngo Gia Tu 071 03817517, kimlancantho.com.vn. This place is decorated in an appealing contemporary style – all modern art and bamboo furnishings. Some of the rooms lack windows but are kept cool by a/c and the showers are heated by solar power. Double **$20**

EATING AND DRINKING

For a local dining experience, head to Nam Ky Khoi Nghia where there are plenty of stalls serving barbecued fish, pork, frog and snake (a local speciality).

Mekong Restaurant 38 Hai Ba Trung. This established favourite is hard to top for its extensive menu of cheap, flavoursome Vietnamese and Chinese meals; the fish stewed in a clay pot (45,000VND) is recommended. Daily 8am–2pm & 4–10pm.

Nam Bo 50 Hai Ba Trung. Munch on snake curry as part of a good-value set menu ("snake menu" 120,000VND), or go for less exotic French-influenced dishes in colonial-style elegant surroundings. Daily noon–2.30pm & 6.30–11pm.

Viva Green 26 Hai Ba Trung. Resembling a cavern for hobbits, this riverfront bar is typically packed; perhaps it's something to do with the two-for-one beer promotion before 6pm. Daily 9am–11pm.

CHAU DOC

Snuggled against the west bank of the Hau Giang River, next to the Cambodian border (see box, p.910), **CHAU DOC** was under Cambodian rule until the mid-eighteenth century and still sustains a large Khmer community. Forays by Pol Pot's genocidal Khmer Rouge into this corner of the delta led to the Vietnamese invasion of Cambodia in 1978 and put an end to Pol Pot's regime. Today Chau Doc is a melting pot of Khmer, Cham, Vietnamese and Chinese communities, with a cluster of interesting sights in and around town, to boot.

WHAT TO SEE AND DO

The town's lively produce **market**, roughly between Quang Trung, Doc Phu Thu, Tran Hung Dao and Nguyen Van Thoi, makes for a good spectacle. A grand, four-tiered gateway deep in the belly of the market announces **Quan Cong Temple**, ornamented with two rooftop dragons and some vivid murals.

Northwest up Tran Hung Dao, long boardwalks lead to sizeable stilt-house communities, and from here, at the junction with Thuong Dang Le, you can take a ferry across the Hau Giang River to the stilt houses of **Con Tien Island**. Cham-dominated **Chau Giang district** lies across the Hau Giang River, 2km northeast of the town. Kampung-style wooden houses, sarongs and white prayer caps betray the influence of Islam, as do the twin domes and minaret of the Mubarak Mosque. *Xe om* and *xe dap loi* will take you there and back for about 40,000VND, including waiting time, or else you can take in Con Tien Island and the floating houses on the river, with mini fish-farms underneath each one, as part of a morning boat tour.

Sam Mountain

Arid, brooding **Sam Mountain** rises dramatically from an ocean of paddy fields 5km southwest of Chau Doc, and Buddhist visitors flock here to worship at its clutch of pagodas and shrines. From town, a road runs straight to the foot of the mountain, reached by *xe dap loi* and *xe lam*, or easily covered by bicycle. A winding, bumpy road leads **up the mountain** for 1km in a clockwise direction; the turn is on the right, just after a large temple; if you don't fancy walking, motorbikes can take you up for around 25,000VND. From the summit, you're rewarded with spectacular 360-degree views of the patchwork of fields below. Along the straight road to the mountain, a large, colourful **temple** on your left, sitting around its own private lagoon, makes for a photogenic stop.

11

11

ARRIVAL AND DEPARTURE

By boat Boats to/from Cambodia dock at a small jetty at the northern end of Tran Hung Dao, 1km from the centre.

By bus Buses offload 2km southeast of town, en route to the bus station on Le Loi, from where *xe dap loi* and *xe om* run into town for about 20,000VND; some minibuses drop off in the centre on Thu Khoa Nghia. Public buses to HCMC depart hourly from the bus station; regular Mai Linh express minibuses to elsewhere in the delta can be booked through your hotel. Futa Express buses offer free minibus drop-off from their bus station to your guesthouse.

Destinations Can Tho (2hr 30min); Ha Tien (3hr); HCMC (hourly; 6–7hr).

INFORMATION

Tourist information Mekong Tours at 14 Nguyen Huu Canh & 41 Quang Trung (daily 8am–9pm; T 076 3562828, W mekongtours.net) offer half-day trips to a fish farm and Cham village (around $12) as well as longer trips through the delta, and can assist with onward travel arrangements to Cambodia (see box below).

Services Agribank, 4–5 Quang Trung, changes dollars and has an ATM. *Trung Nguyen Hotel* offers bike rental for $3/day, and motorbikes for $10.

ACCOMMODATION

Murray Guesthouse 11–15 Truong Dinh T 076 3562108, E nhanghimurray@gmail.com. A 10min walk to the river, this budget boutique choice comes with spacious a/c rooms, rooftop relaxation space with pool table for guests and drinks on an honour system. Onward transport organized. Double $22

Thuan Loi Hotel 275 Tran Hung Dao T 076 3866134, E kshuanloi@yahoo.com. The choice of spacious, clean rooms in this waterfront guesthouse includes bargain fan rooms, some of which have absorbing views of river life drifting by; there's also a floating restaurant. Double $12

Trung Nguyen 86 Bach Dang T 076 3561561, W trungnguyenhotel.com.vn. Bustling, conveniently located mini-hotel popular with tour groups. Rooms are modern and spacious, with balconies overlooking the market. Rates include free breakfast, internet and wi-fi. Double $15

Vinh Phuoc Hotel 12 Quang Trung T 076 3866242, W hotels-chaudoc.com. Brit-run cheapie offering spotlessly clean rooms, some with fans only, a decent restaurant downstairs, and info and advice on travel in the Mekong Delta. Double $10

EATING AND DRINKING

Stalls at the market offer heaped bowls of pho, fresh spring rolls and other Vietnamese dishes for less than 20,000VND. At night, vendors set up food stalls around the pagoda at the central square between Nguyen Huu Canh and Chi Lang.

★ **Bassac Restaurant** 32 Le Loi. The pleasure of eating at Chau Doc's finest doesn't come cheap, but what a pleasure it is. Stir-fried squid with green peppercorns is superb and both the Vietnamese and French mains beautifully executed. Mains from 180,000VND. Daily 9am–11pm.

Bay Bong 22 Thuong Dang Le. This informal, nondescript-looking place serves a particularly good take on the local speciality of pork or stewed fish cooked in a clay pot (*ca kho to*) for 60,000VND, and chunky, fragrant sweet-and-sour soup, as well as other Delta dishes. Daily noon–10pm.

Mekong 41 Le Loi. Brash neon belies the delicacy of the local dishes on offer. The caramelized fish claypot (70,000VND) hits the spot and there are noodle dishes and more. Daily noon–10pm.

RACH GIA

Teetering precariously over the Gulf of Thailand, **RACH GIA** is a booming farming and fishing community. A small islet in the mouth of the Cai Lon River forms the hub of town, its central area

INTO CAMBODIA: VINH XUONG AND TINH BIEN

VINH XUONG

Arguably the nicest crossing into Cambodia is the **Vinh Xuong border crossing** (daily 8am–8pm), 30km north of Chau Doc, as it's done by boat. Sinh Tourist in HCMC (p.901) incorporate it into their Exit to Cambodia tour, and you can also take a daily boat with Hang Chau (W hangchautourist.com.vn), departing at 7.30am from a pier at 18 Tran Hung Dao, returning from Phnom Penh at noon (4hr 30min; $30 one-way). Cambodian visas are available at the border for around $25.

TINH BIEN

A less convenient border crossing near Chau Doc is at **Tinh Bien**, 25km west of Sam Mountain. The road from Chau Doc to Tinh Bien is poor, but local buses from Chao Doc make the trip direct to Phnom Penh daily, departing at 7.30am (5hr; around $20); tickets can be booked through Mekong Tours at 14 Nguyen Huu Canh (W mekongvietnam.com).

shoehorned tightly between Le Loi and Tran Phu. Most visitors simply pass through on their way to or from Phu Quoc island, but it's worth visiting the **Nguyen Trung Truc Temple** at 18 Nguyen Cong Tru; it's dedicated to the leader of a resistance campaign against the French in the 1860s who turned himself in and was executed by them when they took some civilians hostage, including his mother, and threatened to execute them.

ARRIVAL AND DEPARTURE

By plane Flights from HCMC (daily; 50min) and Phu Quoc (daily; 40min) arrive in Rach Soi airport, 7km from Rach Gia. From the airport, you can take a *xe om* (50,000VND) or taxi (around 90,000VND) direct to Rach Gia. If you're coming from town, *xe lam* and minibuses to the airport can be picked up on Tran Phu.

By boat Superdong boats (4 daily; 2hr 15min; ⓦ superdong.com.vn) to Phu Quoc depart from Ben Tau Khach Bien quay on Nguyen Cong Tru, a 10min walk from the centre, daily at 8am, 9am, 12.40pm and 1pm (2hr 20min; 320,000VND). Tickets can be bought in advance from offices along Nguyen Cong Tru or from the dock.

By bus Local buses depart when full from the central bus station along Nguyen Binh Khiem, 500m north of town, at Nguyen Binh Khiem. There are several scheduled departures daily to Can Tho with the plush Futa Express, with onwards connections to other Mekong Delta destinations. Comfortable a/c minibuses to Ha Tien (80,000VND) can be organized through Mai Linh Express (ⓣ 077 3929292). Express buses to HCMC cost 140,000VND, and leave hourly starting from 4pm.

Destinations Can Tho (3hr); Ha Tien (3hr); HCMC, Mien Tay bus station (7hr).

ACCOMMODATION AND EATING

Ao Dai Moi 2 161 Nguyen Hung Son. Run by a local tailor, this simple but popular place cooks up cheap and delicious dishes, some with a Chinese twist. Mains 40,000VND. Daily 11am–9pm.

Hai Au 2 Nguyen Trung Truc. Large restaurant with a pleasant riverside terrace serving somewhat well-executed seafood dishes, including sautéed eel with lemongrass (140,000VND) and Thai cockle salad. Daily 11.30am–9.30pm.

Hong Yen 259–261 Mac Cuu ⓣ 077 3879095, ⓔ hongyen.hotel@yahoo.com. Friendly hotel north of the Cai Lon River, with smart, spacious rooms complete with TV and a/c. Double **200,000VND**

Kim Co Hotel 141 Nguyen Hung Son ⓣ 077 3879610, ⓦ kimcohotel.com. Central hotel offering clean, brightly painted doubles with a/c; most face the corridor. Double **400,000VND**

PHU QUOC

Lying in the Gulf of Thailand 45km west of Ha Tien and just 15km from the coast of Cambodia, **PHU QUOC** is a relatively undeveloped tropical island of almost six hundred square kilometres, much of which is part of a UNESCO Biosphere Reserve. Fringed with golden and powder-white sandy beaches, with the lively Duong Dong town halfway along the west coast, a tropical forested interior, and an archipelago of fifteen small islands off the southern tip – perfect for diving, snorkelling and fishing – the place is currently a low-key alternative to the beach resorts along Vietnam's south coast, though there are plans for further development.

11

WHAT TO SEE AND DO

Besides the island's main beaches and the islets offering **diving** and **snorkelling** opportunities, the network of partially paved but mostly dirt tracks throughout the island makes for bumpy exploration of Phu Quoc's protected forest, waterfalls, and deserted stretches of sand by **motorbike** or **bicycle**.

Duong Dong

The island's only town, **Duong Dong**, is a congested little place with fishing boats bobbing in the harbour and a bustling port-side market, just over the Nguyen Trung Truc bridge. Phu Quoc is famous for its **fish sauce** (*nuoc mam*), and you can check out the enormous vats of fermenting fish at the Hung Thanh factory on Nguyen Van Troi (daily 8–11am & 1–5pm; free). At sunset, locals congregate at **Cau Castle** – a cross between a lighthouse and a temple on Bach Dang.

The beaches

The palm-fringed, 20km stretch of golden grainy sand sweeping down the island's west coast, aptly named **Bai Truong** (Long Beach), is the most accessible and well known of Phu Quoc's beaches. Though the northern end is crammed with hotels and luxury resorts all jostling for their section of the beachfront, the southern 10km is currently deserted.

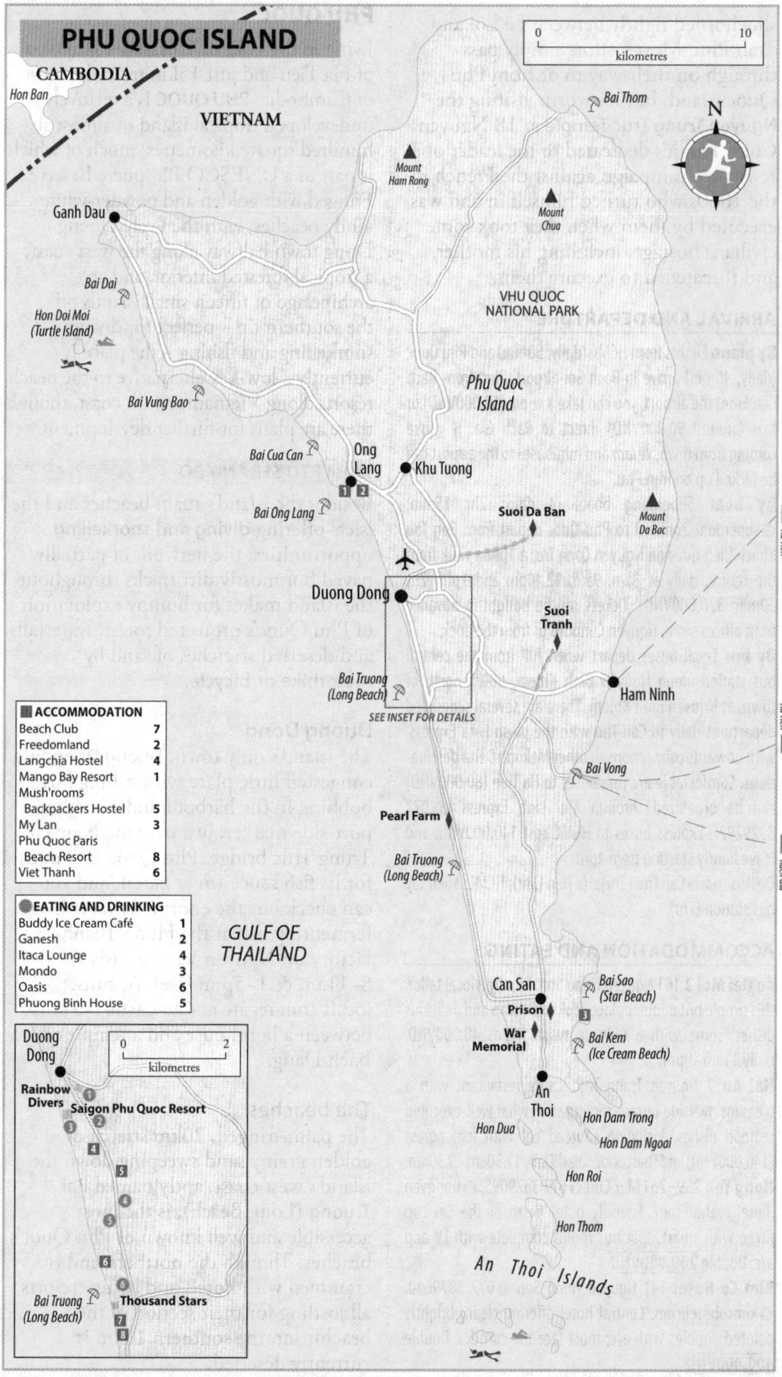

PHU QUOC ISLAND

CAMBODIA
Hon Ban
VIETNAM
0 10 kilometres
N
Bai Thom
Mount Ham Rong
Mount Chua
Ganh Dau
Bai Dai
Hon Doi Moi (Turtle Island)
VHU QUOC NATIONAL PARK
Phu Quoc Island
Bai Vung Bao
Bai Cua Can
Ong Lang
Khu Tuong
Bai Ong Lang
Suoi Da Ban
Mount Da Bac
Ha Tien
Duong Dong
Suoi Tranh
Bai Truong (Long Beach)
Ham Ninh
SEE INSET FOR DETAILS
Ha Tien
Bai Vong
Pearl Farm
Rach Gia
Bai Truong (Long Beach)
GULF OF THAILAND
Can San
Bai Sao (Star Beach)
Prison
War Memorial
Bai Kem (Ice Cream Beach)
An Thoi
Hon Dua
Hon Dam Trong
Hon Dam Ngoai
Hon Roi
Hon Thom
An Thoi Islands

ACCOMMODATION	
Beach Club	7
Freedomland	2
Langchia Hostel	4
Mango Bay Resort	1
Mush'rooms Backpackers Hostel	5
My Lan	3
Phu Quoc Paris Beach Resort	8
Viet Thanh	6

EATING AND DRINKING	
Buddy Ice Cream Café	1
Ganesh	2
Itaca Lounge	4
Mondo	3
Oasis	6
Phuong Binh House	5

Duong Dong
0 2 kilometres
Rainbow Divers
Saigon Phu Quoc Resort
Bai Truong (Long Beach)
Thousand Stars

While lacking the palm fringes of Long Beach, **Bai Ong Lang**, north of Duong Dong town, offers more privacy and seclusion, and its rocky shore is good for snorkelling. To the northeast and northwest, **Bai Thom**, **Bai Cua Can**, **Bai Vung Bao** and **Bai Dai** offer similarly rocky coves; all can be reached by motorbike along dirt paths.

The blindingly white, powdery sand, clean turquoise waters and excellent palm-shaded seafood restaurants make **Bai Sao** (Star Beach) popular for a day-trip, though the road leading down there is currently rough and gravelly. South of here around the rocks lies Phu Quoc's most beautiful beach, **Bai Khem** (Ice-cream Beach); unfortunately, it's hogged by the military and therefore off-limits. Further north of Bai Sao on the island's east coast, **Bai Vong** has more white sand, good shade and shallow waters suitable for paddling.

Phu Quoc National Park

Seventy percent of the island is cloaked in tropical forest. The north is mountainous and heavily forested, while in the south much of the land has been cleared for pepper plantations. As well as its fish sauce, Phu Quoc is known for its pepper and visitors are welcome to have a closer look in places like **Khu Tuong**, inland from Ong Lang Beach – ask permission first.

If you head north up the main road that runs along the coast, you can do a loop through the national park, stop for a short trail walk, and come back towards Duong Dong along the other paved road that runs past some pepper farms. Before you reach town, a signposted dirt trail branches off towards **Suoi Da Ban** – a white-water creek running down some moss-encrusted granite boulders, culminating in some dipping pools. If you head east out of Duong Dong towards the boat jetties, a more accessible track leads to **Suoi Tranh** – another mini-waterfall. Both falls are best visited between May and September (outside those months there's barely a trickle) and admission is 3000VND.

ARRIVAL AND DEPARTURE

By plane The international airport is in Duong Dong. Long Beach is a 10min *xe om* ride (40,000VND) or 100,000VND cab ride away from Long Beach.

Destinations Can Tho (daily; 45min); Hanoi (2 daily; 3hr); HCMC (10 daily; 1hr); Rach Gia (daily; 40min).

By boat Superdong (Ⓦ superdong.com.vn) runs hydrofoils between Vong Beach in the east and Rach Gia (6 daily; 320,000VND; 2hr 20min) at 8am, 9am, 12.40pm and 1pm; Ha Tien boats (8.30am and 1.30pm, 230,000VND; 1hr 10min) dock either here or a little further north at Ham Ninh. Private minivans ply the route to the resorts (60,000VND/person), but are notorious for overcharging. Hydrofoil tickets for the trip back to the mainland can be booked through your hotel.

INFORMATION

Information and tours Resorts and hotels can organize all manner of tours; most can organize motorbike rental (ask for a local map of the island), and assist with booking onward transport. Many work with John's Tours, 4 & 92 Tran Hung Dao (daily 6am–9pm; Ⓣ 091 9107086, Ⓦ johnsislandtours.com), who organize all-inclusive

DIVING AND SNORKELLING AROUND PHU QUOC

When Nha Trang's waters become too murky to dive, Phu Quoc's dive centres are open (October to April), ferrying divers and snorkellers to **Turtle Island** to the northwest and the **An Thoi** archipelago to the south, where you can see hard and soft corals, and a spectacular array of reef fish including scorpion fish, butterfly fish, parrot fish, fairy basslets, damsel fish and huge sea urchins. Rainbow Divers, 17A Tran Hung Dao (Ⓣ 091 3400964, Ⓦ divevietnam.com), offers well-organized and highly recommended diving and snorkelling trips; a day-trip with two boat dives and lunch costs $87 ($30 for snorkellers). They also offer full-day "discover diving" beginners' courses ($124), and PADI certification courses for all levels. Their office is on the main roundabout coming into Duong Dong from the south (Long Beach road). Other reputable dive operators include Searama (48 Tran Hung Dao Ⓣ 077 6291697, Ⓦ searama.com), with English- and French-speaking instructors, and Vietnam Explorer (36 Tran Hung Dao Ⓣ 077 3846372, Ⓦ dive-phuquoc.com); the latter is one of the few dive centres that stays open during the rainy season (May–Sept).

fishing and snorkelling day-trips for $17/person. The website discoverphuquoc.com is a good source of island info.

Services There are a number of ATMs dotted along the length of Tran Hung Dao, and an Agribank at 2 Trang Hung Dao in Duong Dong. There are several pharmacies near the market on Ngo Quyen in Duong Dong. The post office is at Thang 4 in Duong Dong (daily 7am–7pm).

ACCOMMODATION

Prices skyrocket around Dec and Jan, but during low season (May–Sept), prices are slashed by up to two-thirds, making some budget and mid-range resorts fantastic value.

LONG BEACH

11

Beach Club 077 3980998, beachclubvietnam.com. Simple but tasteful beach bungalows and double rooms, with terracotta-tiled floors, white walls and linen, and rustic four-poster beds. The resort is run by a helpful and welcoming Anglo-Vietnamese couple, and also has a decent bar-restaurant. Double $35, bungalow $40

Langchia Hostel 84 Tran Hung Dao 09 39132603, info@langchia-hostel.com. This small hostel, run by a helpful young Vietnamese guy, consists of one large dorm that sleeps sixteen people, and is particularly good for solo travellers. Regular movie nights encourage mingling. Dorm $10

Mush'rooms Backpackers Hostel 170 Tran Hung Dao 09 37942017, mushrooms-phuquoc.com. A 5min walk from the beach, this hostel is cheap and cheerful, with backpackers lingering in the courtyard over a generous breakfast. Dorm $6

Phu Quoc Paris Beach Resort 077 3994548, phuquocparisbeach.com. Bungalows around a pool, simple, comfortable rooms in the main building next to the shaded dining area, delicious food, friendly service and placid dogs underfoot make this a great beachside spot. Double $25

Viet Thanh 118/14 Tran Hung Dao 0122 9866542, vietthanhbungalow.com. Spacious bungalows with porches and hammocks in a friendly family-run compound on the beach. There are also simple rooms on offer in a concrete building out back. Double $20, bungalow $45

ONG LANG BEACH

★Freedomland 077 3994891, freedomlandphuquoc.com. Drowning in greenery down one of the winding dirt paths near Ong Lang Beach, this is a hippie-esque retreat. Accommodation is rustic: fan-cooled bungalows with mosquito nets, cold showers, and no wi-fi, but travellers end up lingering here for days because of the friendly vibe. You're likely to make new friends here over communal dinner, and the beach is a 5min schlep away. Double $45

BAI SAO BEACH

My Lan 077 3990779, vietdung64@yahoo.com. Very basic bungalow accommodation with mattress and fan at the popular *My Lan Restaurant* at the southern end of the beach. Double $25

EATING AND DRINKING

Most resorts have decent bar-restaurants. Places close fairly early; very little is open past 10pm, even at weekends. For the island's best, cheapest seafood, head for the vendor stalls by the lighthouse and the open-air eateries at the night market along Vo Thi Sau in Duong Dong (daily from 5pm, mains from 80,000VND). The basic restaurants on Bai Sao are locally famous for their barbecued seafood and grilled fish.

Buddy Ice Cream Café 26 Nguyen Trai. This congenial café with free computers for guests and a book exchange offers imported New Zealand ice cream (30,000VND/scoop), sublime fruit shakes, fish and chips and toasted sandwiches. Daily 9am–8pm.

Ganesh 97 Tran Hung Dao. Large Indian restaurant specializing mostly in northern Indian cuisine, such as tandoori dishes. Plenty of vegetarian options, and the thalis (veggie or seafood; 180,000VND) make for a gut-busting meal. Daily 11am–10pm.

Mondo 82 Tran Hung Dao. Stylish tapas bar serving delicious gazpacho along with chicken wrapped in banana leaf and other "meal-sized" tapas (from 50,000VND), such

★TREAT YOURSELF

Mango Bay Resort 090 3981693, mangobayphuquoc.com. This beautiful compound of wooden and rammed-earth thatched bungalows, enclosed by deserted beaches and protected forest, is the island's first eco-friendly resort, with solar panels and recycled materials in use. The bungalows themselves are elegantly furnished with four-poster beds, white linen and soft lighting; all have tasteful alfresco bathrooms and a private veranda. High season prices start at $115. Double $60

Itaca Lounge 125 Tran Hung Dao 077 3992022, itacalounge.com. Lanterns in the trees and strings of tiny lights subtly illuminate this open-air lounge, with comfy couches and tables scattered around. The menu is creative international (seared tuna burger, Black Angus rib eye, tabouleh salad, brownie with dragon-fruit coulis), the service is super-attentive and the ambience just lovely. Mains from 210,000VND. Daily 4–11pm.

as meatballs in tomato sauce and *patatas bravas*. Daily 11am–10pm.

Oasis 118/5 Tran Hung Dao. The specialities at this low-key bar/restaurant are their British standbys – think shepherd's pie and fish & chips – as well as Western breakfasts. There's live football on TV on weekends and the music is solid Britpop. Daily noon–10pm.

Phuong Binh House 118 Tran Hung Dao. Excellent grilled fish, seafood and other Vietnamese dishes, a prime beachside location and a cheerful backpacker vibe make this place hugely popular. The downside is that continents may drift before you get served. Daily 11.30am–10pm.

HA TIEN

Right near the Cambodian border and lapped by the Gulf of Thailand, **Ha Tien**, with its riverfront promenade and crumbling colonial buildings, is the most appealing town in the delta.

WHAT TO DO AND SEE

Ha Tien is big on atmosphere, and beyond the lively waterfront **market** there are a couple of appealing pagodas in and beyond town, as well as elaborate tombs and a good stretch of white beach – all of which can be explored by bicycle or motorbike.

Tam Bao Pagoda

A few minutes along Phuong Thanh from the waterfront is the **Tam Bao Pagoda** – a Buddhist nun community founded by feudal lord Mac Cuu in 1730. The cheery yellow, thirteen-storey pagoda is fronted by a statue of the Goddess of Mercy on a lotus blossom, and a large Buddha reclines nearby on a pedestal.

Mac Cuu Family Tombs

Nui Lang, or the Hill of Tombs, where **Mac Cuu**, the seventeenth-century feudal lord who founded Ha Tien, and his family are buried, is found west along Mac Cuu which branches off the main Phuong Thanh. Mac Cuu and his relatives lie buried in peaceful, wooded grounds in semicircular Chinese graves. Mac Cuu's grave is uppermost on the hill, daubed with a yin and yang symbol, and guarded by two swordsmen, a white tiger and a blue dragon. From this vantage point, there are good views down to the river.

Thach Dong Cave Pagoda and Mui Nai Beach

This pleasant circular cycling route takes in Ha Tien's outlying attractions. Strike off west along Lam Son, through rice fields, coconut groves and water palm, past a war cemetery (2.5km from town), from where it's 1.5km to the first of three marked turnings – all with toll gates (5000VND) – to **Mui Nai** peninsula, a relatively peaceful, dark-sand cove, complete with numerous cafés and restaurants.

You'll see the 48m-high granite outcrop housing **Thach Dong** cave long before you reach it – 4.5km past Mui Nai, a right turn deposits you at its base. A monument shaped like a clenched fist and commemorating the 130 Vietnamese killed by the Khmer Rouge near here in 1978 (which prompted the Vietnamese to invade Cambodia and overthrow Pol Pot) marks the entrance (daily 7am–5pm; 5000VND) to Thach Dong, beyond which steps lead up to several Buddhist shrines hidden inside a network of caves, which are also home to a colony of bats. From here, another 3km along the circular road brings you back to Ha Tien.

ARRIVAL AND INFORMATION

By boat Superdong (@superdong.com.vn) hydrofoils depart for Ham Ninh port on Phu Quoc (8am & 1pm daily; 1hr 15min; 230,000VND) from the south bank of the To Chau River; tickets can be booked at the office at 11 Tran Hau (daily 7am–9pm). Ngoc Thanh boats leave daily at 8.15am (1hr 30min; 210,000VND); buy tickets through agencies in town or at the dock.

By bus Buses terminate at the bus station about 2km north of town, though they can often drop you off at the petrol station 400m from the centre. Local buses to elsewhere in the delta depart when full from early morning. Private Mai Linh a/c minibuses can be booked through your hotel.

Destinations Can Tho (5–6hr); Chau Doc (3hr); HCMC (8hr); Rach Gia (3hr).

Services There's an ATM at Agribank, 37 Lam Son. Bikes can be rented from the *Viet Toan* and from the *Tien Trang* café across from the *Hai Van;* both 30,000VND/day.

ACCOMMODATION

Du Hung Hotel 27 Tran Hau ☎077 3951555. This pink hotel has good river views and friendly management. Bicycles and motorbikes available for rent; wi-fi signal weak on upper floors. Double **140,000VND**

11

INTO CAMBODIA: XA XIA

Ha Tien offers an easy crossing to Kep and Kampot on Cambodia's south coast; for travellers coming from Cambodia, it's an easy way of visiting Phu Quoc. Buses leave Ha Tien at noon and 4pm daily for Kep (250,000VND, 1hr), Kampot (300,000VND, 1hr 30min), Sihanoukville (450,000VND, 4hr) and Phnom Penh (430,000VND, 4hr); Ha Tien Tourism arrange bus tickets and visas.

Hai Phuong So 52, Dong Thuy Tram T 077 3852240. The biggest international traveller magnet in town, this basic multistorey hotel features large, spotless, tiled, a/c rooms. Double 220,000VND

Hai Van 55 Lam Son T 077 3852872. A convivial choice offering immaculate, spacious rooms with satellite TV. Superior doubles are available in the mid-range annexe (T 077 3852001; 300,000VND). Double 150,000VND

Hai Yen 15 Duong To Chau T 077 3851580. The staff here are not going to win any prizes for congeniality, but the rooms are spacious and finished in wood, some with waterfront views. Double 300,000VND

EATING AND DRINKING

The stalls around the bustling market on Tran Hau offer cheap Vietnamese dishes from early morning to around 9pm.

Ha Tien Floating Restaurant Tran Hau. Dine out on deck in Ha Tien's most stylish restaurant, a large boat moored behind the imposing *River Hotel* on the waterfront, serving fresh seafood dishes for 90,000–160,000VND. Daily noon–10pm.

★**Oasis** 42 Tuan Phu Dat. Expat Andy and his Vietnamese wife serve up proper English breakfasts (80,000VND), Greek salad with feta cheese, couscous with grilled veg, breakfast dishes such as muesli and omelettes, and filled baguettes (from 25,000VND) for lunch. Andy is a treasure trove of local info and can help arrange motorbike tours of the area. Daily 9am–9pm.

Thuy Tien Dong Ho. This little café built on a floating river raft is the perfect place to enjoy an iced coffee (15,000VND) or beer. Daily noon–9pm.

Small print and index

Rough Guide credits

Editors: Eleanor Aldridge, Lucy Cowie and Emma Gibbs
Layout: Nikhil Agarwal
Cartography: Deshpal Dabas
Picture editors: Emily Taylor and Mark Thomas
Proofreader: Jan McCann
Managing editor: Keith Drew
Assistant editor: Dipika Dasgupta
Production: Charlotte Cade
Cover design: Nicole Newman, Chloe Stickland and Nikhil Agarwal
Editorial assistant: Rebecca Hallett
Senior pre-press designer: Dan May
Programme manager: Helen Blount
Publisher: Joanna Kirby
Publishing director: Georgina Dee

Publishing information

This fourth edition published September 2014 by
Rough Guides Ltd,
80 Strand, London WC2R 0RL
11, Community Centre, Panchsheel Park,
New Delhi 110017, India
Distributed by Penguin Random House
Penguin Books Ltd,
80 Strand, London WC2R 0RL
Penguin Group (USA)
345 Hudson Street, NY 10014, USA
Penguin Group (Australia)
250 Camberwell Road, Camberwell,
Victoria 3124, Australia
Penguin Group (NZ)
67 Apollo Drive, Mairangi Bay, Auckland 1310,
New Zealand
Penguin Group (South Africa)
Block D, Rosebank Office Park, 181 Jan Smuts Avenue,
Parktown North, Gauteng, South Africa 2193
Rough Guides is represented in Canada by Tourmaline Editions Inc. 662 King Street West, Suite 304, Toronto, Ontario M5V 1M7
Printed in Singapore by Toppan Security Printing Pte. Ltd.

936pp includes index
A catalogue record for this book is available from the British Library
ISBN: 978-1-40934-559-6

1 3 5 7 9 8 6 4 2

Help us update

We've gone to a lot of effort to ensure that the fourth edition of **The Rough Guide to Southeast Asia on a Budget** is accurate and up-to-date. However, things change – places get "discovered", opening hours are notoriously fickle, restaurants and rooms raise prices or lower standards. If you feel we've got it wrong or left something out, we'd like to know, and if you can remember the address, the price, the hours, the phone number, so much the better.

Please send your comments with the subject line "**Rough Guide Southeast Asia on a Budget Update**" to mail@uk.roughguides.com. We'll credit all contributions and send a copy of the next edition (or any other Rough Guide if you prefer) for the very best emails.

Find more travel information, connect with fellow travellers and plan your trip on roughguides.com.

Acknowledgements

Emma Boyle Many thanks to Jake Corke and to Jack Bartholomew for sound Cambodia advice. Also to Ducky, Stephane and Dara, and to Jo Crisp for your support. In Kampot, big shout outs to Stephane and Yan for your company and insights, and also to Stephane at Coastal. In Sihanoukville, cheers to The Dive Shop for helping me island hop and to Ana, Mick and the team for travel advice. My appreciation to the Shallow Waters team and to Jason Webb in Koh Kong for keeping my up-to-date with local info. Finally, thanks to Rosie and Ian for your helpful updates on Phnom Penh's dining scene! Last but not least, shout outs to following readers for sharing their tips and updates: Mimosa Nguyen, Andrea Zobec, James Molony, Sandy Schagen, Monica Mackaness and John Garratt.

Kiki Deere Many thanks to Eliane, Jeremy and Casper for their wonderful hospitality and plethora of KL recommendations; my great school friend Biggy whom I managed to team up with after all these years and who introduced me to KL's best fish head curry; Lily, in George Town, for pointing me in the right direction in her quirky hometown; Christina Wee in Singapore, for kindly putting me up again ten years after we first met, and for all her excellent recommendations; Hugh Nolan, for giving me a fun taster of Singaporean nightlife; Budgie, as ever, for his support; Lucy Cowie, Ellie Aldridge and all the team at Rough Guides for commissioning me to work on such great chapters.

Anna Kaminski Many thanks to everyone who assisted me during the course of my travels in Borneo, Hong Kong, Macau and Vietnam. In particular, I'd like to thank Chung-Wah in Hong Kong, Steve in Macau; Tom, Katie, Lupa Masa, Anton, Gert, Wong, Scuba Junkie, Mrs Lee and Donald and Marina in Borneo; Ben, Howard, Tony, Multi, Tung, Sapa O'Chau, Maria and Mayra in Vietnam.

Shafik Meghji Thanks to the many Indonesians and travellers who helped out along the way. A special *terima kasih* must go to Ellie Aldridge and Lucy Cowie at Rough Guides; Jean, Nizar and Nina Meghji; and Sioned Jones for her love, support and companionship on our trip around Bali and Lombok.

John Oates Thanks to Mr Anthony, Gilly Aung San, Dr Chan Aye, Nitti Lay, Lily, Tint Lwin, Maureen Maloney, Jochen Meissner, John Okell, Günther H. Otero, Mike Sein, Moe Set, Tom Tom, Than Tun, Donna Yay and Zinmar. It was a pleasure to travel with Matt Oates for part of the trip, and Christian Desgrippes offered much-needed companionship on the long journey from Myeik to the border. Thanks to Sheryll Sulit for being there on the other side in Thailand, even if she was a day late, and for her support throughout my work on the guide. Back in the UK, I'm particularly grateful to Nicola Frame and Intrepid for their help in Rakhine State. And thanks, of course, to Lucy, Ellie and the rest of the team at Rough Guides.

Readers' updates

Thanks to all the readers who have taken the time to write in with comments and suggestions (and apologies if we've inadvertently omitted or misspelt anyone's name):

Craig Adams, Victor Ashe, Ali Aspden, Katie Burrell, Boris Tierno Becerra, Mandy Berger, Dom Beverley, Wim Beyens, Hiroko Canning, Rosalind Elson, Jennie Fernyhough, Teal Francis, John Garratt, Eva Grimbergen, Liza Hawkins, Rob ter Heine,Tom Hewitt, Paula Higgins, Mark Lane, Melanie Lidman, Monica Mackaness, Natascha Möller, James Molony, Janne Mottlau, Mimosa Nguyen, Helen Peier, Sandie Schagen, Jochen Schlingmann, Svea Schneider, Tricia Score, Elaine Sherwood, Elizabeth Silver, Christine Smith, Oliver Supplie, Wendy Tran, Emily Trumbull, Tine Van den Bergh, Anita Verborgh, Barry Walden and Ineke Willeboordse.

Photo credits

All photos © Rough Guides except the following:
(Key: t-top; c-centre; b-bottom; l-left; r-right)

p.1 AWL Images: Christian Kober
p.2 AWL Images: Walter Bibikow
p.4 AWL Images: Gavin Hellier
p.5 AWL Images: Danita Delimont
p.9 Getty Images: Christian Aslund (b)
p.10 AWL Images: Michele Falzone
p.11 Alamy Images: Robert Harding World Imagery (b); AWL Images: Michele Falzone (t); Katja Kreder (c)
p.12 AWL Images: Michele Falzone (t); Travel Pix Collection (b); Robert Harding Picture Library: Olaf Protze (c)
p.13 AWL Images: Peter Adams (br, tl)
p.14 Alamy Images: Eitan Simanor (b); Aroon Thaewchatturat (c); AWL Images: Gavin Hellier (tr)
p.15 Alamy Images: Simon Reddy (tl)
p.16 Alamy Images: (t); Andrew Bain (cl); WaterFrame (b); AWL Images: Katie Garrod (cr)
p.17 Alamy Images: Travelscape Images (tl); Jan Wlodarczyk (b); Khaled Kassem (cl)
p.18 Alamy Images: Robert Harding World Imagery (t)
p.19 Alamy Images: Hemis (b); Robert Harding Picture Library: Aurora Photos (cl)
p.26 AWL Images: Andrew Watson/John Warburton-Lee Photography Ltd
p.51 Alamy Images: Tibor Bognar
p.119 Corbis: CALLE MONTES
p.159 Robert Harding Picture Library: Matthew Williams-Ellis
p.405 Travel Pictures
p.585 Getty Images: Peter Adams
p.667 Alamy Images: southeast asia
p.695 Getty Images: Flickr RM

Front cover Bagan, Myanmar © Jeremy Woodhouse/ Getty Images
Back cover Longtail boats, Hat Rin, Thailand © Martin Richardson/Rough Guides (t); Akha people weaving, northern Laos © Tim Draper/Rough Guides (bl); Wat Mai, Louang Prabang, Laos © Tim Draper/Rough Guides (br)

Index

Maps are marked in **grey**

ABBREVIATIONS

(B) Brunei
(C) Cambodia
(H) Hong Kong
(I) Indonesia
(L) Laos
(Ma) Malaysia
(My) Myanmar
(P) The Philippines
(S) Singapore
(T) Thailand
(V) Vietnam

A

B

C

D

E

F

N

O

P

R

S

T

U

V

W

X

Y

Map symbols

The symbols below are used on maps throughout the book

- Post office
- Information office
- Telephone
- Hospital
- Embassy
- ATM
- Gate
- Statue
- Point of interest
- Internet access
- Garden
- Golf course
- Bridge
- Ruins
- Border crossing
- Museum
- Chinese temple
- Synagogue
- Campsite
- Pagoda
- Buddhist temple
- Thai temple/stupa
- Monastery
- Tower
- Monument
- Fortress
- Stately Home
- Mountain refuge/lodge
- Cave
- Volcano
- Mountain peak
- Mountain range
- Petrol station
- Helipad
- International airport
- Domestic airport
- Bus/taxi stop
- Parking
- Boat/ship
- Shipwreck
- Viewpoint
- Spring
- Surfing
- Snorkelling
- Swimming pool
- Waterfall
- Lighthouse
- Church (regional maps)
- Church/cathedral
- Building
- Market
- Stadium
- Park/forest
- Beach
- Cemetery
- Swamp/Marsh

Listings key

- Accommodation
- Eating/drinking/nightlife
- Shopping

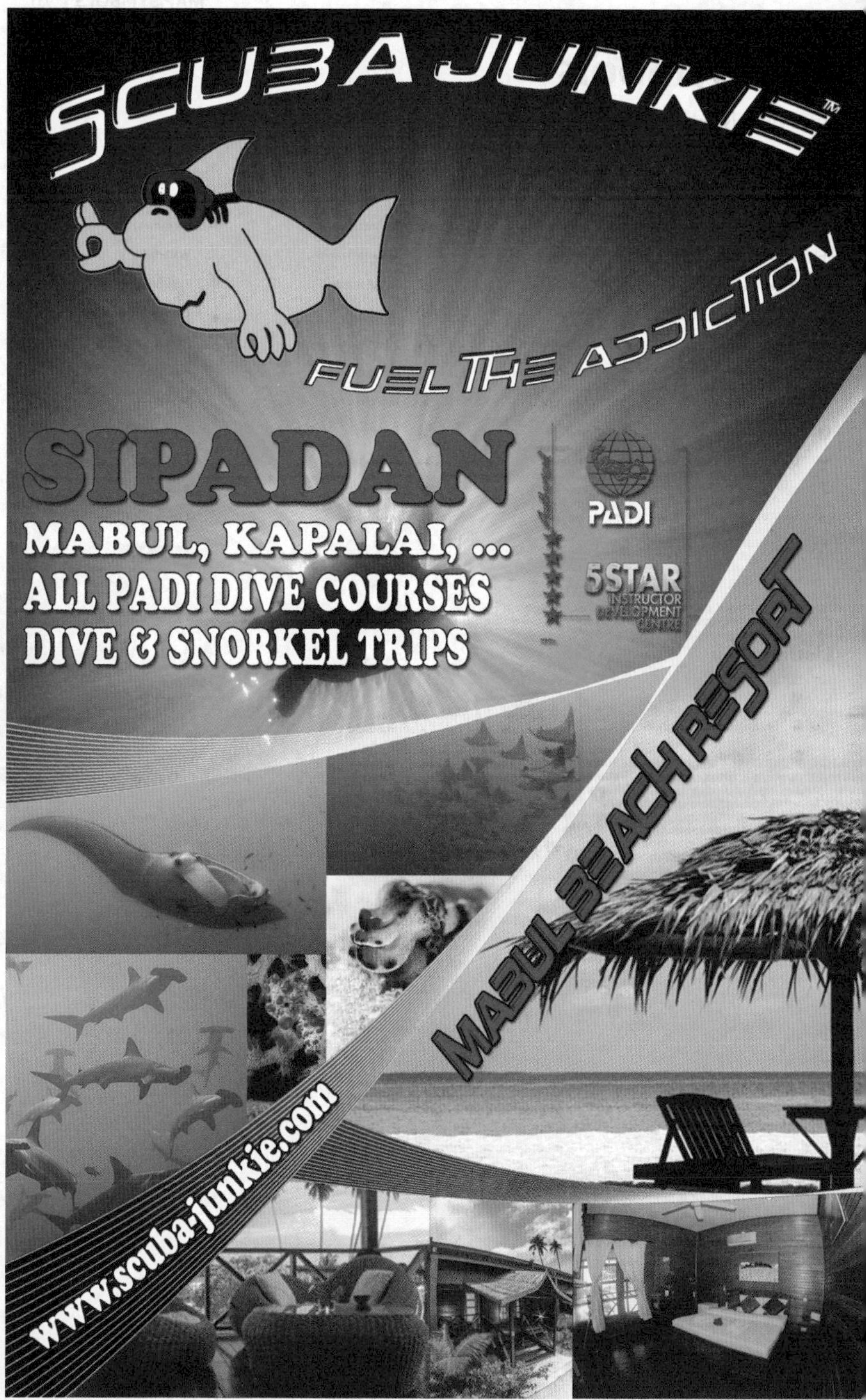
SCUBA JUNKIE™
FUEL THE ADDICTION
SIPADAN
MABUL, KAPALAI, ...
ALL PADI DIVE COURSES
DIVE & SNORKEL TRIPS
PADI
5STAR
INSTRUCTOR
MABUL BEACH RESORT
www.scuba-junkie.com

A ROUGH GUIDE TO ROUGH GUIDES

Published in 1982, the first Rough Guide – to Greece – was a student scheme that became a publishing phenomenon. Mark Ellingham, a recent graduate in English from Bristol University, had been travelling in Greece the previous summer and couldn't find the right guidebook. With a small group of friends he wrote his own guide, combining a highly contemporary, journalistic style with a thoroughly practical approach to travellers' needs.

The immediate success of the book spawned a series that rapidly covered dozens of destinations. And, in addition to impecunious backpackers, Rough Guides soon acquired a much broader and older readership that relished the guides' wit and inquisitiveness as much as their enthusiastic, critical approach and value-for-money ethos.

These days, Rough Guides feature recommendations from shoestring to luxury and cover more than 120 destinations around the globe. Our ever-growing team of authors and photographers is spread all over the world, particularly in Europe, the US and Australia.

Rough Guides now number around 200 titles, including Pocket city guides, inspirational coffee-table books and comprehensive country and regional titles, plus technology guides from iPods to Android. As well as print books, we publish groundbreaking eBooks for every major digital device.

Visit Ⓦ roughguides.com to see our latest publications.

Rough Guide travel images are available for commercial licensing at Ⓦ roughguidespictures.com.

ROUGH
GUIDES